Dictionary

of Canadian English

A Dictionary of Canadianisms

produced for W. J. Gage Limited

by the Lexicographical Centre

for Canadian English,

University of Victoria,

Victoria, British Columbia,

Canada

Director: M. H. Scargill

Associate Director: Walter S. Avis

Research Associate: Douglas Leechman

Editorial Assistant: Joan Hall

on Historical Principles

Editorial Board:

Walter S. Avis / Editor-in-Chief

Charles Crate

Patrick Drysdale

Douglas Leechman

Matthew H. Scargill

Editor until 1960:

Charles J. Lovell

W. J. Gage Limited

Toronto, Canada, 1967

CONSULTANTS

Flora
R. G. H. Cormack, MA, PhD (Toronto), FRSC,
Professor of Botany, University of Alberta.

Fauna
Ian McTaggart Cowan, BA (Brit. Col.),
PhD (California), FRSC,
Dean, Faculty of Graduate Studies,
University of British Columbia.

French-Canadian Etymologies
Gaston Dulong, Licencié ès lettres (Laval),
Professeur agrégé de philologie française,
L'Université Laval.

W. J. GAGE LIMITED EDITORIAL STAFF

Editor:
Patrick Drysdale

Assistant Editors:
Cecil Lancefield
Casimire Pindel

Editorial Assistants:
Joan Compton
Dorothy Schweder

Illustrations by Jean Galt and Mary Guest

Designed by Arnold Rockman

This book is dedicated

to the late

Charles J. Lovell

a pioneer scholar in the field

of Canadian English

Printed and bound in Canada

Foreword

Contents

When man has an experience that he has turned into an idea that stays with him, he invariably gives a name to it. By the instrument of the word he is thus more readily enabled to re-use the experience himself, and to tell other people about it. The study of people's language is thus a study of their experience over the course of time, an intimate study of their history.

By its history a people is set apart, differentiated from the rest of humanity. If, therefore, there is anything distinctive about Canadians, it must be the result of a history of experience different from the histories of the French, the English, the Americans, and all those who have come together to form the Canadian people.

That separateness of experience, in the bludgeoning of the Atlantic waves, the forest over-burden of the St. Lawrence valley, the long waterways to the West, the silence of the Arctic wastes, the lonesome horizons of the prairie, the vast imprisonment of the Cordilleras, the trade and commerce with the original Canadians — all this is recorded in our language.

The publishers hope that, as a contribution to Centennial thinking, the *Dictionary of Canadianisms* will assist in the identification, not only of Canadianisms but of whatever it is that we may call "Canadianism."

W. R. Wees,
Vice-President, Publishing
W. J. Gage Limited

Toronto, Ontario
August, 1967

Preface

A *Dictionary of Canadianisms on Historical Principles* is the product of the vision, hard work, support, and encouragement of a great many people, and its beginning goes back many years.

At the founding meeting of the Canadian Linguistic Association, held at the University of Manitoba in 1954, some discussion was given to the possibility of preparing dictionaries of Canadian English; but it was not until 1957 that the Association established a Lexicographical Committee to begin promoting and co-ordinating lexicographical work in Canada. The membership of the original committee was as follows: M. H. Scargill (Chairman); H. Alexander; W. S. Avis; W. H. Brodie; P. Daviault; R. J. Gregg; C. J. Lovell; J. E. Robbins; G. M. Story; J. P. Vinay; H. R. Wilson. Since 1957, separate committees have been established to deal with French-Canadian and Ukrainian lexicography and with dialect studies.

In 1957 and following years plans were made to prepare three types of dictionaries: a series of dictionaries for use in schools and universities (now completed); a historical dictionary of the English language in Canada; a dictionary of Canadianisms, which was to serve as a pilot project for the larger historical dictionary of the English language in Canada.

In 1958 Mr. C. J. Lovell was invited to prepare a *Dictionary of Canadianisms* for W. J. Gage Limited from materials already assembled by him and other scholars, especially Dr. Avis and Mr. Charles Crate. In order to expedite his work, the Canada Council awarded Mr. Lovell a Visiting Fellowship to Canada in 1960, and he made plans to spend a full year in Canada, editing his materials and consulting with colleagues. However, these plans were never completed, for Mr. Lovell died on March 17th, 1960, at his home in Illinois.

On Mr. Lovell's death, W. J. Gage Limited made arrangements to purchase from his estate his entire lexicographical collection; and at the request of W. J. Gage, Dr. Avis and Dr. Scargill agreed to continue the work that Mr. Lovell had undertaken.

At this time it became essential to have some central location where Mr. Lovell's materials and others being assembled could be housed ready for editing. It also became apparent that the moment had arrived for the acquisition of a budget to provide for secretarial help, for supplies, for filing cabinets, and all the things necessary for the establishment of an editorial office.

During the summer of 1960, Dr. M. G. Taylor, now President of the University of Victoria and then first Principal of the University of Alberta, Calgary (now the University of Calgary), agreed to provide the space and secretarial assistance for what was designated as the "Lexicographical Centre for Canadian English Located at the University of Alberta, Calgary." Dr. Scargill became the Centre's Director and Dr. Avis its Associate Director.

From the summer of 1960 on, materials began to arrive at the Centre in ever-increasing amounts. Particularly valuable was the gift to the Centre of a complete manuscript for a dictionary of terms of the Canadian Northwest collected by Dr. Douglas Leechman.

Until 1963 editorial work proceeded very slowly, and it was obvious that arrangements would have to be made to free one of our colleagues from his normal academic work so that he could devote at least a full year to dictionary editing. Thanks to the co-operation of Canada Council in providing a Senior Fellowship and to the Royal Military College of Canada in granting a sabbatical leave of absence, Dr. Avis was able to spend a full year, 1963-64, at the Lexicographical Centre in Calgary. By the summer of 1964, as a result of his hard work, it was thought possible to advance the publication date of the dictionary from 1970 to 1967, the year of Canada's Centenary. Accordingly, the Lexicographical Centre appointed the Editorial Board which has been responsible for the production of this present dictionary. At the same time, the Board agreed that because other materials in addition to those assembled by Mr. Lovell, notably the collections of Dr. Avis, Mr. Crate, Dr. Leechman, and that of the Centre itself, were being used in the dictionary, the nature and scope of the project as originally conceived had greatly changed and the book should now be acknowledged as compiled from the five collections named above.

In the fall of 1964, Dr. Scargill left the University of Alberta, Calgary, to join the staff of the new University of Victoria, and the Lexicographical Centre was moved to that city. In Victoria the resources of the Centre were increased by the appointment of Dr. Leechman as Research Associate and Miss Joan Hall as Editorial Assistant, positions which both still hold. At the same time the Centre signed a contract with W. J. Gage Limited to produce for them this present dictionary with the Editorial Board named above.

Again thanks to the generosity of Canada Council and to the Royal Military College of Canada, Dr. Avis was able to spend the summer of 1965 at the University of Victoria, where he was joined by Mr. Crate, who spent a further summer there in 1966.

Perhaps there are those who will consider this a rather long prefatory essay; but I do not think that they will be many. I believe that the story of all that has gone into the making of this dictionary is worth the telling, and I am proud to be its narrator on behalf of my colleagues. Several years have elapsed now since our collaboration began. Those years have been enlivened by good humor among a closely knit group of colleagues and marred only by the tragedy of Mr. Lovell's death. We have been aided on all sides and at all times by people in many walks of life. It is with pleasure and with pride that we now offer our

thanks to them in the realization that their good wishes and encouragement will accompany this book that they have helped to make possible.

M. H. Scargill,
Director,
Lexicographical Centre for Canadian English

Victoria, B.C.
June, 1967

Acknowledgments

It is impossible to acknowledge at all adequately the debt that we owe to all those who have helped to make possible *A Dictionary of Canadianisms on Historical Principles*. The following list is by no means a complete record of the names of the people and the institutions providing assistance of varying degrees and kinds, and we apologize for any omissions.

For the financial assistance without which this book could never have been produced we wish to thank the Canada Council, the President and Board of Governors of the University of Victoria, the President and the Board of Governors of the University of Alberta. In this respect our special thanks are due to Dr. M. G. Taylor, President of the University of Victoria, not only for invaluable financial aid but also for encouragement and support of an academic kind.

We are grateful to the Royal Military College of Canada for co-operation in making available the services of Dr. W. S. Avis, not only for a full sabbatical year but at other times as well, and to the School Board of North Island (District #85) for granting occasional leave to Mr. Chas. Crate.

We have received invaluable assistance in checking bibliographical materials and in other ways from the staff of the McPherson Library, University of Victoria; and we thank the Librarian, Mr. Dean Halliwell, for making available to us the services of Mrs. Helen Rodney and Mr. Robin Kerr, Reference Librarians. Thanks for similar assistance are due also to Miss Inez Mitchell, Assistant Provincial Archivist, Provincial Archives, Victoria, B.C., and to the Librarians and their staffs in the following institutions: the University of Alberta, the University of Calgary, the University of British Columbia, the Royal Military College of Canada, the Toronto Public Library, and the Vancouver Public Library. Miss Grace Lewis, Yarmouth, Nova Scotia, has helped us not only in her capacity as Librarian in that city but also as a reader and as a consultant on items of Nova Scotia interest.

It is with special pleasure that we acknowledge the contribution made to this dictionary by students, especially Mr. Terry Klokeid, University of Victoria, for help with Eskimo and Amerindian items, and Mrs. Cheryl Campbell, Alert Bay, B.C., for help with Chinook and Kwakiutl items. Dr. Avis' students in courses at the Summer School of Linguistics, University of Alberta, provided many examples of Canadianisms. Students of Mr. Chas. Crate have given considerable assistance to him with the typing of materials.

We wish to thank also the very many individuals who have helped us in various ways as readers and as occasional consultants. Their names include the following: Mr. H. G. Ambury; Mrs. E. W. J. Avery; Mrs. G. D. Bancroft; Mrs. Geri Pattisson Beddows; Mr. R. W. Bennett; Dr. C. Bida; Rev. L. Braceland; Mr. L. Bunyan; Miss M. I. Buxton; Major S. S. Carroll; Mr. C. Cole; Dr. C. B. Conway; Mr. H. C. Cutbill; Mr. W. Davidson; Mr. B. W. A. Deacon; Mr. H. De Groot; Dr. H. A. Dempsey; Mr. T. Dunbabin; Mr. R. Eaton; Mr. Harold B. Elworthy; Mr. S. J. Ewaniuk; Mr. J. B. Fraser; Mr. N. F. W. Gates; Mr. T. Gilchrist; Miss I. M. Graham; Mr. W. J. Greene; Dr. R. J. Gregg; Mr. A. Harshenin; Mr. E. B. Harvey; Rev. R. B. Horsefield; Mr. Willard Ireland; Lieutenant M. Jacquest; Miss B. A. Johnstone; Mr. R. J. Jones; Mrs. E. Joslin; Mr. R. Keith-Hicks; Mr. J. LeBourdais; Dr. A. R. M. Lower; Miss J. W. Lucas; Dr. N. M. McArthur; Miss D. MacDonald; Mr. C. McAllister; Mrs. J. C. McGibbon; Mrs. K. B. McCool; Mr. H. Michell; Mr. J. S. Moir; Mrs. M. Moore; Mrs. S. Mott; Mr. M. D. Nelles;

Dr. G. N. O'Grady; Mr. T. M. Paikeday; Mr. J. S. Peach; Mr. E. W. Person; Mr. W. Preuss; Mr. E. Pye; Mr. Allen Walker Read; Dr. P. Read-Campbell; Dr. Carroll Reed; Mr. and Mrs. Wallace Roberts; Major N. Sadleir-Brown; Miss M. S. Simpson; Mr. Vernon Simpson; Dr. G. F. G. Stanley; Mr. J. Stein; Miss H. Stevenson; Dr. G. M. Story; Mr. B. Stuart-Stubbs; Dr. J.-P. Vinay; Dr. M. G. Wanamaker; Mr. B. G. Webber; Rev. Gavin White; Dr. H. R. Wilson; Mr. S. F. Wise; Dr. A. J. Wood.

The publishers of any book often play a greater part in its production than readers realize. We should be indeed remiss if we failed to record our appreciation to W. J. Gage Limited for their support and encouragement over many years and, in particular, to Dr. W. R. Wees, whose high ideals and determination helped to make possible the publication of this book and the whole series of which it is a part. In addition, we wish to thank all those members of the publisher's editorial staff who have worked on this book.

Finally, we wish to convey our appreciation to Mrs. C. J. Lovell and her family for their help and co-operation.

W.S.A.
C.C.
P.D.
D.L.
M.H.S.

The Editors

Walter S. Avis, B.A., M.A. (Queen's), Ph.D. (Michigan), is a Professor of English at the Royal Military College of Canada. Born in Toronto, Ontario, in 1919, he has long been interested in English language studies, especially with reference to North American English, both as student and teacher. Dr. Avis has been a teaching fellow at Queen's University and at the University of Michigan and a visiting professor at summer schools of linguistics at both the University of Montreal and the University of Alberta. A founding member of the Canadian Linguistic Association, he was Secretary-Treasurer from 1956 to 1959 and Secretary from 1959 to 1967; he is at present Vice-President of the Association. Since 1955 he has also been Canadian Secretary of the American Dialect Society. Dr. Avis is a co-editor of the *Dictionary of Canadian English* series and compiler of *A Bibliography of Writings on Canadian English (1857-1965)*. He has published various articles in such journals as the *Journal of the Canadian Linguistic Association* (now the *Canadian Journal of Linguistics*), *Language*, *American Speech*, the *Translator's Journal*, and *Culture*. He is also a contributor to the *Encyclopedia Canadiana*, the *Encyclopaedia Britannica, Funk and Wagnall's Standard College Dictionary*, the *Random House Dictionary*, and several other works of reference. He has given several talks about Canadian English on the CBC and has lectured on the subject many times in many places.

Charles Brandel (*"Chuck"*) *Crate* is a teacher at the Quesnel Secondary School, Quesnel, B.C. Born in Weston, Ontario, in 1915, he was educated at York Memorial Collegiate and at the University of British Columbia and the University of Victoria. Mr. Crate has had a varied career and has spent much of his life in the Canadian North. For almost four years, 1952-1955, he published and edited the Yellowknife *North Star* and for nine years directed a program on Radio Station CFYK. Mr. Crate has served as Secretary and Research Director of the Yellowknife District Miners' Union, as a member of the Board of Governors of the Yellowknife Red Cross Hospital, and as Chairman, Friends of the Indians (Northwest Territories). He was twice elected Councillor of the Municipal District of Yellowknife, and in 1954 was a candidate for Northwest Territories Council. He has been a member of the Canadian Linguistic Association for many years, and has written articles and published papers in a variety of fields, including a vocabulary of hardrock mining.

Patrick Dockar Drysdale, M.A. (Oxon.), is a senior editor with W. J. Gage Limited. Born in Shropshire, England, in 1929, he worked for a time in the professional theatre, mainly as a stage manager, before turning to teaching. From 1956 to 1959 he was an Assistant Professor in the Department of English, Memorial University, Newfoundland, and in 1958 taught at the Summer School of Linguistics, University of Alberta. In 1959 he joined W. J. Gage to participate in the preparation and publication of the *Dictionary of Canadian English* series. In addition, he has edited books on English grammar, the theatre, and education. He is a member of the Canadian Linguistic Association, and since 1960 has served on the editorial board of the *Canadian Journal of Linguistics*. He has written articles on lexicography, dialect geography, and general linguistics.

Douglas Leechman, B.Sc., M.A., Ph.D. (Ottawa), F.R.S.C., is Research Associate at the Lexicographical Centre for Canadian English. Born in 1890, he came to Canada in 1908. In 1924 he joined the staff of the Division of Anthropology in the National Museum of Canada and was engaged there till 1955. During this period he attended the University of Ottawa, and in 1941 he was elected a Fellow of the Royal Society of Canada. On leaving the National Museum, he became the first Director of the Glenbow Foundation in Calgary, Alberta. On retiring to Victoria, B.C., in 1957, he devoted much of his time to writing and further work in lexicography, especially in the fields of Canadian slang and terms and expressions used in the fur trade. He joined the staff of the University of Victoria in 1964. He is the author of several books, including *Native Tribes of Canada* and *Eskimo Summer*, and of many technical papers.

Charles Julien Lovell, writer, researcher and lexicographer, was born in Portland, Maine. Orphaned as a small child, he was reared in foster homes in New Bedford, Massachusetts. His life-long interest in words was closely linked to his first love, the out-of-doors. The nomenclature of fauna and flora always fascinated him, and his devotion to Canada and Canadian English grew out of a series of hiking trips in the Canadian Rockies. In 1946 he was appointed research and editorial assistant of *A Dictionary of Americanisms*, to which, in the words of its editor, he made "an outstanding contribution." He worked for the University of Chicago Press until November, 1953, when he suffered a first heart attack. Thereafter he continued his writing and lexicographical work independently. He corresponded and compared notes with Canadian scholars and gradually assembled that impressive collection already referred to in the Preface. His death on March 17, 1960, was a tragic loss to lexicography and to the study of Canadian English.

Matthew Harry Scargill, B.A., Ph.D. (Leeds), is Chairman of the School of Graduate Studies and Head of the Department of Linguistics at the University of Victoria. Born in Yorkshire, England, in 1916, he came to Canada in 1948 and joined the staff of the University of Alberta. In 1959 he became Professor of English at the University of Calgary, and was appointed Dean of Arts and Science there in 1962. Dr. Scargill moved to the University of Victoria in 1964 to head the newly established Department of Linguistics. Dr. Scargill is a founding member of the Canadian Linguistic Association and has served as the Association's Secretary, Editor of the *Journal*, and from 1964 to 1966 as President. He is the author of several articles and books, including *Three Icelandic Sagas*, *An English Handbook*, *The Development of the Principal Sounds of Indo-European*. Together with Dr. W. S. Avis, Dr. R. J. Gregg, and Mr. P. D. Drysdale, he is an editor of the W. J. Gage *Dictionary of Canadian English* series.

Introduction

That part of Canadian English which is neither British nor American is best illustrated by the vocabulary, for there are hundreds of words which are native to Canada or which have meanings peculiar to Canada. As might be expected, many of these words refer to topographical features, plants, trees, fish, animals, and birds; and many others to social, economic, and political institutions and activities. Few of these words, which may be called Canadianisms, find their way into British or American dictionaries, a fact which should occasion no surprise, for British and American dictionaries are based on British and American usage, being primarily intended for Britons and Americans, not for Canadians.[1]

The purpose of *A Dictionary of Canadianisms on Historical Principles* is to provide a historical record of words and expressions characteristic of the various spheres of Canadian life during the almost four centuries that English has been used in Canada. The dictionary is intended to provide the meaning, or meanings, of such terms and, where relevant, their pronunciation, etymology, and scope — both in time and space; moreover, through dated quotations, an extensive cross-referencing system, illustrative drawings, and explanatory notes relating to usage, disputed origins, and other contentious matters, the editors have sought to create an informative, entertaining, and valuable reference work. Finally, the dictionary should demonstrate that a substantial vocabulary relating to both today and yesterday has been developed by Canadians in pursuing their many activities

throughout their vast and varied homeland.

A Dictionary of Canadianisms has been compiled on historical principles in that every term entered is supported by dated evidence from printed sources. In this respect, we are in the well-established tradition of *The Oxford English Dictionary*, *A Dictionary of American English*, and *A Dictionary of Americanisms*, all three of which have been indispensable during the editing process. To follow this tradition, however, is to accept certain restrictions, for it precludes the entering of terms for which there is only oral evidence and of others for which the printed evidence is fragmentary or otherwise inadequate. As a consequence, many interesting items remain in the files, awaiting fuller substantiation in printed sources. Furthermore, since reading for the dictionary has continued during editing and printing, there is in the files a great deal of material that for practical reasons could not be published in the present edition — including additional evidence for entered items as well as evidence for completely new items. It should be added that less stringent limitations of space have made it possible to introduce innovations in format and style affording more ease of reference than was possible in earlier historical dictionaries.

The problem of establishing a definition for *Canadianism* as used in the title of this dictionary was not easy to solve. The term is used in a less inclusive sense than the definition given in the body of the dictionary itself, for we are concerned primarily with vocabulary; on the other hand, it is used in a more inclusive sense than *Americanism* has been used by scholars in the United States. Mitford M. Mathews, for example, defines the term in his Preface to *A Dictionary of Americanisms* as "a word or expression which originated in the United States."[2] Yet in his dictionary he uses a wide variety of Canadian source materials as evidence for a substantial number of "Americanisms," a practice which, to say the least, weakens his definition. After all, Canada is not part of the United States— although she has shared English-speaking North

[1]Walter S. Avis, "Canadian English," *The Senior Dictionary*, Dictionary of Canadian English Series (Toronto: W. J. Gage, 1967), pp. vi-ix.

[2](Chicago: University of Chicago Press, 1951), p. *v*.

America with the United States from the time of the American Revolution. Prior to that time, English speakers in North America held their mother country in common. Consequently, the problem of identifying many terms as specifically "American" or "Canadian" is virtually impossible of solution. Needless to say, the editors of *A Dictionary of Canadianisms* have struggled with this problem since the project began.

In view of the difficulty and, perhaps, pointlessness of trying to identify many words in common use on this continent as being "American" or "Canadian," lexicographers compiling dictionaries of the English used in North America might be well advised to adopt the label *North Americanism*. The arguments for such a solution to this problem are several. In the first place, many terms in this class were current in North America before the United States existed as a political entity. Indeed, the present-day boundary between the United States and Canada was not fixed — especially on the Pacific Coast — until well into the nineteenth century. Furthermore, Canadians and Americans from the late seventeenth century onward have moved back and forth across the border in such numbers and with such regularity that it is impossible to determine exactly where certain terms originated. So much is and has long been similar or identical in the social and economic spheres of Canadian and American life and so much, especially along the border, is shared with respect to natural resources, flora and fauna, topography, and so on, to say nothing of our common contacts with the American Indians, that hosts of terms cannot be claimed by one country or the other with any degree of confidence whatever. As a matter of fact, there is little point in making such claims since these terms reflect a common heritage in many fields of activity, the vocabulary of a people being in a very real sense a record of the history and experience of those who use it.

To meet this problem, we have done our best to confine ourselves to source materials written by persons native to or resident in Canada who were writing about Canadian life or by travellers and other visitors to Canada who were commenting on their experiences in this country. Furthermore, we have found it desirable, perhaps even necessary, to include certain entries in this dictionary which are not Canadian at all. Such entries are intended (1) to clarify terms having numerous extensions of meaning or lending themselves freely to the formation of new compounds, such extensions or compounds being themselves Canadianisms, as *beaver* (defs. 1 and 2); (2) to serve as reference points for synonyms which are themselves Canadianisms, as *wolverine*; (3) to call attention to terms having special interest in various areas of Canadian activity, as *discovery claim*. All words or meanings so entered are marked with a dagger (†); they have, moreover, a special significance and history in Canada and, accordingly, are supported by dated quotations. In addition to easing certain editorial problems, the dagger device has made it possible to include a limited amount of interesting and informative matter that otherwise would not have qualified for inclusion.

Since our approach to our material is clearly quite different from that of lexicographers in the United States, we have chosen to define *Canadianism* less exclusively than they have defined *Americanism*. A Canadianism, then, is a word, expression, or meaning which is native to Canada or which is distinctively characteristic of Canadian usage though not necessarily exclusive to Canada; *Winnipeg couch* falls into the first category, *chesterfield* ("sofa") into the second.

Now that the term *Canadianism* has been defined for our purposes, it is possible to expand on the general nature of the entries in this dictionary. The vocabulary distinctive of Canada has developed along lines characteristic of linguistic groups which become separated from their motherland through emigration to distant and strange shores. The stock of words brought with these emigrants will change as they come into close contact with speakers of other languages, as they encounter novelties of animal life, vegetation, and topography, as they adopt or devise different ways of coping with their new environment, and as they work out new ways of organizing their political, economic, and social life. As a result of these experiences, new terms will be added to the vocabulary, while others will fall into disuse and obsolescence because they have specific reference to things having to do with life in the old country. The result, of course, is a speech community which differs in many respects from the motherland although continuing to share a very extensive common vocabulary. Moreover, the speech patterns in the emigrant community change in other ways: in pronunciation, intonation, syntax, and, often less markedly, in grammatical form. When the extent of such differentiation becomes extreme, the two dialects become mutually unintelligible and are consequently classed as different languages. Such a degree of change has not taken place in North America, and the English spoken in Canada and in the United States is, with relatively minor exceptions largely relating to vocabulary, quite understandable in Britain — and vice versa. Therefore, it is quite erroneous to refer, as some have done, to an American language or a Canadian language.

In colonial times, the English-speakers coming to Canada — first in the sixteenth century as resident fishermen in Newfoundland, then in the seventeenth as fur traders for the Hudson's Bay Company, and eventually in the eighteenth and nineteenth centuries as settlers — came into contact with the Indians, the Eskimos, and the Canadian French. Living among these non-English-speaking peoples, the traders and pioneers borrowed a wide variety of terms, usually referring to things new in their experience, as *pemmican*, *igloo*, and *voyageur*. Another source of new terms lay in the ready-to-hand resources of the parent language, elements of which could be combined in several ways as labels for new concepts, as *fur brigade*, *snowbird*, and *sturgeon-head boat*, compounds which have referents substantially different from the meanings of the parts. Once loanwords from other languages had been assimilated, these too were available for compounding, as *pemmican post*, *portage strap*, and *saskatoon berry*. Still another solution to the problem of labelling

the novelties of the environment was to use already established English words in a new sense, that is, to extend the range of meaning of these words. Thus *buffalo* was extended to refer to the bison of the prairies; and throughout the North *deer* was extended to refer to the caribou. Moreover, assimilated loanwords often took on extended meanings not known in the source languages, as with several of the meanings of *cache*, *shaganappi*, and *siwash* (ultimately from French *sauvage* Indian). Many indeed are the processes of change by which the vocabulary has grown — by borrowing, by compounding, by shortening, by blending, by the generalization of proper names, and by new coinages; moreover, the range of meaning of terms has been altered and expanded by extension, transference, deterioration and amelioration, by generalization and specialization, and by folk etymology. Many of these processes have been applied not only to terms already existing in the parent language, but also to loanwords borrowed and assimilated. Thus *A Dictionary of Canadianisms* offers compelling evidence of the inventiveness of Canadians past and present in the realm of word creation.

Readers of this dictionary will soon become aware that certain areas of activity in the social, political, and economic life of the country have been particularly productive of Canadianisms. In the social and political sphere, the most significant of these include pioneer life, travel, recreation, religion, and education, as well as politics and administration—at the municipal, provincial, and federal levels. In the economic, or commercial, sphere must be included the fur trade, logging, fishing, farming, mining, oil and gas operations, and the maple-products industry. Then, too, there is the large area concerned with relationships between the English-speaking Canadians and the French-speaking Canadians, the Indians, the Eskimos, and, especially in certain regions, the many immigrant peoples who form an important part of the population of twentieth-century Canada. Finally, there is the extensive contribution of terms deriving from the experiences of Canadians in the North American environment, relating to topographical features, weather conditions, and flora and fauna. In fact, the plethora of evidence for local terms and folk-names within the last-mentioned category is both overwhelming and difficult to document. It has been necessary, therefore, to adopt a rather arbitrary policy of selection with regard to such items in the hope of providing a representative rather than definitive listing of the names for plants, shrubs, trees, animals, birds, and fish.

Since most of the areas of activity and experience mentioned above represent situations in which Canadian life differs most markedly from life in the mother country, it should not be surprising that they are well represented in this lexicon. That *A Dictionary of Canadianisms*, in spite of its many entries from many areas of activity, is incomplete goes without saying; it is the fate of all dictionaries, for reasons inherent in the complexity of the subject matter and in the lamentable lack of omniscience among its editors and consultants, to be flawed in this respect. On the other hand, a deliberate decision was taken to omit certain kinds of entries whose relevance to dictionaries is often considered peripheral, namely, biographical and gazeteer entries; also excluded, after much deliberation, were the names of Indian and Eskimo tribes and bands in spite of the wealth of interesting evidence in the files at the Lexicographical Centre. It was decided, however, to include numerous compound terms incorporating proper nouns, terms relating to certain general regions, nicknames of cities, provinces, and regions and their inhabitants (with the exception of common present-day terms such as *Torontonian*, *Montrealer*, and *Vancouverite*), and informal or slang names for people, places, and institutions. In these several categories, special attention has been given to those terms having historical significance justifying definition and illustration.

In the preparation of *A Dictionary of Canadianisms*, constant recourse has been had not only to *The Oxford English Dictionary*, *A Dictionary of Americanisms*, and *The English Dialect Dictionary*, all especially helpful because of their historical evidence, but also to the invaluable *Webster's Third New International Dictionary* and to many other dictionaries and word lists of a more specialized or limited scope. Despite all precautions, however, it is inevitable that certain errors not now known to the editors of this dictionary will be discovered by knowledgeable readers, for any pioneering work is bound to be accompanied by such shortcomings. We shall work to overcome these shortcomings by continuing to add to our files. In this endeavor, we should appreciate the help of interested persons in detecting and rectifying all inaccuracies and omissions; we also need further information concerning terms already entered, including evidence of earlier use, and concerning other terms that we may appear to have overlooked. Any evidence supplied should, of course, be in the form of dated quotations from printed sources, accompanied by full bibliographical details. In this way, through our combined efforts, an improved second edition will be assured.

This first edition of *A Dictionary of Canadianisms* must be regarded as a pioneering work. Nevertheless, in spite of imperfections, it makes available a unique and fascinating record of Canadian history and accomplishment through the medium of the hundreds of terms defined and the thousands of contexts provided to illuminate its terms and definitions. It is in the confidence that this record is sufficiently extensive to constitute a scholarly and valuable contribution that we take pride in offering it to the Canadian people.

Walter S. Avis,
Editor-in-Chief

Kingston, Ontario
June, 1967

Principles of Style

The method and the principles of style followed in compiling *A Dictionary of Canadianisms* have been adopted with two principal considerations in mind: the interests of the reader and the demand for clear and economical presentation. It has been the editors' constant concern to satisfy the latter without detriment to the former. Inasmuch as a uniform pattern of style was followed in putting together each entry, the readers' understanding of these principles will be advanced by a point-by-point description of the parts of an entry.

Entry word

The spelling given for an entry word in current use is the generally accepted form; in the case of many obsolete loanwords having various spellings in the evidence, the principle of frequency and simplicity is followed. Occasionally, where two spellings are clearly in use for current words, both are given, as for *ooloo* or *ulu*, with no implication that one is preferable to the other. To conserve space, certain other measures have been adopted, for example: terms in which the simplex has a meaning identical with that of a compound are occasionally combined, as *bachelor* (*seal*); so with a number of terms having minor variations in form, as *Barren Ground(s) grizzly*; in the alphabetizing of such entries, the parenthetical material is ignored. Where this practice might cause the reader difficulty in locating the entry, a cross-entry has been set up.

When two or more entries have the same spelling but different etymologies, superior numbers are used to observe the distinction, as *boom*[1] and *boom*[2]; superior numbers are also used to distinguish similar forms having the same ultimate origin but arriving in Canadian English by historically different routes, as *voyage*[1] and *voyage*[2].

When two sequential entries differ only in that one normally has an upper-case, or capitalized, initial letter, the upper-case form is entered second, unless it is clearly the antecedent of the lower-case, or generalized, form. Finally, certain terms occur in the evidence in both upper- and lower-case forms; such are treated according to the general practice among modern writers represented in the evidence. Names of flora and fauna are regularly entered as lower-case forms, as *prairie lily*, unless the first element is a word normally requiring a capital letter, as *Canada jay*, *MacIntosh apple*, *Canadian horse*. Furthermore, the names of groups of people are usually entered as proper names, as *Bluenose*, *Doukhobor*, *Métis*; although the "either-or" formula is sometimes used where usage is markedly divided, as *Mountie* or *mountie*. In cases of divided usage in the use of upper- or lower-case forms, no attempt has been made to list as variant spellings the alternative not used in the entry words.

Compound words

Entry words formed by compounding make up such a large part of this dictionary that our treatment of them demands special attention. All compounds appear in proper alphabetical order whether printed as one word (*moosebird*), two words joined by a hyphen (*moose-fly*), or two independent words (*moose maple*). As a rule, such entries represent true compounds in that they have a referent quite distinct from the sum of their parts; thus *pemmican post* is entered because it is not self-explanatory and requires definition, whereas *pemmican shipment*, if it occurred at all in the evidence, would have been used only as an illustration of the word *pemmican*. Decisions as to whether a given compound was to be printed as one word, as a hyphenated word, or as two words were not always easy to make, for the style of treating such compounds has never been consistent in English. Such decisions were based on the evidence (which was not always helpful), on accepted practice (which is unsettled), or on value judgments relating to the appearance of the word as a unit. Moreover, the stress pattern was often taken into account along with other criteria—a sequence of a primary followed by a secondary stress dictating the use of either a block or a hyphenated form and the sequence of primary followed by another primary dictating a two-word entry. The final decision was often somewhat arbitrary although our overall handling of the problem is certainly more rational than was the case in the evidence we worked from. In any event, the forms set up as entry words in such cases are not intended as a reflection of accepted current usage with regard to the treatment of compounds since there is no such thing. Within the confines of our own book, however, the choice of one form or another does have an effect on the degree of detail included in a given entry, as will be seen from the discussion below.

Pronunciation

The pronunciation respelling comes immediately after the entry word and is given in the symbols of the International Phonetic Alphabet within square brackets; a pronunciation key is to be found on page *xxiii*. Such respellings are offered, as a rule, only for words not commonly entered in standard dictionaries, being considered redundant for commonplace words easily looked up elsewhere and for most compounds made up of such words; respellings are not offered for compounds containing words for which the pronunciation is given elsewhere in this dictionary. Moreover, no respellings are offered for terms labelled as obsolete, the pronunciation of many such being a matter of guesswork. Variant pronunciations of current terms are sometimes given; however, in keeping with the position that *A Dictionary of Canadianisms* is not intended as a guide to accepted spelling and pronunciation, most terms are respelled in one form

only, that being, to the best of the editors' knowledge, a currently acceptable variant.

Parts of speech

All entry words consisting of one word or of more than one word joined by hyphens are identified as parts of speech; such is not the case for unhyphenated two-word terms or phrases. Thus *face-off* is labelled *n.* for noun, whereas *face off*, a phrasal verb, is not labelled at all. Where a form has a different set of meanings as a noun, verb, adjective, or other part of speech, a distinct entry has been set up and labelled accordingly. In cases of entry words which have irregular plural forms or which are usually or always construed in the plural form, the appropriate information is given.

Etymology

Wherever relevant, the etymology of a term follows the part-of-speech label, enclosed in square brackets. In the typical entry the symbol < ("derived from") comes first, followed by the word in the source language, if different in form from the entry word, then the English gloss, if different in meaning from the following definition. Few words are traced back farther than the immediate source although for specific words detailed information may be offered. Needless to say, some etymologies are incomplete and others are shown to be uncertain because the facts are not known to the editors. If the origin of a word is a subject of controversy, or of wide speculation, as in the case of *Canada* or *Eskimo*, reference is made to a note occurring later in the entry, where the matter is discussed and, often, illustrated by a number of dated quotations. Indian and Eskimo words are transliterated in a non-technical way in the traditional English alphabet, augmented by macrons to signify long vowels. The evidence for many of these etymologies is based on older sources, most of them by linguistically naïve writers; unfortunately, the present state of Amerindian studies in Canada is quite inadequate to afford a practicable alternative. In any event, such approximations are probably quite adequate for the needs of the general reader and may, indeed, be easier to comprehend than a system of strange symbols representing the many unfamiliar sounds and sequences to be met with in the diverse languages in question.

Restrictive labels

Since many terms are largely confined to certain areas of use, a number of restrictive labels have been regularly employed. These may be grouped into the following categories, each of which is illustrated by examples: sphere (*Fur Trade, Lumbering*), locale (*Maritimes, North*), level (*Informal, Slang*), connotation (*Derog., Humorous*), and currency (*Obs., Hist., Rare*). The distinction between obsolete (*Obs.*) and historical (*Hist.*) terms is not always easy to establish, apart from the fact that all terms so labelled have reference to the past. In this dictionary, a term labelled *Obs.* has a referent solely in the past and is itself no longer in use; a term labelled *Hist.* has a referent in the past but is still used as a current term in historical contexts. Thus the terms *angle* (entrance to a beaver lodge) and *fathom fish* (oolichan) are obsolete, whereas *late-Loyalist* and *York boat* are historical. The absence of a recent quotation from the files does not necessarily mean that a given term has fallen into disuse, for the excerpters may have either looked in the wrong places or simply missed it. Such items known to the editors to be still current have not been labelled. On the other hand, an apparently obsolete term is no less obsolete by virtue of a recent writer's use of it in referring to or in glossing an earlier source. It must be observed that all labels reflect the editors' judgment, based on the evidence in the files and on their own knowledge and experience.

In some instances, special labels have been adopted, as for the few non-English terms entered for various reasons: *Cdn French, Chinook Jargon, Eskimo*. Such entries are not normally given pronunciation respellings or etymologies; the entry word, however, is given an English gloss if the meaning of the components is not directly clear from the definition, as *canot allège* "unburdened canoe." Restrictive labels precede the first definition if applicable to the entire entry; otherwise, they are placed before the definition to which they apply. It might be added that phrases are sometimes used in place of locale labels: "in Upper and Lower Canada," for instance, being preferable to a label for certain historical items current in a restricted area in colonial times. Further, the abbreviation *Esp.* ("especially") may be placed before any label to modify the degree of restrictiveness intended. Certain sets of quotations illustrating the figurative uses of a term are entered as a separate definition and identified either by the label *Figurative use* or by a phrase having the same significance.

Quotations

The quotations selected to illustrate each definition were chosen with the following ends in view: to supply the earliest and, usually, the latest evidence on file; to supply fuller descriptive detail than is possible or desirable in a definition; to supply definitions where acceptable and to which the reader may be referred; and to supply interesting, entertaining, and otherwise appropriate contexts in which the term occurs.

These quotations are, with rare exceptions, presented as grammatical sentences, irrelevant matter in the original usually being displaced by ellipsis dots or editorial interpolations set in square brackets: each is preceded by a brief bibliographical direction which gives year, source, and page number, the quotations for each definition being entered in chronological order. Square brackets are also used within quotations to enclose editorial interpolations intended to clarify ambiguities and obscurities; in addition, they are used to enclose certain quotations—usually early evidence—included as useful information but so set apart for one of the following reasons: (1) the source material is not Canadian or is not clearly Canadian; (2) the quotations explain, describe, or define the term in question without actually using it; (3) the term occurs in some other context not to be classed as evidence for the use of the term in English. The last category includes quotations from early French-Canadian sources and glosses appearing in the writings of early traders and explorers in contact with the Indians and Eskimos.

Although the illustrative quotations have been carefully chosen, a reader may sometimes feel that a given illustration could apply to other definitions as readily as to that to which it has been assigned. It must be remembered, however, that the quotation represents only part of a larger context in the source and that the citation slip usually provides the editor with considerably more information as to the meaning of the term in the larger context than the quotation itself might indicate. In situations where citation slips were ambiguous the deficient quotations have been set aside.

Bibliographical Directions

Special mention should be made of the bibliographical directions which precede each quotation. References to books are made by year, author, short title, and page number; where the author is anonymous, only the short title is given. Periodicals are referred to by year, title, month (or volume number), page, and where relevant, column. The books and periodicals consulted are listed in the bibliography. Newspapers, which are not listed in the bibliography, are referred to by year, title, place of publication (except where identified in the title), province (except for capital and certain other well-known cities), day, month, page, and column (except for advertisements, headlines, and captions, which are identified as such). If the name of the place of publication is obsolete, the current name is inserted in square brackets, as Rat Portage [Kenora], Ont. Finally, where dates are supplied in parentheses, they indicate the date of the edition used, the accompanying volume and page number referring to that edition. Thus a diary written in 1804 but published, say, in 1945 is entered as **1804**(1945). Where a book was first published in 1804 and presumably written at that time, the simple date **1804** is given; if this book was republished in

1900, the date **1804**(1900) is given, indicating that the page reference is to the 1900 edition. In the case of material reprinted in an anthology, a journal, a newspaper, or any other source, the date of the original material is given first and the date of the source in which it was reprinted is given in parentheses.

Sub-Entries

Idioms and phrases are entered in boldface type as numbered definitions under the key word; thus *by acclamation* is entered under *acclamation*. Where there is apt to be doubt as to the key word, a cross-reference is given; thus *bury the hatchet* is entered under *hatchet* and a simple cross-entry set up at *bury the hatchet*. Certain short verbal phrases are, however, listed as main entries in the manner of phrasal verbs — for example, *make fish*, *make fur*, and *make logs*.

Bibliography

The full bibliography of books and periodicals appended to this dictionary follows universally accepted principles of style and should therefore cause little difficulty. Such problems as might arise concerning the entries themselves are discussed in the introductory note to the bibliography on page 881.

General Aids to the Reader

Several additional devices are used throughout the dictionary to give the reader an opportunity to derive a maximum of information from the contents.

Within many entries are short notes (identified by this symbol ☛ and called "fist-notes") which offer various kinds of information relating to complex shifts in the meaning of words, especially complicated or disputed etymologies, expansions of general definitions, and other questions requiring more space for elucidation than is provided in the normal entry.

To conserve space, a system of "focal entries" has been established whereby one term, usually that most commonly used, functions as the focus for a group of synonyms; the entry word for this term carries the definition, all others being cross-referred to it. All entry words are, however, supported by quotations — with the exception of simple cross-reference entries identifying spelling or other variants. At these focal entries, a list of synonyms is provided.

The directive "See also" is used throughout for referring the reader both to synonyms and to certain other related entries having enlightening definitions or quotations.

The abbreviation Cp., used in place of "See also," refers the reader to a term (or terms) having a contrary meaning or a meaning in some way germane to a full understanding of the term being defined.

Other cross-references are made by means of the abbreviation *q.v.* placed within a definition, where it follows a term itself defined and illustrated in the dictionary. This device has permitted the editors to dispense with circumlocutions for Canadian terms having no commonplace synonym.

Economy is often achieved by making quotations do double duty. Thus the instruction "See 1801 quote" (or whatever the relevant year may be) is sometimes used in place of a definition where an adequate definition appears in the designated quotation following. Again, a quotation substitute such as "**1801** [see quote at **lumberjack**]" is sometimes given instead of repeating a quotation which has been entered elsewhere.

Several of the above-mentioned devices are used in the etymologies to direct the reader to entries having related etymologies or other pertinent information.

Finally, there are a substantial number of line drawings included in the dictionary to aid the reader in visualizing the entry concerned. Such drawings are normally placed adjacent to the entry; wherever such is not the case, as when the drawing is located near a synonym elsewhere in the dictionary, the reader is directed to it by a cross-reference.

In these many ways, the editors have striven to produce a reference book in which the information is easy of access as well as interesting and informative. It is our hope that those who make use of the results of our work will find the experience both rewarding and entertaining.

Abbreviations

a	ante (before)	coy	company
abbrev.	abbreviation	cp.	compare
acct	account	C.W.	Canada West
adj.	adjective	*DA*	*Dictionary of Americanisms*
admin.	administration	Dan.	Danish
adv.	adverb	Dec.	December
advert.	advertisement, advertising	def.	definition
Algonk.	Algonkian	dept	department
Alta	Alberta	derog.	derogatory
Am.	America, American	descr.	description, descriptive
Am.E	American English	dial.	dialect
Amer.	America, American	dict.	dictionary
Am. Ind.	American Indian	dim.	diminutive
Am.Sp.	American Spanish	dly	daily
ann.	annual	doc.	document(s)
anthol.	anthology	Du.	Dutch
anthrop.	anthropology, anthropological	E	English
antiq.	antiquarian	E.	Eastern
app.	appendix	East.	Eastern
Apr.	April	econ.	economy, economic
arch.	archive(s)	*EDD*	*English Dialect Dictionary*
art.	article	ed.	edition
assn	association	encyc.	encyclopedia
attrib.	attribute, attributive(ly)	Eng.	English
Aug.	August	Esk.	Eskimo
autobiog.	autobiographical, autobiography	esp.	especially
B.C.	British Columbia	et al.	*et alii* (and others)
biog.	biography, biographical	etc.	et cetera
Brit.	British	ethnol.	ethnology, ethnological
bull.	bulletin	exped.	expedition(s)
bur.	bureau	explor.	exploration(s), exploring
c	circa (about)	F	French
c.	century	Feb.	February
Can.	Canada	fem.	feminine
Capt.	Captain	fig.	figurative
catal.	catalogue	fn.	footnote
Cdn	Canadian	ft	fort
Cdn F	Canadian French	G	German
C.E.	Canada East	gaz.	gazette
cent.	centennial	gen.	general
cf.	confer	geog.	geography, geographic(al)
chron.	chronicle(s)	Gk.	Greek
co.	company	Gmc	Germanic
comm.	commerce, commercial;	gr.	grade
	commission, committee	gt	great
conj.	conjunction	H.B.	Hudson('s) Bay
Corp.	Corporal; corporation	H.B.C.	Hudson's Bay Company
corr.	correspondence	hist.	history, historical

H.M.	His (Her) Majesty's	pl.	plural
H.M.S.	His (Her) Majesty's Ship	pp.	past participle; pages
ibid.	*ibidem* (the same)	prep.	preposition
i.e.	*id est* (it is)	prob.	probability, probably
ill., illust.	illustrated	proc.	proceedings
imp.	imperial	pron.	pronunciation
imper.	imperative	prov.	province, provincial
ind.	industry, industrial	pt	part
Ind.	Indian	pub.	public, publication
infin.	infinitive	pubs	publications
inter.	intermediate; interior	qtly	quarterly
interj.	interjection	Que.	Quebec
Ital.	Italian	q.v.	*quod vide* (which see)
Jan.	January	qq.v.	*qua vide* (which see)
jnl(s)	journal(s)	R.C.M.P.	Royal Canadian Mounted Police
L	Latin	R.M.C.	Royal Military College
Lab.	Labrador	rec.	record(s)
lang.	language	rep.	report(s)
L.C.	Lower Canada	rev.	revised; revue
letts	letters	Rev.	Reverend
lib.	library	roy.	royal
ling.	linguistics, linguistic	R.R.S.	Red River Settlement
lit.	literature, literary; literally	Ry	railway
mag.	magazine	S.	South, Southern
Man.	Manitoba	Sask.	Saskatchewan
Mar.	March	Sat.	Saturday
masc.	masculine	Scand.	Scandinavian
mem.	memoir(s)	sci.	science, scientifical
meteor.	meteorology, meteorological	sec.	section
Mex.	Mexico, Mexican	Sep., Sept.	September
min.	mineral(s)	sing.	singular
mod.	modern	soc.	society
MS	manuscript	S.	South, Southern
MSS	manuscripts	South.	Southern
mtd	mounted	sp.	special
mthly	monthly	Sp.	Spanish
n	note	specif.	specifically
n.	noun	St.	Saint
N.	North, Northern	stat.	statistical, statistics
N.A.	North America	stud.	studies
narr.	narrative	supp.	supplement(s)
nat.	national; natural	topogr.	topography, topographical
N.B.	New Brunswick	Tor.	Toronto
n.d.	no date	trans.	transaction(s); translation, translated
Nfld	Newfoundland	Turk.	Turkish
no.	number	U	university
No.	North	U.B.C.	University of British Columbia
Nov.	November	U.C.	Upper Canada
N.S.	Nova Scotia	U.E.	United Empire
N.W.	Northwest, North West	ult.	ultimately
N.W.Co.	North West Company	univ.	university
N.W.M.P.	North West Mounted Police	U of T	University of Toronto
N.W.T.	Northwest Territories	usu.	usually
obs.	obsolete; observations	v.	verb
Oct.	October	var.	variant, various
OED	*Oxford English Dictionary*	vocab.	vocabulary
ON	Old Norse	voy.	voyage
Ont.	Ontario	W.	West, Western
orig.	originally	West.	Western
p.	page	wkly	weekly
parl.	parliament, parliamentary	vol.	volume
P.E.I.	Prince Edward Island	vols	volumes
phil.	philosophy, philosophical	yr	year
Pg.	Portuguese	Y.T.	Yukon Territory

Pronunciation Key

VOWELS

i	feel, beer, pretty	ə	sofa ['sofə]	u	fool, boor
ɪ	fill		above [əˈbʌv]	ʊ	full
e	fail	ɝ	fur [fɝ]	o	foal
ɛ	fell, fair	ɚ	further [ˈfɝðɚ]	ɔ	form, roar
æ	pal			ɑ	law, father,
a	farm	ʌ	mud, brother		caught, cot
aɪ	file, kite	aʊ	foul, pout	ɔɪ	foil, boy

CONSONANTS

p	pill	θ	thill, thing	dʒ	Jill, judge
b	bill	ð	they'll, then	m	mill
t	till	s	sill	n	nil
d	dill	z	zeal	ŋ	sing, sink
k	kill	ʃ	shill, wish	l	Lil
g	gill	ʒ	rouge, loge	w	will
f	fill	h	hill	r	rill
v	villa	tʃ	chill, church	j	yell

When needed, standard symbols from the International Phonetic Alphabet are used to show the pronunciation of words from French.

STRESS

Three levels of stress are distinguished: primary [ˈ], secondary [ˌ], tertiary (unstressed), the mark symbolizing the first two levels being placed *before* the relevant syllable, that for the third being omitted. Where monosyllabic words are respelled, no stress is given, primary stress being the only one possible under such circumstances. Examples: *pin* [pɪn]; *pinner* [ˈpɪnɚ]; *pinhead* [ˈpɪnˌhɛd]; *pincushion* [ˈpɪnˌkʊʃən]; *kingpin* [ˈkɪŋˌpɪn].

xxiii

A Dictionary of Canadianisms

on Historical Principles

abatteau *n.* See **aboiteau.**

Abegweit ['æbəg,wɪt] *n.* [< Algonk.: Micmac] an Indian name for Prince Edward Island.
1855 *Anglo-American Mag.* 68/1: The country people will not use or adopt that pretty word "Epaigwit," 'the home of the wave' . . . **1962** *Canada Month* Apr. 49/3: Abegweit is the Micmac Indian name for Prince Edward Island; tradition says it was given . . . by the Micmacs' mighty god Glooscap. It means "resting place."

Aberhartism ['ebəˌhartizəm] *n. Hist.* the political and financial policies developed as the basis of Social Credit government by William Aberhart, Premier of Alberta, 1935 to 1943.
1956 *Financial Post* 30 June 6/2: East of Manitoba, where 75 percent of Canadians live, the country is still impervious to Aberhartism.

aboideau *n.* See **aboiteau.**

aboiteau ['æbəˌto] *n.* **-x** or **-s.** [< Cdn F] Also spelled *abatteau, aboideau. Maritimes.*
☞ *The etymology of* **aboiteau** *has not been satisfactorily explained. The following quotations are offered as examples of suggested origins:*
1898 *N.B.Mag.* I 226: I have always understood that the word "aboiteau" came from the French words "aboi," "d'eau"; "aboi"—to keep at bay, "d'eau"— the water. It is a poetical expression taken from hunting—the moose keeping the dogs at bay. . . . *Ibid.* 225: Possibly, [aboiteau] . . . was "une boîte d'eau," but more probably "à la boîte d'eau," or "à boîte d'eau"—at the water-box. . . . *Ibid.* 341: I came to the conclusion that [aboiteau] is a condensation of . . . "l'abée d'eau." Abée is a well-established old French word, whose meaning is a mill-dam, or, simply, a dam.
1 a dike (def. 1) or dam equipped with a gate which functions as a valve releasing flood water from behind but preventing sea water from entering at high tide. See also **bito** and **marsh dike.**
[**1708** (1898) *N.B.Mag.* I 342: On n'arrête pas le cours de la Mer aisément; cependant les Acadiens en viennent à bout par de puissantes Digues qu'ils appelent des Aboteaux. . . .] **1825** *Novascotian* (Halifax) 9 Mar. 86/1: Before half an hour the violence of the water washed away with a fearful rapidity the complete side of the abatteau and left the other a shattered and disfigured monument to their enterprise. **1957** WRIGHT *Blomidon Rose* 126: Beyond Avonport Station, we cross an aboiteau and reach the sands at Oak Bluffs.
2 the sluice-gate, or valve, arrangement in the dike.
1899 *N.B.Mag.* II 22: The dyke and aboideau served the purpose of shutting out the tide from about 600 acres of marsh. **1960** *Cdn Geog.Jnl* Oct. 116/2: The English apparently learned from the Acadians the special arts of building dikes and *aboiteaux.*

above *adj. or adv.* **1** above zero Fahrenheit. Cp. **below** (def. 1).
1881 *Edmonton Bull.* 28 Feb. 1/2: Highest temperature last week was 39 degrees above . . . and lowest 33 below. . . . **1965** *Globe and Mail* (Toronto) 22 Mar. 5/9: Yesterday, springtime brought temperatures to 20 above in both centres.
2 See **above discovery.** Cp. **below** (def. 2).
1898 *Yukon Midnight Sun* (Dawson) 25 July 1/2: Fifteen miles up from the mouth Eldorado creek puts into Bonanza at No. 4 above. . . . **1924** DORRANCE *Never Fire First* 203: . . . Seymour sought out Hoodoo Creek on the map and found the claim accredited to Cato—Thirteen above.

above discovery of a mining claim, located at a position designated as being at a certain distance above or upstream from the original discovery claim, *q.v.*, on a creek. Cp. **below discovery.**
1897 *Slocan Pioneer* (B.C.) 28 Aug. 3/2: They went up to 49 and 50 miles above Discovery, and also staked two claims on the right fork. **1926** DILL *Long Day* 89: There was "No. 1 above discovery," or the land immediately adjoining the claim upon which the gold was first found up the creek. . . .

abroad *adj. or adv. Atlantic Provinces and North* in phrases, of sea ice, broken up and dispersed.
1909 GRENFELL *Adrift on an Ice-Pan* 31: The ice was now "all abroad," which I was sorry for, for there was a big safe pan not twenty yards from me. **1916** DUNCAN *Billy Topsail* 130: As they say on the coast, the ice had "gone abroad."

absentee ballot See 1965 quote.
1957 *Commonwealth* 18 Dec. 7/4: . . . people now are able to vote by absentee ballot in a provincial election, and when a federal election comes along they are completely confused. **1965** *Globe and Mail* (Toronto) 18 Mar. 25/7: . . . a voter who expects to be away

from his home riding at the time of an election should vote in that riding by absentee ballot.

absentee voter 1 *Obs.* a person allowed to vote by proxy in an election.
1859 *Brit.Colonist* (Victoria) 22 Jan. 1/1: It is not generally known that a law exists in this colony by which an absentee voter can vote by proxy.
2 See **absent voter.**

absentee voting voting in an election by persons temporarily away from their ridings.
1953 *Provincial Voters Act* 47: Absentee voting permitted where Returning Officer has not issued transfer certificate. **1963** *Calgary Herald* 17 Dec. 11/8: The commissioner is instructed to make his recommendations about permanent voters' lists and absentee voting. . . .

absent voter a voter who casts an absentee ballot, *q.v.*
1953 *Provincial Voters Act* 48: Where the Deputy Returning Officer is entitled to record his vote as an absent voter under this section, he may make the affidavit before the Poll Clerk. . . .

abuckwan [æ'bʌkwən] *n.* [< Algonk.: Cree] a skin or canvas sheet used as a shelter.
*c*1902 LAUT *Trapper* 119: In this case he uses the *abuckwan*—canvas—for a shed tent, with one side sloping to the ground, banked by brush and snow, the other facing the fire, both tent and fire on such a slope that the smoke drifts out while the heat reflects in. **1913** WILLIAMS *Wilderness Trail* 186: I'd rather battle with winter's cold under an *abuckwan*, and running my line of traps, than live in the finest house in Winnipeg.

Acadia [ə'kediə] *n.* [see 1963 quote (def. 1)]
1 *Hist.* a former French colony on the Atlantic coast of N. America, which included the present Maritime Provinces and adjacent parts of Quebec and New England. See also **La Cadia** and **l'Acadie.**
1684 (1885) RADISSON *Voyages* 259: Wee arrived at Accadia the 26th of november, 1682, and there winter'd. **1963** *Time* (Cdn ed.) 26 Apr. 12/2: France had named its Maritimes possessions *Acadia,* probably after the Greek Arcadia, a one-time "land of happiness."
2 *Hist.* the Maritime Provinces.
1864 *Islander* (Charlottetown) 9 Sep. 2/3: The man in any of the Colonies who has a single objection to offer to a Legislative union of Acadia has as yet failed to state it. **1899** *N.B.Mag.* II 46: Bertrand is another name contained in the census of 1671 which has practically disappeared from Acadia.
3 the areas of French settlement and culture in the Maritime Provinces.
1963 *Time* (Cdn ed.) 26 Apr. 12/3: The creation of the FRENCH University of Moncton deserves to be underlined as a new step in the cultural emancipation of Acadia.
4 a name for a proposed province to be formed through union of the present Maritime Provinces.
1964 *Star Wkly* 12 Dec. 7/2: . . . several names have already been suggested [for the new Maritime province], including Maritopia, Atlantica, Atlanta, Acadia and even New England.

Acadian *n.* a native or inhabitant of Acadia, especially a French-speaking descendant of the early French settlers in what are now the Maritime Provinces.
1760 PICHON *Cape Breton* 96: The settlements on the island of St. John increase every day by the arrival of Acadians and others. . . . **1964** *Chronicle-Herald* (Halifax) 17 June 4/1: Acadians tend to criticize the parochialism and the excesses of the French nationalists.

Acadian *adj.* of or having to do with Acadia, its people, customs, language, etc.
1720 RICHARD *Acadia* I 121: . . . I have thought . . . to send home the Acadian deputies with smooth words and promises of enlargement of time. **1896** *Trans.Roy.Soc.Can.* II 2 254: [Mizzenette Point is] no doubt an alteration of the Acadian Maisonette— little house, used by the Acadians for the Indian houses to the present day. **1964** *Evening Patriot* (Charlottetown) 16 June 4/1: The Canadian Historical Association last night conferred on him an award of merit in recognition of his contribution to Acadian history over the years.

Acadian French 1 See **Acadian,** *n.*
1806 STEWART *Acct P.E.I.* 153: It is not denied by the old Accadian French still resident on the Island, that they were very partial to this savage practice of their neighbours, with whom indeed they were very much assimilated in manners and customs. **1963** *Time* (Cdn ed.) 26 Apr. 12/3: Though New Brunswick is 40% Acadian French, it is only now that the insistent demand . . . for French education is bearing fruit.
2 the dialect of French spoken in areas of French settlement in the Maritimes.
1957 HUTCHISON *Canada* 48: My inquiries elicited from a grizzled man behind a team of black oxen only a skeptical shake of the head, and a torrent of Acadian French.

Acadian Frenchman See **Acadian,** *n.*
1828 MCGREGOR *Maritime Colonies* 56: I have been told by an old Acadian Frenchman, that . . . a vast number of horses were running in a wild state about the east point of the island. **1854** *Anglo-American Mag.* IV 28/1: An Acadian Frenchman with a horse, cart, and a whole bushel of potatoes, was met about seven miles from Richibucto. . . .

Acadian Neutral See **French Neutral.**
1924 *Cdn Hist.Rev.* V 108: Much has been written about the expatriation of the "Acadian Neutrals" in 1775 and about the causes. . . .

Acadian owl a small, brown, eastern sub-species, *Cryptoglaux acadica acadica,* of the saw-whet, *q.v.* See also **sawyer** (def. 2).
1868 *Cdn Naturalist* III 414: The Acadian or little owl makes its abode in barns during the winter. **1922** TAVERNER *Birds Eastern Can.* 138: There are several subspecies of the Saw-whet Owl in Canada; but only one, the Acadian Owl, the type form, is ever found in the east.

Acadian Provinces *Hist.* See **Maritime Provinces.**
1875 *Canadian Mthly* Apr. 292/1: The Acadian Provinces abound in memorials of the French régime. **1948** BORRETT *Historic Halifax* 3: Halifax, the metropolis of Nova Scotia, and the chief city of the

Acadian or Lower Provinces, was founded in the year 1749. . . .

Acadie n. *Archaic or Poetic*. See **Acadia**. Also spelled *Acady*.
1630 (1835) STIRLING *Register* I 104-6: The King of France by his commissione, doeth assure to himself all that part of America which lyeth eleuatione from the fortie to sixty degree, whereby he doeth incluid the River of Canada, all Acady, which incluids all New England and New Scotland, theas lying in lethe by the sea coast some xix hundrithe myllis. **1934** DENNIS *Down in N.S.* 72: They sent a force over the sea from France and one over the land from Quebec, to regain the fortress and at the same time to take all Acadie.

Acadien n. *Cdn French* See **Acadian**.

Accadia n. See **Acadia**.

accepted (bank) cheque a certified cheque.
1886 *Indian* (Hagersville, Ont.) 3 Feb. 6/1: Contractors are requested to bear in mind that an accepted bank cheque for the sum of $600 must accompany each tender. **1902** *High River Times* (Alta) 11 July 2/4: All tenders must be accompanied by an accepted Cheque or Express Order, in favour of the Commissioner of Public Works.

access road 1 a road giving access to areas not served by highways. See also **resources road**.
1953 *North Star* (Yellowknife) Jan.-Feb. 1/2: In anticipation of the expanding operations an access road was completed this year to connect with the Mackenzie Highway at a point 26 miles south of its northern terminus at Hay River on the south shore of Great Slave Lake. **1963** *Cdn Geog.Jnl* Feb. 70/1: The paper companies built access roads for cutting and hauling out the pulpwood, but these seldom helped to connect the communities.
2 a road giving access to a main highway, especially to an expressway.
1958 *Edmonton Jnl* 24 June 3 18/5: The bridge has no access roads as yet, but was built for future requirements. **1964** *Naicam Sentinel* (Sask.) 26 Mar. 2/4: That we ask . . . for assistance in gravelling the access roads into Lac Vert and Pleasantdale.

acclaim (to) v. elect by acclamation.
1955 *Record-Gaz.* 3 Mar. 1/1: The three pictured above were acclaimed to their respective posts. **1964** *Martlet* (U. of Victoria) 8 Oct. 1/1: Also acclaimed were Rosalind Boyd . . . as CUS chairman, Kathy Harvey . . . as secretary, and Joan Mackenzie . . . as social convenor.

acclamation n. **1** the election of a candidate without opposition.
1885 GEMMILL *Companion* 262/2: Mr. Archambault being unseated, a new election took place 19 June 1884: Alfred Lapointe . . . Acclamation. **1964** *Martlet* (U. of Victoria) 8 Oct. 1/1: Acclamations have filled all students' council positions vacated through resignations but one.
2 by acclamation, (elected) without opposition.
1827 *Gore Gaz.* (Ancaster, U.C.) 8 Dec. 161/2: It would appear that the friends of Mr. Papineau intended that the election should be carried unanimously, and by acclamation, in his favor; and, notwithstanding the nomination of Mr. Vallieres, [they] seemed to look down on any division in the body. **1964** *Dly Colonist* (Victoria) 8 Oct. 20/1: Winnipeg Mayor Stephen Juba Wednesday became the first mayor from this city to be elected by acclamation in nearly a quarter of a century.

3 with acclamation, *Now Rare* by acclamation.
1844 *Examiner* (Toronto) 23 Oct. 3/1: Yesterday, the election was held for this County, when Jacob De Witt, Esq. a strong supporter of the late Ministers, was returned with acclamation.

accommodation† n. an accommodation stage or train.
1902 *Gun and Rod in N.B.* 67: Parties can therefore come to Harcourt, 37 miles from Moncton, wire the station agent at Kent Junction to procure supplies and hire guides, and go forward themselves a little later by the freight or accommodation, as may suit their convenience. **1957** WRIGHT *Blomidon Rose* 132: There is another morning train to Halifax, a very leisurely mixed train, the unaccommodating sort of slow train which is known as an accommodation.

accommodation stage† *Obs.* a local stagecoach.
1849 ALEXANDER *L'Acadie* II 86: After leaving Woodstock by what was called the accommodation stage, a long open waggon, holding nine passengers, we had not proceeded far, before we came to a descent and a bridge over a deep ravine. . . .

accommodation train† a local train made up of freight and passenger cars; a mixed train.
1902 *Gun and Rod in N.B.* 67: Express trains do not stop at Kent Junction, but the accommodation train does, as do the regular freight trains. **1907** MILLAIS *Newfoundland* 134: The people of the island regard the "accommodation train" with dread; strangers suffering a single journey resolve never to repeat the experiment.

Ace-away n. See quote.
1956 (1960) NELSON *Northern Lights* 317: In the back room of the Army and Navy Club the Ace-Away game—a hangover from the war days played with three dice—still had its followers.

ace-high adj. highly esteemed.
1910 SERVICE *Trail of '98* 323: . . . You've always been ace-high with me, and there never will come the day when you can't eat on my meal-ticket. . . . **1958** *Citizen* 7 Nov. 4/5: The once very popular CBC Fishermen's Broadcast once again stands ace high with the fishing fleet with word from director Tom Leach that the program has returned to its early morning schedule.

achigan ['æʃɪgən] n. [< Cdn F < Algonk.: Ojibwa *ashigan*] *Rare* the small-mouthed black bass, *Micropterus dolomieu*. Cp. **malachigan**.
1800 (1897) COUES *New Light* I 102: My party went out to seine, and soon came back with a sturgeon, three catfish, eight brim, four achegan, five doré, three pike, and a few lacaishe. **1907** HODGE *Bulletin* I 8/2: Achigan . . . A French-Canadian name of the small-mouthed black bass . . . occasionally found in English writings.

acre n. a linear measurement equal to twenty-two yards, now obsolete except in the Province of Quebec.
1788 (1951) ROE *North Amer.Buffalo* 845: A request of the North West Company for a grant of land one acre in width from Lake Superior to Long Lake. **1830** (1948) McLOUGHLIN *Letters* 72: Your Canoe . . .

was found about an acre below the Mill. **1887** *Senate Report* 125: The length of the dam would certainly be several acres.

across the border in the United States of America. See also **border**.
1865 *Leader* (Toronto) 4 Feb. 1/7: In this respect it is not unlike the people in this part of the country, who in comparison with their neighbors across the border, or even with the Upper Canadians, are slow as a stagecoach of a hundred years ago. **1955** *Lethbridge Herald* (Alta) 4 Mar. 4/1: Uncle Sam has been inclined of late to by-pass such trade agreements by quotas and the like, some of which have injured Canada's sales across the border.

across the line(s) in the United States of America. See also **line** (def. 2).
1825 *Canadian Mag.* IV 214: The landlord was demonstrating his claim to be considered a yankee from having been [a]cross the line on a smuggling expedition where he lost his whole venture. **1849** *Wkly Globe* 16 Nov. 77/6: It was not mere theory. They saw prosperity on the other side of the lines. Products were across the lines worth 20 per cent more than here. Property 50 per cent more. **1958** *B.C.Labour* June 4/1: Unions can't do anything without the okay from across the line.

activity-room *n.* in some schools, a room used for games, folk-dancing, music, meetings, plays, etc.
1958 *Citizen* 30 Oct. 6A/1: Mothers of Norgate School children are providing cakes, pies and cookies for the . . . bake sale to be held in the school activity room Saturday, November 1, at 2 p.m. **1962** *School Building Manual* 41: Activity-rooms will be approved for all elementary schools of more than four or five classrooms.

actual settler† *Hist.* a person improving land he has taken up, as distinguished from a land speculator. Cp. **settler**.
1799 *U.C.Gaz.* (York [Toronto]) 14 Dec. 4/3: Notice is hereby given, that the reserves on Dundas-street are now ready to be Leased; and will be leased to actual Settlers only, on such terms as may be known at the Council-Office. **1909** HUNTER *Simcoe County* I 56: The actual settlers had to open and improve their roads, build the school houses and churches, and otherwise enhance the value of the speculator's land, while the speculator himself was sleeping.

administrative district *N.W.T.* a district having local self-government through a council which is partly elected and partly appointed.
1952 *North Star* (Yellowknife) Dec. 2/1: The campaign for election to the Yellowknife Town Council, still officially termed the Trustee Board of the Yellowknife Administrative District, has been settled for 1953. **1953** *Ibid.* Nov. 1/2: Having obtained the right to local democratic government, the Municipality (formerly an "Administrative District") will elect for the first time all members of its Council.

administrator *n. Hist.* the chief executive officer of an administrative area; sometimes, a deputy for the Governor-in-Chief or for the Lieutenant-Governor.
1796 *U.C.Gaz.* (York [Toronto]) 2 Nov. 3/3: His honor, the administrator, has been pleased to appoint Thos' Ridout, esq. register for the county of York, in this province. **1848** (1866) CHRISTIE *Lower Canada* II 2: Soon after his excellency's arrival, major general Brock was appointed president and administrator of the government in Upper Canada, instead of lieut.-governor Gore, who recently retired. **1932** *Ont.Hist.* I iii: When Hon. Peter Russell became the administrator of the civil government of Upper Canada, he was . . . subject to much ill health.

admiral *n. Hist.* See **fishing admiral**.
1620 WHITBOURNE *Discovrse* 21: And thus they doe, striuing to be there first in a Harbour, to obtaine the name of Admirall that yeere: and so, to haue the chiefest place to make their fish on, where they may doe it with the greatest ease, and haue the choice of diuers other necessaries in the Harbors, which do them little stead: but the taking of them wrongs many others of your Maiesties subiects, which arriue there after the first. **1907** *U of T Stud.Hist.& Econ.* II 271: The democratic English, however, made the admiral change about each week so that each master in turn became ruler. **1965** MACNUTT *Atlantic Provinces* 18: Justice might have been won by the presentation if . . . a flowing bowl of calabogus, a favorite drink of the admirals. . . .

advance poll a poll where an advance vote, *q.v.,* may be cast.
1957 *Commonwealth* 18 Dec. 7/4: . . . there are very few advance polls in rural ridings and a person may have to travel 50 to 100 miles to reach that poll. **1963** *Kingston Whig-Standard* (Ont.) 5 Mar. 22/4: Realization of an advance poll for Kingston is again in the hands of the administration and legislation committee.

advance(d) polling day a day designated for an advance poll.
1963 *Kingston Whig-Standard* (Ont.) 5 Mar. 22/4: The committee will consider . . . a recommendation . . . that Monday and Tuesday preceding election day be designated as advanced polling days.

advances *n.pl.* goods such as ammunition, clothing, tobacco, and knives, as a grubstake advanced to hunters, trappers, and others dealing with fur-trading companies, to be later deducted from the payment for their catches. See also **debt**.
1801 (1897) COUES *New Light* I 186: I gave the . . . men their equipment and advances. **1848** BALLANTYNE *Hudson's Bay* 110: They all proceeded to the trading-room, for the purpose of taking "advances," in the shape of shirts, trousers, bonnets, caps, tobacco, knives, capotes, and all the other things necessary for a long, rough journey. **1947** *Cdn Hist.Rev.* Dec. 402: [The French] introduced the practice of fall "advances" which is still the basis of Canadian fur trade.

advance vote See quote.
1962 *Weekend Mag.* 26 May 22/1: In this election an advance vote may be cast by anyone who believes he will be absent from his polling division on the day of the election.

aeroquay ['ɛrəˌki] *n.* [*aero-* + *quay*] an airport building comprising administrative and operational offices, restaurant, etc. with departure and arrival areas.
1958 *Kingston Whig-Standard* (Ont.) 8 Apr. 12/6: The terminal facilities . . . consist of a central structure for

administrative and operational offices and four circular buildings or aeroquays from which passengers will board and disembark from aircraft. The aeroquays will be circular self-contained buildings from which several aircraft can be loaded and unloaded simultaneously. **1964** *Imperial Oil Rev.* Feb. 23/3: Out of this came what the architects call an aeroquay. It's a multi-storied building within a building, looking like a two-storey ship's wheel with six spokes and an eight-storey rectangular building as its hub.

after man *Fur Trade, Obs.* the paddler in the stern of a canoe.
1806 (1960) FRASER *Letters and Journals* 205: . . . the after man, Saucier, [is] both weak and sickly and scarcely able to perform the duty of middleman. . . .

agency *n.* **1** See **Indian agency** (def. 1).
1958 *Hansard* (4119-29) 31 Jan.: This agency in Yellowknife is covering an area of many thousands of square miles. **1964** *Sask.News* Mar. 4/3: He was a member of the Sakimay Band in the Crooked Lakes Agency and was regarded as a shrewd, wise man, by the rest of the Band.
2 See **Indian agency** (def. 2).
1881 (1910) HAYDON *Riders of Plains* 96: While we were waiting near the Agency for another horse which an Indian had promised to bring in, a minor chief, "Many Spotted Horses," appeared and commenced a violent speech, calling upon the Indians not to give up the horses. **1954** EVANS *Mist* 153: . . . they would file into the Agency office with their hats in their hands and sit down to a white man's business meeting.

agent *n.* **1** See **Indian superintendent.**
1775 *Ont.Bur.Arch.Rep.* IV 76: The said Agents or Superintendents shall have power to Confer such Honors and Rewards on the Indians, as shall be necessary. **1956** KEMP *Northern Trader* 27: None of us knew what he was trying to say until Pat interpreted. Pat told the Agent, "Says his wife has just had a baby, and how about another five bucks." **1965** *Time* (Cdn ed.) 13 Aug. 10/1: . . . Churchill's Indian affairs agents have set up a guide training course and a Tourist Whaling Guide Center.
2 *Hist.* See quotes. See also **eastern partner.** Cp. **wintering partner** (def. 1).
1802 (1900) MASSON *Les Bourgeois* II 466: The said partners shall assume and be stiled Agents of the North West Company and shall be aided and assisted in all occasions by the Wintering partners. . . . *a*1855 (1956) ROSS *Fur Hunters* 69: . . . Mackenzie handed him his instructions, a letter from the Agent at Montreal, with a copy of the minutes of the council at Fort William. **1918** DAVIDSON *North West Co.* 15: Of these [shares] a certain proportion was held by persons who managed the business in Canada and were styled agents of the company. Their duty was to import the necessary goods from England, store them at their own expense at Montreal, get them made up into articles suited for the trade, pack and forward them, and supply the funds that might be wanting for the outfits. . . . **1956** INNIS *Fur Trade* 244: These agents arranged with the partners of the Company in the interior (the wintering partners) each year at Grand Portage for the general management of the business.

aglo or **agloo** *n.* See **aglu.**

aglu ['æglu] *n.* [< Esk.] a breathing-hole in ice, made by seals. See also **air-hole** (def. 2), **blowhole, seal hole,** and **seal igloo.** Also spelled *aglo, agloo.*

[**1836** HUISH *Last Voyage* 701: Seal-hole Ag-loo]
1882 GILDER *Schwatka's Search* 142: . . . no work of any kind . . . can be done upon new skins until the ice has formed sufficiently thickly upon the salt water to permit the hunter to seek the seal at his agloo or blow-hole. **1959** LEISING *Arctic Wings* 310: He does this by going from one hole, or aglu, to another, to keep the holes open as the ice freezes.

agokwa† [ə'gokwə] *n.* [< Algonk.] See **berdash** (def. 1).
1830 (1940) TANNER *Narrative* 105: This man was one of those who make themselves women and are called women by the Indians. There are several of this sort amongst most, if not all the Indian tribes; they are commonly called A-go-kwa, a word which is expressive of their condition. **1951** O'MEARA *Grand Portage* Glossary: Agokwa . . . men who made themselves women.

agrais *n.* See **agrès.**

ag.rep. See **agricultural representative.**
1958 *Kingston Whig-Standard* (Ont.) 14 Jan. 6/8: Don McArthur, "ag-rep" for Frontenac County, will be the principal speaker. **1963** *Sask.News* 15 Jan. 1/1: Greg Barnsley . . . is producer and host along with ag. reps. Don Blackburn [and others].

agrès ['ægre] *n.* [< Cdn F < F *agrès* tackle, rigging] *Hist.* **1** the travelling equipment of a canoe, York boat, etc. See also **agrets** and **tripping kit.**
1814 WENTZEL *Letters* I 111: . . . I saw them . . . in the garret of the Athabaska House mingled with old useless agrès of canoes. . . . **1853** (1953) RAE *Correspondence* 246: The cargo and agres are correct as per Bill of Lading.
2 equipment for any kind of expedition; outfit.
1824 BLACK *Journal* 185: Got our Fishing agres in order & our Nets set. **1855** *Kamloops Jnl* (B.C.) 30 May: Danneau arranging the Horse Agrais.

agrets ['ægre] *n.* [< Cdn F; var. of F *agrès*] *Hist.* **1** See **agrès** (def. 1).
1872 MCDONALD *Peace River* 44n: . . . Agrets is the voyageur word for "outfit" and is applied also to equipment for canoes. . . . **1874** (1956) *Alta Hist.Rev.* Spring 12: Gave out the agrets for the Boats. **1941** *Beaver* June 36/1: Agrets—the travelling equipment of a York Boat; *i.e.,* cooking utensils, portage straps, tarpaulins, tents, tools, etc. **1964** INNIS *Fur Trade* 293: The boats were expected to last two seasons, although the main line, the painter, and some other parts of the *agrets* lasted only one year.
2 See **agrès** (def. 2).
1913 COWIE *Adventurers* 213: . . . at the north end [was] a large [room] for . . . the equipments— called *agrets*—required for sleds and carts on the voyage. **1923** *Beaver* Nov. 53: The guide would look after the "agrets," which means all the requirements for the brigade. . . .

agricultural representative a government official who advises farmers, ranchers, fruit-growers, etc. See also **ag.rep.**

1959 STEWART & FRENCH *No Quarter* 96: The Junior Farmers were government sponsored and, to some extent, government controlled, with the Agricultural Representative in the district a moving spirit in them. **1964** *Globe and Mail* (Toronto) 10 Sep. 25/8: . . . their function is something like that of the various agricultural representatives—Ag Reps—that the provincial government has established in every county.

Ahlied *n.* See **Alaid.**

ahrubahboo *n.* See **rubaboo.**

ahtikameg *n.* See **atikameg.**

ahtook [ˈɑtuk] *n.* [< Esk.] See **caribou** (def. 1). See also **tuktu** (def. 1).
1934 GODSELL *Arctic Trader* 27: They explained to Cotter and the mate that they were following the ahtook, or deer. . . .

air bus an airliner which passengers board without buying tickets in advance.
1963 *Toronto Dly Star* 14 Sep. 10/3: Canada's first . . . airbus service reports early success. . . . **1964** *Calgary Herald* 17 Jan. 22/6: Pacific Western Airlines "air bus" lost a wheel landing at Calgary's McCall Field Thursday afternoon.

air harbo(u)r 1 *Obs.* an airport.
1936 *Cdn Geog.Jnl* XIII 321/1: The first civil air harbour in Canada was then established, and the first practical use of aircraft for civil purposes was then got under way. **1956** BERTON *Mysterious North* 93: Bell likes to use the term "air harbor." The phrase was on his tongue back in 1919 before the word "airport" had been invented.

2 a harbor for aircraft equipped to land on and take off from water.
1954 *Ont.Variety Vacationland* 29/2: For those who enter Ontario by air, whether as private pilots or in chartered aircraft, there are about 175 air fields and air harbours in the province. **1955** *Northern Mail* 11 May 1/2: Lamb had just taken off from Grace Lake air harbor for Moose Lake with 400 pounds of mail, in heavy gusts of wind.

air-hole *n.* **1** a hole in the ice, especially where the water is moving too swiftly to freeze.
1794 (1911) SIMCOE *Diary* 215: One of the horses drawing hay across the bay fell into an airhole and was drowned. **1958** (1960) NELSON *Northern Lights* 504: He stepped into an air hole, a common hazard . . . where the stream, flowing too swiftly to freeze, is covered only by a dome of snow.

2 an opening in the ice, made as a breathing-hole, *q.v.*, by some animal. See also **aglu** and **water-hole** (def. 2).
1852 (1881) TRAILL *Cdn Crusoes* 366: [It] was an air-hole through which the beaver had come up during the night. . . . **1964** *Nat.Geog.* May 722/1: Each seal has several air holes.

3 an opening in rotten, *q.v.*, ice.
1878 *Sask.Herald* (Battleford, N.W.T.) 18 Nov. 1/2: The ice that had formed on Battle River rotted and became so full of air holes that it was dangerous to cross it. **1916** DUNCAN *Billy Topsail* 120: "Rubber ice," said Billy. "Air-holes," said the Doctor.

air-line† *n.* **1** *Obs.* a railway line, especially a through or transcontinental line.
1881 *Edmonton Bull.* 5 Nov. 4/2: The airline between Winnipeg and Portage la Prairie is all under contract, and will be open for traffic on the first of October. **1883** *Prince Albert Times* (Sask.) 19 Sep. 1/3: The quiet serenity which usually prevails in this peaceful region was disturbed on Friday morning by the shrill whistle of the locomotive and people began to wonder if the South Saskatchewan Valley Railway Company had waked up at last, and sent in a special train over the "air" line with those five hundred navvies who were to have commenced work last June.

2 a direct line or route, "as the crow flies"; a beeline.
1854 *Picton Gaz.* (C.W.) 17 July 3/3: The engineer and his assistants should have seen it, as the road at this place is straight as an air-line. **1955** RICH IN BLACK *Journal* liv: From the Kechika Forks to Icy Cape is about 1,200 miles—also in an air line.

An airtight burner

airtight burner or **heater** a lightweight sheet-iron stove which burns wood, the ashes of which are removed by dumping. See also **sheet-iron stove.**
1915 CUMMING *Skookum Chuck* 31: . . . an epidemic of "cold feet" took possession of them, and they retired to warm these extremities at their respective air-tight heaters. **1924** DORRANCE *Never Fire First* 23: [He] arose from his chair beside an "airtight burner" . . . . **1963** *Eaton's Catalogue* (Winnipeg) Spring & Summer 365/2: Wood-burning "Air-Tight" Heater. Blued Steel body, inner steel lining.

aksunai or **auksunai** [ɑkˈsunaɪ] *interj.* *Eskimo* "be strong, wilt thou not?" the traditional Eastern Eskimo greeting and farewell.
1948 *Beaver* Mar. 27/1: . . . the secret of making friends with the Eskimo. All you have to do is say *aksunai* in a real friendly way. . . . **1956** TALLBOOM *Arctic Bride* 247: *Auksunai, Alunasee, Auksunai.* "Goodbye, Goodbye to all."

Alaid [ˈɑled] *n.* [< Tsimshian] See 1923 quote. Also spelled *Ahlied.*
1894 BEGG *Hist.of B.C.* 340: [In May, 1862] Mr. Duncan decided on establishing a village to be known as Met-lah-kat-lah, with the following regulations: (1) To give up "Ahlied" or Indian deviltry; (2) to cease calling in conjurers when sick. . . . **1923** (1961) LA VIOLETTE *Survival* 30: There is among the Nishgas a Society called the Alaid, a semi-secret Society, consisting of four degrees of mysteries to be initiated into which is the ambition of every Indian who can afford it.

alarm bird *Obs.* See 1911 quote.
1771 (1911) HEARNE *Journey* 193: I did not see any birds peculiar to those parts, except what the Copper Indians call the "Alarm Bird" . . . of the owl genus. **1853** REID *Young Voyageurs* 442: Whenever it sees any creature passing . . . it mounts up into the air . . .

keeping up a constant screeching. . . . From this circumstance the Indians of these parts call it the "alarm bird," or "bird of warning". . . . **1911** *Champlain Soc.Pubs* VI 193: The Alarm bird is probably the Short-eared Owl, *Asio flammeus* . . . of the Barren Grounds.

Alaska black diamond hematite, a native sesquioxide of iron; Fe_2O_3.
1958 *News of the North* 13 Nov. 4/1: Come in and compare our quality . . . Genuine Alaska Black Diamond Jewellery. . . .

Alaska pine a species of hemlock, *Tsuga heterophylla,* common on the British Columbia coast.
1905 WIGHTMAN *Our Cdn Heritage* 59: The Pacific Coast is heavily timbered as far north as Alaska, and it is estimated that the Douglas pine, cedar, spruce, Alaska pine, etc., along the railway line, are worth $25,000,000. **1958** *Maclean's* 10 May 56/1: It took the Koerners . . . to appreciate the province's enormous stocks of this scorned wood, give it back its melodious and forgotten name of Alaska Pine, and refine it for the carriage trade.

Alberta District or **Territory** *Hist.* a section of the Northwest Territories, organized in 1875, which became part of the province of Alberta in 1905.
1889 MACLEAN *Indians* 204: The Chinook Belt of the Alberta District is in width about 125 miles. . . . **1946** (1947) FREEDMAN *Mrs.Mike* 24: "A young lady like yourself in Alberta Territory?"

Alberta plain the southeastern part of the province of Alberta, characterized by flat prairie.
1952 PUTNAM *Cdn Regions* 345/1: The outstanding features of the Alberta plain . . . are the deeply entrenched valleys in which flow the main tributaries of the Saskatchewan River system.

Alberta tar sands an extensive sand formation along the Athabasca River impregnated with petroleum oil and tar. See also **Athabasca oil sands, oil sands,** and **tar sands.**
1963 *Canada Month* Nov. 29/2: It stands just about where the Alberta tar sands stand relative to oil wells. . . .

Alberta Territory See **Alberta District.**

Albert coal *Obs.* See **albertite.**
1860 (1861) GESNER *Treatise on Coal* 71: The asphaltum of New Brunswick, now called Albert coal, is one of the richest materials ever discovered for the manufacture of oils.

Albertia *n. Hist.* a name proposed for the Northwest Territories.
1860 *Nor'Wester* (R.R.S.) 28 Sep. 4/3: . . . you might at once connect yourselves with the whole realm, and by the same act commemorate the visit of the heir-apparent, and name it after him "Albertia."

albertite ['ælbɚ̩ˌtaɪt] *n.* [< *Albert* County, N.B.] a bituminous, jet-black hydrocarbon that yields oil and gas, used as fuel.
1876 *Descriptive Catalogue of Econ.Min.* 57: Albertite . . . differs from true coal in being of one quality throughout, in containing no traces of vegetable tissues, and in its mode of occurrence, as a vein, and not as a lead. **1949** LAWSON *N.B.Story* 266: In 1850 . . . erosion of the banks of Frederick Brook at Hillsborough, Albert County, disclosed a large deposit

of a unique mineral, called albertite. **1958** *Encyc.Can.* I 121/2: In the mid-19th century, an asphaltic mineral with a high gas content was discovered here, which came to be known as albertite.

alcool ['ælkul] *n.* [< Cdn F] See **whisky blanc.**
1963 *Maclean's* 27 July 48/2: Quebec, whose commission sells *whisky blanc* (alcool) at a neat profit, has not yet had flavored wines on its shelves at all.

alewife† *n.* [origin obscure] a bony species of herring, *Alosa pseudoharengus,* of the eastern seaboard and Great Lakes. See also **gaspereau, kiack[1],** and **spring herring.**
1817 *Quebec Gaz.* 30 Jan. 3/4: Wholesale Prices at Halifax . . . Alewives, 25 to 27s. . . . **1965** *Globe and Mail* (Toronto) 14 Jan. W10/7: The alewife entered from the ocean and remained inland as the lakes became fresh water.

Alkali Dry Belt See **Dry Belt** (def. 2).

all-Canada *adj.* confined to Canada; all-Canadian.
1955 *Winnipeg Free Press* 1 Feb. 4/4: . . . representations have been made to the federal government . . . regarding the financing of the all-Canada route to eastern Canada. **1957** *Aklavik Jnl* Mar. 4/2: Such a road would be the most direct all-Canada route to northern defence posts.

all-Canadian *adj.* **1** situated wholly within Canada's borders.
1897 *Province* (Victoria) 7 Aug. 486/1: An all-Canadian route, under the circumstances induced by the regrettable attitude assumed by the Americans, is unquestionably to be preferred. **1957** *Star Wkly* 17 Aug. 11/2: He believes that Trans-Canada, which is building the all-Canadian line, will eventually sell to the U.S. middle west anyway.

2 consisting entirely of Canadian people, talents, resources, products, etc.
1957 *Commonwealth* 2 Jan. 1/2: By 1958 one of the greatest all-Canadian engineering achievements should be completed—a microwave radio relay system—longest in the world—will stretch 3,800 miles to link Sydney, N.S., to Vancouver, B.C., making possible a truly national TV network. . . . **1958** *Vancouver Province* 16 Sep. 18/4: . . . it was the first time an all-Canadian fashion show had ever been assembled west of Toronto.

Alliance *n.* See **Lord's Day Alliance.**
1957 *Weekend Mag.* 3 Aug. 19/1: A majority of Vancouverites voted for Sunday sport in a plebiscite but the Alliance was responsible for a situation wherein the Mounties have been selling tickets for Sunday games on Saturdays—none at the box-office on Sundays.

alligator *n.* [< imagined resemblance to an alligator in movement, amphibious character, etc.] *Lumbering* **1** *Hist.* a scow-like raft equipped with a winch and cable, used for towing or hauling logs, breaking up jams, etc.
1947 SAUNDERS *Algonquin* 43: There the individual logs would be moved across by primitive "alligators." A raft . . . served instead of a modern tug for this purpose. A team of horses was hitched to a windlass

in the centre of the raft [and] walked round and round in order to wind up the rope that gradually hauled the raft to the spot where the anchor had previously been dropped. **1950** HAMBLETON *Abitibi* 51: The winches aboard the scow-like alligators pulled craft, logs and all up to the anchor.

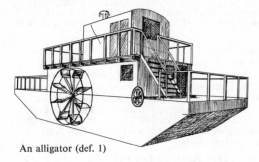

An alligator (def. 1)

2 See 1963 quote. Also called *alligator boat*.
1909 *Gow Ganda Tribune* (Ont.) 17 Apr. 8/1: The alligator boat plying between the Georgian Bay and inland camps will be needed here soon. **1957** *Bush News* (Port Arthur, Ont.) June 1/1: The logs are towed and driven by four alligators, boats especially designed to be at home in this rugged country. **1963** WILKINSON *Abitibi* 3: Alligator: A small gasoline-powered boat used to break log jams on river drives or to transport men and supplies, or to assist in forming the logs into a raft for towing.

allowance *n. Fur Trade* in the Hudson's Bay Company, a specified amount of goods allowed to certain employees in addition to their salary. See also **voyage allowance** and **winter allowance**.
1777 (1951) *Sask.Jnls* 124: . . . the two spare Men at the Sawyers Tent have . . . come Home for Allowance of Provisions. **1907** HUNTER *Cdn Wilds* 70: However, a scale of allowances of a few delicacies was allowed, and these were made up every year at the depot of each district and were for one year. **1933** ROLYAT *Wilderness Walls* 231: With them went their usual Allowances, as well as many special requisitions.

allowance canoe *Hist.* See quote.
1907 HUNTER *Cdn Wilds* 72: The allowances never came up with the general outfit, but were sent up in bulk to the head quarters of the district, and there parceled out for each post in the Factor's territory. The clerks or officers in charge of these out-posts went to headquarters about the 15th of August with a half-sized canoe. This being a special trip, made especially for the allowance of any small thing that might have been overlooked in the indent, was called "The Allowance Canoe."

all-red route or **line** *Hist.* the Canadian Pacific Railway route across Canada, so called because it went entirely through British territory.
1931 MATHEWS *Early Vancouver* 61: . . . the Canadian Pacific Railway had reached Vancouver, closed the last gap in the "All-Red Route" and had raised the obscure settlement on the muddy shore of Water Street . . . to the status of a world port. **1935** SULLIVAN *Great Divide* 189: The all-red line had come to life again and thrust on toward the Rockies.

allumer *v. Cdn French* light up; take a break for a rest. See also **pipe**[1] (def. 2).
1860 (1956) KOHL *Kitchi-Gami* 427: Once we put in to "allumer" at a Frenchman's. . . . The word "allumer" in the Canadian language means, "to call at a person's house while travelling." **1869** KENNICOTT *Journal* 99: In boat voyaging the signal to the crew to stop rowing or hauling the line for a spell is the steersman's cry of "illiume" [sic] which means in voyaging lingo "light your pipes." **1931** NUTE *Voyageur* 50: The order "Allumez!" was given by the guide when he deemed the usual time between smokes had elapsed. . . .

amalgamated school *Nfld* See quotes.
1955 *Western Star* (Corner Brook, Nfld) 12 Mar. Back sec. 1/4: The Amalgamated School Board has become responsible for the education of children of the Church of England, the United Church and the Pentecostal Mission. **1963** *Maclean's* 2 Nov. 49/1: Perhaps the showpiece of the whole camp is a new two-million-dollar school that will have, under Newfoundland's cumbersome system, one wing for Catholic students, one wing for "amalgamated" (everyone else), and a common central section for such secular items as labs and a gym.

amarok [ə'marək] *n. Eskimo* "wolf." a Mountie.
1951 BULIARD *Inuk* 65: Anguyak heard about it and said, "The first Amarok . . . or any other Eyebrow that comes after me will find himself at the wrong end of my rifle."

amaut [ə'maut] *n.* [< Esk.] See 1963 quote. See picture at **atigi**. Also spelled *amowt*.
1897 TUTTLE *Golden North* 227: The women's jacket has a fur-lined "amowt," or large hood, for carrying a child. . . . **1952** MOWAT *People of Deer* 140: There was Ootek, and Howmik his wife, and a child in her womb and another who rode in her amaut. **1963** *Chatelaine* April 58/1: Until he [an Eskimo boy] was three he lived mostly in the *amaut*, a pouch built into the back of his mother's parka.

Ambitious City a nickname for Hamilton, Ontario.
1858 (1955) CRAIG *Early Travellers* 228: The inhabitants of Hamilton call it "ambitious little city;" and its ambition is to be measured by deeds as well as by words. . . . **1891** *Grip* (Toronto) 29 Aug. 132/2: It is another feather in the musical cap of the Ambitious City, and all Canada has a right to feel good over it. **1965** *Globe and Mail* (Toronto) 21 Apr. B5/8: It's hard to be poor in the Ambitious City.

America† *n.* **1** North America, especially Canada and the United States.
☛ *The entries for* **America** *and* **American** *are intended to give some idea of the meaning of these terms in Canada during the past two hundred years. In modern times, it is not usual to include Canada as part of America, which, rightly or wrongly, generally refers to the United States.*
1583 PECKHAM *True Reporte* Bii^v: But hauing the winde fayre & good, they proceeded on theyr course towards the fyrme of Ameryca, which by reason of continuall Fogges, at that time of the yeere especially: they coulde neuer see, till Cox Maister of the Golden Hinde did discerne Lande. **1764** *Quebec Gaz.* 25 Oct. 2/1: Many of us who have served in America since the beginning of the last War . . . have been Witnesses of your irreproachable conduct, of your distinguished Attachment and Zeal for His Majesty's Service. **1836** *Novascotian* (Halifax) 13 Jan. 9/2: St. John is the natural capital of the Bay of Fundy, it will be the

largest city in America next to New York. **1957**
HUTCHISON *Canada* 308: Vancouver . . . is the
damndest, wickedest, bloodiest-awful town in
America!

2 the United States of America, excluding
Canada.
1784 *Moose Ft Jnls* 214: We have heard from
Mishipicoton by Indians that have been there this
Spring that War has broke out again with America.
1829 *P.E.I. Register* (Charlottetown) 29 Sep. 1/2:
It did not appear to me that America has any desire
for the conquest of Canada, for one very good
reason, that she could reap no advantage from it.
1962 *B.C.Digest* Oct. 15/1: Thousands of
rockhounds from Canada and America visit the
Monte Lake digging every year. . . .

American† *n.* **1** *Obs.* the aborigine of North
America; an Indian or Eskimo.
1578 BEST *Trve Discovrse* III 61: They are of the
coloure of a ripe Oliue, which how it may come to
passes, being borne in so cold a climate, I referre to
yᵉ iudgement of others, for they are naturally borne
children of the same couloure & complexiõ that all
the Americans are, which dwell vnder the
Equinoctiall line. **1744** DOBBS *Hudson's Bay* 50: The
French imagine they are descended from Biscayners,
they having Beards up to their Eyes, which the
Americans have not; they are of a white Complexion,
not Copper coloured like the other Americans, having
black, strong Hair. **1784** PENNANT *Arctic Zoology*
clxi: The new-discovered Americans about Nootka
Sound, at this time disguise themselves in dresses
made of the skins of wolves and other wild beasts,
and wear even the heads fitted to their own.

2 *Obs.* an English-speaking native of the British
North American colonies, as opposed to a
French-speaking Canadian or a British
immigrant.
*c*1800 (1955) CURTIS *Voyage* 43: The man that had the
care of this Mill was an American. **1832** (1953)
RADCLIFF *Letters* 120: The usual mode of cleaning the
wheels of the adhesive mud being to strike them, when
dry, on the rims, with a heavy hammer, which,
causing the dirt to drop, restores them, in the eyes of
an American, to a perfectly dandyish appearance.

3 a native or citizen of the United States.
1777 *Quebec Gaz.* 9 Jan. 2/1: The Stamp-Act was
repealed; and from that moment may be dated the
commencement of what the Americans call "an Era
of public ruin." **1831** *Colonial Patriot* (Pictou, N.S.)
2 Apr. 2/3: Americans can't be teachers of common
Schools in some of the districts, and in several
districts no book printed in the Union is allowed in
the schools. **1872** *Cdn Mthly and Nat.Rev.* Jan. 87/1:
The term "American," as applied to themselves by
the people of the United States, is, moreover, a
usurpation against which all the other inhabitants of
our Continent have a right to protest.

American *adj.* **1** *Obs.* of or having to do with
aboriginal languages in North America.
1844 HOWSE *Cree Language* 11: The whole fabric of
language as exhibited in the American idioms,
compared with European tongues, is of a very
peculiar structure, cast, as it appears, in a very
different mould from ours, and offering to the
grammarian a novel and singularly organized system
of speech, and to the metaphysician a new view of the
operations of the human mind.
2 of or having to do with America (def. 1).
1744 DOBBS *Hudson's Bay* 41: The American Oxen, or

Beeves, have a large Bunch upon their Backs, which
is by far the most delicious Part of them for Food, it
being all as sweet as Marrow, juicy and rich, and
weighs several Pounds. **1830** MOORSOM *Letters N.S.*
281: I do not take into account those worthies who,
according to the definition of the term "Squire" given
by the little American boy, " 'tend court and justice
meetings," and on other days "help the mister there
at the tavern." **1845** BEAVAN *Life in Backwoods N.B.*
62: By far the greater proportion of the assembly
have the dark eyes and intellectual expression of face
which declares them of American origin; and,
sprinkled among them, are the features which tell of
England's born.

3 of or having to do with the United States of
America.
1776 *Quebec Gaz.* 29 Aug. 4/1:

United let's live, or united let's die,
If conquer'd let who will survive it, not I;
I'd rather be laid in an untimely Grave,
Than live half an Hour an American Slave.

1879 *Morning Chron.* (Halifax) 4 July 3/1: This is
the "glorious fourth of July," so dear to the hearts of
our American cousins. **1957** *Maclean's* 17 Aug. 45/1:
The "main road" paralleled the Red River, and
warrior, explorer, priest and homesteader plodded the
road, from the American boundary to Fort Garry.

American nightingale *Maritimes, Obs.* a frog.
1820 JOHNSTONE *Travels in P.E.I.* 48: I called it
formerly their yell; but as I heard no bird here sing
so sweet in the night, I shall give them the dignified
name of American Nightingales. **1828** MCGREGOR
Maritime Colonies 38: . . . the frogs, those American
nightingales . . . strain their evening concerts. **1842**
WILLIS *Cdn Scenery* II 95: . . . the American
nightingales, as the frogs are called, commence their
singular evening concerts.

American refugee *Hist.* See **refugee** (def. 1).
1789 *Quebec Herald* 27 Apr. 203/1: At that time the
peaceful inhabitants of Canada were cultivating their
farms, and reaping their harvests in quiet; unmindful
of political disputes, and it would have been better if
the same condition had been pursued by that tribe
called American refugees.

American sleigh *Obs.* a one-horse sleigh having
two double seats, the box being mounted on two
steel-shod runners.
1789 *Quebec Gaz.* 5 Feb. 4/1: We will not reject the
Dutch or American Sleigh and Sled with long high
runners, if found best and most convenient, merely
because they are Dutch or American. **1834** *Vindicator*
(Montreal) 2 Jan. 2/4: Last winter in a "shanty" at
Lassomption a few American sleighs (dragged by one
horse) tracked a road for themselves, which was free
from Cahots. . . .

American wagon *Obs.* See quote.
1845 TOLFREY *Sportsman* I 64: An American waggon
(a light vehicle on springs), which had been chartered
to convey our servants, canteens, and provender,
drove up to the door of the Hotel shortly
afterwards. . . .

American War *Obs.* **1** the American
Revolution.
1796 (1932) RUSSELL *Correspondence* I 69: During the

American War they served as Volunteers under Capt. Brandt. **1817** *U.C.Gaz.* (York [Toronto]) 17 July 115/4: Many of the soldiers serving during the first American war, at its conclusion, received grants of land.

2 the War of 1812.
1883 RYERSON *My Life* 25: At the close of the American War, in 1815, I was twelve years of age. . . .

Americo-Canadian *n.* See quote.
1963 *Kingston Whig-Standard* (Ont.) 23 Jan. 23/4: The Americo-Canadian . . . is a Canadian wholly attached to his situation, cultural and political, right where he is, in North America.

amik ['ɑmɪk] *n.* See **amisk**.
1964 CARROLL *Shy Photographer* 4: Shorty began to work his way back along the float of his plane, which was called a Beaver, after our animal friend, Amik.

amisk ['ɑmɪsk] *n.* [< Algonk.: Cree] See **beaver** (def. 1). Also spelled *amik*.
[**1743** (1949) ISHAM *Observations* 20: A beaver Au misk.] **1949** MCGREGOR *Blankets and Beads* 19: Where there were formerly two Beaver Rivers in Alberta, one of them is now officially the Amisk, which is the Cree name for Beaver. **1951** ANGIER *At Home* 102: "Amisks who bog themselves down on willow," Dudley Shaw explained, "are permeated with a bitterish flavor."

amote or **amute** *n.* [< Chinook Jargon] *Obs.* the wild strawberry.
1855 (1956) ROSS *Fur Hunters* 80: . . . his bark platter [was] filled top heavy with the most delicious melange of bear's grease, dog's flesh, wappatoes, olellies, amutes, and a profusion of other viands, roots and berries. **1899** (1965) *Dictionary of the Chinook Jargon* 3: A-mo-te. The strawberry.

amoutik [ə'mɑutɪk] *n.* [< Esk.] See quote.
1965 *Weekend Mag.* 10 Apr. 33/1: It's a "summer" parka or *amoutik,* as the Eskimos call it, for warmer weather. . . .

amowt *n.* See **amaut**.

anchor ice† See **bottom ice**.
1862 (1932) *Cdn Hist.Rev.* XIII 299: Thursday & Friday last very cold, making anchor ice in the swift water. **1948** *Beaver* Mar. 34: Anchor ice comes to the surface of the lakes amidst swirling waters, and woe betide the man whose canoe is caught on top when a large piece surfaces.

Anchor money *Hist.* See quote.
1963 *Commercial Letter* Jan. 7/1: It [the Magdalen penny] was followed in 1822 by Anchor money, so named from the main device on the reverse. This latter coinage, however, was struck by the Royal Mint for the British Colonies generally and was widely circulated in British North America.

Ancient Company *Obs.* See **Hudson's Bay Company**.
1909 CAMERON *New North* 34: . . . between us and the Arctic lies an unknown country which supports but a few hundred Indian trappers and the fur-traders of the Ancient Company in their little posts.

Anderson chariot *Hist.* See **Bennett buggy**.

1952 (1965) HAMILTON *Cdn Quotations* 225: Anderson Chariots. A two-wheel, horse-drawn vehicle made from a dismantled automobile by farmers of the prairies during the depression of the early 1930's; Dr. J. T. M. Anderson was premier of Saskatchewan, 1929–1934.

angakok or **angekok** ['æŋgə,kɑk] *n.* [< Esk.] an Eskimo shaman. See also **medicine-man** (def. 2) and **shaman**.
1823 *Literary Gaz.* 25 Oct. 675/1: Thus, for example, when they became scarce . . . when the evil genius took away . . . the animals which constitute the principal food of the Enuee, our Angekok was employed to bring them back again. **1906** COMER *Whaling in Hudson Bay* 484: Some of my natives wished to go up to the camping-place of the Southampton natives, and get them to practise their angakok art and see what was the cause of the whale acting so badly. . . . **1964** *North* July 31/2: Apart from the opposition of some angakoks, or conjurers, Christianity had easy play with the ancient Eskimo range of ideas.

angarooka [,ɑŋgə'rukə] *n.* [< Esk.] See **angakok**.
1924 FLAHERTY *Eskimo Friends* 82: To Omarolluk, however, the angarooka's food and the princely wage, eighty-five beavers a month . . . were of small moment. **1936** STRINGER *Wife-Traders* 183: The Angarooka, he was told, was in a rage like a bull walrus.

Anglais [ɑ̃'glɛ:] *n. French* especially among French-speaking Canadians, an English-speaking Canadian. See also **Anglois**.
1953 LOWER *Voyages* 139: The men in the service station were obliging but how could the anglais talk technical motor terms in French? **1964** *Winnipeg Tribune* 6 Feb. 6/6: Ottawa's immigration policy was often painted as simply a dirty plot of the "Anglais" to steadily reduce French-speaking Canadians as a proportion of the population.

angle *n. Obs.* See 1783 quote.
1771 (1792) CARTWRIGHT *Journal* I 85: They opened the beaver house in the lodging, and found the angle firmly frozen up. **1783** (1911) TOWNSEND *Cartwright's Jnl* 299: From the fore part of the house, they [the beavers] build a projection into the pond, sloping downwards all the way, and under this they enter into their house. This entrance is called by the furriers, *the Angle;* nor do they always content themselves with one. . . .

anglicism *n.* any feature of pronunciation, morphology, syntax, vocabulary, or spelling borrowed from English by the Canadian French.
1919 MORLEY *Bridging the Chasm* 153: . . . a study of the speech of Quebec has shown that nine-tenths of the faulty expressions used in that province are "anglicisms" incorporated in the language because of the close contact of the two peoples.

anglicize *v.* assimilate (French Canada or French Canadians) to the customs and language of English-speaking Canada.
1838 *Patriot* (Toronto) 29 May 1/4: That the Lower Province must be anglicised is certain; and if it be not done now, peaceably and with deliberation, it will hereafter be done with confusion and bloodshed. **1916** BRIDLE *Sons of Can.* 31: Some of his [Laurier's] French-Canadian disciples . . . complain that he has Anglicised himself too much.

Anglification *n. Hist.* the political concept of absorbing the French Canadians into the English-

speaking community, a view held by many Canadians of British origins in the 1830's and 40's and finding expression in the Durham Report of 1839 and the Union Act of 1841.
1843 *St.Catharines Jnl* (C.W.) 19 Oct. 2/3: If the great object of the Union is carried out—the Anglification of the French, of who the Tories entertain such a holy horror—we cannot conceive of any readier mode of accomplishing it, than the one which will have the greater tendency to bring the two races the most into each other's society. **1866** BELL *Hist.of Canada* II 480: After sojourning some time in the country, and consulting the British party-leaders, his opinions underwent a change, for he became convinced that under such an arrangement as that just detailed, gradual anglification would have been impossible to effect. **1946** LOWER *Colony to Nation* 248: The gate to "Anglification" was to be opened by the simple device of the union of the two Canadas: the powerful contagion of English example would then do the rest.

anglify *v. Obs.* See **anglicize.**
1828 *Brockville Gaz.* (U.C.) 12 Sep. 2/3: Revolutionary principles and anti-British feelings are spreading . . . by means of the exertions of disguised Yankees and half-anglified Frenchmen. **1866** CHRISTIE *Lower Canada* V: The darling project of his heart, was to anglify, but by means compulsory and distasteful to them, the French Canadian people. . . .

Anglo ['æŋglo] *n.* [< Cdn F] See **Anglo-Canadian,** *n.*
1800 *U.C.Gaz.* (York [Toronto]) 22 Feb. 3/2: The inference to be drawn, is the closest union between the Anglo and trans-atlantic Anglos. **1959** *Maclean's* 14 Feb. 41/1: The scientific, technical and commercial facilities, areas once left to the "Anglos," are booming.

Anglo-American *adj.* Canadian.
1797 (1935) RUSSELL *Correspondence* II 27: All the Anglo-American inhabitants of that part of the Province of Quebec which is now Upper Canada, lived under the most confident expectation that they were eventually to be subject to the Laws of England only. **1871** *Wkly Manitoban* 11 Feb. 2/3: What the Anglo-American public should demand, is a distinct positive measure . . . by which the valleys of the St. Lawrence and the Ottawa . . . and the magnificent roadstead of British Columbia, shall be united by a continuous railroad before 1880.

Anglo-bluenose *n. Obs.* a Nova Scotian. See also **Bluenose** (def. 1b).
1845 BEAVAN *Life in Backwoods N.B.* 49: . . . the Anglo-blue-noses had the choice of uniting the high-aspiring impulses of young America to the more solid principles of the olden world. . . .

Anglo-Canadian *n.* an English-speaking Canadian, especially one of British origin.
1832 (1838) NEED *Six Years in the Bush* 22: The Anglo-Canadian copies the worst and most prominent features of the American character, and the British settler in his turn caricatures the copy. **1963** *Kingston Whig-Standard* (Ont.) 23 Jan. 23/4: "There are French-Canadians," explained the professor, "and Anglo-Canadians. These are the two basic groups in Canada historically."

Anglo-Canadian *adj.* **1** of or having to do with English-speaking Canada.
1833 *Liberal* (St. Thomas, U.C.) 7 Feb. 2/6: . . . the dogmas of which our Anglo-Canadian brethren

appear very much inclined to shake themselves free.
1964 *Canada Month* Jan. 27/3: . . . I had an on-the-spot view of the phenomenon of an Anglo-Canadian nation marching toward unity.

2 of or having to do with Canada and the United Kingdom jointly.
1957 *Commonwealth* 16 Oct. 12/2: Britain's chancellor of the exchequer . . . proposed tariff-free Anglo-Canadian trade.

Anglo-French *adj.* based on mutual respect and accord between French- and English-speaking Canadians with regard to matters of biculturalism and bilingualism.
1964 *Canada Month* Jan. 30/1: The idea of a truly Anglo-French Canada seems to be making some progress. . . .

Anglois *n. Cdn French, Obs.* See **Anglais.**
1833 *Cdn Courant* (Montreal) 2 Jan. 2/5: Among their more peaceable and less assuming fellow subjects "les Anglois," as the British Canadians are styled, are certainly upheld. . . . **1918** DAVIDSON *North West Co.* 246: The Hudson's Bay Company's people were termed *les Anglois.* . . .

Anglo-Saxon *n.* See quote.
1963 *Maclean's* 2 Dec. 79/2: It's natural . . . for English-speaking Canadians to be profoundly disturbed by . . . the French-Canadian habit of lumping all of us under the term "Anglo-Saxons," an uncalculated insult which ignores the great diversity of the country outside Quebec.

Anglo-Saxon Canadian See **Anglo-Canadian.**
1916 BRIDLE *Sons of Can.* 100: What had the habitant or the Anglo-Saxon Canadian to do with such a war at the bottom of the world?

angnacook *n. Obs.* See **angakok.**

ankle-jack *n. Obs.* See quote.
1876 LORD *Wilderness* 143: Hence I always provide myself . . . with a few pairs of strong, [hob]nailed boots of the pattern known as "ankle-jacks," made wide in the sole and laced up the front. . . .

annexation *n. Hist.* the political issue involving union of Canada with the United States.
1849 (1955) CRAIG *Early Travellers* 169: . . . these men are beginning *openly* to propose the question . . . and to weigh and discuss those of *annexation.* **1891** *Grip* (Toronto) 10 Jan. 18/2: They are dreadfully afraid that Free Trade with the States would lead to Annexation. **1963** MORTON *Kingdom of Canada* 284: The action made it clear that annexation talk verged on treason and would be punished.

annexationism *n. Hist.* the policy of annexation, *q.v.*
1921 *Dalhousie Rev.* I 174: He points out that the "Annexationism" of forty years ago has quite died away as a policy. . . .

annexationist *n. Hist.* a person advocating annexation, *q.v.*
1849 *Wkly Globe* 23 Nov. 61/2: The Annexationists of Montreal . . . have now to set forth the reasons for our separation from the British Empire. **1916** SKELTON *Day of Laurier* 265: And while in Canada there might be as yet few annexationists, the tendency of a vast and

intimate trade north and south would be to make many. **1958** GRIFFIN *British Columbia* 37: To the appeal of the annexationists for union with the United States ... the movement for responsible government counterposed the idea of joining the Canadian Confederation, which even then was being shaped in London.

Annexation Manifesto *Hist.* a statement of reasons for annexation, *q.v.*, circulated in 1849. See also **Montreal Manifesto.**
1849 *Wkly Globe* 9 Nov. 74/3: Canada is a ruined country, says the Annexation manifesto. **1948** ANGLIN *Canada Unlimited* 24: They [the supporters of the Chateau Clique] staged riots in Montreal, burned the parliament buildings and ended ingloriously by producing an Annexation Manifesto ... urging a bolt from the British Empire to the United States.

anorak [ˌænəˈræk] *n.* [< Esk.] a waterproof outer coat of skin, often used by the hunter in his kayak.
1937 SHACKLETON *Arctic Journeys* 298: One day David put on a waterproof sealskin anorac which fitted tightly over the ring that surrounds the aperture in the kayak. **1964** *North* Mar.-Apr. 8: The principal article of clothing is the so-called "whole fur-coat," a skin anorak whose lower edge may be fastened around the man-hole without interfering with the freedom of the man to move.

anse [æns] *n.* [< F] a cove or bay (mainly in place names).
1821 (1900) GARRY *Diary* 132: [We] came to a small narrow channel formed by Rocks and in a few Minutes arrived at the Aine [Anse] du Bonnet which is a Portage of ten paces. **1860** (1956) KOHL *Kitchi-Gami* 214: Thus I spoke one day to a half-breed ... on the shore of the Anse. ... **1896** *Trans.Roy.Soc.Can.* II 2 200: Certain topographical terms of Acadian origin occur upon our maps as ... Anse, a cove.

ant bear *Obs.* See **black bear.**
1846 HATHEWAY *Hist.N.B.* 64: The common Ant Bear has very short legs. ...

antelope *n.* **1** the pronghorn, *q.v.*, *Antilocapra americana*, of the southern prairies. See also **cabri** (def. 1), **goat** (def. 1a), **jumping deer** (def. 1), and **wild goat** (def. 1).
1801 (1922) HARMON *Journal* 44: The dancers ... were all clothed with the skins of the Antelope, dressed, which were nearly as white as snow. ... **1964** *Globe and Mail* (Toronto) 31 Dec. 1/3: About 500 head of antelope delayed a CPR Dayliner ... on its run from Medicine Hat to Lethbridge.
2 the meat of the pronghorn.
1916 WOOD *Tourist's N.W.* 332: On a certain Christmas Day the King Edward Hotel, Banff ... served ... antelope, mule deer, bear, moose. ...

anti *n. Hist.* a person opposed to Confederation of the provinces of British North America.
1866 *Islander* (Charlottetown) 12 Oct. 2/6: The Editor of the Patriot was convinced by the eloquent Nova Scotia antis and came out with the following paragraph. **1870** *Mainland Guardian* (New Westminster, B.C.) 30 Mar. 3/3: ... the last advices

from Newfoundland show that the "Antis" have voted want of confidence in their Government by a vote of 21 to 8. **1898** EDGAR *Canada and Capital* 105: The strength of this feeling was made manifest at the first federal elections, when the "antis" swept the Province.

Anti-British *adj. Hist.* opposed to British domination in Canada.
1819 *Cdn Courant* (Montreal) 6 Feb. 3/2: Is then this modern "Lettre de Cachet," this Anti-British persecution intended as the sovereign panacea against Gourlayism. **1871** *Wkly Manitoban* 15 Apr. 2/1: The few who were disloyal were new-comers who had brought their anti-British feelings with them, and joined in Riel's movement for reasons peculiar to themselves.

anti-Canadian *n. Hist.* a person opposed to extending special rights in religious and legal observances to French Canadians.
1808 *Cdn Courant* (Montreal) 6 June 2/4: They proceeded cheered on every side by crowded windows filled with ... the pride of the anti-Canadians, to crown the efforts of the sons of freedom. **1822** *Montreal Herald* 30 Oct. 2/3: In the former this paper is designated by the very honorable distinction of "the paper of the Anti-Canadians."

anti-Canadian *adj.* **1** *Hist.* opposed or prejudicial to the interests of the Canadian French.
1808 GRAY *Letters* 327: The comparison I have made between the Canadians and an ignorant headstrong youth, will no doubt be deemed by them highly Anti-Canadian, yet I think it will hold good in every point. **1850** (1866) CHRISTIE *Lower Canada* III 135: Several officers of the militia ... publicly dissuaded their militiamen from attending muster, haranguing them ... against the existing administration, as inimical to the rights and interests of the *"peuple canadien!"* and as essentially anti-Canadian.
2 opposed or prejudicial to the interests of Canada and Canadians.
1882 *Brandon Mail* (Man.) 22 Dec. 2/2: This is sheer ignorance, and if it were not ignorance, it would be prejudicial to the Dominion, Anti-Canadian, un-British, disloyal, for anything that threatens the integrity of the Confederation, threatens our promising commonwealth.

Anti-Confederate *n. Hist.* an opponent of Confederation, especially one opposed to the Quebec Resolutions of 1865. Also *Anti-Confederationist.*
1866 *Islander* (Charlottetown) 12 Oct. 2/6: Some months since this Island was honored by a visit from prominent Anti-confederates from Nova Scotia. **1960** FOWKE *Story in Song* 105: When the vote [in Newfoundland] was taken in 1869, the Confederates were badly beaten. The Anti-Confederates elected twenty-one out of thirty candidates, and that night they held a great celebration in St. John's.

anti-Confederate *adj. Hist.* opposed to Confederation.
1874 *North Star* (St. John's) 31 Jan. 2/3: And this, we suppose, is the end of the intensely patriotic and anti-Confederate administration, the greatest humbug that was ever perpetrated upon any country in this world. **1957** *Beaver* Spring 13/1: Immediately after Confederation he was plunged into the protracted and delicate business of winning over Joseph Howe and

pacifying the anti-Confederate movement in Nova Scotia.

anti-Confederation *n. Hist.* the political position of being opposed to Confederation.
1874 *North Star* (St. John's) 31 Jan. 2/3: This is what anti-Confederation meant and means. **1963** *Time* (Cdn ed.) 30 Aug. 10/2: . . . few lyrics have the punch of that produced by the anti-Confederation forces in the 1948 Newfoundland plebiscite:

> Her face turns to Britain
> Her back is to the gulf,
> Come near at your peril
> Canadian Wolf.

Anti-Confederationist *n. Hist.* an opponent of Confederation. See also **Anti-Confederate.**
1870 *Mainland Guardian* (New Westminster, B.C.) 19 Feb. 2/1: We feel quite certain that the moderate Confederationists and anti-Confederationists will be satisfied. . . .

Anti-Constitutionalist *n. Hist.* a member of the Anti-Constitutional party.
1832 *Liberal* (St. Thomas, U.C.) 2 Nov. 3/3: He announces his intention . . . of distinguishing them by the cognomen of Constitutionalists and anti-Constitutionalists.

Anti-Constitutional party *Hist.* a party opposed to the constituted political structure of Upper Canada in the 1830's.
1833 *Cdn Courant* (Montreal) 2 Jan. 2/5: I am aware of no more prolific source of discontent and mischief in this Province, than the constant allusion . . . supported by the Anti-Constitutional party, to the difference of origin, of which our population consists. **1837** *Bytown* [Ottawa] *Gaz.* 2 Feb. 2/1: It is singular, that notwithstanding the activity displayed by the Montreal Anti-Constitutional party, every election . . . has turned against them.

anti-highgrading squad a squad of police officers specially organized to prevent the theft of gold by miners at their work.
1963 *Globe and Mail* (Toronto) 23 Apr. 1/3: Inspector Charles W. Wood, of the anti-highgrading squad, said the ring which has been taking large amounts of highgrade gold . . . was far-reaching in its activities.

anti-responsible *n. Hist.* a political group opposed to responsible government for the Canadas; hence, **anti-responsible-ist.**
1840 PRESTON *Three Years' Residence* I 193: Both parties . . . were to blame, but most so the "Anti-responsibles," since they went from Toronto avowedly for the purpose of driving their opponents from the ground. **1844** *Bytown* [Ottawa] *Gaz.* 18 Apr. 3/2: There is nothing in it to irritate its extreme antipodist on either side; for there are uncompromising anti-Responsible-ists as well as Responsibleists of the whole figure, between which two parties is one, outnumbering as we believe, either of the two, and whose sentiments may be fairly assumed to be embodied and represented in the pamphlet before us.

anti-union *adj. Hist.* **1** opposed to the union of Upper with Lower Canada.
1822 *Cdn Courant* (Montreal) 16 Nov. 2/1: The acts and speeches at the Montreal Anti-Union dinner, are of a complexion that must excite wonder and ridicule in the American States. **1840** *Bytown* [Ottawa] *Gaz.* 5 Mar. 1/4: A week or two ago, a petition was carried to the school-house, in the parish of Rivière

du Loup, by an anti-union emissary, and the scholars, to the number of twenty-one, some of whom are about seven years of age, induced to sign it.
2 opposed to Confederation of the provinces of British North America.
1865 *Islander* (Charlottetown) 3 Feb. 2/7: Anti-union meeting at Savage Harbor. **1953** LEBOURDAIS *Nation of North* 25: The government had to contend with the power and prestige of the governor, Hon. Arthur Gordon . . . who openly opposed Confederation, with the result that the government was badly beaten, and an anti-union government under Albert Smith was formed.

Anti-Unionist *n. Hist.* **1** a person opposed to the union of Upper with Lower Canada.
1822 *Cdn Courant* (Montreal) 13 Nov. 2/2: We are aware that in regard to petitioners, the Anti-Unionists will have the greater number; but those who are friend to the Unions, the better arguments. **1848** (1866) CHRISTIE *Lower Canada* II 386: The Canadians of French descent, were almost to a man anti-unionists; those of British origin were, for the greatest part, unionists.
2 a person opposed to Confederation.
1864 *Islander* (Charlottetown) 9 Sep. 2/3: We caution anti-Unionists on the island to beware. **1868** *Ibid.* 3 Apr. 2/7: He censured the course of the Administration as having been ill-advised and hasty; it had created great dissatisfaction in the Maritime Provinces causing strong friends of Union, to become anti-Unionists.

Antkiti Siwash *B.C.* See quote.
1963 SYMONS *Many Trails* 75: Jack used to regale me with weird stories of the Antkiti Siwashes, the Indian giants who lived in bygone days at Chilko Lake, and who, the Indians thought, still turned up unexpectedly.

antlerless season an open season in which does and yearlings may be legally hunted.
1963 *B.C.Digest* Nov.-Dec. 29/1: Also the antlerless season will add considerably to the harvest since many hunters wait to take an antlerless animal.

anvil *n.* either of two iron blocks used for firing a ceremonial salute in the absence of a cannon, the smaller being placed on the larger, an explosive charge being placed between them to be touched off by a blow from a hammer.
1860 (1950) HUTCHISON *Fraser* 158: Cannons and anvils were fired, the British and American flags hoisted in honor of the event. **1959** *Weekend Mag.* 16 May 34: . . . men of The Ancient and Honourable Hyack Anvil Battery are firing their 88th annual Royal Salute. . . . When the powder is properly laid, the right- and left-hand Hoisters, four in number, lift a small anvil by the "beak" and lay it across the big one. The anvil battery is now ready for firing. . . . New Westminster's anvil chorus dates from 1871 . . . the firemen were called by the name used to describe them by the Indians—hyack, meaning "hurry up."

any-sex season an open season during which moose and deer of either sex may be legally hunted.
1962 *B.C.Digest* Oct. 55/2: The any sex season is not the complete answer to our problems in moose and deer management.

apakwa *n*. [< Algonk.: Ojibwa] *Obs*. See quote.
1860 (1956) KOHL *Kitchi-Gami* 9: While I was considering all this, the apakwas had arrived, and my house-skeleton was about to be clothed. This is the name given to the rolls of birch bark, which are generally kept in readiness to cover the wigwams or repair the roofs.

apala *n. Obs*. See **appalat**.

apartment block See 1913 quote.
1913 SANDILANDS *West.Cdn Dict*. 4: Apartment block, a residential block divided up into perfectly self-contained suites, somewhat after the style of the houses of flats in Scotland and in London, England.
1964 *Naicam Sentinel* (Sask.) 26 Mar. 5/4: Mr. and Mrs. W. Souter live in a beautiful apartment block in Vancouver.

apichimo *n*. See **appichimon**.

apishamore *n*. See **appichimon**.

apoulard *n. Obs*. See **appalat**.

appalat *n*. [< F *apala* titbit] *Obs*. a piece of skewered meat grilled over a campfire. See also **en apala**. Also spelled *apala, apoulard*.
1806 (1897) COUES *New Light* I 410: . . . having killed a good fat cow [buffalo], our fire was soon smoking with as many fine appalats as we could crowd upon it. **1863** (1931) CHEADLE *Journal* 116: . . . a period of anxious suspense ensued which we mitigated by eating an apoulard, & a partridge I had shot.

appichimon [ə'pɪʃə,mən] *n*. [< Cdn F < Algonk.] a saddle blanket, usually of buffalo-calf skin, used also as a mat for sitting or lying on. Various spellings.
1804 (1897) COUES *New Light* I 270: They could not remain seated on their epishemaunts on the floor.
1825 (1950) OGDEN *Journals* 77: . . . he also found an appichimon belonging to one of the men. . . . **1876** LORD *Wilderness* 62: First a sheep or goat's skin, or a piece of buffalo "robe," failing either of the former, called an "apichimo[n]," is placed on its back.
[**1914** SCHULTZ *Rising Wolf* 210: . . . we made a lodge lining of our pishimores—pieces of buffalo robe that we used for saddle blankets. . . .]

apple-paring bee See **paring bee**.

apron *n. Lumbering* a platform, usually of heavy timbers, at the bottom of a log chute, used to break the fall of the logs as they enter the water.
1864 (1955) CRAIG *Early Travellers* 283: At the bottom of each separate "shute" there is a wooden platform or "apron" upon which the rafters are precipitated, and so preserved from diving down under the surface by the impetus of their fall. **1942** HAIG-BROWN *Timber* 250: Generally an apron of piles slopes down from it [the log dump] and the logs roll down this when they are dumped from the cars.

arch† *n*. the chamber of the fireplace on which is placed the kettle used in making maple sugar.
1942 CAMPBELL *Thorn-Apple Tree* 98: The snow was cleared off a level place, and flat stones were laid in the shape of a large open-ended rectangle two feet high. The surface of the stone was levelled off with sand. That was the arch. Over it they raised the shelter, and roofed it with bark.

Arctic birch a low shrub, *Betula nana,* growing four to five feet high and having rounded leaves.
1942 TWOMEY & HERRICK *Needle to the North* 242: Sometimes there were . . . a few dense thickets of Arctic birches . . . and some Arctic willows.

Arctic Brotherhood See quote.
1931 LEBOURDAIS *Northward* 118: The Arctic Brotherhood is the fraternal organization of the North. The "A.B.," as it is popularly called, consists of persons who have spent at least one winter in the North. There are branches of it in the principal towns of Alaska and the Yukon.

Arctic char a variety of salmon trout, *Salvelinus alpinus,* found in northern waters. Also spelled *Arctic charr*.
1935 SHACKLETON *Arctic Journeys* 289: While the Eskimos were skinning and cache-ing the meat, I went to look at a little stream and saw many Arctic charr cruising about at the mouth. . . . **1963** *Maclean's* 20 Apr. 3/3: Eskimos who, until recently, couldn't grasp the idea of a restaurant were considering the fluctuations in the price of Arctic char in Montreal.

Arctic cotton a species of cotton grass, *Eriophorum* sp., found in the Far North. See also **Eskimo cotton**.
1936 *Beaver* Mar. 38/2: Arctic cotton plant, the bloom of which, together with the soft sphagnum mosses, is used for wicks of Eskimo lamps. **1951** GILLIS & MYLES *North Pole* 195: The dwarfish Arctic cotton made dots of white against blotches of moss. . . . **1955** BARNETT *World* 215: [Caption] Arctic Cotton Grass annually produces these silky white spheres that rise upward on slender reedlike stems from shallow fresh-water pools. . . .

Arctic crow *North, Informal* the raven, *Corvus corax*.
1951 BULIARD *Inuk* 217: As a trapper, his two enemies are Nanuk, who likes to revenge himself on the trapped fox by slapping the poor beast around with his paw, and the Arctic crows, who steal the bait.

Arctic fox a smallish fox, *Alopex lagopus,* of the northern regions, white in winter but blue-gray to brownish at other times. See also **ice fox** and **white fox**.
1772 *Phil.Trans.Roy.Soc*. LXII 370: Arctic fox . . . are known to stand by, while a trap is baited for them, into which they put their heads immediately.
1896 WHITNEY *On Snow-Shoes* 243: The arctic fox is about half the size of a good big red fox. **1963** *Calgary Herald* 20 Sep. 26/3: On the way back to the RCAF base, two white Arctic fox scurried across the snow. . . .

Arctic grayling a silver-gray freshwater fish, *Thymallus arcticus,* of the trout family, found in northern waters. See also **Arctic trout, Back's grayling, bluefish,** and **grayling**.
1936 STEELE *Policing the Arctic* 31: In the black depths beneath them slept trout and whitefish, "conny" and Arctic grayling. **1963** *Maclean's* 2 Dec. 21/2: Lake trout, arctic grayling and whitefish filled the lakes and rivers. . . .

Arctic hare a species of large hare, *Lepus arcticus,* having white winter fur, found in the Barren Grounds. See also **polar hare**.
1842 *Trans.Lit.& Hist.Soc.Que*. IV 133: The animals frequenting this country, are . . . the Arctic Hare, a

variety of a very large size. . . . **1963** *Maclean's* 2 Dec. 21/2: Arctic hares were very scarce and fleet of foot.

Arctic madness rabies in Arctic foxes.
1958 *Weekend Mag.* 13 Dec. 23/1: Some vets, however, have doubted the wisdom of releasing these foxes, which might not be as healthy as they look or which could become infected by others to spread what is sometimes called "Arctic madness."

Arctic officer an official of the Department of Northern Affairs and National Resources which is responsible for administering the Arctic regions of the Canadian North.
1958 *Edmonton Jnl* 4 19/6: Freeze-dried meat . . . was served at a recent meeting of Arctic officers in Toronto. They did not know they were not eating fresh meat until after the dinner.

Arctic Parliament *Informal* the Council of the Northwest Territories (def. 2b).
1958 *Time* (Cdn ed.) 3 Feb. 12/2: Fortnight ago the "Arctic Parliament" (N.W.T.'s nine-member council) met in Yellowknife to talk conservation. . . .

Arctic prairies See **Barren Grounds.**
1924 DORRANCE *Never Fire First* 68: This was not a rabbit winter on the arctic prairies east of the Mackenzie. **1952** PUTNAM *Cdn Regions* 22/2: In the Arctic prairies, grasses and sedges comprise the bulk of the cover forming a short dense sward. **1963** SYMONS *Many Trails* 180: Here on these Arctic Prairies, a bright picture comes to mind when we think of the snowflakes [buntings]. . . .

Arctic rabbit See **varying hare.**
1897 TUTTLE *Golden North* 96: The arctic rabbit is scarce except once in seven years, when they may be seen in myriads.

Arctic sea smoke See quote.
1958 *Manice* 7: Frost Smoke.—(*Arctic Sea Smoke, Sea Smoke, Water Smoke*). A thick fog rising from the sea surface when relatively warm water is exposed to an air temperature much below freezing. Frost smoke frequently appears over newly-formed cracks and leads.

Arctic trout See **Arctic grayling.**
1897 WILSON *Yukon* 57: Grayling or arctic trout . . . frequent the mouths of small streams and falls. . . . **1962** *Wildlife Rev.* July 16/2: Throw a hook and line, with a bit of coloured cloth as bait, into this swirling pocket and a grayling (arctic trout) will take it the instant it hits the water.

Arctic whale the bowhead, *Balaena mysticetus.*
1909 CAMERON *New North* 282: The members of the Baleen Whale family are the Sulphur-Bottoms, the Finner Whales or Rorquals, the Humpbacks, and the king of all whales, the founder of the municipality of Herschel Island, whom his pursuers call indiscriminately the "Arctic Whale," "Polar Whale," "Greenland Whale," "Bowhead," "Right Whale," or "Icebreaker."

Arctic whiteout See **whiteout.**

Arctic willow a low shrub, *Salix arctica,* of the Barren Grounds, having pale foliage and stalked catkins.
1913 CURRAN & CALKINS *Northland* 246: The island offered a good site for a camp, for although it was treeless, a clump of Arctic willows provided protection for the tent. **1956** SCHERMAN *Spring* 53: The arctic willow, puny as it looks, can live eighty years.

Arctic wolf a large wolf, *Canis lupus tundrarum,* of the Arctic. See also **Barren Ground wolf, Barren Land wolf, caribou wolf, Siberian wolf,** and **tundra wolf.**
1896 WHITNEY *On Snow-Shoes* 239: The caribou . . . has many enemies besides the Indian, and none more implacable than the arctic wolves, which in summer are constantly on its tracks. **1940** *Cdn Geog.Jnl* Feb. 101/2: Arctic wolves are not invariably pure creamy white, but are often of darkish grizzled pelage, especially over the dorsal tract. **1963** *Maclean's* 16 Nov. 66/3: I was peering straight into the amber gaze of a fully grown arctic wolf, who probably weighed more than I did. . . .

arena *n.* an indoor hockey rink built to accommodate spectators. See also **hockey rink** (def. 2) and **rink** (def. 2).
1958 *Time* (Cdn ed.) 11 Aug. 12/1: For recreation there are two beer halls . . . plus the ice arena at the nearby Canadian-U.S. air-and-missile base. . . . **1964** *Calgary Herald* 29 Apr. 52/5: They spelled box-office and Smythe packed the arena. . . .

arena rat *Slang* See **rink rat.**
1957 *Kingston Whig-Standard* (Ont.) 25 Feb. 11/6: . most of the 3,564 fans . . . had wended their ways homeward before a disgraceful episode occurred with Belleville's players opposing Jim McCormick's youthful "arena rats" in a free-for-all.

argali *n.* [< Mongol "the wild sheep of Asia"] *Obs.* See **Rocky Mountain sheep.**
1853 REID *Young Voyagers* 9: The argali, or mountain sheep, with his huge curving horns, is seen there. . . . **1861** *Nor'Wester* (R.R.S.) 15 July 1/4: The declevities of the Rocky Mountains are frequented by herds of the argali, or wild sheep. . . .

Argonaut *n. Hist.* an adventurer who went to the Cariboo country in British Columbia in the 1860's in search of gold. Cp. **Overlander.**
1900 OSBORN *Greater Canada* 82: These particular Argonauts seem to have been a turbulent lot. . . . **1958** WATTERS *B.C.Cent.Anthol.* 161: . . . the argonauts . . . camped in Active Pass on their way to the goldfields from Victoria.

ari-stock-rat *n. Slang, Derog.* See quote.
1962 *Alta Hist.Rev.* Autumn 13/2: "Ari-stock-rats," sometimes "mocassin aristocracy," is a term used to designate the half breeds (or Metis, which they prefer being called).

Armstrong or **armstrong** *adj. Slang.* hand-operated; requiring or worked by strength of arm (as opposed to machine power).
1920 *Rod & Gun in Can.* Nov. 642/1: The motorboat did not put in its appearance so we continued our navigation via the armstrong and elbow grease route. **1922** PRINGLE *Tillicums* 161: At ten feet they had to stop digging operations to make a hand-windlass, an "Armstrong hoist" we called it, and a wooden bucket. **1963** *Western Miner* May 20/1: Hoisting the spoil with old-fashioned windlasses which were facetiously called "Armstrong Hoists" was another tedious chore.

army bill *Hist.* a kind of paper money introduced in Canada during the War of 1812,

circulating for a few years thereafter.
1813 (1891) EDGAR *Ten Years of U.C.* 225: Tomorrow
we shall have . . . in army bills £20,000. **1814** *Quebec
Gaz.* 24 Nov. 2/2: It is probable that every
denomination of Army Bills have been counterfeited
in the States. . . . **1931** CONNOR *Rock and River* 306:
These Army Bills, running from $25.00 upward,
never for a day lost their face value. **1963**
Commercial Letter Jan. 6/2: During the War [of
1812] the need was filled by the issue of "Army
Bills" which the people found so convenient and
reliable that when peace came the clamour for paper
money grew louder.

arpent ['arpənt] *n.* [< F] *Hist.* **1** a French
linear measure equal to approximately 190 feet,
used in areas of predominantly French-Canadian
settlement.
☛ *The linear use seems to have been fairly common
during the early nineteenth century.*
c**1749** (1889) WITHROW *Our Own Country* 207: . . .
the farm houses are never more than five arpents
apart, and sometimes but three. . . . **1841** *Montreal
Transcript* 2 Jan. 421/1: . . . he was discovered near a
fence, frozen to death; his horse was found . . . about
30 arpents from him, well and eating hay. . . . **1936**
Cdn Geog.Jnl XII 5/2: The village was in the form of
a square of forty arpents' side (about 1½ miles).
2 a French land measure equal to about an acre.
1703 LAHONTAN *New Voyages* I 35: An arpent is a
spot of ground containing 100 perches square each of
which is eighteen foot long. **1820** *Montreal Herald* 4
Mar. 1/2: To Sell or Lease, and possession given in
April next, of about one Hundred Arpents, well
fenced, with all good new buildings thereon. **1936**
Cdn Hist.Rev. XVII 395: This pitifully slow
development is also reflected in the meagre amount of
land which was cleared and cultivated, there being in
1628 not more, probably, than twenty-five arpents.

arrival *n. Fur Trade* **1 a.** the arrival of one or
more persons at a post.
1822 (1932) MCLEAN *Notes* 29: Such an uncommon
event as an *arrival* seemed to produce an exhilarating
effect upon them. **1967** *Cdn Geog.Jnl* Jan. 19/2: . . . the
post was a scene of great activity during arrivals and
departures.
b. the person or persons arriving at a post.
1913 COWIE *Adventurers* 271: Day after day these
arrivals took place and the fort presented a busy
scene. Each arrival first reported to the officer in
charge.
2 a drink or other gratuity offered to trappers and
others arriving at a post, to show good feeling
and to promote friendly relations. Cp. **departure.**
1939 GODSELL *Vanishing Frontier* 105: . . . his band
were camped outside with big packs of bear and
beaver skins to trade, and Moir left to give them their
"arrival."

arrow sash *Hist.* a sash, *q.v.*, characterized by
arrowlike markings woven into the border. See
picture at **L'Assomption sash.** See also **ceinture**
and **ceinture fléchée.**
1938 BARBEAU *Assomption Sash* 23: These arrow
sashes were woven in large numbers first for the
North West Company and then for the Hudson's Bay
Company, as they were an important article of barter

all over the northern parts of this continent. **1941**
Beaver June 27/1: The typical arrow sash, with its
inherent finger-weaving, certainly had come into
existence before 1800. . . .

arsean or **arsian** *n.* See **assean.**

artiggi or **artigi** ['artɪgi] *n.* See **atigi.**

ashery *n. Hist.* a place for making potash.
See also **ash-house** and **potashery.**
1825 *Colonial Advocate* (York [Toronto]) 24 Feb. 2/3:
Of asheries there are but few in this country, as it is
too well settled. **1853** STRICKLAND *Canada West* I
170n: The best situation to erect an ashery upon, is
the side of a bank, beside a running stream. . . .
1911 *London & Middlesex Hist.Soc.Trans.* III 11: He
kept an ashery . . . where the farmers dumped the
ashes they obtained from burning the forests they
had cleared, getting their pay in store goods.

ash hat *Obs.* a hat woven from fine splints of
ash.
1877 *Department Interior Ann.Rep.Sessional Paper* 11
23: . . . I think that . . . the ash hats, for men and
women, manufactured by the Abenakis, will rival in
value and quality the Leghorns and Panamas.

ash-house *n. Obs.* See **ashery.**
1853 STRICKLAND *Canada West* I 170n: An ash house,
six or eight leech-tubs, a pot-ash kettle, and three or
four coolers are all the requisites necessary.

ashigan *n.* See **achigan.**

ash-leaf (or -leaved) maple See **Manitoba
maple.**
1852 RICHARDSON *Arctic Exped.* 392: On this day
the sap of the ash-leaved maple . . . ceased to run
altogether, and the sugar harvest closed. **1956** *Native
Trees* 260: Manitoba Maple *Acer Negundo L.*
[is also called] ash-leaf maple, inland box elder,
inland Manitoba maple.

assean or **assian** ['ɑsiən] *n.* [< Algonk.] a
breechclout. Also spelled *arsean, arsian, azion.*
1743 (1949) ISHAM *Observations* 14: a Cloth for the
private parts Ar-se-an. **1801** MACKENZIE *Voyages* xciii:
[He wears] a strip of cloth or leather, called assian,
about a foot wide, and five feet long, whose ends are
drawn inwards and hang down behind and before,
over a belt tied round the waist for that purpose.
1931 NUTE *Voyageur* 13: My man dressed himself in
the habit of a voyageur, that is, a short shirt, a red
woolen cap, a pair of deerskin leggings which reached
from the ankles a little above the knees, and are held
up by a string secured to a belt about the waist, the
azion . . . of the Indians, and a pair of deerskin
moccasins without stockings on the feet.

assemblyman *n.* in P.E.I., one of fifteen
members of the Legislative Assembly elected by
both property and non-property owners. Cp.
councillor (def. 2).
1962 *Globe and Mail* (Toronto) 11 Dec. 1/9: There are
15 constituencies and each elects two members—one
councillor and one assemblyman. **1963** *Ibid.* 15 Mar.
3/7: Unlike other provinces, Prince Edward Island
elects two types of members to the House—
councillors and assemblymen—a system unaltered
since the Legislative Council was merged with the
Assembly in 1893.

Assiniboia [ə'sɪnə,bɔɪə] *n.* [*Assiniboin* <
Algonk.: Ojibwa one who cooks with stones]

Hist. **1** See 1958 quote.
1827 (1829) MacTAGGART *Three Years* I 62: The extensive savannahs of Asnaboyne, where the wild horses and buffaloes range, are beautiful to behold. . . . **1852** RICHARDSON *Arctic Exped.* 277: I was informed that in 1848 the natives at the Red River colony of Osnaboya were paid a high money price for their furs . . . and that they immediately crossed the boundary-line to purchase rum at the American post. . . . **1958** *Encyc.Can.* I 230/2: The earlier Red River Settlement of Lord Selkirk had the official name of Assiniboia.

2 a territory west of Manitoba created as one of the Northwest territories in 1882, now forming part of Alberta and of Saskatchewan.
1882 *Prince Albert Times* (Sask.) 13 Dec. 3/1: Assiniboia includes Qu'Appelle, South Saskatchewan and South River and Forts Pelley and Ellice. **1920** *Cdn Hist.Rev.* I 357: Had this course been pursued—had Assiniboia . . . been in a position to enter Confederation after negotiations upon terms mutually satisfactory to both parties—many of the bitterest controversies of the last fifty years might have been avoided.

3 a proposed province on the prairies.
1884 *Prince Albert Times* (Sask.) 16 Jan. 2/2: It is understood to be the intention of the Dominion Government this session, to create, by Act of Parliament, three provinces in the North West Territory, besides Manitoba, viz.: Alberta, Assiniboia and Saskatchewan.

Assiniboian *n. Hist.* a native or resident of Assiniboia (def. 2).
1884 *Moose Jaw News* (Sask.) 1 Feb. 2/2: In view of this we sometimes wonder what manner of man the future Assiniboian . . . will be. **1935** MORICE *Red River Insurrection* 95: . . . here is a passage from the sworn deposition of a prominent English speaking and Protestant Assiniboian. . . .

Assiniboian *adj. Hist.* of or having to do with Assiniboia.
1963 *Cdn Geog.Jnl* Apr. 118/3: This [Red River] cart was a contribution of the Selkirk settlers adapted to the Assiniboian conditions.

assist *n.* in hockey or lacrosse, the act of helping another player score a goal by setting him up with a pass; also the credit, one point, in the scoring statistics for making such a play.
1955 *Spectator* (Hamilton, Ont.) 25 Jan. 15/4: Montreal Canadiens . . . collect more assists per goal than any other club. **1963** *Kingston Whig-Standard* (Ont.) 17 Jan. 13/5: He made his presence felt by adding a goal and an assist to Kingston's winning cause.

Assomption belt or **sash** See **L'Assomption sash** and picture.
1908 MAIR *Mackenzie Basin* 41: The old Indian [wore] a shirt and corduroy vest to match, a faded kerchief tied around his head, an Assomption sash, and a begrimed body inside it all. . . . **1954** HAMILTON *Prairies* 107: The men wore their hair in what was known as the "Dutch cut" . . . but all were girded with the gaudy "assomption belt" fashioned sash-like in two folds around the waist.

asticameque *n.* See **atikameg.**

ateegi *n.* See **atigi.**

A-tent *n.* a tent with no vertical wall, the canvas

sloping from the ridgepole to the ground on both sides.
1897 TYRRELL *Sub-Arctics* 21: At this time only two small tents were used, an "A" tent for the canoemen and a wall tent, affording a little more headroom, for ourselves. **1954** BEZANSON *Sodbusters* 35: My little A-tent pitched close by on a round knoll beside the creek.

Athabasca [ˌæθəˈbæskə] *n.* [< Algonk.: Cree *athapaskaw* grass or reeds here and there] *Hist.* **1** the general region drained by the upper Athabasca River, a vast area important to the early fur trade. Cp. **Athabasca territory.**
1789 (1801) MACKENZIE *Voy.from Montreal* 70: They were of a small kind, and much inferior in size to those that frequent the vicinity of Athabasca. **1957** FISHER *Pemmican* 31: Colin is going to get brigades ready to go right into the Athabasca.

2 Fort Athabasca.
1860 *Nor'Wester* (R.R.S.) 14 Feb. 3/1: . . . while traversing the whole distance between Athabasca and Fort Pelly Mr. Christie did not meet a single Indian. **1929** MOBERLY *When Fur Was King* 9: One had been in British Columbia, the other at Athabasca.

3 one of the Northwest Territories created in 1882, now forming part of Alberta, of Saskatchewan, and of Manitoba.
1882 *Prince Albert Times* (Sask.) 13 Dec. 3/1: Athabasca takes in the celebrated Peace River districts. **1904** *U of T Stud.Hist.&Econ.* II 152: The fourth provisional district of Athabaska, like Mackenzie, Ungava, and Franklin, is said to be "unorganized," through not being represented in the territorial assembly.

Athabasca boat or **canoe** *Fur Trade, Hist.* an especially light, fast canoe used by the fur traders in the Athabasca country.
1824 (1931) MERK *Fur Trade* 219: Resolved . . . that five canoes containing 115 pieces manned by twenty-six men form part of the current outfit and that the remaining pieces be carried in on freight by the six Athabasca boats. **1954** CAMPBELL *Nor'Westers* 44: Each northern canoe held twenty-five ninety-pound packs instead of the sixty loaded into the Montreal canoes [and] fewer packs were carried in the Athabasca canoes, so as to make better time on the four-thousand-mile Rainy-Fort Chipewyan round trip between spring thaw and autumn freeze-up.

Athabasca department *Fur Trade, Hist.* an administrative district of the fur companies in the far northwest.
c**1799** MCKENZIE *Reminiscences* 19: Mr. Ross being no more, Mr. A. MacKenzie was named for the Athabasca department. . . . **1961** *Edmonton Jnl* 3 July 4/3: This Alexander McKenzie was in charge of the Athabasca Department of the Nor'Westers from 1804 to 1808.

Athabascan [ˌæθəˈbæskən] *n.* **1** *Hist.* a Nor'Wester employed in the Athabasca department.
1954 CAMPBELL *Nor'Westers* 46: . . . the Athabascans boasted that they could outpaddle any crew on Lake Winnipeg.

2 a native of the Athabasca territory, *q.v.*
1923 WALDO *Down Mackenzie* 73: The Athabascans
had brought birch-bark canoes of their own, but in
the hot sun the seams opened and the birch curled up.

Athabasca oil sands See **Alberta tar sands.**
1958 *Edmonton Jnl* 24 June 3 18/3: This area's
big ace-in-the-hole is the fantastic Athabasca oil
sands, and McMurray is right in the heart of them.
Comprising the world's largest known reserve of crude
oil, the black, sticky sands contain an estimated 300
billion barrels waiting to be exploited.

Athabasca scow *Hist.* See quote. See also **scow**
and **scow brigade.**
1938 *Beaver* Mar. 12: The Athabasca scow was . . . a
glorified packing box with just sufficient strength and
sea-worthiness to bring its cargo safely to its
destination where it was broken up and the lumber
used for building. . . .

Athabasca territory the region around Lake
Athabasca and the Athabasca River on the
northern Alberta-Saskatchewan border.
1953 *North Star* (Yellowknife) Jan.-Feb. 3/2: In
1944 he again flew the length of the Mackenzie and
through the Athabasca territory.

atigi ['ætɪgi *or* ə'tigi] *n.* [< Esk.; cf. *attike* a
covering] Also spelled *artigi, artiggi.* **1** an inner
shirt of summer skins with the hair turned
inward against the body, used mainly by Eskimos.
1576 (1889) HAKLUYT *Voyages* XII 81: The language
of the people of Meta incognita . . . attegay, a coate.
1882 GILDER *Schwatka's Search* 140: The women's
outside coats are always made of the short hairs, the
same as are their ar-tee'-gee. **1930** *Keewatin* 70: The
koletuk, or outer coat, is a most important article. It
is practically the same as the artikee, but is slightly
larger to go over it and is worn with the hair outside.
1959 *Camsell Arrow* Jan.-Feb. 23/2: The igloo was
unheated, but the X-ray machine quickly forced the
snow-house's occupants to doff their atigis. . . .

Two kinds of atigi (def. 2), one showing an amaut

2 a hooded outer garment of fur or other
material. See also **dickey, jumper²**, **kapta, kuletuk**
(def. 1), **overparka,** and **parka** (def. 1).
1934 GODSELL *Arctic Trader* 266: She had foresaken
her civilized garb for well fitting mukluks and a blue
cloth ahtegi. . . . **1958** *Edmonton Jnl* 24 June
3 10/8: Wolf or wolverine fur is used to trim the

atigi hoods—wolverine preferably, for ice caused by
condensation of the breath can be easily combed
from the fine fur. **1963** *Beaver* Winter 50/1: His
weatherbeaten face was the colour of old sealskin, but
his tagged artiggi couldn't disguise his blue eyes and
Scandinavian origin.

atikameg ['atɪkə,mɛg *or* a'tɪkəmɛg] *n.* [<
Algonk.: Cree] See **whitefish.** See also **tickameg.**
Various spellings.
1665 (1885) RADISSON *Voyages* 187: . . . if once we
could come to that place we should make good cheare
of a fish that they call Assickmack, wᶜʰ signifieth a
white fish. **1760** JEFFERYS *Descr.New France* 20: The
chief nourishment of the Michilimakinais was fish . . .
such as . . . asticameque, or white fish. **1858** (1860)
HIND *Assiniboine Exped.* II 68: This important source
of food in these regions is well named At-ik-um-aig.
1905 (1954) *B.C.Hist.Rev.* XVIII 169: There is an
excellent food fish in the lakes of that region—the
white fish ("titimeg" or "atikameg" as the Crees
called it). . . . **1909** NURSEY *Isaac Brock* 69: From
these deep cisterns he had seen the Indian fishermen
take whitefish, the *ahtikameg* (deer-of-the-water),
twenty pounds in weight. . . .

atikumaig *n.* See **atikameg.**

Atlantic area that part of Canada bordering
the Atlantic Ocean and the Gulf of the St.
Lawrence.
1962 *Chronicle-Herald* (Halifax) 8 Aug. 3/1: Professor
. . . Cairncross . . . made a study of the Atlantic area
for the Atlantic premiers a few years ago. . . .

Atlantic Provinces 1 *Hist.* the Provinces of
British North America in the Atlantic area.
1855 *Anglo-American Mag.* 87/1: To some persons,
it may seem as absurd thus to connect the Atlantic
Provinces with British Oregon . . . as to connect
them . . . with New Zealand.
2 Nova Scotia, New Brunswick, Prince Edward
Island, and, after joining Canada in 1949,
Newfoundland.
1869 *Mainland Guardian* (New Westminster, B.C.)
15 Sep. 3/3: I readily acknowledge that I am a firm
believer in the benefit of the great scheme of Union,
as applied to the Atlantic Provinces. . . . **1955**
Tribune-Post (Sackville, N.B.) 3 May 1/3: [They]
will make a summer tour of Eastern Canada to
include concerts in all four Atlantic provinces. **1964**
Star Wkly 12 Dec. 6/3: . . . the Atlantic provinces
have been trapped in a backwater of history. . . .

Atlantic salmon 1 a large salmon, *Salmo
salar,* native to the Atlantic Ocean, which enters
many of the rivers draining into that ocean and
which is much prized as a game and food fish.
1951 ANGIER *At Home* 119: [He had] spent some of
his springs fishing for trout and Atlantic salmon in
the . . . northeast. . . . **1964** JENNESS *Eskimo
Admin.* II 41: The Hudson's Bay Company . . .
tried to revive . . . the Atlantic salmon industry,
which had brought it more profit than the fur
trade. . . .
2 See **ouananiche.**
1965 *Globe and Mail* (Toronto) 17 Apr. 29/1: The two
taken last May were found in a hoop net being used
by Lands and Forests biologists studying Atlantic
Salmon (also known as ouananiche or landlocked
salmon) in Trout Lake.

Atlantic time See quotes.
1948 BORRETT *Historic Halifax* 20: . . . Nova Scotia

[stretches] so far toward Europe that "Atlantic Time," an hour in advance of the rest of the Continent, is the standard. **1952** PUTNAM *Cdn Regions* 123/1: The North Shore of the Gulf of St. Lawrence and the Gaspe Peninsula fall in the Atlantic Standard Time Zone, four hours later than Greenwich Mean Time. **1963** *Kingston Whig-Standard* (Ont.) 25 Apr. 14/4: . . . the 68th parallel of longitude [is] the dividing line between Eastern and Atlantic time. . . .

Atlantic Union See **Maritime Union.**
1964 *Star Wkly* 12 Dec. 6/1: I have been thinking about Atlantic Union since . . . 1947.

atluk ['ætlək] *n.* [< Esk.] See **aglu.**

atoca *n.* [< Cdn F *atocas* < Huron] *Obs.* the cranberry, *Vaccinium* sp.
1760 JEFFERYS *Descr.New France* 42: The atoca is a fruit growing in pods, the size of a cherry. **1830** *Trans.Lit.& Hist.Soc.Que.* III 99: This pleasant fruit is yearly collected in autumn, and brought to market under the Indian name of atoca, the proper French name of canneberge not being in use here. **1860** (1956) KOHL *Kitchi-Gami* 321: These ottakas do not require drying or preserving, for they keep through the whole winter in the Indian lodges. . . .

Atti ['æti] *n.* [< Esk.] See quote.
1909 CAMERON *New North* 254: There is an Evil Spirit, Atti, symbolizing cold and death.

attige *n.* See **atigi.**

attihawmeg *n. Obs.* See **atikemeg.**

attikameg *n.* See **atikameg.**

auksunai *n.* See **aksunai.**

auntsary [ˌant'særi] *n.* [< Aunt Sarah] the greater yellowlegs, *Totanus melanoleucas.*
1770 (1792) CARTWRIGHT *Journal* I 31: In the course of the day I shot three curlews, three grouse, and an auntsary.

Aurora trout a species of trout, *Salvelinus timagamiensis,* much prized as a game fish in Northern Ontario, where it was first reported near Kirkland Lake in 1924.
1960 *Kingston Whig-Standard* (Ont.) 21 Nov. 14/1: For 20 years Ontario fishing regulations have listed . . . Aurora trout. Yet only a handful of anglers have ever seen this brilliant blue and silver fish and not one has been legally caught since 1950. **1963** *Globe and Mail* (Toronto) 2 Mar. 30/1: Opening of the season . . . on speckled trout, brown and Aurora trout . . . was greeted [with] enthusiasm by . . . fishermen. . . .

autoboggan [ˌɑtə'bagən] *n.* [< auto + toboggan] See **motor toboggan** and picture.
1964 *Sask.News* Mar. 1/1: [Caption] Ditch duster is mounted on a toboggan and pulled by a gasoline-powered sled known as an autoboggan. **1964** *North* Mar.-Apr. 28: . . . instead of using dog teams many Eskimos travel by autoboggan.

auto camp a place for accommodating tourists, where cabins, cooking facilities, and so on are available for renting.
1925 *Beaver* Sep. 201/2: All our "tourists" report thousands of cars on the road and the auto camps doing a roaring business. **1930** MCCLUNG *Be Good* 27: [We] will one day take the Ford . . . and drive boldly into the gate of the Sunshine Auto Camp. . . .

Autonomist party *Hist.* See quote.
1963 *Sun* (Vancouver) 16 Apr. 4/1: The result was a Quebec Autonomist party which campaigned against any defence expenditure.

auto-stage *n. Obs.* a kind of early bus.
1916 WOOD *Tourist's N.W.* 413: Auto stages run to British Columbia and Washington towns. **1921** MARSHALL *Snowshoe Trail* 20: [He] operated a line of auto-stages during the summer months. . . .

auxiliary road See quote.
1958 *Edmonton Jnl* 18 June 31/5: The request was for a north-south auxiliary road one mile west, presently used by the school van in dry weather to be brought to market road standard. . . .

avalanche lily† *Rockies* any of several alpine plants of the genus *Erythronium* having white or yellow flowers. See also **glacier lily** and **snow-lily.**
1932 WINSON *Weather and Wings* 23: But the glory of the Alpines is the Avalanche Lily that gilds the banks as the snow retreats. . . . **1953** *Cdn Geog.Jnl* Oct. 136/2: . . . the first avalanche lilies are greeted by the piercing whistle of the hoary marmot.

avant de canot *Cdn French* See **bowsman.**
1931 NUTE *Voyageur* 26: [There was] a still larger paddle, which the bowsman or foreman (*avant de canot, devant,* or *ducent*) employed when running rapids or leaping small falls.

avatak ['avəˌtak] *n.* [< Esk.] *North* See **dan** (def. 1).
1966 *North* Mar.-Apr. 5/1: . . . it's all noise and confusion on the boat while the Eskimos work off steam by shouting and aimlessly rushing around: looking at harpoons, at avataks (sealskin bladders), fitting lines, then dropping that and picking up the rifles.

axeman† *n.* a man who makes his living in the bush working with his axe, especially a logger skilled in felling trees. See also **faller.**
1786 (1905) *Ont.Bur.Arch.Rep.* VIII 375: For the future no extra charges for chain or ax-men will be allowed. **1880** GORDON *Mountain and Prairie* 33: A staff of . . . axemen, voyageurs, etc. were to be engaged during the summer in the upper part of the Province. **1964** *Beautiful B.C.* Fall 40/1: The modern feller is an artist with a power saw and the axe-man is becoming almost a legend.

azion *n.* See **assean.**

B an abbreviation on tokens used in the fur trade. See **beaver** (def. 5).

1908 LAUT *Conquest N.W.* I 152: If the hunt exceeded the debt, the Indian might draw either cash or goods to the full amount or let the Company stand in his debt, receiving coins made from the lead of melted tea chests with 1, 2, 3, 4 *B*—beaver—stamped in the lead.

babiche [bə'biʃ, ba'biʃ, *or* 'bæbɪʃ] *n.* [< Cdn F < Algonk.; cf. Micmac *apapish* cord or thread] Also spelled *babich, babish.* **1** strips of leather, or thongs, made from the hide of a moose, caribou, etc. used for laces, threads, netting, etc. See also **battiche, iron of the country,** and **Northland string.** Cp. **shaganappi,** *n.* (def. 1).

[**1683** HENNEPIN *Les Moeurs des Sauvages* 88: Pour coudre leurs souliers, ils ne se servent que de babiche. . . .] **1806** (1960) FRASER *Letters and Journals* 243: Will you be able to send me over some green skins for windows and Babich. . . . **1820** (1938) SIMPSON *Athabasca Jnl* 192: You will trade . . . the large Babiche for Pack cords. . . . **1948** *Beaver* Mar. 16/2: Another important product of caribou skin is babiche, made from the dehaired hide. The skin is spread out flat and a long thong produced by cutting in a spiral, in a clockwise direction, starting from the edge. **1960** *Camsell Arrow* Jan.-Mar. 25: Indians . . . still look for babish, the moose hide thongs for sewing.

2 a rawhide whip.

1942 CAMPBELL *Thorn-Apple Tree* 25: Michael flicked his long babiche over the backs of his horses, while the waggon lurched and bumped over the corduroy. . . .

babine [bə'bin] *n.* [< Cdn F *babine* protruding lip] *Hist.* a labret for the lower lip, formerly used by the Babines and certain other Indian tribes of northern British Columbia.

1834 (1963) TOLMIE *Physician* 300: Crowds of Kittistzoo about the gate & amongst them some good looking women malgré the "babine." **1906** MORICE *Great Déné Race* 728: They [labrets] had for effect to considerably distend the lower lip, giving it a shocking prominence, which recalled that of the larger mammals, such as the moose, which was called *babine* by the French Canadians.

babish *n.* See **babiche.**

baby bonus *Informal* See **Family Allowance.**

1957 HUTCHISON *Canada* 17: " 'Tis all very well, de baby bonus and de like o' dat, and very nice for de wife to buy a bar of soap or a bit of beef, fer ye can't live solid on fish and keep up yer stren'th." **1964** *Calgary Herald* 29 Apr. 17/3: I would sooner see my baby bonus taken away and given to someone who needed it.

bacaloo bird See **baccalao bird.**

baccalao ['bækə‚leo] *n.* [< Pg. *bacalhao* cod-fish] Various spellings. **1** *Hist.* **a.** codfish, *Gadus morrhua.*

1555 (1869) BROWN *Cape Breton* 14: The Brytons and Frenche men are accustomed to take fysshe in the coastes of these landes, where is fownd great plenty of Tunnies which the inhabytauntes caul Baccalaos, whereof the lande was so named. **1841** *Trans.Lit.& Hist.Soc.Que.* IV 30: In the annals of the town of Dieppe, in France, there is authentic evidence to show,

that the inhabitants of that town did carry on Baccalo fisheries, on the coast of Newfoundland, and before the year 1500. **1962** *Cdn.Geog.Jnl* Nov. 148/3: *Bacalhao* survives in its Portuguese form in Bacalhao Island and in a French adaptation of the Portuguese in Baccalieu Island.

b. dried codfish.

1779 (1792) CARTWRIGHT *Journal* II 497: The ship now has on board seven hundred and fifty-eight tierces of salmon, and five hundred and thirty-four quintals of bacaleau, or dried cod-fish. **1905** DAWSON *St.Lawrence* 72: The word bacallaos is a Romance word, found in all the Romance languages for dried cod-fish.

2 See **baccalao bird.**

baccalao bird in coastal Labrador and northeast Newfoundland, any of several birds of the family *Alcidae,* as the puffin, *Fratercula artica,* the razor-billed auk, *Alca torda,* the common murre, *Uria aalge,* and the thick-billed murre, *U. lomvia.* See also **barra-couta.** Also *Baccalieu bird.* Various other spellings.

1819 ANSPACH *Hist.Nfld* 392: This observation . . . that birds did not venture to any considerable distance from land, is not so strictly applicable to the Baccalao and other birds in the vicinity of Newfoundland. **1822** CORMACK *Narr.Nfld* 8: This island . . . is famous for the numbers of sea-fowl that frequent it in the breeding season, principally the puffin, called on this coast the Baccalao or Baccalieu bird. **1861** DE BOILIEU *Labrador Life* 15: From certain movements or "indications" on the part of the bird, known on the coast as the Barcaliau bird . . . we knew it was migrating to the Funk or Bird Island for the purpose of breeding. **1956** MCATEE *Folk-Names* 38: Razor-billed Auk [is also called] Baccaloo, Backalew bird. . . . *Ibid.* 40: Common Puffin [is also called] Baccalieu bird. . . . **1960** TUCK *The Murres* 34: "Baccalieu" (or Baccalo) birds is a traditional name in Newfoundland for the murres nesting on Baccalieu Island, and is usually used only when the birds are in summer plumage.

Baccalaos *n. Hist.* **1** an early name for the region now comprising Newfoundland, Cape Breton, Nova Scotia, Labrador. Cp. **baccalao.**

1555 (1869) BROWN *Cape Breton* 14: The newe lande of Baccalaos is a coulde region, whose inhabitantes are Idolatours and praye to the sonne and moone and dyuers Idoles. **1869** *Ibid.* 15: Immediately after the discovery of the Baccalaos, which embraced Nova Scotia, Cape Breton, and Newfoundland, the fishermen of Normandy, Brittany, and the Basque Provinces, began to frequent the coasts to take cod. **1966** *North* July-Aug. 31/2: It was almost a decade before it was clearly demonstrated that there was no meeting of the waters anywhere within hundreds of leagues of Darien. Cortes suggested a search up the northeast coast towards Bacalaos (Newfoundland).

2 Atlantic codfishing grounds, especially the Grand Banks region.

1936 DENTON & LORD *World Geography* 128: The fishermen manned their little craft, and set sail across the Atlantic, fighting contrary winds, skirting icebergs, and creeping through the fog-blanket to find the "baccalaos," the codfish seas of the new world.

Baccalieu ['bækə‚lu] *n.* See **baccalao bird.**

bachelor (seal) *n.* a young adult male seal or sea lion that has not yet mated.

1936 DENTON & LORD *World Geography* 145: The men land upon the ice floes, kill the bachelor seals with blows from a stout gaff, and drag the carcasses to the water's edge where small boats gather the hides, to which a thick layer of fat adheres. **1960** *Canadian Audubon* Jan.-Feb. 2/2: Breeding localities are known as "rookeries"; breeding adults are "bulls" and "cows"; adults not yet breeding are "bachelors" and "virgins"; young of both sexes are "pups."

bachelors' hall *Hist.* the quarters of unmarried clerks at certain Hudson's Bay Company trading posts.
1848 BALLANTYNE *Hudson's Bay* 25: Bachelors' Hall, indeed, was worthy of its name, being a place that would have killed any woman, so full was it of smoke, noise, and confusion. **1869** (1941) *Beaver* June 14/2: They have seized . . . Bachelors' Hall and all the rooms over the office as their offices and bedrooms. **1957** *Ibid.* Winter 40/1: [The building] on the right is Bachelors' Hall where R. M. Ballantine [sic] lived.

backband *n.* that part of a sled-dog's harness that goes over his back. See picture at **sled dog**.
1900 LONDON *Son of Wolf* 191: There was an ingathering of backbands, a tightening of traces; the sleds leaped forward. . . . **1944** CLAY *Fur Thieves* 116: . . . he took the bells out of the carriole, where they had laid muffled in an old blanket, and fastened them to the backbands of the dogs' harness.

back-block *n.* a block of land in the back country, *q.v.*; hence (*usually plural*) an isolated rural region. See also **back concession** (def. 2a). Cp. **block** (def. 1).
1910 HAYDON *Riders of the Plains* 285: True it is that men and women in the back-blocks sometimes break down under the stress of adverse circumstances and go mad. **1947** TAYLOR *Canada* 464: Members of the Geological Survey in the backblocks of both Ontario and Quebec still travel in canoes. . . . **1956** RADDALL *Wings* 86: He looked more like an old-fashioned back-block preacher of the evangelical kind. . . .

back-board *n.* See **cradle-board**. See also **tikinagan**.
1743 (1949) ISHAM *Observations* 106: As soon as the child is born, they wash itt in Lu'ck warm water, put it in a Rabbit skin and tie itt in a cradle or back board. . . . **1863** WALSHE *Cedar Creek* 265: Perhaps nothing in the camp amused the European young lady more than the infants, the "papooses," in their back-board cradles, buried up to the armpits in moss. . . . **1913** JOHNSON *Shagganappi* 153: The Redskin boy-child . . . is not many hours old before careful hands wrap him about with gay-beaded bands that are strapped to the carven and colored back-board. . . .

back-bush *n.* See **backwoods**.
1946 WOOD *Rockies* 123: The Canada Jay . . . is the Jay-dee of the back-bush youngsters. . . . **1963** *Sun* (Vancouver) 29 May 19/1: The idea we didn't voice as often was the solid family experience that came from tenting. The further into the backbush, the thicker the family cement.

back-channel *n.* See **snye** (def. 2a).
1903 LONDON *Call of the Wild* 78: He . . . crossed a back channel filled with rough ice to another island, gained a third island, curved back to the main river, and in desperation started to cross it. **1933** MERRICK *True North* 315: Late in the morning we pulled out for Mud Lake, only six miles away by a shortcut called the back channel.

backcheck *v.* engage in backchecking.
1964 *Globe and Mail* (Toronto) 22 Dec. 30/1: He is not the complete hockey player, faulted in expert opinion for his reluctance to backcheck.

backchecker *n.* a person who engages in back-checking.
1963 *Hockey Illust.* Dec. 34/2: He . . . is one of the league's best backcheckers. **1965** *Weekend Mag.* 6 Mar. 40/1: In normal action . . . he may shoot fairly long because of a threatening back-checker.

backchecking *n.* in hockey or lacrosse, the practice whereby forwards, having lost the puck or ball to the opposition, attempt to retrieve it by harrying the carrier as he moves towards their goal.
1955 *Herald-Tribune* 4 Mar. 5/3: Heavy backchecking on both sides held down the scoring plays. . . . **1964** *Globe and Mail* (Toronto) 22 Dec. 30/1: . . . they control the puck so much that backchecking is an absolute contradiction.

back concession 1 a concession (def. 2), some distance removed from urban and heavily settled areas, especially one set some distance back from the St. Lawrence River and the Lower Lakes. Cp. **back range**.
1791 (1905) *Ont.Bur.Arch.Rep.* III xciv: Such as have applied for Land . . . will not go back into the back concessions to settle while there is so much waste and unoccupied land in front. **1885** HAIGHT *Country Life* 13: The home we now inhabited was altogether different from the one we had left in the back concession. . . . **1958** *Kingston Whig-Standard* (Ont.) 7 Jan. 4/4: . . . Mr. Stoliker states that back-concession farmers need to be told and advised what farmers should do and when.

2 a. (*often plural*) any rural region. See also **back-block** and **concessions**.
1929 WAAGEN *Wayside Cross* 86: He had been absent for over a fortnight, plying his trade in the back Concessions. **1963** *Globe and Mail* (Toronto) 25 May 8/2: [Calgary dateline] No one had considered . . . the mood of farmers on back concessions [in Alberta]. . . .

b. *Derog.* in attributive uses connoting lack of sophistication, education, etc.
1960 *Press* July 6: Before I am accused of asking fellow socialists to drop their socialism in favour of a nebulous united front with petty nationalists and back-concession statesmen, let me say emphatically that is not my intention. **1963** *Globe and Mail* (Toronto) 21 Feb. 6/3: "Here's Harkness, the only guy probably who could win a clear majority for the Conservatives in this election, if he was the leader, and he's talking like some back-concession reeve, or something."

back country† **1** unsettled regions remote from civilization; the wilderness beyond the explored areas.
1785 HUNTER *Diary* 73: The poor man gave us some account of their expedition into the back country. **1826** (1931) MERK *Fur Trade* 263: The Hunting grounds immediately on the Northern banks of the Columbia are nearly exhausted in respect to Fur bearing Animals but the back country is still productive. . . . **1955** HOBSON *Nothing Too Good* 226: These back-country Indians do not make friends easily. . . . **1964** *Weekend Mag.* 11 July 20/2: . . . devil's club [is] the thorned scourge of hikers in much of British Columbia's back country.

2 a rural region; farm district. See also **outlands**.

1844 *Bytown* [Ottawa] *Gaz.* 8 Aug. 2/6: A road into the interior . . . would not only benefit Kingston, (so much in want of a productive back country) but would open new tracts for settlement. . . . **1965** *Star Wkly* 2 Jan. 37/2: The nearest doctor was 70 miles away over a poor back-country road. . . .

Back Door Route *Hist.* a route to the Klondike gold fields by way of Edmonton and the Mackenzie and Yukon river systems.
1958 *Edmonton Jnl* 18 July 19/6: They called it the "Back Door Route" in 1898 and before a year had passed hundreds of weary, worn and broken men had come back over Edmonton's threshold from the wild and forbidding northland after failing to reach the golden riches of the Klondike.

back East or **east 1** *West* Ontario, especially Southern Ontario; sometimes, also Quebec and the Maritimes. Cp. **down East.**
1903 *Eye Opener* (High River, Alta) 24 Oct. 1/2: . . . I wouldn't live back East again and work for other people. **1954** *North Star* (Yellowknife) Apr. 1/2: Back east . . . Merv Hardie has been gaining a well-deserved reputation for plain speaking.
2 See quote.
1963 *Canada Month* May 13/1: It [B.C.] is the Real West—so far west that Calgary is "back East."

backer *n.* in curling, a rock resting in the back zone of the house and functioning as a buffer for later rocks, preventing them from sliding outside the circle.
1964 *Calgary Herald* 20 Mar. 16/4: He punched Dagg's rock against a backer and allowed Canada to steal one.

backfat *n.* a layer of choice fat found between the skin and muscles of a well-fed animal, especially along the back. See also **depouille.** Cp. **Indian bread** (def. 1). Also **back fat.**
1801 (1933) MCLEOD *Diary* 161: Some of the men [are] at work making horse sledges, others melting or boiling back (Buffaloe) fat to put in the Pimican. . . . **1913** COWIE *Adventurers* 380: We took the tongue, the boss and the backfat and rode back to camp. **1923** (1926) DICKIE *Cdn West* 167: The Indians killed the buffalo recklessly . . . they killed for the tongues and backfats alone. **1965** SYMINGTON *Tuktu* 50: A bull caribou in the autumn may weigh 300 pounds, and a fifth of that weight may be fat—perhaps 40 pounds in a single slab of back fat. . . .

backfire† *n.* a fire deliberately set in an attempt to prevent the spread of a prairie or forest fire by burning off the area in front of it.
1905 (1910) HAYDON *Riders of the Plains* 283: Suddenly the fire appeared . . . rushing down with hurricane force, and jumping the back-fire Mr. Conradi had made. . . . **1959** *Globe and Mail* (Toronto) 23 July 2/1: . . . while setting a backfire against a prairie fire . . . he . . . thought, "I'd sure love to own a farm right here."

backfire† *v.* start a backfire.
1930 COOPER *Challenge of Bush* 237: At other points they back-fired, taking advantage of every change of wind that they might set the forest to blazing and consume the enemy with its own flames. **1963** SYMONS *Many Trails* 42: And so . . . we set to . . . to urge the broncos across the valley with the shares sunk deep, so

that we would have a chance to backfire.

backfire line in forest-fire fighting, a line along which a series of backfires is set.
1953 *Cdn Geog.Jnl* XLVI 49/1: Helicopters placed crew bosses on the back-fire line and removed them as conditions warranted. . . .

back-firing† *n.* the practice or process of setting backfires; also, an instance of this practice.
1909 (1965) *Sask.Hist.* Spring 77: one of our party has just gone to a point of vantage and on his report we shall consider the wisdom of back-firing. . . . A fine method to make flame devour flame. **1955** GOWLAND *Smoke* 179: There was still some equipment to come, including the pumps, gas and oil, and kerosene for back-firing.

back forty the back forty acres, that part of a farm most remote from the house and barn.
1961 MITCHELL *Jake and the Kid* 105: "He was settin' in this here Dooley's back 40 one day an' he looked up and seen one a them there four-engine bombers they're flyin' tuh Roosia. . . ." *Ibid.* 151: There was a little piece saying that Jake Trumper was going to [make] rain on Tuesday next at Tincher's back forty. . . . **1964** *Canadian Wkly* 5 Dec. 9/1: Remember when we used to cut our own Christmas tree in the back forty.

back-forty accent rural or uneducated speech.
1958 *Ottawa Citizen* 25 Aug. 9/3: Whether he was cracking jokes in his best "back forty" accent, or singing . . . he gave the audience what it wanted.

back junk See **backlog.**
1958 HARRINGTON *Sea Stories from Newfoundland* 117: On Christmas Eve, therefore, the "backjunk" blazed higher and brighter than usual in the big, open fireplaces. **1958** *Kingston Whig-Standard* (Ont.) 17 Dec. 27/7: Huge fire places are filled with "back junk"— usually the largest tree in the forest that will burn through the 12 days of Christmas. . . .

back lakes *Hist.* in Upper Canada, the many lakes inland from the north shore of Lake Ontario, such as Lake Simcoe, Rice Lake, etc.
1834 (1926) LANGTON *Early U.C.* 77: One or other of us will go over to Rochester, with a man who knows the points of an ox, and bring over six yoke . . . for ourselves and others on the Back Lakes. **1937** *Cdn Hist.Rev.* XVIII 31: These families not only contributed greatly to the development of the district, but most of them wrote extensively concerning their experiences, and made the "back lakes" region well known in the United Kingdom and the United States. **1964** GUILLET *Pioneer Days* 84: In the early forties the "back lakes" almost as far west as Lake Simcoe were being utilized to float square timber by way of the Trent system. . . .

backlander *n. Hist.* a settler in the back country, *q.v.*
1869 BROWN *Cape Breton* 425: All the best lands fronting on the lakes, rivers, and sea-coast, were taken up previous to the year 1820; since that period the lands to the rear of the front lots have been occupied by the later immigrants, who are in consequence distinguished by the name of "Backlanders."

backlands† *n.pl.* back country (def. 1); wild, unsettled or sparsely settled areas.
1830 MOORSOM *Letters N.S.* 130: The nearest approach that I have observed among this race [negroes] is in a few families who occupy the back-lands of Great Tracadie, an Acadian township near the Gut of Canso. **1960** *New Party Newsletter* Oct.-Nov. 3/2: In the early

1800's people said that these backlands would produce rich lumber fortunes.

backlog† *n.* a large log placed at the back of a wood fire to make it last. See also **back junk.**
1829 MACTAGGART *Three Years* I 52: When the party got to the place, there was a . . . blazing fire with a maple back log. . . . **1956** EVANS *Mountain Dog* 128: At what had been the door of the tent, a charred backlog was grown over with moss.

backpack† *n.* a pack carried on one's back.
1955 GOWLAND *Smoke* 26: Opposite the door was a long table fixed to the wall . . . a rack with various tools and a back-pack water bag with syringes to dowse small fires. **1964** *Canadian Wkly* 13 June 10/3: Reg shook off his backpack.

backpack *v.* carry on one's back. Cp. **pack,** *v.* (def. 2a).
1956 LEECHMAN *Native Tribes* 37: . . . whatever was not carried on the toboggans had to be backpacked. For this, the Algonkians used the tump line. . . . **1965** *Islander* 13 June 12/2: Others found work back-packing supplies from the end of the road to the mine camps . . . 60 to 90 pounds of supplies strapped to their backs.

backpacker *n.* one who carries a pack on his back, especially as a freighter (def. 1).
1950 HUTCHISON *Fraser* 84: Billy Ballou . . . established a fairly regular express service from Victoria to the lower Fraser mines by steamboat, canoe, mule and backpacker.

backpacking *n.* the work of a backpacker, *q.v.*
1921 HAWORTH *Trailmakers* 213: As those who have tried it know, back-packing through the mountains is the hardest work a man ever tried. **1965** *B.C. Digest* Aug. 21/1 : . . . pushing a rail car is easier than back-packing.

back range *Que.* a range of lots located back from the river front. See also **range** (def. 2a). Cp. **back concession** (def. 1).
1872 *Canadian Mthly* Feb. 101/1 : Counties of the South Shore of the St. Lawrence, east of Quebec, [are] peopled chiefly by French-speaking inhabitants, all having "back ranges."

back-setting† *n.* See 1912 quote.
1882 (1883) *Cdn North-West* 18: I arrived at . . . Brandon on the 28th of May, 1881, and commenced to break my land on the 5th of June . . . paying 4 dols. per acre for breaking, and 3 dols. 50c. for back-setting. **1912** SANDILANDS *West.Cdn Dict.* 4: The prairie is first "broken"; that is, ploughed as thin as possible, and back-setting is a second and deeper ploughing, after the original surface sod has rotted.

back settlement† a settlement located some distance back from the shore of a lake, ocean, river, etc. See also **lines** (def. 2). Cp. **back concession** (def. 1) and **back township.**
1766 *Quebec Gaz.* 1 Dec. 1/1 : From the Thinness of the back settlements, would not the Stamp Act be extremely inconvenient to the Inhabitants, if executed. **1805** BOULTON *Upper Canada* 6: Many of the back settlements are well inhabited, and are as near to a market for their superfluous produce as those on the river. **1934** DENNIS *Down in N.S.* 262: Behind Pubnico is the forest. There are no back settlements. The people live along the shore.

backsettler† *n. Obs.* one who lives in a back settlement.
1828 *Cdn Freeman* (York [Toronto]) 31 July 2/5: The good old freeholders of Durham were not to be duped or shaken, however easily the backsettlers might be won. **1845** BEAVAN *Life in Backwoods N.B.* 14: Many beautiful articles are made by them of [birch bark], and to the back settlers it is invaluable.

Back's grayling [< Sir George *Back*, British explorer, 1796-1878] See **Arctic grayling.**
1820 (1823) FRANKLIN *Journey* 248: There are two other species of Coregoni in Winter Lake, Back's grayling and the round fish. . . . **1947** *Beaver* Dec. 24/1 : The Arctic grayling, or Back's Grayling, is to be found in all waters tributary to the Mackenzie.

back stoop a back porch, usually unroofed. See also **stoop.**
1891 *Grip* (Toronto) 1 Aug. 77/1 : Mr Adolphus Hitone, of Jarvis Street, sits around on his back stoop in his shirtsleeves on these fine evenings. **1966** *Globe and Mail* (Toronto) 21 July 21/8 : It's one thing to have [them] looking at you and remarking that the grass is getting a little long, and another to have your reveries on the back stoop rudely interrupted by the sound of a police siren.

back-strap meat See quote. Cp. **backfat.**
1963 PATTERSON *Far Pastures* 212: . . . Jim . . . was busy skinning back the hide [of the moose] and cutting out the tender back-strap meat from each side of the backbone.

back-tilt *n. Lab.* See 1792 quote. Cp. **tilt** and **tilt-back.**
1770 (1792) CARTWRIGHT *Journal* I 50: The wind coming to the eastward, we . . . constructed a back-tilt near the brook. **1792** *Ibid.* II x: A Back-tilt is a shed made of boughs, resembling the section of a roof; the back part is placed towards the wind, and a fire is generally made in the front.

back to the blanket See **blanket** (def. 1b).

back township a township or settlement remote from or isolated from centres of population; formerly, one of the back settlements, *q.v.*, of Upper and Lower Canada. Cp. **back concession.**
1805 BOULTON *Upper Canada* 66: Many of the back townships have been intentionally omitted, as my design was transcribed. **1890** *Grip* (Toronto) 28 June 441/1 : His appearance denoted that he had come in from the back townships to see the Carnival. **1926** LANGTON *Early U.C.* xxix : Mr. B. a native Canadian told Mrs. Jameson that not one person in seventy, in the back townships, could read or write. **1957** GUILLET *Valley of the Trent* xlv n : A grandson of Gilles Stone . . . removed from "the front" to "the back townships". . . .

back trail 1 a. a track leading back to a starting place; the trail back.
1913 WILLIAMS *Wilderness Trail* 53 : Then . . . they "mushed" the dogs on the back trail. . . . **1955** HOBSON *Nothing Too Good* 183 : Twenty tons of pounding beef hit the back trail for their home range.
b. take no back trail, refuse to turn back; never give up.
1912 CONNOR *Corporal Cameron* 305 : McIvor was of the kind that takes no back trail.
2 a track or trace remaining as evidence of something having passed.

1913 WILLIAMS *Wilderness Trail* 113: Morning found them fully ten miles on their way, with no back trail, and the blizzard was lessening perceptibly. **1921** HEMING *Drama of Forests* 225: The back trail will tell him if the animal was travelling fast or slow, whether it was fleeing in fright,or feeding. . . .

back-trail *v.* **1** follow the trail left by a person or animal.
1909 ROBERTS *Backwoodsman* 176: His enemies back-trailed him and caught him off guard.

2 of livestock, turn around and move in the direction opposite to that in which they are being herded.
1955 HOBSON *Nothing Too Good* 64: Cattle would back-trail on us through the timber, singly, in pairs, and in small bunches all night.

back tree *Lumbering* one of the trees to which a skyline, *q.v.*, is attached.
1942 HAIG-BROWN *Timber* 254: In the case of a skidder, a heavy cable [is] stretched from the spar tree out to a "back tree" at the far edge of the setting.

back tripping the moving of goods over a certain route in stages.
1928 WALDEN *Dog-Puncher* 3: There we made our first camp . . . along with about a hundred other men who were getting their provisions up the trail by repeated "back tripping" or relays.

backwoods† *n.pl.* the bush country or back settlements, *qq.v.*; regions remote from well-settled, civilized areas. See also **outlands**.
1834 (1926) LANGTON *Early U.C.* 58: As I am on the subject of eating, you may wish to know how we lived in the backwoods. **1964** *Edmonton Jnl* 11 July 3/6: The raw shanty lad who came out of the backwoods of Quebec . . . would win a place in the mythology of the last frontier.

backwoods or **backwood**† *adj.* **1** of, or having to do with, the backwoods.
1835 (1926) LANGTON *Early U.C.* 147: . . . Dennistoun and I having polished our backwoods integuments a little wrote some letters. **1840** WILLIS *Cdn Scenery* I 99: The tone . . . appears to have been in a great measure given by such Americans as came . . . from the back-wood tracts. **1959** *Star Wkly* 22 Aug. 17/2: In 1953 lobster cops raided a backwoods cannery at Pousette Lake, seven miles south of Shediac, N.B.

2 native to, or living in, the backwoods.
1845 BEAVAN *Life in Backwoods N.B.* 30: . . . on the large airy-looking couches [was] displayed a splendid coverlet of homespun wool . . . the possessing of which is the first ambition of a back-wood matron. **1963** *Weekend Mag.* 16 Nov. 41/1: He [the Canada jay] is a backwoods bird.

3 *Derog.* marked by the absence of taste, tact, sophistication, etc.
1852 MOODIE *Roughing It* 262: Morgan . . . went into the kitchen to light his pipe at the stove, and, with true backwood carelessness, let the hot cinder fall among the dry chips that strewed the floor. **1902** CONNOR *Glengarry* 69: . . . the Front, in all matters pertaining to culture and fashion, thought itself quite superior to the more backwoods country. . . . **1963** *Calgary Herald* 29 Oct. 8/1: Richard's reasoning is backwoods, his public broadcasting of the reasoning is bush.

backwoodser *n.* See **backwoodsman**.
1883 FRASER *Shanty* 318: Their acquaintance with the shanty and the work is limited to an occasional flying visit . . . when they burst in upon the astonished simple-minded backwoodsers with jingling bells and glorious equipages. . . .

backwoodsman† *n.* one who works or lives in the backwoods.
1817 *U.C.Gaz.* (York [Toronto]) 17 July 115/4: The parts of the country they inhabit are rising very fast in wealth and importance, and they are as dextrous in the use of the axe or the gun, as any American backwoodsman. **1963** *Weekend Mag.* 16 Nov. 41/1: He [the Canada jay] is the companion and familiar of the backwoodsman . . .

bad ice thin or rotten, *q.v.*, ice.
1933 MERRICK *True North* 192: At its far end we skirted a small rapid, bordered with bad ice and water under the snow.

bad Indian an untrustworthy Indian, especially one hostile to the whites; a renegade Indian. Cp. **good Indian**.
1791 LONG *Voyages* 104: Among them was an Indian named *Ogashy,* or the horse: he was reckoned, even by his own tribe, a bad Indian. **1824** (1955) BLACK *Journal* 122: I told them . . . that I had seen some bad Indians & had seen them destroyed for bad Indians never lived long. **1963** *Beaver* Summer 37/1: A few years ago he toured with a circus, one of the "bad Indians" who attacked a stage coach.

bad-land caribou See **Barren Ground caribou**.
1930 BEAMES *Army* 288: Billy . . . picked up two bad-land caribou, which are much better eating.

badlands *n.pl.* **1** an arid region in S. Alberta and S.W. Saskatchewan characterized by severe erosion and weird land formations and containing dinosaur and other fossils.
1910 HAYDON *Riders of the Plains* 103: At the same time, a certain amount of horse and cattle stealing . . . was . . . to be laid at the doors of . . . white desperadoes who came up from the border "bad lands." **1962** *Canadian* June 39/2: . . . from the Drumheller Badlands . . . came dinosaur bone jewelry.

2 swampy wasteland characterized by stunted vegetation, and rock; barrens. See also **muskeg**. Also *badland.*
1868 DAWSON *Acadian Geology* 19: They are divisible into two groups, —a lower . . . to which the name "Bad Lands beds" may be given. . . . **1958** WATTERS *B.C. Cent.Anthol.* 236: Across the Fraser . . . the big ranches . . . and, farther west, the badlands of stunted trees and swampy roads seem to have resisted progress. **1966** *Kingston Whig-Standard* (Ont.) 27 Aug. 4/3: By their paddles . . . they forge into . . . badland . . . beyond the smog of civilization.

bad man *West and North* **1** *Hist.* a desperado; outlaw; rustler.
1859 *Brit.Colonist* (Victoria) 22 Jan. 1/3: Now I ask . . . what did the men mean by surrounding the constable . . . it was they who tacitly aided the bad men to rescue the prisoner. **1958** KELSEY *B.C.Rides a Star* 173: On the hill . . . still stands the gnarled pine tree, a frayed rope dangling from it, and graves of badmen who met justice-in-the-rough upon it.

2 a person who becomes disorderly, often breaking the law, while under the influence of liquor.

1898 *Yukon Midnight Sun* (Dawson) 11 June 4/1: Too much "fire water" in town this week after a long dry spell was the indirect cause of several "bad men" visiting the barracks and police courts. **1958** BERTON *Klondike* 23: There were few "bad men" in Fortymile; ... it was a community that hewed surprisingly closely to the Christian ethic.

3 *Slang* in hockey, a player who earns a great many penalties for rough, illegal play.

1958 *Weekend Mag.* 6 Dec. 40/1: [He] had developed into a scoring champ after abandoning a career as hockey "bad man." **1964** *Maclean's* 21 Mar. 49/4: ... Brewer, the Leafs' bad man, speared Stan Mikita. ...

bad medicine 1 in Indian parlance: **a.** misfortune; witchcraft; evil genius. Cp. **big medicine** and **good medicine**.

1825 SIMPSON *Fur Trade* 136: Some of them have it that I am one of the "Master of Life's Sons" sent to see "if their hearts were good" and others that I am his "War Chief" with bad medicine if their hearts were bad. **1955** RICH in BLACK *Journal* xcii: His widow laid his death at Black's door: the bad medicine of the white trader was the cause of it, she said. ...

b. in phrases employing *throw*.

*c*1804 (1890) GRANT *Sauteux Indians* 364: It is very singular that they seldom impute sickness to any natural cause, but ... imagine that some person has ... thrown bad medicine in their way. **1897** YOUNG *Indian Trail* 89: Others were seen rubbing their eyes, as though they feared that by some witchery bad medicine had been thrown in them. ...

c. certain objects believed to have the power to work evil magic against an enemy.

1922 JOHNSON *Legends of Vancouver* 142: About her person she carried the renowned "Bad Medicine" that every Indian believes in—medicine that weakened the arm of the warrior in battle.

2 *Slang* anything worthless or undesirable.

1962 *Alta Hist.Rev.* Autumn 14/2: "Bad medicine," "chaffy" ... and "pizen," are applied to anything worthless on the Eastern slope of the Rockies. ...

bad woods *Obs.* a tract of forest characterized by brush, brulé (def. 1), and down timber, *q.v.*

1827 (1912) ERMATINGER *Express Jnl* 109: Encamped on the banks of the [Athabasca] River, having passed Campment des Vaches and a piece of Bad Woods.

bag *n.* **1** See **taureau** (def. 1).

1800 (1820) HARMON *Journal* 48: This compound is put into bags, made of the skins of buffaloes. ...

2 See **taureau** (def. 2).

1957 FISHER *Pemmican* 189: Just the same he would take ... two ninety-pound bags of pemmican, for a man ate like hell in deep-zero weather.

3 *Lumbering* See **bag boom.**

*c*1963 *New Sounds* 13/2: The river carries the floating logs into a "bag" formed by a necklace of huge logs from Western Canada. When the 10,000 to 12,000 cords of pulpwood have filled the bag the back end is closed and the floating cargo is towed to the mill at the speed of one mile an hour. **1965** *Islander* 6 June 16/1: A fourth raft, called "the Bag," consisted merely of a mass of logs collected without cross-logs as in the old type flat raft. It was used only in sheltered areas.

bag boom *Esp.West Coast* a type of boom (def. 3b) used in towing logs, especially pulp sticks, loosely packed and enclosed by linked boom logs. Such a boom assumes a baglike shape under tow. See picture at **boom.** See also **bag** (def. 2).

1958 KELSEY *B.C.Rides a Star* 24: Bag booms filled with millions of feet of logs pattern their harbours. *Ibid.* 157: Trucks rolling on sixteen powerful tires to dump tons of 20- to 30-foot logs into bag booms pounded its gravel to powder.

baggataway [bəˈgætə,we] *n.* [< Algonk.; cf. Cree *pakahatūwēo* he plays ball] *Hist.* a game formerly played by Indians in eastern Canada, each player having a ball and stick equipped with a netted pouch at one end; an early form of lacrosse, *q.v.* See also **hurdle.**

1763 (1901) HENRY (Elder) *Travels* 77: Baggatiway, called by the Canadians *le jeu de la crosse*, is played with a bat and a ball. The bat is about four feet in length, curved, and terminating in a sort of racket. Two posts are planted in the ground, at a considerable distance from each other, as a mile, or more. Each party has its post, and the game consists of throwing the ball up to the post of the adversary. The ball, at the beginning is placed in the middle of the course, and each party endeavours as well to throw the ball out of the direction of its own post, as into that of the adversary's. **1844** MARRYAT *Settlers in Can.* 45: The Indians are very partial to, and exceedingly dextrous at, a game called the "Baggatiway". ... **1965** *Globe and Mail* (Toronto) 15 Sep. 30/1: The Sacs lost the baggataway war staged for Jack Cartier's benefit, but they got in some good whacks before subsiding.

baidar [ˈbaɪdar] *n.* [< Russian *baidara* < Esk.-Aleut.] a large skin boat resembling an oomiak, *q.v.*, used by the natives of the Alaska coast and adjacent regions. Cp. **baidarka.** Also spelled *bidar, bidarra.*

1838 (1947) HARGRAVE *Correspondence* 260: I ... succeeded in hauling them ashore, and soon obtained one of their large baidars, in which myself and followers embarked. **1963** *Beaver* Autumn 7/1: They were visited by many Eskimos in their baidars. ...

baidarka [baɪˈdarkə] *n.* [< Russian, dim. of *baidara*; see **baidar**] a kayaklike skin boat having two, or occasionally three, cockpits. Cp. **baidar.** Also spelled *bidarka.*

☛*Although nowadays confined largely to the Alaska region, this term seems to have been used first in English by explorers and fur traders in contact with the Russian traders in northern B.C., the Yukon, and Alaska.*

1834 (1963) TOLMIE *Physician* 283: The youth took his departure ... soon after a bidarka approached ... paddled by two men ... the officer sitting in the middle seat. **1947** *B.C.Hist.Qtly* Jan. 24: The *baidarka* was long, narrow, and pointed at each end, varying in length from 12 to 20 feet depending on the number of hatches. The width was 20 to 24 inches and the depth only 20 inches, so that the craft could be propelled swiftly in shallow water.

bain or **bang** *n.* [< Cdn F *beigne* fritter] *Obs.* See quotes.

1862 (1931) CHEADLE *Journal* 45: [He] gave us a loaf of bread ... a nice change after bain. **1869** KENNICOTT *Journal* 116: ... for supper we had a large caribou roasted and some "bangs" —cakes made by frying a batter of flour and water in tallow, improved by the addition of some pounded whitefish roe.

Bain wagon [prob. after the maker-designer] *Hist.* a large freight wagon that was widely used in

the West in the late 19th and early 20th centuries.
1897 *B.C.Mining Jnl* (Ashcroft) 13 Feb. 2/4:
Largest stock in the province and best assortment
American Bain wagons, also Canadian Bain suitable
for freighting and farm purposes. **1934** GODSELL *Arctic
Trader* 113: Every few miles we would overtake strings
of heavily laden Bain wagons hauled by horses, mules,
or even oxen.... **1955** HARDY *Alta Anthol.* 105:
And from the north, east, west, and south, by horse and
buggy, by democrat, in Bain wagons pulled by oxen, on
horseback and on Shanks' mare, thousands of people
flocked into the city.

baiting *n.* the setting out of poisoned bait for
wolves or coyotes (def. 1).
1958 *Alaska Sportsman* Dec. 36/2: [with reference to the
Yukon] We repeated the baiting twenty yards on up
the river, completing the chore by posting poison signs
... through the area....

bait station a site at which poisoned bait is put
out to destroy wolves and other marauding animals.
1956 *Northland News* 17 Dec. 8/4: Poisoned caribou
carcasses are used for bait. All of the bait stations are
clearly marked, and warning notices are posted ... in
three languages. **1957** *Sask.News* 2 Jan. 4/1: In the far-
northern Athabasca region, nearly 100 strychnine-
laced bait stations are located....

bakeapple or **baked-apple** *n. Esp.Atlantic
Provinces* **1** a low bog-dwelling plant, *Rubus
chamaemorus,* having a solitary white flower
followed by a berry that is amber when ripe. See
also **baking apple** and **cloudberry.**
1775 (1792) CARTWRIGHT *Journal* II 96: I saw the first
baked apples. **1822** CORMACK *Narr.Nfld* 19: Here the
prevalent plants are ... the marshberry, and the bakeapple.... **1936** MOWERY *Paradise Trail* 13: Raspberries
... saskatoons, bake-apples ... tangled with the
buckbrush.

2 See **baked-apple berry.**
1778 (1792) CARTWRIGHT *Journal* II 360: After dinner
I went with all my family to Slink Point, where we
picked a bowl full of baked apples. **1955** *Evening
Telegram* (St. John's) 11 Mar. 6/3: They are taking back
with them ... bakeapples which they had never had
before.

baked-apple berry *Atlantic Provinces* the amber-
colored, raspberrylike, edible berry of the
bakeapple.
1818 CHAPPELL *Voyage of Rosamond* 138: In one place
... the dry moss is veriegated by ... what is called, by
the fishermen, the *baked-apple-berry.* **1964** *North* Jan.-
Feb. 45/1: Arctic char cocktail. Labrador baked apple
berry sundae, and wild meat salad were on the menu....

baked wind pills *Slang.* baked beans.
1962 *Alta Hist.Rev.* Autumn 16/1: In the commissariat
department [are] "dope" (butter) ... "baked-wind-
pills" Boston baked beans.... **1963** *Calgary Herald
Mag.* Sec. 21 Dec. 7/1: ... some of the old Western
slang is worth repeating ... "tent pegs," (frozen beef-
steak ribs); "baked wind pills," (baked beans)....

bake kettle a large flat pot of cast iron with a
cover, used for baking bread. See also **bake pan.**

1836 TRAILL *Backwoods* 240: At first I was inclined to
grumble and rebel against the expediency of bake-pans
or bake-kettles. **1961** PRICE & KENNEDY *Renfrew* 46:
The "cookery" consisted of ... seven or eight bake
kettles, "cast iron ovens" that were 14 to 16 inches in
diameter and five inches deep with cast iron covers and
lugs....

bake pan See **bake kettle.**
1834 (1926) LANGTON *Early U.C.* 113: Our oven, or—
as it is called—a bakepan, is a round pan with a flat
bottom and a flat lid, under which a few cinders are put
and a few more on top....

baking apple *Obs.* See **bakeapple.**
1771 (1935) *Cdn Hist.Rev.* XVI 57: The land about is
very woody ... with some currants, raspberrys ... and
baking apples.

baking-powder bannock a kind of dough made
with left-over grease and fried after rising; also,
the bread or loaf made from this dough. Cp.
bannock.
1913 FOOTNER *Jack Chanty* 89: Some finds it hard to
make good baking-powder bannock.... **1966** BAITY
Wilderness Welfare 3: ... after that we would be on
baking powder bannocks for the duration.

baking-powder bread bread made with baking
powder substituted for yeast as a rising agent.
1899 PALMER *Klondyke* 135: A "sour-dough stiff" will,
under no circumstances, eat baking powder bread.
1957 *Beaver* Autumn 40/2: Meals provided the crew
were mostly bacon and beans, baking powder bread,
stewed dried fruits, prepared en route on a stove carried
aboard the scow.

balacada ['bælə,kedə] *n.* See **ballacater.**

bald eagle† See 1958 quote. See also **bald-headed
eagle, fish-eagle** (def. 1), and **white-headed eagle.**
1792 SIMCOE *Diary* 131: We saw a fine bald eagle on the
wing. **1958** *Encyc.Can.* III 327/2: The range of the bald
eagle (*Haliaetus leucocephalus*) includes most of Canada
north to the limit of trees.... Adults have dark brown
bodies with white heads and tails. **1963** *Sun* (Vancouver)
20 July 15/1: Two bald eagles looked down from a snag
above.

bald-face(d) grizzly a color variety of grizzly
bear found in northern B.C. and the Yukon, so
called because the sparse, white hair on its face
suggests baldness. See also **Barren Ground grizzly.**
1900 LONDON *Son of Wolf* 161: Her father had failed to
give a bald-faced grizzly the trail one day, and had died
quickly. **1946** (1947) FREEDMAN *Mrs.Mike* 119: A bald-
faced grizzly was running almost at the horse's flank.

bald-headed *n.* See **bald prairie.**
1922 STEAD *Neighbours* 25: "If you're pushed for money,
work for somebody for awhile the first year, or put up
hay on the bald-headed; you can usually sell it to
settlers next winter".... "On the bald-headed? What
does that mean?" "That means the prairie ... because
it's as bare as a bald head 'cept for a very short grass
which makes wonderful good hay." **1963** SYMONS *Many
Trails* 92: So I wasn't exactly out on what they call the
"bald-headed," but was able ... to enjoy the greenness
of the bush and the presence of woodland birds.

bald-headed eagle See **white-headed eagle.**
1829 MACTAGGART *Three Years* I 22: ... I had seen a
couple of bald-headed eagles the day before. **1957**
Spotter Oct. 9/3: On the way into Aishihik I saw
... a large bald-headed eagle perched on the top of a
tall pine.

bald-headed plain See **bald prairie.**
1936 *Cdn Hist.Rev.* XVII 130: The mention of bones "being also found in hollows" seems to justify the inference that the main masses were on level ground, —but whether on river bottomlands or . . . "bald-headed plains," is left unmentioned. . . .

bald-headed prairie See **bald prairie.**
1889 (1892) PIKE *Barren Grounds* 2: About sixty miles out [of Calgary] the country loses the appearance of what is known among cattlemen as the bald-headed prairie. . . . 1963 PATTERSON *Far Pastures* . . . the squat, sod-walled hovel . . . sat . . . forlornly on the bald-headed prairie. . . .

bald plains See **bald prairie.**
1921 HAWORTH *Trailmakers* 110: They were soon out upon the bald plains, where they were forced to use "buffalo chips" for fuel. . . .

bald prairie the expanse of treeless grassland in the southern third of the Prairie Provinces, lying roughly between Winnipeg and Calgary. See also **bald-headed.**
1903 *Bond of Brotherhood* 5 Dec. 4/1: Every mark of the handiwork of man on the bald prairie had been made by himself. 1958 *Northern Miner* 27 Nov. 25/1: This [the North West] was a vague wilderness near a place called Winnipeg, where you could file on a homestead of 160 acres of bald prairie for free.

balise or **balize** [bə'liz] *n.* [< Cdn F < F *balise* buoy, beacon] one of a series of evergreen shrubs set up as markers at intervals of about 30 feet to outline the edges of winter roads, ice-roads (def. 1), etc.
[1808 (1809) GRAY *Letters* 254: They put up branches of trees on each side the new track, as a direction to others who wish to go that way. These they call *des balises,* or beacons.] 1824 *Canadian Mag.* III 476: . . . the snow storm and drift [render] almost invisible the balises or branched poles set up along the road. . . . 1897 GREENOUGH *Cdn Folk-Life* 182: We did [when sleighing] manage to strike a "balize," which nearly tore the sleeve out of the fur coat of one of the girls. . . . 1904 *U of T Stud.Hist.& Econ.* II 187: The municipal code deals with . . . winter roads—the line of which is marked by means of *balizes* of spruce or cedar. . . .

balise or **balize** [bə'liz] *v.* mark a road with balises. See also **brush,** *v.* (def. 3).
1897 GREENOUGH *Cdn Folk-Life* 182: As soon as the snow becomes deep the roads must be "balized," or after a heavy snow-fall the poor horses would be unable to find them.

ballacarter *n.* See **ballacater.**

ballacater or **ballicater** ['bælə,ketər] *n.* [alteration of *barricado* < F *barricade*] *Nfld* and *E.Arctic* an ice mass formed by pans drifting to shore and being subjected to showers of freezing spray, eventually becoming barricades between the land and the water. See also **barricade** (def. 1), **barricader, barricado** (def. 1), **ice barricade, ice-foot** (def. 2), **ice-wall,** and **shore-ice** (def. 3). Also spelled *ballacarter, ballycadder, ballycater.*
1906 LUMSDEN *Skipper Parson* 61: The rocks were covered with ice, and the shore was bespread with large pans of ice, high and dry—in local phraseology, "balacadas." 1918 GRENFELL *Labrador Doctor* 57: I remember once in Nain the slob ice had already made ballicaters. . . . 1952 BANFILL *Labrador Nurse* 100: We

tore down hills, bolted and swerved round ballacaters. . . . 1963 *Amer.Speech* Dec. 297: BALLYCATER, *n.* Ice formed by spray on the shore.

ballaclauter ['bɑlə,klautər] *n. Nfld* See **ballacater.**
1961 *Nfld Qtly* Spring 43: It is sixty years since I lugged that old portmanteau over the ballaclauters up Clode Sound Reach and on and on.

ballicater *n.* See **ballacater.**

ballotin *n.* [< Cdn F] *Fur Trade, Obs.* See quote.
1814 (1897) COUES *New Light* II 823: . . . only one ballotin [small bale] of their property [was] saved.

ballycadder or **ballycater** *n.* See **ballacater.**

balm (tree)† *n.* See **Balm of Gilead.** See also **bam.**
1922 STEAD *Neighbours* 72: There was no path between the slim, close-growing trunks of poplar and balm, and we had to make progress as best we could. 1958 MCGREGOR *North-west of 16* 29: . . . poplar and balm trees which could be cut and rolled into position for the house. 1962 ONSLOW *Bowler-Hatted Cowboy* 46: Sometimes in the narrow valley the spruce gave place to great black poplar-trees; 'bam-trees' in the vernacular. They are called 'bam' as an abbreviation for Balm of Gilead; well named for the aromatic smell of their buds in springtime.

Balm of Gilead† the balsam poplar, *Populus balsamifera,* found throughout the forested areas of Canada. See also **balm, bam, rough-barked poplar,** and **whitewood** (def. 1).
1817 (1897) DURAND *Reminiscences* 106: [Trees found in the area of Ancaster, U.C., include] white oak . . . balm of Gilead. . . . 1957 HUTCHISON *Canada* 183: All Canadians know the sensual emanation of syringa, the Balm of Gilead's overpowering night redolence by the creek bottom. . . .

Balm of Gilead fir See **balsam.**
1792 (1911) SIMCOE *Diary* 92: Mr. (Lieut.) Grey cut his finger, and applied the turpentine from the balm of Gilead fir, a remedy for wounds greatly esteemed.

Balm of Gilead poplar† See **Balm of Gilead.**

Balm of Gilead tree See **Balm of Gilead.**

balsam (fir)† *n.* **1** a slender evergreen, *Abies balsamea,* found in Canada from northeastern Alberta eastward, the source of Canada balsam (def. 1). See also **sapin, silver fir** (def. 1), **silver pine,** and **var.**
1822 CORMACK *Narr.Nfld* 12: Patches of the balsam-fir grow principally where the steepness does not prevent débris from lodging. 1882 *Prince Albert Times* (Sask.) 22 Nov. 5/1: Amongst the kinds may be mentioned . . . balsam. . . . 1962 *Forest Conservation* 28/2: . . . the balsam woolly aphid [is] a serious pest of balsam fir in the Atlantic Provinces.

2 the wood of this tree.
1854 *Hamilton Gaz.* (C.W.) 14 Dec. 2/7: Green wood should always be sold nearly a third less than dry, and soft, such as cedar . . . balsam, &c. at an equal reduction. 1957 *Bush News* (Port Arthur, Ont.) June 2/5: All of the lumber is spruce, balsam or jackpine from the Longlac limits.

3 See **Canada balsam** (def. 1).
1836 *Vindicator* (Montreal) 6 May 2/3: On Thursday, a woman of the name of Dupre, living in the concession Ste. Rosalie, was occupied boiling gum or Balsam. **1941** LEWIS *Poems Worth Knowing* 338: Sap of the birch and resin of the pine, / Balsam of fir in mountain purity....

4 a fir tree, *Abies amabilis,* of the Pacific Coast. See also **silver fir** (def. 2).
1956 *Native Trees* 68: Amabilis Fir [is also called] balsam fir....

balsam gum See **Canada balsam** (def. 1).
1907 HUNTER *Cdn Wilds* 168: It was quite a work to patch up each separate toe with balsam gum and rag before turning in for the night.... **1912** FOOTNER *New Rivers* 90: His remedy was balsam gum, which he applied to the wound after a thorough chewing. **1957** FISHER *Pemmican* 159: No more berries, no swanskin, no old wolf hides, no wattap roots, no balsam gum.

balsam poplar† See **Balm of Gilead.**
1823 HALIBURTON *General Descr.N.S.* 34: A list of Plants indigenous to Nova Scotia [includes] Balsam Poplar.... **1962** *Forest Conservation* 12/1: The principal trees are white and black spruce, balsam fir ... and balsam poplar.

balsam root the Oregon sunflower, *Balsamorrhiza sagittata,* the roots of which were an important source of food for the Indians in the West.
1925 ANDERSON *Trees and Shrubs* 134: Balsam-Root .. This root is also quite sweet when cooked.... **1950** LYONS *Mighty Fraser* 96: The balsam root had many uses among the natives. **1953** PUTNAM *Cdn Regions* 24/2: The most typical montane landscape ... is a scattered parklike stand of ponderosa pine amidst a steppe vegetation of bunch grass ... balsam root....

bam (tree) *n.* See **balm.**

ban *n.* See **road ban.**

banana belt 1 a region reputed to have a relatively moderate climate (often used facetiously).
1897 *Medicine Hat News* (Alta) 14 Jan. 4/2: This is a truthful pen-picture of a mid-January day in the now far-famed "banana belt" country.... **1958** *Evening Telegram* (St. John's) 25 Apr. 8/4: We called back bantering remarks about the softness of his summer's work in the "banana belt." **1965** *Globe and Mail* (Toronto) 9 Jan. 1/6: The weather office said that the Arctic temperatures and snow that changed Canada's winter banana belt [south-western B.C.] to one of its unhappiest regions are moving inland.

2 *North* the more populated, southerly regions of Canada; outside (def. 1).
1913 BICKERSTETH *Open Doors* 204: Somebody facetiously remarks it looks mighty like snow to him outside and we haven't reached the banana belt yet. **1958** *Edmonton Jnl* 24 June 3 16/3: [Yellowknife's] social life is amazingly active, and its climate, to the surprise of banana belt visitors, is not as severe as rumored. **1962** *Financial Post* 10 Feb. 21/4: Churchill's nearest neighbor, Thompson, is almost indistinguishable from a suburb in the banana belt.

band[1] *n.* **1** *Hist.* a social unit of Indians, smaller than a tribe, who live or hunt together as a group.
1765-75 (1933) POND *Narrative* 57: The other two Bands are North.... **1824** (1955) BLACK *Journal* 14:

This Band are more reasonable than the others we passed, they have killed two Reindeer & gave us the shoulder & the meat of a Beaver & a few small fish. **1963** MACLEOD & MORTON *Cuthbert Grant* 144: These figures ... serve to indicate how impressed the Métis and their companions were by the size of the band.

2 a. a group of Indians in a given area or reserve (def. 2), recognized by the Indian Affairs Branch as a unit for administrative purposes.
1871 (1880) MORRIS *Treaties* 39: Two councillors and two braves of each band were to receive a dress, somewhat inferior to that provided for the Chiefs, and, the braves and councillors of the Portage band excepted, were to receive a buggy. **1963** *Cdn Geog.Jnl* Dec. 186/2: In Ontario, 33 bands ... manage their own welfare services....

b. in attributive uses with reference to legally constituted Indian bands.
1900 OSBORN *Greater Canada* 205: ... the Canadian system of band-reserves was the application of the Imperial maxim *Divide et impera*. **1957** *Vancouver Province* 22 Mar. 3/3: Band corporations should be set up, and all band property rights should be given to them. **1963** *Cdn Geog.Jnl* Dec. 193/2: Six women are band chiefs, many are councillors.... **1965** *Kingston Whig-Standard* (Ont.) 22 Feb. 7/6: Now he sits back in an advisory capacity, encouraging the band council to do as much as it can.

3 a. a herd of buffalo, cattle, horses, caribou, or other such animals.
1824 BLACK *Journal* 73: He was watching all night along the Lake as the Chipeweans do in hopes of the Carribou coming into the waters but ... the band of Carribou is gone farther. **1825** (1950) OGDEN *Journals* 16: The hunters returned having killed 20 Buffaloe all Bulls [;] many large bands were seen by them but no Cows. **1965** *B.C.Digest* June 19/1: This band, however, rallied unexpectedly to follow the old mare's colt, and during three weeks of daily pursuit by men on fresh horses, they could not be approached.

b. *West* a flock of sheep.
1953 *Cdn Geog.Jnl* XLVI 246/2: Herder and "band" (not flock) have lost their lives in blizzards year after year. **1963** SYMONS *Many Trails* 58: A thousand sheep is called a "band"—not a flock; that would be farmer parlance.

band[2] *v. Obs.* place bands of birch bark on the gummed seams of a canoe in order to make it water-tight.
1806 (1930) FRASER *Journal* 118: Buyson was employed making verangues for a small canoe and Mr. Stuart banded the large one but did not render all the verangues. *Ibid.* 131: Sewed the small seams of the first canoe and gummed it inside but in attempting to band it, it broke and could not be mended for want of bark.

band[3] *n. Lumbering, Hist.* a detachable part of a timber raft, comprising about 25 cribs, *q.v.,* each of 20-25 logs or square timbers bound together; dram, *q.v.*
1863 WALSHE *Cedar Creek* 245: ... the raft was infantine compared with its congeners of the great lake and the St. Lawrence. A couple of bonds lashed together—that was all; and a bond containeth twenty cribs, and a crib containeth a variable amount of beams, according to the lumberman's arithmetical tables. **1961** PRICE & KENNEDY *Renfrew* 51: These cribs were again bound together, though in a manner easily to be unloosed, in "drams" or "bands" ... each dram containing about 25 cribs.

band constable See **Indian constable**.
1958 HAWTHORN *Indians of B.C.* 434: The usual
procedure, says everyone, is to notify the Band
Constables if there is any very serious trouble, and the
Constables will decide if it is worth calling the Royal
Canadian Mounted Police.

Band List the list of members of Indian bands
recognized by the federal government. See also
Indian Register. Cp. General List.
1957 *Calgary Herald* 15 Jan. 16/2: We are putting out of
status today people who think they are entirely Indians.
We do not admit to the band lists certain persons
although they may have 15/16 of what you would call
Indian blood. 1964 DUFF *Indian History* 46: The first
[definition], which refers to what are usually called
"registered Indians," is the legal definition used by the
Indian Affairs Branch for the people who come under
the jurisdiction of the *Indian Act,* that is, those whose
names are included on the official Indian Register, either
on a Band List or a General List.

bang *n*. See **bain.**

bang the bush *Obs.* surpass everything.
1835 *Novascotian* (Halifax) 10 Dec. 363/2: "Well, well,"
says he, ". . . if that don't bang the bush."

bank[1] *n.* (*usually plural*) **1** one of the more elevated
portions of the submerged plateau lying off the
Atlantic coast of Canada. See also **Banks.**
1584 (1877) HAKLUYT *Discourse on Western Planting* 83:
. . . Frenchmen . . . brought their banke fishe which
they took on the Bancke, forty or three-score leagues from
Newfoundelande. . . . 1849 ALEXANDER *L'Acadie* II 306:
. . . no fishing boats were sent to the banks of
Newfoundland. 1931 SEARY *Romance* 229: These
platforms over which the sea is shallow are called
"banks". . . . 1959 *Atlantic Advocate* Aug. 109: Ah,
what memories the names of these famous schooners
stir in the hearts of all bank fishermen.

2 *Lumbering* a place at the side of a river or lake
where logs are piled in winter for rafting
downstream after break-up. See also **bank,** *v.*
1829 MACTAGGART *Three Years* I 242: The *Shantymen*
. . . cut down the pine trees, and . . . draw the logs to what
is termed the bank, with oxen. 1912 HEENEY *Pickanock*
83: . . . they began hurling the logs down the bank,
rolling, bumping, splashing into the lake amid the
cheers of the body of young woodsmen. . . .

bank[1] *v. Lumbering* pile logs on a river bank,
lakeshore, etc. ready for rafting.
1883 *Prince Albert Times* (Sask.) 14 Feb. 4/1: . . . there
is now a vast quantity of building logs cut and banked
at Lilly Plain. 1884 *Ibid.* 28 Mar. 1/3: I had no choice
but to leave the logs that I had banked . . . to rot. . . .

bank[2] *n. Maritimes* See quote. See also **banking**[2].
1959 *Star Wkly* 22 Aug. 17/2: A "bank" is a place to
keep lobsters alive until the legal season.

bank barn or **banked barn** a two-storey barn
built into a hill so as to permit entry to the bottom
level from one side and to the top level from the
other side.
1906 CONNOR *Doctor* 26: For many summers the big
boulders were gathered from the fields and piled in a
long heap at the bottom of the lane on their way to their
ultimate destination, the foundation of the bank-barn.
1952 PUTNAM *Cdn Regions* 237/2: In western Ontario,
the bank barn is common with a basement stable for
the animals. In eastern Ontario bank barns are a rarity.

1961 *Ontario Hist.* Mar. 11: In all areas except where
Pennsylvania Dutch settled with their huge banked
barns, the usual outbuildings or "offices" were generally
one two-bay centre-door log barn.

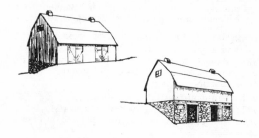

A bank barn, seen from back and front

bank beaver See 1964 quote. See also **land beaver**
and **terrier.**
1918 SCHULTZ *Rising Wolf* 121: There were many . . .
pond beavers and bank beavers, along the stream. 1953
Cdn Geog.Jnl Sep. 88/2: And all along the river we
came upon bank beaver. 1964 *Western Wkly Supp.*
18 Mar. 4/1: There may be no attempt to either erect a
dam or build a lodge. A tunnel or two into some
convenient bank with its entrance below low water mark
is all they require. Some folks refer to these beaver as
"Bank Beavers" as though they were a distinct species.
They are not.

bank burrow a tunnel made by a beaver as an
emergency shelter. See also **bank lodge.**
1948 *Beaver* Sep. 42: In no case does the beaver depend
entirely on his lodge for shelter; he always has emergency
shelters which have been tunnelled into the bank of lake
or stream below water level to rise above water level in
the bank. These are known as bank burrows, and a
beaver colony may have as many as six.

bank diggings *Placer Mining, Hist.* gold-mining
claims on a stream bank rather than on a bar
(def. 1) or bench, *q.v.* See also **dry diggings.** Cp.
bench diggings.
1858 *Brit.Colonist* (Victoria) 11 Dec. 1/1: Within the
fortnight bank diggings have been discovered extending
on both sides of the Fraser to the foot of the mountains.
1860 *Ibid.* 2 June 1/2: Above Hill's Bar they have struck
bank diggings which are paying very good wages.

banker *n.* **1** a vessel engaged in fishing on the
Banks, *q.v.*
1777 (1792) CARTWRIGHT *Journal* II 233: From the boats-
master I was informed, that the Americans had taken
His Majesty's frigate Fox and several bankers upon the
banks of Newfoundland. 1960 *Atlantic Advocate* Nov.
30: New vessels—craft of fifty tons or less, and less than
half the size of latter-day bankers—were soon carrying
Lunenburgers to the offshore banks.

2 a man engaged in fishing on the Banks, *q.v.*
1907 MILLAIS *Newfoundland* 154: The fishermen of all
lands have to encounter the perils of the deep, but none
have to face the risks that the "bankers" do. 1958
RICHARDSON *Tempest* 44: A Banker's life is hard and
dangerous but it's much freer than life on the square-

riggers where a man's very soul can be at the mercy of a bullying mate.

banker's row a number of adjacent gold-mining claims, each of which has a high yield.
1952 WILSON *Chibougamau Venture* 137: My five claims in Dauversiere Township were right in "Banker's Row" . . . and might prove to be of considerable worth later on.

bank fishery 1 the industry or business of fishing on the Banks, *q.v.* Cp. **banking** and **banks fishery**.
1818 CHAPPELL *Voy.of Rosamond* 122: At this time, the war with America had almost annihilated the Bank-fisheries.

2 the fishing grounds on the Banks, *q.v.*
1922 (1958) *Evening Telegram* (St. John's) 4 May 4/6: After taking supplies the Dorothy will go to the bank fishery.

bank fishing See **banking**[1].
1955 *Bulletin* (Bridgewater, N.S.) 9 Mar. 9/2: A number of fishermen . . . have gone sealing out of Halifax, or engaged in bank fishing.

bank herring a variety of herring.
1883 HATTON & HARVEY *Newfoundland* 324: There are two varieties of herring taken on the shores of the island—the Bank (called also the Labrador) herring and the shore herring.

banking[1] *n.* the practice of fishing on the Banks, *q.v.* Cp. **bank fishery**.
1824 *Canadian Mag.* III 350: The inhabitants are desirous that some Legislative regulations be made to prevent the banking vessels from throwing the offal of their fish in to the sea. **1955** *Bulletin* (Bridgewater, N.S.) 9 Mar. 9/3: The Lila B. Boutilier . . . was engaged in banking for some years. . . .

banking[2] *n.* Maritimes the storing underwater of illegally trapped live lobsters until the opening of the season. See also **bank**[2].
1959 *Star Wkly* 22 Aug. 17/2: He rented a light aircraft, spotted two large masses of sunken traps—correctly deciding it was a new "banking" tactic.

bank lodge See **bank burrow**.
1921 HEMING *Drama of the Forests* 123: Several of the passageways led to the bank, where . . . they had what is called "bank lodges"—natural cavities in the river bank to which the beavers had counted on resorting in case their house was raided.

bankman or **banksman** *n.* a fisherman who frequents the Banks, *q.v.*
1907 MILLAIS *Newfoundland* 156: This humane action on the liner's part is agreeably remembered yet among the fishing fleets, for, if the bankmen are to be believed, steamers usually keep on as if nothing had happened, and tell the passengers who may have felt the shock that it was caused by striking loose ice or suddenly changing the course. **1935** *Beaver* Dec. 12/1: On Sunday, unless in some emergency, the banksmen take a welcome rest, patching and darning their mitts and clothes.

bank paper dollar *Obs.* a bank note for four shillings.
1841 *Montreal Transcript* 1 July 2/4: The Bank paper dollar to be considered the fifth of a pound and paid as such in all cases.

Banks *n.pl.* **1** See **bank**[1] (def. 1).
1952 PUTNAM *Cdn Regions* 45/1: The "Banks" are the more elevated portions of this submerged plateau; the most noted of these, the "Grand Banks," lying southeast of Newfoundland, have an area as great as that of the island itself.

2 See **Grand Banks**.
1622 WHITBOURNE *Discovrse* 37: To which Banke our Nation may doe great good in fishing, such as will sail from New-found-land in the latter part of the Summer, when the fish begins to draw from that coast. **1954** *Fishermen's Advocate* (Port Union, Nfld) 5 Feb. 7/3: While a few "bankers" of Newfoundland ownership operated on the Banks, all landings were made in Nova Scotia ports.

banks fishery *Hist.* See **green fishery**. Cp. **bank fishery**.
1963 MORTON *Kingdom of Canada* 12: But from earliest times the fishery developed in two modes, that of the wet fishery and that of the dry. The former was carried on from ships on the Banks where the fish were taken, cleaned and heavily salted on board. In this "wet" or ship or banks fishery, there was little resort to the shores of Newfoundland.

Banksian pine [< Sir Joseph *Banks*, d. 1820, English naturalist] a species of pine, *Pinus banksiana*. See also **gray pine** and **jackpine**.
1852 RICHARDSON *Arctic Exped.* 414: The Banksian pine is more frequently seen in considerable patches, and . . . it offers the prospect of a dry and comfortable encampment. **1947** TAYLOR *Canada* 360: . . . the Banksian pine is fourd to be big enough to be merchantable near James Bay while in the Ottawa Valley it is a shrub.

banksman *n.* See **bankman**.

banlieu *n.* [< F] *Obs.* the suburbs or outskirts of a town; city limits.
1796 *Quebec Gaz.* 11 Aug. 1/1: All that part of it . . . from the Fortifications of the Upper Town to the extreme boundaries of the Banlieue . . . form . . . St. John's ward. **1800** *U.C.Gaz.* (York [Toronto]) 4 Jan. 3/2: . . . when he gets drunk at any brandy-shop or tavern within the banlieus . . . the same disagreeable effects are produced. **1817** *Montreal Police Regulations* 21 June 2/3: All hay and straw sold or delivered within the city and Banlieue of Montreal, shall be weighed . . . at the requisition of either the buyer or seller.

bannik *n.* See **bannock**.

bannock ['bænɪk] *n.* [< Scots Gaelic *bannach* thin oatmeal cake] *Esp.North* See 1913 and 1941 quotes. See also **baking-powder bannock, bush bread, galette, grease bannock**, and **trail biscuit**.
1878 *Sask.Herald* (Battleford, N.W.T.) 2 Dec. 1/2: A Bakery is amongst the latest additions to the industrial enterprises of Battleford. Good-bye to "flap-jack" and "bannock." **1913** COWIE *Adventurers* 121: Flour bannocks, baked with water and a little pemmican grease, without any rising, and, generally, only half "done," by exposing them on twigs and frying pan before the camp fire, were a luxury. . . . **1941** *Beaver* Sep. 36/1: Bannock—The stand-by of the fur country. Flour, lard, baking powder, salt and water; readily made . . . with or without frying pan; does not freeze and is sustaining. Bannock, Scotsmen and furs—all first cousins. **1965** *Globe and Mail* (Toronto) 26 May 3/7: Nobody is starving in the village across Store Creek, although the poorer Indians are eating bannock (flour-and-water pancakes) and drinking tea bross (tea

broth with lard, oatmeal and sugar) while whites eat steak and bacon and eggs.

bannock puncher *Slang* a bachelor cook with some degree of skill.
1951 ANGIER *At Home* 203: These old timers go in mostly for plain cooking, although occasionally you'll meet a bannock puncher with a flair for the exceptional.

baptême *n. Cdn French, Obs.* the practice of "baptizing." See **baptize.**
1784 (1790) UMFREVILLE *Hudson's Bay* 49: [We reached] a stony point which our men called Pointe au Baptême, on account of my paying my baptême there. **1793** (1933) MACDONELL *Diary* 99: The intention of this Bâtême being only to claim a glass[,] I complied with the custom. . . .

baptize *v. Hist.* See quotes.
1761 (1961) PRICE & KENNEDY *Renfrew* 27: On this southern side is a remarkable point of sand . . . on which it is customary to baptize novices. **1800** (1820) HARMON *Journal* 27: By all those on board, who have never passed certain places, they expect to be treated with something to drink; and should a person refuse to comply with their requisitions, he would be sure of being plunged into the water, which they profanely call, baptizing him. **1931** NUTE *Voyageur* 40: Soon after leaving Ste. Anne's all clerks or *bourgeois* who had never before accompanied a brigade into the interior were given to understand that they would be "baptized" in the chilly waters of the river if they did not moisten the whistles of their men.

bar† *n. Placer Mining* **1** a ridge of sand or gravel above the surface or along the shore of a stream in which gold has been found. See also **gold-bar.**
1859 *Brit.Colonist* (Victoria) 12 Feb. 2/1: One of us . . . went down and took up the first unoccupied claims at the lower end of the bar. . . . **1958** LINDSAY *Cariboo Story* 13/2: . . . the miners and Governor Douglas . . . together with the Indians and renegade whites at Yale and some of the bars, did not live together in love and sweetness.
2 (often in place names) a gold-mining camp on or near a productive bar.
1858 *Brit.Colonist* (Victoria) 11 Dec. 1/4: Let miners be allowed to make their own bye-laws and regulations for each bar or district, subject to the approbation of a council of miners. **1958** *Beaver* Summer 48/2: When the word got to Hill's Bar, where the community spirit was strong, there was a great to-do.

bar *v.* prepare fish by cutting slashes in the fillets about an inch apart to allow penetration of smoke and wind in drying or fat in frying.
1828 (1872) MCDONALD *Peace River* 97: . . . fat . . . is allowed to penetrate all parts of the fish by cross-cutting ("barring"), the sides. . . .

barachois ['bærə.ʃwa] *n.* [< Cdn F < F *barachoix* sand bar] *Atlantic Provinces* **1** See 1760 quote. See also **barrasway** and **pond** (def. 1).
1760 PICHON *Cape Breton* 21: They give the name *barachois* in this country to small ponds near the sea, from which they are separated only by a kind of causeway. **1869** BROWN *Cape Breton* 309: On the morning of July 1, a large party, which left the town and approached the Barachois, were attacked by Wolfe with a corps of Light Infantry, and driven back into the town. **1962** *Cdn Geog.Jnl* Nov. 152/1: Such matters as the anglicization of French names, whereby . . . Barachois becomes . . . Barrasway . . . suggest further

possibilities of enquiry for the . . . linguist.
2 a narrow strip of sand or gravel rising above the surface of the adjacent water; causeway.
1964 *Cdn Geog.Jnl* Apr. 137: At Stephenville Crossing, we turned due west to a blob of land connected to Newfoundland only by a barachois of gravel.

barber *n. Obs.* **1 a.** a vapor or mist made up of tiny particles of ice, so called because of its cutting qualities.
1829 MOORSOM *Letters N.S.* 151: Woe betide his fresh shaven visage, if it be upreared above the hatchway! Frozen particles of the atmosphere, aptly termed by the natives "the barber," sweep the surface of the water. . . . **1869** HARDY *Forest Life in Acadie* 332: The "Barber" appears on the harbour in the morning —a dense steam, due to the great differences of temperatures of air and water.
b. the vapor caused by exhaling in sub-zero weather.
1851 OSBORN *Arctic Jnl* 215: . . . with the thermometer . . . at 18° below zero . . . your very breath [forms] into a small snow called "barber," which penetrated into your very innermost garments. . . .
2 See quote.
1832 MCGREGOR *Brit.Amer.* I 133n: The keen northwest wind, during winter, is often called the "Barber" in America.

A barber chair

barber chair *Lumbering* a stump having an upright flange left standing above the undercut when the tree topples.
1944 KOROLEFF *Woodcutter's Handbook* 7/2: It is poor cutting if "barber chairs" are made and butts are very irregular.

barble *n.* [< Cdn F, var. of *barbue*, q.v.] *Obs.* See **barbot.**
1795 (1911) HEARNE *Journey* 249: The fish that are common in this lake . . . are pike, trout, perch, barble, tittameg, and methy.

barbot or **barbotte** ['barbət] *n.* [< Cdn F *barbotte*] *Ont. and Que.* a large catfish, *q.v.*, especially *Ictalurus punctatus.* See also **barbot** and **barbue.**
1901 DRUMMOND *Johnnie Courteau* 28: "He's always ketchin' barbotte, dat's w'at you call bull-pout." **1957** *Ottawa Citizen* 7 June 7/1: Fifty years ago I used to catch pike and barbotte in the Lower Ottawa with lampreys. **1963** *Gazette* (Montreal) 13 June 32/2: . . . most of the fishing up there right now is probably for outsized barbot. . . .

barbotte[1] *n.* See **barbot.**

barbotte² ['barbət] *n.* [< Cdn F *barbote*
< Turk. *barbut*] a gambling game played with
dice, the winning throws being 3-3, 5-5, 6-6, and
6-5; the losing throws being 1-1, 1-2, 2-2, 4-4; the
other combinations being neutral.
1950 PALMER *Montreal Confidential* 48: Wedged
between the brothels, barbotte games and blind pigs
were a handful of licensed night clubs. **1953** (1958)
WALKER *Pardon My Parka* 160: . . . the counterfeit coin
could be used to gamble at red dog, poker, roulette,
barbotte, and for just plain shooting craps. **1959**
Kingston Whig-Standard (Ont.) 2 May 11/4: The law is
not too effective in dealing with this canker . . . because
the bucketeers often pull up stakes and move, like a
travelling barbotte game.

barbue *n.* [< Cdn F < F] *Esp.Northwest, Obs.* See
barbot.
1793 (1933) MacDONELL *Diary* 116: The [Assiniboine]
River is stocked with . . . Cat fish or *Barbue*, Mullets . . .
and Nacaishe.   **1820** (1823) FRANKLIN *Journey* 93: One
of the largest fish is the mathemegh, catfish, or barbue.
1933 GATES *Five Traders* 116n: The catfish, or barbue,
takes its name from its beard appendages (barbes) and
its broad, square head.

barcaliau bird See **baccalao bird.**

bardache *n.* See **berdash.**

bar diggings† *Placer Mining* gold-mining
operations carried out on a bar (def. 1); also, the
defined area of such operations. Cp. **bench
diggings** and **dry diggings.**
1860 *Brit.Colonist* (Victoria) 14 Aug. 3/2: No bar
diggings there, but bench and bed-rock diggings.
1897 GOODMAN *Gold Fields* 7: "Bar diggings" shall
mean any part of a river over which the water extends
when the water is in its flooded state, and which is not
covered at low water. **1960** *Statutes of B.C.* 3584: In
"bar diggings" a claim shall be (*a*) a piece of land not
exceeding 250 feet square on any bar which is covered
at high water. . . . **1962** *B.C.Digest* Oct. 28/1: They had
travelled over the famous Eldorado and Bonanza
creeks to bar diggings beyond. . . .

barge train a number of connected barges drawn
by a tug of shallow draft.
1945 *Beaver* Sep. 36/1: The captain of the barge train
stood on the bridge of his sturdy little tug. . . .

bar harbo(u)r *Maritimes* a harbor, the entrance
to which is partially obstructed by a sand bar.
1830 MOORSOM *Letters N.S.* 27: . . . the coast to the
westward . . . [alternates] with stony beaches and
shallow bar-harbours. **1871** (1878) LEMOINE *Chronicles
of St.Lawrence* 32: Pabos is a bar harbor and very
difficult of access.

bar island a small island, permanently above
water, formed on a sand bar.
1832 BAILLIE *Acct of N.B.* 120: A small bar island on
the southern point, was granted to a person in trade,
who has erected a fish-house and a wharf thereon.

bark (canoe)† *n.* See **birchbark canoe.**
1779 *Quebec Gaz.* 11 Feb. 3/1: The said John
Greaces on the first day of November last set out in a
bark canoe . . . to go to Sorel. **1845** BEAVAN *Life in
Backwoods N.B.* 73: . . . Silas sprung upon the shore,
dashed through the circle, and bore off the Indian bride

to his bark. **1920** *Beaver* Oct. 14: . . . 100 miles of
rapids . . . seemed a dangerous undertaking, but
Captain O'Kelly's handling of the bark soon made it
seem an everyday affair. **1963** *Ibid.* Autumn 44/1:
This was marsh hay, gathered along the lake shore by
Indians working in pairs of bark canoes joined by pole
platforms upon which the hay was piled as it was
removed from the water.

barking crow See quotes.
1840 (1852) RICHARDSON *Arctic Exped.* 384: On the 27th
a gray hawk, and on the 31st a barking crow, *Corvus
americanus*, were seen. **1921** HEMING *Drama of the
Forests* 273: My son, the first birds to arrive are the
eagles; next, the snow-birds and the barking crows
(ravens). . . .

Barnardo boy† a boy or young man from Dr.
Barnardo's Homes, a charitable institution in
England. Cp. **home boy.**
1910 FERGUSON *Janey Canuck* 210: Two Barnardo boys
look on and enjoy the sport. . . . **1920** STRINGER *Prairie
Mother* 152: I was on Paddy the other morning . . .
going like the wind for the Dixon ranch, after hearing
they had a Barnardo boy they wanted to unload. . . .

barn boss† See 1913 quote.
1913 SANDILANDS *West.Cdn Dict.* 5: Barn boss, the man
in charge of the barn (or stables) in a lumber camp, on a
large farm, in a livery, or wherever a large number of
horses are kept. **1947** *Ont.Timberworker* 20 Sep. 4/3:
Barn Bosses . . . will work as many hours during the
week as may be necessary to do the work in hand.
1964 *Outdoorsman* 1/2: One may see a visitor with a
misty look in his eye; an old blacksmith, top loader,
barn boss . . . or river hog who has returned to a
fleeting glimpse of an era long gone by.

barndoor game *Obs.* in hockey, a game in which
all or most shots on goal are blocked by the goalkeeper.
1897 *Medicine Hat News* (Alta) 25 Feb. 1/6: Marshall
in goal seemed to be playing a regular barndoor
game. . . . Several times the puck was forced into close
quarters on the Calgary goal but it did not get through.

barn framer or **raiser** a carpenter skilled in the
construction of barns.
1924 (1933) SLATER *Yellow Briar* 136: He had a grand
reputation throughout the country as a barn framer, a
shingle splitter and a booze artist. **1961** *Alta Hist.Rev.*
Spring 9/1: Ree was a skilled carpenter, and famous as
a "barn-raiser."

barn-raising† *n. Hist.* a community affair at
which the frame of a neighbor's barn was put up,
usually followed by eating, drinking, and dancing.
See also **raising bee.** Cp. **house-raising.**
1886 *Indian* (Hagersville, Ont.) 18 Aug. 188/3: At Chief
John Sickles' barn raising a plate fell and crushed Mr.
Powles' foot. **1959** *Maclean's* 29 Aug. 40/1: Barn-
raisings, corn-huskings, quilting bees and threshings
were community occasions. . . .

Baronet (of Nova Scotia)† *n. Hist.* a hereditary
title conferred by James I on 150 persons granted
extensive land holdings in what is now the
Maritimes. See also **Nova Scotia Knight.** Cp.
barony (def. 1).
1624 (1835) STIRLING *Register* I xix: Everie Baronett is
to be ane Barone of some one or other of the said
Barronies. . . . **1789** *Nova Scotia Mag.* I 5/1: Every one
of his Knight Baronets had, for his hundred and fifty
pounds sterling, heritably disposed unto him, six

thousand good and sufficient acres of Nova-Scotia ground; which, being at the rate of six-pence an acre, could not be thought very dear. **1966** *Globe and Mail* (Toronto) 2 June 8/7: Debrett's records that William Forbes was created a baronet of Nova Scotia in 1630 by Charles I and granted 16,000 acres in what now is New Brunswick.

barony *n. Hist.* **1 a.** the land holdings of a Baronet of Nova Scotia.

1624 (1835) STIRLING *Register* I xix: Everie Baronett is to be ane Barone of some one or other of the said Barronies, and is to haif therein ten thowsand aikars of propetie, besidis his sax thowsand aikars belongeing to his bur[t] of baronie.

b. an early administrative subdivision of Nova Scotia.

1922 *Dalhousie Rev.* I 377: The country was divided into two provinces, each province into several dioceses, each diocese into ten baronies, and each barony into six parishes.

2 the domain of a seigneur, *q.v.*; seigneury, *q.v.*

1764 *Quebec Gaz.* 8 Nov. 3/1: To Be Sold. The Barony of Longeuil, situate opposite the City of Montreal....
1805 *Ibid.* 7 Mar. 3/1: I have seized and taken in execution ... a land situated in the parish of Sainte Marguerite ... in the Barony of Longueil....

3 See **hundred.**

1875 CAMPBELL *Hist.P.E.I.* 10: The forty *Hundreds* or *Baronies* were to be divided into twenty manors of two thousand acres each, which manors were to be entitled to a Court Baron, according to the Common Law of England.

barouge [bə'ruʒ] *n.* [var. of *bois rouge*, q.v.] *Northwest* See **red-osier dogwood.**

1879 ROBINSON *Great Fur Land* 338: The native carries a fire-bag—a long leather bag, containing pipe, tobacco, knife, flint and steel, and *barouge*, the inner bark of the grey willow. **1929** MOBERLY *When Fur Was King* 73: No word was spoken until the interpreter had filled the long-stemmed pipe with tobacco & *barouge*, or red-willow bark.

barra-couta ['bærə,kutə] *n.* the common murre, *Uria aalge.*

1932 MUNN *Prairie Trails* 155: The lead had been black with barra-couta, or looms, near Button Point, a species of sea-bird which nested in immense numbers on the ledges of the high cliffs. ...

barrasway ['barə,swe] *n.* [< Cdn F *barachoix, barachois*] *Nfld Dial.* See **barachois** (def. 1). Also spelled *barrisway.*

1842 JUKES *Excursions in Nfld* I 89: There was a shallow salt lake at the back of the harbour that filled at the rise of the tide, and was called by the people a Barrasway. This was a very common term for a shallow marshy inlet or salt lake along the south coast of Newfoundland. It is spelt in the French charts Barachois, and is, I conclude, a Norman word. **1963** *American Speech* Dec. 298: BARRISWAY, *n.* a lagoon at a river mouth.

Barr colonist *Hist.* a settler in the Barr Colony.

1928 (1955) KING *Sask.Harvest* 108: ... the far-famed Barr Colonists ... led by an unscrupulous Church of England parson, adventured deep into the wilderness of Canada's great northwest.... **1962** *Sask.News* 14 Aug. 1/2: A notable example of the material we received is letters sent from a Barr colonist to his sweetheart in England in 1903.

Barr Colony *Hist.* an ill-starred colonizing venture conceived by the Rev. I. M. Barr, an Anglican clergyman who recruited some 2,000 persons in the south of England to establish a settlement in 1903 in the vicinity of the present Lloydminster, Sask.

1916 BRIDLE *Sons of Canada* 83: They with the Doukhobors ... and the celebrated "Barr Colony," were the Western problem ... in Canada.

barrel boom *Lumbering* a kind of boom (def. 3b) used for towing wood in large lakes and salt water and, sometimes, for holding pulpwood, usually made of four logs or square timbers placed around short core blocks and bolted together.

1961 MACLENNAN *Seven Rivers* 163: Tugs tow mats of them downstream in barrel booms.... **1961** *Maclean's* 29 July 8/1: As the river's current is dead in the lake, the lumbermen must now tow their logs in barrel booms instead of driving them....

barrelman *n.* a man stationed in the crow's-nest of a sealing ship.

1924 ENGLAND *Vikings of the Ice* 313/2: Barrelman. Man who spies for seals. **1944** FAY *Life and Labour* 64: This to my mind is the most important job aboard a sealer, as the barrel man has to watch the movements of the men on the ice and be able to tell the skipper where they are and be able to pick them up in case of a sudden storm. **1961** *Maclean's* 28 Jan. 14/1: ... the barrelman of *Bellaventure,* a Newfoundland sealing ship, spied a huddle of dark shapes on a waste of ice in the North Atlantic.

barren(s) *n.* **1 a.** in the Atlantic Provinces, an elevated tract of exposed land that nourishes only scrubby trees, shrubs, berries, etc. and resembles a moor.

1770 (1792) CARTWRIGHT *Journal* I 21: Early in the morning, I landed on South Head with Ned, and took a walk upon the barrens. **1820** JOHNSTONE *P.E.I.* 20: The *barrens* ... have few or no trees upon them, but are covered with a kind of shrub, they call myrtle.... **1934** DENNIS *Down in N.S.* 281: ... I drove through barren ... until finally the unbroken forest ... was reached. **1964** VARDY *Western Nfld* Folder: Caribou, moose and bear roam the more open sections of the country and partridge are plentiful on the barrens.

b. *N.B.* a tract of peat moss or muskeg, *q.v.* See also **spruce barrens.**

1832 BAILLIE *Acct of N.B.* 21: ... [a] *barren* is an open plain, formed of peat moss, destitute of any covering whatever.... **1948** *Cdn Geog.Jnl* Mar. 149/2: The muskeg, with its mossy surface and occasional spruce. ... would be a *barren* in New Brunswick, or a *savannah* in western Nova Scotia. ...

2 *North* a part of the Barren Ground, *q.v.* Cp. **Barren.**

1913 WILLIAMS *Wilderness Trail* 191: ... the "barrens" about Hudson Bay remained the only country that had successfully kept the independents at bay. **1958** *Maclean's* 10 May 50/3: Sixty-six percent is water, mountain-top, swamp, muskeg, and barren.

Barren(s) *n.* (*usually plural*) See **Barren Ground.**

1896 WHITNEY *On Snow-Shoes* 139: None but the younger and hardiest and most experienced Indians go into the Barrens, and to be a musk-ox hunter is their highest conception of courage and skill and endurance. **1961** *Cdn Geog.Jnl* Jan. 16/2: Skeleton track [was laid] across the "Barrens" to Churchill, spring 1929. . . .

barren goose *Obs.* See **Canada goose.**
1785 (1916) THOMPSON *Narrative* 36: [We saw] a very large species of gray goose—they have a deep, harsh note, and are called Gronkers, by others Barren Geese, from its being assumed that they never lay eggs. **1852** RICHARDSON *Arctic Exped.* 96: The natives observe, that, besides the old birds which rear young . . . there are a considerable number who do not breed, but keep in small bands, and are called "barren geese."

Barren Ground(s) the inhospitable tundra, *q.v.*, of northern Canada. See also **barren** (def. 2), **Barren, Barren Land, Great Barrens, Hudsonian Zone,** and **tundra lands.**
1691 KELSEY *Papers* 13: Now ye manner of their hunting these Beast [musk-oxen] on ye Barren ground is when they see a great parcel of them together they surround them . . . shooting . . . till they break out at some place or other. . . . **1897** GREENOUGH *Cdn Folk-Life* 20: The Barren Grounds extend . . . from the interior of Labrador on the east to Alaska on the west, and from the limit of timber on the south away into the Arctic Circle. **1964** *Time* (Cdn ed.) 27 Nov. 19/2: A thousand or more years ago, a band of Eskimo caribou hunters trekked 200 miles inland to the Barren Grounds, a bleak, God-forgotten plain. . . .

Barren Ground(s) bear See **Barren Ground grizzly.**
1829 RICHARDSON *Fauna Boreali-Americana* I 22: The Indians dread the Barren-Ground bear. . . . **1896** WHITNEY *On Snow-Shoes* 244: The head of this so-called Barren Ground bear looks somewhat like that of an Eskimo dog, very broad in the forehead, with square, long muzzle, and ears set on quite like a dog's. **1908** MAIR *Mackenzie Basin* 219: I . . . saw . . . one enormous and two young Barren Ground bears coming direct for our camp.

Barren Ground(s) caribou 1 a subspecies of caribou (def. 1) native to the tundra of northern Canada, *Rangifer tarandus groenlandicus*. See also **Barren Ground reindeer.**
1829 RICHARDSON *Fauna Boreali-Americana* I 242: The Barren-Ground caribou bears horns twice the size of those of the woodland variety, notwithstanding that the latter is a much larger animal. **1953** *Beaver* Dec. 18/1: The Barren Ground caribou is lighter both in colour and weight than the woodland species. . . . **1965** *Globe and Mail* (Toronto) 27 Dec. 21/2: In Government terminology . . . "tuktu" is a barren ground caribou.
2 in Newfoundland, a similar species, *Rangifer tarandus caribou*.
1958 *Evening Telegram* (St. John's) 26 Apr. 12/7: . . . the spring-time migration of rangifer tarandus (Newfoundland's barren land caribou) . . . to summer grazing grounds in Newfoundland's interior has marked the coming of spring.

Barren Ground(s) deer *Obs.* See **Barren Ground caribou.**
1820 (1823) FRANKLIN *Journey* 242: The weight of a full-grown barren-ground deer, exclusive of the offal, varies from ninety to one hundred and thirty pounds.

Barren Ground(s) grizzly a species of grizzly bear, *Ursus richardsoni,* native to the Barren Grounds. See also **bald-face grizzly** and **Barren Ground bear.**
1965 *Cdn Geog.Jnl* June 187/1: This is also the home of the Barren Grounds grizzly.

Barren Ground(s) reindeer See **Barren Ground caribou.**
1852 RICHARDSON *Arctic Exped.* 290: The flesh that we obtained was the flesh of the small or barren ground reindeer. . . . **1908** MAIR *Mackenzie Basin* 107: The Barren Ground reindeer migrate to the east end of this lake in October. . . .

Barren Ground(s) wolf See **Arctic wolf.** See also **Barren Land wolf.**
1958 *Beaver* Autumn 23/1: Although somewhat smaller than the timber wolf, the barren grounds wolf can still reach large proportions. . . .

Barren Land(s) See **Barren Ground.** Also spelled *Barrenland(s).*
1843 SIMPSON *Narrative* 224: The appellation Barren, or Barren Land, is given to the whole north-east angle of the continent . . . because that extensive region is destitute of wood. **1952** MOWAT *People of the Deer* 89: I . . . begin to understand the libel that is perpetuated by that name—the Barrenlands. **1964** *Calgary Herald* 25 Feb. 11/7: . . . I was fortunate to be flying over some of the "barren lands" where there isn't a tree as far as the eye can see—only gentle rolling country.

Barren Land(s) caribou See **Barren Ground caribou.**
1897 WILSON *Yukon* 54: They are much more strongly built than the barren land caribou. . . . **1963** *Maclean's* 23 Feb. 42/1: So adept was he at killing the Barren Lands caribou that his people felt he had some supernatural power over game.

Barren Land(s) wolf See **Arctic wolf.** See also **Barren Ground wolf.**
1963 *Maclean's* 16 Nov. 69/2: . . . almost all the dens used by the Barren Land wolves were abandoned fox burrows which had been enlarged by the wolves.

Barrens or **Barren** *n.* See **Barren Ground.**
1843 SIMPSON *Narrative* 224: The appellation of Barren . . . is given to the whole north-east angle of the continent. . . . **1908** MAIR *Mackenzie Basin* 161: It . . . is not met with in the "Barrens" proper. . . . **1956** MOWAT *Lost in the Barrens* [book title].

Barrens grizzly bear See **Barren Ground grizzly.**
1956 MOWAT *Lost in the Barrens* 165: They *might* be tracks of the giant Barrens grizzly bear. . . .

barrens partridge *Nfld* the rock ptarmigan, *q.v.*
1933 MERRICK *True North* 191: In a deep gully . . . we came to a company of barrens partridges. They are white, like ptarmigan, only smaller.

barricade *n.* **1** See **ballacater.**
1909 GRENFELL *Adrift on Ice-Pan* 5: . . . I was obliged to keep on what we call the "ballicaters," or ice barricades. . . . **1940** *Beaver* June 21/1: The crew just managed to keep her afloat . . . until she was beached on the barricade ice.
2 a. an overnight camping arrangement consisting of a trench or pit dug in the snow and lined with evergreen boughs which serve, along with a fire, as

protection from the cold.

[**1792** (1911) SIMCOE *Diary* 79: Half the party . . . began felling wood; the rest dug away the snow till they had made a pit many feet in circumference, in which the fire was to be made.] **1946** *Beaver* Mar. 5/1: The barricade was comfortably lined with spruce boughs with a windbreak behind and a cosy fire in front.

b. See quote. Cp. **barricado.**
1941 *Beaver* Sep. 36/1: Barricade—An open camping place formed of small trees and brush.

barricade out camp out in a barricade (def. 2).
1933 MERRICK *True North* 151: "When you barricade out, you got to dig to the ground [in the snow] a big enough hole fer yourself and the fire. . . ."

barricader *n.* *Nfld Dial.* See **ballacater.**
1937 DEVINE *Folklore* 9: Barricaders—The frozen sea ice on the fore shore unmoved by the ebb and flow of the tide. Also spoken Ballacarters.

barricado *n.* *Obs.* **1** See **ballacater.**
1775 (1792) CARTWRIGHT *Journal* II 66: In helping his dog out of the water the barricados broke, whereby he fell in, and was near being drowned.

2 See quote. Cp. **barricade** (def. 2).
1770 (1911) HEARNE *Journey* 78: On our arrival . . . some were immediately employed in making a hut or barracado with young pine trees.

barrier *n.* [< Cdn F *barrière*] *Obs.* See 1897 quote. See also **barrier net** and **Indian fence** (def. 2).
1793 (1933) MACDONELL *Diary* 72: . . . we came to La Parents settlement at the barrier where our guide attempted to hire a man. . . . **1897** COUES *New Light* II 471n: Barrier does not imply any natural obstruction to navigation, but was in those days a usual name of a fish-weir set across a stream.

Barrier *n.* See **Canadian Shield.**
1929 *Cdn Hist.Rev.* X 304: The third class of person to invade the Barrier was the squatter.

barrier net *Obs.* a net set across a stream, replacing a fish weir, or barrier, *q.v.*
1863 WALSHE *Cedar Creek* 355: But the abominable dams, and the barrier nets, and the Indians' spearings, have already lessened it [the salmon run] one-fourth.

barrisway *n.* See **barrasway.**

barrocado *n.* See **barricado.**

barron *n.* See **barren** (def. 1).

Basco ['bæsko] *n.* *Slang* See quote.
1963 SYMONS *Many Trails* 58: . . . the men who are the backbone of the range sheep industry [are] the sheepherders, as we call the Scottish, Mexican, or Basco (Basque) shepherds.

base line† **1** in government surveys, the east-west line that functions as a starting point for the parallel lines demarcating blocks, *q.v.*, townships, *q.v.*, etc. See also **proof line.**
☛ *On the Prairies, base lines run east and west, 24 miles apart, moving northwards, beginning at the 49th parallel; in Old Ontario (Upper Canada) the base lines tend to parallel the St. Lawrence River and the shore of Lake Ontario.*
1871 *Wkly Manitoban* 25 Mar. 3/3: The east and west lines between townships 4 and 5 . . . and 16 and 17, shall be base lines, or standard parallels, in the system. **1962** *Globe and Mail* (Toronto) 12 Dec. 7/3: New Toronto

wants the Municipal Board to give the . . . municipality the northeastern corner of the Toronto Township north of the Base Line and east of the Fourth Line.

2 See **base-line road.**
1934 DENNIS *Down in N.S.* 113: You'll find the Base Line pretty straight. **1958** MCGREGOR *North-west of 16* 153: This [road] came to be called the "Base Line," although in reality the nearest base line was six miles further north.

base-line road or **trail** a road that lies on or near a base line.
1934 DENNIS *Down in N.S.* 113: Take the Base Line Road, then turn to your right. . . . **1961** *Edmonton Jnl* 5 Aug. 4/3: [The] Trail initially followed the old Baseline Trail, which took its name from its route along the base of township 53.

bas-fond *n.* [< F] See 1897 quote.
1811 (1897) COUES *New Light* II 676: We drove briskly until sunrise, which found us at the bas fond where our horses wintered. **1877** GRANT *Ocean to Ocean* 228: . . . the sinuous trail . . . led across grassy bas-fonds under the shadow of the mountains. . . . **1897** COUES *New Light* II 586n: Basfond is hardly a geographical name, being applicable to any piece of low land along a river or about a lake; it is used here in the same sense as we use *bottom.*

basin *n.* See **basin hole.**

basin hole a hole for fishing nets, made in thick ice by chiselling out a basin-shaped depression until a hole is cut through at the centre.
1801 MACKENZIE *Voyages* lxxxix: . . . holes are cut [in the ice] at a distance of thirty feet from each other, to the full length of the net; one of them is larger than the rest, being generally about four feet square, and is called the bason [hole]; by means of them, and poles of proportionable length, the nets are placed in and drawn out of the water. **1888** *Dominion Illust.* 127/2: The Indian dogs or huskies haul the portable canvas house . . . to the "basin holes," and there the nets are "set" and "lifted" in comparative comfort. **1956** KENNEDY *Gt Slave Lake* 13: At the beginning of the season basin holes are relatively easy to open but later, when the ice becomes as much as 6 feet thick, each hole becomes a major chore. To re-open a hole in thick ice calls for less work since a basin hole takes several days to freeze to the original thickness.

basket *n.* **1** *Obs.* a special type of strong durable pannier used by the officers of the fur trade for personal food supplies.
1828 (1872) MCDONALD *Peace River* 43: Also with compartments, and suitable for tin cases, for meats, sugar, and other groceries . . . the frying pan . . . on top of the contents. The basket is made of strong willow, and among Hudson's Bay people, is strong enough for any service or accident. **1841** (1947) *Champlain Soc.Pubs* XXIV 357: The Basket itself you will be pleased to charge to the Montreal Department.

2 a basketwork weir for catching fish.
1830 DAVIES *Northern Quebec* 126: . . . they brought a few hung fish but no fresh ones, for lately neither the basket, nets or hooks have produced anything. **1858** (1860) HIND *Assiniboine Exped.* I 490: We at once ascended the Pike or Jack-fish River to the "basket" or weir erected across it by the Indians . . . for the purpose of procuring fish.

3 See **basket sled.**

1924 DORRANCE *Never Fire First* 34: The sled was braked . . . [and] a tall driver . . . sprang from the basket and waited for them to come up.

basket canoe *Obs.* See quote. Cp. **bull boat.**

1832 MCGREGOR *British America* I 144: The Mic-Mac Indians . . . proceed . . . by East Bay River in their birch-bark canoes, as far as Serpentine Lake; and from thence proceed from lake to lake in their small basket, or wicker-work canoes, covered with skins. These resemble those said to have been used by the ancient Britons.

basket cradle See **cradle-basket** and picture.

1902 MCEVOY *From the Gt Lakes* 178: They [kloochmans] carry their babies in a basket cradle, supported by a band that goes round the mother's forehead in the old style. **1912** (1913) HODGE & WHITE *Indians of Canada* 116/2: On the Pacific slope and throughout the interior basin the basket cradle predominates and exists in great variety. **1953** *Beaver* Mar. 26/1: [Caption] Baby in basket cradle.

basket sled or **sleigh** *North* See 1964 quote.

1900 LONDON *Son of Wolf* 107: "How long since that basket sled, with three men and eight dogs passed?" **1940** FINNIE *Lure of North* 117: In the dead of winter . . . the native komatik reigns supreme, gliding easily where a basket sled would drag. **1964** *Nat.Geog.* May 728/1: The basket sleigh is a toboggan several inches from the ground with runners added. Strong side rails serve as hand-holds for the driver.

bass *n.* See **basswood.**

1783 (1905) *Ont.Bur.Arch.Rep.* III cxxi: . . . the woods in general are maple, bass, hickory, ash, elm. . . . **1852** MOODIE *Roughing It* 243: He observed that the cedars . . . became less numerous, and were succeeded by bass and soft maple.

basswood *n.* the North American lime or linden tree, *Tilia americana.* See also **whitewood** (def. 2).

1795 (1911) SIMCOE *Diary* 269: I was amused by observing . . . the bass wood, the varieties of white and black oak. . . . **1965** *Kingston Whig-Standard* (Ont.) 16 Jan. 7/2: They are most numerous in swampy areas and consist mainly of soft maple, elm, black ash, as well as some basswood. . . .

bastard canoe [trans. of Cdn F *canot bâtard*] *Fur Trade, Hist.* a birchbark canoe about 30 feet long and capable of carrying two tons of freight in addition to its ten-man crew. See also **batard canoe** and **canot bâtard.**

1832 DAVIES *Northern Quebec* 167: Mr. Erlandson and eight men took their departure for the interior in two bastard canoes and a fishing canoe. . . . **1932** *Beaver* Dec. 38/2: Between these two [the Montreal and north canoes] was a hybrid, commonly called . . . bastard canoe. **1952** (1954) JENNINGS *Strange Brigade* 145: The largest at York . . . was . . . the bastard canoe—which seemed to me an enormous craft for one so fragile.

bastard gear *Maritimes* See quote.

1955 WALLACE *Roving Fisherman* 153: Some vessels ran longer skates and some rigged what was known as "bastard gear"—a halibut ganger being alternated with a lighter ganger and hook for taking codfish.

bastard maple See **Manitoba maple.**

1800 (1897) COUES *New Light* I 4: We made sugar of the

bastard maple. **1873** (1904) BUTLER *Wild North Land* 60: In some of the serpentine bends the bastard maple lifts its gnarled trunk. . . . **1951** O'MEARA *Grand Portage* 242: [it was] sweetened with sugar from the bastard maple.

Bastonnais *n.* See **Bostonnais.**

batard canoe *Hist.* See **bastard canoe.**

1931 NUTE *Voyageur* 24: Between these two in size was the *batard,* or "bastard canoe," which was propelled by ten men. **1951** O'MEARA *Grand Portage* 253: [There were] express and batard canoes.

bateau or **batteau** [bæ'to *or* 'bæto] *n.* [< F *bateau*] Also spelled *batto(e).* *Hist.* **1** a boat such as a sloop or large rowboat.

1760 JEFFERYS *Descr.New France* 17: In going up they are obliged to half unload their battoes. . . . **1785** HUNTER *Diary* 28: When he goes to Quebec, it's generally in a bateau of his own, which he prefers to calashes. **1840** *Montreal Transcript* 31 Dec. 421/2: All Passengers [are] to pay their own Ferriage while crossing in Bateaus.

A bateau (def. 2)

2 a flat-bottomed cargo and passenger boat about 30 feet long, tapered to bow and stern, drawing little water, and propelled by oars, poles, or a sail, originally designed for the treacherous river route between Upper and Lower Canada. See also **Canadian boat.**

1765 (1905) *Ont.Bur.Arch.Rep.* III 417: To Sundry Expences . . . Viz.: postage by Landhire or Batteaus. **1806** (1809) GRAY *Letters* 70: Bateaux, and canoes, convey to Upper Canada . . . the European commodities they want. **1963** *Weekend Mag.* 22 June 5/1: Upper Canada village near Morrisburg, Ontario, offers . . . an exciting trip by bateau through "the first lock canal in all of North America."

3 a clumsy, flat-bottomed boat about 19 feet long between tapered ends, propelled by oars, crewed by six men, and capable of carrying about 4,000 pounds of cargo. This prototype for the York boat was widely used throughout the northwest until recent years. See also **pointer** (def. 2) and **upland boat.** Cp. **flat-boat.**

1781 (1954) *Moose Ft Jnls* 358: They had coverings . . . to keep their Goods dry in their Battaux or Canoes. **1938** GODSELL *Red Hunters* 15: In . . . summer [I travelled] by birch-bark canoe, York boat and bateau. . . . **1963** *Beaver* Summer 15/2: Leaving King to bring up the heavy bateaux, Back and McLeod hurried on by canoe. . . .

4 See **York boat** and picture.

1859 *British Colonist* (Victoria) 17 Dec. 3/2: The Hudson's Bay Company's bateau, with a valuable cargo, for Fort Yale, was crushed in the ice, below Six Tree Shoot, about ten days ago. **1898** (1957) *Beaver* Autumn 13/1: Twelve large Battoes [York boats] were sent from Fort Garry to convey the troops up the River.

Each boat had 8 men as a crew—6 oarsmen, one to steer with a long oar, and one at the bow with a long pole and hook with which to shove her clear of a rock ahead or with the hook to catch hold of anything. **1960** BUBLITZ *Dotted Line* 85: For these men it wasn't a pleasant Sunday drive over a black macadam ribbon, but a two-day trudge with heavy "batteaux."

bateau-man *n. Hist.* **1** a man employed on a bateau, usually a skilled riverman.
1783 (1905) *Ont.Bur.Arch.Rep.* III cxx: The batteaux men prefer keeping over on this side, as they can follow the shore without crossing to the islands in their course. **1964** GUILLET *Pioneer Days* 25: The French-Canadian bateaumen on the St. Lawrence and the lakes . . . ate raw pork and hard biscuit, which they appear to have enjoyed.
2 a boatman working on the scows and bateaux in the north-west.
1938 GODSELL *Red Hunters* 173: Scarlet-clad Mounties rubbed shoulders with swarthy moccasined bateaux-men. . . .

bateau yard *Hist.* a place where bateaux were built, repaired, and stored.
1777 *Quebec Gaz.* 8 May 4/1: Lost the 5th Instant at the King's Battoe yard at St. Roch, A Silver Watch, Maker's Name George Lion, London. . . . **1807** (1964) INNIS *Fur Trade* 223: The factory of the Company is situated at the foot of the cascades of Saint Mary on the north side and consists of store-houses, a saw-mill, and a bateaux yard.

bater ['betɚ] *n.* See **beater**.

batiste [bə'tist] *n.* [< Cdn F] *Hist.* See **bateau** (def. 3).
1960 BUBLITZ *Dotted Line* 76: The Hudson Bay Company had to pack their hides from Edmonton to the Thompson River, and then down by rowboats, which Joe called "batistes," to Fort Langley. Those boats were long and heavy; and each took six men to handle and one to steer.

battiche or **battishe** *n. Obs.* See **babiche**.
1847 (1947) *Beaver* June 42/1: . . . they bring no regular axes, only a flat piece of steel shaped something like a plane iron, which the Indians fasten to a crooked stick with battiche. . . . **1848** (1898) JENNINGS *Routes to Yukon* 49: . . . we much wanted . . . Battishe for snow shoes in winter, parchment for windows for our house. . . .

batture [bæ'tɪur] *n.* [< Cdn F] **1** *Obs.* a shoal or rocky shore, usually exposed at low water.
1808 (1960) FRASER *Letters and Journals* 158: A strong Batture on left near beginning of the course, with a very high and rugged rock. **1822** *Montreal Herald* 23 Nov. 2/5: The weather was remarkably cold during last night, & considerable quantities of ice were seen on the battures this morning.
2 *Obs.* an expanse of river beach; strand.
1825 (1931) SIMPSON *Fur Trade* 143: Forded the River twice and Encamped on the Bature at Sun Set. **1873** (1922) MACOUN *Autobiography* 71: Our mode of progress was . . . going ashore and hauling the boat when the wide beach called a "Batture" was on our side of the river. **1912** *Trans.Roy.Soc.Can.* VI 2 79: These "bottoms" were called "battures" by the voyageurs.
3 a sand bar, especially one that forms a small island when the water is low.
1814 (1897) COUES *New Light* II 785: Our people went on a few miles and then camped to dry their packs on a batture (sand bar). **1869** KENNICOTT *Journal* 71: [There were] numerous low islands, and many sand bars, or "battures," as the voyageurs call them. **1909** CAMERON

New North 70: . . . an island or sandbar in a river is a "batture."

4 *Cdn French* See **bottom ice**.
1866 (1873) LEMOINE *Maple Leaves* 218: . . . I noticed him skimming majestically over vast ice fields, *battures,* as they are called. . . . **1941** BUCHAN *Sick Heart River* 250: There was still a broad selvedge of ice—what the Canadian French call a *Batture*—but in the middle the ice was cracking.

bay *n. Nfld* a municipal district serving also as a postal district.
1819 ANSPACH *Hist.Nfld* 428: In the same spring, an unusual number of schooners and boats belonging to that bay were totally lost at the ice. . . . **1963** *Calgary Herald* 2 Oct. 21/2: The island [Nfld] has eight bay sections and each, with its ring of coastal settlements, is a special area.

Bay *n.* **1** (used with *the*) Hudson Bay, its shores, and the vicinity.
1748 (1749) *Proceedings of Comm.* 11: The Petitioners were advised . . . to petition the House of Commons . . . to open the Trade to the Bay, and to incorporate the Petitioners and others their Associates under proper Regulations. **1842** *Trans.Lit.& Hist.Soc.Que.* IV 87: The . . . Hudson's Bay Company . . . are now the only Company that have permanent establishments in the Bay. . . . **1960** *Press* Dec. 13: The title was, however, except for a few isolated posts on the great Bay itself, generally not "pushed" so long as the French held Quebec. . . .
2 the Hudson's Bay Company, *q.v.*; also, one of its trading posts or retail stores.
1812 (1964) INNIS *Fur Trade* 163: Another great advantage of having a House in Canada would be the purchasing of high Wines, Tobacco and Provisions for the Bay. **1824** *Montreal Herald* 3 Nov. 2/5: Petty merchants are encouraged; they receive their outfits from the Bay at cost and charges. **1964** *Calgary Herald* 11 Jan. 1/4: Since the Bay buys its skins from the Eskimo and Indian trappers, it seems fitting that a percentage of the trappers' catch should be used for the benefit of their children.

Bay man an employee of the Hudson's Bay Company.
1776 (1792) CARTWRIGHT *Journal* II 152: Early this morning I sent the Bay-men off. **1957** *Arctic Spotter* Nov. 30: Like Curry, there are hundreds of "Bay" men who, because of their isolated locations, could give the outsider the impression that—why should they worry about defence?

bayman *n. Nfld* See **outporter**.
1964 *United Church Observer* 1 Sep. 12/3: They call the St. John's man a "townie" while the outporter is a "bayman."

bay-noddie *n. Nfld, Slang* See **bayman**.
1907 DUNCAN *Shining Light* 238: "Put the illusions of this designing old bay-noddie away from you," says he.

Bay route See **Hudson Bay route**.
1963 MORTON *Kingdom of Canada* 447: The new challenge by the Bay route to that of the St. Lawrence was to remain for many years a slight and ineffectual one.

bay seal See **harbo(u)r seal**.
1772 (1792) CARTWRIGHT *Journal* I 210: I saw several

bay-seals on the ice there, and shot at two. . . .
1958 *Evening Telegram* (St. John's) 16 May 4/3 : I would also like to mention the bounty for the killing of the bay seals—another step in the protection of the salmon.

bay section See **bay.**

Bayside post one of the Hudson's Bay Company's trading posts on the shores of Hudson Bay, as opposed to the inland posts.
1963 DAVIES *Northern Quebec* xix : The Company's ship-captains . . . knew nothing about the east coast of Hudson Bay because the amount of ice there made them careful to keep well clear of it on their yearly voyages to and from the Bayside posts.

Bay Street a Toronto street on which is located the Toronto Stock Exchange and numerous financial houses, considered the financial centre of Canada ; hence, the moneyed interests of the country, especially of Ontario and eastern Canada, collectively. Cp. **St. James Street.**
1953 (1958) WALKER *Pardon My Parka* 99 : "Where did you meet this Bay Street pal of yours ? Known him long?" **1963** *Calgary Herald* 20 Sep. 4/6 : Bay Street and St. James Street may well have been dilatory in examining the investment prospects offered by this province [British Columbia]. **1965** *Cdn Geog.Jnl* Apr. 119/1 : . . . his success in optioning the . . . claims . . . soon had Bay Street rocking.

B.C.-ite *n.* a native or resident of British Columbia.
1959 *Maclean's* 10 May 8/1 : After all, these things bring money into the province ; and no loyal B.C.-ite wants to attack the basis of our prosperity.

beach *n. Lumbering* a shore from which logs can be floated ; a headquarters camp of a logging outfit.
1908 GRAINGER *Woodsmen* 66 : He worked . . . close to the beach, cutting timber along the frontage of his leases. **1942** HAIG-BROWN *Timber* 249 : . . . the boom camp, where the logs are dumped from the trains into salt water, is . . . likely to be referred to as "the Beach." **1965** *Vancouver Province* 17 June 18/1 : He says they can do basic jobs in the woods and at the beach.

beachcomb *v. Lumbering* See 1958 quote. See also **beachcomber** (def. 2).
1958 WATTERS *B.C.Cent.Anthol.* 253 : When not fishing, Dogfish Johnny and Crazy George go beach-combing. Which means, simply, that they cruise in and out of all the nearby inlets and coves searching for logs that may have broken away from the big log booms towed down the coast to the sawmills. **1965** *Star Wkly* 5 June 16/2 : A man can make a living at beachcombing. . . . With a fishing boat rigged up to handle logs, we cleared $500 a month.

beachcomber *n.* **1** *North* See quote.
1934 GODSELL *Arctic Trader* 257 : Hall had largely favored "beach-combers" as they were called, men who eked out an existence as trappers along the Arctic coast and lived with Eskimo women. . . .
2 *Lumbering, B.C.* a crew member or owner of a small tugboat that collects logs broken loose from booms, getting a commission on each log returned to its owners.
1962 NICHOLSON *West Coast* 331 : Buck fever cost an old beachcomber, living alone, a $20 bounty. **1965** *Star Wkly* 5 June 16/2 : At 35, [he] has worked as a

lumberjack, fisherman, and beachcomber, salvaging logs from broken booms.

beach crawler a boat operator who cruises close to the shore line.
1958 WELLS *Georgian Bay* 22 : These will be hazards to beach crawlers only.

beach-hugger *n.* See **beach crawler.**
1958 WELLS *Georgian Bay* 26 : I have no doubt but that the beach-hugger . . . will gravitate towards the inner and more difficult Cape Hurd Channel.

beach lot *Atlantic Provinces* See **fishing room.**
1824 *Canadian Mag.* III 204 : We humbly suggest . . . beach lots [be granted] in proportion to the number of barges to be employed in the fisheries. . . . *Ibid.* 350 : Among the subjects requiring our most serious attention . . . are the claims for fishing rooms, or beach lots.

bean-cake *n.* a cake or pattie made of beans.
1958 MACGREGOR *North-west of 16* 110 : So, in many cases a schoolboy's menu consisted of beans for supper, bean-cakes for breakfast, and onion sandwiches for lunch.

beanery *n. Slang* a small, usually run-down, restaurant featuring low prices and very ordinary food.
1887 *Grip* (Toronto) 26 Feb. 8/2 : Go to, illustrious reader ; get thee to a beanery. For such is genius! **1950** PALMER *Montreal Confidential* 58 : There are tattoo-ing parlors, Skid Row beaneries, and you can get a haircut for a few cents.

bean-feast *n.* an inexpensive meal of beans forming part of an informal social event at a college, camp, etc.
1964 *Maclean's* 2 Dec. 22/2 : Hand-lettered signs on the pillars advertised the bean-feast that preceded the demonstration.

bearberry *n.* **1** a trailing shrub, *Arctostaphylos uva-ursi,* found on bare, gravelly soils throughout Canada ; kinnikinnik (def. 2). See also **jackashey puck, sagakomi** (def. 2), and **squawberry** (def. 2).
1823 HALIBURTON *General Descr.N.S.* 34 : Bear Berry [*Arbutus Uva Ursi*]. **1877** GRANT *Ocean to Ocean* 169 : The ground was literally covered with bearberries, the *uva ursi.* . . **1958** BERTON *Klondike* 435 : The willows and the aspens, the currant bushes and the bearberries have encroached upon the town.
2 a. the insipid, red fruit of this shrub, much favored as food by bears. See also **sagakomi** (def. 1).
1807 WENTZEL *Letters* 80 : The fruits of this solitary region are the poire . . . bearberry, choak-berry. . . .
1942 TWOMEY & HERRICK *Needle to North* 283 : Even the flat-flavored . . . bearberry was not quite beyond praise, for we . . . felt the result of a long tea-and-flour winter. **1965** SYMINGTON *Tuktu* 24 : . . . crimson bearberries provide flamboyant contrast to the deep green of the alpine cranberry bushes. . . .
b. the fruit of the red-osier dogwood, *q.v.*
1820 (1823) FRANKLIN *Journey* 88 : There is also a berry of bluish-white colour, the produce of the white cornel tree, which is named musqua-meena, bear-berry, because these animals are said to fatten on it. **1946** FERGUSON *Mink, Mary and Me* 38 : Near the water, high-bush cranberries hung in clusters of red brilliance against a background of milk-white bearberries.
c. the luscious, black fruit of the *Arctostaphylos alpina,* a shrub of the Barren Grounds.
1952 *Beaver* June 37/1 : [We find] some of the tundra's

luscious fruits, such as bearberry, Arctic raspberry, and the baked apple.

3 See **bearberry leaf.**
1927 PHILIP *Painted Cliff* 117: He filled it with Indian tobacco, known as kinnikinick or bearberry, lighted the calumet of peace with a coal. . . .

bearberry bush See **bearberry** (def. 1).
1910 (*c*1911) MORICE *Great Déné Race* 420: Nor should we forget to mention the fruit of the kinnikinnik or bearberry bush. **1959** *Sun* (Vancouver) 1 Dec. 16/4: They . . . just munched the leaves of choice kinnikinnik or bearberry bush.

bearberry leaf the leaf of the bearberry bush, dried and used in making Indian tobacco. See also **bearberry** (def. 3).
1820 (1823) FRANKLIN *Journey* 75: He next took up a calumet filled with a mixture of tobacco and bear-berry leaves. . . . **1960** *Alta Hist.Rev.* 3rd Quarter 12/2: [Caption] Bearberry leaves were dried and mixed with other plants or white man's tobacco.

bearded seal a species of seal, *Erignathus barbatus,* characterized by its large size and prominent beardlike bristles about the mouth. See also **square-flipper.**
1854 (1892) KANE *Arctic Explor.* 154: Besides the Hispid seal, the only species which visited Rensselaer Harbour was . . . the large bearded seal. . . . **1963** *Beaver* Winter 24/2: Their umiaks were made of walrus or bearded seal skins and they also had sealskin kayaks.

bear dog *Northwest* a breed of small dog weighing 15 to 20 pounds and piebald in black and white or brown, found among the Indians of northern British Columbia, the Yukon, and the Mackenzie country. See also **crackie** (def. 2), **Hare Indian dog, Mackenzie River dog,** and **Tahltan dog.** Cp. **giddee.**
[**1824** (1955) BLACK *Journal* 35: The Thecannies not being Nimrodians or mighty hunters . . . they have the art of teaching their small Indian Dogs with erect Ears to hunt alone & the little hairy beagles will sometimes go a great distance by themselves & teaze the animal . . . untill the Master come up. . . .] **1905** (1958) *Yukon Telegraph Service* 7 Oct. 41: He reached down and grabbed an ancient bear dog. **1956** *Beaver* Summer 39/2: They were known locally as Bear Dogs because in the past they had been used extensively in the hunting of black bear, especially in the spring when a small dog could move quickly on the crust and hold a bear in deep snow until it was killed with a bow and arrow or muzzle loader. **1963** *Islander* 8 Sep. 2/2: "Too bad, bear dog he nearly all gone now. Dog he no good to us any more. . . . Bear dog, he only get in the way. Kids, they like him for pet."

bear feast *Fur Trade, Obs.* among voyageurs, a meal of fresh meat, such as bear, moose, etc., on the brigade route.
1935 *Beaver* Dec. 66/2: Sometimes a little variety is given to the journey by the killing of a black bear or moose. This is the signal for "cease work," and the whole brigade pitches camp to enjoy what they call a "bear feast."

bear foot an implement of Indian origin roughly resembling a bear's foot with protruding claws, used in harvesting blueberries.
1959 *Star Wkly* 22 Aug. 16/1: If the berries aren't quite ripe . . . the "bear foot" comes into play. This is a handsized rake that cleans off every berry in record time.

bear grease See **bear's grease.**

bear ham† the hind leg of a bear, salted and smoked.
1829 MACTAGGART *Three Years* I 183: In Montreal, bear-hams sell well, and are considered by the *kitcheners* of Canada exquisite in their way. **1952** (1954) JENNINGS *Strange Brigade* 200: They put up pickled fish and jellied venison, made pemmican and salted bear hams, pressed goose and duck. . . .

bear-paw *n.* an almost circular snowshoe, varying considerably in size, used especially by the eastern Algonkians. See also **pas d'ours.**
1811 (1950) THOMPSON *Journals* 145: [I] made a pair of Bear Paws and netted them. **1964** *Atlantic Advocate* June 37/1: He twisted a little on his bear-paws and looked back at his companion. **1965** *Cdn Geog. Jnl* Feb. 62: [Caption] The simplest type of snowshoe [is] the Bear Paw.

bear-paw (snow) shoe See **bear-paw.**
1936 ARMSTRONG *Yukon Yesterdays* 102: All he could obtain was two pairs of "Bear Paw" shoes, which are about the same size as the face of an ordinary tennis racket. . . . **1939** *Beaver* June 45/1: Their white parkas, caribou moccasins, and great, circular bear-paw snowshoes made them a colourful lot. **1964** *Atlantic Advocate* June 37/1: Some of it fell on his bear-paw snow-shoes.

bear's berry weed *Obs.* See **bearberry** (def. 3).
1784-1812 (1916) THOMPSON *Narrative* 365: The tobacco . . . required a great proportion of bears berry weed to be mixed with it.

bear's butter *Obs.* See **bear's grease.**
1873 (1904) BUTLER *Wild North Land* 210: It is the dessert of a Peace River feast; the fat, white as cream, is eaten in large quantities, and although at first a little of it suffices, yet after a while one learns to like it, and the dried Saskootum [sic] and "bear's butter" becomes a luxury.

bears' grape *Obs.* See **bearberry** (def. 2a).
1850 BIGSBY *Shoe and Canoe* II 263: The bears subsist mostly on berries, bilberries, bears' grapes, &c. . . .

bear's grease† the rendered fat of the bear used in cooking, medicine, cosmetics, and for insulating the body against cold. See also **bear's butter.**
*c*1665 (1885) RADISSON *Voyages* 41: The order of making was . . . the corne being dried between two stones into powder, being very thick, putt it into a kettle full of watter, then a quantity of Bear's grease. **1829** (1940) *Minutes of Council* (H.B.C.) 248: That the Gentlemen in Charge of districts be directed to use every exertion to collect Bears Grease as it is likely to become a valuable article of trade. **1948** ONRAET *Sixty Below* 158: I cannot say if there are really any healing virtues in bear grease, but I do know that it makes the dogs lick their wounds, and that this in a roundabout way heals them by keeping the wounds clean. **1964** INNIS *Fur Trade* 308: In 1830 orders were given that bears' grease should be collected at 2/ per pound.

bear tree See quote.
1946 WOOD *Rockies* 29: [Black bears] have a unique habit of marking certain trees with both claws and teeth: such trunks are called Bear-Trees and probably

keep Bruin posted about his immediate neighbours.

bear walker among the Ojibwa Indians, a witch or hoodoo (def. 2).

1959 *Cdn Forum* June 56/1: There is a curious and intricate superstition which many of the Manitoulin Indians believe firmly. When misfortune strikes a brave, he blames it not on bad luck but on a bear walker who has cast a curse on him. *Ibid.* 57/2: An Indian had been killed. She was a bear walker.

beat *n. Obs.* See **yard,** *n.* (def. 1a).
1828 *U.E.Loyalist* 17 May 416/1: . . . after much fatigue they reached the neighbourhood of the yard or beat of the moose-deer.

beater ['bitɚ] *n.* [< *beat* make one's way with persistence in the face of difficulties + *-er*] *Nfld* a young harp seal whose white coat is beginning to show gray tinges and dark spots. Cp. **bedlamer** and **whitecoat.** Also spelled *bater.* Also *beating seal.*
1924 ENGLAND *Vikings of the Ice* 313/2: Bater. a beating seal; young migrating seal. **1933** GREENE *Wooden Walls* 78: Now [the whitecoats] became the "beaters" of the Seal Hunt, and of certain surety every little head will be pointing for the North. **1966** *Weekend Mag.* 19 Mar. 38/1: Baby seals are bought by an English firm and used to make coats; beaters, the harp seals between three weeks and a year old, are bought by a Norwegian firm and used for jackets.

beating seal See **beater.**

beat meat dried meat, beaten into a pulpy mass. See also **piled meat, pounded meat,** and **ruhiggan.** Cp. **pemmican.**
1775 (1934) HEARNE *Journal* 8 Feb. 136: By the middle of January we ware so short that we could not afford more than a Small handfull of Dry'd beat meat . . . and about 4 ounses of other Meat pr Man Each Day. **1872** (1883) BUTLER *Great Lone Land* 153: Pemmican, the favourite food of the Indian and the half-breed voyager, can be made from the flesh of any animal, but it is nearly altogether composed of buffalo meat; the meat is first cut into slices, then dried either by fire or in the sun, and then pounded or beaten out into a thick flaky substance; in this state it is put into a large bag made from the hide of the animal, the dry pulp being soldered down into a hard solid mass by melted fat being poured over it—the quantity of fat is nearly half the total weight, forty pounds of fat going to fifty pounds of "beat meat". . . . **1953** *Beaver* Mar. 48/2: Occasionally the reader . . . may want to know more about "beat meat" than the journals reveal.

beat the path, track, or **trail** break trail, *q.v.,* by going in front of a dog team.
1776 (1901) HENRY (Elder) *Travels* 314: In the van were twenty-five soldiers, who were to beat the path, so the dogs might walk. **1858** (1863) PALLISER *Journals* 122: . . . as the snow was deep two of us [were] always required to go before the dogs to beat the track. **1943** *Beaver* Mar. 48/1: Alexandre, who had the smallest load, beat the trail.

beaver *n.* **1†** an aquatic rodent, *Castor canadensis,* of North America, formerly of first importance in the fur trade and long used as an emblem of Canada.
1584 (1877) HAKLUYT *Discourse on Western Planting* 26: He broughte home a kind of mynerall matter supposed

to holde silver, whereof he gave me some; a kynde of musk called castor; divers beastes skynnes, as bevers, otters . . . all dressed, and painted on the innerside with divers excellent colours. . . . **1962** *Canada Month* May 15/3: The exhibition should give them a better idea of what besides beavers, Mounties and snowfields makes up Ca-na-da.

2† the flesh of the beaver as food.
1754 (1907) HENDAY *Journal* 336: I was invited to a Beaver feast. **1963** *Canada Month* Feb. 26/2: for every [recipe for] roast rabbit . . . there is another for boiled bulrushes . . . fiddleheads (ferns) au gratin, palpation of pigeons or beaver stew.

3† the pelt of the beaver. See also **beaver skin** (def. 1).
1583 STUBBS *Anatomie of Abuses* 22: Beaver became in demand in Europe when hat-makers realized its value for their craft. **1671** (1942) *H.B.C.Minutes* 1: Ordered That upon the first Tuesday in december next about three thousand poundes weight of the bever bee putt to Sale by the candle. . . . **1899** WILLSON *Great Company* 238: The beaver thus received by the chief trader and stored at the factory . . . was classified into eight varieties.

4 *Fur Trade, Hist.* See **made beaver** (def. 1).
1708 (1957) *Beaver* Winter 14/1: One with the other 10 good Skins; that is, Winter Beaver; 12 Skins of the biggest sort, 10 for the mean, and 8 for the smallest. **1765** (1901) HENRY (Elder) *Travels* 184: It is in beaver that accounts are kept at Michilimackinac. . . . **1852** RICHARDSON *Arctic Expedition* 231: To be accounted a chief among the Kutchin, a man must possess beads to the amount of 200 beavers. **1957** *Beaver* Winter 14/2: Kettles . . . sold for one beaver a pound in the earliest list and one and one-half beaver at York Fort in 1715 and 1749.

A beaver (def. 5a)

5 a. *Fur Trade, Hist.* one of the coins or tokens constituting beaver currency, *q.v.* See also **beaver coin, beaverskin token, beaver token, H.B.C. token, Hudson's Bay token, made-beaver token,** and **trade token.**
1908 LAUT *Conquest N.W.* I 152: If the hunt exceeded the debt, the Indian might draw either cash or goods to the full amount or let the Company stand in his debt, receiving coins made from the lead of melted tea chests with 1, 2, 3 or 4 *B*—beaver—stamped in the lead. **1913** WILLIAMS *Wilderness Trail* 190: When the value [of the furs] is determined, the trader pushes over the counter as many "beaver" (lead pellets) as the furs are worth.

b. See quote.
1931 GREY OWL *Last Frontier* 144: Counters were threaded on a string, each worth a dollar, and called "beaver," and as the hunter sold his fur its equivalent in "beaver" counters was pushed along the string.

6 *Slang, Obs.* See quote; swamper (def. 1).
1913 SANDILANDS *West.Cdn Dict.* 6: Beaver, a man engaged on road-making near the lumber camps.

Beaver *n.* **1** *Hist.* the second of four degrees in the Hunters' Lodge, *q.v.*
1926 *Cdn Hist.Rev.* VII 19: The second was the "Beaver" degree; the third was the degree of "Master

Hunter," and the fourth was the degree of "Patriotic Hunter."

2 a famous Canadian bush plane manufactured by DeHavilland Aircraft of Canada Ltd.
1957 *Financial Post* 2 Nov. 62/6: The Beaver first flew in 1947. **1965** *Globe and Mail* (Toronto) 26 Apr. 17/8: First there was the Beaver, which incorporated into its design the suggestions of Canada's highly-respected bush pilots. . . .

beaver blanket 1 a blanket or robe of beaver skins sewn together. See also **beaver coat** (def. 1).
1765-75 (1933) POND *Narrative* 53: I Perseaved five Parsons from the Camp aproching—four was Imployed in Car[ry]ing a Beaver Blanket finely painted—the Other Held in his Hand a Callemeat or Pipe of Peace. . . .
1796 *U.C.Gaz.* (York [Toronto]) 21 Dec. 3/3: In the loss sustained by Mr. Jarvis, was also a Buffalo Skin, which, if returned, with or without the beaver blankets, will be thankfully received and no questions asked.

2 *Fur Trade* the largest size of beaver skin. See also **blanket** (def. 4).
1947 SAUNDERS *Algonquin* 156: A good beaver "blanket" is worth forty dollars.

beaver castor See **beaver medicine.**
1907 HUNTER *Cdn Wilds* 111: The odor of the beaver castor has a very alluring effect on most all animals, and is greatly used by the hunter. **1965** *Islander* 14 Feb. 5/3: . . . with a favorable breeze he probably could smell that mixture of fish oil and beaver castor . . . a half a mile away.

beaver chip See quote.
1946 WOOD *Rockies* 63: . . . the wood chips found near tree stumps after beaver work were once gathered and used for medicinal purposes by pioneers, who labelled them Beaver Chips and attributed marvellous tonic qualities to the shavings.

Beaver Club 1 *Hist.* a social club in Montreal, founded by members of the North West Company.
*c***1799** MCKENZIE *Reminiscences* 58: I shall sound them about the plan of renewing the Beaver Club. . . . **1817** *Montreal Herald* 11 Jan. 1/4: The Beaver Club, social and gay, / With pipe and Paddle combine. **1933** *Beaver* Dec. 6/1: Founded in 1785 by nineteen partners of the Northwest Company, all of whom had wintered in the [North] West, the Beaver Club lived until 1824. . . .

2 a present-day social organization for employees of the Hudson's Bay Company.
1934 *Beaver* Sep. 34/1: So in 1931, when all the employees' welfare and social organizations in Canada were brought into line, no name was more obviously suitable for them than Beaver Club. . . . in 1924, an organization of the same name was formed among the London staff of the Company, and this continues to live and flourish. Let us concern ourselves, however, with the Beaver Clubs that exist in the six large stores, and in Hudson's Bay House, Winnipeg.

beaver coat 1 *Fur Trade, Hist.* five to eight prime beaver skins, from which the guard hairs had been removed, sewn together to make a robe, worn by the Indians with the fur next to the body. The oil-impregnated fur (coat beaver, *q.v.*) made excellent felt and was eagerly bought by the hat-makers. See also **beaver blanket, beaver robe** (def. 1), **coating robe** (def. 1) and **toggy.** Cp. **beaver wool.**
1671 (1942) *H.B.C.Minutes* 14 Nov. 8: That Mr. Rastell take care to put up publick bills upon the

Exchange tomorrow morneing for Sale of lb.3000 weight of beaver coates &. skins. . . . **1754** (1907) HENDAY *Journal* 342: One man narrowly escaped from a Grizzle Bear that he had wounded, by throwing his Beaver coat from him; which the bear tore to pieces, & which the natives always do when forced to retreat. **1954** WALLACE *Pedlars* 17: Tomison had lent to the Indians three beaver coats, stamped with the mark of the Hudson's Bay Company. . . .

2 an overcoat of beaver skins.
1791 (1911) SIMCOE *Diary* 59: They wore large beaver coats and the carriole was filled with buffalo skins.

beaver coin *Fur Trade, Hist.* See **beaver** (def. 5a).
*c***1902** LAUT *Trapper* 191: Montagnais's squaw has only fifty "beaver" coin, and her desires are a hundredfold what these will buy.

beaver country a region in which beaver are numerous and trapping is profitable.
1754 (1907) HENDAY *Journal* 343: The Men must look out for Beaver, as they have no Ammunition & I am resolved to take care of mine, neither would it be prudent to expend Ammunition in a Beaver Country. **1937** *Beaver* June 11/2: It is primarily intended to rehabilitate the beaver country and provide the natives with a steady income. . . .

beaver credit *Obs.* credit established by a trapper in terms of made beaver, *q.v.*
1806 (1960) FRASER *Letters and Journals* 9 May 176: They had a few skins Beaver Credit, and traded 30 with the value of 80 skins [for] dried provisions, and twenty-one orignal [moose] skins.

beaver currency *Fur Trade, Hist.* a fur-trade monetary system in which one made beaver, *q.v.*, was the unit of value. See also **beaver money** and **beaverskin currency.**
*c***1902** LAUT *Trapper* 194: The value of these furs in "beaver" currency varied with the fashions of the civilized world, with the scarcity or plenty of the furs, with the locality of the fort.

beaver cutter See quote.
1941 *Beaver* Sep. 36: Beaver Cutter—A term of ridicule applied to one who fells a tree by cutting around it like a beaver.

beaver cuttings fallen trees, sticks, chips, and pointed stumps left from the activities of beavers.
1770 (1792) CARTWRIGHT *Journal* I 22: I named it Watson Pond, and was greatly surprised to find beaver cuttings by the side of it. . . . **1824** (1955) BLACK *Journal* ix: Few things are more dangerous . . . than the . . . chaos of logs, uprooted trees and beaver cuttings . . . in such places as this. **1937** (1950) STANWELL-FLETCHER *Driftwood Valley* 60: In one place beaver cuttings, along a bank of poplars, extend for a quarter of a mile.

beaver dam a dam built by beavers to maintain a constant water level above their lodge. See also **dam**[1].
1754 (1907) HENDAY *Journal* 342: The Beaver Dams bear people [because frozen], which favors in killing the Beaver. **1880** GORDON *Mountain and Prairie* 212: . . . much of the country is at present covered by swamps and beaver-dams. **1964** *Globe and Mail* (Toronto) 19 Dec. 26/5: [Motor toboggans] will climb over logs, cross beaver dams . . . climb or descend steep hills with amazing ease.

beaver dog a dog specially trained to hunt beaver.
1907 HUNTER *Cdn Wilds* 141 : This is handled (generally at the lake) with a peeled spruce sapling from six to seven feet long, and last but by no means least, is a good beaver dog, and almost any Indian dog is good for beaver, as they learn from the older ones and train themselves. 1948 *Beaver* Sep. 42/1 : . . . if the [bank] burrow is used much in winter, its location is very quickly picked up by the Indian with the help of his "beaver dog."

beaver-eater *n.* the wolverine (def. 1a) or carcajou.
1763 (1904) LONG *Voyages* 76 : The country everywhere abounds with wild animals, particularly bears . . . beaver eaters. . . . 1965 *Islander* 14 Feb. 5/3 : Beaver-eater is one of the wolverine's nicknames.

beaver farm See **beaver preserve.**
1934 *Beaver* June 16/2 : . . . the company operated a very successful Beaver farm on Charlton Island from about the year 1860 until 1902.

beaver flats See **beaver meadow.**
1958 *Beaver* Autumn 48/2 : He was a familiar figure, with . . . his battered old car, which he often drove . . . across pastureland and bumpy beaver flats. . . .

beaver frontier *Hist.* the limits of activity in the fur trade.
1963 MORTON *Kingdom of Canada* 24 : The "beaver frontier" formed and then retreated; the Indians' catches mounted, and the flow of European goods was quickened.

beaver grass See **beaver-meadow hay.**
1896 GOURLAY *Hist.Ottawa* 50 : William Gourlay . . . explored the river through mud . . . ferns, beaver grass and willows.

beaver hay the rank grass that grows in beaver meadows, *q.v.* See also **beaver grass** and **beaver-meadow hay.**
1854 KEEFER *Ottawa* 69 : Beaver hay costs about as much as good hay in agricultural districts, but it is worth only half as much; and as some horses will not eat it. . . . 1896 GOURLAY *Hist.Ottawa* 33 : These could live in the bush in summer, and on beaver hay, brush and sheaf oats in winter. . . . 1967 *Cdn Geog.Jnl* Feb. 51 : And even in 1966, the barns contain a goodly crop of beaver hay. . . .

beaver house See **beaver lodge.**
1691 (1929) KELSEY *Papers* 14 : In these woods there is abundance of small ponds of water of which there is hardly one Escapes without a Beavour house. . . . 1965 *Star Wkly* 23 Jan. 37/2 : Emile Paquette puts a bait of stripped poplar wood near a beaver house . . . and sets his trap in the water below it.

beaver hut See **beaver lodge.**
1943 MILLER *Lone Woodsman* 125 : With them the wolverine could tear open a beaver hut . . . .

beaver lodge a domed structure of mud, sticks, stones, etc. built as a rule in a beaver pond behind the dam and used as a den by a family of beavers. See also **cabane** (def. 3), **cabin, house** (def. 2), and **lodge** (def. 1a).
1789 MCKENZIE *Reminiscences* 33 : I have worked at

beaver lodges, killed a few beavers. 1807 (1890) KEITH *Letters* 69 : For instance, when an Indian discovers one or more beaver lodges, if not already appropriated, he immediately puts a mark upon them. . . . 1964 *Sun* (Vancouver) 15 July 19/1 : Each end of the lake has old beaver lodges, always enthralling to boys, steeped in beaver lore at school.

beaver marsh a marshy area occupied by beavers. See also **beaver swamp.** Cp. **beaver meadow.**
c1902 LAUT *Trapper* 174 : Perhaps a stake stood with a mark at the entrance to a beaver-marsh—some hunter had found this ground first and warned all other trappers off by the code of wilderness honour.

beaver meadow a meadow, often swampy, lying behind an old beaver dam and prized by early settlers for its fertility. See also **beaver flats, beaver prairie**, and **hay meadow.**
1824 TALBOT *Five Years in the Canadas* I 102 : The situation of the town is very unhealthy, for it stands on a piece of low marshy land, which is better calculated for a frog-pond or beaver meadow than for a residence of human beings. 1964 *B.C.Digest* Oct. 57/2 : About 30 miles west of Puntzi Lake they encountered a gang of men cutting hay on a large swamp or beaver meadow. . . .

beaver-meadow hay See **beaver hay.**
1896 GOURLAY *Hist.Ottawa* 48 : The substitute they made for hair in the mortar was cut straw and beaver-meadow hay. . . .

beaver medicine the secretion from the scent glands of the beaver used as a lure or as an ingredient in a lure. See also **beaver castor, beaver pride, castoreum** (def. 1b), and **medicine** (def. 5).
☛ *"Medicine" is used here in the sense of "magic." See* **medicine** (*def. 1*).
1784-1812 (1916) THOMPSON *Narrative* 317 : . . . traps for beaver . . . of which the bait is the castorum of the beaver, called the beaver medicine. 1907 HUNTER *Cdn Wilds* 204 : Beaver medicine and castorum would not allure him [a wily old beaver], and the thought occurred to me to try anise seed oil. . . .

beaver money *Fur Trade* See **beaver currency.**
1944 EVATT *Snow Owl's Secret* 220 : The tokens that are here in this pouch, and of which there are many more on Smallboy's toboggan, are called beaver money! 1967 LEFOLII *Cdn Look* 121/1 : Deprived of beaver money, the gentlemen of central Canada began to have second thoughts about the beaver's squatting rights on their coat of arms.

beaver net a net, usually of the purse type, made of babiche, *q.v.,* and used for netting beaver.
1824 (1955) BLACK *Journal* 161 : We have not found a Beaver skin or Fur of any kind but saw a Beaver Net or a Net for large Fish making also Fishing Nets of small Thong and Sinnew twisted into a Thread.

beaver plu *Fur Trade, Hist.* See **plu.**
1801 (1933) MCLEOD *Diary* 154 : He has now had two hundred & thirteen Skins that is traded Beaver Plus.

beaver pond a small body of water formed by the back-up from a beaver dam, *q.v.,* usually shallow and swampy away from the dam itself. See also **beaver run** and **pond** (def. 4b).
1792 (1905) *Ont.Bur.Arch.Rep.* III 215 : I came to part of the afore said Beaver Pond, low wet land, not the least frozen, which obliged me to discontinue that line. 1962 FRY *Ranch on the Cariboo* 235 : Then I'd take an axe to the beaver ponds in the creek by the meadow to open up the water holes. . . .

beaver prairie See **beaver meadow**.
1937 CONIBEAR *Northland Footprints* 36: Then the farmer calls the corner of his field in which this [a gnawed stick] is found a "beaver prairie", and is happy, knowing that the rich silt dropped there in the still waters....

beaver preserve or **reserve** a preserve where beaver are permitted to flourish without indiscriminate trapping. See also **beaver farm**, **beaver sanctuary**.
1933 *Beaver* Sep. 9/1: Recently the company rented some 7,000 square miles of territory from the Quebec government between the Rupert and the East Main rivers, where a beaver reserve will be established....
1946 *Ibid.* June 50/1: ... an adequate beaver population would be an asset to the whole continent, but complete protection is not the answer... beaver preserves are much nearer the ideal.

One kind of beaver-press

beaver-press *n. Fur Trade* See **fur press**.
1952 *Beaver* June 40/2: He notes the dimensions of the beaver-press, or fur-press, to have been two feet four inches in length, and one foot two inches in breadth....

beaver pride See **beaver medicine**.
1941 *Beaver* Sep. 36: Beaver Pride—Another name for castorum and used extensively as a bait lure.

beaver road a trail made by and used regularly by beavers.
1808 (1950) THOMPSON *Journals* 19: ... we set off to go higher up the River, where we hope to find a few Beaver Roads. **1824** (1955) BLACK *Journal* 195: —this evening put up in an Island where there are some well beat Beaver Roads & quantities of wood cut....

beaver robe 1 See **beaver coat**.
1789 (1801) MACKENZIE *Voyages from Montreal* 106: To these may be added a few dishes ... and old beaver robes, with a small robe made from the skin of the lynx.
1826 (1950) OGDEN *Journals* 156: ... from them we traded a Beaver Robe containing 2 skins....

2 the pelt of an emasculated buffalo, valued for its huge size and glossy, silklike coat.
1890 *Trans.Roy.Soc.Can.* VIII 2 100: Such an animal, with its colossal frame, its vast front, and spreading horns was a striking object in a great herd, and, when killed in season, was greatly prized for its immense size and glossy silklike coat yielded what was known as the "beaver robe."

beaver root a kind of water lily, *Nymphaea odorata*.
1822 (1928) CORMACK *Narr.Nfld* 34: They also subsist on the large roots of the white, scented water-lily, called by the Indians beaver-root. ... **1907** MILLAIS

Newfoundland 236: The Newfoundland beavers subsist largely on the root of the water-lily. ... called by the Indians "beaver root."

beaver run See **beaver pond**.
*c*1902 LAUT *Trapper* 163: The swampy beaver-runs narrowed ... and the dark-shadowed waters came leaping down.

beaver sanctuary See **beaver preserve**.
1937 *Beaver* June 8/1: The Company's first modern beaver sanctuary was established at Rupert's House on James Bay in 1931.

beaverskin *n. Fur Trade* **1** the pelt of the beaver as a staple of the fur trade; specifically, the pelt on which the long, outer guard hairs remain. See also **beaver** (def. 3).
1671 (1942) *H.B.C.Minutes* 8: That Mr. Rastell take care to putt up publick bills upon the Exchange to morrow morneing for the sale of lb.3000 weight of beaver coates and skins.... **1744** DOBBS *Hudson's Bay* 42: They love Pruins and Raisins, and will give a Beaver Skin for twelve of them to carry to their children.... **1958** *Beaver* Winter 54/1: The beaver skin has gone through many vicissitudes apart from clothing the beaver.... In its latest phase it is a "sheepskin" or parchment. This was the inspiration of the Canadian Citizenship Council which wanted a symbolic award for distinguished services in the field of citizenship.

2 See **made beaver** (def. 1).
1744 DOBBS *Hudson's Bay* 193: Standard of Trade carried on by the Hudson's Bay Company at Albany Fort, Moose River, and the East Main, as it stood in the Year 1733, Beaver Skins being the STANDARD. **1896** WHITNEY *On Snow-Shoes* 167: I made him understand that I had no doubt of his willingness to go with me; that it was merely a matter of beaver-skins between us, and I was prepared to pay him liberally. **1963** SPRY *Palliser* 112: They had to pay twenty beaver skins to the Indian who brought him [a strayed horse] in.

beaverskin currency *Fur Trade, Hist.* See **beaver currency**.
1916 BRIDLE *Sons of Canada* 175: There is no money; not even beaverskin currency or military tokens; therefore no banks.

beaverskin token *Fur Trade, Hist.* See **beaver** (def. 5a) and picture.
1963 *Albertan* (Calgary) 4 May 8/8: The Hudson's Bay Co.'s great rival, the North West Co. issued only one token as far as is known. It was a one Beaver skin token and issued in 1820.

beaver standard *Fur Trade, Hist.* a system of values, the unit of which was one beaver skin (def. 2).
1963 *Albertan* (Calgary) 4 May 8/7: It could however be purchased with fox, muskrat, or other skins in their proportional value to the "Beaver" standard.

beaver stone one of the two small sacs in a beaver's groin from which castoreum, *q.v.*, is obtained.
1696 (1929) KELSEY *Papers* 61: To day the governor took from Andrew Johnson all his beaver reason he traded some of it with an indian called whiskers. Likewise some small matter of Beaver stones that is about 6 Beaver and as many stones. **1743** (1949) ISHAM *Observations* 20: Beaver Stone or castorum.

beaver stretcher a roughly circular frame made from a sapling on which to stretch a beaver skin while it is drying. See also **stretcher**. Cp. **busk**.

1948 ONRAET *Sixty Below* 105: For that reason beaver stretchers are made of flexible willows or young birches, bent round like a big hoop and the skin sewn in with stitches about two or three inches apart.

beaver swamp See **beaver marsh**.

1908 LAUT *Conquest N.W.* II 268: In the mountains southward, were the beaver swamps. **1952** INNES *Campbell's Kingdom* 34: He found him as a pup in the beaver swamps the other side of the lake.

beaver tail 1 the broad, fleshy tail of the beaver used as food.

[**1743-49** (1949) ISHAM *Observations* 144: . . . the tail . . . is the finest Eating in the Country, Cutting firm, itts all fat Except a bone in the middle and Very Lucious food. . . .] **1837** (1926) LANGTON *Early U.C.* 182: [I spent] Jan. 1st with Wallis where we had the backwoods delicacy of beaver tails. **1962** *Time* (Cdn ed.) 10 Aug. 10/1: . . . 18th century fur traders . . . washed down beaver tail and buffalo steak with great draughts of Madeira.

2 dough baked on a stick over an open fire. Also spelled *beaver's tail*.

1893 YOUNG *Indian Wigwams* 29: When one side was done brown, it was turned over, and soon the "beaver's tails" were ready for the hungry men. **1896** RUSSELL *Far North* 39: If the traveler has no frying pan the bread is baked in a "beaver tail." Such a loaf is long and narrow and is exposed to the fire upon a stick, the lower end being set in the ground, two or three cross sticks, the size of an ordinary skewer, are required to prevent the loaf from breaking and falling as it breaks.

beavertail beans See quote.

1958 LEWIS *Buckskin Cookery* II 19: BEAVER TAIL BEANS. (Indian) Blister tail over fire till skin loosens. Pull skin off. Boil big black pot of beans. Add beaver tail.

beavertail snowshoe a type of snowshoe used by the Montagnais Indians of northern Quebec, having an oval or circular frame and a short tail. See picture at **snowshoe**. See also **Eastern snowshoe**.

1941 *Beaver* Mar. 27: The Mistassini hunters . . . use the "beaver-tail" pattern. . . . In this snowshoe the smaller end of the oval, which always appears at the tail, has been elongated slightly more and constricted, giving the snowshoe a caudal appendage similar to that of the beaver. **1963** *Ibid*. Autumn 17/1: The strips [of white ash] are steamed and bent around the required patterns, which may be Montagnais, Beavertail, Bear Paw, Cree, Ojibwa, or some other type.

beaver tockey or **tuggy** *Obs*. See **toggy**.

1742 *Gentlemen's Mag.* Nov. 586/2: Our Cloathing is a Beaver or Skin tuggy, above our other Cloaths. **1746** (1949) ISHAM *Journal* 261: Lent them 100 Bricks & some Lime their taylor's a helping our taylors in making Beaver tockeys for their mens use.

beaver token *Hist*. See **beaver** (def. 5a) and picture.

1941 *Beaver* Sep. 14/2: The North-west Company, about 1820, issued beaver tokens, a form of coinage only a few pieces of which, highly valued, have been saved by antiquarians.

beaver wool the fine fur close to the skin beneath the longer guard hairs, formerly, much prized by felt-makers for making beaver hats. Cp. **beaver coat**.

1764 (1948) *Beaver* Sep. 36/2: Once more the felt-makers petitioned . . . a new duty [be] laid upon the exportation of beaver skins and beaver wool unmanufactured. **1958** *Ibid*. Spring 14/2: Then [in winter] the skin carries two kinds of fur; close to the skin is a thick mass of "beaver wool", down or "duvet" as the French called it; on top is a glossy fur of long "guard hairs." **1964** INNIS *Fur Trade* 170: The pressure of hat manufacturers . . . was successful in securing . . . an export duty of . . . 1s, 6d. on every pound of beaver wool.

bechon *n. Obs*. See **bichon**.

bed berth *Obs*. See quote.

1853 STRICKLAND *Canada West* I 30: One door at the end [of the shanty], and two tier of bed berths, one above the other, complete the *tout ensemble*.

bed chesterfield an upholstered couch, or sofa, that is convertible into a double bed.

1955 *Kingston Whig-Standard* (Ont.) 6 Apr. 24/3: The Sklars also design and produce bed-chesterfields, their all-Canadian items. **1957** *Maclean's* 16 Mar. 57/1: A large proportion of the twelve hundred rooms in the CNR's new Queen Elizabeth Hotel in Montreal will be furnished as office bedrooms, with hide-away bed-chesterfields. **1966** *Dly Colonist* (Victoria) 26 Feb. 13/3: Two runaway teenage girls were found in a dazed state on a bed-chesterfield in a downtown apartment Thursday night.

bedding timbers See 1853 quote. See also **sleeper** (def. 1).

1853 STRICKLAND *Canada West* II 280: A gang of men cut down the trees, taking care to throw small trees, called bedding timbers, across the path the tree will fall, for the purpose of keeping it from freezing to the ground or endangering the edge of the workmen's axes against stones or earth. **1863** WALSHE *Cedar Creek* 217: Nearing the sound of the axes, they came to where a group of lumber-men were cutting down some tall spruce-firs, having first laid across over the snow a series of logs, called "bedding timbers," in the line that each tree would fall.

bedlamer *n*. [< F *bête de la mer* sea beast] *Esp.Nfld* the young of the harp, *q.v.*, seal, one or two years of age with brown fur.

1773 (1792) CARTWRIGHT *Journal* I 284: He saw a shoal of bedlamers before his door one day last week. **1880** (1964) *Nfld Qtly* Spring 4: . . . the yearlings and two year olds are called "Young Harps" or "Turning Harps" and also Bedlimers (or Bedlamers). **1966** *Cdn Geog.Jnl* Apr. 132/1: They paid 50 cents for the skin of an adult seal and 25 cents for a bedlamer (young seal) skin. (The word "bedlamer" is a corruption of the French "bête de la mer"—sea beast.)

bed-rock *n*. **1**† the solid rock beneath drift or detritus.

1864 (1962) ANDERSON *Sawney's Letters* 7: Some strike the bed-rock pitchin' in, / And some the bed-rock canna win. . . . **1962** *B.C.Digest* Oct. 28/2: Where bed rock is deep and requires deep holes to be sunk, the ordinary prospector is not prepared in the summer to get to bed rock on account of water.

2 in **get down to bed-rock, a.** impoverished circumstances.

1889 MACLEAN *Indians* 199: When the sombre shades of poverty have entered his old shack, he has in the miner's phraseology, got down to *bed-rock* or *hard-pan*. . . .

b. simple, basic principles; fundamentals.
1923 STRINGER *Empty Hands* 191: . . . there seemed no way of simplifying things, of getting down to bed-rock. . . .

bed-rock creek See quote.
1897 TUTTLE *Golden North* 77: The miners term Forty Mile a "bed-rock" creek—that is, one in the bed of which there is little or no drift, or detrital matter, the bottom of the river being bed-rock.

bed-rock mining See quote.
1887 (1888) LEES & CLUTTERBUCK *British Columbia* 248: . . . he was once hunting gold . . . by a method called, we believe, "bed-rock" mining. This consists in damming or diverting a river by erecting wing dams. . . .

bed-rock pay *Obs*. See quote.
1863 *Islander* (Charlottetown) 18 Dec. 2/1: If gold was taken out of the mine, then I had to pay my share of $10 per day. This was called "bed-rock pay." If the claim pays nothing, then your workman gets only his food.

bed-rock scraper *Placer Mining* a tool having a blade so set as to facilitate clearing gravel from the bedrock floor.
1870 *Cariboo Sentinel* (Barkerville, B.C.) 26 Mar. 2/2: . . . I wish you would bring . . . one small crowbar, a 10-pound sledge[,] three bed-rock scrapers, two shovels. . . .

bed throw a bedspread; coverlet.
1957 *Representative* 19 Dec. 11/2: The bride elect was presented with . . . a lovely bed throw from the staff and wives. **1959** SHIPLEY *Scarlet Lily* 40: The . . . silver candlesticks and snuffer should have appeared incongruous beside the lynx bed throw and white bear rug on the bare plank floor. . . .

bee *n*. in pioneer days especially, a neighborly gathering for various kinds of work, often followed by a party. See also **frolic**.
1814 (1903) CARR-HARRIS *White Chief* 121: Mrs. Chamberlain also had a bee, an apple-drying bee. . . .
1826 (1832) PICKERING *Inquiries* 72: They always contrive to have some whiskey at these "bees," which are a kind of merrymeeting. . . . **1963** *Citizen* 13 June 3/3: Community painting "bees" aren't what they used to be, says municipal councillor Joan Greenwood.

beef boot *Hist*. See **beef shoe**. See also **shoepack** (def. 2).
*a*1880 (1962) *Maclean's* 20 Oct. 36/2: [We wore] beef boots . . . patched on the legs with sundry pieces of leather. . . . **1930** ROLYAT *Fort Garry* 141: The pillar of agriculture . . . thudded into the house in his big beef boots, solid symbols of progress themselves. . . .

beef cut *West* See quote.
1963 SYMONS *Many Trails* 57: . . . the [marketable] beef were cut out of the herd by mounted cowboys, and made into a separate herd called the "beef cut."

beef gather *West* a cattle round-up held in the fall.
1903 *Eye Opener* (High River, Alta.) 24 Oct. 1/4: Worked during the summer till the beef gather and lost all my pay in one disastrous night at poker. **1904** *Eye Opener* (Calgary) 4 Aug. 1/3: Did you ever see the work, on a beef-gather or round-up, of a group of

cowpunchers who had some real or fancied wrong in their heads against the foreman?

beef maker *West, Slang* a steer, etc. being raised for beef.
1962 FRY *Ranch on the Cariboo* 101: Around these cows, these run of the mill Hereford beef makers, had been run a ranch. . . .

beef ring *Esp. West* a co-operative arrangement among members of a community for providing fresh beef. Cp. **meat ring**.
1915 MCCLUNG *Times Like These* 195: The consolidated school and the "Beef-rings" in the country districts are already established facts. . . . **1920** STRINGER *Prairie Mother* 128: As we're in a district that's too sparsely settled for a Beef Ring, we have to depend on ourselves for our roasts. **1965** SHEPHERD *West of Yesterday* 137: We organized a beef ring and did the slaughtering at our place.

beef shoe *Hist*. a boot or shoe of ox or buffalo hide, used by voyageurs, *q.v.*, canoemen, settlers, etc., usually of local manufacture. See also **beef boot**.
1822 (1940) *Minutes of Council* (H.B.C.) 21: That John Clarke Esqre. be authorized to receive of the Buffalo Wool Company 300 Carrying Straps and 200 pairs Beef Shoes. **1944** *Beaver* Sep. 19/2: Most of the shoes meant for the voyageurs and canoe men were of local manufacture . . . called . . . beef shoes.

beef-skin moccasin See **Canadian shoe**.
1896 GOURLAY *Hist.Ottawa* 20: The men wore . . . beef-skin moccasins and coarse boots. **1912** HEENEY *Pickanock* 48: . . . here is Jack Mason patching a hole in the toe of his beef-skin moccasin. . . .

beer high-grade *Mining, Slang* money made by high-grading (def. 1).
1963 *Maclean's* 4 May 30/1: Many people told me that there is hardly a miner in the camp who hasn't at one time or another high-graded enough [gold] to pay for a round or two at his favorite neighborhood taproom. In fact, "beer high-grade" is a common term for money spent in the hotels.

beer licence *Obs*. a saloon or beer parlor.
1846 BONNYCASTLE *Canada and the Canadians* II 93: . . . under the designation "beer-licenses" the most infamous houses for drinking and vice are suffered to exist.

beer parlo(u)r a room in which a hotel is licensed to sell beer; beverage room, *q.v.* See also **parlo(u)r**. Cp. **hotel**.
1925 (1958) TUCK *Pouce Coupe* 14: July 29, 1925 (about) —Beer parlour was opened in Pouce Coupe. **1935** *Calgary Typo News* 26 Apr. 3/1: There is a growing agitation, both in Calgary and Edmonton, against the segregation of women customers of the beer parlors of these two cities in separate rooms. **1965** *Globe and Mail* (Toronto) 13 Oct. 6/5: In Saskatchewan today— hold your breath . . . women hustle the suds in men's beer parlors.

beer-room *n. Rare* See **beer parlor**.
1940 *Temperance Advocate* Jan. 4/1: The beer-room patrons represent for the most part the hard-working proletariat. **1958** WELLS *Georgian Bay* 96: Let the cruising man sit in its beer room, with his mouth shut and his ears open. . . .

beer-slinger *n. Slang* a person who serves beer in a beer parlor.

1962 ONSLOW *Bowler-Hatted Cowboy* 185: He looked at my glass of tomato-juice which the beer-slinger had placed before me with exaggerated courtesy.

behind the glass *Curling* in the spectators' lounge, which is separated from the rink by large windows.

1958 *Chatelaine* Nov. 92: People go "behind the glass," meaning into the club lounge after a game, wearing their curling clothes. . . .

bell *n.* See 1904 and 1937 quotes. See also **brisket bell.**

1904 ROBERTS *Watchers of the Trails* 198: From the lower part of his [a moose's] neck . . . hung a curious tuft of long and very coarse black hair, called among woodsmen the "bell." **1937** ARMSTRONG *Upper Yukon* 29: By the way, one of the distinguishing features of the moose is its "bell"—a sort of hirsute appendage hanging from a position near the animal's throat varying in length from a few inches to about 12 or 14 inches. . . . **1958** *Beaver* Summer 21/2: His bell hung not only to his knee, but rippled like a beard.

below *adj. or adv.* **1** below zero Fahrenheit.

1795 (1911) SIMCOE *Diary* 265: Thermometer [shows] 10 degrees below. **1965** *Globe and Mail* (Toronto) 22 Mar. 5/9: And the lows cast for today were only 23 below at Kapuskasing and 12 below at Timmins.

2 See **below discovery.**

1898 *Yukon Midnight Sun* (Dawson) 18 July 4/3: Shortly afterward application was made by another party to record No. 3 below. **1904** *Yukon Sun* (Dawson) 10 Jan. 3/1: Mrs. Johnson, of 7 below on Bonanza, has taken a trip outside on business. . . .

below discovery downstream from the discovery claim, *q.v.*, on a creek or stream.

1936 ARMSTRONG *Yukon Yesterdays* 31: . . . during the autumn of 1898 . . . I was on No. 4 Below Discovery. **1957** *Saturday Evening Post* 2 Nov. 103/1: Just before the Norseman took off for the Mackenzie, he would . . . point out that the hermits could swarm up there immediately, draw lots for Claims 1 to 5 below discovery, stake them [and] record them. . . .

belt *n. Obs.* **1** *Hist.* See **belt of wampum.**

1765-75 (1933) POND *Narrative* 48: By the Intarpretar I had the Speach Expland and the Intenshun of the Belts. . . . The Counsel when the Commander thought proper to Give Me ye Charge of thre Belts with the Speacheis and the traders of Lake Superer Ware Charged with the Others. **1850** ROY *Hist.of Canada* 85: The Iroquois council sent back the same deputies, with six belts, intimating their resolution, which was expressed in lofty and bitter terms.

2 See **sash.**

1801 (1933) MCLEOD *Diary* 159: . . . one of them stole a Ceinture of Cadottes, [who] overtook them before noon, & threatened to shoot one of them if he did not tell which of them had stolen the Belt. . . . **1912** HEENEY *Pickanock* 30: [The carter] . . . wears only a short, dark, heavy homespun jacket, with a red belt around it which hangs in tasselled ends at his side.

belt of wampum a belt of shell beads used by eastern Indians, especially the Iroquois, as a mnemonic device for recording the terms of treaties etc. or as a mark of honor. See also **wampum.**

1760 JEFFERYS *Descr.New France* 52: Both of them . . . are made into small oblong beads, which are bored and stringed together, and these are called necklaces, or belts of Wampum. **1893** YEIGH *Ont. Parliament* 125: The commissioners were given a belt of wampum, and the council adjourned to Sandusky. . . . **1905** SCHERCK *Pen Pictures* 36: It was quite common for an Indian chief to bestow a belt of wampum upon a white man for favours received.

bench† *n.* a relatively level terrace lying between a river or lake and the nearby hills or plateau, once part of the river or lake bed.

1854 (1885) MOBERLY *Rocks and Rivers* 25: . . . when walking along a high "bench" of the river, I saw smoke arising. . . . **1862** MAYNE *Four Years in B.C.* 108: These flats, or benches as they are called in this country, are found generally at the bends of the river, and are raised some fifty or sixty feet above it. They occur much more frequently on the Thompson and Nicola Rivers, and higher up the Fraser. **1962** FRY *Ranch on the Cariboo* 237: I broke out onto the big bench where the road rises from the valley and spills a man onto the unbroken, open grassland.

bench claim *Placer Mining* a mining claim situated on a bench, *q.v.* See also **bench diggings.**

1897 TUTTLE *Golden North* 282: [quoting Cdn. Mining Regulations] 5. Bench claims shall be 100 feet square. **1942** WIEDERMANN *Cheechako* 211: A bench claim included any claim on the creek bank above rim-rock.

bench diggings *Placer Mining* gold-mining operations on a bench, *q.v.*; also, the defined area of such operations. Cp. **bar diggings, creek diggings,** and **dry diggings.**

1860 *Brit.Colonist* (Victoria) 2 June 1/2: I know of two miles of bench diggings, between Emory's and Texas bars, that if properly worked would yield from $3 to $5 per day to the man. **1897** GOODMAN *Gold Fields* 7: Mines on benches shall be known as "bench diggings," and shall for the purpose of defining the size of such claims be excepted from dry diggings.

bencher *n.* one of the elected officials of a provincial law society.

1812 (1920) *Cdn Hist.Rev.* I 187: It has been found impracticable to get together a quorum of the Benchers of the Law Society to call to the Bar those who were entitled. **1958** *Sun* (Vancouver) 20 Jan. 1/6: The benchers' rulings may be appealed to the B.C. Court of Appeal. **1965** *Globe and Mail* (Toronto) 14 Apr. 6/3: ". . . what else can you expect from a reactionary trade union like the Benchers?"

benchland† *n.* level stretches of land forming benches, *q.v.*

1900 OSBORN *Greater Canada* 84: Meanwhile, however, the auriferous bars and bench-lands in the neighborhood of Hope and Yale on the Lower Fraser were already being worked. **1963** *B.C.Digest* Oct. 19/2: When Scott died in 1878 and was buried on those same fertile benchlands, he had succeeded in growing tremendous crops of tobacco of very high quality.

bench penalty in hockey, a two-minute penalty charged against a coach or one or more players on the bench for any of several infractions, such as abusing officials, and served by a player or players designated by the coach of the team so penalized.

1963 *Globe and Mail* (Toronto) 2 Feb. 26/5: Referee Ed Powers was derided by fans and the Montreal players, Canadiens were called for a bench penalty in the second period. . . . 1963 O'BRIEN *Hockey* 56: If that fails, the referee calls a bench penalty . . . against the team.

Bennett Barnyard [after R. B. *Bennett,* Prime Minister of Canada, 1930-1935] *Hist.* a farm in the Dust Bowl, *q.v.,* during the drought-years of the 1930's.

1965 BERTON *Remember Yesterday* 95: All over Canada, demoralized men are drifting like the prairie soil . . . a future welfare state is in the crucible. But this is small comfort to those who must eke out life here in the "Bennett barnyards."

Bennett buggy *Hist.* See 1960 quote. See also **Anderson cart.**

1950 CAMPBELL *Saskatchewan* 287: The Bennett buggy [was] named for R. B. Bennett. 1960 *Maclean's* 9 Apr. 55/1: Named for R. B. Bennett, who had the misfortune to be prime minister during the first five years of the Depression [1930-35], the buggies were automobiles whose owners could no longer afford gas, oil or licenses. The motors were removed, pairs of trees attached to the front bumpers, and teams hitched on to provide a slow but steady two-horsepower. 1961 *Time* (Cdn ed.) 8 Sep. 17/1: "We're in for another siege of grasshoppers, drought, low prices and Bennett Buggies," muttered one farmer, recalling the motorless, horse-drawn automobiles sarcastically named for the then Tory Prime Minister R. B. Bennett.

berdache *n.* See **berdash.**

berdash *n.* [< MF *bardache* < Ital. dial. *bardascia* < Arab. *bardaj* slave < Pers. *bardah*] Also spelled *berdache, burdash.* **1** among Indians, a homosexual; sodomite; transvestite.

[1674 *Jesuit Relations* [tr.] LIX 129: I know not through what superstition some Illinois . . . while still young, assume the garb of women and retain it throughout their lives. There is some mystery in this, for they never marry and glory in demanding themselves to do everything that women do.] 1806 (1897) COUES *New Light* I 348: [The Mandans] have many berdashes among them, who make it their business to satisfy such beastly passions. 1955 *Amer. Anthropologist* LVII 121: . . . the English word "berdache," or "berdash" . . . was first used, as far as we can discern . . . by early French travellers and explorers, who used it to designate passive homosexuals or, more specifically, those individuals who played a passive role in sodomy.

2 an emasculated buffalo, highly prized for the fine robe made from its skin and its choice meat.

[1858 (1860) HIND *Assiniboine Exped.* II 105: Buffalo emasculated by wolves are often found in the prairies, where they grow to an immense size; the skin of the buffalo ox is recognized by the shortness of the wool and by its large dimensions.] 1957 *Cdn Forum* July 82/1: But perhaps the most notable poem in the volume [*Canadian Poems* by Charles Mair] is "The Last Bison." One day, while lying on the bank of the Saskatchewan River, the author is privileged to hear a burdash, or hermaphrodite bison, burst into song.

berlin [bər'lin] *n.* See **berline.**

berline [bər'lin] *n.* [< Cdn F, adapted from the name of a wheeled vehicle (a kind of sedan) < *Berlin,* Prussia] Also spelled *berlin, burline.* **1** *Hist.* a rude winter vehicle improvised from a

sled or toboggan by erecting a framework to provide a backrest and to support a wrap-around cover and roof, pulled by a horse or by dogs and first used by the French Canadians.

1829 MACTAGGART *Three Years* II 89: The *Burline* is the travelling sleigh of the Canadians; it is just large enough to hold two comfortably. . . . It is on low runners, and not easily upset; it has horns by which the driver balances it; it will glide over very rough roads and untrod snows. 1841 *Montreal Transcript* 9 Nov. 3/3: No cariole, train, berline, or other winter carriage . . . shall be used unless the horse or horses all be harnessed thereto on the manner above mentioned. 1955 *Maclean's* 24 Dec. 18: The wealthy . . . rode majestically around in carioles while their ruder, poorer neighbors raced by in the habitant berlines.

2 *North* See **cariole** (def. 2). See also **dog cariole.**

1896 MCDOUGALL *Saddle, Sled and Snowshoe* 37: I made an improvised, or what was termed a "Berlin," out of my wrapper and sled lashings. . . . 1938 GODSELL *Red Hunters of the Snows* 113: By the simple expedient of erecting two cross-pieces at the rear of my toboggan to form a back-rest, and by utilizing the moose-skin wrapper for a cover, Nazie had succeeded in converting my sled into a berline. . . .

berlot ['bɝlo or bɝr'lo] *n.* [< Cdn F] a kind of sleigh resembling a cutter (def. 1) and having a front and back seat for passengers.

1897 DRUMMOND *Habitant* 18: "But I lak' sit some cole night wit' my girl on ole burleau. . . ." 1942 CAMPBELL *Thorn-Apple Tree* 127: From the window they watched the big berlot swing down the hill and up the road to the west. . . .

berry bank *Atlantic Provinces* a bank or patch where berries are plentiful.

1933 MERRICK *True North* 39: The famous berry banks are just above Mininipi, and when we went ashore to boil [the kettle] we picked nearly a quart. 1964 *Atlantic Advocate* June 29/1: Michelin readily agreed to guide Fry to his "berry bank" and . . . the two men set out over a good path.

berry cake an Indian preparation of dried berries pressed into a cake and preserved for winter use.

1829 (1947) SIMPSON *Dispatch* 19: [We had] a few White Fish in the Winter with an occasional treat of Berry Cake prepared by the Natives. . . . 1896 MCNAUGHTON *Overland to Cariboo* 87: They found a camp of Shuswap Indians and from them obtained dried salmon and berry cakes in exchange for ammunition. . . .

berry pemmican See 1956 quote. See also **fruit pemmican.**

1817 (1939) ROBERTSON *Correspondence* 21: A plate of Berry Pemmican was produced which was approached as [if] they were approaching a piece of bird lime. 1956 LEECHMAN *Native Tribes* 109: An especially nice kind, called berry pemmican, was made by adding crushed choke cherries or berries. The ripe cherries were pounded, just as the meat had been, and the cherry paste, stones and all, was stirred in with the meat and fat. Now and then, as a very special touch, a few crushed leaves of peppermint were added.

berth *n.* **1** *Lumbering* See **timber limit** (def. 1a).

1853 *Mackenzie's Wkly Message* 22 Sep. 4/1: I have seen licenses granted covering both sides of a river, in

defiance of the regulations which say "berths to be confined to one side of rivers wherever practicable".
1962 *Forest Conservation* 9/1: These occupied forests consist of private timber land and government land under various forms of tenure, such as timber leases, licences, berths, and sales.

2 *Hist.* a place on a sealing vessel and the right to share in the profits of the hunt.
1819 ANSPACH *Hist.Nfld* 422: ... the rest generally pay forty shillings for their birth [sic], that is, for their proportion of the provisions during the voyage; and all are to receive each half a man's share of the seals caught, or the value thereof, dividing the amount of the whole produce of the voyage into so many shares as there are men on board. **1905** DUNCAN *Grenfell's Parish* 85: The man who has nothing has yet the labour of his hands. Be he skipper, there is one to back his skill and honesty; be he hand, there is no lack of berths to choose from. **1965** *Nfld Qtly* Spring 7/1: In former years, sealers had to pay from 10 shillings to 30 shillings for a berth.

3 See **berth money.**
1819 ANSPACH *Hist.Nfld* 422: The crews of their largest craft consist of from thirteen to eighteen men; of these some are gunners, who, on finding their own guns, are admitted birth [sic] free. ...

4 *Fishing* a part of a fishery claimed by a vessel and her crew with the exclusive right to fish for the season.
1905 DUNCAN *Grenfell's Parish* 91: ... when he awoke at dawn there were two other schooners lying quietly at anchor near by and the berths had been "staked."

berth money *Sealing, Hist.* the fee paid by each man in the crew for his share of the costs of provisioning a vessel and the right to share in the profits of the hunt. Cp. **shareman.**
1869 MCCREA *Lost Amid Fogs* 183: It's the berth-money the boys is disputing; and Larry ... won't put down a man of us at the same rate as last year. **1965** *Nfld Qtly* Spring 7/1: In former years, sealers had to pay from 10 shillings to 30 shillings for a berth. This was known as berth money and caused friction between the sealers and ship owners.

beverage room See **beer parlo(u)r.**
1936 (1957) SCOTT & SMITH *Blasted Pine* 23:
"Bar" is a nasty, a horrible word.
"Taprooms" and "taverns" and "pubs" are absurd;
Give us a name with a resonant boom,
A respectable name like "Beverage Room". ...
1964 *Globe and Mail* (Toronto) 15 Dec. 31/8: They were rather fussy about their clientele, which is more than you could say for some beverage rooms and cocktail bars.

Bible Bill *Slang, Hist.* William Aberhart (1878-1943), Premier of Alberta from 1935 to 1943, so called because of his widely popular radio sermons. Cp. **Aberhartism.**
1958 *Saturday Night* 27 Sep. 6/1: The Social Credit government of "Bible Bill" Aberhart ... tried to take over the banks and passed the infamous Accurate News and Information Act. ... **1965** *Canadian Wkly* 19 June 5/1: The economic salvation through Social Credit that William ("Bible Bill") Aberhart was offering ... had a broader appeal at that time. **1965** BERTON *Remember Yesterday* 89/2: [Caption] It's 1937 and Bible Bill Aberhart ... is at the height of his power.

biche [biʃ] *n.* [< Cdn F] See **wapiti.**
1800 (1897) COUES *New Light* I 85: This evening the hunters returned, having killed four biches. ... **1806** (1930) FRASER *Journal* 111: Sent Fercier ... to arrange them as La Pistole ... has gone farther on for two small Red Deer (alias Biche). **1952** (1954) JENNINGS *Strange Brigade* 105: There were also red deer or *biche,* and white bears. ...

bichon ['biʃɑn; *French* bi'ʃõ] *n.* [< Cdn F; perhaps related to *biche* red deer (see 1809 quote)] *West* a horse having a fawn or light-bay coat; a buckskin, *q.v.,* pony or mustang.
[**1809** (1950) THOMPSON *Journals* 52: [We] lost abt 40' [minutes] in changing the Load of the Poile de Biche. ...] **1859** (1875) SOUTHESK *Saskatchewan* 130: We also picked out a small light-coloured "bichon" ... a fat, comfortable, lazy little beast. ... **1880** *Edmonton Bull.* 20 Dec. 4/2: Came into my band of horses last September, a small Bichon or Buckskin Horse. ... **1954** CONSTANTIN-WEYER *Half-Breed* 47: He went along the roads on his light bay broncho (*bichon,* as they say in Canada). ...

bidar or **bidarra** *n.* See **baidar.**

bidarka *n.* See **baidarka.**

big chipmunk *Local* See quote. Cp. **chipmunk.**
1946 WOOD *Rockies* 85: In the United States the animal is best known by the name of Say's Spermophile, while in Canada those in the "know" hail it as the Golden Mantled Ground Squirrel. But Park tourists keep right on calling it The Big Chipmunk [*Citellus lateralis*]. ...

big deke *Slang* an extravagant attempt at deception, especially in hockey. Cp. **deke.**
1963 *Calgary Herald* 29 Oct. 8/6: ... this guy likes to try the big deke, this winger is strictly a high shot artist.

Big Dipper *Nfld, Trade Name* [after the name of a bar in Gander Airport] a popular dark rum from the West Indies. Cp. **screech.**
1965 *Globe and Mail* (Toronto) 7 Dec. 6/4: A couple of shots of Newfie Screech or Big Dipper and you get a crying jag on. ...

Big Eyebrow [trans. of Esk. *qablunā*] a white man. See also **Eyebrow** and **Kabloona.**
1955 HARDY *Alta Anthol.* 214: He was so ravaged with tuberculosis that he was even past fearing what the Big Eyebrows Outside would do to him.

Bigfoot *n. West* the legendary Sasquatch, *q.v.,* of the Coast Range.
1963 *B.C.Digest* Nov.-Dec. 14/3: While the prevalence of similar accounts from many parts of the world and the existence of eye-witnesses, footprint cast, etc. might seem to establish the reality of the Sasquatch-Nahanni-Bigfoot-Snowman-Wildman, it is a very strange fact that no specimens have been captured. ...

Bighorn or **Big horn** *n.* See **bighorn sheep.**
1784-1812 (1916) THOMPSON *Narrative* 557: Four sheep, an animal peculiar to these mountains, and by the Americans named Big Horn. **1962** *Canada Month* Sep. 15/3: Geist's lonely vigil was devoted to studying stone sheep, a nearly black race of bighorns living in the Stikine mountains [of northern B.C.].

bighorn sheep See **Rocky Mountain sheep.** See also **large-horned sheep** and **mountain sheep.**
1888 MCDOUGALL *G.M.McDougall* 198: And here I have seen the wild goat upon the mountains, and my party

have killed the big horn sheep. . . . **1964** *Calgary Herald* 5 May 32/3 : Waterton Lakes National Parks officials have weighed, measured and marked 30 Rocky Mountain and Bighorn sheep this spring. . . .

big house *Fur Trade, Hist.* the residence and office of the officer in charge of a fur-trading post. See also **great house** (def. 1).
1910 FERGUSON *Janey Canuck* 299 : Three years ago the Big House at Edmonton was burned down. **1913** COWIE *Adventurers* 211 : Behind and connected by a short passage with the "big house" was another building. **1955** HARDY *Alta Anthol.* 389 : At nightfall Chief Factor Rowand gave a dance in his Big House.

bight *n.* an indentation or bay in the edge of pack ice, *q.v.*
1850 (1851) SNOW *Voyage* 386 : A bight is a bay in the outline of the ice. **1850** OSBORN *Arctic Jnl* 38 : Mr. Gravill had lately ranged the Pack edge as far south as Disco, and found not a single opening except the bight, up which we had been steering last night. **1850** GOODSIR *Baffin's Bay* 106 : We found ourselves in a deep bight of the ice.

big jack *East* See quotes. See also **jack** (def. 5b). Cp. **jack-rabbit.**
1921 *Rod & Gun in Can.* Aug. 348/1 : They were the only shooting we had the last two years, and when it is so convenient for anyone to get out where the game is . . . the "Big Jacks," as they call them, will not last long, I assure you. . . . I think it is a shame to have as good a game animal as the Belgian or Holland Hare exterminated. **1965** *Kingston Whig-Standard* (Ont.) 5 Feb. 11/2 : . . . we understand that the big jack, or European Hare, is not as numerous this year.

big kettle See **kettle**[1] (esp. def. 2).

Big Knife† [trans. of Cree *kichimōkōmān*] *Hist.* See **Long Knife.**
1787 *Quebec Gaz.* 8 Feb. 2/1 : They are determined . . . the Ohio shall be the boundary between them and the Big Knives. **1922** *Beaver* Apr. 21/2 : Jokes against the Big Knives (Yankees) and broad witticisms of all kinds flew from mouth to mouth. **1963** SPRY *Palliser* 30 : . . . an Indian . . . who had been trading in United States territory, said he knew how his people had been treated by the "Kitje Mokomans" (Big Knives, a word for the Americans). . . .

big medicine in Indian parlance, anything of a supernatural nature, especially something considered as an influence for good or evil. Cp. **bad medicine** (def. 1).
[**1805** (1904) LEWIS & CLARK *Journals* I 361 : Everything which is incomprehensible to the Indians they call *big medicine.*] **1952** *Beaver* Sep. 8/1 : A Hamatsa whistle is big medicine.

big mucky-muck *Slang* See **high muckamuck.**
1958 DAVIES *Mixture of Frailties* 285 : You've always been the Big Mucky-Muck around here. . . .

big skate See **go for the big skate.**

binational *adj.* in Canada, consisting of two ethnocultural groups, French and non-French or English-speaking, the meaning of national in this sense being from French *nation,* race or ethnic group.
1964 *Canada Month* Jan. 30/3 : This is where the idea of a bicultural and binational Canada comes in, as opposed to the American "melting pot."

binationalism *n.* the principle or fact of existing in a state that is binational.
1963 *Globe and Mail* (Toronto) 5 Apr. 7/3 : It was in Toronto that he preached bi-culturalism and bi-nationalism, and set out the [NDP] party's program for a Confederation Council to carry out an intensive study of the question that has fired Quebec.

binder twine a coarse, tough cord for tying sheaves in a binder, also used for a variety of purposes around the farm.
1890 *Moose Jaw Times* (Sask.) 18 July 4/6 : The local situation in Binder twine is somewhat interesting. . . . **1957** MOWAT *Dog* 184 : I left him in the yard, perched on the handlebars of my bicycle, and insecurely tied with binder twine. **1960** BLONDAL *Candle* 67 : The chant grew, "What the common people need . . ." until the entire crew shouted in answer, "is bindertwine!"

bingo[1] *n.* See **pingo.**

bingo[2] *n.* [< the interjection *bingo!,* with reference to the quick and thorough effects of drinking cheap wine] *Slang* any cheap wine.
1963 *Maclean's* 6 July 44/1 : And the two boys [stood] amid a litter of paper and bingo bottles in a lane near River Street.

birch *n.* See **birchbark canoe.**
1896 ROBERTS *Camp-Fire* 18 : Running my birch ashore alongside of a mouldering trunk . . . I made my way . . . through the underwood. . . . **1898** EDGAR *Canada and Capital* 176 : For before you could think The birch cracked like a shell, In that rush of hell, And I saw them both sink.

birchbark *n.* See **birchbark canoe.**
1872 DASHWOOD *Chiploquorgan* 92 : In Western Canada, in the neighbourhood of London and Hamilton, there is good duck shooting on the rice lakes, where canoes made of bass wood, beautifully built, very light and shaped like a birch bark, are used. **1957** *Beaver* Winter 59/1 : How different from the old days, when scores of birchbarks would set up that same stretch of river for the far west. . . .

birchbark bugle See **birchbark horn.**
1934 DENNIS *Down in N.S.* 281 : Skilfully the Indian fashions a birch-bark bugle and in the golden September or the mellow October raises it to his lips and there rings through the forest the long, low, plaintive call of the cow-moose.

birchbark canoe a canoe built from the bark of the white birch, *q.v.,* long used by the Indians of eastern Canada.
1829 MACTAGGART *Three Years* II 54 : Thus we can run a rapid of the Rideau River with a birch-bark canoe heavily laden. . . . **1961** *Cdn Geog.Jnl* July 5 : The birch bark canoe must not touch land for fear of damage to its skin. **1965** *Maclean's* 19 June 40/1 : There are no shops with moccasins and totem poles and birchbark canoes. . . .

birchbark horn a device for calling moose. See also **birchbark bugle, birchbark trumpet** and **moose-call** (def. 2).
1888 ST. MAUR *Impressions* 243 : The call is given through a birch-bark horn. **1956** RADDALL *Wings* 183 : "Many's a big bull I called up here . . . through my ol' birch-bark horn, and knockin' 'em down with that ol' rifle. . . ."

birchbark rogan See **rogan.**

1896 WHITNEY *On Snow-Shoes* 98 : Take from the Indian his copper kettle, steel knife, and .30-bore muzzle-loading gun . . . and give him his bow, his birch-bark "rogan" . . . and flintstone knives, and he is just about where he was when the Hudson's Bay Company brought the trinkets of the great world to him.
1956 KEMP *Northern Trader* 245 : They brought us gifts of quill-worked moccasins, birch-bark rogans, and silk-worked slippers.

birchbark talk writings in the Cree syllabic script.

1960 NIX *Mission* 45 : Eagerly did the children of the forest learn to read their own "birch-bark talk."

birchbark trumpet See **birchbark horn.**

1946 *Beaver* Sep. 44/1 : . . . he thought it well to be sure that his birch-bark trumpet was clear and in order, so he put it to his lips and gave the merest whisper of a call.

birch canoe See **birchbark canoe.**

[**1620** WHITBOURNE *Discovrse* 72 : Cannowes are . . . made with the rinds of Birch trees; which they sowe very artificially and close together, and ouerlay euery seame with Turpentine.] *c*1715 (1895) RICHARD *Acadia* I 97 : . . . one hundred of the Accadians . . . can march upon snow-shoes, and understand the use of birch canoes.
1953 LOWER *Voyages* vii : This country was explored from the thwarts of a birch canoe.

birch horn See **moose-call** (def. 2 and 1902 quote).

birch partridge See **ruffed grouse.** See also **partridge** (def. 1).

1823 HALIBURTON *General Descr.N.S.* 31 : The following catalogue contains a list of most of the known birds of the Province with their popular names : . . . Birch partridge. . . . **1958** *In Flight* Summer 12/3 : Game birds [include] . . . birch partridge. . . .

birchrind *n.* **1** the bark of the birch tree, especially of the white birch, *q.v.* ; birch bark.

1692 (1929) KELSEY *Papers* 19 : Their first & Chiefest point is a piece of Birch rine full of Feathers or Divers sorts put on a piece of Leather wch is broad at one End for to tie about their head. . . . **1743** (1941) *Beaver* June 24/2 : . . . a piece of Berch Rhyne Cutt square. . . . **1964** *Ibid.* Spring 40 : . . . the latter place [Moose Factory] was the chief source of supply for birchrind.
2 *Rare, Hist.* a birchbark canoe, *q.v.*
1953 MOWERY *Mounted Police* 56 : The Blood pointed to a clump of whitewoods . . . "Canoe tied up there. My light birchrind."

birchrind canoe *Obs.* See **birchbark canoe.**

1755 (1907) HENDAY *Journal* 352 : Their Birch-rind canoes will carry as much as an India Ships Longboat, and draws little water. **1795** (1911) HEARNE *Journey* 257 : The common deer . . . kick up their hind legs with such violence as to endanger any birch-rind canoe that comes within their reach.

birch rogan See **rogan.**

1896 RUSSELL *Far North* 164 : The sap is collected in birch rogans which are made on the spot and kept there *en cache* during the winter.

birchsap ginger ale a beverage made from the sap of the birch.

1964 *Weekend Mag.* 25 July 18/3 : Beverages Mrs. Moose has tried and enjoyed include . . . juniper beer and birchsap ginger ale.

birch (tree) syrup a sweet syrup made by boiling the sap of the birch tree.

1896 WHITNEY *On Snow-Shoes* 294 : The women had all set off to the woods to make birch syrup. **1934** GODSELL *Arctic Trader* 120 : [We] enjoyed the rabbit stew and purple-colored birch syrup. . . . **1948** *Beaver* Mar. 23/2 : Here she . . . tasted birch tree syrup for the first time.

bird-eye(d) maple *Obs.* See **bird's-eye maple.**

1820 (1823) JOHNSTONE *Travels in P.E.I.* 17 : Of the maple there is white rock or curly, and bird-eye. . . . **1828** MCGREGOR *Maritime Colonies* 21 : Five varieties of the sugar maple are met with . . . [including] the bird-eyed maple. . . .

birdie ['bɜ·di] *n.* a form of clog dance.

1933 MERRICK *True North* 216 : Occasionally they do the "Birdie," and the two opposite men come out to the center of the floor and clog, trying to outdo each other in speed and the intricacy of their steps.

bird of warning *North, Obs.* See **alarm bird.**

bird's-eye maple 1 See **sugar maple.**

1807 GRAY *Letters* 209 : The curled maple and bird's-eye maple make beautiful furniture. **1883** FRASER *Shanty* 20 : He has also on these limites an immense quantity of . . . bird's eye and curly maple.

2 the wood of this tree, much in demand for furniture making because of the attractive patterns formed in the grain by knots.

1792 (1911) SIMCOE *Diary* 161 : Capt. Shaw has given me a tea-chest in bird's-eye maple. **1964** *Indian News* 8/3 : In appreciation they presented the donor with a beautiful pair of Island-made bird's eye maple candlesticks.

birl† *v. Lumbering* maintain one's balance on a floating log by agile footwork which causes the log to revolve.

1957 *Weekend Mag.* 10 Aug. 33/1 : To his surprise, the pup developed a liking for lumbering and in time . . . was birling with the best.

birler *n. Lumbering* a lumberjack who birls logs, often in a contest or competition.

1963 *Weekend Mag.* 6 July 12 : So birlers no longer ask who is going to win the [birling] championship.

birling *n.* the act of birling logs, especially in competition. See also **log-birling** and **log-rolling** (def. 3).

1903 WHITE *Forest* 136 : . . . O'Donnell . . . could turn a somersault on a floating log; of the birling matches, wherein two men on a single log try to throw each other into the river by treading squirrel fashion, in faster and faster rotation. . . . **1963** *Weekend Mag.* 6 July 12 : The object of birling is to see which of two opponents can remain balanced longest atop a log that is twirling and bouncing in the water. **1965** [see quote at **raft** (def. 1)].

biscuit root See **prairie turnip.**

1868 BROWN *Vegetable Products* 381 : The white biscuit root, the *racine blanc* of the Voyageurs . . . is dried, pulverised, and made into cakes baken in the sun. **1891** *Cdn Indian* Mar. 168 : The kouse-root . . . known to Canadians as *racine blanc* and bread or biscuit root, is largely used. **1923** BARBEAU *Indian Days* 150 : . . . they gathered also other nutritious roots and wild fruits, such as caious (a biscuit root) . . . and mountain cherries, which they dried into cakes.

Bishop pippin See 1933 quote.
1879 *Morning Chron.* (Halifax) 1 Nov. 3/2: The lot comprised Baldwins, Russets, Bishop Pippins and other winter fruit. **1934** DENNIS *Down in N.S.* 118: . . . Bishop [John] Inglis selected the little village of Aylesford in Nova Scotia for his country home. Here he . . . grew excellent [apples;] the pippin . . . introduced by him . . . is known to this day as "The Bishop Pippin."

bison† *n.* a North American mammal, *Bison bison,* usually called the buffalo (def. 2).
1786 (1957) *Beaver* Summer 28/2: They [Assiniboines] were all moderately tall, manly looking men . . . well dressed in leather, with a bison robe. . . . **1822** GOURLAY *Upper Canada* I 157: The Bison is an animal of the west regions, scarcely known in the inhabited districts. **1955** MCCOWAN *Upland Trails* 51: Bison and Pronghorn antelope . . . were frequently preyed upon by bands of wolves. . . .

bit *n.* 1† See 1880 and 1913 quotes.
☛ *Originally in American use as a translation of Spanish* pieca *piece of eight, that is, a Spanish dollar. Later, with reference to a* real, *a small Spanish silver coin, or, especially, one of the bits into which physically large coins were sometimes divided. The term took on various senses in different places during the eighteenth and nineteenth centuries. In current North American use, it may be seen in the slang terms* **two bits, four bits,** *and* **six bits,** qq.v., *that is, 25 cents, 50 cents, and 75 cents, respectively.*
1860 *Brit.Colonist* (Victoria) 31 May 3/1: Thinking that whisky selling was the easiest way in which to raise the odd "bit," he had just succeeded in effecting the sale of a bottle of lightning to a Siwash. . . . **1880** GORDON *Mountain and Prairie* 12: Copper currency is unknown, the smallest coin being a "bit"—that is, the English sixpence, whose nearest equivalent is the ten-cent piece. **1913** SANDILANDS *West.Cdn.Dict.* 6: Bit, the old 12½-cent piece of the United States was called a bit, and a defaced 20-cent piece was termed a long bit, while the old York shilling of Canada, valued at 12½ cents, was also known as a bit. **1952** (1965) HAMILTON *Cdn Quotations* 139: . . . old residents of British Columbia prided themselves on using no sum less than a bit, or, twelve and a half cents. In 1861 newspapers were still sold for a bit, either a liberal fifteen cents, or a stingy ten cents.
2 *Obs.* a gold nugget.
1859 (1935) STRANG *Pioneers in Can.* 207: It requires two to work a rocker well, one to dig and the other to wash and collect the "bits."

bitch *n.* See quotes.
1931 WALDRON *Snow Man* 92: The cave had run short of candles once already, and the gloom . . . had been defeated only by Hornby's ingenuity. He devised a "bitch" from a tin-can top and fox fat, with a piece of shoelace for a wick. **1961** *Cdn Geog.Jnl* Jan. 14/2: . . . during the long winter evenings "office" work was done by candlelight and sometimes by nothing better than a "bitch"—a wick in a shallow tin of tallow.

bite-'em-no-see-'em *n.* See **no-see-um.**

bito ['baɪto] *n. Local* See **aboiteau.**
1896 ROBERTS *Camp-Fire* 45: Once a tidal stream, the creek had been brought into subjection by what the country people call a "bito," built across its mouth to shut out the tides. . . . **1898** *New Brunswick Mag.* Oct. 225: "Aboideau" . . . is often corrupted to "bi-to" (like bite-o). . . . **1957** WRIGHT *Blomidon Rose* 81: . . . the

word is pronounced as if spelled Byetoe [on the Peticodiac and Shepody Rivers]. . . .

bit of brown *Slang, Obs.* among the fur traders, an Indian woman kept by a white man in a country alliance, *q.v.*
1831 (1940) *Beaver* Mar. 54/1: Robertson brought his bit of Brown with him to the Settlement this Spring in hopes that she would pick up a few English manners. . . . **1944** *Ibid.* Sep. 48/1: The rough traders and their daily lives, their relations with the Indian women, their "bits of brown," are all there.

bitter berry *Obs.* See **soapberry** (def. 2).
1925 ANDERSON *Trees and Shrubs* 131: Sir Alexander Mackenzie [c1789] refers to it [the soapberry] as the "bitter berry" which he saw mixed with mashed fish-roe by the natives of the sea coast.

black *n.* See **black fox.**
1956 KEMP *Northern Trader* 142: Ten years earlier blacks had fetched a fabulous figure . . . [up to] two thousand dollars apiece.

black bass a game fish common in central and eastern Canada. There are two species: the small-mouth, *Micropterus dolomieu,* and the largemouth, *Huro salmoides.*
1785 HUNTER *Diary* 63: We made a most excellent dinner on some black bass that we caught. . . . **1964** *Outdoorsman* Mar. 14/1: In addition, anglers also fish for speckled trout, black bass and maskinonge.

black bear the most common of the bears of North America, *Ursus americanus.* See also **ant bear, cinnamon bear,** and **ranger** (def. 3).
1743 (1949) ISHAM *Observations* 165: Black bear's . . . have holes or Caves in the ground, or under the snow, where they Live all winter. . . . **1842** WILLIS *Cdn Scenery* II 36: However, the black bear . . . is well known to Canada and is found wherever wooded districts occur. . . . **1964** *Star Wkly* 2 Jan. 37/1: . . . there was one 12-mile road snaking . . . down into a wilderness valley, frequented by mountain sheep and cougars and black bears. . . .

black beaver a rare dark-color phase of the beaver.
1670 (1900) OSBORN *Greater Canada* 188: And further, we do, by these presents for us, our heirs and successors, make, create and constitute the said governor and Company, for the time being, and their successors, the true and absolute lords and proprietors of the same territory, limits, and places aforesaid . . . yielding and paying yearly to us, our heirs and successors, for the same, two elks and two black beavers, whensoever and as often as we, our heirs and successors, shall happen to enter into the said countries, territories and regions hereby granted. **1795** (1911) HEARNE *Journey* 241: Black beaver, and that of a beautiful gloss, are not uncommon . . . but it is rare to get more than twelve or fifteen of their skins in the course of one year's trade. **1939** *Beaver* Mar. 4/1: . . . in 1927 . . . George W. Allan . . . presented two elk heads and two black beaver skins to H.R.H. the Prince of Wales en route to his ranch in Alberta.

black belt *Hist.* a belt of dark purple wampum indicative of hostility, sorrow, death, condolence, and mourning, often used as a declaration of war.

See also **black wampum**.

1798 (1935) RUSSELL *Correspondence* II 168: I am assured from good authority, that a Black Belt, the Emblem of War, was actually sent from the Indian Tribes that are settled within His Majesty's Dominions to the residue of the Six Nations who live in the territories of the United States of America.

black blizzard a dust storm of black prairie soil.

1962 DICKIE *Great Golden Plain* 275: Having no roots to hold it together, the soil turned to dust, and the hot winds carried it off in a "black blizzard." **1964** *Calgary Herald* 25 Nov. 1/4: Nature has conspired to produce ideal conditions for the black blizzards....

black cat See **fisher**.

*c***1902** LAUT *Trapper* 251: This is wuchak the fisher, or pekan, commonly called "the black cat"— who, in spite of his fishy name, hates water as cats hate it. **1946** WOOD *Rockies* 48: In appearance this animal [*Martes pennanti*] looks like a long-bodied black fox and is sometimes nicknamed the Black Cat, but it is a true weasel and a larger cousin of the Marten.

blackcoat *n.* See **blackrobe**.

*c***1665** RADISSON *Voyages* 45: Let us shake off the yoake of a company of whelps that killed so many french and black-coats, and so many of my nation. **1851** (1888) MCDOUGALL *G.M. McDougall* 28: We are glad to see this black coat among us. **1910** FERGUSON *Janey Canuck* 286: The talk drifts on to the redcoats of "the force" who have graduated to the blackcoats of the church.

black cod See **sablefish**.

1888 *Dominion Illustrated* 231/1: The Victoria schooner Theresa has left for the black cod banks off Queen Charlotte Islands. **1897** TUTTLE *Golden North* 124: One of the most delicious of deep water fish is the skil, or black cod, as it is sometimes called. **1964** CARL *Marine Fishes of B.C.* 49: Most [sablefish] are smoked and sold under the name of "black cod."

black devil *Obs.* See **wolverine** (def. 1).

1793 (1937) CAMPBELL *Travels* 73: The Indians in New Brunswick and Lower Canada call him the Black Devil....

black fly a small, winged biting insect especially common in the northern woods, *Simulium* spp. See also **buffalo gnat**.

1821 (1900) GARRY *Diary* 106: After passing a restless Night from the Attacks of Musquitoes and black Fly we embarked.... **1963** *Maclean's* 16 Nov. 54/3: ... the north breeds good fellowship nearly as well as it breeds black flies....

black fox 1 a rare color phase of the North American red fox, *Vulpes fulva*.

[**1583** PECKHAM *True Reporte* E iv v: *Of Beastes for furres*. Martens. Beauers. Foxes blacke and white.] **1744** DOBBS *Hudson's Bay* 49: The East Main ... is least known, there being no Factories fixed there for Trade, altho' the best Sable and black Fox Skins are got there. **1907** MILLAIS *Newfoundland* 301: The Indians say they get one genuine "black fox" in a lifetime.

2 the skin or pelt of a black fox.

1820 (1823) FRANKLIN *Journey* 83: A silver fox, or otter, are [worth] two beavers and a black fox.... **1863** *Nor'Wester* (R.R.S.) 26 Apr. 1/5: The White Fox is very elegant and so is the Black Fox which is a

Canadian fur.... **1924** DORRANCE *Never Fire First* 58: Gently ... he removed the last clutch of O'Malley's fingers from the black fox—probably the pelt of ostensible contention.

black ice 1 thin, new ice on fresh or salt water, appearing dark in color because of its transparency.

1829 MACTAGGART *Three Years* I 66: ... the most compact black ice anywhere to be found, will be about five and three-quarters to five. **1873** *Maritime Mthly* Aug. 117: About two weeks after the ice in this part of the river has been discharged into the Bay, that from the upper part ... makes its appearance in the harbor, and is distinguished not only by the great quantity of driftwood and freshet *débris* which accompany it, but also by its clearness and solidity, hence called the "black ice." **1961** ANDERSON *Angel* 67: October had come with gales and snow and creeping darkness. Black ice had formed upon the Koksoak.

2 similar ice on a road.

1964 *Dly Colonist* (Victoria) 31 Dec. 2/4: Most city streets were clear of snow but extremely hazardous at night, when plunging temperatures turned the melting snow into black ice.

blackjack *n.* **1** strong, black tobacco for chewing or smoking in a pipe, sold in figs, *q.v.*, or plugs.

1896 ROBERTS *Camp-Fire* 56: His hand stole deep into the pocket of his gray homespun trousers, and brought to view a fig of "black-jack," from which he gnawed a thoughtful bite. **1905** ROBERTS *Red Fox* 172: Jabe Smith's long face wrinkled sarcastically, and he bit off a chew of "black Jack" before replying.

2 a. a card game similar to vingt-et-un ("twenty-one") except that any player may become the dealer by drawing an ace and any ten or face card.

1910 SERVICE *Trail of '98* 338: The women with the painted cheeks knew that look; the black-jack boosters knew it: the barkeeper with his knock-out drops knew it. **1935** HALLIDAY *Potlatch and Totem* 149: ... a game of cards commonly known as Black Jack became very popular. **1958** *Northern Miner* 25 Dec. 22/3: Recreations [included] blackjack, stud and giving mine managers insomnia.

b. a combination of an ace and any ten or face card as the first two cards dealt to a player.

1923 GIBBONS *Sourdough Samaritan* 74: When occasionally he turned a Black Jack, as several times occurred, he declined the invitation to "take the bank" if he wanted to.

black jacket a young hoodlum wearing a black leather jacket.

1957 *Maclean's* 9 Nov. 31/2: The Montreal Police later made a survey and of the two hundred young men in black jackets questioned none owned machines [motorcycles], but the name black jacket, as applied to hoodlums, stuck.

Black Jersey See **Canadian cattle**. See also **Canadian Jersey**.

1941 MACEWAN *Farm Live-Stock* 252: ... such names as ... "Black Jersey," sometimes heard with reference to the Canadian breed may have more significance than is usually supposed.

black-man *n.* a dark variety of maple sugar or taffy.

1903 RICHARDSON *Colin* 304: ... he always had his pockets full of sugar sticks, "black man," bulls'

eyes, peppermints, and such like, for the children. . . .
1926 MAIR *Masterworks* XIV 1 iii: The scented forest . . . the new basswood troughs, and cedar spiles, the great fires and steaming kettles, the hot-brown sap, the "black man" and molasses—they haunt an old man's memory still. . . .

black moose *Obs.* See **moose** (def. 1).
1784 PENNANT *Arctic Zoology* 18: The Elk and the Moose are the same species; the last derived from Musu, which in the Algonkin language signifies that animal. The English used to call it the Black Moose, to distinguish it from the Stag, which they name the Grey Moose, the French call it L'Orignal. **1853** REID *Young Voyageurs* 165: Its [the wapiti's] name of "grey moose" is a hunter appelation, to distinguish it from the real moose, which the same hunters know as black moose.

blackout *n.* in bingo, the stage in play of having a marker on every numbered square on the card.
1955 *Mountaineer* (Rocky Mt. House, Alta) 17 Feb. 1/3: There will be a total of eight prizes to be won. To be declared a winner contestant must obtain a BLACKOUT. **1964** *Naicam Sentinel* (Sask.) 26 Mar. 4/1: Donna Gustafson won the blackout.

black pilot *Hist.* See 1933 quote.
1789 (1934) DENNIS *Down in N.S.* 342: Know all men by these presents that we, London Jackson, Richard Leah, James Robertson and Jane Thompson mother of James Jackson, deceased,—black pilots now in Shelburne in the province of Nova Scotia . . . do fully . . . sell . . . a certain tract . . . of land . . . on the east side of McNutt's Island. . . . **1933** *Ibid.* 342: Before the light was built, negroes used to live on the east side [of McNutt's Island]. They piloted vessels in and out of the harbour and were known as "Black Pilots." The building of the light put the black pilots out of commission.

black rat snake See quotes. See also **land black snake.**
1963 *Kingston Whig-Standard* (Ont.) 19 Apr. 14/3: The Elaphe obsoleta, or black rat snake, gets its name obsoleta because a pattern on its back gradually fades away to a soft black hue towards its tail. **1964** *Outdoorsman* Mar. 18/2: . . . Canada's largest snake, the black rat or pilot black snake, which may reach a length of eight feet, is found in Frontenac and Leeds counties [Ont.] as well as occasionally on the Lake Erie shoreline.

blackrobe *n.* originally in Indian parlance, a priest, especially a missionary of the Roman Catholic or Anglican denominations. See also **blackcoat** and **medicine blackrobe.**
1840 WILLIS *Cdn Scenery* I 24: They exhorted her to take it into the woods, where the blackrobes, as they called the Christian priests, would not be able to find her. **1875** *Canadian Mthly* Jan. 46/1: The black-robe, the voyageur, and the red man passed up and down the river in bark canoes. **1959** *News of the North* 16 July 2/5: With his residence established at Fort Good Hope, Father Grollier . . . was the first Blackrobe to meet the Loucheaux and the Eskimos. . . . **1963** SYMONS *Many Trails* 138: "I have heard my friend the blackrobe. What he says is good for the Moonias. I am not a white man."

black salts *Hist.* See quotes.
1819 *Kingston Chron.* (U.C.) 18 June 3/5: Twenty-five Cwt. of clean black salts will make one ton of pearl ash. **1853** STRICKLAND *Canada West* I 170n: After the lye is run off it is boiled down into black salts, which are melted into pot-ash, and packed into air-tight barrels

ready for market. **1904** ERMATINGER *Talbot Regime* 42: . . . "blacksalts" [were] a product of the leached ashes of burnt logs and timber, rendered into potash and pearl ash and brought by the early merchants for export.

black sand *Placer Mining* See 1897 quote.
1862 (1958) LINDSAY *Cariboo Story* 39/1: I got some drifters and started to wash. The black sand was hard to get out of the gold. **1897** TUTTLE *Golden North* 88: Finally all that is left in the pan is whatever gold may have been in the dish and some black sand which almost invariably accompanies it. This black sand is nothing but pulverized magnetic iron ore. **1964** *North* July 7/1: They jiggled and rolled their gold pan, sloshing the water from side to side, washing away the gravel. Soon nothing remained but black sand.

Black settlements settlements of Negroes in Nova Scotia, occupied mostly by the descendants of U.E. Loyalist slaves.
1830 MOORSOM *Letters N.S.* 141: The principal Black settlements, those of Halifax, Preston, Hammond's Plains, Shelburne, and Digby, have schools for the negroes, supported by an English society. . . .

blackskin *n.* the edible skin of narwhal and beluga, called muktuk, *q.v.*, by the Eskimos, eaten fresh and raw by them but usually cooked by whites. See also **cork.**
1862 (1865) HALL *Arctic Researches* 483: We are quite hard up here now, for all the "black skin" is gone, and I have only about ten pounds of whale-meat left. **1952** *Beaver* Sep. 41/1: The cook on our ship had also been busy cooking up large pots full of blackskin, and we gorged ourselves on it, as it is very good eating. It tastes a little like cocoanut.

black-snake† *n.* See **black-snake whip.**
1930 BEAMES *Army* 156: Cooley lashed out with his loaded blacksnake. **1954** HAGELL *Grass Was Free* 3: He also carried the traditional blacksnake.

black-snake whip or **lash** a whip having a long, tapering lash or plaited rawhide, often loaded with shot at the tip. See also **snake-whip.**
1913 JOHNSON *Shagganappi* 203: [With] the whizzing crack of the young driver's "blacksnake" whip . . . the "mountain mail" was away. . . . **1954** HAGELL *Grass Was Free* 3: Long braided or shot-loaded black-snake lashes on a short stock for horses, long stock for bulls— were the standard whip equipment, and either bull whacker or horse skinner had to be able to make his whip talk.

black snow *North* drab, grayish snow soiled by dust in the atmosphere.
1946 *Beaver* Sep. 4/1: . . . old Neovitcheak sent along his first reminder in the form of a tremendous fall of black snow.

blackstrap *n.* **1** See **black-jack** (def. 1).
1897 TUTTLE *Golden North* 202: I then exhibited two plugs of black-strap, and asked in a decided tone of voice, as if it were my last offer, "oomungde?"

2 a liquor made of rum and molasses.
1827 (1832) PICKERING *Inquiries* 93: Let him give out drams of whiskey . . . "bitters" (any kind of liquor taken in the morning ostensibly for procuring an appetite),

"sling," "Black strap," etc. from a tier of yellow painted kegs. . . . **1956** RADDALL *Wings* 49 : . . . what was the service issue ? Good old blackstrap Demerara. A man can fight on that. He can darn near live on it.

3 molasses.
1903 RICHARDSON *Colin* 207 : . . . as for the [maple] syrup, it was far superior to the "black strap" that was sold at the general store. **1963** *Beaver* Autumn 44/1 : He and his playmates were allowed to help . . . receiving in reward a treat of "blackstrap and dumpling."

blacktail *n.* See **blacktail deer.**
1860 *Nor'Wester* (R.R.S.) 15 Oct. 4/3 : We shall . . . then proceed . . . for the Black Tail . . . returning by the head of the Coteau des Prairies. . . . **1912** POCOCK *Man in the Open* 205 : "Wish I'd had a shot," said Billy . . . his mind on the blacktail, our local [Cariboo, B.C.] kind of deer.

blacktail(ed) deer the mule deer, *Odocoileus hemionus,* of western North America, or its smaller relative of the Rocky Mountain region, *O. hemionus columbianus,* the Columbia blacktailed deer, *q.v.*
1858 (1965) *Maclean's* 19 June 39/1 : Our Stoney hunter shot a blacktail deer today. **1887** *Senate Report* 85 : There is just the black tailed deer, the white tailed deer, and the antelope. . . . **1958** CAMERON *Cdn Mammals* 6 : The mule deer and black-tailed deer . . . because of the difference in their size and colour, were once thought to be distinct species.

black tobacco *Obs.* a strong, dark tobacco once sold by the Hudson's Bay Co. See also **brazil tobacco.**
1691 (1929) KELSEY *Papers* 6 : [He] emptied part of it into a leather Bagg so I put one hatchet 2 fathom of Black Tobacco 6 knives . . . into the rundlett. . . . **1743** *Hudson's Bay Record Soc.* XII 86 : . . . give us good (brazl. tobacco) black tobacco, moist & hard twisted. **1799** (1934) HEARNE & TURNOR *Journals* 226 : . . . the Indians had taken from them . . . 5 Cwt of black Tobacco (which is made in imitation of the Honourable Company's but is much smaller).

black wampum *Hist.* See **black belt.**
1814 *Montreal Herald* 2 Apr. 1/3 : This is my parole to the Nations—(Here the Black Wampum is presented to the Newash)—Let them know what I have said—tell them they shall not be forgotten by their Great Father nor by me.

blanket *n.* **1 a.** See **Indian blanket.**
1801 (1922) HARMON *Journal* 40 : Their clothing [includes] a blanket or dressed Buffaloe skin, which they wrap around their bodies, and tie around their waists. **1837** (1952) *Beaver* Sep. 33 : The blanket as an overall, is considered indispensable; it is used [by the Indian] on all occasions. . . . **1873** (1904) BUTLER *Wild North Land* 141 : Lounging at the gate, or on the shore in front, one sees a half-breed in tasseled cap, or a group of Indians in blanket robes or dirty white capotes.

b. the traditional ways of the Indian, symbolized by the blanket as an article of clothing.
1813 *Montreal Herald* 19 June 1/3 : An Indian that lived in Oneida remote, / Was plagu'd by a Parson, to join his dear flock, / To throw off his blanket and put on a coat. **1956** EVANS *Mountain Dog* 12 : Me, with hardly any education, I'm stuck here. Am I supposed to go

back to the blanket ? **1958** HAWTHORN *Indians of B.C.* 303 : A few teachers (as in all other school systems also, of course) conclude that their efforts are wasted. Teachers in Indian schools often phrase this in variants of the "back to the blanket" theme. **1959** *Native Voice* Jan. 4/1 : . . . the younger generation of Indians . . . speaks contemptuously of the old Indian ways and sneers at returning "to the blanket."

c. on the blanket, See quote.
1959 HAYCOX *Earthbreakers* 44 : He made a flat motion with his two hands against the ground. "But I'm on the blanket." "What's that mean ?" she asked. "It's what an Indian says when he's through fighting, running around, raising hell."

2 *Hist.* a unit of barter among traders and Indians in the Northwest.
1859 KANE *Wanderings* 239 : The blanket is the standard by which the value of all articles on the north-west coast is calculated . . . two blankets being equal to a gun. . . . **1958** *Imperial Oil Rev.* Apr. 30/2 : By 1854 another island mill, operated at Nanaimo by the Hudson's Bay Company, was paying the Indians one blanket for every eight big logs. . . .

3 a. *Hist.* a note issued as currency by the Hudson's Bay Co.
1900 OSBORN *Greater Canada* 145 : A hunter's wages consisted in those days of Hudson's Bay "blankets" or notes to the value of £3 sterling. . . . **1923** *Beaver* Jan. 188/2 : Received also H.B.C. "blankets," old-time H.B.C. currency issued from York Factory on Hudson Bay. Denominations are one shilling, five shillings, and one pound. **1952** (1965) HAMILTON *Cdn Quotations* 139 : A blanket. Originally a Hudson's Bay Co. note used in paying wages, during late 19th century. . . .

b. See quotes.
1900 OSBORN *Greater Canada* 44 : Sometimes to-day one hears a dollar-bill described as a "blanket," a reference to the Hudson's Bay Company notes which formed the only currency in the North-West of those days and was so styled by the "old travellers" of the forties. **1952** (1965) HAMILTON *Cdn Quotations* 139 : A blanket. . . . in the West, a term for a dollar bill.

4 See **beaver blanket** (def. 2).
1952 *Beaver* June 33 : Some fine pelts were obtained, ranging up to 76 inches for "blanket" pelts which sold for $24 to $30 each. . . . **1955** HARDY *Alta Anthol.* 308 : Beaver pelts, still on their round frames, are stacked high, and sorted into sizes, the largest called "blankets." **1965** *Islander* 7 Mar. 4 : Any experienced beaver trapper has taken "blanket" male beaver whose otherwise perfect skin has been reduced in value . . . by cuts, scars and sores. . . .

5 *N.S.* a kind of pastry consisting of berries wrapped in a thick crust of dough.
1894 ASHLEY *Tan Pile Jim* 125 : The blueberries were ripening, and "huckleberry" parties, pies, puddings, dumplings, "blankets," "grunts," and sauces were in order.

blanket *v. Mining* **1** stake only the margins of a group of claims so as to give the impression that staking has been done fully and properly.
1913 FOOTNER *Jack Chanty* 51 : I ought to go . . . make sure they don't blanket anything of mine.

2 cover; take in; include.
1953 *North Star* (Yellowknife) Jan.-Feb. 6/1 : The claims are stated to blanket a favorable structure from which high-value assays of uranium have been taken.

blanket aristocracy *Derog., Obs.* Indians.
1882 *Brandon Dly Mail* (Man.) 27 Dec. 4/1 : According

to the custom of the blanket aristocracy aboriginal Red man, a number . . . were up bright and early yesterday. **1883** *Ibid.* 2 Jan. 4/1: The "blanket aristocracy" were around yesterday receiving their usual New Year's demands.

blanket bag a sleeping bag.
1850 OSBORN *Arctic Jnl* 147: Then every man his blanket bag, a general popping thereinto of the legs and body. . . . **1857** MCDOUGALL *Voyage* 315: Frequently, on waking, we found the little animals, rolled up in a ball-like form, snugly ensconced within the folds of our blanket bags; nor would they be expelled from such a warm and desirable position without showing fight.

blanket capote a capote, *q.v.*, made of blanket cloth, much used as winter wear in the North.
1843 LEFROY *Magnetic North* 43: I have been getting winter clothing here to take in, blanket capot etc. . . . **1952** HOWARD *Strange Empire* 164: They yanked off their mittens to thrust freezing hands under their blanket capotes and under their shirts to their warm armpits.

blanket-case *n.* a protective covering of blanket cloth for a gun; gun case; gun coat.
1931 GREY OWL *Last Frontier* 142: I drew the blanket-case off my rifle and pumped a shell into the breech.

blanket coat a warm, usually short coat made of heavy blanket cloth, scarlet, blue, gray, or white, often decorated by needlework at the seams or with fringes. See also **point-blanket coat.**
1761 (1901) HENRY (Elder) *Travels* 35: [He wore] a molton, or blanket coat. **1876** LORD *At Home in the Wilderness* 141: The Canadian "blanket-coats" . . . are admirable in a dry frosty atmosphere. . . . **1955** COLLARD *Cdn Yesterdays* 292: One of them . . . ejected a fellow in a blanket coat who was about to demolish the clerk's table.

blanket Indian† an Indian living remote from civilization and following the traditions of his people; originally, an Indian who dressed in a trade blanket. Cp. **blanket** (def. 1b).
1891 *Cdn Indian* Apr. 190: It seems to me that the proper persons to deal with the wild blanket Indians of the Northwest Territories and British Columbia are these civilized Christian Indians of Ontario and Quebec and some parts of Manitoba.

blanket leggings See **blanket sock.**
1837 (1923) JAMESON *Rambles* 205: . . . there were also a highly ornamented capuchin and a pair of new blanket leggings. **1888** (1890) ST. MAUR *Impressions* 180: They wore bead necklaces and leather bracelets, studded with brass nails; also woollen shirts, and tight blanket leggings, fringed, and reaching half way up their thighs.

blanket marriage among North American Indians, a marriage performed according to local custom, in some tribes by having a blanket placed over the couple. Cp. **longhouse marriage.**
1927 (1928) ROSE *Stump Farm* 156: ". . . there is a good deal of . . . loose living among the Indians and breeds since the white man came into this country. Nearly all of them just have a blanket marriage, and there are so few in here that they'd marry their own sisters if they dared, for the priest." "What's a blanket marriage?" said I. "Oh, a lad sees a girl he wants, and he takes his blanket to her tent, and they're married as long as he leaves it there." **1958** HAWTHORN *Indians of B.C.* 386: The reference to "legitimate child" raised the question in the Committee of the status of a so-called

"blanket marriage," entered into according to local custom.

blanket sock *North* a kind of sock or legging made of duffle or blanketing or wrapped around the feet and legs for warmth in winter. See also **blanket leggings** and **blanket wrapper.**
1748 ELLIS *Hudson's Bay* 188: We likewise began about this Time to put on our Winter Dress, which consisted of . . . two or three pair of Blanket, or thick Duffil Socks. . . . **1938** SULLIVAN *Cycle of North* 171: On his feet she wound great blanket socks and folded his sleeping robe about his shoulders.

blanket staking in mining, registering for all claims over a large area. See also **blanket,** *v.*
1957 *Stettler Independent* 23 Oct. 16/1: First intimations of blanket staking of large tracts of promising ground comes out of the Fort William-Port Arthur area.

blanket suit See quote.
1897 TYRRELL *Sub-Arctics* 219: My brother and I were warmly dressed in deer-skin garbs of the Eskimo, while the rest of the party wore the white blanket suits of the traders.

blanket wrapper See **blanket sock.**
1867 GALTON *Art of Travel* 117: Socks . . . made of thick blanket, and called "Blanket Wrappers," are in use at Hudson's Bay instead of shoes.

blaze† *n.* **1** a white mark made in a tree, usually by chopping off a slice of bark, to indicate a trail or survey line in a forest. See also **trail blaze.**
[**1768** DRAGE *Prob.N.W.Passage* 138: [We] walked a great Way in an *Indian Path*, and saw several marked trees, as is practised among the Southern Indians.] **1842** WILLIS *Cdn Scenery* II 68: These blazes are of as much use as finger posts of a dark night. **1965** *Islander* 14 Feb. 13/1: The snow had come up over many of our blazes and the trapline was hard to follow. . . .
2 a trail marked by blazes.
1833 (1838) NEED *Six Years in the Bush* 75: At length . . . I had the inexpressible comfort of stumbling upon a familiar blaze, which . . . led me to my own clearing. . . . **1946** BIRD *Sunrise for Peter* 211: "We've a plain blaze back to the yard," said Gideon.

blaze *v.* **1** chop a piece of bark from a tree so as to reveal the white wood to serve as a marker.
1788 (1905) *Ont.Bur.Arch.Rep.* III 312: There must be due care to . . . blaze healthy trees. . . . **1793** (1916) *London Hist.Soc.Trans.* VII 9: [LITTLEHALE *Journal*] I observed many trees blazed and various figures of Indians . . . and animals drawn upon them, descriptive of the tribes, nations and numbers that had passed. **1923** STRINGER *Empty Hands* 202: They even marked trails by blazing trees as they went. . . .
2 mark or identify (a trail, property line, etc.) by cutting a series of blazes in trees. See also **blazing.**
1872 DASHWOOD *Chiploquorgan* 114: It took us two or three days to complete this line . . . two of us cutting out a line and blazing the line, the others building and baiting the traps. **1952** BUCKLER *Mountain and Valley* 54: Joseph walked back to the woodlot that day and blazed a road for the fall chopping. . . . **1965** *Maclean's* 3 July 28/2: The trail . . . cleared, blazed, bridged and fence-stiled in a six-month crash program by early 1964.

blazed *adj.* **1** of a tree, marked by the removal of a piece of bark to reveal the white wood. See also **blaze.**

1816 MARSDEN *Narrative* 35: I passed through fifty or sixty miles of wood, by a road chiefly composed of blazed trees.... **1963** SYMONS *Many Trails* 195: Two blazed trees ... will show us the lobstick portage.

2 of a trail, property line, etc., identified by a series of trees, stumps, etc. that have been marked with blazes, *q.v.*

1842 *Trans.Lit.& Hist.Soc.Que.* IV 87: The traps for martens are placed along a blazed path (called a "cat path") leading into the interior.... **1852** *Anglo-American Mag.* I 320/1: Being unused to the bush roads, they had missed the blazed line that led to his clearing. **1965** *Maclean's* 3 July 21/1: I felt a sudden heartening thrill at the knowledge that this modest, blazed footpath went on and on....

blaze out See **blaze** *v.* (def. 2).

1883 FRASER *Shanty* 211: [The road] was not even "blazed out".... **1904** *Ont.Bur.Arch.Rep.* I 49: ... Roger Conant was content with comparatively little and only blazed out some 800 acres altogether.

blaze-trail *n.* a trail marked by blazes.

1904 (1917) *London Hist.Soc.Trans.* VIII 43: The blaze-trail was through a part of the swamp.

blazing *n.* See 1853 quote.

1794 (1905) *Ont.Bur.Arch.Rep.* II 257: May I request ... a report of ... the mode of blazing.... **1853** STRICKLAND *Canada West* I 109n: Blazing is a term used by the backwoodsman for chopping off a portion of the bark from each side of a tree to mark a surveyor's line through the woods. **1963** SYMONS *Many Trails* 165: ... blazing [of] narrow trails ... was undertaken, as well as the putting up of some tiny patrol cabins.

Bleu [blu] *n.* [< Cdn F] a Quebec Conservative, so called because the traditional color of the Conservative party is blue. Cp. **Rouge.**

1885 *Wkly Manitoba Liberal* 25 Dec. 4/4: The *Mail* is frantic over the defection of the rank and file of the Bleus in Quebec. **1946** LOWER *Colony to Nation* 302: Among the French, the word "Bleu" did not necessarily mean "Conservative": George Etienne Cartier insisted on calling himself a "Reformer" as late as 1857, three years after the coalition. **1963** *Globe and Mail* (Toronto) 26 Mar. 7/7: ... the Quebec voters' traditional loyalties have been strained to the limit and the real tug of war no longer is between the rouges and the bleus—the Liberals and the Tories—but between the "old" and the "new" parties.

bleu [blu] *adj.* [< Cdn F] of or having to do with the Quebec Conservative party or its policies.

[**1876** (1965) HAMILTON *Cdn Quotations* 68/1: It is not for me, mes enfants, to tell you for which party you should vote, but I would have you remember that the place on high (pointing to the heavens) is *bleu*, while the other (pointing downward) is *rouge*.] **1900** *Cdn Mag.* Sep. 548/2: There are strong Conservatives who would place the maximum Bleu victories at fifteen. **1963** *Kingston Whig-Standard* (Ont.) 9 Mar. 13/3: This is especially important in the rural ridings where the very low income segment of the population tends to be more bleu than rouge.

blind line *Upper Canada, Hist.* See quote.

1909 HUNTER *Simcoe County* I 41: Yet, still another system came into use in the latest surveys ... in 1832 and 1833, where a side road was placed at every third lot, and the alternative concession lines, called "blind lines," have been usually left unopened.

blind slough or **snye** See **snye** (def. 2a).

blister gum the gum of the Canada balsam, *q.v.*

1905 (1954) *B.C.Hist.Qtly* XVIII 184: To cure a cough they boiled down spruce bark and mixed the liquor with ... a turpentiny smelling liquor. The latter may have been the melted blister-gum that is found under the smooth bark of the balsam.

blizzard *n.* [origin uncertain but probably from English dialect source] a snowstorm accompanied by high winds and intense cold.

[**1866** *British Columbian* (New Westminster) 14 July 1/2: [Advert.] THE BLIZZARD SALOON, Front St., New Westminster.] **1880** GORDON *Mountain and Prairie* 283: ... the stage-driver's description of a blizzard [was] ... "one o' them 'ere mountain storms as gets up on its hind legs and howls." **1936** *Cdn Hist.Rev.* XVII 129: A "blizzard" is not properly a storm of falling snow, though often so called. It is a snow wind-storm, only possible on open plains, and often occurs under a cloudless sky [in the West]. **1963** *Maclean's* 9 Feb. 48/3: Will the occasional shivering Chinese, caught in a Saskatchewan blizzard, cry out that they ought to give the country back to the Canadians?

blizzard cap a warm, tight-fitting cap suitable for use in blizzard weather.

1910 FERGUSON *Janey Canuck* 26: ... one may purchase blizzard caps, hip boots....

blizzard storm See **blizzard.**

1880 YOUNG *Indian Wigwams* 132: ... blinding blizzard storms, added to the bitter cold, made it almost impossible for man to face the dreadful gale. **1946** (1947) FREEDMAN *Mrs.Mike* 35: It was a blizzard storm I was out in. Mighty trees ... crashing down....

block *n.* **1** *Hist.* in Upper and Lower Canada, a subdivision of a newly surveyed township, in turn subdivided into concessions (def. 2) and lots.

1799 *Quebec Gaz.* 5 Dec. Supp. 3/1: There are sixteen blocks in each township, numbered from one to sixteen. **1821** *York Wkly Post* 29 Mar. 23/3: This Lot is part of a block of land lately purchased by Dr. Lyons from Alexander McDonell Esqur. M.P. **1947** TAYLOR *Canada* 324: A few blocks were also occupied in this year at the mouth of the Saugeen River at Southampton [in Upper Canada].

2 an extensive tract of land, especially one granted to or held by the Crown or by a land or railway company, mining or lumbering concern, etc.

1799 (1936) RUSSELL *Correspondence* III 121: When he was in England, the Block of land [that] was called the Mississague Block had been pointed out to him ... as part of the Country properest for his Colony.... **1849** *Wkly Globe* 23 Nov. 82/2: ... these valuable regions were divided out into blocks of *ten square miles* and ceded to certain favoured individuals with exclusive rights of mining! **1964** *Commercial Letter* Mar. 7/1: The belt of nickel uncovered at Thompson is at the southern edge of ... the Churchill block of the Precambrian Shield.

3 a specific tract of surveyed land of considerable extent identified by a proper name.

1827 *Gore Gaz.* (Ancaster, U.C.) 3 Nov. 143/2: The quantity of land already taken up, in the Guelph Block, amounted last week to 12,250 acres. **1963** *Canada*

Month May 14/1: In the extreme north-east lie the wheatlands of the Peace River Block, the only farming district in Canada that has never known a crop failure.

4 a single tract of land or piece of property, small or large.

1820 *Globe* (Toronto) 9 Dec. 2/4: It seems that the Bishop and his friends have set their hearts on the old Parliament House and the four acre block on which it stands.... **1953** MOON *Saskatchewan* 65: He and his associates ... purchased 10,000-acre land blocks from the C.P.R. **1964** *Sun* (Vancouver) 14 Mar. 27/1: A block of 130 acres on the north side of the Cowichan River is being purchased ... for recreational use....

5† one of the tracts, usually rectangular, into which a city or town is subdivided, made up of a number of lots and usually bounded by four streets.

1837 *Times* (Halifax) 24 Oct. 343/1: A whole block of buildings has been totally consumed.... **1959** *Globe and Mail* (Toronto) 23 Apr. 11/2: ... all he had to do was to put up the names of Randolph Scott or George Raft on the marquee of his Downtown Theatre and he'd have a line-up around the block....

6† one side of a block (def. 5), especially when conceived of as a measure of distance.

1891 *Grip* (Toronto) 12 Dec. 373/2: Never have to walk further than a block or so between saloons. **1964** *Vancouver Province* 14 Feb. 10/5: I had four blocks to cover [in canvassing for funds].

7 a. a large single building, especially one containing offices, apartments, or stores.

1890 *Grip* (Toronto) 18 Oct. 247/2: Where Dineen's store stood towered a twelve-story block.... **1961** *Edmonton Jnl* 1 Aug. 1/3: The biggest jump this year has been in the construction of apartment blocks.

b. one of the principal buildings on Parliament Hill in Ottawa, housing the Senate, the Commons, and various offices and committee rooms, now called the East, Centre, and West Blocks, *qq.v.*

1864 (1955) CRAIG *Early Travellers* 282: The Buildings consist of a central block, in which are comprised the House or Chamber of the Legislative Council (the Lords), and a House of Assembly (the Commons), flanked by two wings containing the various Government offices, an arrangement which brings them all together under one roof.... **1963** *Kingston Whig-Standard* (Ont.) 16 Apr. 1/7: ... Mr. Pearson walked the few hundred yards from his office in the Centre Block on Parliament Hill to the East Block....

8 See quote.

1945 CALVIN *Saga* 88: Beyond the outer end of these long piers [in the St. Lawrence timber coves], far enough to give about thirty feet depth at low water, there were square piers called "blocks," at which the sailing-ships, and later the steamers, lay to load timber.

blockpile *n. Lumbering* a large stack of pulpwood logs.

1955 *Bush News* Feb. 7/1: Smooth Rock Falls division has completed ... the haul of more than 100,000 units ... more than 60% on ice or blockpile. **1963** *Canada Month* Nov. 28/3: A blockpile has a lovely chimney effect.... So we wouldn't build blockpiles like that.

Bloc Populaire a political party that flourished in the province of Quebec from about 1941 to 1947.

1946 LOWER *Colony to Nation* 556: During the Quebec election of the summer of 1944, the Union Nationale and Bloc Populaire had deluged the province with flysheets.... **1961** *Edmonton Jnl* 4 Aug. 18/1: Clear Grits, Unionists, Progressives, United Farmers, Bloc Populaire, and now the CCF, are part of the ancestral lore of politics—parties with a past but without a future. **1964** *Globe and Mail* (Toronto) 10 Nov. 1/2: The RIN leader is trying to follow the organizational trail blazed by ... Le Bloc Populaire.

blond Eskimo a member of a tribe of Eskimos, also called Copper Eskimos, reported to have blond individuals among them.

[**1847** PRICHARD *Researches* V 373: M. Charlevoix assures us repeatedly that many of them are of xanthous complexion, or what the French call "blonds."] *c*1912 (1963) LEBOURDAIS *Stefansson* 59: There is no reason for insisting now or ever that the "blond Eskimo(s)" of Victoria Island are descended from the Scandinavian colonists of Greenland, but looking at it historically and geographically, there is no reason why they might not be. **1952** *Natural History* Feb. 60: In the east lay the sealing grounds of the "Blond" Eskimos, as yet undiscovered. **1964** *Cdn Forum* June 71/1: [Stefansson] was reported as having discovered a tribe of "blond Eskimos" with all the implications that such a term implied.

blood brother See **blood-friend**. See also **brother**.

1919 FRASER *Bulldog Carney* 287: I know Standing Bear; he made me a blood brother of his. **1954** CAMPBELL *Nor'Westers* 5: Henry hid under a pile of hides, and even with the help of a blood brother Indian barely escaped scalping.

blood-friend *n.* among Indians, one who has gone through a ceremony of mixing blood with another person and is therefore considered his brother. See also **blood brother**.

1905 (1954) *B.C.Hist.Qtly* XVIII 172: A pole, held at each end by a blood-friend of the deceased husband, was placed across her back under her hands, and she was hoisted into the fire at its fiercest and withdrawn, usually of course much burnt and disfigured.

bloody belt *Hist.* a bloodied belt symbolizing war among certain North American Indians. Cp. **black belt**.

1814 *Montreal Herald* 2 Apr. 1/2: Newash then advanced to His Excellency, and presented him with the Black Wampum and the Bloody belt. *Ibid.* 1/3: Take courage my Children, be strong, and may the Great Spirit preserve you in this day of Battle (Here the Bloody Belt is presented).

bloody hatchet *Hist.* a bloodied hatchet symbolizing war among certain North American Indians. See also **bloody belt**.

1840 MURRAY *British America* I 114: A huge fire was kindled, whereon is placed the great war-cauldron, into which everyone present throws something; and if any allies, invited by a belt of wampum and bloody hatchet to devour the flesh and drink the blood of the enemy, have accepted the summons, they send some ingredient to be also cast in.

Bloody Nose See **Indian paint-brush**.

1910 FERGUSON *Janey Canuck* 189: The *Castillo* [*Castilleja*] is a hot-hued flower. The whites call it "Indian's Paint Brush," but the Indians call it "Bloody Nose."

blowdirt *n.* blown soil, etc. from summerfallow field.

1964 *Sask.News* Mar. 1/1: Use of blowdirt—the unwanted by-product of windswept summerfallow fields—as a means of "clearing" snow-blocked drainage ditches was demonstrated. . . . Sections of ditches spread with blowdirt were open and flowing clear of obstructions, while untreated sections were still blocked with snow and ice.

blowdown† *n.* a tree blown down by wind.
1923 STRINGER *Empty Hands* 212: . . . she came to the upthrust roots of a blow-down. . . . **1947** ROWLANDS *Cache Lake* 170: . . . among the slash and the blowdowns are raspberries bigger and sweeter than any ever grown by man.

blowhole† *n.* See **aglu**. See also **blowing hole**.
1916 DUNCAN *Billy Topsail* 293: . . . they walked warily, . . . in dread of lakes and blow-holes and fissures of water. . . . **1963** *North* May-June 38/1: As we drew near, those seals nearest to us slid quietly into nearby leads and blow holes.

blow in be or become obliterated by snow.
1944 CLAY *Fur Thieves* 127: . . . the trail had blown in, and though Trapper Tom had tried his best to find it he had lost it where it left the bush. . . . **1956** KEMP *Northern Trader* 147: The trails your home-coming customers have made are all blown-in, which means you have to break your own.

blowing hole See **blowhole**.
1861 DE BOILIEU *Labrador Life* 132: For the purpose of obtaining this necessary element [air], holes are kept open by the seals throughout the winter, and are called by the Esquimaux "blowing holes". **1921** *Beaver* Jan. 16/2: Around the seal or blowing holes they [seals] were not in large numbers. . . .

blowout *n.* a workout; a spell of intense effort and application.
1962 *Field, Horse & Rodeo* Nov. 22/3: . . . arena directors . . . are too prone to "save" their good horses for the finals, instead of giving them a good "blowout" earlier in the week.

blowpot *n.* *Slang* a device for cooking on, such as a Primus or Coleman stove.
1963 *North* May-June 10/2: . . . we made coffee and heated two or three packets of soup on the blowpot.

blubberbag *n.* See quotes.
1964 *North* Nov.-Dec. 8/1: On arriving at Thule five collapsible neoprene rubber tanks are installed in each Hercules, permitting 4500 U.S. gallons of fuel to be airlifted on each flight. . . . The five sausage-shaped tanks, nicknamed blubberbags, were used for the first time . . . to airlift 192,260 gallons of fuel-oil to the weather stations . . . on the northern rim of the Canadian Arctic. **1965** *Globe and Mail* (Toronto) 21 Dec. 2/6: A Defense Department spokesman said that RCAF Hercules [air trucks] operating on Arctic manoeuvres have carried 4,000 gallons of oil in rubber blubberbags which fill the interior of the aircraft.

blubber lamp See **kudlik** and picture.
1855 (1892) KANE *Arctic Explor.* 282: I carried in our blubber-lamp, food, and bedding. . . . **1952** *Natural Hist.* Feb. 59: From the snow they built warm houses, heating them with their primitive stone blubber lamps.

Blue *n.* 1 See **Bleu**. Cp. **Red** (def. 2).
1864 *Islander* (Charlottetown) 24 June 2/5: The fact is,

there is to be a coalition between the clear grits of Upper Canada and the Blues of Lower Canada. **1896** GOURLAY *Hist.Ottawa* 39: A Lieut.-Governor and one or two cabinets were dismissed in Quebec because they were not of the blues. . . . **1958** *Time* (Cdn ed.) 31 Mar. 10/2: My family has voted Rouge for years. The Liberals have done more for the average man than the Blues.

2 *Fur Trade, Hist.* See **Sky Blue**.
1947 HARGRAVE *Correspondence* 47n: The officers of the Hudson's Bay Company were formerly known as "Blues" or "Sky Blues" from the colour of their uniforms. The Nor'Westers were similarly known as "Greys." The names were still occasionally used after the union in 1821.

blue *adj.* See **bleu**.
1962 *Chronicle-Herald* (Halifax) 10 Aug. 4/8: Since Confederation we have heard the same old story, have changed from red to blue and blue to red. **1963** *Kingston Whig-Standard* (Ont.) 5 Apr. 1/2: In French Montreal and in constituencies won by the Conservatives last year . . . the big story is the collapse of blue strength.

blueback *n.* **1** a young hood seal, *q.v.*
1842 JUKES *Excursions in Nfld* I 311: The young [hooded seals] . . . have whitish bellies and dark gray backs, which when wet have a bluish tinge, whence they are called "blue-backs". **1883** HATTON & HARVEY *Newfoundland* 312: The young of this species [hood seal] have not the thick woolly coat of the harp seals, and during that season they are called "blue-backs."

2 See **blueback salmon**.

blueback salmon *West Coast* a three-year-old coho, *q.v.*
1907 LAMBERT *Fishing in B.C.* 73: They are . . . the silver and blue-back salmon. . . . **1938** CASH *I Like B.C.* 117: Jack hung around listening to talk of wobblers . . . the best places for bluebacks . . . and a thousand other ramifications of fishing lore. **1963** *Sun* (Vancouver) 20 June 25/1: In these dog days of June salmon slugging, anyone who has two bluebacks to rub together after a trip is doing well.

blue-beech tea a beating with a blue-beech stick.
1925 MCARTHUR *Familiar Fields* 111: . . . blue-beech tea . . . used to be very popular with the teachers of a past generation. It was brewed by making a blue-beech gad about a yard long and as thick as a man's finger and applying it vigorously to the writhing person of an unruly boy.

blue belly *Slang, Obs.* a Yankee, an American.
1827 (1832) PICKERING *Inquiries of an Emigrant* 92: In short "blue bellies" of all sorts and conditions, equal to any of the frontier towns on both sides of the "lines."

blueberry barren *Esp.Maritimes* a tract of untillable land on which blueberries flourish.
1904 ROBERTS *Watchers of Trails* 53: Upward he toiled, through swamps and fir woods, over blueberry barrens and ranges of granite boulders. . . . *c*1963 *Touring P.E.I.* 21: There is good farming land about Mount Stewart and close by are also located some of the Island's finest blueberry barrens.

blue book any of several types of Canadian parliamentary reports, especially financial reports.
1831 *Cdn Courant* (Montreal) 17 Dec. 1/4: The annual returns were included in what was commonly called the Blue Book. **1916** BRIDLE *Sons of Canada* 227: There were too many railways to build . . . trade returns to bulge the blue-books, and election battles to fight. **1964** *Time* (Cdn ed.) 13 Mar. 11/3: Tabling the traditional blue book of estimates in the Commons last week, Finance

Minister Gordon gave notice of what's up in the Government's 1964-65 spending plans: just about everything.

59

bluefish
Bluenose

bluefish *n.* See **Arctic grayling**.

1807 WENTZEL *Letters* 84: The different sorts of fish to be met with in the lakes and rivers of these desserts are . . . inconnu, white fish . . . blue fish, tolliby and Loche. **1924** MASON *Arctic Forests* 159: Bluefish vary considerably in colour, but as a rule they are grey-ish-blue with the under parts silvery. **1962** *B.C. Digest* Oct. 22/2: . . . we discovered the enormous amount of bluefish in this small creek.

blue fox a rare color phase of the Arctic fox, *q.v.* See also **sooty fox**.

1779 (1792) CARTWRIGHT *Journal* II 443: The whole of what we got at this place is as follows, viz. fifteen silver foxes, twenty-eight crosses, nineteen yellows, twenty-six whites, and one blue fox, total ninety-six. **1952** PUTNAM *Cdn Regions* 504/2: Blue foxes, a colour phase (one or two percent) of a white fox litter. . . .

blue goose a white-headed, gray color phase of the snow goose, *Chen hyperborea,* breeding on the Arctic islands. See also **blue wavey**.

1795 (1911) HEARNE *Journey* 441: Blue geese . . . are of the same size as the Snow Geese. . . . **1945** *Beaver* Sep. 16/2: The Blue Goose is by no means a rare bird, yet until 1928 the nesting place of this waterfowl remained undiscovered. **1963** *Globe and Mail* (Toronto) 13 Mar. 2/1: . . . the Cree Indians talk the language of the blue and snow geese and coax them right down to their shotgun muzzles.

blue grouse† a variety of grouse, *Dendragopus obscurus,* of the Rocky Mountain region.

1869 *Mainland Guardian* (New Westminster, B.C.) 10 Nov. 3/2: We only succeeded in getting . . . two blue grouse . . . which we . . . found delicious. **1959** *Tourist Folder* (Duncan-Cowichan Chamber of Commerce, Duncan, B.C.): Wing shooting from September to mid-January, starts with wild pigeons and blue grouse. . . .

blue ice clear, translucent ice that is compact and solid.

1727 (1965) *Letters from Hudson Bay* 127: . . . a ship may with as much safety run against a rock as against . . . a hard blue ice. **1853** (1884) MCCORMICK *Voyages* II 164: I have often seen the strength of the *Erebus* most severely tested between huge dense masses of blue ice, violently grinding past her sides. . . . **1956** SCHERMAN *Spring* 128: Brownish or dark ice, it appeared, was dangerous. Blue ice was all right even if it was covered with water. . . .

blueline *n. Hockey* either of the two blue lines midway between the centre of a rink and each goal. Also spelled *blue line*.

1931 *Vancouver Province* 3 Jan. 7/3: McLean knocked Hutton off his feet with the best shot of the night, a terrific effort from the blue line. **1964** *Maclean's* 21 Mar. 14/2: . . . the Leafs . . . knock a lot of people down at the blue line. . . .

blueline corps *Hockey* a team's defencemen collectively.

1962 *Kingston Whig-Standard* (Ont.) 30 Oct. 8/4: . . . the anchor of the blue-line corps was clipped for four stitches above the eye. . . .

blueliner *n. Hockey* See **defenceman**.

1955 *Evening Telegram* (St. John's) 12 Mar. 19/7: This was the final goal of the Amadio blue liner. **1963**

Kingston Whig-Standard (Ont.) 7 Jan. 8/1: Garfield Ball, a rugged blueliner . . . has missed more than his share of games. . . .

bluelinesman *n. Hockey* See **defenceman**.

1955 *Shawinigan Standard* 12 Jan. 6/1: . . . the burly Chicoutimi bluelinesmen thought it most unfair and the fight was on.

bluemilion *n.* [< *blue* + ver*milion*] laundry bluing, used by some Indians as a pigment.

1941 *Beaver* Sep. 36/1: *Bluemilion.* Vermilion powder is expensive. It is mixed with fish oil and used by the Indians for decorating deerskin coats, snowshoes, choice skins, etc. Ordinary laundry blue in cubes is used in conjunction with the former, but when displayed for sale, the name was automatically changed.

Bluenose *n.* [see note below]

☛ *The origin of the term* **Bluenose** *is uncertain, as shown by the following quotation:*

1942 DUNCAN *Bluenose* 187: As for the nickname *Bluenose* itself, the last person to tell you why he is so called is a Nova Scotian.

Some insist that it comes from the kind of potatoes grown in the province, shaped like a human proboscis and unmistakably blue at the tip.

Others believe it to be an outgrowth of the fishing trade, and the naturally resulting color of the noses of fishermen from the North Atlantic winds.

Sir Charles G. D. Roberts . . . claims that a famous Nova Scotia privateer in the War of 1812 had a cannon in her bow which was painted bright blue. She made a great deal of money for the province by intercepting United States vessels, and she was called the "blue nose" by those who had occasion to keep out of her way. So the name became associated in the United States with Nova Scotians.

1 a. *Hist.* a Nova Scotian residing in that province before the American Revolution and the subsequent arrival of the Loyalists.

1785 (1902) *Acadiensis* Jan. 65: The Blue-noses, to use a vulgar appelation, who had address sufficient to divide the Loyalists, exerted themselves to the utmost of their power and cunning. **1898** *New Brunswick Mag.* Dec. 30: The soubriquet "Bluenose" . . . originated with the Loyalists of Annapolis county, who applied it to the pre-loyalist settlers as a term of "derision" during the bitter struggle to pre-eminence in public affairs between these two sections of the population in the provincial election of 1785.

b. any Nova Scotian (the usual modern sense).

1825 *Novascotian* 4 May 148/2: During the course of the past week I had employed . . . a long blue nose to do the odd jobs. **1959** *Northern Miner* 25 June 26/3: [There were] no fights except among the Irish and "Bluenoses" who fight just anywhere.

c. a New Brunswicker.

1845 BEAVAN *Life in Backwoods N.B.* 2: Of the other original settlers [in New Brunswick], or, as they are particularly termed, "blue noses," they are composed of the refugees and their descendents. . . . **1863** SPEDON *Rambles* 77: To call a New Brunswicker a "Bluenose," he appears neither to feel insulted nor a step lowered in dignity. **1957** *Weekend Mag.* 8 June 55/2: "Break out the hook!"—the first bark of a Bluenose mate [a New Brunswicker] drifted from the water to the shore.

2 a. a ship built in Nova Scotia, specifically a sailing schooner.
1908 QUAYSIDER *Recollections* 48: At the age of eighteen I "signed on" as an ordinary seaman on the full-rigged ship *Celestial Burrel*, 1,800 tons register, at the port of Cardiff. She was a Nova-Scotian, or "a blue nose," as they are oft-times called. **1957** *Maclean's* 28 Sep. 68/1: Twenty Bluenose ships were in harbor in Liverpool. . . .

b. See 1949 quote.
1949 LAWSON *N.B.Story* 229: In those old days all the ships of the Maritime Provinces were known among sailors the world over as Bluenoses. **1957** *Weekend Mag.* 15 June 23/1: In great, relishing gulps, the Bluenose timber drogher [of Saint John, N.B.] was eating up the last of her 14,000 miles to Melbourne.

c. a class of sailboat.
1962 *Chronicle-Herald* (Halifax) 11 Aug. 20/5: This event is for Bluenose class boats.

3 *Obs*. See **bluenose potato**.
1843 HALIBURTON *Attaché* 34: Pray Sir . . . can you tell me why the Nova Scotians are called "Blue-noses"? It is the name of a potato . . . which they produce in great perfection. **1863** SPEDON *Rambles* 75: Some have said, that the people received [the name] from their remarkable tenacity to a species of potato, known by the name of "blue-nose". . . .

bluenosed *adj*. of or having to do with Nova Scotia or Nova Scotians.
1869 MCCREA *Lost Amid Fogs* 99: The skipper . . . backing her sails among the little crafts, soon fills up his venture, at a moderate expense, when away he bowls to Halifax or Boston, to join the Yankee or blue nosed cuckoo-traders in growing fat over the helpless sparrows in Newfoundland.

bluenose potato *Obs*. a variety of potato having a bluish tip. See also **Bluenose** (def. 3).
1807 *U.C.Gaz*. (York [Toronto]) 2 May 1/4: Blue Nose Potatoes, To be sold at Mr. Russell's Farm near York. **1843** HALIBURTON *Attaché* 211: . . . a broiled chicken and blue-nose potatoes. **1942** RADDALL *His Majesty's Yankees* 43: . . . he . . . seemed to get a good deal of satisfaction from . . . the sight of my bold Strang nose as blue as a bluenose potato.

Blue Noser See **Bluenose** (def. 1c).
1863 SPEDON *Rambles* 35: I also felt a sort of quivering curiosity to see a New Brunswick "Blue Noser," as very probably he might differ in some respects from our Canadian "Rouges."

Bluenose Special See quote.
1958 *Edmonton Jnl* 23 July 3/3: George A. Mallet . . . is one of two octogenarians taking part in the CNR's annual "Bluenose Special" excursion from the west to the maritimes this year.

blue pickerel a food fish, *Stizostedion glaucum*, related to the walleye, *q.v.*, and found in the lower Great Lakes.
1952 PUTNAM *Cdn Regions* 248/2: In Lake Erie, which is a shallow lake, the most important fish are herring, whitefish, blue pickerel. . . . **1964** *Outdoorsman* Mar. 14/1: The fish population of Lake Erie has been changing in recent years with the emphasis shifting to smelt and yellow perch, from whitefish and blue pickerel.

blue pie *Obs*. See **Canada jay**.
1824 (1955) BLACK *Journal* 165: We have found all over the Blue Pie Common in the Country & generally knowen under the denomination of the Indian Cree term of Wisky Jan.

bluet *n*. [< Cdn F] *Obs*. the blueberry, *Vaccinium canadense*.
1703 LAHONTAN *New Voyages* I 372: The Bluets are certain little berries . . . black and perfectly round. **1830** *Trans.Lit. & Hist.Soc.Que.* III 97: Whortle Berry. Bluet [is] a small shrub about a foot high, bearing clusters of white or pink flowers . . . followed by a small black or bluish fruit. . . .

blue ticket *Yukon* See 1926 quote.
[**1926** MACBETH *Long Day* 115: . . . it was a piece of blue pasteboard, absolutely blank, handed to a girl by the police . . . and it meant that she must get out in 24 hours.] **1938** BLACK *Seventy Years* 137: She was notorious for "rolling," and finally the police "got the goods on her," and she received a summons, which she knew meant the blue ticket. **1958** BERTON *Klondike* 320: A culprit was either given a "blue ticket" to leave town, or he was sentenced to hard labour on the government woodpile.

blue trunk a hope chest.
1915 MCCLUNG *Times Like These* 128: The well-brought-up young lady diligently prepares for marriage . . . gets her blue trunk ready and—waits.

blue wavey or **wavy** See **blue goose**. Cp. **wavey**.
1743 (1949) ISHAM *Observations* 121: Blew wy'wes, so calld, which they style (Kurskatawawawuck) is of a Blewish Colour intermix't with Black and white feathers. . . . **1932** SUTTON *Southampton Is.* 11: He found great numbers of swans nesting at Cape Low, when he landed there in August, 1902: and during the fall of that year saw great quantities of white and blue wavies.

blue wolf a rare color phase of the timber wolf, *q.v.*
1900 FRASER *Mooswa* x: Blue Wolf is also an actuality. Once in a while one of the gray wolves grows larger than his fellows, and wears a rich blue-gray coat. **1921** *Beaver* Apr. 8/1: As regards the wolves, three varieties are usually available: the prairie or coyote wolf, the large grey or timber wolf, and the blue wolf, which is in great demand on account of its colour.

bluff *n*. **1†** a clifflike bank, often wooded, at the edge of a river or lake.
1744 DOBBS *Hudson's Bay* 88: When they got beyond the N.W. Bluff . . . the Current or Fresh suddenly turned against them. . . . **1842** ATKINSON *Emigrant's Guide to N.B.* 64: Opposite Keswick Bluff, there is a large body of intervale on the right bank of the river. . . . **1963** *Beaver* Autumn 19/1: Here, high on a bluff overlooking Georgian Bay, were found the bones of over 700 Hurons.

2 a low, moundlike hill.
1774 *Moose Ft Jnls* (Hearne's Plan of Albany River): Canoe Hummock or Bluff. **1850** GOODSIR *Baffin's Bay* 146: However, we advanced over the crest of the bluffs with rifles ready cocked, expecting every instant to hear the angry growl of bears.

3 a. See 1957 quote. See also **bunch**, *n*. (def. 2), **hummock** (def. 1), **droke island, poplar bluff**, and **wood island**.
1792 (1934) HEARNE & TURNOR *Journals* 470: All the side of the lake passed has a stony shore and mostly covered with small asps with a few bluffs of pine. **1821** (1824) WEST *Substance of a Journal* 31: . . . the country

we passed presented some beautiful points and bluffs of wood. **1862** *Nor'Wester* (R.R.S.) 23 May 3/2: [We camped] at a stagnant pool in the shelter of a bluff of poplar. **1957** ROBBINS *Canada Between Covers* 7: On the prairies you don't have to be much more than a babe in arms to know that a bluff is a grove of trees and to understand that the village names of Oak Bluff in Manitoba and Poplar Bluff in Saskatchewan prove it beyond a doubt. **1959** *Country Guide* Apr. 71/1: The cabin still stood in the bluff above the pass.

b. See quote.
1960 BLONDAL *Candle* 29: The plains had been stripped so badly that few deer roamed in the tiny clumps of brush and bluff.

bluff country *Prairie Provinces* See **parkland** (def. 1).
1886 *Indian* (Hagersville, Ont.) 18 Aug. 186/3: This piece of land, on which there are some 800 Indians, is one of the finest of bluff country in the world. **1964** *Beaver* Spring 6/2: Some forty steps away it [a wolf] lowered its head and stopped; then it turned and moved into higher bluff country.

bluffie *n.* a practice arrow. Cp. **bunt.**
1913 COWIE *Adventurers* 218: Arrows used in such play and practice were called "bluffies," because the business end was bluff—the full size of the willow instead of being pared down to that of the shaft—not pointed.

bluffy *adj.* having numerous groves of trees.
1909 CONNOR *Foreigner* 245: The difficulties of search are enormously increased by the broken character of a rolling bluffy prairie.

board[1] *v.* offer for sale at a dairy board meeting.
1908 *Observer* (Cowansville, Que.) 17 Sep. 5/1: Twenty-four creameries boarded 1211 packages of butter which brought from 24⅛ to 24¾ cents per pound.

board[2] *v.* in hockey or box lacrosse, bodycheck an opponent into the boards, *q.v.*
1955 *Penticton Herald* 9 Mar. ii 5/5: There was a minor flare-up in this game, John and Newton mixing it up a little after the latter was boarded heavily in the second period. **1963** *Kingston Whig-Standard* (Ont.) 6 Mar. 11/4: Buffey later thumbed off Montreal's Henry Richard for boarding Young.

board cradle See **cradle-board** and picture.
1954 CAMPBELL *Nor'Westers* 32: The old folks, Indians and squaws, squatted along the walls amid black-eyed papooses propped up in board cradles.

board hole *Lumbering* a slot cut by loggers in the trunk of a tree and intended to hold the board on which the fellers stand.
1942 SWANSON *Western Logger* 29: But one forked stump, three "board holes" high, Was sure to hang up e'er the turn went by. . . .

board-ice *n. Maritimes* See quotes. See also **shore-ice** (def. 1).
1904 CROSSKILL *P.E.I.* 96: For about a distance of one mile on each side of the Strait, the ice is attached to the shore and is known as the "board ice." Teams carry the passengers from the edge of the board ice to the Railway stations. **1923** *Dalhousie Rev.* III 207: Often it was difficult to effect a landing from the rushing tide full of tumbling bergs to the solid ice—board ice so called—which extends out from either shore.

boarding *n.* in hockey and box lacrosse, the act or practice of bodychecking, *q.v.*, an opponent into

the boards bordering the playing area. See also **board**[2], *v.* and **boards,** *n.pl.*
1962 *Globe and Mail* (Toronto) 28 Dec. 33/1: Duff . . . received a five-minute penalty for boarding. **1963** O'BRIEN *Hockey* 62: They [the penalties] covered, at a glance: fighting, cross-checking, tripping, elbowing, hooking, holding, charging, spearing, high-sticking, butt-ending and boarding.

boarding house agent *Obs.* a person soliciting patronage for a boarding house.
1883 FRASER *Shanty* 351: As he leaps with a light heart and a heavy pocket from the raft on to the shore he is at once beset with a host of hell-runners in the shape of calash drivers, boarding-house agents, brothel sirens, and crimps and sharpers of the blackest stamp.

Board of Broadcast Governors an independent body appointed in 1961 by the Canadian government to regulate broadcasting and telecasting. *Abbrev.* BBG or B.B.G.
1962 *Time* (Cdn ed.) 19 Jan. 9/2: After their first year on the air, Canada's new private TV stations had a sobering report for the Board of Broadcast Governors.

Board of Control in some Canadian cities, an elected group in the field of civic government, comprised of the mayor and a varying number of controllers, *q.v.*
1962 *Globe and Mail* (Toronto) 28 Nov. 7/1: In one of the most closely fought Board of Control races in recent civic election history, nine candidates are in the running. . . .

board of trustees 1† See **school board.**
1811 *Kingston Star* (U.C.) 12 Feb. 2/3: That our public schools may be endowed with preceptors of approved merit, a board of trustees is appointed for each district whose duty it is to select and appoint such only as a good moral character and learned education render eligible.
2 the body responsible for local government in an administrative district, *q.v.*
1952 *North Star* (Yellowknife) Nov. 2/1: We believe that more of value has been accomplished by this year's Board of Trustees than by any Board since that of 1947.

board pine *Hist.* See **waney pine.**
1860 (1945) CALVIN *Saga* 51: In our next raft we shall probably send Canfield's experimental Board Pine, one dram, about 12,000 [cubic feet]. . . . **1945** *Ibid.* 51: . . . Board Pine quickly became one of the main components of the Quebec export timber trade.

boards *n.pl.* **1** the board fence enclosing a hockey rink or box-lacrosse field. See also **sideboards.**
1931 *Vancouver Province* 8 Jan. 10/2: George Sparrow dashed down the right wing boards and sent the rubber home with a tricky shot. **1963** *Hockey Illustrated* Dec. 14/3: But as I skated to pick up the puck, I lost my balance and my head crashed into the boards.
2 the board flooring adjacent to the playing surface of a curling rink.
1911 KNOWLES *Singer* 282: . . . Murray stepped down from the boards on to the ice—a Rockcliffe man was running a narrow port.

boardwood *n.* See **waney pine.**

boat brigade *Fur Trade, Hist.* See **brigade** (def. 1).
*c*1898 (1957) *Beaver* Autumn 13/2: We came across the other Boat Brigades carrying Settlers merchandise some of which had been 2 years in transit! **1921** *Ibid.* Aug.-Sep. 11/2: . . . Moberly took charge of the boat brigade going on the annual trip east to York Factory. . . .

boat encampment *Hist.* a point at the head of navigable water on a river; specifically, the head of navigation of the Columbia River, where it meets the Canoe River.
1827 (1912) ERMATINGER *Express Jnl* 79: Two of our Iroquois . . . carried snow shoes from the Boat Encampment. . . . **1827** (1914) DOUGLAS *Journal* 70: We had the satisfaction of landing at the boat encampment at the base of the Rocky Mountains. **1859** (1863) PALLISER *Journals* 125: In March . . . the express . . . started from Edmonton . . . and continued on to the boat encampment. . . . **1963** *Beaver* Autumn 26/2: Farther south, a route from . . . the Athabasca River led up a feeder stream . . . to join the Columbia River at the northernmost point of the Big Bend at Boat Encampment.

boater *n. Fur Trade, Obs.* See **tripman.**
1804 (1897) COUES *New Light* I 247: Men not so difficult to hire this year as last, when boaters for Lower Red River refused 700 G.P.Cy. and milieux 500, with extra equipments.

boat guide *Fur Trade, Hist.* the man in charge of a brigade of boats. See also **conductor** (def. 1).
1940 *Beaver* Dec. 24/1: Baptiste Bruce, a celebrated boat guide of the North, was in charge.

boatman *n. Fur Trade, Hist.* a voyageur, *q.v.,* especially a man working with the boat brigades of the fur companies.
1816 (1818) HALL *Travels* 128: Having procured two experienced boatmen, with a bark canoe, I ascended the St. Maurice. . . . **1898** (1957) *Beaver* Autumn 13/2: Indians and halfbreeds make first rate Boatmen [on York Boats]. **1957** FISHER *Pemmican* 250: Colin Robertson preferred Iroquois boatmen to any other. . . .

boat song a chanson sung by the voyageurs, *q.v.,* in rhythm with their paddling or rowing. See also **canoe song** and **paddling song.**
1820 WILCOCKE *Death B.Frobisher* 214: He could occasionally join his men in the chorus of some of the voyageurs boat songs, with which they bequiled [sic] the tediousness of the voyage and the labours of the paddle. **1957** FISHER *Pemmican* 176: The HB men could only listen, for they had no boat song of their own.

boat voyaging *Fur Trade, Hist.* See **tripping** (def. 2).

bob *n.* one of the double-runnered sections of a bobsleigh, *q.v.*
1896 GOURLAY *Hist.Ottawa* 138: The bobs were made with short runners six inches wide shod with steel and slid on the snow leaving scarcely a mark. **1964** *Cdn Geog.Jnl* Mar. 86/2: We find that for economy, many carriages could have their wheels and sled runners or "bobs" bolted on to replace them in winter.

bobbing *n. Lumbering* the process of hauling logs on a bobsleigh (def. 1).
1942 KOROLEFF *Skidding of Wood* 5/2: This booklet deals with chain skidding; but much of its advice

applies to other methods in which log carriers of some kind are used (such as "bobbing," "draying," "boganning," etc.). **1944** *Forestry Course I* 90: Bobbing is used for logs and either the front sleigh or a set of hauling sleighs or a specially built bob is used.

bobbing hole See **air hole** (def. 3).
1923 PRATT *Nfld Verse* 21: The "bobbing holes" within the floes / That neither wind nor frost could close. . . .

bob-jacket *n. Obs.* a small linen jacket.
1830 MOORSOM *Letters N.S.* 261: A little bob-jacket of linen cloth, checked blue and white, with a high waist, is covered at the shoulders with a white or coloured handkerchief, pinned neatly behind.

bobskate *n.* a child's skate consisting of two sections of double runners, the sections being joined in such a way as to be adjustable to the size of the wearer's foot. Cp. **bob.**
1961 MITCHELL *Jake and the Kid* 31: When I knew I was going to talk with my dad in England, I didn't care if I used bob skates till I was as old as Jake. **1966** *Globe Mag.* 8 Jan. 8/2: About the same time . . . his parents bought Eddie a pair of bobskates—you know, two runners and you strap them on your boots.

bobsled *n.* **1** See **bobsleigh** (def. 1) and picture.
1872 DASHWOOD *Chiploquorgan* 104: A crew of lumberers have different occupations assigned to them; the "fellers" cut down the trees . . . the "teamster" and his assistants . . . haul them on a "Bob sled"—two sleds working independently and joined by chains. . . . **1959** *Maclean's* 9 May 82/4: A winded horse, his sleighbells jingling, struggled to pull a real bobsled up the icy slope.

2 See **bobsleigh** (def. 3).
1965 BERTON *Remember Yesterday* 72: [Caption] On Montreal's famous mountain park, the tobogganers are as thick as snowbirds. These specially built, specially iced runs will soon be passé—along with the toboggan and the bobsled.

bob-sledge *n. Rare* See **bobsleigh** (def. 1).
1923 WILLIAMS *Spinning Wheels* 74: Down far-away crossroads bob-sledges were coming after the Hillerites.

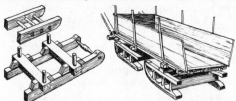

Two kinds of bob   A bobsleigh (def. 1)

bobsleigh *n.* **1** a sleigh made up of one or more (usually two) double-runnered sections called bobs, *q.v.,* having a deck or box mounted on top, long associated with lumbering operations and now also used in tractor trains in the North. See also **bobsled** (def. 1).
1853 STRICKLAND *Canada West* II 283: A large-sized mast, after having been loaded on a bob sleigh, requires from twelve to sixteen span of horses or oxen to draw it. . . . **1961** MITCHELL *Jake and the Kid* 41: . . . her son-in-law took his wife in to have a baby in Crocus, and he made it all right with a bob-sleigh and team.

2 See **bob.**
1873 *Woodstock Sentinel* (Ont.) 12 Dec. 3/2: C. W. Cowan will sell by public auction . . . a good span of

working horses, also a pair of bob sleighs. **1961** PRICE & KENNEDY *Renfrew* 50: Logs were loaded on sleighs (two bobsleighs loosely joined) and hauled to the roll-way.

3 a smaller sleigh having runners and used for coasting and capable of carrying a number of passengers. See also **bobsled** (def. 2).
1958 *Cdn Geog.Jnl* Jan. 4/2: Special events ... include ... bobsleigh races. ...

bobsleigh *v.* use a bobsleigh (def. 3).
1956 KEMP *Northern Trader* 240: Remember Mont and Dennis and I used to bobsleigh down it—and Dad used to worry in case we broke our necks?

bocan(n)e *n.* See **boucan**.

bodewash ['bodə,waʃ] *n.* [alteration of Cdn F *bois de vache*] *Hist.* See **bois de vache**.
1897 COUES *New Light* I 305: We therefore gathered a quantity of dry buffalo dung, (bois de vache or "bodewash"). ... **1953** MOWERY *Mounted Police* 76: If I hadn't heard that crack, we'd all be dead right now! Mashed flatter than a bodewash chip!

bodycheck *n.* in hockey, lacrosse, etc., a defensive play by which a player impedes an opponent's progress by body contact.
1931 *Vancouver Province* 3 Jan. 7/3: ... Sewill twice stopped Cranstoun with stiff body checks. **1963** *Globe and Mail* (Toronto) 14 Mar. 7/7: He says the clean bodycheck has almost vanished. ...

bodycheck *v.* employ a bodycheck.
1963 *Globe and Mail* (Toronto) 14 Mar. 7/7: He says ... players are afraid to bodycheck in case they get a stick in the teeth.

bodychecker *n.* in hockey, lacrosse, etc., a player who checks an opponent by using body contact, especially one skilled at checking in this way.
1957 *Evening Telegram* (St. John's) 17 Dec. 18/5: Barrett [is] one of the circuit's best body-checkers. ... **1964** *Maclean's* 21 Mar. 50/1: Bob Baun [is] a punishing body-checker.

bodychecking *n.* the practice of using bodychecks.
1957 *Record-Gaz.* 19 Dec. 9/2: ... no bodychecking is allowed except by players in their own defensive zone. **1963** *Kingston Whig-Standard* (Ont.) 7 Jan. 8/3: There were lots of goals, hard bodychecking, tremendous goaltending and even a fight.

bogan[1] ['bogən] *n.* [ult. < Algonk.] See quotes. See also **pokelogan**.
1896 *Trans.Roy.Soc.Can.* II 209: bogan—A marshy cove by a stream; called also bogan hole. **1907** HODGE *Bulletin Glossary*: A word very much used by guides and others who go into the New Brunswick woods is *bogan,* a still creek or bay branching from a stream.

bogan[2] ['bɑgən] *n.* [< *toboggan,* q.v.] *Lumbering* a kind of sled used in hauling pulpwood logs. See also **logboggan** and **log sled**.
*c*1939 (1944) *Forestry Course 1* 86: [Caption] Bogan loaded with 4′ bolts [of pulpwood]. **1944** *Ibid.* 89: ... boganning uses a small sleigh (bogan) built in the camp with two natural crook runners made from hardwood trees with a diameter from 6 to 7 inches at breast-height.

boganning ['bɑgəniŋ] *n.* [< *bogan*[2]] *Lumbering* a method of hauling pulpwood. See quotes.
1942 KOROLEFF *Skidding of Wood* 5/2: This booklet

deals with chain skidding; but much of its advice applies to other methods in which log carriers of some kind are used (such as "bobbing," "draying," "boganning," etc.). **1944** *Forestry Course 1* 89: ... boganning uses a small sleigh (bogan) built in the camp with two natural crook runners made from hardwood trees with a diameter from 6 to 7 inches at breast-height. The runners each support three knees, leaning inwards supporting two longitudinal members and cross-members forming a rack. Four-foot wood [pulp sticks] is piled across, a load consisting of 1/3 to 1/2 cord.

bog apple *Obs.* See **bakeapple**.
1823 HALIBURTON *General Descr.N.S.* 34: Bog Apple [*Rubus chamaemorus*].

bog barren *Maritimes* a tract of boggy heath.
1946 BIRD *Sunrise for Peter* 55: Henry loaded his musket with care and led the way to the tip of the bog barren.

bogie or **bogy** ['bogi] *n.* [origin unknown] *Nfld* a small, square stove.
1916 DUNCAN *Billy Topsail* 37: He was discovered hugging a red-hot bogie in his bachelor cottage. ... **1956** STORY *Nfld Dial.Dict.* 5: *bogie,* a small stove used in schooners.

bogus settler a person who takes up land with the pretended purpose of farming it but with the real motive of cutting and selling timber on it; timber pirate. Cp. **lumber squatter**.
[**1883** FRASER *Shanty* 91: ... don't let him attempt to cheat the Government and the merchant by pretending to take out the lot for farming purposes, while all the time he is looking after only the dues on the timber ... pocketing himself a few hundred dollars.] **1936** LOWER *Settlement* 92: ... the chief criticism is that the policy works in favour of that historic figure, the bogus settler, "timber thief" or "timber pirate."

bogy *n.* See **bogie**.

boil *n.* a frost heave.
1955 *Dly Miner* (Flin Flon, Man.) 16 Apr. 6/5: "Boils" are spots where the road has heaved because of the moisture trapped underneath the surface.

boil *v.* See **boil up**.
1933 MERRICK *True North* 39: The famous berry banks are just above Mininipi, and when we went ashore to boil we picked nearly a quart.

boiler *n.* a stretch of seething water, as in a rapids or below a waterfall. See also **boil-up** (def. 1).
1829 MACTAGGART *Three Years* I 95: When a raft of oak arrives at a water-fall, it has to be dragged past it by oxen or horses on the land; for if allowed to run over as other timber is, when it broke up in the cataract and boilers, it would sink. **1889** WITHROW *Our Own Country* 411: Right ahead are seen the white seething "boilers" of the rapids.

boiling-down shack See **sugaring-hut**.
1966 *Kingston Whig-Standard* (Ont.) 19 Mar. 6/8: He noted several farmers ... are using plastic piping to transport the sap from the trees to the "boiling-down" shack.

boiling place 1 See **sugaring-hut**.
1853 STRICKLAND *Canada West* II 302: As soon as the vessel is full of [maple] sap, it is driven to the boiling

place, and emptied into the store-trough.

2 a stopping place on the trail, where the kettle is boiled for tea. See also **boil-up place.**
1956 KEMP *Northern Trader* 218: Perhaps they [wolves] have some doggish instinct or maybe they are just curious; but they certainly like to poke around a camp or a boiling-place after the traveller has pulled away, on the chance of picking up some morsel of food he may have overlooked or discarded.

boil the kettle *North* prepare tea. See **boil up.** See also **kettle²**, and **make tea.**
1785 HUNTER *Diary* 65: At seven we arrived at Pointe au Bodet, where we boiled our kettle and got some milk. **1825** (1931) SIMPSON *Fur Trade* 126: The Weather cold and disagreeable and had much difficulty in collecting sufficient Withered Grass & Horse Dung to Boil our Kettle. **1956** KEMP *Northern Trader* 81: Halfway up the lake we stopped to boil the kettle.

boil-up *n.* **1** See **boiler.**
1912 FOOTNER *New Rivers* 83: We got a bit wet in the boil-up below, but scarcely noticed it in our preoccupation with the whirlpools that were to follow.

2 a stop for tea and a rest on the trail.
1933 MERRICK *True North* 262: Some of the peas we save for Kay to have first thing next evening, or at one of the boil-ups during the day.

boil up stop on the trail to make tea and rest. See also **boil,** *v.*, and **boil the kettle.**
1933 MERRICK *True North* 30: At three we boiled up again. It's wonderful how a cup of tea and a smoke and a rest picks you up. **1943** *Beaver* Mar. 19/1: No let-up in the blustery weather could be predicted, so we "boiled up" to pass the time.

boil-up place See **boiling place** (def. 2).
1933 MERRICK *True North* 52: The most discouraging thing is to fall ... so far behind that when we arrive at a boil-up place, starving for our mug-up, the rest are leaving.

bois blanc *Cdn French* "white wood" *Obs.* basswood or whitewood, *Tilia americana.*
1800 (1897) COUES *New Light* I 112: My men brought a raft of flooring wood of bois blanc split. **1860** (1956) KOHL *Kitchi-Gami* 300: A peculiar Indian mode of cooking turtle is as follows: They thrust a piece of "bois blanc" into the mouth. This wood, when young, contains a sweet and pleasantly tasting pith, of which they also make a soup.

bois-brûlé or **bois-b'rule** ['bwa bru'le] *n.*
[< Cdn F *bois brûlé* charred wood, with reference to the half-breed's dark complexion] *Hist.* a half-breed, *q.v.*, especially one having French blood; Métis. See also **bois grille, Brulé** (def. 1), and **Chicot.**
1815 (1909) BRYCE *Lord Selkirk's Colonists* 120: You will be poor and miserable if the English stay. But we will drive them away, if the Indian does not, for the "Nor'-West" Company and the Bois-brulés are one. **1890** *Cdn Indian* Nov. 33: Bois-brules is explained by referring to the maternal dialect of a large proportion of half-breeds. In the Chippewa [Ojibwa] tongue they are "men partly burnt," *i.e.* tinged with Indian blood, but not quite burned into the coppery complexion. **1960** *Press* Dec. 14: ... the result of the Bay proclamations

was to provoke civil disobedience on the part of the boisbrules and active opposition by the Nor'westers. ...

bois d'arc *Cdn French* "bow wood" *Hist.* the Osage orange, *Maclura pomifera,* used by plains Indians for making bows, and by settlers for hedges.
1858 (1860) HIND *Assiniboine Exped.* I 345: [He was] armed with his bow from the bois d'arc. ... **1953** *Cdn Geog.Jnl* XLVII 229/1: Only a few plants were tried on a large scale, among them ... the Osage orange, or *bois d'arc,* so called because the Indians used it for making their bows.

bois de diable *Cdn French, Obs.* See **devil's wood.**
1825 (1914) DOUGLAS *Journal* 16 Aug. 108: This Acer forms part of the underwood in the pine forests ... 6 to 10 stems rising together which are twisted and crooked in all directions forming growing arches. It is called by the voyageurs *bois de diable* from the obstruction it gives them in passing through the woods.

bois de flèche *Cdn French* "arrow wood" *Obs.* the wood of the saskatoon bush, *Amelanchier canadensis.*
1793 (1933) MACDONELL *Diary* 115: Overtook Mr. Peter Grant and his canoes above the River *au bois de flèche.* **1852** RICHARDSON *Arctic Exped.* 428: Its wood, being tough, is used by the natives for making arrows and pipestems, and has obtained on that account the name of *bois de flèche* from the voyagers.

bois de pelon *Cdn French* "bald wood" *Obs.* See **leatherwood.**
1830 *Trans.Lit.& Hist.Soc.Que.* III 88: Leatherwood, Moosewood, Bois de pelon. A deciduous shrub. ... The whole plant is remarkably pliable, and the bark so strong and flexible as to be frequently used for ligatures, and for straps to carry burdens; it is easily stripped off the plant its whole length when required for use; whence probably the name *Bois de pelon,* usually pronounced *Bois de plomb.*

bois des prairies *Cdn French* "prairie wood" *Obs.* See **bois de vache.**
1859 (1870) SOUTHESK *Saskatchewan* 67: ... dry buffalo dung—"bois des prairies" I believe the French voyageurs call it ... is sometimes also spoken of as buffalo chips.

bois de vache ['bwa də, vaʃ] [< Cdn F, literally "cow wood"] *Hist.* dry buffalo dung used as fuel. See also **bode wash** and **buffalo chip.** Also spelled *bois des vaches.*
1858 (1860) HIND *Assiniboine Exped.* I 343: We kindled a fire with bois de vache, of which there was a vast quantity strewn over the plain. ... **1963** *B.C. Digest* Nov.-Dec. 51/1: In the pre-railway days every traveller on the plains used bois des vaches (buffalo droppings) as fuel, filling it into sacks whenever they found it. ...

bois grille *Cdn French, Obs.* See **bois brûlé.**
1860 (1956) KOHL *Kitchi-Gami* 260: They also call themselves, at times, "Bois brules," or "Bois grillés," in reference to the shades of colour that bronze the face of the mixed breed.

bois inconnu *Cdn French* "unknown wood" *Obs.* the hackberry, *Celtis occidentalis.*
1800 (1897) COUES *New Light* I 155: Bois inconnu is the best wood we have, preferable to birch or any other I know of. It is light, and bends remarkably well. We have none of it N. of this place [45 miles south of Emerson, Man.], but the further S. we go the more plentiful it is. **1951** O'MEARA *Grand Portage* 175: They built snow-shoes of the bois inconnu.

bois picant *Cdn French* "prickly wood" *Obs.*
See **devil's club.**
1793 (1801) MACKENZIE *Voyages from Montreal* 179:
The trees are . . . service tree, bois picant, &c. I never
saw any of the last kind before. It rises to about nine
feet in height, grows in joints without branches, and is
tufted at the extremity . . . it is covered with small
prickles, which caught our trowsers, and working
through them, sometimes found their way to the flesh.
1806 (1960) FRASER *Letters and Journals* 197: . . . with
the exception of the *Bois picant* we saw no other tree or
shrubs.

bois rouge *Cdn French* "red wood" *Obs.* See **red-**
osier dogwood.
1766-8 (1778) CARVER *Travels* 31: About all the great
lakes is found a kind of willow, termed by the French,
bois rouge, in English red wood. 1860 (1956) KOHL
Kitchi-Gami 284: . . . then, a light red willow, called
"bois rouge". . . .

boisson *n.* [< Cdn F *en boisson* drunk] *Fur*
Trade, Hist. a session of heavy drinking that
accompanied the trading activities when Indians
or others visited a post. See also **wabbano** (def. 1b)
and **whisky feast.**
1802 (1897) COUES *New Light* I 196: This was exclusive
of about four kegs of mixed liquor I gave away during
the boisson. . . . 1893 OXLEY *Young Nor'Wester* 60:
There they remained for a fortnight, which was little
better than a prolonged boissons or "drinking match".
. . . 1957 FISHER *Pemmican* 66: David hated trading
because of the grand *wabbana,* the *boisson* or drinking
bout which had become an inseparable part of it.

bois tors *Cdn French* "twisted wood" *Obs.*
bittersweet, a climbing shrub, *Celastrus scandens.*
1801 (1897) COUES *New Light* I 172: There is also an
abundance of bois tors . . . a short shrub that winds up
the stocks of larger trees; the wood is soft and spongy,
with a thick bark, which is often eaten by the natives in
time of famine. 1860 (1956) KOHL *Kitchi-Gami* 284:
They have . . . a creeping plant, called by the Canadians
"bois tors". . . . They smoke the bark. . . .

'boiteau ['bwato] *n.* See **aboiteau.**
1952 RADDALL *His Majesty's Yankees* 175: ". . . Arter
'55 the dikes went down, an' the 'boiteau gates rotted
aout, an' it's on'y lately we've got onto the hang o'
fixin' 'em."

Bo Jo(u) ['bo,ʒu *or* 'bo,ʒõ] [< F *bon jour* good
day] a salutation heard in northern Canada among
Indians, traders, and trappers, long a traditional
greeting.
1837 (1923) JAMESON *Rambles* 291: The form of
salutation in common use between the Indians and
whites is the *bo-jou* borrowed from the early French
settlers. . . . 1903 WHITE *Forest* 97: "Bo' jou', bo' jou',"
we called in the usual double-barrelled North Country
salutation. 1941 *Beaver* Sep. 36/1: "Bo Jo, Bo Jo." An
Indian greeting.

bombardier [,bɑmbə'dir] *n.* [< Armand
Bombardier, of Valcourt, Quebec, the inventor] a
vehicle used for travelling over snow and ice,
equipped with caterpillar tracks at the rear and a
set of skis at the front. See also **skimobile.** Cp.
snowmobile. Also spelled *Bombardier* (originally a
trademark).
1949 *Report of DME Test Team* III 2: DRB Bombardier
snowmobile had two snags drive through [the] bottom
of the vehicle. 1958 *Edmonton Jnl* 24 June 4 16/4:
The Bombardier has the edge from the standpoint of

most drivers . . . because it steers by forward skis,
rather than by its wide tracks. 1962 *Globe and Mail*
(Toronto) 23 Mar. 23/8: We traveled to our fishing hole
in a conveyance known as a bombardier. . . . 1964
Calgary Herald 21 Feb. 19/2: Heated bombardiers
drive their cargo into the packing plants where it is
unloaded and weighed. . . .

A bombardier

bombardier trail *North* a road used by
bombardiers.
1957 *Aklavik Jnl* Feb. 5/2: On the second day he hit
deep snow on the old bombardier trail and was forced
to take snowshoes ahead of his team.

bond *n. Obs.* See **band**[3].

boneyard *n.* **1** *Slang* an old, broken-down horse.
1918 MACKAY *Trench and Trail* 61:

But de glory to God w'en I t'ink of de load
An' de boneyard dat carry it over de road
An' de squeak of de gig, and de squeal of de pig
I don't blame it for laugh w'en he look at de rig.

1920 STRINGER *Prairie Mother* 231: There was a time
when a brave died, they handsomely killed that dead
brave's favorite horse. . . . Now, I find, they have their
doubts, and they pick out a dying old bone-yard whose
day is over. . . .

2 fossil beds, as in the Alberta Badlands.
1962 *Bad Lands of Red Deer River* 29: While on the
trail, to really get the maximum out of the Dinosaur
Boneyards, one should get out of their car and search
for petrified bone and wood specimens.

Bonhomme (Carnaval) *n.* a Quebec City winter-
carnival character.
1963 *Globe and Mail* (Toronto) 1 Feb. 5/1: Bonhomme
Carnaval returned to Quebec tonight none the worse
for his kidnapping by University of Montreal students
24 hours earlier. The Bonhomme—7-foot tall snowman
who symbolizes Quebec City's February winter
carnival [which] includes events ranging from
snowshoe derbies, outdoor dancing, parades, and
ice-canoe races to formal balls. 1964 *College Times* (Pr.
of Wales Coll., Charlottetown) 24 Jan. 4/3: The
appearance here of the Bonhomme in Charlottetown
was a symbol of the good will expressed by Quebec to
us all as we begin our Centennial Year.

Bon Jou See **Bo Jo(u).**

bonne *n.* [< Cdn F] *Obs.* See **pointer** (def. 1) and
picture. See also **bun.**
1891 OXLEY *Chore-Boy* 125: Not much baggage could
be carried so as not to burthen too heavily the three or
four "bonnes," as they call the long, light, flat-bottomed
boats, peculiar to lumbermen. . . .

bonnet bleu *Cdn French* a blue, tasselled tuque, *q.v.,*
traditional wear among rural French Canadians.

1849 ALEXANDER *L'Acadie* II 55: The men are usually clad in thick linen shirts and grey coarse cloth, manufactured by the women; the "bonnet rouge" has now given place to the "bonnet bleu" with a handsome tassel, which has a less republican air than the other. **1853** (1955) CRAIG *Early Travellers* 188: The habitans' [sic] strange dress, with their grey cloth *capots,* with the scarlet sash tied round the waist, and *bonnet bleu,* with Indian moccasins, tastefully worked in beads of various colours, is certainly foreign.

bonnet rouge *Cdn French* a red, tasselled tuque, *q.v.,* traditional wear among rural French Canadians.

1791 (1911) SIMCOE *Diary* 71: The Canadians wear scanty, thick woollen coats, and sometimes leather ones, with hoods to them, over a bonnet rouge, a red bonnet. **1913** PARKER *Money Master* 274: The beaver-hat which Jean Jacques wore on state occasions . . . together with the *bonnet rouge* of the habitant, donned by him in his younger days—they fell to the nod of Mère Langois. . . . **1964** GUILLET *Pioneer Days* 87: The typical costume of the early lumberman,—gray cloth trousers, flannel shirt, blanket coat, fastened around the waist with a red or tri-coloured sash, cow-hide boots with heavy spikes, and a *bonnet rouge* for the head,—formed a picturesque *ensemble.*

bons *n.pl. Obs.* See quote.
1963 *Commercial Letter* Jan. 6/1: An informal paper currency in the form of due bills, called "bons" (an abbreviation of the French "bon pour," and meaning that the notes were good for a specified value) began to be issued by merchants in Lower Canada. *Ibid.* 6/2: These "bons" not only contributed towards filling the urgent need for currency but also helped to pave the way for the subsequent introduction of bank notes.

bonus *v.* offer extra money, property, or stock as an inducement to build or establish something; subsidize.
1883 *Prince Albert Times* (Sask.) 7 Mar. 2/2: In connection therewith it is rumored that the Hudson's Bay Company have bonused the line to the extent of half their land in Goschen. **1896** *Province* (Victoria) 4 Apr. 229/2: The principle of bonussing is abhorrent to most of us. . . . **1955** *Wolfville Acadian* 10 Mar. 4/3: . . . Sweden does bonus milk consumption and . . . most enlightened countries are today seeing that milk . . . is available to schools. . . .

boom[1]† *n. Lumbering* **1** a barrier of logs or other timbers linked by chains and serving to restrain or enclose floating logs, pulpwood, etc. See also **log-boom.**
1828 *Loyalist* (York [Toronto]) 14 June 15/1: The reports from the Coves on the St. Lawrence this morning were distressing, booms broke and timber of an immense value swept adrift. . . . **1831** *Trans.Lit. & Hist.Soc.Que.* II 250: At the head, the lumberers have placed a permanent boom, about three quarters of a mile, and secured midway by two anchors. **1883** FRASER *Shanty* 302: A short distance above the [chute] a strong "boom" is laid across the river in order to keep back the timber, and "knowing hands" are stationed here to let it out gradually, a few sticks at a time. . . . **1958** KELSEY *B.C. Rides a Star* 160: . . . prancing the boom's full length, [he] leaped across water to the back of a recalcitrant log to dance it into place.
2 See **holding boom.**

1805 *Quebec Gaz.* 13 June 1/1: All loose Lumber that may drift upon the said Beach will be taken care of and put within the Boom and delivered to the respective owners on paymenting for trouble and expense. . . . **1846** *Packet* (Bytown [Ottawa]) 21 Nov. 2/7: Timber vessels receiving their cargoes, from any of the coves above the Town, will endeavour to secure a loading berth, as near as possible to the Boom from which they receive their supplies. **1904** ROBERTS *Watchers of Trails* 277: Not for nothing was it, however, that the woodsman had learned to "run the logs" in many a tangled boom and racing "drive." **1964** *Time* (Cdn ed.) 10 July 57/1: In the B.C. coastal waters . . . little "log broncs" herd strays back into the booms. . . .

3 a. a raft of logs or square timber fastened together for transporting by water.
1860 *Islander* (Charlottetown) 13 Oct. 3/4: The booms were broken up and timber cast far up on the beaches, or driven with clipper speed up the Nipisiguit. **1952** GOUGH *Story of B.C.* 185: When the logs are in place, the truck starts off for the booming ground on a lake, a river, or the sea coast where the load is dumped into the water in readiness to be made up into a boom. **1955** CHATTERTON *Canada* 169: So that the logs will not float past the mill they are often made into *booms.* These are made by bringing many logs tightly together. They are held closely packed by outer *boom-sticks.*

A bag boom (def. 3b)

b. a collection of logs or pulpwood gathered to form a tow, *q.v.,* for transporting by water. See also **bag boom, barrel boom, bundle boom, flat boom,** and **raft** (def. 1).
1958 *Evening Telegram* (St. John's) 28 Apr. 5/5: With the drive almost completely underway . . . tug boat engines [will] tow booms of pulpwood to the Exploits Dam. . . .

boom[1] *v. Lumbering* **1** gather or confine (logs, pulpwood, etc.) in a holding boom, *q.v.* See also **boom**[1], *n.* (def. 2).
1883 FRASER *Shanty* 281: The first business of the drive is to collect all these scattered timbers, and "boom" them into the main channel of the river, that is, confine them there. . . . **1966** *Victoria Daily Times* 26 July 7/1: He says he will chip only the small-diameter logs (normally unmarked) and boom the larger floating logs for sale through the gulf log salvage.

2 move or transport logs by means of a raft or tow. See also **boom**[1], *n.* (def. 3).
1933 MERRICK *True North* 347: I've spent some lovely times . . . booming logs, long lonely summer days, on the river, making the water carry on its back tons of wood for puny me. **1958** *Arctic Spotter* Feb. 17/3: The logs were boomed across the water, and there dressed by the sawmill for later use.

boom[2] *n. Rare* the horizontal pieces of a rail fence, *q.v.*
1932 JAMIESON *Cattle in the Stall* 75: There was the rustle fence, with boom on top and centre; the straight rail fence. . . .

boom[3]† *n.* a sudden increase in business activity; entry into a period of prosperity.

1882 *Edmonton Bull.* 3 Feb. 3/1: Winnipeg in common with other Manitoba towns, has been enjoying an unprecedented boom in real estate, and prices have been soaring in the skies. 1964 *Maclean's* 25 Jan. 7/2: The Hamilton Falls power project . . . isn't the first boom that Peter Newman has written about.

boom[3]† *v.* 1 go ahead rapidly in business activity and prosperity.
1882 *Edmonton Bull.* 3 Feb. 3/2: The immediate building of the road would cause this place to boom right along for a while. 1953 *North Star* (Yellowknife) July 2/3: The country . . . sure is booming!

2 call attention to, with a view to inducing investment in or support of, as a town, a company, property; promote.
1883 *Moose Jaw News* (Sask.) 2 Nov. 4/1: Their town is all the better for not having been "boomed" to any considerable extent. 1958 HARRIS & HAWTHORNE *New Denver* 12/2: We had "Windy Young"of The Slocan Bellows trying frantically to boom Slocan city. . . .

boom boat See **log bronc.**
1966 *Cdn Geog.Jnl* June 214/3: Log booms, loose logs, and boom boats were swept out of the bay.

boom camp the camp at a booming ground, *q.v.*
1942 HAIG-BROWN *Timber* 249: Headquarters camp, which is usually also the boom camp, where the logs are dumped from the trains into the salt water, is for this reason likely to be referred to as "the Beach."

boomcat *n. Slang.* See **boom-man.**
1957 BARRATT *Coronets* 245: He had gone native, in the manner of many of the second and third generation Longstockings, working in the logging camps as a boomcat while in his teens and speaking with a Canadian accent.

boom chain a chain linking two boomsticks or boom timbers, *qq.v.*
1883 FRASER *Shanty* 281: The first business of the drive is to collect all these scattered timbers, and "boom" them into the main channel of the river, that is, confine them there by long half-square logs called "boom timber," fastened at the ends by "boom chains." 1956 RADDALL *Wings* 186: . . . a small pile of boom chains abandoned on the shore for some reason [was] now a rusty lump.

boom company a company that contracts to build and tow booms (def. 3).
1897 *Rat Portage* [Kenora] *News* (Ont.) 7 July 1/2: When it is known that almost all the logs sawn at Norman, Rat Portage and Keewatin, are handled by the boom company it will be easily understood that it is work of no little importance. 1955 *North Shore Leader* 18 Mar. 7/4: They were on their way to work at the boom house of the Restigouche Boom Company.

boom crew a gang of boom-men, *q.v.*
1964 *Atlantic Advocate* July 60/2: The pulp mill now is employing on an average 475 to 500 men, without the river and boom crews being taken into account.

boom dozer *West Coast* See **log bronc.** See also **boom scooter** and **dozer boat.**
1958 *Sun* (Vancouver) 9 Dec. 48/1: The ugly vessel [the tug "Snauq") is 22 feet long, almost as wide, and too high for her length. She is what is known as a "boom dozer," popular up and down the coast for working around the [log] booms.

boomed *adj.* brought to public notice; promoted; boosted.
1891 *Grip* (Toronto) 9 May 300/2: Miss Tempest was as handsome as much boomed stage beauties usually are. . . . 1929 JOHNSTON *Beyond Rockies* 112: It has succeeded in living down its notoriety as the most-boomed town in North America. . . .

boomer† *n.* 1 a person who boosts or promotes a town, undertaking, etc. See also **boom**[3], *v.* (def. 2).
1889 (1964) *Calgary Herald Mag.* 13 June 8/6: A Herald reporter was told . . . that the amount of badgering and lying they were subjected to by land speculators and professional boomers along the line . . . was simply torturing. 1898 *Yukon Midnight Sun* (Dawson) 27 Aug. 1/5: At Edmonton he met the effusive and erstwhile boomer, Macdougal, the mayor of the town.

2 a person who moves from one job to another, originally one who took advantage of boomer days.
1893 (1955) MCKELVIE *Pageant of B.C.* 253: "Boomers" of every description were seen coming down the hills and up the valleys. 1960 *Sun* (Vancouver) 19 Apr. 4/2: About one in ten was a boomer, seldom staying in town longer than was required to stake himself to a move to the town beyond. . . . 1966 *Islander* 27 Feb. 13/3: It was the next year, 1866, that . . . Allan arrived in Barkerville with another boomer called Warren Lambert.

boomer days prosperous times, when employment opportunities are exceptionally good.
1948 MOIR *Sinners and Saints* 123: We had some trouble keeping our [telegraph] operators, it being what was called "boomer days," when a man who had any experience could jump his job at will and secure employment with our competitors. . . .

boom-house *n.* a shanty on a log raft or floating wharf, used by boom-men, *q.v.*
1896 ROBERTS *Camp-Fire* 179: Just above the upper end of the wing-boom, at a place widened out a few feet to receive it, was built a little shanty known as a boom-house. 1955 *North Shore Leader* 18 Mar. 7/4: They were on their way to work at the boom house of the Restigouche Boom Company.

booming† *adj.* moving ahead rapidly; growing prosperously and fast.
1882 *Brandon Mail* (Man.) 19 Dec. 3/1: Winnipeg is a "booming" town, but much given to blow. 1965 *Star Wkly* 2 Jan. 37/2: [The] citizens could almost see the reflection of booming Penticton's city lights.

booming *n. Lumbering* the practice of penning logs in booms, *q.v.* See also **logbooming.**
1958 HAWTHORN *Indians of B.C.* 128: The few Indians employed by sawmilling enterprises on the Coast work in local plants situated on tidewater, as in North Vancouver and Port Alberni. They are concentrated in booming and to a lesser extent, green chain and loading gangs, which are about the only jobs in sawmilling that fulfil their preferences for outdoor work. . . . 1965 DOUGLAS *Logging* 3: Clear cut, thinning, pre-logging and salvage operations will be explained [at logging school] as will be the layout of a high lead setting, road grading, industrial road driving and booming.

booming ground[1]† the mating place of prairie chicken, *q.v.*, so called because of the booming sound made by the males.

1962 *Kingston Whig-Standard* (Ont.) 6 Dec. 4/6: In the case of the prairie chicken, the bird likes open ground near the nesting places as "booming sites." In the spring the male birds congregate on the booming grounds to go through the courtship ritual. . . . Hens later walk on the booming grounds and select a male.

booming ground(s)[2] *Lumbering* that part of a river, lake, or ocean where logs are dumped to be gathered into booms (def. 3), or where booms and rafts of logs are held. Cp. **holding boom.**

1883 *Selkirk Herald* (Man.) 22 June 3/2: The raft has now been placed in the "booming" ground in the slough above the mill. **1958** ELLIOTT *Quesnel* 184: . . . Pacific Veneer acquired two acres of land at the junction of the Quesnel and Fraser rivers for use as booming grounds for peeler logs, a collecting place for shipment to Vancouver. **1963** MCKINNON *Forest Activities 1* 10: Truck-load of logs ready for dumping at the booming-ground.

booming place See **booming ground**[2].

1883 *Selkirk Herald* (Man.) 4 May 2/2: The slough south of the mill site becomes narrower for a short distance and then widens out into another deep bay, and forms a natural booming place for millions of logs.

boomlet *n.* a short-lived period of prosperity or increased business activity; a minor boom.

1900 OSBORN *Greater Canada* 68: After all, the Edmonton district is as good as most, and not many suffered loss when the bottom fell out of the boomlet, while the Canadian Pacific Railway sold thousands of acres at prices as high as fifteen dollars an acre. **1940** MACCORMAC *Canada* 269: She [Canada] benefitted from the 1937 boomlet in the United States and did not react so decidedly in 1938.

boom-man *n.* a man who works on or with booms, *q.v.*, of logs. See also **boomcat** and **cat walker.**

1908 GRAINGER *Woodsmen* 28: The work for a practiced boom-man, was now to take a long, light pole, and jumping upon a floating log, to stand upon the log and pole it into the boomstick enclosure. **1932** *Lumber Worker* Sep. 11/1: The whole crew is to get 57½ cents per thousand, this is to be divided among all the workers in the mill from the boomman to loading shingles on kiln trucks. . . . **1966** *Sun* (Vancouver) 30 May 26A: [Caption] THE BIG PUSH of boom men starts logs on way to mill. . . .

boom pool See **pond** (def. 3).

1966 *Dly Colonist* (Victoria) 27 Feb. 8/2: Cross the bridge and keep left for the pump house and boom pools.

boom scooter *West Coast* See **log bronc.** See also **boom dozer.**

1964 *Dly Colonist* (Victoria) 27 Sep. 36/2: . . . a powered boom scooter rides herd on logs in the water where the timber used to be shoved around by a man with caulk boots, a pike pole and the agility of a cougar.

boomster *n.* **1**† a person who creates enthusiasm for an undertaking; a promoter; boomer (def. 1).

1908 MAIR *Mackenzie Basin* 86: Between seven and

eight hundred people had gone up to these regions *via* Edmonton, bound for the Yukon, many of whom, after a tale of suffering which might have filled its boomsters' souls with remorse, had found solitary graves. . . .

2 one of the crowd of people who flock to an area that is booming.

1928 FREEMAN *Nearing North* 52: And so the boomsters fought their way out of the congested purlieus of Saskatchewan and southern Alberta to find breathing-room in the great open spaces of the Peace and the Athabaska.

boomstick† *n. Lumbering* **1** one of the logs or timbers that form a boom (def. 1). See also **boom timber.**

1908 GRAINGER *Woodsmen* 28: The work for a practiced boom-man, was now to take a long, light pole, and jumping upon a floating log, to stand upon the log and pole it into the boomstick enclosure. **1965** *Western Wonderland* Apr. 22/1: . . . the nine sorting categories [of logs] are: hemlock sawlogs . . . peewees . . . and lastly boomsticks.

2 See 1942 quote.

1942 HAIG-BROWN *Timber* 249: BOOMSTICK. A log cut 60-80 feet long instead of the usual 32-40. Coupled by chains passed through holes bored at each end, these hold together rafts of logs to be towed to the mills. **1955** [see cite at **boom**[1], *n.* (def. 3a)].

boom timber See quote.

1883 FRASER *Shanty* 281: The first business of the drive is to collect all these scattered timbers, and "boom" them into the main channel of the river, that is, confine them there by long half-square logs called "boom timber," fastened at the ends by "boom chains."

boondoggle *n.* a device used to take up the slack in a chin-strap, such as a large wooden bead, or a woven knot such as a Turk's head.

1957 *Maclean's* 9 Nov. 62/3: . . . all wore black peaked caps similar to taxi drivers', except that these have a strap under the chin secured by a boondoggle, such as is worn on a cowboy's chinstrap.

booseman *n. Obs.* See **bowsman.**

1886 SCUDDER *Winnipeg Country* 21: He next selected . . . the "booseman," who must be a quick-eyed fellow, ready in emergencies, especially upon the river. . . .

booshway ['buʃwe] *n.* [< Cdn F *bourgeois*] See **bourgeois** (def. 1).

1952 HAYCOX *Earthbreakers* 172: When it was all over the booshway—the leader of the party—came into the tent and gave Kimmel hell.

bordage ['bɔrdɪdʒ] *n.* [< Cdn F < F *bord* river bank + -*age*] See 1807 quote. See also **ice-shelf** (def. 2).

1807 HERIOT *Travels* 267: The ice on the rivers in Canada acquires a thickness of two feet and upwards and is capable of supporting any degree of weight. That on the borders of the St. Lawrence, called the *bordage,* sometimes exceeds six feet. **1849** ALEXANDER *L'Acadie* II 315: We pushed it over the bordage, and launched it in the current. . . . **1898** *Trans.Roy.Soc.Can.* II 4 237: It was to the packing of these leagues of bordage ice . . . that the winter rise of the water was attributed.

Bordeau(x) ['bɔrdo] *n.* [< F] an inferior grade of beaver pelt.

c1735 (1899) WILLSON *Great Company* 238: The beaver . . . was classified into eight varieties. [Third] came in order the dry winter beaver, and the Bordeau, both worth three shillings and sixpence [a pound].

1844 DOBBS *Hudson's Bay* 26: The third the dry Winter Beaver, and fourth the Bordeau, is much the same. . . . **1912** ROE *Whispering Hills* 157: Such furs! Beaver in countless packs, all the fat winter skins,—no Bordeaux, no Mittain.

border *n.* the boundary between Canada and the United States. See also **across the border, boundary,** and **line,** *n.* (def. 2).
1852 *Toronto Mirror* 24 Sep. 3/2: Our neighbors from "over the border" make a respectable appearance, and our Canadian friends are extremely commendable. **1957** *Pacific Tribune* (Vancouver) 18 Oct. 5/3: . . . the supermen south of the border have been heaving the old bull around with unscientific abandon.

borrow pit a pit from which fill is taken as ballast for road and railway building.
1961 *Cdn Geog.Jnl* Jan. 15/1: As much of the embankments crossed wide muskegs, they were built of organic materials excavated from the side borrow pits.

boss *n.* the spinous process on the vertebrae in the hump above the shoulders of a buffalo, much prized as a delicacy. See also **boss rib, buffalo boss, buffalo hump, bunch** (def. 1), **grosse bosse, hump,** *n.* (def. 1), **hunch,** and **wig.** Cp. **petite bosse.**
1801 (1933) MCLEOD *Diary* 155: Collin & the men came back[;] the[y] brought 40 Bladders grease[,] a little pounded meat & the rest of their loads were made up with Bosses & Depouilles. **1887** *Senate Report* 184: The best parts, such as ribs, boss, and backfat, are dried and eaten that way. **1957** *Cdn Hist.Rev.* June 130: The back or boss and tongues were preserved as a great delicacy.

bossbone *n.* any one of several vertebrae forming the boss of the buffalo, used by the Indians for a number of purposes.
1890 MAIR *American Bison* 105: A fluffy or wool-like surface was given to the [buffalo] pelt by rubbing it with a boss-bone or rough stone.

boss-bully *adj.* best, foremost.
1942 CAMPBELL *Thorn-Apple Tree* 119: "You sing, Janet," suggested one. "Sure, we've heard you're the boss-bully singer of the countryside."

boss dog the dog in a dog-team recognized by his owner and his team-mates as the "boss," usually the strongest and most dominant, and usually harnessed nearest the sled. See **steer-dog.**
1942 *Beaver* Mar. 31/2: The boss dog of the team is fed first or else he gives the others no rest until he has had his share. **1942** TWOMEY & HERRICK *Needle to the North* 18: The lead dog pulls on the longest line, far in front of the others; the boss dog pulls nearest the sled and in the midst of the rest.

boss hurdy *Hist.* the manager of a group of hurdy-gurdies (def. 1). Cp. **hurdy.**
1866 *Cariboo Sentinel* (Barkerville, B.C.) 6 Sep. 3/4: They [Hurdy-gurdy girls] are generally brought to America by some speculating, conscienceless scoundrel of a being commonly called a "Boss Hurdy." This man binds them in his service until he has received about a thousand percent for his outlay.

boss logger *Lumbering, Esp.West* a superintendent or manager of a logging outfit; the owner-manager of a small logging outfit.
1908 GRAINGER *Woodsmen* 12: There was a boss logger on board who had been obliged to stop work by the police—they said he had been taking logs from a pulp concession. **1942** HAIG-BROWN *Timber* 229: Just because Ted was a camp-push they'd try to make out he was the same as a boss logger.

boss rib See **boss.**
1914 STEELE *Forty Years* 85: Large quantities of fresh buffalo tongues, humps or "boss ribs," as they were called . . . were purchased. . . . **1918** SCHULTZ *Rising Wolf* 236: Then Little Wolf's wives returned . . . and set food before us . . . big wooden bowls full of boiled boss ribs of buffalo.

Boston *n.* [< Chinook Jargon < Cdn F *Bostonais* an American, orig. a New Englander] *Hist.* on the Pacific Coast, a person from the United States, as opposed to an Englishman or Canadian. See also **Boston man.** Cp. **Bostonnais** (def. 1) and **King George.**
1813 (1945) *B.C.Hist.Qtly* Jan. 4: "Ah," he cried, to Captain Black, spreading a fine sea-otter skin upon the deck, "the Bostons are brave, but they have no ships like this [H.M.S. *Raccoon*]." **1846** *St.Catharines Jnl* (C.W.) 26 Feb. 2/4: When told that the greater part of the chiefs in King George's country, as well as in that of the Boston's, drank, now, nothing stronger than water—he seemed to have a very contemptible opinion of their taste. **1860** *British Colonist* (Victoria) 21 Aug. 3/1: He stated that . . . the King George people . . . would not let the Bostons hurt him.

Bostonais *n.* See **Bostonnais.**

Boston clothing *Obs.* white man's dress. See also **Boston.**
1870 *Mainland Guardian* (New Westminster, B.C.) 16 Apr. 3/3: In the crowd behind are a few dusky natives in Boston clothing . . . some with the remains of an old coat and beaver hat, and some almost naked savagedom.

Boston man *Hist.* See **Boston.**
1829 *Fort Langley Jnl* 28 Aug. 143: Had a visit from a number of Sinnahomes . . . [who] propagate no good here by their continual boasting of Boston man's liberality. **1926** MACINNES *Chinook Days* 27: It was after this affair with the Boston, that all Americans became known in Chinook as Boston men. . . . **1958** *Beaver* Summer 10/2: Moody . . . said that in his grandfather's day three "Bostonmen" (Americans) had a trading post here [Bella Coola River, B.C.].

Bostonnais ['bɑstə,nez] *n.* [< Cdn F *Bostonais*] Also spelled *Bastonnais, Bostonais, Bostonnois.* *Hist.* **1** a person from the United States; a United States citizen. See also **Boston people.** Cp. **Boston.**
1785 HUNTER *Diary* 58: The Bostonnais, as the men call them, have a house here which contains a fine woman and some very fine children. **1808** *Cdn Courant* (Montreal) 18 April 2/2: The pious and loyal Canadian . . . remembers his wars with the Bostonnais. **1963** MORTON *Kingdom of Canada* 164: The Canadians were not moved to spring to arms against this renewed attack; in a quarrel of the English and the "Bastonnais," their interest was uncertain.

2 See **Boston pedlar** (def. 1).
1776 (1901) HENRY (Elder) *Travels* 337: On my remarking to Mr. Frobisher, that I suspected the Bastonnais had been doing some mischief in Canada, the Indians directly exclaimed, "Yes; that is the name, *Bastonnais.*" **1897** *Rev.Hist.Pubs* I 142: It is amusing to read that the American traders, who originally were chiefly from New England, were known by the savages

of the Pacific coast as "Bosten-men," even as the same enterprising traders were known to the French in Canada invariably as "Bastonnais." **1908** LAUT *Conquest N.W.* II 364: Shall we kill—is it good we kill—these Bostonais who come to take our lands?

Boston name *Obs.* on the Pacific Coast, an English word or name as opposed to one that is Indian.
1880 GORDON *Mountain and Prairie* 58: Some of them had retained their old Indian names, some had received "Boston" names, as English words are commonly called by the Coast Indians.

Bostonnois *n.* See **Bostonnais.**

Boston pedlar *Hist.* **1** an American trader, especially on the Pacific Coast. See also **Bostonnais** (def. 2).
1944 *Beaver* Sep. 45/1: Beset by competition on all sides—by the Russians from the north, by the "Boston pedlars" from the sea and by the St. Louis traders from the east—the task seemed almost hopeless.
2 the vessel of such a trader. See also **Yankee pedlar.**
1921 *Beaver* Nov. 2/2: . . . the involved shore line of our province [B.C.], was exploited by the itinerant trading vessels from Boston—"the Boston Peddlers" as they were sneeringly denominated.

Boston people *Obs.* See **Bostonnais** (def. 1).
1846 *Hunt's Merchants' Mag.* XVI 536: Had anyone spoken to them of *American* ships or *American* people, he would not have been understood. We were only known as Boston ships and Boston people. **1923** BARBEAU *Indian Days* 10: . . . he was to show the portraits of all the important Indians to the *King George* and the *Boston* people.

Boston ship *Hist.* an American ship.
1846 *Hunt's Merchants' Mag.* XVI 536: Had anyone spoken to them of *American* ships or *American* people, he would not have been understood. We were only known as Boston ships and Boston people. **1859** (1956) *Beaver* Summer 45/2: They report, having lately visited Victoria, . . . that four Boston ships were here trading furs. **1964** *Fort Langley* 10: . . . he [Geo. Simpson] decided the Hudson's Bay Company should extend its operations along the Pacific Coast and end the competition of the Boston ships.

Boston States *Maritimes* New England.
1948 MACNEIL *Highland Heart* 71: And she would tell of her correspondence, although no one ever saw a letter, with the young bloods of her day, now residing in the Boston States.

botte française *Cdn French* "French shoe" a boot or shoe of tanned leather, as opposed to the soft leather moccasin of the Indians and coureurs-de-bois. Cp. **botte sauvage.**
1889 *Scribner's Mag.* May 530/1: Home-made trousers of the home-woven gray woolen *étoffe du pays* tucked into the wrinkled legs of the long moccasins tied below the knee, which, in contradiction to town-made "bottes françaises," are known as "bottes sauvages."

botte sauvage *Cdn French* "Indian boot" See **Canadian shoe.** Cp. **botte française.**
1889 *Scribner's Mag.* May 534/1: His bottes sauvages, in odd contrast with cassock and birette, show that he has just come in from a long tramp. . . . **1928**

LEROSSIGNOL *Beauport Road* 237: Leon was well prepared for that with his thick coat, his *capuchon,* his *bottes sauvages,* and a good flask of *eau-de-vie.* . . . **1955** COLLARD *Cdn Yesterdays* 287: The canotiers always wore tall boots called "bottes sauvages". . . .

bottom† *n.* the level, low-lying land bordering a stream; interval, *q.v.* See also **flat** (def. 1) and **river flat.**
1793 *Ont.Bur.Arch.Rep.* III 230: The Bottoms or flat lands are overflowed and covered with drifted Wood, the upland only produces White Oak. **1920** FOOTNER *Fur-Bringers* 25: Beyond the fields she could gallop at will over the rolling, grassy bottoms among the patches of scrub and willow.

bottom *v. Placer Mining* excavate down to bed-rock (def. 1).
1869 *Mainland Guardian* (New Westminster, B.C.) 28 Aug. 3/2: It is strange, with the well-known proximity of rich quartz beds in Snowshoe mountain, that Snowshoe creek has never been bottomed. **1900** OSBORN *Greater Canada* 94: There are also many valleys where, though the bed of the existing stream has proved rich in gold, the old channel has never been "bottomed."

bottom bark *Hist.* birch bark of especially high quality, used for the underside of bark canoes, *q.v.* Cp. **side bark.**
1820 (1963) DAVIES *Northern Quebec* 42: One canoe sewed and taken off the bed. The bottom bark of the other laid. **1822** (1940) *Minutes of Council* (H.B.C.) 27: That the following prices be allowed for Country produce . . . Birch Bottom Bark 3*s.* and side Do. 1*s.* 6*d.* **1922** *Beaver* June 6/2: Bark at one time was an important article of trade, and large quantities were collected at the more important posts and canoe building centres for local use as well as shipment to posts unable to obtain it from the surrounding country. It is designated as "side bark" and "bottom bark."

bottom ice See 1958 quote. See also **anchor ice** and **batture** (def. 4). Cp. **frazil.**
1922 *Beaver* Aug. 12/1: Just then the bottom ice I was standing on gave way and down I went. . . . **1958** *Manice* 6: Bottom ice—Ice that has formed on the bottom of shallow rivers and bays [and risen to the surface in great sheets with the coming of warm water], usually identified by the great amount of dirt and grit frozen to it.

boucan [bu'kæn] *n.* [< Cdn F *boucan* place or device for smoking meat] Also spelled *bocanne,* *bocane.* See quotes.
1888 (1948) *Beaver* Dec. 14/1: They passed the *boucannes,* burning seams of lignite. **1894** *Outing Mag.* Nov. 130/1: About ten miles above Fort Norman [N.W.T.] we landed for wood, at the "bocanes." **1909** CAMERON *New North* 200: We came in view of the "boucans" or beds of lignite coal which have been continuously burning here since Mackenzie saw them in 1789 and mistook their smoke for tepee fires.

boudet *n.* [< Cdn F *baudet*] *Obs.* a portable, folding, canvas cot.
1794 (1911) SIMCOE *Diary* 249: The baggage boat was not arrived from Gananowui, and my boudet or canvas stretcher lay in it, I was at a loss what to sleep on. . . . *Ibid.* 256: After drinking tea . . . I dress my hair . . . and lay down on a boudet (or folding bed) before the fire, covered with a fur blanket.

boueau [bu'o] *n.* See quote.
1952 HOWARD *Strange Empire* 335: Unfortunately the prized *boueau*—literally "slop" or "filth"— was now

hard to get. It was a stew of buffalo pemmican and potatoes, and probably got its name from the fact that careless cooks often left some buffalo hair in the pot.

bough bed a makeshift bed in which evergreen boughs function as a mattress, used by Indians, campers, etc. See also **browse bed** and **brush bed.**
1920 MCKOWAN *Graydon* 242: ". . . they don't want to wait around while their guide wastes time making up a fussy bough bed." **1937** *Beaver* Sep. 10/2: . . . the Indians put up tents and build bough beds. . . . **1953** LOWER *Voyages* viii: . . . I can split wood, make a bough bed, snare a rabbit, run a rapids. . . .

bouillon ['bufjɑn *or* 'bujɑ; *French* bu'jõ] *n*. [< Cdn F < F "broth"] a kind of stew.
1887 *Senate Report* 170: In the palmy days when meat was plentiful, the Indians were in the habit of collecting this root [wild turnip, or buffalo root]; as well as being eaten fresh, they used to pound it up and dry it, when it resembled arrow-root; it was then used in thickening their bouillon. **1903** WHITE *Forest* 345: . . . big, medium, and little fellows [trout] mingled in component of the famous North Country *bouillon*, whose other ingredients are partridges, and tomatoes, and potatoes, and onions, and salt pork, and flour in combination delicious beyond belief.

boulder ice large chunks of ice left in a stream bed after a fall in the water level.
1921 *Beaver* May 10/1: . . . the river had fallen about twelve feet since freeze-up and was one mass of boulder ice.

boulder pool a pool scattered with boulders forming lurking places for trout.
1964 *Vancouver Province* 14 Feb. 18/3: Boulder pools have good cutthroat populations in season. . . .

boulevard *n*. **1†** a wide, paved street, usually flanked by strips of grass and rows of shade trees.
1903 *Bond of Brotherhood* 21 Nov. 3/2: Let us have safe streets first; boulevards afterwards. **1906** *Eye Opener* (Calgary) 6 Oct. 4: A magnificent Government boulevard, 200 feet in width, which will eventually be the coaching road to Banff, fronts this property. **1958** *Edmonton Jnl* 28 June 26/3: About 10 years ago the parks department [of Edmonton] began removing poplars from the boulevards and replacing many of them with elms. . . .

2 the strip of grass between the curb and the sidewalk, often furnished with trees.
1891 *Grip* (Toronto) 9 May 297/2: ". . . I saw fish come up oot o' the hydrant an' the cat was eatin' ane o' them on the boolyvard." **1912** BICKERSTETH *Open Doors* 104: The Edmonton . . . streets are beautifully laid out in boul-ey-vards (so pronounced). A boulevard is a street with six feet of grass and a row of trees on each side of the road between it and the paths. **1964** *Oak Bay Leader* (B.C.) 5 Feb. 1/2: We cannot allow frontagers to tell us what will be done with the boulevard.

3 the centre strip of grass, concrete, etc. separating the lines of traffic on a highway or street; median. See also **centre boulevard.**
1958 *Edmonton Jnl* 23 July 3/6: Police said Grasdal's car straddled the centre boulevard near 111 Ave.
1960 *Ottawa Citizen* 15 Sep. 12/5: Following are excerpts from By-Law No. 330-60 of the Corporation of the City of Ottawa. . . . No person shall stop any vehicle on any street . . . adjacent to either side or the ends of any middle boulevard or centre strip separating two roadways. . . .

boulevard *v*. furnish with the characteristics of a boulevard.
1906 *Eye Opener* (Calgary) 6 Oct. 2/5: Say, why don't you boolyvard your streets? **1951** GILLIS & MYLES *North Pole* 6: . . . surprisingly enough, waving maple trees lined two or three boulevarded streets of attractive modern homes.

boulevard strip See **boulevard,** *n*. (def. 2).
1959 *Ottawa Citizen* 1 Apr. 2/1: Prohibition of parking on boulevard strips adjoining sidewalks and boulevards in the center of streets is to be covered in a bylaw to be drawn up by the city.

boundary *n*. See **border.**
1889 DONKIN *Trooper* 270: . . . I left our camp at 8 a.m. in charge of a patrol to the Manitoba boundary. **1923** STEELE *Spirit-of-Iron* 89: He's the biggest horse-thief, cattle-rustler and whisky-smuggler this side of the boundary.

Boundary Country See quotes.
1927 NIVEN *Wild Honey* 131: Boundary Country— Southern Okanagan near U.S. Boundary. . . . **1964** *Sun* (Vancouver) 3 July 6/1: But the Boundary country runs east-west in a narrow strip along the U.S. border, the only real connecting link the Okanagan has with the Kootenays.

Bouquet Sou *Hist*. See quote.
1963 *Commercial Letter* Jan. 7/1: During the period (1820-1840) banks and merchants in Lower Canada also issued a series of sou tokens which were known as Bouquet Sous, from the bouquet of flowers, leaves and wheat on the obverse.

bourassa [bə'ræsə] *n*. [< Cdn F, prob. after the original grower] a variety of eating apple well known in early Canada; also, the tree.
1806 *Quebec Gaz.* 11 Dec. 4/1: The said ground being planted with fruit trees . . . of the best quality, being chiefly bourassa, gris and fameux. **1864** *Canada Farmer* 1 July 188/2: The varieties most cultivated are the Fameuse, St. Lawrence, Pomme Gris, and Bourassa. . . . **1965** [see quote at **gris**].

bourdigneau *n*. [< Cdn F] *Hist*. See 1950 quote. See also **bourdion** and **ice-bank.**
1859 (1925) KANE *Wanderings* 253: . . . how happy I was when I lay down and slept again, instead of clambering over the rugged bourdigneaux! **1950** WHITE in THOMPSON *Journals* 70n: The voyageurs used the term *bourdigneaux* for the perpendicular ridges of ice along rivers.

bourdion *n*. *Cdn French* See **bourdigneau.**
1939 *Beaver* Sep. 13/2: It would be almost impossible to travel over the vast masses of tossed-up ice. . . . As I had . . . already had some experience of *bourdions* I acted on his advice.

bourg *n*. [< F] *Hist*. especially in Quebec, a village, town, or settlement.
1764 *Quebec Gaz.* 26 July 3/1: The said Fief runs . . . from the Brink of the River St. Lawrence to the square Tract of the Royal Borough (or Bourg Royal). . . . **1889** WITHROW *Our Own Country* 223: Not a year, and scarce a month passed in which the ferocious hunters of men did not swoop down upon the little bourg. **1904** *U of T Stud.Hist.& Econ.* II 168: Talon the intendant (1665-1672) indeed established inland villages, Bourg

Royal, Bourg La Reine and Bourg Talon near Quebec, but they did not prosper.

bourgeois ['burʒwa] *n.* [< Cdn F] **1 a.** *Hist.* master; employer; boss. See also **booshway.**
1791 (1904) LONG *Voyages* 106: . . . where great exertion is necessary, all distinction is laid aside, and it is *tel maitre, tel valet,* the bourgeois must work as hard as the engages. . . . *a*1855 (1956) ROSS *Fur Hunters* 198: The Canadians or voyageurs dignify their master by the name of Bourgeois, a turn [of phrase] handed down from the days of the French in the Province of Canada. **1905** (1946) TALMAN *Narratives* 8: My bourgeois, in common with his brother merchants, made a good thing of purchasing U.E. rights. **1961** JONES *Trappers* 67/2: . . . the "bourgeois" [was] the man with enough capital to pay for a trading license and to invest in a quantity of items for barter.

b. *Lumbering* See quotes.
1829 MACTAGGART *Three Years* I 241: *Lumbermen* and *Shantymen* are nearly synonymous; with this difference, that the former are generally the masters, or, what the Canadians call, the *Bourgeois* of the latter. **1854** KEEFER *Ottawa* 54: If you have a little property, you will find a class of gentlemen known among lumbermen as the big *bourgeois* (which is the synonym of *boss*) who will advance you, at least to the value of your property, what are called supplies. . . .

2 a. See **wintering partner** (def. 1).
1793 (1933) MACDONELL *Diary* 97: A head clerk or Bourgeouis is allowed by the concern [N.W. Co.] to have an extra man in his canoe to wait upon him. **1855** (1956) ROSS *Fur Hunters* 9: But here we might well explain what is meant by a "titled charge," according to North West nomenclature, clerks have charge of posts, Bourgeois of districts. **1963** STANLEY *Louis Riel* 5: If these "freemen" . . . no longer had obligations to the companies they had served, many retained a sense of loyalty to their old masters, a loyalty that was encouraged by many a "bourgeois" or factor.

b. See **wintering partner** (def. 2).
1824 (1931) MERK *Fur Trade* 209: Altho' they will not fight for us they always have a warm side to their old Bourgeois, in fact consider themselves under the [H.B.] Coys protection and look up to their representatives as Fathers. **1833** TOLMIE *Physician* 210: [He] exhorted the lazy Bourgeois to put his garden in good trim. **1855** (1956) ROSS *Fur Hunters* 199: [The canoemen] sing to keep time to their paddles. They sing to keep off drowsiness caused by their fatigue, and they sing because the Bourgeois likes it. **1880** BUTLER *Far Out* 33: He was the *bourgeois,* or master of the place, a Scotchman from the Isles. **1955** LEFROY *Magnetic North* xxi: His portage load of gun, barometer, dish, haversack with books and axe was a tolerable burden, even for a *bourgeois.*

3 *Obs.* See quote.
1860 (1956) KOHL *Kitchi-Gami* 184: . . . this shaggy bourgeois—as the Canadians often call the bear. . . .

bourgeois pemmican *Hist.* See quote. See also **fine pemmican.**
1963 MCTAVISH *Behind the Palisades* 89: When the Plains Indians put up a specially prepared lot of pemmican by adding native berries, the product was classified as "Bourgeois" pemmican, suitable only to the palates and supposedly refined tastes of the "Ookimows" (chiefs) among the pale faces.

bout(te) [but] *n.* (*usually plural*) [< Cdn F *bout (de canot)*] *Hist.* either the bowsman, *q.v.,* or the steersman, *q.v.,* in a canoe, bateau, or York boat.
1806 (1960) FRASER *Letters and Journals* 194: My canoe through the awkwardness of the Bouttes was very much endangered and every soul on board near perishing. **1828** (1872) MACDONALD *Peace River* 9: The eight "bouts" (i.e. men of the ends including steersmen and bowsmen, called "boots" from the French word *bout,* end) [carried] the canoes. . . . **1957** FISHER *Pemmican* 250: The crew of each boat comprised the middleman and the boutes, the latter being the bowsman and steersman, who sometimes helped with the paddles.

bow and arrow *Slang* North American Indian.
1923 PINKERTON *Fourth Norwood* 132: "Why, lad, those Mattawa bow-and-arrows is so scared of Cron they won't even listen when you try to tell 'em different." **1923** DE LA ROCHE *Possession* 230: "Yes, they refused me a drink for being an Indian, which was hardly fair for me, as I've told you I can't even speak their language. I may have a dash of the bow and arrow in me, but it's far enough away. . . ."

bowl and beans See **platter.**
1913 JOHNSON *Shagganappi* 157: He excels in the national sports of "lacrosse," "bowl and beans," and "snow snake". . . .

bowman ['baumən] *n.* **1** *Hist.* See **bowsman.**
1775 (1934) HEARNE *Journal* 190: The Bowman have by Frobisher's account from 14 to 16 a Year, and the 2 Men that sets in the Middle of each Canoe have from 10 to 12 L. *c*1804 GRANT *Sauteux Indians* 313: The bowman and the steersman can then carry [during a portage], a duty from which the middlemen are exempt.

2 the paddler whose position is in the bow of a canoe.
1915 WOOD *All Afloat* 36: [The] roaring water . . . drowns the human voice so completely that the bowman can only make use of signals. . . . **1956** *Beaver* Spring 33: . . . the bowman could drive the spike of his pole into a jutting log and pull the canoe up inch by inch or the sternsman could in turn shove against the log.

bowsman *n. Hist.* the crewman of a canoe or York boat, *q.v.,* whose position is in the bow. See also **booseman, bout, bowman** (def. 1), and **foreman.** Cp. **middleman** and **steersman.**
1776 (1951) *Saskatchewan Journals* 10 Mar. 37: . . . he proposes to Visit England next fall, and if he can get an Opportunity to speak to the Hudson's Bay Gentlemen will make a proposal to them for employing Canadians to be engaged by him for a term of years at Montreal to serve as Bowsmen & Helms-men and building large Canoes. **1833** (1932) MCLEAN *Notes* 116: It is the particular duty of the bowsman to attend to the canoe, to repair and pitch it when necessary, and to place it in security when the cargo is discharged. In consideration of these services he is exempt from the duty of loading and unloading, his wages are higher than those of the steersman, and he ranks after the guide. **1954** CAMPBELL *Nor'Westers* 21: As the *voyageurs* neared shore, the bowsman sprang into the water. . . .

box *n.* **1** on a wagon, truck, or sleigh, the rectangular superstructure that functions as a receptacle for the goods to be transported; body.
1824 *Kingston Chron.* (U.C.) 19 Nov. 1/1: [For Sale] Pots and Bake Ovens, Dog Irons, Sleigh shoes, Cart and Waggon Boxes. . . . **1826** (1955) CRAIG *Early Travellers* 76: . . . the body (or box, as it is called . . .)

can be put on or taken off at pleasure. **1964** *Naicam Sentinel* (Sask.) 26 Mar. 5/6: For Sale . . . truck with Woods box and hoist. . . .

2 the sideboard-enclosed playing area on which teams play box lacrosse, *q.v.*
1966 *Globe and Mail* (Toronto) 1 May 32/7: The home box (this is box lacrosse, buster) will be at the new North Toronto arena. . . .

box heater a sheet-metal stove, usually small and flat-topped. Cp. **box stove.**
1938 CASH *I Like B.C.* 10: With an antediluvian furnace, the place was wretchedly cold, so Bruce knocked a pane out of a window and installed a box-heater, round which we clustered gratefully most of the long Okanagan winter.

boxla ['bɑx,læ] *n. Slang* See **box lacrosse.**
1958 *Winnipeg Free Press* 4 June 25/3: The 'Pics knocked the front running Drewrys from the playoff picture in one of the biggest upsets in local boxla history. **1964** *Globe and Mail* (Toronto) 29 Sep. 35/4: Hagersville Captures Senior B Boxla Title.

box lacrosse a form of lacrosse, *q.v.*, played by teams of seven men each on an enclosed playing area roughly the size of a hockey rink. Cp. **field lacrosse.**
1959 *Programme 12th Indian Pow Wow* (Capilano Reserve, North Vancouver, B.C.) 2/2: Councillor Willard Josephs, brother to our famed Indian box lacrosse goal keeper, Stan Josephs, is in the Sports Committee. . . . **1965** *Kingston Whig-Standard* (Ont.) 15 May 8/5: The city has gone mad over box lacrosse. . . .

box phone an early type of telephone, shaped like a box with an opening to speak into.
1961 PRICE & KENNEDY *Renfrew* 126: The "box" phone appeared a year later [1877] and was the first commercial telephone.

box-skin *v.* See quote. See also **case-skin.**
1948 ONRAET *Sixty Below* 103: The marten is box-skinned, which means that the skin is pulled off by pressing the thumbs of both hands between the skin and the flesh, beginning with the hind legs, which are cut open from the rear, being very careful not to break the tail bone at the base.

box-sleigh or **box-sled**† *n.* a large horse-drawn sleigh having a boxlike body, used mainly for carrying goods. See **box** (def. 1).
1896 WHITNEY *On Snow-Shoes* 18: We had two good horses, and a strong box-sleigh, and our load was not heavy, so that I expected to make good time. **1960** BLONDAL *Candle* 28: She . . . had climbed into the box sled . . . before she realized that she didn't want a ride at all.

box social a social event at which boxes (often decorated with colored paper and ribbons) of food are offered at auction to male bidders, the successful bidder having the privilege of eating and dancing with the woman who prepared the lunch. See also **social.**
1908 *Observer* (Cowansville, Que.) 8 Oct. 8/3: The Box Social at Mr. Thos. Jones' on Sept. 24th was a success . . . one going as high as $1.10. **1920** *Beaver* Dec. 29/2: The hall is also used for all sorts of social events, such as dances and box socials. **1966** *Kingston Whig-Standard* (Ont.) 18 Mar. 6/1: [They] sponsored . . . an old-fashioned box social, held in the community hall.

73

box heater
branding

box stove† a large cast-iron stove having a big firebox suitable for burning wood. Cp. **box heater.**
1828 *U.E.Loyalist* (York [Toronto]) 12 Apr. 374/4: He at all times, keeps on hand all kinds of assortments of . . . Box Stoves, Plough Points, to fit almost any Ploughs used in this country. **1963** *Eaton's Catalogue* Spring & Summer (Winnipeg) 355/3: "Favorite" Box Stove. Cast iron, attractively scrolled. For wood burning. Swing fire door. Two cooking holes, removable top section, and six-inch smoke-pipe collar on two larger models. $39.95.

box-trap *n.* a trap consisting of a box with a baited trigger, so constructed that when it is disturbed the box falls and catches the victim.
1779 (1911) TOWNSEND *Cartwright's Jnl* 39: I made a box-trap for martens, and set it on the opposite side of the river. **1956** MOWAT *Lost in the Barrens* 189: The whole affair was really only a large box trap set so that the boys could trip it from the cabin and catch the dogs in the outer porch.

boy cook a cook's helper or apprentice in a camp. See also **choreboy.**
1883 FRASER *Shanty* 52: In marked contrast to old Ned, stood out young Alf, the "boy cook."

boy-hoy *n. Slang, Obs.* in the Maritimes, a low-class tough or ruffian, usually found in gangs.
1872 DASHWOOD *Chiploquorgan* 206: The lower population of the towns—"the boy-hoys" is the local term, answering to the "lambs" in certain manufacturing districts in England, are without exception the most arrant and cowardly scoundrels in existence.

brag load See quote.
1961 PRICE & KENNEDY *Renfrew* 117: Teamsters sometimes tried to outdo each other in the size of their timber loads. The unusually big ones were called "brag loads."

Brahmin(ical) *n. Hist.* in Upper Canada, one of a class of evangelists from the United States, usually Methodists, who publicly expressed their republican sympathies.
1832 *Patriot and Farmer's Monitor* (Kingston, U.C.) 10 Mar. 2/5: The Brahmins have found their Camp Meeting system so fully exposed, as to be no longer tenable, and are obliged, though most reluctantly, to abandon it. *Ibid.* 3 Apr. 2/6: There are not on the face of the earth, a set of more ignorant pretenders than those Brahminicals, who are pouring in upon us from all quarters, and who very obligingly offer to take charge of our temporal, as well as spiritual concerns.

braillet *n.* See **brayet.**

branding *n. Hist.* **1 a.** the clearing away of trees and brush on a tract of land by burning. See also **burning** (def. 1).
1898 (1933) GUILLET *Early Life in U.C.* 277: With a blazing sun overhead and ashes heated like unto a fiery furnace underneath, the men looked like a lot of chimney-sweeps after a day at branding. **1943** FRENCH *Boughs Bend Over* 54: Pushing back the forest to make place for homes and farms meant death to thousands of trees; meant mountainous piles of wood too huge to be left around. They called it "branding," this burning of

the trees. **1953** *Cdn Geog.Jnl* Dec. 220/1: In early summer, in a new settlement, hundreds of piles of burning brush and logs blazed and smoked all night and all day, and the men working at the "branding" as it was called were blistered and scorched, their clothes thick with soot and ashes.

b. See quote.
1933 GUILLET *Early Life in U.C.* 276: The collecting and burning of the half-burnt wood was sometimes called "the branding."

2 the charred wood left after burning.
1924 (1933) SLATER *Yellow Briar* 73: Scarred logs . . . were yanked into fresh piles, with much proddings of the rumps of oxen, and the brandings were thus prepared for a fresh burning.

brand up *Hist.* engage in branding.
1844 (1963) GUILLET *Pioneer Farmer* I 340: My men wanted to go in the morning to brand up the pile we had set on fire the night before. . . .

bran-emptyings *n.pl. Obs.* the yeasty lees of bran soaked in water, used as a home-made leaven in colonial days. See also **bran-rising.**
1852 MOODIE *Roughing It* 129: You are from the old country, I guess, or you would know how to make *milk*-emptyings. Now, I always prefer *bran*-emptyings. They make the best bread.

bran-rising *n. Obs.* a kind of leaven made from bran-emptyings, soaked in water.
1836 TRAILL *Backwoods* 241: Bran-rising . . . is made with bran instead of flour, and is preferred by many. . . .

bras *n.* [< F] *Obs.* a long narrow bay or arm (now only in place-names, as Bras d'Or, N.S.).
1817 *Quebec Gaz.* 29 May 4/1: A land of eight perches and thirteen feet in front . . . beginning at the River St. Lawrence and running to the bras St. Nicholas, to the south of which bras is the land of Jacques Kirouh.

bras(s)e [bras] *n.* [< F] *Obs.* See 1910 quote. Cp. **fathom.**
1754 (1955) *Beaver* Spring 54: If it is your good pleasure to send me 5 brase of Tobacco. **1910** MALHIOT *Journal* 216n: Brasse is a French linear measure, equivalent to 5·318 English feet. . . . There is evidence . . . that in the middle of the eighteenth century a "brasse" was used for a shorter measure, about the length of a forearm. The tobacco was braided or twisted into long strands, and then measured by the brasse.

Brasil tobacco See **Brazil tobacco.**

brave *n.* [< Cdn F] **1** a male Indian, especially a warrior.
1844 MARRYAT *Settlers in Can.* 220: He says he will sing his own death song; that he is the son of a warrior, and he will die like a brave. **1958** *Edmonton Jnl* 19 July 2/3: Cameras clicked and whirred as the colorfully garbed chiefs, braves and squaws advanced. . . . **1964** *Calgary Herald* 9 July 5/2: But a brave from the Tobacco Plains . . . killed him. . . .

2 *Rare* a young male Eskimo.
1936 STRINGER *Wife-Traders* 48: He was glad when he saw the whip taken up by a dusky-skinned brave beside him.

3 (*usually ironic*) any warrior.

1870 *Cdn Illust.News* 4 June 482/2: The massing of Fenian braves along the frontier commenced on Monday. . . . **1935** MORICE *Red River Insurrection* 113: The braves from the East had not counted on this.

brayet *n.* [< Cdn F < OF *brayette*(s) breech(es); cf. F *braie*(s)] *Obs.* See **breechcloth.**
1792 (1918) DAVIDSON *North West Co.* 231n: His . . . equipment [included] two shirts, two brayets . . . 3 carots of tobacco. **1808** (1960) FRASER *Letters and Journals* 156: I gave them each a blanket and a Brayet that they may appear decent. . . . **1808** MCKENZIE *King's Posts* 413: The men dress in a capot, brayet and leggings of carribou skin, prepared in the hair, which they wear, at all seasons, next to skin. . . .

Brazil tobacco *Hist.* a strong, black tobacco twisted into a rope and sold by the fathom, *q.v.*, as an important item of trading goods by the Hudson's Bay Co., beginning in 1685. See also **black tobacco.**
1685 (1948) *H.B.C. Letters Outward* 142: We have made search, what Tobacco the French vends to the Indians, which you doe so much extoll, and have this yeare bought the like (vizt.) Brazelle Tobacco, of which we have sent for each Factorey, a good Quantety. . . . **1743** (1949) ISHAM *Observations* 86: Give us good (brazl. tobacco) black tobacco, moist and hard twisted. Let us see itt before op'n'd. . . . **1801** MACKENZIE *Voyages* ci: The remaining contents of the bag are, a piece of Brazil tobacco . . . and a pipe. **1957** *Beaver* Winter 15/2: "Brazill" tobacco—the kind which came in hanks or "hands"—was introduced at an early date when it was found that the Virginia type was not selling well. . . .

bread-root *n.* See **prairie turnip.**
1852 (1881) TRAILL *Cdn Crusoes* 148: . . . they could not always meet with a supply of bread-roots, as they grew chiefly in damp, swampy thickets. . . .

break *v.* **1** See **break up** (def. 1).
1790 (1964) INNIS *Fur Trade* 137: Here they begin to build their canoes, which are generally compleated very soon after the river ice breaks. **1910** LONDON *Lost Face* 151: The Teelee [River] broke.

2 a. See **break trail.**
1852 MOODIE *Roughing It* 462: Mr. T . . . walked ahead of us, in order to break a track through the untrodden snow. *c*1902 LAUT *Trapper* 218: A man who is breaking the way must keep his eyes on the ground. . . . **1921** HAWORTH *Trailmakers* 252: There come days . . . when every foot of the way must be broken anew.

b. make a way through heavy snow on a road. Also *break open.*
1882 *Prince Albert Times* (Sask.) 6 Dec. 6/1: He was five days from Humbolt and had to break the road to Duck Lake. **1913** CURRAN & CALKINS *Northland* 324: . . . we hoped that the Government road would be broken enough to permit of better speed. **1959** *Maclean's* 29 Aug. 40/1: Farmers had to break open their own road in winter and keep them in repair in summer.

breakaway *n. Hockey* an opportunity to move in on goal without interference, the defensive players all being behind the advancing player.
1955 *Globe and Mail* (Toronto) 31 Jan. 19/4: His goal was an easy effort coming on a breakaway and fired into a vacant net. . . . **1963** *Kingston Whig-Standard* (Ont.) 6 Mar. 12/6: Goddard . . . stopped . . . Gagnon on a breakaway in the first period and made three superb stops on screened shots.

break camp pack up, leave a camp, and go elsewhere. See also **call camp** and **raise camp**.
1896 WHITNEY *On Snow-Shoes* 88: [The squaw] breaks camp and pitches it again where the husband, who has gone on . . . and whose trail she has followed, indicates by sticking up brush in the snow. **1955** GOWLAND *Smoke* 220: The next day I broke camp and decided to go as far south as the desolation allowed.

breaker *n.* an icebreaker.
1959 *Crowsnest* Mar. 14/3: Had the supply fleet tried to bull its way through the ice, even with "breaker" assistance, the chances are inevitable that more than one plate would have been stove in. . . . **1962** *Canada Month* July 12/3: The 'breaker fleet has gone away for the summer—to the Arctic.

breaker plough† See **breaking plough**. Also spelled *breaker plow*.
1930 BEAMES *Army* 54: The settlers hitched their horses to Kent's big breaker plough. **1963** SYMONS *Many Trails* 24: But I won't go into the details of grubbing willow crowns and urging the ox-drawn breaker plow through the heavy sod. . . .

break-head *n.* [trans. of F *cassetête*] *Obs.* See **casse-tête** and picture.
1760 JEFFERYS *Descr.New France* 57: The weapons of the *Indians* were formerly the bow and arrow . . . and the battle-ax, or, as they call it, the break-head.

breaking† *n.* new land prepared for cultivation.
1882 *Edmonton Bull.* 21 Oct. 1/2: The improvements made by Wright before his death consisted of ten acres of breaking with crop and fencing . . . **1955** *Sentinel-Courier* 31 Mar. 4/2: FOR SALE—Selkirk wheat, produced on new breaking from registered seed.

breaking plough† a large plough, especially designed for the heavy work of breaking new land. See also **breaker plough**. Also spelled *breaking plow*.
1929 JOHNSTON *Beyond the Rockies* 194: There are literally . . . millions of acres where a big breaking-plough drawn by six or eight horses, can be put at work without any preliminary. **1957** *Beaver* Autumn 16/2: Making his entry for a half square mile of open prairie, Godfrey Rainville bought an ancient team of oxen, a wagon, some floor lumber for his shack, a breaking plough, cook stove, kitchen outfit and provisions.

breaking-up *n.* **1** See **break-up** (def. 2).
1701 (1929) KELSEY *Papers* 111: I was desirous to winter at Slude river but . . . none is acquainted wth ye breaking up so it is deferr'd till next year. . . . **1925** MCARTHUR *Familiar Fields* 29: . . . when the spring "breaking-up" really began, the country became a series of islands.

2 See **break-up** (def. 1).
1743 (1949) ISHAM *Observations* 64: I[']ll be in at the Breaking up of the Rivers. **1946** (1947) FREEDMAN *Mrs. Mike* 98: . . . the breaking up . . . comes about this time every year.

breaking-up rapid *Obs.* a rapids so violent as to break up a timber raft.
1829 MACTAGGART *Three Years* I 242: When they are passing a *breaking-up rapid,* they live in these lairs, until the raft is new *withed,* and fixed on the still-water below.

break out undertake the break-out.
1964 *Cdn Geog.Jnl* Feb. 67/2: The banks at the dump had been cleared of brush last fall in preparation for the dangerous work of "breaking out the dumps" when spring came.

break-out *n. Lumbering* the removal of key pieces from a pile of logs, permitting them to roll from the landing (def. 1a) into the water for driving or booming. See also **break out**.
1928 PERRY *Two Reds* 109: LeClerk came to her cabin with the announcement that one of the rollways was to be dumped, though the break-out had been set for the following day.

break track *Rare* See **break trail**.
1900 OSBORN *Greater Canada* 172: The custom is for the men to take the lead, "breaking track" as they go, and for the women and children to follow. . . .

break trail move ahead of a dog team, a vehicle, or a party of people, making a way through heavy snow, often on snowshoes. See also **beat the path** and **break,** *v.* (def. 2a).
[**1748** ELLIS *Hudson's Bay* 163: In long Journies, through deep Snows, the Men generally go before them to beat a Path with their Snow Shoes.] **1896** WHITNEY *On Snow-Shoes* 67: It was impossible for me to wear snow-shoes in breaking trail for the dogs. . . . **1936** *Beaver* Sep. 30/2: Such difficulty can be anticipated the first trip of each freighting year, but it can be greatly lessened by having two tractors in operation breaking trail, as they can then assist each other. **1961** *Cdn Geog. Jnl* Jan. 16/2: . . . the reconnaissance engineer, on snowshoes, broke trail ahead with the aid of a small pocket compass. . . .

break up 1 of (ice in) rivers and lakes, melt as a result of the spring thaw. See also **break,** *v.* (def. 1).
1715 (1965) *Letters from Hudson Bay* 51n: The River did break up on the Seventh of May & ye waters forc'd the River to break to before wee had any thaw. . . . **1807** GRAY *Letters* 199: It is brought to Quebec and Montreal as soon as the ice breaks up, and the navigation opens in the river [St. Lawrence]. **1965** *Kingston Whig-Standard* (Ont.) 9 Mar. 1/7: The KFC . . . will be unable to land once the ice begins to break up.

2 of roads, become muddy and often impassable as a result of the spring thaw.
1812 *Montreal Herald* 7 Mar. 3/2: From the thaws in the days and frosts in the nights, it is probable that we shall have a month's communication with the country before the breaking up of the winter roads. **1883** *Prince Albert Times* (Sask.) 14 Feb. 4/1: They appear to be laying in a good supply before the roads break up. **1912** HEENEY *Pickanock* 188: The trip alluded to . . . was one . . . taken when the roads were breaking up. . . .

break-up or **breakup** *n.* **1** the spring thawing of the ice on rivers and lakes, especially the point in time when the ice breaks into pieces that are flushed away by the current. See also **breaking-up** (def. 2) and **open water** (def. 1). Cp. **freeze-up**.
1854 KEEFER *Ottawa* 70: On the first appearance of a break up in March there is a regular stampede among the teamsters. . . . **1965** *Kingston Whig-Standard* (Ont.) 9 Mar. 1/7: Residents of the town gauge the arrival of spring every year by the departure of the ice mantle. Already this year there are signs of a break-up.

2 the melting of the snow and the frozen ground in spring; spring thaw. See also **breaking-up** (def. 1).

1860 *Islander* (Charlottetown) 24 Mar. 2/5: We have every prospect of an early break-up. **1962** FRY *Ranch on the Cariboo* 278: Breakup came early and green grass followed hard on the last of it.

3 See **break-up period.**
1938 *Beaver* Dec. 44: The Mackenzie delta at its mouth is ninety to one hundred and twenty miles wide, and is a vast network of sloughs, lakes and rivers, separated by low-lying land that, during the breakup . . . is completely submerged. **1961** *Edmonton Jnl* 1 Aug. 3/3: The ferry operation across the Mackenzie River at Mile 82 . . . is discontinued during fall freeze-up and spring break-up.

break-up ice the chunks of ice freed during break-up and carried downstream by the current.
1953 MOON *Saskatchewan* 179: But the bridge had barely been opened before the great weight of break-up ice borne by the high river water carried away the centre spans in 1952.

break-up period the period of time taken for the ice in rivers and lakes to soften, crack up, and disappear. See also **break-up** (def. 3), **ice-out season, melt season,** and **open water** (def. 2).
1956 KEMP *Northern Trader* 166: It was at Stanley, during a break-up period when we encountered a particularly vicious bush-fire. **1958** *Edmonton Jnl* 24 June 4 18/1: The small payload capacity, frequent weather delays and the stagnation of all float or ski-equipped planes during the break-up and freeze-up periods in the north contributed to the high cost and relative inefficiency of bush plane transport.

break-up wind the spring winds that hasten break-up in the North.
1955 HARDY *Alta Anthol.* 134: The break-up winds were fingering the frozen northland again.

breathing-hole *n.* See **air-hole** (def. 2).
1854 (1892) KANE *Arctic Explor.* 153: The seal are shot lying by their . . . breathing-holes. **1937** *Beaver* June 72/2: It is only when the sea is in a frozen state that the natives live upon its surface and subsist upon the seals they procure through the breathing holes. **1964** JENNESS *Eskimo Admin.* II 25: Fewer Eskimos now could track down the breathing holes of the seals in the ice. . . .

breathing-place *n. Obs.* See **air-hole** (def. 1).
1829 MACTAGGART *Three Years* I 78: All frozen lakes, toward their outlets, have what are called breathing-places.

breechcloth† *n.* a loin covering of cloth or soft leather. See also **brayet, breechclout,** and **clout.**
1811 (1849) ROSS *Adventures* 91: Instead of the cedar petticoat, the women of some tribes prefer a breech cloth, [which] is nothing more than a piece of dressed deerskin, six inches broad and four feet long, which, after passing between the thighs, is tied round the waist. **1922** *Beaver* Nov. 49/2: The only garment worn was a breechcloth, made either of leather or a piece of blanket about a foot wide. This was placed between their legs, and the ends were passed under the belt fore and aft— the ends being long enough to hang down about a foot in order to keep the cloth in its place.

breechclout† *n.* See **breechcloth.**
1800 (1897) COUES *New Light* I 111: The Indians were standing in the fort with nothing on but their breech-clouts. . . . **1943** *Beaver* Mar. 45/1: When they watered their horses they usually rode into the valley naked except for their breechclouts, with buffalo robes thrown over their shoulders. **1965** *Canadian Wkly* 13 Mar. 9/2: North American Indians are usually pictured as wearing breech clouts or buckskins. . . .

breed or **'breed** *n. Slang, Often Derog.* a half-breed, *q.v.*
1870 *Cdn Illust.News* 26 Feb. 271/3:
McDougall, he was on a Governship bent,
Whom to "boss" no one could tell;
The "breeds" in their ire said on him they'd fire
For him 'twas a regular sell, sell, sell;
He could not at Red River dwell.
1871 *Wkly Manitoban* 1 July 1/2: It is the easiest thing in the world for a few men to . . . denounce the Cabinet and threaten to expel them, and go for the "Breeds" generally. **1956** CRATE & WILLIAMS *We Speak for the Silent* 1: There are, in this area, besides the Indians and whites, a considerable percentage of people with both white and Indian blood, referred to as metis, half-breeds or 'breeds. **1963** STANLEY *Louis Riel* 242: [They] referred to them [Métis] as the "breeds" and the "coyote French."

breed half mile See quote.
1902 (1957) *Sask.Hist.* X 18: The half-mile to the telegraph office seemed exceedingly long. Mr. Thompson contemptuously called it a "breed Half Mile" and maintained that it was fully three times as long as a white man's half mile.

breed trail See quote.
1902 (1957) *Sask.Hist.* X 17: . . . [the trails] ran in every direction. . . . Our guide bore with them for some time, but at last, his patience gave away and "curses, not loud but deep" at the "Breed Trails" gave vent to his feelings.

breeze pole See quote.
1916 WOOD *Tourist's N.W.* 359: When the horses are turned out—bells on leaders and hobbles on those that are hard to catch—the thirteen tepee poles are set, and the two "breeze-poles" that control the ventilation flaps adjusted to catch whatever wind is blowing up or down the valley.

brewis [bruz] *n.* [< Brit. dial. *breawis, brewis* vegetable-and-meat broth] *Nfld* a kind of stew prepared by boiling ship's biscuit with codfish and pork fat, sometimes including potato chunks and wild herbs.
*c*1850 (1960) FOWKE *Story in Song* 164: Tho' Newfoundland is changing fast, some things we must not lose: May we always have our flipper pie, and codfish for our brewis. **1906** LUMSDEN *Skipper Parson* 68: A popular dish in Newfoundland is "brewis," pronounced *broose.* **1964** *Cdn Geog.Jnl* Apr. 135: Only in Newfoundland were we served . . . fish-and-brewis.

bride's boys See quote.
1952 BANFILL *Labrador Nurse* 63: Wedding invitations are issued by young men and boys called "bride's boys" who go from harbour to harbour, inviting the people as these boys had invited us.

bridge *n.* **1** See **ice-bridge** (def. 1a).
1769 (1931) BROOKE *Emily Montague* 188: Before I saw the breaking up of the vast body of ice, which forms what is here called *the bridge,* from Quebec to Point Levi, I imagined there could be nothing in it worth attention. . . . **1849** ALEXANDER *L'Acadie* I 157: At Kingston . . . the "Bridge of Ice," over the lower part

of Lake Ontario, carries him to the French Creek, or Sackett's Harbour. . . .

2 *Nfld* a formation of thick ice over a river, bay, etc., the surroundings being rotten, *q.v.*, ice or water.

1771 (1792) CARTWRIGHT *Journal* I 182: We landed . . . and walked home; for the river was frozen over in bridges. . . . **1916** DUNCAN *Billy Topsail* 262: Archie took one step—and dropped, crashing, with a section of the bridge, which momentarily floated his weight. **1933** MERRICK *True North* 207: By bending close to the ice we could follow their track. The bridge wound. Sometimes we felt that we were surrounded by the black sliding water.

3 See **corduroy bridge.**

bridle *n.* the loop of a snowshoe in which the toes are placed.

1931 GREY OWL *Last Frontier* 64: . . . slipping with deft ankle movements into the bridles of an immense pair of trail breakers (large snowshoes), shoes of an Indian rig, [he] waves his hand and is away.

Brier *n.* [< the name of the trophy, Macdonald *Brier*] the bonspiel for the men's curling championship of Canada.

1958 *Chatelaine* Nov. 92: The Brier is the only name by which the annual Canadian Championship for men is known. . . . **1963** *Sun* (Vancouver) 18 Jan. 15/7: A Brier rhubarb flared around Lyall Dagg's Vancouver Club rink Thursday night in curling playoffs at Marpole Club.

brigade *n.* **1** *Fur Trade, Hist.* a fleet of canoes, bateaux, or York boats carrying trade goods, supplies, and furs to and from the inland posts of the fur companies. See also **boat brigade, canoe brigade, fur brigade,** and **scow brigade.**

1761 (1901) HENRY (Elder) *Travels* 14: To each canoe there are eight men; and to every three or four canoes, which constitute a *brigade,* there is a *guide* or conductor. **1815** BOUCHETTE *Lower Canada* 138: They usually get out in brigades like the bateaux, and in the course of the summer upwards of fifty of these vessels are thus dispatched. **1941** *Beaver* June 36/1: A canoe brigade still connects Senneterre post on the C.N.R. . . . **1963** *Cdn Geog.Jnl* Apr. 118/3: Each June, in brigades of 34-foot [York] boats, Lower Fort Garry despatched its trade goods and its men.

2 *Fur Trade, Hist.* a train of Red River carts, pack horses, dog sleds, etc. employed by the fur companies in transporting trade goods, supplies, and furs overland. See also **fur brigade.**

1863 *Nor'Wester* (R.R.S.) 22 July 3/1: The Hudson Bay Company's monster brigade of carts from Fort Abercrombie arrived here safely last week. **1929** MOBERLY *When Fur Was King* 67: After the last of these trains had departed, a brigade of sixty horse-sleds and thirty dog-trains was sent to the Beaver Hills to haul in three hundred buffalo cows previously killed and staged out of the reach of predatory animals. **1958** ATKINSON *Hist.of Penticton* 19: The term "Brigade" . . . applied to . . . pack horses travelling over the rolling hills of the Interior [of B.C.]. . . . **1967** *Cdn Geog.Jnl* Jan. 19/2: As a brigade included several hundred horses, the post was a scene of great activity during arrivals and departures.

3 *Obs.* a train of wagons; a fleet of bateaux employed in freighting merchandise.

1812 *Montreal Herald* 4 Jan 3/2: We understand that a strong brigade consisting of about 2,000 hogs, arrived

on Thursday . . . to be slaughtered. **1822** HOWISON *Sketches* 48: The supposed Indians were no other than the crew of a brigade of batteaux. . . .

4 a number of canoes on a canoe trip, especially when following the historic routes of the early explorers and voyageurs.

1958 *Edmonton Jnl* 18 June 34/5: Simon Fraser . . . lacked some of the hazards the Fraser brigade faces in its reenactment of that trip. The brigade, 10 men in three canoes headed by veteran riverman Dick Corless of Prince George, now is camped near Lillooet, B.C. . . .

5 a cat-train, *q.v.*, especially one taking supplies to and furs from northern posts of the Hudson's Bay Co.

1958 *Edmonton Jnl* 24 June 4 2/3: The tractor brigades started operating out of Grimshaw for the far north.

brigade trail *Hist.* a route followed by brigades (def. 2) of pack horses.

1860 *Brit.Colonist* (Victoria) 7 Apr. 2/3: At this place [Fort Alexandria, B.C.] is the northern terminus of the Hudson Bay Company's brigade trail, and to this point from the forts still farther north they come in bateaux and canoes. **1953** *Beaver* Mar. 10/1: The "brigade" trails of the Hudson's Bay Company . . . occupied a strategic position in the transportation system of British Columbia from 1812 until the 1860's. . . . **1967** *Cdn Geog.Jnl* Jan. 19/2: . . . the Brigade Trail . . . was a pack-horse trail from Fort Okanagan in the Columbia country to Fort Alexandria on the Fraser River in the Cariboo [B.C.], over which trade goods and furs were carried until 1846 when the boundary settlement defined the international border and caused the fur company to adopt a new route.

brin *n.* [perhaps from older E *brin, brins* colored threads used in making tapestry < F] See quotes.

1941 *Beaver* Sep. 36/2: Brin. Hessians. **1958** *Cdn Geog. Jnl* LVI 76/2: . . . the patterns are traced on a base of coarse brin, which is similar to sack cloth.

brin bag *Lab. and Eastern Arctic* a sack or bag of coarse cloth; gunny sack; burlap bag.

1924 ENGLAND *Vikings of the Ice* 314/1: Brin bag. Gunnysack. **1933** MERRICK *True North* 18: Cecil wants a brinbag to jam some traps in. . . . **1957** *Beaver* Autumn 28/2: He kneels on one knee on a padded brin bag at the "prow" of the *komatik* and uses his free leg for steering.

brisket bell See **bell.**

1951 HOBSON *Grass* 53: Nine bull moose, swinging their dangling brisket bells . . . were walking slowly towards us.

British America *Hist.* the lands in North America colonized by the British or claimed by them; after 1776, the lands now comprising Canada.

*c***1777** (1955) CURTIS *Voyage* 57: I believe he consider'd he had transgrest, the law in his Native Country America, Were it was made death to any Person carrying goods into that part of America call'd British America to Assist the British Troops. **1916** MACMECHAN *Popular Government* 43: In British America itself the Church of Rome was "established" very firmly in Lower Canada.

on a government acceptable to both.

British American *Hist.* a Canadian. See also
British North American.
1837 *Bytown* [Ottawa] *Gaz.* 5 Jan. 1/5: Canadians, or
British Americans—J.B. Robinson, Markland, P.
Robinson, C. Jones. **1866** *Bee* (Ottawa) 2 June 2/3:
Most people, perhaps, are not aware that any great
number of British Americans have gained historical
distinction; but this is because they do not know how
little it takes to give a man a "place in history," or to
constitute him a British American.

British-American *adj. Hist.* of or pertaining to
British America and, after 1776, to Canada.
1765 *Quebec Gaz.* 4 Apr. 2/1: It is now the general
Opinion, that should the British American Colonies be
allowed to send Members to Parliament, such
Gentlemen must be Natives of the Province they
represent.... **1959** *Maclean's* 4 July 37/1: With them
they brought, along with their loyalty to the Crown,
most of the habits, virtues and limitations acquired by
their ancestors in the first century and a half of the
British-American experience.

British American League See **British North
America League.**
1963 MORTON *Kingdom of Canada* 285: In the suddenly
organized and most incoherent British American
League—annexationist, imperialist, nationalist, all at
once—they sought the new orientations together.

British Canada 1 *Hist.* that part of Canada ceded
to the British by the Treaty of Utrecht, comprising
what is now the Maritime Provinces.
1752 BOLTON *Map of North America* 129: [Legend] The
line that parts French Canada from British Canada was
settled by the Commissaries after the Peace of
Utrecht....
2 the English-speaking provinces of Canada, as
opposed to French Canada.
1825 *Cdn Courant* (Montreal) 5 Jan. 1/2: The grumblers
to Southern climes may roam British Canada.... **1839**
Bytown [Ottawa] *Gaz.* 14 Nov. 1/2: It seems
expedient ... that the leading men of ... British
Canada should assemble at the most central spot—say
Montreal—for the purpose of organizing the proposed
agitation. **1927** *Cdn Hist.Rev.* VIII 3: It was not until
near the close of the last century that the spirit of
inquiry, born of a sense of national pride, found
available the raw materials from which to construct the
story of the development of British Canada.

British Canadian 1 a Canadian of British
ancestry.
1850 ROY *Hist.of Canada* 150: In this trying moment
there was nothing to look to but the determined loyalty
of the British Canadians themselves. **1917** MILLER *New
Era* 295: Their scheme appeals to only a portion ... of
the Canadians of British descent; to the remaining
British Canadians it is anathema.
2 an English-speaking Canadian, as opposed to a
French-speaking Canadian.
1837 *Montreal Transcript* 3 Dec. 3/1: The first
paragraph would seem to point to the virtual
disenfranchisement of the British Canadians, and the
unmeasured ambition of the French faction, seen
openly in arms against the constitution. **1953**
LEBOURDAIS *Nation of North* vii: ... the failure of
French-Canadians in Lower Canada (Quebec) and
British-Canadians in Upper Canada (Ontario) to carry

British-Canadian *adj.* associated with or
sympathetic with British Canada or British
Canadians.
1834 *Brit.Amer.Jnl* (St. Catharines, U.C.) 27 May 3/3:
You cannot, nor will you so disgrace the name of
British Canadian Freemen! **1920** *Cdn Hist.Rev.* I 138:
To-day, however, he would be a bold man who would
deny to Canada the existence of a distinctly national
feeling—a national feeling not French-Canadian or
British-Canadian, but all-Canadian.

British Columbia fir See **Douglas fir.**
1905 *Eye Opener* (Calgary) 28 Jan. 4/4: The interior is
all furnished in polished British Columbia fir. **1956**
Native Trees 58: Douglas fir [is also called] British
Columbia fir....

British Columbia maple See quote. See also
broadleaf maple.
1956 *Native Trees* 250: Broadleaf maple, *Acer
macrophyllum,* [is also called] British Columbia maple.

British Columbia pine See quote.
1956 *Native Trees* 20: Ponderosa pine, *Pinus ponderosa,*
[is also called] British Columbia pine.

British connection 1 *Obs.* British ancestry.
1838 *Patriot* (Toronto) 29 May 1/4: The only means
that occur to us are, first, the Legislative union of the
two Provinces, by which a real majority of "British
connexion" would return a British majority to the
United House of Assembly.
2 *Hist.* the relationship that existed between
Canada as a colony and Great Britain as the
mother country. See also **Connectionist.**
1832 *Brockville Gaz.* (U.C.) 8 Nov. 3/1: I trust that
the enemies of Britain and British connexion have run
their race and that another year or two will extinguish
them entirely. **1963** MORTON *Kingdom of Canada* 241:
Reforms many of them desired ... but they wished to
achieve them by British methods and within the British
connection.

British Connectionist *Obs.* a supporter of close
ties between Canada and Great Britain. See also
Connectionist.
1849 *Wkly Globe* 2 Nov. 71/1: The following letter has
been sent us by an elector of the East Riding, who is a
decided British Connexionist, but favourable to the
return of Mr. Perry.

British Constitutionalist *Hist.* a supporter of
the view that the British system of parliamentary
government should be adopted in Canada as
opposed to the congressional system established in
the United States.
1832 *Brockville Gaz.* (U.C.) 5 Apr. 2/2: The British
Constitutionalists carried everything before them, and
Mackenzie and his abettors are put down now and for
ever.

British feeling *Obs.* sympathy with and support
for the British connection (def. 2).
1822 *Montreal Herald* 7 Dec. 3/1: British feeling they
consider as avowedly opposed to those laws that protect
the French Noblesse, in all those rights they continue
to exercise. **1863** *Nor'Wester* (R.R.S.) 16 Sep. 1/1: Such
inquiries would excite no other feelings but those of
admiration at the characteristic enterprise which gives
birth to them, if it were not the unscrupulous action to
which they point, alike neglectful of British feeling and
opposed to the aspirations of the majority of the people
of North America.

British Loyalist See **United Empire Loyalist.**
1899 GARDNER *Names* 3: Large numbers of disbanded officers and soldiers, with civilians who were quitting the United States as British Loyalists, thus became the pioneers of civilization and founders of a new colony.

British North America *Hist.* **1** that part of North America that ultimately came to be called Canada.
1825 *Novascotian* (Halifax) 1 June 179/1: The Subscriber has been requested by the Society lately formed in Glasgow for promoting the moral and religious interests of the Scottish settlers in British North America to make it known . . . that they will be happy to open a correspondence with any body of Settlers. . . . **1955** *Western Star* (Corner Brook, Nfld) 12 Mar. 2 4/1: There are many other attractions however such as a long and colorful history dating back to discovery of British North America. . . .
2 a proposed name for a federal union of the provinces of British North America, now Canada.
1849 *Niagara Chron.* (C.W.) 30 Aug. 2/1: The name of the Canadas to be superceded . . . and the two provinces to be re-divided into the Provinces of Quebec, Montreal, Kingston, and Toronto, which with the Provinces of New Brunswick and Nova Scotia, Prince Edward's Island, and Newfoundland, will in one Federal Union go under the name of British North America.

British North America Act† the act of the British Parliament that created the Dominion of Canada in 1867, uniting the provinces of Ontario and Quebec (formerly United Canada), Nova Scotia, and New Brunswick.
1958 *Saturday Night* 27 Sep. 6/1: They add that . . . Canada already has a written constitution in the British North America Act. **1961** *Canada Month* Dec. 18/3: As an agency of the federal government, EMO [Emergency Measures Organization] must function within the framework of the British North America Act. . . .

British North America(n) League *Hist.* See 1957 quote. See also **Leagueman.**
1957 *Encyc.Can.* II 108/2: British North American League, an association founded in 1849 to counteract the annexation movement. **1961** GREENING *Ottawa* 125: [He was] the British North America League candidate for the Legislature. . . .

British North American See **British American.**
1865 *Islander* (Charlottetown) 6 Jan. 2/3: Well knowing the hatred and horror with which Yankee institutions are viewed by British Americans, we cannot entertain a fear for the repulse of any attempt to seize the lands and later the Government of the Provinces adhering to the mother country.

British Northwest *Hist.* the territories to the west and north of the old province of Upper Canada, north of the U.S. border.
1881 BEGG *Great Cdn N.W.* 17: From this time there existed in Canada a desire to annex the British North West. . . . **1952** HOWARD *Strange Empire* 138: It had become evident to him . . . that the Americans would do anything "short of war" to acquire the British Northwest.

British party *Hist.* a political group in Upper and Lower Canada who supported the traditional British connection (def. 2). See also **English party.**
1832 *Brockville Gaz.* (U.C.) 5 Apr. 2/2: Mackenzie . . .

had the audacity to dare the British party to a meeting. . . . **1860** *Nor'Wester* (R.R.S.) 28 Mar. 2/4: These are the leaders of the British party, par excellence, and they suffer a man like Mr. Cartier to dictate to them what shall be the boundaries of this British Province.

British preference a concept of trading by which British goods could enter Canada at advantageous tariff rates.
1916 BRIDLE *Sons of Canada* 17: Great movements were born during the decade 1901-1911; the new great West, the immigration era, the British Preference—begun in 1897. . . .

British Provinces *Hist.* Canada.
1833 *Liberal* (St. Thomas, U.C.) 10 Jan. 3/3: Then there is the Hamilton Free Press, than which a more staunch, determined and spirited Publication is not to be found in the British Provinces.

Brito-Canadian *n. Rare* See **British Canadian.**
1866 BELL *Hist.of Canada* II 321: . . . in brief, what is denounced as a crime in a Gallo-Canadian shall pass for public virtue in a Brito-Canadian.

A broad axe

broad-axe *n.* a large axe having a broad blade, used for trimming and shaping logs into square timber, planks, etc.
*a*1820 (1838) HEAD *Forest Scenes* 310: Large chips were cut off with the broad axe. . . . **1891** OXLEY *Chore-Boy* 67: . . . the "hewer" . . . with his huge broad-ax, made square the "stick," as the great piece of timber is called. **1964** *Cdn Geog.Jnl* Feb. 67/1: . . . with great skill, the hewer used a broad axe to make one side straight and smooth.

Broadcast Governor a member of the Board of Broadcast Governors, *q.v.*
1959 *Time* (Cdn ed.) 10 Aug. 10/2: The Broadcast Governors . . . are determined to protect Canadianism against cultural and economic pressures from the U.S.

broadleaf (or broadleaved) maple† *West Coast* See **British Columbia maple.**
1894 *Trans.Roy.Soc.Can.* XI 4 15: The broad-leaved maple is a coast species, but [ascends] the Fraser almost as far as its junction with the Thompson. . . . **1956** *Native Trees* 250: The broadleaf maple is the largest species of maple occurring in British Columbia.

brochet [bro'ʃe; *French* brə'ʃɛ] *n.* [< Cdn F < F "pike"] See **northern pike.**
1703 LAHONTAN *New Voyages* II 318: brochet [that is "pike"]. . . . **1804** (1933) CONNOR *Diary* 260: . . . my Indians made several Applications for Liquor which I refused owing to the Brochet (Pike) & Rognion (Kidney) 2 of Cheniers Chiefs that are here & I am determined they shall not taste my Liquor without payment. **1952** WILSON *Chibougamau* 71: The Great Northern Pike (Brochet) can reach forty pounds in weight.

brochet banana [< Lac du *Brochet;* see **brochet**] See **caribou tongue.**
1945 *Beaver* Mar. 11: Posts as far south as Norway

House . . . were certainly supplied with caribou tongues [from Lac du Brochet]. These "Brochet bananas" are still the delicacy today that they were in those far off times.

A Brock copper

Brock copper [< General Sir Isaac *Brock,* 1769-1812, British Commander-in-Chief in Upper Canada] *Hist.* a copper coin, worth about a farthing, that circulated in Canada after the War of 1812 until stopped by law because an influx of American counterfeit coins rendered them worthless. See also **Wellington copper.**
1819 *Kingston Chron.* (U.C.) 29 Jan. 1/2: We, the subscribers, will receive, as small change, the various species of Coppers, which have heretofore been current here, except those denominated Brock Coppers, and Waterloo coppers. **1848** *Examiner* (Toronto) 1 Nov. 2/4: The old "Brock" and "Wellington" coppers are familiar to the recollection of the old settlers; they once formed our only copper circulation although 4 or 5 of them would not balance a British penny!

broken brigade *Obs.* See quote.
1898 *Rev.Hist.Pubs* II 223: The hero . . . falls victim to a land-shark, and becomes "one of the broken brigade" . . . a "remittance man."

broken concession *Obs.* See **broken-front concession.**
1847 *Bytown* [Ottawa] *Gaz.* 6 Nov. 3/6: I have seized and taken in execution . . . Broken Lot H, in broken concession D, on the Rideau [River], in the Township of Nepean. . . .

broken country terrain intersected by ravines and valleys.
[**1922** *Beaver* May 14/1: The country was broken *brule,* tremendous growth of grass with much dead old bottom.] **1947** TANNER *Outlines* I 422: The lynx . . . is found in the southern part of the peninsula in the broken country. **1963** SYMONS *Many Trails* 35: . . . there was still a considerable area of broken country which both the homesteaders and the railways had shunned.

broken fish *Nfld* the lowest grade of cured codfish. See also **dun.** Cp. **salt-burnt.**
1832 MCGREGOR *British America* I 232: . . . the broken fish, dun fish, or whatever will not keep in warm countries . . . is in general equally good for domestic consumption. . . . **1883** HATTON & HARVEY *Newfoundland* 291: When thoroughly dried [cod] have a whitish appearance and are then ready for storing. . . . they are weighted and "culled" or sorted into four different kinds called Merchantable (the best), Madeira, West Indian (intended for . . . the negroes) and Dun, or broken fish, which will not keep, and is intended for home use.

broken front *Hist.* in Ontario, parcels of land of irregular shape, situated along a river or lake, at the front of a concession (def. 2). Cp. **broken lot.**
1793 (1905) *Ont.Bur.Arch.Rep.* III 241: . . . the uneven

patches on account of curvilinear Water boundaries should be distinguished under the name of Broken Fronts. **1834** (1926) LANGTON *Early U.C.* 91: The shores of the lake are surveyed in a very slovenly manner, so that no dependence can be placed in the supposed contents of the broken fronts. . . . **1904** *Ont.Bur.Arch. Rep.* I 49: The lots so blazed were . . . 28 [to] 31 in broken front, Darlington township, Durham County.

broken-front concession a concession (def. 2) of irregular shape lying along a river or lake front. See also **broken concession.**
1842 *U.C.Gaz.* (Toronto) 11 Aug. 87/1: Part of Lot. No. 27, in the broken front concession, township of Whitby. . . . **1963** *Kingston Whig-Standard* (Ont.) 5 Mar. 6/5: The 59-lot development fronts on Lake Ontario in the "broken front concession."

broken lot *Obs.* a lot at the front of a broken-front concession; a lot of irregular shape lying along a river or lake front.
1807 *U.C.Gaz.* (York [Toronto]) 20 June 3/3: Lands for Sale . . . Broken Lot No. 14-9th do.—600 acres in the Township of Gleanford. **1847** *Bytown* [Ottawa] *Gaz.* 6 Nov. 3/6: I have seized and taken in execution . . . part of Broken Lot Number Forty, Concession A of the Township of Nepean, Ottawa Front. . . .

bronc† *n.* **1** See **bronco** (def. 1).
1910 FERGUSON *Janey Canuck* 88: I did not know this particular "bronc". . . . **1964** *Maclean's* 25 Jan. 14/1: [Caption] The cowboy below is on board a bareback bronc.

2 See **bronco** (def. 2).
1942 BOSANQUET *Saddlebags* 166: I am the bronc in the bunch (family) never quite coralled; belonging and yet not quite.

bronc fighter *West* See **bronco-buster.**
1954 HAGELL *Grass Was Free* 59: . . . the same type of animal [was] used by . . . horse-ranny . . . bronc fighter, herd boss or even cook.

broncho *n.* See **bronco.**

bronco or **broncho** ['braŋko] *n.* [< Am. E < Sp. *bronco* rough, unruly] **1†** a wild or semiwild horse. See also **bronc** (def. 1).
1878 *Sask.Herald* (Battleford, N.W.T.) 25 Aug. 1/3: Horses, unbroken (bronchos) only brought $35 to $45 each, which is less than they have ever before sold for. **1961** *Edmonton Jnl* 3 July 21/4: . . . [he] was injured slightly when a bronco he was riding slipped and fell on him.

2 a stubborn, unruly, undisciplined person. See also **bronc** (def. 2).
1919 FRASER *Bulldog Carney* 15: I've saw a man flick his gun and pot at Carney when Bulldog told him to throw up his hands, and all that cuss did was laugh and thrown his own gun up coverin' the other broncho. . . . **1960** *Time* (Cdn ed.) 18 Jan. 6/1: At 14 he quit school ("I presume I was something of a broncho") [and] started to work earning 60¢ for a twelve-hour day. . . .

3 *Slang* an Englishman, especially an English immigrant of the lower classes.
1918 MOORE *Clash* 306: So long as we continue to drink its [racial doctrine's] intoxicating waters we shall never dwell in harmony with the French Canadians, nor any other nationality, not even with the men whom we called "bronchos" and "sparrows" before the war. **1966** *Sun* (Vancouver) 22 Mar. 12/8: Canadians have not been slow to find nicknames for themselves and others. Among them are . . . for the Englishman, bronco and sparrow.

bronco-buster *n.* one who breaks wild horses to the saddle or to harness. See also **bronc fighter** and **bronc stomper.**
1889 MACLEAN *Indians* 198: There are four different occupations in the country the men engage in, which are called bull-whackers and mule-skinners, applied to freighters who drive oxen or mules, broncho-busters and cow-punchers. **1958** *Edmonton Jnl* 19 July 1/6: The day started with a wild west flair when [Princess] Margaret . . . watched bronco-busters bite the dust at a rodeo.

bronco-busting *n.* the breaking of wild horses.
1889 *Regina Jnl* 18 July 1/6: Broncho "busting" and base-ball are the sports most indulged in [in] these times. **1920** *Beaver* Oct. 9/1: There was also an exhibition of "bronco busting" and a pie-eating contest for the boys.

bronc stomper *West, Slang* See **bronco-buster.**
1954 HAGELL *Grass Was Free* 48: . . . his two listeners [were] watching the ranch's bronc stomper working a green colt. **1962** FRY *Ranch on the Cariboo* 122: I shook my head, doubting that I'd ever be a bronc stomper.

brookie ['brʊki] *n. Informal* a brook trout.
1958 *Edmonton Jnl* 8 Aug. 12/1: They averaged 10 inches in length, the largest a 14-inch brookie. **1963** *Globe and Mail* (Toronto) 9 Mar. 31/4: Gary Oram . . . took a string of brookies through the ice of Meach Lake.

broomball ['brʌm,bɑl] *n.* a game played, usually, on a hockey rink, the players, with or without skates, having corn brooms with which to advance a volleyball toward the opposing team's goal.
1933 *Beaver* Mar. 211: . . . the display department team won the broom ball game. . . . **1955** *Bridgewater Bull.* 9 Mar. 2/1: It seems that Brooklyn [N.S.] has been playing Broom Ball for a number of years. . . . **1963** *Kingston Whig-Standard* (Ont.) 23 Jan. 9/2: Preceding the hockey game . . . will be a broomball contest.

broomballer *n.* one who plays broomball.
1963 *Kingston Whig-Standard* (Ont.) 24 Jan. 10/3: "Grundoon" looked exceptionally sharp in his debut as a broom baller and actually scored. . . .

broom game See **curling.**
1921 *Beaver* Mar. 41/2: In the Calgary [HBC] store the broom game was taken up by all employees. . . .

brother *n.* See **blood brother.**
1922 *Beaver* Feb. 35/1: I myself had a "brother" among the Blood Indians, another among the Sarcee, and a son among the Sarcees.

Brother Jonathan† a personification of the United States. See also **Jonathan** (def. 1).
1811 *York* [Toronto] *Gaz.* 26 Sep. 2/4: . . . so great is the terror of Brother Jonathan at another visit from General Brock that . . . they . . . scuttled fifty large boats. . . . **1813** *Montreal Herald* 7 Aug. 3/3: . . . Jonathan is said to have taken all that came into his fangs without discrimination. **1962** *Press* Oct. 10: Big-Brother Jonathan is no longer friendly Uncle Sam to us, but our landlord, adviser and stern disciplinarian.

brow *n. Lumbering* **1** originally, that part of a river bank where logs were piled ready to be rolled into the water at spring break-up; also, the apron, *q.v.* Now also applied to log dumps from which logs are transported by trucks or railway cars. See also **landing** (def. 1a).
1849 ALEXANDER *L'Acadie* II 163: I mentioned a "brow" to which the loggers dragged the logs; they roll them down this to the water's edge, where stakes confine them till the mass of timbers is ready for rafting. **1942** HAIG-BROWN *Timber* 250: [Cables] are passed under the loads and hooked to the cross-log at the brow of the apron.
2 See quotes.
1849 ALEXANDER *L'Acadie* II 164: He had called on his "gang" to work on Sunday, and "cut down the brow" to let the logs into the river. . . . **1896** ROBERTS *Camp-Fire* 203: In lumbermen's parlance, the logs of the winter's chopping, hauled and piled on the river-bank where they can conveniently be launched into the water upon the breaking up of the ice, are termed collectively "a brow of logs."

brow-log *n. Lumbering* See Haig-Brown quote.
1942 HAIG-BROWN *Timber* 11: "What's the brow log?" . . . "It's a big log we set alongside the track," he said. "Between the empty car and the pile on the landing. Makes sure the logs ride up over the car instead of smacking into it and knocking it off the track. It's handy for the loaders too; makes a sort of step up or down for us." **1942** SWANSON *Western Logger* 8: I wish I could stand on a "brow-log" and gawk at the rigger on high. . . .

brown bear any of several North American bears, including the grizzly bear, *q.v.,* and a color phase of the black bear, *q.v.*
1784 PENNANT *Arctic Zoology* 62: Mr. Graham assures me, that the brown Bears, in the inland parts of Hudson's Bay, make great havoc among the Buffaloes. **1958** *Kelvington Radio* 5 June 3/3: [He] shot a large brown bear . . . which had been mauling . . . a calf.

brown biscuit a kind of whole-wheat hardtack.
1849 ALEXANDER *L'Acadie* II 183: . . . it is not advisable for an exploring-party in these woods to take brown biscuit with them. *c***1939** CHAMPION *On the Island* 70: I have stretched my credit to the utmost in procuring salt pork and brown biscuits to support me through the winter.

Brownie *n. Slang, Obs.* a Japanese.
1900 *Prospector* (Lillooet, B.C.) 13 July 2/1: The hired girl had to make way for the "heathen Chinee," and now the little Brownies are ousting John Chinaman from the kitchen.

brown oil See **dark oil.**

brown-sugar house *Slang, Obs.* in Nova Scotia, an inferior hotel or inn.
1830 MOORSOM *Letters N.S.* 269: Barrington is a respectable fishing settlement, but its leading hotel would not receive a better character from a Nova-Scotian traveller than that of a "brown sugar" house. Those houses that are well-frequented are generally supplied with all the requisites for refreshment . . . amongst others, with the best loaf-sugar.

browse bed See **bough bed.**
1951 ANGIER *At Home* 148: "I'll build us a browse bed later on," he promised.

browse line the height to which moose and deer browse the foliage of trees.
1952 PUTNAM *Cdn Regions* 37/2: In Algonquin Park a browse line is quite evident on white cedar. . . .

browse out haul out logs by block and tackle.
1964 *Atlantic Advocate* July 59/1: Trees growing near the stream were "browsed out"—that is hauled with block and tackle to the river's bank.

bruck *n.* [< *b*us + *tr*uck] a type of bus having seats for twenty passengers and a large compartment in the rear for baggage and freight.

1961 *Edmonton Jnl* 1 Aug. 3/3: Last year a bruck was used to cross the ice as long as possible. According to one official, the brucks carry everything from "soup to nuts."

brue [bru] *n.* [< Cdn F *broue* froth, as on beer] *Pacific Coast* See **soapberry** (def. 2). See also **Indian ice-cream.** Also spelled *broue.*

1925 ANDERSON *Trees and Shrubs* 131: The Soapberry or "Brue" . . . is the fruit of a shrub belonging to the olive family.

Brûlé [bru'le *or* 'brule] *n.* [< Cdn F *Bois Brûlé* charred wood] Also spelled *Brule, Brûlé.*
1 *Hist.* See **bois-brûlé.** Cp. **Métis.**
1815 *Kingston Gaz.* (U.C.) 8 July 3/1: It is also reported that several Brules had been made prisoners. . . .
1816 (1817) HALKETT *Selkirk Settlement* xxxiii: . . . Brules, Metifs [Métis], or half-breeds [are] the bastard sons of Indian concubines, kept by the partners or servants of the North-West Company. **1849** MCLEAN *Notes* II 301: There are no better horsemen in the world than the Red River "brulés." **1952** (1954) JENNINGS *Strange Brigade* 238: The horsemen, who seemed to be all Brûlés, turned out toward the prairies. . . .

2 a sub-tribe of the Dakota Indians living south of what is now Saskatchewan; a sub-group of the Sioux.
1912 (1913) HODGE & WHITE *Indians of Can.* 430/1: The Siouan family is divided as follows: . . . 7, (a) Sichangu or Brulés. . . . **1928** EVARTS *Fur Brigade* 61: . . . the Brules undoubtedly had been planning a raid on a Mandan village. . . .

brulé [bru'le *or* 'brule] *n.* [< Cdn F *brûlé, brûlis*] Also spelled *brûlé, brule.* **1** an area that has been burnt out by a forest fire, characterized by charred stumps and rampikes, *q.v.* See also **burn,** *n.* (def. 3), **burnt-out area** (def. 1), **burnt woods, fire-barren, fire-burn, Grand Brulé,** and **rampike country.**
1793 (1933) MACDONELL *Diary* 77: This brulé came to the water's edge. . . . **1824** (1955) BLACK *Journal* 191: Got out of the new burnt Ground & into an old Brule. . . . **1873** (1904) BUTLER *Wild North Land* 240: Thick with brulé and tangled forest lay the base of the mountain. . . . **1965** *Beaver* Autumn 55/2: I had to cross a stretch of brulé. . . .

2 *Hist.* a tract of new land cleared by burning (def. 1) during the early days of settlement. See also **burnt land** (def. 2).
1901 CONNOR *Man from Glengarry* 15: . . . in spring and summer they farmed their narrow fields, and rescued new lands from the brûle. . . . **1942** CAMPBELL *Thorn-Apple Tree* 101: "It would be better if those stumps were cleared out of the brulé," she considered.

brulot *n.* [< Cdn F < F; cf. *brûler* to burn] *Obs.* black fly, *q.v.*; sand fly, *q.v.*
1812 KEITH *Letters* 102: The musquitoes make their appearance about the 15th June and leave us about the end of August, about which time the *brulots* succeed in swarms; their sting is particularly powerful and venemous in this quarter. **1876** LORD *Wilderness* 282: More diminutive is the burning fly, brulot or sand-fly of the trappers and fur-traders.

brush *n.* [< OF *brosse*] **1** low-growing trees and shrubs; undergrowth. See also **brushwood** (def. 1).
1800 (1897) COUES *New Light* I 61: The country . . . is much overgrown with thick brush, poplars, and willows. **1965** *Kingston Whig-Standard* (Ont.) 30 Dec. 17/2: . . . Steel Co. of Canada has awarded a contract for brush clearing on the route of a proposed railway branch. . . .

2† lopped-off branches, especially evergreen boughs. See also **brushwood** (def. 2).
1791 (1934) FIDLER *Journal* 522: Found . . . 1 Brush hut with one family in it when I arrived. **1863** WALSHE *Cedar Creek* 122: . . . when we have a big fire built in front, and a lot of hemlock brush to lie on, we shall be pretty comfortable. **1949** MACGREGOR *Blankets and Beads* 128: [They] covered with a shelter of wood and brush. . . .

3† the woods; the forest or backcountry; the bush. See also **brushwood** (def. 3).
1900 LONG *Wilderness Ways* vi: I was ready enough to quit all claims and take to the brush myself. . . . **1953** SWANSON *Haywire Hooker* 33: It's good level yarding out there in the brush. . . .

brush *v.* **1** clear the brush from land. See also **brush out.**
1863 WALSHE *Cedar Creek* 145: . . . Arthur was "brushing" at a short distance from the shanty. **1896** GOURLAY *Hist.Ottawa* 119: They . . . brushed the road and blazed it after him. . . . **1925** GROVE *Settlers* 25: I've brushed and cleared three acres. . . .

2 cover soft ground with brush to make a trail or road passable for men and horses.
1880 GORDON *Mountain and Prairie* 129: The only route . . . leads . . . over treacherous swamps, where we were . . . delayed by the necessity of "brushing" the trail. **1905** (1910) HAYDON *Riders of the Plains* 278: All boggy and soft places should be brushed and . . . small streams should be bridged. **1913** CURRAN & CALKINS *Northland* 38: . . . the work of brushing the trail was by no means unpleasant.

3 mark a trail, especially by setting small evergreen trees upright along a route across frozen water. See also **balise,** *n.v.,* and **bush,** *v.* (def. 2).
1901 TYRRELL *Annual Report* 17: Artillery Lake was reached . . . more than two weeks after it had been first visited by Fairchild and Acres, when exploring and "brushing" the trail for our voyageurs. **1934** *Beaver* Dec. 48/2: "Brushing" a lake was necessary to mark a trail.

brush bed See **bough bed.**
1922 *Beaver* Nov. 64/2: . . . I made a brush bed under a spreading spruce tree. . . . **1954** EVANS *Mist* 157: Caleb was remembering the pitchy smell from . . . the brush beds on which he and Nettie had lain along the trails. . . .

brush camp† See **brush shed.**
1894 MILES *Boy Life* 313: Mackinnon thought we should save time by carrying it [a tent] instead of making brush camps. **1934** GODSELL *Arctic Trader* 161: Together we walked down the trail past the two Indians who were seated in a brush camp on top of the snow. . . . **1941** *Beaver* Mar. 14/1: In the deep woods, a simple brush camp is made in the shelter of a good wooded bluff. . . .

brush corral *West* a temporary fence made of branches and any such material at hand for forming an enclosure, usually for horses.
1887 (1888) LEES & CLUTTERBUCK *British Columbia* 277: . . . cutting down several fir-trees, with their branches made a "brush corral" all round the windward side of the camp. . . . **1955** HOBSON *Nothing too Good* 92: Gradually a long, rectangular brush corral reached from the timber across the icecap and into the river.

brushed *adj.* cleared of brush.
1955 *Mountaineer* 3 Mar. 10/5: [For Sale] New frame house and buildings. 10 acres broken, 43 brushed. Fenced and cross fenced. Drilled well.

brush fence *Hist.* an early type of fence. See also **brushpile fence** and **bush fence**.
1852 (1881) TRAILL *Cdn Crusoes* 258: After they had piled and burned up the loose boughs and trunks that encumbered the space which they had marked out, they proceeded to enclose it with a brush fence, which was done by felling the trees that stood in the line of the field, and letting them fall so as to form the bottom log of the fence, which they then made of sufficient height by piling up arms of trees and brushwood. **1958** SYMONS *Fences* xii: But probably the earliest pioneer fence of all was known as the brush fence. . . . Presiding in a Caledon township police court, the Squire ruled that a brush fence to be legal "must be forty feet wide, and damned high."

brush fishery *Obs.* a fishery in the backwoods.
1866 KING *Sportsman in Canada* 301: The Shad . . . are seldom taken with the rod, and can barely be classed among the game fish of the country, for they are chiefly taken in "brush fisheries."

brush-hook *n.* a long-handled implement with a sharp cutting edge on a hooked blade, used in cutting brush, lopping off branches, etc.
1832 (1953) RADCLIFF *Letters* 92: The brushwood is cut away with a brush-hook, an instrument constructed here for the purpose. . . . **1963** MCKINNON *Forest Activities 3* 12: Therefore most hand-tools are used in line-building and in mopping-up operations after the fire has died down . . . [including] brush-hook [for] clearing brush. . . .

brushing (out) *n.* the process or operation of clearing the land of brush.
1832 (1953) RADCLIFF *Letters* 48: . . . we had cleared twenty acres of the land for wheat, and during the successive operations of brushing, chopping, logging, burning and fencing—my father was obliged to hire workmen. **1947** SAUNDERS *Algonquin* 152: The rangers did the "brushing out," while especially trained men fastened the lines to convenient trees. **1965** *Kingston Whig-Standard* (Ont.) 30 Dec. 17/3: We have let a contract for railway spur brushing, work that must be done in winter. . . .

brushland *n.* *West* land covered with brush (def. 1).
1963 *Calgary Herald* 4 Oct. 27/7: . . . hunters are urged to take care with the thousands of hunters roaming the scrub brushland.

brushman *n.* a legendary Indian living in solitude in the woods.
1949 LEECHMAN *Indian Summer* 113: Some brushmen were the survivors of bands of Indians which had been nearly exterminated by starvation, living on alone after all the others had succumbed. . . . *Ibid.* 112: She had been afraid it was a "brushman" trapping ground squirrels.

brush out See **brush**, *v.* (def. 1).
1896 GOURLAY *Hist.Ottawa* 42: Fancy, people now, going alone 50 miles, following a road brushed out and blazed and carrying through these solitary forests these necessaries of their lives. **1956** EVANS *Mountain Dog* 52: The old trail to the cabin was overgrown, and he got the ax to brush it out. **1963** SYMONS *Many Trails* 165: It was in order to make patrols in the hills possible that the work of "brushing out"—clearing and blazing narrow trails . . . was undertaken. . . .

brushpile fence See **brush fence**.
1923 WILLIAMS *Spinning Wheels* 25: Reckless with safety in sight, they bounded over the brushpile fence and plunging through the cabin door drew in the latch string.

brush shed a temporary shelter of brush built after the style of a lean-to (def. 1a). See also **brush camp**.
1944 *Beaver* Dec. 30/1: Two three-sided brush sheds, their open faces opposite each other, were built a few feet apart and shared a common fire. . . .

brush tent See **brush shed**.
1832 (1963) DAVIES *Northern Quebec* 163: One of the three Esquimaux families . . . had made a brush tent last fall and surrounded it outside with blocks of snow.

brush up *Logging* pile up (timber) in the process of falling, *q.v.*
1966 *Sun* (Vancouver) 12 Jan. 25/1: He is careful not to "brush up" timber in a tangle which hampers the bucker and scaler.

brush wolf 1 See **coyote** (def. 1).
1937 STANWELL-FLETCHER *Driftwood Valley* 24: A little "brush wolf," or coyote, stared at us from a high bank. **1950** DOBIE *Coyote* 41: "Brush wolf" the trappers of northern Alberta and Saskatchewan were calling the new penetrator into their grounds early in this century. **1966** *Kingston Whig-Standard* (Ont.) 8 Jan. 6: [Caption] The men . . . used purebred Walker hounds as they bagged this 60-pound brush wolf this week [in Eastern Ontario].

2 See **coyote** (def. 2).
1956 KEMP *Northern Trader* 169: Brush wolves are not the fanciest of fur, but I gave him eight dollars for it.

brushwood *n.* **1**† See **brush**, *n.* (def. 1).
1806 (1897) COUES *New Light* I 405: At five o'clock we came to a small lake on which grew brushwood and poiriers. **1933** CAMERON *Twigs* 125: . . . the smaller brushwood had been cut and piled. . . .

2 See **brush**, *n.* (def. 2).
1942 RADDALL *His Majesty's Yankees* 96: We found a Micmac family crouching in a wretched little bark hut, banked with brushwood and sawdust. . . .

3 *Obs.* See **brush**, *n.* (def. 3).
1829 MACTAGGART *Three Years* II 172: . . . they seem to be just as much at home among the thick brushwood, without road or sun, as we are in a cleared country.

buck[1] *n.* See **buck Indian**.
1800 MACKENZIE *Voyages* 385: I . . . kept the woman to be disposed of in the season when the Peace River bucks look out for women, in the month of May. **1900** OSBORN *Warders of the West* 781: [They] were jostled in a . . . crowd of yelling, gun-firing bucks. **1957** FISHER *Pemmican* 309: . . . Sunday had married a buck and was now full of papoose.

buck[2] *v.* **1**† saw wood into lengths, as with a bucksaw, *q.v.*
1912 POCOCK *Man in the Open* 138: . . . he can buck fire-wood if I tend him with spurs and quirt. **1918** MACKAY *Trench and Trail* 112: I can "bark" or "fall" or "buck," / An' w'en whisky's down de cook / I'm "cookee"! **1962** FRY *Ranch on the Cariboo* 117: We felled tree after tree, barked them, skidded them in with horses, bucked them into lengths. . . .

2 gather hay into windrows, as with a buckrake.
1955 HARDY *Alta Anthol.* 114: I've cut, raked and bucked prairie and slough hay (there's a difference) and helped with the stacking. **1959** STOREY *Prairie Harvest* 31: In an hour the men bucked some three or four tons of hay around the framework of the stable where it could be forked into the walls and onto the roof to complete the building.

buck beaver 1 a male beaver (def. 1).
1931 GREY OWL *Last Frontier* 190: The mother . . . lives in a separate lodge built and tended by the male or buck beaver.
2 See quote.
1913 SANDILANDS *West.Cdn Dict.* 6: Beaver, a man engaged on road-making near the lumber camps. Buck beaver, the foreman on such work.

buckboard† *n.* **1** a light, four-wheeled vehicle having a single seat resting on springs that are attached to a springy platform.
1871 (1888) MCDOUGALL *G.M.McDougall* 180: Scarcely had the horse struck the current when he was thrown on his side, and horse and buckboard, with Mr. McDougall standing on the buckboard seat, were carried down the river. **1960** BLONDAL *Candle* 18: At the hotel hitching-rail a team of horses stood dismally, the buckboard creased and dusted with snow.
2 a plank placed across the box of a farm wagon and used as a passenger seat.
1887 *Grip* (Toronto) 4 June 7/2: ". . . I fixed it to go with a lot of young fellers in an old farm wagon with a sort of buckboard for a middle seat. This buckboard, Cap, was a two inch plank and hed no more spring in it than a brick."

buck cop *Slang* See **buck policeman.**
1953 MOWERY *Mounted Police* 90: . . . Holman was a green buck cop then, just out of the Awkward Squad.

bucker *n. Lumbering* See 1963 quote.
1907 *Log of the "Columbia"* March 7/1: With a leap the "buckers" mount the fallen tree. **1942** HAIG-BROWN *Timber* 251: Fallers work in sets of two . . . with one or more buckers following them. **1963** MCKINNON *Forest Activities 1* 5: Once the tree has been felled, the "bucker" will saw the tree into shorter lengths more suitable for hauling.

bucket cable an endless cable stretched across a chasm or gulch and equipped with receptacles for carrying people or materials from one side to the other.
1962 NICHOLSON *West Coast* 152: Some of the cabins are still there, together with the foot bridges the linesmen built across the numerous streams and the bucket cable used for crossing the wider gulches.

buck Indian a male North American Indian. See also **buck**[1], *n.*
1859 *Brit.Colonist* (Victoria) 17 June 2/2: . . . every buck Indian in the country carries one or two shooting irons, and as many knives. . . . **1940** *Beaver* Sep. 45/2: The buck Indians sat like graven images.

bucking *n. Lumbering* the work done by a bucker, *q.v.*
1908 BROWN *Lady of the Snows* 121: The expression of such sentiments as these only makes them dissatisfied with the bucking of wood and breaking of stone, and generates socialism. . . . **1919** *Camp Worker* 28 June 6/2: The cost of falling and bucking by day wages was . . . $1.20 per M log scale. **1966** *Sun* (Vancouver) 12 Jan. 25/1: Falling can be dangerous; 20 of the 64 deaths in the woods in 1964 were in falling and bucking. . . .

bucking horse† at stampedes, rodeos, etc., a horse specially given to bucking and, for this reason, used as a mount in bronco-riding competitions. See also **buck-jumper.**
1919 *Eye Opener* (Calgary) 23 Aug. 4: Miss Tillie Baldwin, World's Champion Lady Bronk [sic] Rider, will ride bucking horses, and also attempt to bulldog a steer from a running horse. **1962** *Canada Month* May 38/1: A top bucking horse is valued from $1000 to $1500 and works, in periods of ten seconds each, for four or five minutes each year.

bucking pole a primitive type of hay loader.
1959 STOREY *Prairie Harvest* 31: He . . . turned his attention to a sweep or bucking pole.

bucking season of range sheep, the breeding season.
1953 *Cdn Geog. Jnl* XLVI 249/1: "Bucking" (breeding) season comes early in December on the plains, when the band is back on the winter range.

buck-jumper *n.* See **bucking horse.**
1900 OSBORN *Greater Canada* 226: The art of breeding and the advantages of breeding something better than the "ten-dollar buck-jumper" are too often disregarded. **1942** BOSANQUET *Saddlebags* 83: Now Scottie Fraser has a good buck-jumper, and . . . I induced him to say I might ride it.

buck policeman a constable, especially a rookie of the R.C.M.P. See also **buck cop.**
1923 STEELE *Spirit-of-Iron* 246: In the course of his meanderings, he killed a settler who refused to help him and shot down a buck policeman. . . .

buck rein a single rope attached to the hackamore of a bucking horse, to assist the rider to keep his balance.
1962 *Canada Month* May 36/1: He gripped the soft cotton buck rein in one hand, raised the other high in the air as a signal to the men holding the chute gate closed, then spurred the horse. . . .

bucksaw† *n.* a saw consisting of a blade set in an H-shaped frame one side of which is extended to form a handle, used for cross-cutting wood.
1885 *Prince Albert Times* (Sask.) 13 Feb. 1/5: "Mother Smoke," a squaw, was tried for having in her possession a buck-saw and axe belonging to a half-breed, but was discharged. **1964** *Atlantic Advocate* July 60/2: It replaces the old bucksaws, and can be operated by one man, doubling his capacity. . . .

buck set often in logging and other camps where there are no women, an all-male square dance; a square made up of men only.
1961 PRICE & KENNEDY *Renfrew* 49: A violin or "fiddle," a mouth organ and the bones provided music for a "buck set" on a Saturday night. . . .

buckskin *n.* See 1885 quote. See also **buckskin horse.**
1885 HILL *Home to Home* 129: The pale yellow horse called by the French "isabelle" is known in the North-West as a "buckskin." **1961** MITCHELL *Jake and the Kid* 120: He says all buckskins are mean because they got Indian [in them].

1963 *News of the North* 28 Feb. 1: A rather unique system of scoring points at the N.W.T. Buckskin Gloves . . . has been developed by the Gloves committee.

buckskin horse or **pony** See **buckskin.**
1880 *Edmonton Bull.* 20 Dec. 4/2: Horse Found.—Came into my band of horses last September, a small Bichon or Buckskin Horse. . . . 1916 WOOD *Tourist's N.W.* 415: One who climbed by the aid of a certain buckskin pony . . . imprinted these scenes in water colours. 1955 HOBSON *Nothing Too Good* 49: I . . . looked up to see that the rider was forking a short-coupled, trim-legged buckskin horse.

buck the brigade *Northwest, Obs.* See quote.
1934 *Beaver* Sep. 37/1: They could never be certain of the irresponsible and excitable *Metis*, who child-like would promise anything in the winter to get an advance on next season's wages, but when in the spring the time came to man the boats the *Metis* would generally refuse and, in local parlance, "buck the brigade."

buckwheat farmer a lazy, improvident farmer.
1944 MOWAT *Carrying Place* 90: It was his settled habit to be late and incompetent; a "buckwheat farmer" who had watched his farm going back. . . .

buckwheat pine *Obs.* the white pine (def. 1a), which has a cone resembling buckwheat flour in color.
1833 *Cdn Literary Mag.* Apr. 1/2: . . . I did not expect to find the Canadians an ignorant people . . . as inaccessible to light as the buck-wheat pines of Dorchester or Galt.

buddy sap maple sap collected late in the season when the buds begin to burst. See also **bud run.**
1951 *Cdn Woods* 225/2: High-grade vinegar may be made from the sugar contained in the wash-water from pans, strainers and other appliances, together with the "buddy" sap, which is not suitable for making syrup.

bud run in sugaring-off (def. 1), the third run of maple sap, which makes inferior syrup and sugar. See also **buddy sap.**
1923 WILLIAMS *Spinning Wheels* 83: Syrup and sugar made from the first or "robin run" are superior to that found in either of the succeeding runs, known respectively as the "frog" and "bud."

buff *n.* [< F *buffle*] See **buffalo,** *n.* (def. 2).
1583 PECKHAM *True Reporte* E iv^r: There is also a kind of Beaste, much bigger than an Oxe, whose hyde is more than 18.foote long, of which sorte a Countriman of ours, one VValker a Sea man, who vppon that Coast, did a trueth reporte, in the presence of diuers honourable and worshipfull persons, that he and his company did finde in one Cottage aboue 240.Hides, which they brought away and solde in Fraunce for xl. shillinges an hyde, and with this agreeth Dauid Ingram, and describeth that beast at large, supposing it to be a certaine kinde of Buffe. 1665 (1885) RADISSON *Voyages* 212: They have very handsome shoose laced very thick all over wth a peece sowen att the side of ye heele, wch was of haire of Buff. 1961 *Alta Hist.Rev.* Winter 2/1: I figured the baby buff would run away if I turned him loose. . . .

buffalo *n.* 1 *Obs.* the musk-ox, *Ovibos moschatus.*
1689 (1929) KELSEY *Papers* 27: In ye Evening spyed two Buffillo left our things & pursued y^m we Kill'd one they are ill shapen beast their Body being bigger than ox leg & foot like ye same but not half so long a long neck & head a hog their Horns not growing like other Beast but joyn together upon their forehead & so come down ye side of their head & turn up till ye tips be even wth ye Buts their Hair is near a foot long. 1795 (1911) HEARNE *Journey* 135: This lake I distinguished by the name of Buffalo, or Musk-Ox Lake, from the number of those animals that we found grazing on the margin of it.

2 the North American bison, *Bison bison.* See also **buff, moostoos,** and **plain buffalo.**
[1665 (1885) RADISSON *Fourth Voyage* 156: The horns of the Buffes are as big as those of an ox, but not so long, but bigger & of a blackish collour; he hath a very long hairy taile; he is reddish, his hair frized & very fine.] 1691 (1929) KELSEY *Papers* 14: This day we lay still ye Indians being willing for to go hunt Buffillo because there is none of these Beast in ye woods. . . . 1743 (1949) ISHAM *Observations* 154: These bufflowe . . . being not so swift footed as Deer . . . I have Known Indian women Kill them by catching them by the tail, and Run fire brans up their —— &c. 1962 *Canada Month* May 36/1: Since the buffalo disappeared from the plains and the West's potential as a ranching country was first recognized, men have spun yarns. . . .

3 the meat of the buffalo.
1843 (1955) LEFROY *Magnetic North* 69: We live upon Whitefish chiefly, varied with dried or fresh moose meat, or buffalo, as the hunters send it in. 1958 *Edmonton Jnl* 8 Aug. 3/5: Monday evening's activities will include a buffalo barbecue, and Indian dance. . . .

4 a buffalo robe.
c1825 (1949) LAWSON *N.B.Story* 172: . . . the two sons lay on the floor in another corner with a buffalo below them and another above them. 1869 MCCREA *Lost Amid Fogs* 45: Thus we sped through the bitter day, crouching beneath the "buffaloes". . . . 1901 DRUMMOND *J.Courteau* 50: "Den w'en he's feex de buffalo, an' wissle to hees pony. . . ."

5 See **buffalo fish.**
1953 MOON *Saskatchewan* 115: Sometimes buffalo fishing is easy, sometimes difficult. Stormy weather and rough water is not the time to hunt buffaloes.

buffalo *v. Slang* **1** run off; evict.
1910 FRASER *Red Meekins* 177: "I'll help salt the mine . . . and if the Englishman gets wise to it an' asks me . . . I'll just get riled and buffalo him off the forty acres by the seat of his pants."

2† puzzle; bluff; intimidate.
1915 *Eye Opener* (Calgary) 3 Apr. 3/5: He's got everybody buffaloed around here. 1960 *Sun* (Vancouver) 26 Jan. 1: [Headline] They're Champs At Hockey But—Russians Buffaloed by Banquets.

Buffalo *n.* a large twin-engined transport plane (CV-7A) designed by de Havilland of Canada for short takeoff conditions.
1965 *Globe and Mail* (Toronto) 26 Apr. 17/8: First there was the Beaver, which incorporated into its design the suggestions of Canada's highly respected bush pilots. . . . Then came the Otter and then the Caribou and now the Buffalo.

buffalo apple *Obs.* See **buffalo bean.**
1887 *Senate Report* 7 June 72: "There is a product of the North-West called the buffalo apple or buffalo fruit: is that [the wild turnip] it?" "No, that is a sort of plum which grows on the prairie on a vine."

these things ... as he loved the smell of buffalo bush and sage.

buffalo apron *Obs.* See **buffalo robe.**
*a*1820 (1838) HEAD *Forest Scenes* 48: I had purchased a buffalo apron, or two skins of the animal sewed together and lined with baize,—an article of the greatest use and comfort....

buffalo bean 1 the buffalo pea, *Astragalus crassicarpus,* a wild pea having yellow blossoms and a pod that is red and fleshy at first, becoming hard and brownish when dry.
1920 STRINGER *Prairie Mother* 232: I told him of our range-lilies and foxglove and buffalo-beans.... **1954** MACGREGOR *Behold the Shining Mountains* 127: [We travelled] through the rolling parklands yellow with buffalo-beans....

2 the fruit or "beans" of this plant. See also **buffalo apple.**
1922 STEAD *Neighbours* 159: Who would think she had a letter from her mother asking if she was canning any buffalo beans? **1965** *Globe and Mail* (Toronto) 13 Oct. 6/4: The coffee they served appeared to have been brewed from dinosaur bones or buffalo beans....

buffalo berry† *West* a shrub of the genus *Shepherdia,* as *S. canadensis;* also, the edible red berry of this shrub. See also **bullberry** and **soapberry.**
1920 SAUNDERS *Wild Plants* 84: I have read that the name Buffalo-berry is derived from the fact that it was a customary garnish to the monotonous buffalo steaks and tongues of those days. **1957** FISHER *Pemmican* 169: He went to the trading room and stared round him, thinking of ... red buffalo berries still on the twigs. **1958** *Globe and Mail* (Toronto) 15 November 16/3: Up in the coulees, you can find a few shrubs of the buffalo berry....

Buffalo Bill See quote.
1942 TWOMEY & HERRICK *Needle to the North* 54: Ross had sent a man down for Old Harold, who came presently in a peaked-front cap of wool, the kind which we used to call a "Buffalo Bill."

buffalo bird See **cowbird.**
1909 BEMISTER *Stories from Prairie and Mountain* 41: One autumn day a young buffalo bird lay almost under his [a buffalo's] feet. **1955** MCCOWAN *Upland Trails* 79: In bygone days when there were no domestic cattle on the plains ... these [cow] birds were seasonal companions of the shaggy buffalo, hence the name buffalo-bird. Later, when the buffalo herds disappeared, they became friendly with the stock on the ranches and farms and have since been known as cowbirds.

buffalo blanket See **buffalo robe.**
1908 LAUT *Conquest N.W.* II 245: Then he realized that he was without either coat or buffalo blanket.

buffalo boss the hump on the shoulders of a buffalo, much esteemed as a delicacy. See also **boss.**
1834 (1947) HARGRAVE *Correspondence* 172: I send you now ... a Buffalo boss which may perhaps be something of a curiosity at York Factory. **1957** FISHER *Pemmican* 7: Pemmican needed plenty of marrow fat, buffalo tongues and bosses, moose noses and beaver tails....

buffalo bush See **buffalo berry.**
1957 FISHER *Pemmican* 322: ... he knew he loved all

buffalo camp *Hist.* a buffalo hunters' camp.
1940 NIVEN *Mine Inheritance* 329: I recalled the winter of the coteau buffalo-camps and the death of Jules....

buffalo chip† *Hist.* a piece of dried buffalo dung, often used for fuel on the prairies. See also **bois de vache, chip,** and **prairie chip.** Cp. **cow chip.**
[**1765-75** (1933) POND *Narrative* 58: They Make youse of Buffaloes dung for fuel as there is but little or no Wood upon the Planes.] **1859** (1860) PALLISER *Journals* 130: We reached "Buffalo Chip Lake" [now Chip Lake] ... and camped on its margin. **1874** (1910) HAYDON *Riders of the Plains* 30: All over this country there is little wood, and snow would hide the buffalo chips, the only fuel available. **1958** *High Prairie Progress* (Alta) 21 May 3/3: Dry buffalo chips were the chief source of fuel on the prairies.

buffalo coat a long winter coat of buffalo skin. See also **buffalo skin** (def. 2b).
1846 (1945) *Beaver* Dec. 16/2: All sentries, by day or night, were provided with buffalo coats kept at each post for their use. **1871** OXENDEN *My First Year in Canada* 49: ... the greater part of the congregation assembled at the door in their buffalo coats and furs.... **1956** YOUNG *Flood* 119: The same old man on the camp chair who'd been there the other night, but now in an old buffalo coat, was holding bags in one team.

buffalo compound See **buffalo pound.**
1965 *Kingston Whig-Standard* (Ont.) 29 Sep. 34/1: A buffalo compound 4,000 years old has been discovered on a farm in this district 100 miles southeast of Edmonton.

buffalo country the prairies, where the buffalo once was plentiful. See also **buffalo grounds, buffalo lands, buffalo plain,** and **buffalo range** (def. 2).
1774 (1934) HEARNE *Journal* 117: This day 3 Cannoes of Grass Indians from the Buffalow Country came with a few wolf skins, some Dry'd meat and a little Buffalo fatt. **1939** *Cdn Hist.Rev.* XX 285: The apparent rapidity with which large areas as in the buffalo country were deforested can in my view be readily explained by the hypothesis of fire.

buffalo days or **period** the time when buffalo were to be found on the praires in their natural state.
1923 *Beaver* May 304/1: Polygamy was very much in vogue among the plains Indians during the buffalo period.... **1933** *Ibid.* Dec. 30/2: ... I asked him to tell me about the buffalo days....

buffalo fish† a species of sucker, *Catostomidae,* resembling a carp and having a humped back. See also **buffalo,** *n.* (def. 5).
1810 SCHULTZ *Travels* I 49: There was no salmon in this bay, but there are pike, maskonangee and buffaloe fish, which will weigh from five to thirty pounds. **1960** *Fisheries Fact Sheet* 47 1: Buffalo fish, native of some waters of the western plains, have a very long dorsal fin with many rays....

buffalo fruit *Obs.* See **buffalo berry.**

buffalo gnat† See **black-fly.**
[**1843** (1868) IRVING *Bonneville* 59: Excessively annoyed by ... buffalo gnats.] **1897** YOUNG *Manitoba Memories* 59: In fact the mosquito, "buffalo-gnat" and "bulldog" seemed to have prairie appetites, and every traveller across these plains knows what that means.

buffalo grass any of several short grasses, as *Buchloë dactyloides,* common on the prairies. See also **buffalo wool** (def. 2).

1788 (1890) EDGAR *Ten Years of U.C.* 340: I received the following memorandum from General Washington, who requested me . . . to send him . . . seeds . . . [of] buffalo grass. . . . **1896** RUSSELL *Far North* 47: It is certainly not an attractive spot in March, surrounded by monotonous, undulating plains, covered with gray buffalo grass. **1964** *Islander* 18 Oct. 12/4: One of the last great areas of arable land, it had produced "buffalo grass" to feed the great herds [of buffalo]. . . .

buffalo grounds See **buffalo country.**

1826 (1950) OGDEN *Journals* 129: Were our horses in good condition in ten days we could reach Buffalo ground. . . . **1908** LAUT *Conquest N.W.* I 342: The Indians' object was to reach the buffalo grounds and lay up store of meat for the winter.

buffalo head *North* See quote.

1934 GODSELL *Arctic Trader* 299: Half-breed and Indian girls had bobbed hair in imitation of the whites, only to be referred to as "buffalo heads". . . . *Ibid.* 303: To the "buffalo heads" and other native ladies of the fur lands the air mail seemed to carry an inestimable boon as each became possessed of a fat mail-order catalogue. . . .

buffalo horse *Hist.* See **buffalo runner** (def. 1).

1933 *Beaver* Sep. 40/1: . . . a trained buffalo horse would generally keep out of the way of furious or wounded buffalo. **1952** HOWARD *Strange Empire* 296: The trained buffalo horse, regarded by frontiersmen as the most intelligent animal that ever lived on the Plains, was high-strung, "spooky," and impossible to hold once the killing run started; he knew his own job and expected his rider to take care of himself.

buffalo hump See **buffalo boss.**

1844 (1955) LEFROY *Magnetic North* 143: The supper was cooking—it was a beautiful kettle of buffalo humps and tongues.

buffalo hunt *Hist.* on the prairies, an organized hunt for buffalo. See also **plain hunt.**

1824 (1931) SIMPSON *Fur Trade* 17: In the event of a failure of the Buffaloe Hunts at Carlton which is not unusual the Brigades are stopped for want of Provisions or the people exposed to the miseries of Famine. **1937** *Cdn Hist.Rev.* XVIII 289: The half-breeds' prairie buffalo-hunt, conducted *en masse* under rude but definite discipline, was a famous institution. . . . **1957** *Beaver* Spring 19/2: Though he had progressed as a farmer . . . he had continued eager for the twice-yearly buffalo hunt.

buffalo hunter *Hist.* a person who took part in buffalo hunts. See **plain hunter.**

1860 *Nor'Wester* (R.R.S.) 15 Nov. 3/2: The carts were ranged round each tent—their number betokening the importance of the owner; for with the buffalo hunters as with the rest of the world, the power of the almighty dollar or its current equivalent in horses and carts, is most keenly appreciated. **1963** *Calgary Herald* 4 Oct. 48/4: Here, Henry Kountz, a whisky trader and buffalo hunter, built a cabin in the early 1870's.

buffalo hunting *Hist.* engaging in a hunt for buffalo; the practice or institution of hunting buffalo.

1754 (1955) HARDY *Alta Anthol.* 49: I went with the young men abuffalo hunting, all armed with bows and arrows; killed seven, fine sport. **1860** *Nor'Wester* (R.R.S.) 15 Nov. 2/3: The occasion is, we think, a

fitting one for the consideration of the bearings and influences of buffalo-hunting, viewed as the business, or regular, ordinary pursuit of a large proportion of the Red River people.

buffalo jump *Hist.* a place where Plains Indians slaughtered buffalo by stampeding them over a precipice. See also **jump,** *n.* (def. 1), **jumping pound, pound** (def. 2), and **piskun.**

1956 LEECHMAN *Native Tribes* 112: Places where these buffalo jumps and pounds once were are still to be found on the prairies; there are thick beds of bones from the hundreds of animals that were killed there. **1964** *Calgary Herald* 6 Jan. 20/1: Recently recovered at the widely-known Old Woman's Buffalo Jump near Cayley [Alta] was a blunt stone axe. . . .

buffalo jumping pound See **buffalo jump.**

1961 MITCHELL *Jake and the Kid* 67: "She's a buffalo jumping pound, the one I'm tellin' you about, the one I figgered out for Chief Weasel Tail of the South Blackfoot in the early days."

buffalo knife a straight, double-edged steel knife about six inches long and three inches wide at the base, tapering to a point.

1934 GODSELL *Arctic Trader* 124: . . . I found a dozen or more black-haired Beavers squatted upon the floor, each of whom was wearing an enormous buffalo knife stuck in a sheath of leather studded with brass headed tacks.

buffalo lands See **buffalo country.**

1954 TYRE *Saddlebag Surgeon* 51: For in 1885 Louis Riel, the Métis rebel, lit the fires of a rebellion which swept across the buffalo lands of the territory later to become the province of Saskatchewan.

buffalo-leather tent a tent made of buffalo leather, especially the teepee, *q.v.*, of the Plains Indians.

1897 YOUNG *Indian Trail* 142: In addition to the buildings already mentioned, we also put up for the sick our large buffalo leather tent. **1953** MOWERY *Mounted Police* 117: The hungry-looking children, the gaunt dogs prowling around the camp, the old buffalo-leather tents —all spoke of poor hunting and short food supplies.

buffalo lick *Obs.* See **salt lick** (def. 2).

buffalo meat the flesh of the buffalo, once the basic meat of the prairie posts and, in the form of pemmican (def. 1a), of the trappers, hunters, and traders on the move.

1819 (1941) *Beaver* Dec. 19/2: . . . a full allowance of Buffaloe meat was served out to them and a pint of Spirits for each man. . . . **1961** *Canada Month* Dec. 28/3: Thus, in January, Bradley will be bringing down buffalo meat from Elk Island Park.

buffalo ox See **berdash** (def. 2).

1858 (1860) HIND *Assiniboine Exped.* II 105: Buffalo emasculated by wolves are often found in the prairies, where they grow to an immense size; the skin of the buffalo ox is recognized by the shortness of the wool and by its large dimensions.

buffalo park See **buffalo reserve.**

1948 ONRAET *Sixty Below* 48: It is illegal to hunt or trap in a buffalo park, and these rangers see to it that nobody with unlawful intentions slips into the prohibited grounds.

buffalo pass or **path** See **buffalo trail.**
1857 (1863) PALLISER *Journals* 56: All these [woods] are traversed by buffalo paths, so that we could ride through them in any direction. **1933** *Beaver* Sep. 39/1: I saw a big herd of buffalo travelling straight toward us. We were camped right on a buffalo pass.

buffalo pemmican *Hist.* pemmican (def. 1a) made from the meat and fat of the buffalo.
1873 (1904) BUTLER *Wild North Land* 58: It was buffalo pemmican from the Saskatchewan. **1890** *Trans.Roy. Soc.Can.* VIII 2 104: I mean, of course, the buffalo pemmican, for it has been made occasionally since by the half-breeds from domestic beef.

buffalo pit See **buffalo wallow.**
1921 *Beaver* Aug.-Sep. 40/2: Buffalo pits worn by ages of pawing and scraping may still be seen.

buffalo placotte See **placotte.**

buffalo plain(s)† See **buffalo country.**
1862 *Nor'Wester* (R.R.S.) 23 May 3/4: Sterile and stony buffalo plain, poor grass, no water for some miles. **1935** *Beaver* Dec. 21/1: The buffalo plains of Alberta were untrodden by white men before 1870. **1952** HOWARD *Strange Empire* 160: He looked out over the shivering thousand, over the snow and the great buffalo plain, and the free, wild, uncompassionate land of the Metis.

buffalo pony *Hist.* See **buffalo runner** (def. 1).
*c*1902 LAUT *Trapper* 71: As soon as the rumbling and pawing began, Colonel Bedson used to send his herders out on the fleetest buffalo ponies to part the contestants.... **1908** LAUT *Conquest N.W.* II 37: The Abbé Dugas tells of another occasion when Marie was riding a buffalo pony—one of the horses used as a swift runner on the chase—her baby dangling in a moss bag from one of the saddle pommels.

buffalo pound *Hist.* an enclosure, corral, or large trap into which the Indians drove buffalo in order to slaughter them. See also **buffalo compound, compound,** and **pound** (def. 1b).
1772 (1908) COCKING *Journal* 108: Did not proceed. The men singing their Buffalo Pound songs. **1820** (1823) FRANKLIN *Journey* 112: The buffalo-pound was a fenced circular space of about a hundred yards in diameter; the entrance was banked up with snow, to a sufficient height to prevent the retreat of the animals that once have entered. **1953** MOON *Saskatchewan* 22: Their tribesmen below would corral the buffalo in a natural ravine buffalo pound and there slaughter them. **1963** SPRY *Palliser* 98: They passed several Indian camps, each near a buffalo pound....

buffalo preserve See **buffalo reserve.**
1927 *Beaver* Sep. 91/2:... the cars of buffalo being transported from the park at Wainwright to the Great Slave Lake buffalo preserve are not picked up until the train arrives at the old Dunvegan yards.

buffalo race See **buffalo run** (def. 1).
1856 ROSS *Red River Settlement* 255: On the third of July [1840]... we came in sight of our destined hunting ground; and on the day following... we had our first buffalo race. **1933** *Beaver* Sep. 39/1: I... told them to

hurry through breakfast, and we would have a good buffalo race.

buffalo racer See **buffalo runner** (def. 1). See also **racer.**
1825 (1950) OGDEN *Journals* 19:... the thieves Started early in the evening [;] they have taken some few Buffalo racers which I do not regret....

buffalo range 1 the normal habitat of the wood buffalo, *q.v.*
1896 RUSSELL *Far North* 103: At the end of the fourth day we reached the northern limit of the buffalo range, perhaps fifty miles south of Great Slave Lake. **1923** WALDO *Down the Mackenzie* 88: The trail to and through the buffalo range starts behind the Roman Catholic Mission at Fort Smith.

2 See **buffalo country.**
1922 *Beaver* Jan. 5/1:... the Indians of the prairies have altered but little from the days of the buffalo range to the present time.

buffalo ranger a warden responsible for the herds on a buffalo reserve.
1923 WALDO *Down the Mackenzie* 87: William McNeill ... is the buffalo ranger, and he has two assistants. **1959** LEISING *Arctic Wings* 65:... Mike finally became a buffalo ranger.

buffalo reserve a tract of land set aside in which buffalo may roam unmolested by hunters, as Wood Buffalo National Park in Northern Alberta. See also **buffalo park** and **buffalo preserve.**
1961 *Alta Hist.Rev.* Winter 1/1: I was range-riding on the Buffalo Reserve at Wainwright on patrol with my favourite saddle horse "Frost."

buffalo road *Hist.* See **buffalo trail.**
1824 (1955) BLACK *Journal* 210: The Country is an extended Plain... and from the number of dry bones & old Buffaloe Roads proclaims it to have been a fine Large animal Country.... **1963** SPRY *Palliser* 118: By following the buffalo roads they escaped getting mired.

buffalo robe† See **robe** (def. 1b). See also **buffalo apron, buffalo blanket,** and **buffalo skin** (def. 2a).
1775 (1901) HENRY (Elder) *Travels* 268: We were obliged to wrap ourselves continually in beaver blankets, or at least in ox-skins, which the traders call *buffalo-robes.* **1957** *Annual Pictorial Rev.* 59: [Caption] Mrs. Lucy Nanertak of Chesterfield Inlet is repairing a 100-year old buffalo robe presented to a Hudson Bay Factor by Chief Sitting Bull. **1967** *Globe and Mail* (Toronto) 26 Jan. 23/2: Lieutenant-Governor... Rowe stepped into the open landau outside the Royal York Hotel and pushed aside the heavy buffalo robe on the seat....

buffalo root See **prairie turnip.**
1887 *Senate Report* 169:... the principal plants would be wild rice, wild turnip or buffalo root, Saskatoon....

buffalo run *Hist.* **1** a buffalo hunt in which the animals were pursued on horseback rather than impounded. See also **buffalo race, course,** and **run,** *n.* (def. 2).
1860 *Nor'Wester* (R.R.S.) 15 Nov. 3/3: Every one has seen or read of a buffalo run so it is needless... to describe it here. *c*1902 LAUT *Trapper* 74: The white blood of the plains' trapper preferred a fair fight in an open field—not the indiscriminate carnage of the Indian hunt; so that the greatest buffalo-runs took place after the opening of spring. **1935** *Trans.Roy.Soc.Can.* III 2 201:... a Hudson's Bay officer... participated in a buffalo run for the first time (1874).

2 See **buffalo trail.**

1910 MCCLUNG *Second Chance* 238: Behind the house . . . was an old "buffalo run," a narrow path, grass-grown now, but beaten deep into the earth by the hoofs of innumerable buffalo. . . . **1933** *Beaver* Sep. 37/1: . . . in the vicinity of the post, where an old buffalo run can still be traced.

buffalo runner *Hist.* **1** a horse or pony trained for hunting buffalo. See also **buffalo horse, buffalo pony, buffalo racer,** and **runner**[1] (def. 2a).

1832 CAMPBELL *Journal* 9: Every spring and fall some hundreds of "Freemen," principally French, half-breeds, were with their families accustomed to leave the Settlement for the plains, taking with them their favorite "Buffalo Runners." **1893** YOUNG *Indian Wigwams* 64: . . . the men mount on their well-trained horses, which are justly called "buffalo runners." **1952** HOWARD *Strange Empire* 302: The price of a good buffalo runner never fell below this figure in forty years and was sometimes as much as $250. **1955** EWERS *Horse* 166: The ideal buffalo runner was a male, at least 8 years of age, fully developed, solidly built, broad backed, long winded, and sure footed.

2 a mounted man, especially a Métis, *q.v.,* who took part in a buffalo run (def. 1). See also **runner**[1] (def. 2b).

1873 BUTLER *Wild North Land* 216: My brother justices [included] two Hudson Bay officials and three half-breed buffalo-runners. . . . **1908** LAUT *Conquest N.W.* II 32: Hosts of freeman—half-breed trappers and buffalo runners—made this their headquarters, refusing allegiance to either company and selling their hunt to the highest bidder.

buffalo-running *n. Hist.* the hunting of buffalo by running them as opposed to impounding them.

1900 OSBORN *Greater Canada* 54: For two years their ordinary occupations (trading, buffalo-running, freighting, and so forth) had been interrupted. . . . **1955** MCCOWAN *Upland Trails* 14: A cayuse trained in all the fine arts of buffalo-running was a priceless possession.

buffalo skin 1 especially among fur traders, a buffalo hide dressed on both sides. Cp. **buffalo robe.** See also **skin** (def. 2).

1754 (1907) HENDAY *Journal* 337: . . . he received us seated on a clear (white) Buffalo skin, attended by 20 elderly men. **1953** MOWERY *Mounted Police* 115: In the middle of the prairillon was a lake, with buffalo-skin tepees pitched around it.

2 a. *Obs.* See **buffalo robe.**

1769 (1931) BROOKE *Emily Montague* 89: . . . we have a large buffaloe's skin under our feet, which turns up, and wraps round us almost to our shoulders. . . . **1837** *Traveller* (Hallowell, U.C.) 10 Feb. 4/5: Ten shillings reward will be paid to any one who has found my Buffalo Skin, and will bring it to me.

b. See **buffalo coat.**

1957 HUTCHISON *Canada* 169: The Royal Canadian Mounted Police, dismounted and bundled in buffalo skins, shivered and stamped their feet on the slippery driveway.

buffalo-skin coracle *Hist.* See **bull boat** and picture.

1953 *Cdn Geog.Jnl* XLVII 88/2: [The Reverend John McDougal] describes many adventures in fording the [Red Deer] river by buffalo-skin coracle, by wagon, and on horseback.

buffalo stone a fragment of a fossil cephalopod, *Bacculites,* valued by Prairie Indians as a charm.

[**1932** JENNESS *Indians of Canada* 177: . . . some Indians on the plains carried curious natural stones shaped like miniature buffaloes to give them good luck and success in hunting.] **1954** MIDDLETON *Kootenai Brown* 2: . . . the "Buffalo Stone" whispers sweet words of encouragement to the faint-hearted. **1965** WORMINGTON & FORBIS *Archaeology Alta* 172: Like many other artifacts, including buffalo stones, they [ribstones] are characteristic of the region as a whole, cross-cutting tribal and linguistic boundaries.

buffalo tongue the tongue of the buffalo, fresh, smoked, or dried, much esteemed as a delicacy.

1754 (1907) HENDAY *Journal* 337: Smoking being over . . . I was presented with 10 Buffalo tongues. **1873** (1952) *Beaver* June 30/2: A banquet of baronial proportions was decreed—Buffalo tongues and humps . . . muf[f]les of Moose deer, the tails of Beaver . . . mingled with the varying civilized cates [delicacies] that the markets of Montreal could furnish. **1922** *Beaver* Apr. 6/1: Early in the spring [c1855] was begun the . . . baling of . . . buffalo tongues which had been salted and smoked.

buffalo trail† a trail made and frequented by buffalo. See also **buffalo pass, buffalo road,** and **buffalo run.**

1880 GORDON *Mountain and Prairie* 158: Their sides are occasionally seamed by old Buffalo trails, for though the buffalo has not been seen on the banks of the Peace for many years, this was once the pasture land for large herds that found here their western limit. **1963** (see quote at **buffalo wallow**].

buffalo wallow† a depression formed by buffalo wallowing in mud or, less often, sand. See also **buffalo pit,** and **wallow.**

1884 *Brandon Mail* (Man.) 6 Mar. 3/1: This illimitable hayfield is everywhere pitted by buffalo wallows. . . . **1963** *B.C.Digest* Nov.-Dec. 51/1: The next day they passed through . . . prairie . . . traversed in all directions by old buffalo trails and wallows.

buffalo wolf *West* See **gray wolf** (def. 1).

1963 SYMONS *Many Trails* xvi: The grey wolf of the plains [is] also known as the buffalo wolf.

buffalo wool 1 the fine hair beneath the coarse outer hair on a buffalo skin. See also **Buffalo Wool Company.**

1913 KELLY *Range Men* 107: During the early days of the Red River settlement . . . an energetic promoter named Pritchard planned an original industry—none other than that of buffalo wool. [**1922** *Beaver* Dec. 112/1: Nothing [was] to be done but to walk out into the Plains, kill buffalo, take their wool, dress and weave it. . . .]

2 See **buffalo grass.** See also **prairie wool.**

1960 MCNAMEE *Florencia Bay* 70: He felt certain that the only heather Dumont had picked had grown among buffalo wool at St. Paul des Métis. . . .

buffalo wool cloth *Hist.* a kind of cloth made from buffalo wool by the Buffalo Wool Company, *q.v.*

1885 BRYCE *Old Settlers* 4/2: It cost $12.50 to manufacture a yard of buffalo wool cloth on Red River, and the cloth only sold for $1.10 in London. **1923** *Beaver* Oct. 5: Large sums were consumed in efforts to manufacture buffalo wool cloth, but it cost many times more than English cloth, to which it was inferior.

Buffalo Wool Company *Hist.* a subsidiary of the Hudson's Bay Company formed in 1821 to manufacture cloth from buffalo wool (def. 1).

1822 *H.B.C.Minutes* 21 : That the Buffalo Wool Company be supplied with seasoned Calves Skins at the rate of 10s. Sterling p. Skin. **1860** *Nor'Wester* (R.R.S.) 14 July 2/4 : The exploits of the Buffalo Wool Company are remembered only to be pitied : we speak of their intentions only to be grieved that they were never carried out. **1922** *Beaver* Dec. 112/1 : The first bubble was the Buffalo Wool Company.

buffer food food that keeps predatory animals satisfied and makes it unnecessary for them to prey on game that the authorities wish to protect.

1962 *Field, Horse & Rodeo* Nov. 19/2 : Rabbits are a famous buffer food ; they may protect pheasants from foxes and antelope kids from coyotes.

bug[1] *n.* [? < F *bougie* lantern, candle] See 1950 quote.

1922 (1924) MASON *Arctic Forests* 239 : In front of me danced the vague shadow of Harry and the dim light thrown before him by the "bug." **1950** HAMBLETON *Abitibi Adventure* 68 : There was a hasty search for flashlights and "bugs," which were simply tin cans with a hole in the side through which a candle protruded.... **1963** *Alaska Sportsman* Mar. 15/2 : In place of flashlights, they made [in the Yukon] what they called bugs out of empty ... syrup cans.

bug[2] *n. Slang* **1** a germ, or microbe ; the cause of an illness.

1919 FRASER *Bulldog Carney* 129 : "Gee! now I will get well," he said ; "I'll beat the bug out now—I'll have heart." **1963** *News of the North* 2 May 1 : This flu bug has been having a hayday [sic], flitting about Discovery....

2 an idea or an obsession with an idea to do or become something.

1909 *Gow Ganda Tribune* (Ont.) 10 Apr. 5/2 : In his speech, Hanley admitted having been unduly urged into running by his friends, but also confessed to having got the bug in his head himself. **1922** STEAD *Neighbours* 57 : "... when you have caught the bug for big farmin', you'll be mighty glad o' the chance to buy Fifteen...." **1955** *Shawinigan Standard* 12 Jan. 2/1 : Men who have succumbed to the do-it-yourself bug have done so through other reasons than avoiding work.

bug-bag *n. Slang* a sleeping bag.

1939 O'HAGAN *Tay John* 141 : I've just been up to where he left his sleeping bag—that bug-bag of his. It's gone, and his rifle too. It's all gone.

buggy *n.* **1** a light four-wheeled carriage, often having a collapsible top and drawn by a single horse.

1841 MCLEOD *Upper Canada* 29 : The clergymen were ... paid by the home government eight hundred dollars each, yearly, for officiating once a week, if the weather would permit his reverence to ride in a cushioned buggy to church.... **1855** (1955) CRAIG *Early Travellers* 204 : We travelled in a buggy, the vehicle generally used in Canada, which although extremely light, successfully resists the terrible concussions arising from the wretched roads. **1958** *Edmonton Jnl* 17 Nov. 4/3 : [We were] hustled into a waiting buggy....

2 a similar vehicle drawn by two horses.

1848 *Sun* (Picton, C.W.) 27 June 2/4 : I happened to be at Norwichville when the Hon. member arrived from Burford ... in a two horse buggy. **1920** WINLOW & POCKLINGTON *Mornin'-Glory Girl* 70 : Not far behind the democrat came a light buggy drawn by a team of greys.

bug-man *n. Slang* an expert on "bugs" ; an entomologist.

1898 CONNOR *Black Rock* 301 : Old "Beetles," whose nickname was prophetic of his future fame as a bugman.... **1955** BIRNEY *Long Table* 38 : There's a bug-man here from Ottawa and he wants college types.

building lot† a plot of land surveyed and zoned for building on.

1816 *Spectator* (St. Davids, U.C.) 25 Oct. 4/4 : The Subscriber offers for Sale Thirty Buildings Lots in Queenston—a reasonable time will be given for payment. **1954** *Peace River Block News* 4 Nov. 7/4 : Two hundred serviced building lots will be sold for homes....

bulk *n. Nfld* a quantity of fish salted and piled in layers. See also **salt-bulk** and **salt pile** (def. 1). Cp. **water-horse** (def. 2).

1777 (1792) CARTWRIGHT *Journal* II 244 : We spread all the green fish, made a large pile, and washed a considerable bulk. **1832** MCGREGOR *Brit.Amer.* I 229 : In salting, the bulks must not be of too great a size, as the weight would injure the lower tiers. **1958** *Evening Telegram* (St. John's) 24 Apr. 4/2 : A good fish can be spoiled in salt bulk or in the wash tub.

bulk carrier a lake boat designed for carrying cargoes of bulk commodities such as ore or grain. See also **bulker.**

1958 *Kingston Whig-Standard* (Ont.) 21 May 18/1 : Finishing touches are being made here to what will be the third largest Canadian bulk carrier plying the St. Lawrence River and the Great Lakes.... **1959** *Weekend Mag.* 5 Sep. 26/1 : Giant bulk carriers will move tremendous tonnages of ore from Northern Quebec, wheat from the West.

bulker *n.* See **bulk carrier.**

1959 *Globe and Mail* (Toronto) 18 June 8/4 : Upper Lakes Shipping hopes to have a new bulker, Seaway Queen, on hand after her maiden trip to the Upper Lakes for ore.

bull[1] *n.* a working ox.

1889 MACLEAN *Indians* 198 : The work-oxen are bulls or stags. **1963** *Western Wkly Supp.* 6 Nov. 3/1 : The homeseekers appear, riding on an ox-drawn wagon piled high with household effects.... As seen, the "bulls" are too fat and well-fed to be in any way typical of the bony critters seen on western homesteads....

bull[2] *n.* See **bullbird.**

1774 (1792) CARTWRIGHT *Journal* II 7 : This day we saw the first penguins and several bulls. **1779** *Ibid.* II 412 : Both myself and others have often found some of these birds, terns, and bulls dead upon the ice, or land, at a great distance from water. **1959** MCATEE *Folk-Names* 39 : Dovekie [is also called] Bull (Said to refer to its thick neck, but may have ironical reference also to its small size. "Labr.")....

bullberry† *n.* See **buffalo berry.**

1918 SCHULTZ *Rising Wolf* 21 : In summer, when in turn the service berries, choke-cherries, and bull berries ripened, we feasted upon them, and the women dried some for winter use. **1959** *Calgary Herald* 31 July 10/2: In shrubs we have . . . wolf willow, wild rose, bullberry, highbush cranberry. . . .

bullbird *n. Nfld* the dovekie, *Alle alle;* little auk. See also **bull²**.
1861 DE BOILIEU *Labrador Life* 191: This year, with the mild weather, there came upon us innumerable quantities of small wild-fowl, called by the settlers "bull-birds." **1958** *Evening Telegram* (St. John's) 7 May 11/4: Many of those Dovekies (locally known as Bullbirds) will later follow the Labrador Current down along the Newfoundland coast.

bull block *Lumbering* a large pulley through which the main line (def. 3) passes in yarding operations.
1943 SWANSON *Lumberjack* 56: In ground lead logging, at first the main line rubbed or *siwashed* around a stump in order to spool it onto the drum, but when the *bull block* was invented, ground lead logging prospered by leaps and bounds, and its inventor, "Tommy" Moore, was crowned with a wreath of salal and made immortal among loggers who know their stuff. **1952** GOUGH *Story of B.C.* 183: Next [after the spar tree is otherwise rigged] the *bull block* is fastened securely in place at the top of the spar tree with steel cable and iron tree-plates. Through it runs the main line which pulls the logs in front of the forest. **1963** *Press* April 9: There's where you'll hear the mainline hum / Through the bullblock, hanging high. . . .

A bull boat

bull boat† *Hist.* a coracle-like boat of saplings and hide used by prairie Indians. See also **buffalo-skin coracle**. Cp. **parchment canoe**.
[**1765-75** (1933) POND *Narrative* 57: The men Cut Down Small Saplens and Made the frames of two Boates— Sowed the Skins toGather and Made Bottoms to thare frames—Rub'd them Over with tallow which Made them tite anuf to Bring the furs Down to me whare I had Canoes to Receve them.] **1858** (1860) HIND *Assiniboine Exped.* I 442: These great prairie-rivers are generally crossed . . . in "bull-boats," or "parchment canoes" by the Indians. . . . **1918** SCHULTZ *Rising Wolf* 13: They had seen . . . few boats other than the round "bull boats" which they hastily constructed when they wanted to cross a river. . . . **1960** *Alta Hist.Rev.* Spring 29/1: It lists well known terms . . . but misses such words as jerky, bull boat. . . .

bull brigade *Obs.* a brigade (def. 2) of Red River carts pulled by oxen.
1860 *Nor'Wester* (R.R.S.) 15 Oct. 4/2: The train was one wing of Mr. Burbank's "bull-brigade," transporting goods from St. Cloud to the head of navigation.

bull bucker *Lumbering, Slang* See 1966 quote.
1948 (1956) ANDREWS *Glory Days* 44: The bull bucker had been celebrating in port and stopped at Goat Ranch to see the landlady. . . . **1966** *Sun* (Vancouver) 30 May 30A/3: The bull bucker is the man in charge of a team of fallers, buckers and a scaler.

bullcook *n.* See 1913 quote. See also **jungle cook**.
☛ *The name probably derives from the handyman's responsibility for preparing and heating ("cooking") the bran mash fed to the bulls (oxen) at a lumber camp.*
1913 SANDILANDS *West.Cdn Dict.* 9/1: Bull-cook, a handyman in a lumber camp, who carries water, splits wood, and does other chores, especially assisting the cookees. **1947** *Ont.Timberworker* 15 Dec. 3/1: The bullcook will be reminded to keep the sinks as clean as possible. **1963** *Maclean's* 16 Nov. 54/2: But even such lowly creatures as laborers and bull cooks and chain men followed the progress of the steel.

bullcook *v.* See quote.
1942 HAIG-BROWN *Timber* 249: Bullcook. This man sweeps out the bunkhouses, makes the beds, packs in wood and water and generally helps out around camp. From this a locomotive switching and straightening around cars is said to be "bullcooking."

bulldog *n.* See **bulldog fly**.
1792 (1934) TURNOR *Journal* 488: A kind of fly about the size of a bee and not much unlike them in colour but flat and resemble the gad fly of England in this country called bull dogs are the most numerous and troublesome I ever knew them and their bite is as sudden as the sting of a bee. **1892** PIKE *Barren Grounds* 7: The large bull-dogs . . . drove the horses about to madness. **1961** *Chatelaine* Mar. 58/3: But in summer, we *do* have black flies and bulldogs (horse-flies) which get into our clothes and take bites the size of a pinhead.

bulldog fly any one of several species of horsefly, especially *Chrysops*. See also **bulldog, bull-fly, caribou fly, deer fly, flesh fly, horse-fly,** and **moose-fly**.
1848 (1890) BALLANTYNE *Hudson's Bay* 176: . . . the whole room was filled with mosquitoes and bulldog flies. **1963** *B.C.Digest* Nov.-Dec. 45/1: Her face was swollen from continuous bites of mosquitoes, bulldog, black and no-seeum flies. . . .

bulldozer† *n.* a powerful machine equipped with caterpillar traction and a horizontal steel blade or ram, used for clearing land, building roads, making firebreaks, etc. See also **'dozer**.
1930 *B.C.Lumberman* Mar. 71/1: The principal lines of machinery covered are compressors, bull-dozers, ditchers, dump wagons, fresnos, graders of all kinds, scarifiers, snow plows, locomotives and saw-rigs. **1960** NELSON *Northern Lights* 309: Out from the airport flies . . . boilers, bulldozers, Diesel engines, children's toys, crockery, the occasional horse, a piano for a mine-owner's wife, a new wing for a stranded Stinson.

bulldozer-plough *n.* a bulldozer equipped with a snow plough.
1954 *Fishermen's Advocate* (Port Union, Nfld) 5 Feb. 1/2: The bull-dozer-plow stationed at Bonavista was unable to do anything with Wednesday's six or more inch snowfall. . . .

bull-driver *n. Obs.* one who drove oxen in a bull train, *q.v.* See also **ox-pusher**.
1876 LORD *Wilderness* 98: A single man, called a "bull-driver," takes charge of eight or ten carts, and manages his team, aided by a whip. . . .

bull-flogger *n. Obs.* a long whip used by the drivers of the bull trains, *q.v.*

1876 LORD *Wilderness* 98: . . . a person requires a vast amount of practice to be able to use a bull-flogger cleverly.

bull-fly *n*. See **bulldog fly.**
1924 DORRANCE *Never Fire First* 55: Not much trade these wintry days and if customers come, they'll stick around like summer bull-flies. 1958 *Herald-Tribune* 10 Feb. 17/1: "Summers, there was . . . those big, furry mosquitoes, the black no-seeums, the bull flies."

bull gang unskilled laborers in a construction crew, road gang, at the surface of a mine, etc.
1939 *Beaver* Sep. 28/1: The "bull gang" are a happy, cursing, hard-working lot of men. 1958 WATTERS *B.C. Cent.Anthol.* 341: Buckley . . . backed out the rotary to let the "bull gang" in with the axes, saws, and shovels.

bull-hook *n*. *Lumbering* See 1958 quote.
1919 *Camp Worker* 26 Apr. 5/2: There are very few railroad camps in this neck of the jungles which do not boast of having the best yarding engineer that ever took the slack out of a bull-hook. 1958 MCCULLOCH *Woods Words* 21: Bull hook—a. An old time heavy, open choker hook. Not satisfactory, chokers were always falling out. b. A skidding hook used on skylines. c. A big hook once used on the butt rigging in some skyline systems.

bull-in-the-ring *n*. a children's game.
1910 MCCLUNG *Second Chance* 21: "Bull-in-the-ring," "squat-tag" . . . are all right for kids that don't have to rise in the world. . . . 1911 KNOWLES *Singer* 52: "We were playing at—we were—oh, we were playing Bull in the Ring, dear," Murray answered, relieved by the fitting title.

bull-nay fence See quote.
1958 SYMONS *Fences* xiii: Then there was the bull-nay fence, which was so called because it could withstand the onrush of a bull. In construction it was much like the straight rail fence. . . .

bull nun *Slang* a monk.
1960 MCNAMEE *Florencia Bay* 121: I thought of my sins and decided that next year I would enter a monastery. "So you want to be a bull nun, Mr. Crogan?"

bull pen *Lumbering* See **booming ground**[2].
1952 GOUGH *Story of B.C.* 186: The men who make up the booms in the "bull-pen" wear sharply caulked boots that enable them to walk and run over the slippery rolling logs as nimbly as cats. They push the logs into place between the side and end boom sticks with long pike poles.

bull pine 1 See **lodgepole pine.**
1890 *Trans.Roy.Soc.Can.* VIII 4 21: Of the black or bull pine . . . the cambium layer is eaten when it is soft and gelatinous, at the time the leaves are still growing. 1955 HOBSON *Nothing too Good* 151: The prairie rolled away to the north where it slid behind a growth of bullpine and giant poplar trees.

2† the yellow pine, *Pinus ponderosa*, of the British Columbia dry belt.
1906 DEFENBAUGH *Lumber Industry* 56: The leading woods of British Columbia are red fir . . . bullpine. . . . 1958 WATTERS *B.C.Cent.Anthol.* 235: The reek of the sea . . . changes . . . to the stinging, medicinal whiff of the bull pine. . . .

bull's ball *Obs.* a stag party; an all male spree, or dance.
1888 (1890) ST. MAUR *Impressions* 205: . . . and the drunken orgie ended in what they call a "Bull's Ball" in this country.

bull's-wool trousers *Maritimes* trousers of heavy cloth.
1956 RADDALL *Wings* 38: He wore a woolen undershirt and what our loggers used to call bull's-wool trousers, made of freize [sic] cloth. . . .

bull team† *Hist.* a team of several pairs of oxen, used for heavy freighting.
1935 SULLIVAN *Great Divide* 35: . . . all bull teams, mind you, with maybe sixteen pair of widehorns yoked to the same drag chain so the darned wagon had to move. 1950 LYONS *Mighty Fraser* 86: Bull teams were made up of patient, plodding oxen. Twelve to sixteen yoke, or pairs, of these animals drawing one load was the common practice. . . . 1964 *Western Wkly Supp.* 24 June 3/2: From that point, it was hauled to Fort McLeod by "bull-team". . . .

bull through force through by great power or exertion.
1941 *Beaver* June 29/1: We spent four days bulling through twenty miles of breaking ice. . . . 1963 *Herald Mag.* 23 Nov. 3/4: In winter you rode huddled around pot-bellied stoves while the steam engine bulled its way through 500 inches of snow.

bulltow *n*. See **bultow.**

bull train† *Hist.* a train of carts or wagons drawn by oxen.
1882 *Edmonton Bull.* 17 June 3/2: On their return trip they passed a bull train in camp on its way to McLeod. 1953 BERRY *Whoop-up Trail* 59: The bull train . . . was made up of six to twelve yoke of oxen, the usual team consisting of eight yoke. 1963 *Calgary Herald* 14 Dec. 3/5: At Fort Calgary, most buffalo hides were loaded on the heavy-duty "bull-train" wagons for shipment to Fort Benton.

bull trout See **Dolly Varden trout.**
1905 WIGHTMAN *Our Cdn Heritage* 163: Bull-trout is distinguishable by its "bull-dog" jaw. 1948 ONRAET *Sixty Below* 68: . . . he caught . . . a bull trout that weighed over eighty pounds. 1965 *Maclean's* 19 June 39/1: Progeny of these trout swim the Kananaskis Lakes: native cutthroat and bull trout.

bullwhacker† *n*. *Hist*. **1** the driver of a bull train of oxen. See also **whacker.**
1870 *Cariboo Sentinel* (Barkerville, B.C.) 21 May 4/1: It scares off the gaim and drives off the fraters [freighters] and bullwhackers and pilgrims. . . . 1962 *Alta Hist.Rev.* Autumn 12/2: The following . . . is largely the soliloquy of Hank, an old bullwhacker. . . .

2 a long whip used by drivers of bull teams, *q.v.*
1884 *Nor'Wester* (Calgary) 10 June 4/2: Bye and Bye he took a chair, laid aside his bull whacker, took a smoke at his calumet, and entered into conversation.

bull work heavy physical labor, as that performed by a bull gang, *q.v.*
1956 RADDALL *Wings* 9: No Indian likes bull work of that kind, carried on day after day without a let up, rain or shine. 1958 *Globe and Mail* (Toronto) 26 July 3/1: They were hired to do the bull work of the camp, and help lug instruments up and down the grim slopes of the New Quebec Crater.

bully (boy) *n. Hist.* in the fur trade, a hired tough whose job it was to intimidate rival traders and to do the fighting for the brigade or post. See also **bullyar.**

1820 (1938) SIMPSON *Athabasca Jnl* 78: St. Picque one of the NW Bullies requested I would sell him a little rum and offered his wearing apparel in payment. **1855** (1956) ROSS *Fur Hunters* 8: . . . here [at Fort William] would the bullies of fighting renown, rendered yet braver by the potent draught, hold their annual exhibitions. **1922** *Beaver* May 6/1: Sir George told me to take a few of our "bullies" with me and give the misbehaving crews a good lesson. . . . **1956** (1957) FISHER *Pemmican* 175: At the head of the pedlar line was Bowman's bully boy. . . .

bullyar ['bʊljɚ] *n.* [< *bully + er*] See **bully.**

1913 COWIE *Adventurers* 129: Long after the plumed and pampered professional "bullyars" had disappeared from the lists the desire to emulate their performances would crop up. . . . **1941** *Beaver* Sep. 36/2: Bullyar. Supposed to be the best man in a boat's crew spoiling for a fight with one of another brigade.

bultow *n.* [? < Brit. dial. (Cornish) *bulter, bultey* a kind of longline] *Nfld* a type of hand line used in coastal fishing. See 1849 quote. See also **long-line.** Also spelled *bulltow.*

1849 (1852) PERLEY *Fisheries N.B.* 11: The "bultow" is described as a long line, with hooks fastened along its whole length, at regular distances, by shorter and smaller cords called snoods, which are six feet long, and are placed on the long line twelve feet apart, to prevent the hooks becoming entangled. **1952** PUTNAM *Cdn Regions* 52/2: The fish are caught by hand lines, trawl lines, "bulltows" or codnets. **1963** *American Speech* Dec. 298: BULTOW, *n.* A line with hooks; a trawl.

bum gun on a sealing vessel, a gun fired periodically to let the sealers know where the ship is.

1958 WATTERS *B.C.Cent.Anthol.* 124: Then would come . . . straining . . . to hear the dull report of the "bum gun" fired periodically for their guidance.

bun [bʌn] *n.* [< Cdn F *bonne*] See **pointer** (def. 1). See also **bonne.**

1960 *Ottawa Citizen* 14 July 42/7: They put the rope on a "bun" (a small rowboat) in an effort to get the rope to Talisman so they could haul her back, but the bun fouled on the rocks.

bunch† *n.* **1** *Obs.* See **boss.**

1819 (1922) HARMON *Journal* 365: On his [buffalo's] back is a bunch or escressence, commencing a little forward of his haunches, the highest part of which is over his shoulders, and which terminates at the neck. **1840** WILLIS *Cdn Scenery* I 53: . . . meeting with a herd of buffaloes in the meadows, I killed a fat one, and took from it the fillets, the bunch and the tongue.

2 a grove of trees. See also **bluff** (def. 3a).

1872 DASHWOOD *Chiploquorgan* 108: A grove, or as they would call it, a "bunch" of pine or spruce, catches the eye sooner than the signs left by a wild animal. **1910** FERGUSON *Janey Canuck* 264: The spruce grows in "bunches" or "stands" along the rivers. . . .

3 a herd of horses or, sometimes, cattle.

1903 (1913) CULLUM *Devil's Keg* 65: Guess I'm reckoned kind of handy 'round a bunch of steers. **1910** WARD *Canadian Born* 93: Bunches of horses and herds of cattle [were] widely scattered over the endless grassy plains. . . . **1962** FRY *Ranch on the Cariboo* 60: Picking a scrubby horse out of the bunch . . . he led him into the infested territory and shot him.

bunch† *v.* of cattle or horses, to round up; to collect into a herd.

1962 *Canadian Wkly* 1 Sep. 9/1: . . . he . . . rode out with his father to bunch the cows and calves in the field. . . . **1963** SYMONS *Many Trails* 44: Dust clouds . . . showed where the horses were being bunched and driven. . . .

bunchgrass† *n.* any of several nutritious grasses, as *Agropyron spicatum,* widely distributed in the West and growing in clumps.

1858 (1863) PALLISER *Journals* 111: The shingle terraces . . . here expand to form an extensive plain free from timber and covered with "bunch grass." **1963** *Beaver* Autumn 50/2: . . . when their wanderings took them . . . to the flats above the Thompson River they were suddenly silent as bunch grass reached above the knees of their horses. . . .

bunchgrass *v. B.C.* of horses or cattle, forage in winter for bunch grass by pawing through the snow.

1963 SYMONS *Many Trails* 63: This "winter rustling," as they call it on the prairies, becomes "bunch-grassing it" in the Chilcotin.

bunch-quitter *n. West* a horse or steer that has a habit of leaving the herd.

1954 HAGELL *Grass Was Free* 19: . . . he's spurrin' like Hell to catch a bunch of range hosses or a bunch-quitter. . . .

bundle boom *West Coast* a raft or boom (def. 3b) of logs bound together in a bundle.

1962 NICHOLSON *West Coast* 151: . . . the logs are brought out in "bundle booms" designed specially to negotiate the [sand] bar. **1966** *B.C.Forest Industries* 1965-66 1: Bundle booms are found safer than flat rafts, towing pay loads are bigger and less time is lost in shelter awaiting calm water.

Bungay *n.* See **Bungee.**

Bungee ['bʌngi] *n.* [< Algonk.; cf. Ojibwa *penkī* small] Also spelled *Bungay, Bungie, Bungy. Hist.* **1** an Ojibwa, or Salteaux, Indian.

1776 (1951) *Saskatchewan Journals* 37: He had been for some years past a Trader . . . on the back of Albany Fort, and often used to see the Bungee Indian Debtors belonging to that place. **1858** (1860) HIND *Red River Exped.* I 333: Our camp received an unexpected addition of six "Bungays." Note: Crees and Ojibways of mixed origin. **1924** *Beaver* Aug. 397: Bungay . . . a common term for the Salteaux Indians . . . is nothing more than a nickname . . . a corrupt Cree word from *Pungey,* meaning "a little," uttered by Indians when they are hungry and . . . begging for something to eat, as "give me a little." **1952** *Ibid.* Mar. 46/2: From all this it is evident that the Bungees were the Ojibway of the Red River—not the Crees. And since the Red River dialect contains Cree words rather than Ojibway, it seems that the historians who maintain that the term Bungee should not be applied to the dialect are right.

2 a lingua franca spoken in the nineteenth century in the Red River area in Manitoba.

1951 *Beaver* Dec. 42/1: Half-breeds of Scottish or Orkney and Cree ancestry [in Manitoba *c*1870] . . . spoke a curious dialect known as "Bungee" or "Bungay" which combined some of the characteristics of both tongues, with the occasional use of a few words of French and other languages. **1952** *Ibid.* Mar. 46/1: ... we have had several enquiries as to the origin of the term *Bungee.* The best guess so far is that it comes from the Ojibway word *punge,* meaning little or few—though why this name should be given to the dialect is not explained.

bunkhouse† *n.* a building in which the men working in a lumber, mining, or other such camp sleep.
1901 *Klondike Miner* (Grand Forks, Y.T.) 18 Oct. 3/4: A separate bunk house has been put up for those who wish to forego the luxury of a spring bed. **1963** *Press* Apr. 7: While toiling manfully on the rigging by day, nonetheless his fertile brain craved employment in the dreary evenings in the bunkhouse.

bunk patrol *Slang* a period of off-duty sleep.
1953 MOWERY *Mounted Police* 165: [He pulled] off his boots and heavy clothing in anticipation of "bunk patrol" that afternoon. . . .

bunt *n.* a blunt arrow used for stunning game without penetrating the skin. Cp. **bluffie.**
1952 *Beaver* Dec. 27: For weapons [the Swampy Cree] used bows and arrows, with chipped stone points or plain "bunts". . . . **1959** *Ibid.* Winter 37/1: [Caption] A cedar bow and "bunt" arrow for stunning small game.

burbot *n. Northwest* See **loche.**
1853 REID *Young Voyageurs* 317: Pike were taken in the net and a species of burbot (Gadus lota). This last is one of the most voracious of the finny tribe and preys upon all others that it is able to swallow. **1964** TURNER *Natural Resources B.C.* 586: The burbot (or ling) is a widespread native fish which provides some winter sport.

burdash *n.* See **berdash.**

bureaucrat *n. Hist.* in Lower Canada, a supporter, whether French Canadian or English, of the English party, against which Papineau and his Reformers were ranged in the 1830's, a situation that led to the Rebellion of 1837-8.
1833 *Cdn Courant* (Montreal) 2 Feb. 2/5: The angry terms which they use in designating each other, are proofs of this feeling Aristocrats, Democrats ... Bureaucrats ... Natives. ... **1870** *Cdn Illust.News* 26 Mar. 334/2: Samuel Varny was suspected of being a bureaucrat. **1963** MORTON *Kingdom of Canada* 240: Papineau and his radicals were striking at the English bureaucrats. . . .

burgess *n.* **1†** *Hist.* a member of a provincial House of Assembly representing an incorporated town.
1808 *York* [Toronto] *Gaz.* 28 May 1/1: We do for that end publish this our Royal Proclamation and do hereby dissolve the said Provincial Parliament accordingly, and the Legislative Council, Counsellors, and the Knights, Citizens and Burgesses of the House of Assembly, are discharged from their attendance and meeting on Monday the Twenty Seventh day of June. **1827** *U.E.Loyalist* 24 Feb. 319/4: The Knights, Citizens, and Burgesses ... are too well acquainted with Constitutional forms and proceedings to interfere. . . .
2 in Saskatchewan, a person who pays municipal taxes; ratepayer.
1957 *Commonwealth* 4 Dec. 24/1: Burgesses in many Saskatchewan cities and towns ... benefit from

the large assets Government Insurance has built up. **1964** *Saskatoon Star-Phoenix* 30 Mar. 14/1: Mr. Rosenberg and Mr. Tiller agreed there should be no division into electors and burgesses, the latter being owners of property and thus eligible to vote on money bylaws.

burgoo ['bɜˣgu] *n.* [< Brit. dial. *burgoo* porridge] *Hist.* thick stew made from whatever meat and vegetable might be available. See also **rubaboo.**
1743 (1949) ISHAM *Observations* 132: There is a sort of Mawse which grows upon the Rocks, which is of a Brownish Colour, which the Indians Eats frequent, they wash itt clean, then Boil itt for a considerable time till itts tender, then mixing it with Ruhiggan[,] Burgoe or other Victuals, and Reckon itt Good Eating. **1931** NUTE *Voyageur* 55: AHRUBUHBOO ... is very much like ... *burgoo.* **1934** *Beaver* Mar. 43/1: [There were] delicacies of the table such as pea soup, burgoo and "Harriet Lane."

burial-tree *n.* a tree (or scaffold) used as a resting place for the dead, especially among the Prairie and West Coast Indians. See also **tree-platform.**
1913 WILLIAMS *Wilderness Trail* 124: "Him I trust, but that old squaw"—he shook his head gravely,—"if she lived on the plains, she would cut down a burial-tree to build a fire. That's the kind she is."

burleau *n.* See **berlot.**

burline *n.* See **berline.**

burn *n.* **1** in clearing land, the process of piling and setting fire to the brush (def. 1).
[**1792** (1911) SIMCOE *Diary* 119: The way of clearing land in this country is cutting down all the small wood, pile it and set it on fire.] **1832** (1953) RADCLIFF *Letters* 95: By these means, in the Canadian phrase, you "get a good burn," upon which the excellence of your crop mainly depends. That part of the field which is not burned black, never produces so good wheat, as that which is. **1955** HOBSON *Nothing Too Good* 97: After the burn, the black ash on the ground added important elements to the coming new growth.
2 a forest fire.
1834 NEED *Six Years in the Bush* 92: A great burn [occurred], during which the wind rose so high as to endanger my shanty and adjoining buildings. **1957** *Northern Affairs Bull.* Jan. 7: The total estimated burn figure is very difficult to arrive at with any accuracy because of the vast areas involved and the infrequency of travel over most parts.
3 See **brulé** (def. 1).
1931 GREY OWL *Last Frontier* 33: Huge burns, of ancient and unknown origin, lie like scars, across the landscape. **1963** *Sun* (Vancouver) 23 Nov. 21/1: The rolling hills along the Kootenay ... are parklike with their copses of fir, tamarack, poplar and willow ... left standing in old log slashes or burns.

burn *v.* **1** clear land by cutting the brush (def. 1) and burning it. See also **burning** (def. 1) and **burn off.**
1833 (1926) LANGTON *Early U.C.* 12: ... instead of being shut up in the forests, you may obtain a healthy, airy frontage to some of the numerous lakes, which ... enables the settlers to burn, when in the confined clearings in the heart of the forest there is not a breath of air stirring.
2 *Mining, Hist.* sink a shaft by means of fire. See also **burning** (def. 3).
c1862 (1958) LINDSAY *Cariboo Story* 35/2: When I came to Pemberton I struck a job there, burning a coal pit for

P. Smith and Company. **1910** SERVICE *Trail of '98* 322:
He burned a hole in the frozen muck. . . . **1964** BERTON
Golden Trail 30: . . . Louis Rhodes was quietly burning
his way down to bedrock.

burned (or burnt) country a tract of forest or
prairie swept by fire. See also **burnt land** (def. 1).
*c*1665 RADISSON *Voyages* 88: It's such a country that the
french calls it ye burned country 20 miles about, and
in many places the same is to be seene where there
weare forests. **1930** MCCLUNG *Be Good* 142: About half
way there, we reached the burnt country, over which the
prairie fire had swept. . . . **1963** SYMONS *Many Trails* 66:
After the dreary burnt country, the hay flats and
bunch-grass hillsides of the valley were a . . . relief. . . .

burned-out *adj.* of veterans, broken in health as a
result of war service. See also **burnt-out pension.**
1946 LOWER *Colony to Nation* 460: It was a good number
of years before authority officially admitted the
situation and made provision for "burned out"
veterans. The phrase was graphic and the condition
behind it real enough: during the late '20's and early
'30's the deaths of ex-service men in their forties were
reported with inescapable frequency.

burning *n.* **1** See 1832 quote. See also **branding**
(def. 1a), **burn,** *v.* (def. 1), and **log burning.**
Cp. **piling.**
1832 (1953) RADCLIFF *Letters* 94: The process of burning
comes next—for this you choose a dry and windy day,
and kindling some of the brush-heaps on the windward
side of the field, the fire is generally communicated to
the rest, by running along the dried leaves on the ground,
or catching from heap to heap. . . . **1924** (1933) SLATER
Yellow Briar Scarred logs . . . were yanked into fresh
piles . . . and the brandings were thus prepared for a
fresh burning.
2 See **burn,** *n.* (def. 3).
1938 *Beaver* June 32/2: Leaving the river at a forks on
a red hot day, August 6, amid swarms of flies, the scent
started over moors and burnings crossed by heavily
bushed water courses.
3 *Mining, Hist.* See 1898 quote. See also **burn,** *v.*
(def. 2).
1897 TUTTLE *Golden North* 90: A great many of the
miners . . . in the winter resort to . . . "burning." **1897**
WILSON *Yukon* 38: This is called burning, and is done
by drifting, melting away the frost by fire and taking out
only the pay dirt, leaving the glacial drift and surface
intact.

burning harrow a heavy harrow used for breaking
up land newly cleared by burning (def. 1).
1961 MITCHELL *Jake and the Kid* 106: Jake says once he
started out with only a cotter pin and he ended up with
a burning harrow, a bull calf, and ten dollars to boot;
he did it in thirty-one trades.

burn off See **burn,** *v.* (def. 1).
1852 MOODIE *Roughing It* 361: Moodie and Jacob had
chopped eight acres during the winter, but these had to
be burnt off and logged up before we could put in a
crop of wheat for the ensuing fall. **1925** MCARTHUR
Familiar Fields 31: . . . in the spring the brush and log
heaps had to be burned off before any crop could be
put in among the stumps.

burnt country See **burned country.**

burnt ground *Obs.* See **burned country.** See also
burn, *n.* (def. 2).
1824 (1955) BLACK *Journal* 191: Got out of the new
burnt ground & into an old Brule. . . .

burnt land(s) Also spelled *burntland.* **1** See
burned country.
1832 MCGREGOR *British America* II 271: If the burnt
lands, as they are termed, were, immediately after being
overrun by fire, brought under cultivation, they would
then be of the same value as those cleared in the usual
way. . . . **1849** ALEXANDER *L'Acadie* II 142: After this,
commenced the most difficult country; "burnt land,"
that is, forest land through which a fire has passed in
1827, two years after the great fire of Miramichi. **1921**
HEMON *Chapdelaine* [trans.] 149: It happened that
François was then in the great burnt lands, where the
fine snow drives and drifts so terribly.
2 land cleared for cultivation by burning off the
trees and brush. See also **brulé** (def. 2).
1896 GOURLAY *Hist.Ottawa* 18: The great winter labour
was chopping, then burn off and hoe or drag the wheat
in the burnt land. **1952** BUCKLER *Mountain and Valley*
27: One spring day . . . your grandfather and I were
planting potatoes in the burntland.

burnt-out area **1** See **brulé** (def. 1).
1959 *Star Wkly* 22 Aug. 16/1: . . . the man
of the house spends days in the bush . . . following
bear tracks into les brules (burnt-out areas) where
blueberries grow thickest. **1964** *Ibid.* 5 Dec. 37/1: The
next day, the hunters . . . reached a ridge in a burnt-out
area. . . .
2 soil damaged by erosion.
1952 PUTNAM *Cdn Regions* 35/2: The agricultural value
of these soils is limited by wind erosion of the surface
soil with the formation of numerous "burnt-out" areas.

burnt-out pension See quote. See also **burned out.**
1958 *B.C.Federation of Labour,* 3rd Convention (Oct.
21-24) Res. 88: . . . a veteran with overseas service is
eligible for what is commonly known as burnt-out
pension . . . granted on the premise that overseas
service shortened his life expectancy. . . .

burnt wheat roasted wheat grains, used as a
substitute for tea or coffee.
1824 *Canadian Mag.* II 317: . . . dried Indian corn or
burnt wheat, (not an uncommon thing among the
poorer classes) is employed in place of the Chinese herb.
1930 BEAMES *Army* 104: Between huge mouthfuls of
pork and onions and gurgling gulps of burnt-wheat
coffee, the man talked to his guests. . . .

burnt woods See **brulé** (def. 1).
1754 (1907) HENDAY *Journal* 327: Level lands and burnt
woods; and there are nothing but stagnated water to
drink. **1888** (1890) ST. MAUR *Impressions* 247: The trail
was very bad, and part of the way led through burnt
woods. **1963** SPRY *Palliser* 139: After desperate climbing
and two days' very hard work in the burnt woods, they
found that the mountains presented one unbroken wall
hemming in the Tobacco Plains.

bury the hatchet See **hatchet** (def. 4).

bush *n.* **1** forested wilderness, especially the
extensive sub-arctic forest of Canada; the largely
unsettled hinterland. See also **bush country** and
bushland (def. 1).
1792 (1937) CAMPBELL *Travels* 222: . . . look after the
Cows, and take care that they should not steal into the
bush; even the endless forests are here termed the bush.
1845 BEAVAN *Life in Backwoods N.B.* 31: The pine table
and the willow-seated chairs are all made in the

"bush".... **1965** *Star Wkly* 23 Jan. 36/1: In many parts of the bush in wintertime, the only manmade tracks to be found are snowshoe prints of the fur trapper and the caterpillar tread of his snowmobile.

2 a tract of land left uncleared on a farm and used as a source of wood, and as a grazing area for cattle. See also **bush lot** (def. 2), **farm woodlot,** and **woodlot** (def. 1).

1793 (1869) CANNIFF *Settlement U.C.* 59: Any person putting fire to any bush or stable, that does not his endeavour to hinder it from doing damage, shall forfeit the sum of forty shillings. **1869** *Mainland Guardian* (New Westminster, B.C.) 29 Sep. 2/2: For Sale. 400 Acres of Land, situated near the steamboat landing at Langley; 280 acres of land is prairie, the remainder bush. **1962** *Forest Conservation* 23/1: From this situation arose the practice, when new farms were being opened up, of making provision for future fuel and lumber needs by setting apart a woodlot, usually known as "the bush," reasonably close to the house and barns. **1966** *Kingston Whig-Standard* (Ont.) 8 Jan. 4/6: In rural Ontario there were two distinct wood splitting jobs. One was in the bush and the other in the woodshed.

3 *West* thinly wooded areas of poplar, birch, and shrubs adjacent to the plains. See also **bushland** (def. 2).

1881 (1957) *Sask.Hist.* X 2 66: Out in the bush, too, the mosquitoes are very thick and very annoying. **1953** MOON *This is Saskatchewan* 22: As you go west, too, there is less bush and more open fields.

4 See **sugar bush.**

1831 PICKERING *Inquiries of an Emigrant* 109: And the sugar maple tree, if growing in what is called bushes, should never be wantonly destroyed, as it is a useful and valuable appendage to a farm. **1903** RICHARDSON *Colin* 214: The McNabb family had a very large bush, and ever since the boys had grown strong enough to attend to the work, they had always tapped a large number of trees. **1966** *Kingston Whig-Standard* (Ont.) 19 Mar. 6/7: Mr. Ostler said the run varies with the kind of bushes. "In sheltered bushes the sap will run early . . ." he noted.

5 in Colonial times, the country back from the settled towns; the back country (def. 1), whether wooded or not.

1820 (1824) *Colonial Advocate* (York [Toronto]) 2 Sep. 4/2: Capt. Mathews of the Royal Artillery, with his family and servants, passed through Ancaster about four weeks ago, on his way to the Bush in Lobo, with six waggons, one cart, 24 horses, a flock of sheep, and some cows. **1852** MOODIE *Roughing It* 87: In the bush, all things are in common; you cannot even get a bed without having to share it with a companion. **1953** RADCLIFF *Letters* xiv: Many friends of the Radcliffs were forced to sell out and seek employment in fields better suited to their capabilities than the bush of Adelaide.

bush *v.* **1** *Rare* cause to become or become fatigued or worn out. See also **bushed**[1] (def. 3).

1912 CONNOR *Corp. Cameron* 309: No man in the camp, not even the chief himself, could "bush" him in a day's work.

2 mark winter roads over ice by placing bushes or small trees along the route. See also **brush,** *v.* (def. 3).

1917 MONTGOMERY *Anne's House of Dreams* 152: The harbour ice grew harder and thicker, until the Four Winds people began their usual travelling over it. The safe ways were "bushed" by a benevolent government....

3 *Obs.* sell (whisky) illegally to Indians by arranging a rendezvous in the bush. See also **bush-whisky.** Cp. **bush-ranger** (def. 3).

1859 *Brit.Colonist* (Victoria) 24 Oct. 3/1: Bushing whiskey is the way in which Indians are supplied. The Indians go to the spot by appointment from the vile wretches engaged in the nefarious trade.

bush ague or **fever** a kind of ague caused by protracted isolation in the bush.

1839 NEED *Six Years in the Bush* 107: On this day I was attacked with an ague, or Bush fever, common to settlers in their second or third year. **1913** JOHNSON *Shagganappi* 224: They reached for their guns, then started to shake and tremble as though the bush ague were upon them. **1966** *Time* (Cdn ed.) 18 Nov. 16/1: To persuade islanders to forsake the comforts of home for the remote forests of Labrador, he now proposes to ease boredom and bush fever by offering volunteers . . . a tidy $400 per man.

bush aircraft See **bush plane.**

1941 *Beaver* Mar. 48/1: All bush aircraft are stocked with rations, tent, rifle, ammunition and stove.... **1958** *Cdn Geog.Jnl* LVII 97/2: Canoe and bush-aircraft are still the main means of transportation....

bush airline a company which operates aircraft on scheduled flights transporting freight and passengers over the largely uninhabited wilderness of Northern Canada. See also **bush company.**

1957 *Maclean's* 28 Sep. 1/1: Two bush airlines, Wheeler and Quebecair, are buying Dutch-designed Fokker Friendships.... **1961** *Time* (Cdn ed.) 25 Aug. 9/2: The roll call would have been impressive for any bush airline.

bush airplane See **bush plane.**

1958 *Edmonton Jnl* 24 June 4 18/2: Before the drone of the first bush airplane shattered the ageless silence . . . almost all movement in the north relied on the dog-team....

bush bread See **bannock.**

1950 HAMBLETON *Abitibi Adventure* 60: René . . . "showed" Bill how to make bannock. There are, of course, scores of recipes for this "bush bread," which is a standby as a replacement for bread.

bush buggy a cross-country vehicle for use in the bush.

1966 *Kingston Whig-Standard* (Ont.) 3 June 13/1: Only too soon on our walk back were we greeted by the familiar face of our . . . bush buggy. Undaunted we headed the penguin in the proper direction.

bush camp the offices, living quarters, cook-houses, and other buildings of a lumbering, mining, or other operation in the bush.

1934 DENNIS *Down in N.S.* 243: She and her parents with other [Acadian] exiles returned to Nova Scotia and lived for a time in the bush camp at Chezzetcook. **1963** *Maclean's* 2 Nov. 25/3: The hotel is the aspect of Wabush that separates it most from the kind of Labrador bush camp I worked in as a student.

bush clearing See **clearing** (def. 1a).

1947 SAUNDERS *Algonquin* 37: . . . since it was hard work to clear the land and to farm on these bush clearings, the depot farmer usually limited his crops to potatoes for the [lumber] camp and oats for the horses. **1965** *Globe and Mail* (Toronto) 12 Jan. 7/2: A few thousand . . . people scratch out a living in bush clearings or on high rocky pastures.

bush coat a heavy, warm coat reaching from the shoulders to the upper legs; Mackinaw coat, *q.v.*
1958 *Liberty* Jan. 25/3: We saw 35-year-olds in bush coats and hats—but the coats were yellow checked, or red.

bush company See **bush airline.**
1958 *Maclean's* 10 May 74/2: When I last knew him he was operating a small bush company with five old planes out of Fort St. James. . . .

bush country the wooded wilderness of Northern Canada. See also **bush,** *n.* (def. 1). Cp. **stick country.**
1913 BICKERSTETH *Open Doors* 246: All day we made good progress through an undulating bush country, broken by several beautiful lakes. **1957** *Saturday Night* 17 Aug. 36/1: Most of Nova Scotia, away from the sea, resembles the Northern Quebec and Ontario bush country. **1965** *Time* (Cdn ed.) 23 Apr. 17/2: . . . it was little more than bush country accessible from Fort St. John, B.C., only by pack train, parachute, or canoe.

bush cowboy a rancher in the bush country, especially that of the interior of British Columbia.
1951 HOBSON *Grass* 31: A top bush cowboy, he built a new ranch ever two years, then always found another meadow bigger than his present one, and moved again.

bushcraft *n.* the knowledge necessary to survival in the bush; woodcraft. See also **bush lore.**
1948 ONRAET *Sixty Below* 107: There is your list of outfit; some notes on bushcraft, and how to skin and stretch fur. **1954** PHILLIPS *Living Legend* 35: . . . he felt he was Johnson's match, either in bushcraft or with a gun.

bush-crew *n. Lumbering* a gang of bushworkers, *q.v.*
1945 CALVIN *Saga* 51: . . . it was not many years until the bush-crews working back from one lake could hear the axes of those who had started in from the other.

bushed[1] *adj.* **1** See 1940 quote.
1890 *Grip* (Toronto) 1 Feb. 70/1: "Say . . . did yez hear that ould Schneider, the contractor, was busht—gone up higher than a kite?" **1940** FINNIE *Lure of North* 5: Though the word "bushed" originally connoted partial or complete insanity from living too long or too much alone in the bush, it is also applied nowadays to any mental quirk or derangement brought about in the treeless areas of the Arctic. **1965** *Time* (Cdn ed.) 12 Feb. 9/1: And at Spartan's bleak Pelly Bay camp in the Canadian Arctic, a bushed cook arose from bed one midnight . . . set about frying every single egg in the stores, and then nailed them all, sunnyside up, to the cookshack wall.
2 bedevilled, frightened through unfamiliarity with the bush.
1910 FRASER *Red Meekins* 123: "I'll trail behind the lord mayor of London—dash him, he's 'bout as near bushed as I ever see a man."
3† exhausted; tired out.
1910 FRASER *Red Meekins* 266: "I was that danged near bushed, toward the last that I was feared I might go right on sleepin'. . . ." **1964** *Star Wkly* 5 Dec. 36/2: Ehricht . . . arrived back at camp bushed.
4 confined to the bush, as when lost or cut off by weather.

1930 BEAMES *Army* 281: "I been bushed all afternoon in this here damn country of yours, an' got so turned around with fences an' bum trails I don't know which end of me's up." **1956** GOWLAND *Sikanaska Trail* 102: I didn't know the country to the West, and I might follow a big creek thinking it would lead to the Yukon River, and thus find myself bushed, again with winter on my neck.
5 living in the wilderness, away from civilization, by choice.
1942 TWOMEY & HERRICK *Needle to the North* 274: Even in Ungava, wandering was considered fit only for "bushed" white folks—the good-for-nothings, the "squaw-men." **1961** *Chatelaine* Mar. 38: [Caption] We're "Bushed" and We Love It. **1961** *Red Deer Advocate* (Alta) 2 Aug. 9/1: Most common symptom of the person who may be called "bushed" is his dislike for the cities, the crowds and the traffic of "outside". . . .

bushed[2] *adj.* heavily wooded; covered with scrub.
1919 FRASER *Bulldog Carney* 40: He clattered down to the hollow he had left, and raced for the hiding screen of the bushed muskeg. **1964** *Edmonton Jnl* 10 July 3/2: Edmonton, being in a section of the province that is well bushed, does not understand such dress.

bushel worker *Lumbering* in lumber camps, fallers, *q.v.*, who work under contract; piece workers.
1942 HAIG-BROWN *Timber* 251: FALLER. The man who cuts the trees down. Fallers work in sets of two, head and second fallers, with one or more buckers following them. Most fallers are contract or "bushel" workers—paid at a rate of so much per thousand board feet of timber felled.

bush farm a farm in the bush country, often one that has much uncleared or waste land on it.
1852 MOODIE *Roughing It* 315: Instead of sinking all his means in buying a bush farm, he hired a very good farm in Cavan. . . . **1881** *Progress* (Rat Portage [Kenora] Ont.) 20 May 1/5: His man . . . most likely had went out to his "bush farm." **1957** HUTCHISON *Canada* 298: At Dutch Lake lived . . . two reformed Vancouver newspaperwomen who, demented at the sight of a worthless bush farm, had made it over into British Columbia's happiest retreat.

bush fence *Obs.* See **brush fence.**
1852 MOODIE *Roughing It* 341: The outer enclosure was a bush fence, formed of trees felled on each other in a row, and the gaps filled with brushwood.

bush fever See **bush ague.**

bush fire See **forest fire.**
1864 (1955) CRAIG *Early Travellers* 280: Since my arrival here we have had some heavy rains, which have extinguished the bush fire, that might, but for this fortuitous downfall, have, I am told, burnt for weeks. **1963** *Globe and Mail* (Toronto) 29 Apr. 5/5: A bush fire near Hammer . . . threatened to destroy 12 houses in the community last night.

bush flier See **bush flyer.**

bush flyer or **flier** See **bush pilot.**
1957 *Beaver* Winter 65/2: . . . judges and explorers, bush fliers and river boatmen . . . patronized the Hudson's Hope Hotel. **1962** DICKIE *Great Golden Plain* 290: The bush flyers found gas on the Peace where they had only to push a stick a foot or so down into the sand of the riverbank to get a tiny gas well. . . .

bush flying flying over and in remote areas.
1936 *Cdn Geog.Jnl* XIII 319/2: "Bush flying" which is the name commonly given to commercial air transport beyond the sphere of the railways, has much romantic interest in its history. **1963** *Globe and Mail* (Toronto) 28 Feb. 17/2: . . . she does an extremely capable job of rounding up a large number of bush flying anecdotes. . . .

bush-French *n.* the French patois spoken in the backwoods, *q.v.*, especially by the Métis.
1936 MOWERY *Paradise Trail* 85: Eutrope said something to him in bush-French. . . .

bush gang men who work in the bush for surveyors, cruisers (def. 1), and others.
1959 *Weekend Mag.* 4 Apr. 4/2: . . . Mike King, a timber cruiser and prospector of considerable repute, had headed off into an area none of his Indian bush gang would enter.

bush horse a horse used in logging camps.
1955 *Bush News* (Port Arthur, Ont.) Feb. 2/1: . . . a proposition was advanced some time ago in Southern Ontario that a fund should be established to finance a "bush horse" control operation under the Society's direction. . . . **1963** SYMONS *Many Trails* 175: Jill gave us very little trouble, for she was an old bush horse and quite accustomed to camp life.

bush Indian 1 one of a band of Indians living in a forested area as opposed to the prairies.
1887 *Senate Report* 54: . . . in these years the Indians are reduced to great distress, the bush Indians depending on the winter time on this food for their existence. . . . **1963** SYMONS *Many Trails* 130: But the Crees . . . were bush Indians and once lived north and east of the plains; but gradually some of them took to the open country. . . .
2 *West Coast and North* an Indian of a region remote from civilization. Cp. **stick Indian.**
1939 *Beaver* Sep. 22/1: These people were bush Indians and did not come to the fort very often.

bushland *n.* Also spelled *bush land.* **1** See **bush,** *n.* (def. 1).
1853 *Anglo-American Mag.* Sep. 276/2: Now old Jim Delany had . . . a barn full of wheat and stacks of hay, the produce of a good lot of bush land. **1947** WELLS *Owl Pen* 67: As the rushing snow invaded the swamps and bushlands, all work stopped there. . . . **1953** *Cdn Geog.Jnl* XLVI 129/2: During the past fifty years most of them have been camping in sordid poverty in the northern bushland. . . . **1965** *Islander* 11 July 10/2: The uncanny stare suggested . . . that maybe this bushland beatnik had stripped his mental gears.
2 See **bush,** *n.* (def. 3).
1963 *Western Wkly Supp.* 13 Mar. 6/3: From there it [a fire] took off through the dry grass and headed for the adjoining bushland.

bush lore knowledge of the woods; woodcraft; the knowledge necessary to survival in the bush. See also **bushcraft.**
1863 WALSHE *Cedar Creek* 122: Sam Holt had evidently become acquainted with "considerable" bush lore at his University of Toronto. **1958** *Arctic Spotter* Feb. 18/3: The course included such subjects as first aid . . . bush lore, codes. . . .

bush lot 1† a holding of uncleared land.
1891 *Elora Express* (Ont.) 22 Jan. 1/2: There was not a tree cut on the 200 acres at the time, so . . . [they] had to undergo the hardships and privations peculiar to early pioneer settlement on a bush lot in the back-woods. **1928** LE ROSSIGNOL *Beauport Road* 80: . . . I'll take a bush lot from the Seminary and be a farmer. . . .
2 See **bush,** *n.* (def. 2).
1947 WELLS *Owl Pen* 68: Trucks can't pick up saw-logs, or cord-wood, in a bushlot that is swimming ankle deep in water and bumper-deep in mud.

bush mail *North* See quote.
1942 *Beaver* Mar. 19/2: One of the most interesting laws requires a traveller to carry the bush mail, either to its destination, or as far along the route as the traveller may be going. When a hunter wishes to send a letter, he writes it on a piece of birch bark or paper and mails it by slipping it into a cleft stick, which he thrusts into the ground alongside a fairly well frequented trail.

bushman *n.* **1** a settler in the bush (def. 5).
1852 *Elora Backwoodsman* (C.W.) 15 July 1/4: One would think that the bushman, ere he made a clearance of this yet, would have enough to do. **1910** BINDLOSS *Thurston* 32: . . . he could assume the bovine stolidity which, though foreign to his real nature, the Canadian bushman occasionally adopts for diplomatic purposes.
2 a person who frequents and is familiar with the bush, as a trapper, prospector, or trader. See also **bush-ranger, bush-rover, bushwacker** (def. 3), and **woods-runner** (def. 2).
1907 HUNTER *Cdn Wilds* 32: During forty years in the [north] country, I never knew an Indian or white bushman to carry a compass. **1960** *News of the North* 14 Jan. 11/2: His hair is messed and long in the approved fashion of all bushmen and northerners in general.
3 a logger; lumberjack; bushworker, *q.v.*
1912 HEENEY *Pickanock* 26: . . . the manager . . . kept . . . a little overcrowded store; there the bushmen might get their winter clothing. . . . **1919** *Camp Worker* 26 Apr. 8/2: We met the Supt. the next day and he stated that the act did not apply to the bushmen, and that we either had to work the full time, or go to the office and get our pay. **1966** *Kingston Whig-Standard* (Ont.) 27 Aug. 4/3: Picking berries on the Mackenzie is more glamorous but not more difficult than picking one's way . . . among . . . the towering log trucks of the bushmen driving hell-bent for Hull.

bushmark *n.* an identifying mark stamped on cut timber by the logging company to show ownership.
1933 GUILLET *Early Life in U.C.* 240: On each log was imprinted the "bush-mark" of the company, important for purposes of identification when more than one group of men are driving logs on one river. **1963** *Cdn Geog.Jnl* Nov. 165/3: . . . years after St. Lawrence rafting ceased, one could see along the southeast coast of England, groynes built of rock elm timber, and find a link with the great river in deciphering the familiar bushmarks and culler's marks still legible upon their solid sides.

bush meat the meat of wild game.
1963 *Weekend Mag.* 16 Nov. 42/2: One day . . . he was in the shed out behind the cook's shanty, chopping up some bush meat for a stew.

bush partridge See **spruce partridge.**
1949 MacGREGOR *Blankets and Beads* 14: On the mat of

yellow leaves the bush partridge patters around. . . .
1958 MACGREGOR *North-West of 16* 111: [We ate] salted breast of bush partridge.

bush people 1 the Woods Cree. Cp. **bush Indian** (def. 1).
1958 *High Prairie Progress* (Alta) 21 May 3/4: The Plains Crees considered themselves superior to their friends and the Bush people never bothered to question this claim.

2 people who live in the bush.
1961 *Chatelaine* Mar. 58/3: Appendicitis is the only thing most bush people really worry about. . . .

bush pilot a pilot who flies commercial aircraft (bush planes) over the trackless wilderness of the northern bush and barrens. See also **bush flyer** and **seat-of-the-pants flyer.**
1936 *Beaver* Mar. 52/2: . . . the northern bush pilot is dependent solely on his own good judgement, resourcefulness and initiative. **1957** *Maclean's* 28 Sep. 1/1: The romantic Canadian bush pilot who flew by the seat of his pants in a crate held together by baling wire will soon join the jet age. **1964** *Calgary Herald* 20 Mar. 3/5: A pilot and two passengers who survived a crash landing . . . were rescued early today by a bush pilot and brought here [Fort Nelson, B.C.].

bush plane a relatively light aircraft flown by a bush pilot and used to carry freight and passengers to isolated points in the northern bush and barrens and usually equipped with pontoons or skis. See also **bush aircraft** and **bush airplane.**
1953 *North Star* (Yellowknife) Mar. 3/5: Pilot Johnny Dapp made the trip in a ski-equipped bush-plane. . . .
1965 *Globe and Mail* (Toronto) 16 Mar. 29/8: . . . that's a mighty large hunk of flying time, especially when it's piled up in bush planes, where you can't lock the aircraft on the beam. . . .

bush-pop *v. B.C., Slang* of cowhands, ride into the bush to round up cattle. See also **bush-popper.**
1964 *Time* (Cdn ed.) 13 Nov. 18/1: Last week, with the last fall roundups underway, cowboys bush-popped cattle out of the forested summer ranges, moved them down to the haystacked meadows for winter feeding.

bush-popper *n. B.C., Slang* a cowhand who bush-pops.
1951 HOBSON *Grass Beyond the Mountains* 103: When animals crashed off the trail into the jungle in an effort to escape, it was up to the bush popper, not only to charge his horse in after them, but also to outrun and manoeuvre them back onto the trail.

bush rabbit See **varying hare.**
1920 *Rod and Gun in Can.* Nov. 740/1: In the Fraser Valley [of B.C.] the bush rabbits, or hares, suffer from the same complaint. **1963** SYMONS *Many Trails* 123: The great majority [of coyotes] live on hares (the so-called jack and bush rabbits of the West), mice, gophers, and carrion of all kinds.

bush ranch *B.C. and W. Alta* a ranch or homestead in the wooded valleys of the interior. See also **bush ranching.**
1909 BINDLOSS *Lorimer* 116: Had a bush ranch in British Columbia and came to grief over it by fooling time away gold prospecting.

bush ranching *B.C. and W. Alta* clearing land for and operating a bush ranch. See also **bushwhacking.**
1948 HOLLIDAY *Valley of Youth* 136: The clearing of

these places with axe and fire, and much muscle and sweat, was known as "bush ranching," or in our local slang "bushwhacking"—the man who did it was a "bushwhacker." *Ibid.* 193: I knew a few men who were bush ranching at that time. . . .

bush-range *v.* travel through the forests.
1849 ALEXANDER *L'Acadie* I 51: In bush-ranging his camping-ground may at one time be among rocks overhanging a clear stream. . . .

bush-ranger *n.* **1** See **bushman** (def. 2).
*a***1855** (1956) ROSS *Fur Hunters* 112: Among the bush rangers . . . was the chief Short Legs, who . . . happened to stumble near where the wounded and enraged bear was concealed. **1883** FRASER *Shanty* 58: These timber roads are often exceedingly bewildering even to old experienced bush-rangers. . . .

2 *Hist.* See **coureur de bois.**
1908 LAUT *Conquest N.W.* I 172: The next time he came to the ship, he was accompanied by the Captain's son, Ben, the poacher, dressed as a bushranger. **1938** *Beaver* June 25/1: Who can this be but young Pierre LeMoyne d'Iberville and his party of bush-rangers on his way to attack Rupert's House.

3 *Obs.* a whisky peddler. Cp. **bush,** *v.* (def. 3).
1860 *Brit.Colonist* (Victoria) 28 Feb. 2/3: It is estimated that the number of Indians who have died within the last eighteen months from drinking whisky prepared by the bush-rangers of Victoria, is full four hundred.

bush rat See **bushy-tailed wood rat.**
1921 WATSON *Spoilers* 267: When they rose, thirty-six dead bush rats lay in a heap directly under the hole in the roof. **1966** BAITY *Wilderness Welfare* 12: The air was so dank and musty smelling that even the bush rats forsook the cabin.

bush road a rough road cut through the bush. See also **bush trail** (def. 2).
1831 (1953) RADCLIFF *Letters* 15: The *master* and his men start before the oxen, to prepare what is termed a bush-road, which is done by felling and drawing aside all trees under five inches diameter, from the line of march, and by cutting a pass through any fallen timber of larger dimensions; thus leaving the great trees standing, round which the other being cleared away, the oxen and sleigh can ply without difficulty. **1916** BRIDLE *Sons of Canada* 150: Since Canadian life grew away from the bush road and the prairie trail, there has never been a man who could so have clung to the inviolable creeds that kept bushmen from going to the devil. **1964** *Globe and Mail* (Toronto) 22 Dec. B3/7: He had three springs on the farm, and a bush road he used for woodcutting.

bush-rover *n. Rare* See **bushman** (def. 2).
1908 LAUT *Conquest N.W.* I 286: Seizing the pistols and knives of the dead men, the Indians crept through the thicket to the fire of the bush-rovers.

bush-runner *n. Rare* See **coureur de bois.**
1938 *Beaver* June 24/1: One can imagine Groseillers returning from a trip, his Indian bush-runners loaded with furs, and Governor Bayly with his fiery red face coming out to welcome him, honestly glad to see old "Gooseberry" back again.

bush searcher *Obs.* an itinerant preacher.
1826 *U.E.Loyalist* (York [Toronto]) 30 Dec. 245/3: The

Methodists he said were the only bush searchers, and but for their exertions the Province would long ago have been on all fours in Religious matters.

bushtail(ed) rat See **bushy-tailed wood rat.**
1905 (1959) *Alaska Sportsman* Mar. 41: At the new halfway refuge I warned Jack to watch out for bushtail rats, but he did not pay much attention. **1958** *Ibid*. Dec. 20/3: The bush-tailed rats have since raised havoc, and empty flour sacks litter the dirt floor.

bush, take to the See **take to the bush.**

bush tavern *Obs*. a drinking establishment catering to lumbermen and raftsmen. See also **shebang** (def. 1).
1896 GOURLAY *Hist.Ottawa* 185: He kept a "bush tavern" and did the honors lordly.

bush tea *Hist*. tea made from the hemlock or any of various wild herbs. See also **hemlock tea, Labrador tea** (def. 1b), and **spruce tea.**
1849 ALEXANDER *L'Acadie* I 150: Our present host treated us to mawkish bush-tea, made from the leaves of the forest. **1964** GUILLET *Pioneer Days* 44: Maple sugar sweetened it . . . and some people added whisky or brandy to make "bush tea" more palatable.

bush trail 1 a path through the bush.
1914 STEELE *Forty Years* 16: These rapids and this place . . . was connected with a main road by a bush trail two miles long. **1965** *Globe Mag*. 11 Dec. 11/3: Family use of motor toboggans is rapidly expanding into winter wanderings on scenic bush trails. . . .

2 See **bush road.**
1947 WELLS *Owl Pen* 94: . . . the patient horses drew a jumper sleigh and a barrel down the bush trails from tree to tree collecting sap from the brimming pails.
1947 SAUNDERS *Algonquin* 36: Only the staples were hauled over the bush trails: beans, salt pork, flour, and blackstrap molasses.

bushwhack *v*. **1**† shoot at from ambush; attack in a stealthy, unfair manner.
1912 LONDON *Smoke Bellew* 128: "You laid among the trees an' bushwhacked him. A short shot." **1959** *Mine-Mill Herald* June 2/1: Following their usual pattern of trying to bushwhack any and all locals where Mine Mill is established . . . [they] found themselves in a blind alley. . . .

2† prowl about the bush, as a hunter does for game.
1956 RADDALL *Wings* 224: I've got a number of surveying jobs for you—they piled up while you were bushwhacking up the river.

bushwhacker *n*. **1** a person who takes up land in the bush, clears it, and makes a home there, back from the centres of civilization; backwoodsman,*q.v.*
1845 BEAVAN *Life in Backwoods N.B*. 35: The bush whacker is nothing of the "bog trotter" in his appearance. . . . *c*1902 LAUT *Trapper* 91: And were the men carving a way through the wilderness only the bushwhackers who have pioneered other forest lands? **1959** *Press* Dec. 6: It is on the subject of pioneers —trailbreakers, bushwhackers, sodbusters, homesteaders—that [he] waxes most eloquent. . . .

2 a country person; a rough, unrefined backwoodsman.
1833 *Novascotian* (Halifax) 20 Nov. 370/2: There are, perhaps, few children of the same age in Halifax that read better than this little bush-whacker of Tatamagouche. **1887** *Grip* (Toronto) 28 May 6/2: There was a lot of country fellows, regular bushwhackers, laying around . . . asking us all sorts of questions. . . .
1916 BRIDLE *Sons of Can*. 5: . . . I am not sure whether it was one of Macdonald's plugs or another sort . . . which furnished bushwhacker wags with the bogus five-cent pieces that sometimes dropped into the collection plate.

3 a person living in the bush and familiar with its ways. See also **bushman** (def. 2).
1910 FERGUSON *Janey Canuck* 9: "Come on, this old bush-whacker ought to be glad to see us, if it's only to hear a voice that isn't his own!" **1963** *Weekend Mag*. 16 Nov. 41/1: [The Canada jay] is the companion and familiar of the backwoodsman, the bushwhacker, the lumber jack and the trapper.

bushwhacking *n*. the activity of a bushwhacker (def. 1).
1826 *Colonial Advocate* (York [Toronto]) 25 May 2/3:
  In thousands in York alone they are flocking,
  On purpose for drawing their land,
  But now they've found out it's no joking,
  Bushwhacking they don't understand.
1953 LOWER *Voyages* 140: English-Canadians, with little tales of pioneer bushwhacking to fall back on for their historical heroisms, will never understand their French fellow-citizens until they realize that this race has passed through deep waters.

bushwhacking *adj*. **1** early; pioneering. See **bushwhacking,** *n*.
1916 BRIDLE *Sons of Can*. 237: That bushwhacking era in finance had been pretty well trail-blazed by a number of shrewd Scotch-brained men. . . .

2 prone to strike from ambush. See **bushwhack,** *v*. (def. 1).
1916 BRIDLE *Sons of Canada* 42: . . . the "good man" was he who could knuckle the bushwhacking bully into a snivel. . . .

bush-whisky *n*. a cheap, potent whisky, usually illegally made. See also **bush,** *v*. (def. 3).
1936 MOWERY *Paradise Trail* 16: He could drink up a half gallon of bush-whisky in two, three zwoops. . . .

bushwork *n*. work done in the bush, specifically logging.
1966 *Sask.Hist*. Winter 27: The [logging] company ran little stores . . . where you could get anything that was required in the line of clothing for bushwork.

bushworker *n*. a person who works in the bush, especially a logger or pulpcutter. See also **bushman** (def. 3) and **woodsworker.**
1913 SANDILANDS *West.Cdn Dict*. 10: [Bushwhacker is] a term occasionally used to denote a ne'er-do-well bush-worker. . . . **1947** *Ont.Timberworker* Sep. 1/1: This organization . . . spoke the plain and to-the-point language of the . . . bushworkers across the province. **1964** *Globe and Mail* (Toronto) 25 Nov. 5/2: [He was] one of the three Indian bushworkers believed to have been drowned in Paquette Lake Monday. . . .

bushy-tailed wood rat a species of wood rat, *Neotoma cinerea*. See also **bush rat, bushtail rat, wood gopher,** and **wood rat.**
1908 MAIR *Mackenzie Basin* 239: Bushy-tailed wood rat. Mr. Moberly states that a wood mouse or rat . . . was

repeatedly seen by him at Fort McMurray, but nowhere else on this side, although not uncommon in New Caledonia, British Columbia, where the people speak of it as the "small wood rat."

busk *n. Obs.* See quote. Cp. **beaver stretcher.**
1792 (1911) TOWNSEND *Cartwright's Jnl* 375: Busk. A piece of board which is pointed at one end and broad at the other. When a furboard is not broad enough to spread a skin properly, the busk is introduced on the belly side to stretch it completely.

bustard *n.* See **Canada goose.**
1744 DOBBS *Hudson's Bay* 20: They have there also all Sorts of Wild-fowl, as Swans, Bustards, Geese, Cranes. . . . **1844** (1955) LEFROY *Magnetic North* 133: The Canada goose or bustard has the weakness always to come back when it is called. **1954** CONSTANTIN-WEYER *Half-Breed* 60: There was the common white goose, the bustard (they called it that, but in reality it was a big Canadian barnacle goose). . . .

bust the sod *Slang* plough, especially on the prairies and for the first time. Cp. **sodbuster.**
1922 STEAD *Neighbours* 123: "[The] fellers that I brung into the bald-headed were busy bustin' the sod. . . . " **1963** *Canada Month* Nov. 36/3: At one time it was the skimpy oasis for a brave band of homesteaders busting the sod of the Peace River country.

butcher bird *Obs.* See **Canada Jay.**
1784-1812 (1916) THOMPSON *Narrative* II 48: At all seasons the Butcher Bird is with us, and called Whiskyjack, from the Indian name, Weeskaijohn.

butin *n.* [< Cdn F; cf. E *booty*] *Obs.* movable goods, especially baggage and personal effects.
1804-5 (1941) *Beaver* June 25: Bazinet arrived last night with the *butin.* **1860** (1956) KOHL *Kitchi-Gami* 308: The sleigh had to be unpacked, and the "butin" was dragged through the river and carried to the ruined hut. . . .

butler *n. Obs.* See 1964 quote.
1899 MACKAY *Pioneer Life* 175: The butler now goes his round with the black bottle and glass. **1964** GUILLET *Pioneer Days* 122: All the settlers living within a radius of fifteen or twenty miles were invited to the [logging] bee, and always brought oxen and implements with them. Sometimes a "butler" or "boss" was placed in charge to give the necessary directions. . . .

butt† *n. Lumbering* See **butt-end** (def. 1).
1932 JAMIESON *Cattle in the Stall* 92: . . . the Boss would pick out a tree for spokes, cut it down, sample the butt cut, and if not satisfied, cut another and let the first one rot. **1957** HUTCHISON *Canada* 116: Men with little axes and hand saws cut pulp logs and marked their names on the butts.

butt† *v. Lumbering* remove a damaged or otherwise unsatisfactory end from a log or length of timber.
1858 (1964) GUILLET *Pioneer Days* 95: [Chas. Perry's sawmill has] . . . in all 130 saws, besides circulars for butting, cutting laths, etc. **1945** CALVIN *Saga* 90: This piece would have a bruised or split end cut off— "butted," as the phrase was. . . .

butte [bjut] *n.* [< Cdn F < F *butte* hillock] **1** a conspicuous isolated hill, often with a flat top, found in many areas, but especially common in southern Alberta.
1804 (1890) CAMERON *Nipigon Country* 272: My canoe got to the Butte de Sable, at the entrance of Osnaburgh Lake. . . . **1852** RICHARDSON *Arctic Exped.* 90: . . . we passed the smaller Balsam Fir Island, below which there is a pretty little bute on the left. . . . **1944** DIESPECKER

Furious Oceans 17: The winding Bow, the dusty Badlands and the Sweetgrass buttes. . . . **1962** *Alta Hist.Rev.* Autumn 14/2: A detached low mountain is a "butte". . . .

2 a low, rounded rock mountain of the Nahani country of northern British Columbia and the Northwest Territories.
1963 *B.C.Digest* Nov.-Dec. 427: . . . I was told by several Metis who spoke the Athapaska dialects that the actual meaning [of Nahani] was "people of the buttes," a butte in that section of Canada being a low, rounded mountain.

butt-end *n.* **1** the thickest part of a felled tree or of a log, being that part of the erect tree nearest the roots. See also **butt,** *n.*
1832 MCGREGOR *British America* II 309: The great bulk of wood exported is in the shape of huge trees reduced by hewing, until the sides form right angles with each other, and tapering from the butt-end to the top, both of which are also cut across at right angles with the sides. **1955** GOWLAND *Smoke* 68: The bear sniffed all along the log until he came to the butt end.

2 *Hockey* a jab or thrust with the handle end of a hockey stick.
1963 O'BRIEN *Hockey* 79: Blair told Ted O'Connor to hand No. 11 of the Swedish national team a butt-end. **1965** *Globe and Mail* (Toronto) 9 Apr. 38/1: Nobody ever gave you a better butt-end.

butt-ending *n. Hockey* the practice of jabbing or thrusting the handle end of the stick into an opponent's body in order to slow him down.
1955 *Telegram* (Toronto) 21 Apr. 6/8: A hockey coach says even youngsters playing hockey are taught kneeing and butt-ending. **1965** *Globe and Mail* (Toronto) 9 Apr. 38/1: The art of butt-ending is almost an obsolete illegality in hockey.

butter-and-egg money money obtained from the sale of butter and eggs, part or all of which by custom goes to the farmer's wife.
1932 JAMIESON *Cattle in the Stall* 15: My little butter-and-egg money and the revenue from my early chickens . . . withered in my hands as I timidly compared it with the price of the dishes. . . .

butternut *n.* **1** the white walnut tree, *Juglans cinerea,* or its wood.
1793 (1911) SIMCOE *Diary* 191: I saw a very fine butternut tree. **1815** BOUCHETTE *Lower Canada* 274: The timber consists of beech, elm, butternut. . . . **1962** *Field, Horse, & Rodeo* Nov. 9/2: . . . I saw [a yellow warbler] while lying on my back looking up into the leaves of the butternut. . . .

2 the fruit of this tree.
1829 *Trans.Lit.&Hist.Soc.Que.* I 46: A very rich and durable brown [is] afforded by the outer husk of the butternut. **1952** BUCKLER *Mountain and Valley* 63: [He remembered] the flat black butternuts. . . .

3 a brown dyestuff made from the butternut. See **butternut** (def. 2) and **butternut,** *adj.*
1903 RICHARDSON *Colin* : ". . . them frum th' Tenth Concession . . . come in flannel frocks . . . dyed in butternut. . . . " **1905** CARTER *Dundas* 51: For brown, butternut was used. . . .

butternut (-colo(u)red) *adj.* dyed brown with butternut (def. 3).
1835 *St.Catharines Jnl* (U.C.) 26 Nov. 3/1: He . . . wore a butternut coloured surtout coat, with a fur collar, all coarse quality. **1889** WITHROW *Our Own Country* 213: . . . he stood on the wharf in a butternut coat. . . . **1924** (1933) SLATER *Yellow Briar* 245: . . . troopers in butternut suits and slouched hats marched off a small batch of us as prisoners.

butter tub or **vat** [< Cdn F *pot au beurre* in similar sense, a term used by the fur traders and voyageurs] *Slang, Hist.* a jail; guard-house, especially at a police post or trading post. See also **pot au beurre.**
1927 ELLIOTT *Hugh Layal* 159: "Did you ever hear . . . of the Butter Vat?" I made no answer . . . for I had indeed heard of the Butter Vat. The "Pot au Beurre," the half-breeds called it. . . . It was the dungeon of the Northwesters, from which prisoners . . . did not often come out alive. **1936** MOWERY *Paradise Trail* 8: . . . he had a sickening vision of himself lying in a Police "butter-tub". . . . **1954** CAMPBELL *Nor'Westers* 103: There was . . . a jail—the *pot au beurre,* or butter tub, the *voyageurs* called it—where unruly young men cooled off after some of the worst brawls.

button *n. Curling* the centre circle of the target area; the house.
1911 KNOWLES *Singer* 290: Then he gave him a shot of great difficulty, a dead draw to the button. . . . **1964** *Calgary Herald* 20 Mar. 16/7: . . . Dagg drew close to the button with his last [shot]. . . .

button blanket among West Coast Indians, a highly ornamented blanket with contrasting color designs and totems outlined with numerous mother-of-pearl buttons. See also **thunderbird cape.**
1935 HALLIDAY *Potlatch and Totem* 53: Early the next morning four messengers went all round the village dressed in button blankets. . . . **1960** *Native Voice* Jan. 1/5: The old chief in his button blanket spoke in his native language.

buttonwood *n.* the sycamore or plane tree, *Platanus occidentalis,* occurring in southern Ontario and southwards.
1793 (1905) *Ont.Bur.Arch.Rep.* III 216: . . . the timber on the good land, Maple, Bass and Button Wood, the soil black and deep. **1958** *Lethbridge Herald* (Alta) 31 May 3/8: Canada has only one species of sycamore tree, also known as the buttonwood or plane tree.

buzz group *Informal* a discussion group.
1958 *Saskatoon Star-Phoenix* 5 June 23/1: Four buzz groups also met to discuss the problems of WA and WMS. **1958** *Rosetown Eagle* 22 May 1/6: Buzz groups were formed in the forenoon to discuss . . . Worship and Bible Study. . . .

buzz session *Informal* a period of discussion following a talk or panel.
1957 *Home and School News* Nov.-Dec. 7/2: This was the subject of a Panel Discussion which took place at the first meeting of the year, followed by a buzz session.

by(e)-boat ['baɪˌbot] *n. Nfld, Hist.* See 1956 quote.

1806 (1956) FAY *Life and Labour* 135: Bye boat fishery wholly laid aside; formerly employed several thousands. **1840** MURRAY *Brit.Amer.* II 111: A considerable quantity were also taken by what were termed by-boats. . . . **1956** FAY *Life and Labour* 43: The by-boat belonged to a merchant or fisherman in England, who employed a crew to operate his boat—the word "by" may refer to its being laid "by" for the winter, or to its being an "extra" to the fishing ship.

by(e)-boat keeper *Nfld, Hist.* See 1793 quote.
1765 *Quebec Gaz.* 31 Oct. 1/1: No Inhabitant of Newfoundland, no By-Boatkeeper . . . shall, on any Pretence whatsoever, go to the Coast of Labradore. **1793** REEVES *Hist.Nfld* 28: The private boat-keepers here spoken of, or *bye boat-keepers,* as they otherwise were called, are described as persons who, not being willing or able to buy a share in a fishing ship, hired servants in the west of England, and carried them as passengers to Newfoundland, where they employed them in private boats to catch and cure fish; and when the season was over, they brought them back to England, or permitted them to take service with the planters, or on board the ships. **1842** BONNYCASTLE *Newfoundland* I 94: Bye-boat keepers were persons who went out to Newfoundland to keep boats for a fishing voyage.

bylaw enforcement officer See quote. See also **green hornet.**
1965 *Globe and Mail* (Toronto) 29 Dec. 5/7: Officially known as bylaw enforcement officers, the green hornets patrol the city [Toronto] on motorcycle or on foot tagging illegally parked cars.

by the seat of (one's) pants See **seat of the pants.**

Bytonian *n. Obs.* See **Bytowner.**
1830 *Cdn Freeman* (York [Toronto]) 4 Nov. 3/4: A Bytonian [a signature]. **1871** *Wkly Manitoban* 5 Aug. 3/3: An old Bytonian can now look around him and . . . he will count but few of the old hearts who first settled. . . .

Bytown *n. Hist.* the original name of Ottawa, so called after Colonel By, builder of the Rideau Canal.
1836 *Bytown* [Ottawa] *Gaz.* [The name of a newspaper]. **1964** *Cdn Geog.Jnl* Feb. 70/2: Yet their wild behaviour in the streets of Bytown was for them a necessary antidote to the isolation of a winter in the bush.

Bytowner *n.* a native or resident of Bytown. See also **Bytonian.**
1964 *Cdn Geog.Jnl* Feb. 71/2: Old Bytowners tell of more than one fight that ended conclusively in the cauldron beneath Chaudière Falls.

bytownite ['baɪˌtaʊnaɪt] *n.* [< *Bytown,* q.v.] a plagioclase feldspar composed of 90-70 per cent anorthite and 10-30 per cent albite.
1884 (1885) *Trans.Roy.Soc.Can.* II 3 41: The feldspars, barsowite and bytownite . . . are as distinct from anorthite as they are from labradorite. **1889** *Ibid.* VII 3 67: Bytownite is the name given by Dr. Thompson to a greenish white felspathic mineral. . . .

caa'ing whale
103
caa'ing whale
caboose

caa'ing (or **ca'ing) whale** [ˈkɑɪŋ or ˈkɔɪŋ]
[< dial. *ca'* call; from the practice of "calling"
or driving such whales ashore for slaughter]
a blackfish, *Globicephala melaena,* of the Atlantic
coast. See also **pothead**[1].
1909 CAMERON *New North* 283: The toothed whales
carry the teeth in their lower jaw, the most valuable of
this lot being the Spermaceti or Sperm Whale or
Cachalot, the Pilot Whale or Ca'ing Whale. . . . **1958**
Beaver Summer 24/2: For generations the small-boat
men of Southern Bay . . . have been chasing the
potheads—commonly known as pilot or caa'ing whales
and blackfish. . . . **1964** *Sun* (Vancouver) 1 Aug. 5/5:
. . . the killer whale does not have as melancholy a
spirit as his cousin the blackfish or Caaing whale.

cabane *n. Cdn French* **1** See **sugaring-hut.**
1836 *Vindicator* (Montreal) 6 May 2/3: Two young
persons of the name of Scott, were nearly killed in their
sugar hut (Cabane) by the fall of a Maple.

2 a cabin or hut.
1843 (1955) LEFROY *Magnetic North* 31: I went to look
for their cabane. **1846** (1955) CRAIG *Early Travellers* 157:
Two large fresh logs were laid across the middle of the
caban, on which was lighted a pile of dry wood. **1901**
DRUMMOND *J. Courteau* 23: you can't see not'ing at all,
but smoke of de leetle cabane.

3 See **beaver lodge.**
1897 GREENOUGH *Cdn Folk-Life* 22: A friend has given
me a sectional sketch of a beaver's *cabane* and many
items of information about their habits. . . .

Cabbagetown *n.* a depressed area on the east side
of downtown Toronto, so called from the supposed
diet of its impoverished Anglo-Saxon population.
1958 *Liberty* Jan. 70/1: In a Cabbage Town tavern
brawl, on a Saturday night, speed is important. **1966**
Globe and Mail (Toronto) 29 July 6/4: I have been
reading quite a lot of articles in the Toronto newspapers
about Cabbagetown taking in Rosedale, the waterfront
and even so far west as Spadina Avenue. This is all
wrong because Cabbagetown is that part of Toronto
lying south of Gerrard Street, north of Queen Street
and east of Parliament Street to the Don River.

cabbagetown *n.* [< *Cabbagetown*] any run-
down urban area; slum.
1959 *Kingston Whig-Standard* (Ont.) 23 Dec. 15/1: [He]
believes Kingston's slums are still about "as depressed
as the worst cabbagetowns in Canada."

caberie *n.* See **cabri.**

cabin *n.* See **beaver lodge.**
1760 JEFFERYS *Descr.New France* 29: These cabbins are
generally capable of lodging eight or ten beavers. . . .
1823 *Canadian Mag.* I 462: Each cabin has its own
magazine, proportioned by the number of its inhabitants,
who have all common right to the store, and never
pillage their neighbours. **1915** SPECK *Hunting
Territories* 5: Beaver were made the object of the most
careful "farming," the numbers of occupants, old and
young, to each "cabin" being kept count of.

cabin dram *Hist.* in rafting lumber, that portion
of a large raft on which the rafters' shanty and
cook-house or the foreman's quarters were built.
See also **dram.**
[**1829** MACTAGGART *Three Years* I 241: On these
rafts they have a fire for cooking . . . and places to
sleep in. . . .] **1874** *Canadian Mthly* Oct. 344/2: A shanty
is built of pine boards on the middle of the dram and
the dram thus honoured is called the Cabin Dram: the
cook's house adjoins the shanty, and in it are stored

barrels of pork, biscuit and bread. **1945** CALVIN *Saga*
74: The raft ran the first two rapids as a unit; for the
others the drams were separated out and went through
one after another, the foreman's "cabin dram" leading.

cabin fever surliness and bad temper resulting
from being confined with someone else in a small,
isolated cabin.
1953 MUNSTERHJELM *Wind and Caribou* 128: Cabin
fever, next to being bushed, is an insidious disease
which creeps unnoticed upon people who are forced to
live together for a long time in cramped quarters. **1955**
HOBSON *Nothing Too Good* 134: "You're just getting
cabin fever with your neighbour," I said. "You fellows
have been seeing too much of each other."

cabluna *n.* See **Kabloona.**

caboose [kəˈbus] *n.* [ult. < Du. *kabuis* < (?)
kaban-huis wretched hut; influenced in Canadian
usage by F *cambuse* camboose, q.v., also
apparently < Du. or LG source]
☞*The term seems to have come into English in the
Dutch maritime sense of "cook's cabin or galley," being
extended to denote a stove on a boat, an open fireplace,
a heated hut, shanty, mobile bunkhouse, etc. The form
cambuse (kãˈby:z) has long been current in French
Canada in several senses (stove, storage place, bunkhouse
on logging trains, etc.). Sense 1 is probably of U.S. origin
but may have been influenced by **camboose**, q.v.*

1† See **camboose** (def. 1).
1853 (1892) KANE *Arctic Explor.* 34: Only yesterday they
were ready to eat the caboose up, for I would not give
them any pemmican. **1913** COWIE *Adventurers* 84: The
cook's caboose on deck was the only place where a fire
was allowed.

2 *Lumbering, Hist.* **a.** on a lumber raft, a simple
shed, often without walls, having a floor of deep
sand and used as a sheltered fireplace for cooking
purposes.
1806 (1903) CARR-HARRIS *White Chief* 94: . . . the
hurricane swept the masts, tents, cabins, and even the
roof of the caboose away down stream, and scattered
the cribs in all directions. **1878** *Canadian Mthly* I 91/1:
The pine-knots . . . have their uses in lighting up the
caboose fires on the lumber rafts. . . .

b. See **camboose** (def. 2).
1883 *Port Moody Gaz.* (B.C.) 29 Dec. 4/3: . . . the
shanty is heated by means of what is called a
"caboose," or open fire place from which the smoke
makes its exit by an opening in the roof. **1891** OXLEY
Chore-Boy 52: . . . the great fire . . . crackled in the
caboose. **1923** (1929) *Selected Stories* 83: He had heard
talk around the caboose. . . .

3† a railway car equipped as living quarters for a
freight-train crew and having a cupola commanding
a view of the train, of which it is the end car.
1879 *Winnipeg Dly Times* 12 Apr. 4/1: A locomotive
train with a large amount of freight and a caboose full
of laborers left this morning for Cross Lake from the
St. Boniface station of the C.P.R. **1966** *Maclean's* 19
Feb. 21/1: My train—a dozen freight cars plus an
antique caboose—was waiting on a siding.

4 a. *West* a bunk-house, such as used by threshing
crews, mounted on wheels in summer and on
runners or bobs in winter. See also **sleeping-caboose.**
1922 STEAD *Neighbours* 140: So the threshing season

wore on. We ate in a cook-car, slept in a "caboose," and worked from dawn until dark. Sometimes, to finish a "set" we would burn a straw pile and work by its light. . . . **1933** *Queen's Qtly* 40 211 : . . . hitching your powerful team to the caboose, you draw it rumbling out of the farmyard for the last time, followed by the parade of ricks . . . and the line thunders along the road like a retreating army. . . .

b. *West* a type of dwelling on runners having some of the functions of a modern house-trailer. See also **van** (def. 2) and **wanigan** (def. 4a).

1912 FERGUSON *Open Trails* 106 : . . . in the later winter one sees, not infrequently, a caboose on a sled, heading for the Peace River district or for some point up north. This is a comfortable way of travelling, and on arriving at his claim the homesteader shifts the caboose to the ground and uses it for a house. **1956** KENNEDY *Gt Slave Lake* 14 : Each team of [winter] fishermen lives in a "caboose," a light well-insulated shack about 12 feet long and 10 feet wide mounted on skids. Each caboose is on the ice near the nets and may be miles from land, even from another fisherman. When the general locality of the nets is changed, the caboose and the fishing gear are towed to a new location by a snowmobile or other vehicle. **1963** SYMONS *Many Trails* 132 : He has a blanketed team drawing a caboose on runners. In this there is a small wood-burning sheet-iron heater. . . .

c. *North* a portable house.

1965 *Sun* (Vancouver) 11 Sep. 33/1 : New Holman [N.W.T.] is a wide scattering of two teacherages, a modern two room school, a powerhouse, a warehouse and many small, square plywood boxes called cabooses which are being built for the Eskimos.

5 *North* **a.** a bunkhouse and cook-house on bobs, *q.v.*, or runners, serving the needs of the crew on a cat-train or other group of vehicles. See also **living wanigan** and **wanigan** (def. 4b).

1934 *Beaver* Dec. 47/1 : Working shifts of six hours on and six off, the crews slept in the heated caboose and prepared their meals *en route*. **1959** *Argosy* (Cdn sec.) July 28/2 : Lamb pulled twelve of his best men off other jobs, fitted them out with four D-t cats, a dozen sleighs, cabooses for eating and sleeping.

b. any enclosed structure on bobs or runners functioning as part of a cat-train, whether for the crew or for perishable freight. See also **sled** (def. 4).

1949 ROBERTS *Mackenzie* 212 : Hauling the cabooses as far as possible, the big caterpillar then doubled back for the freight and blacksmith shop. **1958** *Edmonton Jnl* 24 June 4 16/7 : . . . it was a huge rubber-tired, diesel-powered unit which consisted of two power units towing a string of "cabooses."

6 *Obs.* **a.** a small, dingy bedroom.

1891 *Grip* (Toronto) 29 Aug. 140/1 : [They] put me in some stuffy little caboose way up onto the fourth flat. . . .

b. a small, low-class tavern. See also **shebang** (def. 1).

1916 PARKER *World for Sale* 308 : "He's been lying drunk at Gauntry's caboose ever since yesterday morning. . . ." "Gauntry's tavern—that joint," exclaimed Osterhaut with repulsion.

caboteur [kæbə'tur] *n.* [< F] **1** a French-Canadian wooden coastal vessel ranging from 50 to 500 tons. Cp. **goelette**.

1962 *Imperial Oil Rev.* Apr. 26/1 : His boat, the

Michel Paulecap Emillie, a 500-ton, 100-foot wooden coastal vessel known as a "caboteur," was waiting too. It is a kind of boat and a way of life that reaches back into the very beginnings of Canadian history.

2 a person who operates such a vessel.

1962 *Imperial Oil Rev.* Apr. 28/1 : Perron is a descendant of those first caboteur captains who built the boats to take produce to market. Most of today's caboteurs are also descendants with names like Harvey, Desgagnes, Marais—names mentioned in 17th century charters.

Cabotia [kə'boʃiə] *n.* [< John *Cabot*, 1450(?)-1498] *Hist.* a name proposed for a British province incorporating the general area of the Atlantic Provinces.

1826 *Colonial Advocate* (York [Toronto]) 14 Dec. 2/2 : It would however be the best and safest policy; for England can hold Cabotia only by the ties of friendship, amity and mutual advantage. **1840** *St.Catharines Jnl* (U.C.) 16 July 1/2 : Before Lord Durham's Report appeared, I wrote out and exhibited a scheme dividing British North America . . . into two governments—Canada and Cabotia. . . .

cabree *n.* See **cabri**.

cabri ['kæbri *or* kə'bri] *n.* [see note below]

☛ *The origin is uncertain, but the term probably comes from an Indian word, perhaps through Canadian French, the form undoubtedly being influenced by French* **capri** *kid, for the animal was sometimes called a goat by voyageurs and early writers. The problem is discussed in* American Speech, *Apr. 1941, 125-6 and Feb. 1944, 19-20.*

1 See **antelope** (def. 1).

[1793 (1933) MACDONELL *Diary* 116 : . . . the following animals are natives of [the Assiniboine region]. . . Elks, Red Deer, Cabeniers [?] of various kinds. . . .] *c***1797** (1819) MCDONNELL *Red River* 274 : Those who go up by land . . . have plenty of time to hunt, buffalo, moose deer, caberie. . . . **1801** (1897) COUES *New Light* I 191 : An Indian brought me a large cabbri, which had four inches of fat on the rump. **1859** SOUTHESK *Saskatchewan* 56 : The cabree is . . . in appearance something between a deer, an antelope, and a goat. **1882** *Edmonton Bull.* 4 Nov. 1/2 : They killed several buffalo above the crossing, also some cabri or antelope. **1957** *Encyc.Can.* II 156 : *Cabri* is the Indian word for antelope, and the town was so named because of the presence of these animals in the district.

2 the skin of the pronghorn antelope.

*c***1797** (1819) MCDONNELL *Red River* 279 : Their leggings are also made of dressed leather, those for the young folks are made of wolf, caberie and other skins of a fine quality, which they dress as white and pliable as *chamois.* **1871** (1883) BUTLER *Great Lone Land* 301 : I had slept well; the cabri sack was a very Ajax among roosts; it defied the elements.

3 the meat of the pronghorn antelope.

1827 (1912) ERMATINGER *Express Jnl* 76 : An Indian comes to our camp with a few fish . . . and a small piece of cabris which we exchange for a piece of dried meat.

cabriole *n.* [< F "carriage"] *Obs.* See **cariole** (def. 1). Also spelled *cabriolle*.

1816 *P.E.I.Register* (Charlottetown) 14 Oct. 4/4 : During winter it is a favorite amusement . . . to drive in a cabriolle, a very comfortable open carriage, set on runners. . . . **1827** (1832) PICKERING *Inquiries* 94 : It being Sunday, and the day fine and pleasant, numbers of farmers and others, and fine veiled females in gigs, cabrioles, and Jersey waggons, were dashing along. . . .

cac(c)awee *n.* See **cockawee**.

cache [kæʃ] *n.* [< F *cache* < *cacher* to hide; influenced in several senses by Cdn F use] **1 a.** a secret hiding place.

1804 (1933) CONNOR *Diary* 259: [I] dispatched Mr. Seraphin . . . to examine a Cache of H W [High Wines] to know if all are safe. **1885** TUTTLE *Our North Land* 326: It is believed to this day that there is a cache somewhere in the vicinity where he buried his liquor before taking his departure. . . . **1965** *Islander* 11 July 10/3: Circling out from the tent they found them in a cache 50 or 60 yards away.

b. the contents of a secret hiding place.

[**c1669** (1961) ADAMS *Radisson* 101: One hides a cache of meal, the other his camp iron and all, and all that could cumbersome.] **1879** ROBINSON *Great Fur Land* 93: Small caches of wine and spirits, hoarded away from the meagher annual allowance, make their appearance upon the board, and add to the hilarity of the occasion. **1929** JOHNSTON *Beyond the Rockies* 5: The theory came to be accepted that he had "caches" [of gold] buried on his farm. **1964** *Calgary Herald* 3 Apr. 7/6: Police have recovered a large cache of money believed from the $54,000 robbery of a National Employment Service vault in Vancouver.

c. raise a cache, discover or retrieve a cache or hidden supply of whisky or other goods.

1914 STEELE *Forty Years* 116: . . . many a whisky cache or hiding-place was raised to enable Pat and his many admirers to do honour to the occasion. **1962** *Alta Hist. Rev.* Autumn 10/1: "I raised a cache yesterday," he went on, "but blew it all in last night . . . give me a pick-me-up."

Three kinds of cache (def. 2)

2 a storing place where supplies, furs, equipment and other goods may be deposited for protection from foraging animals and the weather. See also **en cache, hoard,** and **stage,** *n.* (def. 4).

☛ *Such caches may be in the form of holes in the ground, ice, or snow, marked or protected by cairns; they may be enclosed platforms set high in trees or merely the upper fork of a tree; or they may be well-built hutch-like contrivances raised off the ground on posts.*

1578 HAKLUYT *Voyages* XII 100 viⱽ: Going on shoare [we] found where the people of the Countrie had bene, and had hid their prouision in great heapes of stones, being both fleshe and fishe, which they had killed.] **1797** (1964) CHABOILLEZ *Journal* 154: [He] had a large Cash of Provisions at . . . that river. . . . **1808** (1889) FRASER *Journal* 158: Here we put three bales of salmon into *cache* and carried the rest through a very rugged country. **1824** (1955) BLACK *Journal* 155: Here we see a specimen of a Thloadinni cache made in one of the Pine Trees. . . . **1898** (1952) *B.C.Hist.Qtly* XVI 93: At the mouth of the "Pelly" . . . were hundreds of men building "Caches" up on the trees, to store their outfits while they went up river prospecting. **1908** MAIR *Mackenzie Basin* 164: [The Eskimos] always made . . . provision for their return . . . by placing in one or more caches (built on and formed of large blocks of thick ice, well protected from wolves or wolverines. . . . **1929** MOBERLY *When Fur Was*

King 123: The only circumstances in which they [grizzlies] will attack is when they have a dead animal "in cache". . . . **1963** *Weekend Mag.* 5 May 3/1: The Mounties established a cache at Bernard Harbor for their colleagues on the trail from Coppermine. . . .

3 a supply of provisions, gasoline, and equipment stockpiled for future use. See also **gas cache.**

1921 HAWORTH *Trailmaker* 255: Two or three times in the winter he will be visited by bands of hungry Siwash, who . . . will beg everything he has and eat him out of cache and cabin. **1937** *Beaver* Sep. 8/1: Beyond them on shore a cache of gasolene (two hundred barrels) assures them of much winter flying. **1966** *Cdn Geog.Jnl* Feb. 45: . . . Rod Henderson . . . established the smaller caches [on Baffin I.] with the ski-wheel equipped Cessna 185. . . .

4 a hut, tent, lean-to or other structure used as a storehouse. See also **cache house.**

1872 (1873) GRANT *Ocean to Ocean* 274: We made use of the cache or shanty on the bank, opening it for a small quantity of beans or soup. **1912** BICKERSTETH *Open Doors* 126: The stores are then put in large "caches" (i.e. large tents or specially constructed log shelters) at convenient points along the right of way. . . . **1964** *Cdn Geog.Jnl* Mar. 82/2: Vegetation was abundant and various around the yellowish sandstone walls of the cache.

5 a blind used in hunting game.

1866 KING *Sportsman in Can.* 57: Posted on a run, or crouched in his *cache* of green boughs. . . he knows that the bird . . . announces the approach of the wished-for deer. **1907** HUNTER *Cdn Wilds* 146: . . . we fixed a nice brush cache at different angles to the dam, wherein we were to sit and watch.

cache [kæʃ] *v.* [< F *cacher* hide] **1 a.** of things, hide or conceal.

1893 OXLEY *Young Nor'Wester* 85: Let us *caché* their corpses, and get back to the fort as quick as we can. **1909** SERVICE *Cheechako* 71: He's cached away his gold dust, but he's sort of bucking up. . . . **1965** *Beaver* Autumn 30/1: Thomas and two trappers . . . cached their canoe at the mouth of the Unknown and walked westward. . . .

b. of persons, be in hiding.

1918 KENDALL *Benton* 92: "Why, this very beef here was for 'em, while they was up cached in the bush."

2 deposit in a cache (def. 2) for later use.

1854 (1892) KANE *Arctic Explor.* 172: He accordingly cached enough provision to last them back, with four days' dog-meat. **1947** SAUNDERS *Algonquin* 48: . . . each trapper could return year after year to his own trapping grounds, and find his trapping gear undisturbed where he had cached it at the end of the previous season. **1966** *Star Wkly* 12 Mar. 10/2: Meat, blubber and skin were carefully cached and at the end of the season, Eskimos from Pond Inlet came to pick them up as an addition to their winter provisions.

3 deposit (in a safe place).

1963 *Time* (Cdn ed.) 7 Feb. 8/2: [He] ordered the caching of militia arms in central stockpiles so that they would be easier to guard.

cache house See **cache,** *n.* (def. 4).

1898 JENNINGS *Routes to Yukon* 25: As it is likely that the travel will be heavy, with many more animals passing over than the local "feed" to be found by the way will sustain, "cache" houses should be erected at reasonable intervals in which packers doing business on the route may store feed and grain.

Cadborosaurus [ˌkædbərəˈsɔrəs] *n.* [< *Cadboro Bay*] a monster sea-serpent supposed to frequent the waters off Victoria, B.C. See also **Caddy.**
1939 *Vancouver Province* 31 Mar. 4/5: Cadborosaurus has been seen again, this time with a son—or maybe it's a daughter. **1960** *Sun* (Vancouver) 28 Apr. 5/1: One would think that B.C. was already well-stocked with "monsters," what with Ogopogo ripping around the Okanagan, the Cadborosaurus . . . frolicking in the seas around Victoria.

Caddy [ˈkædi] *n.* See **Cadborosaurus.**
1933 (1950) *Sun* (Vancouver) Supp. 6 Mar. 9/5: I believe I am the only person who has been so close to "Caddy," [whose] head was that of a horse without ears or nostrils, but its eyes were in the front of the head. . . .
1963 *Kingston Whig-Standard* (Ont.) 12 July 4/6: Firm believers in sea serpents . . . will take encouragement from the news that Caddy, Victoria's own sea serpent, has been recognized officially by B.C. authorities.

cadge crib [? < *cadge*, v., carry, transport] *Lumbering, Hist.* a raft equipped with a windlass driven by horse-power and having the function of drawing, by means of a cable, booms of logs to a desired anchoring spot.
1947 SAUNDERS *Algonquin* 59: Mort once saw McCoshen getting some of his square timber through the Narrows. His "cadge crib" was a raft worked by horses, and it took a long time to drag the heavy booms out through the East Arm to the flowing waters of the Openongo River.

cadge-sleigh *n.* [? < *cadge*, v., carry, transport] *Lumbering* See **tote-sleigh.**
1966 *Globe and Mail* (Toronto) 11 Oct. 33/8: Usually, a lumberjack who went into camp in the late fall stayed there until the spring, unless he was lucky enough to get a ride out on what was called the cadge sleigh at Christmas.

Cady *n.* See **Caddy.**

cagamite *n.* See **sagamite.**

cahot [kəˈho] *n.* [< Cdn F < *cahoter* jar, bump] *Hist.* one of a series of depressions and ridges caused by impacted snow on a winter road, a source of much jolting and bouncing to passengers in sleighs, carioles, etc. See also **pitch-hole** (def. 1).
1788 *Quebec Gaz.* 27 Nov. 2/1: I found the roads perfectly smooth and even, not a cahot to be seen. . . .
1829 MACTAGGART *Three Years* II 88: The Traineaux are . . . built on low runners . . . drawn from a bar below, which shoves the snows before it, and forms the cahots or waves on the road, which are so troublesome. **1902** CONNOR *Glengarry* 87: These *cahots* . . . only added another to the delights that a sleigh-ride held for the boys.

caiak *n.* See **kayak.**

ca'ing whale See **caa'ing whale.**

caisse populaire [kes pɑpjəˈlɛr] [< Cdn F, lit., "peoples' bank"] a credit union.
1958 *Ottawa Citizen* 12 June 1/7: Three men escaped with an estimated $10,000 in cash after holding up the Sacred Heart Caisse Populaire. . . . **1963** *Time* (Cdn ed.) 9 Aug. 12/2: His first objective was to get Quebeckers' savings out of the mattress, and in particular out of the province's 1,270 *caisses populaires*, a group of credit unions whose assets total $990 million.

'Cajun [ˈkedʒən] *n. adj. Slang* Acadian, *q.v.*
1942 RADDALL *His Majesty's Yankees* 26: "We'd pluck the French off their farms—off the fat red 'Cajun lands around Fundy Bay that we wanted for our own folk— and we'd send their villages up in smoke to show 'em the change o' wind. . . ."

calabogus *n.* See **callibogus.**

calache *n.* See **calèche.**

calash [kəˈlæʃ] *n.* [< F *calèche*] 1 *Hist.* See **calèche** (def. 1).
☛ *When this vehicle was in common use in eastern Canada, the anglicized form* **calash** *was usual among English speakers. The French* **calèche** *took over as the vehicle became less common in the latter part of the 19th century.*
1764 *Quebec Gaz.* 28 June 4/2: To be Sold . . . a Horse Eight Years old, and a new Calash, with English harness. **1828** MCGREGOR *Maritime Colonies* 199: Every Canadian has one or two horses drawing his Calashe in summer, and Cabriolle in winter. **1923** SCOTT *Witching of Elspie* 21: Around came the calash and the quatreroux and away we went to the St. Lawrence landing. . . .
2 See **calèche** (def. 2).

calashe *n.* See **calèche.**

caldron *n.* See **cauldron.**

calèche [kəˈlɛʃ] *n.* [< F] 1 a two-wheeled one-horse carriage, built to carry two passengers and having a seat on the splashboard for the driver. Nowadays the calèche is mainly used for sight-seeing tours in Quebec City and Montreal. See also **calash** (def. 1).
1789 *Quebec Gaz.* 14 Nov. 2/1: No person . . . keeping caleshes, carrioles or other carriages for hire . . . shall ask . . . more than seven shillings and sixpence currency for carrying one or two persons with their baggage to the Post-House at Lorette. **1862** *Nor'Wester* (R.R.S.) 25 June 2/5: [The] Local grandees had ponderous clumsy calèches. . . . **1963** *Holiday Mag.* Apr. 73/2: Nearby are the two-wheeled horse-drawn caleches and victorias . . . which provide an amusing means of touring [Quebec]. . . .
2 *North* See 1954 quote.
1938 *Beaver* Sep. 39: [Caption] A calash, very like a Canadian cariole, is pulled by dogs in double harness. **1954** BEZANSON *Sodbusters Invade the Peace* 142: We drove from the church to the station in a French calèche (a high-backed driving sleigh) and embarked for Montreal.

calendar stick a stick notched each day to keep track of the date, used by trappers and others isolated in the wilderness. Cp. **geesework.**
1943 MILLER *Lone Woodsman* 196: He started a new calendar stick, dating it September twenty-third to be on the safe side.

Calgary redeye a mixture of tomato juice and beer, a drink associated with Calgary, Alberta, and the surrounding area. Cp. **redeye** and **tomalki.**
1964 *Globe and Mail* (Toronto) 16 Oct. 7/3: Along with Anne of Green Gables, Calgary Red Eye and Casa Loma, the Canadian banking system rates right up there among great Canadian accomplishments.

calibogus *n.* See **calibogus**.

calico ball *Obs.* a type of charity ball.
1865 RUSSELL *Canada* 111: The evening was ended at a "calico" ball for the benefit of the poor of [Montreal], which was attended by the townspeople only, the ladies being dressed in calico, which was afterwards, I believe, with receipts, distributed to the indigent. **1897** *Medicine Hat News* (Alta) 11 Mar. 1/4: The calico ball given at the Commercial Hotel on Monday evening . . . was a grand success socially and financially.

calico salmon the chum or dog salmon, *q.v.*, of the Pacific coast, so called because of its mottled summer coloring.
1962 *Co-op Grocery News Bull.* 1 Aug. 1: Formerly known as dog salmon, the chum, with the scientific name *Oncorhynchus Keta,* has also been called the qualla, keta and calico salmon. It is caught all along the coast of British Columbia.

calimut *n.* See **calumet**.

call *n.* **1 a.** See quote. See also **caller** (def. 2), **deer call,** and **moose-call** (def. 2).
1853 REID *Young Voyageurs* 205: It was the celebrated "cow parsnip". . . . Its stem was jointed and hollow and Lucien had heard that the Indians called it in their language "flute stem," as they often used it to make their rude musical instruments . . . [and] a sort of whistle or "call," by which they were enabled to imitate and decoy several kinds of deer.
b. the cry of an animal simulated by a hunter to lure game into range. See also **caller** (def. 1) and **moose-call** (def. 1).
1866 KING *Sportsman in Can.* 52: The instrument by which the "call" is produced is a cone or trumpet of bark. . . . **1955** *Yarmouth Herald* 3 May 5/3: Some years ago, Gordon Hatfield . . . got a recording of Mr. Raynard's call and took it back to the U.S. with him.
2 the words used to direct dancers in following the set of movements in a square dance. See also **call-off.**
1903 RICHARDSON *Colin* 57: I shall here present a few "calls" as I remember hearing them from Goarden's lips at the famous dances that Dooley gave. . . .

call *v.* **1** call game by imitating their cries, either by mouth or by instrument.
1793 (1937) CAMPBELL *Travels* 65: [He was] a great sportsman, and perfectly expert in their manner of . . . calling in the game. **1889** (1892) PIKE *Barren Grounds* 157: A few geese were called up to the camp and killed from the doors of the lodges; the Indians imitate to perfection the cry of any bird, and at this time of year the geese are easy to call. . . . **1957** *Melville Advance* 17 Apr. 4/3: He is an expert on wild life and he can call a mad bull moose up so close you will wonder how things turned out.
2 See **call off.**
1912 BICKERSTETH *Open Doors* 165: Another fellow was calling the dance at the top of his voice, and a number of huge lumberjacks were hopping around like so many ballet girls. **1963** PATTERSON *Far Pastures* 12: . . . he'd gladly have gone fifty miles . . . to hear himself call the square-dances.

call-boy *n. Mining* a boy employed as a helper; nipper, *q.v.*
1930 MCCLUNG *Be Good* 138: Tom went into the mines; a call-boy there.

call camp See **break camp**.

1897 (1908) TYRRELL *Sub-Arctics* 88: Next morning . . . camp was called about four o'clock, and we continued on our way,

caller *n.* **1** a hunter skilled in luring game with a call (def. 1b). See also **moose-caller.**
1866 KING *Sportsman in Canada* 52: The caller . . . retires . . . to the rear of the sportsmen [moose hunting]. . . . **1955** *Yarmouth Herald* 3 May 5/3: . . . one day . . . an incident happened which was to result in considerable fame to himself as a "caller" of deer.
2 See **moose-call** (def. 2). See also **call,** *n.* (def. 1a).
1872 DASHWOOD *Chiploquorgan* 53: Suddenly the Indian pointing with his "caller" towards the end of the barrons, ejaculated in a low voice. . . .
3 See **caller-off.**
1912 BICKERSTETH *Open Doors* 81: The little school filled with dancers, the single fiddler forming the only orchestra, and the caller—in this case a half-breed—shouting out the dance at the far end of the room. **1961** KENNEDY & PRICE *Renfrew* 50: The caller would start off with "Allemande left and the corners all" and the shanty rocked to the tune of "Irish Washerwoman," "Cork Boots" and "Give Her a Calabogie."

caller-off *n.* a person who chants or calls out the changes or movements for square dances. See also **caller** (def. 3).
1929 MACQUEEN *Skye Pioneers* 30: Much of the enjoyment at these gatherings was due to the "caller off." He was responsible for the movement of the various figures, and was often chosen because of special ability to provoke merriment. **1930** BEAMES *Army* 202: And old Dad Croup, silver-haired and silver-voiced, the best caller-off in the country, was floor manager. **1964** GUILLET *Pioneer Days* 156: Above the noises of the dancing could be heard the scraping sounds of the fiddle and the voice of the caller-off. . . .

callibogus [ˌkælə'bogəs *or* 'kælə,bogəs] *n.* [origin unknown] *Atlantic Provinces* See 1963 quote. Also spelled *calabogus, calibogus.*
1771 (1792) CARTWRIGHT *Journal* I 139: They supped with me, and afterwards smoked a few whiffs of tobacco and drank a little callibogus; but they seemed to prefer sugar and water. **1832** MCGREGOR *British America* I 221: Spirits are frequently mixed with spruce beer, to make the drink called Callibogus. **1861** DE BOILIEU *Labrador Life* 162: Then we take copious draughts of drink, christened on the coast "callibogus". . . . **1963** MACNUTT *Atlantic Provinces* 18: Justice might be won by the presentation of . . . a flowing bowl of calabogus, a favorite drink of the admirals composed of rum, molasses and spruce beer.

callimet or **callimut** *n.* See **calumet**.

calling *n.* **1** the practice or method of hunting by luring game with simulated calls. See also **moose-calling.**
1866 KING *Sportsman in Can.* 51: "Calling" [moose] . . . is neither without danger or excitement. **1888** (1890) ST. MAUR *Impressions* 243: Calling [geese] begins with the first full moon in September. . . . **1957** *Northland News* 4 Oct. 3/3: Early "calling" season for moose . . . is from November 11 to December 7. . . .
2 See **calling-off.**
1958 *Neilburg Star* (Sask.) 6 Feb. 1/1: The next

Mix-n-Mingle square dance will be held on Feb. 14 with Art Ziegler doing the calling.

calling hare See **pika**.
1960 *Cdn Audubon* Jan.-Feb. 27/3: For a creature so small, the pika has many names: Coney, Rock Rabbit, Calling Hare, Whistling Hare, and others.

calling-off *n.* the chanting of the changes or movements for a square dance. See also **calling** (def. 2).
1903 RICHARDSON *Colin* 57: It was indeed an inspiring sight to see Goarden standing on a bench and doing the "calling off."

call off chant the changes or movements for a square dance. See also **call,** *v.* (def. 2).
1903 RICHARDSON *Colin* 62: ". . . arter much coaxin', [he] wuz pursuaded t' call off." **1958** SYMONS *Fences* xiii: . . . the local fiddler cleared a space and "called off" for the dancing.

call-off *n.* See **call,** *n.* (def. 2).
1909 CAMERON *New North* 318: In some dancing academy in the woods he has learnt a "call-off" all his own, and proud indeed is he of his stunt.

call one's jaw *West, Slang* See quote. See also **jawbone**.
1885 HILL *From Home to Home* 413: His ready money gone he has nothing to live on but "jawbone" i.e. credit, and "to call his jaw," i.e. live on credit, till he has got further employment and more wages.

calumet ['kæljə,mɛt] *n.* [< Cdn F] See **calumet of peace**.
1665 (1885) RADISSON *Voyages* 215: When we weare together, an old man rises & throws our calumet att our feet. . . . **1743** (1949) ISHAM *Observations* 82: . . . this Callimut (alias wus ka che) is one of their Idols, few being admitted in a meeting but those that has a Lawfull right and title to a callimut. **1890** *Cdn Indian* Dec. 64: The calumet, or pipe of peace, ornamented with eagle's quills, is a sacred pipe, and never allowed to be used on any other occasion than that of peace-making. **1957** *Time* (Cdn ed.) 4 Feb. 63/1: . . . the calumet used at the powwow is supposed to have been sucked by Sitting Bull himself.

calumet dance a ceremonial dance in honor of the calumet, a symbol of peace.
1703 LAHONTAN *New Voyages* I 83: . . . our warriors shall dance the Calumet dance. . . . **1814** *Quebec Gaz.* 24 Mar. 2/3: The Chiefs and Warriors were then conducted into an adjoining room to take refreshments prepared for them, and ended the interview by executing with astonishing energy the Calumet Dance. **1953** *Cdn Geog.Jnl* Sep. 107/2: The calumet (tobacco pipe) dance or *danse du calumet* . . . was an essential feature of all diplomatic relations between the Indians and the white people in charge of government and the fur trade.

Calumet fever *Hist.* among Ottawa Valley lumbermen, fear of riding a crib of logs down the slide at Calumet, Quebec.
1961 PRICE & KENNEDY *Renfrew* 52: If any of the rivermen showed fear of running the slide they were said to have "Calumet fever." **1964** *Cdn Geog.Jnl* Feb. 68/3: Most old-time river drivers know what it meant

to have Calumet Fever, that sudden sickening fear that you couldn't run the Calumet this time and live.

calumet of peace an ornamented ceremonial pipe, used by certain Indian tribes as a symbol of peace and adopted by the white traders in their dealings with these Indians. See also **calumet, peace pipe, pipe**[2] (def. 1), and **pipe of peace**. Cp. **stem** and **war pipe**.
1703 LAHONTAN *New Voyages* I 75: The Calumet of Peace is made of certain stones or of marble. . . . **1774** (1934) HEARNE *Journal* 99: "I presented them with a little Tobacco, and smoak'd my Calimett of Peace with them." **1934** GODSELL *Arctic Trader* 170: . . . talking over the campfire . . . the means of causing erstwhile traditionally hostile tribes to smoke, at last, the calumet of peace together and to seal forever the bonds of friendship with each other.

camas or **camass** ['kæməs] *n.* [< Chinook Jargon < Nootka *kamas* sweet] a plant of the hyacinth family having blue flowers and a nutritious white bulb, used as a staple food by the Indians of the western prairies (*Camassia hyacinthina*) and of the Pacific coast (*Camassia quamash*). Also spelled *commas, kamass*.
1811 (1916) THOMPSON *Narrative* 474: Kamass, a white root, of a slight bitter taste which becomes a favorite, and is agreeable to the stomach. . . . **1923** BARBEAU *Indian Days* 150: In due season they went out with long crooked sticks and dug for the *camass*—the queen of the wild root family in the Creston country. . . . **1958** *Weekend Mag.* 21 June 12/1: The Indian name . . . meant "place for gathering camas," a vegetable resembling an onion but tasting like a potato.

camboose [kæm'bus] *n.* [< Cdn F < F *cambuse,* store, hut, galley] Also spelled *cambuse. Hist.* **1**† a stove, used by voyageurs, explorers, etc. See also **caboose** (def. 1).
☛ *See the note at* **caboose**.
1835 (1945) *B.C.Hist.Qtly* Jan. 63: He sold a . . . ship's cooking Camboose half worn for 2 [beaver].

2 an open fireplace in the living quarters of a lumber camp. See also **caboose** (def. 2b) and **shanty fire**.
1883 FRASER *Shanty* 23: It requires very considerable mechanical ingenuity . . . to construct the camboose and the opening in the roof immediately above it. . . . **1891** OXLEY *Chore-Boy* 48: . . . the fireplace . . . has . . . the very queer name of "camboose". . . . **1947** SAUNDERS *Algonquin* 34: The fireplace, the actual "camboose," was built on a square foundation of stone and sand. **1964** *Cdn Geog.Jnl* Feb. 65/1: The central fireplace or "cambuse" was the remarkable feature of the shanty. Beneath a large hole in the roof, a roaring fire burned day and night from November to April. . . .

3 See **shanty** (def. 1b and picture). See also **camboose camp** (def. 1) and **camboose shanty**.
1923 SCOTT *Witching of Elspie* 169: He had heard talk around the camboose, and at noon in the still, snowy pine woods . . . that the man who married Marie-Louise must be a better man than her father. **1964** *Cdn Geog. Jnl* Feb. 64/3: A camboose was made of the forest at hand, of large pine logs for the sides and "scooped" cedar for the roof.

4 a camboose camp (def. 2). See also **shanty** (def. 2a).
1960 *Ontario Hist.* Dec. 221: The lumbermen of legend, mackinaw-clad, hobnail-shod, this was the lumberjack of the Ottawa; the Spartan life of the

camboose, the giant drive, the roistering plague of Quebec....

5 See **caboose** (def. 1b).
1963 *Chatelaine* Dec. 67/1 : On the [Ottawa] river the men lived on rafts of square-cut logs, with a small cookhouse, called the "caribouse," [sic] in the centre of each.

camboose camp *Hist.* **1** See **shanty** (def. 2). See also **camboose** (def. 3).
1947 SAUNDERS *Algonquin* 32 : These shanties were built with a "camboose" in the centre, and came to be known as camboose camps. **1961** *Ontario Hist.* Sep. 197 : Associated with this museum is the Algonquin Provincial Park Logging Exhibit ... [which] includes a full-size replica of a logging shanty or "camboose camp"....

2 a logging camp, *q.v.* See also **camboose** (def. 4) and **shanty** (def. 3a).
1947 *Cdn Hist.Rev.* Dec. 439 : The author ... has been at pains to describe minutely life in the camboose camps of the lumbering days.... **1964** *Cdn Geog.Jnl* Feb. 63/3 : In the fall the teams would move up the line toward the limits where the camboose camp was being built for the winter.

camboose fire *Hist.* See **camboose** (def. 2) and **shanty fire.**
1883 FRASER *Shanty* 218 : [They] became as cool and self-collected in these mazy depths of the forest, as if they stood by their own camboose fire. **1961** PRICE & KENNEDY *Renfrew* 46 : At night the camboose fire supplied the only light.

camboose shanty *Hist.* See **shanty** (def. 1b). See also **camboose** (def. 3).
1947 SAUNDERS *Algonquin* 33 : According to Mr. Macnamarra, the name "camboose" was originally the French word *"cambuse"*—a store-room, and as in so many other cases where French words were used in Canadian lumber camps, its true meaning had been changed because of the new environment. To the lumberman the camboose was the central fireplace in the log shanty, but since this shanty was the place where the cook made the meals, stored some of his provisions, and fed the workers, the French meaning of the word would still apply. The camboose shanty was more than a store-room in the early lumber camps, since this one building served as dining, sleeping, and recreation centre, throughout the winter's bush operations.
1961 PRICE & KENNEDY *Renfrew* 43 : The typical camboose shanty that housed 50 to 60 men was a low log building about 35 feet by 40 feet with side walls six feet high and gables about ten feet at the peak.

cambuse *n.* See **camboose.**

camp *n.* **1 a.** a temporary shelter, often at a stopping place in the bush. See also **lean-to** (def. 2). Cp. **half-camp.**
1782 *New Brunswick Mag.* II 320 : Men's gear is much wanted such as thick clothes also a few blankets ... as some men are obliged to sleep without blankets in the camp. **1831** (1833) RADCLIFF *Letters* 15 : About an hour before the nightfall preparation is made for sleeping, and what is termed a camp is formed for this purpose, in a summary way, by placing a ridge pole of ten feet upon two forked sticks six feet in length, and stuck firmly in the ground. Against this ridge pole are laid, at one side, a set of poles, obliquely; leaving the other side which forms the front entirely open, not only to admit the heat of a large fire, which is lighted up before it, but the smoke, also, to banish the musquetos.

b. a small and wretched dwelling; hut.
1830 MOORSOM *Letters N.S.* 113 : It is amusing to see a family ... landing near the market-place at Halifax, from their "camp" on the opposite shore. **1849** ALEXANDER *L'Acadie* II 119 : A poor man, his wife and several children, all dwelt in one small "camp," or hut in the forest. **1931** SEARY *Romance* 141 : Log houses and bark "lean-tos," or camps, sheltered most of the civilians ... but the soldiers spent the first winter under canvas.

c. *N.B.* See 1832 quote. See also **shanty** (def. 1b).
·**1832** MCGREGOR *British America* II 299 : They commence by ... building a shanty, or camp of round logs, the walls of which are seldom more than four or five feet high; the roof is covered with birch bark or boards. A pit is dug in the camp to preserve anything liable to injury from the frost. The fire is either in the middle, or at one end; the smoke goes out through the roof. **1872** DASHWOOD *Chiploquorgan* 103 : In front of the fire on one side, and running the whole length of the camp, is a bench, hewn out of spruce or fir....

2 *Rare* See **beaver lodge.**
1888 (1890) ST. MAUR *Impressions* 220 : Judging from the lot of beaver dams here, the number of camps and the amount of work they have done, there must be about thirty or forty beaver.

3† a summer cottage.
1948 BORRETT *Historic Halifax* 195 : [Haligonians] were sitting at their evening meals, some probably planning to spend the evening at the lovely Public Garden or at their camps or at the incomparable North West Arm; when suddenly a terrific blast rent the air. **1959** *Ottawa Citizen* 28 May 3/3 : [He] has a summer cottage at Castleford, on the Ottawa River ... Meanwhile the antique is headed for the camp at Castleford.

4 *Obs.* See **sugar-camp.** See also **camp-house.**
1826 PICKERING *Inquiries of an Emigrant* 51 : A notch is cut or a hole bored into each tree, and a small wooden trough placed to catch the sap, when it is carried in pails or drawn in barrels placed on an ox sled, to the "Camp," and evaporated by boiling down to the proper consistence. **1838** NEED *Six Years in the Bush* 107 : A camp will make ... between three and four hundredweight [of maple sugar].

5 the tents, buildings and general working area of a community (often temporary) of miners, fishermen, etc. in remote areas. See also **campsite** (def. 3).
1859 *Brit.Colonist* (Victoria) 8 Jan. 2/2 : Rose's Bar ... is a small [placer mining] camp about 50 miles above the Forks. **1958** *Fisherman* Aug. 1/1 : At present, her six-man crew is bringing troll fish from camps on the west coast of Vancouver Island.

camp fish fish brought to market from fish camps (def. 2).
1958 *Sun* (Vancouver) 11 Apr. 2/4 : Packers delivered 24,000 pounds of Gulf of Georgia camp fish to Vancouver buyers.

camp-house *n. Obs.* See **sugaring hut.** See also **camp** (def. 4).
1897 DURAND *Reminiscences* 83 : A temporary board camp-house would be built, in which the sugar makers could sit on benches to watch the boiling pots.

camp-push *n. Lumbering, Slang* a foreman, especially one in charge of a logging gang.
1942 HAIG-BROWN *Timber* 229 : Just because Ted was a

camp-push they'd try to make out he was the same as a boss logger. A camp-push is just a working plug getting paid a wage same as anybody else. . . .

camp robber See **Canada Jay.**
1888 LEES & CLUTTERBUCK *British Columbia* 320: At almost every camp . . . we were attended by those delightful birds known as the Camp Robbers. . . .
1963 SYMONS *Many Trails* 64: In the interior [of B.C.] they are often called "camp robbers," in contrast to the universal name of "whiskey jack". . . .

campsite *n.* **1** a stopping place set aside for people to make camp in, usually operated and maintained by the government.
1958 WATTERS *B.C.Cent.Anthol.* 417: The camp-site was nothing more than a stopping-point on a rough trail bulldozed . . . through the bush. **1963** *Sask.News* Oct. 1/3: The Trans-Canada campsites are established on a cost-sharing plan between the Federal and Provincial governments.
2 any place where a camper pitches his tent, or parks his trailer.
1963 *Calgary Herald* 20 Sep. 32/4: He claimed to have had a second look Wednesday morning when the "object" made a brief appearance in front of the campsite.
3 See **camp** (def. 5).
1963 *Weekend Mag.* 7 Dec. 6/2: . . . the farmers began hauling wood from a backwoods campsite. . . . **1963** *Maclean's* 16 Nov. 54/3: . . . the north breeds good fellowship nearly as well as it breeds black flies, and men in the campsites and new towns . . . get along better than their compatriots at the United Nations.

camp stove† a small stove used in camping or in shanties and cabins in the bush.
1933 MERRICK *True North* 18: Finyan is busy with rivets and tin, making a camp stove to replace the one that has been half rusted to pieces. . . . **1963** *Eaton's Spring & Summer Catalogue* 355/1: Sheet Iron Camp Stove. Heavy Sheet Iron. Burns wood and trash. Cooking top 28 x 20 inches with four 6-inch covers. Oven, 13 x 9 x 19 ins. deep. Takes 6-inch smoke pipe. $14.95.

camp tender *West* See quote.
1963 SYMONS *Many Trails* 58: . . . moving the wagon [during roundup] is done by a "camp tender" from the home ranch who comes . . . by team, to bring grub and mail and to move camp.

camp-trade party *Fur Trade, Hist.* a group of traders sent to visit Indian hunting camps to trade for furs. Cp. **en derouine.**
1947 *Cdn Hist.Rev.* Dec. 405: Instead the lessees were content to send out camp-trade parties to gather what they could and with little regard to the well-being of the Indians or the future of the posts.

camp-trader *n. Fur Trade* in a trapping area, an Indian sub-trader who receives a stock of goods on commission and trades with his fellows as agent for the white trader.
1956 KEMP *Northern Trader* 101: Accordingly, to stop your man from heading for the village with the first mink caught, you fall back on the camp-trader.

camp-trading *n. Fur Trade* the practice of trading furs with Indians by means of an agent.
1956 KEMP *Northern Trader* 101: Now camp-trading is

the direct result of the improvident nature of the Indian.

camp wagon a kind of caravan or caboose (def. 4) used on the open range by sheepherders, cowhands, etc.
1953 MOON *Saskatchewan* 64: But when the spring comes every year he goes out once more to his camp wagon home beside his flock on the open range.

Canada ['kænədə] *n.* [< Cdn F < Iroquoian *kanata* village, community]
☛ *The etymology of* **Canada** *is by no means clearly established. During the past three hundred years many solutions to the problem have been offered, most of them fanciful. A few examples follow:*
1754 JEFFERYS *Conduct* 23: [Quoting an earlier source]. . . . certain "Spaniards having entered the Bay of Chaleurs . . . before the time of Cartier . . . [and finding no gold] often repeated the words Aca nada, that is, here is nothing; which the Indians having since then uttered . . . when they saw any Frenchmen, these latter concluded that Canada was the name of the country." **1760** JEFFERYS *Descr.New France* I 1: CANADA, in the *Indian* language, signifies the *Mouth of the country,* from *Can,* Mouth, and *Ada,* the Country. **1789** *Nova Scotia Mag.* Aug. 81/1: . . . some say it was named from Monsieur Cane who early sailed into that river; If so, O caprice! **1791** LONG *Voyages* 2: [Quoting Hennepin, 1698] Such a prospect . . . gave them [Spaniards] a very unfavourable opinion of the country . . . [inducing] them to call it Capa di Nada, or Cape Nothing . . . from which . . . it has derived its present name of Canada. **1811** *Kingston Gaz.* (U.C.) 11 June 3/2: When the French first settled on the banks of the river St. Lawrence, they were stinted by the intendent to a can of spruce beer a day. That people thought this measure very scant, and every moment articulated "can a day." It would be ungenerous in our readers to desire a more rational derivation of the word CANADA. **1861** *Cdn Naturalist* Dec. 432: . . . the erudite author gives *Canada* as another form of the names *Canara,* and *Carnata* . . . in Southern India. . . . [suggesting] to me the possibility, that a part of the mainland was in like manner called Canada in reference to the part of India that was so named, either because the voyagers took it for a portion of India, or because they fancifully chose to transfer the name to the new continent. **1896** CHAMBERS *Ouananiche* 39: "Kanatats! Kanatats! . . ." "They are strangers" . . . exclaimed the aboriginal inhabitants of what is now Quebec when they caught sight of the first European arrivals in the St. Lawrence; and "Kanata," or "Canada," was thus understood by the new-comers to be the name of the country, and was so applied. **1954** BARBEAU *Cdn Folk Songs* 1/1: The name Canada, itself, which means "village dwellers," was that of the Huron-Iroquois, who ranged from the lower St. Lawrence to the bottom lands around the Great Lakes. **1960** *Buzzer* 22 Jan. 1: . . . the Canadian Board of Geographical Names . . . explains that the word "kanata" appeared in the writings of Jacques Cartier in 1534 and referred to the Indian community of Stadacona. **1964** *Dly Colonist* (Victoria) 2 Oct. 4/4: It seems to this writer that, while we are busy on the matter of changing the flag, we ought to do something about changing the name of this country, since Canada is a word derived from a Spanish word meaning gutter. One can see what that implies about the inhabitants.

1 *Hist.* See 1615 quote.
[**1536** (1924) BIGGAR *Voyages* 103: . . . nous les avions prins le premier voyage a Can[a]da. . . . (. . . we had seized them when on our first voyage to Canada. . . .)]

1615 (1890-1901) *Jesuit Relations* [trans.] III 41 : Canada . . . is not, properly speaking, all this extent of country which they now call New France; but it is only that part, which extends along the banks of the great River Canada [The St. Lawrence River] and the Gulf of St. Lawrence. **1708** CLARK *New Description* 174 : Another part of this Tract, is called *Canada* from the River of that Name that Waters it. . . . **1881** RATTRAY *Scots in Brit.N.A.* II 393 : In Canada the King and his officers exercised much greater power even than in France.

2 *Hist.* **a.** after 1759, the British province encompassing what was formerly French Canada. **1769** (1931) BROOKE *Emily Montague* 27 : . . . in Canada, contrary to what we see every where else, the country is rich, the capital poor. . . . **1787** *Account N.S.* 114 : A priest of the Romish communion comes annually from Canada, to baptize, confess, and absolve [the Abenaki].

b. the Provinces of Upper and Lower Canada [1791-1841]. **1793** (1801) MACKENZIE *Voyages from Montreal* 349 : We mixed up some vermillion in melted grease, and inscribed . . . "Alexander Mackenzie, from Canada, by land, the twenty-second of July, one thousand seven hundred and ninety-three." **1905** DAWSON *St.Lawrence* 13 : Canada, in the strict sense of the word, consists of the ancient Province of Quebec, which, in 1791, was divided into the provinces of Upper and Lower Canada.

3 the Province of Canada, a union of Upper and Lower Canada known as Canada West and Canada East respectively [1841-1867]. **1888** *Dominion Illustrated* 258/2 : Within a hundred years . . . Canada, if true to herself, will have a population of 50,000,000 . . . and be the greatest nation on this continent. **1953** LEBOURDAIS *Nation of the North* vii : This led to the union of . . . Nova Scotia, New Brunswick and Canada (Quebec and Ontario) in 1867. . . .

4 after 1867, the confederated provinces of old Canada and the Maritimes, with the later addition of the newly created provinces of the west, of Prince Edward Island, and, in 1949, of Newfoundland. **1869** (1962) ANDERSON *Sawney's Letters* 43 : Said I, I come from Canada / So you can't come over me. **1966** *Globe and Mail* (Toronto) 12 Jan. 6/4 : In this situation (and we see it around us in Canada, as well) the people appointed or elected to lead do not lead. . . .

5 in Newfoundland, the mainland of Canada.
☛ *Although Newfoundland has been a province of Canada since 1949, many older Newfoundlanders continue to call the mainland* **Canada,** *as they did prior to Confederation.*
1957 HUTCHISON *Canada* 19 : "Why, sure the young lads go to Canada or the States."

6 See **Canada goose.**
1955 HARDY *Alta Anthol.* 378 : Then it was mostly drakes you saw, or Canadas that had lost their mates. **1963** *Vancouver Province* 2 Nov. 21/3 : There's been a great migration of Canadas through the Lower Mainland the past 10 days. . . .

Canada balsam 1 the clear resin of the balsam fir, much used as a cement in optical work, formerly used widely as a balm on cuts and minor wounds, and once popular as a chewing gum. See also **balsam** (def. 3), **balsam gum,** and **Canadian balsam** (def. 1).
1811 *Quebec Gazette* 10 Jan. 2/1 : Exportes . . . 6 Casks Canada Balsam. . . . **1893** *Blackwood's Mag.* May 695/2 : Another useful thing one comes across in

walking over the portages is the Canada balsam, which exudes from a species of spruce. . . . **1919** SETON *Woodcraft Manual* 270 : [It is] famous for the blisters on its trunk yielding Canada balsam. . . .

2 See **balsam** (def. 1). See also **Canadian balsam** (def. 2).
1894 *Trans.Roy.Soc.Can.* XI 2 7 : . . . balsam poplar, Canada balsam, paper birch. . . . **1923** STRINGER *Empty Hands* 117 : [He was] coating the entire surface [of a canoe] with . . . Canada-balsam pitch.

Canada bird the white-throated sparrow, *Zonotrichia albicollis.*
1866 (1873) LEMOINE *Maple Leaves* 230 : How eagerly I watched, this spring, for the return from the South of the *Sweet, Sweet Canada bird,* the white-throated sparrow—whose clear, shrill clarion resounds even in the depth of night. **1958** *Albertan* (Calgary) 14 June 4/3 : Best known of Canadian sparrows is frequently nicknamed the Canada bird, the white-throat's clear, silver-arrow song rendered into words as : "Oh, Can-a-da, Can-a-da, Can-a-da!"

Canada boot *Obs.* a high-topped moccasin worn by voyageurs and others in the bush. See also **shoepack** (def. 2). Cp. **English shoe.**
*a*1880 (1962) *Maclean's* 20 Oct. 36/2 : [We wore] beef boots—Canada boots as they are called—torn and roughened all over with scraping on stumps. . . .

Canada bushel *Obs.* See **minot.**
1824 *Canadian Mag.* III 379 : In some of the distant parts of the Districts of Montreal new wheat has been sold at 3s. the Minot, or Canada bushel.

Canada Company *Hist.* See 1963 quote. See also **Canadian Company.**
1825 *U.C.Gaz.* (York [Toronto]) 14 July 4/2 : The Canada Company Bill passed the Commons on the 20th day of May. **1963** MORTON *Kingdom of Can.* 228 : Little was realized from the Reserves, either Clergy or Crown, until in 1824 the Canada Company was formed to invest in the public lands of Upper Canada, including the Reserves, and to place settlers on the land of the Huron Tract.

Canada Confederacy *Hist.* the loyalist Indians from the Six Nations and certain other tribes who supported the British during the American Revolution.
1775 *Quebec Gaz.* 10 Aug. 3/1 : He held a General Congress with the Chiefs and Warriors of the Canada Confederacy, to the Amount of 1700.

Canada corn *Obs.* a variety of Indian corn (maize).
1819 *Kingston Chronicle* (U.C.) 23 Apr. 4/1 : Mr. Porter told me, that it was a fortnight earlier than the little eight-rowed Canada corn.

Canada Day See **Dominion Day.**
1956 *Financial Post* 30 June 7/1 : For the event we celebrate on July 1, Dominion Day, or Canada Day as some prefer to call it, is the birth of the Canadian constitution. **1963** *Observer* 15 Sep. 20/2 : The bill he was referring to was a private member's bill to change Dominion Day to Canada Day. It was passed by the Commons in 1946.

Canada East *Hist.* that part of United Canada [1841-1867] which was formerly the Province of

Lower Canada, embraced in present-day Quebec.
See also **C.E.**
1841 *Bytown* [Ottawa] *Gaz.* 18 Nov. 2/2: It is
proposed to establish a College . . . near Sherbrooke,
and to be called the Diocesan College of Canada East.
1963 MORTON *Kingdom of Canada* 258: In the Union
there was also to be equal representation of the two
sections which were the old Upper and Lower Canada,
now Canada East and Canada West.

Canada First (party) *Hist.* a post-confederation
nationalist movement which urged greater political
attention to domestic problems in Canada as
opposed to the current pre-occupation with such
matters as British trade preference and the
reciprocity issue with the United States. Cp.
Young Canada party.
1875 *Canadian Mthly* July 55/1: In reply to the cry of
"Canada First," it may fairly be asked, In respect to
what countries, and in relation to what authorities it is
proposed to place her so? **1888** *Dominion Illustrated*
390/1: The publication of this essay led to the formation
of what was to be known as the "Canada First" party,
of which Mr. Foster was the acknowledged leader.
1963 MORTON *Kingdom of Canada* 333: McDougall was
something of a mentor to them, and his Young Canada
was soon to be outshone by their Canada First.

Canada First man *Hist.* a supporter or member
of the Canada First party, *q.v.* See also **Canada-ite.**
1963 MORTON *Kingdom of Canada* 334: . . . Schultz and
Mair, and the little coterie of Canada First men in
Ottawa and Toronto . . . did represent a Canadian
"manifest destiny" that was purely British and
Protestant.

Canada First movement See **Canada First.**
1916 SKELTON *Day of Laurier* 40: In Ontario the Canada
First movement, which looked to Blake as its leader,
had strong protectionist leanings.

Canada goose a kind of large gray goose,
Branta canadensis, with a black head and neck and
white cheek patches. See also **barren goose, bustard,
Canada** (def. 6), **Canada honker, Canadian goose,
gray goose, gronker, honker, outarde,** and **wild
goose.**
1795 HEARNE *Journey* 439: Canada goose, or Pisk-a-sish,
as it is called by the Indians, as well as the English in
Hudson's Bay . . . does differ in plumage from the
former. . . . **1959** *Northern Affairs Bull.* Jan.-Feb. 7:
The Canada Goose with its . . . graceful V-formation,
and unforgettable honking cry, is one of Canada's
favourite waterfowl.

Canada grouse See **spruce partridge.**
1866 KING *Sportsman in Canada* 143: The food of the
Canada grouse is wild berries and the buds of different
trees and bushes. . . . **1923** STRINGER *Empty Hands* 202:
They found brackenfields thick with . . . Canada
grouse. . . .

Canada hedgehog See **Canada porcupine.**
1867 PARKMAN *Jesuits* 20: On the inner side, these
robes [of the Hurons] were decorated with painted
figures and devices, or embroidered with the dyed quills
of the Canada hedgehog.

Canada honker See **Canada goose.** See also
Canadian honker.

1958 *Kootenaian* 20 Mar. 3/3: . . . flock after flock of
these large Canada honkers began to descend from
the heavens. . . .

Canada-ite *n. Hist.* a supporter of the Canada
First party, *q.v.*
1916 BRIDLE *Sons of Canada* 226: Foster would as soon
speak about the evolution of the baking-powder era in
China and Japan as about the manifold sins of Liberals
or the shortcomings of little Canada-ites.

Canada jay a gray, crestless jay, *Perisoreus
canadensis.* See also **camp robber, lumberjack**
(def. 2), **moosebird,** and **whisky-jack** (def. 1).
☛ *This bird, common throughout the Canadian forests,
has been known by many names, over thirty of which
have been recorded. Most of these names are entered in
the dictionary, but in the interests of economy only those
most widely used are noted above.*
1772 *Trans.Linnean Soc.* XII 672: The Canada Jay is
confined to the northern parts of America, visiting the
southern parts only in very severe weather, as it does
not regularly migrate. **1863** HIND *Exploring Labrador*
15: They would never permit the Canada Jay . . . to
enter their lodges, lest they should have pains in the
head. **1963** *Weekend Mag.* 16 Nov. 41/1: Without
consulting us Canadian members, they [the American
Ornithologists' Union] have changed the official name
of the whisky jack from Canada jay to grey jay.

Canada Land Company *Hist.* the Canada
Company, *q.v.*
1825 *Colonial Advocate* (York [Toronto]) 14 Apr. 3/1:
The Canada Land Company to which your Address
refers, has not yet been incorporated. **1855** (1955)
CRAIG *Early Travellers* 208: . . . Major Strickland is an
old settler, and moreover agent to the Canada Land
Company.

Canada lynx a North American wildcat, *Lynx
canadensis,* having prominently tufted ears, large
cushioned paws, and a black tail-tip. See also
Canadian lynx, loup-cervier, lucivee, lynx, pichou,
and **wild cat.**
1852 RICHARDSON *Arctic Exped.* 71: In the morning a
Canada lynx was observed swimming. . . . **1964**
Canadian Wkly 5 Dec. 7/3: Unlike the carrion-hungry
wolf, the Canada lynx likes its meat fresh and warm.

Canada Medal a civilian award for outstanding
service to Canada.
1963 *Calgary Herald* 1 Oct. 12/6: . . . if the government
ever decides to grant the Canada Medal Mr. Massey
would probably be the first recipient. . . .

Canadan *n. Obs.* See **Canadian,** *n.* (def. 2).
1703 LAHONTAN *New Voyages* I 402: Canadese or
Canadans are the natives of Canada sprung from a
French father and mother. **1708** OLDMIXON *British
Empire in America* I 381: The *Indians* about *Rupert's
River,* and other Places in the Bay, are more simple
than the *Canadans,* who have had longer commerce with
the Europeans.

Canada paper *Obs.* Canadian bank notes.
1838 *Western Herald & Farmers' Mag.* (Windsor, U.C.)
5 June 126/2: Jist tell your queen when you write to her
that ill jist trouble her to pay me in speshe or Canady
paper, and not in wild cats.

Canada pedlar *Hist.* See **pedlar.**
1953 *Beaver* Mar. 46/1: The "Canada Pedlars," as the
Hudson's Bay Company servants called them
[Northwesters, *q.v.*] were well supplied with trading
goods. . . .

Canada porcupine a porcupine, *Erethizon dorsatum*. See also **Canada hedgehog** and **Indian porcupine**.

113

Canada porcupine
Canadian

1787 PENNANT *Supplement* 54: *The Caqua,* or Canada Porcupine, feeds much on the bark of pines or juniper. **1908** MAIR *Mackenzie Basin* 251: Canada Porcupine . . . are but rarely met with in the wooded country of the northern Anderson River. . . .

Canada Rebellion *Hist*. See **Canadian Rebellion**.
1839 *Western Herald & Farmers' Mag*. (Windsor, U.C.) 1 Jan. 350/1: The Canada Rebellion was the all-engrossing subject for some length of time.

Canada Roll tobacco *Obs*. a kind of twist tobacco, an important item in trade goods.
1852 (1956) COLVILLE *Letters* 159: . . . the Canada Roll of twist Tobacco is spun far too large; it is always sold by measure, and it is considered that it should in no case be thicker than to weigh 7 feet to a lb.

Canadas *n.pl. Hist*. **1** Upper and Lower Canada [1791-1841].
1792 (1955) CRAIG *Early Travellers* 12: The Canadas are not countries of whose cabinets or muses you can expect to hear. **1963** MORTON *Kingdom of Canada* 227: The reunion of the Canadas would solve this problem, as it would restore the unity of the St. Lawrence and strengthen the credit of the Canadas.

2 Canada West and Canada East [1841-1867].
1853 (1955) CRAIG *Early Travellers* 186: Its position is one of great commercial importance, standing as it does, in the centre of all the carrying trade of the Canadas with the Lower Provinces and the United States. **1963** MORTON *Kingdom of Canada* 277: The poverty and anger of the Irish added one more tension to the strain on the public temper of the Canadas in these critical years [1847-56].

Canada stove See **Canadian stove**.
*a*1820 (1838) HEAD *Forest Scenes* 100: There was a small square hole in the centre of the door, as there generally is in all Canada stoves, made to open and shut with a slider as occasion requires. . . . **1833** *Novascotian* (Halifax) 18 Sep. 299/3: The Subscriber has on hand a few Chamber Canada and Franklin stoves, which will be sold on moderate terms. **1899** *N.B.Mag*. II 134: The roaring of a Canada stove on a nipping winter morning was a delightful sound. . . .

Canada thistle a thistle, *Cirsium arvense,* introduced into Canada from France. See also **Canadian thistle**.
1829 *Cdn Courant* (Montreal) 2 May 3/2: The plant is so rank that . . . it has even been said that it will exterminate the Canada thistle. **1964** *Calgary Herald* 10 Mar. 21/1: For some time, weed specialists have sought a chemical that would not only kill the tops of Canada thistle, but would destroy underground growth without sterilizing the soil.

Canada trader *Obs*. See **Canadian trader**.
1770 (1954) WALLACE *Pedlars* 8: These Runners carried printed prohibitions directed against the Canada Traders, not to encroach upon the [Hudson's Bay] Comp^s District by severe penalties.

Canada West *Hist*. that part of United Canada [1841-1867] which was formerly the Province of Upper Canada. See also **C.W.**, **Upper Canada** (def. 1b), and **Western Province** (def. 1).
1842 *Bytown* [Ottawa] *Gaz*. 28 July 2/2: We understand that the Rev. Superintendent of Education for Canada West, has this day commenced his annual

visitations. . . . **1945** CALVIN *Saga* 7: [There was] on the other the fertile southern lands of what became first Upper Canada, then Canada West, and finally the Province of Ontario. **1963** MORTON *Kingdom of Can*. 258: In the Union there was also to be equal representation of the two sections which were the old Upper and Lower Canada, now Canada West and Canada East.

Canada whisky *Obs*. See **Canadian whisky**.
1839 *Montreal Herald* 15 June 75/3: Rum continues so high in price that the consumption is . . . superceded by Canada Whiskey. . . . **1865** *Islander* (Charlottetown) 10 Feb. 3/3: One opponent of Confederation . . . [has stated] that Canada whiskey is "poison": another tells us that it is made from corn cobs.

Canaday *n. Obs*. See **Canada**.

Canadese *adj. Obs*. See **Canadian, n.** (def. 2).
1703 LAHONTAN *New Voyages* I 402: Canadese or Canadans are the natives of Canada sprung from a French father and mother. **1744** (1958) *Autumn* 29/1: With this volume there is also a map . . . and the author is given as "Joseph la France a French Canadese Indian."

Canadia *n. Poetic, Obs*. See **Canada**.
1805 *Quebec Gaz*. 26 Dec. 3/2: That all the joys Canadia's sons can boast / That all the treasures of her teeming coast. . . . **1825** *Gleaner* (Niagara-on-the-Lake, U.C.) 8 Jan. 3/2: When first Canadia's plains I viewed, / My heart heav'd high with sorrow.

Canadian *n*. **1** one of the aboriginal inhabitants of Canada; an Indian or Eskimo.
[**1664** DE CREUX *History of Canada* I 41: [tr. from the French] He transferred to a canoe . . . as the Canadians call their little boats.] **1754** JEFFERYS *Conduct* 74: To bring this about he pretends that the people of Gashepe [Gaspé] and the Baye de Chaleurs near it, are called Canadians. **1852** RICHARDSON *Arctic Exped*. 266: The shafts or galleries lately discovered at the copper mines on the south side of Lake Superior, containing immense quantities of stone chisels, betoken a people more advanced than the Canadians were on the arrival of the French. **1957** *Calgary Herald* 18 Jan. 16/1: We [the Indians] are the only true Canadians on this continent and it is not fair for us to have to leave this reserve.

2 *Hist*. a native of French Canada having French-speaking parents. See also **Canadan, Canadese,** **French Canadian** (def. 1), and **Canadien**.
☛ *Until the 1790's the term was used exclusively of the French in Canada and continued to be so used until well into the 19th century, especially by outsiders travelling in Lower Canada and by Old Country traders in the North and Northwest. After the passing of the Canada Act in 1791, the term took on a wider meaning, referring to natives of both Upper and Lower Canada, an application which gradually displaced the older sense, which is now met with only in historical references, including fiction.*
1746 (1895) RICHARD *Acadia* I 221: Some allowance may likewise be made for their bad situation between Canadians, Indians and English, the ravages of all which they have felt by turns in the course of the war. **1807** GRAY *Letters* 101: The Canadians will not speak English; and Englishmen are weak enough to indulge them so far as to speak French too, which is much to their disadvantage. **1947** *Cdn Hist.Rev*.

Dec. 430: It was not, however, until the latter part of the seventeenth century that the Canadians began their western offensive in earnest.

3 *Fur Trade, Hist.* the traders having their headquarters in Montreal (originally French Canadians but later not necessarily so), especially the partners and employees of the North-West Company. See also **Canadian,** *adj.* (def. 5).
1754 (1907) HENDAY *Journal* 331: They never had traded with any European or Canadian. **1777** (1954) *Moose Ft Jnls* 338: As We find the Canadians carry on their trade Inland by going up the great Rivers & Lakes on the Back of Our Factories & thereby intercept the Natives. . . . **1820** (1963) DAVIES *Northern Quebec* 12: . . . it put it in the power of the men to convey certain formation to the Canadians of the whole extent of the affairs of this district. **1946** *Beaver* Mar. 34/2: English Island preserves in its name the old custom to refer to the Hudson's Bay Company people as English and the North Westers as Canadians.

4 *Hist.* **a.** a native of Upper or Lower Canada or, after 1841, of United Canada, irrespective of racial background.
☛ *Although this sense is largely historical, Maritimers still refer to natives of Ontario especially as Canadians and to Ontario as Canada or Upper Canada.*
1792 (1955) CRAIG *Early Travellers* 12: The sagacity of future ministers . . . will be usefully engaged in estimating that portion of population, which . . . will render it requisite for the Canadians to be permitted to set up for themselves. **1840** *Bytown* [Ottawa] *Gaz.* 1 Oct. 3/1: The native Canadians of French and British extraction, and natives of the British Isles . . . live together in perfect social and political harmony. **1963** MORTON *Kingdom of Canada* 291: The main interest of Canadians [in 1850] . . . was still the trade of the American West.

b. *Northwest* a settler from or a native of Upper Canada, later, Ontario.
1870 (1963) *Beaver* Winter 41/1: . . . the grub was good, the beds were nice and clean, the landlady a Canadian and the baccy plenty. **1939** O'HAGAN *Tay John* 149: Alderson had spoken to his superior, a Canadian by the name of Tatlow, an old-timer who had been through the Riel Rebellion. . . .

c. an English-speaking citizen of Canada, as opposed to a French Canadian.
☛ *After the term* **Canadian** *came to refer to all persons in the Canadas, and later to all citizens of the Dominion of Canada, English speakers often used it (and sometimes still use it) in such a way as to exclude their French-speaking compatriots.*
1813 *Montreal Herald* 20 Feb. 1/3: We must convince our foe [the United States] that a Briton and a Canadian are synonymous terms. **1862** (1955) CRAIG *Early Travellers* 251: As everyone knows, the tone of voice is very different between Americans and Englishmen, but it is also different between Canadians and Englishmen, the Canadians to a slight degree participating in the universal twang prevalent in the northern states. **1887** *Trans.Hist.& Sci.Soc.Man.* 28 14:2: Thirty years ago, we, who speak French, were called by every one purely and simply "Canadians"; others were known as English, Scotch or Irish. Lately the fashion has grown up of calling others Canadians and distinguishing us as French. **1959** *Toronto Dly Star* 21 Dec. 7/2: Across the years Canadians have been

and still are fashioning a distinct kind of English. . . .

5 *Hist.* a member of the Canadian Party (def. 2).
1926 DICKIE *Cdn West* 211: This angered the French group, and when the Canadians gathered at Dr. Schultz' house in Winnipeg, Riel went down with three hundred men, carried them to the fort and locked them up.

6 a native or citizen of Canada, irrespective of racial origin.
1869 *Cdn Illust.News* (Montreal) 30 Oct. 7/3: They do not consider themselves one whit less Canadians because they are also Britons. . . . **1964** *Calgary Herald* 25 Feb. 4/1: There is no doubt about it, Canadians are just plain fed up with elections.

7 See **Canadian English.**
1884 *Nor'Wester* (Calgary) 29 Apr. 4/1: . . . Three Bulls, chief of the Blackfeet, was interviewed to-day . . . and although [he] did not understand Canadian . . . the interview was exceedingly cordial. **1962** *Maclean's* 2 June 24/2: At the very least I expected to emerge able to Say Something in Canadian.

8 a. a cow, steer, etc. bred in Canada.
1909 (1913) KELLY *Range Men* 398: Domesticated Canadians, properly finished, land, as a rule, in excellent condition, and compete closely in price with the best States cattle of the same class.

b. See **Canadian cattle.**
1936 MACEWAN & EWEN *Cdn Animal Husbandry* 53: In conformation, the breed is similar to that of the Channel Islands' breeds. The Canadians are angular in outline, hardy, good grazers, and have large capacity for roughage. **1967** LEFOLII *Cdn Look* 10/1: Quebec farmers long ago bred a strain of cattle they call the Canadian, but to me . . . it looks like just another cow.

9 See **Canadian horse.**
1936 MACEWAN & EWEN *Cdn Animal Husbandry* 83: CANADIAN Type—Draught (small). Place of Origin—Quebec, Canada. . . . Colour—black. Characteristics—The foundations of the breed were introduced to Canada by early settlers from France. Representatives of the breed are smaller than those of the better known draught breeds, but are very muscular and possess great stamina and hardiness. **1941** MACEWAN *Farm Live-Stock* 103: Although not a big horse, the Canadian is well made and rich in quality.

Canadian *adj.* **1 a.** *Hist.* of or having to do with French Canadians; French-Canadian.
1760 JEFFERYS *Descr.New France* 7: Their revenue is besides so small, and the portions they receive with the young Canadian ladies so inconsiderable, that the first time their house was burnt, they were upon the point of being sent back to France. **1924** (1933) SLATER *Yellow Briar* 213: . . . her mother had always spoken highly of the courtesy and good manners of the Canadian children.

b. denoting articles of various kinds associated with or originating among French Canadians.
1795 (1911) SIMCOE *Diary* 265: The Canadian coats, with capots and sashes, look very picturesque. **1942** BOSANQUET *Saddlebags* 231: the bell-cast roofs of the larger houses . . . are allied to the Canadian barn-roof, but hipped at more sharply contrasting angles.

c. of or relating to Canadian cattle, *q.v.*
1764 *Quebec Gaz.* 11 Oct. 3/1: Strayed from His Excellency General Murray's Farm . . . Two Canadian Bullocks. . . . **1842, 1897** [see quotes at **Canadian cow**].

2 a. of, situated in, or characteristic of Canada or of her people.

1769 (1931) BROOKE *Emily Montague* 18: I am going to attend a very handsome French lady, who allows me the honor to drive her *en calache* to our Canadian Hyde Park. . . . **1964** *Calgary Herald* 16 Jan. 6/3: The fact that one-third of the Canadian population is French-speaking greatly contributes to Canada's identity. . . .

b. denoting a native, resident, or citizen of Canada; in older use, with reference to Upper Canada especially.
1840 (1951) *Beaver* Sep. 33/2: . . . George Thorn a Canadian servant [of the H.B.C.], occupied one boat. . . . **1908** MAIR *Mackenzie Basin* 73: . . . if one heard bad language at all it was from the lips of some Yankee or Canadian teamster. . . . **1964** *Calgary Herald* 27 Feb. 4/5: I am afraid that Canadian adults . . . have their attitudes on the Quebec question pretty well fixed.

3 possessed of a sense of loyalty towards Canada and of identification with other Canadians.
1809 *York* [Toronto] *Gaz.* 12 Dec. 4/3:
  Should e'er fierce War's red torrents flow,
  And tinge with blood our fertile plains,
  With joy Canadian hearts would glow
  That dauntless still would be our swains.
1862 *British Cdn Rev.* Dec. 3: Shall we become a united people, truly Canadian in principle, in thought and in action, or shall we remain as we are, a weak and disjointed colony, each and every one of us, adhering to the national names and prejudices of the country from which we sprang? **1883** *Brandon Blade* (Man.) 4 Oct. 1/3: We are Canadian enough in our views to look at Dominion matters from the Federal rather than the Provincial standpoint, though in matters of local self-government we shall be as jealous of Provincial rights as we are of Federal rights.

4 a. characteristic of the French spoken in Canada.
1824 (1931) SIMPSON *Fur Trade* 116: The land is low inside this Shoal and covered with high Grass and Willows which gives it the appearance of an extended Marsh or Swamp (in fact it is so or more properly speaking a quag mire or according to the Canadian phraseology a Ventre de Boeuf as the Weight and Motion of a person Walking thereon shakes it for a considerable distance). **1887** *Trans.Hist.& Sci.Soc.Man.* 28 4/2: Already some of our best Canadian words, such as char-dortoir instead of wagon-lit for "sleeping car" have found their way into that paragon of pocket manuals, Bellows' French and English Dictionary.

b. characteristic of the English spoken in Canada.
1832 DOYLE *Hints on Emigration* 34: Two horses abreast, called in Canadian phraseology a span of horses, will travel from forty to fifty miles a day. **1958** *Maclean's* 4 Jan. 17/3: He's six feet tall and speaks with a snipped Oxford accent, pronouncing "clerk" as "clark" but, oddly, discarding the characteristic "rawtha" for the Canadian "rather."

5 *Fur Trade, Hist.* of or associated with the Montreal traders. See also **Canadian**, *n.* (def. 3).
1820 (1963) DAVIES *Northern Quebec* 49: I found they had among them eleven Canadian nets, seven Canadian guns . . . and all powder and shot they had were Canadian goods. . . . They . . . traded those articles with the Canadian Indians.

Canadiana *n.* **1** things Canadian in a collective sense, especially any collection of literature, records, journals, or letters related to Canadian history and traditions.
1837 WELLS *Canadiana* [The title of a book dealing with Upper Canada]. **1924** *Cdn Hist.Rev.* V 4:

Americana is beyond cavil; but surely *Canadiana* should be *Canadensia*. **1963** *Canada Month* Feb. 26/2: Interested in Canadiana, she began compiling notes. . . .

2 old furniture, glassware, etc. of Canadian origin.
1963 *Maclean's* 9 Feb. 23/1: . . . what begins as an amateur interest in Canadiana ends in a full-time professional occupation. **1965** *Ibid.* 19 June 33/1: The term "antique" has a specific meaning, and is quite often erroneously applied to items that should be listed as Canadiana or Americana.

Canadian balsam *Hist.* **1** See **Canada balsam** (def. 1).
1793 (1801) MACKENZIE *Voyages* 138: The salve I applied was made of the Canadian balsam, wax, and tallow dropped from a burning candle into water. **1923** MACMECHAN *Sagas of Sea* 23: The inventory included . . . three barrels supposed to contain apples, but in reality bottles of Canadian Balsam.

2 See **Canada balsam** (def. 2).
1793 (1801) MACKENZIE *Voyages* 290: They consisted of low walls, with a ridge-pole, covered with the branches of the Canadian balsam tree. **1824** (1955) BLACK *Journal* 81: [There were] low round copsis of great extent of Canadian balsom. . . .

Canadian belt *Obs.* See **L'Assomption sash.**
1821 (1938) SIMPSON *Athabasca Journal* 248: Mr. Perring arrived with . . . some Canadian belts.

Canadian boat *Obs.* the bateau of the St. Lawrence. See **bateau** (def. 2 and picture).
1823 *Kingston Chron.* (U.C.) 24 Jan. 3/5: We will, on the opening of Navigation, have a sufficient number of Durham and Canadian Boats, entirely new and British built. . . . **1829** (1832) PICKERING *Inquiries of an Emigrant* 115: Left Prescott for Montreal, with several other passengers in a batteau or Canadian boat. . . .

Canadian boatman *Obs.* a French-Canadian crewman in a river craft, especially a voyageur (def. 1a).
1816 (1818) HALL *Travels* 154: After admiring the exertions with which the Canadian boatmen, who seem to have exclusive possession of this employment, force their long flat-bottomed barks against the rapids. . . . **1860** (1956) KOHL *Kitchi-Gami* 286: He then proceeded to an explanation of the symbols, with the aid of my Canadian boatman. . . .

Canadian boat-song one of the French-Canadian folksongs sung by the voyageurs; work song. See also **voyageur air** and **voyageur song.**
1816 (1818) HALL *Travels* 101: We returned to Kamouraska in the evening, cheered on our way with the rude harmony of the Canadian boat-song. **1850** BIGSBY *Shoe and Canoe* I 155: This is the scene of one of the most beautiful of the Canadian boat-songs. **1947** *Beaver* Sep. 40/2: It was my father's companion, heartily singing a Canadian boat song.

Canadian breed 1 See **Canadian horse.**
1774 (1935) MCROBERT *North Provinces* 27: Their horses are the Canadian breed, about 14 hands high, very handsome, and mettled. **1836** *Bytown* [Ottawa] *Gaz.* 1 Sep. 4/3: STOLEN OR STRAYED. 3 Bay Horses, one of the Canadian breed and two of the American breed. . . . **1868** (1965) COLLARD *Call Back*

Yesterdays 46: The *charretiers* were smart, attentive French-Canadians, and their horses, being of the pure Canadian breed, were very fast and long-winded.

2 See **Canadian cattle.**
1819 *Kingston Chron.* (U.C.) 23 Apr. 3/1: The Canadian and mixed breed of horned cattle were evidently the best, and were admired by all strangers. **1825** *Novascotian* (Halifax) 11 May 134/1: They were chiefly of the Canadian breed, and if inferior to the American oxen as working cattle, possess many qualities which render them far preferable for the shambles. **1886** (1941) MACEWAN *Farm Live-Stock* 252: The Canadian breed of cattle had excellent qualities; it was adapted to our conditions and it should have been kept pure, without any crosses. **1941** *Ibid.* 252: . . . such names . . . with reference to the Canadian breed may have more significance than is usually supposed.

Canadian Brick a straw-colored cheese.
1963 *Canadian Wkly* 23 Feb. 12/3: Another cousin of Cheddar is Canadian Brick which is even milder and milkier than Colby and more loose and rubbery in texture.

Canadian cart *Obs.* a crude cart having two large wheels and a platform with sides of upright poles and cross-pieces, drawn by a horse or ox.
☛ *This cart was probably the progenitor of the Red River cart, q.v., introduced from Quebec to the West by the North West Company fur traders.*
1814 *Cdn Courant* (Montreal) 24 Dec. 3/2: Each Bateau contained eight Canadian cart loads, including provisions and appurtenances.

Canadian cattle a breed of small cattle developed in Quebec from stock brought to Canada by early French settlers. See also **Black Jersey, Canadian,** *n.* (def. 8b), **Canadian breed** (def. 2), **Canadian cow, Canadian Jersey, French Canadian** (def. 2b), and **Quebec Jersey.**
1936 MACEWAN & EWEN *Cdn Animal Husbandry* 53: The Canadian Cattle Breeders' Association dates to 1895, and administers the publication of the Canadian Cattle Breeders' Herd Book. **1941** MACEWAN *Farm Live-Stock* 252: Jacques Cartier brought cattle to the St. Lawrence on his third voyage in 1541, and some were brought by Champlain in 1608. But of enduring importance were importations between 1660 and 1665 when Colbert sought to introduce some of the best cows from Normandy and Brittany. The Canadian or French Canadian cattle which have been propagated in Quebec province practically in pure form for nearly 300 years, are the direct descendants of those seventeenth century introductions.

Canadian cloth *Obs.* See **Canadian gray.**
1784 (1954) *Moose Ft Jnls* 194: All the Indians that have been in being Cloathed with Canadian Cloth having visited Nishipicoot Settlement either in the Fall or in the Winter. . . . **1849** ALEXANDER *L'Acadie* II 6: Covering our nether man with buffalo robes, our upper being encased in blanket coats, of grey Canadian cloth, with the usual hood attached. . . .

Canadian coat *Obs.* See **capote** (def. 1).
1795 (1911) SIMCOE *Diary* 265: The Canadian coats, with capots and sashes, look very picturesque. **1820** HARMON *Journal* 286: [The Takullies] greatly prefer, and make use of blankets, capots, or Canadian coats, cloth or moose and red deer skin.

Canadian coffee *Obs.* See quote.
1851 JOHNSTON *Notes* I 268: The other was labelled *Canadian Coffee.* It is a species of pea growing in a small inflated pod. It has the flavour of a pea, with a bitterish after-taste, and when roasted, has much the odour and taste of coffee.

Canadian (Land) Company *Hist.* See **Canada Company.**
1824 *P.E.I.Register* (Charlottetown) 25 Sep. 2/4: A new Company, to be called the "Canadian Company," is now being established. . . . **1825** *Novascotian* (Halifax) 16 Mar. 95/1: There seems to be no doubt of the final organization of the Canadian Land Company. . . . **1827** *Colonial Advocate* (York [Toronto]) 12 Apr. 2/3: If the simile holds good here, extensive glass works would tend to enhance the price of the lands of absentees, the military, the clergy, and the Canadian Company.

Canadian Constitution 1 before 1867, the Constitutional Act of 1791 and the Union Act of 1841.
1833 *Vindicator* (Montreal) 8 Jan. 3/1: The framers of the Canadian Constitution forgot the principle that . . . Barons of the Empire could not be affected by any law Canadian Commoners could make. **1853** *Cdn Watchman* 2 Apr. 109/4: . . . he said the Canadian Constitution existed in the hearts of the people. . . .
2 the code of laws determining the relationship between the several provinces and the federal government in Canada; in current use, the British North America Act of 1867.
1869 *Cdn Illust.News* 30 Oct. 7/2: The Canadian Constitution is not yet two and a half years old, but already there is a demand that it should be set aside in favour of still other political relationships. **1958** *Albertan* (Calgary) 12 Aug. 4/1: . . . the Canadian Constitution says what the authorities of the federal and provincial governments are.

Canadian cow See **Canadian cattle.**
1824 *Canadian Mag.* III 217: On arriving from the old country, they rejected the Canadian cows for their starved appearance and diminutive size; and purchased those of a larger breed. **1842** *British-American Cultivator* Jan. 15/3: The young cattle (both Bulls and Heifers) fully demonstrated the great benefit which breeders may derive from putting their Canadian Cows to short horned Bulls. **1897** GREENOUGH *Cdn Folk-Life* 12: Canadian Cows are small but hardy and good milkers. . . .

Canadian cuckoo *Obs.* the whip-poor-will, *Antrostomus vociferus.*
1822 GOURLAY *Upper Canada* I 174: The Canadian Cuckoo is not the bird that bears that appellation in England but has obtained the name here from an imitation of the sound of that word. **1846** TAYLOR *Narrative* 63: A bird, called Whip-poor-will, is called the Canadian cuckoo . . . from the very distinct manner in which it pronounces the words.

Canadian dogwood the dwarf cornel, *Cornus canadensis.*
1947 SAUNDERS *Algonquin* 87: Nor are the woods lacking in flowers; the bunch berry or Canadian dogwood. . . .

Canadian English the kind of English spoken in Canada by English-speaking Canadians. See also **Canadian,** *n.* (def. 7).
1857 *Canadian Jnl* II 344: [Title] "Canadian English" [by] Rev. A. C. Geikie. **1957** *Culture* XVIII 246:

Canadian English . . . is a dialect which resembles American English in some respects and British in others, and which includes a great deal that is singularly Canadian. **1964** *Oak Bay Leader* 5 Feb. 1/1: The purity of Canadian English and French . . . suggests it should be called Canada's Biguttural Commission!

Canadian-English *adj.* See **English Canadian.**
1955 GOWLAND *Smoke* 180: Bentley, Canadian-English, was spending a couple of years in the mines for experience.

Canadian ensign See **Canadian Red Ensign.**
1908 NICHOLSON *In Old Quebec* 52: [Several farms were] flying the Canadian ensign from graceful flag-staffs.

Canadianese *n. Informal* Canadian speech.
1963 *Sun* (Vancouver) 4 June 4/1: What these folks need, maybe, is indoctrination in good Canadianese. Canadian speech . . . is usually intelligible—at least to Canadians it is.

Canadian football a game derived from "rugger" (or rugby, a name still frequently used for the game in Canada), played by two teams of twelve men each on a field 110 by 65 yards; also, the organized activity of games, players, officials, etc.
☞ *The Canadian game differs in the above and several other respects from American football, which, however, it more resembles than it does English rugby.*
1958 *Citizen* 30 Oct. 5A/6: A donation of $120 has been made by the North Shore Canadian Football Club to three high schools. . . . **1964** *Calgary Herald* 25 Feb. 6/1: Jimmy Finks was once known as the Willie Sutton of Canadian football for some of the trades he managed to pull off.

Canadian French 1 the French-speaking people of Canada, especially those of Quebec.
1785 *Quebec Gaz.* 1 Dec. 6/1: The conquest . . . has been the means of accelerating the advancement of the Canadian French. . . . **1840** WILLIS *Cdn Scenery* I 98: The Canadian French, like their forefathers, profess the Roman Catholic religion. . . . **1958** *Encyc.Can.* II 236/2: The population [of Caraquet, N.B.] is of mixed origin: Norman French, with an infusion of native Indian, Canadian French, Acadian, English and Jersey French.
2 the kind of French spoken by French Canadians, especially those of Quebec, or by people descended from the French of Quebec.
1816 MARSDEN *Narrative* 51: Their language is a dialect of the Canadian French; and their general manners about half-way-house between the Indians and the white people. **1948** ONRAET *Sixty Below* 9: His native tongue is Canadian-French; the English that he speaks is crisp, vivid, terse, exact; the English that he writes can be woolly.

Canadian-French *adj.* native to French Canada; French-Canadian.
1822 GOURLAY *Upper Canada* I 169: The horses of Upper Canada are of the American, the English, and Canadian French stocks.

Canadian goose See **Canada goose.**
1832 MCGREGOR *British America* I 112: The common wild goose, of dark greyish colour, with a large white spot under the neck, is best known, and most abundant —the Canadian goose only differs from it in size. **1924** MATHEWS *Wilfred Grenfell* 95: On both sides rose . . . birds of many kinds, eider duck, Canadian goose. . . .

Canadian gray (cloth) *Obs.* a gray, homespun woollen cloth originally associated with the

habitants of French Canada. See also **Canadian cloth.**
1849 ALEXANDER *L'Acadie* II 268: I was dressed in a heavy Canadian grey coat, thick trowsers and boots, with a short Wellington cloak. . . . **1853** STRICKLAND *Canada West* II 293: The common Canadian grey cloth, generally worn by the settlers of the Western Province, is a strong, warm, serviceable fabric, costing about four or five shillings per yard, Halifax currency.

Canadian half-breed *Obs.* See **Métis.**
1861 *Nor'Wester* (R.R.S.) 15 July 3/1: In the spring of the year, when the Europeans are busy, late and early, getting their seed into the ground, the Canadian Halfbreed is often stuck up in the end of his canoe fishing gold-eyes. . . .

Canadian honker See **Canada goose.** See also **Canada honker.**
1947 WELLS *Owl Pen* 96: "Got a Canadian honker," observed a neighbour.

Canadian horse a breed of sturdy, black draught horse developed in Quebec from stock brought to Canada by early French settlers. See also **Canadian,** *n.* (def. 9), **Canadian breed** (def. 1), **Canadian pony, French Canadian** (def. 2a), **French horse, French pony,** and **Quebec horse.**
1798 *U.C.Gaz.* (York [Toronto]) 3 Mar. 4/2: To be Sold . . . a pair of grey cropped Canadian horses. . . . **1832** MCGREGOR *British America* II 481n: . . . when [petite morue] are thrown up, and frozen, the Canadian horses will not only eat them, but they soon become remarkably fond of them. **1907** MILLAIS *Newfoundland* 5: The cabs are a feature of the place, and are drawn by wiry little Canadian horses. **1941** MACEWAN *Farm Live-Stock* 102: The Canadian horse was reinstated in Quebec exhibition prize-lists, and at the Royal Winter Fair at Toronto, classes are now provided for the breed.

Canadianise *v.* See **Canadianize.**

Canadianism *n.* **1 a.** support for or devotion to the concept of Canada as a separate and distinct nation.
1875 *Canadian Mthly* Nov. 429/2: In other words, the feeling of Canadianism is not yet sufficiently strong to override all conflicting local feelings and interests. **1946** LOWER *Colony to Nation* 108: These deep realities will merge into a genuine Canadianism only as Canada itself becomes a political community, a nation with a life and a soul of its own. **1963** *Canadian Saturday Night* Apr. 9/1: Within our sight is the one hundredth year of Confederation, an occasion that will either be marred by a deepening disunity or marked by a resurgence of a strong and vital Canadianism.

b. the nature of Canadian identity or nationhood; the fact of Canada's existence as a distinct and separate nation.
1911 (1912) EWART *Kingdom Papers* I 15: Some Canadian club will some day claim the honor of having been the first to advocate the higher Canadianism. **1964** *Calgary Herald* 22 Feb. 18/1: . . . Mr. Pearson . . . brought his emotions to bear on the question of national unity and the meaning of Canadianism as he saw it.

2 any linguistic feature, as of pronunciation, morphology, syntax, vocabulary, orthography, that is characteristic of Canadian English.

1957 *CBC Times* (East ed.) 14 April 4/4: By all means let us have a list of Canadianisms and jargon, but do not let us honor it by the title of "Dictionary."
1962 *Time* (Cdn ed.) 23 Mar. 12/1: Canadians have made do with imported French-English dictionaries, even though they take no account of such Canadianisms as Socreds and separate schools, the mounties and the muskellunge, or maple taffy in the snow.

3 any instance of behavior that is regarded as Canadian.

1963 *Maclean's* 6 April 59/3: "How good and kind they all had been, chuckling at my Canadianisms and my provincial awkwardness. ..."

Canadianization *n.* **1** the process of bringing persons to adopt Canadian customs, language, and traditions so that they may identify themselves as Canadians.

1929 ENGLAND *Immigrant* 166: ... it is at the root of this matter of assimilation and Canadianization.
1963 MORTON *Kingdom of Canada* 499: The increase in variety of course made more imperative and more challenging the process of Canadianization and also the problem of Canadian identity.

2 the movement to displace American investments in Canada with Canadian capital.

1958 *Time* (Cdn ed.) 21 Apr. 12/1: Yet in proposing "Canadianization" of powerful U.S. subsidiaries in Canada, the commission was more in tune with the Tories than the St. Laurent Liberals. ... **1964** *Calgary Herald* 17 Mar. 8/4: His budget makes some marginal changes in the incentives he offered last year for the expansion and "Canadianization" of the economy.

Canadianize *v.* **1 a.** cause to become Canadian in customs, language, and traditions.

1829 MACTAGGART *Three Years* I 37: Some of the unthinking Scotch ape the manners of the latter [English], and are termed *Canadianized Scotchmen.*
1911 (1914) BICKERSTETH *Open Doors* 25: You could not mistake their Lancashire accent, though in every way except this they have become Canadianised, or rather Westernised. **1953** WALKER *Pardon My Parka* 15: "Holy cats!" I said, having already become Canadianized in my expletives by marriage.

b. render books, especially text-books, more suitable for Canadians by adapting them to the Canadian political, historical, and social scene.

1958 *Saskatoon Star-Phoenix* 5 June 12/2: Better textbooks written for Canadian students, not Canadianized American texts. **1962** DICKIE *Great Golden Plain* 263: In the country, the public schools and the teachers did the most important part of the work of Canadianizing them [books].

c. take foreign designs, ideas, etc. and modify them to suit conditions and tastes in Canada.

1961 BOYLE *Justice* 128: It is most unlikely that the American thesis cited above will be Canadianized, as are most bright ideas which spring up ... in the U.S.
1961 *Time* (Cdn ed.) 30 June 8/2: Similar incentives would go to overseas producers who "Canadianize" these cars.

2 reorganize (a Canadian subsidiary of a foreign company) or be reorganized so as to have Canadian representation at the executive level and a majority of Canadian stockholders, thus qualifying for certain tax concessions and other benefits.

1964 *Calgary Herald* 17 Mar. 8/7: In another section of the budget he smoothed the way for some companies which can't Canadianize because they can't list all classes of voting shares on Canadian stock exchanges.

3 *Cdn Football* make a player count as a Canadian by playing him for five years with a Canadian professional team. Cp. **import** (def. 2).

1964 *Winnipeg Free Press* 19 June 36/4: The chief economic factor is that American players, whether Canadianized or not, still draw more salary. ...

Canadian jay See **Canada jay.**

1872 DASHWOOD *Chiploquorgan* 94: During the winter none remained but the owls, the grouse, some of the wood-peckers, and the cat-birds ... commonly known as the moose bird, the Canadian jay, and a few other minor species. **1937** *Beaver* Mar. 61/3: The dragon-flies were in turn fed upon by the Canadian jays.

Canadian Jersey See **Canadian cattle.**

1958 FRANDSEN *Dairy Handbook* 338/2: CANADIAN (QUEBEC) JERSEYS—said to be the same as French-Canadian [cattle].

Canadian Labrador *Hist.* the eastern part of Labrador, that which borders on the Atlantic Ocean, part of Newfoundland since 1927.

1918 GRENFELL *Labrador Doctor* 60: At Blanc Sablon, on the north coast in the Straits of Belle Isle, the Canadian Labrador begins, so far as the coast-line is concerned. **1952** BANFILL *Labrador Nurse* 218: ... by a Privy Council decree in 1927 the eastern part of Labrador ... was confirmed as part of Newfoundland. This is what was called for many years Canadian Labrador.

Canadian league *Obs.* an old linear measure of French Canada, approximately 3 miles and 110 yards.

1765 *Quebec Gaz.* 14 Feb. 3/1: A Canadian League is 84 Arpents or 2520 Fathom; the Arpent is 30 Fathom 6 French feet, a French Foot is about 13 inches 10 lines English Measure, so that a Canadian League is about 3 miles 55 Fathom English measure.

Canadian Loyalist *Hist.* a supporter of the Canadian party (def. 2). See also **Loyalist** (def. 4).

1870 *Cdn Illust.Mag.* 7 May 426/1: The difficulties and dangers he encountered as a Canadian Loyalist have already been recounted. ...

Canadian lynx See **Canada lynx.**

1820 (1823) FRANKLIN *Journey* 90: Canadian lynx (peeshew) is a timid but well-armed animal, which preys upon the American hare. **1958** WATTERS *B.C. Cent.Anthol.* 191: And as yet they watched the terrifying Canadian lynx. ...

Canadian Northwest in the 19th century, and still in historical reference, the vast area laying west and north of Upper Canada (Ontario), including the present prairie provinces and the territories to the north, exclusive of the colony of British Columbia; in present use, the northern territories and the adjacent areas of the western provinces and northern British Columbia. See also **Northwest.**

1871 (1881) BEGG *Great Cdn N.W.* 126: The very fact that the line now under construction is through American territory, would be a fatal objection to its being made the great trunk line for the Canadian North-West. **1958** *Edmonton Jnl* 27 June 8/8: A far larger nesting population than normal to boost the possible statistics for this fall. Undoubtedly, this will be offset elsewhere in the Canadian northwest, especially on prairie points. . . .

Canadian oyster *Obs.* See quote.
1851 JOHNSTON *Notes* I 115: They are a species known as the Canadian oyster (*Ostrea canadensis*) are very large, and inhabit a shell which is long, narrow, massive, somewhat curved, and often attains a length of eight inches.

Canadian parrot the crossbill, *Loxia* sp.
1959 *Edmonton Jnl* 2 Feb. 4/3: No wonder our cross-bills have been given the nickname of "Canadian parrots."

Canadian partridge See **ruffed grouse.**
1845 TOLFREY *Sportsman* I 251: A Canadian partridge, or at least the thing so called, for it is a libel on our plump and juicy bird to designate it as a partridge is a dry, stringy, tasteless . . . morsel. . . . **1898** EDGAR *Canada and Capital* 144: The loud drum of the Canadian partridge, or ruffed grouse, is echoing through the forest. . . .

Canadian party *Hist.* **1** a political group devoted to the interests of the French Canadians, as opposed to the British ruling party. See also **French party** (def. 1).
1811 *Montreal Herald* 19 Oct. 3/1: It has heretofore been imagined that an English and Canadian party, existed in this Country, contending against each other. **1822** *Cdn Courant* (Montreal) 12 Oct. 3/2: There is too much feeling of this nature harboured by the Canadian party at present.
2 a political group made up of immigrants from Canada to the Red River Settlement who from the early 1860's agitated for the annexation of the region by Canada, their activities playing an important part in the unrest leading to the Northwest Rebellion (def. 1) of 1870. See also **Canadian Loyalist.** Cp. **French party** (def. 2).
1870 *Cdn Illust.News* 12 Mar. 295/1: The late *fiasco* at Fort Garry will, we trust, be sufficient to teach the over-zealous members of the so-called "Canadian" party in the Red River Settlement that their unauthorized attempts to reduce the insurgents to submission to lawful authority are only productive of mischief. . . . **1963** MORTON *Kingdom of Canada* 336: The American annexationists were few and dwindling, and their significance came increasingly to lie in the use the Canadian or colonial party might make of them to help in its own cause.

Canadian pony See **Canadian horse.**
1844 MARRYAT *Settlers in Can.* 126: He had decided to procure a small flock of sheep, and one or two of the Canadian ponies or galloways. . . . **1905** CARTER *Dundas* 65: From Montreal westward goods were conveyed by what were termed "Canadian trains," being composed of a number of short sleighs with long runners, each drawn by one or two Canadian ponies.

Canadian Ranger See quote. Cp. **ranger** (def. 2a).
1959 *Beaver* Autumn 22: The Canadian Rangers are an auxiliary force of the Reserve Militia under the Department of National Defence. They patrol the lonely places of Canada and are a potential guerrilla army.

Canadian Rebellion *Obs.* the abortive rebellion in Upper Canada in 1837-38, led by William Lyon Mackenzie. See also **Canada Rebellion** and **Mackenzie Rebellion.**
1840 *St.Catharines Jnl* (U.C.) 13 Jan. 2/5: Besides

the ordinary calendar, it contains a sketch of the Canadian Rebellion, from its first outbreak, near Toronto, up to the close. **1851** *Voice of the Fugitive* (Sandwich [Windsor], C.W.) 18 June 2/3: [He was the] principal actor in the drama which terminated the Canadian rebellion of 1838.

Canadian Red Ensign See quotes. See also **Canadian ensign.**
1945 (1965) STANLEY *Canada's Flag* 49: . . . until such time as action is taken by parliament for the formal adoption of a national flag, it is desirable to authorize the flying of the Canadian red ensign on federal buildings within as well as without Canada, and to remove any doubt as to the propriety of flying the Canadian Red Ensign wherever place or occasion make it desirable to fly a distinctive Canadian flag [Order-in-Council, Sep. 5]. **1962** *Canada Month* Sep. 6/1: The Canadian Red Ensign, since 1945 officially considered "a distinctive Canadian flag," is the British merchant navy flag, the Red Ensign, with the shield of the Canadian Coat of Arms in the fly. The coat of arms was authorized in 1921; in the upper two thirds it has the arms of England, Scotland, Ireland, and France, in the lower third a sprig of maple on a silver background.

Canadian refugee *Hist.* following the Rebellion of 1837, expatriated rebels who found asylum in the United States.
1838 *Niagara Reporter* (U.C.) 11 Nov. Extra 1/1: We mentioned the other day, our certain belief of the Canadian refugees and Frontier scoundrels organizing to make forays or plundering excursions into this province. **1839** *Montreal Transcript* 4 May 2/5: The Canadian refugees have, by a renewal of their beggarly appeals through the medium of the "Circular," considerably disgusted a portion of our neighbours, who begin to look upon them in their true light.

Canadian Republic *Hist.* a "Republic" established by rebels in 1838.
1904 DECELLES *Papineau* 140: . . . Nelson returned to Vermont [1838] after the collapse of his unfortunate invasion, covered with the ridicule he had richly earned by his proclamation of a Canadian Republic and his own election as president. . . . **1916** MACMECHAN *Popular Government* 29: Durham took ship at Quebec on the first of November [1838]; and Dr. Robert Nelson was declared president of the Canadian Republic at Napierville on the fourth. **1926** WRONG *History of Can.* 231: He [W. L. Mackenzie] set up a so-called "Provisional Government" on Navy Island in the Niagara River above the Falls, under the flag of the Canadian Republic, with two stars, in imitation of those in the Stars and Stripes.

Canadian rice *Obs.* See **wild rice.**
1833 (1926) LANGTON *Early U.C.* 5: . . . Rice Lake . . . as its name would denote, is a low, muddy, swampy, aguish looking place, covered over with Canadian rice and other aquatic weeds.

Canadian rye a Canadian whisky, *q.v.*, made from rye.
1896 *Kaslo Claim* (B.C.) 25 Jan. 5/2: Most of the boys talk American, chew American tobacco, drink Canadian rye, play poker and work for $3.50 a day. **1964** *Maclean's* 8 Feb. 27: [Advert.] For locally grown Alberta rye grain becomes the best-tasting Canadian rye whiskys.

Canadian Shield [so called from its shape] a vast area of mineral-rich, mostly granitic, Pre-Cambrian rock surrounding Hudson Bay and extending as far southward as the Great Lakes. See also **Laurentian barrier, Laurentian plateau, Laurentian Shield,** and **Shield.**
1929 *Cdn Hist.Rev.* X 294: There is no element in the present Dominion of greater significance than the so-called Canadian Shield or Laurentian Barrier. **1963** *Weekend Mag.* 4 May 3/1: The air force ... puts in thousands of flying hours, combing some of Canada's most rugged vastness—the Canadian Shield, the Yukon, the Arctic and the foothills. **1965** *Kingston Whig-Standard* (Ont.) 5 Jan. 12/4: ... carbonatite [is] a rock rare in the Canadian Shield. ...

Canadian shoe a kind of sturdy moccasin having uppers reaching well up the lower leg; shoe pack (def. 1). See also **beef-skin moccasin, botte sauvage, French shoe,** and **Indian boot** (def. 1).
1806 (1905) LEWIS & CLARK *Journals* V 114: ... Frazier ... had previously made him a present of a pair of Canadian shoes or shoe-packs. **1944** *Beaver* Sep. 19/1: Most of the shoes meant for the voyageurs and canoemen were of local manufacture ... some of them were called Canadian shoes.

Canadian sled *North* a large freight-carrying sled designed in Canada and used in tractor trains, *q.v.*
1949 *Report of DME Test Team* IA 1: ... it was found that sufficient fuels ... could not be accommodated in two Canadian sleds.

Canadian stag *Obs.* See **wapiti.**
1863 (1873) LEMOINE *Maple Leaves* 241: One of the greatest enormities perpetrated by the Indian, is the extinction in the eastern and in the greater portion of western Canada, of the Wapiti or Canadian stag ...

Canadian stove See 1899 quote. See also **Canada stove.**
1853 STRICKLAND *Canada West* II 120: The evening was cold, so he proposed a fire in a large double Canadian stove, which stood in the middle of the room. **1899** *N.B.Mag.* II 134: The favorite stove was the Canadian, an oblong iron box, sometimes surmounted by an upper chamber of like shape and dimensions, often used for heating plates, keeping cooked dishes warm, and for kindred purposes. **1924** BLAKE *Chez Nous* 46: And the [wood-burning] Canadian stove is as trusty a custodian of old tradition as ever was the hearth.

Canadian thistle See **Canada thistle.**
1822 GOURLAY *Upper Canada* I 156: It has, likewise, passed from Canada into the United States, where it has received the name of the Canadian thistle, and it is now known by that name even here. **1947** MITCHELL *Who has Seen the Wind* 8: Once they bent down to watch a bee crawl over a Canadian thistle's royal hair. ...

Canadian trader *Hist.* a trader from Quebec other than a Hudson's Bay man, especially a Northwester (def. 1a). See also **Canada trader** and **Montreal trader.**
1778 (1951) *Sask.Jnls* 218: ... Mr. Tomison ... I intent to send ... to wait for the Indians ... to intercept them from going to the Canadian traders. **1820** (1963) DAVIES *Northern Quebec* 49: ... they went for those Canadian Indians who had for a long time past been

supplied with powder and shot from the Canadian trades. ... **1954** WALLACE *Pedlars* 17: Tomison ... had learned that these [beaver] coats had been sold by the Indians to the Canadian traders, and had been taken away by them to the Grand Portage.

Canadian train *Hist.* See 1905 quote.
1833 *Cdn Courant* (Montreal) 21 Dec. 2/5: It is expedient to petition the Legislature at their next ensuing Session, to pass such laws as may be effectual to prevent the using of the Canadian train, as at present constructed, in the public highways. **1905** CARTER *Dundas* 65: From Montreal westward goods were conveyed by what were termed "Canadian trains," being composed of a number of short sleighs with long runners, each drawn by one or two Canadian ponies.

Canadian voltigeur See **voltigeur** (def. 1).

Canadian voyager *Obs.* See **voyageur** (def. 1).
☞ *The Anglicized form was in common use among English traders of the 18th and early 19th centuries.*
1793 (1801) MACKENZIE *Voyages* 280: I was also compelled to put the people up in short allowance, and confine them to two meals a day, a regulation peculiarly offensive to a Canadian voyager. **1820** (1823) FRANKLIN *Journey* 86: It was not very uncommon, amongst the Canadian voyagers for one woman to be common to, and maintained at the joint expense of, two men; nor for a voyager to sell his wife, either for a season, or altogether, for a sum of money, proportioned to her beauty and good qualities, but always inferior to the price of a team of dogs. **1826** *U.E.Loyalist* (York [Toronto]) 2 Dec. 214/3: Here we embarked in two canoes, manned by 24 Canadian voyagers.

Canadian voyageur *Hist.* See **voyageur** (def. 1).
1806 (1809) GRAY *Letters* 89: An Indian or a Canadian voyageur, will discern a path or tract where others have passed, and follow it for many days, where you or I would never have imagined a human being had passed before. **1957** *Beaver* Winter 40/2: ... in the nineteenth century the Canadian voyageur became a familiar sight at York [Factory].

Canadian West from the late 19th century, the general area of the Prairie Provinces.
1888 *Dominion Illustrated* 98/3: The springtime in the Canadian West is served out by the weather clerk, in proportions admirably suited to the needs of the farmer. **1963** *Albertan* (Calgary) 15 Oct. 2/3: ... it is a wonder that the early pioneers didn't give up and abandon the trade that was later to make Calgary famous as the greatest "cowtown" in the Canadian West.

Canadian whisk(e)y whisky distilled in Canada; specifically, blended whisky derived mainly from rye, and called "rye" by Canadians. See also **Canada whisky, Canadian rye,** and **rye.**
1821 *Cdn Courant* (Montreal) 13 Jan. 2/5: Your palsied limbs and water eyes ... your squalid looks and ruined constitutions, may have taught you, to your sad experience ... that one fourth of the Rum, and one fifth of the Gin and Brandy you have drunk, has been nothing else than Yankee or Canadian whiskey. **1965** *Globe and Mail* (Toronto) 6 Jan. B1/4: At the same time ... sales of Canadian whisky increased by about 46,000 gallons.

Canadian wood jay See **Canada jay.**
1907 MILLAIS *Newfoundland* 15: As yet we had not met that delightfully cheeky fellow, the Canadian wood jay, moose-bird, or whiskey jack, as he is variously named.

Canadien [*French* kana'djɛ̃] *n.* [< Cdn F] a French-speaking Canadian.

☛ *This term is largely a spelling device used in printed matter to specify French Canadians as opposed to other Canadians; the form is often italicized.*
1811 *Montreal Herald* 7 Dec. 3/2: Several of his friends carried flags and hat-bands, with the appropriate motto, *Stuart le vrai Canadien.* **1832** *Vindicator* (Montreal) 9 Mar. 2/5: [He] justly remarks that the Canadiens have good grounds for complaining. **1922** *Dalhousie Rev.* II 217: He has once and for all destroyed the popular impression of the Canadien as an amusing individual, speaking hybrid language.... **1964** *Cdn Geog.Jnl* Feb. 71/2: Then the chances that Shiner and Canadien would be fighting on the street ... were good indeed.

Canadien(ne) *adj.* French-Canadian.
1832 *Vindicator* (Montreal) 9 Mar. 2/5: No man who feels as a Briton ought to feel would have thus prostituted a Canadien press. **1963** *Western Wkly Supp.* 13 Mar. 6/1: Louis loved his horses ... almost as much as he did his petite Canadienne wife. **1964** *Cdn Forum* June 69/2: This would require electoral rolls which would be called the Canadien and Canadian roll, to be drawn up.

Canadienne [*French* kanaˈdjɛn] *n.* a French-Canadian woman.
☛ *See note at* **Canadien,** n.
1863 WALSHE *Cedar Creek* 82: The aged Canadienne arose, with the politeness so natural to her Gallic descent, and bade them welcome. **1963** *Maclean's* 6 Apr. 23/2: Miss Gobeil fits neither the cliche about the shy, family-dominated young canadienne who wants only to be married ... or the one about the gay, champagne-drinking flirt.

Canadite *n. Rare, Obs.* a Canadian.
1812 *Kingston Gaz.* (U.C.) 28 Jan. 2/2: ... after all these Canadites are routed out, they are to make an allottment of their lands, as a reward to these modern crusaders, for their valiant achievements.

Canady *n. Obs.* See **Canada.**

canal *n. West Coast* See quotes.
1824 (1931) MERK *Fur Trade* 241: [Is there] any good Roadstead or Harbour in the Portland Canal or between it and the Columbia [?] **1846** *St.Catharines Jnl* (C.W.) 26 Feb. 2/3: The north-west coast of America is intersected by ... canals formed by nature, running far into the interior of the country.... **1936** DENTON & LORD *World Geography* 46: Brawling streams ... pour their ice-cold water into these inlets and canals.... **1966** *Globe and Mail* (Toronto) 14 Jan. B5/6: ... in Stewart [B.C.] ... 600 permanent residents live ... at the end of the 100-mile-long Portland Canal (a fiord and not a man-made waterway).

canaller *n. Hist.* **1** a laborer employed in the building of canals.
1844 *St.Catharines Jnl* (C.W.) 2 Aug. 2/2: The Herald proceeds to complain of "the unlawful and threatening assemblage of two thousand "canallers," many of them armed with destructive weapons, for the purpose of insulting and intimidating the parties forming the excursion." **1846** BONNYCASTLE *Canada and Canadians* II 63: ... the reckless turbulent Irish canal men ... keep the country in constant excitement.... The French Canadians and the Indians cordially detest these canallers.

2 an inland freight boat, stubby, narrow-beamed, and about 250 ft. long, built for the old fourteen-foot St. Lawrence canals and rendered obsolete by the St. Lawrence Seaway.
1959 *Time* (Cdn ed.) 23 Feb. 11/1: From Scott Misener Steamships Ltd. last week, "We regret to inform you" letters went out to captains of the company's 23 aging canallers telling them that the ships would be scrapped. **1963** *Weekend Mag.* 21 Dec. 18/3: There were upper lakers, canallers, packets, side-wheelers and schooners.

Canal Reserve *Obs.* a strip of public land set aside for the construction of the Rideau canal between Kingston and Ottawa.
1815 *Kingston Gaz.* (U.C.) 30 Dec. 3/2: I observe in your number of the 22nd of last month, you take notice of the Settlers on the Canal Reserve; which to a feeling mind is painful indeed, especially at this season of the year. **1822** *Montreal Herald* 24 Dec. 2/3: A Salt Spring ... has just been discovered, and is now in operation, on the estate of Mr. Francis Ireland, one of the English settlers on the Canal Reserve in Murray.

candle *n.* disintegrating ice consisting of prisms formed perpendicular to the original ice surface; also, one of these prisms. Cp. **needle ice.**
1796 (1916) THOMPSON *Narrative* 155: The rest [of the partly melted ice] we call candles, that is, icicles of fifteen to eighteen inches, or more in length, each distinct from the other; it is thus that nature prepares the ice to be broken up by a strong gale. **1913** COWIE *Adventurers* 96: Most of the ice in Hudson Straits was rapidly decomposing, smashing in "candles" on contact with the ship. **1924** MASON *Arctic Forests* 199: Harry pulled me out, shouting with anxiety, for "candle" ice is nerve-wracking stuff.

candle *v.* of ice, form candles.
1924 MASON *Arctic Forests* 195: They were having a bad time, for dogs cannot choose good ice from bad, and continually they fell through the rotten, white, "candled" stuff and had to struggle out again. **1930** *Keewatin* 41: The sun causes the ice to "candle" producing disintigration by vertical weakening while the ice is still thick. **1963** *North* July-Aug. 20: The candling ice would support no burden in its fragmented condition.

candlefish *n.* See **oolichan.** See 1877 quote.
1877 ST. JOHN *Sea of Mountains* I 292: ... there is a little fish called the oolichan or candle fish; so full of oil that it can be lighted at one end and used as a candle, which is found in large quantities on this [Pacific] coast. **1963** *Beaver* Autumn 40/1: This Grease Trail was so named because along it the Nass tribes carried much oolachan (candlefish) oil or grease to the Upper Skeena River country.

Cannibal Society a secret society among some of the Indians of the Pacific northwest; Hamatsa Society, *q.v.*
1932 JENNESS *Indians of Can.* 338: The Tsimshian ... adopted from the Kwakiutl not only the notion of a secret society, but several of the actual fraternities, among them the horrible "Cannibal Society" whose members tore to pieces human corpses and devoured portions of the flesh. **1953** *Beaver* Mar. 26/1: The Carriers in the west had close affiliations with the coast people and adopted many of their customs, including the use of masks, labrets, Chilkat blankets, and such secret organizations as the Cannibal Society.

cannon bunk *Lumbering, Hist.* See **muzzle-loading bunk.**
1919 *Camp Worker* 28 June 7/2: You have in some camps what are known as "cannon bunks."

That is double bunks arranged lengthwise, generally double-deckers, which gives four men about six feet of space to sit down.

canoe† [kə'nu] *n*. [< Sp. *canoa*, ult. < Arawakan] ☞ *Although this word, originally applying to the dugout of the West Indies, was known in England in the sixteenth century, it is probable that its use to refer to the birchbark canoe of the Algonkians derived from that of Cdn F* **canot** *(see the compounds containing this word below). As adapted for the fur trade, these craft played a vital part in the early commerce and exploration of Canada. For this reason, the term is briefly treated here.*

1 any of the various light watercraft propelled by paddles, including the birchbark canoe, *q.v.,* and more modern craft of similar design. See also **express canoe, Montreal canoe** and picture, **Micmac, North canoe,** and **sturgeon-nosed canoe** and picture. Cp. **dugout canoe.**
[**1576** (1889) HAKLUYT *Voyages* XII 48: . . . a Canoa of India could [not] live in those outragious seas without shipwracke. . . .] **1632** (1939) SAGARD *Long Journey* [trans.] 56: The Hurons only group themselves five or six together in each canoe, since these little vessels cannot hold more along with their goods. . . .] **1684** (1885) RADISSON *Voyages* 262: . . . about evening an Indian pursuing a Deere spyed our Canoo. **1761** (1901) HENRY (Elder) *Travels* 13: The canoes, which I provided for my undertaking, were as is usual, five fathom and a half in length, and four feet and a half in their extreme breadth, and formed of birch-tree bark, a quarter of an inch in thickness. **1808** (1889) FRASER *Journal* 189: This morning we traded two canoes for two calico bed gowns. **1936** *Cdn Geog.Jnl.* Jan. 6: [Caption] In Canada the canoe has always been the means of pioneer transport following the water routes. **1966** *Beaver* Summer 44/2: Modern wilderness canoes— canvas, aluminum, and Fiberglass . . . are listed generically by the various canoe makers as Prospector or Guide's model.

2 a canoe and the people or goods carried in it; canoe load.
1697 (1929) KELSEY *Papers* 81: This Evening 4 cannoes of Indians came down the river to the fort upon wch the governer made the signal for M^r kelsey's return to th fort. **1784** (1954) *Moose Ft Jnls* 51: Two cannoes of Eastward Indians came in.

3 *Nfld* See quote.
1952 BANFILL *Labrador Nurse* 215: Canoe or Kinoo. Pronounced "kin-oo." Small hand-rowed boat.

canoe† [kə'nu] *v*. [<*n*.] **1 a.** travel in a canoe.
1905 (1954) *B.C.Hist.Qtly* July-Oct. 181: When canoeing in that locality I often saw beaver traces. . . . **1943** MILLER *Lone Woodsman* 172: "I canoed to the north to learn the ways of your people. . . ."

b. transport (persons or goods) in a canoe.
1909 PARKER *Northern Lights* 87: "What's that about my canoeing a man down to Bindon?" **1924** FLAHERTY *Eskimo Friends* 26: At Moose Factory I secured the . . . 36-foot *Nastapoka* and engined her with a motor we had canoed and packed down from the frontier.

2 canoe it, travel by canoe.
1896 GOURLAY *Hist.Ottawa* 54: The early settlers had to canoe it to Montreal for their goods. **1958** *Herald-Tribune* (Grande Prairie, Alta) 21 Feb. 1/5: He tramped it [the Peace River country], he canoed and he horsebacked it. . . .

canoe bark birchbark suitable for making a canoe.
1804 (1897) COUES *New Light* I 239: Payet off to Lake Winipic in search of canoe bark. **1903** WHITE *Forest* 241: A cache in the forest country is simply a heavily constructed rustic platform on which provisions and clothing are laid and wrapped completely about in sheets of canoe bark tied firmly with strips of cedar bark. . . .

canoe barn See **canoe house.**
1933 ROLYAT *Wilderness Walls* 159: He could see Pecuchie . . . sitting at his ease on the ground near the canoe barn, while his squaws now brought under his firm gaze, sewed with watappe in a quiet, improving fashion.

canoe birch [so called because used by Indians in making bark canoes] See **white birch** (def. 1).
1820 (1823) FRANKLIN *Journey* 87: The canoe birch attains a considerable size in this latitude, but from the great demand for its wood to make sledges, it has become rare. **1966** *Kingston Whig-Standard* (Ont.) 26 Jan. 4/3: After the Indians taught white men its many uses, pioneers called it the Canoe or Paper birch.

canoe brigade *Hist*. a convoy of canoes engaged in transporting trade goods to and furs from the inland trading posts. See also **brigade** (def. 1).
*c***1902** LAUT *Trapper* 198: . . . the canoe brigades still bring the winter's hunt to the forts in the spring. **1960** *Maclean's* 23 Apr. 45/3: Each summer, canoe brigades paddled furs from the interior to the mouth of the Saskatchewan river. . . .

canoe cedar [so called because it was used by coastal Indians for making dugout canoes] *Pacific Coast* **1** See 1936 quote.
1936 *B.C.Lumber Trade* 16: WESTERN RED CEDAR (*Thuja plicata*) [is] also called . . . Canoe cedar, Western Cedar, Shingle Cedar. **1954** EVANS *Mist on the River* 208: Paul had a canoe cedar down near the river, at the lower end of the wood claim. . . .

2 See **yellow cedar.**
1935 WALLACE *Encyclopedia* II 170/2: The yellow cypress . . . is known under various names . . . yellow cedar, Alaska cedar, canoe cedar . . . and is confined to the Pacific Coast. **1956** *Native Trees* 78: YELLOW CEDAR *Chamaecyparis nootkatensis* . . . [is also called] . . . canoe cedar.

Canoe Country *Obs.* an area of land in central British Columbia.
1887 BANCROFT *Hist.of B.C.* 456: The Canoe country so designated from Canoe Creek, in 51° 30', is described as beginning fifty miles above the Fountain, and extending indefinitely to the north, over the undulating plateau, through which the Fraser cuts a deep channel. **1894** BEGG *Hist.of B.C.* 332: In the early mining days, sixty miles above the Thompson country began the "Canoe Country". . . .

canoe country country suitable for canoe travel.
1965 *Cdn Geog.Jnl* June 190/1: The Mackenzie is one of the world's greatest waterways, but it is certainly not "canoe country."

canoe house *Hist*. a building for sheltering, making, repairing, and storing canoes, one of the essentials of many fur-trade posts. See also **canoe barn** and **canoe shed.**
1820 (1939) *Beaver* Dec. 41/1: A canoe house is erected, open at the sides and floored or crossed by several timbers. **1900** WILLSON *Great Fur Co.* 664: Ordinarily, a Company's factory includes a store or trading-house, a

fur house, a factor's house, a clerk's house, the canoe house, and the stable, with a barn.

canoe knife See **crooked knife** and picture.
1940 *Beaver* Dec. 38/2: The curved canoe knives [are] the same articles as are included in the 1748 list of trade goods as mocotaugans. **1948** *Ibid.* Dec. 4/2: [This is] a crooked, curved or canoe-knife blade made in Sheffield and still sold by the [Hudson's Bay] Company.

canoe line *Obs.* a light, strong line used in handling canoes; codline, *q.v.*
1793 (1933) MACDONELL *Diary* 75: The canoe line is not a stout cable such as used by Boats but consists of fine Hambro lines loosely twisted upon one another and is about 60 Yards long.

canoeman *n.* **1** *Hist.* See **voyageur** (def. 1a).
1703 LAHONTAN *New Voyages* I 65: ... the canoe-men sometimes ply on their knees.... **1824** (1955) BLACK *Journal* 30: ... the Canoe men [got] to an opening in the last point over which is a Portage.... **1963** *Maclean's* 23 Feb. 28/1: At the settlement ... there was little difficulty in recruiting Indian canoemen for the next leg of their journey to Ottawa.
2 any person skilled in handling a canoe.
1849 ALEXANDER *L'Acadie* II 221: Our canoe was "set up" with difficulty, though our canoe men ... were very powerful with the pole. **1953** LOWER *Voyages* 44: My canoemen ... were John Panayshees, Jimmie Kenozha Peter....

canoemanship *n.* skill and experience in the art of handling a canoe.
1824 (1955) BLACK *Journal* 30: Although We have got through this bad place with a good dale [sic] of Canoe Manship Manoeuvering, it is at best a horrid Rapid. **1956** EVANS *Mountain Dog* 40: Hal knew that the test of his canoe—and of his canoemanship—lay ahead at Kelta canyon.

canoe moccasin a moccasin with a thin sole, suited for use in a canoe.
1956 RADDALL *Wings* 95: We walked along the street, ... I in canoe moccasins and khaki slacks....

canoe pole See **setting-pole**.
1933 MERRICK *True North* 18: Henry wants a pipe coupling for the business end of his canoe pole.... **1963** PATTERSON *Far Pastures* 223: [I heard] the muffled click of a canoe-pole on the stones....

canoe-raft *n. B.C., Hist.* See quote.
1958 *Beaver* Autumn 44/1: Rafts were common Fraser River transportation even in the early days of this century and of these some of the Indian canoe-rafts were by far the most interesting and handsome. One I had described to me by an old timer consisted of three 35-foot cedar logs four feet at the butt and hollowed out like troughs. These were squared and fastened side by side with a huge dowel pin through each end of the boat. The ends sloped up from the water and the raft was boxed in above with heavy, wide hand-hewn planks.... Thirty men could get away at one time and pole themselves across a river, no matter how wide it was.

canoe rest a pair of brackets, consisting of two poles thrust horizontally into a river bank, each supported by a vertical stake, placed sufficiently far apart to support a canoe.
1883 HATTON & HARVEY *Newfoundland* 210: They observed a "canoe-rest" on which the daubs of red ochre and fibrous roots of trees used to fasten or tie it together, appeared fresh.

canoe road See **canoe route**.
1819 (1890) MASSON *Les Bourgeois* II 219: This obliged us to strike off through the woods to the canoe road. **1889** *Ibid.* 220: The distance from York Factory to Cumberland House is much shorter, but it was probably much lengthened by the sinuosities of the route they had to follow on the canoe road.

canoe route a water route regularly used by canoes, especially by those of the canoe brigades. See also **canoe track**.
1808 MCKENZIE *King's Posts* 445: The canoe route is by the Saguenay.... **1896** RUSSELL *Far North* 105: We followed the canoe route, with which I had become painfully familiar the preceding summer. **1963** SYMONS *Many Trails* 188: Such a mark can be picked out easily, either in summer or when after freeze-up the canoe routes are followed by dog trains.

canoe shed *Hist.* See **canoe house**.
1921 HEMING *Drama of the Forests* 285: On their way to the Indian shop they passed the canoe shed, where skilled hands were finishing two handsome six-fathom canoes for the use of the Fur Brigade. **1953** LOWER *Voyages* 20: ... the old birch freighting canoes were still in the canoe sheds....

canoe song *Hist.* a song or chanson, especially as sung by French-Canadian canoemen as they plied their paddles; boat song, *q.v.*
1828 *U.E.Loyalist* (York [Toronto]) 5 Jan. 255: A company of Canadian North West Voyagers, lately arrived from Red River were introduced and sung their Canoe Songs for the gratification of the Queen. **1904** WHITE *Silent Places* 15: So now he puckered his lips to the sibilance of a canoe-song and waited.

canoe track *Obs.* See **canoe route**.
1765-75 (1933) POND *Narrative* 36: ... we Cam to a Shallo Lake whare you Could Sea water But Just in the Canoe track the Wilde Oates ware so thick that the Indians Could Scarse Git one of thare Small Canoes into it to Geather it.... **1820** (1939) ROBERTSON *Correspondence* 109: They will then make a hunting excursion, and about the middle of September approach the canoe track, and wait the arrival of the canoes....

canot allège *Cdn French* "unburdened canoe" *Hist.* See **express canoe**.
1850 BIGSBY *Shoe and Canoe* I 131: Our canoe was thirty-six feet long, sharp at each end, six feet wide in the middle, and made of birch bark, in sheets sewn together with vegetable fibre, and the seams gummed up close. The sides are strengthened and steadied by four or six cross-bars lashed to the rim of the canoe, and the inside is protected by slender ribs of a light wood, but the bottom by only a few loose poles. It is called a light canoe, or "canot lâche"; because intended to go swiftly, and to carry only provisions and personal baggage. Its usual complement is nineteen—that is, fifteen paddle-men and four gentlemen passengers: the latter sitting each on his rolled-up bed in the middle compartment. **1860** (1956) KOHL *Kitchi-Gami* 34: The principal distinction I heard the Voyageurs make was between canots à lége and canots de charge. **1942** *Beaver* June 15/1: The most celebrated voyageur canoe ... was the ... *canot allege*—unburdened or express canoe.

canot bâtard *Cdn French* See **bastard canoe**.
1952 (1954) JENNINGS *Strange Brigade* 145: The largest

at York, and a rarity there, being used only for heavy cargoes upon wide open waters, was the *canot bâtard:* the bastard canoe—which seemed to me an enormous craft for one so fragile. It measured thirty to thirty-two feet in length and was capable of carrying two tons in addition to its crew of ten.

canot de charge *Cdn French* "freight canoe" *Obs.* See quote. Cp. **Montreal canoe.**
1860 (1956) KOHL *Kitchi-Gami* 34: Their canots de charge are their large heavy goods canoes.

canot du gouverneur *Cdn French, Hist.* See **express canoe.**
1860 (1956) KOHL *Kitchi-Gami* 256: The most celebrated canot allege among my Voyageurs on Lake Superior is the "canot du gouverneur." **1942** *Beaver* June 15/1: The most celebrated voyageur canoe, in the whole history of the Hudson's Bay Company, undoubtedly was the *canot du gouverneur,* the governor's canoe, also called *canot allege*—unburdened or express canoe.

canot du maître *Cdn French* "master's canoe" *Hist.* See **Montreal canoe** and picture. See also **maître canot.**
1828 (1872) MCDONALD *Peace River* 41: The Canot du Maitre was of six fathoms . . . measured within, and the C[anot] du Nord about four, more or less. **1908** MAIR *Mackenzie Basin* 84: . . . the *Canot du Maitre,* as it was called, the largest bark canoe made by the Indians, carrying about six tons and a crew of sixteen paddlers, and which ascended as far as Fort William. Thence further progress was made in much smaller "North Canoes" to all points west of Lake Superior. **1963** *Cdn Geog.Jnl* Dec. 210/3: The bateaux were concealed, and the whole party of twenty-five embarked in a canot-du-maître for Fort Mackinac. **1966** *Ibid.* Apr. 129/2: In 1957 Mr. Bernard supervised the building of a "canot de maître" [sic] for the National Museum. . . .

canot du nord *Cdn French* See **North canoe.**
1828 (1872) MCDONALD *Peace River* 41: The . . . C[anot] du Nord [measured] about four [fathoms]. . . . **1954** RICH in *Moose Ft Jnls* xviii: . . . the *canot du Nord* . . . was ideally suited to the network of small rivers and lakes. **1961** MACLENNAN *Seven Rivers* 46: This single tow of ours moved as much cargo . . . as could have been carried in the old days by nine hundred *canots du nord.*

canotée *n.* [< F] *Obs.* a canoe load.
1794 (1889) MACDONELL *Journal* 290: Met two canotées of South-Men ascending, headed by a Mons. Fournier. **1808** (1897) COUES *New Light* I 428: I sent off the express for Leech Lake, and six men also for their canotées of sugar from that place. . . .

canot lâche See **canot allégé.**

canot Rabasca *Cdn French* "Athabasca canoe" *Obs.* See **express canoe.** See also **canot allégé.**
1860 (1956) KOHL *Kitchi-Gami* 34: The first signifies the light, unladen canoes, employed as post or express boats, and are also known by the name of "canots Rabasca."

cant-hook *n.* [< *cant* a slabbed log + *hook*] *Lumbering* a pole having at the lower end a steel device consisting of an arm equipped with a sharp, hooked point which, when the arm is slipped over a log, permits the user to roll, lever, or to otherwise direct the log. Cp. **peavey.**

1889 WITHROW *Our Own Country* 397: Lighter logs are rolled up with cant-hooks. . . . **1912** HEENEY *Pickanock* 55: . . . then mounting it canthook in hand, he began to roll it on the bunk. . . . **1963** SYMONS *Many Trails* 183: . . . they too await the logs with peevies and cant hooks.

An early type of cant-hook

Canuck [kə'nʌk] *n.* [origin uncertain; see suggestion at 1963 quote (def. 1)]
☞ *It is not clear whether this term was first applied to French Canadians or to residents of Canada in general; in spite of the order dictated by the dates of the Canadian evidence, it is probable that the term first designated a French Canadian since in the early nineteenth century the term* **Canadian** *itself most often referred to a French Canadian.*

1 *Informal* a native or citizen of Canada. See also **Jack Canuck** and **Johnny Canuck.**
☞ *In spite of the definition given in many dictionaries still, the term* **Canuck** *as applied by Canadians to themselves is not at all derogatory, quite the contrary. Nor is the term, in modern use, especially associated with French Canadians; again, quite the contrary.*
1849 ALEXANDER *L'Acadie* I 273: "Come boys and have some grog, I'm what you call a Canuck; a Canadian." **1861** *Cdn Naturalist* Dec. 432: I must add that it is somewhat supported . . . by the analogy of another term, namely *Canuc,* which is used vulgarly and rather contemptuously for Canadian, and which seems to me to come from *Canuchsa,* the word employed by the Iroquois to denote a "hut." Here *Canadian* would mean a "townsman" or "villager," but a *canuc* would be only a "hutter." **1907** KENNEDY *New Canada* 192: "And don't you want to be Americans any longer?" I asked. "No," said they most emphatically, "we're Canucks now." **1963** *Citizen* 30 May 12/5: What is the origin of the nickname Jack Canuck? It probably comes from the name Connaught, the nickname given more than 100 years ago by French Canadians to Canadians of Irish origin. **1964** *Calgary Herald* 19 Mar. 18/6: The Scottish skip missed a wide open takeout in the fifth leaving the Canucks another single.

2† *Slang* a French-Canadian.
1889 DONKIN *Trooper & Redskin* 148: But for pure and unadulterated brag I will back the lower class Canuck against the world. **1900** *North American Notes & Queries* July 64/1: I would very much like to know the origin of the expression Canuck applied to the French Canadians. **1912** ROE *Whispering Hills* 39: On the face of the swarthy Canuck guide who sat in the stern there was a weary contempt.

3 *Rare* a thing made in, or native to, Canada.
1887 *Grip* (Toronto) 19 Feb. 3/2:

"Who'll buy my caller herrin'?
Cod, turbot, ling, delicious herrin',
Buy my caller herrin',
They're every one Kanucks!"

Canuck *adj. Informal* Canadian.
1887 *Grip* (Toronto) 5 Mar. 1/2: "Well, what do you think of the Canuck elections?" **1963** *Globe and Mail* (Toronto) 2 Feb. 6/1: Any trend by the big brother to the south to tell Canadians how to run their affairs can raise Canuck dander very quickly.

Canuckiana *n. Rare, Humorous* See **Canadiana.**
1888 *Dominion Illustrated* 199/1: Canuckiana [used as a heading].

Caouettiste [kauɛ'tist] *n.* [< Cdn F] a follower of Raoul Caouette, leader of the *Ralliement des Créditistes, q.v.,* in the House of Commons during the 1960's. Cp. **Thompsonite.**
1962 *Kingston Whig-Standard* (Ont.) 9 Mar. 1/3: In a few ridings there are reported disagreements ... between the "Creditistes," as Social Credit supporters are called in French Canada, and the so-called "Caouettistes".... *Ibid.* 10 Nov. 3/1: For a few moments it appeared that the rebellious Caouettistes were going to pull the rug out from under the government....

A Cape Ann

Cape Ann (hat) [< *Cape Ann,* Mass.] a type of rain hat having a broad back flap, usually worn with an oilskin raincoat.
1894 MORRIS *Sketches* 41: In a few minutes she is back, bearing with her a seaman's Cape Ann hat. **1936** (1966) *Weekend Mag.* 23 Apr. 4/1: Oh, this is the place where the fishermen gather, / In oilskins and boots and Cape Anns battened down. **1958** *Evening Telegram* (St. John's) 2 May 5/1: One August day back in 1928 a teen-age boy, dressed in "cape ann" and oilskins, was among those who were out on the squid jigging grounds at Change Islands.

Cape drake [< F *Cap de race,* Cape Race, Nfld, by folk etymology] *N.S.* See quotes. See also **cape-race.**
1956 MCATEE *Folk-Names* 2: Red-throated Loon ... Cape drake (... N.S.). **1961** TUFTS *Birds of Nova Scotia* 28: For reasons I have never been able to determine, shore-hunters commonly refer to this bird as "Cape drake." **1965** RICHARDSON *Living Island* 58: ... the smaller red-throated loons [are] known locally (for some unfathomed reason) as Cape drakes.

A Cape Island boat

Cape Island boat [after *Cape Sable Island,* N.S.] *Maritimes* a type of boat used by inshore fishermen of Nova Scotia.
1951 *Yachting* Dec. 56: She closely resembles the Down East type generically referred to as "Cape Island boats." **1963** *Canada Month* Feb. 19/1: The life of the inshore fisherman—the men who take to sea in 40-foot Cape Island boats, some of them powered by old automobile engines—is never an easy one.

cape islander See **Cape Island boat.**
1965 *Time* (Cdn ed.) 23 Apr. 16/1: ... for 24 hours the disabled 38-ft. cape islander was tossed by 50 ft. waves.

capelin *n.* See **caplin.**

cape-race(r) *n.* [after *Cape Race,* Nfld] See quote. See also **Cape drake.**
1956 MCATEE *Folk-Names* 2: Red-throated Loon ... cape-race (... Nfld), cape racer (... N.S., N.B.)....

capette *n.* [< Cdn F; var. of *cassette,* q.v.] *Obs.* a casket.
1812 (1950) THOMPSON *Journals* 195: [I] began wood for Capette or Trunk. **1834** (1947) HARGRAVE *Correspondence* 177: Allow Johnny to see and open my Capette which I left in No. 2[;] there is a small Box and an Hat in it which I wish him to bring up.

capital murder in Canada, murder punishable by hanging, such as premeditated murder or the killing of a policeman, as opposed to non-capital murder, *q.v.*
1962 *Kingston Whig-Standard* (Ont.) 12 Feb. 1/3: Police have charged a wounded man with capital murder in connection with the fatal shooting of a policeman early today. **1963** *Ibid.* (Ont.) 14 Feb. 13/7: Nineteen-year-old Gary McCorkell's bid to have his conviction for capital murder reduced to one of non-capital murder has failed.

caplin ['keplɪn *or* 'kæplɪn] *n.* [< Cdn F < F *capelan* codfish] *Esp.East Coast* a small, edible marine fish, *Mallotus villosus,* much used as bait by cod fishermen. Also spelled *capelin, capling, capline* (older).
1620 MASON *Briefe Discovrse* B[r]: Iune hath Capline a fish much resembling Smeltes in form and eating.... **1784** PENNANT *Arctic Zoology* cxcvi: The bait is small fish of all kinds: Herring, Capelin, Lance, Tom Cod.... **1888** (1908) MAIR *Mackenzie Basin* 477: The capeling is found on the coast of the Arctic Ocean and Hudson Bay, thus implying the presence of cod upon banks nearby.... **1964** JENNESS *Eskimo Admin.* II 111: Other fish too frequented the deep fiords ... particularly the caplin....

capling ['kæplɪn] *n.* See **caplin.**

caplin scull [dial.var. of *school*] *Nfld* the spring swarming of caplin, when large numbers of these fish come inshore to spawn; also, the time when this swarming takes place.
1964 *Imperial Oil Rev.* June 8/1: In vast numbers they stream past the headlands, into the bays, toward the sand and shingle beaches. This is the "caplin scull," the annual miracle which renews the Newfoundland fisheries and makes them the most productive in the world. *Ibid.* 9/1: A few part-time fishermen, who put briefly to sea when the caplin arrive, and quit after three or four weeks, are spoken of contemptuously by the full-timers as "fishing only in the caplin scull."

caplin weather See quote.
1869 HARDY *Forest Life in Acadie* 364: The warm days with light fogs occurring at this season are looked upon by the expectant fishermen as favourable to their [caplin] striking in; they call such days "caplin weather."

capot [kə'po] *n.* See **capote.**

capote [kə'pot] *n.* [< Cdn F < F] **1** a serviceable hooded greatcoat of blanket cloth, moosehide, or other material, long the standard wear among traders and trappers in the North, who took this warm garment over from the habitants and voyageurs of New France. See also **Canadian coat.** Cp. **parka** (def. 2).

1665 RADISSON *Voyages* 110: [He] throws his cappot away, bidding me also to leave my capot. **1789** (1801) MACKENZIE *Voyages* 58: . . . I presented him with one of my capots or travelling coats. **1896** RUSSELL *Far North* 94: The vapor from our heated bodies gathered on the hair of our capotes. . . . **1955** LEFROY *Magnetic North* xxi: Here he equipped himself for the coming winter with a warm *capote* of thick white duffle trimmed with red and with a blue hood.

A capote (defs. 1 and 2)

2 the hood of such a garment. See also **capuchin.**
1795 (1911) SIMCOE *Diary* 265: The Canadian coats, with capots and sashes, look very picturesque. **1893** OXLEY *Young Nor'Wester* 120: A long coat made out of either bison or wolf skin protected the body, and a *capote* of the same material covered the head. **1940** NIVEN *Mine Inheritance* 37: The capot, of course, at that season hung down the back.

3 a winter cap, as a tuque, *q.v.*
1888 (1890) ST. MAUR *Impressions* 254: [The lumberjacks] mostly wear *capotes,* a red cap the same as the *bonnet rouge* at the time of the French Revolution. **1938** SULLIVAN *Cycle of the North* 172: Then over his head she put the capote or hunting cap.

capote coat See **capote** (def. 1).
1913 (1917) CURRAN & CALKINS *Northland* 113: . . . by the time we were opposite the Post it was crowded with dusky men in their blue capot coats. **1952** *Beaver* Dec. 28/1: For winter clothing back in 1905 the men wore capote (hooded) coats either of blue or white duffle.

capoted [ka'potəd] *adj.* wearing a capote.
1873 (1904) BUTLER *Wild North Land* 43: Huts promiscuously crowded together; horses, dogs, women, children, all intermixed in a confusion worthy of Donnybrook Fair; half-breed hunters, ribboned, tasselled, and capôted, lazy, idle, and if there is any spirit in the camp, sure to be intoxicated. **1934** GODSELL *Arctic Trader* 82: . . . there were far more long-haired, capoted bucks around than he had ever anticipated. . . .

capotries *n.pl. Obs.* a trader's stock of capotes or materials for making them.
1804 BURPEE *Journal de Larocque* 309: My getting skins at the Big Bellies' since my arrival was owing to my having such goods as pleased the Indians, i.e., strouds, capotries, iron works, etc., which my opponent had not.

captain *n.* **1** *Hist.* an Indian chief or band leader.
1691 (1929) KELSEY *Papers* 13: This day still waiting for a post wᶜʰ came in yᵉ afternoon from yᵉ Capt: of the Mountain Poets Named Washa so yᵉ Substance of their news was yᵗ he desired we would meet him when we pitch again so I told yᵐ I would. **1795** (1911) HEARNE *Journey* 35: Here also we met a Northern Indian leader, or Captain, called Keelshies, and a small party. . . . **1941** *Beaver* Sep. 36/2: Captain. A term applied to the chief man in a band of Indians in the early years.

2 the leader and spokesman of a band of Indians trading at a fur post, often appointed by the factor and rewarded with a captain's coat. See also **chief, Indian captain,** and **leader** (def. 1).
1723 (1923) *Beaver* Mar. 234/1: [He] was Imploy'd to make Peace with: the Northern Nation for wch. he was made a Capn; and Expects Greater Privileges Still than I can well afford him. . . . **1785** (1954) *Moose Ft Jnls* 114: Six Canoes of uplanders came in, seemingly well Gooded, made the Principal of them a Captain. **1958** *Encyc.Can.* V 183/1: . . . the Indian bands under "captains" made their way down the rivers each summer, often from far inland.

3 *Hist.* See **war captain.**
1965 JENNESS *Indians* 298: Both Hurons and Iroquois . . . made the raising of levies . . . a matter for individual "captains," who bought the services of volunteers with presents, outlined the objective and plan of attack, and, as far as they possessed the authority, disposed of any prisoners that were taken.

captain's coat *Obs.* a gaudy garment or outfit of clothing presented to an Indian leader or "captain" (def. 2) as an inducement to trade furs. See also **clothing, Indian coat,** and **trading coat.** Cp. **Henry VII coat** and **treaty coat.**
[**1748** DRAGE *Voyage* I 228: These Leaders are called Captains by the Factory People; and when these Captains are down at the factory are presented by the Governors with a Tinsel-laced Coat, much like a Drummer's, with a Tinsel-laced Hat, and a painted Feather stuck in it; will have English Stockings of two Colours, and, perhaps, an Indian Shoe on one Foot, and an English one on the other.] **1784** (1954) *Moose Ft Jnls* 236: I'd recommend to you not to be too hasty in making a Leader of any of the Indians that may Visit you but reserve the Captain's Coat &c. for the Indian that may seem to you to have the most sway among his countrymen bring you the most Furs & prove most serviceable to you.

capuchin or **capuchon** [kə'putʃɪn] *n.* [< Cdn F < F *capuchon*] the hood of a capote, *q.v.*; sometimes the entire garment. See picture at **capote.**
1837 (1923) JAMESON *Rambles* 205: . . . there were also a highly ornamented capuchin and a pair of new blanket leggings. **1928** LEROSSIGNOL *Beauport Road* 237: . . . Leon was well prepared for that with his thick coat, his *capuchon,* his *bottes sauvages,* and a good flask of *eau-de-vie,* from which he took a little now and then to warm his heart and keep up his courage.

caraboo *n.* See **caribou.**

caracajou *n.* See **carcajou.**

caragana [ˌkærə'gænə] *n.* any one of a number of shrubs of the genus Caragana, the Siberian pea, used widely in hedges on the prairies as a windbreak.
1894 *Trans.Roy.Soc.Can.* XII 4 144: The Caragana arborescens, or Siberian pea tree, which can be readily grown from seed, also makes a very good hedge. **1958** *Sask.Highway News* 30 Jan. 10/2: Caragana . . .

is famous for stopping snow from blowing. . . .
1963 *Maclean's* 5 Oct. 41/1: There was simply nothing to do but sprawl in the . . . shade . . . eat clover heads and caragana flowers.

caraquette [ˌkærəˈkɛt] *n.* [< Cdn F < *Caraquet*, N.B.] See 1870 quote.
1870 *Cdn Illust.News* 19 Mar. 318/2: "Have you Canadians any national variety of the mollusk?" "Yes, the Caraquette, a small oyster, rather salt, but very succulent." **1901** DRUMMOND *J.Courteau* 19: Is becos de oyster schooner she's sailin' up de bay / An' de caraquette an' malpecque will quickly melt away. . . .

carat *n.* See **carrot.**

carcajou [ˈkarkəˌdʒu] *n.* [< Algonk.; prob. Montagnais *kākachu* through Cdn F]

1 a. the wolverine (def. 1a), a cunning robber of traps and caches, found in most parts of the Canadian forest. See also **quincajou.** Also spelled, in early records of fur traders especially, *carcajon, carcaseu, casacajou, carcassause.*
1703 LAHONTAN *New Voyages* I iii: [We saw] the Holes and Dens of the Carcaioux. . . . **1822** GOURLAY *Upper Canada* I 157: The Wolverene, sometimes called the Carcajou, is about two feet nine inches long. **1952** *Beaver* Sep. 22/1: The word wolverine is a diminutive of wolf. Sometimes this animal is called skunk-bear because its size, build and colour suggest a cross between the two. The French named it the *carcajou,* the English *quiquehatch,* names derived from the Cree *kwekwuhakayo.* The Chipewyan name is pronounced knockeye, but usually these people refer to it as "the devil."

b. the fur of the carcajou.
1806 (1930) FRASER *Journal* 112: They brought 22 Beaver skins, 2 carcassause, and six Pechause. . . .
1896 RUSSELL *Far North* 142: Their clothing was trimmed with the white-haired Asiatic reindeerskin, carcajou and wolfskin.

2 *Obs.* the badger, *Taxidea taxus.*
☛ *In Canadian sources, this word is found only in reference to the wolverine. However, in some parts of the northern U.S.A., the term has been used for both the badger and the lynx.*
1823 FRANKLIN *Journey* 650: [badger] in this also Buffen agreed, describing the American animal under the name Carcajou.

3 a treacherous, dishonest person; a thief, a rogue.
1793 (1937) CAMPBELL *Travels* 73: . . . when a merchant cheats or circumvents them in a bargain, they call him a Carcaseu. **1953** MOWERY *Mounted Police* 80: "Somebody robbed us, the low-down carcajou."

card money *Hist.* a kind of paper currency issued in New France by the Intendant Bigot to meet the pay of the garrison while awaiting funds from France and made from playing cards which were cut in quarters, each quarter being marked as having a certain value and each being signed by the Governor and the Intendant.
1840 WILLIS *Cdn Scenery* I 51: . . . a paper currency termed card money . . . enabled Bigot to conceal for a long time his waste and peculations. **1963** *Commercial Letter* Jan. 5/2: The expedient was resorted to on several subsequent occasions and at one time "card money" constituted the chief currency of Canada.

Carey *n.* See **Mother Carey's chicken.**
Also *Carey('s) chick.*

1953 MILLS *Folksongs of Nfld* [Booklet]: They went batting Carey's Chicks and said that they were puffins. **1956** MCATEE *Folk-Names* 4: White-rumped petrel [is also called] Carey (N.S.); Carey chick (Nfld, Que.); Mother Carey's chick (Nfld); Mother Carey's chicken (Nfld, N.S., N.B.) Middle term spelled also "Carew's" and "Cary's." . . . one [explanation] having dictionary sanction (NID) is that the term is an Anglicization of the Latin *Mater Cara* (esteemed Mother) applied to the Virgin Mary, patroness of sailors. As these birds are regarded as portents of trouble, however, the explanation does not seem too clear.

cargodor† [ˌkargəˈdɔr] *n.* [< Am.E < Sp.] the foreman of a pack-train, *q.v.* Also spelled *cargador, cargodore.*
1912 POCOCK *Man in the Open* 322: Pete only cut from the plug into his palm, and rolled the tobacco small for his corn-cob pipe. His winter servitude was ended, and he was master, the cargador before whom all men bow in the dread northlands. **1923** *Beaver* Sep. 454: Every year from May to August he acts as cargodor on a packtrain, which means that he is the head man on the train. **1958** *Alaska Sportsman* Dec. 34/3: The "cargodore" is Chinese, two of the packers are Tahitan natives and the cook . . . is Chinese.

cariboo *n.* See **caribou.**

Cariboo [ˈkærəˌbu] *n.* **1** an extensive region in south-central British Columbia, originally that region between the junction of the Quesnel and Fraser Rivers and the Cariboo Mountains, but later, especially in popular usage, a much larger region, extending from Lillooet almost to Prince George.
☛ *The Cariboo was the scene of a famous gold rush which began in 1860.*
1860 *Brit.Colonist* (Victoria) 27 Oct. 2/2: Victoria may yet turn out to be a regular Cariboo, as far as regards hidden treasure. **1964** *Time* (Cdn ed.) 13 Nov. 18/2: But this year, where once there was only campfire smoke on the trail, the Cariboo horizon was dotted also by the smoke from sawmill burners.

2 *Slang, Obs.* (*usually plural*) a name given to the Reformers in Upper Canada in the 1830's.
1838 HALIBURTON *Sam Slick* 28: The Toronto folks call 'em Carriboo, 'cause they are ontamed wild critters from the woods, and come down in droves to the legislatur'. *Ibid.*: I have often wish't . . . that I have performed the feat of killing a Carriboo.

Cariboo country See **Cariboo** (def. 1).
1860 *Brit.Colonist* (Victoria) 27 Sep. 3/2: The news from the Cariboo Country is very encouraging.
1963 SYMONS *Many Trails* 62: . . . this plateau does have a general level, rolling away east to the Cariboo country and westward to lap the feet of the mountains.

Cariboo fever *Obs.* the urge to seek gold in the Cariboo.
1867 (1962) ANDERSON *Sawney's Letters* 40: Ted, he took the Cariboo fever . . . and started up the river. . . .

Caribooite *n.* **1** *Hist.* a person who went into the Cariboo Country during the gold rush, especially a placer miner.
1862 *Nor'Wester* (R.R.S.) 22 Jan. 1/2: Victoria will

be . . . inundated with successful Caribooites. **1894** BEGG *History of B.C.* 368: Driven from their work by the severe climate in the winter, the "Caribooites" spent some time and much money in that town. . . .

2 a resident of the Cariboo.
1869 *Mainland Guardian* (New Westminster, B.C.) 25 Sep. 3/2: The Victorians have an apple weighing 1½ pounds, and a pear weighing 1 pound 2 ounces, for the exhibition; the Caribooites send turnips.

Cariboo Road a historic road from Yale to Barkerville, B.C., built in 1862-65 to facilitate travel to and from the gold fields.
1929 MOBERLY *When Fur was King* ix: Walter Moberly also built a section of the famous Cariboo Road.
1962 FRY *Ranch on the Cariboo* 39: Johnnie Wright . . . had arrived on the Cariboo Road in 1865 at ten years of age. . . .

Cariboo slum See **slum.**
1952 (1958) WATTERS *B.C.Cent.Anthol.* 71: Ah Bau was a Chinese who panned for gold in that same slippery mud called Cariboo Slum that was to plague two generations of railroad builders who followed him. **1958** LINDSAY *Cariboo Story* 47: Despite the dread "Cariboo slum" which bedevilled miners on Lightning Creek, some $13,000,000 was taken from it.

Cariboo Trail See **Cariboo Road.**
1953 LOWER *Voyages* 147: Sixty years after Fraser, British engineers hacked out a wagon trail from those very cliffs, the famous Cariboo Trail.

caribou or **cariboo** ['kærə,bu] *n.* **caribous** or **caribou.** [< Cdn F < Algonk.; cf. Micmac *halibū pawer, scratcher*] **1** any of several species of North American reindeer, genus *Rangifer,* native to Canada, Alaska, and formerly to Maine and Mass. See also **carreboeuf, moose-deer** (def. 3), **reindeer, tuktu** (def. 1), and **tundra deer.**
1665 (1885) RADISSON *Voyages* 202: We killed severall . . . Carriboucks. . . . **1744** DOBBS *Hudson's Bay* They . . . live by Fishing, and a kind of Deer they call *Cariboux.* . . . **1888** PHILLIPPS-WOLLEY *Sportsman's Eden* 243: In Quebec two moose, two cariboo, three deer was the largest bag allowed per man per annum. . . .
1964 *Globe and Mail* (Toronto) 12 Dec. 8/7: Some fear the herds will disappear from the province [New Brunswick] entirely, as the caribou did early in this century.

2 the flesh of the caribou; caribou meat.
1896 WHITNEY *On Snow-Shoes* 125: Caribou, I may say in passing, I consider of all wild meats the one that one tires of least. **1957** *Aklavik Jnl* Mar. 2: The last two places in N.W.T. where the PEOPLE should be denied their daily bread—caribou, should be the Hospitals for their sick and the schools for their children. It is forbidden by the Game Law to serve the patients caribou!

3 the skin or hide of the caribou.
1808 (1960) FRASER *Letters and Journals* 132: . . . their clothing consisted of dressed leather . . . with robes of . . . Carribo. . . . **1898** *Medicine Hat News* (Alta) 8 Dec. 5/4: Her parkee, made of Caribou, it is a lively fit. / And she's all right from muck-a-luck unto her dainty mit. / This lovely Klooch is fond of Hooch, and makes it very well. **1947** GILLHAM *Raw North* 77: The trousers were of caribou. . . .

4 *Que., Slang* a potent mixture of whisky-blanc, *q.v.,* and red wine. See also **whisky-wine.** Cp. **loup-garou** (def. 2).
1952 *Chicago Tribune* 25 Dec. 5/1: Traditional drink of the season [in French Canada] is caribou. . . .
1960 *Maclean's* 7 May 56/4: . . . this is filled with that formidable Quebec concoction, Caribou. . . . **1965** *Kingston Whig-Standard* (Ont.) 15 Apr. 17/1: In the old days, when . . . caribou overcame one reporter, Pop pieced together a . . . story . . . and wired it off to save the reporter's neck.

Caribou *n.* **1** See **Caribou.**

2 a. *Hist.* one of a branch of the Abenaki Indians of the Maritimes.
1845 HAWKINS *Missions* 361: Mr. Wood . . . offered up some prayers in the Micmac language, which is understood by the three tribes of the province: the Micmacs, the Marashites, and the Carribous.

b. See **Caribou Eskimo.**
1966 *North* Mar.-Apr. 11/1: Father Ducharme then told us of Magoose Lake. . . . There a single family of Caribou, or inland-dwelling Eskimos, of the Padlermiut group had their igloo.

3 a twin-engined aircraft designed and produced in Canada, used by the armed services and for low-cost passenger and freight service in areas not having first-rate airports with long runways, the Caribou being able to take off and land on strips less than 500 feet long.
1956 *Cdn Aviation* Feb. 3/2: The United States army has asked for authority to increase its order for de Haviland of Canada Caribou to 12 aircraft. **1965** *Globe and Mail* (Toronto) 26 Apr. 17/8: The Caribou . . . is now doing a splendid workhorse job in Vietnam.

caribou barrens See **caribou plain.**
1855 HARDY *Sporting Adventures* I 20: Situated in the heart of the forest, and surrounded by the woods as by a wall, lie these little plains, covered with a soft and often swampy carpeting of mosses and lichens, which from their being the favourite feeding grounds of the American rein-deer, have obtained the name of Carriboo Barrens, or Bogs. **1920** *Rod and Gun in Can.* Nov. 737: All along the route of the Railway are . . . Caribou barrens.

caribou bird See **Canada jay.**
1892 PIKE *Barren Grounds* 123: This bird [Canada jay] is common throughout the wilder parts of Canada, and has acquired many names in different places; in the mountains of British Columbia he is the Hudson Bay bird or grease bird, and far away in the East the moose bird, caribou bird, Rupert's bird, and camp robber.

caribou bog *Obs.* See **caribou plain.**
1850 JOHNSTON *Notes* I 23: It rises very gently . . . till it reaches an immense bog—called in these provinces a Carriboo bog or Cariboo plain—which is the water-shed from which flow both the Cornwallis river and that of Annapolis.

caribou crossing (-place) a shallow stretch in a river or lake where caribou habitually cross, often usable by man as a ford. See also **deer crossing.**
1911 SETON *Arctic Prairies* 219: The place we had selected for camp proved to be a Caribou crossing.
1923 STRINGER *Empty Hands* 66: From the lay of this land there ought to be a caribou-crossing somewhere in the neighborhood. . . . **1965** SYMINGTON *Tuktu* 50: Leading to the caribou crossing-places on lakes and rivers . . . are seen drift fences. . . .

caribou deer See **caribou** (def. 1).

1849 ALEXANDER *L'Acadie* II 125. On them we saw the tracks of the caribou deer, whose broad feet are well adapted to moving across the barrens without sinking into them. . . . 1889 WITHROW *Our Own Country* 62: The fine engraving which accompanies this article gives a graphic view of some of the magnificent moose and caribou deer of the forests of Nova Scotia. . . .

Caribou Eater 1 a. a member of a sub-tribe of the Chipewyan Indians. See also **Deer Eater.**
[1807 WENTZEL *Letters* 78: The only information I can get concerning these Natives is that they inhabit these rocks, live upon carribou and goat flesh and make war upon one another.] 1821 SIMPSON *Journal* 371: The Carribeau Eaters are those who confine themselves to their own barren lands and are so called from the circumstance of their devoting the whole of their attention to hunting the Carribeau or Reindeer, which are very numerous. 1892 PIKE *Barren Grounds* 18: A large band of Indians, known as the Caribou-Eaters, whose hunting ground lies between the two big lakes, get their supplies from here. 1956 *Beaver* Summer 57/2: The first part of it, he points out, tells of life among the Caribou Eaters at the east end of Lake Athabasca, where, he says, "I set my hand to the oar, whip, or axe, or to the handle of a frying pan more often than I did to a pen."

b. the Athapaskan dialect spoken by the Caribou Eaters.
1894 *Outing Mag.* Nov. 124/2: As they spoke no English, and we no Caribou Eater, we naturally did not converse.

2 See **Caribou Eskimo.**
1962 WHALLEY *Hornby* 1: . . . relics of little traditional camps could be seen, made by the inland Eskimo—the Caribou-eaters—at the deer-crossings. . . .

Caribou eater a person whose principal food is caribou, specifically an Indian or Eskimo.
1911 SETON *Arctic Prairies* 260: Of these the Hay River and Liard Indians, numbering about 500, can scarcely be considered Caribou-Eaters, so that the Indian population feeding on Caribou to-day is about 3,000, less than half what it was 100 years ago.

caribouer ['kærə,buər] *n.* See **Caribou Eskimo.**
1958 *Camsell Arrow* Christmas 79/3: The minister, who gave the details of the tragedy in reply to questions . . . said the Garry Lake Eskimos were "caribouers"— Eskimos who are mainly dependent on caribou for food.

Caribou Eskimo one of a group of Eskimos living inland in the District of Keewatin, west of Hudson Bay. See also **Caribou** (def. 2b), **Caribou Eater** (def. 2), and **Deer Men.**
1929 BIRKET-SMITH *Caribou Eskimos* I 9: "Caribou Eskimo" is the name which the Fifth Thule Expedition has attached to a group of Eskimo tribes in the southern part of the extensive Barren Grounds west of Hudson Bay. 1958 *Time* (Cdn ed.) 25 Aug. 9/1: In its search over mountains, bush and tundra, the R.C.A.F. so far this year has responded to about 1,200 alerts . . . including a mercy mission to fly starving Caribou Eskimos to welfare centers.

caribou fence See **deer hedge.**
[1852 RICHARDSON *Arctic Expedition* 232: On the open hilly downs frequented by reindeer, the Kutchin have formed pounds, toward which the animals are conducted by two rows of stakes or trunks of trees extending for miles. These rows converge, and as the space between them narrows, they are converted into a regular fence by the addition of strong horizontal bars.] 1956 *Spotter* July 4/2: Before the use of firearms for

hunting purposes in the Yukon, the natives would construct a caribou fence . . . sometimes three miles long and 10 feet high. . . .

caribou fly *Nfld* See **deer fly.**
1835 AUDUBON *Ornithological Biography* III 486: . . . musquitoes, although plentiful enough, are not accompanied by carraboo flies. . . .

caribou lice the larvae of the warble, *Oedemagena tarandi.*
1940 *Beaver* Mar. 5/2: He lived with the natives . . . he even tried their chief delicacy, caribou lice!

caribou moss a whitish-gray lichen, *Cladonia rangiferina,* a staple food of the caribou. See also **reindeer lichen, reindeer moss,** and **snow moss.**
[1744 DOBBS *Hudson's Bay* 47: Near the Rivers and Sea-coast, there was small shrubby Woods, but for many Miles, at least 60 farther into the Country, they had nothing but a barren white Moss upon which the Rain-Deer feed. . . .] 1857 (1860) HIND *Red River Exped.* I 134: Moving on to a spot more favourable, perhaps because it is level, small batches of caribou moss began to show themselves. 1963 *Kingston Whig-Standard* (Ont.) 2 Apr. 7/1: They didn't know . . . how to brew a stew of wild roots to make a meal of caribou moss.

caribou plain *Maritimes* a tract of low-lying peat bog at one time frequented by caribou; savanna, *q.v.* See also **caribou barrens** and **caribou bog.**
1832 MCGREGOR *British America* II 591: Caraboo Plains . . . and lands formerly laid waste by fire, or that from some natural cause produce little wood. They are also called *Barrens.* 1849 ALEXANDER *L'Acadie* II 130: . . . we were on the edge of the large cariboo plain of a hundred or more acres. . . . 1902 *Gun and Rod in N.B.* 22: Along the Gaspereau river are caribou plains which stretch away four or five miles without a break, and on these it is no rare sight to see a herd of from 75 to 100 caribou. . . .

caribou tongue the tongue of the caribou, considered a delicacy in the North. See also **brochet banana.**
1682-3 (1885) RADISSON *Voyages* 302: The Indians being present after my arrival laid out their presents before me, being Beavors' tailes, cariboux tongues dry'd, Greas of Bears, Deere, & of Elks. 1896 RUSSELL *Far North* 110: We usually made a few fresh caribou tongues each Sunday . . . and a ball of freshly made pemmican. 1958 *Cdn Geog.Jnl* Jan. IV/1: A visitor may find himself . . . dining on beaver-tail soup and caribou tongues. . . .

caribou uplands the summer range of the mountain caribou in the mountainous regions of central and northern British Columbia.
1952 *Beaver* June 13/1: There we had cached our outfit and made a sashay on foot westwards . . . into the blue immensity of the caribou uplands.

caribou wolf See **Arctic wolf.**
1963 *Maclean's* 23 Feb. 43/1: We don't want to exterminate the caribou wolf, but too many wolves preying on too few caribou could have had only one end result.

cariole or **carriole** ['kæri,ol *or* 'kæri,al] *n.*
[< Cdn F *carriole*]
☛ *The term* **cariole** *seems to have been used for a wide*

variety of horse-drawn sleighs, becoming a common
word from the Maritimes to the Pacific Coast:
1808 (1809) GRAY *Letters* 247: The cariole, in short, is
the name for all sorts of vehicles used in winter, from a
market cart, up to a state coach.
The extension to the one-man sleigh drawn by dogs seems
to have taken place very early (see 1791 quote, def. 1a).

1 a. originally, a light open sleigh used in French
Canada, drawn by one or two horses (sometimes
by dogs), and having a seat for the driver. See
also **cabriole.**
1765 *Quebec Gaz.* 18 Apr. 3/1: To be sold at Publick
Vendue . . . a Horse, Cariolle and Harness, and sundry
other Articles too tedious to mention. **1791** (1911)
SIMCOE *Diary* 54: Mastiffs draw loads of provisions,
and very small dogs carrioles, with children in them.
1816 MARSDEN *Narrative* 42: [Some were] in little
carioles; (a few boards nailed together and fastened
to a horse). . . . **1964** *Cdn Geog.Jnl* Mar. 89/1: [Caption]
A single carriole said to have been made by Derocher of
Montreal about 1890.

b. a light passenger sleigh usually accommodating
two passengers and a driver, ordinarily drawn by
two horses and widely used for pleasure in many
parts of Canada from the 18th to the early 20th
century. See also **carryall** (def. 1), **covered carriole,**
and **horse carriole.**
1769 (1931) BROOKE *Emily Montague* 87: There is
something exceedingly agreeable in the whirl of the
carrioles, which fly along at the rate of twenty miles an
hour. . . . **1861** *Nor'Wester* (R.R.S.) 1 Feb. 2/3: Should
there not also be a rule for carrioles meeting on the
highway, as to which side should be taken? **1914** STEELE
Forty Years 42: The bridal party drove in carrioles,
another reason for not celebrating weddings in the
summer months, as it would not be becoming to see
twenty or thirty well-dressed couples going to church in
squeaking Red River carts. **1965** *Star Wkly* 2 Jan.
21/2: In La Perade [Quebec] fur-coated cariole
drivers sing as they drive the fishing parties to and
from . . . the fishing huts.

A cariole (def. 2a)

2 a. in the North and Northwest, a light
tobogganlike dog sled into which a single
passenger or a load is laced securely, the dog-
driver following behind. See also **carryall** (def. 2a),
dog cariole, dog-toboggan, Hudson Bay toboggan,
tabanask, toboggan (def. 4), **toboggan cariole,**
toboggan-sled, train (def. 1a), and **traineau** (def. 2).
1761 (1901) HENRY (Elder) *Travels* 9: I discerned a
cariole, or sledge, moving our way, and immediately
sent my guide to the driver. . . . **1844** LEFROY *Magnetic*
North 93: They have been building a cariole, a light
sled to be drawn by three dogs; in these one is laced and
secured. **1929** MOBERLY *When Fur Was King* 67: Each

officer had his "carriole," a sled of birch boards,
twelve feet long, the sides covered with parchment skins
and handsomely painted. Four dogs went to a sled.
1966 *Maclean's* 19 Feb. 32/1: Six white Mackenzie
River malemutes would race over the snow, drawing
a flame-red carriole decked with long colored streamers.

b. a similar sled pulled by a horse. See also
toboggan (def. 3).
1801 (1897) COUES *New Light* I 192: Went to the hills
with a horse and carriole, low and surrounded with
parchment buffalo skin; it weighed only twenty pounds,
but was large enough for one person and his bedding.
1927 *Cdn N.W.Hist.Soc.Pubs* I 2 56: Mr. McKay used
his train of "husky dogs," while the Bishop was
conveyed . . . in a carriole or toboggan, drawn by a
horse.

3 the upper framework and leather or canvas sides
of the sled; the structure mounted on the toboggan.
See also **carryall** (def. 3).
1820 (1823) FRANKLIN *Journey* 95: The cariole used by
the traders is merely a covering of leather for the lower
part of the body, affixed to the common sledge, which is
painted and ornamented according to the taste of the
proprietor. **1944** CLAY *Phantom Fur Thieves* 88: A
carriole . . . is made with a frame of sticks and ropes
fastened to a toboggan. Over this a canvas is spread to
form a bath-tub shaped affair.

cariole or **carriole** ['kæri,ol] *v.* drive or ride in a
cariole.
1767 *Quebec Gaz.* 31 Dec. 3/1:
    Not Venus with the winged Loves,
    Drawn by her Sparrows or her Doves,
    So gracefully and swiftly moves,
    As Ladies Carioling.
1936 *Bytown* [Ottawa] *Gaz.* 27 Oct. 2/3: We see one
youngster carioling behind a horse and another driving
a dog-team.

carioling or **carrioling** *n. Hist.* driving or riding
in a cariole, especially a horse-drawn cariole;
sleighing (def. 1).
1769 (1931) BROOKE *Emily Montague* 87: Emily . . .
wants me, every time we make a carrioling-party, to
invite all the Misses of Quebec. . . . **1806** (1890) EDGAR
Ten Years of U.C. 16: There has been very little
carioling hitherto. . . .

carot *n.* See **carrot.**

carpenter cloth thin iron-wire mesh; screening.
1964 *Western Wkly Supp.* 18 Mar. 7/4: . . . No one
calls it carpenter cloth anymore. It is called hardware
cloth. You can purchase the wire mesh in black or
galvanized. . . .

carpet bowling a type of bowling played indoors
on a carpet.
1928 *Beaver* Dec. 127/1: Carpet Bowling.—This new
game has started in the capable hands of Mr. Nichols.
. . . The association has bought bowls, carpets, and
has rented Hampton Hall. . . .

carpet parlo(u)r *Obs.* the best room in a house.
1813 (1890) EDGAR *Ten Years of U.C.* 212: There is an
astonishing run of white-cuffed ensigns and lieutenants
at the house, and the carpet parlour is adorned the
whole day with red.

carreboeuf *n.* [< Cdn F] *Obs.* See **caribou**
(def. 1).
1793 (1801) MACKENZIE *Voyages* 14: We saw some
reindeer on one of the islands, [which . . .] was

accordingly named Isle de Carreboeuf. **1859** (1863)
PALLISER *Journals* 161: . . . Carriboeufs frequent this
part of the country in large numbers. **1924** MASON *Arctic
Forests* 104: The French-Canadian name for the
American reindeer is said to come from "carré boeuf"
(square ox), or more likely from "Kalibu" (the
scratcher), Algonquin, referring to the animal's habit
of pawing the snow away to reach the moss below. **1958**
ELLIOTT *Quesnel* 5: The name Cariboo is a corruption
of "Car-boeuf," or Elk.

carriage *n. Obs.* **1** See **portage**, *n.* (def. 2a). See
also **carry**, *n.* (def. 1).
*c*1669 (1961) ADAMS *Radisson* 86: We were come above
three hundred leagues, always against the stream, and
made sixty carriages, besides drawing, besides the swift
we overcame by the oars and poles to come to that little
Lake of Castors. . . . **1760** PICHON *Cape Breton* 25: At
the further end of this lake we made a carriage of
fourscore fathoms. . . .

2 See **portage**, *n.* (def. 1a). See also **carry**, *n.* (def. 2).
1690 (1929) KELSEY *Papers* 2: Through Rivers wch run
strong with falls [there were] thirty three Carriages five
lakes in all. **1717** (1932) KNIGHT *Journals* 165: That was
sev^{ll} Great hills that way as they was forc'd to Cross w^{th}
their Canoos & Goods Upon their backs, wch makes
it very Difficult for them, Especially one Carriage w^{ch}
is Allmost a Days Travell for them to Carry their
Bundles on their backs.

carrier *n. Fur Trade, Obs.* a person who took
trading goods inland and carried furs back to a
post. See also **trader** (def. 2).
1795 (1911) HEARNE *Journey* 84: I have often heard it
observed, that the Indians who attend the deer-pounds
might, in the course of a winter, collect a vast number of
pelts, which could well serve the attention of those who
are called carriers or traders.

carriole *n.* See **cariole**.

Carron stove a collapsible, portable cast-iron
stove originally made at the Carron Iron Works in
Scotland. Also spelled *Caron*.
[**1827** (1927) DICKIE *How Canada Grew Up* 70: A
manufactory of carron ware is carried on here [Three
Rivers, Quebec].] **1914** STEELE *Forty Years* 38: . . . Jack
Kerr was busy polishing the Carron Stove when this
fellow came upstairs. **1946** *Beaver* Dec. 23/2: As
the old woman sat in front of the Carron stove, trying
to get warm, my father found out her sad plight,
through his interpreter. **1963** MCTAVISH *Behind the
Palisades* 28: These Caron stoves were ungainly, closed
in iron oblong receptacles for long billets of wood,
showed no light from the fire, excepting when the sides
became red hot but . . . radiated heat efficiently. . . .

carrot *n.* [< Cdn F *carotte* (de tabac)] *Hist.* **1** a
bundle of carrot tobacco, *q.v.*
1778 (1904) LONG *Voyages* 128: I gave him two gallons
of rum, and a carrot of tobacco. . . . **1809** (1897) COUES
New Light II 526: A common horse can be bought here
[among the Blackfeet] for a carrot of tobacco, which
weighs about three pounds, and costs in Canada four
shillings. **1961** JONES *Trappers* 91: [Caption] Hudson's
Bay Company traded many things to the Indians.
Among the most popular items . . . were "carrots" . . .
or packages of tobacco wrapped in cloth and twine. . . .

2 See **carrot tobacco**.
1944 *Beaver* Mar. 39/1: As more and more natives
became cigarette smokers, carrot and twist (or
"niggerhead") were going into the discard.

carrot tobacco *Hist.* tobacco packaged in carrot-
shaped bundles wrapped in cloth and twine,

weighing about three pounds and about eighteen
inches long, prominent among trade goods of the
fur companies. See also **carrot**.
1766 *Quebec Gaz.* 17 Nov. 3/1: Manufactured and
to be sold by Mathew Gemmil, Tobacconist . . . Roll
Tobacco in all its different Kinds . . . likewise Carot
Tobacco. . . . **1878** *Sask.Herald* (Battleford, N.W.T.)
4 Nov. 1/3: Tea is sold at 40c to 50c; sugar 20c; carrot
tobacco $2.25 per roll. **1947** *Beaver* Dec. 9/1: "Carrot
tobacco" was not tobacco made from carrots, but
tobacco put up in the shape of carrots.

carry *n.* **1** See **portage**, *n.* (def. 2a). See also
carriage (def. 1).
1912 FOOTNER *New Rivers* 14: At Giscomb Portage there
is a six-mile carry over the height of land to Summit
Lake, one of the sources of the Peace. **1928** FREEMAN
Nearing North 105: Where the first *voyageurs* had made
a carry of a hundred and twenty paces it would now
have been possible, had we only enough power, to have
driven right up the deepest part of the rapid. **1963**
PATTERSON *Far Pastures* 98: . . . Portage la Loche [is]
a twelve-mile carry over the Hudson's Bay-Mackenzie
divide.

2 See **portage**, *n.* (def. 1a). See also **carriage** (def. 2).
1921 HAWORTH *Trailmakers* 268: When we got to
Giscome Portage, it was clear that it would take a
long time to get all the stuff over the eight-mile carry.
1952 HOWARD *Strange Empire* 201: . . . there were days
. . . when the men sank to their knees in the sodden
black muskeg or were hauled half-drowned from the
icy rivers, and an hour later were dripping with sweat
under a blazing sun on a high rock "carry."

carry *v.* **1** See **portage**, *v.* (def. 3a).
1775 (1951) *Sask.Jnls* 5: We passed five falls, leading
Canoes over two and carrying at two. **1781** (1934)
TURNOR *Journal* 355: Then [we] . . . carried 350 yards
through burnt woods on south side. **1824** (1955) BLACK
Journal 124: The Old Slave has a pain in his side & his
wife is sick & not able to carry. **1921** HAWORTH
Trailmakers 212: . . . we had to carry around great
log-jams. . . . **1933** MERRICK *True North* 175: There were
more than thirty portages to carry over.

2 carry tobacco, *Obs.* Of Indians, visit other bands
to try to persuade them to join forces for war, the
tobacco being carried to be smoked in the councils
of deliberation.
1800 (1897) COUES *New Light* I 160: They [three
Indians] had been to all the Indian camps to carry
tobacco concerning war. . . . **1801** *Ibid.* 163:
Berdash . . . arrived from the Assiniboine, where he had
been with a young man to carry tobacco concerning
war.

carryall ['kæri,al] *n.* [by folk etymology < F
carriole] **1** *Obs.* See **cariole** (def. 1b).
[**1714** (1933) STODDARD *Journal* in *N.E.Hist.and Gen.
Reg.* V 27 [O.E.D. Supp.]: Mr. Longuille sent a carryall
for us.] **1821** (1823) JOHNSTONE *Travels in P.E.I.* 37:
The next step is to cut down as many more, (rooting
out the stumps,) so as to allow a carryall or slay
(sledge) to pass.

2 a. See **cariole** (def. 2a and picture).
1897 TYRRELL *Sub-Arctics* 248: My brother and I were
now warmly rolled up in robes and blankets and lying in
our carryalls. **1938** ELLS *Northland Trails* 58: An hour
later the carryall stood loaded before the door, the
shaggy dogs harnessed and curled in the snow. . . .

b. one of a number of vehicles so called because of their ability to carry many passengers or things.
1861 *Nor'Wester* (R.R.S.) 1 Apr. 1/1: The carry-all was of a soberer sort, imported from England by way of Hudson's Bay and York Factory, and of a pattern not now in fashion here and there—low heavy wheels, thick, substantial whiffle-trees, high dash-board, and a body like that of the carriages of well-to-do English squires half a century ago. **1949** *Report of DME Test Team* IA 2: As "Carry-alls" for a mobile repair team, the Canadian Sled (10 cwt) proved unsatisfactory. . . .
1963 PATTERSON *Far Pastures* 250: . . . I had now travelled with a dogteam . . . with pack-horses, in a U.S. Army carry-all. . . .
3 See **cariole** (def. 3).
1948 ONRAET *Sixty Below* 117: The loading begins with a carry-all . . . a buck-skin thing [which holds] all that I want. . . . **1959** LEISING *Arctic Wings* 121: His body was jammed . . . tightly in the carryall of the dog sled. . . .
1963 PATTERSON *Far Pastures* 67: Securely laced into the canvas carry-all of the dog sled . . . Mam [a bitch] screamed monotonously.

carrying *n.* the process of transporting canoes and equipment over a portage.
1793 (1933) MACDONELL *Diary* 106: The River winipoc is full of shocking rapids which occasions this frequent carrying. **1921** HAWORTH *Trailmakers* 59: Much trouble was experienced in carrying round the many bad rapids which abound in this stream.

carrying-path *n. Obs.* the trail along a portage.
1789 (1927) MACKENZIE *Voyages* 5: The carrying path is very bad, and five hundred and thirty paces in length.

carrying place See **portage** (def. 1a).
1760 JEFFERYS *Descr.New France* 17: From the church of the Cedar Hills across the point . . . there is a carrying place of about six or seven miles. **1954** CAMPBELL *Nor'Westers* 55: He had persuaded . . . his . . . men to paddle and portage kegs of rum and bales of trade goods over all the rough water and carrying-places from Montreal three thousand miles away.

carrying-road *n. Obs.* See **carrying path**.
1828 *P.E.I.Register* (Charlottetown) 19 Jan. 1/1: The "portage" or carrying-road, extends to Chippewa Creek to which place goods are transported in waggons, on account of the Falls, and there put again into boats or canoes.

carrying-strap *n.* See **tumpline** and picture.
1847 (1947) *Beaver* June 42/1: The boat they had was made of . . . *dressed parchment,* similar to the men's carrying straps which he saw here. **1893** YOUNG *Indian Wigwams* 273: My load, which I carried on my back, supported by the carrying-strap from my forehead, was heavy, but my heart was light. . . . **1939** *Beaver* Mar. 46/1: He . . . threw his canoe cross-wise on his shoulders and suspended it from his forehead by a carrying strap, keeping it steady with his hand.

carry-place *n. Obs.* See **portage** (def. 1a).
1798 (1957) *Ont.Hist.* XLIX 91: The country at the carry-place is open and dry, and the surrounding country soft and level.

cart brigade *Hist.* a brigade of Red River carts, *q.v.,* carrying furs, supplies, trading goods, personal effects, etc. See also **cart train**.
1861 *Nor'Wester* (R.R.S.) 1 Oct. 2/3: The Company's

two grand cart-brigades to Carlton have returned.
1963 MORTON *Kingdom of Canada* 366: The resistance of the Red River métis had not . . . preserved the buffalo hunt, the cart brigade, the semi-nomadic way of life. . . .

carter *n.* **1** *Obs.* See **chartier**.
1832 MCGREGOR *British America* II 481: The Canadian carter is not the pugnacious animal that the man of similar occupation in England is. . . . **1889** WITHROW *Our Own Country* 151: I was complimenting one of the French "carters," as they are called—a corruption of *charretier*—on the steadiness of his little runt of a Canadian pony. . . .
2 *Nfld* a dog driver.
1918 GRENFELL *Labrador Doctor* 138: . . . I have enjoyed the luxury of a driver, or a "carter" as we call them. . . .

cartouche knife [karˈtuʃ] *Hist.* a kind of knife traded to the Indians by the Hudson's Bay Company.
1824 (1955) BLACK *Journal* lxxvi: Donald Manson Dr. June 8th. To 1/2″ Tobacco [,] To 1 Cartouch Knife. . . .
1862 (1923) *Beaver* Apr. 260/2: He also took all the cartouche knives on hand. **1941** *Ibid.* Sep. 36/2: Cartouche knife. An all-purpose knife popular with the Indians.

cart trail *Hist.* in the old Northwest, a track travelled by or intended for the use of a cart brigade, *q.v.*
1898 *Yukon via Prince Albert* 18: We were exploring for a new cart trail in order to ship the Company's goods from the Peel to the Yukon, and found no particular difficulty. **1913** COWIE *Adventurers* 284: Mr. Finlayson was in charge of the neighbouring post at Touchwood Hills, only forty-five miles north of Qu'Appelle by a beautiful cart trail.

cart train *Hist.* See **cart brigade**.
1934 *Beaver* Sep. 37/2: The cart trains travelling west across the prairies by Fort Ellice and Qu'Appelle to Edmonton carried the produce of the buffalo hunting wanted in the West for the hunters' shoes.

case *v.* skin (an animal) without slitting the hide; prepare (a pelt) by case-skinning, *q.v.* See also **cased** and **case-skin**.
1712 (1965) *Letters from Hudson Bay* 16: I shall encourage the Indians to case the fox, cats and otters as they do the martens. . . **1885** *Indian* (Hagersville, Ont.) 30 Dec. 11/2: Ermine, Fisher, Foxes, Lynx, Martin, Mink, Oppossum, Otter, and Skunk, *must be "cased"* that is, not cut open. **1950** DOBIE *Coyote* 35n: "Cased wolf"became the trade name for the animal [coyote], from the fact that the pelt was cased—peeled off without slitting the body—and dried over a frame. . . .

case(d) cat *Obs.* the skin of the Canada lynx, so called because the pelt was removed by case-skinning, *q.v.*
1755 (1907) HENDAY *Journal* 352: The Natives received from the Master ten Gallons of Brandy half adulterated with water; and when intoxicated they traded Cased Cats, Martens, & good parchment Beaver skins, refusing Wolves & dressed Beaver. **1800** (1933) MCLEOD *Diary* 145: The old Pass au Travers came to the Fort, with 20 Cass'd Catts & 8 Beavers.

cased *adj.* skinned by the process of case-skinning, *q.v.* See also **case** and **case cat**. Cp. **open,** *adj.* (def. 1).
1783 (1918) DAVIDSON *North West Co.* 269: Exports [included] Cassed catts 5536, Open Catts 4197. . . .
1807 *Quebec Gaz.* 22 Jan. 4/1: Exports from the Port of Quebec, 1806 [included] 5,286 cased and open Cat. . . . **1864** *Nor'Wester* (R.R.S.) 20 May 3/4: Opossum

were only saleable at very low rates say cased large good 9 to 10d. . . . **1948** *Sask.Fur Marketing Service* 18: For "cased" pelts use a wedge-shaped stretcher, made of soft wood, rounded on the edges.

case-skin *n*. a pelt that has been removed by case-skinning, *q.v.*

1921 HEMING *Drama of the Forests* 230: All case skins are stretched over wedge-shaped boards of various sizes—all save muskrat skins which are more often stretched over a hooped frame or looped stick.

case-skin *v*. See quote. See also **box-skin** and **case.**

1921 HEMING *Drama of the Forests* 230: To case skin an animal . . . the skin is cut down the inner side of each hind leg until the two cuts meet just under the tail, and then the pelt is peeled off by turning it inside out.

case-skinning *n*. the process of removing an animal's pelt by peeling it off without slitting the body (much as a sock is removed from a foot); box-skinning. See also **case-skin.** Cp. **split-skinning.**

1921 HEMING *Drama of the Forests* 230: In the forest there are several different ways of skinning animals: one is called "case skinning" and another is called "split skinning."

casette *n*. See **cassette.**

case(d) wolf *Obs*. See **coyote** (def. 1).

1857 (1863) PALLISER *Journals* 63: I saw great numbers of the case wolf . . . prowling about. This is the wolf proper to the partially wooded country, and is about twice the size of a fox, with a tail shaped like the brush of that animal. **1950** DOBIE *Coyote* 35n: "Cased wolf" became the trade name for the animal [coyote], from the fact that the pelt was cased—peeled off without slitting the body—and dried over a frame. . . .

cash district *Hist*. a settled area where money is the usual medium of exchange, as opposed to a backwoods area, where barter is usual.

1842 WILLIS *Cdn Scenery* II 23: . . . it becomes a highly important question what are the market or cash districts (as they are sometimes called), in contradistinction to those in the bush.

casseau [kæ'so] *n*. **-eaux** or **-s**. Also *cassot*. [< Cdn F] a birch-bark box used for collecting the sap of the sugar maple, and also for storing maple syrup and maple sugar. Cp. **mocock.**

1822 (1932) MCLEAN *Notes* 61: An old squaw brought to our house several casseaux of [maple] sugar. . . . **1928** LEROSSIGNOL *Beauport Road* 204: . . . Louis sent the lads to the woods to gather balsam and spruce gum, sarsaparilla, gold-thread, moss, and birch-bark for caseaux in which to pack the maple sugar in the following spring.

casse-tête *n*. [< Cdn F "head-breaker"] *Hist*. See quotes. See also **break-head, gunstock club, pogamagan,** and **war club.**

1776 (1901) HENRY (Elder) *Travels* 304: They have still another weapon, formed of a stone of about two pounds weight, which is sewed in leather, and made fast to a wooden handle, two feet long. This primitive weapon was known to the traders as a *casse tete,* or war club, and was gradually superceded by those of wood . . . with a spike of iron imbedded in the ball or bulb at the end. *c*1804 GRANT *Sauteux Indians* 317: The dress of the men consists of a molton capot, or coat, in the Canadian fashion, which comes down to the knees . . . they tighten it round the body with a worsted belt, in which the cassetête and knife are occasionally worn. **1933**

GATES *Five Traders* 146n: The "cassetette" (casse-tête) was a club or tomahawk that was used as a weapon.

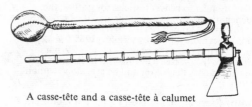

A casse-tête and a casse-tête à calumet

casse-tête à calumet *Cdn French* "tomahawk pipe" *Obs*. a trade tomahawk with a metal, hatchet-shaped head, the poll of which forms a tobacco pipe, smoke being drawn through the hollow stem, used for ceremony and show.

1800 (1933) MCLEOD *Diary* 145: Mr. McGillis takes from here 4 large Capots, 3 New Guns, 10 Pr Tranches, 1 Buffaloe robe, 4 Cassetettes à Calûmet, 1 Pr Large Steelyards, & a Fort Flag. **1805** (1911) BURPEE *Journal de Larocque* 309: Being in want of horses I took him at the following price: 1 blanket, 1 casse-tête-à-calumet, 100 balls and powder, 1 pair leggings, 1 lance, 1 knife, 1 hoe, 1 eyed bag, and a few beads.

cassette [kæ'sɛt] *n*. [< F "a small chest"] *Hist*. a strong, light, waterproof box used among the fur traders for carrying personal effects. Cp. **travelling box.**

1791 (1947) *Beaver* Dec. 11/2: You will observe I have ordered some trunk locks, they are for cassettes & I am not sure but the right name for them is cupboard locks. . . . **1821** (1900) GARRY *Diary* 96: Our Boxes and our Cassettes become our Chairs and Tables. **1963** MCTAVISH *Behind the Palisades* 106: Our worldly possessions just about filled a small easily portable cassette, an honestly made, by old country mechanics, receptacle. . . .

cassot *n*. See **casseau.**

castor *n*. [< Cdn F] **1 a.** *Hist*. a beaver pelt.

1769 (1898) *N.B.Mag.* I 73: We have sent all the furs and everything received except about 60 lbs. Castor and a quantity of Musquash skins that could not be brought down. **1964** *Wildlife Rev.* Dec. 7: Accordingly, the Hurons and Algonquins had to explain to the Iroquois that the supply of Castor was "disproportionné."

b. a unit of barter equivalent to one made beaver, *q.v.* Cp. **beaver** (def. 5).

1848 (1859) BALLANTYNE *Hudson's Bay* 39: The number of castors that an Indian makes in a winter hunt varies from fifty to two hundred, according to his perseverance and activity, and the part of the country in which he hunts. **1871** (1935) *Beaver* June 63/2: A beaver skin was worth two castors, or one dollar. A black fox skin usually brought twelve castors in trade and a silver fox about four. **1926** DICKIE *Cdn West* 128: If they [furs] were worth fifty castors he gave the Indian fifty little pieces of wood which the latter returned in payment for the goods which he wanted.

2 a. See **castoreum** (def. 1a).

1946 WOOD *Rockies* 64: Castor refers to the beaver's secretion or castoreum, which Vergil believed smelled like castor oil.

b. See **castoreum** (def. 2).
[**1955** Verbal communication from J. MacNeish to D. Leechman: Castor—This is the term used by Slavey Indians to refer to beaver testicles (or, rather, the attached scent sacs). They sell them to the Hudson's Bay Company. Sometimes the Indians add little stones inside to get more money by weight.] **1965** *Islander* 7 Mar. 5: How come the beaver's castors? What purpose do they serve? The muskrat lives much the same life as does the beaver and he gets along without castors.

Castor ['kæstər] *n.* [< Cdn F] *Hist.* a faction of Quebec Conservatives of the period 1882-1900.
1904 DECELLES *Cartier* 79: In this case the danger sprang from among the most advanced Conservatives of his following, those whom Protestants called Ultramontaines, and loyal Conservatives nicknamed Castors. **1963** MORTON *Kingdom of Canada* 422: As a result, Bourassa's nationalism became ever more a defensive, Quebec *nationalisme,* resembling that of the Castors which preceded it. . . .

castoreum† or **castorum** *n.* **1 a.** See 1908 quote. See also **castor** (def. 2a).
1685 (1931) *Beaver* Sep. 283: Castoreum is a proved remedy for ear-ache. **1783** (1918) DAVIDSON *North West Co.* 269: Exports [included] . . . Castoreum 1106 lb. **1908** MAIR *Mackenzie Basin* 260: The substance contained in two pyriform sacs situated near the organs of reproduction in the beaver, and commercially well-known as "castorum," has always been traded from the natives. **1946** (1947) FREEDMAN *Mrs.Mike* 73: "The only bottles I ever carry north are empty bottles," said Baldy solemnly, "for castoreum." He turned to me and explained that this was a panacea made by the Indians from two small glands under the beaver's tail. **1966** *Beaver* Spring 11/1: Finally an attempt was made to catch male beaver by using the *castoreum* (a secretion contained in the scent glands) of the female, beaten up with green aspen buds. Surprisingly, this caught both males and females.

b. See **beaver medicine.**
1797 (1916) THOMPSON *Narrative* 204: All of them were infatuated with the love of the Castorum of their own species, and more fond of it than we are of fire water [an Indian being reported]. **1834-43** (1955) RUSSELL *Journal* 150: The trapper . . . sets his trap in the water near the bank . . . throws a handful of mud on the bank about one foot from it and puts a small portion of the castorum thereon. . . . **1921** HEMING *Drama of Forests* 97: The bait used is made by rubbing beaver castorum on a bit of rabbit skin placed in a split stick. . . . **1964** INNIS *Fur Trade* 263: The exhaustion of the beaver fields was apparently hastened by the use of steel traps and the discovery of the use of castoreum as bait.

2 the scent sac or sacs of the beaver. See also **castor** (def. 2b).
1743 (1949) ISHAM *Observations* 144: Beavers have three pair of stones, or bladders, as the Gendering stones, the Castorum, [which contains] the oyly Substance the Natives usses in trapping [,] Rubbing the baits with itt. . . . **1907** HUNTER *Cdn Wilds* 84: On a twig 9 in. high and set back about a foot from the trap he placed a small piece of castorum. The smell of this attracts a beaver.

castor gras [< F "greasy beaver"] *Fur Trade, Hist.* See **coat beaver.** See also **gras.** Cp. **castor sec.**

[**1696** (1956) INNIS *Fur Trade* 48: [translated from French] It is much to be feared that our company could not be successful in saving the best furs of Canada since certainly the greater part of the "castor gras" comes from the North. . . .] **1958** *Beaver* Spring 15/1: This made them dependent on *castor gras,* or in English, "coat beaver." These were skins which the Indians had worn for a season and which in the process had lost their guard hairs and had become so thoroughly greasy that they fully earned the title *castor gras.* **1964** *Wildlife Rev.* May 22: Castor Gras was a beaver robe that had been worn to a sufficient degree of greasiness . . . to be acceptable to the peculiar demands of the hat trade.

castor sec [< F "dry beaver"] *Fur Trade, Hist.* See **parchment beaver.** See also **sec.** Cp. **castor gras.**
1942 *H.B.C.Minutes* 14 Nov. 8n: [Beaver skins were] called *castor sec* by the French. The guard hairs were still on the skin and the fur did not have the downy quality of *castor gras,* which was the result of long wear. **1964** *Wildlife Rev.* May 22: The Hurons and Algonquins started up a brisk trade in worn-out kettles and second-hand axes for the Castor Gras of the Iriquois and in a short time, had them all wearing Castor Sec too. . . .

castorum *n.* See **castoreum.**

cast up [< Scottish dial.] *Fur Trade, Hist.* arrive at a place, especially a trading post.
1834 (1909) CAMERON *New North* 111: A party of Isle à la Crosse Indians with old Nulooh and Gauche cast up. **1860** *Kamloops Jnl* (B.C.) 19 Sep.: Late this evening an Indian cast up with a letter from Gov. Douglas. **1941** *Beaver* Sep. 37/1: Cast up—To arrive at a point.

cat[1] *n.* **1** *Archaic* the lynx. See **catamount** (def. 1).
1743 (1949) ISHAM *Observations* 142: Catt's are a fierce Creature to Look at, and about as big as a small sheep, their Skins are the finest and softest furr in the Country. **1859** (1863) PALLISER *Journals* 126: As the mountain mutton was very lean at this season, while the cats were fat, we used to combine them by stuffing the cat with minced mutton, and roasting it whole. . . . **1933** MERRICK *True North* 188: . . . he turned to see a big cat bound over the ice and . . . make straight for Lizzie.

2 *Obs.* the pelt of the lynx.
1681 (1945) *H.B.C.Minutes* 4 Nov. 142: One Lott of Catt skins. . . . **1716** (1965) *Letters from Hudson Bay* 43: . . . I have traded all the cats that has been traded here at two beaver per cat, and have promised to trade our 4 foot guns at six cats per gun. . . . **1820** (1922) HARMON *Journal* 286: Their [Takullies'] clothing consists of a covering made of the skins of beaver, badger, muskrat, cat or hare. **1964** INNIS *Fur Trade* 196n: The first winter they got 23 packs of furs. In 1779-80 they got 44 packs in which there were 34 packs of beaver, 3 of otter, 3 of cats. . . .

cat[2] *n. Obs.* See **clay cat.**
1853 STRICKLAND *Canada West* II 181: There is another kind of chimney which . . . answers very well for a shanty, if constructed with cats. **1863** WALSHE *Cedar Creek* 143: . . . he inquired abruptly why they hadn't built their chimney of "cats." "Mine is of cats," said Mr. Logan. "Cats is clay," he continued sententiously, "kinder like straw an' clay mixed up. . . ."

cat[3]† *n.* **1** a caterpillar tractor; a bulldozer, *q.v.*
1934 *Beaver* Dec. 46/1: The North . . . awoke to the challenging roar of the "cats" as they hustled their heavy burdens over the cumbrous frozen land. **1952**

the fabulous transportation system of the Canadian north. **1963** *Albertan* (Calgary) 23 Dec. 3/4: Use of traditional cats for snow removal would allow speeds of only up to three miles an hour.

2 *North, Informal* See **cat-train**.
1952 KNOTT *Harnessing the Giant* 14/2: The life line of the northland, which makes it possible for people to live in tiny, isolated settlements . . . are the "tractor trains" called by the north people "cat swings" or "cats." *Ibid.* 12/1: . . . dogs and "cats" between them have transported men, materials and supplies to the isolated settlements or lonely shacks.

catamaran *n.* **1**† a small raft. See 1849 quote.
1845 BEAVAN *Life in Backwoods N.B.* 61: . . . old and young, "off they come" from Miramichi from Acadia and the Oromocto, in shay and waggon, steam-boat and catamaran, on horse back and on foot, as best they can.
1849 ALEXANDER *L'Acadie* II 164: Our plan was to construct a couple of catamarans or small rafts of spruce trees. The five logs for each catamaran were cut 8 feet long, and then a double row of auger holes were bored into the logs near their ends; cross pieces were laid between the holes; a withe of twisted hazel was passed through the holes and over the cross pieces, and was then firmly pegged down. A seat raised on pegs in the middle served to keep things dry, and this primitive craft was completed with 10 feet poles for propelling it.
1958 *Saturday Night* 25 Oct. 16/2: This . . . involved travelling by boat along the coast or by catamaran (raft) in the summertime and by komotick and dog team in winter.

2 *Nfld* **a.** a heavy sledge used in hauling lumber.
1819 ANSPACH *Hist.Nfld* 383: The principal use of this animal [dog] . . . is to assist in fetching from the woods lumber . . . on sledges, or catamarans. **1842** BONNYCASTLE *Newfoundland* II 25: The common dogs used in the catamarans . . . are of every variety of colour and fur. **1869** MCCREA *Lost Amid Fogs* 101: On they came in succession, five or six sleighs, or lumbering catamarans.

b. See 1933 quote. See also **slide** (def. 4) and **catamaran sledge**.
1933 MERRICK *True North* 329: Ed had a catamaran (a light sledge with wide runners) and a powerful hauling dog to help him. **1954** *Fishermen's Advocate* (Port Union, Nfld) 17 Sep. 5/1: Send Us Your Specifications for Steel Slide Shoes for Komatiks, Bobsleds or Catamarans.

catamaran *v.* **1** join two boats or kayaks together to gain stability in rough water.
1924 FLAHERTY *Eskimo Friends* 128: Our boat, sixteen feet long, and the kayak, we would catamaran if we came upon rough weather. **1936** STRINGER *Wife-Traders* 42: . . . kayaks were catamaraned and . . . a bevy of battered old canoes were launched.

2 *Rare* move or travel in a boat or kayak rigged in this way.
1924 FLAHERTY *Eskimo Friends* 121: For three days an endless chain of them plied the ship's dories, and their own kayaks catamaraned between ship and shore. . . .

catamaran sledge *Nfld* See **catamaran**, *n.* (def. 2b).
1933 MERRICK *True North* 185: Since arriving, Harvey has built the new cabin, made a catamaran sledge, a great long toboggan, and a whole set of new fur boards.

catamount ['kætə,maunt] *n.* **1** any of various wild cats, especially the lynx or the cougar, *qq.v.* See

also **cat** (def. 1) and **cat of mountain.** Cp. **mountain cat** (def. 1).
1822 GOURLAY *Upper Canada* I 162: The Catamount, or Tiger Cat, sometimes improperly named the panther, is of the cat kind, very distinct from the wildcat, although there has been a confusion in the description of the two. **1852** (1881) TRAILL *Cdn Crusoes* 123: Deer . . . were plentiful, and . . . the Canadian lynx, or catamount, as it is here commonly called, a species of wild cat or panther. **1904** ROBERTS *Watchers of the Trails* 142: The cook of the camp, in telling his comrades about the fate of the dog, spoke of the great wildcat as a "catamount", to distinguish him from the common cat of the woods. **1965** *Wildlife Rev.* Mar. 19: Cougars, also known as . . . catamounts . . . are large unspotted cats.

2 See quote.
1835 *Novascotian* (Halifax) 10 Dec. 363/3: Well, she was a dreadful cross grained woman, a real catamount, as savage as a she bear that has cubs.

catch *v.* *Esp.Nfld* **1** freeze in; to become frozen in by the ice.
1850 GOODSIR *Baffin's Bay* 136: A party of her crew volunteered to remain with her during the winter, the rest going home in the other ships, which lying further out, had not been "caught."

2 of a body of water, freeze over, especially to a degree to permit travel over the surface.
1952 BANFILL *Labrador Nurse* 229: The plane could not land at Mutton Bay, so I would have to go down at the next village . . . if the ice were "caught" enough for a plane to land.

3 freeze.
1920 GRENFELL & SPALDING *Le Petit Nord* 125: . . . we had to face the full fury of a living winter gale. I "caught" both my cheeks on the way, or in common parlance I froze them.

catch over *Nfld* See **catch** (def. 2).
1878 *North Star* (St. John's) 30 Mar. 3/1: The bay here was caught over last week, and a string of "slob" made its appearance across the mouth, but the heavy sea of Thursday broke it all up. **1916** DUNCAN *Billy Topsail* 96: Anxious Bight was caught over with rotten ice from Ragged Run Cove to the heads of Our Harbour.

catch-pen *n.* *West* See 1963 quote.
1962 *Field, Horse & Rodeo* Nov. 32/2: The boys never knew why Red and I carried them to the catch-pen before we let him down. . . . **1963** SYMONS *Many Trails* 37: There was also a catch pen for branding, and for holding or roping out cattle stock.

cat driver a person who drives a caterpillar tractor or a bulldozer, *q.v.*; catskinner (def. 1).
1959 *News of the North* 22 Jan. 2/2: Ernie Balsillie and brother Walter . . . are both employed as Cat Drivers at Providence and Ft. Smith respectively.

caterpillar[1]† *n.* a caterpillar tractor; a bulldozer, *q.v.*
1929 *Beaver* Mar. 161: Prior to 1913, all the posts in British Columbia district had their supplies delivered overland by pack horses, but today there is no need for this method, as trucks and caterpillars have taken their place. . . . **1946** *Ibid.* June 4/2: [His] Caterpillar turned over and crushed him. . . .

caterpillar[2] *n.* a bed made from a collection of evergreen boughs or brush.
1943 MILLER *Lone Woodsman* 55: Night was now coming on fast. Dan cut a withe with a fork on it and went into the brush to make a balsam "caterpillar." This consisted of radiating balsam-sprays, hooked round the withe, in layers above the fork. It was dark by the time the caterpillar was three feet high, a thick green bundle of balsam fronds two feet in diameter.

caterpillar-tractor train *North* See **cat-train**.
1934 *Beaver* Dec. 46: (Caption) Arctic "Caterpillars." An account of man's fight with winter and his ingenuity in keeping a caterpillar tractor train running in the face of great difficulties. **1953** MOON *Saskatchewan* 228: Another kind of arduous northern work is done by the men on the caterpillar tractor trains. Every winter these trains travel over northern lake and river ice, pulling heavy supplies into remote mining and fishing and trading communities.

catfish *n.* any of a number of North American fish, family *letaluridae,* having barbels suggesting a cat's whiskers. See also **barbue**.
1620 MASON *Briefe Discovrse* B[r]: What should I spake of . . . Catfish, Millers, thunnes, &c. **1791** LONG *Voyages* 81: There are few fish except eels, cat fish, and pike. . . . **1852** MOODIE *Roughing It* 431: At the next stake he found upon the hooks a large eel and a catfish. **1965** *Globe and Mail* (Toronto) 14 Jan. W10/5: Most Canadians dismiss . . . catfish, alewife and others as impossible to eat. . . .

cat-house *n.* among trappers, a protective housing placed over a trap or a bait; trap-house. Cp. **cat-trap** and **cubby**.
1770 (1792) CARTWRIGHT *Journal* I 70: The furriers took four traps out of cat-houses near home, and carried them down the river, where they tailed them for foxes. **1819** ANSPACH *Hist.Nfld* 378: Over the whole is a cat-house, or hut of boughs, to defend the trap from the snow. **1955** ADTIC *Glossary*: cat-house. . . .

cat-killer *n. Obs.* a kind of deadfall trap, *q.v.*
1819 ANSPACH *Hist.Nfld* 377: The cat-killer has one end turning upon a nail driven into a long stake, whilst the other is supported high up by a line which passes over a crutch on the top of a stake, and then comes down to another at the bottom, where one end of the tongue is fixed.

cat of mountain *Obs.* a wild cat, especially the lynx (def. I). See **catamount** (def. 1).
[**1505** *Privy Purse Expenses of Henry VII* 25/8: catts of the mountaigne. . . .] **1665** (1885) RADISSON *Voyages* 202: We killed several other beasts, as Oriniacks, staggs, wild cows, Carriboucks, fallow does and bucks, Catts of mountains, child of the Devill; in a word, we lead a good life. **1844** MARRYAT *Settlers* 38: "Why, there's painters, and bears, and cata'mountains."

cat-path *n. Obs.* a trapline.
1775 (1792) CARTWRIGHT *Journal* II 113: I went to Friend's Point, and there met with another cat-path, with twenty-six traps in it. **1842** *Trans.Lit.& Hist.Soc. Que.* IV 87: The traps for martens are placed along a blazed path (called a "cat-path") leading into the interior, and varying in length from one to three day's walk, according to the address and activity of the hunter.

cat-skin *n.* the pelt of a lynx, *q.v.* or bobcat.
1748 DRAGE *Voyage* I 162: Those who do not use Caps, have Martin or Cat-skin Wigs. **1795** (1911) HEARNE *Journey* 176: Thus, a hatchet that is bought at the Factory for one beaver-skin, or one cat-skin, or three ordinary martins' skins, is sold to those people at the advanced price of one thousand percent. . . . **1908** LAUT *Conquest N.W.* 158: . . . when the Company wanted favors it openly sent purses of gold or beaver stocking or cat-skin counterpanes.

catskinner *n.* [after *mule-skinner,* q.v.] **1** See 1947 quote. See also **skinner** (def. 2).
1934 *Beaver* Dec. 47/1: Crews were made up consisting of two drivers, or "cat skinners" as they were called, and two brakemen. **1947** DICKIE *Gay Adventurers* 245: Mr. Boodleman . . . said that it was another kind of catskinner he was wanting, drivers for the big caterpillar tractors they use in the woods. They're called catskinners, just as teamsters are called muleskinners. **1964** *Calgary Herald* 24 July 19/4: "I'm a catskinner," one man was saying. "Home is where I park my trailer."

2 the man in charge of a cat-train, *q.v.*
1952 KNOTT *Harnessing* 14/1: "Cats" and "catswings," "cat skinners" and "brakies" are all part of the fabulous transportation system of the Canadian north. **1953** MOON *Saskatchewan* 229: The cat-skinners, as the train bosses are called, like it when the temperature is between forty and sixty degrees below zero.

cat spruce the white spruce, *q.v.*
1917 *Native Trees of Canada* 30: Common names [include] White spruce . . . cat spruce (Nova Scotia). **1925** ANDERSON *Trees and Shrubs* 45: The young shoots and leaves have when crushed a very unpleasant odour, which has earned for the tree the name of Cat-Spruce. **1952** BUCKLER *Mountain and Valley* 65: Joseph himself stopped to examine . . . a cat spruce and quite useless as a Christmas tree. **1956** RADDALL *Wings* 96: She made a fast drive of it . . . winding through a wood of cat-spruce trees.

cat-swing *n. North* See **cat-train**. See also **swing** (def. 2).
1948 *New Deal for Sask.Fisheries* 20: These "cat swings," travelling across frozen lakes in the winter months, carry more than 2,000,000 pounds of fish annually and transport supplies for development projects. . . . **1958** *CBC Times* (Prairie ed.) 23-29 Mar. 6/3: An important aid in the development of Manitoba's northland has been the "cat swing"—12 to 15 sleighs pulled by a team of tractors. **1962** DICKIE *Great Golden Plain* 289: The stretch from God's Lake to Ilford is a regular tractor train route used by many cat swings which then branch out to all the mines and trading posts in that part of the north.

cattalo ['kætəlo] *n.* [a blend of *cattle* and *buffalo*] an experimental cross between buffalo and domestic cattle.
1958 *Kootenaian* 26 June 6/4: The development of the "Cattalo," a cross between the Buffalo and domestic beef breeds, is the result of attempts by research men of the Canada Department of Agriculture to breed a range beef animal from Western and North Western Canada. **1964** *Western Wkly Supp.* 1 July 3/3: It is true that experiments have been made to cross the bison with domestic beef cattle. The offspring from this mating are known as "Catello."

cattle boss *West* a ranch foreman.
1955 HOBSON *Nothing Too Good* 40: I knew that whatever this clear-thinking and long-experienced cattle boss had

to say would weigh mighty heavy, and I was half shamefaced at my breathless and excited approach.

cattle keeper *Fur Trade, Obs.* a fur-company employee charged with looking after the livestock.
1784 (1954) *Moose Ft Jnls* 38: Two out hunting, Cook and Cattle keeper as usual, Paqueteerers, Fishermen, Trappers, and hunters, as yesterday. **1855** (1924) *Beaver* Dec. 31: Fishermen, cooks and cattle keeper [employed] as usual.

cattle-lifter *n. Slang* a rustler; a cattle thief.
1927 LONGSTRETH *Silent Force* 123: Cattle-lifters, red white, and mixed, could scarcely hide their jubilation at the rapid growth of ranching.

cattle reeve *N.S.* a municipal official responsible for the proper control of cattle in the community. Cp. **hog reeve.**
1955 *Wkly Monitor* 4 May 2/3: List of Ward Officers— ...Cattle Reeves...Fence Viewers...Sheep Valuers....

cattle wrangler *West* a cowboy; ranch hand. See also **wrangler** (def. 2).
1957 *Maclean's* 9 Nov. 70/1: Come lunch time we sat down with twenty-odd wolf-hungry cattle wranglers at a long table stacked with food.

cat-track *n.* a caterpillar tractor.
1959 *Maclean's* 11 Apr. 58/3: ...the Northern Transportation Company, after lengthening the old portage by another ten miles...was using cat-tracks to haul their barges across.

cat tractor a caterpillar tractor.
1959 *Argosy* (Cdn sec.) July 25: [Caption] Big cat tractors are the work horses for Tom Lamb.

cat (-train) trail *North* See **tractor road.**
1958 *Globe and Mail* (Toronto) 3 July 3/4: [the drilling rig] is the reason for the huts and the isolation and the long cat-train trails....**1964** *North* May-June 6: This winter, some of the heaviest equipment to be used in the mining operation was shipped over the same cat trail....

cat-train *n. North* a tractor-drawn train of sleds and cabooses (def. 5), the principal means of transporting freight, supplies, etc. in the Canadian North in winter. See also **cat**[3] (def. 2), **caterpillar-tractor train, cat-swing, sled train, swing** (def. 2), **tractor brigade, tractor swing, tractor train,** and **train**[3] (def. 2).
1946 FERGUSON *Mink, Mary and Me* 221: Throughout the winter of 1942-43 freight moved north. Cat-trains, half-tracks, giant trucks, loaded to capacity with everything from shingle nails and four-inch pipe to gigantic pieces of machinery for the Imperial Oil Company's wells and refinery. **1962** DICKIE *Great Golden Plain* 288: ...all must be skillfully loaded so as not to slide or roll off as the cat train rocks and plunges over the hummocks and pitch holes in the ice and snow roads.

cat-trap *n. Obs.* a trap for lynx. Cp. **cat-house.**
1777 (1792) CARTWRIGHT *Journal* II 276: Jack went to the cat-traps, but they were so covered with snow, that they could not strike up.

catwalk *n.* a narrow platform running the length of a boxcar to facilitate walking on the roof.
1955 BIRNEY *Long Table* 165: He lay belly-flat, fingers clamped on the swaying catwalk on the top of the wind-tormented boxcar....

cat walker *Lumbering* See **boom-man.**
1958 HAWTHORN *Indians of B.C.* 133: A sample of 121 Indian logging and sawmill workers registered in the regional office of the National Employment Service at Prince George revealed the following classifications: ...Cat walker (booming) 2 [,] Green chainman 2....

cauldron *n.* [an extension of *cauldron* a large kettle or boiler] the churning, seething mass of white water at the foot of a cataract. See also **chaudière** and **kettle**[1] (def. 1). Also *caldron.*
1826 (1829) MACTAGGART *Three Years* I 327: ...down they [the waters] tumble, in some places more than one hundred feet, into the cauldrons or kettles beneath....**1877** GRANT *Ocean to Ocean* 53: Beyond that it breaks into curling, gleaming rolls which end off in white, boiling cauldrons, where the water has broken on the rocks underneath. **1964** *Cdn Geog.Jnl* Feb. 71/2: Old Bytowners tell of more than one fight that ended conclusively in the cauldron beneath Chaudière Falls.

cauldron pool See **ca(u)ldron.**
1936 MOWERY *Paradise Trail* 70: ...the main overfalls, plunging over a seventy-foot cliff into a big caldron pool, gave a faint quivering tremble to the rock they sat on....

caulk *n.* **1** one of a number of sharp spikes set into an iron plate that fits over a shoe or boot, or set in the sole of the boot itself; also, the fitted patten. See also **creeper spike.**
1805 *Naval Chron.* XII 113: In Canada it is customary during the winter season...to wear on the feet a sort of patten, called caulks. **1941** *Beaver* Sep. 37/1: Creepers [are] bands of iron fitted with caulks....
2 a. See **caulked boot.**
1942 HAIG-BROWN *Timber* 249: The logger is careful to keep his caulks in good shape....**1943** SWANSON *Lumberjack* 26: Not with guns we fought that meet, but with fists and caulk-shod feet....
b. *Figurative use.* See quote.
1942 HAIG-BROWN *Timber* 249: Quitting the woods for good a logger is likely to talk about "hanging up his caulks"....

caulk boot or **shoe 1** See **caulked boot.**
1930 (1963) *Press* Jan.-Feb. 8: Oh Friends and choker setters, I know it will be tough; / Our caulk shoes will be heavy, the ground is steep and rough. **1966** *Globe and Mail* (Toronto) 18 Jan. B5/7: [The logger] was a pack-sack citizen and appeared on Skid Row streets complete with dirty Stanfields and caulk boots which would be later hocked for the last bottle.
2 *Figurative use.* See quote.
1964 *Victoria Dly Times* 8 Feb. 1/1: In the course of the budget debate, I look for Mr. Gibson to launch a caulk-boot attack on this move....

caulked boot or **shoe 1** a strong boot the sole of which is studded with steel spikes, or caulks, used by loggers to keep from slipping on wet or sloping logs. See also **caulk** (def. 2a), **caulk boot, cork boot, river boot,** and **spiked boot.**
1943 SWANSON *Lumberjack* 57: About this time...loggers landed in town clad in stagged-off pants, their caulked shoes flashing sparks on the...pavements....
1964 *Cdn Geog.Jnl* Feb. 68/2: Caulked boots with a row

of steel nails down the sides gave a certain traction on the slippery logs. . . .

2 *Figurative use.* See quote.

1942 HAIG-BROWN *Timber* 249: Quitting the woods for good a logger is likely to talk about . . . "throwing his caulked boots in the stove."

cayeuse or **cayoose** *n.* See **cayuse.**

cayote *n.* See **coyote.**

cayuse ['kaɪjus] *n.* [< the *Cayuse* Indians of parts of Washington and Oregon, U.S.A.]. Originally, a wild pony, a mustang; later generalized in the West as a name for any horse, often with a derogatory or contemptuous connotation. See also **Indian horse, Indian pony, shaganappi pony,** and **squaw horse.**

1860 *British Colonist* (Victoria) 26 June 1/1: A few uninitiated Oregonians . . . had rode over on Keyuse poneys from the Willamette valley. **1863** *Norfolk Reformer* (Simcoe, C.W.) 8 Jan. 3/1: We were amused by observing a drove of "Kioush" horses that had been driven from the mountains in a wild state, and were enclosed in a yard. . . . **1962** *Field, Horse & Rodeo* Nov. 30/1: "Well, chances are Mr. Dude, you've been getting a silent horse laugh yourself from your own trusty cayuse."

cayuse ['kaɪjus] *v. Rare* ride a cayuse.

1916 BRIDLE *Sons of Canada* 219: He believed in its future more sanely than the trailsters, who camped on the survey lines of new railways, along trails he had buckboarded and cayused in the 'eighties.

CCF or **C.C.F.** the Co-operative Commonwealth Federation, *q.v.*

1935 *Cdn Hist.Rev.* XVI 387: Perhaps the unrest which has shown itself in the Progressive movement of the 1920's, and in the C.C.F. and other movements of political protest in the 1930's has pointed in the same direction. **1961** *Edmonton Jnl* 4 Aug. 18/1: The CCF was born in Calgary in 1932 and held its first national convention in Regina in 1933. **1964** *Calgary Herald* 23 Apr. 1/6: The Saskatchewan people defeated the CCF not decisively, but almost reluctantly. . . .

CCFer a member or supporter of the CCF.

1944 *Cdn Seaman* Nov. 8: Maybe he is a Labor-Progressive—a Liberal—a CCFer or perhaps he is still "thinking it over." **1962** *Canada Month* May 13/2: Could it be, rumored CCFers, that Canada's Tory government regretted seeing socialist Saskatchewan score first.

CCP the Canadian Communist Party.

1962 *Kingston Whig-Standard* (Ont.) 12 Feb. 3/5: . . . it would not be right for the CCP to endorse the NDP. . . .

C.E. *Hist.* See **Canada East.**

1852 *Anglo-American Mag.* I 363/1: Mr. Orvis Ball, of Hatley, C.E., has recently discovered . . . a rich and extensive vein of silver ore. **1867** *Islander* (Charlottetown) 4 Jan. 2/4: Five vessels loaded at Three Rivers, C.E., this year, with sugar shooks for Cuba, and four for Buenos Ayres.

cedar *n.* See **cedar canoe.**

1897 TYRRELL *Sub-Arctics* 39: Our light cedars, though partly filled by the foam and spray, rose buoyantly on the waves, and again we breathed freely.

cedar bird† the cedar waxwing, *Bombycilla cedrorum.*

1873 LEMOINE *Maple Leaves* 207: Be careful, however, not to confound him with the Cedar or Cherry Bird—our summer visitor. . . . **1956** MCATEE *Folk-Names* 56: Cedar Waxwing . . . cedar bird (From frequenting red cedars and feeding on their "berries," General). . . .

cedar canoe a light, seaworthy canoe made of cedar and capable of carrying a sail. See also **Chestnut.**

1852 MOODIE *Roughing It* 263: My husband had purchased a very light cedar canoe, to which he attached a keel and a sail. **1898** EDGAR *Canada and Capital* 140: They are mostly cedar canoes of Rice Lake or Peterboro' make, as the birch-bark are not so suitable for sailing. **1967** *Cdn Geog.Jnl* Jan. 29/3: The children would later be exchanged by the Nisgahs to the Haidas, as payment for cedar canoes.

cedar scoop a roof timber of half a cedar log, the inner part of which is scooped out to form a trough. See also **scoop** and **scoop roof.**

1935 SULLIVAN *Great Divide* 388: He . . . stared at his ceiling of cedar scoops.

cedar shake a thick shingle split from cedar used to roof cabins and other buildings. See **shake.**

1925 *Cdn Labor Advocate* Nov. 6/4: The Haslam Lake Camp, being constructed of cedar shakes, are old buildings. **1966** *Kingston Whig Standard* (Ont.) 8 Jan. 11/7: If cedar shakes are used for a roof finish, . . . solid sheathing . . . could be used.

cedar swamp† See 1832 quote.

1793 (1933) MACDONELL *Diary* 81: After passing the last of the musiques we proceeded about a quarter of a mile in a ditch not much wider than the canoe, which nature seems to have made through the centre of a cedar swamp for the convenience of the North West Trade. . . . **1832** MCGREGOR *British America* II 591: *Cedar Swamps* . . . are deep mossy bogs, soft and spongy below, with a coating sufficiently firm to uphold small cedar or fir-trees, or shrubs. Such lands are much more difficult to reclaim than any of our bogs in the United Kingdom. **1960** *Weekend Mag.* 10 Dec. 55/1: There's a lot of cedar swamps north of here in a few miles. . . .

ceinture [sɛ̃'ty:r] *n. Cdn French* See **sash.**

1801 (1933) MCLEOD *Diary* 159: . . . one of them stole a Ceinture of Cadottes, [who] overtook them before noon, &, threatened to shoot one of them if he did not tell which of them had stolen the Belt, they restored the Sash & proceeded quietly on their journey. **1941** *Beaver* June 26/2: The pattern in the ceintures, with very few exceptions in the trade variety consisted of a wide red band or core in the centre that ran from one end to the other; this band was barbed along the edges, like a series of continuous arrow points.

ceinture à flammes *Cdn French* "flame sash." a kind of sash, *q.v.*, having a flamelike design woven into it. See also **L'Assomption sash.**

1941 *Beaver* June 26/1: . . . sashes of different descriptions and names appear on the invoice books of this company; like, worsted sashes, or belts . . . *ceintures a flammes* (flame-like), ceintures a fléches (arrow sashes). . . .

ceinture fléchée *Cdn French* "arrow sash." a kind of sash, *q.v.*, having an arrowlike design woven into it. See also **L'Assomption sash** and picture.

1931 NUTE *Voyageur* 42: . . . the old voyageur, dressed in his big blue capote, wearing his ceinture fléchée (sash) . . . sang in a staid manner. . . . **1941** *Beaver* June 24/1: The arrow sash or *ceinture fléchée* of General Sir Isaac Brock is the oldest dated specimen, its owner having died while wearing it on the battlefield in 1812.

cellar *n*. an underwater cavern or deep hole at the foot of a rapid.
1854 KEEFER *Ottawa* 33: The requisites for an examination of the Ottawa are . . . to paddle a bark canoe, run a rapid, and . . . swim when your canoe is swamped in a "cellar," or riddled on a rock.

cens *n. Cdn French, Obs.* See **cens et rentes.**
1777 *Quebec Gaz.* 30 Jan. 3/1: It is chargeable with only Cens and Seignorial Rights. **1832** MCGREGOR *British America* II 425: Under this [seigneurial] system estates are held nobly as *fiefs,* or *franc aleu noble;* and in *villainage,* subject to *cens* or *censive,* and *franc aleu villain.*

cens et rentes *Cdn French, Hist.* in New France and in Lower Canada, a ground rent of feudal nature.
1806 *Quebec Gaz.* 20 Mar. 1/1: I have seized and taken in execution . . . the appurtenances particularly of the Banel Mills, rights and privileges, and of all cens et rentes, lots et ventes and all other profits and pecuniary advantages. . . . **1905** *Ont.Bur.Arch.Rep.* III xlviii: Cens et rentes. A ground rent composed of two parts, the cens payable in money, the rentes payable in kind or equivalent in money. The cens corresponds to the superiorite, or the first right of the lord in the lands held by the vassal or tenant. **1960** RYERSON *Founding of Canada* 108: First there was the payment of feudal dues of *cens et rentes.* The cens was a small payment made in recognition of the seigneur's overlordship; it was generally from one to eight French *sols* or sous. The *rentes* or annual rent was more substantial, varying from one to five *livres.*

censitaire [ˌsɛnsəˈtɛr] *n.* [< F] *Hist.* a tenant paying cens et rentes.
1796 *Quebec Gaz.* 14 Jan. 4/1: Two petitions were presented to the House . . . setting forth the hardships that would attend the raising of the Lots et Ventes due by the Censitaires of the King's Domains in this Province. . . . **1831** *Brockville Gaz.* (U.C.) 19 Jan. 2/3: Resolved that the said Commissioners be authorized to exempt such of the said Censitaires as may be in a state of poverty, from any expenses to be incurred for the purpose of making the declarations for the Land Roll. **1960** RYERSON *Founding of Canada* 107: The seigneur extracted surplus-labor from his censitaires in numerous ways.

censive [ˈsɛnsɪv] *n.* [< F] *Hist.* the right of collecting *cens et rentes, q.v.,* and other feudal dues; the income from such payments; the seigneury or fief from which such income accrues.
1796 *Quebec Gaz.* 14 Jan. 4/1: The House in Committee proceeded to the further consideration of the Lots et Ventes due in the Censive of the King's Domains in this Province. **1822** *U.C.Gaz.* (York [Toronto]) 24 Oct. 251/1: And be it further enacted, that it shall and may be lawful for His Majesty, His Heirs and Successors, to commute with any Person holding Lands at Cens et Rentes in any Censive or Fief of His Majesty within either of the said Provinces. . . . **1886** (1887) *Trans Roy.Soc.Can.* IV 2 47: The habitant or censitaire held his property by the tenure of en censive, on condition of making annual payments in money or produce known as cens et rente, which were ridiculously small in the early times of the colony.

cent *n.* a bronze coin valued at one hundredth part of a Canadian dollar, adopted officially as Canadian currency in 1858; also, the value of this coin.
[**1825** *Kingston Chron.* (U.C.) 4 Feb. 3/3: . . . now because the New York State counts in dollars and cents, we, forsooth, you choose to think should follow their example.] **1853** *British Colonist* (Victoria) 2 Sep. 1/1: And be it enacted, that the denominations of money in the Currency of this Province, shall be pounds, dollars, shillings, pence, cents, and mills: the pound, shilling and penny shall have, respectively, the same proportionate values as they now have, the dollar shall be one-fourth of a pound, the cent shall be one-hundredth and the mill one-tenth of a cent. **1963** *Commercial Letter* Jan. 7/1: . . . the currency reformers in Canada already strongly favoured the system which has since been adopted, namely a special silver and copper coinage for North America, expressed in the American decimal system of dollars and cents.

Cent Belt *Obs.* See quote.
1952 (1965) HAMILTON *Cdn Quotations* 139/1: The Cent Belt. A term common in British Columbia, middle 19th century, in reference to Ontario and Quebec; old residents of British Columbia prided themselves on using no sum less than a bit, or, twelve and a half cents.

center *n.* See **centre.**

centralized school in Alberta, a centrally located rural school accommodating the pupils from several older, smaller country schools in the district.
1958 *Edmonton Jnl* 24 June 3 12/3: Several hundred children from the Barrhead district are vanned into centralized schools here each day. **1958** *Herald-Tribune* 10 Jan. 2/5: A huge crowd attended the Xmas concert which was put on by the centralized school at Elmworth.

Central Provinces Upper and Lower Canada, now Ontario and Quebec.
1954 RADDALL *Muster of Arms* 90: You have the look of the Bluenose regarding the ill-gotten wealth of the central provinces and ready to quote Joe Howe at the drop of a balance sheet. . . . **1963** *Commercial Letter* Jan. 8/1: Although the foregoing history refers mainly to the Central Provinces, the history of currency in the Maritime Provinces until the time of Confederation is very similar in its main outlines.

centre *n.* in hockey or lacrosse, the team position between the two wings in the forward line; the person playing this position. See also **centreman.**
1902 CONNOR *Glengarry School Days* 306: But before the latter could get up speed, Hughie was upon him, and ignoring the [lacrosse] ball, blocked and bothered and checked him, till one of the Twentieth centers, rushing in, secured it for his side. **1963** *Kingston Whig-Standard* (Ont.) 17 Jan. 13/7: Kingston's centres . . . consistently beat their Sudbury counterparts on the faceoffs, the puck was thrown back to the defencemen on the point and all the Kingston goals were started from there.

centre *v.* in hockey or lacrosse, act as centre for two wingers; to play as the centre man in the forward line.
1963 *Kingston Whig-Standard* (Ont.) 23 Jan. 9/1:

Imlach says he intends to use Horvath in the spot he played Sunday—centring Bob Fulford and Shack.

Centre Block the middle building of the three that make up the Parliament Buildings in Ottawa; the building in which the Commons and the Senate chambers are located. Cp. **East Block, West Block.**
1964 *Time* (Cdn ed.) 13 Nov. 17/2: But for the majority of the press gallery members, "the office" is a cluttered desk on the Centre Block's third floor, halfway between the Commons and the Senate chambers.

centre boulevard See **boulevard,** *n.* (def. 3).
1958 *Edmonton Jnl* 31 July 17/6: . . . the monument and its foundation, set in the centre boulevard, were smashed in an auto accident.

centre ice *Hockey* the general area midway between the ends of the rink, specifically the central point of the ice surface, where the puck is faced off at the start of a period and after each goal.
1963 *Kingston Whig-Standard* (Ont.) 22 Jan. 8/7: [They] were sent to the penalty box . . . after a minor tussle at centre ice.

centre-ice man *Hockey* a centre, *q.v.*
1955 *Vancouver Province* 6 Jan. 15/1: The bread-and-butter guy on the heralded new line of the Canucks is a deft centre ice man named Phil Maloney.

centreman *n.* See **centre,** *n.*
1916 WALLACE *Shack Locker* 294: The center man, relying on Stream no more after spoiling the last shoot on goal, shot himself and missed. **1963** *Kingston Whig-Standard* (Ont.) 17 Jan. 13/5: Jim Kozie, Kingston Frontenacs rookie centreman, has been placed on waivers.

C form in hockey, a contract signed by a young amateur agreeing to play for a specified professional team and for that team only.
1962 *National Hockey Annual* 69/2: Johnson played three years of Junior A . . . with the Three Rivers Flambeaux, where he signed a C form for Les Canadiens. **1963** *Globe and Mail* (Toronto) 12 Mar. 7/7: If a youngster signs a "C" tryout form, then changes his mind, he can be thrown out of all hockey.

cha [tʃɑ] *interj.* See **chaw.**

chain-lightning *n. Slang.* inferior whisky.
1843 HALIBURTON *Attaché* I xv: The drinks ain't good here [England]; they hante no variety in them nother: no white-nose, apple-jack, stone-wall, chain-lightning. . . . **1860** *British Colonist* (Victoria) 19 July 3/1: His stock is said to have been "chain-lightning" of the truest description. **1869** *Mainland Guardian* (New Westminster, B.C.) 8 Dec. 1/4: We found them well supplied with flour, rice, molasses, beans, tobacco, and "chain lightning" in spite of our legislation to the contrary.

chain of lakes a series of lakes connected by rivers.
1784 PENNANT *Arctic Zoology* 106: The traffic carried on in *Hudson's Bay* is chiefly brought from the chain of lakes and rivers that empty themselves into the bay at *Nelson's* river. **1896** RUSSELL *Far North* 75: The Yellow Knife River is simply a chain of lakes connected by rapids and falls. **1964** *Weekend Mag.* 11 July 18/2: Jack's attention was drawn to a chain of lakes and

rivers in what is now Bowron Lake Provincial Park, north of historic Barkerville. . . .

chain stake in trapping, the stake to which the chain of a trap is secured.
1933 MERRICK *True North* 193: This [trap] he unsets and hangs up on its chain stake, for he is "striking up" his path. . . .

chalking *n.* the process of marking logs about to be cut into square timber.
1961 PRICE & KENNEDY *Renfrew* 96: . . . poplar and alder were gathered nearby (and suitably charred) for "chalking" or marking square timber.

Champ de Mars [< F] a parade square; specifically, in late use, a place in Montreal which was formerly a parade square.
1807 *Quebec Gaz.* 10 Sep. 2/1: On Monday last, the chosen men of the 2d and 3d Battalion met on the Champ de Mars. . . . **1963** MORTON *Kingdom of Canada* 371: On the Champs [sic] de Mars that day the oratory was torrential.

chantecler *n.* [< Cdn F] a breed of white poultry developed by the Trappist monks at Oka, Quebec. Also spelled *chanticler.*
1936 *Cdn Geog.Jnl* XII 215/1: Here I was met by the famous monk Brother Wilfred, the originator of the first all-Canadian chicken "The Chantecler." It took from 1908 to 1918 of continuous experimenting to produce this superlative fowl. The breeds crossed to result in the Chantecler were the Cornish, White Leghorn, Rhode Island Red, Wyandotte and White Plymouth Rock. **1947** WELLS *Owl Pen* 74: They were very special chicks, Chanticler chicks, a distinctively Canadian breed of poultry. . . .

chanter *n.* in lumber and other camps, a ballad singer; a singer of chanteys.
1909 ROBERTS *Backwoodsman* 120: If McWha chanced to be singing, for he was a "chanter" of some note, he would appear so utterly absorbed that Rosy-Lilly would at last slip away. . . .

chanticler *n.* See **chantecler.**

chantie *n.* [< Cdn F] *Obs.* **1** See **shanty** (def. 2a). See also **chantier** (def. 2).
1824 *Canadian Mag.* III 202: the oxen and horses . . . are either driven up through the woods to the Chanties in the fall of the year, or after the ice takes. . . .

2 See **shanty** (def. 1a). See also **chantier** (def. 1).
1871 *Wkly Manitoban* 28 Jan. 2/6: We . . . dined at Mr. Murray's the owner of the only chantie between Macaulayville and that point.

chantie-man *n. Obs.* See **shantyman.**
1823 *Montreal Herald* 12 July 2/5: . . . I think you will agree with . . . an old Ottawa River Chantie-man. . . . **1824** *Canadian Mag.* III 204: Should these Chanty men happen to meet with a grove of Timber . . . they will cut it down without remorse.

chantier ['ʃænti,e; *French* ʃɑ̃'tje] *n.* [< Cdn F "logger's cabin or camp" < F "timber yard, dock"]
1 *Obs.* See **shanty** (def. 1a). See also **chantie** (def. 2).
1822 (1932) MCLEAN *Notes* 30: . . . he usually halted at a Chantier. . . . We . . . concluded that the *shanty* must be close at hand. **1859** MCDONALD *Autobiographical Notes* 14: Here we were fixed for the winter, in new and comfortable *chantiers,* with plenty of firewood and good accessories.

2 *Obs.* See 1958 quote. See also **shanty** (def. 2a) and **chantie** (def. 1).

1824 (1947) HARGRAVE *Correspondence* 9: Cap. John & an other brother were trying their fortunes in the Chantier line last winter. **1837** (1960) *Ontario Hist.* Dec. 229: . . . we have every reason to suppose that said sheep were taken up in Gatineau River to the chantiers where the rioters . . . are employed. **1854** (1960) *Ibid.* 230: For some years past, intoxicating liquors have been vigorously excluded from almost all the chantiers (shanties) . . . and . . . the result of the experiment has been entirely satisfactory. **1958** *Citizen* 18 Dec. 4/1: The word "shanty" developed as an equivalent for the French-Canadian word chantier, a lumber camp.

3 *Fur Trade, Obs.* **a.** See quote.
1902 (1954) CHITTENDEN *Amer.Fur Trade* I 47: Near most of the larger river posts there was some spot selected where timber was abundant at which the pickets and lumber for the posts were manufactured, the mackinaw boats and the canoes built, and such other work done as the establishment required. These places were called *chantiers*. . . .

b. an article made at such a building yard.
1834 TOLMIE *Physician* 280: During the day with the people at Point Duncan carting Chantieres.

4 *N.Ont.* a co-operative of independent loggers. Cp. **settler** (def. 3).
1963 *Weekend Mag.* 7 Dec. 9/1: Largest of the co-operatives in the area is the *Chantier Co-operative Val Rita.* . . . "The *chantier*," he says, "is very careful in its choice of members."

chant the cock [< Cdn F] *Obs.* among voyageurs, the traditional way to invite a fight.
[**1822** (1932) MCLEAN *Notes* 21: Our hut was first completed, when our champion clambered aloft, and crowed defiance; three times he crowed (aloud), but no responding voice was heard from the opposite camp.] **1913** COWIE *Adventurers* 129: The challenger would parade, "chanting the cock" (chantant le coq), in defiance of the best man (le meilleur).

chanty *n.* See **chantie.**

chanty-man *n.* See **chantie-man.**

charbon *n.* [< F] *Obs.* See quotes.
1829 MACTAGGART *Three Years* II 20: *Charbon* is a disease which seems to afflict the poor French peasants: it is something of the nature of the *yaws.* A small *black spot* appears on some part of the body,—hence the French name *charbon,* or charcoal: this is commonly on the *arm,* and there is no remedy but that of almost instantly cutting out the infected part. It is reported that they are tainted with this loathsome complaint from their handling cadaverous animals, skinning and eating such, as they frequently do,—the same as the poor Scotch moor farmers do their braxy sheep, which is the root of their *sibbans,* or yaws. **1903** CARR-HARRIS *White Chief* 75: The charbon was a disease that afflicted many of the French settlers in Canada at that time [1808].

charge *n.* [< Cdn F] *Fur Trade, Hist.* the normal load carried by a voyageur on a portage, usually two pieces of ninety pounds each.
1828 MCDONALD *Peace River* 5 Sep. 19: . . . we had but three loads over and above the *charge* of each man.

charging *n. Hockey* an illegal check involving a direct, forward-moving attack of more than two steps or strides against an opponent's person in an attempt to take him out of the play.

1963 O'BRIEN *Hockey* 62: [The rules] covered at a glance: fighting . . . hooking . . . charging . . . and boarding.

charity bandage unroll one's charity bandage, display sympathy; find excuses (for someone else's shortcomings).
1894 ASHLEY *Tan Pile Jim* 118: "That was because you were kept up so late last night taking care of the fish and game," interposed Ruth, who always unrolled her charity bandage whenever there was the slightest occasion for its use.

charivari [ˌʃɪvəˈriˈ] *n.* [< Cdn F < F] See 1791 quote. See also **shivaree.**
1786 *Quebec Gaz.* 12 Jan. 4/1: Friend, hast thou hear'd a strong North-easter roar,/ Or the harsh discord of Charivari, or Cat's wild scream ere them to love agree? **1791** LONG *Voyages* 35: Sometimes I distinguish myself at a charivari, which is a custom that prevails in different parts of Canada, of assembling with old pots, kettles, &c. and beating them at the doors of new married people; but generally, either when the man is older than the woman, or the parties have been twice married: in those cases they beat a charivari, hallooing out very vociferously, until the man is obliged to obtain their silence by a pecuniary contribution, or submit to be abused with the vilest language. **1852** MOODIE *Roughing It* 228: The charivari is a custom that the Canadians got from the French, in the Lower Province, and a queer custom it is. **1958** *Edmonton Jnl* 30 Oct. 3/2: . . . for the following year town council passed a bylaw prohibiting charivaries—"serenading of rough music made with kettles, pans and teatrays."

Charlottetown Conference or **Convention** *Hist.* the initial convention relating to the proposed union of the British North American Provinces, held at Charlottetown in 1864. See also **Confederation Conference.**
1864 *Nor'Wester* (R.R.S.) 21 Nov. 2/3: It was agreed at the Charlottetown convention that provision should be made for the admission of the far west of this Territory. **1886** GEMMILL *Companion* 344: [He] was one of the delegates to the Charlottetown Conference. . . . **1964** *Calgary Herald* 17 Mar. 31/4: The resolution said the visit, because of its connection with the centenary of the 1864 Charlottetown and Quebec conferences leading to confederation, makes the Queen a propaganda instrument on behalf of confederation. . . .

charrette *n.* [< F] *Obs.* a two-wheeled cart related to, and probably the model for, the Red River cart, *q.v.*
1862 *Nor'Wester* (R.R.S.) 25 June 2/5: We are also beginning to use waggons instead of old fashioned Lower Canada charrettes.

chartier *n.* [Cdn F < F *charretier* a carter] *Obs.* the driver of a charrette. See also **carter** (def. 1).
1836 *Montreal Transcript* 22 Dec. 2/3: A cariole was proposed to passengers . . . but all the world was singing out for canoes, and the "chartiers" made a bad speculation.

chaser *n. Lumbering* See 1966 quote.
1926 *Cdn Labor Advocate* I Apr. 1/1: On Tuesday a chaser was hit by the haul back line on one of the loaders, and after being thrown 15 or 20 feet in the air, landed head first on a log. **1966** *B.C.Logging* 9/1: At

the landing, a Chaser unhooks the logs. At intervals he inspects the rigging and splices wire ropes needing repairs. His job name originated many years ago when he had to clear the chokers as they became hung-up on obstacles while returning to the Chokerman. He sometimes "chased" the lines for several hundred feet.

chat-cervier *n.* [< Cdn F] *Obs.* See **Canada lynx.** See also **loup-cervier.**
1823 *Canadian Mag.* I 38: The Canadian lynx is known by the name of chat-cervier, because this animal, like all others, is smaller in the New than the Old Continent.

château† *n.* [< F] *Hist.* in French Canada, the residence of a governor or a seigneur, *q.v.*
c1821 (1840) WILLIS *Canadian Scenery* I 123: The grand entrance to the château is flanked on one side by this grim mouldering pile, and on the other by the stables.... 1839 HALIBURTON *Bubbles of Canada* 41: The eldest son, by right, takes the chateau, and the yard adjoining it.... 1889 WITHROW *Our Own Country* 183: Durham Terrace... is built on the foundation arches of the old Palais Saint Louis, the chateau of the early French Governors.

Château *n. Hist.* See **Château St. Louis.**

Château Clique *Hist.* the name given to the governing class in Lower Canada after 1791, comprising the English officials and the French seigneurs and leaders who supported their policies. Cp. **Family Compact** (def. 1).
1915 WALLACE *Family Compact* 116: It was on this occasion that William Ewart Gladstone, then a brilliant young Tory of twenty-seven years of age, stood up in the House and championed the cause of the Family Compact in Upper Canada and the Château clique in Lower Canada. 1963 MORTON *Kingdom of Canada* 259: The Family Compact and the Château Clique had never been more than small groups of officials and lawyers, together with a few business men.

Château St. Louis *Hist.* the Château St. Louis (or Lewis) in Quebec City, the former residence of the Governors of Quebec.
1774 *Quebec Gaz.* 2 June 3/1: As His Majesty's Birthday falls upon a Saturday, the Ball, intended to be given at the Château St. Louis in Honor of it, is put off by the Lieutenant-Governor to Monday next. 1904 DECELLES *Papineau* 41: He lacked force of character and fell under the influence of the coterie who reigned at Château St. Louis and who, under cover of the governor, had ruled and exploited our province for forty years.

chaudière [ˌʃodiˈɛr] *n.* [< Cdn F] See **ca(u)ldron.**
[1632 CHAMPLAIN *Carte de la Nouvelle France* [trans.] No. 77: *Sault de la Chaudière* [is] on the river of the Algonquins, some eighteen feet high and descending among rocks with a great roar.] 1826 *Kingston Chron.* (U.C.) 3 Nov. 2/5:... a cow one morning tumbled into the little kettle, or Chaudiere, and came up again at Gox Point, ten miles down the river. 1927 (1954) PATTERSON *Dangerous River* 84:... two fast riffles sprang out, one from each side of the canyon, and met in a boiling chaudière of wild white water. 1965 *Cdn Geog.Jnl* Dec. 202/3:... the water had hollowed out a deep basin... which the Indians called Asticou (the boiler) and so it became known by the French translation, Chaudière.

chaw [tʃɑ] *interj.* [origin uncertain] *North* a call directing a team of dogs to swing to the left. Cp. **chee.** Also spelled *cha.*
1896 RUSSELL *Far North* 15: *Hu* and *chac,* anglicized to "you" and "chaw" are words necessary to turn the foregoer to the right or left. 1913 WILLIAMS *Wilderness Trail* 164:... Mistisi, responding to the cry of "chaw," swerved into the... underbrush. 1953 OSGOOD *Winter* 64:... the people in this country [Great Bear Lake] use the expressions "hew" and "chaw" to signal a turn to right and left. Most of the time, their dogs pay no attention to them anyway.

cheap penalty *Hockey* a penalty imposed for an illegal action carried out in retaliation; a pointless penalty. See also **chippy penalty.**
1962 *National Hockey Annual* 92/1: Pete was still rough but he didn't get the cheap penalties.

cheater *n. Lumbering, Slang* See quote.
1948 (1956) ANDREWS *Glory Days* 25: "You th' new cheater?" he asked. I told him yes, that I was the new timekeeper and scaler.

Chebacco boat† [< Am.E, named after an early fishing village in Massachusetts] *Hist.* a type of fishing boat formerly used in the Maritimes. See also **Chebucto boat.**
1898 *N.B.Mag.* I 284: The "Chebacco" boat was one with a half deck forward, extending back to about midships, with the after part of the boat open, and it had one mast... was brought here by the Massachusetts Loyalists, who had been accustomed to the use of it.

Chebucto boat [var. of *Chebacco boat,* q.v., probably influenced as to form by *Chebucto,* an early name of Halifax and its bay < Micmac "great long harbor"] *Maritimes, Obs.* See **Chebacco boat.**
1818 LOCKWOOD *Nova Scotia* 10: Their Chebucto boats, from 25 to 70 tons, ride in the middle of the ocean, with buoyancy and ease....

chechako or **chechaqua** *n.* See **cheechako.**

che-che-guy *n.* See **shishiquoi.**

checker *n.* See **checkerboard.**
1916 WALLACE *Shack Locker* 207: "D'ye think halibut can stay in the checkers when a vessel rolls down to her hatches?"

checkerboard *n. Maritimes* See 1958 quote.
1916 WALLACE *Shack Locker* 202: The two of them had scarce shipped the checkerboards to receive the fish before the weather dory had an oar up. 1958 *Weekend Mag.* 28 June 27/2: [The raft] was a crude, makeshift affair, made up of checker boards (wooden bins used for dressing the fish) and floats salvaged from the trawls.

chee [tʃi] *interj.* a dog-driver's command calling for a turn to the right. See also **hew,** *interj.,* and **yea.** Cp. **chaw.**
1944 CLAY *Phantom Fur Thieves* 141: "... An' the leader must have an ear for the driver's commands." "I know," said Dave alertly, "*chee* for going to the right and *cha* for going to the left!"

cheechako [tʃɪˈtʃako] *n.* -s or -es. [< Chinook Jargon *chee* new + *chako* come] *Orig. Northwest* a newcomer; greenhorn; tenderfoot, *q.v.* Cp. **pilgrim** (def. 1). Also spelled *chechako, chechaque.*
1897 HARRIS *Gold Fields* 41: In speaking of the miners who came out on the Portland, Captain Kidston was

enthusiastic. "These men are every one what the Yukoners call "Chechockoes" or newcomers, and up to last winter they had nothing." **1923** WALDO *Down Mackenzie* 248: The "cheechaco" (the man who has never seen the ice go out) and the "sour-dough" (the man who has learned to save a little of his bread to be the leaven of the next baking) do not talk the same language. **1963** *Western Miner* Aug. 16/2: To many Cheechakos a shipment of a quarter ton of gold bricks represents most fabulous wealth.

cheechako [tʃɪ'tʃako] *adj.* [< n.] from or associated with the "outside," *q.v.* Also spelled *chechako, chechaqua,* etc.
1899 (1957) GOWLAND *Return to Canada* 113: "For two dollars apiece in Chekaco money, I unite this couple in matrimony." **1922** PRINGLE *Tillicums* 56: We had . . . parsnips and potatoes. These were good "chechako spuds" shipped in from the South. **1926** DILL *Long Day* 90: Although "cheechako" money or currency was rapidly making its way into the Yukon, it was no infrequent sight to see a poke of gold thrown on the scales.

cheemo *interj.* See **chimo.**

cheese block *Lumbering* a wedge-shaped steel or wooden block placed on the bunks of cars to prevent the loaded logs from rocking.
1942 HAIG-BROWN *Timber* 250: Perhaps the most usual [method of dumping] is the "parbuckle"—cheese blocks are knocked out on the water side, cables are passed under the loads and hooked to the cross-log at the brow of the apron.

cheese factory *Esp.Ont.* a small cheese-making plant making use of milk produced on local farms.
1869 *Cdn Illust.News* 18 Dec. 98/2: . . . whoever shall sell to a butter or cheese factory, skimmed adulterated or tainted milk, shall be liable to a fine for each offence. . . . **1871** OXENDEN *First Year* 71: . . . the milk is deposited in zinc pails, and placed on a platform, and a cart comes trotting by, picks up the various contributions, and carries them to the nearest cheese factory. . . . **1966** *Globe and Mail* (Toronto) 15 Jan. 30/5: These were . . . farmers who ship milk to cheese factories.

chemanis ['tʃɛmənɪs] *n.* [< Algonk.; cf. Ojibwa *chīmān* canoe, boat] a light canoe.
[**1768-82** (1904) LONG *Voyages* 242: cheeman canoe.] **1860** KOHL *Kitchi-Gami* 256: . . . "jimans"—so they [Ojibwa Indians] call their canoes. . . .] **1955** SHIPLEY *Anna* 36: Sometimes I go in my chemanis if the water is good.

chemin du large *Cdn French* "road of the open plains" *Obs.* a prairie trail; a route across the plains.
1810 (1897) COUES *New Light* II 637: We came to the pretty plain, where we found that the Sarcees had separated; a part had passed by the chemin du large to avoid the strong wood, while the others had continued to follow the Rocky mountains route.

chemoo(n) *interj.* See **chimo.**

chenail [ʃə'na:j] *n. Cdn French* (especially in place names) a channel. Cp. **chenal.** See note at **snye.**
1779 *Quebec Gaz.* 11 Mar. 3/1: To be Sold . . . Another piece of ground . . . by the High Road and behind the Chenail du Moine. **1886** *Indian* (Hagersville, Ont.) 7 July 146/2: The band known as the Chippewas

of Chenail Ecarte and St Clair . . . raised crops far in excess of those of any previous year.

chenal [ʃə'nal] *n.* **-aux.** *Cdn French* "channel" (often in place names) *Northwest* See **snye** (def. 2). Cp. **chenail.**
1793 (1933) MACDONELL *Diary* 77: [The river] has changed its course back to what it was at the entrance of the Chenaux 5 Leagues below the Grand Calumet. **1896** RUSSELL *Far North* 73: We continued through the winding *chanals* (anglicized as "schnys"). . . . **1928** FREEMAN *Nearing North* 158: . . . the great western river had already received a considerable portion of the discharge of the Athabasca through the Chenal des Quatre Fourches.

Chenook *n.* See **Chinook.**

cherry bird† the cedar waxwing, *Bombycilla cedrorum.*
1823 HALIBURTON *General Descr.N.S.* 31: The following catalogue contains a list of most of the known birds of the Province . . . Cherry Bird . . . Towhe Bird. . . . **1955** MCCOWAN *Upland Trails* 56: The Cedar waxwing is sometimes called the Cherry bird because of its pronounced fondness for this sort of orchard fruit.

cherry-picker *n. Lumbering, Slang* **1** See quote.
1942 HAIG-BROWN *Timber* 249: Cherry-picker. A small donkey engine loaded on to a skeleton car or flat car and taken out along the track to pick up logs or loads dropped from cars on the way down to the Beach.
2 a large machine, mounted on a caterpillar tractor, for picking up long, heavy logs.
1962 *Canada 1962* 158: [Caption] This fabulous machine for loading the enormous logs from the British Columbia forests onto trailers is nicknamed the "cherry-picker."

cherry-tree tea an infusion of twigs of the wild cherry, prepared by certain Indian tribes.
1905 MOTT *Jules of the Great Heart* 166: The water in the pannikin on the fire bubbled, and Jules dropped some cherry-tree tea in it, then munched chunks of pemmican slowly. . . .

chessaquoy *n.* See **shishiquoi.**

chesterfield† ['tʃɛstər,fild] *n.* [< Lord *Chesterfield*, 1694-1773] a long upholstered seat or couch having back and arms and often forming part of a suite; sofa.
☛ *Not originally Canadian, this term has become the generic word in Canada for this kind of couch, and, indeed, is often used for any kind of couch. It is still occasionally used in England and is heard locally in the United States, as in the northern counties of California.*
1903 (1913) CULLUM *Devil's Keg* 1: He was leaning over the cushioned back of the Chesterfield upon which an old lady was seated. . . . **1918** *Globe* (Toronto) 24 Oct. 14: [Advert.] Chesterfields, all-over upholstered frame, deep spring back, roll-shaped arms, and spring seat and edge covered in floral tapestry and velour, Reg. $110. for $85.00. **1939** GROVE *Two Generations* 58: Enjoying the privileges of a lifelong familiarity, he went to the chesterfield . . . and lay down flat on his back. **1965** *Dly Colonist* (Victoria) 14 Aug. 1/5: [Caption] Looter carries out chesterfield on back.

chesterfield chair a capacious upholstered chair forming part of a chesterfield suite.

1956 KEMP *Northern Trader* 65: He waved me to a chesterfield chair, took another himself, and proceeded to give me the facts of life. **1966** *Globe and Mail* (Toronto) 3 June 27/8: My wife asked me if I wanted another cup of coffee when I climbed into my special chesterfield chair after turning on the television. . . .

chesterfield suite a set of upholstered furniture comprising a chesterfield, *q.v.*, and one or two large chairs.
1961 *Edmonton Jnl* 29 July 34/6: [Advert.] 2-piece Chesterfield Suites. **1966** *Kingston Whig-Standard* (Ont.) 18 Feb. 21/4: [Advert.] NEW two-piece chesterfield suite, foam cushions, zippers, . . . $99.95.

chesterfield table a long, low table for placing in front of a chesterfield; a coffee table.
1927 *Toronto Dly Star* 8 Oct. 2: [Advert.] The Chesterfield Table and End Table are in walnut finish.

Chestnut *n. Trademark* See **cedar canoe.**
1922 FLAHERTY *My Eskimo Friends* 2: A seventeen-foot "Chestnut" . . . a few simple instruments, and a carbine Winchester, comprised the outfit. **1933** MERRICK *True North* 27: Our canoes are both eighteen-foot Chestnuts, very strong and deep, excellent in rough water. **1963** PATTERSON *Far Pastures* 123: The canoe . . . was a sixteen-foot Chestnut, made of eastern cedar, canvas-covered. . . .

chev(e)reau *n.* -eaux. [< Cdn F, var. of *chevreuil*, q.v.] *Obs.* See **chevreuil.**
1808 (1960) FRASER *Letters and Journals* 149: Mossu, Red Deer, and Chevereau, and Beaver are likewise said to be numerous. . . . **1859** *Kamloops Journal* (B.C.) 28 Feb.: Traded . . . four Chivereaux Skins from the Indians. **1887** *Senate Report* 182: Chevreux [are found in the] same country as the black tail deer.

chevreuil *n.* [< Cdn F < F "roebuck"] *Obs.* See 1950 quote.
1800 (1897) COUES *New Light* I 127: . . . we saw numerous tracks . . . of the . . . chevreuil. . . . **1824** (1931) MERK *Fur Trade* 248: The Country is said to abound with Red deer and Chevriel. . . . **1833** TOLMIE *Physician* 221: Have been pestered all day by fellows trading rats and chevreuil skins. . . . **1950** WHITE in THOMPSON *Journals* 11n: Although the word *chevreuil* is the feminine for the roe-deer of Europe, the French-Canadian voyageurs commonly applied this term to the mule deer [*q.v.*].

chewee [tʃəˈwi] *n.* [imitative] the eastern towhee, *Pipilo erythrophthalmus.* Also called *cheweek, chewink, pewee.*
1823 HALIBURTON *General Descr.N.S.* 31: The following catalogue contains a list of most of the known birds of the Province . . . Towhe Bird (or Pewee or Cheweek). . . . **1897** DURAND *Reminiscences* 58: Again I would hear . . . the chewee, crying "Chewee, chewee," as it starts from a brush heap.

Chicago heavy mess See **Chicago rattlesnake.**
1961 PRICE & KENNEDY *Renfrew* 48: [Lunch] consisted of boiled salt pork—very fat Chicago heavy mess—and bread and tea.

Chicago rattlesnake *Slang* salt pork.
1947 SAUNDERS *Algonquin Story* 37: Many are the stories told about "Chicago rattlesnake," as the salt pork was affectionately called by the shantymen, whose mainstay it was.

chicamin [ˈtʃɪkəmɪn] *n.* [< Chinook Jargon *chikamin* iron, metal; cf. Nootka *tsikimin* iron, steel] *West and Northwest* money; coins. Various spellings.
1860 *British Colonist* (Victoria) 26 July 1/2: The accomodating engineer [agreed] to extend to the government . . . three year's grace, or, in other words, await the expiration of that time for the "chickyman." **1927** PHILIP *Painted Cliff* 38: "It would be different if it was ol' J.B.'s chicamin, 'cause he's got barrels o' money. . . ." **1953** MOWERY *Mounted Police* 53: "I think he's got your furlough papers and your *chickamin* ready." **1963** SYMONS *Many Trails* 74: "Mebbeso," Charlie went on, "helo chickamun stop I come back," meaning that he might return broke.

chichicoe or **checheckquoi** *n.* See **shishiquoi.**

chickamin or **chickamun** *n.* See **chicamin.**

chickaree [ˈtʃɪkəˌri] *n.* [imitative] a species of squirrel, *Tamiasciurus hudsonicus.*
1833 TYLER *Progress of Discovery* 340: The chickaree or Hudson's Bay squirrel . . . inhabits the forests of white spruce-trees which cover so vast a portion of the fur countries. **1911** ROGERS *Wild Animals* 190: "Chickaree" is a nickname which imitates his scolding, chattering conversation.

chicken *n. West* See **prairie chicken** (def. 1).
1860 *Nor'Wester* (R.R.S.) 28 Feb. 4/1: During the entire day, the whole party were engaged as busily in "picking" our chickens as was Peggy in the *Low-Backed Car*. **1959** *Calgary Herald* 1 Aug. 19/1: He has seen a chicken isolated from others by sagebrush dancing in perfect harmony.

chickimin or **chickyman** *n.* See **chicamin.**

chico(t) [ˈtʃiko *or* ˈʃiko] *n.* [< Cdn F < F *chicot* stump] a tree stub, especially a rampike, *q.v.*, or deadhead, *q.v.*
1832 COX *Adventures* 120: Great caution is required to avoid sunken trees, called snags or planters, and by the Canadians chicots. . . . **1931** GREY OWL *Last Frontier* 119: I climbed the knoll, and there . . . sat my friend and mentor at the foot of one of the chicos. . . .

Chicot [ˈtʃiko *or* ˈʃiko] *n.* [< Cdn F] See **bois-brûlé.**
1860 (1956) KOHL *Kitchi-Gami* 260: Frequently, too, pure-blooded French Voyageurs, if they live entirely among the Indians, and inter-marry with them, are counted among the Chicots. **1942** *Beaver* June 18/1: Some of the singers, particularly among the *Bois-Brules* or *Chicots*, were endowed with a gift for song-making. . . .

chief *n. Fur Trade, Hist.* an industrious leader of a band of Indian hunters, rewarded with coat, tall hat, trousers, and flag, as symbols of headship. See also **captain** (def. 2) and **trading chief.**
1795 (1929) MCGILLIVRAY *Journal* 74: And before night/I/clothed the following Chiefs. . . . **1801** (1933) MCLEOD *Diary* 176: I clothed [the corpse] with a chief's cloathing, vizt coat, shirt, Hatt & Trowsers. **1908** MAIR *Mackenzie Basin* 144: Her father . . . was a fur company's Chief, and, in his youth, a noted hunter. . . .

chief clerk *Fur Trade, Hist.* an officer junior to a trader.
1922 *Beaver* April 9/1: A chief trader received half the quantity [of provisions], and a chief clerk half as much as a chief trader.

Chief commissioner See **commissioner** (def. 1).

chief electoral officer a government official who is responsible for the organization and operation of federal elections in Canada.
1958 *Edmonton Jnl* 26 June 15/2: It has been the custom to refer the report of chief electoral officer Nelson Castonguay to the committee after each general election. **1962** *Weekend Mag.* 26 May 20/2: The man responsible for Canada's election machinery is the Chief Electoral Officer . . . The Chief Electoral Officer has the rank of a deputy minister, holds office until the age of 65 and can be removed only by impeachment.

chief factor *Fur Trade, Hist.* a senior commissioned officer who was in charge of a main post and usually a department or district, especially of the Hudson's Bay Company. See also **factor.**
1680 (1948) *H.B.C.Letters Outward* 5: . . . let Mr. John Bridger, who is chief factor . . . know wee have great expectations. . . . **1723** (1923) *Beaver* July 381/1: You are to deliver to Mr. Thos. Macklish . . . (or, in case of his Death to ye Chief Factor). . . . **1824** (1931) SIMPSON *Fur Trade* 19: Saw several bands of Indians but they were all starving being quite destitute of Ammunitions which reflects much discredit on the Chief Factor in charge of the District. **1923** *Beaver* Nov. 40: Archibald McDonald, the last chief factor in the service to hold the title, was born . . . in 1836. **1962** DICKIE *Great Golden Plain* 36: Each post [factory] was ruled by a governor or chief factor. . . .

chief factorship *Hist.* the position and duties of a chief factor.
1905 (1954) *B.C.Hist.Qtly* XVIII 190: No other than a clerk could be promoted to a chief tradership . . . and only a chief trader to a chief factorship. **1955** RICH in BLACK *Journal* xci: There is no mention of the Chief Factorship which Black received dating from November 15.

chieftainess *n.* a female Indian chief.
1837 (1923) JAMESON *Rambles* 320: . . . they . . . call me the white or fair English Chieftainess (ogima-quay). **1899** PARKER *Translation* 11: The next morning Lali . . . the chieftainess of a portion of her father's tribe . . . was introduced . . . as Mrs. Frank Armour. **1942** NIVEN *Flying Years* 36: A squaw with a marriage certificate in her hand is apt to become heap big chieftainess.

chief trader *Fur Trade, Hist.* a commissioned officer a grade lower than a chief factor, *q.v.*, and usually in charge of a trading post.
1821 (1900) GARRY *Diary* 133: We found here Mr. J. W. Dean a Chief Trader to whom I delivered his Commission. **1955** RICH in BLACK *Journal* xxv: There were also two lower ranks of Gentlemen—men with sufficient education and, it was hoped, ability to rise to the positions of chief trader and chief factor—clerks and apprentice clerks.

chief tradership *Hist.* the position and duties of a chief trader.
1858 (1955) BLACK *Journal* 240: I have therefore . . . made up my mind to resign my C[hief] Tradership and to settle down. . . . **1905** (1954) *B.C.Hist.Qtly* XVIII 190: No other than a clerk could be promoted to a chief tradership . . . and only a chief trader to a chief factorship.

Chilkat blanket or **robe** a D-shaped blanket woven of mountain goat wool with a warp of yellow cedar bark, into which are worked symbolic designs, originally made by the Chilcat Indians and later adopted by other tribes of the west coast. See also **Haida blanket.**

1890 BOAS *Masks and Head Ornaments* 8: Thus the beautiful raven rattles of the *Tsimshean* frequently imitated by the *Kwakiutl* and the beautifully woven Chilkat-blankets are used as far south as Comox. **1924** *Beaver* Jan. 143: Securing and preparing the materials for the manufacture of the Chilkat blanket took about six months and weaving about the same time. **1958** *Native Voice* Sp.ed. 8: He carried to Her Majesty on the occasion of her Coronation in London, a Chilkat Blanket or Robe which is of symbolic and historic interest and is as fine an example of these now cherished and invaluable robes as can be found anywhere in the world.

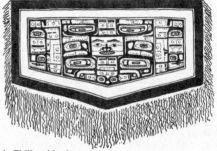
A Chilkat blanket

chimo ['tʃaɪmo *or* 'tʃimo] *interj.* [< Esk.] *North* an Eskimo greeting. See also **tima.**
1748 DRAGE *Voyage* I 24: The Person in the Canoe . . . shewed a Piece of Whale-bone, repeating *Chima,* and moving his Left-hand circularly upon his left Breast. . . . **1812** (1819) MCKEEVOR *Hudson's Bay* 27: When they had got within a short distance of the vessel, they all set up a loud cry, every one repeating the word chimò, chimò, which, in their language, signifies trade. **1858** BALLANTYNE *Ungava* 238: . . . Chimo (the i and o of which are sounded long) is an Esquimaux word of salutation. . . . **1938** *Beaver* June 28: Chimo is a mixed Indian and Eskimo word, and has been taken to have several meanings. Andrew Graham in 1768 writes . . . The Eskimos "rub their breast with their open hand, calling in a pitiful tone, Chimo! Chimo! which is a sign of peace and friendship." In 1814 Lieut. Edward Chappell writes that "Chymo" means to barter. The Eskimos today use it as a greeting. **1964** *Edmonton Jnl* 11 July 1/3: Chimo Cheeckakos. (That's pronounced chee-mo).

Chinaman *n.* See **oatmeal Chinaman.**

Chinaman's hat a cap for the exterior end of a stovepipe, designed to shed rain and snow.
1933 MERRICK *True North* 345: The house is a gray, weather-beaten structure with a sharp-peaked roof and a crooked stovepipe . . . capped with a Chinaman's hat.

China plague *Hist.* See quote.
1935 SULLIVAN *Great Divide* 32: . . . he held a position of considerable importance, having secured the contract for burying Chinamen dead of the China plague, a mysterious malady, little understood, which began in the legs that immediately turned black, then mounted to the heart and carried off its victims in a few hours: it did not attack the whites. . . .

Chinatown† *n.* that part of a town or city where the Chinese dwell.

1869 (1960) RAMSAY *Barkerville* 61 : Chinatown is universally voted a nuisance in Barkerville in every shape, sense or manner. **1963** *Sun* (Vancouver) 28 Jan. 4/3 : I do not see any reason why we cannot build a new Chinatown on an ambitious scale like that of San Francisco, Los Angeles or New York City.

Chinese café See **Chinese restaurant.**
1934 GODSELL *Arctic Trader* 134 : . . . I found it smelling strongly of . . . Chinese cafés and places.

Chinese Freemason a member of the Chinese Masonic Order, *q.v.*
1960 RAMSAY *Barkerville* 60 : The Chinese Freemasons are in no way connected with the A.F. & A.M. rites, being an independent order, going far back into Chinese history.

Chinese gin or **rum** *B.C.* a cheap potent liquor made and sold by Chinese.
1919 FRASER *Bulldog Carney* 99 : "He'd seen me down in the Del Monte joint, and thought—well, he was filled up on Chinese rum. He wasn't none too much like a man in anything he said or done, but I was standin' for him as long as he don't get plumb Injun." **1935** SULLIVAN *Great Divide* 33 : . . . he distilled a potent liquor from a mash of pounded rice and other ingredients whose identity passed beyond common understanding; it was known as Chinese gin. . . .

Chinese laundry a small neighborhood laundry run by Chinese.
1884 *Brandon Blade* (Man.) 28 Feb. 3/3 : A sample of the water used by its inhabitants was taken at hazard from a passing water cart and analyzed by a competent chemist with the following result : Solution of dead cat, ·13 . . . Attar of Chinese laundry, ·04. . . . **1889** *Rat Portage* [Kenora] *News* (Ont.) 28 June 3/1 : What Rat Portage Has. One Bank, Six Hotels; Two Saloons . . . A Chinese laundry. **1959** MOON *Saskatchewan* 11 : It plunged into a Chinese laundry taking a door casing along.

Chinese Masonic Order an independent rite of Masons established about 1869 in Barkerville, B.C. and having roots deep in Chinese tradition. See also **Chinese Freemason.**
1959 *Northwest Digest* Nov. 15/1 : The Chinese and White Masonic Orders could take over or else finance the restoration of their respective lodge buildings [in Barkerville].

Chinese restaurant a restaurant operated by a Chinese, especially one of the small cafés that are found, particularly in the West, in most Canadian small towns.
1920 GIBBON *Conquering Hero* 151 : . . . there were also hotels, stores, a lumber concern, a pool room and a Chinese restaurant. **1962** ALLEN *Peace River* 64 : After that, the abstemious members of the visiting party would step into the Chinese restaurant for Denver sandwiches.

Chinese rum See **Chinese gin.**

Chinese wash shop *Obs.* See **Chinese laundry.**
1897 *Medicine Hat News* (Alta) 14 Jan. 4/2 : It is an open question whether or not some of the Chinese wash shops in town should not be counselled to find another way of disposing of their refuse and dirty water besides slopping it out into the most used thoroughfare in town.

chin grist *Slang, Obs.* talk, especially talk of little consequence.
1891 *Grip* (Toronto) 24 Oct. 266/2 : . . . I hadn't got but five dollars for all the chin grist I had peddled about so long.

Chink stuff *Slang* in placer-mining areas, ore deposits of low concentration, so called because Chinese often worked such deposits.
1936 MOWERY *Paradise Trail* 29 : The place is not staked or posted. Gary fancied that the deposit must be "chink stuff," of low concentration.

Chinook [ʃəˈnuk, ʃəˈnuk, *or (rarely)* tʃəˈnuk] *n.* [< Salishan (Chehalis) *chənukw*] **1** *Hist.* (one of) a relatively small group of Indians who lived north of the Columbia River on the Pacific Coast.
1824 (1931) SIMPSON *Fur Trade* 98 : The Chinooks never take the trouble of hunting and rarely employ their Slaves in that way, they are however keen traders and through their hands nearly the whole of our Furs pass. **1957** *Encyc.Can.* II 358/1 : Four-fifths of the Chinook were wiped out by a fever epidemic in 1829.

2 See **Chinook Jargon.**
1833 (1963) TOLMIE *Physician* 210 : Have begun making a vocabulary of the Chenooke gibberish, by which we communicate with the indians . . . it is a vile compound of English, French, American & the Chenooke dialect. **1859** *British Colonist* (Victoria) 12 Sep. 2/2 : From the prospectus we learn that it will be printed in English and not in Chinook, the diplomatic language of the northern courts. **1963** *Calgary Herald* 1 Oct. 12/1 : [George] used Chinook, the language [of] conversation between whites and Indians in fur-trading days. . . .

3 See **Chinook wind.** Also spelled *chinook.*
1879 *Sask.Herald* (Battleford, N.W.T.) 13 Jan. 3/1 : On the evening of the fourth, however, a chinook sprang up and sent the cold snap to seek its old haunts. **1963** *Calgary Herald* 12 Oct. 6/1 : I'm thankful for breezy Chinooks that make our city the envy of all Canadian cities. . . . **1966** *Globe and Mail* (Toronto) 30 Jan. 8/3 : The weather still hasn't broken—no chinook has made its appearance [in S. Alberta]. . . .

4 See **Chinook salmon.** Also spelled *chinook.*
1932 SHIELS *Seward's Ice Box* 74 : Salmon is, of course, principally canned though there is a limited quantity salted each year and there is also a considerable business done in mild curing, principally of Kings or Chinooks. **1964** *Islander* 27 Sep. 3/3 : Spring salmon . . . have become extinct through the modern terminology of science and will from now on be known . . . as Chinooks.

chinook [ʃəˈnuk *or* ʃəˈnuk] *v.* blow a Chinook wind, *q.v.*
1947 FREEDMAN *Mrs.Mike* 16 : But that night it chinooked, and I threw off all my blankets, for it blew hot and warm. **1954** PATTERSON *Dangerous River* 223 : it never Chinooked again till early March. . . . **1957** HUTCHISON *Canada* 257 : If the weather took to Chinooking, the temperature could rise by eighty degrees in a few hours.

Chinook arch a cloud formation that often attends or presages the Chinook winds, observed as an archlike strip of blue sky above the western horizon, often between the peaks of the Rockies and the surrounding overcast. Cp. **Chinook sky.**
1941 *Beaver* Mar. 43 : [Caption] The dark cloud is the "Chinook Arch," forerunner of the warm wind of winter. **1964** *Calgary Herald* 6 Jan. 1/1 : This Chinook arch appeared in the western sky Sunday but its usual

promise of warm air sweeping in from the west is not expected to come true.

Chinook belt that part of southern Alberta and Saskatchewan most influenced by Chinook winds. See also **Chinook country.**

1889 MACLEAN *Indians* 204: The Chinook Belt of the Alberta District is in width about 125 miles. . . . **1963** *Calgary Herald* 23 Dec. 2/1: In the Chinook belt of southwestern Alberta the warm air hit with a tremendous blast especially at Pincher Creek where peak winds reached 65 with gusts of 90.

Chinook canoe a large dugout canoe used by the Indians of S.W. British Columbia and N.W. Washington.

1858 (1921) LAUT *Cariboo Trail* 13: Every party that starts from the Sound should have their own supplies to last them three or four months, and they should bring the largest size chinook canoes, as small ones are liable to swamp in the rapids. **1907** CROSBY *An-ko-me-nums* 141: The canoes of the Pacific Coast are of the type called "dugouts," that is . . . they are mostly cut out of a cedar log. In the south, the large ones were spoken of as "Chinook canoes, with rather a stub or short stern and a very high bow or neck. **1964** *B.C.Digest* Oct. 59/2: In the morning we got on board a large Chinook canoe, with five Indians and four white men.

Chinook clouds the cloud waves (*lenticularis*) forming the leading or western edge of the Chinook arch, *q.v.*, the constant movement of which is caused by the rising and falling air currents of the Chinook winds pouring over the crest of the Rockies. See also **Chinook sky.**

1954 PATTERSON *Dangerous River* 210: Summer clouds they were, Chinook clouds, spinning because Chinook clouds always spin, though no man has ever been able to tell me why.

Chinook country the region in which Chinook winds prevail. See also **Chinook belt.**

1927 *Beaver* Dec. 117: . . . the buffalo migrated south . . . never to return . . . as the . . . Indians set fire to the prairie, thus preventing their trek to the chinook country in Southern Alberta. . . .

Chinook fever a kind of malaise resembling spring fever, said to be felt by newcomers in Calgary during the balmy winter days brought on by the Chinook winds.

1963 *Calgary Herald* 6 Dec. 4/5: "You're suffering from a typical case of Chinook fever," the doctor said . . . "People coming here from the coast are particularly vulnerable."

Chinook Jargon a relatively simple trade language used by the Indians of the Pacific Coast in their dealings with whites and Indians of other tribes, based on the language of the Chinook Indians; words from Nootka, Salish, French, English, and other languages were adapted to the jargon. See also **Chinook** (def. 2), **jargon, Siwash tongue,** and **trade jargon.**

[**1849** ROSS *Adventures* 348: Besides the foregoing language [Chinookan], there is another lingo, or rather mixed dialect, spoken by the Chinook and other neighbouring tribes; which is generally used in their intercourse with the white.] **1862** MAYNE *Four Years in B.C.* 244: The southern tribes, as a rule, understand the Chinook jargon, in which almost all the intercourse between Indians and whites is at present carried on. **1958** *Beaver* Winter 27/1: Actually, the Chinook jargon

was older than any of the white men. Neither the traders nor missionaries invented it, but both expanded the vocabulary and extended its use. **1964** DUFF *Indian History* 91: . . . Father J. M. Le Jeune . . . printed books and the weekly journal "Kamloops Wawa" in Chinook jargon.

Chinook salmon† a large salmon, *Onchorhynchus tshawytscha,* of the Pacific Coast, much valued as a game fish. See also **Chinook** (def. 4), **king salmon, quinnat, spring salmon,** and **tyee** (def. 3).

1907 LAMBERT *Fishing in B.C.* 74: The king or tyee, quinnat, spring or chinook salmon . . . is the most important from the sportsman's point of view, but owing to the white or very pale pink flesh not so useful to the canner. **1963** *Sun* (Vancouver) 16 Feb. 17/1: Kelly started mooching a herring, caught himself a 10-pound chinook salmon.

Chinook shorthand *Hist.* a set of signs used for writing and printing Chinook Jargon, adapted about 1891 from a French (Duployé) system of shorthand and used as late as 1910. See also **shorthand Chinook.**

1958 *Beaver* Winter 26/2: [Caption] The column in Chinook jargon is repeated in phonetic Chinook shorthand, English, and in a French phonographic version.

Chinook sky a sky characterized by the striking cloud formations framing the Chinook arch, *q.v.* See also **Chinook clouds.**

[**1810** (1897) COUES *New Light* II 661: . . . in the S.W., directly over the Rocky Mountains . . . I have observed the sky to be perfectly clear for many days past, while every other part of the heavens is overcast with thick black clouds.] **1958** *Beaver* Spring 28/1: [The] vaguely luminous cloudscapes of the Pacific have here given way to the riotously magnificent Chinook skies of the eastern foothills.

Chinook wind a warm, usually dry, west or southwest wind, commonest during winter and spring, that moderates the weather in the region east of the Rockies, including much of the western prairies on occasion, but regularly in the foothills from the Peace River to Colorado. See also **Chinook** (def. 3) and **snow-eater.**

1878 *Sask.Herald* (Battleford, N.W.T.) 2 Dec. 2/2: On Saturday, the Chinook wind began to blow. **1966** *Kingston Whig-Standard* (Ont.) 8 Jan. 1/7: In Alberta warm chinook winds allowed many rural schools to open again . . . after a four-day holiday enforced by the cold snap.

Chip *n. Informal* a Chipewyan Indian.

1948 *Beaver* March 13/2: There is today probably no tribe of Canadian Indians more primitive than these northern Manitoba "Chips." **1962** *Time* (Cdn ed.) 20 Apr. 12/2: Said one young [Indian] maiden . . . "I'm a quarter Cree, a quarter Chip, a quarter French, and a quarter Mounted Police."

chip *n. West* a cake of dried buffalo or, later, cow dung, formerly much used on the prairies for fuel. See also **buffalo chip.**

1884 *Brandon Mail* (Man.) 6 Mar. 3/1: This illimitable hayfield is everywhere pitted with buffalo wallows, seamed by . . . buffalo trails, sprinkled with their chips or droppings and whitened with their bones.

c1902 LAUT *Trapper* 175: The free trappers went alone or in pairs . . . cooking meals on chip fires, using slow-burning wormwood bark for matches. . . . **1960** BUBLITZ *Dotted Line* 98: There were no chips or wood around. so we meandered into the schoolhouse.

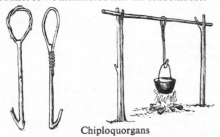

Chiploquorgans

chiploquorgan [ˌtʃɪpləˈkwɔrgən] *n.* [< Algonk.] *N.B.* See quotes. See also **pot-bow** and **squaw pole** (def. 2). Cp. **kettle-stick.**
1872 DASHWOOD *Chiploquorgan* Preface: The word "chiploquorgan" is the Indian name in the Milicite language, for the stick on which the kettle is suspended over the camp fire. . . . *Ibid.* 156: In a double camp the chiploquorgan is different to that used in a single one. . . . A stick is cut of birch or cherry, with a crook in the bottom, the twigs being left at the top, these are twisted so as to form a loop, by which the stick is suspended over the fire from a crossed pole at the top of the camp. **1896** ROBERTS *Around the Camp-Fire* 323: We fixed up the camp to look natural and secure, hung our wet clothes to dry on the cheep lah-quah-gan, closed the tent-door for the night to keep out the mosquitoes, and retired. **1961** *Nfld Qtly* Spring 27/2: The Indians attach a certain degree of superstition to the chiploquorgan, and it is considered most unlucky to burn or remove it on leaving a camp.

chipmunk *n.* [< Algonk; cf. Ojibwa *atchitamon* head first, applied originally to the red squirrel from its way of descending a tree trunk]
☛ *Earlier recorded forms such as* chetamon, chitmunk, *q.v.,* chipmonk, *etc. indicate the influence of folk etymology in shaping the now general form.*
any one of several small striped rodents, resembling squirrels, of the family Sciuridae. See also **hackee** and **striped squirrel.** Cp. **big chipmunk.**
[**1791** (1907) HODGE *Bulletin* I: The Chippewa vocabulary of Long (1791) gives for squirrel *chetamon*. . . .]
1832 (1838) TRAILL *Backwoods of Canada* 112: With the exception of the aforesaid chipmunk, no living thing crossed our path during our . . . journey in the woods. **1961** GREENING *Ottawa* 103: . . . one man had seen a chipmunk playing around the shanty. . . .

Chipmunk *n. Trademark* the first commercial airplane designed and built in Canada.
1957 *Financial Post* 2 Nov. 62/4: In the early postwar years de Havilland was faced with a cutback. But by this time design and development had advanced to the stage where the company was ready with its own airplane—the DHC-1 Chipmunk. This was the first all-Canadian designed and built aircraft. It underwent flight tests in May, 1946. It found immediate favor with the air forces of the world.

chippiness *n. Slang* readiness to fight. See **chippy.**

1962 *National Hockey Annual* 38/2: Mikita has been drawing a great many senseless penalties due to outright chippiness. . . .

chippy *n. Slang* See quote.
1960 *Time* (Cdn ed.) 21 Nov. 79/1: Moore has mellowed since he came up as a 20-year-old "chippy" (jargon for a player with a chip on his shoulder), but he still approaches the game as though it were football on ice.

chippy *adj. Slang* **1** spoiling for an argument; argumentative.
1891 *Grip* (Toronto) 9 May 299/1: Sir John [A. Macdonald was] on hand, chippy as ever. . . .
2 characterized by bad tempers and rough play.
1962 *Kingston Whig-Standard* (Ont.) 8 Feb. 8/6: . . . it was a chippy game which featured some questionable officiating. **1965** *Globe and Mail* (Toronto) 27 Dec. 22/1: Spearing is the sort of chippy crime Shack might commit. . . .

chippy penalty *Hockey, Slang* See **cheap penalty.**
1963 *Globe and Mail* (Toronto) 2 Feb. 23/3: He [the referee] lets everything go and then he calls a chippy penalty against us.

Chirper *n.* [by association with the (*English*) *sparrow*] *Slang* an Englishman, especially a Cockney. See also **Sparrow.**
1965 *Globe and Mail* (Toronto) 15 Nov. 6/6: Has your writer considered the possibility that, in their hesitance to become Canadian citizens . . . a lot of Chirpers are smarter than most people think?

chisel *v.* See 1941 quote. See also **trenching.**
1907 HUNTER *Cdn Wilds* 144: If the lake has drained a foot or two since the ice took it is useless to attempt to chisel, as the beaver can go ashore under the ice anywhere and breathe. **1941** *Beaver* Sep. 37/1: Chiselling Beaver. A method of impounding beaver under the ice and spearing them alive.

chitmunk or **chitmunck** *n. Obs.* See **chipmunk.**
1842 WILLIS *Cdn Scenery* II 70: . . . the shrill whistling cry of the little striped squirrel, called by the natives "chitmunk," was every sound that broke the stillness of the wild. **1853** STRICKLAND *Canada West* I 303: The chitmunck . . . or ground squirrel, is much smaller and more mischievous than any of the former species.

chivaree, chivariri, chivarie *n.* See **shivaree.**

chivirease *n. Obs.* See **chevreuil.**

chix *n.pl.* "chicken" halibut; small halibut, *Hippoglossus stenolepis,* up to ten pounds in weight.
1958 *Fisherman* 15 Aug. 7/4: Halibut landings were fairly heavy and 12 boats landed a total of 688,000 pounds. Chix were sold on the exchange for 14c. . . .
1963 *Ibid.* 7 June 1/1: Fish Prices Chix . . . lb. 16-18c.

choc *interj.* a call to a team of sled dogs. See also **choo.**
1934 GODSELL *Arctic Trader* 39: Then to the vociferous accompaniment of the medley of yells from the Indian drivers—"Choc! Choc! Gee, muchistem!!" . . . the teams sped one by one through the gateway and soon were lost to sight.

chock-and-log fence See quotes.
[**1953** *Cdn Geog.Jnl* Dec. 224/2: Comparatively slender logs, fifteen feet or so in length, were selected and these were supported at each end by "chocks," which were sections of slightly thicker logs, about three feet long. Each chock had two wide notches cut in it, deep enough

to hold the logs, which were so laid that each end of each log was supported by a chock.] *Ibid.*: [Caption] In this chock-and-log fence the logs are held by additional supports.

A chock-and-log fence

chocolate root the purple or water avens, *Geum rivale.*
1822 (1928) CORMACK *Narr.Nfld* 20: And in the running waters are the willow-leaved meadow-sweet, water avens or chocolate root, and so on. **1828** MCGREGOR *Maritime Colonies* 23: ... a decoction of a root, called chocolate root, is used by the Indians as a certain remedy for the severest attack of cholic.

choke *n.* the freezing up of a waterway, choking off traffic.
1920 *Beaver* Dec. 5/2: We were none too early to avoid being locked in the [Hudson] Bay for nine months. Fox Channel is where the "choke" comes earliest.

chokeberry *n.* **1** a species of wild pear, *Pyrus arbutifolia.*
1807 WENTZEL *Letters* 80: The fruits of this solitary region are the ... choakberry, and another berry, the name of which I do not know. ... **1852** RICHARDSON *Arctic Exped.* 428: *P. arbutifolia,* choke-berry, is common in the damp thickets of the Northern States, in Newfoundland, in Canada, and onward to the Saskatchewan.

2 See **chokecherry.**
1852 (1881) TRAILL *Cdn Crusoes* 360: When first lost, she had a large trout, which was the only food she ate, except choke-berries, the first week. ...

chokecherry† *n.* **1** an astringent wild cherry of the genus *Prunus,* especially *P. virginiana.* See also **chokeberry** (def. 2).
1793 (1933) MACDONELL *Diary* 116: The wild plumb ... choak and sand cherries ... are also natives of this [Assiniboine] country. **1886** *Indian* (Hagersville, Ont.) 26 May 111/1: He poured over the meat a thick, reddish-colored ... sauce, which I ... recognized as boiled dried choke-cherries. **1954** PATTERSON *Dangerous River* 174: Cranberries, choke-cherries and the tall wild roses strewed their reds and scarlets in amongst the gold and green. ...

2 the shrubby tree these cherries grow on.
1809 MACKENZIE *Mississouri Indians* 378: ... cutting a green branch of chokecherry and passing it through a piece of fat dried meat, they planted it in the ground close to each pipe. **1961** *Telegram* (Toronto) 19 May 17/1: A ... pair of brown thrashers have taken over a bushy bunch of choke cherries.

choker *n. Lumbering* See 1942 quote. See pictures at **high-lead system** and **skyline.**
1925 *Cdn Labor Advocate* 16 Oct. 11/4: Lights go out at 9 p.m., which means that we all should be in bed recuperating our strength to "wrestle chokers" on the following day. **1942** HAIG-BROWN *Timber* 250: CHOKER. A short length of heavy cable coupled to the main cable (sky line or mainline) and having a hook

attached at the free end. The hook is passed under the log and brought round to hook back on to its cable, thus making a running noose which is drawn tight by the mainline when the engineer starts to bring in the turn. **1963** *Press* Apr. 7: In his salad days, before the War, the irrepressible Grogan took a whirl at setting chokers at Cumeshaw Inlet in the Queen Charlottes.

chokerman *n. Lumbering* the logger who sets the chokers. See also **choker setter.**
1930 *B.C.Lumberman* April 48/1: ... shall the conversation of chokermen and buckers (including the Scandinavian) be charted as to subject matter and then put into graphs? **1958** *Globe Mag.* 5 July 21/1: It isn't necessary here to go into the jobs that a riggin' slinger and his chokerman hold down in the B.C. woods.

choke-rope *n. Hist.* a length of rope used in choking (def. 1).
1795 (1911) SIMCOE *Diary* 269: When Governor Simcoe was driven ... to Detroit he carried these "choke ropes" and had occasion to use them. **1955** COLLARD *Cdn Yesterdays* 302: Some experienced travellers on the river-roads even carried "choke-ropes" to rescue their horses should the sleigh fall through. These ropes were fastened around the horses' necks. If the ice gave way and the passengers succeeded in saving themselves, they would try to seize hold of these ropes and draw them tight. The tightened ropes would prevent the water from rushing into the horses' lungs.

choker setter See **chokerman.**
*c***1930** (1963) *Press* Jan.-Feb. 8: For on the morrow I'll be setting chokers in the snow / Oh! Friends and choker setters, I know it will be tough; / Our caulk shoes will be heavy, the ground is steep and rough.

choking *n.* **1** *Hist.* the practice of temporarily choking off with a rope the breath of a horse floundering in water so that it will not take water into the lungs and drown. See also **choke-rope.**
*a***1820** (1838) HEAD *Forest Scenes* 55: In this dilemma the driver ... slipped a noose of rope round the drowning animal's neck, upon which we pulled till he seemed to be nearly strangled: and this operation is called in the country, very properly, "choking." Whether it was that he floated by means of the air thus forcibly retained in his lungs, as the driver asserted, or whether our united efforts caused him to rise, I cannot say; but so he did; and we had not continued to tug long, before out he slipped on his side, and after a few kicks and struggles, stood frightened and shivering once more on his feet.

2 *Lumbering* the process of handling logs by means of a choker, *q.v.*
1948 *Ont.Timberworker* 15 Aug. 1/2: Choking and Skidding is wholly mechanized by means of Arches or Sulky's pulled by Caterpillars, mostly on level ground.

choo or **chook** *interj.* a call to sled dogs. See also **choc.**
1902 LONDON *Daughter of Snows* 268: "... Ah! Would you? Go on! Chook, Miriam! Chook! The thing is to get the first one [sleigh dog] across." **1913** COWIE *Adventurers* 248: Seresto ... swerved, in spite of my yelling "Choo", to the right, off the trail he had been following. ...

chop *v. Obs.* clear a farm in the bush by removing the trees.

1821 (1960) McCULLOCH *Stepsure Letters* 21: The house and barn could stand for a year; and, instead of chopping upon his farm, he could have another great lot of timber ready by the spring. **1832** PICKERING *Inquiries* 107: If not preserved at all, land can be hired, to be chopped, logged, burned, and fenced at from 45s to 52s per acre.

chopper *n.* **1** a man employed to fell trees and clear bush land for cultivation.
1828 (1832) PICKERING *Inquiries* 107: A good chopper will chop an acre of moderately heavy timber in a week. . . . **1960** NIX *Mission* 16: Hitherto he had had local fame [in Upper Canada] as a "chopper"—a mighty man with an axe. . . .
2 *Lumbering* a skilled axeman, *q.v.*
1854 KEEFER *Ottawa* 60: The hay cutters then proceed to the timber grove to make ready for the choppers, hewers and scorers. . . . **1881** *Progress* (Rat Portage [Kenora], Ont.) 5 Nov. 4/1: About fifty choppers arrived by Wednesday's train, en route for the tie camps. **1964** *Cdn Geog.Jnl* Feb. 66/3: Felling was done with an axe by men called choppers.

chopping *n. Hist.* **1** the operation of cutting down trees in clearing a farm in the bush.
1832 (1953) RADCLIFF *Letters* 48: . . . we had cleared twenty acres of the land for wheat, and during the successive operations of brushing, chopping, logging, burning and fencing—my father was obliged to hire workmen. **1912** HEENEY *Pickanock* 195: . . . at this moment in sprang Harry, black from the chopping. **1963** GUILLET *Pioneer Farmer* I 335: A logging bee logically followed a chopping, but it was often delayed till summer.
2 a holding of bush land cleared or being cleared of trees to make it ready for cultivation; also, the trees felled on such land.
1834 (1926) LANGTON *Early U.C.* 108: My choppers had not yet returned and as we had a few days of dry weather I was afraid to lose the opportunity and resolved to burn their chopping without them. **1852** *Elora Backwoodsman* (C.W.) 1 Sep. 2/5: The spring was middling dry and I had a good burn on the highest part of the chopping. **1896** GOURLAY *Hist.Ottawa* 116: . . . he hastily constructed a block house of a few logs from the chopping.

chopping bee or **frolic†** *Hist.* **1** a communal land-clearing accompanied or followed by eating, drinking, and dancing. See also **bee** and **frolic.**
1821 (1960) McCULLOCH *Stepsure Letters* 19: . . . Jack was a likely, clever-handed fellow, and could chop more in a day than any of his neighbours. But this was a kind of work of which, except at a chopping frolic, he was never very fond. **1828** McGREGOR *Maritime Colonies* 74: When a farmer or a new settler wants a piece of wood cut down, he procures a few gallons of rum to drink on the occasion, and sends for his neighbours to assist him in levelling the forest: this is . . . called a chopping frolic.
2 See 1931 quote.
1890 *Regina Jnl* 18 Dec. 1/2: Come to the chopping bee and bring your axe. **1931** SEARY *Romance* 177: There were . . . "chopping frolics" for chopping and piling the winter's supply of firewood.

chopstuff *n.* ground or chopped feed for livestock.
1932 JAMESON *Cattle in the Stall* 2: [The trough] still held

chopstuff from the last feeding—and the geese were at it, as though they had never left it.

choreboy *n.* a handyman, especially around a lumber camp, ranch, etc. See also **boy cook.**
1891 OXLEY *Chore-Boy* 26: "I don't quite like the idea of his being a chore-boy. . . ." **1957** *Fish and Game* 30 Aug. 11/2: [He] accompanies him on fishing trips and . . . has gradually slipped into the role of camp-cook and chore-boy. **1967** *Globe and Mail* (Toronto) 14 Mar. B7/9: For example, with the substantial adoption of the new machines . . . there will be sharp declines in requirements for pulpwood cutters, teamsters, roadmen and swampers, laborers, cooks, cookees, and choreboys. . . .

Chouayen *n.* [< Cdn F; see 1904 quote] *Hist.* a derogatory name given to the French-Canadian supporters of the British governing group in Lower Canada.
1848 (1866) CHRISTIE *Lower Canada* I 313: The province, by this time, from the agitation that had arisen, was divided into two distinct parties . . . the one set characterising their opponents by the odious cant terms of *"anti-canadiens, choyens,* or *anglais"*—those of *"frenchmen, democrats, bouteféus,"* being as freely and indeed angrily bestowed in return by the other class. **1904** DeCELLES *Papineau* 68: As to those of the French Canadians who sided with the Bureaucrats and l'oligarchie, they were dubbed Chouayens. The origin of the word is thus explained: At the taking of Oswego, called Chouagen, by the French led by Montcalm, some militiamen deserted, and were afterwards called Chouauens. . . . Etienne Parent was the first to apply this soubriquet to those pusillanimous or cowardly countrymen who refused to follow Papineau.

chou creux *Cdn French* "hollow cabbage" the cow parsnip, *Heracleum lanatum.*
1824 (1955) BLACK *Journal* 12: They have a large Bundle of a kind of Water Hemlock (but not poisonous) & what the Canadians call Chou Creux. **1925** ANDERSON *Trees and Shrubs* 127: This plant, called "Chou Creux" by the French-Canadians, belongs to the Umbelliferae.

choyen *n.* See **Chouayen.**

Christian pack *Fur Trade, Obs.* a white man's pack, as opposed to an Indian's.
1793 (1937) CAMPBELL *Travels* 196: . . . having put my furs and other goods, consisting of five Christian packs, chiefly Deer-skins a-board of my boat, proceeded with them to Niagara.

Christie *n.* See **Christy.**

Christie stiff See **Christy.**
1909 CAMERON *New North* 162: With one accord come off their Glengarry bonnets, smoking caps, and Christie stiffs, and a row of brown hands is extended to greet us. **1965** BERTON *Remember Yesterday* 65: The popular derby hat, or Christy Stiff, will be in vogue until 1915.

Christmas Boy *Local, Obs.* See quote.
1948 BORRETT *Historic Halifax* 30: One of these bands of young men and boys had adopted the name of "Christmas Boys" and had been roaming the streets at that season molesting citizens.

Christmas tree a party held at Christmastime and sponsored by a church, school, etc.
1882 *Brandon Dly Mail* (Man.) 26 Dec. 4/1: The children . . . intend having a Xmas tree . . . at the church. **1916** BRIDLE *Sons of Canada* 28: No, he is up at the Hospital Christmas tree. . . . *c***1958** TUCK *Pouce Coupe*

26: Money for School Christmas Trees, which always ended in a dance, was raised by means of box socials mostly. **1965** *North* Nov.-Dec. 26/2: They . . . went to the hall for [the] Christmas tree. . . . all the kids were excited. . . .

Christmas tree plantation a farm devoted to the growing of evergreen trees to supply the demand for Christmas trees.

1958 *Edmonton Jnl* 31 July 20/3: . . . thousands of farmers in all parts of Canada where Christmas tree plantations are a lively . . . business are right now out in the blazing sun. . . . **1964** *Canadian Wkly* 5 Dec. 1/2: Delighted youngsters drag their choice from a Christmas tree farm at Aurora, Ont.

Christy or **Christie** ['krıstı] *n.* [prob. < *Christy* & *Co.*, an English hat manufacturer] a derby or bowler hat. Also spelled *christy*.

1887 *Grip* (Toronto) 26 Feb. 11/2: When this poser is speaking, I look one of the supporters to rise and hang his christy upon one of the extended limbs. **1958** ALLEN *Peace River Country* 89: He hung his new Christie on the wall and took a seat halfway down the empty lunch counter.

chuck[1] [tʃʌk] *n.* [< Chinook Jargon < Nootka *ch'a'ak* fresh water] *West Coast* **1** water.

1860 *British Colonist* (Victoria) 17 May 2/2: The engine seemed to work well, and threw a very fair stream, although the "chuck" was not of the sweetest description. **1958** WATTERS *B.C.Cent.Anthol.* 214: "Chuck" is a Chinook jargon for "water". . . .

2 a. any body of water.

1880 DAWSON *Queen Charlotte Is.* 30: The most considerable is that which has been called the Slate Chuck on the chart. **1958** *Beaver* Winter 26/2: A mother in Stanley Park [Vancouver] scolds, "Johnny, throw that dirty stick in the *chuck*."

b. See **salt-chuck.**

1926 *Cdn Labor Advocate* 15 Apr. 4/4: The "chuck" could be greatly improved by "chucking" the cook in the "chuck." **1954** EVANS *Mist* 55: Pay no attention to him; tell him to go jump in the chuck. **1959** *Northwest Digest* Dec. 38/3: . . . the logger speaks of dumping logs in the chuck.

chuck[2] [tʃʌk] *n.* *West* food; grub; a meal.

1889 *Rat Portage* [Kenora] *News* (Ont.) 22 Feb. 1/7: Why don't they put up at a regular hotel, and not go around "bumming their chuck" on private people, and on those "good sisters" and "good brothers." **1963** *B.C.Digest* Nov.-Dec. 63/1: For all those 53 years he . . . ate chuck that would give a dietician ulcers.

chuck driver *Informal* a driver in a chuckwagon race, *q.v.*

1964 *Calgary Herald* 8 July 25/3: Now 36, Hally has been a chuck driver since he was 18. . . .

'chucker ['tʃʌkər] *n.* See **salt-chucker.**

1963 *Sun* (Vancouver) 25 June 15/1: Mrs. Eileen Tobias . . . caught her first salmon . . . among the flurry that brought joy to many another surprised 'chucker Sunday. . . .

chuckwagon† *n.* **1** *West* a wagon used by ranch hands for carrying cooking gear and provisions needed while camping on the trail or on the open range.

1923 STEELE *Spirit-of-Iron* 252: In a little gully beside the chuck-wagon, the cook was boiling coffee. **1963** *Maclean's* 9 Feb. 26/2: Stringer was . . . at home

eating sow-belly off the tailboard of an Alberta chuck wagon.

2 a wagon used in chuckwagon races, *q.v.*

1957 HUTCHISON *Canada* 251: It was a fine chuckwagon, in perfect order, gaily painted and quite useless on a modern ranch. **1964** *Albertan* (Calgary) 7 July 1/6: At night chuck-wagons bogging in heavy mud buckled wheels and several teams fell.

chuckwagon dinner a western-style dinner of beef and vegetable stew.

1964 *Maclean's* 4 Apr. 23/1: The Johnstons . . . are fond of ten-gallon hats, chuck-wagon dinners and hootenanny music.

chuck-wagon outfit the wagon, horses, driver, outriders, *q.v.*, and equipment constituting an entry in a chuckwagon race.

1958 *Edmonton Jnl* 24 June 2 20/1: At least 20 to 25 chuck-wagon outfits have indicated their intention to enter. **1964** *Albertan* (Calgary) 7 July 15/6: He's driving two chuckwagon outfits [and] will probably outride for a couple more. . . .

chuckwagon race a type of race popular at the stampedes and rodeos of Western Canada. See 1950 quote.

1950 SUTTON *Footloose in Canada* 211: In a chuck wagon race the entrants are required at a given signal to break an entire camp—including a burning stove—load all the paraphernalia in a wagon, do a series of figure eights around barrels, and then ride once around the track. **1962** *Kingston Whig-Standard* (Ont.) 9 Oct. 6/1: A special feature of the Kingston Harness Horsemen's final meet of the season was a chuck wagon race at the Memorial Centre Monday.

chum[1] *n.* [prob. < Chinook Jargon *tzum* spotted] See **dog salmon.**

1920 *Book of Canada* 121: . . . the large dog-salmon, or "Chum," 4 lbs. to 15 lbs., dies at the end of three, four, five or six years. . . . **1962** *Co-op Grocery News Bull.* 1 Aug. 1: Formerly known as dog salmon, the chum . . . has also been called the qualla, keta and calico salmon. It is caught all along the coast of British Columbia.

chum[2] *n.* See **chummie.**

1883 FRASER *Shanty* 126: And so the trapper has always to be on guard as to his fur property, both about his camp and in the traps—hence the "chum" business. They always trap in couples. **1925** CLARKE *Chris in Can.* 208: It might be that his chum was working down that side of ridge. . . .

chummie *n.* one of two men who join forces on the trail or in the bush, as two trappers who always work together. See also **chum**[2].

1965 *Islander* 30 May 6/2: As these trail companionships were styled, these two were "chummies."

chum salmon See **dog salmon.**

1954 EVANS *Mist* 80: Most were chum salmon, hook nosed, dark of belly, and soon to spawn. . . . **1964** *Dly Colonist* (Victoria) 6 Oct. 7/8: Chum salmon landings at Prince Rupert last week were more than triple the number reported for the same week in 1963. . . .

chunking *n.* *Obs.* See quote.

1905 SCHERCK *Early Pioneer Life* 48: The chunks which remained after this second burning were collected by the farmer and his men (the women folks and children often assisted at the "chunking") into little piles, and once more set afire and kept burning by heaping up the burning fragments and pieces of log until they were all reduced to ashes.

Churchill buffalo *Obs*. See **musk-ox.**
1784 PENNANT *Arctic Zoology* 10: These are called Churchill Buffaloes, to distinguish them from the last species, which are in Hudson's Bay called Inland Buffaloes, of which only the tongues are brought as presents.

church parlo(u)rs *West* in some churches, the room or rooms used for social gatherings, as a waiting room, etc.
1957 *Melville Advance* 17 Apr. 12/4: A busy afternoon was spent by the ladies of St. Paul's Lutheran Church when they served their final coffee of the Lenten season, in the church parlors, on Friday afternoon. **1958** *Edmonton Jnl* 14 Aug. 36/1: The congregation of Stettler United Church gathered in the church parlors to bid farewell to [them].

Church Reserves *Hist*. See **Clergy Reserves.**
1798 (1935) RUSSELL *Correspondence* II 60: The immediate consequence of such a plan will be, to raise the value of the Crown and Church Reserves. . . .

chute *n*. [< F] **1** See **shoot** (def. 1).
1793 (1933) MacDONELL *Diary* 71: [We] slept at the *chute a Blondeau*. **1824** (1955) BLACK *Journal* 206: These high banks prevail to the approach of the Chutes or falls in Peace River. **1883** FRASER *Shanty* 302: These places are called "chutes," and are generally narrow, crooked, and precipitous descents of the river. . . . **1965** *Islander* 14 Nov. 13/1: The river leaves Isaac Lake by a short fast chute. . . .
2 See **riffle** (def. 1c).
1819 (1939) ROBERTSON *Correspondence* 87: I perceived the canoe avoid the rapid and enter a shute. **1956** KEMP *Northern Trader* 37: [We met with] a long, oily chute, black as frozen molasses, white water on each side of us and white water ahead.
3 *Lumbering* See **slide,** *n*. (def. 1a).
1903 WHITE *Forest* 136: . . . a dozen rivermen, one after the other, would often go through the chute of a dam standing upright on single logs. **1947** SAUNDERS *Algonquin* 44: On Porcupine Lake a dam had been built to control the flow of water, and the chute itself was nineteen hundred and fourteen feet long.

Chyma or **Chymo** *interj*. See **chimo.**

cigarette dude *West, Slang* a city slicker. See also **dude.**
1910 FRASER *Red Meekins* 98: "Don't look much like one of 'em cigarette dudes, does he?" Peloo commented. "A chaw of niggerhead tobaccer'd be more in his line."

cinereous crow *Obs*. See **Canada jay.**
1795 (1911) HEARNE *Journey* 405: The Cinereous Crow, or . . . Whisky-Jack . . . is in reality so small, seldom as to weigh three ounces. **1820** (1823) FRANKLIN *Journey* 247: The summer birds by this time had entirely deserted us, leaving for our winter companions, the raven, cinereous crow, ptarmigan, and snow-bird. **1853** REID *Young Voyageurs* 388: On looking up, they beheld . . .

the "cinereous crow" . . . or, as it is better known, the "whiskey jack."

cinnamon bear a subspecies of the black bear, *q.v.* See 1964 quote. See also **yellow bear.**
1821 (1823) FRANKLIN *Journey* 648: Individuals vary in colour from black to different shades of brown, and are known to the traders under the different names of Black, Brown, Cinnamon, and Grey Bears. **1956** CAMERON *Guide to Mammals* 18: Black Bear . . . Black or dark brown is the usual colour, but there is a rarer colour phase known as the "cinnamon bear," which is light buff. **1964** *Wildlife Rev.* Dec. 21: [The] cinnamon bear of the interior of British Columbia is another geographic race of the same species [*Ursus americanus*], one of its subspecific characteristics is the occurrence of a brown colour phase.

circle *n*. **1** *Hist*. in colonial Canada, an electoral district; riding; constituency.
1790 *George III* c.31 s.XIV: [Act of Parliament] [The Governor or Lieutenant-Governor of each of the provinces is authorized] to issue a Proclamation dividing such Province into Districts, or Counties, or Circles, and Towns or Townships, and appointing the Limits thereof, and declaring and appointing the Number of Representatives to be chosen by each of such Districts, or Counties or Circles, and Towns or Townships, respectively. . . . **1805** *U.C.Gaz.* (York [Toronto]) 26 Jan. 3/1: Mr. Weeks avails himself of this public manner of soliciting the support of the FREE and INDEPENDENT Electors . . . to represent the inhabitants of this Circle in Parliament. **1828** *Vindicator* (Montreal) 23 Dec. 1/4: Nothing [is] herein contained to prevent the courts of the King's bench from proceeding to the trial before juries of the circles. **1902** *London and Middlesex Hist.Soc.Trans.* I 21: These districts were sub-divided into counties, or "circles," though the latter title appears to have been used only in some official documents.
2 *North, Informal* the Arctic Circle.
1920 *Beaver* Oct. 15/1: We saw no stars from early June until leaving the "circle" again August 7th.

cisco† ['sɪsko] *n*. [< Cdn. F, shortening of *ciscoette, ciscaouette, sisquoette* < Ojibwa; cf. **siskawet**] any of several varieties of whitefish, *Leucichthys* sp., especially *L. artedi,* found in central and northern Canada. Also spelled *siscoe.*
1917 *Grit* (Toronto) 7 Dec. 2/7: The fish man had as today's special . *:.* ciscoes 20 cents a pound. **1958** *Cdn Geog.Jnl* Sep. 96/2: The 1944 surveys [in Great Slave Lake were] based mainly on whitefish . . . lake trout . . . and ciscoes. . . .

citizen court See quote.
1961 *Telegram* (Toronto) 19 May 46/1: Citizen courts are perhaps the only courts in Canada Canadians are proud to attend for they are the courts where New Canadians take the oath of allegiance to the Queen and become full Canadian citizens.

citizen picket a person who, though not a union member, pickets in sympathy with union members forbidden to picket by injunction. See also **mystery picket.**
1962 *Oily Bird* Dec. 2/2: Naturally the employers and the provincial government disapprove very strongly of the united support that has developed in labor's ranks. They don't like the citizen picket lines. . . . **1963** *Canada Month* Apr. 29: . . . when an injunction is slapped on a striking union, we . . . often move in as unpaid citizen pickets.

civic block the building in which a City Hall and other municipal offices are located.
1958 *Edmonton Jnl* 31 July 3/4: Edmonton's archives and landmarks committee Wednesday urged the civic administration to secure someone to supervise the historical exhibit being established in the civic block.

civic holiday a holiday established by a city ordinance.
1883 *Selkirk Herald* (Man.) 3 Aug. 3/2: It is thought that arrangements could be made to have the celebration take place on the same day that Winnipeg civic holiday will be held. **1903** *Eye Opener* (High River, Alta) 22 Aug. 1/6: It was thought better to play two games today as Thursday is a civic holiday.

civil *adj. Nfld* of weather, fair or good.
1905 DUNCAN *Grenfell's Parish* 109: It was a mere puff on a "civil" evening—but a swift, wicked little puff, sweeping round Breakheart Head. . . . **1907** MILLAIS *Newfoundland* 212: "No, I think it's goin' to be civil," argued Frank. . . . **1944** *Beaver* Sep. 23/1: [Caption] On a "civil" day in October, Baxter John and his boys arrive . . . to sell their dried fish.

civil list *Hist.* in colonial Canada, a list of monies to be appropriated for the civil administration of a province, including the salaries of the governor, executive councillors, judges, civil servants, under the control of the British Parliament.
1819 *Kingston Chron.* (U.C.) 23 Apr. 2/5: The discussion on the new Civil List commenced last evening and will be resumed on Saturday. **1963** MORTON *Kingdom of Canada* 231: In the matter of supply it [the Select Committee] recommended that the Assembly be given full control except for a "civil list" to cover the salaries of the governor, the executive councillors and the judges, the amount to be voted for the life of the king and not annually.

clah-how-yah *n.* See **klahowya** (def. 1).

clamon or **clemen(t)** *n.* [< Salish: Tillamook] *Hist.* See quotes. Also spelled *clemal.*
1811 (1849) ROSS *Adventures* 89: Their war garments are of two kinds, one is termed clemal, of elk-skin, dressed and worked to the thickness of nearly half an inch and arrow proof. The clemal nearly covers the whole of the body, with an opening left on the right side to allow the arm free action in combat. **1814** (1897) COUES *New Light* II 858: They [the Tillamook] brought to trade some clemens, or war garments of thick red deer skins, dressed in the grain with urine. **1834** (1963) TOLMIE *Physician* 296: . . . several clement skins were also bestowed amongst the guests—this is a dressed elk skin of great size—it must come originally from the interior —two are equal in value to a blanket. **1942** *B.C.Hist. Qtly* July 165: They [Pacific Coast trading ships] even dealt in the products of the Coast itself: clamons, (native armour of tanned elk or moose hide). . . .

clamper *n.* one of the large chunks of ice that pile up on the shore, especially during spring break-up. See also **clumpet** and **ice clamper.**
1960 *Maclean's* 9 Apr. 22/1: When the break-up comes, it is the most awaited moment in the seasonal life of the Saskatchewan. The ice cracks, the clampers sometimes pile up a dozen feet high. . . .

classical college *Que.* an educational establishment at the secondary-school and college levels that offers a seven- or eight-year course, mainly in the classics and liberal arts, leading to the B.A. degree, which is conferred by the university to which the college is affiliated. The Séminaire de Québec, founded in 1663, was the first classical college. See also **collège classique.**
1957 PHILLIPS *Education* 203/1: The traditional secondary school was the college classique, or classical college, offering to entrants who had had elementary education, a course of about eight years leading to the baccalaureate, or a shorter course of much less prestige including some commercial subjects. The classical colleges were financed by fees, by contributions of former pupils, especially clergy, and by income from property or from agriculture. They were controlled by regents, including professors, who were almost all members of the clergy. **1965** *Globe and Mail* (Toronto) 21 Jan. 2/5: Pierre Boucher . . . testified . . . there was tension among his fellow students at the Roman Catholic classical college here after the college receptionist-doorman was beaten to death last April.

classical education *Que.* an education received in a classical college, *q.v.*
1962 *Globe and Mail* (Toronto) 13 Dec. 6/1: A classical education doesn't tend to fit into our type of situation. Most young French graduates have wanted a profession. **1965** KILBOURN *Making of Nation* 36/1: Besides his French classical education he [Laurier] had gone for two years to an English-speaking school, and had read law at McGill.

clatawa *n.v.* See **klatawa.**

clay belt a large tract of land in Northern Ontario and Quebec lying south of James Bay and north of the Laurentian Plateau.
1916 SKELTON *Railway Builders* 239: This railway, striking up from North Bay into the mineral region and clay belt beyond the height-of-land, was begun by the Ontario government in 1902 as a colonization road. **1961** GREENING *Ottawa* 144: B. J. Mulligan . . . was impressed by the fertility of the clay belt . . . near the present-day town of Haileybury.

clay cat *Obs.* rolls or blocks of wet clay used as bricks in the building of one kind of chimney in colonial times. See also **cat²**. Cp. **mud chimney.**
1853 STRICKLAND *Canada West* II 181: The clay-cats are then kneaded strongly round the rings, and all the interstices well filled up; some well-tempered clay is plastered inside the chimney, which . . . soon hardens and reddens by the heat of the fire.

clean *adj. Nfld* See quotes.
1883 HATTON & HARVEY *Newfoundland* 91: It is no uncommon occurrence for a hundred vessels to be thus beset by heavy ice, through which no passage can be forced. Some are "nipped," some crushed to atoms, and the men have to escape . . . over the ice. Others are carried into the great northern bays, or borne in the heavy "pack" up and down on the ocean for weeks, returning to port "clean"—that is without a single seal. **1933** GREENE *Wooden Walls* xvi: CLEAN [is] the term used when no sculps at all are taken. . . .

clean house *Curling* knock all the opponents' rocks out of the scoring ring, or house.
1964 *Calgary Herald* 20 Mar. 16/8: After that the Canadians cleaned house and Torrance was heavy with his last draw.

clean the ring See **clean house.**
1911 KNOWLES *Singer* 277: . . . you may be asked, at a

distance of near one hundred and forty feet . . . to clean the ring with a stone.

clearance *n. Hist.* a tract of bushland cleared for cultivation or settlement; also, a settlement on such land. Cp. **clearing** (def. 1).

1822 *U.C.Gaz.* (York [Toronto]) 23 May 47/3: Afterwards, when the whole projected clearance was made . . . it became necessary to attack the reserved, and standing trees. . . . **1852** *Elora Backwoodsman* (C.W.) 15 July 1/4: The little *clearance,* as they call it, what a very state of confusion it is! **1908** *London & Middlesex Hist.Soc.Trans.* 31: The logs gathered from the clearance were piled around.

Clear Grit [< Am.E *clear grit* obstinate, unflinching] *Hist.* a supporter of the movement which took form as the Clear Grit Party; an adherent of the Clear Grit Party, *q.v.* See also **Grit**.

1849 *Dundas Warden* (C.W.) 9 Aug. 2/7: Though it is highly desirable to carry some of the objects of the "clear grits" into effect, the circumstances of their coquetting with the ULTRA TORY party is sufficient to excite suspicion, and to put real Reformers on their guard. **1906** LEWIS *George Brown* 40: Yet in all the history of a quarrelsome period in politics there is no more violent quarrel than that between Brown and the Clear Grits. **1963** *New Democrat* Jan. 8/1: The Clear Grits [1850's] were the first to hear the cry: "Why don't you merge with the Liberals?"

Clear Gritism *Hist.* the principles and policies of the Clear Grits; the platform of the Clear Grit Party. See also **Gritism**.

1850 *Wkly Globe* 25 Oct. 3/2: This is terrible, and seems as if the Globe itself were turning towards "Clear Gritism." **1857** *Vindicator* (Quebec) 12 Dec. 2/1: Mr. Holton's address is now before the public and we have a gentle hint of what Clear-Gritism means—at least, in Montreal.

Clear Grit Party *Hist.* a liberal reform party in Upper Canada, beginning as a faction of the Reform party in the late 1840's and fielding candidates in the elections of the 1850's and ultimately merging with the Liberal Party, *q.v.,* which is still known informally as the Grits. See also **Grit Party**.

1851 (1924) *Cdn Hist.Rev.* V 260: The clear-grit party will either make a sweep or a smash. **1963** *Time* (Cdn ed.) 1 Mar. 12/2: The Mulocks swung their weight in the Clear Grit party, ran an iron works and accumulated millions.

clearing *n.* **1** *Hist.* **a.** a farm on cleared land in the bush. See also **bush clearing**.

1822 (1960) MCCULLOCH *Stepsure Letters* 69: [The constable's] little clearing was not in good order; and one day when he was from home, serving an ejectment, Mr. Bullock's oxen came along, and . . . took peaceable possession of his grain. **1852** *Anglo-American Mag.* Sep. 198/2: An emigrant, intending to farm and having some means at his command, will find it advisable to rent a "clearing" for some time before purchasing. **1926** LANGTON *Early U.C.* xxxiii: The gentlemen's topics were:—crops and clearings, lumber, price of wheat, road mending, deer shooting, logburning, etc.

b. a settlement, village or town in the bush.

1855 *Hamilton Gaz.* (C.W.) 29 Oct. 2/6: The Times of little London announces that the citizens of that thriving village have it in contemplation to apply to Parliament for a less ambitious, and mock heroic name for the clearing. **1916** BRIDLE *Sons of Canada* 150: Carman was born in a clearing in eastern Ontario.

2 a stretch of bush land devoid of trees for some natural reason.

1902 ROBERTS *Kindred of the Wild* 145: . . . in the heart of the same deep-wooded wilderness, stood a long, low-roofed log cabin, on the edge of a narrow clearing. **1948** ONRAET *Sixty Below* 94: Most of the time while hunting a moose, he will hear or smell you before you see him, and then he is away like a streak, crashing through bush and undergrowth unless he happens to cross a small lake or clearing. **1956** EVANS *Mountain Dog* 41: Hal poled close to the bank, which hid him from anyone who might be in the clearing.

clearing pass *Hockey* a forward pass of the puck intended to get it out of the defending team's end of the rink.

1963 *Globe and Mail* (Toronto) 12 Jan. 27/6: He scored on a pass from Tremblay who had trapped a clearing pass by McNeill inside the Detroit blue line. **1967** *Globe and Mail* (Toronto) 2 Jan. 20/7: A Leaf clearing pass was halted by Mohns, who shot the puck to Makita.

clemal *n.* See **clamon**.

clergy-block *n. Obs.* See **Clergy Reserve** (def. 1).

1853 STRICKLAND *Canada West* I 217: Mr. Galt and the accountant both expressed themselves much pleased with what I had done, especially with the bridge connecting the clergy-block (now called the township of Puslinch) with the town of Guelph.

Clergy Lands *Hist.* See **Clergy Reserves**.

1836 *St.Catharines Jnl* (U.C.) 3 Nov. 3/1: In the first place, a long anonymous feeler, on the subject of the Clergy and School Lands in Upper Canada, comes out. . . .

clergy lot *Obs.* See **Clergy Reserve** (def. 1).

1847 *Bytown* [Ottawa] *Gaz.* 6 Nov. 3/6: I have seized and taken in execution . . . what is commonly known as the Clergy Lot to the Concession Line C.

clergy reservations *Obs.* See **Clergy Reserves**.

1815 BOUCHETTE *Lower Canada* 258: The remainder of it is more irregularly divided and appropriated in Crown and clergy reservations, in large portions, or blocks, as they are technically termed.

Clergy Reserve *Hist.* **1** a lot or subdivision of land belonging to the Clergy Reserves, *q.v.*

1813 (1955) CRAIG *Early Travellers* 41: The rent of these lots, called Clergy reserves, is given to the Clergy to the amount of $800 a year. **1855** (1926) LANGTON *Early U.C.* 229: Clergy reserves are sold on ten years credit.

2 in British Columbia, a tract of land set aside for the support and maintenance of the clergy.

1854 (1894) BEGG *Hist.of B.C.* 331: But from returns to the Imperial Parliament just received, it appears that a Clergy Reserve of two thousand one hundred and eighteen acres of land has been set apart in Victoria district alone. . . .

clergy-reserve block *Obs.* See **Clergy Reserve** (def. 1).

1853 STRICKLAND *Canada West* I 235: . . . I came upon a tolerably fresh blazed line, which I suspected was the boundary between the townships of Guelph and the Clergy-reserve-block of Puslinch.

Clergy Reserves *Hist.* those lands, comprising one-seventh of each township in Upper Canada and parts of Lower Canada, reserved by the Crown in the Canada Act of 1791 for the support and maintenance of the clergy of the Church of England. See also **Church Reserves, reserve** (def. 1), and **Reserve.** Cp. **school lands.**

1799 *U.C.Gaz.* (York [Toronto]) 28 Sep. 4/3: The Townships ... in the Western District of this Province, are to be sold in lots of three thousand Acres each, exclusive of the Crown and Clergy Reserves. **1831** *Colonial Patriot* (Pictou, N.S.) 7 May 1/3: We are told that the Clergy Reserves, are intended only to endow the clergy of the Established Church, and that no Presbyterians or other dissenters have anything to do with them.... **1963** MORTON *Kingdom of Canada* 295: The new ministry [1854] at once carried the secularization of the Clergy Reserves and the abolition of seigniorial tenure, with compensation....

clerk *n.* **1** *Fur Trade* a junior officer of a company, often appointed to the charge of a small trading post; occasionally in charge of a substantial district. See also **commis.**

1765-75 (1933) POND *Narrative* 44: I had Nine Clarks which I Imploid in differant Rivers that fel into the River. **1852** RICHARDSON *Arctic Exped.* 274: Many of the young men so educated have entered the Hudson's Bay Company service as clerks, and some have attained the rank of chief traders and chief factors. **1905** (1954) *B.C.Hist.Qtly* 167: My present position was that of a $500 a year "clerk" in charge of a station of some importance.... The next highest grade was that of a chief trader. The next grade in the service, lower than that of "clerk" was "postmaster"—a class of non-commissioned officers, usually from the rank and file....

2 *Obs.* the purser on a passenger boat.

1834 *Canadian Freeman* (York [Toronto]) 24 July 4/2: All baggage and small parcels are to be considered at the risk of the owners, unless delivered on board in charge of the Clerk.

climbing skins See quote.

1958 *Evening Telegram* (St. John's) 28 Apr. 5/4: Equipment includes a knapsack for food and extra clothing, and climbing skins—strips of fur or plush strapped to the bottom of the skiis. They give traction in climbing slopes that otherwise would have to be mounted in the arduous herring-bone or side-step.

clod-buster *n. Slang* a farmer.

1954 TYRE *Saddlebag Surgeon* 141: You'll ... end up marrying a clod-buster's daughter and spend the rest of your life raising chickens....

clod-busting *adj. Slang* farming.

1961 MITCHELL *Jake and the Kid* 98: "... You are the biggest ... two-handed ... clod-busting liar I have ever known!"

cloosh *n.* See **kloshe.**

Clootchman *n.* See **kloochman.**

close season *Obs.* See quote.

1897 GOODMAN *Gold Fields* 7: "Close season" shall mean the period of the year during which placer mining is generally suspended.

clo(o)sh *adj.* See **kloshe.**

Clote Scarpe See **Glooscap.**

clothe *v. Fur Trade, Obs.* invest an Indian hunter as a captain (def. 2). See also **clothing.**

1773 (1908) COCKING *Journal* 118: The French man ... cloathed 2 Leaders with a Coat & Hat. **1795** (1929) MCGILLIVRAY *Journal* 74: And before night [I] clothed the following Chiefs.... [**1929** *Ibid.* 74n: This ceremony consisted in giving a coat, usually of calico, and other garments and a tall hat and flag, the symbols of headship. Chiefs whose bands had been indolent and had not hunted and were not able to pay their credits were deprived of their position by withholding these symbols of office.]

clothing *n. Fur Trade, Obs.* a gaudy outfit (tall hat, coat laced with tinsel, and so on) presented to the leading hunter of a band as an inducement to bring in more fur. See also **captain's coat.**

1794 (1929) MCGILLIVRAY *Journal* 50: A young Chief desirous of tracing the footsteps of his father; And as a first mark of his quality Mr. Shaw has indulged him with a cloathing. **1801** (1933) MCLEOD *Diary* 176: I clothed [the corpse] with a chiefs cloathing, vizt coat, shirt, Hatt, & Trowsers.

cloudberry *n.* See **bakeapple.**

1892 (1948) *Beaver* June 44/2: Later on I came to the muskeg ... cranberries and cloud-berries.... **1942** HARDY *Edible Plants of B.C.* 23: Cloud Berry ... when fully ripe is juicy and pleasant to the taste.

cloudhopper *n. Slang* an airplane pilot, especially a bush pilot, *q.v.*

1959 LEISING *Arctic Wings* 170: Remember, it is better to have a red face with a few scars of humiliation, and live to be an old pilot than to die a bold smooth-faced young cloudhopper.

clout *n. Obs.* See **breechcloth.**

1824 (1955) BLACK *Journal* 113: They rose to great animation or rather fury springing up loosing & droping now & then part of their cloathing until naked to the clout when they began to dance with such vigour & spirit their bunches of Feathers & matted hair moving time, writhing & twisting themselves into such antic positions & such ferocious contortions of countinance that they perhaps fairly undo the War dances of the Iroquois....

clucker *n.* the two shells of a scallop still joined at the hinge after the scallop has died naturally.

1955 *Fisheries Research Board Jnl* XII 811: Numbers of empty shells, called "cluckers" by the fishermen, are brought up in the drags among the living scallops.... *Ibid.*: The size of the population of living scallops and cluckers may be judged from the catches of each.

clumpet ['klʌmpət] *n.* [< *clump, clumper* a shapeless mass, a lump] *Nfld* one of the large chunks of ice formed during break-up. See also **clamper.**

1835 WIX *Journal* 62: I came out at Bay de l'Argent, by three P.M. down a rapid brook, which had a fall of water in it, and marks of a recent freshet in immense "clumpets" of ice, a yard and a half thick, which had been carried a hundred yards into the woods on each side.

clutch goal in hockey and lacrosse, a goal scored at a crucial time in the play, that is, when needed to decide or tie the game.

1958 *Weekend Mag.* 6 Dec. 40/1: [He has] a fighting reputation as "clutch" goal artist—for the last two seasons he has been the great team's top scorer of winning goals. 1963 *Kingston Whig-Standard* (Ont.) 7 Mar. 27/1: Mike Corbett . . . set up another clutch goal in the final period. . . .

coalie ['koli] *n. Informal* the coalfish or pollock, *Pollachius virens.*

1936 *Cdn Geog.Jnl* Jan. 149/1: There were also a few stray "dogs," a nice showing of ling, cod, halibut, "coalies," "dabs," bream, and catfish. . . .

coal limit *Obs.* a tract of land on which a company or an individual had the legal right to mine coal. Cp. **timber limit** (def. 1a).

1882 *Edmonton Bull.* 29 April 1/1: S. Lucas arrived from up the river above the White Mud where he had been surveying a coal limit on Thursday.

coal oil† See **kerosene oil.**

1860 (1861) GESNER *Treatise on Coal* 89: The great number of impurities contained in the oils distilled from coals, whether from coal tar or crude coal oil, renders their purification somewhat difficult, expensive, and uncertain. 1966 *Islander* 27 Feb. 13/1: . . . the editor . . . by the light of a coal oil lamp . . . set up line by line the announcement. . . .

coarse grain any grain other than wheat, such as oats and barley.

1929 *Beaver* Mar. 168: Wheat, all coarse grains, roots, vegetables and flowers can be cultivated in abundance. 1959 STOREY *Prairie Harvest* 163: . . . the Toreys chopped their coarse grain and sold it to the owner of a feed lot near Saskatoon.

coast *v.* slide down a snow-covered hill, as on a sleigh or toboggan.

1828 (1830) MOORSOM *Letters N.S.* 105: Sometimes on a clear frosty night . . . I have watched these little sleds coasting (as it is termed) down the hills. . . . 1879 *Morning Chron.* (Halifax) 27 Dec. 3/1: On Christmas day a little girl was coasting with some companions in a field off Pleasant Street, when she coasted over a stone wall on to the street, and was . . . badly hurt. 1903 CARR-HARRIS *White Chief* 122: The young people were having a gay time coasting down hill over the "crust" on Dudley Moore's traineau. . . . 1934 WENTWORTH *Amer. Dial.Dict.* 122/1: coast, U.S. and Canada.

Coast *n.* 1 See 1958 quote.

☞ *This meaning is general among Westerners. Easterners often use the term to refer to the Atlantic Coast, especially Halifax.*

1903 *Eye Opener* (High River, Alta) 24 Oct. 4/1: High River race horses have been turning tricks in good shape at the coast. 1938 CASH *I Like B.C.* 97: Some of the mines in the district had recently closed down, and it was filled with miners and their families trying to get to the Coast. 1958 KELSEY *B.C.Rides a Star* 12: Here, I should insert that the coast of British Columbia and "The Coast" are birds of two different feathers. The coast extends from the International Boundary to Prince Rupert, more than five hundred miles north. "The Coast," according to popular British Columbian geography, begins with Point Atkinson at the junction of the northwest waters of Burrard Inlet and Gulf of Georgia. The southern fragment, including Vancouver, is known as Lower Mainland. 1962 *Canada Month* Apr. 25/2: Jones is employed by . . . a pioneer chopper

firm on the coast that helped in the construction of the pipeline. . . .

2 *Local* the southern coast of Labrador.

1861 DE BOILIEU *Labrador Life* 155: We generally wear what on the coast are called "creepers," which are made in the shape of a cross with thick "starts," and which are much the same as cricketers wear in England. 1952 BANFILL *Labrador Nurse* 153: His grandmother, who had raised thirteen children, had left the Coast the previous fall and had seen, for the first time, the same things that her grandson now saw: streets, roads, cows. . . .

Coast or **coast** *adj.* associated with or native to the Coast Country. See also **coaster**[2].

1926 SULLIVAN *Under Northern Lights* 86: I saw but one caribou—a coast caribou. 1938 SULLIVAN *Cycle of North* 119: The salt shores are fringed with her hungry sisters, with tall coast wolves and white and red foxes, all seeking the dead things from the sea.

Coast Country See quote.

1921 HEMING *Drama of Forests* 15: The several zones of the Canadian wilderness are locally known as the Coast Country—the shores of the Arctic Ocean and Hudson Bay; the Barren Grounds. . . .

coaster[1] *n.* a sleigh used by children for coasting down hills. See also **coast,** *v.* and **coasting,** *n.*

1870 *Cdn Illust.News* 9 Apr. 363/2: William Henry Dart . . . [invented an] improvement on coasting Sleighs and Steering apparatus called "Dart's Improved Hand Steering Coaster." 1922 STRINGER *Prairie Child* 63: I could see myself sky-hooting down that icy slope on my coaster. . . .

coaster[2] *n.* an Indian or Eskimo of the coast of Hudson Bay or the Arctic shore. See also **Coast country.** Also spelled *Coaster.*

1835 (1947) HARGRAVE *Correspondence* 197: If you were to allow these Indians (I mean Coasters) a few skins of Debt in fall . . . it would be the means to enable them to withstand the cold. . . . 1924 FLAHERTY *Eskimo Friends* 9: Hungry coasters came filtering into the post during the first week in December, bringing little or no fur, so the factor complained, but with the usual tales of want and distress on their hungry lips.

Coast Indian an Indian living on the Pacific Coast of North America, especially north of the Columbia River.

1824 (1931) SIMPSON *Fur Trade* 71: The Coast Indians are such keen traders that many of them would even bring their Skins as high as the Cascades at appointed times in order to obtain our supplies. 1908 LAUT *Conquest N.W.* II 108: The coast Indians pursued, pillaging packs when the white men camped, threatening violence when the voyageurs embarked. 1966 *Native Voice* Apr. 3/2: He [Chief Hemos Johnson of Kingcome] was affectionately called Womby by all the coast Indians because Womby means father and he lavished the impartial love of a wise father upon them.

coasting† *n.* the practice or pastime of sliding down a snow-covered hill, as on a sleigh or toboggan. See also **sliding** (def. 2).

1896 *Times* (Niagara-on-the-Lake, Ont.) 30 Jan. 1/2: The small boys and girls now enjoy themselves coasting. c1902 LAUT *Trapper* 249: . . . here was nekik the otter at the favourite amusement of his kind—coasting down a snow bank. 1966 *Atlantic Advocate* July 46/3: They adapted to Canadian conditions with enthusiasm, to winter sleigh-rides and coasting, skating up at the rink—and snow. . . .

coast sledge *Arctic* See **komatik**.
1895 MONROE *Snow-Shoes and Sledges* 78: They were to use the ingalik, or regular Yukon sledge, which is much lighter than the Eskimo, or coast sledge, but heavier and stronger than the Hudson Bay toboggan commonly used in the interior.

coast telegraph See **mocassin telegraph**.
1964 *Islander* 5 July 4/1: . . . the Indians on this coast had what the early white settlers referred to as "coast telegraph."

coat beaver *Fur Trade, Hist.* beaver pelts from a beaver coat (def. 1). See also **castor gras**. Cp. **parchment beaver**.
1679 (1945) *H.B.C.Minutes* 23 Dec. 16: Resolved Upon Debate that all our Beavor both Coat and Parchment shall be exposed at the same time to Publique sale. . . .
1795 (1911) HEARNE *Journey* 239: The sixth is the Coat beaver, which is worn till it is half greased, and is worth 4s. 6d. per Pound. **1958** *Beaver* Spring 15/1: It was *castor gras,* the greasy coat beaver, which was promised from Hudson's Bay. . . .

coating *n. Obs.* See **beaver coat** (def. 1).
1826 (1950) OGDEN *Journals* 171: . . . traded 4 Beaver Skins in coating.

cobalt bomb a device for the use of Cobalt-60 in the treatment of disease. See quotes.
1953 MOON *Saskatchewan* 137: At the Chalk River atomic pile, meanwhile, the cobalt, after a year of bombardment by billions of neutrons from the uranium, had become highly charged—one cobalt bomb unit has more than half the power of all the radium units used in medical work throughout the world. **1959** *Maclean's* 14 Feb. 19: Ivy may not yet grow in its walls, but the University of Saskatchewan has already turned out the world's first cobalt bomb, our current prime minister and the best Rhodes scholars from anywhere.

cock and hen the soft clam, *Mya arenaria*. Also called *long clam*.
1842 JUKES *Excursions in Nfld* II 190: The animals of this species are called "cocks and hens" by the fishermen, who sometimes use them as bait for the cod.

cockawee ['kɑkə,wi] *n.* [< Algonk., perhaps through Cdn F; cf. Micmac *kakawegech* wild duck] See **old squaw**. Also spelled *cac(c)awee*.
1760 PICHON *Cape Breton* 103: The coast around these islands swarms . . . with all sorts of wild fowl, as bustards, crevans . . . cacaouis. . . . **1853** REID *Young Voyageurs* 264: There is the "old wife" or "old squaw" . . . called by the voyageurs "caccawié," from its fancied utterance of these syllables. . . . **1896** RUSSELL *Far North* 150: Red-throated loons and cacawees were the most abundant of the water birds. **1904** CROSSKILL *P.E.I.* 33: Of the sea-duck there are many varieties . . . loon, teal, and cock-a-wie. . . . **1959** MCATEE *Folk-Names* 15: OLD SQUAW . . . cockawee (Spelled in numerous other ways . . . Nfld., "Labr.," Que., Ont., "N.W.T.," B.C.). . . .

cock of the woods† the pileated woodpecker, *Dryocopus pileatus*. See also **logcock**.
*a*1820 (1838) HEAD *Forest Scenes* 246: I shot one of the large species of woodpeckers, in size rather larger than a carrier pigeon, with a bright scarlet crest, called by the Canadians, "cocks of the wood." **1897** DURAND *Reminiscences* 230: Bluejays do not all stay with us; woodpeckers do. The large red-headed kind, sometimes called the cock-of-the-woods, does. **1954** MACGREGOR *Behold the Shining Mountains* 20: Through that gap in the hills we will walk to the drumming of partridge and the tattoo of the cock of the woods.

cod-flake *n.* See **flake**.
1907 MILLAIS *Newfoundland* 5: On one side of the beautiful harbour are endless cod-flakes and a few sealing vessels, and on the other is the main town, built on the side of a steep hill, where electric trams and lights add the one jarring note.

cod hooker a sailing vessel used in cod fishing.
1953 RADDALL *Tidefall* 41: Inside six months a whole fleet of ships was playing it, everything from old cod hookers to swank steam yachts.

cod jigger *Nfld* a hand-line with many baited hooks used for inshore cod fishing.
1958 *Evening Telegram* (St. John's) 9 May 20/3: . . . there is a very good sign of fish with the cod jigger.

cod-jigging *n. Nfld* fishing for cod with a jigger (def. 1).
1964 *Holiday* Apr. 177/4: While your ship is at dock, you can take trips out with local fishermen for cod-jigging.

codline *n.* a strong 18-thread line, used in cod fishing and also as an all-purpose cord.
1800 (1897) COUES *New Light* I 89: My horse . . . is a headstrong, powerful beast and requires a strong double codline to hold him. **1934** GODSELL *Arctic Trader* 32: . . . two Indians walked along the shore towing, or "tracking" the boat with a long cod-line. **1958** WATTERS *B.C.Cent.Anthol.* 144: Oars, cod-line, coffee-can and all, the hand-liner is gone now.

cod-stage *n. Nfld* See **stage** (def. 1).
1861 DE BOILIEU *Labrador Life* 29: In large establishments the cod-stage is usually a permanent building built over the water, with generally a good depth of water in front, in which is cast the offal fish.

cod-trap *n. Nfld* a large netted trap about 100 feet square, with a bottom, a door, and a leader to direct fish into the trap. See also **trap net**.
1904 (1929) DUNCAN in *Canadian Prose* 236: Long ago, when young Luke Dart, the Boot Bay trader, was ambitious for Shore patronage, he said to Solomon Stride . . . "Solomon, b'y, an you be willin', I'll trust you with twine for a cod-trap." **1907** MILLAIS *Newfoundland* 152: In shape a cod-trap is very like a house, with a large door at which the fish can enter. **1944** *Beaver* Sep. 20/2: Before the fishing season begins, the cod traps—which are boxlike nets—are dyed with bark and mended. . . .

coffee-head *n.* the cowbird (def. 1), so called because of the color of its head.
1953 MOWERY *Tales of the Mounted Police* 125: A huge flock of "coffee-heads" accompanied the herd, perching on the backs of the shaggy animals and flying around them incessantly.

coho ['koho] *n.* **-hoes.** [prob. of native origin] a silvery salmon, *Oncorhynchus kisutch,* of the northern Pacific. See also **fall fish** and **silver salmon**.
[1808 (1960) FRASER *Letters and Journals* 153: However our Indian Guides say . . . that the large salmon (Cace) already begin to come up.] **1859** *British Colonist* (Victoria) 29 July 1/2: Lastly, there is the genus

known by the Indian name of coocouse a hybrid bastard sort of fish, half trout, half salmon. **1869** *Mainland Guardian* (New Westminster, B.C.) 25 Sep. 2/1: The second of salmon in class is the Cohose, which comes in September and continues to run until November. **1926** MCKELVIE *Huldowget* 101: Overhead expenses could be made from the coho pack but sockeyes signified success. . . . **1963** *Sun* (Vancouver) 25 July 25/1: Peculiar how the fish run to sexes. First five cohoes I caught were cockfish; all the rest but one have been hens.

cold deck *Lumbering* See 1952 quote. Cp. **hot deck.**
1938 CASH *I Like B.C.* 67: But the fire swept towards the "cold decks" on a dirt road, where they had been piled during the winter waiting till the ground had dried enough to truck them out. **1952** GOUGH *Story of B.C.* 185: Logs which are piled together for loading immediately make up a *hot deck,* those left in a pile to be moved later form a *cold deck.*

cold-deck *v. Lumbering* build a cold deck; pile (logs) to make a cold deck. See also **deck,** *v.* Cp. **hot-deck.**
1930 *B.C.Lumberman* April 48/1: Gasoline logging equipment has been developed to a point where it is now recognized as the standard of efficient methods of cold decking logs, yarding the odd corner or helping in the loading out of a few extra. **1966** *B.C.Logging* 10/1: The processes of yarding and loading, usually go on simultaneously unless the felled and bucked timber is to be "cold-decked," or "windrowed," that is piled for future loading.

cold-decking *n. Lumbering* piling logs to make a cold deck.
1952 *Beaver* Sep. 14/1: Everybody was too tired after nine hours of falling, bucking, loading, track-laying, cold-decking, scaling, sawfiling, flunkeying, or whatever the job was. . . .

cold dip *Obs.* See **cold snap.**
1885 *Prince Albert Times* (Sask.) 25 Dec. 3/1: The first real cold dip passed over this district the beginning of this week—thermometer down to 10° below, it said. **1896** *Trans.Roy.Soc.Can.* II 3 41: From March 6th to 10th there was warm weather, to be followed on March 11th by another cold dip, —8°F.

cold draw *Curling* a rock that is curled into an open house or into the house without rubbing or knocking out another rock.
1964 *Calgary Herald* 20 Mar. 16/6: Another cold draw to the four-foot with the last rock by Dagg bailed out Canada. . . .

Cold Maker in Indian mythology, the spirit responsible for cold weather; in later use, the north wind. Cp. **Keewatin.**
1909 PARKER *Northern Lights* 111: . . . it was like the day we first met, old Coldmaker hitting the world with his whips of frost, and shaking his ragged blankets of snow over the wild west. **1918** SCHULTZ *Rising Wolf* 210: . . . we sat back of our rye grass couches and were truly comfortable, and very thankful that Cold Maker had not overcome us!

cold skidding *Lumbering* See quote at **hot skidding.**

cold snap† a short period of unusually cold weather.
1887 (1888) LEES & CLUTTERBUCK *British Columbia* 356: The "cold snap" which had come on continued. . . . **1963** *Calgary Herald* 20 Nov. 27/1: . . . the ducks that are going south moved out ahead of the . . . cold snap.

collar *n.* [prob. influenced by F *collier* in this sense] **1** *Obs.* a snare.
1778 (1904) LONG *Voyages* 96: I asked the Indian where she was gone; he smiled, and told me, he supposed into the woods to set a collar for the partridge.

2 *North* See quote. See also **collar ice.**
1939 MONTAGUE *Eskimos* 16: We were on the ice—what we call the *collar* because it is attached to the cliff edge of the land, and runs out maybe twenty feet before you come to the ocean ice and the tide-flow under it.

collared lemming a rodent, *Dicrostonyx groenlandicus,* of the Arctic, brown in summer and of a light color in winter.
1952 STANWELL-FLETCHER *Tundra World* 110: The collared lemming, incidentally, is the only species of mouse that changes color in winter, sometimes becoming light platinum gray or pure white.

collar ice See **collar** (def. 2).
1937 *Beaver* Mar. 9/2: The water was calm in the lee of the collar ice, with skin ice forming in the little bays.

collar iron See **standing iron.**
1922 *Beaver* Aug. 12/1: He [a dog] dodged and I struck the collar irons at the back of his neck and drove them nearly through my hand.

collar wire *Obs.* a light wire, usually brass, for making snares, or collars, *q.v.*
1829 *Fort Langley Journal* 8 July: The three principal articles indented for came—namely Duffles, Beads & Collar wire.

collège classique *Cdn French* See **classical college.**
1957 PHILLIPS *Education in Canada* 221: We have seen how the *collèges classiques* were founded and how they increased in number after 1840. They were taught by regular or secular clergy, who received only nominal salaries, so that fees were kept low. **1963** MORTON *Kingdom of Canada* 218: . . . the *collèges classiques* of Lower Canada [in 1820's] were turning out lawyers, journalists, and doctors. . . . **1963** *Gauntlet* 11 Oct. 5/3: In Quebec, 21 tertiary educational colleges, the College Classique, may now join CUS because of the change.

college farmer *Derog.* a farmer who has attended an agricultural college but has little practical experience.
1939 GROVE *Two Generations* 39: You want to show some executive ability. Otherwise he'll call you a college farmer.

collegiate *n.* **1** See **collegiate institute.**
1853 (1965) HAMILTON *Cdn Quotations* 66/2: . . . Common School, grammar school and collegiate [are] free from sectarianism and open to all on equal terms. . . . (Toronto *Globe,* Oct. 1, 1853). **1912** WHITE *Wildcatters* 6: . . . he sent me through collegiate and university without a murmur. **1964** *Maclean's* 25 July 38/2: I took high school at the collegiate in Yorkton, Saskatchewan. . . .

2 loosely, any high school.
1965 *Globe and Mail* (Toronto) 29 Apr. 5/2: I was a science teacher in a collegiate [in B.C.] for 10 years. . . .

collegiate and vocational institute or **school** in Ontario, a secondary school where pupils may undertake a program in either academic studies or vocational training in commercial courses and shop work.
1963 *Kingston Whig-Standard* (Ont.) 28 Feb. 17/3: The teachers are needed . . . for . . . Loyalist Collegiate and Vocational School.

collegiate department *Hist.* See **collegiate school.**
1957 PHILLIPS *Education* 227: As for full-fledged high schools, in 1882 there was a collegiate department only in Winnipeg. By 1913 there were seven centres in the province outside Winnipeg with collegiate departments of four or more teachers, six centres with collegiate departments of three or more teachers, and thirteen centres with high schools.

collegiate institute in Ontario, Manitoba, and Saskatchewan, a secondary school that meets certain provincial requirements with regard to curriculum, facilities, and specialist staff over and above those required in a high school, *q.v.* See also **collegiate** (def. 1).
1861 *Nor'Wester* (R.R.S.) 1 Oct. 3/1: The Red River Academy was a High School or Collegiate Institute, in which along with a thorough English education, the higher classics and mathematics were taught. **1963** *Kingston Whig-Standard* (Ont.) 13 May 1/7: We have bought hundreds and hundreds of defence planes, each of which has cost the price of an educational institution such as our new collegiate institute in Napanee.

collegiate school 1 *Hist.* in Manitoba, a high school having special academic facilities and superior staff. See also **collegiate department.** Cp. **collegiate institute.**
1860 *Nor'Wester* (R.R.S.) 28 Feb. 3/4: A collegiate school had opened a year before. **1871** *Wkly Manitoban* 1 July 2/5: St. John's Collegiate School broke up for the midsummer vacation of Friday. . . .
2 *N.S.* a school affiliated with a college or university.
1832 MCGREGOR *British America* II 122: A very respectable academy, built of free-stone, and called the Collegiate School, stands within the [King's] college grounds [Windsor, N.S.]. **1927** HAMILTON *Maritime Provinces* 68: About nine hundred students attend the college and its affiliated seminary and collegiate school, making Wolfville [N.S.] a real university town.

collet *n.* [< F] *Obs.* a snare. See also **collar** (def. 1).
1824 (1955) BLACK *Journal* 184: [We] camped on the other side, here we saw some Siffleu Collets newly set.

collier *n.* [< F "collar"] *Cdn French* See **tumpline** and picture.
1860 (1956) KOHL *Kitchi-Gami* 168: Du Roy thrust all our indispensable articles into his blue woollen "couverte," tied it round with his leathern "collier," and hung the whole on his back, while fastening the broad band of the "paqueton" round his head, for the Voyageurs. . . . **1872** MCDONALD *Peace River* 44: The best *"colliers"* are made with the broad part, and two or three feet of the string, all of one piece. . . .

Colonial Assembly *Hist.* the assembly of representatives from the various ridings or constituencies in Upper and Lower Canada, 1791-1841.
1822 *Montreal Herald* 11 Dec. 2/3: When admitted to a fair participation in the Colonial Assembly, the

Townships would anxiously coalesce with the rest of the population of the Province without distinctions of any kind. **1826** (1832) PICKERING *Inquiries of an Emigrant* 75: This place, I am told, mostly belongs to one of four brothers, Scotchmen, of the name of Crooks, who have all been members of the colonial assembly.

colonial produce *Fur Trade, Obs.* local produce as opposed to imported foods and other goods.
1843 *Standing Rules* (*H.B.C.*) Marginal Note to No. 1: . . . but all country and colonial produce at the depot inventory tariff. Red River or Colonial Produce at 12% on Inventory Prices.

colonist *n.* **1** See **colonist car.**
1911 KNOWLES *Singer* 36: "He sho' raised de debbil in de Colonist last night when he seed a sharper doin' up a fellah. . . ."
2 *Now rare* one of the persons making up a colony, *q.v.*
1879 *Winnipeg Dly Times* 14 Apr. 3/3: The colonists bring with them farm implements, machinery, horses, cattle, and all the mechanical tools required for manufacturing industries. **1909** BINDLOSS *Lorimer* 328: . . . there is the tale of a hard fight for this mine between two Englishmen, one of whom championed the cause of an oppressed colonist.
3 a farmer in a remote area recently opened for settlement. See also **settler** (def. 3).
☛ *The Cdn French* colon *in this sense is undoubtedly the source of this meaning.*
1963 *Weekend Mag.* 7 Dec. 8/3: These were the men they once called colonists but whom the almost-exclusively French-Canadian population of several villages now refer to as *les fermiers* (the farmers). Some came from the Lake St. John area of Quebec 30 years ago and some of the older men are sons of fathers who moved in soon after the railroad.

colonist car *Hist.* a railway coach having wooden seats and rough berths for sleeping, sometimes also having cooking facilities. See also **colonist sleeper.** Cp. **immigrant car** and **tourist car.**
1887 *Our Forest Children* Nov. 2/1: In these colonist cars the upper berth is simply a strong wooden tray hinged on one side and held in horizontal position by two strong chains. **1922** STEAD *Neighbours* 26: We travelled in a colonist car, and it was lucky that there were four of us, as we occupied just one section. **1966** *Weekend Mag.* 31: [Caption] Going by train to settle the West, the immigrants rode in colonist cars.

colonist (-type) sleeper *Hist.* See **colonist car.**
1891 *Medicine Hat Times* (Alta) 10 Dec. 1/6: The special transport train consisting of six colonist sleepers, one pullman, a mess car and a baggage car . . . steamed into the station at 20:30 Sunday evening. **1966** *Kingston Whig-Standard* (Ont.) 1 Sep. 3/1: We were paid . . . $2.25 a day, out of which we were docked 90 cents for board and bunk in an old wooden Colonist-type sleeper.

colonist ticket *Hist.* a ticket entitling the holder to ride on a colonist car, *q.v.*
*c*1900 (1965) KILBOURN *Making of Nation* 36: [Advert.] Holders of COLONIST or SECOND-CLASS TICKETS are allowed FREE USE OF THESE CARS FROM THE BEGINNING TO THE END OF THEIR JOURNEY OVER THE CANADIAN PACIFIC RAILWAY.

colonization company *Hist.* a company acting as an agent in bringing colonists to their destination in Canada.

1880 GORDON *Mountain and Prairie* 298: Colonization Companies may serve for the North-West the same purpose, as immigration agents, that has been served by the Railway Companies in the Western States. **1909** HUNTER *Simcoe County* I 50: Large grants of land to colonization companies and others have been a feature of the settlement of some counties in this Province. **1935** *Trans.Roy.Soc.Can.* III 2 25: Colonization companies were given grants [in Saskatchewan in the early 1880's].

colonization highway See **colonization road**.

1933 THOMPSON & EDGAR *Cdn Ry Development* 126: It is related that the British Columbia delegates, during negotiations with the Dominion Government, urged Cartier to the effect that a railway be built across the prairies to the foot of the mountains, and that a colonization highway be laid out thence to the Pacific Coast.

colonization lands *Hist.* lands held by a colonization company for sale to settlers.

1883 *Brandon Daily* (Man.) 13 Feb. 4/1: It is the intention of the company to build from fifty to eighty houses on their colonization lands during the coming summer.

colonization line *Hist.* See **colonization railway**.

1933 THOMPSON & EDGAR *Cdn Ry Development* 289: Commenced as a colonization line by the Provincial Government, with the object of enabling the clay belt to be settled, valuable mining interests were later established along a portion of this route.

colonization railway *Hist.* a railway line built to facilitate the colonizing of unsettled areas; also, the company building or operating such a line.

1883 *Prince Albert Times* (Sask.) 14 Feb. 5/1: A meeting of the share holders of the ... Colonization Railway was held in Montreal on Wednesday. **1933** THOMPSON & EDGAR *Cdn Ry Development* 211: The superintendent ... lent his aid in handling traffic, this being fundamentally a colonization railway.

colonization reserves *Hist.* land set aside for settlement, usually owned by a colonization company.

1882 *Prince Albert Times* (Sask.) 6 Dec. 5/3: Is he at liberty to settle upon and homestead the seven sections in the Colonization Reserves, or must he be placed thereon, and take up his claim by the express consent of the society?

colonization road *Hist.* a road built into an unsettled area to make it accessible for settlement. See also **colonization highway** and **settlement road**.

1855 (1957) *Ont.Hist.* XLIX 6: According to a memorandum with the title "Colonization Roads in Upper Canada," signed by Andrew Russel, dated Quebec, 20 February, 1855, Gibson had been placed in charge of the roads to be constructed.... **1920** *Rod and Gun in Canada* Nov. 733: Already there are thousands of miles of colonization roads and steam railways spreading like a spider's web over a huge part of that immense forest-robed territory. **1961** PRICE & KENNEDY *Renfrew* 113: To accomplish this, the immigration department built the famous "colonization roads."

colonization society *Hist.* a society which bought land for settlement by its members.

1878 *Sask.Herald* (Battleford, N.W.T.) 30 Dec. 2/3: The Hudson's Bay Company has intimated to an Ontario colonization society that it will carry its members as passengers on the river steamboats if they will settle on the Saskatchewan. **1929** *Cdn Hist.Rev.* X 297: The colonization society, which made its appearance about 1850, was a prominent result.

colonize *v. Obs.* accustom (someone) to the hardships and privations of a colonist.

1863 WALSHE *Cedar Creek* 91: "I forgot you were a fresh importation," observed Mr. Holt with a satisfied chuckle. "You ain't colonized yet...."

colony *n.* a settlement formed under the auspices of a land company or by a group of persons of the same nationality or religion, or having similar principles.

1799 RUSSELL *Correspondence* III 121: When he was in England, the Block of land called the Mississague Block had been pointed out to him ... as the part of the Country properest for his Colony. **1878** *Sask.Herald* (Battleford, N.W.T.) 30 Dec. 2/2: A Colony is to be organized at Hamilton (Ont.) and vicinity, to move into the North-West Territories. **1964** *Western Wkly* 29 Jan. 6/2: [Advert.] PALLISER BARLEY – PEARLING – yielded 95 bushels per acre this year.... Contact Hutterite Colony ... Ponoka, or write.

colony work *Obs.* See quote.

1861 *Nor'Wester* (R.R.S.) 1 Apr. 4/1: Some of them had been employed in what was called "Colony work" —road-making, house-building, tripping and the like; and at such work had earned a good deal of money which was to have been placed to their credit in reduction of their debts.

colo(u)r *n.* **1** evidence of gold; traces of gold.

1859 *British Colonist* (Victoria) 25 May 2/3: We learn ... that there have been about 20 men prospecting in the locality, and that they have succeeded in obtaining "the color" of the precious metal. **1880** GORDON *Mountain and Prairie* 75: Should this "colour" be plentiful, it may lead to further exploring, and perhaps to successful mining. **1963** SYMONS *Many Trails* 67: There was colour to be found in all the little creeks on his trap line....

2 a minute speck of gold. See also **fine gold**.

1864 (1962) ANDERSON *Sawney's Letters* 7: But ne'er a color can they see, / Until they saut it first a wee.... **1910** SERVICE *Trail of '98* 339: Ruefully he turns his poke inside out—not a "colour." **1960** *Weekend Mag.* 8 Oct. 28/1: They had panned one or two colors and they wanted to get down to bedrock to see if she would pay, so they set to sinking a shaft.

colo(u)red fox the red fox, *Vulpes fulva*. See 1921 quote.

1921 HEMING *Drama of Forests* 93: The "coloured" foxes, including the red, the cross, the silver, and the black—the latter three being merely colour phases of the former and not separate species.... **1966** *North* March 30/1: Arctic or White Fox (Alopex Lagopus) ... is about two-thirds the size of the coloured fox....

colo(u)red fur the fur of the colored fox.

1966 *North* March 27/1: The main items purchased [by the Moravian Mission] were seal and cod liver oil, sealskins and fox skins (mostly coloured fur from the interior of Labrador), and ivory carvings.

Columbia *n. Hist.* **1** See **Columbia Department**.

1824 (1931) SIMPSON *Fur Trade* 105: The Climate of

the Columbia is temperate regular and salubrious; on New Years Day I have seen at Fort George Pease, Carrots and Radishes in blossom and up to that Date we had neither Frost nor Snow.

2 a. before Confederation, the general area now designated as British Columbia, including New Caledonia.

1859 *British Colonist* (Victoria) 22 June 2/2: But not so long as that curious despotism exists in Columbia, or the de facto despotism exists here. **1872** *Canadian Mthly* Oct. 368/1: Prince Edward Island, now that it shows a tendency to follow the example of Columbia, will, probably, be the subject of a supplementary competition.

b. *Rare* British Columbia.

1922 MURPHY *Black Candle* 194: The figures are indicative of the sums of money at the disposal of these aliens, and maybe the figures show incidentally why there is so much unemployment in Columbia by the Sea.

Columbia(n) blacktailed deer See 1958 quote.

1911 ROGERS *Wild Animals* 322: The Columbian black-tailed deer of British Columbia, Washington, and Oregon has a full right to the name.... **1924** SHERMAN *Mother Nature Stories* 61: The columbia black-tailed deer has also reached the vanishing point in some districts. **1958** *Encyc.Can.* III 222/2: The Columbian black-tailed deer (*Odocoileus hemonius columbianus*) inhabits the coastal regions of British Columbia.

Columbia Department or District *Hist.* the administrative district of the Hudson's Bay Company occupying approximately what are now Oregon, Washington, and southern British Columbia. See also **Columbia** (def. 1).

1821 WENTZEL *Letters* 140: A kind of demi-official report is in circulation that the Company have come to the conclusive resolve of evacuating the Columbia Department altogether. **1921** *Beaver* July 15/2: The country was also known as Columbia District.... **1946** *Ibid.* Mar. 8/2: ... the Columbia Department extended over the whole vast watershed of the Columbia River, which includes most of the states of Washington and Oregon.

Columbia leprosy *Obs.* a euphemism for some disease, probably syphilis.

1841 (1963) TOLMIE *Physician* 342: Poor Angus is affected with the Columbia leprosy, and will no doubt fall a martyr to it.

Columbian *n. Hist.* 1 an employee of the Hudson's Bay Company in the Columbia Department.

1824 (1931) SIMPSON *Fur Trade* 30: This is merely a temporary Summer post for the convenience of the Columbians in crossing. **1929** (1931) MERK *Fur Trade* xxvi: It had been the practice of the Columbians to import for their own use quantities of European provisions.

2 a native or resident of Columbia (def. 2), later British Columbia.

1859 *British Colonist* (Victoria) 5 Feb. 3/2: Why are not Columbians up and doing, advocating union of the two colonies,—and a House of Assembly formed from the united representatives of both? **1883** *Prince Albert Times* (Sask.) 10 Jan. 4/2: It seems to be part of the religion of every Columbian to laud the climate of his country.

Columbian *adj. Hist.* associated with or characteristic of Columbia (def. 2), later British Columbia.

1861 *Nor'Wester* (R.R.S.) 1 Mar. 3/3: When, therefore,

the Columbian Government has finished the roads it is now making from Derby (Fort Langley) and when that of Canada shall have opened one from Lake Superior and the Selkirk Settlement, the means of communication will be complete across the whole continent. **1958** WATTERS *B.C.Cent.Anthol.* 410: The Victoria *Colonist* of the time described the architecture as neither "Doric, Ionian, nor Corinthian, but decidedly Columbian."

Columbian candle *Obs.* See quote.

1825 (1940) *B.C.Hist.Qtly* Oct. 223: His journal he wrote by the light of his camp-fire or his "Columbian candle"—a stick containing resin.

combine *n.* a farm machine which cuts and threshes grain in one operation.

1940 MACCORMAC *Canada* 235: Not for him the reapers and harvesters and combines of the West, nor the hope of sudden riches. **1953** MOON *Saskatchewan* 58: The first combine on the North American prairies for cutting and threshing grain in one operation was tried out on the Swift Current station in 1922. **1964** *Family Herald* 12 Mar. 13/1: Bill and Fred Streich of Clandeboye, Manitoba and Frank McBain ... built a combine that resembles traditional machines only from the pick-up to the rear of the cylinder assembly.

Combines Act (in full, the Combines Investigation Act) legislation passed in 1911, re-enacted in 1923, and since revised periodically, permitting the government to control practices in restraint of trade arising from combines.

1956 *Mine-Mill Herald* July 8/5: 1 It is our contention that use of the Combines Act in regard to said Union, or any Union, is in direct contravention of the original intent of the Act. **1958** *Edmonton Jnl* 8 Aug. 7/5: Frank Howard (CCF—Skeena) suggested hiring of more staff to police provision of the Combines Act.

come out *North* leave the North, the bush, to return "outside," *i.e.,* to civilization.

1929 *Beaver* Dec. 315: ... where he remained for ten years ... before coming out. **1938** *Ibid.* Dec. 28/1: Strange old men appear there [in Bachelors' Hall]—old servants of the Company who, after a lifetime in the interior, finally "come out" on their way home across the seas. **1951** GILLIS & MYLES *North Pole* 136: Afterwards, when we had "come out" and were in Toronto....

comers and goers *Fur Trade, Hist.* voyageurs plying between Quebec and the fur country, especially the porkeaters (def. 1a). See also **goers and comers.**

1665 (1885) RADISSON *Voyages* 192: The way was well beaten because of the comers and goers, who by making that passage shortens their passage by 8 dayes by tourning about the point that goes very farr in that great lake. **1913** COWIE *Company of Adventurers* 227: Arrivals and departures of all "comers and goers" ... were all fully noted.... **1931** NUTE *Voyageur* 62: ... he followed the portage route already well marked by the feet of the "comers and goers." This epithet was sometimes used as the English equivalent of *mangeurs de lard*.

come York over *Obs.* play the superior, as if from York (Toronto); behave as if a superior.

1852 (1923) MOODIE *Roughing It* 131: You are not going to come York over me in that way, or Yankee either.

commander *n. Obs.* See quote.

1801 MACKENZIE *Voyages* iv: A number of able and respectable men retired from the army, prosecuted the [fur] trade in person, under their respective licences, with great order and regularity. . . . These gentlemen denominated themselves commanders, and not traders, though they were entitled to both those characters.

commercial-vocational school a school for training pupils in non-academic subjects.

1958 *Edmonton Jnl* 27 June 31/4: A commercial-vocational school for students completing Grade 9 and located in the Peace River area was suggested here Thursday before the Cameron Royal Commission on Education.

commet(t)ek *n.* See **komatik.**

commis [kə'mis] *n.* [< Cdn F] *Fur Trade, Hist.* a clerk (def. 1).

[**1804** (1889) MASSON *Les Bourgeois* I 395: Liste des "bourgeois," commis, engagés, et "voyageurs" de la Compagnie du Nord-Ouest, après la fusion de 1804.] **1918** DAVIDSON *North West Co.* 47n: The guides, *commis,* and interpreters . . . were . . . not of the best. **1947** *Beaver* Mar. 4/1: It was growing late and the *commis* was trying to pluck up enough courage to make his round of inspection. **1951** O'MEARA *Grand Portage* Glossary: Commis—Clerk but not in the usual sense of the word. The clerks of the North West Company were often men of great responsibility, with districts as large as a modern Canadian province.

commissary *n. Fur Trade* the man in charge of the stores.

1913 WILLIAMS *Wilderness Trail* 203: When the commissary had left him, Charley Seguis's brow clouded with annoyance. . . . **1913** BICKERSTETH *Open Doors* 209: We found the Commissary playing poker with a number of other men, and he readily consented to put me up.

commissioned gentleman or **officer** *Fur Trade, Hist.* in the Hudson's Bay Company, any officer of the rank of assistant clerk or above. See also **gentleman** and **Company's gentleman.** Cp. **people.**

1828 (1872) MCDONALD *Peace River* 1: Doctor Hamlyn and myself, were accompanied down to our craft by fourteen commissioned gentlemen and about as many clerks. **1907** HUNTER *Cdn Wilds* 5: I entered the service of the Hudson's Bay Company in 1863 as a clerk and retired in 1903 a commissioned officer of twenty years' standing. **1942** *Beaver* June 4/1: He belonged to that splendid group of "Commissioned Gentlemen" who during the nineteenth century built up the great traditions of the Hudson's Bay Company. . . .

commissioner *n.* **1** *Hist.* in the fur companies, the senior of all the commissioned officers.

1907 HUNTER *Cdn Wilds* 12: Sir George Simpson held the position of Governor of the fur trade of the Hudson's Bay Company for very many years and was followed by Governors Dallas, McTavish, Graham and Sir Donald A. Smith . . . after the latter's term of office the title of this position was altered to "The Commissioner." **1940** *Beaver* June 22/2: Perhaps no greater tribute could be paid him than that with his retirement the title of Fur Trade Commissioner should cease to exist.

2 the chief executive officer of a territorial government.

1953 *North Star* (Yellowknife) Oct. 2/1: The North-west Territories is still governed by an appointed Commissioner and a Territorial Council on which the majority are appointed. **1961** *Canada Month* Dec. 31/1: This non-partisan group works with the commissioner, who is an appointed official of the northern affairs department.

3 the senior official of the Royal Canadian Mounted Police.

1958 *Edmonton Jnl* 24 June 3/8/2: The commissioner of the RCMP is one of the appointed members.

4 one of various officers having special functions under different levels of government.

1822 (1960) MCCULLOCH *Stepsure Letters* 37: . . . poor Mrs. Castup curses the day which made her husband a commissioner of roads. **1889** DONKIN *Trooper and Redskin* 226: The entire North West is divided into Indian Districts, each of which is under the supervision of an agent, who is again responsible to the Indian Department at Regina, controlled by the Commissioner of Indian Affairs. **1904** *Ont.Bur.Arch. Rep.* I 21: The Commissioner of Crown Lands has control of the sale or management of Crown, Clergy lands.

commoner *n. Obs.* an animal permitted to graze on community pasture land.

1820 (1887) HIGGINS *Life J.Gould* 134: Voted—That Horses shall not be commoners.

Commoner† *n.* a member of the House of Commons or, in earlier times, of a legislative assembly. Cp. **Commons.**

1833 *Vindicator* (Montreal) 8 Jan. 3/1: The framers of the Canadian Constitution forgot the principle that the Dukes of Devonshire, of Cornwall, &c. and the other Barons of the Empire could not be affected by any law Canadian Commoners could make. **1916** BRIDLE *Sons of Canada* 29: When he first became a Commoner . . . he was too passionately chivalrous to be aware of his place on the stage of professional politics. **1957** *Record-Gaz.* 19 Dec. 6/6: . . . he had not been in office long enough to answer his fellow-Commoners questions.

Commons† *n.* **1** *Hist.* See **Commons House of Assembly.**

1816 *Montreal Herald* 20 Jan. 3/1: The Commons in Canada, as in Britain, dispose of the public money as they may see fit and of the lands of individuals as they may see constitutional when great public benefit is acknowledged.

2 a. the House of Commons, the lower house of Parliament.

1867 (1965) GAETZ *Diary* 11 Sep. 95: . . . the following persons were nominated for the "Commons" at Ottawa, Confederate, H. A. N. Kaulbach; Anti-Confederate, Edwd. McDonald, of Halifax. **1881** BEGG *Great Cdn N.W.* 50: It . . . gave the people the right to elect four members to the Commons of Canada, and entitled them to two representatives in the Senate. **1957** *Camsell Arrow* Christmas 68/1: There is little likelihood of an Indian being elected to the Commons at an early date, but the appointment of one or more to the Senate would give Indians representation in Parliament.

b. the members of this house collectively.

1962 *Chronicle-Herald* (Halifax) 11 Aug. 1/6: After electing a speaker at a morning sitting, the Commons moves into the Senate chamber in the afternoon.

common school† *Hist.* an elementary school open to the children of all the inhabitants of a town or district.

☛ *In Ontario, the name of such schools was officially changed in 1871; it remained current for some time afterwards in other parts of Canada.*

1810 *Kingston Gaz.* (U.C.) 25 Sep. 3/1: The importance of Common Schools for the education of children is generally admitted, but not sufficiently realized. **1881** BEGG *Great Cdn N.W.* 77: In addition to the common schools there are three colleges. **1953** LEBOURDAIS *Nation of North* 35: Grammar or common schools were responsible for education up to the age of 21.

Commons House of Assembly *Hist.* the lower house (of elected representatives) in the colonial Parliament. See also **Commons** (def. 1).

1798 *U.C.Gaz.* (York [Toronto]) 23 June 3/2: We ... the Commons House of Assembly of Upper Canada, in parliament met, beg leave to return your Honor the thanks of this house for your Honor's speech. **1824** *Wkly Register* (York [Toronto]) 12 Feb. 54/2: ... we have no reluctance to declare our sentiments as to the degree of propriety, there may be in sending a certain number of Lawyers to the Commons House of Assembly....

commoosie [kə'musi] *n.* [< Algonk.] *N.B.* See quotes.

1900 LONG *Wilderness Ways* 26: ... then we built our houses, Simmo a bark *commoosie,* and I a little tent.... *Ibid.* 110: You steal away towards the cry, past the little *commoosie,* or shelter, that you made hastily at sundown....

community centre a building or complex of buildings, usually operated by a community or municipality and often equipped with an arena, swimming pool, and other recreational facilities, serving as a centre for public entertainments, fairs, sporting events, political rallies, etc. Cp. **community hall.**

1955 *Vancouver Province* 6 Jan. 5/1: Christmas time the White Cane people called Mr. Emery to see if he could whip up a concert party for the blind. There was little more than a day to arrange this but the man whose work with "Kitsilano Show Boat" and the Community Centre is well known was glad to go to work. **1962** *Chronicle-Herald* (Halifax) 8 Aug. 19/8: ... the Liberal nominating convention [was] held at the Community Centre....

Community Doukhobor See **Sons of Freedom.**

1929 ENGLAND *Immigrant* 54: It is important to distinguish between the independent Doukhobors and the Community Doukhobors known as the "Sons of Freedom." **1964** *Weekend Mag.* 26 Dec. 2/2: [The] peaceful Doukhobors ... belong to the sect's other two factions, the orthodox or Community Doukhobors, and the most Canadianized, the Independents.

community hall a hall supported by the community for holding dances, meetings, and so on. Cp. **community centre.**

1928 FREEMAN *Nearing North* 63: For the Police Barracks and Land Office a turn to the left would have to be made at a certain pond or patch of woods, while for the Community Hall the turn was to the right and along half a mile of new-graded road. **1966** *Kingston Whig-Standard* (Ont.) 18 Mar. 6/1: ... an old-fashioned box social [was] held in the community hall.

community league an organization of persons in a particular district interested in providing social and recreational activities for themselves and their families.

1958 *Edmonton Jnl* 19 Sep. 31/7: ... one community league has established a $30 membership fee this year....

Compact *n. Hist.* **1** See **Family Compact** (def. 1).

1823 *Wkly Register* (York [Toronto]) 9 Oct. 327/1: A vast column of innoxious vapour has issued from the "Compact" through the Observer last week.... **1903** CONANT *Life in Canada* 101: A farmer living near Oshawa, being the son of a United Empire Loyalist, seemed to have all the Compact's hate and suspicion centred upon him, simply because his father came from Massachusetts. **1956** *New Frontiers* Summer 14/1: The whole affair raised such a stench / That even Compact noses swore / They'd never sniffed the like before....

2 See **Family-Company-Compact.**

1859 *British Colonist* (Victoria) 12 Feb. 1/4: Latterly, however, though with a few exceptions chiefly under Compact influence ... it has shown a disposition to meet the wants of the people ... and answer the end of its institution.

Company† *n.* **1** *Hist.* one of the fur trading companies, especially the Hudson's Bay Company or the North West Company.

1820 (1823) FRANKLIN *Journey* 86: The masters of posts and wintering partners of the Companies, deemed this criminal indulgence to the vices of their servants necessary to stimulate them to extortion for the interest of the respective concerns.

2 the Company, the Hudson's Bay Company.

1697/8 (1908) LAUT *Conquest N.W.* I 272: The Humble Peticon of Peter Esprit Radisson Humbly sheweth ... That during the late Reign a Price was set upon your Petr head by the French & several attempts were made upon him to assassinate him & that for none other reasons but for quitting his owne country & serving the compy. **1752** ROBSON *Hudson's Bay* 6: The Company have for eighty years slept at the edge of a frozen sea; they have shown no curiosity to penetrate further themselves, and have exerted their art and power to crush that spirit in others. **1870** (1883) BUTLER *Great Lone Land* 38: The Company—not the Hudson Bay Company, but *the* Company—represented for him all law, all power, all government. **1963** *Beaver* Winter 28/1: From there, with two Loucheaux and six Company servants ... he rafted down river....

Company Indian an Indian trading exclusively with the Hudson's Bay Company. See also **English Indian** and **Hudson's Bay Indian.**

1931 *Beaver* June 220: The Company Indian of today is the Indian who consistently trades with the Company in good or bad times and whose faith in the Company remains always unshaken. **1953** LOWER *Voyages* 36: Every Indian was thus either a "Company Indian" or a "French Company Indian."

Company man an employee of the Hudson's Bay Company. See also **servant.**

1913 KELLY *Range Men* 86: There was little difference between the free men and the Company men.... **1938** GODSELL *Red Hunters* 66: They showed the deep respect for the "Company" man that characterized all the Crees[,] refusing to let me work around the camp at night, since this is considered demeaning to an

Okemow. **1961** ANDERSON *Angel* v: In time Jim Watt became what has been known for two hundred and fifty years as a "Company man," his chief loyalty, aside from his family, to serve the best interests of the Hudson's Bay Company.

Company of (Gentlemen) Adventurers† an abbreviation of the charter name of the Hudson's Bay Company, often misquoted.
1670 *Hudson's Bay Company Charter* 1: We Doe . . . grant to . . . the said Governor and Company of Adventurers of England Tradeing into Hudson's Bay. . . . **1880** MORRIS *Treaties with the Indians* 9: The predecessors of Canada—the Company of Adventurers of England trading into Hudson's Bay, popularly known as the Hudson's Bay Company—had, for long years, been eminently successful in securing the good-will of the Indians. . . . **1930** ROLYAT *Fort Garry* 212: Groups of boats left regularly during the time of open waters for points in the wilderness, following the ordered schedule of the orderly Company of Gentlemen Adventurers.

Company of New France *Hist.* See quote.
1926 WRONG *History of Can.* 44: Thus was formed in 1627 the Company of New France, called also The Company of One Hundred Associates, or partners.

Company's gentleman *Hist.* See **commissioned gentleman.**
1933 *Beaver* Sep. 30/2: . . . and apprentices of every grade who were entitled to the name of "Company's gentlemen."

Company's mark *Fur Trade, Obs.* See quote.
1820 (1938) SIMPSON *Athabasca Journal* 198: . . . several of the dogs are frost bitten, and many of the people have what is called "The Company's mark"; Frozen noses.

Company's medal any one of various medals awarded by the Hudson's Bay Company to long-time Servants on their retirement and to deserving Indians.
1934 GODSELL *Arctic Trader* 206: He added that they did not want the Company's medals which were being presented to the leading natives to commemorate the 250th Anniversary. . . .

company town a settlement or town built by and maintained by a company for its employees, sometimes in a remote part of the bush. Cp. **open town.**
1929 *Beaver* June 222: . . . never losing sight of land until we reached Ocean Falls, a regular company town. **1962** *Time* (Cdn ed.) 18 Dec. 16/3: Even today the Gaspe company town of Murdochville . . . is a scabrous word to Quebec labor unions.

composite high school in certain provinces, a centralized high school which offers academic, commercial, and vocational courses.
1958 *Rosetown Eagle* 29 May 10/4: Prior to the graduation exercises of the Rosetown Composite High School, the Kinsmen entertained the members of the graduating class. **1965** *Canadian Wkly* 2-8 Jan. 11/3: . . . Strathcona composite high school . . . holds its Sweetheart's Swirl in February. . . .

composite school See **composite high school.**
1955 HARDY *Alta Anthol.* 174: In Senior High, the new

Composite School is changing the educational picture again; large school plants are being designed for the teaching of technical, commercial and academic subjects, so that the student has a wide range of subjects from which to choose. **1964** *Kingston Whig-Standard* (Ont.) 10 Dec. 6/3: A new composite school . . . would cost in the neighborhood of $900,000. . . .

compound *n.* See **buffalo pound.**
1965 *Kingston Whig-Standard* (Ont.) 29 Sep. 34/1: Stories told by trappers and traders suggest that compounds may have been used by successive groups of Indians.

comp school *Informal* See **composite high school.**
1958 *Progress* 28 May 1/1: Advantages offered students in the local comp school . . . are on a par with those available in city schools.

comtax *v.* See **kumtux.**

Con. or **con.** See **concession.**
1816 *Spectator* (St. David's, U.C.) 25 Oct. 4/4: Home District, Township of Pickering, No. 25, 1st Con. **1850** *Watchman* (Port Hope, U.C.) 12 Dec. 4/3: For sale, an excellent farm of 150 acres, being part of Lots Nos. 19 and 20, in the 3rd Con. of the Township of Cavanagh. **1909** HUNTER *Simcoe County* I 76: Owing to this boom, a township called Port Powell was surveyed in 1846 on lots 9 & 10, Con. 9 Tay, and building lots placed on the market.

concession *n.* [< Cdn F < F "a grant of land"] *Abbrev.* Con. **1** in earliest use in French Canada, one of the ranged lots into which a seigneury was divided, these being held by tenants under feudal custom. See also **range** (def. 2a).
1764 *Quebec Gaz.* 23 Aug. 4/2: The said Seigneurie [is] capable of containing upwards of 500 Plantations in more than 3 Concessions Depth on each Side the River. . . . **1911** PRINGLE *Home of Evangeline* 185: The apple culture a few miles inland is comparable to the best of the Annapolis valley; and the orchards of our Acadians of these Concessions recall the most flourishing to be found in Normandy.

2 in Upper Canada and post-seigneural Lower Canada, one of the ranges (def. 2b) of thirty-two 200-acre lots into which each new township was subdivided.
☞ *Although this term is largely confined to Ontario and Quebec, it occurs in related senses in other provinces and it had some early use in the West.*
1790 (1905) *Ont.Bur.Arch.Rep.* III 65: The Concessions were to run parallel to each other, the Ranges to contain a certain number of Lots of 200 Acres each, the front of every Lot to run parallel to the front of the Township. **1846** TAYLOR *Narrative* 98: Property, in Canada, is divided by what is called concessions, which means a range of land that extends from east to west, through the whole length of a township. The first range from the south is called the first concession; that behind, the second, and so on. **1965** *Kingston Whig-Standard* (Ont.) 22 Jan. 5/7: This growth is reasonably rare in Frontenac County . . . appearing only in the first, second and third concessions.

3 See **concession road.**
1842 *Montreal Transcript* 3 Mar. 1/4: What is the number and Concession, (or street) of the Lot on which the house you inhabit stands? **1932** JAMIESON *Cattle in the Stall* 43: Now, it is some brave lady with a car who takes all chances of a flat tire on a remote concession, or a broken axle. . . . **1963** *Globe and Mail* (Toronto) 26 Apr. 5/1: The areas, locations and fish are . . . Heart

Lake, five miles north of No. 7 Highway on Second Concession, east of Brampton, rainbow trout.

concessional line *Obs.* See **concession line** (def. 1).
1787 (1905) *Ont.Bur.Arch.Rep.* VIII 379: You will lay out the concessional lines that are not already run out, the distance between each lot to be 19 chains.

concessioner *n. Rare* a person living on or owning land on a concession.
1902 (1916) *London & Middlesex Hist.Soc.Trans.* VII 10: A thirteenth concessioner, Mr. Robinson, is now a very influential member of Parliament.

concession line 1 a survey line, indicated by blazed trees or other markers, establishing the boundaries of a concession (def. 2), the number of the several lots appearing on fixed posts. See also **line** (def. 4a).
1794 (1905) *Ont.Bur.Arch.Rep.* III 257: May I request you will be pleased to procure from the persons employed under your Board as Surveyors, a report of their method of opening their Concession lines and those of Townships, &c. . . . **1863** WALSHE *Cedar Creek* 115: The new townships in Upper Canada are laid out in parallel lines, running nearly east and west, sixty-six chains apart, and sixty-six feet in width, which are termed concession lines, being conceded by Government as road allowances. **1962** ALLEN *Peace River Country* 142: "I'm sorry," Chris panted, "but I ran off the road at the concession line."

2 See **concession road**. See also **line** (def. 4b).
1832 *Canadian Freeman* 26 Oct. 3/2: The concession lines and side-roads are being cut out at the expense of the Home Government. **1960** *Ontario History* June 90: This occurred because the ninth concession . . . became a more frequently travelled route than the tenth concession line which was the road to Lloydtown.

concession road a road built on the road allowance between concessions, following the concession line and connected to other concession roads by side roads, the distance separating each being, as a rule, 1¼ miles. See also **concession** (def. 3), **concession line** (def. 2), and **line** (def. 4b). Cp. **section line** (def. 2) and **side-road** (def. 2).
1811 *Kingston Gaz.* (U.C.) 28 May 3/3: Such persons as may be disposed to contract for building a Bridge over the Little Cataraqui River, on the Second Concession Road, are requested to send their proposals in writing to the subscriber. **1922** PICKTHALL *Bridge* 223: He recrossed the wide pasture and went back along the track until it entered at right angles the concession-road. . . . **1965** *Maclean's* 3 July 26/2: It was reasonably close to Ontario's main centres of population and accessible from concession roads along most of its course.

concessions *n.pl.* the rural or bush districts as opposed to the urban centres; back concessions, *q.v.*
1924 BLAKE *Chez Nous* 27: Back in the concessions the houses are scattered, and the distance from one to another is covered at a rattling pace. **1961** *Press* July 7: "Guaranteed Employment" can take the New Party into the outlands of darkest Quebec and into the under-privileged, low-standard coves and concessions of the Atlantic Provinces. . . .

conch-shell road *N.S.* See quote.
1934 DENNIS *Down in N.S.* 113: Take the Base Line Road, then turn to your right. . . . You'll find the Base Line pretty straight. This road you're on is a conch-shell road [which] was marked on the base road and at an opposite point on the Bay, then blazoned

through the forest from one point to another by the sound of a conch-shell used as a horn. There are numbers of conch-shell roads on this side of the mountain.

Concordia *n.* Montreal, Quebec.
1936 CROSS *Cross Roads* 11: Concordia (from the civic crest "Concordia Salus") is noted for its women newsies. *Ibid.* 1: [Montreal] is the second largest French-speaking city in the world, and is familiarly known to intimates as Concordia.

conductor *n.* [< Cdn F *conducteur*] *Obs.* **1** the pilot or guide in charge of a brigade of canoes or other vessels, or of one vessel only. See also **guide** (def. 1).
1761 (1901) HENRY (Elder) *Travels* 14: . . . to every three or four canoes, which constitute a *brigade*, there is a *guide* or conductor. **1821** HOWISON *Sketches of U.C.* 43: The whole equipment was under the command . . . of an individual who was styled the *conductor*.

2 a person engaged in effecting the escape of slaves by way of the Underground Railway, *q.v.*
1852 *Voice of the Fugitive* (Sandwich [Windsor], C.W.) 22 Apr. 1/3: I was formerly, while residing East, a conductor of a car on the Underground Railroad, I felt a desire to get the perusal of said paper, so that I might be able to keep track of the progress that is being made by a portion of mankind who were so unfortunate as to receive their birth in a land of slavery.

coney[1] *n.* See **connie**.

coney[2] or **cony** *n.* See **pika**.
1936 MOWERY *Paradise Trail* 39: On a talus slide they spotted a cony, solitary little denizen of bleak high places, and paused to watch him industriously making hay. . . . **1960** *Cdn Audubon* Jan.-Feb. 27/3: For a creature so small, the pika has many names: Coney, Rock Rabbit, Calling Hare, Whistling Hare, and others.

Confederacy *n.* See **Confederation**.
1864 *Nor'Wester* (R.R.S.) 21 Nov. 3/3: The Confederation conference has decided in reference to members of the Legislative Council to the new Confederacy, that they be selected from the members of the Legislative Councils of the several provinces instead of elected by the people. **1940** MACCORMAC *Canada* 181: The British North America Act, which constituted the confederacy, gave her a system of government thoroughly English. . . .

Confederate *n.* a supporter of Confederation, *q.v.* See also **Confederationist**.
1867 (1965) GAETZ *Diary* 95: . . . the following persons were nominated for the "Commons" at Ottawa, Confederate, H. A. N. Kaulbach; Anti-Confederate, Edwd. McDonald, of Halifax. **1867** *Islander* (Charlottetown) 4 Jan. 2/6: We believe . . . the Confederate members of the . . . House of Assembly might commit the Island to Confederation after the example of Nova Scotia. **1869** *Mainland Guardian* (New Westminster, B.C.) 13 Nov. 3/3: Where are the two hundred thousand dollars per annum that the Confederates say we are to receive from Canada. **1875** *North Star* (St. John's) 18 Sep. 3/1: The Newfoundlanders have begun to see that Canada can do a great deal better without them than they can do without Canada, and that the Confederates were not so far wrong. **1958** *Evening Telegram* (St. John's) 24 Apr. 4/4: I agree, as far as a Confederate can, the dastardly

conspiracy was equal to anything Hitler or Stalin could think up.

Confederated Provinces *Hist.* the provinces entering Confederation.
1865 *Islander* (Charlottetown) 27 Jan. 2/7: The subjects of national debts, and public works, in the case of the Confederated Provinces have considerable affinity. **1883** LAWRENCE *Foot-Prints* vi: A railway connecting the Confederated Provinces, by the terms of the Imperial Statute, had to be built; but its location was left for future determination.

Confederation *n.* the joining in federal union, under the British North America Act, of the several provinces consituting the Dominion of Canada, inaugurated in 1867. See also **Confederacy** and **Union** (def. 2).
[**1825** *Colonial Advocate* (York [Toronto]) 27 Jan. 3/5: By an article in the Canadian Spectator . . . a confederation of all the British provinces is mentioned as the substitute which the English government have in contemplation.] **1863** *Wkly Manitoban* 11 Nov. 1/1: From Halifax to Huron the question of the Confederation to the British North American provinces is being discussed. **1869** *Cdn Illust.News* 30 Oct. 7/2: Confederation was rather the work of the politicians than of the people. **1964** *Canada Month* Jan. 27/2: As for the western provinces, we know that they only came into being after Confederation.

Confederation Conference See **Charlottetown Conference**.
1864 *Nor'Wester* (R.R.S.) 21 Nov. 3/3: The Confederation conference has decided in reference to members of the Legislative Council to the new Confederacy, that they be selected from the members of the Legislative Councils of the several provinces instead of being elected by the people. **1957** HUTCHISON *Canada* 72: A committee compiling a booklet to celebrate Charlottetown's centennial could think of nothing to record since the Confederation Conference, but plenty happened before that.

Confederation Day See **Dominion Day**.
1928 *Beaver* June 42/2: Our illustration is that of the flag display on Confederation Day at Cumberland House. **1963** *Observer* 15 Sep. 20/2: It was called Confederation Day, Dominion Day, and Canada Day. "Surely," he said, "some definite title could be selected so that a minister of the Crown would not have to refer to it as the 1st of July." And he added that "If that could be done, it would be something to celebrate."

Confederation Father See **Father of Confederation**.
1954 *Fundy Fisherman* 23 June 4/1: We like to think of that day long ago when the Confederation Fathers resolved that provincialism would be put aside for the sake of the country, fair and wide they envisioned in the future.

Confederationist *n.* See **Confederate**.
1869 *Mainland Guardian* (New Westminster, B.C.) 29 Sep. 3/3: During the interview the Governor is believed to have said; That he personally was a confederationist. . . . **1958** *Fisherman* 10 Oct. 6/6: . . . MacDonald fought for a railroad to the Pacific, when the B.C. Confederationists urged joining the new dominion. . . .

Confederation Square the site of the National War Memorial in Ottawa, near the Parliament Buildings.
1959 *Kingston Whig-Standard* (Ont.) 2 May 11/6: The recommendation that Sparks street be closed to vehicles for five blocks west from the central Confederation Square was made last December. . . . **1962** *Canada Month* Feb. 18/1: As winter bit in, nary a spot in a Canadian city was as deuced uncomfortable as the open stretch of Confederation Square between the Chateau Laurier and Parliament. . . .

congé [kɑn'ʒe] *n. Cdn French, Hist.* a permit to enter Indian country, issued by the Governor of New France.
1931 NUTE *Voyageur* 5: Licenses (*congés*) to enter Indian country were required. **1956** INNIS *Fur Trade* 98: . . . a partner of M. de la Marque secured two *congés* in 1739, one for three canoes and eighteen men . . . and one for four canoes and twenty-eight men. . . .

conibear (trap) *n.* [after *F. Conibear,* a Canadian expert on trapping] a kind of trap that kills its victims instantly. Also spelled *Conibear*.
1965 *Star Wkly* 23 Jan. 36/3: Emile Paquette uses small traps most of the time, but he likes a newer device called the Conibear trap. . . . **1966** *Toronto Dly Star* 30 Apr. 65/6: There is a more humane trap [than the leghole trap], known as the conibear, which kills large animals, such as beavers, instantly and humanely.

conie *n.* See **connie**.

conjurer or **conjuror** *n.* **1** See **medicine man** (def. 1a).
1784-1812 (1916) THOMPSON *Narrative* 90: For to acquire this important knowledge, they have recourse to Dreams and other superstitions; and a few of their best conjurers sometimes take a bold method of imposing upon themselves and others. **1907** CROSBY *An-ko-me-nums* 114: When becalmed on a fair day the conjurer or "Windmaker" would volunteer to raise the wind. **1964** *North* July 49/2: I had heard unbelievable stories about the uncanny performances of native conjurers in different parts of the north where I had been but never thought I would sometime become the object of their deliberations.

2 *Obs.* See 1865 quote.
1852 SUTHERLAND *Baffin's Bay* II lxvii: Roused the cook at four A.M.; had breakfast comfortably, but our conjurer is rather small to supply seven. **1865** HALL *Arctic Researches* 328: . . . this they did by taking a whale-boat, a "conjuror" (a portable cooking apparatus), two guns and ammunition. . . .

conjurer's lodge among Indians, a small, hut-like structure used by a medicine man (def. 1a) to demonstrate his magical powers by freeing himself from bonds and conversing with spirits. See also **conjuring-box, jonglerie, juggling machine, medicine tent** (def. 2), and **shaking lodge**.
1945 *Beaver* June 17/1: . . . the magician would build, a small circular conjuror's lodge of poles thrust into the ground and covered with skins. . . . **1956** LEECHMAN *Native Tribes* 50: A more elaborate way of seeing into the future was by means of the Conjuror's Lodge, a hut built of sheets of birch bark or of mats. Into this the medicine man was carried, often bound hand and foot.

conjuring-box, -house, or **-lodge** *n.* See **conjurer's lodge**.
1771 (1911) HEARNE *Journey* 210: On such extraordinary occasions a conjuring-house is erected. **1784-1812** (1916)

THOMPSON *Narrative* 91: On one of these occasions . . . we found the above Indian preparing his conjuring box. . . . **1903** WHITE *Forest* 328: Had it been a question of Rupert's River Crees with their . . . conjuring-lodges . . . the affair might have been different. **1935** JENNESS *Parry Island* 65: The conjuror . . . derived his power from a vision at puberty, when a *manido* visited him and conferred upon him the special gift of divining by means of the conjuring lodge.

conjuring dance among Indians and Eskimos, a ritual dance led by a shaman with the purpose of propitiating the spirits.
1924 FLAHERTY *Eskimo Friends* 123: Igloo building, conjuring dances, sledging, and seal-hunting were run off as the sunny days of February and March wore on.

conjuring duck 1 the bufflehead, *Glaucionetta albeola.* See also **spirit duck.**
1823 FRANKLIN *Journey* 701: The Buffel-headed Duck of Catesby . . . is known to the Canadian settlers also as the Conjuring Duck.

2 the common goldeneye, *Glaucionetta clangula.*
1959 MCATEE *Folk-Names* 14: Common Goldeneye [is also called] conjuring duck (In reference to its "magical" ability in diving at the flash of an old-time gun or the twang of a bow-string quickly enough to evade the missile. "N.W.T."). . . .

conjuring feast *Obs.* See quote.
1804 CAMERON *Nipigon Country* 254: They likewise make feasts from which boys, women and children are excluded; these they call their "Medicine" or conjuring feasts, at which they observe a number of ridiculous ceremonies, such as eating without a knife, striving who can finish his share first.

conjuror *n.* See **conjurer.**

Connectionist *n. Hist.* a supporter of the British connection (def. 2).
1849 *Wkly Globe* 2 Nov. 71/5: The *Examiner* seems to think it would have been better to let Mr. Perry slip in, Annexationist or Connectionist, to affect public opinion in "England and the world."

connie or **conny** ['kɑnɪ *or* 'konɪ] *n.* [reduction of F *inconnu* unknown] *North* See **inconnu.** Also spelled *con(e)y.*
1936 STEELE *Policing the Arctic* 31: In the black depths beneath them slept trout and whitefish, "conny," and Arctic grayling. **1947** *Beaver* Dec. 24/1: The "unknown fish," or "conny" as it is more often called, looks like an overgrown whitefish and turns the scales between twenty and forty pounds. **1961** FERGUSON *Tuktoyaktuk* 15: Common species are whitefish, at least two varieties of herring, smelts, and the large fish—inconnu or connie.

conscriptionist *n.* a person who favored a policy of compulsory military service during the First World War.
1917 *Grit* (Toronto) 13 Dec. 2/5: Graham is a conscriptionist, too.

conservation officer an official of a government department concerned with the conservation of game. See also **game warden.**
1962 *Canada Month* Nov. 9/2: Bill was caught pit-lamping deer on the Otter Point Road . . . by conservation officer Jack Lenfesty and RCMP Cpl. I. W. Demsey. **1965** *Kingston Whig-Standard* (Ont.) 5 Feb. 11/2: The local conservation officers and their wives were literally beset with telephone calls.

conservation road a road giving access to a forest conservation area.
1959 *Country Guide* May 61/1: The southern half of the conservation road begins at Coleman, a mining town on Alberta Highway No. 3, about 60 miles west of Fort Macleod.

Conservatism *n.* the body of principles held by Conservatives; the platform of the Conservative Party or, more recently, the Progressive-Conservative Party.
1836 (1965) HAMILTON *Cdn Quotations* 49/2: Never did we see such an assemblage of long-visaged Tories. They appeared as if they were following . . . conservatism to the grave (*Bathurst Courier*, Feb. 5, 1836). **1958** *Herald-Tribune* (Grande Prairie, Alta) 11 Mar. 2/1: . . . when the CCF and Social Credit parties claim that there is no appreciable difference between Liberalism and Conservatism it is evident that they have something different in mind. . . .

Conservative *n.* **1** *Hist.* in colonial times, a supporter of the British connection (def. 2) and of colonial constitutions; a member of the political party endorsing these views; Tory.
1839 *Bytown* [Ottawa] *Gaz.* 7 Nov. 3/2: The Conservatives succeeding in choosing Francis Boyde, Esq. of George street, against Lieut. Steel, R.N., who was put in nomination by the Durhamites. **1853** *Hamilton Gaz.* (C.W.) 29 Jan. 3/3: He is a Conservative of the progressive school. **1963** MORTON *Kingdom of Canada* 264: . . . the only members to leave the council were two pronounced Conservatives, William Draper and Henry Sherwood. . . .

2 a member of the Conservative Party of Sir John A. Macdonald and succeeding leaders, a party nowadays known officially as the Progressive Conservative Party. See also **Progressive Conservative.**
1889 *Rat Portage* [Kenora] *News* (Ont.) 1 Mar. 2/1: Conservatives and Reformers are thoroughly disgusted with his actions, and are most anxious to show it at the polls. **1964** *Calgary Herald* 9 July 5/7: . . . the Conservatives showed signs of digging in for a long fight against the amendment. . . .

Conservative Party formerly, the official name for one of the political groups in Canada, later used informally for the Liberal-Conservative Party and nowadays for the Progressive Conservative Party.
1852 *Voice of the Fugitive* (Sandwich [Windsor], C.W.) 29 Jan. 2/3: The colored people were in former times, generally supposed to vote with the Conservative party, from a belief, unfounded it is true, that the Reformers were disposed towards Annexation. **1963** *Globe and Mail* (Toronto) 26 Mar. 7/1: "It's a queer campaign," key figures in the Liberal, Conservative and New Democratic Parties have commented in almost identical terms in the north.

Conservative Unionist party *Hist.* the Conservative group sharing in the Union Government of 1917 under Sir Robert Borden.
1917 *Grit* (Toronto) 12 Dec. 3/5: The street railway men are up in arms against the Conservative Unionist party.

consolidated high school See **consolidated school.** Cp. **union school.**
1958 *Edmonton Jnl* 28 June 3/5: Much of the afternoon was taken up with questions directed to Dr. Byrne on the advantages of large consolidated high schools. **1962** *Gleaner* (Fredericton) 2 Aug. 5/2: She will teach French next year in the Woodstock [N.B.] Consolidated High School.

Consolidated Revenue Fund See quote.
1963 *Toronto Dly Star* 23 Nov. 7/2: Consolidated Revenue Fund—This is the name that is applied to the gigantic pool of money into which all federal government bills are paid.

consolidated school especially in rural districts, a centrally located school taking the place of several smaller schools. See also **consolidated high school** and **regional school.**
1915 MCCLUNG *In Times Like These* 195: The consolidated school and the "Beef-rings" in the country district are already established facts, and have opened the way for this larger scheme of coöperation. **1957** PHILLIPS *Education* 271: . . . in 1912, the Macdonald Consolidated School at Hillsboro, the first of its kind in Canada, closed for financial reasons after nine years of operation. **1964** WILSON *Barrett's Landing* 13: Kids . . . are picked up by bus and taken to a large modern consolidated school in a nearby town.

Constitutional *n. Hist.* See **Constitutionalist.**
1904 DECELLES *Papineau* 152: Their language was strong . . . excitement was greatly enhanced by the virulence of the opposite party, who called themselves the Constitutionals, or Conservative party, i.e., the conservators of existing abuses.

Constitutional *adj. Hist.* of or associated with the Constitutional party, *q.v.*
1834 *Niagara Reporter* (U.C.) 2 Dec. 2/2: We rejoice that another engine of the Radicals has thus been annihilated, and the Constitutional press in this city may take some part of the credit for bringing it about. **1837** *Times* (Halifax) 4 July 210/3: We have taken from the Lower Canada Constitutional papers, several extracts which will show the disposition with which the British portion of the population regard the proceedings of the Revolutionists.

Constitutional Act *Hist.* the act passed in 1791 which created Upper and Lower Canada on the basis of a British Constitution and with all the machinery of a British colonial province.
1828 BIDWELL *Tor.Pub.Lib.MSS B 104* 47: Some colour was lent to this view by the language of the Constitutional Act; and from the earliest times the government clique was then composed of members of the Church of England. **1915** WALLACE *Family Compact* 1: The Constitutional Act seemed on the surface a very liberal measure. **1963** MORTON *Kingdom of Canada* 183: . . . in 1791 the British parliament passed the Constitutional Act.

Constitutionalist *n. Hist.* a supporter of the Constitutional party; a Tory or Conservative. See also **constitutionist.**
1822 *Canadian Courant* (Montreal) 30 Nov. 3/1: The poor inhabitants of the Townships, have received a heavy broadside of artillery from this champion of the Constitutionalists. **1873** *Maritime Mthly* July 81: The "Sons of Liberty," with their silken banners and bands of music, openly paraded the thoroughfares of Montreal, and frequent conflicts occurred between these agitators and a body of loyal citizens calling themselves "Constitutionalists."

Constitutional party *Hist.* the political group supporting the Constitutional Act of 1791 with its implicit safeguards for the British connection; the Tory Party, precursors of the Conservative Party in Canada.
1834 *British-American Jnl.* (St. Catharines, U.C.) 20 Nov. 3/2: . . . the late Speaker [is] the candidate of the administration and Mr. Midwell of the constitutional party. **1837** *Times* (Halifax) 18 July 230/1: The regular organs of the Constitutional Party have . . . advised their adherers not to attend it. **1847** *Montreal Transcript* 18 Dec. 2/2: A public meeting of the Conservatives has been held in that town, for the purpose of selecting from the several nominees the one most likely to meet with the undivided support of the constitutional party.

Constitutional Reformer *Hist.* in Upper Canada, a supporter of reform by constitutional means; a moderate Reformer.
1836 *Bytown* [Ottawa] *Gaz.* 16 June 4/3: The editor avows himself a Constitutional Reformer, in the true sense of the phrase, and ardent admirer of the institutions of the mother country, and of the Constitution of this Province given by the parent state as a pledge of affectionate regard. **1881** RATTRAY *Scots in Brit.N.W.* II 455: He was a constitutional Reformer; yet his programme was moderate enough.

Constitutional Reform Society in the 1830's in Upper Canada, an organization dedicated to the movement for reform, in opposition to the Family Compact (def. 1).
1836 (1961) *Ont.Hist.* June 102: . . . this meeting do resolve itself into a society to be called the "Constitutional Reform Society of Upper Canada." **1961** *Ibid.* June 97: Sometime during the 'twenties [1820's] . . . a Reform organization called the Constitutional Reform Society of Upper Canada was established.

Constitutional Society *Hist.* a society of Tories organized in 1836-37 with the purpose of maintaining the British position in Lower Canada, then in ferment because of the Patriotes, *q.v.*
1963 MORTON *Kingdom of Canada* 247: The English of the bureaucratic party [in Lower Canada] . . . had organized a Constitutional Society. . . .

constitutionist *n. Hist.* See **Constitutionalist.**
1893 YEIGH *Ont.Parliament* 81: By June of 1836 he had tendered his resignation to Lord Glenelg, though the change in the complexion of parties, resulting from the election of 1836, when the "constitutionists" were forty-five in number, and the "republicans" seventeen, raised his spirits and his hopes of a speedy settlement.

consumption vine *Obs.* a plant of the wintergreen family, *Pyrola americana,* used as a medicine in colonial times.
1796 (1911) SIMCOE *Diary* 328: . . . consumption vine [is] a pretty creeper.

continental bed a bed having a box spring and mattress but no head or foot boards.
1955 *Globe and Mail* (Toronto) 31 Jan. 30/6: An English family has accommodation for 2 young men,

share comfortable room, continental beds, packed lunches, privileges. $15 each.

continental divide the great watershed in the Rockies which divides the rivers flowing west to the Pacific from those flowing east and north; the Great Divide, *q.v.*
1889 *Trans.Roy.Soc.Can.* VII 130: They returned to ascend a second branch and finally reached the continental "divide" on February 25th. **1958** *Edmonton Jnl* 18 Oct. 4/3: The path lay via the Athabasca, Mackenzie and Liard Rivers to the continental divide. ...

continental watershed See **continental divide**.
1905 OUTRAM *Cdn Rockies* 265: And the familiar forms of the great peaks of the Continental watershed, Stephen and the Cathedral ... with the great ice-clad helmet of Mt. Temple shining resplendently above the line of giants. ...

continuation school in rural Ontario, a small secondary school coming under the jurisdiction of a municipal public-school board.
1955 *Manitoulin Expositor* 26 May 14/5: TEACHER WANTED. Manitowaning Continuation School (Manitoulin Island) (2 room school with attendance of approximately 37 pupils) requires qualified assistant, male or female, protestant, to teach French, Latin, Art, English and Geography. **1955** *Tweed News* 14 Apr. 9/2: A special meeting of the Flinton Continuation and Public School trustees was held in the school building. ...

contraband beaver beaver skins trapped contrary to the provisions of the game act.
1934 GODSELL *Arctic Trader* 135: Hidden in the depths of the surrounding woods were many heavy packs of "contraband" beaver ... which had to be smuggled past the alert game authorities and shipped to England.

contract worker *Lumbering* See quote.
1942 HAIG-BROWN *Timber* 251: Most fallers are contract or "bushel" workers—paid at a rate of so much per thousand board feet of timber felled.

controller *n.* See 1960 quote.
1960 WARD *Government in Canada* 57: In Ontario, the larger cities have a board of control, and controllers are elected at the same time as the mayor and aldermen. Controllers are members of the city council as well as being members of the board of control. **1962** *Globe and Mail* (Toronto) 28 Nov. 7/1: Three sitting controllers are conducting strong campaigns for re-election with Controller Donald Summerville making his first bid for the mayoralty in an attempt to unseat Nathan Phillips. **1966** *Toronto Dly Star* 18 Apr. 27/8: Since acquiring the land after World War II the Toronto controller has planted 60,000 trees there.

coo *n.* See **coup**.

coocouse *n.* See **coho**.

cook boat See **cook scow**.
1909 CAMERON *New North* 54: The third craft [of a "flotilla"] we observe with due respect as "the cook boat."

cook camp† a cookhouse, *q.v.*, in a logging, construction, or other camp.
1935 SULLIVAN *Great Divide* 194: ... there was ... the cook camp with its log annex for supplies and fresh beef.

cook car a mobile cookhouse used by threshing crews, cat-swing crews, and other workers.

1922 STEAD *Neighbours* 140: So the threshing season wore on. We ate in a cook-car, slept in a "caboose," and worked from dawn until dark. Sometimes, to finish a "set" we would burn a straw pile and work by its light. ... **1956** KEMP *Northern Trader* 211: There would be either a sleeping car or a big stove-heated tent for the men to sleep in and the cook car to take care of their bodily needs. **1964** *Calgary Herald* 10 Mar. 21/6: A cook car and two wagon loads of lumber ... followed.

cookee ['kʊki *or* kuˈki] *n.* [< *cook* + dim. suffix *-ee*] *Esp.Lumbering* a cook's helper. See also **cook's mate** and **flunkey** (def. 1). Cp. **cookie**.
1896 ROBERTS *Camp-Fire* 81: The cook had the camp all to himself for a while; for the teams and choppers were at work a mile away, and the "cookee," as the cook's assistant is called, had betaken himself to a neighboring pond to fish for trout through the ice. **1957** *Bush News* (St. Catharines, Ont.) June 2/1: Since this photo was taken, it is understood that an additional cook and cookee have been added to the staff to look after the appetites of some 260 employees. **1965** *Islander* 16 May 6/2: Food was laid out in "dishups" scattered along the table and "cookees" watched to see that they were well filled.

cookery *n.* **1** in work camps, a place where meals are cooked and eaten; cookhouse; kitchen.
1748 DRAGE *Voyage* I 128: This Part ... called the Plantation, is separated from the Factory by two Rows of High Palissades, between the first of which and the second, are Store-Houses, the Cookery, and some Work-shops, low-built, and so placed as they would be of little Service to an Enemy to cover an Attack of the Place. **1854** KEEFER *Ottawa* 67: The raft being ready, all hands, with provisions, cook and cookery, are embarked. ... **1964** *Globe and Mail* (Toronto) 17 Nov. 31/8: I suppose it is partly to ... get the meal over with quickly so the cookery staff can get on with the dish-washing.
2 the rendering plant on board a whaling ship.
1954 RADDALL *Muster of Arms* 203: You have to be a good man born with fins to have a job in a hunting ship, and on the voyage home they are like kings to the mess-boys and butchers and lemmers and flensers and the others who work in the cookery.

cookery crib *Hist.* a strongly built raft for accommodating the cook's caboose (def. 1b), gear, and supplies, used for preparing meals during a timber drive.
1883 FRASER *S'hanty* 341: If you can manage to get on the "cookery crib," which carries all the provisions and cooking utensils, then you may consider yourself quite safe, as it is constructed with all the skill and care that the most experienced raftsmen can bestow. **1933** ROLYAT *Wilderness Walls* 10: How long ... since they had left behind the jolly river drivers, the gay cookery cribs. ...

cookhouse *n.* in a work camp, a building where cooking is done and meals are served. See also **cook-shack, cook-shed, grub camp,** and **grub-house**.
1904 ROBERTS *Watchers of the Trails* 141: The cook was in the cook-house, rattling tins. **1942** TWOMEY & HERRICK *Needle to the North* 10: The cookhouse, perhaps thirty by seventy feet, was full of crude long tables and benches. ... **1959** *News of the North* 22 Jan. 7/5: We have a considerable quantity of new

cook house utensils suitable for a bush camp.

cookie or **cooky**† ['kʊki] *n.* a camp cook. Cp. **cookee.**

1912 FOOTNER *New Rivers* 90: The jolly cooky at Summit Lake . . . threw together the materials of his culinary successes with a delightful nonchalance, holding forth meanwhile as uninterruptedly as his pot of beans simmering over the fire. **1920** GIBBON *Conquering Hero* 129: If ever you come to the point where you are looking for a job, I'll hire you as cookie at fifty dollars a month. **1962** FRY *Ranch on the Cariboo* 149: "Jack, you go with the boy and see Cookie gives him something to eat."

cook-room *n. Esp.Nfld, Hist.* See 1898 quote.

1633 *Commission for well Gouerning* 7: Thirdly, That no person whatsoeuer, either Fishermen or Inhabitants doe destroy, deface, or any way worke any spoyle or detriment to any Stage, Cookeroome, Flakes, Spikes, Nayles, or any thing else, that belongeth to the Stages whatsoeuer, either at the end of the voyage when hee hath done, and is to depart the Countrey, or to any such Stages as hee shall fall withall at his comming into the Countrey. **1793** REEVES *Hist.Nfld* 8: No person was to deface or spoil any stage, cook-room, or other building. **1898** *Rev.Hist.Pubs* II 160: When one of the companies controls a fishing-station it brings fishermen for the summer season from the Gaspé coast . . . and lodges the men in large buildings called "cook-rooms," of which the upper story is a huge dormitory. **1964** *Nfld Qtly* Summer 15/1: Also with a large enough lot of non-resident hands, there would be a "cook room". . . .

cook scow *Hist.* in the scow brigades, *q.v.,* of the Northwest, a scow equipped for the preparing and serving of meals. See also **cook-boat.**

1914 DOUGLAS *Lands Forlorn* 28: To exchange a bed of boughs in the open for a small and usually stuffy cabin was of doubtful benefit, but this was offset by the comfortable saloon for meals, although of the cramped table on the cook scow, where you sat on a sack of pork with the grease ozzing through it, and thought yourself lucky if you could find room for your feet in a half empty sugar barrel under the table. **1936** *Cdn Geog.Jnl* Jan. 142: Ultimately in 1887, the Hudson's Bay Company introduced the use of a cook scow.

cook-shack† *n.* See **cookhouse.**

1912 BICKERSTETH *Open Doors* 157: [Being] kept waiting for their dinner . . . is a most unpardonable offence in their eyes, and they were ready to pull down the cook-shack over his ears. **1965** *Time* (Cdn ed.) 12 Feb. 9/1: And at Spartan's bleak Pelly Bay camp in the Canadian Arctic, a bushed cook arose from bed one midnight, purposefully set about frying every single egg in the stores, and then nailed them all, sunnyside up, to the cookshack wall.

cook-shed *n.* See **cookhouse.**

1898 CONNOR *Black Rock* 2: The grub camp, with cook-shed attached, stood in the middle of the clearing; at a little distance was the sleeping-camp with the office built against it, and about a hundred yards away . . . stood the stables, and near them the smiddy.

cook's mate See **cookee.**

1883 FRASER *Shanty* 27: . . . they must be men . . . who know experimentally every detail of the [logging] business from "cook's mate" up to hewer. . . .

cook's shovel a long-handled shovel used to

bury bake kettles in hot sand in a camboose (def. 2). See also **Irish miner's shovel.**

1961 PRICE & KENNEDY *Renfrew* 46: The "cook's shovel" used to bury the kettles was round-pointed with a short socket into which the cook fitted a long straight handle.

cooky *n.* See **cookie.**

coolee, cooley, or **cooly** *n.* See **coulee.**

coon *n.* See **raccoon.**

cooney[1] ['kuni] *n.* [< Esk. *kuni(a)* wife < Danish *Kone*] *Arctic* **1** a woman, especially a wife. Also spelled *kuni.*

1850 *Arctic Miscellany* 93: I like this species of madness, especially when the pretty Koonahs made me jump about with them. **1860** (1865) HALL *Arctic Researches* 161: Tookoolito informed me to-day that the words pickaninny, for infant; cooney, for wife; pussy, for seal; Husky, for Innuit; smoketute, for pipe, and many other words, are not Esquimaux, though in use among her people. [**1910** HODGE *Bulletin* II 484/1: The presence of a few Scandinavian words, for example, *kunia,* "wife," in the jargon of the Point Barrow Eskimo and whites, is due to Danish rather than to Norse influence.] **1938** *Beaver* Mar. 24/1: They told me there was even a square dance, the numbers called by John L. Sullivan [an Eskimo]. When it came to "Ladies in the center," John L. called out "Bunch your coonies." "Coonies" I found out was whaler-Eskimo for ladies. **1961** ANDERSON *Angel of Hudson Bay* 39: "It can't be," murmured the old lady, who had never known a Company trader without a beard and a bald head. "Whatever will the *kunis* think of them curly locks!"

2 a caribou doe.

1882 GILDER *Schwatka's Search* 25: He had shot two deer [caribou], a "cooney" and an "isaacer"—that is, a doe and a buck—and he had their warm, bloody skins on his back.

cooney[2]† ['kuni] *n.* [< Am.E < Sp. *cuna* cradle] *West* a sheet of cowhide or, nowadays, canvas, lashed under the bed of a chuckwagon, *q.v.,* and used to carry fuel.

1963 SYMONS *Many Trails* 55: Under the wagon was commonly slung a cowhide "cooney" into which dried brush or cow chips were chucked in the event of a shortage of fuel.

Co-operative Commonwealth Federation a farmer-labor-socialist party founded 30 July, 1932, in Calgary, Alberta, its original principles being embodied in the Regina Manifesto, *q.v.* The party was best known as the C.C.F. and was superseded in the early 1960's by the New Democratic Party, *q.v.* See also **CCF.**

1934 *New Commonwealth* 28 July 1/3: Endorsation of a brief, fighting platform, the establishment of a national C.C.F. movement . . . featured the second annual convention of the Co-operative Commonwealth Federation. **1953** MOON *Saskatchewan* 35: There are some who say there is a direct connection between that sad July day in 1935 and the 1944 election of the Co-operative Commonwealth Federation—more commonly, C.C.F.—government of Saskatchewan, the first Socialist administration in North America. **1963** MORTON *Kingdom of Canada* 461: In 1932 the U.F.A. members of Parliament, labour politicians, farmer leaders, trade-union leaders and left-wing intellectuals began the organization of a new party, the Co-operative Commonwealth Federation.

coot-sac *n.* [< F *cul de sac*] See quote.

1941 *Beaver* Sep. 37/1: Coot-sac—A bay or cove that
has no outlet.

cop owl *N.B.* See **Acadian owl.**
1959 MCATEE *Folk-Names* 44: SAW-WHET OWL . . . cop
owl (A common call is a repeated "kup, kup." N.B.). . . .

Copenhagen snoose See **snoose.**
1961 *Western Miner & Oil Rev.* Aug. 20/1: The trio . . .
surveyed the pile . . . increasing its volume the while by
regular parabolic ejections of copenhagen snoose-juice.
1964 *B.C. Digest* 8/2: The smell of a pine-knot fire /
From a stovepipe that's come loose / Mingles sweetly
with the boot grease / And the Copenhagen snoose.

copper *n.* **1 a.** *Hist.* in colonial times, a copper coin
valued at one half-penny in York currency, *q.v.* See
1844 quote.
1767 *Quebec Gaz.* 2 Feb. 4/1: Just published, and to be
Sold . . . at Eighteen Coppers each, or One Dollar per
Dozen, A Sheet Almanac . . . fitted to the Latitude of
Quebec. 1844 *Bytown* [Ottawa] *Gaz.* 8 Feb. 2/4: The
Shilling currency is subdivided into twenty-four copper
coins, called Coppers. Coins of this metal, of Colonial,
British and American origin, and of various
denomination, are common, and each is pretty
generally taken as the equivalent of a copper, without
much reference to its intrinsic value. 1905 SCHERCK *Pen
Pictures* 68: The penny of the New York currency was
equivalent to our present cent, but the name "copper"
was generally used then instead of cent.

b. a Canadian one-cent piece, first minted in 1858.
See also **cent.**
1863 WALSHE *Cedar Creek* 109: No you didn't stare
about as they did, as if the house and fixins was a show
at a copper a head. 1916 WOOD *Tourist's N.W.* 320:
Coppers are not in general circulation west of Calgary.
Employés at railway news and curio stands are
instructed to refuse them, and tourists relate incidents
of their being declined at Government post offices.
1954 LYSENKO *Yellow Boots* 31: . . . he opened his huge
fists and tossed fifty shining new coppers into the air.

2 a shield-shaped sheet of copper used by West
Coast Indians as a symbol of wealth or distinction,
often prominent in gift-giving ceremonies.
1912 HODGE & WHITE *Indians of Canada* 113/1: Perhaps
the most noteworthy product is the unique, shield-like
"coppers" made of sheet metal and highly esteemed as
symbols of wealth and distinction. The origin of these
"coppers" and of their peculiar form and use is not
known. 1926 MCKELVIE *Huldowget* v: The potlatch . . .
has been banned, and the bartering of coppers declared
illegal. 1956 LEECHMAN *Native Tribes* 303: He would
take a "copper," a shield-shaped sheet of copper [at a
potlatch], and break it up, throwing the pieces away, or
giving them as presents to his rivals. This has more
meaning when we understand that these "coppers"
were symbols of great wealth.

3 *Slang* a Copper Eskimo.
1942 TWOMEY & HERRICK *Needle to North* 13: West-
coast *coppers,* the caribou Eskimos of central Canada,
with girlish hair-bobs and dickey-flaps on their parkas,
resemble the Eskimos of Greenland. . . .

Copper Eskimo See quotes.
1884 (1913) HODGE & WHITE *Indians of Canada* 241/1:
KIDNELIK. A tribe of Central Eskimos living on
Coronation gulf, Arctic ocean [called] Copper Eskimo.
1922 JENNESS *Life of the Copper Eskimos* 11: The main
sources of information for all that relates to the
ethnology of the Copper Eskimos are the works of Mr.
V. Stefansson, the commander of the Canadian Arctic

Expedition. 1965 *News of the North* 11 Nov. 4/1: The
Holman artists are a small group of five in an isolated
community of 125 Eskimos. A part of this group is
known as the Copper Eskimos because they fashioned
their tools and weapons from native copper.

coppermine region the region of the Coppermine
River, Mackenzie District, where native copper is
to be found.
1963 OLSEN *Runes of the North* 140: To the north was a
bleak and barren land once occupied by a tribe known
as the Yellowknives, natives who in the long ago had
fashioned spears and knives from the strange yellow
metal they found in the coppermine region to the
northeast.

copper store *Nfld* a co-operative store; a co-op.
1918 GRENFELL *Labrador Doctor* 100: . . . he would come
around seeking a private interview, and inquire after
the health of "the copper store". . . .

copy *v. Nfld* engage in copying, *q.v.*
1933 GREENE *Wooden Walls* 38: . . . you will see the
merry young lads "copying" as they call it—jumping
from pan to pan till far out in the Cove. . . . 1958
HARRINGTON *Sea Stories* 86: Driven to seek a stronger,
larger pan they had to "copy" with great speed on the
smaller ones. . . .

copying *n. Nfld* See 1933 quotes.
1933 GREENE *Wooden Walls* xvi: COPYING Denotes the
passage on foot of loose ice and the use of small bits of
bigger ice to reach the bigger pans. 1945 LEECHMAN
Eskimo Summer 1: Copying is an exciting and risky
business, for the floating cakes of ice, close jammed
though they are, rock and tilt as you leap from one to
the other.

cordeau *n.* [< Cdn F] *Obs.* See **cordelle,** *n.*
1807 (1930) FRASER *Letters* 155: Maitres will serve as
well as codline for a cordeau.

cordelle [kɔr'dɛl] *n.* [< Cdn F] See **tracking line.**
[1792 (1911) SIMCOE *Diary* 91: The current becoming
very strong, the men were obliged to *tirer à la
cordelle,* or drag the boat by ropes on a narrow beach
under high, woody banks.] 1836 (1868) IRVING *Astoria*
196: The boats in general had to be propelled by oars
and setting poles . . . or towed by the long cordelle, or
towing line. 1931 NUTE *Voyageur* 27: A rope or
cordelle, for towing purposes, sixty yards in length, also
found a place in every canoe.

cordelle [kɔr'dɛl] *v.* See **track,** *v.* (def. 1 and note).
1931 NUTE *Voyageur* 48: To pass a décharge it was
necessary to *cordelle,* that is, tow the canoe by means of
a rope (*cordelle*) or cable.

corduroy ['kɔrdə,rɔi] *n.* [< its resemblance to the
ribbed cloth called *corduroy*] **1** See **corduroy road.**
[1796 (1911) SIMCOE *Diary* 319: . . . we had five miles of
that terrible kind of road where the horses' feet are
entangled among the logs amid water and stumps.]
1829 MACTAGGART *Three Years* I 110: These turnpikes
are fancied to resemble the famous King's cloth, called
Corduroy—hence their name. 1930 BEAMES *Army* 89:
Crossing the runway the oxen showed considerable
distrust of the corduroy, stopping, despite Pierre's
frantic objurgations, to snuff at the poles before
venturing forward. 1958 MACGREGOR *North-west of 16*
216: Many a trip Henry and I took in this shaking
steed, bumping over the corduroy at a snail's pace.

2 the logs composing such roads.
1829 MOORSOM *Letters N.S.* 246: However well the interstices may be filled with gravel, the wear and tear soon carries it down below, and the corduroys remain in their pristine simplicity, alike insensible to the maledictions of all impatient travellers, and to the furious assaults of their waggon-wheels. **1948** HOLLIDAY *Valley of Youth* 132: Along the western shore of the lake rambled a rough track which we called the stage road, on which a democrat bumped and wallowed over the narrow rock cuts or swampy bits bridged by corduroy, with the mail and an occasional passenger.
1961 *Cdn Geog.Jnl* Jan. 10/1: Saturated fine-grained clay is very difficult to excavate and handle; where timber is available, corduroy is helpful.

corduroy ['kɔrdəˌrɔi] *v.* surface or bridge a swampy place with logs laid side by side at right angles to the way. See also **corduroy road.** Cp. **skid,** *v.* (def. 3).
1861 *Nor'Wester* (R.R.S.) 15 Aug. 2/4: Here and there the rolling prairie makes little "slews" as they are termed, which require to be corduroyed or rudely bridged after the spring freshets. **1962** DICKIE *Great Golden Plain* 69: They built forts to protect it, a wharf, store and bunk houses, mess rooms, kitchens, and stables; and they corduroyed the portage road.

corduroy bridge 1 a short stretch of corduroy road, *q.v.*, bridging a swamp, muskeg, etc. See also **log crossway.**
☛ *The terms* **corduroy, corduroy bridge,** *and* **corduroy road** *seem often to be used interchangeably by early writers to refer to a stretch of road made passable by a surface of transversely placed logs. The relatively late quotes for* **corduroy road** *and* **corduroy bridge** *(def. 2) suggest that a need for a distinction between them arose only when the latter term became widely used.*
[**1792** (1911) SIMCOE *Diary* 104: It is certainly necessary to have a horse of the country to pass the bridges we everywhere met with, whether across creeks (very small rivers) or swamps.] **1824** *Colonial Advocate* (York [Toronto]) 2 Sep. 4/1: Here . . . [is] the swamp, where there is enough of corduroy breeches [sic] . . . stump and rut paths, as any I have travelled in the province of the same length. . . . **1825** *Kingston Chron.* (U.C.) 7 Jan. 3/1: The honest farmer . . . has hitherto been compelled by want of snow, to plod his weary way over rough roads and corduroy bridges in his four-wheel wagon, instead of gliding smoothly to market in his sleigh. **1952** BANFILL *Labrador Nurse* 15: From there I . . . hobbled down a corduroy bridge made of uneven small, round peeled poles. . . .
2 a bridge having a surface of transversely placed logs.
1875 *Canadian Mthly* May 403/1: The stage rolled on across corduroy bridges, and through deep, gorgeously tinted woods. **1960** *Cdn Bank of Commerce Calendar for 1961*: Bridges had to be built on the spot from available material and so on, from the corduroy road, the corduroy bridge was evolved. Of log construction, the bridges were also surfaced with unhewn logs.

corduroyed *adj.* **1** of a road or bridge surfaced with corduroy (def. 2).
1866 (1958) ELLIOTT *Quesnel* 52: We built bridges over all small streams, that were not fordable, corduroyed swamps. **1958** MACGREGOR *North-west of 16* 22: For four days she sat in that wagon lurching in the mud holes, swaying over the corduroyed sloughs.
2 of logs, laid close together to form a corduroy road, *q.v.*
1942 BOSANQUET *Saddlebags* 117: . . . we went on along the power line, first across a very large swamp, where the trail lay over "corduroyed" logs. . . .

corduroy log one of the logs making up a corduroy road, *q.v.*
1953 BANFILL *Labrador Nurse* 16: Legs dangling behind, we sat flat on the floor of that springless, cushionless cart and bumped through black muck and over corduroy logs to the Post. **1964** *Cdn Geog.Jnl* Feb. 63/2: All but the largest boulders remained on the trail and it plunged into swamps on shifting corduroy logs.

corduroy road a road over swampy or muddy terrain built of logs laid side by side at right angles to the way. See also **corduroy** (def. 1), **corduroy bridge** (def. 1), **log causeway, logged road, log-way** (def. 1), and **pole bridge.** Cp. **faggot road.**
1829 MACTAGGART *Three Years* II 111: . . . when the members of Parliament travel to their public business, the *Road Bill* and *Turnpike Act* are strongly forced upon their recollections; the Corduroy roads send in their own petitions in earnest. **1961** *Edmonton Jnl* 1 Aug. 1/1: Floating muskeg surrounded the lake, so we moved onto higher ground and built a corduroy road back down to the lake.

cork *n. North* See **blackskin.**
1942 *Beaver* Mar. 7/1: The protective "cork" or outer covering of the whale, whether it be bowhead, white whale or narwhal, is highly prized and regarded as a delicacy by the Eskimo. This *muktuk* is eaten raw or cooked and has the flavour characteristic of shell fish.

cork(ed) boot or **shoe** See **caulked boot** (def. 1).
1901 CONNOR *Man from Glengarry* 28: The Frenchman . . . bore him down and jumped with his heavy "corked" boots on his breast and face. **1912** HEENEY *Pickanock* 255: This time it was by the river "boss" and his "gang" who came with their cant-dogs and pike-poles and cork-shoes, to roll in the saw logs and float them down . . . to the markets of the world. . . . **1965** *Maclean's* 1 May 24/2: George Street on a Saturday night is awash with visiting bushworkers, many of them still in hard hats or cork boots. . . .

Corktown *n.* a district in Ottawa (*c*1830-50) where Irish canal laborers and loggers lived in a shacktown.
1833 (1903) CARR-HARRIS *White Chief* 222: Near the works is a place called Corktown, where the workmen have burrowed in the sandhills. **1946** BRAULT *Ottawa* 34n: Corktown was named after Cork, Ireland, by the Irish majority originating from that city or probably on account of the great number of corks which were made to fly from liquor bottles. **1960** *Ont.Hist.* Dec. 228: Establishing themselves in the area of Bytown known as "Cork Town", centred about the picturesque "Mother McGinty's Tavern," the Shiners soon made their presence felt.

corn bake See **corn roast.**
1958 *Maple Ridge-Pitt Meadows Gaz.* (B.C.) 7 Aug. 6/1: Thousands of cobs have been purchased for the largest corn bake and free dance ever staged in the valley.

corn boil See **corn roast.**
1943 RADDALL *Pied Piper* 312: There was a memorable . . . corn-boil on a wooded point in the moonlight where Dougie demolished fifteen luscious cobs. . . . **1958** WATTERS *B.C.Cent.Anthol.* 395: When we had a

corn boil on the beach we did not count out a careful few cobs for each expected child. . . .

corner-blaze *n.* a blaze (def. 1) cut in a tree to mark the corner of a lot or limit.
1954 BRUCE *Channel Shore* 13: Areas of almost unbroken woods, unmarked except for the grey scar of a corner-blaze on an ancient beech. . . .

cornerer *n. Hist.* See **corner-man.**
1925 MCARTHUR *Familiar Fields* 40: . . . anyone who examines one of the buildings cannot but marvel at the skilful dovetailing done by the old-time cornerer.

corner-man *n. Hist.* an axeman who shaped the corners of log buildings.
1873 CROASDAILE *Pacific Shores* 52: The ends of the logs are dovetailed into one another. This is done by the corner-men, who have the hardest work, and require to be well skilled in the use of the axe. **1965** *Sask.Hist.* Spring 42: When a log building was being raised . . . "good corner men were in demand, and there was rivalry to see who could put up the best corner."

corner mound *West* a mound of earth used on the prairies to mark the corner of a section or other subdivision of land.
1963 SYMONS *Many Trails* 91: Of course the "locators" had good maps . . . and were expert at finding the corner mounds.

corn-husking† *n. Hist.* See **corn-husking bee.**
1897 DURAND *Reminiscences* 80: Some of these were raccoon hunting at night with dogs . . . corn husking, house and barn raisings. . . . **1908** BROWN *Lady of the Snows* 222: . . . It is like going back to chaos and a chapter of Dante's "Inferno" after the pumpkins and peaches and corn huskings of Fernwylde. . . .

corn-husking bee† *Hist.* an affair where neighbors gathered to husk corn and to enjoy social activities. See also **bee.** See also **corn-shelling bee** and **husking bee.**
1863 WALSHE *Cedar Creek* 356: The young people from Cedar Creek had gone to a corn-husking bee at Vernon's. . . . **1923** WILLIAMS *Spinning Wheels* 23: The early settlers used to combine work and pleasure by having quilting, corn-husking and barn-raising "bees" followed by dancing and refreshments.

Cornish pump or **water wheel** *Placer Mining* a pumping device consisting of a large wheel overshot from a flume, used for draining placer claims. See also **Davis water wheel.**
1958 ELLIOTT *Quesnel* 77: . . . Lieutenant-Governor Randolph Bruce had unveiled a Cornish pump which had been donated by W. H. Boyd as a reminder of Quesnel's heritage of gold. **1960** RAMSAY *Barkerville* 46: [Caption] Davis, or Cornish water wheel and flume [used in] hydraulic operations at Morning Star Claim.

corn roast† an outdoor party where cobs of corn are cooked and eaten. See also **corn bake** and **corn boil.**
1923 *Beaver* Oct. 29/2: Girls of the office staff spent an enjoyable time . . . the occasion being a corn roast. **1958** *Edmonton Jnl* 31 July 37/2: Members also decided to hold their annual corn roast at Sandy Lake on Sunday, Aug. 24.

corn-shelling bee *Obs.* See **corn-husking bee.**
1863 WALSHE *Cedar Creek* 358: This very evening, her father coming late to Mrs. Vernon's corn-shelling bee, had told her that Zack would be propitiated no longer. . . .

corpse plant† See **Indian pipe.**
1912 (1913) HODGE & WHITE 220: Indian pipe. The corpse-plant or ghost-flower. . . . **1962** *Maclean's* 10 Mar. 17/1: It was a palely sprouting parasite called Indian pipe, or corpse plant, which extrudes almost overnight from rotting compost and lives only briefly.

corral† [kə'ræl] *n.* [< Am.E < Sp. (in most senses); cf. Afrikaans *kraal*] *Esp.West* **1** *Hist.* a temporary enclosure of wagons, Red River carts, etc. set up overnight or under conditions of danger on the trail.
1862 (1956) *New Frontiers* Summer 42/2: After supper "a meeting was held in the centre of the correll of all musicians both vocal and instrumental. . . . **1874** (1910) HAYDON *Riders of the Plains* 23: About midnight . . . our horses stampeded from the corral . . . knocking over some of the wagons which encircled them. **1913** COWIE *Adventurers* 213: The square served as a corral in which to round up the horses and oxen required for a brigade.

2 a fenced enclosure for horses or cattle.
1877 GRANT *Ocean to Ocean* 291: Small log cabins of the new settlers, each with an enclosure called "the corral" close to it, next gladdened our eyes. . . . **1960** NELSON *Northern Lights* 707: Would we find wild horses tomorrow? And, if we did, how many could be pushed off the mountainside and hazed down into the corral on the flats?

3 a trap for game or fish.
1954 PATTERSON *Dangerous River* 215: The corral itself was there for two reasons—first to get the marten coming in from the right direction, and secondly because the curious little beast would be instantly attracted by the very novelty of the thing and would go in to see what it was all about. **1958** ATKINSON *Hist.of Penticton* 14: . . . and at one side of the river they formed an enclosure or corral by interlacing the stakes with pliable whips to form a trap into which the fish could be driven and captured.

4 *Figurative use.* See quotes.
1904 CONNOR *Prospector* 116: "You can't keep an eye on all the fools unless you round 'em up in a corral." **1910** *Eye Opener* (Calgary) 1 Jan. 1/7: Yes, the individual opinions of the whole caboodle of Grit members of parliament . . . do not vary one hair's breadth from the opinions arbitrarily laid down for them by the boss of the corrall. **1958** *Saturday Night* 1 Mar. 5/1: . . . droves of disgruntled Tories who had seceded to this new party are now moving back to their old political corral. . . .

corral† [kə'ræl] *v.* **1** *Hist.* enclose horses or cattle in a temporary ring of wagons or carts.
1832 (1851) CAMPBELL *Journal* 9: On camping the carts were formed in a circle and at dark all horses &c. were corralled inside. **1884** *Prince Albert Times* (Sask.) 27 June 4/1: Parties at Maple Creek and Medicine Hat should be on their guard and keep their horses corralled, as these are their objective points. **1963** MACLEOD & MORTON *Cuthbert Grant* 110: [The captain] rode between the two or four columns of carts, proceeding in formation over the prairies so that any moment they could halt sharply, or wheel into formation to corral horses and oxen, and stand off the Sioux.

2 drive horses or cattle into a fenced enclosure.

1877 GRANT *Ocean to Ocean* 297: On such occasions, the whole guard has to be corralled or penned, and the selection made. It would be impossible for a thief to steal one except by corralling the band. **1964** *Calgary Herald* 20 July 20/3: Soon he widened his business and started shipping cattle from Manitoba to Calgary, corralling them on a half section of land that now forms the Regal Golf Course.
3 drive fish into a trap or barrier.
1937 *Beaver* Dec. 52/2: [Caption] Large stone fish trap at mouth of River Nadluktak, where Arctic char and salmon trout running upstream corral themselves.
4 *Slang* to catch; apprehend; get hold of; collect.
1878 *Sask.Herald* (Battleford, N.W.T.) 18 Nov. 3/2: "Why," said the old man, as he slyly reached up and corralled the most active of the two flies, "times have changed most 'mazingly." **1916** BRIDLE *Sons of Canada* 48: Steele and his men went out north to corral Big Bear. **1945** PUGSLEY *Saints* 101: Corralling funds from the whole eastern "moneyshed," she organized an outstandingly attractive club for ratings. . . .

correction line *West* See 1952 quote.
1884 *Prince Albert Times* (Sask.) 16 Jan. 3/1: The section of country which was surveyed extends from Moose Jaw and the Touchwood Hills to Calgary, and from the third base line north to the ninth correction line.
1952 PUTNAM *Cdn Regions* 372/1: Along each base line, points are established at six mile intervals and from them lines are surveyed 12 miles due north and 12 miles due south. These lines . . . are true meridians and converge towards the north; consequently, they are not directly in line with corresponding offsets from the next base line. Thus all north-south lines have a jog every 24 miles. The line along which these jogs occur, lying midway between the base lines, is known as the "correction line." **1962** ALLEN *Peace River Country* 140: He knew he was almost sober because it was not even necessary to walk back to the road for him to ascertain that he had missed the jog of a correction line.

Corruptionist *n. Hist.* a derogatory name for the Tory Party in the Canadas.
1833 *Liberal* (St. Thomas, U.C.) 23 May 3/2: In this Country and in the Province generally there can be only one division of party;—Whig against Tory—Reformists against Corruptionists—Economy against Extravagance—public good against private interest—the natural rights of the many against the usurped rights of the few. **1865** *Leader* (Toronto) 23 Jan. 1/9: The *Globe's* scoundrels, the *Globe's* corruptionists, the *Globe's* political harpies that preyed upon the vitals of this country, so frightened the people of this fine county that every story was swallowed without salt, and they voted blind for the *Globe's* Mahomet.

corvée† [kɔr'veɪ] *n.* [< F] *Hist.* **1** in French Canada, the obligation of a tenant to perform a certain amount of manual labor for the seigneur as one of the conditions of holding land, usually involving the repair of roads and bridges or the supplying of building stone and wood.
1791 (1905) *Ont.Bur.Arch.Rep.* III 117: The board called on Trudelle to state his Services and Loyalty, who says, he has always done the directed Corviés &c., in common and with as much Chearfulness as others in the Company. **1832** *Cdn Courant* (Montreal) 22 Dec. 2/3: Secondly, certain feudal and degrading services, such as . . . performing days of ignoble servitude . . .

called corvée days, on the Seignior's farm or domain, as it is usually called. **1960** RYERSON *Founding of Canada* 108: The *corvée* of so many days' compulsory, unpaid labor for the seigneur, was a more burdensome exaction.
2 a body of men doing unpaid work on roads and bridges, usually in lieu of paying taxes.
1815 BOUCHETTE *Lower Canada* 558: The remainder of the way to Lake Timiscouata has been much improved by *corvées* of several hundreds of militiamen.

cosh [kɑʃ] *n. Nfld* See quote.
1842 JUKES *Excursions in Nfld* I 42: Here a brook empties itself into the sea, having run for about three miles through a narrow pond, or "cosh," as my men call it.

cossack *n.* See **kossack.**

côte¹ [kot] *n.* [< F *côte* side, coast] *Hist.* (*except in place names*) a canton or settlement along a river on the outskirts of a town or city.
☛ *See* **côte²**: *in some quotes* **côte** *in place names is ambiguous in the evidence.*
1703 LAHONTAN *New Voyages* I 34: Some cantons or quarters in the neighborhood of Quebec . . . planters call . . . cotes. . . . **1883** *Trans.Roy.Soc.Can.* III 48: These various settlements became known in local phraseology as Côtes, apparently from their natural situation on the banks of the river. **1904** *U of T Stud.Hist.& Econ.* II 168: I cannot find that the word cote has ever been applied to river settlements in the province. **1964** GUILLET *Pioneer Days* 1: The *côtes* [along the Detroit River in U.C.], or long, straggling villages resembled . . . the settlements along the St. Lawrence in Quebec.

côte² [kot] *n.* [< F *côte* slope, hill] (*especially in place names*) a canton or district, often on the slope of a hill. See 1934 quote.
1904 *U of T Stud.Hist.& Econ.* II 168: Near Quebec where côtes also abound the same restricted use of the word to the slopes of Cape Diamond as to the slopes of Mount Royal near Montreal, is to be observed. **1934** *Cdn Hist.Rev.* XV 397: His widow, a devout Roman Catholic, at once applied for permission to bury his remains in the cemetery of the Côte des Neiges.

coteau [kə'to] *n.* [< F *côteau* hillock] **1** *Obs.* (*except in place names*) a small hill; also, the slope of a low hill.
1767 *Quebec Gaz.* 5 Jan. 3/1: Also another Lot of Land, situate at the Grande Coteau, One Acre in Front and about Thirty Acres deep. **1875** BEMISTER *Ry Routes from Montreal* 10: The saving on the line by St. Esprit is much reduced by the heavy work required at "the coteau." **1924** *Cdn Hist.Rev.* V 43: An attempt was made to ascertain the actual consumption of goods by Upper Canada, by stationing a joint inspector at the Coteau du Lac, at whose office all boats and carriages passed from Lower Canada into Upper Canada.
2 *West* an elevated plateau or a series of such plateaus having the appearance of a range of hills or ridges when viewed from the adjacent prairie. See also **high prairie.**
1843 SIMPSON *Narrative* 43: For seven miles our route led west-north-west . . . it then changed to west . . . through a more open country, consisting of rising grounds, or "côteaus," with bare ridges, and sides clothed with dwarf poplar and brushwood. **1872** BUTLER *Great Lone Land* 279: Warned by tradition of the frightful losses of earlier times from the ravages of small-pox, the Assineboines this year kept far out in

the great central prairie along the coteau, and escaped
the infection altogether. **1938** FETHERSTONHAUGH
R.C.M.P. 17: . . . the Force . . . climbed the coteau
twice in the next few days. . . . **1963** SYMONS *Many Trails*
36: Except for the great cattle country of the Cypress
Hills and Milk River, only the wrinkled Coteau [des
Prairies] remained as isolated range. . . .

175

côte de boeuf
council

côte de boeuf *Cdn French, Obs.* a bag made from
the flank skins of buffalo and used for carrying
pemmican. See also **taureau.**
1806 (1960) FRASER *Letters and Journals* 164: He brought
two Coté de Bouff full of pounded meat.

cottage† *n.* an unpretentious residence built, as a
rule, on or near a lake or river; a summer cottage.
1878 LEMOINE *Chronicles of St.Lawrence* 189: In a trice,
a sitting-room and cabinet for sleeping apartment was
rented in one of the white roofed cottages lining the
shore, at the rate of $10 per month, including board.
1961 *Edmonton Jnl* 28 July 1/4: A man who has
lived on Crown land at Garner Lake provincial park . . .
without permission will be asked to move the cottage.

cottage roll a prepared ham, boned, rolled, and
sometimes cooked.
1958 *Cut Knife Grinder* (Sask.) 3 Apr. 8/4: We have a
good supply of . . . Buffet Style Cottage Rolls (Ready-
to-Eat). . . .

cotton plant or **sedge** cotton grass, *Eriophorum*
sp.
1931 LEBOURDAIS *Northward* 98: Farther along was the
corral [for reindeer]; and beyond, stretching away for
five miles or so to the hills, was rolling tundra, now white
with waving cotton sedge. **1934** GODSELL *Arctic Trader*
272: They lighted their igloos with pieces of sea ice in
lieu of windows, and heated them with their dish-shaped
stone lamps in which seal oil was used for fuel and a
piece of moss, or cotton-plant, for wick.

cottontail (rabbit)† *n.* the common N. American
rabbit, *Sylvilagus floridanus.*
*c*1902 LAUT *Trapper* 153: Out from the gray thicket
bounds a cotton-tail. **1966** *Globe and Mail* (Toronto)
15 Jan. 29/1: And the cottontail rabbit is everywhere
when the days are mild and sunny.

cottonwood (tree)† *n. Esp.West* **1** any of several
trees of the genus *Populus* especially the black
poplar, *P. trichocarpa.*
1877 GRANT *Ocean to Ocean* 219: [We went] through
thick underbrush of willows and aspens that had sprung
up round the burnt spruce and cotton-wood. **1959**
STOREY *Prairie Harvest* 182: . . . the house stared with
broken windows upon the dying cottonwood trees. . . .
2 the wood of such trees.
1910 HAYDON *Riders of Plains* 90: The original Police
quarters, built of cotton-wood, roofed with poles, and
thatched with grass and earth, were being done away
with. **1958** *Maclean's* 10 May 52/1: . . . the Indians had
found [the Douglas fir] too big to handle, and hewed
their dugouts and totem poles from the more malleable
Red Cedar or [from] Cottonwood.

cottonwood canoe a dug-out canoe fashioned
from the trunk of the black cottonwood, *Populus
trichocarpa,* used by the Indians of the interior of
British Columbia.
1873 (1904) BUTLER *Wild North Land* 219: . . . it is
glorious work for the *voyageur* to launch his cottonwood
canoe on the rushing water and glance down the broad
bosom of the river. **1880** GORDON *Mountain and
Prairie* 109: . . . strong wind . . . made the lake so rough
as to be unsafe for the cottonwood canoes. [**1958**
BERTON *Klondike* 8: . . . pushing down the Peace River in
canoes hacked out of cottonwood poplar trunks. . . .]

couers actuel *French* legal tender; acceptable
money.
1836 *Montreal Transcript* 6 Oct. 2/2: Now in Canada it is
customary to stipulate for payment in *Couers Actuel,*
which means any of the various monies before
mentioned, but none of them in particular; and it often
happens that this nominal "Couers Actuel" is not to be
had.

cougar† ['kugar] *n.* a large, wild cat, *Felis
concolor,* once common but now confined to
southwestern Canada. See also **catamount** (def. 1),
great cat, hill lion, lion, mountain cat (def. 2),
mountain lion, painter, panther, puma, and **tiger.**
1853 *Anglo-American Mag.* I 83/1: The cougar is
called a cowardly animal; some naturalists even assert
that it will not venture to attack man. **1965** *Star Wkly*
2 Jan. 37/1: . . . there was one 12-mile road snaking
. . . down into a wilderness valley, frequented by
mountain sheep and cougars and black bear, only to
peter out into nothing.

cougar dog or **hound** a dog trained to hunt
cougars.
1916 WOOD *Tourist's Northwest* 348: On Vancouver
Island the latter are very numerous, but you must have
a man with a regular cougar-dog, as there is very little
use trying to stalk them. **1958** *Time* (Cdn ed.) 14 Apr.
18/2: Ed Burton, 58 . . . raised Hereford cattle, quarter
horses and cougar hounds on his . . . ranch in the
foothills of southern Alberta.

couillon [kui'jɔ] *n.* [< Cdn F] *Hist.* a double-ball
game somewhat resembling lacrosse and played by
Indian women in eastern Canada on the ice or in a
natural clearing.
1801 (1897) COUES *New Light* I 169: This is delightful
weather for the Indian women to play their favorite
game of couillon on the ice. **1951** O'MEARA *Grand
Portage* 195: He even tried his hand at the women's
game of couillon on the river ice.

coulee ['kuli] *n.* [< Cdn F *coulée*] *Prairies* **1** See
1962 quote.
1804 (1911) LAROCQUE *Journal* 302: At sunset removed
a little higher upon the coulee to a better place for the
feeding of our horses, where we kept them tied to
pickets all night. **1857** (1863) PALLISER *Journals* 53: At
sunset they fell upon the young Crees, surrounded them
in the Coulee in which the men encamped, and killed
17 of them on the spot. . . . **1962** *Alta Hist.Rev.* Autumn
14/2: The dry bed of a stream when deep is a "gulch"
or "coulee," its inclined sides distinguishing it from a
canyon, the sides of which are perpendicular.
2 See quote.
*c*1902 LAUT *Trapper* 175: On the high rolling plains,
hostiles could be descried at a distance, coming over
the horizon head and top first like the peak of a sail,
or emerging from the "coolies"—dried sloughs—
like wolves from the earth.

council† *n.* an elective administrative body at the
municipal level, as for a village, town, city,
township, county, or district.

1852 (1853) STRICKLAND *Canada West* II 273n: [They] choose from among the council a town reeve, and in certain cases a deputy town reeve, the same as in townships. **1958** *Edmonton Jnl* 6 Nov. 29/5: ... the councils of the town of Leduc, the Municipal District of Strathcona. ...

council bluff *Hist.* a natural elevation, such as a hill or bluff (def. 2), on the prairie, affording a vantage point for an encampment of Indians holding pow-wows, looking for herds of buffalo, etc.
1856 (1923) BROADUS *Cdn Prose and Verse* 215: Had I judged of things by the lively conversation and cheerful countenances I saw on the little council bluff [where the buffalo hunters were encamped], I had been greatly deceived indeed. ...

council house among Indians, a building in which leaders meet to discuss matters of importance to the band.
1798 *U.C.Gaz.* (York [Toronto]) 12 May 3/1: The day was spent with the greatest conviviality, and finished with several Indian dances at the council house. **1959** *Kingston Whig-Standard* (Ont.) 2 May 11/5: Six Nations Indians vote today at their council house in Ohsweken to decide whether or not they want the right to buy liquor, beer and wine for consumption in their homes. **1965** BERTON *Remember Yesterday* 37: Here, Sir John A. Macdonald ... is honoured by the Six Nations Indians in a ceremony at the Brantford Council House.

council lodge a temporary council house erected for a particular occasion, such as an intertribal pow-wow.
1889 (1935) STRANG *Pioneers in Can.* 317: A large council lodge is erected fully 100 feet in diameter [for the Sun Dance]. The sides are formed of poles, with boughs of trees interlaced. The roof is constructed in the same manner with strong cross beams. In this place all the tribe and their visitors assemble. ...

councillor *n.* **1** in pre-Confederation days, an appointed member of the Executive Council or Legislative Council, the second chamber of the legislature; now in Quebec only. Also spelled *counsellor.*
1836 *Vindicator* (Montreal) 5 Feb. 1/4: While the public lands and their revenues are lavished on Councillors and government favorites, the sufferers by the late American War must be paid out of taxes raised from their productive fellow country men. **1844** *Globe* (Toronto) 9 July 1/3: The Home Government assent entirely and unreservedly to responsible Government Resolutions of September, 1841, but not to the anti-Responsible Government demands of the late Counsellors. **1963** *Globe and Mail* (Toronto) 10 July 1/1: At present, councillors are appointed for life. Under the new bill, those named after July 1, 1963, will be forced to retire at 75.
2 in Prince Edward Island, one of that half of the members of the Legislative Assembly, elected by special provisions. See 1962 quote. Cp. **assemblyman.**
1962 *Kingston Whig-Standard* (Ont.) 10 Dec. 3/5: The house is made up of 15 councillors and 15 assemblymen, each with equal rights. Only property owners, their wives or husbands, and over-seas war veterans and clergymen may vote for councillors. **1963** *Globe and Mail* (Toronto) 15 Mar. 3/7: Unlike other provinces, Prince Edward Island elects two types of members to the House—councillors and assemblymen—a system unaltered since the Legislative Council was merged with the Assembly in 1893.

3 an elected member of a council, *q.v.*
1852 (1853) STRICKLAND *Canada West* II 270n: Townships or union of townships [will have] five councillors. **1963** *Globe and Mail* (Toronto) 9 May 13/2: Etobicoke councillors voted to support North York by appointing counsel.

4 a. an Indian sub-chief.
1871 (1880) MORRIS *Treaties* 39: Two councillors and two braves of each band were to receive a dress, somewhat inferior to that provided for the Chiefs, and the braves and councillors of the Portage band excepted, were to receive a buggy. **1929** JEFFERSON *Saskatchewan* 102: [Pound-maker] had been what is called a councillor, or head man under a chief.
b. an Indian, below the rank of chief, elected to band council. See also **councilman.**
1963 *Press* Dec. 12: This is the second time I've been Counsellor for the Band. The first time I was elected for two years. ... **1964** *Indian News* 2/4: Mr. Paupanekis is an elected Councillor of the Norway House Band, president of the Norway House Social Club, and has taught school for two years.

councilman *n.* See **councillor** (def. 4b).
1964 *Camsell Arrow* Summer 35/2: B.R. funeral rites took place at the St. Paul's Anglican Church for Councilman Fred Tail Feathers. ... he ... has been a Councilman for 32 years. He was first elected Councilman in 1927.

Council of Assiniboia *Hist.* the governing council of the Red River Colony (Assiniboia) from 1835-1870, made up of a president, namely the Governor of the Hudson's Bay Company, and councillors appointed by the Company.
1913 COWIE *Adventurers* 450: The proper course for Governor McTavish and the Council of Assiniboine to have taken was to have suppressed the Nor'wester newspaper for seditious libel against the constituted authorities. **1921** *Beaver* Apr. 17/1: So in 1835 he [Sir George Simpson] asked permission of the company's executive in London and secured the appointment of the "Council of Assiniboia," consisting of himself as president and fifteen influential members of the Red River colony as councillors. **1963** MACLEOD & MORTON *Cuthbert Grant* 85: ... Alexander Macdonell [was] now a member of the Council of Assiniboia.

count coup or **coo** See **coup.**

country *n.* **1** See **live off the country.**
2 See **in the country.**

country alliance *Hist.* among fur traders and pioneers, a common-law marriage between a white man and an Indian girl. See also **country marriage, country wife, fur-trade marriage.**
[1806 (1964) INNIS *Fur Trade* 277: ... no man whatsoever ... belonging to the Concern shall henceforth take or suffer to be taken ... any woman or maid from any of the tribes of Indians ... to live with him after the fashion of the North West, that is to say to live with him within the Company Houses or Fort and be maintained at the expence [sic] of the Concern.] **1948** *Beaver* Dec. 10/1: He was doing an almost unbelievable thing, not according to Company usage, to terminate an unhappy "country" alliance.

country elevator *Esp.West* a specially designed building equipped to unload grain from trucks, carry it to a storage area, and, when required, transfer it to railway cars. See also **elevator** (def. 2a and picture) and **grain elevator** (def. 1). Cp. **terminal elevator.**
1921 *Dalhousie Rev.* I 237: There two farmers' companies own and operate 632 country elevators and 4 terminal elevators at the head of the lakes. **1964** *Calgary Herald* 8 May 28/1: The Canadian Wheat Board . . . will put extra delivery quotas into effect next week at most country elevator points in the Prairies.

country food See **country provisions.**
1919 (1923) *Beaver* July 372/1: . . . no more will we depend on "country food" to see us through a trip. **1959** BODSWORTH *Strange One* 249: Without a steady supply of country food . . . the store food could not last out the winter. **1966** *North* March-April 2/1: The economic life of the Eskimo almost entirely hinges upon the plentifulness of country food (meat).

country-made *adj. North, Hist.* made in Canada; not imported (with special reference to things manufactured for trade with the Indians).
1878 (1921) *Beaver* July 3/2: That the country-made articles for English River District for Outfit 1879 be provided at Fort Garry, Summer 1878. **1913** COWIE *Company of Adventurers* 105: The "country-made articles" consisted chiefly of articles made at the Factory, such as . . . ice-chisels, fish and muskrat spears, ironwork for boats. . . . **1923** *Beaver* Mar. 236/1: First he dug a grave, then fastened heavy country-made beaver traps on her hands and feet, threw her into the grave and covered her with stones.

country marriage *Hist.* See **country alliance.**
1939 GODSELL *Vanishing Frontier* 83: In earlier days they [traders] had handled the situation more conveniently by contracting a so-called "country marriage" which in reality, was no marriage at all. . . .

country produce *Fur Trade, Hist.* **1 a.** all local produce of a region except furs.
1822 (1940) *Minutes of Council* (H.B.C.) 27: That the following prices be allowed for Country produce . . . Birch Bottom Bark 3s. . . . **1963** MCTAVISH *Behind the Palisades* 21: The "Ocean Nymph" was piloted out of Churchill River . . . when the furs, oil, and country produce (including goose feathers and quills) were loaded on board.
b. loosely, local produce in general, including furs.
1966 *North* March-April 27/1: Trading with the Moravian Mission at the permanent establishment protected the people from dealing with fly-by-night traders who sometimes cheated them, and paid for country produce in rum.
2 See **country provisions.**
1907 HUNTER *Cdn Wilds* 236: These people were brought up on country produce: i.e., fish and flesh, therefore found it no hardship to be without flour, etc.,—the white man's food. **1966** *Western Wkly* 4 May 3/2: The food stocks brought in canoe and portage from Fort Garry in those decades were meagre enough and had all to be supplemented by "country produce."

country provisions *Fur Trade, Hist.* game and other food available from the forests and streams of the country. See also **country food** and **country produce** (def. 2). Cp. **English provisions.**
1717 (1932) KNIGHT *Journals* 123: The Country Provisions is very scarce here at present. **1853** (1944) *B.C.Hist.Qtly* July 186: I would impress upon your

mind the great importance of securing as large a stock of country provisions as possible seeing that the stock here [Fort Victoria] is quite inadequate to meet all the demands upon it. **1963** DAVIES *Northern Quebec* 265: [At] an alternative site to the south of Cape Jones . . . country provisions could be obtained to supplement European fare. . . .

country rates† *N.S., Hist.* a tax on property.
1952 BUCKLER *Mountain and Valley* 125: When Joseph came home . . . there were ten-dollar bills . . . but those all went for the country rates, the tote-load of flour and feed, things like that.

country ship *Obs.* a large iceberg, often mistaken for a ship.
1852 SUTHERLAND *Baffin's Bay* II 332: Many of them [icebergs] were of a very dirty colour, from accumulations of mud, gravel, and larger fragments of rock which had taken place in them in the glaciers, and not infrequently very dark seams (the closed up crevasses) could be seen traversing them throughout their whole extent, causing the most illusory and fantastic appearances. These the whalers sometimes mistake for ships, and then they call them "country ships."

country sled *Obs.* See **stoneboat.**
1872 DASHWOOD *Chiploquorgan* 89: Thousands of country sleds, fit to transport the heaviest guns could have been bought in a week. . . .

country store a general store catering to local farmers and country people, often on a credit basis. See also **general store** (def. 2).
1825 (1923) BROADUS *Cdn Prose and Verse* 10:
Woolcards and stockings, hats for men and boys,
Mills-saws and fenders, silks, and infants' toys;
All usefull things and joined with many more,
Compose the well assorted country store.
1923 WILLIAMS *Spinning Wheels* 35: Other stores in the village changed the "things" in the windows. The Country Store never did.

country-style *adv. Hist.* after the manner of a country alliance, *q.v.*
1953 LOWER *Voyages* 53: She was the daughter of an old Scot, who had come out in his youth, had never been off the Bay, and had married "country style."

country tea *Obs.* **1** See **Labrador tea** (def. 1a).
1791 (1934) FIDLER *Journal* 529: [There is] plenty of the Country tea or Wis sa kay puck kay—a small shrub. **1821** (1823) FRANKLIN *Journey* 449: We had no *tripe de roche* that day, but drank an infusion of the country tea plant, which was grateful for its warmth, although it afforded no sustenance.
2 See **Labrador tea** (def. 1b).
1887 *Senate Report* 166: The Labrador or country tea . . . was used very extensively in the country before our entrance into Confederation. In the hay and harvest fields it was considered by many of the old settlers of the Red River colony to be superior to any other beverage in allaying thirst. I know homes in this country where this tea is still used.

country wife *Fur Trade, Hist.* an Indian or Métis woman who was a trader's common-law wife. See also **country alliance** and **wife of the country.**
1948 *Beaver* Dec. 9/2: In 1829 these two men, each of

whom had a "country" wife, decided to visit Britain, to find wives there and to make a trial of bringing gently reared women to live in Rupert's land. **1966** *Beaver* Winter 48/2: . . . James Sutherland and his country wife Jane Flett were formally married in May 1828. . . .

country wool *Maritimes* homespun.
1956 RADDALL *Wings* 76: He always wore . . . a pair of long country-wool stockings.

county *n.* in certain provinces, the largest political subdivision having its own municipal government.
☞ *The internal structure of a county varies from province to province and not all provinces employ the county system. In Upper and Lower Canada, the county also functioned as a riding (def. 1) See also* **circle** *(def. 1).*
1832 (1953) RADCLIFF *Letters* 127: John Brant [the Mohawk chief] was returned as a member for his county to the last parliament, and made some excellent speeches in the house, but on a petition lost his seat, by some trifling informality of the Election. **1872** (1965) HAMILTON *Cdn Quotations* 67/2: We have expended our strength in aiding outlying counties and helping our city candidates. **1948** ANGLIN *Canada Unlimited* 66: . . . the number of municipal governments run to that large total of nearly 4,000. In the first place, each province is divided into large rural municipalities. These are known as . . . counties in Ontario (subdivided into townships); counties in Quebec (divided into townships and parishes); counties (and parishes) in New Brunswick; and in Nova Scotia simply municipalities. **1964** *Guardian* (Charlottetown) 18 June 1/8: The firm . . . dealt with factors influencing the development of the county.

county council in certain provinces, the elected administrative body of a county.
1850 *Wkly Globe* 15 Feb. 131/3: The following is a list of the names of the Town Reeves and Deputy Town Reeves, from several Townships composing the County Council. **1945** BROWN *Cdn Democracy* 89: In Ontario and Quebec the county councils are not elected directly and the system therefore requires a brief explanation. The county councils in Ontario are made up of reeves and, in most cases, deputy reeves who have already been elected to serve on the councils of towns, villages and townships which make up the county. **1964** *Kingston Whig-Standard* (Ont.) 10 Dec. 6/3: An election for a new warden will be conducted at the January session of county council.

county councillor in Nova Scotia, an elected member of a county council; elsewhere an elected town or township reeve sitting on such a council.
1903 RICHARDSON *Colin* 85: Jock, the drover, opined that if he ever attained to the high office of a county councillor, it would be necessary to provide him with a double expansion hat or let him go bare-headed. **1962** *Time* (Cdn ed.) 17 Aug. 8/1: . . . Flemming rode his political career from Carleton (N.B.) county councillor in 1921 to provincial premier in 1952.

county court the court having jurisdiction over matters relating to a county and dealing with civil actions. See also **district court**.
1891 *Grip* (Toronto) 31 Jan. 69/2: A bill supplementary to this will also be presented making sheriffs, registrars, county court clerks, etc., elective by ballot of the

people. . . . **1948** MACNEIL *Highland Heart* 151: They are going to sell his farm from the steps of the county court in Baddeck.

county road a secondary road, the maintaining of which is the responsibility of the county, as opposed to a highway maintained by the provincial or federal government.
1964 *Kingston Whig-Standard* (Ont.) 10 Dec. 6/1: The Palace road is one of six county roads which are included in a roads reconstruction program started last March.

county seat See **county town**.
1852 *Welland Advocate and Rev.* (Port Robinson, C.W.) 13 Feb. 2/7: The Reeves of Lincoln may protest and get up what addresses to the Government they please, they will not prevent the inhabitants of Welland from establishing their County seat, and having their County business under their own control. **1962** *Canada Month* Sep. 16/1: Except for the Shriners' county-wide shindigs, there are few conferences that draw the attendance the Mennonites got, and it nearly overwhelmed Kitchener, the county seat.

county town† See 1945 quote. See also **district town** and **shiretown**.
1789 (1905) *Ont.Bur.Arch.Rep.* III 31: The Scite of the county town agreed upon, you will direct the Surveyor for the district to lay out the township and proceed to receive applications and issue certificates for Town and Farm lots therein . . . as soon as may be. **1945** BROWN *Cdn Democracy* 90: In each county there is a county town with a court house and jail, and accommodation for the county offices and the meetings of the county council. **1959** STEWART & FRENCH *Ask No Quarter* 121: Durham was the centre of political activity for Agnes, though Owen Sound was the county town.

county warden in Ontario, the chairman of the county council, *q.v.*, himself a township reeve, selected for the chair by his fellow reeves on the council. See also **warden** (def. 2).
1851 *Watchman* (St. Thomas, C.W.) 8 Feb. 3/1: The said debentures . . . shall be signed by the County Warden, and countersigned by the County Treasurer. **1964** *Kingston Whig-Standard* (Ont.) 10 Dec. 6/3: Warden Brown . . . retires as reeve and county warden at the end of this year.

coup† [ku] *n.* [< Cdn F in this sense < F *coup* a blow] *Hist.* among the Plains Indians: **1** the act of striking or touching an enemy in warfare with the bow, the gun, or a ceremonial coupstick (def. 2).
1907 HODGE *Bulletin* I 354/1: Coup . . . The French-Canadian term adopted to designate the formal token or signal of victory in battle, as used among the Plains tribes. **1956** LEECHMAN *Native Tribes* 132: A warrior's bravery was not measured by the number of scalps he had taken, but by the number of coups he had counted. . . .

2 count coup, a. gain prestige for striking an enemy (dead or alive) in battle with a weapon or with a coupstick (def. 2).
1928 EVARTS *Fur Brigade* 59: "You two warriors counted plenty coos," Brady said, eyeing the seven scalps. "Counting coos" was a custom and a term prevalent among all Western tribes, the expression no doubt having been derived from the French word "coup" of the early French voyageurs. **1952** HOWARD *Strange Empire* 500: Significantly, it was not necessary to kill to "count coup"; it was even more glorious to

ride into danger, humble the enemy by striking him down and taking his horse or an article of his apparel, and escape unscratched, than it was to bring back a scalp.

b. recount one's coups, or acts of bravery.
1918 SCHULTZ *Rising Wolf* 111: The warriors, gathered in front of the great lodge, were one by one counting their coups, their deeds of bravery. . . .

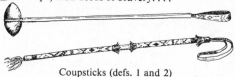

Coupsticks (defs. 1 and 2)

coupstick *n. Hist.* **1** See 1914 quote.
1914 STEELE *Forty Years* 107: "Coup" sticks are weapons having an egg-shaped stone secured to a stick by raw hide tied round a groove in the stone, with a loose end at the other extremity which was coiled round the wrists like a sword knot. **1953** MOWERY *Mounted Police* 117: The warriors, tall and powerful men, all had magazine rifles, some Enfields, some Sharpes and Winchesters, and some Springfield Cavalry carbines. Most of them wore vicious coupsticks in their belts.

2 a slender stick bedecked with feathers and used in ceremonies and for counting coup, that is, striking an adversary in battle. Cp. **coup.**
[**1765-75** (1933) POND *Narrative* 43: As I Aprocht the Banks of the Villeag I Perseaved a Number of Long Pa[i]nted Poles on which Hung a Number of Artickels. . . .] **1907** (1913) HODGE & WHITE *Indians of Can.* 115/1: In ceremonial parades . . . an ornamental quirt or rod was sometimes carried and used as a coup stick. **1934** GODSELL *Arctic Trader* 168: The gaudy war-bonnets and coup sticks of the Sioux . . . formed a strange contrast to the Governor in his frock coat and silk hat. . . . **1963** *Beaver* Summer 33/2: But in the lodges that are entered for the best tipi contest . . . are to be seen priceless treasures; decorated parfleches (rawhide bags made something like an envelope); a medicine bundle . . . befeathered coup stick (to touch an enemy or count coup was a braver act than killing him).

coureur [ku'rœr] *n.* [< F] *Hist.* See **coureur de bois.**
1900 OSBORN *Greater Canada* 21: His store of peltries was turned over to the merchant who had supplied the goods, and he for his part handed over their value (minus the price of his goods and as much again for his risk) to the *coureur*. **1908** LAUT *Conquest N.W.* II 162: Once, the coureur brought word that a northern tribe was coming down with furs.

coureur de bois [ku'rœrdə'bwa] *n.* -s de bois. [< Cdn F "woods ranger"] *Hist.* **1** an unlicensed trader who ranged the forest in search of furs. See also **bush-ranger** (def. 2), **bush-runner, French pedlar, wood-ranger** (def. 2), **woodrover,** and **woods-runner** (def. 1).
☛ *Although long used in English in Canada, this term is often treated as a French word still.*
1703 (1905) LAHONTAN *New Voyages* I 403: Coureurs de Bois, i.e. Forest Rangers, [are] so called from employing their whole life in the rough exercise of transporting merchandise goods to the lakes of Canada . . . to trade with the savages. . . . **1898** *Rev.Hist. Pubs* II 64: After the British conquest enterprising Scotch traders began to organize the considerable trade that the coureurs de bois had created. **1963** MORTON *Kingdom of Canada* 85: The licenses had been

multiplied by Frontenac, and the need for them ignored by the outfitting merchants and the coureurs de bois alike.

2 an independent fur trader allied with the Montreal fur companies.
1801 MACKENZIE *Voyages* ii: Hence they derived the title of *Coureurs des Bois*, became a kind of pedlars, and were extremely useful to the merchants engaged in the fur trade. . . . **1907** HUNTER *Cdn Wilds* 10: . . . after the French regime several Scotch Merchants of Montreal prosecuted [the fur trade] with more vigor than heretofore. This they did under the name of "The Northwest Company." Their agents and "Coureur des Bois" [sic] were ever pushing westward and had posts strung from Ottawa to the Rocky Mountains. **1938** GODSELL *Red Hunters of the Snows* 50: Overnight there sprang up a demand for these cast-off and dispossessed voyageurs and coureurs de bois as guides, and once again their lilting chansons awakened the echoes of the Ottawa valley.

course *n.* [< Cdn F] *Obs.* See **buffalo run** (def. 1).
1849 (1955) MCCOWAN *Upland Trails* 15: A first rate runner not infrequently secures ten buffaloes at a "course"; from four to eight is the usual number.

couteau croche [ku'to'krɔʃ] [< Cdn F] See **crooked knife** and picture.
1789 MCKENZIE *Reminiscences* 33: I make *traines,* bend snow-shoe frames, and with perseverance, I'll perhaps learn to handle the *couteau croche.* **1932** MUNN *Prairie Trails* 78: Flett was one of the cleverest workers with the "couteau croche" or crooked knife (very like a saddler's knife) I have ever seen.

Coutume de Paris† *Hist.* originally the common law of northern France, a code of laws instituted in New France in 1663 and contributing much to the civil code in force in modern Quebec. See also **Custom of Paris.**
1799 *U.C.Gaz.* (York [Toronto]) 7 Dec. 3/2: What can the law of Canada mean? It must be the coutume de Paris, modified as it has been by the ordinances of the province. **1840** MURRAY *Brit.Amer.* I 309: In regard to property and civil jurisdiction, the *coutume de Paris,* with the ordinances of the French kings, though forming a complicated, perplexed, and inconvenient system, had been so interwoven with the habits of the settlers, that they could not be persuaded to prefer one decidedly better. **1963** MORTON *Kingdom of Canada* 57: By royal decree of 1663 the Coutume de Paris, the common law of northern France, was established as the law of New France.

cove *n.* **1** *Hist.* See **timber cove.**
1818 PALMER *Journal* 223: Several rafts lay in the cove [at Quebec]. . . . **1829** MACTAGGART *Three Years* II 87: The timber-merchants regret that they were not found to answer; as they had cleared their ponds and coves of lumber. . . . **1945** CALVIN *Saga* 89: The best coves were those which needed long containing piers; that is they were situated at places where the river bottom sloped out gradually, leaving a wide space of tidal flats between high and low water. Coves were not established where the water deepened suddenly, for this would have given little or no area for working or for storage.

2 *Nfld, Local* See quote.
1958 *Maclean's* 27 Sep. 18/1: Yet, when you stand on

the street itself [Water Street, St. John's, Nfld] and look down one of the coves, the name given to the short sharply pitched streets leading to the waterfront . . . you do get a glimpse of days gone by.

coveman *n. Hist.* a man who worked in a timber cove. See also **cove** (def. 1).
1963 *Cdn Geog.Jnl* Nov. 165/2: . . . all loose wood and the framework of the raft, became the prey of the covemen whose work it was to break up the raft and prepare the timber for shipment to Britain.

cover *n.* in hockey, a forward assigned to follow and check constantly the opposing player on the line facing him.
1963 O'BRIEN *Hockey* 74: But if his opposing covers have totalled as much as he has, the over-all result is poor.

covered bridge† a roofed wooden bridge, long a characteristic of the eastern provinces.
1895 PARKER *Adventurer of North* 131: Brydon's eyes were now on the covered bridge. **1955** *Pictou Advocate* 24 Feb. 2/5: The covered bridges of Nova Scotia are fast disappearing. Only two are left, which reminds me that these covered bridges . . . were considered swell spots for spooning. **1961** PRICE & KENNEDY *Renfrew* 171: [The] Covered bridge at Fort Coulonge [Ottawa Valley] . . . was built in 1885.

covered carriole *Obs.* an expensive and superior type of horse-drawn sleigh. See also **cariole** (def. 1b).
1769 (1931) BROOKE *Emily Montague* 89: Our covered carrioles too have not only canvas windows (we dare not have glass, because we often overturn), but cloth curtains to draw all round us. . . . **1791** (1911) SIMCOE *Diary* 54: General Clarke's covered carriole, a small chaise on runners instead of wheels, was ready to carry me to the inn in Upper Town.

cover-point *n. Obs.* **1** in ice hockey and lacrosse, one of two defensive players (the other called the point) who take up positions just in front of the goalkeeper; also, the position of this player.
1894 *Blackwood's Mag.* 410/2: See how grandly those cover-points work; each man laboring for his colors like a beaver, always covering the puck, and swiftly and surely returning. **1898** EDGAR *Canada and Capital* 128: The players on each side [of a hockey team] are: a goal keeper, point, cover point and four forwards. **1965** *Canadian Wkly* 2-8 Jan. 7/2: The team lining up in a T-formation with two defencemen (called "point" and "coverpoint") in single file in front of the goal, then the rover, then the centre, with wingmen to right and left.
2 the position played by this player.
1896 *Times* (Niagara-on-the-Lake, Ont.) 20 Feb. 1/4: The play was very even, and decidedly rough, and it looked as though they were evenly matched when Hartley came from coverpoint and scored in 2 minutes.

cow bell the wood anemone, *Anemone quinquefolia*.
1910 FERGUSON *Janey Canuck* 187: The air is heavy with the honeyed odour of the wood anemone. For so white a blossom it has a suspicious number of aliases; the Wind-flower, Cow Bell, Herb Trinity, and Pasque Flower.

cowbird† *n.* **1** a small, black bird, *Molothrus ater,* having a short bill and bright eyes, noted for its practice of laying eggs in the nests of other birds and for its symbiotic attendance on cattle.
1908 MAIR *Mackenzie Basin* 385: The cow bird . . . imposes its eggs on several of our smaller flycatchers. . . .
1955 MCCOWAN *Upland Trails* 78: The cowbirds [were] formerly called buffalo-birds. . . .
2 *Slang* a sponger; freeloader; grafter.
1910 FRASER *Red Meekins* 238: ". . . I'll take the law into my own hands an' wallop seven kinds of daylight out of that cowbird."

cowboy *n.* **1**† a man who works as a rider on a cattle or horse ranch. See also **cow hand, cowpoke, cow-puncher,** and **puncher** (def. 1).
1882 *Edmonton Bull.* 4 Mar. 1/1: Davy, chief cowboy in . . . this place, says his birthday always comes on Easter Sunday. **1912** BICKERSTETH *Open Doors* 106: But you must not think of Edmonton as a rough primitive place with cow-boys "shooting up the town," and so forth. **1962** *Canada Month* May 36/3: Many of the early cowboys . . . remained on the open ranges of the Canadian territories. . . .
2 *Slang* in mining, a greenhorn.
1959 *Press* Aug. 13: *Cowboy* alone has acquired a romantic connotation (except in the mines where it is a synonym for "greenhorn").

cowboy *v.* **1** work as a cowboy (def. 1).
1960 *Sun* (Vancouver) 11 Jan. 3/3: All these things, said Joe, he found out in the past 19 years. Although he cowboyed as a lad and has bought and sold horses all his life he wasn't even sure of the name of the first spotted horse he bought in 1940. **1964** *Ibid.* 11 Feb. 4/4: . . . Mooney told the court that he has had 20-odd years experience cowboying in Arizona, Utah, Wyoming and B.C. . . .
2 bring under control, as an unbroken horse, a wild steer, etc.
1927 (1929) JOHNSTON *Beyond Rockies* 88: Rider must hook 'em in the shoulder and holler first jump and then cowboy him in the best way he knows how. **1962** FRY *Ranch on the Cariboo* 242: "Can'tcha cowboy a little yearling like that 'thout trouble?"

cowboy hat† a felt hat having a high crown and a broad brim.
1888 (1890) ST. MAUR *Impressions* 172: We were not much to look at, as Adela and I dressed with regard only to perfect comfort: woollen petticoats and tweed jackets, cowboy hats and long thick boots, the only suitable dress for roughing it out here. **1958** *Edmonton Jnl* 24 July 9/6: Princess Margaret will see a miniature rodeo in which some of Canada's top cowpokes will perform, but whether she gets the cowboy hat at the start of her visit may depend on the style of clothes she is wearing.

cowboy round-up *Rare* a rodeo or stampede.
1916 WOOD *Tourist's N.W.* 361: The organised celebrations of Western Canada principally consist of Indian games and cowboy round-ups, which are advertised in the summer and fall at Calgary, Banff, Vancouver, and other centres.

cow-call *n.* See **moose-call** (def. 2).
1946 *Beaver* Sep. 42/2: I have never used cow-calls for two good reasons: it is in execrable bad taste, and it is rarely effective.

cow camp *West* a seasonal camp some distance from the main buildings of a ranch, used at roundup time for branding, vaccinating, etc.
1897 *Medicine Hat News* (Alta.) 8 Apr. 1/5: Mr. Fawcett

has put up a new stable and house at his cow camp and Mrs. Fawcett will reside there during the summer months. **1954** BEZANSON *Sodbusters* 149: My partner, S. J. Webb, and I have purchased . . . the "cow camp" on a spring-fed creek at the head of Bear Lake. **1962** FRY *Ranch on the Cariboo* 21: How much more he suffered, then, in the hard school of the hayfield and the cow camp where only performance counted. . . .

cow chip *West* dried cattle dung used as a fuel. Cp. **buffalo chip.**
1944 *Canadian Cattlemen* Mar. 159: An old Half-breed once told me that in his youth it was considered quite correct to burn buffalo chips for a camp fire, but cow chips—"Phew, they stink!" **1960** BUBLITZ *Dotted Line* 22: . . . with the help of the children, we'd go and gather these cow chips to do our cooking.

cow corn a variety of maize, *Zea mays tunicata,* having an envelope of husk around each kernel as well as around the entire cob.
1832 MCGREGOR *British America* II 316: A plant called *cow-corn* abounds on the hardwood uplands, on which cattle, that are turned out very lean in the spring to range the woods for food, fatten rapidly. **1963** *Western Wkly Supp.* 27 Feb. 6: [Caption] Cow-corn is harvested in Joyceville Institution [Ont.]—a modern farm-type, minimum-security prison.

cow country 1 western range land used in raising beef cattle.
1929 *Beaver* Sep. 284/1: . . . a store in the cow country . . . for saddles and chapps, and spurs . . . form a conspicuous portion of the goods for sale. **1963** SYMONS *Many Trails* 15: Most English greenhorns are called "Charlie" in the cow country.
2 *Obs.* in Indian parlance, areas settled by white men, so called because of their apparent dependence on dairy cattle.
1850 BIGSBY *Shoe and Canoe* II 319: Great was the enjoyment of returning to the comforts and amenities of civilised life. Milk was a luxurious novelty. The Indians call the land of the pale-faces "the cow-country."

cowgirl† *n.* a woman who works on a ranch, takes part in rodeos, etc., dressing in western-style clothes.
1913 *Eye Opener* (Calgary) 1 July 3: [Headline] Cowgirls Comely Charming. **1923** STEELE *Spirit-of-Iron* 196: "[Her] father's a rancher an' she wears cow-gal clothes an' thinks she owns the place. . . ." **1958** *Edmonton Jnl* 24 July 9/6: The hat itself [is] said to be the finest "cowgirl" hat ever devised. . . .

cow hand† *West* See **cowboy** (def. 1).
1903 (1913) CULLUM *Devil's Keg* 32: They were "cow" hands belonging to the ranch. **1964** *Time* (Cdn ed.) 13 Nov. 18/2: But on most of the Cariboo's 1000-odd spreads, the need is for cowhands who can also run farm machinery. . . .

cowhole *n. Obs.* See **cahot.**
1864 (1965) COLLARD *Call Back Yesterdays* 122: At every crossing, where the snow was trodden down hard, there would be a dip, which gradually became deeper and deeper, forming what was called a "cahuat" (called by the boys cowholes), and which gave the occupants of sleighs a good jolt. . . .

cow horse† a horse trained to work with cattle; a cowboy's horse. See also **cow pony.**
1902 [?] *High River Times* 11 July 1/1: The next race was . . . a cow horse binding race, a zigzag course around posts. **1962** FRY *Ranch on the Cariboo* 24: A good cow horse will get the cow, while the cowboy looks after himself.

Cowichan (Indian) sweater [ˈkaʊətʃən] a heavy sweater of gray, unbleached wool, knitted by the Cowichan Indians of southern Vancouver Island, distinguished by symbolic designs, originally black and white, now sometimes multi-colored. See also **Indian** (def. 5), **Indian sweater,** and **Siwash sweater.**
1945 *Beaver* Dec. 18/2: Distinguished visitors to Vancouver Island have not been received with due honor if they are allowed to leave without a Cowichan sweater. **1964** *Time* (Cdn ed.) 17 Jan. 11/1: He donned a borrowed Cowichan Indian sweater. . . .

cow-kick *v. West* of horses, kick outward and upward as a cow does.
1954 HAGELL *Grass Was Free* 59: Among them were stampeders, kickers, strikers and the odd one that would cow-kick or bite.

cowman† *n.* a man whose business is raising cattle; a cattle rancher.
1919 *Eye Opener* (Calgary) 9 Aug. 4: The "Big Four" namely, Messrs. Lane, Burns, Cross and McLean, the gentlemen who are responsible for you getting this wonderful opportunity to see this celebration are COWMEN. **1957** HUTCHISON *Canada* 259: Its [Calgary's] mind is the mind of an overgrown cowtown. I say that with no disrespect, for I can think of nothing better than a cowtown and a race of cowmen.

cow outfit† *West* a cattle ranch and its staff; a company owning a cattle ranch.
1920 KENDALL *Luck of the Mounted* 280: I punched for one or two cow-outfits awhile, and then came a time when a deputation of citizens came. . . . **1962** FRY *Ranch on the Cariboo* 16: I was proud . . . to feel I was part of his cow outfit. . . .

cow parsnip a wild plant, *Heracleum lanatum.* See also **wild parsnip** (def. 1).
1853 REID *Young Voyageurs* 205: It was the celebrated "cow parsnip." Its stem was jointed and hollow and . . . the Indians called it in their language "flute stem," as they often used it to make their rude musical instruments. . . . **1880** GORDON *Mountain and Prairie* 143: The Parsnip [River is] so called from the abundance of cow-parsnip that grows near its banks. **1934** HASKIN *Wild Flowers* 233: To those who wish to vary . . . their spring diet by an occasional taste of wildlings, I recommend the common cow parsnip.

cowpoke† *n. West* See **cowboy** (def. 1).
1955 HOBSON *Nothing Too Good* 193: One good drink for every cowpoke—just one slug, remember—not half a bottle. **1964** *Time* (Cdn ed.) 13 Nov. 18/1: North of Williams Lake . . . lone cowpokes still plunged through willow thickets.

cow pony† *West* See **cow horse.**
1888 (1890) ST. MAUR *Impressions* 184: A clever cow pony will never come to grief with a lariat, and can generally unwind himself by going the reverse way. **1960** *Sun* (Vancouver) 6 Feb. 5/8: There is nothing—no, not so much as the doff of a hat—to the cowpony, the packhorse, the mustang, the Indian horses, the quarter horse, the pinto, the hundreds of thousands of animals which opened up the Canadian west and which to this day, remain one of the most useful and used animals over vast sections of British Columbia and Alberta.

cowpunch† *v. West* work as a cowboy (def. 1).
1903 *Eye Opener* (High River, Alta) 1/4: I packed my things in a large envelope and hit the blind baggage for the West where I went cowpunching.

cow-puncher† *n. West* See **cowboy** (def. 1).
1889 MACLEAN *Indians* 198: There are four different occupations in the country the men engage in, which are called bull-whackers and mule-skinners, applied to freighters who drive oxen or mules, broncho-busters and cow-punchers. **1955** GOWLAND *Smoke* 201: The men who looked after the cattle were variously referred to as cow-hands, hired men and sometimes as cow-punchers, but only once in a very long while were they referred to as cowboys.

cow's breakfast *Slang* a hat, especially a straw hat.
1900 OSBORN *Warders of the West* 777: Nothing looks more out of place than a pallid face under a policeman's "cow's breakfast" (as the slouch hat was sometimes styled). **1959** *Weekend Mag.* 1 Aug. 28/3: . . . he returned through the streets . . . quite oblivious of the very un-naval "cow's breakfast" [straw hat] still on his head.

cow's tongue *Cariboo* an oval, water-worn cobblestone, resembling a cow's tongue in shape, often found in numbers and forming a kind of pavement in a stream bed, believed by placer miners to indicate the probable presence of gold.
1958 LINDSAY *Cariboo Story* 41/2: And many an old timer waits eagerly and tries desperately to be the one to startle the villages and towns with that ancient cry. "Cow's tongues and the bed-rock pitchin', get away girls, get away." **1963** *B.C. Digest* May-June 10/3: Cow's tongues are the round, smooth boulders found along rivers and streams.

Cowtown *n.* Calgary, Alberta.
[**1945** GARD *Johnny Chinook* 253: The second charge was that they had conspired to form a so-called University in their "cow town" of Calgary.] **1955** HARDY *Alta Anthol.* 60: Calgary is still "Cowtown" . . . and the Stampede, the Ranchmen's Club and the palatial homes in the heart of the city are part of the imprint left by that unfettered era. **1963** *Calgary Herald Mag.* 5 Oct. 7/5: And, like most Calgarians, they're quick to boost Cowtown as "a most progressive city."

cowtown† *n. West* a town largely dependent on the cattle business; a shipping point for cattle. See also **ranching town.**
1916 WOOD *Tourist's N.W.* 424: Macleod, site of the first station of the Royal North-West Mounted Police, has had fame for forty years as a typical "cow-town." **1953** MOON *Saskatchewan* 67: On into the southwest near the Alberta border is Maple Creek, Saskatchewan's cow town. **1962** DICKIE *Great Golden Plain* 293: Southern Alberta still has many ranches, and Calgary is still a cowtown. . . .

coyote† [kaɪˈoti *or* ˈkaɪot] *n.* [< Am.E < Am.Sp. < Nahuatl *koyotl*] **1** a small wolf, *Canis latrans,* usually associated with the prairies but found across Canada, mainly in the region south of the range of the larger timber wolf, *q.v.* See also **brush wolf** (def. 1), **case wolf, gray wolf** (def. 2), **loper, mishagunis, prairie wolf,** and **togony.**

1860 *Sask. Herald* (Battleford, N.W.T.) 25 Aug. 1/4: As yet, the wolves and cayotes howl their dreary requiems around its vast solitude, while an occasional grizzly comes out from his lair to see if the white man has yet invaded his favorite gulch. **1950** DOBIE *Coyote* 177: The first biologist to observe the coyote, Thomas Say, in 1819, regarded the animal as "probably the original of the domestic dog so common in the villages of the Indians." **1963** *Globe and Mail* (Toronto) "Outdoors" 13 Mar. 7/3: An animal newcomer to Ontario is the coyote . . . now found from Manitoba to the Quebec border.

2 the skin of the prairie wolf.
1924 MASON *Arctic Forests* 47: Lynx and coyote are not warm enough for sleeping in comfort in open camp on a very cold night, and the fur rubs off.

3 *Slang* a cowardly, contemptible person.
1890 *Grip* (Toronto) 4 Oct. 2/2: Some of the boys done it while he was drunk, the mean coyotes. **1919** FRASER *Bulldog Carney* 23: . . . she pleaded for the "wayward boy," as she euphemistically designated this coyote.

4 *Military Slang, Obs.* a second lieutenant.
1900 *Medicine Hat News* (Alta) 4 Oct. Supp. 1/5: Strictly speaking, a "shavetail" is a "giffin" or "coyote" or "rooster," but frequently is called a "piebiter" and perhaps known even more widely as a "ringtailed snorter."

Coyote *n.* See **coyote French** (def. 2).
1953 CUSHMAN *Stay Away Joe* 217: [He was] speaking French of the highly nasal Coyote variety, its small vocabulary pieced out by sign language done in the grand manner. . . .

coyote French *West, Slang, Derog.* **1** See **Métis.**
1963 STANLEY *Louis Riel* 242: [They] referred to them [métis] as the "breeds" and the "coyote French."
2 a mixture of Canadian French, Cree and, sometimes English spoken by the Métis of the older generation.
1953 CUSHMAN *Stay Away Joe* 3: "Did you use spurs on those bronc?" his father called in his excitable Coyote French.

coyote hound See 1916 quote.
1916 WOOD *Tourist's N.W.* 361: The Calgary Hunt Club pursues the coyote of the prairies with coyote hounds, bred for fleetness from the Russian wolfhound and the greyhound. **1963** *Calgary Herald Mag.* 26 Oct. 3/3: He was a big, strong man who lived alone with, his horses, cattle and coyote hounds.

C.P.R. strawberries *Slang* prunes (originally so called in derision by railway work gangs). See also **lumberman's strawberries.**
1919 *Camp Worker* 17 May 5/2: What do you want real strawberries for, when you have a big supply already of C.P.R. strawberries? **1964** *Sun* (Vancouver) 9 Apr. 4/4: When I suggested we might have a little fruit for breakfast Jack laughed uproariously and asked if I expected CPR strawberries with 50-cent-a-day board. I understood he meant prunes.

crack an egg *Curling* See quote.
1960 *Weekend Mag.* 26 Nov. 34: To crack an egg on a stone is to touch it lightly.

cracker *n.* **1** *Slang* anything extraordinary; a crackerjack.
1890 *Grip* (Toronto) 15 Mar. 184/1: I'm clean gone on that fly head-gear of yours. She's a cracker. **1922** FLAHERTY *Eskimo Friends* 63: "'Tis the land of the gales, sir," said Salty Bill. "In the last nine days you has

been gone but one day come clear. In the cracker last night, rifle shots woke me. 'Twas the big provision tent strippin' to pieces. . . ."

2 the lash of a dog-whip, which can be made to crack like a pistol shot.
1896 RUSSELL *Far North* 179: The cracker is 11.5 inches long of three-ply twisted babiche.

cracker hopper a grasshopper. See also **crackler**.
1924 (1933) SLATER *Yellow Briar* 201 : . . . the crazy hens [turkeys] . . . would lead the tender creatures [poults] off to chase cracker hoppers over the blistering hillsides. . . .

crackie ['kræki] *n.* Also spelled *cracky.* **1** *Nfld and Maritimes* any small, yapping dog, so-called by reason of its bark.
1895 (1944) WENTWORTH *Am.Dial.Dict.* Cracky— A small hybrid dog. 1895 E.Canada, N.B., N.S., Newfoundland 1921. c**1928** (1966) *Weekend Mag.* 23 Apr. 4/2: There was . . . / Pig's feet, cat's meat, dumplings boiled in a sheet, / Dandelions and crackies' teeth at the Kelligrew's Soiree. **1959** ENGLISH *Newfoundland* 39: [Nfld] Figures of Speech [include] . . . Saucy as a crackie. . . .

2 an Indian hunting dog. See also **bear dog**.
1933 MERRICK *True North* 220: They [huskies] have none of the instinctive intelligence of the little Indian "cracky" dogs that look so small and useless, and are so valuable to a hunter. **1956** *Beaver* Summer 19/1: . . . the yip-yi-yipping of a dozen "crackies," the small Indian hunting dogs tethered along the edge of the plateau.

crackler *n. Maritimes* See **cracker hopper**.
1947 BIRD *Judgment Glen* 164: Grasshoppers raised in swarms about her in the grassy clearing, the kind Moses called cracklers, so different, she thought, from the black ones in the burntland.

cracky *n.* See **crackie**.

cradle *n.* among Indians, a cradle-board or cradle-basket, *qq.v.*
1743 (1949) ISHAM *Observations* 106: As soon as the Child is born, they wash itt in Lu'ck warm water, put it in a Rabbit skin and tie itt in a cradle or back board as aforemention'd. **1956** LEECHMAN *Native Tribes* 37: Some cradles were highly decorated, and the mothers took great pride in them. . . .

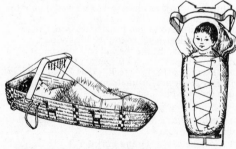

A cradle-basket and cradle-board

cradle-basket *n.* a cradle woven of vegetable fibres, used by the Indians of central British Columbia. See also **basket cradle**. Cp. **moss basket**.
1922 JOHNSON *Legends of Vancouver* 93: "My daughter —who is barely out of her own cradle-basket—give her to you, whose hands are blood-dyed with the killing of a score of my tribe? You ask for this thing?" **1939** O'HAGAN *Tay John* 32: Many cradle baskets were hung

up in the trees around the [Shuswap] village that winter, where the women, sorrowing had put them to be used no more. . . .

cradle-board *n.* a thin, rectangular board to which a moss bag, *q.v.*, is fastened and in which infants are carried. See also **board cradle, Indian cradle, papoose board,** and **papoose-carrier**.
[**1791** LONG *Voyages* 61: The board, on which the child is placed, is slung to the mother's forehead with a broad worsted belt, and rests against her back.] **1885** *Trans.Roy.Soc.Can.* III ii 68: The mode of nursing the Indian papoose, by bandaging it on a cradle-board, is specially adapted to the vicissitudes of a nomad forest life. **1966** *Kingston Whig-Standard* (Ont.) 6 Feb. 4/6: Tools and equipment made from forest products included . . . birch bark containers, wooden utensils, cradle boards. . . .

cradle-heap *n.* See **cradle-hill**.
1963 GUILLET *Pioneer Farmer* I 328: Great stones often came to light after clearing, and there were cradle-heaps at the sides of trees that had been unearthed and blown over.

cradle-hill *n. Esp.Maritimes* a small hill or mound of earth. See 1820 quote. Cp. **cradle-hole**.
1820 (1955) HARVEY *Island St.John* 102: But there is another impediment to travelling in the woods: many of the trees have been torn up by the roots with high winds, which have raised little hills of earth, which the natives call cradle hills. **1855** HALIBURTON *Nature and Human Nature* II 374: The stanhope is in the coach-house, but the bye-road was so full of stumps and cradle-hills, it was impossible to drive in it. **1955** *Pictou Advocate* 24 Feb. 3/2: All rigged up, the good man . . . sat among the ferns on a cradle hill . . . and took a little nip from his bottle.

cradle-hole *n.* a cradle-shaped hole left in the ground when a large tree is overthrown by a gale, carrying the soil from the hole in its roots. Cp. **cradle-hill**.
1826 (1832) PICKERING *Inquiries of an Emigrant* 54: Ploughing prevented by the water standing on the land, in what are termed cradle-holes, formed by trees being blown up by the roots, and are found only on a wet, or a loose soil. **1925** MCARTHUR *Familiar Fields* 103: It was no easy matter to make rail-fences "horse-high and hog-tight," when they had to be built over cradle-holes. . . .

cradle-name *n.* among Indians, a name given a child at birth, often changed later.
1909 CAMERON *New North* 163: . . . I like best to think of him by the cradle-name his mother gave him, Tenny Gouley, which means "A man born."

Cradle of (Canadian) Confederation See 1952 quote.
1952 (1965) HAMILTON *Cdn Quotations* 35/1: Charlottetown, P.E.I.—The Cradle of Confederation (From the conference held in 1864 by delegates of the Maritime Provinces to discuss union . . . which delegates from the Canadas attended.) **1964** *P.E.I. Tourist Guide* (Travel Bureau folder, Charlottetown): Prince Edward Island is the Cradle of Canadian Confederation. . . . **1965** *Globe and Mail* (Toronto) 8 Sep. 6/4: . . . the only Canadian city not served by Canada's national airline is the Cradle of Confederation itself.

process of selective cutting or "creaming", whereby the best trees were logged at the sacrifice of all the rest in the area.

cradle-rocker *n. Placer Mining, Obs.* See **rocker**[1].
1859 (1935) STRANG *Pioneers in Can.* 200: . . . as he rocks away at his cradle-rocker, and gathers the glittering treasure presented to his eye, he thinks of those to whom he is endeared. . . .

crafts officer a federal government official who advises and assists Indians and Eskimos in producing and marketing handicrafts.
1963 *Globe and Mail* (Toronto) 1 Feb. 9/6: . . . in Great Whale . . . the local fishermen have kept their crafts officer supplied with speckled trout, white fish, and the odd char.

cramiere ['kræmi,ɛr] *n.* [< Cdn F *cramière* < F *crémaillière* pothook] *Hist.* a device consisting of an upright axle and a horizontal arm to swing kettles and pots on and off an open fire.
[**1854** KEEFER *Ottawa* 61: . . . a wooden crane renewed when burnt through, swings over the fire and suspends the family pot, tea and bake kettle.] **1947** SAUNDERS *Algonquin* 34: Mr. Pennock also ran across the camboose pile and old "cramiere" of another camp, which he says may still be seen. . . . **1964** *Cdn Geog.Jnl* Feb. 65/3: From one of the four posts that supported the chimney [of the camboose] swung the "cramiere" or crane that held the big pots over the fire.

cranberry tree See **highbush cranberry**.
1852 RICHARDSON *Arctic Expedition* 79: It is distinguished as a species from the very common cranberry tree . . . its fruit has an orange color, is less acid, more fleshy, and more agreeable to the taste. **1910** FERGUSON *Janey Canuck* 187: The flowers on the cranberry tree are white, too.

crannick *n.* See **crunnick**.

Crawler *n.* [perhaps after the Rev. Edmund A. Crawley, a leading Methodist minister of the time] *Maritimes, Hist.* a Methodist.
1965 MACNUTT *Atlantic Provinces* 161: Their insistence on observation of the Lord's Day excited the bitter hostility of merchants. By the vulgar their adherents were [c1814] derisively termed "Crawlers."

crazy oats *Obs.* See **wild rice**.
1963 *Sask.News* Nov. 4/1: The French settlers came closer to the truth when they called it "crazy oats" since it is a close relative to the oat family.

crazy-water *n.* in Indian parlance, alcoholic liquor; firewater (def. 1).
1950 STEELE *Ghosts Returning* 19: Then came the Stone-hearts killing us with great sickness, driving us to kill our buffalo for crazy-water, taking our lands, shutting us up on reserves, like bulls in a piskun (trap), so that today nothing is left and we must all depend on you.

cream *v. Slang* **1** *Hockey* body-check heavily so as to knock sprawling and shake up seriously.
1962 *Kingston Whig-Standard* (Ont.) 30 Oct. 10/4: It makes a player keep his head up, thus he isn't as liable to get creamed by a bodychecking forward or defenceman. **1964** *Calgary Herald* 3 Apr. 12/3: Jean Beliveau had missed the final period after being creamed by Edward Shack. . . .

2 *Lumbering* See quote.
1958 *Imperial Oil Review* April 31/2: Little concern was ever voiced . . . over the waste that occurred in the

crease *n.* in hockey and lacrosse, the marked area in front of the goal reserved for the goal tender and prohibited to attacking players except when the puck or ball is inside it; goal crease.
1963 *Kingston Whig-Standard* (Ont.) 22 Jan. 9/8: It's just, that, if he persists on leaving his crease, he must accept the possibility of bodily contact the same as other players. **1964** *Globe Mag.* 7 Nov. 2/2: The referee . . . gave Bower a penalty, for holding the puck outside the crease.

credit *n. Fur Trade* goods advanced to Indians and Eskimos to be paid for from their catch. See also **debt**.
1739 (1965) *Letters from Hudson Bay* 293: . . . it is confessed that the Indians have considerable credit given them at the southern factory but here [Fort Prince of Wales] it is a trifle, and shall take care to break that custom as much as is possible. **1800** (1801) MACKENZIE *Voyages* 379: The Beaver sent by these young men twenty-two skins of his credits and also three skins worth fresh meat; gave them each a piece of tobacco, a flint, &c, and sent the Beaver 1½ foot of tabacco. **1889** MASSON *Les Bourgeois* I 15: In order to economise freight, and to enable the Indians to hunt at a distance, credits were often given payable at another fort.

Creditiste *n.* [< Cdn F *Créditiste*] a supporter of the Quebec wing of the Social Credit party; specifically, a Member of Parliament representing this group. See also **Ralliement des Créditistes**.
1962 *Kingston Whig-Standard* (Ont.) 10 Nov. 3/1: How many of the Creditistes could have voted for the government . . . is a matter they must . . . explain to the voters back home. **1965** *Ibid.* 11 Jan. 3/6: He told reporters that the Creditistes will demand that the government give aid to Quebec farmers. . . .

creek [krik; *often* krɪk] *n.* **1** any freshwater stream smaller than a river. See also **crick**.
☛ *In the Atlantic Provinces, and occasionally on the West Coast, the older sense of* **creek**, *"tidal estuary, saltwater inlet," has been retained, a small freshwater stream usually being called a brook.*
1691 (1964) WARKENTIN *West.Interior* 25: Today . . . we went through a little creek were [sic] we were forc'd to track our Cannoes. . . . **1863** WALSHE *Cedar Creek* 142: When I'm writing to Linda, I shall date from Cedar Creek which will give her an exalted idea of our location: at the same time she will be convinced it is situated on the seashore, if I forget to say that in Canada every stream is a "creek." **1964** *Family Herald* 12 Mar. 50/2: We are fortunate enough to have a creek running through our land which has a good bottom and can serve as a swimming pool.

2 the creeks, *Placer Mining* streams and adjacent diggings yielding gold.
[**1901** *Klondike Miner* (Grand Forks, Y.T.) 18 Oct. 3/1: Being above all things a creek paper, we will endeavor to acquaint ourselves and our readers . . . with the doings of those . . . "shoveling gravel" in all parts of the Klondike. . . .] **1907** *U of T Stud.Hist.& Econ.* II 198: During the first two or three years their work was confined mainly to Dawson and its immediate environment, "the creeks." **1958** *Northern Miner* 27 Nov. 25/2: He made his usual small stake at Dawson City. We wanted to know all about life on the creeks.

creek claim† *Placer Mining* See 1907 quote. See also **river claim**.
1900 LONDON *Son of Wolf* 128: At the base of the French Hill lay Eldorado Creek, and on a creek claim stood the cabin of Clyde Wharton. **1907** *U of T Stud. Hist.& Econ.* II 201: In the early days a creek claim extended 500 feet up and down the creek and from rimrock to rimrock in width or, later, from the base of the hill on one side of the valley to the base of the hill on the other side in width.

creek diggings† *Placer Mining* a mine on or near a creek bed, as opposed to bench diggings, *q.v.*
1960 *Statutes of B.C.* 3584: In "creek diggings" a claim shall be 250 feet long. . . .

Creek-women *n.* in West Coast Indian beliefs, the spiritual beings who control the creeks.
1956 LEECHMAN *Native Tribes* 318: The Creek-women controlled the streams and brooks, and among the most powerful of the spiritual beings were the Killer Whales.

Cree medicine a love charm.
1958 *Beaver* Autumn 41/1: Actually there were many varieties of Cree medicine prepared by different tribesmen skilled in the concoction and use of love charms.

creep *v.* stalk moose or other big game; engage in creeping, *q.v.*
1872 DASHWOOD *Chiploquorgan* 67: The Nova Scotia Indians are the only men I know who can "creep" moose without snow. **1945** MOORE *Castle Buck* 125: "You have proved to me that you can creep a herd of deer. Then you go and scare 'em off."

creeper *n.* one of a pair of metal bands or plates equipped with caulks (def. 1) or spikes and attached to boots or overshoes for walking on icy surfaces. See also **ice-creepers**.
*a*1820 (1838) HEAD *Forest Scenes* 15: I saw an old gentleman carefully picking his way across a steep street with creepers (spikes made to buckle under the sole) on his feet and a pointed walking stick in his hand. . . . **1861** DE BOILIEU *Labrador Life* 155: We generally wear what on the coast are called "creepers," which are made in the shape of a cross with thick "starts," and which are much the same as cricketers wear in England. **1950** *Beaver* Dec. 9/1: The climb became too rough and steep for snowshoes so we exchanged them for creepers, made of light steel bands with sharp prongs under the ball of the foot. **1955** COLLARD *Canadian Yesterdays* 136: He would go out walking on Montreal's uneven sidewalks . . . with his feet spiked with "creepers," which reminded him of the "crampons" used in Switzerland for crossing the glaciers.

creeper spike *Lumbering* See **caulk** (def. 1). Cp. **creeper**.
1910 BINDLOSS *Thurston* 71: The logs rolled, groaned, and heaved beneath them and Thurston, trusting to the creeper spikes upon his heels, sprang from one great tree trunk to another behind his companion, who had a longer experience of the perilous work of log-driving.

creeping *n.* a method of hunting moose by stalking. See also **moose-creeping** and **still-hunting**. Cp. **creep**, *v.*
1866 KING *Sportsman in Canada* 56: "Creeping," or "still-hunting" . . . may be followed both in autumn and in winter. . . . **1888** (1890) ST. MAUR *Impressions* 244: Still-hunting, or creeping, is really the most

sportsmanlike way of killing moose, and likewise the most difficult, and consists of stalking him in his feeding ground, which is generally of a swampy nature. **1945** MOORE *Castle Buck* 115: . . . a genuine stealthy hunter . . . can approach almost near enough to a bob-cat to whisper in its ear. This sort of patient "creeping" must be done up wind.

creeping irons *Obs.* climbing irons.
1849 ALEXANDER *L'Acadie* II 75: We got linen bags made for sugar, and flannel ones for tea, also creeping-irons, to ascend the trees and look out. These irons are of peculiar construction; they are like the letter L, are flat, and about one inch broad; the feet rest on the lower part, two leather straps bind the irons round the mid-leg and the ankle, over the lumberer's boot. At the bottom of the long leg of the L, which rests against the inner part of the leg, is a sharp spike at an angle of 45 degrees; this is stuck into the bark of the tree, like the claw of a wild beast. . . .

Cree shoe a type of snowshoe used by the Cree Indians. See quote. See picture at **snowshoe**.
1963 *Beaver* Autumn 17/1: Since the Crees, in their country, had no white ash that could be bent easily, they used the more brittle yellow birch—thus producing the long, tapered Cree shoe, which is still made in two pieces.

BE CAREFUL ABOUT FIRE
THE FOREST IS YOUR
MEANS OF LIVELIHOOD

ᔕᐱᕐᔾ ᒐᑐᐃᐧᑯᐤ
ᒥ ᐃᓬᕑᐊᐃᓬ ᐧᐊᐧᕑᐣᐁᑯᐸᐧ

Cree syllabics

Cree syllabics a syllabary devised by the Reverend James Evans, a Wesleyan missionary, for the Crees (about 1840) and adapted to Eskimo toward the end of the nineteenth century. See also **syllabic** and **syllabics**. Cp. **Eskimo script**.
[**1859** (1863) PALLISER *Journals* 145: The Stoneys are all Christians, and some of them can read and write in their own language, using the Cree syllabic characters, which were invented by Wesleyan missionaries.]
1925 *Beaver* Dec. 19: In June, 1841 . . . [Evans] had so far perfected his Cree syllabics that he wrote: The men women and children at Norway House write and read it with ease and fluency. . . . **1961** *Cdn Geog.Jnl* Jan. 34/1: [The Reverend E. J. Peck, an Anglican missionary] had translated the Gospels and some hymns from Cree syllabics into the Eskimo language [1903-4].
1965 *Maclean's* 24 July 34/4: . . . with this [fur press] he printed five thousand birchbark pages in Cree syllabics.

Cree symbols See **Cree syllabics**.
1913 WILLIAMS *Wilderness Trail* 97: This was, indeed, a message from Peter Rainy, and written in the only language the old Indian could use—the Cree symbols into which the Bible had been translated by the zealous missionary, James Evans, back in the [eighteen-] fifties. **1961** ANDERSON *Angel of Hudson Bay* 83: Indians used Petitsikapau as a crossroads post exchange where messages could be left in Cree symbols on the blazed bole of a tree.

crematory *n. Obs.* an incinerator for the disposal of garbage.
1887 *Grip* (Toronto) 30 Apr. 10/1: Last year the Board of Health introduced a crematory which serves a good purpose. This year it is hoped they will introduce a lavatory, as the streets are in a horrible condition.

crest *n.* among West Coast Indians: **1** the symbol of a social group such as a clan or phratry. See also **totem crest.**
1888 *Report N.W.Tribes* 5: The Kwākiutl and Salish tribes are not distinguished by animal totems, but derive their origin each from a man who was sent down from heaven by the deity, and who, in some way or other, obtained his crest from a spirit. **1916** WOOD *Tourist's N.W.* 384: A totem is a "crest column." **1964** DUFF *Indian History* 54: One well-known authority . . . believes that much of what is commonly believed to be aboriginal in coast Indian culture, such as the clan system, the use of crests, and the carving of totem poles, did not exist before the time of contact, but was in a sense a product of the fur trade.

2 the social group identified by this symbol.
1954 EVANS *Mist* 126: On top of that we know the parents of the two boys. One is of our crest, from Kitwancool. *Ibid.* 184: He was seeing Elora as she was now . . . the lissome, bright-eyed, teasing little girl he could not have because she was of his crest.

crested seal See **hood seal.**
1850 GOODSIR *Baffin's Bay* 144: I had often before shot these seals, and the crested or bladder nose (*Cystophora cristata*), on the east side; but if they happened to be killed outright, they invariably sank. **1945** RAND *Mammals of Yukon* 42: The crested seal . . . an Atlantic species has been recorded at the mouth of the Mackenzie. . . .

crew *n. Obs.* a family of beavers.
1770 (1911) TOWNSEND *Cartwright's Journal* 50: I had the satisfaction of finding a large new beaverhouse, which appeared to be inhabited by a numerous crew. **1792** CARTWRIGHT *Journal* III Glossary iii: Crew of Beavers. The two old beavers, and all their young ones which have not yet begun to breed, if there are more breeding pairs than one in the same house, it is said, to be inhabited by a double or treble crew.

crib *n. Lumbering* **1 a.** *Hist.* in the Ottawa Valley especially, one of the small units or assemblages of logs that, in groups of 25 or 30, formed a raft of timber, used in driving from the camps to the mills or shipping points. See also **log crib** and **timber crib.** Cp. **dram** and **raft** (def. 2 and note).
1806 (1903) CARR-HARRIS *White Chief* 90: It is an immense flotilla . . . made up of numerous sections or cribs of timber, lashed together by green withes, which are easily detached from the flotilla or raft, and which are capable of being rowed by long rude oars. **1829** MACTAGGART *Three Years* I 241: When spring draws on, they form the lumber into small rafts, called *cribs*, and drop away down the rapids to market. **1864** (1955) CRAIG *Early Travellers* 284: . . . down we shot at a terrible pace, till . . . we lodged upon the first "apron" with a bump and a crash that sent the timbers jumping beneath our feet, and deluged the fore part of the crib with spray and foam. **1963** *Cdn Geog.Jnl* Nov. 159/3: . . . the Ottawa raft was a different species, built for different conditions. Most of the Ottawa rapids were passed by slides, and the Ottawa "cribs," which went down them, could not safely have run the St. Lawrence rapids.

b. *West* a small raft of logs.
1916 PARKER *World for Sale* 222: Tied up to the Manitou shore were a half-dozen cribs or rafts of timber which should be floating eastward down the Sagalac. **1959** SHIPLEY *Scarlet Lily* 142: Beamish's Company . . . had built a channel or series of steps to the river below down which "cribs" of lumber could be guided.

2 *Hist.* a framework made of floats (def. 1) and traverses, *q.v.*, into which staves were stowed for rafting down the St. Lawrence River from the Great Lakes.
1945 CALVIN *Saga* 6: . . . some general standards for "merchantable" timber were set up [and] rules of pilotage from "Chateauguay to Montreal," for rafts of timber and cribs of staves, were drawn up.

crib navigation or **slide** *Lumbering, Ottawa Valley, Obs.* See **timber slide.**
1854 KEEFER *Ottawa* 68: One of the disasters to which lumbermen are subjected in driving their timber, and one which induces them to go to great expense in forming a crib navigation where it can be obtained, is what is called a "jam." *Ibid.* 66: In this simple manner . . . are formed the "cribs," one of which will carry all the provisions and many men in safety down any navigable rapid or crib slide.

crib-sucker *n.* a horse that has the habit of biting his manger or other object and noisily sucking in his breath; crib-biter.
1924 (1933) SLATER *Yellow Briar* 188: Not, perhaps, that the schoolmaster was really amatory-minded; nor that the jealous plow-boys of Mono, with rustic waggery, were justified in calling him a kisser, which was as approbrious an epithet in those days, as calling a horse a crib-sucker.

crick† [krɪk] *n.* See **creek** (def. 1).
☛ *This spelling represents a pronunciation long established in Canada at the popular, especially rural, level; the variant exists in many British dialects and goes back several centuries. See note at* **creek.**
c1777 (1955) CURTIS *Voyage* 49: "Geo Hardt now inform'd us their was a french Wigwam up a Crick about half a mile off. . . ." **1832** (1953) RADCLIFF *Letters* 141: . . . it's well that ever we got to this place, with them roads, and the floods, and the cricks, and the axes going . . . and the mistress almost destroyed, and the children as bad. **1960** *Weekend Mag.* 30 Apr. 63/1: We have even eaten a couple of gift trout taken from Bick's Crick.

criée sale [< F *criée* auction + E *sale*] *Obs.* a sale ordered by a court; auction sale.
1812 *Quebec Gaz.* 2 Apr. 1/1: On Saturday the Eighteenth of April, next, at Quebec aforesaid, in the said Court House, Court Sitting, at ten o' clock in the morning, will be made the third and last Criée sale and Adjudication of the said land. **1817** *Ibid.* 12 Sep. 4/1: There will, by order of the Honorable Court of King's Bench . . . be proceeded on the Fourth and last Criee sale and adjudication to the last offerer . . . on Tuesday . . . in the Court House. . . .

crimson snow snow reddened by an alga, *Protococcus nivalis,* found in Arctic and Alpine regions.
1850 (1852) OSBORN *Arctic Journal* 85: I was neither interested . . . in Arctic Highlanders or "Crimson Snow!"

crocus *n. West* the pasque flower, *Anemone patens.* See also **prairie crocus, prairie smoke, sandflower,** and **windflower.**

1893 *Wkly Manitoban* Apr. 110/2: Behold a pleasant landscape aglow with April sun. . . . Where purple crocus blows and downy willows wave. **1961** MITCHELL *Jake and the Kid* 65: You . . . can look at the crocuses and they're purple, not out-and-out purple, but not blue either.

A crooked knife

crooked knife ['krʊkəd *or* krʊkt] a wood-working knife usually having a crooked handle and, often, a hook at one end of the blade, used widely in the north, especially by the Indians, for making snowshoes, fur stretchers, canoes, and all woodwork. See also **canoe knife** and **mocotaugan.**
☞ *Known also by the French-Canadian name* **couteau croche,** *q.v., this tool was an important article of trading goods, although it was often homemade from old files or trap springs.*

[**1681** (1945) *H.B.C.Minutes* 177: Ordered that Rich. Mauhlin make ready . . . 500 of the large crooked steel blades. . . .] **1743** (1949) ISHAM *Observations* 105: They make a board . . . which they cutt out of a large tree with only a Hatchet and crooked Knife. **1896** RUSSELL *Far North* 194: The crooked knife with the Eskimo, as with the Indian, is an important tool, which he uses with considerable skill in carving and wood-working. **1942** TWOMEY & HERRICK *Needle to the North* 89: An Indian depends for almost all his accomplishments in manufacture upon the crooked knife. **1966** *Cdn Geog.Jnl* Apr. 125/2: His most important implement is the "crooked knife"; this has a cutting blade about six inches long with an abrupt hook at the end. First made by a cutlery firm in Sheffield, England, and used as barter by the pioneering fur traders, this knife is still distributed in Canada by the Hudson's Bay Company.

crop *n. Nfld* equipment and supplies to outfit a ship for a sealing, whaling, or fishing voyage.
1906 LUMSDEN *Skipper Parson* 116: The voyage had been a failure; the men had hardly earned enough to pay for their "crop," or outfit, and had nothing coming to them.

cross¹ or **crosse** *n.* [Cdn F *la crosse*] *Obs.* **1** the game of lacrosse (def. 1).
1760 JEFFERYS *Descr.New France* 78: The Game of the Cross . . . is played with a ball and sticks bent, and smoothed like racquets. **1893** OXLEY *Young Nor'Wester* 48: . . . the broad level stretch at the other side of the fort made a fine ground upon which to play the game of Crosse, out of which the modern game of Lacrosse had been developed.

2 See **lacrosse stick** and picture.
1820 (1823) FRANKLIN *Journey* 73: When a nimble runner gets the ball in his cross, he sets off towards the goal with the utmost speed, and is followed by the rest, who endeavour to jostle him and shake it out. **1869** *Cdn Illust.News* 30 Oct. 6/3: Prince Arthur . . . proceeded to open the Tournament by tossing the ball off his crosse into the field.

cross² *n.* **1** See **cross-fox.**
2 the skin of the cross-fox.
1933 MERRICK *True North* 117: I got . . . forty weasels, 139 muskrats, two crosses and a red. **1956** KEMP *Northern Trader* 142: Red foxes, crosses and silvers are holding up, but black foxes are not in demand.

cross-check *v. Hockey* engage in cross-checking.
1963 *Kingston Whig-Standard* (Ont.) 29 Jan. 9/1: Late in the game Ted Green . . . cross-checked an attacker against the boards. . . . **1965** *Globe and Mail* (Toronto) 19 Apr. 15/9: . . . the Hawk centre . . . had cross-checked him near the goal.

cross-checking *n. Hockey* an illegal manner of checking an opponent. See 1963 quote.
1958 *Herald-Tribune* (Grande Prairie, Alta) 28 Feb. 5/6: Derf Swanston sat out two minutes at 4.08 for cross-checking. . . . **1963** *Calgary Herald* 15 Nov. 14/2: The rule on cross-checking calls it "a check delivered with both hands on the stick and no part of the stick on the ice." **1966** *Hockey News* 1 Jan. 17/2: . . . during some cross-checking he cut John's lip to earn a five-minute penalty.

crosse *n.* See **cross¹.**

crossed fox *Obs.* See **cross-fox.**
1812 KEITH *Letters* 103: This is a poor beaver country, but there are plenty of martens and musk-rats, with a diversity of foxes, such as red, white, black, silver, crossed foxes.

cross-fence *n.* a type of rail fence in which the horizontal rail is set in the crotch of two crossed uprights, the ends of which are driven into the ground.
1870 *Cdn Illust.News* 19 Mar. 314/2: . . . a passenger was expected to pay his stage fare, and then arm himself with a rail from the nearest cross-fence to assist in prying the coach out of the mud-holes.

cross-fox *n.* a color-phase of the red fox, *Vulpes fulva,* marked with a cross over the shoulders. See also **cross²** and **patch fox.**
1771 (1792) CARTWRIGHT *Journal* I 82: I examined the traps and deathfalls near Fox Pond, and upon the river, and had a good cross fox. *c*1902 (1912) LAUT *Story of the Trapper* 259: The value of the cross fox depends on the markings that give him his name. If the bands running diagonally over his shoulders in the shape of a cross, shade to grayish blue he is a prize, if to reddish russet, he is only a curiosity. **1958** *Alaska Sportsman* Dec. 11/1: We trap for red fox on land, same as we do for white fox. Use fish and squirrel for bait. Red fox stay on land, also cross fox and silver.

cross-fox skin the pelt of the cross-fox.
1771 (1792) CARTWRIGHT *Journal* I 92: The man whom I sent to the tilt yesterday, returned this morning, accompanied by Ned, who brought two cross-fox skins. **1928** FREEMAN *Nearing North* 86: The rickety Peterboro belonged to his brother while the synthetic Elto he was holding as security for the price of a cross fox skin another Indian had sold him.

crossing *n.* See **traverse¹** (def. 1a).
1956 KEMP *Northern Trader* 28: From the mouth of the Beaver to Ile a la Crosse settlement calls for a "crossing" of five miles.

crossing-stringer *n.* See **stringer** (def. 1).
1902 PATTILLO *Moose-Hunting* 3: But the crossing-stringer (an old tree) did not seem over safe.

cross of the north See quote.
1947 ROWLANDS *Cache Lake* 165: Somehow, when you are on a portage with a pack on your back and you meet a fellow and stop to speak, you just naturally lean forward on your paddles to ease the load of your pack, and so the blades cross between you making what we call "the cross of the north."

cross road a road running at right angles to and joining two concession roads, or other main roads; side road.
1835 *Novascotian* (Halifax) 23 Dec. 379/3: If there bant a road made up to every citizen's door . . . why he says the House of Assembly have voted all the money to pay great men's salaries, and there's nothing left for poor settlers, and cross roads. **1909** HUNTER *Simcoe County* I 48: In all the townships there were "jogs" in the middle of the concessions, causing obstructions and deviations on the side roads, or "cross roads," as they are called in some localities. **1926** *Dalhousie Rev.* V 205: On the crossroad approaches a span drawing an ornate buckboard filled with belated tourists.

cross-slate *n.* a number of candidates chosen from opposing political parties or groupings; a non-partisan group of candidates.
1961 *Press* Oct. 11: . . . non-partisan organizations began to call for election of a "Jan-Jango" cross-slate.

cross-tree pack-saddle *West* a pack-saddle resembling a saw-horse, much used in pack trains.
1876 LORD *Wilderness* 52: Some persons, for example the Hudson Bay Company's traders, stick to and swear by the cross-tree pack-saddle, from which they hang their bales of fur-peltries by loops.

crotch or **crutch** *n.* See 1898 and 1912 quotes. Cp. **travois** (def. 3).
1896 GOURLAY *Hist.Ottawa* 72: Think of boards drawn from the mill by oxen on two crotches, then put into cribs in the river. . . . **1898** (1963) GUILLET *Pioneer Farmer* II 30: "Crotch? Why that was a thing my old man made to haul logs on. It quirled up at the nose like a sled and sprauled out so-fashion. You see one end of the logs laid on the crotch an' tother end drug behind." **1912** HEENEY *Pickanock* 54: A rough tongueless sled, made out of the fork of a tree and called a "crutch," was used for drawing the logs on.

crowbar palace *Slang* a jail.
1963 *News of the North* 29 Aug. 2/1: Three months in Fort Smith's crowbar palace may have a most salutary effect on the young man concerned. . . .

crow-beater *n.* [< Cdn F; see 1959 quote] the eastern kingbird, *Tyrannus tyrannus,* from its habit of driving other birds from its nesting site.
1866 (1873) LEMOINE *Maple Leaves* IV 485: Allow me to introduce you to a brave, indomitable fellow—the King Bird; . . . schoolboys know him as the Crow-beater. **1959** MCATEE *Folk-Names* 48: EASTERN KINGBIRD . . . *Batteur de corbeaux* (Crow beater. It attacks, sometimes even alighting upon and pecking larger birds that invade its nesting territory. Que.). . . .

crowboot *n. North* a lined mukluk or boot usually having a short upper of muskrat fur and thick soles of moosehide.
1963 *News of the North* 2 May Back page: [Advert.] Aklavik Fur Garment Co-operative. Eskimo Native Handicrafts Now On Display! Womens Parkas size 14 & 16 $175.00. Crowboots All Sizes $19.95. Muskrat Rug Matching Skins $35.00. **1966** *North* May-June 39/2: The flowers that blaze in the scrawny boreal forest near Fort Franklin are the kind that you wear on your feet. They bloom on moccasin, mukluk and crowboot; bright bold designs worked with silk or beads on stroud, a sturdy felt material.

crow duck the double-crested cormorant, *Phalacrocorax auritus,* so called because its color suggests a crow and its habits a duck.
1792 (1934) TURNOR *Journal* 476: This day we took some eggs of the Crow duck . . . a large black kind of duck with a beak like a crow and lives upon fish. **1938** *Beaver* Sep. 13/1: The cormorants, known also as shags and water turkeys, are large black divers nearly the size of a wild goose, known to the Crees as crow ducks. **1959** MCATEE *Folk-Names* 5: Double-crested Cormorant . . . crow duck (In allusion to its colour and somewhat duck-like appearance. . . .).

crowhop *v.* make a series of stiff-legged little jumps. See also **crow-hopping**.
1922 STRINGER *Prairie Child* 206: I'm a she-devil crow-hopping around in skirts. **1954** PHILLIPS *Living Legends* 55: They [horses] sunfish and they crowhop, trainees fly in all directions. **1961** MITCHELL *Jake and the Kid* 126: When he [a mustang] started crow-hopping that finished me. I lit right in the middle of the duck-pond.

crow-hopping *n.* a horse's way of arching the back and making a series of stiff-legged little jumps as if about to buck. See also **crowhop**.
1951 HOBSON *Grass* 68: He ran sideways around the corral trying to scrape me off on the logs, made a poor job of crow-hopping, then stopped in his tracks and looked about him. **1960** NELSON *Northern Lights* 709: He [a horse] gets his head roughly snapped back and has to settle for a little crow-hopping.

crown *n. West* especially of willows, that part of a tree where the root system merges with the trunk.
1934 BETTANY *Valley of Lost Gold* 219: He took an axe and disappeared into the bushes, emerging with a willow root, a tough old crown, hardened by fire. **1963** SYMONS *Many Trails* 24: But I won't go into details of grubbing willow crowns and urging the ox-drawn breaker plow through heavy sod. . . .

crown(up)† *v.* of forest fires, burn in the tops of trees rather than along the ground.
1951 ANGIER *At Home* 172: The fires mostly burn slowly and deliberately, crowning only occasionally. **1964** *Calgary Herald* 28 July 29/3: The blaze . . . crowned as high winds carried the flames from one tree top to another.

Crown company or **corporation**† a company owned and operated by the government, federal or provincial.
1863 *Nor'Wester* (R.R.S.) 22 July 3/1: Feast one day, fast the next; rich one year, poverty-stricken and woe-begone the next; annexation to Canada one day, annexation to the States the next; a Crown Company the third day, and smash the jail on the fourth. **1958** *Edmonton Jnl* 8 Aug. 4/1: The report contained strong criticism of the defence and defence production departments and five Crown companies. **1963** *Globe*

and Mail (Toronto) 2 May 8/4: Maple Leaf Services is a Crown Corporation established to operate canteens, grocery stores and other outlets at army establishments in Canada and abroad.

crown fire a forest fire that spreads by jumping from the top, or crown, of one tree to that of another.
1943 SWANSON *Lumberjack* 9: Crown fires sweep the lofty tree tops, leave behind stark desolation. **1958** *Edmonton Jnl* 1 Aug. 1/2: The pitch in spruce heated by sun and wind or by ground fires from underneath, can explode like a bombshell and become a crown fire, travelling at a rate at least equal to the speed of the wind that fans it.

Crown land(s)† unsettled land held by the state in the name of the Crown; in earlier use, often a synonym for Crown reserve, *q.v.*
1791 (1905) *Ont.Bur.Arch.Rep.* VIII 393: You are to divide the front into lots of two hundred acres each and mark every third line of concession, reserving the cite of the town, the glebe, and the Crown lands. **1830** MOORSOM *Letters N.S.* 177: Crown-land is obtained on application to the Commissioner, Halifax, at the rate of about £5 currency for 100 acres.... **1964** *Family Herald* 12 Mar. 16/4: He leases a further 85 acres of Crown land on a year to year basis for maple production.

Crown reserve(s) 1 *Hist.* a tract of land set apart to assure the Crown a source of revenue free from the control of the colonial legislature.
1802 *Niagara Herald* (U.C.) 7 Aug. 2/2: For Sale, that valuable Farm, adjoining the crown reserve at Fort Erie, containing 498 acres.... **1832** (1953) RADCLIFF *Letters* 105: There are still crown, and clergy reserves, which will be sold next year to *gentlemen* settlers, but after that, the lots here will be closed to everyone, except by private purchase.... **1963** MORTON *Kingdom of Canada* 228: Little was realized from the Reserves, either Clergy or Crown, until in 1824 the Canada Company was formed....

2 in certain provinces, lands reserved by the provincial government, which retains the rights while offering leases for sale to oil companies, lumber companies, etc.
1958 *Edmonton Jnl* 9 Aug. 24/4: The Saskatchewan department of natural resources has accepted ... cash bonuses for crown reserve leases offered this week. *Ibid.* 14 June 9/2: The Alberta government is beginning to reap returns through the sale of oil rights in the area and the first three proven parcels of rights offered as such are up for tender at a July 22 Crown reserve sale.

cruise *n.* **1** an exploratory tour through a region. See also **cruise**, *v.* (def. 1).
1775 (1792) CARTWRIGHT *Journal* II 62: I took a cruise over Lyon Head and Eyre Island and, after a good course, killed a yellow fox.... **1962** *B.C.Digest* Oct. 28/1: If the prospector has time in summer, he will make a cruise to see the country, to study and locate the creek wash....

2 *Lumbering* See **timber-cruise**. See also **cruise**, *v.* (def. 2).
1961 PRICE & KENNEDY *Renfrew* 39: These explorers were equipped as lightly as possible but carried rifles and enjoyed several weeks roughing it while on the "cruise."

cruise *v.* **1** travel through the country to appraise its potential in natural resources.

189

1834-43 (1955) RUSSELL *Journal* 56: I was cruising with another Trapper thro. the timber....

2 *Lumbering* examine a tract of forest to estimate the value of the timber on it, especially for a logging company. See also **cruiser** (def. 1), **cruising, cruise-line, range**, *v.*, and **sight**.
1912 RATHBORNE *Canoe Mates* 238: Stackpole and Dubois had sense enough to cruise in other timber than that surrounding the trading post. **1956** EVANS *Mountain Dog* 90: They're going to work on shares, getting out some timber they've been cruising.

3 *Nfld* See quote.
1933 GREENE *Wooden Walls* xvi: CRUISING THE FLOE Denotes the search for the seals on foot, often over many miles of ice.

cruise-line *n.* *Lumbering* one of the lines marked out by a cruiser (def. 1) while assessing a stand of timber. See also **cruise**, *v.* (def. 2).
1954 BRUCE *Channel Shore* 198: His pencil ran down the figures recording the diameter of trees sampled along the cruise-lines. *c*1963 *New Sounds* 6/1: The accuracy of the map, which is drawn by men skilled at copying information from aerial photographs, is checked in the areas photographed, by Foresters who travel a compass-route or "cruise-line" designed to cover all possible timber-types of forest in the proposed cutting area.

cruiser *n.* **1†** *Lumbering* See 1942 quote. See also **prospector** (def. 2), **timber-cruiser**, and **wood-ranger** (def. 1).
1942 HAIG-BROWN *Timber* 250: CRUISER. A man who goes out in the woods to estimate the volume of timber standing on a given acreage. He does a good deal more than this and submits his work in the form of a map divided into 40-acre squares and showing the contours and general physical features of the country as well as the volume and type of timber. **1947** SAUNDERS *Algonquin* 74: The company, he says, "spent millions of dollars" on it, out of a misguided faith in the cruiser's glowing reports. **1964** *Cdn Geog.Jnl* Feb. 66/2: The site of the winter cutting had been chosen in advance by a man known as the cruiser....

2 a boot having a high laced top and used in rough country.
1903 WHITE *Forest* 183: He brought to light ... oil-tanned shoepacs, with and without the flexible leather sole; "cruisers" of varying degree of height— each and every sort of footgear in use in the Far North....

3† a police patrol car.
1955 *Globe and Mail* (Toronto) 31 Jan. 4/1: They gave chase in their cruiser and radioed for assistance. Speeds between 60 and 70 mph were recorded along Queen St. toward Sunnyside. **1958** *Liberty* Jan. 25/2: We were parked in the yellow cruiser, about 75 yards beyond a stop sign that Toronto's east-end motorists love to ignore.

4 See **Snow Cruiser**.
1965 *Kingston Whig-Standard* (Ont.) 5 Feb. 11/1: Since it is about two miles off the road to the lake, I figure the cruiser will have an opportunity to prove itself.

cruiser cloth *Maritimes* a thick woollen cloth suitable for Mackinaw coats, *q.v.*, and similar heavy garments.

1964 *Atlantic Advocate* July 77/1: By 1934 William M., a third generation Humphrey, was operating the mill and producing a large red and black check design for Mackinaw or cruiser cloth. Three grades of Canadian wool, fine, medium and coarse, called "one-half," "three-eights" and "quarter blood" respectively, were used in its manufacture.

cruiser gang the party accompanying a cruiser (def. 1).
1947 *Ont.Timberworker* 15 Nov. 4/4: The $7.00 per day applies to small crews, such as a cruiser gang surveying the bush, etc.

cruising *n. Lumbering* See **timber-cruising.** See also **cruise,** *v.* (def. 2) and **cruiser** (def. 1).
1922 ROBERTS *More Animal Stories* 25: Being a dead shot with the revolver, he seldom troubled to carry a rifle in his "cruisings." 1954 BRUCE *Channel Shore* 183: Dan and I'll do the cruising tomorrow.

cruising horse *West* a horse trained to work its way through scrubland, brush, etc.
1966 *Sask.Hist.* Winter 33: On this trip locating and looking over this timber we used a buckboard and a good team of cruising horses.

crummy ['krʌmi] *n.* [prob. < *crumb* body louse] *Esp. West Coast, Slang* See 1942 and 1964 quotes.
1942 HAIG-BROWN *Timber* 250: Crummy . . . A box car or an old caboose converted to passenger carrying by the addition of a few wooden benches, and used to carry the men to and from work. 1957 HUTCHISON *Canada* 323: Most of these men live in towns and travel perhaps forty miles to work in a "crummy." 1964 *Sun* (Vancouver) 30 May 5/2: Loggers ride in cold and heat in old trucks called crummies, which are "crummy."

crunnick ['krʌnək] *n. Atlantic Provinces* See quotes. Also spelled *crannich, crunnock*.
1895 (1944) WENTWORTH *Amer.Dialect Dict.* 146/2: e.Canada, N.B., N.S., Newfoundland "To spell (gather) a yafful (armful) of crunnocks (kindling). 1921 Newfoundland. 1964 *Imperial Oil Rev.* Apr. 1: And, by the way, if you're still wondering what crunnicks are, they're dry, twisted pieces of wood. *Ibid.* Apr. 23: If turr-shooting is your favorite sport, if you love nothing better than a kettle of tea boiled over a fire built of crunnicks on the barrens. . . .

crust *n.* a layer of frozen snow overlying softer snow, formed by the melting and refreezing of the surface, aided by wind compaction. See also **snow-crust.**
1776 (1792) CARTWRIGHT *Journal* II 158: It was exceedingly bad walking to-day, and also very bad for the eyes; the snow having a crust on it which reflected as much as cut glass, and every tree had assumed a most brilliant lustre, from the effect of the silver thaw. 1826 *Cdn Courant* (Montreal) 18 Jan. 3/1: It was impossible for any animal to travel, whose feet were not armed with points to penetrate the crust, or heavy enough to break it, in which case, its legs were wounded and in constant danger of being broken. 1955 GOWLAND *Smoke* 124: Over the crisp crust of the day before my snowshoes had made some noise, and I had paid the matter no attention.

crust coffee *Obs.* a beverage made by boiling burnt or scorched crusts.

1853 STRICKLAND *Canada West* I 251: . . . mine hostess placed before me a piece of dirty-looking Indian meal-bread, and a large cake of beef-tallow, and . . . a dish of crust coffee without either milk or sugar. . . .

crusting† *n. Obs.* See quotes.
1866 KING *Sportsman in Canada* 51: Moose hunting lasts throughout autumn and winter, and there are several different methods of pursuing the sport, as "calling," "driving," "creeping," and "tracking," or hunting on snow-shoes, sometimes called "crusting." 1892 DAUNT *Land of Moose* 130: This [the exhaustion of the pursued moose] occurs all the sooner if the snow be covered with a thin icy crust, which breaks beneath the weight of the animal, and lacerates his legs. . . . This method [of hunting] is called "crusting."

crutch *n.* See **crotch.**

cubby ['kʌbi] *n.* [< obs. E *cub* pen, stall] See 1943 quote. Cp. **cat-house** and **trap house.**
1939 PINKERTON *Wilderness Wife* 94: "You don't know how to build a cubby, set a trap or snare a bait." 1943 *Beaver* Dec. 23: For marten, the trapper builds a small enclosure of stakes at the base of two trees, sets his trap inside, places some scented bait beyond it, covers the trap with grass, and lays some brush over the "cubby."

cud [kʌd] *n.* [abbrev. of *cuddy,* a cabin abaft in a large ship] *N.S.* the cosy, built-in forward part of a fishing boat.
1945 RICHARDSON *We Keep a Light* 215: The boats that fish from Mud Island, and have to be hauled up over skids there, must sacrifice the comfort of the "cud" . . . for lightness in weight. 1960 *Weekend Mag.* 29 Oct. 30/1: Then I noticed an inch or two of water on the cud floor.

cull *n. Lumbering* a log below the marketable standard; a reject.
1829 MACTAGGART *Three Years* I 245: The refuse wood is called *culls,* and brings an inferior price. 1883 FRASER *Shanty* 302: Some refractory stick generally some worthless "cull," or rotten, twisted piece . . . is the cause of the whole mischief. 1964 *Victoria Dly Times* 9 Oct. 4/2: They are not always economic because cutting takes place at some distance from a ready market for what the loggers consider undersized or cull sticks.

culler ['kʌlər] *n. Obs.* **1** an inspector of fish.
1907 *U of T Stud.Hist.& Econ.* II 242: In 1762 the grand juries in sessions were employed to appoint cullers and surveyors of dry fish, surveyors of lumber, and surveyors of cordwood. 1957 *Nfld Qtly* Sep. 4/1: He used to be a culler on Strickland's room across the harbour.

2 *Lumbering* an inspector of logs.
1808 *Canadian Courant* (Montreal) 23 May 3/2: His Excellency the Governor in Chief has been pleased to make the following appointments, viz: Master Cullers and Measurers of Staves, for the Port of Montreal. William England, Alexander England. . . . 1829 MACTAGGART *Three Years* I 245: At Quebec, there are people called Cullers, who are appointed to select lots of timber according to quality. 1963 *Cdn Geog.Jnl* Nov. 165/3: . . . years after St. Lawrence rafting ceased, one could see . . . culler's marks still legible upon their solid sides.

cultus ['kʌltəs] *adj.* [< Chinook Jargon *kultus* < Chinook] *West Coast* worthless, insignificant, useless, bad.
[1849 ROSS *Adventures* 346: Idle talk . . . Kaltash

wa-wa.] **1904** MORICE *Northern Interior B.C.* 322: Oh! your companion is a "cultus" man, while I know that you are a chief. **1948** HOLLIDAY *Valley of Youth* 164: Mary wasn't letting any cultus white man put anything like this over on her. . . . **1962** *Alta Hist.Rev.*Autumn 14/2: "Bad medicine," "chaffy," "snide," "jim-crow," and "pizen," are applied to anything worthless on the Eastern slope of the Rockies while "cultus"—a Chinook Indian word—is most frequently employed with like significance upon the B.C. side.

cultus coulee ['kʌltəs 'kuli] [< Chinook Jargon; *cultus,* q.v. and *coolee* < F *courir* to run] *West Coast* a stroll or ride for pleasure. See 1963 quote.
1894 PHILLIPPS-WOLLEY *Gold* 171: "I'm taking a 'cultus coolee,' " replied he. . . . **1912** POCOCK *Man in the Open* 96: I hustled the ponies just in case Mrs. Trevor might be taking her *cultus cooly* along toward Soda Spring. **1963** SYMONS *Many Trails* 75: These Indians [Chilcotin] always seemed to be travelling "cultus coulee," which means moving about with no set destination, and stopping wherever there was good hunting or fishing.

cultus potlatch a gift for which nothing is expected in return, especially one of little value. See also **potlatch,** *n.* (def. 1).
1862 MAYNE *Four Years in B.C.* 100: All that is expected being that you should give them a "cultus-patalatch" (literally, a useless present). **1894** *Port Moody Gaz.* (B.C.) 12 Jan. 3/4: In answer to the Bench it was admitted that the whisky was a "cultus potlatch" on the part of the prisoner. **1937** ANDREWS *Wrangell* 16: A cultus potlatch is a little gift, too small to mention. . . . **1940** *B.C.Hist.Qtly* July 200: At Christmas-time Chief Gregior would come and receive . . . tobacco as a *cultus potlatch.*

cumtux *v.* See **kumtux.**

cunner† ['kʌnɚ] *n. Maritimes* a small fish of the wrasse family, *Tautogolabrus adspersus.*
1945 RICHARDSON *We Keep a Light* 47: The morning was silky calm, and we thought we would try our hand at catching a few small fish, cunners or frost fish, so we went out in the skiff with our lines. **1963** HARRIS *Northern Exposure* 27: It was also various wharves, five in number, the short brokendown ones where we fished for cunners and the long one piled with lumber where the beautiful tall ships came.

curé† ['kjure] *n.* [< F] in French Canada, a parish priest.
1765 *Quebec Gaz.* 28 Feb. 4/1: And that no Person or Persons may plead Ignorance thereof His Excellency and Council, Have thought fit to Order and Direct, That for the Future, the Curés of each Parish respectively, shall cause the said Gazette to be sent home weekly. **1896** PARKER *Romany* 128: They both had a whimsical turn, and the curé did not ask Tarboe how he came by such perfect liquor. **1962** *Maclean's* 6 Oct. 71/1: He teases, but never offends, the curé.

curled maple 1 See **curly maple** (def. 1).
1800 WELD *Travels* I 381: The swamp maple . . . yields a much greater quantity of sap . . . but this sap does not afford so much sugar as that of the curled maple.

2 See **curly maple** (def. 2).
1830 (1837) *Trans.Lit.& Hist.Soc.Que.* III 105: It is in much request with the cabinet-maker and house carpenter, especially that variety which is so beautifully marked with dots and rings surrounding them, known by the name of bird's eye maple; and that with undulations, or the curled maple.

curlew-berry *n.* the crowberry, *Empetrum nigrum.*
1895 TABOR *In Rugged Labrador* 18/1: Even the outlying islands furnish the curlew-berry and bake-apple in profusion.

curling† *n.* a winter sport first popular in Scotland, played by two teams of four players, each of whom slides, in turn, two stones down the surface of a sheet of ice, a team's object being to finish with its stones closest to the "tee" in the centre of the target area. See also **roaring game.**
1818 PALMER *Journal* 216: Curling matches are sometimes made [in Montreal]. **1827** (1829) MACTAGGART *Three Years* II 222: Notwithstanding the numbers of lakes and rivers which abound in Canada, and all the intensity of the winter frost, still the game of curling, the great ice amusement of Scotland, is unknown. **1841** *Montreal Transcript* 12 Jan. 438/4: The Montreal Club was instituted in January 1807, thirty-four years ago; and Curling was kept up there with great spirit for several years, until a temporary relaxation was occasioned, for three winters, by war with the United States, which broke out in 1812; when the Curlers had to bear arms and assist in defending the country. **1966** *Globe and Mail* (Toronto) 2 Mar. 26: [Headline] Saskatchewan upset in women's curling.

curling iron *Obs.* a curling stone, so called because earlier "stones" were often made of iron.
1841 *Montreal Transcript* 12 Jan. 438/4: . . . they are sometimes called Curling Irons, a term used chiefly by Hairdressers, which was soon laid aside, and now they are always named stones or stanes.

curly maple 1 See **sugar maple** (def. 1). See also **curled maple** (def. 1).
1827 (1829) MACTAGGART *Three Years* I 172: Let the local names be given, as *prickly ash, spotted alder, pitch pine, curly maple.* . . . **1883** FRASER *Shanty* 20: He has also on these limits an immense quantity of bird's eye maple and curly maple. **1956** *Native Trees* 240: "Curly" and "Bird's-eye" maple . . . are unusual forms occasionally met with.

2 the wavy-grained wood of this tree, much valued for furniture making and interior finish. See also **curled maple** (def. 2).
1828 *Gore Gaz.* (Ancaster, U.C.) 12 Feb. 4/3: The subscriber is willing to contract for any quantity of . . . curly maple lumber. . . . **1952** *Cdn Geog.Jnl* XLVI 181: [Caption] Body and drawer are handcarved from a block of curly maple.

current sail See quote.
1928 WALDEN *Dog-Puncher* 227: They evidently had a "current sail" out. . . . A current sail is made by dropping a piece of canvas under the boat with rocks tied to the two lower corners. The under-current catching this, will carry the boat against any wind. . . .

curricle *n. Obs.* a light sleigh drawn by two horses, usually abreast.
1849 ALEXANDER *L'Acadie* I 183: Twice a week we had sleigh meets, when curricles, and tandem, and cutters, or sleighs of one horse power, turned out with steeds gaily decked with party-coloured streamers, and alive with bells.

curtain-wall school See quote.
1957 *Maclean's* 17 Aug. 3/3: Curtain-wall schools that can be enlarged to suit student requirements are now

being built in answer to pleas from harassed boom-town school boards. Two-inch insulated steel walls are simply bolted together and can be moved to insert additional partitions and provide more space.

cushion *n.* See **hockey cushion.**
1965 *Globe and Mail* (Toronto) 5 Jan. 27/4: However, shinny players make use of five cushions in the area.

Custom of Paris See **Coutume de Paris.**
1897 *Rev.Hist.Pubs* I 100: The Custom of Paris, which had been the law of Canada under the French, was now made valid in all civil affairs. **1905** *Ont.Bur.Arch.Rep.* III lxvii: By the Quebec Act of 1774 the Custom of Paris was to be continued in disputes relative to property and civil rights, but in criminal matters the law of England.

cut *n.* **1**† a way cut through rock or gravel in building a road, canal, or railway.
1826 *U.E.Loyalist* (York [Toronto]) 24 June 30/4: . . . the slopes of the Deep Cut above the tow-path, are at an angle of 45′. **1961** *Cdn Geog.Jnl* Jan. 16/2: Materials from the cuts were pushed . . . in cars over a track of poles to build adjacent embankments.

2 a natural gully or ravine, serving as a pass.
1905 (1954) *B.C.Hist.Qtly* July–Oct. 161: What struck me most was the "cut" of the Peace river through the Rocky mountains, which, as to its main range, narrows in that quarter. **1965** *B.C.Digest* Dec. 56/3: Late that afternoon we came to the top of the Peace River cut. When I saw the steepness of the road as it zig-zagged down the hillside, I demanded to be lifted out of the sleigh.

3† the amount of timber cut in one season.
1901 CONNOR *Man from Glengarry* 11: Dan Murphy was mightily pleased with himself and with the bit of the world about him, for there lay his winter's cut of logs in the river below him snug and secure and held tight by a boom across the mouth, just where it flowed into the Nation. **1957** *Evening Telegram* (St. John's) 17 Dec. 17/8: To provide therefore for an annual cut of say 25,000 cords, would mean an initial capital investment of over half a million dollars. . . .

4 a holding of timber for lumbering purposes.
1883 FRASER *Shanty* 91: And if he is an honest man . . . let him go to the merchant . . . and make an open bargain with him, either for a job, or to buy a "cut," or purchase out and out the whole lot for a stated sum. . . . **1895** (1929) THOMSON *Old Man Savarin* 192: They never knew the direction from which he might come—an ignorance which kept them all busy with axe, saw, cant-hook and horses over the two square miles of forest comprising his "cut."

5 *Sealing* See 1933 quote at **patch** (def. 2).

cutbank† *n.* **1** a precipitous river bank, eroded by the current.
1897 *Medicine Hat News* (Alta.) 28 Jan. 1/6: While on his way home from the Rosebud in the frost and storm the horse on which he was riding went over the cut bank near the iron bridge on the Bow. **1954** PATTERSON *Dangerous River* 253: The cabin stood on a high cutbank looking straight north across the Liard. **1962** *B.C.Digest* Oct. 40/1: . . . I couldn't remember just which of the cut banks along the lake was the one where I had seen the nodules in place.

2 either one of the two banks of a river that has eroded a course deep into its bed. Cp. **cut-rock.**
1897 TYRRELL *Sub-Arctics* 22: The banks were high, towering in some places three, four or five hundred feet above the river; here abrupt and precipitous, consisting of cut banks of stratified clay; in other places more receding, but by a gradual slope rising, beneath dense foliage, to an equal elevation. **1962** *Alta Hist.Rev.* Autumn 14/2: . . . a narrow bridge of land is known as a "hog's back" and the precipitous escarpments of clay bordering on a river are "cut-banks."

3 a hill having a steep front resulting from erosion. See also **cuthill.**
1889 *Our Forest Children* Dec. 97/2: Our delight was to make corrals for the buffaloes, and to drive them over the cut bank and let them fall. **1934** GODSELL *Arctic Trader* 119: Along lovely jackpine ridges, down one cutbank and up another . . . our cayuses followed the guide with tireless gait. **1955** *Beaver* Spring 21/1: We turned south into a long stretch of shale cutbanks.

cut country *West, Slang* take a short cut across country.
1963 SYMONS *Many Trails* 76: So they were going to go like hell and "cut country."

cuthill *n.* *West* See **cutbank** (def. 3).
1958 *Globe and Mail* (Toronto) 15 Nov. 16/5: Dried roots of juniper were abundant back in the draws and cuthills of the ranch. . . .

cutline *n.* a survey or other line cut through bush.
1958 MCGREGOR *North-west of 16* 26: The cutline . . . stood out clearly, a gash in the forest three feet wide with all trees cut to fall right and left of the line. **1958** *Edmonton Jnl* 12 Aug. 2/5: Wolter and Solomon were working on a cutline by themselves when they went to get some water for camp.

cut money *Obs.* coins cut into halves, quarters, or eighths to make change.
1799 *Cdn Constellation* (Niagara-on-the-Lake, U.C.) 30 Aug. 3/1: The cut money in circulation has, within a few days, been cried down.

cut-off† *n.* **1** a road or trail that cuts off a loop or bend in an older road, thus reducing the distance to be travelled.
1859 *British Colonist* (Victoria) 29 Jan. 1/4: During the past season individual enterprise has done much towards improving this trail, cut offs have been discovered which have shortened it some 20 miles. **1958** *Arctic Spotter* Mar. 12/2: Leaving Fort Nelson, we set off for Beatton River, and were soon on the cut-off that leads from the Highway in to the airport.

2 a channel resulting from a change in the course of a river.
1859 *British Colonist* (Victoria) 17 Dec. 3/2: The ice was packed ten feet high, below Six Tree Shoot, and the Maria cut off,—where a portage of a mile had to be made, with a whale-boat, over the ice. **1900** LONDON *Son of Wolf* 112: Watch out for the open water on the Thirty Mile River, and be sure to take the big cut-off above Le Barge. **1952** PUTNAM *Cdn Regions* 485/2: Between the channels are innumerable shallow lakes and cut-offs of all sizes and shapes.

cut out† *Esp.West* separate one or two or more animals from a herd.
*c*1895 (1966) *Alta Hist.Rev.* Winter 14/1: I wanted to cut out some cattle that were required and to let the rest go.

1908 LAUT *Conquest N.W.* II 37: ... Marie's pony took the bit in his mouth and bolted, wheeling ... and cutting out the biggest of buffaloes for the hunt. ...
1962 *Canada Month* May 37/1: In the afternoon, they rode straight into the herd, dexterously cutting out the cows and calves belonging to each rancher.
1964 JENNESS *Eskimo Admin.* II 106: ... a third herd [of reindeer] was to be cut out and placed under Eskimo ownership. ...

cut over† *Lumbering* remove the trees from. See also **log**, *v.* (def. 2).
1961 *Maclean's* 29 July 42/1: The lumbermen of the Ottawa cut over a territory and then moved on, leaving the cut-over land alone while a new generation of trees grew up.

cut-over† *adj. Lumbering* cleared of timber; logged.
1928 PERRY *Two Reds* 9: ... he could reforest the sandy wastes, the burned-over, cut-over bush which he had picked up with timbered acreage. ... 1961 *Edmonton Jnl* 5 Aug. 36/1: "I am not asking for good land," says Mr. Bancroft, "any old waste or cut over timber lands would do."

cut-rock *n. West* the steep side of a river channel through rocky terrain. Cp. **cutbank** (def. 2).
1908 LAUT *Conquest N.W.* II 270: There, the cut rocks, steep as a wall and sharp as knives, crowded the pack horses to the edge of bottomless precipices where one misstep meant instant death for rider and horse.
1926 DICKIE *Cdn West* 126: Each day Tom McKay with his band of hunters scoured the cut-rocks [for beaver]. ...

cutter *n.* **1**† a low, light one-horse sleigh having an upholstered seat. See also **sleigh-cutter.**
1826 (1832) PICKERING *Inquiries of an Emigrant* 49: A sleigh is drawn by two horses abreast, here called a "span"; a cutter is drawn by one horse. 1849 ALEXANDER *L'Acadie* I 183: Twice a week we had sleigh meets, when curricles, and tandem, and cutters, or sleighs of one horse power, turned out with steeds gaily decked with party-coloured streamers, and alive with bells.
1948 HOLLIDAY *Valley of Youth* 235: ... Jake [was] fast asleep in the arms of Bacchus, with his horse and cutter, stranded in a fence corner by the side of the road.
1966 *Globe and Mail* (Toronto) 6 Jan. 5/4: The six, square-timbered barns ... [contain] a museum of pioneer equipment—cutters, wagons, broad axes. ...

2 *Esp. West* a low two-horse sleigh having narrow runners and, usually, a front and back seat.
1920 KENDALL *Luck of the Mounted* 51: ... as he spoke the "off" horse suddenly slipped and fell, and, plunging to its feet again, a leg slid over the cutter's tongue.
1934 BETTANY *Valley of Lost Gold* 40: ... with a team and cutter, fur robes, hot stones at her feet ... their continued journey had been warm and comfortable by comparison. 1960 BUBLITZ *Dotted Line* 28: ... my trip of twenty-two miles was made by team and cutter.

cut throat *n.* **1** in preparing fish for salting, the person who guts the fish and all but severs its head, making it ready to be snapped off by the header, *q.v.* See also **throater.** Also *cut-throat.*
1818 CHAPPELL *Voy. of Rosamond* 127: Each salting-house is provided with one or more tables, around which are placed wooden chairs and leathern aprons, for the cut-throats, headers, and splitters. 1861 DE BOILIEU *Labrador Life* 30: The first person on the stage engaged in curing fish is the "cut-throat," with his double-edged knife; the next is the "header," who dislocates the neck, and forces the head of the fish off, which falls into the water through a hole cut in the table. 1965 LEACH *Songs* 5: The man nearest the box, the "cut-throat," reaches down, grasps a fish and holding by a finger in each eye ... he makes a lightning-quick cut across the throat from gill to gill and then a second longitudinal cut, ripping down the belly and allowing the entrails to spill out. He then pushes the fish over to the "header."

2 See **cutthroat trout.**
1907 LAMBERT *Fishing in B.C.* 43: The cut-throat is unknown to me. I have never caught it in British Columbian waters, unless some fish mentioned later in the accounts of the Nicola River belong to this species.
1963 *Sun* (Vancouver) 28 Mar. 29/1: The cutthroats could start feeding on the first hatches of pink salmon fry in the sloughs and lower reaches of the rivers.

cutthroat trout† a large trout of western Canada, *Salmo clarkii,* so called from a red streak under each side of the lower jaw.
1918 SCHULTZ *Rising Wolf* 77: ... these lakes are full of cutthroat trout, and what the whites call Dolly Varden trout, and whitefish. 1966 *Dly Colonist* (Victoria) 27 Feb. 8/2: ... the sand pool ... at this time of year is often filled with cutthroat trout and sometimes is holding water for steel head.

cutting *n.* a stand of timber; the site of a logging operation.
1902 WHITE *Blazed Trail* 191: It's a fine country ... with a fine cutting of white pine. 1928 PERRY *Two Reds* 13: Surrounding the settlement was a tangle of second-growth timber, penetrated in every direction by the old roads where, at one time, great loads of logs had been hauled out from the cuttings. 1964 *Cdn Geog. Jnl* Feb. 63/2: [It was] known to every shantyman of the Ottawa as the route to the Madawaska and Bonnechère cuttings.

cutting horse† *West* a horse specially trained to separate cattle, one by one, from a herd.
1955 HOBSON *Nothing Too Good* 139: [He] was astraddle his buckskin cutting horse, dangerously close to the caved-in end of the porch. 1962 ONSLOW *Bowler-Hatted Cowboy* 199: ... "cutting" horses ... by instinct and by training ... will bring out a beast from the herd without disturbing the rest of the cattle, or they may be required to hold a bunch from breaking back. 1962 *Canada Month* May 37/1: This practice originated today's cutting-horse competitions.

C.W. *Hist.* See **Canada West.**
1845 *Niagara Argus* (C.W.) 29 Oct. 3/2: A new Reform journal entitled the Western Globe, has just been started in London, C.W. 1863 *Nor'Wester* (R.R.S.) 2 June 2/4: We have the following in reply to a letter from J. F. Moore, Stratford, C.W. 1924 (1933) SLATER *Yellow Briar* 175: The McLaughlins had a flouring and grist mill on a branch of the Humber at Mono Mills, C.W. ...

cyprès *n. Cdn French* See **cypress** (def. 1).
1784 (1790) UMFREVILLE *Hudson's Bay* 44: Then [we] crossed a small bay 3/4 mile S. by W. to portage Cyprès. ... 1823 FRANKLIN *Journey* 765: Banksiana: the Canadian voyagers term it Cypres. ... 1896 RUSSELL *Far North* 103: Early in the afternoon we entered an extensive grove of pines ... the cyprès of the métis.

cypress *n.* **1** one of several species of pine tree, especially the Banksian and the lodge-pole, *qq.v.* See also **jackpine.**

1793 (1801) MACKENZIE *Voyages from Montreal* 179: The trees are spruce, red-pine, cypress, poplar. . . . **1872** (1873) GRANT *Ocean to Ocean* 161: Near Victoria was a sandy ridge producing scrub pine, or as the people here called it "cypress." **1953** MOON *Saskatchewan* 70: French-speaking fur traders found the high lands first and named them Cyprès, their word for the jack pines they found. Through the years the word became changed to Cypress, misleading because no cypress trees can be found there. **1956** *Native Trees* 16: Jack Pine [is also called] Banksian pine . . . grey pine . . . cypress, juniper.

2 *East* See **pitch pine.**

1767 *Quebec Gaz.* 8 Dec. 3/1: They are hereby forbid to cut down . . . White Pine, Red Pine, Cypress, or White Oak Trees, on the lands above described. **1921** HEMON *Chapdelaine* [trans.] 121: Nothing remained but cord the split wood in the shed beside the house where it was sheltered from the snow; the huge piles mingling the resinous cypress which gives a quick hot flame, spruce and red birch, burning steadily and longer, close-grained white birch with its marble-like surface, slower yet to be consumed. . . .

3 *Pacific Coast* See **yellow cedar.** See also **Nootka cypress.**

1869 *Mainland Guardian* (New Westminster, B.C.) 11 Dec. 1/4: A quantity of cypress bark . . . is teased into oakum. . . . **1905** WIGHTMAN *Our Cdn Heritage* 155: . . . Menzies spruce, western hemlock, and cypress are the principal trees, all of which grow in plenty, and of immense size. **1917** (1920) *Native Trees of Canada* 48: . . . The Western Cypresses. . . . Only one species, *Chamaecyparis nootkatensis,* occurs in Canada. **1966** *B.C.Logging* 4/2: Estimated annual production . . . Cypress 10.2 [million cubic feet]. . . .

dag [dæg] *n.* [< Cdn F < F *dague* dagger] *Now Rare.* See 1859 quote. See also **hand dag.** Cp. **snow-knife.**

1797 (1964) CHABOILLEZ *Journal* 171: Laganast ... very near stabed him but luckyly Macsathy Mouse took the Dag. **1859** (1870) SOUTHESK *Saskatchewan* 164: I bought from a half-breed a knife of what is called the "dag" pattern, a heavy flat, double-edged blade about eight inches long, of triangular shape, tapering to a point from a width of some two and a half inches at the base. **1938** SULLIVAN *Cycle of the North* 87: So ... the spear broke in his body, and I struck with my dag till he died with his mouth open to slay me.

A dag

dague *n.* [< F] *Obs.* See **dag.**

1812 KEITH *Letters* II 109: They make use of the axe or hatchet, butchers knife, crooked knife and dagues, with iron trenches for fishing or working beaver.

Dahl sheep See **Dall sheep.**

Dall [dɑl] *n.* See **Dall sheep.**

1954 PATTERSON *Dangerous River* 166: Something moved in the field of vision, and two Dall rams came grazing into view on the grass and talus slopes along the foot of the precipice. **1958** *Beaver* Spring 31/2: There you will find the magnificent Stone sheep, merging slowly into Fannin's sheep and then the Dall.

dalle [dæl] *n.* [< Cdn F "trough, flume" < F "flagstone"] **1** *Obs.* a smooth flume or artificial slide for floating logs.

1832 MCGREGOR *British America* II 453: From the mill the deals are floated down a *dall* or *trough* to the basin for shipment, part of the distance being cut through soil and rock fourteen feet deep. **1834** (1955) DOMETT *Cdn Journal* 8: The deals are floated down in a raised trough just wide enough for one to pass, which runs for miles across the country and terminates at the wharf. It is called a "dalle." God knows how they spell it.

2 See **riffle** (def. 1c). See also **flat rapid.**

1789 (1801) MACKENZIE *Voyages* lix: I estimate its winding course to the Dalles eight miles. **1821** (1900) GARRY *Diary* 131: After 10 minutes paddling we came to a small Rapid which we run and in a few Minutes arrived at the Dalles or Straits between Rocks which is a Décharge of a few Paces. **1912** ROE *Whispering Hills* 248: Northward along Nelson River went the concourse ... turning westward into the chain of little dalles above Winnipeg ... sweeping forward over portage and dalle. ...**1963** MACLEOD & MORTON *Cuthbert Grant* 55: They found Keveny above the Dalles of the Winnipeg River....

3 a narrow stretch of river between high rock walls, characterized by whirlpools, rapids, and treacherous currents.

1793 (1933) MACDONELL *Diary* 85: After passing a narrow Racy rapid named the Dalles we saw an Island on which ... the Irroquois in former days ... tried to cut off a strong Brigade of trading canoes. **1808** (1916) THOMPSON *Narrative* 386: Dalle ... a name given to where the river is contracted by high steep rocks. **1948** *Cdn Geog.Jnl* March 151: Another obscure appellative dalles is of Canadian origin although it is now for the most part used in the United States, particularly along the Columbia River.

Dall sheep [< W. H. *Dall*, 1845-1927, Alaska naturalist] the white sheep, *Ovis dalli*, of the mountains of the Northwest. See also **Dall, white buffalo** (def. 2), **White Dall sheep,** and **white sheep** (def. 2).

[**1908** MAIR *Mackenzie Basin* 169: Dall's Mountain Sheep: It is probably this recently-determined variety or species of wild sheep which inhabits the Rocky Mountains of the lower Mackenzie River to the Arctic coast, while the true Bighorn ... exists in the ranges to the south.] **1948** CAMERON *Cdn Mammals* 26: The white or "Dall" sheep occur in northern British Columbia, the Yukon and Northwest Territories, and the grey or "Stone" sheep occur in British Columbia. **1966** *Maclean's* 1 Jan. 7/2: We are speaking of a harvest of one dall sheep, one bear, etc. per thousand square miles.

dam[1] *n.* See **beaver dam.**

1907 HUNTER *Cdn Wilds* 84: After placing the trap on the dam[,] Wa-sa-Kejic opened another ready for setting, tied the poles, and had everything ready.... **1948** ONRAET *Sixty Below* 153: Some of these lengths [the beaver] use for dams....

dam[2] *n. Prairies* See **dugout** (def. 3). See also **pothole** (def. 3b).

1957 *Maclean's* 25 May 27/3: "Dam," in prairie usage, refers to both the retaining wall of the dam and the waters within it, and covers everything from true irrigation dams, which, though fed periodically with fresh water, become very warm in summer, to stock-watering dugouts in farmers' fields.

damper† *n.* [< Australian E] a kind of bannock, *q.v.*

1850 BIGSBY *Shoe and Canoe* II 272: Our fare in the Fort was primitive—chiefly damper (scorched balls of dough), potatoes, and fish wine, coffee, and tea. **1962** NICHOLSON *West Coast* 114: ... now a meal consisted of tea and "damper," with the Indians reduced to eating roots and fern.

dan† *n.* [origin uncertain] *North* **1** a sealskin bag used as a buoy or float. See also **floater** (def. 1) and **poke** (def. 3a).

1831 (1963) DAVIES *Northern Quebec* 153: ... they returned pursuing a whale which they had harpooned and which we observed by the dan attached to the harpoon line. **1940** *Beaver* Mar. 7/1: We steered for the float or "dan" and picked it up, and by hauling on the line, soon brought the walrus to the surface.

2 a sealskin bag used by Eskimos for storing or transporting seal or whale oil. See also **poke** (def. 3b).

1847 NEVINS *Two Voyages* 16: The Esquimaux fill these dans with seal or whale oil, and bring it to the ships for sale. **1941** *Beaver* Dec. 50/2: ... the fat [of a seal] is later pushed back in one great creamy roll. This is later packed into a sealskin bag or "dan" where it will render itself down into blubber.

dance hall 1† a building used for public dancing.

☛ *In frontier times, usually a place of entertainment where gambling, drinking, and more fleshly pleasures were available.*

1898 *Yukon Midnight Sun* (Dawson) 17 Sep. 4/2: In relation to the dance halls, they would be classed as one of the conditions in vogue in mining camp life, and will not be molested, provided that there is no indecent exposure of person by the girl occupants, and strict order maintained without noise or vulgarity.

1921 HEMING *Drama of Forests* 189 : Instead of lurching into the dance hall and blazing away at the ceiling, picture the "old-timer," the hardened miner of a hundred camps, planking down his pistols on the counter of the pawnshop and asking "How much?" **1958** *Edmonton Jnl* 24 June 1 3/8 : The proposed change would put premises used for teen dances, "controlled by a responsible organization that has been approved by city commissioners," outside the classification of "dance hall."

2 See **dance house.**
1936 *Cdn Geog.Jnl* Jan. 54/1 : . . . behind the pow-wow house, or dance-hall, was a long birch-bark structure, surmounted with a white cross and a white flag.

3 an area where prairie chicken perform mating dances. See also **dancing ground.**
1959 *Calgary Herald* 1 Aug. 19/1 : The prairie chicken have four "dance halls" on Moore's place. He has approached within 30 yards to watch the annual rites.

dance-hall girl *Hist.* in frontier days, a woman employed in a saloon or dance-hall, ostensibly to serve as a dancing partner for male clients.
1910 SERVICE *Trail of '98* 369 : It was the régime of the dance-hall girl. . . . **1926** DILL *Long Day* 153 : A dance-hall girl staked him and he applied himself cautiously, grimly, to the business of beating the wheel.
1960 RAMSAY *Barkerville* 39 : A new and far different type of dance hall girl appeared on the scene in 1866, when Madame Fannie Bendixen brought in the first of the hurdy-gurdy girls. . . .

dance house among Indians and Eskimos, a large structure where communal dancing is performed. See also **dance hall** (def. 2) and **dancing lodge.** Cp. **singing house** and **snowhouse** (def. 2).
1853 SEEMANN *H.M.S.Herald* II 59 : It is rare to find a village without its accompanying dance-house . . . a building erected by the united efforts of the whole community, and constructed on the same plan as the common dwellings, but larger, and, the floor being raised some three feet from the ground, more free from wet. **1948** *Beaver* Sep. 10/2 : . . . the whole population of the village quickly gathered together in the large village dance house to discuss the matter. **1964** DUFF *Indian History* 101 : The dance houses are large barn-like structures with dirt floors and tiers of benches round the walls, heated by two large bonfires. **1965** JENNESS *Eskimo Admin.* III 49 : Lack of any definite organization . . . did not deprive the Eskimos of a social and religious life. . . . It centred on the dance-house, which in Hudson Bay, and probably also in Labrador, was no more than an enlarged snow hut that provided a home for two or three families, and possessed a forecourt into which other families could squeeze for conversation, dances, and religious ceremonies.

dancing booth *Obs.* in pioneer days, a structure serving as a temporary dance hall.
1908 MAIR *Mackenzie Basin* 53 : . . . we were speedily surrounded by a bustling crowd, putting up trading tents and shacks, dancing booths, eating-places, etc. . . .

dancing girl *Obs.* See **dance-hall girl.**
1866 (1962) ANDERSON *Sawney's Letters* 46 :
We are dancing girls in Cariboo,
And we're liked by all the men. . . .

dancing ground a well-worn patch of elevated prairie where prairie chickens habitually congregate for their mating ritual or dance. See also **dance hall** (def. 3).
1958 *Kootenaian* 3 Apr. 2/5 : Good dancing grounds are often almost bare of grass. . . . Finding a dancing ground in good sharptail country is not difficult, and the experience of watching a dance . . . will more than repay the observer for very early rising.

dancing lodge See **dance house.**
1914 RADIN *Myths of the Ojibwa* 7 : Then he built them a dancing-lodge of branches and leaves, and when everything was ready, he picked up his drum and started to sing.

dancing tent *Obs.* a special tent or tepee in which Indians performed ceremonial dances.
1926 *Battleford Hist.Soc.Pubs* I 26 : As it was reported that the culprit was among the dancers, Crozier and the rest of us pushed our way through the crowd of armed Indians into the dancing tent.

dark oil or **brown oil** *Sealing* See quotes.
1832 MCGREGOR *British America* I 225 : The first that runs off the seal blubber is the virgin, or pale oil, and the last the brown oil. **1966** *Cdn Geog.Jnl* Apr. 133/1 : The resultant oil, classified according to colour and quality as "pale oil," "straw oil," and "dark oil," sells for an average price of about 50 cents per gallon.

dark spell *North* the winter darkness in the Arctic regions.
1951 GILLIS & MYLES *North Pole* 156 : "Have you noticed the 'dark-spell' much? I didn't mind it nearly as much this year as last. . . ."

dasher [ˈdæʃɚ] *n.* the enclosing fence of a hockey rink; the boards.
1962 *National Hockey Annual* 54/3 : The Red Wing players on the nearby bench leaped up and leaned over the dasher, shouting encouragement to their teammates.

date *n.* (*usually plural*) *Obs.* a news dispatch (of a specified date).
1798 *Quebec Gaz.* 13 Dec. 3/1 : The London dates in the New York Papers, reach down to the first October. **1828** *Loyalist* (York [Toronto]) 7 June 6/1 : Our latest dates are from Liverpool, to 28th April, but they did not contain any very important news. **1875** *Harbor Grace Standard* (Nfld) 4 Sep. : Dates from Long Island to the 27th ult. say that fishing has somewhat improved from that place south—with a very fine prospect of herring.

Davidite *n. Obs.* See 1837 quote.
1828 *Loyalist* (York [Toronto]) 23 Aug. 86/1 : The Davidites, too, of Yonge Street notoriety, would doubtless sympathize in the exclusion of their Chief from an office—say, the premiership. . . . **1837** WILKIE *Sketches* 202 : One of the most remarkable of the bodies alluded to at present is the one in Canada denominated "Children of Peace," or popularly "Davidites." Their chief teacher, and I believe the founder also, is an old man named David Wilson. Their leading doctrine, as far as I could understand, is equality in everything, both temporal and eternal.

Davis raft *West Coast* an ocean-going raft constructed of layers of logs, used mostly for short tows.
1942 SWANSON *Western Logger* 54 : . . . raft (Davis raft) —invented by Davis at Port Renfrew, B.C.; a boom of logs capable of being towed in heavy seas bound up

with cables. **1944** (1952) ROBINS *Pocketful of Canada* 20:
. . . you are the donkey man, / The sky line and the
Davis raft; the high rigger and the tug-towed boom of
logs. . . . **1965** *Dly Colonist* (Victoria) 6 June 16/1:
Then the Davis raft was designed in 1913. Logs were
wrapped in bundles by wires and chains. This proved
for many years the best raft to withstand rough seas,
and served for forty years. The Davis was 475 feet long,
30 feet deep, 16 feet above sea level, and carried
3,600,000 board feet.

Davis water wheel [perhaps after a Cornish
miner named *Davis,* who worked one of the early
claims in the Cariboo goldfield] *Hist.* a large wheel
(about 20 feet in diameter) having buckets on the
rim and used in placer mining to operate a pump
to keep the workings dry. See also **Cornish pump.**
1960 RAMSAY *Barkerville* 46: [Caption] Davis, or
Cornish water wheel and flume [used in] hydraulic
operations at Morning Star Claim.

davy-man *n.* [< affi*davit*] *N.S., Hist.* a prisoner
taken from a captured vessel and made to swear an
affidavit before Admiralty Court that the vessel
taken was legitimate prey for privateers.
1958 RADDALL *Rover* 126: ". . . Cap'n, pick a good
davy-man for the love o' truth, or we'll all be
condemned as liars by our own wives, let alone the
Admiralty Court."

Dawson caribou [< G. M. *Dawson,* 1849-1901,
Canadian geologist and surveyor] an extinct subspecies of caribou (def. 1), *Rangifer torandus
dawsoni,* found only on Graham Island of the
Queen Charlotte Islands.
1964 *Wildlife Rev.* May 6: For example, the Dawson
caribou seems to have been "on the way out" naturally;
man's appearance on the scene only hastened the
process slightly.

Dawson route, road, or **highway** a road and
water route from Fort William to Fort Garry,
recommended by Simon J. Dawson, a Canadian
engineer, after an exploration trip in 1857-9, the
first leg of a proposed trans-Canada highway.
☛ *Surveying for this undertaking led to conflict with the
Métis and was one of the incidents that triggered the
Red River Insurrection of 1869-70.*
1885 GEMMILL *Companion* 108: In 1868, called
upon by the Gov't to commence the construction of the
route to Red River, now known as the "Dawson Route."
1921 *Beaver* Dec. 7/1: In the fall [of 1871] he was
appointed to take charge of the North West Angle
post. . . . This post had been established when the
"Dawson Road" was opening as an immigration route
from eastern Canada. **1954** CONSTANTIN-WEYER
Half-Breed 7: It was then the news came that two
English surveyors, Snow and Mair, had obtained the
necessary sum from the Canadian government for the
construction of the Dawson highway, which was to
cross the continent from one ocean to the other.

day camp a summer camp which young people
attend only during the daytime, returning to their
homes each night.
1957 *Cdn Home and School* June 2: Local . . .
organizations may have day camp programmes and
would be grateful for further parent interest and support.
1963 *Globe and Mail* (Toronto) 16 May 17/1: Day
camps are located as far away from densely populated
urban areas and commercial resorts as possible.

dayliner ['deˌlaɪnɚ] *n.* a self-driven express train

of one or more coaches travelling daily between
two cities. See also **railiner.**
1958 *Edmonton Jnl* 27 June 45/3: Mr. Herridge said he
had been informed that communicable-disease patients
could be carried in the baggage section of the Budd
cars—or dayliners—on the CPR'S Kettle Valley run
in British Columbia. **1965** *Kingston Whig-Standard*
(Ont.) 13 Dec. 23/1: Railroad enthusiasts . . . got a look
at the Canadian National Railway's new dayliner
Saturday.

deacon seat† a long bench in a bunkhouse, *q.v.,*
especially in a lumber camp.
1872 DASHWOOD *Chiploquorgan* 103: In front of the
fire on one side, and running the whole length of the
camp, is a bench, hewn out of spruce or fir; this bench
is termed the "deacon seat"; behind it the men sleep in
a row, on fir boughs, with one long rug under and
another over them. **1925** CLARKE *Chris in Canada* 172:
. . . when the food was cleared away to one end of the
[lumber shanty's] table, some of the men sat down again
and played poker, for matches, while others sat on the
Deacon seat, and joked or told stories. **1965** STEVENS
Incompleat Canadian 36: Along three sides of the single
room ran double or even treble tiers of bunks, below
which stood the benches or "deacon seats" on which the
men sharpened their tools, mended their harness, ate
their meals and took their ease. . . .

deacon's nose *Slang* the broad lobe of a chicken,
turkey, etc. which corresponds to a mammal's
tail and which serves as a base for the tail-feathers;
the pope's nose.
1855 HALIBURTON *Nature* II 8: "Mr. Slick, what part
shall I help you to—a slice of the breast, a wing, a
side-bone, or the deacon's nose, or what?" Everybody
laughs at that last word, especially if there is a deacon
at table. . . .

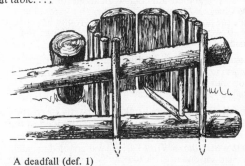

A deadfall (def. 1)

deadfall *n.* **1** a kind of animal trap. See 1853 quote.
See also **deadfall trap, deathfall, fall-trap, figure-
four trap,** and **log trap** (def. 1).
[**1771** (1911) TOWNSEND *Cartwright's Jnl* 89: These people
. . . do not trouble to catch furs, not being furnished with
traps; nor do they understand the use of deathfalls.]
1853 STRICKLAND *Canada West* I 158n: The method
pursued by the trappers and Indians is to blaze a line
through the bush for several miles. Along this line is
set, at intervals of one or two hundred yards, a kind of
trap, called a dead fall which is constructed thus:—
Two rows of short sticks are driven into the ground
about one foot apart, open only at one end, the top
being covered with brush-wood at the entrance. A piece
of wood two or three feet long is bedded into the

ground, or snow, as the case may be. The falling pole is supported immediately over this by three pieces of stick notched together in the form of a figure of four. The centre-stick is made long and sharp at the point, to which the bait is attached, and projects well into the miniature house. The marten or fisher, allured by the bait, reaches in to snatch it, which springs the trap, and causes the pole to fall across the neck of the animal, which is instantly killed by the blow. **1956** LEECHMAN *Native Tribes of Canada* 28: The commonest type of trap was a deadfall, in which the animal, trying to take the bait, disturbed a trigger which let a heavy log fall on its back, killing it.

2 a tract of forest cluttered with dead and fallen trees. Cp. **dead stand timber** and **timberfall.**
1912 POCOCK *Man in the Open* 12: The little trees, a cut here, a slash there ... cross the crick, first deadfall, more lops, a number one trap empty.... **1963** *Calgary Herald* 20 Nov. 27/1: Walking in heavy snow and deadfall is too hard work for me.

3 a single dead tree that has been blown to the ground.
1921 *Beaver* Feb. 6/2: After ... climbing over dead falls and crossing many creeks, I struck the lake....
1962 FRY *Ranch on the Cariboo* 220: Herbie ... struck out at once with a short crosscut saw and an axe to clear the trail of any deadfalls....

deadfall or **deadfallen** *adj.* of trees, downed by wind, disease, or age.
1908 MAIR *Mackenzie Basin* 126: Though a tough spot to get up to, the flat proved to be a prime place for our camp, with plenty of dead fallen and standing timber....
1912 POCOCK *Man in the Open* 165: But it doesn't say ... what to say when Jones kicks me in the morning, or in deadfall timber ... or any unusual accident in this vale of tears; and there ain't one word about robbers.
1963 SYMONS *Many Trails* 165: There for yards at a time the poor dogs never put foot to ground but have to climb over a succession of tangled deadfall logs, the legacy of a forest fire or high winds....

deadfall trap See **deadfall** (def. 1 and picture).
1953 FLUCKE *Déné* 16: In general the Sekani preferred loop snares to deadfall traps, though the latter were used to some extent [to catch caribou].

deadhead *n.* a water-soaked log partly or entirely submerged, usually with one end embedded in the bottom. See also **snag** (def. 1).
1902 WHITE *Blazed Trail* 380: He was enabled to catch the slanting end of a "dead head" log whose lower end was jammed in the crib. **1924** FLAHERTY *Eskimo Friends* 3: Trunks, branches, and foliage of the wreckage swayed like dead heads at midstream. **1963** *Globe and Mail* (Toronto) 20 Apr. 42/3: In lakes try [fishing] beside shoreline deadheads, fallen trees and logs.

dead lodge *Obs.* See **death teepee** (def. 1).
1933 HIGINBOTHAM *When the West Was Young* 232: The preceding year [1869] smallpox had swept through the Blackfoot tribes and left in its wake whole camps of "dead lodges," the mortality being estimated ... at forty or fifty percent.

deadman *n.* **1** *Obs.* one of two series of converging objects, such as posts, piles of turf, large upright stones, forming a funnel into which big game, such as buffalo, were driven into a pound for slaughter.

See also **deer hedge** and **watching waiter.** Cp. **deer drive.**
1858 HIND *Assiniboine Exped.* 356: [They set up] a lane of branches of trees, which are called "dead men" to the gate or trap of the pound. **1859** KANE *Wanderings* 118: At one side [of a buffalo pound] an entrance is left, about ten feet wide, and from each side of this, to a distance of half a mile, a row of posts or short stumps, called deadmen, are planted, at a distance of twenty feet each, gradually widening into out the plain from the entrance.

2 any solidly fixed object to which a block and tackle can be hitched. See 1954 quote.
1883 *Prince Albert Times* (Sask.) 9 Aug. 4/1: On the 25th the steamer was still aground on a sand bar and had to plant a "dead man." **1923** WALDO *Down the Mackenzie* 151: A "dead man" is a pole driven into the bed of the lake or stream, to which block and tackle may be affixed for the purpose of hauling off the stranded vessel. **1954** PATTERSON *Dangerous River* 117: We got out of that mess by building a series of deadmen out into the main river on a submerged bar and then windlassing the scow up the chute from one deadman to another out into the stream. The deadmen were constructed of heavy poplar logs held down in the water by boulders and slabs of rock as large as we could carry—a "deadman" being some solid object from which a pull can be taken. **1966** *Cdn Geog.Jnl* July 21/1: Turning in midstream, Capt. Simpson headed his tow upstream and nosed into the bank, where he tied on to the anchored "deadmen." These are looped cables, attached to the middle of short, squared timbers which are then planted like coffins, deep in the river bank.

dead stand timber dead trees that remain standing. Cp. **deadfall,** *n.* (def. 2).
1949 *Report of DME Test Team* II 4: Tasks such as cooking ... cutting dead stand timber for fuel, etc. occupy most of the working day....

dead water(s) [trans. of Cdn F *eaux mortes*] a region characterized by sluggish, muddy streams, marsh, muskeg, etc.; also, the sluggish streams and ponds found there.
1793 (1933) MACDONELL *Diary* 74: Above the *portage des Chiens* we entered the *Lac des Chaudiers*[,] a piece of dead water.... **1804** (1933) FARIES *Diary* 196: After breakfast we walked up to the dead water—met a canoe with 4 men a little above the paresseux from Lac des chiens. **1872** DASHWOOD *Chiploquorgan* 38: In summer time they hang about the neighbourhood of muddy lakes and sluggish brooks—called "dead waters" to which they repair.... **1953** MOWERY *Mounted Police* 126: Their strategy was to let the herd work north ... toward a swamp country known as the *Eaux Mortes* or Dead Waters. In that maze of muskeg and boggy streams, a hundred warriors summoned from the camps could slaughter the herd to the last hoof.

deadwood *n. Obs.* See **rampike.**
1853 REID *Young Voyageurs* 277: It [the osprey's nest] can be seen when the woods are open ... and the more easily, as the tree upon which it is built is always a "dead wood," and therefore without leaves to conceal it.

deadwood fence a fence constructed of the brush and deadfalls taken from the clearing of land.
1953 *Cdn Geog.Jnl* Dec. 220/2: The brush fence, or deadwood fence as it was sometimes called, though the least efficient, was a direct product of the clearing of the land.

dealer *n. Nfld.* a trapper or other person who receives advances on his catch and undertakes to bring it to the store giving him the advances. Cp. **debt.**
1918 GRENFELL *Labrador Doctor* 59: It was no salve to his fretfulness when I assured him that I had paid in good English gold, and that his "dealer" would be as honest with the money as the system had made him.

dealing settler *Obs.* a storekeeper in a new settlement.
1898 (1957) *Beaver* Autumn 14/1: The dealing Settlers [at Red River] sent their orders every year 12 mos in advance.

deathfall *n. Lab.* See **deadfall** (def. 1 and picture).
1770 (1792) CARTWRIGHT *Journal* I 46: In our return we found two old furriers' tilts, and snow deathfalls; which appeared to be of Canadian construction. **1792** (1911) TOWNSEND *Cartwright's Jnl* 374: [Glossary] Deathfall. A trap made of logs. They are chiefly used to catch martens, but they will kill any beast, by erecting them in proportion to his size and strength.

death song a dirge sung by or for an Indian at the time of his death.
1760 JEFFERYS *Descr.New France* I 63: Before they begin to burn him, he sings his death-song for the last time; next he makes the recital of his valiant feats, and almost always in the manner that is most insulting to the by-standers. **1938** FETHERSTONHAUGH *Royal Canadian Mounted Police* 93: Accordingly, he was found guilty of murder, was led from his cell to the scaffold, and, with his death-song on his lips paid the penalty for his savage crime.

death teepee *Hist.* **1** a teepee in which those dead from disease were abandoned. See also **dead lodge.**
1888 *Our Forest Children* Dec. 9/1: A death teepee is a horrible place to enter.
2 a teepee erected in honor of a prominent person who has died.
1952 *Beaver* Sep. 27: The [Blackfoot] dead were usually deposited in trees or on scaffolds, but sometimes a special death teepee was erected on a prominent hill-top.

Death Trail See **Long Traverse.**
1913 WILLIAMS *Wilderness Trail* 47: Then, his father had added some description as to the nature of this rumored Death Trail: how a man with a knife, but no gun; snowshoes, but no dogs; and not even a compass, was turned loose in the forest with a few day's food on his back and told to save himself.

débâcle† *n. Cdn French* See **ice-shove** (def. 2).
1852 SUTHERLAND *Baffin's Bay* II clx: Violent débâcles entering Assistance Bay from the lakes. **1870** *Cdn Illust.News* 19 Mar. 318/4: The ice-shove or *débacle* is always an event ,. . . in Lower Canada. . . .

déboulé *n.* [< Cdn F < F *débouler* roll down] *Obs.* a rock slide; avalanche.
1806 (1960) FRASER *Letters and Journals* 155: In these last courses is a large Deboulle on right. . . . **1824** (1955) BLACK *Journal* 95: These Deboules, Avalanches are very common here abouts. . . . The Word Deboulé [is] a common term in this Country . . . the meaning of the word is any part or portion of a Mountain or Bank of Rock Earth, Snow Stone &c tumbled down. . . . **1904** MORICE *Northern Interior B.C.* 208: . . . the Babines . . . were in the habit of trading . . . with their own congeners of what was then called the Fallen Rock— now Ackwilgate or Rocher Deboulé. . . .

debt *n. Fur Trade* **1** credit extended to hunters and trappers in the form of supplies to be paid for out of the coming year's catch. See also **credit, grubstake,** *n.* (def. 2), and **trust,** *n.*
1738 (1965) *Letters from Hudson Bay* 269: . . . if he [an Indian] should be sick and not able to get goods his debt must increase and if he dies the debt is totally lost for here is no executors. **1835** (1947) HARGRAVE *Correspondence* 197: If you were to allow these Indians . . . a few skins of Debt in fall . . . it would be the means to enable them to withstand the cold. . . . **1955** (1964) JENNESS *Eskimo Admin.* II 165: It is the man of the household who lays in the stores. Firstly, he [Eskimo] goes for "debt" in the fall to the Hudson's Bay Company office. . . .

2 a. *Obs.* the supplies advanced.
1743 (1949) ISHAM *Observations* 48: I did see him[;] he Brought your Debt.

b. the value of such supplies; the amount owing.
1844 LEFROY *Magnetic North* 113: This is about the season when the Indians gather round the Forts, to subsist upon muskrats, to pay their debts of furs, and to purchase ammunition for summer expenditure. **1947** *Cdn Hist.Rev.* Dec. 404: In addition, they were not burdened with the necessity of collecting "debt" and could resort to tricks and manoeuvres which were denied the legitimate traders of the post.

3 get (or take) debt, obtain credit for supplies to be paid for out of the coming season's catch.
1783 *Moose Ft Jnls* 159: My Indians in general took very large Debts when they went away in the Fall, I wish they may be able to pay, but from the scarsity of Martins near the Factory I very much fear it. **1800** (1898) COUES *New Light* I 58: This is customary on their taking debts; we generally give them some liquor to encourage them to hunt and pay us. **1909** CAMERON *New North* 70: When you obtain credit from a Hudson's Bay store, you "get debt." A Factor's unwillingness to advance you goods on credit would be expressed thus, "The Company will give me no debt this winter."

4 give debt, extend credit in the form of supplies to trappers who will pay out of the coming season's catch. See also **trust,** *v.*
1809 (1897) COUES *New Light* II 553: Indians still drunk. I equipped those who were sober, and gave them debts, but with a sparing hand, as I feared they would make no great hunts. **1934** GODSELL *Arctic Trader* 129: The Wolf had attempted to stab him in the back for refusing to give him debt. . . .

debtor *n. Fur Trade* a person taking debt at a trading post.
1776 (1951) *Saskatchewan Journals* 37: He has been for some Years past a Trader . . . on the back of Albany Fort, and often used to see the Bungee Indian Debtors belonging to that Place. . . . **1801** (1933) MCLEOD *Diary* 149: They are come from the Beaver Mountain where there are some of my debtors. . . .

décharge [de'ʃarʒ] *n.* [< Cdn F < F *décharger* unload] *Hist.* **1** a shallow place where a boat or canoe had to be partly unloaded before it could proceed. See also **demi-charge** (def. 2), **discharge,** *n.* and *v.*, **launcher,** and **lightening place.**
1761 (1901) HENRY (Elder) *Travels* 23: In this distance, there are four carrying-places, besides three or four

decharges, or *discharges,* which are places where the merchandize only is carried, and are therefore distinguishable from *portages,* or carrying-places, where the canoe itself is taken out of the water, and transported on men's shoulders. **1821** (1900) GARRY *Diary* 95: A Décharge is a place where the Goods are carried, a Portage where both the Goods and Canoe [are carried]. **1965** *Cdn Geog.Jnl* Sep. 89: [Caption] The voyageurs called such places *décharges.*

2 make a décharge, unload a boat or canoe to permit passage through a shallow stretch of water. See also **lighten.**
1804 (1897) COUES *New Light* I 247: Water exceedingly low. We made continual décharges and half-loads. **1909** CAMERON *New North* 139: Until within a few years every ounce of freight for the lower Mackenzie River posts had to negotiate this turbulent waterway, making seven portages and many décharges. **1961** *Cdn Geog.Jnl* July 3: Coming downstream they would, depending on its degree of danger or difficulty, run the rapid, make a "décharge," or portage.

deck *n. Lumbering* **1** a pile of logs ready for driving or hauling. See also **log-pile.**
1928 PERRY *Two Reds* 100: The break-out was to begin the next day. Far up at the end of the trail, which turned away from the river at the first deck of logs, stood the boss, superintending the construction and placing of a huge skidway which was to extend from the foot of the rollway down to the water's edge and down which the logs would go thundering and plunging. . . .

2 See **log deck.**
1947 ENGLEBERT *Men & Trees* 19: . . . guided by the sawyer, it [the steam nigger] tosses the [log] . . . like a match stick from the deck to the carriage.

deck† *v. Lumbering* pile up logs ready for driving or hauling. See also **cold-deck.**
1912 SANDILANDS *West.Cdn Dict.* 44/1: Stack, a pile of lumber; a rollway of logs decked on the banks of the river ready for the drive. **1957** *Kootenaian* 14 Nov. 4/4: There will be offered for sale at public auction . . . the Licence X76189, to cut 874,000 cubic feet of Standing, Felled and Decked, hemlock, fir. . . .

deck passenger *Obs.* a passenger on a steamboat travelling at the lowest rate on the deck, often providing his own food and bedding.
1819 *Kingston Chron.* (U.C.) 30 Apr. 1/1: Deck Passengers will pay 15s. and may either bring their own Provisions, or can be furnished by the Steward. **1832** *Brockville Gaz.* (U.C.) 3 May 3/3: Cabin passengers from Kingston to Bytown—Five Shillings each.— Deck Passengers to be charged half price.

declaration day the day on which the official count of ballots for an election is announced and the successful candidates declared legally elected.
1855 (1965) GAETZ *Diary* 14: Declaration Day; the above named persons declared duly elected. **1959** *Kingston Whig-Standard* (Ont.) 2 Sep. 1/1: Premier Matheson . . . said he would be ready to relinquish power on Declaration Day, Sep. 15. . . . **1963** *Ibid.* 30 Apr. 11/5: Monday's declaration day proceedings, a week after the New Brunswick elections, confirmed narrow-margin victories for three Progressive Conservatives and one Liberal in Saint John City.

declare out *Armed Forces Jargon* withdraw from service; resign one's commission.
1959 *Globe and Mail* (Toronto) 10 July 8/6: Those who come in from university enter on permanent commissions, but may declare out if they wish after four years. . . .

deer *n.* [< *(rein)deer*] *North* See **caribou** (def. 1). See also **reindeer.**
1577 (1938) SETTLE in *Frobisher's Voyages* II 23: Howbeit, there is great quantitie of Deere, whose skinnes are like unto Asses, their heads or hornes doe farre exceed, as wel in length as also in breadth, any in these oure partes or Countrie: their feete likewise, are as great as oure oxens, whiche we measured to be seven or eight ynches in breadth. **1696** (1929) KELSEY *Papers* 46: . . . sent one cannoe up ye river to see if deer crost. . . . **1738** (1965) *Letters from Hudson Bay* 260: . . . 'tis a maxim with the natives to destroy what deer they can . . . for the tongues alone. **1821** (1900) GARRY *Diary* 164: Three canoes came in from the North River with Deer. Report they are crossing in great Numbers. **1965** SYMINGTON *Tuktu* 10: With the winds of late September driving chill from the northwest . . . the scattered deer bunch into groups once more and move toward the timberline.

deer call an instrument for imitating the call of deer to entice them within shooting range. See also **call,** *n.* (def. 1a).
1955 *Yarmouth Herald* 3 May 5/3: The Raynard "natural" deer call has also been used with considerable success in the hunting grounds of Maine.

deer crossing See **caribou crossing.**
1937 *Beaver* June 31/2: They simply wait at known deer crossings and spear the herds in the water from kayaks.

deer drive a formerly-used method of hunting deer or caribou by driving them through a pair of converging fences into a pound (def. 1). Cp. **deadman** (def. 1), **deer hedge, deer-pound,** and **drive,** *v.* (def. 2).
1954 *B.C.Hist.Qtly* XVIII 44: The gun came to replace the bow and arrow for single hunters hunting larger land game, but the deer drive with the net may have been used longer.

Deer Eater See **Caribou Eater** (def. 1a).
1956 MOWAT *Lost in Barrens* 12: . . . Jamie asked, "Who are the Deer Eaters, Awasin?" Awasin was frowning. "They are the Idthen Eldeli, a band of Chipewyans . . ."

deer fence See **deer hedge.**
1832 MCGREGOR *British America* I 271: On the north side of the lake, opposite the river Exploits are the extremities of two deer fences, about half a mile apart, where they lead to the water. **1953** FLUCKE *Déné* 16: . . . the most abundant supply of meat was obtained by means of contrivances similar to the deer-fences of the Interior Salish. These were set at converging angles, culminating in narrow openings. Whereas the method used by the Salish people ended in the slaughter of the animals by bow and arrow, that used by the Sekani . . . ended in the animals being caught in loop snares. Often as many as forty snares would be set at the narrow end of these funnel-shaped corrals. **1962** *Cdn Geog.Jnl* Nov. 157/3: The Beothuks showed marked ingenuity in their deer-hunting methods. They built deer fences made of trees felled in such a way as to form an impassable barrier extending sometimes for as far as forty miles. The purpose of these fences was to divert the caribou . . . and force them toward the rivers. . . .

deer fly a blood-sucking horsefly of the genus

Chrysops. See also **caribou fly**. Cp. **bulldog fly**.
1903 WHITE *Forest* 150: The question of flies—using that, to a woodsman, connotive word in its wide embracement of mosquitoes, sand-flies, deer-flies, black flies, and midges—is one much mooted in the craft. **1962** *Weekend Mag.* 5 May 11/2: But in addition, the bogs of the region abound with mosquitoes, deer flies, snapping turtles, lizards and snakes.

deer-grass† *n*. meadow beauty, *Rhexia* sp.
1832 (1838) TRAILL *Backwoods* 62: The deer resort hither in great herds for the sake of a peculiar tall sort of grass with which these plains abound, called deer-grass, on which they become exceedingly fat at certain seasons of the year. **1852** *Anglo-American Mag.* I Nov. 419/2: Twined among the tall stalks of the deer-grass . . . we find vetches of all the most delicate hues. . . .

deer hedge *Hist*. two converging lines of fencing, as poles, piles of turf or brush, etc., used in early times in deer drives, *q.v.* See also **caribou fence**, **deadman** (def. 1), **deer fence**, **drift fence** (def. 2), **hunting fence**, and **Indian fence** (def. 1). Cp. **hawk fence**.
1843 (1935) STRANG *Pioneers in Can.* 133: In the evening, we descended to the borders of some lakes, where the natives had constructed a deer hedge set with nooses. **1957** *Beaver* Winter 42/1: In the early years the Company's employees set up deer hedges at points up the Hayes River . . . and in addition to the deer meat obtained from these hedges . . . a certain amount of trade in provisions was carried on with Indians.

deer lick See **lick**.

deer lodge a lodge or camp for deer hunters.
1947 SAUNDERS *Algonquin* 48: His sons . . . expert guides . . . have built widely known deer lodges.

Deer Men See **Caribou Eskimo**.
1909 CAMERON *New North* 215: The Eskimo of the Arctic foreshore are of two tribes: the Kogmollucs to the east of the Mackenzie mouth, the Nunatalmutes, Dwellers in the Hills, or Deermen, originally from the interior to the West. . . .

deer-pass *n*. a migration route followed by caribou. See also **reindeer pass**.
1836 (1935) STRANG *Pioneers in Can.* 80: This . . . was soon after agreeably confirmed by the spot which I have described as a Deer Pass of a cache containing more than three whole animals. . . . **1939** *Beaver* June 25/2: None knew so well the deer-passes and the retreats of the caribou. . . .

deer post *Hist*. a trading post near a plentiful supply of caribou. Cp. **fish post** and **meat post**.
1896 (1898) RUSSELL *Far North* 227: Rampart House was a "deer post," being situated in a pass traversed semiannually by the caribou.

deer-pound *n*. *Hist*. an enclosure in which deer or caribou were driven for slaughter. Cp. **deer drive**.
1795 (1911) HEARNE *Journey* 84: I have often heard it observed, that the Indians who attend the deer-pounds might, in the course of a winter, collect a vast number of pelts, which would well serve the attention of those who are called carriers or traders.

deerskin *n*. 1 caribou hide, widely used for clothing and tents by Indians and Eskimos in the North.
1735 (1965) *Letters from Hudson Bay* 208: Our powder we keep wrapped up with deerskins which being a very safe method has been well approved of. . . . **1774** (1934)

deer-grass
dégradé

HEARNE & TURNOR *Journals* 119: Traded a little Meat and some Parchment Deerskins for Snow shoe Netting. **1895** PARKER *Adventurer of North* 80: Then again he offered the Great Slave women to marry, and fifty tents of deerskin for the making of a village. **1963** MCTAVISH *Behind the Palisades* 199: . . . I had enough to do to keep from freezing, tho' I had on a hairy deerskin coat, and was warmly clad.

2 a robe or blanket made of caribou hide.
1931 *Beaver* Mar. 163: A platform about two feet above the floor . . . was covered with deerskins. **1958** WILSON *Northern Treasury* 15: Frequently the writer has encountered native trappers with two deerskins and two Hudson's Bay "Point" Blankets on the front of the sled. . . .

deerskin bag a sleeping-bag made of caribou hide.
1916 BRIDLE *Sons of Canada* 253: He slept in deerskin bags and four-point blankets and talked Cree with a Scotch burr. **1940** FINNIE *Lure of the North* 109: Our eiderdowns and deerskin bags kept us warm enough.

deer's tongue *North* the blazing star, *Liatris* sp.
1952 *Beaver* Mar. 48/1: . . . the contraband goods were simply the dried leaves of a plant called "deer's tongue," which grows in the North and is used for flavouring tobacco.

deer yard See **yard**, *n*. (def. 1a).
1959 *Globe and Mail* (Toronto) 6 Mar. 9/4: Tastier bundles of food are being scattered in deer yards. . . .

defence *n*. in hockey and lacrosse, the players stationed in front of the goalkeeper to help him prevent the opposing team from scoring. Also spelled *defense*.
1902 CONNOR *Glengarry* 310: . . . Hughie moved up two of his centers nearer to the Front defense. **1966** *Hockey News* 16 Apr. 19/4: He [the goalkeeper] needed and received help from his defense, handling only 25 shots. . . .

defenceman *n*. in hockey and lacrosse, one of the players who constitute a team's defence. Also spelled *defenseman*.
1895 *Athletic Life* Feb. 78/1: You will generally find it easiest to skate past a defence man if such tactics are necessary, by tiling straight at him and at the critical moment severing [sic] to his right hand side. **1966** *Hockey News* 16 Apr. 6/3: Toronto Maple Leafs suffered a crippling blow when it was announced that Allan Stanley, best defenseman on the club, would be sidelined for the balance of the playoffs. . . .

degrade *n*. [< Cdn F *dégradé* < F *dégrader* of ships, be turned off course by wind, tide, etc.] *Fur Trade, Obs.* a stop-over enforced by high winds, etc. (often in the phrase *make a degrade*).
1793 (1933) MACDONELL *Diary* 103: [We] Left the place of our Degrade and made five Leagues which brought us to the end of the lake. . . . **1933** GATES *Five Traders* 103n: When the Canadians were forced by adverse winds to land and wait for more favorable sailing conditions, they were said to have made a "degrade."

dégradé *adj*. *Cdn French* See **degraded**.
1900 MASSON *Les Bourgeois* II 215: The French Canadians, to this day, make use of the word *"dégradé"* whenever stopped on their journey by unfavorable weather. **1961** *Cdn Geog.Jnl* July 17: The last defence

the voyageurs had against such big lakes was retreat— to give up, land, and wait. This was termed being "dégradé."

degraded *adj.* [< Cdn F *dégradé;* see *degrade*] *Fur Trade, Obs.* See 1820 quote. See also **dégradé.**
1819 WILCOCKE *Death B.Frobisher* 215: Degraded at the Old House. 1820 WILCOCKE *Death B.Frobisher* 215: "Degraded" is a *voyageurs* term for being prevented from proceeding by the weather; being weatherbound. 1931 NUTE *Voyageur* 39: The voyageurs' term for this state of affairs [windbound] was *dégradé,* and "degraded" soon become a part of the vocabulary of English-speaking travellers.

deke [dik] *n.* [< *decoy*] *Hockey, Slang* a fake shot or movement intended to draw a defending player out of position. Cp. **big deke.** Also spelled *deek*.
1960 *Time* (Cdn ed.) 21 Nov. 79/1: On the ice, Moore is one of the league's best players in the split-second art of faking a goalie out of position. "I've developed a little play of my own," he says. "It's a kind of fake shot —we call them 'deeks' for decoys." 1966 *Globe and Mail* (Toronto) 8 Nov. 34/6: "I went in [on the goalie] but he wouldn't move. I gave one-two-three-four dekes. Finally on the fourth deke he moved and I fired her [the puck] into the corner."

deke [dik] *v.* [< *decoy*] Also spelled *deek*. *Hockey, Slang* **1** draw (a defending player) out of position by feinting, thus getting in a better position to score.
1962 *Kingston Whig-Standard* (Ont.) 12 Feb. 8/6: The big Irishman . . . deked [the defenceman] almost out of his uniform, and ripped a deadly backhand shot past the helpless Hull netminder. . . . 1963 O'BRIEN *Hockey* 74: We try to get our forwards into the habit of lifting their eyes for a quick peek after lowering them for the shot, just hoping the opposing defenceman has been deked into falling early.
2 manoeuvre oneself (or the puck) by feinting so as to outsmart a defending player.
1961 *Kingston Whig-Standard* (Ont.) 23 Oct. 8/6: He deked around a Soo defenceman but was spun off balance from behind before he could get his shot away. *Ibid.* 14 Nov. 11/4: Brown . . . made no mistake[,] faking the shot to the right of goal tender Gord Parker and deking it past him in the left-hand corner.

delayed penalty *Hockey* a penalty call for which the referee delays stopping play until the offending team gets possession of the puck, the imposition being signalled by the referee's raised arm.
1963 O'BRIEN *Hockey* 62: . . . the "delayed penalty" comes into force when an infraction has been committed by the team not . . . in possession. 1963 *Calgary Herald* 12 Dec. 66/1: It is the habit . . . of [goalies] rushing off the ice so a forward can take their place when the referee raises his arm, signalling a delayed penalty on the opposition.

de Meuron [də'murən] [< Col. A. *de Meuron,* commander of a Swiss-German regiment in the service of Great Britain] *Hist.* See 1938 quote. See also **Meuron.**
1822 (1889) *Trans.Hist. & Sci.Soc.Man.* 33: Mr. Halkett knows nothing of any regular tariff formed, as the de Meurons say, by the late Earl of Selkirk, to regulate the prices of goods and grain in the colony. 1938 SIMPSON *Athabasca Jnl* 71n: . . . the De Meurons, a regiment of

Swiss and German mercenaries raised during the Napoleonic Wars. They were taken to Canada during the Anglo-American War of 1812, and were disbanded in 1816. Lord Selkirk took 140 of them for his [Red River] colony in 1818. 1954 CAMPBELL *Nor'Westers* 136: . . . Selkirk had engaged a private army of Swiss mercenary troops, de Meurons, under a Captain D'Orsonnens.

demi-canot *n. Cdn French* "half canoe" See **half canoe.**
1952 (1954) JENNINGS *Strange Brigade* 146: In addition to these were the *demi-canot,* or half canoe, which might be twenty feet long and carried a crew of four to six. . . .

demi-charge *n.* [< Cdn F < F "half load"] *Obs.*
1 that part of a canoe's load that was unloaded at a décharge (def. 1). See also **demi-decharge.**
1804 (1933) FARIES *Diary* 196: [T]hey set off after dinner for the Barrier, and return'd about 8 oclock with the last demi charge. 1933 GATES *Five Traders* 196n: A *demi-charge* was a part of the loading of a canoe. It was carried around a *décharge* while the canoe itself, thus lightened, was towed past the rapids.
2 See **décharge** (def. 1).
1884 *Prince Albert Times* (Sask.) 14 Mar. 4/2: Above the Demicharge, the current was strong to Clear Lake and the boats had to be pulled and pulled as best they might. 1963 PATTERSON *Far Pastures* 52: But what in the world was a demi-charge? Some sort of a rapid, but what?

demi-decharge *n.* [< Cdn F] *Obs.* a partial unloading of a canoe to enable it to pass a shallow or dangerous place. See also **demi-charge** (def. 1), **half cargo, half-lead,** and **half portage.**
1825 (1931) SIMPSON *Fur Trade* 141: Made a demi decharge at Rapid aux Morts where I picked up some curious specimens of Stone to be sent home.

democrat† *n.* See **democrat wagon.**
1885 *Wkly Manitoba Liberal* 6 Nov. 5/6: Headquarters for Buggies, Buckboards, Phætons, Democrats, Sleighs and Cutters New and Second Hand. 1916 PARKER *World for Sale* 198: Some were skimming along in . . . double or triple-seated light wagons— "democrats" they were called. 1964 *Islander* 4 Oct. 5/2: When the democrat, successor to the Red River cart, had to be abandoned, the cayuse accepted a life he had been accustomed to as a pack horse.

democrat wagon† a light, two-horse wagon, having springs and two, sometimes three, seats. See also **democrat.**
1880 GORDON *Mountain and Prairie* 255: The light waggon . . . the two-horse spring waggon similar to the ordinary "democrat" waggon of Ontario, and the double buck-board are the greatest favourites. 1927 *Cdn N.W.Hist.Soc.Pubs* I iii 61: As he and those with him in the "democrat" wagon were going down the steep hill at Edmonton, the horses became unmanageable. . . .

demoiselle [‚dɛmə'zɛl] *n.* [< Cdn F] a curiously-shaped pillar of clay, or cemented gravel, or other material, caused by erosion. See also **hoodoo** (def. 3) and **pingo** (def. 2).
1940 *Cdn Geog.Jnl* Feb. 90/1: In Hoodoo Valley opposite Leanchoil rain-water has cut the cemented boulder clay into fantastic forms called "hoodoos" or "demoiselles" similar to those in Banff and Jasper Parks. 1952 *Ibid.* Apr. 161/2: In places along Medicine Lake highway the thick deposits of glacial drift or boulder clay have been cut into high, fantastic earth

pillars called "hoodoos" or "demoiselles," similar to those near Banff.

Demoiselles

department *n. Fur Trade, Hist.* the largest of the administrative districts of a fur company.
1765-75 (1933) POND *Narrative* 47: After all the Bisness Was Dun . . . thay Began to Draw of[f] for thare Differant Departments and Prepare for the Insewing winter. **1837** (1931) MERK *Fur Trade* 337: The country in which the Hudson's Bay Company now trade is divided into four great districts, known by the names of the Northern, Southern, Columbia and Montreal Departments, in which there are 136 establishments. **1957** *Beaver* Winter 55/1: The Northern Department had been relieved of the greater part of its troublesome brigades—and York Factory of her crown.

departmental store See **department store.**
1897 *Medicine Hat News* (Alta) 1 Apr. 4/2: The big departmental stores . . . are absorbing the trade of both city and country merchants, and concentrating in one spot the business which a few years ago was distributed over a large area and among a great number of people. **1922** *Beaver* April 17/1: The purchase by the Hudson's Bay Company of the Saskatoon departmental store . . . was announced on March 28th.

department store† a large store organized into departments, each one of which sells a particular type of merchandise.
1907 *Eye Opener* (Calgary) 12 Jan. 1/1: Every person wrongfully arrested and searched in one of those confounded department stores should place the matter in a lawyer's hands immediately, within the hour. **1955** *Edmonton Jnl* 4 Jan. 24/2: You can buy them in any hardware or department store but before you spend the money, try what you can do for nothing.

departure *n. Fur Trade, Hist.* **1** the departure of one or more persons from a post. Cp. **arrival** (def. 1).
1967 *Cdn Geog.Jnl* Jan. 19/2: As a brigade included several hundred horses, the post was a scene of great activity during arrivals and departures.
2 a token of friendship, such as a drink of rum or brandy, given to Indian trading parties on their departure from a post. Cp. **arrival** (def. 2).
1929 (1965) INNIS *Fur Trade* 375: At Resolution the [gratuity] system was said to have been abolished in 1922. "Departures" are said to have also disappeared, but there remains the "arrival."

deposit *n.* a sum of money required to be put up by a candidate for election to Parliament or to a Legislature as evidence of his good faith, the money to be forfeited to the Crown should the candidate fail to poll half as many votes as the person elected.
1917 *Grit* (Toronto) 11 Dec. 1/6: In fact, if Lavergne escapes without the loss of his deposit he will do well. **1957** *Commonwealth* 23 Oct. 10/1: There were five candidates, the Liberal candidate losing his deposit.

depot *n.* Also spelled *depôt.* **1** *Fur Trade, Hist.* a trading post which also served as a warehouse for supplies for other posts.
1784-1812 (1964) INNIS *Fur Trade* 233: The greatest use of the Winepeg House is for a depot of Provisions, which are brought to this place by the canoes and boats from the Bison countries of the Red and Saskatchewan Rivers, and distributed to the canoes and boats for the voyages to the several wintering furr trading Houses. **1836** (1851) CAMPBELL *Journal* Spring: In Spring Mr. McPherson went off with the brigade . . . leaving me in charge of the Depot. **1952** (1954) JENNINGS *Strange Brigade* 146: We were told that in the Great Lakes' service, between the Northwest depot at Fort William and Montreal, there was an even larger type in regular use: the canot du maitre. . . .
2 *Obs.* See **cache** (def. 2).
1852 SUTHERLAND *Baffin's Bay* II xli: A depôt of one bag of dog pemmican, a small bag of bread, and one case, 90 lbs., of pemmican, was left, partly for our return, but principally because all the sledges had full allowance without them.
3 *Lumbering, Hist.* See **depot farm.** Cp. **forest depot.**
1883 FRASER *Shanty* 65: He generally makes his habitat about the farm or depot of the [lumbering] concern. **1891** OXLEY *Chore-Boy* 36: This depot was simply a large farm in the midst of a wilderness of trees, and forming a center from which some half dozen shanties, or lumber camps, placed at different distances in the depths of the forest . . . were supplied with all that was necessary for their maintenance. **1961** PRICE & KENNEDY *Renfrew* 93: He began clearing land on what was later referred to as "The Farm," although it was a depot for lumbering rather than agriculture.

depot farm *Lumbering, Hist.* a farm, operated by a lumber company or privately owned, supplying fresh meat and vegetables, oats, etc., to lumber camps and often serving as a repository for supplies. See also **depot** (def. 3), **farm depot, lumber depot,** and **shanty farming.**
1947 SAUNDERS *Algonquin* 37: When there was a depot farm run in connection with the camp, it was sometimes possible to obtain a limited supply of fresh vegetables. **1964** *Cdn Geog.Jnl* Feb. 63/1: Depot farms such as the Egan Estate . . . were supply centres for the larger logging companies.

depot farmer *Hist.* the owner or the man in charge of a depot farm.
1947 SAUNDERS *Algonquin* 37: . . . since it was hard work to clear the land and to farm on these bush clearings, the depot farmer usually limited his crops to potatoes for the camp, and oats for the horses.

depouille [de'pwi] *n.* [< Cdn F < F "skin" or "hide"] *Hist.* See **backfat.**
1793 (1929) MCGILLIVRAY *Journal* 46: I have seen one of this tribe employ a ½ hour in bartering a Dozen Wolves and twice as many *Depouilles.* . . . **1800** (1897) COUES *New Light* I 122: The racoons were very fat, having depouilles two or three inches thick, and are excellent eating. **1892** PIKE *Barren Grounds* 50: By the middle of September this back-fat, or *depouille* as it is called in Northern patois, has reached a length of a foot or more forward from the tail, and, as it is sometimes a couple of inches thick and extends right across the neck, it is a

great prize for the lucky hunter. **1957** FISHER *Pemmican* 91: Indians were fond of the *depouille,* or back fat, which they melted to make pemmican. . . .

deputy *n.* [< Cdn F] *Que.* a member of the Legislative Assembly.
1963 *Time* (Cdn ed.) 8 Mar. 11/3: "The people would glance at the headlines and say proudly, 'That's my deputy'."

deputy reeve in a municipality headed by a reeve, *q.v.,* a member of council who acts as chairman in the reeve's absence.
1852 (1853) STRICKLAND *Canada West* II 271n: Counties,—the several township, village, and town councils in each county, choose their reeves, and deputy reeves where the population admits of it, and these form the county council. **1884** *Brandon Mail* (Man.) 7 Feb. 8/2: They met and on votes for the Wardenship found themselves a tie; and as they were unable from the reading of the statute as applied in their case to decide which municipality was entitled to the deputy reeve, they adjourned without appointing a warden. **1966** *Kingston Whig-Standard* (Ont.) 22 Apr. 6/3: Deputy Reeve Thompson also reported that department officials had pointed out possible discrepancies. . . .

deputy sheriff a court official who acts as assistant to a sheriff, *q.v.*
1921 *Beaver* Mar. 13/2: Mr. Thompson is taking a position as deputy sheriff. **1927** LONGSTRETH *Silent Force* 337: Sergeant Joy, in his final transformation as deputy sheriff, Corporal Jakeman, orderly to the judge, and Constables Fairman and Fielder, escort to the prisoners, are brilliant in scarlet and glitter of button.

deputy town reeve *Obs.* See **deputy reeve.**
1850 *Wkly Globe* 15 Feb. 131/3: The following is a list of the names of the Town Reeves and Deputy Town Reeves, from several Townships composing the County Council.

derby ['dɜˑbi] *n.* [< the *Derby,* a famous British horse race, first run in 1780 under the patronage of the Earl of Derby] **1** a race with dog-sleds, canoes, etc. See also **dog derby.**
1928 FREEMAN *Nearing North* 338: It was the home of the most famous of Canadian dog-team racers, he explained—a French half-breed with several winnings of the great Pas Derby to his credit. **1959** *Weekend Mag.* 18 April 68/3: . . . the Voyageurs planned to stage a canoe and kayak derby. . . . The derby includes down-river races and slaloms, with "gates" to shoot through.

2 a competition of almost any kind.
1929 JOHNSTON *Beyond Rockies* 87: There is as much keenness about the Cariboo Derby [a rodeo] as there is on Epsom Downs on the first Wednesday in June. **1957** *Sask.News* 5 Nov. 4/1: The derby is an annual sportfisherman's classic. . . . **1958** *Ottawa Citizen* 6 Oct. 40/2: More than 100,000 people are expected to visit the "tented city" during the four-day plowing derby. **1962** *B.C.Digest* Oct. 6: We welcome photos of outdoor activities, news about derbies, shoots and similar Rod and Gun Club events. . . . **1963** *Globe and Mail* (Toronto) 1 Feb. 5/1: The Quebec winter carnival . . . includes events ranging from snowshoe derbies, outdoor dancing, parades, and ice-canoe races to formal balls.

derouine *n.* [< Cdn F (*courir*)*en derouine* < F

en derouine on the move, gadding about] *Fur Trade, Obs.* a trading trip for furs; trade carried on at an Indian camp away from the post. See also **en derouine** and **tripping** (def. 1). Cp. **runner**[2].
1801 (1897) COUES *New Light* II 579: Two of my men returned from derouine well loaded with furs.
1820 (1938) SIMPSON *Athabasca Jnl* 178: It is usual for the servants of both Companies to assist each other when short of provisions on their return from Derouinne's and as Bouche has frequently been supplied in this manner I found no fault for rendering assistance on the present occasions. **1955** RICH in BLACK *Journal* xxxix: Simpson was buoyed up by the successful inroads he was making among North West Company Indians, by "Lazette's derouine" which produced five packs of fur, and by the sense of power and empire that plans for invading New Caledonia cannot have failed to confer.

Deserted Acadian *Hist.* one of the colonists abandoned in Acadia by the French after the signing of the Treaty of Utrecht in 1713. See also **Deserted French.**
1755 (1895) RICHARD *Acadia* II 33: The deserted Acadians are delivering up their arms. **1895** *Ibid.* 101: In this letter of November 30th Lawrence explains at considerable length what he understood by the "deserted Acadians."

Deserted French *Hist.* See **Deserted Acadian.**
1755 (1884) SMITH *Acadia* 171: The people . . . were by us commonly called the Deserted French Inhabitants, because they were universally, as well as the other inhabitants, the descendants of those French left in Nova Scotia at the treaty of Utrecht; and had taken the Oath of Allegiance to his Majesty at the time of General Philips' government, with the reserve of not bearing arms! **1755** (1895) RICHARD *Acadia* II 90: It is observed by your letter of the 28th of June, that you had given orders to Colonel Monckton to drive the deserted French inhabitants at all events out of the country. **1884** SMITH *Acadia* 179: The Council were of opinion that the return of these Deserted French families, and their voluntarily taking the oath without any reservation, would have a good effect; they therefore granted them permission to return to their possessions, and allowed the most needy among them provisions for the winter.

destitute rations relief issues of food made available to needy Indians.
1954 *North Star* (Yellowknife) Aug. 2/4: He stated also that, while he didn't wish to be thought a complainer, the Indians receiving "destitute rations" were being denied them if they didn't call for them on the days assigned.

detachment *n.* in the North West Mounted Police and the Royal Canadian Mounted Police, the smallest administrative unit; a police post.
1889 (1935) STRANG *Pioneers in Can.* 310: Leaving a detachment on this spot, the officer was to move westward with the rest of his command. . . . **1929** *Beaver* Dec. 316: A detachment of the Northwest Mounted Police was stationed there [Fort Pitt]. **1945** *Ibid.* Sep. 6/2: Both [Arctic] districts have a number of widely separated detachments, each usually manned by a non-commissioned officer and a constable, who are responsible for the policing of their particular detachment area. **1958** *Edmonton Jnl* 24 June 3 8/3: Canada's sovereignty in the north has been maintained by the Royal Canadian Mounted Police since 1903, when the first police detachment in the eastern Arctic was established at Cape Fullerton, near Chesterfield Inlet.

detroit [də'trɔit] *n.* [< Cdn F < F; cf. *étroit* narrow] *Obs.* **1** narrows; a strait.
1793 (1933) MACDONELL *Diary* 103: . . . we camped at the petit detroit about three P.M. to wait the canoes behind. **1833** (1835) ROSS *Last Voyage* 177: The canoe was immediately carried to its stream, which is narrow in some parts, and connected with a chain of small lakes by detroits and rapids. **1853** CAMPBELL *Two Journals* 27 Jan. 148: Weather warm and thawing—come on well—campd detroit Lac Mac-ca-coise—still very ill.

2 specifically, the strait between Lakes Erie and Huron.
1768-82 (1904) LONG *Voyages* 50: The Detroit is so called from being a strait between Lake Erie, and Lake Huron. . . . **1789** (1905) *Ont.Bur.Arch.Rep.* III 4: . . . Mr. McNiff [is] to lay out a range of Townships . . . commencing . . . at the centre of Long Point in Lake Erie and moving on round the Lake towards the Detroit.

Detroiter *n. Hist.* a person in the employ of the Gregory, McLeod Company, a fur-trading concern having its base at Detroit, absorbed by the North-West Company in 1787.
1954 CAMPBELL *Nor'Westers* 58: As a result, McTavish was able to convince the Detroiters, especially Alexander Mackenzie, that the opposition was dangerous to both interests.

devant *n.* [< Cdn F *devant* (*de canot*)] *Obs.* the bowsman, *q.v.*, in a canoe; one of the two bouts, *q.v.* See also **ducent**.
1767 (1964) INNIS *Fur Trade* 211: Settled—Aimable Rouillard Feauybourg de Ricollet to go as above, devant de Cannote for 320 livres. **1860** (1956) KOHL *Kitchi-Gami* 35: Gendron was gouvernail and one of his boys acted as devant. **1930** *Cdn Hist.Rev.* XI 130: Beads were given to the devants but not to the milieux.

development road one of a system of access roads intended to advance the development of natural resources.
1958 *Edmonton Jnl* 18 Sep. 1/2: It will be a development road, part of the government's "roads to resources" programme. **1958** *Northern Affairs Bull.* Apr.-May 10: From Marian Lake near Fort Rae a road now runs some 30 miles north to serve local mining developments, and this section of the road will become part of the development road system. **1966** *Kingston Whig-Standard* (Ont.) 14 Apr. 7/3: Prince Edward county roads committee is preparing to call for tenders for the North Marysburgh development road.

devil *n.* See **Indian devil**.
[**1907** HUNTER *Cdn Wilds* 152: He [the wolverine] is to all intents a part of the tree limb, and the knowledge that all things "come to him who waits" is strongly fixed in his devil brain.] **1911** ROGERS *Wild Animals* 112: It is one of the tricks that has earned for the animal the name of "devil!"

Devil of the Woods See **wolverine** (def. 1a). See also **Indian devil**.
1900 FRASER *Mooswa* 202: This is terrible. It's that Devil of the Woods, Carcajou, who has robbed me, I suppose—he stole the bacon before.

devil's club a shrub, *Oplopanax horridus,* of western Canada, having large leaves, a prickly stem and conspicuous red berries. See also **bois picant**.
[**1824** (1955) BLACK *Journal* 11: In this point saw a plant or Tree full of joints & prickles all over with a Tuft of large Green leaves at the top, it resembles the water Trefoil or Lilly but grows on drie land but thrives best in wet places.] **1887** ROBERTS *Western Avernus* 10: . . . the prickly devils' clubs [sic] made things unpleasant for us. . . . **1895** *Canadian Mag.* Aug. 365/2: The "Devil's Club" . . . might almost be called the emblem of British Columbia, for there is scarcely a spot where it is not. **1963** *B.C.Digest* Oct. 34/2: From Rainbow Lake a switchback trail climbs steeply upwards through buckbrush and devil's club, 2,600 feet to alpine country and Peters Lake.

devil snatcher See quote.
1955 GOWLAND *Smoke* 167: It was she who . . . informed us that there would be many fish at the north end of the lake for a few days feeding on devil snatchers, which, I guess you'll know, are the larvae of the dragon fly. The few there were elsewhere would take nothing but devil-snatchers.

devil's tobacco *Obs.* See quote.
1784-1812 (1916) THOMPSON *Narrative* 365: The tobacco they [Piegans] raised had a very hot taste in smoking, and required a great proportion of bears berry weed to be mixed with it. The white people gave it the name of the devil's tobacco.

devil's whiskey-jack the great northern shrike, *Lanius borealis.*
1882 *Trans.Roy.Soc.Can.* I 4 53: The great northern shrike . . . called the "Devil's Whiskey-jack," is common on the western side of Hudson's Bay. **1959** MCATEE *Folk-Names* 57: Northern Shrike [is also called] . . . Devil's whiskey-jack (From its preying upon other birds and from its slight resemblance to the grey jay or whiskey-jack. "Hudson Bay"). . . .

devil's wood [trans. of Cdn F *bois de diable*] *Obs.* the vine maple of British Columbia, *Acer circinatum.* See also **bois de diable**. Also called *mountain maple.*
1833 TOLMIE *Physician* 171: "the Govr. pointed out to me a tall slender tree having a profusion of large syngenesious flowers called here Devil's Wood."

dewatter-berry *n.* [origin unknown] *Obs.* See **bakeapple**. Also spelled *dewotter-berry.*
1744 DOBBS *Hudson's Bay* 12: They saw no Grain there, but many Gooseberries, Strawberries, and Dewotter Berries. **1795** (1911) HEARNE *Journey* 450: Bethago-tominick, as it is called by the Indians, or the Dewater-berry . . . flourishes best . . . in swampy boggy ground covered with moss. . . .

dewberry *n.* any one of several species of *Rubus* having a raspberry-like fruit.
1796 (1911) SIMCOE *Diary* 328: I gathered a great many plants [including] dewberries; wild turnip, which cures a cough—it is like aram. **1823** HALIBURTON *General Descr. N.S.* 34: Shrubs . . . Dew-berry [Rubus Saxatilis]. . . . **1960** BLONDAL *Candle* 76: They came home one day for lunch with dewberries they had picked in the cool still woods. . . .

DEW Line [*Distant Early Warning Line*] a 3,000-mile network of radar stations and airstrips for interceptor aircraft, extending from Point Barrow, Alaska, to Baffin Island and intended for defence against attack by air. See also **Distant Early Warning Line.** Also *Dewline.*
1957 *Maclean's* 28 Sep. 4/1: Some thought the

just-finished Dewline and nearly all the rest of our defense apparatus had become obsolete. **1965** *Ibid.* 24 July 2/4: Conditions are even worse now than in the early '50s, when there was heavy air traffic to the DEW Line, Ungava and other regions.

dewotter-berry *n.* See **dewatter-berry.**

dew worm a large earthworm, *Lumbricus* sp.
1889 *Rat Portage* [Kenora] *News* (Ont.) 9 Aug. 4/2: Live minnows, frogs, dew worms and crawfish are more attractive to bass than any amount of phantoms. **1963** *Globe and Mail* (Toronto) 20 Apr. 42/4: A willowleaf spinner and dewworm will work, so might a junebug spinner and worm in deeper water. **1965** *Kingston Whig-Standard* (Ont.) 27 Dec. 1: [Caption] This was the scene Christmas Eve when Fireman James O'Donnell found several dew worms in his garden during warm rain.

diable *n.* [< Cdn F < F "porter's dolly"] *Obs.* a stone boat; drag; go-devil, *q.v.*
1810 (1897) COUES *New Light* II 604: Men began to . . . haul stones, and made a diable to cart with.

diamond hitch† **1** a complicated hitch used in securing a pack on a horse, about forty feet of rope being thrown back and forth over the animal in such a way that it forms a diamond pattern on top.
1872 (1873) GRANT *Ocean to Ocean* 187: . . . and then the triangular shaped load is bound in one by folds of shaganappi twisted firmly but without a knot, after a regular fashion called the "diamond hitch." **1963** SYMONS *Many Trails* x: . . . he learned the diamond hitch on the Chilcotin pack trails.

2 throw a diamond hitch, See note.
☞ *Since the rope used is thrown from one side of the horse to the other, a diamond hitch is said to be "thrown" and not "tied."*
1911 BICKERSTETH *Open Doors* 69: We took a pack pony, and I was shown how to throw the diamond hitch, quite a complicated business if you don't know how. **1957** LARGE *Skeena* 59: My partner . . . thought he knew how to throw a diamond hitch.

diamond willow an abnormal growth of the stem of any species of willow, resulting in a diamond or diaper pattern in the grain, much favored for making walking-sticks.
1953 CUSHMAN *Stay Away Joe* 25: Even Grandpere, standing bowed over his diamond willow walking stick, was laughing. **1957** FISHER *Pemmican* 86: . . . he could smell the first yellow on cottonwood and aspen and . . . the smoky sweetness of . . . diamond willow. **1964** *Dly Colonist* (Victoria) 19 Aug. 17/5: There, they made a living making and selling canoes; making their own furniture of Diamond Willows and their clothes of Moose hide.

dickey ['dɪki] *n.* [by folk etymology < Esk. *attike* a covering] *North* See **atigi** (def. 2 and picture). Also spelled *dickie, dicky.*
1916 HAWKES *Labrador Eskimo* 38n: . . . the word dicky, in common use among the white trappers and settlers of Labrador is a corruption of the Eskimo word atigi. . . . **1933** *Beaver* Mar. 208: The men regularly wear dickey, trousers and boots, the material being either sealskin or duffle. . . . **1952** BANFILL *Labrador Nurse* 71: Sealskin

boots replaced rubber ones, summer clothing was packed away and heavy woolen socks, water-proof dickies and mittens replaced it.

dickey-flap *n.* a protective flap at the neck-opening of a dickey.
1942 TWOMEY & HERRICK *Needle to the North* 314: A pathetic bit of bright red yarn, procurable only at a post, tied back a strand of hair just above her forehead, and all around the dickey-flap of her feather parka was an edging of empty ·22 shells, highly polished and ornamented. **1949** *Nat.Geog.* Oct. 475/2: The *artiggi,* or "dickey" flap, is gaily ornamented with braid, beads, coins, sometimes spoons.

Digby chicken [< *Digby,* N.S.] *Maritimes* a small smoke-cured herring. See also **Digby herring.** Cp. **Digby chips.**
*a*1820 (1838) HEAD *Forest Scenes* 40: A small species of herring afforded the inhabitants a staple commodity. They are extremely delicate, and are salted in great quantities every year. They have gained the nick-name of Digby chickens, and are exported to different parts of the province in barrels. **1894** ASHLEY *Tan Pile Jim* 145: The Dove lay at Liverpool wharf taking in dried cod, tubbed mackerel, pickled herring, smoked alewives, digby chickens—a smoked herring—maple syrup, maple sugar and apples, and potatoes. **1958** *Encyc. Can.* III 267/1: Digby is noted . . . for fish, including cured herrings known as "Digby chickens"; and for the world's largest scallop fleet.

Digby chips [< *Digby,* N.S.] fillets of herring, dried and salted. Cp. **Digby chicken.**
1959 *Sun* (Vancouver) 8 Jan. 3/1: Or would you rather stick to Digby chips. . . . You eat these "as is" and right good they are, but so salty you shouldn't consider munching them without at least a bottle of beer at your side.

Digby herring [< *Digby,* N.S.] *Obs.* See **Digby chicken.**
1832 MCGREGOR *British America* II 111: The fame of the small fat smoked or red Digby herrings . . . has spread over the continent of America. **1839** *Montreal Transcript* 1 Aug. 115/2: For Sale by the Subscribers . . . 50 boxes Fresh Digby Herrings. **1861** BAGSTER *Progress P.E.I.* 96: What made the Digby herring what it is?

digging stick a specially shaped implement, usually of yew wood, used by western Indian women for digging up roots and clams, and in primitive agriculture.
1912 SMITH *Southern B.C.* 12: Perforated pieces of antler, found in the graves, are exactly like the handles of the digging-stick of to-day. **1926** MCKELVIE *Huldowget* 37: . . . every morning she took her clam digging-stick, and her clam basket, and went down on the beach. . . . **1958** ATKINSON *Hist. of Penticton* 14: The roots were harvested by the women of the tribe who used a "digging stick." These implements were regarded as special tools and were highly prized by their owners, usually about two feet long with a curved point and handles made from antler often decorated with incised designs.

dig up the hatchet See **hatchet** (def. 5).

dike *n.* Also spelled *dyke. Maritimes* **1**† an earthwork embankment equipped with aboiteaus, *q.v.,* to protect the land from the high tides of the Bay of Fundy.
1876 CAMPBELL *Yarmouth, N.S.* 5: The river . . . in 1810, was again closed by a good dyke, with substantial

sluices. . . . **1889** WITHROW *Our Own Country* 45: With remarkable industry the Acadians reclaimed from the sea by dikes many thousands of fertile acres . . . and on the sea meadows, at one time, grazed as many as sixty thousand head of cattle.

2 See dike land.
1835 (1838) HALIBURTON *Sam Slick* 5: ". . . The Deacon has a hundred acres of dyke." **1957** WRIGHT *Blomidon Rose* 78: In everyday speech, we make no distinction between the dykes and the dyked lands, but call them both dykes.

dike(d) land(s) *Maritimes* the fertile sea meadows protected by a dike (def. 1). See also **dike** (def. 2), **dike marsh, marsh,** and **marsh lands.** Also spelled *dyke-land, dikeland,* etc.
1851 JOHNSTON *Notes* I 21: Advancing twelve or fifteen miles further to Horton and Wolfville, I found myself on the edge of the richest dyke-land in the province. **1896** ROBERTS *Camp-Fire* 271: ". . . to our right lay far unrolled those rich diked lands which the vanished Acadian farmers of old won back from the sea. . . ." **1936** DENTON & LORD *World Geography* 138: This is an area of fertile dyke lands. . . .

dike(d) marsh *Maritimes* See **dike land.** Also spelled *dyke(d) marsh.*
1823 HALIBURTON *A General Description of Nova Scotia* 32: These birds are most numerous in large dyke marshes. . . . **1830** MOORSOM *Letters N.S.* 189: About Annapolis, we first meet with dyked marsh, which is not however equal in quality to that higher up the bay shores. **1892** (1908) DAWSON & SUTHERLAND *Geography* 70: There are besides some large tracts of marsh lands along the shores of the Bay of Fundy with soil of almost inexhaustible fertility. These are classed as "salt marsh" and "dyked marsh," the first named being subject to occasional overflow by the sea and therefore useful only for . . . fodder and for pasturage.

dilworth ['dɪl,wɚθ] *n.* [< Thomas *Dilworth,* English schoolmaster, d. 1780] *Hist.* a school textbook, "A New Guide to the English Tongue," long used in the Maritimes.
1845 BEAVAN *Life in Backwoods N.B.* 52: Each little black-eyed urchin, on his wooden bench and dog-eared dilworth in hand must be treated by his teacher as a free enlightened citizen.

dime† *n.* [< Am.E] **1** an American ten-cent piece.
1835 *Brit.Amer.Jnl* (St. Catharines, U.C.) 5 Feb. 2/4: Change received according to the present system, 1 dime or a ten cent piece, value 6d, and 8 coppers, valued 4d. Loss 4 coppers on the half dollar.
2 a Canadian ten-cent piece; a silver coin valued at one-tenth part of a dollar.
1864 [see quote at **dime party**]. **1902** CONNOR *Glengarry* 166: "Six pennies and two dimes," was Hughie's disconsolate reply. **1965** *Kingston Whig-Standard* (Ont). 4 Jan. 13/1: Some . . . had to settle for a dime or even a nickel.

dime party *Obs.* a social affair, entry to which required a donation of a dime, usually for charity.
1864 *Elora Observer* (C.W.) 15 Jan. 2/5: One of the great "institutions" of the day, are the Dime Parties now being given in this Village.

dime society *Obs.* a society that held dime parties, *q.v.,* in aid of charity.
1866 *Ottawa Free Press* Aug. 3/1: A NEW TAX BILL. For kissing a pretty girl, one dollar. . . . Seeing a lady home from the dime society, five cents, the proceeds to be devoted to the relief of disabled army chaplains.

direct action man *Hist.* a strong-arm bully employed during elections in colonial days to intimidate supporters of an opposing political party.
1965 *Globe and Mail* (Toronto) 4 Oct. 7/3: Each party had its share of mobsters, known euphemistically as "direct action men," who were not above beating the brains out of more timid citizens on their way to the hustings.

dirt-igloo *n.* an Eskimo house built of rocks and sod, often with a driftwood roof.
1902 LONDON *Daughter of Snows* 220: And an Epicurus, in the dirt-igloo of the Eskimos, will wax eloquent over the whale oil and walrus blubber, or die.

dirty ice *East Coast* See **slob.**
1918 GRENFELL *Labrador Doctor* 75: This ice is of very different qualities. Now it is "slob" mixed with snow born on the Newfoundland coast. This is called "dirty ice" by the sealers.

Dirty Thirties *Hist.* the depression years of the 1930's, so called in reference to the dust storms and drought on the prairies. See also **dust-bowl days.** Cp. **Hungry Thirties.**
1958 *Time* (Cdn ed.) 13 Jan. 9/3: To some of the prairie provinces last month, the weather looked like a recipe for disaster, possibly even a repeat performance of the "Dirty Thirties," when high winds roaring over bare, parched earth sheared off millions of tons of topsoil, forced abandonment of 30% of the land in south Saskatchewan alone. **1963** *Canada Month* Nov. 17/1: And it was during those depression days, the dirty Thirties, that Jodoin met trade unionists. . . . **1966** *Cdn Geog.Jnl* June IV: [Book-Review] This book gives a very sharp portrait of the Province of Saskatchewan in those terrible "dust-bowl" years, the dirty thirties, as they were called.

disallow *v. Hist.* invoke disallowance, *q.v.*
1834 *Brit.Amer.Jnl* (St. Catharines, U.C.) 6 May 3/2: Neither does it deny the right of His Majesty's Government to disallow provincial acts, when they operate to the prejudice of other portions of the empire, or in contravention of treaties. **1958** *Encyc.Can.* III 274/1: Before Canada attained full autonomy, it was possible for the British Government—i.e., the Sovereign in Council—to disallow by Order in Council any act of the Canadian Parliament within two years of its original enactment. . . . In fact, only one Canadian Act was disallowed (in 1873) on the ground that the act was beyond the powers of the Parliament of Canada.

disallowance *n. Hist.* the power, formerly held by the British government to veto provincial or federal legislation, ordinances, appointments, etc., made in Canada.
1763 (1906) *Ont.Bur.Arch.Rep.* IV 4: And you are forthwith to transmit unto our Commissioners for Trade and Plantations, in order to be laid before Us for Our Approbation or Disallowance, the Names of the Members of the Council so to be appointed by you as aforesaid. **1778** *Quebec Gaz.* 5 Nov. 1/1: His Majesty . . . hath been pleased to signify His Royal disallowance of, and declare void and of none effect, a certain Law and Ordinance made and passed in the Castle of St. Lewis, in the said City and Province of Quebec. . . . **1841** *Montreal Transcript* 24 Dec. 2/2: The same Gazette also contains . . . another Proclamation declaring the

disallowance by Her Majesty of the Provincial "Act to establish a College by the name and style of the University of Kingston." **1958** *Encyc.Can.* III 274/1: Although Section 56 of the BNA Act has never been repealed, the exercise of the power of disallowance was declared to be obsolete by the Imperial Conference of 1926.

discharge *n.* [trans. of Cdn F *décharge*] *Hist.* See **décharge.**
1761 (1901) HENRY (Elder) *Travels* 23: In this distance, there are four carrving-places, besides three or four *decharges,* or *discharges,* which are places where the merchandize only is carried, and are therefore distinguishable from *portages,* or carrying-places, where the canoe itself is taken out of the water, and transported on men's shoulders. **1793** (1933) MACDONELL *Diary* 79: Left the *Grand River* at *Mattawin* in which we made eighteen portages and about as many discharges. **1824** (1939) ROBERTSON *Correspondence* 177: The first step . . . is the repairing of portages, discharges and other impediments. **1931** NUTE *Voyageur* 48: Sometimes it was not necessary to portage around an obstruction, but merely to remove some of the lading from the canoe. Such spots were termed *décharges,* which promptly became "discharges" in the English vocabulary of the clerk, proprietor, and passenger.

discharge *v. Hist.* unload part of the cargo of a canoe in order to get over a shallow place or to avoid bad water; make a discharge. See also **decharge** (def. 2).
1784 UMFREVILLE *Hudson's Bay* 24: [We] entered lac about 1 mile long, after which portage Noir, 1430 yards; discharged on right side of rock. . . . **1827** (1912) ERMATINGER *Express Jnl* 71: Encamp above the little Dalles (discharged part of our baggage) at 6 p.m.

discovering party *Obs.* a group of scouts; a reconnaissance party. See also **discovery** (def. 1).
1800 (1897) COUES *New Light* I 75: At five o'clock the discovering party returned. . . .

discovery *n.* **1** *Fur Trade, Hist.* a scouting or exploring trip.
1775 (1954) *Moose Ft Jnls* 350: . . . the Indians whose Country lies between the Canadians & us, are averse to our making any discovery or Settlement where the Pedlars are. . . . **1800** (1897) COUES *New Light* I 74: Two of them set off with one of my men on horseback, on discoveries. **1810** *Ibid.* II 594: Beaver Hill Crees were on discoveries.

2 *Placer Mining* See **discovery claim.**
1898 *Yukon Midnight Sun* (Dawson) 29 Oct. 4/5: The last news from Quartz and Sulphur is that both creeks are panning out up to expectations, and especially is this so above the discoveries.

discovery claim† *Placer Mining* the first or original claim staked on a creek, all other claims being recorded as above discovery or below discovery, *qq.v.*
1898 *Yukon Midnight Sun* (Dawson) 20 June 8/1: George Harvey, who has been working on discovery claim Bonanza, is making preparations to pole up the river en route for Douglas City. **1958** LINDSAY *Cariboo Story* 16/2: But the men from Keithley and the men from Antler all of whom were apparently real gold hounds were also good sports about the matter and staked whatever they wanted as a discovery claim.

Discovery Day *Yukon* See quotes.
1956 (1960) NELSON *Northern Lights* 329: On Discovery Day (August 17), which commemorates the finding of gold on Bonanza Creek, the Pioneers don their purple and gold sashes and parade through the town. **1958** *Edmonton Jnl* 24 June Sec. 3 2/2: Discovery Day celebrations will be held at Dawson City. . . . **1964** *North* July 7/1: This simple event triggered the great Gold Rush, and gave the name "Discovery Day" to August 17th, 1896, the day they found the rich yellow metal in the valley of the Klondike.

discovery post the first of four squared posts marking the limits of a mineral claim, which shows the name of the claimant and the date of discovery.
1910 FRASER *Red Meekins* 194: When we've grubbed, we'll plant this discovery post, an' first thing in the mornin' we'll hike to the outside and file the claim. **1956** KEMP *Northern Trader* 63: We hewed our discovery posts, ran our boundaries, named our claims.

discovery well the first successful well drilled in a new oil field.
1923 WALDO *Down Mackenzie* 193: Seven miles above the original "discovery" well is a derrick, and the only horse in the region—a pet like a dog—was grazing along the beach in front of it. **1958** *Dawson Creek Star* (B.C.) 3 Jan. 1/3: The finding of similar light oil in two discovery wells in a new geological formation—and some 25 miles apart—electrified Canadian oil industry circles this past summer.

disking *n.* a game patterned on curling and played on a marked polished floor with wooden disks, 8 inches in diameter and an inch thick.
1954 *Fishermen's Advocate* (Port Union, Nfld) 2 Apr. 11/3: Disking, first cousin to curling, was originated in Fort William in 1921 by Canon H. A. Sims, once a rector at Kirkland Lake. It is played like curling on a marked floor, with disks initialed by their owners.

disloyalist *n. Obs.* a resident of Canada who left for the United States during the War of 1812.
1897 DURAND *Reminiscences* 22: My father had got the privilege of occupying a large forfeited farm three miles from Dundas, once owned by a person named Mills . . . who at the commencement of the war of 1812 left the country as a disloyalist, and joined the Americans, forfeiting his farm.

Distant Early Warning Line See **DEW line.**
1955 (1964) JENNESS *Eskimo Admin.* II 115: The employment opportunities for local labor, created by the construction of the Distant Early Warning line . . . have provided some much needed additional income. . . . **1965** SYMINGTON *Tuktu* 60: The construction of the Distant Early Warning (DEW) Line and the Mid-Canada Line in the mid-1950's, with their great freight movements throughout the North, gave impetus to the activity of the governments, both federal and provincial.

district *n.* **1** a large unorganized or partly organized frontier area established primarily for judicial purposes. See also **provisional district** and **provisional territory.**
☛ *The term has been used in Canada from the start of British rule and has undergone varied modifications of specific meaning and application, the common denominator being its creation for judicial purposes. There are now both federal and provincial districts.*
1789 (1905) *Ont.Bur.Arch.Rep.* III 31: The Scite of the county town agreed upon, you will direct the Surveyor for the district to lay out the township . . . as soon as

may be. **1963** *Maclean's* 23 Feb. 42/2: Mikkie was a fine hunter of the caribou at Henik Lake in the District of Keewatin.

2 See school district.
1811 *Kingston Star* (U.C.) 12 Feb. 2/3: As encouragement for the acquisition of teachers of distinguished respectability, the sum of 100 pounds is annually appropriated to each district, as a salary in part compensation for the services of its public instructor. **1860** *Islander* (Charlottetown) 30 Mar. 1/2: Where 40 Children reside in the District, average daily attendance should be kept at the present standard, viz. 20: and where upwards of 40, then half the number in all cases to be the standard average attendance. **1958** ATKINSON *Hist.of Penticton* 68: "With this new classification put into effect the district was required to pay half of all teachers' salaries."

3 in B.C., a rural municipality; one of the administrative sub-divisions into which rural British Columbia is divided, corresponding to a township or parish in other provinces.
☛ *In B.C. a county is a sub-division of the province for judicial purposes only and rarely coincides with a district in boundaries.*
1856 *Royal Proclamation* 16 June: "You [Sir James Douglas] are therefore for the purpose of electing the Members of such Assemblies hereby authorized to issue a proclamation declaring the number of representatives to be chosen by such freeholders to serve in the said General Assembly, and if you should see fit, dividing our said Island and its Dependencies, into Districts or Counties, Towns or Townships, and declaring the number of representatives. . . . We have divided the said Island and its dependencies into Districts as follows. . . ." **1948** ANGLIN *Canada Unlimited* 66: In the first place, each province is divided into large rural municipalities. These are known as districts in British Columbia; municipal districts in Alberta; rural municipalities in Saskatchewan and Manitoba.

4 See quote.
1958 *Encyc.Can.* III 279/2: Today the term "district" (or "territory") is reserved in Quebec for the partially organized areas of Abitibi, Mistassini and New Quebec (Ungava).

district council *Hist.* in United Canada, the elected administrative body of a district, as established by the Municipal Act of 1841.
1841 *Bytown* [Ottawa] *Gaz.* 11 Nov. 1/2: And be it enacted, that there shall be a district council in each such district as aforesaid, which district council shall consist of a warden and councillors, to be appointed and elected as herein-provided. **1916** *London & Middlesex Hist.Soc.Trans.* VII 23: In the discharge of his duty, he called the attention of the District council to the facts and figures. . . .

district court† a court dealing with minor criminal and civil cases within a specific area. See also **county court.**
1800 *U.C.Gaz.* (York [Toronto]) 12 Apr. 4/2: "An act to extend the jurisdiction and regulate the proceedings of the District Court and the Court of Requests." **1953** MOON *Saskatchewan* 8: At one time, seven Moosomin lawyers were judges of the Queen's Bench, appeal and district courts, which is a good record for a town of 1,200 population.

district master *Fur Trade, Hist.* See 1937 quote.
1821 (1938) SIMPSON *Athabasca Jnl* 251: The proposition I made . . . was 120 p. annum for 3 Years with all the privileges of a District Master. **1937** *Beaver* Sep. 37/2:

In 1814-19 "district masters" first appear on record, this being the rank next to Chief Factor; evidently corresponding approximately to the more important of the old "masters," though apparently with widened powers and higher pay, since a few of them received the same salary as a Chief Factor.

district school† *Hist.* a publicly supported elementary school. See also **division school** and **public school.**
1808 *York* [Toronto] *Gaz.* 6 Aug. 4/1: On Wednesday . . . the examination of the scholars in the District Grammar school, was held. . . . **1825** *Novascotian* (Halifax) 30 Mar. 109/3: The Trustees for such District Schools [shall] be appointed and chosen by the people. **1905** SCHERCK *Pen Pictures* 76: The public schools were at one time called "common" and "district" schools. **1955** *Western Star* (Corner Brook, Nfld) 10 Mar. 6/1: Tonight at 8 o'clock the United Church Service Men's Club will entertain patients at the West Coast Sanatorium with their delightful play, The District School at Blueberry Corners.

district town *Hist.* the town in which the seat of municipal government is located. See also **county town.**
1827 *Gore Gaz.* (Ancaster, U.C.) 11 Aug. 94/2: It deserves to be noticed that not less than thirteen tavern licenses were granted at Perth (the district town), for this place and its neighborhood, at the last meeting of the Quarter Sessions. **1841** *Montreal Transcript* 27 Nov. 2/2: We have received the first number of the "Ottawa Advocate," a paper published at Aylmer, the intended District Town of the New District of Sydenham.

district warden *Hist.* the presiding officer of a district council, *q.v.,* equivalent to the modern county warden, *q.v.*
1841 *Western Herald* (Sandwich [Windsor], C.W.) 24 Dec. 3/3: "Who is to be the Disttict Warden?" is a question frequently asked but which as yet remains unanswered.

ditch duster a machine for blowing dust into frozen ditches to free them from ice and snow.
1964 *Sask.News* Mar. 1/1: Ditch duster is mounted on a toboggan and pulled by a gasoline-powered sled. . . .

divide† *n.* a watershed.
1853 REID *Young Voyageurs* 239: Making their first portage over a "divide," they reached another small stream that ran in quite a different direction. . . . **1957** *Aklavik Jnl* Feb. 6/2: They followed the headwaters of Cash creek right over the divide into Yukon Territory and finally got caribou on Slim Mountain.

dividend *n.* in Alberta, a payment made to citizens of ten years' residence, paid by the Social Credit government from gas and oil royalties.
1957 *Commonwealth* 20 Mar. 11/1: Albertan's may be able to have a double laugh at Social Credit "dividends" recently announced. **1958** *Edmonton Sun* 5 June 5/5: In 1957 the Alberta Social Credit government paid out about $540,000 in dividends.

divisional point a place where a railway has its

headquarters for a given administrative district, usually at the boundary of two such districts or divisions. See also **division station**.

1927 *Beaver* Dec. 121: Setting Lake is now an important divisional point on the Hudson Bay railway.... **1958** *Edmonton Jnl* 24 June Sec. 4 12/1: As a sizeable railway divisional point a sizeable payroll is available and spent in the town's modern stores and other businesses.

division court a lesser court concerned with minor civil actions only.

1916 *London and Middlesex Hist.Soc.Trans.* VII 21: Then the Division Courts as they exist were substituted for "Courts of Request." **1958** *Encyc.Can.* III 135/2: The division courts (10) try civil cases only and the presiding judge hands down the decision.

division point See **divisional point**.

1936 MACKENZIE *Living Rough* 230: The best thing we can do ... is ride into Hanna, the division point....

division school *Hist.* See **district school**.

1854 *Guelph Advertiser* 16 Nov. 5/3: Teacher Wanted Immediately, To take charge of Division School No. One in the Township of Eramosa.

division station See **divisional point**.

1947 TAYLOR *Canada* 147: Every hundred miles or so there is a 'Division' station, where a little town of a hundred or so inhabitants has grown up around the railway yards.

doater *n.* See **doter**.

do down preserve, as fruit and vegetables.

1932 JAMIESON *Cattle in the Stall* 112: Last Summer when the mulberries were at their best, Aunt Caroline came over to help me do some down, as she expressed it.

dog *n.* **1** See **prairie dog** (def. 2).

1853 REID *Young Voyageurs* 214: The "dogs" live in large settlements, many hundreds of them in one place.

2 See **dog salmon**.

1916 WOOD *Tourist's N.W.* 377: The spring, the cohoe, dog and hump-back varieties are inferior to the sockeye in quality and numbers.

3† *Lumbering* See **log dog**.

1918 MACKAY *Trench and Trail* 112:

Dare is notting lak a jog
Do'n dat mo'nta'n on a log
Clinging to an iron dog,
Hully gee!

1956 ANDREWS *Glory Days* 14: These were ... doggers who drove in dogs and linked the logs together [so that they could be hauled in a string]....

dogan ['dogən] *n.* [? < *Dogan*, an Irish surname] *Slang* an Irish Roman Catholic.

☛ *In older use, often a derogatory term for a low-class Irish Roman Catholic; in present use, any Roman Catholic, and, frequently, any Catholic. The connotation of the term is only mildly offensive in itself, if at all.*
1854 *Hamilton Gaz.* (C.W.) 15 May 2/7: I would be overly liberal if I estimated their number as a couple of Dogans! [Irish Catholics]. **1875** *Canadian Mthly* Dec. 533/2: The "Dogans" were taken into favour, and the priests and nuns ceased to be vile and unprincipled. **1924** (1933) SLATER *Yellow Briar* 28: He was a harsh

taskmaster over me, and many a time I got a smart clout on the lug and was told to take that for a dirty little dogan. **1965** *Kingston Whig-Standard* (Ont.) 1 May 13/8:... he [was] a drunken Orangeman at peace with his "dogan friends"....

dog bear a male bear.

1910 FRASER *Red Meekins* 128: "A man that wouldn't find dog-bear meat rank enough, but wanted walrus, must have a pickled palate." **1942** *Beaver* March 7/1: During the winter months, few bears are encountered, but occasionally an old dog bear, unable to hunt sufficient food in open water through impaired faculties, and consequently debarred from hibernating by the pangs of hunger, will be encountered.

dog-bell *n.* one of the bells on a sled-dog's harness.

*c*1902 LAUT *Story of Trapper* 263: If the fine powdery snow-drifts are glossed with the ice of unbroken sun-glare, the runners strap iron crampets to their snow-shoes, and with a great jingling of dog-bells, barking of the huskies, and yelling of the drivers, coast away for the leagueless levels of the desolate North. **1962** (1964) INNIS *Fur Trade in Canada* 373: The Eskimo along the Mackenzie delta began to demand ... rat-tail files, horse bells, dog bells—following the visit of American whalers ... after 1890.

dog-boot *n.* See **dog shoe**.

[**1852** SUTHERLAND *Baffin's Bay* II 4: The sailmakers had to make ... two pairs of canvas "boots" for each dog, to protect their feet from the rough ice, after being several days out.] **1871** (1883) BUTLER *Great Lone Land* 348: The dog-boot is simply a fingerless glove drawn on over the toes and foot, and tied by a running string of leather round the wrist or ancle of the animal; the boot itself is either made of leather or strong white cloth. Thus protected, the dog will travel for days.... **1942** TWOMEY & HERRICK *Needle to the North* 218: The little pups never did any asking, and when at last it was absolutely necessary, Bob simply caught them and forcibly held them when he tied on the leather dog-boots.

dog brigade a brigade of dog teams. See also **dog-train** (def. 4).

1921 HEMING *Drama of Forests* 181: All were to sleep in the open, for dog brigades never carry tents but bivouac on the snow with nothing but a blanket between the sleeper and the Aurora Borealis—though the thermometer may fall to sixty below zero.

dog cariole or **carriole** See **cariole** (def. 2a and picture).

1861 *Cdn Naturalist* Dec. 437: Of parchment, as such, the Chipewyans make, little use; but the residents avail themselves of it, in place of glass for windows, for constructing the sides of dog-carioles, and for making glue. **1914** TUPPER *Recollections* 109: A dog-cariole is a large canvas shoe on a toboggan in which a man can lie down, and the driver stands on the open part behind him. **1962** DICKIE *Great Golden Plain* 113: For winter travel, the dog cariole was used. The cariole was rather like a wooden shoe with the toe turned up to form a dashboard.

dog corral an enclosure in which sled dogs are penned when not working. See also **dog-yard**.

1956 KEMP *Northern Trader* 16: Facing the sward and the river, buildings range themselves in a hollow square —a sprawling, low-raftered store, a residence converted to offices; fur rooms, a warehouse a hundred feet long, a high-picketed dog corral, and a huge barn. **1963** PATTERSON *Far Pastures* 95: Gordon and McIntyre were out there in the dog corrals, dishing out the feed....

dog derby **1** a race in which the contestants are dog teams and drivers. See also **derby, dog race, dogsled race, dogsleigh race,** and **dog-team race.**
1926 *Beaver* Mar. 87/2: At The Pas (Manitoba) dog derby of 1923 a train of dogs ran the course of 200 miles in 24 hours, 51 minutes. **1958** *Cdn Geog.Jnl* Jan. IV/1: The main event is the dog derby, which is run over a course about 140 miles long. This race was first held in March of 1915. **1966** *Kingston Whig-Standard* (Ont.) 28 Feb. 10/1: In all respects, this dog derby represented a resounding triumph for the tiny isolated village of Old Crow.

2 a winter carnival or exhibition featuring dog-team races and other contests.
1958 *Edmonton Jnl* 24 June 4 17/3: Yellowknife Dog Derby. Held under the sponsorship of the Yellowknife Fish and Game Association, the derby's main event is a 30-mile dog-team race on the ice of Yellowknife Bay. . . .

dog-driver *n.* a person who drives a dog team. See also **dog-musher, dog-puncher, dog-runner, dog-skinner, dog teamster driver** (def. 2), and **musher** (def. 2).
1857 MCDOUGALL *Voyage* 370: This time, however, Thompson (who had proved the excellence of his qualities as dog-driver under Captain Penny . . .) had installed himself as master of the hounds, and on taking office, substituted for the old harness some of his own, lighter, more simple, and better adapted for the service in every respect. **1965** *Beaver* Autumn 56/1: The dog drivers . . . had been instructed to locate the caches ten miles apart.

dog-eating *n.* See **dog feast.**
1966 *Native Voice* April 2/2: They [missionaries] did away with many heathen customs such as "dog eating." A medicine man would fast in the woods and eventually come out with a live dog in his hands. The one who could eat the most live dog was declared the bravest.

dog feast *Hist.* among certain Indian tribes, a ceremonial feast in which dogs were eaten to propitiate evil spirits. See also **dog-eating.**
[**1755** (1907) HENDAY *Journal* 349: Each tent killed two Dogs & had a Grand Feast.] **1857** (1860) HIND *Red River* I 202: The heathen Indians [at Fort Garry] held their dog feasts and medicine dances on the open plain. In one instance five dogs were slaughtered cooked and devoured. . . . **1940** *Beaver* Sep. 9/2: The year 1873, which saw the last Indian dog feast at Point Douglas, saw also the . . . cluster of buildings . . . incorporated as Winnipeg. **1963** MACLEOD & MORTON *Cuthbert Grant* 90: It was known as the *coteau des festins,* because the local Indians from time immemorial had held dog feasts on the site.

dogger *n. Lumbering* a worker responsible for fixing and adjusting log dogs, *q.v.*
1956 ANDREWS *Glory Days* 14: These were . . . doggers who drove in dogs and linked the logs together. . . .

doggery *n. Slang* **1†** *Obs.* a low-class drinking place; a cheap saloon.
1852 *Voice of the Fugitive* (Sandwich [Windsor], C.W.) 29 Jan. 2/2: This we believe to be the outline of a law that will shut up many a "doggery" doubtless.

2 *Lumbering* an open bunk house.
1910 FERGUSON *Janey Canuck* 86: He gave me his bunk last night and betook himself to the sleeping camp, which bears also the opprobrious name of "the doggery."

doggie *n.* See **dogie.**

dog harness the gear by which sled dogs are harnessed to sleds.
1852 SUTHERLAND *Baffin's Bay* II 4: The sailmakers had to make . . . sledge-covers eight, of which two were for dog sledges . . . forty sets of dog harness. . . . **1965** SYMINGTON *Tuktu* 53: The Indians made babiche. . . for . . . snares and dog harness.

dog-hood *n.* an adult male hood seal, *q.v.*
1883 HATTON & HARVEY *Newfoundland* 313: Instances have occurred where a fight between an old dog-hood and five or six men, has lasted for an hour, and sometimes a hunter is fearfully torn and even killed in the encounter. **1906** LUMSDEN *Skipper Parson* 108: The male, called by sealers "the dog-hood," chivalrously attends and defends his female.

dogie† ['dogi] *n.* [< *dough-guts,* with reference to a bloated belly resulting from poor feeding] *West*
1 a range-herd calf that has lost its mother. Also *dogy.*
1897 *Medicine Hat News* (Alta) 14 Jan. 4/2: There were a few losses among dogies, but these represent an infinitesimal fraction of one per cent. of the entire number of cattle in the district. **1963** *Calgary Herald* 16 Oct. 29/8: Under normal weather conditions the cowboys find the dogies sunning themselves in the clearings at fall round-up time and have little difficulty finding them.

2 of cattle, a young animal acquired to build up a new herd; a stocker.
1897 *Medicine Hat News* (Alta) 1 Apr. 4/1: Owners of dogie cattle—stockers—who have brought their bands through the winter of 1896-7 with any degree of success need not fear that their business will not prove a successful one. **1952** MCNEIL *Between the Red* 131: About 1890 some of the ranchers decided upon a policy of importing young cattle of the stocker order, called "dogies" or "barnyard cattle."

dog-leg fence a type of rail fence.
1953 *Cdn Geog.Jnl* Dec. 226/1: One of the strangest and least familiar of the rail fences is the dog-leg which has been recorded from Nova Scotia, New Brunswick, and Australia . . . its essential feature is a series of crossed posts, set in post holes, with rails laid in the crotches.

dog-line *n.* **1** *Obs.* one of the leather or webbing traces by which dogs are hitched to a sled.
1854 (1892) KANE *Arctic Explor.* 149: It was only after appropriating an undue share of his seal-skin breeches that the leader of the party succeeded in patching up his mutilated dog-lines.

2 a strong rope or line to which sled dogs are tethered when not working.
1941 *Beaver* March 12/1: The dog line is placed in a sack and loaded last. **1951** BULIARD *Inuk* 255: He always tried, after the first gallop, when the sled was moving well, to sweep around in a great curve and return to the dog line where he could take his ease.

dog moccasin See **dog shoe.** See also **moccasin** (def. 2).
[**1867** LORD *At Home in the Wilderness* 235: I always put on the dog's moccasins (merely bags made of leather or stout hide) if I anticipate rough travelling.] **1912** LONDON

Smoke Bellew 326: Smoke spent the morning in camp, sewing dog-moccasins and repairing harness.
1954 PATTERSON *Dangerous River* 278: And if we lost dog moccasins that was the least of our worries—the trail was littered with them, scattered by those ahead of us.

dog-musher *n.* See **dog driver**. Cp. **mush,** *v.*
1906 LONDON *White Fang* 215: Dog-mushers' cries were heard ... up the trail.... **1966** *Kingston Whig-Standard* (Ont). 28 Feb. 10/1: The new champion dog-musher of the Yukon is a stubble-jumper from Brandon, Manitoba.

dog-pack *n.* a bag, usually one of a pair, carried by a pack dog, *q.v.*
1924 MASON *Arctic Forests* 37: The best dog packs are made of caribou skin, the outsides being the shanks sewn together. The Eskimaux ... make them of sealskin. **1954** PATTERSON *Dangerous River* 291: Gordon was busy down at the cabin doing some baking and mending one of the dog-packs that had got torn.

dog packet *Obs.* a small dog-train (def. 4) broken off from a brigade for a side trip to small posts.
1873 (1904) BUTLER *Wild North Land* 78: During the succeeding months it [the brigade] hold steadily along its northern way, sending off at long, long intervals branch dog packets to right and left.

dog-path *n.* a trail used by sled dogs. See also **dog-road** and **dog-trail**.
1939 *Beaver* Sep. 22: The dog-paths through the woods were bright with colored leaves and berries.

dog pemmican inferior pemmican, *q.v.*, prepared for use as dog-feed.
1852 SUTHERLAND *Baffin's Bay* II 136: At 2 A.M. we came to the depot at Point Separation, where the dogs did get a feed of the small quantity of "dog pemmican" that had been left there for our return. **1915** (1922) JENNESS *Copper Eskimos* 125: Kanneyuk and her cousin Kesullik freighted some blubber and my dog-pemmican towards the shore in preparation for a migration the following day. **1956** WENTWORTH *Dried Meat* 7: After a few weeks' experience ... the men exchanged their ration for the "dog pemmican," and the dogs got the "cake" variety.

dog-puncher *n.* *Slang* See **dog-driver**.
1899 PALMER *Klondyke* 3: "I hear you're looking for a dog-puncher," he said, awkwardly. **1928** WALDEN *Dog-Puncher* 32: ... I made up my mind I would become a freighter, or what was called locally a "dog-puncher." **1964** BERTON *Golden Trail* 37: ... Arthur Treadwell, a young dog-puncher, arrived from Dawson with a load of mail.

dog race See **dog derby** (def. 1).
1953 MOON *Saskatchewan* 202: During the 1930's snowmobile races were held and dog races of forty-mile courses have been held. **1966** *Kingston Whig-Standard* (Ont.) 25 Feb. 12/1: ... the piece de resistance of this folk-carnival is the dog race—this is the Epsom Derby of the canine world.

dog-road *n.* See **dog-path**.
1956 KEMP *Northern Trader* 50: Instead of becoming a trader, living on the dog-roads and sleeping out under the stars, I was a mere store man.

dog-runner *n.* See **dog-driver**.

1911 SETON *Arctic Prairies* 290: They were young men and dog-runners; I was left behind and was getting so tired now I could not keep warm. **1939** GODSELL *Vanishing Frontier* 83: In earlier days they had handled the situation by contracting a so-called country marriage ... marrying their half-breed daughters to dog-runners or hunters.

dog salmon† a large salmon of the Pacific coast, *Oncorhynchus keta*. See also **calico salmon, chum[1], chum salmon, dog** (def. 2), and **keta.**
1884 CHITTENDEN *Queen Charlotte Is.* 39: Large schools of dog salmon were rushing in and out at the time of our arrival. **1900** LONDON *Son of Wolf* 31: ... we are proud to have thee our *potlach*-guest; but the king-salmon does not mate with the dog-salmon.... **1962** *Co-op Grocery News Bull.* 1 Aug. 1: Formerly known as dog salmon, the chum ... has also been called the qualla, keta and calico salmon.

dog shoe a simple leather or canvas bag tied on the feet of sled dogs to protect their paws. See also **dog-boot** and **dog moccasin.**
1880 (1893) YOUNG *Indian Wigwams* 153: We let them huddle on our blankets and robes before the fire, and we put on their dog-shoes to save their feet from freezing. **1952** BANFILL *Labrador Nurse* 99: ... I did not think that one day part of my nursing duties would be making dog shoes!

dog-skinner *n.* [< *(mule-)skinner*] See **dog-driver**.
1921 *Beaver* Aug.-Sep. 46/1: There was to be a railway! No more dog-skinners! No more voyageurs! **1941** *Ibid.* Sep. 37/1: Dog Skinner. A superman in dog driving and dog lore in Manitoba.

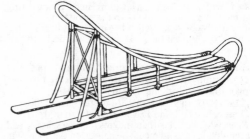

One kind of dog-sled

dog-sled *n.* a sled drawn by a team of dogs. See also **dog-sledge, dog-sleigh, sled** (def. 1), **sledge,** and **sleigh,** *n.* (def. 2).
1697 (1929) KELSEY *Papers* 62: Took 2 hands along with mee to try to draw home plank but could not so came with one upon the dogs slead to the Rivers side. **1844** (1955) LEFROY *Magnetic North* 97: I was extremely restricted as to baggage for the journey ... from the small size of the dog sled, and the space required for provisions. **1923** WALDO *Down Mackenzie* 214: Caribou skins dangled below the dog-sleds in the rafters, almost tickling the noses of the dancers. **1965** *Globe and Mail* (Toronto) 6 Jan. 1/2: Make and use a bow and arrow, run a trapline, learn to drive a dog sled, and take part in a seal hunt.

dog-sledge *n.* See **dog-sled** and picture.
1794 (1929) McGILLIVRAY *Journal* 49: They carry on Dog Sledges, 5 Kegs High Wines.... **1856** BALLANTYNE *Young Fur Traders* 30: ... the rafters sustained a miscellaneous mass of materials, the more conspicuous among which were snow-shoes, dog-sledges, axe-handles and nets. **1952** PUTNAM *Cdn Regions* 505/1: Air transport is the

only means, except for dog sledge, of reaching the Arctic in winter.

dogsled race See **dog derby** (def. 1).
1961 *Time* (Cdn ed.) 22 Dec. 6/2: On the ice there will be dogsled races and in the HBC storage shed the Eskimo drum dances. **1964** *Kingston Whig-Standard* (Ont.) 23 Dec. 16/3: Then came the traditional dogsled races. . . .

dog-sleigh *n*. See **dog-sled** and picture.
1859 MCDONALD *Autobiog.Notes* 25: I order Mr. King to get ready and set off next morning with a couple of men and as many dog sleighs. **1957** *Explorer* 16 June 190/2: Your minister may have more than one church in his charge, but we doubt if he travels between them by dog-sleigh.

dogsleigh race See **dog derby** (def. 1).
1965 *Star Wkly* 2 Jan. 21/2: There are ice-carving contests, dogsleigh races . . . every night.

dog-team *n*. a number of sled dogs (2 to 20) hitched to a sled or toboggan. See also **dog-train** (def. 3) and **train²** (def. 1b). Cp. **sled-team.**
1897 TYRRELL *Sub-Arctics* 247: Two of the dog-teams procured at Oxford had been intended to haul my brother and myself. . . . **1966** *Kingston Whig-Standard* (Ont.) 25 Feb. 12/1: Miller quoted his latest prices on the field of eight dog-teams. . . .

dog-team race See **dog derby** (def. 1).
1964 *Weekend Mag.* 19 Dec. 20/3: By far the most popular event during Christmas was the dog-team races. Thirty teams—five dogs in each—took part in the men's race, a distance of 16 miles.

dog teamster See **dog-driver.**
1954 TYRE *Saddlebag Surgeon* 60: At winter's end he had added to his experience, first as a dog teamster on fish hauls between Lake Manitoba and Raeburn. . . . **1966** *Kingston Whig-Standard* (Ont.) 25 Feb. 12/1: Wilfred Sharlie, the demoniac dog-teamster from the Carmacks band of Yukon Indians, has been installed as a torrid 8-to-5 favorite to win the fourth annual running of the Sourdough Stakes.

dog-team taxi(cab) a dog-sled employed as a taxi.
1953 MOON *Saskatchewan* 234: In 1935 Goldfields had electric lights . . . dog-team taxicabs, and a schoolma'am. **1958** *Cdn Geog.Jnl* Jan. 4/1: A visitor may find himself taking a dog-team taxi, wearing a foxtail hat, dining on beaver-tail soup and caribou tongues. . . .

dog-toboggan *n*. See **cariole** (def. 2a and picture).
1954 PATTERSON *Dangerous River* 222: He loaded the dog toboggan on the raft and poked and lugged the clumsy thing upstream to gain height for his crossing. **1956** KEMP *Northern Trader* 75: We loaded the living woman and child onto the flat-sleigh, the man into the dog toboggan. **1961** MACLENNAN *Seven Rivers* 48: There was a pile of dog-toboggans in the apron of the front barge.

dog-trail *n*. See **dog-path.**
1908 MAIR *Mackenzie Basin* 140: What could be supplied, however, is a waggon-road from Wahpooskow to Athabasca Landing, instead of the present dog-trail. . . . **1956** KEMP *Northern Trader* 116: Drop a whip on the dog-trail or forget your coat on a portage, and it will be there, probably hanging in a tree, the next time you come along.

dog-train *n*. **1** a dog-sled and the dog-team together. See also **dog traineau** and **train²** (def. 1c).

1793 (1889) MACDONELL *Journal* 285: Five men, five loaded horses and five dog trains started with goods for Mr. Grant's. . . . **1875** *Cdn Mthly* July 7/2: Instances are known of men and dog-trains having been completely buried by such storms for several days, and who yet came out alive. **1960** NIX *Mission* 44: John acquired a fine train of sleigh dogs, and a dozen dog trains swung off down the ice of the Saskatchewan River. . . .

2 *Obs.* See **dog-sled.**
1854 *Trans.Lit.& Hist.Soc.Que.* IV 332: Their travelling in summer is performed by water, in winter by dog-trains called "commetteks."

3 See **dog-team.**
1836 *Bytown* [Ottawa] *Gaz.* 27 Oct. 2/3: We saw one youngster carioling behind a horse and another driving a dog-train. **1913** WILLIAMS *Wilderness Trail* 32: Voudrin, with the dog-train and sledge, was already ashore on the beach. . . . **1938** ELLS *Northern Trails* 57: The interpreter and dog driver had carried the body of the murdered man back to the carryall and, with the dog train, had disappeared around a bend in the river.

4 a number of dog-teams and sleds forming a brigade that moves in single file. See also **dog brigade** and **train³** (def. 1a).
1872 (1883) BUTLER *Great Lone Land* 340: During five days our course lay through vast expanses of stiff frozen reeds, whose corn-like stalks rattled harshly against the parchment sides of the cariole as the dog-trains wound along through their snow-covered roots. **1913** WILLIAMS *Wilderness Trail* 203: Arrangements had been made, however, to send a great dog-train of ten sledges north, loaded with supplies, that the hunters might replenish their failing stores. **1963** SYMONS *Many Trails* 188: . . . after freeze-up the canoe routes are followed by dog trains.

dog traineau *Obs.* See **dog train** (def. 1). See also **traineau.**
1888 (1890) ST. MAUR *Impressions* 27: One foolhardy passenger with several guides attempted, with the aid of a dog traineau, to reach the land. . . . **1905** DRUMMOND *Voyageur* 2: An' off on de home of de great white bear, I'm seein' hees dog traineau.

dog travail *Obs.* See **travois** (def. 1 and picture). See also **dog travois.**
1867 GALTON *Art of Travel* 83: In a dog travail the cross of the poles rests on the back of the neck, and is kept in place by a . . . neck strap; the poles are wrapped with pieces of buffalo robe where they press against the dog.

dog travois See **travois** (def. 1 and picture).
1913 COWIE *Company of Adventurers* 323: The dog-travois was, and is still, in the forests of the north, a smaller implement of the same model. **1966** *Kingston Whig-Standard* (Ont.) 6 Feb. 4/5: Toboggans were made of hardwood and the dog "travois" consisted simply of a couple of sticks tied together over the neck of a dog, the other ends of the sticks trailing behind to serve as a resting place for the load which was lashed to it.

dog-wolf *n*. an adult male wolf.
1919 FRASER *Bulldog Carney* 153: The dog-wolf, with a snarling twist of his head, sprang into the bushes just as Carney dropped a hand to his gun. . . . **1926** SULLIVAN *Northern Lights* 25: It was always an old dog wolf, tenanted by some evil and human spirit, endowed with wild powers of murder and revenge.

dogy *n.* See **dogie**.

dog-yard *n.* See **dog corral**.
1934 GODSELL *Arctic Trader* 51: Next, a gaudily painted carriole, hauled by five big hounds, dashed madly into the fort, while a pandemonium of yelping and barking came from the dog-yard.

dollar† *n.* **1** *Hist.* in colonial days (until 1858 officially), the Spanish dollar, *q.v.*, a silver coin valued at so many shillings Halifax currency, *q.v.*, or York currency, *q.v.* See also **silver dollar** (def. 1). Cp. **half-dollar**.
☛ *The currency system in colonial Canada was in a highly disorganized state until 1858, when legislation came into effect in United Canada requiring that government accounts be kept in dollars and cents, i.e., in the decimal system, which had been in unofficial use in many quarters for some years.*
1764 *Quebec Gaz.* 19 July 2/1: Whoever will discover the Offender, or Offenders, for that they may be convicted thereof, shall receive a reward of FOUR DOLLARS, by Application to Mr. Sills, in the Lower-Town. **1852** MOODIE *Roughing It* 40: Girls, who were scarcely able to wash a floor decently, talked of service with contempt, unless tempted to change their resolution by the offer of twelve dollars a month. **1863** WALSHE *Cedar Creek* 334: The franchise is almost universal throughout Canada. In 1849 it was lowered to thirty dollars (six pounds sterling) for freeholders, proprietary, or tenantry in towns, and to twenty dollars (four pounds) in rural districts.
2 the Canadian dollar, a monetary unit of 100 cents, taken over from the decimal system used in the United States and officially adopted in 1858 in United Canada; also, the equivalent of this unit in paper money or coin.
[**1835** *Novascotian* (Halifax) 1 Oct. 288/1: We [Americans] reckon hours and minutes to be dollars and cents. **1854** *Hamilton Gaz.* (C.W.) 27 Apr. 2/7: But mainly do we protest against the use of the monetary term dollar, at all! It always conveys to us the impression that the person who thus expresses himself has a longing to exchange the red cross of Saint George, for the Goose and Gridiron of brother Jonathan.] **1859** *British Colonist* (Victoria) 29 Aug. 2/1: We cannot look with favor on any system which is designed as a substitute for the dollar and cent, and we think the dollar should be taken as the unit, instead of the pound. **1872** DASHWOOD *Chiploquorgan* 250: Even in the Dominion the value of the dollar varies in different provinces. **1965** *Dly Colonist* (Victoria) 8/6: If every wage earner gets an extra dollar a week, then there are at least $5,000,000 extra spending dollars going around in Canada every week.

dollar bill a bank note having the face value of one dollar.
1813 *Kingston Gaz.* (U.C.) 7 Sep. 3/3: . . . the above sum [shall] be struck off in the following manner, viz. The sum of twelve hundred & fifty pounds in three Dollar Bills, two hundred and fifty pounds in Dollar bills, and two hundred and fifty pounds in half Dollar Bills. **1913** (1914) BICKERSTETH *Open Doors* 219: Pat was sitting on the farther side, and seemed in his element—his "Stettson" hat pushed to the back of his head; his face, on which grew a short stubbly beard, flushed with excitement, and a substantial heap of dollar bills in front of him.

Dollardom *n. Slang, Obs.* the United States, so called because of the reputed love of the dollar among the citizens of that country. Cp. **Dollar Yankee**.
1852 *Hamilton Gaz.* (C.W.) 20 May 3/2: Of recent years the mercurial Demon of Republicanism, hath been urging the matrons and maidens of Dollardom to the perpetration of strangely preposterous pranks. **1855** *Anglo-American Mag.* VI 66/2: Are you aware that there was published some years ago in Dollardom, an edition of the Bible for family reading . . . purified from all coarse expressions and indelicate passages.

dollar house *Obs.* an inn or rest house at which any meal costs a dollar.
1965 *Islander* 31 Oct. 3/3: . . . always managed to get a meal of some kind at one of the resthouses [in the Cariboo, c1865]. It generally consisted of beans and fat bacon, with bread or biscuit, and very thick coffee. Every house was what was called "a dollar house," and whatever the meal consisted of, or whether or not it was good or bad, it was always a dollar.

dollar native *Arctic, Local* an Eskimo of the Mackenzie delta region who demands high pay for his services.
1952 *Beaver* Sep. 36/2: Even Knud Rasmussen . . . speaks of the "dollar natives" of the Western Arctic, in 1925.

dollar piece a silver dollar.
1917 MILLER *New Era* 420: Let us walk in our old boots on the old boards, patriots all, with dollar pieces jingling in our pockets adding up to twenty-five for the latest patriotic loan. **1958** *Evening Telegram* (St. John's) 7 May 19/4: Twenty-five dollar pieces have been inserted into the white and silver cake. . . .

Dollar Yankee *Slang, Obs.* a citizen of the United States. Cp. **Dollardom**.
1839 *Montreal Transcript* 11 July 118/4: Was Mr. Papineau contemplating a union with the United States, those "Dollar Yankees" that he derided in debate, in the House of Assembly?

Dolly *n.* See **Dolly Varden trout**. Also spelled *dolly*.
1938 STANWELL-FLETCHER *Driftwood Valley* 182: We're catching more and more trout in the river. Beautiful fat things, eight- and ten-pounders. Most are Dollies, the pink spots on their silver bodies reminding one of the Eastern brook trout. **1963** *Sun* (Vancouver) 16 Apr. 15/1: Some dollies taken, too, on the tidal reaches of the Squamish.

Dolly Varden† See **Dolly Varden trout**.
1916 WOOD *Tourist's N.W.* 349: At all these streams you can also obtain sport with Dolly Varden and a few sea trout, but the fly-fishing will not be on until later. **1965** *B.C. Digest* June 28/2: Bluff Lake . . . does support a good population of excellent Dolly Varden, claimed by many to be the best dollies in the Chilcotin.

Dolly Varden trout or **char**† [perhaps from a character in Dickens' *Barnaby-Rudge,* a coquette who wore a flowered dimity dress] a char, *Salvelinus malma spectabilis,* characterized by reddish-orange spots on an olive-green skin, found in western lakes and rivers and on the Pacific coast. See also **bull trout**, **Dolly**, **Dolly Varden**, **salmon trout** (def. 2), and **sapi**.
1918 SCHULTZ *Rising Wolf* 77: . . . these lakes are full of cutthroat trout, and what the whites call Dolly Varden trout, and whitefish. **1960** *Fisheries Fact Sheets* 76 2:

The Dolly Varden char . . . is found nearly everywhere
. . . from the Queen Charlotte Islands to the Rockies. . . .

domain(e) [dəˈmen] *n.* [< F *domaine,* estate,
hereditary land] *Hist.* in Quebec, a farm belonging
to a seigniory; manorial farm.
1764 *Quebec Gaz.* 25 Oct. 3/1: On said Seigneurie there
is a Domaine, on which may be sown yearly 50 Bushels
of Corn, with a good Dwelling-house, two Barns, a
Stable and a good Wind-mill built with Stone. **1804**
Ibid. 30 Aug. Supp. 3/1: I have seized and taken
in execution . . . a lot or piece of land . . . bounded in
front . . . by the road of the cote Saint Louis, in the rear
by the domain of the said Seigniory. . . .

dominie† [ˈdamə͵ni] *n.* [< Scots] **1** a school-
teacher, especially a Scot.
1829 MACTAGGART *Three Years* I 196: . . . the parents
blame the dominie for want of attention, he leaves the
parish, finds teaching elsewhere, and no one is found to
replace him. **1883** FRASER *Shanty* 186: Never did school-
boy get a more stinging "lick" from an irate dominie
than did Tauton from that thick jagged strap. **1964**
B.C.Teacher Mar. 304/1: Ex Dominie's caustic letter
discussing Mr. Hamm's "orgy of overgeneralization"
is somewhat deplorable. . . . I am disappointed that
Ex Dominie finds it necessary to adopt a tone which
criticizes a person rather than ideas.
2 a. a Presbyterian minister.
1909 CAMERON *New North* 17: Straight from Aberdeen,
the young Dominee coming into Winnipeg little dreamed
that the Church of Rome had established its Mission
on the Red River decades ago. **1947** *Beaver* Dec. 34/1:
Company records show that in 1808 there arrived at
Fort York three young dominies. . . . **1952** (1954)
JENNINGS *Strange Brigade* 133: "Mister MacLean is to
be dominie of the Red River Parish," I put in quickly.
b. any Christian minister.
1930 *B.C.Lumberman* Feb. 44: "I repeat, the game of
checkers has no place in a Christian home," said the
dominie [the Rev. Axel Borg, Lutheran].

Dominion *n.* See **Dominion of Canada.**
[**1859** *British Colonist* (Victoria) 13 June 1/3: In the
language of Roebuck, "The language of England went
from Halifax to Vancouver's Island, the institutions of
Britain would reach thence as far as habitable land, even
to the pole; and we shall have such a dominion as the
world never saw."] **1870** (1963) *Beaver* Winter 34/1 . . .
on account of his being son of the Dominion Premier,
he . . . has been appointed over the heads of older and
more experienced volunteer officers. . . . **1889** (1965)
HAMILTON *Cdn Quotations* 63/1: [Sir John A.
Macdonald, letter from Riviére-du-Loup to Lord
Knutsford, July 18, 1889] On reading the above [letter]
over I see that it will convey the impression that the
change of title from Kingdom to Dominion was
caused by the Duke of Buckingham. This is not so.
It was made at the instance of Lord Derby, then (1867)
foreign minister, who feared the first name would
wound the sensibilities of the Yankees. **1963** MORTON
Kingdom of Can. 355: In these varied accomplishments
the government was responding to public pressures and
applying party principles rather than implementing
a national policy such as the unfinished state of the
Dominion demanded.

Dominion Day a statutory holiday celebrated
annually on July 1 in commemoration of the
creation of the Dominion of Canada, July 1, 1867.
See also **Canada Day, Confederation Day,** and
First of July.

1867 (1965) GAETZ *Diary* 1 July 94: Dominion Day !!
This first day of July, in the year of our Lord, 1867, is the
Birth Day of the Dominion of Canada. Nova Scotia has
entered to day into a new state of things, having now
entered into partnership, for ever, with New
Brunswick and the Canadas. **1868** *St.Catharines
Constitutional* (Ont.) 28 May 2/6: We hope the
arrangements for Dominion Day celebration will be
more perfect, and more in keeping with what should be
done at such a time. **1876** *Thunder Bay Sentinel* (Port
Arthur, Ont.) 22 June 3/1: Attention is invited to the
excursion on Dominion Day for the benefit of the
Presbyterian Church Fund. **1964** *Globe and Mail*
(Toronto) 16 Dec. 6/5: On or about Dominion Day, you
would go and watch the ice breaking up in the river.

Dominion Government the Government of
Canada; the federal government whose seat is in
Ottawa.
1870 (1883) BUTLER *Great Lone Land* 43: . . . it is an
undoubted fact that warning had been given to the
Dominion Government of the state of feeling amongst the
half-breeds, and the phrase, "they are only eaters of
pemmican," was so cutting to the Metis, was then first
originated by a distinguished Canadian politician. **1962**
Canada Month Sep. 14/2: That cenotaph belongs to the
dominion government and what is done with it is their
responsibility.

Dominion Holiday *Obs.* See **Dominion Day.**
1867 *Islander* (Charlottetown) 5 July 2/5: We present
our readers with some notices of the way in which
what was virtually the first Dominion Holiday was spent
in the City and elsewhere.

Dominion note *Obs.* a bank note issued by the
federal government.
1869 *Cdn Illust.News* 30 Oct. 3/1: Dominion notes in
circulation on the 6th October 1869, $5,050,000.

Dominion of Canada the name of the
Confederation of Canada as created by the British
North America Act in 1867. See also **Dominion.**
1867 (1965) GAETZ *Diary* 94: At sunset [July 1st]
another salute of 21 guns was fired which ended the
programme for the day, and all wished Peace,
Happeness [sic] & Prosperity to the Dominion of
Canada. **1872** DASHWOOD *Chiploquorgan* 213: With
respect to the confederation of the provinces of Upper
and Lower Canada, New Brunswick and Nova Scotia,
into what is now termed the Dominion of Canada, there
is a good deal to be said on both sides. **1924** DORRANCE
Never Fire First 60: Nowhere in the civilized world,
perhaps, is there more respect paid to the coroner and
his inquests than in the Dominion of Canada. **1958**
Encyc.Can. III 290/1: In the BNA Act the word
Dominion is used officially to describe the Union, and
Dominion of Canada became accepted as the formal
designation of the nation.

Dominion Parliament the House of Commons
and Senate in Ottawa; the federal Parliament.
1868 *Niagara Mail* (Ont.) 1 Jan. 2/2: The matters
entrusted to the Local Assembly, are such as more
nearly affect the interests and every day business of the
people than those legislated by the Dominion
Parliament. **1939** *Thunderbolt* Mar.-Apr. 9/1: The
problem, moreover, has been brought forward time after
time in both the Dominion Parliament and the British
Columbia Provincial Legislature.

Dominion Police *Hist.* a federal police organization absorbed in 1920 into the Royal Canadian Mounted Police, *q.v.*

1963 *Globe and Mail* (Toronto) 26 Apr. 7/6: In 1904 King Edward VII gave the force [N.W.M.P.] the prefix Royal and in 1920 it absorbed a federal organization known as the Dominion Police. The new organization was named the Royal Canadian Mounted Police.

donation feast See **potlatch** *n.* (def. 2a).

1877 *Department Interior Ann.Rep.Sessional Paper* 11 36: The Indians were holding one of their old-time donation feasts.... **1890** *Trans.Roy.Soc.Can.* VIII 4 14: The "potlatch" or donation feast, which is everywhere among the tribes of the littoral of British Columbia most important, does not seem to have occupied a prominent place among the customs of the Shuswaps.

donation party† *Obs.* a social gathering held by members of a church at which donations were made for the support of the minister. See also **donation visit.**

1847 *St.Catharines Jnl* (C.W.) 7 Jan. 3/2: The Ladies of the Presbyterian Church and Congregational propose to have a Donation Party, at the residence of their Pastor.... **1895** *Times* (Niagara-on-the-Lake, Ont.) 11 Apr. 8/1: Our churches and leagues owe much to the press for its free advertising of all donation parties, tea meetings, picnics....

donation visit *Obs.* See **donation party.**

1850 *Watchman* (Port Hope, C.W.) 5 Dec. 2/3: We are requested to intimate that a Donation Visit, in favour of the Rev. G. Goodson will be held in the Methodist Parsonage, on Monday evening, the 8th Inst. **1879** *Morning Chronicle* (Halifax) 4 Dec. 3/1: "Donation visits" to pastors are being reported in the country papers.

donkey jammer or **puncher** *Lumbering, Slang* the operator of a donkey engine; donkeyman. See also **puncher** (def. 2).

1930 *B.C.Lumberman* April 48/1: Shall bull-cooks and donkey-punchers be checked as to whether they use a knife or a fork...? **1953** SWANSON *Haywire Hooker* 41: I'm a donkey jammer from hell and back, / With a Humboldt yarder a "Cracker Jack".... **1956** ANDREWS *Glory Days* 43:... if... he didn't like the donkey puncher... he would roll his blanket and head for town.

donnaconna(board) [ˌdɑnəˈkɑnə] *n. Trademark* a type of fibreboard.

1958 HAWTHORN *Indians of B.C.* 235: The lean-to kitchen, a step higher than the main room of the house, is lined with donnaconna. **1965** *Sun* (Vancouver) 21 Apr. 37/2:... the steam from the oil can sweats on the grey donnaconnaboard walls of Father Veyrat's small house behind the church of Our Lady of the Snows.

Dook *n.* See **Douk.**

doozer [ˈduzər] *n. Slang* [cf. Brit. dial. *douse* a heavy blow] something extraordinary in size, interest, or strength; often in the phrase "a doozer of a..."; whopper.

1949 PETERSON *Chipmunk* 231: "Paying for three World Wars now. Next one'll really be a doozer, and expensive." **1953** *Cdn Geog.Jnl* XLVI 73/2: This time

he not only grew a "doozer" [of a wheat crop] but is reaping a handsome financial reward as well. **1962** *National Hockey Annual* 52/2: The finale was a doozer.

dope *n.* **1** a preparation for applying to the skin to repel insect pests such as mosquitoes and black flies. See also **fly-dope** and **mosquito-dope.**

1903 WHITE *Forest* 156: Next in order come the various "dopes." And they are various. From the stickiest, blackest pastes to the silkiest, suavest oils, they range, through the grades of essence, salve, and cream. **1947** GILLHAM *Raw North* 20: The fact that the dope leaks over spare socks, blankets and reading matter does not detract from the worth of the equipment.

2 *Slang* butter.

1889 MACLEAN *Indians* 199: Some of the old timers feast occasionally on hardtack covered with dope—butter—and in their tea or strong coffee they use the tin-cow—condensed milk.

doré [ˈdɔre *or* ˈdɔri] *n.* [< Cdn F (*poisson*) *doré* gilded fish] See **walleye pike.** See also **dory** and **poisson doré.** Also spelled *dore, doree.*

1775 (1901) HENRY (Elder) *Travels* 265: There are also pickerel, called *poissons dorés* (gilt-fish), and sturgeon. **1793** (1933) MACDONELL *Diary* 116: The [Assiniboine] River is stocked with the following fish viz—Sturgeons... Breams, suckers or carpes, Pike, Doré.... **1859** DAWSON *Lake Superior* 17/2:... the fish... are very abundant in the rivers and lakes; sturgeon, white-fish, pike, doré and various other kinds are found in Lake Winnipeg. **1963** *Gazette* (Montreal) 13 June 32/2: Also he'd like to have reported to him the taking of any dore which were tagged by him and his staff during the spawning run of this species.

dormeuse *n.* [< Cdn F] *Obs.* a modification of the cariole (def. 1b), adapted for sleeping.

1795 (1911) SIMCOE *Diary* 265: Lord Dorchester sent his dormeuse, a travelling carriage adapted for sleeping.... It is like an open carriole, with a head made of sealskin, and lined with baize; a large bear or buffalo skin fixes in front, which perfectly secures you from wind and bad weather, and may be unhooked if the weather is fine or mild. **1955** COLLARD *Cdn Yesterdays* 301: The vehicle in which Mrs. Simcoe travelled was somewhat unusual. It was called a "dormeuse". Within was a feather bed on which the passenger could sleep.

dory [ˈdɔri] *n.* See **doré.**

1792 (1911) SIMCOE *Diary* 104: They are... as firm as a dory and of very good taste.... **1893** *Blackwood's Mag.* May 691/2:... after passing the Rapids, we got with a minnow two very game fish called dories or dorés; they being, their French name implies, of a golden hue. **1952** (1954) JENNINGS *Strange Brigade* 105: There was also another, smaller species of pike that was called dory....

doter or **doater** [ˈdotər] *n.* [< *dotard* < *dote*] *Nfld* an old seal, especially a harp, *q.v.*

1771 (1792) CARTWRIGHT *Journal* I 171: I killed a doater with a ball, shot another through, and killed three water fowl with shot. **1963** *American Speech* Dec. 298: DOTER, *n.* an old seal.

double bark camp See **double camp.**

1872 DASHWOOD *Chiploquorgan* 56:... we built a double bark camp in the woods, a mile from the lake.

double-bee *n. Obs.* See quotes.

1905 CARTER *Dundas* 48: Often the logging-bee was linked with the quilting-bee and the two known as a double-bee, followed by the usual dance, which lasted until the "wee sma' hours." **1964** GUILLET *Pioneer Days* 137: Logging and quilting were sometimes combined into a "double bee", and in the same manner the quilting in the afternoon often preceded the husking in the evening, in which the men participated.

double buckboard *Obs.* a buckboard drawn by two horses.
1880 GORDON *Mountain and Prairie* 255: The light waggon . . . the two-horse spring waggon similar to the ordinary "democrat" waggon of Ontario, and the double buck-board are the greatest favourites. *Ibid.* 281: I left Battleford at noon on Monday . . . being passed along through the kindness of Major Walker of the N.W. Mounted Police, who was sending one of his men with a double buck-board to Duck Lake.

double camp *Obs.* See **double tent.** Cp. **half-camp.**
1872 DASHWOOD *Chiploquorgan* 145: In addition should be supplied . . . a piece of canvas to serve as a door for a double camp, together with resin to be used in mending bark canoes.

double decker See **double-decker bunk.**
1919 *Camp Worker* 28 June 7/2: You have . . . double bunks arranged lengthwise, generally double-deckers, which gives four men about six feet of space to sit down.

double-decker bunk two bunks built one above the other.
1919 *Camp Worker* 3 Oct. 3/4: Accommodation poor: one bunk house for twenty-two men with double decker bunks. **1948** *Ont.Timberworker* 10 Nov. 3/4: We, the Quebec bushworkers, must return at night after a heavy day's work, to camps which are small and over-crowded with double-decker bunks. **1966** [see quote at **long-handled underwear**].

double-fronted township a township two of whose boundaries are base lines of different concessions.
1899 GARDNER *Nothing But Names* 123: What are known as the double-fronted townships, in the range of Sherbrooke, Oso, Olden, Kennebec and Kaladar, were surveyed under contract from the old Canadian Government to Elmore and Smith, commencing as far back as 1829, and supposed to be completed in 1835.

double-jack *n.* [from its use in double-jacking, *q.v.*] *Mining* a heavy long-handled sledgehammer.
1944 *Prospecting in Can.* 161: double jack—an 8-pound striking hammer as used in hand drilling. **1961** *Press* 1 Sep. 11: The mechanization of mines in 1890 —the replacing of hand-steel, single-jack and double-jack, by drilling machines—had created new problems and the mine owners had attempted to lower wages on the grounds that less skill and energy was required.

double-jacking *n.* [< *double* + *jack* fellow, laborer] *Mining* a method of drilling in which one man strikes with a double-jack a drill-steel held and rotated by his mate.
1944 *Prospecting in Can.* 52: [Caption] Double-jacking. Drilling a down hole with an 8-pound hammer. **1963** *Western Miner and Oil Rev.* Mar. 20: There were no Yukon engines to create compressed air. Double jacking was the order of the day, the heavy sledges driving steel deep into the native rock.

double kayak a two-man kayak with two separate cockpits. Cp. **kayak**[1].
1931 LEBOURDAIS *Northward* 254: After dinner the

captain and two Eskimos went out again in the double kayaks and killed twenty walruses.

double mooley [? < *muley* hornless (of cattle)] *Obs.* a kind of skate having double runners and resembling a bobskate, *q.v.*
1918 COPELAND *Trail of Swinging Lanterns* 59: Sixty years ago, over the same surface James Charlton skated and scudded on an old pair of "double mooleys" with screws in their heels and he enjoyed this sport ever after.

double north canoe *Hist.* See **Montreal canoe.**
1929 MOBERLY *When Fur Was King* 11: I may mention that at Fort William we had exchanged our large "double north" canoe used on the great lakes, for smaller ones. . . .

double sleigh *Hist.* **1** a wide passenger sleigh having double front and back seats, drawn by one or two horses and riding on two sets of bobs, *q.v.*
1813 *Montreal Herald* 31 Dec. 3/3: The evil complained of will never be remedied, until the use of double sleighs or trains [is banned]. . . . **1819** *Kingston Chron.* (U.C.) 19 Feb. 3/4: On Sunday, two men . . . who had been from Mill Creek over to Fish Point, and were returning in a double sleigh drawn by one horse, drove into a crack [in the ice]. **1931** CONNOR *Rock and River* 17: . . . behind a spanking pair of French Canadians in a double sleigh the party drove down through the Lower Town . . . out upon the ice course on Le Fleuve. . . .
2 *Lumbering* a large sleigh consisting of one or two sets of four bobs, *q.v.*, chained together and having bunkers of squared timbers traversing the paired bobs, used for hauling logs, which were held in place by stakes fitted into sockets in the bunkers. Cp. **hauling sleigh.**
1882 *Edmonton Bull.* 1 Apr. 3/2: At Qu'Appelle the engineers left the party, and the mode of conveyance was changed from double sleighs to single jumpers. **1896** GOURLAY *Hist.Ottawa* 165: They had considerable trouble with teams and their wide double sleighs on the train roads. . . . **1912** HEENEY *Pickanock* 172: Going out of doors, he placed himself in the rear seat of the long double sleigh, where he wrapped himself about with the buffalo robe and sat waiting. . . . **1966** *Globe and Mail* (Toronto) 6 Jan. 5/4: The six, square-timbered barns that surround the farmhouse . . . [contain] a museum of pioneer equipment—cutters, wagons, broad axes, double sleighs. . . .

double spruce See quotes.
1853 REID *Young Voyageurs* 139: The "black" or "double spruce" (*P.nigra*), is that species from the twigs of which is extracted the essence that gives its peculiar flavour to the well-known "spruce beer." **1917** (1921) *Native Trees* 28: PICEA MARIANA (Mill.) B.S.P. BLACK SPRUCE Common names: Black spruce, red spruce, double spruce, water spruce, swamp spruce. **1956** *Ibid.* 40: Black Spruce [is also called] double spruce. . . .

double takeout *Curling* a shot which hits two of an opponent's rocks, driving both out of the house.
1963 *Calgary Herald* 31 Dec. 21/4: In contrast, Woolley was in fine form, rattling off double takeouts, hit-and-rolls and delivering cool draws with heady abandon.

double tent a bivouac shelter large enough to hold two persons. See also **double camp.** Cp. **half-tent.**

1872 DASHWOOD *Chiploquorgan* 152: In the way of tents, a light "lean-to" or "half tent"—of cotton or canvas is preferable to a double tent, as in the latter the fire cannot be made in front. A lean-to is much lighter to carry, and in case you stay long in one place, a double-camp can generally be built.

double-trip *v.* take part of a load, leave it, and return for the rest; transport a load in two trips.
1962 *B.C. Digest* Oct. 29/1: The old prospectors had already begun to mush their outfits by dog sleds, having to double-trip it, pulling a load up ten miles, leaving that load and returning to camp the same day.

double window a storm window; a removable glazed frame put on in the fall and taken off in the spring, to help keep out the cold.
1837 (1961) *Ontario Hist.* Mar. 29: Toward the end of October Anne wondered whether the house would be cold in the winter because of the lack of "double windows". 1871 OXENDEN *First Year* 49: On entering the room I found a scorching stove, and the temperature up to about 70°; and as there were double windows, and no aperture for the ingress of fresh air, and the place was crammed full, I began to fear lest we should be stifled. 1958 *Journal of the Cdn Linguistic Assn* Fall 74: It is possible that the prevalence of *double window* in Montreal English is reflected in the speech of French-speaking Montrealers since many of them use the term *fenêtre double* to refer to a window placed over another for extra protection during the winter.

Douglas *n.* See **Douglas fir.**
1888 MCDOUGALL *G.M. McDougall* 241: Now these great hills attract our attention, their wooded slopes and summits finely shaded by Douglas and spruce trees.... 1917 PHILLIPPS-WOLLEY *Songs* 47: Lurid and loud the smelter rose / In the place where the Douglas grew....

Douglas Day in British Columbia, November 19, a day commemorating Sir James Douglas, 1803-1877, Governor of British Columbia 1858-1864.
1958 *Sun* (Vancouver) 5 Nov. 1/1: November 19, or Douglas Day as it is known among Native Sons, historians and a few others looks as though it may become an annual provincially celebrated major date on the calendar. 1959 (1960) *Douglas Day Observance* 1: In each year the nineteenth day of November shall henceforth be observed as Douglas Day throughout the Province of British Columbia.

Douglas fir [< David *Douglas,* Scottish botanist, 1799-1834] 1 *Pseudotsuga taxifolia,* the largest tree native to Canada. See also **Douglas, false hemlock,** and **Oregon pine.** Also called *red fir, yellow fir, B.C. fir.*
1877 GRANT *Ocean to Ocean* 259: The hillsides and the country beyond support a growth of splendid spruce, black pine, and Douglas fir.... 1958 *Maclean's* 10 May 56/1: ... the survival of the wonderful Douglas Fir as a Canadian species ... seems assured through the forest-management licenses of recent years. 1963 *Canada Month* Nov. 21/2: We plundered the lordly pine of eastern Canada and even now we are slaughtering the giant Douglas firs of the Pacific coast.

2 the wood of this tree.
1888 *Dominion Illustrated* 38/2: The hotel is furnished throughout in red and yellow Douglas fir and white pine, oiled and varnished. 1952 PUTNAM *Cdn Regions*

440/1: Douglas fir is one of the best structural timbers, and is used in the construction of buildings and bridges. 1958 *Maclean's* 10 May 86/4: ... his is perhaps the only building in Canada paneled in B.C. softwoods—in cedar, pine and hemlock and ... plain Douglas Fir ply....

Douglas pine See **Douglas fir.**
1873 (1904) BUTLER *Wild North Land* 333: Many isles lie upon their surface; from tiny promontories the huge Douglas pine lifts his motionless head. 1956 *Native Trees* 58: DOUGLAS FIR [is also called] Douglas pine....

Douglas spruce† See **Douglas fir.**
1936 *B.C. Lumber Trade* 16: DOUGLAS FIR ... [is] Also Known as ... Douglas Spruce. 1956 *Native Trees* 58: DOUGLAS FIR [is also called] Douglas spruce....

Douk [duk] *n.* [< *Douk*hobor] *Slang* See **Doukhobor.** Also spelled *Dook.*
1899 *Medicine Hat News* (Alta) 16 Feb. 5/5: In the train of which he was in charge every coach was swept, scrubbed and aired regularly by the Douks themselves. 1907 KENNEDY *New Canada* 149: There is a general impression that the "Dooks," as their neighbours call them, are a troublesome lot. 1962 *Maclean's* 10 Mar. 50/1: "It's a joke all over the rest of Canada, isn't it?" he said. "Fun and games. Cops and Douks. Douks and cops."

Doukhobor ['dukə,bɔr] *n.* [< Russian "spirit wrestlers"] a member of a Christian sect founded in Russia in the 18th century, several thousand of whom settled in Western Canada at the end of the 19th century. See also **Independent Doukhobor** and **spirit-wrestler.** Also *Dukhobor.*
1899 *Medicine Hat News* (Alta) 16 Feb. 1/5: The Doukhobor reservation as originally located, was in Assiniboia, with the exception of range 29, comprising three townships which extended eastward into Manitoba. 1916 BRIDLE *Sons of Canada* 91: It is years now since the fanatical Doukhobors gave any trouble to the authorities. Mavor's experiment has succeeded. 1964 *Sun* (Vancouver) 3 July 6/4: "The Doukhobors have just started to vote provincially," says Stan Orris, editor of the Grand Forks Gazette. 1966 *Kingston Whig-Standard* (Ont.) 19 Apr. 17/7: Two Doukhobor women who refuse to eat on their own are being forced to take nourishment the hard way in the Canadian Forces Hospital today.

down† *n. Cdn Football* one of the three attempts a team has to advance the ball ten yards from the place where the ball was previously grounded; the duration of such an attempt.
1958 *Edmonton Jnl* 7 Aug. 7/2: ... London kicker Legg fumbled a snap on the third down and the Riders took over at the London four....

down below *Obs.* See **down East** (def. 2).
1884 *Prince Albert Times* (Sask.) 22 Feb. 1/2: Leap year surprise parties are quite the rage "down below" (we don't mean literally in warmer climate, but down East), in which the position of the sexes is reversed and the ladies get up the parties and go round and pick up the young gentlemen and select their partners afterwards at the dance.

down East or **east** 1 in or to the Maritimes, especially Nova Scotia (particularly from the point of view of someone in Central Canada). See also **East** (def. 1).
1834 *Brit.Amer.Jnl* (St. Catharines, U.C.) 20 May 3/2:

Now Nab is a real cute girl, and has got so much larnin . . . for her father sent her sicks weeks down east to bordin skool. **1891** *Grip* (Toronto) 18 Mar. 254/1: An enterprising down East Hustler lately conceived the idea of crowding the "Best Fifty Books" into one volume, and selling the same by subscription. **1962** *Canada Month* Feb. 32/2: Nobody forces it [a family], though it's of course too bad if it can no longer make a livelihood Down East.

2 in or to central Canada or the Maritimes, usually Ontario (from the point of view of persons in the West and Northwest). See also **back East** (def. 1) and **East** (def. 2).
1881 *Edmonton Bull.* 28 Feb. 4/1: The weather we have experienced so far this winter has been as summer compared to that down east. **1912** POCOCK *Man in the Open* 268: We gossiped of Captain Taylor's half-bred child, Wee James at school down East. . . . **1962** *Canada Month* April 26/3: The traditional style favored down east, the old draw game, had the curlers trying to place their stones "in the house"—somewhere inside a 12-foot circle at the other end of the ice sheet.

Down-Easter *n.* a native of eastern Canada. See also **down East.**
1865 *Leader* (Toronto) 30 Jan. 2/4: [At the masquerade] Jean Baptiste was represented by more than one habitant, and there were Indian Chiefs, some looking more terrible than the great Tecumseh himself, a Down-Easter in bed-gown, Sam Slick, [and] John Bull. **1916** BRIDLE *Sons of Canada* 218: In many a growing town on or near a new railway these Rip Van Winkles croaked over the menace of immigrants and colonist cars and down-easters hanging out business signs on the streets of the furpost and cowboy towns. **1958** MACGREGOR *North-west of 16* 91: There were two kinds of Down-Easters, those from the Maritimes and those from Ontario; each was as much superior to the other as the way they did things down east was superior to the way people did things out here.

down logs† See **down timber.**
1954 BEZANSON *Sodbusters* 95: One serious barrier appeared; a long slough filled with down logs, their limbs broken and jagged. . . . **1959** *Alaska Sportsman* Aug. 37/1: . . . a forest fire . . . had left the little valley [in B.C.] a maze of down logs—hard enough to get through on horse in daylight.

down North or **north 1** *Nfld* to, or northward along, the Labrador coast.
1905 DUNCAN *Dr.Grenfell's Parish* 86: When, at last, word comes south that the ice is clearing from the coast, the vessels spread their little wings to the first favouring winds; and in a week—two weeks or three—the last of the Labradormen have gone "down north." **1920** GRENFELL & SPALDING *Le Petit Nord* 24: Neither do you go north if you know what you are about; you go "down North"; and your friend is not bound for Labrador. She is going to "the Labradore."

2 in, or to, the north country (used by northerners, where most "outsiders" would say "up north"); in the regions where the rivers flow "down" to the Arctic Ocean.
[**1776** (1951) *Sask.Jnls* 50: . . . for even now it is full early for Paddling in the Lakes down to the Northward.] [**1887** *Senate Report* 142: . . . if the post was situated down in the north, the servant received so much moose meat. . . .] **1943** *Beaver* Sep. 14: [Caption] These great machines are of inestimable value in levelling the landing strips which make possible year-round flying down north. **1954** BEZANSON *Sodbusters* 26: "We

learned in Edmonton to say 'down north,' but it was hard to get accustomed to." **1965** SYMINGTON *Tuktu* 17: The land slopes gradually "down north" from a height of land roughly coinciding with the northern limit of the settlement.

down timber† trees that have been blown down or felled by other natural causes. See also **down logs, fallen timber,** and **windfall** (def. 1b).
1895 SOMERSET *Muskeg* 170: [Caption] Horses in Down Timber. **1951** HOBSON *Grass* 136: There was no feed. Windfalls or down timber lay piled up between the trees.

'dozer *n.* [abbrev. of *bulldozer*] See **bulldozer.**
1950 HAMBLETON *Abitibi Adventure* 81: Later, through Rene, he met one of the 'dozer drivers, a young French Canadian from the LaSarre region, and managed to talk his way into being allowed to try out the machine. . . . **1958** *Edmonton Jnl* 24 June 4 6/2: Often, the 'dozer will hit ridges of heavy timber where each tree has to be taken out separately. . . . **1966** *Sun* (Vancouver) 27 April 3-6: [Advert.] COMPLETELY UNRESERVED AUCTION . . . CONSTRUCTION & LOGGING EQUIPMENT . . . Some of Major Items from Cattermole Timber: . . . 1963 Models Hyd. Angle Dozers and Hyster D89A Winches. . . .

dozer boat *Lumbering* See **boom dozer.**
1966 *B.C.Logging* 13/1: Other men operate quick turning steel hulled "dozer boats" nosing logs by grade and species into boom formation.

draegerman ['drægəˑmən *or* 'dre-] *n.* [< A.B. *Dräger,* died 1928, a German physicist, who invented a mask effective in gas-filled mines] *Maritimes* a coal miner trained in underground rescue work and the use of special equipment; a mine rescuer.
1918 DRUMMOND *Mining in N.S.* 343: Draeger men were soon ready but exploration was somewhat impeded by the jamming of the cage at the bottom of the shaft. **1958** *Edmonton Jnl* 24 Oct. 2/8: The draegermen—the name comes from the German-made equipment they originally used—are hand-picked for size, health, intelligence and temperament.

drag *n.* **1†** *West* See **drag end.**
1951 HOBSON *Grass* 115: The men followed tracks for days; once they had the thrill of jumping the band, and they gave their saddle horses a hard run for several miles at the flank of some of the mares and colts in the drag. **1962** FRY *Ranch on the Cariboo* 25: . . . I moved along behind the drag, pushing the odd late-born calf that grew reluctant to keep up. . . .

2 *Nfld* a chain or rope used to brake a dog sled. See also **drogue** (def. 2).
1952 BANFILL *Labrador Nurse* 215: Drag. Chain of steel links or rope carried by dog-team drivers to throw under komatic runners to stop the dogs.

drag end *West* the tail of a moving herd of cattle or horses.
1962 FRY *Ranch on the Cariboo* 28: . . . we were on the drag end where fully half the herd was hanging out, looking for a chance to break.

dragger† *n. Atlantic Coast* See 1963 quote.
1954 *Fishermen's Advocate* 5 Feb. 12/3: Moreover, the turnover of personnel on some of the industry's

largest draggers . . . placed added curbs on the output of frozen groundfish. **1961** *Weekend Mag.* 5 Aug. 3/2: . . . Mrs. Alfred Anderson tuned in her radio and heard two dragger skippers talking about the storm. **1963** *Globe and Mail* (Toronto) Dec. 21 6/6: The dragger was introduced to provincial fishermen in 1947. It is a pocket edition of the trawler (under 100 feet long) which tows a conical net along the sea bottom to harvest cod and other groundfish—haddock, pollock, plaice and so on.

dragline *n.* See **tracking line.** Cp. **draw line.**
1963 *Beaver* Winter 25/2: . . . one woman would pull on the dragline tied to the bow, with four to six dogs pulling ahead of her.

dram [dræm] *n. Lumbering, Hist.* a detachable component of a timber raft, those on the Ottawa drives comprising some 25 cribs made up of logs or square timbers lashed or chained together and of appropriate size to shoot the timber slides. See also **band**[3] and **cabin dram.** Cp. **crib** (def. 1a), **raft** (def. 2) and note.
1846 BONNYCASTLE *Canada and Canadians* I 70: A raft a quarter of a mile long . . . is curious enough; but to see it in drams, or detached portions, sent down . . . the timber slides of the Ottawa . . . is still more so. **1874** *Canada Month* Oct. 344/2: For going through the canals, the drams are built about twenty-four by one hundred and twenty, and in a less secure manner than those intended to take their chances of the rapids. **1964** *Cdn Geol.Jnl* Feb. 68/1: Until these were passed, the men kept the logs in cribs waiting to tie cribs into drams and rafts once the dangerous slides were passed.

draught *n. Nfld* a load of dried codfish equal to two quintals.
1944 *Beaver* Sep. 23/2: When the load [of dry codfish] on the barrow reaches a "draught" (two quintals), it is placed on the scales and checked.

draw† *n. Esp.West and Northwest* a gully; ravine.
1909 SERVICE *Cheechako* 45: In cabin or dance-hall, camp or dive, muckiucks or patent shoon; / On velvet tundra or virgin peak, by glacier, drift or draw. . . . **1963** *B.C.Digest* Nov.-Dec. 63/1: Joe knew every acre of it, every draw, every coulee, every bluff, and every mud-hole.

draw *v. Hist.* receive a grant of land from the government.
1767 *New Brunswick Mag.* I 266: The lots in Gage Town are drawn, Moses and William Hazen Nos. 53, 54, Mr. Simonds No. 12, none of them either the best or worst in the Township. **1873** (1883) RYERSON *My Life* 4: Near the close of the last century my Father, with his family, followed an elder brother to Canada, where he drew some 2,500 acres of land from the Government for his services in the army, besides his pension. **1902** *London & Middlesex Hist.Soc.Trans.* I 29: He went to Colonel Talbot's and drew one hundred acres of land, about eight miles north of this city.

draw game *Curling* a style of play in which the curlers aim their stones with a view to having them curl into the house, as opposed to aiming with intent to knock the opposing stones out of play.
1962 *Canada Month* Apr. 26/3: The traditional style favored down east, the old draw game, had the curlers trying to place their stones "in the house". . . .

draw line *North* the main line by which a dog sled is drawn, the traces of the several dogs being attached to this line in what is called a fan hitch, *q.v.* See picture at **fan hitch.**
1941 *Beaver* March 11/1: Seven to twelve dogs are hitched to the main draw line, each by a single trace.

drawmaster *n. Curling* the official in charge of organizing a bonspiel.
1956 *Northland News* 17 Dec. 2/2: Seventeen completed rinks are reported by the Curling Club drawmaster. **1964** *Calgary Herald* 3 Apr. 14/3: Drawmaster Dick Kelly had 14 rinks down to the 16s of the primary after the firing died down Thursday night.

draw treaty of Indians, qualify for and receive treaty money, *q.v.*
1909 CAMERON *New North* 163: A father "draws treaty" for his olive-skinned branches until each marries and erects a tepee for himself.

Dreamer *n.* **1 a.** *Hist.* an Indian who claimed the power of divination.
1784-1812 (1916) THOMPSON *Narrative* 366: Others turn Dreamers, and tell what other tribes are doing and intend to do; where the Bisons and Deer are most plenty; and how the weather will be; and the boldest Dreamers point out the place of the camp of their enemy, and what they intend to do.
b. a member of an Indian religious cult that flourished in the Oregon Territory in the mid-19th century, popularly called "the Dreamers."
1910 HODGE *Bulletin* II 603: "Smohalla has recently died, but, in spite of occasional friction with agency officials, the "Dreamers", as they are popularly called, maintain their religious organization, with periodical gatherings and an elaborate ceremony." **1952** HOWARD *Strange Empire* 275: . . . the Dreamers believed that someday all the dead warriors would arise and help the living to recapture their country.
2 a member of a fanatical Russian sect in southern Alberta.
1910 HAYDON *Riders of Plains* 233: Even more troublesome have been the fanatics known as the "Dreamers."

dreaming stage *Hist.* a tree platform used by Indians to commune with their special spirits during the ritual marking progress from puberty to manhood.
1955 SHIPLEY *Anna and the Indians* 31: They are the old dreaming stages. Once it was the custom in these parts for young men to build shelters for themselves in the trees when they reached puberty and here live without food or water for a week or until their special spirit or Bowakunak appeared to them.

dress *n. Hist.* an outfit of clothing presented to an Indian on a ceremonial occasion by a fur company or a government agency as a mark of recognition. See also **clothing.**
1871 (1880) MORRIS *Treaties* 39: Two councillors and two braves of each band were to receive a dress, somewhat inferior to that provided for the Chiefs. . . .

dressing-shack *n.* a heated shack near an outdoor skating rink in which to change clothes.
1963 *Kingston Whig-Standard* (Ont.) 4 Mar. 13/1: He will walk back and forth in his dressing-shack [at an outdoor rink] not unlike a ship's captain. . . .

dried fish or **dry fish** *Esp.North* dried and, sometimes, smoked fish, as whitefish, long used for food for both men and dogs by the Indians and Eskimos. See also **fish** (def. 2) and **hung fish**. Cp. **drying stage** (def. 2) and **green fish** (def. 2).

c1665 (1885) RADISSON *Voyages* 36: After came a company of women . . . that brought us dry fish and Indian corn. **1785** (1954) *Moose Ft Jnls* 273: James Robinson is here now and . . . going up nodway River to fetch his stock of dry'd Fish. . . . **1847** (1910) BURPEE [Ed.] *Yukon* 23 June 86: Their stock of provisions, consisting generally of dried fish, is kept outside in a "cache" made of branches and snow, open above on which are placed their sleighs. **1921** HAWORTH *Trailmakers* 50: Even to-day it is so difficult to obtain forage at some of the northern Hudson's Bay posts that it is not uncommon to feed cows during the winter on dried fish. **1962** *Favorite Recipes* 37: Pounded Dry Fish Pudding. Pound up 5 or 6 dry fish and throw away the skin. Add sugar to taste, a small amount of grease, and cranberries . . . Bertha Allen.

dried meat 1 *Hist.* See 1857 quote. See also **dry meat**.

1765-75 (1933) POND *Narrative* 46: In Jany thay Began to Aproach us & Brot with them Drid & Grean Meet, Bever . . . Raccone & other Skins to trade. **1800** (1933) MCLEOD *Diary* 148: Collin came back [bringing] a little dryed and Green Meat. **1857** (1860) HIND *Red River Exped.* 312: Dried meat is the flesh of the buffalo cut into long, broad, and thin pieces about two feet by fifteen inches, which are smoked over a slow fire for a few minutes and then packed into a bale of about sixty pounds. **1956** WENTWORTH *Dried Meat* 4: When fully dried, a buffalo cow was estimated to yield 45 pounds of dried meat which was quite a saving in weight in comparison with the original carcass.

2 the flesh of caribou, moose, etc. cured by smoking and exposure to the sun. Cp. **drying stage** (def. 2). **1774** (1934) HEARNE *Journal* 127: I gave him a little Dryd meat &c to carry home. . . . **1896** RUSSELL *Far North* 88: I loaded my sled with thirty whitefish, three days' provision for the dogs, and fifteen pounds of dried meat for the boy. **1963** MCTAVISH *Behind the Palisades* 88: The "dried meat"—Indians of the far north used the rib or side-meat, with bones extracted, of the reindeer almost exclusively to earn this name— was preserved at the season when the animals were at their best condition. . . .

dried salmon salmon filleted, smoked, and dried, once a staple in the diet of the British Columbia Indians.

1808 (1889) FRASER *Journal* 158: Went ashore on an island and secured a bale of dried salmon for our return. **1897** *B.C.Mining Jnl* (Ashcroft) 27 Feb. 2/2: Dried salmon is comparatively light and a dog team can quite easily draw a sufficient amount for its own feed and the provisions of a man, and camping outfit, from Circle City to Dyea. **1900** LONDON *Son of Wolf* 17: The whole stock of dried salmon had been devoured. . . .

drift boat *Maritimes* a small fishing boat used in tending drift nets.

1879 *Morning Chron.* (Halifax) 10 July 3/1: The drift boats are doing extremely well, some of the boats taking as high as five or six hundred [shad] a night. **1953** *Cdn Geog.Jnl* July 40/1: Where others have turned to using "drift" boats to tend their nets, he alone fishes with horse and ladder.

drifter *n.* See **drift storm**.

1922 FLAHERTY *Eskimo Friends* 8: Then came snow, the winter's first big "drifter," and for three days there was no land or sea or sky. **1942** TWOMEY & HERRICK *Needle to the North* 79: There we met our first blast, not a

drifter but a steady and almost unbearable wind, drumming in our ears like the roar of the sea until we could hear nothing else.

drift fence 1† *West* a fence erected to prevent cattle or horses from straying.

1951 HOBSON *Grass* 89: Billy Dagg had dropped in for coffee on his way to help Eddie Collet and Tim Drainey finish a drift fence. **1964** *Sun* (Vancouver) 11 Feb. 4/3: . . . Dorsey . . . once ran a drift fence between his ranchhouse and the toolshed without any gate whatever in it. . . .

2 See quotes. See also **deer fence**.

1965 SYMINGTON *Tuktu* 50: Leading to the caribou crossing-places on lakes or rivers, or at right angles to deeply worn caribou trails, are seen drift fences—rows of stone columns fifty yards or more apart, made by setting rock upon rock to form a man-like silhouette. Some of the drift fences are close to six miles long. *Ibid.* 51: The Indians made similar drift fences, using spruce saplings instead of stones, and the circular pound might be made into a maze of passages between rows of trees, with snares set to capture the animals.

drift-ice *n.* small ice masses drifting in the sea.

1829 MACTAGGART *Three Years* I 315: . . . even the heaviest drift ice rushing before a flood would not be able to sweep them away. **1902** (1964) *Nfld Qtly* Summer 29/1: . . . we had a remarkably striking view of drift-ice streaming west-south-west into the strait. . . . The Labrador current was a vivid reality to us as we watched the truly majestic procession of these dazzling migrants from a polar sea. **1965** *Fisherman* 19 Mar. 25/1: . . . a hunter was carried out to the Gulf of Georgia and drowned by being caught in drift ice in a small punt.

drift-pan *n.* a piece of drift-ice.

1916 DUNCAN *Billy Topsail* 247: . . . with an accumulation of Arctic bergs and drift-pans, blown in by the last nor'easter, it was sluggishly moving into the black shadows of the open sea.

driftpile *n.* a large pile of driftwood in a river. See also **embarras** and **jam-pile**.

[**1858** (1863) PALLISER *Journals* 77: We halted at noon . . . upon an enormous island of driftwood, one of many that block the centre of the channel. . . .] **1927** WOOLLACOTT *Mackenzie and His Voyageurs* 37: Many rocky islands break up the [Slave] river into intricate channels. Log-jams and drift-piles are numerous and troublesome. **1955** RICH in BLACK *Journal* lxi: Yet, balancing the canoe between the two currents that divided on the driftpile . . . they somehow poled, paddled and shoved themselves across to the main shore and slack water.

drift storm a snowstorm in which the snow is whipped into drifts by the wind. See also **drifter**.

[**1743** (1949) ISHAM *Observations* 66: Itt oft'n happens we shall have fine moderate weather, in a winter morning w'n before night approches, a sudden gale will spring up with Drift & snow to that Degree, that if men happen's to be out, and drest for warm weather, they Run a great Resque of their Lives,—Several having perrishd.] **1946** *Beaver* Sep. 3/1: Harold Luca, HB apprentice, perished there [King William Land] in a drift storm.

driftwood pile See **driftpile.**
1963 *Beaver* Winter 23/2: . . . further progress seemed impracticable as the driftwood piles were too large.

drill hall a building with a spacious open floor where the militia perform marching and other exercises. See also **drill shed.**
1906 *Eye Opener* (Calgary) 8 Sep. 1/1: The city council had invited his excellency to a reception at the drill hall and only two of them showed up.

drilling reservation a permit granting drilling rights on a defined area of land.
1958 *Edmonton Jnl* 12 Aug. 11/1: The drilling group also holds an Alberta government drilling reservation and lands in that tract are all in close proximity to the farmout half-section and scheduled "deep test" well.

drill shed *Obs.* See **drill hall.**
1867 *Islander* (Charlottetown) 4 Jan. 2/6: The Georgetown Drill Shed has been finished for a considerable time, and the contractor has not yet received the price of the materials bought for it. 1899 MACKAY *Pioneer Life* 162: . . . two hundred stalwart men presented themselves in Embro ready for drill. Crittendom's distillery was extemporized for a drill-shed.

drinking bar *Obs.* See **saloon.**
1859 (1958) WATTERS *B.C.Cent.Anthol.* 103: I heard the voices of men in the drinking-bars shouting and singing. . . .

drips *n. Slang* a kind of syrup.
1909 BINDLOSS *Lorimer* 36: . . . though the meal was frugal—potatoes, pork, green tea, flapjacks and drips, which is probably glucose flavored with essences—they gave me of their best, as even the poorest settlers do.

drivable *adj.* of a river, suitable for driving logs.
1933 GUILLET *Early Life in U.C.* 239: The first men to enter the limit . . . pick out the site for the camps and shanty, and lay out the course of the roads to the most convenient watercourse or "drivable" creek, where the "roll-way" is to be located.

drive† *n.* **1** *Lumbering* **a.** a specific collection of logs being floated downstream at high water from the timber limits to a mill or shipping point. See also **log drive, logging drive, log run, river drive,** and **timber drive.**
1872 DASHWOOD *Chiploquorgan* 106: . . . the men working at the head of the "drive" earn more than those at the tail, where there are no jams; the smartest men therefore go to the front. 1964 *Cdn Geog.Jnl* Feb. 70: If the drive was to go on, some one man had to go out there, find the key log and cut it away.
b. the process or practice of floating logs downstream at high water. See also **driving** (def. 1).
1926 MAIR *Masterworks* XIV liii: These raftsmen are nimble on timber beyond belief. To-day, when it is mainly saw-logs that are cut, the fully improved streams make the drive easy; but in the old days I speak of, the unimproved streams were very dangerous. . . . 1964 *Cdn Geog.Jnl* Feb. 71/1: Log jams on the Ottawa which held up the drive and filled taverns with rival gangs of Irish and French, were almost certain to brew trouble.
2 See **drive hunting.**

1921 HEMING *Drama of Forests* 233: One of the most ancient methods of hunting and one which is still in vogue in some remote places is the "drive." At those driving grounds in the right season—even if a drive of only a few miles were made—the Indians could count on securing two or three bears, three or four moose, and twelve or fifteen caribou.

3† *West* **a.** the driving of cattle or other animals from one place to another.
1955 HOBSON *Nothing Too Good* 93: There's not many cow outfits would have landed this drive! 1957 HUTCHISON *Canada* 251: To know what cattle would do in a pinch, to foresee their next move on a drive, to understand their minds—that was a skilled trade not to be learned under half a lifetime.
b. the herd of livestock being driven from one place to another.
1955 HOBSON *Nothing Too Good* 60: The horse cavvy with Rob and Ed Striegler had flashed past the drive into the frozen haze of the early dawn.

drive *v.* **1** *Lumbering* **a.** move a mass of logs by floating them downstream at high water in the spring; manage or control logs being moved in this way. See also **run,** *n.* (def. 3).
1848 LANMAN *Adventures* 192: They obtain their living by "driving" logs, and are as happy as they are ignorant. 1917 MILLER *New Era* 83: Most of the logs to supply these mills must now be brought from distances of fifty to a hundred and fifty miles . . . often requiring two years to drive them. 1960 *Ont.Hist.* Dec. 222: A series of slides along the Ottawa River completed the system, making it a matter of only six weeks to drive from Bytown to Quebec.
b. take part in the activity of driving logs on a river.
1854 KEEFER *Ottawa* 68: [Though] there is very little sympathy among lumbermen . . . necessity compels them often to "drive" together. 1964 *Cdn Geog.Jnl* Feb. 67/3: His father and grandfather drove the Petawawa and Madawaska rivers for men like Gillies and Booth.
2 take part in drive hunting, *q.v.* Cp. **deer drive.**
1832 RADCLIFF *Letters* 156: This is in my estimation an unsportsmanlike method, and is effected in the vicinity of the lakes, by driving the deer with dogs, who pursue the animal through the woods, till he is obliged to take refuge in the water. There a canoe is waiting; and as the hunted deer comes bounding along, and boldly dashes into the lake . . . [and when the deer weakens from fatigue, he is killed]. 1853 STRICKLAND *Canada West* I 178: Deer-hunting is a very exciting sport; but I prefer still-hunting (or deer-stalking, as it is called in the Highlands of Scotland) to driving them into the lakes and rivers with hounds.
3 cut a road through a forest.
1849 ALEXANDER *L'Acadie* II 100: . . . to "drive" this new road through a wilderness, would cost at least £30,000, and then, they thought, it never could be kept clear in winter.
4 *West* move cattle or other livestock from one place to another.
1955 HOBSON *Nothing Too Good* 35: We would be driving cattle until well in January, through an uninhabited, little-known country.
5 See quote.
1915 SPECK *Myths* 67n: To drive beaver is to hunt them by driving them from their cabins beneath the ice.

drive-barn *n.* See **drive-shed.**
1931 RORKE *Lefty* 50: He and Lefty made their way across the yard to the closed doors of the drive-barn.

driveboat *n.* a shallow-draft rowboat used in driving logs. See also **driving boat** and **pointer** (def. 1 and picture).
1948 *Ont.Timberworker* (Sudbury, Ont.) 30 May 6/5: The Driveboat, manned by four men, was drawn into the raging centre of the Chute and disappeared.

drive camp *Lumbering* a temporary camp set up during a drive, *n.* (def. 1b).
1948 *Ont.Timberworker* (Sudbury, Ont.) 30 May 6/4: Logging camps have not been saved for Drive camps, and the drive crews live in tents. **1957** *Bush News* June 2/2: We travelled through some fine-looking country to Malcolm's Rapids drive-camp where we enjoyed one of the finest meals of the entire tour.

drive-house *n.* See **drive-shed.**
1886 *Indian* (Hagersville, Ont.) 21 July 162/2: Mr. Joseph Marale has started to erect a new drive-house. **1939** GROVE *Two Generations* 17: Having gone through . . . the workshop and the drive-house with its one big carriage, its democrat, and its two buggies, he glanced at his dollar watch. . . .

drive hunting a method of hunting deer by which the animal is driven, usually by dogs, until it seeks refuge in a stream or lake, where, at the point of exhaustion, it is easily killed. See also **drive,** *n.* (def. 2) and *v.* (def. 2), and **driving** (def. 2).
1921 HEMING *Drama of Forests* 233: Two famous places for drive hunting in olden days were Point Carcajou on Peace River, and Grand detour on Great Slave River.

driver *n.* **1** *Lumbering* a man who takes part in the process of floating or driving logs. See also **log driver, river-driver, river-hog, riverman** (def. 2), **river rat, stream-driver,** and **white-water man** (def. 2).
1853 *Anglo-American Mag.* II 180/1: Then the logs are apt to get jammed together between the rocks, and the driver has constantly to be on the alert to preserve his raft, or what he values at less rate, his own life. **1964** *Cdn Geog.Jnl* Feb. 68/2: In the old days drivers worked from the logs more than they can now that logs are smaller.

2 See **dog-driver.**
1871 (1883) BUTLER *Great Lone Land* 321: The dogs were good ones, the drivers well versed in their work. . . . **1956** SHERMAN *Spring in the Arctic* 35: A good driver . . . can with a single word make his dogs stop and lie down in their traces.

drive-shed *n.* a shed in which farm vehicles and machinery are stored when not in use. See also **drive-barn, drive-house, driving-shed.** Cp. **machine shed** and note.
1899 PARKER *Lane* 197: If they missed him they must have thought him gone to the barn, or in the drive-shed sharpening his axe. **1947** DUMBRILLE *Deep Doorways* 163: Jackson had dug the potatoes, and the bags were in the driveshed, ready to be stored in the cellar.

drive steel *Mining* work with a steel drill and sledge; hence, work as a miner.
1963 *Inside Reports* 4 June 2/2: The field man who located the property for GANDA is an old Cobalt hand who drove steel himself, there, thirty years ago.

driveway *n.* **1** a scenic highway, especially a city thoroughfare, the sides of which are landscaped and planted with trees and flowers.

1909 *Gow Ganda Tribune* (Ont.) 1 May 1/1: . . . the big "County Council" in Queen's Park is considering the advisability of spending three hundred thousand dollars in building a driveway and boulevard along the Canadian side of the Niagara River. **1958** *Saturday Night* 27 Sep. 7/1: What Ottawa needs most sorely though is not more trees, parks and driveways as handouts from the taxpayers of Canada, but certain civilizing amenities which its own inhabitants, particularly the city officials and businessmen, can supply.

2 a private way by the side of a house, often giving access to a garage; a side drive.
1955 *Coast Guard* (Shelburne, N.S.) 10 Mar. 11/2: As a car was driving along the highway, a dog suddenly came out of a driveway and in order to avoid killing the dog, he had to ditch his car and damaged it quite badly. **1966** *Globe and Mail* (Toronto) 9 May 7/3: Friday . . . [I] shovelled gravel to make a new driveway.

3 a lane leading from a road to a house.
1939 GROVE *Two Generations* 3: . . . Ralph Patterson appeared on the driveway behind the barn. **1963** *Weekend Mag.* 7 Dec. 8/3: But I saw farmers shovelling their driveways. . . .

driving *n.* **1** *Lumbering* See **drive,** *n.* (def. 1b). See also **river-driving** and **stream-driving.**
1849 (1926) LANGTON *Early U.C.* 205: The men follow them down clearing everything before them, which is called driving. Each stick they release of course is soon brought up by some other lower down, and as you advance the jams, as they are called, of course get worse and worse. **1883** FRASER *Shanty* 307: Some of the most narrow escapes from mutilation and drowning are of everyday occurrence during driving season. **1958** *Evening Telegram* (St. John's) 5 May 14/4: Pulpwood cutting and hauling for this year's delivery to the papermill at Grand Falls has been brought to a close and driving is now in full swing. . . .

2 See **drive hunting.** See also **drive,** *v.* (def. 2).
1832 (1953) RADCLIFF *Letters* 155: The fourth method is that of *Driving the Deer.* **1866** KING *Sportsman in Can.* 51: Moose hunting lasts throughout the autumn and winter, and there are several different methods of pursuing the sport, as "calling," "driving," "creeping," and "tracking," or hunting on snow-shoes, sometimes called "crusting." **1921** HEMING *Drama of Forests* 233: At those driving grounds . . . the Indians could count on securing two or three bears, three or four moose, and twelve or fifteen caribou.

driving boat *Lumbering* See **driveboat.** See also **pointer boat.**
1964 *Cdn Geog.Jnl* Feb. 67/3: If you ask Emmett Chartrand about the driving boat or "pointer" he has a faraway look when he answers, "—used them, wore them out, broke them."

driving-shed *n.* See **drive-shed.**
1832 BARCLAY *Letters* 26: George and Charles has built two houses, and they have got a driving shade [sic] 50 feet square, and a genteel cottage to build this winter. **1905** SCHERCK *Pen Pictures* 56: Over the driving-shed . . . there was usually a large hall, in which the annual ball was held.

drogue [drog] *n.* [< *draw*] **1** See **droke.**
1921 (1934) WENTWORTH *Am.Dial.Dict.* 181/2: drogue, droke, drook, or drove, *n.* A cluster of fir or spruce.

1921 Nfld. **1936** MOWERY *Paradise Trail* 75: The sun had inched down behind the western peakline, and the first shadows of twilight were creeping into the denser drogues of the valley. **1946** BIRD *Sunrise* 4: He knew every pond and barren and drogue all the way to Old Woman Tickle. ...

2 *Nfld* See **drag** (def. 2).

1957 *Beaver* Autumn 28/2: ... if the hill is very steep he lets go the "drogue," which is a heavy piece of rope looped around the left runner. This slides underneath the runner and brakes the *komatik*. On level ground it will stop it.

droke [drok] *n.* [var. of *draw*] a clump of trees, especially evergreens; a copse. See also **bluff** (def. 3) and **drogue**. Also spelled *drook*.

☞ *Usually associated with Newfoundland, this term does occur elsewhere in the Atlantic Provinces and in the Hudson Bay area.*

1772 (1792) CARTWRIGHT *Journal* I 210: I then went over Lower Table to the Droke; where I observed much old slot of deer. **1907** MILLAIS *Newfoundland* 65: ... as we stops to look we hear a faint call from a droke o' spruce close by—a' runs up, and there lies Baxter 'most froze. **1934** DENNIS *Down in N.S.* 340: "Look at the barrens and drokes," said the light-keeper. "Drokes?" "Yes, little stumps of trees. The word is an Old Country one handed down to us by our ancestors." **1941** *Beaver* Sep. 37/1: Droke—A bluff or grove of woods.

drop-log *n.* in a deadfall (def. 1), the log which falls on the animal taking the bait. See also **falling pole** and **neck log**.

1956 KEMP *Northern Trader* 179: The drop-log was heavy enough itself, but to increase its crushing power, the boy cut and leaned across it half a dozen other logs. ... The drop-log, one end resting on the ground and the other end in the air, was held in position by a trigger arrangement.

drop pass *Hockey* a type of passing play in which a puck-carrier leaves the puck for a team-mate following him, after the defending players have been drawn out of position.

1963 *Kingston Whig-Standard* (Ont.) 6 Mar. 11/4: He left a drop pass and then went in to screen Plante, jostling the goalie.

Drought Area See **droughtlands** and **Dust Bowl**.

1955 HARDY *Alta Anthol.* 127: The Dust Bowl of Southern Alberta, where I spent much of my earlier life, is not really a dust bowl at all. That's just the fancy name given to it by someone who's never been there. It's also known as the Dry Area, the Drought Area and —since the government took notice of it and formed a Board to administer it—The Special Area.

droughtlands *n.pl.* a term applied to the southern regions of the Prairie Provinces, especially during the 1930's. See also **Drought Area**.

1954 TYRE *Saddlebag Surgeon* 247: In the wake of the grasshopper a new invader marched across the droughtlands of the south.

drouine *n.* See **derouine**.

drowned lands low-lying areas liable to flooding.

[**1790-96** (1961) PERKINS *Diary* 18: The Sawmills are Drowned with the freshet. There is not much Lumber on hand.] **1883** FRASER *Shanty* 281: ... where the ground is low-lying ... the country on both sides is completely submerged, forming what are called "lagoons" in the Southern States, and in our backwoods "drowned lands."

druggist store† *Obs.* See **drugstore**.

1820 *U.C.Herald* (Kingston) 21 Mar. 3/5: The Building next door south of the Subscribers Druggist Store, will positively be sold at Auction without reserve on the Premises the 30th March inst. at 12 o'clock, unless previously disposed of at private sale.

drugstore† *n.* a shop in which prescriptions are filled and patent medicines sold, often having a great variety of other goods for sale.

1859 *British Colonist* (Victoria) 12 Dec. 2/5: [Advert.] W. Zelner, Surgical and Mechanical DENTIST Drugstore Government street, between Yates and Johnson **1915** *Eye Opener* (Calgary) 12 June 4/3: It is unlawful for an injured person who has been carried into a drug store to drink liquor, even if ordered by a physician. **1966** *Victoria Dly Times* 2 Mar. 1/7: "This wasn't done by the same guys who knocked over the corner drug store," he added.

drum *n.* See **drum stove** (def. 1).

1931 HENDRYX *Outlaws* 163: "Mebbe you'd like to go up now, mam? She'll show you the way. You'll find the room warm. It's het by a drum from the kitchen stove."

drum *v.* of the male ruffed grouse, produce a loud reverberating noise by beating the wings.

1873 (1904) BUTLER *Wild North Land* 227: Butterflies fluttered in the clear, pure air; partridges drummed in the budding thickets. **1957** HUTCHISON *Canada* 304: Grouse drummed and hooted here, woodpeckers hammered, squirrels chattered, insects murmured in the nuptial flight of evening. **1967** *Wildlife Rev.* Mar. 9: ... the sound of drumming grouse or bugling elk. ...

drum dance 1 an Eskimo dance accompanied by drums. Cp. **drum song**.

1942 *Beaver* March 4/1: The Eskimo enjoys community life with its simple pleasures. ... The drum dance is an interesting spectacle and the genius of the Eskimo for descriptive gesticulations is given full play. **1964** *Kingston Whig-Standard* (Ont.) 23 Dec. 16/4: Drum dances in the western Arctic are performed by three or four men. They sing as they dance.

2 an Indian dance accompanied by drums, especially a tea dance, *q.v.*

[**1928** *Beaver* Sep. 90/1: ... the G.O.M. of drum dancing, John Duck, set to work building a suitable tent. ...] **1959** *News of the North* 25 June 3/3: An Indian Drum Dance was staged Sunday night in the field behind the Mission.

drumming *n.* of the male ruffed grouse, the making of a loud reverberating noise by beating the wings, especially in the mating ritual.

1853 REID *Young Voyageurs* 109: ... after listening a while, I knew it was ... the drumming of the ruffed grouse. **1921** HEMING *Drama of Forests* 315: Back deep in the birch thicket partridges are drumming, and all the woodland is musical with the song of birds.

drum oven a cylindrical bake-oven built into a stove pipe. Cp. **drum stove** (def. 1).

1937 (1958) WATTERS *B.C.Cent.Anthol.* 108: In addition to bannock, which I bake daily either in the drum oven or in an open fry pan on top of the stove, I made tarts of strawberry jam and a chocolate cake.

drum song among Eskimos, a song accompanied by drum music. Cp. **drum dance** (def. 1).
1946 *Beaver* Mar. 20/1: Every Eskimo man has at least one song which he makes up and teaches to his wife, who in turn teaches the other women in the camp. The women sing while the man drums and dances. Some of the men have several songs, and there are Eskimos with as many as twenty or thirty.

drum stove† [< G dial. *drumm*] **1** *Obs.* a heating device used in German pioneer homes. See note at **dumb stove**. See also **drum,** *n.* Cp. **drum oven.**
1899 *New Brunswick Mag.* II 134: In the upper halls, dumb or drum stoves, cylindrical in form and made of sheet iron, through which the smoke pipe ran, served to collect heat for the benefit of those portions of dwellings including passage and general bed-rooms.
2 a stove made from an empty oil drum.
1966 ST. PIERRE *Quarter Horse* 24: . . . his cigarette was now sodden at the end and would not draw. He dropped it through a hole in the top of the drum stove. . . .

drunken forest in permafrost regions, a group of trees tilted in various directions by natural forces acting on their shallow root systems.
1957 *Maclean's* 14 Sep. 92/4: High winds or earth movements sometimes capsize whole areas of these unstably based trees, causing what are known as "drunken forests."

dry *n.* **1**† a person who advocates prohibition of the sale of intoxicating beverages.
1920 *Eye Opener* (Calgary) 7 Feb. 1/3: The drys cannot pretend much longer that Alberta is "prohibition".
1957 *Saturday Night* 17 Aug. 36/1: Since my last visit, Halifax has thumbed its nose at the drys, and if Angus L. Macdonald did nothing else he should be remembered with gratitude for the introduction of taverns.
2 a type of slide or avalanche.
1958 WATTERS *B.C.Cent.Anthol.* 340: It was the kind of slide oldtimers called a "dry" or "Whistler." The kind that often follows a fresh snowfall on crust, gathering force and volume with lightning speed, bending or snapping off stray trees like matchwood.

dry† *adj.* **1** forbidding the sale and use of intoxicating beverages.
1915 *Eye Opener* (Calgary) 12 June 1/7: Should the Prohibition Act have passed in the meantime, you will take up your permanent abode in the dry province of Alberta. **1959** *Native Voice* June 4/3: Six Nations Indians voted early in May to end the "dry" status that has always prevailed on the reservation five miles south of here.
2 (quasi-adverbial use, as in *vote dry, go dry*, etc.) against the sale and use of intoxicating beverages.
1910 *Eye Opener* (Calgary) 1 Jan. 1/7: At the recent local elections the town of Newmarket, Ont., went dry.
1922 *Beaver* Feb. 42/1: . . . the Dominion government . . . had legislated the whole country dry. **1938** CASH *I Like B.C.* 110: When local option was exercised here, Victoria voted dry.

Dry Area See quote.
1955 HARDY *Alta Anthol.* 127: The Dust Bowl of Southern Alberta, where I spent much of my earlier life, is not really a dust bowl at all. That's just the fancy name given to it by someone who's never been there. It's also known as the Dry Area, the Drought Area and —since the government took notice of it and formed a Board to administer it—The Special Area.

dry-bag *n.* a waterproof bag in which spare clothing is kept while on the trail.
1943 MILLER *Lone Woodsman* 6: Dan . . . picked out two stout, brown, waterproof duffel bags. Into them went his red . . . Hudson's Bay blanket . . . a dry-bag containing thick socks . . . and a sleeping toque.

dry beaver *Fur Trade, Hist.* See **parchment beaver.**
[**1790** (1934) HEARNE & TURNOR *Journals* 323: They brought a few Summer Beaver, some dry, and a little fresh Moose flesh. . . .] **1962** (1964) INNIS *Fur Trade in Can.* 65: The sale of surplus dry beaver in Holland and other markets reduced the price and prejudiced the position of the fermier.

dry bee *Hist.* a bee at which no liquor was served.
[**1836** *Cdn Temperance Advocate* June 16/1: Several "raisings" have taken place this Spring, at which scarcely any liquor has been seen, and at which there has been no drunkeness; and it is to be immediately tried whether a "bee" cannot be mustered at which no spirits will be used. Men who stated as their only reason for not joining, was that they could get no men to come to a raising without spirits, have been told to try, and if none will come the members of the Temperance Society will do the work.] **1960** *Ont.Hist.* June 95: To combat the liberal dispensing of liquor at the bees which accompanied the raisings of buildings like barns and mills, the township's Quakers instituted "dry bees" which became more common with the spread of temperance societies.

Dry Belt 1 on the Prairies, an extensive region of low precipitation, roughly bounded by Moose Jaw, Saskatchewan, and Medicine Hat, Alberta. See also **dry-land.** Also *Alkali Dry Belt.*
1902 (1957) *Sask.Hist.* Spring 13: We sped on towards Moose Jaw, traversing a district recently settled by homesteaders who seem to have much faith in the future of this gumbo region at the outskirts of the dry belt. **1952** PUTNAM *Cdn Regions* 403/1: The Dry Belt has no population nucleus or regional centre, although Swift Current and Medicine Hat might be considered as rivals for this function.
2 in British Columbia, a long tract of arid broken country stretching from the United States border to Prince George and lying between the Monashee Range (east of the Okanagan Valley) and the Coast Range.
1887 ROBERTS *Western Avernus* 137: . . . we had now passed out of the up-country Wet Belt, and were in the Dry Belt, where the rain did not fall all the year round.
1957 HUTCHISON *Canada* 297: Now the last black skeletons of Wallachin's orchards confirm the decisive fact of vegetable life in the Dry Belt—its absolute dependence on a trickle of moisture.

dry diggings† *Placer Mining* gold claims away from the bed of a stream. See also **bank diggings.** Cp. **bar diggings.**
1858 *British Colonist* (Victoria) 11 Dec. 1/2: These are in fact a species of dry diggings, but it is beyond doubt that the other kind of dry diggings exist plentifully in the north. **1897** GOODMAN *Gold Fields* 7: "Dry diggings" shall mean any mine over which a river never extends.
1960 *Statutes of B.C.* 3584: In "dry diggings" a claim shall be 250 feet square.

dry farm† a farm in a semi-arid region operated without irrigation.
1952 PUTNAM *Cdn Regions* 376/2: The irrigated farms of southern Alberta are, of course, smaller than the non-irrigated but, on a small scale map, they are outweighed by the extra size of the dry farms and grazing areas.

dry farming† a technique of farming in a semi-arid region without recourse to irrigation.
1945 HAIG *Brave Harvest* 165: "Furthermore, the Mormons did not 'discover the system of dry farming'; neither did they bring the method to western Canada. The system of summer cultivation and the packing of the soil to hold the moisture was first advocated in western Canada by Angus MacKay, a Scottish-Canadian superintendent of the Dominion Government Experimental Farm at Indian Head, Saskatchewan, as early as 1889. . . ." **1965** *Modern Instructor* April 461: The "dry farming" type of agriculture as practised in Saskatchewan some years ago, resulted in the development of methods . . . to increase the moisture content of the soil and control weeds.

dry fish 1 See **dried fish**.
2 *Maritimes* cod that have been full weather-cured on flakes. See also **dry fishery**. Cp. **green fish**.
1905 DUNCAN *Grenfell's Parish* 92n: A quintal is, roughly, a hundred pounds. One hundred quintals of green fish are equal, roughly, to thirty of dry, which at $3, would amount to $90.

dry fishery *Nfld* a method of commercial fishing involving the drying of the catch on flakes, *q.v.*
1960 RYERSON *Founding of Can.* 74: There were two methods employed in the fishery. In the "green" or "wet" fishery, the catch was salted directly on board ship; in the "dry" or "shore" fishery, the catch was taken ashore and dried on specially built stagings or "flakes." **1965** MACNUTT *Atlantic Provinces* 4: Their [New Englanders'] own "dry" fishery . . . became a power in its own right.

dry fishing See **dry fishery**.
1930 (1964) INNIS *Fur Trade in Canada* 9: Increasing demands for improvement in handling fish led to the development of dry fishing which reduced the outlay on such commodities as salt, and economized shipping. . . . Dry fishing stimulated the search for harbours suitable for drying and preferably with supplies of bait.
1963 MORTON *Kingdom of Canada* 12: In dry fishing, the fish were dried on platforms called flakes before being lightly salted and shipped, and this of course required landing, and a brief season's residence on shore.

dry goods† clothing, yard goods, etc.
1765 *Quebec Gaz.* 24 Jan. 4/1: Hunter & M'Fie . . . imported a Parcel of Dry Goods, agreeable to this market, last Fall; such as road-cloths, Velvets, Plushes, Thicksets. **1876** LORD *Wilderness* 65: . . . it will sooner or later get broken, if used for the conveyance . . . such for instance as "dry goods," meaning trans-Atlantically drapery, hosiery and clothing in general, or what is called by packers, "Jews freight." **1959** MOWAT *Desperate People* 221: Ellen was impressed by the number of unpainted and false-front stores offering all sorts of hardware and dry goods.

dry herd *West* See quote.
1926 DICKIE *Cdn West* 254: To make a rapid trip Strong divided the herd, sending the steers, the dry herd as it

was called, first, and letting the cows and calves follow.

drying-beach *n. Nfld* a beach for curing the catch taken by fishermen engaged in the dry fishery, *q.v.*
1965 MACNUTT *Atlantic Provinces* 8: . . . it was not until 1662 that France established a military, naval, and commercial base at Placentia which was said to offer the best drying-beach in Newfoundland.

drying house *Obs.* a building, such as a smokehouse, for drying and curing fish.
1829 MACTAGGART *Three Years* I 10: Drying-houses should be built on this coast where so much timber grows, and these valuable fish properly cured. . . .

drying stage 1 *Nfld* See **flake**.
1907 MILLAIS *Newfoundland* 148: The women work on the drying stages as well as the men, laying out the fish whenever the sun shines, and piling into heaps under layers of bark whenever it threatens to rain.

2 *North* a platform of poles, usually high enough to be out of reach of dogs or predatory animals, on which fish or meat are placed to dry. See also **stage**, *n.* (def. 3) and **staging** (def. 1). Cp. **dried fish** and **dried meat** (def. 2). Cp. **fish-stage** (def. 1).
1922 *Beaver* Aug. 14/2: . . . put up on the drying stage some four or five hundred whitefish and trout. . . .
1963 SPRY *Palliser* 139: They stocked up with meat but had to travel for two days before they found poplar trees big enough to make poles for drying-stages on which it could be exposed. . . .

dry-ki† ['drɑɪki] *n.* See **dry-kill timber**.

dry-kill timber† See quote.
1947 ROWLANDS *Cache Lake* 48: That is what they call dry-ki, a shortening of "dry-kill timber"—trees killed by fire, but still standing. Dry-ki has also come to mean timber killed by the backwater when they raise the level of the lakes for lumbering.

dry-land *n.* an area of low precipitation, such as the Dry Belt (def. 1).
1917 *Eye Opener* (Calgary) 6 Jan. 3/5: Jan Johnson and Katrina Jensen married and took up a dry land homestead. **1953** *Cdn Geog.Jnl* June 241/2: . . . the development of such an irrigation area does materially help the nearby dry regions . . . by providing a market for dry-land cattle for finishing, by providing a sure source of feed and seed in drought cycles, and by bringing nearer to the dry-land farmer the superior service facilities of the more densely occupied irrigation districts.

drylander *n.* a person who settled in a region of low precipitation, especially the Dry Belt (def. 1).
1963 *Western Wkly Supp.* 6 Nov. 3: [Caption] All-too-familiar to many a pioneer of the prairies is this shot from the "Drylanders"—the moving story of courage in the Canadian west now being shown by the National Film Board through Columbia Pictures. **1963** *Time* (Cdn ed.) 11 Oct. 16/2: At the Tivoli theater in Saskatoon last week, surviving drylanders could be heard telling the youngsters: "That was the way it was."

dry meat *Hist.* See **dried meat** (def. 1).
1864 *Nor'Wester* (R.R.S.) 9 Nov. 3/2: The dry-meat hunters [of buffalo] are dropping in daily and we are happy to state that in general they are well loaded.
1929 JEFFERSON *Saskatchewan* 27: [In 1878] . . . I found a small sheet of "dry meat" on the road. It was almost like a piece of leather, and did not look appetizing in the least, but it served me to munch for many a mile. This

comestible, if it be not expedient to crisp it on a fire—when it is much improved—must simply be gnawed like a piece of rawhide.

dry permafrost See quote. Cp. **permafrost.**
1957 *Maclean's* 14 Sep. 90/4: Recent tests have shown that there is a condition known as "dry permafrost"—that is, permanently frozen soil or gravel containing no moisture.

dry portage a portage which one can traverse dry-shod.
1939 *Beaver* March 47/1: Our dogs hauled our goods—we had packs of furs and meat now—over the dry portages. Sometimes on the trail these huskies fought. These fights, though often serious, were comical too—the dogs with packs strapped to their backs dashing back and forth and getting tangled.

dry sink See quote.
1963 *Maclean's* 9 Feb. 22/3: A dry sink is a pioneer's wooden cabinet with a sunken top in which sat the family dishpan. Today dry sinks are usually filled with liquor bottles, records, or plants. *Ibid.* 20/3: . . . Ontario dry sinks [are] worth seventy-five dollars. . . .

dry snye *Obs.* a dry side channel which, when deepened and filled with water from a snye-dam, *q.v.*, served as a by-pass enabling raftsmen to avoid rapids. Cp. **snye** (def. 1b).
1826 *Kingston Chron.* (U.C.) 3 Nov. 2/5: We are also busy forming a channel through the rapids, for the sake of the raftsmen—this is done by building two strong dams, and deepening what is called a *dry snie.*

dry summer beaver *Fur Trade, Hist.* unprime, or inferior, skins of parchment beaver, *q.v.* See also **summer beaver.**
c**1735** (1899) WILLSON *Great Company* 238: The dry summer beaver, not much valued [bring] about one shilling and ninepence [a pound]. **1962** (1964) INNIS *Fur Trade in Can.* 105: . . . arrangements were made January 4, 1733, to receive dry summer beaver for the following year at 20 sols, and fat summer beaver at 35 sols la livre.

dry the pot finish what remains of the food.
1933 MERRICK *True North* 116: Kay had just baked, and Victor said the rose bread was the best thing he ever ate. John and Victor "dried the pot," splitting the last partridge.

dry wash† *West* a gully cut by erosion but with no stream in its bed.
1962 *Bad Lands of the Red Deer River* 25: The pieces that have eroded out of their original position and are lying scattered at the base of the cliffs or in dry washes where they have been carried by run-off are of no value scientifically but are highly prized by the finder.

dry winter beaver *Fur Trade, Hist.* prime skins of parchment beaver, *q.v.* See also **winter beaver.**
1962 (1964) INNIS *Fur Trade in Can.* 105: On June 6, 1746, as a result of the war, prices of beaver were increased . . . dry winter beaver 55 sols to 3 livres 16 sols;—other beaver, summer and late autumn, 20 sols to 30 sols *la livre.*

D'Sonoqua *n.* See **Tsonoqua.**

dual-member constituency See **two-member constituency.** See also **dual riding.**
1963 *Globe and Mail* (Toronto) 11 May 8/5: One of the two remaining dual-member constituencies in Canada, Halifax . . . is entitled on a population basis to an additional member at the present time.

dual nomination meeting one party meeting to nominate candidates for both federal and provincial elections.
1963 *Kingston Whig-Standard* (Ont.) 7 Feb. 6/2: He has been attempting to contact Transport Minister James Auld (MPP for Leeds) to check on the holding of a dual (federal-provincial) nomination meeting.

dual riding an electoral district that is represented in the House of Commons by two Members of Parliament or Members of the Legislative Assembly.
1963 *Globe and Mail* (Toronto) 2 Mar. 8/1: The PCs should hold both seats in the dual riding of Queens [P.E.I.]. . . . **1965** *Ibid.* 29 Apr. 5/3: In addition to the present dual riding of Queen's . . . P.E.I. has the ridings of Kings . . . and Prince. . . .

dubshot *n.* See quote.
1941 *Beaver* Sep. 37/1: Dubshot. In pitsawing, the end of the log not sawn through.

ducent *n. Cdn French, Obs.* See **bowsman.** See also **devant.**
1800 (1897) COUES *New Light* I 49: Jacques Barbé: Voyageur, bowman (ducent). **1810** *Ibid.* II 610: At daybreak two canoes set off for the Columbia. The first contained: Delcour, ducent; Methode, guide; Delcour and Roberge, middlemen. . . . **1931** NUTE *Voyageur* 26: [There was] a still larger paddle, which the bowsman or foreman (*avant de canot, devant,* or *ducent*) employed when running rapids or leaping small falls.

duck camp a hunting lodge providing accommodation for duck hunters.
1966 *Globe and Mail* (Toronto) 14 Jan. 45/5: [He] operated the Albany Goose and Duck Camp at Fort Albany on James Bay.

duck factory *Slang* in the southern prairies, an area of sloughs where ducks nest.
1964 *Guardian* (Charlottetown) 18 June 1/3: The duck factory is the name wildlife people give a southern prairie region, which is the breeding ground for the majority of North America's hunted waterfowl.

ducks and drakes *Obs.* See quote.
1846 BONNYCASTLE *Canada and the Canadians* II 234: . . . the real and dangerous lake . . . is everywhere beset with "ducks and drakes", as its rocky and treacherous islets are called.

dude† [dud *or* djud] *n.* [origin unknown]
☛ *This word has had many subtle meanings, almost all of them derogatory and often connoting distrust on the part of the user.*

1 *Esp.West* a non-westerner or a newly-arrived settler who affects stylish eastern clothes.
1883 *Prince Albert Times* (Sask.) 4 July 5/1: The dude is one of those creatures which are perfectly harmless, and are a necessary evil to civilization. **1962** *Field, Horse & Rodeo* Nov. 30/1: Well, chances are Mr. Dude, you've been getting a silent horse laugh yourself from your trusty cayuse.

2 a dandy; an elegant person, or one who affects elegance; snob.
1900 OSBORN *Greater Canada* 75: Is not the West a free country, and must not a man shun the soap-dish and hair-brush, except on festal occasions, if he wants to be

known as a worker and not a "dude"? **1910** MCCLUNG *Second Chance* 19: Camilla . . . took them for Mrs. Francis to see, and also for the boys to see themselves in the long mirror. . . . Danny sidled up to Mrs. Francis and said in a confidential whisper: "Ain't I the biggest dood in the bunch?" **1918** MACKAY *Trench and Trail* 26:

> You have often sold a daughter
> To some dude across the water,
> While the title high which bought her
> You so seemingly ignore;
> Why not send us a cotillion
> Of those girls who own a million
> For our hardy northern gillian
> On the old Canadian shore?

3 an inexperienced person; greenhorn.
1912 LONDON *Smoke Bellew* 33: He's going down to Dawson with a couple of dudes and another gentleman's man—camp-cook, boatman, and general all-round hustler. **1951** HOBSON *Grass* 51: I don't like to see these dudes or smart Indians taking these three hundred yard shots, unless there's no other way. **1958** *Edmonton Jnl* 12 Aug. 15/6: The election was held following the return of some 60 dude and veteran members from their six-day camp. . . .

dude ranch† *West* a ranch which takes paying guests, providing riding, barbecues, square dances, etc.
1962 FRY *Ranch on the Cariboo* 214: Pete was trying to make a dude ranch out of a place that wasn't big enough or suitable for stock.

Duffield(s) *n. Obs.* See **duffle** (def. 1).
1741 (1932) KENNEY *Fort Churchill* 101: No person Could Endure the Cold in this Country without this Contrivance. The Shoes they were here are of the Leather of deer-skins or Canvas, made big enough to contain their feet when cover'd with Yarn Stockings and three pair of socks of coarse Duffield over them.
1749 *Short State of North America* 19: [If] Duffields, Strouds, Blankets, and other coarse Woolen, and Iron and Copper Manufactures, which would serve them for Coverings Cloaths, and for other Conveniences, were carried to them, that then the remaining three 4ths, now lost to *Britain,* would come to Market.

duffle or **duffel** ['dʌfəl] *n.* [< *Duffel,* a town near Antwerp] **1** a very closely woven woollen cloth. See also **Duffield.** Cp. **stroud.** Earlier also *duffles*.
1674 (1942) *H.B.C.Minutes* 108: Ordered . . . that Mr. Holmes provide 4 pieces of duffals. . . . **1784** (1954) *Moose Ft Jnls* 204: Red Duffle all gone long ago, Blankets nearly so. **1896** WHITNEY *On Snow-Shoes* 61: The Indian gets his duffel by the yard, and when he has cut it into strips—about six inches wide by eighteen inches long his socks are completed. **1958** *Edmonton Jnl* 24 June 3 9/8: When it is warmer, he wears a parka of duffel. . . .

2 (*usually plural*) **a.** See **duffle sock** (def. 1). Cp. **duffle sock** (def. 2).
1913 CURRAN & CALKINS *Northland* 311: No matter how careful he is, there is bound to be more or less moisture in his moccasins and duffels (socks made in the shape of moccasins out of blanket material, and worn over light stockings and under heavy outside ones) and if they are not dried out daily sore feet are sure to be the result. **1964** *Nat.Geog.* May 722/2: An inner shoe, known as "duffle," is worn in cold weather, as well as ordinary woolen socks.

b. See **duffle stocking.**
1884 *Prince Albert Times* (Sask.) 21 Mar. 3/3: Before going to bed, dry duffels moccasins and duffels are put on the feet, the leggings and over coat taken off, the cap tied on firmly and sometimes it is a case of shiver all night. **1926** DICKIE *Cdn West* 147: The duffels reached up to the knee and were tied there to keep the snow out. Moccasins were worn over the duffels. **1962** DICKIE *Great Golden Plain* 118: In the winter the children wore coats made of Hudson's Bay blankets with a strip of leather for a belt, leggings called "duffels" made of blanket cloth, with moccasins over them, and woollen caps pulled down over their ears.

3 personal belongings such as were carried in a duffle-bag, *q.v.*; personal gear carried on the trail.
1938 *Beaver* Sep. 16/1: Perhaps Harry Paull had a pack of cards somewhere in his duffle, but he did not carry a gun. **1964** *Weekend Mag.* 11 July 20/3: They emptied the canoe of duffle and food and eagerly ran the rapids.

4 See **duffle-bag.**
1946 *Trail Riders* Oct. 10/1: Duffles are packed and we are still sitting about. . . . **1957** FISHER *Pemmican* 32: In the next moment he had let his duffel slip off his shoulder and over his head.

duffle-bag *n.* a large bag of heavy cloth or canvas, used for carrying personal belongings. See also **duffle** (def. 4).
1924 FLAHERTY *Eskimo Friends* 145: He smiled "good morning," as he took up my duffle-bag and eiderdown and handed them out to be lashed aboard the sledge. **1964** *Atlantic Advocate* July 62/2: We found it cramped going, prodded from all sides by duffle bags, fishing rods and elbows.

duffle dickie a parka or atigi (def. 2) made of duffle.
1916 HAWKES *Labrador Eskimo* 39: Over the fur or duffle dickey a cotton slip . . . is drawn. **1933** *Beaver* Mar. 208: The Canadian Eskimo woman's dress consists usually of a sealskin artiggi or duffle dickie equipped with a hood, sealskin trousers (north of the circle) . . . and sealskin boots terminating below the knees with a pucker string.

duffle moccasin or **slipper** See **duffle sock** (def. 1).
1884 *Prince Albert Times* (Sask.) 21 Mar. 3/3: Before going to bed, dry duffel moccasins and duffels are put on the feet. . . . **1933** MERRICK *True North* 284: On the side of the bank we built a fire, got dry socks and duffel slippers and moccasins off the sled and sat on a blown-down tree to put them on. **1942** TWOMEY & HERRICK *Needle to the North* 59: They were in soft skin boots, well mattressed with the inside duffle moccasins and several pairs of wool socks.

duffle neap See **duffle sock** (def. 1).
1921 HEMING *Drama of the Forests* 212: Over the rabbit pelts, I wore my regular woollen socks, duffel neaps, and caribou-skin mitten moccasins.

duffle sock 1 a warm ankle-length sock, or liner, of duffle worn inside moccasins, mukluks, etc. and usually folded down at the top. See also **duffle** (def. 2a), **duffle moccasin, moccasin sock,** and **Siwash sock.** Cp. **German sock.**
☛ *It is difficult to know which specific kind of duffle sock or stocking is being referred to in many contexts, the commonest term nowadays being* duffles, *which most often refers to ankle-length socks or slippers.*

1933 MERRICK *True North* 193: Then he remembers he forgot to put on his duffel sock and has to take off his moccasin and legging. **1941** *Beaver* Dec. 24/1: I had . . . duffle socks, with a thin pair of worsted socks next to my feet. . . . **1958** *Evening Telegram* (St. John's) 24 Apr. 17/1: As my "trail clothes" were not yet ready, I borrowed duffle socks, a pair of matik (skin boots) and a huge pair of duffle pants from Corporal Johnson.

2 *Obs.* one of a pair of wrap-around, puttee-like leg coverings made of long strips of duffle, and worn inside moccasins, etc. Cp. **duffle** (def. 2a).
[**1741** (1932) KENNEY *Fort Churchill* 101: No person Could Endure the Cold in this Country without this Contrivance. The Shoes they were here are of the Leather of deer-skins or Canvas, made big enough to contain their feet when cover'd with Yarn Stockings and three pair of socks of coarse Duffield over them.]
1748 ELLIS *Hudson's Bay* 158: . . . we wore two or three Pair of Blanket, or thick Duffil Socks to prevent our Feet freezing. . . .

duffle stocking a long stocking of duffle worn over inner socks inside moccasins, mukluks, etc. See note at **duffle sock** (def. 1). See also **duffle** (def. 2b). Cp. **German sock**.
1888 (1890) ST. MAUR *Impressions* 255: They also wear over their ordinary clothing long red duffel stockings, and over them, boots lined with flannel.

duffle vamp *Lab.* See **duffle sock** (def. 1).
1933 MERRICK *True North* 18: The women are busy these days . . . making duffel vamps and mitts. . . .

dugout *n.* **1** See **dugout canoe**.
1840 *St.Catharines Jnl* (U.C.) 6 Aug. 1/2: We have travelled by rail-road, stage, steam-boat, schooner and dug out. **1966** *Kingston Whig-Standard* (Ont.) 6 Feb. 4/5: Dugouts were sometimes used, made from a hollow tree if possible, to avoid the work of burning and chopping out the wood.

2 a shelter made by excavating, usually in the side of a hill, often serving as a temporary dwelling.
1888 (1890) ST. MAUR *Impressions* 45: All the people here, who have poultry, find the necessity of keeping them very warm, and either make them "dug-outs" or else comfortable wooden houses. **1958** SCOTT *Prairie Provinces* 134: In some cases the first "house" was a "dug-out." This was a cave that was dug in a low hillside. The front was built up of stones and sod.

3 *Prairies* a large shallow excavation intended to hold the spring run-off and rain, serving as a reservoir. See also **dam²**, **farm dugout**, **pothole** (def. 3b), and **scoop-out**.
1947 TAYLOR *Canada* 229: If there are streams they can be dammed, if not then the pioneer has to rely on "dug-outs" cut in clay soil, in which he can collect surface water or winter snow. **1953** MOON *Saskatchewan* 77: The water-filled dugouts on thousands of Saskatchewan farms bear its imprint. **1964** *Albertan* (Calgary) 7 July 17/8: [She] . . . drowned Saturday in a dugout on a farm near this [Alberta] community. . . .

A Nootka dugout canoe

dugout canoe† a canoe, *q.v.*, hewn from a single log. See also **dugout** (def. 1) and **log canoe**.

1859 (1863) PALLISER *Journals* 153: . . . a couple of Shouswap Indians . . . had come up the river in a rough "dug-out" wooden canoe, in search of us. **1938** (1950) STANWELL-FLETCHER *Driftwood Valley* 170: It is one of Charlie's dugout canoes . . . thirty feet long and is made, as are all dugouts in this country, from the trunk of a huge balsam poplar. After a careful selection of the tree the Indians fell it, and then start a slow fire inside. When the fire has partially hollowed out the trunk, the rest of the shaping and cleaning process is continued by axe and knife until there is a smooth, shapely interior. Wooden stretchers are wedged across the two ends and middle, and it is ready for use. If the boat is badly balanced, big stones are placed in its bottom. **1966** *Native Voice* Apr. 2/2: He [Rev. Thomas Crosby] . . . surveyed the whole area from Cape Mudge to Victoria and up the Fraser River to Yale in a dugout canoe.

Dukhobor *n.* See **Doukhobor**.

dumb stove† *Obs.* See **drum stove** (def. 1).
☛ *Possibly so called by folk etymology since the "stove" had no fire in it, being simply an expansion in a stovepipe.*

dump *n.* **1** *Placer Mining* **a.** the pile of gold-bearing dirt excavated and waiting to be washed in the sluice boxes.
1898 *Yukon Midnight Sun* (Dawson) 11 June 1/1: There are other men on Eldorado who are not obtaining as much from their dumps as expected, and these estimate the total yield of the creek much lower. **1913** OGILVIE *Yukon* 187: An estimate of the value of the dump—pile of pay dirt taken out—placed it at one hundred and thirty thousand dollars. **1958** BERTON *Klondike* 67: He and Stander began to hire men to help them haul the dirt up by windlass and pile it on the great "dump" which, when the spring thaw came, would be shoveled into sluiceboxes so that the gold could be washed free of the clay and gravel.
b. See **tailings** (def. 1).
1897 LADUE *Klondyke Facts* 129: Two ladies, Mrs. Lippi . . . and Mrs. Berry, picked out of a dump $6,000 each in a few days after their arrival. **1915** CUMMING *Skookum Chuck* 28: He engaged others to take charge of the tail race and dump, with which he would not trust his brother on previous occasions.

2 *Lumbering* a place where logs are piled, as on the bank of a river, by a railway siding, road, etc., ready for moving out to the mill. See also **log dump** (def. 2).
1910 FERGUSON *Janey Canuck* 97: The men at "the dump" were piling the logs on huge skidways, thirty feet high. **1942** HAIG-BROWN *Timber* 250: A log dump, or "the dump", is commonly a trestle built out over water. Generally an apron of piles slopes down from it and the logs roll down this when they are dumped from the cars. **1964** *Cdn Geog.Jnl* Feb. 67/1: From here, logs would be taken to a "dump" at the river's edge where they waited in great log piles for the spring drive.

3 on a portage, a staging point or resting place, where pieces of cargo are dropped before being packed to the next point; a **pose** (def. 2).
1941 *Beaver* June 38: This is the longest of the three big portages and the freight is relayed across in three dumps.

4† a place where waste is dumped, as slag from mines, refuse from cities, and other detritus. See also **garbage dump**.

1923 MACMECHAN *Sagas of Sea* 119: Even in a dump exposed to the air, coal generates heat and gas.
1966 *Sun* (Vancouver) 27 May 1/2: The striking Vancouver Civic Employees Union (Outside Workers) will pull their pickets from the dump for a 24-hour period starting at midnight today.

5 a waterfall.
1945 MOORE *Castle Buck* 108: The line was still going out when the fish went over the dump and made a slicing scoot for that old windfall. *Ibid.* 195: It [a large salmon] was now heading for a fall, or "dump", that I could not attempt to navigate and live.

dump *v.* **1** *Lumbering* drop a pile of logs from the bank into the water. See also **dump,** *n.* (def. 2).
1928 PERRY *Two Reds* 109: Leclerk came to her cabin with the announcement that one of the rollways was to be dumped, though the break-out had been set for the following day. The big skid had been completed and they were going to try it out.

2 of a sleigh, boat, etc., overturn or capsize, throwing out its passengers.
1945 HAIG *Brave Harvest* 5: This latter was more chancey, for you might dump into the banks of soft snow. **1960** *Ottawa Citizen* 14 July 42/8: A dozen 14-foot International dinghies started the race and more than half "dumped." They were righted by their crews however, and when the storm had passed they returned to harbour safely.

dump-box *n. Placer Mining, Hist.* a box used in washing the dump (def. 1a).
1868 (1962) ANDERSON *Sawney's Letters* 34: Wash! Wash! Wash!/And rattle the rocks around,/Is the song the Dump-box sings. . . , **1869** (1960) RAMSAY *Barkerville* 45: . . . the dance now most appreciated is that which is induced by the monotonous music of the water as it runs over a glittering dump-box.

dump car a self-unloading gondola railway car; also, in mining, a smaller car made to drop its load by levers or by tipping.
1912 BICKERSTETH *Open Doors* 141: As the train was a mixed passenger and freight, we were constantly stopping at various places to take on or put off "flat-cars" full of gravel, or "dump-cars" full of "dirt" deposited there by the steam shovel, trucks loaded with rails or ties, "box-cars" full of provisions, coal or lumber. **1956** *Ont. Dept of Mines Rep.* 5 Jan.: They were using a 1½-ton Manchu battery-operated electric trammer with five 1-ton end dump cars.

dun *n. Nfld* an inferior grade of cured codfish, soft and dingy brown. See also **broken fish.** Also *dun fish.*
1819 ANSPACH *Hist. Nfld* 440: Some people prefer this dun fish for present use; but it will not stand the voyage. **1840** MURRAY *Brit. Amer.* II 127: There remain the dunfish and others discoloured, broken, and otherwise damaged, which nevertheless may be as fit as others for immediate consumption, to which they are therefore applied. **1883** HATTON & HARVEY *Nfld* 291: When thoroughly dried [cod] have a whitish appearance and are then ready for storing. In due time they reach the merchant's wharf or store, where they are weighed and "culled" or sorted into four different kinds called Merchantable (the best), Madiera, West India (intended for the consumption of the Negroes) and Dun,

or broken fish, which will not keep, and is intended for home use.

dun *adj. Nfld* **become (or go) dun,** of cured codfish, turn dingy brown and soft.
1819 ANSPACH *Hist. Nfld* 440: To mention one defect more, it may become *dun,* if left too long in the pile, which happens sometimes from want of sufficient store-room and of an opportunity to ship it off in the proper time: the weather beating into the piles softens the fish and gives it a black, snuffy, or dun colour. **1958** *Evening Telegram* (St. John's) 24 Apr. 4/2: A good fish . . . can be sunburned on the flake, go slimey in the pile or dun in the store.

duplex *n.* **1** a building consisting of two dwellings under one roof, either side by side or one below the other. Cp. **fiveplex, fourplex,** and **triplex.**
1958 *Dawson Creek Star* (B.C.) 3 Jan. 1/2: Permits for three duplexes, $38,000. **1963** *Kingston Whig-Standard* (Ont.) 2 Jan. 1/8: Mr. Sullivan . . . yelled down to . . . [the] owner of the two-storey frame duplex. . . .

2 one of the dwellings of such a building.
1959 *Ottawa Citizen* 17 Jan. 12/4: Emile Groulx, 68, living in the upstairs duplex, also smelled smoke. . . .

3 *Lumbering* See 1942 quote.
1942 HAIG-BROWN *Timber* 256: A yarder may be a single-purpose donkey or it may be a "duplex" machine, having loading drums as well as mainline and haulback drums fed their steam from the same boiler. **1960** SWANSON *Railroad Logging* 5: Most old-time loggers will remember Bloedel, Stewart and Welch's big logging camp . . . near Powell River. This camp started operations also in 1911 and the superintendent's name was Reilly, who . . . invented the steam duplex system of loading and used railways to a larger extent than ever before used in the woods. **1963** *Press* Apr. 9: There's where you hear the duplex shrill / As it roars, screams and whines. . . .

A Durham boat

Durham boat† [from a similar craft designed about 1750 by Robert Durham of Pennsylvania] *Hist.* a river-boat having a false keel and shallow draught, somewhat less than 100 feet in length and propelled by sails or poles, much used in the early 19th century on the St. Lawrence and its tributaries for freight and passengers.
1812 *Kingston Gaz.* (U.C.) 19 Sep. 3/3: They had two large Durham Boats filled with men, one of them with a six-pounder on board, and two smaller Boats. **1846** BONNYCASTLE *Canada and Canadians* I 93: . . . the Durham boat, a long decked barge, square ahead, and square astern, has now vanished. . . . It was neither invented by nor named after Lord Durham. . . . **1900** *Trans. Roy. Soc. Can.* VI 2 35: In 1835, there were 800 Durham boats and 1500 batteaux engaged in the navigation of Lake Ontario and the St. Lawrence river. **1961** GREENING *Ottawa* 80: There were also the

Durham boats, of similar design [to the bateau] but somewhat larger.

Durhamite [ˈdɜˑrəmˌaɪt] *n. Hist.* a person supporting the reforms advocated by Lord Durham in his *Report* of 1839.

1839 *Bytown* [Ottawa] *Gaz.* 24 Oct. 1/1: (Patriot) Whose heart's as false as his liver's white, / Be sure that man is "A Durhamite". **1937** *Cdn Hist.Rev.* XVIII 34: A volley of stones put the "Durhamites" to flight, one being carried off wounded, and others hiding in cellars, in the woods, or among the rushes of the lake-shore.

dust *n.* gold dust.

1859 (1935) STRANG *Pioneers in Canada* 220: . . . the average yield of "dust" was no less than four ounces each man, equal to about sixty-four dollars (£12 16s.), besides the nuggets. **1958** *Fisherman* 10 Oct. 6/2: Here the miners . . . lost their hard-earned dust in gambling.

Dust Bowl a region subject to dust storms in arid years, specifically the Dry Belt (def. 1). See also **Drought Area.** Also spelled *dust bowl.*

1953 *Cdn Geog.Jnl* July 70/2: The first year is 1937, the year of the worst crop failure, the climax year of the "dust-bowl." **1955** HARDY *Alta Anthol.* 128: What little they had, they shared with one another; and somehow, in doing so, their humble little shacks became palaces in the Dust Bowl.

dust-bowl days or **years** *Hist.* See **Dirty Thirties.**

1953 *Cdn Geog.Jnl* July 73/2: It is the land which, in 1952, fulfilled its promise . . . which had a hollow ring in the dust-bowl days of the hungry thirties. **1964** *Maclean's* 2 May 1/2: [This] is considerably higher than the national average and several times more than farmers earned during the harsh, dust-bowl years of the 1930s. **1966** *Cdn Geog.Jnl* June IV: This book gives a very sharp portrait of the Province of Saskatchewan in those terrible "dust-bowl" years, the dirty thirties, as they were called.

dust hawk *Slang* a horse driven in sulky races.

1916 PARKER *World for Sale* 221: ". . . I wasn't off my feed, nor hadn't lost my head neither. I wanted that dust hawk and he knew it; but I got it on him with the harness and the sulky."

Dutch† *n.* See **Dutchman** (def. 1).

1829 MACTAGGART *Three Years* I 311: The Dutch copy the Canadians: have their houses small and comfortable. **1830** MOORSOM *Letters N.S.* 307: The settlers of German extraction throughout Nova Scotia are commonly called "Dutch," although there are but few to whom that national appellative is strictly appropriate.

Dutch† *adj.* of or having to do with settlers of German extraction. See also **Dutchman** (def. 1).

1816 (1818) HALL *Travels* 94: We returned through the village, which is one of the neatest in the province; the houses are placed in the Dutch fashion, with the gable end to the road. **1860** *Grumbler* (Toronto) 7 Apr. 1/3: O Lager-beer, fine Lager-beer, I likes it vera much; I likes it, 'cause it's Lager-beer. I likes it, 'cause it's Dutch. *c*1916 (1922) WALLACE *Shack Locker* 43: "I'm Dutch and can't pronounce my yays—I cal'late dat oder feller was Dutch, too. . . ." **1942** RADDALL *His Majesty's Yankees* 23: The girl spoke distinctly but in the rich Dutch accent of the Lunenburgers.

Dutch *v.* provide with a Dutch-cut, *q.v.*

1922 STRINGER *Prairie Child* 86: The barber, in fact,

refused to take any money for Dutching my small daughter's hair. . . .

Dutch barn† a type of bank barn, *q.v.*, used by settlers in Upper Canada, a style introduced by American settlers, who learned the design from the Pennsylvania Dutch.

1961 *Ont.Hist.* Mar. 21: This is an excellent example of a "Dutch" barn and will be used eventually as a farm museum [at Edgeley, Ont., built 1809].

Dutch-cut *n. Hist.* a style of haircut such that the hair, combed straight back, is bobbed on a level with the ear lobes.

[**1922** STRINGER *Prairie Child* 85: I escorted Pauline Augusta to Hunk Granby, the town barber, to have her hair cut Dutch.] **1954** HAMILTON *Prairies* 107: The men wore their hair in what was known as the "Dutch cut." **1958** *Weekend Mag.* 28 June 39/1: Though he was in his seventies, his hair was still jet black, and he wore it combed straight back and cut in the original Ojibway fashion, bobbed just below his ears—Dutch-cut they used to call it.

Dutch lever *Hist.* See quote.

1829 MACTAGGART *Three Years* I 311: . . . above the well [of a Dutch settler] is sure to be placed the long Dutch lever, a large spar, often nearly thirty feet long, balanced on a fulcrum of about twelve feet high; a chain is fixed to the upper end, and a hook, by which the can or pail is let down to the well, and when full, the lever, to return to its equilibrium, assists the drawer of water to bring it up—a simple and useful invention.

Dutchman† *n.* **1** a settler of German extraction, especially during colonial days, as a Pennsylvania Dutch Loyalist or as in the Lunenburg region of Nova Scotia. See also **Dutch,** *n.* and *adj.*

1829 MACTAGGART *Three Years* II 5: Water may attract the *willow* to a certain extent, which may account for the Dutchman's art in discovering spring-wells with a forked stick. **1853** STRICKLAND *Canada West* II 141: I hired a Dutchman from the settlement with his lumber-sleigh and span of horses to move my family. . . . **1903** RICHARDSON *Colin* 102: "Th' only man es I've iver heered on, es could beat Nathan at th' table wuz Schmidt, th' Dutchman. . . ." **1916** WALLACE *Shack Locker* 43: ". . . I'm a Nova Scotia Dutchman, but I can spot an old country Deutscher ten faddom away. . . ."

2 *Obs.* a keg of liquor.

1830 (1953) *Beaver* Dec. 51/1: There is also a keg of liquor (called the Dutchman) from which the people are drammed three or four times a day, according to the state of the Weather.

Dutch mess See quote.

1959 *Maclean's* 28 Mar. 27/1: [Lunenburg] is continentally famous for its cooking and for its dozens of local recipes, including . . . Dutch mess (potatoes and salt codfish covered with a dressing of pork scraps and onions). *c*1963 (1965) STEVENS *Incompleat Canadian* One *must* go down to the sea again, if only to tuck the napkin under the chin and to have a go before it is too late at a Dutch Mess . . . or a Solomon Gundy (which is the rich sea-change salmagundi has suffered in these parts).

Dutch oven† a cast-iron pot with a tight-fitting lid for baking food in the hot ashes of a fire.

1877 GRANT *Ocean to Ocean* 42: Bread . . . was baked in Dutch ovens, buried in the hot embers of a huge fire outside, near the door. **1903** WHITE *Forest* 241: In this receptacle we left all our canned goods, our extra clothing, and our Dutch oven. **1913** OGILVIE *Yukon* 300: Cooking [is done in] bake kettles, or dutch-ovens, a cast-iron pot, with a closefitting top of the same metal.

Dutch sleigh *Obs.* a two-seater sleigh on long, high runners.
1789 *Quebec Gaz.* 5 Feb. 4/1: We will not reject the Dutch or American Sleigh and Sled with long high runners, if found best and most convenient, merely because they are Dutch or American.

dyke *n.* See **dike**.

ear *n.* a head or spike of Indian corn, *q.v.*, together with its kernels.

c1665 (1885) RADISSON *Voyages* 78: Each takes an ear of corne and putts in their mouths, wch is properly as milke, chawes it, and when their mouths are full, spitts it out in their hands, wch possibly they wash not once a yeare. **1833** (1926) LANGTON *Early U.C.* 38: . . . finding some ears of corn we roasted them also and made an admirable breakfast. **1914** RADIN *Myths of the Ojibwa* 1: . . . he could make his corn-stalks yield as many as ten to twelve ears of corn apiece. **1958** *Edmonton Jnl* 26 July 39/4: . . . the staff of the dominion experimental farm at Beaverlodge, reported harvesting about 300 ears of Altagold corn. . . .

ear pad an ear flap on a winter cap.

1871 OXENDEN *First Year* 56: A fur coat, and cap with ear-pads, completely protect one. **1955** COLLARD *Cdn Yesterdays* 230: A fur coat, and ear-pads, and rugs provided complete protection.

earth *v. North* See **mud**, *v.* (def. 2).

1942 TWOMEY & HERRICK *Needle to North* 68: On earthed runners and over smooth surfaces our load would have bothered nobody, but twelve hundred pounds over the rocky Bay ice was another story. Our runners were earthed, but no one expected the earthing to last long.

earthing *n. North* the process of applying mud to dogsled runners.

1942 TWOMEY & HERRICK *Needle to North* 67: Earthing . . . is done by moistening peat—decayed leaf-mould from the muskegs—and smearing it along the runner, where it freezes solidly and can be smoothed to form a fine, icy surface. Earthing . . . is always resorted to by careful and skillful Eskimos under the right conditions.

East (the) *n.* **1** See **down East** (def. 1).

1890 *Grip* (Toronto) 18 Oct. 245/2: The two Sir Johns had done Haligonians the compliment to study Sam Slick before going East. . . .

2 See **down East** (def. 2).

1884 *Prince Albert Times* (Sask.) 14 Mar. 6/1: I have been in churches where a dog would not be allowed inside under any considerations, but the idea is peculiar to the old straight-laced societies of the *East*. **1957** HUTCHISON *Canada* 280: The east hasn't heard about it, but, then, the east doesn't know any more about the north than a pig knows Sunday.

3 any part of Canada (except the far north) east of the Rocky Mountains.

1963 *Canada Month* May 14/3: Canadians from all parts of the East (including Alberta!) now retire to Vancouver. . . . In fact, nearly ten percent of Vancouverites are over 70.

East Block the most easterly of the three structures making up the Parliament Buildings in Ottawa and the one in which the Prime Minister has his office. See also **Eastern Block.** Cp. **Centre Block** and **West Block.**

☛ *Often used figuratively to mean the federal government.*

1957 HUTCHISON *Canada* 174: Behind the double doors of the East Block it is only a coalition of rival forces in constant disagreement, tension, and compromise. **1964** *Time* (Cdn ed.) 13 Nov. 17/1: At the East Block's invitation, military officers and diplomats from 23 countries gathered in Ottawa to exchange experience and ideas. . . .

Eastern Block *Obs.* See **East Block.**

1870 *Cdn Illust.News* 2 Apr. 346/1: The Eastern Block of the Departmental Buildings is in the same style and material as the Parliament Buildings but of an irregular and picturesque shape. **1888** *Dominion Illust.* 19/3: Next to the right is the "Eastern Block" of Government offices. *Ibid.* 226/1: The Governor-General, although in love with Quebec citadel, has left it at last and gone to Rideau Hall and his office, in the "Eastern Block," for the winter.

Eastern District *Hist.* the eastern region of Rupert's Land.

1897 TUTTLE *Golden North* 108: The territory east of Keewatin and south of Hudson's Bay, known as the Eastern District, contains 196,800 square miles.

Easterner *n.* a person from the East of Canada. Cp. **down East.**

1958 *Edmonton Jnl* 24 June 1 4/1: An easterner visiting Edmonton has made a special trip to *The Journal* to compliment Edmonton's motorists. **1962** *Cdn Saturday Night* Aug. 34/1: . . . it should be said that these are Easterners who know nothing about the West. . . .

Eastern Indian or **Eastward Indian** *Obs.* an Indian living to the east of Hudson Bay, as the Montagnais and Naskapi.

1783 (1954) *Moose Ft Jnls* 23: The Eastward Indian who came in yesterday is so much froze in his thighs and legs, that he is incapable of returning to his family. **1784** *Ibid.* 77: Received 35 Made Beaver from Moosominan, Quemess, & Cheman, Eastern Indians.

eastern partner *Hist.* See **agent** (def. 2).

1929 (1931) MERK *Fur Trade* x: Two classes of shareholders were in it: eastern partners, merchants of substance in Montreal and Quebec, who supplied the capital, and the so-called "wintering partners," who contributed the skill and experience which went into leadership in the field.

Eastern Province *Obs.* See **Canada East.**

1904 DECELLES *Cartier* 25: They would probably have conquered him long before had they not been . . . compromised by their "clear Grit" allies of Upper Canada, who were then clamouring against the institutions of the Eastern Province.

Eastern Provinces 1 *Obs.* See **Maritime colony.**

1848 *Sun* (Picton, C.W.) 3 Oct. 3/3: All the golden anticipations, therefore, connected with this important undertaking, so fondly indulged in by the people of Lower Canada and the Eastern Provinces, are apparently frustrated. **1879** *Canadian Mthly* II 244/1: Liberalism in Quebec and the Eastern provinces has always been bolder and more genuine than in Ontario, where it is narrowed and benumbed by oppressive influences, clannish and sectarian.

2 the provinces of Canada lying east of Manitoba.

1871 (1881) BEGG *Great Cdn N.W.* 75: The completion of the Telegraph line to Fort Garry . . . forms a fresh and most important link between the Eastern Provinces and the North West, and is a happy augury for the future. **1957** *Commonwealth* 2 Oct. 3/1: It was the trainloads of fruit, vegetables and clothing that came into this province, donated by the eastern provinces and B.C. that did the greatest part in keeping life and soul together in this province. **1966** *Toronto Dly Star* 30 Apr. 68/7: At this period [1847] in Canada, the eastern provinces had their own stamps, and New Brunswick was one of them.

Eastern Shore *N.S.* that part of the Atlantic seaboard stretching from Halifax to the beginning of Cape Breton Island.

1955 *Dartmouth Free Press* 14 Apr. 1/3: Described as a "mild epidemic," Dartmouth and the Eastern Shore are suffering from the 'flu this week and many business houses limped along on small staffs. **1963** *Using the Marine Forecast:* Eastern Shore [map area].

Eastern snowshoe See **beavertail snowshoe.**

1941 *Beaver* Mar. 27: The Montagnais shoe is the commonest form used throughout the Labrador Peninsula and is usually known simply as the Eastern snowshoe.

Eastern Townships eleven Quebec townships lying south of the St. Lawrence River and east of the Richelieu River, an area settled in large part by Loyalists and other American immigrants but now populated largely by French-speaking Canadians. See also **Lower Townships** and **Townships.**

1815 STEWART *Short View Eastern Townships* 3: Eastern Townships, is a general name frequently given to all the Townships extending East from the River Richelieu to the Eastern boundary of the Province, which divides it from the States of New-Hampshire and Massachusetts, of which last State Maine forms a part. **1849** ALEXANDER *L'Acadie* II 56: Now many young French Canadians move away, and occupy new lands at a distance from the banks of the St. Lawrence; or remove to the Eastern townships, that fertile country as yet but little appreciated, bounded on the States of New York, Vermont and New Hampshire. **1913** WILLSON *Quebec* 198: Very pathetic pictures have been drawn of the English-speaking depopulation of the Eastern Townships. **1966** *Globe and Mail* (Toronto) 8 Jan. 5/3: Three thousand teachers in Quebec's Eastern Townships threatened yesterday to resign at the end of the current school year.

Eastmain *n.* See 1929 quote. See also **Main** (def. 1). Cp. **West Main.** Also spelled *East Main.*

1689 *H.B.C.Minutes* II 140n: Wee judge it necessary that you always keep up that old Factory It being a kind of an Outwork to prevent any inroad of the French upon that part of the East Main. **1752** ROBSON *Hudson's Bay* 20: At Cape-Diggs the captain expected more Eskimaux; but none appearing, he conjectured that the Indians from the east-main had cut them off. **1808** MCKENZIE *King's Posts* 447: A light canoe, well manned and well piloted, may perform the journey from East Main to Tadousac in twenty days. **1929** *Beaver* Dec. 301: Roughly stated, Eastmain is the west side of the Labrador peninsula and at the same time the east shore of Hudson's Bay. Its extent is from Cape Jones on the south to Hudson's Straits on the north, a distance of between five and six hundred miles. **1963** DAVIES *Northern Quebec* xviii: . . . the enhanced value in a period of beaver glut of the martens and other small furs of the Eastmain . . .

Eastward Indian See **Eastern Indian.**

eat *v. Slang* chew (tobacco). See also **eating tobacco.**

1922 STEAD *Neighbours* 34: "I'm your gazabo," said Jake, stuffing a fist in a trouser pocket and bringing forth a half-eaten plug of tobacco. . . . **1961** MITCHELL

Jake and the Kid 135: ". . . I guess next to eatin' tobacco yer maw hates gamblin'."

Eater of Caribou See **Caribou Eskimo.**

1963 *North* May-June 39/1: The people are called the "Eaters of Caribou" or the "People of the Deer". They are the only Eskimos that make their living entirely from the land. . . .

eating tobacco *Slang* chewing tobacco.

1959 *Globe and Mail* (Toronto) 28 May 28/9: The sawyer would stand in chewing away thoughtfully on his wad of "eating tobacco". . . .

échoueries [eʃuˈriz] *n.pl.* [< Cdn F < F *échouer* run aground] rocky slopes on shore where walruses haul out. See also **hauling grounds** and **uglit.**

1784 PENNANT *Arctic Zoology* 149: The *Echoueries,* are formed principally by nature, being a gradual slope of soft rock, with which the *Magdalene* islands abound, about eighty or a hundred yards wide at the waterside, and spreading number so as to contain, near the summit, a very large number of these animals. **1862** *Islander* (Charlottetown) 30 May 3/1: At length the sea cows in the front are driven up the back as far so far in the echourie, that the last of them, then assembled has sufficient room to rest, when they usually sleep, if not disturbed. **1966** *Cdn Geog.Jnl* Mar. 89/2: Molineux Shuldham [1775] has left a full account of . . . the *échoueries* or hauling-out sites. . . .

ectas *n.* See **iktas.**

eel grass† a marine plant with long slender leaves, *Zostera marina,* usually growing in large beds.

1828 MCGREGOR *Maritime Colonies* 34: During winter eels live under the mud, within the bays and rivers, in places where a long marine grass (called eel grass) grows, the roots of which, penetrating several inches down through the mud, constitutes their food. **1934** DENNIS *Down in N.S.* 227: For centuries the busy Atlantic had been tossing eel grass on the Nova Scotia shore. But little use was made of the lowly weed, although pioneer settlers were aware of the value of eel grass as an insulator, for they used it for banking their houses and stuffed it in the sheathing spaces of their walls. **1959** BODSWORTH *Strange One* 40: The water was dotted with thousands of geese, most of them with heads and necks submerged as they fed on the eel grass under the surface. . . .

eenerksook *n.* See **inukshuk.**

egg-beater *n.* any very small outboard motor.

1956 *Beaver* Winter 16/2: We ran across the four miles of lake under power, having brought with us a 3 h.p. Johnson. . . . People were rude to this small machine in that land of big riverboats and 20 and 25 h.p. kickers— they called it an egg-beater and burst into laughter at the sight of it.

egloo *n.* See **igloo.**

eiderdown *n.* See **eiderdown sleeping-bag.**

1924 FLAHERTY *Eskimo Friends* 12: Beans and bacon were frying on the stove, and my eiderdown was unrolled on the tent's snow floor and spread over robes of deerskin. **1956** KEMP *Northern Trader* 144: We cooked supper and fed the dogs, but when I went to fetch my eiderdown from the sleigh I could find no bedding belonging to Kitimakis.

eiderdown sleeping-bag a sleeping-bag insulated with eiderdown, or similar stuffing.

1964 *Weekend Mag.* 11 July 18/3: They chose

eiderdown sleeping bags, took a complete change of clothing. . . .

eight-ender *n. Curling* an end, or frame, in which one team counts all eight of its rocks to the utter exclusion of the opposing team; eight points scored by one team in one end, *q.v.*
1958 *Chatelaine* Nov. 83: The maximum obviously would be eight rocks, which sets up an "eight ender," curling's equivalent of golf's hole in one.

elbowing *n. Hockey* the illegal action of jabbing one's elbows into an opponent's body.
1963 *Kingston Whig-Standard* (Ont.) 22 Jan. 8/7: [They] were sent to the penalty box for roughing, elbowing and slashing after a minor tussle at centre ice. . . .

elbow snowshoe See quote. See also **swallow-tail snowshoe.** Cp. **bear-paw.**
1941 *Beaver* March 27: Assuming that the bearpaw was the original pattern, we have a slight departure from it in the "elbow" snowshoe. . . . it is merely a bearpaw snowshoe which has had the tail elongated slightly, giving it an oval rather than an elliptical outline.

Eldorado [ˌɛldəˈrado] *n.* [< Sp. *el dorado* the gilded (place)] **1** a place where much gold is being mined or is reported to be in abundance; a rich goldfield.
1861 *Nor'Wester* (R.R.S.) 15 July 3/4: That mighty monarch "the Press" has recently presented another El Dorado to the wonderous gaze of that great potentate the public . . . the Saskatchewan Diggings. **1937** ARMSTRONG *Upper Yukon* 14: The average man who thinks of the Yukon recalls the famous gold rush and pictures the scenes . . . of ice wastes and tremendous hardships over trails where thousands of men and horses lay down to die before ever the *El Dorado* was reached.

2 a rich strike; bonanza.
1912 WHITE *Wildcatters* 48: And you were afraid we would pinch the Graham eldorado on him? **1954** PATTERSON *Dangerous River* 81: I wondered whether they had won through in the end to their Eldorado on the Yukon River, or whether the Nahanni or the Indians could best tell what became of them.

3 rich and rewarding quantities of anything.
1889 WITHROW *Our Own Country* 96: On a bright and beautiful Sabbath morning, he struck one of those El-Dorados; hundreds of thousands of seals surrounded his ship. **1916** BRIDLE *Sons of Canada* 247: It is a fact that we scarcely heard of Colonel Pellatt till Canada began to be prosperous with great railways, fabulous mines, eldoradoes of arable land, the rise of marvellous power plants on the brink of Niagara with transmission lines stretching over half a province, and the bumptious, parabolic curves of real estate that would persist in going up and up regardless of what the land was worth in rent.

elector *n. Sask.* a non-property-holding voter, as opposed to a burgess (def. 2), in the municipal electoral scheme.
1964 *Saskatoon Star-Phoenix* 30 Mar. 14/1: Mr. Kreutzweiser said three times more burgesses than ordinary electors demonstrated an interest in elections by voting.

electoral district a district encompassing a body of electors entitled to return a member to the House of Commons or to a legislative assembly. See also **riding** (def. 2).

[**1859** *British Colonist* (Victoria) 18 May 2/2: The manner in which the bill proposes to divide up the country into small electoral districts, requires modification.] **1879** *Canadian Mthly* II 478/1: "The Legislative Assembly of Ontario," says the B.N.A. Act, section 70, "shall be composed of eighty-two members, to be elected to represent the eighty-two electoral districts set forth in the first schedule of this Act." **1963** *Kingston Whig-Standard* (Ont.) 5 Mar. 16/6: Among them are Chief Electoral Officer Nelson Castonguay and the returning officers in the 263 electoral districts.

electoral division See **electoral district.**
1907 *U of T Stud.Hist.& Econ.* II 235: The "Electoral Division" to-day is the constituency which is represented in Parliament.

elephant's head the lousewort or wood betony, *Pedicularis groenlandica.*
1938 *Beaver* Mar. 42/2: These were the elephants' heads or Lapland Pediculars, and they were accompanied by a larger bright yellow form and a deep purple one [and] grew abundant in the willow thickets.

elevator† *n.* **1** a device, especially an endless chain of cups or buckets, used to move grain from one level to another.
1864 (1955) CRAIG *Early Travellers* 272: By means of elevators a barge can be loaded or unloaded in an hour. . . .

Elevators (defs. 2a and 2b)

2 a. See **country elevator.**
1902 (1956) *Sask.Hist.* IX 2 74: At some of the stations three or four elevators were in course of erection. **1956** *New Frontiers* Summer 40: The mind that visioned this unending chain / Of elevators rising from the wheat / And sleepy hamlets sprawling on the plain.
b. See **terminal elevator.**
1868 SMALL *Chronicles* 156: Another important branch runs from Komoka to Sarnia, on Lake Huron, where and at Hamilton the Company owns fine grain stores and elevators. **1922** *Beaver* Nov. 67/1: Canada's system of handling grain through elevators is being investigated by delegates from South Africa and India.
c. the people who own and operate a grain elevator; an elevator company.
1907 *Eye Opener* (Calgary) 26 Jan. 5/1: Five elevators in Leduc combined to sandbag the farmer. **1958** *Edmonton Jnl* 24 June 4 14/5: For instance a leading elevator here handled only a few bushels of barley. Now one such elevator alone ships out more than 140,000 bushels of this crop.

elk† *n.* **1 a.** See **moose** (def. 1).
*c*1665 (1885) RADISSON *Voyages* 31: There is to be seen 300 wild cowes together, a number of Elks and Beavers, an infinit of fowls. **1760** PICHON *Cape Breton* 100: A great many are of opinion that this [moose] is the same

animal as in other places is called the elk. **1863** WALSHE
Cedar Creek 215: "It was a sharp idea to make the elk
his own butcher's boy," quoth Argent. **1930** QUANCE
Cdn Speller 6 39: [Caption] The elk nipped the leaves
off the trees. **1937** CONIBEAR *Northland Footprints* 38:
The larger island . . . had been for some years much
favoured by Moose as the Elk as a place in which to bear
and rear her fawns.

b. See **elk skin** (def. 1).

1962 (1964) INNIS *Fur Trade in Can.* 120: In 1679 the
returns of furs included [from what is now Northern
Ontario] 10,500 beaver, 1,100 marten, 200 otter, 700 elk,
and smaller furs.

2 See **wapiti**.

1832 MCGREGOR *British America* I 102: The horns of the
elk are not palmated, and are longer than those of any
other quadruped. Probably not one of these immense
animals is now to be met with east of Lake Superior. . . .
1877 GRANT *Ocean to Ocean* 228: [There] formerly the
wood buffalo, and the elk, and now the moose, bighorn
and bear find shelter. **1966** *Globe and Mail* (Toronto)
7 May 41/1: Why has there been a drastic drop in the
birthrate among deer and elk in the East Kootenay, one
of the largest big game hunting areas in the province?

elk deer *Obs.* See **moose** (def. 1).

1743 (1949) ISHAM *Observations* 154: Moose or Elk
Deer, more in Land to the So.—their is plenty these
are for shape and make much Like other Deer, but
Larger, with short tails &c.

elk skin or **hide 1** *Obs. or Hist.* moosehide. See
also **elk** (def. 1b).

1748 ELLIS *Hudson's Bay* 158: We likewise began
about this Time to put on our . . . Shoes of soft-tanned
Moose or Elk-Skin, under which we wore . . . thick
Duffil Socks. . . . **1792** (1911) SIMCOE *Diary* 82: The
racket is made of deer or elk skins. **1930** (1964) INNIS
Fur Trade in Can. 346: Dog harness of the best
manufacture, lined with elk skin, is sold at $40 a set for
four dogs. . . .

2 the skin of the wapiti, *q.v.* See also **elk** (def. 2).

1853 REID *Young Voyageurs* 185: Lucien knew how to
dress the elk-hide, and could make leather out of it as
well as any Indian squaw in the country. **1905** (1954)
B.C.Hist.Qtly XVIII 173: The old man wore constantly
. . . a large elk skin coat that came down to his heels,
and of this coat, he was very proud.

elm canoe *Obs.* a type of canoe made of the bark
of the white elm, used by the Iroquois and the
Ojibwas.

1853 STRICKLAND *Canada West* II 49: The Chippewas,
near Goderich, are the only Indians I ever saw use the
elm-canoe.

embarras *n.* [< Cdn F] *Obs. (except in place
names)* a tangle of logs and brush obstructing a
stream. See also. **driftpile**.

1793 (1801) MACKENZIE *Voy. from Montreal* 226: In
passing over one of the embarras, our dog . . . fell
in. . . . **1808** (1950) THOMPSON *Journals* 7: . . . the first
part of this Rivulet had water enough for us & plenty of
beaver—the mid part full of embarras which took us
much time to get a passage through. . . . *c*1902 LAUT
Trapper 174: The greatest risk of travelling after
dark during the spring floods arose from what the
voyageurs called *embarras*—trees torn from the banks
sticking in the soft bottom like derelicts to entangle the

trapper's craft; but the *embarras* often befriended the
solitary white man.

emigrant agent *Hist.* See **immigration agent**
(def. 1).

1837 *Bytown* [Ottawa] *Gaz.* 16 Aug. 3/3: The minute
in Council of the 20th July . . . places a sum of money
at the disposal of the Emigrant Agent to enable him to
open a road through some of the townships in the rear
of Kingston. **1934** *Cdn Hist.Rev.* XV 27: A. C.
Buchanan, chief emigrant agent, estimated that of the
total number of immigrants arriving at Quebec and
Montreal in 1856, forty-one per cent. went to the
United States.

emigrant car *Hist.* a railway car that carried
emigrants to their new places of settlement. See
also **immigrant car**.

1895 *Rat Portage* [Kenora] *News* (Ont.) 5 Apr. 5/2:
A special train of six emigrant cars passed through
here about five o'clock this morning from the east. **1913**
FOOTNER *Jack Chanty* 82: He came West on an emigrant
car.

emigrant depot or **house** *Obs.* See **immigration
shed**.

1821 *Kingston Chron.* (U.C.) 8 June 3/3: An Emigrant
House . . . has been provided at Cobourg for the
accomodation of settlers—and will no doubt be found
very useful. **1871** *Wkly Manitoban* 15 Apr. 3/4: I
hope the Dominion Government has made the unused
barracks at London and elsewhere, habitable as
emigrant depots. **1876** *Thunder Bay Sentinel* (Port
Arthur, Ont.) 8 June 2/2: The former boat had some
800 hungry Mennonites, who immediately took
possession of the N.P. emigrant house. . . .

emigrant shed *Obs.* See **immigration shed**.

1836 *Bytown* [Ottawa] *Gaz.* 8 Sep. 2/4: We yesterday
did ourselves the pleasure of visiting for the first time
the emigrant-sheds, and were hugely gratified by the
general air of cleanliness and comfort. **1885** *Nor'Wester*
(Calgary) 19 Feb. 3/1: The work on the Emigrant Shed
is already advancing rapidly, a gang of competent
workmen being employed.

emigrant society *Obs.* See **immigration society**.

1819 *Kingston Chron.* (U.C.) 6 Aug. 4/4: We shall publish
the Rules and Regulations of the Quebec Emigrant
Society in our next. **1836** *Bytown* [Ottawa] *Gaz.* 22 Dec.
2/5: The operations of the Emigrant Society have been
closed for the season.

emigrant train *Hist.* **1** a train of wagons taking
emigrants to the West in the early days of
settlement.

1963 SPRY *Palliser* 133: That this was the right entrance
to the pass was later confirmed by Blakiston, who
reported that he had seen on the banks of the
Kananaskis the remains of the carts that Sinclair's
second emigrant train had abandoned. . . .

2 *Obs.* See **immigrant train**.

1864 *Nor'Wester* (R.R.S.) 3 Aug. 1/2: A serious
accident happened this morning about half-past one A.
m. to the emigrant train from Quebec. **1889** *Rat
Portage* [Kenora] *News* (Ont.) 10 May 1/4: A special
emigrant train from Quebec on the C.P.R. arrived at
the Union Depot last night about 8.30.

emigration agency or **office** *Obs.* the
headquarters of the immigration agent (def. 1) of a
district.

1860 *Islander* (Charlottetown) 26 Oct. 2/5: Other
Colonies have Emmigration Offices and Officers. **1879**
Morning Chron. (Halifax) 1 July 2/1: Others have an

Emigration Agency or a Prothonotaryship, or a Post Office, but none of them is in Parliament today.

emigration agent *Obs.* See **immigration agent** (def. 1). See also **emigrant agent.**
1884 (1965) HAMILTON *Cdn Quotations* 105/1: The best kind of emigration agent is the successful settler in the new districts. (Thomas White. H. of C. Debates, Mar. 4, 1884.)

Empire Loyalist See **United Empire Loyalist.**
1961 *Canada Month* Dec. 13/2: Ever since the Empire Loyalists fled across the border with their Yankee twangs and expressions, Canadians have been accused of speaking a verbal mish-mash of something between British English and American English.

emplacement *n.* [< Cdn F] *Obs.* in Quebec, a small parcel of surveyed land in a town; lot.
1777 *Quebec Gaz.* 8 May 4/1: It is ordered that every House-keeper, and every owner of an empty house or emplacement in the Upper and Lower-towns, shall within five days after the publication of the regulations herein contained by the public Cryier or Bellman, clean or cause to be cleaned, one half of the width of the street opposite to his or her house, hangard, outhouse or emplacement. **1832** *Cdn Courant* (Montreal) 26 Dec. 4/2: A Ground Plane exhibiting the emplacements and their situation in respect to each other, and to the streets in which the above may be seen on application at the Office of the undersigned. **1836** *Montreal Transcript* 26 Nov. 3/1: It consists of a lot of ground or Emplacement ... the whole surrounded by very high walls.

en apala *Cdn French* See **appalat.**
1824 (1955) BLACK *Journal* 132: ... the little singed Squirrels ranged round the Fires en apala adds another dish to the Feast this evening.

en cache [< Cdn F "in a hiding place"] See **cache,** *n.* (def. 2 and picture).
1794 (1929) McGILLIVRAY *Journal* 16: [We] embarked ... with the greatest care of the baggage, leaving the rest behind *en cache.* **1874** (1956) ROSS *Athabasca* 11: Cust accompanied us some distance down the River to where Dacoigne had the Beaver skins en cache. **1925** GRAHAME *Bompas* 16: The canoe was dragged ashore, and placed en cache on the bank with their baggage.

en censive or **encensive** *adj.* [< Cdn F < F] *Hist.* pertaining to a form of tenure enjoyed by the habitant in Quebec, by the terms of which he held land from the seigneur in return for *cens et rentes, q.v.*
1886 (1887) *Trans Roy.Soc.Can.* IV 2 47: The habitant or censitaire held his property by the tenure of en censive, on condition of making annual payments in money or produce known as cens et rente, which was ridiculously small in the early times of the colony. *Ibid.* 48: As the lots of a grant en censive were limited in area—four arpents in front by forty in depth—the farms in the course of time assumed the appearance of a continuous settlement on the river. **1905** *Ont.Bur.Arch. Rep.* III xlvii: Some encensive grants were made by the Crown direct. Grantee could not sublet.

end *n. Curling* one of the frames, or divisions of a game, during which each of the four players of both teams curls two stones.
1884 *Prince Albert Times* (Sask.) 28 Mar. 1/3: Four rinks of eight ends each were played, at the conclusion of which the score stood—Argyle's 21, Saskatchewans 24, leaving the latter club winners by three points. **1911** KNOWLES *Singer* 282: The last "end" was about to be

played—and Rockcliffe was still four shots down. **1965** *Globe and Mail* (Toronto) 5 Jan. 27/9: Mrs. Salter forced an extra end by counting a two on the eighth end as she made a takeout and stayed with her final rock.

en derouine *Cdn French, Obs.* See 1933 quote. See also **derouine.** Cp. **camp-trade party.**
1800 (1933) McLEOD *Diary* 144: I sent Collin & Seven men off *en Derouine* to where the Vent du Nord came from.... **1801** (1897) COUES *New Light* I 192: Lac la Pluie Indians arrived, for people to go *en derouine* on the upper part of Two Rivers. **1933** GATES *Five Traders* 144n: Traders were said to *courir en derouine* when, instead of waiting at their established posts for the Indians to come in and trade their furs, they went out to the Indian hunting camps to get the peltries. **1962** (1964) INNIS *Fur Trade in Can.* 269: A large number of men was necessary to secure provisions to engage in trapping furs, to go about among the Indians collecting furs en derouine, and to protect the forts.

end-man *n. Fur Trade, Obs.* one of the two paddlers occupying either the bow or the stern of a canoe. See also **bowsman** and **steersman.**
1761 (1901) HENRY (Elder) *Travels* 14: Skilful men, at double the wages of the rest, are placed in the head and stern.... They engage ... the middle-men at one hundred and fifty livres and the end-men at three hundred livres, each.

end of steel 1 a. the farthest point to which railway service extends; the terminus of a railway. See also **head of rail, head of steel** (def. 2), **railhead** (def. 1b), and **steel** (def. 1).
1909 CAMERON *New North* 21: Edmonton is the end of steel. Three lines converge here: the Canadian Northern, the Canadian Pacific, and the Grand Trunk Pacific. **1938** *Beaver* 19 Sep. 20/2: The "Muskeg" was just pulling out, headed not south for The Pas but north for Mile 214, which was then the "end of steel" on the Hudson Bay Railway. **1962** SLOBODIN *Kutchin* 12: The railroad terminus—the "end of steel"—is at Waterways, Alberta....

b. See **head of steel** (def. 1).
1933 THOMPSON & EDGAR *Cdn Ry Development* 247: Winter, therefore, had scarcely gripped the country, when an engine drawing a train of ballast trucks and two steam shovels steamed to the end of steel.... **1964** *Calgary Herald* 18 Apr. 11/4: The end of steel now is 140 miles from its terminal point at the Hay River, N.W.T....

2 See **end-of-steel town.**
1913 FOOTNER *Jack Chanty* 136: The weather had favored them and eventually they had found themselves in Athabaska, end-of-steel! **1935** *Cdn Geog.Jnl* Sep. 126/1: It is a drama which finds its foci on those days when ... trains leave for that most eloquent place-name to be found in any railway guide—"the end-of-steel." **1961** *Alta Hist.Rev.* Spring 22: It was on April 5th, 1902, that my husband and I arrived at Strathcona, Alberta, the end of steel....

end-of-steel town or **village** a community at the end of a railway line.
1912 BICKERSTETH *Open Doors* 199: An end-of-steel town is a wicked place. **1913** *Prince George Herald* 20 Sep.: An "end of steel" village is made up of booze, billiards, and belles. **1960** *Ont.Hist.* June 93: For

several glorious months [Aurora] was the end-of-steel town and the future looked very rosy.

end of the steel *Obs.* See **end of steel** (def. 1b).
1912 FOOTNER *New Rivers* 276: After following this for a mile or so, we came to the end of the steel, but there was no construction work going on, and indeed no sign of life anywhere about. **1916** BRIDLE *Sons of Can.* 49: All the battalions thus far organised in the two chief cities of Canada would not equal in number the army of men employed by the C.P.R. from the President's anteroom to the outposting end of the steel, round the world and back.

end of track See **end of steel** (def. 1b).
1884 *Prince Albert Times* (Sask.) 4 July 3/1: A number of leading citizens of Calgary waited on Inspector Steele last Monday evening on the eve of his departure to End of Track, and presented him with a neat casket containing a cigar case and match receptacle. **1923** STEELE *Spirit-of-Iron* 106: The "end of track," by this time, had reached Regina. . . .

endorsation [ˌɛndɔrˈseʃən] *n.* evidence of support or approval of a policy or action.
1869 *North Wellington Times* (Elora, Ont.) 24 Dec. 2/1: Their re-election is an endorsation of their conduct at the Council board this year. **1914** *Eye Opener* (Calgary) 27 June 7/5: We wish to thank the public for the hearty endorsation and support our first two issues of 200,000 shares have received, same being fully subscribed. **1957** *Native Voice* July 4/1: There was no question of the Progressive-Conservative position at that time, a position of principle which won the warm endorsation of Canadian Natives.

enfarge or **enferge** *n. and v.* [< Cdn F] *Obs.* of horses or cattle, hobble or fetter.
1840 (1955) EWERS *Horse* 39n: The Osage, on their summer hunt in 1840, unloaded their horses each night and set them free "after their forelegs had been fastened with enferges or horse locks." **1862** (1931) CHEADLE *Journal* 52: [We] camped near a large swamp . . . enfarged the horses and cooked ducks.

enforcement trail a trail used by the Mounted Police in their law-enforcement duties.
1953 MOON *Saskatchewan* 73: Enforcement trails radiated out across the northwest from that time until 1882 when the railway came across the plains and the headquarters [of the RCMP, or then the NWMP] was moved to Regina.

enfranchised *adj.* no longer having status as an Indian with band membership and rights as an Indian.
1939 (1942) ANGER *Cdn Commercial Law* 26: An enfranchised Indian has all the rights and liabilities of any other British subject. **1958** HEALEY *Alert Bay* 60: Now we find the old community house a thing of the past, many of the Indians in individual homes of their own, some marrying amongst the white people, and moving away to other towns or cities, some being enfranchised and accepting the white man's burden. **1961** *Camsell Arrow* Summer 10: On her mother's marriage to a non-Indian Denise was enfranchised, but on her own marriage to John, she became a Treaty Indian again.

enfranchisement *n.* the removal of a person from the list of registered Indians, *q.v.*, whereby he relinquishes his band membership and rights as an Indian.
1912 (1913) HODGE & WHITE *Indians of Can.* 182/1n: But a thorough comprehension of the Indian nature has led the Canadian Government to make haste slowly in the matter of enfranchisement. **1958** HAWTHORN *Indians of B.C.* 385: The first is that, while the point is not covered in the Indian Act, the Department follows the policy of refusing an application for enfranchisement from an Indian woman living apart from her husband unless he consents to being enfranchised at the same time. **1964** DUFF *Indian History* 47: Indian status is given up by "enfranchisement," which is automatic for women marrying non-Indian husbands, and otherwise voluntary, by application.

engagé [ãgaˈʒe] *n.* [< Cdn F < F servant] *Hist.* a fur-company employee, originally a French Canadian hired in Montreal to work in the inland trade. See also **voyageur** (def. 1).
1765-75 (1933) POND *Narrative* 31: But all way in the Spring . . . the Engashea often went to Confes & git absolution. **1796** *Quebec Gaz.* 24 Mar. 3/1: Leave was also given to bring in a Bill for regulating the Engages to the Indian Country, &c. **1824** (1931) MERK *Fur Trade* 238: While at the Depot they shall be allowed per week four days ordinary rations as issued to Engages besides three loaves of Bread three pounds of Pork 1/4 lb Tea 1 1/4 lb sugar and one pint Rum. **1955** RICH in BLACK *Journal* xxv: After them came the engagés—postmasters, interpreters, tradesmen, guides, steersmen, bowsmen, voyageurs and labourers. **1966** [see quote at **engagement**].

engage *v. Obs.* sign an engagement or agreement to work for a fur company in any capacity. See also **engagé**.
1852 (1942) *Beaver* Dec. 24/2: . . . I had two men and two engaged Indians with me. . . . **1874** (1956) ROSS *Athabasca* 11: . . . Roy and John Flett got each the offer of $500 to engage with him but all refused.

engaged servant *Obs.* See **engagé**.
1815 (1948) *Beaver* June 20/1: Bollant who accompanies him is one of the Company's engaged Servants. . . .

engagement *n. Hist.* the contract agreed to by an engagé, *q.v.*
1791 LONG *Voyages* 75: The "bourgeois" was the chief trader, to whom the voyageurs were bound by engagements for service. The term was also often applied to the trader's agent or clerk, when the latter was in command of the expedition. **1806** (1960) FRASER *Letters and Journals* 183: . . . as I had not his engagement I was obliged to take him on his word. . . . **1931** NUTE *Voyageur* 36: As soon as the agent had come to terms with his *engagé,* an engagement was signed. **1966** *B.C. Digest* Dec. 44/3: . . . voyageurs in general were mentioned as engages, or men who had engagements with the bourgeois.

English *n.* **1** (*usually plural*) *Hist.* the Hudson's Bay Company or its employees, a designation used by the North West Company and other fur companies based in Canada. See also **English Company.**
1784 PENNANT *Arctic Zoology* 18: The English used to call it the Black Moose, to distinguish it from the Stag, which they name the Grey Moose, the French call it L'Orignal. **1794** (1929) MCGILLIVRAY *Journal* 16: The English are so apprehensive of being attacked . . . that they would certainly remain here. . . . **1820** (1938)

English were completely extirpated and not a vestige of them would ever be permitted to cross Portage La Loche again. **1946** *Beaver* March 34/2: English Island preserves in its name the old custom to refer to the Hudson's Bay Company people as English and the North Westers as Canadians.

2 an English-speaking Canadian.
[**1800** (1965) COLLARD *Call Back Yesterdays* 6: . . . principal people in the town . . . are either English, Scotch, Irish, or their descendants, all of whom pass for English with the French inhabitants.] **1870** *Wkly Manitoban* 5 Nov. 2/4: Are we going to have a French party and an English party; I say no. **1953** WALKER *Pardon My Parka* 26: Later I discovered that in Canada, English means anyone who isn't French-Canadian. **1966** *Globe and Mail* (Toronto) 32: Despite their continual search for talent, the Canadiens' lineup today is more than half English. . . .

3 *Rare* the Anglican Church or its members (in full, English Church).
1898 (1960) ELLIOTT *Klondike* 13: Hazleton is an extremely one horse place consisting chiefly of the Hudson's Bay Co.'s store, and another store, an Indian Agent's residence, and an English church mission of sorts. **1911** KNOWLES *Singer* 85: "Well, I mean as how we used to be Methodys—you know that—an then we joined the English. You used to go to class-meetin', Martha—you know you did. An' I often wish I was back with the Methodys . . . they were far more sentimentaller than the English. . . ."

English brandy *Obs.* inferior trade alcohol.
1784-1812 (1916) THOMPSON *Narrative* 53: The Company has the Bay in full possession, and can enforce the strictest temperance of spirituous liquors, but the ships at the same time bringing out several hundred gallons of vile spirits called Eng. Brandy no such morality is thought of.

English breed See English half-breed.
1900 OSBORN *Greater Can.* 39: During the conversation an old Irishman pointed out that for one English "breed" there were ten Scotch and fifty French, but "niver an Oirish half-breed at all."

English Canada that part of Canada where English-speaking people predominate, as distinct from French Canada, especially Quebec.
1888 *Dominion Illustrated* 275/3: If the fecundity of "the French" were a danger to English Canada, how would the alarmed Smashers proceed to avert that danger? **1964** *Canada Month* Jan. 27/3: If French Canada has been in existence for over three centuries, it can be said that English Canada, as we know it today, is the product of Confederation.

English Canadian a Canadian who speaks English and who is identified with English Canada. See also Canadian-English.
*a*1820 (1838) HEAD *Forest Scenes* 307: There was an old man among them, an English Canadian, called Mr. Weller. . . . **1882** LEMOINE *Quebec* 60: The hon. gentleman then in language of forcible eloquence referred to the pleasure shown by English-Canadians at the success of Mr. Frechette. **1965** *Kingston Whig-Standard* (Ont.) 9 Jan. 22/2: It may not help the English Canadian and the French Canadian politician to speak one another's language if they do not share the same understanding of the tongue that money talks.

English Company *Hist.* the Hudson's Bay Company, with headquarters in England, as

opposed to other fur companies with headquarters in Canada or the United States. See also **English** (def. 1).
1905 (1954) *B.C.Hist.Qtly*. July 152: That was the year [1821] of the coalition of the Hudson's Bay Company, or "English" company, as some called it, dating from 1670 . . . with its famous rival. . . .

English half-breed a half-breed having an English-speaking father and an Indian mother. See also **English breed** and **English metis**.
1820 (1938) SIMPSON *Athabasca Jnl* 136: A few attached English halfbreeds would therefore be of the utmost importance to us. **1860** *Nor'Wester* (R.R.S.) 14 Apr. 3/5: Whenever an opportunity offered for sending home, I would see the French Half-breed running round a circle of carts, very often upwards of a thousand in number, in search of an English Half-breed to pen a few lines for him. **1963** MORTON *Kingdom of Canada* 281: There a quarrel between private traders and the some officers of the Hudson's Bay Company had blown up into an agitation by the half-caste people of Red River— the French métis and the English half-breeds—against the monopoly. . . .

English Indian *Obs.* See **Company Indian.**
1795 (1929) MCGILLIVRAY *Journal* 75: The *English Indians* on the contrary complain bitterly of their treatment and threaten to return no more to that House.

English Line *Obs.* in Upper Canada, a settlement area taken up by emigrants from England. Cp. **Scotch Line.**
1852 MOODIE *Roughing It* 444: This place, so named by the migrants who had pitched their tents in that solitary wilderness, was a long line of cleared land, extending upon either side for some miles through the darkest and most interminable forest. The English Line as inhabited chiefly by Cornish miners, who, tired of burrowing like moles underground, had determined to emigrate to Canada, where they could breathe the fresh air of Heaven, and obtain the necessaries of life upon the bosom of their mother earth. **1853** STRICKLAND *Canada West* I 142: A few years ago . . . a meeting was held in a school-house on the English line, in the township of Dummer.

Englishman *n*. **1** *Fur Trade, Hist.* a person working for the Hudson's Bay Company, as opposed to one working for any non-English company.
1772 (1964) INNIS *Fur Trade in Can.* 151: I find they consider an Englishman's going with them as a person sent to collect Furs; and not as an encouragement to them to trap furs, and come down to the Settlements. . . . **1821** (1938) SIMPSON *Athabasca Jnl* 285: A valuable Officer must necessarily be esteemed and it is quite immaterial whether he is an Englishman or a Canadian. **1952** (1954) JENNINGS *Strange Brigade* 153: "Hallo, Messieurs! Hallo, Charles!" he cried. "Belly, ye've the manners of an Englishman," and it was only much later that I learned that when a Northwester spoke of an "Englishman" he meant an employee of the Bay Company.

2 an English-speaking Canadian, as distinct from one whose language is French.
1899 PARKER *Lane* 34: He was fond of music for an Englishman, and with a ravishing charm she sang for him a bergerette of the eighteenth century. . . . **1954** CONSTANTIN-WEYER *Half-Breed* 36: ". . . I'd like

to see him, the Englishman who's the equal of a *metis*. I've got boys of my own, sapristi!. . . ."

English métis See **English half-breed.**
1896 RUSSELL *Far North* 2: "Old" Joe Atkinson, an English métis from Hudson's Bay, would watch me by the hour, te-heeing with delight as each specimen was prepared and placed in its fluffy, cotton shroud on the drying shelves.

English milk *Obs.* in Indian parlance, rum. See also **milk** and **new milk.** Cp. **moose milk** (def. 2).
1761 (1901) HENRY (Elder) *Travels* 45: Minavavana requested that his young men might be allowed to taste what he called my *English milk* (meaning *rum*) . . . observing that it was long since they had tasted any. . . . **1926** DICKIE *Cdn West* 18: . . . they [Indians] welcomed him as a brother, offered him the pipe, and asked for English milk (rum).

English party *Hist.* in Lower Canada, a group of influential bureaucrats and merchants who sought to keep the British connection strong and, in so doing, to keep the English element dominant in British North America. See also **British party.**
1806 (1809) GRAY *Letters* 81: If Upper and Lower Canada had had but one house of assembly, the English party would have always kept the majority.
1904 DECELLES *Papineau* 196: On one occasion . . . Colonel Gugy, a Swiss by origin, and a tool of the English party, declared in the House at Quebec, that he preferred to see in office a ministry composed of citizens born in the country. **1963** MORTON *Kingdom of Canada* 227: The English party therefore went to work quietly in London to use the problem of the division of customs duties to bring about a union of the provinces.

English provisions *Fur Trade, Obs.* provisions imported from England, as opposed to country provisions, *q.v.*
1714 (1965) *Letters from Hudson Bay* 32: I have had a great many starved Indians come in upon me the last winter which caused me for to expend more English provisions than I should otherwise have spent. . . . **1798** (1927) *Beaver* June 18: A Stock of English Provisions will be sent to Gordon House by the Fall Boats.

English ranter *Obs.* a member of a fundamentalist sect of Methodists in Upper Canada.
1897 DURAND *Reminiscences* 114: In 1826 to 1830, in Hamilton, and generally in Upper Canada, there were four divisions—the Episcopal Methodists, in connection with the American body; the Ryanites, as they were called, or Canadian Wesleyans of that day; the New Connexion body, who had a church on Main, near Walnut Street; and the Old Primitives—the extremists, or some called them English ranters. . . .

English shoe *Hist.* a factory-made shoe, local or imported, as opposed to moccasins. Cp. **Canada boot.**
1778 (1934) TURNOR *Journal* 201: For my own part I wore two pair of English Shoes intirely out in the tracking ground in walking a long the shore. . . . **1862** *Nor'Wester* (R.R.S.) 25 June 2/5: To some extent also, the moccasin is giving way to the "English shoe." **1930** ROLYAT *Fort Garry* 153: Margaret chose a pair of "English shoes" as all footwear other than moccasins were designated. Her first pair of English

shoes which she prized greatly were small gaters with elastic sides.

English-speaking *adj.* of or associated with that part of Canada or her population that is not French Canadian.
1959 *Maclean's* 9 May 8/3: The contrast between this attitude and the attitude of the rest of English Canada brings to mind a question; "Have we in Quebec a special brand of English-speaking citizen?" **1966** *Globe and Mail* (Toronto) 32/3: "I can honestly say that . . . I've never seen a problem between French and English-speaking players on our teams."

entrave *n.* [< Cdn F] *Obs.* a thwart of a canoe.
1806 (1960) FRASER *Letters and Journals* 201: As it was late before everything was ready to begin the canoe, we only laid the bottom and fixed the maitres and entraves.

Enuit *n.* See **Innuit.**

enumeration *n.* the process of making up the voter's lists before an election.
1963 *Globe and Mail* (Toronto) 9 Mar. 11/7: In spite of such secrecy, enumeration went much more smoothly this year than in 1962, probably because the enumerators were more experienced.

enumerator *n.* a person employed to make up voters' lists before elections.
1930 MCCLUNG *Be Good* 159: . . . the Enumerator called at the front door, and she gave him the information he wanted. . . . **1962** *Weekend Mag.* 9 June 17/1: The candidate for the party that holds the seat selects the first of each pair of enumerators and the candidate for the party that came next in the previous election, selects the second. **1964** *Saskatoon Star-Phoenix* 30 Mar. 3/5: . . . the Hanley enumerator is liable to a fine and imprisonment of one year under the Saskatchewan Elections Act. . . .

Epagweit or **Epaigwit** *n.* See **Abegweit.**

Ephraim *n. Jocular* a bear, especially a grizzly bear. Also called *Old Eph(raim).*
1854 *Hamilton Gaz.* (C.W.)14 Sep. 1/7: For all that, whar the timmer's clost and brushy, and the ground o' that sort whar a hoss must stummel, it are allers the safest plan to let old Eph'm slide. **1876** LORD *Wilderness* 220: "Old Ephraim" (the trapper's usual sobriquet for a grizzly bear), was next to be lassooed. . . . **1921** MARSHALL *Snowshoe Trail* 184: Ephraim was an old bear, used to every hunting wile, and his disposition hadn't improved with years. He was the undisputed master of the forest, and he couldn't think of any particular enemy that he would not encounter with a roar of joy.

epinette *n.* [< Cdn F *épinette*] **1** any of the various species of spruce.
1793 (1801) MACKENZIE *Voy.from Montreal* 239: A river also flowed from the right, and the land was high and rocky, and wooded with the epinette. **1853** REID *Young Voyageurs* 152: The gum of the épinette had to be boiled and mixed with a little grease, so as to form a species of wax [suitable for paying a canoe].

2 spruce gum.
1883 (1955) LEFROY *Magnetic North* 98: He then bathed the wound with a decoction of epinette, which is much used in the country for external applications.

epishamore or **epishemaunt** *n. Obs.* See **appichimon.**

equalization *n.* (usually attributive, with *grants, payments, policy,* etc.) See 1964 quote. See also **tax-sharing agreement.**

1963 *Globe and Mail* (Toronto) 15 May 6/6: By moving Ontario to the Prairies, Life has settled once and for all the problem of equalization grants. **1963** *Calgary Herald* 28 Nov. 1/8: His proposal to revise the equalization formula, basing it on the per-capita yield of the wealthiest province rather than as at present on the national average, was broached in terms that suggested this might be all the provinces would get at this conference. **1964** DAWSON *Government of Canada* 119: The equalization grants were unconditional grants to the poorer provinces based on fiscal need. They were designed to enable the less affluent provinces to provide a moderate level of provincial services without the necessity of carrying an abnormal load of taxation; and computed on a set formula designed to bring the per capita yield of the three "standard taxes" up to the *per capita* yield of the same standard in the two most wealthy provinces in each year. **1966** *Globe and Mail* (Toronto) 12 Aug. 7/1: Equalization is a relatively new word—it first appeared in the 1956 agreement—but the principle it represents goes back to the earliest days of Confederation.

Equal Righter *Obs.* a member of the Equal Rights Association.

1890 *Grip* (Toronto) 18 Oct. 248/1: My mind reverted to the stalwart Equal Righters who but yesterday so nobly championed the cause of civil and religious liberty.

Equal Rights (Association) *Hist.* an association of Protestants against the alleged encroachments of the Catholic Church.

1890 *Grip* (Toronto) 25 Jan. 56/2: Equal Rights has been defeated in its stronghold—Toronto—headquarters of Orange fanaticism. **1963** MORTON *Kingdom of Canada* 380: In the summer of 1889 the Equal Rights Association was organized to protect the rights of Protestants against the alleged encroachments of the Roman Catholic Church.

Ermite ['ɚmaɪt] *n.* [< Cdn F < F "hermit"] a type of blue cheese made in the Eastern Townships of Quebec.

1963 *Canadian Wkly* 23 Feb. 12/3: Benedictines at St. Benoit-du-lac in the eastern townships make a sharp, salty blue cheese called Ermite, now the only blue cheese made in Canada. **1964** LEE *Foods and Textiles* 72: Oka and Ermite are also typically Canadian cheeses.

Eskimo† ['ɛskə,mo] *n.* [< Algonk., probably through Cdn F *Esquimau* with spelling influenced by Danish *Eskimo*; cf. Cree *askimowew* he eats it raw; Ojibwa *askkimē* raw-flesh eater]

☛ *Although several other etymologies have been advanced (see quotes below), the evidence unquestionably supports the Algonkian source. The remarkably large number of variant spellings in early writings of the Labrador-Hudson's Bay region suggest constant reinforcing from contact of the English traders with the Crees. See also* **Husky.**
(a)**1748** ELLIS *Hudson's Bay* 138/9: The very Orthography of the Word *Eskimaux* plainly proves it an *Indian* Appellation, with a *French* termination, and we are told by a celebrated Writer of that Country, that it is derived from the Words *Abenaqui Esquimantsic,* which is as much as to say, *an eater of raw Flesh.* **1860** (1956) KOHL *Kitchi-Gami* 324: To my surprise, the Ojibbeways on Lake Superior are all acquainted with the raw flesh eaters, or, as they call them, "Ashkimeg." **1956**

SCHERMAN *Spring* 12: The Eskimos traditionally despise the Indians (*Irkrekret*-"Lice") and the Indians fear the barbaric little northern men (*Eskimo* is Indian for "Eaters of Raw Meat.") (b) **1616** (1858) BIARD *Relation de la Nouvelle-France* 1 7/2: Quelques peuples ont maintenant une implacable guerre contre nous, comme Excomminquois, qui habitent au costé boreal de grand golfe S. Laurens, et nous font de grands maux. **1950** *American Anthropology* Oct.-Dec. 564: The usual etymology given for the word Eskimo [French *esquimau(x)*], whereby it is derived from Algonkin Indian language *aske* "raw meat," and *moho* "to eat," is probably wrong. Originally the form of the name, as found in the *Jesuit Relations,* was *Excomminquois* or *Excomminqui.* . . . The name was first used by the Jesuits who, in 1605, began missionary work particularly among the Algonkin Indians, their friendly allies. These Indians often had encounters with the coastal tribes of Labrador, wild seal hunters who for a long time remained hostile to the Jesuits and their Indian friends. The missionaries invented the name of *Excomminquois* (pronounced *Excomminqué*) for their pagan neighbors to the north-east, and this name was later, by degrees, altered to *Escoumains* and *Esquimaux.* The original meaning is probably connected with the fact that the hostile pagans were interdicted from the church and the sacrament: Latin *excommunicati.* Therefore the etymology of Eskimo is not "eaters of raw meat," but "the excommunicated ones." (c) **1852** RICHARDSON *Arctic Exped.* 202: This appellation is probably of Canadian origin, and the word, which in French orthography is written *Esquimaux,* was, probably, originally *Ceux qui miaux* (*miaulent*), and was expressive of the shouts of *Tey-mō,* proceeding from the fleets of kaiyaks, that surround a trading-vessel in the straits of Hudson, or coasts of Labrador. (d) **1879** HALL *Second Exped.* 62: The word Esquimaux—better written Eskimo—is derived from a root indicating, in the language of the Northern tribes, a sorcerer. The Innuit name *Kag-uskeeme* means the house where the *shamans,* sorcerers, conduct their dances and incantations.

1 a member of a large group of North American aborigines inhabiting the Arctic and northern coastal areas from Greenland to Siberia. See also **Eskimo Indian, Husky** (def. 1), **Innuit** (def. 1), **'Skimo,** and **Suckemo.** Also spelled *Esquimau* (*pl. -aux*), *q.v.*

[c**1500** (1850) HAKLUYT *Divers Voyages* 23: This yeere also were brought vnto the king three men, taken in the new founde Iland, that before I spake of in William Purchas time, being Maior. These were clothed in beastes skinnes, and ate rawe fleshe, and spake such speech that no man coulde understand them, and in their demeanour like to bruite bestes, whom the king kept a time after.] **1584** (1887) HAKLUYT *Discourse on Western Planting* 269: What shoulde I speake of the customes of the greate multitudes of course clothes, Welshe frise, and Irishe ruggs that may be uttered in the more northerly partes of the land amonge the Esquimawes of the Grande Bay, and amonge them of Canada, Saguynay, and Hochelaga, wᶜʰ are subjecte to sharpe and nippinge winters, albeit their somers be hotter moche then oures. **1684** (1885) RADISSON *Voyages* 260: Wee put into Harbour to avoide the Danger of it, as also to take in fresh Water & some other Provisions at the Coast of the Indians called Esquimos, the most cruel of all the salvages when the meet an advantage to surprize Persons. **1743** (1949) ISHAM *Observations* 155:

To the Northward among'st the Northward Indians, and Ehuskemay's they have neither of these beast's. **1871** (1883) BUTLER *Great Lone Land* 296: The Esquimaux in the far-North run their dogs abreast. **1965** *Beaver* Spring 4/1: . . . the Eskimo's ancestors prevailed over a vast expanse from easternmost Siberia to the Strait of Belle Isle and to Denmark Strait between Greenland and Iceland.

2 the language of these people. See also **Husky** (def. 2) and **Innuit** (def. 2).
1819 ROSS *Voyage of Discovery* 80: When we arrived within hail, Sackheuse called out to them in his own language; some words were heard in return, to which a reply was again made in the Eskimaux, but neither party appeared to be in the least degree intelligible to the other. **1885** TUTTLE *Our North Land* 58: It was originally, and the place is still, called New-nan-go, which, in Eskimo, means a hidden place. **1965** *Globe and Mail* (Toronto) 6 Jan. 1/6: If the [Wolf] Cub is an Eskimo he must be able to translate from Eskimo to another language and understand the system of Eskimo syllabics.

3 See **Eskimo dog**.
1853 (1892) KANE *Arctic Explor.* 95: My dogs, that I had counted on so largely, the nine splendid Newfoundlanders and thirty-five Esquimaux of six months before, had perished. **1940** *Cdn Geog.Jnl* Feb. 94/1: . . . the Eskimo dog . . . is known by such names as "husky" and "wolf dog," though in the Eastern Canadian Arctic it is customarily referred to simply as the "Eskimo," or by the native name, "Kingmik." **1944** CLAY *Fur Thieves* 136: The dogs o' the Yukon an' Alaska are as different from Manitoba dogs as ours are different from the Eskimos!

Eskimo boot in the western Arctic, a mukluk (def. 1); in the eastern Arctic, a kamik, *q.v.*
1768 DRAGE *Prob.N.W.Passage* 145: A Person aboard had bought a Pair of *Eskemaux* Boots. . . . **1852** RICHARDSON *Arctic Exped.* 212: The Eskimo boots are also peculiar to the nation, being made of seal-skin so closely sewed as to be water-tight, and coming up to the hips like those used by fishermen in our own land. **1942** TWOMEY & HERRICK *Needle to the North* 213: When you walk in a pair of Eskimo boots, you must remember that the ridges of rocky hills are too sharp for a boot to endure many miles without coming to pieces.

Eskimo canoe See **kayak**[1] and picture.
1749 DRAGE *Voyage* II 39: Both these Kind of Canoes, the Eskemaux Canoes and those of these Indians were in Use amongst the Antients. **1857** MCDOUGALL *Voyage* 30: The Esquimaux canoes are well worthy of notice, being proofs alike of the ingenuity and neat workmanship of the builders.

Eskimo cotton See **Arctic cotton**.
1936 STRINGER *Wife-Traders* 115: The redberries shone coral-bright against the caribou-moss. The Eskimo-cotton and the twin-flowers were thinning out between the rocky slopes. The Innuit girls were busy gathering the last of the cloudberries. . . .

Eskimo devil See **Torngak**.
1912 POCOCK *Man in the Open* 11: I wished . . . the bush didn't look so wolfy, and what if I met up with the Eskimo devil! *Ibid.* 5: We kids used to play at Newf'nlanders up in the hold, when the winter storms

were tearing the tops off the hills, and the Eskimo devil howled blue shrieks outside.

Eskimo dog one of an aboriginal breed of dog, *Canis familiaris borealis,* probably originating in Siberia, trained by the Eskimo to draw sleds and carry packs. See also **Eskimo** (def. 3), **husky**[1], **kingmik**, and **wolf dog**. Cp. **malemute**.
1577 (1889) HAKLUYT *Voyages* XII 89: Thier . . . Dogges [are] like unto wolves, but for ye most part black. . . . **1774** LA TROBE *Mission* 29: The great number of Esquimaux dogs, that must seek their own maintenance, prevent the success they [Eskimos] might have in catching fish, as these half-starved dogs, at low water, run into the nets, tear out and devour the fish, and morever [sic] tear the nets to pieces. **1851** (1917) GOULD *Inasmuch* 126: Sometimes they are playing and fondling each other and persons of their acquaintance, although there is less personal attachment in the Eskimo dog than in any others; and, again, I have seen Eskimo dogs lying dead, killed by their companions in terrible battles. **1949** *Beaver* Mar. 36/1: The Eskimo dog is not built for the hunt but for the pack.

Eskimo fan hitch See **fan hitch** and picture.
1936 STEELE *Policing the Arctic* 220: [They preferred] to draw those sleds with large teams of dogs on the Eskimo fan-hitch, not exhaust personnel by the hard man-haul. **1936** *Beaver* Mar. 39/2: But beyond doubt the Eskimo fan hitch is the superior of any other for the open treeless regions of the Arctic.

Eskimo hunt *Obs.* an organized foray by the Northern Indians to seek out and destroy Eskimos. See also **Eskimo hunting**.
1785 *Moose Ft Jnls* 306: Just at the writing of this the Albany Indian arrived here for the Esquimauix hunt, and yours returned with them again. **1845** (1914) DOUGLAS *Lands Forlorn* 3: An Eskimo Hunt has always been a favourite diversion among the Border Indians. **1914** *Ibid.* 3: That they reached the Coppermine River at all was due to the decision of Hearne's Chipewyans, who had been joined by a number of Copper Indians, to have an "Eskimo Hunt," evidently a popular form of amusement with the Northern Indians at that time.

Eskimo hunter *Obs.* an Indian who took part in Eskimo hunts.
1830 (1963) DAVIES *Northern Quebec* 105: . . . an old Esquimaux hunter used all his eloquence to persuade us to return. . . .

Eskimo hunting *Obs.* See **Eskimo hunt**.
*c*1752 (1852) COATS *Geography of H.B.* 56: These powerfull people are such a terrour to the servile tribes, that although they do not constantly go annually a Usquemow hunting for their bloody inhumane sacrifice, these poor creatures do this for them, or are sure to be that sacrifice themselves. **1963** DAVIES *Northern Quebec* XXXV: Numerous examples can be found in the post records of Company servants along the Eastmain coast standing by helplessly as bands of Indians bent on the murderous pursuit of "Eskimo hunting" passed the posts on the way north. . . .

Eskimo ice cream See quotes.
1913 HAWKES *Inviting-in Feast* 9: The visiting tribe also has the privilege of demanding any delicacy . . . which fancy may suggest. This usually takes the form of meat out of season, or Eskimo "ice-cream"—a concoction of reindeer tallow, blueberries, and chunks of whitefish kneaded in the snow until it is frozen. **1962** *Favorite Recipes* 39: *Eskimo Ice Cream*. Grind up cooked meat. Melt tallow and while still warm mix well by hand.

Keep adding meat until not able to stir anymore. This is good to eat with meat and bread . . . Sadie Simon.

Eskimo Indian *Obs.* See **Eskimo** (def. 1).
1742 (1744) DOBBS *Hudson's Bay* 96: What was still as unpardonable as neglecting the Discovery, was his putting the two *Northern Indians* ashore on *Marble Island* against their Inclinations . . . in a very bad Boat he got at *Churchill,* which they did not know how to manage, in an Island 3 Leagues from their supposed Way, the *Eskimay Indians,* their Enemies, living upon that Coast. **1848** LANMAN *Adventures* 213: During one of my national expeditions down the St. Lawrence, I chanced to be wind-bound for a couple of days at the mouth of a river on the north shore, where I found a small encampment of Esquimaux Indians.

Eskimo (oil) lamp See **kudlik** and picture.
1864 HALL *Life with Esquimaux* I 183: The Esquimaux lamp is the "all in all" to these people. **1938** *Beaver* Dec. 14: The Eskimo oil lamp and the primus stoves were soon going and a meal well under way.

Eskimoland *n.* the Arctic regions inhabited by Eskimos.
1853 SEEMAN *H.M.S.Herald* II 49: Indeed, a rough estimate of merely the coast of Eskimo-land—for of the interior we are ignorant, would give no more than three souls for every two square miles, or a total number of 2500. **1916** BRIDLE *Sons of Canada* 209: Introduced to a young explorer from Eskimoland he at once heckled him for positive, reliable, and strictly ethnological information concerning the Eskimos. . . . **1964** *North* July 47/2: My standing with the Gods of the ethereal regions surrounding Eskimo-land may have been on a sound footing but my position with the natives themselves was none too firmly established.

Eskimo roll See quote.
1959 *Weekend Mag.* 18 Apr. 69/1: . . . in the case of kayaks, there is a good chance they will capsize. When this happens, the kayak contestant must execute the "Eskimo roll," which is a means of righting himself with his paddles. . . .

Eskimo salad the half-digested moss found in the stomach of a caribou and highly prized as food by the Eskimos.
[**1882** GILDER *Schwatka's Search* 141: He then regales himself with some of the spinach-like contents of the paunch, and by way of filling in the time and the little crinkles of his stomach, cuts off and eats such little portions of fat as are exposed in the process of butchering.] **1942** *Beaver* Dec. 19/2: Removing the stomach [of a caribou] full of "Eskimo salad". . . . **1948** ONRAET *Sixty Below* 129: Some Eskimo tribes even eat the half digested contents of the stomach. It is chewed-up moss and we call it Eskimo salad.

Eskimo script or **syllabics** a modification of the Cree syllabics, *q.v.,* used by the Eskimos.
[**1964** JENNESS *Eskimo Admin.* II 16: In 1876 the Anglican missionary, E. J. Peck, took over a mission on the east coast of Hudson Bay at Little Whale River, and for the benefit of the Eskimos in that region transcribed in Evans' syllabic script parts of the New Testament that had been translated into Eskimo by a Moravian missionary on the Labrador coast.] **1965** *North* Nov.-Dec. 12: The chapter received thank you letters from the children written in English and Eskimo script and signed, "your nieces and nephews," under such names as Eleesapee, Jukee, Ooleepeeka and Elijah. **1966** *Ibid.* May-June 44/1: The talks on co-operative operation and a guide book of fur have been translated into Eskimo syllabics.

Eskimo sled or **sledge** See **komatik** and picture.
1770 (1792) CARTWRIGHT *Journal* I 71: An Esquimau sled . . . is made of two spruce planks, each twenty-one feet long, fourteen inches broad, and two inches thick, which are hewn out of separate trees (because they are not acquainted with the use of the pitsaw). **1852** (1855) BELLOT *Journal* II 82: It has also the advantage of not sinking in the snow when it is soft; whereas the Esquimaux sledges would sink to their full depth in it. **1914** DOUGLAS *Lands Forlorn* 146: Above Hanbury's Kopje we came on the track of an Eskimo sled and pushed on fully expecting to find the Eskimos at the lake.

Eskimo tent See **tupek.**
1749 DRAGE *Voyage* II 220: We saw also at our first landing a round of Stones, which we supposed had been the Foundation of one of the Eskemaux Tents. **1852** RICHARDSON *Arctic Exped.* 160: Soon afterward we saw two Eskimo tents on the extreme point of this island. **1914** DOUGLAS *Lands Forlorn* 226: At the edge of the spruce woods on the western slope we saw some Eskimo tents and a number of musk-ox skins spread out over the big boulders, but there was no one in sight.

Esquimau *n.* -aux. See **Eskimo.**
☞ *This form which came into English through French, has been current for several centuries and is still in wide use. The plural form* Esquimaux *is often used in singular contexts.*

étoffe du pays *Cdn French* strong, gray woollen homespun, much used in the bush.
1889 *Scribner's Mag.* May 530/1: Home-made trousers of the home-woven gray woolen *étoffe du pays* tucked into the wrinkled legs of the long moccasins tied below the knee, which, in contradiction from town-made "bottes francaises," are known as "bottes sauvages". . . . **1933** ROLYAT *Wilderness Walls* 22: . . . the voyageurs [were dressed] in checked shirts and trousers of thick *étoffe du pays*. . . . **1951** O'MEARA *Grand Portage* 307: *Étoffe du pays:* a coarse woolen material.

eulachon *n.* See **oolichan.**

Europe *n. Obs.* See quote.
1845 TOLFREY *Sportsman* II 14n: Europe-shop is a Colonial saying; everything imported from England is designated as Europe—for instance, Europe porter, Europe pickles—to distinguish the commodities from indigenous articles. The word Europe also carries with it a carte blanche as to price, of which the Europe shopkeeper knows how to avail himself.

Europe-shop *n. Obs.* See quote. See also **Europe.**
1845 TOLFREY *Sportsman* II 13: . . . we engaged and fitted up for the purpose a large store or shop, termed by all Colonial residents a Europe-*shop,* that is a shop for the exclusive sale of European goods, in contradistinction, I presume, to the *store,* where Native commodities are disposed of.

Ex [ɛks] *n.* [shortening of *exhibition*] an exhibition, especially the Canadian National Exhibition held each summer in Toronto.
1958 *Weekend Mag.* 23 Aug. 6/3: . . . Toronto youngsters add one more red-letter day to the calendar. It's the annual day at the "Ex"—the Canadian National Exhibition, which runs the latter part of August and into September. **1959** *Ottawa Citizen* 13 Aug. 3/5: Lansdowne Park is a busy spot these days with workmen putting up . . . structures which will play a vital role

during the Central Canada Exhibition. The "Ex" opens Aug. 21. **1962** *Kingston Whig-Standard* (Ont.) 4 Sep. 13/1: ... this reporter paid a flying trip to Toronto ... to find out if the "Ex" of this year was "up to scratch."

exchange† *n.* See **exchange paper.**
1837 (1938) *Cdn.Hist.Rev.* XIX 15: No news establishment in British America pays so high a price as we do for paper. Yet nineteen-twentieths of our exchanges are printed on a fairer quality [paper]. ...
1904 *Eye Opener* (Calgary) 25 June 1/5: The following poem appears in Eastern exchanges, signed "Scotch but nae Foreigner."

exchange paper† a newspaper sent free by one publisher to another in return for a like service.
1838 *Western Herald & Farmers' Mag.* (Sandwich [Windsor], U.C.) 23 Jan. 13/3: The Toronto Patriot is the only exchange paper that has as yet come to hand.
1842 *Bytown* [Ottawa] *Gaz.* 26 May 2/4: In looking over our exchange papers, we find the following account of a meeting which has been held in Kingston, relative to this important subject.

excursionist *n. Hist.* a person taking part in the harvest excursion, *q.v.,* to the wheatlands of the West.
1966 *Canadian* 30 Apr. 7/2: This gave the excursionists further opportunity for highjinks.

executive council 1 *Hist.* during colonial times, a group of advisors appointed by the governor and responsible to him.
1789 (1866) CHRISTIE *Lower Canada* VI 20: Your Lordship will also state to me for His Majesty's information, the number and names of those persons whom you may think proper to recommend to His Majesty for seats in the Executive Council.
1870 *Mainland Guardian* (New Westminster, B.C.) 8 Jan. 2/1: In any case the Executive Council is not a responsible Council, but is the Governor's Council, and therefore, we presume it to be advisable that he should have members representing different views, because no one will contend that all parts of the country desire the same, or would be satisfied with a similar line of policy.
1963 MORTON *Kingdom of Canada* 183: A clear structure of government, modelled exactly ... on the British Constitution in church and state, was provided in governor, executive council, legislative council, and representative assembly to correspond with King, Privy Council, Lords, and Commons.

2 the body of ministers forming the cabinet of a provincial government.
1875 (1905) BIGGAR *Oliver Mowat* II 572: It was in consequence of the policy adopted by my colleagues in the conduct of the reciprocity negotiations that I felt compelled to resign my position as President of the Executive Council. **1958** *Encyc.Can.* IV 55/1: At Confederation the Governor-General's council was designate the Queen's Privy Council for Canada, but the term Executive Council remains for the executives in the provinces.

exemption money *Obs.* in Upper Canada, a fee charged those persons in each riding who obtained certificates excusing them from voting.
1801 *Niagara Herald* (U.C.) 23 May 3/3: All quakers, menonists or tunkers within the said riding are hereby required to attend at the time and place above

mentioned, with such certificates as the law requires, and pay the exemption money.

Exovedate [ˌɛksovəˈdet] *n.* [< *Exovede,* q.v.] *Hist.* the provisional government established under Louis Riel in 1885 during the Northwest Rebellion.
1885 (1963) STANLEY *Louis Riel* 330: The Exovedate are of the opinion that Middleton and his troops ought not to be treated as extraordinary. **1952** HOWARD *Strange Empire* 385: It was intended to designate him as "one of the flock," as were all members of the council, which he called the "Exivodat," and was a specific disavowal of personal leadership. **1963** STANLEY *Louis Riel* 315: The Exovedate had ... talked about occupying Fort Carleton, but no preparations had been made for doing so. ...

Exovede [ɛksˈovid] *n.* [coined by Louis Riel: L *ex* from, and *ovede* flock] *Hist.* a member of the Exovedate.
1885 (1927) LONGSTRETH *Silent Force* 150: Yours, LOUIS "DAVID" RIEL, EXOVEDE. *Ibid.* 149: McKay, with a gesture worthy of Cyrano, ventured to say that Riel would have it, whereupon the Exovede rose abruptly, mentioned a committee meeting, and left the room. **1963** STANLEY *Louis Riel* 307: Riel remained aloof. ... But he did make his own special contribution by giving the new body a name. Each man was called an *exovede,* and the council itself the *Exovedate.*

experimental farm one of a number of farms operated by the federal government for the purpose of making available to Canadian farmers the results of scientific research and experiment in agriculture and keeping them informed on agricultural developments. See also **experimental station.**
1894 *Trans.Roy.Soc.Can.* XII 4 143: Six years ago the testing of trees and shrubs suitable for planting on the Northwest plains was begun at the experimental farms at Brandon, Manitoba, and at Indian Head, N.W.T.
1921 *Beaver* June 10/1: The first experimental farm in Manitoba was started in 1831 by the Hudson's Bay company. **1958** *Edmonton Jnl* 26 July 39/4: Horticulturalist R. E. Harris, on the staff of the dominion experimental farm at Beaverlodge, reported harvesting about 300 ears of Altagold corn on Tuesday, July 22.

experimental station See **experimental farm.**
1912 FOOTNER *New Rivers* 155: The corn and tomatoes do not always ripen fully, but the experiment station is only three years old and the superintendent is confident of getting them yet. **1958** ATKINSON *Hist.of Penticton* 29: ... and as the Dominion Experimental Station was not established until 1914, they did not play a part in laying out the early plantings.

exploration camp the headquarters in the field for a mining company's prospectors.
1964 *Calgary Herald* 25 Feb. 11/7: One of the main stop-over points on the trip was an exploration camp some 200 miles from the closest living person.

Expo ('67) [< *exposition*] the world's fair held in Montreal during Canada's Centennial Year.
1965 *Saturday Night* July 11: ... these towns, in their way, are as accurate a reflection of the Canada we've become as Expo '67. **1966** *Vancouver Province* 10 Sep. 37/3: In the services department, you can get ... a shopping spree at a supermarket, a year's parking downtown, a week at EXPO in Montreal. **1967** *Globe and Mail* (Toronto) 19 Apr. 3/1: Two Belgian gendarmes were disarmed yesterday as Expo moved to enforce

Canadian law that no foreign nationals carry firearms on Canadian soil.

express† *n. Hist.* **1** a party of special messengers travelling light by foot, canoe, or dog team and entrusted with conveying messages, correspondence, and other documents between posts; also, the system of employing such messengers. See also **inland packet** and **winter express**.

1794 (1929) MCGILLIVRAY *Journal* 40: Mr. Tomison is much disappointed that no goods are sent him by this express. **1820** (1938) SIMPSON *Athabasca Jnl* 193: I expect some trains of dogs by the return Express from St. Marys. . . . **1918** DAVIDSON *North West Co.* 219: There was a regular system of expresses to carry correspondence, reports, and news to and from the different posts in the Northwest. Masson states that there were two expresses annually. The winter express left the farthest posts in the north about the end of November, passed through the whole country on sledges and snow-shoes and reached Sault St. Marie in March. The summer express hurried down to the place of rendezvous with the results of the winter's trade, apparently in advance of the canoes with the furs. **1949** ROBERTS *Mackenzie* 122: But in the golden years, Simpson's "express" was regarded as a speed-up of revolutionary proportions typical of the efficient trader who inaugurated it. **1962** (1964) INNIS *Fur Trade in Canada* 317: In 1832 the southern express went via Fort Pelly and Norway house.

2† a runner, especially an Indian runner.
1806 (1893) LEWIS & CLARK *Journals* V 103: To day the Indians dispatched an express over the mountains to the travellers rest. **1896** WHITNEY *On Snow-Shoes* 21: Once past here, the most rapid means of communication is the "express," as the Indian runner is called.
1921 HEMING *Drama of Forests* 137: In the meantime, an express had been despatched to Prince Albert to summon a doctor; but the old Indian women could not bear to wait so long for the coming of relief, so filing a big knife into a fine-toothed saw, they cut away the bruised flesh and sawed off the broken bones.
1957 FISHER *Pemmican* 223: Colin had then seized the pedlar express and found, in writing, absolute proof of a plot to wipe out the entire colony. . . .

express canoe *Fur Trade, Hist.* a fast light canoe (def. 1) used by the fur-traders for speedy delivery of officials, communications, correspondence, and special goods. See also **canoe** (def. 1), **canot allégé**, **canot du gouverneur**, and **canot Rabasca**. Cp. **small canoe**. Also *express boat*.

1824 (1931) MERK *Fur Trade* 248: A larger supply of Fish than usual will be required at this place as the extra men who accompany the Express canoe in Spring so much earlier than customary will remain here a considerable time. **1827** (1912) ERMATINGER *Express Jnl* 70: The Express Boat leaves Fort Vancouver at 1/4 before 6 o'clock p.m. **1870** *Mainland Guardian* (New Westminster, B.C.) 26 Jan. 3/1: The Express canoe arrived at this city on the afternoon of Sunday last, after a delay that began to give rise to inquietude. **1954** CAMPBELL *Nor'Westers* 51: Paddling an express canoe was the highest honour for a canoeman. With four or five picked men he would rush the mail or a *bourgeois* at twice the usual speed.

Expulsion *n. Hist.* the mass deportations in 1755 of French Acadians who refused to take an unconditional oath of allegiance to the British flag.
1950 BIRD *This Is N.S.* 25: Masstown was once an Acadian village called "cobequid," and the Acadians had a large place of worship there, the Church of St.

Peter and St. Paul. It was burned at the time of the *Expulsion*. . . . **1963** *Time* (Cdn ed.) 26 April 12/2: Today, the Acadians' only popular preference in art are paintings and prints of the Expulsion, which is also the source for their melancholy folk songs.

extra gang in railway construction, a gang of laborers employed for various kinds of heavy work, usually involving road-bed repairs, replacement of rails or ties, and other work not handled by the section crew.
1923 (1926) DICKIE *Cdn West* 298: He had all the ties hauled up the grade the night before, and he brought up an 'extra' gang of men. **1927** NIVEN *Wild Honey* 2: There was what was called an Extra Gang there, employed upon shovelling gravel out of a hillside into dump-cars that took it away to fill in gulches under trestle bridges. **1954** LYSENKO *Yellow Boots* 186: . . . the speech of the Boukovinian homesteaders made constant reference to their experience on the extra gang. **1966** *Kingston Whig-Standard* (Ont.) 1 Sep. 3/1: I was a gandy-dancer on the extra gang lifting and reballasting the main line in the McAdam, N.B., subdivision.

eye *n.* [trans. from Ojibwa] *Rare* See **toe-hole**.
1860 (1956) KOHL *Kitchi-Gami* 335: They [Ojibwa] call this hole "oshkinjig," or the "eye of the snowshoe." *Ibid.* 336: In many parts they only take a long board, which they cut in the shape of a fish, but, of course, the "eye" of the shoe [snowshoe] must be made in this.

eyeberry *n.* a plant, *Rubus acaulis,* of the northern regions; also, its fruit.
1795 (1911) HEARNE *Journey* 453: The Eye-berry grows much in the same manner as the Strawberry, and though smaller, is infinitely superior in flavour. **1821** (1900) GARRY *Diary* 154: Fine Berry, called by the Indians Eye Berry, like a Strawberry in Appearance with the Taste of a Blackberry. . . . **1900** *Ibid.* 154n: *Eyeberry* is mentioned by Franklin . . . but no Latin name is given and I cannot trace it elsewhere.

Eyebrow *n.* See **Big Eyebrow**.
1951 BULIARD *Inuk* 65: Anguyak heard about it and said, "The first Amarok (Wolf Police) or any other Eyebrow that comes after me will find himself at the wrong end of my rifle. I'll shoot him like a rabbit."

fabrique ['fæbrɪk] *n*. [< Cdn F] *Hist*. in French Canada, a local parish body responsible for the maintenance and management of church property; vestry.
1767 *Quebec Gaz.* 30 Apr. 3/1: Consequently, it belongs to the Managers of the Fabrick Lands, and not to any other Persons, to repair the said wall. **1836** *Vindicator* (Quebec) 19 Jan. 2/2: Remember how the Fabrique question was treated by the Tory party. **1887** *Trans. Roy.Soc.Can.* IV 2 55: The old institution of the fabrique—which still exists in all its vigour—enabled them to meet together whenever it was necessary to repair a church or presbytery. **1963** MORTON *Kingdom of Canada* 259: The only kind of local government left [1830's] was the ecclesiastical *fabrique*, the parish vestry charged with the upkeep of the church edifice.

face *v. Obs*. See **face off**.
1897 *Medicine Hat News* (Alta) 25 Feb. 1/6: Ben Niblock scored the first goal for Medicine Hat a few seconds after the puck was faced.

face off begin play in hockey, lacrosse, etc. by a face-off (def. 1).
1958 *Vancouver Province* 12 May 11/5: Reeve John Stolberg *faced off* the ball.... **1963** O'BRIEN *Hockey* 67: In accordance with the rules, Storey skated over to the penalty bench, lifted the minor penalty to a major penalty and skated away to face off the puck.

face-off *n*. in hockey, lacrosse, etc.: **1** the putting of the puck or ball into play by dropping it between the sticks of two opposing players facing each other. Also spelled *faceoff*.
1896 *Times* (Niagara-on-the-Lake, Ont.) 20 Feb. 1/4: In the face-off Bishop lost, and Gilmore scored in 10 minutes. **1902** CONNOR *Glengarry School Days* 309: ... when in the face-off he secured the ball, Hughie clung so tenaciously to his heels and checked him so effectually, that he was forced to resign it to the Reds, who piercing the Twentieth center, managed to scurry up the ice with the ball between them. **1966** *Globe and Mail* (Toronto) 11 Jan. 30/6: ... Horton is probably the strongest man in the league on faceoffs.
2 the start of a game.
1899 *Medicine Hat News* (Alta) 23 Mar. 5/5: From the face off till the finish the home team showed to better advantage in combination and general team work. **1964** *Maclean's* 21 Mar. 11/2: By curtain, or face-off, time the house was about three-quarters full, and when Frank Mahovlich scored after five minutes of the first period there was a loud roar of appreciation.

factor† *n. Hist*. a Hudson's Bay Company employee in charge of a trading post, ranking higher than a chief trader, *q.v.*, but below a chief factor, *q.v.* See also **second** (def. 1). Cp. **post manager**.
1671 (1942) *H.B.C.Minutes* 4: That Mr. Rastell take and account ... of all orders & Commissions given to the Commanders & factors abroad.... **1743** (1949) ISHAM *Observations* 85: When Light the factor takes the Callimutt by the midle, and points the small End first to the sun's Rising, then to the highth or midle of the Day, then at the suns setting, then to the Ground, and with a round turn presents itt again to the Leader, when they all and Everyone cry ho! (which signifies thanks). **1893** OXLEY *Young Nor'Wester* 43: From the curse of firewater the factor of Fort Chipewyan had kept his

skirts clear. **1962** DICKIE *Great Golden Plain* 32: Then Factor Verner surrendered.

factory† *n. Hist*. a fur-trading post, especially one of the larger trans-shipment posts operated by the Hudson's Bay Company, for example, York Factory.
1671 (1942) *H.B.C.Minutes* 4: That an account bee taken also ... of ... the bills of Ladeing & factoryes. **1765-75** (1933) POND *Narrative* 39: This factoery Belongd to the French traders of Canaday. **1861** *Nor'Wester* (R.R.S.) 1 July 1/2: They are distributed over 152 trading-posts and factories, scattered at distances of 300 or 400 miles apart over the whole country from the Atlantic to the Pacific. **1907** HUNTER *Cdn Wilds* 46: The so-called factories were not places in which fabrics or other goods were manufactured, but more rightly speaking great depots where an entire year's supplies were stored in advance in case of a mishap to either of the ships. **1963** *Beaver* Autumn 44/1: However, it may be assumed that the clearing of land and importation of livestock from Moose Factory began soon after the union of 1821.

faculty jacket in certain Canadian universities, a windbreaker or jacket worn by students of the several faculties, as Arts, Science, Medicine, identified by color and lettering, which usually indicates the year the wearer expects to graduate.
1963 *Kingston Whig-Standard* (Ont.) 8 Feb. 4/4: She suggested that the Queen's undergraduate with his faculty jacket and generally unkempt appearance set the tone to which the high school student tried to conform.

faggot *n. Nfld* a stack of codfish so built as to shed rain. See also **fish pile** and **flacket**.
1777 (1792) CARTWRIGHT *Journal* II 249: We turned up yesterday's water horse and in the evening made it up into large faggots. **1832** MCGREGOR *British America* I 230: ... men, women, and children ... even run, if on Sunday, out of places of worship, to collect the fish into fagots or piles. **1963** *American Speech* Dec. 298: FAGGOT, *n*. A pile of half-dried fish.

faggot *v. Nfld* pile codfish into faggots.
1779 (1792) CARTWRIGHT *Journal* II 469: We heaved part of the fish that was re-packed last; but were obliged to faggot it upon the flakes immediately, on account of rain coming on.

faggot road *West, Obs*. a road surfaced with bundles of saplings. Cp. **corduroy road**.
1956 INNIS *Travellers West* 24: The Council [of Assiniboia] was concerned with the building of faggot roads and bridges, probably related to the corduroy roads and bridges in the more heavily forested backwoods of Canada West....

fairy shoe a pink orchid, *Calypso bulbosa*.
1938 STANWELL-FLETCHER *Driftwood Valley* 171: Beds of pink Calypso orchids—"fairy shoes"—are scattered through the woods.

fall† *n*. autumn.
1697 (1929) KELSEY *Papers* 95: Yᵉ french man told me he found a dead man in yᵉ marsh so sent 4 hands to see it proved to be Thoˢ. Bullears boy & yᵗ died of yᵉ rivers mouth last fall. **1767** *Quebec Gaz.* 5 Jan. 3/1: To be Sold Cheap ... A Few Barrels of pickeled COD FISH, taken [late] last Fall.... **1849** ALEXANDER *L'Acadie* II 10: A week at Loughborough in the "fall" is delightful. Then the woods put on their coats of many colours, the sugar maple displayed all the shades of red—from deep crimson to bright orange.... **1958** *Edmonton Jnl* 22

July 23/4: Meanwhile, it will be sometime this fall before any new outlets can be opened in Edmonton.

fall *v. Lumbering* work as a faller, *q.v.*
1918 MACKAY *Trench and Trail* 112:
I am call' de "Skookum Kid," Rosemarie;
I'm grease lightning on de skid Yes siree;
I can "team" or "tend de hook,"
I can "bark" or "fall" or "buck,"
An' w'en whisky's down de cook
I'm "cookee!"

fall debt See **debt.**
1952 *Beaver* Dec. 29/1: Some hunters would get their "fall debt" or a portion of it, as early as August, transporting the heavier goods to their trapping grounds and returning to the post in September for the balance of their debt.

fallen timber See **down timber.**
1824 (1931) SIMPSON *Fur Trade* 34: Our Road was rugged and bad frequently covered with fallen Timber the country having been over run by Fire. **1936** *Cdn.Geog. Jnl* Jan. 15: [Caption] Often the portage trails are blocked by fallen timber or cross muskegs where the packers sink down half way to the knee in moss and mud.

faller *n. Lumbering* a person whose work is to fell trees. See also **feller.**
1908 GRAINGER *Woodsmen* 84: The "fallers" had worked along the slope . . . and all the trees of value had been felled criss-cross. . . . **1966** *Dly Colonist* (Victoria) 4 Feb. 17/6: Mr. Peterson is employed as a faller by Butler Brothers.

fall fair a fair held each fall in many Canadian communities for the exhibiting and judging of livestock, home-baking, etc., often accompanied by horse races, dancing, and other forms of entertainment.
1903 RICHARDSON *Colin* 304: Goarden usually sang with special gusto upon his return from the county town late in the evening of a fall fair-day. **1949** DE LA ROCHE *Wakefield* 245: . . . a man in a gig training a trotter for the Fall Fair trotting races. **1960** *Ontario History* June 97: . . . the first Township Fall Fair [King, Ont.] was organized in 1852. **1965** *News of the North* 23 Sep. 4/1: The 15th. Annual Fall fair at Fort Simpson held last week, brought exhibits from other northern settlements including Fort Franklin, Jean Marie River, Fort Providence and Nahanni Butte.

fall fish or **salmon** *West Coast* See **coho.**
1907 LAMBERT *Fishing in B.C.* 74: The cohoe, silver or fall salmon (*O. kisutch*) is also canned, weight 3 lb. to 8 lb., light green and silver in colour. **1954** EVANS *Mist* 78: . . . Caleb had hoped that when the sockeye season ended, and the cannery went on to fall fish, a transfer could be arranged. . . .

fall goose See **wavey.**
1959 BODSWORTH *Strange One* 198: And soon the fall geese, the waveys, are here from the Arctic. . . .

fall hunt *Fur Trade* **1** the period of hunting and trapping before winter sets in.
1783 (1954) *Moose Ft Jnls* 151: I am sorry I have to Echo back your Complaints of Geese this Fall necessity having obliged me almost all the Season to serve the Men salt Geese the remains of [the] last fall Hunt. **1896** RUSSELL *Far North* 108: Since they had given up the fall hunt, owing to the severity of the season, it became the more necessary that they should succeed in the spring. **1921** HEMING *Drama of Forests* 258: The Indians divide their annual hunt for fur into three distinct hunting seasons: the fall hunt—from autumn until Christmas; the winter hunt—from New Year's Day until Easter; and the spring hunt—from Easter until the hunters depart for their tribal summer camping ground.

2 the furs taken in this period.
1907 HUNTER *Cdn Wilds* 234: . . . hunters . . . will sell their fall hunts less a skin. This reserved skin may be only a musquash. They keep this . . . to draw other skins when next they go trapping.

falling† *n. Lumbering* the felling of trees.
1943 SWANSON *Lumberjack* 12: So huge they were (both cedar and fir) that days were spent in their falling. **1952** *Beaver* Sep. 14/1: Everybody was too tired after nine hours of falling, bucking, loading, track-laying, cold-decking, scaling, saw-filing, flunkeying, or whatever the job was. . . . **1960** *Citizen* 10 Mar. 10/1: Men who have known forehead strain of tump-line . . . / Swinging balance and cut of keen falling-saw / Bite of falling-axe, tap of falling-wedge. . . .

falling pole See **drop-log.** See **deadfall,** *n.* (def. 1) for full quote.
1853 STRICKLAND *Canada West* I 158n: . . . a kind of trap, called a dead fall which is constructed thus. . . . A piece of wood two or three feet long is bedded into the ground, or snow, as the case may be. The falling pole is supported immediately over this by three pieces of stick notched together in the form of a figure of four. . . . The marten or fisher, allured by the bait, reaches in to snatch it, which springs the trap, and causes the pole to fall across the neck of the animal, which is instantly killed by the blow.

fallow† *n. Hist.* **1 a.** a tract of land on which the trees and brush have been chopped down for burning (def. 1).
1826 (1916) SELLAR *Narrative* 104: On Jabez telling me we would need somebody to teach us how to handle oxen and to burn a fallow, I went to see Sloot, and bargained with him for a week's work. **1845** BEAVAN *Life in Backwoods N.B.* 18: After this first burn, a *fallow* presents a blackened scene of desolation and confusion. . . . **1852** (1923) MOODIE *Roughing It* 341: A logging-bee followed the burning of the fallow as a matter of course. **1905** SCHERCK *Pen Pictures* 48: During a dry spell in summer, a day was set for the "burn," when the piles in the "fallow" were set on fire.

b. a tract marked off for chopping (def. 1).
1853 (1959) MOODIE *Life in Clearings* 198: "We set sail the first o' May, an' were here in time to chop a sma' fallow for our fall crop." **1902** (1957) GUILLET *Valley of the Trent* 273: A fallow of ten acres was staked off into one acre parcels and when a teamster and a gang got their acre logged the day's work was . . . at an end with that gang.

2 a tract of land that has just been cleared of trees and is in crop or ready for planting.
1826 (1916) SELLAR *Narrative* 105: All week we worked at getting crop into the fallow. **1845** BEAVAN *Life In Backwoods N.B.* 18: . . . our fallow [is] fenced and filled . . . the buckwheat spreading its broad leaves, and the vines of the pumpkin and cucumbers running along the rich soil. . . .

fall salmon† See **fall fish.**

fall-trap *n.* See **deadfall** (def. 1 and picture).
1867 LORD *Wilderness* 313: Two or three different kinds of fall-traps are employed to catch pine martens.

fall wheat† wheat sown in the fall, ripening during the following spring or summer.
1823 *Cdn Mag.* I: Notwithstanding the failure of Fall wheat sown last year, considerable quantities have again been sown this fall. . . . **1836** *Bytown* [Ottawa] *Gaz.* 13 Oct. 4/1: The best fall wheat, sold by Messrs. Woods and Davidson, weighed 62 lbs per bushel. **1960** RYERSON *Founding of Canada* 98: With the exception of fall wheat (the development of which aroused some interest on the part of the French authorities), the practice of farming in New France differed little from that in the Old World.

false heath or **heather** a shrub, *Phyllodoce empetriformis,* found in northern regions and in the Rocky Mountains; pink mountain heather.
1830 (1837) *Trans.Lit.& Hist.Soc.Que.* III 96: False Heath [is] a delicate little shrub about six inches high, resembling some species of heath. **1952** PUTNAM *Cdn Regions* 436/2: Red and yellow heaths, false heathers and blueberry bushes are common plants.

false hemlock See **Douglas fir.**
1956 *Native Trees* 56: The Douglas firs (or "false hemlocks", as their botanical name implies) are a small genus of 4 or 5 species of which 2 are natives of Western North America. . . . The name "false hemlock" is derived from the resemblance of the flexible, flattened, bluntly-pointed leaves to those of the true hemlock.

false ice a surface layer of thin ice formed over the thick under-surface and separated from it by a layer of water, slush, or air of varying depth.
1858 (1863) PALLISER *Journals* 77: We had a good deal of trouble getting past several great rapids, where there was much false ice, through which our dogs broke several times.

false sugar maple *Obs.* See **Manitoba maple.**
1863 PALLISER *Journals* 11: Only a few trees of the false sugar maple, from which the Indians make a coarse kind of sugar, being found in certain places [on the prairies].

fameuse [fə'muz *or* fa'mø:z] *n.* [< Cdn F < F "famous"] **1** See **snow apple.**
1814 *Quebec Gaz.* 13 Jan. 1/1: For Sale . . . at the Mariner Store, Lower Town—20 Bbls. Montreal Apples, Grisse, Bourassa and Fameaus, of superior quality and in prime order. **1888** *Dominion Illustrated* 130/2: Canada has the finest table apple in the world, and it is not generally known that the Island of Montreal, and, notably, the Royal Mountain behind it, yields the best of these—the Fameuses,—giving rise to the theory that there is the original *habitat* of this great fruit. **1923** WILLIAMS *Spinning Wheels* 239: And to few of us is it given . . . to get a whiff of a fragrant Russet or Fameuse without being taken back to the days of "hoards" in queer, unfrequented places. **1965** (see quote at **gris**].

2 the tree this apple grows on.
1806 *Quebec Gaz.* 11 Dec. 4/1: The said ground being planted with fruit trees . . . of the best quality being chiefly, bourassa, gris and fameux. **1883** *What Farmers*

Say 67: It has been proved that apple trees do thrive in this country, and there is ground to believe that the celebrated "Fameuse" of Quebec could be produced.

Family Allowance a monthly allowance paid to the parents or trustees of children under 16 years of age. See also **baby bonus, Family Allowance Act,** and **Mothers' Allowance.**
1952 *Cdn Geog.Jnl* Jan. 15/2: Since the casual trading of children between families makes the administration of Family Allowance difficult, Ottawa has now ruled "no more adoptions." **1959** MOWAT *Desperate People* 231: . . . they were also given a month's supply of flour and other food paid from their Family Allowance credits. **1963** *Maclean's* 23 Feb. 3/1: Canada's family allowances—$72 a year for each child under the age of ten and $96 for each child between ten and sixteen. . . .

Family Allowance Act a federal act, passed in 1944, which provides for the payment of a monthly allowance to the parents or trustees of each child under sixteen years of age, later amended to continue such payments to eighteen, provided that the child remains in school, this payment being known as the youth allowance, *q.v.*
1945 *Beaver* Dec. 43/2: . . . at every [HBC] post visited, arrangements were made for the distribution of benefits under the Family Allowance Act. **1964** JENNESS *Eskimo Admin.* II 150: . . . in August 1944, parliament had passed the Family Allowance Act ordaining that the parents or trustees of all children under 16 years of age, whether Eskimo, Indian, or white, should receive a monthly allowance. . . .

Family Compact 1 *Hist.* the name applied to the governing class in Upper Canada prior to 1837, and in particular to the executive and legislative councils of that province. See also **Compact** (def. 1). Cp. **Château Clique.**
☛ *The term is attributed to Wm Lyon Mackenzie, the most vocal opponent of this group, which was predominantly made up of Loyalist families who had grown into positions of great influence. See 1833 quote.*
1828 *Tor.Pub.Lib.MSS B104* 153: I shall be happy to consult with yourself and Mr. Rolph on the measures to be adopted to relieve this province from the evils which a family compact have brought upon it. **1833** (1885) DENT *U.C.Rebellion* I 76: This family compact surround the Lieutenant-Governor, and mould him, like wax, to their will; they fill every office with their relatives, dependants, and partisans; by them justices of the peace and officers of the militia are made and unmade. **1839** HEAD *Narrative* 464: The *family compact* of Upper Canada is composed of those members of its society who, either by their abilities and character, have been honoured by the confidence of the executive government, or who by their industry and intelligence have amassed wealth. **1917** *Grit* (Toronto) 14 Dec. 3/7: After some time he came back to Canada, and was the means of breaking up the Family Compact, and giving us responsible government. **1965** *Kingston Whig-Standard* (Ont.) 9 Jan. 9/8: . . . he wrested the leadership of the old Family Compact from the Anglican Tories of muddy York and made it into the Conservative party.

2 *Obs.* See **Family-Company-Compact.**
1859 *British Colonist* (Victoria) 2 Nov. 1/1: The Legislative Council in Vancouver Island is the closest of Family Compacts.

3 any group which in its political influence and reactionary objectives resembles the Family Compact of Upper Canada.

1860 *Islander* (Charlottetown) 3 Feb. 2/5: "Family Compacts" and "designing Proprietary Agents," have by some means lost the dreaded and selfish properties with which these ingenious appellations were ingeniously invested. **1881** RATTRAY *Scots in Brit.N.A.* II 504: Both in New Brunswick and Nova Scotia, the same system prevailed, the "family compact" party ruled throughout the years succeeding the war, with undisputed authority, yet the progress of freer constitutional views was silent, though not less secure. **1904** DECELLES *Cartier* 2: In no other section of the country did the feeling against the hated bureaucrats— the family compact of Lower Canada—run so high as along the Richelieu. **1963** *Time* (Cdn ed.) 12 Nov. 12/2: The principal trouble with the Canadian Establishment as a latter-day Family Compact is that no one has ever really defined it. **1966** *Globe and Mail* (Toronto) 9 May 4/5: Ontario Liberal Leader Andrew Thompson said Saturday the New Democratic Party in Ontario has all the aspects of a family compact.

Family Compactism *Obs.* the doctrine and principles of the Family Compact (def. 1).
1849 *Journal and Express* (Hamilton, C.W.) 2 Jan. 3/1: Witness the granting of Responsible Government to Canada instead of a Family Compactism. **1850** *Wkly Globe* 11 Oct. 59/4: We suppose they followed the usual fashion of land-claim buyers, whether in the good old days of Family Compactism, or in these days of sharper practice.

Family Compactite *Obs.* a person belonging to the Family-Company-Compact, *q.v.*
1859 *British Colonist* (Victoria) 2 Apr. 1/4: They know how the Family-Compactites have fattened and grown lazy on the public purse.

Family-Company-Compact *n. Hist.* a group, dominated by officers of the Hudson's Bay Company, that controlled the Crown Colonies of Vancouver Island and British Columbia in the 1850's under the governship of Sir James Douglas.
1859 *British Colonist* (Victoria) 12 Feb. 1/2: Does the Family-Company-Compact of Vancouver's Island tend to build up public confidence, and promote the harmony and prosperity of the country? **1921** *Cdn Hist.Rev.* II 346: De Cosmos was . . . the champion of political reform, and one of the greatest opponents of Douglas and his administration, which he denounced as the "Family-Company-Compact." **1958** GRIFFIN *British Columbia* 31: From its first issues the influence of the earlier Reform movement on the new paper was apparent. It was reflected in the name DeCosmos coined for Douglas, his governing clique and the Hudson's Bay Company—the Family-Company Compact—and in the allusions he made to illustrate the colonists' demands.

fan *n. North* **1** a train of sled dogs harnessed in the fan hitch, *q.v.*
1924 FLAHERTY *Eskimo Friends* 145: By nightfall the wild fan of dogs were scrambling like a pack of wolves up the slope of the last igloo village on the coast, miles beyond the point we had hoped to make.

2 See **fan hitch.**
1936 *Beaver* Mar. 39/2: In Baffin Island the Eskimos hitch their dogs to the sledge by means of long individual single traces, which centre in a long bridle of heavy sealskin attached about three feet to the rear of the forward end of the runners. This arrangement is known as "the fan" in contradistinction to the method of single file hitch used in the forest and referred to as "the tandem." **1942** TWOMEY & HERRICK *Needle to the North* 18: The dogs were hitched in fan formation, the only one possible in the rough Hudson Bay country.

fan hitch *North* a method of harnessing sled dogs. See 1956 quote. See also **draw line, Eskimo fan hitch,** and **fan** (def. 2). Cp. **Nome hitch** and **tandem hitch.**
[**1770** (1792) CARTWRIGHT *Journal* I 72: They make use of any number of dogs, as occasion may require: and their thongs are of different lengths; always minding that the dog which is best trained, has the longest.] **1936** *Beaver* Mar. 39/2: . . . and there can be no doubt in rough difficult climbing, or while on thin or broken ice and on detached floes of open leads, the fan hitch ranks supreme. **1956** LEECHMAN *Native Tribes of Canada* 177: In the eastern Arctic the fan hitch is used, the lead dog having the longest trace and running out in front of the others; they, on shorter traces, fan out on each side.

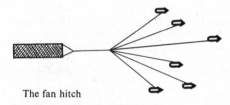

The fan hitch

Fannin('s) sheep a vari-colored intermediate between the Stone and the Dall sheep, *qq.v.*, of the Yukon Mountains.
1958 *Beaver* Spring 31/2: There you will find the magnificent Stone sheep, merging slowly into Fannin's sheep and then the Dall. *c*1959 *Fish and Game Bulletin:* THE FANNIN SHEEP may be found along the Yukon-B.C. border near Atlin and Teslin Lakes. It . . . separates the Dall sheep from the Stone sheep.

far (out) *adv. West and North* of caribou and, formerly, of buffalo, a long distance away from their customary feeding grounds.
1858 (1934) *Cdn Hist.Rev.* XV 7: Hector . . . records them as "far out" at Rocky Mountain House, in January, 1858. **1871** (1883) BUTLER *Great Lone Land* 229: . . . for the buffalo were "far out," on the great prairie, and that phrase "far out" applied to buffalo, means starvation in the North-west. **1957** *Aklavik Jnl* Apr. 3/2: Up around Norman Joe Blondin reports that the people have been living on moose meat all winter as the caribou were far.

farm *v.* of trappers, conserve the fur-bearing animals on a trapline by working only certain parts of it at one time, allowing the game to flourish in other areas. See also **farming.**
1929 JOHNSTON *Beyond Rockies* 180: He told me that since the trap-line registration had come into effect it was worth his while to "farm" his beaver, for instance. Before this Act came in there was no object in a trapper trying to conserve the fur; some other trapper would come along and jump his line and he had no redress. **1934** GODSELL *Arctic Trader* 197: The professional trapper does not make an occasional short trapping journey as does the Indian . . . neither does he "farm" his territory as was done by many Indians until just a few years ago.

farm depot *Lumbering, Hist.* See **depot farm.**
1912 HEENEY *Pickanock* 29: With the return of winter another change came over the farm depot, which this

time took on the appearance of a busy market centre. Thither the settlers betook themselves, bringing their oats, hay, pork, beef and other products of their little farms to convert into money or exchange for the necessaries of life. . . .

farm dugout *West* See **dugout** (def. 3).
1958 *Edmonton Jnl* 11 Nov. 12/3: Farm dugouts used for storing water for livestock were so low. . . .
1961 *Ibid.* 4 Aug. 1/1: . . . drowned Thursday in a farm dugout three miles north of the Peace River community.

farmer *n. Hist.* See **fermier.**
1947 *Cdn Hist.Rev.* Dec. 405: The Sieur Cugnet, agent of the Farmers, was well aware of the necessity of re-establishing a permanent post in the Nikabau region. . . .

Farmer-Labo(u)r Party a political party founded in Saskatchewan, one of the original groups forming the Co-operative Commonwealth Federation, *q.v.*
1957 *Commonwealth* 4 Dec. 13/1: The Sask. Farmer-Labour Party, which was formed in July of 1932, was the uniting of the Labour Party and the Farmer Party, the organization of both of which had been going on since 1929. **1959** STEWART & FRENCH *Ask No Quarter* 162: In Saskatchewan a joint meeting of delegates from the United Farmers of Canada and the Independent Labour Party was held in Saskatoon . . . and the Saskatchewan Farmer-Labour Party came into being.

farming *n.* a system for conserving beaver and other fur-bearing animals. See also **farm,** *v.*
1915 SPECK *Hunting Territories* 5: Beaver were made the object of the most careful "farming," the numbers of occupants, old and young, to each "cabin" being kept count of.

farm instructor an officer of the Indian Affairs Branch who serves as a resident agricultural adviser on an Indian reserve.
1920 *Beaver* Dec. 29/2: The Indian Department keeps a resident farm instructor on the reserve. . . . **1945** *Ibid.* Dec. 5/1: These included . . . John Delaney, government farm instructor. . . .

farm lot† *Hist.* a tract of land, usually 200 acres, set off for farming and sold or granted for use as a farm.
1789 (1905) *Ont.Bur.Arch.Rep.* III 31: The Scite of the county town agreed upon, you will direct the Surveyor for the district to lay out the township and proceed to receive applications and issue certificates for Town and Farm lots therein . . . as soon as may be. **1827** *Gore Gaz.* (Ancaster, U.C.) 29 Sep. 123/1: Purchasers of Farm Lots are required to commence improvements thereon within 12 months from the date of purchase. **1908** LAUT *Conquest N.W.* II 137: The farm lots were small so the colonists could be together in case of danger.

farmout *n.* a sub-lease granted by an oil company, permitting a person or group to drill in a prescribed area.
1955 *Vancouver Province* 6 Jan. 17/4: Both the indicated oil strikes are on farmout from Canadian Superior Oil of California Ltd. and are shared by Dome and the private group, the farmout acreage is shared

50 percent by Dome et al and 50 percent by Canadian Superior. **1958** *Edmonton Jnl* 12 Aug. 11/1: The drilling group also holds an Alberta government drilling reservation and lands in that tract are all in close proximity to the farmout half-section and scheduled "deep test" well.

farm-partner *n. Obs.* an immigrant buying a partnership in a farm before arriving in Canada to settle. Cp. **farm-pupil.**
1890 *Grip* (Toronto) 22 March 197/1: . . . poor Benwell will have been the last English gentleman to come to Canada as a farm-partner without first having assured himself that the alleged farm had an existence.

farm-pupil *n. Obs.* an immigrant induced to pay money before coming to Canada on the understanding that he be taught how to farm after his arrival.
1890 *Grip* (Toronto) 22 March 197/1: Meanwhile, if the tragedy results in the complete destruction of the "farm-pupil" nets spread in every corner of England by wily scamps, great good will be done.

farm woodlot See **bush** (def. 2).
1955 *Edmonton Jnl* 4 Jan. 2/6: The development is all the more unusual since in most of the area the natural forests, as preserved in farm woodlots, are of hardwood such as maple, oak, hickory, elm and ash. **1960** *Weekend Mag.* 8 Oct. 63/1: "Not 40 miles east of the city," said Pete, "there's a whole series of big farm woodlots, all connecting. . . . The farmers have it all posted. . . ."

Far North the Arctic and sub-Arctic regions of Canada. See also **North Country.**
1860 *Nor'Wester* (R.R.S.) 14 Mar. 4/5: A journey of twelve hundred miles in the Far North, during a severe winter, would in the opinion of many be an undertaking sufficiently arduous to entitle them to write a book of travels. **1963** *Globe and Mail* (Toronto) 21 Feb. 4/7: He added that Canada's Far North had its best year yet in 1962.

Far West 1 *Obs.* until about 1840, that part of Upper Canada now known as Western Ontario. See 1845 quote at def. 2.
1836 *Bytown* [Ottawa] *Gaz.* 13 Oct. 3/2: Being in the "far West" at the time I cannot enter into the particulars. **1839** *Montreal Transcript* 4 July 2/4: We regret to learn that many of our discontented inhabitants, still persist in selling out their properties, and running a wild goose chase in search of wealth and happiness in the "far west."

2 after about 1840, the territories west of Upper Canada, progressively Manitoba, Saskatchewan, Alberta, and British Columbia, as settlement moved westward; in present-day use the term usually refers to the region west of the Prairies.
1845 *Globe* (Toronto) 14 Oct. 1/3: The Committee does not consider it out of order briefly to define in this place the term "Far-West," inasmuch as what was formerly known as such is not now even thought of in connexion with that term. **1915** PRESTON *Strathcona* 28: This trade had gradually declined, so that the merchants were all the more anxious to establish permanent relations with the tribes in the Far West. **1949** (1965) HAMILTON *Cdn Quotations* 242/2: To the native of the prairies Alberta is the far West; British Columbia the near East.

fascine ['fæsin] *n.* [< Cdn F] a kind of fish trap used on the Lower St. Lawrence.
1959 *Cdn Geog.Jnl* August 50/1: At low tide they

construct on the wet surface the framework of their complicated "fascines". The fascine is a large circular trap, resembling a palisade enclosure, into which the fish find their way by a narrow passage and remain imprisoned.

fast† *adj.* frozen solid. Cp. **fast ice.**
1743 (1949) ISHAM *Observations* 179: The Lakes and Rivers near the ocean some affirm, are fast all the Summer; the Ice never breaking up. **1854** (1924) *Beaver* Dec. 31: We have had the pleasure of seeing the river fast this morning; in fact, so strong that Cameron crossed his horses safely.

fastball *n.* a variety of softball played with a relatively small ball, the players wearing gloves.
1949 *News of the North* 10 June 8/5: Much more practice is needed before the fast-ball comes up to the standard of Yellowknife nines. **1955** *Crag and Canyon* 17 June 1/5: A fastball game was held on Sunday, June 12 at Teepee Town between Canmore and Maclin Motors (Calgary). **1964** *Calgary Herald* 20 May 15/3: Dates for the Alberta finals . . . were released by Alberta Fastball Commissioner Ed Corbett Tuesday.

fast ice See 1958 quote. Cp. **fast.**
1853 (1892) KANE *Arctic Explor.* 26: Step by step, as the year advances, its outer edge breaks off; yet its inner curve frequently remains unbroken through the entire summer. This is the "fast ice" of the whalers, so important to their progress in the earlier portions of the season; for, however it may be encroached upon by storms or currents, they can generally find room to track their vessels along its solid margin. . . . **1958** *Manice* 6: Fast Ice—All types of ice, either broken or unbroken, attached to the shore, beached, stranded in shoal water or attached to the bottom of shoal areas.

fast snye *Northwest* a snye open at both ends. Cp. **snye** (def. 2b).
1954 PATTERSON *Dangerous River* 113: The scow came to the head of an island where a fast snye ran off into the woods. *Ibid.* 127: . . . and then, suddenly, near the head of a fast snye that wound like a small river through the forest. . . .

fast time† daylight-saving time. Cp. **slow time.**
1953 MOON *Saskatchewan* 14: "When do we eat? Slow time. Fast time. Doctor's time. Methodist's time. When do we eat."

fast water swift-moving water flowing over rapids.
1905 MOTT *Jules of the Great Heart* 295: . . . the canoe settled lower and lower, then it struck the first fast water; it lurched and plunged soggily, cleared one big wave, hovered staggering on the next crest, disappeared in the hollow beyond and came in sight no more. **1957** *Cominco Mag.* Feb. 12/1: I learned how to "track" a canoe up fast water. . . . **1964** *Canadian Wkly* 13 June 12/1: We . . . shot the fast water below the camp.

fast-water man a person skilled in handling a canoe or boat in fast water, *q.v.* See also **white-water man** (def. 1).
1964 *Canadian Wkly* 13 June 12/2: The water boiled for three-quarters of a mile below us but . . . Reg is a good fast-water man.

fat *n. Nfld* **1** *Sealing* **a.** seal blubber.
*c***1850** (1960) FOWKE *Story in Song* 162: There's a noble fleet of sealers being fitted for the ice./ They'll take a chance again this year tho' fat's gone down in

251 **fast**
Father of Confederation

price. . . . **1933** MERRICK *True North* 255: How could they handle 300-pound harps, even get them in the boat? But they did. And every now and then they'd take a loat [sic] of fat and skins to North West River. . . . **1965** *Kingston Whig-Standard* (Ont.) 3 Apr. 4/4: . . . 2- to 3-week-old pups that are clubbed and skinned . . . for their white fur and fat.

b. sealskins and the attached blubber. See also **sculp** (def. 2).
1925 *Beaver* Mar. 74: . . . coils of small ropes . . . cut up into suitable lengths and used by the men as hauling lines when hauling a tow of "fat" to the ship. **1933** GREENE *Wooden Walls* XV: SCULPS, PELTS OR FAT. These are the sealers' names for the skin and attached blubber of the Seals.

2 *Sealing* **a.** seals, especially whitecoats, *q.v.*, as the object of the hunt.
1918 GRENFELL *Labrador Doctor* 74: Advantage is also taken of the maternal instinct to get the mothers as well as the young "fat," if the latter is not obtainable in sufficient quantities. **1964** *Nfld Qtly* Spring 12/3: For the skeleton ships and crews of the once great sailing armada of wooden hulls who have gone forth to look for the "fat" we give the toast of sixty odd years ago. "God Speed, bumper trip, and long may your big jib draw."

b. in the fat, among the seal herds.
1964 *Time* (Cdn ed.) 20 Mar. 20/3: Once "in the fat" (among the herds), the hunters . . . all work at speed.

3 small immature herring.
1915 (1916) *Commission of Conservation* 39: From the study of the growth of the Newfoundland herring it is evident that the three-, four-, five- and six-year-old herring, which to a larger or smaller degree may belong to the immature "fat" schools, must possess the esteemed qualities of the Norwegian "fat" which are caught by hundreds of thousands of barrels.

father *n.* in Indian parlance, a government official, especially the governor of a colony or province as representative of the king; also, the king himself.
1727 *Pub.Col.Soc.* VIII 282 [*DA*]: When the Governor of Canada speaks to us . . . he calls us *Children,* and saith *I am your Father. . . . I will protect you as a Father doth his Children.* **1793** (1916) *London Hist.Soc.Trans.* VII 7: On our arrival at the Mohawk village the Indians hoisted their flags and trophies of war, and fired a feu-de-joie in compliment to his excellency, the representative of the king their father. **1840** *Bytown* [Ottawa] *Gaz.* 20 Feb. 1/5: The Governor-General has been made a father,—although a patron of the happy state of single-blessedness, and our young Queen has been made "a great mother."

Father of Confederation any of the delegates to the conferences at Charlottetown, Quebec, and London, which resulted in Confederation in 1867. See also **Confederation Father.**
1888 *Dominion Illustrated* 67/1: After complimenting his friend, Sir Charles Tupper, on his patriotic allusions to his native land, he recalled the fact that he himself, with the Honourable the Agent-General, had attended the conference of 1864, and that they were, therefore, both among the Fathers of Confederation—a title to glory and remembrance quite enough for any man. **1898** EDGAR *Canada and Capital* 104: Canada, in the

year of grace 1897, has still a group of public men whose services in connection with the founding of the Dominion entitle them to be called the "Fathers of Confederation." **1962** *Chronicle-Herald* (Halifax) 11 Aug. 1/8: Put a father of Confederation and a former prime minister of Canada on the list of Ottawa's forgotten men.

fathom† *n. Hist.* a linear measure of six feet, widely used in colonial and fur-trade days for measuring rope, wampum, cloth, tobacco, dried oolichan, nets, canoe bark, canoes, as well as for water depth, for which the official fathom is 6.08 feet. Cp. **brase.**
1728 (1949) ISHAM *Observations* xxvii: I offer'd 10 Guns, and 40 fathoms of Tobacco, 14 Gallons of Brandy, to carry as Presents.... **1794** MCGILLIVRAY *Journal* 17: The Men put ashore to raise a few fathoms of bark of which we had great need.... **1799** (1897) COUES *New Light* I 3: [He traded] at the low price of four skins for a fathom of common blue strouds.... **1963** *Commercial Letter* Jan. 2/1: The unit of the [wampum] money was the fathom, consisting of 360 white beads and at one time worth sixpence, or about fourteen cents.

fathom-fish *n. Pacific Coast, Obs.* See **oolichan.**
1849 ROSS *Adventures* 95: To prepare them [oolichan] for a distant market, they are laid side by side, head and tail alternately, and then a thread run through both extremities links them together, in which state they are dried, smoked, and sold by the fathom, hence they have obtained the name of fathom-fish. **1897** COUES *New Light* II 787n: Another name of these "smelts" was fathom-fish, given because they were strung on strings and sold by the fathom.

fat pine† pine wood having a high content of resin, used for light, torches, or kindling.
1838 TRAILL *Backwoods of Canada* 160: This is filled with a very combustible substance called fat-pine, which burns with a fierce and rapid flame, or else with rolls of birch-bark, which is also very easily ignited. **1866** KING *Sportsman in Canada* 91: A blazing light of birch bark and "fat pine" is kindled in an iron cresset fixed in the bows of a canoe.... **1905** SCHERCK *Pen Pictures* 206: The Jack-light was made of fat pine knots (knots full of pitch), or hickory bark placed in a basket made of hoop iron hung up to a pole at one end of the boat.

fat summer beaver *Fur Trade, Hist.* unprime or inferior skins from a beaver coat, *q.v.* See also **summer beaver.**
1735 (1899) WILLSON *Great Company* 238: The beaver ... was classified into eight varieties.... The second sort was the fat summer beaver, worth two shillings and sixpence [a pound]. **1962** (1964) INNIS *Fur Trade* 105:... arrangements were made January 4, 1733, to receive dry summer beaver for the following year at 20 sols, and fat summer beaver at 35 sols *la livre.*

fat winter beaver *Fur Trade, Hist.* a prime skin from a beaver coat, *q.v.* See also **winter beaver.**
1962 (1964) INNIS *Fur Trade* 105: On June 6, 1746, as a result of the war, prices of beaver were increased; fat winter beaver 55 sols to 4 livres....

faubourg *n.* [< Cdn F < F] *Obs.* in Quebec, a community outside the original city limits; suburb.

Also spelled *fauxbourg.*
1785 (1943) HUNTER *Diary* 31: Our driver pretended to know all the girls in the *fauxbourgs* and called to them to wake them with some of his impertinent talk as he went past. **1830** *Vindicator* (Montreal) 15 Oct. 1/1: The 1st Bat. of Infantry will be composed of the Militia residing within the Fauxbourg Ste. Marie.... **1851** JOHNSTON *Notes* I 339: Near Kamouraska church and faubourg, the lower bay of this name also contains good flat land, and, with occasional interruptions, similar land stretches along the shore as we descend.

feather *n. North* (used attributively) of articles of clothing made by the Eskimos from bird skins.
[**1578** (1889) HAKLUYT *Voyages* XII 214: They haue also some garments of feathers, being made of the cases of Foules, finely sowed and compact togither.]
1942 TWOMEY & HERRICK *Needle to the North* 311: In winter, the islanders all wear two separate feather parkas, the inner one with feathers next to the body, the outer one with the feathers outside to shed the rain and snow. **1947** *Beaver* Dec. 16/1: It didn't take me long to slip into my caribou-skin parka and feather pants....

feathers *n.pl. Esp.Maritimes* small branches, especially of evergreen trees.
1849 ALEXANDER *L'Acadie* II 20: (On the ridge-pole) rested ... other poles and on them were carefully disposed "hemlock feathers," or small branches of the hemlock-pine, broken off and laid like a thatch on the sloping roof of our wigwam.... **1945** MOORE *Castle Buck* 8:... he washed the few dishes, stowed the food in the pack-sack and put it in the lean-to behind him. He cut an armful of spruce "feathers" and that sufficed for a mattress.

federal *adj.* of, associated with, or under the jurisdiction of the government of Canada.
1883 *Brandon Blade* (Man.) 4 Oct. 1/3: We are Canadian enough in our views to look at Dominion matters from the Federal rather than the Provincial standpoint, though in matters of local self-government we shall be as jealous of Provincial rights as we are of Federal rights. **1925** GROVE *Settlers* 299: The verdict read for ten years in the federal prison, with hard labour. **1966** *Globe and Mail* (Toronto) 3 May 31/2: [He] warned ... that in federal debates a stagnation has set in that could destroy Parliament.

Federal Building in many Canadian cities and towns, a building in which regional offices of federal government departments are located, often including a post office.
1953 *North Star* (Yellowknife) Aug. 3/4: Work is going ahead rapidly on the large new Federal Building, which occupies a city block in the centre of down-town Whitehorse. **1963** *Canada Month* Jan. 26/2: On his feet again, he jogs ... to the Federal Building where he takes a brief look into Magistrate Adams' police court....

federal government the government of Canada.
1945 HAIG *Brave Harvest* 28/9: "Mr. David Horn, the assistant, is really in charge," Cora explained to Aunt Alice that 1884 day. "The head, Mr. Clarke, has gone to England for the federal government." **1955** *Dly News* (St John's) 2 Mar. 1/1: Two opposition parties Tuesday called for the overthrow of the federal government because of rising unemployment. **1966** *Globe and Mail* (Toronto) 2 May 7/1:... water development and planning comes under provincial jurisdiction, with some assistance coming from the federal government.

Federal Parliament the members of the Canadian

House of Commons and of the Senate collectively; the Parliament of the Dominion of Canada.
1876 (1877) ST. JOHN *Sea of Mountains* I 146: The personal intercourse I have had with your Parliamentary representatives at the capital of the Dominion still further confirmed my desire to visit a population who in the person of their members contributed so materially to enhance the dignity, the eloquence, and the intellectual reputation of the Federal Parliament. **1953** *North Star* (Yellowknife) Aug. 1/4: He now makes his first bid for a seat in the Federal Parliament.

feed-alley *n.* in a stable, a passageway behind the stalls, used when carrying feed to the mangers.
1942 BOSANQUET *Saddlebags* 77: I would sleep with the pony in the feed-alley behind his manger.

feed(ing)-bed *n.* the place near a beaver dam, *q.v.*, where the beavers anchor the sticks intended to feed the colony during the winter.
1946 FERGUSON *Mink, Mary & Me* 94: Upon reaching the feed-bed site they would dive with their burden and, by some unknown skill, anchor it securely in the deep water, where it would be easily accessible after freeze-up. **1948** ONRAET *Sixty Below* 153: Some of these lengths they use for dams, and others as eating stuff, adding it to their feeding bed for next winter.

feeding-house *n.* See quote.
1956 KEMP *Northern Trader* 57: Among the reeds and the rushes, he indicated several muskrat houses, pointing out the three varieties—the living-house, the feeding-house, and the little "pushup". . . .

feeding platform See **pushup.**
1940 *Beaver* Dec. 18/1: Then we discovered a lone individual [muskrat] perched upon a bulrush feeding platform busily chewing on the white tender end of a bulrush stem.

feed line the line along which a moose, deer, etc. browses.
1945 MOORE *Castle Buck* 87: Within an hour after breakfast I found myself (still on the feed line and big track) within a mile of where I started the day before.

feller *n. Lumbering* See **faller.**
1872 DASHWOOD *Chiploquorgan* 104: A crew of lumberers have different occupations assigned to them; the "fellers," cut down the trees and trim them; the "swampers," who "swamp"—cut roads—to the felled trees to enable the "teamster" and his assistants to haul them on a "Bob sled"—two sleds working independently and joined by chains. . . . **1964** *Beautiful B.C.* Fall 40/1: The modern feller is an artist with a power saw and the axe-man is becoming almost a legend.

fence viewer† a municipal official whose duty it is to see that fences meet legal specifications as to construction and location. See also **judge of fences.**
☛ *Although in general use in colonial Canada, the term is now confined to Nova Scotia; it came to Canada from New England.*
1793 (1869) CANNIFF *Settlement U.C.* 454: The following persons were chosen to officiate in their respective offices, the ensuing year, and also the regulations of the same. . . . Abraham Mayvee and Peter Rutland, fence viewers. The height of fence to be 4 feet 8 inches; water fence voted to be fenced. **1846** BONNYCASTLE *Canada and Canadians* II 93: All freeholders above twenty-one years of age are entitled to a vote, and choose the undermentioned officers, viz.—one assessor and a collector . . . and from three to eighteen fence-

viewers, whose duty it is to regulate fences. *a*1894 (1960) *Ont.Hist.* June 107: Bad boundary fences were then, as now, a fertile source of misunderstanding between neighbors; I had been warned of this, and desired . . . to avert the necessity for the services of those municipal officers, known as "fence viewers," who are lawful and absolute arbiters in case of dispute. **1955** *Wkly Monitor* 4 May 2/3: List of Ward Officers . . . Cattle Reeves . . . Fence Viewers . . . Sheep Valuers. . . . **1963** GUILLET *Pioneer Farmer* II 17: . . . in fact one of the municipal offices at one time was that of fence-viewer.

fencible† ['fɛnsəbəl] *n. Hist.* a militiaman having obligations to serve in his home region only.
1805 *Quebec Gaz.* 6 June 3/1: Lieut. Colonel Shank and several Officers of the Canadian Fencibles have arrived with intent to commence raising men immediately. **1896** GOURLAY *Hist.Ottawa* 116: His three hundred men were the Canadian fencibles and Voltigeurs. **1949** LAWSON *N.B.Story* 159: In the meantime their departure left New Brunswick undefended, so General Coffin raised a regiment of Fencibles—so called because they enlisted for home defence only.

Fenian† ['finiən] *n.* [alteration of Irish Gaelic. *feinne,* pl. of *fiann* band of Fenians; cp. *Feni* ancient people of Ireland] *Hist.* a member of a militant secret brotherhood of Irish-Americans and their sympathizers in Canada, advocates of Irish independence, who sought to advance their cause by attacking Canada, carrying out abortive raids in 1866, 1870, and 1871. Cp. **Hunters' Lodge.**
1865 *Islander* (Charlottetown) 27 Jan. 2/1: Every mail brings us tidings of the organization and arming of Fenians and Orangemen in all the chief cities of Upper Canada. **1870** *Cdn Illust.News* 2 June 499/3: To squelch these Fenian scamps right out / Would glorify our nation. **1963** *Beaver* Winter 32/1: Bumptious Fenians, operating out of bases in the United States, seemed determined once again to attempt the conquest of Canada.

Fenianism† *n. Hist.* the policies of the Fenians; the movement itself.
1858 (1965) HAMILTON *Cdn Quotations* 77/1: In Toronto one extreme is made auxiliary to the other; Orangeism has been made the pretext of Fenianism, and Fenianism is doing its best to justify and magnify Orangeism. **1958** *Encyc.Can.* IV 117/2: By 1871 Fenianism was doomed to failure.

fermier *n. Cdn French, Hist.* in New France, a fur trader holding a lease on a certain trading post and having the sole right to trade in the defined vicinity. See also **farmer.**
[**1676** (1924) *Canada Public Archives* II Pt 1 72-80: . . . the beaver shall be taken for all its weight by the "fermier" and not taken only for a pound and a half although it sometimes weighs up to two pounds.] **1956** INNIS *Fur Trade in Canada* 98: In the same year (1742) the general policy of leasing posts was changed and all the posts were farmed out to traders reserving a certain allowance for the officers, but apparently the *fermiers* or traders were given little encouragement by the officers in full control.

fertile belt 1 *Hist.* the wide belt of fertile land stretching from the Red River to the foothills of the

Rockies and from the North Saskatchewan River to the American border.

1861 *Nor'Wester* (R.R.S.) 1 Mar. 3/3: Among the means of future wealth and prosperity they will find within the limits of the Fertile Belt, or on its eastern borders . . . iron ore widely distributed, of great purity, and in considerable abundance. **1936** *Beaver* Sep. 5/2: A city-bred crowd, or even people from "the fertile belt," could not have the same sympathy with Henry Kelsey's effort as these people who live on the new frontier. **1963** MORTON *Kingdom of Canada* 334: Finally Granville decided the Company must be compelled to settle, and practically forced them to accept the Canadians' reluctant agreement to have Canada . . . grant . . . one twentieth of the "fertile belt" of the north-west. . . .

2 any tract of fertile land, especially one in the generally inarable expanse of the Canadian Shield.

1883 HATTON & HARVEY *Newfoundland* 30: Only of late have people been convinced that the island contains fertile belts, noble pine-forests, extensive coal-fields, and vast mineral treasures. **1921** HEMING *Drama of Forests* 2: It was the heart of a vast fertile belt that was rapidly becoming the greatest of all farming districts. **1957** HUTCHISON *Canada* 194: The fertile belt of clay, the rich fields, big barns, and sleek cattle around the dairy town of Earlton, about one hundred miles within the Shield, looked almost unbelievable after the sterile rock north and south of it.

festin *n.* [< Cdn F < F < Ital. *festino* feast] *Obs.* a feast, especially one of large proportions.

1869 KENNICOTT *Journal* 106: When we arrived at Peel's River we gave the dogs a *festin*, [and] ate two suppers ourselves. . . . **1893** OXLEY *Young Nor'Wester* 111: We could have a festin à tout manger, once a week, and still have plenty to last until spring. // A festin à tout manger, it may be explained, is a very popular institution among the Indians. The literal meaning of the term is a feast at which everything must be eaten up. . . . **1896** RUSSELL *Far North* 23: The wedding "festin" reduced one or two families to the point of starvation, but at New-year the whole settlement became bankrupt.

fiddlehead† *n.* the edible, tightly furled young frond of certain ferns, so called because of its shape.

☛ *The fiddlehead is chiefly associated in Canada with the Maritimes, especially New Brunswick, where the fronds of the ostrich fern are harvested and packaged for export as a delicacy.*

*c*1820 (1949) LAWSON *N.B.Story* 147: "We ate fiddle-heads, grapes, and even the leaves of trees." **1932** WINSON *Weather and Wings* 29: The fronds, unfurling, resemble bishop's crooks, though the country folk [in B.C.] call them "fiddleheads." **1964** *Maclean's* 16 Nov. 2/2: The Canadian booth with its . . . "mountie" dolls, maple syrup and maple sugar [and] cans of New Brunswick fiddleheads . . . is invariably a big attraction at the [International Food] fair. **1965** *Globe and Mail* (Toronto) 9 Nov. 7/2: Here she had been happy . . . getting together with the neighbors . . . for dulse sandwiches and moose milk (one part emulsified fiddleheads, one part clam juice, three parts catawba). . . .

fiddler *n.* *Maritimes* an Atlantic salmon weighing less than eight pounds.

1964 *Star Wkly* 5 Dec. 16/1: It represented a catch of 60 salmon, many of them fiddlers (under 8 pounds).

fiddler's elbow a sharp crook in a road.

1950 *Beaver* Sep. 18: "Narrow, curving, and unblessed with gravel, it [the road to Hudson's Hope] has many a switchback and 'fiddler's elbow' too slippery to negotiate in wet weather."

fief† [fif] *n.* [< F] **1** *Obs.* See **seigneury** (def. 1a).

1775 (1905) *Ont.Bur.Arch.Rep.* III xliv: It is therefore our will and pleasure, that all lands . . . be granted in fief or seigneurie, in like manner as was practiced antecedent to the conquest of the said province . . . omitting, however, the reservation of any judicial powers whatever, the properties of which seigneuries or fiefs shall be and remains vested in us, our heirs and successors.

2 a lease to a tract of land; also, the land itself.

1807 *Quebec Gaz.* 2 July 3/1: Labrador Fiefs and Fisheries for sale. **1953** MOWERY *Mounted Police* 59: On the death of her uncle, who had homesteaded this tract along the Bear River and staked a float-gold claim up the tributary creek, she had come here to live out the two remaining years of the fief and nurse her brother Paul back to health.

field day 1 a day on which the people of a community enjoy themselves by entering into various games, races, dancing, etc.; a sports day.

1953 *North Star* (Yellowknife) Jan.-Feb. 5/4: The annual Union Labour Day Picnic, held the first Monday in August each year, has become the "big day" not only for miners and their families but for all the children of Yellowknife who are provided with free treats and a first-class field-day, as guests of the Union. **1960** BUBLITZ *Dotted Line* 40: In those times a big field day was held in July or August in Shaunavon.

2 a day on which livestock are shown and judged and where breeding programs are discussed.

1953 *Fur Trade Jnl* Mar. 8/1: Prior to the provincial mink show, a number of field days are held both in the northern and southern part of the province. **1958** *Edmonton Jnl* 28 June 13/3: The field day was staged at Lacombe experimental farm where swine herds, Yorkshire, Lacombe and crossbreds were inspected.

field ice† See 1954 quote.

1850 (1851) SNOW *Voyage* 102: Far and near, east, north, and west, the eye met nothing but one uniform glare of dazzling whiteness, proceeding from immense bodies of field ice, broken floes, and bergs. **1924** *Beaver* Dec. 9: Field ice is almost always to be met in the [Hudson] straits, sometimes loose and easy to force a passage, but often a tight jam. . . . **1954** *Labrador and H.B.Pilot* 3: FIELD ICE is a large area of flat ice, the extent of which may not be seen from the masthead.

field lacrosse a form of lacrosse, *q.v.*, played on a large field with ten players on each team, largely displaced in Canada by box lacrosse, *q.v.*

1959 *Programme of the 12th Annual Indian Pow Wow* (Capilano Reserve, North Vancouver, B.C.) 2/2: Councillor Willard Josephs, brother to our famed Indian box lacrosse goal keeper, Stan Josephs, is in the Sports Committee and active member of our Squamish Field Lacrosse Team. **1966** *Globe and Mail* (Toronto) 30 June 26/5: It will mark the first time in 35 years that a Canadian team has played against the United States in a 10-man field lacrosse match.

field nurse a public health and registered nurse assigned for general duty in a remote part of Canada.

1965 WILSON *No Man Stands Alone* 26: The position meant being field nurse for the 3,000 Indians in the Yukon Territory and Northern British Columbia, an area covering roughly 200,000 square miles.

field officer 1 See **soldier bird.**
*a*1820 (1838) HEAD *Forest Scenes* 275: The inhabitants give this bird the *sobriquet* of "Field Officer." 1866 KING *Sportsman in Can.* 113: . . . and flocks of the red-winged starling, or Field-officer, with jetty plumage and flashing epaulets of red and yellow, chatter round the marshy pools. 1959 MCATEE *Folk-Names* 59: Red-Winged Blackbird [is also called] *Field officer, field officer bird* (the red patches on the wings of the male suggest military insignia. Ont.).
2 *Fur Trade, Hist.* a senior commissioned officer of the Hudson's Bay Company.
1934 *Beaver* June 36/1: One of these [practices] was the admission of field officers (chief factors and chief traders) to partnership in the concern. 1945 *Ibid.* March 12/1: . . . James Cumines, erstwhile trader, now field officer. . . .

field pitcher on a threshing crew, the person forking sheaves from the stook to the wagon for delivery to the threshing machine.
1955 HARDY *Alta Anthol.* 433: "Go by a field an' see alla them spikers an' field pitchers working without no pants . . ." 1963 SYMONS *Many Trails* 116: . . . but luckily they gave us some field pitchers to help us load.

Fife wheat [< David Fife ?1804-1877, of Otonabee, U.C., who developed it] a variety of rust-resistant spring wheat. See also **Red Fife.**
1851 *Watchman* (St Thomas, C.W.) 1 Feb. 2/4: In another column will be found an article on the "Fife Wheat" which is held in such high estimation by the farmers of Newcastle and Colborne districts, and in fact by all who have tried it. 1881 *Edmonton Bull.* 3 Dec. 3/1: Do all you can to get the farmers to grow Fife wheat, and pay the price for it when pure. 1958 *Encyc. Can.* IV 123/1: From these grains Fife developed the variety known as Fife (later Red Fife), the first Canadian wheat to be resistant to rust.

fifty-cent piece a large silver coin worth half a Canadian dollar.
1897 TUTTLE *Golden North* 152: During the present year the lowest standard of value in actual use there, has been the fifty-cent piece, or, in the parlance of the town, "four bits." 1955 *Coast Guard* (Shelburne, N.S.) 10 Mar. 1/6: "It now means that the 1955 dollar will not buy more gasoline than the 1939 50-cent piece," said the Provincial Treasurer.

fifty-eighter *n. Hist.* one of those taking part in the gold rush to the Fraser River Valley, B.C., in 1858.
1900 OSBORN *Greater Canada* 87: The "fifty-eighter" was, and is, in his way, as romantic a character as the typical Argonaut. . . .

fig *n.* a plug of tobacco, especially chewing tobacco, probably so called because it resembled a slab of dried figs.
*a*1836 (1838) HALIBURTON *Sam Slick* 187: How are you off for tobacco? said Mr. Slick. Grand, said he, got half a fig left yet. 1880 GORDON *Mountain and Prairie* 237: The stakes were small, usually a fig of tobacco. 1956 RADDALL *Wings* 39: "All I can offer you right now is a chaw off my fig o' tobacca."

figure-(of-)four trap a kind of deadfall (def. 1) or other trap having the triggers set in a figure 4,

first used by the Indians. See picture at **deadfall.** Also spelled *figure-4, figure-of-4,* etc.
1743 (1949) ISHAM *Observations* 162: One more trap their is a figure of 4 trap, which is 2 Logs Squar'd for the sides, and a Log for the top of one foot wide, which is call'd a figure of 4 trap being sett up with 3 sticks in the shape of a figure of 4 the top Log falls upon the Vermin which is the safest trap to Keep Vermin from being Eat. 1867 *Canadian Naturalist* III 54: Others are caught in a kind of figure-of-4 trap, but by far the larger number are speared. 1907 HUNTER *Cdn Wilds* 101: In the "figure-of-four" traps, before the animal is caught it must seize the bait with its teeth and pull strong enough to set off the trap, whereas with the steel trap the mere fact of his coming to the doorway to smell insures his putting his foot in it. . . . 1936 MOWERY *Paradise Trail* 58: The signs of that figure-4 trap could all be smoothed out. . . .

file *v. Mining* **1** register (a claim) for a staked piece of land.
1910 FRASER *Red Meekins* 194: . . . first thing in the mornin' we'll hike to the outside an' file the claim. 1912 FOOTNER *New Rivers* 115: At intervals we came to square posts driven into the earth, with inscriptions in lead pencil to the effect that so-and-so hereby gave notice of his intention to file a claim, etc., etc., with dates thirteen years old and upwards.
2 file on, make application for a mining claim or other tract of land.
1900 LONDON *Son of Wolf* 128: . . . Edwin Bentham . . . filed on Bench Claim 23, second tier, of French Hill. 1945 HAIG *Brave Harvest* 64: Miss Hind knew of the homesteaders standing in queues for a day and a night and a day and a night, that they might "file" on the quarter section of their choice. 1963 SYMONS *Many Trails* 25: Amos had filed on a quarter by the creek, and had a small log shack sheltered against a cut bank. . . .

fill *v.* furnish (snowshoes) with webbing; string.
1954 EVANS *Mist* 201: Matt had a pair of snowshoe-frames which he had long meant to fill and . . . he brought in the bucket of rawhide. . . .

Fils de la Liberté *Hist.* an organization of republican-minded Lower-Canadian Reformers established at Montreal in August 1837 and outlawed in November of that year. See also **Sons of Liberty.**
1837 (1866) CHRISTIE *Lower Canada* IV 430: A fracas occurred at Montreal, on the 6th November, between the young men styling themselves "Sons of Liberty," (les fils de la liberte) and the Constitutionalists. 1904 DECELLES *Papineau* 127: Combat broke out in the streets on the seventh of the month between the Constitutionals of the Doric Club and the *Fils de la Liberté,* followed by the sacking of the office of the Vindicator, and an attack on the residence of Papineau. 1963 MORTON *Kingdom of Canada* 247: Then, when fighting between the Doric Club and the Fils de la Liberté began, the government decided to arrest the leaders of the Fils.

fin boom *Lumbering* See quote. See also **boom[1]**, *n.* (def. 1).
1966 *Sask.Hist.* Winter 33: In order to take the logs out of the Saskatchewan River and run them through the Sipcinok Channel we would use fin booms. . . .

Each unit of the boom was made of three 12 x 14 inch 40 feet long timbers; bolted together on their edge. On each one of these hinges, we bolted a plank 16 feet long, 12 inches wide, four inches thick at one end and tapered to two inches thick at the other end. We would bolt the thick end to the hinges. In the centre of these planks or fins you could put out a boom at any angle you wished.

fine gold† *Placer Mining* tiny particles of gold. See also **flour gold** and **colo(u)r** (def. 2).
1859 *British Colonist* (Victoria) 12 Feb. 2/1: The coldness of the water thickens the quicksilver so much as to prevent full half of the fine gold being taken up or amalgamated as it would be when the weather is warm. **1935** SULLIVAN *Great Divide* 90: . . . these Orientals being admitted experts at catching fine gold on claims that more impatient and less skilful whites abandoned in contempt.

fine pemmican *Obs.* See 1890 quote. See also **bourgeois pemmican.**
1847 NEVINS *Two Voyages* 41: What is called gentleman's or fine pimmikin, is made of buffalo marrow, dried meat, and a kind of black berry, which grows in abundance in the woods. **1890** *Trans.Roy.Soc. Can.* VIII 2 104: From the siftings of the dried meat the "fine pemmican" was made in which marrowfat was used instead of tallow; and the "berry" pemmican, the most highly valued of all, consisted of these two and a due proportion of Saskatoon berries, or of choke-cherries, if the other could not be had.

finger wharf *Nfld* See quote.
1960 *Cdn Geog.Jnl* March 81/1: The backs of these mercantile premises face the water and each premise has a number of finger wharves which, in earlier days, were of prime importance for docking schooners which loaded fish and unloaded supplies of various kinds for the large-scale coastal traffic which focuses on the harbour of St. John's. . . .

fire† *v. Slang* discharge an employee in a summary fashion; dismiss.
1887 ROBERTS *Western Avernus* 183: "Why, I nearly fired him the first morning. . . ." And "fired" means in that oversea, overland language, being discharged. . . . **1955** *Globe and Mail* (Toronto) 31 Jan. 8/6: Six mechanics were fired because they joined a trade union.

fire-bag *n. Hist.* a soft leather pouch, usually decorated, used by the Indians of the old Northwest to carry flint-and-steel, tinder, tobacco, etc. See also **skipertogan** and **smoking bag.**
1819 (1939) ROBERTSON *Correspondence* 69: The Indian . . . tying up his Fire bag very composedly gave two or three *hems.* . . . **1879** ROBINSON *Great Fur Land* 338: The native carries a fire-bag—a long leather bag, containing pipe, tobacco, knife, flint and steel, and . . . the inner bark of the grey willow. **1957** FISHER *Pemmican* 134: "An Indian never admits anything, even if you catch him with your scalp on his medicine pole and your teeth in his fire bag."

fire-barren *n. Maritimes* See **brulé** (def. 1).
1956 RADDALL *Wings* 77: . . . there were patches of old fire-barren that had come up with a pure stand of young poplar or of wire birch. . . .

fire-bird† *n.* the Baltimore oriole, *Icterus galbula,* so called because the flash of its orange breast through the tree leaves suggested the glow of a fire.

1910 FERGUSON *Janey Canuck* 258: The orioles have several names too. The Indians call them "fire-birds," and the settlers "hang-birds," because of their pendant nests. **1924** SHERMAN *Nature Stories* 109: In the swaying boughs of a drooping elm the fire-bird builds her nest. **1959** MCATEE *Folk-Names* 60: Baltimore Oriole [is also called] *Fire Bird.*

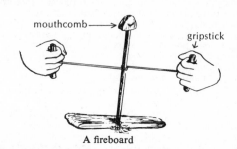
A fireboard

fire-board *n.* a flat piece of wood used in making fire by friction.
1943 MILLER *Lone Woodsman* 46: This time Dan used the fire-making method of the Ojibways. He tied a short grip-stick to each end of his cord, put his teeth on the fire-board, and stooped over it with the socket in his teeth. *Ibid.* 188: Out of his fire bag Dan took the Ojibway socket with the mouth comb, a thong with grip sticks on its ends, his drill, fire board and curls of yellow birch mixed with shredded cedar bark.

fire bomber a cargo plane especially equipped for carrying large quantities of water to be used in extinguishing forest fires. See also **water-bomber.**
1961 *Canada Month* 6 Oct. 42/1: Tools used for forest firefighting range from rolls of toilet paper to the spectacular new fire bombers, mobile water tankers. . . .

fire-boss[1]† *n. Mining* a mine foreman responsible for the observation of all safety regulations.
1898 CONNOR *Black Rock* 87: But in six months, mother and baby . . . transformed "Old Ricketts" into Mr. Shaw, fire-boss of the mines. **1955** GOWLAND *Smoke* 180: There's a Greek who used to be a fire boss in the mine.

fire-boss[2] *n.* See quote.
1965 MARTIN *Alberta Story* 14/1: Members of the general public selected by forestry personnel as key fire fighters receive training and certification as "Fire Bosses."

firebreak *n.* **1** any device for preventing the spread of fire.
1841 *Nfld House of Assembly Jnl App.* 178: There are two streams crossing the street between Queen Street and the lane opposite Messrs. Codner & Jennings's firebreak, over which bridges similar to the above are required to be built.

2 See **fireguard** (def. 1).
1889 *Regina Jnl* 12 Sep. 4/3: Fires are raging around and the captain of the fire brigade had a fire break put round the village as he said prevention was worth two chemical extinguishers.

3 in the bush, a strip of land cleared of trees and brush and intended to stop the advance of a forest fire. See also **fireguard** (def. 2), **fire-line** (def. 2), **guard** (def. 3b), and **guard line.**
1935 *Beaver* Sep. 62/2: The fire started . . . and a fire break had to be cut. **1959** *Time* (Cdn ed.) 17 Aug. 13/2: Smoke billowed . . . along the Gaspe, where 600 men

hacked out firebreaks to control two of Quebec's worst blazes this year.

fire-burn *n*. See **brulé** (def. 1).
1947 SAUNDERS *Algonquin* ix: Up on the hill is an old fire-burn where he stops to stuff himself with luscious blueberries. . . .

fire camp a camp for men engaged in or prepared for fighting forest fires.
1953 *Cdn Geog.Jnl* XLVI 47/1: He landed at the fire camps, and discussed his plans with the Deputy Ranger.

fire district a region specifically organized with officials and equipment as protection against fire.
1886 (1904) *U of T Stud.Hist.& Econ.* II 155: According to the ordinance of 1886 respecting fire districts, the majority of residents . . . may petition to be formed into a fire district under fire guardians or a fire guardian. **1953** *Cdn Geog.Jnl* XLVI 50/2: That portion of Ontario under organized fire protection today is designated as the "fire district." **1955** *Tweed News* 14 Apr. 5/1: No person shall set out fire for clearing land, disposal of debris or inflammable waste or for industrial purposes on Crown or private lands within the Fire District during the fire season April 1st to October 31st, except under authority of a Fire Permit.

fire-face *n*. See **fire-front**.
1955 GOWLAND *Smoke* 183: There was not a flame to be seen at the fire-face.

fire-front *n*. the point of farthest advance of a forest fire, where the firefighters work. See also **fire-face** and **fire-line**.
1953 *Cdn Geog.Jnl* XLVI 48/2: By noon the wind was blowing steadily from the south-west and the fire front was less than a mile from Paradise Lake. **1958** WATTERS *B.C.Cent.Anthol.* 267: . . . suddenly McGilvary pointed through the smoke towards the fire front.

fireguard *n*. **1** a strip of land, usually ploughed but sometimes burned free of grass, intended to stop the advance of a grass fire or a prairie fire. See also **firebreak** (def. 2) and **guard** (def. 3a).
1890 *Medicine Hat Times* (Alta) 3 July 1/5: The action of the C.P.R. in plowing fireguards along each side of their roadbed between here and Swift Current is worthy of praise. **1925** OSTENSO *Wild Geese* 346: He had thought a fire guard between the bush and the flax would be a waste of land. . . . **1954** *Ghost Pine* 161: We tried to light a fire guard and after lighting a box of matches finally had a strip burned on which we stood.
1963 SYMONS *Many Trails* 40: For days the smoky air had been redolent of sage and prairie herbs, and it choked us as we feverishly plowed fireguards.

2 See **firebreak** (def. 3).
1955 GOWLAND *Smoke* 184: The immediate task was to get the fire guard finished, soaked as much as possible with the pumps and perhaps backfire. **1961** *Canada Month* 6 Oct. 43/1: They know the dangers when these splinters of flame . . . jump fire guards and set woods ablaze behind them.

fireguard *v*. make a **fireguard** (def. 1).
1954 *Ghost Pine* 103: About 1 a.m. I was fire-guarding my own shack.

fire guardian *Obs*. See **fire warden** (def. 1).
1886 (1904) *U of T Stud.Hist.& Econ.* II 155: According to the Ordinance of 1886 . . . the majority of residents . . . may petition to be formed into a fire district under fire guardians or a fire guardian.

fire hall the headquarters of a fire brigade.
[**1849** (1961) *Ont.Hist.* Sep. 210: Hook and Ladder Co. No. 1 (Toronto)—Fireman's Hall Church Street.] **1881** BEGG *Great Cdn N.W.* 103: For the protection of property there is an efficient Fire Department with two steam fire engines and hook and ladder apparatus, ready for use at a moment's warning, in a handsome fire hall centrally located. **1891** *Grip* (Toronto) 21 Nov. 333/2: Whereas there are 4 chiefs and 19 firemen in the fire brigade and only 15 fire halls, it is recommended that 8 more fire halls be built to provide those 8 lonely officials with proper accommodation. **1953** *Pictou Advocate* 24 Dec. 14/5: Bylaws governing fire fighting going back to 1869 were reviewed amidst laughter here last Thursday night as present day firemen marked the opening of their new fire hall. **1966** *Kingston Whig-Standard* (Ont.) 26 Jan. 6/3: Council decided to increase the insurance on the fire hall. . . .

fire-hunting *n*. a method of hunting deer and moose. Cp. **jacklighting**.
1889 WITHROW *Our Own Country* 61: Fire-hunting, or hunting by torchlight, is practised by exhibiting a bright light formed by burning bunches of birch bark, in places known to be frequented by moose. The brilliant light seems to fascinate the animals, and he will readily approach within range of the rifle. **1896** RUSSELL *Far North* 9: I suggested fire-hunting to my companions, who declared that they would immediately leave the neighborhood, if we attempted it. **1934** DENNIS *Down in N.S.* 282: "There are three kinds of hunting," said an Indian who had many moose to his credit, "Still hunting, fire hunting, and calling."

fire-keeper *n*. a member of an Indian Council, such as that of the Six Nations, charged with the care of the ceremonial Council Fire.
1886 *Indian* (Hagersville, Ont.) 8 Sep. 198/1: The proceedings were commenced by a speech by Chief George Buck, the fire-keeper of the great council, who welcomed Sir John Macdonald on behalf of the Six Nations.

fire-line† *n*. **1** See **fire-front**.
c**1902** LAUT *Trapper* 147: The four trappers, running short of rations, decided to try to flank the fire coming around far enough ahead to intercept the game that must be moving away from the fire line. **1953** *Cdn Geog.Jnl* XLVI 46/1: The fifth and sixth fires appeared out of control and reports from portable radios on the fire line indicated that much more of everything . . . would be required to win control.

2 See **firebreak** (def. 3).
1958 WATTERS *B.C.Cent.Anthol.* 266: Dropping our packs we raced as fast as we dared down a narrow game trail, glutted with dead-falls and small jack pine. There was no chance of reaching the Babine Lake fire lines now. **1961** *Canada Month* 6 Oct. 43/1: Firefighting in B.C. is often referred to as war on the fire lines. **1963** MCKINNON *Forest Activities 3* 12: When possible, the first thing to do on a fire is to build a fire-line right around it, or at least across the advancing head of the fire. A fire-line is simply a wide path cleared of all underbrush and cover of all kinds and scraped down to mineral soil. When the fire reaches the line, there is no material for it to burn, and if it can be kept from "jumping" the line, control can be established.

3† a barrier erected by firemen to restrain curious onlookers.

1957 *Kingston Whig-Standard* (Ont.) 28 Sep. 1/5: One man was arrested and charged with obstructing police when he refused to move behind fire lines.

fire patrol a patrol carried out to detect and locate fires, especially forest fires.
1900 OSBORN *Warders of West* 775: A carbine and revolver are always carried when the policeman is looking for trouble, but the former is generally left at barracks when it is a question of "fire patrol" or some other purely civilian duty. 1924 *Beaver* Sep. 460: The seaplanes from Victoria Beach can be seen daily passing over the post on fire patrol. 1965 *Vancouver Province* 17 June 18/1: ... the daily fire patrol in a small airplane takes an hour and a half.

fire-ranger *n.* a government official engaged in the prevention and control of forest fires. See also **fire warden** (def. 2) and **ranger** (def. 4).
1909 CAMERON *New North* 82: The Fire-Ranger of the district, Mr. Biggs, has his barley and rice spread out on sheeting.... 1966 *Globe and Mail* (Toronto) 18 July 15/8: [He] was a wise and courteous old fire ranger who for years minded the tower near the northern end of the lake.

fire-ranging *n.* the office or occupation of a fire-ranger.
1899 GARDNER *Nothing But Names* 497: Mr. White devised and applied the system of fire ranging which is now used for the preservation of Ontario's forests.
1911 BICKERSTETH *Open Doors* 69: Like so many other appointments ... fire-ranging is a Government job, and if the Government changes Bury is likely to lose his post. 1923 WALDO *Down Mackenzie* 43: The ruling spirit of the place—or perhaps dividing the honor with the fire-ranging justice of the peace and his wife—is Mrs. Sutherland at the Hudson's Bay Post.

fire-reels *n.pl.* a fire engine; fire truck. See also **hose reel** and **reels.**
☛ *Formerly applied to a hand-drawn vehicle equipped with a reel of hose, the term persists in modern urban usage in the Toronto area, to some extent in Montreal and to some extent elsewhere.*
1898 (1958) WATTERS *B.C.Cent.Anthol.* 46: The hub-and-hub race was a dash of one hundred and fifty yards with the fire reels drawn by twelve men. 1957 *Kingston Whig-Standard* (Ont.) 2 Oct. 6/4: A century of grape-growing in the Niagara peninsula inspired a parade of old-time cars, fire reels and costumes in the Grape Festival at St. Catharines. 1958 *Weekend Mag.* 29 Nov. 47/1: Three things will bring me hustling to my window: fire reels; the screech and crunch of a motor collision; and voices raised in angry altercation.

fire rig a fire engine; fire truck.
1958 *Edmonton Jnl* 11 Aug. 3/4: Fire rigs from Edmonton arrived about 15 minutes after the fire was discovered....

fire sale† a sale of merchandise allegedly damaged by fire.
1899 *Yarmouth Herald* 27 Jan. 4/4: The Fire did not reach us and we are not running a FIRE SALE, but we are going to close out a lot of stock before spring goods arrive at prices that will make your money burn your pockets. 1955 *Dly News* (St. John's) 2 Mar. 3/1: People started lining up on LeMarchant Road shortly after 7 o'clock yesterday morning to get a chance at the bargains offered in Parker & Monroe's fire sale which started when the store opened at 9 o'clock.

fire-spotter *n.* a person employed to watch for and locate forest fires. See also **towerman.**
1962 *Sask.News* 19 June 2/1: For a fire-spotter life from early May to October is a constant dawn-to-dusk vigil. 1965 *Star Wkly* 23 Jan. 37/3: He works in the summer months as a fire spotter at the Montgomery lake tower in the Petawawa forestry reserve.

fire tower† a high tower from which a member of the forestry service watches for forest fires. See also **lookout tower** and **tower.**
1958 *Arctic Spotter* Feb. 19/1: From the top of his 60-foot fire tower in Nova Scotia, this watchman phones in an Aircraft Flash report. 1964 *Herald Mag.* 8 Aug. 4/1: The Alberta lands and forests department has a Fort McMurray office, responsible for 22,600 square miles of forest lands spotted with 14 fire towers and scanned by two forestry helicopters stationed in town.

fire trail *Esp.B.C.* a bush trail constructed for use by fire-fighting crews. See also **fireway.**
1942 HAIG-BROWN *Timber* 256: Sparks and burning embers of a forest fire, caught by its up-draft and driven by the following wind, set small fires far ahead of the main fire. These are the fire fighter's main concern once he has a good fire trail built. 1955 GOWLAND *Smoke* 100: On my next trip to Sikanaska I found evidence of a camp having been made there at the end of the fire trail.

fire-wagon *n.* in Indian parlance, a steam locomotive.
1926 SULLIVAN *Northern Lights* 138: "... Great Spirit tell me last night fire-wagon no good for Land of Little Sticks." 1963 *Herald Mag.* 14 Sep. 1/4: ... the Indians ... believed it [the smallpox] was caused by the smoke from the "demon fire-wagons" sticking in their throats.

fire-wagon hockey a way of playing hockey that is characterized by hard, fast, offensive teamwork accompanied by heavy body checking and sharp passing.
1963 O'BRIEN *Hockey* 53: Despite the immense increase in goalkeeping skills, fire-wagon hockey has resulted in what produces the cheers and packs the pews—namely, goals, more goals.

fire warden 1 an official responsible for fire protection and control.
1817 *U.C.Gaz.* (York [Toronto]) 12 June 95/5: The said Fire Warden shall ... carry about with him on occasion of Fires, a staff or some other visible distinguishing badge of office. 1859 *British Colonist* (Victoria) 15 Jan. 2/3: He will carry out the necessary measures, such as the appointment of Fire Wardens and Engineers, the building of cisterns, the storing of gunpowder, and other improvements, without delay. 1934 DENNIS *Down in N.S.* 235: "The apparatus is to give warning if a dry spell is coming. If it is, I keep a sharper look-out and tend my tower sharper, for I'm the fire warden."

2 See **fire-ranger.**
1917 MILLER *New Era* 84: ... the fire wardens at any of the outlooks seeing the smoke of a bush fire can at once get together a sufficient number of men to extinguish the fire in its incipient stages. 1938 CASH *I Like B.C.* 67: It was the summer the Provincial

Government in an "economy" programme had cut down on fire wardens.

firewater† *n.* [prob. trans. of an Algonk. term; cf. *scuttaywabo*] **1** See quotes. See also **scuttaywabo.** Also, earlier, *fire waters.*
[1757 (1965) HAMILTON *Cdn Quotations* 63/2: Fire water. Term (trans.) used by Indians to describe brandy given them in exchange for furs; good liquor blazed up when poured on a fire, diluted liquor quenched it. Paradise for them is to get drunk. (Montcalm, *Journal des campagnes,* Aug. 29, 1757. . . .) **1791** LONG *Voyages* 69: It is very hard for us Indians, who have not the sense of the white people to know when we have had enough of the strong fiery water.] **1833** *Brit.Colonial Argus* (St. Catharines, U.C.) 21 Sep. 3/3: They doubted not, from what they had seen of the effects of fire-water, that it was the very MANITOU (or the DEVIL) and would not touch it. **1861** *Nor'Wester* (R.R.S.) 1 Aug. 3/5: I cannot leave the Settlement without expressing my hearty concurrence in the resolve to which the Honorable Hudson's Bay Company have come viz. that they will not take any more "fire-water" into the Saskatchewan. **1927** LONGSTRETH *Silent Forces* 47: Some tribes would stand for a smaller quantity of spirits than others, but the sophisticated Blackfeet demanded something that would ignite if you put a match to it—fire-water. It was colored with black tea to look more devilish yet. **1962** *Canada Month* Jan. 27/3: Some made moccasins and snowshoes, others spruce beer, the original fire-water.
2 See quote.
1950 CREIGHTON *Lunenburg County* 110: When fishing for albacore or tuna, at night, when there is a glow of phosphorescence about the moving fish, the men call it firewater.

fireway *n.* See **fire trail.**
1938 CASH *I Like B.C.* 65: Fortunately, creeks were full and many, but we all knew they must be having an awful time up there; working inadequate, little, old pumps; cutting fireways through the forest and wetting them down.

fireweed *n.* a plant of the genus *Epilobium,* especially *E. angustifolium,* the floral emblem of the Yukon. See also **French willow, giant willow herb,** and **mooseweed.**
1820 (1823) JOHNSTONE *Travels in P.E.I.* 22: If the land is not directly cleared and cultivated . . . a weed they call fire-weed, springs up as rank and strong as hemp, which entirely impoverishes the land. **1833** (1955) DOMETT *Cdn Journal* 1: A beautiful weed with a pink flower grows plentifully in the parts thus cleared— they call it fireweed here [Lower Canada]. **1905** OUTRAM *Cdn Rockies* 297: The weird relics of tall, blackened poles and the accompaniment of tangled stems lay in thick confusion among the rocky outcrops, sparse grass and bushes, and luxuriant fireweed, made the scene rather desolate. . . . **1965** *Maclean's* 21 Aug. 24/1: Yukon's Fireweed blooms like the heather in late northern spring.

firewood tree *Nfld* a tree, usually a conifer, that has been killed by girdling, *q.v.,* and left standing as a reserve source of firewood.
1933 MERRICK *True North* 77: Often when everything close around has been cut, you will see a couple of dry firewood trees still standing beside the tilt. They are there in case of sickness. Most trappers girdle a good many trees around their tilts each year. . . . they die, and in three years make excellent firewood.

fire-works *n.pl. Obs.* flint and steel or other equipment for making a fire.

1743 (1949) ISHAM *Observations* 19: a bag to put fire works in . . . Skip pa to gan. **1822** (1932) MCLEAN *Notes* 30: The night was dark, and to make our situation as cheerless as possible, it was discovered that my companion had left his "fire-works" behind—a proof of his inexperience.

first goose *North* See quotes. See also **goose hunt.**
1888 (1948) *Beaver* Dec. 14/1: On May 5, 1888, the first goose was shot, "the successful marksman receiving, according to immemorial custom at the Hudson's Bay establishments, a present of a pound each of the two luxuries of the country, tea and tobacco." **1941** *Ibid.* Sep. 37/2: First Goose—At the Bay posts where the geese usually came in thousands, it was an old custom to reward the hunters who brought in the first goose in the spring with a payment of five shillings or one fathom of tobacco.

first ice the winter's first formation of ice permitting travel on lakes and streams.
1821 (1938) SIMPSON *Athabasca Jnl* 247: "He can get up in the Fall or by the first ice." **1929** *Beaver* Dec. 318: . . . awaiting first cold day to cross they arrived on very first ice on straits.

First Meridian *West* See quote.
1963 *Citizen* 31 Jan. 14/6: WHAT IS THE FIRST MERIDIAN? This is the basic north-south line from which lands are surveyed in the prairie provinces. It is at 97 degrees 27 minutes west, just a few miles west of Winnipeg. From this line townships are surveyed and numbered east to the second initial meridian, [e]ast, at 94 degrees west, just east of the Lake of the Woods, and west to the second initial meridian west, at 102 degrees west, not far west of the Manitoba-Saskatchewan boundary. Here township numbers begin again then again at the third meridian west (the Saskatchewan-Alberta boundary), at the fifth meridian west, near Calgary, and at the sext meridian west near Jasper.

First of July See **Dominion Day.**
1884 *Nor'Wester* (Calgary) 27 May 1/6. All over the Dominion . . . the first of July is taking the lead, though from what we saw yesterday it would be advisable for our citizens to drop the celebration business altogether for a year or two so that people will have a chance to get their breath. **1932** JAMIESON *Cattle in the Stall* 48: "Well, we heard some sort of rumour about great doings in Dundas on the First of July." **1958** *Native Voice* Jan. 6/1: I often wonder why we even participate in First of July celebrations because it's a date commemorating the complete capitulation of the Canadian Indians.

first timber or **wood** *North* See **timber line** (def. 2).
1867 (1913) COWIE *Adventurers* 270: We made the first woods early and had tea and something to eat. . . . **1916** (1936) STEELE *Policing the Arctic* 185: Thawed out, Beyts put his comments on paper explaining that because of the exhaustion of the dogs and because "none of the natives, so far, will go beyond the first timber," he no longer thought it possible to reach Bathurst Inlet that winter.

fish† *n.* **1** especially in Newfoundland, cod.
1861 DE BOILIEU *Labrador Life* 38: As the reader may suppose, fish is, in Labrador, a standing—or, rather, the standard—dish. **1909** ROBINSON *Unknown Land* 30: A salmon is a salmon, and a trout is a trout, but

cod, and cod only, is spoken of as fish. "Will you have salmon or fish?" you are asked at the dinner table, and you soon get into the same way of talking.
1957 HUTCHISON *Canada* 7: "Me fadder . . . worked all of his life and not a penny to show fer it. And his fadder before him. And his fadder, too. 'Tis always dat way wid fish."

2 *North* See **dried fish.**
1897 YOUNG *Indian Trail* 48: Well, first of all, as word has come that the wolves have been visiting our fish-cache, Martin Papanekis and I have arranged to drive over there with the dogs to see the extent of the damage. **1956** KEMP *Northern Trader* 133: In early October, Mooneas asked me what I was going to do about fish. He meant winter fish, dog-feed. I knew we would require some "Hung fish"—semi-dried fish— for winter travel. . . .

fish barrier See **barrier.**
1913 COWIE *Adventurers* 235: He had been born at the fish barrier, about a quarter of a mile below the fort.

fish camp *Esp. North* **1** a camp used as headquarters for a fishing party. See also **fishing camp** (def. 1).
1900 *Yukon Sun* (Dawson) 6 Feb. 1/2: The tragedy occurred at a fish camp on a small lake about fifty miles up the Pelly river. **1962** SLOBODIN *Kutchin* 19: In the summer of 1789 . . . Alexander Mackenzie . . . came upon two small fish-camps of Indians. . . .

2 a commercial fishing establishment operating seasonally in a remote area, often equipped with dressing and packing facilities. See also **fishing camp** (def. 2) and **fishing station** (def. 1).
1953 *North Star* (Yellowknife) Mar. 3/4: Only one thing to do, and they started on their long, pain-ridden walk to the nearest source of help, the watchman's cabin at the fish camp, Gros Cap, five miles away. **1956** KENNEDY *Gt Slave Lake* 10: Some fish companies have built ice houses at favorite temporary bases and there is a tendency for other shore facilities to be built near such ice houses and for such bases to become permanent fish camps. **1958** *Sun* (Vancouver) 11 Apr. 4/2: Latest reports we have from good authority are that the fish camps will be paying better prices for troll fish this year, for springs, anyway.

fish-club *n.* a decorated club used by Pacific Coast Indians to kill fish.
1952 *Tsimshian* 22: Fish-clubs were made from wood and were carved in various intricate designs representing birds and animals which normally preyed on the sea-creatures. **1956** LEECHMAN *Native Tribes* 315: A fish club was designed first of all for killing fish when they were pulled alive into the canoe so that they would not flop about and upset things, and the decoration had to come second.

fish collector a vessel equipped for picking up fish catches for transporting to a cannery. See also **fish-packer.**
1966 *Fisherman* 6 May 14/3: [Advert.] WANTED— GOOD SKIPPER TO RUN fish collector in Alert Bay area. Can hire his own deck hand. Union wages.

fish derby See **derby** (def. 2).

fish-eagle *n.* **1** See **bald eagle.**
1905 OUTRAM *Cdn Rockies* 13: Fish-eagles are by no

means rare, as are fish hawks, and golden eagles . . . are sometimes seen. **1956** MCATEE *Folk-Names* 22: Bald Eagle [is also called] fish eagle (N.B.). . . .

2 See **fish-hawk.**
1956 MCATEE *Folk-Names* 22: Osprey [is also called] . . . fish eagle (rather general). . . .

fish-eater *n. Slang* **1** an Eskimo.
1936 STRINGER *Wife-Traders* 104: "I've found these fish-eaters rustling some pretty rough chow," he said as he took a final drag at his cigarette. . . .

2 a Nova Scotian.
1950 BIRD *This is N.S.* 130: "You a fish eater?" We took it that he meant a Nova Scotian, and nodded assent.

fished out See **fish out.**

fisher† *n.* **1** a weasel-like fur-bearer, *Martes pennanti.* See also **black cat, pekan, wejack,** and **woodshock.**
1774 ROBINSON & RISPIN *Journey N.S.* 43: Here are also otters . . . fishers. . . . **1862** *Nor' Wester* (R.R.S.) 22 Jan. 1/1: And when I mention that the most valuable fur bearing animals abound in the Mountains,—such as bears, foxes, fishers and marten in great numbers,—I need scarcely add that such a winter's work would pay well. **1965** *Islander* 14 Feb. 13/1: It was an extra-small female, not much larger than a big fisher.

2 the valuable pelt of this animal.
*c***1800** (1964) INNIS *Fur Trade in Canada* 264: The animal is first mentioned, the skins of which amount to the smallest sum . . . Beaver, otter, muskrat, martin, bear fox, lynx, fisher, mink, wolf, buffaloe. **1807** *Quebec Gaz.* 22 Jan. 4/1: Exports from the Port of Quebec, 1806 . . . 6,578 Fisher . . . 125,622 Raccoon, etc. **1908** MAIR *Mackenzie Basin* 204: For the period 1858 to 1884, Athabasca District turned out 5,138 fishers.

fishery *n.* **1**† the fishing business or industry.
1765 *Quebec Gaz.* 9 May 3/1: A Practice, for some Time, has been carried on by Fisher-men and others . . . of throwing the Offals of the Fish on the said Fishing-Banks and other places, to the great prejudice of the Fishery. *c***1860** (1953) MILLS *Folk Songs of Nfld:* Such constant strain might crack the brain; / the fishery game I'm leavin'. **1958** *Encyc.Can.* IV 164: [Caption] The salmon is today the basis of the nation's most valuable commercial fishery.

2 an area for fishing, often including buildings, sometimes held on lease. See also **fishing-berth.** Cp. **fishing post.**
1807 *Quebec Gaz.* 2 July 3/1: Labrador Fiefs and Fisheries for sale. **1946** *Beaver* March 34/2: There was the island to the west, back of which was the fishery. There were old fishermen's huts and ruins of log buildings at the fishery. . . . **1958** *Encyc.Can.* IV 159/1: With the advance of settlement . . . some of these [northern] fisheries were depleted.

3 an organized effort to catch fish in quantity.
1807 (1820) HARMON *Journal* 160: We sent people to the other end of this lake, to make a fall fishery. They will take whitefish, trout, pike, carp, [etc.]. **1952** PUTNAM *Cdn Regions* 496/1: The Mackenzie River has sufficient fish for local use . . . [and] important "fisheries" are held every fall at all settlements to catch enough fish for winter dog-feed. **1956** *Albertan* (Calgary) 27 July 8/1: A goldeye fishery was recently concluded at Lake Clare in the Wood Buffalo Park. . . .

fishery inspector or **officer** a government official whose duty is to inspect commercial fishing operations.
1927 *Beaver* Sep. 92/2: [He] was a fishery inspector

for the Dominion government for a number of years. . . .
1963 SYMONS *Many Trails* 134: The fishery officer, making his rounds, checks the mesh of nets, the yardage, and the permit number.

fish-flake† *n.* *Nfld* See **flake.**
1818 CHAPPELL *Voy.of Rosamond* 128: On the following day, the cod are removed to the fish-flakes, where they are spread in the sun to dry: and from thence forward thay are kept constantly turned during the day, and piled up in small heaps, called flackets, at night.
1963 *Kingston Whig-Standard* (Ont.) 20 Feb. 21/1: They build fish flakes, piers and storage sheds . . . from timber cut in the surrounding countryside.

fish gurry *Maritimes* See **gurry.**
1934 DENNIS *Down in N.S.* 180: Towner was hunted up and driven out of town to the accompaniment of fish gurry, mud and rotten eggs. **1942** RADDALL *His Majesty's Yankees* 339: When at last we stumbled up a boat slip of peeled poles slippery with fish gurry . . . we were greeted by people who took us for rebel privateersmen on another raid.

fish-hawk† *n.* the osprey, *Pandion haliaetus.* See also **fish-eagle** (def. 2) and **fishing eagle** (def. 1).
1853 REID *Young Voyageurs* 274: . . . another incident occurred to our voyageurs, which illustrated the habits of a very interesting bird, the "osprey," or fish-hawk, as it is more familiarly known [in the Northwest].
1902 ROBERTS *Kindred of Wild* 63: All at once, the fish-hawk was seen to poise on steady wing [New Brunswick]. **1940** NIVEN *Mine Inheritance* 328: . . . there were the plunging fish-hawks and the patient hunched herons standing on one leg [Manitoba]. **1965** RICHARDSON *Living Island* 29: The osprey's local name is fish-hawk, and the "hawk-nest tree" became a landmark [Nova Scotia].

fish house 1 *Maritimes* a shore building where offshore fishermen store gear and sometimes cure their fish. See **fishing shack, fish shed,** and **store** (def. 2).
1934 DENNIS *Down in N.S.* 316: In one spot are numerous little fish-houses with fishing paraphernalia galore and infinitely more lobster pots than could be seen by most people in a lifetime. **1963** *Canada Month* Feb. 19/3: On the exposed Digby Neck . . . towering waves . . . poured over the village's tiny breakwater, tearing boats from their moorings and smashing over fish houses on the shore.
2 *North* a shack for storing dried fish, *q.v.*
1934 GODSELL *Arctic Trader* 63: The third building was the fish house in which were a few sticks of frozen fish for dog-feed.

fishing admiral *Nfld, Hist.* a title given to the captain of the first fishing vessel to reach a harbor on the Newfoundland coast each year, a title that carried with it authority as magistrate for the fishery in the area of his jurisdiction, a form of justice that endured from the early seventeenth century until the late eighteenth. Cp. **rear admiral.**
1718 (1793) REEVES *Hist.Nfld* 79: But what I would more particularly represent to their lordships, is the clandestine and illegal commerce carried on between the New England men, and several of the British masters, especially the fishing admirals; who after they have, according to the act, qualified themselves in England for fishing ships, depart for France, Spain, or Portugal, which they freight with wines and brandies. . . .
1840 (1860) MURRAY *Brit.Amer.* II 119: The captain who first arrives here is dignified with the title of fishing-

admiral, and enjoys a certain jurisdiction over the coast.
1907 *U of T Stud.Hist.& Econ.* II 271: The local government of that day and for many years later is known as the rule of the "fishing admiral," one of the most grotesque forms of government ever devised.
1965–66 *Dalhousie Rev.* Winter 545: Their fishing "admirals" ruled the roost in whatever harbour they chose to anchor, and theirs was the only law.

fishing banks an extensive offshore shelf where fish abound, specifically the Grand Banks, *q.v.*, off Newfoundland and Labrador.
1765 *Quebec Gaz.* 9 May 3/1: A Practice, for some Time, has been carried on by Fisher-men and others, fishing on the Banks and other Places in this Province, of throwing the Offals of the Fish on the said Fishing-Banks and other places, to the great prejudice of the Fishery. **1818** CHAPPELL *Voy.of Rosamond* 51: In the fishing season, it is resorted to by at least 10,000 people, on account of the fishing banks. **1958** *Evening Telegram* (St. John's) 7 May 13/5: This is the Nova Scotia trawler Sheila Patricia that caught fire off the east coast on her way to the fishing banks.

fishing-berth *n.* See **fishery** (def. 2).
1916 DUNCAN *Billy Topsail* 175: . . . it is a long way for fame to carry—north to the uttermost fishing-berths of the Labrador.

fishing camp 1 See **fish camp** (def. 1).
1934 *Beaver* June 48/1: This island is a fishing camp where the trappers come in summer to set nets and get fish for dog feed during the winter.
2 See **fish camp** (def. 2).
1936 ARMSTRONG *Yukon Yesterdays* 52: The broken-down debris, as one might call them, of the Pacific Coast mining and fishing camps, such as Juneau, Ketchikan, Wrangel and a dozen more, came in over the Skagway trail and Chilcoot Pass.
1958 *Edmonton Jnl* 12 Aug. 17/3: By the same token, he went on, "the minister of transport could occupy a disused wharf as a fishing camp."
3 See **fishing lodge.**
1955 *Winnipeg Free Press* 1 Feb. 21/4: Kitchen girl twenty or over, for work from May 1st to October 1st at fishing camp on Lake of the Woods at Sioux Narrows, Ontario. **1965** *Globe and Mail* (Toronto) 12 Jan. 7/3: . . . one farmer has turned a bad farm into a good little fishing camp. . . .

fishing derby See **derby** (def. 2).

fishing eagle 1 See **fish-hawk.**
1795 (1911) HEARNE *Journey* 398: Eagles of several sorts are found in the country bordering on Hudson's Bay during the Summer; but none, except the common brown Fishing Eagle, ever frequent the Northern parts. **1963** SPRY *Palliser* 254: Hector was fascinated by the great fishing eagles—as he called the ospreys—perched on the tops of dead trees. . . .
2 See **bald eagle.** See also **fish-eagle** (def. 1).
1853 REID *Young Voyageurs* 455: Had it been a fishing eagle—such as the bald-head—the case would have been different, for these last . . . taste rank and disagreeable.

fishing hole a hole cut in the ice of a lake or river for catching fish in winter.
1783 (1954) *Moose Fort Jnls* 18: Armourer and one man making spikes, two at the fishing holes, two

brewing. **1962** *Globe and Mail* (Toronto) 23 Mar. 23/8: We traveled to our fishing holes in a conveyance known as a bombardier, an ingenious vehicle with runners on the front and caterpillar tracks at the back.

fishing light See **jacklight** *n.* (def. 1).
1832 (1953) RADCLIFF *Letters* 129: At night the shore was brilliant with the fishing lights in the canoes; and I had to walk but twenty paces to mine, to enjoy as fine sport as the most enthusiastic fisherman could desire.

fishing lodge an establishment providing accommodation and, usually, boats for sport fishermen. See also **lodge** (def. 4a).
1956 KEMP *Northern Trader* 250: The Hudson's Bay post still stood—that new, streamlined establishment—but around it I saw fishing lodges and a service station, restaurants, a building where movies were shown and a poolroom. **1966** *Kingston Whig-Standard* (Ont.) 15 Jan. 4/3: [She] maintained . . . a fishing lodge in the New Brunswick wilderness.

fishing lot *Maritimes, Obs.* See **fish lot.**
1869 BROWN *Cape Breton* 369: This meagre list embraces all the heads of families in Cape Breton in 1768, according to the best information Mr. Francklyn could obtain; but there is every reason to believe that it was very incorrect, as many families undoubtedly occupied lands and fishing lots in remote and secluded places, who escaped observation.

fishing post 1 *Obs.* the buildings, flakes, and stages belonging to a fishery (def. 2).
1807 *Quebec Gaz.* 2 July 3/1: Also . . . The Fishing Posts or Establishments on the said coast, with two vessels, and all the craft, utensils and effects belonging to that Fishery, which shall remain at the close of the present season. **1832** MCGREGOR *British America* I 352: [They] never made any permanent settlement on the island, except trifling fishing posts at two or three places.

2 *Hist.* See **fish post.**
1824 (1955) BLACK *Journal* 40: . . . no other fisherman could be had none having been provided from the Fishing Posts. . . . **1926** MAIR *Masterworks* XIV 271: "Huskies," a corruption of the word Esquimaux, are train dogs which are summered in large numbers at fishing-posts in the interior.

fishing room *Nfld* a beach lot, *q.v.*, from which a fisherman may operate and where he may set up flakes, *q.v.*, and stages (def. 1). Cp. **fish lot.**
1713–14 (1793) REEVES *Hist.Nfld* 76: In such case should the ships fishing rooms of that harbour be taken up before he arrives, they often remove some planter or other for him, pretending that the planter's title is not good to the room he possesses, when the commanders of men of war, some years before, adjudged it to be the said planter's right. **1824** *Cdn Mag.* III 350: Among the subjects requiring our most serious attention, and which we probably shall find the most difficult of adjustment, are the claims for fishing rooms, or beach lots. **1952** PUTNAM *Cdn Regions* 65/2: The places of business, fishing rooms, stages and flakes are close along the water's edge separated from the houses by a narrow, winding and often rough and grass grown road which, however, does not extend beyond the settlement. **1965** MACNUTT *Atlantic Provinces* 12: Placentia saw the coming of a British garrison; and British officers purchased from their withdrawing French

counterparts, the ownership of the best fishing-rooms in the harbour.

fishing shack or **shanty** See **fish house** (def. 1).
1918 COPELAND *Trail of Swinging Lanterns* 59: Hamilton Bay . . . stretches a way to beach and bar, with a colony of fishing shanties squatting in the cove not far from the location of the awful "Des jardins Canal" wreck. **1934** DENNIS *Down in N.S.* 285: The little fishing shacks on the beach where the fishermen dress their fish were deserted.

fishing stage *Esp.Nfld* **1** See **stage** (def. 1).
1715 (1883) HATTON & HARVEY *Newfoundland* 111: On the 19th September a storm of unexampled severity swept over the island, causing an immense destruction of shipping, houses, fishing stages and flakes, fences and bridges, and engulfing in many instances the fruits of the fishermen's toil during the previous summer. **1944** *Beaver* Sep. 22/2: Boats are loaded down to the water's edge and then headed for the fishing stage for the dressing of the fish. **1958** *Evening Telegram* (St. John's) 7 May 10/2: Each year high seas came in and smashed the fishing stages and equipment, and each year the sturdy fishermen would go as far as seven miles into the forest for wood to rebuild.

2 *Rare* See **flake.**
1842 BONNYCASTLE *Newfoundland* I 295: The consumption of all the spruce tribe in the formation of fishing stages, or places to dry the fish on, is enormous; as, in consequence of nature having denied this iron-bound shore the necessary beaches, man has been obliged to substitute stages or platforms, which are very ingeniously formed along the steep descents of the hills on the edges of harbours, by using upright stakes of great length, and attaching others from the hill side to them, and then covering the platform thus formed in ribs longitudinally with the boughs and branches of the pines.

fishing station 1 *Hist.* See **fish camp** (def. 2).
1832 BAILLIE *Account of N.B.* 123: There are only seven of these islands which are in any way capable of settlement, and that only with the chief purpose of fishing stations. **1927** *Beaver* Sep. 70: . . . in 1850 . . . the Company used the island [San Juan Island] as a fishing station, putting up annually two or three thousand barrels of salmon. **1955** ENGLISH *Newfoundland* 20/2: Apparently the French had used the harbour [Renews, once Rougenoust] as a fishing station as early as 1506.

2 *Obs.* a place to angle for game fish.
1872 DASHWOOD *Chiploquorgan* 20: Two miles over rough waters are the Round Rocks, which is a very fair fishing station when the river is high and the fish are running.

fish ladder† a device constructed at a waterfall to facilitate the upstream migration of fish to their spawning grounds. Cp. **fish pass.**
1870 *Cdn Illust.News* 9 Apr. 363/2: James Wyeth King [of Shubenacadie, N.S.] [invented] improvements in machines by which fish are enabled to surmount and pass dams, cascades and other obstructions in water courses, called "The King Fish Ladder." **1947** *Game Trails in Can.* Aug. 14: [Subheading] Fish ladders at Fraser River bottleneck promise boost to salmon industry of British Columbia.

fish lot *Maritimes* a beach lot from which fishermen may operate. See also **fishing lot.** Cp. **fishing room.**
1934 DENNIS *Down in N.S.* 276: The land in Barrington was not allotted when the grant was issued in 1763. It

was divided so as to furnish each grantee with a homestead and a fish lot.

fish-making *n. Nfld* the process of preparing and drying codfish. Cp. **make fish.**
1964 *Nfld Qtly* Spring 27/1: These sharemen were and are sometimes chargeable with a part of certain items . . . [as] when a Labradorman's voyage of fish has to be "made," i.e. sun dried by the planters and/or neighbours with flake-room and time to spare, a prior pre-quintal charge is reserved from the entire voyage's value to pay for this labour called "fish-making". . . .

fishocracy *n. Nfld, Hist.* **1** See quote.
1878 (1965) HAMILTON *Cdn Quotations* 147: Fishocracy. Term used to describe well-to-do merchants opposed to self-government. (P. Toque, *Newfoundland, as it was,* 1878, 86.)
2 the social and economic pyramid built on the fisheries, *q.v.*
1940 INNIS *Cod Fisheries* 387n: The "fishocracy" comprised in descending order: (1) the principal merchants, high officials, and some lawyers and medical men; (2) small merchants, important shopkeepers, lawyers, doctors, and secondary officials; (3) grocers, master mechanics, and schooner holders; and (4) fishermen.

fish oil *West Coast* See **oolichan oil.**
1884 (1926) MOSER *Reminiscences* 139: [There was] Hayou makmak: 12 baskets of herring spawn; two barrels of molasses, and one barrel of fish oil.

fish out depopulate (a stream, lake, etc.) of fish through fishing operations.
1907 HUNTER *Cdn Wilds* 180: Lakes were all about us and when one was fished out we moved our nets to another. **1956** KENNEDY *Gt Slave Lake* 48: Sometimes they have the skill but because they think the lake is "fished out" . . . they fail to put forth the extra effort required to handle nets in the most efficient way. . . .

fish-packer *n.* a comparatively large boat that collects the fish caught by smaller fishing boats and packs them in ice for taking to cannery or market. See also **fish-collector.**
1954 EVANS *Mist* 19: A big fish-packer was moving slowly toward the head of the bay and more men came from the office to watch it. **1959** *Native Voice* May 4/5: He'll be an ordained minister and no longer a fisherman. But he intends to keep his fish packer.

fish pass an artificial lock built to assist fish in passing a waterfall or other obstruction on their way upstream to spawn. See also **fishway.** Cp. **fish ladder.**
1879 *Morning Chron.* (Halifax) 7 July 2/2: The principle of this scheme is, I may say at once and without hesitation, the very best which can be devised for an artificial fish pass. **1959** *Cdn Geog.Jnl* Aug. 62/1: The Hydro Board has adopted an ingenious fish pass, operating on the principle of a canal lock.

fish pemmican *Hist.* a preparation of dried, pounded fish and fish fat made after the fashion of pemmican (def. 1).
1860 HIND *Assiniboine Exped.* I 487: On stopping to cook breakfast we were greatly disappointed to find that the fish pemmican which we were so thankful to get, was nearly all rotten. **1956** WENTWORTH *Dried Meat* 7: For fish pemmican, salmon was dried . . . and then pounded fine in stone mortars. These dried fish could be stored in baskets or fish fats could be added to make standard type pemmican.

fish pile *Nfld* See **faggot.**
1861 DE BOILIEU *Labrador Life* 37: When sufficiently dry, a fine warm day is chosen to lay the fish out, singly, on a large stage; and during the hottest hours they are made up into a "fish pile,"—which is a large quantity of dry fish, built up in the form of a round haystack.

fish post *Fur Trade, Hist.* a northern post where the principal food was fish and where fish were caught for supplying to other posts. See also **fishing post** (def. 2). Cp. **deer post** and **meat post.**
1821 (1938) SIMPSON *Athabasca Jnl* 243: The same precaution [to have an adequate supply of twine] is applicable to all our fish posts. **1938** *Ibid.* 31n: Whitefish were the usual mainstay of the "Fish Posts" in the interior.

fish shed *Maritimes* See **fish house** (def. 1).
1956 RADDALL *Wings of Night* 10: And then . . . you saw those . . . gray weathered cottages and fish sheds, the small wharves and stagings. . . .

fish stage 1 *North* a platform of poles on which fish are hung to dry. Cp. **drying stage** (def. 2).
1792 (1923) MENZIES *Voyage* 66: We soon after rounded out a deep Bay, on the West side of which we saw a great number of fish stages erected from the ground in a slanting manner, for the purpose of exposing the fish fastened to them to the most advantageous aspect for, drying. **1818** CHAPPELL *Voy.of Rosamond* 75: We also perceived great quantities of stinking fish and bones lying scattered about their wigwams; together with canoes, and large fish-stages. **1939** *Beaver* Sep. 22/1: The frozen white-fish . . . hung on fish-stages, high platforms made out of reach of the dogs.

2 *Nfld* See **stage** (def. 1).
1910 (1947) DUNCAN *Billy Topsail* 28: Half-way to the fish stage . . . Jimmie Grimm came to a startled full stop. **1963** *Imperial Oil Rev.* Dec. 10/1: . . . past the crazy legs of the wharves and fish stages and a clutch of tidy salt-box houses, fading finally into the bare and brooding hills.

fish-stick *n.* an oblong bar of frozen fish, often breaded, pre-cooked, and marketed in packages.
1955 *Kingston Whig-Standard* (Ont.) 6 Apr. 25/2: The newly developed frozen fish fillets [are] known as fish sticks. **1957** *Time* (Cdn ed.) 25 Feb. 78/3: In 1953 they were among the first to produce and market the highly popular fish sticks. **1962** *Commercial Letter* Oct. 4/2: Technological advances have continually given rise to new products . . . Examples include fish-sticks, which are at present very popular. . . .

fish warden an official appointed locally, especially on Indian reserves, to supervise fishing for domestic use and distribution of fish to the aged and infirm.
1958 HAWTHORN *Indians of B.C.* 216: The fish warden was supposed to be present to record the catch.

fishway† *n.* See **fish pass.**
1866 KING *Sportsman in Can.* 260: Were this carried out, and, as the Superintendent says, all the mill-dams removed, or fishways constructed adjacent to them, protection being also afforded to spawning fish, most of the rivers in this district would ere long be plentifully stocked with salmon once more. **1950** HUTCHISON *Fraser* 307: Essentially the Gate fishway was to consist of two gigantic concrete flumes, one on each side of the

canyon, through which the water would flow quietly enough to offer the fish sure passage. **1961** *Time* (Cdn ed.) 18 Aug. 11/1: [The Commission] completed a fishway around Hell's Gate barrier.

fish wheel a mechanical device for catching fish, consisting of several scoop nets on a circular frame which is driven by the force of the current. See also **salmon wheel**.
1965 *B.C. Digest* June 23/2: The Dawson residents use fish wheels to take Kings [salmon] and then sell the better ones for human consumption and use the others for dog food.

fit-out *n.* **1** clothing, provisions, and equipment; outfit.
1829 MOORSOM *Letters N.S.* 49: Those engaged in the pursuit were persons of the poorest description, who, commencing without capital, without any thing, in fact, but the power of bodily labour, had to procure credit in the first instance, and then fight up-hill under an accumulation of debt for their fit-out, their annual equipment, and their winter-stores, which keeps the greater part of them at this moment in arrear on the books of the merchant. **1852** RICHARDSON *Arctic Exped.* 294: ... they came *en masse* to the fort, with their sledges and all their movables, to receive another fit-out. **1954** *Fishermen's Advocate* 2 Apr. 12/2: Aid to the men ranged from a new blanket to a new fitout, including a new dress suit to the value of $25.
2 *Nfld* of a ship, the process of taking on gear, provisions, and crew.
1955 *Fishermen's Advocate* 18 Feb. 1/4: [Headline] Local Sealer Begins Fitout Many Seek Berth Aboard.

fitter *n. Lumbering, Hist. or Obs.* the member of a gang who selected the trees to be felled for fashioning into square timber.
1947 SAUNDERS *Algonquin* 30: The fitter came first, selecting trees large enough to make a stick, and sound from top to base. **1964** *Cdn Geog. Jnl* Feb. 66/3: The fitter ranged the forest selecting timber that was large enough and sound enough to be economically floated to Quebec.

five-cent piece a Canadian coin worth five cents; nickel, *q.v.*
1862 *Nor' Wester* (R.R.S.) 30 Apr. 1/2: Canada never stirred a finger, and to-day she is not, as she deserves not to be, a five-cent piece better off for her near proximity to Red River than she would have been had that country remained inaccessible save through Hudson's Bay. **1953** LEBOURDAIS *Nation of North* 204: To most, such discussions lacked a sense of reality, especially in the light of Mr. King's expression not to contribute a five-cent piece toward their relief.

Five Nations† the original Iroquois Confederacy of Senecas, Cayugas, Onendagas, Oneidas, and Mohawks, later (c1722) joined by the Tuscaroras to form the Six Nations, *q.v.* See also **Great Confederacy**.
1703 LAHONTAN *New Voyages* I 58: [It was a] pipe of the five nations. **1834** (1926) LANGTON *Early U.C.* 125: As we advanced in intimacy during the day, though our only medium of communication was imperfect French and a still more imperfect Missisauga interpreter, the old chief Uraguadire intimated his intention of making me a member of the Five Nations. **1907** *Ont.Bur.Arch.*

Rep. V 6: As to the relative positions of the Hurons and their mortal enemies, the Five Nations or Iroquois, Huronia lay 150 miles about from the Senecas, who were the nearest, and 250 from the Mohawks, who were the most remote.

fivepin bowling a game of bowls, first played in 1909, in which the players attempt to knock over five pins, each of different scoring value, by rolling three large balls, one at a time, down an alley.
1929 *Beaver* June 228/2: A successful five pin bowling season was concluded at a banquet held in the Georgian Restaurant.... **1957** *Kingston Whig-Standard* (Ont.) 10 Oct. 42/5: An estimated 1,000,000 Canadian players are engaged in fivepin bowling as this truly native Canadian game gets into full swing on some 7,000 alleys across the country.

fivepinner *n. Slang* a person who engages in fivepin bowling, *q.v.*
1964 *Calgary Herald* 23 Jan. 16/1: I don't know whether or not you've noticed, but there's a minor revolution taking place in Calgary bowling circles. The five pinners, once complete rulers of the local picture, are facing a real challenge from the ten pinners and with good reason.

fivepins *n. pl.* See **fivepin bowling**.
1962 *Weekend Mag.* 17 Feb. 6/1: There are several types of bowling games, from duckpins in Quebec to candlepins in the Maritimes, but most people prefer fivepins. **1963** *Calgary Herald* 23 Jan. 16/1: He [the bowler] does not, for instance, have to knock over a certain pin to count, as is the case in five pins.

fiveplex ['faɪvplɛks] *n.* [by analogy with **duplex**, *q.v.*] a small apartment block having five self-contained apartments. Also spelled *5-plex*.
1964 *Enterprise* (West Hill, Ont.) 14 May 3/2: The application had been made by O. E. Crockford on behalf of Dr. Stephen Sovis, who wants to operate from his home at Aylesworth and Midland Avenues, which is a 5-plex.

fix (someone's) flint *Slang* get even with; dispose of; take care of; spoil (someone's) chances.
1836 *Novascotian* (Halifax) 27 Jan. 25/2: Oh no, if I didn't fix his flint for him in fair play, it's a pity. **1856** BALLANTYNE *Young Fur-Traders* 12: "Yes, I'll fix both their flints to-morrow...." By "fixing their flints" Mr. Kennedy meant to express the fact that he intended to place his children in an entirely new sphere of action, and with a view to this he ordered out his horse and cariole on the following morning. **1942** RADDALL *His Majesty's Yankees* 242: "This day's the thirteenth o' November. Thank God it ain't a Friday or we'd ha' fixed our flint for keeps...."

flacket ['flækət] *n.* [related to *flake* and Norwegian *flak* disk] *Nfld* See **faggot**.
1818 CHAPPELL *Voy.of Rosamond* 129: By degrees, the size of these *flackets* is increased, until . . . they assume the form of large circular stacks; and in this state the *cod* are left for a few days, so the fishermen say, "to sweat." **1840** MURRAY *Brit.Amer.* II 127: At night they are piled above each other, with the backs uppermost, in heaps called fagots or flackets, which often accumulate until they resemble haystacks.

flag day *Northwest, Obs.* one of certain specified days on which a river boat made stops for freight and passengers at points not on the regular schedule.
1916 WOOD *Tourist's N.W.* 411: Leaving the head of the lake about two in the afternoon, the journey is ended at eight, or a little later on "flag days."

flag football a game based on rugby-football but in which tackling is outlawed, the ball-carrier being stopped in his advance when a handkerchief is snatched from his back pocket.
1963 *Calgary Herald* 28 Oct. 32/1: Junior high school flag football matches are coming to a close . . .

flagpole *n.* a ceremonial pole used by the Indians of the eastern woodlands on which to suspend the skulls of bears and other animals they have killed to prevent their being desecrated by dogs or by careless handling.
1925 *Beaver* Sep. 175: This pole will be from twelve to fifteen feet in height, with the bark cut off and trimmed with ribbon and a kind of weather vane at the top. This is called the flag-pole (*mistik-ko-khan*). This pole is used for hanging bear skull bones, beaver head bones . . . killed by the hunter . . . to preserve the luck of the hunter.

flake *n.* *Atlantic Provinces* See 1883 quote.
See also **cod-flake, drying stage, fish-flake, fishing stage** (def. 2), and **stage** (def. 2).
1620 WHITBOURNE *Discovrse* 63: There are also some, who arriuing first in Harbor, take away other mens Salt that they had left there the yeere before . . . and some teare downe Flakes, whereon men yeerely dry their fish, to their great hurt and hinderance of many other that come after them. **1771** (1792) CARTWRIGHT *Journal* I 133: We got one raft on shore there, and I fixed on the place for the stage, flakes, and the shoreman's house. **1883** HATTON & HARVEY *Newfoundland* 291: The flake consists of a horizontal framework of small poles, covered with spruce-boughs, and supported by upright poles, the air having free access beneath. Here the cod are spread to bleach in the sun and air. . . . **1963** *Globe and Mail* (Toronto) 25 July 19/8: In L'Anse-A-Beaufils [Quebec] you will still see the cod drying on the flakes, instead of being fast-frozen and packed in fancy plastic bags.

flambeau [flæm'bo] *n.* [< Cdn F < F "torch"] a torch made of birchbark or resinous wood used as a jacklight (def. 1) in spearing fish at night.
1784–1812 (1916) THOMPSON *Narrative* 117: The Fir is resinous and makes good flambeaux's for spearing fish at night. **1929** MOBERLY *When Fur Was King* 86: The run commenced about dusk and finished round midnight, when, the fish growing scarce, we left off spearing. We used birchbark flambeaux for torches, and seldom secured less than a thousand each calm night during the whole spawning period.

flank company *Hist.* one of a number of militia companies raised in Upper Canada in 1811, who saw much service in the War of 1812. See also **flanker¹** (def. 1).
1963 MORTON *Kingdom of Canada* 204: In Upper Canada the volunteers were embodied, under an Act procured by Brock in 1811, as the famous "flank companies" which fought in the line with the British regulars and from which the battalion of Incorporated Militia was drawn.

flanker¹ *n.* *Hist.* **1** a soldier in a flank company, *q.v.*
1826 *Colonial Advocate* (York & Queenston, U.C.) 25 May 2/3: The English have drawn in Toronto. Trafalgar and Nelson also;—Chingacousy all sorts have got into;—the flankers in Nassagua. **1833** *Liberal* (St. Thomas, U.C.) 4 July 3/2: Many a U.E.'s grant for 200 acres was sold for a horse—and the Flanker's 100 acre right for 20 dollars.

2 in a palisade fort, a corner building serving as a bastion and as a storehouse and bunkhouse.
1695–6 (1954) *Moose Ft Jnls* 176: You . . . to whom the Charge of Each Watch is given are to take it Successively one from the Other, and are to watch four Hours, keeping a Man on the No. East flanker, One on the Southwest, one Walking in the Yard and another at the gate not Suffering any to leave Their Post before such time they are relieved. **1779** (1934) TURNOR *Journal* 256: The Flanker in which the Men resides and was in a decaid rotten state I found rebuilding upon a larger scale. **1874** (1910) HAYDON *Riders of Plains* 36: [This post was] of the stockyard type, almost square, and with two bastions, or "flankers" as they were generally called on the frontier.

flanker² *n.* [< obs. *flanker*, v., glow, sparkle] *Nfld* a bright spark from a chimney or fire.
1835 WIX *Journal* 59: I had discovered this cabin by the "flankers," or bright sparks, which flew up his chimney in the clear starlit sky, from his brisk birch fire. **1955** ENGLISH *Newfoundland* 30: flankers [are] sparks from a chimney[.]

flasher *n.* a bright piece of metal used to attract fish to a lure or bait.
1955 DAWSON *Ahoy There!* 70: This was a fishing line almost as thick as a small clothes line and about one hundred fathoms long, equipped with two bent oblongs of nickel-plated metal, known as "flashers." **1961** *Sun* (Vancouver) 17 Aug. 23/3: Comfortably leading all other combinations as a Sun Derby prize-getter is the old herring dodger (flasher) and herring strip (or jack herring).

flat† *n.* **1** (*often plural*) See **bottom** and **mud-flat**.
1765–75 (1933) POND *Narrative* 53: Earley in the Morning the wind took the Canew up in the Air—Leat hir fall on the frozen flat and Broke hir in Pecis. **1832** (1953) RADCLIFF *Letters* 89: A creek or small river winding nearly through its entire length, between rich *flats*, as they are here called. . . . **1908** MAIR *Mackenzie Basin* 32: A long hill leads down to the flat, and from its brow we had a striking view of the . . . noble river. . . . **1963** *Beaver* Autumn 50/2: . . . their wanderings took them over the old trails . . . to the flats above the Thompson River. . . .

2 *Maritimes* a small flat-bottomed boat used for fishing near shore.
1954 BRUCE *Channel Shore* 35: . . . Lon rowed the flat ashore and he and Anse brailed up the canvas. *Ibid.* 60: . . . his eyes would be alert for . . . a white pine to watch and hoard until it was big enough to be sawed and planed into planking for a lap-seam flat.

flat-boat *n.* *Hist.* a boat having a flat bottom and pointed bow and stern, used for inland freight traffic. Cp. **bateau** (def. 3) and **York boat**.
1859 (1932) *Beaver* June 14: A flat boat was built and they all embarked on it to drift down the river, as they had no crew. **1870** *Cdn Illust.News* 23 Apr. 391/2: The construction of flat boats for river navigation and other preparations for the North-West expedition are actively going forward. **1936** *Natural Hist.* Nov. 290: Leaving the end of steel in their scows and flat-boats they floated down the Athabasca, the Slave and the Mackenzie rivers, carrying to the native the "blessings" of civilization. . . . **1963** STANLEY *Louis Riel* 196: In only five years [from 1858] the S.S. Selkirk would arrive with

a flatboat bearing the "Countess of Dufferin," the first locomotive to enter the Canadian North-West.

flat boom *Lumbering* a simple boom (def. 3b) or raft in which one layer of floating logs is held by chained boomsticks (def. 2) and spaced cross-logs. See also **flat raft**.
1930 *B.C. Lumberman* May 17/1: Flat boom towing over the rough waters of the open Pacific is impossible. **1945** *Intermediate Booming Grounds B.C.* 3: There are various ways of protecting flat booms [from storms] in intermediate booming grounds. **1965** *Islander* 6 June 16/1: Ninety years ago, and during 50 following years, flat booms very loosely held by chains and with covering lighter logs, were constantly broken and logs scattered far and wide, causing great losses.

flat raft See **flat boom**.
1965 *Islander* 6 June 16/1: A fourth raft, called "the Bag," consisted merely of a mass of logs collected without cross-logs as in the old type flat raft. It was used only in sheltered areas.

flat rapid See **riffle** (def. 1c).
1849 ALEXANDER *L'Acadie* II 162: What I took for a ford at a distance was a "flat rapid" with a considerable depth of water running over a smooth bed of rock.

flatroofer *n. Maritimes* See quotes.
1955 WALLACE *Roving Fishermen* 28: "In wintertime we sends 'em down and we sails as a flatroofer—nawthin' but the four lowers—winter rig we calls it." *Ibid.* 50: The working rig of a fishing schooner of the period was the "four lowers"—mainsail, foresail, jumbo (or fore-stag sail) and jib.... In winter months, the vessels sent down their topmasts and stored their light sails ashore and went to sea as "Flat-roofers."

flat sled 1 a runnerless, tobogganlike sled usually drawn by dogs.
1831 (1963) DAVIES *Northern Quebec* 132: ... John Hay and Mr. Taylor making flat sleds etc. **1897** TYRRELL *Sub-Arctics* 243: The dog-sleds were not the same as those we had used in traversing the hard driven snow of the plains, but were what are known as "flat sleds" or large toboggans, they being better suited to woodland travel. **1922** *Beaver* July 10/2: Everything an Indian requires ... is made with this knife—canoes, flatsleds, snowshoes....

2 a similar, somewhat larger sled, drawn by one or two horses.
1880 *Edmonton Bull.* 27 Dec. 1/2: On Christmas Eve Mr. Brunette's horse ran away with the flat sled scattering the contents over the whole length of Ross' new grade. **1929** MOBERLY *When Fur Was King* 43: Sometimes I was off to the plains with horses and flat sleds for buffalo meat, sometimes shooting prairie chickens.... **1958** *Edmonton Jnl* 18 July 19/7: The gold seekers set out with horse-drawn flat sleds eventually.

flat-sleigh *n.* See **flat sled** (def. 2).
1956 KEMP *Northern Trader* 75: We decided ... we should take two strings of dogs, and a pony hitched to a flat-sleigh.

flaw lead See quote. Cp. **shore lead**.
1958 *Manice* 7: Flaw Lead—The Shore Lead just outside the Landfast Ice.

flesh fly *Obs.* See **bulldog fly**.
1743 (1949) ISHAM *Observations* 131: Flesh flies are still more troublesome and offencive, than those aforemention'd, which the Natives styl's (au'mo,) they taking a peice wherever the Bite, the Hotter the weather the plentier they are.

flipper dinner or **supper** *Nfld* a traditional meal of seal flippers.
1933 GREENE *Wooden Walls* 49: Endless are the stories of the Wooden Walls, of laughter ... of tragedy and of loss ... once heard in the days gone by at "F'ipper suppers," on board the early arrivals.... **1958** *Evening Telegram* (St John's) 5 May 13/1: The April 29 meeting of the Bell Island Lions Club was highlighted by a delicious flipper dinner....

flivver† ['flɪvɚ] *n.* [origin unknown] *Slang* **1** a cheap light car, especially a Ford of early make.
1910 FRASER *Red Meekins* 22: "... You stick to me an' you'll be travellin' 'round the country in a flivver." **1939** MONTAGUE *Eskimos* 52: [We were] trundling round the country in a flivver with Mr. Fiddler at the wheel. **1958** *Globe and Mail* (Toronto) 21 June 16/1: "The term flivver, for example, used in this book to describe any ancient motor car, was never used to describe a car other than a Model T Ford."

2 *Obs.* (attributive uses) cheaply made; small; insignificant; of little account.
1917 *Grit* (Toronto) 11 Dec. 6/6: [He is] the greatest little flivver statesman in captivity. **1936** *Beaver* Mar. 9/1: Numerous successful experiments are being conducted with so-called "flea" or "flivver" types [of aeroplanes].

float *n.* **1** *Lumbering* a length of buoyant wood forming part of the framework of a crib (def. 2) used in rafting oak and other timber. See picture at **raft** (def. 2).
1854 KEEFER *Ottawa* 66: [Cribs] are formed by placing two round logs, called "floats," about twenty-four feet apart, and bringing the squared timber between them; across the whole, four or five rather large sized poles called "traverses" are laid and pinned at each end to the floats. **1896** GOURLAY *Hist. Ottawa* 137: The floats on the sides were generally round sticks bored to take two and a half inch pins to secure the cross pieces (traverses).... **1945** CALVIN *Saga* 65: The materials for the wooden framework of the rafts, as they were built forty years ago, were very simple. They were: "floats," 42' long, 7" diameter at the top and flatted to 7" thickness at the butt; traverses, 32' long, 3" or 4" at the top, not flatted; "pickets," or pins, about $1\frac{1}{2}$" diameter.

2 *Mining* fragments of rock, especially mineral-bearing rock, separated from the original bedrock.
1905 (1963) *North* May-June 4/1: Iron ore occurs merely as float in the wash of both the Bonnet Plume and Snake Rivers. **1936** MOWERY *Paradise Trail* 29: Though green at the business of hawking float, he walked over to the tom rocker, a shallow cradle-like contraption with galvanized lining and two handles, and studied it. **1966** *North* May-June 37/1: Attention was then transferred to ... an area of know[n] float, some ten miles north west of the Vangords [lead-zinc] deposit.

3 See **floathouse**.
1953 SWANSON *Haywire Hooker* 26: In the hot afternoon he slipped down to the float, / Cooked a scheme up in secret, he'd be round with a boat....

4 *Esp. North* a floatplane.
1965 *Maclean's* 24 July 2/3: An Ontario flying service wanted a pilot with float (seaplane) experience.

floater *n.* **1** *North* See **dan** (def. 1).
[**1578** BEST *Trve Discovrse* III 64: When they shoote at a greate fishe with any of theyr Dartes, they vse to tye a bladder thereunto, whereby they may the better finde them agayne, and the fishe not able to carrie it so easily away, for that the bladder dothe boy the darte, will at length be weerie, and dye therewith.]
1942 TWOMEY & HERRICK *Needle to North* 318: Flashing out with her slim, sharp tusks, she ripped the precious floater to bits.

2 *Nfld* **a.** a fisherman who establishes no shore base but remains at sea following the fish from place to place. Cp. **liveyere** (def. 1) and **stationer**.
1909 BROWNE *Where the Fishers Go* 67: The "Floaters" leave the Newfoundland ports about the 1st of June, and fish in the Straits of Belle Isle, from Mecatina Islands to Greenly. **1924** ENGLAND *Vikings of the Ice* 316/1: Floaters. Labrador codders who move during the summer. **1942** GOUGH *New World Horizons* 182: The "floaters," who come here to fish for cod in the summer are five times as numerous [as the liveyeres]. **1965** JENNESS *Eskimo Admin.* III 19: . . . Grenfell's Mission was ministering to both the "floaters" and the shore fishermen.

b. a person who lives at home and travels some distance each week to work.
1930 SMALLWOOD *Newfoundland* 148: These, coming from their homes to work in and about the mines, and returning each week end, are called "floaters."

floaterman *n.* *Nfld* See **floater** (def. 2a).
1954 *Fishermen's Advocate* 29 Jan. 2/1: A floaterman for some years, he soon got around to Labrador and the dogs.

floathouse *n.* *Pacific Coast* a dwelling built on floats at the shore, and usually so built that it can be towed from one mooring to another. See also **float** (def. 3) and **scow-house**.
1938 CASH *I Like B.C.* 165: Before we left Cowichan Lake though, we visited people who lived on a floathouse . . . fifty feet long, had a living-room twenty feet square, five bedrooms, bathroom, kitchen, water supply. . . . **1958** WATTERS *B.C.Cent.Anthol.* 214: The wrenching of its tides loosens the nails in their float-houses and their children wear lifebelts all day as insurance against its uncertain temper. **1965** *Islander* 18 Apr. 14/1: The floathouse was of great advantage when the work took him away from base since it was necessary only to be towed by the government tug to the area under study. . . .

floating bog or **muskeg** a layer of muskeg (def. 3) floating on the surface of the water near the shores of a river or lake.
1946 *Beaver* Sep. 42/2: They got well into some bushes while I, acting as guide, went gingerly out on the floating bog at the lake inlet to look. . . . **1961** *Edmonton Jnl* 1 Aug. 1/1: Floating muskeg surrounded the lake, so we moved onto higher ground and built a corduroy road back down to the lake. **1963** SYMONS *Many Trails* 187: . . . the approach to the lake itself . . . was simply a floating bog, so soft that a tussock stepped upon sank a foot or more. . . .

floating mess hall *Lumbering* a large raft or barge fitted out as a place for loggers to eat in.
1957 *Bush News* (St.Catharines, Ont.) June 1/1: Three wanegans, a floating mess hall and cook shack, and six drive camps are maintained to keep the wood moving.

floating surrogate *Nfld, Hist.* a judge who made

an annual visit to hold court at the fisheries, often the captain of a man-of-war. See also **surrogate**.
1819 ANSPACH *Hist.Nfld* 143: These Judges were afterwards called Foating Surrogates. **1964** *Nfld Qtly* Summer 35/1: In 1792, "the Supreme Court of Judicature of the Island of Newfoundland" (London 1793-Chief-Justice Reeves) . . . were established in Newfoundland. They were called "Floating Surrogates," because perhaps they spent most of their time aboard of vessels covering legal business around the Island.

floating swamp a detached mass of swamp vegetation floating on the surface of the water.
1829 MACTAGGART *Three Years* II 82: We are led to think that the enormous quantities of drift wood, floating swamps . . . soils of all kinds, &c. hurried into Lake Ontario annually, would conduce towards the formation of islands and shoals in the same. . . .

floatwood *n.* driftwood.
1908 MAIR *Mackenzie Basin* 50: The stream is almost choked at its discharge by a conglomeration of slimy roots, weeds and floatwood. . . .

flood *n.* *Esp.Que.* the annual spring break-up, especially the ice shove (def. 2), on the rivers.
1894 BLOUET *John Bull & Co.* 10: The people speak of this annual breakup of winter as "the flood". . . . **1931** LEBOURDAIS *Northward* 153: In some instances it is due to river "flood ice," in others, to sea ice, snow drifts, or frozen tundra lagoons. . . . **1965** COLLARD *Call Back Yesterdays* 181: The flood of April, 1885 was the greatest in twelve years.

flood *v.* build up a rink surface by applying water and allowing it to freeze.
1872 (1891) DUFFERIN *Journal* 14th Dec.: We are working at our outdoor rink, and find it difficult to manage. An Englishman exclaims, "Flood it!" but this is just the difficulty as the water freezes as it touches the ice. . . . **1955** WATSON *Curling to Win* 82: The ice surface [of a curling "sheet"], as a result of more frost, milder weather or another flooding, will have changed, even though slightly. . . .

floor hockey an indoor team-sport derived from hockey, in which the players, on foot, use a long stick to carry and pass a rope or felt ring resembling a quoit with a view to directing it into a goal.
1963 *Calgary Herald* 12 Oct. 20/4: Innisfail Eagles hockey coach . . . held a floor hockey session . . . to get players "into shape." **1964** *Marker* (R.M.C., Kingston, Ont.) 10 Apr. 10/1: The league standings are practically immaterial . . . in the finer arts of floor hockey.

floor-price *n.* a minimum price set on a commodity by the government to protect the producer from losses due to a drastic decline in market prices.
1953 LEBOURDAIS *Nation of the North* 173: With the prospect of a return to a free market in the post-war years, the farmers began agitating for a floor-price to protect them against a drastic decline. **1957** *Mine-Mill Herald* Oct. 9/5: I asked the Prime Minister if he would be prepared to carry out his promise to consider the question of stock piling base metals and maintaining a floor price on those metals, that is to say, lead, zinc, copper and so on, metals which have depreciated in price. . . .

flossy *adj. Informal* showy; overembellished.
1908 HAVERSON *Sour Sonnets* 32: You bet if he would fall in love wid me / An' tell it to me in that flossy way, / I'd hold me arms an' ast him in to stay . . .
1910 SERVICE *Trail of '98* 355: ". . . Come on boys! Here you are for the nice, glossy floor and the nice, flossy girls. Here you are!" **1958** *Fisherman* 15 Aug. 2/3: The fact [was] not mentioned in the flossy propaganda issued by the CMA. . . .

flour gold† See **fine gold**.
1900 OSBORN *Greater Canada* 55: As often happened in the North-West, those who came to find "flour gold" were content to remain and raise flour. **1963** *Placer-Mining B.C.* 18/1: Subsequently, fine and flour gold has been found on many bars and low benches of the Finlay, Parsnip, and Peace Rivers.

fluff out *Slang, Obs.* leave; depart.
1922 FOOTNER *Huntress* 186: Wafted. Vamosed. Fluffed out. Beat it for the outside.

flunkey *n.* **1** *Lumbering* See **cookee**. Also spelled *flunky*.
1908 GRAINGER *Woodsmen of the West* 91: ". . . I know the bosses say that it costs them more than five a week to feed a man, taking into account the wages of the cook and flunky. . . ." **1956** GOWLAND *Sikanaska Trail* 177: "You're a flunkey," he said. "Report to the cook." **1959** *Press* Aug. 13: A *flunky* (a "stooge" or subservient person) was a sideman in the days of liveried servants and the word still occasionally appears in occupational lists as equivalent to "cookee" or "choreboy."
2 *Maritimes* an apprentice fisherman assigned the menial tasks.
1923 MACMECHAN *Sagas of Sea* 146: He had learned the fisherman's strenuous trade, as "flunkey," "trouter," "header," and then . . . he was considered fit to take the bow oar of a dory.
3 *West* See quote.
1954 *Journal of the Cdn Linguistic Assn* Oct. 21: . . . the general farm worker is known as a *hired man*, a *flunkey*, a *chore-boy*, or just a *labourer*.

flunkey (around) *v.* do odd jobs. See **flunkey,** *n.*
1908 GRAINGER *Woodsmen* 195: ". . . Just cook and clean up the bunk-house, and saw wood for the stoves and flunkey around to fill in time." **1949** *Cominco Mag.* Jan. 8/3: The steamshovel pilot never tried to fly again. After many weeks he hobbled back to the hotel on crutches and made a dicker to flunkey around for his board until he got strong.

flunkeying *n.* the work done by a cook's helper or choreboy in a lumber camp.
1952 *Beaver* Sep. 14/1: Everybody was too tired after nine hours of falling, bucking, loading, track-laying, cold-decking, scaling, saw-filing, flunkeying, or whatever the job was. . . .

fly *n.* a sheet of canvas or hide erected for protection against the weather.
1910 LONDON *Burning Daylight* 23: ". . . No bring um tent. Mebbe bring um fly? um little fly?" / "No fly," Daylight answered decisively. **1947** *Beaver* Dec. 20/2: . . . we cut some poles and with our toboggan wrappers made a fly. **1960** MCNAMEE *Florencia Bay* 129: Next to them a frame of saplings supported a canvas fly.

fly-beer *n. Maritimes* a kind of beer brewed from potatoes and hop yeast mixed with molasses or sugar and water.
1959 MILLS *Songs of the Maritimes* 5/1: There was the Widow Whinney, she sold ale and cockaninny, / She sold whiskey, gin and fly-beer. . . .

fly camp a temporary camp away from the main camp, so called because flies, *q.v.*, were carried as the only shelter.
1964 *Imperial Oil Rev.* Dec. 5/2: Outside on the river bank . . . Hughes moved one helicopter . . . off to the nearest fly camp, 35 miles southwest. **1965** *Beaver* Autumn 56/2: I started back to the fly camp with one plug of chewing tobacco. . . .

fly-dope† *n.* any insect repellant.
1903 WHITE *Forest* 34: A few minor items, of practically no weight, suggest themselves—toilet requisites, fly-dope, needle and thread. . . . **1930** SMALLWOOD *New Newfoundland* 73: . . . the flask or bottle . . . full of what is usually termed "fly dope" . . . is sufficient to ward off the flies. **1966** *Globe and Mail* (Toronto) 30 July 23/7: The fly dope simply inflamed the insects to attack still more fiercely.

fly-in *adj.* of or associated with sportsmen who fly or are flown in to remote hunting and fishing areas.
1963 *Globe and Mail* (Toronto) 13 Mar. 6/4: It costs a lot to operate a fly-in camp with a guide to every two hunters and you can expect to pay accordingly. *Ibid.* 18 May 31/1: After the talk in this corner last Saturday about a fly-in secret lake . . . Dr. C.W.A. Coop . . . plunked down photo proof of the luck in another secret lake. **1965** *Cdn Geog. Jnl* Sep. 89/1: . . . fly-in "sportsmen," as even the most rapacious fish-hogs are called, make their easy way into hitherto unspoiled areas.

flying boxcar *Slang* a freight plane, especially the C119 used by the R.C.A.F.
1932 *Beaver* Mar. 393: The new Junkers freight plane "JU-52," "flying boxcar," belonging to the Canadian Airways Limited, aroused a great deal of interest. . . . **1942** TWOMEY & HERRICK *Needle to the North* 30: The flying "box car" rested and the mechanic fastened the door. **1958** *Arctic Spotter* Jan. 4: Santa Claus headed north . . . driving a sleigh, in the shape of a C-119 Flying Boxcar, from 435 (Transport) Squadron at Namao, Alberta.

flying level See 1829 quote.
1829 MACTAGGART *Three Years* I 49: . . . we were enabled to take, what is called in surveying a flying level, which is a rough guess to a foot, more or less, of the rise or fall of the country above any fixed data. *Ibid.* II 94: [We took] what is termed *flying* levels through the dark woods. . . . **1903** CARR-HARRIS *White Chief* 235: We were taking a flying-level between Rafting Bay and the Rideau—a distance of about four miles.

flying post *Fur Trade, Hist.* a temporary post for trading with hunters at the hunting grounds, the location moving with the scene of hunting operations. Cp. **outpost** (def. 1).
1820 (1939) ROBERTSON *Correspondence* 113: I hope Mr. Williams will not be deterred from following up the plan I suggested of a flying post about Lac Winipec either on land or water. **1867** (1913) COWIE *Adventurers* 191: Fort Ellice had a regular winter outpost at Riding Montain, besides flying posts wherever the buffalo were numerous, at such places as Turtle and Moose Mountain. **1921** HEMING *Drama*

of Forests 297: Meanwhile, canoes laden with furs and in charge of Hudson's Bay traders or clerks from outlying "Flying Posts" had arrived.

269

flying weevil
foothill country

flying weevil *Obs.* See **Hessian fly.**
1788 (1789) *Nova Scotia Mag.* I 16/1: The Hessian Fly, or, as is more generally called, the Flying Weevil, was first observed in the Southern Provinces about 50 years ago. . . .

flying wing *Cdn Football* a player whose position is variable behind the line of scrimmage.
1895 (1964) *Kingston Whig-Standard* (Ont.) 27 Oct. 9/3: . . . the wings which are seven in number correspond to the American guards, tackles and ends and the extra man is called a flying wing. **1958** *Time* (Cdn ed.) 15 Sep. 15/1: Topflight U.S. players quickly adapt to the roomier field (110 yds. between goal lines), a fifth man (called a flying wing) in the backfield, the point-scoring (one point) "rouge." **1964** *Kingston Whig-Standard* (Ont.) 27 Oct. 9/3: Again in the same article Mr. Rodden says that "in 1907 Rev. Father Stanton of the University of Ottawa . . . introduced the flying wing."

fly-line *n.* a point or line above which flies do not commonly fly.
1947 *Beaver* June 26/1: If you are a horseman, the southern reaches will claim you . . . above timberline, above the fly-line. **1963** MCTAVISH *Behind the Palisades* 39: Another method [of keeping flies off meat] was to tie game or meat to a tall pole and elevate it beyond the fly line, where the sun and air were cooler than nearer the ground.

fog-eater *n.* a phenomenon resembling a rainbow, occurring in a fog about to dissipate. See also **fog scoffer.**
1935 *Cdn Geog.Jnl* Apr. 167/2: We could now see almost a hundred yards about us; above the fog the sun was shining from a cloudless sky, forming the sun-bow on the fog called a "fog-eater." **1958** KELSEY *B.C.Rides a Star* 166: Whenever you see a fog-eater, the fog is going to lift. **1963** *North* Mar.-Apr. 11/1: With the calms come fog bows—the "fog eaters" of the Eskimo. This peculiar phenomenon resembles a rainbow in the fog, mainly made up of thick, grey fog. On some days, this arch will revolve completely around an observer as the sun turns in the sky.

fog mull *Maritimes* a long, continuous fog during mild weather.
1965 RICHARDSON *Living Island* 15: A visitor from Florida (who arrived during one of our "fog mulls" and never once in her week's stay saw beyond the blurred shoreline) was also disturbed by wild night cries.

fog scoffer *Obs.* See **fog-eater.**
1748 ELLIS *Hudson's Bay* 288: Our Sailors fancy, that these drive away the Fogs, and have therefore bestowed on them the Name of Fog Scoffers; whereas in reality that are the last remnants of the Fog, that by a Reverberation of the Sun Beams, produce these Appearances.

folder *n. Obs.* an item of trading goods, seemingly a small envelope used for carrying tobacco, vermilion, etc.
1800 (1897) COUES *New Light* I 97: I . . . then gave out to the Indians . . . an assortment of small articles gratis, such as one scalper, two folders, and four flints apiece. **1826** (1961) OGDEN *Journals* 154: ". . . we gave our new Guide a folder and two inches of Tobacco. . . ." **1829** *Fort Langley Jnl* 12 Aug.: ½ doz. Folders.

folle avoine *Cdn French* See **wild rice.**
1800 (1897) COUES *New Light* I 143: A few miles above . . . is Riviere a la Folle Avoine (Wild Rice River), navigable for small Indian canoes. **1852** RICHARDSON *Arctic Exped.* 411: In 1847 multitudes of caterpillars . . . destroyed the folle avoine on Rainy Lake, but left untouched some wheat that was just coming into ear. **1890** MASSON *Les Bourgeois* II 156: Folle avoine was often substituted for Indian corn. **1963** GUILLET *Pioneer Farmer* I 7: Among the lakes noted for wild rice was Rice Lake, known in the French period as Folle Avoine (wild oats), the two plants being quite similar.

following pole *Obs.* a long, strong pole used for raising the heavy bents, or crossbeams, in building a house or barn.
1832 (1953) RADCLIFF *Letters* 46: A *Bee,* which means an assemblage of the neighbours, is then called; and a person well skilled in the business, and termed a *Boss,* takes active leadership of the active party, who, with the mere mechanical aid of a *following,* or *raising,* pole, gradually elevates the mighty bents, until the tenants (connected with each other by tie beams,) drop into their mortices in the sill, to which, as well as to each other, they are immediately afterwards secured by pins, and in a few hours the skeleton of the house, with its rafters, &c. is ready for shingles and clap boards.

fool hen the spruce partridge, *q.v.,* and certain related species of grouse. See also **Franklin's grouse** and **tree-grouse.** Cp. **galoot.**
[**1760** PICHON *Cape Breton* 35: They fare best towards Gabarus, where there is plenty of game, and where the woodcocks are so extremely tame, that you may knock them down with stones.] **1872** (1873) GRANT *Ocean to Ocean* 281: The spruce partridge or fool hen, that is oftener knocked over with a stick than shot. **1921** MARSHALL *Snowshoe Trail* 48: ". . . They are fool hens—Franklin's grouse—and that means that they'll set all day and let you pepper at 'em. . . ." **1956** LEECHMAN *Native Tribes of Canada* 240: The fool hen, a kind of grouse, was so called because it would sit quite still while a hunter came up close with a long thin stick on the end of which was a noose of fine sinew. This noose he would slip gently over the sitting fool hen's neck and pull the bird down. **1965** *Islander* 14 Feb. 13/3: It wasn't the least bit like grabbing a fluttering fool hen.

football *n.* See **rugby-football** and note.
1896 ROBERTS *Camp-Fire* 263: "But what I'm thinking about is his refusal to play foot-ball last fall. He's quick, and sharp, and tough; just the man the team wanted for quarter back. . . ." **1958** *Edmonton Jnl* 24 June I 11/4: Calgary Stampeders of the Western Interprovincial Football Union Monday night announced the signing to [sic] two imports. . . .

foot burner See **foot warmer.**
1954 *Ghost Pine* 154: Having erected the shack, the next thing was to get some breaking done. The usual outfit was the walking plow or "foot burner," drawn by four horses or four oxen or two of each.

foothill country the area of rolling grassland on the east side of the Rockies, especially that in southwest Alberta. See also **foothills.**
1913 KELLY *Range Men* 53: There is no doubt that the southern foothill country . . . is the finest pasture . . . in all North America. **1923** (1926) DICKIE *Cdn West* 300:

... the train approached the up-grades of the foothill country.

foothills *n.pl.* the rounded, rolling hills, largely grassland, lying between the prairies and the Rocky Mountains proper. See also **high country**[2].
1853 REID *Young Voyageurs* 102: ... the great prairies stretch westward, even to the "foot-hills" (piedmont) of the Rocky Mountains. **1916** BRIDLE *Sons of Canada* 171: The outward trail over the prairie petering off into the foot-hills and the Rockies is to him not a mere waggon road. ... **1966** *Globe and Mail* (Toronto) 15 Jan. 9/3: The scheme would trap water in the Rocky Mountains and foothills of western Alberta and distribute them [sic] easterward to the Saskatchewan border.

foot warmer *West, Slang* a walking plough. See also **foot burner**.
1954 *Ghost Pine* 61: Afterwards we broke 20 acres of gumbo with the John Deere "foot warmer."

Force, the See **Royal Canadian Mounted Police**.
1910 SERVICE *Trail of '98* 182: "... I joined the Force in Regina. It's altogether different 'outside,' patrol work, a free life on the open prairie." **1958** (1960) NELSON *Northern Lights* 503: He was a young man with pink cheeks, newly in the Force, and was not drinking but merely keeping warm and passing the time until the local came by to take him to his destination.

forecheck *v. Hockey* check an opponent in his own defensive zone, to prevent the opposing team from organizing an attack.
1963 O'BRIEN *Hockey* 81: One night ... the ... coach approached me ... to ask if it were usual in Canada to do as the Whitby team was doing in sending two players in to forecheck a puck-carrier in the latter's zone? **1964** *Maclean's* 21 Mar. 14/2: But when the Leafs are going well, there's a doggedness about their play; they forecheck ferociously; they knock down a lot of people at the blue line, and they grab and hold a lot more people in front of the goalmouth.

forechecking *n.* the practice or skill of one who forechecks, *q.v.*
1962 *National Hockey Annual* 25/3: Sometimes I get more tired just fore-checking for a minute or so because it's like stops and starts, than I do when I'm out there for four minutes. **1966** *Kingston Whig-Standard* (Ont.) 16 Apr. 10/3: ... thanks to the forechecking of Cherry ... the Athletics managed only three shots on Ace's goalie Tom Mercer during the penalty.

foregoer *n.* **1** See **leader** (def. 2).
1873 (1926) DICKIE *Cdn West* 219: It is the business of the "foregoer" to keep the track however faint it may be on the lake or river. **1921** HEMING *Drama of Forests* 174: With a final rush the gaunt, travel-worn dogs galloped through the driving snow, and, eager for the shelter of the trading room, bolted pell-mell through the gathering in the doorway, upsetting several spectators before the driver could halt the runaways by falling headlong upon the foregoer's back and flattening him to the floor. **1963** MCTAVISH *Behind the Palisades* 202: Of the remaining three [dogs] ... Carlo, the foregoer and Wolf, the steerer, showed symptoms of the disease.

2 See **forerunner**.
1934 GODSELL *Arctic Trader* 39: Already the Indian

foregoer had slid his moccasined feet into his snowshoe thongs and was headed for the gateway. ... **1955** SHIPLEY *Anna and the Indians* 58: [He was] a fore-goer, a hardy runner who trotted ahead of the dog-teams to break trail after a snowfall or in unmarked country.

forehead strap See **tumpline** and picture.
*a*1820 (1838) HEAD *Forest Scenes* 302: She carried this ... by means of a forehead strap. ... **1913** WILLIAMS *Wilderness Trail* 158: Then, he took the light pack from the little sledge, fastened the forehead straps around it, and tucked Jean in its place.

fore-lock *n.* See **scalp-lock** (def. 2).
1922 STRINGER *Prairie Child* 267: They took his fore-lock and his teepee and his last string of wampum. And the old snob, of course, would never forgive them.

foreman *n. Hist.* See **bowsman**.
1774 (1934) HEARNE *Journal* 122: The Pataroon or Steersman of each Cannoe has 50£ pr annom, the foresman £40 and the rest of the Crew 20 and 25£ according to their goodness. **1821** (1900) GARRY *Diary* 144: Our Foreman placed his Arms on the Bows, but the Water rushed over them. **1894** BEGG *Hist.of B.C.* 64: The foreman caught some overhanging branches, but was jerked out of the boat in an instant and swung on shore. **1931** NUTE *Voyageur* 26: [There was] a still larger paddle, which the bowsman or foreman (*avant de canot, devant,* or *ducent*) employed when running rapids or leaping small falls.

forerunner *n.* a man on snowshoes who runs ahead of a dog team making a passable track in new or deep snow. See also **foregoer** (def. 2), **run**, *v.* (def. 5), **runner**[1] (def. 3), **track-beater, track-breaker, tracker** (def. 2), and **trail-breaker** (def. 1).
[**1748** ELLIS *Hudson's Bay* 163: In long Journies, through deep Snows, the Men generally go before them to beat a Path with the Snow Shoes; the Dogs soon grow accustomed to whatever thay are taught, and being docil and tractable are very useful.] **1936** STEELE *Policing the Arctic* 30: When the trail was bad and snow deep, they marched on snow-shoes, sometimes with a "forerunner" to break trail. Generally they ran or walked, occasionally they rode on the sleds. **1954** PATTERSON *Dangerous River* 268: The two policemen were travelling with two dog teams and two Indian fore-runners, making patrol up the Liard to the British Columbia boundary.

Forest City See 1952 quote.
1858 (1955) CRAIG *Early Travellers* 231: Thus we have in this "Forest City," as it is sometimes called ... and the use of which, coupled with the word "London," very often leads to serious mistakes in the post-office. ... **1952** PUTNAM *Cdn Regions* 285/1: London [Ont.] "The Forest City," is situated at the forks of the Thames River, 115 miles southwest of Toronto.

forest depot *Nfld* a lumber camp. Cp. **depot** (def. 3).
1957 *Cdn Geog.Jnl* Oct. 135/1: Many of the forest depots of Bowaters, such as Main Brook and Baie Verte on the north-east coast, are modern communities.

forest district or **division** one of a number of large areas in the northern forest set apart for such purposes as fire control and game conservation.
1958 *Edmonton Jnl* 31 July 1/1: ... aircraft are still being used to transport crews and supplies in the Lac la Biche and Slave Lake forest divisions. **1964** *Calgary*

Herald 15 May 47/8: Six fires are in the Whitecourt
forest area . . . and one in the Lac La Biche forest district.

271

**forester
fort trapper**

forester *n*. **1** a person knowledgeable in forestry
who works as a timber cruiser, *q.v.*

1922 *Dalhousie Rev*. II 96: The lumberman is not a
forester and never will be. **1956** RADDALL *Wings* 63:
"He had his forester, Pemberton, go over the list and
check the titles at the county records office. . . ."

2 a government employee who looks after forests
and Crown lands.

1956 EVANS *Mountain Dog* 148: If only Belile will leave
us alone a few days till that chief forester gets back!
1964 *Star Wkly* 19 Dec. 13/1: The first of these
open-air snowmobiles was the Skidoo, originated by
the late Armand Bombardier of Valcourt, Que., seven
years ago and intended to make life easier for trappers,
foresters, and Arctic missionaries.

forest fire a raging fire that sweeps through a
forest. See also **bush fire**.

1868 *Canadian Naturalist* III 411: If, as already
suggested, forest fires, in the uncultivated state of the
country, be a provision for removing old and decaying
forests, then such changes as the above detailed must
have an important use in the economy of nature.
1964 *Calgary Herald* 15 May 47/8: There are nine
forest fires in Alberta, all of them under control.

forest ranger See 1955 quote. See also **ranger**
(def. 4).

1884 *Prince Albert Times* (Sask.) 4 July 3/1: Mr. G. F.
Clarke, of Toronto, who has been appointed Forest
Ranger for this District, in place of Mr. Swan,
promoted, arrived on Wednesday's train. **1955** GOWLAND
Smoke 45: The Forest Ranger is responsible for all that
takes place in his district, being in large degree a law
unto himself, and possessing powers exceeding those of
the police. He looks after the game, guards against
abuse of fishing rights, clears trails, builds bridges, does
all he can to prevent fires, deals with those which do
start, or supervises the fighting of large outbreaks, when
maybe hundreds of men are conscripted to deal with
such emergencies. **1960** NELSON *Northern Lights* 502:
At Bisco, in those days, trappers, hunters, traders,
rivermen, and forest rangers . . . met, pitched their tents
beside the lake . . . and danced. . . .

forest reserve a tract of forested land set aside by
the government.

1955 GOWLAND *Smoke* 45: A Forest Reserve differs
from a National Park slightly, although the job of a
Forest Ranger is almost identical with that of a Park
Warden. The great National Parks are administered by
the Federal Government of Canada, and have been set
aside as such for all time. The Forest Reserves, which
often adjoin the Parks, allow, where conditions are
suitable, the grazing of cattle and the cutting of timber.
1961 GREENING *Ottawa* 161: In 1895 the Quebec
Government . . . created the Laurentide Park, north of
Quebec City, as a game refuge and forest reserve.

forestry reserve See **forest reserve**.

1965 *Star Wkly* 23 Jan. 37/3: He works in the summer
months as a fire spotter at the Montgomery lake tower
in the Petawawa forestry reserve.

forest township reserve See quote.

1958 *Cdn Geog.Jnl* July 45/1: . . . forest township
reserves [were] established in 1911 for the purpose of
providing settlers with building and fencing material
and fire-wood which they cannot get on their own land.

forked tongue, speak with† originally in
Indian parlance, speak falsely; lie.

1871 (1883) BUTLER *Great Lone Land* 312: "You speak
with a forked tongue," answered the Blackfoot,
dividing his fingers as he spoke to indicate that the
other was speaking falsely. **1954** MCGREGOR *Shining
Mountains* 260: Now Henday found that his Crees had
been lying all the time. Someone had spoken with a
forked tongue.

fort *n. Fur Trade* a trading post, so called because
many early posts were fortified. See also **fur fort**
and **trading fort**.

1670 (1900) OSBORN *Greater Canada* 195: The Governor
and his Council of the several and respective places
where the said Company shall have plantations, forts,
factories, colonies, or places of trade within any of the
countries, lands or territories hereby granted may have
power to judge all persons belonging to the said
Governor and Company, or that shall live under them,
in all causes, whether civil or criminal, according to
the laws of this kingdom, and to execute justice
accordingly. **1743** (1949) ISHAM *Observations* 114: Their
has been and is Still men that wou'd undertake such a
Land Voyage with good Encouragem't Either to bring
them to the English forts to trade; or to give such a
Discription of the Country that a Setlement might be
made their. **1848** (1859) BALLANTYNE *Hudson's Bay* 24:
The fort (as all establishments in the Indian country,
whether small or great, are called) is a large square, I
should think about six or seven acres, inclosed within
high stockades, and built on the banks of Hayes River,
nearly five miles from its mouth. **1938** GODSELL *Red
Hunters* 173: God's Country . . . even had a language
of its own. Civilization became the "Outside" . . . an
aggregation of mudded huts a fort. . . . **1964** *Edmonton
Jnl* 10 July 37/1: Edmonton's first fair was held in two
rough rooms in the old Hudson's Bay Company fort on
Oct. 15, 1879.

fort captain *Fur Trade, Hist.* a person in charge of
a trading post.

1913 WILLIAMS *Wilderness Trail* 11: The only men she
had ever known were Indians, half-breeds, French-
Canadians, and a few pure-white fort captains like
himself.

fort hunter *Fur Trade, Hist.* a hunter, usually an
Indian, employed by a fur company to provide
meat for a fort. See also **hunter** and **Indian hunter**.
Cp. **fort trapper**.

1820 (1938) SIMPSON *Athabasca Jnl* 107: Our Fort
Hunters have lived on Babiche and Leather for several
days. . . . **1822** (1940) *Minutes of Council* (H.B.C.) 26:
That all Servants employed as Fort Hunters, be allowed
half the price that is given to Indians, and paid with
goods out of the shop. **1921** HEMING *Drama of Forests*
173: But before the fort-hunter had returned with the
telescope, the snowy veil suddenly thinned and revealed
the gray figure of a tripper coming up the bank.

fort lot *Obs.* a parcel of land set aside for the
building of a fortification.

1861 SUTHERLAND *Geography P.E.I.* 23: Charlottetown
and Royalty occupy 7,300 acres; and a reserved Fort
Lot at the entrance of Charlottetown harbor, 520 acres.

fort trapper *North* a trapper, usually an Indian,
who sets out trap lines near a trading post at which
he deals. Cp. **fort hunter**.

1938 GODSELL *Red Hunters* 261: When they surrendered
their nomadic hunting existence to become "fort

trappers" this no-man's-land widened into a vast uninhabited area. . . .

forty-rod† *n.* cheap, strong spirits, especially whisky. See 1958 quote.

1878 LEMOINE *Chronicles of St.Lawrence* 152: "Forty Rod" was the name of the wine of the country—the balm of Giliad of the railway navvy on a Saturday night. **1927** LONGSTRETH *Silent Force* 113: On one occasion word came that Tin Cup Joe was heading for Fort Walsh with a cargo of "40 Rod." **1958** BERTON *Klondike* 23: It [hootchinoo] was sometimes referred to as Forty-Rod Whisky because it was supposed to kill a man at that distance.

forwarder *n. Hist.* See quotes.

1829 MACTAGGART *Three Years* II 50: There are a class of people living on the banks [of the St. Lawrence], called *Forwarders:* these have the care of conducting goods and chattels up the river. **1838** *Niagara Reporter* (U.C.) 11 Nov. Extra 1/3: We are requested to mention, for the information of the Upper Canadian Merchants that the Forwarders below are using their utmost exertion to send forward all the goods in their possession, if they can do so with safety.

foule *n.* See **la foule.**

found-in *n.* a person arrested for being present in a brothel or an illegal drinking or gambling establishment.

1958 *Ottawa Citizen* 28 Aug. 1/3: Liquor Commission Police early today raided six alleged illegal drinking establishments and arrested 48 men and six women as keepers and found-ins. **1960** *Maclean's* 26 Mar. 18/1: Found-ins from a raided Toronto gambling club are taken by paddy wagon to face charges. **1963** *News of the North* 2 May 3: R.C.M.P. had raided the house about a week earlier [and] seized a quantity of liquor and questioned the "guests" who had been there at the time of the raid. Names of the "found-ins" were not disclosed to the court.

four bits† *Slang* fifty cents; a fifty-cent piece. See also **bit** (def. 1 and note).

1860 *Brit.Colonist* (Victoria) 22 Mar. 2/3: It was mighty hard to charge a poor fellow $1.25 for lodging in the street, without blankets, when he could sleep between sheets at the best hotel in town for only four bits. **1897** TUTTLE *Golden North* 152: During the present year the lowest standard of value in actual use there, has been the fifty-cent piece, or, in the parlance of the town, "four bits." **1961** MITCHELL *Jake and the Kid* 134: "I don't really need a four-bit haircut, Repeat."

four-foot wood *Lumbering* short logs for use as pulpwood, so called because they are usually sawn into four-foot lengths.

1944 KOROLEFF *Woodcutter's Handbook* 13/1: In four-foot wood, bucking usually takes about one-fifth of the working time and in logs about one-tenth.

four per-cent *Slang, Obs.* a mild beer sold in the West in early days.

1962 *Alta Hist.Rev.* Autumn 16/1: Under the general term liquor we have "Old Alky" . . . for whiskey, and "four per-cent" for a milder variety of beer.

fourplex ['fɔrplɛks] *n.* [by analogy with **duplex,** q.v.] a small apartment block having four self-contained apartments. Also spelled *4-plex.*

1963 *Globe and Mail* (Toronto) 3 Aug. 8/7: Kenneth Bryden, NDP member for Woodbine, owns a fourplex that pays his rent. **1965** *Ibid.* 9 Jan. 5/2: . . . Mr. Smith, Skey, and Eileen Griffith were joint owners of a $60,000 4-plex in Brampton.

four-point blanket a famous woollen blanket first used as trading goods at the Hudson's Bay Company posts. See also **point blanket.** Also spelled *4-point blanket.*

1787 *Quebec Gaz.* 1 Feb. 2/1: For Sale by Public Auction . . . A Parcel of New Goods not yet unpacked, consisting of 15 pairs of 4 point Blankets, 10 pieces of Red Strouds. **1884** *Prince Albert Times* (Sask.) 21 Mar. 3/2: In the way of bedding, two pairs of four-point H.B. blankets which are very light and warm, are considered to be necessary for each man, and two men sleep together using the double allowance of blankets. **1921** HEMING *Drama of Forests* 238: When she saw that I had nothing but a double "four-point" Hudson's Bay blanket, she offered to make me a complete suit. . . . **1954** BEZANSON *Sodbusters Invade the Peace* 10: First was a bedroll with attached mattress, Hudson's Bay 4-point blanket, mosquito net large enough to cover the bed amply, a set of nested copper kettles, four to a set, cutlery, dishes, etc.

four-pointer *n.* See **four-point blanket.**

1946 *Beaver* March 5/1: John set about making his blankets into a sleeping robe, only to discover that, while they were sufficient in weight, they were lacking in size. They should have been "four-pointers" instead of three and a half. . . .

four-point Hudson-Bay See **four-point blanket.**

1920 STRINGER *Prairie Mother* 299: I sat there wrapped up in one of Dundy-Dunk's four-point Hudson-Bays. . . .

four-poster *n.* an open steeple belfry the roof of which is supported by four columns, found in the architecture of certain older churches, especially in the Maritimes.

1896 ROBERTS *Camp-Fire* 121: "Soon the crest of the hill was passed, and the four-poster on the top of Second Westcock Church sank out of sight. . . ."

foutereau or **foutrau** *n.* [< Cdn F < F *foutre* < L *futuere* copulate] *Obs.* the North American mink, *Mustela vison.* See also **jackash.**

[**1801** (1933) MCLEOD *Diary* 184: Jabouran (the young Foutrau) arrived from Lac La course soon after the Canoes went off.] **1852** RICHARDSON *Arctic Exped.* 73: It is the Shakweshew or Atjakashew of the Crees, the "Mink" of the fur-traders, and the Foutereau of the Canadians. **1933** GATES *Five Traders* 184n: Foutrau was another name for the vison or mink of the Northwest.

foxberry *n.* the cowberry, *Vaccinium vitis-idaea,* or mountain cranberry, *V. vitis-idaea* var. *minus.* See also **ground cranberry.**

1796 (1911) SIMCOE *Diary* 301: I gathered fox berries. They grow like small red currants on a delicate plant. **1950** BIRD *This is N.S.* 287: "We've three things to brag about here," said a man at a filling station. "First, Newcomb, then the quarry, and then fox berries. . . ." **1964** *Maclean's* 16 Nov. 36/3: And to this day I don't know just what a foxberry is, either. All I know is that foxberries grow wild on low bushes, and they taste quite like ordinary cranberries, only with more flavor.

foxy *adj.* of rotten ice, discolored.

1886 *Trans.Roy.Soc.Can.* IV 3 87: In the middle of summer, the surface having thawed, the whole of this ice becomes "foxy," as it is termed, or shows discoloration.

fraction *n. Mining* a parcel of land that remains unclaimed after roughly staked claims are properly surveyed.
1898 *Prospector* (Lillooet, B.C.) 22 July 4/1: In all fractions surveyed from now on, whether staked correctly or not, the surveyor may adopt the boundary lines of the surrounding claims, provided no side exceeds 1,500 feet in length. **1963** *Western Miner* Feb. 23/2: He advised Dick Low who was rodding for him to stake the fraction.

fractional township† *West* a township of less than statutory size (36 sections), the irregularity being due to natural obstacles.
1881 BEGG *Great Cdn N.W.* 72: Provision was made for fractional townships, and others broken by lakes, and the terms of the Act as thus laid down were accepted by the Hudson's Bay Company. **1884** *Moose Jaw News* (Sask.) 30 May 1/4: The Lieut-Governor has issued his proclamation erecting certain townships and fractional townships into the electoral district of Calgary.

frame† *n.* (used attributively) constructed of plank siding, or clapboard, as distinct from logs, bricks, etc. See also **framer**.
1820 (1955) HARVEY *Island St. John* 97: Others have the wood set perpendicularly, and fixed to beams above and below, previously framed together, the whole size of the building. This is called a frame-house. **1825** *Colonial Advocate* (York [Toronto]) 5 Jan. 1/4: For Sale . . . A Frame Barn with Stabling, Forty by Forty-two. **1961** *Weekend Mag.* 5 Aug. 27/1: It was . . . a characteristic hamlet, with a church, a general store, a few frame houses, one brick house, a gas station and, down at the far end, a motel. . . .

frame *v. Fur Trade, Rare* put (the hide of a deer, caribou, etc.) on a board or frame for stretching. Cp. **fur board** and **stretcher**.
1853 REID *Young Voyageurs* 185: While Lucien was framing the skin [of the wapiti] Basil and Norman occupied themselves in cutting the choice pieces of the meat into thin slices and hanging them up before the fire.

framer *n.* a person skilled in erecting the structure of a frame building. See also **frame**, *n.*
1832 (1953) RADCLIFF *Letters* 46: The mode of forming such a house is as follows:—A framer, on receiving the dimensions and plan, cuts out the mortices and prepares the frame. A Bee, which means an assemblage of the neighbours, is then called.

franchise *v.* of Indians, be enfranchised, *q.v.*
1963 *Press* Dec. 12: I don't think anyone wants to franchise and I don't think anyone wants to sell outright. You can franchise off the reserve—that means you get your per cent of the capital of the Band's funds. . . . When they married the white boys they automatically left the Band, and so they franchised out.

Franco-Canadian *n. Archaic* See **French Canadian** (def. 1).
1841 *Montreal Transcript* 30 Oct. 2/4: It would wreak its vengeance upon every thing English in order to raise upon its ruins a monument to the vanity of the Franco-Canadians. **1881** RATTRAY *Scots in Brit.N.A.* II 404: . . . under the Constitutional Act of 1791, the Franco-Canadians were, if not quite satisfied, at least tranquil and submissive.

Franco-Canadian *adj. Archaic* See **French-Canadian** (def. 1).
1837 *Niagara Reporter* (Niagara-on-the-Lake, U.C.) 24 Sep. 2/3: We understand that a meeting was held on Tuesday evening last, of the Franco-Canadian clique, at the Nelson Hotel: Dr. Robert Nelson in the Chair. **1873** (1952) *Beaver* June 31/1: . . . the wild choruses of the Franco-Canadian voyageurs. . . .

Franco-Indian *n. Rare* See **Métis**.
1947 *Cdn Hist.Rev.* Dec. 429: . . . it is with the Franco-Indian, or métis, that the book is principally concerned.

Franglais [frɑnˈglɛ] *n.* [*français* + *anglais*] *Jocular* a mixture or blend of French and English.
1964 *Calgary Herald* 2 Jan. 5/4: As they say in Franglais—that curious French-English mixture popular among newly "bilingual" English-speaking Montrealers these days—la preuve is in le pudding.

Franglish [ˈfrɑnglɪʃ] *n.* [*français* + *english*] *Jocular* See **Franglais**.
1964 *Calgary Herald* 2 Jan. 4/1 [Headline]: Not Even Franglish.

Franklin[1] *n.* [< Sir John *Franklin*, English explorer, 1786-1847] a district in the Northwest Territories, embracing all islands in Hudson Bay and Strait, and the Arctic Ocean, north to the Pole. Also called *Franklin District*.
1923 WALDO *Down Mackenzie* 248: A man's foot may freeze; or his ax may slip; or his canoe may sink; or his dogs may die; and the pain of "Marie Chapdelaine" is the pain of Keewatin, Franklin, and Mackenzie as well as of Ontario. **1962** *Time* (Cdn ed.) 2 Mar. 8/3: Yukon Tory Erik Nielson . . . introduced a bill to extend the franchise to the Districts of Keewatin and Franklin by adding their 777,413 sq.mi. of Arctic wastes to the Mackenzie electoral district.

Franklin[2]† *n.* See **Franklin stove**.
1833 (1926) LANGTON *Early U.C.* 20: Franklins, cooking and common stoves, have each their advocates. **1869** MCCREA *Lost Amid Fogs* 76: It was, he afterwards learnt, one of those charming Yankee contrivances for giving heat at the expense of every other comfort, called a "Franklin," very common in former days in the western hemisphere.

Franklin fireplace or **heater** a kind of Franklin stove, *q.v.*
1963 *Eaton's Catalogue* (Winnipeg) Spring and Summer 355/4: "Early Canada" atmosphere with abundant warmth for your cottage, home or den. Franklin Fireplace is made of heavy cast iron ornately decorated. Will burn either wood or coal. Doubles as a small stove, too. Doors swing out and slide back along sides of heater out of the way. Each door has sliding draught. Size about 27 inches high by 31 inches wide by 23 inches deep. Black finish.

Franklin ground squirrel [< Sir John *Franklin*, English explorer, 1786-1847] a gray ground squirrel, *q.v.*, *Spermophilus franklini,* found on the prairies.
1941 SETON *Trail of an Artist-Naturalist* 189: The gray or Franklin ground squirrel [is] notable for its loud, ringing, musical call-note. **1955** HARDY *Alta Anthol.* 208: Apparently he was even more interested in nature study, for he described many plants, animals, and birds of Alberta, which he named for himself and Sir John Franklin—the Franklin ground squirrel, the

common Franklin gull, the Richardson kangaroo rat. . . .

Franklin's grouse [< Sir John *Franklin*, English explorer, 1786-1847] a species of grouse, *Canachites franklinii*, found throughout the West and Northwest. See also **fool hen** and **mountain grouse.**
1908 MAIR *Mackenzie Basin* 340: Three eggs of Franklin's grouse and one egg of the Canadian ruffed grouse were found in one nest by an Indian near Lake Babine post. . . . **1963** SYMONS *Many Trails* 66: The bird I shot was . . . slightly different from the spruce grouse of the Saskatchewan woods. I got to know this variety as Franklin's grouse, with the tail darker and narrowly tipped with dingy white rather than buff.

Franklin stove† [< Benjamin *Franklin,* American inventor, 1706-90] any of several kinds of iron heating stoves resembling a fireplace and patterned on a stove invented by Benjamin Franklin. See also **Franklin²** and **Franklin fireplace.**
1797 *U.C.Gaz.* (York [Toronto]) 4 Nov. 3/3: For Sale—A Franklin Stove Complete. **1833** (1838) TRAILL *Backwoods of Canada* 142: Our parlour is warmed by a handsome Franklin stove. **1954** BRUCE *Channel Shore* 28: Across the hall Anse got up and stretched and threw a cigarette butt at the Franklin stove.

frazil ['fræzəl *or* frə'zil] *n.* [< Cdn F *frasil* or *frazil* < F *frasil* cinders] ice crystals in the form of flakes occurring in rapidly moving, turbulent water, often caused by the rising of anchor or bottom ice, *q.v.* See also **frazil ice** and **lolly.** Cp. **candle** and **sish.**
1870 *Cdn Illust.News* 12 Feb. 236/4: It is when the frasi [sic] or floating snow, interspersed with small ice, is thick on the river that the greatest trouble is met with in crossing. . . . **1886** *Trans.Roy.Soc.Can.* IV 3 88: When the weather becomes milder, or the sky overcast, the frazil rises to the surface or floats off like a mixture of snow and water. **1962** *Canada Month* Apr. 28/3: Their crews talk glibly . . . during the winter of such phenomena of their trade as ropak, polynya, stamukha, bergy bit, and frazil.

frazil (or frazzle) ice ice formed from frazil and often accumulating in great banks on the shoreline.
1955 *Albertan* (Calgary) 17 Dec. 1/5: Frazzle ice has been pouring down the river steadily. . . . **1959** *Ottawa Citizen* 19 Mar. 21/6: This year . . . there is no ice jam on the river. In the past, frazil ice has piled up as high as 18 feet and as far up river as 2,000 feet from the city's waterfront. **1963** *Cdn Geog.Jnl* Nov. 150: [Caption] A crack near the summit of the ice hump, looking west towards Greece's Point. The dark band is clear river ice. Below is the frazil ice extending some 35 feet to the surface of the river.

free *adj. Fur Trade, Hist.* See 1941 quote. See also **free hunter, freeman,** and **free trader.**
1809 (1820) HARMON *Journal* 177: These Canadians came up into this part of the world (Dunvegan), free, to hunt the beaver. . . . **1941** *Beaver* Sep. 37/2: "Free"— quite a common expression at one time and relates to engaged servants whose contracts expired and who chose to remain in the country.

Freedomite ['fridəm,aɪt] *n.* See **Sons of Freedom.**

1958 *Time* (Cdn ed.) 24 Feb. 10/3: No non-Doukhobor could quite account for the latest signs of unrest from the Freedomites, who traditionally dramatize their resentment of authority by staging nude parades and touching off fires and explosions. **1964** *Sun* (Vancouver) 4 July 13/5: Now, with the core of the Freedomites gone, Doukhobors are building new houses. . . .

free fur-trader *Hist.* See **free trader** (def. 2a).
1929 JEFFERSON *Saskatchewan* 77: In the Lake Winnipeg region, while the Hudson's Bay Company and the Free Fur-traders used the water routes of the North-West in going to-and-fro between the settlements and their winter quarters, it was common practice to fee a conjuror for the production of a fair wind.

free gold *Mining* See **free-milling.**
1913 FOOTNER *Jack Chanty* 144: There's a good chance of finding free gold in the bed of the creek. . . .
1960 RAMSAY *Barkerville* 21: When he had driven in 60 feet he cut a small vein which showed substantial values and several sizeable fragments of free gold.

free grant *Hist.* a grant of land given gratis to a settler on condition that he settle and improve the land in a set time.
1856 (1957) *Ont.Hist.Winter* 8: The Agents on the "Free Grants" roads report, that the settlers are prosperous and well satisfied with their locations. . . .
1926 POLLARD *Pioneering* 84: Script, or official writing entitling the holder to locate land in free grant sections, was given to the half-breeds descended from the Indians, in the years 1899 and 1900.

free grass or **range** *West, Hist.* unsettled public grasslands on which livestock could be pastured without charge.
1884 *Nor'Wester* (Calgary) 3 June 2/2: In its issue of the 17th May it advocates free ranges, and in its issue a week later it says the ranges are free in all but name.
1955 HOBSON *Nothing Too Good* 250: They would never know that this gallant herd of old cows had trailed across the last of the free-grass cattle frontiers of our continent, more than a half-century later than their ancestors of the Chisholm Trail days.

free hunter *Fur Trade, Hist.* a trapper or hunter not in the employ of the fur companies, often a former company servant. See also **freeman** (def. 2) and **free trapper.** Cp. **freeman** (def. 1a).
1812 (1916) THOMPSON *Narrative* 551: [The] two men . . . were the sole survivors of about three hundred and fifty free hunters, almost all of them of french origin. *c*1902 LAUT *Trapper* 173: Going out alone, or with only one partner, the free hunter encumbered himself with few provisions. **1923** BARBEAU *Indian Days* 33: Many stories from the lips of other Indians, of catholicized half-breeds from the east . . . may have reached his ears, possibly through the "free hunters" who resorted by the score to the Rocky Mountains even before the time when Thompson, in 1807, first wintered at Lake Windermere.

freeman *n. Fur Trade, Hist.* **1 a.** a former employee of a fur company who elected to remain in the interior as a free hunter or, sometimes, as a free trader (def. 1).
1793 (1889) MacDONELL *Journal* 285: Peltier, old Robert Taylor, (freeman from the Missouri) . . . and Belair started for Pine Fort. **1824** (1931) SIMPSON *Fur Trade* 45: In the next place by laying at the Flat Head Post such a length of time the Freemen consume in the course of the Winter their ammunition and other supplies which they

receive in the Fall and will not start in the Spring until they have a second outfit which they cannot afford to pay for. **1860** *Nor'Wester* (R.R.S.) 14 May 3/5: These persons [former company servants] resolve themselves into two classes—the hunter, who follows the pursuits both of bartering for furs and hunting for them—in most cases doing very little in either line of business; and the "freeman," who confines himself almost exclusively to the trade of selling goods to the Indians, receiving their furs in payment. **1921** HEMING *Drama of Forests* 49: ... the only white man living in all that beautiful region was old Malcolm MacLean, a "freeman" of the H.B.Co., who had married an Indian woman and become a trapper. **1963** SPRY *Palliser* 191: These were freemen—that is, men not in the service of the Hudson's Bay Company—who had been trappers for the North-West Company before its merger in 1821.

b. See 1880 quote. Cp. **tripman.**
1832 (1851) CAMPBELL *Journal* 9: Every spring and fall some hundreds of "Freemen," principally French, half-breeds, were, with their families accustomed to leave the Settlement for the plains, taking with them their favorite "Buffalo Runners." **1880** GORDON *Mountain and Prairie* 230: A number of Indians,— "free-men," that is, men not in the regular service of the Company,—live in the neighbourhood, being employed by the Company as occasion may require. **1963** *Beaver* Autumn 38/1: ... the consensus of opinion among the Company men, missionaries and "freemen" (mostly half breeds) ... was that the "Boundary, Kootenay and Sinclair Passes" presented fewest difficulties.

2 See **free hunter.**
1953 *B.C.Hist.Qtly* XVII 187: In the Snake country, where the freemen and engagés called him "M'sieu Pete," he complained that the hard life he led had reduced him to skin and bone. **1961** JONES *Trappers* 8: [They were] a tough, colorful, sometimes cruel, always superbly skilled breed of men called by the French coureurs de bois, by the English woods runners, by the Russians promyshlenniki, and by the American trappers, free men, and mountain men.

Free Man's Tariff *Fur Trade, Hist.* See quote. See also **free trader** (def. 1).
1907 HUNTER *Cdn Wilds* 15: The barter tariffs at each of the posts was made out in two columns, i.e., Indian Tariff and Free Man's Tariff. Say, for example, a pound of English tobacco was bartered to the Indian at the posts for one dollar a pound, the [H.B.Co.-approved] Free Trader would get it in his outfit for 75 cents. ...

free-milling† *adj. Mining* of ore, not requiring costly treatment for recovery of the gold. See also **free gold.**
1910 SERVICE *Trail of '98* 333: "... they knew of a ledge of high-grade, free-milling quartz somewhere out there in the Land Back of Beyond." **1926** SULLIVAN *Under Northern Lights* 2: To a mining man it would have been a sample of high-grade, free-milling gold ore. **1951** SHORT *Barren Land Murders* 28: The ore is free milling.

free miner *Esp.B.C.* a person holding a Free Miner's Certificate.
1898 *Placer Miner's Certificate* (on display in the offices of Chamber of Mines, Vancouver, B.C.): This is to Certify that F. Woodside of Rossland, has this day paid me the sum of Five Dollars and is entitled to all the rights and privileges of a Free Miner, for one year from 21st. June, 1898. **1910** SERVICE *Trail of '98* 174: Franchises were being given to the favourites of those in power, concessions sold, liquor permits granted, and abuses of every kind practised on the free miner. **1960** *Statutes of B.C.* 3580: Every free miner ... has the right to enter, locate, and prospect, and mine for minerals upon any lands in this Province. ... **1965** *Cdn Geog.Jnl* Dec. 205/1: In British Columbia a free miner has very strong rights under the Placer Mining Act. ...

Free Miner's Certificate *Esp.B.C.* a licence bought by an individual or a group permitting prospecting on unstaked lands and the right to register and develop claims while remaining free of any poll tax.
1866 *Cariboo Sentinel* (Barkerville, B.C.) 6 Aug. 3/3: Ah Coon, a Chinaman from Kiethleys Creek was charged by officer Coney with being found mining without a Free Miner's Certificate. **1898** LANDREVILLE *Appeal of Yukon Miners* 93: Before a person can have any privileges in the District he must pay an annual tax of $10 (companies must pay more) for a "free miner's certificate." **1960** *Statutes of B.C.* 3617: For each free miner's certificate issued to an individual—$5.00. For each free miner's certificate issued to a corporation—$100.00. **1965** *Cdn Geog.Jnl* Dec. 205/1: Of course you will need a free miner's certificate but that will cost you only a few dollars.

free prospector *Obs.* See **free miner.**
1905 BINDLOSS *Alton* 2: A mixed company of ... free prospectors ... and miners lounged outside in picturesque disarray. ...

free run *Obs.* See quote. See also **buffalo run** (def. 1).
1952 HOWARD *Strange Empire* 305: For the benefit of the needy, families which had no hunter, the riders made "free runs" through the herd [of buffalo]. *Ibid.* 308: On the hunt he habitually made a "free run" and donated eight or ten buffalo to the poorer families in his camp.

free school† *Hist.* a school supported by the municipality through payment of school taxes; a public school.
1839 HALIBURTON *Bubbles of Canada* 65: Among the topics insisted upon in the governor's speech, was a recommendation for a grant of money for free schools for the instruction of the rising generation in the first rudiments of useful learning, and in the English tongue. **1899** MACKAY *Pioneer Life* 242: At length Egerton Ryerson introduced the "Free School" system. This system, where adopted, did away with the fee formerly charged, and provided for the expenses of schools by levying a tax on every acre of land, occupied or unoccupied, within the section. **1942** CARR *Book of Small* 167: It took a generation and a'half for English settlers in Victoria to accept the Canadian public school which they insisted on calling the "free school." They turned their noses up at public schools. ...

free township *Hist.* in Quebec, a township in which the farmers were not subject to seigneurial obligations as was the case until 1854 on the older seigneuries.
1929 CUDMORE *World's Commerce* 230: Farther east they founded "free" townships instead of feudal seigneuries to the south of the St. Lawrence and on the lower Ottawa.

free trade *Fur Trade* See **free trading.**
1920 FOOTNER *Fur-Bringers* 51: "... I say I t'ink I go East to Lake Miwasa. There is free trade there."

free trader *Fur Trade* **1** *Hist.* a former servant of the Hudson's Bay Company who travelled amongst the Indians, especially in the hunting grounds, trading necessary articles for furs and usually getting his outfit from the Company. Cp. **freeman** (def. 1a).

1872 (1883) BUTLER *Great Lone Land* 108: These "houses" were the trading posts of the first English Free-Traders.... **1907** HUNTER *Cdn Wilds* 14: The origin of the term "Free Trader" dates back considerably over three-quarters of a century and was first used as a distinction by the Hudson's Bay Company between their own traders, who traded directly from their posts and others who in most cases had been formerly in their employ, but had turned "Free Traders." **1940** NIVEN *Mine Inheritance* 180: Local métis and French Canadians—free-traders—cabined in the neighbourhood, were happy enough to assist McLeod in a task to which he had set himself. **1965** *Maclean's* 19 June 15/1: James Sinclair, a métis free trader... nearly lost his life going over the Kananaskis Pass.

2 a. a fur trader operating independently of and in opposition to the fur companies. See also **free fur-trader**.

1864 *Nor' Wester* (R.R.S.) 21 Nov. 2/3: Another circumstance which strengthens this probability is that the plains are lined with Free traders, who are well-supplied with goods and provisions. **1934** GODSELL *Arctic Trader* 34: The bitterness aroused in their breasts if a "free trader" ventured to defy the might of the "Gentlemen Adventurers" by attempting to trade on their own was almost inconceivable. **1947** *Cdn Hist. Rev.* Dec. 401: Its founder, Nicolas Peltier, a native-born Canadian of French parentage, and one of the first free traders to follow in the footsteps of Pierre Esprit Radisson... first came into the Saguenay in 1672 under a congé, or permit, from the Governor, de Frontenac. **1965** *Globe and Mail* (Toronto) 27 May 8/9: Bill Anderson [is] a veteran free trader at Fort Albany on James Bay....

b. *Hist.* See **whisky trader.**

1881 *Edmonton Bull.* 28 Mar. 2/1: Whiskey was the great staple article of trade, both of the Hudson's Bay Company and the free traders in this district, and the horses and fur of the Indians and gold of the miners went to purchase it. **1957** *Beaver* Spring 272: Being somewhat remote, they were never overrun with whisky-peddling "free-traders." **1960** NIX *Mission* 55: [Between 1868 and 1874] there was an invasion of American "free traders," bringing in raw whisky in their trade with the Indians.

free trading *Fur Trade* trading independent of the fur companies.

1909 CAMERON *New North* 94: At the other gibbous horn of this Athens of the Athabasca rise the steeples and convent-school of the Roman Church, with the free-trading-post of Colin Fraser. **1928** LeROSSIGNOL *Beauport Road* 28: "Not that he considered free trading a great sin, as we do now." **1960** NIX *Mission* 55: This free trading... had as its accompaniment acts of lawlessness and violence.

free trapper *Fur Trade* See **free hunter.**

*c*1902 LAUT *Trapper* 168: The free trapper went among the Indians with no defence but good behaviour and the keenness of his wit. *Ibid.* 173: Indeed, rival hunters have not hesitated to bribe the savages to

pillage and murder the free trapper; for there was no law in the fur trading country, and no one to ask what became of the free trapper who went out alone into the wilderness and never returned. **1955** RICH in BLACK *Journal* 243: He then became a free trapper until 1841, when he became a settler.

freeze-up *n.* the freezing up of bodies of water and the topsoil of land in the late fall or early winter; also, the period during which this freezing takes place. Cp. **break-up.**

1910 LONDON *Lost Face* 116: The freeze-up came on when we were at the mouth of Henderson Creek.... **1933** MERRICK *True North* 97: They had never seen a white woman in the country at freeze-up time.... **1954** BEZANSON *Sodbusters Invade the Peace* 195: "... we must set our time according to my experience and observation of freeze-ups and snow fall...." **1966** *Globe and Mail* (Toronto) 8 Feb. 10/7: They go on foot, by canoe before the freeze up, and by other crude means....

freight *n.* (used attributively) of or having to do with the transporting of goods, especially in the North and West.

1879 ROBINSON *Great Fur Land* 225: The vehicles to which dogs are harnessed in the Fur Land are of three kinds—the passenger sledge, or dog-cariole, the freight-sledge, and the travaille. **1938** *Beaver* June 25/2: Freight brigades would come and go, the store would be crowded with Indians, men, women, and children. **1965** *Modern Instructor* Dec. 250: When the Metis boys became men they often worked for the fur traders as interpreters, guides, and freight drivers.

freight canoe a large canoe (from 20 to 30 feet long), used for transporting goods, especially in the North. See also **freighter** (def. 5), **freighter canoe, freighting canoe,** and **luggage canoe.**

1914 DOUGLAS *Lands Forlorn* 234: The Aldebaran was a big "freight" canoe made by the Peterborough Canoe Co. **1927** (1958) WATTERS *B.C.Cent.Anthol.* 26: ... the raft [was] lashed alongside Gordon's 20-foot freight canoe. **1966** *Cdn Geog.Jnl* Mar. 93/1: But the use of fragile canvas and wood freight canoes [in hunting walrus] is increasing....

freighter† *n.* **1** a person engaged in the transporting of goods, especially in the North and, formerly, in the West.

1859 (1964) INNIS *Fur Trade in Canada* 315: Many of them... will not go as far as York, it's the Lower River that is the stumbling block for procuring freighters. **1860** *Nor' Wester* (R.R.S.) 14 Mar. 4/3: The system on which the freighters deal with their trip men is, I believe, injurious both to the employed and the employer. **1908** MAIR *Mackenzie Basin* 109: Here... they sold the horses, and with the proceeds hired local freighters to carry them and their supplies to Peace River Crossing.... **1963** *Western Wkly* 13 Mar. 6: [Headline] Life In The North Was Good For Freighter And His Team.

2 *Nfld* a passenger or crew member on a coastal vessel.

1905 DUNCAN *Grenfell's Parish* 96: The schooners take many passengers north in the spring. Such are called "freighters" on the coast; they are put ashore at such harbours as they elect, and, for passage for themselves, families, and gear, pay upon the return voyage twenty-five cents for every hundredweight of fish caught. **1964** *Nfld Qtly* Summer 16/1: Cruiser. John Eagan, 8 November, 1819. Member of the crew of a vessel engaged in local coastal transportation.... Other more modern synonyms are freighter, coaster, trader (but the last as a thorough misuse, as a trading vessel was a floating shop).

3 a large dog-sled used in the North for transporting supplies.
1910 LONDON *Burning Daylight* 47: Also he saw the heavy freighters pulling down the main street and heading up the frozen Klondike. . . .

4† a heavy wagon for carrying goods.
1918 LOWREY *Young Canada Boys* 52: ". . . I wuz a'sittin' up there on the freighter a'toting boxes and bales up over thet there mountain, my old black snake whip a'snappin' an' a'crackin'. . . ."

5 See **freight canoe.**
1928 FREEMAN *Nearing North* 349: Because his big twenty-foot freighter was overloaded and undermanned, he had been permitted to use an outboard motor—for the first time in his life. **1956** KEMP *Northern Trader* 121: Travelling upstream and carrying an eighteen-foot freighter or a two-hundred-pound pack, the portage seems interminable; but the labor is less than poling the canoe up those eight miles of rapids.

freighter canoe See **freight canoe.**
1942 TWOMEY & HERRICK *Needle to North* 236: In the big twenty-six-foot freighter canoe, with the old outboard motor attached, we would go over to the Sound where the ice floe was thickest and there find netchek, the hair seal, sporting among and resting on the ice blocks. **1963** *Globe and Mail* (Toronto) 16 Feb. 26/7: The [James Bay] trip they made without a guide, using their own freighter canoe and camping on the shores of the bay.

freighting† *n.* the transporting of goods and supplies, especially in the North, and, formerly, in the West.
1909 CONNOR *Foreigner* 189: These left the great riverways and freighting trails, and pressing up the streams to distant head waters, there pitched their camp. . . . **1909** CAMERON *New North* 340: They all to some extent cultivate the soil, varying their farm operations by hunting, trapping, and freighting. **1926** DICKIE *Cdn West* 137: A brigade might include several hundred carts, one freighter being in charge of three carts. Sixteen to eighteen shillings per hundred pounds was paid for freighting. **1942** TWOMEY & HERRICK *Needle to North* 27: He had a freighting ship, a Fairchild, splendid for Northern travel and the only plane of its type in the whole eastern Arctic.

freighting canoe See **freight canoe.**
1897 TYRRELL *Sub-Arctics* 119: Placing him in our third or freighting canoe, and accompanied by an escort of three kyacks, we departed, amid a generous exchange of salutes. **1953** LOWER *Voyages* 20: . . . the old birch freighting canoes were still in the canoe sheds. . . .

freight shed† a building for storing goods to be transported.
1882 *Brandon Mail* (Man.) 22 Dec. 4/1: There is a good deal of activity in and around the freight sheds. **1954** *Pictou Advocate* (N.S.) 3 June 1/5: The new freight shed . . . on the Pictou waterfront was used for the first time over the week end.

freight train 1† a railway train transporting goods.
1854 *Guelph Advertiser* (C.W.) 16 Nov. 1/5: We grieve to learn that another collision occurred on the Great Western Railway, between a passenger train and a freight train, near Thamesville, on Friday last. **1916** BRIDLE *Sons of Canada* 69: Rivers and York boats and trail-carts were being superceded by freight trains and

passenger coaches. **1955** *Dly News* (St John's) 2 Mar. 6/4: Cargoes must now be unloaded at North Sydney, put aboard the ship and discharged at Port aux Basques to be reloaded on freight trains.

2 *Hist.* a wagon train, as of Red River carts, *q.v.*, or larger vehicles, transporting goods.
1880 GORDON *Mountain and Prairie* 237: When the freight train from Edmonton had come, the Indians from the lake and those in charge of the carts spent the evening in the red man's favourite recreation, gambling. **1926** DICKIE *Cdn West* 260: The freight trains were imposing bodies of great wagons and boiling bulls. Eight yoke made a team, and four teams made a train, a foreman being in charge of each brigade and each train being supplied with cook and mess-wagon.

French *n.pl.* See **French Canadian** (def. 1).
1784 PENNANT *Arctic Zoology* 18: The English used to call it the Black Moose, to distinguish it from the Stag, which they named the Grey Moose, the French call it L'Orignal. **1872** (1883) BUTLER *Great Lone Land* 124: And "the French" was at that time altogether a new name in my ears for the Red River natives. **1919** MORLEY *Bridging the Chasm* 3: The English and French in Canada have not yet attained to the state of brotherly love.

French *adj.* **1** See **French-Canadian** (def. 1a).
1908 LAUT *Conquest N.W.* II 3: French habitants were no more anxious to have their heads broken in other men's quarrels than the Orkneymen of the Old Country. . . . **1963** MORTON *Kingdom of Canada* 334: The attitude . . . spread to the French element in Red River, the French-Canadian traders and the metis buffalo-hunters and freighters.

2 See **French-Canadian** (def. 1b).
1673 (1942) *H.B.C.Minutes* 59: That Mr. Kirke bee desired to treate for provideing Such french goodes as may be necessary. **1799** (1955) CRAIG *Early Travellers* 25: No sooner were we in sight of it, than the postmaster, his wife in her close French cap, and all the family came running out to receive us. **1842** *Montreal Transcript* 15 Nov. 2/2: It is our firm conviction that the murderer of lieut. Weir, if supported by the leaders of the Canadian party, could be returned as member for any French County in Lower Canada, so abject is the submission of Canadian constituencies to the advice of their leaders. **1916** BRIDLE *Sons of Canada* 56: He spoke of the French question. **1966** *Maclean's* 2 May 2/3: Throughout Quebec it's the French, not the English, doctors who are making the most noise in favor of birth control.

French-Acadian *n.* a French-speaking settler in Acadia or one of his descendants, especially one who still speaks French.
1829 MOORSOM *Letters N.S.* 342: The French Acadians, who seldom formed a settlement except in the most advantageous situations, built a small fort at Sherbrooke, from the ruins of which were very lately dug up two iron guns, of old French manufacture. **1898** *New Brunswick Mag.* I 121: There is no denying the fact that in point of antiquity the French Acadians of the Maritime Provinces ante-date all the inhabitants of British origin. **1934** DENNIS *Down in N.S.* 55: Canute was not the only one who commanded the waves, for these French Acadians said to the invading sea: "Thus far shalt thou come and no further."

French-Acadian *adj.* of or associated with French Acadians.
1890 *Trans.Roy.Soc.Can.* VIII 2 15: In the maritime provinces of Nova Scotia, New Brunswick and Prince Edward Island, there was a small French Acadian population still living in favoured localities.
1964 *Evening Patriot* (Charlottetown) 16 June 4/1: He has long been regarded as the prime source of knowledge on French Acadian history in this area. . . .

French Canada 1 that part of Canada which was formerly known as New France; the province of Quebec.
1844 *Patriot* (Toronto) 5 Nov. 3/1: We thus see proof abundant, that in twelve Counties in French Canada, there is not merely a division, but a considerable division. **1966** *Saturday Night* Apr. 29/2: A recent survey of sex-attitudes in French Canada indicated that the male presence in the home is practically nil.

2 the people of Quebec collectively.
1888 *Dominion Illustrated* 114/2: We said, a couple of weeks ago, that French Canada, without distinction of party, was opposed to the scheme of Imperial Federation. **1916** BRIDLE *Sons of Canada* 39: Quebec . . . must have a leader of French Canada outside the old parties in the person of Henri Bourassa. **1964** *Time* (Cdn ed.) 31 Jan. 8/3: Pearson . . . gave French Canada perhaps the strongest voice it has ever had in a Federal Cabinet.

3 French-speaking Canadians collectively.
1895 *Rat Portage* [Kenora] *News* (Ont.) 26 Apr. 4/1: French Canada and the Separate schools forsooth, when will those frothy writers and talkers give us a rest on this seemingly inexhaustable subject and confine themselves to something practical, something of immediate interest? **1961** *Time* (Cdn ed.) 24 Mar. 15/2: "No one seriously imagines," Premier Jean Lesage assured the Quebec legislature a fortnight ago, "that French Canada ends at the territorial limits of Quebec province." In fact, Lesage does not even concede that French Canada ends at the territorial limits of Canada. **1964** *Calgary Herald* 25 Feb. 25/1: There are another 1,750,000 viewers in French Canada. **1966** *Kingston Whig-Standard* (Ont.) 14 Apr. 4/6: "French Canada extends from the Maritimes to British Columbia. But you people insist on keeping us in the reserve of Quebec. . . ."

French Canadian 1 a French-speaking descendant of the settlers of New France or Acadia; a Canadian of French ancestry. See also **Franco-Canadian**, *n.*, **French**, *n.*, and **Frenchman**.
1758 *Description Cape Breton* 4: According to his own Description of these *French* Canadians, whom he represents as an indolent People . . . it is not in the least probable that *Quebec* should be raised to this greatness by them? **1823** *Kingston Chron.* (U.C.) 28 Mar. Supp. 1/3: An hon. Member said the French Canadians will be gradually melted down and in a few generations be reduced to one language. **1887** *Trans. Hist.& Sci.Soc.Man.* 28 14: If people don't choose to call us simply "Canadians," though we are the original emigrants from Europe, then let them at least call us French Canadians. **1966** *Saturday Night* Apr. 14/2: She . . . had married a French Canadian, had learned his language completely, adopted his faith and now wanted to know what the hell was going on in Quebec.

2 *Hist.* **a.** See **Canadian horse.** See also **French-Canadian** (def. 2).
1901 CONNOR *Man from Glengarry* 209: But even as it heaved, he heard Aleck's call and the answering crash, and before he could get his team a-going, the French-Canadians were off for their pile at a gallop, with the lines flying in the air behind them. **1931** CONNOR *Rock and River* 17: . . . soon behind a spanking pair of French Canadians in a double sleigh the party drove down through the Lower Town. . . . **1941** MACEWAN *Farm Live-Stock* 102: . . . the French-Canadian Horse Breeders' Association was formed in 1895.

b. See **Canadian cattle.**
1936 MACEWAN & EWEN *Cdn Animal Husbandry* 53: Canadian cattle, formerly called French-Canadian, represent a remarkable survival of a type brought to this continent by the early French settlers. **1941** MACEWEN *Farm Live-Stock* 253: The name of the breed was changed officially from French Canadian to Canadian at the annual meeting of the [Canadian Cattle Breeders'] Association in 1930. **1958** FRANDSEN *Dairy Handbook* 573: *French-Canadian*—A minor breed of dairy cattle, the forbears of which were brought to Canada by French settlers more than 250 years ago, but the breed was developed in Canada. The cattle . . . are about the same size as Jerseys, are active, vigorous and able to withstand long winters. They are black in color or black with a fawn or orange colored strip down the back and around the muzzle. . . . the yield is about equal to that of the Jersey.

3 See **Canadian French** (def. 2).
1929 CONSTANTIN-WEYER *A Man Scans* [trans.] 203: He hailed me in French Canadian. So it was David! The Prairie came to life again.

French-Canadian *adj.* **1 a.** descended from the settlers of New France. See also **French**, *adj.* (def. 1).
1779 (1934) TURNOR *Journal* 235: A French Canadian Servant to McCormack was at the same tent. **1873** (1877) GRANT *Ocean to Ocean* 299: Four hours after, we reached Cache Creek, having rested only ten minutes on the way at the house of a French Canadian settler. **1958** *Edmonton Jnl* 6 Aug. 9/1: . . . Mr. and Mrs. Isreal Rondeau . . . were among the original French-Canadian families of Morinville [Alta].

b. of or associated with French Canada, especially Quebec, or with French Canadians. See also **French**, *adj.* (def. 2).
1822 *Kingston Chron.* (U.C.) 23 Nov. 3/4: The tempting nature of the subject might lead us astray from the path we have marked out for ourselves, and insensibly betray us into the commission of indecencies similar to those which have disfigured the pages of some French Canadian papers. **1913** LLOYD *Real Canadian* 3: It is no idle boast, the familiar saying, that the last shot in defence of the British Empire, will be from a French Canadian rifle. **1965** *Kingston Whig-Standard* (Ont.) 9 Jan. 22/2: It may not help the English Canadian and the French Canadian politician to speak one another's language if they do not share the same understanding of the tongue that money talks.

2 *Hist.* of or associated with the Canadian horse, *q.v.* See also **French Canadian** (def. 2a).
1853 STRICKLAND *Canada West* I 39: One pair of our horses were French Canadian . . . rough-looking beasts with shaggy manes and tails, but strong, active, and stout for their size. **1883** *Edmonton Bull.* 6 Jan. 1/2: A thoroughbred French-Canadian stallion, which he purchased in Battleford and brought with him, is a desirable and much needed acquisition to the stock of

this district. **1902** CONNOR *Glengarry* 298: ... there appeared Alphonse le Roque driving his French-Canadian team, the joy and pride of his heart, for Alphonse had taught his French-Canadians many extraordinary tricks.

French Canadianism attachment to and support of French Canada, its people, language, and culture.
1916 BRIDLE *Sons of Canada* 33: One might have naively surmised that ... he had renounced some of his French Canadianism. **1953** HUTCHISON *Incredible Canadian* 36: Already the Liberals of Ontario and the West had quarrelled with him, some secretly, some openly, on the question of bilingualism in the Ontario schools which he had forced into Parliament, against their advice, to demonstrate his French Canadianism.

French-Canadian party *Hist.* See **French party** (def. 1).
1881 RATTRAY *Scots in Brit.N.A.* II 407: During Sir James Craig's administration, there was a critical struggle between the advanced spirits of the French Canadian party and the Executive.

French coast See **French shore** (def. 1).
1842 BONNYCASTLE *Newfoundland* II 243: Very little is known of the French coast or of the French settlers; the policy of France excludes them from our ports, and the part of the island near or on which they dwell, is situated beyond the thinnest portion of our population. **1911** GOSLING *Labrador* 360: Being asked if the Americans employed vessels in the fishery on the French coast as well as on the other coasts of Newfoundland, he stated that they were not allowed to come round to that part of the French coast or the front of the island.

French Company 1 *Obs.* See **North West Company.**
1923 SCOTT *Witching of Elspie* 102: When Pierre Loudet, of the French Company—this was in the year 1808—appeared before his fort, laid peaceful siege to it, and endeavoured to undermine its trade, he was at his wits' end.
2 *Hist.* Revillon Freres Trading Co., a Paris-based fur company operating in Canada from 1905 to 1936, when absorbed by the Hudson's Bay Company. See also **Revillon.**
1939 *Beaver* Sep. 31/2: Revillon Frères, known locally as "The French company," had established posts in this area. ... **1953** LOWER *Voyages* 36: Every Indian was thus either a "Company Indian" or a "French Company Indian." **1956** KEMP *Northern Trader* 50: I joined the ranks of the deviationists and went over to the "French Company" myself.

French currency *Hist.* the system of currency deriving from New France and in use for many years in Lower Canada.
1938 SIMPSON *Athabasca Jnl* 186n: ... from 1796 onwards the dollar was equivalent to five shillings, Halifax (i.e. four dollars were equal to a pound Halifax), whilst five livres, French money, were equal to five shillings, Halifax, or one dollar. The sterling guinea was equivalent to one pound, three shillings and fourpence, Halifax, or twenty-eight livres, French currency.

French Fours a kind of square dance, popular among the voyageurs and the Métis of the Northwest.
1853 STRICKLAND *Canada West* I 82: After tea, dancing commenced, to the music of two fiddles, when country dances, reels, and French fours were performed, with

much spirit. **1908** MAIR *Mackenzie Basin* 75: "French Fours" and the immortal "Red River Jig" were repeated again and again. ...

French halfbreed See **Métis.** See also **Brulé** (def. 1).
1860 *Nor'Wester* (R.R.S.) 28 Apr. 3/3: It does not contain a single word in the way of a comparison between the English and the French Halfbreeds. **1963** MORTON *Kingdom of Canada* 148: Urging them on were French half-breeds among them, and French traders behind them in the Illinois country. ...

French horse *Obs. or Hist.* See **Canadian horse.**
1829 (1832) PICKERING *Inquiries* 116: This was the first time I saw the pluck and spirit of the little Canadian or French horse. **1845** BEAVAN *Life in Backwoods N.B.* 34: ... when the snow was well beaten down, with his little French horse and light sled he soon drew it to the place from whence the boats are loaded in the spring. **1931** CONNOR *Rock and River* 81: "Fitz-Gibbon was telling me about it. French horse. By the way, it is your horse, Fraser?"

Frenchie or **Frenchy** *n. Slang* **1** See **French Canadian** (def. 1).
1891 OXLEY *Chore-Boy* 74: I wouldn't give him for half a dozen of those *parlez vous* Frenchies. ... **1910** FRASER *Red Meekins* 278: "Lamonte was his name. He was a Frenchy." **1966** *Maclean's* 2 May 50/4: In those three months ... I was constantly laughed at, pointed at and corrected, as a stupid Frenchy.
2 *Obs.* a member of the French Company (def. 2).
1913 WILLIAMS *Wilderness Trail* 189: ... they've bargained with a French fur company, as far as I can gather. The Frenchies have been successful in the Rockies and on the Mackenzie, and they're figuring on starting a post or so in this territory.

Frenchified *adj. Derog.* French-Canadian (def. 1b) in customs, traits, or sympathies.
1832 *Novascotian* (Halifax) 24 Jan. 26/2: The Governor General lives in Canada, and is called *All Marr*, from marring all by giving up every thing to *Puppy now,* and those Frenchified Canadians. **1836** *Bytown* [Ottawa] *Gaz.* 8 Sep. 2/5: Let us for a moment suppose (Providence forbid,) that these Frenchified politicians attain the upper hand. ... **1870** *Cdn Illust.News* 26 Feb. 271/3:
> Now John on his farm has raised human stock
> Of a Frenchified Indian breed,
> Who became very bold, when they were all told
> To depend on Canadian feed, feed feed—
> To this they replied—no, indeed!

Frenchify *v. Derog.* make French-Canadian in customs, traits, or sympathies.
1703 (1965) *Letters from Hudson Bay* 8: ... there came abundance of Indians down who used the French and were so much Frenchified that they asked for the goods which they traded in French, among whom there were two or three canoes of the Ottawas. ... **1836** *Bytown* [Ottawa] *Gaz.* 17 Nov. 2/2: Some people are incredulous as to Lord Gosford's intention of Frenchifying the Legislative Council.

French Indian *Hist.* an Indian from territory controlled by New France, or one who hunted for and dealt with French-Canadian traders, as opposed to the Hudson's Bay Company.

1724 (1965) *Letters from Hudson Bay* 101: . . . the French Indians . . . shall be in very great hopes of a good trade next spring. . . . *c*1752 (1852) COATS *Geography of H.B.* 56: The contests between the English and French Indians have so depeopled the stocks, that it hardly affords either beaver, or martins, or porcupines, or other family creatures. **1912** (1913) HODGE & WHITE *Indians of Canada* 172/2: French Indians. A term used by early English writers to designate the tribes in the French interest, especially the Abnaki and their congeners on the New England Frontier.

French Loyalist *Hist.* a United Empire Loyalist, *q.v.,* of French-Canadian origin.
1799 (1936) RUSSELL *Correspondence* III 122: He had good reason to believe that the Messessagues were now well disposed to sell to Government a part of their land for the accommodation of those French Loyalists to whom His Majesty their common Father had given an asylum in Upper Canada. **1893** YEIGH *Ont.Parliament* 129: The Count de Puissaye, on the other hand, failed in his attempt to settle a colony of French loyalists.

Frenchman *n.* See **French Canadian** (def. 1).
1856 (1926) LANGTON *Early U.C.* 264: I know that all the Frenchmen in the ministry without exception are very indignant at me. **1883** FRASER *Shanty* 40: . . . one of the men, a Frenchman, resolved to assert his independence and defiance of Bob on these points. **1943** SWANSON *Lumberjack* 38:

Dees foreman, he's mad at dees li'l Frenchman,
He is all feegure out for to geeve heem de can.
But de boat, she is late an' de hooker he's mad,
An' for one chokair-man, he is ver' mooch glad . . .

French Métis See **Métis.**

French Métisse See **Métisse.**

French money See **French currency.**

French Neutral *Hist.* one of the Acadian French who, after the signing of the Treaty of Utrecht in 1713 had brought Acadia under British rule, refused to take the oath of allegiance, preferring to remain neutral in the strife between British and French. See also **Acadian Neutral.**
1755 (1895) RICHARD *Acadia* II 77: We are now hatching the noble and great project of banishing the French Neutrals from this province; they have ever been our secret enemies, and have encouraged our Indians to cut our throats. **1823** HALIBURTON *General Descr.N.S.* 11: Acadians, who in submitting to a new yoke, had sworn never to bear arms against their former standards, were called the French neutrals. **1884** SMITH *Acadia* 216: We defy all past history to present a parallel case, in which an unarmed and peacable people have suffered to such an extent as did the French Neutrals of Acadia at the hands of the New England troops.

French party *Hist.* **1** in Lower Canada, a faction serving the political interests of French Canadians.
1822 *Montreal Herald* 6 Nov. 2/4: The French party knew they could rely upon these men, for it was their interest, to oppose the re-union. . . . **1858** *Brit.Colonist* (Victoria) 11 Dec. 2/7: Mr. Cameron stands, in regard to the French party, in a still worse position even than Dr. Rolph—He is simply despised by them. **1923** *Cdn Hist.Rev.* IV 259: William Grant had sat in the Legislative Council since 1778 and had won the especial dislike of the French party, in the days of Hamilton and Pope. **1963** MORTON *Kingdom of Canada* 197: The controversy became bitter [c1805] when two English newspapers . . . attacked the French party for its stand on taxation.

2 in the Northwest, a faction serving the interests of the French-Canadians and Métis in their opposition to annexation of the territories by Canada without guarantees of their civil and religious rites. Cp. **Canadian party** (def. 2).
1870 *Wkly Manitoban* 5 Nov. 2/4: Are we going to have a French party and an English party; I say, no. **1952** HOWARD *Strange Empire* 152: The French party, he declared, had indicated willingness to negotiate a settlement with Canada.

French pedlar *Hist.* See **pedlar** (def. 1a).
1772 (1908) COCKING *Journal* 101: . . . in the afternoon passed by an old Trading house, belonging to the French pedlars before the conquest of Quebec. . . .
1960 *Press* Dec. 13: The defeat of France in America did not mean the end of the "French Pedlars," as they were disdainfully called by the British Company.

French pony *Hist.* See **Canadian horse.**
1871 *Niagara News* 9 Aug. 1/2: In those days the land carriage between Quebec and Montreal was only on horse back or by Calashe drawn by compact French Ponies with Jean Baptiste on the box, with pipe, as driver. **1913** PARKER *Money Master* 33: . . . Jean Jacques worked "like a little French pony," as they say in Canada of every man with the courage to do hard things in him. . . .

French régime *Hist.* the pre-British period in Canada; the period in New France before 1759.
1945 CALVIN *Saga of the St.Lawrence* 4: There had been little export of timber from the St. Lawrence under the French régime. **1966** *Saturday Night* Apr. 27/2: Once Quebec fell it seems that everyone forgot about the gay, coquettish, dance-mad creatures remarked on by every traveller to Quebec during the French regime.

French shoe *Hist.* See **Canadian shoe.**
1948 *Beaver* June 21/2: The simple voyageur Leger lost only . . . a pair of French shoes, and a cotton shirt.

French shore 1 that part of the Newfoundland coast, since 1783 from Cape St. John northward on the east and the entire west coast down to Cape Ray, where by the Treaty of Utrecht in 1713 the French were granted fishery and shore-drying rights, an arrangement that lasted until 1904. See also **French coast, Petit Nord,** and **Treaty Shore.**
[**1793** REEVES *Hist.Nfld* 53: Placentia, and all the parts occupied by the French, were now ceded to the king of Great Britain, in full sovereignty; the French retaining nothing more than a licence to come and go during the fishing season.] **1806** (1956) FAY *Life and Labour* 134: These go sealing in March: then to the N/E of the Island on the French shore. **1907** MILLAIS *Newfoundland* 57: Up there along the French shore the youngsters is born web-footed, and the old folk watch the ebb-tide. **1963** MORTON *Kingdom of Canada* 412: The Anglo-French colonial settlement in 1904 ended the regime of the "French Shore" in Newfoundland.

2 *N.S.* that part of the coast of the Bay of Fundy lying between Yarmouth and Digby, inhabited almost entirely by Acadian French.

1899 *Yarmouth Herald* 13 July 1/4: "Almost the whole French shore of Digby county," he told the Herald, "is a small edition of St. Pierre." **1938** GIBBON *Cdn Mosaic* 54: This was done, and eventually six thousand removed, but gradually a considerable number returned to take the oath of allegiance, and their descendants may be found today along what is known as the 'French shore' between Digby and Yarmouth.

French willow See **fireweed**.

1823 HALIBURTON *General Descr. N.S.* 37: Plants [include] ... French willow [*Epilobium angustifolium*]. ...
1868 *Cdn Naturalist* III 408: Pre-eminent among these is the specie of Epilobium, known in Nova Scotia as the fire-weed or French willow.

Frenchy *n*. See **Frenchie**.

fresh fisherman *Maritimes* a fishing vessel that brings a catch of fish back fresh, rather than salted, from the Grand Banks, *q.v.*

1961 *Atlantic Advocate* Jan. 55: A group of Halifax and Lunenburg men realized that the problem was to produce a salt banker with a cargo-carrying capacity combined with the speed of a fresh fisherman.

fresh-water seal See **harbo(u)r seal**.

[1828 (1963) DAVIES *Northern Quebec* 84: Saw two or three seals. N.B. These are fresh water seals and their skins of fine quality. ...] **1922** FLAHERTY *Eskimo Friends* 19: "And here . . . is where he caught the rare fresh-water seal and made his salmon kills. 'Tis a lake, sir," said Miller. ... **1939** *Beaver* June 48/1: Here [Lower Seal Lake] the Indians said that we might find the freshwater seal, the main objective of our inland trip.

Frog *n. Slang, Derog.* See **French Canadian** (def. 1).

1966 *Globe and Mail* (Toronto) 14 Apr. 23/8: "I hope the Canadians [sic] or Frogs as you call them, beat the hell out of your Hogtown heroes." *Ibid.* 19 Apr. 6/6: ... their [French Canadians'] waspish counterparts in Quebec always refer to "pea-soupers" or "Joes." The word "Frog" in that connection went out of fashion 50 years ago.

frog *v*. push a canoe through shallow water while wading behind or beside it.

1952 *Beaver* Dec. 33/1: For a whole day long, I poled, lined and "frogged" the outfit up the river, shoving the canoe and load over a huge cottonwood ... portaging the outfit up a sandbar in the middle of the stream at a point where dangerous driftpiles lined both banks. Luckily it was warm, for "frogging," in Finlay River parlance, means wading the canoe upstream. **1966** PATTERSON *Trail* 45: They were travelling against the latter end of the flood by the old-time methods of pole, line and "frogging"—that is, wading upstream and lugging the canoe by hand up the riffles.

frogeater† *n. Slang, Derog.* See **French Canadian** (def. 1).

1923 (1929) SCOTT *Witching of Elspie* 98: "The like o' you in league with that frogeater—to steal the good tea-pails, and then to lie about it!" **1954** CONSTANTIN-WEYER *Half-Breed* 40: ... They frightened the Frenchmen, and so we won the battle of the Alma for the frogeaters, with nothing but our bayonets.

frog-eating *adj. Slang, Derog.* See **French-Canadian** (def. 1).

1903 RICHARDSON *Colin* 88: But Goarden ... contented himself ... with talking about what he would have done with that "frog-eatin' furriner". ...
1943 SWANSON *Lumberjack* 38: "Buck de tree into logs wi' de beeg bucking-saw, / You frog-eating felloe from Eas' Canadaw!"

Froggie *n. Slang, Derog.* See **French Canadian** (def. 1).

1966 *Globe and Mail* (Toronto) 19 Apr. 6/6: Our only hope may lie with our Froggies whose strength is drawn from their unqualified pride in their side.

frog run in sugaring-off operations, the second run of sap in the maple trees, inferior to the first or "robin run" for making sap or sugar.

1923 WILLIAMS *Spinning Wheels* 83: Syrup and sugar made from the first or "robin run" are superior to that found in either of the succeeding runs, known respectively as the "frog" and "bud."

frolic† *n*. See **bee**. See also **milling frolic**.

1822 (1960) MCCULLOCH *Stepsure Letters* 67: But a little consideration showed me that the profit of a frolic would be dearly purchased. ... a number attend principally for amusement. **1827** *Gore Gaz.* (Ancaster, U.C.) 11 Aug. 94/2: The parties, it appeared, had been out together on a "Frolic" or "Bee" and on their return toward home in the evening, in a state of intoxication, the Prisoner beat his wife, first with a Rail, and afterwards with a Switch. **1952** BUCKLER *Mountain and Valley* 50: "Better ask her how she's off for wood," he said. "Maybe we would get her up a frolic." **1964** GUILLET *Pioneer Days* 120: All bees provided entertainment and social intercourse as well as hard work. On that account they were usually called "frolics" in New Brunswick and the United States.

frolicker *n. Obs.* a person taking part in a frolic or bee, *q.v.*

1845 BEAVAN *Life in Backwoods N.B.* 43: Again we meet the frolickers returning rather earlier than is usual on such occasions. ...

front or **Front, the** *n*. **1 a.** *Ont.* the settled land along the shores of Lake Ontario and, sometimes, Lake Erie.

☛ *The "front" along the Lake Ontario shore expanded inland with advancing settlement, bringing about the extended meanings below.*

1799 SMYTH *Topogr. Descr. U.C.* 6: Lancaster ... extends nine miles, which is the ordinary size of all townships, and extending back 12 miles from the front. **1835** (1926) LANGTON *Early U.C.* 140: Even those who are only five or six miles from Peterborough call themselves backwoodsmen and Peterborough itself the great Metropolis is reckoned amongst semibarbarous regions by the dwellers in the front. **1902** CONNOR *Glengarry* 69: ... the Front, in all matters pertaining to culture and fashion thought itself quite superior to the more backwoods country of the Twentieth. **1953** LOWER *Voyages* 7: All the way along the Front, as the shores and the lower lakes were termed, settlement worked back into the bush. ... **1964** GUILLET *Pioneer Days* 84: Many an early settler hired out as a chopper for a farmer along "the front", or worked at a saw-mill. ...

b. the transcontinental railway and the communities along and south of it, the farthest advance of civilization for many years.

1913 (1917) CURRAN & CALKINS *Northland* 301: On the fourteenth of December, a prospector, who had been working in the vicinity of Rupert House, arrived in Moose Factory with his partner, a guide, and a dog team, en route for the "front." **1931** GREY OWL *Last Frontier* 21: I remember being of a party where one of the guides was asked how he could go such long periods without news from the "front," as the railroad is called.

c. the settled, civilized part of the country. See also **frontier** (def. 3).

1913 JOHNSON *Shagganappi* 113: "Cariboo gold," his father had called it, and said that it was sent down in numberless bags to "the front," and the stage brought it. **1933** ROLYAT *Wilderness Walls* 243: Few books were well read and wherever possible sons and daughters were sent to College either abroad or "at the front."

2 *Obs.* See **front concession**.

1786 (1905) *Ont.Bur.Arch.Rep.* III 376: In the Townships surveyed on River La Fenche I found twenty eight Families settled in front, some with very considerable Improvements. **1829** MACTAGGART *Three Years* II 283: The townships are farther divided into *concessions*, by lines running parallel to the river, lake, or settled township, which is called the *front*. **1834** (1926) LANGTON *Early U.C.* 80: The land after all was not to be had, but McCall determined to buy the front and be contented with the remainder of his land behind at some distance.

3 *Nfld* See quotes. See also **ice,** *n.* (def. 1).

1933 GREEN *Wooden Walls* 9: . . . on the "Front"—as the Seal Fishery on the east coast of Newfoundland is termed (in contradistinction to that of the "Gulf," which is the smaller west-coast Seal Fishery). . . . **1935** *Beaver* June 62/3: All steamers with the exception of the *Ranger* sailed for the "front" of the island, while the latter is prosecuting the hunt in the Gulf of St. Lawrence. **1956** FAY *Life and Labour* 60: The "Front," as the ice-hunters call the stretch of sea between Funk Island . . . and the Straits. For this Front is the whelping ground, on which the babes will be born and where the ice-hunters will go after them—babes and grown-ups—with batt and gaff, hitting them on the head and dragging them to a "pan" or store-pile on the ice. **1966** *Globe and Mail* (Toronto) 9 Mar. 3/7: No quota on the number of pelts taken is imposed on the Front, and the hunters may kill adults, something not allowed in the Gulf at this time of year.

4 in eastern Ontario, the part of a township fronting on the St. Lawrence River and having a separate council.

1966 *Kingston Whig-Standard* (Ont.) 3 Jan. 6/2: The Front of Escott was given the approval to take possession of Hill Island by the Ontario Municipal Board in December, 1964. The Front of Leeds and Landsdowne protested and took back the island in July of last year.

frontage *n. Obs.* See **front concession**.

1834 (1926) LANGTON *Early U.C.* 77: . . . but it would seem that in this operation Fortune contrived to get one eye from under the bandage, for the frontages are generally the lots first drawn.

front concession the block or range of lots laid out along the river, lake, or base line marking the beginning of a township; also, the line of this boundary. See also **concession** (def. 2), **front** (def. 2) and **frontage.**

1791 (1905) *Ont.Bur.Arch.Rep.* III 125: The Settlers on the front Concessions would find the Lots from the Surveyor's numbers, and those on the Second and

others, might readily measure them off from the sideline. . . . **1807** *Cdn Courant* (Montreal) 1 June 1/1: [Such] is already the case with that part of the proposed road which is already made in the front concession of St. Armand from the North to the South boundary, for which there is a Process verbal existing. **1834** *Reformer* (Cobourg, U.C.) 16 Dec. 3/5: [For sale] At the upset price of 25s currency, per acre. Front concession, numbers 13, 14. . . . **1946** HARKNESS *Dundas and Glengarry* 560: Most of these trees would be in the front concessions of Matilda, Williamsburg and Osnabruck.

frontier† *n.* **1** *Obs.* the Canada-United States border.

1766 *Quebec Gaz.* 1 Dec. 1/1: The Frontier Counties, all along the continent, having been frequently ravaged by the enemy, and greatly impoverished, are able to pay very little tax. **1811** *U.C.Gaz.* (York [Toronto]) 17 Aug. 3/1: The taking [of] a prisoner has alarmed the frontier extremely, as it is a sure indication of war.

2 the thinly populated regions forming the border between the settled and unsettled parts of the country; a region of pioneer settlement beyond the centres of population.

1838 *Western Herald* (Sandwich [Windsor], U.C.) 24 Apr. 78: Our frontier towns, occupying positions on the banks of navigable rivers and lakes, are in a state of utter stagnation. **1841** MCLEOD *Upper Canada* 30: The legislature, in place of encouraging settlers, by expending the public moneys, on opening roads and lines of communication between the newly surveyed townships and the old frontier settlements, sought only plausible pretensions, to apply them to their own selfish purposes. **1885** HAIGHT *Country Life* 71: An isolated community like that which stretched along the frontier of our Province, cut off from the older and more advanced stages of society . . . could not be expected to keep up with the march of either social or intellectual improvement. **1940** MACCORMAC *Canada* 200: . . . Canada, unlike the United States, still has a frontier. **1960** *Weekend Mag.* 2 Apr. 18/2: These two frontier towns were separated by 170 miles of muskeg. . . .

3 *Rare* See **front** (def. 1c).

1862 (1888) MCDOUGALL *G.M.McDougall* 138: Since that date we have had no communication with the frontier world and now expect none until January. **1907** HUNTER *Cdn Wilds* 77: Prior to 1865, furs at inland posts were made up in packs of ninety pounds for transport to the frontier. . . .

Frontier College an educational institution, founded in 1899, which, through correspondence courses and field teachers, provides educational opportunities for workers in frontier lumber and mining camps.

1958 *Globe and Mail* (Toronto) 15 Sep. 8/5: One of the most interesting and constructive educational enterprises in Canada . . . is the Frontier College. **1964** *Calgary Herald* 5 Aug. 54/2: By day the teacher swings pick and shovel for the same pay as other laborers. But in the evening he becomes an instructor for Frontier College, one of 90 students sent out for the summer to work and teach across the country. **1966** *Martlet* 17 Feb. 6/2: Recruiting will take place for the Frontier College on Tuesday, February 22.

frontier pants dress pants of high quality material modelled after tightly fitting levis or jeans.

1955 HOBSON *Nothing Too Good* 102: He wore an

expensive 3X beaver Stetson, frontier pants, custom-built riding boots and homemade, beaded moosehide jacket.

frontiersman† *n. Hist.* a person who lives on the frontier (def. 2), especially one who is knowledgeable in its ways. Also spelled *frontierman*.

1882 *Edmonton Bull.* 3 June 4/2: If this boundary manipulator, claim-staker, smudge verifyer, sproutee, frontiersman thirteen years out has by the success of his artifices deluded himself to the zenith of consequentiality, he must not count on a quiet walk in over my shanty. **1960** RAMSAY *Barkerville* 5: In 1862, Richard Willoughby, an experienced frontierman, found the Lowhee, which he named after a secret society formed by the miners in 1858 at Yale. **1963** STANLEY *Louis Riel* 242: In the words of the frontiersman, the half-breed was "the meanest creature that walks."

front lot *Hist.* a lot in a front concession, *q.v.*
1835 *Dundas Wkly Post* 1 Dec. 3: [For sale] the Front Lots reserved from the last sale, in the Front Concession of the tract of land adjoining the Townships of Eldon and Fenelon, north of the Balsam Lake. **1841** WARD *River St.John* 23: The front lots are generally settled on both sides; there is however much ungranted land in the rear.

front road the road fronting the first concession of a township; the first concession road of a township. See also **front** (def. 1a).
1822 GOURLAY *Upper Canada* I 122: The allowance for the front road was generally 60 feet, and for the other Concession roads 40 feet. **1952** PUTNAM *Cdn Regions* 152: Each lot is divided on the cadaster as a long strip one mile deep and 600–700 feet wide on the front road.

Front Road *Ont.* the road (now Highway 2) running along the north shore of Lake Ontario and the St. Lawrence River. Cp. **front** (def. 1a).
1965 *Globe and Mail* (Toronto) 15 Oct. 7/2: The Front Road, as some local residents call it, [joins] the string of villages along Highway 2 between Trenton and Coburg.... **1966** *Kingston Whig-Standard* (Ont.) 3 Jan. 13/6: A Kingston couple escaped uninjured early in the New Year when their car skidded off the Front road into Lake Ontario.

front stoop a veranda, usually roofed and often equipped with chairs, a couch, etc. See also **stoop** (def. 1).
1887 *Grip* (Toronto) 4 June 5/1: Trees should be ... prohibited within 500 yards of the front stoop, and a potatoe patch should occupy the place of the lawn. **1897** DURAND *Reminiscences* 30: A front stoop looking east fronted the house.

front township *Hist.* one of the townships along the front (def. 1a).
1822 *Scribbler* (Montreal) 4 July 15: The subscriber offers for sale SEVERAL THOUSAND ACRES OF LAND situated in well-settled front townships, in lots to suit purchasers. **1955** CRAIG *Early Travellers* 202: It was often remarked that the society in this backwoods region, and in some others like it in the province, had a tone not to be found in the longer settled "front" townships.

front train in railway building, the first train to pass over newly laid track, carrying materials for further construction.
1923 (1926) DICKIE *Cdn West* 296: On August 11, 1883, the "front" train reached the "eleventh siding," or what is known to-day as the city of Calgary.... the front train

was the construction train, the train that never went back. **1962** DICKIE *Great Golden Plain* 223: As soon as the track was down, the "front train" inched its way along the new-laid rails, carrying the materials for another mile of track—ten cars of ties, six cars of rails, two cars of bridge material, two cars of telegraph line material, two sleeping cars with four tiers of berths, and several cook cars, the whole hauled by two engines.

frost barrel *West* a barrel kept outside in winter and used for storing meat and other perishable food.
1934 BETTANY *Valley of Lost Gold* 16: "I'll stoke up!" announced Lacey shortly, going over to the small cookstove. "See if you can find some grub—there's likely a frost barrel outside." *Ibid.* 76: "I've put a jackrabbit in the frost barrel outside, and it's going to bliz, May: it's going to snow like hell!"

frost boil a place in a paved road where the pavement has heaved as a result of the expansion of trapped moisture frozen during the cold weather.
1955 *Flin Flon Dly Miner* (Man.) 16 Apr. 6/5: The worst outbreak of "frost boils" in history was reported today on Manitoba highways.... **1959** *Ottawa Citizen* 23 Dec. 7/8: More layers of pavement will be laid in the spring after expected frost boils are repaired. **1966** *Sun* (Vancouver) June 6 27/1: We drove around the new town of Fort Fraser ... the car clawing its way through the frost boils of the new streets.

frost dry *Fur Trade* cure (animal skins) by exposing them to frost.
1941 *Beaver* Sep. 37/2: Frost Dried—Newly netted snowshoes, babiche, otter skins, etc., were hung in the cold frosty air in order to whiten and improve their appearance. **1948** *Ibid.* 42: Most of the beaver pelts are frost dried; that is, they are stretched and placed outside to freeze, then brought in to be scraped, washed and dried a little. This process is repeated until the pelt is perfectly dry and the leather is very light in colour. **1959** BODSWORTH *Strange One* 110: ... she must learn to paddle, to frost-dry the beaver pelts, to snare rabbits....

frosted lung *North* frozen lung tissue resulting from breathing air at very low temperatures. See also **frost one's lungs.**
1919 CURWOOD *River's End* 5: "... I've seen this frosted lung business a dozen times.... I've got two sure days ahead of me, possibly a third...." *Ibid.* 16: "... tell McDowell how you got your man and how he died up here with a frosted lung...."

frost fish *Maritimes* See **tommy-cod.**
1861 SUTHERLAND *Geography P.E.I.* 68: The Frost Fish, or Tom Cod ... may be caught in many parts of the Island.... It attains its name from the time of year in which it makes its appearance in creeks—generally after the *frost* has set in in the month of December. **1866** KING *Sportsman in Can.* 315: The Tom-cod, sometimes called also the Frost-fish. .. the Petite Morue Fraiche, Tacaud, and Gode Mollet of the French-Canadians, is peculiar I believe to North America. **1945** RICHARDSON *We Keep a Light* 47: The morning was silky calm, and we thought we would try our hand at catching a few small fish, cunners or frost fish, so we went out in the skiff with our lines.

frost leak condensation and freezing of moisture

on the inside of a wall, caused by the penetration of intensely cold air.
1949 *Report of DME Test Team* II 2: The Wannegan showed a number of "frost leaks" which manifested themselves at night as large patches of condensation and frost, which, when the fire was started next morning, proceeded to drip over everything below.

frost one's (or the) lungs See **frosted lung.**
1965 WILSON *No Man Stands Alone* 34: . . . the thermometer . . . registered 68° below zero. . . . Old timers say the horses "frost their lungs" if you drive them when the weather is too cold.

frost smoke† See 1958 quote.
1748 ELLIS *Hudson's Bay* 172: In the Winter, there arises a very thick Vapour, commonly called Frost Smoak; this Vapour Freezing is driven by the Wind in the Form we see it. **1851** OSBORN *Arctic Jnl* 276: A dark, misty-looking cloud which hung over it (technically termed frost-smoke) was indicative of much open water in that direction. **1958** *Manice* 7: Frost Smoke—(*Arctic Sea Smoke, Sea Smoke, Water Smoke*). A thick fog rising from the sea surface when relatively warm water is exposed to an air temperature much below freezing. Frost smoke frequently appears over newly-formed cracks and leads.

Frozen North the Arctic regions.
1958 *Edmonton Jnl* 24 June 3 9/8: . . . the Arctic Islands are traditionally considered the real "Frozen North". . . .

Frozen Ocean the Arctic Ocean.
1801 (1927) MACKENZIE *Voyages* 488: The climate . . . is extreme on the coast of Hudson's Bay, and proceeds from its immediate exposure to the north-west winds that blow off the Frozen Ocean. **1959** *News of the North* 19 July 2/5: At the same time (1864–1878) Father Petitot could be found anywhere between Great Bear Lake and the Frozen Ocean, the first European to live among the Eskimos alone and unarmed.

fruit pemmican See **berry pemmican.**
1923 STRINGER *Empty Hands* 147: . . . he wanted large crocks . . . for their fruit-pemmican . . . for their stores of wild rice and starch-bulbs . . .

fruit ranch† *Esp.B.C.* a fruit farm; a commercial orchard. See also **ranch¹**, *n.* (def. 2c).
1911 SMITH *Is It Just?* 48: "Yes, you are quite right about that, especially when a person has to be man and woman both on a fruit-ranch. . . ." **1953** LOWER *Voyages* 146: The Okanagan with its pleasant little towns and its fruit ranches—everything is a ranch in B.C. . . . constitutes a good big stretch of settled countryside.

fruit rancher *B.C.* the owner or operator of a fruit ranch, *q.v.*
1911 SMITH *Is It Just?* 72: ". . . I am a fruit rancher, or rather, I am trying to be one!" **1966** *B.C. Digest* June 34/2: . . . I am in agreement with . . . your contention that there are a lot more whitetail around this area [South Okanagan] than most hunters (or fruit ranchers) realize.

frying-pan bread *Maritimes* See **bannock.**
1945 MOORE *Castle Buck* 10: With the remains of the frying-pan bread he made a sandwich with some strips

of dried venison and fried pork.

fuel sloop *North* a unit of a cat-train, *q.v.*, for carrying reserve fuel such as diesel oil or gasoline.
1958 WATTERS *B.C.Cent.Anthol.* 421: First was the "Meal Train" with the kitchen, the diner, the utility, and three sleepers. In the other group were the office, two sleepers, the workshop, and the fuel sloop.

fuke [fjuk] *n.* [? var. of F *fusil* gun, musket < Ital. < L *focus*] *Fur Trade, Hist.* a light flintlock musket important as trading goods in the early fur trade. Cp. **Indian gun** and **Northwest gun**
1933 HIGINBOTHAM *When the West Was Young* 232: The South Piegans were well armed with repeating rifles. . . while the Crees and Assiniboines had had only old muskets, Hudson's Bay "fukes" and bows and arrows to depend on. **1955** SHARP *Whoop-up Country*: A gun, or fuke in Hudson's Bay trading, might [c1865] be worth fifteen skins while a blanket would fetch ten. **1956** *Alta Hist.Qtly* Spring 5: . . . the North West gun and the earlier Hudson's Bay fuke or fusil were essentially the same weapon.

fullblood† *n.* an Indian of unmixed blood.
1900 LONDON *Son of Wolf* 195: "You see, when the 'breeds' rose under Riel the full-bloods kept the peace, and they've not lost much love for one another since." **1953** CUSHMAN *Stay Away Joe* 19: Connie Shortgun, a slatternly fullblood . . . got out and started for the house.

full-blooded† *adj.* of Indians, of unmixed blood.
1832 LUNDY *Diary* 12: He is a full-blooded Indian, well-educated, and as the white people say, "very much of the gentleman." **1958** HEALEY *Alert Bay* 29: These two good citizens were not full-blooded Indians, but they always lived among them.

fungy ['fʌndʒi] *n.* [origin unknown] *N.S.* a kind of deep blueberry pie. Cp. **grunt.** Also spelled *fungee.*
1952 BUCKLER *Mountain and Valley* 48: They never made blueberries into a fungy, as Mrs. Canaan did—they just stewed them. **1953** *Dutch Oven* 28: Apparently the same dish (blueberry grunt] is called Fungy, Fungee . . . in Yarmouth County. It is pronounced Fun'jee.

funny Canadian *Jocular* in Canadian football, an American player classed as a Canadian for football purposes after playing in Canada for five years. Cp. **import.**
1964 *Winnipeg Free Press* 19 June 36/3: . . . the Canadian Football League's nine teams choose sides in the battle over "funny Canadians."

funny-money *adj. Slang* having to do with the Social Credit principles of free credit and monetary reform, especially with the issue of scrip in Alberta.
1958 *Time* (Cdn ed.) 15 Sep. 16/3: After 21 years on the hustings, Solon Earl Low, 58, provincial treasurer in Alberta's first Social Credit government, later leader (after 1944) of the "funny-money" party's national representation in Parliament, returned to Raymond (pop. 3,000) High School, where he taught from 1926 to 1934. **1963** *Globe and Mail* (Toronto) 28 Feb. 1/7: ". . . . the election in 1961 of joint chairmen of the party which enabled Robert Thompson to maintain the conservative face of the party in nine provinces and permitted Real Caouette to advocate the Aberhart free credit or funny-money policies . . . in Quebec," Mr. Kierans said.

fur† *n.* **1** (used attributively) **a.** denoting regions where fur-bearing animals are hunted commercially.

1809 JOHNSTON *Lake Superior* 147: The express words of the treaty are . . . drawn with a degree of absurdity and ignorance hardly to be conceived, and which has wantonly given away several thousand leagues of the richest fur country to which the Americans had no more right than they had to the Province of Bengal.
1879 ROBINSON *Great Fur Land* 40n: The term "half-breed" is applied indiscriminately in the Fur Land to all persons having Indian blood in their veins, and bears no especial reference to quantity. **1896** RUSSELL *Far North* 40: All is included in the "Northern Department" of the Hudson's Bay Company, which has subdivided it into some half dozen fur districts. **1933** MERRICK *True North* 22: Picking out good fur ground is an art.
1949 MacGREGOR *Blankets and Beads* 82: Not only did the beaver abound in the fur forest of the Saskatchewan, but the farther north and west the traders went, the better the quality of the fur became. **1960** *Press* Dec. 14: If farmers were to invade the Fur Country, the Bay was determined that any loss must be borne by their rivals.

b. denoting persons or groups occupied in the fur trade.

1820 (1823) FRANKLIN *Journey* 82: We shall merely add a few remarks on the manner in which the trade is conducted at the different inland posts of the Fur Companies. **1907** HUNTER *Cdn Wilds* 207: Opposition became keen and fur buyers from Quebec, Boston, New York and Paris, came to the different places of resort of the Indians, bidding up raw furs to prices out of all reason. **1934** GODSELL *Arctic Trader* 309: The Fur Lords no longer rule the Red Men. . . . **1949** ROBERTS *Mackenzie* 107: The first attack was driven off but the furmen put undefended houses in the settlement to the torch. **1966** *Canadian* 29 Jan. 13/1: . . . Grant ruled the métis when the Red River Valley was a bloody battleground for competing fur companies and the métis hunting rights were being threatened.

2 fur-bearing animals or their pelts.

1928 ROSE *Stump Farm* 128: As the rabbits get too thick, lack of feed or cold gives them a contagious sickness and soon all are dead. The fur leaves, that fed on them. **1933** MERRICK *True North* 88: Some believe it is all right to skin and scrape and spread fur on Sundays, but Harvey spoiled his luck one year that way. **1951** ANGIER *At Home* 81: Fur doesn't move any more than necessary in weather like this, anyway. . . .

fur *v. Nfld* hunt fur-bearing animals; run a trapline. See also **furring**.

[**1799** *Labrador & Banks Pilot* fr: . . . it is not a mile broad there, as I was informed by planters at Bonaventure, who usually go a furring there in the winter.] **1912** POCOCK *Man in the Open* 5: You see he worked the bones through his hide, furring all winter and fishing summers, and what he earned he'd got in truck from the company. **1933** MERRICK *True North* 71: He used to fur the path that cuts in over the hills from Grand Lake, near Cotter's Point. . . .

fur board *Fur Trade* a thin board inserted in a cased skin to hold its shape till dry. See also **fur stretcher**.

1771 (1792) CARTWRIGHT *Journal* I 106: Charles and I were engaged all day in altering the furboards, and making new ones after the Canadian form. **1933** MERRICK *True North* 185: Since arriving, Harvey has built the new cabin, made a catamaran sledge, a great long toboggan, and a whole set of new fur boards. . . .

fur book *Fur Trade, Hist.* a ledger for keeping a record of furs acquired by trade.

1913 COWIE *Adventurers* 225: At the head of each column in the fur book the names of each kind of skin and whether large or small, prime or common, were written alphabetically across the double page, beginning with badgers and ending with wolves.

fur brigade *Fur Trade, Hist.* a brigade, *q.v.*, of canoes, York boats, Red River carts, etc. transporting furs from the interior posts.

1862 MAYNE *Four Years in B.C.* 122: . . . a message [was] received from the officer in charge of the Fur Brigade, which was expected to arrive daily. **1959** *Cdn Geog.Jnl* Mar. 87/1: Fifty years before Confederation the Columbia River . . . was a vital link in the annual route of the fur brigade which brought the pelts from the West to Montreal.

fur canoe *Fur Trade* a large canoe used for transporting furs. See also **fur freighter**.

1908 LAUT *Conquest N.W.* I 135: The brigades of fur canoes can yet be seen at remote posts like Abbittibbi. **1956** KEMP *Northern Trader* 191: For years it had been the practice of the men of the fur canoe to leave their own rifles at home and take with them an old ·44-40 carbine that was kept at the post.

fur debt See **debt** (def. 1).

1934 GODSELL *Arctic Trader* 101: . . . I faced half a thousand hungry Indians who had been waiting for their fur debts.

fur farm 1 an establishment where certain fur-bearing animals, such as mink and fox, are bred and raised for their pelts, usually in pens or protected runs. See also **fur ranch** and **ranch**[1], *n.* (def. 2a).

1923 WALDO *Down Mackenzie* 133: Been a-wonderin' if a fur-farm would pay better on a island in Slave Lake or in Athabasca. **1928** FREEMAN *Nearing North* 16: The Company can advise you about plans for everything from starting a fur farm on Lake Athabaska to a four-year expedition to the Arctic. **1963** SYMONS *Many Trails* 43: For the plan was to transform the pony carcasses into concentrated meal for sale to the fur farms. . . .

2 See **fur preserve** (def. 2).

1937 *Beaver* June 10/1: Next in importance as a conservation measure comes the Charlton Island beaver sanctuary, which, although revived in 1934, was nevertheless the first fur farm in Canada, having been established by the Hudson's Bay Company in the year 1851.

fur farmer a person engaged in operating a fur farm (def. 1).

1953 *Fur Trade Jnl* Mar. 12/1: It is rather interesting sometimes to know how fur farmers get started in the business, so I will give my experience.

fur-farming *n.* **1** the operating of a fur farm (def. 1). See also **fur ranching**.

1934 GODSELL *Arctic Trader* 198: Fur farming will undoubtedly gradually take the place of primitive trapping and trading. **1964** JENNESS *Eskimo Admin.* II 15: Fur-farming was still in its infancy [c1900]. . . .

2 See quote. See also **fur farm** (def. 2).

1958 HAWTHORN *Indians of B.C.* 105: Such a

programme involves such measures as ... "fur-farming" in the full sense of the word, that is flooding or draining areas as the case may be, and transplanting beaver and muskrat to areas of plentiful food supply so as to increase the fur-bearing animal population. ...

fur fort See **fort.**
1873 (1904) BUTLER *Wild North Land* ix: Written by camp fire, or in cañon, or in the little log-house of a northern fur fort, when dogs and men rested for a day or two in the long icy run, that narrative will be found, I fear, to bear many indications of the rough scenes 'mid which it has been penned. **1938** GODSELL *Red Hunters* 64: [The Indians] hunted and trapped as their forefathers had done before them; bartering the pelts of beaver, lynx and silver fox at the fur forts from Labrador to the Pacific.

fur freighter See **fur canoe.**
1908 LAUT *Conquest N.W.* II 130: The old fur freighters wallowed in the waves like water-logged tubs, straining to the pounding seas as if the timbers would part, sails flapping to the wind tattered and rotten as the ensigns of pirates.

fur highway *Fur Trade, Hist.* the route by which furs from the inland posts were transported to ports for shipment to markets abroad.
1946 *Beaver* Dec. 15/1: ... only the lower part of the valley from the Big Bend down became a part of the fur highway.

fur house See **fur-loft.**
1900 WILLSON *Great Fur Co.* 664: Ordinarily, a Company's factory includes a store or trading-house, a fur house, a factor's house, a clerk's house, the canoe-house, and the stable, with a barn.

fur hunter a person who hunts or traps fur-bearing animals. See also **furrier** (def. 1).
1842 *Trans.Lit.& Hist.Soc.Que.* IV 129: They are not fur hunters, nor is the mode of life they lead favourable to it. **1921** HEMING *Drama of Forests* 145: Years ago many wolves were destroyed with poison, but nowadays it has gone out of use—that is, among the fur-hunters of the forest.

fur-hunting *n.* the trapping of fur-bearing animals for sale of their pelts. See also **furring.**
1819 ANSPACH *Hist.Nfld* 378: This fur-hunting employs a great number of persons, not only within the limits of the Hudson's Bay Company, but also on the coast of Labrador and in the northern parts of Newfoundland. **1862** *Nor' Wester* (R.R.S.) 11 Sep. 2/3: The Company's policy will drive scores if not hundreds into the fur business who would not otherwise have gone, and who, while they could make a tolerable living here, would never have dreamt of going out a fur-hunting.

fur-loft *n. Fur Trade* that part of a trading post where furs are stored, folded, and baled for shipment. See also **fur house** and **fur shed.**
1921 HEMING *Drama of Forests* 172: In the morning a miserable north-easter was blowing a heavy fall of snow over the country, and the Factor offered to show me the fur-loft where the clerk and a few half-breed men-servants were folding and packing furs. **1936** STRINGER *Wife-Traders* 8: Beside it was a storage-shed and fur-loft, flanked by a smokehouse and a net-reel and a pyramid of spindly firewood cut into stove-lengths.

fur mould *Fur Trade* a device used for shaping folded furs into 90-pound packs during pressing. See also **mould.** Cp. **fur press.**
1874 (1956) ROSS *Athabasca* 15: ... the fur mould and pack press at this post are both very bad and not the same size as the presses at the other posts in the District. ...

fur nail a special type of nail used for fixing pelts to a fur stretcher, *q.v.*
1933 MERRICK *True North* 18: ... Fred forgot to get a bit of resin and some paint and fur nails from the Hudson's Bay Company store.

fur pack See **piece** (def. 1).
1908 LAUT *Conquest N.W.* II 90: Up on Canoe River, Thompson and his voyageurs worked feverishly —building canoes, and getting the fur packs ready against spring. **1938** GODSELL *Red Hunters* 54: A fleet of ... North canoes ... conveyed the trading goods into the interior and the fur packs back to Montreal.

fur path 1 See **trapline** (def. 2a).
1921 HEMING *Drama of Forests* 209: The reason the brute is so persistent in following a hunter's fur path is that it usually affords the wolverine an abundance of food. **1933** MERRICK *True North* 140: A fur path is, of course, not a path at all. It is a trap line. ... the "path" is just like the rest of the forest, unless there are blazes.
2 See **trapline** (def. 2b).
1933 MERRICK *True North* 22: A fur path in these parts is handed down from father to son. It consists mainly of a hazily defined territory. ... that land is his to hunt, and no one else's.

fur pedlar *Derog., Obs.* See **fur trader.** Cp. **pedlar** (def. 1).
1858 *Brit.Colonist* (Victoria) 18 Dec. 2/1: Their rulers have been the tools of a company of "fur pedlers," [sic] who have used the country for hunting grounds instead of the purposes of colonization.

fur post a trading establishment of a fur company.
1820 (1823) FRANKLIN *Journey* 116: A considerable quantity of it is also kept for winter use, at most of the fur-posts. **1957** *Beaver* Spring 49: There were several fur posts he had to keep away from until the heat had cooled a bit.

furposter *n. Obs.* See **fur trader.**
1916 BRIDLE *Sons of Can.* 179: Indians, furposters, and railwaymen had gone over the great Canadian West.

fur preserve 1 a region reserved for the hunting and trapping of fur-bearing animals.
1880 GORDON *Mountain and Prairie* 172: During their tenure of the land, it had been the policy of the Company to retain it as a great fur-preserve, and therefore, they kept the outer world as far as possible in ignorance of its resources and capabilities. **1929** (1931) MERK *Fur Trade* xviii: There was material wreckage in the form of exhaustion of fur preserves, the duplication of trading posts and the multiplication of equipment and men. **1953** LEBOURDAIS *Nation of North* 16: The greatest cause for concern, however, lay in the territories under the jurisdiction of the Hudson's Bay Company, and which, in conformity with that company's desire to keep the country a vast fur-preserve, were still almost empty.
2 a large tract in the fur country where fur-bearing animals live in their natural habitat, being trapped in a controlled way under sanctuary conditions. See also **fur farm** (def. 2) and **ranch**[1], *n.* (def. 2b).

1946 *Beaver* June 47/2: Leonard Butler, Ph.D., the Company biologist, has been making a study for some years of fur cycles and the wild life of the fur preserves.

fur press *Fur Trade* a heavy press (of several types) for compressing furs into 90-pound bales. See also **beaver-press** and picture, and **pack press**. Cp. **fur mould.**
1913 COWIE *Adventurers* 277: And then commenced the lively scene of packing the robes and furs in the big lever fur press in the middle of the square. **1938** *Beaver* Sep. 66: Eskimo helpers at Port Harrison pile white foxes into a fur press. **1963** *Herald Mag.* 14 Dec. 1/4: The base for the fur press—used for putting furs into large bales—was also found.

fur ranch See **fur farm** (def. 1).
1957 *Farm News Press* 3 July 1: At the Experimental Fur Ranch, Summerside, P.E.I., it has been found that 45 per cent fish can be used during the mink season. . . .

fur ranching See **fur-farming** (def. 1).
1953 *Fur Trade Jnl* Mar. 8: A report on fur ranching in Canada would not be complete without a few words about the industry in this great expanse of prairie, forest, and lakes we call Saskatchewan. **1966** *Wildlife Rev.* Mar. 21: Early in the 20th century fur ranching took form and has since developed, particularly in respect of mink, into a scientific live-stock operation that today contributes two-thirds of the value of Canadian raw-fur production annually.

furrier *n.* **1** *Esp.Nfld* See **fur hunter.**
1770 (1792) CARTWRIGHT *Journal* I 46: In our return we found two old furriers' tilts, and snow death-falls; which appeared to be of Canadian construction. **1829** MACTAGGART *Three Years* II 31: As yet, she has been viewed only by the eyes of lumberers and furriers, the former with their hatchets, the latter with their guns. **1918** GRENFELL *Labrador Doctor* 59: One day a Northern furrier . . . came to me as a magistrate to insist that a trading company keep its bargain by paying him in cash for a valuable fox skin. **1962** *Cdn Geog.Jnl* Nov. 158: . . . the hostile action . . . may well have been due to Beothuk suspicion of their inveterate foes, the white furriers, several of whom accompanied Buchan as guides.
2 *Obs.* a person engaged in the fur trade.
1789 *Quebec Herald* 10 Aug. 332/2: It is therefore not improbable that the enterprising spirit of our Canadian furriers may penetrate to this coast . . . and add to the comforts and luxuries of Europe, this invaluable fur, which in warmth, beauty, and magnificence, exceeds the richest furs of Siberia. **1860** *Brit.Colonist* (Victoria) 21 Feb. 2/1: The ex-chief factor is characterized as a "Governor in whom the people of British Columbia have never placed confidence,"—as controlled in his public and private course by the interests of the "Furriers,"—and as eminently qualified to "retire from public life."

furriery *n. Nfld, Obs.* See **fur-hunting.**
1770 (1792) CARTWRIGHT *Journal* I 72: The furriers began to build a tilt of boards, which is to be sent to Eyre Island, for the convenience of furriery and shooting.

furring *n. Esp.Nfld* See **fur-hunting.** See also **fur,** *v.*
1778 (1792) CARTWRIGHT *Journal* II 373: I fitted out Joseph for a furring voyage to White-bear River, at which place he is to reside by himself during the winter. **1822** CORMACK *Narr.Nfld* 96: Like the people of St. George's Harbour they are industrious and frugal; the extent of their salmon fishery and furring has already

been noticed. **1907** MILLAIS *Newfoundland* 227: "Furring" was his sole means of livelihood. . . .
1920 GRENFELL & SPALDING *Le Petit Nord* 48: In the winter the northern people move up the bays and go "furring."

furring grounds *Lab.* a region in which fur-bearing animals are numerous and where commercial trapping is carried on.
1933 MERRICK *True North* 15: Soon they will be gone too, bound up the rivers "into the country" to the furring grounds hundreds of miles away.

fur-runner *n. Fur Trade* See **runner**[2].
1921 HEMING *Drama of Forests* 154: They chopped a hole and, after placing the fish in, filled it up with water, which they allowed to freeze, with the tail of a single fish protruding, in order to show the fur-runner what was cached below. **1934** *Beaver* June 13/1: The Indian [c1894] now told Mackenzie that he wanted him to send the "fur runners" to him with supplies in ten weeks' time. . . . **1936** *Cdn Geog.Jnl* XII 30: The freighter and the fur runner found travel possible and profitable in this season as in no other.

fur-running *n.* the occupation of a fur-runner.
1921 HEMING *Drama of Forests* 161: Besides, it would give me a chance to do my own fur-running in winter, and in that way I believe I could double, if not treble, our income.

fur shed See **fur-loft.**
1905 (1954) *B.C.Hist.Qtly* XVIII 152: Then having acted for a spell as clerk to the managing factor at York Factory, I was made superintendent of the fur shed at the latter place.

fur ship a vessel carrying furs, usually from Canada to Europe.
1859 (1890) MCDONALD *Autobiog.Notes* 43: I left Quebec in the "Isaac Todd," fur ship, with a valuable cargo, under convoy with the fall fleet numbering about forty sails, from Bique. **1936** *Beaver* June 52/2: Now the red ensign with its white HBC initialling was hoisted to her mainmast-head and alterations were begun for her new employment as a fur ship.

fur station *Fur Trade, Obs.* a fur post, *q.v.,* especially a small one in a remote district.
1873 (1904) BUTLER *Wild North Land* 90: They came generally from the remote isles or highlands of Scotland, they left home young, and the mind tires when it thinks upon the remoteness of many of their fur stations.

fur stretcher See **stretcher** and picture. See also **fur board.**
1922 *Beaver* July 10/2: Everything an Indian requires in wood is made with this [crooked] knife—canoes, flatsleds, snowshoes, paddles, net floats and fur stretchers. **1954** PATTERSON *Dangerous River* 282: Then I sharpened a knife, hunted up a fur stretcher of the right size and sat down to fix up the marten.

fur trade the business of trading in furs, especially with the Indians and Eskimos.
1743 (1949) ISHAM *Observations* 104: But now their is no method Can be taken to break them from itt, without the Entire Ruing of the small fur trade in these parts. **1760** PICHON *Cape Breton* 4: During the winter the inhabitants of Acadia resorted thither for the sake of the fur-trade with the savages. **1860** *Nor'Wester*

(R.R.S.) 14 Mar. 4/3: As the Company's outfit for the fur-trade has been lost with the Kitty, very little, if any, of their goods in store this winter at York Factory, will be taken to this place. **1962** (1964) INNIS *Fur Trade in Canada* 10: Although of minor importance, the fur trade in the area tributary to the Gulf of St. Lawrence began at an early date.

fur trade commissioner See **commissioner** (def. 1).

fur-trade marriage *Hist.* See **country alliance.**
[**1940** *Beaver* Dec. 10/2: These two had already been married without benefit of clergy in the old fur trade way....] **1942** *B.C.Hist.Qtly* Jan. 20: Others were bound together by the so-called fur-trade marriages, the legal validity of which was upheld in later years by the Supreme Court in Quebec.

fur trader a person engaged in the fur trade, *q.v.* See also **trader** (def. 1).
1815 *Kingston Gaz.* (U.C.) 8 July 1/3: Thirty years ago, these Lakes were navigated only by Indian Canoes, Batteaux, and 2 or 3 small vessels, chiefly employed in conveying goods for the fur traders. **1966** *Cdn Geog.Jnl* Apr. 129/3: The commerce of the fur traders demanded a larger boat than the usual Indian canoes, and for this purpose the 36-foot freighter canoes were constructed.

fur-trading *n.* trading in furs; the fur trade, *q.v.*
1880 GORDON *Mountain and Prairie* 174: This responsibility rests mainly upon the Indian hunters, while Dumas himself attends to fur-trading.
1896 WHITNEY *On Snow-Shoes* 313: This is the island, by-the-way, where in the earliest days of fur-trading the Northwest Company had its headquarters. **1964** JENNESS *Eskimo Admin.* II 10: ... numerous fur-trading posts sprang up along the south-west shore of Hudson Bay....

fur trail 1 See **trapline** (def. 2a).
1921 HEMING *Drama of Forests* 44: As to the Indian mode of dressing meat and skins—more anon, when we are finally settled upon the fur trail. **1938** *Beaver* Sep. 53/2: But death stalked the fur trails in other districts too.
2 a route followed by persons engaged in the fur trade.
1966 *Sun* (Vancouver) 30 May 32A/1: A fur trail led east on the Anderson Creek from near modern-day Boston Bar and connected with the Nicola and Okanagan regions.

fur train *Fur Trade, North* a dog-sled transporting packs of furs.
1921 HEMING *Drama of Forests* 176: The four dogs comprising each of the fur trains hauled three hundred pounds of fur besides the camp outfit and grub for both driver and dogs—in all, about five hundred pounds to the sled. **1938** *Beaver* Sep. 19/1: Travelling to "Steel" with the fur trains! This was the very pinnacle of boyhood aspirations.

fur vote *B.C.* a fund established by the government to aid British Columbia trappers.
1958 HAWTHORN *Indians of B.C.* 195: In trapping, capital aid is supplied from the separate "Fur Vote" in the Branch's annual appropriations.

fusil† *n.* [< F] *Obs.* See **fuke.**

Fyfe *n.* See **Fife wheat.**

Gabby Islander *Slang* See quote.
1939 MONTAGUE *Eskimos* 217: The residents of
Newfoundland are sometimes called by the nickname,
Gabby Islanders.

gable-end *n. Obs.* a summer kitchen, wood-shed,
etc. attached to a house.
1830 MOORSOM *Letters N.S.* 175: A hut formed of rough
logs, or long, straight trunks, placed one upon the
other as they are cut from the forest, has now become
the gable-end, or, (as we should deem it in England),
the "wash house" to a neatly boarded cottage.

gadnipper *n. Obs.* See **bulldog fly.**
1829 MACTAGGART *Three Years* I 186: The *gadnipper,* a
large species of gadfly, is also common, but not so
troublesome as those above described.

gaff [gæf] *n. Sealing, Nfld* See 1883 quote. See also
sealing club.
1883 (1889) WITHROW *Our Own Country* 88: Each of
them carries a bundle of spare clothing over his
shoulder, swinging at the extremity of a pole six or
seven feet in length, which is called a "gaff," and which
serves as bat or a club to strike the seal on the nose
where it is most vulnerable. **1916** DUNCAN *Billy Topsail,
M.D.* 108: . . . Up St. John's way . . . you couldn't
touch tea nor pork nor flour with a ten-foot-sealing
gaff. **1966** *Globe and Mail* (Toronto) 8 Mar. 1/2: The
Minister borrowed a gaff and poked the [seal's]
carcass.

Gagging Bill *Hist.* a bill passed in Upper Canada
in 1819, prohibiting the holding of political
conventions.
1824 *Advocate* (Queenston, U.C.) 8 July 3/1: Though
I were not to speak of the gagging bill, yet a disgrace to
our statute book. **1832** *Liberal* (St.Thomas, U.C.)
8 Nov. 3/4: Were the disgraceful Gagging Bill of 1818—
the appropriation of THREE THOUSAND POUNDS of the
people's money to Governor Gore, in 1816, for the
purpose of buying a service of Plate—in accordance
with the views and wishes of the yeomanry of
Middlesex ? **1893** YEIGH *Ont.Parliament* 39: The
"Gagging Bill" of 1819, as "the Act to prevent certain
meetings within the Province," was called, was
repealed in 1820.

galais *n.* See **galet.**

galet or **galais** *n.* [< Cdn F < F *galet* < OF *gal*
pebble] *Obs.* a rocky place; a gravel bank.
1793 (1933) MACDONELL *Diary* 104: [We] Camped at
Mr Frobisher's Galais about the Dalls. **1800** (1897)
COUES *New Light* I 30: [We] proceeded to Grand Galet,
where we put up for the night. **1801** MACKENZIE *Voyages*
lx: From thence to another galet, or rocky portage is
about two miles.

galette [gə'lɛt] *n.* [< Cdn F < F "pancake"] a
flat, unleavened cake made by baking in a frying
pan or by covering with hot ashes in a fireplace.
See also **bannock, river cake,** and **stove cake.** Also
spelled *gelette.*
1843 (1955) LEFROY *Magnetic North* 69: . . . bread is
unknown but we indulge in a sort of gallette. . . .
1930 ROLYAT *Fort Garry* 100: Madelaine's gelettes
were better than their own bannock though of similar
ingredients exactly. **1963** STANLEY *Louis Riel* 18:
Without doubt Louis shared in the . . . feasts of galettes,
tickameg (whitefish), buffalo steaks and boiled tea. . . .

Galician [gə'lɪʃən] *n.* [< *Galicia*] *Hist.* **1** one of
the many Slavic immigrants, particularly
Ukrainians, coming to Canada from central

Europe in the late 1800's and later. See also
Ruthenian (def. 1). Cp. **Sifton's Sheepskins.**
☞ *The term came to be used in a derogatory sense to
mean any Central European immigrant; it is little used
nowadays except among older people in the West.*
1903 *Eye Opener* (High River, Alta) 25 July 3/3: The
lost tribes of Israel, in the dishevelled shapes of
Galicians and Doukhobors, are getting the south
branch of the C. and E. into splendid condition,
ballasting with gravel and giving it a complete over-
hauling. **1912** (1914) BICKERSTETH *Open Doors* 197: "Say,
Parson, I'm not lousy," said Harry, "but I can't answer
for them darned Galicians [in the bunk] above."
1953 LOWER *Voyages* 17: I once tried to get from a
simple man, his notion of a "bohunk." Were Galicians,
"bohunks"?

2 the language of such people, especially Ukrainian.
See also **Ruthenian** (def. 2).
1909 CONNOR *Foreigner* 77: "He does not understand
Russian," said Paulina. "Speak in Galician."

galley ['gæli] *n.* [origin uncertain; ? ult. < obs.
dial. *galligaskins* leggings] See **Ojibwa snowshoe.**
See also **gillie.**
1743 (1949) ISHAM *Observations* 138: Galley shoes are in
two pieces Narrow at the top and turns up a Little, and
sharpe at the Hee'l. **1775** (1949) GRAHAM *Observations*
312: Their Snow Shoes are like the Gallies described
before only the inside part of the frame is in a streight
line. **1957** *Beaver* Autumn 54/1: The form of these
"galleys" or "gillies" is traditional, but the front and
rear panels are woven of fine twine instead of babiche.

galley-devil *n. Slang* a cook's helper on a whaler.
1909 CAMERON *New North* 287: . . . every one on board
a whaler from captain to galley-devil works on a lay.
The captain gets one-twelfth of the take, the first mate
one twenty-second, the second mate one-thirtieth. . . .

galoot [gə'lut] *n.* [< "silly galoot"; so called
because of its lack of fear] See **Ross's goose.** Cp.
fool hen.
1945 *Beaver* Sep. 17/2: . . . the Ross goose is in some
quarters known as "galoot". . . .

galyette *n.* See **galette.**

gambling stick a small stick used by many
Indian tribes to keep score when gambling. Those
of the Pacific coast were beautifully made and
decorated.
1880 GORDON *Mountain and Prairie* 134: They [divide]
their leisure time between listening to the priest and
rattling their gambling-sticks, for all Indians seem to be
born gamblers.

gambling stone a small stone, often having a
carved design, used by Indians in gambling games
such as bowl and beans, *q.v.*
1893 YOUNG *Indian Wigwams* 106: Since we have become
Christians we have flung all our dice and gambling
stones into the fire. **1943** MILLER *Lone Woodsman* 163:
Then, lower down, the stake threw up pottery shards,
broken bones . . . some gambling stones, and arrow
points of flint. . . .

game guardian See **game warden.**
1884 *Brandon Mail* (Man.) 14 Feb. 3/1: Look out for
the game guardians. **1958** *Edmonton Jnl* 24 June 3 8/4:
The police are game guardians in the N.W.T.

game inspector *Obs.* See **game warden**.
1886 *Indian* (Hagersville, Ont.) 14 Apr. 77/3: It shall be the duty of every such game inspector to institute prosecutions against all persons found infringing the provisions of this Act.

game misconduct (penalty) *Hockey* a penalty which, when imposed, banishes a player from the ice for such time as remains after the infraction. Such a penalty is automatic after three major penalties in one game and carries with it a fifty-dollar fine.
1963 O'BRIEN *Hockey* 55: A third major penalty brings a Game Misconduct Penalty (remainder of the game) plus a $50 fine. **1964** *Globe and Mail* (Toronto) 7 Dec. 24/1: . . . each was given game misconduct penalties and 10 minute misconduct penalties for their fight in the penalty box. . . .

game of the platter See **platter, game of the**.

game preserve or **reserve** a large tract of land and forest set aside by the government for the protection of wildlife. See also **game refuge**.
1915 (1916) *Commission of Conservation* 121: . . . the Forestry Branch of the Dept. of the Interior . . . has delineated four proposed game preserves. . . . **1955** GOWLAND *Smoke* 70: This was, in fact, the provincial boundary, being used only by hunting parties in the late summer and autumn, as there was no game reserve in that part of B.C. **1965** *Globe and Mail* (Toronto) 12 Jan. 7/1: Other economic use could be made of the land, for example, or parks and game preserves. . . .

game refuge or **sanctuary** See **game preserve**.
1961 GREENING *Ottawa* 161: In 1895 the Quebec Government . . . created the Laurentide Park, north of Quebec City, as a game refuge and forest reserve. **1965** WILSON *No Man Stands Alone* 69: But you hunters with itchy fingers—don't shoot! This is still part of the game sanctuary.

game trail† a path beaten by wild animals.
1905 OUTRAM *Cdn Rockies* 308: A few rods below Glacier Lake we turned up a game-trail leading steeply upward, and found an ideal camping-ground on the slopes about three hundred feet above the lake. **1963** PATTERSON *Far Pastures* 265: I waded off the island and followed the game trail to the outlet of the lake. . . .

game warden a government official whose duties include the enforcing of hunting and fishing regulations. See also **game guardian**.
1915 (1916) *Commission of Conservation* 111: But the police, although *ex officio* game wardens, are few in number and have other duties that largely prevent them from taking an important part in game protection. **1965** WILSON *No Man Stands Alone* 48: The Game Warden was at the field . . . and he took us twelve miles to the Indian camp. . . .

gang *n. Lumbering, Hist.* a work-crew of loggers (def. 1).
1832 MCGREGOR *Brit.Amer.* II 300: Immediately after breakfast, they divide into three *gangs*; one of which cuts down the trees, another hews them, and the third is employed with the oxen in hauling the timber. . . . **1854** KEEFER *Ottawa* 64: Three men and a cook form a "gang";—two cut down the tree, *line* and *score* it, that is, split out the outer slabs so as to make it four-sided. . . . **1945** CALVIN *Saga* 44: A gang was counted upon to

"make" about 30,000 cubic feet in a season. **1964** *Cdn Geog.Jnl* Feb. 71/1: Log jams on the Ottawa which held up the drive and filled taverns with rival gangs of Irish and French, were almost certain to brew trouble.

gap *n. Esp.Ont.* an entrance between two islands (or an island and the mainland) to a harbor or inner bay.
1853 (1959) MOODIE *Life in the Clearings* 150: Just after you pass the island and enter the Lower Gap, there are three very small islands in a direct line with each other, that are known as the three brothers. **1937** CLARK *So What?* 107: "We'll go out the eastern gap, mate," hailed Jim. "Aye, aye, sir," I replied, bailing another three canfuls. **1945** CALVIN *Saga* 137: There is only a brief exposure to the lake winds at "the upper gap" between Prince Edward County and Amherst Island. . . .

gap *v. Nfld* cross by boat.
1964 *Cdn Geog.Jnl* Apr. 138: A small boat can be hired "to gap the waters" between Flowers Cove and the Labrador. . . .

garbage dump† a place where garbage and other refuse are disposed of. See also **dump** (def. 4).
1958 *Edmonton Jnl* 24 Sep. 38/2: Garbage dumps attract bears to inhabited areas. **1966** *Sun* (Vancouver) 27 May 1/1: . . . Saturday's the day to head for the Kerr Road garbage dump to unload that three-week accumulation of trash.

garbage fish fish of no commercial value, such as coarse fish or lampreys.
1963 *Kingston Whig-Standard* (Ont.) 9 May 9/6: The only way to put commercial fishing on the Great Lakes on a sound economic footing is to start wiping out "garbage fish" which abound in these waters. . . .

garbage rack a raised platform for garbage cans, protected on three sides by a fence and intended to prevent dogs and other animals from upsetting the cans.
1958 *Edmonton Jnl* 26 Sep. 6/7: . . . he stopped the mower when it came up against a garbage rack in front of the [house].

Garden Island schooner *Hist.* a sturdily built, schooner-rigged vessel made in the shipyards at Garden Island, off Kingston, Ontario, and used in the timber trade during the latter part of the nineteenth century, especially on the Great Lakes.
1945 CALVIN *Saga* 55: It was said that a Garden Island schooner could be recognized by the weight of her spars, and especially by the long "doublings" between lower masts and topmasts.

Garry oak [< Nicholas *Garry*, 1781-1856, an officer of the Hudson's Bay Co.] a species of oak, *Quercus garryana*, native to southwestern British Columbia and the Pacific coast to the south; Pacific oak. See also **western white oak**.
1952 PUTNAM *Cdn Regions* 465: In the driest areas, around Victoria, a more open forest prevails, in which such trees as madrona and Garry oak indicate a similarity to some Mediterranean environments. **1956** *Native Trees* 170: The quantity of Garry Oak is too small for the tree to be of much importance commercially in Canada.

gas boat a boat powered by a gasoline engine. See also **gasoline boat**.
1919 *Camp Worker* 28 June 8/1: Gas boat brings mail once a week, which makes news late. **1959** *Native Voice* Jan. 2/5: Chief Assu had four fine sons, each of whom he set up with a house and gas boat.

gas cache a supply of gasoline stored in drums, used especially for refuelling aircraft. See **cache** (def. 5). See also **gasoline cache.**
1936 *Beaver* Mar. 48/1: Fuel now became a problem as the gas caches at Cambridge apparently had not been arranged for. **1960** BLANCHET *Search in the North* 175: Carburetor trouble on setting out cost them precious gasoline and time, so that instead of making Bathurst in one day, they only reached the Beverly gas cache.

gas-car *n.* See 1934 quote. See also **gasoline car, gasoline speeder, gas speeder, jigger** (def. 3), and **speeder** (def. 1a). Cp. **hand-car.**
1928 FREEMAN *Nearing North* 344: Captain Johnston . . . ran me over on his gas car to the trading post of Luke Clemons at Kettle Rapids. **1953** *Cdn Geog.Jnl* XLVI 46/2: Shortly before midnight, two railway gas cars . . . set out over a logging railroad.

gasher *n. Lab.* See quote.
1895 *St. Nicholas* Apr. 448/2: Here [Blanc Sablon, Labrador] . . . I saw . . . the dapper little Labrador gasher—a small fishing craft not much longer than a dory, but with sharp prow and stern, and two masts fitted with reddish-brown sails. . . . *Ibid.* The gashers [were] dashing in and out among the punts and jacks (stoutly built two-stickers larger than gashers).

gasoline boat See **gas boat.**
1909 *Gow Ganda Tribune* (Ont.) 10 Apr. 6/3: Gasoline Boat Service on Elk Lake, and Mountain Lake, between Mountain Chute and India Chute.

gasoline cache See **gas cache.**
1939 *Beaver* March 31/1: One of the first flights to use a solar compass was from Baker Lake to set a gasoline cache at Dubawnt Lake.

gasoline canoe a canoe driven by an outboard motor.
1921 *Beaver* Aug.-Sep. 15/2: . . . three scows arrived, propelled by gasoline canoes. . . .

gasoline car See **gas-car.**
1928 FREEMAN *Nearing North* 380: Engineer Cecil Johnson took me on to the end of steel in his gasoline car.

gasoline speeder See **gas-car.**
1923 WALDO *Down Mackenzie* 24: A "gasoline speeder" put on in emergencies can beat the train to and fro by a day, its inconsiderable weight enabling it to pass over the unstable roadbed without risk at from twenty to thirty miles an hour.

gaspereau ['gæspə,ro] *n.* [< Acadian F *gasparot, gaspareau*] *Esp.Maritimes* See **alewife.** Various spellings.
[**1672** DENYS *Descr.Geographique* 28: Pour du Hareng, il n'en ont pas beaucoup, mais bien du Gasparot, qui est une espece qui n'est pas si bon à beaucoup pres.] **1703** (1905) LAHONTAN *New Voyages* I 358: Gasperots [are] a small fish like a Herring. **1912** *Sea Fisheries East.Can.* 105: The gaspereaux . . . is mostly used as a bait fish, but considerable quantities are salted for food. **1964** *Chronicle-Herald* (Halifax) 1 July 4/6: Your editorial . . . of May 22, "They're Running," concerning the migration of the "kayak or gaspereaux," attracted my attention.

Gaspesia *n.* [< F *Gaspésie*] *Obs.* the Gaspé. See **Gaspesian,** *n.*
1754 JEFFERYS *Conduct* 75: On this false foundation some geographers give the name of Canada to the country, which in De Mont's patent of 1603, is termed Gaspe or Gaspesia, as it has generally been called ever since. **1871** (1878) LEMOINE *Chronicles of St.Lawrence* 18: C.R.C. is really a grand, a glorious name, a tower of strength in Gaspesia, though it may mean a monopoly.

Gaspesian [gæs'pezɔn] *n.* [< Cdn F *Gaspésien*] a native or inhabitant of the Gaspé, a peninsula in southeast Quebec, lying between Chaleur Bay and the Gulf of St. Lawrence. Also spelled *Gaspésian.*
1905 DAWSON *St.Lawrence* 181: There is no reason to believe, with some, that these Gaspésians were a separate race or tribe of Indians, or in the myth that they had been, from old times, worshippers of the cross. **1950** SUTTON *Footloose in Canada* 127: In full view of thousands of Gaspesians, a white cross, presumably in smoke, appeared at the top of the chimney, and although the priest insisted that it had formed through natural causes, many local folk still consider it a miracle. **1963** *Globe and Mail* (Toronto) 12 Mar. 7/3: Living in one of the poorer and more underdeveloped areas of the country, Gaspesians have found it fairly easy to ask . . . what have we got to lose?

Gaspesian [gæs'pezɔn] *adj.* [< Cdn F *Gaspésien*] of or adjacent to the Gaspé.
1958 *Cdn Fisherman* Aug. 28/2: Cod fishermen in Gaspesian waters have experienced quite a successful period of fishing since the opening of the season. . . .

gas speeder See **gas-car.**
1938 CASH *I Like B.C.* 28: He went there and back, morning and evening, on a gas speeder and made enough money to cover our board . . . and a bit over.

Gastown *n. Hist.* See 1964 quote.
1869 *Mainland Guardian* (New Westminster, B.C.) 11 Sep. 3/2: The village of Gastown was then visited after which the party again returned to the Leviathan and proceeded to the logging camp of Mr. Jeremiah Rogers at English Bay, where the admirably constructed logging roads elicited high encomiums. **1952** (1965) HAMILTON *Cdn Quotations* 37: *Vancouver, B.C.*—. . . Gas Town. (From Captain John "Gassy Jack" Deighton, builder of a hotel on Burrard Inlet, 1867.) **1964** *Time* (Cdn ed.) 10 July 9/2: When the historical arrival of the CPR's first locomotive virtually created Vancouver in 1887, the city was little more than a bush-clearing of 2,000 called by the undignified name of Gastown (after popular Saloon Keeper "Gassy Jack" Deighton).

gauffre *n. Obs.* See **gopher** (def. 1).

gear *n. Fishing, West Coast* a commercial fishing vessel and its crew collectively.
1958 *Fisherman* 15 Aug. 1/4: A lot of gear was concentrated in Johnstone Straits and fishing was good . . . especially for sockeye. *Ibid.*: Open meetings for gillnetters, reef netters, drum seiners and vessel owners have been called for Sunday to ask support from all gears.

geddie ['gɛdi] *n.* See **giddee.**
1869 KENNICOTT *Journal* 94: The geddies look a good deal like a fox, only heavier and stronger in every way. **1921** HEMING *Drama of Forests* 311: "Yes, that's right; they were blowin'; for *geddies* don't bark like other dogs when they're frightened."

gee [dʒi] *v.imper.* [origin obscure, taken over from command to other draft animals] "wheel to

the right," a command to sled-dogs. See also **hew,**
interj.

1900 LONDON *Son of Wolf* 191: "Gee! Gee!" the men
cried . . . as their sleds abruptly left the main-trail,
heeling over on single runners like luggers on the wind.
1934 GODSELL *Arctic Trader* 39: Then to the vociferous
accompaniment of the medley of yells from the Indian
drivers: "Choc! Choc! Gee, muchistem!!" . . . the
teams sped one by one through the gateway and soon
were lost to sight.

gee-pole ['dʒi,pol] *n.* [? < *gee*, q.v.] *North* a
strong hardwood pole, six to seven feet long,
attached to the side of a dog-sled and extending
ahead at an angle, used by the driver as a guiding
device and as a support while the sled is in motion.
See also **handle bar** and **sled rail.**

1899 PALMER *Klondyke* 14: Jack snapped the long lash of
his whip, shook the "gee-pole" to free the runners, cried
"Mush!". . . . **1928** WALDEN *Dog-Puncher* 36: On one
side of the leading sled was what would correspond to a
wagonpole, called the 'gee-pole! [**1940** MARSHALL
Arctic Village 82: In most cases a person [steers] by
pressure on a pole extending forward and upward from
the right side of the front end.]

geesewark ['gis,wark] *n.* [< Algonk.] in Indian
parlance, a measure of days; calendar. Cp. **calendar
stick.**

1921 (1923) BROADUS *Cdn Prose* 275: The Indian now
told the trader that he wanted him to send the "Fur
Runners" to him with supplies in ten weeks' time and
that he must have a "geese-wark," or measure of days,
in order to know exactly when the Fur Runners would
arrive at his camp. So the Factor made out the calendar
on the following pages.

gelette *n.* See **galette.**

Gemini *n. Trademark* a small tractor-trailer
specially designed for cross-country hauling, as
over muskeg, much of its weight being supported
by an air cushion produced by a gas-turbine fan.

1961 *Kingston Whig-Standard* (Ont.) 13 Sep. 5/2: The
Gemini is a new off-highway vehicle developed by the
Avro Aircraft division of A. V. Roe of Canada.

General List the list of Indians who receive
treaty money but are not attached to a band
recognized by the federal government. See also
Indian Register. Cp. **Band List.**

1964 DUFF *Indian Hist.* 46: The first [definition], which
refers to what are usually called "registered Indians," is
the legal definition used by the Indian Affairs Branch
for the people who come under the jurisdiction of the
Indian Act; that is, those whose names are included on
the official Indian Register, either on a Band List or a
General List.

general store 1 *Fur Trade, Obs.* See quote.

1918 DAVIDSON *North West Co.* 21: In 1779 a
partnership, termed a "General Store," was formed at
Michilimackinac. According to an undated list,
probably compiled in 1780, this store was composed of
thirty-eight individuals and companies who contributed
an estimated number of 34¾ canoe-loads of goods.

2† *Esp. Rural* a store carrying a wide variety of
goods—groceries, dry goods, hardware, etc.
See also **country store.**

1860 *Nor' Wester* (R.R.S.) 28 Sep. 2/5: A wood outbuilding, which served as a general store, was consumed
with all its contents. **1963** *Globe and Mail* (Toronto)
"Outdoors" 13 Mar. 16/1: On the way in we rode
merrily down the main village street, up to the general
store and tethered the dogs without trouble.

Gens *n. Cdn French, Fur Trade, Hist.* people (used
in various combinations by the traders and
voyageurs to identify Indians of certain regions
and fur-company men associated with certain
departments). See quotes.

1794 (1929) MCGILLIVRAY *Journal* 31: This with little
difference is ye manner in which the Beaver Hunters are
treated, but the *Gens du large* [Plains Indians] consisting
of Blackfeet, Gros Ventres, Blood Indians, Piedgans &,
are treated with less liberality. **1847** (1910) BURPEE
Yukon 21: "Gens du Fou" . . . inhabit a wide country
which extends from the sources of the Porcupine and
Peel to those of the River of the Mountain Men.
1887 DAWSON *Tribes of Yukon* 12: They are the Gens de
Bois or Wood Indians of the fur-traders. **1913** COWIE
Adventurers 129: . . . the challenge was generally
addressed to *"le meilleurs"* of the offending district,
the men of which were known by such nicknames as
"Les Blaireaux," or badgers of Saskatchewan; "Les
Cygnes," or Swans of Swan River; "Les Rabisca," of
Athabasca; or "Les Gens de la Grande Riviere," of
Mackenzie River. **1918** DAVIDSON *North West Co.* 246:
The Hudson's Bay Company's people were termed *les
Anglois* or *les Gens de la Baie d'Urson* [sic] or *les Gens
du Petit Nord.* The North West Company's people were
called *les Gens du Nord-Ouest.* **1951** O'MEARA *Grand
Portage* 42: Gens du large [are] the mounted Indians of
open land.

gentleman *n. Hist.* See **commissioned gentleman.**

1800 (1820) HARMON *Journal* 45: In the former part of
the day, we overtook several gentlemen . . . on their
way to their winter quarters. **1835** (1945) *B.C.Hist.Qtly*
Jan. 61: [He was] threatening to stab one of the men in
revenge, which he no doubt would have done, either to
a gentleman or a man. . . . **1955** RICH in BLACK *Journal*
xxv: There were also two lower ranks of Gentlemen . . .
clerks and apprentice clerks.

gentleman's pemmican *Obs.* See **fine
pemmican.**

Gentlemen Adventurers *Hist.* a common
misnomer of the Hudson's Bay Company, "The
Company of Adventurers of England Trading into
Hudson's Bay."

1934 GODSELL *Arctic Trader* 158: . . . a Hudson's Bay
man to push even his own brother to the wall if he
happened to be trading in opposition to the "Gentlemen
Adventurers." **1958** *Native Voice* Oct. 6/3: He was in
the employ of the Hudson's Bay Company, the
Gentleman Adventurers trading into Rupert's Land.

German sock one of a pair of long over-
stockings having drawstrings at the top, used for
protection against cold. Cp. **duffle sock** and **duffle
stocking.**

1910 SERVICE *Trail of '98* 297: I wore heavy sweaters,
mackinaw trousers, thick German socks and moccasins.
1956 GOWLAND *Sikanaska Trail* 176: The thick, almost
felt-like German socks that came up to the knees and
fastened with a tasselled cord—an almost indispensable
garment for the bush—sold for forty cents, while larger
items such as a Mackinaw jacket or windbreaker cost as
little as four dollars.

get into the ice *Obs.* go through river or lake

ice into the water, especially when in a horse-drawn vehicle.
1827 (1829) MACTAGGART *Three Years* II 40: We got *into the ice*, as the saying is, in crossing the bay of Quinty in a covered sleigh. . . .

get out *North* get a radio signal to the outside, *q.v.*
1951 GILLIS & MYLES *North Pole* 154: At times we had complete radio black-outs—and Joe would be unable to "get out" at all.

ghost car an unmarked automobile used by policemen in plain clothes to apprehend persons who are speeding or breaking the law in other ways.
1962 *Albertan* (Calgary) 26 Nov. City Page: Opposition to the use of ghost cars operated by policemen without uniforms was expressed at the annual meeting of the directors of the Alberta Motor Association in the Palliser Hotel Saturday.

ghost flower See **Indian pipe.**
1860 *Trans.Lit.&Hist.Soc.Que.* IV 4 41: The Ghost Flower, Indian Pipe or Monotropa, is a white plant springing up from decayed leaves now very plentiful. . . . **1932** *Cdn Geog. Jnl* IV 150/1: The Indian Pipe, Corpse Plant, or Ghost Flower (Monotropa uniflora), Pyrola family, appropriately deserves its alternative names, standing as it does in ghastly whiteness in the shadowed woods.

giant willow herb See **fireweed.**
1909 CAMERON *New North* 122: Fighting our way . . . through a pungant bocage of ground pine, wild roses, giant willow-herb . . . we reach the H.B. garden. . . .

giddé [gɪ'de] *n.* See **giddee.**
1896 RUSSELL *Far North* 15: Most of them are of the wolfish breed known as Indian dogs, or, in the far North,—giddés; these are smaller and more uniform in color than those kept by the whites. **1896** WHITNEY *On Snow-Shoes* 106: These dogs are certainly notable travellers, from the best fed down to the puniest of the Indian species, which are contemptuously called *giddés* by the half-breeds, and are not a great deal larger than a big fox. **1913** MASON *Notes on Northeastern Athabascan Culture*: Dogs are now indispensable beasts of burden in the north and each family possess a team. These are generally known as "giddés," being of a different strain from and somewhat inferior to the Eskimo "husky." **1921** (1928) HEMING *Drama of Forests* 179: . . . there were few real "huskies," as Eskimo dogs are called, for most of the brutes were the usual sharp-nosed, heavy-coated mongrels that in the Strong Woods Country go by the name of *giddes;* some, however, had been sired by wolves.

giddee ['gɪdi] *n.* [origin unknown] *Northwest* a breed of dog used by certain Athabascan Indians as a draft animal. See also **geddie** and **giddé.** Cp. **bear dog, Indian dog,** and **Siwash dog.**
1905 (1954) *B.C.Hist.Qtly* July-Oct. 173: The well-bred English horse detained at Fort Severn . . . ran eagerly for his dinner of goose-bones, but I never knew him to dine off a coat, as a "giddee", or Indian dog did, at a way-camp of mine in 1824. The odd fact . . . was that the dog ate the coat off his master's back while he slept. **1958** ELLIOTT *Quesnel* 153: Meat of a young bear was a welcome change or, if nothing else, "giddee" or Indian dog was variety for the menu.

gig, gigger, gigging See **jig, jigger, jigging.**

gillie or **gilly** ['gɪli] *n.* See **galley.**

1941 *Beaver* Sep. 37/2: Gillies—Long, narrow snow-shoes. **1957** *Ibid.* Autumn 56/2: On one tree hangs a finely-made pair of "gillies," on others hang beaver skins on willow stretchers.

gilpoke *n.* See **jill-poke.**

Ginger Group 1 *Obs.* See quote.
1952 (1965) HAMILTON *Cdn Quotations* 174: The Ginger Group. . . . The phrase was earlier used to denote a group of Conservative members, including W. F. Nickle, during the term of Union Government, 1917-21. **2** *Hist.* a number of progressives (six, later ten) in the House of Commons from 1924-1932, so called because of their spirited questioning of government policy and for their energetic championing of the interests of the farmer and of labor.
1953 LEBOURDAIS *Nation of North* 220: After the disintegration of the Progressives, the Alberta members, soon to become known as the "Ginger Group," had found themselves more and more thrown into association with Woodsworth and his Labour associate, or associates . . . and, as a rule, finding themselves members of the same minority in divisions. **1963** MORTON *Kingdom of Canada* 443: Two members of the "Ginger Group," as it was dubbed, were labour politicians. . . .

girdle† *v.* See quotes. See also **ring.**
1766 *Quebec Gaz.* 24 Nov. 3/1: The Boundary Line . . . is distinguished by Openings . . . where several Trees are girdled and square Posts set up. . . . **1863** WALSHE *Cedar Creek* 139: . . . the trees may be "girdled;" that is, a ring of bark from the trunk near the base, which causes death in so far that no foliage appears next spring. . . . **1964** *Atlantic Advocate* Aug. 79: Their tender bark could not withstand such wear and tear and sometimes the young trees were "girdled."

girdling† *n.* the process of cutting a ring through the bark of a tree, thus cutting off the flow of sap and eventually killing it.
1821 HOWISON *Sketches* 264: The easiest and most economical system is that named girdling. **1842** (1911) *London & Middlesex Hist.Soc.Trans.* III 48: Among innumerable stumps blasted by fire and girdling, were seen wide streets at right angles to each other. **1899** MACKAY *Pioneer Life* 168: Another way to clear the bush was by "girdling." This consisted in hacking the tree all around, so that in the course of six or seven years it would decay and fall.

Gitchi Manitou [< Algonk. "Great Spirit"] the supreme deity of the Crees, Ojibwas, and related tribes, identified by some whites and Christian Indians with God. See also **Manitou** (def. 2) and **Master of Life** (def. 1). Cp. **Great Spirit** and **Matchi Manitou.** Also spelled *Kitchee Manitoo, Keche Manitou,* etc.
1791 LONG *Voyages* 7: At the entrance of this lake is a high rock, somewhat in the shape of a man, which the Chippeway Indians call "Kitchee Manitou," or the Master of Life. **1792-1807** JOHNSTON *Lake Superior* 169: After examining it for some time, it occurred to the eldest girl that it belonged to the *Gitchi Manitou,* the Great Spirit, upon which they abandoned the place with precipitation. **1860** *Nor'Wester* (R.R.S.) 14 Mar. 3/2: It was lit by a spark struck from a piece of flint, and the stem having been presented to the north, to the south,

surface of a waterway.

to the east, to the west, and then upwards to Gitche Manito, or the Master of Life, it was passed round to the assembled councillors, beginning with the chiefs. **1910** FERGUSON *Janey Canuck* 177: A certain northern chronicler relates that Kitch Manitou became angry when, one day, all the men married all the women. . . . **1926** (1958) *Camsell Arrow* Christmas 34: Twas in the moon of winter-time / When all the birds had fled, / That mighty Gitchi-Manitou / Sent angel-choirs instead. . . . **1956** KEMP *Northern Trader* 38: The Christ-theme was missing, but Jehovah and the Devil were represented by *Keche Munito,* the Great Spirit, and *Muche Munito,* the Evil Spirit.

give-away dance or **festival** *Esp. Pacific Coast* See **potlatch,** *n.* (def. 2b). See also **pow-wow** (def. 1d). **1916** WOOD *Tourist's N.W.* 361: Alert Bay and other Indian villages of the British Columbia coast are occasionally enlivened by Potlatch or Give-away festivals, at which the Indian host bestows his worldly goods upon his invited guests amid formal dancing and feasting beneath rows of totem poles. **1927** (1928) ROSE *Stump Farm* 157: The races kept up till six o'clock and after that there was an Indian dance that is very popular. It is called the "Lame Dance," and sometimes the "Give-away Dance." They just jump up and down around a fire to the beat of drums. It is odd, because they give away nearly everything they have. A man with a nice pair of fancy moccasins will hold them out to another Indian, who grabs hold of them, and then they dance awhile together. The second Indian gives the other man something, probably a hat or a pair of gaily embroidered gloves of deerskin. Away they go again. **1940** *Beaver* Sep. 45/1: In the give-away dance you present some person, male or female, with a handkerchief, which he or she grabs. You then fall in line with the others, making the round of the lodge, weaving in and out among the sacrificial fires. . . . **1963** SYMONS *Many Trails* 74: He [a Chilcotin Indian] . . . told me he was on his way to a potlatch or "give-away dance" at the Nemiah Valley.

Giver of Life See **Great Spirit** (def. 1). **1814** *Montreal Herald* 2 Apr. 1/2: It consisted of a number of short sentences, expressive of gratitude to the "Giver of Life" for having given them spirits and strength to travel so far to see their Father.

glacier or **glacière** *n.* [< Cdn F *glacière* ice-box] *Obs.* a cold-storage pit for preserving food, especially meat and fish. See also **ice-pit** and **ice-vault.** Cp. **hangard** (def. 2). **1809** (1916) THOMPSON *Narrative* 400: As there was now plenty of shore ice of sufficient thickness, we made a glacier for frozen meat. This is a square of about twelve feet, the bottom and the sides lined with ice. . . . In these meat Glaciers, a layer of Meat is laid on the ice, and then a layer of ice, and thus continued. **1810** (1950) THOMPSON *Journals* 77: 54 lbs of Meat in the Glacier. **1950** CAMPBELL *Saskatchewan* 161: [In] the glacière or ice-pit . . . were placed quarters of buffalo.

glacier lily See **avalanche lily.** **1952** HOWARD *Strange Empire* 358: All about him patterns of color sprang suddenly from the sod, as if they had been evoked by the viewer . . . the first glacier lilies, slim and regally yellow. **1964** *Wildlife Rev.* May 17: Up where the Glacier Lilies blow / Late May and June still sees fresh snow. . . .

glade† *n.* an open stretch or patch in the frozen

1953 BANFILL *Labrador Nurse* 195: Six inches from an open, dangerous glade we just missed a huge ballacater, then catapulted onto the risky ice. **1959** *Ottawa Citizen* 10 Feb. 30/6: (Caption) The triangular patch at the upper right and the black patch at left center show open stretches of water—the "glades" which are avoided as danger spots by all winter river travellers.

gladed ice an ice surface broken by glades. **1924** DORRANCE *Never Fire First* 85: Three days ago, crossing lake on gladed ice . . . Dogs sight a stray wolf.

glare *adj.* of ice, smooth, translucent and slippery. See also **glare ice** (def. 1). **1829** MACTAGGART *Three Years* II 210: When the ice of the lake is *glare*—that is, sleek and clear—ice-boats run about with great velocity. . . . **1957** *Aklavik Jnl* (N.W.T.) Apr. 7/1: Simigiak's father Sabgut went immediately to search but because the ice was glare up to the open water there remained not even a trace of the sled tracks.

glare *n.* See **glare ice.** **1905** MOTT *Jules of the Great Heart* 62: . . . the sledge often whirled sidewise on the turns, because the bone runners could get no hold on the glare surface. **1965** WILSON *No Man Stands Alone* 128: The road was a glare of black ice. It had rained and then frozen.

glare-crust *n.* the shiny, slippery surface that forms on a layer of snow the top of which has melted and re-frozen. **1905** MOTT *Jules of the Great Heart* 28: Jules took off his snowshoes once more, and glided away to the southward, leaving no trace, not a sign on the glare-crust at the edge of the timber.

glare ice 1 smooth, translucent, slippery ice on lakes and rivers. See also **glare,** *adj.* and *n.,* and **glib ice.** **1829** MACTAGGART *Three Years* I 181: I . . . once beheld a large [wolf] in close pursuit of a buck on the *glare ice* of the Mississippi Lake. **1872** (1873) GRANT *Ocean to Ocean* 233: The lake freezes, but there is so little snow that the travellers prefer fording the river to trusting to the glare ice. **1939** (1951) TWEEDSMUIR *Hudson's Bay Trader* 145: Patches of glare ice showed bottle green all over it and the wind chased rills of blown snow across it, twisting and dancing as they went. **1963** SYMONS *Many Trails* 125: . . . one cannot put brakes on in a hurry with just a light covering of snow over the glare ice. . . .

2 smooth, slippery ice formed on the ground after a fall of freezing rain or sleet. See also **glare,** *n.* Cp. **silver thaw** (def. 2). **1872** DASHWOOD *Chiploquorgan* 116: On our return we had not to face the wind, but the glare ice—from which the slight covering of snow had been blown off. . . . **1954** *Fundy Fisherman* 3 Mar. 1/7: While regular chains are not as effective as the reinforced type on glare ice, they do provide good traction on snow and, to some extent, on ice. **1965** *Kingston Whig-Standard* (Ont.) 2 Feb. 1/3: The road along the waterfront between the three causeway spans was glare ice in sections adding to the woes of the motorists.

3 any formation of smooth, translucent ice. **1956** SCHERMAN *Spring* 51: Over us leaned a slim, graceful tower of glare ice fifty feet high, shaped by wind and sleet into beautiful curves and carved with delicate ridges.

glareness *n. Obs.* the quality of being glare, *q.v.* **1849** ALEXANDER *L'Acadie* I 230: Now our curling in Canada East is practised with iron "stones" of 56 pounds, from that up to 80 pounds, owing to the "glareness" of the ice; and as real stones are apt to break with the frost, iron is used instead.

glaze *v. North* See **ice,** *v.* (def. 2).
1965 *North* Nov.-Dec. 12: They call the earth "ibyo" and its only use, according to 13-year-old Luke Issaluk, is to melt it in the igloo, mix it with boiling water and glaze sledge runners.

glib ice *Now Rare* See **glare ice** (def. 1).
1837 (1952) *Beaver* Sep. 35/2: While we were enjoying the scenes around us, a fellow with a showy horse and gay cariole shot past us on the glib ice like lightning. . . . **1952** *Ibid.*: [Caption] The carriole is driving on the "glib ice" of the Assiniboine's mouth.

glitter *n. Nfld* **1** See **silver thaw** (def. 1).
1868 (1873) REEKS *Nfld Meteor.Obs.*: [Jan.] 8: 7 a.m. "Glitter," wind ENE. (Note: "Glitter," rain freezing and coating everything with a layer of ice.) **1955** *Evening Telegram* (St. John's) 14 Mar. 3/3: The "glitter" storm of late last night . . . cost St. John's thousands of dollars. . . . *Ibid.* 3/5: Weather Office reported the glitter would turn to snowshowers this afternoon.

2 See **silver thaw** (def. 2). Cp. **glare ice** (def. 2).
1879 *North Star* (St. John's) 5 Apr. 3/1: Whilst going towards the well, situated near a steep cliff, the snow being covered with a glitter of ice, it is supposed that he lost his balance and fell over the cliff upon the rocks beneath.

glitter over *Nfld* become coated with ice as a result of a silver thaw (def. 1). See also **glitter.**
1955 *Evening Telegram* (St. John's) 14 Mar. 3/5: The highway from St. John's to Carbonear, glittered over early this morning, was reported safe about 10.30 a.m.

Glooscap ['gluskæp] *n.* [< Algonk.] a legendary demi-god of the Micmacs, Malecites, and kindred Indian tribes, revered as a mighty warrior and magician. See also **Groscap.** Also spelled *Gluscap, Glusecap.*
1887 *Trans.Roy.Soc.Can.* II 3: All these groups have the same legends, and honour the same mythical personages, Glooscap, Mikwumpwees, etc., though under different names. **1891** *Cdn Indian* (Owen Sound, Ont.) Sep. 332: Such a one was Glooscap, the saviour of the Milicetes, and who, I think, was also venerated as such by the Micmacs. **1963** *Weekend Mag.* 9 Nov. 54: The third such book is Glooscap and his magic, legends of the Wabanaki Indians of Nova Scotia, which Haligonian Kay Hill found on her own doorstep.

Glorious Twelfth† July 12, celebrated annually by Orangemen in commemoration of King William's victory at the Battle of the Boyne.
1889 *Regina Jnl* 11 July 1/5: Owing to some misunderstanding about securing the services of the Band for the celebration of the "Glorious Twelfth" the ireful manager of the Orange hall has refused to allow it to be used by the Band for practice. **1959** *Maclean's* 29 Aug. 39/1: As evidence of its good faith, the Orange Order would allow the citizens of Quebec to abandon June 24th and celebrate their national holiday on the Glorious Twelfth of July—the only date in the calendar worth mentioning—on the sole condition that the Quebec festival be known by its proper English name of St. John the Baptist Day.

glory-fit *n. Nfld* a state of emotional frenzy inspired by religious fervor.
1905 DUNCAN *Grenfell's Parish* 107: [He] was a cheerful Methodist, too, and subject to "glory-fits." **1946** BIRD *Sunrise* 5: He had not the religion of some of the

outport Newfoundlanders who were subject to "glory fits" and loud repentances.

Glus(e)cap *n.* See **Glooscap.**

glutton† *n.* [see 1912 quote] See **wolverine** (def. 1a).
1784 PENNANT *Arctic Zoology* 67: I have reason to think that the Glutton of the old writers is the same with this animal. . . . **1823** *Canadian Mag.* I 496: The rosomack or glutton, though not so numerous, is a more dangerous enemy. **1912** (1913) HODGE & WHITE *Indians of Can.* 80/1: By a freak of popular etymology this animal received the name of "glutton." Its Finnish name is *fiael-frass,* "dweller among rocks," corrupted by the Germans into *vielfrass,* 'glutton.' **1926** SULLIVAN *Northern Lights* 61: Carcajou—the wolverine and glutton—stared at the pack-sack, then slid down and began tearing it. . . .

go-ahead goal in hockey, etc., the goal necessary to give one's team the victory; the winning goal.
1963 *Kingston Whig-Standard* (Ont.) 7 Mar. 27/1: He also made the play for the go-ahead goal with a sweep which set up slapshooting Ray Dupont.

go astray *Maritimes* See quote.
1923 MACMECHAN *Sagas of Sea* 146: He had "gone astray" from his vessel once, that is he had been lost in his dory, been picked up and taken to St. Pierre.

goat *n.* **1 a.** *Fur Trade, Obs.* See **antelope.**
1754 (1907) HENDAY *Journal* 336: Two young men brought in 3 Goats: they are not so large as the Welsh ones. **1853** REID *Young Voyageurs* 100: What Norman had shot, then, was an antelope; and the reason why it is called "cabree" by the voyageurs, and "goat" by the fur-traders, is partly from its colour resembling that of the common goat, but more from the fact, that along the upper part of its neck there is a standing mane, which does in truth give it somewhat the appearance of the European goat.

b. See **Rocky Mountain goat.**
1888 (1890) ST. MAUR *Impressions* 223: About 4.30 in the afternoon we reached the creek we meant to camp on; excellent water, wood, and lots of grass again, added to which it looked good goat country. **1905** OUTRAM *Cdn Rockies* 340: Here more than thirty goats were scattered over a small area—goats of all sizes and apparently all ages, from shaggy patriarchs to tiny kids only a few weeks old. **1957** HUTCHISON *Canada* 264: Midwinter in the Rockies and the tracks of moose, deer, elk, sheep, and goat circle the lower hills in criss-cross webbing.

2 *Hist.* a kind of locomotive (U-class) built in 1905 and used in certain coal mines.
1964 *Calgary Herald* 15 May 26/2: . . . the Canmore "goat" is receiving a more thorough check.

3 See **rigging goat.**

goat-antelope *n. Obs.* See **antelope.** See also **goat** (def. 1a).
1852 RICHARDSON *Arctic Expedition* 111: The goat-antelope (*Antilocapra americana* [sic]), which is covered with a fine long-stapled wool, has its northern limit on the River of the Mountains.

go-devil *n.* a crude sled formerly used in drawing logs out of the bush and in transporting goods over rough terrain. See also **diable.** Cp. **crotch.**

1897 COUES *New Light* II 604n: [A diable is] what we
should call a "go-devil"—a rude sort of drag or sled for
hauling logs and the like. In some places called a "tie-
boy." **1964** *Cdn Geog.Jnl* Feb. 67/2: The first device used
to move logs was a crude sort of sleigh known as a
"go-devil." It was simply the crotch of a birch tree
to which the log was fastened and then dragged over
the snow. Bob-sleds eventually replaced the go-devils.
1964 *Western Wkly* 29 Jan. 3: [Caption] Lead horse,
with lightly loaded "go-devil", breaks trail for rest of
the string.

God's steamboat *West Coast* a small steamer
plying the coast of British Columbia.
1958 WATTERS *B.C.Cent.Anthol.* 216: These big-souled
men in their little ships—God's Steamboats, some
oldtimers call them—can be seen any day of any year
braving Bute winds, Qualicums, Squamish squalls, as
they buck through Beware Pass. . . .

A goelette

goelette [ˌɡoə'lɛt] *n.* [< Cdn F < F *goélette*
schooner] a flat-bottomed, motor-driven vessel
built mainly on the Ile aux Coudres and used for
carrying freight on the St. Lawrence River and
occasionally on the Lower Lakes. Cp. **caboteur**
(def. 1).
1958 *Weekend Mag.* 22 Mar. 3/1: Goelettes mostly
carry pulpwood and sometimes sail as far as the Great
Lakes. **1958** *Crowsnest* May 21/3: "There is something
for everyone here, a sense of music . . . and some new
words to think about—goelette, bugalet rig, arquebuses-
a-croc, tillac, toise and carroy." **1959** *Weekend Mag.*
21 Mar. 38/2: And the more than 500 people who sail
the goelettes . . . see these ports and those of the Great
Lakes. **1959** *Maclean's* 23 May 4/4: Being partly a
lower St. Lawrence River man I would like to
compliment John Little on his cover (April 25). . . .
Unfortunately the spelling of the name of the type of
boat is incorrect. This should be *goelette* not *geolette*.

goers and comers *Fur Trade, Hist.* See **comers
and goers.**
1843 *Standing Rules* (H.B.C.) 32: That persons
retiring from the Service, likewise Goers and Comers,
or others leaving the Country be permitted to take with
them not exceeding 20 pairs of Indian shoes. **1908** LAUT
Conquest N.W. II 21: Fifteen days at the most it
takes the "goers and comers" of Montreal to exchange
their cargo of provisions for the Northerners' cargo of
furs. **1943** FRENCH *Boughs* 213: "Northmen" they were
called or "goers and comers" depending on what
company they were working for.

go for the big skate *Hockey, Slang* See quote.
1963 *Maclean's* 23 Mar. 32/4: Keon's accomplishments

and promise would not be as interesting as they are if
he were the type of hockey player who goes for what
the players call "the big skate"—who coasts around the
rink waiting for an opportunity to add to his scoring
total.

go free *Fur Trade, Hist.* become a freeman (def. 1).
1832 (1939) *B.C.Hist.Qtly* Apr. 117: He was "allowed
to go free," in the phrase of the time, on June 1, 1832.
1913 COWIE *Adventurers* 362: "It was the fixed policy of
the Company whenever any of their employees 'went
free' and then started as 'free-traders',—to put forth
even greater exertions to crush their competition than
was the case against any other of their opponents."

go in *North* enter the Far North, especially by
the rivers flowing into the Arctic Ocean. Cp. **go
outside.**
1896 RUSSELL *Far North* 50: To "go in," by the way, is
to descend the Athabasca; to return to civilization is to
"go outside." **1937** *Beaver* June 37/2: The Klondike gold
rush brought in more people, outfitting there before
going "in" from the Cariboo.

go Indian of white men, adopt the ways of the
Indian.
1934 GODSELL *Arctic Trader* 91: The Indians, though
nominally Christians, were utter savages at heart, and
close contact with primitive life and passions, and the
almost complete absence of moral sense amongst those
with whom I was so closely associated had a disquieting
effect. Only the strictest self-discipline could prevent
one "going Indian," with all that it implies.

gold-bar *n. Placer Mining* See **bar** (def. 1).
1873 (1904) BUTLER *Wild North Land* 271: I talked the
matter over with Jacques, as we sat camped on the
gold-bar opposite Pete Toy's house. **1880** GORDON
Mountain and Prairie 24: The Fraser . . . starts on its
winding course some 800 miles above this, in the upper
slopes of the Rocky Mountains, cleaving its way through
many a wild cañon, skirting rich gold bars and fertile
valleys.

Gold Colony *Hist.* British Columbia.
1921 *Cdn Hist.Rev.* II 352: One cannot . . . turn away
from the legal enactments and resultant correspondence
which set up the new Gold Colony, without pausing to
comment on its name. **1958** ORMSBY *B.C.History* 173:
All the major policies for the Gold Colony were then
determined by the Governor himself and announced in
the form of proclamations.

gold commissioner See 1930 quote.
1859 *British Colonist* (Victoria) 15 Jan. 2/2: New
Appointments.—Geo. W. Heaton, Sherif of
Vancouver's Island; Charles Brew, Chief Gold
Commissioner of British Columbia. **1930** ROBERTSON
Yukon Memories 52: A Gold Commissioner attends to
the granting of mining claims, titles, permits for cutting
timber and the settlement of disputes between
conflicting claimants. **1964** *Weekend Mag.* 27 June 22/2:
They include such colorful landmarks as . . . the Gold
Commissioner's office.

gold country a region in which gold is present, or
believed to be present, in paying quantities.
1748 ELLIS *Hudson's Bay* 13: It is very justly observed
by Capt. Fox, that from the Accounts we have of
these three Voyages, it looks as if they had a mind to
keep this Gold Country to themselves. **1863** *Nor'Wester*
(R.R.S.) 9 Feb. 3/5: The miners who are flocking down
the Fraser to take up their quarters in Victoria, bring
abundance of intelligence about the gold country.
1910 HAYDON *Riders of Plains* 287: Later on he went

over the cañon trail of the Peace River into the gold country of British Columbia.

Golden Bowler *Informal* a compulsory retirement plan, instituted in 1965, whereby surplus servicemen in the Canadian forces were discharged with a substantial bonus and pension; also, such a discharge.
1966 *Globe and Mail* (Toronto) 13 Oct. 6/1: The Golden Bowler was announced originally as a cash and pension salve for people with whom the government was breaking its contract.

golden eagle a large North American eagle, *Aquila chrysaetos.*
1784 PENNANT *Arctic Zoology* cxciii: A variety of the Golden Eagle is also a native of the same place.
1935 *Beaver* Dec. 56/1: The head-dress of golden eagle feathers swaying in the wind still symbolizes, for imaginative youth, "trailing clouds of glory."
1964 *Western Wkly* 24 June 7/3: . . . he actually succeeded in carrying alive two eagles, a golden, and a bald, only to have them die when two-thirds of the journey were ended!

Golden Horseshoe See quotes.
1959 *Cdn Geog.Jnl* April 104: It [the Niagara fruit belt] shares with the "Golden Horseshoe" (a popular name given to the urban complex around the western end of Lake Ontario) a rich agricultural hinterland, cheap water transportation, an excellent network of highways and railroads, and an abundant supply of fresh water.
1966 *Globe and Mail* (Toronto) 2 May 5/8: The regions of this province outside the Golden Horseshoe (the area surrounding Metro Toronto from Oshawa to Niagara Falls) must have proper provincially supported education centres.

golden pass See quote.
1965 *Kingston Whig-Standard* (Ont.) 15 Apr. 17/4: Mr. Couture has been given a rare "golden pass" which enables him and his wife to travel free on CNR trains and at half-fare on United States railways.

Golden Spike a golden spike used in the ceremony of driving the last spike of a railway line.
1928 FREEMAN *Nearing North* 370: So high was enthusiasm and confidence that there is said to have been a proposal that the Golden Spike be driven at the beginning [of the Hudson Bay Railway] rather than at the finish. **1958** *Kootenaian* 8 May: It's your year . . . to see the Golden Spike re-enactment at Craigellachie. . . .

Golden West the Prairie Provinces.
1936 MACKENZIE *Living Rough* 228: They all figured they would make a million in the Golden West. . . .

goldeye *n.* a small edible fish, *Hiodon alosoides,* native to the Lake Winnipeg region, but now found over a wider range in the Northwest. See also **lacaishe, Lake Winnipeg goldeye, nacaishe,** and **Winnipeg goldeye.** Cp. **mooneye.**
*a*1811 (1909) BRYCE *Lord Selkirk's Colonists* 48: The buffalo comes to the fords of the Assiniboil, besides in these rivers are plenty of sturgeon, catfish, goldeyes, pike and whitefish—the latter so common that men have been seen to catch thirty or forty apiece while they smoked their pipes. **1828** (1872) MCDONALD *Peace River* 5: Stopped on shore at the *Passe* . . . when we got a few "gold-eyes" (a kind of fresh herring about a foot long, with bright iris, large and yellow—Indian name Nacaish). **1964** *Commercial Letter* March 7: Manitoba's most famous fish, the goldeye, which often appears on distant menus as "Winnipeg

goldeye," has in recent years been playing a decreasing role commercially.

gold-eyed carp or **herring** *Obs.* See **goldeye.**
1857 (1863) PALLISER *Journals* 33: Some of our men . . . obtained several perch and gold-eyed carp. **1890** MASSON *Les Bourgeois* II 310: The gold eyed herring [is] so named on account of its large yellow eyes, and called by the French Canadians, laquaiche.

gold-hunter *n.* a person who prospects for gold.
1859 *British Colonist* (Victoria) 29 July 2/2: On Wednesday the Queen Charlotte gold-hunters to the number of about 100, went on board the Island Queen, at Kindler's Wharf, and dropped down near the mouth of the harbor. **1924** DORRANCE *Never Fire First* 61: . . . on the bunks in the living room of the post sat . . . the three gold hunters from Prospect. . . .

gold king a miner striking it rich in the goldfields.
1898 *Yukon Midnight Sun* (Dawson) 1 Aug. 4/4: Gay and gorgeous was the scene, as party after party of gold kings, their wives, daughters and friends passed through the side entrance of the Hotel Fair View last Wednesday evening and upstairs to the reception and dressing rooms, so cosily and artistically furnished.

gold pan† *Placer Mining* a shallow iron pan used for washing gold from gravel.
1898 LANDREVILLE *Appeal of Yukon Miners* 7: It is outside the range of language to picture the trials that encompass the explorer who goes forth here with pick, shovel, and gold-pan to search for gold. **1964** *North* July 7/1: They jiggled and rolled their gold pan, sloshing the water from side to side, washing away the gravel. Soon nothing remained but black sand.

gold rush† a vast movement of persons to a new goldfield. See also **gold stampede, rush,** and **stampede,** *n.* (def. 1c).
1900 LONDON *Son of Wolf* 119: They were specimens of the many strange waifs which ride the breast of a gold rush. . . . **1964** *Edmonton Jnl* 11 July 3/6: Mike subsequently took part in half a dozen gold rushes in the Yukon and Alaska, and got luckier every time.

gold stampede See **gold rush.**
1908 LAUT *Conquest N.W.* I xvii: In Manitoba, the passing of the Company was marked by the Riel Rebellion; in British Columbia, by the mad gold stampede. **1954** PATTERSON *Dangerous River* 285: It now became apparent that, failing the gold stampede to the Flat River for which we were all poised, they had a plan in reserve.

gold strike the discovery of gold.
1937 *Beaver* Sep. 10/1: Another gold strike has been made one hundred miles still farther east. **1958** *Albertan* (Calgary) 7 June 28/7: The mining recorder's office Thursday confirmed a small flurry of staking activity in what may be a gold strike on the Athabasca river, 275 miles north of Edmonton.

gold town a town whose economy is based on neighboring gold mines.
1952 *North Star* (Yellowknife) Oct. 2/1: The ten-thousand-population-in-three-years predicted for the expanding gold town proved to be a myth. **1955** *Cdn Mining Reporter* 8 Apr. 3/3: "In a country growing as rapidly as Canada and in a region with the prospects

which seem ahead for Northern Ontario, it would be a hardy pessimist who would firmly deny the gold towns a future," the report continues.

gold trail the route leading to a goldfield or to a hoped-for gold strike.
1921 HAWORTH *Trailmakers* 264: Such a man may spend his last cent on the gold trail, but, just as soon as he can, by trapping or otherwise, make a new grubstake, he is off again into the mountains after the golden will o' the wisp. **1963** *Herald Mag.* 23 Nov. 3/4: The narrow-guage railway . . . follows the shore of Lake Bennett, following a path beaten so hard by the thousands of sourdoughs that the gold trail is still visible today.

G.O.M. *Obs.* Grand Old Man, with reference to Sir John A. Macdonald in his later political career.
1891 *Grip* (Toronto) 7 Feb. 86/2: "Well, no," replied the G.O.M. . . . **1895** *Rat Portage* [Kenora] *News* (Ont.) 24 May 4/1: Such funny business is scarcely in keeping with the masterly political moves of the G.O.M.

gondola ['gɑndələ] *n.* a broadcasting booth rigged near the roof of an arena, *q.v.*, for the use of play-by-play announcers of hockey games, etc.
1960 *Ottawa Citizen T.V.Wkly* 16 Apr. 13/1: . . . he took eight-year-old Bill Hewitt up to the broadcast gondola of Toronto's Maple Leaf Gardens.
1965 *Maclean's* 4 Sep. 46/3: The winter I was eleven, an uncle of mine . . . arranged for me to watch a hockey game from the gondola at Maple Leaf Gardens.

good Indian an Indian friendly to the whites; a peaceful Indian. See also **white Indian.** Cp. **bad Indian.**
1791 LONG *Voyages* 146: It is true the Master of Life has sent me here to those Indians whose hearts are full of poisoned blood, and as they mean to change my climate, I shall go with courage to a better trading ground, where I shall find good Indians. **1860** *Nor'Wester* (R.R.S.) 28 Feb. 3/3: Peguis was always a good Indian—the best that was ever known in the colony. **1926** *Battleford Hist.Soc.Pubs.* I 30: At this juncture William McKay, a Hudson's Bay man . . . rode amongst the still excited crowd and brought up to the shack Indian after Indian whom McKay vouched for as "good Indians" and to whom bags of flour and sides of bacon were dished out by Crozier's orders. **1966** BAITY *Wilderness Welfare* 170: They were good Indians . . . and . . . they had adjusted to the white man's rigid laws remarkably well. . . . **1967** *Maclean's* Apr. 107/1: But at least Charlie Wenjack died an Indian—not a slavish, obsequious, pandering, "good" Indian.

good medicine in Indian parlance, any auspicious action, event, or thing; good luck. Cp. **bad medicine** (def. 1).
1858 (1935) STRANG *Pioneers in Canada* 242: I gave a bundle [of matches] to Mis-tick-oos, who wrapped them carefully in a piece of deerskin, and said he should keep them safely: they were "good medicine." **1893** YOUNG *Indian Wigwams* 221: When specially fortunate in hunting or warfare or in more quiet duties of life he was said to be under the influence of "good medicine." **1923** WALDO *Down Mackenzie* 230: He could not have gone to heaven had he died with his eyes open; and for themselves it would not have been "good medicine" to leave him. **1965** STEVENS *Incompleat Canadian* 18: . . . if an Indian's horse romped home in a race, the winner cared little whether the shaman had come to his aid

with good medicine or the sorcerer had assisted him by putting a curse on the losers.

goods *n.pl. Fur Trade* items to be bartered for furs. See also **trading goods.**
1671 (1942) *H.B.C.Minutes* 10: That Mr. Forster . . . doe give an account . . . of all goods outwardes by them sould in the Countrey. . . . **1808** (1950) THOMPSON *Journals* 5: [We] began to carry the Goods to the Junction of the Rivers. . . . **1872** (1937) *B.C.Hist.Qtly* July 181: I . . . remember . . . the "stockades" . . . large enough for three or four hundred horses, for the horse brigades for the transport of "goods in" and "returns out" for the [Kamloops] District. . . . **1921** HEMING *Drama of Forests* 35: It was one of the boats of "The Goods Brigade" transporting supplies for the northern posts of the Hudson's Bay Company.

goods price *Obs.* in pioneer days, a price set on an article of merchandise to be bought by trade or barter rather than for cash.
1830 MOORSOM *Letters N.S.* 291: Such a thing as hard cash is now seldom met with. Two scales of value, the "cash price" and "goods price," are established, and the various gradations thereof distinctly marked in all transactions between employers and labourers.

good water in rivers or lakes, water that makes for easy canoeing.
1754 (1907) HENDAY *Journal* 325: The River in general good water. **1811** (1950) THOMPSON *Journals* 158: this Branch is abt 30 yds wide & sharp Current always good water for the Canoe. . . . **1828** (1872) MCDONALD *Peace River* ix: About 16 miles above Island and Pine Portage . . . "Good water."

goolie ['guli] *n.* [origin unknown] *Man., Slang* a person of Icelandic extraction.
1960 BLONDAL *Candle* 260: In those days a boy had to fight for his corner. I mean fight—fists and bleeding noses and black eyes and the gangs screaming kike or bohunk or goolie.

go on timber *Lumbering, Obs.* move on to the logs floating downstream in a drive (def. 1a), especially during a jam (def. 2).
1883 FRASER *Shanty* 273: In his easy going way . . . he hopped about from stick to stick . . . no doubt thinking it no great matter after all "to go on timber."

goose camp *North* a camp used for the hunting of geese.
1959 BODSWORTH *Strange One* 140: Do you know if anyone is going up to the goose camps today? **1966** *Globe and Mail* (Toronto) 14 Jan. 45/5: Their Fort Albany goose camp has been the northernmost temporary hunting camp in Eastern Canada. . . .

goosefoot maple† See **striped maple.**
1924 SHERMAN *Nature Stories* 77: The Striped Maple of the east and the Vine Maple of the west are scarcely more than shrubs. The former is also known as the Goosefoot Maple, or Moosewood.

goose-grass *n.* any of several herbs supposedly eaten by geese, especially silverweed, *Polygonum aviculare,* and horsetail, *Equisetum* sp.
1810 (1897) COUES *New Light* II 667: The snow prevented them [horses] from filling their bellies with that small goosegrass, which is the only thing for them in these swamps. **1888** (1890) ST. MAUR *Impressions* 225: I woke about midnight, and heard something splashing in the creek, but thinking it was only some of the ponies drinking, or crossing the water to another bank of goose-grass we had come through from the other

side, I slept until morning. **1957** FISHER *Pemmican* 198: It had taken its way through goose grass and juniper and scrub pine and willow. . . .

goose ground *North* a region where geese are plentiful.
1896 RUSSELL *Far North* 258: A much smaller number than formerly is obtained at Big Island, a famous "goose ground," and they are surely passing away.

goose hunt *Hist.* at the Hudson Bay trading posts, an organized shoot during the spring and fall migration to lay in a supply of geese to be salted or frozen for food. See also **first goose** and **salt goose**.
1784 (1954) *Moose Ft Jnls* 41: . . . packing and getting things in readiness for the Goose hunt at the Eastward. . . . **1834** (1947) HARGRAVE *Correspondence* 151: . . . upon the Fall "Goose Hunt" as it is called, the living of the people at the different posts on the sea coast depends. **1963** DAVIES *Northern Quebec* 266: The fall of 1816, even at Big River, was a bad one for country provisions as the goose hunt had proved indifferent. . . .

goose month [trans. < Cree; see 1965 quote] the month in which the spring migration of geese occurs, roughly from mid-March to mid-April. Cp. **goose moon**.
1784 PENNANT *Arctic Zoology* cxciii: The savages, in some respects, regulate their months by the appearance of birds; and have their Goose month from the vernal appearance of Geese from the south. **1939** *Beaver* Sep. 34/1: Spring arrived in April—the goose month. . . . **1965** *Globe and Mail* (Toronto) 24 May 4/1: April in the Cree dialect of this area is Niskapesim, goose month. That means Canada geese; and September is Wawaypesim, wavy goose moon ("wavy" being English-Cree slang for blue and snowy goose).

goose moon See 1749 quote. Cp. **goose month**.
1749 DRAGE *Voyage* II 30: There is a certain Season when these Birds are expected on their Journey Northward, and they are expected at York Fort and Churchill near at the same time, for which Reason, at both Places the[y] call the New-Moon nearest the twenty-fifth of March, or the Spring Moon with us, the Goose Moon. **1921** HEMING *Drama of Forests* 257: Yes, truly, the long-tarrying but wonderous Goose Moon had at last arrived, and at last, too, the spring hunt was on.

goose stand a type of blind used in hunting geese.
1743 (1949) ISHAM *Observations* 150: I have Known the Natives when sitting in a goose stand to Kill bushels of them, and Carry to the tent for Childn. to play with, not Eating them but in Case of Necessity. **1921** HEMING *Drama of Forests* 274: The next day the hunters built a "goose stand" on the sandy beach of Willow Point by making a screen about six feet long by three feet high of willow branches. . . . **1963** MCTAVISH *Behind the Palisades* 92: Sitting in a goose-stand all day . . . is a tiresome task, but must be persevered in to obtain results.

goose tent *Obs.* a shelter of wood or of willow branches used as a blind in a goose hunt.
1697 (1929) KELSEY *Papers* 75: . . . one hand came from the goose tent for provision[s]. . . . **1785** (1954) *Moose Ft.Jnls* 115: Mr. Brand, the shipwright and Linklater with one of the Batteaux fetched home the Powder Shot &c. from the East Bluff Goose Tent.

goose winter *North* a spring storm of wet snow arriving in the goose month, *q.v.*
1921 HEMING *Drama of Forests* 273: Then, as likely as

not, a few days later, what is called a 'goose winter'—a heavy, wet snowstorm followed by colder weather—may come along and try to drive the birds all back again. . . . *Ibid.*: Before the bad weather completes its useless work a timely south wind may arrive, and with the aid of a milder spell, will utterly destroy the "goose winter."

go out 1 of ice, break up in the spring and move with the current until melted.
1743 (1949) ISHAM *Observations* 72: I have Known the Ice when going out of the Rivers, to appear Like a wood or grove of trees with the perdigious Quantity of wood, which has been brought of the shores by the water and Ice, when these floods has happn'd. **1904** ROBERTS *Watchers of Trails* 275: It [the river ice] appeared placid . . . but the woodsman's practised eye perceived that it might break up, or "go out," at any moment. **1963** PATTERSON *Far Pastures* 78: I met Kenai Creek, its ice covered with muddy water and odd flotsam, flowing upstream against itself, and in the distance was a muttering as if of thunder—The Sikanni Chief [River] had "gone out."

2 See **go outside**.
1909 CAMERON *New North* 139: The older man had been in the North for years and was "going out." **1948** *Beaver* Sep. 14/1: They [H.B.C. officers and men] thought and wrote much of promotion ("getting the parchment") and of "going out" for their furloughs. **1963** SYMONS *Many Trails* 68: . . . I asked him why he was going out.

go outside *Esp.North* leave the North to visit or return to more settled areas. See also **go out** (def. 2) and **outside,** *n.* (def. 1). Cp. **go in.**
1896 RUSSELL *Far North* 50: To "go in," by the way, is to descend the Athabasca; to return to civilization is to "go outside." **1945** GARD *Johnny Chinook* xiv: The people of the Peace country always speak of "going outside" when they visit Edmonton or Vancouver.

gopher ['gofɚ] *n.* [< Cdn F *gaufre gris* < F *gaufre* honeycomb, from the structure of the gopher's burrow] *West* **1** one of several kinds of small ground squirrels.
1853 REID *Young Voyageurs* 8: [The prairie] is the favourite home of . . . the gauffres. . . . **1873** (1962) *Maclean's* 20 Oct. 40/2: On the prairies the little gopher or ground squirrel is almost equally abundant. . . . **1905** OUTRAM *Cdn Rockies* 12: A chipmunk, with its bright-striped coat, or a more soberly clad gopher will sometimes dash across the trail or make remarks from the security of a snug retreat. **1958** CAMERON *Canadian Mammals* 59: Besides the Richardson ground squirrel, which is the commonest "gopher" on the Canadian prairies, there are several other species, such as the thirteen-lined, Franklin, Columbian, Parry's and mantled. **1964** *Maclean's* 2 May 22/1: [It was] probably a Saturday morning on a return from a gopher hunt in the prairie beyond.

2 *Slang, Obs.* a member of the North West Mounted Police, *q.v.*
1927 LONGSTRETH *Silent Force* 154: . . . the Force objected to their name of "gophers," the gopher being an animal that takes to its hole at the first intimation of peril, and stays there till it is past. . . .

gopher-getter *n.* a poison for exterminating gophers.
1961 *Edmonton Jnl* 3 July 16/1: The gopher-getter is being used successfully in a liquidation program in the Okanagan Valley.

gopher hawk *West* the ferruginous rough-leg hawk, *Archibuteo ferrugineus,* whose principal food is gophers.
1952 PUTNAM *Cdn Regions* 39: Among the breeding birds of the prairie may be mentioned the . . . prairie falcon . . . gopher hawk. . . .

gophering *n. Slang* the digging of small mines; prospecting and digging.
[**1944** ADAMS *Western Words* 67: gophering. Digging for something. I once heard a cowman characterize a certain old prospector by saying he'd "been gophering in them hills as far back as an Injun could remember."]
1958 *Northern Miner* 27 Nov. 25/4: The mining fields in Canada were painfully restricted at that time to Eastern Ontario, Kenora, Sudbury and some gophering in Nova Scotia and British Columbia.

gopher ranch *Jocular* a ranch or farm having more gophers than cattle; a place that produces more gophers than anything else.
[**1905** *Eye Opener* (Calgary) 28 Jan. 1/4: Well, I am happy to inform you that I now have no fewer than 1800 head of gophers on my place.] **1905** (1951) ROBINS & RAY *Cdn Humour* 5: [title given to article] THE GOPHER RANCH. **1922** STEAD *Neighbours* 122: "Well, how goes it on the gopher ranch?"

G.O.P. of Canada *Obs.* See **Grand Old Party.**
1896 *Kootenaian* 6 June 2/2: Ye Gods! to what straits must the G.O.P. of Canada be reduced when it picks up an ex-bookmaker, ex-publisher of an indecent sheet which the authorities were forced to suppress, to do its carpet-bagging.

gore† *n. Hist.* in Upper Canada: **1** a parcel of land remaining after a region had been surveyed into townships, concessions, and lots of uniform size, such parcels being usually unassigned and frequently a bone of contention.
1791 (1905) *Ont.Bur.Arch.Rep.* III 130: Such a direction if extended . . . throughout the Settlement will cast the whole country into Confusion, by cutting the farms . . . into small gores, or Angles, besides not agreeing to the general course of the Lake for any distance. **1821** *U.C. Gaz.* (York [Toronto]) 28 May 60/1: Four hundred and twenty-five acres of Land, for sale, in a Gore between the Townships of Kingston and Earnestown, bounded on the East by the Township road, and on the north by a small lake. **1896** GOURLAY *Hist.Ottawa* 137: North Gower is one of the three gores in the County of Carleton containing about 33,000 acres.

2 often **Gore,** a specific tract of such land.
1833 *Canadian Freeman* (York [Toronto]) 5 Sep. 4: For Sale. The North West Half of Lot No. 97, in the 10th Concession, Gore of Toronto, containing 100 acres. **1853** *Hamilton Gaz.* (C.W.) 8 Aug. 3/1: The expression of the public is evidently in having the Gore unencumbered by buildings of any kind and that it be converted into a park, or promenade. **1909** *London & Middlesex Hist.Soc. Trans.* II 10: In the old days this street was the scene of a hot contest between citizens and soldiers, when the latter extended their pine stump fence across the street and enclosed the gore in their barrack grounds.

go to ice *Sealing, Nfld* See **ice** (def. 1b).

Gourlayism *n. Hist.* the principles and policy of Robert Gourlay, 1778-1863, an outspoken Scot who publicly opposed the oligarchy in Upper Canada in 1818, being imprisoned and deported for his pains. Hence *Gourlayite.*
1819 *Canadian Courant* (Montreal) 6 Feb. 3/2: Is then this modern "Lettre de Cachet," this Anti-British persecution intended as the sovereign panacea against Gourlayism? **1824** *Colonial Advocate* (York [Toronto]) 18 May 4/2: We are not disappointed land-speculators; and as we were not in Canada when Mr. Gourlay's convention took place, we are, of course, not Gourlayites.

Government House the official residence of the monarch's representative, in modern use that of the Governor General (Rideau Hall in Ottawa) or of the Lieutenant-Governor of a province.
1785 *Quebec Gaz.* 28 Dec. 2/1: He was welcomed on shore by Major General Campbell and his Excellency Governor Parr, by whom he was conducted to the Government House. **1893** YEIGH *Ont.Parliament* 83: The first Government House in York was the canvas tent erected by Governor Simcoe when he first visited York, and which he occupied temporarily until his residence was built on the banks of the Don, known as Castle Frank. **1962** *Weekend Mag.* 9 June 2/1: "We're not going to land in the poorhouse just because you insist on giving a reception like a Government House levée." **1966** *Globe and Mail* (Toronto) 15 Jan. 8/8: The perils of Government House, one of Alberta's most intriguing tales, may have its finale written by . . . the new Lieutenant-Governor.

government liquor store See **liquor store.**
1938 CASH *I Like B.C.* 110: Within the city limits, beer can only be sold in dozens to people with a twenty-five cent permit in the Government Liquor store, where they also sell every other kind of intoxicant. **1966** *Globe Mag.* 11 June 3/4: . . . the tiny weather-beaten, peaked-roofed building sits humbly in the shadow of a shiny Government liquor store. . . .

government reserve *Hist.* a tract of unsettled land belonging to the Crown.
1828 BIDWELL *Tor.Pub.Lib.Mss B104* 59: He had encroached upon the government reserve which ran along the bank of the river, had enclosed it with a fence, and had built a blacksmith's shop on it. **1889** WITHROW *Our Own Country* 600: About midnight I stopped off at Banff Springs, where there is a Government reserve . . . which is being converted into a national park. . . .

governor *n.* **1** *Hist.* the person in charge of a fort or factory, *qq.v.,* of the Hudson's Bay Company.
1739 (1744) DOBBS *Hudson's Bay* 116: I was this Year at Churchill Factory, where Mr. Norton is Governor. **1819** WENTZEL *Letters* 124: Some of the Hudson's Bay Company's clerks have three hundred pounds sterling, others less, and I believe few have more except those who are styled "Governors," these have five hundred. **1937** *Beaver* Sep. 37/1: Though the strictly official designation of these officers was "Chief Factor," the officer in charge of such a fort or factory at this period was generally designed "Governor" or "Chief," while the officer commanding an "inland" or subordinate trading post was usually styled "inland trader" or "master at So-and-So House."

2 the principal officer of the Hudson's Bay Company in Canada. See also **governor-in-chief** (def. 2).

1894 BEGG *Hist.of B.C.* 114: In 1856, the affairs of 152 establishments were managed by a governor, 16 chief factors, and 29 chief traders, assisted by 5 surgeons, 87 clerks, 67 postmasters, 500 voyageurs, and 1,200 permanent servants, besides sailors on sea-going vessels and persons temporarily employed—about three thousand men in all.

3 *Obs.* See **governor general.**
1845 *Niagara Argus* (Niagara-on-the-Lake, C.W.) 5 Feb. 1/3: That Civil List was secured by the Union Bill, and the Governor's Salary fixed at £7000 sterling a year, a larger income than that of the President of the United States.

governor general† the representative of the monarch in executive control in one of the provinces of British North America; in modern use, the representative appointed on the advice of the Canadian government to act on behalf of the Queen (or King) of Canada. See also **governor-in-chief** (def. 1).
1764 *Quebec Gaz.* 16 Aug. 2/1: We the British Merchants of the City of Quebec, beg leave to congratulate Your Excellency on being appointed Governor General of this Province. **1844** *Bytown* [Ottawa] *Gaz.* 4 Jan. 2/2: The Governor-general of Canada is about to prorogue the House preparatory to a dissolution. **1887** *Grip* (Toronto) June 15/2: . . . while we are all pleased that the Governor-General has been *feted* and made much of in Toronto, to keep well in mind, at the same time, that he is but a figure-head. **1958** *Edmonton Jnl* 28 June 30/2: CBC radio and television will carry a message from the governor-general at 5:45 p.m. EDT Tuesday over the Trans-Canada network. . . .

governor-general-in-council *n.* the governor general acting with the advice and consent of the Privy Council of Canada as a formal instrument for legalizing cabinet decisions.
☛ *In present-day practice the term* **Governor-General-in-Council** *refers to the cabinet acting with the formal approval of the Governor General.*
1885 GEMMILL *Companion* 33: Petitions of this nature should be addressed to "His Excellency the Governor-General in Council." **1902** [?] *High River Times* 11 July 1/4: He gave notice he would offer an amendment entrusting the protection of navigation to the governor-general-in-council. **1959** *Maclean's* 1 Aug. 7: It is true that lately the Governor-General-in-Council has commuted to life imprisonment about ninety percent of death sentences. **1963** MORTON *Kingdom of Canada* 258: The members of the second chamber, the Legislative-Council, were appointed by the Governor General in Council for life.

governor-general's warrant a legal device by which a government after dissolution and prior to an election may raise money to meet its current bills in the interim preceding the convening of a new parliament.
1963 *Kingston Whig-Standard* (Ont.) 28 Jan. 3/3: In the face of such a prospect, the government might dissolve Parliament for a new election, financing its operations until a new Parliament meets through governor-general's warrants—in effect, cabinet orders.

governor-in-chief *n.* **1** *Hist.* See **governor general.**
1823 *P.E.I.Register* (Charlottetown) 26 July 2/3: His Excellency the Governor in Chief, the Earl of Dalhousie . . . arrived at Halifax on the 3d inst. from Quebec. **1839** *Montreal Transcript* 19 Nov. 342/1: Yesterday

morning, his Excellency the Governor-in-Chief and suite left this city on his way to the Upper Province.

2 See **governor** (def. 2).
1962 DICKIE *Great Golden Plain* 96: The business in Canada was to be carried on by a governor-in-chief with a council of chief factors. Some of the shares were distributed among the chief factors, the chief traders, and retiring partners.

governor-in-council† *n. Hist.* in Canada, a colonial governor acting with the advice but not necessarily the consent of the executive council (def. 1).
1871 *Wkly Manitoban* 25 Mar. 3/5: At anytime after the first of May, A.D. 1874, the Governor in Council may, subject to the then existing rights, withdraw from the operation of the above system land to the width of three townships on each side of the line, finally sanctioned, for the inter-oceanic railway. **1883** HATTON & HARVEY *Newfoundland* 444: Two legislative Chambers were appointed, the House of Assembly, to be elected, the Legislative Council to be nominated by "The Governor in Council."

G.P.C. or **G.P.Currency** *Obs.* See **Grand Portage Currency.**
1800 (1933) MCLEOD *Diary* 132: I Sold the Grey Colt to La Rose for 100 lb G.P.C. **1804** (1897) COUES *New Light* I 247: Men not so difficult to hire this year as last, when boaters for Lower Red River refused G.P.Cy. and milieux 500, with extra equipments. **1810** (1950) THOMPSON *Journals* 94: [I] engaged Pierre Gignon to work at the House &c for 400 Livres G.P. Currency pro Ann. . . .

Grade 13 *Esp.Ont.* a fifth year of secondary school.
1963 *Globe and Mail* (Toronto) 21 May 7/3: Ontario has had a fifth year in its secondary school program for a long time. It has gone under different names—the one best known to older people was the Upper School—but it is now known far and wide as Grade 13. **1964** *Ibid.* 30 Dec. 6/2: Most schools find it difficult to persuade their students to stay on until Grade 13.

graduand† ['grædju,ænd] *n.* a person qualified for and about to receive a graduation diploma or a degree.
1958 *Edmonton Jnl* 14 June 28/4: About 215 graduands were awarded diplomas Friday at the 55th commencement exercises of Alberta College, held in the college auditorium. **1958** *Lethbridge Herald* (Alta) 31 May 7/5: Shirley Housenga expressed the thanks of the graduands. **1966** *R.M.C.Review* (Yearbook) 8: My pleasure today is completed by your choice of the other two honorary graduands.

grain elevator† **1** See **country elevator.**
1877 GRANT *Ocean to Ocean* 28: Now, there is a thriving town . . . with a grain elevator. . . . **1963** *Canada Month* Feb. 9/1: Small railway towns dot the flat prairie landscape, each with its tall grain elevator, grimy railroad shed and general store. . . .

2 See **terminal elevator.**
1882 *Edmonton Bull.* 25 Nov. 4/1: A grain elevator having a capacity of 80,000 bushels and to cost $2,000 is to be erected at Brandon. **1958** WELLS *Georgian Bay* 19: With its bustle of busy, gaily-painted and self-important little tugs . . . and the white columns of the grain elevators rising behind, it is something good

for the cruising man to sit and look at when the cruising day is done.

grain fair a fair where wheat, barley, oats, etc. are exhibited and judged.
1960 BUBLITZ *Dotted Line* 38: We held the grain fair at our place that fall.

grain king *West* a successful producer of grain, especially wheat, on a large scale.
1957 *Herald-Tribune* (Grande Prairie, Alta) 17 Dec. 1/8: Mayors from other Peace River centres, former grain kings and prominent oldtimers will be among the special guests.

grain tank *West* a large, high box built on a wagon or truck bed and used for hauling grain.
1963 PATTERSON *Far Pastures* 69: The grain tanks were each drawn by four horses and the teamsters sat high. . . .

grammar school† *Hist.* a tax-supported secondary school; high school, *q.v.*
1808 *York* [Toronto] *Gaz.* 6 Aug. 4/1: On Wednesday . . . the examination of the scholars in the District Grammar School, was held in the presence of the Committee. . . . **1876** CAMPBELL *Yarmouth N.S.* 166: The Grammar School . . . provided in some measure for the wants of all who lived in the vicinity of the County Town. **1914** *London and Middlesex Hist.Soc. Trans.* V 34: The Educational Act of 1871 substituted for the title of Grammar School that of High School. **1953** LEBOURDAIS *Nation of North* 42: Despite the fact that schools in Canada West in 1865 contained 179,332 girls, it was not till 1868 that girls could legally attend grammar schools.

Grand Banks the extensive shoals, or bank (def. 1), lying southeast of Newfoundland, famous as cod-fishing grounds. See also **Banks** (def. 2) and **Great Banks**.
1935 *Beaver* Dec. 8/2: To the south and east of the island [Newfoundland] one hundred miles or so lies the famous Great Grand Bank . . . some eighty thousand square miles in area. . . . **1962** *Time* (Cdn ed.) 2 Mar. 9/1: Doughty Nova Scotian sailors loaded their schooners with codfish from the Newfoundland Grand Banks and timber from the forests of the Maritimes. . . .

Grand Brulé *Cdn French* a large area of burnt-over forest land (latterly only in French-Canadian place names). See also **brulé** (def. 1).
1793 (1933) MACDONELL *Diary* 77: At intervals through the pines we could see like a large clearing apparently made by fire and which the Canadians would call a Grand-Brulé. **1854** *Quebec Observer* 10 Oct.: With the exception of the Grand Brule (where the soil is sandy) the land continues of a similar character. . . .

grand calumet or **pipe** *Obs.* a calumet, *q.v.*, used on ceremonial occasions.
1754 (1907) HENDAY *Journal* 337: Our Leader set on several grand-pipes, and smoked all round, according to their usual custom: not a word was spoke on either side. **1755** (1907) *Ibid.* 348: All hands employed building Canoes & in the Evening Smoking the Grand Calimut &c. *c*1804 (1890) GRANT *Sauteux Indians* 336: The *Grand Calumet* dance is only performed on some extraordinary occasion. . . .

Grand Carrying Place *Obs.* See **Grand Portage**.

1776 (1951) *Sask.Jnls* 29: . . . this Year no less than Sixty Canoes with Goods came from the Grand Carrying Place.

grand marais See **marais**.

grand medicine *Hist.* among certain Indian tribes, a solemn initiation ceremony admitting novices to higher knowledge of medicine (def. 1). See also **midewewin**.
1801 (1897) COUES *New Light* I 182: [We] found the Indians busy making the grand medicine—a ceremony performed every spring, when they meet and there is some novice to be admitted into the mysteries of this solemn affair. **1834** *Nor'Wester* (R.R.S.) 31 May 1/1: Last evening we went over to the Lodges to see a "Grand Medicine Dance." **1956** LEECHMAN *Native Tribes* 51: Among the Ojibwa and, to a lesser extent, among their neighbors the Cree, membership in the *midewewin,* or Grand Medicine Society, was eagerly sought.

Grand Medicine Society See **midewewin**. See also **grand medicine**.

grand muskeg See quote. See also **muskeg** (def. 1).
1959 *Edmonton Jnl* 7 Feb. 4/3: . . . the country between Fort Assiniboine and Lesser Slave Lake was known as the "grand muskeg". . . .

Grand Old Party *Hist.* the Conservative Party, especially under the leadership of Sir John A. Macdonald. See also **G.O.P. of Canada**.
1891 *Grip* (Toronto) 3 Jan. 5/1: We congratulate Sir John that, this being so, he has one annexationist less in the Grand Old Party. **1906** *Eye Opener* (Calgary) 6 Oct. 2/1: They visited Calgary, among other places, all yelping and bawling for the Grand Old Party.

Grand Pays See **le Grand Pays**.

grand pipe See **grand calumet**.

Grand Portage *Hist.* a rendezvous point for fur traders at the Lake Superior end of the long portage to the Rainy River waterway, used by the North West Company as the main entrepôt between Montreal and the inland posts of the Northwest.
1773 (1908) COCKING *Journal* 119: . . . have sent two [canoes full of furs] down to the Grand portage. . . . **1793** (1933) MACDONELL *Diary* 92: The Grand Portage is situated in the bottom of a shallow Bay perhaps three miles deep and about one league and a half wide at its mouth. . . . **1850** BIGSBY *Shoe and Canoe* II 182: Ninety years, however, have produced no change at the Grand Portage, where such an event would have been readily detected. **1939** *Beaver* June 15/1: After Great Britain and the United States signed a treaty of peace in 1783, Grand Portage on the northwest shore of Lake Superior, "the Great Carrying Place" for canoes of the fur trade route from Montreal to the Rockies, was placed in United States territory.

Grand Portage currency *Hist.* a scale of currency reckoned in French livres, *q.v.*, and used by the North West Company in their inland fur trade up to 1820, originally used by the French-Canadian traders. See also **G.P.C.** and **North West Currency**. Cp. **Michilimackinac currency**.
1793 (1933) MACDONELL *Diary* 93: . . . the currency of the North west is double that of Canada which currency had its origine, I presume, from the men's wages being formerly paid in peltries and it was supposed that one *liver's* worth of Furs would be worth two livers to the person that took it to Montreal to be paid. **1930** *Cdn*

Hist.Rev. XI 130: Grand Portage currency was reckoned as twelve livres to the pound. **1933** GATES *Five Traders* 94: Grand Portage currency was reckoned by units designated as G.P.C. Twelve of these units were equal to a pound sterling.

Grand River *Hist.* an early name of the Ottawa River, taken over from the French-Canadian explorers.
1792 (1911) SIMCOE *Diary* 99: [We] saw the junction of the Ottawa or Grand River which divided Upper and Lower Canada with the St. Lawrence. . . . **1883** FRASER *Shanty* 339: It is quite a common thing when you are speaking to these backwoods river-men about the Ottawa, for them to ask "is it the Grand River you mean?" for by this and no other name will they recognize and designate it. **1933** ROLYAT *Wilderness Walls* 10: How long since they had left behind the huge rafts of square timber . . . on the smooth bosom of "the grand river," as it was often called. . . .

Grand River canoe *Hist.* See **Montreal canoe** and picture.
1793 (1933) MacDONELL *Diary* 97: These N.W. canoes are about half the size of the Montreal or Grand River Canoes and when loaded to the utmost can carry a Tun and a half. **1918** DAVIDSON *North West Co.* 218: Fewer men were required to carry a North canoe than an Ottawa or Grand River canoe.

grand voyageur *Obs.* See **porkeater** (def. 1a).
1792 (1911) SIMCOE *Diary* 93: This practice has been learned from Grand Voyageurs or Canadians who are hired by the North-West Company to take canoes to the Grand Portage beyond Lake Superior.

grand voyer [< Cdn F < F] *Que., Hist.* a municipal official responsible for the surveying, building, and maintenance of the roads and road allowances in a district; a road commissioner, *q.v.*
1765 *Quebec Gaz.* 30 May 3/3: Grand-Voyer Francois Joseph Cugner. . . . **1777** *Ibid.* 17 Apr. 1/1: Standing pickets shall nevertheless be permitted to remain in places where the said Grand Voyer shall be of opinion that the same can be of no prejudice to the road adjoining thereto. **1832** *Vindicator* (Montreal) 9 Mar. 2/6: The powers heretofore vested in the Grand Voyers and their Deputies are to be vested in Road Commissioners. **1904** *U of T Stud.Hist.& Econ.* II 174: Under the French regime the *grand voyer* was subject to the control of the intendant.

gras *n.* See **castor gras.**
1964 *Wildlife Rev.* May 22: Not only did he have to catch the beaver but he was expected to wear three-quarters of his catch. You no sooner got comfortable in a Gras than you had to start breaking in a Sec.

grass hockey *B.C. and Alta, Informal* field hockey (as opposed to ice hockey).
1960 *Ubyssey* (Vancouver) 12 Oct. 6/1: Important men's Grasshockey practice Thursday, October 13, at 13:30. **1962** *Globe and Mail* (Toronto) 1 Sep. 21/8: . . . he chose to further belittle the scheme by suggesting UBC really meant "grass hockey." **1964** *Maclean's* 16 Nov. 81/2: I . . . do solemnly swear never to waste company time arguing . . . or raving about . . . lawn bowling and grass hockey. . . .

grass-line *n.* **1** *Lumbering* a light line used to haul back heavier lines. See also **straw-line.**
1919 *Camp Worker* 26 Apr. 5/2: There are innumerable firms that have monopolized the services of the best hooker that ever gave signals for the high-rigger, while his short-handed crew changed the haul-back without the assistance of a grass-line.

2 a line of grass, sedge, etc. showing above ice and snow and marking the margin of a river, lake, etc.
1944 MARTIN *Cdn Wilderness* 22: I make these sets as soon as the ice will carry me. I put them about three or four rods from shore, or beyond the grass line, and make them in pairs about six rods apart.

grass roots† **1** *Placer Mining* the top stratum of gravel immediately below the grass roots.
1909 SERVICE *Cheechako* 17: We were rich in a day beyond our dreams, it was gold from the grass-roots down. . . . **1958** LINDSAY *Caribou Story* 14: . . . they made the richest strike up to that time with gold running from the grass roots.

2 *Politics* the base of the political pyramid, as the voting public, the riding associations, etc.
1956 *Financial Post* 30 June 13/4: Now, after diligent research in the grass roots of democracy, I know better. **1957** HUTCHISON *Canada* 76: Our purpose in North Rustico was to attend a political meeting and inspect real democracy in action at the grass roots. **1963** *Globe and Mail* (Toronto) 24 Mar. 7/7: Just how much these have seeped down to the grass-roots level will likely be indicated when the counting is completed on election day.

gravel puncher *Placer Mining, Slang* a miner using primitive equipment.
1951 ANGIER *At Home* 197: Hard long work might have paid me a dollar a day, which was what the few remaining gravel punchers managed to gross on some of the better bars upriver.

Graveyard of the (North) Atlantic See 1958 quote.
1892 (1908) DAWSON & SUTHERLAND *Geography* 72: It [Sable Island] is . . . sometimes called the "Graveyard of the North Atlantic." **1931** SEARY *Romance* 8: Even as early as 1598, Sable Island had begun to earn its title of "The Graveyard of the Atlantic." **1958** *Citizen* 31 Dec. 4/7: One hundred and eighty miles east of Halifax lies . . . Sable Island . . . for long known as the graveyard of the Atlantic.

Gray *n.* See **Grey.**
☛ **gray.** *Compounds having this adjective as the first element are entered with this spelling, though* **grey** *is perfectly acceptable as an alternative form. Compounds based on proper names spelled* **Grey** *are entered under that spelling.*

grayback *n. Maritimes* a large ocean wave.
1916 WALLACE *Shack Locker* 104: A seething grayback struck the dory and piled over the low gunnel. **1964** *Atlantic Advocate* July 25/1: A languid "greyback" sea crawled under the dory's stern; the . . . craft yawed and slid . . . a little cloud of spray from the breaking crest of the following sea blew over.

gray bear *Obs.* **1 a.** See **grizzly bear.**
1819 (1922) HARMON *Journal* 367: The grey bear differs but little in shape, from those of a smaller kind and of a different colour . . . a beautiful lively silver grey. **1950** MCCOWAN *Animals of the Cdn Rockies* 4: Dr. Richardson, naturalist to the Franklin Expedition of 1830, tells of a man at Edmonton being scalped by a Grey Bear.

b. the hide of this animal.

1855 (1924) *Beaver* Dec. 31: The freemen traded a few rats and a grey bear.

2 a color phase of the black bear, *q.v.*

1821 (1823) FRANKLIN *Journey* 648: Individuals vary in colour from black to different shades of brown, and are known to the traders under the different names of Black, Brown, Cinnamon, and Grey Bears.

gray birch See **wire birch.**
1823 HALIBURTON *General Descr.N.S.* 26: Natural forest trees are elm, cherry; white, black, yellow, and gray birch.... **1956** *Native Trees* 138: Wire Birch *Betula populifolia* [also called] Grey birch....

gray cod *Pacific Coast* the Pacific cod, *Gadus macrocephalus.*
1958 *Sun* (Vancouver) 11 Apr. 2/2: ... also graded as minkfeed were 20,000 pounds of the grey cod.
1964 CARL *Marine Fishes B.C.* 41: This species is known as "grey cod" by commercial fishermen.

gray crow *West* Clarke's nutcracker, *Nucifraga columbiana.*
1953 MOWERY *Mounted Police* 64: They climbed out of the hardwoods into the big conifers, where the gray crow was at home; out of these into the storm-gnarled tamarack and ground pines.... **1955** MCCOWAN *Upland Trails* 64: But magpies ... loot the larders of the Grey crows, thus compelling the wrathful owners henceforth to hide their emergency rations in secret nooks under the snow.

gray deer *Obs.* See **moose.**
1791 (1934) TURNOR *Journal* 444: They saw only grey Deer and wild Fowl upon the flat country. **1820** (1938) SIMPSON *Athabasca Jnl* 49: [The Chipewyan] may devote their attention to the more easy mode of subsistence by following the Grey Deer.

grayfish† *n. Pacific Coast* the dogfish, *Squalus suckleyi.*
1962 *Commercial Letter* Oct. 4/1: Other fish, caught commercially off the Pacific coast include sole, greyfish, ling cod and sablefish. **1964** CARL *Marine Fishes B.C.* 17: Another name for this small shark is grayfish.

gray goose 1 See **Canada goose.**
1717 (1932) KNIGHT *Journals* 126: The Indians ware out & brought home 4 Grey Geese. **1896** RUSSELL *Far North* 258: The "gray goose" is common throughout this region, at least during the migratory season, and furnishes food in the spring for many natives. **1942** TWOMEY & HERRICK *Needle to North* 215: The five big gray geese ... were wearily walking among the rocks and gravel that edged the ice-fringed creek. **1959** MCATEE *Folk-Names* 8: Eastern Canada Goose [is also called] ... grey goose (Rather general)....

2 See **white-fronted goose.**
1922 TAVERNER *Birds of Eastern Can.* 79: Genus—Anser. Grey Goose. White-Fronted Goose.... **1954** HAMILTON *Prairies* 200: Mr. Hamilton brought in a handsome grey goose that he said was identical with the variety known as the "grey Lag" in the far away Shetland Islands.

gray jay† See **Canada jay.**
1938 (1950) STANWELL-FLETCHER *Driftwood Valley* 109: We were a mile from the cabin by noon and then our

fluffy gray jays suddenly appeared from nowhere.
1963 *Weekend Mag.* 16 Nov. 41/1: Canada jay is being blacked out [by the American Ornithologists' Union], and the disgusting name of grey jay is being substituted.

grayling *n.* See **Arctic grayling.**
1897 TUTTLE *Golden North* 190: Whitefish, losh and graylings are found in large quantities in the Yukon, and afford more food for the natives than the salmon.
1963 *Globe and Mail* (Toronto) 23 Mar. 32/1: The fishing there would make your eyeballs loll out on stocks—lake trout and pike ... and grayling that are nudging the world's record of 4 pounds 9 ounces.

gray moose *Obs.* **1** See **moose** (def. 1). See also **gray deer.**
1784 PENNANT *Arctic Zoology* 28: In most parts of North America they are called the Grey moose.... **1823** HALIBURTON *General Descr.N.S.* 30: The native animals [include] Grey Moose, Carraboo....

2 See **wapiti.**
1853 REID *Young Voyageurs* 165: [The wapiti's] name of "grey moose" is a hunter appelation, to distinguish it from the real moose, which some hunters know as the "black moose."

Gray Nun See **Grey Nun.**

gray-out *n. North* See quote. Cp. **white-out.**
1965 SYMINGTON *Tuktu* 20: When the sun is low in the sky and there is a low overcast, the bane of the northern traveller occurs—the dreaded grey-out. The muted greys of the snow blend into the dull greys of the overhanging cloud, obscuring the horizon and baffling perspective. A hump in the snow may look like a distant hill, whereas if may be merely a snow-covered stone a few yards away. Small hummocks and hollows cause walkers to stumble and fall, and airplane pilots may make serious errors in judgement of distance.

gray pine† See **Banksian pine.**
1824 (1890) MASSON *Les Bourgeois* II 447: The fort was built of red spruce and grey pine, of which there is some hereabouts. **1956** *Native Trees* 16: Banksian pine [is also called] grey pine....

gray rabbit *Obs.* See **cottontail.**
1866 KING *Sportsman in Can.* 31: The "Grey-Rabbit" ... in general appearance very much resembles our common rabbit [of England].

gray seal a large seal of the North Atlantic, *Halichoerus grypus.* See also **horse head.**
1894 *Trans.Roy.Soc.Can.* XI 2 6: They are of two species, the large grey or Greenland seal and the common or harbour seal. **1965** *Cdn Geog.Jnl* Sep. 93/1: In January ... grey seals, largest and rarest of all Canadian seals (*Phocidae*) haul out on this island [Basque I., off Cape Breton] to bear their young.

gray sheep See **Stone sheep.**
1811 (1897) COUES *New Light* II 680: These are the gray sheep which have been seen about this place [Rockies], and which delight to dwell among precipices and caverns, where they feed on a peculiar sort of clay.
1948 CAMERON *Cdn Mammals* 26: The white or "Dall" sheep occur in northern British Columbia, the Yukon and Northwest Territories, and the grey or "Stone" sheep occur in British Columbia.

Gray Sister See **Grey Sister.**

gray trout See **lake trout.**
1896 ROBERTS *Camp-Fire* 70: I wanted to set night-lines for the gray trout, or *togue,* which haunt the

waters of Big Squatook.... **1938** *Beaver* June 33/2: Grey trout as well as speckled made fishing at the head waters of the Rupert well worthwhile. **1958** *Evening Telegram* (St. John's) 29 Apr. 16/3: The open season for ... grey trout: April 15-Sept. 15 [in Nova Scotia]....

gray wavey See **white-fronted goose.**
1890 *Trans. Hist.& Sci.Soc.Man. 39* 12: A considerable number of nests of this Grey Wavy was discovered in the vicinity of fresh water lakes in timbered tracts, as well as along the lower Anderson river to the sea. **1959** MCATEE *Folk-Names* 9: White-fronted Goose [is also called] ... grey wavey....

gray wolf† 1 the great wolf of the plains, *Canis lupus nubilus.* See also **buffalo wolf.**
1895 PARKER *Adventurer* 102: Skins hung along two sides, with bullet-holes and knife-holes showing ... of the great grey wolf.... **1920** SCHOOLING *Hudson's Bay Co.* 60: The Grey Wolf is one of the shyest of wild animals, and, though often heard at night, it is seldom seen until it has been caught or killed....

2 See **coyote** (def. 1).
1963 SYMONS *Many Trails* 42: They too had known the long night vigils over their herds, when the calves were coming and the grey wolves were abroad. *Ibid.* 119: ... it had certainly been the best coyote hunting I had had for ages, for the little grey wolves had increased with the abundance of the prey.

grazing lease *West* a tract of land set aside for the grazing of livestock and leased to ranchers by the government. See also **lease.**
1888 (1963) *Herald Mag.* (Calgary) 14 Dec. 8/1: ... a certain portion of the press in the east is proclaiming that Alberta is closed to settlement; being parcelled out in grazing leases upon which settlers are not allowed to locate. **1963** PATTERSON *Far Pastures* 3: ... these ranchers with their warnings of dry seasons and long years of drought, are liars one and all, thinking only of hanging on to their grazing leases, worried for their creeks and springs.

grease *n. Fur Trade, Hist.* the rendered fat of large mammals, especially the bison, used as food, in pemmican, *q.v.,* and in the making of soap and candles.
1794 (1929) MCGILLIVRAY *Journal* 37: ... a band of Assiniboines arrived with a small quantity of pounded meat & Grease. **1820** (1938) SIMPSON *Athabasca Jnl* 194: Do me the favor to send . . . a few bladders of grease. **1931** NUTE *Voyageur* 213: ... the train wound its slow way back to Pembina laden with ... 166 boskoyas, or bags of grease; and 556 bladders of marrow grease.

grease bannock *North* a kind of bannock, *q.v.,* having animal grease as an ingredient.
1897 TYRRELL *Sub-Arctics* 75: At first John had confined his baking to the making of grease bannocks, which, after being formed in a pan, were removed and cooked before the fire on a stick. **1962** *B.C.Digest* Oct. 25: The moose tallow, used for filling up the seams in the patches on the boat, we also used for cooking our grease bannock.

grease bird *B.C.* See **Canada jay.**
1891 (1892) PIKE *Barren Grounds* 123: This bird is common throughout the wilder parts of Canada, and has acquired many names in different places; in the mountains of British Columbia he is the Hudson's Bay bird or grease bird, and far away to the East the moose bird, caribou bird, Rupert's bird, and camp robber.

grease cake *Nfld* See **grease bannock.**

1933 MERRICK *True North* 94: I ... sometimes bake bannock or fry grease cakes.

grease ice See quote.
1958 *Manice* 5: Grease Ice: Formed from the congelation of ice crystals in the early stages of freezing. It gives the sea surface a greasy appearance.

grease trail *Hist.* any of a number of ancient trails leading from the Pacific Coast into the interior of British Columbia, used by Indians for the trade in oolichan oil, *q.v.,* and other items.
1879 *Trans.Roy.Soc.Can.* VII 83: By the second of the above routes oolachen oil was carried far into the interior; and the old trail from Bella Coola and Fraser River is still known to the inland Indians as the "Grease Trail." **1932** *Cdn Hist.Rev.* XIII 410: It was an article of trade in great demand along the many "grease trails".... **1963** *Beaver* Autumn 40: This Grease Trail was so named because along it the Nass tribes carried much oolachan (candlefish) oil or grease to the Upper Skeena River country.

greasewood *n.* the antelope bush, *Purshia tridentata.*
1859 (1958) WATTERS *B.C.Cent.Anthol.* 246: I climbed mountains and got covered with wood-ticks as I ploughed through the sage-brush and greasewood.... **1953** MOON *Saskatchewan* 86: Low exposed ground may be covered with sagebrush, greasewood and prickly pear cactus. **1964** *B.C.Digest* Sep.-Oct. 4/1: Chukkars have spread through the desert hills around here just as they did west of Savona. In the greasewood draws between Okanagan Falls and Oliver, these nimble-footed chickens sound like a barnyard full of laying hens, especially around sunset.

Great Banks See **Grand Banks.**
1955 *Western Star* (Corner Brook, Nfld) 14 Mar. 5/2: For 400 years its menfolk have gone down to the sea in small ships to snatch a bare and uncertain living from the famous Great Banks and to market their catches as best they could.

Great Barrens (or Barren) Ground See **Barren Ground.**
1900 LONDON *Son of Wolf* 74: The canoe and bateau answered to the swift current of the Mackenzie, and they plunged into the Great Barren Ground. **1924** DORRANCE *Never Fire First* 120: No difficulty was there in guessing whose fire—not in the Great Barrens!

great bend an extensive curve in a river's course, used often as a point of reference.
1801 MACKENZIE *Voyages* lxviii: From this lake the Saskatchiwine may be considered navigable to near its sources in the rocky mountains, for canoes, and without a carrying-place, making a great bend to Cumberland House, on Sturgeon Lake. **1929** (1931) MERK *Fur Trade* 34: Committee's Punch Bowl, still so known, is in reality a pair of tarns or mountain pools, one of which empties into Whirlpool River, the headstream of the Athabasca, the other into Wood River, a tributary of the Canoe River, which flows into the Columbia at the great bend.

Great Canada Road *Obs.* the first overland road to Lower Canada from New Brunswick and Nova Scotia.
1832 BAILLIE *Account of N.B.* 104: ... the Great

Canada Road on the bank of the St. John may be used for carriages as far as Presqu'Isle.

great cat *West* See **cougar.**
1938 CASH *I Like B.C.* 132: Bob Smith is an American and he's killed panther, cougar, great cats, call them what you will, among the mountains of the Pacific, all the way from Alaska to Mexico.

Great Company See 1963 quote.
1914 STEELE *Forty Years* 41: The rivers during the summer were the highways for their boats, and those of the Great Company. . . . **1963** SYMONS *Many Trails* 130: . . . not even the "Great Company," the Hudson's Bay Company, ever successfully invaded their [Blackfoot] territory.

Great Confederacy *Hist.* See **Five Nations.**
1954 BARBEAU *Cdn Folk Songs* 1: The leader of this thanksgiving ritual song is a Cayuga member of the Little Bear Clan and a hereditary chief whose title descends from a founder of the Great Confederacy.

Great Divide See **continental divide.**
1905 OUTRAM *Cdn Rockies* 89: Abbot Pass is a narrow V-shaped notch, cut deep between the lofty walls of Mt. Lefroy and Mt. Victoria, upon the Great Divide.
1958 *Edmonton Jnl.* 18 Oct. 4/3: The former chief, after many hardships, joined a band of refugees on the Dease River near the Great Divide.

Greater Ontario *Hist.* See **New Ontario.**
1908 NICHOLSON *In Old Quebec* 102: We are still in the "banner province" of the Dominion, for the vast country to the north and West of Lake Nipissing and the French River is known as "New" or "Greater Ontario."

greater snow goose See **white wavey.**
1908 MAIR *Mackenzie Basin* 319: Greater snow goose—*Chen hyperborea nivalis.* **1958** *Evening Telegram* (St. John's) 7 May 3/1: [St. Joachim, Que.] a federal government biologist is trying to establish how big the world's only flock of greater snow geese should be.

Great Father *Hist.* in Indian parlance, the King of England. See also **Great Leader** and **Great White Chief.** Cp. **Great Mother.** Also *Great White Father.*
1796 (1932) RUSSELL *Correspondence* I 44: I am happy that our great Father has brought us together to shake hands. **1861** *Nor'Wester* (R.R.S.) 15 Mar. 2/5: It's the 'Great Father' who is farmer here; and if the 'Little Father,' his agent, don't keep things just so, in this ship-shape and British fashion, the chances are that the 'Little Father' will be shipped himself—which would be too painful for his pockets to contemplate. **1942** RADDALL *His Majesty's Yankees* 17: . . . his harsh voice startled us so. "Let your light so shine before men that they may see your good works!" Silence, and then Luke's gibing voice, "And glorify the Great White Father which is in London?"

great furs *Fur Trade, Obs.* the pelts of large animals such as beaver, bear, and moose. Cp. **small furs.**
1723 (1923) *Beaver* May 307/1: We hope to receive from you a Good Cargoe, of Great & Small Furrs.

great horned owl a common North American owl, *Bubo virginianus.* See 1748 quote.

1748 ELLIS *Hudson's Bay* 40: The great Horned Owl is also common in this Country, which is a very singular Bird, with a Head very little inferior in Size to that of a Cat, and what are called the Horns, composed of Feathers, rising just above the Bill, intermixed at the Bottom with white, becoming of a red brown by Degrees, and tipped with black. **1863** (1873) LEMOINE *Maple Leaves* 247: And if, perchance, camped for the night out on the mountain brow in a deserted sugar-hut, you hear the terrible hooting of the great horned owl, fear nothing; it is not the evil one. **1957** MOWAT *Dog* 168: . . . it was his ambition to take a series of pictures of a great horned owl.

great house 1 *Hist.* See **big house.**
1946 *Beaver* March 35/1: They [palisades] enclosed the store and warehouse, the great house of the factor and the mess.

2 *West Coast* See **plank house.**
1872 POOLE *Queen Charlotte Is.* 112: They received me in a "great house" not unlike that of the Skiddans. . . .

Great House *Obs.* in Indian parlance, the home of the Great Father, *q.v.*
1860 *Nor'Wester* (R.R.S.) 14 Feb. 2/3: I Peguis, (his mark), Saulteaux Chief of the Indian Settlement at Red River, wish to make my statement to the Great House across the great waters.

great lake *Obs.* one of the Great Lakes, *q.v.*
1863 WALSHE *Cedar Creek* 244: . . . for the raft was infantine compared with its congeners of the great lake [Ontario] and the St. Lawrence.

Great Lake *Obs.* in Indian parlance: **1** Lake Superior.
1772 (1954) WALLACE *Pedlars* 10: . . . the Indians reported to Andrew Graham at York Factory that they had met Corry "in the Great Lake on his way to the Grand Fort [Grand Portage] with seven large canoes loaded with Beavers."

2 the Atlantic Ocean.
1796 (1932) RUSSELL *Correspondence* I 44: Our Father the Governor is gone over the Great Lake to see his & our Great Father the King, he has left me here to represent him. **1814** *Montreal Herald* 2 Apr. 1/2: I am . . . delighted to hear my Red Children declare their attachment to the King our Father Great beyond the Great Lake, and to myself and to my Warriors. **1848** (1866) CHRISTIE *Lower Canada* II 180: But we hope, although we are few, and are here as it were upon a little island, our great and mighty father who lives beyond the great lake, will not forsake us in our distress, but will continue to remember his faithful red children.

Great Lakes Lakes Ontario, Erie, Huron, Michigan, and Superior. See also **inland seas** and **Lakes.**
1665 (1885) RADISSON *Fourth Voyage* 187: These great lakes had not so soone comed to our knowledge if it had not been for those brutish people. **1748** ELLIS *Hudson's Bay* 151: This is the finest River in Hudson's-Bay, navigable for many Leagues, having a Communication with the great Lakes behind Canada. **1836** *Hamilton Free Press* (U.C.) 24 July 1/2: The project of a ship and steamboat Canal from the Great Lakes to the Atlantic, is attracting the public attention more and more every day. **1966** *Cdn Geog.Jnl* Apr. 113/2: The abnormally low water levels on the Great Lakes over the past two or three years have generated demands that something be done to control the levels of the lakes.

Great Leader *Hist.* See **Great Father.**
1954 MCGREGOR *Shining Mountains* 152: The Great

Leader had given strict orders that the camp was to be on its good behavior.

Great Lone Land the Canadian Northwest.

1872 BUTLER *Great Lone Land* [Book title]. **1875** *Cdn Mthly* Nov. 371: "Great Lone Land" as applied to the Nor'-West is a misnomer, in that it conveys the idea of an empire of nothingness through whose amazing vastness the bewildered traveller might wander with the loneliness of a deserted Siberian miner. **1915** PRESTON *Strathcona* 33: It was from this source that the first clarion sounded for the right of Canada to hold undisputed sway over the Great Lone Land of the west. **1955** COLLARD *Cdn Yesterdays* 145: "This has truly been called the Great Lone Land," he would say.

Great Mother *Hist.* in Indian parlance, Queen Victoria. Cp. **Great Father.** Also *Great White Mother.*

1871 *Wkly Manitoban* 25 Mar. 1/3: Your Great Mother knows that *fire-water* does great harm to her Red subjects, and desires to keep it away from them. **1912** CONNOR *Corp.Cameron* 399: Chief Red Crow, too, returned to his band with a chastened mind, it having been made clear to him that a chief who could not control his young braves was not the kind of chief the Great White Mother desired to have in command of her Indian subjects. **1963** *Herald Mag.* 14 Sep. 1/2: Many years ago our Great Mother made a treaty with the Indians far away by the great waters to the east.

Great Plain(s)† See **Prairies** (def. 1).

1825 (1931) SIMPSON *Fur Trade* 159: Continued our route through the Great plain keeping in a South Easterly direction. **1880** GORDON *Mountain and Prairie* 276: The country to the south of Battleford from the Hand Hills to the valley of the Qu'Appelle has hitherto been known as the Great Plain, and has been regarded as sterile, barren and useless. **1938** *Cdn Labour Herald* Nov. 1/1: Whether the farmers of the Great Plains remain in Confederation, form a separate dominion or found a republic they will still be forced to play the game of commerce according to capitalist rules. **1952** PUTNAM *Cdn Regions* 6: The Great Plains are, for the most part above or very close to the 2,000 foot level.

Great Plains grizzly a huge grizzly bear, *Ursus horribilis horribilis,* once found on the prairies and now probably extinct. Cp. **grizzly bear.**

1958 *Weekend Mag.* 26 Apr. 9/1: Where they came from is also a mystery . . . for not since the Great Plains grizzly became extinct has any of its size been seen.

Great Spirit a literal translation of Gitchi Manitou, *q.v.,* considered by Christian Indians and whites as the Indian manifestation or concept of God. See also **Manitou** (def. 4), **Master of Life** (def. 2), and **Wakanda.**

1703 (1905) LAHONTAN *New Voyages* II 434: [There is] a Being superior—which they call the Great Spirit. . . . **1831** (1886) *Indian* (Hagersville, Ont.) 17 Mar. 59/3: If you should see any of my Indian brethren, I would thank you to tell them that I pray for them every day, that the Great Spirit, through Christ, may keep them in the good way. **1921** HEMING *Drama of Forests* 77: They took not the Great Spirit's name in vain; nor did they mention it save in a whisper, and with bowed head. **1958** *Native Voice* Sp.ed. 48/1: "Woe! Woe! My children," cried the wise Chief, "Do you not know that those who harm one of the Great Spirit's creatures will suffer in a like way."

great war chief See **war chief.**

Great West *Hist.* See **Northwest** (def. 1a).

1854 *Hamilton Gaz.* (C.W.) 16 Jan. 2/3: He . . . warned them to expect an avalanche of friendly Americans who would seek this thoroughfare to and from the Great West. **1916** SKELTON *Day of Laurier* 73: Long before the Great West was more than a name to any but a handful in older Canada, hardy French voyageurs and Scottish adventurers had pushed their canoes or driven their Red River carts to the foot of the Rockies and beyond.

Great White Chief See **Great Father.**

1936 *Beaver* Sep. 64/3: To whatever degree such abstractions as British justice or "the Great White Chief across the water" may have penetrated into the Indian mind, these things were personified for them almost entirely by the Hudson's Bay Company throughout vast territories.

Great White Father See **Great Father.**

Great White Land See **Far North.**

1910 SERVICE *Trail of '98* v: It is the voice, inexorably scornful of the Great White Land.

Great White Mother See **Great Mother.**

green *adj.* relating to the green fishery, *q.v.* See also **green fish.**

1965 MACNUTT *Atlantic Provinces* 2: . . . they [the French] had . . . resorted to what was called the wet, green, or mud branch of the industry.

greenback† *n. Slang* a banknote; a bill of paper money.

☛ *Although only one-dollar bills have green backs in Canada, this term has been applied to all bills after the usage in the United States, where all bills have green backs.*

1870 *Wkly Manitoban* 22 Oct. 2/1: Subscription. Ten Shillings Sterling ($2.50) per annum; greenbacks, $3. **1903** (1913) CULLUM *Devil's Keg* 137: ". . . Here's your fifty," he went on, taking a roll of bills from his pocket, and counting out the coveted greenbacks. **1950** STEELE *Ghosts Returning* 175: Smelly oil-lamps gleamed over hard-eyed men, their drinks and their notched guns, glinted on silver coins, flickered on greenbacks and on the red, black, blue, white and yellow of stacked chips and falling cards.

greenchain *n. Lumbering* an endless-belt system carrying cut-and-marked lumber from the sawyer to the sorters, so called because the lumber is unseasoned, or green.

1947 ENGLEBERT *Men and Trees* 22: The trimmer machine . . . squares off the ends of the boards . . . before passing on to a long, slowly moving conveyor, called a greenchain. **1958** HAWTHORN *Indians of B.C.* 128: The few Indians employed by sawmilling enterprises on the Coast work in local plants situated on tidewater, as in North Vancouver and Port Alberni. They are concentrated in booming and, to a lesser extent, green chain and loading gangs, which are about the only jobs in sawmilling that fulfil their preferences for outdoor work. . . .

Green Chamber the Canadian House of Commons, so called because of the color scheme of the chamber. Cp. **Red Chamber.**

1938 BLACK *Seventy Years* 9: Two weeks before my seventieth birthday . . . I took my place in the "green chamber" at Ottawa. **1966** *Globe and Mail* (Toronto)

19 Jan. 7/1: The House of Commons is sometimes called the Green Chamber and the Senate the Red Chamber because the carpet, the leather chair bottoms, and the desk blotters are all green, whereas in the Senate they are red.

green cheese See quote.
1852 MOODIE *Roughing It* 327: Besides venison, pork, chickens, ducks, and fish of several kinds, cooked in a variety of ways, there was a number of pumpkin, raspberry, cherry, and currant pies, with fresh butter and green cheese (as the new cream cheese is called), maple molasses, preserves, and pickled cucumbers, besides tea and coffee.

green Christmas† A Christmas Day devoid of snow and characterized by mild weather.
1947 DUMBRILLE *Deep Doorways* 10: I like a white Christmas. Remember what Mother used to say, "Green Christmas, fat graveyard!" 1965 *Kingston Whig-Standard* (Ont.) 27 Dec. 17/7: Prospects of a "green Christmas" had worried authorities.

green cod *Hist.* See **green fish** (def. 1).
1942 RADDALL *His Majesty's Yankees* 332: ". . . she's the Two Friends, out o' Ragged Island, that's jist run in a cargo o' green cod, split an' slack-salted, to certain merchants o' Salem. . . ."

greener *n. Slang, Obs.* a newly arrived immigrant.
1905 FRASER *Canada As It Is* 120: He was what the Canadians call a "greener."

green fish 1 *Nfld* See 1965 quote. See also **green,** *adj.* Cp. **dry fish** (def. 2) and **mud-fish.**
1777 (1792) CARTWRIGHT *Journal* II 249: We heaved a pile, piled some green fish, and washed out two bulks. 1832 MCGREGOR *Brit. Amer.* I 232: . . . mud-fish, or green fish, is generally understood to be cod-fish, either wholly or partially split and pickled. 1965 LEACH *Songs* 5: After the fish [having been headed, gutted and split] are washed, they are forked into the home-made wooden. wheelbarrows and taken to the 'rooms' at the head of the wharf where they are stacked in heavy rock salt to pickle. At this stage they are referred to as 'green fish.' After proper curing in the salt, the green fish are spread, split side up, on long racks, called flakes to dry in the sun.
2 *North* fish that have not been cured. Cp. **dried fish.**
1940 FINNIE *Lure of North* 207: Maggots were swarming over bales of dried fish, and "green" fish that had been frozen but was frozen no longer.

green-fish catcher *Nfld* 1 a fisherman.
1905 DUNCAN *Grenfell's Parish* 61: He is the only doctor . . . most of the 'liveyeres' and green-fish catchers of the middle coast can reach, save the hospital physician at Indian Harbour.
2 a fishing vessel engaged in the green fishery.
1929 (1930) *Beaver* June 16: Owing to the change from the old floating green-fish catchers, it has become necessary in our work to change our methods also. . . .

green fishery *Esp.Nfld, Hist.* See quote. See also **banks fishery, green fish, ship fishery,** and **wet fishery.**
1960 RYERSON *Founding of Can.* 74: There were two methods employed in the fishery. In the "green" or "wet" fishery, the catch was salted directly on board

ship; in the "dry" or "shore" fishery, the catch was taken ashore and dried on specially built stagings or "flakes."

green hand 1 *Fur Trade, Hist.* See **greenhorn** (def. 1).
1859 (1870) SOUTHESK *Saskatchewan* 296: Met a party from Carleton bringing the mail, and likewise the "green hands"—as the newly engaged men are called. 1913 COWIE *Adventurers* 113: I especially resented the rule prohibiting any "green hand" to get into a canoe. . . .
2 in lumbering, fishing, etc., an inexperienced man. See also **greenhorn** (def. 2) and **green man.**
1835 DAVIES *Northern Quebec* 244: . . . I need not tell you that *green hands* must always pass a season or two with experienced fishermen. . . . 1883 FRASER *Shanty* 272: It is time for the "green hands" to exercise themselves on the loose timber and logs. 1927 WALLACE *In the Wake of the Windships* 7: Life in such craft was so monotonous, so jail-like, and the cruises so lengthy that naught but graduate whalemen and "green" hands were carried. 1961 GREENING *Ottawa* 103: This was also the time when the "green hands"—the young men who had been hired for the drive for the first time—would practise on the loose timber and logs. . . .

greenhide *n.* 1 undressed hide; rawhide.
1934 BETTANY *Valley of Lost Gold* 148: When the framework was completed to Jimmy's satisfaction, the skins were laced to it with strips of the green-hide so as to cover it completely, the hair inside. 1950 BIRD *This is N.S.* 95: The farm had been self-sufficient then, with everything from candles for lighting to greenhides for footwear, produced on the place.
2 *N.S.* See 1950 quote. Cp. **green moccasin.**
1946 BIRD *Sunrise for Peter* 155: "Ma says I'm better'n her with the bake kettle, and I—I kin make greenhides and skin eels." 1950 BIRD *This is N.S.* 53: Grandfather had retired leaving his greenhides—moccasins made with the hairy side inward—by the fire to dry.

greenhorn *n.* 1 *Fur Trade* See 1920 quote. See also **green hand** (def. 1).
1830 (1851) CAMPBELL *Journal* 14 Aug.: During the day a boat came out to us from York Factory, manned with a mixed crew of Indians, Halfbreeds & French Canadian Voyageurs, all different in appearance, dress and language to anything we "greenhorns" had ever run across before. 1920 *Beaver* Dec. 14/1: We were "greenhorns", a name applied to men during their first year in the service. 1939 *Ibid.* 24: Trading parties were going out. . . . The year was 1862. I was a greenhorn.
2† See **green hand** (def. 2).
1854 KEEFER *Ottawa* 64: A cheaper class of men, generally the "greenhorns," are employed as road cutters. 1896 ROBERTS *Camp-Fire* 291: There is nothing that so cheers the heart of the lumberman as to play a practical joke on one whom he calls a "greenhorn," or, in other words, any one unused to the strange ways and flavor of the lumber-camps. . . .

green hornet *Local* See quote.
1965 *Globe and Mail* (Toronto) 29 Dec. 5/7: Officially known as bylaw enforcement officers, the green hornets patrol the city [Toronto] on motorcycle or on foot tagging illegally parked cars. . . . The bylaw enforcement officers, first hired in 1964, received their nickname because of their green uniforms and the noise of their motorcycles.

green ice salt-water ice in a melting state. See also **rotten** and **slush ice** (def. 2).

1916 DUNCAN *Billy Topsail* 123: It would be slow . . . on the treacherous reaches of green ice between the floe and the Spotted Horses. **1930** *Keewatin* 39: Salt-water ice does not "candle" in melting but remains solid green ice, perforated by holes and broken by cracks.

green man† *Esp.Nfld* See 1964 quote. See also **green hand** (def. 2).
1832 MCGREGOR *British America* I 241: . . . one-third, or at least one-fourth, of the men employed . . . were "green men," or men who were never before at sea; and by this trade they [the French] bred up from 4000 to 6000 seamen annually. **1964** *Nfld Qtly* Summer 15/1: Youngster. An immigrant apprentice to the fishery, or "green man." **1965** MACNUTT *Atlantic Provinces* 5: An attempt was made by English ordinances in 1670 to enforce the long-standing custom of annually introducing "green men" to the [Newfoundland] fishery and ensuring their return to England where they would be available for the purposes of the navy.

green meat *Obs.* fresh meat, as opposed to dried meat or pemmican, *qq.v.*
1765-75 (1933) POND *Narrative* 46: In Jany thay Began to Aproach us & Brot with them Drid & Grean Meet, Bever . . . Raccone & other Skins to trade. **1800** (1933) MCLEOD *Diary* 148: Collin came back [bringing] a little dryed and Green Meat. **1887** *Senate Report* 111: The fall hunters returned with carts heavily laden with what was termed "green meat," this being the choicest portions of the animal with all the inferior portions cast away.

green moccasin See quote. Cp. **greenhide** (def. 2).
1955 SHIPLEY *Anna* 100: Green moccasins [are] footwear of moosehide with fur left on the soles, to maintain better balance on glare-ice and to withstand the jagged edges.

greenshank moccasin See **green moccasin**.
1946 BIRD *Sunrise for Peter* 115: From the hide of the steer she made greenshank moccasins, and with shears and thread she fitted garments for the little ones. . . .

green-spruce tea See **spruce tea**.
1909 SERVICE *Cheechako* 79: . . . they brewed me the green-spruce tea, and nursed me there like a child. . . .

greenwoods *n.pl.* forest that has not been affected by fires, as opposed to burnt woods, *q.v.*
1849 ALEXANDER *L'Acadie* II 149: They first took us 5 miles by a lumber-road through the burnt woods. After which we steered North East by compass through "greenwoods," on very good land. **1872** DASHWOOD *Chiploquorgan* 124: We took up our quarters in a double bark camp situated in some "green" woods, a quarter of a mile from a large barren. **1933** MERRICK *True North* 142: In the greenwoods, far from lakes and brooks, marten traps replaced mink traps.

grey (in compounds) See under **gray**.

Grey *n. Fur Trade, Hist.* a partner or engagé of the North West Company. Cp. **Sky Blue**.
1820 (1938) SIMPSON *Athabasca Jnl* 175: If our Grey friends had been a little more attentive [to business]. . . . **1928** *Beaver* June 11: Chief Factor Samuel Black was one of the famous "Greys" of the Nor'West Company. **1955** RICH in BLACK *Journal* lxxxiii: The North Westers were similarly known as "Greys."

Grey Cup [< A.H.G. *Grey*, 4th Earl, 1851-1917] the cup, first presented in 1909, awarded annually to the champion professional football team in Canada; also, the game played to decide the winner of this cup.

1953 MOON *Saskatchewan* 37: . . . its beloved Roughriders [have gone] to the Grey Cup finals accompanied by hundreds of loyal home town supporters. . . . **1961** *Maclean's* 26 Aug. 17/2: Football, or, more specifically, the Grey Cup game, gives bookmakers the most concentrated action of any Canadian sports event. . . . **1963** *Albertan* (Calgary) 19 Nov. 11/1: Shortly after Nov. 30, this year, the Grey Cup will become unique in sports. It will be the first spectacle which will be able to advertise: "the only game ever played on land, sea, and in the air."

2 the festivities accompanying the Grey Cup game, together with the game itself.
1964 *Globe and Mail* 28 Nov. 4/2: . . . each year at this time there was a national gathering called the Grey Cup. **1964** *Kingston Whig-Standard* (Ont.) 30 Nov. 1/4: . . . Grey Cup 1964 was a weak version of past blowouts.

Grey Nun See **Grey Sister**.
1817 *Montreal Police Regulations* 21 June Art. 38: No person shall bathe in any part of the river between the Grey Nuns' House, called Point St. Charles, and Mr. Molson's Brewery below St. Mary Suburb, under the penalty of five shillings. **1873** BUTLER *Wild North Land* 101: Four ladies of the order of Grey Nuns have made their home here, and their school already contains some thirty children. **1964** *Herald Mag.* 8 Aug. 3/1: Catholic Father Lesage, a distant relation of the Quebec premier, is responsible for a large Metis church fold, a separate school and the town's hospital administered by an order of Grey Nuns.

Grey Sister a member of a congregation of nuns founded in 1747 in Montreal, devoted to social service. See also **Grey Nun**.
1765 *Quebec Gaz.* 30 May 4/1: It is said 8 or 9 sick Persons in the Grey Sisters' Nunnery were burnt to death. **1823** (1955) CRAIG *Early Travellers* 56: We first called at the Convent of the Gray Sisters, containing a Mère Superieure and twenty four nuns. **1958** *Encyc. Can.* IX 75: Placed in charge of the Hôpital Général in Montreal in 1747. Mother d'Youville founded the order of Grey Sisters or Grey Nuns.

grid road *Sask.* a rural road built under the grid system, *q.v.*
1957 *Sask.News* 2 Jan. 1/1: In its first year, Saskatchewan's 10-year Grid Road Program exceeded expectations both in mileage completed and in the quality of the grid roads constructed. . . . **1958** *Edmonton Jnl* 6 Aug. 5/1: About 1,300 miles of grid roads will be built in Saskatchewan by the end of this year. . . . This is the third building season of the grid road program, which has seen more than 3,000 miles of road built. **1964** *Naicam Sentinel* 26 Mar. 2/3: That we apply . . . for $50,000 . . . for the purpose of accelerating and extending additional Grid Road. . . .

grid(road) system a method of laying out new roads such that the distance between them will be two miles north to south and one mile east and west.
1958 *Edmonton Jnl* 24 June 2 1/5: Two other roadways that do not conform to the grid system also require names. . . . **1964** *Calgary Herald* 24 June 17/5: Saskatchewan . . . has the best municipal road system in Canada and other provinces were moving to copy the grid road system, Archie Campbell, director of the provincial grid road authority, said Tuesday night.

Grievance, the *Maritimes* the complaint that the Maritime provinces lost out economically as a result of Confederation, their home markets being opened up to the producers of central Canada and their U.S. markets being sealed off by tariff barriers.

1964 *Star Wkly* 12 Dec. 6/2: This complaint has been recited so often here it is known simply as the Grievance. . . .

grievance monger *Obs.* a name applied by their opponents to the early Reformers (def. 1) of Upper Canada, from the list of thirty-one grievances presented by William Lyon Mackenzie in 1829.

1828 BIDWELL *Tor.Pub.Lib.MSS B 104* 41: Like William Lyon Mackenzie, he was a confirmed grievance-monger. **1832** *Patriot and Farmer's Monitor* (Kingston, U.C.) 6 Mar. 1/5: Between 11 and 12 o'clock, the business of the day commenced, with choosing a genuine grievance monger chairman. **1832** *Cdn Courant* (Montreal) 1 Aug. 2/5: Demagogues and grievance-mongers will soon find their business to be but a poor one.

grillade *n.* [< Cdn F] *Hist.* or *Obs.* meat, especially salt pork, fried in grease.

1892 DAUNT *Land of Moose* 94: [He] found time . . . for a *grillade* of the juicy tongues of the bison. . . . **1947** SAUNDERS *Algonquin* 36: This meal consisted of beans, fried salt pork, known as "grillades". . . . **1961** PRICE & KENNEDY *Renfrew* 48: One Sunday special was "des grillades," mess pork cut into slices and fried.

grinder *n. N.S.* See quote.

1950 BIRD *This is N.S.* 197: As traffic continued to increase several "grinders" were put in service, small paddle boats, having paddles at each side which were turned by women operating a large crank.

grip-stick *n.* a short length of wood attached to each end of the thong used to rotate a firedrill (a stick used for making fire). See picture at **fireboard**.

1943 MILLER *Lone Woodsman* 46: This time Dan used the fire-making method of the Ojibways. He tied a short grip-stick to each end of his cord . . . and stooped over it with the socket in his teeth.

gris *n. Obs.* See **pomme gris.**

1806 *Quebec Gaz.* 11 Dec. 4/1: The said ground being planted with fruit trees . . . of the best quality being chiefly, bourassa, gris and fameux. **1822** *Cdn Courant* (Montreal) 16 Nov. 1/2: For Sale by the subscriber, Femeuses, Bourrassas and Grises . . . Apples will be delivered in the finest possible condition in Barrels. **1965** COLLARD *Call Back Yesterdays* 79: The fameuse, the grise . . . the bourassa . . . [were apples] which could not be found anywhere as perfect as here [Montreal].

grisel bear See **grizzly bear.**

grisley (or grisly) bear See **grizzly bear.**

Grit *n.* See **Clear Grit**. See also **Liberal** and **Loyal Grit.**

1852 *U.E.Loyalist* (Toronto) 16 Sep. 2/5: Will the Grits desert him in this; and allow him to be accused by the government "of leaving his slime upon everything that he crawled over?" **1896** *Kootenaian*

23 May 1/1: The proposal for a loan in aid of the Crow's Nest Pass railway had been blocked by the "Grits" also, he said. **1906** LEWIS *George Brown* 40: "Grit" afterward became a nickname for a member of the Reform or Liberal party, and especially for the enthusiastic followers of George Brown. **1964** *Maclean's* 7 Mar. 2/1: Of course the Grits know that Diefenbaker is a formidable campaigner, but they regard him as a known quantity.

Grit(t)ism *n. Hist.* See **Clear Gritism.**

1858 (1905) BIGGAR *Oliver Mowat* I 75: The charge of "Gritism" or "Brownism," I thought nothing of, just as I had made up my mind to disregard any and every other party name as only embarrassing. **1884** *Nor'Wester* (Calgary) 1 July 2/2: If their howling be analyzed it will be found to consist of Mischief 24, Grittism, 65, Wind 10, Patriotism 1. **1908** CLARKE *Sixty Years* 105: From the early days of Ontario Gritism I had . . . urged the adoption of the ballot. . . . **1935** *Cdn Hist.Rev.* XVI 375: In Toronto the Grit movement found an incomparable leader with an incomparable organ through which the gospel of Grittism might be preached—George Brown and his *Globe*.

Grit Party *Hist.* See **Clear Grit Party.**

1884 *Toronto Wkly News* 8 Aug. 1/3: The Grit party, who have been politically on the tramp for some time, have come to a fork in the road. **1909** O'DONNELL *Manitoba* 86: Most of the "old Grit party" do not believe in a second term and think it should be discontinued.

Gritty *adj. Obs.* reflecting Clear Grit political views.

1882 *Progress* (Rat Portage [Kenora], Ont.) 18 Mar. 4/1: . . . the political proclivities of its editor were so strong that every other article in the paper was as Gritty as the old *Globe* itself.

grizzle (grizel or **grisel) bear** *Obs.* See **grizzly bear.**

1743 (1949) ISHAM *Observations* 165: Black bear's their is a pretty many and some Very Large, Espetially the Grizel bears which will Seize a man if Come in his way having Known an Indian tore in a Sad manner with one **1824** (1955) BLACK *Journal* 159: The men tell me that last night 2 huge Grisel Bears visited our camp quite near, but got off. **1825** (1931) SIMPSON *Fur Trade* 160: In the even^g saw a Grizzle Bear, his sense of smelling must be very acute as from the distance of more than a Mile he came towards us at a canter. . . .

grizzled bear *Obs.* See **grizzly bear.**

1752 ROBSON *Hudson's Bay* 48: There is no beast truly dangerous but the grizzled bear; and he always keeps up the country in a warmer climate, where indeed he makes dreadful ravages, devouring whole families in a short time. **1807** (1890) KEITH *Letters* 66: The lesser species or fur kinds are: the black and grizzled bear, the latter inhabits the Rocky Mountains or thereabouts, and are apparently not so ferocious as those in the Peace River.

grizzly ['grɪzli] *n.* [< *grizzle* gray + -*ly*] **1** See **grizzly bear.**

1854 *Hamilton Gaz.* (C.W.) 14 Sep. 1/7: I've seed a grizzly pull down as good a hoss as ever tracked a prairy, where the critter had got bothered in a thicket. **1963** *B.C.Digest* Oct. 34/2: We watched a huge grizzly root up the sod and tear a mound of solid rock to pieces to catch a groundsquirrel or a whistler.

2 the meat of the grizzly bear.

1937 STANWELL-FLETCHER *Driftwood Valley* 87: And we traded flour and sugar which he wanted for some dry old moose meat and a piece of tough, but delicious, frozen grizzly.

3† Placer Mining a. See 1966 quote.
1881 *Edmonton Bulletin* 7 Feb. 2/1: The boiler and force pumps are on a scow and the "grizzly" on a raft close by, and the whole aparatus can be easily floated from one part of the river to another.
1966 BAITY *Wilderness Welfare* 48: There are many different rigs . . . but perhaps the one that has best stood the test of time is the grizzly. It evolved from the old rocker, which the Chinese introduced to the Western world during the California gold rush.

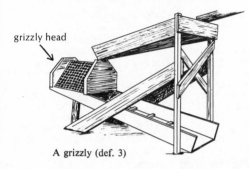

grizzly head

A grizzly (def. 3)

b. See **grizzly head.**
1881 *Progress* (Rat Portage [Kenora], Ont.) 30 Apr. 3/1: The dirt is shovelled into the dump box and water is poured on it, which washes it on the grizzley, and into and through the sluice box, the gold catching on the blanket as it passes through. **1963** *Placer-Mining B.C.* 30/1: A grizzly is a set of parallel steel bars or rails, or even poles, set in a 2- by 4-inch rack. . . .

4† Hardrock Mining a screening device, usually a grid, of steel bars on which ore or rock is broken by means of a sledge hammer.
1955 *Mining Explained* 149: GRIZZLY—a grating (usually steel rails) placed over the top of a chute or ore pass for the purpose of stopping the larger pieces of rock or ore. **1964** *Vancouver Times* 3 Nov. 17/6: The grizzlyman breaks up rock by hammering on a steel grid known as a grizzly.

grizzly bear a large and, often, ferocious bear, *Ursus horribilis,* nowadays largely confined to the northern Rockies. See also **gray bear** (def. 1), **grizzle bear, grizzled bear, grizzly** (def. 1), **mountain bear, silvertip,** and **white bear** (def. 2).
[**1691** (1929) KELSEY *Papers* 12: This plain affords Nothing but short Round sticky grass & Buffilo & a great sort of a Bear wᶜʰ is Bigger than any white Bear & is Neither White nor Black But silver hair's like our English Rabbit.] **1793** (1801) MACKENZIE *Voyages* 160: The Indians entertain great apprehension of this kind of bear, which is called the grisley bear. . . . **1860** *Nor'Wester* (R.R.S.) 14 June 2/5: They are to go west to Fort Chesterfield, where they hope to fall in with the grizzly bear. **1958** CAMERON *Cdn Mammals* 33: The grizzly bear is the largest land carnivore on earth. The largest specimen on record weighed over half a ton and was over nine feet in total length.

grizzly head *Placer Mining* See quote. See also **grizzly** (def. 3b) and **shed grizzly.**
1966 BAITY *Wilderness Welfare* 48: The grizzly head was a grid made of the three-sixteenth inch iron rods I had bought and fitted over the upper end of the box in the shape of a small pitched roof.

grizzlyman *n.* See 1964 quote at **grizzly** (def. 4).

grocery† n. Obs. See **grocery store** (def. 2).
1837 *Cdn Temperance Advocate* Sep. 43/1: There is a fearful array of groceries, as they are called, or drunkeries as they should be designated. **1841** MCLEOD *Upper Canada* 259: They shot a woman dead, who kept a grocery near the mill, because she furnished them cider.

grocery store† 1 a shop where groceries may be bought.
1834 *Cdn Courant* (Montreal) 15 Jan. 2/5: On Sunday night last, some thieves broke into the grocery store of Mr. Wm. Scott, Wellington Street, St. Anne Suburbs, and carried away goods to a considerable amount. **1960** BLONDAL *Candle* 15: Before Jacob there had been five grocery stores, the prices the same in each. . . .

2 Obs. See quote. See also **grocery** and **groggery.**
1837 (1927) DICKIE *How Canada Grew Up* 100: Besides the seven taverns, there is a number of little grocery stores which are, in fact, drinking-houses.

groceteria *n.* a self-service grocery store.
1925 *Cdn Labor Advocate* 18 Sep. 8/1: Kirkham's Grocerteria Ltd. The Working Man's Store. **1934** *New Commonwealth* 18 Aug. 7/1: On 39 groceterias in Ontario, Eatons are losing money. **1958** *Evening Telegram* (St. John's) 14 May 11/6: Mercer's Self-Service Groceteria Merrymeeting Road.

grog-boss *n. Hist.* the person in charge of serving the whisky or other liquor at a bee, *q.v.* See also **whisky-boy.**
1853 STRICKLAND *Canada West* I 35: A man with a pail of spring water . . . and a bottle of whiskey . . . is the most important personage at the "Bee" and is known by the appellation of the "Grog-bos." **1905** CARTER *Dundas* 49: During the progress of the work the "grog boss" was quite busy dispensing his favors, and very few declined his calls. **1964** GUILLET *Pioneer Days* 137: During the day the "grog-boss" dealt out plenty of refreshment from a pail, while a couple of meals were served. . . .

groggery† n. Obs. a low-class tavern. See also **grocery store** (def. 2).
1860 *Nor'Wester* (R.R.S.) 14 June 2/5: The case was clearly proved by a Frenchman, who had purchased over a pint of bad whiskey at Herveyworth's unlicensed groggery, and "consumed it on the premises." **1894** BEGG *Hist.of B.C.* 348: He then asked me to come with him to the little groggery he was staying at, and have a drink, I wondering if he would pay me. **1909** HUNTER *Simcoe County* I 46: It is said the surveying party were too much inclined to hang around some low groggeries on the Penetanguishene Road, and did their work badly.

grogman *n.* See **grog-boss.**

gronker ['grɑnkɚ] *n.* See **Canada Goose.**
1785 (1916) THOMPSON *Narrative* 36: [We saw] a very large species of gray goose—they have a deep harsh note, and are called Gronkers, by others Barren Geese, from its being assumed that they never lay eggs. **1959** MCATEE *Folk-Names* 8: Eastern Canada Goose [is also called . . . gronker. . . .

Groscap ['gros,kæp] *n.* See **Glooscap.**
1900 LONG *Wilderness Ways* 155: Clote Scarpe, a legendry hero, like Hiawatha, of the Northern

Indians, Pronounced variously, Clote Scarpe, Groscap, Gluscap, etc.

grosse bosse *Cdn French* "large hump" *Hist.* See **boss.**

1808 (1897) COUES *New Light* I 446: Buffalo are cut up into the following 20 pieces by the hunter: 1 grosse bosse; 1 petite bosse; 2 depouilles; 2 shoulders; 2 lourdes épaulettes [shoulder pieces]; 2 fillets; 2 thighs; 2 sides; 1 belly; 1 heart; 1 rump; 1 brisket; 1 backbone; 1 neck. The tongue usually belongs to the hunter. **1952** HOWARD *Strange Empire* 298: [They sought] the tongue, the thirty-pound *grosse bosse* or hump, and the dépouilles, two layers of tender flesh along the ribs.

ground birch the dwarf birch, *Betula glandulosa.*

1897 TYRRELL *Sub-Arctics* 111: Just beyond this, much to our surprise and pleasure, we suddenly came upon abundance of drift-wood—not little sticks of willow or ground birch, but the trunks of trees six or eight inches in diameter, as heavy as two men could carry. **1957** PORSILD *Flora of the Arctic* 70: Where abundant, the ground birch provides a valuable source of fuel for outdoor cooking.

ground cedar one of several species of club moss, especially *Lycopodium complanatum* or *L. tristachyum.*

1832 (1838) TRAILL *Backwoods* 120: In my rambles in the wood near the house I have discovered a trailing plant bearing a near resemblance to the cedar, which I consider has, with equal propriety, a claim to the name of ground or creeping cedar. **1954** PATTERSON *Dangerous River* 179: A warm autumnal smell rose from the ground cedar, the kini-kinik and the fallen leaves.

ground chuck *Obs.* See **groundhog** (def. 1)

1828 *Methodist Mag.* 74: There various furs for caps are found: The beaver, coon . . . ground chuck. . . .

ground cranberry *North* the mountain or rock cranberry, *Vaccinium vitis-idaea* var. minus. See also **foxberry.**

1945 *Beaver* Sep. 44: Atamaoya is the Eskimo substitute for tobacco. It is made of the leaves of the ground cranberry. . . .

ground cruising surveying on the ground as opposed to in the air.

1946 *Beaver* June 43/1: They continued to fly on daily survey trips whenever the weather was good, and spent their time ground cruising when this was impossible.

ground-drift *n. North* snow driven along the surface by wind.

1777 (1951) *Sask.Jnls* 198: Weather clear with a ground drift and freezing yard. **1883** (1963) MCTAVISH *Behind the Palisades*: . . . there is a great prospect of remaining here tomorrow yet, on account of the ground drift and wind. **1937** *Beaver* Mar. 29/2: . . . recordings on the Kittigazuit reindeer reserve last winter often sank to fifty and sixty degrees below zero, accompanied by high winds that set up a dangerous blinding ground-drift. **1946** *Ibid.* Mar. 36/1: It was bitterly cold with a hard nor'west wind sweeping the ground-drift before it. . . .

ground-drifter *n. North* a cold wind that creates ground-drifts.

1942 TWOMEY & HERRICK *Needle to North* 148: What would we not have given for a biting wind that day, a scouring blast of a good ground-drifter, to turn all that

sop and flow and splash into a bleak, white, icy waste once more!

ground hemlock the Canadian yew, *Taxus canadensis.*

1822 (1928) CORMACK *Narr.Nfld* 88: The soil and shelter are so good here that the ground-hemlock, bearing its red berries, constitutes the chief underwood, as in the forests of Canada and Nova Scotia. **1926** SULLIVAN *Northern Lights* 1: Close to the ridge, in a clump of ground hemlock, was [a] stream on whose banks the snow lay a few inches deep. **1956** *Native Trees* 2: Two species, the western yew, and the Canada yew or ground hemlock . . . occur in Canada.

groundhog *n.* **1** a large burrowing rodent, *Marmota monax,* common in eastern and central Canada. See also **ground chuck, weenusk,** and **woodchuck.**

1789 (1801) MACKENZIE *Voyages* 51: We saw a fox and a ground hog on the hill. . . . **1883** FRASER *Shanty* 276: A ground-hog had issued forth from his winterquarters and had been worried by a dog. **1957** *London Free Press* (Ont.) 12 Feb. 6/3: Any groundhog who is crazy enough to get out of a nice warm bed to see what the weather is like should be shot at sunrise. **1963** SYMONS *Many Trails* 171: . . . it was a very large pine marten attacking a ground hog.

2 *B.C.* See **hoary marmot.**

1807 WENTZEL *Letters* 81: The other animals are the beaver, otter, wolverine, wolf, lynx; red, grey, white and black foxes, porcupine, ground hog, marten, mink; common red, ground and flying squirrels; hares, bats and mice. **1824** (1955) BLACK *Journal* 16: The Old Slave says there are Siffleu or the Ground Hog . . . on some of these bare mountains. **1954** EVANS *Mist* 157: And across the divides the groundhogs whistling down at them and the flocks of little birds coming and going in swirls of cheery sound. . . . **1959** *Native Voice* Jan. 7: I watched ground hogs swimming for their lives. . . .

groundhog day† February 2, the day on which the groundhog (def. 1) is supposed to come out of his burrow to determine the length of time remaining till spring; the legend being that he will anticipate an additional six weeks of hard winter if he should see his shadow and a relatively mild period if he should not.

1955 *Mountaineer* 3 Mar. 12/1: Feb. 2, that fateful day when the groundhog frightened by his own shadow, retreated for another nap, is about six weeks past. . . . **1965** *Kingston Whig-Standard* (Ont.) 2 Feb. 11/1: Today is groundhog day.

ground juniper the dwarf juniper, *Juniperus horizontalis.*

1793 (1933) MACDONELL *Diary* 114: There are two sorts of Juniper in the plains, one of which grows in tufts while the other runs on the ground like a vine. The berries of each are so alike that I find no difference; the leaf of the latter is verry like Red Cedar. **1861** SUTHERLAND *Geography P.E.I.* 57: There are some short species of little use, such as, the Ground Hemlock; and the Ground Juniper which yields berries. **1955** ENGLISH *Newfoundland* 43: The ground juniper boiled was supposed to be a panacea for stomach ills.

ground lead *Lumbering* a method of yarding logs by dragging them along the ground by means of a cable and a donkey engine. Cp. **high-lead.**

1943 SWANSON *Lumberjack* 56: Soon the system known as the ground lead was developed due to this improved yarding donkey.

ground pine a type of club moss, *Lycopodium obscurum.*
1861 SUTHERLAND *Geography P.E.I.* 53: Ground-pines . . . are trailing plants found in swamps and bogs and moorlands. **1953** MOWERY *Mounted Police* 64: They climbed out of the hardwoods into the big conifers, where the gray crow was at home; out of these into the storm-gnarled tamarack and ground pines. . . .

grounds *n.pl.* a region where hunting, trapping, and fishing is carried on. See also **hunting grounds.**
1913 WILLIAMS *Wilderness Trail* 21: "He stopped here on his way up, and said he was looking for better grounds." **1954** EVANS *Mist* 179: The grounds had been held by his family for many generations, long before the first whites came. . . .

ground sleigh See **stoneboat** and picture.
1909 BINDLOSS *Lorimer* 91: Some of our horses are not much to look at, and others are hard to drive, but the way they can haul the light wagons or even the humble ground sleigh along league after league would surprise those not used to them.

ground squirrel† any of several squirrel-like animals living largely on the ground, usually applied to the genus Spermophilus. See also **marmot** (def. 1).
1743 (1949) ISHAM *Observations* 150: Ground squrls' are as big as a small house catt, which harbour's in trees and Lives upon pine aple's [cones], another squr'l, the size & colour as in England, here is Numerious. **1853** STRICKLAND *Canada West* I 303: The chitmunck, or *Siriatus,* or ground squirrel, is much smaller and more mischievous than is any of the former species. *c*1902 LAUT *Trapper* 236: The gopher, or ground squirrel, is smaller than the wood squirrel, while the badger is larger than a Manx cat. **1963** *B.C.Digest* Oct. 34/2: We watched a huge grizzly root up the sod and tear a mound of solid rock to catch a ground squirrel or a whistler.

group box one of a number of mail boxes tiered on one frame or stand, used on rural routes for the convenience of persons in small suburban communities.
1963 *Herald Mag.* 5 Oct. 1/1: Some mail boxes . . . swing around . . . Others are called "group boxes."

grove *n. Lumbering, Now Rare* a timber stand.
1854 KEEFER *Ottawa* 61: When the grove is selected, the shanty is commenced; this is built of logs, nearly square. . . . **1896** GOURLAY *Hist.Ottawa* 21: . . . the road [was] at first that cut to reach the shanty to get in provisions for the work, the timber roads crossing this as they led from the groves to the river. . . .

growler *n. Esp.Nfld* See 1958 quote.
1920 GRENFELL & SPALDING *Le Petit Nord* 2: There is no chart for icebergs, and "growlers" are formidable opponents to encounter at any time. **1958** *Manice* 9: Growler—A small fragment of ice awash, smaller than a bergy bit, usually of glacial origin, and generally greenish in color. A typical growler is about the size of a grand piano. **1965** *Dly Colonist* (Victoria) 16 May 14/2: The only thing that one could do to protect the thin-hulled ships of the escort group was to place them astern of the heavier merchant ships, and this I proceeded to do once we began to encounter the first growlers inside the Straits [of Belle Isle].

grub(b) *n. Lumbering, Obs.* See quotes.
1853 STRICKLAND *Canada West* II 282: In squaring the butt-end, a large mortice—or grub-hole as it is termed—must be left to pass the chain through to draw the mast.

1945 CALVIN *Saga* 84: One of the components of the stave-crib was the "grubb" or "stave grubb"—the name occurs constantly (with "floats" and "traverses") in the records, but what they were is now unknown.

grub(b) *v. Lumbering* secure the pieces of a raft together with grubs.
1896 GOURLAY *Hist.Ottawa* 137: Oak rafts had to be floated by the lightest material and the ends grubbed and withed to the traverses, and were not loaded on.

grub-bag *n.* a bag or sack in which to keep provisions while on the trail. See also **grub-sack** and **tote-bag.** Cp. **grub-box.**
1913 CURRAN & CALKINS *Northland* 308: Others busied themselves in loosening the lashings of the toboggans in order to get the "grub" bag, which was placed at the end of the load so as to be easy of access. **1946** BIRD *Sunrise for Peter* 208: . . . only Nathan and old Gideon . . . went on, with the one musket, the sled to drag, and not much more than the bone of the ham in their grub-bag.

grub-box *n.* a special box for carrying cooking utensils and food on any sort of expedition. Cp. **grub-bag.**
1911 SETON *Arctic Prairies* 290: I plunged into the water, ice-cold and waist-deep—and before the merciless one could snatch it along, I had the grub-box safe. **1942** TWOMEY & HERRICK *Needle to North* 173: The grub box (with a hinged lid) stood open and revealed nested plates and cups of white enamel and the common necessities of each meal: salt, sugar, flour, dried fruit, and packages of 'Hudson Bay Red Label Tea.' **1963** *Chatelaine* Apr. 57/2: I pack his "grub box" when he goes hunting.

grub camp *Lumbering* See **cookhouse.**
1898 CONNOR *Black Rock* 2: The grub camp, with cook-shed attached, stood in the middle of the clearing; at a little distance was the sleeping-camp with the office built against it, and about a hundred yards away . . . stood the stables, and near them the smiddy.

grub-hole *n. Lumbering* See **grub,** *n.*

grub-house *n.* See **cookhouse.**
1912 CONNOR *Corp.Cameron* 332: The icy cold woke Cameron as the grey light came in through the dirty windows and the cracks between the logs of the grub-house.

grub-pile† *n. Slang* **1** a store of provisions.
1903 *Eye Opener* (High River, Alta) 24 Oct. 1/1: Over in the States a man who expected to appeal to the masses and to suggest extra taxes on their grub-pile, wouldn't dare to have the gout. **1919** FRASER *Bulldog Carney* 248: "Two men ain't got no chanct on that grub-pile, no chanct." **1954** PATTERSON *Dangerous River* 246: I then bought some odds and ends of grub from Jack to throw into his grub pile, so as not to be a burden on him in that way.

2 time to eat; a summons to a meal.
1892 DWIGHT *Life in N.W.M.P.* 27: "That means 'grub pile' that does," said a ravenous-looking individual of whom I made enquiry. **1893** *Wkly Manitoban* Apr. 93/2: It was "grub pile" with him, for the hind legs of a jackrabbit were still sticking out of his mouth. **1936** ELLS *Northland Trails* 87: Now his half defiant, wholly triumphant, "Grub Pile," echoed back from green valley walls. **1962** *Alta Hist.Rev.* Autumn

16/1: When the "layout" is complete the cook calls: "grubpile!", "wire in!", "grab-a-root!" or "come a-runnin you hungry hunters."

3 a meal.
1892 DWIGHT *Life in N.W.M.P.* 89: We were anxious for the time when we might parade our guests before the "grub pile" which had been provided for the occasion, and thus show the unbounded hospitality of our ideas in this direction. **1927** LONGSTRETH *Silent Force* 14: Every "grub-pile" seemed a feast, every sleep in the tarpaulin shelter was at least a change.

grub-rider *n. West* See 1962 quote.
1922 FOOTNER *Huntress* 50: For the masters to be bearded by a humble grub-rider was incredible. **1962** *Alta Hist.Rev.* Autumn 17/2: That itinerant . . . personage known in the East as the tramp has a counterpart in the west under the cognomen of "grub-rider."

grub run a trip made for the purpose of carrying provisions.
1958 *Beaver* Summer 16: Two hours earlier we had taken advantage of the Lands and Forests "grub run" piloted by Al Stewart. . . .

grub-sack *n.* See **grub-bag**.
1912 LONDON *Smoke Bellew* 16: He mopped his forehead, and across a heap of grub-sacks saw John Bellew gazing at him, wintry amusement in his eyes. **1956** KEMP *Northern Trader* 218: [The wolves] ripped his rabbit robe, dug into his grubsack, ate even a chunk of meat he had cooked in a pot.

grub-sled *n. North* a sled carrying provisions. See also **grub train**.
1934 GODSELL *Arctic Trader* 214: I was accompanied by . . . a young native named Sibbeston who drove the "grub-sled" containing food, dog-feed, bedding and baggage.

grubstake ['grʌb,stek] *n.* [< *grub* food + *stake*]
1† an arrangement by which a person or company provides money to outfit a prospector with food and equipment in return for a share (often one half) in any strike the prospector may make; also, the money or supplies involved in such an arrangement.
1899 PALMER *Klondyke* 97: They . . . were determined to return to their old stamping grounds, where any honest prospector can get a grubstake from a speculative city man. . . . **1928** FREEMAN *Nearing North* 234: The leader, too embittered to go back into the ministry, borrowed a grubstake and turned prospector. **1958** BERTON *Klondike* 37: But Henderson stayed on, lured by Ladue's promise of a grubstake, and for the next two years he stubbornly combed the Indian and its tributaries for gold.
2 *Fur Trade* an advance in the form of food and other supplies, to be paid for out of the coming season's catch. See also **debt** (def. 1).
1900 FRASER *Mooswa* 149: "What fur we keel now? Not enough to pay fer de grub stake." **1963** *Cdn Geog.Jnl* Dec. 191/3: Trappers are assisted by provision of grubstakes and equipment to enable them to reach and remain on their traplines during periods of peak production when the pelts are prime.
3 the money or the means to obtain food and other

necessaries for a certain period of time. See also **stake,** *n.*
1897 TUTTLE *Golden North* 76: . . . no place is very rich, but no place is very poor; every man can make a "grub stake" (that is enough to feed and clothe him for a year), which is more than I can say of the other places I have been in. **1912** BICKERSTETH *Open Doors* 134: Some spend their life going from one camp to another as labourers, others are homesteaders and farmers, and are here for a few months to make a "grub-stake." **1936** ARMSTRONG *Yukon Yesterdays* 59: He seemed quite cheerful over it all so I gave him back his job and he started to amass another "grub stake." **1963** *B.C. Digest* Apr. 51/2: My partner and I relocated a claim at that first midnight session that afterward turned out to be our grubstake, our bank, so to speak. . . . We could always go out to the claim if a grubstake was wanted and pound out an ounce a day; that is, $16.00.

4 a. a store or supply of provisions.
1909 SERVICE *Cheechako* 84:
The men who can't remember when they learned to swing a pack,
Or in what lawless land the quest began;
The solitary seeker with his grub-stake on his back,
The restless buccaneer of pick and pan.
1912 FOOTNER *New Rivers* 86: He built a fire on the bank and spread his meager grub-stake in a score of dirty little canvas bags to dry beside it. **1953** *North Star* (Yellowknife) Mar. 3/5: The Indian agency will help this pair to obtain new equipment and grubstake and clothing; no old age pension for Maurice, even if he is 68!
b. the food itself.
1923 WALDO *Down Mackenzie* 139: So he kicked over the traces of respectable conformity, and took to the woods with an outfit of seasoned "sour-doughs," wearing the clothes they wore and dividing the high cost and the tough chewing of their grub-stake.

5 See **grubstake claim**.
1909 SERVICE *Cheechako* 85: It's wine and painted women and the things that do me hurt,/Till I crawl back, beggared, broken to the Wild./ Till I crawl back, sapped and sodden, to my grubstake and my tent . . . . **1958** HARRIS *New Denver* 3/1: Thomas Latheen had seventy-five grub stakes here and went to Victoria to get permission to build a tunnel one mile long, as in Denver, Colorado.

grubstake ['grʌb,stek] *v.* **1 a.†** provide with a grubstake (def. 1).
1897 HARRIS *Gold Fields* 444: . . . by mining law, the "angel" receives one-half of all the grub-staked one discovers. **1958** BERTON *Klondike* 28: For years he and Harper had been grubstaking men to seek out the legendary "Preacher's Creek."
b. provide with a grubstake (def. 2).
1936 *Natural Hist.* Nov. 291: Airplane companies have grub-staked trappers, transported them into the heart of the Indian hunting grounds, with adequate supplies of traps and other equipment, picking them up at the end of the season and allowing them twenty-five per cent on the gross value of their fur catch.
c. provide with a grubstake (def. 3). See also **stake,** *v.* (def. 2).
1956 KEMP *Northern Trader* 101: You may outfit him and grubstake him, but being of a race that has to depend for breakfast on the yield of the early-morning fish net, the Indian thinks nothing of eating up his winter grubstake long before he reaches the winter camp. **1964** JENNESS *Eskimo Admin.* II 41: Revillon

Frères consistently grub-staked the [Eskimo] trappers who were threatened with famine. . . .

2 provide with food and other necessaries.
1919 FRASER *Bulldog Carney* 38: "I'm goin' to grubstake you," he said, "leave you rations for three days; that's more than you'd do for me." **1955** GOWLAND *Smoke* 95: I'm several years older than you are, and I've pretty near enough to grub stake myself for the rest of my life. **1964** *North* July 48: . . . she had departed with her son and his family, whom I had grubstaked for the season's fishing in Andrew Gordon Bay.

3 *B.C.* finance under the grubstake program, *q.v.*
1964 *Western Miner* July 14/2: [He] reports some fifty men have been grubstaked this year. . . .

grubstake claim a mining claim providing a modest income; a claim that produces a relatively small amount of gold. See also **grubstake,** *n.* (def. 5).
1963 *B.C.Digest* Apr. 51/2: . . . Mr. Dobbin never found anything better than a grubstake claim.

grubstake program a program by which money is provided in varying amounts as an incentive to prospectors to search for minerals in specified areas and over a minimum period of time.
1964 *Western Miner* July 14: Douglas H. Rae, field engineer for the prospectors' grubstake program financed by the Provincial Department of Mines & Petroleum Resources, Victoria, reports some fifty men have been grubstaked this year. . . .

grubstaker† *n.* **1** the recipient of a grubstake (def. 1).
1897 HARRIS *Gold Fields* 444: Grub-stakers proved one of the most ample crops of the craze [the gold-rush]. . . . A grub-staker is a man who wants someone to stake him with grub, and "grub" is Klondike for beans, bacon and tea.
2 the person who provides a grubstake (def. 1).
1918 COPELAND *Swinging Lanterns* 101: Vein sampling engineers, grubstakers, rock-worms, mine captains, prospectors and agents in coats of "astrachan goose" . . . strut about and add to their kit, each man jack of them probably thinking he has a "nose for ore" and inside information. **1967** *Cdn Geog.Jnl* Jan. 9/1: Once back in Haileybury [Ont.], Hollinger and his grubstaker, McMahon . . . discussed the situation with Alphonse Paré. . . .

grubstaking system the practice of providing trappers with a grubstake (def. 2).
1962 (1964) INNIS *Fur Trade in Canada* 374: Improved transportation and consequent competition has led to a marked decline at Peace River of the "credit" system and the "grubstaking" system.

grub train *Obs.* See **grub-sled.**
1896 MCDOUGALL *Saddle, Sled and Snowshoe* 3: Billy drove the baggage and "grub train."

grunt† [grʌnt] *n.* [prob. imitative of the sound made while boiling] *Maritimes* a steamed pudding or dumpling made with small fruits, such as blueberries or huckleberries. Cp. **fungy.**
1894 ASHLEY *Tan Pile Jim* 158: Jim had three small jugs of preserved huckleberries in reserve and with these he went to work intending to make a "grunt" after Ruth's most approved recipe. You place a batch of well-kneaded dough at the bottom of a kettle; over this you pour a layer of berries until the kettle is two-thirds full. Over the whole you place a nice whitecap of dough and a tight cover to shut the whole thing out of sight

until it sees fit to show itself . . . the kettle is set over a steady fire. . . . **1950** CREIGHTON *Lunenburg County* 68: Blueberry grunt or slump or fudge. Put berries in a pot, cover well with water and cook. Cool and add sugar. Drop baking powder dough in it. This may also be done with raspberries or apples. **1964** *Maclean's* 16 Nov. 34/3: My mother made another dessert . . . called a Foxberry Grunt.

guard *n.* **1** *Hist.* See **horseguard** (def. 1).
1857 (1863) PALLISER *Journals* 63: Despatch the horses to the Company's 'guard,' distant 10 miles down the other side of the river. **1872** (1873) GRANT *Ocean to Ocean* 148: Every station of the Hudson's Bay Company has a "guard," or judiciously selected spot, well supplied with good water, wood, pasturage, and shelter, where the horses are kept. **1956** INNIS *Travellers West* 42: From the seventy horses grazing in the guard he chose a number for riding and drawing wagon and carts. . . .

2 *West* See quote.
1963 SYMONS *Many Trails* 57: Usually everyone did a two-hour spell of night herd, or "guard" as it was sometimes called. . . .

3 a. See **fireguard** (def. 1).
1902 *High River Times* 11 July 2/4: The guard must be disked, so that all the weeds and grass are cut off. **1905** (1910) HAYDON *Riders of Plains* 283: When Mr. Conrad arrived he promptly helped me with the plough, and we finished the furrow. He, thinking the guard was large enough, got the horses inside.

b. See **firebreak** (def. 3).
1955 GOWLAND *Smoke* 181: I told them I would show them just where the guard had to be cut, as I had already decided on a likely spot while surveying the position. **1958** *Edmonton Jnl.* 23 July 8/1: One blaze . . . jumped its guards Monday night and 35 men were attempting to stop it.

guard hair† the coarse, glossy hair protecting the soft under-hair on a fur-bearing animal. Cp. **king hair.**
[**1703** (1964) INNIS *Fur Trade* 4: . . . a beaver has two lays of hair; one is long and of a shining black color, with a grain as big as that of a Man's Hair; the other is fine and smooth and in Winter fifteen lines long. In a word, the last is the finest Down in the world.] **1930** HODGSON *Muskrat Farming* 63: [Caption] Muskrat fur with the long (guard) hairs plucked. **1956** LEECHMAN *Native Tribes* 287: It took the wool from three [mountain] goats to make one blanket and, after it had been pulled from the hide, the coarse guard hairs had to be pulled out leaving the finer and softer wool. **1962** (1964) INNIS *Fur Trade* 4: The fur of the beaver, like that of other animals, may be divided into two parts: the guard hair, up to two inches in length, and the underhair or fur, at most an inch.

guard line See **firebreak** (def. 3).
1958 *Edmonton Jnl* 23 July 8/1: Two bulldozers were cutting guard lines.

guard room *Fur Trade, Hist.* See 1941 quote. See also **bachelors' hall.**
1801 (1920) *Beaver* Oct. 31/1: Oct'r 14th . . . Cloudy weather . . . Mended the chimney. Mended the guard room stove. Finished repairing the North gates. **1941** *Ibid.* Sep. 37/2: Guard Room—Bachelors' quarters.

guide *n.* [< Cdn F < F] *Fur Trade, Hist.* **1** See
conductor (def. 1).

1761 (1901) HENRY (Elder) *Travels* 14: To each canoe
there are eight men; and to every three or four canoes,
which constitute a *brigade*, there is a *guide* or a
conductor.... **1821** (1900) GARRY *Diary* 93: Our party
consists in Mr. William McGillivray, Mr. Simon
McGillivray and myself, (?) Mornis an old Canadian
Voyageur as McG's servant, an English Boy servant to
his Brother and my man Raven, one Guide[,] Langue,
12 Canadian Voyageurs.... **1923** *Beaver* Nov. 52/1: The
principal man of the brigade was the "guide" in charge
of the whole works. **1956** KEMP *Northern Trader* 121:
The fault lay with the "guide," the oldest man of the
four who, by tacit agreement and prevailing custom,
was appointed leader of the sorry expedition.

2 the head driver of a train of dog-sleds.
1921 HEMING *Drama of Forests* 175: "M-a-r-r-che!"
(start) shouted the guide—as the head dog-driver is
called.

3 an experienced woodsman who conducts
sportsmen on hunting, fishing, or other expeditions,
piloting the party and looking after the gear and the
camp.
1903 WHITE *Forest* 309: Undoubtedly among the
half-breed and white guides of Lower Canada ... are
many skilful men. **1920** GIBBON *Conquering Hero* 9: To
the casual eye there was little to choose between "sports"
and guide, for, after a fortnight in the woods, chins and
cheeks were unkempt with whiskers, shoepacks were
muddy, clothes were torn and untidy. **1966** *Globe and
Mail* (Toronto) 29 Aug. 6/4: Some of the jobs most
suitable for Indians are: ... fire rangers, timber
cruisers, scalers ... lumbermen, game wardens ... park
wardens and guides....

guide *v.* act as a guide (def. 3) (for).
1921 *Rod and Gun in Can.* Aug. 380: I have guided
parties on the famous Nipigon waters for the past 25
years. **1966** *Globe and Mail* (Toronto) 18 May 6/1: He
uses his time off from the railroad to guide fishermen
and hunters in summer and autumn.

guiding *n.* employment as a guide (def. 3).
1921 *Rod and Gun in Can.* Aug. 380: [Advert.]
... Canoeing and guiding for trout are my specialties.
1945 MOORE *Castle Buck* 99: "I pay this buck three
dollars a day for guidin' and one certificate extra for
them clothes and that line o' guff." **1965** *Globe and Mail*
(Toronto) 26 Nov. 7/2: Fishing, hunting and trapping,
plus guiding ... provided some sort of livelihood for
them.

Guignolée [gɪnjɔ'le] *n.* [< Cdn F < F *guignol*
marionette] See 1959 quote.
1955 COLLARD *Cdn Yesterdays* 62: If you have nothing
to give us/ Just say so./ We will take the eldest girl,/
and roast her feet for her,/ The "guignolée," the
"guignolée"/ To grease our pockets. **1959** *Citizen*
(North Vancouver) 4 June 6A/3: The "Guignolee" is
the custom of groups of young men, the "Guignoleux,"
to dress in gay attire and go from house to house singing
and begging for the poor. This is the traditional
celebration of French Canada and has been carried on
for many years on New Year's Eve.

guignoleux [gɪnjɔ'lu] *n.pl.* [< Cdn F
< *Guignolée*, q.v.] groups of young men taking
part in a Guignolée, *q.v.*

1955 COLLARD *Cdn Yesterdays* 62: So it was in many a
town and village on the St. Lawrence when the
"guignoleux" used to set out on New Year's Eve ...
[and] with long sticks would knock on each door,
keeping time by their knocking to the rhythm of their
song.

gulch† [gʌltʃ] *n.* [prob. < Brit. dial. *gulch, gulsh,*
drink noisily; of land, sink in] **1** a ravine or large
gully in a hillside, especially one flooded by
freshets. Older, *gulsh.*
1835 WIX *Journal* 140: I was put across La Hune Bay in
a boat, and walked about two miles, across some
mountainous ridges, in the "gulshes," between which
the hardened snow was still thirty or forty feet high, to
Western Cul de Sac. **1860** *Sask.Herald* (Battleford,
N.W.T.) 25 Aug. 1/4: As yet, the wolves and cayotes
howl their dreary requiems around its vast solitude,
while an occasional grizzly comes out from his lair to
see if the white man has yet invaded his favorite gulch.
1934 DENNIS *Down in N.S.* 406: More sandy hillocks
and we enter a gulch. "This is 'Smoky Hut Gulch',," the
Superintendent says. **1963** SYMONS *Many Trails* 62: Then
we come to a series of grass benches cut by coulees
(called gulches in this province [B.C.]).... **1965** *Maclean's*
3 July 23/1: According to one story, a party of [Ontario]
trailbuilders came to a gulch with steep limestone cliffs
surrounding it and saw a bearded fellow hoeing a
garden beside a shanty below.

2 a gully in which placer gold has been found.
1859 *Brit.Colonist* (Victoria) 15 Aug. 2/2: Men have
arrived at Lytton from Alexander, who state positively
they can make fifty dollars per day, to the hand,
anywhere—that the diggings are extensive, and that all
the gulches and ravines are rich with gold. **1877** GRANT
Ocean to Ocean 271: John Glen calculated ... that he
might strike a new bar or gulch that would pan out as
richly as Williams' Creek, Cariboo.... **1924** DORRANCE
Never Fire First: [He] could wait until he learned what
"richer than gold" was being gleaned up the gulch.

Gulf Islander *B.C.* a native or resident of one of
the many islands lying between Vancouver
Island and the mainland in the Gulf of Georgia.
1960 *Sun* (Vancouver) 11 Apr. 3/1: "That's right," said
the Gulf Islander. "He witches for wells." In the
language of the trade, smelling for water. **1961** *Canada
Month* Dec. 45: [Caption] Government ferry "Motor
Princess" alarms Gulf Islanders as a sign of possible
increase in both taxes and tourists.

Gulf shore the shore of the Gulf of St. Lawrence.
1830 MOORSOM *Letters N.S.* 215: Between Pictou and
Truro it is connected with another chain [of hills] ...
running nearly parallel from Tatamagouche on the
Gulf-shore to Chignecto Head on the Bay of Fundy....
1832 BAILLIE *Account of N.B.* 72: The French have
exclusive occupation of the whole Gulf shore in this part
of the province, and although they are good, peaceable
subjects, they are the worst of agriculturists. **1963**
DAVIES *Northern Quebec* xv fn2: Hudson's Bay Company
men tended to refer specifically to the different regions
with which they were concerned rather than to the
peninsula as a whole: to the Eastmain (the Hudson Bay
and James Bay coast north of Rupert River) ...
Ungava ... Labrador ... and the Gulf Shores (the
southern part bordering the Gulf of St. Lawrence).

gulsh *n.* See gulch.

gum *n.* **1** a resinous substance exuded from certain
evergreen trees, especially the spruce, as used for
waterproofing the seams of birchbark canoes,
q.v. See also **Indian pitch.**

1749 DRAGE *Voyage* II 37: When the Canoe is made with two Pieces, then one Piece is sewed to the other with the Rind; the Inside and Outside of both which Pieces they dress with Gum, in such a Manner as to make them appear to be one Piece. **1830** (1954) *Beaver* Mar. 16: . . . covering the seam with melted Pine Pitch, or "Gum," which rendered it perfectly water-tight. **1921** HEMING *Drama of Forests* 318: After a little burning, the stick opened like a fork; and, placing it over the broken seam, the voyageur blew upon the crotch, thus melting the hardened "gum"; then, spitting upon his palm, he rounded it off and smoothed it down. **1953** MOWERY *Mounted Police* 63: At each camp Itai-Po produced a gum pot and smeared cracks in his birchbark.

2 See **gumboot.**
1912 POCOCK *Man in the Open* 165: If ever I get to a town I'm to take the outside of the sidewalk, wipe my gums on the mat, and wash before I use them roller towels.

gum *v.* render (a birchbark canoe) water-tight by applying gum (def. 1) to the seams.
1765-75 (1933) POND *Narrative* 40: After Two Days Hard Labor We Gits our Canoes . . . and Gund [gummed] our Canoes fit to descend that River. **1793** (1911) SIMCOE *Diary* 209: An Indian woman came to-day with pitch . . . to gum the canoe. . . . **1857** (1863) PALLISER *Journals* 23: . . . the voyageurs gummed the canoes, an operation necessary at almost every encampment. **1921** HEMING *Drama of Forests* 318: In the half light of early day, and while breakfast was being prepared, the men "gummed" afresh the big canoes.

gum bed *Obs.* See quotes.
1876 (1888) BESANT & RICE *Golden Butterfly* 100: Sometimes you came upon patches of "gum-beds," as they called them, where the ground was like tar, and smelt strong. **1889** WITHROW *Our Own Country* 360: In the neighbourhood of Oil Springs are situated the 'gum beds.' These are tracts of about four acres each— there are two of them—covered by a crust varying from two or three inches to about as many feet in thickness; the accumulation, it may be supposed of ages, being a residuum from the oil forced to the surface. . . .

gumbo† ['gʌmbo] *n.* [< Am.E "okra" < a. Bantu word] **1** *West and Northwest* See 1902 quote.
1902 (1957) *Sask.Hist.* X 11: As we neared Regina the soil took on the character of what in western parlance is called "gumbo." This gumbo is a very fine-grained soil, rich in alkaline compounds, which, when saturated with water, becomes as sticky as glue and impervious to moisture, whilst it cracks and bakes as hard as bricks when thoroughly dry. **1923** WALDO *Down Mackenzie* 116: When it rains, the first half of the road, from Fitzgerald, is turned to a liquid mud or "gumbo," profound and tenacious. **1964** *Calgary Herald* 24 July 19/3: There is a bank, 'though a bandit with a flair for the spectacular could make the getaway of the century by putting wheels back under it and pulling out in a cloud of dust, or gumbo.

2 any thick, sticky mud.
1909 CONNOR *Foreigner* 202: The team stuck fast in the black muck, and every effort to extricate them served only to imbed them more hopelessly in the sticky gumbo. **1966** *Islander* 27 Feb. 13/1: . . . this little press had once been taken apart and packed on the backs of men through 40 miles of gumbo and jack pine.

gumboot *n.* **1** a rubber boot, reaching to just below the knee. See also **gum,** *n.* (def. 2).
1860 *Brit.Colonist* (Victoria) 26 Oct. 2/3: At the Cariboo, gum boots were selling at $25 per pair. . . . **1909** CAMERON *New North* 27: The girlish figure of a

teacher struggling through the awful mud in gum-boots indicates that we have not travelled beyond the range of the little red schoolhouse. **1955** HOBSON *Nothing Too Good* 137: That big Rooshin stands with his dirty gumboots on my outhouse seat. **1964** *Sun* (Vancouver) 4 July 1: "He'll need socks, gum boots, work pants . . . hard hats, bone dry jackets. . . ."

2 See **hip-wader.**
☛ *Other references to gumboots during the gold-rush days may well refer to hip-waders.*
1873 JOHNSON *Very Far West* 118: His large feet were encased in india-rubber boots . . . (called gum-boots in the vernacular), which covered the thighs and fastened around the waist.

gum-stick *n. Obs.* a stick of pine saturated with pitch or gum (def. 1), carried on the trail for kindling campfires.
1867 LORD *Wilderness* 201: The best material I have ever met for kindling a fire, is known to the fur-traders . . . as gum-stick; nearly every Indian Tribe employs it.

gum-sugar *n.* a kind of maple sugar, *q.v.* See quotes.
1860 (1956) KOHL *Kitchi-Gami* 324: A third variety [of maple sugar] is the "gum," or "wax sugar." This is produced by throwing the thick-boiled sugar into the snow and cooling it rapidly. **1863** WALSHE *Cedar Creek* 231: An Indian girl was making what is called gum-sugar, near the kettles: cutting moulds of various shapes in the snow, and dropping therein small quantities of the boiling molasses [maple sap], which cooled rapidly into a tough yellowish substance, which could be drawn out with the fingers like toffy.

gunk-hole ['gʌŋk,hol] *n.* [origin obscure] *Local* a tiny cove having deep water right to the rock face which constitutes the shore.
1958 WELLS *Georgian Bay* 94: And then you may cruise back to your hidden gunk hole near the inlet entrance and enjoy peace, and quietude and privacy again. **1958** *Globe and Mail* (Toronto) 23 Aug. 9/4: When reviewing Cruising the Georgian Bay, I remarked that I didn't know what a gunk hole is. I dislike ignorance of Canadian words. **1960** WELLS *North Channel* 102: This [the North Channel] is an area rich in gunk-holes and little coves.

gunk-hole ['gʌŋk,hol] *v. Local* move from one gunk-hole to another, fishing and idling.
1958 WELLS *Georgian Bay* 101: If I was seeking, on the Georgian, a summer base from which to explore and laze, and gunk-hole, and fish, the French would be it.

gunnybag *v. Local* beat out a prairie fire with wet sacks.
1882 *Prince Albert Times* (Sask.) 6 Dec. 1/4: The men had to turn out and "gunnybag" the fire, as they call it, i.e. beat it out with bags.

gunnysack *n.* (used attributively) *Esp.Northwest, Slang* among miners and loggers, second-rate; unattractive; stingy; badly equipped; poorly organized. See also **haywire,** *adj.* (def. 2).
1958 LINDSAY *Cariboo Story* 18: They had a gunnysack show to start off with, greasy gravel and slippery clay. . . .

gunstock club See **casse-tête** and picture.
1943 MILLER *Lone Woodsman* 67: The woods Indians

preferred the gunstock club that looks something like a hockey stick with a stone blade jutting from the angle.

gurdy ['gɜ˞di] *n.* [< *hurdy-gurdy*] a hand- or machine-operated winch that winds fishing line on a drum as fish are hauled in. See also **hauler-head.**
1936 MACKENZIE *Living Rough* 26: "Yah," he replied, looking up at us. "I bane making some gurdies. Sometimes when I catch salmon he get tangled in other lines so I make gurdies to stop too much jerking, and make fish more steady to haul lines in." **1955** WALLACE *Roving Fisherman* 153: But as halibut were tougher fish to pull in than are cod and haddock the hand-winch, known as the "gurdy", affixed across the bow of the dory was frequently employed to haul up the line and fish. **1959** *Time* (Cdn ed.) 6 July 10/1: As an electric "gurdy" hauled in the line, the fish, weighing five to fifty lbs., were gaffed at the rail's edge, gutted, flipped in the hold.

gurry† ['gɜ˞i] *n.* [? Brit.dial. *gurry* diarrhea] *Atlantic Provinces* the waste from cleaning fish; fish offal. See also **fish gurry.**
1791 (1961) PERKINS *Diary* 112: Scraped off the Gurrey that was put on the tallow, & scraped part of what was Tard. We tallow it affresh. **1922** WALLACE *Shack Locker* 18: Ye trimmed Jack Hemsley an hove him inter th' gurry-scow?

gusperot *n. Obs.* See **gaspereau.**
1807 HERIOT *Travels* 518: The fish produced in the river Saint Lawrence are whales of different kinds, sea-cows . . . mackarel, gusperot, herring, pickerell.

gut sausage See 1958 quote.
1858 (1863) PALLISER *Journals* 86: We halted in the neighbourhood to enjoy a feast of moose meat, moofle, and gut sausage, dishes which our hunters and half-breeds prepared with great skill. . . . **1958** LEWIS *Buckskin Cookery* II 30: [Moose] Gut Sausage (Indian, Nazko). Take a big gut with all fat on. Now wash good. Turn inside out, and scrape and wash good again. Tie with string every little ways. Dry and smoke over camp fire. Sure good for eat.

gutskin *n. North* a kind of leather made from the large intestines of seals and whales.
1916 HAWKES *Labrador Eskimo* 40: A kayaker's suit, consisting of a gutskin coat and trousers, was obtained at Wolstenholme.

gyp(p)o ['dʒɪpo] *n.* [< *Gypo* (slang) gypsy] *Slang* a small operator or contractor. Also spelled *jippo.*
☛ *The source of this term indicates the mobile character of such operators and does not necessarily have derogatory connotations, although the association with* **gyp,** *suggesting dishonest or shoddy work, is often made.*
1912 FOOTNER *New Rivers* 66: It appeared that at this end of the road there were no "Gyppos" or "wheel-barrow outfits," as they call the independent freighters, and the contractors . . . refused to carry a pound that was not their own. **1948** *Ont.Timberworker* 15 Jan. 4/2: The traditional gypo-contractor and small jobber still lives in his dog-house and talks about the "good old days, when men were men." **1959** *Sun* (Vancouver) 26 May 4/5: This office did offer me the usual dime a dozen jobs selling thingamajigs door-to-door on commission for the gyppo firms. **1960** *Ibid.* 16 Feb. 2/2: Now we got the tree farm licence, designed to protect the inefficiency of the big

boy, and maybe the race of gyppos is going to be wiped out.

gyp(p)o logger *Lumbering* a logger who works on a small scale, often on piecework or on land leased from a big lumber company. See also **gypo.**
1925 *Cdn Labor Advocate* 21 Aug. 6/5: Our foreman was an ex-jippo logger, named D. McDonald, formerly of Glengarry, Ontario. McDonald suffered from all a "jippo's" complexes and inhibitions, including a complete ignorance of the nature and structure of a square meal. **1960** *Sun* (Vancouver) 16 Feb. 1/1: Joe Garner is a gyppo logger who was born in a dirt-floored log cabin. . . . **1964** *Fisherman* 8/5: [The] gyploggers skidded their logs down creeks ripping up spawning beds. . . .

gypsy machine *Lumbering, Hist.* a portable donkey engine.
1953 SWANSON *Haywire Hooker* 70: [Caption] The first steam donkey to log in the woods. This was a vertical spool or gypsy machine and was moved around with horses or oxen. Picture was taken on Vancouver Island about 1901.

Hab [hæb] *n. Slang* **1** See **habitant** (def. 2).
1966 *Globe and Mail* (Toronto) 19 Apr. 6/6: To be a
Hab, one only needs to play on the Hab team.
2 See **Habitant.**

habitan *n.* See **habitant.**
1762 (1908) *Champlain Soc.Pubs* III 202: The Canadians
may be ranked under four different classes: The
Gentry . . . The Clergy . . . The merchants . . . The
Peasantry, or what are here styled *habitans*. **1849**
ALEXANDER *L'Acadie* II 55: The habitans, dark and
thin, are a contented and amiable race of people, when
restless demigods do not excite them. **1956** INNIS *Fur
Trade* 63: The company began with an attempt to
exercise the full rights of the chapter in the control of
trade, but because of complaints from the *habitans* . . .
it was unsuccessful. . . .

habitant ['hæbətənt *or* 'hæbɪtã; *French* abi'tã] *n.*
[< Cdn F] **1** a farmer in French Canada,
originally a person holding land from a seigneur
(def. 1).
1791 LONG *Voyages* 167: The Canadians are particularly
fond of dancing, from the *seigneur* to the *habitant*. . . .
1886 (1887) *Trans.Roy.Soc.Can.* V 4 47: The habitant
or censitaire held his property by the tenure of a
censive, on condition of making annual payments in
money or produce known as cens et rente, which was
ridiculously small in the early times of the colony.
1931 SEARY *Romance* 101: The *habitants,* on the other
hand, being a stubborn people, refused to take any
oath of allegiance unless it contained a special clause
promising them that they would not have to fight for
the British king. **1938** GODSELL *Red Hunters* 24: And so
they continued to swagger round the dram shops . . .
while despising the humble habitants from whose ranks
they had sprung. . . . **1963** *Globe Mag.* 16 Mar. 5:
From almost its earliest beginnings, the colony [New
France] was under the joint tutelage of church and state,
with each reinforcing the other in dealings with the
Habitants.
2 any French Canadian, especially one from rural
Quebec.
1789 *Quebec Gaz.* 5 Feb. 4/1: When the experiment shall
have been fairly made, my Brother Habitants will be so
convinced of the expediency of the regulation, that they
will universally give it their support. **1891** *Grip* (Toronto)
17 Jan. 50: "La Presse," of Quebec, intimates that the
habitants of that Province fail because they do not run
their households economically. **1916** BRIDLE *Sons of Can.*
104: The habitant prefers to be let alone. In defence of
Quebec he would fight like a wild cat. **1963** *Globe and
Mail* (Toronto) 16 Feb. 19/7: Old-time suppers, square
dances, habitant sports will be interspersed with ice
skating contests. . . . **1966** *Kingston Whig-Standard* (Ont.)
27 Aug. 4/3: As the old habitant joke had it, it's okay to
t'row out de hank [anchor], but suppose there's no
rope on the hank?
3 See **habitant French.**
*c*1902 LAUT *Trapper* 146: Then the grass strands
would tremble with excitement and the little French
hunter's body would quiver and he would begin pouring
forth a jumble, half habitant half Indian with a mixture
of all the oaths from both languages, pointing and
pointing at his hidden face and bidding you look at
what the bear had done to him. . . .
4 *Local* on the southern coast of Labrador, a
French-speaking fisherman.
1947 TANNER *Outlines* II 727: On the southern coast a
distinction is also made between *liveyeres,* English-
speaking, semi-settled fishermen[,] and *habitants,*
semi-settled fishermen who speak French.

Habitant *n.* (*usually plural*) a member of the
Montreal Canadians, a professional hockey club.
1950 PALMER *Montreal Confidential* 116: Back in those
days Howie Morenz starred for Les Canadians. . . .
Other Habitants around at that time were the Mantha
brothers . . . and Art Lesieur.

habitant French the dialect or patois spoken by
rustic or backwoods French Canadians. See also
habitant (def. 3).
1889 *Scribner's Mag.* May 528/1: Thereupon ensued a
wordy war between the carter and the passenger whose
command of habitant French was most nearly equal to
the occasion.

habitant penny *Hist.* a coin in circulation in
Lower Canada during the early 1800's, properly
the Bank of Montreal copper token.
1900 *Canadian Mag.* Dec. 115/2: From this the coins
are called "Habitant pennies," but among the French
Canadians, "Papineaus," because the Hon. L. J.
Papineau, the leader of the patriots, affected this
costume.

hackee† *n.* [imitative] *Obs.* See **chipmunk.**
1887 *Trans.Roy.Soc.Can.* IV 175: The Chipmunk,
Chipping Squirrel or Hackee, has his abode
underground in a specially constructed burrow; the
Red Squirell, or Chickaree, lives in nests in trees.

hackmatack ['hækmə,tæk] *n.* [< Algonk.; cf.
Abnaki *akemantak* wood for snowshoes]
Esp.Maritimes any of several evergreens,
especially the common larch, or tamarack, *q.v.*;
also, the wood of such trees. Various spellings.
[**1774** (1945) ROBINSON & RISPIN *Journey N.S.* 34:
This town . . . affords great store of fine timber
[including] tackamahacka, or juniper. . . .]
1823 HALIBURTON *General Descr.N.S.* 26: Natural
forest-trees are elm . . . white and yellow pine . . .
hackmatack or juniper. . . . **1840** *Bytown* [Ottawa] *Gaz.*
18 June 1/3: the hackmatac . . . is found in the largest
quantities in New Brunswick, Nova Scotia and Prince
Edward Island. **1949** LAWSON *N.B.Story* 13: "Well . . .
first we took roots of the spruce or hackmatack, about
so thick. . . ." **1957** *Ukrainian Canadian* 15 Apr. 4/3:
"Hackmatack" to an Easterner is a shipbuilding term,
but to the Westerner it is a larch or tamarack.

ha-ha-wie or **hah-wee-a** *n.* [< Algonk.] *Obs.*
a pintail duck.
1795 (1911) HEARNE *Journey* 170: I also observed several
flocks of sea-fowl flying about the shores; such as, gulls,
black-heads, loons, old wives, ha-ha-wies, dunter geese,
arctic gulls, and willicks. **1882** *Trans.Roy.Soc.Can.* I 4 50:
The long-tail (*Dafila acuta,* Linn.) was obtained from
Fort George, and is not uncommon in the interior part
of Hudson's Bay where it is called the "hah-wee-a."

Haida blanket See **Chilkat blanket** and picture.
1891 *Trans.Roy.Soc.Can.* IX 2 47: Such blankets were
made only by the Chilkats of the Alaskan coast, and
although often called Haida blankets, the term is
erroneous, as the Haida never practised the art of
weaving wool or hair.

Haida canoe *West Coast* a sixty-foot dugout

canoe, *q.v.*, used by the Haida Indians for raids on the mainland.
1869 *Mainland Guardian* (New Westminster, B.C.) 30 Oct. 3/2: We bought a large Hydah canoe for $50, and hired ten siwashes (nine Hydahs and one bog-will Indian), for $10 a month and board, to stop with us where we chose, and to go with us at least as far as their own villages. **1955** MCCOWAN *Upland Trails* 153: There is a specimen of a Haida canoe in the Natural History Museum in New York, sixty-four feet long and eight feet wide. . . .

haiqua *n.* See **hiaqua.**

hair *n. Fur Trade* See **in the hair.**

hair seal† one of several seals, such as the harbor seal, *q.v.*, whose coat lacks underfur and is of little commercial value.
1872 DASHWOOD *Chiploquorgan* 255: . . . these are the hair seals. . . . **1929** *Beaver* June 209: The framework [of a kayak] is made entirely by the men, who leave the covering to their women-folk, and, as the green hides of the hair seal have to be sewn on before drying. . . .
1964 *Sechelt Peninsula Times* 22 Apr. 3/3: [Caption] Bergliot Solberg of Sechelt with a small 75-pound hair seal she shot in Sechelt Inlet. The hair seals are not so numerous in the inlet as formerly.

hair stick See quote.
1940 *Beaver* Dec. 46/1: One or two [Eskimo women] wore hair-sticks. These appendages hung from each side of the forehead, the hair being drawn down the side of the stick of wood, by no means light in itself, and was wound kept in place by a band of heavy cloth, which was on in the same way as a soldier puts on his puttees.

half axe *Obs.* a light axe for use on the trail and in camp.
1948 *Beaver* Dec. 6/2: The history of hatchets and axes [must include] the half axe, the broad axe, the squaw axe and the almost endless variations of the metal tomahawks. **1964** *Weekend Mag.* 11 July 18/3: Important was a half-axe with heavy head. . . .

half beaver *Fur Trade, Obs.* the skin of an immature beaver, $\frac{1}{4}$, $\frac{1}{2}$, and $\frac{3}{4}$ beavers being 1, 2, and 3 years old respectively. See 1743 quote.
1682 (1945) *H.B.C.Minutes* 37: Ordered the beavor and skins be put up as Foll. at the Sale: The Coate Beavor . . . the parchment beavor . . . the halfe beavor. . . .
1743 (1949) ISHAM *Observations* 147: They [beaver] are four years before they Come to the full growth, Distinguishing by Whole, $\frac{3}{4}$, $\frac{1}{2}$ and $\frac{1}{4}$ beaver.
1791 (1934) FIDLER *Journal* 522: Yesterday . . . at a Beaver house . . . killed one $\frac{3}{4}$ & one $\frac{1}{2}$ Beaver.
1962 (1964) INNIS *Fur Trade* 127: Beaver . . . was sold as coat beaver . . . parchment beaver . . . and as half-beaver, or stage beaver, or poorer quality beaver.

half blood *n.* See **half-breed.**
1910 FERGUSON *Janey Canuck* 240: Perhaps Louis Riel, the ill-starred half-blood is among them. **1964** *Fort Langley* 13: French-Canadians and Iroquois from Eastern Canada, Scottish employees of the company, Kanakas from the Islands of Hawaii, and Coast Indians and half-bloods worked at the fort as boatbuilders, carpenters, coopers, blacksmiths, hunters, trappers, boatmen, clerks, and labourers.

half-breed† *n.* **1** a person of mixed Indian and white ancestry. See also **half-Indian, half-white, Métis,** and **mixed-blood.**
1815 (1940) NIVEN *Mine Inheritance* 151: Article of Agreement entered into between the Half-Breed Indians of the Indian Territory on the one part and the Honorable Hudson's Bay Company on the other. . . .
1862 *Nor'Wester* (R.R.S.) 22 Oct. 2/4: In this country, in fact, the name applies to all who have Indian blood in greater or less degree. This is the general acception of the term, and, in this sense nine-tenths or more of the civilised people of Rupert's Land are "Half breeds."
1903 *Eye Opener* (High River, Alta) 24 Oct. 1/4: I am married to a half-breed and have three ornery looking, copper-colored brats. **1962** *Alta Hist.Rev.* Autumn 13/2: "Ari-stock-rats," sometimes "moccasin aristocracy," is a term used to designate the half-breeds (or Metis) which they prefer being called.

2 See 1920 quote.
1842 *Trans.Lit.& Hist.Soc.Que.* IV 88: Their number may be on an average, about forty-five souls, of these eight are white men, the remainder half-breed Esquimaux. **1920** GRENFELL & SPALDING *Le Petit Nord* 49: In the Home we have only one pure Eskimo, a few half-breeds (Indian and Eskimo), and the remainder are of English descent.

Half-breed Rebellion *Hist.* See **Northwest Rebellion** (defs. 1 and 2).
1888 (1890) ST. MAUR *Impressions* 28: Little [was] to be seen except the fort and a small settlement of about 250 to 300 people, chiefly known then as the centre of the half-breed rebellion under Louis Riel. **1900** OSBORN *Greater Canada* 41: Of the many descendants of these people—those "Men of the Movement" who rebelled against civilization under the leadership of Louis Riel and Gabriel Dumont—the writer will have something to say later on, when he comes to deal with those much misunderstood episodes, the half-breed rebellions of 1870 and 1885. **1953** MOWERY *Mounted Police* viii: When the Half-Breed Rebellion broke out, the Mounted Policeman fought alongside the militia till the rebellion was quelled.

half-breed scrip *Hist.* See **land-scrip** (def. 2). See also **old settlers' scrip.**
1878 (1963) STANLEY *Louis Riel* 260: Your petitioners would humbly represent that their rights to a participation in the issue of the half-breed or old settlers' scrip are as valid and binding as those of the half-breed and old settlers of Manitoba. . . . **1945** HAIG *Brave Harvest* 24: . . . up from the Bank came much business, especially land business, especially that concerning the settlement of deeds for half-breed script [sic], sold by their owners during the boom of the previous years.

half-breed scrip millionaire *Hist.* See **scrip millionaire.**
1956 *Sask.Hist.* IX 1 5: Instead, the operation was a principal factor in creating a class of rich speculators, "the half-breed scrip millionaires," whose fortunes were built upon the dispossession of a group of men who were victims of their own ignorance, their weakness and their ill-adaptation to the new economy.

Half-breed Uprising *Hist.* See **Northwest Rebellion** (def. 2).
1885 *Qu'Appelle Vidette* 26 Mar. 2/3: Wild rumors are prevalent here to-day respecting the Half-breed uprising in the North-west. **1935** *Trans.Roy.Soc.Can.* III 2 19: The half-breed uprising was the only serious interruption to good order in the history of the [Northwest] Territories. . . .

half-camp *n. Obs.* See **lean-to** (def. 1a). Cp. **double camp.**
1872 DASHWOOD *Chiploquorgan* 157: A half camp is covered only on one side, the other being left open, and the fire place in front.

half(-sized) canoe *Fur Trade, Hist.* a light canoe about 20 feet long, used on certain low-water routes. See also **demi-canot.**
1820 (1938) SIMPSON *Athabasca Jnl* 30: [We] proceeded and met a half sized canoe from Isle à la Crosse with supplies for the Indians. **1824** (1931) SIMPSON *Fur Trade* 18: Learning that the Beaver River was unusually low I got a half sized Canoe from Mʳ Heron and two Men, with whom I put in two of our own Crew and part of the Baggage to lighten us. **1929** (1931) MERK *Fur Trade* 346: Besides North canoes, there were in use in the fur trade half canoes and single canoes. . . .

half cargo *Fur Trade, Obs.* See **demi-decharge.**
1810 (1950) THOMPSON *Journals* 118: At 1 PM the Canoes came half Cargoe—they crossed us & went to fetch the rest of the Furrs. *Ibid.* 125: . . . went down to the Forks—here half Cargoe over the Rapids—dangerous. . . .

half-caste† *n. Rare* See **half-breed** (def. 1).
1819 (1823) FRANKLIN *Journey* 53: This, however, could hardly have been expected from persons who have permitted their own offspring, the half-casts, to remain in lamentable ignorance on a subject of such vital importance. **1935** MORICE *Red River Insurrection* 43: . . . Mr. Coldwell remained in full possession of the little sheet ["The Nor-wester"], which he edited in conjunction with an able half caste native, James Ross. . . .

half-cent *n. Hist.* a copper coin having a brief period of circulation in New Brunswick and Nova Scotia.
1891 *Trans.Roy.Soc.Can.* IX 2 40: A coinage of cents, of the same design, was also ordered in 1861 for New Brunswick and, although this order required no half cents, a quantity were struck and sent out with those ordered for Nova Scotia. **1964** TAYLOR *Cdn Coins* 70: Before Nova Scotia and New Brunswick, then British colonies, entered Confederation, they had struck money of their own . . . Nova Scotia ordered half-cent pieces from the mint in London, but New Brunswick did not. Owing to an error some 220,000 were minted and sent along with those for Nova Scotia. . . .

half-dime *n.* a coin worth five cents; nickel, *q.v.*
1870 *Cdn Illust.News* 30 Apr. 407/1: It was decided that the following should be the rates at which the depreciated coinage should be current:—Half-dollar, 47c.; quarter, 23c.; dime, 9c.; half-dime, 4c. **1959** *Maclean's* 29 Aug. 46/4: He joined almost the total juvenile population of the day in reading all the "half-dime" novels he could get.

half-dollar *n.* 1† *Hist.* half a Spanish dollar, *q.v.*
1764 *Quebec Gaz.* 25 Oct. 2/1: A Search-Warrant being immediately granted, several pieces of counterfeit Dollars and half Dollars, together with two Crucibles, were found in his Apartments. **1836** *Bytown* [Ottawa] *Gaz.* 21 July 2/2: The boy who found the [counterfeit] half dollars disposed of 50 of them for two shillings and sixpence and attempts have since been made to pass them.

2† a United States fifty-cent piece.
1836 *Montreal Transcript* 15 Oct. 2/2: . . . will they give you two American half-dollars for every dollar note? I guess not. **1870** *Cdn Illust.News* 12 Feb. 227/2:

The Governor-General will issue his proclamation immediately, as authorized by law, ordering that American silver shall only be a legal tender at rates mentioned in the Finance Minister's circular: half-dollar, 40 cents; quarter, 20 cents; and so on for other coins. . . .

3 a Canadian fifty-cent piece.
1909 BINDLOSS *Lorimer* 59: Harry, forgetting he was in Western Canada, tried to slip a silver half-dollar into the waitress' hand, who dropped it on the floor, perhaps because in that region wages are such that the hireling is neither dependent on nor looks for a stranger's generosity. **1964** *Canadian Wkly* 28 Nov. 11/1: Although Confederation came in 1867, Canada's first half-dollar was not issued until 1870.

half-dried or **half-dry** *adj. North* pertaining to meat or fish dried on the outside by exposure to the sun and wind, a process which forms an airtight sun-glazed envelope that protects the moist inner flesh from deterioration.
1777 (1951) *Sask.Jnls* 128: Our half dried Meat here [Cumberland House] is such as is called dried meat at York Fort. The same kind traded here in the Warm Weather is much dried to preserve it after we receive it. **1811** (1950) THOMPSON *Journals* 135: Vallade and Cote arrived[;] they brought 6 Bundles of half dried Meat, the whole they could preserve of the Animals killed. **1835** (1945) WORK *Journal* 53: A Canoe arrived from Pearl Harbour and traded about a hundred salmon, mostly half dried. **1956** WENTWORTH *Dried Meat* Jan. 5: Not much has been written aout half-dry meat. Stefansson states that this is the favorite form of preparation when the caribou are fat, over Canada from Lake Athabasca northward.

half gentry *Fur Trade, Obs.* Hudson's Bay Company officials intermediate in position between engagés and commissioned gentlemen, *qq.v.*
1820 (1939) ROBERTSON *Correspondence* 271: There are a number of half Gentry of lesser note. **1821** (1938) SIMPSON *Athabasca Jnl* 243: . . . the Half Gentry (a useful class of people if kept at a respectable distance) are however not in such a state of discipline as could be wished. . . .

half home (guard) Indian *Fur Trade, Hist.* a half-breed home-guard Indian. See **home-guard** (def. 1).
1774 (1934) HEARNE and TURNOR *Journals* 112: . . . about Noon 4 Cannoes of half home guard Indians came to the Tent. . . . *Ibid.* 113: . . . this day fitted out the half home Indians for their Returning to the Fort. . . . **1780** (1951) *Sask.Jnls* 27: [He] informed me of Cumberland House being destroyed airly in the fall by a party of half home-guard Indians. **1959** RICH *Hudson's Bay Co.* II 62: Hearne was little better provided with canoes at the end than at the beginning of his winter at Cumberland, and was most thankful that Jacobs had managed to get some of the "Half-home Indians" at York to build for him.

half-Indian *n.* See **half-breed** (def. 1).
1823 (1931) MERK *Fur Trade* 198: The Red River Settlers from the portrait I have of them are a distinct sort of beings somewhere between the half Indians and overgrown children. **1873** (1904) BUTLER *Wild North Land* 204: No man save the Indian, or the half Indian,

can hunt the moose with chance of success. **1940** NIVEN *Mine Inheritance* 179: "I'm taking the Qu'Appelle half Indians off," said Grant. . . .

half-Indian *adj.* of mixed Indian and white ancestry.
*c*1777 (1955) CURTIS *Voyage* 30: One of the Sailors was half Indian & could speak their language so as to be understood. **1844** (1955) LEFROY *Magnetic North* 132: Mrs. Lewis, a half Indian woman, made the fifth. **1956** KEMP *Northern Trader* 143: Philip McLeod . . . himself half-Indian, stated that when he was a young man . . . the winter attire of the Indian [included] unlined moccasins and unlined gloves.

half-joe† *n. Obs.* See **half-Johannes.**
1772 *Quebec Gaz.* 28 May 3/1: The Quantity generally taken from every Half-Joe is from two to three Penny Weight. **1826** *U.E.Loyalist* (York [Toronto]) 4 Nov. 184/1: The following gold pieces were found in his possession: 2 doubloons 2 half do. 4 quarter do. 11 half Joes, 1 quarter do. . . . 10 half Eagles.

half-Johannes *n. Obs.* half a Portuguese Johannes, a gold coin worth about $8.00, in circulation during colonial days.
1772 *Quebec Gaz.* 21 May 3/1: The Public are caution'd to beware of receiving clipt and light Gold, chiefly in Half Johanneses, lately brought into this Province from New York. **1780** *Ibid.* 11 Mar. 3/1: We also hear that several other robberies were committed the same week, particularly towards St. Roch, where a man had been stopp'd in the Street and robb'd of a half Johannes, another of two Dollars.

half-load *n.* See **demi-decharge.**
1804 (1897) COUES *New Light* I 247: Water exceedingly low. We made continual décharges and half-loads. **1884** *Prince Albert Times* (Sask.) 14 Mar. 4/2: The Demi-charge or Half load rapid was about fifteen miles above the Roche rouge.

half portage *Obs.* See **demi-decharge.**
1852 (1853) JACOBS *Journal* 13: After an early breakfast we started off again, and during the forenoon we made three half portages, that is, the men taking out part of the luggage, and then pulled up the canoes by lines, or pole up the rapids with the half-loaded canoes.

half-section *n. West* 320 acres of land, 640 constituting a section (def. 2).
1911 BICKERSTETH *Open Doors* 21: Occasionally one finds a man and his son holding a half section between them, namely half a square mile. **1958** *Edmonton Jnl* 12 Aug. 11/1: The drilling group also holds an Alberta government drilling reservation and lands in that tract are all in close proximity to the far-out half-section and scheduled "deep test" well.

half-sized canoe *Obs.* See **half canoe.**

half-tent *n. Obs.* See **lean-to** (def. 1a). Cp. **double tent.**
1849 ALEXANDER *L'Acadie* II 42: The back part of the tent was pegged to the ground, and the whole formed a half tent as it were, whilst the long wood fire was made opposite the open front. In winter, two of these sheds put face to face, with a fire between, would afford comfortable shelter. **1872** DASHWOOD *Chiploquorgan* 40: Having left my "half-tent" and all other superfluous baggage behind, I started for Campbellton. . . .

half-white *n.* See **half-breed** (def. 1).
1853 (1942) *B.C.Hist.Qtly* July 203: The force for field operations consisted of 130 seamen and marines . . . and a body of 11 half whites, enlisted in the Colony for that service. **1933** MERRICK *True North* 99: The Indians never get as much fur as the whites or half-whites. . . .

half-york *n. North, Obs.* a flat-bottomed boat patterned on the York boat, *q.v.,* but about half its size.
1897 *To Klondike Via Edmonton* 2: A better, but more expensive boat, is what is known as a half-york.

Halifax *n. Hist.* See **Halifax currency.**
1764 *Quebec Gaz.* 4 Oct. 1/1: From the Date of the Publication hereof. . . Forty-Eight Sols Marqués shall be deemed to be equal to One Shilling Halifax; and Thirty of said Sols Marqués equal to One Shilling York Currency. **1827** *U.E.Loyalist* (York [Toronto]) 17 Mar. 336/4: Just Published, and for Sale by Edward Leslie & Sons, price 2s. 6d. C'y, Computation Tables, for reducing British Sterling to Halifax Currency (the Dollar at 4s 4d) and Halifax to Sterling, by Robert Adams. **1938** SIMPSON *Athabasca Jnl* 186n: . . . from 1796 onwards the dollar was equivalent to five shillings, Halifax (i.e. four dollars were equal to a pound Halifax), whilst five livres, French money, were equal to five shillings, Halifax, or one dollar. The sterling guinea was equivalent to one pound, three shillings and fourpence, Halifax, or twenty-eight livres, French currency.

Halifax currency *Hist.* a standard of exchange which served as a system of account in colonial times, being officially adopted in Lower Canada and later in Upper Canada, where York Currency, *q.v.,* had long predominated. See also **provincial currency.**
1764 *Quebec Gaz.* 1 Nov. 3/2: Every Subscriber shall pay Six-pence per Week, Halifax Currency. **1836** *Montreal Transcript* 6 Oct. 2/1: The only metallic currency which this ill-fated colony can boast, is what is termed Halifax Currency—falsely so called—for Halifax, either has no currency of its own, or, if it has, it does not find its way here—the only currency we can boast of is, what the law terms, "Cours Actuel." **1963** *Commercial Letter* Jan. 6/2: In 1777 Halifax currency was established as the official standard of the colony of Canada, but York currency continued in use in Montreal and in what was then known as Upper Canada. Later when Canada was formally divided into two provinces, Upper and Lower Canada, each was given jurisdiction over its own currency and York currency enjoyed recognition in Upper Canada. In 1821 the York unit was replaced by Halifax currency although it continued for many years as a popular unit of account with the rural population.

Halkett (air-)boat [< John *Halkett,* 1768-1852] *Hist.* an inflatable rubber boat. See 1850 quote.
1850 (1953) RAE *Correspondence* 18n: John Halkett, Esq., one of the Directors of the Hudson's Bay Company, whose son (Lieut. P. A. Halkett, R.N.,) is the ingenious inventor of the portable air-boat, which ought to be the travelling companion of every explorer. . . . During the whole of our spring [1847] fishing Halkett's air-boat was used for setting and examining the nets. . . . **1964** *Cdn Geog.Jnl* Mar. 77/3: M'Dougall put ashore eighteen items of boatswain's stores from H.M.S. *Resolute,* including . . . one of the very interesting, inflatable "Halket's boats."

halo or **halu** *adj. adv.* See **helo.**

hamatsa [həˈmætsə] *n.* [< Kwakiutl *hāmatsʼa;* cf. *haem* eat] *Hist.* **1** a member of the Hamatsa Society, *q.v.* See also **hanata.**

1907 CROSBY *An-ko-me-nums* 109: The hamatsa or medicine man, when he first comes from the woods, carries a dead body in his arms professing to have lived on such things while in the woods, and as soon as the hamatsa comes in the house, the other hamatsas all get up and go and tear the body to pieces, among them, like dogs.... **1958** *Native Voice* Sp.ed. 29/1: ... "shamens" or witch-doctors and ascetic "hamatzas," all of whom alone still stand for the ideal remnant, so deeply versed in the cult of their ancient and almost forgotten Indian rituals, ceremonies and ancestor worship.

2 See quote.

1958 HEALEY *Alert Bay* 14: One dance, the hamatsa, was a form of cannibalism and flesh eating was connected with it.

Hamatsa *attrib. Hist.* See **Hamatsa Society.**

1952 *Beaver* Sep. 8/1: A Hamatsa whistle is big medicine. **1958** *Native Voice* Sp.ed. 18/1: This bird was also used in Hamatsa (cannibal) dances showing that "Nan-wa-kaw-i's" people used both kinds in their festivals.

Hamatsa Society *Hist.* a secret society of the Kwakiutl Indians of the Pacific coast which indulged in the eating of human flesh. See also **Cannibal Society.**

1956 LEECHMAN *Native Tribes* 309: ... one of the young initiates of the Cannibal Society might be heard approaching ... running up to people and pretending to bite, or actually biting, pieces out of their arms. Many men bore scars showing where one of the *Hamatsa* (Cannibal) Society members had bitten him.

Hambro line *Obs.* a strong light line made in Hamburg, Germany, used for tracking canoes.

1793 (1933) MACDONELL *Diary* 75: The canoe line is not a stout cable as used by Boats but consists of fine Hambro lines loosely twisted upon one another and is about 60 yards long. **1798** (1918) DAVIDSON *North West Co.* 217: Each canoe had ... a few Hambro lines [and] a bundle of watap.... **1933** GATES *Five Traders* 75n: Hambro lines were, according to Landmann, part of the standard equipment of every canoe, but neither he nor Macdonell gives any description of them.

Hamburg bread *Nfld* See quote.

1906 LUMSDEN *Skipper Parson* 68: "Hamburg bread," or hard biscuit (not to be confounded with pilot or sailor biscuit as popularly known, being thick and cake-like in shape and extraordinarily hard), is in constant use on the vessels and in the houses of the fishermen. **1917** *Christmas Echo* II 19: [In the cookroom] the bill of fare consisted of pork and duff, Hamburg bread and butter, tea....

hammock *n.* See **hummock.**

hanata *n.* See **hamatsa** (def. 1).

1900 *Canadian Mag.* July 205/1: He said that a Hanata was one who dances and eats a human body.

hand *v.* drag a canoe upstream by hand, walking ahead, hand on gunwale. See also **lead,** *v.*

1809 (1950) THOMPSON *Journals* 33: ... then up the little River which had also good Water, except the upper part which is rapid & shoal, here we handed much. **1934** TYRELL in *Champlain Soc.Pubs* XXI 204n: Lutit was evidently "handing" the canoe up the rapid, walking in the water in front of it, and dragging it up after him.

1950 THOMPSON *Journals* 33n: In "handing," the men waded in the stream, keeping hold of the gunwale of the canoe and dragging it upstream against the swift current.

hand-car† *n.* a small car used by section hands on a railway and driven by a geared hand-lever which is pumped up and down. Cp. **gas-car** and **speeder** (def. 1a).

1865 *Grand Trunk Railway Rules* 38: No hand car, or lorry, must be used on the track, under any circumstances, during a fog or snow storm, or within fifteen minutes of the time of a train being due. **1933** SPINKS *B.C.Frontier* 8: "So you stole the handcar and came away with it?" said Moore.... **1963** *Weekend Mag.* 21 Dec. 9/1: ... the Myrtle And Maude was a small paddle-wheel tug.... Them big paddles on her was cranked by a walking beam that went up and down like the pump on a railroad hand car.

hand dag or **dague** *Obs.* See **dag** and picture.

1802 (1897) COUES *New Light* I 194: In a drinking match at the Hills yesterday, Gros Bras in a fit of jealousy stabbed Aupusoi to death with a hand-dague. **1829** *Fort Langley Jnl* 11 Aug. 2: Hand Dags ...

hand game† See 1907 quote. See also **lahal.**

1834-43 (1955) RUSSELL *Journal* 58: Some were gambling at Cards some playing the Indian game of hand and others horse racing.... **1907** HODGE *Bulletin*: Games ... Hand Game. The commonest and most widely distributed of Indian guessing games. Two (or four) bone or wooden cylinders, one plain and one marked, are held in the hands by one player, the other side guessing in which hand the unmarked cylinder is concealed. The game is commonly counted with sticks and is played to the accompaniment of songs and incantations. **1966** *Beaver* Winter 54: [Caption] Playing the hand game at Rae, 1962; a six to eight hour session is followed by several hours of tea dancing.

handing *n.* See **hand,** *v.*

handliner† *n.* a fisherman who uses a handline. See also **hook-and-line** man.

1955 DAWSON *Ahoy There!* 144: The hand-liner fishes from a rowing-boat, using lines like thin clothes lines to which are attached not only lures but also heavy lead weights to take the lures fathoms deep. **1958** WATTERS *B.C.Cent.Anthol.* 139: ... he once spent a season or two as a hand-liner ... with his hands on the oar looms of a patched rowboat and the end of his lines wrapped around his legs.

handlining *n.* fishing with handlines.

1946 BIRD *Sunrise* 21: ... she was but one of those Irish wastrels up the Bay who made a living of sorts by hand lining and, on shore, hunting out of season. **1954** BRUCE *Channel Shore* 40: He spent the days running traul and hand-lining, splitting fish and turning them on the flakes he had set up behind Stewart's hut on the beach.

hand-log *v.* engage in hand-logging, *q.v.*

1958 HEALEY *Alert Bay* 45: About 1905, a man named Oscar Soderman handlogged on Minstrel Island and built the first shack on the present-day site of the small settlement. **1961** *Sun* (Vancouver) 7 Feb. 4/1: Somewhere he has a stump ranch, a little mining claim, a few range cows or a bit of timber he can hand-log.

hand-logger *n.* one who engages in hand-logging, *q.v.*

1908 GRAINGER *Woodsmen* 12: ... hand-loggers are prosecuted for stealing logs whose existence has been denied. **1966** *Islander* 21 Aug. 4/1: The picturesque hand loggers are almost gone. These men, with axes, saw, wedges and lifting jacks, once cut down trees in sheer places; with seeming miracles of ingenuity moved the logs down steep, rough mountain-sides into the water.

hand-logging *n.* logging with hand tools only, such as axes, peavies, and jacks.

1952 PUTNAM *Cdn Regions* 439: Hand logging in the 19th century gradually gave way to widespread cutting in the 20th century, and the forests were penetrated beyond the coastline. **1956** ANDREWS *Glory Days* 40: Their 'boom' (in loggers speech) was 'hung'. They were now ready to start hand logging.

hand method *Placer Mining* the process of separating gold from sand and gravel by using a pan (def. 3a).

1897 TUTTLE *Golden North* 88: This [panning of gold] is called the 'pan' or 'hand' method, and is never, on account of its slowness and laboriousness, continued for any length of time when it is possible to procure a 'rocker,' or to make and work sluices.

handsled† *n.* See **sleigh** (def. 3a).

1923 WALDO *Down Mackenzie* 147: He came along with his hand-sled—not even with dogs—and drew the fallen timbers unaided, and worked here and at four other points all winter long for his few hundred dollars far from men, or any passer-by, or the sound of a cheerful settlement. **1938** *Beaver* Sep. 20/2: Part of the way to "the line" I pulled my outfit on a handsled.

handsleigh *n.* **1** See **sleigh** (def. 3a).

*a*1820 (1838) HEAD *Forest Scenes* 203: [The trees] had been felled, cut into lengths, and removed by means of small hand sleighs purposely prepared for them. ... **1836** TRAILL *Backwoods* 110: We were overtaken ... by S—with a handsleigh, which is a sort of wheelbarrow, such as porters use, without sides, and instead of a wheel, is fixed on wooden runners, which you can drag over the snow and ice with the greatest ease, if ever so heavily laden. **1961** *Cdn Geog.Jnl* Jan. 13/1: The personnel ... detrained ...; then native birch was whittled to build hand sleighs, which were pulled over deep wet snow until Spring 1912. **1964** GUILLET *Pioneer Days* 67: ... for some years the settlers had to make a journey of several weeks in open boats—or with hand-sleighs upon the ice in winter—to the nearest mill at Long Point.

2 See **sleigh** (def. 3b).

1852 *Hamilton Gaz.*(C.W.) 19 Aug. 3/2: There was a time when we could in winter sleigh, on our handsleighs, down from the Court House door to Mr. Cooch's "Emporium." **1932** JAMIESON *Cattle in the Stall* 183: We know it is not safe practice for children to run and hook their little handsleighs on behind some big bob sleigh. ... **1947** WELLS *Owl Pen* 76: Soon ... two little girls ... joined us with their hand-sleighs.

hand-toboggan *n.* [see **toboggan**] a toboggan (def. 1), pulled by hand, as opposed to one pulled by dogs or horses.

1873 (1904) BUTLER *Wild North Land* 195: They come, a motley throng; men, women and children; dogs, sleds and hand-toboggans, bearing the precious freight of fur to the trading-post. **1933** MERRICK *True North* 263: But, unfortunately, they are too bulky for a hand toboggan.

hang (up) *v. North* string fish up for drying.

1922 *Beaver* Mar. 35/2: The head fisherman ... was sent to Lac. St. Anne with orders to "hang up" thirty-six thousand fish, for the use of the dogs and for rations at the post when necessary. **1956** KEMP *Northern Trader* 222: Ever since old Amos Charles had hung those four thousand fish for us, the matter of winter dog-feed at Stanley had been a problem.

hangard ['hæŋgərd] *n.* [< Cdn F *hangar(d)* < F *hangar*] *Hist.* **1** a shed, warehouse, or outbuilding.

1777 *Quebec Gaz.* 8 May 4/1: Every person shall clean the street before his house, outhouse, hangard or emplacement every Saturday, under penalty of five shillings. **1806** (1809) GRAY *Letters* 52: Those next the river have attached to them very extensive warehouses (called, in the language of Quebec, hangards), and vessels come close to the wharfs to discharge their cargoes. **1808** *Cdn Courant* (Montreal) 1 Feb. 3/3: The next morning at 6 o'clock, a large Hangard of 140 feet in length by 40 in depth, belonging to Mr. Alex. Munn, ship builder, was crushed to pieces by an enormous mass of snow which fell from the Cape near the same place. **1940** NIVEN *Mine Inheritance* 26: Inside the palisade were ... a trading store, two "hangards" or stables. ...

2 an outbuilding serving as an ice-house (def. 1) at a fur post. Cp. **glacier**.

1794 (1929) MCGILLIVRAY *Journal* 41: The Hunters have been very successful for some time past and there is a fine quantity of fresh meat in the Hangard. ... **1806** (1960) FRASER *Letters and Journals* 240: What plausible reason can he give for not arranging the hangard before you got there. ... **1809** (1950) THOMPSON *Journal* 76: Made a door for the Hangard—& put Snow & Water to form Ice to lay Meat on. ... **1950** WHITE in THOMPSON *Journal* 36n: The use of the term hangard was common among men of the North West Company.

hang up 1 *Lumbering* **a.** (usually as pp.) of the movement of logs, slow down or stop en route from forest to deck, water, or mill. See also **hang-up**, **hung-up**, and **stick**[3], *v.* (def. 1).

1872 DASHWOOD *Chiploquorgan* 217: By this means they would have their employers on the hip, as on the water falling, the lumber would be "hung up" and could not possibly be got down until the following spring. **1896** *Trans.Roy.Soc.Can.* II 2 231: Local tradition states that many years ago a drive was "hung up" below its mouth, and there at a dance, during which the big Irishman, in his enthusiasm, shouted, "We'll make Dungarvon shake". ... **1945** CALVIN *Saga* 44: ... a mild winter, with bad "hauling," might mean that the timber was "hung up in the woods," as the phrase went. ...

b. of a tree or log, become caught on a snag while being felled or yarded. See also **hang-up**.

1909 ROBERTS *Backwoodsman* 133: When the logs were running in any numbers, the bend had to be watched with vigilance lest a jam should form, and the waters be dammed back, and the lumber get "hung up" all over the swamps of the upper reaches. **1942** SWANSON *Western Logger* 29: But one forked stump ... / Was sure to hang up e'er the turn went by. ... **1966** *B.C. Lumber Worker* Nov(2nd issue) 4/5: [Caption] How'd ya like to Shinny Up an' Trim a Couple of Limbs— seems to Have Hung up!

c. of a person, have one's load snagged so as to halt operations.

1953 SWANSON *Haywire Hooker* 42: Well, it happened once I hung up on a chunk / When the ground was rough and the crew was punk / And the signalman was asleep on a log.

2 See **hang.**

hang-up *n. Lumbering* a log caught on a snag or obstruction when being transported. See also **hang up** (def. 1).

1942 KOROLEFF *Skidding of Wood* 15/2: [Caption] Avoid hang-ups . . . the load is likely to become hung-up on a stump with a protruding root. . . . **1943** SWANSON *Lumberjack* 24: . . . Old Rough House Pete lay down his weary head; / For his rough house days were over, and his last hangup was fought. . . .

Hansard† ['hænsəd] *n.* [< Luke *Hansard,* d. 1828, printer of the journals of the British House of Commons] the day-to-day official record of speeches and debates in the House of Commons in Ottawa and in certain provincial legislatures.

1860 *Nor' Wester* (R.R.S.) 28 Apr. 3/2: With regard to the debates in the Legislature, so far, I refer you to the Mirror of Parliament, an excellent Canadian Hansard, got out here by your old confereres, Taylor, Harvey, and others, and published by Thompson, of the Colonist. **1885** HAIGHT *Country Life* 133: The expense of Hansards would not be very considerable if the legislators of the present day followed the example of such brevity as his. **1948** ANGLIN *Canada Unlimited* 60: Debate may be carried on in either language in Parliament at Ottawa; Hansard the official parliamentary record is published in both languages, as are all bills and acts of Parliament. . . . **1963** *Kingston Whig-Standard* (Ont.) 7 Mar. 6/3: Mr. Alkenbrack said it was true his name was not on Hansard but explained that as a new MP he was "sitting, listening and learning."

hap *v.* [< dial. "cover up"] *Obs.* trap.

1754 (1907) HENDAY *Journal* 344: I asked the Natives why they did not Hap wolves; they made answer that the Archithunue [Blackfeet] would kill them, if they trapped in their country. *Ibid.:* An Indian told me that my tent-mates were angry with me last night for speaking so much concerning Happing. . . .

hap *n.* [< v.] *Obs.* a trap.

1754 (1907) HENDAY *Journal* 344: Travelled none: got two Wolves from my Haps.

harbo(u)r lot a specified piece of ground underwater, leased for fishing purposes.

1964 *Star Wkly* 5 Dec. 17/2: For his underwater harbor lot, Richard paid $40 at the triennial auction. . . .

harbo(u)r seal 1 a small seal, *Phoca vitulina,* common on the East Coast. See also **bay seal, fresh-water seal, kasagea, leopard-seal, ranger** (def. 1), and **wandering seal.**

1832 MCGREGOR *Brit.Amer.* I 106: There are apparently five or six varieties of seals that frequent the coasts of America . . . [including] the harbour seal. . . . **1891** OXLEY *Wreckers* 79: The common harbor seal was there all the year round. **1958** CAMERON *Cdn Mammals* 55: Apart from the grey seal, the harbour seal is the only member of the tribe that ordinarily spends the summer in southern Canada.

2 the fur of this seal.

1908 MAIR *Mackenzie Basin* 230 xxx: There is reason to believe that other species of seals besides the harbour seal are embraced in the foregoing sales statement. **1933** MERRICK *True North* 217: It is an odd thing that Labrador people never have fur coats, unless they be of harbor seal which is stiff and bristly. . . .

hard-cut *adj. Slang* tough; hard-living; rough.
1962 FRY *Ranch on the Cariboo* 39: . . . the gold fields to the north were ajump with hard cut miners. . . .

hardfist ['hard,fist] *n. North, Slang* a rough person who is prone to violence.
1901 (1955) COLLARD *Cdn Yesterdays* 40: That, and the hearts of the hardfists. . . . **1917** PHILLIPPS-WOLLEY *Songs* 65: Where through endless silent spaces reckless bands of hardfists plod / By this map and by the compass to the gold they make their god. **1955** COLLARD *Cdn Yesterdays* 38: Among the "hardfists" of the wilderness he had been . . . a good companion.

hard hat a protective hat having a metal or hard plastic crown, worn by construction workers, loggers, miners, etc.
1953 *Giant Yellowknife Agreement* 3: (a) Protective devices and other equipment considered necessary by the Company to protect employees from injury shall be provided by the Company, but this shall not include personal necessities such as hard hats, hard toed boots and gloves, which will be sold to the employees at cost. **1955** *Bush News* (Port Arthur, Ont.) Feb. 6/2: Earlier in the safety meeting, delegates . . . talked over "beefs" of men in the bush against certain types of hard hat liners. . . . **1964** *Oily Bird* Apr. 3/2: The Gent who wore no goggles / When tapping in a pot and / One who wore no hard hat / Both, use the "I forgot[.]"

hardhead† *n.* a round rock or boulder.
1918 COPELAND *Swinging Lanterns* 101: At this juncture an Indian guide from out the forest surrounding Lady Evelyn Lake came aboard at Temagami's commodious, artistically conceived depot of split hardheads. **1959** LEISING *Arctic Wings* 148: The keg hit a "hard head." Most of this moss was two feet deep, but a few boulders showed their bald heads, and they picked one!

hard maple the sugar maple, *Acer saccharum,* or the black maple, *Acer nigrum;* also, the wood of either of these trees.
1790 (1905) *Ont.Bur.Arch.Rep.* III 70: Timber, Hard Maple, Bass, and Black walnut, from this place to River la French, 22 miles. **1863** WALSHE *Cedar Creek* 233: "This 'ere sugar bush is . . . mostly hard maple, an' the right age. Soft maple don't make nothing but molasses, hardly—them with whitish skin; so you are safe to chop 'em down." **1957** HUTCHISON *Canada* 102: Hard maple and its magic contents are concentrated in the Laurentian valley, with offshoots into the Maritimes and New England.

hardpan† ['hard,pæn] *n.* **1** a compacted layer of hard soil, especially clay, lying beneath the subsoil.
1887 *Trans.Hist.& Sci.Soc.Man.* 27 5: The boulder clay is cemented together into a solid mass like concrete, and the well drillers call it hard pan. **1961** *Cdn Geog.Jnl* Jan. 17/1: Stationmen excavating by hand cut of hardpan and boulders on Hudson Bay Railway, 1914.

2 any hard, cement-like ground.
1951 HOBSON *Grass* 23: He unhooked his horses and pulled the Bloater to safety on a dry patch of hardpan road. **1954** PATTERSON *Dangerous River* 36: Somewhere, in a patch of hardpan, they found the track of a hobnailed boot—a right foot with nine nails in it.

3 *Fig.* rock bottom; lowest limit; the basic part or issue.

1871 *Niagara News* (Ont.) 5 Apr. 2/2: We have decided to cut all "dead advertisements," and come down to "hard pan." **1886** *Indian* (Hagersville, Ont.) 8 Sep. 204/2: If You Want to Purchase Fall Goods Away Down at Hard Pan Prices, go to Daniel J. Lynch's One Price Cash Store. **1889** MACLEAN *Indians* 199: When the sombre shades of poverty have entered his old shack, he has in the miner's phraseology, got down to *bed rock* or *hard pan.* . . . **1920** STRINGER *Prairie Mother* 112: It took me just about ten minutes to get down to hard-pan, with him, once he was convinced I meant business.

hardrock ['hard͵rak] *n.* **1** *Mining* **a.** mining in solid rock, especially quartz. See also **quartz mining.**
1936 MOWERY *Paradise Trail* 14: "People wouldn't look at hard-rock in them days. Hard-rock takes machinery and money."
b. (attributive uses) pertaining to such rock or the mining of it.
1936 MOWERY *Paradise Trail* 5: . . . he was looking upon Mona Casper and young Hugh Ludlow, heirs to these mills and timber limits and the precious hard-rock veins in the range yonder. **1957** *Ottawa Citizen* 26 Feb. 6/3: No trouble getting work out there if you can claim experience as a catskinner, high rigger, hardrock mucker, sidehill gouger, or bullcook. **1963** *Western Miner* Sep. 9: . . . this traditional hardrock miner's union can do a better job on behalf of mine employees than either Steel or the craft unions.
2 *Slang* **a.** a strong, rough person of great endurance.
1950 BIRD *This is N.S.* 19: One night in Parrsboro he ran up against a hardrock from Spencer's Island, and when the fracas ended he had been completely thrashed for the first time in his life. **1964** *Calgary Herald* 3 Apr. 12/8: Murray Balfour, a Chicago Black Hawk hardrock, will accept goals in any form, even if they're scored off his backside.
b. (attributive uses) characterized by strong, rough, durable behavior.
1962 *National Hockey Annual* 72/2: He is truly a hard-rock competitor assuming "policeman" role for [the] Maple Leafs. **1965** *Globe and Mail* (Toronto) 6 Jan. 24/9: Page [is] a hard-rock defensive back. . . .
3 *Slang* (attributive uses) unyielding; difficult to reason with; hard-headed.
1963 *Kingston Whig-Standard* (Ont.) 28 Mar. 13/1: Old-line, hardrock Tory Protestants cannot vote for "the Party of the Pope"—that is, the Liberals. . . .

Hare Indian dog *Northwest* See **bear dog.**
1833 TYLER *Progress of Discovery* 330: We can here afford space only for a few lines regarding the Hare Indian, or Mackenzie River Dog. . . . **1861** *Cdn Naturalist* Feb. 13: The Hare Indian dog, [*Canis familiaris*] *var. Lagopus,* is the race domesticated among the Indians of the Mackenzie River District. It is characterized by a narrow, elongated and pointed muzzle, by erect sharp ears, and by a bushy tail not carried erect but only slightly curved upwards, as well as by a fine silky hair mixed with thick under fur. **1949** (1956) DAVIS *Modern Dog Encyc.* 11/1: The Hare Indian Dog (*Canis lagopus*), was found only with the Indian tribes which lived along the borders of Great Bear Lake and the Mackenzie [and] was much like the

Collie in appearance. **1963** *Islander* 8 Sep. 2/1: Richardson's Hare Indian Dog is undoubtedly of the same breed as those we find in B.C. and the Yukon.

harp (seal) *n.* a large grey seal, *Phoca groenlandica,* so called because of the harp-shaped markings on its back. See also **ragged jacket, turning harp,** and **voyage seal.**
1771 (1792) CARTWRIGHT *Journal* I 89: I had the fat of two harps melted, which produced eighteen gallon of oil. **1819** ANSPACH *Hist.Nfld* 325: Five kinds of seals frequent these shores, namely, the common, the great, the rough, the hooded, the harp, and an obscure species, called by the Laplanders, fatuc vindac, with a round and a long snout bending like the proboscis of an elephant. **1901** *Cdn Mag.* Jan. 195/2: The Harps are mild, civilized and gregarious. **1965** *Kingston Whig-Standard* (Ont.) 3 Apr. 4/5: Off the north-east coast of Canada lives one of the most appealing of animals, the Harp seal.

harp mark *Sealing* the saddle, or markings, by which the harp seal is characterized.
1880 (1964) *Nfld Qtly* Spring 4/2: The harp seal, like the Crested Seal (the Hood Seal) presents characters at least in the male sex, that readily attract the attention . . . the one by its "Saddle" or "Harp Mark" of black on a light ground, the other by its inflatable hood.

harse *n.* [< Cdn F < F *herse* harrow] *Fur Trade, Obs.* See quote.
1833 (1932) MCLEAN *Notes* 123: I was surprised to observe his frowning aspect on landing, and ascribed it to the circumstance of his being the "harse" or harrow, a term of derision applied to the slowest canoe.

harvester special *Hist.* See **harvest special.**
1966 *Canadian* 30 Apr. 7/4: There was the prim, elderly spinster who was put aboard a harvester special by mistake.

harvest excursion *Hist.* a low-fare railway trip for field-workers travelling to the West to harvest grain.
1925 MONTGOMERY *Kilmeny of the Orchard* 212: "Why, us folks at the station knew there must have been a to-do of some kind when Neil Gordon went off on the harvest excursion the way he did." **1966** *Canadian* 30 Apr. 3/1: The wheels began to turn and the first Harvest Excursion got underway. The date was July 28, 1891.

harvest special or **train** *Hist.* a train taking part in the harvest excursion, *q.v.*
1954 *Ghost Pine* 34: It was a new land we were looking for, and a future home, so it was a good-bye to all, and board the harvest trains for Winnipeg. **1965** BERTON *Remember Yesterday* 70: [Caption] The harvest special, rolling west, briefly dumps its human cargo at Winnipeg.

hatchet *n.* in phrases where the hatchet symbolizes war; originally an Indian metaphor:
1 *Obs.* **heave up the hatchet against,** threaten or promise to make war on.
c**1665** (1885) RADISSON *Voyages* 61: In those feasts my father heaves up his hatchet against the Algonquins.
2 *Obs.* **send a hatchet,** invite to join an alliance for making war.
1796 (1932) RUSSELL *Correspondence* I 40: The last accounts from the Westward inform us that the Creeks have sent a hatchet to the Hurons and the other Indian tribes of that confederacy. **1814** *Montreal Herald* 2 Apr. 1/2: . . . when you sent the hatchet, we took hold of it, Father, and made use of it, Father, as you know.

3† *Obs.* **take up the hatchet,** declare war; make war.
1812 *Quebec Gaz.* 20 Feb. 1/4: If we took up the hatchet it was in vain. . . . **1812** *Montreal Herald* 26 Sep. 2/1: They were the first to take up the hatchet, the first to begin the war dance. **1912** (1913) HODGE & WHITE *Indians of Can.* 195: To "take up the hatchet" was to declare war. . . .

4† **bury the hatchet,** stop fighting; make peace; end a quarrel. See also **tomahawk** (def. 2).
[**1703** LAHONTAN *New Voyages* I 80: Burying the axe signifies peace.] **1850** ROY *Hist.of Canada* 60: It was at length announced that a great deputation was coming from all the cantons, with the intention of "uniting the whole earth," and "of burying the hatchet so deep that it might never again be dug up." **1908** BROWN *Lady of the Snows* 57: "And to see us . . . kiss the hatchet and bury it as we spoke," added another. **1942** RADDALL *His Majesty's Yankees* 26: "There wasn't any god in Nova Scotia in '49. Only the Injun god Muntoo—him the French priests called the devil. We gave 'em Muntoo, from '49 to '61, when they buried the hatchet at last." **1956** KEMP *Northern Trader* 135: When freeze-up came we were going to cut each other's throats in business, but the hatchet would be buried until that time came around.

5† **dig up the hatchet,** resume hostilities; break a peace agreed to by burying the hatchet.
1840 MURRAY *Brit.Amer.* I 123: This agreement is often accompanied with professions, at the moment perhaps sincere, of maintaining the sun always in the heavens, and never again digging up the hatchet. **1913** SANDILANDS *West.Cdn Dict.* 22/1: To dig up the hatchet, to recall the cause of strife or to renew the quarrel.

hat trick *Hockey* the feat of scoring three goals in one game.
☞ *The term is of British origin, a cricket bowler who takes three wickets on three successive balls being bought a new hat by his team-mates.*
1957 *Kingston Whig-Standard* (Ont.) 25 Feb. 11/1: Bud Aylesworth led the Kingston scoring with a hat trick and Doug Senior and Dennis O'Donnell each had two [goals]. **1966** *Hockey News* 16 Apr. 18/5: Trottier had a hat trick in the opening game.

haul *n.* *Lumbering* the operation of moving logs from the felling area to the dump, either by transporting or skidding, *q.v.*, or by a high-lead system, *q.v.* See also **haul-off.**
1909 ROBERTS *Backwoodsman* 108: It was heavy sledding on the Upper Ottanoonsis trail. The two lumbermen were nearing the close of the third day of the hard four day's haul in from the Settlements to the camp. **1942** SWANSON *Western Logger* 35: A twelve-mile haul was nothing at all [for the donkey-engine], her exhaust made clouds in the sky. . . . **1955** *Bush News* (Port Arthur, Ont.) Feb. 1/4: . . . the haul is now going along fairly well and is pretty much on a par with last year's operations.

haul† *v.* **1** drag or draw a load, such as coal, grain, or logs.
1743 (1949) ISHAM *Observations* 171: For our firing we use all wood which is fell in the winter and hawl'd out. . . . **1804** (1933) FARIES *Diary* 220: Azure [is] hauling logs. **1928** PERRY *Two Reds* 13: Surrounding the settlement was a tangle of second-growth timber, penetrated in every direction by the old roads where, at one time, great loads of logs had been hauled out from the cuttings. **1955** *Western Star* (Corner Brook, Nfld) 12 Mar. I 6/5: . . . it is beginning to look as though very little wood will be left to haul at the end of the present month. **1960** DOWNS *Wagon Road* 42: [Caption] The

first attempt to haul freight to Cariboo by mechanical means was made by F. J. Barnard and J. C. Beedy.
2 travel with a load.
1872 DASHWOOD *Chiploquorgan* 117: . . . we had fifteen miles to haul along a lumber road to the mouth of Rocky brook. . . . **1933** MERRICK *True North* 338: We hauled across lots of yellow, slushy places. . . .

haulback† ['hɔl,bæk] *n.* *Lumbering* See 1942 quote. See picture at **high-lead system.**
1919 *Camp Worker* 26 Apr. 5/2: There are innumerable firms that have monopolized the services of the best hooker that ever gave signals for the high-rigger, while his short-handed crew changed the haul-back without the assistance of a grass-line. **1942** HAIG-BROWN *Timber* 251: HAULBACK. A lighter line coupled to the mainline which hauls the logs in from the woods, operated from a second drum on the donkey through an arrangement of blocks. Its function is to draw the mainline and chokers back out of the woods to pick up a fresh "turn" of logs. **1966** *Dly Colonist* (Victoria) 3 Aug. 28/2: Whether the mainline was to be pulled in, or the haulback to go out . . . or stop all operations depended on the correct number of whistles.

hauler *n.* See **sled dog** (def. 1 and picture). See also **hauling dog.**
1908 MAIR *Mackenzie Basin* 189: At times, long after he became a hauler, Keskayoo seemed to delight in beginning a fight with other dogs.

hauler-head *n.* See **gurdy.**
1945 RICHARDSON *We Keep a Light* 162: Morrill had a hauler-head installed in the bow of his boat and had it geared to his engine. The hauler-head is a wooden cylinder, about six inches in diameter, which revolves when in use.

hauling *n.* *Lumbering* the process of conveying logs from the cutting area to the dump. See also **haul,** *n.*
1854 (1945) CALVIN *Saga* 44: . . . push on with all speed making and hauling. **1909** ROBERTS *Backwoodsman* 129: Everyone was working with feverish haste to get the logs all out to the "landings" on the river banks before the hauling should go to pieces. **1955** *Bush News* Feb. 7/3: . . . hauling is going along nicely and about two-thirds of the wood cut has been hauled to river landings.

hauling dog *North* See **sled dog** (def. 1).
1871 (1883) BUTLER *Great Lone Land* 295: . . . so does this perversion of the dog from his true use to that of a beast of burthen produce in endless variety traits of cunning and deception in the hauling-dog. **1933** MERRICK *True North* 96: In the middle of their load sat a mongrel hauling dog, his nose tied up tight with a *babische* thong.

hauling grounds See **échoueries.** See also **hauling-out site.**
1960 *Cdn Audubon* Jan.-Feb. 2/2: Localities where sea lions come ashore for purposes other than breeding or pupping are called "hauling grounds."

hauling-line *n.* See **tracking line.**
1908 MAIR *Mackenzie Basin* 183: When tracking on the beach the woman is attached to the cord hauling-line next to the bow of the umiak. . . .

hauling-out site See **échoueries.**
1966 *Cdn Geog.Jnl* Mar. 90: [Caption] Kaalukta . . . is a favoured hauling-out site for walruses in the summer.

hauling place *Obs.* See **tracking ground.**
1827 (1912) ERMATINGER *Express Jnl* 94: Made another
short hauling place and entered the still water about
6 o'clock. **1828** (1872) MCDONALD *Peace River* 7: After
dinner we made a number of hauling places before
coming to Trout Portage.

hauling-road *n. Esp.Atlantic Provinces* See
logging road.
1954 RADDALL *Muster of Arms* 28: "Then you'll see
a hauling-road running off to the north, with our tire
marks in the snow. . . ." **1954** BRUCE *Channel Shore* 13:
As Hazel walked down the crooked hauling-road her
ears caught the slight rushing murmur of the Black
Brook. . . .

hauling sleigh *Lumbering* a sleigh usually
consisting of four bobs, *q.v.*, used in a series to form
a long sleigh for hauling logs. Cp. **double sleigh**
(def. 2).
1944 *Forestry Course 1* 90: Bobbing is used for
[hauling] logs, and either the front sleigh of a set of
hauling sleighs, or a specially built bob is used.

haul-off *n. Nfld* See **haul,** *n.*
1955 *Western Star* (Corner Brook, Nfld) 12 Mar. 6/5:
The pulpwood haul-off, in the Deer Lake jurisdiction . . .
has now reached an interesting stage, and it is beginning
to look as though very little wood will be left to haul at
the end of the present month.

haul out of seals and walruses, come ashore at the
échoueries, *q.v.*
1966 *Cdn Geog.Jnl* Mar. 90/2: . . . the walrus herds then
haul out onto several traditional *uglit.*

haul-out *n.* of seals and walruses, the periodic
coming ashore at the échoueries, *q.v.*
1966 *Cdn Geog.Jnl* Mar. 90/1: The spring haul-out at
Coats Island appears to concentrate on one promontory
and adjacent beach.

haul road *Lumbering* See **logging road.**
1966 *Cdn Forest Industries* June 38/2: Most of the
company's 650 mi [sic] of haul road has been built
during the last five years.

haul-up† *n. Lumbering* See **jackladder** and **log
haul-up.**
1964 *Atlantic Advocate* July 59/2: They had [c1870]
patent edgers, endless haul-ups, jump-up saws, steam
canters to roll the logs on the saw carriage, transfer
chains.

Haute Terre See **Hauteur des Terres.**
1931 GREY OWL *Last Frontier* 30: To those who dwell in
the region that lies north of the Haute Terre . . . the
settled portions of the Dominion are situated in another
sphere.

Hauteur des Terres *Cdn French* See **Height of
Land** (def. 1).
1800 (1897) COUES *New Light* I 11: Having passed this
we came to Portage des Hauteur des Terres [Land's
Height], which is about 700 paces. **1897** *Ibid.* 11n:
Hauteur des Terres (or de Terre) is a more general
name of the high land, full of small lakes, which
occupies the region between the waters of the Pigeon r.,
flowing eastward, and those of Rainy r. taking the
opposite direction.

hawk [hauk *or* hɑk] *v.* [< Brit. dial. *hawk* [hauk]
search out, hunt through < Scand.; cf. Swedish
hålka] *Placer Mining* examine loose rocks and
stones of an area in search of gold or other
minerals.
1869 (1962) ANDERSON *Sawney's Letters* 37: The rough
but honest miner . . . / Seeking for the yellow gold, / Hid
amang the clay— / Howkin' in the mountain side.
1936 MOWERY *Paradise Trail* 29: Though green at the
business of hawking float, he walked over to the tom
rocker, a shallow cradle-like contraption with
galvanized lining and two handles, and studied it.

hawk bell† *Fur Trade, Hist.* a small spherical bell,
originally used in falconry, much prized by the
Indians as ornaments.
1684 (1946) *H.B.C.Minutes* 304: . . . one Rest for a
hand saw, 250 Hawkes bells, 1 pestell. . . . **1791** LONG
Voyages 36: I also made makissins, or Indian shoes, of
deer skins, drest and smoked to make the leather soft and
pliable, and worked with porcupine quills and small
beads, to which are sometimes suspended hawk bells.
1811 (1950) THOMPSON *Journals* 147: Account of the
Goods now with us [includes] 7 groce of hawks Bells.
1913 COWIE *Adventurers* 258: . . . and hawk bells to
jingle as they walked. . . .

hawk's-eye *n. Local, Obs.* the golden plover,
Pluvialis dominica.
1795 (1911) HEARNE *Journey* 427: Plovers, commonly
called Hawk's Eyes, from their watchfulness to prevent
a near approach when sitting. **1813** WILSON *Ornithology*
VII 42: It is said, that at Hudson's Bay it is called the
Hawk's-eye on account of its brilliancy.

hay cache *West* a supply of hay put out on the
range for winter cattle-feed. Cp. **hay corral.**
1959 *Time* (Cdn ed.) 5 Jan. 10/3: Near Waterton Lakes
National Park, 1,300 elk, each one eating almost as
much grass as a prize beef steer, spend the winter
foraging on the hay caches ranchers set out for their
cattle, break through barbed-wire fences and shoulder
cattle out of the way to get at the feed.

hay camp† *West* a camp, often temporary, where
hay is cut and stacked for cattle feed.
1934 *Beaver* June 42/2: . . . soon after dinner we stopped
at the main base there, the government hay camp, a
collection of buildings in a wide clearing. **1962** FRY
Ranch on the Cariboo 146: [He was] no other than the
ornery boy he had known so well in the Old Man's hay
camp.

hay corral *West* an enclosure in which hay is
stored. Cp. **hay cache.**
1884 *Nor'Wester* (Calgary) 10 June 1/4: There are upon
the land a dwelling-house, granary, blacksmith's shop,
cattle and hay corrals, [and] sheds. **1963** SYMONS *Many
Trails* 173: The doe never stopped till she came to the
hay corral behind my barn. . . .

hay-flats *n.pl. West* low-lying meadows near a
river or slough. Cp. **hay meadow** and **hay slough.**
1934 BETTANY *Valley of Lost Gold* 30: She could almost
see those cattle straggling through the hay-flats. . . .
1959 *Country Guide* April 72/4: [The old elk] bugled the
starving herds down, at last, to the rancher's hay flats.

hay-knife *n.* See 1962 quote.
1909 BINDLOSS *Lorimer* 49: When [the stack] has
settled into shape and solidity it is both frost and rain
proof, and often requires a hay-knife to get into it.
1962 FRY *Ranch on the Cariboo* 67: The three of us
trudged down to the far end of the meadow, carrying

shovels, a fork, a scythe, and a hay knife, a contraption like a straight-ended shovel only jagged and sharp which one uses by thrusting downward into the stack to cut the hay when one wishes to use one end of a stack and leave the remainder untouched.

haymaker n. Placer Mining, Slang, Obs. a miner choosing to work only rich deposits, leaving the poorer dirt. Cp. **high-grading** (def. 2).
1900 OSBORN Greater Canada 94: Even now, in spite of the cost of labour . . . companies formed for the purpose of utilizing the poorer gravels and tailings left by old-time "haymakers" in Cariboo and elsewhere are doing more than paying expenses.

hay meadow See **beaver meadow**. Cp. **hay-flats**.
1954 BEZANSON Sodbusters 4: You might have a small ranch, if you can locate a good hay meadow. Ibid. 177: Our hay meadows were made by beaver dams long since dried up and grown to grass.

hay privilege Hist. in the Red River Settlement:
1 the right enjoyed by settlers to cut hay on the untilled land lying to the rear of each river lot.
1871 Wkly Manitoban 22 July 2/2: It was a question of hay privilege that was on the tapis[;] besides the old cry is a little stale. **1935** MORICE Red River Insurrection 305: At next day's meeting, O'Donoghue gave notice that he would introduce a bill providing that the hitherto prevailing two-mile hay privilege be converted into fee simple ownership. . . . **1963** MACLEOD & MORTON Cuthbert Grant 164 (n45): While settlers on the Red River had hay privileges, so far as is known these settlers of Grantown are the only people who had sugar privileges also.
2 the land to which this right applied.
1952 HOWARD Strange Empire 95: The "hay privilege," though uncultivated, was an integral part of each farm. **1963** STANLEY Louis Riel 59: When the survey team . . . started running their lines over the "hay privilege"—the land to the rear of the long river farms on which each farmer cut his hay—which belonged to André Nault, a group of métis . . . quickly appeared on the scene.

hayseed ['he,sid] n. Slang a farmer, especially a rustic, countrified one; yokel. See also **hay-tosser**.
1883 Prince Albert Times (Sask.) 28 Dec. 3/1: One section in three you've left quite alone, where the hay seeds may work at their farming. **1919** Camp Worker 16 Oct. 3/2: These "hayseeds" . . . cannot see that their interests are identical with the interests of all workers. . . . **1963** Maclean's 24 Aug. 16: Here are the secrets of success of the deceptive hayseed who's now the Conservatives' strongest figure.

hayseedy ['he,sidi] adj. Slang having the characteristics of a hayseed.
1918 COPELAND Swinging Lanterns 116: A "hayseedy" looking man with field mice jumping out of his whiskers, walked up to the lunch counter, seated himself on a stool, placed his bright-colored carpet bag on the next stool, and partook of a hearty lunch.

hay slough† [slü] Prairies a low-lying damp depression where wild hay grows abundantly. Cp. **hay-flats**.
1925 GROVE Settlers 292: He could not go to the hay-slough alone this morning. **1955** RUSSELL Carlton Trail 74: In the hollow beyond the telephone post is a "hay slough" surrounded by a ring of willow bushes.

hay-tosser n. Slang See **hayseed**.
1920 STRINGER Prairie Mother 41: We were just rubes and hicks and clodhoppers and hay-tossers in those

days and we weren't staying awake nights worrying about land-speculations. . . .

hay trail B.C.Interior a trail leading to an upland meadow.
1963 SYMONS Many Trails 16: The hay trail back of the corrals winds steeply up through the timber to the bench on top. . . .

haywire n. smooth, light flexible wire used for binding bales of hay or straw.
1919 Camp Worker 19 Sep. 8/1: . . . a number of small logging outfits that start with a ball of haywire and a number of small, dirty and evil smelling shacks. . . . **1957** Maclean's 17 Aug. 4/3: . . . haywire is extinct on farms, its place being taken by binder twine. . . . **1965** Islander 14 Feb. 5/1: He can break a single strand of haywire in a straight pull so at least two strands must be used, or a heavier wire.

haywire adj. [< n.] Slang **1** Esp. Lumbering poorly organized and equipped; less than efficient; second-rate. See also **gunnysack**.
1925 Cdn Labor Advocate 26 June 6/3: One hay-wire sawmill, Nice location, Ten mile haul To shipping station. **1942** HAIG-BROWN Timber 251: HAYWIRE. An allusion to the farm practice of repairing machinery with the light wire used to bale hay and straw. Any piece of equipment not up to the peak of operation efficiency is haywire to a logger. **1960** Sun (Vancouver) 16 Feb. 2/1: Neither does it [gyppo] denote shoddy equipment. There's another name for that—the haywire outfit.
2 make-shift; temporary; hasty. See also **gunnysack** and **shaganappi**, adj.
1954 PATTERSON Dangerous River 107: Next morning we ran on into the Splits, and when we hit the fast water it became clear that the haywire repair job on the kicker was not going to stand up to this sort of thing.

haywiredom ['he,waɪrdəm] n. Nonce shoddy, ill-equipped firms or groups collectively. See also **haywire**, adj.
1925 Cdn Labor Advocate 21 Aug. 6/5: The camp, built on floats situated on Saginaw Lake, was in accord with the best traditions of haywiredom.

H.B., H.B.C., H.B.Co., H.B.Company, H.B.Coy the Hudson's Bay Company, q.v.
1794 (1889) MACDONELL Journal 289: Auge has sad complaints against his H.B. opponent, Mr. Donald. . . . **1819** (1890) WILCOCKE Death B.Frobisher 204: Mr. Frobisher, myself and the men who were with us were suddenly confined to even more narrow limits and to a space nearly square, between our buildings and the range of buildings occupied by the H.B. Co. **1824** (1931) SIMPSON Fur Trade 80: Such a facility might be an additional inducement for them to fall in with the H.B. Coy's views. **1843** (1955) LEFROY Magnetic North 16: Rather than send a son of mine to become a clerk in the H.B. Company I would see him a day labourer at home. **1962** Canada Month Jan. 28/3: The trapper, the missionary, the HBC storekeeper and later the government may all have acted in reasonable ways, by their own lights.

H.B.C. Jocular See quotes. See also **Here Before Christ**.

1907 HUNTER *Cdn Wilds* 8: This [H.B.C.] flag is known from Labrador to the Pacific . . . Several would-be wits have given these mysterious letters odd meanings. Among several I call to memory, "Here Before Christ," "Hungry Belly Company" and "Here Before Columbus." **1933** ROLYAT *Wilderness Walls* 163: "H.B.C. (hell's blackest curse), H.B.C. (half-breed credit), H.B.C. (heaven's bad charter), H.B.C.," rushing to an hilarious climax he flung his pen to the other end of the room. . . .

H.B.C. token See **beaver** (def. 5a and picture). **1965** [see quote at **made beaver** (def. 2)].

H.C. *Obs*. See **Halifax currency**.
1825 *Novascotian* (Halifax) 16 Feb. 3/1: Mackarel . . . pr. bbl. . . . 20s. to 25s. H.C.

head *n. Obs*. See **niggerhead tobacco**.
1835 (1944) *B.C.Hist.Qtly* July 242: It remained with us now to either lose the beaver or rise our price . . . and we accordingly offered 5 gal. Mixed run & 10 heads tobacco, with a blanket per beaver. . . . **1835** (1958) WATTERS *B.C.Cent. Anthol*. 56: These two deer cost ½ pint Rum, 1 quart Molasses, 6 lbs Buckshot & 2 Heads Tobacco, which altogether amount to 2s 7d. . . .

header *n*. in preparing cod for salting, the person who beheads the fish receiving it from the cut-throat (def. 1) and passing it on to the splitter, *q.v.*
c1777 (1955) CURTIS *Voyage* 62: My next Station was to Work in the Stage as Header for 2 or 3 Weeks. **1818** CHAPPELL *Voy. of Rosamond* 127: Each salting-house is provided with one or more tables, around which are placed wooden chairs and leathern aprons, for the cut-throats, headers, and splitters. **1965** LEACH *Songs* 5: He then pushes the fish over to the 'header.' The header, wearing a 'headin' palm' (pam), grasps the fish by the dangling head, pulls out the liver and throws it in the bucket at his feet, and then bending the head against the edge of the table, he rips it off and casts it on the pile on the wharf.

head guide *Fur Trade, Hist*. the man in charge of a brigade, *q.v*. See also **conductor** (def. 1) and **guide** (def. 1).
1921 *Beaver* Dec. 11/2: The head guide was chosen on account of his being an old steersman who knew the route well, was a good judge of both water and weather, and being a good fighter, could if occasion arose enforce his orders with a dose of elbow grease. **1935** *Ibid*. Dec. 16/2: The head guide brings out the tobacco ration, and while the canoes cluster around he distributes to every man half a plug of the Hudson's Bay Imperial twist tobacco.

headlifting *n*. among certain Eskimo shamans, a method of divining the future by lifting the suppliant's head as if weighing it.
[**1922** JENNESS *Copper Eskimos* 216: . . . she asked me to let her divine by lifting my head . . . Higilak slipped her belt round my head, and told me to close my eyes. Then they both questioned me, and Higilak lifted my head from time to time for the answers. The whole ceremony lasted perhaps a quarter of an hour.] **1956** LEECHMAN *Native Tribes* 190: Sometimes they [Eskimo] tried to foretell the future by a curious form of fortune telling, known as head-lifting.

headline *n. North* a strong leather line attached to the front of a dog-sled, *q.v*., to permit the driver to aid the dogs when the difficult terrain requires it. Cp. **tail-line**.
1924 MASON *Arctic Forests* 30: Others [toboggans] have the tanned leather wrapper with the head and tail lines. **1956** KEMP *Northern Trader* 148: Then will come another portage, an uphill portage. You'll grab the headline of the sleigh, pull with the dogs. . . .

head-man *v. Hockey* pass (the puck) to a team-mate who is closer to the opposing team's goal than the passer.
1963 *Calgary Herald* 24 Dec. 8/3: We're always told to head-man the puck, pass it to the player ahead of us, because the puck can travel faster than you can skate. **1966** *Canadian* (Toronto) 29 Jan. 7/2: What occurs to almost every veteran hockey fan who's seen the Russians play, is how closely their play resembles the Canadian game of 20 . . . years ago; shorter passes, no slapshots, no head-manning the puck. **1966** *Kingston Whig-Standard* (Ont.) 11 Feb. 12/1: Why is it when a power play is on, the offensive team . . . [takes] the puck . . . back of its own net instead of head-manning it and charging in?

head of rail See **end of steel** (def. 1a).
1952 PUTNAM *Cdn Regions* 496/1: The fish from Great Slave Lake are frozen . . . and shipped southwards . . . to the head of rail in Alberta.

head of steel 1 the most recently laid tracks of a railway under construction; the farthest point to which tracks have been laid. See also **end of steel** (def. 1b). See also **railhead** (def. 1a).
1912 BICKERSTETH *Open Doors* 126: The head of steel is the point where, for the time being, the actual steel rails end. **1963** *Maclean's* 2 Nov. 26/3: To a man who has seen labor gangs living in boxcars at the head of steel . . . these rooms still looked comfortable. *Ibid*. 16 Nov. 57/1: For a week or so, the survey party to which I was attached worked around the gang laying the head of steel at about Mile 30. The steel gang lived in railway cars, pulled up by a locomotive along one or two miles of the track they had laid that day.

2 See **end of steel** (def. 1a).
1939 *Beaver* Dec. 15/2: From this post the letter will go out by dog team with the rest of the winter mail to Moosonee and the head of steel.

Head of the Lake *Hist*. the western end of Lake Ontario: the vicinity of Burlington, Hamilton, and Niagara-on-the-Lake. See also **Lakehead** (def. 1).
1793 (1911) SIMCOE *Diary* 211: They left Niagara [and] slept a few hours at Jones' farm at the "head of the lake." **1824** *Advocate* (Queenston, U.C.) 1 July 3/4: My absence at the Head of the Lake was prolonged by ill health. . . . **1911** ROBERTSON in SIMCOE *Diary* 323: Richard Beasley . . . was the first settler at the "Head of the Lake." **1958** JOHNSTON *Head of the Lake* 19: The region long known as the fond du lac was shortly re-named the "Head of the Lake," a new British colony of settlement.

Head of the Lakes See **Lakehead** (def. 2).
1910 *Eye Opener* (Calgary) 18 June 1/7: The Sifton bunch are omnipresent and partially omnipotent at the head of the lakes. **1956** *Northern Miner* 29 Nov. 85/3: In the hassle which ensued when the Ontario Government decided in 1890 that a school of mines was a necessity, the choice quickly narrowed to Port Arthur at the Head of the Lakes and Kingston at the foot.

head of the line *North* the point on a river at the end of a stretch where boats or canoes were pulled by tracking lines, *q.v.*; specifically, such a point on the Mackenzie River. Cp. **line,** *n.* (def. 1b).
1808 (1897) COUES *New Light* II 486: At eleven we reached the head of the line where we put ashore to gum and repair our canoes. **1940** *Beaver* June 28/2: After Providence we travelled eighty-nine miles downstream to the "head of the line" . . . this part of the river is called the "line" because, in the days before steamers, the scows, boats and canoes had to be tracked upstream with tow-lines. **1943** *Ibid.* Mar. 35: At the Head of the Line, eight miles above Simpson, we camped.

headstrap *n.* See **tumpline** and picture.
1933 MERRICK *True North* 27: The head strap across the top of one's head supports the first bag, which goes lengthwise on one's back. **1964** CARROLL *Shy Photographer* 9: Then Mad Pierre . . . hoisted him with his pack . . . to *his* shoulders, and without even a headstrap, started off.

head-swamper *n. Hist.* the supervisor of a gang of swampers (def. 1).
1961 PRICE & KENNEDY *Renfrew* 50: The head-swamper or road-maker extended the roads into the forest as work progressed so teamsters could haul back to the roll-way. **1964** GUILLET *Pioneer Days* 85: The "head-swamper" and his gang then cleared a bush road from the interior to the roll-way.

heap *n. Obs.* See **plan-heap.**
1852 MOODIE *Roughing It* 298: Could he have found an opening through the burning heaps, we could not have seen our way through the dense canopy of smoke.

heart seal *Nfld, Obs.* See **harp.**
1784 PENNANT *Arctic Zoology* 165: The *Newfoundland* Seal hunters call it the *Harp,* or *Heart* Seal, and name the marks on the side, the saddle.

heath cock or **hen** *Obs.* See **prairie chicken** (def. 1).
1749 DRAGE *Voyage* II 319: There are Abundance of . . . wild Fowl, Heath-Cocks and Hens, likewise Partridges, and Turkeys, and Sea Fowl in great Plenty. **1823** FRANKLIN *Journey* 679: This species is an inhabitant of woody countries only, in which it differs from the Pinnated grouse of America . . . better known to the Sportsmen of the New World under the appellation of the Prairie hen and Heath hen.

heavy *adj.* of drift-ice, *q.v.*, thick and close-packed, making it difficult for a ship to make headway.
1850 SNOW *Voyage* 386: Heavy and light are terms attached to ice, distinguishable of their thickness. **1958** *Evening Telegram* (St. John's) 26 Apr. 3/8: She became jammed in heavy ice off Grey Islands, northern Newfoundland, and her operations were greatly hampered.

hedging *n.* See **milking the bushes.**
1852 CAMPBELL *Two Journals* 140: Mild and cloudy— camped at the grand bay—but little tracking and hedging.

hee-hee[1] ['hi,hi] *n.* [< Chinook Jargon] laughter; fun.
1884 (1926) MOSER *Reminiscences* 139: In the afternoon hayou hihi [much merriment]. **1894** PHILLIPPS-WOLLEY *Gold* 17: ". . . Where are you going to—the hee-hee house?" "No, no. Hee-hee house no good. No makee money there. Pay all the time. Me go gamble."

hee-hee[2] ['hi,hi] *n.* [origin unknown] *West Coast* See quote.
1964 CARL *Marine Fishes B.C.* 53: The Indian method of fishing for lingcod was ingenious. A lure called a "hee-hee," of wood and fibres in the shape of a shuttle-cock, was pushed down toward the reef with a long three-tined spear. When the spear was sharply withdrawn, the "hee-hee" spun slowly to the surface followed by the curious or hungry lingcod.

heeler† *n.* **1** *Politics, Slang* a subservient party worker who comes to heel readily when ordered.
1890 *Grip* (Toronto) 18 Oct. 245/1: When Orange toughs meet / For a row on the street, / Stirred up by political heelers. **1943** (1959) STEWART & FRENCH *Ask No Quarter* 268: "Judges," she said, "are all political heelers or they would not be judges."
2 *West* See quote.
1963 SYMONS *Many Trails* 56: For each such crew was a "heeler," a mounted cowboy who would go into the heat and dust and noise of the herd to rope out the calves one at a time by the heels and drag the bawling and protesting infants up to the fire. . . .

height *n. Obs.* See **height of land.**
1768 DRAGE *Prob.N.W.Passage* 134: In ascending this Heighth, saw many Moose Deer Paths. **1835** (1947) SAUNDERS *Algonquin* 15: The height or dividing ridge consisted of land covered with a fine growth of timber.

height of land a watershed. See also **Height of Land** and **land's height.**
☛ *Perhaps a translation of the Canadian-French term* hauteur des terres.
[1732 (1947) *Cdn Hist.Rev.* Dec. 406: . . . since these people live in the neighbourhood of the height of land, they go sometimes to Trois Rivières. . . .] **1791** *Ont.Bur. Arch.Rep.* III 415: His Majesty's ungranted lands . . . from the Height of Land passing through the Junction of the River St. Johns and Madawasca, and intersecting the River St. Lawrence is 11,936,163 Acres. **1870** *Wkly Manitoban* 31 Dec. 2/3: On one side it is sheltered by the chain of hills which forms the height of land, while on the other it is far enough removed from the coast to be exempt from the injurious sea breezes. **1965** *Globe and Mail* (Toronto) 15 Jan. 7/5: [It] is one of eight ARDA-designated "rural research regions" . . . on a height of land above the only incorporated town in the county, Alexandria.

Height of Land 1 a region of high ground forming a watershed to the north of the western end of Lake Superior. See also **Hauteur des Terres.**
1800 (1922) HARMON *Journal* 18: In the former part of the day, we crossed small lakes and ponds, connected by several portages, and then came over the height of land. **1821** (1900) GARRY *Diary* 116: Kamanistiquia River takes its Rise from the Height of Land towards Lake Nipigan. **1922** *Beaver* June 12/2: All over the Lake Superior country, from the height of land north of the lake as far south as Minnesota. **1958** *Weekend Mag.* 28 June 39/2: A lot of water has flowed this way and that way off the Height of Land since I last saw Nahdaweh.
2 the elevated plateau forming the western boundary separating Labrador and Quebec.
1887 *Trans.Roy.Soc.Can.* IV 1 79: The latter portion of Ungava dist. is an elevated plateau, more or less broken yet nowhere abruptly so, and known throughout the entire country as the "Height of Land." **1905** DUNCAN

Grenfell's Parish 68: Trappers who have caught sight of the 'height of land' say that it is for the most part a vast table-land, barren, strewn with enormous boulders, scarce in game, swarming with flies, with vegetables surviving only in the hollows and ravines—a sullen, forsaken waste. **1963** *Maclean's* 16 Nov. 57/1: The height of land is at Mile 150; there the southbound trains start their long run down to Seven Islands. . . .

Height-of-Lander *n. Lab.* a trapper whose traplines are in the region of the Height of Land (def. 2).
1933 MERRICK *True North* 17: Tomorrow the first bunch of Height of Landers leaves and I hope we will not be too far behind to catch them.

height of the country *Obs.* See **Height of Land** (def. 2).
1820 (1963) DAVIES *Northern Quebec* 24: I expect . . . to go . . . over the height of the country towards Labrador.

hei-ho *n.* See **high-hole.**

hellery ['hɛləri] *n.* [< *heller* mischief-maker] *Slang* mischief; trouble; wild behavior.
1910 FRASER *Red Meekins* 54: "He's got me guessin'; some hell'ry on [that] we ain't doped out yet."
1930 BEAMES *Army* 114: We don't have to bother what hellery they'll be into next till we get back home.
1965 *Globe and Mail* (Toronto) 17 Feb. 31/8: For years . . . I have been craftily awaiting the chance to write a column about women's brassieres, just for the (wink! wink!) hellery of it.

hell-hole *n.* an underground cave. See also **pothole** (def. 6).
1965 *Kingston Whig-Standard* (Ont.) 10 May 6/2: The present hell-hole at first casual glance appears to be only a large crevice in the limestone.

hell-runner *n. Slang, Obs.* a person soliciting business for saloons, brothels, gambling houses, etc.
1883 FRASER *Shanty* 351: As he leaps with a light heart and a heavy pocket from the raft on to the shore he is at once beset with a host of hell-runners in the shape of calash drivers, boarding-house agents, brothel sirens, and crimps and sharpers of the blackest stamp.

Helluland† ['hɛlu‚lænd] *n.* [< ON "land of boulders"] *Hist.* See 1958 quote.
1869 BROWN *Cape Breton* 17: The country called Helluland, or Slateland in the Saga, was evidently Newfoundland; that called Markland, or Woodland, was Nova Scotia and Cape Breton. **1958** *Encyc.Can.* V 111/1: Helluland, the most northerly of three regions on the E. coast of North America names in Icelandic literature of the 11th century. The other two were Markland and Vinland. Helluland may have been on Baffin Island. See Norse Voyages.

helo ['hɛlo] *adj. adv.* [< Chinook Jargon] *B.C.* no; none. Also spelled *halo, halu.*
[*c*1846 (1849) ROSS *Adventures* 347: "It's done . . . Hi-low."] **1860** *Brit.Colonist* (Victoria) 17 July 2/2: Garretson replied that he had "halu chicamun," when the Tongass presented a musket at his breast, and threatened to shoot. **1894** PHILLIPPS-WOLLEY *Gold* 185: "What keeps the old man? You halo comtax

anything, Chance. . . ." **1963** SYMONS *Many Trails* 74: "Mebbeso," Charlie went on, "helo chicamun stop I come back," meaning that he might return broke.

hemlock feathers See **feathers.**

hemlock pine *Obs.* See **hemlock spruce.**
1796 (1911) SIMCOE *Diary* 298: Mr. McGill drinks tea made of hemlock pine. **1849** ALEXANDER *L'Acadie* II 20: [On the ridge-pole] rested . . . other poles and on them . . . small branches of the hemlock-pine, broken off and laid like a thatch on the sloping roof of our wigwam. . . .

hemlock spruce the Canadian hemlock, *Tsuga canadensis.* See also **hemlock pine.**
1833 *Trans.Lit.& Hist.Soc.Que.* III 226: The little block of wood exhibited, . . . was lately chopped out of a standing Hemlock Spruce, by a surveying party, in the township of Halifax. **1956** *Native Trees* 50: EASTERN HEMLOCK [is also called] hemlock spruce.

hemlock tea *Hist.* a beverage made from steeped hemlock needles and twigs. See also **bush tea, high Hyson,** and **Yankee tea.** Cp. **spruce tea.**
[**1796** (1911) SIMCOE *Diary* 298: Mr. McGill drinks tea made of hemlock pine.] **1821** HOWISON *Sketches* 199: After supping on bread and hemlock tea. . . I went to bed at an early hour. **1853** STRICKLAND *Canada West* I 231: I recommend, from experience, a hemlock-bed, and hemlock-tea, with a dash of whiskey in it, merely to assist the flavour, as the best preventive. **1964** GUILLET *Pioneer Days* 39: . . . hemlock "tea" and burned Indian corn "coffee" were the substitutes for the real articles, which were too expensive.

Henry VIII coat *Fur Trade, Obs.* See quote. Cp. **captain's coat.**
1929 MOBERLY *When Fur Was King* 71: The Company carried in stock in those days a quantity of military coats, adorned with gilt braid and buttons of the period of Henry VIII. A Henry VIII coat cost a good horse.

Hepburn's Hussars *Slang, Derog., Hist.* See 1965 quote.
1946 LOWER *Colony to Nation* 525: A body of police was specially organized for the occasion on military lines, "Hepburn's Hussars," as they were dubbed. **1965** HAMILTON *Cdn Quotations* 174: Hepburn's Hussars. Popular name for police body organized by Premier Mitchell Hepburn at the time of the Ontario Automobile Workers' strike, Oshawa, 1937.

herd bull *Slang* the chief boss; manager.
1960 *Sun* (Vancouver) 16 Feb. 1/4: . . . I wheeled through the brick gateposts and down the paved driveway to the Garner mansion on the shore of Cadboro Bay here and saw Joe, the herd bull of the Garner enterprises. . . .

herd-camp *n. West* See **horseguard** (def. 1).
1923 STEELE *Spirit-of-Iron* 78: Hector was in charge of the Police herd-camp a few miles from the fort. *Ibid.* 85: I went to the herd-camp and hid all day under a tarpaulin. . . .

Here Before Christ *Jocular* a play on the initials H.B.C. for Hudson's Bay Company. See also **H.B.C.**
1872 JOHNSON *Very Far West* 35: "Waall now, what's that ar flag, with them letters?" Bill's attention thus directed, fastened itself on the prominent piece of bunting. After some consideration, and much expectoration, he slowly replied: "Le'ss see, 'B.C.' in

ancient history means 'Before Christ,' I b'lieve—'tleast so the school-marm used to tell when I was to school—tharfore, I calc'late 'H.B.C.' to mean 'Here before Christ;' fur this 'tarnal location don't 'pear to've bin much overrun with strangers since that period." **1936** *Beaver* Dec. 48/1: The above cheque, drawn as a bet, cost the payer $100, much, we understand, to his surprise. He did not believe the bank would recognize "The Here Before Christ Co." as the Hudson's Bay Company. **1966** *Islander* 17 July 4/3: An American prospector . . . once studied the flag for a moment then enquired what the letters meant. "Here before Christ" was old McPherson's reply.

Here-Before-Christer *n.* See quote. See also **Here Before Christ.**
1958 (1960) NELSON *Northern Lights* 502: Here the Hudson's Bay Company—the "HBC" or the "Here-Before-Christers" . . . had long ago established a post.

Here Before Columbus See **H.B.C.**

hereditary chief a chief of an Indian band through hereditary right, as opposed to an elected chief.
1959 *Kingston Whig-Standard* (Ont.) 2 May 11/5: . . . a small vote is expected because the hereditary chiefs and their supporters never vote—believing to do so would mean the loss of their Indian treaty rights.

here's a ho See **ho** (def. 2).

Herring-Choker *n. Slang* a Maritimer, *q.v.*, especially one from New Brunswick.
1899 *Yarmouth Telegram* (N.S.) 20 Oct. 1/1: I am down among the "herring chokers" and "blue noses" for a few weeks. **1927** LONGSTRETH *Silent Force* 4: Behind a raised blanket a French Canadian and a "herring-choker" were tilting a bottle unespied. **1954** *Fundy Fisherman* 3 Mar. 4/4: But talking to New Brunswick senators (male) some of them rather fancy that Premier High John can make or has made a better dicker with Maurice Duplessis. These Herring Choker senators point out that Duplessis has already peddled a lot of horse power to Ontario and indeed is selling plenty to Premier Frost et al right now. **1962** *Time* (Cdn ed.) 23 Mar. 12/3: To keep the listings within bounds, the editors omitted regionalisms but included such Canadian originals as the derogatory *pea-souper* (for French Canadian), *komatik* (an Eskimo sled) and *herring choker* (for a Nova Scotian).

herring-hog *n. Maritimes* a common porpoise of the north Atlantic and Pacific, *Phocoena phocoena.*
1883 HATTON & HARVEY *Newfoundland* 233: Another variety is called puffing-pig and herring-hog by the fishermen.

A herring rake

herring-rake *n. Northwest Coast* See quotes.
1932 JENNESS *Indians of Can.* 63: . . . they used [c1790] for both herring and oolakan a pole about 18 feet long, with a blade 6 feet long by a foot [an inch] wide fitted with a number of bone spikes; almost every stroke of this curious club into a shoal of herring brought up three or four fish. **1953** FLUKE *Kwakiutl* 16: For gathering herring, a very ancient implement was used. It was called a herring-rake and consisted of a long, flat piece of cedar or fir set with 2-inch teeth along 3 or

4 feet of one end. **1958** WATTERS *B.C.Cent.Anthol.* 162: The herring rake—a long stick with spikes on one side—still remains a favourite weapon among the humbler fishing-folk, as it was before the white man came.

herring salmon or **whitefish** *Obs.* See **whitefish.**
1849 (1852) RICHARDSON *Arctic Exped.* 315: On taking up our nets (which we laid carefully on the rocks for the Eskimos), they were found full of herring-salmon, in fine condition. **1866** KING *Sportsman in Can.* 295: The absence of teeth . . . and the presence of the adipose fin in this fish, place it among the Coregoni, and I believe it to be the C. Clupeiformis described by Cuvier under the local name of "Herring Salmon." **1880** BELL *Churchill and Nelson Rivers* 60: The herring white-fish . . . is caught in abundance at the mouths of the Nelson and Hayes rivers. . . .

Hessian fly† a small flying insect, *Phytophaga destructor,* whose larvae does much damage to wheat crops.
☛ *This pest was so named because of the mistaken belief that it was imported into North America in the straw bedding of Hessian troops during the American Revolution.*
1788 (1789) *N.S.Mag.* I 16/1: The Hessian Fly, or, as is more generally called, the Flying Weevil, was first observed in the Southern Provinces about 50 years ago, and since that time has regularly extended itself to the Northward, without quitting a place where it has once got possession. **1855** *Hamilton Gaz.* (C.W.) 14 June 3/2: Some of the farmers in this vicinity assure us of the presence of the Hessian fly. **1947** (1957) SCOTT & SMITH *Blasted Pine* 76:
I used to think the cut-worm and the weevil,
Were things that blindly come and go by chance,
And Hessian-fly an undiluted evil,
To make the farmer shudder in his pants. . . .

hew or **hu** [hju] *interj.* [origin uncertain] *North* a call directing a team of dogs to swing to the right. See also **chee, gee, huddy, ou,** and **ouk.** Cp. **chaw.**
1896 RUSSELL *Far North* 15: *Hu* and *chac,* anglicized to "you" and "chaw" are the words necessary to turn the foregoer to the right or left. **1956** MOWAT *Lost in Barrens* 196: The dogs worked with great energy and endurance, and they began to learn to answer the forest-country driving cries—"Chaw" and "Hew" for left and right.

hew *v. Lumbering, Obs.* work as a hewer.
1883 FRASER *Shanty* 20: In each of these [gangs] a full complement of men . . . are busy at work, felling, scoring, hewing, sawing and drawing onto the ice.

hewer† *n. Lumbering, Hist.* See 1947 quote.
1853 STRICKLAND *Canada West* II 281: The tree is now ready for the hewer's gang, which generally consists of the hewer and three, or at most four, axe-men, all of whom stand on the prostrate trunk of the tree, except the hewer. **1891** OXLEY *Chore-Boy* 67: . . . the "hewer," . . . with his huge broad-ax, made square the "stick," as the great piece of timber is called. **1947** SAUNDERS *Algonquin* 30: The hewer, standing on top of the log, wielded a broad axe with a large head and razor-keen edge, trimming first one side and then the other till *each was almost as smooth as a planed board.*

H.H.B.C. or **H.H.B.Co.** the Honourable Hudson's Bay Company.

1852 (1956) COLVILLE *Letters* 93: The renewal of the claim after the liberality of the H.H.B. Co. . . . seems to me very reasonable. *Ibid.* 96: [signed] John Chapman Chap. H.H.B.C. **1871** (1951) *Beaver* June 207/2: I . . . was en route for Pembina with the H.H.B.C. Mounted Rifles, cart horse and all.

hiak *v.* See **hyak.**

hiaqua ['hiakwə] *n.* [< Chinook Jargon < Nootka]
Pacific Coast, Hist. the shell of a mollusc, *Dentalium indianorum,* used by the Coast Indians as money and ornaments. See also **hykwa.** Various spellings.
1816 (1849) ROSS *Adventures* 95: The circulating medium in use among these people is a small white shell called higua, about two inches long, of a convex form, and hollow in the heart, resembling in appearance the small end of a smoking pipe. **1824** (1931) SIMPSON *Fur Trade* 96: The Ears are perforated all round and Beads or Hyaques suspended therefrom in quantity according to the rank or taste of the party. **1829** (1948) MCLOUGHLIN *Letters* 59: . . . if you buy for us the Value of Thirty Blankets of hiaquois it would be desirable. . . . **1859** KANE *Wanderings* 238: . . . iaquas . . . are valuable to their length, and their value increases according to a fixed ration, forty shells being the standard number to extend a fathom's length; which number . . . is equal in value to a beaver skin; but if thirty-nine be found long enough to make the fathom, it would be worth two beavers' skins; if thirty-eight, three skins; and so on, increasing one beaver skin for every shell less than the standard number. **1923** *Cdn Hist.Rev.* IV 37: The shell *dentalium indianorum,* commonly called hiquia, is much esteemed by the coast Indians, and amongst them has fulfilled some of the functions of money.

hiaqua shell See **hiaqua.**
1862 *Nor'Wester* (R.R.S.) 5 Mar. 4/3: Instead of the nose jewels being "of tin" they were composed of the Hyaqua shells which [give] the expression of the face a singular appearance. **1867** GIBBS *Notes on Tinneh* 320: Both fringe and band were in former times made of Hiagua shells (*Dentalium*) or of wooden beads made from willows.

hias *adj. adv.* See **hyas.**

High Arctic the polar regions.
1958 *Evening Telegram* (St. John's) 2 May 23/1: Our first knowledge . . . of the existence of a large sea-bird colony in that high Arctic region was a reference to a "loomery" (an old word for murre colony) in the journal of Captain M'Clintock . . . in 1858.
1964 JENNESS *Eskimo Admin.* II 73: In 1947 other radio and meteorological outposts arose in the High Arctic. . . .

highball *adj. or attrib.* [< *highball,* n., an early type of railway signal to proceed] *Esp.Lumbering, Slang* operating on a speeded-up schedule; working at top speed.
1919 *Camp Worker* 26 Apr. 5/2: I sometimes think they have hit the nail on the head, more especially so when I see some of our high-ball hook-tenders moving the "Old Pot" to a new landing and leave her setting so that when the boiler is full of water the glass will show a gauge or less. **1925** *Cdn Labor Advocate* 12 June 6/1: This outfit would be "high-ball" if the super had his way, but owing to his ignorance of logging he is not able to

put it over. **1948** (1956) ANDREWS *Glory Days* 25: ". . . you gotta be good to last. She's highball."

Highball Express See Hudson Bay Railway.
1952 (1965) HAMILTON *Cdn Quotations* 194: Railways (Nicknames) . . . *Hudson Bay*—The Highball Express. The Muskeg Special. The Muskeg Unlimited.

highbush cranberry a shrub, *Viburnum opulus;* also the reddish, tart berry of this shrub. See also **cranberry tree, mooseberry,** and **pembina.**
1833 (1838) NEED *Six Years in Bush* 99: The high-bush cranberry, by far the most delicate and admired of all our native fruits, was not yet ripe. **1912** FOOTNER *New Rivers* 208: The "high-bush" cranberry . . . is not highly regarded as an article of human diet, but we found its acrid tartness very refreshing, when there were no currants or gooseberries to be had along the trail. **1958** *Edmonton Jnl* 20 Oct. 4/3: . . . and I'll get a few suckers from the highbush cranberries. . . .

high climber See **rigger.**

high country[1] [trans. of Cdn F *haut pays*] the hinterland; the forests of the North and Northwest; the fur country.
1903 WHITE *Forest* 278: The second day, however, we came to a surveyor's base-line cut through the woods. Then we followed that as a matter of convenience. The base-line, cut the fall before was the only evidence of man we saw in the high country. **1942** CAMPBELL *Thorn-Apple Tree* 152: "Eh, bien. Well, some time again we winter in the high country, maybe. . . ."

high country[2] *West* the foothills, *q.v.,* of the Rockies.
1960 NELSON *Northern Lights* 707: It was good that October night in the high country of western Alberta with the supper-fire burning a bright hole in the dark and the talk of the roundup hands drifting here and there with the smoke.

high-grade *adj. Mining* denoting or containing gold-bearing ore of a high assay value. See also **high-grade**[1], *n.* (def. 1).
1910 SERVICE *Trail of '98* 333: . . . they knew of a ledge of high-grade, free-milling quartz somewhere out there in the Land Back of Beyond. **1913** OGILVIE *Yukon* 121: . . . Klondike . . . now considered a fairly good creek with, if not high-grade dirt, plenty of paying stuff. **1958** *Northern Miner* 25 Dec. 17/2: At one property The Northern Miner was shown no less than 10 sample bags containing high grade gold ore that has been recovered this year.

high-grade[1] *n.* Also *high-grade ore. Mining*
1 gold-bearing ore that is of high assay value.
1910 FRASER *Red Meekins* 167: A massive-jawed fighting bulldog was turned loose nightly in the ore-house to guard the sacks of high grade ore; but Red Meekins . . . went on high-grading. **1963** *Maclean's* 4 May 18/3: On rare occasions, after a dynamite blast, this visible gold falls out of the rock in pure nuggets. If the miners are honest, they send for the shift boss and the security guards. Then everybody watches everybody else while they fill a canvas sack with the high-grade and take it straight to the refinery. If the miners are dishonest, they hide the high-grade and start scheming to get it out of the mine.

2 high-assay gold-bearing ore stolen from a mine. See also **high-grade**[1], *v.* (def. 1).
1948 ONRAET *Sixty Below* 80: "Someone's suspicious; I guess he's got high-grade. He wants to git the dope on and won't let us in on it." **1963** *Time* (Cdn ed.) 18 Jan. 10/2: One dealer once got a job as a milk-driver, so he

could collect high-grade ore along his route.

high-grade[1]† *v.* **1** *Mining* steal high-grade ore from a mine.
1910 FRASER *Red Meekins* 167: A massive-jawed fighting bulldog was turned loose nightly in the ore-house to guard the sacks of high grade ore; but Red Meekins . . . went on high-grading. **1963** *Time* (Cdn ed.) 18 Jan. 10/2: Some Timmins stores have been known to accept high-graded ore in payment for grocery bills.
2 *Lumbering* remove only the best timber from a stand.
1964 *Victoria Dly Times* 9 Oct. 4/1: "We've been living high off the hog. We've been high-grading the forests," Mr. McKee said, adding that in British Columbia some operators have been wasting half of the wood and in other provinces, due to improvident practices, yields were but a fraction of possible maximums.

high-grade[2] *v.* in road making, build on a bed of ballast and so grade as to shed water.
1958 MACGREGOR *North-west of 16* 95: Even in prosperous communities it was another twenty or thirty years before such roads were "high graded" and partially gravelled.

high-grader† *n.* a person who steals or traffics in high-grade ore from a mine. See also **high-grade**[1], *v.* (def. 1).
1953 (1958) WALKER *Pardon My Parka* 20: . . . when the police raided the basement of the post office on a hot tip that high-graders were using it as a smelter, the lining of the furnace assayed at $18,000 per ton.
1963 *Maclean's* 4 May 18/1: At the time, the heat was supposed to be on Timmins' high-graders, the men who steal, refine and sell gold from the local mines.

high-grade squad a police detail whose special function is to track down high-graders, *q.v.*, and recover stolen gold.
1963 *Maclean's* 4 May 30/2: The high-graders are more than romantic swashbucklers to the local provincial police high-grade squad.

high-grading *n.* **1** *Mining* See 1958 quote. See also **high-grade**[1], *v.* (def. 1).
1910 FRASER *Red Meekins* 167: This high grading was a peculiarly fine point in the ethics of stealing; it was looked upon as something akin to beating the customs. **1958** *Northern Miner* 25 Dec. 17/2: Highgrading [is] the common term for theft of gold bullion, nuggets, fines or precipitates. . . . **1963** *Time* (Cdn ed.) 18 Jan. 10: To the Porcupine's 10,000 gold miners, high-grading is . . . more an art than a crime.
2 *Mining* the practice of recovering only high-grade or easily separated ore. Cp. **haymaker**.
1966 *North* Jan.-Feb. 21/1: The pattern of mining development in the Yukon to date has been characterised by "high grading" by the first comers using hand-labour; then a slow but steady decline in output as the lower grade minerals came into production.
3 *Lumbering* the removal of only the best timber from a stand. See **high-grade**[1], *v.* (def. 2).
1948 *Ont.Timberworker* 28 Feb. 2/3: Put to work in poor timber stands left after shameless high-grading of timber during the war, these inexperienced newcomers find it impossible to make a living wage.

high-hole *n.* [< Brit.dial. *highhoe, haihow,* the green woodpecker] the flicker, *Colaptes auratus*.
1793 (1937) CAMPBELL *Travels* 33: Also shot two other

beautiful birds called Hei-ho. . . . **1926** MACKAY *Blencarrow* 226: The tap-tapping of an industrious high-hole sounded loudly in the quiet. **1941** SETON *Autobiography* 77: He had a golden-winged woodpecker that he had shot—he called it a high-hole.

high Hyson [cf. *Hyson* a coarse green Chinese tea < Cantonese *hei-ch'un* bright spring] *Obs.* See **hemlock tea**.
1910 FERGUSON *Janey Canuck* 221: It [Labrador tea] is said to be palatable as a tea and was used for that purpose by pioneers, just as the early settlers in Ontario used "High Hyson," which was only a well-sounding name for hemlock needles.

high-lead *n.* *Lumbering* the cable, or main line (def. 3), used to haul in logs when using a high-lead system, *q.v.* See also **skyline** and picture. Cp **ground lead**.
1925 PHILIP *Crimson West* 144: He yawned sleepily. "Got to fix a 'spar-tree' for a 'high-lead' to-morrow, so I better hit the hay." **1957** HUTCHISON *Canada* 322: The caterpillar tractor is replacing the high lead. **1965** *Star Wkly* 13 Feb. 7: We high-lead-logged the slopes of the Iskut, tractor-logged the river bottom [and] built a road up the south shore. . . .

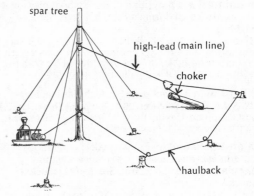

A high-lead system

high-lead system or **method** *Lumbering* any method of high-line logging, *q.v.*; specifically and originally, a system using only one spar tree. See also **high-lead yarding**.
1930 *B.C.Lumberman* Apr. 61: Slackline gasoline yarders are also being used to advantage as the extra drum of skyline permits the yarding distance to be extended and logs brought in across canyons . . . more efficiently than by high lead methods. **1939** BEAULIEU & BARTON *Lumber Science* 35: The High-Lead is the most common method of yarding by steam. It is a modification of the old ground method and has a radius of operation from 500 to 800 feet (maximum 1400 feet). **1942** SWANSON *Western Logger* 52: high-lead —system of logging using spar-tree. **1966** *B.C.Forest Industries* C13/1: The "high lead" system of logging and the "McLean loading boom" combined with an enlarged market to revolutionize the industry.

high-lead yarding See **high-lead system**.
1937 MULHOLLAND *Forest Resources B.C.* 71: Logging in this district is done almost entirely with machinery; steam, oil, and gasoline engines and high-lead

yarding bring in most of the logs direct. . . . **1966** *B.C. Logging* 8/1: High-Lead Yarding is most common in the Coast Region. One metal spar is used, its main line and haul-back line rigged to a stump or "back" spar 600 to 800 feet distant.

highline† *n.* See **highliner.**
1890 *Grip* (Toronto) 5 Apr. 233/2: Always "high line," he was always "filled up" with the split mackerel of the North Bay. **1899** *Yarmouth Herald* 6 Jan. 2/3: The Annie Greenlaw is commanded by Capt John Greenlaw, one of the smartest and best-known skippers in the haddocking fleet, who is certainly high line of the fleet this year.

high-line logging *Lumbering* any method of yarding logs by means of one or more spar trees, *q.v.*, and a cable system. See also **high-lead system, high-lining, high-rigging,** and **skyline.**
1965 *B.C. Digest* Sep.-Oct. 19/1: Mobile spar trees, which are monstrous self-propelled cranes whose thick booms bear a multiplicity of sheaves and cables, are used in modern high-line logging to replace the spar tree used until recently as the focal point for the complicated system of cables and pulley-blocks.

highliner† *n.* a fisherman or fishing boat making the largest catch during a specified time. See also **highline.**
1916 WALLACE *Shack Locker* 65: ". . . I ain't a highliner this season, but we've got one thing to brag about when it comes to fishin'." **1957** *Explorer* 2 June 170: With two of us working, we'll be highliner for the day.

high-lining *n.* *Lumbering* See **high-line logging.**
1965 *B.C. Digest* Sep.-Oct. 20/1: But many [high-riggers] just disappeared, as did the giant trees they had topped, limbed and rigged for high-lining.

high muckamuck† ['mʌkə,mʌk] [< Chinook Jargon *hyiu muckamuck, q.v.*] *Slang* a leading person in a group; big-shot. See also **big mucky-muck.**
1903 (1913) CULLUM *Devil's Keg* 32: . . . they reckon as they're the high muck-i-muck o' this location. . . .
1927 PHILIP *Painted Cliff* 14: "J. B. Smith is the high-muck-a-muck, the tyee of the mining business of British Columbia." **1965** *Time* (Cdn ed.) 16 Apr. 14/3: Not all the Liberal high muckamucks were as warmly defended as Favreau.

high north the far north, especially the Arctic.
1923 MACMECHAN *Sagas of Sea* 14: The bitter cold of the high north set in. **1963** *Maclean's* 23 Feb. 2/1: . . . Northern Affairs recently lopped $40,000 from a $100,000 program of grants for private research in the high north.

high-pole cache *North* a cache raised off the ground on poles. See also **cache,** *n.* (def. 2).
1955 BEAVER *Yukon Trader* 165: I noticed a group of log structures and high pole catches [sic] set off from the rest.

high prairies See **coteau** (def. 2).
1900 OSBORN *Greater Canada* 145: In the fifties there were years when as many as fifteen hundred carts and waggons and more than two thousand men, women, and children came to the time-honoured trysting-place on the high prairies about two days' journey from Fort Garry.

high-rigger *n.* *Lumbering* See **rigger.**
1919 *Camp Worker* 26 Apr. 5/2: There are innumerable firms that have monopolized the services of the best hooker that ever gave signals for the high-rigger, while his short-handed crew changed the haul-back without the assistance of a grass-line.
1963 MCKINNON *Forest Activities I* 6: [Caption] A "high-rigger" topping a spar tree. He climbs the tree with the aid of spurs, belt, and climbing rope (a rope with a steel core), cutting off the branches as he goes.

high-rigging *n.* *Lumbering* See **high-line logging.**
1958 HARRIS & HAWTHORNE *New Denver* 17: The method of logging is high-rigging, the spar tree covering about two acres.

high school a secondary school having four or five grades, the number of grades and the nature of the curriculum varying from province to province. Cp. **collegiate institute.**
1849 *Journal of Education for U.C.* I 47: The proposition we understand, to purchase two lots from the Odd Fellows, was entertained, by the Council, and a High School is to be erected thereon immediately.
1889 WITHROW *Our Own Country* 344: The Educational system of Ontario is one of the best in the world. It consists of Public Schools, High Schools and the University, an organic whole, each part fused into the other. **1955** *Western Star* (Corner Brook, Nfld) 10 Mar. 4/2: Even this year there are young Corner Brook ladies, graduates from High School, who have had to go elsewhere for training in secretarial work.
1962 *Globe and Mail* (Toronto) 26 Sep. 7/3: It is true that some high schools of good quality are now being called "Secondary Schools," but this indicates that they have classes in technical and commercial subjects under the same roof as those in academic (now called arts and science) subjects.

highstick *v.* in hockey and lacrosse, strike an opposing player with one's stick raised to an illegal height, normally so that it extends above shoulder level.
1962 *National Hockey Annual* 26/2: "I high-sticked him," Bert said, "but that sometimes happens in hockey." **1966** *Kingston Whig-Standard* (Ont.) 19 Mar. 10/7: I elbowed a couple of guys, high sticked another and blinked on the faceoffs.

highsticking *n.* in hockey and lacrosse, the illegal practice of striking an opponent with one's stick raised above shoulder level.
1955 *Pictou Advocate* 24 Feb. 4/6: . . . Melanson was forced to send some of the boys to the "cooler" for high sticking and elbowing. **1963** *Albertan* (Calgary) 10 Dec. 11/2: Paul Thompson . . . agreed that the high-sticking "art" has increased in recent years.
1966 *Globe and Mail* (Toronto) 20 June 19/1: Excelsior's offenders were led by Gord Thompson with a five minute high sticking penalty.

hightail (it) *v.* *Informal* move as fast as possible, usually in departing or retreating from a place.
1928 FREEMAN *Nearing North* 157: A glimpse through my binoculars of a string of red-brown bodies high-tailing it through the bush was all that could be seen of the disembarkation. **1953** CUSHMAN *Stay Away Joe* 24: "I want to hightail. I'm not staying where I'm treated like dirt." **1958** *Weekend Mag.* 13 Sep. 29/1: . . . the surviving pilots jettisoned their bombs on a Sunderland housing development and hightailed back

to Norway. **1960** *Press* Dec. 3: Many of them, as soon as they can scrape together their return fare, hightail it back to their native lands where . . . breadlines for the jobless are unknown and unimaginable. . . .

337

high-toned
ho

high-toned† *adj. Derog.* affecting a superior attitude.

1824 (1931) SIMPSON *Fur Trade* 31: Were more firm and decided conduct observed to freemen generally throughout the Country it would be much to our interest as their present independence and high toned importance is very injurious and in my opinion frought with danger to the concern. **1955** HOBSON *Nothing Too Good* 45: The Bear, who was as discerning of character and high-toned in his choice of friends, had taken an equal liking to Joe.

High Toryism *Hist.* the principles and policies of the far right of the colonial Tory party, epitomized in the Family Compact and the oligarchic arrogance associated with it.

1885 DENT *U.C.Rebellion* I 224: He was voluble, and made many verbose speeches, the matter of which never rose above the veriest commonplace, but as it was always charged with emphatic High Toryism it was applauded to the echo by the official party. **1963** MORTON *Kingdom of Can.* 284: The chief results . . . of the flaring passions of 1849 were that the old High Toryism and the old democratic radicalism had reached their historic terms in Canada.

high wine (*usually plural*) *Hist.* spiritous liquor, specifically a mixture of alcohol and flavored water, widely traded to the Indians by fur traders. See also **H.W.** and **Indian liquor.**

1794 (1929) MCGILLIVRAY *Journal* 49: They carry on Dog Sledges, 5 Kegs High Wines. . . . **1872** (1883) BUTLER *Great Lone Land* 213: Whisky, alcohol, high wine, and poison, which . . . mean death to the Indian. **1883** FRASER *Shanty* 335: Highwines diluted with water, and then charged with the oil of vitriol to disguise the water, was the only, and continuous drink. **1957** FISHER *Pemmican* 18: "Mucha high wine," he said, using Alexander Henry's term for it "Firewater."

Hill, the *n.* See **Parliament Hill** (def. 2).

1955 *Pictou Advocate* (N.S.) 24 Feb. 1/1: Meanwhile Fearless Dave Fulton, who earns his keep here [Ottawa] on the Hill just by the rumpuses he stirs up, has charged the Liberal regime with holding down immigration. . . . **1965** *Kingston Whig-Standard* (Ont.) 3 Mar. 34/6: Mr. Cassels said it was one thing for a person to argue in court that he was immune from arrest on the Hill, but wondered whether this could be pleaded afterwards.

hill lion *Obs.* See **cougar.**

1895 PARKER *Adventurer* 102: Skins hung along two sides, with bullet-holes and knife-holes showing—of the great gray wolf, the red puma, the bronze hill-lion, the beaver, the bear, and the sable; and in one corner was a huge pile of them.

hillside lay a hillside claim worked in partnership with the owner. See **lay,** *n.* (def. 1).

1909 SERVICE *Cheechako* 66: 'Twas in the fall of nineteen four—leap-year I've heard them say—/When Hard-Luck came to Hunker Creek and took a hillside lay.

hip-wader *n.* a long rubber boot reaching to the hips. See also **gumboot** (def. 2).

1963 *Chatelaine* April 58/1: My four pairs of *kamiks* range from knee-high white sheepskin to sealskin appliqued in a flower pattern. When the snow melts, I switch to rubber boots or hip waders. **1964** *Star Wkly* 20 June 9/1: There were not enough hip waders to go around.

hit *v.* reach; arrive at; meet.

1873 (1904) BUTLER *Wild North Land* 205: In the morning "Twa-poos," or the Three Thumbs, sets forth to look for a moose; he hits the trail and follows it. . . . **1919** FRASER *Bulldog Carney* 88: "Cayuse Braun has passed to the Happy Hunting Ground—he can't talk; Seth, of course, won't; and the Wolf will never stop running till he hits the border. . . ." **1961** *Sun* (Vancouver) 10 Jan. 10/1: . . . the Little Qualicum, which hits the saltchuck north-west of Qualicum Beach, has sizeable Cameron Lake on its headwaters. . . .

hit-and-roll *n. Curling* a play in which a curled rock glances off a stationary rock and slides into a better position.

1963 *Calgary Herald* 31 Dec. 21/4: In contrast, Woolley was in fine form, rattling off double takeouts, hit-and-rolls and delivering cool draws with heady abandon.

hitch *n. Slang* a period of time, especially a period of service in the armed services.

1835 *Novascotian* (Halifax) 12 Nov. 332/2: That remark seemed to grig him a little, he felt oneasy like and walked twice across the room, fifty fathoms deep in thought; at last he said, which way are you from, Mr. Slick, this hitch. **1945** PUGSLEY *Saints* 234: . . . they do see a very real attraction in doing a single five-year hitch. . . . **1959** *Ottawa Citizen* 13 June 2/3: NAVY REDUCES FIRST "HITCH" TO THREE YEARS. As of July 6, the initial term of engagement of men recruited into the Royal Canadian Navy as new entries will be three years instead of the present five.

hit the trail *Informal* take to the trail; leave; depart.

1898 (1930) ROBERTSON *Yukon Memories* 211: It is now clearing so I must "mush on," hike or hit the trail, in hieroglyphist parlance. **1964** *B.C.Digest* Sep.-Oct. 10/3: When the winter of 1898 set in, Kate Ryan acquired a sleigh dog team, and travelling alone hit the trail for Atlin by the old Teslin Trail.

hivernant [iver'nã] *n. Cdn French, Hist.* See **winterer** (def. 2).

1897 COUES *New Light* I viii: Alexander Henry was established as a winterer or *hivernant* in a post he had built on the Red River of the North. **1944** *Beaver* Sep. 18: It was at Montreal . . . that the . . . Hudson's Bay Company managed to procure most of the foods . . . required for . . . their . . . *hivernants* or wintering partners. **1954** WALLACE *Pedlars* 74: Fort William became a teeming town with a population of over three thousand persons, in which the *hivernants,* or winterers, mingled with the *mangeurs de lard,* or *voyageurs* from Montreal. **1966** *B.C.Digest* Nov.-Dec. 46/2: There they met the "hivernants" (winterers) from the Far West, received their packs, supplied them with trade goods from Montreal, and returned to Montreal the same season.

hiyu *adj.* See **hyiu.**

ho [ho] *interj. Hist.* **1** See 1952 quote.

1900 OSBORN *Greater Can.* 149: But at ten o'clock the next morning the hunters were made to fall into line, and the crier was ordered to cry the "ho!" which was the signal for a general attack. **1952** (1965) HAMILTON *Cdn Quotations* 63 : . . . the signal to attack in the great buffalo hunts was the cry of "Ho!"

2 See 1952 cite.

[**1856** BALLANTYNE *Young Fur-Traders* 137 : "Ho! What cheer?" said Jacques, taking him by the hand after the manner of Europeans, and accosting him with the phrase used by the fur-traders to the natives.] **1900** OSBORN *Greater Canada* 149 : The quaint expression, "Here's a ho!" which old-fashioned North-Western folk utter before gulping down the dram or "horn" of whisky, is really a reminiscence of this ancient [buffalo-hunt] signal to begin the fun, and not as some authorities say, a silly reference to the opening phrase of Isaiah lv. **1903** (1965) HAMILTON *Cdn Quotations* 233 : So I drink this toast / To the "Queen of the Coast." / Vancouver, here's a Ho! **1952** (1965) *Ibid.* 63 : Here's a ho, boy! A drinking term popular in the West, 19th century; in the early days the commonest form of cup was a buffalo horn; the signal to attack in the great buffalo hunts was the cry of "Ho!"

hoard *n. Hist.* See **cache**, *n.*(def. 2 and picture).
1784-1812 (1916) THOMPSON *Narrative* 41 : A Hoard is made of logs well notched into each other about eight feet in length, six feet wide at the bottom, five feet in height, and the top narrowed to two feet covered with Logs to secure our provisions and game from carnivorous animals. **1809** (1916) *Ibid.* 31 : . . . to the Hoard at 10 AM—where thank God I found all well & safe. . . . **1926** DICKIE *Cdn West* 82 : Each dog's load had to be reduced one-third; the rest of the goods they left in a log hoard.

hoary marmot a large marmot, *Marmota caligata,* of the western mountains. See also **groundhog** (def. 2), **marmot** (def. 2), **mountain marmot**, **rock whistler**, **siffleur** (def. 1), **whistler** (def. 1), **whistling badger**, **whistling marmot**, and **whistling pig**.
1781 PENNANT *Quadrupeds* II 398 : [The] Hoary [marmot] . . . Inhabits the northern parts of North America. **1829** RICHARDSON *Fauna* I 150 : Hoary marmot, with long coarse fur, particularly on the chest and shoulders, where it is hoary. **1963** SYMONS *Many Trails* 82 : At first I thought it was a whistler, one of the hoary marmots of the mountainside.

hockey† ['hɑki] *n.* [< *hock* bent stick, a variant of *hook*. See 1527 quote.] a sport played on ice on a board-enclosed rink by two teams of six men each whose object is to shoot a puck, *q.v.*, into the opponents' goal. See also **ice-hockey** and **shinny** (def. 2).
[**1527** (1934) BULL *From Rattlesnake Hunt to Hockey* 402 : The name [hockey] which is apparently derived from the French *hoquet* meaning shepherd's crook, is found in Murray's Dictionary of 1527 where it is defined as "the horlinge of the litill ball with hockie sticks or staves."] **1895** *News* (Rat Portage [Kenora], Ont.) 11 Jan. 1/2 : Hockey is the most popular winter sport in Canada, taking the place of lacrosse. **1916** BRIDLE *Sons of Can.* 23 : He was himself an expert amateur athlete, famous at hockey—baseball not yet being invented. **1954** LONGSTRETH *Force Carries On* 162 : Boys' clubs started, hockey games filled in the winter, ball diamond opened—and juvenile courts closed. **1963** O'BRIEN *Hockey* 30 : Evidence was presented to the effect that Members of Her

Majesties Royal Canadian Rifles, an Imperial Army Unit, had played ice hockey to the rear of Tete du Pont barracks [Halifax] in 1855. *Ibid.* 32 : In 1885 Queen's University and the Royal Military College played Canada's first organized hockey game. . . .
1964 *Globe and Mail* (Toronto) 4 Nov. 30/1 : Enlarged newspaper clippings referring to hockey played here [Halifax] in 1833 "proves that this is where it all started," says Ahern, who claims the game was born here in 1828.

hockey baron See quote.
1963 *Globe and Mail* (Toronto) 13 Mar. 7/7 : The jeers were a sign that the hockey barons—the men who rule the NHL and all hockey in North America—are not as solidly planted in their position of command as some people imagine.

hockey cop *Slang* See **policeman** (def. 2).
1963 *Maclean's* 9 Mar. 20 : But mostly, the hockey cops are on the ice to settle fights, not start them.

hockey cushion a hockey rink (def. 1) especially an outdoor rink of natural ice. See also **cushion**.
1965 *Globe and Mail* (Toronto) 5 Jan. 27/4 : Etobicoke Township has 40 hockey cushions with natural ice and five artificial rinks.

hockeyist ['hɑkiɪst] *n.* a person who plays hockey, *q.v.*
1895 *Athletic Life* Mar. 121 : In his stead was elected an equally capable young man in the person of A. B. Code, an enthusiastic hockeyist and vice-president of the Victoria club. **1963** *National Hockey Annual* 36/2 : Shack . . . was actually a reluctant hockeyist and was thrust into the game by his father.

hockeyite ['hɑki‚aɪt] *n. Obs.* a person who plays hockey, *q.v.*
1899 *Medicine Hat News* (Alta) 2 Mar. 8/1 : It appears as though the Moose Jaw hockeyites were not inclined to give our boys a match this season.

hockey puck See **puck**.
1964 *Globe and Mail* (Toronto) 15 Dec. 41/8 : Tom White has produced . . . a "mobile hockey puck," [and] a "hockey stick road adapter."

hockey rink 1 the ice surface, usually surrounded by a board fence, on which hockey, *q.v.*, is played. See also **rink** (def. 1).
1953 *Cdn Geog. Jnl* XLVI 138/2 : The children maintain their own open air hockey rink on the ice of Green River. . . . **1956** YOUNG *Flood* 74 : [He was] a boy who had a good fast body on the hockey rink and a surging need to be really good at something. . . .

2 a place at which hockey games are played and which has seating accommodation for spectators.
1945 PUGSLEY *Saints* 90 : . . . in the early months of the war . . . ratings lived in a converted hockey rink. **1964** *Globe and Mail* (Toronto) 4 Nov. 30/1 : Evidence that the Halifax Public Gardens had the first indoor hockey rink in 1863 . . . will also be included, he says.

A hockey stick

hockey stick a stick specially designed for playing hockey, *q.v.*, having a flat blade at the lower end so angled as to permit the effective control and shooting of a puck.

1897 *Kootenaian* 1 Dec. 1/5: If the mercury will only remain passive . . . the Hockey stick and the puck will be resurrected from their last years hiding place, and sport begin. **1955** *Penticton Herald* (B.C.) 9 Mar. 8/2: The hockey stick was autographed by all the players.

hock-moccasin *n. West, Hist.* See quote. Cp. **shanks.**
1965 SHEPHERD *West of Yesterday* 125: Members of a hunting camp wore hock-moccasins as footwear. These consisted of the skin from the hocks of slaughtered buffalo.

hog reeve† *Maritimes, Hist.* a municipal officer responsible for rounding up stray pigs and assessing whatever damage they may have done to the property of others. Cp. **cattle reeve** and **reeve.**
1825 *P.E.I.Register* (Charlottetown) 17 Feb. 23/2: I am inclined to think, Sir, that the appointment of Hog Reeves will not suffice to remove this increasing nuisance. **1829** *Colonial Patriot* (Pictou, N.S.) 28 Jan. 5/3: We hope at the present sitting of the Session's measures will be to compel the Hog grieves [sic] to do their duty. **1907** *U of T Stud.Hist.& Econ.* II 243: The justices of the peace were appointed to appoint . . . hogreaves, surveyors and weighers of hay. **1942** RADDALL *His Majesty's Yankees* 208: "Gentlemen, this isn't a town meeting selecting a hog reeve; it's a council of war. . . ."

Hogtown ['hɑg,taʊn] *n.* [so called because outsiders accuse Torontonians of taking everything unto themselves] *Slang* Toronto, Ontario.
1959 *Press* Feb. 4: The Sergeant Major had been a Toronto policeman. He suspended KRO as far as guard duty was concerned; we stood watch a straight eight because that was the hours of work for the coppers back in Hogtown. **1963** *Calgary Herald* 28 Nov. 42/1: "Trust it won't take you long to get back into harness . . . after living it up in Hog Town." **1965** *Maclean's* 7 Aug. 38: This, then, is . . . his image . . . a cocky, loud-mouthed, Baptist-baiting, overpaid old blowhard from Hogtown. **1966** *Globe and Mail* (Toronto) 14 Apr. 23/8: "I hope the Canadians [sic], or Frogs as you call them, beat the hell out of your Hogtown heroes."

A carving of a hohoq

hohoq or **hoh-hok** ['ho,hok] *n.* [< Kwakiutl *hūkhwhukw*] *Pacific Coast* See 1964 quote. Cp. **thunderbird** (def. 1a).
1937 *Beaver* Sep. 42/1: What could it matter to the storekeeper whether his [totem] pole was crested with a hoh-hok, a thunderbird, or a raven? **1954** *Ibid.* Mar. 8: [Caption] Mungo Martin . . . paints one of the two rear houseposts he has carved for his new house. Top figure is Ho'hoq, lower is a bear holding a child. **1964** WHERRY *Totem Pole Indians* 83: Hohoq . . . is a very special spirit bird of the mountains. Sometimes he

looks like a white owl; at other times he has an extraordinary long beak. Those who own him as guardian spirit are particularly skilled as sturgeon fishermen.

holding *n.* in hockey, lacrosse, etc., an illegal act in which a player grasps an opponent or his stick so as to hamper his movements.
1963 *Kingston Whig-Standard* (Ont.) 23 Mar. 10/3: Of the 63 minors [Brewer] has served, 18 have been for holding.

holding boom *Lumbering* a large enclosure formed by logs chained together and used for holding floating logs, pulpwood, etc. until ready for transporting to a mill. See also **boom**[1], *n.* (def. 2). Cp. **booming ground**[2] and **pond** (def. 3).
[**1799** SMYTH *Topogr.Descr.U.C.* 32: They are cut upon the banks of the river Welland, and floated down to its mouth, where there is a reservoir made by a chain of logs.] **1958** *Evening Telegram* (St. John's) 6 May 19/1: J. D. Roberts, woods manager, pointed out that the portion which broke was the lead or "sheer" boom and not the main holding boom . . . into which the floating logs are funnelled by the lead booms. **1964** *Atlantic Advocate* July 60: When the flow of the river is down to about 50,000 to 60,000 cubic feet per second, they are allowed to go to the holding boom at Maugerville, near Fredericton. There the logs are sorted from the pulpwood, and both logs and pulpwood are towed separately in booms down river to the mill.

holding ground or **pasture** *West* an enclosure where cattle are temporarily penned during a drive (def. 3a) or round up (def. 1).
1955 HOBSON *Nothing Too Good* 187: We strung the long, snaky, trail herd past two holding grounds this first day of the drive to take some of the snoose out of the ringy Batnuni bunch. **1962** FRY *Ranch on the Cariboo* 171: Soon I reached the main holding ground where a dozen riders ringed a herd of several hundred cows and calves. . . . *Ibid.* 173: . . . we camped on Louie Lake, up the Pinantan road a mile from the holding pasture.

holding water water backed up by some kind of obstruction in a stream so as to create a relatively placid and deep pool.
1964 *Vancouver Province* 14 Feb. 18/3: Most real "holding water" can be easily fly fished. **1966** *Dly Colonist* (Victoria) 27 Feb. 8/2: . . . the sand pool . . . sometimes is holding water for steelhead.

hole† *n.* **1** See 1961 quote. See also **pothole** (def. 5) and **park** (def. 2).
1834-43 (1955) RUSSELL *Journal* 18: This valley is called Jackson hole. . . . **1961** JONES *Trappers* 96: They trapped the beaver streams of the mountain "holes" and "parks," the open, partially wooded valleys of the Rockies.

2 *North, Obs.* a stretch of water free from ice.
1850 (1852) OSBORN *Arctic Jnl* 50: With the "Pioneer's" sharp bow, we broke through the first of these barriers, and carried the "Resolute" into a "hole of water," as it is called. **1852** SUTHERLAND *Baffin's Bay* II 151: One immense floe had toggled across the channel on Hamilton Island, and a little hole of water had made under lee of it to the W.N.W.

holey dollar *P.E.I., Hist.* a Spanish dollar, *q.v.*, having a hole punched in the centre. See also **ring dollar.**
1957 *Maclean's* 3 Aug. 50/3: By a proclamation issued in 1813 the coins were called into Charlottetown, and the centres were punched out and given the value of a shilling. The remainder—a doughnut-shaped piece that came to be called a "holey" dollar—was worth five shillings. **1963** *Commercial Letter* Jan. 6/2: An illustration of such expedient is the "Holey Dollar." In order to prevent the citizens from taking the coins off the Island to areas where the exchange rate was higher, the authorities punched out the centre. The punched out disc was used as a shilling while the outer rim retained the 5s. Halifax currency value. **1964** TAYLOR *Cdn Coins* 19: The Holey Dollar is now a rare collector's item.

A holey dollar

home-and-school *attrib.* of or having to do with the Home and School Association.
1959 *Star Wkly* 22 Aug. 14/2: I had been in his home a few times at home-and-school executive meetings. . . . **1963** *Globe and Mail* (Toronto) 16 May 17/3: Members of home and school associations may like to plan a talk on camping. **1964** *Calgary Herald* 15 May 28/1: This . . . shocked the normally lethargic home and school groups into action. . . .

Home and School Association an organization founded in Toronto in 1919 to promote the well-being of school children through co-operation and the exchange of ideas between parents and teachers.
1955 *Western Star* (Corner Brooke, Nfld) 12 Mar. Back sec. 1/4: An organization which does much to further the educational interests in Deer Lake is the Home and School Association. **1957** *Aklavik Jnl* Apr. 3/1: The Home and School Association nominated four young ladies of the E-3 settlement to run for the title of "MISS ICE QUEEN OF 1957". **1965** *Canadian Wkly* 2-8 Jan. 11/2: . . . post-dance parties [are] organized by the home and school association [in Montreal]. . . .

Home-and-Schooler *n.* a member of the Home and School Association.
1957 *Alta Home and School News* Sept.-Oct. 1/3: Hello to all Home and Scholers in Alberta and the North West Territories.

home boy *Hist.* See 1913 quote. Cp. **Barnardo boy.**
1913 FRANCIS *Cdn Home Boy* iii: The Canadian reader will need no explanation of the title "Home Boy," but to the British reader this term will convey little meaning . . . English readers will understand the stigma that would attach to a boy who has been reared in a workhouse, or a charity school. "He is only a workhouse boy" would be the contemptuous estimation of his position and chances in life. Something of the same meaning is attached to the term "home boy" in Canada. It denotes a boy who has been brought up in some charitable "Home," and from whom little that is good is expected. **1932** JAMIESON *Cattle in the Stall* 192: [A] lonesome little English home boy [was] playing his mouth organ softly in the dusk. . . .

homebred *n. Slang* **1** See **homebrew** (def. 1a).
1958 *Edmonton Jnl* 7 Aug. 7/3: . . . he named no less than six homebreds to the starting offensive lineup for Friday's battle.

2 See **homebrew** (def. 1b).
1962 *National Hockey Annual* 68/2: Perhaps we filled in around our own homebreds with more good men who came in deals—Bob Goldham, for instance.

homebrew *n. Slang* **1 a.** in Canadian professional football, a native-born player. Cp. **import** (def. 2).
1957 *Star Wkly* 17 Aug. 9/1: The Leos still are short of homebrews and are plagued by a problem at quarterback they have never succeeded in solving. **1964** *Winnipeg Free Press* 19 June 36/4: The chief economic factor is that American players, whether Canadianized or not, still draw more salary than homebrews.

b. a local player in any sport; a player trained by the team for which he plays.
1958 *Edmonton Jnl* 18 June 12/3: To make room for import talent en route from the States, Edmonton Eskimos announced the release of 16-year-old homebrew third sacker Gene Kinesewich today. **1962** *Kingston Whig-Standard* (Ont.) 3 Oct. 23/3: We are strictly a homebrew [hockey] club and all positions on the club are wide open. **1964** *Weekend Mag.* 27 June 12/2: . . . the kid boom in British Columbia is the most forceful evidence of "home brew" soccer potential I have encountered.

2 any person or thing of native origin.
1963 *Sun* (Vancouver) 26 Feb. 21/7: Rebel members of the International Brotherhood of Pulp, Sulphite and Paper Mill Workers at Crofton on Vancouver Island have led the first in what could be a series of breakaways from the International union and the formation of a strictly homebrew union to cover 5,000 pulp mill workers in B.C. **1963** *Ubyssey* (Vancouver) 11 Oct. 3/1: I attended the Tuesday noon showing of the production before there was any hint of grief for the home-brew effort, and came to a few personal conclusions about it. **1966** *Globe and Mail* (Toronto) 29 Mar. 14/2: Some of this [applause] can be attributed to local enthusiasm for the home-brew [a playwright].

Home County any of the several counties of the Toronto (Ontario) region. Cp. **Home District** and **Home Riding.**
1963 *Globe and Mail* (Toronto) 26 Mar. 8/4: Mr. Middleton enjoys the distinction of being the only Original Canadian nominee in the Home Counties. He is a Plains Indian.

Home Defence Force *Hist.* during World War II, the force conscripted for service in Canada only.
1959 *Legionary* June 5/4: I refer to the Home Defence Force—the "conscripts" of the last war.

Home District *Hist.* in Upper Canada, the district that included York (Toronto) and adjacent townships. Cp. **Home County** and **Home Riding.**
1798 *U.C.Gaz.* (York [Toronto]) 23 June 3/3: We readily see the necessity of the Home district being divided, and of York being made the capital of a new

district. **1846** TAYLOR *Narrative* 39: Toronto lies in the home district, and is the capital of the Western Province of the United Canadas. **1964** *Cdn Journal of Corrections* Oct. 4: Regarding the condition of the Jail. Thomas Ridout . . . laid before him the Court a letter addressed to him from the Sheriff of the Home District. . . .

Home Government† *Hist.* the British government.
1825 *Colonial Advocate* (York [Toronto]) 14 Apr. 64: The home government correctly estimates our situation. **1921** *Cdn Hist.Rev.* II 357: The Home Government was . . . by no means ready to give Douglas too free a hand in the appointment of officers for the new colony.

home guard 1 See **home-guard. 2** *Lumbering, Slang, Derog.* a logger who works consistently in one camp, especially a family man who becomes a resident logger. Also *homeguard.*
1919 *Camp Worker* 19 Sep. 8/3: Camp poorly organized; too many home guards. **1942** SWANSON *Western Logger* 35: You talk of your drums! you home-guard bums should have seen the size of her 'main'!

home-guard (Indian) *n. Fur Trade, Hist.* **1 a.** an Indian, usually a Cree, living in or near a fur post on Hudson's Bay and employed by the traders. See 1965 quote. See also **half home Indian.** Cp. **Home Indian** and **upland Indian.**
1743 (1949) ISHAM *Observations* 310: . . . a remnant [of Crees] remain'd about the Factories and at present constitute what we call the Home-guard Indians who are become dependant on the English and retain'd by them to procure provisions and perform any other Services. . . . **1784** (1954) *Moose Ft Jnls* 163: Some few of my Homeguard whom have been in have done tolerably well & others as bad indeed the bad outweighs the good. **1959** RICH *Hudson's Bay Co.* I 494: . . . there had also arisen a considerable body of Indians dependent on the posts in a different manner, 'home-guard' Indians who hunted in spring and fall to provide geese and partridges for the English to live on. **1965** *Letters from Hudson Bay* xxiii: The traders divided the Indians into two broad classes, the "Home Guards" and the "Uplanders." The Home Guards, as Samuel Hearne put it [1795], were "certain of the natives who are immediately employed under the protection of the Company's servants, reside on the plantation and are employed in hunting for the Factory."
b. any Indian who lived in or near a fur post, especially those employed as hunters. See also **home hunter** and **post native.**
1849 (1932) MCLEAN *Notes* 99: "Home Guards,"—a term generally applied to the Indians attached to a trading post. . . . **1957** *Beaver* Winter 30/2: The "home guard" Indians who lived in or near a post became the constant friends and familiars of the trader and his staff, and the Indian women helped with the daily chores.

2 See **Home Indian.**
1777 (1954) *Moose Ft Jnls* 345: To me it appears a matter of much consequence to our Welfare as it may happen & Time may prove us only to be fighting about a few Home Guards or Shore Indians, rather confounding the Company's Interest more than we annoy the Inland Pedlars. **1783** (1954) *Ibid.* 19: A family of home guard Indians came in, paid their debts in Rabbits and brought only 5 Martin skins. **1795** (1911) HEARNE *Journey* 49: However, the Northern Indians had address enough to talk my home-guard

Indians out of all they had: so that before we left them, they were as cleanswept as myself, excepting their guns, some ammunition, an old hatchet, an ice-chissel, and a file to sharpen them. **1908** MAIR *Mackenzie Basin* 44: Indeed, he says the [Crees] were called by the Hudson's Bay Company's officers at York Factory "their home guards." **1938** GODSELL *Red Hunters* 36: . . . the place was alive with . . . the "home guard Indians," as the Crees were called, in fringed leggings and bright capotes. . . .

home-guard camp *Lumbering, Slang* a main camp; depot (def. 3) camp.
1956 ANDREWS *Glory Days* 44: Curley also drove a lokey at Daddy Lamb's homeguard camp at Menzies Bay—around 1921. . . .

home-guard language *Obs.* See quote. See also **home-guard** (def. 1b).
1791 LONG *Voyages* x: It may not be amiss to observe, that the Chippeway tongue, as spoken by the servants of the Hudson's Bay Company, is somewhat different, though not essentially so, and is called by them the *Home-Guard* language.

home hunter *Fur Trade, Obs.* a Home Indian, *q.v.*, employed as a hunter supplying meat to a fur post.
1831 (1963) DAVIES *Northern Quebec* 131: Rocher brought five partridges and home hunters ten.

home ice *Hockey* the rink, *q.v.*, where a team plays its home games.
1955 *Shawinigan Standard* 12 Jan. 6: Chicoutimi . . . kept Cats from scoring a victory on their home ice. . . . **1958** *Chauvin Chron.* (Alta) 5 Mar. 9/6: Last Wednesday night on home ice the Regals skated to an easy 11-2 victory. . . .

Home Indian *Fur Trade, Hist.* a Cree Indian from the vicinity of the fur posts on Hudson Bay. See also **home-guard** (def. 2) and **Shore Indian.**
1690 (1929) KELSEY *Papers* 3: Nor none of those home Indians did I see / Untill that they their murder all had done. **1723** (1923) *Beaver* Mar. 234/2: . . . the Last night 2 of our home Inds came here with their families. . . . **1932** KENNEY *Ft Churchill* 53: Knight made a feast for the "Home" Indians, the Crees of the neighbourhood of York Factory, and proposed that they should arrange a peace with their northern neighbours. **1952** MALKUS *Little Giant* 9: When the Home Indians came into the Fort with their furs, he listened to every word of the strange musical Arabeck tongue spoken around Hudson's Bay. . . .

home native *Fur Trade, Obs.* See **home-guard** (def. 1b).
1775 (1951) *Saskatchewan Jnls* 4: . . . arrived at the Place where several Home Natives are waiting to kill Deer, several crossing the River here at times.

home-print *adj. or attrib. Obs.* denoting a newspaper that is set up and printed entirely on the publisher's own equipment.
1896 *Kootenaian* 24 Sep. 2/3: Here you are, a seven-column, all-home-print newspaper, the largest and handsomest paper ever printed in Kaslo. **1898** *Yukon Midnight Sun* (Dawson) 18 July 3/3: The new MIDNIGHT SUN; four pages, seven columns, no boiler plate; no patent inside; all home print . . . nicest souvenir of the Klondike to send home to friends.

home (or homestead) quarter *West* the quarter-section, *q.v.*, on which a homestead (def. 1) is located; the quarter-section first homesteaded.
1881 *Edmonton Bull.* 17 Dec. 2/2: Any occupant of a homestead quarter section having no timber on his own may, upon application, obtain a permit to cut such quantity of building timber, fencing timber or fuel as he may require for use on his homestead.
1954 *Ghost Pine* 30: Charlie . . . filed on the quarter west of ours, and as soon as possible Dad pre-empted the one east of the home quarter.

homer *n. Slang* **1** a supporter of the home-town team.
1961 *Kingston Whig-Standard* (Ont.) 17 Apr. 8/1: The . . . Ontario Intermediate semi-final hockey series isn't for homers. **1964** *Sun* (Vancouver) 10 Apr. 21/3: It's all right to be a homer. I'm in favor of that all the way. But what about the reputation that Toronto fans have for being fair-minded . . . and having a kind word for the underdog?

2 a player or team that plays well in home games.
1962 *Kingston Whig-Standard* (Ont.) 7 Nov. 11/7: In fact, strong "homers" like the Montreal Canadians and Toronto Maple Leafs just didn't lose at home.
1963 *Ibid.* 14 Dec. 10/2: My first impression of Ottawa's Auditorium was a homer's paradise. Last Friday Bill Carter, playing the point, fired a shot into one of the rink's round corners . . . and it caromed right in front of the goal.

3† a referee, umpire, etc. who favors, or is said to favor, the home team.
1963 *Globe and Mail* (Toronto) 11 May 28/7: Emms . . . said the official was strictly a homer and his actions were dictatorial.

Home Riding one of the constituencies in the greater Toronto area. Cp. **Home County** and **Home District.**
1963 *Globe and Mail* (Toronto) 26 Mar. 8/4: 83 to Contest Seats In 21 Home Ridings.

homestake *n. Placer Mining* enough gold to enable a miner to go home and buy a farm or business.
1900 OSBORN *Greater Can.* 111: All those who got far enough down the river found it easy enough to make a "grub-stake," and though a "home-stake" . . . was not so easily found, the Yukon gold-fields obtained a fair reputation among the placer-miners of the coast.
1926 DILL *Long Day* 51: He'll likely go out to the creeks and make a home-stake . . . and then we want his trade.

homestead† *n.* **1** a piece of farmland, including a house and outbuildings, where a family makes its home.
1755 (1895) RICHARD *Acadia* II 77: If we can accomplish this expulsion, it will have been one of the greatest deeds the English in America have ever achieved; for, among other considerations, the part of the country which they occupy is one of the best soils in the world, and, in that event, we might place some good farmers on their homesteads. **1957** *Maclean's* 3 Aug. 48/2: Last year, at fifty-three, he gave his son the Parker homestead and one hundred acres in Ellice first tilled in 1853 by his English-born grandfather.

2 a. a tract of government land taken up by a settler as a grant, especially under the conditions of homestead laws. See **Homestead Act** (def. 2), **Homestead Law** (def. 1), and **location** (def. 1a).
1827 *Gore Gaz.* (Ancaster, U.C.) 2 June 55/1: 1st Capital Prize will consist of . . . part of the homestead of the Subscriber, in the flourishing village of Dundas.
1884 *Moose Jaw News* (Sask.) 9 Jan. 1/5: The majority of the settlers are engaged in getting out logs for houses to be erected on their homesteads next summer.
1966 *Weekend Mag.* 8 Jan. 31: [Caption] These prairie schooners brought Canadians back from Montana to homesteads in the Peace River Country.

b. the house raised on such a piece of land.
1877 (1880) MORRIS *Treaties* 255: In short, I have very little doubt that this portion of the territories, before many years, will abound with herds of cattle, and be dotted with a not a few comfortable homesteads.
1966 *Weekend Mag.* 8 Jan. 31: [Caption] This grassland homestead near Lloydminster, Alta . . . was made out of mud bricks.

homestead† *v.* take up public lands under the conditions of the Homestead Act (def. 2). See also **locate.**
1913 SANDILANDS *West.Cdn Dict.* 23: Any person who is the sole head of a family, or any male over 18 years old, may homestead a quarter-section of available Dominion land in Manitoba, Saskatchewan, or Alberta. **1953** MOON *Saskatchewan* 61: He homesteaded in 1910 near the town of Success. . . . **1962** DICKIE *Great Golden Plain* 263: They [eastern Europeans] homesteaded the poorer, outlying lands; they cleared, dug, ditched, and drained them, using their first money to buy modern machinery. . . .

Homestead Act 1 *Obs.* See **Homestead Law** (def. 1).
1870 *Edmonton Bull.* 11 Feb. 3/1: Why he did so is not very clear, as he being an American citizen must not be entitled to the privileges of the homestead act, and it was under cover of this act that the jump was to be made.

2 an act of Parliament passed in 1872, in full called the Free Land Homestead Act, governing the conditions under which government land was to be settled, especially in the Canadian West. See also **homestead** (def. 2a) and **Homestead Law** (def. 2).
1949 MacGREGOR *Blankets and Beads* 179: . . . The Homesteads Act was actually brought into force in 1882 [sic]. . . . **1964** *Calgary Herald* 10 July 21/1: The department of lands and forests . . . administers the Homestead Act. . . .

homestead entry the process of applying for and taking up land under the Homestead Act (def. 2). Cp. **homestead patent.**
1883 *Brandon Dly Mail* (Man.) 26 Jan. 4/2: To-day an application was made to cancel a homestead entry under circumstances, which promises to make it a test case. **1953** LEBOURDAIS *Nation of North* 117: Homestead entries, numbering 7,800 in 1900, were 22,000 by 1902, and by 1906 reached 41,000.

homesteader† *n.* a settler, especially one who takes up land under the Homestead Act (def. 2).
1882 *Brandon Dly Mail* (Man.) 23 Dec. 4/3: A few days ago some of the neighbors found the old homesteader near his tent dead. **1925** GROVE *Settlers* 29: "Believe an old homesteader like me. By the time you are ready to prove up, in the bush, you've paid for the place in work three times over." **1966** *Maclean's* 19 Feb. 32/4: Up

there [High Level, Alta] Canadian homesteaders are sod-busting in the space age.

homesteaders' Bible *Slang, Hist.* See quote.
1965 SHEPHERD *West of Yesterday* 44: It is said that many a foreign-born settler and his family learned about the way of life, prices of things, and even the art of reading from the mail-order catalogue. Small wonder that it has been called the homesteader's Bible.

homesteader's fiddle *Jocular* a crosscut saw. Cp. **Swedish fiddle.**
1954 PATTERSON *Dangerous River* 174: . . . the monotonous swish of the crosscut saw which, away down south in the Peace River country, I had come to know as "the homesteader's fiddle."

homesteading *n.* settling on land under the conditions of the Homestead Act (def. 2).
1891 *Grip* (Toronto) 13 June 377/1: Mr. Dabin moved that certain settlers in the North-West be granted the privilege of second homesteading. . . . **1960** *Maclean's* 9 Apr. 55/1: Hundreds of families abandoned their farms and . . . crowded the roads in their desperation to reach the parklands or forest belt to the north[,] where a fresh start was made at homesteading—with nothing.

homestead inspector a government official responsible for seeing that homesteaders meet the conditions of the Homestead Act (def. 2).
1883 *Prince Albert Times* (Sask.) 19 Sep. 3/2: The tour of the Government Homestead Inspector amongst the settlers of the locality to find out whether the conditions of the homestead law are being fulfilled is causing a good deal of excitement in the rural districts. **1913** (1914) BICKERSTETH *Open Doors* 244: The homestead inspector for those parts . . . told us that in his opinion there was nothing more remarkable than the way in which English people . . . adapted themselves to the new conditions of life.

homestead land tracts of land set aside by the government for settlement under the Homestead Act (def. 2).
1902 (1956) *Sask.Hist.* IX 2 70: As we rapidly travelled over the country, we could not help noticing that all the homestead lands had been taken. . . . **1961** *Edmonton Jnl* 17 July 3/1: Alberta farmers, caught in drought-parched areas, are also increasing the demand for homestead land in the northwest.

Homestead Law 1 *Hist.* one of the several pieces of legislation governing settlement on government land in Canada prior to the passing of the Homestead Act (def. 2) of 1872.
1848 *Niagara Mail* (Niagara-on-the-Lake, C.W.) 11 Mar. 2/2: Among the important laws that date from this Parliament are the Free Land Grant and Homestead Laws. **1868** *St.Catharines Constitutional* (Ont.) 2 Jan. 2/6: The announcement that the enactment of the Homestead Law with free grants of land to actual settlers, will be included amongst the Ministerial measures, shows that the Government is fully alive to the popular feeling on this question.
2 See **Homestead Act** (def. 2).
1880 GORDON *Mountain and Prairie* 306: He has availed himself of the liberal homestead law, and has pre-empted an adjoining quarter-section, so that he is now the possessor of a farm of 320 acres. **1963** STANLEY *Louis Riel* 262: There were demands . . . for exemption from the operation of the Homestead Law. . . .

homestead patent a legal acknowledgment from the government that a homesteader has met the

requirements of the Homestead Act (def. 2) and is thus the legal owner of the land Cp. **homestead entry.**
1879 *Winnipeg Dly Times* 12 Apr. 4/3: Thus, at the end of three years when their homestead patents are received from the Crown, we frequently find four well fenced farms, each having a house, and stocked with teams, cows, and the necessary farm implements. **1913** SANDILANDS *West.Cdn Dict.* 23: [Homesteaders]— Must reside six months in each of six years from date of homestead entry (including time required to earn homestead patent) and cultivate 50 acres extra.

homestead quarter See **home quarter.**

homestead right the right of a citizen to file on a tract of land under the conditions of the Homestead Act (def. 2).
1871 *Wkly Manitoban* 25 Mar. 3/4: No other person shall be entitled to more than one homestead right. **1954** BEZANSON *Sodbusters* 81: With his family using their homestead rights, plus a scrip or two of a half-section each, they could gain a big farm for an expenditure of a comparatively little besides their labour.

hommack *n.* See **hummock.**

homme du nord *Cdn French, Hist.* See **winterer** (def. 2a).
1918 DAVIDSON *North West Co.* 230: These men were called north men, *hommes du nord,* or winterers.

hommock *n.* See **hummock.**

hone *n.* [< Brit.dial. "swelling"] *Obs.* See **pink salmon.**
1869 *Mainland Guardian* (New Westminster, B.C.) 25 Sep. 2/1: The Oleys or Hones appear every alternate year; they are known as the Humpback salmon, from a peculiar protuberance on the back.

honey bucket *Slang* a receptacle for excreta, as in an outdoor toilet.
1962 VALLEE *Kabloona and Eskimo* 48: ". . . And where do they get the money? From emptying honey buckets for the Whites and mostly sitting on their butts—no sweat for them. . . ." **1964** *Nat.Geog.* May 734/1: In Inuvik there are flush toilets. Here [Sachs Harbour] there is only the "honey bucket" to empty.

honey-house *n.* a shed or other outbuilding equipped with boxes and trays in which bees build up honeycombs.
1947 WELLS *Owl Pen* 40: We would build a honey-house, and a poultry house, and a goat pen.

honey-pot *n. Obs.* See 1835 quote.
1835 *Novascotian* (Halifax) 19 Nov. 339/3: Well, every now and then, when a feller goes to look for his horse— he sees his tail a sticking out on eend, from one of these honey pots, and wavin like a head of broom corn. . . . Most of them are dyke marshes have what they call "honey pots" in them, that is, a deep hole all full of squash, where you cant find no bottom. **1860** (1936) KOHL *Kitchi-Gami* 173: We clambered or stumbled over a chaos of trees six thousand years old, which the Canadians call a "renversi," and through various bottomless swamps and "honeypots". . . .

honker† ['haŋkɚ] *n.* [< the cry made by this bird] See **Canada goose.**

1896 WHITNEY *On Snow-Shoes* 311: There are four kinds of geese: the "honker," or Canadian gray goose; a smaller gray goose; a large white goose, not quite so large as the "honker"; and a smaller white goose. **1963** *Globe and Mail* (Toronto) 13 Mar. 2/2: Four honkers swung in from the bay and followed the coastline past our blind. . . .

hono(u)r box an unattended newspaper stand equipped with a slotted receptacle for coins.
1963 *Albertan* (Calgary) 19 Nov. 1/3: But the street vendor's who operate The Albertan's honor boxes aren't too happy about the 1,100 papers for which they pay out of their own pockets every day. **1965** *Globe and Mail* (Toronto) 6 Jan. 23/2: Frequent thefts of papers and honor boxes have been reported to police since July 9. . . .

hono(u)rs course in certain Canadian universities, a special program of study, usually taking four years after matriculation, offered to better-than-average students who wish to specialize in certain major fields.
1946 LOWER *Colony to Nation* 413: In Ontario . . . the "honours courses" of the Universities exerted an influence present nowhere else. . . . **1955** BIRNEY *Long Table* 41: "Canada, a territory in the far, far north, the continent's roothouse. They have their certain academic skirmishes of a sort which Wasatch College would consider quaint, quaint as bows and arrows. Honours Courses." **1965** *R.M.C. of Canada Calendar* 1965-1966 221: A cadet in Honours Arts in the Third Year must pass in all his courses and . . . maintain a 66% combined average in the courses of his Honours Course of Study, with a mark of at least 60% in each of those Honours courses. . . .

hooch *n.* See **hootch.**

hoochino *n.* See **hootchinoo.**

hood *n.* See **hood seal.**
1859 *Brit.Colonist* (Victoria) 27 July 1/1: The best known . . . are . . . the Harp . . . the Hood . . . and . . . the Squareflipper. **1956** FAY *Life and Labour* 59: The Hoods (now rare) . . . have a hood of loose black skin over the head of the male that it puffs out when angry. **1966** *Weekend Mag.* 19 Mar. 39/1: This year the government has ruled that the hoods will not be killed. This is a major conservation move.

hoodoo ['hudu] *n.* [of African origin, related to *voodoo*] **1** something associated with bad luck, as an evil, malignant spell.
1892 *Medicine Hat Times* (Alta) 15 Dec. 1/3: An Indian woman in the Sioux camp south of town recently gave birth to a child with two heads . . . A dog feast to counteract the "hoodoo" was held on the day following. **1932** KENNEY *Ft Churchill* 67: The hoodoo that seemed to wait on Captain Knight was already at work, for the want of a sailing vessel seriously crippled his movements.

2† a person or thing that brings bad luck; a jinx or Jonah.
1913 SANDILANDS *West.Cdn Dict.* 23/2: Hoodoo, something that brings bad luck; the opposite of mascot. **1924** SHERMAN *Nature Stories* 26: Need we wonder, then, that Jake got it into his head that Jacko was a "hoodoo," as he called it?

3† See **demoiselle** and picture.

[**1793** (**1801**) MACKENZIE *Voy.from Montreal* 233: The banks were here composed of high white cliffs, crowned with pinnacles in very grotesque shapes.] *c***1902** LAUT *Trapper* 160: The gnomes, called in trappers' vernacular "hoodoos" great pillars of sandstone higher than a house, left standing in valleys by prehistoric floods—were to the Crows and Blackfeet petrified giants that only awakened at night to hurl down rocks on intruding mortals. **1940** *Cdn Geog.Jnl* Feb. 84/2: This similarity extends even to such peculiar phenomena as the presence in Jasper Park of a group of hot springs of medicinal value, and earth pillars or "hoodoos" similar to those at Banff. **1962** *Bad Lands of the Red Deer River* 32: Approximately 500 feet across the highway [8 miles east of Drumheller] the fascinating Hoodoos can be seen and examined.

Hoodoo ['hudu] *n.* [< *hoodoo*] a supernatural creature of dangerous and malignant tendencies, as the famed Sasquatch of British Columbia.
1958 KING *Golden Memories* 24: Fear of the enormous Hoodoo that was supposed to haunt the Columbia River Valley made the Indians reluctant to expose themselves to the danger of an encounter with the dreaded monster. **1963** *B.C.Digest* Nov.-Dec. 14/3: To return to B.C., I have read an account by a Golden [B.C.] oldtimer of a giant "Hoodoo" that terrorized the Indians of the region many years ago.

hood seal a large seal of the North Atlantic, *Cystophora cristata.* See also **crested seal, dog-hood** and **hood.** Also *hooded seal.*
1784 PENNANT *Arctic Zoology* 162: Our Seal-hunters name it the Hooded Seal, and pretend they cannot kill it till they remove that integument. **1883** (**1889**) HATTON & HARVEY *Newfoundland* 95: The old male harps appear to be indifferent about their young. The male hood seal, on the other hand assists his mate in her maternal guardianship. . . . **1966** *Weekend Mag.* 19 Mar. 39/1: Last year I surveyed the hood seals and discovered that only a few hundred were still alive; this magnificent animal had been hunted to the brink of extinction.

hoo-haw ['hu,hɑ] *n.* [imitative] *Slang* a dispute; altercation; furor. See also **hoo-raw.**
1959 *Globe and Mail* (Toronto) 13 May 17/8: Yesterday it was tables the participants were concerned about. . . . Today there was a hoo-haw about chairs.

hook *n. Hockey* an instance of hooking, *q.v.*
1965 *Globe and Mail* (Toronto) 3 Dec. 14/1: . . . press box witnesses saw the infraction as more of a hook or slash.

hook¹ *v.* [< *hook* take without permission; steal] **1** See quote.
1934 DENNIS *Down in N.S.* 18: Sometime after Halifax was founded, Bedford Basin was frequently visited by hookers, whose crews came to these shores to "hook" stones for ballast and who were prone to take (or "hook") stones from any beach, regardless of ownership, when they had failed to obtain a return cargo.
2 *Slang* **hook a ride,** beg a ride; hitch a ride.
1958 *Citizen* (Vancouver) 18 Sep. 2/1: He left me . . . and I had to hook a ride home.

hook² *v.* **1** *West, Slang* rake (a horse) with spurs.
1927 (**1929**) JOHNSTON *Beyond Rockies* 88: Rider must hook 'em in the shoulder and holler first jump and then cowboy him in the best way he knows how.
2 *Hockey* check by hooking, *q.v.* See also **hook,** *n.*

1962 *National Hockey Annual* 28/3: "I hate fighting. It doesn't belong in hockey. But this guy Kyle holds and hooks and plays so dirty."

hook-and-line man *Nfld* See **handliner**.

1905 DUNCAN *Grenfell's Parish* 109: Often . . . the hook-and-line man fishes his eighty years of life, and dies in his bed as cheerfully as he has lived and as poor as he was born. **1916** DUNCAN *Billy Topsail* 106: "With me, Tom?" said Sam. "That's a saucy notion for a hook-an'-line man."

hook-check *n. v. Hockey* See **sweep-check**, *n*. and *v*.

1963 O'BRIEN *Hockey* 72: . . . if a defender hook-checks a puck-carrier, knocks the puck away and, in so doing, trips him, it's legal. But if the puck is so far ahead of the defender that he can't reach it, yet he tries a hook-check that trips, he's out.

hooker[1] *n.* **1** *Lumbering* See **hooktender**.

1919 *Camp Worker* 26 Apr. 5/2: There are innumerable firms that have monopolized the services of the best hooker that ever gave signals for the high-rigger, while his short-handed crew changed the haul-back without the assistance of a grass-line. **1960** *Sun* (Vancouver) 2 June 50/8: We invite enquiries from Hookers & Riggers, Head Loaders, Yarder Engineers, etc., who are available now. Call Don Stevenson at B. C. Forest Products. . . .

2 See **stone-hooker**.

1934 DENNIS *Down in N.S.* 17: Sometime after Halifax was founded, Bedford Basin was frequently visited by hookers, whose crews came to these shores to "hook" stones for ballast. . . .

hooker[2] *n.* [< Brit.dial. "large amount"] *Slang* a drink of liquor, especially a generous one.

1887 *Grip* (Toronto) 21 May 12/2: We went in and were served out with a pretty stiff hooker each. . . . **1910** FRASER *Red Meekins* 125: "I'd give up my diamonds for a hooker of whisky. . . ." **1954** KELLY *Black Donnellys* 63: Danny was quiet enough until he got about six hookers under his belt.

hookey *n.* See **hooky**.

hooking *n. Hockey* an illegal check made by using the blade of the hockey stick as a hook to impede a puck-carrier's progress. See also **hook**[2] (def. 2).

1931 *Vancouver Province* 3 Jan. 7/3: Wanderers were reduced to four men against five when McLean was banished for hooking. . . . **1963** *Globe and Mail* (Toronto) 14 Mar. 7/7: [They should] decree sterner and more certain punishment for such offenses as tripping and hooking—the tactic that mediocre players use to stop speedy opponents.

hook-nosed trout *Obs.* See **pink salmon**.

1852 RICHARDSON *Arctic Exped.* 368: Salmon and hook-nosed trout . . . ascend the river, but are not found in the Mackenzie, or rivers falling into the Arctic Sea.

hooktender *n. Lumbering* See 1942 quote. See also **hooker**[1] (def. 1).

1906 *Log of the "Columbia"* June 7/1: "I've been swamper, line-horse man and riggan-slinger for this layout for over 8 years an' now when a chanst comes along to get on hook-tender they put on a bloomin' blue nose, who hasn't been on the coast over a year. . . ." **1942** HAIG-BROWN *Timber* 251: [The] Hooktender or "hooker" [is] in charge of the chokermen and the whole operation of hauling logs from the woods to the railroad track. **1966** *Sun* (Vancouver) 12 Jan. 25/5:

Furthering his point, Moore said the industry needs more managers, logging operators, hook-tenders, machine operators, power saw fallers "and even chokermen."

hooky[1]† [ˈhʊki] *n.* [< Brit.dial. *hook* make off; run away] **play hooky**, stay away from school without permission; play truant. Also spelled *hookey*.

1909 TOWNLEY *Opinions* 54/5: . . . these days you can't play hookey like that. If you're away half a day there's a note from the teacher chasing you up. **1925** OSTENSO *Wild Geese* 102: "Salt of the earth: a school teacher. I was one myself for about a month. Got fired for encouraging the kids to play hookey," he laughed. **1965** *Globe and Mail* (Toronto) 22 Apr. 23/8: It was certainly interesting to read . . . that youngsters who play hooky are not really naughty but are merely afraid of their classrooms.

hooky[2] [ˈhʊki] *n.* [< *hook*, v.] *Lab.* a brittle crust that forms on snow, such that the foot sinks through it causing a person to trip. Also spelled *hookey*.

1933 MERRICK *True North* 218: Another kind of crust [on the snow] is brittle. It trips you every step. The men call it "hookey."

hoop game an Indian game in which a hoop is rolled in such a way as to fall on an arrow slid along the ground just behind it.

1950 STEELE *Ghosts Returning* 104: Children enjoyed their last pre-bedtime Hoop Game, Kit-Foxes danced for their headman. . . .

hooping crane See **whooping crane**.

hoo-raw [ˈhuˌrɑ] *n.* [imitative; influenced by *hurrah*?] *Slang* See **hoo-haw**.

1958 *Herald-Tribune* (Grande Prairie, Alta) 21 Feb. 2/5: . . . pretty soon Canada will have a "Social Register," although not without considerable hoo-raw and the odd "exposure" about its founders.

hooshum (berry) [ˈhuʃəm] *n.* [? < Athapascan] *B.C.* See **soapberry** (def. 2).

1955 TAYLOR *Blackboard* 47: The wild berries were plentiful: Saskatoon berries . . . and "hooshum" berries. . . . **1963** *Sun* (Vancouver) 23 Sep.6/1: The latest weapon in the Lillooet election campaign is whipped hooshum berries. **1965** WILSON *No Man Stands Alone* 79: . . . the soapberry [is] sometimes called Soapallala or Hooshum.

hootch [hutʃ] *n.* [< *hootchino*, q.v.] *Slang* **1** *Yukon* See **hootchinoo**.

1897 HAYNE *Pioneers* 91: The manufacture of "hooch," which is undertaken by the saloon-keepers themselves, is weirdly horrible. **1898** *Medicine Hat News* (Alta) 8 Dec. 5/4: Her parkee, made of Caribou, it is a lovely fit./ And she's all right from muck-a-luck unto her dainty mit./ This lovely Klooch is fond of Hooch, and makes it very well. **1913** OGILVIE *Yukon* 286: Hootch [is] the name given a kind of whisky distilled from the fermentation of flour and molasses. **1958** BERTON *Klondike* 23: Hootch, like everything else, was paid for in gold dust. **1966** BERTON *Centennial Food Guide* 58/2:

Tappen Adney, the Maritimer who was sent to cover the Klondike gold rush by Harper's Illustrated Weekly, reported on that most native of all Canadian drinks, Yukon "hootch," as it was manufactured in 1897-98. . . .

2 any alcoholic drink, especially inferior whisky.
1910 SERVICE *Trail of '98* 216: I can't hold my hootch so well as I could a few summers ago. . . . **1917** *Eye Opener* (Calgary) 6 Jan. 3/5: "I ducks my nut out o' there like a bat outer hell and connects up with a bunch of rough-necks that had some hooch and we puts a touch of real colour into the old town." **1936** MACKENZIE *Living Rough* 239: I guess they had bummed some money some place and invested it in hootch. **1964** *Globe and Mail* (Toronto) 15 Dec. 31/8: The least the authorities could do when they make a raid would be to pack the confiscated hootch and ship to some underprivileged country.

hootchinoo ['hutʃi,nu] *n.* [< Tlingit *khutsnuwu,* literally, grizzly bear fort, an Indian people and village on Admiralty Island, where it was first made] *Yukon* **1** a kind of home brew. See 1937 quote. See also **hootch** (def. 1).
*c***1898** (1966) BERTON *Centennial Food Guide* 58/2: Whenever whisky runs short the Yukoner falls back upon a villanous decoction . . . known as "hootchinoo," or "hootch." **1904** *Yukon Sun* (Dawson) 2 Jan. 4/4: Three-Tongued Lightning from the Peel River did the left alaman with the brown-skinned maiden from the Tanana, while the hootchinoo-soaked son of the Fortymile forest led the grand right and left with the walrus-greased lass from the McKenzie. **1937** ANDREWS *Wrangell* 49: The white man sold them "Forty Rod" whiskey, then taught them to manufacture "Hooch." They were instructed in this art by a discharged soldier named Doyle, who went to Hootznahoo, showed them how to distill a villainous compound from molasses, yeast, berries, sugar, or other compounds. It was first so called from the village, "Hootznahoo" paraphrased as "Hoochinoo," then shortened to "Hooch," and the name lives even until this day. **1958** BERTON *Klondike* 27: Another was to collect the excise duty on all locally made hootchinoo.

2 *Slang* a drinker of hootchinoo; any heavy drinker.
1910 LONDON *Burning Daylight* 35: "And I'm sure going to win, and sixty days is a long time between drinks, so I pay now. Name your brand, you hoochinoos! Name your brand!"

hop-rising *n. Obs.* a homemade leaven made from hops and used in baking a kind of bread.
1836 TRAILL *Backwoods* 137: She must know how to manufacture *hop-rising* or *salt-rising* for leavening her bread. **1852** (1923) MOODIE *Roughing It* 246: But they were out of tea, and the hop-rising had failed, and there was no bread in the house.

hop-yeast bread *Hist.* bread made from hop-rising, *q.v.*
1836 TRAILL *Backwoods* 194: The *salt-rising* makes beautiful bread . . . far whiter and firmer than the hop-yeast bread. **1932** JAMIESON *Cattle in the Stall* 86: Think of . . . the bread-troughs (I had a man of seventy tell me that one had been his cradle!) with their frequent, regular great burdens of hop-yeast bread. . . .

horiniack *n. Obs.* See **orignal**.
1665 (1885) RADISSON *Voyages* 164: The 2nd day att

evening after we landed & boyled an horiniack wch we killed.

horizon ground mist a low mist that extends to the horizon but does not hamper vertical vision.
1946 *Beaver* Dec. 10/2: . . . visibility was impaired, due to the full brilliance of the moon being obstructed by horizon ground mist. . . . At that time the horizon ground mist had slowly crept over the sea and land, and for about half an hour visibility was poor.

hornbeam† *n.* the blue beech, *Carpinus caroliniana;* also, the wood of this tree.
1823 HALIBURTON *General Descr.N.S.* 34: Hornbeam [Carpinus Ostia]. **1832** (1953) RADCLIFF *Letters* 90: Ours [timber] consists of maple, beech, butternut, elm, white ash, hornbeam, a sprinkling of oak, and some cherry and bass wood. **1956** *Native Trees* 124: Blue-Beech *Carpinus caroliniana* . . . [also called] hornbeam.

horned wavey *Obs.* See **Ross's goose**.
1795 (1911) HEARNE *Journey* 442: Horned Wavey. This delicate and diminutive species of the Goose is not much larger than the Mallard Duck. **1945** *Beaver* Sep. 17/1: Described quite accurately by Samuel Hearne . . . —he called it [Ross's Goose] the Horned Wavey from the numerous warts on the bill—nearly a century elapsed before this little goose received a name.

Hornerite movement *Hist.* an evangelical offshoot of the Methodist church, founded by Ralph Horner, a native of Renfrew, Ont.
1961 GREENING *Ottawa* 167: But the old revivalist methods still kept their appeal in some districts, as is shown by the remarkable rise of the Hornerite movement in the Ottawa Valley in the 1890's.

horn-fish *n. Obs.* See **sauger**.
1820 (1823) FRANKLIN *Journey* 93: The occow, or river perch, termed also horn-fish, piccarel, or doré is common, but is not so much esteemed as the attihhawmeg. **1882** JORDAN & GILBERT *Synopsis Fishes N.A.* 526: *Stizostedium canadense* . . . Sauger; Sand-pike; Gray-pike; Horn-fish.

horse-boat† *n. Hist.* a boat propelled by horses working a treadmill that drove the paddle-wheel(s). See also **team-boat** (def. 1).
1829 *Brockville Gaz.* (U.C.) 28 Aug. 2/5: In crossing the lake . . . the Steamboat Montreal and the horse-boat came in contact with each other, but both running in the same direction, neither received injury. **1863** (1930) *Cdn Hist.Rev.* XI 41: During the time that I lived in Laprairie there were no steamers used as ferry boats, nor even a horse boat; we had to cross both at Laprairie and Longueuil in batteaus. **1909** HUNTER *Simcoe County* I 69: The inauguration of steamboats on Lake Simcoe took place in 1832, and a "horseboat" was tried in 1838, but did not work well.

horse brigade *Fur Trade, Hist.* a train of pack horses used in transporting furs and trading goods, especially in the Rockies.
1908 LAUT *Conquest N.W.* II 331: It became apparent that it would be cheaper for the Hudson's Bay Company to ship some of its New Caledonia furs by sea south to the Columbia than to send the packs inland and south by the horse brigades. **1953** *Beaver* Mar. 15: The era of the horse brigades came to an end with the building of the Cariboo Road up the Fraser Canyon and on to the gold mines of the interior. . . .

horse-bun *n. Slang* one of the roundish pieces of the feces of a horse.
1959 *Maclean's* 26 Sep. 37/4: Pinsky caught a frozen

horse-bun on the cheek. **1960** *Ibid.* 27 Aug. 28/4: You could throw snowballs packed with ice or frozen horse-buns. . . .

horse cariole *Hist.* See **cariole** (def. 1b).
1820 (1823) FRANKLIN *Journey* 114: Mr. Back was speedily thrown from his vehicle, and had to join me in my horse-cariole. **1859** (1863) PALLISER *Journals* 122: They had two horse carioles and several dog sleds with provisions for the pic-nic.

horse collar *Slang* a clerical collar.
1958 *Weekend Mag.* 28 June 39/2: I found that out when he got into conversation with the passenger in the chair across the aisle, opposite, who was a clergyman, as could be seen from his horse collar.

horse-drawing *n.* a contest in which teams of horses draw increasingly heavy weights on a stoneboat, *q.v.*, over a ten-foot space until all but the winner are eliminated, the initial weight being 1,000 pounds, additional weights of 500 pounds being added in successive heats. See also **horse-hauling contest.**
☛ *Such contests are said to have originated among logging teamsters in the bush.*
1961 *Can.Month* 6 Oct. 40/2: I don't know a sport that is more disgusting than horse-drawing. **1965** *Kingston Whig-Standard* (Ont.) 16 Sep. 2/4: Two Canadian records were set yesterday by a . . . man who drove his horses to win all three divisions in the horse-drawing competition at the Kingston Fall Fair.

horse-fly *n.* See **bulldog fly.**
1849 ALEXANDER *L'Acadie* II 117: In short . . . the closeness is often times terrible to bear, especially as it is accompanied with . . . the horse-fly, which seems to take the bite out of the flesh. . . . **1963** *B.C.Digest* Nov.-Dec. 41/1: There I was . . . pushing aside Devil's Club with one hand . . . trying to swat aggressive horseflies at the same time. . . .

horseguard *n. Fur Trade, Hist.* **1** an enclosed pasture near a fur post or fort where spare horses were kept under surveillance. See also **guard** (def. 1), **herd-camp** and **horse park.**
1859 (1870) SOUTHESK *Saskatchewan* 129: [I] rode over to the "horse-guard," about three miles away . . . to leave [four horses] who were to be kept there till my return. **1881** *Edmonton Bull.* 3 Jan. 4/2: Strayed from the H.B.C. horse guard, near Sturgeon river, about the 15th of August, a sorrel mare, 4 or 5 years old, white star on the forehead about the size of a half dollar piece, 14 hands high, branded WF on nigh shoulder and nigh hip. **1963** SPRY *Palliser* 94: It was the custom to tie their forelegs together with a soft leather band to keep them from wandering, but at the company horseguard the band had been kept too tight. . . .

2† *Obs.* See **horsekeeper.**
1880 GORDON *Mountain and Prairie* 198: The horses . . . were running wild upon the plateau, and the "horse-guards" moved slowly in search of them. . . .

horse-haul *n. Lumbering* the operation of hauling logs from the bush by means of horses. Cp. **horse-skid.**
1955 *Bush News* (Port Arthur, Ont.) Feb. 7/3: At the present rate, it's expected that the haul will be finished by March 1. Some 250 persons are engaged in the operation plus 55 teams for the horse-haul and several tractors. . . .

horse-hauling contest See **horse-drawing.**
1962 *Dly Gleaner* (Fredericton) 2 Aug. 5/5: The

concluding day's activities features morning and afternoon horse-hauling contests.

horse head *N.S.* See **gray seal.**
1965 *Cdn Geog.Jnl* Sep. 93/1: But despite their impressive size and arrogant Roman noses, which have earned them the local name of "horse heads," the great bulls are rather cowardly and hump down to sea as soon as the seal-taggers land.

horse Indian *Hist.* **1** a Kootenay Indian of the interior of Southern B.C., so called from the practice of travelling by horse rather than canoe.
1888 (1890) ST. MAUR *Impressions* 172: . . . she like all Kootenay women, carried her "quirt," or riding-whip, for they are horse Indians and rarely walk. **1948** HOLLIDAY *Valley of Youth* 150: And for some unknown reason the Indians around Okanagan Lake neither made nor used canoes. Probably they belonged to a different tribe; they were sometimes referred to as horse Indians, and those round the Shuswap Lake as canoe Indians; however in other ways their customs were much the same.

2† See **Plain Indian.**
1954 *Proud Procession* 409: For the Blackfeet, the Piegans and the Bloods kept the land. They were the Horse Indians, war-like, proud, without fear of the white man.

horsekeep *n. Obs.* See **horsekeeper.**
1825 (1931) SIMPSON *Fur Trade* 147: The Coy required no transport it is therefore quite unnecessary to keep a band of Horses, Horsekeeps and Hunters as Single Gentlemen can or ought to be able to Walk.

horsekeeper *n. Fur Trade, Hist.* the person in charge of a horseguard (def. 1). See also **keeper**[1].
1809 (1897) COUES *New Light* II 546: Having purchased a number of horses, I sent three men with them to the horse-keeper's tent. **1824** (1931) SIMPSON *Fur Trade* 69: From thence the Horses should cross over to the Athabasca Portage in charge of 2 Horsekeepers and an Indian hunter, there to remain until Fall. **1859** (1863) PALLISER *Journals* 122: The Horse-keeper gave up his log hut for our use, and we passed a very merry evening. **1949** MACGREGOR *Blankets and Beads* 94: These [horses] he sent out to his horse-keeper some miles up the river to graze. . . .

horse latitudes *Jocular* those parts of Canada where horses, as opposed to dogs, are used as draft animals.
1909 CAMERON *New North* 359: Mrs. Harvey is one of the best horsewomen in the North, and it is clear delight, with her as pilot, to find ourselves once more in the "horse latitudes". . . .

horseman *n.* **1** *West* a rancher who raises horses.
1954 HAGELL *Grass Was Free* v: Then came the empire of the cattleman, the horseman and the unfenced ranch, with its saloons and six-shooters, its branding irons and lariats, its mavericks and slick ears.

2 *Slang* a member of the Royal Canadian Mounted Police, *q.v.*
[*c***1878** (1928) ROSE *Stump Farm* 111:
. . . Our horsemen when they ride.
The sense of duty well discharged
All idle thought sustains;
No other spur to action need
The Riders of the Plains.]

1957 *Maclean's* 7 Dec. 60: "Does she think you're taking him to the army road to wait for the horseman?" **1960** MCNAMEE *Florencia Bay* 21: He had over three hundred dollars in his wallet and he shuffled the edges of the bills to make sure the horseman would realize he was not dealing with a vagrant. **1963** *Calgary Herald* 12 Nov. 21/2: "Here we are with a dozen set of threads [stolen suits] and a good drop [fence] and in walks the horsemen [RCMP]."

horse park *Hist*. See **horseguard** (def. 1).
1941 *Beaver* June 12/1: Here there was a large horse park, one thousand acres in cultivation, a considerable number of cattle and a large dairy.

horse ranch *West* a ranch specializing in the raising of horses.
1888 (1890) ST. MAUR *Impressions* 40: Algernon went for a ride with Mr. Kerfoot, and in the afternoon we all rode over to his horse-ranche. **1910** HAYDON *Riders of Plains* 128: The Blackfeet tribes, also well armed, were less a source of anxiety, but they were in close and tempting proximity to cattle and horse ranches, and it was just possible that the younger chiefs of the Bloods and Blackfeet might kick over the traces. **1934** *Beaver* Sep. 38/1: . . . headquarters were at Fort Kamloops, where in those days the Company maintained a large horse ranch of some two thousand to three thousand animals.

horse scraper See **scraper**.

horse-skid *v. Lumbering* skid logs out of the bush by means of horses. Cp. **horse-haul**.
1957 *Bush News* (Port Arthur, Ont.) June 3/2: The wood is horse-skidded to the road and then truck-hauled to the dump.

horse-skinner *n.* [after *mule-skinner*] *West, Slang* a teamster.
1954 HAGELL *Grass Was Free* 3: Long braided or shot-loaded black-snake lashes on a short stock for horses, long stock for bulls—were the standard whip equipment, and either bull whacker or horse skinner had to be able to make his whip talk.

horse sled or **sleigh** *Hist*. a kind of sled or toboggan drawn by horses. See 1859 quote. See also **horse-toboggan**.
1859 (1870) SOUTHESK *Saskatchewan* 293: Instead of pack-saddles, we were now provided with horse sleds . . . of the simplest nature, nothing more than three thin elastic boards, turned up in front with a strong curve, and firmly fastened together, so as to form a platform about ten feet long, by one and a half wide. A single horse works each of them in shafts, and draws a considerable load without difficulty. **1929** MOBERLY *When Fur Was King* 67: After the last of these trains had departed a brigade of sixty horse-sleds and thirty dog-trains was sent to the Beaver Hills to haul in three hundred buffalo cows previously killed and staged out of the reach of predatory animals. **1956** KEMP *Northern Trader* 15: Men have crossed the Montreal Portage in dog sleighs and horse sleighs, in motor trucks and Caterpillar tractors, but only once in history has man crossed it in a pair of patent-leather shoes.

horse snowshoe a circular snowshoe fitted to horses that have to work in snow. See also **snowshoe** (def. 2).

1919 FRASER *Bulldog Carney* 250: "When the men who were working this mine pulled out they left a lot of heavy truck behind," Carney continued. "There's a forge, coal, tools, and, what I'm thinking of, half a dozen sets of horse snowshoes back there. . . ."
1964 *Western Wkly* 29 Jan. 4/3: The unknown inventor of the first horse snow shoes chose for his model the 'Salish Bear Paw' type as best suited to meet the conditions in the B.C. terrain. . . . The usual human "Bear Paw" was 48 inches diameter; while that which successfully carried a horse was only 12 inches.

A horse snowshoe

horse-toboggan *n. Hist*. See **horse sled**.
1940 *Beaver* March 48/2: The work was done on snowshoes and transportation was carried out with horses and horse-toboggans. **1960** NIX *Mission* 79: At Pitt . . . the snow was now so deep as to be impassable for their wheeled vehicles, so they left these behind and proceeded with horse toboggans.

horse travail(le) *Obs*. See **travois** (def. 2 and picture).
1800 (1897) COUES *New Light* I 142: We saw also . . . old broken horse-travailles. . . . **1867** GALTON *Art of Travel* 56: In a North American Indian horse "travail," the crossing of the poles . . . usually rests on a rough pack-saddle or pad, which a breast-strap keeps from slipping backwards.

horse wrangler† *West* See **wrangler** (def. 1).
1916 WOOD *Tourist's N.W.* 339: Here horses cost $3 a day each, the wages of a guide are $7.50 a day and board, a packer who is also the horse-wrangler, must be hired at $5 a day. **1963** SYMONS *Many Trails* 54: Commonly . . . these tasks had to be performed by the horse wranglers.

hose *v.* [transferred use of a vulgarism referring to the male role in copulation] *Slang* take advantage of; treat unfairly; defeat convincingly, as in a hockey game; trounce.
☞ *Many persons today use this term in complete ignorance of its vulgar origin.*
1964 *Globe and Mail* (Toronto) 15 Dec. 32/1: "I'm sick and tired the way the Rangers get hosed by the officials in this league."

hose reel See **fire-reels**.
1966 *Weekend Mag.* 16 July 31/1: The hose reel being first to arrive, had to roar to a furious halt, its siren moaning low, because of the dog fight in the middle of the pavement.

Hosky *n.* See **Husky**.

hospital district in certain provinces, a district established for purposes of administration of local hospital and medical services.
1955 *Sentinel-Courier* 31 Mar. 5/1: A contract was signed Tuesday between the governing Board of Crystal City Hospital District No. 22 and Hoffman Construction of Morris, Man., for the building of an addition to the present Memorial Hospital in Crystal City. **1958** *Progress* 28 May 2/1: A decision to increase

the bed capacity of the Reston hospital to fifteen beds was the outcome of the meeting of the central board of the Virden hospital district, held in the Court Room at Virden on Friday night.

hospitality centre or **room** *Ont.* a large room or other public place where, under the terms of the liquor laws, alcoholic drinks may be served under a special temporary licence during the holding of some special function, as a carnival, convention, or exhibition.
1963 *Kingston Whig-Standard* (Ont.) 31 Jan. 17/8: One hotel owner . . . suggested . . . the Community Centre as a hospitality Centre so as not to favor any particular hotel. *Ibid.* 17/6: Both the Hotel LaSalle and the Commodore Hotel had the city's only two hospitality rooms, secured by the winter carnival committee.

hostel *n. North* **1** a residential boarding house for Eskimos or Indians attending school away from home. See also **Indian residential hostel.**
1958 *Edmonton Jnl* 24 June 3 17/3: Last January we opened a new school and hostel at Fort Smith. Construction is now underway at the new town of Aklavik of a school and hostel which will be opened sometime next year. **1965** *Globe Mag.* 24 Apr. 19/2: At Fort George . . . there is an Anglican hostel and federal school. . . .

2 See **hostel school.**
1958 *Beaver* Autumn 6/1: Schools are now being built throughout the north, and hostels for children to live in who cannot go to day school near their own homes. **1964** *Kingston Whig-Standard* (Ont.) 17 Dec. 21/1: As well as the children at the school, others at . . . a government hostel in Whitehorse will receive gifts.

hostel school *North* See **residential school.**
1958 *Edmonton Jnl* 24 June 4 8/5: [Coppermine's] federal day school . . . and tent hostel school . . . are attempting to fit Eskimo children into the new way of life that lies ahead of them. **1961** *Time* (Cdn ed.) 25 Aug. 9/2: For Ottawa's Indian Affairs branch, they also fly a school-bus service from remote Indian and Eskimo settlements to federal hostel schools, as well as medical missions.

hot *adj. Mining, Slang* characterized by rich ore finds; potentially rich in minerals.
1953 *North Star* (Yellowknife) July 4/2: The staking rush is not hitting a very high pitch at present, although there are lots of rumors flying around about hot stuff. **1957** *Financial Post* 2 Nov. 58/1: Air survey aircraft specially modified for their earth-probing instruments . . . have criss-crossed many areas of the country to find economically "hot" mineral areas which have become focal points for mining booms (the Bathurst mining area in New Brunswick). **1958** *Admiral Securities Ltd Prospectus* (Regina) 18 July: We will even go further and say that its properties are located IN THE "HOTTEST" MINING DISTRICT IN CANADA TO-DAY . . . an area that is commanding the attention of speculators both in Canada and the United States.

hot-blood *n.* a thoroughbred horse.
1954 HAGELL *Grass Was Free* 84: . . . When you find a hot-blood that knows his way around, that's the baby to tie to. . . . **1961** MITCHELL *Jake and the Kid* 133: "I knew a real smart horse once," Jake said. "Wasn't no hot blood neither—just an ordinary work horse."

hot deck *Lumbering* See quote. See also **hot-deck.** Cp. **cold deck** and **hot pond.**
1952 GOUGH *Story of B.C.* 185: Logs which are piled

together for loading immediately make up a *hot deck;* those left in a pile to be moved later form a *cold deck.*

hot-deck† *v. Lumbering* move logs out of the woods as soon as they are cut. Cp. **cold-deck.**
1939 BEAULIEU & BARTON *Lumber Science* 38: In some places the tractors "hot deck" the logs as they lie scattered.

hotel *n. Informal* a place where alcoholic beverages are sold by the glass. Cp. **beer parlo(u)r.**
☞ *Many of these establishments meet only the minimal requirements for accommodation under the provincial liquor laws.*
1825 *Colonial Advocate* (York [Toronto]) 14 Apr. Supp. 39: New and spacious hotels, at short distances have taken the place of small log hut beer houses. **1888** LEES & CLUTTERBUCK *British Columbia* 35: . . . here every pothouse calls itself an "hotel," and most of the first-rate hotels are dignified by the title of "house." **1935** *Calgary Typo News* 26 Apr. 3/1: Something like 90 per cent of the hotels are in favor of abolishing the regulation and bringing about a situation where men and their wives can sit down together as they do elsewhere. **1963** *Maclean's* 4 May 32/1: After the hotel closed, we went out for coffee.

hot pond *Lumbering* **1** a pond where logs are held for immediate use. Cp. **hot deck.**
1966 *Cdn Pulp and Paper Industry* July 45/1: Sawlogs go directly to the sawmill yard to be unloaded into the hot pond or on to storage piles.

2 See quote.
1966 *Cdn Forest Industries* Nov. 33/2: When winter comes, the frozen logs will be thawed in the hot pond which will be heated by two Eclipse gas-fired heaters. . . . Openings between bays at both ends of the pond allow the water to circulate in the heating process.

hot skidding *Lumbering* See quote.
1942 KOROLEFF *Skidding of Wood* 5/1: It is "hot" skidding if done jointly with cutting wood and "cold" skidding if done later, separately from the cutting.

hot-stove *adj. or attrib.* designating discussions of sports, especially and originally hockey, usually taking place between periods of play.
1959 *Ottawa Citizen* 25 June Supp. 7/1: The auto industry has its own hot-stove league—the off-season gatherings of stylists, planners and engineers who talk of what might have been or what might yet be. **1962** *Hockey Canada* Nov. 12/2: . . . things we have missed may be mulled over in Hot Stove sessions which are as old and as popular as the sport of hockey itself. **1965** *Globe and Mail* (Toronto) 13 Jan. 26/4: King Clancy . . . joined Bower . . . on the Hot Stove panel yesterday. . . .

houlican or **houlikin** *n.* See **oolichan.**

hound *n.* [see 1956 quote] See **old squaw.**
1779 (1792) CARTWRIGHT *Journal* II 440: There were several hounds and gulls, with some pigeons and black-divers among them. **1861** DE BOILIEU *Labrador Life* 160: The bird called the Hound—a graceful fowl, rather larger than a teal—is very abundant. **1956** MCATEE *Folk-Names* 14: Old Squaw [is also called] hound (the Chorus of sound from a number of these birds suggests the baying of a pack of hounds. Nfld., "Labr.", N.S.). . . .

house *n.* **1** *Fur Trade* a trading post, especially, in later years, an inland post.

1690 (1929) KELSEY *Papers* 2: Distance from hence by Judgement at ye lest From ye house six hundred miles southwest. **1779** (1934) TURNOR *Journal* 255: Good Pine or Poplar might be got near the House fit for Planking and Birch or a kind of Hickery fit for Knees and Timbers. **1828** (1872) MCDONALD *Peace River* 20: They [Sicanee] seem to deserve a house somewhere, for their country is rich in beaver. **1873** (1883) BUTLER *Great Lone Land* 108: Finlay's House, and Mackay's House. These "houses" were the trading posts of the first English Free-traders, whose combination in 1783 gave rise to the great North-West Fur Company. **1966** *Globe and Mail* (Toronto) 18 May 6/1: He's . . . a Cree from the Cumberland House region of Saskatchewan. . . .

2 *Obs.* See **beaver lodge**. See also **beaver house**.

1743 (1949) ISHAM *Observations* 144: they [beaver] have a house they build mostly by creeks or Rivilets, the strength & Curiousness of which house would puzle a good workman to do the Like. . . . **1748** DRAGE *Voyage* I 139: The Plenty of Water was not natural to the Place, but owing to its being kept up by Dams, the Work of the Beavers; which Animals had also built a House on the Side of this Creek.

3 See **trap house**.

1965 *Star Wkly* 23 Jan. 36/3: For mink, fisher or marten Mr. Paquette makes a "house" of sticks and stones containing a bait of meat or fish, with the trap in the entrance.

house-moccasin *n.* a soft, comfortable moccasin (def. 1) for wearing indoors; moccasin slipper.

1900 LONDON *Son of Wolf* 172: Madeline raised a foot and regarded her shapeless house-moccasin dubiously. **1902** LONDON *Daughter of Snows* 43: She put her wet shoes on a pile of wood at the back of the stove, substituting for them a pair of soft and dainty house-moccasins of Indian make.

House of Assembly 1 a. *Hist.* the legislative body in a province of British North America, usually the lower of two bodies, the upper, called the Executive Council, sometimes being included in the designation. See also **House of Commons** (def. 1), **House of Parliament** (def. 1), and **Lower House**.

☛ *Such assemblies had varied composition and power during the colonial period.*
1789 (1905) *Ont.Bur.Arch.Rep.* II 23: The new-comers from the States have again raised a cry for a House of Assembly, and wish to put an end to the "Quebec Bill," under which the great body of the people, the Canadians, live happily. **1811** *Montreal Herald* 23 Nov. 3/3: Canada abounds with men of abilities . . . who would be an honour and an ornament to our House of Assembly. . . . **1832** BAILLIE *Account of N.B.* 126: The House of Assembly consists of 28 members, who are chosen by the freeholders. . . . **1948** BORRETT *Historic Halifax* 146: He stated that the House of Assembly had addressed him, requesting that a patent might be issued toward carrying into effect the purposes intended in the said petition. . . .

b. *Nfld* the provincial legislative assembly.

1832 *Liberal* (St. Thomas, U.C.) 25 Oct. 3/1: St. Johns, N.F. Sept. 5 . . . In consequence of an application from the inhabitants of Newfoundland, the island is to have

a Miniature Legislature, with a House of Assembly composed of sixty members. **1883** HATTON & HARVEY *Newfoundland* 443: The system did not work well, and in 1842 the constitution was suspended, and the council abolished as a distinct branch of Legislature, and its members were authorised to sit and vote in the House of Assembly, on the same footing as if they were elected members. **1958** *Evening Telegram* (St. John's) 2 May 4/7: Hon. John Stone . . . will be sworn in at the session of the House of Assembly this afternoon.

2 the chamber or building in which such an assembly meets. See also **House of Parliament** (def. 2).

1808 (1866) CHRISTIE *Lower Canada* 117: There is reason to apprehend that the time is fast approaching when the House of Assembly of Lower Canada will become the centre of sedition, and a receptacle for the most desparate demagogues in the Province. **1858** *Brit. Colonist* (Victoria) 11 Dec. 3/1: In the conference between the Executive and the House of Assembly [B.C.] a different position was affirmed. . . . **1863** WALSHE *Cedar Creek* 56: . . . in 1840 the provinces of Upper and Lower Canada were legally united; their representatives met in the same House of Assembly. . . . **1955** *Bridgewater Bull.* 9 Mar. 1/7: . . . all letters or communications forwarded to either of us at The House of Assembly, Halifax, N.S., will receive our earnest and careful attention.

House of Commons 1 *Obs.* See **House of Assembly** (def. 1a).

1835 (1838) HALIBURTON *Sam Slick* 10: ". . . If he was in your House of Commons, I reckon he'd make some of your great folks look pretty streaked—he's a true patriot and statesman. . . ."

2 since 1867, the lower house of the Canadian Parliament.

1867 *Islander* (Charlottetown) 8 Mar. 2/5: The Upper House is to be styled "Senate," and the Lower House "House of Commons." **1963** *Globe and Mail* (Toronto) 2 Feb. 2/5: I got to Ottawa and discovered the House of Commons rules were only in English, but not one French member had asked for a translation.

House of Parliament *Hist.* **1** See **House of Assembly** (def. 1a).

1825 *Colonial Advocate* (York [Toronto]) 20 Jan. 2/5: A corn broom, or a hot brick, has turned the House of Parliament out of doors, and here is the Gazette, threatening destruction to the market-square, some windy morning. **1893** YEIGH *Ontario Parliament* 87: Baldwin audaciously insisted that a member of the House was not entitled to the privilege of non-arrest, as it was a House of Assembly only, and not a House of Parliament.

2 See **House of Assembly** (def. 2).

1904 DECELLES *Cartier* 32: When Lord Elgin gave the royal assent to the Indemnity Bill, he was not with the mob that . . . burned the house of parliament. . . .

house-pole *n.* See **house-post**.

1885 *Trans.Roy.Soc.Can.* III 2 82: The symbols of the four clans—the eagle, beaver, dog-fish, and black duck,—are represented in conventional style on the carved house-pole, along with their individual or family totems.

house-post *n.* *Pacific Coast* one of several posts supporting the framework of an Indian building, often carved and decorated to symbolize identification with a certain clan or family. See also **house-pole** and **lodgepole** (def. 2). Cp. **totem pole**.

1906 HOLMES *Anthropological Papers* 180: Among the

Northwest Coast tribes, totem-poles, house-posts, mortuary columns, masks, batons, pipes, and various implements and utensils, represent the forms of beasts, men, and monsters, in relief and in the round.
1964 *Camsell Arrow* Summer 84/3: The two short totems surmounted by Thunderbirds are twin house-posts which supported beams in the home of Kwakiutl Chief Tsa-wee-nox, of Kingcome Inlet.

house-raising† *n. Hist.* in colonial times especially, a community gathering, or bee, *q.v.*, for the purpose of helping a neighbor to build a house. See also **raising bee**. Cp. **barn-raising.**
1829 *Vindicator* (Montreal) 22 Dec. 3/2: A man, of the name of Redmons, who, with some others, attended at a house-raising six miles from this town, was, whilst returning to his home, murdered. **1834** (1926) LANGTON *Early U.C.* 104: . . . we were obliged to spend a long evening at the tavern, which was unusually full in consequence of a house-raising in the neighbourhood. . . . **1912** POCOCK *Man in the Open* 128: Of course our house-raising was a celebration, with a dance, camp-fire, water-butt full of punch, and headaches.

how† [haʊ] *interj.* [cf. Siouan *hâo*] in Indian parlance, an expression used for several purposes, as when greeting someone, thanking him, registering approval, etc.
1886 *Indian* (Hagersville, Ont.) 26 May 111/1: A chorus of "How! How! How!" followed every appeal the medicine man made to the circle of half-naked and battle-scarred warriors. **1913** COWIE *Adventurers* 317: The tea and tobacco which La Pierre and I measured out to them was received with many a "How How" of thanks. **1956** *Beaver* Summer 34/1: An ill-founded legend insists that Indians are inarticulate, content to make "How!" a conversation. **1962** *Alta Hist.Rev.* Autumn 11/1: The Blackfoot Indians usually greet a white man with "How, How!" sometimes, "How wa-pe," perhaps an imitation of the English "How do you do?"

howk *v*. See **hawk.**

hu *interj.* See **hew,** *interj.*

huchemaw *n. Obs.* See **ogema.**

huckleberry [ˈhʌkəlˌbɛri] *n.* [prob. a variant of *hurtleberry*] **1** a shrub of the genus *Gaylussacia;* also its edible, bluish-black berries.
☛ *This term is also used to refer to the blueberry, Vaccinium sp., as may, in fact, be the case in some of the following quotations.*
1743 (1949) ISHAM *Observations* 26: a Huckle Berrie Mis ke ma na. **1852** (1881) TRAILL *Cdn Crusoes* 266: "We shall have neither huckleberries nor strawberries this summer," she said, mournfully. . . . **1902** ROBERTS *Kindred of Wild* 70: The point he chose was where a dense growth of huckleberry and withe-wood ran out to within a few feet of the water's edge, and where the sand of the beach was dotted thickly with tufts of grass. **1958** HEALEY *Alert Bay* 76: They . . . lived off the land, utilizing fish . . . salmon berries, silver currants and huckleberries (blue, red, to jet black). . . . **1959** *Chatelaine* July 64/2: A few huckleberries glimmered frostily blue among the russet leaves.

2 *Slang* a trite saying; cliché.
1957 *UE Cdn News* 1 Nov. 2/3: "Things could always be worse" is another of the old huckleberries usually uttered by folk who never had it better.

huddy [ˈhʌdi] *n.* [origin unknown] See **hew,** *interj.*
1957 *Beaver* Autumn 28/2: He does not know the origin of most of these words but he tells me that "keebaw" stands for "keep off" and means "keep to the right" (keep to the "off" or right side, as with a horse?) and that "huddy" means "keep left." "Fa!" which seems to be the driving word, may have had its origin in the French word *"Va"* (go!).

Hudson Bay See **Hudson's Bay** and combinations.
☛ *In modern usage the body of water in northern Canada is referred to as Hudson Bay, but the trading company is properly called the Hudson's Bay Company. All entries referring to this company are entered under the traditional **Hudson's** form; other entries are shown under **Hudson**, even though the longer form may have been used for them in earlier times. See also **H.B., H.B.C.,** etc.*

Hudson Bay bird 1 *Rare* the great northern shrike, *Lanius borealis.*
1888 (1890) ST. MAUR *Impressions* 273: My friend of the woods, the moose-bird. . . . I found his real name was the great northern shrike, *Lanius borealis;* he has many aliases, being also called the Hudson's Bay bird.

2 See **Canada jay.**
1891 (1892) PIKE *Barren Grounds* 123: This bird is common throughout the wilder parts of Canada, and has acquired many names in different places; in the mountains of British Columbia he is the Hudson Bay bird or grease bird, and far away to the East the moose bird, caribou bird, Rupert's bird, and camp-robber. **1910** FERGUSON *Janey Canuck* 93: This was the Whisky Jack of which I had heard so much. He is a cross between the shrikes and the jays. He has several names, such as Hudson's Bay bird, Oregon jay, and moose bird. **1959** MCATEE *Folk-Names* 50: Grey Jay [is also called] Hudson Bay bird (B.C.). . . .

Hudson Bay fashion or **style** See quotes.
1880 GORDON *Mountain and Prairie* 164: Thankful for such an unexpected conveyance, we were ready to adopt what is called the Hudson's Bay fashion,—that is, to use anything you can get which will serve your turn, and let the next man forage for himself.
1935 *Beaver* Sep. 6/1: "Hudson Bay style for them," he said, "Kick, bite and scratch". . . ."Hudson Bay style" was a reference not to the Company but to the old-time free-for-all fighting among boatmen and voyageurs where there were no rounds, rings or Marquis of Queensbury rules.

Hudson Bay Railway the first railway into the Canadian North, from Winnipeg to Churchill, Manitoba, completed in 1932. See also **Highball Express** and **muskeg railway** (def. 1).
1927 *Beaver* Dec. 121: Setting Lake is now an important divisional point on the Hudson Bay railway . . . Roundhouses, yards, water tanks, freight sheds, etc., have been erected by the Canadian National Railways. **1931** *Ibid.* 383: The completion of the Hudson Bay railway to Churchill marks another step in the opening of the great Northland.

Hudson Bay route *Hist.* the proposed route for the Hudson Bay Railway, *q.v.*
1908 MAIR *Mackenzie Basin* 110: If the Hudson's Bay route were developed, a short line of rail from the western end of Chesterfield Inlet would tap the mining regions prospected. . . . **1913** SANDILANDS *West.Cdn*

Dict. 24/1: [The] Hudson Bay route [is] a proposed new route to reduce the length of the journey between the wheat fields of the West and the markets of Europe. **1932** MUNN *Prairie Trails* 218: The Dominion Government have now nearly completed the railway to Hudson Bay, and "the Hudson Bay route" will soon be an accomplished fact. . . .

Hudson Bay sable the fur of the marten, *q.v.* (a trade name).
1909 CAMERON *New North* 150: Included in these London sales [of fur] are some hundred thousand martens, or Hudson Bay sables, and probably four times that number of mink. **1951** ANGIER *At home* 137: There was the finest marten in the world, with a glossy and luxuriant fur sold by some retailers as Hudson Bay Sable.

Hudson Bay salt side *Hist.* a kind of salt pork.
1963 SYMONS *Many Trails* 169: . . . they were introduced to the salted variety, known as "Hudson Bay salt side."

Hudson Bay Seal See **Hudson seal.**
1914 JONES *Fur Farming in Canada* 7: When the furdressers and dyers produced a clipped and dyed muskrat skin that resembled sealskin almost perfectly, it was found that it would not sell under its own name . . . [the] high-priced fur is now sold as 'Hudson Bay seal.'

Hudson Bay squirrel *Obs.* the red squirrel, *Sciurus hudsonicus.*
1826 GODMAN *Am.Natural History* II 138: The Hudson's Bay Squirrel . . . is very common in the northern and western parts of this Country. **1833** TYLER *Progress of Discovery* 340: The chickaree or Hudson's Bay squirrel . . . inhabits the forests of white spruce-trees which cover so vast a portion of the fur countries.

Hudson Bay style See **Hudson Bay fashion.**

Hudson Bay tea See **Labrador tea** (def. 1).
1948 *Beaver* Mar. 14/2: . . . a tea used to be made from Hudson's Bay tea or Labrador tea (*Ledum*). . . . **1957** LEWIS *Buckskin Cookery* I 31: "HUDSON BAY TEA" (Nazko Indian) Pick whole bush and hang up to dry in shed. Take leaves off and boil in water. Needs more tea than white man's tea. **1960** CRONIN *Cross* 67: . . . the Indian food consisted of baked moss, dried berries and roots, washed down by a brew made from the Hudson's Bay tea shrub (*Ledum Groenlandicum*). . . .

Hudson Bay toboggan *North* See **cariole** (def. 2a and picture).
1895 MUNROE *Snow-Shoes* 78: They were to use the ingalik, or regular Yukon sledge, which is much lighter than the Eskimo, or coast sledge, but heavier and stronger than the Hudson Bay toboggan commonly used in the interior.

Hudsonian [hʌd'soniən] *adj.* [< *Hudson* Bay] of or associated with Hudson Bay. See combinations that follow.

Hudsonian chickadee† a brown-headed chickadee, *Parus hudsonicus,* common in northern Canada.
1908 MAIR *Mackenzie Basin* 431: [List] Hudsonian chickadee. **1939** *Beaver* June 48/1: The Hudsonian chickadees and Canada jays would come near, making

life a bit more cheerful. **1956** *Explorer* 9 Dec. 396/1: Chicadees are never far from our yard, both the brown-headed Hudsonian and the more numerous Blackcaps.

Hudsonian curlew a short-billed curlew, *Numenius phaeopus hudsonicus,* that breeds in northern Canada.
1890 *Trans.Hist.& Sci.Soc.Man.* 39 17: Hudsonian Curlew . . . is by no means rare in the "Barrens" to the west of the lower Anderson, where the Esquimaux discovered some thirteen well identified nests with eggs. **1952** STANWELL-FLETCHER *Tundra World* 42: . . . I was startled by a series of loud, wild "tit-tit-tit-tit-tit" notes from a big brown bird which leapt into the air a few feet in front. A Hudsonian curlew of course.

Hudsonian godwit a blacktailed godwit, *Limosa haemastica,* that breeds in the Barren Grounds.
1908 MAIR *Mackenzie Basin* 334: [List] Hudsonian godwit. **1937** *Beaver* Mar. 48/1: The stilt sandpiper, Hudsonian curlew, yellow-legs, Hudsonian godwit and buff-breasted sandpiper all make a round trip to the Argentine. **1952** STANWELL-FLETCHER *Tundra World* 198: The Hudsonian godwit is an interesting bird. . . .

Hudsonian zone a biogeographic zone stretching from Labrador to Alaska, bounded on the south by the timber line (def. 2) and being roughly co-terminous with the Barren Grounds, *q.v.*
1942 TWOMEY & HERRICK *Needle to North* 79: The south banks are strictly transition territory, from the last of the bush to the true barren land—a no-man's country between Hudsonian zone and the northern tundra. **1952** PUTNAM *Cdn Regions* 139/1: The Hudsonian Life Zone . . . extends from the timber limit to the south of James Bay, Lake Mistassini and Pointe de Monts on the North Shore.

Hudson's (or Hudson) Bay
☞ *See note at* **Hudson Bay.**
1 a. See **Hudson's Bay Company.**
1912 POCOCK *Man in the Open* 5: All us Liveyeres owed to the Hudson's Bay. . . . **1958** *Native Voice* Sp.ed. 16: As the loss of life mounted, the old people claimed the Hudson's Bay had put germs in the sugar to kill off the Indians.
b. (attributive uses) of or associated with the Hudson's Bay Company.
1793 (1933) MACDONELL *Diary* 108: The Hu[d]son's Bay Party is here with us. **1873** (1904) BUTLER *Wild North Land* 223: Spanker and his six companions here passed from my hands, and remained at St. John's to idle through the approaching summer, and then to take their places as Hudson Bay hauling-dogs. **1934** GODSELL *Arctic Trader* 200: . . . members of the staff [were] all wearing their best suits and nautical caps decorated with Hudson's Bay badges. **1966** *Islander* 27 Feb. 13/2: When he sensed the overburdening opinion of Hudson's Bay men in the Island legislature, he plumped for reform.

2 an officer or servant of the Hudson's Bay Company.
1893 OXLEY *Young Nor'Wester* 211: ". . . If he isn't, we're all wrong, Virginie. Could the Hudson Bays have interfered with him, I wonder?" and the factor knitted his brow perplexedly.

3 See **Hudson's Bay blanket** (def. 1a).
1920 STRINGER *Prairie Mother* 299: I sat there wrapped up in one of Dunky-Dunk's four-point Hudson-Bays. . . .
1943 (1953) SWANSON *Haywire Hooker* 51:
The stranger smiles and then he says:
"Why, them is four point Hudson Bays!

I hated to leave them back down there,
They're worth 'bout eighteen bucks a pair."

Hudson's Bay bateau or **boat** *Hist.* See **York boat** and picture.

1871 (1883) BUTLER *Great Lone Land* 174: . . . we came suddenly upon four large Hudson Bay boats with full crews of Red River half-breeds and Indians. . . . **1913** ROTHROCK *Collin's Overland Exped.* (*MSS*): August we left Fort St. James in a Hudson Bay bateau for Lake Takla.

Hudson's Bay bill *Hist.* paper currency issued by the Hudson's Bay Company in the amounts of five shillings and five pounds. See also **Hudson's Bay blanket** (def. 2b). Cp. **Hudson's Bay token.**

1870 *Wkly Manitoban* 26 Nov. 2/6: Our currency . . . Hudson's Bay Bills, Canada Provincial Notes and U.S. Greenbacks.

Hudson's Bay blanket 1 a. a durable woollen blanket long sold by the Hudson's Bay Company. See **Hudson's Bay** (def. 3) and **point blanket.**

1900 LONDON *Son of Wolf* 181: Prince wrapped a Hudson Bay blanket about her with a mock reverence more real than feigned. . . . **1921** HEMING *Drama of Forests* 161: It is my experience that there is no easier way to get rid of a bad cold than to sleep out in the snow, wrapped in a Hudson's Bay blanket, a caribou robe, or a rabbit-skin quilt, when the thermometer is about fifty below zero. **1963** *Globe and Mail* (Toronto) 13 Mar. 17/1: I recall a motel in Manitoba that insisted we bring our muddy dogs indoors where they slept on scarlet Hudson's Bay blankets at the foot of the beds.

b. *Figurative use.* See quote.

1939 (1951) TWEEDSMUIR *Hudson's Bay Trader* 85: The blizzard is your greatest enemy. Then the fall of heavy flakes—which obliterates tracks and wipes out visibility—which in the North they call "Snowing Hudson's Bay blankets," has brought many of the hardiest travellers to losing their way.

2 *Hist.* **a.** See quotes.

1897 *Rev.Hist.Pubs* I 65: The company had its own paper currency after 1825—"Hudson's Bay blankets" the notes were called. **1923** *Beaver* Oct. 5/2: The currency of the time [c1821] consisted largely of "Hudson's Bay blankets," which were notes for one pound, five shillings, and one shilling each. **1963** *Albertan* (Calgary) 4 May 8/8: The York factory, of the Hudson's Bay Co. also issued paper currency in the denominations of one Shilling, five Shilling and 1 Pound Notes. [These] . . . four and three quarters inches by nine and three eighths inches . . . known as "Hudson's Bay Blankets," were used extensively throughout Western Canada.

b. See **Hudson's Bay bill.**

1896 MCDOUGALL *Saddle, Sled and Snowshoe* 147: I handled, in making my purchases, the first "Hudson's Bay blankets" I had every seen. These were large 5s. and £5 notes, issued by the Company. . . . **1955** RUSSELL *Carlton Trail* 37: He also saw "Hudson's Bay blankets" for the first time. These were large five-shilling and five-pound notes issued by the Company.

Hudson's Bay blanket coat a warm woollen coat made of the same material as Hudson's Bay blankets. See also **point-blanket coat.**

1912 CONNOR *Corp.Cameron* 438: Tall, she looked . . . lithe and strong, her close-fitting Hudson Bay blanket coat revealing the swelling lines of her budding womanhood. **1955** HARDY *Alta Anthol.* 85: In his last days, the old warrior was a familiar sight in his Hudson Bay

blanket coat and was often pointed out as the surviving link with a great bygone era of buffalo hunts, war parties and scalp dances.

Hudson's Bay boat See **Hudson's Bay bateau.**

Hudson's Bay canoe *Hist.* See **Montreal canoe** and picture.

1961 PRICE & KENNEDY *Renfrew* 30: Matt Bernard . . . supervises the launching of a large Hudson's Bay type canoe (canot du maître or Montreal canoe) which he completed Sept. 28, 1957.

Hudson's Bay cap a distinctive cap formerly worn by servants of the Hudson's Bay Company, characterized by a soft crown of blue cloth and a visor with a shiny leather peak, and resembling a seaman's peaked cap.

[**1913** COWIE *Adventurers* 116: It appeared the approved uniform [in 1867] for clerks on the boat journey was a greyish blue cloth "Illinois" capote with silverplated buttons, and a broad scarlet worsted sash, the regulation headgear being a fine navy blue cloth cap with a leather peak.] **1939** *Beaver* Sep. 23: The oarsmen wearing Hudson's Bay caps with shiny peaks and a squirrel tail stuck in the gold band. **1943** *Ibid.* Mar. 19: On shore only one man kept, Willie Smith in his cocky Hudson's Bay cap.

Hudson's Bay capote *Hist.* a heavy blue capote (def. 1) furnished with metal buttons and worn as a part of the winter uniform by servants of the Hudson's Bay Company. See also **Illinois capote.**

1880 GORDON *Mountain and Prairie* 191: Some wore the old Hudson's Bay capote of navy-blue cloth with brass buttons.

Hudson's Bay Company the popular and traditional name of the Company of Adventurers of England trading into Hudson's Bay, chartered by Charles II in 1670. See also **Hudson's** (def. 1a), **John Company,** and **Old Company.**

1684 (1885) RADISSON *Voyages* 252: At the time my Brother-in-Law and I were dissatisfy'd with the Hudson's Bay Company, wee were severall times invited by the laste Monsieur Colbert to return back for france, with large promises that wee should bee very kindly entertain'd. **1744** DOBBS *Hudson's Bay* 2: The Reason why the Manner of living there at present appears to be so dismal to us in Britain, is intirely owing to the Monopoly and Avarice of the Hudson's Bay Company, (not to give it a harsher Name) who, to deter others from trading there, or making Settlements, conceal all the Advantages to be made in that Country, and give out, that the Climate, and Counutry, and Passage thither, are much worse, and more dangerous, than they really are. **1861** *Nor'Wester* (R.R.S.) 1 Feb. 2/4: The Magna Carta of the Hudson's Bay Company dates not exactly from 1215, nor does it bear the signature of the despicable King James; still it dates back far enough to be respectable for years if not for its master or its author. **1965** *Globe and Mail* (Toronto) 12 Jan. 31/8: . . . the paddles of the great trade craft . . . carried the brigades of the North West and Hudson's Bay companies into the far northern wilderness.

Hudson's Bay Company store a trading post of the Hudson's Bay Company. Also *Hudson's Bay Store.*

[**1898** (1960) ELLIOTT *Klondike* 13: Hazleton is an extremely one horse place consisting chiefly of the Hudson's Bay Co.'s store, and another store, an Indian Agent's residence, and an English church mission of sorts.] **1930** ROLYAT *Fort Garry* 68: ... she turned to the door of the Hudson Bay store which had all at once opened stiffly with a sharp, whizzing report.... **1963** *Maclean's* 23 Feb. 43/1: Their village was now abandoned, and the deserted, ghostly buildings, including the Hudson's Bay Company stores and the Anglican church, were a depressing reminder of what we were there for.

Hudson's Bay dollar See **Hudson's Bay token.**

Hudson's Bay fashion See **Hudson Bay fashion.**

Hudson's Bay harness See **tumpline** and picture.
1922 *Beaver* July 10/1: The hardy voyageur of the paddle and tumpline, or "Hudson's Bay harness" as it is termed in York boat parlance. **1941** COTTER *Fur Trade Glossary*: Hudson's Bay Harness—[is] A sarcastic allusion to the portage strap.

Hudson's Bay Hymn Book *Jocular* the ledger in which the Hudson's Bay Company recorded debt, *q.v.*, taken by trappers.
1941 COTTER *Fur Trade Glossary*: Hudson's Bay Hymn Book—The Indian ledger.

Hudson's Bay Indian See **Company Indian.**
1887 DAWSON *Tribes of Yukon* 9: The Kaska are still more closely allied by language and marriage to the Indians of the Lower Liard, who are commonly referred to as the "Hudson Bay Indians," from the circumstance that they trade with that company. **1933** MERRICK *True North* 59: Arch told me they were old juniper sticks that Louie and his H.B.C. Indians put there long ago.

Hudson's Bay land See **Hudson's Bay reserve.**
1925 GROVE *Settlers* 125: He bought a half section of Hudson's Bay land, just across the creek, north of the bridge.

Hudson's Bay pointer *Fur Trade, Hist.* See **pointer** (def. 2).
1909 CONNOR *Foreigner* 189: Down these streams and rivers floated the great fur brigades in canoe and Hudson's Bay pointer with priceless bales of pelts to the Bay in the north or the Lakes in the south....

Hudson's Bay reserve *Hist.* one of a number of tracts of land surrounding fur posts, reserved for the Hudson's Bay Company when its claim to sovereignty in Rupert's Land was transferred to Canada by the Manitoba Act of 1870; also, these tracts collectively. See also **Hudson's Bay land.**
1883 *Prince Albert Times* (Sask.) 16 May 2/1: These with the odd numbered sections, the school and Hudson's Bay reserves, form a large part of the country.... **1912** (1914) BICKERSTETH *Open Doors* 110: Not long ago the Hudson's Bay Reserve was put on the market. **1946** *Beaver* Dec. 35/2: All the land seen on this side of the Assiniboine formed part of the old Hudson's Bay Reserve, surrounding Fort Garry.

Hudson's Bay start a short first leg of a long journey, a term originating among the fur traders of the old Northwest.

1914 STEELE *Forty Years* 65: The first camp was merely a "pullout," commonly called a "Hudson's Bay Start," very necessary so that before launching into the unknown, one could see that nothing had been forgotten, or that if one had taken too much, being so near the base, the mistake could easily be corrected. **1927** LONGSTRETH *Silent Force* 26: The day came— July 8—and they moved to a lake two miles away on a trial, a Hudson's Bay start. **1940** *Beaver* June 23/2: "We leave camp at 3.30 p.m. ... and start our march across the prairies." As any reader might surmise from the hour of departure given, this was only a march-out, or, as it was then known, a "Hudson's Bay start," designed to rest horses, oxen, harness, and wagon loads before the real march began. **1966** ST. PIERRE *Quarter Horse* 100: Then about eight P.M. he would make a Hudson's Bay start for Namko, pausing for a partial night's sleep about one hundred miles west of town.

Hudson's Bay store See **Hudson's Bay Company store.**

Hudson's Bay strouds See **stroud.**
1804 LAROCQUE *Journal* 308: Bought a stout mule for which I paid: 1 gun, 1 large axe, 1 awl, 1 looking glass, 1 fathom Hudson's Bay red strouds, 1 fathom tobacco, 3 strings pipe beads, 300 balls and powder, 2 knives, 2 workers, and a little vermillon. **1913** COWIE *Adventurers* 242: He exchanged his "fall robes" and leather for the strong cloth called "Hudson's Bay strouds"—taking dark blue for gowns and red cloth for leggings for his wives.

Hudson's Bay style See **Hudson Bay fashion.**

Hudson's Bay suitcase *Slang* See quote.
1909 CAMERON *New North* 25: What have we? Tent, tent-poles, typewriter ... a flour-bag or "Hudson's Bay suit-case" (containing tent-pegs, hatchet, and tin wash-basin) ... the kodak films....

Hudson's Bay token or **dollar** See 1963 quote. See also **beaver** (def. 5a and picture) and **made-beaver token.** Cp. **Hudson's Bay bill.**
1918 GRENFELL *Labrador Doctor* 66: ... one lonely-looking brave came on board, and explained to me by signs and grunts that during the entertainment a white counter, or Hudson Bay dollar, had rolled out of the lining of his hat into our wood-pile. **1963** *Albertan* (Calgary) 4 May 8/7: Hudson's Bay Tokens were issued for use in the St. Lawrence-Labrador Districts in denominations of ... 20 "Made Beavers," 10 "Made Beavers," 5 "Made Beaver" and 1 "Made Beaver."

Hudson's Bay wind [waɪnd] *Obs.* a method of lashing loads to pack-horses, presumably used in the horse brigades, *q.v.*, of the Hudson's Bay Company.
1887 (1888) LEES & CLUTTERBUCK *British Columbia* 232: Then there is the "Hudson Bay Wind," which we never tried, but which we are informed consists of winding a few score yards of rope round pack and horse, as if you were putting splints on a broken arm.

Hudson seal dyed muskrat fur (a trade name). See also **Hudson Bay Seal.**
1920 *Eye Opener* (Calgary) 11 Sep. 1/4: The jackpot is to be the real thing in Hudson seal coats this coming winter. **1936** *Natural Hist.* Nov. 291: Those posts which, a few years ago, shipped out thousands of these small [muskrat] pelts to be converted into Hudson Seal found their shipments reduced to mere hundreds. **1945** MACLENNAN *Two Solitudes* 217: Paul looked

out the window and saw . . . women in black Hudson seal coats with their hands in black muffs, men with fur caps. . . .

huldowokit or **huldowget** [hǝl'daʊ(wǝ)gǝt] *n.* [< Tsimshian] *Pacific Coast* a conjurer of evil spirits; also, the evil spirit conjured.
1926 MCKELVIE *Huldowget* 66: "I can get rid of the huldowget in the young woman." *Ibid.* 113: When the Indians think funny things are being done that they don't know the reason for—and perhaps it's a bad spirit or something—why they just say "It" instead of saying it's a bad spirit or a "huldowget."
1958 *Native Voice* Sp.ed. 17: Redcoats embarked in war canoes and arrived at Kitammax—the measles had subsided. Meanwhile, there was an Indian to whom we will refer as Huldowokit, a dreaded word, which does not mean a medicine man but means a witch doctor or craft killer, a sender of bad thoughts or strong evil mental power.

hummock ['hʌmǝk] *n.* [< older *hammock* a hill or knoll, often wooded, standing apart] **1** *Obs.* a small stand of trees, usually one surrounded by prairie, barrens, etc. See also **bluff** (def. 3a). Also spelled *hammock, hommock,* etc.
☛ *This term, displaced by* bluff *in the West, was in general use among the fur traders and explorers and seems to have survived longest among their half-breed descendents. See 1858 quote.*
1717 (1932) KNIGHT *Journals* 150: He was once Actually within 8 or 9 Leagues of the Factory . . . up as farr as the Eastermost hammock of Woods. **1754** (1907) HENDAY *Journal* 345: Ridgg land with hommocks of wood and creeks. **1786** (1916) THOMPSON *Narrative* 324: Our road lay through . . . fine short grass and hummocks, or islands of wood, almost wholly of Aspin. . . . **1827** (1912) ERMATINGER *Express Jnl* 87: [He] tried to escape by running across a small plain to shelter himself . . . in a hammock of woods. . . . **1858** (1860) HIND *Assiniboine Exped.* I 308: Small "hummocks" of aspen [Footnote: A half-breed expression].

2 See quotes. See also **hummock(ed) ice** and **ice hummock.**
1850 (1851) SNOW *Voyage* 385: A Hummock is a protuberance raised upon any plane of ice above the common level. Hummocks are likewise formed by pieces of ice mutually crushing each other, the wreck being heaped upon one or both of them. **1883** HATTON & HARVEY *Newfoundland* 301: The whole mass opens and expands and then the broken fragments are dashed against one another with resistless violence, and piled on each other, forming "hummocks" or hills of ice.
1934 DENNIS *Down in N.S.* 302: While the geese are getting gravel, they appoint sentries to be on the lookout for danger. These sentries are posted on hummocks or rocks. **1958** *Manice* 6: Hummock— Hard remnants of old ridges usually snow-covered and slightly rounded.

3 See **niggerhead** (def. 2).
1931 GREY OWL *Last Frontier* 32: Moss stands in waist-high hummocks, around which detours must be made.

hummock(ed) ice See **hummock** (def. 2).
1855 (1892) KANE *Arctic Explor.* 349: . . . this will prevent her rocking and pitching when crossing hummocked ice, and enable us to cradle her firmly to the sled. **1937** *Beaver* Mar. 6/2: . . . they had a good load to haul over a long stretch of hummock ice which fronted the shore. . . . **1954** *Labrador and H.B.Pilot* 3: HUMMOCK ICE is result of marginal crushing, which heaps up the ice.

hummocky ['hʌmǝki] *adj.* of ice, marked by hummocks (def. 2).
1850 GOODSIR *Baffin's Bay* 102: The refraction had caused a hummocky piece of ice to assume these forms. **1906** LUMSDEN *Skipper Parson* 207: Wind and tide had jammed together masses of floating ice, now frozen solid, but with a surface rough and uneven— "hummocky," as Newfoundlanders call it—and liable to have treacherous spots to catch the unwary. **1939** MONTAGUE *Eskimos* 21: [Soon] they were out of sight round the first of the hummocky ice. . . .

hump *n.* **1** See **boss.**
1820 (1823) FRANKLIN *Journey* 115: The meat which covers the spinal processes themselves, after the wig is removed, is next in esteem for its flavour and juiciness, and is more extensively termed the hump by the hunters. **1887** *Senate Report* 111: The hump was a special tid bit, the unused muscle alternating with layers of fat, which constituted it a dish, if either boiled, fried or roasted, fit for a king. **1958** DOBIE *Mustangs* 136: They shot buffaloes and lived on hump.

2 *B.C., Slang* See **humpback salmon.**
1963 *Sun* (Vancouver) 13 Aug. 14/1: Any resident or tourist who's ever had an urge to catch a salmon, should get out to one of our local boat rentals and "hook a coupla humps," as the boys put it.

hump *v.* **1**† *Informal* carry (something) with much effort, especially on one's back.
1912 POCOCK *Man in the Open* 142: My wife humped this widow to the barn, and got warm clothes from her trunks for both of them. She fired out her baggage and the puppy piano, bedded down the widow in clean hay . . . and hit the trail for home. **1933** *Beaver* Mar. 206: Here, as everywhere else in the North, the women smoke briar pipes and hump freight as easily as the men. **1959** *Weekend Mag.* 4 Apr. 4/2: The editor of the Inland Sentinel inopportunely chose this month to hump his newspaper and his presses up the canyon from Yale to Kamloops. . . .

2† put forth one's best efforts; hasten.
1908 *Observer* (Cowansville, Que.) 1 Oct. 1/6: As a matter of fact the Laurier government keeps us all humping to pay for its extravagance. **1918** LOWREY *Young Canada Boys* 133: "An' by heck! et kept ole General Riall a'humpin' to hold 'em. Dinged if thum Yanks didn't hev four thousand blue coats agin' ourn two thousand. . . ."

humpback† *n.* **1** See **humpback whale.**
1819 ANSPACH *Hist.Nfld* 397: [List] . . . humpback. . . . **1909** CAMERON *New North* 282: The members of the Baleen Whale family are the Sulphur-Bottoms, the Finner Whales or Rorquals, the Humpbacks, and the king of all whales, the founder of the municipality of Herschel Island, whom his pursuers call indiscriminately the "Arctic Whale," "Polar Whale," "Greenland Whale," "Bowhead," "Right Whale," or "Icebreaker." **1965** *Islander* 4 July 7/1: Among the several types of whales caught in this period were sperm, blues . . . bottle-nose, humpback and finback. . . .

2 See **humpback salmon.**
1963 *Sun* (Vancouver) 13 Aug. 14/1: Humpback is the old and still popular name for the pink salmon.

humpback salmon See **pink salmon.** See also **hump,** *n.* (def. 2) and **humpback** (def. 2).
1869 *Mainland Guardian* (New Westminster, B.C.)

25 Sep. 2/1: The Oleys or Hones appear every alternate year; they are known as the Humpback salmon, from a peculiar protuberance on the back. **1960** *Fisheries Fact Sheets* 6/1: A peculiarity of the pink salmon is that when it is on the way to spawn . . . it develops a large hump on its back. Because of this it [is] known as humpback salmon.

humpback whale† a large whale, *Megaptera nodosa*. See also **humpback** (def. 1).
1832 MCGREGOR *Brit.Amer.* I 203n: A vast number of hump-back whales . . . have been taken this season, 1830, by the fishermen belonging to this establishment. **1965** *Islander* 4 July 6/3: The schooner Kate captured 12 "humpback" whales in quick succession. . . .

humpie *n. B.C., Slang* See **humpback salmon.**
1963 *Sun* (Vancouver) 13 Aug. 14/1: Typical are reports phoned in by two boat liveries adjacent to the hotbed for the humpies. . . .

Hun *n. Esp.West, Informal* See **Hungarian.**
1955 HARDY *Alta Anthol.* 255: What hunter hasn't finished such a day walking up "Huns" through the rolling countryside? The gleam of their bronze feathers against the hazy autumn sky . . . the surprise and thrill one feels. . . . **1964** *B.C.Digest* Sep.-Oct. 4/1: Quail are plentiful in that same cover, with the grassy benches along the west side of the valley apparently the best location for Huns, although I have seen a few coveys out Oliver way.

hunch *n. Obs.* See **boss.**
1859 KANE *Wanderings* 84: The upper part of the hunch of the buffalo, weighing four or five pounds, is called by the Indians the little hunch.

hunchback salmon *Obs.* See **pink salmon.**
1835 (1945) *B.C.Hist.Qtly* Jan. 57: . . . they were all the hunch back salmon and so poor and bad that but few of them were eatable. **1859** *Brit.Colonist* (Victoria) 29 July 1/2: The humpback salmon is regularly intermittent in its visits, only coming to fresh water every second season.

hundred *n. Hist.* one of a number of proposed land grants in Prince Edward Island, the recipients of which were to have baronial rights and obligations. See also **barony** (def. 3).
1765 (1875) CAMPBELL *Hist.P.E.I.* 15: For yourself, you may be assured of your Hundred, as formerly intended, if I have anything to do in the direction of the affair,—which probably I shall have in the same mode and manner. **1875** *Ibid.* 10: Each Hundred was to have a fair four times a year, and a market twice in every week. **1886** *Trans.Roy.Soc.Can.* IV 2 68: Each hundred or barony was to consist of somewhat less than eight square miles, and the lord of each was bound to erect and forever maintain a castle or blockhouse as the capital seat of his property, and as a place of retreat and rendezvous for the settlers. **1965** STEVENS *Incompleat Canadian* 104: Each hundred would be protected by a castle armed with cannon.

Hungarian (partridge) *n.* a European partridge, *Perdix perdix,* introduced from Europe, many of the original birds coming from Hungary. See also **Hun.**
1925 (1958) *Beaver* Autumn 49/2: Rooney sent me four Hungarians picked up dead on the railway track near Blackfalds [Alta]. **1955** HARDY *Alta Anthol.* 255:

Ever since 1909, when the Hungarian partridge was first introduced—to spread in spectacular increase across central and southern Alberta—the population has risen and fallen in the same mysterious pattern that affects others of our northern game-birds.
1965 *Globe and Mail* (Toronto) 9 Jan. 9/6: Hundreds of thousands of pheasants and Hungarian partridges have been lost.

hung-by-tail *n. North, Obs.* See **hung fish.**
1887 *Senate Report* 56: They call [these fish] "hung-by-tail" from the manner in which they are preserved.

hung fish *North* fish, especially whitefish, partially dried and cured in the sun and wind by being hung by their tails to a pole, used as winter feed for sled-dogs. See also **dried fish.**
1830 (1963) DAVIES *Northern Quebec* 126: . . . they brought a few hung fish but no fresh ones. . . .
1839 (1947) HARGRAVE *Correspondence* 278: If you want Pemican . . . I have an over abundance . . . and plenty of hung fish. **1956** KEMP *Northern Trader* 133: I knew we would require some "hung fish"—semi-dried fish—for winter travel, but how many would we need in all?

Hungry Belly Company See **H.B.C.**

Hungry Thirties *Hist.* the period 1930-39, when many people were unemployed and on relief; the Great Depression of the 1930's. Cp. **Dirty Thirties.**
1950 MCCOURT *Home* 187: . . . they had resisted him stubbornly from the time of his in-coming, retreating now, now re-asserting their domination as in that bleak period of drought and depression called the Hungry Thirties. **1960** UBYSSEY (Vancouver) 12 Oct. 2/4: . . . it was there in the beginning and in the "Hungry 30's," and again in the student-veteran days of the immediate post-war period. **1966** *Kingston Whig-Standard* (Ont.) 12 Aug. 4/5: "We [were] asking for . . . floor prices so that prices could not go back to the level of the hungry thirties."

hung-up *adj. Lumbering* of the movement of logs, slowed down or stopped en route from forest to mill. See also **hang up** (def. 1).
1942 KOROLEFF *Skidding of Wood* 15/2: [Caption] . . . the load is likely to become hung-up on a stump with a protruding root. . . . **1957** *Bush News* (St. Catharines, Ont.) June 2/1: Along the shore are clumps of hung-up logs which will be reared through in the Fall.

hung whitefish *North* See **hung fish.**
1942 *Beaver* Dec. 42: [Caption] Mr. Arnold about to feed the dogs with a couple of hung whitefish.

hunt *n. Fur Trade* the catch of furs of a trapper or hunter, either for a season or one trip.
1767 (1898) *N.B.Mag.* I 72: They are very numerous at this time but have made bad hunts. **1809** (1897) COUES *New Light* II 576: Desnoyers arrived with his fall hunt, bringing 50 skins. **1913** COWIE *Adventurers* 273: In case the hunt did not come up to or exceed the amount of the hunter's debts, the master arranged with him how much should be paid on account. . . . **1933** MERRICK *True North* 185: . . . Harvey has . . . set out his traps and made a better than average hunt. **1962** (1964) INNIS *Fur Trade* 320: The Indians' hunt varied from 50 to 200 beaver, the largest . . . being 250.

hunter *n. Hist.* See **fort hunter.**
1800 (1933) MCLEOD *Diary* 132: I sent 4 men for the

four red Deer that are in our Hunters lodges, to whom I sent some Amunition &. to the *Petit Corbau* a Strip'd Blanket. **1929** MOBERLY *When Fur Was King* 60: We had . . . sixty-five regular servants, including boat-builders, carpenters and blacksmiths, and about fifty temporary servants—hunters, horse-keepers, meat-haulers and fishermen. They formed the regular staff for Edmonton.

Hunter *n. Hist.* a member of the Hunters' Lodge, *q.v.* See also **Patriot** (def. 1b).
1838 *Western Herald* (Sandwich [Windsor], U.C.) 14 Mar. 23/2: This information is from a sworn Hunter. **1935** SULLIVAN *Great Divide* 343: "Have either of you ever heard of the Hunters?" "Somewhere," said Schreiber, "when I was a boy: the original Fenians, weren't they, and behind some kind of an invasion?" "It was before your time, back in '38. . . ." **1958** *Encyc. Can.* V 201/2: Early on Dec. 4, 1838, the Hunters' second invasion occurred at Windsor.

Hunters' Lodge† *Hist.* a secret society organized in Vermont in 1838 and having branches in Canada and the northern United States, its purpose being to support those in Canada who wished to be free of British rule. See also **Hunter.**
1840 *St.Catharines Jnl* (U.C.) 9 Jan. 2/3: A "Hunters' Lodge" seems to have been in existence . . . in Cobourg [Ontario]. . . . **1861** CROIL *Dundas* 109: All along the Frontiers, secret associations under the name of "Hunter's Lodges," were organized. **1963** MORTON *Kingdom of Can.* 248: Soon the Hunters' Lodges were formed to liberate Canada from British tyranny. . . .

hunter's swan *Obs.* See quote.
1866 KING *Sportsman in Canada* 188: The first among the numerous host, from its size, importance and great beauty, is the Trumpeter Swan (*Cygnus buccinator*), known also as the "Hunter's Swan," which is peculiar to North America, and is a magnificent bird, in size exceeding the European Hooper.

hunting-bag *n. North* a game-bag of woven babiche (def. 1) used by Indian hunters.
1894 *Outing Mag.* Nov. 127/1: The hunting-bag which is used by all the Indians of the far north [is] made from "Babiche," or narrow strips of reindeer skin woven into a fine mesh, and trimmed with little tassels of thong headed with porcupine-quills. **1949** LEECHMAN *Indian Summer* 102: . . . the charred, blackened little corpse thrust its head ludicrously out of the babiche hunting bag she had slung over her shoulder.

hunting brigade *Fur Trade, Hist.* a party on an excursion to hunt for provisions.
1908 LAUT *Conquest N.W.* II 262: Three classes, the Company divided each of the hunting brigades into—gentlemen, white men, hunters.

hunting camp 1† *Fur Trade, Hist.* the headquarters of a party of Indian hunters.
1897 YOUNG *Indian Trail* 82: So great a comfort and solace is it to them in their solitary wigwams and lonely hunting-camps, that nothing will induce them to leave it out of their pack. **1900** OSBORN *Greater Can.* 20: Before long the actual trading in peltries fell into the hands of a peculiar class of men, the *coureurs des bois,* hardy, dare-devil adventurers, with a knowledge of Indian language and character, who travelled alone to the far-off hunting camps and bartered canoe-loads of goods bought on long credit for furs and skins. **1965** SHEPHERD *West of Yesterday* 125: Members of a hunting camp wore hock-moccasins as footwear.

2 a camp operated to accommodate sportsmen wishing to hunt.
1964 *Star Wkly* 5 Dec. 37/1: Ezra Ames . . . operates a fishing and hunting camp there. . . .

hunting canoe a canoe used on hunting trips, especially by Indians.
1921 HEMING *Drama of Forests* 58: . . . Oo-koo-hoo, slipping away in his hunting canoe, paddled up a little creek into a small lake in which he knew a colony of beavers lived. **1948** ONRAET *Sixty Below* 96: For that purpose you want a thirteen-foot hunting canoe.

hunting fence *Hist.* See **deer hedge.**
1953 *Cdn Geog.Jnl* XLVII 218/2: The Indians of North America . . . used hunting fences, built in a rather casual way of whatever happened to be most convenient. . . . These were intended to lead big game, such as moose and deer, in a desired direction, either to a circular corral . . . or past gaps in the fence where slip nooses were set to catch those animals which attempted to break through at these points.

hunting ground(s) a region frequented by Indians in search of game and furs. See also **grounds** and **hunting territory.** Cp. **trapping-grounds.**
1773 (1954) *Moose Ft Jnls* 344: The Pedlars increase all over the Country, and Actually drove one of Your Eastmain Indians off his hunting ground, after taking away his hatchets. **1812** *Quebec Gaz.* 20 Feb. 1/4: This is because Red-Men have been fools and given up their hunting grounds. **1965** *Globe and Mail* (Toronto) 26 May 3/3: Comparatively few [Indians] landed jobs with the industrial firms that invaded their hunting grounds.

Hunting Indian *Fur Trade, Hist.* a Montagnais or Naskapi Indian from the region between Hudson Bay and Labrador coast.
1784 (1954) *Moose Ft Jnls* 82: Two Men returned with part of the hunting Indians from the Eastward. **1818** CHAPPELL *Voy.of Rosamond* 103: There are few tribes of *Hunting Indians* in Labrador that do not profess the *Catholic* religion; but the whole of their faith consists in paying a stupid homage to those little pictures of the Crucifixion that are strung about their swarthy necks by the *Canadian* Missionaries. **1848** LANMAN *Adventures* 212: Of these the more famous tribes are the Red Indians (now almost extinct), the Hunting Indians, the Mikmaks, and the Esquimaux.

hunting lodge 1 *Obs.* a wigwam (def. 1) or other habitation used by an Indian on the hunt. See also **hunting tent** and **hunting wigwam.**
[**1800** (1933) MCLEOD *Diary* 132: I sent 4 men for the four red Deer that are in our Hunters lodges. . . .]
1852 (1881) TRAILL *Cdn Crusoes* 322: The Indian only visits the town, once the favourite site for his hunting-lodge, to receive his annual government presents, to trade his simple wares of basket and birch-bark work . . . to supply wants which have now become indispensable, before undreamed of. **1897** YOUNG *Indian Trail* 83: During these long waitings in their wigwams, or hunting lodges, the Indians have not much with which to interest themselves; the result is, the Bible has come to them as a wonderful benediction.

2 a cabin or cottage used by a sportsman while on a hunting expedition. See also **lodge** (def. 4a).

1869 *Cdn Illust.News* 27 Nov. 50/3: . . . Mr. Sandford has a hunting lodge [at Clearwater]. . . . **1965** *Globe and Mail* (Toronto) 9 Jan. 2/5: All told more than 100 properties were expropriated, including a number of hunting and fishing lodges.

hunting lot See **hunting territory**.

hunting scrape *Maritimes, Obs.* a hunting expedition.

1849 ALEXANDER *L'Acadie* II 17: During the last week of deer-shooting . . . we engaged in another hunting "scrape," and this time on show-shoes. *Ibid.* 25: A hunting "scrape," as it is called in these western regions, is pleasant enough when you see deer and shoot them. . . .

hunting shoe See **hunting snowshoe**.

hunting sled See **hunting toboggan**.

hunting snowshoe See 1924 quote. Also *hunting shoe*.

1680 *H.B.C.Minutes* II 73: Mar. Letton is to Deliver Foure Moose skins to the *Albemarle* Friggt. for the use of those who goe for New Severne, for to make them hunting shoes. **1867** GIBBS *Notes on Tinneh* 309: . . . the Indians . . . on their large hunting snow-shoes, almost skimmed over the surface of the snow. . . . **1921** HEMING *Drama of Forests* 179: The track-beater's snowshoes, which were the largest used by any of the brigade, were Wood Cree "hunting shoes" and measured nearly six feet in length. **1924** MASON *Arctic Forests* 33: The "hunting" snowshoes are very large. A big man will wear shoes of at least six feet by twelve inches. The Takudh Kutchin make them of willow. They are not used for breaking trail, but for running over the unbroken snow, hunting or exploring. They only sink three or four inches in the powdery snow, and a man can follow the moose all day over deep drifts and through thick brushwood impassable in any other fashion.

hunting tent *Obs.* See **hunting lodge** (def. 1).

1801 (1920) *Beaver* Dec. 8/2: The 2 men at the hunting tent made 2 trips to the house with 5 Horses each time. . . .

hunting territory *Fur Trade* See 1915 quote. See also **hunting ground**. Cp. **hunting tract**.

1915 SPECK *Hunting Territories* 4: These hunting "lots" or territories . . . are more or less fixed tracts of country whose boundaries are determined by certain rivers, ridges, lakes, or other natural landmarks, such as swamps and clumps of cedars or pines. Hunting outside of one's inherited territory was punishable occasionally by death. **1935** JENNESS *Parry Island* 3: . . . murder called for a compensating life unless the deed were compounded with goods or hunting territory.

hunting toboggan or **sled** See 1872 quote.

1872 DASHWOOD *Chiploquorgan* 101: A hunting toboggin is six feet long, composed of two sidepieces of spruce, six inches wide, and one inch in thickness, rounded off in front, and square behind; these are placed parallel to each other, at the distance of two feet, and joined at the upper sides by wooden benches of maple or other hard wood. Strips of thin sheet iron, two inches wide, and turned up in front to serve as runners,

are then nailed or screwed to the bottom of the sidepieces; thin pieces of wood are placed over the benches, on the top of which the load is fastened, by ropes or thongs of hide. **1921** HEMING *Drama of Forests* 160: Our domestic outfit was loaded upon two hunting sleds. . . .

hunting tract *Obs.* a region in which a fur company had the right to trade for furs. Cp. **hunting territory**.

1829 MACTAGGART *Three Years* II 309: . . . it is not known why the Hudson's Bay Company has any reason to assume as a right, various extensive "Hunting Tracts," which have no connection with "Hudson's Bay." In many instances, they are thought to overleap their charter.

hunting wigwam *Obs.* See **hunting lodge** (def. 1).

1872 DASHWOOD *Chiploquorgan* 110: We only got about five miles that day, and camped at night in an old hunting wigwam.

hurdle *n.* [cf. *hurley*, an Irish stick-and-ball game] *Obs.* the stick used in playing Indian lacrosse or baggataway, *q.v.*; also, the game itself.

1832 (1923) BROADUS *Cdn Prose and Verse* 155: For an instant a dense group collected around the ball, which had been driven to within a hundred yards of the gate, and fifty hurdles were crossed in their endeavors to secure it, when the warrior, who formed the solitary exception to the multitude . . . came rapidly up to the spot where the well-affected struggle was maintained. At his approach the hurdles of the other players were withdrawn, when at a single blow of his powerful arm, the ball was seen flying into the air. . . . **1905** (1954) *B.C. Hist.Qtly* XVIII 161: After . . . nearly 2,000 miles of journeying, via Île-à-la-Crosse, Athabaska and Peace river (the first named an Indian resort for the favourite "hurdle" game), we reached Fort McLeod at the north end of McLeod's lake in New Caledonia, on the 10th of October.

hurdy ['hɝdi] *n. Hist.* See **hurdy-gurdy** (def. 1). Cp. **boss hurdy**.

1866 *Cariboo Sentinel* (Barkerville, B.C.) 30 Nov. 3/3: It seems that during his preliminary trial, Barry stated that one of the Hurdies had given him a pin. **1958** ELLIOTT *Quesnel* 30: Nothing indicates that the Hurdies were anything more than dancers.

hurdy-gurdy ['hɝdi,gɝdi] *n.* [after the musical instrument] *B.C., Hist.* **1** a dance-hall girl who frequented the saloons and dance-halls of mining camps during the Cariboo gold rush. See also **hurdy** and **hurdy-gurdy girl**.

1866 (1914) HOWAY *British Columbia* II 112:
Bonnie are the hurdies O,
The German hurdy-gurdies, O!
The daftest hour that e'er I spent
Was dancing wi' the hurdies, O!

1935 SULLIVAN *Great Divide* 43: From the dance halls . . . came fair, flaxen-haired, straight-bodied girls arm-in-arm, most of them German or Scandinavians, popularly known as the 'Hurdy Gurdies', with whom for a dollar and a drink one might dance, but nothing more. . . . **1950** HUTCHISON *Fraser* 73: There were plump, painted German dance hall girls, the "hurdy-gurdies" who demanded pay for every dance.

2 See **hurdy house**.

1937 ANDREWS *Wrangell* 56: The native dance hall girls had gone to their villages, and the hurdy-gurdy had closed its doors.

hurdy-gurdy girl *B.C., Hist.* See **hurdy-gurdy** (def. 1).

359

hurdy-gurdy girl
Husky

1914 HOWAY *British Columbia* II 112: An anomalous class of females known as the hurdy-gurdy girls made their appearance in the Cariboo. **1958** WATTERS *B.C. Cent.Anthol.* 411: The fire is reputed to have been caused by a drunken miner lunging towards a hurdy-gurdy girl who was ironing her petticoats in the canvas-covered shed. . . . **1962** *Wildlife Rev.* July 21/1: Anderson tells of the rich gold strikes, the town gamblers, the Hurdy-Gurdy girls and all the colourful excitement, the heartache and the joy of the gold rush days. . . .

hurdy(-gurdy) house *West, Hist.* a low-class dance hall where dancing-partners could be hired. See also **hurdy-gurdy** (def. 2).
1873 (1904) BUTLER *Wild North Land* 305: It was not a hurdy-house; music and dancing were both wanting. **1955** SHARP *Whoop-up Country* 192: Freighting . . . was a series of dull assignments, broken only by infrequent visits to the saloons and hurdy-gurdy houses of Benton, Macleod, and Calgary.

Huronia ['hjuroniǝ] *n.* See quotes.
1912 (1913) HODGE & WHITE *Indians of Can.* 206/1: A confederation of . . . Iroquoian tribes . . . occupied a limited territory, sometimes called Huronia, around lake Simcoe and S. and E. of Georgian Bay. **1947** SAUNDERS *Algonquin* 6: With the Hurons . . . occupying the region between Lake Simcoe and Georgian Bay, named after them "Huronia," Champlain was more familiar. **1963** *Beaver* Autumn 15/1: Before that, snowshoe-making with deerhide and white ash was common around the longhouses of the old homeland of *Wendake*—which later inhabitants now call Huronia—in the Georgian Bay region of Ontario.

Huron reserve or **territory** *Hist.* See **Huron Tract.**
1799 SMYTH *Topogr.Descr.U.C.* 60: There is a fine limestone quarry . . . nearly in the centre of the Huron reserve. **1832** DOYLE *Hints on Emigration* 17: The soil in the Huron territory is a rich sandy loam—suited to the culture of tobacco, of which much is grown there.

Huron route *Hist.* the route to Georgian Bay by way of the Ottawa River, originally a trade route of the Huron Indians.
1854 KEEFER *Ottawa* 51: . . . it has been surveyed by Mr. Logan as high as Lake Temiscaming, upon the main stream, and as far as Lake Nipissing, upon the Huron Route. . . .

Huron Tract *Hist.* an extensive tract of land (one million acres) in western Upper Canada, opened for settlement after 1828 by the Canada Company, *q.v.* See also **reserve** (def. 1).
1829 MACTAGGART *Three Years* II 114: . . . in such places as the great swamp in the Huron tract, they would be found most beneficial. **1832** (1953) RADCLIFF *Letters* 71: I have, for the present, bought four hundred acres for two hundred pounds, land of superior quality, in the Huron track, London district, township Adelaide, named after the Queen, within twenty miles of Lake Huron, and thirty of Lake Erie. **1963** MORTON *Kingdom of Canada* 228: Little was realized from the Reserves, whether Clergy or Crown, until in 1824 the Canada Company was formed to invest in the public lands of Upper Canada, including the Reserves, and to place settlers on the land of the Huron Tract.

hurricane deck *West, Slang* the back of a bucking bronco.

1910 FERGUSON *Janey Canuck* 87: I have heard the back of a bronco spoken of in the West as "the hurricane deck of a cayuse." **1962** FRY *Ranch on the Cariboo* 163: He'd been athletic and the hurricane deck came to him like a football does to the city youth. . . .

Huskey or **Huski(e)** *n.* See **Husky.**

huskimaw ['hʌskǝ,mɑ] *n.* [see **Husky**] *Nfld* See **Eskimo.**
1921 (1944) WENTWORTH *Am.Dial.Dict.* 196/1: Eskimo . . . 1921 Newfoundland huskimaw. **1924** MASON *Arctic Forests* 11: Esquimaux [are also called] . . . Huskemaw (Labrador). . . .

husking† *n. Obs.* See **husking bee.**
1905 SCHERCK *Pen Pictures* 195: The men, women, boys and girls in the neighborhood who had been invited to the "husking" would assemble about six or seven o'clock, and spend the evening in stripping the husks off the ears of corn.

husking bee *Hist.* a community gathering where neighbors husked corn and had a party. See also **bee, corn-husking bee,** and **husking frolic.**
1832 DOYLE *Hints on Emigration* 45: This kind of work is called a raising Bee, and in the same way assistance is mutually given in beating out the Indian corn from its husks, in what is called a husking Bee. **1884** *Toronto Wkly News* 24 Oct. 2/1: And at a husking bee we were a power. Five hundred bushels of corn was nothing for us to undress. **1964** GUILLET *Pioneer Days* 137: Perhaps the husking bee provided most pleasure to the participants.

husking corn Indian corn, *Zea mays.*
1952 PUTNAM *Cdn Regions* 241/1: Husking corn is, and has long been, an important crop.

husking frolic or **party†** *Obs.* See **husking bee.**
1832 MCGREGOR *Brit.Amer.* II 190: In New Brunswick, and other parts where husking Indian corn is a matter of some moment, the young men and women assemble for the purpose of performing the job. On these occasions, which they call "husking frolics," they have rare frolics indeed; tumbling and kissing each other among the corn, forming a prominent share of the amusement. **1836** *Novascotian* (Halifax) 3 Feb. 37/2: I won't consent to Sall's goin to them huskin parties and quiltin frolicks along with you no more, on no account, for you know how Polly Brown and Nancy White. . . .

Husky ['hʌski] *n.* [abbrev. of some early variant of *Eskimo,* q.v.; see 1743 quote; cf. **huskimaw**] Various early spellings. *North* 1 *Slang, Often Derog.* See **Eskimo** (def. 1).
[**1743** (1949) ISHAM *Observations* 155: Among'st the Northward Indians, and Ehuskemay's they have neither of these beasts.] **1830** (1963) DAVIES *Northern Quebec* 115: . . . there was a cry that the river was full of *Hoskies* (Esquimaux); I went to the landing place and saw six kyaks and two large skin boats full of people. **1891** PACKARD *Labrador Coast* 249: He personally knew only by hearsay received information that the Eskimos, by whalers called "Huskies," lived as far south as St. Lawrence Bay. **1923** WALDO *Down Mackenzie* 177: But one of the Eskimo lads replied: "Some of the huskies"—he did not hesitate to use the term—"live so far from everybody that they have never heard of God." **1952** MOWAT *People of Deer* 285: These sky pilots . . . smash up the Huskies' religion,

then they feed 'em a damn great Book we've been arguing and fighting over for about two thousand years.
2 the Eskimo language. See also **Eskimo** (def. 2).
1864 HALL *Life with Esquimaux* I 66: Carl Petersen no speak Husky.... **1949** LEECHMAN *Indian Summer* 72: "Alapah!" I would agree and hug my shoulders even though the day promised to be hot, and the old man would then rattle off some more "Husky," grinning and chuckling with delight.

husky[1] ['hʌski] *n.* [< *Husky*, q.v.] See **Eskimo dog.** See also **husky dog.** Also spelled *huskie.*
[**1852** (1889) COLLINSON *Journal* 218: On his way to the ship [the dog] was kidnapped by the natives, and not being of a pure huski breed, would most likely be prized by them.] **1872** *Canadian Mthly* Oct. 307/1: The "huskie," or Esquimaux dogs ... are only fed once a day, that is in the evening, the meal consisting of fish or about a pound of pemmican. **1924** MASON *Arctic Forests* 5: On the Arctic tundras the "Huskies" use long runner-sleds with the little short-legged "husky" dogs who can run all day over the iron-like crusted snow. **1966** *Kingston Whig-Standard* (Ont.) 28 Feb. 10/2: Even Whitehorse city dogs, jealously maddened by the adulation that the visiting sled-dogs were receiving, fell upon Washington's two huskies and reduced them to a state, nigh onto hamburger.

husky[2] ['hʌski] *adj.* [< *husky* dry, coarse, strong] big; strong; well-built.
1906 *Eye Opener* (Calgary) Aug. 1/6: Watty himself is a husky all-round athlete, being a shining light in the boxing arena, the wrestling game and the baseball diamond. **1957** *Record-Gaz.* 19 Dec. 16/3: Several husky newcomers appeared in their opening lineup....

husky boot *North* a kind of mukluk (def. 1).
1924 MASON *Arctic Forests* 48: A form of snow boot, generally called "husky" boot, is worn by the Takudh Kutchin, which I prefer for winter use as the snow does not get in the tops.

husky dog See **Eskimo dog.** See also **husky**[1].
1878 *Sask.Herald* (Battleford, N.W.T.) 18 Nov. 3/1: I had with me a "Huskie" dog/As lively as the "jumping frog,"/Although he'd feed—well, like a hog,/ On shaganappi. **1916** HAWKES *Labrador Eskimo* 68: The Labrador "husky" dog is not different in appearance from the Alaskan "malemute." **1963** *Globe and Mail* (Toronto) 13 Mar. 16/1: The husky dog is still the workhorse of numerous areas of the north....

husky goose *North* **1** See 1957 quote.
1921 HEMING *Drama of Forests* 274: And last of all may come the little husky geese that travel farther north to breed their young than do those of any other kind. **1959** MCATEE *Folk-Names* 8: Lesser Canada Goose (*Branta canadensis leucopareia*) ... [is also called] husky goose (Also spelled "huskie" =Eskimo goose. "N.W.T.").

2 See quote.
1959 MCATEE *Folk-Names* 9: Pacific Brant (*Branta bernicla nigricans*) ... [is also called] husky goose (That is Eskimo goose. "N.W.T.").

husky mouse *North* one of several voles of the tundra.
1938 SULLIVAN *Cycle of North* 173: So the [Arctic owl] sat warmly on the eggs while his bare-fleshed wife killed rabbits and ptarmigan, and husky mice and

lemming, and fed her lord....

hustle† ['hʌsəl] *v.* **1** exert oneself in order to succeed or get ahead.
1889 *Regina Jnl* 8 Aug. 1/5: We have the making of a good club, and with practice they will make the other clubs in the Territori[e]s hustle. **1911** BICKERSTETH *Open Doors* 55: A fellow's got to hustle a bit if he's going to make good in this blamed country.

2 *Slang* be employed in selling or serving (something); sell (something) in an aggressive manner.
1887 *Grip* (Toronto) 5 Mar. 6/2: She hustled the hash at Gilhooley's on Blank St. **1894** DEWAR *Round the Globe* 84: Almost every second man you meet is said to be a university man, or the son of some high and mighty family at home, and is now either 'hustling lumber' or farming at four or five dollars a week. **1902** *Eye Opener* (High River, Alta) 6 June 1/3: Some weeks ago we took a run down to Macleod to hustle up business for The Eye Opener. **1963** *Sun* (Vancouver) 1 June 21/5: Canadian Pacific Airlines chief Grant MacConachie is not above hustling tickets on his airline.

hustler† *n.* a person who works energetically to achieve or sell something.
1891 *Grip* (Toronto) 18 Mar. 254/1: An enterprising down East Hustler lately conceived the idea of crowding the "Best Fifty Books" into one volume, and selling the same by subscription. **1954** BEZANSON *Sodbusters* 194: But Chris was a hustler, and brought to our partnership a type of aggressiveness I lacked, so we got along well enough.

hutte *n. Cdn French* [< F *hutte* hut] a blind used in hunting ducks or geese.
1845 TOLFREY *Sportsman* I 144: Before I proceeded to join my companions, I inspected the two ponds in both of which I found decoy-ducks tethered to stakes about fifteen or twenty yards in front of the "huttes," and so admirably did these gay deceivers act their parts ... I was nearly taken in....

Hutterite† ['hʌtə,raɪt] *n.* a Christian sect of frugal farmers living (since 1918) in communities in the Prairie Provinces. See 1963 quote. See also **Hutterite colony.**
1955 *Winnipeg Free Press* 1 Feb. 1/1: The meeting was an unofficial gathering of Hutterite leaders and councillors of some of the municipalities in which Manitoba's 22 colonies are located. **1960** *Cdn Geog.Jnl* Nov. VIII/1: One reads of the Hutterites, the Mormons and the remittance men "who may have been green but were never yellow".... **1963** *Canada Month* Mar. 22/1: The Hutterites sprang from the Anabaptist movement in Switzerland in 1528, taking their name from Jacob Hutter, a leader who was burned at the stake in Tyrol in 1535.

Hutterite colony or **community** a farming community (*Brüderhof*) of Hutterites, operated as a Christian commune under elective superiors.
1953 MOON *Saskatchewan* 75: To the northwest of Shaunavon are Hutterite communities. **1958** *Edmonton Jnl* 8 Oct. 49/2: Under the Communal Properties Act [1944], Hutterite colonies must be at least 40 miles apart.

H.W. or **H.Wine** *Obs.* See **high wine.**
1800 (1933) MCLEOD *Diary* 135: Bellile told me about the keg of H. Wines they made free with when they remained behind ... I mean to charge it to the account of La France as he was the foreman of the Canoe.

1804 (1933) CONNOR *Diary* 259: ... dispatched Mr Seraphin ... to examine a Cache of H W to know if all are safe.

hyack *v. adv.* See **hyak**.

Hyack ['haɪæk] *n.* [see **hyak**] *Local* a volunteer fireman (a term now preserved in tradition in the Honourable Hyack Battery of New Westminster, B.C.).
1869 *Mainland Guardian* (New Westminster, B.C.) 8 Sept. 3/1: The Hyacks turned out in full force and presented a fine appearance; their bright scarlet uniforms gave the assemblage a picturesque effect. **1870** (1958) WATTERS *B.C.Cent.Anthol.* 24: Captain Fisher of the Hyacks then decorated them.... **1959** *Weekend Mag.* 16 May 34: [Caption] ... men of The Ancient and Honourable Hyack Battery firing their 88th annual Royal Salute....

hyak ['haɪæk] *v.* [< Chinook Jargon] *B.C.* hurry up; hasten. Also spelled *hyack, hiak.*
1936 MOWERY *Paradise Trail* 82: The 'breed spoke again. "... you wise lak trap-line carcajou, an take differen' trails on way home ... Skunk-Bear wen' after you wan tam an he didn' come back ... So we tie you op an den hyak to camp...." **1959** *Weekend Mag.* 16 May 34/1: ... the firemen were called by the name used to describe them by the Indians—hyack, meaning "hurry up."

hyak ['haɪæk] *adv.* [< Chinook Jargon] *B.C.* quickly; right away. Also spelled *hyack, hiak.*
1915 CUMMING *Skookum Chuck* 21: "Klatawa!" (Go!) he commanded. "Hiak!" (Quick!) he shouted. **1927** PHILIP *Painted Cliff* 22: "I seen hyak that I ain't got no chance o' gettin' the best in an exchange o' gay reparty with a jane that slings the wau-wau like she does." **1936** MOWERY *Paradise Trail* 119: "Did you tell these other fellows about this?" "Non, I come hyak right to you."

hyaqua(u) or **hyaque** *n.* See **hiaqua**.

hyas ['haɪæs] *adj. adv.* [< Chinook Jargon; cf. Nootka *ĩh* big, large] *B.C.* large; big; very. Cp. **hyiu**. Also spelled *hias, hyass.*
1860 *Brit.Colonist* (Victoria) 5 July 1/1: San Diego, he used to say, was a hyas klosh (very good) city—for at that time (he said) it was much larger than San Francisco. **1915** CUMMING *Skookum Chuck* 20: Hias Peter had a hias gun, and he raised it to his shoulder.... **1953** MOWERY *Mounted Police* 53: This evening we pitch off. We leave *hyas* quick—in half a pipe. **1958** *Beaver* Winter 28/2: But moosmoos is not a moose; it means cattle. Moose is *ulchey* or *hyas mowitch*, big deer.

hyas tyee [< Chinook Jargon *hyas* big and *tyee* chief, king] *Pacific Coast* a great or mighty chief; an important person.
1860 *Brit.Colonist* (Victoria) 26 June 2/2: Seven hyas yhees, of the Hyder tribe of Northern Indians, accompanied by their families, waited upon Governor Douglas at the Government House, on Saturday last. **1866** LORD *Naturalist* I 161: Having handed my letters of introduction ... to the chief trader, I was presented to the chiefs as a Hyas tyee (great chief), one of "King George's" men. **1937** ANDREWS *Wrangell* 33: ... he landed on a bar ... at a place he called Shakesville, after old Shakes, the hyas tyee of the Stikines. **1956** *Beaver* Summer 44: Tom Hastie told me his employer, Col. Ebey, was a *hyass tyee* (Mighty Chief).

Hydah, Hyder, Hyter *n.* See under **Haida**.

Hydro ['haɪdro] *n.* [abbrev.] *Informal* **1** Hydro Electric Commission of Ontario, a publicly owned corporation created in 1906 to produce and distribute electricity. See also **Hydro-Electric**.
1916 BRIDLE *Sons of Canada* 185: ... there is a real masculine person at the back of the Hydro movement in Ontario. **1926** *Canada Forward* 15 Nov. 2/1: The Hydro will be in a position where they will have to pay whatever price is asked or seek elsewhere for power. **1966** *Imperial Oil Rev.* June 9/1: Hydro uses muskeg vehicles for road construction to its sub-stations, and in maintenance work along its right-of-way.

2 any of several similar corporations in other provinces.
1964 *Winnipeg Tribune* 6 Feb. 24/7: Speakers will be Robert Shearer from Manitoba Hydro, another Hydro representative in each district, and a district home economist. **1964** *Guardian* (Charlottetown) 18 June 12/1: In awarding contracts, Hydro doesn't hesitate to favor Quebec enterprises in order to stimulate the economy. **1965** *Globe and Mail* (Toronto) 9 Jan. 9/6: B.C. Hydro asked [him] to search for a competent man....

hydro ['haɪdro] *n.* [abbrev.] **1** hydro-electric power. See also **hydro power**.
1916 BRIDLE *Sons of Can.* 185: The product of Niagara, according to [Sir Adam] Beck, is Hydro-Electric—familiarly abbreviated to Hydro.... **1952** PUTNAM *Cdn Regions* 387/2: The cities of Alberta, also, have good sources of power, including coal, natural gas and hydro. **1962** *Canada Month* Nov. 13/1: The advice to Nova Scotia's two major power companies [was]: forget about hydro development. **1964** *Victoria Dly Times* 8 Feb. 18/1: The B.C. government has introduced safety valve legislation in case its hydro laws are repudiated by the courts.

2 electricity as a utility distributed by a power company or commission.
1939 GROVE *Two Generations* 230: "... the telephone and hydro wires are down." **1942** *Gazette* (Glace Bay, N.S.) 21 Sep. 4/3: The sparkle left the streets of cities and towns in Ontario and Quebec Sunday night as new dim out regulations went into force and centres turned out all but essential lights in an effort to conserve hydro. **1949** PETERSON *Chipmunk* 149: Claude wrote out the address ... on the envelope of the hydro bill he'd forgotten to pay. **1964** *Globe and Mail* (Toronto) 9 Dec. 1/1: Added to these costs would be a minimum of $650 to $700 for winter berths, hydro and water service....

Hydro-Electric *n.* *Obs.* See **Hydro** (def. 1).
1909 *Eye Opener* (Calgary) 4 Dec. 3/1: Port Arthurites, just pin your faith to the Hydro-Electric. **1916** BRIDLE *Sons of Can.* 191: Toronto street lighting was taken out of private corporation hands and placed in the hands of the hydro-electric....

hydro power See **hydro** (def. 1).
1955 *Bridgewater Bull.* 9 Mar. 4/2: [Canada is] second in production of hydro power, wood pulp, gold.... **1962** *Cdn Saturday Night* Aug. 7/3: ... due to cheap hydro power, the Niagara Peninsula became one of the most industrialized parts of Canada.

hydro-stone *n. N.S., Local* a type of artificial
stone made in Halifax from sand pressed into
building blocks.
1934 DENNIS *Down in N.S.* 11 : The area is covered with
new and different-looking houses. All are made of
hydro-stone, which gives to the district its name and
is a home product made of sand from Eastern
Passage.

hyiu ['haɪju] *adj. adv.* [< Chinook Jargon]
Pacific Coast much; many; great; very. Cp. **hyas.**
Also spelled *highu, hiyou, hiyu,* etc.
1859 (1958) ELLIOTT *Quesnel* 19 : I think there is hiyou
gold up here. . . . **1927** PHILIP *Painted Cliff* 10 :
"Klahowya, little girl." "Me and him has been
tillikums for a hyiu long time." **1966** *Islander* 27 Feb.
6/1 : "Gee!" he added. "I bet they make hiyu potlatch
tonight!"

hyiu muckamuck *Pacific Coast* lots to eat;
a good big meal. See also **hyiu** and **muck-a-muck,** *n.*
Cp. **high muckamuck.**
1860 *Brit.Colonist* (Victoria) 27 Sep. 3/2 : The Indian
ought to be kept in prison when convicted, as the other
Indians think he has a good time and hiyu muck-a-
muck. **1884** (1926) MOSER *Reminiscences* 139 : Hayou
makmak : 12 baskets of herring spawn, two barrels of
molasses, and one barrel of fish oil. **1888** *Dominion
Illust.* 265 : For Breakfast.—"*Hyiu Muckamuck.*"

hyiu-skookum ['haɪju,skukəm] *adj. Pacific Coast
and Northwest* very great, strong, or important.
See also **hyiu** and **skookum,** *adj.*
1898 *Medicine Hat News* (Alta) 8 Dec. 5/4 : Down in
Dawson on the Klondyke, there's a lady in command/
Who rules the good old pioneers and the great
Cheechacah band./She's a hyiu-skookum lady, she's
the Dawson City Belle. **1910** LONDON *Lost Face* 150 :
. . . he knew that Dave Walsh was a big man, worth
lots of money, a hi-yu skookum chief.

hykwa ['haɪkwə] *n.* See **hiaqua.** Also spelled *hai-
qua.*
1862 MAYNE *Four Years in B.C.* 281 : The northern
tribes wear also very generally a small round shell,
called the "hai-qua," in appearance not unlike a piece
of clay-pipe stem one or two inches long, stuck into
their lower lips at an angle of 45° with the chin.
1922 JOHNSON *Legends of Vancouver* 66 : Of all his
wealth of fish and furs, of game and hykwa (large
shell-money) he gave to the boys who had none. . . .

iaqua *n*. See **hiaqua.**

ice *n*. **1 a.** *Sealing, Nfld* **the ice,** the seal-hunting grounds on the edge of the icefields in the North Atlantic. See also **front** (def. 3) and **sea-ice** (def. 2).
1819 ANSPACH *Hist.Nfld* 428: In the same spring, an unusual number of schooners and boats belonging to that bay were totally lost at the ice.... 1916 DUNCAN *Billy Topsail* 226: "He's young for the ice," Bill observed. 1961 *Maclean's* 28 Jan. 17/1: Hedley Payne ... who had wangled his very first berth to the ice, walked for two days to Gambo railway station to catch the sealers' car into the capital in time to sign on.

b. leave home to engage in the seal hunt.
1964 *Time* (Cdn ed.) 20 Mar. 20: Seal hunting is known to Newfoundlanders as "going to the ice," and they have taken to the floes every March for two centuries.

2 *Hockey* the sheet of ice on which the game is played.
1955 *Shawinigan Standard* 12 Jan. 6/4: The Shawinigan Cataracts ... are still undefeated by Chicoutimi on Shawinigan ice.... 1966 *Hockey News* 14 May 3/3: The little centre was flying every minute he was on the ice....

3 *Curling* the sheet of ice over which the stones are curled.
1911 KNOWLES *Singer* 281: The ice was capital—for the floor was a wooden one and twenty-four hours' frost had been quite enough.... 1956 *Northland News* 17 Dec. 8/2: In the nine o'clock draw on ice number one Hemmingson vs Cochrane....

ice *v*. **1** *Hockey* **a.** put a team on the ice, equipped and ready to play.
1955 *Star* (Val d'Or, Que.) 15 Apr. 11/2: Counting the three teams, the Kiwanis themselves have iced for inter-service club play, the total comes to 37.
1963 *Kingston Whig-Standard* (Ont.) 5 Feb. 10/1: McGill iced many potent and colorful teams but none ever won the Canadian title.

b. shoot (a puck) from behind one's own blueline past the red line at the opposing team's end of the rink. Cp. **icing** (def. 2).
1965 *Kingston Whig-Standard* (Ont.) 7 Apr. 12/1: If that puck had slid behind the Montreal goal, the Leafs would have been called for "icing the puck"....
1966 *Canadian* 29 Jan. 5/3: Some of the most exciting moments ... come during the killing of penalties, when the defending team, not allowed to ice the puck into the attacking team's end, must stickhandle or pass to waste ... time.

2 *North* put a glaze of ice on dog-sled runners to reduce friction when the sled is in motion. See also **glaze.** Cp. **icing** (def. 1).
1942 TWOMEY & HERRICK *Needle to North* 67: Lastly, the runner is 'iced.' A hare's foot or a piece of hairy dog fur is dipped into the warm liquid and run swiftly down the length of the runner. When several layers of ice have been added, the earthing is over. The komatik has been 'shod.' 1951 BULIARD *Inuk* 159: Dressed at last, Ayallik took a little pot of water with him and went outside to ice his sled.

ice anchorage an engineering technique for slowing down the flow of a river during break-up, involving the dredging of holes into the river bottom so that the ice will build up, forming a barrier. See also **ice-trap.**
1963 *Calgary Herald* 16 Oct. 30/1: Acting City

Engineer Charles Howarth describes the provincial project as an ice anchorage system to cut down the danger of spring floods. 1963 *Albertan* (Calgary) 19 Nov. 3/2: Dredges dig out ice anchorages in the Bow River by Princes Island. The idea is to form an ice bridge, prevent pile-ups, flooding.

ice-angling *n*. See **ice fishing.**
1962 *Globe and Mail* (Toronto) 23 Mar. 23/8: One reason for this outdoor mode of fishing was that we were after lake trout, a type of ice-angling which requires that the fishermen be fairly well separated.

ice-axe *n*. See **ice-chisel** and picture.
1775 (1955) CURTIS *Voyage* 44: Then one of us took the Ice axe[,] this being upright with a long handle.
1905 OUTRAM *Cdn Rockies* 105: The ice-axe ... serves as a balancing pole when crossing streams on fallen logs, or as a balustrade for timid folks, chops wood for fires and boughs for beds, is a distinct success as a can-opener, and, on an emergency, comes in handy as a camera stand, two making a most effective substitute for the conventional tripod.

ice-ball *n*. a ball-like bit of ice that forms on the paws of sled dogs, under the hooves of horses, etc.
1931 GREY OWL *Last Frontier* 54: ... whilst the dogs take the opportunity to bite the ice balls off their feet.
1956 KEMP *Northern Trader* 148: Meanwhile, the dogs are down, chewing at the ice-balls between their toes.

ice-bank *n*. See **bourdigneau.**
1870 *Cdn Illust.News* 19 Mar. 318/4: Rumours had come from Montreal that the current was rapidly swelling, and that ice-banks were forming on the eastern end of St. Helen's island.

ice-bar *n*. See **ice-chisel** and picture.
1875 *Cdn Mthly* Feb. 139/1: It is then firm enough to walk over and work upon without showing the least sign of weakness, while at the same time, it is so sufficiently cut through that it can be easily divided into separate lengths and blocks by a few strokes of the ice bar.

ice barricade See **ballacater.**
1854 (1892) KANE *Arctic Explor.* 148: Deep cavities filled with snow intervened between lines of ice-barricades, making their travel as slow and tedious as the same obstructions had done to the party of poor Brooks before their eventful rescue last March.
1909 GRENFELL *Adrift on Ice-Pan* 5: The first rain of the year was falling when I started, and I was obliged to keep on what we call the "ballicaters," or ice barricades, much farther up the bay than I had expected.

ice-belt *n*. *Arctic, Obs*. See **shore ice** (def. 1).
1854 (1892) KANE *Arctic Explor.* 128: I am going this time to follow the ice-belt (Eis-fod) to the Great Glacier of Humboldt, and there load up with pemmican from our cache of last October.

ice-blind *n*. See quote.
1934 DENNIS *Down in N.S.* 302: In this case the hunters [of wild geese] shoot from boats, ice-blinds, and from the ledges between the two sanctuaries. The ice-blinds are built of blocks of ice. The hunter hides behind them.

ice-blind *adj*. temporarily blind from exposure to the glare from expanses of ice. Cp. **snow-blind.**

1961 *Maclean's* 28 Jan. 48/1 : It was Hearn, the
stowaway, delirious and ice-blind.

ice-blink† *n.* See 1954 quote.
[1773 (1774) PHIPPS *Voyage* 71 : [We saw a] bright
appearance near the horizon, which the pilots called the
blink of the ice.] **1850** (1852) OSBORN *Arctic Jnl* 99 : We
were pained to see, from the strong ice-blink to the S.W.,
that a body of packed ice had been driven up the straits
by the late gales. **1954** *Labrador and H.B.Pilot* 4 : Ice
blink is the whitish glare of the clouds on or near the
horizon produced by the reflection of large areas of
sea ice in the vicinity.

iceboat *n.* **1** *Hist.* **a.** a small boat rigged to travel
over ice.
*c*1752 (1852) COATS *Geography of H.B.* 18 : I have made
upwards of twenty voyages without a small ice-boat,
yet I do not deny the use of them. **1857** MCDOUGALL
Voyage 246 : One of the boats (whale) he had deposited
on Cape Lady Franklin, the other (an ice boat) on the
west shore of Byam Martin Channel. **1945** CALVIN *Saga*
150 : During these few days, necessary trips to Kingston
or Wolfe Island were made in "the iceboat," a big
heavy punt on runners.
b. See quotes.
1853 SLEIGH *Pine Forests* 116 : . . . it was justly argued
that the "ice-boat" had not been able to cross the
[Northumberland] Straits. **1883** *Brandon Dly Mail*
(Man.) 26 Feb. 4/1 : The mails have been carried by the
old ice-boat line from Cape Traverse to Cape
Tormentine, while travellers have often been unable to
cross. **1923** *Dalhousie Rev.* III 207 : Passengers who
crossed the Straits . . . were carried [until 1915] in little
amphibious ice-boats fitted with runners, oars and
sails, and plying between Cape Traverse, P.E.I., and
Cape Tormentine, N.B. **1939** CHAMPION *On the Island*
10 : In the winter the cold and heavy ice-boats took
the place of the row-boats.

2 a strong, often triangular, frame mounted on
runners and equipped with a sail and rudder, used
as a pleasure craft on frozen lakes and rivers.
1821 *Montreal Herald* 7 Mar. 2/1 : Ice Boat—A
gentleman, at Chambly, having made a boat of this
description, (running on skates, one on each side and
a third near the rudder,) was lately sailing on the
basins, when the wind shifted violently, and carried the
vessel at an inconceivably swift rate towards the rapid.
1846 (1927) DICKIE *How Canada Grew Up* 192 : Ice-boats
come into play on these occasions. These boats are
fixed on a triangular frame, with runners like those of
skates at each corner. They are propelled by sails. . . .
1849 ALEXANDER *L'Acadie* I 228 : Ice boats, or sail
boats, mounted on a large pair of runners, with an
iron rudder, used to be in fashion in the winter in
Toronto, but I saw none on this occasion.
1964 *Canadian Wkly* 12 Dec. 7/4 : Today iceboats are
getting smaller and faster, and much easier to handle.

3 See **scoot** and picture.
1963 *Globe and Mail* (Toronto) 3 May 4/6 : He was
with three other men in February when their ice boat
ran out of gas on a lake north of here. **1963** *Kingston
Whig-Standard* (Ont.) 1 Feb. 17/7 : The ice boat passed
under the plane's wing and its propellor caused an
estimated $200 damage to the aircraft.

4 *Fisheries* a commercial fishing boat equipped with
facilities for icing, or refrigerating, caught fish.

1878 *Sask.Herald* (Battleford, N.W.T.) 29 Jul. 4/1 :
The crew of the Lady Ellen are building an ice-boat for
the fishing trade this winter. **1966** *Fisherman* 6 May
14/2 : [Advert.] Ice-Boat Wanted, Preferably larger class
to charter for trolling season. Coastwise experience,
good producer.

iceboater *n.* one who sails an iceboat (def. 2).
1964 *Canadian Wkly* 12 Dec. 7/4 : Iceboating is
essentially a racing sport, yet many iceboaters race very
seldom.

iceboating *n.* the recreation of sailing an iceboat
(def. 2). See also **ice-yachting.**
1887 (1888) LEES & CLUTTERBUCK *British Columbia* 34 :
There is tennis and boating in summer, and in winter
ice-boating, snow-shoeing. . . . **1898** EDGAR *Canada
and Capital* 121 : The ice-boating in Toronto Bay is
probably the best to be found anywhere, owing to the
number of times during the winter that fresh ice is
formed, either by a clean sheet of new ice, or by a
sharp frost after the flooding of the surface snow in a
thaw. **1965** *Weekend Mag.* 6 Mar. 33/1 : Iceboating is
no easy sport and the Ghost Dam . . . is no place for
beginners.

ice-bridge *n.* **1 a.** a bridge across a river, bay, etc.,
formed by the natural freezing of the water and
used as a means of crossing from one shore to the
other. See also **bridge** (def. 1), **ice-road** (def. 1),
and **pont.**
☛ *This use of the term is doubtless a translation of the
Canadian French* **pont** *in this sense.*
[1781 *Quebec Gaz.* 11 Jan. 2/1 : . . . the icy bridge over
the Great River St. Lawrence before Quebec has stood
fast, and may . . . continue passable till the . . . 30th of
April next.] **1792** (1911) SIMCOE *Diary* 77 : Col. Simcoe
and I were going to walk on the ice bridge. **1873** (1904)
BUTLER *Wild North Land* 223 : By the 22nd all
preparations were declared complete, and we began to
cross the river over the doubtful ice-bridge. **1963** *Cdn
Geog.Jnl* Apr. 126/3 : . . . a very gay and animated water
colour of the Winter Carnival in Quebec City, with
crowds of people on an ice bridge extending across the
St. Lawrence. . . .

b. a natural bridge of ice reinforced by flooding,
corduroying, *q.v.*, or artificial refrigeration.
1957 *Herald-Tribune* (Grande Prairie, Alta) 17 Dec.
9/3 : Once the river has frozen solidly, highway crews
will start flooding operations to build up an ice bridge
as the base for the winter road across the river.
1958 *Edmonton Jnl* 24 June 4 6/2 : They had made an
ice bridge over the Kakisa [River] earlier, corduroying
its surface with logs and then pumping water over the
logs to sheath them in ice and provide a surface three
or four feet thick over the river ice. . . . **1959** *Time* (Cdn
ed.) 2 Mar. 7/3 : Then the company consulted the
University of Alberta's famed Engineer Robert M.
Hardy. His startling $30,000 proposal : build a thicker
ice bridge with artificial refrigeration.

2 a bridge of ice formed by the jamming of ice-
cakes in a river or other channel.
1889 WITHROW *Our Own Country* 335 : When the river
below is running full of ice, sometimes a "jam" occurs
at the narrowest part ; and when intensely cold it
speedily "takes" or becomes firmly frozen. Sometimes,
however, several winters pass without the formation
of an ice-bridge. **1903** CARR-HARRIS *White Chief* 27 :
. . . the volume of water, tossed, broken, dashed into
foam, which floated down like miniature icebergs on
the mighty rushing current till the natural ice-bridge
was reached, made a scene not soon to be forgotten.
1964 *North* July 39/2 : Now in November, it [the river]

was nearly choked; a mad race of water in the middle flung rafts of ice to the sides, burrowed under ice bridges, and showed in roils and slicks as far as could be seen.

3 *Arctic* See quote.
1920 (1939) *Beaver* Sep. 45/1: The officers on the ice bridge, which was rigged up high so that ice could be seen farther off, were busy zigzagging the ship to avoid being caught again.

ice-cake *n.* a piece or slab of ice. Cp. **ice-pan.**
1870 *Cdn Illust.News* 26 Mar. 334/1: One ice-cake after another struck her boat. . . . **1953** *Cdn Geog.Jnl* July 150/1: . . . a strip of open water stretched between shore and ice-cake which still filled most of the bay.

ice-canoe *n.* a sturdy small boat long used in crossing the St. Lawrence in winter, its trained crew propelling it, often loaded with freight and passengers, through swift currents choked with ice-cakes and manhandling it over the sharp, uneven ice banks, or bourdigneaux, *q.v.* See also **winter canoe.**
1958 *Kootenaian* 27 Feb. 6/1: Separate races are run for "professional" and "amateur" ice canoe enthusiasts. **1959** *Weekend Mag.* 21 Mar. 36/3: Ice canoes have been crossing the deep channel that separates the nine-mile-long island from the mainland for more than 200 winters.

ice-canoe race an exhausting race across the St. Lawrence River by crews in ice-canoes, nowadays a traditional spectacle at Quebec City's annual winter carnival.
1958 *Cdn Geog.Jnl* Jan. iv/2: Special events . . . include the international dog sled derby . . . an ice-canoe race and the crowning of a carnival queen. **1963** *Globe and Mail* (Toronto) 1 Feb. 5/1: The Quebec winter carnival . . . includes events ranging from snowshoe derbies, outdoor dancing, parades, and ice-canoe races to formal balls.

ice carnival See **winter carnival.**
1930 MCCLUNG *Be Good* 127: [We saw] . . . the pictures of the ice-carnival in Montreal which came in the Family Herald. **1957** *Aklavik Jnl* Apr. 3/1: Both E-3, D.P.W. and the Aklavik Constructor camps will have a half-holiday to attend the Ice Carnival and visitors and participants are welcomed from Old Aklavik and the Delta country.

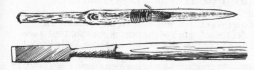

Ice chisels

ice-chisel *n.* an ice-cutting tool. See 1848 quote. See also **ice-axe, ice-bar, ice-cutter,** and **trench.** Cp. **needle bar.**
1689 (1929) KELSEY *Papers* 28: This day finding our Burdens heavy concluded to leave some things for a mark so left 1 Bottle of Powder & some shott 2 Ice Chizzels 4 hatchets on yᵉ top of a flatt stone. **1748** ELLIS *Hudson's-Bay* 204: On the 23d on this Month, Orders Were given to cut the Ice from about our Ships; which was performed with Ice Chissels, and Pick-axes. **1848** (1859) BALLANTYNE *Hudson's Bay* 68: Things being arranged to his entire satisfaction, he takes an instrument called an ice-chisel, which is a bit of steel about a foot long, by one inch broad, fastened to the

end of a stout pole, wherewith he proceeds to dig through the lodge. **1960** *Northern Affairs Bull.* May-June 41/2: . . . when sufficient distance is reached for a net "set," another hole is chopped with an ice chisel. . . .

ice clamper See **clamper.**
1945 MACLENNAN *Two Solitudes* 216: "He dragged me up out of that water across the ice clampers and the rocks. . . ."

ice-cream festival *Obs.* See **ice-cream social.**
1879 *Morning Chron.* (Halifax) 9 July 3/1: There will be a Strawberry and Ice Cream Festival, with concert in the evening, in aid of the Organ Fund of St. Mark's Church, at the School House in rear of the Church.

ice-cream parlo(u)r† a shop which sells ice-cream, sodas, sundaes, etc.
1887 *Grip* (Toronto) 4 June 6/1: The ice cream parlor, the boating excursion, the reserved seats in the grand stand . . . are separately "terrors" in themselves to the average young man who has undertaken to entertain a sweet girl with the love for all good things. **1954** BRUCE *Channel Shore* 62: She saw herself slipping away from them, away from the crowd at Carter's ice-cream parlour, slipping down the street to Dr. Brickley's house. **1959** *Star Wkly* 8/3: There is no theatre, hotel or ice-cream parlor.

ice-cream social *Obs.* a social gathering, as of a church group, at which ice cream is served.
1889 *Rat Portage* [Kenora] *News* (Ont.) 2 Aug. 4/2: The Ice Cream Social came off last evening in the Music Hall and was well attended. **1899** *Medicine Hat News* (Alta) 28 June 8/2: The Methodist church purpose giving an ice-cream social on the parsonage lawn Thursday July 6th commencing 2 o'clock.

ice-creepers *n.* See **creepers.**
1889 *Montreal Dly Star* (Carnival No.) 5/1: Ice-creepers [took] the place of wading boots. **1910** SERVICE *Trail of '98* 115: The men wore ice-creepers, so that their feet would clutch the slippery surface.

ice cruiser *North* See **snowmobile** (def. 1).
1948 ONRAET *Sixty Below* 124: Dogs are able to penetrate into nooks and crannies of the Canadian wilds absolutely unreachable by ice cruisers, tractors, or planes.

ice crust See quote.
1958 *Manice* 5: Ice Crust; Formed by the freezing of slush on a quiet sea surface. Thickness less than 2 inches.

ice-cutter *n. Obs.* See **ice-chisel** and picture.
*a*1791 (1904) LONG *Voyages* 120: The fishing party [were] natives of Canada, who [were] provided with axes, ice-cutters, and fishing materials. . . .

ice field *Obs.* an expanse of fresh-water ice from which ice blocks are taken for refrigeration purposes.
1875 *Canadian Mthly* Feb. 139/2: The length of the skid depends upon the distance of the ice field from the shore.

icefish *v.* engage in ice fishing, *q.v.*
1963 *B.C.Digest* Nov.-Dec. 31: . . . it'll be nothing less

than wonderful if I manage to make one good steelhead trip and icefish in three lakes all winter!

ice-fisherman *n.* a person who engages in ice fishing, *q.v.*
1962 *Globe and Mail* (Toronto) 23 Mar. 23/8: There's nothing that restores the flagging energy of an ice-fisherman more rapidly than the sight of a fat lake trout lying there in the snow. **1964** *Star Wkly* 19 Dec. 13/2: Twelve thousand were sold in Canada last year . . . to ice fishermen who can try several frozen lakes in a day. . . .

ice fishing the practice of fishing through holes in the ice, either for sport or commercially. See also **ice-angling.**
[**1752** ROBSON *Hudson's Bay* 11: They sometimes make large openings in the ice, where they angle with a hook and line, and catch salmon. . . .] **1962** *Globe and Mail* (Toronto) 24 Feb. 28/1: . . . ice fishing has been a mite slow, but [is] expected to pick up any old time. **1965** *Globe Mag.* 11 Dec. 11/3: Ice fishing . . . now calls hundreds of thousands of persons . . . to lakes and rivers across Canada.

ice-fishing hut a small building towed onto the ice in winter and used by ice-fishermen as shelter while angling through holes cut in the ice "floor." See also **ice hut.**
1963 *Globe and Mail* (Toronto) 1 Feb. 37/8: When the raw winds of winter howl around the ice-fishing hut, it is rum which does the best job of taking the bite out of it.

ice flood *Obs.* See **ice-shove** (def. 2).
1898 *Trans.Roy.Soc.Can.* LV 3 3: The winter ice floods on the St. Lawrence are distinguished from those produced in other rivers more to the south, in that the latter are the direct result of thaw and rain . . . whereas those of the St. Lawrence occur when there is the least water in the river as well as less ice than at a later period of the winter.

ice-foot *n.* [trans. of Dan. *eis-fod*] *North* **1** See **shore-ice** (def. 1) and 1954 quote.
1854 (1892) KANE *Arctic Explor.* 103: I must reserve for my official report the detailed story of this ice-foot and its changes. The name is adopted on board ship from the Danish "Eis-fod," to designate a zone of ice which extends along the shore from the untried north beyond us almost to the Arctic circle. . . . a perennial growth, clinging to the bold faces of the cliffs, following the sweeps of the bays and the indentations of rivers. **1937** SHACKLETON *Arctic Journeys* 130: The ice-foot indeed is one of the most interesting phenomena in the Arctic. It is that part of the sea ice which has frozen to the coast, and is therefore unaffected by tidal movements. *Ibid.* 131: The nature of the ice-foot varies tremendously according to the locality, and while in some places it may form a broad highway over a hundred yards wide, in other places there may only be a few feet of rough ice clinging against the cliffs. **1954** *Labrador and H.B. Pilot* 3: LAND ICE (shore floe or ice foot) is field or floe ice attached to the coast.

2 See **ballacater** and 1958 quote.
1924 FLAHERTY *Eskimo Friends* 161: We see-sawed over the ice foot into land and struck up the Cape's big slope. **1958** *Manice* 7: Ice Foot—Heavy ridges of ice formed along a shore caused by tidal action and

spray. The base may be below the water line at high tide.

ice fox *North* See **Arctic fox.**
1939 MONTAGUE *Eskimos* 126: [There was] a fight between an ice fox and a land fox, which are counted to be bitter enemies.

ice-grind *n.* the eroding action of ice in contact with shore rock.
1936 STRINGER *Wife-Traders* 5: It threw a chill over the dark masses of tide-washed rock, scarred and rounded by ice-grind, that marked the outer fringe of the Inlet.

ice harvest the annual cutting and storing of blocks of ice used for refrigeration.
1896 (1898) RUSSELL *Far North* 21: All the Indians at the post and a few from the river reserves were engaged in the ice harvest from the middle of November until New-year. **1955** *Coast Guard* 10 Mar. 1/2: Shelburne Fisheries Ltd., have completed their Ice harvest at Swansburgs Lake. They have 20,000 tons of ice in their Ice House. . . .

ice hockey See **hockey.**
1906 CLARKE *All Abroad* 281: What made the West wild was the result of a series of ice hockey games at Ottawa, between the team of that city (holders of the Stanley Cup) and . . . Indian Jaw. **1948** ONRAET *Sixty Below* 81: Some people say he invented ice-hockey, getting the big idea from that frying-pan and the guys with greasy bacon on their feet. **1961** *Canada Month* Dec. 34/2: To the world of sport Canada contributed the peculiarly Canadian game of ice hockey.

ice-house *n.* **1** a structure usually having insulated walls and roof, used as a storage place for meat and other perishables, the refrigerant being blocks of ice. See also **hangard** (def. 2).
1792 (1911) SIMCOE *Diary* 98: They use the ice to cool liquors and butter, and the ice houses are used for larders to keep meat. **1832** (1953) RADCLIFF *Letters* 47: When we had completed the house, we raised a barn . . . with an ice-house, root house, and summer dairy beneath it. . . . **1934** *Beaver* Sep. 39/2: . . . there was always a large ice-house full of ice so that everything brought in could be kept fresh. **1963** *Cdn Geog.Jnl* Apr. 120/1: The southeast and northwest bastions were ice-houses.

2 See **igloo** (def. 1a) (a misnomer, for igloos are made of blocks of snow rather than ice).
1857 MCDOUGALL *Voyage* 426: The remains of two ice houses yet existed, but were rapidly thawing away, under the influence of the heat of the sun. **1961** *Time* (Cdn ed.) 22 Dec. 5/2: As in years past, Pelly Bay's 125 Eskimos will build an ice house for their Christmas Mass. As children watch, the men tramp out a circle in the snow, then make six igloos of ordinary size. They fill the spaces in between with snow blocks, raising a dome 15 feet high. Then the inside walls are cut away.

ice hummock *North* See **hummock** (def. 2).
1933 *Beaver* Sep. 45/2: . . . we . . . struck out through the ice hummocks into the obscurity of the Queen Maud sea.

ice-hunter *n. Nfld* See **seal hunter.** Cp. **ice,** *n.* (def. 1).
1861 DE BOILIEU *Labrador Life* 198: One of the shipwrecked men saved from the schooner had been an ice-hunter, and whiled away many an hour by relating the mode of catching seals in the spring of the year on the coast of Newfoundland. **1896** (1965) LEACH *Songs* 187: From Trinity, Ship Cove, Trouty . . . and other

small places, the daring ice hunters set off with high hopes . . . to chase the wary seal. . . . **1964** *Nfld Qtly* Spring 27/1 : The large credits in the spring are obviously for marine ironwork, gunsmithing, etc., etc. done for Ridley's ice-hunters.

ice-hunting *n. Nfld* See **sealing.** Cp. **ice-hunter.**
1905 GRENFELL *Harvest of Sea* 120 : Though we made very little by it, somehow we all looked forward to the "ice-hunting," as we called it.

ice hut See **ice-fishing hut.**
1966 *Globe and Mail* (Toronto) 15 Jan. 29/3 : After an unexpected delay because of mild weather the ice huts began to move onto Lake Simcoe this week.

ice-jam *n.* a pile-up of ice-cakes, *q.v.,* in a river or other narrow watercourse. See also **jam,** *n.* (def. 1).
1846 BONNYCASTLE *Canada and Canadians* II 3 : I have mentioned that, in the spring of 1845, an ice-jam, as it is called here, occurred, which suddenly raised the level of the Niagara thirty and forty feet above its ordinary floods. . . . **1898** *Yukon Midnight Sun* (Dawson) 11 June 4/2 : Captain Mariner says the boat was landed high and dry by the pressure of the ice jam, but that he relaunched her without any damage whatever. **1962** *Weekend Mag.* 5 May 3/2 : Near Matty Island, the ice jam reached from shore to shore. . . .

ice-jammed *adj.* blocked by an ice-jam.
1958 *Edmonton Jnl* 24 June 4 15/4 : . . . the ice-jammed river broke into a raging torrent of water, completely isolating the hospital.

ice-land *v. Lumbering* stack pulpwood or logs on the ice in winter so that they will be ready for driving at the break-up (def. 1) in spring.
[1822 (1932) MCLEAN *Notes* 30 : . . . finding a quantity of timber collected on the ice, [we] concluded that the *shanty* must be close at hand.] **1955** *Bush News* (Port Arthur, Ont.) Feb. 1 : Some 6,000 cords of pulp from Lake of the Woods Concession is being truck hauled to ice landings near Kenora and the balance including tie bolts and logs is ice landed at different camps.

ice-landing *n. Lumbering* the place where logs are ice-landed, *q.v.* See also **river landing.**
1966 *Cdn Forest Industries* June 38/2 : Each of the five company camps contributes about 25,000 cords for the spring river drive. This is trucked from the bush to ice landings on the Kapuskasing River.

ice lanes *Slang* hockey, *q.v.,* (with reference to the players' movements up and down the ice while playing his position).
1966 *Kingston Whig-Standard* (Ont.) 16 Apr. 9/1 : Frank Nighbor, magician and gentleman of the ice lanes, has gone to his last resting place. *Ibid.* 28 June 9/1 : Harvey "Busher" Jackson, storied left wing star of the hockey ice lanes [died] in Toronto last Saturday. . . .

ice-ledge *n.* See **shore-ice** (def. 1).
1908 MAIR *Mackenzie Basin* 42 : In the morning we passed several ice-ledges along shore, the survivals of the severe winter. . . . **1936** STRINGER *Wife-Traders* 168 : And, once free, he went lurching out across the ice-ledge. He reminded Stendal of a wounded seal as he slipped and fell, tumbling headlong across the first small pressure-ridge.

ice lens a layer of ice in permafrost, *q.v.*
1957 *Maclean's* 14 Sep. 90/4 : . . . the permafrost in clay or fine silts . . . may contain up to six times as much water as solid matter, usually in layers of ice known as "ice lenses."

ice-lip *n.* See **shore-ice** (def. 1).
1936 STRINGER *Wife-Traders* 169 : "Are you all right ?" asked Winslow, hobbling out on the ice-lip to meet them.

iceman *n.* a sailor or sealer experienced at moving about on the ice or in the ice fields.
1850 (1851) SNOW *Voyage* 302 : Ten men formed the number of the working seamen ; there were no "ice-masters," nor regular "ice-men :" but most of the sailors were long accustomed to the ice. **1907** MILLAIS *Newfoundland* 47 : This little 'tickle,' as it is called, was not quite open water, but a space of slushy, fine fragments of ice on which none can run except the most experienced ice-men.

ice-master *n.* See **ice-pilot.**
1853 INGLEFIELD *Summer Search* 39 : . . . the ice-masters carefully looked out for a lane, and we succeeded, about a mile and a half to the eastward, in getting into a fine opening, which gave every prospect of leading us into open water. **1921** *Beaver* Apr. 4/1 : Captain Bishop was . . . a skilled ice-master, and a navigator of rare good judgment.

ice-mate *n. Nfld* the man in charge of a party of sealers on the ice (def. 1).
1857 MCDOUGALL *Voyage* 323 : The same evening, another (calf) was shot by Mr. Newton (Ice mate).

ice-motor *n. North, Obs.* See quote.
1949 BECKER *Klondike* 59 : [Caption] Ice motors leaving Bennett for Dawson on March 16, 1899. The motorized sled was guided by means of a disk controlled by a steering wheel with a bar attachment to give greater leverage.

ice-out season *North* See **break-up period.**
1957 *Time* (Cdn ed.) 6 May 17 : With the ice-out season beginning this week, the surface of Trout Lake will be frothing for almost a month, after which the warming water will send the ouananiche back down to the seclusion of the bottom of the lake.

ice-pack† *n.* an expanse of ice made up of many small pans or floes tightly packed together. See also **pack,** *n.* (def. 2). Cp. **pack ice.**
1855 (1892) KANE *Arctic Explor.* 386 : A single gale might convert the precarious platform, over which we were travelling, into a tumultuous ice-pack.
1912 POCOCK *Man in the Open* 19 : We lay in the big ice pack off Cape Breton, getting a load of seal pelts.
1962 *Weekend Mag.* 5 May 4/3 : The ship was still fast in the grip of the ice pack and she stayed there till the beginning of August. . . .

ice palace 1 a building made of blocks of clear ice.
1889 WITHROW *Our Own Country* 235 : The Montreal Ice Palace was the first ever tried in the New World.
1905 WIGHTMAN *Our Cdn Heritage* 38 : The ice palaces and winter carnivals, once so popular in the chief cities of the Dominion . . . have aided in this work of peculiar education to a surprising degree. . . .
1957 *Herald-Tribune* (Grande Prairie, Alta) 17 Dec. 1/8 : In rapid-fire succession during the day, events, running the gamut from a snow man contest for the children to construction of an ice palace on Richmond avenue, will be run off.

2 *Slang* See **arena.**
1955 *Winnipeg Free Press* 14 Jan.: . . . Robertson should have an attraction tonight at the ancient Whitehall ice palace that should be well worth taking in.

ice-pan *n.* **1** a fairly substantial slab of ice broken off from a large expanse of ice; an ice floe. See also **ice-raft** and **pan,** *n.* (def. 1). Cp. **ice-cake.**
1918 GRENFELL *Labrador Doctor* 76: Jumping from the side of the ship as she goes along, scurrying and leaping from ice-pan to ice-pan, and then having killed, "sculped," and "pelted" the seal, the exciting return to the vessel. **1939** (1951) TWEEDSMUIR *Hudson's Bay Trader* 163: An elderly herring-gull sat on an ice-pan, head under its wing asleep. **1963** *Calgary Herald* 20 Sep. 26/1: Turquoise ice pans (last year's ice) cluttered the water just off shore.

2 an extensive expanse of ice.
1953 *Cdn Geog.Jnl* July 161: . . . we were able to make the first part of the journey by boat . . . between the rocky shores and the ice pan which still covered most of the bay.

ice-pilot *n. North* an experienced seaman who cons a ship through sea ice. See also **ice-master.**
1934 GODSELL *Arctic Trader* 266: Alex Seymour, the ice pilot, has his Eskimo wife on board, also his half-caste daughter, a very pretty girl who had been educated at a Ladies' College in San Francisco. . . . **1937** *Beaver* June 20/1: . . . with Captain John Ford . . . as ice pilot and supercargo.

ice-pit *n. Obs.* See **glacier.**
1859 KANE *Wanderings* 367: . . . the ice-pit . . . is made by digging a square hole, capable of containing 700 to 800 buffalo carcases.

ice-pole *n.* a long, strong pole used by seamen for levering and thrusting against ice floes, etc.
1850 (1851) SNOW *Voyage* 154: The slackest and thinnest part of the floe, or fragment, was cut into with the axes and chisels until some fortunate blow or prise of the ice-pole rent and loosened it. **1906** LUMSDEN *Skipper Parson* 107: This useful instrument [a sealing gaff] also serves as an ice pole, enabling the daring sealer . . . to leap from "pan to pan."

ice pool a sweepstake, the winner being the person who makes the closest guess as to the date of the break-up (def. 1) in spring, as marked by the actual movement of the ice.
1910 SERVICE *Trail of '98* 428: "Chances in the ice pools. Funny thing I don't remember buying them."

ice-pounder *n. Nfld* See quote.
1835 WIX *Journal* 17: We took a heavy mallet, with a long handle, which the people call an ice-pounder, and escaped some hours of very laborious walking, by crossing in a boat to Bay Roberts.

ice racket *Obs.* See **ice-scoop.**
1795 (1916) THOMPSON *Narrative* 158: [An] ice racket [is] a netted scoop for cleaning bits of floating ice out of a hole prepared for fishing through the ice.

ice-raft *n. North* See **ice-pan** (def. 1).
1856 (1892) KANE *Arctic Explor.* II 228: The transporting forces of the ice-raft [were considerable]. **1893** YOUNG *Indian Wigwams* 178: . . . an ice-raft is an awkward,

unwieldy thing with a tendency to crack in pieces at very critical moments in the passage. **1931** LEBOURDAIS *Northward* 221: Would their ice-raft continue its drift ashore? Or would it float away to sea again?

ice-railway *n. Hist.* a winter railway built in 1880 on the ice of the St. Lawrence River between Montreal and Longueil, Quebec, the tracks being taken up in April each year until 1882, when the service was discontinued.
1955 COLLARD *Cdn Yesterdays* 310: The ice-railway was an ingenious device to break the monopoly of the Grand Trunk.

ice-road *n.* **1** a winter route across a river, lake, etc. See also **ice-bridge** (def. 1).
1845 TOLFREY *Sportsman* II 3: Experienced "ice-road" makers are then selected to cut and prepare a carriage and foot-way across the river, to define which large branches and stems of the fir-tree are placed at legitimate distances to indicate the path a well-conditioned Canadian should travel. . . . **1884** DAWSON *Canada* 122: The ice-roads [across the St. Lawrence] are always marked-out by spruce-trees stuck in the snow. **1955** COLLARD *Cdn Yesterdays* 305n: The "shove" menaced anyone still trying to cross the St. Lawrence on the ice-roads, and year by year there would be rescues or casualties.

2 a route following the course of a frozen river. See also **river road** and **winter road** (def. 3).
1963 *Weekend Mag.* 7 Dec. 6/2: The forest is criss-crossed by good solid ice roads all winter, but a thaw can come quite suddenly in March.

ice-roller *n. Arctic* one of a number of low ridges from 30 to 40 feet high that are characteristic of shore-ice (def. 1).
1963 *North* Mar.-Apr. 13/1: While sledging through the fog, he had noted "hard sastrugi" and "ice rollers". . . .

ice-run *n.* See **ice shove** (def. 2) and **run,** *n.* (def. 4).
1900 LONDON *Son of Wolf* 72: The first break-up of spring found the party following the ice-run of Elk River.

ice-scoop *n.* a device for scooping ice fragments from fishing holes to keep them from freezing over. See also **ice racket.**
1948 *Beaver* Mar. 32/1: Each hunter sets out armed with traps, an ice chisel, and an ice scoop. The scoop is usually a piece of barrel iron hammered to the shape of a spoon, and is indeed often known by that name.

ice-scooter *n.* See **scoot** and picture.
1966 *Kingston Whig-Standard* (Ont.) 13 Jan. 2/6: A provincial police diver today located an ice-scooter owned by a local insurance agent who vanished here [Cayuga, Ont.] last night.

ice-shelf *n.* **1** See **shore-ice** (def. 1).
1940 *Beaver* June 22/1: . . . the men worked with feverish energy to repair the damage caused by the treacherous ice shelf. . . . **1963** *North* Mar.-Apr. 13/1: The rolls are the characteristic features of the ice shelves attached to this [Arctic] coast. These shelves, defined as "floating ice sheets rising more than two metres above sea level," differ from the ordinary pack ice on the Arctic Ocean in that they are much thicker, have rolls on their surface, and are attached to the land, and do not drift with the currents.

2 a shelf of ice anchored to the bank of a river otherwise open. See also **bordage, rim-ice, shelf, shore-ice** (def. 2).

1957 FISHER *Pemmican* 303: They stood on the ice shelf and stared at the water . . . but there was no sign of beaver or of any kind of life.

ice-shove *n.* 1 *Obs.* See quote.
1829 MACTAGGART *Three Years* II 102: Mr. Wright termed these wavy rocks, ice-shoves: he agreed that they had once been the channels of rapids, and were scooped out by the spring floods, laden with ice. . . .

2 *Hist.* the annual thrusting forward and expansion of river ice during break-up, with special reference to the St. Lawrence River, where the phenomenon was accompanied with much flooding and considerable danger. See also **débâcle, ice-flood, ice-run, shove,** *n.* (def. 2), and **shove,** *v.*
1865 PARKMAN *Champlain* 334: He built a wall of bricks . . . to measure the destructive effects of the "ice-shove" in the spring. **1870** *Cdn Illust.News* 26 Mar. 334/1: . . . it will give us a vivid idea of the dangers attendant on the ice-shove of the St. Lawrence. . . . **1955** COLLARD *Cdn Yesterdays* 305n: As in a monstrous game of leap-frog, the huge blocks of ice are sliding over one another in the ice-shove on the Montreal waterfront in 1873.

ice-storm† *n.* 1 See quote.
1886 GEIKIE *Outline Geology* 50: By repeated thawings and regelations the boughs and branches are gradually loaded with ice and snow. . . . Should one [tree] be overthrown it collides against its neighbour, and this in turn falls upon another, until shortly the trees are seen crashing to the ground in all directions. This is what is known in North America as an ice-storm.

2 See **silver thaw** (def. 1).
1955 *Spectator* (Hamilton, Ont.) 25 Jan. 29/1: She takes off all the make-up and slaps a quart of cold cream over her face so that trying to plant a kiss is like trying to drive your car around a 90-degree turn during an ice-storm—you're due for one heck of a skid. **1965** *Kingston Whig-Standard* (Ont.) 13 Dec. 19/1: Nearly every cloud has a silver lining and Sunday's ice-storm was no exception.

ice-strip *n.* *North* a landing strip on ice.
1959 LEISING *Arctic Wings* 129: Mike flew low over the steel-domed huts of the camp and we landed quickly and smoothly on the river icestrip.

ice time *Hockey* the amount of time actually spent on the ice by a player taking part in the game.
1965 *Globe and Mail* (Toronto) 5 Jan. 27/2: Shinny also gives a youngster plenty of ice time. . . .

ice-trap *n.* See **ice anchorage.**
1963 *Albertan* (Calgary) 19 Nov. 3/4: The ice trap first was dug several years ago. . . .

ice-vault *n.* *Obs.* See **glacier.**
1831 (1963) DAVIES *Northern Quebec* 152: The people boating home clay, squaring posts for an ice vault, etc. **1833** *Ibid.* 173: . . . Milette . . . after stowing by the green meat in the ice vault, cut firewood.

ice-velocipede *n.* *Obs.* See quote.
1870 *Cdn Illust.News* 19 Feb. 250/1: The ice-velocipede has but one wheel, armed with short spikes, which catch in the ice and considerably lessen the chances of slipping. . . . Our illustration represents an everyday scene on the river near Montreal, where the ice-velocipede is in very general use.

ice-wall *n.* *Maritimes* See **ballacater.**
1934 DENNIS *Down in N.S.* 321: Sometimes the ice-walls were thirty feet in height, sometimes as high

as sixty feet. Sometimes, when the winter was a mild one, the ice-walls would be low enough to step over. **1953** RADDALL *Tidefall* 291: It's low—most of it's barely above the tide on the springs—so there's no ice wall to bother us if we want to get ashore there.

ice-worm *n.* 1 a mythical creature born as a practical joke in the Yukon during the Klondike gold rush.
☛ *Although the evidence given here for* **ice-worm** *refers to an imaginary creature, the term also refers to a worm of the* Oligochaeta *family,* Mesenchytraeus solifugus, *found on mountain snow and ice fields, which almost certainly was not identified when the term appeared in the* Klondike Nugget *and the writings of Robert W. Service.*
1901 *Klondike Nugget* (Dawson, Y.T.) 10 Apr. 2/2: As usual the doctor had with him his medicine case, likewise a bottle of fluid extract of rye, for in a country where ice worms abound there is no telling but that deadly serpents may also be found. **1910** SERVICE *Trail of '98* 209: Nothing like ice-worm oil for salads. **1953** RADDALL *Tidefall* 203: I think they have a theory that after a certain number of years in the North without a break a man's apt to get bitten by the ice worms. **1964** *Edmonton Jnl* 11 July 27/1: The Klondike ice worm, immortalized in Robert Service's The Ice Worm Cocktail, has been imported to Edmonton. Royal Canadian Legion insiders report the Kingsway branch will feature the Service beverage with prime adult worms brought "directly from the Arctic (Their suspicious macaroni flavor undermines the Klondike romance element somewhat.)"

2 in the phrase **when the ice-worms nest again,** popularized by Robert W. Service, 1876-1958, and sometimes used as a farewell in the North.
1910 SERVICE *Trail of '98* 209: Oh, my Heart, my Life, my Soul,/ I will meet thee when the ice-worms nest again. **1948** ONRAET *Sixty Below* 86: We shook hands, and said, each to each other: "I'll be seeing you, when the ice worms nest again." **1958** *Cdn Geog.Jnl* Jan. IV/1: A visitor may find himself . . . singing "When the Ice-Worms Nest Again," a song introduced during the 1949 festival.

ice-worm cocktail a cocktail, originally served in the Klondike, having as a basic ingredient ice-worms, *q.v.*—actually bits of spaghetti or macaroni.
1910 SERVICE *Trail of '98* 209: You've never had an ice-worm cocktail? We must remedy that. **1954** BERTON *I Married Klondike* 16: As we ate dinner a waiter came in with a tray of what he called "ice-worm cocktails," to the intense annoyance of the teetotalling Miss Lawson. Sure enough, the white worms, which we were told were considered a prime delicacy, could be seen at the bottom of each glass. They turned out, of course, to be spaghetti. **1966** *Kingston Whig-Standard* (Ont.) 25 Feb. 12/1: Miller . . . paused briefly from his arduous task of mixing the two local opiates—moose milk and ice-worm cocktails—for clamorous customers in his warm bistro on Whitehorse's main drag.

ice-yachting *n.* See **iceboating.**
1964 *Canadian Wkly* 12 Dec. 7/4: You won't go on any ice-yachting picnics either, because you go too fast to relax, or else you have to get out and push.

icing *n.* 1 *North* the layer of ice that is built up

when water is applied to a dog-sled runner. Cp.
ice, *v.* (def. 2).
1942 TWOMEY & HERRICK *Needle to North* 69: In the
warmth of the weather, the icing on the sled runners
was already going bad.
2 *Hockey* the infraction committed when a player
ices the puck, thus causing play to be stopped and
the puck brought back to be faced off in the
offending team's end. Cp. **ice,** *v.* (def. 1b).
1958 *Evening Telegram* (St. John's) 24 Apr. 14/7:
Icing violations do not mean too much to the sprites
as yet as they don't have the strength to fire the puck all
the way down.... **1965** *Kingston Whig-Standard* (Ont.)
7 Apr. 12: With that gesture, he automatically
nullified the prospective "icing" call.

ictas, icties, ictus *n.pl.* See **iktas.**

idiot stick *Slang* a small, carved replica of a
totem pole, *q.v.*, sold widely to souvenir buyers in
British Columbia and elsewhere.
1964 DUFF *Indian History* I 83: The talented carver has
to choose between volume production of low-priced
souvenir [totem] poles (called by some "idiot sticks")
and works of high quality which must be sold at high
prices.

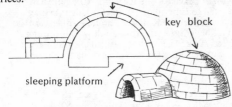

key block

sleeping platform

An igloo (def. la)

igloo ['ɪglu] *n.* [< East Esk. *iglu* dwelling] **1 a.** a
domed structure built of blocks of hard snow; an
Eskimo snowhouse. See also **ice-house** (def. 2),
snowhouse (def. 1), **snow hut,** and **snow igloo.** Also
spelled *iglu.*
[1771 (1935) *Cdn Hist.Rev.* XVI 58: Yes, veritably made
of snow, without either stone or wood—this house the
indians call aneo-iggilo, which litterally is snow house.]
1832 (1963) DAVIES *Northern Quebec* 162: Average
thermometer, −35°. Very sharp; were obliged to get
iglou porches (made of hardened snow) to the dwelling
houses. which made them much warmer. **1864** HALL
Life with Esquimaux I 131: During the last few years
Esquimaux live almost entirely in igloos—"snow-
houses"—through the winter season. **1958** *Edmonton
Jnl* 24 June 3 16/4: The domed igloo of the Eskimo is a
familiar picture to most Canadians—yet only about
one-third of Canada's Eskimos live in igloos.
b. any other Eskimo house, except the tent, or
tupek, *q.v.*
1824 LYON *Private Jnl* 447: The natives term them, as
well as the whole island, Igloolik; and Igloo being a
house, the huts may have been the means of naming
the country. **1849** MCLEAN *Notes* II 161: These
buildings are generally formed of stakes driven into
the ground, chinked with moss, and covered with bark;
they are always warmed with stoves, otherwise the
igloe would afford more comfort. **1885** TUTTLE *Our
North Land* 233: In summer the Eskimos live in conical
skin tents, and in winter in half underground huts

(igloos) built of stone, turf, earth, etc., entered by a
long tunnel-like passage which can only be traversed
on all fours. **1916** HAWKES *Labrador Eskimo* 60: There
still remain at Hebron, Okkek, and Killinek old stone
iglus roofed with turf, some of which are inhabited.
1938 *Beaver* Sep. 39: The igloos are made of rough
wooden poles, and covered with reindeer skins.
1958 *Evening Telegram* (St. John's) 29 Apr. 13/1: Many
people are still under the impression that Eskimos live
in "igloos." Actually, the word igloos to an Eskimo
means any type of home which cannot be moved—a
snow house or a wooden one. **1966** *Kingston
Whig-Standard* (Ont.) 28 Feb. 10/1: ... the presiding
steward ... retired to his igloo to compile the results. ...
2 *Obs.* See **aglu.**
1864 HALL *Life with Esquimaux* II 242: While Koojesse
kept hold of the line, four or five fathoms long, the seal
worked itself hastily back into the igloo, its birthplace,
and there made a plunge down the seal-hole into the
sea.

ikkumer or **ikomer** *n.* [< Esk. *ikoma* candle]
North, Obs. a kudlik, *q.v.*, or other lamp.
1865 (1960) MOWAT *Ordeal by Ice* 339: [Water] is made
only by melting snow or ice over the ikkumer
(fire-lamp), which is an expensive heat and light when
oil and blubber become scarce.... **1882** GILDER
Schwatka's Search 27: During the night we were
visited by a severe thunder-storm, which frightened
my tent-mates because unused to it, and they lighted
an ikomer to take the sharp edge off the lightening.

iktas ['ɪktas] *n.pl.* [< Chinook Jargon] *Pacific
Coast* goods; belongings; things. Also spelled
ectas, ictas, ictus, iktahs, iktus, etc.
1870 *Mainland Guardian* (New Westminster, B.C.)
8 Jan. 3/3: Some little "iktas" were disposed of by
lottery when the good Dane's back was turned.
1892 (1941) *B.C.Hist.Qtly* Oct. 302: They chiefly took
their pay in blankets and provisions and other ectas—
the balance in coin. **1951** HOBSON *Grass* 101: We got
eighteen horses, a summer's grub and all the ictus we
need for the time being. **1957** LARGE *Skeena* 58: We
had not gone far before the ground was covered with
our various "iktus."

Ile St. Jean *Hist.* See **Isle St. Jean.**

illahie ['ɪlə͵hi] *n.* [< Chinook Jargon] Also
spelled *illahee, illiha(e), illihee,* etc. *Pacific Coast*
1 country; field; homeland; place.
1833 (1963) TOLMIE *Physician* 167: "Passed a canoe
fastened to the trunk of a tree in the bank about 5 yards
from margin, containing the ashes of a Chenooke
[Chinook]. The indians call these sepulchres Nimilush
elihe 'the Place of the Dead'." **1915** CUMMING *Skookum
Chuck* 70: A message was sent to the Lillooet illihae
(country) with the glad tidings, and at the close of two
days a swarm of smootlatches (women), and keekas
(girls), rushed into camp breathless.... **1957** LARGE
Skeena 66: Took trail for the Omineca and the Tahltan
illahie.
2 home; lodge.
1869 *Mainland Guardian* (New Westminster, B.C.)
27 Nov. 1/4: Here we paid off Sambo who was much
delighted to reach his own illihee. **1904** HERRING *In the
Pathless West* 226: So it was taken in hand by the
klootchmen in the Chief's illehee. **1915** CUMMING
Skookum Chuck 17: Peter had nothing: he had no
illiha, no icties of any kind; he was broke morning,
noon and night. Johnny had a sixty dollar saddle, a
five dollar bridle, a two and a half quirt and the best
cayuse in Spence's Bridge. ...

Illinois capote *Hist*. See **Hudson's Bay capote**.
1798 (1964) CHABOILLEZ *Journal* 178 : [These] articles [were] over charge in the Recapitulation received from the Agents—Vist :—. . . 1 Illinois Capo. . . .
1913 COWIE *Adventurers* 116 : It appeared the approved uniform for clerks on the boat journey was a greyish blue cloth "illinois" capote with silverplated buttons, and a broad scarlet worsted sash, the regulation headgear being a fine navy blue cloth cap with a leather peak.

immigrant car or **coach** a railway car carrying immigrants, as on an immigrant train, *q.v*. See also **emigrant car**. Cp. **colonist car**.
1883 *Brandon Dly Mail* (Man.) 20 Apr. 4/1 : The regular train west yesterday had a new immigrant coach attached, crowded with immigrants for the west.
1935 (1951) GRAHAM *Golden Grindstone* 16 :
. . . they travelled west from Winnipeg in an immigrant car. **1959** *Maclean's* 18 July 56/4 : The immigration department recently ordered out of its immigrant coaches the vice-president of a German-Canadian club in Toronto. . . .

immigrant house or **shed** *Obs*. See **immigration shed**.
1879 *Winnipeg Dly Times* 14 Apr. 3/3 : On arriving on the Winnipeg side of the river they scattered among the hotels and boarding houses, a few taking up quarters in the Immigrant Sheds. **1883** *Brandon Dly Mail* (Man.) 19 Jan. 4/1 : The Firemen's concert came off last night at the Immigrant House. **1885** *Prince Albert Times* (Sask.) 9 Oct. 1/4 : The buildings in the vicinity, including the immigrant sheds, had a narrow escape, but were saved by the prompt attention of the firemen.

immigrant society *Obs*. See **immigration society**.
1841 *Montreal Transcript* 27 Nov. 2/1 : The benefits to the Colony of immigration . . . are such as to make it the interest of all to assist in forwarding the aims of Immigrant Societies.

immigrant train *Hist*. a railway train carrying immigrants at low rates to their new places of settlement. See also **emigrant train** (def. 2) and **immigration train**.
1895 *Rat Portage* [Kenora] *News* (Ont.) 19 Apr. 3/2 : At the time of my arrival everything was bustle and excitement, as an immigrant train was expected with several settlers for the Bay. **1911** *Eye Opener* (Calgary) 20 May 1/7 : In the last issue we asked the C.P.R. why they didn't put on a coffee-and-sinker layout on their immigrant trains. **1953** LEBOURDAIS *Nation of the North* 95 : Soon the spectacle of long immigrant trains shuttling across the country was a typical sight, and Winnipeg, the first distribution-point for these new Canadians, became a polyglot metropolis of diverse accents and nationalities.

immigration agent 1 a government official appointed to assist immigrants to find land or employment on their arrival in Canada. See also **emigrant agent** and **emigration agent**.
1880 GORDON *Mountain and Prairie* 298 : Such companies, spurred into activity by the prospect of profitable land sales, will probably be more zealous than Government immigration agents. **1904** (1917) *London Hist.Soc.Trans*. VIII 37 : There were no immigration agents, no one to lead and guide the pioneers to their locations, which were chosen and taken up in Little York without even seeing them.
1965 BERTON *Remember Yesterday* 53 : [Caption] These people in Langenburg, Saskatchewan, have just finished

helping Mr. Riedle, the immigration agent . . . finish his home.
2 a Canadian official in another country who promotes immigration, screens applicants, etc.
1900 OSBORN *Greater Canada* 67 : The best immigration agent is a contented settler. **1923** *One Big Union Bull*. (Winnipeg) 22 Mar. 5/3 : A Canadian immigration agent, hailing from Calgary, Alberta, attempted to give a lecture in Lincolnshire, England, explaining the wisdom of workers migrating from the Old Land to Sunny Alberta.

immigration officer See **immigration agent** (def. 1).
1909 BINDLOSS *Lorimer* 27 : A wheat-grower's dwelling thirty miles back from the railroad was registered as wanting assistance, the immigration officer said.

immigration shed a building equipped to shelter immigrants newly arrived in the country. See also **emigrant depot, emigrant shed** and **immigrant house**.
1882 *Progress* (Rat Portage [Kenora], Ont.) 10 June 1/5 : The Grand Trunk station and sheds and the Dominion, Quebec and Ontario immigration sheds at Levis were burned last Saturday. **1926** *Dalhousie Rev*. V 318 : Altogether, the immigrant is seldom more than two or three hours at the immigration sheds. **1932** *Cdn Labor Defender* Sep. 6 : The ten active working class fighters . . . are now putting in their fourth month in the immigration detention shed in Halifax.

immigration society *Hist*. a charitable organization dedicated to looking after immigrants and watching out for their interests. See also **emigrant society**.
1883 *Brandon Daily Mail* (Man.) 8/2 : The Immigration society is a good institution in its place, but the nervous energy and honest industry peculiar to the young Northwest made it no longer necessary.

immigration train *Obs*. See **immigrant train**.
1879 *Winnipeg Dly Times* 14 Apr. 4/1 : The regular train came in on time last night, also a special immigration train at 11 p.m.

import *n. Slang* **1** *Sports* **a.** a player who is brought in from elsewhere to play for a team representing a town, company, etc.; a player who is not a native or product of the area his team represents.
1949 PETERSON *Chipmunk* 76 : "Be glad to see more of the employees on the [softball] team . . .' Stead of all these imports." **1955** *Western Star* (Corner Brook, Nfld) 12 Mar. I 2/2 : Taking item by item it was agreed that the senior 'A' group be classed as open league, which would allow the use of imports and paid playing coaches. **1958** *Kingston Whig-Standard* (Ont.) 30 May 13/1 : Imports are adding color to soccer in Canada just as they did for football. **1962** *Hockey Canada* Nov. 12/2 : One of the greatest of all the imports was Bill Cowley, a smoothie from Ottawa.

b. any competitor who is not native to the area in which he is competing.
1958 *Edmonton Jnl* 20 June 8/4 : Up to now the Edmonton drivers, long acclaimed the best in Canada, have proven patsies for the United States imports who have come up for the past two stock car races at Speedway Park.

2 *Cdn Football* a non-Canadian professional player (in practice, an American) who has not played for five years in Canada. Cp. **homebrew** (def. 1a) and **non-import.**

1958 *Edmonton Jnl* 18 June 13/4: It is understood he may receive his citizenship papers this year and not be classed as an import on Stamp's roster. **1964** *Winnipeg Free Press* 19 June 36/3: ... the group ... favors limiting each team to a certain number of imports who have gained Canadian status through five year residence. **1966** *Globe and Mail* (Toronto) 29 June 40/3: If he had known two years ago what he knows now, Atamian would be playing as a Canadian for Ottawa Rough Riders, not as an import for Argos.

3 a company that is non-Canadian.

1955 *Maclean's* 1 Feb. 48/1: When Simpson-Sears was called an import firm, Eaton's became Eaton's of Canada.

improve *v. Hist.* **1†** increase the value of land by preparing it for cultivation, erecting buildings, enclosing with fences, etc., often as a condition required by the government in making a grant. See also **improvement** (def. 1a). Cp. **prove up.**

1759 (1876) CAMPBELL *Yarmouth, N.S.* 28: The grantees will be obliged by their said grants to plant[,] cultivate, improve or enclose one third of their land in ten years. **1769** *Quebec Gaz.* 16 Feb. 3/1: The Possessors of such Concessions shall be entitled to such Part of them as shall be proportioned to the Improvements they have made thereon, at the Rate of fifty Acres they shall have improved. **1958** *Sun* (Vancouver) 20 Jan. 35/2: In fact, in 1868, it was disputed. By a civil servant's error, Kanakas with Indian wives living at the "Kanaka rancherie" on Coal Harbor and working at the inlet mills were allowed to pre-empt and improve a part of the Morton-Brighouse-Hailstone land.

2 clear trees and underbrush from land in preparation for seeding. See also **improvement** (def. 1b).

1791 (1905) *Ont.Bur.Arch.Rep.* III 117: How many children have you capable of improving lands? **1827** *Gore Gaz.* (Ancaster, U.C.) 13 Apr. 27/1: There are about 20 Acres improved, and under good fence.

improved† *adj. Hist.* See 1913 quote. See also **improve.**

1911 SMITH *Is it Just?* 13: ... the Pierces became purchasers of a partly-improved ten-acre lot at Ortgeard for the sum of $3,000. "Dirt cheap" it was, according to Mr Masson.... **1913** SANDILANDS *West. Cdn Dict.* 24: [An] improved farm [is] cultivated or partly cultivated, and having some of the necessary buildings or barns on it.

improved Britisher *Jocular* an immigrant from the British Isles, especially an Englishman, who has been in Canada long enough to have lost some of his native shortcomings. Cp. **improved Scotsman.**

☛ *This term is still heard although it seldom appears in print.*

1913 SANDILANDS *West.Cdn Dict.* 24/2: A person born in the Old Country, but of long residence in Canada.

improved Scotsman *North, Slang* a half-breed, especially a Scotch half-breed, *q.v.* See also **Smoked Scotchman.**

1934 GODSELL *Arctic Trader* 189: There were Mounted Police ... and "Improved Scotsmen" as the mixed bloods were facetiously known. **1938** *Beaver* June 25/1: The Indians had intermarried with Scots for nearly two hundred years and may well be what Skipper Neilson calls them, improved Scotsmen. **1966** *Sun* (Vancouver) 22 Mar. 12/8: Canadians have not been slow to find nicknames for themselves and others. Among them are: Spud Islander ... improved Scotsman....

improvement† *n.* **1** *Hist.* **a.** the clearing of land, provision of fences, buildings, etc. as required of settlers receiving grants of land or, later, holding land under the homestead laws. See 1824 quote. See also **improve** (def. 1).

1789 (1905) *Ont.Bur.Arch.Rep.* III lxx: ... the petitioner shall ... begin the improvement and cultivation thereof within one year from the date of such assignment. **1824** *Cdn Mag.* II 503: In Canada, what is called improvement consists in merely chopping down the trees, collecting and burning them with such other impediments upon the surface as the fire will consume, such as under-brush, leaves, etc. **1827** *Cdn Freeman* (York [Toronto]) 18 Jan. 4/5: Upon this farm there are 20 acres of land under fence and in a good state of improvement, and 200 acres of unimproved land.

b. into (or **under**) **improvement,** of land, cleared of trees and underbrush and ready for farming. See also **improve** (def. 2).

1799 *Canada Constellation* (Niagara-on-the-Lake, U.C.) 20 Sep. 4/3: A valuable and pleasant situation at Burlington Bay ... containing 975 acres of land, 150 of which are under good improvement. **1811** *Kingston Gaz.* (U.C.) 7 May 1/4: A few years ago I purchased a lot of land in this neighborhood, which I have now brought into a good state of improvement. **1821** HOWISON *Sketches* 208: Their object is, to have a great deal of land under improvement, as they call it; and ... they go on cutting down the woods on their lots, and regularly transferring the crops to the soil last cleared, until they think they have sufficiently extended the bounds of their farms.

2 (*usually plural*) **a.** things done to improve (def. 1) land.

1769 *Quebec Gaz.* 16 Feb. 3/1: The Possessors of such Concessions shall be entitled to such Part of them as shall be proportioned to the Improvements they have made thereon, at the Rate of fifty Acres they shall have improved. **1824** *Cdn Mag.* II 504: Numbers of farmers from the old country come here with wives and families, and they often to avoid the sufferings and privations which they must endure by going at once into the woods, purchase or rent a farm with what is here termed improvements. **1869** *Mainland Guardian* (New Westminster, B.C.) 29 Sep. 2/2: The improvements comprise a dwelling house and barn, with about 70 acres under fence. **1882** *Edmonton Bull.* 21 Oct. 1/2: The improvements made by Wright before his death consisted of ten acres of breaking with crop and fencing, partially in each of the quarters forming the west half of the section, and the walls of a house on one of the same quarters. **1910** MCCLUNG *Second Chance* 105: This unpretentious log house had been the first home of Mr. and Mrs. Steadman, and was part of the "improvements" specified by the Government to show that a homestead had been entered in good faith. **1958** STEGNER *Making Paths* 37: I remember it as it originally was, for my brother and I, aged eight and six, accompanied my father when he went out to make the first "improvements." **1966** *Globe and Mail* (Toronto) 30 Nov. 1/4: "Tonks ... could have no honest belief that he was making improvements on land that was his own."

b. *Obs.* the lands so improved.

1796 *U.C.Gaz.* (York [Toronto]) 26 Oct. 3/1: Some of you have as large improvements as 50 acres, or more, and the crops you get scarcely worth harvesting. **1824** *Canadian Mag.* II 503: When this [clearing and burning] is done, the land is fit to receive the seed without the application of any implement of agriculture, and is called an improvement of so many acres. . . .

3 *Obs.* of land, enhancement in value resulting from the making of improvements (def. 2). See **improve,** *v.* (def. 1).

1805 BOULTON *Upper Canada* 7: Sometimes . . . the obligee in the bond . . . takes back the land with four or five years improvement upon it, and resells it to a fresh purchaser to a great profit.

improvement district See **local improvement district.**

1954 *Peace River Block News* (Dawson Creek, B.C.) 4 Mar. 6/2: If the improvement district trustees wish to raise a sizable sum to finance the community's share of the cost of a large project such as constructing and equipping a hospital, such an amount may be included in one money by-law. **1961** *Edmonton Jnl* 17 July 28/1: The type of service and form of government provided in an improvement district was designed for pioneer districts or areas which cannot support people in sufficient numbers to make municipal government practical. **1964** *Maclean's* 25 July 1/1: [He] is chairman of the board of trustees of the improvement district of White River [Ont.].

inconnu ['ɪŋkə,nu] *n.* [< Cdn F < F "unknown"] a fresh-water food fish, *Stenodus mackenzii,* native to the rivers and lakes of the Yukon and the Northwest Territories, having pinkish flesh when prime and averaging about twelve pounds, though occasionally running as high as forty. See also **connie, poisson inconnu, shee,** and **unknown fish.**

1806 (1960) FRASER *Letters and Journals* 231: The Indians also state that there are plenty white fish uncanu some trout carp Jub, &c. in the fall of the year. **1844** (1955) LEFROY *Magnetic North* 99: I tried the Inconnu there, but it is far inferior to the Trout. **1952** PUTNAM *Cdn Regions* 496: One of the species found in the Mackenzie River is the distinctive "coney", or inconnu, so named by Alexander Mackenzie, because the fish was not known in other parts of Canada. **1966** *Commercial Letter* Jan.-Feb. 6: Lake trout up to forty pounds, northern pike, whitefish, inconnu and other species are found in the waters of the Yukon river.

incorporated village a village that has an independent form of local government, separate from surrounding townships.

1958 *Encyc.Can.* VIII 289: There are [in New Brunswick] 19 incorporated towns and 3 incorporated villages. **1965** *Globe and Mail* (Toronto) 14 Jan. W1/1: The area, which is a fraction of what was an incorporated village a hundred years ago, is gradually spreading. . . . **1965** *Canada Year Book* 94: . . . all fully incorporated cities, towns, and villages are regarded as "urban" municipalities.

indemnify *v.* pay an indemnity (to), *q.v.*

1850 CHRISTIE *Lower Canada* III 314: The members of the assembly were now [in 1823], for the first time since the establishment of the constitution, indemnified for attending to their legislative duties.

indemnity *n.* **1** the money received by a member of parliament or of a legislative assembly in return

---

for his services and in compensation for loss of personal income. See also **sessional indemnity.**

1831 *Vindicator* (Montreal) 6 Dec. **3**/3: We see that the indemnity bill underwent further discussion, and has received the concurrence of the House. . . . **1871** *Wkly Manitoban* 6 May 2/3: A rather discreditable discussion took place in the House of Assembly, on the subject of the members' indemnity. **1947** DAWSON *Government of Canada* 394: Members of the House of Commons and the Senate are not paid a salary, but rather what they are pleased to call an indemnity. **1965** *Kingston Whig-Standard* (Ont.) 6 Apr. 4/3: I imagine that one day we shall see independent commissions recommending on the indemnities of members.

2 a similar remuneration received by elected municipal officials.

1907 *U of T Stud.Hist.Econ.* II 217: The indemnities payable are not to exceed $2,000 to a mayor, $400 to an alderman, and $100 to a reeve or councilllor. **1964** *Leader* (Oak Bay, B.C.) 5 Feb. 1/3: The new indemnities compare with Esquimalt's $2,400 for the reeve, and $900 for councillors. . . .

Independent Doukhobor one of a group of Doukhobors, *q.v.,* who do not subscribe to violence.

1962 DICKIE *Great Golden Plain* 239: . . . and a large number who accepted naturalization and with it education and other Canadian customs. These "Independent Doukhobors" usually left the colonies and settled in other places. **1964** *Weekend Mag.* 26 Dec. 2/2: [The] peaceful Doukhobors . . . belong to the sect's other two factions, the Orthodox or Community Doukhobors, and the most Canadianized, the Independents.

Indian† *n.* **1 a.** any member of the Mongoloid aboriginal stock of America, including legally, the Eskimos. Also dial. *Injin, Injun.*

1576 (1889) HAKLUYT *Voyages* XII 54: So that it plainely appeareth that those Indians (which as you haue heard in sundry ages were driuen by tempest vpon the shore of Germanie) came onely through our Northwest passage. **1711** (1920) *Cdn Hist.Rev.* I 51: At Lorett which makes yᵉ Little River of Quebeck about Four Leagues From sᵈ Town, is an Indian Town, about fifty men. **1856** BALLANTYNE *Young Fur-Traders* 83: "Difficult to say, monsieur. Perhaps Injins, though I thought there were none here just now. . . ." **1962** *Canada Month* May 29: North American Indians number more than 500,000: 180,000 in Canada, more than half of whom live in B.C., Saskatchewan, and Ontario, and 350,000 in the U.S. . . .

b. See **registered Indian.**

1965 *Globe and Mail* (Toronto) 26 May 3/4: Those whose names are in a register kept by the federal Indian Affairs Branch are officially Indians; others are not. If your father had Indian status your name goes on the list, but you can apply to have it removed. The Indians have special rights. **1966** *Ibid.* 12 Jan. 9/2: An Indian is defined in law as any person registered with the Indian Affairs Branch as an Indian. . . .

2 any of the various aboriginal languages spoken by Indians.

1717 (1932) KNIGHT *Journals* 170: I send Wᵐ Stewart to be Assistant to my Depᵗʸ In case he Should doo otherways than well, their not being a Man their as Understandeth one Word of Indian. **1852** (1923)

MOODIE *Roughing It* 273: Indian, till after he knew your people, never swore—no bad word in Indian. **1958** *Camsell Arrow* Jan.-Feb. 1: Although [the sisters] are French and the children speak Indian, English is the language of the school.

3 Indians, a children's game in which one group plays the part of Indians on the warpath, another group playing their adversaries, often "cowboys." **1902** CONNOR *Glengarry* 157: He organized the game of "Injuns," some of the boys being set apart as settlers who were to defend the fort . . . the rest to constitute the invading force of savages.

4 *Slang* a person prone to fighting and getting into trouble; a wild-tempered, undisciplined fellow. See also **Indian,** *adj.* *c*1914 (1916) WALLACE *Shack Locker* 276: . . . among the college crowd he was known as an "Indian," a reputation which was well enough in college fights and differences with authorities but detrimental to his prospects with the faculty.

5 *Slang* See **Cowichan sweater.** **1945** *Beaver* Dec. 18/2: To-day there is scarcely a man, woman or child who does not own his "Indian".

Indian *adj. Slang* wild with drink; unruly. See also **Indian,** *n.* (def. 4). **1919** FRASER *Bulldog Carney* 99: "He'd seen me down in the Del Monte joint, and thought—well, he was filled up on Chinese rum. He wasn't none too much like a man in anything he said or done, but I was standin' for him as long as he don't get plumb Injun." *Ibid.* 119: "You've got too much booze. If you want to bet on your horse sit there and cut out this Injun stuff."

Indian Act a federal act governing Indian affairs, first passed in 1876 and revised in 1951. **1878** *Sask.Herald* (Battleford, N.W.T.) 4 Nov. 1: On the 24th ult., Basil Lafonde was convicted before the Stipendiary Magistrate of having given liquor to an Indian, contrary to the "Indian Act." **1886** *Indian* (Hagersville, Ont.) 3 Feb. 5/2: The Dominion Government in a cast-iron act had decided how we should be managed and anything coming in court was regulated by it, "The Indian Act," an act absurdly made in every particular, to apply to the uncivilized pagan tribes, as well as to the civilized and Christian bands of this Province. **1964** JENNESS *Eskimo Admin.* II 40: . . . Quebec's inhabitants unless they were Indians . . . did not come under the Indian Act.

Indian affairs† all matters arising out of the government's relations with the Indians. **1766** *Quebec Gaz.* 3 July 1/1: [Trade] should be carried on at certain Posts, expressed in the Plan for regulating Indian Affairs. **1899** *Prospector* (Lillooet, B.C.) 20 Jan. 1/4: When the Dominion government took control of the Indian affairs of British Columbia, they certainly assumed the burdens, along with the blessings. **1965** *Globe and Mail* (Toronto) 2 Sep. W1/5: Many separate Indian day schools are still operated by the Indian Affairs Branch of the Department of Citizenship and Immigration. . . .

Indian agency 1 the government agency responsible for the well-being of Indians in a given area, especially those on a reserve; also, the area of jurisdiction of this agency. See also **agency** (def. 1).

1921 *Beaver* Aug.-Sep. 13/2: The Indian agency of the government was represented by Mr. H. A. Conroy, who will make treaty with the different Indian tribes along the Mackenzie. **1963** *Calgary Herald* 20 Sep. 32/8: Norman E. Whitehead, officer in charge of the Okanagan Indian Agency, said arrangements . . . had already been made between the band and a Vernon bank and auditor.

2 the actual compound, buildings, etc. where the Indian superintendent, *q.v.,* or Indian agent, makes his headquarters. See also **agency** (def. 2). **1885** *Battleford Hist.Soc.Pubs* I-III 53: Chief Poundmaker and his Indians raided the settlement and burned the Indian Agency. **1958** *Edmonton Jnl* 26 Sep. 9/1: [There is] a teachers' residence and a powerhouse at the Athabasca Indian Agency, Fort Chipewyan.

Indian agent See **Indian superintendent.** **1789** (1905) *Ont.Bur.Arch.Rep.* III 5: Board adjourned until the arrival of Alex. McKee, the Indian agent from the Ottawa River, in order to consult respecting the intended purchase of a Tract from the natives on the east side of the Streight. **1881** *Edmonton Bull.* 3 Jan. 3/1: The Indian Agent is establishing soup kitchens at Victoria, Saddle Lake, White Fish Lake and Lac La Biche. **1965** *Kingston Whig-Standard* (Ont.) 22 Feb. 7/6: In the past the Indian agent directed the reserve's business.

Indian awl a square, double-ended awl of steel, used in canoe-making, leather-working, etc. See also **square awl.** **1821** (1938) SIMPSON *Athabasca Jnl* 142: Awls, Indian, doz. 12. **1942** *Beaver* June 25: Holes are made in the bark with an Indian awl, and the root pulled through in a tight cross-stitch.

Indian blanket† a blanket made for or by Indians, formerly much used by them as a robe. **1782** *Quebec Gaz.* 19 Dec. 4/1: For Sale. . . . A Large assortment . . . Indian blanket Rugs. . . . **1824** *Advocate* (Queenston, U.C.) 2 Sep. 4/3: There was nothing fanciful about his dress or horse furniture, save an Indian blanket, which was wrapped up like a horseman's cloak and fastened behind the saddle. **1907** CROSBY *An-ko-me-nums* 83: Of course, in later years the common garment was the "Indian Blanket," sold by the Hudson's Bay Co. **1966** *Islander* 27 Feb. 7/1: We smelled perfume and talcum from many Indian blankets. . . .

Indian boarding school a mission school where Indian students live in. Cp. **residential school.** **1926** *Beaver* June 105: There are two missions at Cross Lake—Methodist and Roman Catholic, the latter having a large Indian boarding school. **1927** *Ibid.* Mar. 73: The United Church mission . . . has a large Indian boarding school, accommodating about one hundred pupils.

Indian boot See **Canadian shoe.** **1770** (1792) CARTWRIGHT *Journal* I 73: The Indians . . . brought me a pair of stockings; the legs of which are made of deer-skin, with the wool on the inside: they are intended to wear with Indian boots. **1852** RICHARDSON *Arctic Exped.* 212: Neither have these Indian boots, but merely shoes or mocassins, with soft tops that wrap round the ankle, and are unconnected with the leggins or trowsers. **1921** HEMON *Chapdelaine* [trans.] 53: His high Indian boots were caked with mud to the knee. . . .

Indian brandy *Fur Trade, Hist.* See **Indian liquor.** **1747** (1949) ISHAM *Journal* 300: It's suffitient to give them one gallon Indn. Brandy soon after they come, or before any game is to be had, & no more tell the Season is Done. **1748** DRAGE *Voyage* I 121: Three Indians came, with their Canoe, Alongside, telling us, they had Geese, and when Aboard, brought three out of a large greasy Laether Satchel, picked and dressed; for which they had a Bottle of Indian Brandy, the Name given for two Thirds of Brandy, and one of Water.

Indian bread *Obs.* **1** See quote. Cp. **backfat.**
1944 ADAMS *Western Words* 82: Indian bread . . . was a tasty strip of fatty matter starting from the shoulder blade and extending backward along the backbone of a buffalo. When scalded in hot grease . . . then smoked, it became a tidbit the buffalo hunter used as bread. When eaten with lean or dried meat it made an excellent sandwich.
2 a food prepared from tree moss by certain British Columbia Indians.
1954 *B.C.Hist.Qtly* XVIII 261: Indian bread made from moss was also cooked in similar fashion.

Indian bread-root See **prairie turnip.**
1852 (1881) TRAILL *Cdn Crusoes* 126n: This plant appears to be a species of the *Psoralea esculenta,* or Indian bread-root, which it resembles in description, excepting that the root of the above is tuberous, oval, and connected by long filaments. **1912** (1913) HODGE & WHITE *Indians of Can.* 219/1: Indian bread-root. The prairie turnip, or pomme blanche (*Psoralea esculenta*).

Indian camp an Indian encampment or village.
1771 (1792) CARTWRIGHT *Journal* I 142: Early this morning I went to Cape Charles, and there pitched my tent upon the continent, directly opposite the Indian camp. **1824** (1955) BLACK *Journal* 72: Last night I was wakned by a hubbub in the Indian camp it was one of the Thecannies beating his wife with a stick.
1957 *Arctic Spotter* Dec. 11/1: . . . an Indian camp squats near the airfield, beside the White River.

Indian captain *Fur Trade, Hist.* See **captain** (def. 2).
1686 (1932) KENNEY *Fort Churchill* 29: The design of sending Englishmen up to the heads of rivers should be dropped as impracticable and instead the Indian captains who lived at a great distance off should be employed to persuade the Indians to come to the factories. **1738** (1965) *Letters from Hudson Bay* 271: I must further acquaint your honours that the Indian Captain of this river, as the Indians calls him . . . has been too familiar . . . he having of two wives and a great sway amongst all the Indian women. . . .
1774 (1934) HEARNE *Journal* 122: The Indian captain who brought me from the Fort . . . was so affected with the smell of the Canadians New England rum that he and his crew embark'd and followe'd after them. . . .

Indian carrot See **prairie turnip.**
1887 *Senate Report* 84: This Indian turnip or carrot is one of the first vegetables they get in the spring. The Indians commence to dig them out of the ground as soon as the frost is out.

Indian clock See quote.
1922 *Beaver* Sep. 17/2: Alongside the track was an Indian clock . . . a circle drawn in the snow with a stick stuck upright in its centre, and a line traced from the stick to the line of circumference to indicate where the shadow of the stick had fallen at the time the clock was made.

Indian coat *Fur Trade, Obs.* See **captain's coat.**
1785 (1954) *Moose Ft Jnls* 305: Should have sent James Folster now had we been able any way to have spared him, he being the only one left to cook for us or the

Indians the Armourer being mending the trading guns and the Indians, the Taylor making Indian Coats, and that poor helpless creature Halcrow to mind the gates.

Indian collar *North* See quote.
1924 MASON *Arctic Forests* 32: The Indian collar [for sled-dogs] is a piece of willow, heavily padded by a moose-hide cushion stuffed with moose-hair. The two objections to this collar are that the snow is apt to stick on the rough moose-hide and that they are always made without a space for the windpipe.

Indian Commission *Hist.* a government commission having the responsibility of dealing with the Indians, making treaties, establishing reserves, etc.
1881 *Edmonton Bull.* 3 Jan. 2/1: Besides this, some $4,000 of expenses that had been incurred by the former Acting Indian Agent had to be paid and a general feeling of discontent, caused by broked promises and previous neglect on the part of the Indian Commission had to be allayed.

Indian Commissioner *Hist.* an officer of the Indian Commission, *q.v.*
1871 *Wkly Manitoban* (Winnipeg) 22 July 2/1: When the news reached the people of the settlement that the Indian Commissioner had arrived, every one breathed more freely, more especially since the Indian tribes for the last few months have been evidently restless.
1893 YEIGH *Ont.Parliament* 125: In 1793, three great councils were held at Newark, in the presence of the Governor, the Indian Commissioners and the officers of the garrison, 50 chiefs coming via Fort Erie to attend it. **1916** PARKER *World for Sale* 14: . . . he had been checked and rebuked before his tribe by the Indian Commissioner for being drunk.

Indian constable an Indian employed by the R.C.M.P., earlier the N.W.M.P., as a constable with limited authority on a reserve or in other regions occupied by Indians. See also **band constable** and **policeman** (def. 1).
1886 *Indian* (Hagersville, Ont.) 17 Feb. 32/3: When the Indian constable went to put him out, he produced a revolver. **1935** HALLIDAY *Potlatch and Totem* 177: The Indian constables had been two weeks in close confinement, but were still convinced that they were in the right over the whole affair.

Indian corn† maize, *Zea mays.*
*c*1665 (1885) RADISSON *Voyages* 36: After came a company of women . . . that brought us dry fish and Indian corn. **1842** *Bytown* [Ottawa] *Gaz.* 17 Feb. 1/4: Charles and I gathering Indian corn, at night had a "bee" a term used for a mustering together of the neighbors, to assist in any work, which would puzzle them to do alone, when all the young people came to help me to husk it. **1963** GUILLET *Pioneer Farmer* I 6: The first agricultural products at Quebec were Indian corn, squashes and kidney-beans, grown Indian fashion.

Indian country 1 a region inhabited by Indians. See also **Indian territory** (def. 1).
[**1690** (1929) KELSEY *Papers* 2: But making all ye hast I could upon our way Gott on ye borders of ye stone Indian Country.] *c*1752 (1852) COATS *Geography of H.B.* 37: Wether they came thro the northern Indian country . . . our interpriters are not clear in.

1812 (1906) *Ont.Bur.Arch.Rep.* IV 254: All White persons are forbidden to establish themselves or reside in an Indian Village or country within this province, without such License, under a Penalty for the first Offence, of Ten Pounds. **1948** ONRAET *Sixty Below* 130: I have mentioned the caribou in relation to the Eskimos and Indians because he is to be found in both the Eskimo and Indian country, though they are very distinct peoples, live far apart and differently, and neither encroaches on the territory of the other.

2 *Hist.* See 1948 quote. See also **Indian territory** (def. 2), **inland** (def. 1), **interior** (def. 1), and **Pays Sauvages.** Also *Indian countries.*

1749 *Short State of North America* 17: If . . . People were allowed to go into the Indian Country to trade, by the Rivers and Lakes in Summer, and upon Sledges in Winter, the Trade might be increased Ten-fold. **1824** (1931) SIMPSON *Fur Trade* 28: He had amassed a fortune of about £7,000 & returned to Canada but so enchanted was he with the roving life of a Freeman and the charms of some half Doz Wives (natives of the Soil) that he could not sit down quietly at Home to enjoy his good fortune but must revisit the Indian Country since which time he has met with nothing but reverses. **1948** *Beaver* Sep. 14: The "Indian countries" is a term one often encounters in reading the old journals and letters of the early fur traders of the west. "Canada" at that time lay entirely to the east of the Great Lakes. All West and north of that to the far distant Pacific and Arctic oceans, was called "the Indian Countries." **1957** *Cdn Red Cross Junior* Dec. 16: He was a little homesick, for the fur traders were often away in the Indian country for two or three years. . . .

Indian cradle† See **cradle-board** and picture. See also **moss bag.**
1852 RICHARDSON *Arctic Exped.* 295: She then set out dragging a sledge, and having her first-born suspended between her shoulders, in a bag or Indian cradle. **1952** *Beaver* Mar. 42: A greater part of the baby's first year is spent in a tickhenaghen or moss bag (Indian cradle). It is made from a board a couple of feet or so long with a piece of cloth tacked over the top, pocket fashion.

Indian cup See **pitcher plant.**
1823 HALIBURTON *General Descr.N.S.* 37: Indian Cups [Sarracinia Purpurea]. **1849** ALEXANDER *L'Acadie* I 257: Among the plants is to be distinguished the rare and most curious Indian cup or pitcher plant (*Sarracenia purpurea*), the leaves of which [are] united together, so as to form a deep cup filled with water, distilled probably from the moss in which the plant is found. **1861** SUTHERLAND *Geography P.E.I.* 57: The Sarracenia is the beautiful Indian Cup, seen in the bogs or swamps.

Indian Days an exhibition during which Indians revive tribal customs, as traditional dress and dances, often in conjunction with a stampede or rodeo.
1923 BARBEAU *Indian Days* 5: Picturesque stampedes take place every summer in the July celebrations at Banff, when the Stony warriors . . . mount their broncos and caracole in parades which are reminiscent of the buffalo hunt and the traditional challenges of ancient native warfare. These are the "Indian Days" as we now understand them. . . . **1956** LEECHMAN *Native Tribes* 146: The old men remember the tales their fathers told them, and the Calgary Stampede, the Indian Days at Banff, and the occasional country fair and rodeo revive those dear, warm memories. **1964** DUFF *Indian History* 104: The Indian "pow wows" held in recent years at North Vancouver, the "Indian Days" at Kamloops, and other gatherings such as the Williams Lake stampedes are similar occasions for Indians to enjoy renewed social contacts and gain recognition as Indians.

Indian day school a mission or government school, usually on a reserve, attended in the daytime only. Cp. **residential school.**
1926 *Beaver* June 120/2: Last summer a nice new house was built on the reserve for use of the teacher of the Indian day school. **1965** *Globe and Mail* (Toronto) 2 Sep. W1/5: In comparison with public schools for whites, the Indian day and residential schools were of poor quality.

Indian debt *Fur Trade* See **debt** (def. 1).
1784 (1954) *Moose Ft Jnls* 252: Inclosed is a list of Indian Visitors and Indian Debts. **1941** *Beaver* Dec. 25: I was three days at the post getting my business arranged, exchanging lists of Indian debts with Taylor. . . .

Indian debt book *Fur Trade* the ledger in which debt (def. 1) was recorded together with furs and other payments credited against that debt.
1913 COWIE *Adventurers* 225: In the Indian debt book every article had to be strictly itemized, whether debtor or creditor. . . . **1934** GODSELL *Arctic Trader* 216: Then followed three days of . . . looking over the Indian Debt Book and holding counsel with the Slavey hunters in the dim light of candles for, as we neared the Arctic Circle, the hours of daylight became very short indeed.

Indian deer *Obs.* See **woodland caribou.**
1795 (1911) HEARNE *Journey* 224: Indian deer (the only) species found in those parts, except the moose) are so much larger than those which frequent the barren grounds to the North of Churchill River, that a small doe is equal in size to a Northern buck.

Indian Department *Hist.* the government agency responsible for relations with Indians (now the Indian Affairs Branch).
1775 *Quebec Gaz.* 19 Oct. 3/1: We cannot help recommending the behaviour of Mr. Johnson and Mr. Butler of the Indian department. . . . **1812** *Kingston Gaz.* (U.C.) 19 Sep. 1/3: Colonel Elliot and Major McKee and the Officers of the Indian Department, are entitled to his best thanks for their judicious management of the Indians. **1956** KEMP *Northern Trader* 22: Making up the personnel of the government party would be the Paying Agent, a clerk appointed by the Indian Department, a doctor, and a cook.

Indian devil 1 See **wolverine** (def. 1a). See also **Devil of the Woods.**
[**1665** (1885) RADISSON *Fourth Voyage* 202: We killed severall other beasts, as Oriniacks, staggs, wild cows, Carriboucks, fallow does and bucks, Catts of mountains, child of the Devill; in a word, we lead a good life.] **1853** *Anglo-American Mag.* II 181: It is popularly and significantly called "Indian devil." **1950** BIRD *This is N.S.* 155: "I reckon," we heard him say, "you'll get pictures of about everything from a moose to an Injun devil."

2 any of several wild cats, especially the cougar.
1896 ROBERTS *Camp-Fire* 324: I replied that the voice, in my opinion, came from the dangerous Northern panther, or 'Indian devil.' **1902** ROBERTS *Kindred of Wild* 264: . . . he had a quarrel with all lucifees or

lynxes,—"Injun devils," he called them. **1965** *Wildlife Rev.* Mar. 19: COUGARS, also known as panthers, pumas, catamounts, mountain lions and Indian devils, are large unspotted cats. Adult males weigh up to 180 pounds and measure as much as 9 feet in length with a tail of 30 inches.

3 See **loup-garou** (def. 1).
1907 BAIRD *Roger Davis* 173: . . . I had heard from the old inhabitants on the river, of the dread Loup-garoue or Indian devil as many called it.

Indian dog† any of various breeds of dog found among the Indians, as the giddee, *q.v.*
1771 (1792) CARTWRIGHT *Journal* I 90: Haines went up the river for four traps, in one of which he found an Indian dog almost dead. **1829** MACTAGGART *Three Years* II 72: The Indian dogs are small prick-eared little fellows, not unlike some of the smaller English terriers; they are bred from a certain kind of fox. . . . **1850** (1958) WATTERS *B.C.Cent.Anthol.* 501: Often the Indian dogs would swim over from the Indian village oppsite the fort. . . . The dogs I refer to were handsome white animals resembling a Pomeranian but larger, with long woolly hair which was regularly shorn and woven into blankets and articles of clothing. **1958** ELLIOTT *Quesnel* 153: Meat of a young bear was a welcome change or, if nothing else, "giddee" or Indian dog was variety for the menu.

Indian drum a drum consisting of a sheet of parchment leather stretched on a wooden hoop.
1946 *Beaver* Mar. 4/2: [There was] an orchestra consisting of two violins and an Indian drum. . . .

Indian fence 1 *Obs.* See **deer hedge.**
1827 (1911) TOWNSEND *Cartwright's Journal* 23n: But what arrests the attention most . . . is the extent of the Indian fences to entrap deer.

2 a kind of fish weir. See also **barrier.**
1956 EVANS *Mountain Dog* 119: That afternoon Moses and Eli laid out stringers and poles and started to nail their Indian fence together.

Indian file† one after another; single file.
1791 LONG *Voyages* 55: The rest of the Savages then came into my house, one by one, which is called Indian file, singing war songs, and dancing. **1945** MACLENNAN *Two Solitudes* 143: They walked in Indian file down to the river. . . .

Indian grant *Hist.* a grant of land in a region formerly inhabited by Indians.
1791 (1905) *Ont.Bur.Arch.Rep.* III xciii: The various and almost unlimited claims made by Individuals to Tracts of Land by virtue of Indian Grants have been a great cause of keeping the Country unsettled and will so long as they are suffered to exist.

Indian grass *Obs.* a species of North American grass, *Sorghastrum nutans,* used for basket-making by eastern Indians; sweet grass.
1826 (1832) PICKERING *Inquiries* 57: As the month advanced . . . the harvest was got in; the Timothy grass pretty good, but the Indian, or wild grass of the pea species, a poor crop to mow. **1850** BIGSBY *Shoe and Canoe* II 154: There is a grass, abundant here, of a strong and agreeable perfume, and called Indian grass. It is often made into ornaments for sale. **1916** *Wentworth Hist.Soc.Papers & Records* VII 35: They landed at the place where Hamilton now stands, a swamp district overgrown with Indian grass.

Indian guest room *Fur Trade* See **Indian hall.**
1946 *Beaver* Mar. 27: [Caption] Kotah and family,

natives from Liard River, in Indian guest room, Fort Simpson.

Indian gun† *Fur Trade, Hist.* a type of muzzle-loader prominent among the trading goods of the fur companies. See also **trade gun** and **trading gun.** Cp. **fuke** and **Northwest gun.**
1784 (1954) *Moose Ft Jnls* 38: Two picking oakum, Armr. mending Indian guns. **1913** COWIE *Adventurers* 197: I never did get up to the use of the "Indian gun" nor get over my surprise at the fine shooting the natives did with it.

Indian hall *Fur Trade, Hist.* the building or room in which Indians were received when bringing furs or other goods to trade. See also **Indian guest room, Indian house, Indian room,** and **Siwash house.** Cp. **Indian shop.**
1804 (1897) COUES *New Light* I 249: Climbed up into a sort of half garret over the men's bedrooms in the Indian hall. **1855** (1956) ROSS *Fur Hunters* 190: Here is seen the counting room, the mess room, the kitchen and pantry, the cellars, and Indian hall. . . . **1962** DICKIE *Great Golden Plain* 71: In the middle of the space inside the stockade, they built the trader's house and the store or "Indian hall." This was connected by a walled passage with the river gate, so that the Indians could trade without entering the inner part of the fort.

An Indian hammer

Indian hammer a globular stone having a groove chipped out around the smaller circumference for the attachment of a handle, used as a pounding instrument by the early Indians.
1953 MOON *Saskatchewan* 199: Today Yorkton remembers its founders with a cairn erected by the city in 1933. Fittingly, forty Indian hammers and numerous arrowheads are embedded in it.

Indian hen See **marsh bittern.**
1866 KING *Sportsman in Canada* 168: The American Bittern is known in most parts of the country by the name of "Indian Hen," and is not an easy bird to approach. **1956** MCATEE *Folk-Names* 6: Indian hen . . . A widely used name known from "Eastern Canada."

Indian horse† See **cayuse,** *n.*
1825 (1931) SIMPSON *Fur Trade* 161: Started before Day break and was very much inclined to give the Indian Horses the benefit of a few Miles exercise in order to relieve our Weary limbs but ascertained the proprietors could track us and not knowing their Strength thought it was as well to let be for let be. **1960** *Sun* (Vancouver) 6 Feb. 5/8: There is nothing—no, not so much as a doff of the hat—to the cowpony, the packhorse, the mustang, the Indian horses, the quarter horse, the pinto, the hundreds of thousands of animals which opened up the Canadian west. . . .

Indian house *Fur Trade, Hist.* See **Indian hall.**
1771 (1792) CARTWRIGHT *Journal* II 107: I shifted the sawyers into the Indian house which is in the cove below. **1834** (1963) TOLMIE *Physician* 293: [It was] the all engrossing topic of conversation amongst the loungers

in the Indian House (an apartment adjoining the front gate set apart for the use of the natives). **1899** *N.B. Mag.* II 150: The Indian House was finished in the course of the winter by James Woodman.

Indian hunter *Fur Trade, Hist.* See **fort hunter.**
1824 (1931) SIMPSON *Fur Trade* 69: From thence the Horses should cross over to the Athabasca Portage in charge of 2 Horsekeepers and an Indian hunter, there to remain until Fall. **1884** *Prince Albert Times* (Sask.) 21 Mar. 3/2: In the spring the H.B. Co. used to send a party of Indian hunters and several white men to the northern side of the Hudson's Bay, where the Indians would shoot the geese and the white men salt them in barrels. *c***1902** (1912) LAUT *Trapper* 62: A case is on record at Moose Factory, on James Bay, of an Indian hunter and his wife who were literally brought to the verge of starvation by a wolverine that nightly destroyed their traps.

Indian ice-cream *B.C.* a pinkish, frothy substance having a somewhat bitter taste, made from beating soapberries (def. 2). See also **brue, hooshum, soapolallie** (def. 1), and **soapolallie ice-cream.**
1923 *Beaver* Dec. 104: Indian Ice Cream.—In Central British Columbia it was made by working to a lather the dried soap berry, and this, when well made has a very tempting appearance. **1965** WILSON *No Man Stands Alone* 80: "What did you eat today," I questioned . . . "Nothin' but Soapolalla." Seeing that I was bewildered by that answer, she said, "Indian Ice Cream."

Indianize *v.* **1**† cause (someone) to become like an Indian in manner, dress, outlook, etc.
1849 ALEXANDER *L'Acadie* II 234: When [the children] were recovered, they were quite Indianized, and one of them having children, would not stay with their friends, but preferred the woods, the blanket, and mocassins to civilized habits. **1923** STRINGER *Empty Hands* 48: He found something vaguely fortifying in the thought of how such exposure had already partly Indianized her. . . .
2 adopt (words) into an Indian language in such a way that they follow the phonological and morphological patterns of that language.
1909 HUNTER *Simcoe County* I 11: Various words in the Algonquin vocabulary are but the early French words Indianized, and this name of Lake Simcoe is so suspiciously like the French "chien" for "dog" as to suggest some connection with it.

Indian leaf *Obs.* See **kinnikinik** (def. 1).
1855 (1956) ROSS *Fur Hunters* 198: He then puffs the Indian leaf in curling clouds.

Indian leggings See **leggings.**
1952 (1954) JENNINGS *Strange Brigade* 155: I noticed he wore, like Cuthbert Grant and Bostonnais Pangman, Indian leggings,—pants, without a seat and only a broad loincloth dangling fore and aft to cover his intimates. Not to put too fine a point upon it—like his comrades', his arse hung out with painful immodesty.

Indian liquor *Fur Trade, Hist.* brandy, rum, whisky, or high wines, *q.v.* (often diluted and sometimes spiced with pepper, Tabasco, tobacco, or weak acids) traded to the Indians. See also **Indian brandy, Indian rum, Indian whisky, rum**

(def. 2a), **Saulteur liquor,** and **trade whisky.**
1835 (1944) *B.C.Hist.Qtly* July 230: Traded only 3 or 4 beaver for which we had to raise our price 1 gall. Ind. liquor per beaver. **1912** (1913) HODGE & WHITE *Indians of Can.* 221/1: Indian liquor, a Western term for whisky or rum adulterated for sale to the Indians.

Indian list 1 See 1913 quote. See also **interdict list.**
1913 SANDILANDS *West.Cdn Dict.* 25: Indian list, the black list, or the list of interdicts, people who have been barred by the magistrates, on the request of an employer or near relative from purchasing drink. All Indians are supposed to be on the list, and any person supplying them with intoxicants is liable to a heavy fine. **1923** DE LA ROCHE *Possession* 225: "He was wanting a drink but, of course, we had tae order him out as he is on the Indian List. He objected, and contended that he was white." **1960** *Ottawa Citizen* 22 June 10/1: Mr. Sopha said he knew of persons placed on the "Indian List" by a wife, a relative, and even a member of the provincial government.
2 *Slang* the list of those refused further servings of liquor.
1958 DAVIES *Mixture of Frailties* 13: "She was drunk" said Sally, "What on earth did you give her?" . . . "Well —she had seven. I couldn't put her on the Indian list. . . ."

Indian lodge See **lodge** (def. 2a).
1789 (1801) MACKENZIE *Voyages* 82: At eight we landed at three large Indian lodges. **1957** *Beaver* Spring 52/1: Moose Factory [was] just a tiny village of a few wooden houses—and many Indian lodges.

Indian longhouse See **plank house.**
1959 *Sun* (Vancouver) 16 July 23/2: Another attraction . . . will be the famed Indian Longhouse, built last year by Capilano Indians as their centennial project.

Indian mark *Obs.* See quote.
1768 DRAGE *Probability N.W.Passage* 139: Several of the People . . . had rambled from the Vessel, got on the Heights, rolled down the Indian Marks, which are Stones that they put one upon the other on the Knolls and Summits of Hills, to direct them in their journeying. . . .

Indian moccasin† **1** See **moccasin** (def. 1 and picture).
1844 (1955) LEFROY *Magnetic North* 155: I have some diminutive Indian moccasins made expressly for her. **1942** TWOMEY & HERRICK *Needle to North* 21: I selected heavy wool shirts, heavy wool underwear, wool pants, duffle socks, and Indian moccasins—the Indian *winter* moccasin with high canvas tops to keep snow out.
2 See **moccasin flower.**
1912 (1913) HODGE & WHITE *Indians of Canada* 220/1: Indian moccasin. The stemless lady's-slipper or moccasin flower (*Cypripedium acaule*).

Indian office *Obs.* See **Indian agency** (def. 1).
1879 *Battleford Hist.Soc.Pubs* I-III 62: It has been impossible for the Indian Office to supply the destitute with meat to any extent.

Indian outfit See **outfit** (def. 1b).
1860 *Nor'Wester* (R.R.S.) 14 May 1/4: The good and well-worked stuffs always found a ready sale at the store of the Company, who seemed desirous of furnishing their Indian outfits with goods of home manufacture.

Indian pack *Fur Trade, Obs.* a package of furs weighing about 60 pounds, smaller than the normal piece (def. 1) which weighed 90 pounds. Cp. **inland piece.**
1823 (1932) MCLEAN *Notes* 77: The Iroquois passed early in the spring with eighteen Indian packs in their canoes,—each pack might be estimated at 60 *l*.

Indian pad *Obs.* See quote.
1876 LORD *Wilderness* 89: . . . the only type of saddle I should ever venture to use is that usually designated by hunters 'the Indian pad,' which, in point of fact, is simply two cushions or small pillows, fastened together by stout pieces of leather, and firmly 'synched' on to the horse. . . .

Indian paint *Obs.* red and yellow iron pigments.
1755 (1951) *Saskatchewan Jnls* 9: . . . a Narrow Lake called Uthamun Sackaeagan or Paint Lake, from there being some Indian Paint found here.

Indian paint-brush† any of various wild flowers, *Castilleja* sp., having bright scarlet to orangey floral bracts. See also **paintbrush, painted cup, painter's brush,** and **painter's flower.**
1910 FERGUSON *Janey Canuck* 189: The Castillo is a hot-hued flower. The whites call it "Indian's Paint Brush," but the Indians call it "Bloody Nose."
1938 (1950) STANWELL-FLETCHER *Driftwood Valley* 171: Scarlet columbine and red and orange Indian paintbrush cover the open places. **1959** *Calgary Herald* 31 July 10/1: There is no finer feature of the autumn landscape in Alberta . . . than the roadside aster, goldenrod, blue lupins, brown-eyed susan, Indian paint brush and wild geranium.

Indian paint fungus a brightly-colored tooth fungus, *Echinodontium tinctorum,* of the Rocky Mountain region that attacks trees such as fir and spruce.
1964 *Beaver* Summer 16: Such injuries provided infection courts for the fungi that Al and I had been encountering all day, among them the red ring rot fungus and the Indian paint fungus used by the Tlinkits for facial painting.

Indian parlo(u)r *Fur Trade, Obs.* See **Indian hall.**
1882 (1926) MOSER *Reminiscences* 103: "He now put them [trousers] on and solemnly walked into the Indian parlor of my house."

Indian pass a mountain pass used by the Indians.
1873 (1904) BUTLER *Wild North Land* 355: The full importance of this Indian pass, as a highway to the Pacific through the Rocky Mountains, will be easily understood. **1963** SPRY *Palliser* 7: Rumours of good Indian passes were none the less persistent, and in 1848 Palliser had met 'a . . . half-breed gentleman' from Red River, James Sinclair, who had already crossed the mountains at least once with a party of emigrants from the Red River to the Columbia River.

Indian pay-list See **Indian Register.**
1886 *Indian* (Hagersville, Ont.) 8 Sep. 194/3: Of the 43 who did not vote the most of them were the pagan chiefs and warriors who had been told that if they did so, they would endanger other treaty rights and be struck off the Indian pay list.

Indian pear *Esp.Eastern Canada* **1** See **serviceberry** (def. 2). See also **pear** (def. 1).
1818 *Description P.E.I.* 6: A fruit in this Island, called the Indian Pear, is very delicious. **1872** (1873) GRANT *Ocean to Ocean* 156: The sasketoon are simply what are known in Nova Scotia as "Indian pears". . . .

1921 HEMON *Chapdelaine* [trans.]: The forests of Quebec are rich in wild berries; cranberries, Indian pears. . . .
2 See **serviceberry** (def. 1).
1822 (1928) CORMACK *Narr.Nfld* 19: On the skirts of the forest, and of the marshes, are found . . . Indian pear or shadbush. . . . **1956** RADDALL *Wings* 12: Then came the long reach of scrub woods, wire birch and poplar mostly, with blossoming clumps of Indian pear, like patches of snow on the slopes. . . .

Indian pig *B.C.. Obs.* See quote.
1862 (1958) LYONS *Milestones* 216: A passerby in a canoe in the year 1862 had this comment to make: "Further on we passed Denman Island, where Comox Indians used to live. . . . Here on the sands were many seals, which are much relished and are known as 'Indian Pig'. The flesh was not unlike bacon, but whites soon tire of it."

Indian pipe† a pale parasitic plant, *Monotropa uniflora,* found in compost in damp places. See also **corpse plant** and **ghost flower.**
1860 *Trans.Lit.& Hist.Soc.Que.* IV 4 41: The Ghost Flower, Indian Pipe or Monotropa, is a white plant springing up from decayed leaves. . . . **1923** SQUIER *Autumn Trails* 32: It is an Indian pipe . . . an orchid that one rarely finds in these woods. The Micmac Indians call it the Death Plant. **1962** *Maclean's* 10 Mar. 17/1: It was a palely sprouting parasite called Indian pipe, or corpse plant, which extrudes almost overnight from rotting compost and lives only briefly.

Indian pitch *Fur Trade, Obs.* See **gum,** *n.* (def. 1).
1785 (1954) *Moose Ft Jnls* 294: The craft were obliged to be tarred all over for want of paint Oil which has quite exhausted our pitch and Tar notwithstanding I got near 1 Cwt. of Indian pitch from the Natives to eke it out with.

Indian place-congregation *Obs.* an independent community of Christian Indians living on lands belonging to the Moravian Brethren.
1798 (1957) *Ont.Hist.* XLIX 95: Should, in case of any future Indian wars, or the unfavorable disposition of the chiefs, the messenger of the gospel, or their converts, be under the necessity of seeking places of refuge, they would now, in every case, find them in Indian place-congregations, built on lands belonging to the [Moravian] Brethern, in Canada or in the United States, or in both.

Indian placement-officer an official of the Indian Affairs Branch who tries to provide Indians with employment opportunities outside the reserve.
1958 *Edmonton Jnl* 9 Aug. 24/5: R. Murray Sutherland . . . has resigned to take over the duties of Indian placement officer in the regional office of the department of Indian affairs here.

Indian pony† See **cayuse,** *n.*
1865 *Nor'Wester* (R.R.S.) 21 Sep. 2/3: Our hardy Indian ponies found many purchasers at good prices. **1955** MCCOWAN *Upland Trails* 15: It is a far cry from the days of the stolid little Indian ponies so common among the prairie tribes in the early days of the West.

Indian porcupine *Obs.* See **Canada porcupine.**
1852 (1881) TRAILL *Cdn Crusoes* 231: The Indian porcupine is a small animal, not a very great deal larger than the common British hedgehog; the quills, however, are longer and stronger, and varied with

alternate clouded marks of pure white and dark brownish grey; they are minutely barbed, so that if one enters the flesh it is with difficulty extracted....

Indian post[1] *Fur Trade, Hist.* a fur post trading with Indians.
1902 (1957) *Sask.Hist.* X 1 22: Ascending the south bank of the Battle, we obtained a fine view of Battleford, which is situated on an ideal place for an Indian post.

Indian post[2] *Fur Trade, Hist.* a method of postal delivery in which a letter was given to an Indian who took it as far as he was going, passing it to another, and so on until it eventually reached the addressee.
1930 MACINNES *Rockies* 191: Thompson describes what was known among the fur-traders as the Indian post, which appears to have been a fairly sure, if not particularly rapid, method of postal delivery.

Indian potato† any of several tubers used as food, especially by the Indians, as the wapatoo, *q.v.*
[1843 (1868) IRVING *Bonneville* 55: Game was scanty, and they had to eke out their scanty fare with wild roots and vegetables, such as the Indian potato, the wild onion, and the prairie tomato.] **1912** (1913) HODGE & WHITE *Indians of Can.* 220/1: *Indian potato.* (1) The groundnut (*Apios apios*). (2) A western name for the squirrel corn (*Bikukulla canadensis*). **1927** PHILIP *Painted Cliff* 131: She taught them to distinguish the small, pinkish-white flower of the Indian potato, whose root, when eaten raw, is somewhat the flavour of a chestnut, and is highly prized by the natives for its food value. **1947** MCKELVIE *Ft Langley* 3: There had been but little else discussed when the Cowichans met that autumn on the Saan-a-sant (Pitt) River where the Katzies were hosts each year during the digging of Indian potatoes, amid great festivity.

Indian price an exorbitant price, with reference to the high cost of beer or liquor illegally sold to the Indians. Cp. **Indian tariff.**
1953 CUSHMAN *Stay Away Joe* 89: Thirty-five cents is the Injun price for beer, take it or leave it.

Indian rack *West* a small rack used for hauling sheaves to a barn or threshing machine.
1963 SYMONS *Many Trails* 115: ... if he noticed this he'd tell the man with the "Indian rack," as we called the small ones, to load high....

Indian racket *Obs.* See **racket.**
1779 (1792) CARTWRIGHT *Journal* II 408: ... the snow was so deep and light, that it was with the greatest difficulty I could follow him even in Indian rackets.

Indian rancheria See **rancheria.**

Indian rancherie See **rancherie.**

Indian Register the record kept by the Indian Affairs Branch of the federal government for all Indians in receipt of treaty money, *q.v.*, or equivalent payment. See also **Band List, General List, Indian pay-list, treaty list,** and **treaty roll.** Cp. **registered Indian.**

1964 DUFF *Indian History* 46: The first [definition], which refers to what are usually called "registered Indians," is the legal definition used by the Indian Affairs Branch for the people who come under the jurisdiction of the Indian Act; that is, those whose names are included on the official Indian Register, either on a Band List or a General List.

Indian remittance man See quote. See also **remittance man.**
1959 *Weekend Mag.* 4 Apr. 33/2: Indian remittance men: Social outcasts from West Coast tribes who have been driven to lone-wolfing it away from established communities.

Indian reservation† See **Indian reserve.**
1859 (1959) *Native Voice* Feb. 5: "Has the Government of this Island [Vancouver] the power to remove the Indians (by purchase) from that piece of land inside Victoria Harbour known as the Indian Reservation?" **1954** EVANS *Mist* 43: She said that this fall or next, when Stevie was old enough, she would try to get him into an Indian reservation school. ...

Indian reserve a tract of land set aside by the government for the exclusive use of a band of Indians, usually by treaty. See also **reserve** (def. 2).
1792 (1905) *Ont.Bur.Arch.Rep.* III 215: Every farm of good land, in that part of the Country, is comprehended within the Indian reserve. **1859** *British Colonist* (Victoria) 15 Jan. 3/2: If the Victoria bridge remains, and the Indian reserve sold for town lots to the highest bidders, not less than three hundred thousand dollars would be added to the colonial revenue. **1958** *Edmonton Jnl* 18 June 31/7: Through his efforts, conditions on the two Indian reserves have improved greatly.

Indian residential hostel See **hostel** (def. 1).
1965 *Globe and Mail* (Toronto) 26 May 3/1: It is also the site of ... a federally financed Indian residential hostel, where young Indians and Eskimos who don't speak a word of English come to learn from teachers who don't speak a word of Eskimo or Cree.

Indian residential school See **residential school.**
1966 *Weekend Mag.* 18 June 27/1: "I was at the Indian residential school [in Southern Manitoba in 1912] and I never had done any running."

Indian rhubarb a herb of the western mountain region, *Peltiphyllum peltatum*, with edible leaf stalks. See also **Siwash rhubarb.**
1932 *Cdn Hist.Rev.* XIII 407: Ferns and Indian rhubarb [were] in the underbrush.... **1958** BERTON *Klondike* 226: There was still no grass for the horses— only leaves and ... Indian rhubarb.

Indian rice *Obs.* See **wild rice.**
1822 (1940) *Minutes of Council* (H.B.C.) 22: That Rodk. McKenzie ... be directed to grind all the wheat he may raise, which together with all the Indian Rice and Corn he may collect be brought to Norway House. **1852** (1881) TRAILL *Cdn Crusoes* 138: ... those rush beds, as you call them, must be Indian rice that we have seen the squaws make their soup of.

Indian room *Fur Trade* See **Indian hall.**
1872 (1883) BUTLER *Great Lone Land* 283: Within the fort all preparations have been completed, communication cut off between the Indian room and the rest of the buildings ... then the outer gate is thrown open, and a large throng enters the Indian room. **1921** HAWORTH *Trailmakers* 158: The Indian room and the trading room were connected by a narrow passage, each end of which was closed by a heavy door.

Indian rum *Fur Trade* See **Indian liquor.**
1768-82 (1904) LONG *Voyages* 171: . . . having a very
small portion of rum, and no prospect of encreasing
my stock; I was therefore obliged to dilute it so as to
make it about one-fifth part weaker than usual, which
made twenty gallons of very passable Indian rum.
1793 (1933) MACDONELL *Diary* 101: Mixed nine
Gallons of Indian rum[,] it being customary for
Bourgeois to wet the whistle of every Indian they meet
on the way. **1835** (1944) *B.C.Hist.Qtly* Apr. 140: We
were induced to offer a blanket i gall: Ind. Rum & a
head of tobacco per beaver. . . . **1944** *Ibid.* 140n:
"Indian rum" was rum diluted with water.

Indian salad the water leaf, *Hydrophyllum
virginianum,* the young shoots of which are highly
prized as a salad.
1778 (1792) CARTWRIGHT *Journal* II 319: Indian salad
now springing up. **1779** *Ibid.* 436: Observed that Indian
salad has made an appearance.

Indian sash See **sash.**
1849 ALEXANDER *L'Acadie* II 64: He was well got up
as a woodsman for appearance at the settlements,
wearing a glazed hat, red shirt, grey clothing,
embroidered Indian sash, silver hilted knife in his
belt, and pipe in his button-hole. **1893** YOUNG *Indian
Wigwams* 265: [The coat] is good for at least nine years
of hard service yet, and nothing would give its owner
greater joy than to have the pleasure of again fastening
it around him with an Indian sash. . . .

Indian shoe† **1** See **moccasin** (def. 1 and picture).
1696 (1929) KELSEY *Papers* 49: Gave our men out
Indian shoes. **1791** LONG *Voyages* 36: I also made
makissins, or Indian Shoes, of deer skins. . . .
1862 *Nor'Wester* (R.R.S.) 25 June 2: We cannot but
think that consumption and other maladies are very
much festered by the use of this "Indian shoe," and we
rejoice to see it gradually discontinued for boots and
shoes proper.

2 See **moccasin flower.**
1912 (1913) HODGE & WHITE *Indians of Canada*
220/2: Indian shoe. The large yellow lady's-slipper
(*Cypripedium hirsutum*). **1947** BIRD *Judgment Glen* 270:
She talked of . . . the good that could be brewed from
yellow dock, Indian shoe, gold thread and five fingers.

Indian shop *Fur Trade* See **trading room.** Cp.
Indian hall.
1799 (1801) MACKENZIE *Voyages* 371: Took an inventory
of all the goods remaining in the Indian shop, and
afterward suspended them in the garret. . . . **1921**
HEMING *Drama of Forests* 286: After leaving the Indian
shop, the hunter returned to his camp to talk matters
over with Amik and the women. **1934** *Beaver* June 9:
. . . I might look them over while they were getting their
supplies in the Indian shop. . . .

Indian slave *Obs.* an Indian held as a slave,
either by another Indian or a white person.
1802 *Niagara Herald* (Niagara-on-the-Lake, U.C.)
28 Aug. 3/3: All persons are forbidden harboring,
employing or concealing my Indian slave called SAL,
as I am determined to prosecute any offender. . . .

Indian sled or **sleigh** See **toboggan** (def. 1a and
picture).
1771 (1792) CARTWRIGHT *Journal* I 81: The tilt being
taken to pieces and stowed upon the Indian sled, the
sawyers, with the assistance of the Indians and their
dogs, carried it to Eyre Island. **1828** *U.E.Loyalist* (York,
[Toronto]) 17 May 416/1: The next morning the pair set
out on their arduous task: Mr. Rodgers having been

laid on an Indian sleigh, well secured and defended by
several blankets.

Indian slipper 1 See **moccasin** (def. 1 and picture).
1785 (1943) HUNTER *Diary* 36: They wear the same dress
summer and winter, which consists of a pair of scarlet
leggings, Indian slippers, a short calico jacket without
breeches, crimson cloak finely ornamented with rich
fringe, and a kind of a helmet instead of a hat.

2 See **moccasin flower.**
1912 (1913) HODGE & WHITE *Indians of Canada* 220/2:
Indian Slipper. The pink lady's-slipper, or moccasin-
flower (*Cypripedium acaule*).

Indian squaw See **squaw** (def. 1).

Indian stockings† *Obs.* See **leggings.**
1748 ELLIS *Hudson's Bay* 158: We likewise began about
this Time to put on our Winter Dress, which
consisted of a Robe of Beaver Skin, with the Furr on,
which reached to our Heels, and two Waistcoats under
it, a Cap and Mittens of the same, lined with Flannel,
a Pair of Indian Stockings, over our Yarn ones, made
of Broad Cloth or Leather, which reached up to the
mid Thigh, with Shoes of soft-tanned Moose or
Elk-Skin, under which we wore two or three Pair of
Blanket, or thick Duffil Socks to prevent our Feet
freezing, which is a thing that nevertheless frequently
happens. **1820** (1823) FRANKLIN *Journey* 81: These hose,
or as they are termed Indian stockings, are commonly
ornamented with beads or ribands, and from their
convenience, have been universally adopted by the
white residents, as an essential part of their winter
clothing.

Indian storehouse *Fur Trade* See **trading room.**
1796 (1932) RUSSELL *Correspondence* I 45: If you will go
down to the Indian store house you will receive some
things and I wish you all a very good journey.

Indian summer† a period of mild weather in late
fall, often accompanied by a slightly smoky haze.
Cp. **Indian winter** and **squaw winter.**
1796 (1911) SIMCOE *Diary* 351: There is a fog like our
Indian summer, with insufferable heat. **1830** MOORSOM
Letters N.S. 167: . . . in November, and sometimes until
the middle of December, the waning season, like the
expiring efforts of a lamp, which now and then glimmers
fitfully yet brilliantly in the socket, presents us with
days to which there is no parallel in England. This sort
of weather is called the Indian summer, and varies in
duration, from a few unconnected days in some years, to
as many weeks in others. **1965** *Maclean's* 19 June 40/4:
A few had packsacks; some carried lunch pails with
thermos bottles. A mercifully unseasonable Indian
summer spared them all.

Indian superintendent an official representing
the Indian Affairs Branch of the federal
government in its dealings with and
responsibilities toward the Indians in a certain
agency, reserve, or district. Formerly called
Indian agent, *q.v.,* as still in popular usage. See also
reserve agent and **superintendent.**
1958 HAWTHORN *Indians of B.C.* 171: They expect this
to happen, because of support the Indian superintendent
has offered. . . .

Indian sweater See **Cowichan sweater.**
1942 CASH *Million Miles* 84: We lay on our tummies

in the sun at the edge of the pool, three middle-aged women in dirty slacks and Indian sweaters. . . .
1956 *Native Voice* (Vancouver) Dec. 1/1: Hard at work by the light of her kerosene lamp is this Indian mother helped by her little children as she knits an intricately patterned Indian sweater, the very one which was presented to Canada's star swimmer, Marilyn Bell.

Indian tariff *Fur Trade, Hist.* See 1907 quote. Cp. **Indian price.**
1826 (1950) OGDEN *Journals* 183: For the Past I rewarded him to the amount of eight Skins Indian Tariff. . . . **1907** HUNTER *Cdn Wilds* 15: The barter tariffs at each of the posts was made out in two columns, i.e., Indian Tariff and Free Man's Tariff. Say, for example, a pound of English tobacco was bartered to the Indian at the posts for one dollar a pound, the Free Trader would get it in his outfit for 75 cents, and when he bartered it to some hunter . . . he would charge one and half to two dollars. . . .

Indian tea 1 See **Labrador tea** (def. 1a).
1771 (1792) CARTWRIGHT *Journal* I 100: But as I judged, that Indian tea was of the same nature with the herbs which are recommended by that author, I had some gathered from under the snow in the woods, and gave her a pint of the strong infusion of that plant sweetened with sugar. **1823** HALIBURTON *Gen.Descr.N.S.* 34: Shrubs [include] . . . Labrador or India [sic] Tea. . . . **1938** *Beaver* June 23/1: Light springing feet of youths and maidens would make little impression on the tough bushes of Indian Tea.

2 the creeping snowberry, *Chiogenes hispidula.*
1861 *Cdn Naturalist* Apr. 128: Chiogenes hispidula . . . (Indian Tea). Abundant in rocky and sandy woods and swamps, amongst moss.

Indian tea-plant See **Labrador tea** (def. 1a).
1821 (1823) FRANKLIN *Journey* 363: Since our departure from Point Lake we had boiled the Indian tea-plant . . . which produced a beverage in smell much resembling rhubarb. **1858** (1860) HIND *Assiniboine Exped.* II 53: The fragrant Indian tea plant (*Ledum latifolium*) abounded in the moss bordering this elevated sheet of water.

Indian teepee See **teepee.**

Indian teepee ring See **tent ring.**
1963 *Herald Mag.* 26 Oct. 3/4: That these stone emplacements were of Indian origin is pretty well accepted but their exact purpose is open to doubt. The smaller ones, called teepee rings, may well have served to give stability to the leather-covered shelters.

Indian territory 1† See **Indian country** (def. 1).
1821 *York Wkly Post* 22 Nov. 159: The Governor or person administering the Government of Lower Canada, is empowered to appoint any Justices of the Peace, for the Indian territories, as Commissioners for carrying into effect the processes, &c. of the above Courts. **1908** LAUT *Conquest N.W.* II 203: You can do what you like here! There is no law in the Indian Territory!

2† See **Indian country** (def. 2).
1807 (1809) GRAY *Letters* 153: The largest [canoes], however, are used by the North-West Company, for conveying goods into the Indian territory, and bringing down furs. **1927** WOOLLACOTT *Mackenzie* 2: The stage on which this romantic drama was enacted covered more than half a continent, and was variously referred to in

the literature of the fur-trade as *le pays d'En Haut,* the Indian Territory, the Interior, and by a more recent public as the North-West.

3 *Hist.* See quotes.
1820 (1938) SIMPSON *Athabasca Jnl* 96: That a Constable of the District of Montreal should arrest a person in the Indian Territories of British America and detain him a Prisoner . . . is certainly an absolute mockery of all Law and Justice. **1838** (1931) MERK *Fur Trade* 342: The country denominated "Indian Territories," comprehended in the Royal License, is principally situated on the west side of the Rocky Mountains. **1860** *Nor'Wester* (R.R.S.) 28 Apr. 2/4: An act was passed last year, authorising the appointment of Justices for the Indian Territory—meaning the territory not covered by the charter of the Hudson's Bay Company. **1886** *Trans.Roy.Soc.Can.* IV 2 91: The wide expanse of country lying west and north of Rupert' Land was technically known as the "Indian territories." Fur trading license, 1821-1838 renewed. **1937** *Beaver* June 56/1: James Anderson, a Chief Factor and experienced officer of the Indian Territory, was appointed to the command of the party.

Indian title† *Hist.* the claim by Indians to rights of ownership of land by virtue of its being occupied by Indians before the coming of the white man.
1791 *Ont.Bur.Arch.Rep.* III xciii: Others of them . . . were under the necessity of purchasing land of . . . those persons claiming large Tracts under Indian Titles at the enormous price of £100 for 100 acres of wild land. **1859** *British Colonist* (Victoria) 4 July 2/1: We want farmers,—and the best way to get them is to open the lands of Cowitchen to actual settlers by extinguishing the Indian title. **1935** HALLIDAY *Potlatch and Totem* 134: This was finally settled by a parliamentary commission in 1927, which decided that the Indian title did not exist. . . . **1964** DUFF *Indian History* 65: First there was the question of recognizing and extinguishing the aboriginal possessory rights or "Indian title."

Indian tobacco 1 a. a poisonous plant, *Lobelia inflata,* used as tobacco.
1860 *Trans.Lit.& Hist. Soc.Que.* IV 4 45: . . . Indian Tobacco, a plant of some medicinal value, is also now in flower.

b. a plant, *Nicotiana attenuata,* of the western mountain region, used with other plants in preparing smoking mixtures.
1880 DAWSON *Queen Charlotte Is.* 114: Before the introduction of the potato, the only plant cultivated was one which has been described to me as 'Indian tobacco.' **1950** LYONS *Mighty Fraser* 89: Indian tobacco . . . was used by the Thompson Indians from time immemorial. The leaves were gathered, dried and greased. Before being used they were blended with bear-berry leaves which had been dried or roasted over a fire.

2 any of several mixtures prepared by Indians for smoking, especially kinnikinik (def. 1).
[**1805** (1904) LEWIS & CLARK *Journals* III 278: All of which we purchased for a few fishing hooks and a Small Sack of Indian tobacco.] **1915** CUMMING *Skookum Chuck* 40: And he could always [have] a few long draws at his kin-i-kin-nick (sort of Indian tobacco) pipe. **1956** GOWLAND *Sikanaska Trail* 61: By early fall I was almost ready for the winter, I had stored all my berries, roots and leaves, and I had an ample supply of Indian tobacco.

Indian trade† trade with the Indians, especially for furs.

1744 DOBBS *Hudson's Bay* 68: Besides, the Company allows them no time to learn, by confining them to their Factories whilst the Indian Trade continues, and the Navigation is open. **1833** (1963) TOLMIE *Physician* 176: . . . at all the outposts the goods are advanced in price 33⅓ pct. for the Indian trade as every servant of the Coys is expected to supply himself at headquarters. **1957** *Beaver* Autumn 38/2: This included all of the merchandise required to outfit trappers, prospectors and miners, and the traditional Indian trade.

Indian trader† a person engaging in trade with the Indians, especially a fur trader.
1773 *Quebec Gaz.* 26 Aug. 3/1: The Reason given for the Indian Traders keeping up the Prices of their skins so long is, because they daily expect an eminent Merchant . . . to purchase of those Commodities. . . . **1811** *Kingston Gaz.* (U.C.) 4 June 2/1: Before the American war our great contractor Mr. E was an Indian trader of low credit and indifferent reputation. **1912** CONNOR *Corp.Cameron* 333: In the days of the early eighties there were weird stories floating about through the Western country of outlaw Indian traders whose chief stock for barter was a concoction which passed for whiskey. . . . **1964** *Fort Langley* 4: The others [buildings] were the residences of the supervisor and Indian trader, the cooper, the boatbuilder, the blacksmith, the dairyman, the three labourers and the stewards, the depot storehouse, the shops of the Indian trader . . . and storerooms.

Indian trading room See **trading room.**

Indian treaty 1 See **treaty** (def. 1a).
1880 GORDON *Mountain and Prairie* 203: The Government are not in a position to offer for settlement any of the country north of the Athabasca, that being the present boundary, in this direction, of the territory embraced by the Indian treaties. **1957** *Beaver* Spring 58/2: The 1871 Indian treaty by no means covered the then North West Territory; and the "last spike" of the C.P.R. was not a golden one.

2 See **treaty money.**
1883 *Prince Albert Times* (Sask.) 3 Oct. 6/1: We were aware that they were called upon to perform escort duty in the carriage of large sums of money about the country for the payment of Indian treaties.

3 See **Treaty Day.**
1883 *Selkirk Herald* (Man.) 13 July 2/2: I am a steadfast admirer of fashion, and it being fashionable last week to visit the Indian treaty at St. Peters, why, of course I was one of the very many who spent a short time there, ostensibly studying aboriginal life and character.

Indian turnip 1 *West* See **prairie turnip.**
1858 (1860) HIND *Assiniboine Exped.* I 319: The lower prairie consisted of sandy loam, in which the Indian turnip was very abundant. **1887** *Senate Report* 84: This Indian turnip or carrot is one of the first vegetables they get in the spring. The Indians commence to dig them out of the ground as soon as the frost is out. **1912** (1913) HODGE & WHITE *Indians of Can.* 220/2: Indian turnip . . . the prairie potato . . . (*Psoralea esculenta*).

2 See quotes.
1912 (1913) HODGE & WHITE *Indians of Can.* 220/2: *Indian turnip* . . . The jack-in-the-pulpit (*Arisaema triphyllum*), also called three-leaved Indian turnip. **1930** JONES *Wild Flowers* Plate 265: JACK IN THE PULPIT. Indian Turnip. *Arisaema triphyllum. Per.* Wet woods. Fruit brilliant scarlet. Peppery bulb edible if boiled.

Indianware *n.* articles made by Indians after the fashion of their traditional culture.
1963 *Maclean's* 9 Mar. 65/3: The government's delicate role in all this is to promote a boom in Indianware but not promote it so well that the Indians with good jobs will quit work. . . .

Indian whisky *Hist.* See **Indian liquor.**
1859 *British Colonist* (Victoria) 19 Sep. 2/1: The officers brought in two or three bottles and a pail full of Indian Whisky which were taken from him. **1952** HOWARD *Strange Empire* 260: From then until the commerce was summarily extinguished by the North West Mounted Police fifteen years later, a steady stream of "Injun whiskey"—unspeakably vile compared to the Hudson's Bay Company product— flowed north across the border.

Indian wigwam See **wigwam** (def. 1).

Indian winter a cold spell following the onset of spring. Cp. **Indian summer.**
1937 CONIBEAR *Northland Footprints* 308: The early catkings shrivelled and dropped. . . . The "Indian Winter," as MacIvor called it, had come, making a last stand against the powers of Nature and Summer.

Indian wrestling† one of several forms of wrestling formerly used in trials of strength by the Indians and involving two persons who, by locking hands or legs, attempt to overpower each other.
1920 *Beaver* Oct. 7/2: Other events included foot races, Indian wrestling, tug-of-war. . . .

indications *n.pl. Mining* evidence of mineral deposits of economic value.
1836 *Bytown* [Ottawa] *Gaz.* 29 Sep. 4/1: Are there any mines or mineral indications in your district? **1860** *British Colonist* (Victoria) 29 May 3/1: The indications here for gold are more favorable. **1909** *Gow Ganda Tribune* (Ont.) 17 Apr. 6/2: My own idea is to keep a lookout for indications as soon as the real thaw comes, and I can get about more, and try and get something where the other fellow hasn't been.

indignation meeting a public meeting at which citizens express themselves regarding government actions that are regarded as abuses.
1828 BIDWELL *Tor.Pub.Lib.MSS B104* 82: During the remainder of the winter he busied himself in holding indignation meetings throughout the country and obtaining signatures to petitions which he intended presenting to the king and the parliament in England. **1883** *Brandon Dly Mail* (Man.) 24 Feb. 4/2: We must have an old-time indignation meeting and let every man be his own mouth-piece.

indoor trapping *Fur Trade, Slang* stealing furs from a fur-company's warehouse.
1934 GODSELL *Arctic Trader* 284: ". . . he was working for a tradin' outfit at the time and was doin' quite a lot of indoor trappin'."

indorsation *n.* See **endorsation.**

indulgence passage passage on a trans-Atlantic vessel at a special rate for persons connected with the armed services; hence, *indulgence passenger.*
1953 LOWER *Voyages* 66: I was crossing on what is known in the Service as an "indulgence passage" (by which you pay a stated daily rate). . . . *Ibid.* 67: All the indulgence passengers . . . being nobodies, they were not kept informed. . . .

infidel dish *Hist.* See quotes. See also **richeau.**
1886 SCUDDER *Winnipeg Country* 48: But the "infidel dish," as we termed rousseau, is by comparison with the others palatable, though it is even then impossible to so disguise it as to avoid the suggestion of tallow candles; and this and the leathery, or India-rubbery, structure of the meat are its chief disqualifications. **1954** *Beaver* Summer 36/1: The latter [rousseau] the travellers nicknamed the infidel dish.

Injin or **Injun** *n. adj.Dial.* See **Indian.**

inland *n. Hist.* **1** See **Indian country** (def. 2).
1913 KELLY *Range Men* 71: . . . canny men and good traders, built posts in the great inland, and soon controlled a huge native trade.
2 used attributively to denote persons or things associated with the fur trade in the Indian country (def. 2).
1777 (1954) *Moose Ft Jnls* 345: To me it appears a matter of much consequence to our Welfare as it may happen & Time may prove us only to be fighting about a few Home Guards or Shore Indians, rather confounding the Company's Interest more than we annoy the Inland Pedlars. **1820** (1963) DAVIES *Northern Quebec* 13: . . . only one man came here last fall for inland service. . . . **1927** *Beaver* June 18: From about the year 1794 onwards, he was employed as an inland trader from York. **1937** *Ibid.* Sep. 37: . . . the officer commanding an "inland" or subordinate trading post was usually styled "inland trader" or "master at So-and-So House."

inland boat *Fur Trade, Hist.* **1** See **York boat** and picture.
1859 (1932) *Beaver* June 14: The young ladies came in an open inland boat across Lake Winnipeg. **1891** *Wkly Manitoban* Dec. 31/1: In winter travellers are confined solely to the use of dogs, and in summer . . . to boats— York or inland boats of the style of the McKinnaw build. **1943** *Beaver* Mar. 28: "York" or "Inland" boats were introduced between 1820 and 1821. . . .
2 any of several kinds of flat-bottomed boat used in the Indian country (def. 2).
1889 (1892) PIKE *Barren Grounds* 6: These inland boats, as they are termed, are extraordinary specimens of marine architecture, classified according to shape as York boats, sturgeon-heads, and scows, capable of carrying a load of ten tons, manned by a crew of eight oars and a steersman, rowed downstream and tracked up, running rapids and bumping on rocks.

inlander *n. Fur Trade, Obs.* a fur-company employee working in the Indian country (def. 2).
1843 *Standing Rules* (H.B.C.) Index: Rations and regales to Inlanders, Scale of.

Inlander *n.* See **Inland Eskimo.**
1935 EVANS *Reindeer Trek* 179: He had rushed terrified from the spot to tell a tribe of passing Inlanders. **1958** *Beaver* Autumn 22: There was a time . . . when the term *Nunamiut* (Inlanders) applied to well over half the people living in the central arctic Coppermine area of Coronation Gulf. . . .

Inland Eskimo one of a group of Eskimos living in the Central Arctic inland from the west coast of Hudson Bay.
1954 *North Star* Feb. 2/1: An additional point of interest volunteered by the Inlander (Inland Eskimo)

. . . was that the Barren Lands are now literally infested with wolves.

inland packet *Fur Trade, Hist.* See **express** (def. 1).
1931 NUTE *Voyageur* 215: For years voyageurs had been used to carry the mail from the interior posts to Canada, and from one post to another. Even more famous was the "Inland Packet" . . . perilous and lonely enterprises.

inland piece *Fur Trade, Hist.* a package of furs or goods weighing 100 pounds, as opposed to the standard 90-pound piece (def. 1). Cp. **Indian pack.**
1937 *B.C.Hist.Qtly* Apr. 77: Goods came from Fort Langley by water and were there made up for carriage by the brigade, probably . . . in packages of one hundred pounds, called "inland pieces."

inland seas† See **Great Lakes.**
1829 MACTAGGART *Three Years* II 322: The great inland seas of Canada. **1858** (1965) HAMILTON *Cdn Quotations* 164: True Wizard of the Wild! . . . Columbus of the inland seas. **1963** *Weekend Mag.* 9 Nov. 58: The sailors of the inland seas have long memories, and they know how bad the weather can get during the closing weeks of navigation.

in meat See **in the meat.**

inner cabinet See **Treasury Board.**

Innuit ['ɪnjəwət] *n.* **Innuit** or **Innuits** [< Esk. "mankind, people, men"; pl. of *innuk, inuk* man]
1 See **Eskimo** (def. 1). Cp. **Inuk.** Also spelled *Inuit.*
1774 LA TROBE *Mission* 10: Formerly, they were bold and impudent, and looked upon the Europeans as upon dogs, giving them the appellation, Kablunets, that is, Barbarians, but called themselves Innuit, which signifies men. **1835** (1948) *Beaver* Sep. 12/1: . . . being informed that we were Europeans (Kablunae), they answered that they were men Innuit. **1882** GILDER *Schwatka's Search* 30: Not far from this same spot were the ruins of a cairn which had been built by white men and torn down by Inuits. **1963** *North* May-June 34: We are masters here; we are filled with power/Without us the Innuit go hungry/Or on rough journeys to better hunting grounds. . . .
2 the language of the Eskimos. See also **Eskimo** (def. 2).
1861 (1865) HALL *Arctic Researches* 476: The word 'wich-ou,' in Innuit has two significations. **1877** DALL *Tribes of N.W.* 95: Linguistically, no ultimate distinction can be drawn between the American Innuit and the American Indian.

inshore ice See **shore ice** (def. 1).
1946 *Beaver* Mar. 37: . . . the pent-up rising water had suddenly burst out with a rush through one of those cracks which generally divides [sic] the inshore ice, anchored to the rocks below, from the main body of floating sea ice.

inside *n. North* the sparsely settled regions of the Far North, especially the Yukon and Northwest Territories. Cp. **outside,** *n.*
1902 LONDON *Daughter of the Snows* 17: And then you went away, over the Pass, to the Inside, and we never heard a word of you. **1928** WALDEN *Dog-Puncher* 216: Native dogs were spoken of as "inside dogs." **1935** *Cdn Geog.Jnl* X 16/1: . . . the "inside" is a prohibition country where Nature enforces the law.

inside *adv.* in the sparsely settled regions of the Far North. Cp. **inside,** *n.,* and **outside,** *adv.*

1957 *Arctic Spotter* Oct. 9: Not once did I meet anyone who was sorry to be "inside."

385

inside lot
interdiction

inside lot *Obs.* See quote.
1913 SANDILANDS *West.Cdn Dict.* 25: Inside lots [is] a term used in the real estate business to indicate lots or property inside the city limits, or on land which must necessarily come within the city limits with the city's early expansion.

insider *n. North* a person who lives in the Far North. See also **inside,** *n.* Cp. **outsider.**
1923 WALDO *Down Mackenzie* 248: The Outsider cannot know: the Insider never can make clear to him the grip that holds, the urge that stirs and never sleeps.

inspectioneer [ɪn,spɛkʃəˈnir] *n. Whaling, North* See quote.
1897 TUTTLE *Golden North* 209: On the approach of the vessel, the whale is made fast to her side, tail forward, so that the large open mouth will not fill with water in case of the advance of the ship, and the work of sculping is begun. This is done under the superintendence of an official called "the Inspectioneer."

in store See **store** (def. 2).

insulin [ˈɪnsələn] *n.* [< NL *insula* island + E -*in*] an extract from the islets of Langerhans in the pancreas, used in the treatment of diabetes.
1922 BEST *Am.Journal of Physiology* Sep. 175: Purified alcohol extract of pancreas, for which we suggest the name insulin, when injected subcutaneously into normal rabbits, cause the percentage of sugar in the blood to fall within a few hours. 1948 ANGLIN *Canada Unlimited* 96: 1921 . . . Frederick Banting and Charles H. Best administer the first injection of insulin given to a human diabetic—"insulin," a word that is to become a synonym for "miracle" to millions of diabetic sufferers who would otherwise be doomed to die. 1958 *Evening Telegram* (St. John's) 29 Apr. 17/8: . . . the required insulin dosage can be more accurately determined when a patient is ambulant with routine similar to normal daily activity.

insurance goal in certain sports, a goal that puts the scoring team two goals ahead of its opponents.
1963 *Kingston Whig-Standard* (Ont.) 17 Jan. 13/7: Randy Miller back-handed the insurance goal . . . 22 seconds after Gilbert scored.

integrated school a school attended by the children of both whites and native Indians who are charges of the federal government, which pays the tuition of the Indian children by arrangement with the provincial department of education. See also **joint school.**
1958 HEALEY *Alert Bay* 81: Many others, both Indian and non-Indian, share this dream with him and with the success of such things as integrated schools and enfranchisement for Indians who live away from the reservation, this dream may become a reality.
1964 *Camsell Arrow* Summer 61: Indian reservations may need to become school units or portions thereof if effective, integrated schools are to develop, it was suggested today at conclusion of the second "Schools in the Forest Conference" being held in Prince Albert.

integration *n.* the policy or action of integrating the three armed services in areas of administration and operation where effort was formerly duplicated and therefore uneconomical. Cp. **unification.**
1966 *Globe and Mail* (Toronto) 1 Aug. 7/3: Most of the concern over integration stems from uncertainty about the future.

intendant† [ɪnˈtɛndənt] *n.* [< F] *Hist.* the head of the civil administration in New France.
1711 (1920) *Cdn Hist.Rev.* I 50: And as you turn up, at yᵉ Intendants, there is a Gate and a little above yᵗ Gate is three Guns west, & a small Clockhouse upon yᵉ works. 1857 ROGER *Quebec* 13: The gentlemen who have the management of the Police and the civil power, meet here, and the Intendant generally presides. 1904 *U of T Stud.Hist.& Econ.* II 168: The Intendant in New France was a kind of business manager for the King, a combined Minister of Finance, Justice and Police, the most important man in the colony, next to the governor, upon whom, to tell the truth, he was a spy, or at least a check. 1962 *Canada Month* Jan. 38/2: The first came from Jacques de Meulles, Intendant of New France, in 1686.

intercolonial railway *Hist.* a railway linking the Maritimes with Quebec and Ontario, the beginnings of the transcontinental railway.
1887 (1888) LEES & CLUTTERBUCK *British Columbia* 16: . . . many of our passengers [left] at Rimouski, where the mail tender meets the steamer, and the inter-colonial railway is available. . . . 1953 LEBOURDAIS *Nation of the North* 15: For twenty years previous to Confederation, the people of Nova Scotia and New Brunswick, led by Howe, had been attempting to build an intercolonial railway connecting them one with the other and with Canada.

interdict *n. Esp.B.C.* a person who has been placed on the interdict list, *q.v.*
c1956 (1958) HAWTHORN *Indians of B.C.* 359: We have about ten interdicts, usually on for a six month period. They don't like to be on the interdiction list. The interdicted person is a social failure as he cannot go into the beer parlour. For many drunk charges where wife beating is involved, we have them interdicted. 1965 *News of the North* 23 Sep. 4/3: Drink charges meant fines of $10 apiece for Christine Abel and Peter Stevens and Noah Kemajak, but Mary Drybones who is an interdict paid $25.00 on the same charge.

interdict *v.* **1** of a district, have laws forbidding the sale of wine and spirits.
1913 COWIE *Adventurers* 500: "Luxuries"—in the ante-steam transport days this fur-trade term was applied to the voyaging and wintering allowances given to the officers and missionaries, and consisted of mustard, pepper, pimento, Hyson and Souchong tea, sugar, rice, raisins, currants, vinegar and flour, also of wine and spirits in non-interdicted districts."

2 have (someone) placed on the interdict list, *q.v.* See also **siwash,** *v.* (def. 2a).
1930 MCCLUNG *Be Good* 80: "He'll not vote for Mrs. Banks. You know it was Mrs. Banks who got his wife to interdict him. . . ." 1964 *News of the North* 30 July 1/4: . . . Sophie Football is now spending 30 day term for consuming liquor whilst interdicted and may face other charges.

interdicted list See **interdict list.**
1967 *Kingston Whig-Standard* (Ont.) 29 Mar. 33/1: An additional charge of possessing liquor while on the interdicted list was dismissed. . . .

interdiction *n. Esp.B.C.* legal restraint from buying, selling, or using liquor.

1958 HAWTHORN *Indians of B.C.* 359: Interdiction is effective only in the smaller centers where the police know everyone. **1963** *Sun* (Vancouver) 5 Nov. 2/4: Interdiction then was a restraint imposed on a person incapable of managing his own affairs. In B.C. today it is a ban against the purchase, use or supply of liquor.

interdiction list *Esp.B.C.* See **interdict list**.
*c***1956** (1958) HAWTHORN *Indians of B.C.* 359: They don't like to be on the interdiction list.

interdiction order *Esp.B.C.* a legal instrument placing a person or persons on the interdict list, *q.v.*
1966 *Sun* (Vancouver) 19 Apr. 1/1: He said the interdiction order will be signed as soon as the names of all the band members are obtained from the Indian Affairs department.

interdict list *Esp.B.C.* a list of persons who have been placed under legal restraint in the buying, selling, or consuming of liquor. See also **Indian list** (def. 1), **interdicted list, interdiction list,** and **Siwash list**.
1963 *Sun* (Vancouver) 5 Nov. 2/4: By placing [drunken drivers] on the interdict list he is invoking a form of prohibition adopted by the courts as far back as 1579. *Ibid.* 2/5: . . . there are between 4,500 and 5,000 British Columbians on the interdict list now. **1966** *Ibid.* 19 Apr. 1/1: He believed it is the first time in the history of the province that an entire Indian community will be placed on the interdict list.

interior *n.* **1** *Hist.* See **Indian country** (def. 2).
1800 (1820) HARMON *Journal* 25: The goods intended for the interiour, or upper countries, are here put on board of canoes. **1855** (1956) ROSS *Fur Hunters* 16: . . . you will have heard that the spring brigade is to leave in a few days for the interior. **1927** WOOLLACOTT *Mackenzie* 2: The stage on which this romantic drama was enacted covered more than half a continent, and was variously referred to in the literature of the fur-trade as *le pays d'En Haut,* the Indian Territory, the Interior, and by a more recent public as the North-West.
2 that part of British Columbia lying inland, particularly the more southern portion between the Coastal Ranges and the Rocky Mountains.
1927 *Beaver* June 32/2: As this was the first one [orthophonic Victrola] imported into the interior, it caused great interest. . . . **1964** *Dly Colonist* (Victoria) 12 Sep. 1/3: . . . the controversial Freedomites . . . had been blamed for violence in the Interior for years.

interoceanic *adj. Obs.* from the Atlantic to the Pacific coast of Canada; transcontinental.
1858 *British Colonist* (Victoria) 11 Dec. 4/1: The inter-oceanic road will, in the course of time, be built step by step, as the continent fills up with population and wealth, the joint product of its natural resources and human labor. **1873** (1904) BUTLER *Wild North Land* 343: We must now glance at the mountains themselves, which form the real obstacle to interoceanic lines of railroad.

interprovincial *adj.* between two or more provinces of Canada; from province to province.
1895 *Times* (Niagara-on-the-Lake, Ont.) 4 Apr. 5/2: The object of the meeting was . . . to push the inter-provincial bridge scheme. **1962** *Chronicle-Herald* (Halifax) 8 Aug. 1/8: . . . whatever happens in the

interprovincial exchange of electric power, each province should be responsible for ownership and maintenance of installations within the province.

interval or **intervale**† ['ɪntəvəl *or* 'ɪntɚˌvel] *n.* *Esp. Atlantic Provinces* the low-lying land adjacent to a river, usually of rich soil because of alluvial deposits left by spring freshets. See also **interval land** and **riverbottom**.
☞ **Interval** *and* **intervale** (*a variant arising by popular etymology*) *both came from New England, being widely disseminated in colonial Canada and the Maritimes, where the term is still in general use.*
1799 *U.C.Gaz.* (York [Toronto]) 7 Dec. 4/3: Those Lots are remarkable for their extent of intervale, the Upland being no less inferior, comprized for the most part of hard timber, and being of a deep black soil, with not more than from ten to fourteen acres of pine.
1825 *Novascotian* (Halifax) 13 July 226/2: The extensive tract of interval and meadows at the Forks [is] terminated at one side by the lake and its out-let. . . .
1896 ROBERTS *Camp-Fire* 56: . . . It was a new farm, which father was cutting out of the woods; but it had good bit of 'interval,' so we were able to keep a lot of stock.
1954 BRUCE *Channel Shore* 213: Here there are lonely lakes, swamps tucked between wavelike hills, aimless brooks and still waters in which are sourced the creeks that slip through hidden intervales. . . .

interval(e) island *Obs.* an island caused by the settling of alluvial soils behind some obstruction in a river.
1846 HATHEWAY *Hist.N.B.* 57: The intervale islands in the rivers appear, generally, to have been made by trees and other substances grounding on shoals.

interval(e) land See **interval**.
*c***1780** (1949) LAWSON *New Brunswick Story* 124: The interval lands on the St. John are wonderful, not a stone, and black mold six feet deep. **1883** HATTON & HARVEY *Newfoundland* 381: The "interval land" along the river made excellent meadow ground.
1923 WILLIAMS *Spinning Wheels* 63: . . . coming out into the open of intervale lands . . . the footprints of yesterday lead you.

in (or into) the country *North* in or into the wilderness of the northern forests or barrens (def. 2).
1933 MERRICK *True North* 15: Soon they will be gone too, bound up the rivers "into the country" to the furring grounds hundreds of miles away. **1944** *Beaver* June 39: To the average person "outside," and even to those who have spent a considerable time "in the country" the thought of finding himself lost . . . would inspire feelings of extreme helplessness. . . .

in the hair *Fur Trade* with the hair intact. See 1921 quote.
1771 (1911) HEARNE *Journey* 190: Their tents are made of parchment deer-skins in the hair, and are pitched in circular form. . . . **1921** *Beaver* Oct. 4/1: . . . they [furs] may be what is termed "cased in the hair", which means that the natural dimensions of the animal's skin are retained, with the fur showing outside and the pelt within. . . .

in the meat *Fur Trade, Obs.* of furs or skins, attached to the animal's body. Also *in meat.*
1797 (1964) CHABOILLEZ *Journal* 161: [He] brought two Deers in Meat for which I paid him Ten Pints Mixed Rum, & the Boisson Begun. **1801** (1897) COUES *New Light* I 175: Came down Park river in a skin canoe, with 25 Beaver skins, 12 of which were still in the meat.

Inuit *n.* See **Innuit.**

Inuk ['inuk] *n. Eskimo* a man, especially one superior to other men. Cp. **Innuit.**
1824 NIAGUNGITOK *Esquimeaux Words* 22: Innuk[:] Esquimeaux Indians. **1951** BULIARD *Inuk* 60: The Eskimo is different, quite different. What is he, this Inuk, this man of the men *par excellence*? **1959** LEISING *Arctic Wings* 122: And Billy Trasher is a real Inuk (man above other men).

Inukshuks

inukshuk ['ɪnuk‚ʃuk] *n.* [< Esk. "something acting in the capacity of a man," pl. *inukshuit*] a cairn constructed by Eskimos to resemble a man's outline and serving as a landmark, or, in some parts of the Arctic, as one of the deadmen (def. 1) in a deer hedge, *q.v.*
[**1939** *Beaver* Sep. 26/1: The Eskimos use what they call *eenevsook* or stone men: piles of rocks for guides.]
1951 BULIARD *Inuk* 199: The Eskimos used to build avenues, miles long, of rocks that looked like men— Inuksoit, they called them. **1953** *Cdn Geog.Jnl* XLVI 162: Inukshuks . . . were built to frighten the caribou herd into certain channels where hunters with bows and arrows would wait for them. **1966** *Ibid.* LXXIII 87: It is fairly conclusive that the large figures made in the shape of a man were at one time of only ceremonial significance. They were originally called inunguaks which means 'like a man' as distinct from inukshuk which means 'acting in the capacity of a man'. In other words, the large man-like figures, although they were found at the entrance to the migration routes, may have served, not as navigational beacons, but as gods which had to be appeased before one undertook a long and dangerous journey.

Irish miner's shovel See **cook's shovel.**
1961 PRICE & KENNEDY *Renfrew* 46: In the hardware store the implement [cook's shovel] was known as an "Irish miner's shovel."

ironbender *n. Slang* a strict disciplinarian.
1956 GOWLAND *Sikanaska Trail* 42: Dad was a good man, but a real ironbender. He was as strict as a monk, and he thought of little else but work.

iron chink a machine for cleaning and dressing fish, so called because this work was often done by Chinese in the West Coast salmon factories.
1913 *Heaton's Guide to Western Canada* 11: In the salmon canneries the introduction of a machine called the "Iron Chink", for cleaning and cutting the fish has made a great economy in the cost of labor. **1926** MCKELVIE *Huldowget* 101: . . . garnering the silver harvest of the sea for the insatiable maws of the "Iron Chinks" at the Sliam cannery. **1963** *Sun* (Vancouver) 5 Apr. 34/1: [Advert] Fishing company requires qualified iron chink operator. Also filling machine operator. Apply to Box 1617, Sun, for interview.

iron horse† a railway locomotive.
1852 *Anglo-American Mag.* I 464: A considerable number of persons congregated near the Queen's wharf, to witness the trial, and appeared much pleased with the "Iron Horse," as he snorted along the track. **1887** *Our Forest Children* Feb. 1: The advance of the iron horse into the prairies of the North West had probably as much to do with the Indian rising of 1885 as had the insidious influence of Louis Riel and his half breeds. **1955** CHATTERTON *Canada* 75: Early 'Iron Horses' had names, but to-day they have numbers.

iron-nose *n. B.C., Slang* See **steelhead,** *n.*
1963 *B.C.Digest* Nov.-Dec. 30: I took a picture that day of Kamloops steelheader Doug Lyons holding a nineteen pound iron-nose. . . .

iron of the country *North* See **babiche** (def. 1).
1909 CAMERON *New North* 338: —Babiche, or rawhide of the moose or caribou—"the iron of the country."

Iron Stone See **Manitou Stone.**
1927 *Beaver* Dec. 116: . . . the Iron Stone of Alberta [a meteorite] which lay on the prairie near a beautiful stream, named after this circumstance, Iron Creek.

ironwood† *n.* a hardwood tree, *Ostrya virginiana,* native to central and eastern Canada; also its wood.
1795 (1911) SIMCOE *Diary* 269: I was amused by observing the . . . regular marked iron wood. . . . **1855** (1955) CRAIG *Early Travellers* 208: Hard wood stumps, such as Beech, Maple, Oak, Iron-wood . . . wrought out in that period, but pine stumps remained sound much longer, and require to be either burnt out or extracted by the aid of oxen or horses. **1956** *Native Trees* 126: The ironwood produces one of the hardest and toughest of native woods.

isaacer ['aɪzəkɚ] *n.* [? < Esk. *isaq* something ancient + E *-er*] *North* an adult male caribou (def. 1).
1882 GILDER *Schwatka's Search* 25: He had shot two deer, a "cooney" and an "isaacer"—that is, a doe and a buck—and he had their warm, bloody skins on his back.

Ishmaels of the prairies *Hist.* the Blackfoot Confederacy. See quotes.
1936 (1960) STANLEY *Birth of Western Can.* 196: [The Blackfoot] were the "Ishmaels of the prairie" and lived in a state of desultory warfare with their neighbours. **1955** JENNESS *Indians of Can.* 318: So the Blackfoot became the Ishmaels of the prairies, their hands being raised against every neighbour except the insignificant Sarcee, and occasionally the Gros Ventre, who sought the shelter of their confederacy.

island *n.* a clump of trees on the prairie, in a meadow, etc. See also **bluff** (def. 3a) and **islet de bois.**
1691 (1929) KELSEY *Papers* 15: . . . having travelled to day near 30 miles in yᵉ Evening came to a small poplo Island wᶜʰ standeth out from yᵉ main ridge of woods. . . . **1776** (1901) HENRY (Elder) *Travels* 287: We were in sight of a wood, or island, as the term not unnaturally is[,] as well with the Indians as others. **1888** MCDOUGALL *G.M.McDougall* 240: Islands of timber and fields of prairie, artistically arranged, and so placed that however cultivated your taste, you would

not change them if you could. **1962** FRY *Ranch on the Cariboo* 70: Bill worked from bunch to bunch near one of the islands of timber in the middle of the meadow.

Island of St. John('s) *Hist.* See Isle St. Jean.

1755 (1955) CURTIS *Voyage*: [Title] A Narrative of the Voyage of Thos. Curtis to the Island of St. John's. . . . **1960** *Press* Dec. 13: . . . he had . . . followed this with resettlement,—a moderately succesful settlement on the Island of St. John (P.E.I.) and two failures in the Lake Erie-St. Clair districts of Upper Canada.

isle d'arbres *Acadian French* See **island.**

1955 *Time* (Cdn ed.) 31 Jan. 25/2: They use scores of Acadian idioms, such as isle d'arbres (literally: island of trees) for a forest grove.

Isle (or Ile) St. Jean *Hist.* the early French name for Prince Edward Island. See also **Island of St. John.**

1923 MACMECHAN *Sagas of Sea* 18: At first, the watchers thought that they descried Isle St. Jean, and hope sprang up of finding a port of assistance. **1940** NIVEN *Mine Inheritance* 387: For those in Prince Edward Island, that used to be called the Ile St. Jean, although there had been preliminary hardship, the tide had turned. *c*1963 *Touring P.E.I.* 9: This little settlement was named after an old resident, Noel Pinet . . . who migrated to the Isle St. Jean and settled here.

islet de bois *Cdn French* See **island.**

*c*1797 (1819) MCDONNELL *Red River* 269: All the wood here, as in the rest of the plains, being only small tufts, here and there, called by the French Ilêts de bois, surrounded by the plains the same as an isle encompassed by water, and slips that grow on the richest lands, on low points near the river and on its banks. **1873** *Cdn Mthly* May 376: At intervals, lower spots occur in the prairie, which in wet seasons are filled with water, and in which thin belts of trees usually spring up; these receive the name "Bluffs" or "Islets de Bois." **1897** COUES *New Light* I 66n: Not necessarily implying that the river has small wooded islets, but that it is bordered at intervals by patches or clumps of trees, commonly called islettes de bois by the voyageurs.

isletin [ɪzˈlɛtən] *n.* [< F *islet* isle + E *-in*] an early name for insulin, *q.v.*

1929 BANTING *History of Insulin* 5: At the end of this time we had used up all the available supply of what we then called "isletin." **1959** *Today's Health* Aug. 67/1: The digestive enzymes of sweetbreads were too abundant to permit the isolation of the elusive isletin.

jack *n.* **1** See **northern pike**. See also **jackfish**.
1696 (1929) KELSEY *Papers* 54: To day 5 of our men came from the fourteens which brought 7 Jacks and 20 patridges likewise two from french Creek with 2 Jack and two trout. **1792** (1934) TURNOR *Journal* 476: Tuesday at 4 AM took up our nets got as many small Jack and Suckers as made a meal. **1897** COUES *New Light* II 456n: *Brochet* is F. name of the pike, a fish, otherwise called jack; and the *tete du brochet* is literally jackhead, another name of the same fish. **1959** *Calgary Herald* 31 July 14/2: Plenty of jacks and pickerel but no trout.

2 See **jacklight**, *n.* (def. 1).
1842 WILLIS *Cdn Scenery* II 90: It is a very pretty sight to see these little barks . . . rendered visible in the darkness by the blaze of light cast on the water from the jack—a sort of open grated iron basket, fixed to a long pole at the bows of the skiff or canoe. This is filled with a very combustible substance, called fat-pine, which burns with a fierce and rapid flame, or else with rolls of birch-bark, which is also very easily ignited. **1878** *Canadian Mthly* I 91/1: Its dark pine-clad shores used to be enlivened with the canoes and skiffs of the fisher, stealing out from the little bays and coves, with the red glare of the fat-pine all ablaze, casting its stream of light upon the dark surface of the waters, from the open-grated iron basket or jack, as it was called, raised at one end of the little vessel on a tall pole. **1885** HAIGHT *Country Life* 41: Three or four would set out with spears, with a man to carry the jack, and also a supply of dry pineknots. . . . **1903** CONANT *Life in Canada* 137: Hear their shouts as they race up and down the stream for suckers, pike, mullet, and eels. "Here he goes . . . plague on your jack—you missed that big fellow."

3 *Nfld* See **jackboat**.
1895 *St.Nicholas* Apr. 448/2: . . . the gashers [were] dashing in and out among the punts and jacks (stoutly built two-stickers larger than gashers). **1937** *Beaver* June 29/2: Bill had a nice little jack (small fishing schooner, in this case with outriggers on the quarters instead of booms) which took my fancy, and which he guaranteed had a pitchline-oak bottom, whatever that might be.

4 See **lumberjack** (def. 1).
1910 FERGUSON *Janey Canuck* 106: The "jacks" do not dine on half a pasteboard package of chips. . . . **1961** GREENING *Ottawa* 101: The jacks who felled the trees and the workers who stripped them were called *piqueteurs*. . . .

5 a. See **jack-rabbit**.
1923 WALDO *Down Mackenzie* 54: "The jacks o' the prairies is twice the size." **1964** *B.C.Digest* Dec. 36/1: [Caption] The jack's ears flop back in annoyance.

b. See **big jack**.
1947 WELLS *Owl Pen* 84: "My young lad has been hunting for jacks all winter, and he ain't got one yet." **1962** *Kingston Whig-Standard* (Ont.) 28 Dec. 11/1: During the first drive I had a jack come directly towards me along a fence.

6 *B.C.* a salmon that matures early, usually in its third year.
1958 WATTERS *B.C.Cent.Anthol.* 136: Some precocious fish, usually males, return as three-year-old "jacks". . . . The jacks average nineteen inches in length and about three pounds in weight. . . . **1959** CARL *Fresh-Water Fishes B.C.* 83: A few sockeye, for the most part males, mature at 3 years of age and are frequently referred to as grilse and sometimes "jacks." **1961** CLEMENS *Fishes of Pacific Coast* 121: Anadromous sockeye salmon usually mature in their 4th or 5th year of life, but

sometimes large numbers of males mature in their 3rd year, when they are known as "jack" sockeye. Fewer individuals spawn in their 6th or 7th year. **1964** CARL *Marine Fishes B.C.* 28: Some [Chinook] males become sexually mature in their second or third years, while still quite small; these are commonly called "jacks" or "jack springs."

jackash *n.* [< Algonk.: ? Cree *atchakas* genitals] *Fur Trade, Obs.* the North American mink, *Mustela vison*. See also **foutereau**.
1743 (1949) ISHAM *Observations* 165: Jackashes is the size, shape, make & colour of a martin, Excepting the tail, not being so Bushy and full of hair. **1795** (1911) HEARNE *Journey* 374: I never saw a hollow tree that was capable of affording shelter to any larger animal than martins, jackashes, or wejacks; much less the quiquehatch or Bear, as some have asserted. **1907** HODGE *Bulletin* I Glossary: Jackash. A name of the American mink . . . in use in the fur country. . . .

jackasheypuck *n.* [< Algonk.] *Obs.* See **bearberry** (def. 1).
1743 (1949) ISHAM *Observations* 132: Jac'kashepuck, so call'd by the natives, is a Leaf Like unto a box Leaf, itt Grow's about 2 foot high, and Run's in Long branches spreading itt Self upon the Ground, the Stalk's not being of Substance to bear itt up. **1771** (1911) HEARNE *Journey* 188: . . . some jackasheypuck, which the natives use as tobacco. **1819** MCKEEVOR *Hudson's Bay* 69: There is also an herb, called by the Indians, jackasheypuck, found here, though rather in sparing quantity. It much resembles creeping-box; and is only used by the English, or Indians, to mix with tobacco, which makes it smoke mild and pleasant.

jackboat *n.* *Nfld* a small two-masted fishing schooner, sometimes equipped with outriggers. See also **jack** (def. 3) and **two-sticker**.
1951 *9th Census of Canada* IX Fisheries A-2: Jack boats . . . Bateaux "Jack." **1962** *Kingston Whig-Standard* (Ont.) 14 Aug. 8/1: [Headline] Jackboat Race Course Will Include Kingston.

Jack Canuck See **Canuck** (def. 1).
1898 (1967) LEFOLII *Canadian Look* 13: [Caption] Uncle Sam to Jack Canuck—"I hate to see any of the folks leaving home. But when they *do* go I like to see 'em go to Canada where they'll feel at home and get square treatment." **1908** *Observer* (Cowansville, Que.) 1 Oct. 1/6: The Toronto Globe has a cartoon wherein Jack Canuck is walking arm in arm with Laurier and saying, "I like to walk with a man who can set the pace for me." **1963** *Citizen* 30 May 12/5: What is the origin of the nickname Jack Canuck?

jackfish *n.* See **northern pike**. See also **jack** (def. 1).
1743 (1949) ISHAM *Observations* 22: a Jack fish Ke no shue. **1784** (1790) UMFREVILLE *Hudson's Bay* 14: The Indians . . . had killed several fine jackfish on our arrival. **1896** WHITNEY *On Snow-Shoes* 313: The white-fish are prepared for eating, while the jack-fish and others are dried for the dogs. **1961** *Time* (Cdn ed.) 18 Aug. 9/2: "None of this jackfish stuff," he said. "I want pickerel."

jackfish twine *North* heavy, strong twine used mainly for making nets to catch northern pike and other large fish.
1775 (1951) *Sask.Jnls* 22: We are obliged to make our

Sturgeon Nets all of Jack Twine, the fishing Twine we have being two Weak two Thread to hold a fish of any size. . . . **1896** RUSSELL *Far North* 275: Nets intended for their capture are made of "jackfish twine," somewhat heavier than that in other nets, but they are rarely used. *Ibid.* 248: The rabbit [is] caught in snares made from "jackfish twine."

jack herring *B.C.* small male herring used as bait in angling.
1961 *Sun* (Vancouver) 17 Aug. 23/3: Comfortably leading all other combinations as a Sun Derby prize-getter is the old herring dodger (flasher) and herring strip (or jack herring). **1963** *Ibid.* 28 May 15/1: We prowled the shoreline, armed with about 50 live herring and two packs of frozen jack herring.

jack-jay *n.* See **Canada jay.**
1946 WOOD *Rockies* 123: The Canada Jay has more names than a debt collector. It is the Whisky Jack of the early settlers, the Moose-bird and Meat-bird of the hunters, the Jay-dee of the back-bush youngsters, the Camp-robber of the resentful picknicker, while some confuse the issue even more by calling it the Jack-jay.

jack-knife *v. North* of a tug, push (barges) ahead in a zigzag fashion.
1949 BECKER *Klondike* 77: Captains "jacknifed" the barges ahead of them by means of ropes and tackles.

jack-knife saw See quote.
1950 BIRD *This is N.S.* 23: In 1860 two of the Fulton men built a sawmill near the mouth of Bass River, utilizing the stream to operate a home-made jack-knife saw which moved upward and downward as the log was fed to it by a low-geared ratchet.

jackladder *n.* See 1963 quote. See also **haul-up** and **log tack.**
1944 *Beaver* June 29/2: [Caption] . . . this seasoned river man guides them [logs] towards the jackladder of the sawmill. **1957** *Cdn Geog.Jnl* Feb. 56/2: The giant pulpwood operations in the Lake Superior region are indicated by this view of a jackladder and surrounding booms of logs at Terrace Bay. **1963** WILKINSON *Abitibi* 4: Jack Ladder. An escalator-type moving iron belt that carries the logs from the mill pond into the mill's conveying system or to the mill's slasher where the logs are cut smaller.

jacklight *n.* **1** a light used at night to attract fish. See also **fishing light, jack** (def. 2), and **light-jack.** Cp. **flambeau.**
☛ *In Canada both the practice and the device were taken over from the Indians, who used torches, often shielded by basketlike hoods, to lure fish into position to be speared easily.*
[**1793** (1911) SIMCOE *Diary* 209: Large torches of white birch bark being carried in the boat, the blaze of light attracts the fish, when the men are dextrous in spearing.] **1849** ALEXANDER *L'Acadie* I 264: The night was calm, which was favourable for the jack-light. **1905** SCHERCK *Pen Pictures* 206: The Jack-light was made of fat pine knots (knots full of pitch), or hickory bark placed in a basket made of hoop iron hung up to a pole at one end of the boat. **1956** LEECHMAN *Native Tribes* 214: Some fish were taken at night with jacklights from a canoe or even through the ice. . . .
2 a light used at night in hunting deer, intended to daze the quarry.

[**1827** (1829) MACTAGGART *Three Years* I 61: Deluding deer at night with a lantern and candle, and then lodging a slug in their vitals, seems to be a favourite murdering kind of sport with the traversing tribes of the wild rivers of Canada.] **1883** FRASER *Shanty* 147: In this respect it stands far ahead of . . . shooting him by the jack-light after night by the marshy side of river or lake where he comes to drink. . . . **1958** *Ottawa Citizen* 18 Oct. 2/2: Two Masham men were fined $100 each, plus costs and their hunting equipment was confiscated after they were found guilty of jack-light hunting. . . .

jacklight *v.* hunt with a jacklight (def. 2). See also **jacklighting.**
1960 *Weekend Mag.* 2 July 39/1: They had been out jack-lighting deer, paddling their canoe up the creeks at midnight, shining their flashlights in the eyes of does and fawns, shooting them. **1963** *Sun* (Vancouver) 23 Nov. 21/1: After four days of seeing only the aggravating flick of the white brush that these wary species of deer wear for tails, I was almost ready to buy or jack-light a deer, illegal though both methods are.

jacklighter *n.* one who uses a jacklight (def. 2) to hunt deer.
1964 *Globe and Mail* (Toronto) 12 Dec. 8/7: Poachers and jacklighters are being blamed by some and increasing wood-cutting operations by others.

jacklighting *n.* the practice of hunting or fishing at night by using a jacklight, *q.v.* See also **pitlamping.** Cp. **fire-hunting.**
1956 LEECHMAN *Native Tribes* 28: Sometimes they used to fish at night, using a bright light in the bow of a canoe. The fish were attracted by the light and would swim towards it. The fisherman would spear them when they came close enough. This way of fishing, known as jacklighting, is against the law now.

jackpine† *n.* **1** one of several varieties of pine, especially the Banksian pine, *q.v.*
1897 TYRRELL *Sub-Arctics* 62: Finding an inviting camping-ground in the open jack-pine wood, we went ashore. **1904** CONNOR *Prospector* 248: . . . they camped . . . in a little sheltered dell all thick with jack pines. . . . **1966** *Islander* 27 Feb. 13/1: . . . this little press had once been taken apart and packed on the backs of men through 40 miles of gumbo and jack pine. . . .
2 the wood of any of these trees.
1955 *Edmonton Jnl* 4 Jan. 2/6: Development of techniques which make it possible to use jackpine, red and Scottish pine in making newsprint—once almost wholly a spruce and balsam product. **1962** FRY *Ranch on the Cariboo* 4: And I skidded rails, gathering them in bundles where the men had split them into fifteen foot lengths of jack pine. . . .

jackpot *n.* a difficult or embarrassing situation; predicament.
1887 *Grip* (Toronto) 21 May 10/2: I think that the fact of the travellers being commercial men . . . leans toward the theory that what was written of . . . was a jack-pot. **1905** *Eye Opener* (Calgary) 28 Jan.: Now I come to think of it he helped me out of quite a jackpot at one time. **1927** LONGSTRETH *Silent Force* 279: And now his rival was in a jack-pot and he had been chosen to pull him out. **1942** SWANSON *Western Logger* 52: jack-pot—a hell of a mess. **1959** *Maclean's* 4 July 34/3: Like all Canadian embassies, but more often than most, Canada House receives SOS messages from "distressed Canadians" the official designation for those who get themselves into various jackpots.

jackpress *n. Fur Trade* See **jackscrew.**
1925 *Beaver* Dec. 19: . . . with an old jackpress used for packing furs he printed five thousand pages. . . .

jack-rabbit *n.* any of several large North American hares found in the West, as *Lepus americanus* and, especially, *L. townsendii.* See also **jack** (def. 5a), **prairie plain hare,** and **varying hare.**
1882 *Edmonton Bull.* 25 Feb. 4/1: A cache of 35 gallons of whisky was discovered lately in the Pelly River Valley . . . by a policeman while hunting a jack rabbit. **1905** *Eye Opener* (Calgary) 24 June 1/3: So they all went to the shed and found five live jack-rabbits which this athletic Etonian had run down, thinking they belonged to the sheep. **1963** SYMONS *Many Trails* 118: The big prairie jack-rabbits were congregating for their evening meal.

jackscrew (press) *n. Fur Trade, Hist.* a type of press used for baling furs, force being applied by a screw-operated jack. See also **jackpress** and **pack press.**
1941 *Beaver* Sep. 37/2: Various sorts [of fur presses] were used—the jack screw press, the lever and tackle, the windlass press. . . . **1953** WOODLEY *Bible in Can.* 54: His press was a jack-screw used by the traders in baling furs.

jack-snipe *n.* any of several shore birds, as the pectoral sandpiper, *Pisobia maculata,* and, especially, Wilson's snipe, *Capella delicata.*
1795 (1911) HEARNE *Journey* 425: Jack Snipes . . . visit Hudson's Bay in Summer in considerable numbers. **1910** FERGUSON *Janey Canuck* 151: I shot at a jack-snipe in the sleigh to-day, but I missed him. **1928** TAVERNER *Birds of Eastern Can.* 97: *Wilson's Snipe.* Jack Snipe . . . *Gallinago delicata.* **1940** *Beaver* Dec. 17/1: Jacksnipe move through their haunts . . . always as solitary birds. . . . **1956** MCATEE *Folk-Names* 28: Almost any shore bird may be called a snipe or jacksnipe.

jack spring See **jack** (def. 6).

jack twine See **jackfish twine.**

Jacobin *n. Hist.* a follower of Judge Robert Thorpe, an Irishman who led dissident elements of Upper Canada (1805-1807) in opposition to the oligarchy.
1828 BIDWELL *Tor.Pub.Lib.MSS B104* 17: In the first place, he denied the "Jacobins," as Thorpe's party now came to be called, the freedom of the press. **1958** *Encyc.Can.* X 76/1: In Upper Canada he became the leader of the so-called Jacobins in their campaign against the Governor and the Family Compact.

Jacob's ladder See quote.
1921 LAUT *Cariboo Trail* 15: Then he had pushed on up the river to the Cariboo, travelling by the Indian trails over 'Jacob's Ladders'—wicker and pole swings to serve as bridges across chasm's—wherever the "float" or sign of mineral might lead them.

jail boom *Lumbering* See quote. See also **log trap** (def. 2).
1966 *Sask.Hist.* Winter 30: We put a jail boom in a bend in the river six miles downstream to catch any stray logs.

jam *n.* **1** See **ice-jam.** Also, earlier, spelled *jamb.*
1771 (1792) CARTWRIGHT *Journal* I 121: We had clear water till we passed Camp islands; but on observing a jamb of ice which extended from Table Point towards

391 **jackpress**
jam ice

Belle Isle, we endeavoured to go on the outside of it. **1863** WALSHE *Cedar Creek* 375: . . . for the edges of the vast [ice] field set in motion the previous day had ploughed into the earth, and piled itself in immense angular "jambs." **1948** ONRAET *Sixty Below* 25: The fast receding water, after the jam had given way, had left bold banks and beaches, piled with ice and debris, in places hundreds of feet high.
2 *Lumbering* a massing together of logs, as in a river drive, as a result of some obstruction to their forward progress. See also **log-jam** (def. 1) and **timber jam.**
1836 *Bytown* [Ottawa] *Gaz.* 9 June 4/3: On the morning of the 30th ult, while a canoe with nine men, in the employ of Messrs. Wells and McCrae of this town, were engaged in taking some timber in a jam at the head of Colton's shoots, on the river Madawaska, the canoe unfortunately upset, and seven out of the nine perished. **1952** BUCKLER *Mountain and Valley* 359: He was in the kitchen . . . that day they were talking about the drive . . . and suddenly he rushed out and broke the jam. **1961** GREENING *Ottawa* 104: Sometimes the key logs of the jam could be pried loose. . . .

jam *v.* **1** of ice, form into an ice-jam, *q.v.*
1771 (1911) TOWNSEND *Cartwright's Journal* 76: The ice [was] firmly jammed quite across. . . . **1846** *Niagara Mail* (Niagara-on-the-Lake, C.W.) Apr. 3/2: The ice still continues firmly jammed opposite the New Market. . . . **1924** FLAHERTY *Eskimo Friends* 154: Constantly comes the boom and thunder of the icefields as they jam and raft high along the coast.
2 of ships in ice, become caught in an ice-jam, *q.v.*
1784 (1954) *Moose Ft Jnls* 83: The boat (they tell me) they had left at Matapooswom the Ice having so jam'd her in the 23 Instant, that their utmost endeavours for getting her out proved fruitless. **1961** *Maclean's* 28 Jan. 47/1: A couple of miles away, Captain Wes had finally got Newfoundland free, though a short time later she jammed again.
3 of logs, become hung up in a jam (def. 2).
1836 *Bytown* [Ottawa] *Gaz.* 7 July 4/1: Intelligence has been received in Town . . . that a large quantity of Timber which had been jammed on the Rapids there in coming down, and left dry by the falling of the water, had been set fire to. **1966** *B.C. Digest* Oct. 39/1: A limited number of railroad ties were floated down [the Stellako River] until 1957. The ties, of course, are sawn, have no bark that peels off and covers the bottom, are shorter than saw logs and less liable to jam.

jam crew *Lumbering* a gang of loggers trained and equipped to deal with jams (def. 2).
1963 SYMONS *Many Trails* 183: Already the jam crews have established their camps at strategic places along the bank, and they too await the logs with peevies and cant hooks.

jam dragger *Lumbering* an arrangement of ropes attached to a key-log (def. 1) so it could be pulled free to release a log jam.
1961 GREENING *Ottawa* 104: Sometimes the key logs of the jam could be pried loose from the shore with the jam dragger, a series of ropes attached to the key logs.

jam ice *Obs.* See 1792 quote.
1775 (1792) CARTWRIGHT *Journal* II 74: The main body of jam ice being not more than four miles off, rendered

it very dangerous to keep the sea. **1792** *Ibid.* II
Glossary v: Jam Ice. The low ice with which the whole
face of the ocean is covered every winter, and until
late in the summer.

jammer *n. Lumbering* a hoist used in loading logs.
1955 *Bush News* (Port Arthur, Ont.) Feb. 7/3: Some
200 men have been working since early Fall and this
force will be maintained until the end of the haul. About
28 teams of horses, 20 trucks, 6 tractors, two
draglines, and two jammers are being used. **1966** *Sask.
Hist.* Winter 27: We loaded with a jammer and logs
were hoisted onto the sleigh by a cross haul team.

jam-pile *n.* See **driftpile.**
1963 *Alta Hist.Rev.* Autumn 1/2: Near evening luck
was with us [in a scow] in getting by a large jam-pile
of big uprooted trees lodged on rocks.

January thaw† a spell of mild weather occurring
in January and causing the snow to melt.
1853 STRICKLAND *Canada West* I 85: The sleighing was
good from the middle of December to the middle of
March, with the exception of the January thaw, which
continued for upwards of a week, and took away
nearly all the snow. **1925** *Dalhousie Rev.* V 315: Nor
could a flood much change the appearance of a January
thaw.

jar (seal) *n.* See **ring seal.**
1832 MCGREGOR *Brit.Amer.* I 108: Five kinds . . . come
down to the coasts of Labrador, Newfoundland, and to
the Gulf of St. Lawrence: the harp seal (phoca
Groenlandica), the hooded seal (phoca leonina) . . . the
square flipper, the blue seal, and the jar seal.
1861 DE BOILIEU *Labrador Life* 97: The "Jar" is a seal
of social habits, like the beaver, living in large
communities under the ice in winter, and in numerous
bays along the coast in summer. **1959** *Northern
Affairs Bull.* Sep.-Oct. 45/2: Although they had the
opportunity of fishing for Arctic char, they spent much
of their time hunting for jar and bearded seals.

jargon *n.* See **Chinook Jargon.**
1912 (1913) HODGE & WHITE *Indians of Can.* 94/1: Hale
in 1841 estimated the number of words in the jargon at
250; Gibbs, in 1863, recorded about 500; Eells, in 1894
counted 740 words actually in use. . . . **1957** FISHER
Pemmican 131: *Totoosh* was jargon for breasts.

Jasper House Iroquois *Hist.* one of numerous
Iroquois who travelled West as voyageurs, settling
in Alberta and intermarrying with whites and Crees,
some of their descendants now living on the
Driftpile Reserve.
1929 MOBERLY *When Fur Was King* 94: Meanwhile, the
Shushwaps had been going to the west side of the
Rockies for their supplies, while the Jasper House
Iroquois came to Lac Ste. Anne and Fort Assiniboine.

jaw *n.* See **jawbone.**
1962 *Alta Hist.Rev.* Autumn 16/2: In western parlance
. . . credit is "jawbone" sometimes abbreviated into
"jaw".

jawbone *n. West, Slang* credit (presumably
because the jawbone had to be exercised in
speaking to win over the creditor). See also **call
one's jaw.**
1865 (1867) *Cariboo Sentinel* (Barkerville, B.C.)
22 July 2/2: Flour is selling at 45 cents; beans, 50;

sugar, 75; bacon, 75; fresh beef, 25 and 30, on
jaw-bone; clothing is cheaper here than at Yale.
1908 GRAINGER *Woodsmen* 9: Jawbone is the western
word for credit. I lack the art of using mine
persuasively. **1923** WALDO *Down Mackenzie* 201: I
have to extend "jawbone" credit, much as I would like
to do business on a cash basis. **1957** *Beaver* Autumn
41/1: Indians were constantly seeking "jawbone," or
credit and this raised a continuing economic problem
for post operation. **1966** ST. PIERRE *Quarter Horse* 98:
The mower parts would have been charged or, in the
language of the country, put on his jawbone.

jay-bird or **jay-jack** *n.* See **Canada jay.**
1959 MCATEE *Folk-Names* 50: [The Canada jay is also
called] jay-bird ["Labr.", N.S.); jay-jack (. . . N.S.). . . .

jay-dee ['dʒe̩di] *n.* [imitative] See **Canada jay.**
1946 WOOD *Rockies* 123: It [Canada Jay] is the Jay-dee
of the back-bush youngsters. . . .

Jean Baptiste a personification of the French
Canadian. See also **John Baptiste** and **Johnny
Courteau.** Also spelled *Jean Batiste.*
1818 HALL *Travels* 65: The sharp, unchangeable
lineaments of the French countenance, set off with a
blue or red night-cap . . . give undeniable testimony of
the presence of Jean Baptiste. **1832** MCGREGOR *Brit.
Amer.* II 461n: Jean Baptiste is as frequently a *nom de
guerre* for Canadian *habitans*, as John Bull is for the
English, or Saunders for the Scotch. **1878** *Canadian
Mthly* I 92/1: Your Jean Baptiste has a specially keen
eye for a good stick of timber. **1960** *Beaver* Autumn
57/1: These Nile men were rather the shanty-boy
variety of Canadian riverman, just as much at home
on certain Canadian rivers as Jean Baptiste had ever
been but more skilled with the raft, the pike and the
peavey than with the paddle and packsack.

jerk† [dʒɝ·k] *v.* [back formation from *jerky,*
q.v.] preserve meat by cutting it into strips or
flakes and drying it in the sun. See also **jerky.**
1770 (1911) TOWNSEND *Cartwright's Journal* 23: [The
Boethuk] take care to provide for . . . scarcity . . . by
jerking venison, seal's flesh, and fish. . . . **1852** (1881)
TRAILL *Cdn Crusoes* 147: Instead of cutting the meat in
strips, and drying it, (or jerking it, as the lumberers
term it), she roasted it before the fire. . . . **1963** *B.C.
Digest* Oct. 55/2: . . . the meat can be "jerked" and
temporarily preserved until the nearest wild game
storage centre can be reached.

jerkline† *n. West* See 1960 quote.
1950 LYONS *Mighty Fraser* 86: Such a system gave rise
to the driver being known as a "jerk-line driver."
1953 BERRY *Whoop-up Trail* 61: Mule teams . . . hooked
in a tandem arrangement . . . six to eight span in a
team . . . were controlled by a jerk-line. . . .
1960 DOWNS *Wagon Road* 43: Sometimes there were so
many horses or mules hitched to a freight wagon that
the use of reins was impractical. Under these
circumstances a "jerk-line" was used. This was a
single line connected to the bridles of the lead horses.
The teamsters then 'telegraphed' directions to the
trained leaders, who would turn left or right according
to the number of jerks on the line.

jerky† ['dʒɝ·ki] *n.* [< Am.Sp. *charqui* < Quichua
(Peruvian) *echarqui*] meat that has been cured by
jerking. See **jerk.**
1921 MARSHALL *Snowshoe Trail* 273: The last of the
meat is gone, except one little piece of jerky.
1963 SYMONS *Many Trails* 137: If an animal is killed in
summer, the meat is cut in long strips and hung in
racks to dry into "Jerky."

jewellery or **jewelry** *n. Slang* **1** *Lumbering* See quote.

1942 SWANSON *Western Logger* 52: jewelry—rigging, hooks, knobs, etc.

2 *Northwest* See quote.

1963 *Weekend Mag.* 6 Apr. 28/1: He climbs out and puts on the "jewelry"—the tire chains—and we wait till the pilgrim is untangled and on his way . . . It is slow going, with or without the jewelry, but we pull into Dawson Creek, on schedule as usual.

Jew's freight *Slang, Obs.* See quote.

1876 LORD *At Home in Wilderness* 65: . . . it will sooner or later get broken, if used for the corveyance . . . such for instance as "dry goods," meaning trans-Atlantically drapery, hosiery and clothing in general, or what is called by packers, "Jews' freight."

jick† [dʒɪk] *n.* [< the suffix common to many Cree names] *Slang, Obs.* an Indian.

1933 ROLYAT *Wilderness Walls* 196: They were at best transients, those about now consisting of several families of jicks whose hunting territory abutted on the post property and other families who spent the summer holidays in the neighbourhood, convenient to the islands on the lake, which were kept as summer preserves, the property of all, the hunts thereon being communal and for festive purposes rather than for births.

jig† *n.* See 1956 quote. Cp. **jigger** (def. 1). Also, earlier, spelled *gig*.

1956 LEECHMAN *Native Tribes* 344: JIG—A hook used to catch fish by jigging it up and down where fish are believed to be numerous. **1964** *Canadian Wkly* 13 June 12/2: While Reg laid a fire I tossed out a bait in a bid for dinner. I let the jig sink, but before it touched bottom I felt a fish hit it. . . .

jig *v.* Also, earlier, spelled *gig*. **1**† *Nfld* fish with a jigger (def. 1).

1859 *Brit.Colonist* (Victoria) 25 July 1/1: It [squid] is made no use of except for bait; and as it maintains itself in deeper water than the capelin, instead of nets being used to take it, it is jigged. **1958** *Evening Telegram* (St. John's) 18 May 8/1: After jigging a few small, ordinary fish, young Bob's jigger jabbed into "something real big". . . . **1965** LEACH *Songs* 4: On each fish day in spring and summer the men go out in their small boats to net, trap, jig, and trawl capelin, cod, and herring.

2 fish with a jig, *q.v.*

1939 *Beaver* Sep. 33/1: . . . we cut a hole in the ice and sat on a seat of boughs and jigged with a hook baited with salt pork. **1960** MCNAMEE *Florencia Bay* 54: An Indian woman, iron-grey hair in braids, her dress a checkerboard of blue and yellow, was jigging for sea bass.

Jig *n.* See **Red River jig**.

1908 MAIR *Mackenzie Basin* 75: No sooner was the fiddler heard lowering his strings for the time-honoured "Jig" than eyes brightened, and feet began to beat the floor . . . The dance itself is nothing . . . so far as steps go. The tune is everything; Did it come from Normandy, the ancestral home of so many French Canadians and of French Canadian song? Or did some lonely inspired voyageur on the banks of the Red River [compose it]? **1929** MOBERLY *When Fur Was King* viii: . . . he still upon occasion shuffles a lively toe in "The Jig."

jigger *n.* Also, earlier, spelled *gigger*. **1**† *Nfld* See 1832 quote. Cp. **jig**, *n.*

1778 (1792) CARTWRIGHT *Journal* II 340: The Stag brought in seven quintals of fish this evening, which were killed with jiggers. **1832** MCGREGOR *Brit.Amer.* I 226: A jigger is a piece of lead made into the form of a small fish, with two hooks fixed into its mouth, and turned outwards in opposite directions. It is made fast to a line, which is thrown over into the sea, and by jerking it up and down, the hooks frequently fasten into the cod or other fish. . . . *c***1936** (1966) *Weekend Mag.* 23 Apr. 4/1: All sizes and figures, with squid lines and jiggers, / They congregate here on the squid-jiggin' ground.

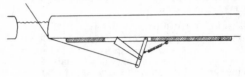

A jigger (def. 2)

2 *North* See 1958 quote.

1946 *Beaver* June 17/1: The jigger is a wooden plank with a slot in the middle through which a wooden arm controlled by a metal lever, moves. **1958** *Encyc.Can.* IV 152: [Caption] the jigger . . . is used to hang [gill] nets under the ice. Inserted through a hole cut for the purpose, the jigger floats against the ice and is driven ahead by a lever worked with a line. The rig is recovered at another hole and the line is used to thread the net. **1964** *Commercial Letter* Mar. 7/2: During the summer the fishermen set their gill-nets and tend them daily by boat. In the winter, the gill-nets are set under the ice surface with a device called a "jigger."

3 a hand-car, *q.v.*, or gas-car, *q.v.* Cp. **steam jigger**. Also, earlier, spelled *gigger*.

1934 GODSELL *Arctic Trader* 156: . . . and it was arranged with Mr. Gafer . . . to take me to Long Lake on his gas-car, or jigger, which was fitted with a motor and flanged wheels and ran on the railroad track. **1947** SAUNDERS *Algonquin* 45: Two of them . . . travelled by jigger along the line to Headquarters. . . . **1958** *Globe Mag.* 9 Aug. 18/1: A few days before I boarded the WP & Y, a jigger carrying eight men came belting around the mountains and ran smack into a moose.

jigging† *n.* Also, earlier, spelled *gigging*. **1** fishing with jigs, *q.v.*, or jiggers (def. 1). Cp. **jugging**.

1859 *Brit.Colonist* (Victoria) 20 July 1/3: When bait is scarce, considerable numbers of cod are caught by jigging. . . . **1948** WALWORTH *Cape Breton* 146: The jigging of all game fish is strictly forbidden. **1962** *Globe and Mail* (Toronto) 23 Mar. 23/8: When this happened the rest of us resumed our jigging at a furious rate.

2 See quote.

1942 TWOMEY & HERRICK *Needle to North* 232: The waiting fisher, from above, could drift his hand out . . . and run the fingers caressingly along the belly, his hand moving tenderly toward the fish's head. At the head, the fingers suddenly and viciously could clasp into the open gills as though they were handles. Such was the game. To take the prey this way is known among the east-coast men as 'gigging' (perhaps corruptly for "gilling' the fish). Only when they were sluggish from the spawning could the salmon be taken by 'gigging.'

jigging ground *Nfld* See **squid-jigging ground.**
1966 *Weekend Mag.* 23 Apr. 2/3: "Squid-Jiggin'
Ground" describes the scene on the local jigging
grounds. . . .

jigging line a fish-line to which a number of jigs,
or hooks, are attached.
1959 *Maclean's* 31 Jan. 42/4: As Halo took his ice
chisels and fought his way against the gale toward the
lake, there to laboriously chop through the new-made
ice which covered his fishing hole, he too knew that
the time had come to move. He came to his decision
as he squatted, back to the whining wind, keeping his
jigging line in motion.

jill-poke or **gilpoke** ['dʒɪl,pok] *n.* [origin
unknown] *Lumbering* **1** *Maritimes* See quote.
1908 DAY *King Spruce* Frontispiece: A "jill-poke," a
pet aversion of drivers, is a log with one end lodged
on the bank and the other thrust out into the stream.
2 *Esp.B.C.* See quotes.
1942 SWANSON *Western Logger* 52: [A] jill-poke [is] a
prop, which when motion is started will cause an
object to move in another direction. **1945** *Intermediate
Booming Grounds* 4: Jill Pokes or single sticks are
used . . . from time to time [to keep flat booms from
grounding] but are usually considered a temporary
arrangement. **1965** *Islander* 18 Apr. 14/1: The
floathouse was of great advantage . . . since it was
necessary only to . . . run a couple of lines to trees on
the shore, rig a couple of long poles, "gilpokes," to
keep the float away from the beach. . . .

jim crow *West, Slang* See 1962 quote.
1859 (1958) WATTERS *B.C.Cent.Anthol.* 243: My present
dress consists of a very bad jim crow, a red serge shirt
with pockets, a blue serge pair of trousers, stockings
and moccasins, a huge gauze bag over my head, and a
short pipe puffing to try and keep the 'squitors off.
1962 *Alta Hist.Rev.* Autumn 14/2: "Bad medicine,"
"chaffy," "snide," "jim-crow," and "pizen," are
applied to anything worthless on the Eastern slope of
the Rockies. . . .

jinker ['dʒɪŋkɚ] *n.* [origin unknown; ? related to
jinx] *Nfld* **1** See quotes.
[**1902** WRIGHT *English Dialect Dict.*: jinker—Nfld.
An unlucky fellow, one who does not succeed at
anything.] **1953** MILLS *Folksongs of Nfld*: Two jinkers
in our harbour dwell, adventuresome and plucky. . . .
1962 *Kingston Whig-Standard* (Ont.) 4 May 3/4:
Things got so bad Thursday that people were saying a
"jinker"—a Newfoundland term for one who brings
bad luck—must have been responsible.
2 an imaginary creature to whom bad luck is
attributed; gremlin.
1962 *Time* (Cdn ed.) 11 May 6/2: The visit was
plagued by "jinkers" (a Newfoundland variant of
gremlins).

jippo *n.* See **gypo.**

joan *n.* See **jone.**

jobber *n. Lumbering, East* See 1944 quote.
1895 (1929) *Selected Stories* 192: The shanty was eighty
miles from any settlement; ordinary teamsters were not
eager to work for a small speculative jobber, who might
or might not be able to pay in the spring. **1912** HEENEY
Pickanock 82: Meanwhile he had gone to the Gatineau

to follow lumbering, first as a workman in the camps
and then as a jobber in a small way on the Danford.
1944 *Forestry Course 1* 10: . . . the company may
make a contract with an independent operator, often
called a "jobber," who undertakes to log a specified
area for a certain price per thousand board feet or per
cord. Under such an arrangement, the jobber may
undertake to build camps and roads, provide horse,
equipment and supplies, and find the necessary men. . . .

Joe *n. Slang* See quote.
1966 *Globe and Mail* (Toronto) 19 Apr. 6/6: . . . their
[French Canadians'] waspish counterparts in Quebec
always refer to "pea-soupers" or "Joes." The word
"Frog" in that connection went out of fashion 50 years
ago.

John† *n. Slang* a Chinese. See also **John
Chinaman.**
1858 *Brit.Colonist* (Victoria) 27 Dec. 4/3: The legs were
accordingly cut off, and the Johns had a high time,
drinking brandy and eating fried hog. **1921** WATSON
Spoilers 310: John always was a better truck farmer
anyway. He can make a fortune off a piece of land that
a white man would starve on. . . .

John Baptiste See **Jean Baptiste.**
1865 *Nor'Wester* (R.R.S.) 8 Nov. 2/4: The grand "take"
is in the fall when just before the ice makes, for a
couple of weeks in the golden October "John
Baptiste" and our "Swampy" friend may be seen urging
their skiff and canoes towards Lake Winnipeg.

John Chinaman† *Slang* See **John.**
1877 ST. JOHN *Sea of Mountains* I 172: Victoria . . . is in
that respect like a miniature San Francisco, and as in
the city of the golden gate, John Chinaman is a large
element in the population. **1921** WATSON *Spoilers* 310:
. . . John Chinaman is beating them to a frazzle at their
own game. . . .

John Company *Slang* See **Hudson's Bay Company.**
1870 *Cdn Illust.News* 26 Feb. 271/3:
John Company once owned a very large firm
Extending from sea to sea,
Where he drove his own curs, and traded in furs—
A very rich man was he, was he—
A monopolist was he.
1963 MCTAVISH *Behind the Palisades* 235: John Company
is still—like Johnny Walker—going strong, and the
old class guides are getting fewer.

John Dory [< *John* + *dorée* turbot] the pickerel.
1887 *Senate Journal* XXI App. 171: The fish I know of
are the whitefish, pickerel (sometimes called John
Dory there [in Manitoba]). . . .

John Down [? < *John* + *down* feathers] *Nfld* any
of several large oceanic birds such as the fulmar.
1852 *Arctic Miscellanies* 10: On the banks of
Newfoundland, where this bird is known by the name
of 'John Down,' it attends the fishing vessels for the
offal of the cod fish. **1959** MCATEE *Folk-Names* 4:
Fulmar . . . John Down (Sailor's name, significance
unknown. Nfld). . . .

Johnnie (in compounds) See **Johnny.**

johnnycake† *n.* [< Am.E; origin obscure] **1** a
thin, flat cake made of cornmeal. See also
journey cake.
☞ *American evidence for* **johnnycake** *is somewhat
earlier than that for* **journey cake** *which has often been
suggested as the source of this word. Other suggested
sources are the name* **Johnny** *and* **jonakin** *a thin wafer*

(*see* Dictionary of Americanisms), *perhaps of Indian origin.*
1826 (1832) PICKERING *Inquiries* 61: Indian meal is also sometimes made into cakes, which are called Johnny cakes.... **1942** CAMPBELL *Thorn-Apple Tree* 102: "Think of all the johnny-cake we'll grow on that patch." "You'll be planting corn, then." **1964** GUILLET *Pioneer Days* 28:... Johnny cake [was made] except in those ultra-loyal sections where an American dish was considered disloyal.
2 *Obs.* a similar cake made of wheat flour.
1852 MOODIE *Roughing It* 113: First, I want you to lend me ten pounds of flour to make some Johnnie cakes. **1887** (1962) *United Church Observer* 15 Oct. 29/3: Some of the wheat we took turns grinding in the coffee mill for porridge, sifting some for johnny cake, as the corn meal is all used.

Johnny Canuck 1 a. See **Canuck** (def. 1).
1910 HAYDON *Riders of Plains* 113: "Thar ain't no Johnny Canuck kin arrest me." **1953** ROCHE *Hockey Book* xvii: There were baseball, football & lacrosse games during other seasons, but in winter there was nothing but idleness for red-blooded, sports-loving Johnny Canucks.
b. a Canadian soldier.
1957 *Cdn Red Cross Junior* Nov. 17: John comes into many nicknames, here are a few of them. John Bull... Johnny Canuck, a Canadian soldier, and Johnny Raw, a new recruit.

One representation
of Johnny Canuck

2 a personification of Canada.
1909 CAMERON *New North* 260: Failing any or all of these [desired trade goods], it was in vain that the Factor displayed before them the wares of John Bull, Uncle Sam, or Johnny Canuck, or any seductive lure made in Germany. **1959** *Maclean's* 1 Aug. 1/2: Millions of Asians, Africans and Europeans who'll never see a travelling hockey team or a cartoon of Johnny Canuck, have only one image: the men and women of our foreign service. **1964** *Canada Month* Jan. 38/2: That's the spirit of USA which Johnny Canuck will never catch up with. **1967** LEFOLII *Canadian Look* 10/3: As far as I know, Johnny made his first appearance as a cartoon character in an 1869 copy of Grinchuckle (page 12), a new Montreal journal that billed itself as "a magazine of mirth and opinion." The cartoonist had already translated Johnny into a Western hat and vaguely British field uniform and used him as a symbol for young Canadians regardless of language.

Johnny Courteau *Obs.* a personification of the French Canadian. See also **Jean Baptiste.**
1901 DRUMMOND *Johnnie Courteau* [Title]. **1916** BRIDLE *Sons of Canada* 100: Johnnie Courteau loves a great speech, especially when he may not know what half of it means.

Johnny Crapaud or **Crapeau** [< F *crapaud* toad (dial. "frog")] *Slang, Derog.* a French Canadian.

1851 JOHNSTON *Notes* II 6:... but these Ayrshire emigrants appear to be shrewd enough to buy out Johnny Crapaud, when he happens to possess good or easily available and improvable land. **1913** PARKER *Money Master* 323: Yet, raged as he was, and ready to take the Johnny Crapaud... by the throat, he was not yet sure that Jean Jacques was not armed. **1919** FRASER *Bulldog Carney* 70: "The trickiest damn bunch that ever come into these mountains are them Johnnie Crapeaus from Quebec—they're more damn trouble to the police than so many Injuns." **1965** STEVENS *Incompleat Canadian* 142:... wherever forests were being cut or railways and harbours built, or mines were being dug there would be found "Johnny Crapeau," esteemed alike for his good temper, great physical strength and ebullient spirits.

joint school *B.C.* See **integrated school.**
1964 DUFF *Indian History* 73: Of great and growing importance in recent years has been the development of "joint" or "integrated" schools.

Jonathan† *n. Obs.* **1** See **Brother Jonathan.**
1813 *Montreal Herald* 7 Aug. 3/3:... Jonathan is said to have taken all that came into his fangs without discrimination.
2 an American settler in Canada.
*c*1833 (1964) GUILLET *Pioneer Days* 14: It is almost needless for me to say that this is the mansion of Jonathan, or the U.E. Loyalist....

jone (pole) [dʒon] *n.* [? perhaps a variant of *gin* (aphetic form of *engine*) device, contrivance] *Maritimes* a long pole set upright in the water, its butt-end anchored in a block of concrete, a buoyed hawser being attached to the top for the mooring of boats. Cp. **pryor.** Also spelled *joan.*
1945 RICHARDSON *We Keep a Light* 160: Now came a time when we kept our boat on a joan-pole about a hundred yards off-shore from the landing place. **1953** RICHARDSON *Desired Haven* 7: No houses nor fish-stores had stood among the rocks, no small boats had ridden at jone-poles, no vessels at anchor, when Prince Nickerson and his bride came to town. **1965** RICHARDSON *Living Island* 8:... the larger fishing-boats which bring visitors to the island must tie up at the jone, a hundred and fifty yards offshore, then transfer their passengers to a skiff and row them to the slip.

jonglerie ['dʒɑŋgləri] *n.* [< Cdn F < F *jonglerie* sorcery; trickery] See **conjurer's lodge.** Cp. **juggler.**
1859 KANE *Wanderings* 439: In the evening our Indians constructed a jonglerie, or medicine lodge, the main object of which was to procure a fair wind for the next day. **1955** LAMBERT *Supernatural* 33:... a Canadian once had the temerity to peep under the covering which enclosed the Jonglerie, but that he got such a fright that he never fairly recovered from it.

jongleur *n. Cdn French* See **juggler.**
1763 (1901) HENRY (Elder) *Travels* 117: The multitude believe that these physicians, whom the French call *jongleurs,* or jugglers, can inflict as well as remove disorders. **1912** (1913) HODGE & WHITE *Indians of Can.* 270/1: The Nipissing were called Jongleurs by the French on account of the expertness in magic of their medicine men.

joual [jwal] *n.* [< dial. pron. of F *cheval* horse]
Cdn French uneducated or dialectal Canadian
French considered as debased or inferior by
educated French Canadians, characterized by
regional pronunciations, non-standard grammar,
and often, especially in cities, by numerous English
words and syntactical arrangements.
1963 *Maclean's* 16 Nov. 54/3: [I] have less trouble
with workers' *joual* than with Montreal cabdrivers. . . .
Ibid.: *Gaspesiens* with their thick, gutteral *joual* accents,
make up, after Newfoundlanders, the predominant
labor force for the newly opened areas of Northern
Quebec and Labrador. . . .

journal of (daily) occurrences *Fur Trade*
a journal of all activities taking place at a post,
including arrivals and departures, births, deaths,
marriages, receipts of furs, employment of servants,
and notes on the weather.
1843 *Standing Rules* (H.B.C.) 34: That Gentleman
in charge of Districts be directed to furnish . . .
Journals of Occurrences at the several posts. **1913** COWIE
Adventurers 227: The Journal of Daily Occurrences . . .
was, like the log of a ship, supposed to contain a
complete record of everything taking place at the post.

journey cake See **johnnycake** (def. 1 and note).
1848 *Niagara Mail* (Niagara-on-the-Lake, C.W.)
4 Oct. 1/3: Receipts for Making . . . Common Journey,
or Johnny Cake. **1959** *Sun* (Vancouver) 15 Aug. 27/1:
Maple syrup reminds me of johnny cake . . . [,] first
called "journey cake," because it was made in
easy-to-pack flat slabs, suitable for travellers to carry
on trips.

jowler ['dʒaʊlə] *n.* [? < Brit. dial. *jowl* knock on
the head + *-er*] *Sealing, Nfld.* a lucky or successful
person, especially a captain bringing home a large
catch.
1924 ENGLAND *Vikings of Ice* 317/2: Jowler. Lucky or
successful person. **1933** GREENE *Wooden Walls* XV: A
JOWLER . . . the name given to the most famous of the
sealing Captains. It is the greatest honour the Seal
Hunt can bestow. **1958** HARRINGTON *Sea Stories* 80:
They found "Cap'n Art'ur" keeping up his long-
established tradition as one of the seal fishery's leading
"jowlers"; the Resolute was loaded to the hatches and
about to bear up for home [St. John's].

judge of fences *Obs.* See **fence viewer**.
1825 *Kingston Chron.* (U.C.) 7 Jan. 3/3: Bulls and Oxen
to run at large—Fences 5 feet high. Road Masters
to be Judges of Fences.

judicial district in certain provinces, a subdivision for purposes of holding district courts,
q.v. (known as county courts in certain other
provinces).
1958 *Wilkie Press* 5 June: Wilkie is still the centre
of the Wilkie Judicial District; all legal services
which were formerly rendered at the old Court House
building will still be rendered here. **1963** *Calgary
Herald* 23 Sep. 22/1: Charles W. Mason, recently
retired sheriff of the Judicial District of Macleod, whose
grandfather was a Lord High Sheriff of County Galway,
Ireland, will be honored at the next sitting of the
Supreme Court at Lethbridge.

jug *n.* *Slang* among oil drillers, a geophone.

1958 WATTERS *B.C.Cent.Anthol.* 419: The cable truck
is manned by "jug-hustlers," so-called because
geophones are nicknamed "jugs."

jugging† *n.* See quote. Cp. **jigging**.
1958 *Evening Telegram* (St. John's) 29 Apr. 16/1: In
New Brunswick "jugging" and "jigging" are specifically
prohibited. Jugging involves attaching a line to a bottle
or can and letting it drift, while jigging refers to hooking
a fish on parts of its body other than the mouth.

juggler *n.* [< Cdn F *jongleur* medicine-man < F
"trickster"; mountebank] *Obs.* See **medicine-man**
(def. 1a). See also **jongleur**. Cp. **jonglerie**.
1748 DRAGE *Voyage* I 235: These Juglers pretend to an
intimacy with Vitico [Weetigo], erect a Tent which
will just hold them, and is shaped much like a
Butter-Churn; black their Faces, and then go alone
into such Tent where they will make a great Variety
of Noises in imitation of Animals, jump about, and
make a great Stir. **1847** PRICHARD *Researches* V 417:
Like all the other Indians, they put more faith in their
dreams, omens, and jugglers, in the power of imaginary
deities of their own creation, and of their consecrated
relics, to which the Canadians have given the singular
appellation of *medicine*.

juggling machine *Obs.* See **conjurer's lodge**.
Cp. **juggler**.
1802 (1897) COUES *New Light* I 199: Before his
conversation with the spirit his juggling machine always
appeared in motion, bending to and fro as if shaken by
the wind. . . .

jug-hustler *n.* *Slang* among oil-drillers, a member
of a cable-car crew, especially a geophone
operator.
1958 WATTERS *B.C.Cent.Anthol.* 419: The cable truck
is manned by "jug-hustlers," so-called because
geophones are nicknamed "jugs."

jumbo sweater a sweater knitted of thick strands
of heavy wool.
1962 ONSLOW *Bowler-Hatted Cowboy* 283: So cold was
the winter that Susan decided to knit me a thick
'jumbo' sweater.

jump *n.* **1** See **buffalo jump**.
1964 *Calgary Herald* 6 Jan. 20/1: Archaeologists have
unearthed about 20 of these jumps within 50 miles of
Calgary and estimate some were in use before Christ
was born.

2 See **jump fire**.
1963 MCKINNON *Forest Activities 3* 11: The back-pack
pump is . . . mainly used for initial action on smaller
fires, patrolling fire-lines to stop "jumps," and in
mopping-up operations.

jump *v.* run or sail through (a rapids).
1903 WHITE *Forest* 300: Often while "jumping" a
roaring rapids in two canoes, my companion and I
have heard our men talking to each other in quite an
ordinary tone of voice.

jumper[1] *n.* **1 a.** See 1921 quote. See also **jumper
sleigh**.
1812 (1903) CARR-HARRIS *White Chief* 119: They had
not gone far when the Indian drew their attention to
the tracks of a jumper in the snow. **1834** (1926) LANGTON
Early U.C. 81: . . . after five or six miles we fell in
with a sort of vehicle called a jumper which we
purchased for the enormous sum of one dollar.
1921 HEMING *Drama of Forests* 308: In winter time,
travel was by way of snowshoes, dog-sled, or jumper.

A jumper is a low, short, strong sleigh set upon heavy wooden runners and hauled by ox, horse, men or dogs. **1964** GUILLET *Pioneer Days* 74: . . . early settlers from the vicinity of Meaford and Owen Sound brought their grists in home-made sleighs called jumpers, which were hauled by oxen. . . .

b. a similar vehicle used as a stoneboat, *q.v.* Cp. **travois** (def. 3).
1905 SCHERCK *Pen Pictures* 173: When ripe it was cut with the sickle, bound in sheaves, and taken on the umper to the threshing-floor.

2 See **mule deer.**
1948 RAND *Eastern Rockies* 210: When going at full speed the [mule] deer travels with a peculiar bounding gait that has given to it the name of "jumper". **1958** *Encyc.Can.* III 222/2: When alarmed, mule deer have the habit of making vertical jumps; this has gained for them the name "jumper."

3 a jumping mouse, *Zapus princeps,* of the Rocky Mountain region.
1946 WOOD *Rockies* 101: During the winter the Jumpers are said to go underground for greater warmth, their hibernation period lasting six months.

jumper[2] *n.* See **atigi** (def. 2 and picture).
1854 (1892) KANE *Arctic Explor.* 120: His dress was a hooked *capôte* or jumper of mixed white and blue fox-pelts, arranged with something of fancy, and booted trousers of white bear-skin, which at the end of the foot were made to terminate with the claws of the animal. **1924** MATHEWS *Wilfred Grenfell* 85: Dressed in skins and snow-white jumpers, topped by long pointed curls standing high up over their heads, and with gleaming black eyes, some sat cross-legged on the bulwarks or hatches. . . .

jumper road *Maritimes* See **skidroad** (def. 1).
1950 BIRD *This is N.S.* 181: All his firewood, and the cordwood he sold, was hauled over a "jumper road" which was a trail cut through the forest on which was placed peeled skids about three feet apart.

jumper sleigh See **jumper**[1] (def. 1a).
*c*1902 (1912) LAUT *Trapper* 221: The rutted marks of a "jumper" sleigh cut the hard crust. **1955** HOBSON *Nothing Too Good* 64: Baxter had a small jumper sleigh which had been unloaded at the Dry Lake camp.

jump fire a forest fire started by burning material carried ahead by wind from another blaze. See also **jump,** *n.* (def. 2).
1953 *Cdn Geog.Jnl* XLVI 47/2: The team could be seen tackling a hot spot on the fire line which could give further trouble but at least all the jump fires had been caught and extinguished. **1962** *Ottawa Citizen* 9 June 1/3: A few smaller "jump fires" spread flames from the main blaze. . . .

jumping deer 1 *Obs* See **antelope** (def. 1).
1806 (1897) COUES *New Light* I 305: Herds of cabbrie or jumping deer were always in sight. **1908** LAUT *Conquest N.W.* I 345: The jumping deer [Henday, 1754] describes as a new kind of goat. **1921** HAWORTH *Trailmakers* 110: They were soon out upon the bald plains, where they were forced to use "buffalo chips" for fuel, and where they saw many "jumping deer," i.e., antelope.

2 See **mule deer.**
1819 (1922) HARMON *Journal* 372: One of these [is] designated the jumping deer. . . . **1860** *Nor'Wester* (R.R.S.) 28 June 4/4: My provision has . . . been almost as varied as it could well be, consisting at times of moose, red deer, jumping deer . . . and almost every

species of the feathered tribe. **1937** CONIBEAR *Northland Footprints* 137: . . . a jumping deer was caught [in the mire] and slowly sank, struggling to the last to keep his head above water. . . .

jumping-off place 1 a point on a trail, waterway, etc. where the route changes in nature or direction, marking a new leg of the journey. Cp. **leavings.**
1887 (1888) LEES & CLUTTERBUCK *British Columbia* 268: At last we came to a "jumping off" place, and here the trail turned sharply down. . . . **1934** *Beaver* Sep. 18/1: . . . the village at the rapids' head continued to be the "jumping off place" for the canoe brigades. . . . **1958** *Evening Telegram* (St. John's) 6 May 30/5: Beautiful Tay Bay [is the] jumping-off place for the Tuck harbor. . . .

2 a. *Esp.North* a place, usually a town, where one leaves the railway or other link with civilization to proceed into the wilderness. See also **jumping-off point** (def. 1), **jumping-off spot, jump-off point, jumping-off town,** and **kicking-off place.**
1903 WHITE *Forest* 36: Were you . . . to be transported direct to it from the heart of the city, you could not fail to recognize it. "The jumping-off place!" you would cry ecstatically, and turn with unerring instinct to the Aromatic Shop. **1951** ANGIER *At Home* 23: The end of steel! The jumping-off place! Dawson Creek, British Columbia, was these. **1963** SYMONS *Many Trails* 162: The nearest town is The Pas, in Manitoba, famous as a jumping-off place for Hudson Bay.

b. any starting place. See also **jumping-off point** (def. 2).
*c*1939 CHAMPION *On the Island* 12: I walked from Carleton Shore to the "jumping-off-place" of the new cable.

3† any place considered the ultimate in isolated, undeveloped wilderness.
1922 CODY *King's Arrow* 28: "But I can't see de Lo'd's hand in dis racket. It doan seems nat'ral to me fo' de Lo'd to let King George lose a good an' beau'ful country, an' den gib him sich a jumpin'-off place as dis instead. . . ." **1937** (1964) JENNESS *Eskimo Admin.* II 14: Archdeacon Stuck described Herschel Island during the whaling period as "the world's last jumping-off place, where no law existed and no writs ran".

jumping-off point 1 See **jumping-off place** (def. 2a).
1953 LOWER *Voyages* 8: This egregious place, not far from the wilderness of the Canadian Shield, grew up as a "jumping off point" for the bush. . . . **1966** *Star Wkly* 12 Mar. 17/2: The city [Edmonton] was one of the main jumping-off points . . . for the long trek to the gold country.

2 See **jumping-off place** (def. 2b).
1958 *Kootenaian* 19 June 5/1: Prince George is your jumping-off point for another great excursion. . . .

jumping-off spot See **jumping-off place** (def. 2a).
1936 *Beaver* Sep. 46/1: Lac du Bonnet, one of the jumping off spots for northern air travel, is an interesting little place. **1966** *Beautiful B.C.* Spring 23/1: Prince Rupert, known as "The Halibut Capital of the World," is a jumping-off spot for the Queen Charlotte Islands.

jumping-off town See **jumping-off place** (def. 2a).
1958 *Edmonton Jnl* 24 June 3 4/4: Fairview is the

jumping off town to the famous Dunvegan Crossing which at present has a ferry for summer crossing and an ice bridge in the winter.

jumping pound See **buffalo jump.**
1888 (1890) ST. MAUR *Impressions* 41: On the other side of the Bow river is a cañon known as "the jumping pound," over the edge of which the hunters used to drive the buffalo, and in this cañon their bones still lie in places two or three feet deep. **1949** MACGREGOR *Blankets and Beads* 36: Many places on the prairies were known as Jumping Pounds, and at the foot of these cliffs, large quantities of buffalo bones may be disinterred.

jump off begin a journey into the northern wilderness. See also **jumping-off place** (def. 2a).
1924 FLAHERTY *Eskimo Friends* 2: We jumped off for the North from a tiny settlement outlying the northern Ontario frontier, Ground Hog by name.

jump-off point See **jumping-off place** (def. 2a).
1958 *Herald-Tribune* (Grande Prairie, Alta) 10 Feb. 18/1: [Grande Prairie] has been the jump-off point for many seismic and drilling crews pushing the search throughout the south Peace and on its fringes. **1966** *Globe and Mail* (Toronto) 18 July 15/8: Oxtongue Lake . . . was once one of the main jump-off points for .canoe trips into the great preserve [Algonquin Park]. . . .

jump the line See quote.
1913 SANDILANDS *West.Cdn Dict.* 26/1: . . . [to] jump the line (or boundary) [is] stealing across the international border line (or boundary) between Canada and the States, evading the customs and immigration regulations, etc.

jump-trap *n.* a strong spring trap having wide-spread jaws.
1937 CONIBEAR *Northland Footprints* 281: Peeshoo was held by an old jump-trap, large, but too weak to be used for less docile animals. **1965** *Islander* 14 Feb. 5/1: The No. 14 jump trap meets these requirements. . . .

June beetle or **bug**† a large beetle of the genus *Phyllophaga*, often in flight in great numbers on warm June nights.
1920 STRINGER *Prairie Mother* 150: ". . . I'll put a June-bug down your neck if you don't let me stay here!" **1965** *Globe and Mail* (Toronto) 24 Mar. 27/8: June bugs would come through the crack in the screen door and bump against the green metal cones that shaded the bulbs. . . .

juneberry† *n.* **1** See **serviceberry** (def. 1).
1853 REID *Young Voyageurs* 356: The berries . . . are known as . . . "June-berries," [or] "service-berries. . . ."
1928 LeROSSIGNOL *Beauport Road* 274: The chief attraction . . . was along the fences and hedgerows where, in season, were strawberries, June berries . . . dew berries . . . pin cherries . . . choke-cherries . . . and the orange-red berries of the mountain ash. . . .

2 See **serviceberry** (def. 2).
1913 COWIE *Adventurers* 327: . . . a grizzly bear [was] found among the saskatoon (Juneberry) bushes. . . .
1956 *Native Trees* 212: The serviceberries, also known as juneberries, shad-bushes, and, in the West, the Saskatoons, are deciduous species with simple alternate leaves and slender unarmed twigs.

June fever *North* spring fever.
1920 FOOTNER *Fur-Bringers* 4: "Twenty-five years old," murmured Peter, "in the pink of condition! I'm telling you what's the matter with you. It's a plain case of the June fever. Ask any of the fellows up here."

jungle *n. Lumbering, Slang* the woods; bush.
1943 SWANSON *Lumberjack* 24: In the days of bull-team logging, when they hauled logs on the skid,/And they cut the stumps away up above the swell;/It was then I hit the jungles—I was only just a kid. . . . *c***1945** (1956) ANDREWS *Glory Days* 31/1: He's fresh in from the jungles dear, with a great big load of hay,/ So stick right close beside him, and make that sucker pay.

jungle cook *Lumbering, Slang* See **bullcook**, *n.*
1966 *Sask.Hist.* Winter 26: The "jungle" cook as he was called cut wood and kept seven or eight fires going for warmth. . . .

jungle hound *Lumbering, Slang, Derog.* See **logger** (def. 1). See also **jungle.**
1953 SWANSON *Haywire Hooker* 35:
And it's jungle hound, and timber beast
And give these bums a ride,
But it's—"Have one on the house, Old Boy,"
When you're stepping with the tide.

junior chief trader *Fur Trade, Hist.* a company officer a grade lower than a chief trader, *q.v.*
1878 (1921) *Beaver* July 2/2: The following Factors, Chief Trader and Junior Chief Trader were also invited to attend. . . . **1921** *Ibid.* Dec. 5/2: . . . Mr. Rae had received his first commission as junior chief trader. . . .

junior matric See **junior matriculation.**
1958 *Lethbridge Herald* (Alta) 31 May 6: Are you getting your Junior Matric this summer?

junior matriculation in certain provinces, the successful completion of a secondary-school course one year short of the full requirements for university entrance. Cp. **senior matriculation.**
1939 GROVE *Two Generations* 2: . . . he had finished middle school with first-class honours, taking his junior matriculation. . . . **1963** *Globe and Mail* (Toronto) 21 May 7/3: Prior to that time [1932], the ordinary junior matriculation (now called Grade 12) with some special questions, was accepted by universities for admission. **1964** *Maclean's* 25 July 38/3: Requirements for grades vary from province to province . . . some provinces have junior and senior matriculation, some do not.

junk [dʒʌŋk] *n.* [var. of *chunk*] *Esp.East* a length of sawn log, stovewood, etc.
1827 (1829) MACTAGGART *Three Years* II 119: Landing on the shore . . . we came upon pieces of junk pinewood split up in thin pieces. . . . **1832** McGREGOR *Brit.Amer.* II 310: Lathwood . . . consists of roughly split junks, three, four, and six feet long. . . . **1954** BRUCE *Channel Shore* 91: He had told himself that . . . he should be thinking of lumber . . . planking, sill logs, shingle junks.

junk [dʒʌŋk] *v. Obs.* in clearing land, cut trees into lengths for burning.
1820 (1955) HARVEY *Island of St.John* 108: As the trees are cut the branches are to be topped off, and the trunks cut into lengths of 12 or 14 feet. This operation they call junking them; if they are not junked before the fire is applied, they are much worse to junk afterwards.

Kabloona or **kabluna** [kə'blunə] *n.* [< Esk. *kablunā(k),* pl. *kablunet* person with big eyebrows] *Arctic* a European; white man. See also **Kadloona**.

☛ *The term occurs in a host of spellings* (**Kablunak, Kablunat, Kablunan, Kablunait,** *and, older,* **Cabluna(k),** *etc.*) *resulting from the English-speaking writers' transcriptions of various regional and grammatical variants; plural forms vary, the word being uninflected usually, but sometimes taking English* **-s,** *and, less often, Latin* **-ae.**

1774 LA TROBE *Mission* 10: Formerly, they were bold and impudent, and looked upon the Europeans as upon dogs, giving them the appellation, *Kablunets,* that is, Barbarians, but called themselves *Innuit,* which signifies men. **1823** *Canadian Mag.* I 528: Yet he attended very sedulously to the proceedings of the Cablunae. **1865** *Nor'Wester* (R.R.S.) 4 Nov. 1/2: We now know that he remained through the next winter with the Esquimaux, and then started for the land of the Kablunas. **1922** FLAHERTY *Eskimo Friends* 56: For hours at a time they watched the crew build the kablunak's big igloo. **1962** VALLEE *Kabloona and Eskimo* 159: In the past, except for the few Eskimos who worked for Kabloona agencies, there was no situation requiring the rigid scheduling of activities.... **1966** *Kingston Whig-Standard* (Ont.) 17 May 19/1: Chances are Eskimo mothers have never heard of baby-sitters. If they have, they've probably rejected the idea as another crazy practice of the kabluna.

kadjak or **kagak** *n. Obs.* See **kiack**[1].

Kadloona or **Kadluna** [kəd'lunə] *n.* [< Esk.] *Arctic* See **Kabloona.** Also spelled *Kodlunar, Kudloonah.*

1864 HALL *Life with Esquimaux* I 302: Five Innuits were also killed by the kodlunas. **1897** TYRRELL *Sub-Arctics* 118: As we drew nearer they soon observed by our canoes and personal appearance that we were not Indians, as they had supposed, but were "Kudloonahs." **1965** *Toronto Dly Star* 16 Oct. 35/6: The only white man working for them is a Kadloona called Brian Pearson.

kahmatik, kahmotick, etc. *n.* See **komatik.**

Kaila ['kaɪlə] *n.* [< Esk.] the supreme nature god of the Eskimos.

1956 MOWAT *Lost in Barrens:* [Blurb] Here is a picture of a primitive civilization shaped by the unrestrained forces of nature which the People call Kaila, the god of weather and sky. **1959** LEISING *Arctic Wings* 220: "We have many small gods, but really only one big God, Kaila. Are there many gods and many churches?"

Kallispellem canoe [< *Kallispel* (Indians)] *B.C.* a canoe made of the bark of western white pine, now largely confined to the Kootenay Valley.

1866 LORD *Naturalist* II 178: Their canoes are of a most singular shape, not unlike the Kallispellem canoe shown in the illustration of Syniakwateen. **1876** LORD *Wilderness* 191: The 'Kallispellem' canoes used by the Columbia River Kootanie and other inland Indians, are made of large sheets of bark....

kalsominer ['kælsə,maɪnɚ] *n.* [< *kalsomine,* var. of *calcimine* a kind of whitewash] *Slang* **1** *Obs.* a person who attempts to gloss over or cover up (evil, corruption, etc.).

1890 *Grip* (Toronto) 17 May 328/1: From a letter over this talented kalsominer's signature ... we gather that it is quite impossible that Gen. Middleton could have appropriated Bremner's furs....

2 *Mining* a person claiming mining experience and

skills he does not possess.

1964 *Western Miner & Oil Review* April 18/2: "Don't Flo me, you dammed kalsominer. Two months ago ... your rounds weren't breaking. ..."

kamas *n.* See **camas.**

kamik ['kɑmɪk *or* 'kæmɪk] *n.* [< Esk.] *Eastern Arctic* a type of knee-length waterproof boot made of sealskin. See also **Eskimo boot, moccasin** (def. 3), and **skin boot.** Cp. **mukluk** (def. 1).

[**1744** DOBBS *Hudson's Bay* 203/1: Boots, Cam-meke] **1861** (1865) HALL *Arctic Researches* 327: Puto and Miner's wife have been mending my *kum-ings.* **1937** *Beaver* Mar. 9/2: This was a cold job waiting for seal in the raw air by the open water with the temperature about 25 below zero, and my feet were cold, notwithstanding the polar bear hide on the soles of my "kamiks." **1940** *Ibid.* Sep. 17: In the Eastern Arctic one speaks of skin-boots or *kumik* never mukluks. **1963** *Chatelaine* April 33: [Caption] ... the child's mother chats with Sally as she busily mends Batiste's kamiks. ...

Kamloops (trout) *n.* [< *Kamloops* (< Salishan "meeting place of waters"), B.C.] a large game fish, *Salmo gairdneri kamloops,* native to the upper Columbia and Fraser Rivers; a landlocked steelhead, *q.v.* See also **silver trout** (def. 1).

1905 WHEELER *Selkirk Range* I 364: In the Illecilewaet and other streams may be found the trout of the Upper Columbia—the Kamloops trout. **1938** (1950) STANWELL-FLETCHER *Driftwood Valley* 183: A few, which are rather like rainbows, are the Kamloops. **1964** *Weekend Mag.* 11 July 20/2: The big Kamloops stood on his tail and skittered all over the bay for 55 minutes before Jack was able to get him into the canoe.

kamotik, kamutik, etc. *n.* See **komatik.**

Kanaka [kə'nækə] *n.* [< Polynesian "man"] *Hist.* a native of the South Sea Islands, especially a Hawaiian in the service of the Hudson's Bay Co. on the Pacific Coast, most of whom settled in British Columbia.

1833 (1963) TOLMIE *Physician* 181: Our crew consisted of four Kanakas, stout fellows, who paddled lustily.... **1843** (1948) MCLOUGHLIN *Letters* 153: ... and that [was] again corroborated by the deceased calling out to the Kanackas to fire on the Canadians. ... **1958** WATTERS *B.C.Cent.Anthol.* 160: The Islands have been a haven to ... naval deserters, Kanakas, remittance men ... and everyday fishermen.

kanhanwee *n.* See **ha-ha-wie.**

kapta ['kæptə] *n.* [< Esk.; cf. Coronation Gulf *kapitaq*] *Arctic* See **atigi** (def. 2 and picture). Also spelled *kapetah.*

1855 (1892) KANE *Arctic Explor.* 279: Underneath the kapetah is a similar garment, but destitute of the hood, which is put on as we do an inner shirt. **1934** *Beaver* Mar. 64/1: The preparation was now in its final stages. Tents and tools were ready. Tanned hides and sleeping bags and kaptas were in order. **1935** EVANS *Reindeer Trek* 101: Always were the women scraping new skins and fashioning boots and kaptas.

kasagea *n.* [< Esk.; cf. Barrow Esk. *qasigiaq*] See **harbo(u)r seal.** Also spelled *kashogiak, kossegear, kussegear.*

1852 RICHARDSON *Arctic Exped.* 494: Spotted seal kassigi-ak. **1864** HALL *Life with Esquimaux* II 120: The skins were of a kind of seals called by the natives *kus-se-gear*, which has softer hair than some other species, and visits salt and fresh water alike.
1882 GILDER *Schwatka's Search* 174: The finest quality of kossegear skins I have seen were killed in Hudson's Strait. **1942** TWOMEY & HERRICK *Needle to North* 142: When the inlanders hunt kasagea in summer, they lie in ambush and shoot those animals that come to sun on shore.

kashim *n.* [< Lab.Esk. *kashiminiwik*] *Obs.* men's council house.
1852 RICHARDSON *Arctic Exped.* 217: On the murder of a relation, retaliation is decided upon at a council held in the kashim, and is generally blood for blood.

A kayak

kayak¹ ['kaɪæk] *n.* [< Esk.] Various spellings.
1 a light sealskin boat completely decked except for a cockpit to accommodate the hunter, who propels the craft with a double-bladed paddle. See also **Eskimo canoe, skin boat** (def. 2), and **skin canoe** (def. 3). Cp. **double kayak.**
[**1576** (1889) HAKLUYT *Voyages* XII 79: Their boates are made all of Seales skinnes, with a keele of wood within the skin: the proportion of them is like a Spanish shallop, saue only they be flat in the bottome, and sharpe at both ends.] **1770** (1792) CARTWRIGHT *Journal* I 42: At nine o'clock, Attuiock, Tooklavinia, his brother . . . and Etuiock, the nephew, a youth of fifteen; came up here in their kyacks, and breakfasted with me. **1897** TUTTLE *Golden North* 219: The Eskimos use . . . its bones for kayak frames and other purposes. **1942** *Beaver* Mar. 9/2: The natural genius of Eskimo workmanship is exploited fully in the building of a kyak, those light, buoyant seaworthy craft, which are truly capable of crossing the Atlantic . . . The capable hands of the Eskimo measure the boat for beam and draft with outspread fingers, crosspieces are fitted and securely lashed with rawhide to the main skeletal framework, which is covered with sealskins in a wet state. When dry, the skins have a drum-like tension, supply rigidity to the framework, and are waterproofed at the seams with seal blood. **1960** BLONDAL *Candle* 203: Do you know that when Eskimos go on a hunt they take lactating women with them? Think of it, so much nimbler than a cow or a goat, can be packed in a kayak; have teats will travel. **1965** *North* Nov.-Dec. 41: A considerable amount of evidence of transitory historic occupation was found in the area: tent rings, a variety of fox traps and meat caches, markers and kayak rests.
2 any boat fashioned after the Eskimo canoe.
1958 *Edmonton Jnl* 29 July 19/1: Two daring experts of the Kayak [sic] . . . are practising the handling of this light craft in preparation for a proposed trip to South America. **1964** *Ibid.* 11 July 2/5: They will be followed by several power boat races, kayak races, water skiing demonstrations by the Wizard Water Ski Club and a host of other aquatic events.

kayaker ['kaɪækɚ] *n.* one who paddles a kayak, *q.v.* Also spelled *kyacker*.
1855 (1892) KANE *Arctic Explor.* 247: Almost in an instant the animal charged upon the kayacker, ripping him up, as the description went, after the fashion of his sylvan brother, the wild boar. **1963** *Beaver* Winter 25/2: In the evening, fifteen kayaks overtook his canoes. Most of the kayakers wore coats of mountain goats . . . and they were in fact Mackenzie Delta Eskimos.

kayaking ['kaɪækɪŋ] *n.* travelling by kayak, *q.v.*
1922 FLAHERTY *Eskimo Friends* 120: . . . even now there are Eskimos there, and the camps of half-a-hundred more . . . are less than a day's kayaking away. **1966** *Cdn Geog.Jnl* Mar. 93/1: [Hunting walrus in freight canoes] is as exhilarating to the modern Eskimo as kayaking was to his grandfather. . . .

Keche Manitou See **Gitchi Manitou.**

keekwil(l)ie (house) ['kikwɪli] *n.* [< Chinook Jargon, adv., below, underneath < Chinook *gigwalix*] *B.C.* a large semisubterranean winter dwelling formerly used by certain Indian tribes, a typical example being 10-12 feet deep and 25-40 feet in diameter, covered with split logs and a layer of mud, and accommodating 12-15 persons. See also **kikili.** Also spelled *kekuli, kikwilly,* etc.
1907 CROSBY *An-ko-me-nums* 80: Besides this type of house they constructed for winter use an underground hut usually spoken of as a "keekwillie house"— "keekwillie" being Chinook for deep underground. **1915** CUMMING *Skookum Chuck* 41: The interior of his "dug-out" was more like an Indian kik-willy (ancient Indian house) than the dwelling of a modern Anglo-Saxon. **1949** LEECHMAN *Indian Summer* 8: . . . thirty or forty people would live together in the "keekwillie" houses, great semi-subterranean structures, warm and snug, safe from the below-zero temperatures. **1958** WATTERS *B.C.Cent.Anthol.* 404: Just at that moment, August Gillard was emerging from his keekwillie.

keekwil(l)ie hole See **keekwilie.**
1950 LYONS *Mighty Fraser* 56: Keekwilie holes . . . very old Indian dwellings . . . distinguished by the semi-subterranean portion of the conically-shaped houses. **1965** STEVENS *Incompleat Canadian* 173: [When] settlers first arrived in what is now British Columbia they found the native tribes addicted to steam baths, which they prepared with heated rocks in a "keekwillie hole," after the fashion of the Finnish *sauna.*

keeper¹ *n. Fur Trade, Hist.* See **horsekeeper.**
1956 INNIS *Travellers West* 277: The keeper's lodge, a large one made of fourteen buffalo skins, had a fire in the centre and the family slept round it. . . .

keeper² *n.* a fish large enough to keep, being of the legal minimum size.
1957 *Maclean's* 25 May 57/1: Similarly, Alberta scrapped the regulation saying "keeper" trout had to be at least eight inches long. **1963** *Globe and Mail* (Toronto) 3 Aug. 21/2: A survey of the lake four years ago showed that the annual catch of keeper muskies (28 inches and up) was between 1,000 and 1,100.

keep-over *n.* [cf. Brit. dial. *keep* lodge, reside] *Ottawa Valley, Obs.* See **stopping-house.**
1961 PRICE & KENNEDY *Renfrew* 50: A bush super-intendant travelled from gang to gang supervising the work. Often one will hear the remark, "that place

is an old 'keep-over' or 'half-way.' " They became landmarks and often villages grew up beside them thus advancing settlement in the wake of the lumber trade.

Keewatin [ki'wetən] *n.* [< Algonk. (Cree)] **1** the North Wind.
1910 FRASER *Red Meekins* 291: A wind blew in their faces now; it chilled as though beyond lay snow. "We're gettin' there," Red called back to Slack. "I'm gettin' ol' Keewatin's breath." **1934** GODSELL *Arctic Trader* 39: For Keewatin, the dreaded north wind, plays no favorites but treats one and all alike, often searing the face as though with a hot iron.

2 *Hist.* **a.** a large territory of the Northwest (def. 1a), lying west and south of Hudson Bay.
1880 MORRIS *Treaties* 10: The District of Kee-wa-tin, "the land of the north wind," was also established, comprising the eastern and northern portions of the Territories, and placed under the control of the Lieutenant-Governor of Manitoba, and an Executive and Legislative Council. **1908** LAUT *Conquest N.W.* I 291: The dispute came as a heritage to modern days when Quebec and Ontario wrangled out their boundaries, and Ontario and Manitoba competed for Keewatin. **1963** MORTON *Kingdom of Canada* 372: These [North-West Territories] now consisted of three, Assiniboia, Saskatchewan, and Alberta, organized in 1882, as well as the unorganized territory which was to become the districts of Athabasca, Franklin, Mackenzie, Ungava, and Yukon in 1895, Keewatin remaining under the Lieutenant-Governor of Manitoba until 1912.

b. since 1912 (modified in 1920), the most easterly of the three Northwest Territories. See 1958 quote.
1913 SANDILANDS *West.Cdn Dict.* 26/1: [Keewatin is] a District of the North-west Territories, part of which lying south of the 60th parallel, was, in 1912, divided and added to the Provinces of Manitoba and Ontario. **1958** *Encyc.Can.* V 390/2: Thus Keewatin District ... embraces all of Hudson and James bays as well as the mainland N. of 60° N. and E. of 102° W. except Boothia and Melville peninsulas. **1963** SYMONS *Many Trails* 196: ... the world wherein we move—even this far-off Keewatin—is still tied to it by the questing of the mind's eye.

3 *Hist.* a proposed name for the province of Manitoba.
1886 *Indian* (Hagersville, Ont.) 8 Dec. 235/2: In Kee-wa-tin, the name at present applied to an incipient province west of Manitoba, the authorities cannot be said to have been very happy. The word is very deficient in dignity.

keg *n. Slang* See **muskeg**.
1903 (1913) CULLUM *Devil's Keg* 67: There is only one approach to it, and that's across the keg. In winter that can be crossed anywhere, but no sane person would trust himself in the foot-hills at that time of year.... **1934** *Beaver* Dec. 47/2: For a diver to reach the wreck, he would have to penetrate twenty feet or so of sticky muskeg and though ... a diver had forced his way down through twenty-eight feet of "keg," it was a risk fraught with dire possibilities.

keg angel *West, Slang, Obs.* See **whisky trader**.
1963 *Herald Mag.* (Calgary) 21 Dec. 7/1: ... some of the old Western slang is worth repeating: ... "tent pegs," (frozen beef steak ribs); "baked wind pills," (baked beans); "paperweights," (hot biscuits); "keg angels," (whisky traders).

kekeele or **kekuli** *n.* See **keekwilie**.

401   **Keewatin**
kerosene lamp

kenik-kenik *n.* See **kinnikinik**.

Kentycooker *n. Slang, Obs.* See quote.
1829 (1830) MOORSOM *Letters N.S.* 317: This part of Hants may be deemed to Nova Scotia what Kent is to England: "a regular Kentycooker," is a term used to express a native Nova-Scotian of the true breed; a being raw-boned, gaunt, keen-eyed, and lantern jawed; greatly resembling ... his own half-savage hog, and obstinate withal as the same animal, if you attempt to drive him in any given direction.

kepling *n. Obs.* See **caplin**.

Kermode bear [< Francis *Kermode,* 1874-1946, former Director of the B.C. Provincial Museum] **1** a subspecies of the black bear, *Ursus americanus kermodei.*
1964 *Sun* (Vancouver) 22 May 14/3: Best said the bear is a Kermode bear, found only on Princess Royal and surrounding islands. About 2½ years old, he weighs more than 200 pounds. **1964** *Wildlife Rev.* Dec. 21: The Kermode bear has been written up in a number of "popular" articles, none of which mention that most Kermode bears are black.

2 the white or creamy-white color phase of this bear. See also **white bear** (def. 3).
1958 *Beaver* Spring 28/2: .... it involves a transition from the sea otter, the hair seal, and the little cream-coloured Kermode bear to the Stone sheep, the moose, and the grizzly bear of the Rockies.
1964 *Wildlife Rev.* Dec. 21: .... a habitat group of white phase Kermode bears at the Provincial Museum [Victoria] ... no doubt contributed to the generally held, but erroneous belief that all Kermode bears are white. **1966** *B.C.Digest* Dec. 20/3: And so Stanley Park obtained its rare "Kermodes" bear, the second of its kind to be exhibited in any zoo.

kerosene ['kɛrə,sin] *n.* [a coined word based on Gk. *kēros* wax + *-ene*] See **kerosene oil**.
☛ *This term was coined by Dr. Abraham Gesner, 1797-1864, of Halifax, N.S., who developed a process for distilling kerosene from the coal-like mineral albertite, q.v.*
1852 *Wkly Globe* 4 June 1/7: [Headline] The Kerosene Gas. **1854** (1861) GESNER *Treatise on Coal* 97: The product is kerosene, the lightest of which is called A kerosene, and the two succeeding parts B and C kerosene. **1865** *Canada Farmer* 1 Apr. 109/3: If Kerosene has any such destructive effect on trees it would be well for those in the habit of using it indiscriminately to bear the fact in mind. **1912** MONTGOMERY *Avonlea* 232: "Well, I noticed the kerosene demijohn wasn't very hefty the last time I filled the can." **1965** SYMINGTON *Tuktu* 70: They killed deer constantly for themselves and their dogs, and for fat to supplement kerosene and willow-twig fuel for their heating lamps.

kerosene lamp a lamp that burns kerosene.
1870 *Wkly Manitoban* 31 Dec. 1/4: A spoiled child—the one that played with the kerosene lamp. **1964** *Globe and Mail* (Toronto) 17 Nov. 31/8: .... a group of men sat in the light of an ordinary kerosene lamp in the bunkhouse....

kerosene oil a distillant of petroleum, used for heating, illumination, and various other purposes. See also **coal oil** and **kerosene**.

1860 (1861) GESNER *Treatise on Coal* 8: The first successful attempt to manufacture oils from coals in America was made by the author of this work. Oil from coal was made and consumed in lamps by him in his public lectures at Prince Edward's Island, in August, 1846, and subsequently at Halifax, Nova Scotia, accounts of which are still extant. The patents afterwards obtained for his improvements were sold to the North American Kerosene Gas Light Company, and the oils are now manufactured and sold under the denomination of "Kerosene Oil." **1894** *Trans.Roy. Soc.Can.* XII 4 145: Kerosene oil was found to be the most satsifactory fluid for preserving strawberries, having just about the right density to allow them to settle to the bottom of the jar. **1964** WILSON *Barrett's Landing* 78: It was better to go to school . . . than . . . take the risk of being given . . . a large dose of kerosene oil. **1966** *Kingston Whig-Standard* (Ont.) 28 May 4/3: Born in Cornwallis, the son of a Loyalist, he [Dr. Abraham Gesner] is remembered as the inventor of the process which gave the world kerosene oil. As such he merits wider recognition than is likely to be accorded him in this electrically-oriented age.

keta (salmon) ['ketə *or* 'kitə] *n.* [< Russian] See **dog salmon**.

1824 (1955) BLACK *Journal* 52: In Bears River near the Lake they speared a kind of salmon he names Keth [sic] in the Rapids but not in quantities. **1933** SHIELS *Seward's Ice Box* 83: Chums or keta are plentiful in all districts. **1962** *Co-op Grocery News Bull.* 1 Aug. 1: Formerly known as dog salmon, the chum, with the scientific name Oncorhynchus Keta, has also been called the qualla, keta and calico salmon. It is caught all along the coast of British Columbia.

Ketchee-Maneeto *n.* See **Gitchi Manitou**.

kettle[1] *n.* [trans. of Cdn F *chaudière* in similar senses] **1** See 1903 quote. See also **cauldron**.

1793 (1933) MACDONELL *Diary* 104: In sight of the fort of Lake La Pluie is the Kettle fall, causing a portage. **1826** (1829) MACTAGGART *Three Years* I 327: . . . down they [the waters] tumble, in some places more than one hundred feet, into the cauldrons or kettles beneath. . . . **1903** CARR-HARRIS *White Chief* 108: . . . he saw a cloud of mist rising from the falls, which the Indians called the "Asticou," which means "Chaudiere" in French, or "kettle" in English, for the water has worn a deep basin into which it rushes with a swirling motion which boils up in the midst like a kettle. **1964** *Cdn Geog.Jnl* Feb. 68/3: . . . a lot of young shantymen ended their journey short of Quebec in the Big Kettle at the foot of the falls.

2 See 1824 quote. See also **pothole** (def. 1a).

[**1790** (1905) *Ont.Bur.Arch.Rep.* III 81: Commencing at the mouth of the River au Chaudière or Kettle Creek . . . to the first south Fork. . . .] **1824** (1955) BLACK *Journal* 64: There are also found at some parts of this River small round regular cavities in the Rocks, the Canadians call Kettles somes of them far above the present level of the River they are formed I imagine by the waters hollowing the softer substances of the Rock often of a round form & the round stones geting into these hollows & keep in a circular motion form these Cavities or Kettles. **1873** (1904) BUTLER *Wild North Land* 247: Some of these kettles are tiny as a teacup; others are huge as the tun of Heidelberg. **1954** PATTERSON *Dangerous River* 153: . . . I had panned . . . the gravel and sand from the great potholes and "kettles" worn in the walls of the canyon. . . .

kettle[2] *n. Obs.* tea; the pause for making tea. See also **boil the kettle**.

1800 (1897) COUES *New Light* I 102: Our situation appeared more comfortable and my people began to enjoy their kettle more than heretofore.

kettle-stick *n.* a stick of green wood, often resting on two crotched uprights, used to hold kettles over a campfire. Cp. **chiploquorgan**.

1933 MERRICK *True North* 289: John had left us some warm tea hanging on the blackened kettle-stick over the fire.

kettlestone *n. North* See quote.

1914 STEFANSSON *Eskimo* 25: The above-mentioned tribes that come to "Big Stick island" embrace most of the people who seek the kettlestone (soapstone) quarries on the Kogluktualuk (Tree river). . . .

key *v. Lumbering* obstruct as a key-log (def. 1) does.

1910 BINDLOSS *Thurston* 71: But he worked his way forward towards the center of the fir which keyed the growing mass. *Ibid.* 70: "I'm going to try to chop through the king log that's keying them."

key-block *n. Arctic* a polygonal block of snow dropped into place in the centre of an igloo dome and serving to lock the structure firmly together. See picture at **igloo**. See also **keystone**.

1823 *Canadian Mag.* I 527: The huts themselves, are entirely made of square blocks of solid snow, with a larger key-block at the top of the rotunda. **1957** *Beaver* Spring 49/2: The walls usually fell in just as I was about to fit the key-block in the top.

key-log *n. Lumbering* **1** the log which when released will free a jam (def. 2). See also **key-piece, key-stick,** and **lock-stick**.

1853 *Anglo-Amer.Mag.* II 180/1: It may be thought best to cut off the key-log, or that which appears to be the principal barrier. **1894** ASHLEY *Tan Pile Jim* 200: Every hour's delay increased the tangle, and the difficulty of breaking the jam. The first thing necessary was to find the key log of the jam. **1964** *Cdn Geog.Jnl* Feb. 68/1: We watched it [the driving boat] . . . go into quick action where river drivers loosened key logs in jams along the river.

2 the log retaining a pile of logs at the water's edge. Cp. **brow** (def. 2).

1964 GUILLET *Pioneer Days* 87: When spring arrived the timber was released from its position on the shore; this was usually effected by moving the "key-log", located in such a position that it held all the others in place.

key-piece *n.* See **key-log** (def. 1).

1891 OXLEY *Chore-Boy* 133: The "keypiece" of the jam was fully exposed, and, once it was cut in two, would no longer hold the accumulation of logs together. **1964** GUILLET *Pioneer Days* 87: Many a man risked his life in breaking up these [lumber] blockades with the handspike by skilfully extracting the key-piece of the jam. . . .

key-stick *n.* See **key-log** (def. 1).

1883 FRASER *Shanty* 177: For three days the combined crews had been prying, and pinching, and tugging at the key sticks.

keystone (block) *n*. See **key-block**.
1864 HALL *Life with Esquimaux* II 237: Then commenced
the "spiraling," allowing each tier to fall in,
dome-shaped, till the whole was completed, and the
key-stone of the dome or arch dropped into its place,
the builders being within during the operation.
1930 *Beaver* Mar. 363: . . . the arch gradually closing
over the builder's head, until at length nothing but a
square hold is left, which receives the last block—the
keystone—cut somewhat wedge-shaped and dropped
into its place from without. . . . **1958** *Edmonton Jnl*
24 June 3 16/6: Finally, the igloo is complete except for
one snow block, the keystone block, at its top. . . .

keyuse *n*. See **cayuse**.

khabloonak *n*. See **Kabloona**.

kiack[1] ['kaɪæk] *n*. [prob. < Algonk. (Micmac)]
N.S. See **alewife**. Also spelled *kayak, kiak*.
1849 GESNER *Ind.Resources N.S.* 121: Sometimes a
hundred men, among whom is a sprinkling of Indians,
are engaged in taking the "kiacks" from the stream.
1894 ASHLEY *Tan Pile Jim* 60: "Yes, they belong to the
herring family, but we call them kyacks or alewives."
1956 RADDALL *Wings* 55: When the salmon come up
our river in the month of May they have companions
of another kind, the rough-scaled and bony fish we call
kiacks. The flesh of the kiack is white and sweet, but it
is a chore to eat because of the bones. **1965** *Cdn Geog.
Jnl* June 209/1: "Alewives" is the common name used
in Britain and New England, while the MicMac
Indians called the fish "kayaks," and in Latin it's
Pomolobus pseudoharengus.

Kiack ['kaɪæk] *n*. [see **kiack**[1]] *N.S., Slang, Derog*.
a term of derision directed at persons eating
alewives.
1956 RADDALL *Wings* 56: . . . when the loggers and mill
hands went to Port Seaforth for rum and a look at the
movie show, the townmen could start a fight just by
yelling "Kiacks!" in the street.

kiack[2]**, kiak,** etc. *n*. See **kayak**[1].

kickaninny *n*. See **kickininee**.

kicker *n*. **1 a.** a small outboard motor. See also
kicker engine.
1928 FREEMAN *Nearing North* 132: In such cases the
kicker is hung in a hole cut at a proper height in the
long overhang of the stern. **1963** SYMONS *Many Trails*
165: Travelling down-stream with a good "kicker"
(outboard motor) pushing the canoe at a good speed
is easy.
b. any gasoline-driven boat-motor of low
horsepower.
1931 *Cdn Geog.Jnl* II 391/1: Our "two-sticker with a
kicker" lies in Sandy Bay harbour, Nova Scotia,
outward bound for Labrador, that terra incognito even
to the Maritimers.
2 a boat driven by a **kicker** (def. 1a).
1929 JOHNSTON *Beyond Rockies* 163: This is the Judge's
twelfth trip over the rivers, so he knows the ropes.
Seymour appears to understand the "kicker."
1947 SAUNDERS *Algonquin* ix: An isolated sectionman's
shack flashes by, or a little lake on which a lonely
"kicker" put-puts its way. **1963** *North* July-Aug. 43:
Crafts in the air and kickers in the water get people
long distances in a hurry.

kicker engine See **kicker** (def. 1a).
1958 HEALEY *Alert Bay* 76: Jim and Laurette Stanton
travelled up the coast from Seattle in a double-ended
rowboat powered by a 2½ horsepower kicker engine.

kicking-off place See **jumping-off place** (def. 2a).
1911 BICKERSTETH *Open Doors* 12: Lake la Nonne will
be my kicking-off place for still farther journeys
north-west into a country which we have reason to
think is well settled, but where services have never yet
been held. **1921** HAWORTH *Trailmakers* 17: The
important point is that well before the end of the
seventeenth century white men had become acquainted
with Hudson Bay and Lake Superior, two of the three
important "kicking off" places for the remote
Northwest.

kickininee ['kɪkə,nɪni] *n*. See **kokanee**. Also
spelled *kickaninny*.
1875 (1953) *Okanagan Hist.Soc.Rep.* 17: There we
would fill our basket with the shining kik-e-ninnies.
Then would my mother take me by the hand and
swinging a basket over my shoulder, lead me forth to
my father's fish trap. **1963** *Globe and Mail* (Toronto)
2 Mar. 8/6: The kokanee (or kickininee) is a sockeye
salmon that does not migrate to the ocean. Its life
span is similar to that of the sockeye in that it returns
to the nursery stream after three or four years, at
which time it weighs about a pound. **1964** *Ibid*. 22 Dec.
3/4: Officials . . . say the fish being transplanted from
British Columbia . . . is known as the kokanee, the
kickaninny, the silverfish, or the redfish, depending on
where you're fishing for it, and at what time of year.
1965 *Wildlife Rev.* Mar. 17: KOKANEE, LITTLE REDFISH
or KICKININEE of catchable sizes are familiar to many
anglers.

kieyak *n*. See **kayak**[1].

Kika-nisei ['kikə,nise] *n*. [< Japanese] See quote.
1962 *Maclean's* 28 July 4/3: Now Toronto has more
Japanese-Canadians—about 7,000—than any city in
Canada. A small percentage of these are Kikanisei,
Japanese-Canadians who were born here but went to
Japan before World War II and didn't return until
they were well into their teens and twenties.

kikili (hole) *n*. See **keekwilie**. Also spelled
kekeele.
1958 ATKINSON *Hist.of Penticton* 15: Close examination
of this old village before it was destroyed revealed
numerous winter houses "Ke-ke-e-le." **1963** SYMONS
Many Trails 74: In the old days . . . they [Chilcotin
Indians] lived underground in community dwellings
called *kikiliholes*—a type of which has been in use in
quite recent times among their relatives the Carriers.

kikwilly *n*. See **keekwilie**.

kill (off) a penalty in hockey or lacrosse, attempt
to prevent the opposition from scoring by
controlling the play while one's own team is
short-handed.
1963 O'BRIEN *Hockey* 29: . . . replacements were few and
speed lagged at the end or when players "ragged" the
puck in mid-ice to kill off penalties. **1966** *Globe and
Mail* (Toronto) 10 Jan. 20/1: He kills penalties, plays
the point on the power play and when all our other
defensemen got hurt, he hung in there, holding our
blueline together.

killer *n. Obs.* the cross-log that falls on and kills
the animal caught in a deadfall (def. 1). See **drop-
log**.
1771 (1792) CARTWRIGHT *Journal* I 176: We then went

to Wolf Cove where we finished the deathfall except fixing the killers.

killer claw See quote.
1962 *Weekend Mag.* 8 Sep: 4/3: The tremendous striking power of their [cougars'] jaws and legs fells their prey; the *coup-de-grace* is adminstered by the "killer claw," a fixed talon often two inches long, a few inches below the hind elbow.

killick† ['kɪlək] *n.* [origin unknown] *Esp.East Coast* See 1957 quote. Also spelled *killock*.
1774 (1792) CARTWRIGHT *Journal* II 29: Having filled up the boat with . . . pryor-poles and killick-rods, at highwater we sailed home. **1835** *Novascotian* (Halifax) 12 Nov. 332/3: So what with Marm Lecain's corsets in the house, and other folks waistcoats in the Street, its too nice a location for me, I guess, so I shall up killock and off. . . . **1957** HUTCHISON *Canada* 14: The captain showed me the two boats left in a port which once supported fifty, a crude winch to drag them from the water, and the eight-hundred pound killicks of long, thin stones tied to wooden crosses that serve as anchors.

killick-claw ['kɪlə,klɑ] *n.* [*killick*, q.v. + *claw*] *Nfld* See 1952 quote.
1774 (1792) CARTWRIGHT *Journal* II 32: Four hands brought the traps from Atkinson Pond, hauled up the flat which is there, cut some killick-claws, and pulled rods. **1952** SMITH *Nfld Holiday* 33: A killickclaw is a several-pronged anchor bound round a rock for weight and used to hold fish-nets when set in the sea.

killikenek *n. Obs.* See **kinnikinik**.

killock *n.* See **killick**.

kill off a penalty See **kill a penalty**.

kimo *interj.* See **chimo**.

Kinchotch man ['kɪntʃatʃ] *n.* [< Chinook Jargon] *Hist.* See **King George Man** (def. 1). Also spelled *Kintshautsh man*.
[**1848** *Trans.Amer.Ethnol.Soc.* II 64: Kintshotsh, English, Englishman] **1897** *Rev.Hist.Pubs* 142: The philologer will be interested in knowing that the term for Englishman among the Northwestern Indians, "Kintshautsh man," is only the result of an attempt on their part to say "King George man." **1958** *Beaver* Winter 28/1: An Englishman was a *Kinchotch* man. . . .

Kinchotch wawa ['kɪntʃatʃ'wawa] [< Chinook Jargon] *Hist.* the English language. See **King George** and **wawa**².
1958 *Beaver* Winter 29/2: Not being a tribal language, Chinook is rarely used in Indians homes. Nor is it needed between the tribes, for most Indians use the *Kinchotch wawa* as a common tongue.

king *n.* **1** an Indian chief.
1778 CARVER *Travels* 107: Here I met a large party of the Killistinoe and Assinipoil Indians, with their respective kings and families. **1824** (1931) SIMPSON *Fur.Trade* 86: Nearly the whole of the Furs got now at this place pass through the hands of [the] . . . King or Chief of the Chinooks at Point George. . . . **1927** MCKELVIE *Black Canyon* 17: "Did you see King Freezy . . . the big tyee, or head man . . . ?"
2 *Maritimes* See quote.
1965-66 *Dalhousie Rev.* Winter 545: The oldest ship

fisherman in each harbour was often called "the King" a clear indication of the kind of authority he wielded.
3 See **king salmon**.

king duck the king eider of the Arctic, *Somateria spectabilis*.
1775 (1792) CARTWRIGHT *Journal* II 63: The ice being driven four or five miles off shore, three flocks of king-ducks were seen flying to the northward. **1854** (1892) KANE *Arctic Explor.* 160: They saw reindeer, and brought back a noble specimen of the king duck. It was a solitary male, resplendent with the orange, black, and green of his head and neck. **1956** MCATEE *Folk-Names* 17: King Eider [is called] king duck (Nfld., "Labr.", Que., Ont.). . . .

King George *Hist.* (used attributively) of or having to do with Englishmen or subjects of King George, the English king when white traders first appeared on the Pacific coast, the term being adopted with this meaning into the Chinook Jargon and used in contrast to *Boston*, *q.v.* See also **Kinchotch wawa** and **King George man** (def. 1).
1813 (1849) ROSS *Adventures* 256: See those few King George people who come down the river? **1860** *Brit. Colonist* (Victoria) 21 Aug. 3/1: He stated that he was not afraid, for he had a hundred dollars, and if he was put into jail, he could pay his hundred dollars to the King George people, and they would not let the Bostons hurt him. **1958** *Beaver* Summer 44: The Indians had respected the promises of the Great White Queen—or as she was known "King George's Klootchman"—and they relied upon the word of the Hudson's Bay Company.

King George('s) man *Hist.* **1** an Englishman, as opposed to an American. See also **Kinchotch man** and **King George**.
1846 *St.Catharines Jnl* (C.W.) 26 Feb. 2/4: The first question he asked was—"Are you a King George man, or a Boston man?" **1862** BARRETT-LENNARD *Travels in B.C.* 113: The crew turned out to be Americans, not Englishmen, it being a ruse on their part to describe themselves as "King George's men" to the Indians, in order to secure their good services. **1913** JOHNSON *Shagganappi* 236: "So the little King Georgeman comes tomorrow, eh, Tillicum?" asked the old Lillooet hunter. **1966** ST. PIERRE *Quarter Horse* 21: . . . when he surrendered in the expectation of pardon and was ordered to give us his musket he broke it against a tree instead and said, "King George man big liar."
2 a trader or servant of the Hudson's Bay Company, as opposed to an American trader, or, sometimes, a Northwester (def. 1a).
1862 MAYNE *Four Years in B.C.* 149: The Indians [inquire] constantly when the Boston and King George men may be expected. **1869** *Mainland Guardian* (New Westminster, B.C.) 11 Dec. 1/3: Thieves by profession, trusting none and being trusted by none among themselves, they have however, a strong belief in the honesty of "King George man" and many of them have their whole worldly possessions lying in the Queen Charlotte Company's store. **1940** NIVEN *Mine Inheritance* 31: "That no doubt explains why the Indians—who know its history—look upon the Hudson's Bay Company's men as being King George men but do not look so upon the Nor'-Westers." **1957** *Beaver* Summer 17/2: After his arrival here he became very friendly with the men of the Hudson's Bay Company—the King George Men he [Chief Peguis] called them.

3 an Indian who considers himself a citizen of
Canada.
*c*1863 (1888) McDOUGALL *G.M.McDougall* 152: Then
there is still a lingering love for the Union Jack.
Many of the Crees call themselves "King George's
men," and they all dread American encroachment.
1930 ROBERTSON *Yukon Memories* 80: The Indians
were Canadian Indians, or King George men, as they
proudly called themselves. **1963** *B.C.Digest* Oct. 54/1:
He proclaimed himself a King George Man—the
Chinook term for Englishman—and always flew a
Union Jack in front of his house.

king hair *Nfld, Obs.* See 1819 quote. Cp. **guard
hair.**
1776 (1911) TOWNSEND *Cartwright's Jnl* 192: Jack . . .
brought a rabit; on examining it, I find the white coat
is an additional one . . . composed of long coarse,
king-hairs. **1819** ANSPACH *Hist.Nfld* 376: All, even
the dogs and cats which have been but very lately
carried there, acquire a much softer and thicker coat
than they had originally: this coat is covered with long
white glossy hairs, known there by the name of
king-hairs. . . .

king log *Lumbering, Now Rare* See **key-log.**
1910 BINDLOSS *Thurston* 70: "I'm going to try to chop
through the king log that's keying them. It's rather
more than you bargained for, but will you stand by
me, Tom?"

kingmee, kingmek, kingmiak *n.* See **kingmik.**

kingmik ['kɪŋmɪk] *n.* [< East Esk. *qimmiq*,
dog] the Eskimo dog, *q.v.*, native to the Canadian
Arctic.
[**1824** *Literary Gaz.* 16 Oct. 667/3: Canis (Arcticus)—
Linn. Arctic or Siberian Dog—*Pennant.* King-miak—
Esquimaux.] **1939** MONTAGUE *Eskimos* 25: . . . let
alone the kingmik, that strange dog of the northeast
Arctic and sub-Arctic regions, half Arctic wolf and
half dog, the origin of which nobody knows, and which
never seems to respond to an offer of kindness from
man. It's an entirely different animal from the husky
dog of the Northwest, which is half timberwolf and
half dog, and which may be made a pet. **1940** *Cdn
Geog.Jnl* Feb. 94/1: At the present time the Eskimo
dog is universally employed by the various tribes over
the whole of the vast hinterland indicated above. It is
known by such names as "husky" and "wolf dog,"
though in the Eastern Canadian Arctic it is
customarily referred to simply as the "Eskimo," or
by the native name, "Kingmik." **1963** *North* May-June
42/1: "Kingmik," he shouted and pointed to his mouth
and then across the lake, He was going to his
permanent camp on the opposite shore to feed his
dogs.

king-nipper *n. Mining, B.C.* See quote. See also
nipper².
1964 *Vancouver Times* 3 Nov. 5/2: The king-nipper is
boss of the nippers, men who transport materials in the
mine with a compressed air hoist known as a tugger.

king salmon† *Pacific Coast* a Chinook salmon,
q.v. See also **tyee** (def. 3).
1900 LONDON *Son of Wolf* 31: . . . we are proud to have
thee as our *potlach*-guest; but the king-salmon does
not mate with the dog-salmon. **1916** WOOD *Tourist's
N.W.* 344: In mid-summer the tyee or king salmon
also runs strong in Valdez Straits north and south of
the mouth of the Campbell River. **1959** *Sun* (Vancouver)
15 July 22/1: Thirty big . . . kings met their fate, about
80 per cent of them from fishermen using pearl pink

Lucky Louis plugs. **1963** *Ibid.* 28 Aug. 5/1: Fall is
also in the return of the salmon to their rivers—not
in the early king salmon runs that come to a few
rivers in May. . . .

King's Domain [< F *Domaine du Roi*] *Hist.* a
vast tract of land lying north of the Lower St.
Lawrence and originally belonging to the French
kings, who leased the trading rights to traders, a
practice taken over by the British government after
1760. See also **King's post** (def. 2) and **Tadoussac
Trade.**
1765 *Quebec Gaz.* 14 Mar. 3/1: His Excellency the
Governor and Council have this Day received a
Petition from Messrs. Thomas Dunn and John Gray,
praying that they would be pleased to secure unto
them a peaceable Possession and Enjoyment of their
Lease of the Posts of the King's Domain in this
Province according to the Conditions therein
mentioned. **1923** *Cdn Hist.Rev.* IV 321: In 1762,
Murray had given Thomas Dunn and John Gray a
lease of the King's Domain, or the King's Posts, the
most important of which were Tadoussac and
Chicoutimi. **1958** *Encyc.Can.* V 413/2: King's Posts
[is] a name applied to the trading and fishing posts on
the north bank of the St. Lawrence River, within the
limits of what was known as the Domaine du Roi
(King's Domain).

King's girl [trans. of F *fille du roi*] *Hist.* one of
the women sent to New France by Louis XIV as
wives for settlers.
1940 MACCORMAC *Canada* 170: To enable the bachelor
to escape such punishments a thousand young women
were sent out from France in eight years to find
husbands. They were known as "the King's girls". . . .

King's Pine *Hist.* choice white pine marked with
a broad arrow and claimed as government property
for use as spars and masts for the navy. See also
King's Woods.
1945 CALVIN *Saga* 2: These "King's Pine" were
reserved for use as naval masts and spars. The policy
was pursued in Nova Scotia from 1721; in 1774 the
timber growing on great tracts of land in the valley of
the St. John River, in what afterwards became New
Brunswick, was similarly reserved for the navy.

King's post *Hist.* **1** one of a number of fur-
trading and fishing posts in Quebec, most of them
in the King's Domain, *q.v.* See also **lessee post**
and **Queen's post.**
1787 (1905) *Ont.Bur.Arch.Rep.* II 22: They are
mostly thriving, in so much that they have been able to
supply the King's posts with bread, and very soon
they will be able to be a good saving to Great Britain,
as the expense of transporting provisions and stores
to the upper posts is immense. **1832** MCGREGOR *Brit.Amer.*
II 447: Here [Sept Iles] there is a king's post rented to
the Hudson Bay Company. **1963** *Beaver* Autumn 17/1:
The Hudson's Bay Company took over the old King's
Post in 1831 and has operated it continuously ever
since.

2 King's Posts, *pl.* such posts collectively, the
term often being used as a synonym for King's
Domain, *q.v.*
1786 (1906) *Ont.Bur.Arch.Rep.* IV 153: The lease under
which His Majesty's Domain Lands . . . known by the

name of King's Posts, and the Fisheries belonging to the Same, are held by Thomas Dunn, Wm. Grant; Peter & Stuart, Esquires, expires on the last day of October next. **1837** *Bytown* [Ottawa] *Gaz.* 13 Apr. 2/3: There has been a recent report in town for some days; last, that the Hudson's Bay Company has obtained permission to cut timber within the limits of the King's posts, of which they have a lease for the Fur Trade, which will expire in 1841. **1948** *Beaver* June 32/2: This vast territory was variously known as the "Tadoussac Trade," the "King's Domain," or simply the "King's Posts."

King's Posts Company *Hist.* See quote.
1947 *Beaver* Sep. 45/1: The English "King's Posts Company" took over at the Cession where the French left off, to be followed, in turn, by the North West Company and the Hudson's Bay Company.

King's Printer† **1** *Hist.* See **Queen's Printer** (def. 1).
1798 (1935) RUSSELL *Correspondence* II 144: Resolved . . . That the King's Printer do print in the Town of York at his own expence a weekly paper called the Upper Canada Gazette. . . . **1882** RATTRAY *Scots in Brit. N.A.* II 490: As the *Quebec Gazette* was the vehicle of governmental notices, the proprietor, in order to be unshackled as a member of the Assembly, made over the journal to his son, who became King's Printer. **1958** *Encyc.Can.* IX 119: In 1799, Ryan succeeded Sower as King's printer and took over publication of the *Royal Gazette and New Brunswick Advertiser.*

2 See **Queen's Printer** (def. 2).
1908 *Observer* (Cowansville, Que.) 24 Sep. 1/6: We are glad that Chas. Parmelee, Esq., M.P. for Shefford, has been made King's Printer.

King's steer *North, Slang* a moose taken out of season (a euphemism).
1938 *Beaver* Sep. 45/2: Their inroads on supplies were offset by their skill in hunting by which "the King's steers" supplied the meat pot.

King's Woods *Hist.* tracts of timberland in British North America set aside as a source of lumber, especially for masts and spars. See also **King's Pine.**
1964 *Atlantic Advocate* July 58/2: The British Parliament of George I passed an act, in 1722, prohibiting the cutting or destroying of white pine trees twelve inches in diameter and upward in the King's Woods in North America.

kinikinik *n.* See **kinnikinik.**

kink [kɪŋk] *n.* [? < *kink* cramp, stiffness] *Maritimes, Slang* a short sleep; nap.
1955 WALLACE *Roving Fisherman* 78: . . . I took a somewhat ridiculous pride in the reputation I had acquired . . . as the "hard guy that kiled (coiled) down on the locker for a kink (sleep)".

kinnikinik [ˌkɪnəkəˈnɪk] *n.* [< Algonk.: Cree or Ojibwa "that which is mixed"] Various spellings.
1 a smoking mixture varying as to ingredients from tribe to tribe and place to place, but including bearberry or sumac leaves, the inner bark of red-osier dogwood, *q.v.,* and, often, tobacco. See also **Indian tobacco** (def. 2).

1858 (1860) HIND *Assiniboine Exped.* I 315: A sandy ridge . . . was covered with the bear-berry from which kinnikinnik is made. **1863** WALSHE *Cedar Creek* 225: . . . husband and sons looked on tranquilly, and smoked 'kinne-kanik' in short stone pipes. **1920** FOOTNER *Fur-Bringers* 139: The air was suffocating to white lungs—what with human emanations combined with the thick fumes of kinnikinnik. **1960** *Alta Hist.Rev.* 3rd Quarter 12/2: [Caption] Bearberry leaves were dried and mixed with other plants or white man's tobacco. This was known as kinnikinik.

2 the bearberry, *q.v.,* especially its leaves as used for smoking. See also **Yukon holly.**
1863 (1958) WATTERS *B.C.Cent.Anthol.* 280: We had not had tobacco for months, but now obtained the flavour of it by pounding up one or two black and seasoned clays, mixing the dust with "kinnikinnick." But this was killing the goose with the golden egg, and as pure kinnikinnick did not satisfy the craving, we laid our pipes by for a happy day. **1906** (1910) MORICE *Great Déné Race* 128: Nor should we omit . . . the berry of the kinnikinik . . . which is prepared for eating by roasting in a frying pan and mixed with salmon oil or the grease of any animal. **1963** *Sun* (Vancouver) 23 Nov. 21/1: The rolling hills along the Kootenay, Bull and Elk rivers are parklike with their copses of fir, tamarack, poplar and willow, dotted through open stretches of bitterbrush and kinnikinnik, or left standing in old log slashes or burns.

3 certain other shrubs from which a smoking mixture is made, such as the red-osier dogwood, *q.v.*
1878 (1955) RUSSELL *Carlton Trail:* The Indians were inveterate smokers and the odour emitted from that horrid weed they smoke (the dried bark of the red willow, called kinnikanic) is very unpleasant. **1890** *Cdn Indian* (Hagersville, Ont.) Dec. 64: . . . the bark of the red willow [is] known amongst them as "K'nick K'neck," corrupted into Killikinek in English. **1954** CONSTANTIN-WEYER *Half-Breed* 15: The half-breed then seated himself . . . and filled his red-clay pipe with Kenik-Kenik, the bark of red dogwood. **1957** FISHER *Pemmican* 276: . . . they went another day, and another, eating nothing but rose hips, leaves, kinnikinnik bark, moss, water cress.

kinoo *n.* See **canoe,** *n.* (def. 3).

Kintshautsh or **Kintshotsh (man)** *n.* See **Kinchotch man.**

Kirmess† *n.* [< Am.E < Du. *kirmes* < *kirk* church + *mis* mass] *Obs.* a fair or bazaar held to raise money for charity.
1887 *Grip* (Toronto) 19 Mar. 6/1: The Kirmess in aid of the infants' home being the first ever attempted in Toronto, there are probably many people who not unnaturally will be thankful for a few suggestions as to how they ought to conduct themselves at it. **1889** *Rat Portage* [Kenora] *News* (Ont.) 3 May 1/3: The "Kirmess" was the social subject of last week's talk. It was a huge bazaar gotten up by charitable and fashionable ladies, for the benefit of the Infants Home.

kissing dance a dance at the end of which the dancing couples kiss, popular at New Year's parties.
1896 RUSSELL *Far North* 23: The ball closed with the kissing dance, a ceremony I did not stay to witness. **1923** WALDO *Down Mackenzie* 217: There were the Reel of Four and the Duck Dance, the Rabbit Dance and the Handkerchief Dance, the Kissing Dance and the Drops of Brandy, but the favourite was the simple,

old-time Square Dance.

kit[1] *n.* the young of any of the smaller fur-bearing animals, especially of the fox. See also **kit fox** (def. 2). Cp. **kit fox** (def. 1).
1907 HUNTER *Cdn Wilds* 114: Musquash breed twice in the summer, and bring forth at each litter from six to eight. In the fall the large ones fetch the hunters ten cents, and the kits or small ones, five cents. **1948** RAND *Eastern Rockies* 108: Any information on the occurrence of kit foxes is worthy of record, and any specimens should find their way to a Museum, but it must be kept in mind that a fox kit (= a young fox) is not necessarily a kit fox. **1958** CAMERON *Cdn Mammals* 49: Foxes mate in February or March, and the four to nine kits are born in April or May. **1963** *Commercial Letter* Feb. 3/1: Minks have but one litter each year, and a fertility rate of over four kits per litter is generally required for a profitable operation.

kit[2] *n.* the killer whale, as characterized on the totem poles of West Coast Indians.
1958 *Native Voice* Sp.ed. 23/1: Now every time that *Nan-wa-kaw-i* struck the big cedar box, painted with signs and used as a base-drum, the great Thunder-bird, carved life-like at the end of his stick, would energetically flap both wings, while the "kit" or killer whale, faithfully shaped true to nature, resting below on the same stick, would straighten out full length, vigorously stretching itself and blowing out fire.

Kitchee Manitoo See **Gitchi Manitou.**

kitchen *n. Fur Trade* **1** *Obs.* See quote.
1806 (1897) COUES *New Light* I 382: The camp consisted of about 120 leather tents (exclusive of small ones, or, as we call them, kitchens) . . . a small [tent] which appeared to be the remains of an old one cut down—that is, the lower parts, having become rotten and damaged by the weather, had been cut off, reducing the former size by about one-half. Such tents appear to be for the women's necessary occupations, such as cooking, preparing meat, dressing leather, etc.
2 See quote.
1933 MERRICK *True North* 232: . . . he was in charge of the Company's "kitchen," a small wooden building, still standing, where any one who comes to the post to trade can put up free.

kitchen dresser *Slang, Obs.* See quote.
1887 (1888) LEES & CLUTTERBUCK *British Columbia* 139: [A Douglas fir] . . . was lumbering up the camp, and its stump would make a good kitchen dresser (i.e. a chopping block). . . .

kitchen horse *West, Slang* a pack-horse that carries the cooking utensils and the grub-box, *q.v.*
1916 WOOD *Tourist's N.W.* 358: The cook catches the "kitchen-horse," ties it to a tree near the fire-place, and pretty soon bacon and coffee scent the air.

kit fox 1 a. a small fox, *Vulpes velox hebes,* once common on the prairies. See also **kitt** (def. 1), **prairie fox** (def. 2), and **swift.** Cp. **kit**[1].
1801 MACKENZIE *Voy.from Montreal* xxv: The produce of the year of which I am now speaking, consisted of the following furs and peltries: 106,000 skins, [including] 4000 Kit fox Skins. . . . **1836** BACK *Arctic Land* 481: The prairie wolf, the kit-fox and various marmots are peculiar to the plains. *c*1902 (1912) LAUT *Trapper* 258: It matters not to the trapper that the little kit fox or swift at run among the hills between the Missouri and Saskatchewan is the most shapely of all the fox kind. **1958** *Encyc.Can.* IV 246/1: The kit fox is a very small fox found in the Prairie Provinces and B.C.

b. the fur of this fox, gray on the back, shading to reddish yellow on the belly and legs, the tail being tipped with black. See also **kitt** (def. 2).
1801 MACKENZIE *Voy.from Montreal* xxvi: [There were] 1724 kit foxes. **1823** FRANKLIN *Journey* 658: [The] grizzled skins of this species are imported by the Hudson's Bay Company, under the name of Kitt Foxes.

2 a fox cub; a young fox. See also **kit**[1].
1873 (1904) BUTLER *Wild North Land* 57: "L'homme capable" ran round our line of traps, returning with a couple of kit foxes, the fattest of which he skinned and roasted for his supper. **1956** TURNER *Mounted Police* 9: Gossip also said he was putting on airs, parading boastfully with two "kit-fox" tails attached to the heels of his moccasins. . . .

kitt *n.* **1** *Obs.* **a.** See **kit fox** (def. 1a).
1793 (1933) MACDONELL *Diary* 116: The . . . Assinibouan River is the part most abounding in all the north west, the following animals are natives of it . . . Lynx, Wolves, Foxes, Kitts, the common Red wood squirrels, and the striped Swiss. . . . **1933** GATES *Five Traders* 116n: Professor Innis thinks that *kitts* may have reference to the small prairie fox known as the kit fox.
b. See **kit fox** (def. 1b).
1786 (1918) DAVIDSON *North West Co.* 269: Exports [included] . . . Kitts 296, Pichoux 882. . . . **1800** (1933) MCLEOD *Diary* 135: The Stone Indians traded half a Doz^n Buffaloe robes &. a few kitts &. and went off. . . .

2 the skin of a small or young muskrat. Also *kit skin.*
1907 HUNTER *Cdn Wilds* 116: The "kit skins" are used in large number in the manufacture of kid gloves. **1966** *Fur Market Bulletin* Nov. 1: Muskrat . . . Early falls, Kitts & Dged. at the HIGHEST MARKET PRICE.

kitty-bar-the-door *adj. or attrib. Slang* in sports, a strongly defensive style of play, often adopted by a team already ahead in goals.
1963 *Kingston Whig-Standard* (Ont.) 17 Jan. 14/2: It is generally agreed, however, that defensively the kitty-bar-the-door Ottawa Senator brigade was in a class all alone. **1966** *Ibid.* 16 Apr. 9/1: Thus there came to the fore Ottawa's kitty-bar-the-door system, an invention of the late Art Ross. . . .

kiya(c)k *n.* See **kayak**[1].

klahowya(h) [klə'hauʒə] *n.* [< Chinook Jargon] *Pacific Coast* **1** (a salutation) Greetings! How are you? Also spelled *clahowya(h), klahowa,* etc.
[**1849** ROSS *Adventures* 349: How are you?—Thla choea.] **1862** MAYNE *Four Years in B.C.* 313: I was greeted by . . . the principal personages with "clah-how-yah," which is the complimentary term used in the trading jargon. **1908** DORR *Sunset Shore* 153: O'er the bay float shrill "cla-how-yas"/Through the dusk. . . . **1957** HARRIS *Cariboo Trail* 174: "Kla-how-ya!" he called cheerily, raising one hand in a salutation of friendship. **1964** *Maclean's* 25 July 47/1: Klahowya! My tribe with wisdom of forefathers, has observed lack of unity in native land. . . .

2 See quote.
1956 MCATEE *Folk-Names* 15: Old Squaw [is also called] kla-how-ya (Siwash Indian name adopted by whites in

British Columbia; it is in imitation of the bird's notes)....

klatawa [klət'awə] *v.* [< Chinook Jargon < Nootka *tlatw'ā* paddling] *Pacific Coast* go; travel. Also spelled *clat(t)awa, klattawa.*
1859 *Brit.Colonist* (Victoria) 9 Apr. 1/4: The rush for the upper country continues unabated, and the fever seems to have seized upon all conditions of society—miners and traders "clatawa-ing" alike. **1915** CUMMING *Skookum Chuck* 21: "Klatawa!" (Go) he commanded.

klatawa [klət'awə] *n.* [< *v.*] *Pacific Coast* a journey. Also spelled *clat(t)awa, klattawa.*
1927 PHILIP *Painted Cliff* 38: "... It will be a hyas klattawa [long journey] but we can travel light an' take our time." **1963** SYMONS *Many Trails* 75: ... to "go klatawa" is to go visiting at some special place—perhaps one of the rancheries—and they [Chilcotin] like to travel straight through, not even stopping for camp unless forced to.

Klondigger ['klɑndɪgɚ] *n.* [< *Klon*dike + *digger*] *Obs.* See **Klondiker.**
1900 OSBORN *Greater Canada* 6: Secondly, the Transcontinental railways began to compete for the privilege of carrying the would-be Klondigger to his port on the Pacific—a competition which led not only to the issue of millions of pamphlets, but also to a general cutting-down of rates.

Klondike ['klɑndaɪk] *n.* [< Kutchin *tron-duik* hammer river, a tributary of the Yukon River]
1 a region in the Yukon Territory, including the Klondike river and its tributary creeks, scene of the great gold rush of the late 1890's. Also spelled *Klondyke.*
1896 (1897) OGILVIE in GOODMAN *Klondyke Gold Fields* 13: Klondak, Klondyke, or Clondyke, as it is variously spelled, is "a mispronunciation of the Indian word or words Thron-dak or Duick...." **1897** TUTTLE *Golden North* 1: The gold deposits of the Klondike are probably unequalled in any part of the world either as to their extent or the significance of their discovery.
1964 *Edmonton Jnl* 11 July 3/6: However, the past 60 years have obscured or distorted the extraordinary strength and endurance, and the Klondike wealth of the erstwhile sourdough who became a legendary character during his own lifetime.
2 See **Klondike game.**

Klondike bicycle *Obs.* See quote.
1897 *Official Guide to Klondyke Country* 192: The Klondyke bicycle is specially designed to carry freight, and is in reality a four-wheeled vehicle and a bicycle combined.

Klondike(-type) chimney See **Yukon chimney.**
1959 *Sun* (Vancouver) 2 Jan. 26/2: Regulations prevent installation in Vancouver of this Klondike-type chimney which incorporates two pipes with insulation between.

Klondike fever *Hist.* the excitement and lust for gold generated by the Klondike gold rush.
1897 *Slocan Pioneer* (B.C.) 31 July 4/2: The Klondike fever has struck Slocan City in a mild form. **1958** *Encyc. Can.* VI 15: [Caption] Hundreds watch as the *Australia* ... leaves Seattle for the North at the height of the Klondike fever.

Klondike game a game of solitaire in which 28 cards are laid out in seven piles, the first of which has one card face up, the second two cards with the top one face up, and so on, the player using the rest of the deck and the exposed cards to build runs of alternating colors in an attempt to use up all the cards and thus make four complete runs. Also *Klondike.*
1910 SERVICE *Trail of '98* 183: In one corner was a very ornate bar, and all around the capacious room were gambling devices of every kind. There were crap-tables ... the Klondike game, Keno, stud poker, roulette and faro outfits. **1953** (1958) WALKER *Pardon My Parka* 127: We sat around ... and we played a vicious gambling patience called Klondike, morning, noon, and night, which cost me a vast amount of money....

Klondike gold rush *Hist.* the great stampede of gold-seekers to the Yukon beginning in 1897. Also *Klondike rush.*
1912 FOOTNER *New Rivers* 192: The little trees had been cut with strokes from one side only as white men chop, and we guessed that we were upon the spot where our last white predecessors had made camp in the year of the Klondike rush. **1965** *Star Wkly* 2 Jan. 37/2: ... Mrs. MacCleave was a young girl at the height of the Klondike gold rush.

Klondike heater See **Klondike stove.**

Klondike king *Slang, Hist.* one of the gold miners in the Klondike who struck it rich.
1910 SERVICE *Trail of '98* 183: "The Klondike Kings are in there, hard at it. They've been playing now for twenty-four hours, and goodness knows when they'll let up." **1938** CURTIN *Yukon Voyage* 291: No matter how crowded the boats were, there was always room for a "Klondike King" and his sweetheart or wife.

Klondike marriage a common-law marriage.
1910 SERVICE *Trail of '98* 156: "Of course he's married," she went on, "but that doesn't matter up here. There's such a thing as a Klondike marriage, and they say he behaves well to his discarded...."

Klondike Night a social affair where people dress as sourdoughs, hurdy-gurdy girls, etc., men often growing beards for the occasion, which includes numerous games of chance played with stage money.
1958 *Edmonton Jnl* 24 June 3 2/1: Discovery Day celebrations will be held at Dawson City ... and summer fairs, picnics, fish frys, and Klondike Nights.

Klondiker ['klɑndaɪkɚ] *n.* [*Klondike* + *-er*] a person who took part in the Klondike gold rush, *q.v.* See also **Klondigger.**
1897 *B.C.Mining Jnl* (Ashcroft) 9 Oct. 1/6: The venturesome Klondiker who may select this valley as his road to the diggings may rest assured that his daily bill of fare will not only be ample but of good variety.
1908 MAIR *Mackenzie Basin* 32: At the Landing we pitched our tents in front of the Hudson's Bay Company's post, where had stood, the previous year, a big canvas town of "Klondikers." **1954** BEZANSON *Sodbusters* 4: "There's an old trail that some Klondikers tried to take their outfits over...."

Klondike rush See **Klondike gold rush.**

Klondike sleigh *Northwest* See quote. Cp. **Yukon sled.**
1966 PATTERSON *Trail* 88: We had seven Klondike sleighs with us on which to transport our outfit. These sleighs are about seven feet long by eighteen inches

wide and eight inches high, the runners being of wood about four inches wide.

Klondike stove or **heater** See 1922 quote. See also **Yukon stove.**
1910 MCCLUNG *Second Chance* 115: A cheerful fire was burning in the Klondike heater.... **1922** PRINGLE *Tillicums* 53: [It was] a sheet-iron one-chambered affair with an oven in the pipe, a simple, small Klondike stove which was not much to look at but capable of great things when rightly handled. **1938** BLACK *Seventy Years* 117: We cooked our meals on a little sheet-iron Klondyke stove....

Klondike Trail *Hist.* a route through the western prairies and B.C. leading to the Klondike.
1954 BEZANSON *Sodbusters* 29: We were now on the old trail to Dunvegan, which had become a part of the so-called Klondike Trail the Mounties had blazed and cut out where tree clumps intervened, clear to Ft. Grahame.

klooch or **klootch** [klutʃ] *n.* See **kloochman** (def. 1).
1861 (1948) MAIDEN *Lighted Journey* 1: "...I perceived two clootch-vimmen a'standin' outside of a 'ouse, and they was a-laughing at me. So I haxes myself—is 'eathens to be allowed to laugh at Christians in this blessed country?" **1897** HAYNE *Pioneers* 25: The half-breed women wear skirts, but the klütch (short for klütchman, the local name for squaws) dress exactly like the men, and have not the smallest pretence to looks or figure. **1921** HAWORTH *Trailmakers* 262: A few trappers and prospectors find their lives so lonely that they mate with the dusky klooches of the country. **1963** SYMONS *Many Trails* 83: ... the good breakfast of fried mowitch and bannock [was] being cooked by Henry's klootch.

kloochman or **klootchman** ['klutʃmən] *n.* -**mans** or -**men.** [< Chinook Jargon *klütchman* female, wife < Nootka *lhūtsma*] Also spelled *cloo(t)chman, klu(t)chman. Pacific Coast and Northwest* **1** an Indian woman; wife; squaw. See also **klooch.**
[**1849** ROSS *Adventures* 349: Mixed dialect ... Woman Tlutchè-men.] **1860** *Brit.Colonist* (Victoria) 24 Mar. 2/3: About 75 Cape Flattery Indians arrived in canoes yesterday, from their home, on a visit to the Songish tribe, for the purpose of buying a *clootchman* for their chief. **1872** POOLE *Queen Charlotte Is.* 81: I had found sleeping utterly impracticable on account of the four Klootchmen (Indian women), who chattered and quarrelled unceasingly. **1895** *Trans.Roy.Soc.Can.* I 2 104: I found it hard to believe difficult that the enormous mass of shell-fish whose remains enter so largely into the composition of these piles had been laboriously brought up against the stream in canoes or "packed" on the backs of the patient "klutchmans." **1915** CUMMING *Skookum Chuck* 17: Peter got married, and then the trouble began, because they both wanted the same klootchman. **1964** *Islander* 4 Oct. 6/3: ... one or two of his Indian seamen had brought along their Indian wives. Usually as handy as men aboard ship, one was a young klootchman called Amy.

2 a white man married to or living with an Indian woman; squawman (def. 1a).
☛ *An erroneous usage resulting from folk etymology—* **klooch** + **man.**
1938 CURTIN *Yukon Voyage* 88: A "kluchman" is a man with a squaw. **1942** CARR *Book of Small* 179: The

Kloochman's was an even grander race than the Indian men's.

kloshe [kloʃ] *adj.* [< Chinook Jargon < Nootka *tlulh*] *Pacific Coast* good. Various spellings.
[**1788** (1958) *Beaver* Winter 28/1: John Meares, trading at Nootka in 1788, notes one word of the Chinook jargon—*cloosh*, meaning good.] **1860** *Brit.Colonist* (Victoria) 5 July 1/1: San Diego, he used to say, was a hyas klosh (very good) city.... **1931** *B.C.Hist.Qtly* Oct. 257: My kloshe tillicum (friend) who, collaborates with me in producing this modest volume.... **1942** *Ibid.* Jan. 7: He gave the grace in good Chinook. It was very short and consisted of the words, *Tyee papa mahsie* (from the French, *merci*) *kloshe muck-a-muck*—Great Chief Father thanks for the good food.

klutch or **klutchman** *n.* See **klooch** and **kloochman.**

knight† *n. Hist.* the representative of a riding (def. 1) in a provincial house of assembly.
1804 *U.C.Gaz.* (York [Toronto]) 26 May 4/2: I shall attent on Monday ... at the Government Buildings, at the Town of York, and proceed to the election of one Knight to represent the said County Riding and County in the said House of Assembly. **1805** *Ibid.* 9 Feb. 3/2: And whereas by a Certain Writ under the Great Seal of Upper Canada, by me received, I am thereby directed to Cause one Knight, girt with a Sword, the most fit and discreet, to be freely and indifferently chosen to represent the said County Riding and County in Assembly, by those who shall be present at the day of Election. **1824** *Advocate* (Queenston, U.C.) 5 Aug. 2/1: The reader will therefore scarce wonder, that four knights, girt with swords, should be found necessary in the 19th century, to guard the interests of the hardy yeomanry who are settled upon its Western banks.

Knight of the Red Wig *Obs.* William Lyon Mackenzie, 1795-1861, leader of the radical Reformers responsible for the 1837 Rebellion in Upper Canada (a derogatory allusion to his red hair). See **knight.** See also **Red Wig.** Cp. **little Mac.**
1831 *Canadian Freeman* 8 Sep. 2/3: We see by the Gore papers that the little Knight of the Red Wig is carrying on his mountebank capers in that neighbourhood ... in conjunction with his saddlebag coadjutors the Ryersonians.

Kodiak bear [< *Kodiak* Island, Alaska] an enormous grizzly bear, *Ursus middendorfi* of N.W. Canada and S. Alaska.
1936 MACKENZIE *Living Rough* 42: After we had taken care of all the stations around Cook Inlet we went over to Kodiak Island where are found the famous Kodiak brown bears, the largest in the world. **1964** *Islander* 4 Oct. 6/3: When a boat's crew went ashore to bury her above the Unimak shoreline ... a couple of Kodiak bears ... disputed their right to land.

Kodluna(r) *n.* See **Kabloona.**

kokanee ['kokəni] *n.* [< Interior Salish *kikinee*] a dwarf landlocked salmon, *Oncorhynchus nerka kennerlyi,* native to southern British Columbia. See also **kickininee, little red fish, redfish** (def. 1), and **silver trout** (def. 2).
1937 *Kootenay and the City of Nelson, B.C.* 62: The Kokanee or "Silver Trout," which is in reality a landlocked Sockeye salmon abounds in the larger

lakes of the district. . . . **1964** *Globe and Mail* (Toronto)
22 Dec. 3/5: Officials say there isn't enough experience
on record to predict for certain the reaction of kokanee
to water the size of the Great Lakes. **1966** *Islander*
27 Feb. 2/2: . . . here live some of the largest rainbow
trout in the world . . . along with the kokanee on which
the rainbows feed themselves to their fine, fat, fit
condition.

koletuk *n.* See **kuletuk** (def. 1).

komatik ['kɒmətɪk] *n.* [< East Esk. *qamutik*,
dual of *qamut* sled runner] *North* an open Eskimo
dog-sled. See also **Eskimo sled.** Also spelled
ka(h)motik, kamutik, kumotik, earlier *commetik,*
etc.
[**1824** NIAGUNGITOK *Esquimeaux Words* 25: Kamotik—
Sledge] **1853** *Trans.Lit.& Hist.Soc.Que.* IV 337: They
are short and well made, are fed principally on seal
and blubber, and are so hardy that six or eight of them
tackled to a heavily laden sledge or 'commettek' will
travel as much as twenty leagues in a day.
1905 GRENFELL *Harvest* 118: Making their harness and
the komatik, or sleigh, and feeding the dogs and driving
them to and from the woods, was always more play
than work to me. **1965** *Globe and Mail* (Toronto)
6 Jan. 1/3: The dog sled, or komatik, has replaced the
bicycle for northern Cubs.

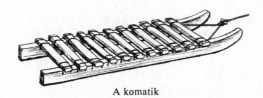

A komatik

komatik ['kɒmətɪk] *v.* [< n.] travel in a komatik.
1934 SUTTON *Eskimo Year* 233: When the gale had
spent itself Jack and I decided we would *komatik* to the
head of the bay to set traps and locate some fox-dens.

komik *n.* See **kamik.**

koodleook, koodlik, koogli *n.* See **kudlik.**

kooleta(h) ['kulə,ta] *n.* [< Esk.; cf. Coronation
Gulf *qulitaq*] *North* See **atigi** (def. 2). See also
kuletuk (def. 1). Various spellings.
1882 GILDER *Schwatka's Search* 138: In cold or wintry
weather, when out of doors, the native puts on another
coat, called a koo'-lee-tar, which is made of skin with
heavier fur, from the animal killed in the fall.
1922 FLAHERTY *Eskimo Friends* 137: I did secure for
my own wear a much-worn kooletah (hooded coat)
and an old pair of deerskin trousers. . . . **1939** *Beaver*
Mar. 7: These primitive people, dressed in sealskin
and eider-duck kulitas, were very friendly.

koonah *n.* See **cooney**[1].

kossack or **cossack** ['kɒsæk] *n.* [< East Esk.;
perhaps related to *kasagea,* q.v., harbor seal]
1 *Eastern Arctic and Lab.* a short sealskin jacket of
the pullover type. Cp. **atigi.**
1884 STEARNS *Labrador* 168: A cossack is a loose short
jacket. **1918** GRENFELL *Labrador Doctor* 88: The kossak

should be made with, so to speak, no neck through
which the heat one produces, can leak out. The
headpiece must be attached to the tunic, which also
clips tight round the wrists, and round the waist, to
retain the heat. The edges may be bound with fur. . . .
1924 MATHEWS *Wilfred Grenfell* 89: Their [Eskimos']
dress consists of an upper garment of skin called a
"kossack." **1939** *Beaver* Sep. 30/2: She dressed Eskimo
fashion for this, with sealskin breeches and sealskin
cossack with the usual long tail.
2 a similar garment of deer or caribou skin.
1939 *Beaver* Sep. 34/1: The Nascopie men wore no
trousers but they had long scarlet cloth leggings. The
upper garment was a deerskin cossack pulled over the
head. The outside was usually painted in bright designs,
and the hair was inside. When they bought shirts, the
shirts were worn outside the cossack.

kossegear *n.* See **kasagea.**

kotluk *n.* See **kudlik.**

Krabloonak, Krablouma *n.* See **Kabloona.**

krang† [kræŋ] *n.* [< Du. *kreng* carcass] *Arctic*
the carcass of a whale; whale meat.
1850 GOODSIR *Baffin's Bay* 146: We soon passed the
first point of the inner harbour, and landed between it
and the second, intending to creep quietly over towards
the "krang," and have a snug shot at Master Bruin.
1864 HALL *Life with Esquimaux* I 214: Ebierbing and
Koodloo did not return until the next evening bringing
with them some black skin and krang. . . .
1963 MCTAVISH *Behind the Palisades* 211: The
residue [after rendering oil from blubber] or "Krang"
was reserved for dog feed. One winter the Esquimaux
were starving when they arrived at the Fort, and we
saved their lives with this "Krang," having nothing else
to give them.

kuaalutuh *n.* See **kuletuk.**

A kudlik

kudlik ['kudlɪk] *n.* [< Esk.; cf. East Esk. *qulliq*]
Arctic a shallow, crescent-shaped dish of soapstone
in which seal-oil or caribou fat is burned to
provide light and heat for cooking in an Eskimo
home. See also **blubber lamp, Eskimo lamp, seal
lamp, seal-oil lamp, stone lamp.** Also spelled
koodlik, kotluk, kudeli, kudleh, kudlic, etc.
[**1748** ELLIS *Hudson's Bay* 234: They also make use of
this Oil for their Lamps, which are made of Stone,
hollowed out with some Difficulty, and as artificially
as can be well expected, considering the Tools they
work with; and for the Wick, instead of Cotton, which
we use, they have recourse to dryed Goose Dung, a
very poor Shift indeed, but still better than none.
1824 NIAGUNGITOK *Esquimeaux Words* 26: Kollik—
Lamp] **1855** (1892) KANE *Arctic Explor.* 335: The
kotluk of each matron was glowing with a flame
sixteen inches long. **1933** *Beaver* Mar. 209: Heating and
cooking is done over a seal-oil kudlik. **1952** *Cdn Geog.
Jnl* Jan. 2/2: The stone kudeli filled with caribou fat or
seal oil has given place to the more efficient, though

more costly, primus stove which consumes kerosene. **1965** *North* Nov.-Dec. 29/2: They moved their families inside and soon the kud-lik, the seal oil soapstone lamp . . . would be burning. Its wick of moss, trimmed by a capable woman, gave off a warm glow fairly free of smoke, and a white pleasant flame.

Kudlunah *n*. See **Kabloona.**

kuletuk ['kulǝ,tʌk] *n*. [East Esk.; cf. *koliktar* (over)coat] **1** *East.Arctic* See **atigi** (def. 2 and picture). See also **kooleta.** Also spelled *koletuk, koolitak, kulatuk, kulutuk,* etc.
1897 TUTTLE *Golden North* 201: . . . after a moment's pause he shouted out 'ko-le-tuk,' meaning a woman's dress of deer skin. He exhibited two of these, made of beautifully dressed skins, with shoulder hoods for papoose, and the inevitable long tails, the only distinguishing mark between the dress of the men and that of the women. **1904** HANBURY *Sport and Travel* 82: The ordinary winter dress of the Husky is an inner deerskin coat (u-u-pak), worn hair inside, and a thicker deerskin coat (kūl-i-tak) over this, with the hair outside. **1933** *Cdn Geog.Jnl* VII 108/1: An Eskimo woman in winter "kuletuk", showing the character of the back with the long tail embellishments. **1941** *Beaver* Mar. 9/1: A pull-over skin shirt with hair on and a hood trimmed with fur is generally called an *artiggi, artikie, dickie, koolitak* or what you will; but to avoid confusion it will be referred to in this article as a parka. **1965** *Kingston Whig-Standard* (Ont.) 27 Sep. 17/7: Both kulatuks were made by Eskimo women patients in the Moose Factory Indian-Eskimo hospital.

2 a parka of commercial make patterned on the Eskimo garment and styled primarily for women.
1959 *Weekend Mag.* 22 Aug. 9/2: This year a group of manufacturers decided that since the Eskimo has always been far ahead of the rest of us when it comes to keeping warm, they would use his basic design and his name for parka (*kul-e-tuk*) for their cold-weather garments. **1960** *Camsell Arrow* Jan.-Mar. 15: This time of year (February) Hope wears a flame-red kulutuk—Eskimo style parka trimmed with wolverine fur—and moccasins. **1963** *Weekend Mag.* 28 Dec. 15/2: [Caption] "Walking-out" ensemble combines stretch slacks with a Kul-e-tuk (parka) made by Lydia, Deep-pile Orlon is used, and hood is trimmed with fox.

kultus *adj*. See **cultus.**

kulutuk *n*. See **kuletuk.**

kumatick, kumotik, etc. *n*. See **komatik.**

kumik, kuming *n*. See **kamik.**

kumtux *v*. [< Chinook Jargon; cf. Nootka *kamitah'ks* known, definite] *Pacific Coast* understand; know; believe. Also spelled *cumtux, kumtuks.*
[**1862** MAYNE *Four Years in B.C.* 256: Wake cumtux Sivash muckermuch cushon (Indians do not understand how to eat pork).] **1894** PHILLIPPS-WOLLEY *Gold* 185: What keeps the old man? You halo comtax anything. . . . **1953** MOWERY *Mounted Police* 56: "You go put canoe to water and paddle up Bear River to landing . . . You *kumtux?*" **1963** SYMONS *Many Trails* 75: "Me no savvy see-um that fellow before—me hyu cumtux (guess) him Ankiti Siwash!"

kuni *n*. See **cooney**[1].

kusegear *n*. See **kasagea.**

kweekwillie *n*. See **keekwilie.**

kwunusela ['kwunus(ǝ)lǝ] *n*. [< Kwakiutl] *Pacific Coast* See quote. See also **thunderbird** (def. 1a).
1958 HEALEY *Alert Bay* 12: "That is the very reason why I come from above," replied Kwunusela, the Thunderbird, for that was his name. . . .

kya(c)k *n*. See **kayak**[1].

kyack *n*. See **kiack**[1].

Lab [læb] *n. Informal* See **Labrador retriever.**
1963 *Globe and Mail* (Toronto) 13 Mar. 2/1 : In fact,
they were just about as nervous of the Labs as the
hunters were of the mean-looking animals tied to the
stakes in the Indian camp.

La Belle Province *Cdn French* Quebec.
1963 *Drop in Anytime Neighbour* 10 : You'll never lack
for something out-of-the-ordinary to see in la belle
Province . . . and the French touch makes it more so.
1964 *Canada Month* Jan. 27/1 : . . . I met people who
were open-minded, receptive, very curious about what
is going on in *la belle province*. . . .

Labrador ['læbrə,dɔr] *n.* **1** See **Labrador tea**
(def. 1a).
*c*1820 (1949) LAWSON *N.B.Story* 147 : We greatly missed
our tea. Sometimes we used an article called Labrador,
and sometimes steeped spruce or hemlock bark for
drinking, but I despised it.

2 a. See **Labrador dog** (def. 1).
*a*1820 (1838) HEAD *Forest Scenes* 41 : The dog was of
the Labrador breed, extremely powerful, and of
enormous stature. **1907** MILLAIS *Newfoundland* 145 :
The pure Newfoundland dogs are curly, and are a little
higher on the leg than are the Labradors.

b. See **Labrador retriever.**
1957 *Representative* 19 Dec. 5/4 : The ribbons indicate
first prize for the best in the Labrador group. . . .
1966 *Globe and Mail* (Toronto) 15 Jan. 29/1 : He wants
fast, sporty . . . shooting at . . . birds that keep his
springer or labrador in top form.

3 See quote.
1966 *Maclean's* 20 Aug. 17/4 : . . . the Labrador-born
people, or "labradors" as they are often called locally.

Labrador dog 1 a breed of dog from which the
Labrador retriever, *q.v.*, was developed. See also
Labrador (def. 2a) and **lesser Newfoundland.**
1842 BONNYCASTLE *Newfoundland* II 24 : [These
water-dogs] are of two kinds; the short, wiry-haired
Labrador dog, and the long, curly-haired Newfoundland
species, generally black, with a white cross upon the
breast. **1910** HAYDON *Riders of Plains* 212 : For Police
purposes many Labrador dogs have been bought, these
averaging over seventy pounds in weight when in
condition.

2 a sled-dog of the Labrador Eskimos.
1957 *Beaver* Autumn 28/1 : They have no name but are
called "Newfoundland" dogs, I suppose to distinguish
them from the "Labrador" dogs, that is, the huskies.

Labrador feldspar See **labradorite.**
1824 *Canadian Mag.* III 380 : Mr. Smillie, Lapidary, of
Quebec, brought up some beautiful specimens of a
sky-blue variety of the Labradore feldspar, a mineral
first, and as yet almost exclusively found on that coast.
1829 *Trans.Lit.& Hist.Soc.Que.* II 77 : Of the
productions of the Kiglapyed we have no account, but
to the south of this chain the district commences, where
the Labrador feldspar is found.

Labrador herring See quote.
1866 KING *Sportsman in Can.* 302 : The common
herring, generally called in Canada the Gulf Herring
and Labrador Herring, constitutes one of the most
important articles of commerce in the country. . . .

labradorite ['læbrədɔr,aɪt] *n.* [*Labrador* + *-ite*]
n. a feldspar shot with blue, green, and other
colors. See also **Labrador feldspar** and **Labrador
spar.**
1864 *Cdn Naturalist* II 301 : Huge blocks of gneiss and
labradorite lie in the channel of the river, or on the
gneiss domes which here and there pierce the sandy
tract through which the river flows. **1963** *Cdn Geog.Jnl*
Mar. 100/1 : They have unearthed semi-precious stones
the length and breadth of the country from
Newfoundland's labradorite to malachite in Yukon. . . .

Labradorman ['læbrə,dɔrmən] *n.* **1** a
Newfoundland fisherman who summers on the
Labrador coast, spending the winters at home.
See also **visiting fisherman.** Cp. **liveyere.**
1905 DUNCAN *Grenfell's Parish* 98 : Withal, the
Labradormen are of a simple, God-fearing,
clean-lived, hardy race of men. **1935** *Beaver* Dec. 66/3 :
Mid-June sees the Labradorman setting sail from his
home port on the northern coast of Newfoundland.

2 a resident or native of Labrador.
1918 GRENFELL *Labrador Doctor* 60 : Labrador is owned
by Newfoundland, so that legally the Labradormen are
Newfoundlanders, though they have no representation
in the Newfoundland Government. **1933** MERRICK *New
North* 56 : It is something that has to do with their
Labradorman's code that says, "I am not tired, I am
not hungry, I am steel."

3 a fishing vessel of a Labradorman (def. 1).
1905 DUNCAN *Grenfell's Parish* 86 : . . . in a week—two
weeks or three—the last of the Labradormen have gone
"down north." **1964** *Nfld Qtly* Spring 27/1 :
. . . sharemen were and are sometimes chargeable . . .
when a Labradorman's voyage of fish has to be "made,"
i.e. sun dried, by the planters.

Labrador Ranger Force *Hist.* a police force
patterned on the Royal Canadian Mounted
Police, formed in 1935 and absorbed by the
R.C.M.P. in 1954. See also **ranger** (def. 2b). Cp.
ranger (def. 2a).
1965 JENNESS *Eskimo Admin.* III 76 : [In 1954] the Royal
Canadian Mounted Police, absorbing the Labrador
Ranger Force, posted one policeman in Nain. . . .

Labrador retriever a hunting dog developed
from a breed originating in Labrador and
Newfoundland, characterized by short, thick,
usually black hair, broad head and chest, and
outstanding performance as a retriever of game,
both in water and on land. See also **Lab** and
Labrador (def. 2b). Cp. **Labrador dog** (def. 1).
1907 MILLAIS *Newfoundland* 217 : Each of the brothers
possessed a starved-looking Labrador retriever, clever,
amiable beasts, scarcely less hungry than their masters.
1963 *Globe and Mail* (Toronto) 23 Mar. 32/4 : The
other native Canadian dogs are the Nova Scotia Duck
Tolling Retriever, a comparative newcomer, and the
Labrador Retriever, a relative of the Newfoundland.
1966 *Ibid.* 15 Jan. 29 : [Caption] Ron Bowman of
Oshawa tests his aim and trains a Labrador retriever.

Labrador shrub *Obs.* See **Labrador tea** (def. 1a).
1828 MCGREGOR *Maritime Colonies* 23 : The indian tea,
or Labrador shrub, is grateful to the taste, and
considered an effectual antiscorbutic.

Labrador spar or **stone** See **labradorite.**
1787 PENNANT *Supplement* 44 : The curious body the
Labrador stone, which reflects all the colors of the
peacock, is found there in loose masses. **1835** (1836)

in this bay, and of a white friable stone resembling talk [sic] or Labradore spar, in the manner in which it breaks off into plates. **1861** DE BOILIEU *Labrador Life* 237 : Labrador abounds in white spar, and also in small specimens of that beautiful one called "Labrador spar."

Labrador tea 1 a. either of two closely related evergreen shrubs, *Ledum groenlandicum* and *L. decumbens* var. *palustre*. See also **country tea** (def. 1), **Hudson Bay tea**, **Indian tea** (def. 1), **Indian tea-plant**, **Labrador tea** (def. 1), **Labrador tea plant**, **muskeg tea** (def. 1), **squaw tea**, **swamp tea** (def. 1), **wild tea**, and **wishakapucka**. Cp. **woolly Labrador tea**.
1822 CORMACK *Narr.Nfld* 19 : On the skirts of the forest, and of the marshes, are found . . . the Indian or Labrador Tea, sweet-gale, and two species of roses. **1830** (1837) *Trans.Lit.& Hist.Soc.Que.* III 100 : Labrador tea [is] an evergreen shrub two or three feet high, with dark brownish green leaves, rust colour ˸ beneath. **1910** FERGUSON *Janey Canuck* 221 : Labrador tea, which belongs to the heath family, grows along the road. **1951** ANGIER *At Home* 126 : Labrador tea, the curling, rusty-bottomed leaves of the short perennial shrub we'd noticed in muskegs, is another favourite tobacco substitute. **1965** SYMINGTON *Tuktu* 23 : Between and among the sparse conifers is a shrub layer, usually of dwarf birches or Labrador tea.
b. an infusion made from the leaves of *L. groenlandicum* or from the flowers of *L. palustre*. See also **bush tea**, **country tea** (def. 2), **muskeg tea** (def. 2), **swamp tea** (def. 2), and **wishakapucka tea**.
1833 (1963) TOLMIE *Physician* 241 : Had some Labradore tea for dinner yesterday. . . . **1897** *B.C.Mining Jnl* (Ashcroft) 25 Sep.1/2 : So all we had for 62 hours was two small rabbits (at least we thought them small) and Labrador tea with snowballs and mountain scenery, and a few moose tracks for dessert. **1963** *Beaver* Winter 28/2 : Living entirely off the country—on deer, fish . . . and Labrador tea—the men worked well. . . .

2 See **woolly Labrador tea**.
1955 MCCOWAN *Upland Trails* 82 : The most widespread flowering shrub in Canada is in all probability that known as Labrador Tea. There are two varieties of this plant but the one best known in the Canadian Rockies is that known as Woolly Labrador tea, the glossy leaves having a rusty-red wool on the underside.

Labrador tea plant See **Labrador tea** (def. 1a).
1821 (1823) FRANKLIN *Journey* 43 : Not being able to find any tripe de roche, we drank an infusion of the Labrador tea plant (ledum palustre) and ate a few morsels of burnt leather for supper. **1858** (1863) PALLISER *Journals* 101 : . . . the bottom of it [was] occupied by an extensive morass overgrown with scrubby pines, and the *Labrador Tea plant*. **1869** *Cdn Illust.News* 30 Oct. 6/2 : The Labrador tea plant might also be found to be a not unacceptable luxury.

La Cadia or **La Cadie** *Hist.* See **Acadia** (def. 1).
1754 JEFFERYS *Conduct* 3 : [The French] made settlements in the country then called La Cadia. . . . **1835** STIRLING *Register* I xxvi : On the counsel of Cardinal Richelieu, the French had determined to re-assert their title to La Cadie, which included every portion of New Scotland. **1923** LUCAS *Hist.Geography* I 36 : The Maritime Provinces of the present Dominion, or at any rate Nova Scotia, were not in Canada properly so called, but bore the name of La Cadie or Acadia, and

the great North-West was an unknown land.

l'Acadie [laka'di] *n.* [< F] See **Acadia** (def. 1).
1789 *Nova Scotia Mag.* I 81/2 : Anno 1604, Henry IV. of France made further discoveries in L'Acadia, now Nova Scotia. . . . **1961** *Telegram* (Toronto) 19 May 7/1 : This is your day across the land. The day of the southshore schoonerman, prairie wheatgrower, "l'Acadie" market gardener, "Spud Island" farmer. . . .

lacaishe [lə'keʃ] *n.* [< Cdn F < Algonk. *nacaysh*] *Hist.* See **goldeye**.
1793 (1933) MACDONELL *Diary* 116 : The men call these latter [fish] Lacaiche. . . . **1800** (1897) COUES *New Light* I 42 : [They] caught a great many lacaishe, a small fish about a foot long. . . . **1952** (1954) JENNINGS *Strange Brigade* 196 : At the same time there were catfish and sturgeon of immense size in the river, as well as pike, piccano brim, pois d'oile, male achegan, lacaishe and such.

lacrosse [lə'krɑs] *n.* [< Cdn F *la crosse* < F "hooked stick"] **1** a game originating among the Indians and played by two teams, the players passing a ball to each other on the run or throwing it at the opponents' goal by means of a lacrosse stick, *q.v.* See also **baggataway**, **box lacrosse**, **cross**[1] (def. 1), **field lacrosse**, and **hurdle**.
[**1791** LONG *Voyages* 52 : Playing at ball, which is a favourite game, is very fatiguing. The ball is about the size of a cricket ball, made of deer skin, and stuffed with hair; this is driven forwards and backwards with short sticks about two feet long, and broad at the end like a bat, worked like a racket, but with larger intersticies : by this the ball is impelled, and from the elasticity of the racket, which is composed of deers' sinews, is thrown to a great distance : the game is played by two parties, and the contest lies in intercepting each other, and striking the ball into a goal, at the distance of about four hundred yards, at the extremity of which are placed two high poles, about the width of a wicket from each other; the victory consists in driving the ball between the poles. . . .] **1821** (1900) GARRY *Diary* 111 : They were preparing to play the Game of de la Crosse or Baggatiway and had painted their Cheeks with Vermilion and their Bodies with the most fantastic colors. **1870** *Cdn Illust.News* 18 June 515/3 : It is perhaps not generally known here that Lacrosse was imported into England a few years back, but beyond a few games played by a couple of Indian teams it had no success. **1956** LEECHMAN *Native Tribes* 41 : In some tribes, the men played lacrosse, which is a native Indian game. Catlin, who visited the western Algonkians about 1830 to 1840, saw lacrosse games in which there were eight hundred or a thousand men on each side, the goals were as much as half a mile apart, and there were practically no side boundaries. **1965** *Globe and Mail* (Toronto) 15 Sep. 30/1 : It is refreshing . . . to discover that Indians are not altogether extinct from lacrosse, a game the Canadian aborigines played for its robust charm.

2 See **lacrosse stick** and picture.
1763 (1901) HENRY (Elder) *Travels* 77 : *Baggatiway*, called by the Canadians, *le jeu de la crosse*, is played with a bat and ball. The bat is about four feet in length, curved, and terminating in a sort of racket. **1869** *Cdn Illust.News* 30 Oct. 6/3 : . . . he was received by the Committee, presented with an address, accompanied by a very handsome gold-mounted Lacrosse, and an

elegantly bound copy of Mr. Beer's work on the game.
1906 *Cornwall & United Counties:* [Advert.] More
Lally's Lacrosses sold than all other makes combined.

lacrosse box the board-enclosed playing area
used in box lacrosse, *q.v.*
1965 *Globe and Mail* (Toronto) 5 Jan. 27/4: Toronto
Township has converted five lacrosse boxes into natural
ice rinks.

A lacrosse stick and ball

lacrosse stick a stick hooked at one end and
strung with leather thongs crosshatched by strings
of gut to form a kind of pouch for carrying and
throwing a ball in the game of lacrosse, *q.v.*
See also **crosse**[1] (def. 2).
1884 *Echo of Niagara* (Niagara-on-the-Lake, Ont.)
17 May 6/4: Capt. Bill's lacrosse sticks [are] on hand.
1966 *Kingston Whig-Standard* (Ont.) 6 Feb. 4/6: At
playtime . . . the young men [used] wooden lacrosse
sticks.

Ladies' Aid (Society) an organization of
women who raise funds and contribute other help
in supporting the work of a church.
1873 *Woodstock Sentinel* (Ont.) 5 Dec. 3/1: The Ladies'
Aid Society in connection with the Baptist Church in
this Town will hold a social this evening. **1895** *Times*
(Niagara-on-the-Lake, Ont.) 4 Apr. 1/2: The Social
[was] under the auspices of the Ladies Aid of the
Methodist Church. . . . **1964** *Herald Mag.* (Calgary)
21 Mar. 8/9: Good management . . . and a jolly party
combined to make a complete success of the "Apron
Social" and tea given in the basement of the Knox
Church last evening under the auspices of the Ladies'
Aid Society of the congregation.

lady *n.* See **lord and lady.**
1770 (1792) CARTWRIGHT *Journal* I 42: I shot a bird
called a lady. **1777** *Ibid.* II 255: I killed five ladies and
a duck.

Lady of the Snows† [a term coined by Rudyard
Kipling] Canada.
1905 WIGHTMAN *Our Cdn Heritage* 18: Kipling came
to Canada in winter and visited Quebec City when the
snow was piled high. He has ever since called this
country "Our Lady of the Snows." **1918** COPELAND
Swinging Lanterns 73: The majority—whether Briton,
Frank or Celt—accept this dictum and make obeisance
to the inexorable law: wherefore, the sons of "Our
Lady of the Snows" cheerfully caught hold and lifted
with their cousins.

la foule [la'ful] [< Cdn F < F "crowd"] *North*
See quotes.
1892 PIKE *Barren Grounds* 45: It was late in October,
immediately after the rutting season, that the great
bands of caribou, commonly known as *La Foule*, mass
up on the edge of the woods, and start for food and
shelter afforded by the stronger growth of pines
farther southward. **1932** MUNN *Prairie Trails* 57: A

week or two later . . . "la foule," the great migration
of cariboo from the Arctic Ocean to the woods
overtook us. **1936** *Beaver* Sep. 25: The greatest sight
of all is of "la foule."

lahal [lə'hɑl] *n.* [< *slahal* < Chinook *etlaltlal*]
Esp.Pacific Coast an Indian gambling game taking
various forms, the winner being the player to
whom falls a marked object (as a disc) mixed with
several similar but unmarked objects. See also **la
hille, pagessan** (def. 3), **slahal,** and **stick game.**
See note at **platter.** Also spelled *la halle, lahelle,
lehal.*
1906 TEIT *Tahltan Indians* 347: Lehal, which appears to
be played in the same way as among the southern
tribes, is also in vogue. **1934** GODSELL *Arctic Trader*
124: . . . as (the gamblers) played their ancient game,
La halle. . . . **1963** *Citizen* 13 June 3/5: Performances
include the Swai-Swai dance, Lahal or stick game,
Salish Mask dance, medicine, paddle and masked
dances.

la hille [lə'hɪl] [var. of *lahal*] See **lahal.**
1963 SYMONS *Many Trails* 74: [La hille] is played with
tremendous enthusiasm, the players sitting in a circle
and chanting the *la hille* song long into the night.

lair *n. Lumbering, Obs.* a kind of portable bunk
used by lumbermen on a drive.
1829 MACTAGGART *Three Years* I 242: On these rafts
they have . . . places to sleep in, formed of broad
strips of bark, resembling the half of a cylinder, the
arch about four feet high, and in length about eight.
To these *beds,* or *lairs, trams* or handles are attached,
so that they can be moved about from *crib* to *crib,* or
from crib to shore, as circumstances render it necessary.
Ibid.: When they are passing a breaking-up rapid, they
live in these lairs, until the raft is new withed, and fixed
on the still-water below.

lake boat a vessel designed for service on the
Great Lakes. See also **laker** (def. 2).
1936 MACKENZIE *Living Rough* 202: I'm going to try to
make the lake boats for the summer. **1954** *Fishermen's
Advocate* 5 Feb. 9/2: . . . the past two or three years he
followed the trade of sailor on the Lake Boats on the
mainland.

lake carrier a freighter designed for service on
the Great Lakes.
1957 *Time* (Cdn ed.) 16 Dec. 12/2: . . . the *Alexander
Wood* will be able to make up the difference by going
to sea at the beginning of December, plying coastal
routes during the four months when less sturdy lake
carriers are idled by ice.

lake char See **lake trout.**
1961 *Sun* (Vancouver) 17 Aug. 23/1: The laker
(mackinaw trout) is a record. Largest Canadian
sport-caught lake char . . . is an 87 pounder. . . .

lake fever *Obs.* a fever resembling typhoid and
contracted from drinking the polluted water of
lakes and rivers.
1808 *York* [Toronto] *Gaz.* 13 Aug. 4/1: The month is
fast approaching, which in this part of the country, is
understood to be the Ague and Lake Fever season.
1829 MACTAGGART *Three Years* II 18: The *Lake Fever*
prevails at Kingston, York, and other towns and
villages on the borders of the great lakes. **1863** WALSHE
Cedar Creek 329: Lake fever and ague broke out
among the low-lying log-houses, and Zack's highly
adulterated and heavily priced drugs came into great
demand.

Lakehead *n.* **1** *Obs.* See **Head of the Lake.**

1827 *Gore Gaz.* (Ancaster, U.C.) 25 May 50/4: It appeared, that a person at the Lake Head, had furnished the York Garrison with 800 bbls. of Flour last year. . . .

2 the twin cities of Port Arthur and Fort William, Ont., and the surrounding region on the northwest shore of Lake Superior. See also **Head of the Lakes.** Also spelled *lakehead.*
1955 *Beaver* Summer 37: From the deck of the loaded freighter, bound for the Sault and Welland Canals, the grain strongholds of the lakehead stand like castles against the sunset. **1965** *Globe and Mail* (Toronto) 30 Dec. 3/2: . . . one large corporation refused to set up a business in the Lakehead because of the constant history of bickering between the two cities.

3 a proposed province to be established in northwestern Ontario.
1952 PUTNAM *Cdn Regions* 574/2: Even a future population of half a million, however, would hardly justify the setting up of a separate province of the Lakehead as is sometimes advocated.

lake man a sailor who sails the Great Lakes.
1958 WELLS *Georgian Bay* 30: Fog is a thing that might touch you. It is called bay smoke by the lake men and is most frequent in the month of May and in the early part of June.

laker *n.* **1** See **lake trout.**
1957 *Sask.News* 5 Nov. 4/1: Second place in the trout class went to Allan Nachtegale of North Battleford, with a 33½-pound "laker" caught in Lac la Ronge. **1965** *Kingston Whig-Standard* (Ont.) 5 Feb. 11/1: . . . he does know of another lake where lakers and perch have a very agreeable relationship.

2† See **lake boat.**
1958 *Kingston Whig-Standard* (Ont.) 21 May 18/1: The 681.25-foot long laker, built at Port Weller Dry Docks Limited, will be an addition to the fleet of the Upper Lakes and St. Lawrence Transportation Company Limited of Toronto. **1963** *Maclean's* 18 May 19/3: A deckhand on a Canadian laker now draws more than $315 a month. . . .

3 a sailor on a lake boat, *q.v.*
1936 MACKENZIE *Living Rough* 274: When the deep-water sailor goes on the lakes, he has a tendency to criticize the methods and refer to the lakers as farmers, niggerhead sailors, and other salt-water jokes.

Lakes *n.pl.* See **Great Lakes.**
1812 *Quebec Gaz.* 12 Nov. 2/4: They know that if they command the Lakes, upper Canada must fall. **1901** CONNOR *Man from Glengarry* 11: In the Canada beyond the Lakes, where men are making empire, the sons of these Glengarry men are found. **1936** [see quote at **laker** (def. 3)].

lake salmon *Obs.* See **lake trout.**
1822 GOURLAY *Upper Canada* I 177: I think the proper name of this fish is the *lake salmon.* **1829** MACTAGGART *Three Years* II 130: Lake Salmon are found weighing from twenty to sixty pounds, are good to eat, although not so finely flavoured as those that live in the salt seas.

lakeshore line *Obs.* a long line used in the timber trade for getting logs from the shore to the vessels which were to carry them to market.
1945 CALVIN *Saga* 58: Boats were lowered and long "lake shore lines" run from vessel to beach. The timber-men would set the timber afloat, the vessel men then "dogged" it together, a few pieces at a time. To reach their vessels they stood or sat on each little lot of

timber and hauled it out by means of the "lake shore line."

lakeshore loading *Obs.* the practice of loading timber onto vessels directly from the shore by means of lakeshore lines.
1945 CALVIN *Saga* 58: "Lake shore loading," as it was called, was a special part of the Island firm's timber carrying.

lake trout a North American char, *Cristivomer namaycush,* having important commercial value. See also **gray trout, lake char, laker** (def. 1), **lake salmon, Mackinaw trout, namaycush, salmon trout** (def. 1), **togue, touladi,** and **white trout.**
1897 TUTTLE *Golden North* 96: Lake trout are caught in most of the lakes. They take a troll bait readily. **1924** FLAHERTY *Eskimo Friends* 104: The one dependable source of food supply for the natives who travel the interior in summer is fish, particularly the namaycush, the great lake trout, and a finer-eating fish does not exist. **1965** *Globe and Mail* (Toronto) 14 Jan. 10/5: These unwanted species clutter the lakes . . . affecting the highly regarded whitefish and lake trout.

Lake Winnipeg goldeye See **goldeye.**
1958 *Maclean's* 24 May 1/1: The prized Arctic Char, a well-known but little-tasted delicacy in most of Canada, is going to start muscling into gourmet circles once sacred to Lake Winnipeg goldeye and Restigouche salmon.

la loche [la'laʃ] [< Cdn F] See **loche.**
1852 RICHARDSON *Arctic Exped.* 72: The Methy River, Lake, and Portage, are named from the Cree designation of the Burbot (*Lota maculosa*), (*La Loche* of the Canadians), which abounds in these waters, and often supplies a poor and watery food to voyagers whose provisions are exhausted. **1936** *Cdn Geog.Jnl* XII 142: Both "La Loche" and "Mithey" signify the humble "tommycod."

lambing pen *West* a pen or corral where ewes and lambs are protected.
1953 *Cdn Geog.Jnl* June 246/1: When the ewes drop their lambs, both are transferred from the open range to lambing pens, in the "lamb wagon."

lamb wagon *West* See quote at **lambing pen.**

La Montée or **La Montie** See **Montée.**

lampfish *n.* See **oolichan.**
1953 *Beaver* Dec. 41/1: *Thaleichthys pacificus* of the family *Salmonidae,* also called lampfish or candlefish, is closely related to the smelt.

land *v.* enter or be permitted to enter Canada as a landed immigrant, *q.v.*
1962 *Canada Month* Aug. 16/3: They arrived from an Italian refugee camp in three groups around mid-month, were duly "landed" by immigration officials.

land agency (or agent) office *Hist.* the office of a land agent (def. 1).
1798 *U.C.Gaz.* (York [Toronto]) 12 May 3/3: To facilitate the buying and selling of lands . . . he has established . . . a Land Agent Office where all applications of that nature will be duly attended to. **1832** *Patriot* (York [Toronto] 7 Dec. 1/6: Fortunately hearing of Mr. Allison's Land Agency

Office, I applied to him and received much valuable and interesting information together with the most gentlemanly and honorable treatment. **1965** SHEPHERD *West of Yesterday* 25: The prospective homesteader could obtain information from the land agency office.

land agent *Hist.* **1** a broker who assists settlers in obtaining or selling land. See also **land-guide**.
1828 BIDWELL *Tor.Pub.Lib.MSS B104* 28: He settled in Upper Canada, and immediately set up in business as a land-agent. **1858** *Brit.Colonist* (Victoria) 11 Dec. 1/3: Over speculation is at an end, and land agents in despair. **1916** PARKER *World for Sale* 31: It . . . became the home of all adventurous spirits—land agents, company promoters . . . saloon keepers. . . .
2 a government official or the representative of a land company, *q.v.*, who is responsible for assisting settlers to occupy new land.
1832 *Liberal* (St. Thomas, U.C.) 13 Dec. 3/1: Now hear the passions that self interest puts in motion, "If I oppose the bill, I incure the displeasure of the "executive, and lose my office of "——of what? "Of Surveyor, Post-Master, Registrar, Collector of Customs——of Col., of Magistrate, of Land Agent &c, &c, &c.
1900 OSBORN *Greater Canada* 68: The Canadian Pacific Railway land agents had no interest in Prince Albert (where the land is owned by another company), and said as much, refusing to give any information about the Saskatchewan country.

land beaver *Obs.* See **bank beaver**.
1760 JEFFERYS *Descr.New France* 29: Those pretended exiles were probably no other than the land beavers, who really live separate from the others, do no manner of work, and lodge underground, where they have no other care but to make themselves a secret passage to the water. **1844** MARRYAT *Settlers in Canada* 128: "But there is another sort of beaver, Ma'am, called the land-beaver, which is more easily taken," observed Martin; "they make holes in the earth like rabbits. The Indians say that these beavers are those who are lazy and idle, and have been driven out by the others for not working."

land black snake See **black rat snake**.
1963 *Kingston Whig-Standard* (Ont.) 19 Apr. 14/7: In Frontenac county, the black rat snake is frequently referred to as the land black snake to distinguish it from the common water snake which appears black when submerged but is actually dark brown with darker dorsal markings.

land board *Hist.* in Upper Canada, a body of officials appointed in each district to receive and report upon applications for land. See also **land council**.
1789 (1905) *Ont.Bur.Arch.Rep.* III 316: There being then no land Board instituted those tickets were merely to give the Settlers the satisfaction of knowing the number of their lots. **1833** *Liberal* (St. Thomas, U.C.) 29 Aug. 2/4: It was proposed to establish a land board in each District, for the accommodation of persons having claims for grants of Lands in this province. **1904** ERMATINGER *Talbot Regime* 122: The courts for the western district . . . were held at Detroit, where the land board also sat. . . .

land-board certificate *Obs.* **1** a certificate issued to a person granted land by a land board.
1821 *Kingston Chron.* (U.C.) 30 Mar. 2/4: There was

also a great difference between these Land Board Certificates at that time, and the Location Tickets at present.
2 the holder of such a document.
1821 *Kingston Chron.* (U.C.) 30 Mar. 2/4: At the time the Land Board certificates were allowed to vote, there were not sufficient votes without them.

land carriage *Obs.* See **portage**, *n.* (def. 2).
1744 DOBBS *Hudson's Bay* 30: He had 36 Land Carriages before he got to *Nepising*.

land cod *Obs.* the burbot, *Lota lota*.
1784 PENNANT *Arctic Zoology* cxci: Allied to this is the Mathemeg of the natives, the Land Cod of the English, a fish abundant in the northerly lakes; it grows to the length of three feet, and the weight of twelve pounds: has three beards on the lower jaw; the middlemost the longest: the back is brownish, the belly grey.

land company† *Hist.* a company holding extensive blocks of land for sale to settlers.
1841 WARD *River St.John* 55: The vacant land in the vicinity of this river, belongs to the Land Company; but farms can be obtained without difficulty by persons who are desirous of purchasing either cleared or unimproved. **1916** BRIDLE *Sons of Canada* 7: Optimistic promoters of mining companies, land companies, gas and power companies never got much encouragement from Macdonald. **1952** PUTNAM *Cdn Regions* 372/2: Other railway systems also received large grants of land which they offered for sale or disposed of to land companies which sold them to settlers.

land council *Obs.* See **land board**.
1818 *Gleaner* (Niagara-on-the-Lake, U.C.) 2 July 488/1: The three next Land Council days will be on Wednesday the 1st and 22d of July and 12th of August.

land-crossing *n. North* a definite crossing place over land between two sea-ice routes. See also **land portage** and **portage**, *n.* (def. 7).
1938 *Beaver* Dec. 16/1: Off at an early hour, as we hoped to reach the land-crossing by evening.

landed immigrant a person admitted to Canada as a potential settler and citizen of Canada.
1963 *Maclean's* 20 Apr. 18/3: The only black people freely admitted to Canada as landed immigrants are a limited number of women. . . . **1964** *Calgary Herald* 4 May 25/3: If he is to see his child, he will have to . . . be accepted as a landed immigrant. **1966** *Globe and Mail* (Toronto) 12 Mar. 1/4: . . . she came to Canada in 1955 . . . and obtained landed-immigrant status.

land fever† *Hist.* a strong desire to obtain title to public lands offered for settlement.
1860 (1960) *Ontario Hist.* June 80: Let us remember the land fever and take care to avoid catching a complaint of a somewhat similar character under the name of "oil fever". **1900** OSBORN *Greater Canada* 60: Many years passed before the North-West recovered from the commercial lethargy which followed this attack of land-fever.

land-floe *n.* See **shore-ice** (def. 1).
1850 (1852) OSBORN *Arctic Jnl* 66: The land-floe was still fast, reaching twenty-five or thirty miles off shore, and the pack had drifted off some ten or fifteen miles.
1857 MCDOUGALL *Voyage* 58: There is generally along the land a body of compact ice fixed to the shore, occasionally extending many miles to seaward; this is termed the land floe, the edge of which—unless compelled by adverse fortune—is never quitted by the experienced Arctic navigator. **1939** *Beaver* June 31: By

May literally hundreds of thousands [of eider ducks] have arrived to feed in the sea and rest idly on the edge of land-floe and ice-pan.

land God gave (to) Cain the rocky, barren coast of Labrador.
1952 PUTNAM *Cdn Regions* 67/1: In 1534 parts of the coast were charted by Jacques Cartier who designated it "the land that God gave Cain." **1953** BANFILL *Labrador Nurse* 5: "The land God gave to Cain . . . not a cartload of earth on the whole of it." Thus Jacques Cartier described the Labrador Coast in 1534.

land-grabber† *n.* a person who buys up large amounts of land usually intending to profit by speculation. See also **land-jobber, land shark** and **landsharp.**
1871 *Mainland Guardian* (New Westminster, B.C.) 6 May 2/1: The resources of the colony are not playthings for the amusement or profit of a clique composed of Island land-grabbers. **1908** NICHOLSON *In Old Quebec* 92: . . . it struck him during his visit that some light or cursory account of what he saw, written by one who is in no way interested in either the refined art of the land grabber or the modest and veracious employment of the land agent, might be of interest to eastern Canadians. . . .

land-grabbing *n.* the activity of a land-grabber, *q.v.* See also **land-jobbing.**
1909 HUNTER *Simcoe County* I 52: Although there were thus more than six hundred location tickets granted within the first year after the survey of those townships, there were not one-tenth that number of actual settlers in the county, land-grabbing having been a common practice then as later. **1952** PUTNAM *Cdn Regions* 149/1: That section of the country was the scene of land grabbing, not by the settlers who were not granted more than 1,200 acres each, much less in most cases, but by speculators, who were often government officials.

land grant *Hist.* **1**† a grant of public land made as part payment to a company contracting to build a railway.
1881 BEGG *Great Cdn N.W.* 128: While the building of the road north of Lake Superior is necessary to the success of the whole line yet it would be unfair to compel the Syndicate to take their land grant in a country where it is chiefly rock and forest. **1916** SKELTON *Day of Laurier* 229: No more land-grants were given, and when cash subsidies were bestowed, the companies so aided were required to carry free government mails, materials and men, up to three per cent on the subsidy.
2 a grant of public land made to an individual as a reward for service to his country.
1893 YEIGH *Ont.Parliament* 129: Among the recipients of land grants, Simcoe himself received 5,000 acres as a colonel of the Queen's Rangers. **1903** *Eye Opener* (High River, Alta) 5 Sep. 4/3: For his services during the rebellion he received a medal and ribbon (but no land grant.)

land-guide *n. Hist.* during the settlement of the West, an official of the government or a land company who met settlers and directed them to available homesteads. See also **land agent** (def. 1), **land locator,** and **locator** (def. 2).
1881 BEGG *Great Cdn N.W.* 110: No land guide is to leave a new comer while under any difficulty, but is to remain until such is overcome, or good provision made. **1911** (1914) BICKERSTETH *Open Doors* 40: The man finds suitable land—often a very expensive job through

unscrupulous land-guides. **1954** *Ghost Pine* 60: While there [at Didsbury, Alta] I contacted Bert Smith, the land guide, who drove me out here.

land-ice *n.* See **shore-ice** (def.1).
1850 GOODSIR *Baffin's Bay* 70: After "flensing" the whale, we proceeded in to the land ice, and there made fast. **1954** *Labrador and H.B.Pilot* 3: LAND ICE (shore floe or ice foot) is field or floe ice attached to the coast.

landing† *n.* **1** *Lumbering* **a.** See **brow** (def. 1). See also **skidded landing.**
1896 ROBERTS *Camp-Fire* 203: A brow of logs is a "landing" when the logs were piled from the water's edge. A landing may be either a "rough-and-tumble" or a "skidded" landing. **1942** HAIG-BROWN *Timber* 226: "If we had to start on that new tree with bad tongs we'd have a pile on the landing that we wouldn't see the bottom of in weeks." **1963** SYMONS *Many Trails* 184: These landings are strips along the river banks from which all trees and stumps have been removed, so that logs can be unloaded and put into the river without so much as a rose brier to obstruct the work.

b. See quote.
1942 HAIG-BROWN *Timber* 252: LANDING. An area of ground directly around the base of a spar tree, where logs are piled to be loaded on cars.

2 *Fisheries* the bringing into port and discharging of a catch of fish.
1954 *Fishermen's Advocate* 5 Feb. 7/3: While a few "bankers" of Newfoundland ownership operated on the Banks, all landings were made in Nova Scotia ports. **1958** *Fisherman* 24 Oct. 4/5: One black cod landing last week, the Capella I with 16,000 pounds of black cod.

landing camp *Lumbering* See quote. See also **landing** (def. 1a).
1963 SYMONS *Many Trails* 184: The work of putting the logs into the river has already been accomplished by the crew at the landing camp, which is a camp established at a point on the river as near as possible to where the logs are being cut in the hills by the men in the logging camps.

landing snye *Northwest* a river side-channel used by bush pilots for landing aircraft equipped with floats or, in winter, skis. See also **snye** (def. 2c).
1959 LEISING *Arctic Wings* 174: The landing snye at McMurray is a challenge to any pilot.

land-jobber *n. Obs.* See **land-grabber.**
1863 WALSHE *Cedar Creek* 80: "One of the most noted land-jobbers in the country—a man who buys wild lands at three shillings an acre, to sell them again at ten or fifteen, if he can. . . ."

land-jobbing *n. Obs.* See **land-grabbing.**
1841 MCLEOD *Upper Canada* 9: The public lands [are] frittered away by thousands to partizans and parasites;—three millions of acres sold to a company of land-jobbing speculators, residing in London, for forty-three cents per acre, and resold by their agents, to the poor emigrant, at five, ten and twenty five dollars per acre.

land-jumping *n. Obs.* the practice of taking over another person's land by illegal or dishonest means.
1883 *Brandon Daily Mail* (Man.) 3 Feb. 2/1: Several

cases of land jumping being brought up involving great hardship to those whose entries had been cancelled.

land locator† See **land-guide.**
1957 *Beaver* Autumn 41/2: Timber cruisers and land locators passed through, buying big jags of supplies.

landlock (salmon) [ˈlændˌlɑk] *n.* See **landlocked salmon.**
1897 WILSON *Yukon* 57: Throughout the summer months landlock salmon, similar to those of Maine and Canada, abound in the lakes. **1957** *Time* (Cdn ed.) 6 May 16/3: Although Trout Lake boasts some of the largest landlocks on the continent . . . it is known to only 200 or 300 devoted anglers.

landlocked salmon† any of various freshwater salmon, as the ouananiche and the kokanee, *qq.v.* See also **landlock** and **landlocker.**
1888 (1890) ST. MAUR *Impressions* 167: The land-locked salmon is found in these waters, also the red and white charr. **1933** MERRICK *True North* 70: . . . the net which had been supplying us . . . with trout, landlocked salmon, and whitefish was gone. . . . **1965** *Globe and Mail* (Toronto) 17 Apr. 29/1: . . . Lands and Forests notes that several areas . . . stock millions of smelt annually as a forage fish for the landlocked salmon.

landlocker [ˈlændˌlɑkɚ] *n.* See **landlocked salmon.**
1964 *Atlantic Advocate* July 67/1: "So that's the fighting landlocker," Glenn mused, holding up his puny prize before he threw it back.

land-miner *n. Esp. West, Slang* See 1920 quote. See also **mine,** *v.,* and **soil miner.** Cp. **wheat miner.**
1920 STRINGER *Prairie Mother* 119: All this talk of mine about wheat sounds as though I were what they call out here a Soil Robber, or a Land Miner, a get-rich-quick squatter who doesn't bother about mixed farming or the rotation of crops, with no true love for the land. . . . **1940** MACCORMAC *Canada* 232: In his good days he had been an optimist and a speculator, a land-miner rather than a farmer, a businessman in agriculture.

Land of Evangeline the region of Grand Pré, on the west shore of Nova Scotia, the home of Evangeline, the heroine of Longfellow's poem concerning the expulsion of the Acadians.
1958 *Cdn Geog.Jnl* LVII 62/1: Driving to the famous Land of Evangeline by way of Highway One from Halifax. . . .

land office† a government office that handles business relating to public lands.
1790 (1905) *Ont.Bur.Arch.Rep.* III 74: The Complete execution . . . of the Rules and Regulations for the conduct of the Land office department, being prevented . . . the following order . . . is submitted. . . .
1859 *Brit.Colonist* (Victoria) 1 Jan. 3/2: I am glad you have found out that Augean stable the Land Office.
1960 BUBLITZ *Dotted Line* 11: I later went into the local land office to work. . . .

Land of (the) Little Sticks a sub-arctic zone of stunted spruce and dwarf willow lying between the forests and the Barren Grounds in northern Canada. See also **little sticks.** Cp. **sticks** (def. 1).
1896 WHITNEY *On Snow-Shoes* 186: No man may

consider himself an expert until he has driven dogs and handled a sledge over such country as that approaching the Land of the Little Sticks. **1922** PICKTHALL *Bridge* 248: And it had swept south across the musk-ox pastures, across the desolate tundra, and the caribou-moss, and all the Land of Little Sticks. . . . **1965** SYMINGTON *Tuktu* 9: Urged by the high suns of May, the snow retreats through the land of the Little Sticks and the caribou pour out on the tundra. . . .

Land of the Midnight Sun Cp. **midnight sun.** the Far North, *q.v.*
1925 *Beaver* June 120: . . . the very rim of the world, the home of the Eskimo, the Land of the Midnight Sun. **1942** GOUGH *New World Horizons* 19: This "land of the midnight sun" is larger than Canada's Prairie Provinces put together but there is hardly a person on it.
1966 *Beautiful B.C.* Spring: North of the 60th parallel is "The Land of the Midnight Sun." Days are long and nights short in summer and temperatures range from about a low of 40 degrees at night to 80 or even 90 on some days.

Land of the North Wind the district of Keewatin (def. 2), the Cree name for the north wind.
1880 MORRIS *Treaties* 10: The District of Kee-wa-tin, "the land of the north wind," was also established, comprising the eastern and northern portions of the Territories, and placed under the control of the Lieutenant-Governor of Manitoba, and an Executive and Legislative Council. **1910** HAYDON *Riders of Plains* 52: The first-named favoured the Province of Manitoba and the district of Keewatin ("the land of the north wind"), having migrated thither in previous years after the settlement of Quebec and Ontario. **1964** *Time* (Cdn ed.) 27 Nov. 19/3: . . . the carvings are a brooding testament to the human endurance in the Keewatin, the Land of the North Wind.

land otter the Canadian otter, *Lutra canadensis.*
1828 (1931) MERK *Fur Trade* 307: We are willing in order to relieve you from all further concern respecting it, to take it off your hands, at what we consider to be its utmost value here, say . . . Beaver at 3 $ p Skin Land Otters at 2 $ pʳ Skin and Sea Otters at 10 $ pʳ Skin.
1908 MAIR *Mackenzie Basin* 213: [The] land otter [or] Canada otter is but very sparingly present on the lower Anderson, nor could it be truthfully stated that it was very abundant in the far north. . . . **1944** *Beaver* Dec. 20/2: To the Indians of Alaska . . . the land otter . . . was gifted with uncanny powers.

land pack See **shore-ice** (def. 1).
1853 INGLEFIELD *Summer Search* 73: . . . the thick fog and mist . . . precluded our seeing any distance before us, and thus we imperceptibly drew too near the land pack off the western shore.

land portage *North* See **land-crossing.**
1951 BULIARD *Inuk* 93: Perhaps we were not too smart to try the land portage. We seem to have exchanged rough ice for rocks. Sometimes the slopes are so steep we have to pull the dogs; the next moment we plunge down into a gully, where our sleds disappear in the soft snow.

land-scrip *n. Hist.* **1**† a government certificate which entitled the holder to locate on a stated amount of public land. See also **scrip** (def. 1a).
1856 (1926) LANGTON *Early U.C.* 243: With the Crown Lands I am also at present at a standstill, except that I discovered the other day forgeries of land scrip to the extent of £6,000.

2 a certificate issued following the Northwest Rebellions, *q.v.*, to Metis as compensation for lost lands and entitling the bearer to 240 acres. See also **half-breed scrip, old settlers' scrip, scrip** (def. 1b), and **scrip certificate.** Cp. **money-scrip.**

1923 WALDO *Down Mackenzie* 153: If you have taken land-scrip or money-scrip—that is, if you have accepted 240 acres or $240 from the Government—your status as a "breed" is legally fixed. **1935** SULLIVAN *Great Divide* 339: The Metis, he says, ask for landscrip to give them title, also that the Government sell a certain amount of land and use the proceeds for schools and hospitals. . . . **1956** *Sask.Hist.* IX 2: To métis children born before July, 1870, was given the choice between a "scrip" valued at $240, which they could either negotiate or use for the purchase of federal lands, and a "land scrip" which authorized them to pick out a piece of property of 240 acres on unoccupied Dominion lands.

land shark† See **land-grabber.**

1882 *Edmonton Bull.* 18 Feb. 2/3: If the country is to be handed over to land sharks of every shade and kind, what is the use of prolonging the agony. **1935** SULLIVAN *Great Divide* 342: . . . the Metis are being stirred up by the land sharks to demand their scrip, then the sharks will swallow them: what's paid for scrip will go in whisky, and they're left no better off.

landsharp *n. Slang, Obs.* See **land-grabber.**

1909 PARKER *Northern Lights* 262: "You say he was a landsharp in the South, and he had to leave. . . ."

land's height See **height of land.**

1815 BOUCHETTE *Lower Canada* 36: On the north side of Lake Huron many rivers of considerable size run from the Land's Height down to it.

land sky *Arctic* See quote. Cp. **water sky.**

1958 *Manice* 8: Bare land and open water reflect little or no light and for this reason the clouds above these surfaces are relatively dark (*Land Sky, Water Sky*).

landsman *n. Sealing, Nfld* a sealer who goes to the ice (def. 1) on foot rather than on a ship.

1958 *Evening Telegram* (St. John's) 2 May 3/7: Bowring's second vessel . . . leaves port today to join the Algerine in collecting landsmen's seals. **1966** *Globe and Mail* (Toronto) 9 Mar. 3/6: No quota is placed on the landsmen, [but] each must have a license to hunt.

la poudre *n.* See **poudre.**

laragan *n.* See **larrigan.**

Large Canoe *Fur Trade, Obs.* See **Montreal canoe** and picture.

1767 (1954) WALLACE *Pedlars* 5: They informed me . . . that they were gone down with fur to Montreal . . . an Englishman and 8 Servants who mans two Large Canoes. . . . **1793** (1933) MACDONELL *Diary* 95: M^{rss} Robert Grant . . . and Wm Thorburn set out in two Large Canoes for Montreal. **1801** (1933) MCLEOD *Diary* 182: I embarked in the Bark or Large Canoe well loaded. . . .

large-horned sheep *Obs.* See **bighorn sheep.**

1822 *U.C.Gaz.* (York [Toronto]) 25 Apr. 14/1: Very little is known of the large horned sheep of the Rocky Mountains in the north western regions of this continent.

large plains or **prairies** *Obs.* the great plains of the West.

1802 (1820) HARMON *Journal* 99: Two of our people, whom I sent a few days since into the large prairie, have just returned. . . . **1804** *Ibid.* 111: Those Indians

who reside in the large plains or prairies, are the most independent. . . .

lariat ['læriət] *n.* [< Am.E < Sp. *la riata, reata* rope, tether] **1**† originally, a long halter or tether of braided rawhide or horsehair; now, usually, a lasso, *q.v.*

[**1835** IRVING *Tour on Prairies* 34: Coils of cordage at his saddle-bow, which [we] were told were lariats, or noosed cords, used in catching the wild horse.] **1873** (1904) BUTLER *Wild North Land* 53: Its skin gave him a house, its robe a blanket and a bed, its undressed hide a boat . . . its leather a lariat for his horse, a saddle, bridle, rein, and bit. **1919** FRASER *Bulldog Carney* 81: . . . Carney dropped the rein from over the horse's head to the ground, took his lariat from the saddle-horn, hung the two pack-bags over his shoulder, and . . . slipped through the bush. . . . **1962** FRY *Ranch on the Cariboo* 11: Already Marvin was rolling down his lariat.

2 *Obs.* any long rope.

1909 NURSEY *Isaac Brock* 44: At times these lightened boats were poled or tracked through the broken water, towed by the men, from such foothold as the rocky banks afforded, by means of a long lariat tied to the boat's bow, with loops over each trackman's shoulder, one man steering with a long sweep.

larigan *n.* See **larrigan.**

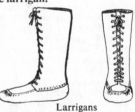

Larrigans

larrigan ['lærəgən] *n.* [origin unknown] a type of moccasin of oil-tanned cowhide having uppers reaching almost to the knee and, usually, flexible soles. See also **shoepack** (def. 1). Also spelled *laragan, larigan.*

1898 *Hints for Intending Klondikers* 12: For clothing, then, take . . . 1 pair Canadian laragans or shoe-packs; 3 pairs seamless felt ankle moccasins. . . . **1905** WALLACE *Labrador Wild* 266: The snow clogged in all that was left of my cowhide mocassins (larigans) and I took them off. . . . **1950** BIRD *This is N.S.* 99: The cook said after, it was lucky they had been cold enough to leave their larrigans on, else they'd run in their sock feet. **1961** *Sat. Night* 23 Dec. 18/1: After breakfast that day I rode to school on the rear runner of a fishmonger's sleigh wearing a pair of cowhide larrigans greasy with linseed oil.

larriganed *adj.* shod with larrigans.

1904 ROBERTS *Watchers of Trails* 287: Then turning on his larriganed heels, he strode up the trail. . . .

lash† *n.* a long rope used to secure the load on a pack animal, sled, etc. See also **lash-line.** Also *lashing-rope.*

1887 (1888) LEES & CLUTTERBUCK *British Columbia* 229: The lash rope is from thirty to forty feet long, terminating at one end in a synch (girth) of ordinary size, the end of which remote from the lash rope is

furnished with a large smooth wooden hook, in which
a rope can run easily. **1912** POCOCK *Man in the Open* 92:
By loading-time they've got such grass bellies on them
that I has to be quite severe with the lash ropes. They
hold their wind while I cinch them, and that's how their
stomach's get kicked. **1941** *Beaver* Mar. 10/2: Lashing
ropes for the load are necessary. . . .

lashed-boats *n.pl. North* See 1938 quote.
1929 *Beaver* Mar. 154: . . . the winches on the ship out
in the bay [were] discharging the cargo into the
"lashed-boats". . . . **[1938** *Ibid.* Mar. 20/1: The ship
sometimes anchored over a mile from the post, and
supplies were unloaded on two ship's boats lashed
together and towed by a steam launch.]

lash-line *n.* See **lash.**
1933 MERRICK *True North* 139: Outside the [sled]
wrapper the gun was tied to the crisscrossing lashline.
Ibid. 200: The lash line . . . came loose and the load was
spilling . . . all over the snow.

lasso† [læ'su] *n.* [< Am.E < Sp. *lazo* noose] a
long rope, often, in earlier days, of braided
rawhide or horsehair, having a running noose at
one end, used for roping cattle, horses, etc. See
also **lariat** (def. 1). Also spelled *lassoo.*
1856 BALLANTYNE *Young Fur-Traders* 20: "If you had
travelled farther south, friend," replied Mr. Grant,
"you would have seen the Spaniards of Mexico break
in their wild horses in a very different way; for after
catching one with a lasso, a fellow gets on his back and
gives it the rein and the whip—ay, and the spur too;
and before that race is over, there is no need for a
curb." **1927** LONGSTRETH *Silent Force* 77: Men were at
once told off into squads, some to collect the arms from
the outlying traders . . . so that if the Indians pulled
down parts of the stockade by lasso, as bravado
prompted, there would still be a line of protection.
1965 SYMINGTON *Tuktu* 30: The pilot of the plane
lassoed a yearling caribou with a mooring rope as the
herd rushed past him at a distance of about five yards.

lasso† [læ'su] *v.* [< n.] **1 a.** catch with a lasso.
1853 REID *Young Voyageurs* 125: It was this that
suggested my plan, which was no other than to lasso the
bull, and tie him to the tree! **1935** SULLIVAN *Great
Divide* 132: . . . the Blackfoot lassoo their horses and
ride towards me very fast.

b. *Figurative use.*
1961 *Time* (Cdn ed.) 10 Nov. 15/3: Alberta's cattlemen,
lassoing an expanded U.S. market for their beef, have
never had it so good.

2 *Obs.* tie up (an animal) to prevent bucking and
kicking.
1876 LORD *At Home* 62: Let us imagine a horse
lassooed up awaiting the operation of packing.

L'Assomption belt See **L'Assomption sash.**

L'Assomption sash [læ'sʌmʃən] a colorful sash,
q.v., 4 to 6 inches wide and 8 to 10 feet long,
so called because the best such sashes were made in
L'Assomption, Quebec, and widely distributed as
trade goods by the fur companies, especially in
the design known as the arrow sash, *q.v.* See also
Assomption belt.

1892 (1948) *Beaver* June 46/1: The men have kept
little of the picturesque costume of the *voyageur* of the
old days, only the bright handkerchief on the head, the
moccasins, and an occasional fire bag and *L'Assomption*
sash. **1896** RUSSELL *Far North* 27: The best are called
l'Assomption belts; they are woven from heavy
threads and are from four to six inches wide and eight to
ten feet in length. **1934** GODSELL *Arctic Trader* 54: Next
day was spent in a round of visiting by red and white
people alike, all attired in their best capotes . . . belted
with gaudy L'Assomption sashes at the waist. . . .
1956 KEMP *Northern Trader* 89: While I stared in
amazement, one of the older men pulled a "fire-bag"
from beneath his *l'assomption* belt and produced flint-
and-steel.

L'Assomption sashes

L'Assomption sash or **belt** See **L'Assomption**
sash.

last frontier the Canadian North.
1924 DORRANCE *Never Fire First* 223: To escape further
discussion he hurried into the fallen night. Pondering
the marvelous complexities of the women met in a day
on the "Last Frontier," he nearly plumped into a mud
hole which lay out front. **1964** *Edmonton Jnl* 11 July
3/6: The raw shanty lad who came out of the backwoods
of Quebec at the age of 14 to carve some sort of future
out of the American West hardly resembled the man
who, in a few short years, would win a place in the
mythology of the last frontier.

last ice the ice that permits travel just prior to
break-up, *q.v.*
1819 (1939) ROBERTSON *Correspondence* 107: Mr.
Miles . . . will remain at Fort Wedderburne untill the
last ice. **1821** (1938) SIMPSON *Athabasca Jnl* 263: The
twelve bags . . . I hope you will be able to forward by
the last ice to Lac La Loche. **1937** *Beaver* June 29/2:
By the last ice, he had accompanied Dr. Paddon to the
summer hospital. . . .

last woods See 1955 quote.
1896 WHITNEY *On Snow-Shoes* 274: How cold, I cannot
adequately describe; and our wood was going stick by
stick, and we had begun on our lodge poles, all but two
of which had been consumed by the time we reached
the "last wood." **1913** COWIE *Adventurers* 244: . . . a bend
in one of the branches of the Souris River where the
last woods occurred on the route between Pile of Bones
Creek and the Old Wives' Lakes. **1955** ADTIC *Glossary*:
last woods. A popular term applied to small, scattered
groves and thickets above or north of timberline.

lateer [lə'tir] *n.* [< Cdn F < F *la tire* toffee
< *tirer* draw, pull] See **taffy** (def. 1). Also *la tire.*
1903 CARR-HARRIS *White Chief* 128: . . . the gentlemen
served each lady with a block of hard snow upon which
had been poured some of the boiling [maple] sugar,
which immediately hardened into "lateer," or "taffy."

1959 TAYLOR *Canada and her Neighbours* 77/2: Then ... we pass around, pouring out this hot [maple] syrup onto the snow. We call this syrup on snow *la tire,* and how good it tastes!

421

late Loyalist
lay

late (or later) Loyalist *Hist.* an American settler who moved into Canada (1790-1800) after the influx of the true refugees, the motive usually being to take advantage of the Crown lands being opened for settlement. See also **Loyalist** (def. 2) and **post-Loyalist.** Cp. **Pre-Loyalist** and **United Empire Loyalist.**
1931 CONNOR *Rock and River* 219: "On the other hand we have some twenty thousand 'later loyalists' as they are called, American Colonists who, loyal enough to Canada, have no great affection for Britain. They will likely swing to the winning side." **1943** CRAIG *Upper Canada* 43: The first wave of these people has sometimes been described as "late loyalists," a term of limited accuracy since most of them did not migrate for political reasons. **1963** MORTON *Kingdom of Canada* 196: The migration of the late loyalists was ... part of this great [land] speculation. ...

latigo† ['lætəgo] *n.* [< Am.E < Sp. *làtigo*] *West*
See 1962 quote.
1912 POCOCK *Man in the Open* 106: "Kneel on the mare's head, reach under the pannier, find the latego, and cast off." **1951** ANGIER *At Home* 146: Joe drew the latigo up two more notches. **1962** *Alta Hist.Rev.* Autumn 16/2: A "latigo" is a long leather thong about an inch and a half wide used for tying the "cinche". ...

la tire See **lateer.**

laughing goose [from its harsh call, resembling laughter] See **white-fronted goose.**
1743 (1949) ISHAM *Observations* 122: Laug'hing geese are of the size of a weywey. ... **1833** (1963) TOLMIE *Physician* 234: "Large flocks of the Laughing Goose have passed southward since dusk." **1921** HEMING *Drama of Forests* 274: Then, after that, the sky soon becomes mottled with flying birds of many kinds: gray geese, laughing geese, waveys, and white geese, as well as great flocks of ducks of many kinds. **1956** MCATEE *Folk-Names* 9: White-fronted goose [is also called] laughing goose (... Early use Edwards 1750. "N.W.T.," Man, Sask.). ...

launcher *n. Fur Trade, Hist.* See **décharge** (def. 1).
1827 (1912) ERMATINGER *Express Jnl* 94: Leaving Morgan's Rock ... we went to the Rocky Launcher and encamped at 10 p.m. **1923** *Beaver* Oct. 19: In localities where there was a large number of "launchers" and the boats were hauled over portages, 28 to 30 feet was the length [of a York boat]. On routes where there were no "launchers", the length was 38 to 40 feet.

Laurentia [lə'rɛnʃiə] *n.* [< fem. form of Latin *Laurentius* Lawrence] *Often Poetic* the region north of the St. Lawrence River, formerly New France and its hinterland.
1761 (1965) HAMILTON *Cdn Quotations* 48/2:
Happy Laurentia, to thy farthest shore,
Lavish of life, a chosen band she led;
And to those royal towers her standard bore,
Whence fell Oppression, Gallic tyrant fled.
1889 POCOCK *Laurentides* 355: Laurentia! Superb Laurentia! / Thy mountains in the garment of the cloud. ... **1963** *Globe and Mail* (Toronto) 11 May 19/4: Because so much of the story deals with trips here and there around Laurentia and Acadia, the need for a guide should have been obvious.

Laurentian barrier or **belt** See **Canadian Shield.**
1887 *Trans.Hist.& Sci.Soc.Man.* 27 3: The Laurentian belt or lowest rock-step in the ladder of time, is mainly a barren unproductive region here as elsewhere, and scarcely any land fit for settlement is to be found on it. **1929** *Cdn Hist.Rev.* X 294: There is no element in the present Dominion of greater significance than the so-called Canadian Shield or Laurentian Barrier.

Laurentian coalition *Hist.* See quote.
1963 MORTON *Kingdom of Canada* 23: This alliance was the beginning of the "Laurentian coalition" of Algonkians, Hurons, and French that was to dominate the history of New France until 1701.

Laurentian plateau See **Canadian Shield.**
1917 MILLER *New Era* 64: ... the peculiar significance of the Laurentian plateau in its relation to the development of Canadian history lies in the fact that, speaking generally, it is a great tract of barren country incapable of supporting an agricultural population, and thus splits the Dominion into two parts, Eastern and Western Canada. **1926** *Beaver* June 96: East of a line drawn from the Lake of the Woods to Great Bear lake in the far northwest lies the ancient Laurentian plateau. ... **1952** PUTNAM *Cdn Regions* 126/2: The Pleistocene glaciation is nearly as evident here as in the Laurentian Plateau.

Laurentian Shield See **Canadian Shield.**
1940 MACCORMAC *Canada* 244: Wherever railroads have been built through the Laurentian Shield, minerals have been discovered. **1963** MORTON *Kingdom of Canada* 23: They committed themselves to the exploitation of the Canadian (or Laurentian) Shield, the ancient rock plateau which lay north of the St. Lawrence. ...

Laurierite ['lɔrie,aɪt] *n.* [< Sir Wilfrid *Laurier,* 1841-1919, French-Canadian statesman and Prime Minister of Canada from 1896 to 1911] *Hist.* a supporter of the political views and principles of Sir Wilfrid Laurier, specifically with regard to the issue of conscription during World War I.
1916 BRIDLE *Sons of Canada* 98: Most of the French-Canadian members were Laurierites out-and-out. **1917** *Grit* (Toronto) 11 Dec. 7/4: A Borden Government organ gives the Laurierites twelve seats in Ontario, eighteen more than the law allows, to get an even break with the Liberals.

lawn social a garden party.
1886 *Indian* (Hagersville, Ont.) 8 Sep. 197/1: The lawn social, held on Saturday last, was the most successful one of the season. **1932** JAMIESON *Cattle in the Stall* 41: There will be lawn socials and strawberry festivals and garden parties and Sunday school picnics. ...

lay *n. Placer Mining, Hist.* **1** a lease to work a gold claim for a share, usually half, of the proceeds.
1898 *Yukon Midnight Sun* (Dawson) 11 June 1/2: Some of these lay holders say they have not made wages, and many of them claim they have not even made expenses. **1926** DILL *Long Day* 52: Ole had been offered a lay on a supposedly rich piece of ground, and he was violently agitated at the prospect of acquiring it. "Working on lay" was the Yukoner's manner of saying working on a percentage. **1958** BERTON *Klondike* 84: He began by acquiring half of Thirty Eldorado for a few groceries. He made no move to mine it, but instead let a section of it out on lease or "lay," as it was called, to Charley

Myers and Dick Butler, receiving from them a percentage of the take.

2 a. the actual land covered by such a lease.
1899 PALMER *Klondyke* 98: The number of applications quite exceeded the number of lays to be let, and all through the winter the laymen on Bonanza were the envy of their fellows.

b. a mining operation carried out on such a lease.
1898 *Klondyke Miner* (Dawson, Y.T.) 1 Oct. 3/1: The layman on a Rich Hill claim is rocking out the refused dirt of last year's lay and is making $100 a day.

lay *v. Lumbering* haul (logs) from the cutting site and pile them ready for dumping into the river in the spring.
1896 GOURLAY *Hist.Ottawa* 100: They . . . with yoke chain and crotch, could lay many pieces [of lumber] a day on the river. **1912** HEENEY *Pickanock* 41: "I laid my logs on it last winter," he went on.

layman *n. Placer Mining* a person holding a lay (def. 1).
1898 *Yukon Midnight Sun* (Dawson) 9 Dec. 1/6: The last few days several laymen have arrived from Sulphur well pleased with their prospects. **1901** *Klondike Miner* (Grand Forks, Y.T.) 18 Oct. 3/4: Discovery claims and Nos. 1 and 2 on Bonanza will be worked by laymen the coming winter. **1926** DILL *Long Day* 53: Old-timers will remember the trio who took out an 80% lay from the North American Trading Company, and each man received over sixty thousand dollars as his share of the winter's work. Thereafter, they were known as "the lucky laymen."

lay on the lumber See **lumber** (def. 4b).

lay over *Placer Mining, B.C., Obs.* suspend enforcement, usually during winter, of the law requiring a miner to work his claim without interruptions of more than three consecutive days.
1870 *Cariboo Sentinel* (Barkerville, B.C.) 21 May 2/4: Representation Day—yesterday the general laying over of claims ceased, and all miners possessing claims were required to represent them.

lay up See **lay,** *v.*
1912 HEENEY *Pickanock* 27: . . . there were chains lying in piles—strong chains for laying up logs in the woods. . . .

lazarus *n.* [origin unknown] *Nfld, Obs.* a variety of seal.
1774 (1792) CARTWRIGHT *Journal* II 34: At noon I went in a skiff and hauled the nets under the Lyon Head, and had a lazarus in one of them. **1861** DE BOILIEU *Labrador Life* 97: The next seal I have to catalogue (there is nothing special in it to describe) generally loiters on the coast later than the Harp, and frequents it sooner in the spring: it is called the Lazarus.

L.C. *Hist.* 1 See **Lower Canada** (def. 1).
1815 *Quebec Gaz.* 9 Feb. 2/3: His Excellency . . . has been please to appoint [him] Surveyor of Lands for the Province of L.C. **1850** *Toronto Dly Express* 8 Apr. 2/1: It is now quite certain that the Ministers of L.C. will sustain the Radicals of Upper Canada in all their measures.

2 See **legislative council** (def. 2).
1885 GEMMILL *Companion* 234: Resigned his seat in the Latter on his appointment to L.C., Quebec, 1867.

lead† [lid] *n. North* an opening in an icefield. See also **tickle** (def. 2).
1850 (1852) OSBORN *Arctic Jnl* 55: As anything was better than standing still, I was heartily glad to see the "Chieftain," a bonnie Scotch whaler, show us the road by entering a lead of water, and away we all went, working to windward. **1958** *Evening Telegram* (St. John's) 28 Apr. 2/1: [Caption] Catching a full-grown seal alive is quite a stunt. . . . Finding the animal some distance from a "lead" he managed to get between it and open water, then making a short dash he seized it by the hind flippers.

lead [lid] *v. Obs.* See **hand** and **leading place.**
1775 (1951) *Sask.Jnls* 5: We passed over several Falls leading Canoes in Places. . . . **1778** (1931) TYRRELL *Documents* 203: Willm Lutit in attempting to Lead the Canoe up a fall was taken off his Legs by the Current and carried into the stream. . . .

lead boom [lid] *Lumbering* See **sheer-boom.**
1958 *Evening Telegram* (St. John's) 6 May 19/1: J. D. Roberts, woods manager, pointed out that the portion which broke was the lead or "sheer" boom and not the main holding boom . . . into which the floating logs are funnelled by the lead booms.

lead dog See **leader** (def. 2).
1934 GODSELL *Arctic Trader* 215: . . . I leapt from the carriole, held the team while John circled the dangerous air-hole and grabbed the lead-dog of the other train, dragging him upon the ice. **1965** *Kingston Whig-Standard* (Ont.) 8 Feb. 8/7: The 38-year-old civil servant, who has been a musher for three years, claims that the key to a successful team is a good lead dog.

leader *n.* 1 *Fur Trade, Hist.* See **captain** (def. 2).
1754 (1907) HENDAY *Journal* 326: At night I went to my tent . . . and told my Leader. **1772** (1908) COCKING *Journal* 100: Here I met with a York Fort Leader who had not been down this summer. **1954** MacGREGOR *Shining Mountains* 199: There were certain Indians who brought in more furs than their colleagues, and who for various reasons pleased the English and the French fur traders. The traders called them Leaders and made special presents to them. . . .

2 in a dog team, the dog, sometimes a female, who leads the team, setting the pace and carrying out the driver's commands. See pictures at **fan hitch** and **tandem hitch.** See also **foregoer** (def. 1), **lead dog, leader dog,** and **train-leader.**
1818 CHAPPELL *Voy.of Rosamond* 143: Two of the most sagacious and best-trained dogs are placed in front, as leaders; no reins being necessary; for the animals will naturally follow a beaten track through the snow; and they are easily guided by a long whip, the lash of which extends to the foremost dogs. **1864** HALL *Life with Esquimaux* II 286: Barbekark was my leader, and, by dint of hard blows, I managed to keep him in a right position. **1956** KEMP *Northern Trader* 157: He was my spare leader, but any time I went to harness him, he hung his head and dropped his tail and registered his disgust.

3 See quotes.
1907 MILLAIS *Newfoundland* 152: The trap is set in 10 to 12 fathoms of water, and a long net stretching landwards, and called a "leader," guides the fish in at the front door. **1944** *Beaver* Sep. 21/1: A long net hung vertically, called a leader, is fastened to the shore, extending out to the cod trap.

leader dog See **leader** (def. 2).
1880 (1893) YOUNG *Indian Wigwams*: Three of my dogs were St. Bernards, but the fourth was old Voyageur, a

long-legged cross-breed, the grandest leader-dog I ever drove. **1953** BANFILL *Labrador Nurse* 198: When I stepped out into the inky blackness I could barely distinguish the leader dogs.

leading place *Obs.* a shallow or rocky place in a river, where a canoe had to be pulled along by hand. See also **lead,** *v.*
1778 (1931) TYRRELL *Documents* 206: . . . came to a bad leeding place about 100 yds long . . . went 5 Miles very crooked and came to a very bad leeding place. . . .

league *n.* [< Cdn F < OF *ligue;* cf. F *lieue*] *Hist.* See 1933 quote.
1765-75 (1933) POND *Narrative* 44: . . . St. Peters River . . . was a Hundred Leags up the River. . . . **1793** (1933) MacDONELL *Diary* 72: From the long Sault we have twenty leagues of still water to navigate. **1933** GATES *Five Traders* 72n: David Thompson found that the "league" of the canoemen averaged about two miles in length.

Leagueman or **Leagueite** *n. Hist.* a member of the British North America League, *q.v.*
1849 *Wkly Globe* (Toronto) 7 Nov. 92/1: It is only necessary to remind them that the evils complained of by the *Leagueites* and the *Gowanites,* or Annexationists, are evils of their own making. *Ibid.* 7 Dec. 92/1: The "ruin and decay" with which the *Leaguemen* and the *Annexationists* have been devastating Canada for the last six months, will bear a fair comparison with the downfall of the Laigh Kirk of Kilmarnock.

leaning fence an old-fashioned rail fence having all the posts set at an angle of 40 degrees.
1953 *Cdn Geog.Jnl* XLVII 235/2: It takes your car off the highway and into quiet and little-visited byways where you might come across a "dog-leg" to add to your collection or even a Bloomer, whatever that was, or a leaning fence. . . .

lean-to *n.* **1 a.** See 1966 quote. See also **brush shed, half-camp, half-tent,** and **shed tent.**
1872 (1877) GRANT *Ocean to Ocean* 185: Tents, for the sake of carrying as little weight as possible, were discarded for the simple "lean to." **1910** FERGUSON *Janey Canuck* 235: With Walter Barrie, his guide, he was ranging timber up north. They built a lean-to of boughs (with nothing to lean-to). . . . **1966** *Kingston Whig-Standard* (Ont.) 6 Feb. 4/5: Lean-tos were overnight shelters just large enough for one or two men to sleep in, made by laying poles against some support as a fallen tree and covering them with bark or boughs to check the wind.
b. a portable canvas shelter having a sloping roof from ridgepole to ground and being open on three sides.
1913 FOOTNER *Jack Chanty* 253: Jack opened the cache for an additional supply of grub, and what else he needed: his cherished leather chaps, and a canvas lean-to, and mosquito bar. **1963** *Weekend Mag.* 21 Dec. 6/2: . . . it was a real pleasure to see him tending his camp, his bedroll laid on pine boughs beneath a canvas lean-to.

2 See **camp** (def. 1a).
1912 POCOCK *Man in the Open* 28: "How are we going to stow all our furniture in that shack, I wonder?" were Helen's first words when she saw the frame "lean-to" which was the only building on the place. **1931** SEARY *Romance* 141: Log houses and bark "lean-tos," or camps, sheltered most of the civilians . . . but the soldiers spent the first winter under canvas. **1964** *Sechelt Peninsula Times* 22 Apr. 5/3: [Caption] The lean-to beyond was the logging camp of the

"Mosher" who logged the timber off the slopes behind.

lease *n.* See **grazing lease.**
1962 FRY *Ranch on the Cariboo* 35: The only chance to find them was to scour the Milk Ranch field and the big lease, hoping they might have drifted in there in the last few weeks.

leather *n. Fur Trade* See 1904 quote. See also **moose leather.**
1806 (1897) COUES *New Light* I 382: The camp consisted of about 120 leather tents. . . . **1836** (1932) MCLEAN *Notes* 166: Mr. Linton . . . was directed to wait the arrival of the party sent to Jasper house for a supply of leather. . . . **1904** MORICE *Northern Interior B.C.* 154: The object of that expedition was to get a supply of leather, *i.e.* dressed moose or cariboo skins, which, scarce in the west, Indians and *engagés* needed to make moccasins, bags, ropes, pieces of attire, etc. **1933** *Beaver* Sep. 47: I gave him . . . two large leather lodges for his reception room.

leather brigade or **party** *Fur Trade, Hist.* a special party which carried buffalo, caribou, and moose hides to the New Caledonian posts of the Hudson's Bay Co. from the prairies. See also **leather** and **Leather Pass.**
1836 (1932) MCLEAN *Notes* 167: . . . no accounts having been received of the leather party, he determined to embark for his destination. **1924** *Beaver* Feb. 184: The leather brigade of earlier times used the Peace, Parsnip and Pack rivers as their route from Chipewyan to B.C. points. . . . **1934** *Ibid.* Sep. 38: Fort Edmonton . . . was the starting point for the important "Leather" brigade using pack horses, canoes and boats, and carrying the necessary buffalo and moose hides to the Far West for making the hunter's shoes, without which the Indians refused to hunt.

Leather Pass *Fur Trade, Hist.* The Yellowhead Pass. See 1906 quote. See also **leather track.**
1828 (1872) MCDONALD *Peace River* 113: Tete Jaune's Cache . . . called . . . by the Hudson's Bay people . . . *Leather Pass.* . . . **1904** MORICE *Northern Interior B.C.* 158: The object of that expedition was to get a supply of leather, *i.e.,* dressed moose or cariboo skins, which, scarce in the west, Indians and *engagés* needed to make moccasins, bags, ropes, pieces of attire, etc. The original Tete Jaune Cache, also called Leather Pass from the above mentioned circumstance, was at the first forks of the Fraser. . . . **1934** *Beaver* Sep. 38/1: . . . part of the brigade turned up the Miette, and then crossing the "Leather" pass (the Yellowhead), reached the headwaters of the Fraser river. . . .

leather track or **trail** *Fur Trade, Hist.* the route through the Leather Pass, *q.v.*
1829 (1947) SIMPSON *Dispatch* 241: . . . requesting that a proportion of the Tobacco expected from York factory should be sent for this district by Okanagan, should none have been forwarded by the Leathertrack. . . . **1965** *Beaver* Autumn 27/1: This so-called "leather trail" was necessary because moose and caribou were scarce in the west, but their hides were needed for moccasins, bags, clothes, and ropes at all the posts.

leatherwood† *n.* a small tree or shrub, *Dirca palustris,* having tough, pliant bark. See also **bois de pelon** and **moosewood** (def. 2).
1829 MACTAGGART *Three Years* I 307: The *timbers* [of

the bark canoe] ... are sewed with stripes of the leatherwood-tree.... **1852** (1881) TRAILL *Cdn Crusoes* 77: ... Louis pointed to the strips of leather-wood. ...

leavings *n.pl. West, Obs.* (*except in place names*) a point where travellers left a water route to take a trail leading across the plains. See also **Montée.** Cp. **jumping-off place** (def. 1).
1884 *Edmonton Bull.* 20 Dec. 4/1: Rev. C. Scollen is erecting Roman Catholic mission buildings at Coyote's place at the leavings of Battle River. **1913** KELLY *Range Men* 272: ... small irrigation schemes were planned and put into effect at Leeds and Elliott's Ranch at The Leavings.... **1928** *Beaver* June 15: ... we still had about twenty miles to travel to the Leavings [between Calgary and Macleod, Alta], where we should find food and shelter.

ledge *n. Obs.* a long, narrow strip (of trees).
1691 (1929) KELSEY *Papers* 16: This day we pitcht again & got through ye woods[,] this ledge not being above 30 Miles through.... **1754** (1907) HENDAY *Journal* 330: Came to a ledge of Poplars and sweet water.
1773 (1908) COCKING *Journal* 114: We proceeded ... travelling over barren ground [prairie]: pitched at a small ledge of willows and a few straggling poplars.

legal Indian See **registered Indian.**
1958 HAWTHORN *Indians of B.C.* 439: Again there are a number of White women who have legally married Indians, and who are resident on reserves and participate in Indian life as full band members, some of them taking office on or under the band council. This mixture through intermarriage is considerable, and, racially speaking, the legal Indians are becoming assimilated to the general population. **1959** *Northern Affairs Bull.* Sep.-Oct. 32/2: The present number of legal Indians (i.e., Indians coming under the Indian Act as registered members of official bands) is nearing 160,000. **1966** *Indian-Eskimo Assn Bull.* Jan.-Feb. 6/1: There are probably as many Indian people in Canada who are not legally Indian as there are of those who have legal Indian status.

leggings ['lɛgɪŋz] *n.pl.* a pair of coverings for the legs, usually made of dressed skins and often reaching from ankles to hips, where they are fastened to a belt, originally used by the Indians. See also **Indian leggings, Indian stockings,** and **mitashes.** Also spelled *leggins.*
1764 (1901) HENRY (Elder) *Travels* 147: ... a pair of leggings ... of scarlet cloth, which with the ribbon to garnish them *fashionably*, cost me fifteen pounds of beaver.... **1820** (1922) HARMON *Journal* 286: They [Takullies] seldom use either leggins or shoes, in the summer. **1893** YOUNG *Indian Wigwams* 60: [The Métis'] moccasined feet and brilliant-colored scarf-belt, beaded cap, fire-bag and leggins, and distinct Indian face seemed to so ally him to the native tribes that too many never for a moment thought he could have any grievances to be redressed.
1954 CAMPBELL *Nor' Westers* 31: Every pork-eater appeared in a clean shirt and with his brightest hand-woven sash about his waist; northmen [appeared] in new buckskin short shirts and leggings.

legislative assembly since Confederation, the elected legislative body in each Canadian province, forming the total legislature in all provinces except

Quebec, where it is the lower house in a bicameral system. See also **legislature.** Cp. **legislative council** (def. 2).
1867 *Islander* (Charlottetown) 8 Mar. 2/5: Ontario, formerly Upper Canada, is to have but one chamber, to be known as the "Legislative Assembly of Ontario." **1922** *Cdn Hist.Rev.* III 60: The legislative councillors had to take their pay in the honour of their position, but the members of the Legislative Assembly were not so particular. **1963** *Globe and Mail* (Toronto) 30 Jan. 5/8: An Australian attended a session of the Quebec Legislative Assembly today and set off anew the discussion over the use of the word state in referring to Quebec Province.

legislative building in each Canadian province, the building housing the legislative assembly.
1916 BRIDLE *Sons of Canada* 33: ... a portrait of Sir Wilfrid ... now hangs in the Legislative Building at Quebec. **1958** *Edmonton Jnl* 24 June 1/6: A fire which threatened the public works building annex in the Legislative Building grounds late Monday was brought under control in about 40 minutes by the city fire department.

legislative council 1 *Hist.* in colonial times, a body of persons, usually appointed by the governor to act as his advisors, first acting as a unicameral legislature and later as the upper house of a bicameral body, the lower house being an elective assembly. See also **Upper House** (def. 1a).
1789 *Quebec Herald* 13 Apr. 182/2: In February 1777 the Legislative Council convened for the purpose of framing such laws as should secure the property of the subject. **1832** BAILLIE *Account of N.B.* 126: The executive council also constitutes the legislative council, and forms some branch in the constitution of the province as the House of Lords in England.... he is assisted by an executive council of twelve, whenever he thinks proper to call from those gentlemen for their advice and opinion. **1863** *Islander* (Charlottetown) 30 Jan. 3/1: If the Conservative party wish to insure their success at the approaching Legislative Council Election, let them beware of allowing to their opponents such opportunities as we have here alluded to. **1963** MORTON *Kingdom of Can.* 183: A clear structure of government, modelled exactly ... on the British Constitution in church and state, was provided in governor, executive council, legislative council, and representative assembly to correspond with King, Privy Council, Lords, and Commons.

2 in Quebec, the upper house of the bicameral legislature, the 24 members of which are appointed for life by the government in power. See also **L.C.** (def. 2) and **Upper House** (def. 1b). Cp. **legislative assembly.**
1963 *Globe and Mail* (Toronto) 2 Mar. 9/2: The Quebec Liberal Federation's annual convention recommended abolition of Quebec's Legislative Council—only provincial upper house remaining in Canada—and unspecified pay increases for provincial cabinet ministers and members of the Legislative Assembly. **1966** *Ibid.* 2 May 5/5: The party platform [Union Nationale] calls for the abolition of Quebec's Legislative Council, the provincial Upper House, without reference to Ottawa or to the British Privy Council for the required constitutional amendments.

legislative councillor 1 *Hist.* a member of a legislative council (def. 1).
1811 *Kingston Star* (U.C.) 1 Jan. 3/3: Entreat your legislative councillors not to withhold from it their sanction. **1885** GEMMILL *Companion* 389: Legislative

Councillors in the Provinces not in future to have that title; but gentlemen who were Legislative Councillors at the time of the Union (1st July, 1867) to retain their title of Honourable for life. **1922** *Cdn Hist.Rev.* III 60: The legislative councillors had to take their pay in the honour of their position, but the members of the Legislative Assembly were not so particular.

2 in Quebec, a member of the legislative council (def. 2).
1963 *Calgary Herald* 24 Sep. 1/7: Charges of defrauding the province of Quebec were laid today against two former Union Nationale cabinet ministers, one legislative councillor and a former high-ranking civil servant.

legislature *n.* See **legislative assembly.**
1869 *Islander* (Charlottetown) 4 May 3/3: His Excellency the Lieutenant Governor, with the usual ceremonies, prorogued the Legislature on Wednesday. **1958** *Saturday Night* 26 Apr. 44/3: In Manitoba, the Legislature voted to ask Ottawa to call a conference of provincial representatives to work out a national code for liquor advertising.

le Grand Pays *Cdn French, North* See **outside,** *n.* (def. 1a).
1892 PIKE *Barren Grounds* 76: The old man was keen to hear about the doings of the white man in the Grand Pays, as the half-breeds indefinitely term the whole of the outside world. **1909** CAMERON *New North* 70: The land we have come from is known as "Outside" or "Le Grand Pays."

lehal *n.* See **lahal.**

leopard seal See **harbo(u)r seal.**
1958 CAMERON *Cdn Mammals* 55: The dark markings are responsible for another name often applied to him— "leopard seal." To most fishermen he is known as the "bay seal," but in Newfoundland he bears the unusual name "ranger."

le Petit Nord See **Petit Nord.**

les Anglais *n.pl.* See **Anglais.**

lessee post *Hist.* See **King's post** (def. 1).
1830 (1963) DAVIES *Northern Quebec* 108: . . . our guide says they were Indians from the Lessee Posts. . . .

lesser Newfoundland See quote. See also **Labrador dog** (def. 1).
1883 HATTON & HARVEY *Newfoundland* 232: It is generally admitted that there are two distinct types of the Newfoundland dog, one considerably larger than the other, and reckoned as the true breed; the other being named the Labrador, or St. John's, or Lesser Newfoundland.

lesser snow goose See **white wavey.**
1882 *Trans.Roy.Soc.Can.* I 4 51: The lesser snow-goose, which is very rare on Hudson's Bay, is more probably a distinct species. **1939** *Beaver* Mar. 18/1: In the southern wintering area, the proportion is about nine Lesser Snow Geese to seventy Blue Geese.

let pass *West, Hist.* a permit issued by the North West Mounted Police, permitting the bearer to cross the Canada-United States border.
1966 *Sask.Hist.* Spring 62: The Department of Inland Revenue prevailed upon the police to establish and operate outposts along the frontier . . . to issue "let" passes to those individuals wishing to cross from one country to the other.

leve [lɛv] *imper.v.* [< Cdn F < F *se lever* rise] *Fur Trade, Hist.* the traditional voyageur summons to awake and get ready for the trail, shouted several times by the guide.
1833 (1932) MCLEAN *Notes* 117: The guide roused the men in the morning; the moment the call is heard, "Leve, leve!" the passengers spring up upon their feet. . . . **1869** KENNICOTT *Journal* 51: Lève. Call to arouse men in morning. **1935** *Beaver* Sep. 8/1: It was a similar admonition to the "'leve, 'leve" which disturbed the short rest of the voyageurs when they were toiling up the rivers from Hudson Bay with their cargoes of supplies for interior posts.

levee† ['lɛvi] *n.* [< F *levée*] **1** in Canada, a formal reception, usually for men only, held New Year's morning by the Governor General, lieutenant-governors, and, sometimes, mayors. See also **New Year's levee.**
1844 (1955) LEFROY *Magnetic North* 69: I wish you a happy new year—la bonne Année as the Canadians say. . . . It is a day of great fête in which the gentlemen hold a kind of levée in the morning and give a dance in the evening. . . . A separate levée or drawing room is held for the ladies. . . . **1860** (1955) CRAIG *Early Travellers* 236: At 11 a levee was held at the Court-house, at which nearly 1,100 persons attended. **1960** *Ottawa Citizen* 31 Dec. 36/5: Mayor Nelms held his own levee at city hall yesterday afternoon. **1964** *Calgary Herald* 2 Jan. 8/1: A few service women . . . entered the receiving lines at some of the levees but only in Ontario was the male-only custom not held sacred.

2 a formal reception held on New Year's morning by the members of a military mess.
1964 *Calgary Herald* 2 Jan. 31/6: On New Year's morning officers of the permanent and reserve forces of the three armed services held the traditional New Year's levees.

level crossing a place where a railway line crosses a public road or highway.
1853 *Anglo-Amer.Mag.* 325/2: "Level-crossings" have always been a source of danger, and should at any cost be avoided, if possible in crowded thoroughfares. **1909** HUNTER *Simcoe County* I 202: The railway track at a level crossing in Allandale was used as a shunting yard by the railroad company and the crossing was considered to be unsafe to the travelling public. **1964** *Kingston Whig-Standard* (Ont.) 14 Sep. 1/4: A teen-age Brockville girl . . . was instantly killed at a district level crossing Sunday night when a Montreal-Toronto passenger train struck her boy friend's car.

level rail crossing See **level crossing.**
1964 *Calgary Herald* 21 July 23/3: Police said Mrs. Baker . . . saw her mother trip at a level rail crossing, went back to help her and was struck by a CNR freight.

liard ['liɚd] *n.* [< Cdn F < F "black poplar" < OF *liard* gray] *Hist.* (*except in place names*) See 1955 quote and **Balm of Gilead.**
1789 (1927) MACKENZIE *Voy.from Montreal* 73: The low land is covered with wood, such as . . . three kinds of willow, and the liard. **1806** (1960) FRASER *Letters and Journals* 224: . . . the Liard is the most stupendous I ever saw, as for any other wood or anything else. . . . **1888** (1908) MAIR *Mackenzie Basin* 478: . . . the

alluvial portion has upon it (on the river of its name and elsewhere) the "Liard," a balsam poplar, sometimes called Balm of Giliad or rough bark poplar. . . .
1955 RICH in BLACK *Journal* 149: The liard, a term . . . applicable only to *Populus deltoides* [eastern cottonwood], was evidently applied by the Canadian voyageurs to the balsam poplar (*Populus balsamifera*), which ranges from Labrador into northeastern British Columbia and down the Mackenzie, reaching its greatest size on the Peace and Liard Rivers.

Liberal *n*. **1** *Hist*. in colonial times, a member of the faction opposing the governor and his Tory followers. See also **Reformer** (def. 1).
1832 *Liberal* (St. Thomas, U.C.) 20 Sep. 3/4: We shall first notice the slanderous imputations cast upon the Liberals, that they are a discontented set of men, ever on the watch to find occasion for complaint and clamour. **1858** *Dly Colonist* (Victoria) 11 Dec. 1/4: The Tories and Liberals are working lustily for the "loaves and fishes."
2 in modern contexts, a member or supporter of the Liberal Party (def. 2).
1867 *Islander* (Charlottetown) 1 Mar. 2/6: They will have a working majority of clear grit Liberals, independently of a tail composed of "loose fish," "middle-men," or "independent members,"—varieties of an order of politicians of which Mr. Cornelius Howatt is the type. **1927** LONGSTRETH *Silent Force* 314: Ominously for the Force, the Liberals, as opposition in 1919, had criticized the Conservative policies, especially their handling of the strike, and consequently, the Force. **1963** *Kingston Whig-Standard* (Ont.) 28 Jan. 1/4: Ken Brydon [said] that the Liberals continue to play "on again, off again Finnegan" with medicare.

Liberal *adj. or attrib*. supporting, associated with, or belonging to the Liberal Party (def. 2).
1900 *Prospector* (Lillooet, B.C.) 7 Dec. 1/2: Every province but one in the recent elections has supported Laurier, and nearly all of them went more Liberal in proportion than Ontario went Conservative. **1913** (1914) BICKERSTETH *Open Doors* 229: One of the leading Liberal papers had a most caustic article on the giving of titles to Canadians, which it said must be tolerated, owing to human weakness, although it was altogether against the best interests of the country. **1958** *Sat.Night* 27 Sep. 7/1: When it was being used as a private jitney by a now-unfrocked Liberal cabinet minister, one of the government's big transport planes developed leaks in its gas tanks.

Liberal-Conservative *n. Hist*. a member or supporter of the Liberal-Conservative Party, *q.v.*
1852 *Elora Backwoodsman* (C.W.) 30 Sep. 3/2: The Inspector General is a politician of circumstances— yesterday a Tory, to-day a Reformer, to-morrow a Liberal Conservative. **1935** *Cdn Hist.Rev*. XVI 369: Over against the Liberal-Conservatives, the various groups and individuals who found themselves wandering in the wilderness of opposition gradually in their turn coalesced into a new Reform or Liberal party. . . .

Liberal-Conservative *adj. or attrib. Hist*. supporting the Liberal-Conservative Party, *q.v.*
1882 *Brandon Dly Mail* (Man.) 19 Dec. 2/1: It is needless to say that the MAIL in its political views will be Liberal Conservative. . . . **1909** *Eye Opener* (Calgary) 18 Dec. 1/6: The Conservatives should cut out the hybrid "Liberal-Conservative" title.

Liberal-Conservative Party *Hist*. a political group that developed in the last half of the nineteenth century, claiming to occupy a position between reactionary Tories and radical Reformers. See also **Liberal-Conservative**, *n*. and *adj*.
1916 *London Hist.Soc.Trans*. VII 60: The new-school conservative John A. McDonald was the leading spirit under whom the moderate reformer and the new-school conservative coalesced into what has since been known as the Liberal-Conservative party. **1953** LEBOURDAIS *Nation of North* 30: Although Liberals constituted the official opposition in parliament and in the country, the party of which Macdonald was the head, despite the obvious contradiction in terms and the fact that its membership consisted almost wholly of Conservatives, called itself the Liberal-Conservative party.

Liberal Party 1 *Hist*. in colonial times, the reform group. See also **Liberal** (def. 1) and **Clear Grit Party.**
1834 *Brit.Amer.Jnl* (St. Catharines, U.C.) 22 Apr. 3/1: Mr. Mackenzie was then considered the nominal, if not official, head of the liberal party. **1864** *Nor'Wester* (R.R.S.) 3 Aug. 4/1: The Government, with the aid of almost the entire Liberal party, of Upper Canada, has taken in hand the task of settling forever the sectional difficulties between Upper and Lower Canada.
2 in modern contexts, the political party descended from the moderate reform groups and generally considered a middle-of-the-road party in modern Canadian politics; also, any of the several related provincial parties.
1966 *Victoria Dly Times* 28 May 5/6: The usually homogeneous Liberal party is splitting up into two factions. . . .

Liberal-Progressive *n*. in Manitoba, a political party made up of a coalition of Liberals and Conservatives.
1940 MACCORMAC *Canada* 190: [This group] was elected in Manitoba in 1922 and is still there although it now calls itself Liberal-Progressive. **1958** *Edmonton Jnl* 28 June 30/1: Premier D. L. Campbell was willing to form a coalition with the CCF after his Liberal-Progressives were defeated in the June 16 Manitoba election. . . .

licensed house† *West* a hotel licensed to sell beer and liquor on complying with certain government regulations. See 1915 quote.
1915 MCCLUNG *Times Like These* 173: There was a licensed house in one of the small prairie towns, which complied with all the regulations; it had the required number of bedrooms; its windows were unscreened, the license fee was paid; the bartender was a total abstainer, and a member of the union; also said to be a man of good moral character; the proprietor regularly gave twenty-five dollars a year to the Children's Aid, and put up a cup to be competed for by the district hockey clubs. **1958** ELLIOTT *Quesnel* 34: All the amenities were there, even "gamblers and courtesans, and strange to say, one of the latter keeps a licensed house."

lick† *n*. **1** See **salt spring.**
1825 (1832) PICKERING *Inquiries* 49: Deer will go miles to the salt spring, or "licks" as they are called.
2 See **salt lick** (def. 2).
1832 MCGREGOR *Brit.Amer*. II 556n: Buffalo, or deer licks, are prairies or marshes rendered salt by the overflowing of numerous salt springs; both buffalo and deer resort to them for the purpose of licking the salt off the shrubs hence the name *lick*. **1957** *Beaver*

Summer 37/2: ... the goat evidently was headed for the same lick from which the sheep were returning.

licking place

licking place *Obs.* See **salt lick** (def. 2).
1784 PENNANT *Arctic Zoology* 30: Such spots are called *licking-places*.

licorice (root) *n.* See 1955 quote. See also **maso.** Also spelled *liquorice* (*root*).
1789 (1801) MACKENZIE *Voy. from Montreal* 89: On the upper part of the beach, liquorice grew in great abundance and it was now in blossom. **1821** (1823) FRANKLIN *Journey* 378: Dr. Richardson found ... a large quantity of the liquorice root of Mackenzie (*hedysarum*) which is common on these shores. ...
1955 ADTIC *Glossary*: liquorice-root, *n.* a perennial herb, *Heydysarum alpinum,* 1 to 2 feet high, having erect, branching leafy stems, odd-pinnate leaves, and half-inch thick, sweet, carrot-tasting, edible root tubers. It occurs in the Arctic along river and lake shores. Also called "masu."

lieutenant-governor† *n.* **1** *Hist.* in colonial times, the chief executive officer in a colony or province, subordinate to the governor general.
1766 *Quebec Gaz.* 24 Nov. 3/1: His Excellency, and General Carleton, Lieutenant-Governor of Quebec, were each attended by several Gentlemen from their respective Governments. **1832** BAILLIE *Acct of N.B.* 126: ... forms part of the general government of the North American provinces, being included in the Governor-General's commission; but, except when he is present in the Province, the Lieutenant-Governor, who is appointed to the command of New Brunswick by a separate commission, is in every respect a governor.... **1878** *Sask. Herald* (Battleford, N.W.T.) 30 Dec. 2/3: Among the Hallowe'en pranks at Winnipeg a live pig was hoisted on a flag-staff at the residence of Lieutenant-Governor Cauchon.

2 in modern contexts, the official head of a provincial government, appointed by the Governor-General-in-Council for a term of five years to act as the representative of the Crown.
1869 *Islander* (Charlottetown) 4 May 3/3: His Excellency the Lieutenant Governor, with the usual ceremonies, prorogued the Legislature on Wednesday. **1966** *Globe and Mail* (Toronto) 15 Jan. 8/8: The perils of Government House, one of Alberta's most intriguing tales, may have its finale written by ... the new Lieutenant-Governor.

lieutenant-governor-in-council *n.* the executive government of a province, considered as the lieutenant-governor acting with the advice and consent of the provincial cabinet. Cp. **governor-general-in-council.**
[**1796** (1905) *Ont. Bur. Arch. Rep.* III cxii: Others of the said applicants who have received orders of Councils preparatory to his Majesty's grant under the seal of the Province, subject to the terms aforesaid, from the Lieutenant-governor in Council, have sinfully perverted his Majesty's most gracious intentions signified in the proclamation aforesaid.] **1871** *Wkly Manitoban* 15 July 2/4: It was provided that the Board of Education should have power to alter and subdivide with the sanction of the Lieutenant-Governor-in-Council, and school district established by that Act. **1915** *Eye Opener* (Calgary) 12 June 4/1: The Lieutenant Governor in Council (viz., the political party in power) will appoint vendors and establish them wherever advisable throughout the Province. **1937** *Memorandum* 5: The Provisions of this Acct referring to the Lieutenant-Governor in Council shall be construed as referring to the Lieutenant-Governor

of the Province acting by and with the Advice of the Executive Council [i.e. Cabinet] therefore.

life-line *n.* *West* a stout rope running from a settler's house to his stable, necessary during blizzards as a guide and support.
1912 POCOCK *Man in the Open* 133: This morning, after rigging a life-line to the stable because of this continuing blizzard, I went to the lady's home. **1934** BETTANY *Valley of Lost Gold* 77: "After supper I'll get some cordwood piled on the veranda, and run a life-line out to the stable. Best give Snowman a three-day ration. ..."

lift *n.* **1** *Fur Trade, Hist.* See **pose** (def. 2).
1824 (1931) SIMPSON *Fur Trade* 62: The Portage ... is crossed in two poses or lifts.... **1929** (1931) MERK *Fur Trade* 11: Such a load was carried by the voyageur at a kind of a dog trot, by "poses" or "lifts" of 500 to 800 yards if the portage was a long one.

2 *Obs.* See quotes.
1853 STRICKLAND *Canada West* I 89: Land speculators would employ a third party to perform their settlement duties, all they required to obtain the deed or "lift" as it is called in Canadian parlance, was the sworn certificate for cutting the road allowances, and the payment of certain fees to Government. **1963** GUILLET *Pioneer Farmer* I 277: And as a result of this racketeering collaboration the men received their pay, the speculator his deed or lift as it was commonly called, and the forest lot remained practically in a state of nature.

light boat See **light canoe** (def. 2).

light canoe *Fur Trade, Hist.* **1** See 1952 quote.
1791 (1947) *Beaver* Dec. 11/2: ... I consented to his departure, in consequence of which I made one light canoe serve us to come down. **1804** (1897) COUES *New Light* I 249: Payet arrived in a light canoe. **1952** (1954) JENNINGS *Strange Brigade* 146: In addition to these were the demi-canot, or half canoe, which might be twenty feet long and carried a crew of four to six, and the light canoe which ran from ten to fifteen feet long, and was generally used by the Indians to transport themselves and their families.

2 See **express canoe.** Also *light boat.*
1798 (1964) CHABOILLEZ *Journal* 216: Mr. Thorburn set off ... for the Grand Portage in a light Canoe. **1807** (1930) FRASER *Letters* 156: ... it may go out to headquarters in the light canoe. *a*1855 (1956) ROSS *Fur Hunters* 200: A light canoe ... leaving the Pacific reaches Montreal in a hundred days ... thus performing a journey of many thousand miles, without delay, stoppage, or scarcely any repose, in the short period of little more than six months. **1929** MOBERLY *When Fur Was King* 84: We were much disappointed not to see the "old boss," Chief Factor William Sinclair, aboard the light-boat. **1931** NUTE *Voyageur* 25: Ordinarily, however, a "light canoe" was merely one dispatched without freight.

3 See **North canoe.**
1828 (1872) MCDONALD *Peace River* 1: ... the crews of two "Light Canoes," consisting of nine men each.... **1872** *Ibid.* 41n: Light Canoes—specially made and adapted for speediest travel ... were generally known under the name of "North Canoes"....

lighten *v.* *Obs.* make a décharge (def. 2).
1829 (1947) SIMPSON *Dispatch* 34: The whole of these Rapids we shot down, and only lightened at two of

them, where it was necessary to run altho' dangerous, as there was no possibility of making a portage. . . . **1830** (1963) DAVIES *Northern Quebec* 108: . . . ran twelve strong rapids, two of which we lightened at. . . .

lightening place *Obs.* See **décharge** (def. 1).
1827 (1912) ERMATINGER *Express Jnl* 95: [We] then make the Upper Portage and a lightening place which hold us till about noon. **1852** RICHARDSON *Arctic Exped.* 63: Afterward we passed the lightening-place of the Rapid River, and encamped five or six miles further on, at half-past eight o'clock.

light-jack *n. Obs.* See **jacklight,** *n.* (def. 1).
1859 (1925) KANE *Wanderings* 21: . . . the strong red glare of the blazing pine knots and roots in the iron frame, or light-jack, at the bow of the canoe. . . . **1903** CONANT *Life in Canada* 137: See how their forms are increased in size until they look like veritable giants in the haze of the blazing light-jack.

light wagon *Hist.* a one-horse vehicle having two seats in front and a space for light freight in the back.
1836 (1923) JAMESON *Rambles* 121: At Hamilton I hired a light *wagon* as they call it, a sort of gig perched in the middle of a wooden tray wherein my baggage was stowed. . . . **1880** GORDON *Mountain and Prairie* 255: The light waggon . . . [and] the two-horse spring waggon similar to the ordinary "democrat" waggon of Ontario, and the double buck-board are the greatest favourites, **1909** BINDLOSS *Lorimer* 91: Some of our horses are not much to look at, and others are hard to drive, but the way they can haul the light wagons or even the humble ground sleigh along league after league would surprise those not used to them.

lily-pad ice *North* See quote.
1958 *Manice* 5: Small cakes up to about 18 inches in diameter are occasionally called *Lily Pad Ice.*

lime-heap *n. Obs.* a great heap of logs surmounted by a frame holding broken pieces of limestone which were rendered into lime when the logs were set on fire, a by-product of the burn (def. 1) in land clearing.
1853 STRICKLAND *Canada West* I 97: My first step towards it was to build a lime-heap.

limit *n.* (*usually plural*) See **timber limit** (def. 1a).
1836 *Bytown* [Ottawa] *Gaz.* 21 July 2/5: They entered into an agreement to effect the necessary improvements for the passage of timber . . . far beyond where others had previously obtained limits near the mouth. **1881** *Edmonton Bull.* 3 Dec. 2/1: Limits are sold at the rate of $20 per square mile as bonus, $2 per square mile as rental, and five percent royalty on all timber cut and sold. **1964** *Cdn Geog.Jnl* Feb. 63/3: In the fall the teams would move up the line toward the limits where the camboose camp was being built for the winter.

line *n.* **1 a.** See **tracking line.**
1794 (1929) MCGILLIVRAY *Journal* 18: [We] mounted the Grand Rapid by the line without accident. **1872** MCDONALD *Peace River* 44n: A descent of over three feet per mile in the river flow generally requires the line. **1955** STEPHEN *Winged Canoes* 218: They pulled the rope over their shoulders and so towed the boat by "line."
b. *Local* See quote. Cp. **head of the line.**

1940 *Beaver* June 28: It should be explained that this part of the [Mackenzie] river is called "the line" because, in the days before steamers, the scows, boats and canoes had to be tracked upstream with tow-lines.
2 the border, *q.v.,* between Canada and the United States. See also **lines** (def. 3).
1812 *Kingston Gaz.* (U.C.) 28 Jan. 2/2: . . . we may therefore conclude that those who have set up the war-whoop, on the other side of the line, have yet the trade to learn. **1860** *Brit.Colonist* (Victoria) 12 Jan. 2/1: But why is the British Columbian settler to pay double for land worth no more than that on the other side of the line? **1962** *Field, Horse & Rodeo* Nov. 32/3: "I never saw a horse like him," marvelled a rider from across the line, "Kickers or whirlers or straight buckers are all the same to him."

3 a. *Obs.* See **lines** (def. 2).
b. a settlement road in Upper Canada, especially one identified with settlers of a certain origin. See 1896 quote.
1828 *Brockville Gaz.* (U.C.) 26 Dec. 3/4: . . . a teamster by the name of M'Pherson from the Scotch line, lost his span of horses and sleigh on Tuesday last. . . . **1853** (1959) MOODIE *Life in Clearings* 202: George Desne . . . lived about three miles from the clearing known as the English line. [**1896** GOURLAY *Hist.Ottawa* 21: . . . the line of settlement went on merely as a line, not spreading out till long afterwards, so that as the land pleased them they sat down beside one another on both sides of the line rather than go back from it. The line was prolonged with settlers into Bristol, which was chiefly taken up by Scotchman.] **1961** PRICE & KENNEDY *Renfrew* 110: McNaughton's Plan of 1836 shows Queen's Line as an opened road. **1965** *Globe and Mail* (Toronto) 12 Jan. 7/3: True, there are highly visible shack-towns . . . the French Line up in Lanark and, over a larger area of the Shield, the Ozarks of Ontario. **1966** *Weekend Mag.* 16 July 28/2: Their murder was the climax to a feud that raged among the Irish immigrants along the Roman Line of Biddulph township [near London, Ont.]

c. a road, especially one built through the bush.
☛ *Probably a reduction of* **line of road,** *as in:*
1832 MCGREGOR *Brit.Amer.* II 257: Another line of road . . . was pointed out . . . as a great military road from Halifax to Quebec.
☛ *This usage seems commonest in areas of Irish and Scots settlement and may derive from older dialectal usage in the British Isles. See* W. Kirwin, "Lines . . . in Newfoundland Names," American Speech (*Oct., 1965*), 163-5.
1830 MOORSOM *Letters N.S.* 344: The greater part of this line is either a rough horsepath, or in the same state as that described under the name of a "new cut." **1832** MCGREGOR *Brit.Amer.* II 257: This line would be a continuation of the road from Halifax to the bend of the River Petit Coudiac, thence to the gulf coast. . . . **1947** SAUNDERS *Algonquin* 52: Whatever they could produce was easy to market, and if they didn't want to farm they could work farther up the line on the timber limits, which are now inside the Park boundaries.

4 a.† *Hist.* a line of blazed trees, stakes or cairns marking the boundary of a concession, lot, or other surveyed piece of land. See also **concession line** (def. 1).
1833 (1926) LANGTON *Early U.C.* 18: We found it almost impossible to ascertain our exact position, for the blazes which denote the lines of the lots and concessions are obliterated by time—if they were ever properly marked. **1846** (1927) DICKIE *How Canada GrewUp* 161: Each settler was allowed to cut down

the timber on that part of the line which adjoined his lot. **1954** RADDALL *Muster of Arms* 39: "Years ago," he said, "I worked for a summer in the bush with a survey party, cutting lines."

b. *Ont.* See **concession road.**
1863 WALSHE *Cedar Creek* 103: They wished even for the corduroy expedient a little farther on, when the line became encumbered with stumps left from the underbrushing.... **1924** (1933) SLATER *Yellow Briar* 172: ... this grain was hauled down the 6th line and stored till the spring in Isaac Chafee's warehouse at Tullamore. **1963** *Globe and Mail* (Toronto) 9 May 5/1: A 67-year old retired farmer was found dead ... yesterday when a neighbor called at their cottage on the 12th Line of Brooke Township....

5 See **trapline** (def. 1).
1853 REID *Young Voyageurs* 190: Moreover, he [the wolverine] will follow the tracks of the trapper from one to another, until he has destroyed the whole line. **1872** DASHWOOD *Chiploquorgan* 109: We followed an old "sable line" ... a line of traps set for that animal. **1946** FERGUSON *Mink, Mary and Me* 78: We paddled fifteen miles further upriver, and there, where a turbulent creek empties into Horn River from the west or mountain side, we built another small line cabin. **1964** *Calgary Herald* 22 July 17/7: During the slim years ... trappers left their lines and sought employment in business and industry.

6 a.† *Football* the seven players ranged along the line of scrimmage at the beginning of each down.
1912 WHITE *Wildcatters* 15: He bucked the line in fine shape. But it wasn't the full back or the scrimmage either. If the quarter had been right, it would have been different. **1960** *Weekend Mag.* 9 Jan. 27/2: And like a line plunger, he just whirled and crushed through the guests toward the door.

b. in hockey and lacrosse, the line of three forwards.
1966 *Hockey News* 9 Apr. 4/3: The line of Jean Beliveau, Claude Provost and Gilles Tremblay figures to remain intact.

7 See 1953 quote. See also **main line** (def. 2).
1907 HUNTER *Cdn Wilds* 19: They [smalltime "free-traders"] could almost always "dead-head" their way up the line on a construction train. **1938** *Beaver* 19 Sep. 20/2: Part of the way to "the line" I pulled my outfit on a handsled. **1953** LOWER *Voyages* 14: ... provincial policemen carefully inspected the men who were going up to "the line" (transcontinental railway then being built, now the northern line of the Canadian National).

8 the rope by which sled-dogs are hitched to a sled, often made of rawhide.
1951 BULIARD *Inuk* 257: We tried Chasseur, who was ... now back on the line and pulling like a Trojan....

line *v.* **1** *Lumbering, Obs.* mark a log for cutting into square timber, *q.v.* See also **line-mark** and **liner.**
1853 STRICKLAND *Canada West* II 280n: Taking off the bark [rossing] a few inches in width along the entire length of the trunk on the space that is to be lined, so that the black mark may be more distinctly seen by the scorers. **1854** KEEFER *Ottawa* 64: Three men and a cook form a "gang";—two cut down the tree, *line* and *score* it, that is, split out the outer slabs so as to make it four-sided....

2 engage in tracking (def. 1). See also **line through** and **lining.** Cp. **line down** and **line up.**

1924 *Beaver* Aug. 412: The remainder of the crew were lining a loaded York boat up the Athabasca river.... **1961** *Cdn Geog.Jnl* July 3: Attacking a rapid upstream, the voyageurs would ... paddle the canoe, "demi-charge," line or pole the canoe, make a "décharge," or portage.

line down draw or haul a canoe downstream. See also **line,** *v.* (def. 2).
1907 MILLAIS *Newfoundland* 305: Several times they packed everything for a mile or two, but negotiated most of the worst rapids by 'lining' down them, whilst one man kept the nose of the canoe straight with a long spruce pole. **1948** ONRAET *Sixty Below* 37: The skiff was too heavy for carrying, and to line it down as we had done in the rapids above was impossible, owing to a huge rock jutting out at a sharp angle from the shore. **1963** *Beaver* Autumn 22: Rapids after rapids disappeared behind us and where there was any doubt, we waded the shallows and lined the canoes down with ropes rather than portage.

line fence† a fence on a property line, as between two farms or next to the road allowance.
1893 YOUNG *Indian Wigwams* 34: One morning I arose very early and went off to help a couple of Indians about their line fences. **1954** BRUCE *Channel Shore* 12: From there a person could look east and west along the northern fields ... separated by line fences....

line-horse *n.* *Lumbering, Hist.* a horse used in skidding logs from the cutting area to the landing.
1906 *Log of the "Columbia"* June 7/1: "I've been swamper, line-horse man and riggan-slinger for this layout for over 8 years an' now when a chanst comes along to get on hook-tender, they put on a bloomin' blue nose, who hasn't been on the coast over a year." **1943** SWANSON *Lumberjack* 24: ... the line-horse days had gone beyond recall....

line-mark *n.* *Lumbering, Obs.* the mark made by the liner, *q.v.* See also **line,** *v.* (def. 1).
1853 STRICKLAND *Canada West* II 281: One man then cuts a row of notches as deep into the side of the tree as the line-mark will allow, or nearly so, between two and three feet apart....

line of road See **line,** *n.* (def. 3c).

line post *Fur Trade* a fur post close to a railway line. See also **line,** *n.* (def. 7).
1921 *Beaver* Mar. 16/1: ... even now Long Lake cannot be classed as a "line post," owing to the distance of two miles from the station.... **1931** *Ibid.* June 255/1: ... visiting at North Bay ... besides visiting the "line" posts on the C.N.R., belonging to Superior-Huron district. **1961** *Chatelaine* Mar. 61/1: I guess "roughing" is the right word to describe the year we started at the line post of Nakina....

liner *n.* *Lumbering, Obs.* See quotes. See also **line,** *v.* (def. 1).
1853 STRICKLAND *Canada West* II 280: As soon as the tree is felled, a person, called a liner, rosses and lines the tree on each side, and the axe-men cut the top of the tree off, at the length determined on by the liner.... **1863** WALSHE *Cedar Creek* 217: Immediately on its fall, the 'liner' commenced to chop away the bark for a few inches wide all along the trunk before marking with charcoal where the axes were to hew in squaring the timber....

line rider *West, Hist.* a horseman patrolling the Canada-U.S. border to head off whisky-traders, rustlers, and other undesirables.
1910 HAYDON *Riders of Plains* 305: The "line riders," whether Mounted Policemen or special men engaged by stock-owners for this service, have plenty to do in frustrating their wiles.

lines *n.pl.* **1** *Obs.* the outer limit of a town; the open area at the edge of a town.
1792 (1911) SIMCOE *Diary* 83: After church we repaired to the lines with Mr. Talbot. . . .
2 *Obs.* the strips of settlement in the back country, *q.v.* See also **back settlement.** Cp. **line** (def. 3b).
1811 *Cdn Courant* (Montreal) 28 Jan. 3/2: A grant was made by the Provincial Parliament, three or four years ago, to enable a number of persons to open a Turnpike Road from St. John to Pike River and through St. Armand to the Lines. **1816** MARSDEN *Narrative* 100: [There was not] another Methodist preacher in the whole province, save good old Mr. M'Coll, who, living upon the *lines*, seldom or never quitted his mission. . . . **1822** (1960) MCCULLOCH *Stepsure Letters* 26: . . . he had excellent plaster upon his lot, [so] it would be easy for him, when he had nothing else to do, to build a vessel which would carry it to the Lines.
3 *Hist.* See **line,** *n.* (def. 2).
1870 *Cdn Illust.News* 4 June 482/2: On the 25th of May the Fenians . . . crossed the lines . . . and attempted to effect a lodgement near Pigeon Hill. . . . **1922** *Cdn Hist.Rev.* III 38: . . . Prevost states . . . it being near the lines, they could defend the frontier in case of future attack.

linesman *n.* *Hockey* an official who assists the referee by calling offsides and certain other infractions of the rules.
1955 *Globe and Mail* (Toronto) 31 Jan. 19/1: . . . Flaman tried desperately to break loose from linesman Bill Roberts, who had put the clutch on the rampaging Bruin defenseman. **1963** *Ibid.* 22 Apr. 18/1: Does it occur to the average fan that referees and linesmen skate 60 minutes every game?

line through See **line,** *v.* (def. 2).
1929 JOHNSTON *Beyond Rockies* 175: . . . Some "ride" the rapids, I believe . . . we "lined" the boat through. **1956** EVANS *Mountain Dog* 44: When the ledge was covered, the water was too deep for poling, and a canoe must be lined through.

line up draw or haul a canoe upstream. See also **line,** *v.* (def. 2).
1912 FOOTNER *New Rivers* 125: No one has ever descended it alive, but there is a tradition that a party of Iroquois Indians in the "company's" employ once lined a boat up. **1953** LEBOURDAIS *Nation of North* 44: The hardy voyageurs who paddled or lined the heavily-laden canoes up the streams and carried their loads over the numerous portages were nearly all *Canadiens,* but no *Canadien* trader was tolerated.

line-up† *n.* a line of persons waiting with a common objective, such as buying tickets.
☛ *The usual North American term, as opposed to British* **queue.**
1912 (1914) BICKERSTETH *Open Doors* 172: Guess I'm in the line up for hell all right—with no return ticket either. **1955** *Globe and Mail* (Toronto) 31 Jan. 13/4:

There will be a long line-up of guests so you can't miss going to the right place.

ling† *n.* **1** See **loche.**
1905 (1956) *B.C.Hist.Qtly* July-Oct. 179: There are whitefish, ling and varieties of trout in the waters. . . . **1956** LEECHMAN *Native Tribes* 345: LING—A fish, common in Canada, used by the Indians for food.

2 See **ling cod.**
1964 *Cdn Geog.Jnl* Mar. 92/1: The early Indians too, made good use of the ling's inquisitive nature in their cod fishery.

ling cod *West Coast* a species of cod, *Ophiodon elongatus,* native to the North Pacific.
1955 DAWSON *Ahoy There!* 205: Besides salmon, we catch cod . . . ling-cod of up to (in our case) twelve pounds. **1964** *Cdn Geog.Jnl* Mar. 91/3: This is particularly true in the case of the ling cod, the spear-fisherman's favourite quarry. . . .

lining *n.* See **tracking** (def. 1). See also **line,** *v.* (def. 2).
1955 STEPHEN *Winged Canoes* 218: He explained that "lining" meant dragging a canoe along by a rope. **1967** *Cdn Geog.Jnl* May 158/3: In lining a canoe, whether upstream or down, both bow and stern lines are used.

link [lɪŋk] *n. Dial.* See **lynx.**
☛ *A common form among trappers in the Northwest, a back-formation from* **lynx** [lɪŋks] *to form an unhistorical singular.*
1896 RUSSELL *Far North* 240: . . . in the Great Slave Lake region . . . the "pishew" or "link" was by no means common. **1920** FOOTNER *Fur-Bringers* 1: "How many link skins in the bale you made up, to-day?" asked Peter Minot. **1966** ST. PIERRE *Quarter Horse* 84: ". . . let's go into the link money." In the long previous winter Rappaport had trailed and treed four lynx which Smith had shot, skinned and sold.

linx *n.* See **lynx.**

lion *n.* See **cougar.**
1914 RADIN *Myths of the Ojibwa* 18: Once Nenebojo was out hunting. He was hunting for lions and beaver. **1962** *B.C.Digest* Oct. 45/1: In every-day language the species is known as cougar, puma, painter, panther, mountain lion, catamount and simply lion.

liquor commission in a territory, a regulatory body having functions similar to those of a liquor control board, *q.v.,* in a province.
1954 *North Star* (Yellowknife) Apr. 2/1: He is NOT responsible for the patronage appointment of a Territorial Liquor Commissioner, nor for the bureaucratic set-up of the new liquor commission.

liquor control board a government board regulating the distribution and sale of alcoholic beverages within a province.
1966 *Victoria Dly Times* 28 May 18/1: [Advert.] This advertisement is not published or displayed by the Liquor Control Board or by the Government of British Columbia.

liquorice *n.* See **licorice.**

liquor store an outlet for the sale of liquor, beer, and wines, operated by the liquor control board of a province or the liquor commission of a territory. See also **government liquor store.**
1939 GROVE *Two Generations* 39: "Anyone of the fellows around here will sell you his seed and take the proceeds

to the liquor store." **1964** *Calgary Herald* 24 July 23/2: A liquor store on the site would devalue residential property to the immediate west.

lisse *n.* [< F] *Obs.* See 1897 quote.
1804 (1933) FARIES *Diary* 223: Amelle finished the lises of 90 Canoes. Fn.: The French expression for the ribs of a vessel is *lisses*. **1805** (1930) FRASER *Journal* 132: Before the Canoes were dry and *liehes* [sic] put upon one of them it was late so that the last of them gummed wet. **1897** COUES *New Light* Index: Lisses are certain strakes of woodwork about a birch-bark canoe, as distinguished from the *varangues* or flooring.

little-chief (hare)† *n.* See **pika.**
1896 RUSSELL *Far North* vi: The timid squeak of the little chief hare was often heard, but, owing to its wariness only one specimen was obtained. **1908** MAIR *Mackenzie Basin* 251: Indians informed Mr. Ross that little-chief hares were common in the mountains of the Liard River.... **1960** *Cdn Audubon* Jan.-Feb. 28/3: The industrious little pika has yet another name, the Indian name, "Little Chief Hare."

Little Company *Fur Trade, Hist.* See quotes. See also **pottie** (def. 1) and **X.Y. Company.**
1889-90 MASSON *Les Bourgeois* 389n: [Potties] Name given in the Athabasca district to the people of the X.Y. Company,—the "Little Company,"—by their opponents. **1897** COUES *New Light* I 233n: The "X.Y. Co." [was] also styled in derision the "Little Company."....

Little Emperor *Fur Trade, Hist.* Sir George Simpson (d. 1860), Governor of the Hudson's Bay Co. from 1826 to 1860.
1860 (1934) *Beaver* Dec. 51/1-2: "The little Emperor's light has gone out," wrote chief Trader Dugald MacTavish, "Just after he basked in a final blaze of glory." *Ibid.* Dec. 35/1: ... his elder brother ... may very well have driven the "Little Emperor" in his dog carriole.

Little Haymaker See **pika.**
1966 *Modern Instructor* Sep. 40: From where he sat, Joey could see the Little Haymakers (a name often given to the Rocky Mountain Pika) nipping off mosses and lichens which grew at the edge of broken rocks.

little Mac(k) *Obs.* William Lyon Mackenzie, 1795-1861 (a derogatory allusion to his small stature). Cp. **Knight of the Red Wig.**
1832 *Patriot and Farmer's Monitor* (Kingston, U.C.) 27 Mar. 1/2: Little Mac, fell ... like a cat—on all fours, and the wig went under the bench—the little man gathered himself up, picked up his wig, and ran for his life. **1834** *Brit.Amer.Jnl* (St. Catharines, U.C.) 22 Apr. 2/5: How annoying it must be ... to the muckle rampart boys of Toronto, to see his lordship little Mack ... seated on the throne ... as King William the First. **1836** *St.Catharines Jnl* (U.C.) 7 Jan. 3/2: "And little Mac may burn his ain 'Canawl' [Quesnel tobacco], "His grievance budget, fiery wig, and all."

little parliament *Obs.* See quote.
1843 *Statesman* (Kingston, C.W.) 12 July 1/4: In Western Canada [i.e. in Western Ontario], the Municipal Councils are familiarly termed among the people, "little parliaments," and there certainly is much in their organization of a Parliamentary character.

Little Potties *Fur Trade, Obs.* See **pottie.**
1800 (1889) MCKENZIE *Journal* 395: The Crees went and encamped before the Little Potties who borrowed fish this day of an old Montagner woman.

little red fish See **kokanee.**
1907 LAMBERT *Fishing in B.C.* 62: There is another smaller form of the sockeye salmon, found in many of the interior waters, that appears to be a permanently small form which is known to writers as "the little red fish." **1965** *Wildlife Rev.* Mar. 17: KOKANEE, LITTLE REDFISH or KICKININEE of catchable sizes are familiar to many anglers.

Little Rockies *Obs.* See quote.
1878 *Sask.Herald* (Battleford, N.W.T.) 18 Nov. 2/2: About the same time a prominent Blackfoot chief was killed at the head of Sheep Creek, among the Little Rockies or Foot Hills, by the Mountain Assiniboines.

little sticks *North* the stunted trees on the edge of the barrens. See also **Land of Little Sticks.**
*c*1902 LAUT *Trapper* 266: The regular Northern hunters do not go so far as the Arctics, but choose their hunting-ground somewhere in the region of "little sticks." **1947** *Beaver* Dec. 26/1: The far Northern part of Manitoba, where the forests peter out into the "little sticks" on the edge of the barrens, is inhabited mainly by a few bands of Chipewyan Indians.... **1956** MOWAT *Lost in Barrens* 238: ... big generous fires were a source of surprise and pleasure to them after the "little sticks" of the Barrens.

Little York *Hist.* York, U.C., now Toronto, Ont.
☛ *This epithet was, like Muddy York, q.v., often used contemptuously in colonial times.*
1822 *Wkly Register* (York [Toronto]) 20 June 92/3: There is one hint, however, we wish to give Mr. W. Patton ... which is, that although there may be many "Little" York's in the United States, we know of no place labled "Little York," in Canada, and beg that he will bear that little circumstance in his recollection, when he again addresses us. **1885** HAIGHT *Country Life* 51: Father drove him twice to Little York one winter, a distance of over one hundred and fifty miles, accomplishing the trip both times inside of a week. **1955** COLLARD *Cdn Yesterdays* 67: The danger became too much for ... Shaver, a member of the provincial parliament, who was on his way to attend a session in Little York.

live off the country (or land) *Esp.North* subsist on the food available in a region, as game, fish, berries.
1913 FOOTNER *Jack Chanty* 68: The Indians ... live off the land during the summer. **1914** DOUGLAS *Lands Forlorn* 8: The Indians have proved that one can live off the country, but it keeps them busy hunting and fishing from one year's end to another, ever following the movements of the game. **1944** *Beaver* Dec. 6/2: At times they were near starvation, for they lived "off the country" and were entirely dependent on the goodwill of the Indians.... **1966** *Globe and Mail* (Toronto) 5 Jan. 25/3: Eskimos in the area [Boothia Peninsula] live off the land.

live on the country (or land) See **live off the country.**
1942 TWOMEY & HERRICK *Needle to North* 56: They were said to live largely on the country, hunting ptarmigan and catching fish. **1953** LOWER *Voyages* 31: There were no human beings within fifty miles, but the dogs, living on the country, were fat as butter. **1965** SYMINGTON *Tuktu* 43: Without this wild reindeer

the country would be uninhabitable by Eskimos and
Indians living "on the land"....

livere *n.* See **liveyere.**

liveyere† ['lɪvjɑ] *n.* [see note below] Also spelled
liv(i)er(e), livyer, Liveyere, etc. *Nfld Dial.* **1** a
permanent resident of the coast of Labrador, as
opposed to the fishermen coming from
Newfoundland for the fishing season. See also
planter (def. 2d). Cp. **floater** (def. 2a),
Labradorman (def. 1), **longshoreman,** and
winterer (def. 1).
☞ *Although usually regarded as* <live here, *this term
may be* <livier < *OF* livree (*cp.* livery), *formerly in
English villages a manorial worker having certain
hereditary rights to a cottage and a small piece of land,
thus being regarded as a permanent resident.*
1905 DUNCAN *Grenfell's Parish* 71: The 'liveyeres' of
the north dwell in huts, in lonely coves of the bays,
remote even from neighbours as ill-cased as
themselves; there they live and laugh and love and
suffer and die and bury their dead—alone. **1912** POCOCK
Man in the Open 3: She's married a sailorman before
the mast, a Liveyere from the Labrador....
1924 MATHEWS *Wilfred Grenfell* 60: It shows how
different the life of Labrador is winter and summer to
recall that only four thousand people live on the
Labrador all the year round (liveyeres, they are called,
of whom about seventeen hundred are Eskimo), while
in summer there are about twenty-five thousand people
on her coasts. **1947** TANNER *Outlines* II 727: The
resident white fishermen of the outer coast are mostly
known under the title liveyeres, a West of England
word supposed to be a corruption of "live here". On
the southern coast a distinction is also made between
liveyeres, English-speaking, semi-settled fishermen[,]
and *habitants,* semi-settled fishermen who speak French.
The former are also termed "planters" or "settlers."
1964 JENNESS *Eskimo Admin.* II 98:... there is
developing a pattern of life similar to that... of most
"liveyers" in southern Labrador....

2 (by extension) a permanent resident of the
isolated outports (def. 1) of Newfoundland or the
North Shore of the Gulf of St. Lawrence.
1946 TAYLOR *Newfoundland* 13: Around 1700 of the
settlers (known as 'liviers') had built their huts as
far north as the Bay of Exploits; and Fogo and
Twillingate were new fishing centres. **1958**
HARRINGTON *Sea Stories* 37: They were just four
miles from Cape St. John where some "liveyers"
(resident families) lived; only six miles from the little
settlement of Shoe Cove. **1963** *Globe and Mail* (Toronto)
5 Sep. 16/2: There are two Kingston-born sisters on
the upper St. Lawrence who have been chipping away
at the primitive conditions among the Liveyeres since
1930.

livier(e) *n.* See **liveyere.**

living-house *n.* of the several houses built by a
muskrat, the one he sleeps in. See also
muskrat house.
1956 KEMP *Northern Trader* 57: Among the reeds and
the rushes, he indicated several muskrat houses,
pointing out the three varieties—the living-house, the
feeding-house, and the little "pushup" wherein the
muskrat would come to sun himself in the warmer
days.

living wanigan See **caboose** (def. 5a). See also
wanigan (def. 3b).
1949 *Report of DME Test Team* I 1: This convoy
consisted of three D-6 Caterpillars and two TD-14
International Tractors, each towing trains of two
10-ton Cargo Sleighs and one 10-ton Living Wannegan,
or three 10-ton Cargo Sleighs.

livre† ['livɑ *or* 'livrə] *n.* [< F] *Hist.* **1** an old
French unit of currency used in New France and in
Quebec for some time after the advent of the
British regime. See also **Montreal livre.**
1703 (1956) INNIS *Fur Trade* 62:... they are paid in
French livres, which are twenty Sols, whereas a *Canada*
livre is but fifteen sols. **1820** (1963) DAVIES *Northern
Quebec* 56:... some wolves were black for which the
Canadian traders gave 10 MB (i.e. livres). **1927** DICKIE
How Canada Grew Up 91: One of the most efficient of
the early women teachers, who died in 1897 at the age
of ninety-four years, taught school for four livres (a
livre is about 16½ cents) a week. **1964** TAYLOR *Cdn
Coins* 19: In Canada, the sol had a value of about one
penny, 20 sols making one livre, the 12 denier piece
being equivalent to one sol.

2 See **North West livre.**
1761 (1901) HENRY (Elder) *Travels* 187: Beaver... was
worth, at Michilimackinac, two shillings and sixpence a
pound, in the currency of that place; that is six livres,
or a dollar. **1806** (1960) FRASER *Letters and Journals*
182: Hired Wananshish for the term of six years at the
rate of 300 livres per annum. **1930** *Cdn Hist.Rev.* XI
130: Grand Portage currency was reckoned as twelve
livres to the pound.

livyere *n.* See **liveyere.**

loach [lotʃ] *n.* [< Cdn F] See **loche.**
1952 WILSON *Chibougamau* 82: They had caught a
loach (petit barbot) near the shoreline....

loaded ice *N.S., Obs.* See quote.
1845 LYELL *Travels* II 146: In Nova Scotia the term
"loaded ice" is in common use for large sheets of ice
several acres in area, which are sometimes floated off
from the rivers as the tide rises, with sedge and other
salt-marsh plants frozen into their lower surfaces; also
with mud adhering plentifully to their roots.

loader *n. Lumbering* See 1942 quote.
1942 HAIG-BROWN *Timber* 252: LOADER. Loads logs
from the landing on to the cars. Normally a crew of one
head and two second loaders, working to a close
routine, keeps pace with the logs brought in by one
yarding machine. When yarding from a cold-deck pile
at the rate of forty to sixty loads a day two crews are
used, each consisting of one head and one second
loader. These alternate through the day, spelling each
other off. **1963** MCKINNON *Forest Activities 1* 7: After
the logs have been yarded to the "side," a loader places
the tongs on the log at a point somewhat behind its
centre of gravity.

loading timber *Lumbering, Obs.* See quotes.
1854 KEEFER *Ottawa* 66: To secure this [the crib] four
heavy sticks called loading timbers—generally those
which are too crooked to fit well between the floats—
are dragged on top of the traverses and by their weight
sink the floating timbers lower in the water; the friction
thus created against the under side of the traverses
(arising from the floatation of the timbers which are in
the water) effectually prevents the latter from moving
backward or forward, while the loading timbers are
fairly shipped high and dry and have no tendency to
move. **1896** GOURLAY *Hist.Ottawa* 137: The oars were
long, the men using them stood one on each side of the

loading timber in the middle of the crib. This middle stick had a rowlock on each end for the men to steer by.

lob-shot *n. Hockey* a deceptive, slow-moving shot on goal.
1964 *Maclean's* 21 Mar. 50/1: Carl Brewer, who may be the fastest defenseman and who is almost as good at his specialties of shoulder-fakes, lob-shots and holding sweaters as Stanley is at his. . . .

lobster cop *Maritimes, Slang* a government official who enforces the laws governing lobster trapping.
1959 *Star Wkly* 22 Aug. 3/1: The mosquitoes also found Allan Robichaud, tall, spare-framed veteran fisheries protection officer—a "lobster cop."

Lobster Lad *Slang* a Prince Edward Islander.
1955 *Pictou Advocate* 24 Feb. 4/1: That leaves Nova Scotia and Prince Edward Island presumably in the bag. As long as the opiate of patronage is efficiently operated by Handsome Bob Winters for the Bluenoses and by Watson Macnaught for the Lobster Lads, no trouble is in sight.

lobster pound *Maritimes* See quote.
1934 DENNIS *Down in N.S.* 292: The large wooden arrangement we are coming to is the "Lobster Pound." Lobsters are caught in season and impounded here until they are sold and shipped away.

lobster spearing *Maritimes* See quote.
1862 DENNYS *Cruise of St.George* 170: When I speak of lobster spearing, do not imagine . . . that a sharp-pointed steel weapon is the instrument of capture . . . [but] a long-forked pole, which, when pressed hard over the back of the fish, holds him in its embrace till you can draw him from the water.

lobstick or **lopstick** ['lɑb,stɪk *or* 'lɑp,stɪk] *n.*
1 (originally associated with the northern Indians) a tall, conspicuous spruce or pine denuded of all but its topmost branches to serve as a mark of honor for a friend, as a monument, or often as a living talisman of the man for whom it was made. See also **maypole** (def. 1) and **nob stick**.
1821 (1900) GARRY *Diary* 149: After Dinner we observed that two of our Men had lopped away the Boughs and all the Lower Branches of two Trees leaving a Top. This is called a Lop-Stick and the Voyageurs named it Garry's Point. **1847** NEVINS *Two Voyages* 90: Two gentlemen were travelling a short time since, and lobsticks were out for them; but they professed tee-total principles, and could not think of encouraging intemperance, by giving rum. **1908** MAIR *Mackenzie Basin* 126: The Indians lop-stick, called by the Crees piskootenusk, is a sort of living talisman which he connects in some mysterious way with his own fate, and which he will often go many miles out of his direct course to visit. **1923** *Beaver* Aug. 421: To commemorate this great battle, three lobsticks were cut on each side of the river. **1964** *Islander* 18 Oct. 1/12: There was a tradition among the Northern Indians that a lobstick honouring an individual would fall when its sponsor died.

2 such a tree serving as a landmark. See also **mai** and **maypole** (def. 2).
[1789 (1801) MACKENZIE *Voy.from Montreal* 69: We observed a great number of trees, in different places, whose branches had been lopped off to the tops. They denote the immediate abode of the natives and probably serve for signals to direct each other to their respective winter quarters.] **1819** (1923) FRANKLIN *Journey* 39: At

this place we observed a conspicuous lop-stick, a kind of land-mark, which I have not hitherto noticed, notwithstanding its great use in pointing out the frequented routes. **1896** WHITNEY *On Snow-Shoes* 321: The "lop stick" is always made on a very high point of ground, and stands as a kind of traveller's guide-post in this wilderness. **1928** FREEMAN *Nearing North* 174: The lobstick (originally lop-stick, from the fact that it is a tree with all but the topmost branches lopped off close to the trunk) serves the North for everything from a mark of navigation to a flagpole, tombstone and monument. **1963** SYMONS *Many Trails* 188: We located and headed towards the lobstick which marked the portage into Shorson Creek.

local assembly *Hist.* See **local legislature**.
1867 *Niagara Mail* (Niagara-on-the-Lake, Ont.) 14 Dec. 2/2: The nomination for the Local Assembly of a member to represent Niagara, takes place at twelve o'clock noon, to-morrow.

local government board a provincial-government body charged with overseeing the activities of the various municipal governments.
1953 MOON *Saskatchewan* 47: The civic administration . . . has . . . been under the close surveillance of the Provincial government's local government board ever since.

local house *Hist.* See **local legislature**.
1871 *Wkly Manitoban* 4 Mar. 2/2: It will be recalled that there was no voting in nine of the Divisions during the contest for the Local House,—the members being returned by acclamation. **1904** DECELLES *Cartier* 79: His presence in the local House at Quebec during the first parliament of that province, and his many absorbing duties at Ottawa left him very little time to devote to those attentions which a leader of men must bestow on his followers in order to keep his popularity.

local improvement district 1 *Prairie Provinces* a district administered by provincial-government officials because it is too thinly populated to merit a municipal government of its own. See also **improvement district**.
1899 *Medicine Hat News* (Alta) 9 Feb. 1/6: A settler in the Dunmore district . . . states that the feeling among the few settlers in Township 12 is "very strongly against having this township by itself made into a local improvement district." **1954** *Ghost Pine* 173: In 1908 a Local Improvement District was formed. We notice in the school records that a Local Improvement District election was held in Sarcee Butte School on Jan. 10, 1910. **1958** *Edmonton Jnl* 31 July 37/3: He was speaking to . . . about 50 representatives of the County of Grande Prairie, municipal districts and local improvement districts.

2 a form of local government having appointed municipal boards of limited powers. See also **improvement district**.
1958 *Encyc.Can.* VII 202/1: There are several special forms of local government, usually with limited powers, though in some cases with full municipal powers, but with appointed rather than elected boards. Such are the New Brunswick local improvement districts, Ontario Police villages and improvement districts, etc.

local legislature *Hist.* a colonial or a provincial legislature. See also **local assembly, local house** and **local parliament**.

1774 *Quebec Gaz.* 10 Nov. 3/1: Indeed the restraints laid by this act upon the local legislature confine its discretionary powers within very narrow bounds, and almost reduce it to a necessity of exercising its authority for the general good only. **1836** *Niagara Telegraph* (Niagara-on-the-Lake, U.C.) 16 Nov. 2/4: The Local Legislature is divided against itself, one of the Houses seeking the destruction of the other for several years past. **1867** *Islander* (Charlottetown) 8 Mar. 2/5: The local legislatures are to be known as the Provincial Legislatures of Ontario, Quebec, Nova Scotia and New Brunswick, respectively. **1916** SKELTON *Day of Laurier* 238: In 1888 a local legislature was created, with limited powers, later somewhat enlarged.

local parliament *Hist.* See **local legislature.**
1715 (1883) HATTON & HARVEY *Newfoundland* 47: We have proof of this in the fact that, finding there was no redress of their wrongs to be expected from the home authorities, the inhabitants of St. John's organised a local parliament, composed of the more intelligent and influential of their number, including the commanders of merchant-ships and some of the merchants. **1841** *Chatham Jnl* (C.W.) 30 Oct. 3/1: As the time is fast approaching for the election of District Councillors ... we think it is well to state the mode in which ou future local Parliaments will be constituted. **1881** BEGG *Great Cdn N.W.* 76: On the 15th March, 1871, the first meeting of the Local Parliament took place, and from that day representative Government commenced in Manitoba.

local premier *Obs.* the chief executive officer of a local legislature, *q.v.*; a provincial premier.
1884 *Moose Jaw News* (Sask.) 2 Jan. 2/2: There can be no question that if it is decided to give Manitoba a representative in the Ottawa ministry, the Local Premier is the most likely man for the position.

locate *v.* **1** (*often passive*) establish (someone) legally as a settler on land under terms of settlement set by the government. See also **homestead**, *v.*, and **location** (def. 2).
1790 (1905) *Ont.Bur.Arch.Rep.* III 44: The board then examined John Snider's ticket for Lot No. 1 73, New settlement, and finding no reason why he should not be located, they proceeded to take his solemn affirmation of and subscription for the oaths of Allegiance, etc. and granted him a certificate for a single Lot. **1801** *U.C. Gaz.* (York [Toronto]) 5 Sep. 1/3: Notice is hereby given to all persons located upon Yonge Street, that the 16th day of September next is appointed to hear the Defaulters. **1819** *Ibid.* 16 Sep. 153/4: No vacant land being found in the District of Niagara, it is not expedient to appoint a Board to locate desirable Settlers therein. **1930** BEAMES *Army* 34: "I figure on locatin' Mr. Kent on the northwest of eight, just across the slough," said Webb. "It's just about as good a quarter as I know of."

2 a. legally occupy (land) under government-established conditions of settlement. See also **homestead**, *v.*
1822 GOURLAY *Upper Canada* I 13: As the sons and daughters of those whose names are on the U.E. list become of age, they petition the lieutenant-governor, in council, stating the facts and verifying them by their own oath, and the affidavit of one witness, and upon such petitions obtain orders for the land, which they locate in some of the new townships, and then take out their patents without cost. **1926** POLLARD *Pioneering* 84: Script, or official writing entitling the holder to locate land in free grant sections, was given to the half-breeds descended from the Indians, in the years 1899 and 1900. **1954** BEZANSON *Sodbusters* 171: By both of us taking homesteads and locating scrip we can get a whole section for what one quarter would cost us here.

b. take up residence, especially as a settler under a Homestead Law, *q.v.*
☛ *The general sense of* **locate** *"take up residence, settle," which has been in American use since the 17th century, seems to have become common among Canadians somewhat later than the more technical senses associated with homesteading; early writers in Canada* (*usually British in origin*) *attribute the term to "Yankees," classing it as a barbarism.*
1888 (1963) *Herald Mag.* (Calgary) 14 Dec. 8/1: ... a certain portion of the press in the east is proclaiming that Alberta is closed to settlement; being parcelled out in grazing leases upon which settlers are not allowed to locate. **1958** *Citizen* (North Vancouver) 11 Dec. 5A/1: We must be prepared to supply their needs if they locate in North Vancouver City. **1964** *Alta Hist. Rev.* Summer 27/1: After finishing the panning of the gold he located on that piece of land, later securing the homestead.

3† establish (a town).
1830 MOORSOM *Letters N.S.* 272: This splendid harbour was the bauble that dazzled the eyes of those by whom the town [Shelburne] was (to use an appropriate American expression) first located. **1882** *Edmonton Bull.* 2/2: [It] appears to be the intention of the Ottawa Government to abandon Battleford and locate some other place as the capital of the north-west—probably the C.P.R. crossing of the South Branch.

4 *Obs.* open up for settlement; arrange for the establishing of settlers on new land.
1832 *Brockville Gaz.* (U.C.) 24 May 3/2: Major Campbell, of Seymour, will locate the Township of Seymour and its Neighborhood.

5 a. *West* act as a land-guide, *q.v.*, for. See also **locating.**
1912 POCOCK *Man in the Open* 274: "She's been locatin' settlers along them old clearings in the black pine and, judging by samples I'd seen, she's swept the jails."

b. *West* find the exact location and boundaries of a tract of land.
1963 SYMONS *Many Trails* 91: ... the business of locating a certain quarter section in an unsettled area boiled down to finding the "corner mounds" of the section in question.

6 survey and establish the route for (a railway line). See also **location** (def. 4).
1880 GORDON *Mountain and Prairie* 115: Were it necessary to locate a line across this northern part of the Province more than one favourable route might be found connecting Port Simpson with the Pine River Pass. **1883** *Prince Albert Times* (Sask.) 3 Jan. 2/2: Westward from Leopold the line has been located to Calgary, 120 miles, leaving a distance of 140 miles to the summit of the Rockies, to be finally decided upon next year.

7† *Mining* stake and register a claim. See also **location** (def. 5) and **locator** (def. 1).
1897 HARRIS *Gold Fields* 444: Then the "angel" when the mine was located would reap the reward of his childlike trust and implicit faith. ... **1964** *North* Nov.-Dec. 6/2: Henderson ... had prospected and located on the same branch [Gold Bottom], a few claims above where Hunker staked at a later date.

located *adj.* of land, taken up legally by settlers; homesteaded. Cp. **unlocated.**
1826 *U.E.Loyalist* (York [Toronto]) 14 Oct. 160/2: The Reserves are scattered in lots of 200 acres each over all the located and cultivated townships in the province. **1912** HEENEY *Pickanock* 83: Luke's logs, which had been cut on his own "located" land, were still unsold. . . .

locatee *n. Obs.* a person having a location (def. la). See also **location ticket** (def. 2).
1820 *U.C.Gaz.* (York [Toronto]) 15 Feb. 25/5: Unless the representatives of John Bless, the original Locatee of the West half of Lot number Sixteen, in the Third Concession of the Township of Fredericksburgh, in the Midland District, do Claim within one Year from this date, the Patent will issue to Martin Salisbury.
1840 *Montreal Transcript* 24 Dec. 407/1: An assignment, or attempt to assign any ticket of location, will also be considered as a forfeiture of all right in the Locatee or Assignee.

locating *n. Hist.* See quote. See also **locate** (def. 5a) and **locator** (def. 2).
1963 SYMONS *Many Trails* 89: Teams went out over the prairie, came back to the town barn, were fed, and went out again, taking homesteaders to their grants. This was called "locating," and a pretty good fee was charged. . . .

location *n.* **1 a.** a parcel of government land applied for and granted for purposes of settlement. See also **homestead,** *n.* (def. 2a). Cp. **location ticket** (def. 1).
1789 (1905) *Ont.Bur.Arch.Rep.* III lxx: But the said certificate shall nevertheless have no effect if the petitioner shall not enter upon the location and begin the improvement and cultivation thereof within one year from the date of such assignment. **1849** ALEXANDER *L'Acadie* II 101: . . . a short run across the Atlantic brings the emigrant, at once, to his "location" without ruinous expense. **1959** STOREY *Prairie Harvest* 29: Now the house building began. They had planned it carefully, and Henry had already dug the hole in the centre of the location to serve as a root cellar.
b. *Obs.* the legal grant to such land.
1789 (1905) *Ont.Bur.Arch.Rep.* VIII 313: I have not as yet been able to keep my Book of Locations one week without three or four alterations, which arise from the above recited reasons. **1801** *U.C.Gaz.* (York [Toronto]) 5 Sep. 1/3: If they cannot show good cause why further time should be given to them, their Locations will be rescinded, and the Lots thrown open.
2 *Obs.* the process of settling persons on government land. See also **locate** (def. 1).
1791 (1905) *Ont.Bur.Arch.Rep.* III 165: The Location of the District hitherto has, perhaps, been retarded by a rigid adherence to the Rules and Regulations for the Board's Guidance, and it is mortifying to foster the idea of deviating from them. **1816** (1899) GARDNER *Names* 196: A new township in the rear of Darlington, in the district of Newcastle, has been surveyed and is now open for the location of U.E. Loyalists and military claimants. **1833** (1926) LANGTON *Early U.C.* 15: The mode of location is this:—I go to the Government office, and upon showing my title, put down the name of my loyalist upon any unoccupied lot I please.
3† a site, especially with regard to its surroundings.
1835 *Novascotian* (Halifax) 12 Nov. 332/3: So what with Marm Lecain's corsets in the house, and other folks waistcoats in the Street, its too nice a location for me, I guess, so I shall up killock and off. . . . **1957** *Herald-Tribune* (Grande Prairie, Alta.) 17 Dec. 1/1: Crews working from both sides of the river are pushing as

quickly as possible to complete the 500-foot temporary span in the same location as the one taken out by grinding ice last week.
4† the surveying and establishing of a route for a railway. See also **locate** (def. 6).
1880 GORDON *Mountain and Prairie* 10: True, there was far more work involved than was at first anticipated, in the location of the line. **1961** *Cdn Geog.Jnl* Jan. 13/1: During break-up canoes were carved . . . for further travel . . . until location was completed and the party assigned to construction. . . .
5† *Mining* a claim, or block of claims, staked and registered. See also **locate** (def. 7), **location notice, mining location,** and **mining lot.**
1883 *Brandon Dly* (Man.) 15 Feb. 2/2: Work has commenced on the Pine Portage location known as "The Whale." **1963** *Insider Reports* 4 June 2/1: After scouring the whole Cobalt area for some time in search of an attractive reactivation program to help finance, I've settled for the oldest and largest of the Hitchcock properties—a 43-claim spread on one location. . . .

location certificate *Obs.* See **location ticket.**
1791 (1905) *Ont.Bur.Arch.Rep.* III 137: The Board will be thankful to you, Sir. if you will have the Goodness to direct, a few more Location certificates, for Single Lots, to be forwarded. . . .

location notice *Mining* a document relating to the staking and registering of a legal claim. See **location** (def. 5).
1897 *Slocan Pioneer* (B.C.) 15 May 4/2: A number of prospectors in the city are watching the operations of an individual who, they claim, is making a business of following them and dating back their location notices.

location ticket 1 *Hist.* See 1822 quote. See also **location certificate** and **ticket.** Cp. **location** (def. 1a).
1821 HOWISON *Sketches* 259: Whenever the emigrant has obtained from the government a location ticket, which is a sort of certificate that empowers him to take possession of the portion of land he has selected, he ought to commence operations immediately.
1927 DICKIE *How Canada Grew Up* 42: The settler must clear five acres upon each hundred granted to him, open a road in front of his lot, and build a loghouse of certain dimensions. These settling duties, if performed within eighteen months after the location ticket has been issued entitle the emigrant to a deed from the Government which makes the lot his forever. **1963** *Cdn Geog.Jnl* Nov. 147/3: The first inspection of the lands of the Ottawa for purposes of settlement was made in 1783, and the first location tickets were issued in 1788.
2 *Obs.* a holder of such a ticket. See also **locatee.**
1821 *York Wkly Post* 8 Mar. 11/3: A distinct motion immediately afterwards set at rest the question of the right of Location Tickets having a vote; a majority was of opinion that the Location Tickets were not entitled to vote.

locator† *n. Hist.* **1** *Mining* a person who stakes and registers a mining claim. See also **locate** (def. 7).
1898 *Yukon Midnight Sun* (Dawson) 10 Sep. 3/1: He visited the Atlin lake strike and states that four miles of Pine creek is turning out satisfactorily to the locators.

2 See **land-guide.** See also **locate** (def. 5a).

1963 SYMONS *Many Trails* 91: Of course, the "locators" had good maps, knew the country well . . . and were expert at finding the corner mounds. . . .

loche [loʃ] *n.* [< Cdn F < F] a freshwater cod, *Lota lota maculosa;* burbot, *q.v.* See also **la loche, ling** (def. 1), **loach, mari, maria, mathemeg,** and **methy.** Also spelled *loch, louche,* etc.

1808 (1890) KEITH *Letters* 81: The active squirrel commanded his attention, a pike, a loche and a mouse [moose]. **1869** (1942) KENNICOTT *Journal* 96: Loche [is] a kind of fish resembling the cod . . . the liver of which is a great delicacy. **1897** TUTTLE *Golden North* 190: Whitefish, losh and graylings are found in large quantities in the Yukon, and afford more food for the natives than the salmon. **1962** *Favorite Recipes* I: Fried loch—Cut loch up and put in frying pan with a little lard and cover tightly. Cook until loch is soft.

loci(e) ['loki] *n.* [shortening and alteration of *locomotive*] *Slang* any of several kinds of hauling engines used in mining and logging operations. See also **loco².** Also spelled *lokey.*

1943 SWANSON *Lumberjack* 57: . . . as the roaders could not reach further than a mile or so, rails were laid on the skid road and a weird type of locomotive developed that would climb hills, rails, or practically anything. This mechanical abortion dragged the logs for miles between the rails, which were merely laid on a skid road; this *locie,* due to its climbing ability, was called a *Climax.* **1956** ANDREWS *Glory Days* 44: Curley also drove a lokey at Daddy Lamb's homeguard camp at Menzies Bay—around 1921. . . . **1964** CRATE *Hardrock Mining* 4: The trammer now, however—and he has other titles—is the driver of a battery or trolley-powered engine known as an electric mule, a motor or (more frequently) a "*loci.*"

lock-stick *n. Lumbering* See **key-log** (def. 1).

1926 MAIR *Masterworks* XIV liii: Real peril there was in "jams" at unslided chutes, where the timber piled up to a great height, and the lock-sticks had to be cut to set the jam going.

loco¹† ['loko] *n.* [< Am.E < Sp. "crazy"] *West* See **locoweed.**

1919 FRASER *Bulldog Carney* 130: "If Slimy Red got wise to anything he'd slip him a twig of locoe or put a sponge up his nose." **1958** *Ghost Pine* 25: Evidently we had moved onto a loco range.

loco² ['loko] *n.* [shortening of *locomotive*] *Lumbering, Slang* See **loci.**

1936 *B.C.Lumber Trade* 73: ELCO LOGGING CO., LTD.— Youbou, B.C. . . . Three Sides; Three High Leads . . . 1.45 ton Loco; 1.80 ton Loco; 45 Skeleton Cars; 4 Skidders, 5 Donkey Engines, 1 Steam Shovel, 1 Gas Shovel.

locoweed ['loko,wid] *n.* [see **loco¹**] a weed, *Oxytropis sericea,* poisonous to grazing animals. See also **loco¹.**

1906 (1959) *Alaska Sportsman* Mar. 52: [Northern B.C. locale] Dick . . . had recently lost his own mare to loco weed. . . . **1952** PUTNAM *Cdn Regions* 23/1: On the upland north of Great Bear Lake . . . are found . . . loco-weed . . . and rhododendron. . . . **1954** TYRE *Saddlebag Surgeon* 233: [Grasshoppers] came by the crawling, hopping millions and somewhere along the

way they must have dined on locoweed, for they were the most vicious little brigands I have ever encountered.

lod *n.* See **lods et ventes.**

lode mine *Esp.B.C. and Northwest* a hardrock mine, as opposed to a placer mine.

1958 ELLIOTT *Quesnel* 166: Perhaps the lode mine most interesting to Quesnel people has been in the Hixon Hills. **1963** *Western Miner* Oct. 52: [Caption] Most northerly lode mine in the western hemisphere. A view of the surface plant of Tundra Gold Mine Ltd. at Mathews Lake, N.W.T.

lode-mining *n. Esp.B.C. and Northwest* the operation of lode mines, *q.v.*

1905 WIGHTMAN *Our Cdn Heritage* 148: . . . prospectors have been deterred from going into the country because of the lack of transportation facilities, which are absolutely necessary to the success of lode-mining. **1952** PUTNAM *Cdn Regions* 443/1: Lode mining, depending on heavy equipment, is now predominant in the industry. **1963** *Western District Union* 2: In this period of 10 years, the working force in the lode-mining industry has been reduced from 9610 to 3993. . . .

lodge [lɑdʒ] *n.* [< ME < OF *loge* hut, of Gmc origin; influenced in some meanings by Cdn F *loge* hut, of similar origin] **1 a.** See **beaver lodge.**

1744 DOBBS *Hudson's Bay* 40: He says these Skins are extremely white, and have a fine Lustre, no snow being whiter, and have a fine long Fur or Hair; he has seen 15 taken of that Colour out of one Lodge or Pond. **1821** (1900) GARRY *Diary* 195: The Beaver is easier taken in his Lodge. . . . **1955** GOWLAND *Smoke* 205: Around the lodge were rafts of poles gnawed into handy lengths, waiting to be taken below.

b. See **muskrat house.**

1896 RUSSELL *Far North* 216: Wisagatchak blew upon the muskrats driving them back, saying, "Go, build lodges for your children, and wherever there is a people they shall know where you live and shall use your skins." **1921** HEMING *Drama of Forests* 259: The muskrat's little island lodge among the rushes is erected upon a foundation of mud and reeds that rises about two feet before it protrudes above the surface of the water.

2 a. an Indian dwelling, as a teepee, *q.v.,* or wigwam (def. 1a). See also **Indian lodge.**

1765-75 (1933) POND *Narrative* 41: If there be aney Young Garl in this Lodg or hut that aney Man of a Differant Hut Has a Likeing for he will Seat among them. **1849** ALEXANDER *L'Acadie* II 233: In winter the lodges are removed to sheltered situations in the depth of the wood. **1908** MAIR *Mackenzie Basin* 52: Teepees were to be seen in all directions from our camp—the lodges of the Indians and half-breeds. **1966** *Kingston Whig-Standard* (Ont.) 6 Feb. 4/5: The peaked lodge differed in having a ridge pole like a modern tent. . . .

b. *Hist.* See **tent** (def. 1).

1820 (1823) FRANKLIN *Journey* 78: A large tent or lodge, was prepared for the important occasion, by the men of the party, none of the women being allowed to enter. **1896** WHITNEY *On Snow-Shoes* 250: Our lodge was blown full of snow, burying us and the dogs in its driftings, and was finally blown down altogether, and would have been blown away had we not clung to it. **1932** KENNEY *Ft Churchill* 117: . . . "tent" in the parlance of Hudson's Bay journals was applied to a small hut or shanty of any construction, and especially to the lodges, probably built of logs, earth and moss, in which the Company's servants lived while hunting, trapping, fishing or lumbering during the winter.

3 See **tent** (def. 2).
1789 (1801) MACKENZIE *Voy. from Montreal* 41: These people informed us that we were close to another great rapid and that there were several lodges of their relations in the vicinity. **1879** *Winnipeg Dly Times* 18 Apr. 3/2: The Indians number over one-hundred lodges; all Siouxs. **1939** *Beaver* Mar. 39/2: Next year, Mr. Christie went out to Qu'Appelle to pay the treaty money, but to his amazement he found nearly 500 lodges assembled there.

4 a.† See **hunting lodge** (def. 2) and **fishing lodge.**
1955 MCCOWAN *Upland Trails* 90: [The porcupine] may frequently be found around woodland cabins and lodges.... **1966** *Globe and Mail* (Toronto) 14 Jan. 45/5: Their Fort Albany goose cap has been the northernmost temporary hunting camp in Eastern Canada and the lodge at Little Abitibi Lake ... the northernmost permanent camp.

b. a hotel for accommodating guests in a resort area.
1958 *Edmonton Jnl* 23 July 29/1: ... Mr. and Mrs. O'Brien ffrench ... elected to create a lodge and ranch buildings in the midst of their wilderness beauty spot five miles from Banff township. **1964** *Atlantic Advocate* July 68/2: When I wrote later to explain that fishing in New Brunswick is really much better than the sample of it we had at Landlocker Lodge, I don't think he believed me.

lodge leather *Obs.* dressed skins of buffalo, moose, or caribou, used for making lodges (def. 2a). See also **leather.**
1913 COWIE *Adventurers* 248: We had six sleds with large lodge leather wrappers....

lodgepole *n.* **1 a.** one of the poles forming the framework for a teepee or wigwam, *qq.v.*
1872 (1883) BUTLER *Great Lone Land* 89: ... twenty years ago the Sioux lodge-poles were the only signs of habitation. **1963** *Beaver* 33/2: Nineteen poles hold up this mass of canvas.... Cross poles between the lodge poles serve as hanging racks.

b. *Obs.* the dwelling itself.
1873 (1904) BUTLER *Wild North Land* 209: The beaver brought many a white man's scalp to the red man's lodge-pole; and many a red man's life went out with the beaver's.

2 See **house-post.**
1885 *Trans. Roy. Soc. Can.* III 2 83: The decorations of the Haida lodge-poles admit at times of a much more homely interpretation.

3 See **lodgepole pine.**
1936 MOWERY *Paradise Trail* 47: ... he passed rapidly through the storm-twisted balsams, the squat spruces hugging the ground, and lodgepoles gnarled and stunted.... **1955** MCCOWAN *Upland Trails* 44: These [cones] may remain attached to the tree for several years, a factor which permits of burnt-over areas of Lodgepole woodland being quickly re-forested.

lodgepole pine† a slim, straight pine, *Pinus contorta* var. *latifolia,* common in the Rocky Mountain region, so called because the young trees make good lodgepoles. See also **bull pine** (def. 1) and **white pine** (def. 2).
1916 WOOD *Tourist's N.W.* 456: Descending the road ... through a forest of white spruce and lodge-pole pine, Cascade Mountain, Aylmer, Stony Squaw Mountain and Mt. Edith come more prominently into the picture. **1955** MCCOWAN *Upland Trails* 43: By a strange twist ... the most perpendicular species of tree in Canada is known to botanists and foresters as Pinus

Contortus—the contorted pine ... first discovered by ... David Douglas, over one hundred and twenty years ago. He found it in swampy soil near tidewater where, exposed to winds from the ocean, it was stunted and scrubby.... Thereupon the learned men ... at Kew Gardens ... bestowed upon it the aforementioned name ... now best known as Lodgepole pine....
1964 *Beaver* Summer 13: The new, fresh look at the old Skagway sites will be due to the fact that Alaska coast or Kenai birches and lodgepole pines have appeared following the destruction of the original darker green Sitka spruce and hemlocks by fire about 1912.

lodgepole spruce See **lodgepole pine.**
1937 *Beaver* Sep. 13/1: Masts of lodge-pole spruce are cut, and sails from tarps and tent floors rigged for each canoe.

lods et ventes† *French, Hist.* in New France, one of several seigneurial rights transplanted with the Coutume de Paris, namely, the right to a twelfth part of the purchase price of every estate changing hands by sale or transfer, abolished with the institution of seigneurial tenure in 1854. See also **losivants.** Also *lots and ventes.*
1764 *Quebec Gaz.* 25 Oct. 3/2: The Lots and Ventes, or Alienation Fines, on the Purchases made by the Inhabitants, one from the other ... may amount yearly to about £2000. **1831** *Brockville Gaz.* (U.C.) 19 Jan. 2/3: It is just and necessary to grant, in certain cases, an abatement and a delay to those who owe Lods and Ventes in His Majesty's Domain in the said suburbs. **1963** MORTON *Kingdom of Canada* 40: The lord's economic rights ... consisted in the main of the rights to *lods et ventes,* a charge on transfers; the right of *banalité,* the exaction of a charge for services, such as milling; the customary rent of *cens et rentes,* a fixed payment for tenure.

log *n.*
☛ *Combinations having* **log** *as the first element are extremely numerous and largely self explanatory. For the most part, the entries that follow have some special significance as a combination, over and above the mere attributive use of the word* **log** *denoting structures made of logs.*

log *v.* **1** *Hist.* in clearing land, remove trees by felling, cutting into lengths, and piling ready for burning, splitting, etc. See also **logging** (def. 1a and note), **logging bee,** and **log up** (def. 1).
1829 MACTAGGART *Three Years* II 206: ... when the large wood is hewn down and *logged,* that is, cut into lengths and laid round these stacks in a rude pile, the fire can more readily be applied to them. **1832** (1838) TRAILL *Backwoods* 101: After the trees have been chopped, cut into lengths, drawn together, or logged, as we call it, and burned, the field must be fenced, the seed sown, harvested, and thrashed before any returns can be obtained. **1963** GUILLET *Pioneer Farmer* I 318: ... some men were known to log several acres a year entirely alone—without even oxen.

2 *Lumbering* (often with *off*) remove timber for commercial use. See also **cut over, logged-off,** and **lumber,** *v.* (def. 1).
1919 SINCLAIR *Burned Bridges* 302: As fast as the land is logged off it is open for soldier entry. There is room here for five hundred families. **1928** PERRY *Two Reds* 11: He had resolved only to log off enough to make his

reforestation project pay for itself.... *Ibid.* 62: "... what is being logged there will just about take care of things. If I'm going to cash in on any money, it means opening the Black River tract." **1964** *Sun* (Vancouver) 10 Apr. 23/1:... a logging road leading into the valley, whose upper part isn't logged, eventually should lead to access from the Aloutette recreation and campsite area, just south.

log barge *Lumbering* a huge barge onto which logs are loaded for transporting from the dump (def. 2) to the mill.
1963 MCKINNON *Forest Activities 1* 12: Self-dumping log barges are used primarily for open-water, long-distance hauling and have replaced the historic Davis raft. **1964** *Beautiful B.C.* Fall 40/1: The era of huge log booms is being superceded by huge log barges....

log-bee *n.* See **logging bee.**
1916 BRIDLE *Sons of Canada* 270: There is the suggestion of the axe and the crosscut saw, the ox-team and the log-bee....

log birler See **birler.**
1966 *Cdn Forest Industries* Oct. 50/3: For the past several years either Arne or Jube [Wickheim, of Sook, B.C.] has been the world's champion log birler.

log-birling *n.* See **birling.**
1965 *Dly Colonist* (Victoria) 10 July 17/3: Log-birling ... and sawing events will occupy the rest of the day.

logboggan ['lɑg,bɑgən] *n.* [< *log* + to*boggan*] See quote. See also **bogan**[2].
1951 ANGIER *At Home* 42: Numerous flat slabs of clay-ironstone were at hand from the previous building operations. We skidded them over on a logboggan, improvised one evening by setting the ends of three light boards in a slot sawed and then chiseled from a short poplar log.

log-boom *n.* See **boom**[1], *n.* (def. 1).
1912 HEENEY *Pickanock* 13: Now ... on the left the river is gliding, a wide glassy tide spreading away to where dusk is thickening on the log-booms.... **1966** *Cdn Geog.Jnl* June 4/3: Log booms, loose logs, and boom boats were swept out of the bay.

logbooming *n.* See **booming.**
1958 HEALEY *Alert Bay* 35: He did not know anything about logbooming, but being quick and active and having fallen in a few dozen times, he grew accustomed to his work.

log bronc *Lumbering, B.C.* a small tug used to control a boom of logs under tow or in the booming grounds. See also **boom boat, boom dozer, boom scooter.**
1964 *Time* (Cdn ed.) 10 July 57/1: In the B.C. coastal waters ... little "log broncs" herd strays back into the booms....

log burning *Hist.* See **burning** (def. 1).
1926 LANGTON *Early U.C.* xxxiii: The gentlemen's topics were:—crops and clearings, lumber, price of wheat, road mending, deer shooting, logburning, etc.

log camp† See **logging camp.**
1888 (1890) ST. MAUR *Impressions* 68: Near here is the oldest log-camp in the Mountains, where a Government engineering party, under Mr. Walter Moberly, C.E., spent the winter of 1871. **1919** *Camp Worker* 28 June

7/3: As every real lumberjack knows, this element is almost impossible to organize, being for the most part homesteaders on the prairies in summer, and they go to short log camps in B.C. during the winter.

log canoe† See **dugout canoe** and picture.
1828 MCGREGOR *Maritime Colonies* 15: Upwards, the meandering river, on which one may now and then see passengers crossing in a log canoe, or an Indian with his family paddling in a bark one. **1896** GOURLAY *Hist. Ottawa* 72: Think of boards drawn from the mill by oxen on two crotches, then put into cribs in the river and pushed by poles, or towed by a log canoe or hurriedly constructed boat....

log causeway *Obs.* See **corduroy road.**
1828 *Gore Gaz.* (Ancaster, U.C.) 18 Oct. 134/2: The stumps are all taken out—and the log causeways, where these are necessary—are covered with a thick coat of earth.

log chain See **logging chain.**
1827 *Gore Gaz.* (Ancaster, U.C.) 2 June 55/1: 1 Prize of a lot of log chains, 2 10 Dundas Lottery. **1904** *Eye Opener* (Calgary) 1 Nov. 2/3: Robinson was handed a biff that made him drop in a heap like six feet of log chain.

logcock† *n.* See **cock of the woods.**
1900 LONG *Wilderness Ways* 54: He killed them all, tasting the brains again, and hunted the tree over for the father bird, the great black logcock that makes the wilderness ring with his tattoo. **1956** MCATEE *Folk-Names* 47: Pileated Woodpecker [is also called] logcock (As a striking bird frequenting trees, General)....

log crib See **crib** (def. 1a).
1928 WALDEN *Dog-Puncher* 181: The rafts were made of a series of log cribs thirty feet square yoked together one behind the other....

log crossway *Obs.* See **corduroy bridge.**
1908 CLARKE *Sixty Years* 36: What can the settler of to-day, in any section of old Upper Canada, tell of corduroys, log crossways and culverts, jolting mud-holes wide and deep....

log deck *Lumbering* See quotes. See also **deck**, *n.* (def. 2).
1944 *Forestry Course 1* 145: *Log-deck men.* One or two men may be employed in rolling logs from the jack-ladder chain into the log deck and two or more may be needed to roll them from the deck onto the carriage [which bears them into the saw]. **1947** ENGLEBERT *Men and Trees* 19: The log is caught by the dogs, and hauled up into the mill where it waits on the log deck before being placed in the carriage.

log dog *Lumbering* See 1947 quote. See also **dog** (def. 3).
1944 *Forestry Course 1* 145: The setter, in a [saw-]mill of this size [moderately large] will ride on the carriage and adjust the setworks after each cut in accordance with the signalled instruction of the sawyer. He may also operate the leading set of log dogs. **1947** ENGLEBERT *Men and Trees* 19: This moving chain [jackladder] is equipped at intervals with steel grips, called log dogs. ... The log is caught by the dogs and hauled up into the mill where it waits on the log deck before being placed on the carriage.

log drive See **drive,** *n.* (def. 1).
1894 ASHLEY *Tan Pile Jim* 173: In due time the chains were hitched to them and they were drawn to the shore, where they were canthooked upon the ice and

left to await the spring freshets and the log drive.
1964 *Atlantic Advocate* July 56/2: As a boy in
Buctouche, Kent County, he had often heard the old
lumbermen talk of Big John Glasier, who was the
first man to bring a log drive over Grand Falls.

log driver See **driver** (def. 1).
1909 ROBERTS *Backwoodsman* 34: Black Angus
MacAllister, the Boss . . . one of the gang of log-drivers
—had his ideas already pretty well formed. . . .
1958 *Evening Telegram* (St. John's) 2 May 4/7: . . . the
log drivers claim they would not make more than 22
cents an hour.

log dump† See **dump,** *n.* (def. 2).
1942 HAIG-BROWN *Timber* 250: A log dump, or "the
dump," is commonly a trestle built over the water.
1966 *Globe and Mail* (Toronto) 21 Feb. 1/6: [He] said
lumber camps and log dumps should be 600 feet from
all lakes and waterways. . . .

log flume *Lumbering* a wooden water trough for
floating logs from one point to another. See also
log sluice.
1963 *B.C.Digest* Nov.-Dec. 34/3: Logs came to the
mill pond by a 19-mile log flume, the second largest on
the continent at that time.

logged *adj.* See **logged-off.**
1919 SINCLAIR *Burned Bridges* 299: Beyond that [the
logging operation] there was a logged space, littered
with broken branches, stumps, tops, cut with troughs
plowed deep in the soil, where the donkey had skidded
out the logs.

logged-off† *adj. Lumbering* cleared of timber
through logging operations. See also **log,** *v.* (def. 2)
and **lumbered-over.**
1932 WINSON *Weather and Wings* 26: Old settlers in the
coast districts that have been "logged off," as the land
is described when the trees have been cut, are heard to
assert that the summers are drier than they used to be.
1963 MCKINNON *Forest Activities 2* 7: The various steps
in producing a seedling: . . . (8) two-year-old seedlings
ready for planting-out on logged-off land.

logged-out *adj.* See **logged-off.**
1954 RADDALL *Muster of Arms* 30: The forest was
mostly logged-out land covered with second-growth
spruce and fir.

logged road *Obs.* See **corduroy road.**
1816 (1818) HALL *Travels* 215: My friend having
returned to Queenston by water, I left York with no
companion but my dog, frequently repeating, as my
wain dragged heavily over the logged roads, which
cross the swampy woods round the Mocaco and
Etobico, the verses of Petrarca. . . .

logger† *n. Lumbering* **1** a person whose occupation
is logging (def. 2). See also **log-rider, lumberer**
(def. 2), **lumberjack** (def. 1), **lumberman** (def. 2),
timber-beast, timberjack, and **timber-maker.**
1853 *Anglo-Amer.Mag.* II 178/2: They are generally
known by the name of Lumber-men, or Loggers. **1963**
MORTON *Kingdom of Canada* 248: In Lower Canada
. . . scores hid out in the sugaring huts and loggers'
shanties in the bush. **1966** *Globe and Mail* (Toronto)
1 Jan. 24/3: Several thousand loggers are affected [by
delays caused by snow in B.C.].

2 a tracked vehicle used for hauling logs. Cp.
skidder (def. 3c).
1955 *Western Star* (Corner Brook, Nfld) 12 Mar. 5/6:
These broad-tracked loggers are geared to the ground,

can go into mud-clogged stands and come out with
money-making loads.

logging *n.* **1** *Hist.* **a.** See quotes. See also **log,** *v.*
(def. 1) and **log-rolling** (def. 1a).
☛ *The clearing of land in pioneer days involved at
least three operations: the chopping down of trees and
the removal of brush; the cutting of the trunks into
lengths and the piling of the logs and brush; the burning
of the log-heaps,* q.v. *The term* **logging** *was applied to
either or both of the first two of these operations, but
especially to the second. See* **burning, chopping, fallow,
improvement** *(def. 1),* **niggering, plan-heap,** *and* **slashing**
(def. 1b).

1807 *U.C.Gaz.* (York [Toronto]) 25 July 4/2: To be
Sold . . . 16 acres chopped down and ready for logging.
1832 (1953) RADCLIFF *Letters* 48: Before the house was
ready for our reception, we had cleared twenty acres of
the land for wheat, and during the successive
operations of brushing, chopping, logging, burning
and fencing—my father was obliged to hire workmen.
1863 WALSHE *Cedar Creek* 239: The logging can wait
for a couple of months. . . . **1898** CONANT *U.C.Sketches*
34: They spent the days "logging" (felling the trees)
and the nights burning. **1963** GUILLET *Pioneer Farmer*
318: In the absence of any mention in the use of the
cross-cut saw in logging, it must be assumed that the
trees . . . were almost always chopped into lengths, not
sawn.

b. See **logging bee.**
1905 SCHERCK *Pen Pictures* 181: The oxen, with a big
chain dragging behind them, could be seen coming
from different directions along the side-roads and
concessions, and as many as a dozen yoke of oxen at a
time might sometimes be seen at a "logging."
1908 CLARKE *Sixty Years* 34: . . . there were few
"bees," "loggings," or "raisings" at which [whisky]
was not more freely dispensed than water, and there
was a prevalent opinion that it was much more
wholesome.

2† the business or occupation of felling and sawing
trees and of transporting them to sawmills,
lumberyards, etc. See also **lumbering** (def. 1 and
note). Cp. **lumbering** (def. 2).
1838 NEED *Six Years in Bush* 112: At home, the old
winter work of chopping wood and logging for the
supply of the lumberyard afforded me exercise.
1883 FRASER *Shanty* 83: Why it would . . . buy him a
yoke of steers to do his "logging" for him. . . .
1938 CASH *I Like B.C.* 58: The reason Englishmen and
Canadians often couldn't make money logging was
because they expected to sit behind a glass-covered,
mahogany desk in a city, wear good clothes and
direct operations from afar. **1966** *Globe and Mail*
(Toronto) 1 Jan. 24/3: . . . for several years, logging
on Vancouver Island . . . has proceeded through the
winter with few snow problems.

logging bee *Hist.* a gathering of neighbors to
clear land by logging (def. 1). See also **log,** *v.*
(def. 1), **log-bee,** and **log-rolling** (def. 1b).
1832 DOYLE *Hints on Emigration* 48: The timber of
4 or 5 acres will (through the kind medium of the
logging Bee) be drawn off the ground in a single day.
1897 DURAND *Reminiscences* 80: Some of these
[sports in 1820] were . . . house and barn raisings,
logging bees and sugar making, and lastly, camp-

meetings. **1961** GREENING *Ottawa* 69: . . . he and his neighbors would organize a logging bee, heaping up the logs in big piles and then setting fire to them.

logging camp† See **shanty** (def. 2a). See also **log camp, lumber camp,** and **woods camp.**
1869 *Mainland Guardian* (New Westminster, B.C.) 11 Sept. 3/2: The village of Gastown was then visited, after which the party again returned to the Leviathan and proceeded to the logging camp of Mr. Jeremiah Rogers at English Bay. . . . **1903** RICHARDSON *Colin* 53: [He] . . . declared it was so cold in the "shanty" (the logging camp) that he used to trap foxes by just turning his bob-sleighs upside down and putting grease on the steel shoeing. **1965** *Victoria Dly Times* 21 July 39/7: [He] is accused of battering his wife . . . to death . . . following a party at a logging camp.

logging chain a strong chain used for hauling logs, pulling stumps, etc. See also **log chain.**
1825 (1916) SELLAR *Narrative* 103: Walked to Toronto [to buy a] logging-chain and an ox-sled. **1841** *Bytown* [Ottawa] *Gaz.* 17 Feb. 1/2: A plough $17, 2 axes 8s each—harrow teeth 8s—2 logging chains 10s each. **1955** HOBSON *Nothing Too Good* 160: [He] had a winch on his truck, logging chains, ropes, and every kind of jack and tool to help him make the journey.

logging division *Lumbering* an area in which logging is being carried on; logging camp, *q.v.*
1965 *Vancouver Province* 17 June 18/1: At Kelsey Bay and two other logging divisions . . . the company is spending $1 million this year. . . .

logging drive See **drive** (def. 1).
1966 *Kingston Whig-Standard* (Ont.) 2 June 38: [Caption] Rivermen keep the flow of logs moving downstream during logging drive down the Loup river north of Joliette, Que.

logging road† *Lumbering* a bush road made for hauling logs from the cutting area. See also **lumbering road** and **lumber road.**
1869 *Mainland Guardian* (New Westminster, B.C.) 11 Sep. 3/2: . . . the party proceeded to the logging camp . . . where the admirably constructed logging roads elicited high encomiums. **1966** *Globe and Mail* (Toronto) 14 Jan. B5/9: And there are hopes that Stewart [B.C.] may be connected soon with Prince Rupert, through a series of logging roads.

logging-shirt *n. Obs.* See quote. See also **logging** (def. 1a).
1832 (1838) TRAILL *Backwoods* 209: He learns to chop down trees . . . in a coarse over-garment of hempen cloth, called a logging-shirt.

log-guard *n. Lumbering* See **sheer-boom.**
1910 BINDLOSS *Thurston* 77: "I'm considerable indebted to you for the way you tackled the late crisis, and approve of the log-guard's extension. How much did the extra cost you?"

log haul-up See **haul-up.**
1964 *Atlantic Advocate* July 56/3: There will also be the facilities for a log haul-up, mooring piles and a wharf on the south shore of the Salmon River.

log-heap *n. Hist.* a great pile of logs for burning when clearing land, as at a logging bee, *q.v.*

1822 *U.C.Gaz.* (York [Toronto]) 23 May 47/3: If, in making the clearance the top and under brush only, were burnt in the field and the heavy timber was cut into cordwood, or split for rails, instead of being burnt in large log-heaps, in one universal conflagration . . . several generations must appear and disappear before any serious inconvenience could arise from want of fuel. **1852** (1923) MOODIE *Roughing It* 304: The Devil sat on a log heap, A Log heap, a log heap—A red hot burning log heap—A-grinning at the bee. **1933** GUILLET *Early Life in U.C.* 277: In new settlements during July the whole countryside was illuminated by the burning of log heaps.

log-jam *n.* **1 a.** *Lumbering* See **jam,** *n.* (def. 2).
1889 WITHROW *Our Own Country* 126: Just below there was a huge log-jam which must await the next freshet before it could be released. **1965** *Islander* 11 July 11/3: Quite a number of these tough, two-fisted characters died unnoticed, either by falling into rivers or being caught in log jams.

b. *Figurative use.*
1966 *Vancouver Province* 12 Dec. 25/2: "Once we get back the regular rhythm I'd say the log jam among the general cargo vessels will start to disappear sometime next week."

2 *North* a protective framework of logs intended to keep ice from damaging a ship's hull.
1908 LAUT *Conquest N.W.* I 82: To-day there are no forests within miles from the rocky wastes of Churchill, but at that time, the country was timbered to the water's edge, and during the ebb tide the men constructed a log jam or ice-break around the ship.

log-load *n. Sealing, Nfld* a capacity load.
1933 GREENE *Wooden Walls* 43: . . . Owners and crews alike would always look . . . with implicit confidence in their skill and intuition to set the courses aright, and to bring a log-load home.

log-load *v. Sealing, Nfld.* See first quote. See also **log-load,** *n.*
1933 GREENE *Wooden Walls* xvi: LOG LOADED This term is only used when every cranny in the ship is filled with the sculps. *Ibid.* 12: She log-loaded twice within sight of the City's cliffs.

log-maker *n. Lumbering* See 1947 quote. See also **log-making.** Cp. **timber-maker.**
1912 HEENEY *Pickanock* 58: Soon the road-cutters and log-makers arrived and all began to satisfy their woodsmen's appetites. . . . **1947** SAUNDERS *Algonquin* 30: The log maker took over next, trimming to log off its branches, and cutting off the top to a specified length. **1964** *Cdn Geog.Jnl* Feb. 66/3: Then the log maker trimmed off the branches and cut off the top.

log-making *n. Lumbering* See quotes. See also **log-maker.** Cp. **make logs** and **making**
1944 *Forestry Course 1* 79: *Log-making.* This term includes, falling, trimming as required, and cross-cutting or bucking into the desired lengths. **1964** *Cdn Geog.Jnl* Feb. 72/2: A large tractor takes two or three logs at once to the log-making area where log-maker and cut-control man work together to cut the tree into logs.

log off See **log,** *v.* (def. 2).

log pen 1 *Obs.* See **boom¹,** *n.* (def. 1).
1805 BOULTON *Upper Canada* 57: They are cut on the banks of the river Welland, and floated down to its mouth, where there is a reservoir made to receive them by a chain of log pens, as they are called.

2 *Obs.* a structure of logs forming a kind of cache (def. 2).

1896 RUSSELL *Far North* 274: Several families were "starving" before February, that is, either living on hares, owls, martens and other fur-bearing animals from the traps, or stealing from the log pens in which their more industrious neighbors had cached their fish along the lake shore.

3 a kind of trap. See also **log trap.**

*c*1902 (1912) LAUT *Trapper* 217: As the rabbits decreased, Koot set out many traps for the bob-cats now reckless with hunger, steel-traps and dead-falls and pits and log pens with a live grouse clucking inside.

log-pile *n.* See **deck** (def. 1).

1901 CONNOR *Man from Glengarry* 198: At each log-pile stood a man with a hand-spike to help the driver to get the log into position, a work requiring strength and skill, and above all, a knowledge of the ways of logs which comes only by experience.

log pond *Lumbering* See **pond** (def. 3).

1964 *Powell River News* 7 May 5/6: Jack Kliever, Mahood woods superintendent, said that westerly winds last year caused considerable damage to the company's log pond at the mouth of Kelly Creek.

log-pond man *Lumbering* a man who works at a pond (def. 3).

1964 *Powell River News* 7 May 5/5: Log pond men at Mahood's Logging Co. at Stillwater won't curse westerly winds as heartily this year, thanks to the extension of the company's breakwater.

log-pool *n. Lumbering* See **pond** (def. 3).

1953 *Harmac News* Oct. 14/2: In 1935 Ed was transferred to Somass Division, where he later became log-pool manager.

log-rider *n. Slang* See **logger** (def. 1).

1900 OSBORN *Warders of West* 776: [There are] Western broncho-busters and Eastern log-riders . . . Scotch half-breeds whose fathers served "The Company. . . ."

log-roller *n. Lumbering, Slang, Obs.* a logger, especially one who worked with sawlogs rather than square timber.

1901 CONNOR *Man from Glengarry* 19: For the Glengarry men, who handled only square timber, despised the Murphy gang as sawlog men; "log-rollers" or "mushrats" they called them, and hated them as Irish "Papishes" and French "Crapeaux."

log-rolling† *n.* **1 a.** *Obs.* See **logging** (def. 1a).

1796 *U.C.Gaz.* (York [Toronto]) 9 Nov. 2/2: One other field of six acres, three of which are wheat stubble and potatoe land; the rest wanting a few days of log rolling to make it a good piece for corn.

b. *Hist.* See **logging bee.**

1946 LOWER *Colony to Nation* 191: . . . the great virtue was neighborliness, manifesting itself in bees, barn-raisings, log-rollings. . . .

2 the practice of exchanging favors for political ends.

☛ *The term derives from the pioneer practice of neighbor helping neighbor in the work of clearing land. See* **logging bee.**

1854 KEEFER *Ottawa* 45: Under the good old log-rolling system which prevailed in the Upper Canada legislature before the Union, such works as the Welland and St. Lawrence Canals could only obtain votes upon the principle of perfect reciprocity.

1916 SKELTON *Railway Builders* 18: . . . the system of provincial grants for road-building too often meant

log-rolling and corruption. . . . **1946** LOWER *Colony to Nation* 232: Members tried to serve the interests of their constituents by obtaining cash grants towards this local project or that: thus was built up the famous practice of "log-rolling." Just as the neighbors got together to roll up the newly-cut logs from a clearing into piles for burning, so the members "rolled up" each others' financial logs.

3 See **birling.**

1925 PHILIP *Crimson West* 225: The sports committee had arranged a . . . list of events [including] a log-rolling contest between a man from the State of Maine and a citizen of New Brunswick. **1957** *Weekend Mag.* 10 Aug. 33/1: Horizontally inclined is Bill Fontana, a lumberjack who taught his pet Dalmation log-rolling in the Ontario bush. **1966** *Cdn Forest Industries* Oct. 53/2: [Caption] June and Arne Wickheim demonstrate log rolling skill. The Sooke, B.C., brothers will organize logging sports at Expo '67 World's Fair.

log run See **drive** (def. 1).

1957 *Weekend Mag.* 23 Mar. 41/1: . . . his father took him along to help on the annual log run. . . .

log shack a shack, *q.v.,* built of logs.

1910 FRASER *Red Meekins* 233: . . . now the plenitude of rock and trees had its primeval contours thrown out of joint by the aggressive squares of logshacks and canvas tents. **1952** PUTNAM *Cdn Regions* 321/2: Sudbury was founded in 1883 as a collection of log shacks on Federal Government land, a mile north of Lake Ramsay.

log shanty 1 See **shanty** (def. 1a).

1848 LANMAN *Adventures* 191: We retraced our steps back to the log shanty where we had stopped. **1952** PUTNAM *Cdn Regions* 237/1: The original log shanties were probably much of the same type, so also were the squared-log houses which followed them.

2 See **shanty** (def. 1b and picture).

1957 *Beaver* Spring 38/2: In most camps before the First World War they slept and ate under one roof, in log shanties forty or fifty feet square.

log sled See **bogan**[2].

1897 GREENOUGH *Cdn Folk-Life* 36: And if it is hard to get up hills with the empty log-sled it is not easier to get down with a load, for the way is steep, and crooked in places. . . .

log slide *Lumbering, East* See **slide** (def. 1a).

1958 *Encyc.Can.* X 149/1: New activity started in 1852, when a log slide was built at Shawinigan Falls. . . . **1961** PRICE & KENNEDY *Renfrew* 51: The cribs were suitable in size for sending down log slides; the drams were sent down rapids.

log sluice See **log flume.**

1952 PUTNAM *Cdn Regions* 211/2: Small settlements of forest workers are found in coves along the shore, each with its wharf and log sluice.

log tack See **jackladder.**

1961 GREENING *Ottawa* 117: Most of them [sawmills] were equipped with a log tack having an endless chain which took the logs out of the water and raised them to the level of the saws. . . .

log tent 1 *Obs. or Hist.* an A-shaped shed made by laying logs up to a ridgepole and chinking with moss and clay. Cp. **lean-to.**

☛ *These structures, much simpler to build than a cabin, were used for temporary dwellings and storehouses.*
1743 (1949) ISHAM *Observations* 90: Log tents or huts are us'd in these parts by the English only, these they make in length and Weddth according to the Quantity of men that is to Live in them. **1887** (1932) *Beaver* Dec. 139: Our log tent is almost buried in snow-drift. **1954** RICH in *Moose Ft Jnls* 331: On December 14 a start was made on a log tent in which to live during the winter of 1776-77.
2 See quote. See also **shack-tent**.
1942 *Beaver* Mar. 19: [Caption] An Indian log tent. Canvas and spruce boughs cover the pyramidal framework and poles.

log tow *Lumbering* See **tow**.
1955 *Star Wkly* 5 June 17/3: Now they [old concrete-hulled ships] form a breakwater, sheltering the booming grounds where log tows are assembled.

log trap 1 a kind of deadfall (def. 1). See also **log pen** (def. 3). See picture at **deadfall**.
1743 (1949) ISHAM *Observations* 141: Wolvereen's . . . are catch't in Log traps chiefly, and are Eat by the natives, tho not by the English, they are Very strong Rank food. **1784** PENNANT *Arctic Zoology* 104: They are taken in several ways: sometimes in log-traps, baited with poplar sticks, laid in a path near the water. [**1921** HEMING *Drama of Forests* 133: [The deadfall] was set for bear, and was of the "log-house" kind, with walls nearly six feet high, and a base that was eight feet long by five feet wide in front, while only two feet in width in the rear.]
2 *Lumbering, B.C.* a boom set at the mouth of a river to prevent logs from drifting out to sea. See also **jail boom**.
1906 *Log of the "Columbia"* May 9/1: At high tide the "Columbia" was admitted through the gap into the log trap and proceeded up the river, and after some difficulty with the bar arrived at the camp.

log-trough roof See **scoop roof** and picture.
1924 *Beaver* Sep. 431: . . . when he saw the log trough roof . . . he was intensely interested. . . .

log up 1 *Hist.* See **log**, *v.* (def. 1).
1829 (1957) GUILLET *Valley of the Trent* 355: . . . after this we logged up and cleared three acres. . . .
1832 TRAILL *Backwoods* 132: The wind fallen trees are chopped through in length, to be logged up in the spring with the winter's chopping. **1853** STRICKLAND *Canada West* I 169: The remainder of the fallow should be burnt off and logged up in July, the rail-cuts split into quarters and drawn off to the site of the fences, ready for splitting into rails. **1957** GUILLET *Valley of the Trent* 1: Finding no demand for weavers . . . he hired out to "log up."
2 *Obs.* construct (of logs), as a cabin.
1897 YOUNG *Indian Trail* 44: The houses are built with a framework of squared timber which is well logged up, and the chinks well packed with moss and mud.

log village a small settlement having cabins, stores, etc. built of logs.
c**1902** LAUT *Trapper* 201: We think of these northern streams as ice-jammed, with mean log villages on their banks. **1923** WALDO *Down Mackenzie* 31: The "end of steel" came at Waterways, a log village too new for paint, with steel rails for a station platform.

log-way† *n. Obs.* **1** See **corduroy road**.
1832 (1953) RADCLIFF *Letters* 119: . . . in the meantime, a school-house is to be formed in the log-way, to be used for Divine Service till the church is prepared.
2 *Lumbering* an inclined trough for carrying logs from one level to another at a sawmill.
1881 *Progress* (Rat Portage [Kenora], Ont.) 15 July 1/5: The upper story or saw floor contains . . . one double edger, one trimmer and two log ways, all fitted with the latest improvements and conveniences.

lokey *n.* See **loci**.

lollacapop ['lɑləkə‚pɑp] *n.* [origin unknown] a kind of insect repellant; mosquito dope.
1923 WALDO *Down Mackenzie* 39: The familiar preparation known as lollacapop seems to be the best discourager.

lolly ['lɑli] *n.* [< Brit. dial. *lolly* < *loblolly* thick soup or porridge] *Orig.Nfld* See **frazil**.
1771 (1792) CARTWRIGHT *Journal* I 180: There being much lolly in the river, it was with great difficulty that I could cross it in a punt. **1889** WITHROW *Our Own Country* 68: The distance to Cape Traverse is about nine miles, part solid ice, part drifting ice, part water, and sometimes a great deal of broken ice or 'lolly.'
1963 *American Speech* Dec. 299: LOLLY, *n.* Soft ice beginning to form in a harbor.

Lombard sock See quote. See also **German sock**.
1910 FERGUSON *Janey Canuck* 105: The lumberman's stocking is known as the "Lombard sock." It comes up to his knees, and is held by a gay cord running through and round it.

Lone Land 1 *Hist.* the immense, sparsely populated prairies prior to 1900.
1872 (1883) BUTLER *Great Lone Land* 351: . . . it needs but little cause to recall again to the wanderer the image of the immense meadows where, far away at the portals of the setting sun, lies the Great Lone Land. **1878** *Sask. Herald* (Battleford, N.W.T.) 30 Dec. 8/1: The westerly end of the Pacific Telegraph flashes a kindly greeting to the Capital of the Lone Land, and to the inhabitants wishes a Merry Christmas and many returns, which will doubtless be fulfilled if the murderous scalping knife can be educated to operate on plum duff instead of human skulls. **1963** *Herald Mag.* 5 Oct. 4/1: Thus [in 1873] opened the modern history of the lone land, the southern portion of the territory which was to become Saskatchewan and Alberta 32 years later.
2 (in more recent use) the Northland of bush and barrens.
1900 OSBORN *Greater Canada* 41: "Although what they consider good eating and drinking is their chief god," says that wanderer in the Lone Land, "yet, when necessity compels them to it, they submit to great privation and hardship, not only without complaining, but even with cheerfulness and gaiety." **1934** GODSELL *Arctic Trader* 309: The Fur Lords no longer rule the Red Men; the erstwhile silence of the Lone Land is now broken by the sirens of ocean freighters carrying grain from Churchill to Europe, and the rumble and shrieks of freight and passenger trains as they speed swiftly across the Barren Lands.

long campfire See **long fire**.
1941 *Beaver* Mar. 14/1: . . . a long camp fire is made for cooking supper and keeping the traveller warm while he sleeps.

longer ['lɑŋgɚ] *n.* [*long* + *-er*] *Atlantic Provinces* long poles or timber in the rough, used

for building fishing stages, fences, floors, etc.; stringer. See also **longer fence.**
1772 (1792) CARTWRIGHT *Journal* I 215: At noon I . . . searched the woods . . . where I found some good longers, and boat-hook staffs. **1837** *Times* (Halifax) 25 July 235/1: On Thursday last the skeleton of a man was found in the woods a short distance from the Block House, at the entrance of this harbour, by a man and boy who were cutting longers. **1878** *North Star* (St. John's) 30 Mar. 3/2: On the afternoon of their death, the deceased . . . left home for the woods to draw "longers" across the pond. **1963** *American Speech* Dec. 299: LONGERS, *n.* Rails for a fence.

longer *v. Obs.* build or repair with longers.
1775 (1792) CARTWRIGHT *Journal* II 96: We longered part of the salt-room.

longer fence *Atlantic Provinces* See 1832 quote. See also **longer,** *n.*
[**1832** (1955) LEWELLIN *Emigration* 197: Fences are made with poles called longers, 14 to 15 feet long, eight in number, placed one above another in a diagonal form, and secured at the angles . . . by stakes driven into the ground . . . the topmost pole or longer, stouter than the others, rests in the crutch made by these stakes . . . when [they] angle.] **1842** BONNYCASTLE *Newfoundland* I 292: The other mode [of fence building] is to set up a strong stick every eight or ten feet, and then to nail three or four longer ones of less diameter to them; this is called a longer fence, and the poles of spruce are called 'longers.' **1925** (1936) MONTGOMERY *Kilmeny* 203: As he crossed the pasture field before the spruce wood he came upon Neil Gordon building a longer fence.

long fire See 1921 quote. See also **long campfire.**
1900 LONDON *Son of Wolf* 24: Down the centre a long fire was built, while either side was carpeted with spruce boughs. **1921** HEMING *Drama of Forests* 182: The "long fires" were huge structures, twelve or fifteen feet in length, so that each man might bask in the heat without crowding his neighbour.

long-handled underwear *Slang* warm underwear having ankle-length legs and, usually, long sleeves.
1937 (1950) STANWELL-FLETCHER *Driftwood Valley* 83: I wear light wool "long-handled" underwear. . . . **1947** GILLHAM *Raw North* 93: On shelves, behind the counter, is long handled underwear that men and women alike purchase and wear. **1966** *Globe and Mail* (Toronto) 11 Oct. 33/8: All around me, in their double-decker bunks, lay sleeping lumberjacks clad in their sweaty long-handled underwear. . . .

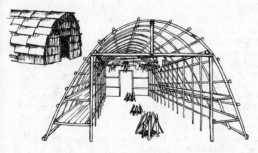

A longhouse (def. 1)

longhouse *n.* **1**† among the Indians of the Five Nations (Iroquois) and the Hurons, a communal dwelling and council house about 20 feet wide and varying in length, the centre of political and religious life.
1883 (1895) *Trans.Roy.Soc.Can.* I 2 48: He will therefore be unable to accompany me to the Onandaga "Long-House," where the council is to be held. **1913** JOHNSON *Shagganappi* 119: . . . he would accompany his parents to the "Longhouse" (which was their church), and take his little part in the religious festivities. **1963** *Beaver* Autumn 15/1: Before that, snowshoe-making with deerhide and white ash was common around the longhouses of the old homeland of *Wendake*—which later inhabitants now call Huronia—in the Georgian Bay region of Ontario.
2 See **plank house** and picture.
1958 GRIFFIN *British Columbia* 6: Yet Marpole was a flourishing village of cedar longhouses built by a food-gathering neolithic people around the time of the Roman conquest of Britain. **1959** *Native Voice* Feb. 7/2: The longhouse used for tribal celebrations was erected with massive cedar timbers. The longest known in history was 1,000 feet long. It was built by the grandfather of Chief Dominic Charlie of the Squamish tribe on the Capilano reserve in North Vancouver. **1964** *Canadian Wkly* 4 Jan. 9/2,3: I met Mungo Martin, the chief, and he took me into the longhouse where they were celebrating the end of the salmon catch.

longhouse marriage among non-Christian Iroquois, a marriage ceremony conducted according to the ancient tribal traditions. Cp. **blanket marriage.**
1957 *Kingston Whig-Standard* (Ont.) 13 Mar. 2/6: Harry Nixon (L—Brant) said the government's earlier refusal to recognize longhouse marriages was an insult to the Indians.

longhouse religion the ancient pagan religious beliefs of the Iroquois people.
1959 *Native Voice* July 4/1: Until 1923 the Canadian government left them pretty much to run their own affairs. They were ruled by their hereditary chiefs, had their own police, administered their own laws, and practised the "Long House Religion" of their ancestors. **1963** *Weekend Mag.* 4 May 7/1: . . . she taught me the Longhouse religion, which is really the practice of a way of living, with emphasis on symbols from nature, animals and plants and so on.

Long Knife† [trans. of an Algonk. expression; cf. Ojibwa *kechchi* big, long and *mōkkumān* knife] *Hist.* in Indian parlance, originally, a Virginian; in Canada, an American; U.S. citizen. See also **Big Knife.**
1836 (1923) JAMESON *Rambles* 31: "Hah! what is the matter with the young Long-knife?" **1909** NURSEY *Isaac Brock* 100: "My object," said Brock, addressing the Indians, "is to assist you to drive the 'Long-knives' [Americans] from the frontier, and repel invasion of the King's country." **1959** SLUMAN *Blackfoot Crossing* 33: But Crowfoot says that the border—the medicine line—protects his people from the Long Knives.

long-line† *n. Fisheries* a long fishing line having many baited hooks, used for deep-sea commercial fishing.
1947 TAYLOR *Canada* 341: Each large boat uses small 'dories,' from which the actual fishing is done by means

of trawls or baited long-lines. **1963** *Globe and Mail* (Toronto) 20 Nov. B5/2: [This was] a switch from chasing and harpooning the fish to catching them on long-lines, with baited hooks.

longliner *n. Fisheries* a fishing vessel that uses long-lines, *q.v.*
1955 *Fishermen's Advocate* 14 Jan. 10/5: Three new longliners are now under construction. . . .
1959 *Globe Mag.* (Toronto) 12 Sep. 21/2: Ground-fishing operations—draggers with their great, bottom-scraping nets, and longliners with multiple lines armed with hundreds of baited hooks—were the principle targets. **1966** *Weekend Mag.* 5 Mar. 18/1: Three fishermen from Nova Scotia aboard the 42-foot longliner Maureen Rose set their lines in the North Atlantic fishing grounds, and turned in for the night.

longlinerman *n.* a fisherman on a longliner, *q.v.*
1955 *Fishermen's Advocate* 14 Jan. 7/3: The courses, while aimed at longlinermen, were made available to all who wished to attend. . . . **1956** *Saturday Night* 8 Dec. 16/1: And since when have Americans or British freely discussed Clear Grits, Digby chickens, Socreds, the Land of Little Sticks, separate schools, nitchies, longlinermen?

long-line skinner *Hist.* a teamster skilled in driving several span of horses or mules by means of long reins.
1958 WATTERS *B.C.Cent.Anthol.* 558: Smoothy Morrow, the stage-driver, who was a tinsmith who graduated to be a long-line skinner, then finally became the ace of the profession of the Cariboo a stage driver.

longlining† *n. Fisheries* fishing with a long-line, *q.v.*
1868 SPROAT *Savage Life* 225: The mode of fishing for halibut is by 'long-lining.' **1954** *Fundy Fisherman* (Black's Harbour, N.B.) 13 Oct. 1/4: An experiment is underway in Lunenburg County which might well revolutionize Long Lining. . . . **1960** *Cdn Geog.Jnl* July 28/2: Canada supplied 40 engines to establish a revolving fund and at the same time longlining was introduced by the Canadian instructors.

Long Night the Arctic winter.
1919 CURWOOD *River's End* 64: "Were you ever up there—through the Long Night—alone?"

longshoreman *n. Local* in northern Labrador, a person who lives along the coast. Cp. **liveyere** (def. 1).
1891 PACKARD *Labrador Coast* 141: The houses of the "long-shore-men," or those of the permanent residents, were clapboarded and a little better looking than the tilts. **1947** TANNER *Outlines* II 745: A specialist among the traders told to me that he reckons that a little family of these 'longshoremen' south of Cartwright required an annual average income of $160.

long slide *Curling* a style of play in which the curler takes a long slide along the ice when delivering his stone from the hack.
1962 *Canada Month* Apr. 26/3: The west . . . introduced the long slide now about twice the distance the old-style curler slides before launching his stone. *Ibid.* 27/2: The long slide and knockout game are becoming more and more common in the east.

Longstocking *n. B.C., Slang, Hist.* See 1957 quote.
1955 *Maclean's* 2 Apr. 31/2: These are the heads of old English households . . . [who] live at peace with their neighbors and are known somewhat affectionately as Longstockings . . . from their habit of wearing knickbockers . . . short puttees and sturdy ankle boots. *Ibid.* 80/2: Ex-officers of the British imperial forces still trickle into the Cowichan [Valley, B.C.], but they are different than the old Longstockings. **1957** BARRATT *Coronets* 16: "Guess they think they're Longstockings. At Skomish the upper class English were called Longstockings because most of the men and boys wore knickers or riding breeches, with long knitted stockings."

long stoop *Obs.* See quote. See also **stoop** (def. 1).
1885 HAIGHT *Country Life* 80: Very often the roof projected over, giving an elliptical shape to one side [of the house], and the projection of about six feet formed a cover for what was then called a long stoop, but which now-a-days would be known as a verandah.

longtailed duck See **old squaw**.
1795 (1911) HEARNE *Journey* 447: The Mallard and Long-tailed Duck visit Hudson's Bay in great numbers, and extend from the sea-coast to the remotest Western parts. **1850** GOODSIR *Baffin's Bay* 20: They said there were also plenty of the eider, and the long-tailed duck. **1958** *Evening Telegram* (St. John's) 29 Apr. 13/8: Here we had snow geese, eider ducks and long-tailed ducks in a lagoon nearby.

long tom† *Placer Mining* See **sluice-box** and picture.
1852 *Elora Backwoodsman* (C.W.) 17 June 2/4: The plough is a far more profitable instrument than "the long Tom" or "the rocker." **1963** *Placer-Mining B.C.* Plate III (A): [Caption] A long-tom with one man bailing water and the other shovelling gravel. Coarse coco-matting covers the bottom of the sluice-box.

Long Trail *Fur Trade, Hist.* **1** the long route into the fur country of the Northwest (def. 1a).
1903 WHITE *Forest* 36: For here is where begins the Long Trail. Whether it will lead you through the forests . . . or over the plains, or by invisible water paths . . . these things matter not a particle.

2 See **Long Traverse**.
1905 MOTT *Jules* 6: He was a thorn in the factor's side, as he stole fur from the traps of the Company's Indians, and they could never catch him to send him over the "long trail." **1908** LAUT *Conquest N.W.* I 65: So passed Henry Hudson down the Long Trail on June 21, 1611!

Long Traverse *Fur Trade, Hist.* (a euphemism for death) See **1931** quote. See also **Death Trail** and **Long Trail** (def. 2).
1924 *Beaver* Jan. 148: His shack was burnt, his provisions were taken away, and he was sent on "the long traverse." **1931** GREY OWL *Last Frontier* 19: This affair was a modification of the old "Longue Traverse," a scheme adopted by the despotic representatives of a big fur company in earlier days, whereby undesirables, such as freetraders, encroaching trappers and others, were captured, their outfit confiscated, and themselves turned loose with a rifle and a few rounds of ammunition, to find their way on foot, hundreds of miles, to the nearest town.

lookout *n.* **1** See **lookout tower**.
1952 PUTNAM *Cdn Regions* 330/1: The whole landscape may easily be seen from the Lands and Forests lookout on the "back road." **1961** *Canada Month* 6 Oct. 42/3:

However, the forestry people want money to buy greater preparedness through more lookouts, men, planes and equipment.

2 See **lookout man.**

1955 GOWLAND *Smoke* 16: The look-out had to be an expert woodsman, be able to read meteorological instruments, have an excellent degree of physical fitness and good eyesight, and, the advert stated, preference would be given to an ex-serviceman.

lookout man a forester who mans a lookout tower, *q.v.*

[**1953** *Cdn Geog.Jnl* Feb. 50/2: Mechanics . . . lookout towermen and pump operators are also directed by the Chief Forest Ranger.] **1958** *Lethbridge Herald* (Alta) 31 May 5/1: The fire was spotted by Bill Clarke, lookout man on the Livingstone Lookout in the Gap area. . . . **1963** MCKINNON *Forest Activities 3* 3: The lookoutman takes readings on all his weather· instruments hourly between 8 a.m. and 8 p.m. in hazardous weather and relays this information to his Ranger.

lookout tower a high tower from which a trained forestry employee watches for forest fires and reports the position so that action may be taken to fight them. See also **fire tower** and **lookout.**

1958 *Edmonton Jnl* 25 July 28/3: In the Slave Lake division, three lumber roads . . . are closed, along with the . . . Flattop trail leading from Highway 2 south to Flattop lookout tower. . . . **1962** *Sask.News* 19 June 2/1: It's a lonely life for a man confined to a glass dome atop a lookout tower.

loper ['lopɚ] *n.* [< *lope* move with an easy, bounding gait + *-er*] *West* See **coyote** (def. 1).

1963 SYMONS *Many Trails* 39: The few ranchers . . . had overcome . . . the depredation of the "lopers," the grey wolves of the plains.

lopped stick *Obs.* See **lobstick.**

1830 (1954) *Beaver* June 17: The Voyagers agreed among themselves to cut a "May Pole," or "Lopped Stick" for me. . . .

lopstick ['lɑpˌstɪk] *n.* See **lobstick.**

lord *n.* See **lord and lady.**

1771 (1792) CARTWRIGHT *Journal* I 123: The two furriers came up from the tilt, and brought an otter and a lord. **1779** *Ibid*. II 490: After breakfast I went to Green Island, where I saw a white fox, and killed a pair of lords. **1959** MCATEE *Folk-Names* 16: Harlequin Duck [is also called] lord (Nfld. N.S.) . . . old lord (The fully adult male. Nfld.). . . .

lord and lady (duck) a harlequin duck, *Histrionicus histrionicus.* See 1956 quote. See also **lady.**

1771 (1792) CARTWRIGHT *Journal* I 170: After dinner I went down the river, shifted one of the traps from Furriers Cove to another rubbing place higher up, and killed three lords and ladies. **1835** WIX *Journal* 162: I had a fine view of a patch fox in my walk, saw several seals, and some of those very beautiful birds, called by the people of Newfoundland "lords and ladies." **1930** *Cdn Geog.Jnl* I 32/2: The Harlequin Duck . . . is known to trappers and prospectors in the far west as "Lord and Lady Duck." **1959** MCATEE *Folk-Names* 16: Harlequin Duck [is also called] lord and lady (Usually in the plural, "lords and ladies." In allusion to the handsome plumage. While these terms refer basically to the sexes, they are customarily used together to indicate the species. Nfld., "Labr.," N.S., N.B., B.C.). . . .

Lord's Day Act (of Canada) an act passed by the federal government in 1906 to prevent the introduction of non-essential commerce and commercial entertainment on Sunday.

[**1949** PETERSON *Chipmunk* 267: The Lord's Day Alliance, which defied everybody to enjoy himself on Sunday, seemed to have been repealed.] **1958** *Encyc.Can.* VI 203/1: To this end the alliance gave effective leadership in the campaign that led to the passing in 1906 of the Lord's Day Act of Canada. . . . **1964** *Calgary Herald* 30 July 26/5: Never on Sundays, says the Lord's Day Act "is it lawful, except as provided herein, for any person to sell, offer for sale, or purchase any goods or chattels, or other personal property, or any real estate, or to carry on any business, or employ any person to do work, business, or labor."

Lord's Day Alliance (of Canada) an interchurch body founded in 1888 to preserve Sunday as a day of rest, prominent in the movement leading to the passing of the Lord's Day Act, *q.v.*

1897 *Ledge* (New Denver, B.C.) July-Aug. 1/4: It is about time a contingent of the Lord's Day Alliance went over there and made the Scotch be mum on the Sabbath. **1962** *Time* (Cdn ed.) 2 Mar. 10/3: Surprisingly, the Calgary campaign earned no opposition from the strait-laced, Toronto-based national Lord's Day Alliance.

Lords of the North *Hist.* See **North West Company.**

1903 WHITE *Forest* 185: . . . this had been on the route of the voyageurs from Montreal and Quebec at the time when the lords of the North journeyed to the scenes of their annual revels at Fort Williams. **1962** DICKIE *Great Golden Plain* 62: The pedlars . . . formed a great company. "The Lords of the North," people called them, and lords of the prairie they proved to be.

losh *n.* See **loche.**

losivants *n.pl. Obs.* See **lods et ventes.**

1770 *Quebec Gaz.* 1 Nov. 2/1: It is required of the Tennants of said Seigneurie to come and satisfy the present Proprietor of whatever may be due of Rents, or Arrears of Rents, Losivants &c. at or before the 11th of November next.

lot† *n.* **1** *Hist.* **a.** in colonial Nova Scotia, one of the 100-acre parcels of land making up a surveyed division.

1750 JEFFERYS *Fishing Banks*: [Map of s. N.S.] Shewing the Number of Lotts in Each Division. **1763** (1876) CAMPBELL *Yarmouth, N.S.* 41: . . . Each Lot of Land ajoyneing the harbour . . . shall containe Eighte Rods and Run so far back as to containe one hundred acors.

b. in Upper Canada and parts of Lower Canada, one of the 200-acre parcels of land into which a surveyed concession (def. 2) was divided.

[**1783** (1959) PRESTON *Kingston* 37: Every Township will have 25 Lots in front [and] contain 175 Lots of 12 acres.] **1806** BOULTON *Upper Canada* 7: The lands are usually divided into lots of two hundred acres each, forming a complete farm. **1842** WILLIS *Cdn Scenery* II 56: These concessions are subdivided into lots of 200 acres of which there are 32 in each. **1921** HEMON *Chapdelaine* [trans.] 196: . . . I have two lots of my own, paid for out and out, and you know the soil is good.

2 *P.E.I., Hist.* See 1904 cite.
1783 (1876) CAMPBELL *Hist.P.E.I.* 31: I did more: I prevented all the lots from being sold belonging to proprietors who I knew were inclined to improve their lands, and this I did by taking the debt upon myself, which was not required by the law, nor perhaps in justice to my own family. **1821** (1823) JOHNSTONE *Travels in P.E.I.* 39: The main road passing through the remainder of lot 49, to the head of Vernon River, divides, one branch on the right; leads to Murray Harbour, through seventeen miles of wood, without a house. **1904** CROSSKILL *P.E.I.* 11: A survey was begun by Captain Samuel Holland in 1764 and completed in 1766, by which the Island was divided into 67 lots or townships of about 20,000 acres each and granted by means of a lottery to persons . . . who were considered to have claims upon the British Government.
1955 HARVEY *Island of St.John* 5: In 1765 it was surveyed by Captain Samuel Holland and divided into 67 lots or townships of 20,000 acres each.

3 any small parcel of land, especially in an urban area.
1797 *U.C.Gaz.* (York [Toronto]) 18 Jan. 1/2: As an encouragement to trades men a number of lots will be leased for 900 years, subject to an annual ground rent of six percent. on the price, and ten per cent purchase money. **1899** GARDNER *Names* 510: James Wilkes, as a boy, used to ride a pony across lots from the present Simpson corner to the post office, which was then east of the St. Lawrence market, the population of Toronto being then about 1,600. **1912** BICKERSTETH *Open Doors* 110: During the rush to Klondyke he went off seeking gold, and after travelling round in many parts of the West returned, after about fifteen years, to find his fifty-dollar lot had sold for 100,000 dollars. **1966** *Globe and Mail* (Toronto) 30 June 30/5: [Advert.] Rustic 7 room ranch bungalow on 1/2 acre lot, trees galore!

lot line *Hist.* the survey line marking each of the four sides of a lot (def. 1b).
1853 STRICKLAND *Canada West* I 88: Cross lines run at right angles with the former every thirty chains, and are called lot-lines: they subdivide the township into two hundred acre lots; every fifth cross line is a road allowance. **1863** WALSHE *Cedar Creek* 115: He looked again at the landmark—an elm tree at the junction of the lot line and the concession road, which bore numbers of each, "Nine Fifteen" . . . on opposite sides.

lots et ventes See **lods et ventes.**

louche *n.* See **loche.**

loup-cervier ['lusəfi; *French* lusɛr'vje] *n.* [< F < L *lupus cervarius* wolf that hunts stags] See **Canada lynx.** See also **lucivee.**
1744 DOBBS *Hudson's Bay* 41: The Loup Cervier, or Lynx, is of the Cat Kind, but as large as a great Dog; it preys upon all the Beasts it can conquer, as does the Tyger, which is the only Beast in that Country that won't fly from a Man. *a*1820 (1838) HEAD *Forest Scenes* 41: [It was] a species of lynx or wild cat, which the natives call the loup-cervier, or, as they pronounce it *lousifee.* **1825** *P.E.I.Register* (Charlottetown) 15 Apr. 1/1: The sum of Five Shillings shall be paid to any person or persons who shall bring to said Treasurer the snout of any Loup-Cervier killed within said Island. . . . **1955** ADTIC *Glossary*: loup cervier. A

French Canadian term for the lynx. **1962** (1964) INNIS *Fur Trade* 90: This quality [castor gras] of beaver being necessary [in 1720] for the consumption of the hat-trade, they would have their furs which consist principally in the most beautiful martens and "loups cerviers". . . .

loup-garou [ˌlugə'ru] *n.* [< Cdn F < F *loup* wolf + *garou* < OF *garoul* < Gmc, whence also E *werewolf*] **1** a werewolf. See also **Indian devil** (def. 3).
☛ *This term and the superstition came to New France with the first settlers; in later use among the voyageurs and the French half-breeds, the loup-garou was confused with the* **Weetigo,** *q.v., of the Algonkian peoples.*
1901 DRUMMOND *J.Courteau* 24: "But lissen dat win', how she scream outside, mak' me t'ink of de loup garou. . . ." **1910** FRASER *Red Meekins* 30: The canoe rose in the air as if the ghost paddlers of the Loup Garou had lifted it. . . . **1923** SCOTT *Witching of Elspie* 19: The neighbours' gossip about him, that he were a werewolf, a loup garou, he had never heeded, and to requite him this power had struck into his own family. **1928** PERRY *Two Reds* 77: . . . it was on a par with Indian superstitions of the dread *loup garou,* or werewolf, who was able, so the stories go, to travel hundreds of miles in a single night. **1961** ANDERSON *Angel* 11: The black wilderness to the northward . . . was the source of terrifying tales told by the Indian children of the *loup-garou,* of Tache and of Windigo.

2 *Que.* See quote. Cp. **caribou** (def. 4).
1959 *Time* (Cdn ed.) 19 Jan. 8/1: Some 225 people attended the affair, dined on buffalo steak, guzzled *loups-garous* ("were-wolves," hot red wine laced with rum), smoked peace pipes, toasted everything worth toasting.

loup-marin *n. Cdn French* "marine wolf, sea wolf" a seal.
1889 WITHROW *Our Own Country* 152: . . . Rivière du Loup. Its name is said to be derived from the fact that many years ago it was the resort of great droves of seals— *loups-marins*—who frequented the shoals at the mouth of the river. **1901** DRUMMOND *J.Courteau* 68: But he'll bring de fines' presen' from upper St. Maurice/ De loup marin an' black-fox from off de Hodson Bay/. . . .

Louse Town *Slang, Hist.* Klondike City, Y.T. See also **L-town.** Also spelled *Lousetown.*
1897 *Medicine Hat News* (Alta) 30 Sep. 7/5: We pitched camp on the south side, on what is known as Louse Town. **1938** BLACK *Seventy Years* 121: We squatted on the hill above Lousetown, described by the Sourdoughs as "The lousiest place on God's earth, for any day the lice might walk away with them buildin's." **1963** *Alaska Sportsman* Mar. 34/3: Poking through the ruins of Lousetown, the old red light district across the river from Dawson City, antique collector Gradelle Leigh of Fairbanks came up with a real find.

low-bush cranberry a shrub, *Viburnum edule;* also, its fruit. See note at **mooseberry.**
1833 (1838) TRAILL *Backwoods* 144: The low-bush cranberries are brought in great quantities by the Indians to the towns and villages. **1958** *Edmonton Jnl* 26 July 39/6: For the most part, housewives pick high and low bush blueberries . . . and in the fall, low bush cranberries.

Lower Canada 1 *Hist.* **a.** from 1791-1841, the official name of the province lying between the Ottawa River and New Brunswick, now included in Quebec. See also **L.C.** (def. 1).

1787 *Account N.S.* 195: The whole of the vast province of Canada ought to be viewed as forming two grand divisions, distinguished by the names of Upper and Lower Canada. **1791** (1911) SIMCOE *Diary* 69: Dec. 26— This day the division of the Province of Quebec into Upper and Lower Canada, and the new constitution given to the former, was announced by proclamation. **1836** *Bytown* [Ottawa] *Gaz.*1 Sep. 2/4: Judging from the Lower Canada newspapers, which, as in other countries, are the organs of and fomenters of party and faction, we should conclude that parties are breaking up in this country. **1963** MORTON *Kingdom of Canada* 258: In the Union there was also to be equal representation of the two sections which were the old Upper and Lower Canada, now Canada West and Canada East.

b. from 1841-1867, the popular name for Canada East, *q.v.*
1841 *Chatham Jnl* (C.W.) 7 Aug. 3/1: The Solicitor General testified that in Upper Canada the schools educated only one in eight of the population, and that in Lower Canada there were 120,000 of the youth of both sexes who receive not the slightest description of elementary education. **1863** *Nor'Wester* (R.R.S.) 2 Sep. 2/2: It could not be expected that the language of "la belle France" should maintain its classified purity and beauty out here, when it does not even in Lower Canada.

2 since 1867, an unofficial traditional name for Quebec. Cp. **Upper Canada** (def. 2).
1868 *Niagara Mail* (Niagara-on-the-Lake, Ont.) 18 Mar. 2/1: The law in *Lower Canada* respecting caterpillars has just been strengthened by a decision in a case brought by a party to recover damages against a neighbor who carelessly allowed caterpillars to breed in his garden. **1917** *Grit* (Toronto) 7 Dec. 4/3: If the priests of Lower Canada were, in a body, to advise their parishioners to vote for Laurier, what a howl would be raised by the press of Ontario! **1966** *Globe and Mail* (Toronto) 14 Jan. 45/4: Upper and Lower Canada came together with a head-table flourish last night amid the rocking rhythms of old Canadian folk music. . . .

Lower Canadian a native or resident of Lower Canada, especially a French-speaking Canadian.
1798 (1935) RUSSELL *Correspondence* II 73: This looks like a continuance of the War, & is accompanied by a hint that the Lower Canadians are not so quiet as they should be. **1853** *Mackenzie's Wkly Message* 22 Sep. 2/5: Up to 1849, you Lower Canadians had the meanest, shabbiest, most deceitful executive administration of any I know. **1963** MORTON *Kingdom of Can.* 242: . . . but Lower Canadians also, following their own political genius, had advanced from the position of 1809.

Lower-Canadian *adj.* of or having to do with Lower Canada or Lower Canadians.
1812 *Kingston Gaz.* (U.C.) 24 Mar. 2/1: Your Excellency . . . may rely upon . . . an early attention . . . to every measure which can tend to enable His Majesty's Lower Canadian subjects to assist in repelling any sudden attack. **1861** *Nor'Wester* (R.R.S.) 14 Dec. 2/3: The French spoken here is of the Lower Canadian species, for the French speaking population consists mainly of Lower Canadians and their descendants. **1963** MORTON *Kingdom of Canada* 227: The tension in Lower Canadian politics was suddenly increased in 1822 by a secret and unexpected attempt to reunite the Canadas.

Lower-Canadian breed *Obs.* See **Canadian horse.**
1872 POOLE *Queen Charlotte Is.* 2: Our team consisted of two diminutive horses. These belonged to the Lower

Canadian breed, and were wretched objects to look at; for all of which, they really could do a deal of work. . . .

Lower City *Obs.* See **Lower Town** (def. 1).
1857 ROGER *Quebec* 11: The Church in the Lower City was built in 1690, after the town had been delivered from the English, and is called *Notre Dame de la Victoire.*

Lower Colonies *Hist.* See **Lower Provinces** (def. 1).
1835 *Novascotian* (Halifax) 2 Apr. 110/1: New Brunswick is the only one of the Lower Colonies yet favored with Legislative and Executive Councils. **1856** (1932) *Cdn Hist.Rev.* XIII 4: I do not now believe in the practicability of the federal or legislative union of Canada with the three "Lower Colonies."

lower countries *Fur Trade, Obs.* the trading region to the south and west of the Great Lakes in the headwaters of the Mississippi and Missouri Rivers. Cp. **Upper Country** (def. 1).
1761 (1901) HENRY (Elder) *Travels* 41: Michilimackinac is the place of deposit, and point of departure between the upper countries and the lower.

Lower House *Hist.* See **House of Assembly** (def. 1a). Cp. **legislative assembly.**
1792 (1955) CRAIG *Early Travellers* 10: The Houses of Assembly meet at Niagara. The Upper one consists of seven or eight members, the Lower one of sixteen. These have been increased by the Governor, for the time being, with the increasing population of the country. The Chief Justice is the Speaker of the Upper House, and a Mr. McDonnell of the Lower. **1858** *Brit.Colonist* (Victoria) 11 Dec. 1/4: The late election for two members of the Lower House, resulted in favor of the Liberals. **1863** WALSHE *Cedar Creek* 334: This is with reference to the hundred and thirty representatives in the Lower House of the Provincial Legislature.

Lower Lakes Lakes Ontario and Erie, two of the Great Lakes, *q.v.* See also **Upper Lakes** (def. 1).
1953 LOWER *Voyages* 7: All the way along the Front, as the shores of the St. Lawrence and the lower lakes were termed, settlement worked back into the bush. . . . **1964** *Edmonton Jnl* 9 July 2/3: Water levels in the lower lakes are at one of their lowest levels in history.

Lower Province *Hist.* See **Lower Canada** (def. 1).
1791 (1866) CHRISTIE *Lower Canada* I 73: The population of Upper Canada amounted to only ten thousand inhabitants, and that of the Lower Province to not more than a hundred thousand. **1852** MOODIE *Roughing It* 234: I have been told a story of a lady in the Lower Province, who took for her second husband a young fellow, who, as far as his age was concerned, might have been her son. **1955** CRAIG *Early Travellers* xxviii: [The] Lower province . . . was not an attractive goal for British settlers.

Lower Provinces *Hist.* **1** the Atlantic provinces, especially Nova Scotia and New Brunswick, as opposed to the Canadas, *q.v.* See also **Lower Colonies.**
1825 *Novascotian* (Halifax) 16 Mar. 95/1: We have certainly equal . . . advantages, as regards shipbuilding, to the Lower Provinces; yet one hundred and twenty vessels were built in New Brunswick in 1824, and near

seventy during the year just ended. **1829** MOORSOM *Letters N.S.* 95: The lower provinces, by which I mean New Brunswick, Nova Scotia, Prince Edward Island, and Newfoundland, are as essentially distinct from the Canadas, as (to use a home phrase) the "West End," from the "City" of our British Metropolis. **1948** BORRETT *Historic Halifax* 3: Halifax, the metropolis of Nova Scotia, and the chief city of the Acadian or Lower Provinces, was founded in the year 1749....

2 *West* the eastern provinces, from Ontario to the Maritimes.
1879 *Winnipeg Dly Times* 12 Apr. 1/1: The Employment Bureau connected with The Times has been established for the purpose of opening up a direct and reliable medium of communication between employers of all kinds in the North-West and those seeking employment in the Lower Provinces.

Lower Provincial *Obs.* of or having to do with the Lower Provinces (def. 1); also a native or resident of these provinces.
1852 *Hamilton Gaz.* (C.W.) 23 Feb. 2/6: Mr. Young, one of the Lower Provincial authorities, received for some negotiations of his ... three thousand pounds. **1859** *Brit.Colonist* (Victoria) 20 May 2/2: If the Canadians and Lower Provincials would keep their Bibles and religious questions out of their Legislatures and politics, it would be a desirable improvement, for they are eternally quarrelling about the way to go to Heaven.

Lower Town 1 the part of a town lying closest to the water front, usually the oldest part of the town and that where many business establishments are located; specifically, this part of Quebec City. See also **Low-Town.** Cp. **Upper Town.**
1711 (1920) *Cdn Hist.Rev.* I 49: There is in Quebeck Town Two hundred and fifty men of ye Melitia, and One hundred and fifty soldiers in ye kings pay, two batteries in ye Lower Town.... **1815** BOUCHETTE *Lower Canada* 142: [Quebec City] is divided into the upper and lower town, although the elevation of one above the other is scarcely perceptible. **1957** HUTCHISON *Canada* 127: As it happened, I was jerked violently back into the twentieth century by a wild ride, with a mad taxi-driver, through the teeming labyrinth of Lower Town, where laundry hung and women gossiped between the noisome tenements ... and tourists gaped at what they took to be the charming quaintness of a foreign civilization.

2 *Local* in Ottawa, Ontario, that part of the city lying downstream from the point where the Rideau Canal meets the Ottawa River, nowadays a predominently French-Canadian district.
1843 *Bytown* [Ottawa] *Gaz.* 9 Feb. 3/2: We were very much pleased to observe a substantial looking Pump, of the latest and most approved construction, has been inserted into the Public Well, in the Market Place Lower Town. **1959** *Ottawa Jnl* 12 July 4/4: The area referred to in the Journal item (Sparks, between Elgin and Bank) is clearly downtown ... Editor's note: ... local custom has recognized a "lower town" and "up town". The "lower town" boundaries did not extend further west than Sussex Drive. The business area west of Sussex by common usage has been known as "up town"; this despite any lexicographer's definition.

Lower Townships See **Eastern Townships.**
1965 STEVENS *Incompleat Canadian* 131: Hugh Graham came out of the Lower Townships and fetched up in the House of Lords....

low runner *Obs.* a type of sleigh having two low wooden runners which barely raised the box off the surface of the snow; a crude type of cariole (def. 1).
1818 HALL *Travels* 68: ... An attempt was once made to correct this evil, by prohibiting all low runners, as they were called, from coming within a certain distance of Quebec....

Low-Town *n. Obs.* See **Lower Town** (def. 1).
1764 *Quebec Gaz.* 18 Oct. 2/2: Alexander Mackenzie & John Grant, Have to sell at their Store, in the Low-Town of Quebec, A Great Variety of Goods.... **1766** *Ibid.* 12 June 3/1: This is to acquaint the Public, That Simon's Coffee-House, in the Low-Town, was open'd on Friday last; where Gentlemen will always meet with good Entertainment.

Loyal Grit *Hist.* See quote. See also **Grit.**
1954 BERTON *I Married Klondike* 119: Thus, during my early years in Dawson, every government position grand or humble was held by a Loyal Grit, as the Liberals were then called.

Loyalist *n. Hist.* **1 a.** See **United Empire Loyalist.**
1779 *Quebec Gaz.* 11 Feb. 3/1: Mr. John Greaves was appointed by His Excellency the Commander-in-Chief to attend the Loyalists residing at Mischish as Surgeon. **1805** BOULTON *Upper Canada* 13: A great mass of land has been granted by His Majesty's patent, free of expense, to officers, old soldiers, loyalists and others. **1966** *Kingston Whig-Standard* (Ont.) 28 May 4/3: Born in Cornwallis [N.S.], the son of a Loyalist, he [Gesner] is remembered as the inventor of the process which gave the world kerosene oil.

b. occasionally still, a descendant of a United Empire Loyalist.
1883 LAWRENCE *Foot-Prints* 51: Though not a Loyalist, he felt that the terms Canadian and Loyalist were identical, and that all true Canadians would throw themselves into the celebration.

2 See late **Loyalist.**
1833 (1917) *London Hist.Soc.Trans.* VIII 25: I am a Loyalist, but not a U.E. Loyalist; we did not draw land from the King, when we came to the country.

3 a person remaining loyal to the Crown during the rebellions of 1837-38 in the Canadas, *q.v.*
1837 *Kingston Chron.* (U.C.) 15 Nov. 2/4: The Loyalists then marched through the principal portion of the town and suburbs seeking for the "Sons of Gaineeroy" but in vain—they seemed to have evaporated like ghosts into thin air. **1924** *Cdn Hist.Rev.* V 244: Ogle R. Gowan, then of Brockville, as ... a conservative and an active loyalist of 1837.

4 a supporter of the Canadian party (def. 2). See also **Canadian Loyalist.**
1871 *Wkly Manitoban* 6 May 2/1: When we examine the counts of the indictment, we find the first and main one to be that stale grievance—appointment of "rebels" to office, neglecting the "loyalists." **1909** CAMERON *New North* 77: Philip is a Loyalist. During the half-breed rebellion of 1885 he carried dispatches to Middleton and Otter, going seventy-five miles one day on foot. **1963** STANLEY *Louis Riel* 139: Rebuffed by the Prime Minister, the "loyalists" turned to the Governor-General....

Loyalist Province New Brunswick, because originally settled by United Empire Loyalists.
1895 *Trans.Roy.Soc.Can.* I 2 101: The movement meant more to New Brunswick than to the other provinces—it is truly "The Loyalist province."
1931 SEARY *Romance* 139: [Title] The Birth of New Brunswick, "The Loyalist Province."

L.P.P. Labor Progressive Party, a former name of the Communist party in Canada.
1944 *Cdn Seaman* 18 Aug. 3/2: Since the membership of any union is neither all Liberal, CCF, Social Credit, nor LPP, it is clear that the work of a political action committee, serving the best interests of the whole membership, must be based upon the advancement of progressive policies of social and economic reconstruction, rather than upon parties.
1957 *Maclean's* 6 July 36/2: The eclipse of the LPP is credited to prosperity by most of the Strip's citizens. . . .

L-town *n.* See **Louse Town.**
1926 DILL *Long Day* 32: Nevertheless, L-town enjoyed the distinction of having two saloons while Dawson, proper, had only one, of which Joe Ladue was the proprietor.

lucerver *n.* See **lucivee.**

lucifee ['lusə,fi] *n.* See **lucivee.**

lucififer *n.* See quote. See also **lucivee.**
1900 LONG *Wilderness Ways* 118: He had a dog, Grip, a big brindled cur, of whose prowess in killing "varmints" he was always bragging, calling him the best "lucififer" dog in all Canada. Lucififer, by the way, is a local name for the lynx on the upper St. John where Grip and his master lived.

lucivee ['lusə,vi] *n.* [< *loup-cervier,* q.v.] *Esp. Maritimes* See **Canada lynx.** See also **lucififer.** Also, the pelt of the lynx. Also spelled *luce(r)vi, lucerver, lucifee,* etc.
1774 (1945) ROBINSON & RISPIN *Journey N.S.* 43: The lucovie, or wild cat, is also an inhabitant of this country. . . . **1861** BAGSTER *Progress P.E.I.* 86: The Lynx or Lucifee, or more properly the Loup-cervier is in the doomed list of animals. **1900** LONG *Wilderness Ways* 120: The lucivee tracks now showed different tactics. They crossed and crisscrossed the trail. . . .
1949 LAWSON *N.B.Story* 256: In the year 1781, Simonds, Hazen, and White sent a consignment of furs to Halifax to be shipped to England. It consisted of moose skins, caribou . . . "lucervers," red fox, cross fox, bear skins.

luggage-boat *n. Obs.* See **oomiak** and picture.
1748 DRAGE *Voyage* I 32: These Boats move very slowly, and are called Luggage-Boats, by those who use Hudson's Streights, this seem to be for the Convenience of transporting their Families and Provisions, as their Fishing and Hunting makes it necessary. **1820** (1963) DAVIES *Northern Quebec* 57: . . . the Indians spied an Esquimeau luggage boat coming in and waylaid the Esquimeaù behind rocks. . . . **1885** TUTTLE *Our North Land* 234: The umiak is a flat-bottomed skin luggage boat, open at the top, generally rowed by women.

luggage canoe *Obs.* See **freight canoe.**
1779 (1954) *Moose Ft Jnls* 355: Arriv'd here with 3 Indians & 7 Canadians in a Luggage Canoe & 3 small Ones.

lully *n.* See **lolly.**

lumber *n.* **1**† rough-sawn or finished planks, boards, etc.

1773 (1948) PERKINS *Diary* 50: Lumber sold at £4, and fish at 16 shilling. **1889** CHURCH *Making a Start* 209: They pulled it out and about 9 hundredweight of lumber with it. **1965** *Globe and Mail* (Toronto) 5 Jan. B5: The formation of a company that will manufacture pre-fabricated homes in the United Kingdom with Canadian lumber has been announced.

2 a. logs, square timber, etc.
1811 (1959) PRESTON *Kingston* 221: The large returns heretofore made in lumber have occasioned an immense Quantity of goods to be poured into this Country. . . . **1836** (1923) JAMESON *Rambles* 33: In the summer it is a frequented harbor, and carries on a considerable trade in lumber, for so they characteristically call timber in this country.
1964 *Atlantic Advocate* July 56/1: By 1913 about 125 million feet of lumber were floating down the St. John River.

b. *Obs.* **in the lumber,** engaged in lumbering (def. 2).
1896 GOURLAY *Hist.Ottawa* 66: The Shiners were raftsmen, chiefly Irish, employed in the lumber, rough and ready for a conflict when mellowed with poteen.

3 *Obs.* baggage; gear; belongings.
1804 (1890) CAMERON *Nipigon Country* 255: The man carries his canoe, his gun and his medecine bag. The women and children must carry all the rest of their lumber. **1820** (1963) DAVIES *Northern Quebec* 60: These [Indians] had only two canoes which contained most of their lumber.

4 *Hockey, Slang* **a.** a hockey stick.
1963 *Calgary Herald* 15 Nov. 14/2: . . . when he used to keep the lumber low they used to run right over the top of him.

b. **lay on the lumber,** check heavily with a hockey stick, legally or illegally.
1966 *Canadian* 29 Jan. 7/2: . . . they do not hesitate, as hockey men put it, to lay on the lumber. **1966** *Kingston Whig-Standard* (Ont.) 8 Feb. 10/4: Lumley would lay the lumber on his own players, when they came into the goal crease.

lumber *v.* **1** See **log,** *v.* (def. 2).
1831 *Trans.Lit.& Hist.Soc.Que.* II 269: His intention, he said, was to clear land and lumber some; and, he might have added, to keep a rum and whiskey shop, when he could obtain a supply. **1849** ALEXANDER *L'Acadie* II 85: She said her husband was lumbering in the woods for ten months in the year, during all which time she never saw him. No wonder, then, that lumbering is attended with demoralizing consequences. **1896** GOURLAY *Hist.Ottawa* 21: [They] lumbered and built beautiful houses and made fine farms. . . .

2 (usually with *over*) exploit for timber. See also **lumbered-over.**
1872 DASHWOOD *Chiploquorgan* 60: This part of the country has never been "lumbered," being too difficult of access. . . . **1936** LOWER *Settlement* 77: . . . the title to most of the surface of Eastern Canada, even to those parts which have been "lumbered over" for a century[,] remains with the Crown.

lumberboat *n.* See **pointer** (def. 1 and picture).
1961 PRICE & KENNEDY *Renfrew* 41: Lumbermen left for the woods in the autumn months with horses, sleighs, lumberboats and everything necessary for the season's operations.

lumber camp See **logging camp**.

☞ *See note at* **lumbering** (*def. 1*).

1872 DASHWOOD *Chiploquorgan* 51: Our stock of provisions again becoming small, I sent off . . . to a lumber camp distant about thirty miles. **1903** *Eye Opener* (Calgary) 24 Oct. 1/4: After a long hard winter working as a cook in a lumber camp I struck for Peace River country where I now am, knocking life out to keep life in. **1963** MORTON *Kingdom of Canada* 221: Here [in New Brunswick] developed the river drive of the squared timber and the masts down the river, the lumber camp, the lumberjack. . . . [See **Main John** for full quote.]

lumber claim See **timber limit** (def. 1a).

1883 *Selkirk Herald* (Man.) 16 Feb. 3/3: The dwellers in the Icelandic settlement on the west side of the lake are beginning to feel the benefit of the increased travel to and from the lumber claims.

lumber dam See **pond** (def. 3).

1872 DASHWOOD *Chiploquorgan* 7: Here was a lumber dam, and a large crew of men engaged in "driving" the timber brought down the lake in large rafts. **1921** HEMON *Chapdelaine* [trans.] 99: "I am going down to Grand'Mere next week . . . to work on the lumber dam."

lumber (or lumbering) depot *Hist*. See **depot farm**.

1883 FRASER *Shanty* 123: Some weeks after . . . Gandron was seen at a lumbering depot some distance off. . . . **1961** GREENING *Ottawa* 103: . . . it was almost impossible to smuggle in *whisky blanc* or rotgut because of the distances of the lumber depots from the towns and villages along the shore.

lumbered-over *adj*. See **logged-off**. See also **lumber,** *v*. (def. 2).

1957 WRIGHT *Blomidon Rose* 30: . . . we went, by rock and lake and many a mile of lumbered-over and burned-over country, and at last we reached the head of St. Margaret's Bay.

lumberer *n*. **1** See **lumberman** (def. 1a).

1824 *Canadian Mag.* III 406: Where would you find labourers or hired men if the lumberers did not bring people into this country? **1896** GOURLAY *Hist.Ottawa* 139: The lumberers and their hands soon discovered the quality of the lands, and settlements followed.

2 See **logger** (def. 1).

☞ *This term is being displaced by* **logger**. *See note at* **lumbering** (*def. 1*).

1826 *U.E.Loyalist* (York [Toronto]) 29 July 71/3: In the North West, we understand, the fires have been greatest in the vicinity of the little Sevogle, where many excellent groves of timber were untouched by the axe of the Lumberer. **1846** BONNYCASTLE *Canada and Canadians* I 63: The lumberers, who are the cutters and conveyors of timber, pass a short and excited existence. **1933** ROLYAT *Wilderness Walls* 47: "Did you notice, Sir . . . any indications on our lake of that singular human species, calling themselves 'lumberers'?"

lumber flat a railway car having a flat bed and staked sides, used for transporting lumber.

1955 BIRNEY *Long Table* 167: Loaded lumber flats, on the other hand, offer the quietest of all rides. . . .

lumbering *n*. **1** See **logging** (def. 2).

☞ *The terms* **lumberer** *and* **lumbering** *relating to the felling and hauling of timber are apparently giving way to* **logger** *and* **logging**. *In earlier use, the first set of terms was typical of the East.*

1821 (1960) MCCULLOCH *Stepsure Letters* 21: Without a little spirits, the fatigue of lumbering would be intolerable. **1847** *Packet* (Bytown [Ottawa]) 11 Dec. 2/6: The Government ought to survey no Lumbering territory; that is, to reserve and conserve the pine limits for the uses to which they are now applied, and in no case interfere with the present system of licensing. **1891** OXLEY *Chore-Boy* 34: "Whether I like lumbering or not, I'm going to stick out the winter. . . ." **1964** *Atlantic Advocate* July 58/2: The enormous lumbering operations carried on upon the St. John River and its tributaries in modern times had their small beginning with that load.

2 the wide field of exploiting forest products, including logging, milling, etc.

☞ *In this dictionary, the label* **Lumbering** *is used with reference to this wide area.*

1849 (1926) LANGTON *Early U.C.* 207: I learned from the manager of one of the larger lumbering firms at Quebec that the annual demand is only for about 2,000 pieces. . . . **1892** (1908) DAWSON & SUTHERLAND *Geography* 119: Lumbering, in all its branches, stands next to agriculture in importance. . . . **1946** LOWER *Colony to Nation* 421: . . . the exploitive urge had been applied . . . in the fur trade, in lumbering, ship-building and especially in the Montreal complex of forwarding and finance. . . .

lumbering counties See quote.

1946 LOWER *Colony to Nation* 292: But everywhere from the Saguenay to the Georgian Bay, the settlers were now in contact with "the rough country," "the lumbering counties," by which terms was meant the Canadian Shield.

lumbering depot See **lumber depot**.

lumbering party *Obs*. See 1832 quote.

1825 *P.E.I.Register* (Charlottetown) 20 Oct. 3/2: The number of lives that have been lost in the remote parts of the woods, among the lumbering parties, cannot be ascertained for some time to come; for it is feared that few are left to tell the tale. **1832** MCGREGOR *Brit.Amer.* II 299: Several of these people from what is termed a "lumbering party," composed of persons who are all either hired by a master lumberer, who pays them wages and finds them in provisions, or of individuals, who enter into an understanding with each other to have a joint interest in the proceeds of their labour.

lumbering road See **logging road**.

1961 GREENING *Ottawa* 154: [They] have been spending a great deal of money in the construction of first-class year-round lumbering roads through the bush.

lumbering wagon See **lumber wagon**.

lumberjack *n*. **1** See **logger** (def. 1). See also **jack** (def. 4).

1831 (1957) GUILLET *Valley of the Trent* 236: But my misfortunes have been brought upon me chiefly by an incorrigible, though perhaps a useful, race of mortals called LUMBERJACKS, whom, however, I would name the Cossacks of Upper Canada, who, having been reared among the oaks and pines of the wild forest, have never been subjected to the salutary restraint of laws. **1923** WALDO *Down Mackenzie* 139: "Slim" signed on for the job of lumber-jack because he was sick, like Huckleberry Finn, of being civilized. **1964** *Cdn Geog. Jnl* Feb. 72/1: Average earnings for lumberjacks are from $15 to $25 a day. **1966** *Globe and Mail* (Toronto) 11 Oct. 33/8: All around me, in their double-decker bunks, lay sleeping lumberjacks clad in their sweaty long-handled underwear....

2 See Canada jay.
1959 MCATEE *Folk-Names* 50: [The Canada jay is also called] lumberjack (From its frequenting areas where lumbering is in progress. Alta.) **1963** *Weekend Mag.* 16 Nov. 41/1: His [Canada jay's] names, all Canadian, are: whisky jack, whisky john, moose bird, meat bird, camp robber, meat hawk, and lumberjack.

lumber jacket See **Mackinaw coat.**
1956 RADDALL *Wings* 70: I pulled on my old lumber jacket and went out to do the firewood chore. **1966** *Globe and Mail* (Toronto) 4 Nov. 29/3: The members of Local 43 ... were clad in ... mechanic's overalls, lumber jackets, hunting jackets, windbreakers, and rubber boots.

lumberjack's breakfast a remarkably big breakfast.
1965 *Victoria Dly Times* 20 July 13/2: Monday was Canada Day at the village and so after the Maple Leaf was hoisted and a "lumberjack's" breakfast dispatched, [they] went outside....

lumber king a large-scale operator in lumbering (def. 2), especially in logging (def. 2). See also **sawdust nobility, timber baron,** and **timber king.**
1889 WITHROW *Our Own Country* 372: At Keswick is seen the charmingly situated resort of one of the great lumber-kings of the country.... **1891** OXLEY *Chore-Boy* 144: [He was] the most popular and respected "lumber-king" on the river. **1964** *Cdn Geog.Jnl* Feb. 72/1: To the Ottawa lumber kings these ideas were unusual to indeed.

lumberman *n.* **1 a.** an owner or manager of a company engaged in lumbering (def. 2). See also **lumberer** (def. 1) and **timberman.**
1823 *Montreal Herald* 12 July 2/5: The crown ought to dispose of timber to honest lumbermen at one farthing per foot. **1829** MACTAGGART *Three Years* I 241: *Lumbermen* and *Shantymen* are nearly synonymous; with this difference, that the former are generally the masters, or, what the Canadians call, the *Bourgeois* of the latter. **1897** TUTTLE *Golden North* 124: The immense value of this industry, also comparatively new, is beginning to interest eastern lumbermen both in Canada and the States. **1963** *Canada Month* Nov. 22/2: The old-time lumber man plundered the forest....

b. a lumbering company as an entity.
1964 *Powell River News* 7 May 5/3: Take notice that CANADIAN COLLIERIES RESOURCES LIMITED of Vancouver, B.C. occupation Lumberman intends to apply for a lease of the following lands....

2 See logger (def. 1).
1824 *Canadian Mag.* III 201: The people employed in what they call The Lumber Trade, that is in preparing the timber in this country for shipment, are denominated Lumber Men; and possess a rather doubtful character in many parts of the country.... **1839** *Western Herald* (Sandwich [Windsor], U.C.) 7 Mar. 9/3: The Governor of New Brunswick has sent an agent to the Arrostook, to persuade the lumbermen there to give up the arms stolen from the Arsenal, and to return as peaceable citizens and loyal subjects of the Queen. **1900** LONG *Wilderness Ways* 65: Somewhere above me I knew that a crew of lumbermen were at work.... **1958** *Edmonton Jnl* 25 July 28/3: ... the

roads are little more than bush trails, seldom travelled except by lumbermen.... **1966** *Globe and Mail* (Toronto) 29 Aug. 6/4: Some of the jobs most suitable for Indians are ... fire rangers, timber cruisers, scalers ... lumbermen, game wardens ... park wardens and guides....

3† See timber ship.
1912 POCOCK *Man in the Open* 37: ... liner, tramp, fisher, lumberman, geordie, greaser was all the same to him.

lumberman's strawberries *Slang* prunes. See also **C.P.R. strawberries.**
1947 FREEDMAN *Mrs.Mike* 79: She set prunes on the table. "These here are known as lumberman's strawberries."

lumber out denude of timber through logging (def. 2).
1936 LOWER *Settlement* 59: By 1867 the St. Lawrence plain had been practically "lumbered out" and had passed under the plough....

lumber over See **lumber,** *v.* (def. 2).

lumber raft *Hist.* See **raft,** *n.* (def. 2 and picture).
1878 *Canadian Mthly* I 91/1: The pine-knots still however have their uses in lighting up the caboose fires on the lumber rafts.... **1961** GREENING *Ottawa* 62: Never before had lumber rafts from the Ottawa River region been floated to Quebec City from any point above the Long Sault Rapids....

lumber road See **logging road.**
[**1822** (1932) MCLEAN *Notes* 30: Wee accordingly followed the lumber track until we reached the hut....] **1868** SMALL *Chronicles* 158: The Brockville and Ottawa Railway, is almost exclusively a lumber road, bringing down timber from the Ottawa country, and carrying up supplies for the lumberers. **1958** *Edmonton Jnl* 25 July 28/3: In the Slave Lake division, three lumber roads in the vicinity of Slave Lake town are closed.

lumber shanty *Hist.* **1 See shanty** (def. 1b and picture).
1853 STRICKLAND *Canada West* I 30: The lumber-shanty differs both in size and shape, being much larger, and the roof sloping both ways, with a raised hearth in the centre of the floor, with an aperture directly above for the escape of the smoke. It has no window. One door at the end, and two tier of bed berths, one above the other, complete the tout ensemble. **1863** WALSHE *Cedar Creek* 215: It proceeded from the lumber shanty; a long, windowless log-hut with a door at one end, a perpetual fire in the centre, on a large open hearth of stones; the chimney, a hole in the roof. Along both sides and the farther end was a sort of dais, or low platform of unhewn trees laid close together, and supporting the "bunks," or general bed, of spruce boughs and blankets. **1923** WILLIAMS *Spinning Wheels* 30: They ... in summer camped in lumber shanties....

2 See shanty (def. 2a).
1883 *Brandon Dly Mail* (Man.) 7 Apr. 3/1: Grey backs [lice] of "prodigious size" are said to form a source of amusement in a certain lumber shanty in the Shell River Country. **1910** MCCLUNG *Second Chance* 83: ... I've railroaded and worked in lumber shanties. **1967** *Cdn Geog.Jnl* Mar. 79/3: During the four months of winter snow the men frequently worked at a lumber shanty for wages of £2.10s.0d. a month....

lumber sled or **sleigh** *Obs.* a sleigh used in
hauling logs.
1829 MACTAGGART *Three Years* I 252: For some years,
the Americans . . . were in the habit of running the
Canadians off the road, their lumber-sleighs being much
heavier. **1841** MCLEOD *Upper Canada* 223: In Monroe
they disguised him for a night in a ladies dress, in the
morning they dressed him as a sturdy beggar, and
shipped him under our eyes, in an old crazy lumber sled,
and he escaped the vigilance of all the Marshals.
1852 MOODIE *Roughing It* 335: The wood of this oak is
so heavy and hard that it will not float in the water,
and it is in great request for the runners of
lumber-sleighs, which have to pass over very bad roads.

lumber slide *Obs.* See **slide** (def. 1a).
1826 (1903) CARR-HARRIS *White Chief* 180: . . . the north
side [of the river] is not available owing to the
existence of our lumber slides.

lumbersole *n. West* See quote.
1965 SHEPHERD *West of Yesterday* 44: Charlie tried
out a much-heralded type of boot known as lumbersoles.
These were shoes with wooden soles about an inch
thick and leather uppers lined with felt. They looked
fine but were too heavy, and snow built up on the
wooden soles. . . . They were not a success.

lumber squatter *Hist.* a person who engaged in
logging on Crown lands without a licence. Cp.
bogus settler.
1961 PRICE & KENNEDY *Renfrew* 88: Two years later
came Joseph Brunette, [who] remained for some years
as a lumber squatter.

lumber trade See 1824 quote.
1824 *Canadian Mag.* II 305: They were . . . engaged in
what is termed the Lumber Trade, that is cutting down
timber, preparing it for the market, and carrying it
down to Quebec where it is shipped. **1963** *Canada
Month* Nov. 22/1: The lumber trade furnished
employment for thousands of lumber jacks, river
drivers, and sailors.

lumber trust a combine of logging companies.
1903 *Bond of Brotherhood* 19 June 1/2: For instance,
we have before us now a lumber trust that dominates
the region extending from Vancouver as far east as
Rat Portage. **1919** *Camp Worker* 28 June 6/2: Any
apparent concession the Lumber Trust makes to labor
will be paid by labor while the system remains.

lumber wagon *Hist.* a heavy, springless, horse-
drawn wagon of a type used for hauling lumber.
[**1829** MACTAGGART *Three Years* I 110: In passing over
them in a lumbering waggon, the poor human frame is
jolted to pieces.] **1849** ALEXANDER *L'Acadie* I 126: We
now mounted a lumber waggon without springs, and
jolted over a road which was rather trying for a lady.
1912 CONNOR *Corp.Cameron* 159: The stable yard
attached to his hotel was lined three deep with buggies,
carriages, and lumber waggons which had borne in
the crowds of farmers from the country. **1961** *Edmonton
Jnl* 24 July 11/7: They [in 1892] forded the North
Saskatchewan River in a lumber wagon, and
homesteaded at Sturgeon.

lumber-woods *n.* timberlands.
1896 ROBERTS *Camp-Fire* 202: "Three winters ago, as
some of you will remember, Stranion and I took a

month in the lumber-woods. . . ." **1927** DICKIE *How
Canada Grew Up* 166: He . . . had driven oxen, cut and
hauled cordwood . . . teamed in the lumber woods,
hauled logs to the lake front and the mill, fired in the
Cobourg tannery, and attended Victoria College.
1960 FOWKE *Story in Song* 202: The verses probably
date from about 1890, when a railway was being built
through the northern lumberwoods from Ottawa to
Parry Sound.

lumberyard† *n.* **1** a yard where lumber (def. 1) is
stored and sold.
1801 *Niagara Herald* (Niagara-on-the-Lake, U.C.) 28
Nov. 3/4: On examining the plank, it was found to be
of black walnut, and stolen from the subscriber's
lumber yard. **1961** GREENING *Ottawa* 108: . . . the
district close to the lumberyards was full of waterfront
dives. . . .

lun [lʌn] *n.* [< Brit. dial. "a lull"] *Nfld* a spot
providing shelter from the wind; lee.
1933 MERRICK *True North* 42: After a while, when
Harvey gets across, there will be the dog, sitting behind
a point or under the trees waiting "in the lun."
1958 HARRINGTON *Sea Stories* 93: He had no alternative
to the slim chance of safety offered by the "lun" of Cat
Harbour, Northern Island.

lun [lʌn] *v.* [< *lun*, n.] of wind, die down.
1946 MERRICK *Northern Nurse* 213: "We'll have to wait
till the storm lunns [sic] down," said Jim.

lunatic patrol *West* See quote.
1945 HAIG *Brave Harvest* 117: She knew also of their
care of the homesteaders, and of the "lunatic patrols"
when the police went out to bring to hospital some man
or woman whose reason has toppled before the
loneliness of the prairies.

lunge† [lʌndʒ] *n.* [shortening of *muskellunge*,
q.v.] See **maskinonge.** Also spelled *'lunge.*
1896 *Trans.Roy.Soc.Can.* II 2 138: The lake trout,—
forked tail,—lunge or touladi is fortunate in the
almost universal maintenance for the name of its
variety, of the original French orthographical
illustration of the Indian sound represented by the
pronunciation of namaycush. **1953** *Cdn Geog.Jnl*
XLVII 17/1: Recently, thanks to government
hatcheries, 'lunge has been added to the menu.

luxury *n. Fur Trade, Hist.* one of a listed number
of provisions making up part of the allowances,
q.v., of company officers and missionaries on trips
to and from the interior.
1822 (1940) *Minutes of Council* (H.B.C.) 25: . . . the
allowance of Luxuries applicable to a Chief Trader
[may] be granted to him. **1913** COWIE *Adventurers* 500:
"Luxuries"—in the ante-steam transport days this
fur-trade term was applied to the voyaging and
wintering allowances given to the officers and
missionaries, and consisted of mustard, pepper,
pimento, Hyson and Souchong tea, sugar, rice,
raisins, currants, vinegar and flour, also of wine and
spirits in non-interdicted districts. **1940** *Beaver* Dec.
25/1: We had no luxuries. Three pounds was the gross
weight of food allowed each man on the bill of lading
[of a boat brigade from Lower Fort Garry, 1863]. It
consisted of a little pemmican, tea, a bit of flour,
tobacco; no luxuries.

lynx† *n.* **1** See **Canada lynx.**
1760 PICHON *Cape Breton* 102: They have a great
number of lynxes, whose flesh tastes like veal.
1849 ALEXANDER *L'Acadie* II 153: In these woods
occasionally is seen the lynx, with its stout active mate,

cat-like face, tufted ears, spotted legs and short tail. **1966** *Kingston Whig-Standard* (Ont.) 8 Jan. 6/1: A well-known trapper . . . discovered a lynx in one of his beaver traps this week.

2 the fur of the Canada lynx.

1820 (1823) FRANKLIN *Journey* 83: Three marten, a musk-rat, or a single, lynx, or wolverine skin are equivalent to one beaver. **1964** *Calgary Herald* 22 July 17/6: . . . the price of white fox has risen to $25 from $10 in the 1950s. Lynx prices have gone up to $15 from $3.

3 the flesh of the Canada lynx used as food.

1858 (1958) WATTERS *B.C.Cent.Anthol.* 105: Lynx also makes a good stew if you do not think of cats, and squirrels make *un grand ragoût*. **1921** HEMING *Drama of Forests* 166: The dishes included the choice of moose, caribou, bear, lynx, beaver, or muskrat.

lynx-paw robe See 1896 quote.

[**1896** RUSSELL *Far North* 241: The Crees make a very warm and serviceable robe from the fur of lynx's feet when the animals are abundant.] **1921** *Beaver* May 16/2: . . . there was little discomfort if, in addition to blankets and an eiderdown robe, one has a lynx-paw robe between one and the ground. **1954** BEZANSON *Sodbusters* 124: I laid a lynx-paw robe down on the straw, put the hot stone on it, and, after Lois was seated . . . spread another lynx-paw robe over her. . . .

Mac [mæk] *n. Informal* See **McIntosh Red.**
1958 *Herald Tribune* (Grande Prairie, Alta) 10 Jan. 3/4:
... whether you are serving B.C. "Macs" fresh ... or
in your favorite cooked dishes, you can do so with
complete confidence....

macassin *n. Obs.* See **moccasin.**

maccaron *n.* [prob. < *macaroon* a small cake or
biscuit < F *macaron* < Ital. *maccarone* (now
maccherone) macaroni; cf. *macaroni* medley,
mixture] *Fur Trade, Hist.* See 1922 quote.
1797 (1964) CHABOILLEZ *Journal* 143: Received the
loadings of four Canoes for River Painbinat ... 4 Bales
Carrot Tobacco ... 1 Maccaron Rum.... **1827** (1912)
ERMATINGER *Express Jnl* 103: Passengers, pieces and
baggage being as follows: ... 1 bale portage
straps ... 1/2 Maccaron.... **1836** (1843) *Standing
Rules* (H.B.C.) June 164: Scale of winter allowances ...
"Maccarons Contg. 4 two Gall. Kegs of Brandy,
Fruits, Molasses, Rice, Vinegar. **1922** *Beaver* April
9/1: These provisions were put in two gallon kegs, four
of which were laced together and called a maccaron.
1929 MOBERLY *When Fur Was King* 82: The chief
factor's portion was one maccaron, of biscuit, ham,
tea, sugar, chocolate, salted tongues, butter and flour.
The clerks got half a maccaron, and each man might
take what he preferred of the four beverages.

Macdonald Brier the Canadian national curling
championship, name for the trophy donated by the
Macdonald Tobacco Company.
1959 *News of the North* (Yellowknife) 15 Jan. 8/3: It
was voted to enter a rink in the MacDonald Brier
playoffs. **1959** *Maclean's* 15 Aug. 27/1: He broadcasts
such periodic events as the Manitoba bonspiel and the
Macdonald's Brier in curling....

Macdonaldian *adj. Hist.* having to do with or
supporting the policies of Sir John A. Macdonald,
1815-1891. See also **Macdonaldite.**
1890 *Grip* (Toronto) 1 Feb. 66/2: It appears that Mr.
Mercier, the Macdonaldian leader of the Quebec
Government, has for some time been practising a new
and highly effective scheme of bribery of his own
invention.

Macdonaldite *n. Hist.* a supporter of the policies
of Sir John A. Macdonald, 1815-1891; a Conservative.
1872 *Canadian Mthly* Oct. 372/1: In truth, the theory
that all men are born Nationalists or Realists would be
more tenable than the theory that they are born
Macdonaldite or Grits. **1916** BRIDLE *Sons of Canada* 17:
... Borden had the magnificent moral courage to take
the leadership of the Macdonaldites in Canada....

machecoti *n.* See **matchcoat.**

Machi Manitou See **Matchi Manitou.**

machinaway *n. Obs.* See **mishiniway.**

machine man *Hardrock Mining* a driller.
1900 *Lardeau Eagle* 28 Mar. 1/3: Good miners and
machine men can find work in any white man's mining
camp.... **1964** CRATE *Hardrock Mining* 3: ... in others
[mines] all are miners, and drillers are listed as such or
as "machine-men" on the payroll or in the Collective
bargaining agreement.

machine shed a farm building in which implements
are kept.
☞ *This term is perhaps commoner in the West than in
the East, where* **drive-shed,** q.v., *or* **driving-shed** *is usual.*
1958 *Edmonton Jnl* 11 June 4/3: A bamboo binder whip
was "posh" and its owner was regarded as somewhat
of a dare-devil for the whip probably was filched from
the machine shed where the father had stored it the
fall before.

machison *n. Obs.* See **moccasin.**

MacIntosh *n.* See **McIntosh Red.**

Mackenzie (district) *n.* the most westerly of the
Northwest Territories (def. 2b), named after the
explorer Alexander Mackenzie, 1764-1820.
1883 *Trans.Hist.& Sci.Soc.Man.* II 2/2: His lot was cast
in the far-off Mackenzie district, and here he gained
his acquaintance with the fur trade and the company's
affairs, so useful to him in his after career. **1953** *North
Star* (Yellowknife) July 1/1: It is my belief that many
measures could be introduced by the Federal
Government, through the Northwest Territories
Administration, which would better the lot of the
residents of Mackenzie. **1966** *North* July-Aug. 42/2:
The rapidly increasing pace of development in the
Northwest Territories, especially in the Mackenzie
District, now began to suggest even more fundamental
changes in the structure of Territorial government.

Mackenzie dog or **husky** See **Mackenzie River
husky.**
1923 WALDO *Down Mackenzie* 90: Yet the Mackenzie
dogs are as restless and as full of fight as their distant
kinsdogs of the Atlantic seaboard, and the tufts of
hair all along the lowest barbed wire of the fences about
the Hudson's Bay Company headquarters betray their
eagerness to be in every fight that is started.
1928 WALDEN *Dog-Puncher* 34: The "Porcupine River"
or "Mackenzie" Husky ... originated a great many
years ago from a cross of the Eskimo with some large
domesticated dog, and were the best freight dogs I have
ever seen, being far superior to the Eskimo and much
larger and stronger.

Mackenzieite *n. Upper Canada, Hist.* a supporter
of the policies of William Lyon Mackenzie,
1795-1861.
1832 *Cdn Freeman* (York [Toronto]) 5 Apr. 2/3: But
when some of the Mackenzieites told this to a wag
of an Irishman in town, he made an excellent reply—
"How many soup-kitchen men attacked you, and ran
away with your waggon, chairman, Secretary, and all?"
said Pat. **1840** *St.Catharines Jnl* (U.C.) 31 Dec. 2/5: Mr.
Rykert ... may very easily ... call all Responsible
Government men, or Durhamites, rebels and
Mackenzieites....

Mackenzie Rebellion *Hist.* See **Canadian
Rebellion.** Also *Mackenzie's Rebellion.*
1838 *Western Herald & Farmers' Mag.* (Sandwich
[Windsor], U.C.) 28 Aug. 213/1: Why are Hume,
Roebuck, Leader, Moleworth, and others, who advised,
rejoiced, encouraged and [?] in the Mackenzie, and
Papineau Rebellions, allowed to go unpunished?
1838 *Dominion Illust.* 163/2: The first election was held
in the same month of March, and resulted in the return,
as first Mayor, of the renowned William Lyon
Mackenzie, whose exploits in 1837-38 gave the
uprising in Upper Canada the title of "Mackenzie's
Rebellion." **1912** (1916) *London Hist.Soc.Trans.* VII 37:
There is no record in the office as to the carrying out of
the sentence, which was imposed no doubt, on the

Mackenzie River dog 1 *Obs.* See **bear dog.**
1833 TYLER *Progress of Discovery* 330: We can here afford to spare only a few lines regarding the Hare Indian, or Mackenzie River dog. (Canis familiaris, var. lagopus).

2 See **Mackenzie River husky.**
1896 WHITNEY *On Snow-Shoes* 107: Some great stories are told of the loads drawn by the Mackenzie River dogs, whose tails are docked short, to give a more workman-like appearance, and keep the meek and lowly from advertising their shrinking nature and spoiling the appearance of the train by sticking the offending member between their legs.

Mackenzie River husky See 1963 quote. See also **Mackenzie dog, Mackenzie River dog** (def. 2), and **Porcupine River husky.**
1928 WALDEN *Dog-Puncher* 72: I saw hamstringing done next summer in Dawson by a band of five Mackenzie River Huskies. **1963** *Alaska Sportsman* Dec. 45/1: The Mackenzie River Husky, first used extensively by the Northwest Mounted Police in patrol work, was in the main as large or larger than the Alaskan Malamute. We would say, therefore, that while some Siberian Husky blood may have been infused into the Mackenzie River Husky strain, it is more likely that larger breeds of dogs, with possibly the added mixture from the Arctic wolf, figured in the development of the Mackenzie River freighting dog.

Mackenzie Territory See quotes.
1962 *Maclean's* 6 Jan. 1/4: A new territory in the Canadian north. ... If Ottawa approves, it could come into existence in 1964. ... Probable name Mackenzie Territory. **1963** *Globe Mag.* 12 Jan. 17/1: Already decided upon is the formation, government and boundaries-to-be of the new western territory, to be called the Mackenzie Territory. Embracing a 580,000-square-mile area extending east from the Yukon to a line bisecting Saskatchewan's northern boundary and north to the Arctic Ocean islands of Victoria and Banks, it will be governed by a nine-man council, five of them elected and four appointed. The seat of the council will be located within the territory, probably at Fort Smith.

Mackina, Mackinac, Mackinau *n.* See **Mackinaw.**

Mackinaw ['mækənɑ] *n.* [< Cdn F *mackinac* < Ojibwa; see 1761quote] Also spelled *mackinaw.*
1 a heavily napped and felted woollen cloth from which blankets and articles of clothing are made, nowadays usually of plaid design. Cp. **mackinaws.**
[**1761** (1901) HENRY (Elder) *Travels* 38: The land, in the centre of this island, is high, and its form somewhat resembles that of a turtle's back. Mackinac, or Mickinac, signifies *turtle,* and michi(*mishi*), or *missi,* signifies *great,* as it does also *several,* or *many.* The common interpretation, of the word *Michilimackinac* is the Great Turtle.] **1841** *Western Herald* (Sandwich [Windsor], C.W.) 31 Mar. 3/2: They have also a large assortment of Blankets ... of the real Mackinaw, assorted from 2 to 3 points to suit the Indian trade. **1896** *Kaslo Claim* (B.C.) 22 Feb. 4/2: Oh! Their Mackinaw garments are wooly and wet,/Their gunny-sack leggings are smelly, and yet/We admire them; not for their beauty you bet! **1910** SERVICE *Trail of '98* 347: He was dressed in mackinaw, and wore a fur cap with drooping ear-flaps. **1964** *Atlantic Advocate* July 77/1: By 1934 William M., a third generation Humphrey, was operating the mill and producing a

large red and black check design for Mackinaw or cruiser cloth. Three grades of Canadian wool, fine, medium and coarse, called "one-half," "three-eights" and "quarter blood" respectively, were used in its manufacture.

2 See **Mackinaw blanket** (def. 2).
1854 *Hamilton Gaz.* (C.W.) 14 Sep. 1/7: "I soon toort o' a dodge, an' went back to camp for my blanket, which wur a red mackinaw." **1909** SERVICE *Cheechako* 109: We built our boats and we launched them. Never had been such a fleet;/ A packing-case for a bottom, a mackinaw for a sheet.

3 *Hist.* **a.** See **Mackinaw boat** (def. 1).
1891 *Wkly Manitoban* (Winnipeg) Dec. 31/1: In winter travellers are confined solely to the use of dogs, and in summer time to boats—York or inland boats of the style of the McKinnaw build. **1908** LAUT *Conquest N.W.* II 48: The boats of the English traders from Hudson Bay were ponderously clumsy, almost as large as the Mackinaws. **1915** WOOD *All Afloat* 36: The rather barge-like 'Mackinaw' ... was a useful but humdrum cargo boat, laboriously poled along shallow, quiet waters, or rowed with lumbering sweeps; or sometimes even sailed, when it shovelled its way through the water with a very safe wind dead aft. **1960** GRANT *Amer.Indians* 191: A mackinaw is a kind of bateau or flatboat used by traders.

b. See **Mackinaw boat** (def. 2).
1923 SMITH *Pioneers* 264: The journey was made in mackinaws,—open boats with a schooner rig, and the sugar was carried in mococks,—containers made of birch bark, each holding from twenty to thirty pounds. **1958** WELLS *Georgian Bay* 29: That is why the fishermen of the old schooner and mackinaw days loved Tobermory.

4 See **Mackinaw coat.**
1913 JOHNSON *Shagganappi* 55n: A mackinaw is a short, rough coat of material much like a grey horse blanket. It is worn by most lumberjacks, explorers, miners and woodsmen in the regions north of the great Canadian lakes. **1965** *Islander* 14 Feb. 13/3: I ... put on a mackinaw and a fur cap and took a turn down to the RR track and back. ...

5 (in euphemistic exclamations) See quotes.
1927 PHILIP *Painted Cliff* 36: "By the holy mackinaw, if we don't hit her, I ain't goin' to see that kid lose a cent, if I have to work my fingers to the bone to get it!" **1954** PATTERSON *Dangerous River* 93: Now, by the holy mackinaw, was the time to lay on that paddle as never before!

Mackinaw blanket 1 See **Mackinaw** (def. 1).
1853 (1892) KANE *Arctic Explor.* 67: The personal equipment of the men was a buffalo-robe for the party to lie upon, and a bag of Mackinaw blanket for each man to crawl into at night.

2 a blanket of Mackinaw (def. 1). See also **Mackinaw** (def. 2).
1960 GRANT *Amer.Indians* 191: A heavy blanket is known as a machinaw blanket. ...

Mackinaw boat *Hist.* **1** a heavy, flat-bottomed freight boat. See also **Mackinaw** (def. 3a). See also **York boat** and picture.
1861 *Nor'Wester* (R.R.S.) 1 Apr. 1/3: Besides the merchants, there is another class, called freighters, who

row the heavy Mackinaw boats, and haul them and their loads over the portages between York Factory and Red River. **1871** (1883) BUTLER *Great Lone Land* 155: This is the regular Hudson Bay Mackinaw boat, used for carrying trade of the great Fur Company on every river from the Bay of Hudson to the Polar Ocean. [**1902** (1954) CHITTENDEN *Amer.Fur Trade* I 47: Near most of the larger river posts there was some spot selected where timber was abundant at which . . . the mackinaw boats and the canoes [were] built. . . . **1965** *Beaver* Spring 45/2: On 30 June [1848] they left the Sault, travelling in two canoes and a mackinaw boat—a cross between a dory and a mudscow.

2 a schooner-rigged boat formerly in use on the Great Lakes. See also **Mackinaw** (def. 3b).
[**1860** (1956) KOHL *Kitchi-Gami* 167: It was four o'clock . . . when one of the elegant steamers which now traverse Lake Superior by the side of the Indian canoes and the old brown "Mackinac barks" put us ashore on the sandy beach of the great peninsula of Keweena.] **1903** WHITE *Forest* 130: A dozen wharves of various sizes, over whose edges peeped the double masts of Mackinaw boats, spoke of a fishing community.

Mackinaw coat or **jacket** a short belted coat made of Mackinaw (def. 1). See also **bush coat, lumber jacket,** and **Mackinaw** (def. 4).
1910 FRASER *Red Meekins* 10: The . . . khaki pants, brown leather shoe packs, and short Mackinaw coat contrasted with the elaborate tourist gear that his companion had evidently acquired of a London outfitter. **1935** *Beaver* June 47: The original mackinaw coats were made from Hudson's Bay "Point" blankets for the British soldiers who, during the war of 1812, fought in the neighbourhood of Mackinaw. Captain Charles Roberts was unable to obtain greatcoats for his men, so commandeered a supply of "Point" blankets and coats were designed and made by one of his men. **1956** GOWLAND *Sikanaska Trail* 44: Sure enough, a guard in plain clothes brought along my mackinaw jacket and hat and invited me to come along with him.

Mackinaw Company *Hist.* a fur-trading company established in the Michilimackinac region by British interests.
1836 (1868) IRVING *Astoria* 49: A new association of British merchants was formed. . . . The chief factory was established at the old emporium of Michilimackinac, from which place the association took its name, and was commonly called the Mackinaw Company. **1934** WALLACE *Documents N.W.Co.* 9: . . . about 1795 the first Mackinac Company was formed.

mackinaws *n.pl.* clothing made of Mackinaw (def. 1).
1902 LONDON *Daughter of Snows* 316: He was interrupted by a warm-complexioned man clad in faded mackinaws. **1947** FREEDMAN *Mrs.Mike* 59: . . . the wet penetrated my heavy mackinaws.

Mackinaw trout† See **lake trout**.
1845 *Bytown* [Ottawa] *Gaz.* 24 Apr. 1/2: No more delicious repast can be offered than a fine Mackinaw trout, caught from the depths of his cool retreat. **1866** KING *Sportsman in Canada* 287: There are several varieties of Lake trout, though very similar to one another in habit and qualities; the Mackinaw-trout (*Salmo amethystus*) being the chief in point of excellence as it is in size; attaining frequently enormous

proportions. **1961** *Sun* (Vancouver) 17 Aug. 23/1: The laker (mackinaw trout) is a record. Largest Canadian sport-caught lake char . . . is an 87 pounder. . . .

Mackintosh *n.* See **McIntosh Red**.

mackisin or **mackison** *n. Obs.* See **moccasin**.

macock *n.* See **mocock**.

Madawaska tobacco a kind of tobacco formerly grown in the Madawaska region of southern Quebec.
1896 ROBERTS *Camp-Fire* 290: We procured, moreover, some native Madawaska tobacco—which we smoked once, and never smoked again.

made beaver *Fur Trade, Hist.* **1** a unit of exchange equivalent to the value of one prime beaver pelt, used in buying furs and bartering provisions, more usually referred to be trappers as a skin (def. 1). *Abbrev.* M.B. or MB, *q.v.* See also **beaver** (def. 4), **beaver skin** (def. 2), **MBeaver,** and **plu** (def. 1) and note. Cp. **marten** (def. 2b).
1723 (1965) *Letters from Hudson Bay* 96: . . . I understand their last year's trade did not exceed 12,000 skins everything made beaver. . . . **1830** (1909) CAMERON *New North* 110: Poitras, a Chipewyan half-breed, arrived, and delivered 81 made beavers in prime furs, though he says he has been sickly all winter. **1965** *Beaver* Autumn 48/1: Although the "made beaver" . . . has been replaced by dollars and cents, the language of trade is still Cree.

2 See **beaver** (def. 5a).
1896 WHITNEY *On Snow-Shoes* 11: Thus, an Indian having brought in a parcel of furs was told that they amounted to so many "made beaver." Soon it was found more convenient to have a token which should represent the "made beaver." **1928** FREEMAN *Nearing North* 191: Later brass discs were substituted for convenience, values as low as "1/4 Made-Beaver" being issued. **1965** *North* Nov.-Dec. 29/2: Foxes were valued and an equivalent amount in "Made Beaver" or shiny round HBC tokens was spread out on the counter.

made-beaver token *Fur Trade* See **beaver** (def. 5a and picture).
1939 *Beaver* June 4/1: A "made beaver" token . . . requires some explanation. Until not so many years ago these tokens were the coinage used at posts. . . . Various objects were used as tallies. . . . To simplify the system "made beaver" coins were introduced in various denominations. . . . One "made beaver" equalled the skin of an adult beaver in prime condition and of good quality.

Madeira (fish) *n. Nfld* See 1832 quote.
1818 CHAPPELL *Voy.of Rosamond* 130: *Madeira fish;* which are nearly as valuable as the former. This sort is chiefly exported to supply the Spanish and Portuguese markets. **1832** MCGREGOR *Brit.Amer.* I 232: First, the merchantable, which are [codfish] of the finest quality and colour; second, the Madeira, which are nearly equal to the first; third, West India fish . . . lastly, the broken fish, dun fish, or whatever will not keep in warm countries, but which is in general equally good for domestic consumption. . . . **1954** *Fishermen's Advocate* 29 Jan. 1/3: This trend has been influenced by the production in experimental dryers of a top quality product indistinguishable from the best sun-cured Maderia. **1965** MACNUTT *Atlantic Provinces* 3: The second grade, classified as Madeira, were slightly damaged [cod] fish but still salable.

Madji Manido See **Matchi Manitou**.

Magdalen penny *Hist.* See quote.
1963 *Commercial Letter* Jan. 6/2: In 1815 an unofficial copper coin, called the Magdalen penny, was issued by Sir Isaac Coffin for the Magdalen Islands, which had been granted to him after the American Revolution as a reward for his public service. The Magdalen penny thus became the first coin ever to be struck specifically for use in Canada.

magpie *n.* **1** *Prairies* a black-and-white horse; a piebald.
1961 MITCHELL *Jake and the Kid* 120: ". . . He says all buckskins are mean because they got Indian—"Some is," said Jake, "So's a lotta blacks an' magpies. Take a dally round that there set post with the rope. Colour ain't got a hell of a lot to do with it. . . ."

2 See **Canada jay.**
1959 MCATEE *Folk-Names* 50: [The Canada jay is also called] magpie (Perhaps from its pilfering habits, there being hardly any other resemblance. Ont.) . . . pie (Short for magpie . . . N.S.). . . .

mai *n. Cdn French* See **maypole.**
1793 (1933) MACDONELL *Diary* 102: Killed a cub Bear on an Island in Lac la Crois and slept in sight of the *Mai.* **1951** O'MEARA *Grand Portage* Glossary: Mai. lobstick; pine or spruce with lower branches trimmed away, as landmark.

mail-order bride or **wife** *Slang* a wife courted by correspondence, as through a matrimonial agency.
1958 HEALEY *Alert Bay* 32: Some of the women were "mail order" wives and appeared to be quite content with their choice. **1962** *Canada Month* May 38/1: Some of them were mail-order brides who answered advertisements inserted by ranchers in the lonely hearts columns of eastern newspapers. **1965** BERTON *Remember Yesterday* 35/1: Only with the coming of the women, many of them mail-order brides, did the amenities of civilization begin to appear.

mail road *Obs.* a main road kept open and in good repair to ensure the prompt distribution of mail.
1854 *Guelph Advertiser* 16 Nov. 2/3: Mr. Donaldson moved, and Mr. Dobbin seconded,—that a grant be made of £100, towards improving the mail road leading from Orangeville to Fergus, in the township of Garafaxa.

main *n. Lumbering* See **main line** (def. 3).
1942 SWANSON *Western Logger* 35: You talk of your drums! you home-guard bums should have seen the size of her 'main'!/ A twelve-mile haul was nothing at all, her exhaust made clouds in the sky . . .

Main *n.* **1** *Obs.* See **Eastmain.**
1682 (1945) *H.B.C.Minutes* 243: I did send Richard Nalridge . . . over to the maine with a pacquet. . . .

2 in Montreal, St. Lawrence Boulevard.
1950 PALMER *Montreal Confidential* 57: Sometimes it is called "The Oriental Main." No one seems to know where the tag "Oriental" comes in, but it is easy to see why the term "Main" applies. The city's numbering system east and west springs from the street. North of Ontario [St.] the Main becomes the Jewish district. **1964** *Marker* 23 Oct. 1/1: "If somebody roll me on the main, Daddy I stay rolled."

main drag *Slang* the principal street of a village or town; the main street of a city.
1945 PUGSLEY *Saints* 64: Uptown one night on the main drag, he ran smack into a P.O. . . . **1966** *Kingston Whig-Standard* (Ont.) 25 Feb. 12/1: Miller quoted his latest prices . . . in his warm bistro on Whitehorse's main drag.

Main John *Lumbering, Hist.* See quotes. See also **woods superintendent.**
1952 (1965) HAMILTON *Cdn Quotations* 127: The Main John. Lumbermen's expression for woods bosses; originated in New Brunswick, from John B. Glasier (1809-1894) N.B. lumberman and Senator. **1963** MORTON *Kingdom of Can.* 221: In New Brunswick, the St. John and Miramichi River trade gave rise to the logging industry as it was to be in the northern pine zone from Fundy to the Mississippi. Here developed the river drive of the squared timber and the masts down the river, the lumber camp, the lumberjack, the peavey, the term "Main John" for the woods boss.

main line 1 *North, Hist.* See 1941 quote. See also **tracking line.**
1827 (1912) ERMATINGER *Express Jnl* 78: [We] dry the main line as well as we can first by the sun and afterwards by the fire. **1892** (1948) *Beaver* June 45/1: Six men drew the boat along, a stout leather band passing around the chest and being attached to the main line. The latter was about two hundred feet long and the boat was drawn along the stream at quite a distance from the shore. **1941** *Ibid* Sep. 38/1: Main Line. The large Manilla rope by which York Boats were taken upstream.

2 See **line**, *n.* (def. 7).
1921 *Beaver* Feb. 9/2: Now they are looking forward to the two hundred miles of snowshoeing to the main line and let their wives and families know they are well.

3 *Lumbering* See 1942 quote. See picture at **high-lead system.** See also **main.** Also spelled *mainline.*
1939 BEAULIEU & BARTON *Lumber Science* 35: The main line from the donkey (skidder) is reeved through a great block at the head of the spar tree. . . . **1942** HAIG-BROWN *Timber* 252: MAINLINE . . . the heavy cable which hauls the logs from the woods to the landing. **1966** *Dly Colonist* (Victoria) 3 Aug. 28/2: Whether the mainline was to be pulled in, or the haulback to go out . . . depended on the correct number of whistles.

main patch *Sealing, Nfld* See quotes. Cp. **patch** (def. 2).
1933 GREENE *Wooden Walls* XV: THE MAIN PATCH The largest communal birthplace on the Newfoundland Floe of the Harp Seal. **1953** *Nfld Qtly* March 18/2: The use of scouting aeroplanes . . . has helped the fleet to more easily locate the main herd commonly called the "Main Patch."

mainstreeting *n.* the practice of promenading the main street of a town, especially by a politician wishing to meet and greet potential supporters.
1959 *Time* (Cdn ed.) 17 Aug. 11/1: There were handshakes all round, a quiet afternoon walk that Dief loves to call "Main-streeting," then a ball game after dinner. **1963** *Ibid.* 8 Mar. 11/3: He flew into hometown Rouyn to open his campaign, [and] got in a few hours mainstreeting. . . .

maitre *n.* [< Cdn F *maître*] *Obs.* **1** a canoe gunwale.
1806 (1960) FRASER *Letters and Journals* 201: As it was late before everything was ready to begin the canoe, we only laid the bottom and fixed the maitres and entraves. **1814** (1897) COUES *New Light* II 838: Men preparing

wood for canoes . . . making maitres, verrangues, etc.
2 a strong line or cord.
1806 (1960) FRASER *Letters and Journals* 240:
The nets had maitres enough and no stones or floats
were tied with maitres when I came away. **1807** (1930)
FRASER *Letters* 155: Maitres will serve as well as
codline for a cordeau.

maître canot *Cdn French, Hist*. See **Montreal
canoe** and picture. See also **canot du maître.**
1791 LONG *Voyages* 43: Having . . . exchanged my
large canoes, or maître canots, for smaller ones . . . we
proceeded to the Falls of St. Mary. **1836** BACK *Arctic
Land* 32: Both our *maitre-canôt*, and the other, which
was of smaller dimensions, were rather lumbered than
loaded.

maître de poste *Cdn French, Obs*. in colonial
Lower Canada, a person in charge of a road
station, often an inn, on a public road. See quote.
1832 MCGREGOR *Brit.Amer*. II 458: . . . the *maitre de
poste* is obliged to keep a certain number of horses,
caleches, and cabrioles, ready at all hours of the night
or day, for the accomodation of travellers.

major (penalty) *n. Hockey* a penalty called
against a player for certain infractions of the rules,
including fighting and drawing blood with an
illegal stick check, and punished by banishment
from the ice for five minutes.
1962 *Kingston Whig-Standard* (Ont.) 28 Dec. 9/7:
Kingston took 21 penalties and Gananoque sat out 14
sentences, including a misconduct to James McGlade
for incurring his second major of the game.
1963 *Calgary Herald* 11 Nov. 9/2: Alex Faulkner was
in the penalty box serving a major penalty for
high-sticking Montreal's Ralph Backstrom and
drawing blood.

makak, makuk, etc. *n*. See **mocock.**

make *n. Obs*. the state of timber that has been
made ready for rafting or driving. See also **making.**
1945 CALVIN *Saga* 52: In the autumn of 1878, Calvin
and Breck sent James Butler . . . to improve the "make"
of the timber.

make *v*. **1** *North* of ice, form.
1817 *Montreal Herald* 8 Feb. 2/5: The ice having made
in the bay, has added greatly to the gaiety of the place,
by affording an easy access to his Majesty's ship,
Charell. **1888** MCDOUGALL *G.M.McDougall* 114: . . . as
soon as the snow falls and ice makes, dogs will become
the means of transport for the most part; at any rate,
all long distances and quick journeys must be made by
these hardy animals. **1933** MERRICK *True North* 86:
. . . a gray day, ice making everywhere.
2 See quote.
1859 KANE *Wanderings* 324: On arriving at the head of
the rapids, the guide gets out on the rocks and surveys
the whirlpools. If they are filling in or "making," as
they term it, the men rest on their paddles until they
commence throwing off, when the guides instantly
re-embark, and shove off the boat, and shoot through
this dread portal with the speed of lightning.

make beaver *Fur Trade, Obs*. See **make fur.**
1824 (1955) BLACK *Journal* 14: They say they are going
up a small River to pass the Summer & think to make
Beaver.

make camp set up shelters, make a fire, etc. when
stopping for a time on the trail.
1849 ALEXANDER *L'Acadie* II 192: We forded the river
. . . and began "making camp," so as to save the carriers
as much as possible when they came up.
1912 (1914) BICKERSTETH *Open Doors* 191: What's the
best camp to make to-night?

make cod *Nfld* See **make fish.**
1967 *Nat.Geog.Mag*. May 632: [Caption] But despite
diminishing catches, a few men of the sea still
laboriously "make cod" by hand.

make debt *North* draw winter supplies on credit
from a trading store. See also **debt.**
1933 ROLYAT *Wilderness Walls* 95: Not until September
would the Indians come in great numbers to "make
debt." *Ibid*. 255: The next day the Indians began to
come to the Fort for their winter's supplies, to "make
debt."

make fish *Esp.Nfld* cure fish by drying it in the
sun. See also **make cod.** Cp. **fish-making.**
1620 WHITBOURNE *Discovrse* 21: And thus they doe,
striuing to be there first in a Harbour, to obtaine the
name of Admirall that yeere: and so, to haue the
chiefest place to make their fish on, where they may doe
it with the greatest ease, and have the choice of diuers
other necessaries in the Harbors, which do them little
stead: but the taking of them wrongs many others of
your Maiesties subiects, which arriue there after the
first. **1842** JUKES *Excursions in Nfld* I 230: Lastly, many
families in some of the outports, instead of "making,"
or curing, their own fish, bring it as it is caught to the
merchants' stores and stages, where it is cured by his
own men. **1909** ROBINSON *Unknown Land* 30: A fisherman comes here to "make" fish, not to catch them.
1965 LEACH *Songs* 5: There are no fish plants on the
coast; the fish must therefore be processed and dried
by the fishermen themselves. As soon as a returning
fishing boat is sighted, the women and children rush to
the wharf to assist in "making the fish."

make fur *Fur Trade* See 1909 quote. See also
make beaver.
1806 (1960) FRASER *Letters and Journals* 241: . . . I am
afraid that they will not make any furs. **1909** CAMERON
New North 70: Trapping animals is "making fur."
"I made no fur last winter and The Company would
give me no debt," is a painful picture of hard times.

make good succeed in an undertaking; become a
success.
1907 *Eye Opener* (Calgary) 27 June 2/5: As a member
for Calgary during the present parliament he had *made
good*. **1938** CASH *I Like B.C*. 1: All at once there were . . .
opportunities, not particularly for "making good" in
the accepted sense of the phrase, but for living.

make good time travel at a swift pace; advance at
a satisfactory rate.
1874 *Canadian Mthly* Oct. 348/1: So there is good
reason for our raft making good time onwards—it is
going down the first pair of stairs. **1955** *Cdn Mining
Reporter* (Toronto) 8 Apr. 2/1: In a telephone
conversation from the mine to local officials of the
company, President Pierre Beauchemin reported work
proceeding on schedule with good time being made in
surface building construction and installation of
equipment.

make land cultivate the soil; till.
1913 (1929) *Selected Stories* 210: Chapdelaine, his
three sons and man, proceeded then to "make land."

1925 GROVE *Settlers* 108: "She keeps chickens, cows, and pigs. The man makes the land."

make logs *Lumbering* cut, trim, and pile logs ready for driving or hauling. Cp. **log-making** and **make timber.**
1897 GREENOUGH *Cdn Folk-Life* 34: ... the logs are made by jobbers who cut and draw them to the water's edge.... 1912 HEENEY *Pickanock* 34: They had known each other from boyhood and had made logs together for three winters in succession....

make medicine See **medicine** (def. 3).

make muck-(a-) muck eat; prepare a meal. See also **muck-a-muck,** *v.*
1924 DORRANCE *Never Fire First* 74: "We're hitting the trail," explained the missionary. "We've just pitched camp and are about to make muck-muck."

make tea *North* See **boil the kettle.**
1909 CAMERON *New North* 28: At noon it clears, and as we "make tea" at Sturgeon Creek ... the Doctor has his will....

make timber *Lumbering* cut and trim trees ready for rafting (def. 1) or driving (def. 1). See also **making** and **timber-maker.** Cp. **make logs.**
1821 (1960) MCCULLOCH *Stepsure Letters* 22: The large lot of timber was at last made and delivered. 1829 MACTAGGART *Three Years* I 240: In winter they make it [timber] on the remote banks of small streams.... 1896 GOURLAY *Hist.Ottawa* 40: He cleared land, made timber, built houses and mills. 1945 CALVIN *Saga* 44: A gang was counted upon to "make" about 30,000 cubic feet in a season. 1964 GUILLET *Pioneer Days* 85: To "make timber" the lumberman had first to secure a "limit" from the government....

make track break trail, *q.v.*
1846 (1955) CRAIG *Early Travellers* 160: The Indians took it in turn to go in front and "make track," this being ... most fatiguing....

make tracks (for)† leave; start out (for a place), usually in haste.
1849 ALEXANDER *L'Acadie* II 22: ... we divided the baggage, and each carrying a portion ... we "made tracks" for Horse-shoe Lake. 1873 CROASDAILE *Pacific Shores* 47: At length I tired of my continued rise and fall, and, gold being found at Carriboo, I made tracks for that land of promise, determining to drop speculation. 1953 LOWER *Voyages* 65: "If I'm to get there on time, I'll have to make tracks, won't I?"

make up a mail *Obs.* See quote.
1931 WADE *Overlanders* 83: Writing to his friends at home, Alexander made use of a plan formerly adopted by travellers in that country, the process being known as "making up a mail," and consisted of leaving the letters "conspicuously sticking" where they would be most likely to catch the eye of the "passing traveller," and so be taken on to Fort Garry; but, he comments, "the odds are greatly against such letters ever reaching their destinations...."

making *n. Lumbering, Obs.* the process of cutting and trimming trees, especially for square timber, *q.v.* See also **make,** *n.* and **make timber.** Cp. **log-making.**
1853 STRICKLAND *Canada West* II 281: ... the same process is gone through ... which finishes the operation of "making," as the lumber men term squaring the timber. 1854 (1945) CALVIN *Saga* 44: ... push on with all speed making and hauling.

makings† *n.pl.* fine-cut tobacco and paper with which to roll one's own cigarettes. See also **rollings.** Cp. **tailor-made,** *n.*
1910 SERVICE *Trail of '98* 15: "... Glad I came, even if it's to do the horny-handed son of toil stunt. Got the makings?" 1936 MACKENZIE *Living Rough* 221: "... I rolled a cigarette and went over and handed Slim the makings." 1962 FRY *Ranch on the Cariboo* 190: "Can you spare a smoke?" "Makin's. Here, help yourself." I passed him the tobacco and papers.

makissin *n.* See **moccasin.**

makmak *n.* See **muck-a-muck.**
1884 (1926) MOSER *Reminiscences* 139: [There was] Hayou makmak: 12 baskets of herring spawn; two barrels of molasses, and one barrel of fish oil.

maktak or **maktuk** *n.* See **muktuk.**

makuk *n.* See **mocock.**

malachigan *n.* [< Cdn F *malachegané* < Algonk.] *Obs.* the sheepshead, *Aplodinotus grunniens.* Cp. **achigan.** Also spelled *male achigan* and *malichigan.*
1793 (1933) MACDONELL *Diary* 116: The [Assiniboine] River is stocked with the following fish viz—Sturgeons ... Millets, Mâe Achigan called by the Men Male Achigan and Nacaishe. c1804 (1889) GRANT *Sauteux Indians* 310: The principal fishes are: sturgeon, cat-fish ... tullibee, Malachigan.... 1912 (1913) HODGE & WHITE *Indians of Canada* 271/1: Malashaganay. A name of the sheepshead or fresh-water drum (*Haplodinotus grunniens*). Through Canadian French *malashigané* or *malashigane,* from *manashigan* in the Chippewa-Nipissing dialects of the Algonquian stock, signifying "ugly ashigan." The *ashigan* is the black bass of Canadians. 1933 GATES *Five Traders* 116n: The malashegane is mentioned by Tache as having the peculiar power of producing a noise like a distant beating as a drum deep in the water.

malamute *n.* See **malemute.**

malashaganay or **malashegané** *n.* See **malachigan.**

mal de raquette [< Cdn F] a painful state of inflamed joints and muscles affecting snowshoers, caused by undue strain on the tendons of the leg. See also **snowshoe evil, snowshoe fever, snowshoe lameness, snowshoe sickness.**
1821 (1910) GARRY *Diary* 156: (Mal de Raquet a Pain in the Nerves of the Leg from the Pressure of the Snow Shoe. The Indians cure this by putting a live Coal on the Part affected and burn it to the Bone.) 1859 (1925) KANE *Wanderings* 247: The morning I found I had what the voyageurs call mal de racquet. 1955 GOWLAND *Smoke* 113: These induced such a bad attack of mal de racquette that I could hardly walk the next day.

male achigan See **malachigan.**

Malecite (canoe) ['mælə,sit] *n.* a canoe of the design used by the Malecite Indians of New Brunswick. Cp. **Micmac.**
1872 DASHWOOD *Chiploquorgan* 11: I was astonished at the ease and skill with which the Indians paddled their bark canoes which were of the Malecite pattern—long, narrow, and crank. *Ibid.* 30: A Milicite canoe is much more crank than a Micmac, and is difficult to

stand up in at any time, unless thoroughly accustomed to it. **1942** JEFFERYS *Picture Gallery* I 30: [Caption] MALECITE . . . New Brunswick . . . ends slightly decked and with side flaps.

malemute ['mælə,mjut] *n*. [< *Malemiut,* an Eskimo people of western Alaska] a sled-dog of a type first bred by the Malemiut Eskimos. Cp. **Eskimo dog.** Also spelled *malamute.*

[**1874** *Annual Report Smithsonian Institution* 27: Maglemut] **1898** *Yukon Midnight Sun* (Dawson) 1 Oct. 2/5: I have the first man to find in the country who owns a dog, it matters not whether he is malamute, husky, St. Bernard, or even a short-haired, measly, little mongrel, that won't tell you he is the best leader in the country; yes, and believe it himself. **1924** *Beaver* May 296: Each [Eskimo] family owned its five or six malemutes, which were tied at intervals to a rope pegged to the ground. **1960** *Weekend Mag.* 23 Jan. 9/1: Some trappers . . . use dog teams to tend their territory. Oliver's six sturdy malemutes enable him to cover up to 20 miles a day.

Malemute ['mælə,mjut] *n*. [< *malemute,* q.v.] *Slang, Derog.* See quote. Also spelled *Malamute.*
1910 SERVICE *Trail of '98* 102: He triumphantly threw down a straight. "There, now," he snarled [addressing a Métis], "beat that, you stinking Malamute."

malichigan *n*. See **malachigan.**

mall *n*. See **shopping plaza.**
1966 *Kingston Whig-Standard* (Ont.) 22 Oct. 15/1: The entire mall will be temperature controlled, restaurants will also eventually serve the mall.

Malpeque (oyster) ['mælpɛk] *n*. [< *Malpeque* Bay, P.E.I. < Cdn F < Micmac *makpāk* large bay] a famous oyster of Prince Edward Island.
1901 DRUMMOND *J.Courteau* 19: Ain't dey got de noder oyster more better dan malpecque/Or caraquette, dat leetle wan from down below Kebeck? **1915** (1916) *Commission of Conservation* 75: The bulk of oysters sold to-day as Malpeques are not really such.
1964 *Time* (Cdn ed.) 18 Dec. 14/3: [They enjoyed] a stag dinner of Malpeque oysters, Brome Lake duckling and maple mousse at 24 Sussex Drive. . . .

mamaloos(h) ['mɑmə,lus *or* 'mɑmə,luʃ] *v. adj.* [< Chinook Jargon *memaloost* < Chinook *memalust* die, dead] *Pacific Coast* die; kill; dead; dying.
☛ *Many small islands in British Columbia are locally known as "Mamaloos Island," having been used as burial grounds. "Deadman's Island," off Stanley Park in Vancouver, is one of them.*
1858 (1937) *B.C.Hist.Qtly* 249: . . . each in his turn had to keep watch, with revolver in hand, that the Indians did not steal our provisions, as well as Mamaloose us while asleep. **1926** MOSER *Reminiscences* 42: I asked him what the matter was . . . and pulling the skin of his leg, he answered "Memeloust—small pox." **1956** RELANDER *Drummers* 197: The Reverend Thomas Pearne, an Indian, said, "Moses, memaloose (dead)." I knew Moses. **1963** SYMONS *Many Trails* 78: "My papoose going mamaloosh I t'ink."

mamaloosh ['mɑmə,luʃ] *adj.* See **mamaloos.**

mamateek ['mɑmə,tik] *n*. [< Beothuk, i.e., the language of the Red Indians (def. 1)] *Nfld, Hist.*

See quotes.
1832 MCGREGOR *Brit.Amer.* I 265: Here remains one of their [Beothuk] villages, where the vestiges of eight or ten winter mamateeks, or wigwams, each intended to contain six to eighteen or twenty people, are distinctly seen close together. **1907** MILLAIS *Newfoundland* 25: On the lakes near New Bay were the remains of winter mamateeks or wigwams. . . . **1962** *Cdn Geog.Jnl* Nov. 157/2: In summer they frequented the coasts and in winter they retired to their wigwams in the interior. These they called "mamateeks." Some of them were circular in shape while others were rectangular.

mamelle *n*. [< F "breast"] *Cdn French* an isolated rounded hill, sometimes one of two adjacent peaks resembling breasts.
1744 DOBBS *Hudson's Bay* 33: Then there is a Fork where two Branches meet, and on each Side, and at a considerable Distance, are two round Hills detached from the others, which they call Le deux Mamelles, or two Paps. **1760** JEFFERYS *Descr.New France* 3: Another land-mark of the Southern shore, is the double-headed mountain, called Les Mamelles de Matane, or Paps of Matane. . . .

mameloos(e), mameloost, etc. *v. adj.* See **mamaloos.**

man-catcher *n. Slang, Obs.* a hiring agent.
1912 (1914) BICKERSTETH *Open Doors* 183: Every big bunch of men has a "man-catcher" of this sort in charge.

maneater *n. Cariboo, Slang* a low-class prostitute, specifically an Indian woman.
1935 SULLIVAN *Great Divide* 44: These were . . . Hurdy Gurdy, fluzie and maneater, representing the descending order of female relaxation in the town of Yale.

Maneto *n*. See **Manitou.**

mangeur de lard *Cdn French, Fur Trade, Hist.*
1 See **porkeater** (def. 1a). Also *mangeur du lard.*
1794 (1929) MCGILLIVRAY *Journal* 6: A strong contrary wind obliged us to put ashore on an Island in Lac de la Pluie, where the Mangeurs de Lard from the Fort passed us under Sail. **1884** *Prince Albert Times* (Sask.) 11 Jan. 5/1: They looked contemptuously on the voyageurs from Montreal to Grand Portage, whom they called "mangeurs de lard," pork eaters from the dried provisions used in the absence of game coming up the lakes. **1961** PRICE & KENNEDY *Renfrew* 33: There was a day, no doubt, when Oiseau Rock echoed the voices of the "Mangeurs du Lard" as they sang their favorite songs. . . .

2 See **porkeater** (def. 1b).
1836 BACK *Arctic Land* 32: In our case, however, there was an unavoidable mixture of old hands and "mangeurs de lard," or green-horns; and there was scarcely one who had failed to take advantage of the last opportunity of getting drunk. **1843** (1932) MCLEAN *Notes* 329: [He was] the ablest mangeur de lard we have had in the country for a number of years.
1955 STANLEY in LEFROY *Magnetic North* xxi: It was as significant as crossing the Equator; henceforth he and Henry might call themselves voyageurs; no longer were they still novices in northern travel, mere mangeurs de lard.

3 *Northwest* the men employed in operating rafts and barges, as distinct from the trappers and canoemen, who considered themselves much higher in station.
*c*1902 LAUT *Trapper* 5: That threw an army of some two

thousand men—voyageurs, coureurs des bois, mangeurs de lard, famous hunters, traders, and trappers—on their own resources. *Ibid.* 167: For the mangeurs de lard, as they called the fur company raftsmen, they had a supreme contempt.

Manito *n.* See **Manitou**.

Manitoba [ˌmænəˈtobə] *n.* [< *Manitoba,* the province] See 1964 quote. Also *No. 1 hard Manitoba wheat.*

1888 *Dominion Illust.* 99/1: In the middle two men are absorbed by the duty of loading the No. 1 hard Manitoba wheat into waggons as fast as the bags are filled. **1945** HAIG *Brave Harvest* 28: "Mr. David Horn, the assistant, is really in charge," Cora explained to Aunt Alice that 1884 day. "The head, Mr. Clarke, has gone to England for the federal government. Six grades have been set up, the first one, like these grains, is called Manitoba No. 1 Hard,"—Manitoba No. 1 Hard still the hall mark of quality among wheats. **1946** LOWER *Colony to Nation* 410: The small quantities of western wheat exported before the end of the century had already made so good an impression on buyers in the Liverpool market that the term "Manitobas" had become well known. **1964** LEE *Foods and Textiles* 91: All the hard red spring wheats grown in any of the prairie provinces are called "Manitobas," but each variety within this class has a name of its own as well.

Manitoba fever *Hist.* in the early 1880's, the excitement in eastern Canada which led to extensive migrations to the newly opened-up province of Manitoba.

1883 *Brandon Dly Mail* (Man.) 24 Feb. 4/2: The infernal row you are all making up there about grievances[,] monopolies, squatter's rights, etc. has, together with your last spring's floods and Winnipeg speculations, cooled off the Manitoba fever prevalent in Ontario last year. **1883** FRASER *Shanty* 56: George, like many of his young compatriots, is smitten with the Manitoban fever, and is off to the land of the setting sun. . . . **1963** MORTON *Kingdom of Canada* 260: In the rural districts of the old province [Ontario] . . . the "Manitoba fever" was burning and settlement "parties" were being organized. . . .

Manitoba maple a deciduous tree, *Acer negundo,* common in western Canada; box elder. See also **ash-leaf maple, bastard maple, Red River maple,** and **sugar maple** (def. 2).

1887 *Senate Jnl* XXI App. 11: I have a good sized bag of Manitoba maple, as it is called, the Negunda Acreoids or ash leaved maple. **1913** ROSS *Tree Planting* 48: The Manitoba Maple . . . is generally found growing in river or creek bottoms, or on rich moist soil. **1963** SYMONS *Many Trails* 94: Separated from the farmyard by a fine grove of Manitoba maples and Russian poplars . . . stands an eight- or ten-roomed house. . . .

Manitoba Republic See **Republic of Manitoba**.

Manitoba School(s) Question *Hist.* a public controversy that raged in Canada between 1890 and 1919 and arose out of the enactment of provincial laws denying French-speaking Catholics the right to receive instruction in their own language in church-run schools, an issue which became national in scope because these laws were in defiance of the Manitoba Act (1870). See also **school question**.

1894 EWART *Manitoba School Question* [Title].

1946 LOWER *Colony to Nation* 416: Laurier's first job was to get the Manitoba School question settled. **1963** MORTON *Kingdom of Canada* 381: The strife of race and culture which was involved in the Manitoba Schools Question was the most strident of political issues, excepting only that of commercial union.

Manitou [ˈmænəˌtu] *n.* [< Algonk.; cf. Ojibwa *manitō*] Various spellings. **1 a.** a spirit; deity.

[**1613** (1932) CHAMPLAIN *Voyages* 320: Il y a de certaines personnes entr'eux qui font les Oqui ou Manitous (ainsi appellez par les Algommequins & Montagnais) lesquels se meslent de guarir les malades, penser les blessez, & predire les chose futures.] **1703** (1905) LAHONTAN *New Voyages* II 448: Matchi [is] the word for evil and Manitou for spirit. . . . **1789** (1801) MACKENZIE *Voyages* 45: We are now informed, that behind the opposite island there was a Manitoe or spirit, in the river, which swallowed every person that approached it. **1886** *Indian* (Hagersville, Ont.) 21 July 164/1: The Manitos who live in the air, the earth, and the water, became jealous of their great power and conspired against them. **1936** *Cdn Geog.Jnl* XII 54/2: That hapless primal being, personification of winter, built a fire to warm himself before the wigwam he might not enter; a lodge built in the clouds by the jealous manitos of earth, air and water.

b. See quote.

1811 (1891) EDGAR *Ten Years of U.C.* 371: This compass . . . not being able to comprehend its action, they called . . . a "Manitou," by which they mean "spirit," or something incomprehensible and powerful.

2 See **Gitchi Manitou**.

1748 DRAGE *Voyage* I 235: It is a received Opinion amongst the Indians in those Parts, that there are two Spirits, one whom they call Manitou, to which Spirit, they attribute all the Perfections of the Deity. . . . **1863** WALSHE *Cedar Creek* 356: They believe that these flashes are the spirits of the dead dancing before the throne of the Manitou, or Great Spirit. **1952** HOWARD *Strange Empire* 295: In the sixties the medicine men told their tribes they had been warned in dreams that such brutal processes as the piskun offended the buffalo and Manito, who had stocked the Plains for His people. **1965** *Kingston Whig-Standard* (Ont.) 29 Sep. 36/4: "The white man is getting to[o] big and rich. Manitou does not like this and he gave bad weather.

3 an idol, charm, or fetish.

1760 JEFFERYS *Descr.New France* 58: If there are too many manitous to be contained in one bag, they are distributed into several. . . . **1863** (1888) MCDOUGALL *G.M.McDougall* 142: For ages the tribes of Blackfeet and Crees have gathered their clans to pay homage to this wonderful manitoo. **1921** HAWORTH *Trailmakers* 116: Upon it usually lay a pair of bull's heads, which were esteemed a great Manitou and protection.

4 the Christian God. See also **Great Spirit**.

1893 OXLEY *Young Nor'Wester* 80: His constant companionship . . . had given this Indian boy a comprehension . . . and the mention of God, the mysterious and all-powerful Manitou of the white men, to whom Mr. M'Kenzie prayed so often, calmed and comforted him. **1926** (1958) *Camsell Arrow* Christmas 37:

O children of the forest free,
O songs of Manitou,
The Holy Child of earth and heaven
Is born to-day for you.

1962 *Maclean's* 20 Oct. 46/1: If so they would soon become followers of the white man's good Manitou.

5 a priest or spiritual adviser.
1962 *Field,Horse & Rodeo* Nov. 26/1: ". . . It is true that they broke off the battle because they feared our Manitou, Father Lafleche, but that won't hold them off long."

6 See **Manitou wheat**.

Manitou Stone See quotes. See also **Iron Stone**. Cp. **medicine stone**.
1952 HOWARD *Strange Empire* 252: The Manito Stone was . . . sacred to most of the Plains tribes, for obviously it was no ordinary stone; their legends said it had come down from the sky. 1962 DICKIE *Great Golden Plain* 181: . . . the Manitou Stone was a large meteorite which had lain on a hill top in southern Alberta so long that rain and the reverent hands of pilgrims had polished it till it shone like silver in the moonlight.

Manitou wheat See quote.
1966 *Western Wkly* 23 Mar. 5: [Caption] Last year, yields of 40 and 50 bushels per acre were not uncommon in the increase fields of Manitou wheat one of which, near Regina, is shown being swathed. However, seed of this variety is in too short supply because of the great demand for it throughout most of the prairies. Manitou, developed by the Canada Department of Agriculture and released in 1965, is resistant to both leaf and stem rust.

manning depot a district depot where recruits of the Royal Canadian Air Force receive basic training.
1962 FRY *Ranch on the Cariboo* 252: Appearing before an examining board at the Jericho Beach manning depot in Vancouver, I qualified. . . .

manning pool a central pool, or replacement depot, of seamen, airmen, etc.
1944 *Cdn Seaman* 24 Nov. 1/3: The CSU executive meeting seriously criticized the present system of administration of the Manning Pools. *Ibid.* 4/1: When he arrives in port, a manning pool flop is arranged for him while he awaits his turn to be shipped out on another vessel.

Man of the North *Fur Trade* 1 *Hist*. See **winterer** (def. 2a). See also **Northman** (def. 1).
[1843 (1868) IRVING *Bonneville* 39: The voyageurs or boatmen were the rank and file in the service of the trader, and even the hardy "men of the north" . . . were fain to be paddled from point to point of their migrations.] 1952 (1954) JENNINGS *Strange Brigade* 153: ". . . Ye'll forgive my fellows, I hope, but we are 'Men o' th' North' an' somethin' inclined t' boast about it."

2 a man who has lived in and is familiar with the Northland, especially a trader or trapper.
1888 (1948) *Beaver* Dec. 14/1: . . . even articles for washing [are] dispensed with by those who are desirous of being styled "men of the north." 1940 *Ibid.* Mar. 2/1: His eldest son, John, who succeeds to the title [Tweedsmuir], is also a man of the North.

man-pack *v*. carry supplies, etc. on one's back.
1965 *Beaver* Autumn 55/1: We man-packed from there on, some hundred miles to the Mackenzie River.

man-packer *n*. one who man-packs, *q.v.*

man-packing *n*. carrying supplies, etc. on one's back. See also **man-pack**.
1938 *Beaver* Sep. 45/2: Transport along the line varied. . . . In the lake country of northern Manitoba it was handled by canoe, man-packing, and dogs. . . .

manta *n*. [< Sp.] *West, Obs*. See **mantle**.
1912 POCOCK *Man in the Open* 321: Around him in a horseshoe stood fifty complete aparajeos, each with . . . sovran helmo and cinchas, sweat pad, blanket, and corona, while the head-ropes strapped the mantas over all.

mantle *n*. [trans. of Sp. *manta*] *West, Obs*. See quotes. See also **manta**.
1887 (1888) LEES & CLUTTERBUCK *British Columbia* 230: Cover all [the horse packs] with the mantle (generally a strong waterproof sheet) to protect it from the elements. 1951 HOBSON *Grass* 102: This rope is used for the diamond hitch that is tightly lashed about the complete pack over the top of a twelve-ounce, six-foot-square canvas tarp called a pack mantle.

maple bush See **sugar bush**.
1954 BEATTIE *Along the Road* 2: Guarding it was our neighbour's maple bush. . . . 1966 *Kingston Whig-Standard* (Ont.) 19 Mar. 6/7: He said he had heard from three farmers who noted the sap run was fairly good in their maple bushes.

maple cake a block or mould of maple sugar.
1945 HAIG *Brave Harvest* 4: There was the sugaring-off with the fires, over which great pots of syrup were boiled, and finally the storing of maple cakes in the house.

maple camp See **sugar-camp**.
1955 *Star* 15 Apr. 3/1: [Advert.] Good road leading to maple camp of Lucien Gagnon. . . .

maple candy† candy made from maple sap. See also **taffy** (def. 1).
1879 *Morning Chron.* (Halifax) 2 July 1/8: The average boy and a good sized lump of maple candy, form the materials from which we might deduct self-evident conclusion regarding the facility with which attachments are formed in early life.

maple crop† the produce of a sugar bush; annual production of maple sugar and maple syrup.
1964 *Family Herald* 12 Mar. 18: . . . the maple producer's thoughts turn to dairying or other outdoor activities, and they're glad to cash in their maple crop, at any price.

maple grove See **sugar bush**.
1835 (1947) WELLS *Owl Pen* 91: "As soon as the sap begins to rise, the squaws betake themselves in families . . . to maple groves, or sugar bushes, as they are called. 1877 O'LEARY *Travels* 205: A large quantity of maple sugar is made in the eastern townships, and is an article of considerable value to the manufacturers or proprietors of a maple grove.

maple juice *Obs*. the sap of the maple, used for making syrup.
1804 (1933) CONNOR *Diary* 274: [We] gave up Sugar Makeing [for] the Maple Juice is turned quite Bitter.

maple leaf a representation of the leaf of the maple tree, long used as an emblem of Canada.
1860 *Trans.Lit.& Hist.Soc.Que.* IV 20: The Mayflower . . . I am told is the emblem of Nova Scotia, as the

Maple leaf is of Canada. **1950** QUANCE *Canadian Speller* Grade Six 4: During the war of 1812-14, the scarlet jacket of Canadian and British soldiers made a perfect target for the enemies. Therefore, when fighting in the woods, each soldier cut slips in his blouse and inserted a twig of maple leaves to bluff the enemy. This was the first time that the maple leaf had been specifically identified with Canadians or with Canada. **1964** *Globe and Mail* (Toronto) 29 Oct. 1/9: A single maple leaf on a white field flanked by red bars will be recommended to the House of Commons today as Canada's new flag.

Maple Leaf (flag) the flag of Canada (see 1964 quote at **maple leaf**).
1965 *Victoria Daily Times* 20 July 13/2: Monday was Canada Day at the village and so after the Maple Leaf was hoisted and a "lumberjack's" breakfast dispatched, [they] went outside. . . . **1966** *Kingston Whig-Standard* (Ont.) 21 July 4/5: . . . every Canadian must regard the maple leaf flag as the symbol of our nation.

maple molasses See **maple syrup**.
1840 WILLIS *Cdn Scenery* I 100: Three copious meals . . . are daily served up . . . consisting generally of the same component parts; among which are . . . maple-molasses, pease-pudding, gingerbread, and sour crout.
1848 LANMAN *Adventures* 193: The supper was laid on the table at ten o'clock, and consisted principally of dried beaver-tail and cariboo meat, fried and boiled salmon, rye-bread, maple molasses and tea.
1897 DURAND *Reminiscences* 83: . . . we made our household sugar, and luscious maple molasses, not mixed as it is now too often with water and common Muscovado sugar.

maple producer a person who operates a sugar bush, *q.v.*, producing maple sugar and maple syrup.
1964 *Family Herald* 12 Mar. 18: . . . the maple producer's thoughts turn to dairying or other outdoor activities, and they're glad to cash in their maple crop, at any price.

maple season See **sugaring season**.
1966 *Kingston Whig-Standard* (Ont.) 19 Mar. 6/8: We have to have both frosty nights and warm days to have a good maple season.

maple sucrerie See **sugary**.

maple sugar† sugar obtained by boiling the sap of certain maple trees, especially the sugar maple, *q.v.* See also **sugar,** *n.*
1765-75 (1933) POND *Narrative* 30: Hear I Met with a Grate meney . . . trading with the tribes that Came a Grate Distans with thare furs, Skins & Mapel Suga &c to Market. **1767** (1901) HENRY (Elder) *Travels* 211: In the beginning of April, I prepared to make maple-sugar. **1849** *Wkly Globe* 16 Nov. 78/7: In 1848 nearly four million lbs. of maple sugar were manufactured in Upper Canada! **1966** *Kingston Whig-Standard* (Ont.) 6 Feb. 4/4: Maple sugar was made by many tribes of Ontario.

maple-sugar making† See **sugaring-off** (def. 1).
1926 MAIR *Masterworks* XIV lii: There were also such ideal pastimes as . . . visiting Indian encampments . . . and maple-sugar making in the dense woods in spring. **1960** *Cdn Geog.Jnl* Nov. 171: [Caption] An exhibit of maple sugar-making equipment in the Dalziel Barn museum, containing a sled for transportation of the cap tank, oxen yoke, burl dipper, skimmer, large iron pots, sap buckets and maple sugar moulds.

maple syrup a syrup made from the sap of certain maple trees, especially the sugar maple,

q.v. See also **maple molasses, molasses, syrup, taffy** (def. 2), and **treacle**.
[**1703** (1905) LAHONTAN *New Voyages* I 70: . . . a Syrup of Maple beat up with water. . . .] **1849** ALEXANDER *L'Acadie* II 123: They . . . brought us . . . a present of butter, and buck-wheat cakes, and a bottle of maple syrup. **1921** LAUT *Cariboo Trail* 105: The fare consisted of ham . . . slapjacks, known as "Rocky Mountain dead shot," in maple syrup that never saw a maple tree and was black as a pot. . . . **1965** *Kingston Whig-Standard* (Ont.) 28 Dec. 4/3: Ontario maple syrup production dropped from 500,000 gallons in 1942 to 125,000 gallons in 1964.

maple water [trans. of F *eau d'erable*] *Obs.*
1 See **maple syrup**.
1703 (1905) LAHONTAN *New Voyages* I 249: 'Tis but a few of the inhabitants that have the patience to make Mapple-Water.
2 the sap of the maple tree, used in making maple syrup.
1947 WELLS *Owl Pen* 90: The "maple water" dripped from these crude spiles into scooped out basswood logs or birch-bark baskets.

marais [ma're] *n.* [< F] *Hist.* (*except in place names*) See 1933 quote.
1793 (1933) MACDONELL *Diary* 77: Opposite to this marais on the south shore there is a fine sandbank. . . . **1800** (1897) COUES *New Light* I 39: I went duck shooting, having seen great numbers in the marais during my walk. **1933** GATES *Five Traders* 77n: The French word marais means swamp or marsh. The phrase grand marais was descriptive of many places along the canoe routes of the Canadian Northwest and in early times was not used as a specific place name.

march *n.* [< v. (def. 1)] *North* a journey of any kind, especially by canoe, dogsled, etc.; also, a leg of a journey. Cp. **mush,** *n.*
1801 (1820) HARMON *Journal* 77: Sent five men with a canoe, two days march up the river. **1820** (1938) SIMPSON *Athabasca Jnl* 6: . . . Brunelle's Canoe . . . was unable to keep company with Magnions Brigade, in consequence of his wife being taken in labour on the march two days ago. **1905** (1954) *B.C.Hist.Qtly* XVIII 214: There were two feet of snow on the ground during the first part of our trip of 270 miles, and after a long week of almost incessant travel, or "march" as the word was, we reached our destination. . . . **1931** NUTE *Voyageur* 61: Once again the long marches were resumed as the little hamlets . . . faded from sight.

march *v.* [< Cdn F < F *marcher* walk] **1** See 1905 quote. See also **march,** *n.* and **mush,** *v.* (def. 2b).
1794 (1929) MCGILLIVRAY *Journal* 5: Camped at Lac la Croix . . . there being no necessity for marching more expeditiously. . . . **1819** (1890) WILCOCKE *Death B. Frobisher* 197: Marched the whole day and did not encamp "until dark"—"To march" is the Canadian term for travelling, and is as frequently, if not oftener, applied to express the progress of a canoe or boat as of a pedestrian. **1905** (1954) *B.C.Hist.Qtly* XVIII 161: Some peculiar expressions used by the French-Canadians also have vogue in the service—"to march" for instance, generally, is applied to any progression—including canoe and boat travel.

2 a. See **mush,** *v.* (def. 1). See also **marche**.
1873 (1904) BUTLER *Wild North Land* 144: Once more

the sleds were packed, once more the Untiring Cerf-Vola took his place in the leading harness, and the word "march" was given. **1921** *Beaver* Nov. 13/2: "In all sections of Canada east of the Rockies the terms used in driving dogs were taken from the French language—'marche', commonly used as 'march', to start; 'yea' for 'gee' and 'chaw' for 'haw'. In this country west of the mountains they tried to copy from the east, but made a failure. The terms they used are 'mush,' 'gee' and 'haw.' **1959** LEISING *Arctic Wings* 37: "Redzie, march," Leo barked at him, and that red face turned and gave me an ornery look.

b. See **mush,** *v.* (def. 3a).
1959 LEISING *Arctic Wings* 34: The trappers, which included Indians, Metis and whites, gathered their supplies, hitched their dog teams, and "marched them" out across the frozen river to their trap lines.

marche(donc) *imper.v. Cdn French* [< F *marche(donc)!* a command to horses < *marcher* go, walk] See **mush,** *v.* (def. 1). See also **march,** *v.* (def. 2a).
1880 (1893) YOUNG *Indian Wigwams* 130: When well harnessed the driver shouts, "March!" and the three well-trained dogs ahead spring off on the jump.
1913 WILLIAMS *Wilderness Trail* 78: Voudrin climbed into the sledge, and, shouting, "Marche donc, marche donc," started the dogs around the headland.
1947 DICKIE *Gay Adventures* 422: MARCHE . . . The early French trappers in the North used this word when driving their dog teams.

marche-donc *n. Cdn French* **1** See **calèche** (def. 1).
1799 (1955) CRAIG *Early Travellers* 25: From the frequent use made by the drivers of these words, the calashes have received a nick-name of "marche-doncs."

2 a French-Canadian driver of a caleche or cart.
1845 TOLFREY *Sportsman* II 133n: Marche donc is a sobriquet bestowed on all Habitans from their vehement and invariable ejaculation of the words when applied to their ponies as an incentive to increased speed. **1850** BIGSBY *Shoe and Canoe* I 173: . . . and the narrow Norman carts of the "marche-doncs," as their drivers are nicknamed, from their perpetual use of that "cry" to their cattle. **1916** SKELTON *Railway Builders* 20: [The] driver, or *marche-donc,* usually exceeded this rate.

marguillier *n.* [< F] *Que., Obs.* a churchwarden.
1831 *Vindicator* (Montreal) 13 Dec. 1/1: No one could tell what might happen if the Marguilliers were allowed to perpetuate themselves without the suffrages of the parishioners. **1832** *Cdn Courant* (Montreal) 26 Dec. 2/5: The Marguillier (Church Wardens) are men who are generally held in much esteem in their respective Parishes.

mari [məˈraɪ] *n.* [origin uncertain; perhaps related to *mathemeg,* q.v.] See **loche.**
1858 (1863) PALLISER *Journals* 282: A squaw . . . caught a fine sturgeon, and a fish called by the Canadians a Marry (Burbot). **1887** *Senate Jnl* XXI App. 121: Next in quantity would come . . . gold-eye, mari or methy (dog fish or ling), yellow perch. . . . **1939** GODSELL *Vanishing Frontier* 91: She'd been there quite a while, got quite a few maris, and was about ready to go home. . . .

maria [məraɪə] *n.* [var. of *mari,* q.v.] See **loche.**
1909 CAMERON *New North* 329: The net yields seven fish and they are of five different species,—trout, ling, sucker, jack-fish, and something else that Tom calls a "Maria." **1938** *Beaver* Sep. 32/1: [Caption] A poor haul, whitefish, red suckers and marias. **1964** *Fur Trade Jnl* Oct. 8/1: Early in 1964 two groups of mink . . . were used for 100% diets of tullibee and marias. The fish were caught early in December and in January, and kept in a commercial cold storage. **1964** [see quote at **methy**].

marine highway a connected series of waterways, as the St. Lawrence Seaway.
1954 *Cdn Geog.Jnl* Feb. 55/3: The new marine highway is, in a very real sense, a huge financial gamble. **1962** *Canada Month* Sep. 17/2: A joint federal-provincial-state enterprise, the marine highway is the key link in a huge new transportation system.

marine railway† a device consisting of a cable-drawn cradle equipped to run on rails up and down a ramp, used for launching and landing boats or for moving boats from one water level to another.
1836 ROLPH *Brief Account* 155: A marine rail-way has been formed, and a great deal of business is carried on in the dock yard. **1860** *Islander* (Charlottetown) 3 Feb. 2/3: A Marine Railway, for the rapid repair of vessels, is wanted at this port. **1963** *Toronto Dly Star* 29 June 17/2: I mean the marine railways on the Severn river portion of the Trent waterway. They carry pleasure boats, even up to 20 tons, over the tops of two big hydro-electric power dams and lower them gently into the river 60 feet below.

marionette *n.* See quote.
1946 *Beaver* Sep. 13: In some regions they [northern lights] are called "marionettes."

Maritime [ˈmɛrəˌtaɪm *or* ˈmærəˌtaɪm] *n.* **1** *Rare* See **Maritime Provinces.**
1904 CROSSKILL *P.E.I.* 10: Like the rest "of the Maritime" the Island of Prince Edward received its quota of loyalists.

2 (used attributively) of or having to do with the Maritime Provinces or Maritimers, *qq.v.*
1957 HUTCHISON *Canada* 82: He knows it . . . if he is an eastern man, when the native orchids dance in lady-slippers, the swamp maples spill arterial blood, and the succulent fiddlehead excites the Maritime palate. **1959** *Star Wkly* 22 Aug. 17/1: Maritime lobstering began in the 1850's and by 1870 the delectable crustacean had appeared on dinner tables from Maine to California. **1964** *Kingston Whig-Standard* (Ont.) 16 Nov. 18/6: He said Maritime union would result in a two per cent saving in administrative costs. . . .

Maritime colony *Hist.* any of the provinces of British North America lying on the eastern seaboard; the present Atlantic Provinces (def. 2). See also **Eastern Provinces** (def. 1).
1953 LEBOURDAIS *Nation of North* 12: In 1858, Alexander T. Galt, an English-speaking member of parliament from Lower Canada, had moved a series of resolutions calling for a committee to sound out the people of the Maritime colonies and the British government on the question of union.

Maritime Confederation *Hist.* See **Maritime Union.**
1872 DASHWOOD *Chiploquorgan* 251: The Canadians are inclined to put the screw on the non-Confederating colonies in the shape of heavy duties on their produce, in order to compel them to join the Confederation. As has before been mentioned, a Maritime Confederation would have been the best course to have commenced with.

Maritime province 1 *Obs.* See **Maritime colony.**

1863 *Islander* (Charlottetown) 24 June 2/5: It is probable that a general Union may be proceded by the Union of the "Maritime" Provinces. **1872** DASHWOOD *Chiploquorgan* 246: The island of Newfoundland was the least settled of any of the Maritime provinces of Canada.

2 any of the Maritime Provinces, *q.v.*

1924 MACMECHAN *Provincial Tales* 285: There might be seventeen captains of clan MacKenzie at one time sailing out of Pictou, but nothing ever shook the primacy of Yarmouth as the most maritime county of a maritime province. **1942** DUNCAN *Bluenose* 80: In a few moments . . . a Nova Scotia sunset of no mean proportions was attempting to outdo every other impression I had received from my first holiday in this Maritime Province. **1954** *Fundy Fisherman* 31 Mar. 1/5: There is narrative verse, too, to be enjoyed, particularly by readers who cherish memories of Maritime Province neighborliness and friendliness.

Maritime Provinces the Canadian provinces of Nova Scotia, New Brunswick, and Prince Edward Island. See also **Maritimes.**

☛ *Traditionally the term refers to the listed provinces although Newfoundland is occasionally included by some modern writers. This dictionary uses the term* **Atlantic Provinces** *to include the Maritime Provinces and Newfoundland.*
1850 ROY *Hist.of Canada* 165: These Provinces are of two classes—first, the Inland Portions, watered only by great lakes and rivers, and, secondly, the Maritime Provinces. **1890** *Moose Jaw Times* (Sask.) 7 Nov. 3/1: They will take a trip through Ontario, on their way to the Maritime Provinces. **1966** *Kingston Whig-Standard* (Ont.) 27 July 36/1: The Maritime provinces' famous lobster catch may have an up-and-coming rival in the North Atlantic queen crab. . . .

Maritimer *n.* a native or resident of the Maritime Provinces. See also **Herring-Choker.**

1931 *Cdn Geog.Jnl* II 391/1: Our "two-sticker with a kicker" lies in Sandy Bay harbor, Nova Scotia, outward bound for Labrador, that terra incognito even to the Maritimers. **1964** *Canada Month* Jan. 11/1: The memory of the great sailing vessels swooping across the waves and sliding into port has stayed with Maritimers.

Maritimes *n.pl.* See **Maritime Provinces.**

1806 (1956) FAY *Life and Labour* 134: Schooners come from the Maritimes with much needed provisions and lumber. **1964** *Star Wkly* 12 Dec. 6/1: We in the Maritimes are sick of hand-outs. . . . **1966** *Kingston Whig-Standard* (Ont.) 29 July 5/1: Attempts were being made to locate Mr. Walsh and his wife who are presently on vacation in the Maritimes.

Maritime(s) Union a proposed union or federation of the Maritime Provinces and Newfoundland. See also **Maritime Confederation.**

[**1863** *Islander* (Charlottetown) 24 June 2/5: It is probable that a general Union may be preceded by the Union of the "Maritime" Provinces.] **1923** *Dalhousie Rev.* III 211: We can understand why Maritime Union might find favour in Nova Scotia, as that fine province . . . would dominate the Acadian Government and Parliament absolutely. **1964** *Star Wkly* 12 Dec. 7/1: He reminded them that the 1864 meeting . . . had originally been called to promote a Maritimes Union.

marker *n.* an automobile licence plate.

1949 *Globe and Mail* (Toronto) 13 Apr. 17/9: Another place . . . is the average automobile license office a couple of days before the deadline for new markers.

market boat *Obs.* in colonial New Brunswick, a boat used for shipping produce and goods down river from the clearings to the towns.

1845 BEAVAN *Life in Backwoods N.B.* 8: . . . when the spring opens, the reeds and other spare produce are quickly shipped (boated would be a better expression) into large open boats, called market boats. *Ibid.* 96: The proprietors . . . had deposited the butter and oats equivalent to her hire, in the market boat. . . .

marketman *n.* a commercial fisherman who markets his own fish.

1942 GOUGH *New World Horizons* 187: If the crew are "marketmen" they wash the fish in tubs of sea water and pack them in ice to be sold fresh in a day or two's time.

market road *West* a rural road maintained by the provincial Department of Highways for year-round use.

1958 *Edmonton Jnl* 18 June 31/5: A petition from Pipestone community residents requesting the relocation of a market road was turned down here by county councillors.

market sleigh *Obs.* a farm sleigh having a large open box for carrying produce to market.

1816 (1818) HALL *Travels* 68: The markets both of Montreal and Quebec exhibit several hundred market sleighs daily.

marmot *n.* **1** See **ground squirrel.**

1821 (1823) FRANKLIN *Journey* 378: Dr. Richardson found in the stomach of this animal the remains of a seal, several marmots. . . . **1897** TYRRELL *Sub-Arctics* 187: We were not altogether unsuccessful, assembling in the evening with five marmots (little animals about the size of squirrels).

2 See **hoary marmot.**

1955 GOWLAND *Smoke* 29: Crossing to the door, I opened it hesitantly, and in tumbled four fat marmots, the size of badgers which, except for colour, they somewhat resembled.

maron *adj.* [< F *marron;* cf. **Maroon**] *Obs.* wild; untrained.

1859 *Kamloops Jnl* (B.C.) 11 Mar.: Exchanged two maron mares for two trained ones.

Maroon† *n. Hist.* one of a number of Negroes brought to Nova Scotia during the building of Halifax in 1749.

1796 (1895) *Trans.Roy.Soc.Can.* XI 2 87: The dogs had nothing to do with it; it was not, I apprehend, known to the Maroons that they were with us, for the Maroons had moved the day before we did. **1832** MCGREGOR *Brit.Amer.* II 204: Some time after, three ships, with the rebellious Maroons of Jamaica, arrived at Halifax. **1955** *Huntingdon Gleaner* 13 Apr. 6/3: Nova Scotia has the largest Negro community in Canada, and in Halifax the colored race has been prominent since the Maroons helped build the city in 1749.

Marquis wheat a famous strain of hard, fast-ripening wheat developed in Canada in 1903, by Dr. Charles E. Saunders.

1936 DENTON & LORD *World Geography* 85: Dr. Charles E. Saunders, the Dominion cerealist, had been experimenting for several years, trying to produce a new wheat which would ripen earlier than Red Fife. In 1903 his efforts were crowned with success. The new wheat was named "Marquis." **1960** BUBLITZ *Dotted Line* 51: Marquis wheat was chosen as their crop that first year.

marrow fat or **grease** *Hist. or Obs.* a choice butterlike substance rendered from the bones of buffalo and other large animals and used by the Indians and traders as butter and as an ingredient of pemmican.
1717 (1932) KNIGHT *Journals* 164: These Indians gave me a Side of Moose flesh, Dry'd, & Another of Deers flesh, & 2 pretty bigg bladders of Marrow fatt. . . . **1862** (1931) CHEADLE *Journal* 60: Send to Fort for potatoes, milk & marrow fat. **1931** NUTE *Voyageur* 213: . . . the train wound its slow way back to Pembina laden with . . . 556 bladders of marrow grease. **1947** *Beaver* Dec. 21: Clean Marrow fat rendered down like white butter.

marsh *n. Maritimes* reclaimed marshland. See also **dike land.**
1821 (1960) MCCULLOCH *Stepsure Letters* 15: . . . a few acres of Mr. Gosling's best marsh passed into the hands of Saunders Scantocreesh, a hard-faced, hard-working Scotchman. . . . **1889** WITHROW *Our Own Country* 110: In the foreground were fields of yellowing grain, and stretching to the landward horizon was the vast expanse of the green Tantramar and Missiguash marshes, not less, it is said, than 50,000 fertile acres. **1957** WRIGHT *Blomidon Rose* 79: In Westmoreland and Cumberland counties, too, the dyked land was marsh. . . .

marsh bittern the American bittern, *Botaurus lentiginosus.* See also **Indian hen, marsh hen,** and **meadow hen.**
1823 HALIBURTON *General Descr.N.S.* 31: The following catalogue contains a list of the known birds of the Province . . . Marsh Bittern. . . . **1905** MOTT *Jules* 255: . . . the dull, booming calls of the marsh bittern floated up out of a distant valley stream.

marsh broadleaf *Maritimes* See **marsh hay.**
1946 BIRD *Sunrise* 198: Hay was a light crop, mostly marsh broadleaf.

marsh dike or **dyke** See **aboiteau** (def. 1).
1822 (1960) MCCULLOCH *Stepsure Letters* 28: . . . a great storm in the Bay . . . broke through a weak portion of his marsh dyke which . . . he had neglected to mend.

marsh greens *N.S.* See quote.
1952 PUTNAM *Cdn Regions* 28/1: Characteristic of this "salt marsh" are fox grass (*Spartina juncea*), black grass (*Juncus gerardii*) and marsh greens (*Plantago juncoides*). The latter, as its name implies, is commonly eaten in the same manner as spinach.

marsh hare See **marsh rabbit.**

marsh hawk a slate-gray or brownish hawk, *Circus cyaneus hudsonius.*
1772 *Linnean Soc.Trans.* XII 671: The legs of the Marsh Hawk are remarkably long and slender. **1903** SETON *Animal Heroes* 136: A brown Marsh Hawk came skimming over the river flat as the sun began his color play. **1963** SYMONS *Many Trails* 189: A marsh hawk floated overhead.

marsh hay a kind of broadleafed grass, *Spartina* sp., common in marshes and used as hay. See also

marsh broadleaf.
1821 (1955) HARVEY *Island of St.John* 130: New Settlers, unless they get marsh hay along with their farms at first, get slowly on in keeping stock. **1924** *Beaver* Sep. 460/2: There is every indication of a poor [hay] crop. . . . The Indians who depend upon the marsh hay have the same cry. **1945** *Ibid.* June 55/2: [Thatch] was made with "a rank sort of grass growing in the marshes, much like the flags which are everywhere in our English brooks". (To-day at Rupert's House it is known as "marsh hay", and is used for feeding the cattle).

marsh hen See **marsh bittern.**
1956 MCATEE *Folk-Names* 6: American Bittern [is also called] marsh hen (a widely used name known from "Eastern Canada"). . . .

marsh lands *N.S.* See **dike land.**
1889 WITHROW *Our Own Country* 49: The Acadians reclaimed the fertile marsh lands from the sweep of the tides, by constructing dikes with much labour by means of wattled stakes and earthen embankments. **1957** WRIGHT *Blomidon Rose* 79: Officially, then, the eight thousand five hundred acres of dyked lands around Minas Basin are marsh lands. . . .

marsh rabbit or **hare** See quotes. See also **swamp rabbit.**
1930 HODGSON *Muskrat Farming* 324: Thousands of Muskrats have been served in the dining room of prominent hotels as "Marsh Hare" and "Diamond Back Terrapin." **1946** WOOD *Rockies* 93: Today, city restaurants handy to the large muskrat farms of the East sometimes feature "Marsh Rabbit" on their menus and find that patrons are fond of the delicious oddity.

marsh rat See **muskrat** (def. 1). See also **mushrat** (def. 1).
*c*1902 (1912) LAUT *Trapper* 225: The owl is flapping blindly through the flags to another hiding-place, while the wriggle-wriggle of the waters tells where the marsh-rat has darted away under the tangled growth.

marten *n.* **1** the pine marten, *Martes americana.* See also **pine marten.**
1697 (1929) KELSEY *Papers* 88: The indians brought some deers flesh and tongues & had given yᵉ Govʳ. 2 young foxes & one young martin. **1776** (1951) *Sask. Jnls* 29 Feb.: I gave the Leader a small present desiring them to be diligent in Trapping Martens having told me they are plentiful. **1872** DASHWOOD *Chiploquorgan* 181: The marten, commonly known as the sable . . . is about the same size as the mink, and differs little from it in form, save that its feet are larger, and hairy to the toes; the tail is also somewhat larger. **1957** *Aklavik Jnl* Mar. 2: Although he traps near the headwaters of the Anderson River where the marten are thick he may only take thirty five per year. . . .

2 a. the pelt of the pine marten.
1784 (1954) *Moose Ft Jnls* 28: They brought 5 martins only, a Fox having tore their traps and ate almost all the martins that were caught. *c*1948 *Sask.Fur Marketing Service* 11: Fisher, marten, lynx and otter are sold individually, unless well matched.

b. *Fur Trade, Hist.* See 1907 quote. Cp. **made beaver** (def. 1).
*c*1771 (1964) INNIS *Fur Trade* 150: For a small brass kettle of two pounds, or two and a half weight, they pay sixty martins, or twenty beaver in other kinds of furrs. . . . **1907** HUNTER *Cdn Wilds* 50: So that the Indian might know the amount of his means of trade the furs were taken in first and valued at a certain well-known currency of that particular part of the

country in which he resided, i. e., "Made Beaver" or so many "Martens."

467

marten road
Master of Life

marten road *North* See **trapline** (def. 1).
1900 FRASER *Mooswa* x: It is a well known fact that many a trapper has had to abandon his "marten road" and move to another locality when Carcajou has set up to drive him out. *Ibid.* 100: François and Rod shouldered each a bag of Traps and started to lay out the Marten Road, as was called a big circle of Traps extending perhaps thirty miles, for the Winter's hunt.

marthy *n.* See **methy.**

mash *v.* See **mush.**

mashimonge *n.* See **maskinonge.**

mashquemcate or **mashquemincte** *n.* See **muskimoot.**

maskalonge, maskalongy, maskelongé *n.* See **muskellunge.**

maskinonge ['mæskɪˌnɑnʒ] *n.* [< Cdn F *masquinongé* < Algonk.; cf. Cree *mashkkinonche* great pike.]
☛ *Other etymologies have been proposed for this much-used word, for example:*
1866 KING *Sportsman in Canada* 307: One of the most remarkable inhabitants of the Great Lakes belongs to this family, namely, the celebrated Masq'allongé . . . erroneously called Maskinongé, Mascalongé, Muskalinge, Maskalunge, and other barbarous corruptions of two simple French words, signifying "long face." **1896** *Trans.Roy.Soc.Can.* II 2 138: According to Mgr. Lafleche, "maskinongé" is derived from *mashk* deformed, and *kinongé*, a pike, and was applied to *esox nobilior* by the Indians because it appeared to them a deformed or different kind of pike from that to which they had been accustomed.
a large species of pike, *Esox masquinongy*, weighing up to 80 pounds, found principally in the Great Lakes system. See also **lunge, muskellunge** and **muskie.** Many spellings.
[**1703** LAHONTAN *New Voyages* II 318: '*kinongé*, brochet [northern pike]] **1761** (1901) HENRY (Elder) *Travels* 30: Among the pike, is to be included the species, called, by the Indians, *masquinonge.* **1826** (1832) PICKERING *Inquiries* 54: Hauled the seine yesterday in the lake, and caught nine maskinonge (a large fish, very like a pike) from five to thirty pounds each. **1928** *Beaver* Sep. 59: The giant maskinonge (the muskellunge, or "lunge") known to reach a length of eight feet and a weight of one hundred pounds. **1963** *Globe and Mail* (Toronto) 13 April 5/6: He is also an officer of the Outdoor Writers of Canada and only in one respect might he come into conflict with his companions on that body— by using the U.S. term muskellunge instead of the accepted, original Canadian name, maskinonge.

maso or **masu** *n. Eskimo* See **licorice.**
1951 BULIARD *Inuk* 167: In the fall, the women and children search for berries, if they don't mind endless hours of labor for a few ounces of food, and they also dig from the ground a root called "maso," insipid and quite diuretic, but nevertheless appreciated. **1955** ADTIC *Glossary* 51/2: masu *n.* Liquorice-root.

masquenunja, masquinongé, masquinongie, etc. *n.* See **maskinonge.**

Massasauga (rattler) [ˌmæsəˈsɑgə] *n.* [an irregular form of a river name in S.W. Ontario: *Missisauga* < Algonk.] a relatively small rattle-snake of the genus *Sistrurus*.
1837 *Trans.Lit.& Hist.Soc.Que.* IV 25: The fangs of the "Massasaugua", through which the poison distils, are two in number, one on each side. **1959** WELLS *Trent-Severn* 14: There is . . . the Massasauga, a runty type of rattlesnake whose bite is ordinarily no more dangerous than a bee sting. **1963** *Kingston Whig-Standard* (Ont.) 3 July 23/1: It was the third case in the last ten days of attacks by Massasauga rattlers. **1964** *Outdoorsman* 18/1: The Pacific rattler is found in parts of British Columbia, the prairie rattler in sections of Alberta and Saskatchewan and the small Massasauga in Ontario. The Massasauga is found chiefly within 20 to 30 miles of the Georgian Bay, Lake Erie and Lake Huron shorelines and is fairly common on the Bruce Peninsula. Although the Massasauga has claimed two lives since 1956, with prompt and proper treatment, this need not be the case.

master *n. Fur Trade, Hist.* a senior officer in a fur company, such as a wintering partner or factor, *qq.v.*, as opposed to a servant, *q.v.* See also **master pedlar.**
1769 (1954) WALLACE *Pedlars* 8: Edward Lutit & the other men tell me they see one of the Pedlers wᵗʰ some French & Indians wᵗʰ him, he is one [of] the Masters & his Name is Jamˢ Finley. . . . **1775** (1951) *SaskJnls.* 16: It seems that Twenty three Canoes of Pedlers intent to Winter up the River Saskachiwan Under several Masters, 18 of Which are gone past. **1819** (1823) FRANKLIN *Journey* 22: He introduced me at once to Messrs. Charles, Swaine, and Snodie, masters of districts, who, from long residence in the country, were perfectly acquainted with the different modes of travelling, and the obstructions which might be anticipated. **1896** RUSSELL *Far North* 99: It was cold work for the "master," measuring dry goods and counting bullets in the storeroom without any fire. **1954** WALLACE *Pedlars* 12: Jacobs wrote on July 18, 1773, to the master at Churchill. . . .

master-ditch *n. West* See quote.
1925 GROVE *Settlers* 304: The road followed a straight line now . . . flanked by ditches which were drained by huge master-ditches running crosswise and carrying the water to the lake.

master dog *Arctic, Obs.* See **leader** (def. 2).
1854 (1892) KANE *Arctic Explor.* 232: Tudla, our master dog, was already hors de combat; he had been tossed twice.

Master Farmer *West* an honorary title bestowed annually upon outstanding farmers and their families.
1958 *Edmonton Jnl* 14 Oct. 17/5: Three Alberta farm families . . . have been named Master Farmers of 1958.

master lumberer *Maritimes, Obs.* See **lumberman** (def. 1a).
1832 MCGREGOR *Brit.Amer.* II 299: [They are] hired by a master lumberer, who pays them wages and finds them in provisions. . . . **1849** ALEXANDER *L'Acadie* II 84: After saluting the master lumberer, who was superintending his sturdy people at work among the logs, rafting them, with their piked poles, or gaffs, and handspikes, I asked him what quantity of timber . . . had gone down this spring. . . .

Master of Life in Indian parlance: **1** See **Gitchi Manitou.**

1769 (1931) BROOKE *Emily Montague* 34: They anciently believed in one God, the ruler and creator of the universe, whom they called The Great Spirit and the Master of Life. **1886** *Indian* (Hagersville, Ont.) 21 July 158/1: The Master of Life had, however, decreed to let them pass, for the thoughts and acts of neither of them had been bad.

2 the Christian God. See also **Great Spirit.**
1791 LONG *Voyages* 7: Their religion is Catholic, and they have a French priest, or, as the Chippeway Indians term it, "The Master of Life's Man," who instructs them, and performs divine service in the Iroquois tongue. **1844** (1955) LEFROY *Magnetic North* 90: Many of them refrain from hunting etc. on a Sunday, knowing nothing more than that it is a day sacred to the Master of Life. **1921** HEMING *Drama of Forests* 202: Every one in that whole brigade of wild men of the wilderness ... knelt down, and with bowed head, said his evening prayer to The Master of Life.

master pedlar *Fur Trade, Hist.* See **wintering partner** (def. 1). See also **master.** Cp. **pedlar.**
1954 WALLACE *Pedlars* 7: The first master pedlar to reach the Saskatchewan was Franceway, who seems to have gone there in 1767.... **1955** HARDY *Alta Anthol.* 40: But, before the Company could catch its breath, the "Master Pedlars" had arrived. These were fur-traders, chiefly Scottish-born, operating out of Montreal.

master strand See 1941 quote.
1940 *Beaver* Dec. 36/1: ... in the making of snowshoes the women did the lacing as a rule but the frames were bent and prepared by the men, whose task it was also to lace the "master strands" which bear the greatest strain. **1941** *Ibid.* Sep. 38/1: Master strand—The large transverse strands in a snowshoe that carry the weight of the body.

masting† *n. Lumbering, Hist.* the felling and trimming of trees for ships' masts.
1899 *N.B.Mag.* II 214: The masting business was a very important one in the early days of New Brunswick. **1907** BAIRD *Roger Davis* 144: "Were you not up the river? Did you not see the magnificent forests of pine and spruce? These make the best masts in the world. Masting on this river must become a great industry."

mast road *Lumbering, Obs.* a logging road, *q.v.,* along which mast pine were hauled to the river for rafting (def. 1).
1896 GOURLAY *Hist.Ottawa* 38: Mr. John Smith took us to see the old mast road, down which to the river were drawn the stately pines, hewn on Torbolton hills, to mast the fleets that rule the waves.... **1902** (1957) GUILLET *Valley of the Trent* 269: The last monster pine was yet lying prone in the mast-road at the foot of a ridge....

matayway *n.* See **midewewin.**
1859 KANE *Wanderings* 4: ... their medicine dances [are] called Matayway.

matchcoat† *n.* [< Algonk.; cf. Ojibwa *manchikōten* skirt] *Obs.* See 1907 quote.
☛ *First recorded in John Smith,* Works, *1607-9, as* matchcore, *apparently from Powhatan, an Algonkian language of E. Virginia, with reference to a short fur mantle, this word evolved by folk etymology into* matchcoat, *which is cited by the* Dictionary of Americanisms *from 1638. The term appears to have* been applied to various garments of several materials *from place to place, the early Canadian references being to a kind of woman's petticoat worn among the Ojibwas.*
1768-82 (1904) LONG *Voyages* 137: A hut was prepared, and the girl stripped to her *matchee-coaty* or under petticoat.... **1832** (1929) RICHARDSON in *Cdn Prose* 36: Each of these females in addition to the machecoti or petticoat, which in one solid square of broadcloth was tightly wrapped around the loins, also carried a blanket.... [**1907** HODGE *Bulletin* I 819/2: During the era of trade with the Indians almost throughout the Algonquian seaboard certain garments supplied in traffic were called by the English "matchcoats," a corruption of a name belonging to one of the cloaks or mantles of the natives. The Algonquian word from which it was derived is represented by the Chippewa matchigoté, Delaware wachgotey, "petticoat."]

Matchi Manitou [< Algonk. "bad spirit"] the evil spirit of the Algonkian Indians. Cp. **Gitchi Manitou.** Also spelled *Machi Manitou, Matchee Manitou, Muche Maneto,* etc.
1800 (1922) HARMON *Journal* 39: ... the Natives ... leave ... some other article of little value to appease the Devil, or Muchamunatoo.... *c***1804** (1890) GRANT *Sauteux Indians* 354: ... as to *Matchi Manitou,* he is as terrible and disgusting in his person as he is wicked in his dispositions, and will remain so to the end of time. *Ibid.* 355: The wicked Indians he delivers over to *Machi Manitou,* who receives them under the earth in a wretched dungeon swarming with serpents, and where the poor souls endure every degree of misery, while the good are immediately released from any future dread of pain, and enjoy every pleasure which the heart of man can desire. **1935** JENNESS *Parry Island* 29: Occasionally the Parry Islanders speak of a Madji Manido, Bad Spirit, referring either to some lesser being malignant to man (most commonly the great serpent or water spirit), or else to some vague evil power that is apparently independent of the Great Spirit. **1966** *North* July-Aug. 17/2: ... when I saw the lashing tail in full play I knew without a doubt that I had been talking to none other than the Mutchee Manitou himself.

match misconduct or **penalty** *Hockey* a penalty that banishes the offending player from the ice for the remainder of the game and carries with it an automatic fine and an investigation by league officials.
1962 *Kingston Whig-Standard* (Ont.) 28 Dec. 9/7: Assistant captain Peter Mantrop ... wound up with a match misconduct for commenting on the refereeing.... **1964** *Globe and Mail* (Toronto) 7 Dec. 24/1: [He] was suspended indefinitely for taking a match penalty in the third period....

mathemeg *n.* [< Algonk.; Cree *mathemek*] *Obs.* See **loche.** See also **methy.**
1784 PENNANT *Arctic Zoology* cxci: Allied to this is the Mathemeg of the natives, the Land Cod of the English, a fish abundant in the northerly lakes; it grows to the length of three feet, and the weight of twelve pounds: had three beards on the lower jaw; the middlemost the longest: the back is brownish; the belly grey. **1820** (1823) FRANKLIN *Journey* 93: One of the largest fish is the mathemegh, catfish, or barbue.

mathii, mathy, mathyi *n.* See **methy.**

matric [mə'trɪk] *n. Informal* matriculation, that is, high-school graduation.
1945 PUGSLEY *Saints* 224: He got his matric., sure, but so did the rest of us. **1955** BIRNEY *Long Table* 106: "I spend my time working for a living, while you sit home

and moon over Rosa Luxembourg, when you ought to be boning for that Matric supp you haven't written off." **1958** *Time* (Cdn ed.) 25 Aug. 9/2: . . . the teachers' federation . . . calls for merely one year of training beyond "matric."

maul in goal *Obs.* in early Canadian rugby-football, a score resulting from wresting the ball away from an opponent while behind his goal line, such a score counting four points.
1904 CONNOR *Prospector* 40: I am thinking it is what they will be calling a *maul in goal*, and it is a peety we cannot be seeing it. **1964** *Kingston Whig-Standard* (Ont.) 27 Oct. 9/3: The article [1895] also mentions, a "maul in goal" which counted four points.

mayapple† *n.* a North American herb, *Podophyllum peltatum;* also, its egg-shaped, yellow, edible fruit. See 1866 quote.
1795 (1911) SIMCOE *Diary* 290: The May apples are now a great luxury; I have some preserved and the hurtleberries are ripe. Baron La Hontan says the root of the May apple (or, as the French call them *citrons sauvages*) is poisonous. **1866** KING *Sportsman in Can.* 113: . . . broad-leaved May-apple . . . [has] a delicious and refreshing wild fruit, of a deep yellow colour, and about the size of a bantam's egg, somewhat similar in appearance to the loquat. When stripped of its outer skin it presents a mass of juicy pulp and seeds, not unlike pine-apple in flavour. The plant is of low growth, and has deeply indented broad leaves and a simple white blossom. **1952** PUTNAM *Cdn Regions* 26/2: A few of the commoner species are mayapple . . . lily of the valley. . . .

mayflower† *n.* the trailing arbutus or ground laurel, *Epigaea repens,* of eastern Canada and the U.S., the floral emblem of Nova Scotia.
1792 (1911) SIMCOE *Diary* 136: I send you May flower seeds. **1830** *Novascotian* (Halifax) 18 Nov. 366/3: Our contemporaries have spoken of . . . Mayflowers in full bloom. . . . **1964** WILSON *Barrett's Landing* 90: We celebrated by going into the woods . . . to pick arbutus, or mayflower, the flower of Nova Scotia.

mayflower picnic *Maritimes, Obs.* a social outing for the picking of mayflowers.
1872 DASHWOOD *Chiploquorgan* 190: In the early spring, may-flower picnics are got up, as the plant is by no means general, and only grown in certain localities.

maypole *n.* [trans. of Cdn F *mai,* q.v.] *Hist.*
1 See lobstick (def. 1). See also **mai.**
[**1801** MACKENZIE *Voy. from Montreal* 56: There was the singular appearance of a spruce fir, stripped of its branches to the top like an English may-pole.]
1811 (1849) ROSS *Adventures* 79: On Mr. M'Kay's return . . . he ordered one of his men to climb a lofty tree and dress it for a May-pole. **1859** (1869) KENNICOTT *Journal* 59: It is customary for the voyageurs to make what they call a "lob stick" or "may pole," in honor of any gentlemen who may be passengers with them; and on Cross Lake ours made one for Mr. Hubbard and myself.
2 See lobstick (def. 2).
1850 BIGSBY *Shoe and Canoe* II 261: It may be distinguished by a tall pine-tree trimmed into a Maypole. **1933** GATES *Five Traders* 102n: The *Mai* was probably a lobstick, or maypole, a favorite landmark of voyageurs. Such a pole was made by cutting away all but a few branches of a tree, usually one which stood on a headland or promontory.

M.B. or **MB** *Hist.* See **made beaver** (def. 1).

469

maul in goal
meadow

1896 RUSSELL *Far North* 235: . . . experience has taught the hunter that he will get 50 MB for the robe be it large or small, so he cuts it down in order to make room on the sled for a larger number. **1958** ELLIOTT *Quesnel* 153: The skin, as a unit of value, was presumed to weigh one pound and was called, technically, a "Made Beaver", or "M.B." Merchandise was priced in "M.B.'s" or fractions thereof.

MBeaver *Hist.* See **made beaver.**
1784 (1955) *Moose Ft Jnls* 161: Many of my Indians have been in since my last, some have done well others indifferent & some very bad indeed only paying 15 out of 65 MBeaver their Debts. **1794** (1954) WALLACE *Pedlars* 85: . . . all the Furrs I saw would not amount to 1000 MBeaver . . . but as the large Canoes are returned to Montreal some time since much must have gone down by them. . . .

McIntosh ['mækɪn,taʃ] *n.* [< John *McIntosh* (born 1777) of Matilda, Dundas County, U.C., on whose farm the original tree was discovered and cultured] See **McIntosh Red.** Also spelled *Macintosh* and *Mackintosh.*
1910 WOOLVERTON *Cdn Apple Grower's Guide* 190: McIntosh [is] a very fine dessert apple for early winter use. **1963** *Calgary Herald* 4 Oct. 48/4: Indications are the McIntosh harvest . . . will take up most available packing house space. . . . **1966** *Globe and Mail* (Toronto) 1 Apr. 10/2: . . . a private member's bill [was] introduced . . . to declare the McIntosh apple Canada's national fruit.

McIntosh Red (apple) a highly popular eating apple having a ruddy skin and juicy, white flesh. See also **McIntosh** and **Mac.**
1878 *Cdn Horticulturist* Mar. 42: Winter apples; here my list will be small, but I think reliable: Talman's Sweet, Pomme Grise, American Golden Russet, and McIntosh Red. **1923** WILLIAMS *Spinning Wheels* 226: Artistically stacked oats eke out asparagus very successfully as a background against which to heap . . . Ponderosa tomatoes, Mackintosh Red apples and braided strands of Golden Bantam corn. **1964** GUILLET *Pioneer Days* 43: John McIntosh, an early settler in Dundas County, transplanted a number of wild apple trees in 1796, and one of them lived to allow grafts to be distributed throughout the province, the McIntosh Red earning the reputation of being one of the best apples.

MD or **M.D.** See **municipal district.**
1958 *Edmonton Jnl* 14 Aug. 36/1: The regular meeting of the council of the MD of Peace was held Saturday in the Secretary's Office. **1961** *Ibid.* 17 July 28/2: As for the MD of Spirit River and the MD of Fairview . . . it would be possible to enlarge them. . . .

meadow¹ *n.* [trans. of F *pré, prairie* meadow] *Obs.* See **prairie** (def. 1).
1795 (1929) MCGILLIVRAY *Journal* 23: . . . we mounted our Horses and sett off across the meadows.

meadow² *n.* *B.C.* an expanse of grassland, usually more or less surrounded by trees, in the uplands and valleys of the mountains. See also **slough meadow.** Cp. **outpost meadow.**
1951 HOBSON *Grass* 31: A top bush cowboy, he built a new ranch every two years, then always found another meadow bigger than his present one, and moved again.

1962 FRY *Ranch on the Cariboo* 58: But within a year or two of the time when we visited them, they quit their piece of meadow and came out to civilization to stay. **1964** *Time* (Cdn ed.) 13 Nov. 18/1: Last week, with the last fall roundups underway, cowboys bush-popped cattle out of the forested summer ranges, moved them down to the hay-stacked meadows for winter feeding.

meadow hen† *N.B.* See **marsh bittern.**
1896 ROBERTS *Camp-Fire* 46: Ditches, dikes, and fences were of small concern to me, and I went craning it over the country like a huge meadow-hen. **1956** MCATEE *Folk-Names* 6: American Bittern [is also called] meadow hen (. . . in a country where a marsh is a meadow, N.B.). . . .

meadow lark† any of several North American songbirds, *Sturnella* sp.
1792 (1911) SIMCOE *Diary* 141: The Governor went to the Landing, and I went to the Fort to see Capt. Darling's stuffed birds . . . a meadow lark, the size of a blackbird, the colour the richest yellow, shaded to orange intermixed with black. . . . **1957** HUTCHISON *Canada* 224: The burble of meadowlarks did not break but only seemed to enforce the silence of this vacuum, and a cleansing wind carried all the perfumes of Eden.

meadow turnip *Obs.* See **prairie turnip.** Cp. **meadow¹.**
1806 (1897) COUES *New Light* I 369: He instantly made a place for us near himself, presented the pipe, some meadow turnips, and a few ears of very hard, dry corn. . . .

meal train a cat-train, *q.v.*, made up of sleds carrying the cooking, eating and sleeping quarters of a work-party in the wilderness.
1958 WATTERS *B.C.Cent.Anthol.* 42: First was the "Meal Train" with the kitchen, the diner, the utility and three sleepers. In the other group were the office, two sleepers, the workshop and the fuel sloop.

meat *n. Fur Trade* See **in the meat.**

meat bird† See **Canada jay.**
1903 MCLEOD *Markland* 563: This is the common "meat bird" of Nova Scotia. . . . **1944** CLAY *Fur Thieves* 100: They belong to the Jay family. I guess their right name would be Canada Jay, but they have others, too: moose bird, camp robber, meat bird, and, of course, whiskey jack. **1963** *Weekend Mag.* 16 Nov. 41/1: His [Canada jay's] names, all Canadian, are: whisky jack, whisky john, moose bird, meat bird, camp robber, meat hawk, and lumberjack.

meat hawk or **jay** See **Canada jay.**
1956 MCATEE *Folk-Names* 50: [The Canada jay is also called] meat hawk (. . . N.S., Ont.); meat jay (. . . N.S.). . . . **1963** [see quote at **meat bird**]

meatkind *n. Local* See quote.
1937 *Beaver* June 24/2: They [supplies of fish] had disappeared, leaving us pretty short of what is known in James Bay as "meatkind," which included fish.

meat post *Fur Trade, Hist.* a post established by a fur-trading company to accommodate hunters responsible for supplying meat to trading posts in the district. See also **meat station** and **provision post.** Cp. **fish post** and **pemmican post.**
1821 (1938) SIMPSON *Athabasca Jnl* 236: I intend

providing even the meat posts with one or more [fishermen] and a good supply of twine for nets. **1896** WHITNEY *On Snow-Shoes* 241: It is a fact that several of the Hudson's Bay Company forts originally established as meat posts and once the centre of caribou migration are now many days' journey to the side of it. **1962** SLOBODIN *Kutchin* 22: . . . Fort McPherson remained primarily a "meat post" until the last two decades of the century . . . useful primarily as a source of caribou and moose meat for other northern trading posts. . . .

meat ring a co-operative arrangement for buying and butchering livestock. Cp. **beef ring.**
1929 ENGLAND *Immigrant* 96: Meat rings could not be run owing to petty jealousies, lack of a good butcher, or because of diseased cattle.

meat station *Hist.* See **meat post.**
1909 CAMERON *New North* 129: Rae was the old meat-station for the Far North, and the records show that after supplying local needs three thousand tongues were often exported in one season.

meatsu(k) *n.* See **meetsu.**

medé *n.* See **midé.**

medicarchy *n. Obs.* a proposed association of doctors to provide medical service in Upper Canada.
1832 *Reformer* (Cobourg, U.C.) 16 Dec. 1/2: Be it therefore enacted . . . That this Medicarchy be composed of an Archdoctor, who shall be established in the Metropolis; of eleven doctors, of whom one shall be established in each District; and of a sufficient number of physicians and surgeons, of whom two, a physician and a surgeon, shall be located in each township.

Medicare ['mɛdə,kɛr] *n.* [< *medi*cal + *care*] the medical-care plan put into operation by the Saskatchewan Government in 1962. See also **medicare.**
1962 *New Democrat* Aug. 3/3: Doctors wishing to work under Medicare were denied operating facilities, even in grave cases. **1963** *Maclean's* 5 Jan. 48/2: Remember 1962? . . . Medicare joined the language for keeps. . . .

medicare ['mɛdɛ,kɛr] *n.* [< *Medicare,* q.v.] a program, usually government-operated, for providing medical care for all citizens of a country, province, etc.
1962 *Maclean's* 28 July 42/4: The party . . . had no campaign strategy except to . . . stress medicare and nuclear policy on the hustings. . . . **1964** *Sun* (Vancouver) 25 July 1/2: Alberta implemented its own free-enterprise version of medicare—Albertans call it Manning care—on Oct. 1, 1963.

medicine *n.* in Indian parlance: **1** something believed to have power over the forces of nature; magic or supernatural powers believed to have the means of healing or harming. See also **strong medicine.**
1763 (1901) HENRY (Elder) *Travels* 116: In his hand, he had his *shishiquoi,* or rattle, with which he beat time to his *medicine song.* **1792** (1934) TURNOR *Journal* 479: We informed them that we had a better Medicine and are not fearfull of them as they must get every thing from our Country. **1844** (1955) LEFROY *Magnetic North* 90: The Indians generally are losing most of their old superstitions without acquiring anything better. "Medicine" is hardly heard of. **1952** HOWARD *Strange Empire* 267: The tribal medicine men were helpless

because small pox was a white man's importation and they had no myth to account for it, therefore no "medicine." **1966** *Beaver* Winter 53/1: Even now you can't talk to a man about his medicine. If a man talks about his medicine, his medicine gets weak.

2 an object or practice believed to endow its owner with power to withstand illness or defeat; a fetish or talisman. See also **medicine bag.**
1847 PRICHARD *Researches* V 417: Like all the other Indians, they put more faith in their dreams, omens, and jugglers, in the power of imaginary deities of their own creation, and of their consecrated relics, to which the Canadians have given the singular appellation of *medicine*. **1880** DAWSON *Queen Charlotte Is.* 123: A ska-ga has his hair long and tangled, as, in obedience to custom, it is neither allowed to be cut or comb passed through it. This constitutes a part of his "medicine." **1957** *Beaver* Winter 30/1: . . . every [Indian] hunter carried a medicine bag with as wide an assortment of "medicines" as any fly-fisherman ever dreamed of.

3 make medicine, a. enter upon certain rituals intended to gain the help of the gods in warding off evil or sickness, in ensuring a good hunt or successful war, in bringing harm to enemies, etc.
1802 (1897) COUES *New Light* I 199: An Indian made medicine to ask his Manitou whether a certain sick person would recover. **1896** WHITNEY *On Snow-Shoes* 34: They thought we were making "medicine" against them, but were won over by Heming drawing the moose and caribou, while they watched the animals they knew so well develop under his pencil. **1923** WALDO *Down Mackenzie* 213: The medicine man makes medicines (i.e., symbols, or inimical thoughts) against a man, and promptly that unlucky individual falls ill.

b. *Figurative use.* See quotes.
1956 KEMP *Northern Trader* 86: When I dropped around to make medicine with him, the girl in the office told me he had left the Company. **1957** *Beaver* Summer 46/2: "If he [an angry bull] makes medicine, so will I!" retorted the postie.

4 throw medicine, *Obs.* cast a spell over, usually an evil spell, as against enemies in war; seek to bring harm (to).
1789 (1801) MACKENZIE *Voy. from Montreal* 118: This man had conceived an idea, that the people with whom he had been at war, had thrown medicine at him, which had caused his present complaint, and that he despaired of recovery. **1820** (1938) SIMPSON *Athabasca Jnl* 107: "They have lived on Babiche and Leather for several days, and imagine that our Opponents have 'thrown bad Medicine on them'."

5 See **beaver medicine.**
1861 *Cdn Naturalist* Feb. 7: The gin covered inside the jaws, with a well fitting "pallet" of birch bark, is placed indifferently either under or upon the snow, and on the pallet a piece of hair skin, well rubbed with the "medicine" is tied.

medicine bag a bag or pouch, often decorated with beadwork, used by the Indians to carry various objects believed to have magical powers in protecting the bearer from harm. See **medicine** (def. 2). See also **medicine box, medicine pouch,** and **powahgen** (def. 2). Cp. **medicine bundle.**
1797 (1964) CHABOILLEZ *Journal* 155: [I] made him consent to go for his Medecine Bag that was at the English [post] and not return any more to them. . . . *c***1804** (1890) GRANT *Sauteux Indians* 363: [They] pretend, by virtue of their medicine bags, to baffle all

the secret machinations of their most inveterate enemies, and even to kill them at pleasure without being detected. **1956** GOWLAND *Sikanaska Trail* 130: Each carried across one arm a medicine bag made of otter or some other fine skin and embellished with a wonder fully designed beaded piece of pure white leather, like a stole.

medicine blackrobe See **blackrobe.**
1935 SULLIVAN *Great Divide* 123: "Albert Lacombe, if perhaps you cannot make these poor Indians believe the word of the white-man's God, you can at least be a medicine blackrobe to assist hunger and disease."

medicine box *Obs.* See **medicine bag.**
1791 LONG *Voyages* 149: It is always observable that the Indians take out the bag which contains . . . the poison of this venomous reptile, and carry it alive in their medicine box when they go to war.

medicine bundle among the Plains Indians, a bundle of objects believed to have magical powers for protecting the bearer or band against harm. Cp. **medicine bag.**
1936 *Cdn Geog.Jnl* XII 98/2: Wherever they went they carried with them a medicine pipe and bundle upon the back of a milk-white steed. **1949** LEECHMAN *Indian Summer* 29: Weeks later, Mrs. Prairie Fire's medicine bundle lay with dozens of other specimens on the long study table in my laboratory. **1965** WORMINGTON & FORBIS *Archaeology Alta* 170: Frequently, pairs [of buffalo stones] were kept in medicine bundles, where it is thought that they would procreate.

medicine drum a drum used by medicine-men (def. 1a) in their incantations.
[1801 (1897) COUES *New Light* I 162: The fellow came accordingly with his drum and medicine bag. . . .] **1861** *Nautical Mag.* XXX 29: The sick woman was lying in a buffalo skin tent; the conjuror, painted and decorated, employed himself in beating a medicine drum within a few feet of her. **1896** RUSSELL *Far North* 36: His medicine drum was very similar in shape to an old fashioned dasher churn.

medicine feast See **conjuring feast.**

medicine line *West, Hist.* in Indian parlance, the Canada-U.S. border.
1910 HAYDON *Riders of Plains* 95: The Indians, as a matter of fact, called the International Boundary the "Medicine Line," assuming that in the absence of any agreement between the two Governments relative to this crime, they were perfectly safe on one side of the line with regard to what had been done on the other. **1959** SLUMAN *Blackfoot Crossing* 33: But Crowfoot says that the border—the medicine line—protects his people from the Long Knives.

medicine lodge 1 See **medicine tent** (def. 1).
1808 (1889) MACKENZIE *Mississouri Indians* 354: The women were directed to go into the woods for branches to cover the Medecine lodge, while the men were occupied in dressing themselves. **1959** SLUMAN *Blackfoot Crossing* 198: After he had left the medicine lodge, Sikimi forced himself to walk to Anow hawk's teepee.

2 See **midewewin.**

medicine-man *n.* **1 a.** an Indian magician or shaman who practises healing by means of charms and the exorcism of evil spirits or by practical remedies such as administering herbs and sweat baths. See also **conjurer** (def. 1), **juggler, medicine tyhee, midé,** and **tamanawous.**

1801 (1897) COUES *New Light* I 162: An Indian who pretended to be a medicine man was employed by Maymiutch to cure his sick brother. **1860** *Nor'Wester* (R.R.S.) 14 June 3/4: The "medicine-men" had all been posed by the disease: and the "powers of the air" had been invoked to no purpose. **1958** *Native Voice* Sp.ed. 41/1: Now there is a great difference between a Medicine Man and a Witch Doctor—the Medicine Man aims to heal, the Witch Doctor aims to kill, now we have this right.

b. anyone who prescribes or administers remedies for illness, etc.

1893 OXLEY *Young Nor'Wester* 215: None of those at his post knew anything about applying remedies, and Mr. M'Kenzie's reputation as a "medicine man" being founded upon many successful cures by the aid of a well-furnished medicine-chest, his rival . . . had sent over for him. . . . **1966** *Cdn Geog.Jnl* July 26/1: One receives the impression that his reputation as a medicine man had preceded him over the mountains, for . . . the sick were brought forth for his skill.

2 among Eskimos, an angakok, *q.v.*

1896 MACLEAN *Savage Folk* 99: The angakok or medicine man, is a man of influence. **1940** FINNIE *Lure of North* 145: He was one of the last practising Eskimo medicine-men, and I could not suppress a sneaking liking for him. **1945** LEECHMAN *Eskimo Summer* 137: Here the medicine man, the *angakok,* would stand when he was repeating incantations to bring good weather, to ensure a catch of seals, to speed the recovery of a sick woman.

3 an itinerant quack doctor, especially one who sells nostrums and panaceas to the accompaniment of a crowd-gathering show. Cp. **medicine show.**

1901 PARKER *Right of Way* 180: There was one person in the crowd surrounding the medicine-man's wagon who had none of that superstitious thrill. . . . **1965** BERTON *Remember Yesterday* 54/2: [Caption] Here comes the medicine man, plying his potions in Saskatchewan, unrestricted by any food and drug regulations. He can and probably does advertise sure cures for everything from cancer to chilblains—with a free show thrown in.

medicine piece *Obs.* See quote.

1804 (1890) CAMERON *Nipigon Country* 263: Every Indian has what they call his "medecine piece" of all the game he kills, such as the snout of the moose, the tongue and heart of the deer, the paws of the bear, and so on; this piece is always cooked by itself and no female, young or old, ever dare taste it, if she did, she would either die or turn as black as jet and lose all her nails.

medicine pipe† a pipe or calumet, *q.v.*, believed to have magical properties and used in certain Indian rituals and ceremonies.

1898 (1910) HAYDON *Riders of Plains* 239: The wife of an Indian, named "Heavy Shield," at one time on her death-bed, as she thought, vowed that she would purchase a certain Medicine Pipe in the event of her recovery, and so become a member of the society. **1946** *Beaver* Dec. 8/2: [Caption] The medicine pipe stem belonging to the head chief of all the Crees . . . is now in the Manitoba Museum.

medicine pole† among the Plains Indians, a pole set upright in the ground, decorated with feathers, and bearing numerous tribal fetishes as well as enemy scalps.

1957 FISHER *Pemmican* 134: An Indian never admits anything, even if you catch him with your scalp on his medicine pole and your teeth in his fire bag.

medicine pouch See **medicine bag.**

1931 GREY OWL *Last Frontier* 217: Great fighting chiefs of former days carried medicine pouches containing a few bits of feathers and small bones. . . .

medicine rattle See **shishiquoi** and picture.

[**1842** *Montreal Transcript* 27 Jan. 2/1: The medicine-bag, rattle, and juggling tricks of the priest were, however, the ordinary hopes of restoration.] **1934** GODSELL *Arctic Trader* 42: For days he (medicine man) had howled and shouted, waved his medicine-rattle and pounded his tom-tom close to the girl's body in hopes that the noise would drive the evil spirits out, but all to no avail.

medicine robe *Obs.* among Plains Indians, an animal hide, as that of a buffalo, on which were symbolically represented the wearer's war deeds.

1873 (1904) BUTLER *Wild North Land* 53: Its tail formed an ornament for his tent, its inner skin a book in which to sketch the brave deeds of his life, the "medicine robe" of his history.

medicine show† **1** *Hist.* a travelling show with attractions intended to lure a crowd of spectators, who were then asked to buy medicines, often said to have been ancient Indian remedies. Cp. **medicine-man** (def. 3).

1954 TYRE *Saddlebag Surgeon* 123: The appearance of a travelling medicine show one day in August brought a measure of colour and excitement to the dull routine of life in Dominion City. **1959** *Maclean's* 14 Mar. 16/2: The days of the medicine show are over. . . .

2 *Figurative use.*

1965 BERTON *Remember Yesterday* 62/2: The [western] boom was the result of what Ralph Allen has called "one of the largest, noisiest and most successful medicine shows of all time"—the Canadian government's European campaign to attract settlers.

medicine stone *Hist.* any of a large number of stones, usually glacial erratics, on which sacred designs had been carved, formerly held in reverence by certain Plains Indians. See also **ribstone** and **spirit stone.**

[**1805** (1904) LEWIS & CLARK *Journals* I 264: Several men of their nation was gone to Consult their Medison Stone about 3 days march to the South West to know what was to be the result of the ensuing year. They have great confidence in this stone, and say that it informs them of everything which is to happen, & visit it everry Spring & Sometimes in the Summer.] **1886** *Indian* (Hagersville, Ont.) 23 June 139/2: This was one of the famous "medicine" stones of the Blackfeet Indians.

medicine tent 1 a wigwam, teepee, etc. erected for use by a medicine-man (def. 1a).

1806 (1897) COUES *New Light* I 388: The affair went on very slowly, and it was not without many speeches, smoking-matches, and persuasive arguments, that the medicine-tent was prepared. **1939** *Beaver* Dec. 26/1: The inner, or "medicine" tent, was enclosed by a great outer tent one hundred feet in circumference covered with the leather lodge coverings borrowed from the assembled tribes.

2 See conjurer's lodge.
1859 (1870) SOUTHESK *Saskatchewan* 81: There are Indian conjurors who will allow themselves to be bound from head to foot with nets, cords, straps, or anything; then, entering their small "medicine tent," it is seen to heave violently for about five minutes . . . and the wizard steps forth perfectly free.

medicine tyhee *Pacific Coast* a chief, or head, medicine-man (def. 1a). See also **tyee** (def. 1).
1884 CHITTENDEN *Queen Charlotte Islands* 70: He told me he was a medicine Tyhee, and inviting me into his house, showed me the curious medicine dance-dresses, wands, rattles, charms, etc., worn and used by him when practicing his healing art.

medicine wheel a circle of stones found at old Indian encampments on the prairies and believed to be associated with the religious life of those who constructed them.
1963 *Herald Mag.* 26 Oct. 3/4: Under the direction of friends who found them or saw them previously, I had opportunity in recent weeks of inspecting three well-defined and well preserved circles of stones, best known as Indian tepee rings or medicine wheels.

medicine woman among Indians and Eskimos, a female angakok or medicine-man, *qq.v.*
1935 JENNESS *Parry Island* 36: The girl became a great medicine-woman and lived to a very old age. Often she restored the dying to life, and was summoned from great distances to heal the sick. **1953** *Cdn Geog.Jnl* Apr. 162: [Caption] Obeluk was one of the few remaining medicine women, who still communed with the spirits. . . .

meesasscootoomeena *n. Obs.* See **misaskatomina.**

meetchwop ['mitʃ,wɑp] *n.* [< Algonk.] *Lab.* a shelter, as a shack, hut, tent-frame, or wigwam. See also **tilt** (def. 1) and **wickiup.**
1933 MERRICK *True North* 145: We stuffed up the holes with our coats and caps and mitts and the little *meetchwop* began to get hot. **1936** STRINGER *Wife-Traders* 6: Along with the uncovered framework . . . made of well-bleached whale ribs, and a couple of meetchwops, they tended to give a graveyard melancholy to the straggling village-end.

meetsu(k) ['mit,su(k)] *n.* [< Algonk.; Cree; cf. Ojibwa *mĭchit* he eats it] a meal; mealtime. See also **mitshim.** Also spelled *meatsu(k), metsook.*
1896 RUSSELL *Far North* 5: After our "metsook" of bacon, bread and tea, Napasis spent the evening in making "cakes." *c*1900 (1963) *Beaver* Summer 28/1: He did not have much hair on his head and when it was *meet-su,* when the Bishop eat his fish, he shoo that mosquito away. . . . **1909** CAMERON *New North* 78: In the scow next us the two young Crees who are preparing the food for our evening "meat-su" carry on a religious controversy as they slice the sow-belly. **1934** GODSELL *Arctic Trader* 219: "Meetsuk! Meetsuk" —yelled Robillard as he swung a frying pan full of steaming beans towards us, and lifted the copper tea kettle off the roaring fire with a stick.

melt season *North* See **break-up period.**
1964 *Beaver* Spring 21/2: The return journey was made during the height of the melt season with men, dogs and equipment constantly soaked by the icy water of pools and streams on the surface of the shore-fast ice. . . .

men in sheepskin coats *Hist.* See **Sifton's Sheepskins.**
[**1922** (1965) HAMILTON *Cdn Quotations* 105/1: "When I speak of quality I have in mind, I think, something that is quite different from what is in the mind of the average writer or speaker upon the question of immigration. I think a stalwart peasant in a sheep-skin coat born on the soil, whose forefathers have been farmers for ten generations, with a stout wife and a half-dozen children, is good quality." Sir Clifford Sifton, speech to Toronto Board of Trade, March 1922.] **1965** BERTON *Remember Yesterday* 71: [Caption] Thousands will make a stake, and head east again. But the men in sheepskin coats will stick and build the west.

menominee† [mən'ɑmə,ni] *n.* [< Algonk.: Ojibwa. See 1907 quote] See **wild rice.**
[**1744** DOBBS *Hudson's Bay* 62: Above them [is] a small Lake called *Malominis;* upon the Sides of it grows a Kind of wild Oats, from which the Natives get plentiful Crops.] **1779** (1791) LONG *Voyages* 155: We were reduced to a few fish and some wild rice, or *menomen* (which are kept in *muccucks,* or bark boxes), to support myself and seventeen men. [**1905** DAWSON *St.Lawrence* 365: The last-named people are the Folles Avoines of the French narratives, and their river, still called the Menominee, reaches far into the rice-producing region. **1907** HODGE *Bulletin* I: Menominee (*meno,* by change from *mino,* "good," "beneficent"; *min,* a "grain," "seed") the Chippewa name for the wild rice.]

Menzies spruce [< Archibald *Menzies,* who discovered the species during the Vancouver expedition of 1792] See **Sitka spruce** (def. 1).
1894 *Trans.Roy.Soc.Can.* XI 4 14: It is in the lower Fraser valley that we first see the Pacific coast forest and are lost in wonder at the height of the Douglas fir, Menzies spruce and the western cedar. **1956** *Native Trees* 46: SITKA SPRUCE [is also called] Menzies spruce. . . .

merchantable *adj. Esp.Nfld* See 1883 quote.
1779 (1911) TOWNSEND *Cartwright's Journal* 496: [They] turned out two hundred and eighty-seven quintals of merchantable fish. **1837** *Montreal Transcript* 11 Nov. 3/1: Merchantable Dry Cod is selling in Halifax at 17s. 6d. **1883** HATTON & HARVEY *Newfoundland* 291: When thoroughly dried [cod] have a whitish appearance and are then ready for storing. In due time they reach the merchant's wharf or store, where they are weighed and "culled" or sorted into four different kinds called Merchantable (the best), Madiera, West India (intended for the consumption of the Negroes) and Dun, or broken fish, which will not keep, and is intended for home use. **1957** *Nfld Qtly* Sep. 5/1: Durned old fool got lippy about the cull. Trying to tell me his sunburned fish should have gone merchantable.

mercy flight an airplane flight to an isolated community to fetch a sick or injured person to hospital for treatment.
1944 *Beaver* Dec. 40/2: The aeroplane has ceased to be a novelty and is proving of the greatest value as a means of conveying medical assistance . . . Such "mercy flights" are increasing annually. . . . **1957** *Arctic Spotter* Nov. 9: Notification of the requirement for a mercy flight is passed to the RCC from many sources, in many instances coming directly from doctors in outlying districts.

merry dancers *North* See quote.

1946 *Beaver* Sep. 13/2: In some regions they [northern lights] are called . . . "the merry dancers."

merthy *n.* See **methy.**

meskatomina *n. Obs.* See **misaskatomina.**

mess beef or **pork**† *Hist.* salted beef or pork, prepared in barrels made up of assorted cuts.
1770 *Quebec Gaz.* 1 Nov. 2/1: Just imported, from Cork . . . a few Barrels and Half Barrels of Irish Pork and Mess-Beef, and a few Firkins of Hog's Lard.
1824 *Colonial Advocate* (York [Toronto]) 2 Dec. 4/5: Prime Mess Beef shall consist of pieces of fat cattle, with the ends of the hocks, and half of the neck taken off. 1961 PRICE & KENNEDY *Renfrew* 47: One Sunday special was "des grillades," mess pork cut into slices and fried.

meter maid *Informal* a policewoman who patrols city streets, her main task being to check meters for parking infractions.
1964 *Globe and Mail* (Toronto) 30 Dec. 5/3: No decision has been made yet whether to provide headgear for the meter maids, policewomen who cruise the city on motor scooters. 1965 *Kingston Whig-Standard* (Ont.) 26 Mar. 2/6: Advertisements will be placed next week for four meter maids for Kingston. 1966 *Ibid.* 21 Mar. 11: [Caption] This Ottawa meter maid had a hard decision to make, but make it she did and stuck to the letter of the law.

methy ['mεθi] *n.* [< Algonk.; prob. a shortening of *mathemeg*, q.v.] *Northwest* (*now mainly in place names*) See **loche.** Various spellings in older writings.
1743 (1949) ISHAM *Observations* 169: Mer'thy (as the Natives styles itt,) are a fish Resembles an Eal in taste, they are muddy fish and skin's—the Same as an Eal, but of a Different shape, these are plenty, they are fine Eating in a pye with pork &c. 1770 (1911) HEARNE *Journey* 73: [It was] a coarse kind of fish known in Hudson's Bay by the name of Methy. 1887 *Senate Jnl* XXI App. 121: Next in quantity would come . . . goldeye, mari or methy (dog fish or ling), yellow perch. . . .
1957 FISHER *Pemmican* 275: Just north of the small lakes was the Methy Portage, the most man-killing of all. . . . 1964 TURNER *Nat.Resources B.C.* 586: The Burbot . . . is known by a variety of names, but Burbot, Ling, Maria (the prevailing name in Manitoba), Loche (French-Canadian) and Methy (Cree Indian) appear to be the most commonly used.

Metif† *n.* [< Cdn F < OF *metif* (of) mixed breed] *Obs.* See **Métis.**
1817 HALKETT *Selkirk Settlement* 17: Recourse was had to the aid of a lawless banditti, technically termed, *Metifs, Bois Brulés* or *Half-breeds.* 1821 (1938) SIMPSON *Athabasca Jnl* 388: . . . the North West Coy . . . are allied [with] and have Meitiff progeny with all the other Tribes in North America. 1840 (1860) MURRAY *Brit. Amer.* II 215: On the 28th June he embarked with a motley group, composed of "an Englishman, a man from Stornoway, two Canadians, two metifs (or half-breeds), and three Iroquois Indians."

metiffe *n.* [< Cdn F < OF *métiffe,* fem. of *métif* mongrel; mixed breed] *Obs.* See quote.
1791 (1911) SIMCOE *Diary* 59: I eat part of a metiffe, a bird between a wild goose (the outarde) and a tame one.

Métis or **Metis** [me'tis, me'ti, *or* 'mitɪs] *n.* [< Cdn F < F "mongrel; half-breed"] *Esp. West and Northwest* a person of mixed Indian and European, especially French, parentage; half-breed. See also **Canadian half-breed, French halfbreed, half-breed** (def. 1), and **Metif.** Cp. **Brulé** (def. 1).
☛ *This well-established term reflects much divided usage in Canada, both with regard to spelling and pronunciation.*
1816 (1939) ROBERTSON *Correspondence* 248: Your European Servants and Metiss are in many places deserting over to the North West Company.
1841 NICOLLET *Report* 49: The Metis call themselves "free people," (*gens libres;*) but by their neighbours they are designated as *"Metis of the Red river," "the Red-river people," "the People of the North."*
1886 *Indian* (Hagersville, Ont.) 26 May 111/2: In all his experience on the plains, Johnny had never been called on to eat dog flesh, and in despair he turned to McGillies, the French Metis, (many of the French half-breeds have Scotch names,) who was eating away most unconcernedly, and asked him what was to be done, for he would not eat any more of the mess.
1913 COWIE *Adventurers* 501: Metis (pronounced Mee-tees; has same form in singular and plural). It is applied to all half-breeds of Indian blood, but more especially to those whose ancestry is French, for those of British descent are always designated by the French as Metis "Anglaise". . . . 1934 GODSELL *Arctic Trader* 188: Old Angus Brabant had employed methods all his own in handling these Indian and Metis freighters.
1966 *Kingston Whig-Standard* (Ont.) 29 July 6/3: Mr. Anderson . . . flew north to a settlement of about 1500 Cree Indians and 300 Metis.

Métisse or **Metisse** [me'tis] *n.* a female Métis, *q.v.*
1935 MOWERY *Resurrection River* 83: "You don't load her into no plane weelly-neelly, lak if she was some . . . *métise.*" 1952 HOWARD *Strange Empire* 60: Riel's mother was a Metisse, half French, half Montagnais. *Ibid.* 346: She may have been a very pretty girl, as so many of the Metisse were. 1963 STANLEY *Louis Riel* 268: Thomas Scott [was] a Scottish farmer married to a French *métisse.* . . .

Metro ['mεtro] *n.* [< *Metropolitan*] **1** Metropolitan Toronto, an administrative federation of the city proper and suburban municipalities to provide certain common services, such as police protection.
1957 *Maclean's* 17 Aug. 3/3: The payoff came one day this summer when Metro chairman Fred Gardiner said a Bloor Street subway was a mistake; Metro would study others, among them Mary Young's.
1963 *Kingston Whig-Standard* (Ont.) 24 Jan. 26/8: Billed as "Tory night in Metro," the event was described by a party spokesman as a "means to get the ball rolling". . . . 1966 *Toronto Dly Star* 30 Apr. 63/1: Mr. Wilson said that separate schools are able to serve from 40 to 90 per cent of the Roman Catholic population in any given area of Metro.

2 any similar form of city government elsewhere.
1962 *Time* (Cdn ed.) 26 Jan. 10/2: Canada's second experiment with metropolitan government scarcely seemed controversial when Winnipeg put the scheme into effect a year ago. The Metro did not follow Toronto Metro's example of taking over the police or fire departments or the school systems. 1966 *Globe and Mail* (Toronto) 25 June 3/4: [He] faced an indirect challenge during the election campaign from a so-called ginger group of eight Liberal in metro Winnipeg ridings.

metropolitanization *n.* the state or condition of being formed into a metropolitan administrative area, as in Metropolitan Toronto. Cp. **Metro.**

1955 *Vancouver Province* 6 Jan. 6/2: This newspaper doubts if Vancouver and its neighboring municipalities can afford to ignore the trend toward metropolitanization making itself felt all over the continent.

metropolitan town *Obs.* the town designated as the seat of the district courts and other offices of municipal government in each of the districts of Canada West.

1853 (1959) MOODIE *Life in Clearings* 30: Belleville had just been incorporated as the metropolitan town of the Victoria District, and my husband presided as Sheriff in the first court ever held in the place.

metsook *n.* See **meetsu.**

Meuron *n. Hist.* See **de Meuron.**

1817 (1939) ROBERTSON *Correspondence* 12: He was in a canoe which upset and drowned . . . two Meurons and six Indians. **1821** (1900) GARRY *Diary* 141: I found her at the Colony happily married to Sergeant-Major Veitch of the Meurons, a most excellent Man, and the Mother of two Children. **1935** MORICE *Red River Insurrection* 224: Despite his German name, due to his descent from one of Lord Selkirk's Meuron soldiers, Georges Klyne passed for a Métis or French half-breed, as do many. . . . **1963** MACLEOD & MORTON *Cuthbert Grant* [trans.] 57: Meurons, without delay, / Please play us something gay, / A lively tune to start our happy ball [from an old Métis folk-song].

M.H.A. *Nfld* Member of the House of Assembly (def. 1b).

1961-62 *Nfld Qtly* Winter 24/3: [Caption] Claude Sheppard M.H.A., (Harbour Grace). Born July 21, 1916 at Spaniard Bay, Nfld.

Michilimackinac currency *Hist.* a system of exchange in use during the latter part of the eighteenth century in the fur-trading regions of the upper Great Lakes. Cp. **Grand Portage currency.**

1765 (1901) HENRY (Elder) *Travels* 184: It is in beaver that accounts are kept at Michilimackinac; but in defect of this article, other furs and skins are accepted in payments, being first reduced unto their value in beaver, Beaver was at this time at the price of two shillings and sixpence per pound, Michilimackinac currency; otter skins, at six shillings each; marten, at one shilling and sixpence, and others in proportion.

michiniwais *n.* See **mishiniway.**

mickey ['mɪki] *n.* [origin uncertain] *Slang* See 1950 quote.

☛ *This term is often assumed to derive from* **Mickey Mouse,** *the reference being to a bottle of small size. However, Disney's character did not appear till 1928, and the term is shown below to have been in use before then.*

1927 NIVEN *Wild Honey* 200: "We takes a chase round a block and gets a mickey of de demon, which put us on our way rejoicing. . . ." **1950** SUTTON *Footloose* 5: An American pint holds 16 ounces, a Canadian "mickey," 12 ounces of rye, or 13 ounces of Scotch. **1962** *Sun* (Vancouver) 17 Dec 4/1: But even then very few of the electorate went reeling to the polls with $3—the price of their votes—in one hip pocket and a mickey of rye in the other. **1966** *Kingston Whig-Standard* (Ont.) 21 July 6/2: Bradley said the four . . . had gone through two mickeys of whiskey.

Micmac (canoe) ['mɪkmæk] *n. Maritimes* a small, two-man canoe (def. 1) of the design used by the Micmac Indians of the Maritimes. Cp. **Malecite.**

1872 DASHWOOD *Chiploquorgan* 16: Having here hired three Micmac canoes and six Indians, we chartered a schooner to drop us at the moat of the Cascapediac. . . . *Ibid* 239: On my arrival at Halifax I set about the purchase of two canoes, but was only able to procure one small Micmac of a suitable size for "portaging."

midawin *n.* See **midewewin.**

1925 *Beaver* Mar. 81: In the ceremony of the midawin of the Ojibwas, the chief medicine man makes a smoke offering.

Mid-Canada line a system of radar stations stretching across Canada and designed to give early warning of hostile attack through the air.

1957 *Maclean's* 7 Dec 2/4: . . . the Mid-Canada Line of early warning stations is now almost finished. . . . **1965** SYMINGTON *Tuktu* 60: The construction of the Distant Early Warning (DEW) Line and the Mid-Canada Line in the mid-1950's, with their great freight movements throughout the North, gave impetus to the activity of the governments . . . federal and provincial.

middle ice *Arctic* an extensive field of sea ice in the middle of Baffin Bay.

1938 *Beaver* June 43/2: Soon they became entangled with the eastern edge of the middle ice, which has a mean breadth of one hundred and fifty miles, and confines itself to the centre of Baffin's Bay.

middleman *n. Fur Trade, Hist.* in a freight canoe, York boat, or bateau, one of the crewmen who worked the paddles or oars from a middle position in the craft, a rank inferior to that of the bowsman or steersman, *qq.v.* See also **midman** and **milieu.**

1761 (1901) HENRY (Elder) *Travels* 14: They engage . . . the middle-men at one hundred and fifty livres and the end-men at three hundred livres, each. **1806** (1960) FRASER *Letters and Journals* 184: St. Pierre, that was here as *boute de canot* above, was reduced to a middleman. . . . **1957** FISHER *Pemmican* 250: The crew of each boat comprised the middleman and the *boutes,* the latter being the bowsman and steersman, who sometimes helped with the paddles.

middle school *Hist.* in Ontario, third and fourth form in high school, equivalent to Grades 11 and 12. Cp. **Upper School.**

1939 GROVE *Two Generations* 2: . . . he had finished middle school with first-class honours, taking his junior matriculation.

middle wing *Obsolescent* in Canadian rugby-football, a position between the inside and the outside wing on each side of the line, now usually called a tackle; also the player functioning in one of the two middle-wing positions.

1958 *Kingston Whig-Standard* (Ont.) 24 Oct 11/2: A plunging middle wing, now known as a tackle, was handed the ball by a halfback or acted as a decoy with an end run in motion **1962** *Ibid.* 10 Oct. 23/1: . . . his father . . . was a tackle or middle wing when he made his ORFU [Ontario Rugby-Football Union] junior debut with Toronto YMCA in 1918.

midé or **medé** [mə'de] *n.* [< Algonk.; cf. Cree *mitēō* conjurer, *q.v.*] See **medicine man** (def. 1a).

the largest, weighing over 20 pounds Many of these are "mild-cured," but a large portion are sold fresh.

Cp. **midewewin**. Also spelled *mittay*.
1804 (1933) CONNOR *Diary* 261: Indians performed the superstitious Mittay ceremony, which continued the whole day. **1860** (1956) KOHL *Kitchi-Gami* 245: At length . . . he summoned the other Jossakids, and Midés, and the Ogimas (chieftains) of the tribe together. . . . **1914** RADIN *Myths of the Ojibwa* 24: He was a very good hunter, and he killed all kinds of game. He was a midé. **1935** JENNESS *Parry Island* 69: . . . the Grand Medicine Society . . . is extinct in Georgian Bay and . . . children will never join it and become genuine *medé*.

midewewin ['mɪdəwəwɪn] *n*. [< Algonk.: Ojibwa; cf. Cree *mitēwewin*] See quotes. See also **grand medicine, matayway,** and **midawin.** Cp. **midé.** Also spelled *midewiwin, mitawiwin*.
1860 (1956) KOHL *Kitchi-Gami* 41: Midewiwin is the Indian term for what the Canadians call "la grande medicine," that is, the great fraternity among the Indians for religious purposes. [**1910** HODGE *Bulletin* II 495/2: According to Hoffman, the Grand Medicine society, or Midewiwin, of the Chippewa and neighboring tribes, was a secret society of four degrees, or lodges, into which one could be successively inducted by the expenditure of a greater and greater amount of property on the accompanying feasts. As a result of these initiations the spiritual insight and power, especially the power to cure disease, was successively increased, while on the purely material side the novitiate received instructions regarding the medicinal virtues of many plants.] **1932** JENNESS *Indians of Canada* 160: The Ojibwa usually celebrated their *Midewiwin* or "medicine lodge" in the summer at the ripening of fruits and berries, and friends and relatives gathered from all the surrounding districts to witness the initiation of candidates into the society of medicine-men. **1935** JENNESS *Parry Island* v: He and his cousin . . . were the only surviving Indians on the island who had been initiated into the Midewiwin or Grand Medicine Society. **1956** LEECHMAN *Native Tribes* 51: Among the Ojibwa and, to a lesser extent, among their neighbors the Cree, membership in the *midewewin*, or Grand Medicine Society, was eagerly sought. **1964** *Sask.Hist.* Winter 17: Before he adopted Christianity . . . he had been well up in the ranks of those who belonged to the secret society of medicine men, called Mitāwiwin.

midman *n. Hist.* See **middleman.**
1800 (1897) COUES *New Light* I 29: . . . the other midman remained in the canoe **1921** HEMING *Drama of Forests* 320: We midmen sat upon dunnage sacks and braced our moccasined feet against the ribbing.

midnight sun *North* See 1960 quote. Cp. **Land of the Midnight-Sun.**
1909 SERVICE *Cheechako* 51: . . . And I smoke my pipe and I meditate in the light of the Midnight Sun,/And sometimes I wonder if they was, the awful things I done. **1960** *North* July-Oct 17/1: In the Arctic, the "Midnight Sun" is . . . the nocturnal sun in summer.

mild *n. Lab.* a spell of mild weather.
1933 MERRICK *True North* 219: Generally in January or February each winter there comes a two or three day "mild" when the snow thaws.

mild-cured *adj.* of fish, slightly cured.
1952 PUTNAM *Cdn Regions* 447/2: The spring salmon is

mile-belt *n. Obs.* on the Prairies, the first tier of sections on each side of the Canadian Pacific Railway line within the railway belt, *q.v.*, so called because each section was a mile deep and those closest to the line were first opened to settlement.
1883 *Prince Albert Times* (Sask.) 28 Dec. 2/2: The mile belt—that is the even numbered sections along and on both sides of the Canadian Pacific Railway. **1883** *Moose Jaw News* (Sask.) 2 Nov. 2/1: It is mysteriously hinted that the rights of squatters on the mile-belt will be finally conceded, if they but hold fast to their lands and improvements.

mile house *B.C., Hist.* See quotes.
1950 HUTCHISON *Fraser* 85: At every stopping place a hotel sprang up, the rude but well-fed mile houses of the Cariboo road. . . . *Ibid.* 250: Starting first from Lillooet, as the jumping-off place of the Harrison route, and then from Ashcroft when Douglas's road was built, every stopping place along the way was called a "mile house." It had no name but its number. Even now you speak of stopping at the Seventy, or the Hundred, or the Hundred and Fifty. **1966** CROSS *B.C. Source Book* 159: . . . several farms and ranches were established, mainly at way points along the Cariboo wagon-road, such as the well-known 70 Mile, 100 Mile, and 150 Mile Houses. These "mile houses" were spaced about a horse-team's change apart along the Cariboo Road and were numbered as distances from Lillooet.

Milicite *n.* See **Malecite.**

milieu *n*. **-x.** [< Cdn F] *Hist.* See **middleman.**
1804 (1897) COUES *New Light* I 247: Men not so difficult to hire this year as last, when boaters for Lower Red River refused 700 G.P. Cy. and milieux 500, with extra equipments. **1930** *Cdn Hist.Rev.* XI 130: Beads were given to the devants but not to the milieux. **1966** *B.C.Digest* Dec. 44/3: The men in the middle of the canoes were referred to as a group as the milieux. . . .

military grant *Hist.* a parcel of land granted to discharged soldiers in compensation for military service.
1852 MOODIE *Roughing It* 341: On the way, I explained to him the object of my visit, which was to mark out, or "blaze," the sidelines of a lot of land I had received as part of a military grant, immediately adjoining the beaver-meadow.

military reserve *Hist.* a tract of land reserved by the Crown for the use of military establishments.
1797 *U.C.Gaz.* (York [Toronto]) 5 Apr. 3/1: Military reserve. The digging of Holes or Pits for loam on the common, is forbidden. **1839** (1955) LEFROY *Magnetic North* xvi: The college ground possesses the advantage of being dry and healthy, where the Military Reserve will probably remain for some time longer little better than a swamp. **1932** RUSSELL *Correspondence* I iv: He bought a house at Niagara, situated on the military reserve, enlarged it, and obtained a lease of the land on which it stood.

military township *Hist.* in colonial times, a township made up of concessions which were granted to disbanded soldiers.
1829 MACTAGGART *Three Years* I 275: . . . when the . . . Duke of Richmond . . . came up the Ottawa River to establish his military townships, he was perfectly surprised to meet with such a neat furnished cabin in the heart of the wilderness.

militia *n.* an organized army of citizen-soldiers distinct from the regular army and trained on a part-time basis as a reserve force for service in time of national need.

1816 (1818) HALL *Travels* 209: . . . her son had served in the militia, in token of which he was most obstreperously loyal, both in speech and song, during the whole evening. **1890** *Grip* (Toronto) 15 Feb. 100/2: The Militia Department were preparing, he said, for an insurrection of the Equal Righters, Orangemen, Jesuits and Opposition Members of the House combined. **1964** *Time* (Cdn ed.) 28 Feb. 9/3: Regular army men tend to question the militia's professionalism, and with some reason.

milk *n. Obs.* See **English milk**.

1775 (1901) HENRY (Elder) *Travels* 242: What they most long for, is a taste of his rum, which they uniformly denominate *milk*. **1802** (1897) COUES *New Light* I 203: . . . the Indians were anxiously awaiting me, to taste the "new milk," as they generally call rum when speaking in a ceremonious style.

milk emptyings† *Obs.* fermented or sour milk used as a leaven.

1852 MOODIE *Roughing It* 127: Those stingy wretches had just baked a fine batch of bread, and they would neither lend nor sell a loaf; but they told me how to make their milk-emptyings.

milk house a farm outbuilding where milk is kept, usually under some degree of coldness.

1796 *Quebec Gaz.* 11 Feb. 3/1: To be disposed of, six years lease of . . . a good House pleasantly situated, comprising eight Rooms, Garrets, and Kitchen, with a Milk House Barns and Stables, adjoining. **1826** (1955) CRAIG *Early Travellers* 74: Milk will now hardly keep sweet some days from morning to night, through having a bad "milk house" (dairy) situated above ground and without shade. **1959** STEWART & FRENCH *Ask No Quarter* 21: And then, too, they had no proper place to ripen the cream. The earthen rooms called milk houses came later.

milk-ice *n.* patches of thin, whitish ice that form in depressions in fields.

1952 BUCKLER *Mountain and Valley* 3: Islands of milk-ice speckled the brown fields where the withered aftergrass held the snow longest. . . .

milking the bushes *North, Slang* See quote. See also **hedging**.

1940 MARSHALL *Arctic Village* 85: The most primitive method is to pull the boat upstream by grasping bushes along the shore. This is known as "milking the bushes."

milkshed† *n.* a milk-producing region, the produce from which comes to a specific market.

1950 HUTCHISON *Fraser* 179: . . . every inch of fertile alluvial soil is under cultivation . . . and thickly inhabited by dairy cattle . . . The estuary . . . supports the milkshed of Vancouver. **1958** *Co-operative Consumer* 10 Jan. 3/2: The Winnipeg District Milk Producers Co-operative Association does not figure in the report since it is essentially a service type organization and does the bargaining for approximately a thousand in the Winnipeg milk shed.

mill† *n.* the smallest unit of reckoning in the Canadian monetary system, calculated as one-tenth of a cent but not now represented by any coin.

1853 *Brit.Colonist* (Victoria) 2 Sep. 1/1: And be it enacted, that the denominations of money in the Currency of this Province, shall be pounds, dollars, shillings, pence, cents, and mills: the pound, shilling

and penny shall have, respectively, the same proportionate values as they now have, the dollar shall be one-fourth of a pound, the cent shall be one-hundredth, and the mill one-tenth of a cent. **1958** *Edmonton Jnl* 29 Sep. 37/5: Tax rate here is 57 mills.

mill-grant land *Hist.* See **mill site**.

1958 *Sun* (Vancouver) 21 Apr. 8/3: By 1873 . . . [they] were squatting on mill-grant lands along False Creek.

milling frolic *Cape Breton* (*N.S.*) See quotes. See also **frolic**.

1948 MACNEIL *Highland Heart* 57: When large bolts were available the family would have a "milling frolic" to "mill," or soften, the heavy, warm but coarse cloth and give it a nap. The leader would start a long lilting song and as she did the "milling" would begin, the girls along the sides joining lustily in the chorus, and all beating and thumping the cloth against the bench in time to the tune. **1954** BARBEAU *Cdn Folk Songs* 3/2: In Cape Breton. the people call these community work sessions "milling frolics" and they take place in the autumn or winter, when there is time for singing, working and dancing together.

mill lot *Hist.* See **mill site**.

1763 (1876) CAMPBELL *Yarmouth, N.S.* 42: . . . the Land [is] Granted to John Charles for a mill lot. **1804** *Quebec Gaz.* 2 Aug. Supp. 4/1: They will sell . . . The Mill and Mill Lot . . . equal to manufacture 50 to 60,000 minots of wheat annually. . . .

millpond hockey ice hockey played by youngsters on a frozen mill pond or river. Cp. **shinny** (def. 1a).

1964 *Star Wkly* 19 Dec. 13/1: As Canadian as cold fronts and millpond hockey, these pint-sized snowmobiles . . . are turning previously deserted lake and cottage country into new winter playgrounds.

mill seat† *Obs.* See **mill site**.

1796 (1932) RUSSELL *Correspondence* I 10: Read the Petition of John Laurence Esquire, praying for a Mill Seat on the River Humber. **1816** (1818) HALL *Travels* 133: The number of abandoned mill-seats, particularly in parts of the country recently settled, as well as the difficulty of working many of those still in use, shew the same process of draining to be still continuing. **1829** MACTAGGART *Three Years* I 198: These engines he obtains by procuring for himself . . . a *mill-seat*, or what the Yankees call a *hydraulic privilege*, which he enjoys by setting himself down by the side of a rapid of some river or other, as there he may erect as many mills as he pleases. **1833** (1963) TOLMIE *Physician* 195: The fort is to be erected along the bank of a streamlet, which in its devious course through plain presents points well adapted for Mill-seats. . . .

mill site *Hist.* a piece of land on which a flour mill was or could be built; specifically, a lot granted to a person who undertook to build and operate a flour mill there. See also **mill-grant land, mill lot,** and **mill seat**. Cp. **water privilege** (def. 1).

1825 *Colonial Advocate* (York [Toronto]) 29 Dec. 3/3: There is also unoccupied Mill-Scites on the Credit . . . sufficient to drive a number of Mills and Machines. **1833** (1926) LANGTON *Early U.C.* 19: . . . I bought about 300 acres . . . including the creek, which McDonell, the agent at Peterborough, who knows the country well, tells me has a fall of 20 feet, a good mill site. **1956** EVANS

Mountain Dog 107: Earth and stones had been bulldozed to the water's edge to form a millsite.

mine *v.* See quote. Cp. **land-miner.**
1955 *Christmas Tree Farming*: In other words, the Christmas tree lands were "mined" rather than "farmed" with little or no thought or care given to future crops or a permanent production basis.

mine captain a superintendent of underground work in a mine.
1918 COPELAND *Swinging Lanterns* 101: Vein sampling engineers, grubstakers, rock-worms, mine captains, prospectors and agents in coats of "astrachan goose" . . . strut about and add to their kit, each man jack of them probably thinking he has a "nose for ore" and inside information. **1964** CRATE *Hardrock Mining* 3: By tradition, an underground superintendent is known as a *Mine Captain:* his principal assistants in supervision being the *shift-bosses* or *shifters.* This last term has come to mean not only the supervisor during a shift of working hours, but the foreman of workers in a given area of the mine.

mine muck waste from a mine, often used for roadbeds or as fill.
1961 *News of the North* 27 July 5/3: Tenders are invited by Yellowknife School District No. 1 for the following: 1. Supplying approximately 90 yards of rock fill (*mine muck*) and 40 yards of sand at a site immediately behind the school.

mineral indications See **indications.**

miners' law *Obs.* See **miners' meeting law.**

miners' meeting *Hist.* a meeting of the miners at a camp to pass laws governing behavior, to try offenders, to settle disputes, etc.
1858 (1921) *Cdn Hist.Rev.* II 356: A "Miners' Meeting" was held, which proceeded to legislate against the sale of liquor without a license and the sale of fire-arms to the Indians. **1860** *British Colonist* (Victoria) 16 Oct. 2/4: A miners' meeting had been called to determine a dispute between men named Myers and Merrit, with regard to the right of the former to run a tail race through the latters' claim. **1907** *U of T Stud.Hist.& Econ.* II 201: Before the organization of government in the Yukon, the miners themselves, at miners' meetings, framed and adopted certain primitive regulations, which were strictly adhered to. **1948** MOIR *Sinners and Saints* 29: Meanwhile, on August 22, a miners meeting was held on the hillside opposite a claim, No. 17.

miners' meeting law *Hist.* the law in effect in early goldmining communities, established and enforced by miners' meetings, *q.v.* Also *miners' law.*
1899 PALMER *Klondyke* 72: "Miners' meeting law" is unscientific and rarely commendable, but here it served its purpose well because its methods made it so seldom required. **1900** OSBORN *Greater Canada* 112: In the old times . . . Miners' Law prevailed; that is to say, in cases of stealing or murder . . . a meeting of miners was called, before whom the plaintiff and defendant and the witnesses were examined by the old-timers.

mining camp a mining area and the settlement it includes.
1859 *Brit.Colonist* (Victoria) 1 Jan. 2/2: On my return down I called at Foster's Bar, a very considerable

mining camp, situated 8 miles below Rose's.
1955 *Western Star* (Corner Brook, Nfld) 12 Mar. I 2/1: A jam packed, breath holding, 3000 or more fans watched the men from the mining camp and the paper town rocket up and down the ice with thrilling pattern plays. . . .

mining location *Hist.* See **location** (def. 5).
1883 *Brandon Dly Mail* (Man.) 15 Feb. 2/2: Two mining locations were surveyed on the lake Wednesday. **1900** OSBORN *Greater Canada* 202: A special feature of this sequence of Treaties was the adjustment of claims preferred by the Indians to receive the amount paid to the government for the sale of mining locations.

mining lot *Obs.* See **location** (def. 5).
1865 *Cdn Naturalist* II 199: Mining-lots were laid off by the Government, fifty by twenty feet, for which high rentals were asked.

mining recorder† a government official whose duty is the recording of claims.
1899 *Greenwood Miner* (B.C.) 18 Aug. 9/2: We want a local Mining Recorder with the powers of a Gold Commissioner. **1957** *Northern Affairs Bull.* Jan. 14: There were no great finds or staking flurries during the year, but there was a steady run of business for the Mining Recorders.

minor *n. Hockey* a two-minute penalty awarded for any of a wide variety of infractions of the playing rules relating to checking, sticking, etc.
1958 *Herald-Tribune* (Grande Prairie, Alta) 11 Mar. 5/3: Jim Hudson of the Mustangs and Fluky Kjemhus both got minors for kneeing and tripping. **1963** *Maclean's* 23 Mar. 32/3: Keon—perhaps accidentally—bonked Young on the head with his stick and was given a minor.

minot *n.* [< F] *Hist.* in Lower Canada, a unit of dry measure equal to 1.07 Imperial bushels. See also **Canada bushel.**
1764 *Quebec Gaz.* 8 Nov. 3/1: The yearly Rents and chief Rents they pay in Cash amount to 694 Minots and a Half of Corn. . . . **1833** *Cdn Correspondent* (York [Toronto]) 16 Mar. 4/4: Lower Canada Wheat of very superior quality is selling at 5s [and] 5s 3d per minot weighing about 65 lbs. **1905** *Ont.Bur.Arch.Rep.* III xlviii: The rentes corresponded to the ordinary tenants' rent, and consisted generally of one-half minot of corn . . . for each superficial arpent. . . .

misaskatomina *n.* [< Algonk.: cf. Cree *misākwatomin* berries of the *misākwat,* tree of many branches] Various spellings. *Obs.* **1** See **saskatoon** (def. 1).
1801 (1922) HARMON *Journal* 53: Different kinds of berries are now ripe [including] what the Canadians call paires, which the Natives denominate Mis-sas-qui-to-min-uck. **1820** (1823) FRANKLIN *Journey* 88: Under the name of meesasscootoomeena it is a favourite dish at most Indian feasts, and mixed with pemmican it renders that greasy food actually palatable.

2 See **saskatoon** (def. 2).
1858 (1960) HIND *Assiniboine Exped.* I 345: His arrows [were] from the mesaskatomina. **1870** *Cdn Illust. News* 29 Jan. 198/3: . . . the Misaskatomina is no longer a bush, but a tree from 18 to 20 feet high, and loaded with most luscious fruit. **1883** *Trans.Hist.& Sci.Soc.Man.* III 51: The Misasquitomunuck (service berry) berries receive, as it is proper their meed of praise.

mischechogonis *n.* See **mishagunis.**

misconduct (penalty) *n. Hockey* a penalty awarded for misbehavior such as verbal abuse of the referee and involving banishment of the player from the ice for ten minutes, substitution being allowed.

1963 O'BRIEN *Hockey* 55: Now a second major penalty in the same game automatically adds a Misconduct Penalty (ten minutes added to five) plus a $25 fine. **1964** *Globe and Mail* (Toronto) 7 Dec. 24/1: ... each was given game misconduct penalties and 10 minute misconduct penalties for their fight in the penalty box. ...

misery fiddle a cross-cut saw. Cp. **Swedish fiddle.**

1961 *Sun* (Vancouver) 18 July 32/4: Cross-cut saws, once called misery fiddles, and horses, are what today's old loggers recall when they talk of the good old days which they'd never return to. ...

mishagunis [məˈʃɑgənɪs] *n.* [< Algonk.; cf. Cree *māstuchakunis*] See **coyote** (def. 1).

1857 (1963) PALLISER *Journals* 63: I saw great numbers of the case wolf (mischechogonis or togonie) prowling about. This is the wolf proper to the partially wooded country, and is about twice the size of a fox, with a tail shaped like the brush of that animal. **1963** SYMONS *Many Trails* 121: In daylight a silently flitting shadow on the grass, at night a mournful voice, Mishagunis is the very spirit of the plains.

mishiniway *n.* [< Algonk.] *Obs.* among Prairie Indians, an underchief whose duty it was to prepare and pass around the medicine pipe at ceremonial occasions. Also spelled *mishiniwais, machinaway.*

c1799 (1889) MACDONELL *Journal* 286: The Machinaway du Chien Fou and associate came in. ...
1801 MACKENZIE *Voy.from Montreal* ci: The Michiniwais, or Assistant, takes up the pipe, lights it, and presents it to the officiating person, who receives it standing and holds it between both his hands.
1806 (1897) COUES *New Light* I 388: At nine o'clock the ceremony began by three of Le Borgne's principal mishinaways or secretaries, taking their seats in the center of the tent which faced the open space.

One representation
of Miss Canada

Miss Canada *Hist.* See 1966 quote.

1912 *Jack Canuck* 28 Dec. 1: [Caption] MISS CANADA— "That can't make this waterway more undrinkable than it has been for many a long year." **1914** (1918) MACKAY *Trench & Trail* 97:

They would settle in a trice.
But Miss Canada is frigid
And Columbia [U.S.A.] is cold,
So in presence of the couple
There's an iciness untold.

1967 LEFOLII *Canadian Look* 10/3: In the High Victorian period some cartoonists found Johnny [Canuck] too crude a figure to convey Canada's moral superiority in her quarrels with the U.S., the U.K., or the Metis of the Red River. They introduced a new symbol, Miss Canada, to stand for Canadian virtue.

missionary station *Obs.* See **mission station.**

mission boat, scow, or **ship** a vessel plying the coastal inlets and islands or the inland rivers carrying spiritual and medical services to isolated communities.

1897 TYRRELL *Sub-Arctics* 26: Mission scows, loaded with freight for Fort Chippewyan and other points, were expected, and free-traders' outfits were liable to arrive at any time. **1905** GRENFELL *Harvest* 143: So this was the mission-ship! We had heard some talk of one coming, but had thought it only one of the idle rumours of the coast. **1958** KELSEY *B.C.Rides a Star* 14: Church and medical profession also join, by way of mission boats, to bring spiritual and physical aid to the coast. **1959** *Native Voice* May 4/5: "Since 1933 there has been no ordained minister at Klemtu," he explains. "We had to depend on services from the mission boat Crosby IV and it had many places to serve."

mission Indian *Hist.* an Indian brought up near a mission and under the guidance of missionaries.

1889 WITHROW *Our Own Country* 253: In the month of June, he collected, at Montreal, a force of four hundred men, including mission Indians. ... **1905** (1954) *B.C.Hist.Qtly* XVIII 214: An Indian named Lolo, but as a "mission" Indian who preached about St. Paul, commonly called "Paul" ... appeared soon, to sympathize with us. ...

mission (or missionary) station 1† the headquarters of a church mission among the Indians or Eskimos.

1844 (1955) LEFROY *Magnetic North* 148: The existing missionary stations are as follows. ... **1873** (1966) *Sask. Hist.* Spring 75: ... Prince Albert ... is occupied as a Mission Station by the Presbyterians. **1897** TYRRELL *Sub-Arctics* 30: On the morning following our arrival at the Grand Rapid, being the 4th of June, a number of mission scows, loaded with goods for Chippewyan and other mission stations, arrived.

2 *Hist.* a meeting-place where itinerant preachers held periodic religious services in the backwoods or bush, as for the men of the early lumber camps.

1947 SAUNDERS *Algonquin* 40: Before that time there were only mission "stations" in the district. ...

Missouri cattle *Slang, Obs.* See **plain buffalo.**

1890 *Trans.Roy.Soc.Can.* VIII 2 95: The southern or "Missouri cattle," as they were called by the plain hunters, varied in some degree from those of the Saskatchewan. They were long-backed and heavy, the full grown cow often dressing to five hundred pounds and over of clean meat.

Missouri tobacco *Obs.* a kind of tobacco, *Nicotiana attenuata,* grown by the Plains Indians.

1806 (1897) HENRY (Younger) *Journals* 327: The young men ... pass the day ... eating corn and smoking Missourie tobacco.

mitashes or **mitasses** *n.pl.* [< Cdn F < Algonk.; see 1791 and 1947 quotes] *Obs.* See **leggings.**

[**1732** (1947) *Cdn Hist.Rev.* Dec. 407: [Trans.] And these people ... do not realize that these Frenchmen to whom they trade their peltries give them goods, such as bonnets, capots, *mistashes,* etc., which are worth less than half those obtainable at this post.]
1763 (1901) HENRY (Elder) *Travels* 112: My legs were covered with *mitasses,* a kind of hose, made ... of

scarlet cloth. [**1791** LONG *Voyages* 225: *English* Leggons, or stockings *Chippeway* Mitasse] **1832** COX *Adventures* 240: The dress of the [Flathead] men consists solely of long leggings, called *mitasses* by the Canadians, which reach from the ancles to the hips, and are fastened by string to a leathern belt round the waist **1862** (1931) CHEADLE *Journal* 74: The Old Boy & the hunter come in just before dinner, bringing the mitlas [sic] we had left with them to be made. **1947** *Cdn Hist.Rev.* Dec. 407: Mitlashes: long leggings or gaiters often reaching to the thigh. Modern Montagnais word for "stockings."

mitawiwin *n*. See **midewewin**.

mitshim ['mɪtʃɪm] *n*. [< Algonk.] See **meetsu**.
1941 *Beaver* Sep. 38/1: Mitshim—This word, meaning food, is at some places used in an English sense.

mittain (beaver) *n*. [< Cdn F] *Fur Trade, Obs. or Hist.* the lowest grade of beaver pelt. See 1735 quote.
*c***1735** (1899) WILLSON *Great Company* 238: "The beaver . . . was classified into eight varieties . . . Lastly on the list figured the Mittain beaver, which were utilized in the manufacture of mittens, being worth one shilling and ninepence [a pound]." **1744** DOBBS *Hudson's Bay* 26: The eighth is the Mittain beaver, cut out for that Purpose to make Mittains, to preserve them from the Cold, and are greased by being used, and are worth 1 s. 9 d. per Pound. **1912** ROE *Whispering Hills* 157: . . . "Such furs! Beaver in countless packs, all the fat winter skins,—no Bordeaux, no Mittain."

mittaine *n*. [< Cdn F] *North, Obs.* heavy fur gloves.
1872 (1883) BUTLER *Great Lone Land* 201: I was well found in blankets, deer-skins, and moccasins; all the appliances of half-breed apparel had been brought into play to fit me out, and I found myself possessed of ample stores of leggings, buffalo 'mittaines' and capôts, wherewith to face the biting breeze of the prairie and to stand at night the icy bivouac. *Ibid.* 213: . . . the large moose-skin "mittaines" [were] taken into wear. . . . **1880** BUTLER *Far Out* 10: . . . its rapid movement has done more to make the blood course freely through their bodies than capote or mittaine or fur-cap could ever achieve on such a [cold] morning.

mittay *n*. See **midé**.

mitten moccasin *North* See quotes.
1921 HEMING *Drama of Forests* 107: Among other work that was well under way was the making of the moccasins, known as the "mitten moccasin"—by far the best for snowshoeing, as the seam runs round only the outer side of the foot and leaves no puckering above the toes to cause blistering. *Ibid.* True, the mitten moccasin is not of the Ojibway style, but Mrs Oo-koo-hoo had learned to make it when she and her husband formerly sojourned among the Wood-Crees on the upper Athabasca.

mixed-blood† *n*. See **half-breed** (def. 1).
1863 (1888) MCDOUGALL *G.M.McDougall* 148: A large number of Crees and mixed bloods have signed an address to the new Governor, asking for a peaceable settlement. **1960** *Press* Dec. 13: The traders and their "servants" liked the land and the free life and, mingling with the Indians and with Metis bands, within a generation formed a new and dominant element, the mixed bloods, descended from French and Scottish

fathers and Indian mothers, speaking a dialect of French intermixed with Cree, living as canoemen and runners for the fur-trade, as buffalo hunters and makers of pemmican, with cabins . . . along the river fronts.

mixed liquor *Fur Trade, Obs.* See **Indian liquor**.
1800 (1897) COUES *New Light* I 71: "I made them a present of three kegs of mixed liquor and sent them to enjoy themselves at their cabins."

M.L.A. or **MLA** Member of the Legislative Assembly. See **legislative assembly**. See also **M.P.P.**
1897 *Medicine Hat News* (Alta) 8 Apr. 4/2: Another of our M.L.A.'s is to join his confreres in the new Western Eldorado, the marvellously rich Kootenay. **1918** JENKINS *Cdn Civics* App. ii: In the provinces of Quebec and Nova Scotia, where there are two houses in the legislature, members of the legislative council and those of the legislative assembly are sometimes given the distinguishing titles M.L.C. and M.L.A., respectively. Occasionally but improperly, the form M.L.A. is used with the names of members of the legislature in the other provinces, where there is but one legislative chamber. **1966** *Globe and Mail* (Toronto) 15 Jan. 8/9 . . . a Calgary Liberal MLA suggested putting it [a new Government House] in Calgary. . . .

M.L.C. *Hist.* Member of the Legislative Council.
1849 *Niagara Chron.* (C.W.) 25 Oct. 3/2: J. Leslie, M.L.C. **1870** *Mainland Guardian* (New Westminster, B.C.) 5 Feb. 2/1: Of course an immaculate creature like our remarkable representative, could not be to blame; or if such could be for a moment supposed, it would never do to sacrifice such a rara avis as the M.L.C. for New Westminster, at least he thinks so. **1958** *Evening Telegram* (St. John's) 22 Apr. 4/6: The other was Michael Power, later the Honourable Michael Power, M.L.C.

mobile column in civil defence, one of a number of groups specially trained for the work of rescuing and evacuating people from stricken areas during attack, as by nuclear weapons.
1961 *Time* (Cdn ed.) 15 Sep. 20/1: The mobile columns will be staffed by the trained civilians and 50,000 more men drawn from the regular army and militia.

Moccasins (def. 1)

moccasin ['mɑkəsən] *n*. [< Algonk.; cf. Ojibwa *makisin*] **1**† a flat-soled shoe of soft leather, originally worn by the Indians. See also **Indian moccasin, Indian shoe,** and **Indian slipper**.
☞ *Spelling variants in earlier writings are very numerous indeed: mackassin, mockison, mogison, mowkisin, etc.*
1765-75 (1933) POND *Narrative* 53: After smoking they toock of my shoes and Put on me a pair of fine Mockasans or Leather shoes of thare One [own] make Raught in a Cureas Manner. . . . **1791** (1911) SIMCOE *Diary* 69: We saw two Indians from the village of Lorette, who had mocassins to sell. . . . **1825** *Novascotian* (Halifax) 1 June 182/2: Her dress was completed by a handsome pair of Mogasins, adorned with porcupine

quills. **1827** (1927) DICKIE *How Canada Grew Up* 72: Mogozeens, which are only worn by Canadians, are cheap. **1965** *Maclean's* 19 June 40/1: There are no shops with . . . moccasins and totem poles and birchbark canoes. . . .

2 See dog moccasin.
1867 LORD *Wilderness* 235: I always put on the dog's mocassins (merely bags made of leather or stout hide) if I anticipate rough travelling. **1903** LONDON *Call of Wild* 77: Also, the dog-driver rubbed Buck's feet for half an hour each night after supper, and sacrificed the tops of his own moccasins to make four moccasins for Buck. **1956** KEMP *Northern Trader* 161: On rough ice in the spring, all dogs wear moccasins, but Bill had to wear them a lot of the time.

3 *Obs.* **See kamik.**
1852 SUTHERLAND *Baffin's Bay* II 90: Next to india-rubber, seal-skin moccassins or boots suit very well; but only so long as the oil remains in the substance of the skin, after which they become as porous as ordinary leather.

moccasin aristocracy *West, Slang* See 1962 quote.
1889 DONKIN *Trooper and Redskin* 93: Many of the "moccasin aristocracy"—as we dubbed the French half-breeds, in barrack parlance—lived in huts for the winter. . . . **1962** *Alta Hist.Rev.* Autumn 13/2: "Ari-stock-rats," sometimes "moccasin aristocracy," is a term used to designate the half-breeds (or Metis) which they prefer being called.

moccasin dance a dance where the couples wear moccasins, popular at winter carnivals and other forms of outdoor winter entertainment.
1958 *News of the North* 31 Mar. 2 1/1: Moccasin dance and 100 pounds of fireworks will follow! **1964** *Western Miner* April 27/1: Some of the . . . occasions requiring music in Dawson were . . . Bobby Burns Day concerts . . . Hard Time dances, Moccasin dances (held in the curling rink). . . .

moccasined ['mɑkəsənd] *adj.* [< *moccasin*, q.v.] shod in moccasins.
1893 YOUNG *Indian Wigwams* 60: Then his moccasined feet and brilliant-colored scarf-belt, beaded cap, fire-bag and leggins, and distinct Indian face seemed to so ally him to the native tribes that too many never for a moment thought he could have any grievances to be redressed. **1954** PATTERSON *Dangerous River* 277: Breakfast was eaten at dawn and the party sat around on the edges of the vertical-sided pit, toasting its moccasined feet above the glowing embers down below.

moccasin flower† one of several varieties of lady's slipper, as *Cypripedium acaule* or *C. parviflorum*. See also **Indian moccasin** (def. 2), **Indian shoe** (def. 2), **Indian slipper** (def. 2), and **moccasin slipper** (def. 2).
1832 (1838) TRAILL *Backwoods* 91: I am told the spring and summer produce . . . the orange lilly . . . the moccasin flower or ladies' slipper. . . . **1923** WILLIAMS *Spinning Wheels* 309: Like the fragile pink Moccasin Flower or Lady's Slipper, surprised in cloistered ravines near, it will not survive transportation. **1930** JONES *Wild Flowers* Plate 191: LADY'S SLIPPER, STEMLESS. Moccasin Flower. *Cypripedium acaule. Per.* June-July. Moist Places. Slightly fragrant. The most common Lady's Slipper.

moccasin game† See 1921 quote. See note at **platter.**

1871 *Wkly Manitoban* 29 July 2/3: A near approach to these groups will show the gambler playing the moccasin game, or some other, with the stakes—generally clothing—lying close at hand. **1921** HAWORTH *Trailmakers* 146: Here a small but excited circle, gathered under the shade of a cart, are deeply engaged in gambling by what is known as the "moccasin game." In an empty moccasin are placed sundry buttons and bullets, which, being shaken up, involve the guessing of the number in the shoe. **1965** *Cdn Geog.Jnl* Sep. 80/1: Here . . . one can still see . . . a modern variation of the ancient moccasin game.

moccasin rubbers *North* heel-less rubber overshoes worn over moccasins or duffle socks (def. 1).
1940 *Beaver* Dec. 49/2: Rubber boots of all descriptions, together with moccasin rubbers, worn over duffles, have . . . ousted boots of their own make. . . . **1966** PATTERSON *Trail* 116: . . . and so we parted, I to buy some moccasin rubbers at Thorman's Taku Trading Post. . . .

moccasin slipper 1 a soft leather slipper for wearing indoors, similar in design to a moccasin.
1954 EVANS *Mist* 190: Caleb shuffled his moccasin slippers and made consoling sounds.

2 See moccasin flower.
1956 TAYLOR *Pine Roots* 172: Moccasin Slippers we call them. . . . **1963** *Canadian Wkly* 4-10 May 18/1: A native orchid is the popular choice as provincial flower of Prince Edward Island—the moccasin or pink lady's slipper.

moccasin sock See **duffle sock** (def. 1).
1943 MILLER *Lone Woodsman* 7: He now wore an outdoor shirt and loden-cloth trousers, with the moccasin socks underneath them. . . .

moccasin telegram *Esp.North* See **moccasin telegraph.**
1908 LAUT *Conquest N.W.* II 35: Word of the white woman ran before the advancing traders by "moccasin telegram," and wherever pause was made, Indians flocked in thousands to see Marie Gaboury. **1934** GODSELL *Arctic Trader* 81: "Moccasin Telegram again," muttered Constable Cashman disgustedly. "It sure beats me how news travels in this North country."

moccasin telegraph *Esp.North* the spreading of news by word of mouth, originally by Indian runner. See also **coast telegraph** and **moccasin wireless.**
1909 CAMERON *New North* 349: And now, apprised by moccasin telegraph, we are all on the *qui vive* to catch sight of a floating bride. **1933** *Beaver* Dec. 32/1: . . . word drifted by moccasin telegraph . . . that there were many signs of moose. . . . **1957** *Bay News* July 3/2: Post personnel keep in touch with the "outside" by means of radio communication which has taken the place of "moccasin telegraph." **1965** *Sun* (Vancouver) 17 Apr. 29/1: . . . as the Moccasin Telegraph spread the news through the bush, it became known that the Russian armoured divisions were already moving.

moccasin trail *Hist.* any of the trails followed by explorers and fur traders in the Northwest (def. 1a).
1957 HUTCHISON *Canada* 107: In less than two hundred years the French Canadians . . . have burst the bounds

mokock or mokok *n.* See mocock.

moktok *n.* See muktuk.

molasses *n. Obsolescent* See maple syrup.
1834 (1926) LANGTON *Early U.C.* 103: "I might indeed collect a keg of the molasses of the maple sugar, and having flavoured it with wild herbs, I might make honey such as my father loveth, but I am afraid my father would detect the cheat." **1863** WALSHE *Cedar Creek* 235: The dark amber-coloured molasses had stood and settled for some days in deep wooden troughs, before his other avocations . . . allowed him to come up to the Cedars and give the finishing touch. **1926** MAIR *Masterworks* XIV liii: The scented forest . . . the new basswood troughs, and cedar spiles, the great fires and steaming kettles, the hot-brown sap, the "black-man" and molasses—they haunt an old man's memory still. . . .

mole *n. West* See quote.
1964 *Calgary Herald* 25 May 23/1: While the pests colloquially are called "moles" they are really pocket gophers and our "gophers" are ground squirrels.

molly-hogan deal *Lumbering, Slang* See quotes.
[**1966** *Cdn Forest Industries* Oct. 50/2: Suddenly, logging sports seem to have become the "in" thing, attracting hordes of ardent admirers among west coast "civilians," most of whom firmly believe Molly Hogan is the young colleen responsible for causing Clancy to get careless with the boom.] **1966** *Sun* (Vancouver) 30 May 30A/3: . . . the Logging industry had evolved a jargon of its own that was as fascinating as it was baffling to the uninitiated. . . . A molly-hogan deal was a deal with a catch, something amiss.

molton *n.* [< F *molleton*] *Fur Trade, Obs.* a coarse broadcloth or blanketing carried as trade goods, often made up into capotes. Also spelled *mol(l)eton.*
1761 (1901) HENRY (Elder) *Travels* 154: Being no longer in the society of Indians, I laid aside the dress, putting on that of a Canadian: a molton or blanket coat, over my shirt; and a handkerchief about my head, hats being very little worn in this country. **1784-1812** (1916) THOMPSON *Narrative* 80: The dress of the Men is simply of one or two loose coats of coarse broad cloth, or molton, a piece of the same sewed to form a rude kind of stockings to half way up the thigh, a blanket by way of a cloak. **1820** (1939) ROBERTSON *Correspondence* 270: The *white* Molton capotes were of so superior a quality last year that a considerable augmentation of that article will be required for the outfit of 1820.

moneas, monias *n.* See mooneas.

money-scrip *n. Hist.* a certificate issued following the Northwest Rebellions, *q.v.*, to Métis as compensation for lost lands and entitling the bearer to the sum of $240.00, either in cash or as an allowance against the purchase of government lands. See also scrip (def. 2). Cp. land-scrip (def. 2).
1885 (1956) *Sask.Hist.* IX 3: Almost all the people are taking money scrips. **1923** WALDO *Down Mackenzie* 153: If you have taken land-scrip or money-scrip— that is, if you have accepted 240 acres or $240 from the Government—your status as a "breed" is legally fixed. **1956** *Sask.Hist.* IX 3: In the Fort Qu'Appelle area, their inclination first expressed, under the influence of the clergy, to refuse "money scrips" and instead to claim land concessions, was not long in being dissipated.

mongrel whitefish See tullibee.
1912 *Trans.Roy.Soc.Can.* VI ii 77n: Tullibee; a species of whitefish (*Goregonus tullibee*) of the Great lakes and

---

of Quebec, resumed the old westward march on the moccasin trails of their fathers, and colored the whole life of Canada. **1958** *Beaver* Summer 12/2: The old "moccasin trails" of Mackenzie's day were in much better condition than the horse trails that have superceded them.

moccasin wireless *Esp.North* See moccasin telegraph.
1938 *Beaver* June 23/2: The squaws . . . would peer at the white men from behind bushes, and the tales would travel far, the moccasin wireless working overtime.

mockasin, mockesin, etc. *n.* See moccasin.

mock goose *Obs.* a decoy fashioned to attract wild geese.
1784 (1916) THOMPSON *Narrative* 35: Each hunter has about ten mock geese which are sticks made and painted to resemble the head and neck of a gray goose, to which is added a piece of canvas for a body.

mocock ['mɑkɑk *or* mə'kɑk] *n.* [< Algonk.: Ojibwa *makak*] a box or container made of birchbark, often used to hold maple sugar, wild rice, berries, etc. Cp. casseau and rogan. Also spelled *makak, makuk, mokock, mokok,* etc.
[**1748** DRAGE *Voyage* I 215: They now have by Trade from the Factories Brass Kettles by which they boil, otherwise they make use of Nockins, which are of Birch-Bark, take a square Piece, slash it at the four Corners some Way in, then there are four Sides which they can set up, and they sew together with a Rim, round the Top they put an Edge of Porcupine Quills, these they make of various Sizes.] **1779** (1791) LONG *Voyages* 155: We were reduced to a few fish and some wild rice, or *menomen* (which are kept in *muccucks,* or bark boxes), to support myself and seventeen men. **1804** (1933) CONNOR *Diary* 273: Margoe sent a Mocock Sugar 70 lb Net. **1859** KANE *Wanderings* 8: They make their mohcocks, or kettles, of birch-bark, in which they cook fish and game. **1923** SMITH *Pioneers* 264: The journey was made in mackinaws,—open boats with a schooner rig, and the sugar was carried in mococks,— containers made of birch bark, each holding from twenty to thirty pounds. **1951** O'MEARA *Grand Portage* 141: There was a small makuk of sugar also. . . .

mocotaugan *n.* [< Algonk.: Cree] *Obs.* See crooked knife and picture.
1716 (1957) *Beaver* Winter 15/2: . . . Baggonetts, Mocotawgons, Sword Blades. . . . **1795** (1911) HEARNE *Journey* 169: This last was rivetted onto a piece of ivory, so as to form a man's knife, known in Hudson's Bay by the name of *Mokeatoggan,* and is the only instrument used by them in shaping all their woodwork. **1940** *Beaver* Dec. 38: The curved canoe knives, the same articles as are included in a list of 1748 trade goods as *mocotaugans.* **1957** *Ibid.* Winter 15/1: "Mocotawgons" are the curved knives, still used by the Indians.

mogasin, mogason, moggasin, etc. *n.* See moccasin.

mohcock *n.* See mocock.

mojak *n.* See moyaque.

mokeatoggan *n.* See mocotaugan.

mokeson, mokesson, etc. *n.* See moccasin.

the waters of the Canadian Northwest; the mongrel whitefish.

Moniyas ['moni‚æs] *n.* [see **mooneas**] See quote. See also **mooneas** (def. 2).
1926 MAIR *Masterworks* XIV 271: "Moniyas." This is the Cree word for Canadian; but it means, as well, any newcomer, or "green horn." Moniyas stands for Canada, and, as in the Cree alphabet the letters "l" and "r" are wanting, it is probably the Indians effort to pronounce the word Montreal as the French voyageurs did. . . . The word is in common use on the Saskatchewan, even among whites who have mingled much with the natives of the country.

monkey-French *n. Slang, Derog.* non-standard regional speech of French Canada. See also **bush French** and **joual.** Cp. **coyote French.**
1916 PARKER *World for Sale* 94: ". . . and I said likewise in my best *patois.* They liked that. I've got a pretty good stock of monkey-French, and I let it go."

Montagnais shoe a style of snowshoe associated with the Montagnais Indians of Northern Quebec and Labrador.
1916 *Trans.Roy.Soc.Can.* X 1 314: It is somewhat peculiar in shape and is possibly a transition between the Ojibwa and Montagnais snowshoe. **1941** *Beaver* Mar. 27: The Montagnais shoe is the commonest form used throughout the Labrador Peninsula and is usually known simply as the Eastern snowshoe. **1964** *Western Wkly Supp.* 3/1: Montagnais and Naskapi [shoes are] all made wide for travel in deep snow through underbrush.

Montée *n.* [< Cdn F *montée* mounting place < F *monter* mount] *Obs. (except in place names)* See **leavings.** Also *La Montée, La Montie, Monte, Mounte.*
1794 (1929) MCGILLIVRAY *Journal* 22: Arrived the *Mounte* where the road goes to the S.B. Fort. . . .
1854 *Kamloops Jnl* (B.C.) 30 Nov.: In the evening the Men returned with the Square wood from the Monte.
1949 MACGREGOR *Blankets and Beads* 124: On September 5th they reached La Montee. This place was so named because it was here that the traders took to horses, or mounted and rode either to the houses along the South Branch or westward up the River towards Alberta.

A Montreal canoe

Montreal canoe *Fur Trade, Hist.* a large freight canoe, measuring about 40 feet and capable of carrying 4 to 5 tons, used for the voyage from Montreal to the Grand Portage. See also **canoe** (def. 1), **canot du maître, Grand River canoe, Hudson's Bay canoe, Large Canoe, maître canot,** and **Ottawa River canoe.** Cp. **canot de charge.**
1793 (1933) MACDONELL *Diary* 94: Part of the Company's Furs are sent Round the Lakes in Shipping, but the major part goes down the ottawa in montreal canoes.
1794 (1954) WALLACE *Pedlars* 86: There are three of the large Montreal canoes lying here which are about 36 Ft long, 2½ deep, and 6 wide in Midships, carry 70 Bales,

Bags, and Kegs each, and are navigated by 8 Men.
1961 PRICE & KENNEDY *Renfrew* 30: Matt Bernard . . . supervises the launching of a large Hudson's Bay type canoe (canot du maître or Montreal canoe) which he completed Sept. 28, 1957.

Montreal canoeman *Fur Trade, Hist.* See **porkeater** (def. 1a).
1918 DAVIDSON *North West Co.* 230: The north men . . . pointed with derision to the use of pork by the Montreal canoemen.

Montreal Company *Fur Trade, Hist.* See **North West Company.**
1947 *Beaver* Dec. 34/2: . . . the demise of the Montreal Company in 1821 was to accelerate that development. . . .

Montreal Department *Fur Trade, Hist.* an administrative division of the Hudson's Bay Company. See 1929 quote.
1929 (1931) MERK *Fur Trade* xii: The Montreal Department comprised whatever business was done in the Canadas, and included the Kings Posts, and at a later date part of Labrador. **1956** INNIS *Fur Trade* 333: In 1842, 3,000 prime otter and 150 fisher were sold to the Russian American Company. Otter skins were brought from the Montreal department and from Albany and disposed of in this market.

Montreal livre *Hist.* See 1950 quote. See also **livre** (def. 1).
1950 RICH in OGDEN *Journals* xvi n.: (Sterling) was worth 26⅔ Montreal livres or 13⅓ North West livres. Halifax Currency equalled 24 Montreal livres or 12 North West livres. **1955** RICH in BLACK *Journal* 218: A contract dated Norway House, June 28, 1822, shows that he engaged to serve in the Athabaska District as a middleman for two years for 800 Montreal Livres per annum, and that as equipment he received a 3-point blanket, a 2½-point blanket, 2 shirts, 2 yards of common cloth and 6 lbs. of tobacco.

Montreal man *Fur Trade, Hist.* See **Northwester** (def. 1a).
1957 FISHER *Pemmican* 2: The Montreal men could act, at once, decisively, and with terrifying energy. . . .

Montreal Manifesto *Hist.* See **Annexation Manifesto.**
1849 *Wkly Globe* 16 Nov. 78/7: The misstatements and false reasoning of the Montreal Manifesto are here so universally admitted that we had begun to think it unnecessary to pursue our dissection of it further.
1849 (1924) *Cdn Hist.Rev.* V 254: I would remark that whatever may have been the latent feeling in Upper Canada at the time the Montreal Manifesto was published there was no organized or concentrated opinion on the subject.

A Montreal ship copper

Montreal ship copper *Obs.* a half-penny token in circulation in the Canadas in the early 19th century, issued in Quebec about 1816.

1820 *Kingston Chron.* (U.C.) 8 Sep. 1/3: Such immense quantites of . . . spurious Coppers have been imported . . . that it has become absolutely necessary to [prohibit] the circulation of the Waterloo Harp, the Half penny tokens, having Britania on the one side and a ship on the other, and Montreal ship coppers.

Montreal trader *Fur Trade, Hist.* See **Canadian Trader.**
1963 MORTON *Kingdom of Canada* 367: Quarrels there had been . . . as when the Indians . . . turned on the Montreal traders on the Saskatchewan in 1781.

mooch [mutʃ] *v.* [prob. < F dial. *muchier* hide, lurk] *West Coast* to engage in mooching, *q.v.*
1961 *Sun* (Vancouver) 17 Aug. 23/3: . . . most anglers troll, rather than mooch or strip-cast with light, sporty but riskier tackle **1963** *Ibid.* 16 Feb. 17/1: Kelly started mooching a herring, caught himself a 10-pound chinook salmon.

mooched herring herring used as bait in mooching, *q.v.*
1961 *Sun* (Vancouver) 17 Aug. 23/3: . . . taking 11 prizes each are plugs . . . and mooched or trolled herring . . . the latter as strip, plug-cut or whole bait. *Ibid.* 29 Aug. 16/1: . . . wise in the ways of a mooched, whole herring [he] took two quick salmon 13 miles down the inlet. . . .

moocher ['mutʃɚ] *n.* [see **mooch,** v.] *West Coast* a person who fishes by mooching, *q.v.*
1960 *Duncan Cowichan Leader* 28 Apr. 7/1: A moocher does not require expensive rods, reels, lines . . . and other tackle. . . .

moochigan ['mutʃəgən] *n.* [< Algonk.: Cree] *North* See quotes.
1948 ONRAET *Sixty Below* 61: When the Indians . . . have done their trading, and enjoyed a few "moochigans" and tea dances, they load up. . . . **1963** PATTERSON *Far Pastures* 9: Or there would be a moochigan (in English, a dance. . . .)

mooching ['mutʃɪŋ] *n.* [see **mooch,** v.] See 1960 quote.
1960 *Duncan Cowichan Leader* 28 Apr. 7/1: . . . mooching just consists of dropping a line over the side of a boat with a weight attached to take it to the required depth, and a herring strip attached to a hook for bait. **1963** *Sun* (Vancouver) 3 July 19/1: And before you ask, by "mooching" I mean mostly drifting with light tackle for heavy fish; not mooching gas.

moo-moo maker *Slang* See quote.
1962 *Chronicle-Herald* (Halifax) 10 Aug. 1/8: And later last night another offer was made—this time for a "moo-moo maker"—official title of a cattle caller.

moon† *n.* in Indian parlance, a lunar month.
1665 (1885) RADISSON *Voyages* 202: I can say that we wᵗʰ our comrades, who weare about 60, killed in the space of 2 moons and a halfe, a thousand moons we wanted not bear's grease to annoint ourselves, to runne the better. **1743** (1949) ISHAM *Observations* 57: When will she arrive [? . . .] in one month or moon I believe. **1856** BALLANTYNE *Young Fur-Traders* 122: ". . . Redfeather has been following in the track of his white friends. He has not seen his nation for many moons." **1964** *Maclean's* 25 July 47/1: "My tribe . . .

after work of ten moons now offers this humble symbol. . . ."

mooneas or **moonias** ['munjæs *or* 'muni̩æs] *n.* [< Algonk.: Cree] Various spellings. *Derog.* especially in Indian parlance: **1** a newcomer; tenderfoot; greenhorn.
c1880 (1966) *Alta Hist.Rev.* Winter 21/1: There was always an extra cake put on for appearance, and it was a sure sign of a "tenderfoot" or a "moonias" to eat that extra cake. **1908** MAIR *Mackenzie Basin* 46: If a monias (a greenhorn) took the bow pole . . . the orders of our steersman, Cyr, were amusing to listen to. **1959** SHIPLEY *Scarlet Lily* 16: He was constantly involved in some transportation difficulty, and earned for himself among the half-breeds and Indians such unflattering appellations as "moonias" and "kipooch," epithets reserved for blundering tenderfeet. **1966** *R.M.C.Review* (Yearbook) 134/2: . . . I was the assistant surveyor and the moneas (tenderfoot) of the outfit.

2 a European; a white man. See also **Moniyas.**
1885 MOBERLY *Rock and Rivers* 84: . . . we came upon the main trail and saw the track of boots, which the Indians at once said were "Moneasses," or men of the east, unaccustomed to mountain travelling. **1913** COWIE *Adventurers* 235: I ordered him to get out immediately, which he did promptly, amid the jeers of the people before whom he had been bragging how he could "play over a Moonyass" a minute before. **1956** KEMP *Northern Trader* 128: Mooneas is the Cree word for White Man. He obtained the sobriquet due, not to his blood, but to his grey eyes. **1963** SYMONS *Many Trails* 156: A *moonias*—a white man—sees but a great thundercloud black and menacing. . . .

mooneye† *n.* a freshwater fish, *Hiodon tergisus,* related to the goldeye, *q.v.,* and found in the Lower Great Lakes.
1866 KING *Sportsman in Canada* 294: A fish of another family, which is exceedingly abundant in the Upper Lakes, and is becoming in many other parts of the country, is the so-called "Lake herring," otherwise Shiner, Moon-eye, or Shad-waiter. **1958** *Encyc.Can.* VII 153/1: The mooneye does not smoke well and is of little commercial value.

moose† [mus] *n.* [< Algonk. "browser, stripper"] **1** a large ruminant mammal, *Alces alces,* of the northern forests. See also **black moose, elk, gray moose** (def. 1), **moose-deer** (def. 1), **mooswa,** and **orignal.**
1680 (1946) *H.B.C.Minutes* 67: Mar. Letton to Deliver 4 Dressed Mouse skins to Thos. Garland to make Snowe Shooes. **1717** (1932) KNIGHT *Journals* 164: These Indians gave me a Side of Moose flesh, Dry'd, & Another of Deers flesh, & 2 pretty bigg bladders of Marrow fat. . . . **1820** (1823) FRANKLIN *Journey* 89: The quadrupeds that are hunted for food in this part of the country, are the moose and the reindeer, the former termed by the Crees, mongsoa, or moosoa, the latter attekh. **1964** *Globe and Mail* (Toronto) 12 Dec. 8/7: A few point to the slow resurgence of moose, particularly in the southwest of the province. . . .

2 the flesh of the moose used as food. See also **moose-deer** (def. 2), **moose-meat,** and **moose venison.**
1784 PENNANT *Arctic Zoology* 19: The Indians say, that they can travel three times as far after a meal of Moose, as after any other animal food. **1954** PATTERSON *Dangerous River* 67: One could get up and dress now, and light the fire and have breakfast with the day well begun; Faille would probably be along soon and there would be moose for everybody—moose galore.

3 See **moose-skin.**

1748 ELLIS *Hudson's Bay* 181: They live in Tents covered with Moose, and Deer-Skins sewed together. **1933** ROLYAT *Wilderness Walls* 134: "The moose shoes suit capitally."

4 *Slang* See quote.

1925 *Dalhousie Rev.* V 321: There is much meandering in the neighbouring woods; and if it is desired to cloak this fondness for the bush in the guise of a rational activity, it is known as the game of "moose."

mooseberry *n.* See **highbush cranberry.**

☛ *In the west, the terms* **mooseberry** *and* **pembina** *are often applied to the low-bush cranberry,* q.v.
1789 (1801) MACKENZIE *Voyages* 111: The women gathered large quantities of the fruit . . . cranberries, crowberries, mooseberries. . . . **1852** RICHARDSON *Arctic Exped.* 79: It is distinguished as a species from the very common cranberry tree, or moose berry (*Mongsöa meena* of the Crees), by the obtuse sinus of its leaves; and its fruit has an orange color, is less acid, more fleshy, and more agreeable to the taste. **1957** SCOGGAN *Flora of Manitoba* 503: Mooseberry. Pimbina. Woods, thickets, shores, and gravel ridges throughout the province. . . .

moosebird *n.* **1** *Esp.East* See **Canada jay.** See also **moose-jay.**

1849 ALEXANDER *L'Acadie* II 121: At our evening meals the moose bird, the size of a pigeon, with a black and white head and soft flight would sometimes perch singly or in pairs on the branches above us, and flit down familiarly near us to peck up a chance morsel. **1892** (1948) *Beaver* June 46/1: The only sound was the low whistling of Baptiste at the helm . . . or the note of a chickadee or moosebird from the shore. . . . **1964** *Atlantic Advocate* Oct. 67/1: This time of year there were always a pair of moosebirds on the maple tree almost killing themselves with curiosity.

2 a local name used for several birds at various times. See quotes.

1872 DASHWOOD *Chiploquorgan* 94: During the winter none remained but the owls, the grouse, some of the wood-peckers, and the cat-birds . . . commonly known as the moose bird, the Canadian jay, and a few other minor species. **1888** (1890) ST. MAUR *Impressions* 273: My friend of the woods, the moose-bird. . . . I found his real name was the great northern shrike, *Lanius borealis;* he has many aliases, being also called the Hudson's Bay bird. **1908** MAIR *Mackenzie Basin* 384: The Indians call them [phoebe, *Sayornis sayus*] "Moose birds," as they often use moose hair in lining their nests. **1958** BERTON *Klondike* 96: Robins warbled among the birches, woodpeckers drummed against the spruce bark, moosebirds and chicken hawks wheeled and hovered in the sky.

moose brush See **moose-willow.**

1948 ONRAET *Sixty Below* 46: He handed us a handful of knick-a-knick, which is the dried under-bark of a red willow we call moose brush.

moose-call *n.* **1** See 1849 quote. See also **call,** *n.* (def. 1b).

1849 GESNER *Ind.Resources N.S.* 222: The hunter enters the deep recesses of the forest, and imitates [a moose's] lowing in what is termed the "moose-call." c**1902** (1912) LAUT *Trapper* 121: Neither moose call nor birch horn, of which wonders are told, will avail now. **1964** *Kingston Whig-Standard* (Ont.) 10 Nov. 3/1: They could entice it [the magnetic pole] over into Siberia by setting up a battery of big magnets . . . putting out a sort of magnetic moose call.

2 a device for making such a call, especially a bark horn. See also **birchbark horn, call,** *n.* (def. 1a), **caller** (def. 2), **cow-call,** and **moose horn.**

1904 ROBERTS *Watchers of Trails* 321: . . . an old hunter . . . had made his joy complete by the gift of the bark "moose-call" itself, a battered old tube with many "kills" to its credit. **1965** *Globe and Mail* (Toronto) 29 Nov. 6/6: I'd suggest you go to your nearest sporting goods store and buy a moose call. . . .

moose-caller *n.* a hunter skilled in moose calling. See also **caller** (def. 1).

1892 DAUNT *Land of Moose* 131: It is an exciting moment for the moose-caller on a still autumn night when he hears the distant bellow of the bull and the noise of crashing branches. . . . **1902** *Gun and Rod in N.B.* 20: Good accommodation is furnished at Cole's Island at the house of Richard Cole, a veteran moose caller and guide. **1966** *Globe and Mail* (Toronto) 14 Jan. 45/5: He was . . . known as Bull Moose because he was a noted moose caller.

moose-calling *n.* the art or practice of simulating a moose's call. See also **calling** (def. 1) and **moose-call** (def. 1).

1872 DASHWOOD *Chiploquorgan* 63: I shall here say a few words in answer to those who declare that moose calling is no sport, and is taking an unfair advantage of the animal. **1923** SQUIER *Autumn Trails* 44: "I'm going to invite him to go moose-calling with us". . . . **1966** *Kingston Whig-Standard* (Ont.) 28 Feb. 10/2: Lamentably, the annual moose-calling contest was cancelled this year.

moose camp See **moose-yard** (def. 1).

1905 (1954) *B.C.Hist.Qtly* XVIII 152: I sought in every direction for a moose camp without success. The habit of the animal is to spend most of the winter season in a particular selected spot, where its food of branches is plentiful.

moose country a region in which moose are numerous. See also **moose-grounds.**

1880 GORDON *Mountain and Prairie* 174: Throughout the Peace River country the moose is to the Indian almost everything that the buffalo is the the hunter of the plains, for this is the best moose country in Canada. **1966** *Globe and Mail* (Toronto) 30 July 23/6: It looks much like good moose country with small marshy lakes and a few woodcutter's trails.

moose-creeping *n.* See **creeping.**

1866 KING *Sportsman in Canada* 56: Few sports . . . more test the skill of the hunter than Moose-creeping. **1872** DASHWOOD *Chiploquorgan* 100: It is better . . . to call moose in September, spend October in . . . moose creeping, and wait until the snow falls . . . to hunt cariboo.

moose-deer† *n. Obs.* **1** See **moose** (def. 1).

1765-75 (1933) POND *Narrative* 57: . . . the Read and Moose Deer are Plentey hear, Espeshaley the former. **1872** BALLANTYNE *Pioneers* 17: But the sight of a bear or moose-deer had the effect of waking him up in a way that caused his dark eyes to flash. . . . **1901** DRUMMOND *J.Corteau* 66: But de swallow will fly, an' de beeg moose

deer/ An' caribou too, will go long way/ To drink de sweet water of Lac Grenier.
2 See **moose** (def. 2).
1807 (1890) KEITH *Letters* II 69: They assist one another with provisions when in want, and their principal food consists of hares, beavers and moose deer, generally roasted. **1880** (1893) YOUNG *Indian Wigwams* 175: The dinner consisted of the head of a moose-deer, which had been cut up into large pieces and then boiled.
3 See **caribou** (def. 1).
1789 *Quebec Herald* 27 Apr. 201/2: North America supplies us with skins of the Stag, the Deer, and the Roe-Buck; of the Mooze deer, called there CARIBOU; and of the Elk, which they call ORIGNAL. **1793** (1933) MACDONELL *Diary* 115: The . . . Assinibouan River is the part most abounding in all the north west, the following animals are natives of it, viz—Buffaloes, Moose Deers, Orignals, Elks, Red Deer, Cabeniers of various kinds. . . .

moose-deer berry *Obs.* See **mooseberry.**
1807 (1889) WENTZEL *Letters* 80: The fruits of this solitary region are the poire . . . moose deer berry . . . crowberry . . . juniperberry. . . .

moose-fly *n.* See **bulldog fly.**
1849 ALEXANDER *L'Acadie* II 117: In short . . . the closeness is often times terrible to bear, especially as it is accompanied with . . . the horse-fly, which seems to take the bite out of the flesh; and the large moose or speckled-winged fly. **1953** LOWER *Voyages* 43: Further south, where they are never so numerous, they [bulldogs] are called horse-flies, or moose-flies.

moose-grounds *n.pl.* See **moose country.**
1902 *Gun and Rod in N.B.* 9: The best moose grounds are found to the east and north of the River St. John, north of Kings County. **1916** WOOD *Tourist's N.W.* 347: By the third week in September you should have got both your sheep and goats and have moved your camp to the moose-grounds, which are generally in close proximity to the sheep.

moose hair† See 1956 quote.
1846 (1927) DICKIE *How Canada Grew Up* 192: Their moccasins . . . are decked with elaborate embroidery of stained moose-hair. . . . **1862** (1931) CHEADLE *Journal* 27: Moose hair work and bead do. at Bazaar. **1956** LEECHMAN *Native Tribes* 43: . . . some [Indians] used moose hair for embroidery. There is a tuft of pale, stiffish hair about seven inches long, between the shoulders of the moose. These hairs were dyed in various colors and used for decorating snowshoes, moccasins, and many other things.

moosehide† *n.* See **moose-skin.**
1897 TYRRELL *Sub-Arctics* 25: After the space of an hour or so my brother and the men returned, well loaded with fresh meat and a fine moose-hide. **1954** EVANS *Mist* 77: Oolichan grease from the coast villages was exchanged for the up-river people's dried soapberries or beaded moose-hide. . . . **1966** *Globe and Mail* (Toronto) 18 May 6/2: When he is racing [on snowshoes], he wears moosehide moccasins made by some of his friends around Cranberry.

moose horn See **moose-call** (def. 2).
1922 *Beaver* June 7/1: . . . many a moose . . . has been lured to his death through the adroit use of the birchbark "moose horn." **1941** *Ibid.* Sep. 38/1: . . . Cape

Horn, the birch-bark "moose horn," the "horn" of rum, the powder horn, and the famous forebuck horn cutlery, have all played their part in the annals of the fur trade.

moose-jay *n.* See **Canada jay.** See also **moosebird.**
1905 MOTT *Jules* 269: Birds fluttered to and fro over the stream, and gray and white moose-jays floated on the air with open wings, calling harshly.

moose leather See **moose-skin.** See also **leather.**
1754 (1907) HENDAY *Journal* 343: Women making Shoes of Moose leather: I have as yet only wore Shoes with the hair on the inside, so moderate hath the weather been. **1896** RUSSELL *Far North* 172: Dressed moose leather is the best material obtainable by the Northern Indians for the manufacture of moccasins.

moose-lick *n.* a salt lick, *q.v.*, frequented by moose.
1922 PRINGLE *Tillicums* 217: This pond . . . was a "moose-lick," a place to which for years, at certain seasons, the moose came at night from miles around, because the water and soil had in them some salty substance which they liked or needed. **1938** BLACK *Seventy Years* 198: The experienced hunter knows where to find himself a moose lick, and, having found one, builds himself a look-out in some tree. . . .

moose lily the yellow, or pond, lily, *Nuphar advena.*
1934 DENNIS *Down in N.S.* 282: There is a lily called the moose lily which they [the moose] wade out and get in July before it grows tough.

moose maple See **striped maple.**
1917 (1920) *Native Trees* 118: Common names [are] Striped maple, moosewood, moose maple. **1952** (1954) JENNINGS *Strange Brigade* 123: . . . to our left lay the woodsy thickets . . . beech and chokecherry and moose maple. **1956** *Native Trees* 240: The buds and twigs provide winter food for deer and moose, and the latter eat the leaves in summer, hence the names moosewood and moose maple.

moose-meat *n.* See **moose** (def. 2).
1797 (1964) CHABOILLEZ *Journal* 163: The People returned, they brought 1 Bear skin—2 Beaver Skins—1 Bear in Meat—8 pieces Mouse Meat half Dryed & three Beaver in Meat. **1829** (1830) MOORSOM *Letters N.S.* 121: The moose-meat, though by some compared to venison, would not stand competition with the poorest haunch from Whittlebury, being both dry, devoid of fat, and insipid. **1965** *Kingston Whig-Standard* (Ont.) 15 Apr. 17/3: "You have to ask for a steak epais," Pop advised. Steak epais was the password for moose meat, sale of which was forbidden in restaurants in the Saguenay county.

moose milk 1 *North, Slang* home-distilled liquor.
1957 *Weekend Mag.* 23 Mar. 49/1: [He brought to trial] a man who had drunk too freely of the native "moose milk" homebrew and started fighting.
2 one of several mixed drinks, the main ingredients of which are rum and milk. Cp. **English milk.**
1958 LEWIS *Buckskin Cookery* II 31: MOOSE MILK 2 OZ. rum, or 1 oz. of overproof rum in 8 oz. glass. Fill with half and half, i.e. half cream and half milk. For: Any ailment. **1966** *Kingston Whig-Standard* (Ont.) 25 Feb. 12/1: Miller . . . paused briefly from his arduous task of mixing the two local opiates—moose milk and ice-worm cocktails—for clamorous customers in his warm bistro on Whitehorse's main drag.

moose misse See **mozo-mish.**

moose muffle or **moufle** See **moose nose.**
1872 (1877) GRANT *Ocean to Ocean* 230: The verdict
was favourable throughout; the [beaver] meat tender,
though dry, the liver a delicious morsel, and the tail
superior to moose-muffle. 1873 (1904) BUTLER *Wild
North Land* 119: No more dog-driving . . . nothing but
endless wood buffalo steaks, fried onions, moose
moufle . . . rest and sleep. 1950 BIRD *This is N.S.* 88:
[She] was a large handsome woman . . . famous for
her moose muffle soup, which was so good that some of
it was exported to England.

moose nose the nose and upper lip of the
moose used as food, considered a delicacy. See
also **moose muffle, mouffle,** and **muffle.**
1697 (1929) KELSEY *Papers* 71: Today 3 indians came
from mr. kelsey they having kill'd no deer as yet but
brought some dryed flesh four moose tongues & noses
ditto &c. 1754 (1907) HENDAY *Journal* 329: I dressed a
lame man's leg. He gave me a Moose nose, which is a
delicate dish, for my trouble. 1837 (1909) CAMERON
New North 192: . . . we had in addition to our usual
dinner a roasted swan and a moose-nose. . . .
1957 FISHER *Pemmican* 7: Pemmican needed plenty of
marrow fat, buffalo tongues and bosses, moose noses
and beaver tails. . . .

moose pasture 1 *Slang* worthless or unproven
mining claims. See also **moose-yard** (def. 2).
1896 (1964) *North* Nov.-Dec. 6/1: . . . some miners, led
on by a Mr. Whipple, started in to stake Eldorado
branch, up to that time "Reserved as a moose pasture,"
as a wag put it. . . . 1909 (1962) THOMAS *Trail of
Ninety-Eight* 83: "Moose pasture!" sneered Kink
Mitchell. But Bill gravely paced off five hundred feet up
the creek and blazed the corner-stakes. 1962 *Press*
Jan. 5: When prospecting lagged and the bottom
fell out of the "moose-pasture" market, Ernie took a
semi-skilled job with a local mining company. . . .

2 *North* terrain having little value except for
browsing moose.
1965 SYMINGTON *Tuktu* 17: The timberland is
interspersed with . . . willow-and-aldergrown "moose
pasture."

moose-run *n.* See quote.
1894 ASHLEY *Tan Pile Jim* 182: . . . Sam explained to
Jim that a "moose-run" was a path beaten by the moose
through the snow to give them access to their drinking
and feeding grounds among the high sedge or the low
birches. . . .

moose shanks See **shanks.**

moose-skin *n.* the hide of the moose, valued as
leather, *q.v.* See also **moose** (def. 3), **moosehide,**
and **moose leather.**
1671 (1942) *H.B.C.Minutes* 16: Any of the Committee
have power to Sell the ottar & mouse Skins as they shall
see fit. 1717 (1932) KNIGHT *Journals* 166: I took the
Oppertunity & told them abt Scrapeing of their Moose
Skins so thin. he Said it was because of the Long
Carriages they had to bring them they was forced to
make them Light. 1805 (1933) CONNOR *Diary* 269:
. . . Seraphin with 1 Man went to pay a visit to Chenier
[to] get a Moose Skin and probably will pay a visit to
Laprairie. 1909 CAMERON *New North* 107: [Caption]
Watch-pocket of smoked moose-skin, embroidered in
silkwork, made by a Cree girl. . . . 1957 HARRIS *Cariboo
Trail* 174: But the mooseskin-trousered [one] looked at
him darkly.

moose-snare *n.* See 1903 quote.
[1807 (1889) WENTZEL *Letters* 89: Their economy

consists in hoarding up as many provisions as possible
for the winter and in obtaining a great quantity of
orignal snares.] 1903 CARR-HARRIS *White Chief* 119:
They then followed a trail which led down the little
Chaudiere, where Machecawa had a moose snare. He
had driven two pegs into two large pine trees, about six
feet from the ground, on opposite sides of the trail. On
these he hung a cord about the size of a cod-line,
formed of thirty-strands of the green skin of a moose
and arranged as a noose, one end of which was securely
attached to a fallen log, so that when the moose would
come down hill for a drink he would run his head into
it and the strip would slip off the pegs and tighten
round his neck. . . . 1904 ROBERTS *Watchers of Trails*
179: What he saw before him was a great, gaunt
moose-cow reared upon her hind legs, caught under the
jaws by a villainous moose-snare.

mooses-potting *n.* See quote.
1962 *Globe and Mail* (Toronto) 24 Feb. 28/3: There had
been talk of longer moose seasons and of permitting
moose-spotting from aircraft.

moose thumb the dewclaw and fibula of a moose
used as a pin to hold together the flaps of a teepee.
1963 *Beaver* Summer 33/2: John Hunter fastens the
tipi cover with moose thumbs.

moose-tongue† *n.* the tongue of a moose used as
food.
1697 (1929) KELSEY *Papers* 71: Today 3 indians came
from mr. kelsey they have kill'd no deer as yet but
brought some dryed flesh four moose tongues & noses
ditto &c. 1923 WALDO *Down Mackenzie* 212: You
must not feed a woman moose-tongue . . . because her
tongue will then let the moose know that the hunter
is after them.

moose-veal *n.* the meat of a moose calf.
1902 ROBERTS *Kindred of Wild* 113: Then, there was the
calf—no meat like moose-veal.

moose venison See **moose** (def. 2).
1873 (1904) BUTLER *Wild North Land* 119: In the small
fort at the Forks, luxuries unseen during many a day
met the eye; choice vegetables, the produce of the
garden; moose venison. . . . 1925 GARRIOCH *Furry
North* 204: "Father sends his compliments and asks you
to accept this piece of moose venison," and the
younger one speaking equally good English, handed
him a birch bark rogan full of berries. . . .

moose-walk *n. Obs.* a hunt for moose. Cp.
creeping.
1849 GESNER *Ind.Resources N.S.* 223: The Indians are
remarkably cunning upon a moose-walk, and creep
upon their prey with the subtlety of serpents.

mooseweed *n. Esp.North* See **fireweed.**
1900 FRASER *Mooswa* 9: I get tired of the purple-headed
Moose-weed, and the leaves and twigs.

moose-willow *n.* See **red-osier dogwood.** See also
moose brush.
1910 FERGUSON *Janey Canuck* 48: The moose "yard up"
for the winter. Their chief food is the branches of the
moose-willow. Indeed their name is derived from the
Indian word *mouswah,* meaning wood eater.

moosewood† *n.* **1** See **striped maple.**
1822 (1928) CORMACK *Narr.Nfld* 14: Also . . . the red
maple and the striped maple, known as the moose-

wood of Canada. **1924** SHERMAN *Nature Stories* 77: The Striped Maple of the east and the Vine Maple of the west are scarcely more than shrubs. The former is also known as the Goosefoot Maple, or Moosewood. **1956** *Native Trees* 240: The buds and twigs provide winter food for deer and moose, and the latter eat the leaves in summer, hence the names moosewood and moose maple.

2 See **leatherwood**.
1830 *Trans.Lit.& Hist.Soc.Que.* III 88: Leatherwood, Moosewood, Bois de pelon. A deciduous shrub of four or five feet in height, with light gray bark; and leaves oval, entire, alternate, on long footstalks. **1852** (1881) TRAILL *Cdn Crusoes* 75: ... these he bound on with strips of the leathery bark of the moose-wood. **1933** CAMERON *Twigs* 129: The under-growth consisted of ... moosewood, dogwood. ...

moose-yard *n.* **1** See **yard**, *n.* (def. 1a). See also **moose camp**.
1846 (1955) CRAIG *Early Travellers* 160: [The] guide told us we were at the place for stopping that night, and within two miles of the "Ravage," or moose-yard. **1921** HEMING *Drama of Forests* 221: A moose yard is usually composed of a series of gutters from one foot to eighteen inches wide, intersecting one another at any distance from ten to fifty feet or more apart, and each gutter being punctured about every three feet with a post hole in which the moose steps as it walks. **1946** BIRD *Sunrise* 209: Nathan plunged to join him and almost fell into a well-trodden moose-yard. It had been travelled that day.

2 *Slang* See **moose pasture** (def. 1).
1910 FRASER *Red Meekins* 188: "There ain't no silver in this God-forsaken corner of the earth, Pete! It's a mooseyard, that's what it is." Meekins growled.

moostoos ['mustus] *n.* [< Algonk.: Cree] See **buffalo**, *n.* (def. 2).
1772 (1908) COCKING *Journal* 107: [There is] very little grass, mostly wild wormwood which the Natives name Mustoose or Buffalo-liking: from that Animal being very fond of this Herb. **1820** (1823) FRANKLIN *Journey* 89: The buffalo or bison, (moostoosh) ... are not found in the neighbourhood of Cumberland House. **1916** BRIDLE *Sons of Can.* 217: He deplored the passing of the "moostoos," but so far as we know never tried to hold up the "Oogamous" Donald A. Smith and Van Horne with their conquering transcontinental that cut clean through the dry belt. ... **1957** FISHER *Pemmican* 25: And in the end they had all fled like a moostoos with a fire in its tail. **1963** SYMONS *Many Trails* 156: "Moostoos," he said softly, and drew on his pipe. ...

moosu(e) *n.* See **mooswa**.
1743 (1949) ISHAM *Observations* 20: a moose or Elk Moo sue. **1808** (1960) FRASER *Letters and Journals* 149: Mossu, Red Deer, and Chevereau, and Beaver are likewise said to be very numerous. ...

mooswa(h) ['muswɑ] *n.* [< Algonk.: Cree] See **moose** (def. 1).
1896 RUSSELL *Far North* 13: Aleck ... pointed ... and said "mooswa." **1910** FERGUSON *Janey Canuck* 48: Indeed their name is derived from the Indian word *mouswah*, meaning wood-eater. **1951** ANGIER *At Home* 218: Ted Boynton spoke of mooswa which, of course, is moose.

moouch *n.* See **mowich**.

mooyak *n.* See **moyaque**.

Moravian *n. Hist.* See **Moravian Indian**.
1793 (1905) *Ont.Bur.Arch.Rep.* III 230: The Moravian Village is nearly at commencement of the 4th Township. **1832** (1902) LUNDY *Diary* 19: This act has been justly condemned, even by warriors, as the Moravians were a peaceful people, and it is believed they took no part in the contest. **1886** *Indian* (Hagersville, Ont.) 7 July 146/3: The small band of Indians known as the Moravians of the Thames, whose reserve is situated in the Township of Orford, in the County of Kent, appear to be making pleasing progress.

Moravian Grant *Hist.* a grant of land made to the Moravian Brethren in 1792 (25,000 acres on the Thames River near Lake St. Clair). See also **Moravian Indian**.
1827 *Gore Gaz.* (Ancaster, U.C.) 22 Sep. 118/5: He always stood high in the estimation of his neighbours, as an honest man, and one to whom the public of that day was much indebted for opening Road of about 70 or 80 miles, through a wilderness, from Oxford to the Moravian Grant.

Moravian Indian one of a small band of Christianized Delaware and Muncee Indians brought to Upper Canada by the Moravian Brethren from Pennsylvania and occupying the Moravian Grant after 1792. See also **Moravian**.
1798 (1957) *Ontario Hist.* XLIX 66: The fact is, the so called Moravian Indians are accounted the best of neighbors, especially for new settlers. **1897** DURAND *Reminiscences* 141: Chatham town now contains nearly 10,000 people. There were, in 1817, a good many Indians—the Delawares and Moravians. **1958** *Edmonton Jnl* 6 Nov. 7/3: The Moravian Indians consist for the most part of descendants of Munsees and Delawares who migrated to Canada in 1791 from Ohio following a massacre at the missionary village of Muskingum.

Moravian post one of several trading posts in the Labrador peninsula in locations first settled by Moravian missionaries in the 18th century.
1934 *Beaver* Sep. 63/3: The district manager is now on the northern section of Labrador making his inspection tour of the Moravian posts.

mortgage lifter *Slang, Obs.* See quote.
*c*1900 POLLARD *Life on the Frontier* 57: Hogs, known as "mortage lifters" in the old Province of Ontario, were among the "fruits" that were realised by the early settlers in these regions.

mortuary pole See quote.
1964 *Imperial Oil Rev.* April 17/2: Reid suggested instead that they reconstruct part of a traditional Haida village. He and Doug Cranmer spent three years carving totems, mortuary poles (these were erected to the memory of particularly powerful chiefs and held the remains of the chiefs in a box at the top of the pole), a long house and a mortuary house.

mosquenonge *n.* See **maskinonge**.

mosquito-dope *n.* insect repellent.
1903 WHITE *Forest* 383: Pack one, or absolute necessities for hard trip ... knife; mosquito-dope; compass; match box. ... **1911** SHAFFER *Indian Trails* 66: [We applied] a highly advertised mosquito "dope" which was grey and greasy. ... [**1928** FREEMAN *Nearing North* 32: There was not a glove, net or bottle of antimosquito dope in the party.]

mosquito fan *Obs.* See quote. Cp. **mosquito wig.**
1749 DRAGE *Voyage* II 62: The Indians bring down to the Factory, what is call'd a Musketoe Fan, made of the long black Hair of a Buffalo [i.e., musk-ox], tied to the End of a short Stick, with which you wisk the Musketoes off the Face.

mosquito hawk† **1 a.** *Obs.* See quote.
1743 (1949) ISHAM *Observations* 131: Musketo hawk's (alias) Suacanappasish is Like for shape and make what we call a horse fly in England, these does Rather good than harm, killing a great quantity of musketoes and flesh flies. **1959** MCATEE *Folk-Names* 44: Common Nighthawk [is also called] mosquito hawk (Que., "Hudson Bay," P.E.I., N.S., N.B., Man., Sask., B.C.).
b. a dragon-fly.
1826 (1832) PICKERING *Inquiries* 59: Thousands of long large flies, similar to the English dragon fly, but a little smaller, are flying about the fields; they are called musquito hawks, on account of their killing and living on those insects. **1923** WALDO *Down Mackenzie* 78: The brilliant dragon-flies, black and green, banded like sounding-poles used for the shallows, are called mosquito-hawks. **1933** HIGINBOTHAM *West Was Young* 299: [They were] dragon-flies (mosquito hawks as they are called here). . . .
2 the nighthawk, *Chordeiles minor.*
1796 (1911) SIMCOE *Diary* 335: I saw mosquito hawks' nests, at least the eggs and young birds lying in pieces of bark on the ground. **1866** KING *Sportsman in Can.* 108: . . . the somewhat rare swallow-tail or musquito-hawk, in the neighbourhood of St. Davids, soaring in pursuit of insects, and performing the most singular and graceful evolutions. **1938** CASH *I Like B.C.* 187: A mosquito hawk zoomed belatedly overhead.

mosquito-smudge *n.* See **smudge** (def. 1).
1909 CAMERON *New North* 169: At three o'clock in the morning we haul into the Hay River Mission, where the familiar mosquito-smudge greets us at the Landing. **1953** MOWERY *Mounted Police* 26: Cluttered around several mosquito smudges, they were cleaning their guns and sharpening their long, wicked skinning knives.

mosquito wig *Obs.* a kind of cap having a long fringe of musk-ox hair, used as protection against mosquitoes, etc. Cp. **mosquito fan.**
1795 (1947) *Beaver* Sep. 16/2: Hearne . . . says the long hair used for these "musketto wigs" came from the throat and breast [of the musk-ox] where it "hangs down like a horse's mane inverted." **1832** MCGREGOR *Brit.Amer.* I 104: Their [musk-oxen's] hair is very long . . . and . . . of this . . . the Esquimaux make their mosquito wigs.

mossback *n.* *Slang* an oldtimer, often one having unprogressive, old-fashioned ideas.
1884 *Nor'Wester* (Calgary) 3 June 4/1: The local mossback refers to the recent picking up of stones on Stephen Avenue, and the piling of the same in the middle of the avenue. **1959** LEISING *Arctic Wings* 97: Many evenings at the mission I listened to old mossbacks, prospectors, and trappers unfold the scroll of their experiences. **1963** *Maclean's* 9 Feb. 2/2: He is not, however, a member of the mossback rump in the Liberal caucus, a group led by Yvon Dupuis, MP for Sain-Jean. . . .

moss bag among certain Indian tribes, a kind of bag that is laced in front and sometimes attached to a cradle-board, *q.v.*, used for carrying a baby and so called because the bag is lined with dry moss, which serves as a diaper. See picture at **cradle-**

board. See also **papoose bag** and **tikinagan.** Cp. **moss basket.**
[**1743** (1949) ISHAM *Observations* 105: For clouts they use white mawse, twice a Day trying Drying itt well before the fire, or putt a Burning Coal, into the mawse which Dry's itt as well,—which is an Excellent thing Keeping the Child Constantly Dry, the soft mawse sucking all the Damp up,—Not being at the trouble and Charge other Nations are at, in Washing, Drying and Bying Cloth for clouts.] **1867** GIBBS *Notes on Tinneh* 304: Cradles are never used; but this machine, called a "moss bag," is an excellent adjunct to the rearing of children up to a certain age, and has become almost, if not universally adopted in the families of the Hudson's Bay Company's employés. **1963** *Beaver* Summer 37/2: It is an event for the whole family, from the 15-day-old baby sleeping in a moss bag to the old lady of a hundred years. . . .

moss basket a moss bag, *q.v.*, attached to a cradle-board. Cp. **cradle-basket.**
1927 (1928) ROSE *Stump Farm* 173: . . . I saw a squaw fix up her baby in a moss basket as they are called in here [N. Alta]. The foundation is a board a little longer than the baby. The board is very smooth and smaller at each end. The top end has a hole to put a rawhide thong through to hang it by. On both sides are holes to lace it up after the baby is in it. The squaw . . . laid the board on the ground in the teepee and took some moss out of a big sack . . . She spread a layer of the moss four to six inches thick very evenly on the board. Then she placed her little newborn naked baby boy on it and put another layer of moss on up to his armpits. Next she laid a piece of Hudson Bay four-point blanket over him and tucked it in good . . . There were two long rawhide strings at the bottom and now she laced it up good and tight, the strings crossing. . . .

moss heather the white heather, *Cassiope Mertensiana).*
1952 PUTNAM *Cdn Regions* 25/1: Many of the plants of the alpine tundra are the same as those of the Arctic; others, however, are found only in the Cordilleran region, including . . . moss heather. . . .

Mother Carey's chicken† *Atlantic Provinces* a petrel. See 1829 quote. See also **Carey.** Also spelled *Mother Cary, Mother Carew.*
☞ *For another explanation of this term, see the 1956 quote at* **Carey.**
1791 (1911) SIMCOE *Diary* 47: [We saw a] number of gulls and shearwaters and Mother Carey's chickens flying about. Mother Carey is Matara Cara [Portuguese]. **1818** LOCKWOOD *Nova Scotia* 81: On one of these Islands thousands of Pettrels, or Mother Carey's chickens, annually hatch their young. **1829** MACTAGGART *Three Years* I 11: When fully out to sea, we fall in with the stormy petrels, better known by the name of Mother Carew's chickens. — *Ibid.* I 12: Mother Carew was an old witch . . . good at raising the wind . . . The sailors would not shoot [petrels] on any account; they pay them great respect that their mother's wrath may not be roused. **1953** RADDALL *Tidefall* 198: And I know a place on the west side of the Head, a turfy spot above a high bank, where Mother Carey's chickens still make their burrows.

Mother Hubbard *North* See 1964 quote.
1961 FERGUSON *Tuktoyaktuk* 60: These teen-agers differentiate themselves from the adult population by a

distinctive dress: the men wear "motorcycle" jackets, the women slacks and short parkas, unlike the otherwise universal "Mother Hubbards." **1964** *North* Jan.-Feb. 32/1: The older women and the young girls wear the Mother Hubbard, a parka made from duffle cloth, covered with a cotton cover in a bright print, edged at hood and cuffs with wolverine fur.

mother lode *Placer Mining* the rich vein or lode which has "mothered" the gold found below as float (def. 2).

*c*1860 (1927) MCKELVIE *Black Canyon* vi: After working for some time . . . they started up-stream in search of the mother-lode. **1897** *B.C.Mining Jnl* (Ashcroft) 27 Mar. 1/4: A theory has been advanced, that in the center of this mountain exists what is termed a "mother lode," and that the lodes appearing on either side are simply veins thrown out of the "mother." **1958** KELSEY *B.C.Rides a Star* 174: Their appetites whetted for the mother lodes, the majority pressed on up the Fraser's terrifying canyons.

Mothers' Allowance See **Family Allowance.**
1961 *News of the North* 27 July 1/5: The committee does not recommend payment of a supplementary allowance for old age pensioners nor Mothers' Allowance.

motorized sled See **motor toboggan.**
1967 *Kingston Whig-Standard* (Ont.) 23 Mar. 12/2: The thing she misses most is a modern contraption that the South introduced into the North—the motorized sled.

motorized toboggan See **motor toboggan.**
1958 *Edmonton Jnl* 24 June 4 16/6: Motorized toboggans have made their appearance in the Mackenzie River delta where an enterprising Aklavik pair are operating a charter service in winter. **1966** *Globe and Mail* (Toronto) 1 Jan. 23/1: A significant factor in the development of winter recreation is the relatively recent popularity of the snowmobile (or motorized toboggan), which is just starting to occupy the place in winter that the outboard motor does in summer.

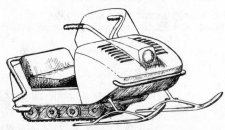

A motor toboggan

motor toboggan a small over-snow vehicle equipped with skis at the front and powered by a motor driving a treaded endless track. See also **autoboggan, motorized sled, motorized toboggan, power toboggan, skidoo, ski-scooter, ski-sled, snow-bug, snow-buggy, Snow Cruiser, snowmobile** (def. 2), **snow scooter,** and **toboggan,** *n.* (def. 5).
1948 *New Deal for Sask.Fisheries* 20: . . . replacing the old-fashioned dog team and sled, [are] . . . motor toboggans and "snow tractors" which attain a speed up to 35 miles per hour and manoeuver in almost any kind

of terrain. **1963** *Globe and Mail* (Toronto) 9 Mar. 31/1: Whizzing through the bush on a motor toboggan is an adventure. These machines, which cost $700 or $800, travel up hill, down dale and across frozen lakes with ridiculous ease.

mouche *v.* See **mush.**

mouf(f)le *n.* [< Cdn F *mufle* < F "muzzle"] See **moose nose.** See also **muffle.**
1791 (1911) SIMCOE *Diary* 66: I ate part of the moufle of the orignale, or elk [i.e., *moose*]. **1858** (1863) PALLISER *Journals* 86: We halted . . . to enjoy a feast of moose meat, moffle, and gut sausage, dishes which our hunters and half-breeds prepared with great skill. **1872** DASHWOOD *Chiploquorgan* 38: One of the chief characteristics [of the moose] is the mouffle, or over hanging lip, which gives to his head an ugly appearance . . . The mouffle is considered a great delicacy. **1892** DAUNT *Land of Moose* 180: "Jest to think o' bein' done out o' steak and mouffle by that rotted critter. . . ."

mould *n.* See **fur mould.**
1921 HEMING *Drama of Forests* 297: Now in the fur loft many hands were busily engaged in sorting, folding, and packing in collapsible moulds—that determined the size and shape of the fur packs—a great variety of skins.

moulin banal *French, Hist.* in Old Quebec, the mill of the seigneur, where tenants were obliged to take their grain for milling. Cp. **mouture.**
1815 BOUCHETTE *Lower Canada* 11: They are also bound to grind their corn at the moulin banal, or the lord's mill, where one-fourteenth part of it is taken as his use for mouture, or payment for grinding. **1886** *Trans.Roy. Soc.Can.* IV 3 47: The intendant issued an ordinance forbidding the Dame de la Forêt from turning her mill in the county of St. Laurent while there was a *moulin banal* in that place.

mounder *n.* a member of a surveying team responsible for setting up boundary markers. See note.
☛ *When the prairies were being surveyed in the early days of this century, corners of townships and other important points were marked by a pit dug in the middle of a square with a mound of earth at each corner. This was done because of a shortage of wood with which to make stakes, and also because Indians would pull up stakes for firewood. The men who did this work were called "mounders" and the term was later extended to include those who erected any kind of a boundary marker.*
1965 *Beaver* Autumn 55/2: I was first assigned to break in the chainmen, then the "mounders," who were to erect survey monuments along the line. . . .

mouniac *n.* See **muniack.**

mountain bear *B.C.* See **grizzly bear.**
1920 FOOTNER *Fur-Bringers* 232: "See my children, white man! Brave as the white-face mountain bear!"

mountain beaver† See **sewellel.**

mountain caribou a species of caribou, *Rangifer arcticus montanus,* native to the mountainous region of the Northwest.
1908 MAIR *Mackenzie Basin* 162: . . . the variety of woodland caribou found in the Rocky Mountains of northern Canada may belong to the mountain caribou discovered in the Selkirk Range of British Columbia and made known to science by Mr. Ernest Thompson Seton, in 1899. It is said to be darker in colour than Maine and other eastern specimens. **1963** *B.C.Digest*

Nov. 31/2: Pat Brady . . . had the honor of bagging the first mountain caribou calf to be captured in the world.

mountain cat 1 *East* See 1947 quote. Cp. **catamount** (def. 1).

*c*1665 (1885) RADISSON *Voyages* 42: He came with us to our Cottage, where we mett our companion after having killed one beare, 2 staggs, and 2 mountain catts. **1861** DE BOILIEU *Labrador Life* 171: This gives us more time for sport, for another cruize or two up the bay, to gather eggs or rinds, or to try and secure one of the large seals for boot-bottoms for the ensuing winter, and to shoot a mountain-cat or two. **1947** TANNER *Outlines* I 422: The lynx or mountain cat . . . is found in the southern part of the peninsula in broken country.

2 *West* See **cougar**.

*c*1902 (1912) LAUT *Trapper* 150: Some soft oozy moss-padded lair . . . sets Ba'tiste's pulse hopping—jumping—marking time in thrills like the lithe bounds of a pouncing mountain-cat. **1911** KNOWLES *Singer* 166: "I guess—that was a mountain-cat, back in the woods. . . ."

mountain cutthroat *B.C.* a small cutthroat trout, *Salmo clarkii.* See 1960 quote. See also **mountain trout**.

1932 DYMOND *Game Fishes of B.C.* 34: The mountain cut-throats are similar in their qualities as game fish to the coastal forms. **1960** *Fisheries Fact Sheets* 76: Certain small, fine-scaled types of cutthroat—the "Yellowstone" and "Mountain" cutthroats—provide good fishing in the southeastern and central parts of the province. . . .

mountain devil *Gaspé* (*Que.*) See **wolverine** (def. 1).

1935 *Cdn Geog.Jnl* Jan. 36/2: Otter, fisher, wolverine ("mountain devils," the guides called them), and mink showed themselves on rare occasions.

Mountaineer ['maʊntə‚nir] *n.* [so called because they lived in the highlands] **1** *Hist.* one of an Algonkian-speaking people of eastern Quebec and Labrador, the Naskapi.

☛ *The closely related Montagnais and Mountaineers were so named in colonial times by the French and the English respectively; the former people retain this name still; the latter are now generally known as Naskapi.*

1770 (1792) CARTWRIGHT *Journal* I 28: I then landed on the south side, and saw very recent marks of Mountaineer Indians. **1849** MCLEAN *Notes* I 305: The Nascopies, or mountaineers of Labrador, speak a mixture of Cree and Sauteux, the former predominating. **1907** MILLAIS *Newfoundland* 217: They had probably heard, perhaps from the Mountaineer Indians of the Labrador, who are themselves a branch of the Algonquins, of the excellent trapping and hunting to be found in the island, and had come for that purpose.

2 a. *Obs.* one of a group of woods Crees living to the northwest of Lake Superior.

1832 *Cdn Courant* (Montreal) 1 Aug. 2/5: During the past winter a band of Mushkegons, or Mountaineers, speaking a dialect of the Chippewas language fell upon a trading post, situated on the Nipigon river, belonging to the Hon. Hudson Bay Company, and murdered indiscriminately, all the traders occupying the post.

b. one of several Athapaskan-speaking peoples in the Northwest, as the Kasha, Sekani, Nahani, and, earlier, the western Chipewyans.

1880 MORRIS *Treaties* 192: Ken-oo-say-oo, or The Fish, was a Chippewayan or mountaineer, a small band of whom are in this region [now south-central Saskatchewan]. **1932** MORICE *Carrier Language* xi: The

Sékanais, or Mountaineers . . . call them Arêtnê, which means Carriers, by allusion to the practice of their widows to *carry* on their back, those of the bones of their late husbands which may have withstood the flames of ritual cremation.

mountain fever See **Rocky Mountain fever**.

1898 CONNOR *Black Rock* 322: He had had mountain fever, whatever that may be, and he will not pull up again. . . . **1933** SPINKS *B.C. Frontier* 43: . . . Mike fell sick of mountain fever, a kind of typhoid, that curse of the mountains. **1958** ELLIOTT *Quesnel* 24: Cunningham died at Soda Creek on June 21, 1864, from mountain fever. . . .

mountain goat See **Rocky Mountain goat**.

1888 (1890) ST. MAUR *Impressions* 144: The time is closed for the shooting of mountain sheep and goat till September, and it is somewhat aggravating, for poor Algernon to feel so near and be unable to have a few days with them. **1966** *Globe and Mail* (Toronto) 7 May 41/2: Mountain goat also abound in the mountainous region . . . in . . . southeastern British Columbia.

mountain grouse† See **Franklin's grouse**. Cp. **mountain partridge**.

1913 JOHNSON *Shagganappi* 201: And here are some mountain grouse Roy and I got. . . . **1921** LAUT *Cariboo Trail* 28: A 'fool-hen' or mountain grouse comes out and bobbles her head at the passing pack-train.

mountain lands *N.S.* See quote.

1832 MCGREGOR *Brit.Amer.* II 7: Some of the uplands, lying between the hilly ground and the *intervales,* or rivers, are light and poor, while the high, or what the inhabitants call the mountain lands, are rich, and very productive.

mountain lion† See **cougar**.

1895 PARKER *Adventurer* 209: Pourcette had shot two mountain lions. . . . **1963** SYMONS *Many Trails* 81: One wild animal of the Chilcotin interested me greatly—the cougar or mountain lion.

mountain marmot See **hoary marmot**.

1858 (1863) PALLISER *Journals* 101: Among the blocks of rock the sifleurs or mountain marmots kept whistling in a very loud shrill note answering one another. . . . **1932** WINSON *Weather and Wings* 9: Its green slopes pasture . . . mountain marmots of the rocks and slides. . . . **1962** ONSLOW *Bowler-Hatted Cowboy* 255: A fat . . . mountain marmot had taken up his abode beneath the house, and Susan spent much time in stalking him with cameras. . . .

mountain mutton† the flesh of the Rocky Mountain sheep used as food.

1921 HAWORTH *Trailmakers* 205: And I might add here that "mountain mutton" is the best game meat I have ever tasted. **1954** PATTERSON *Dangerous River* 187: He seemed to have struck an Eldorado of partridges, however, and the living was good in those days—arctic grayling and Dolly Varden, partridges, wild duck and cranberry sauce and mountain mutton.

mountain oyster† *West, Slang* a testicle of a lamb or calf used as food.

1962 *Alta Hist.Rev.* Autumn 15/2: In the commissariat department [are] "dope" (butter) . . . "Mountain oysters" (calves fries).

viewpoint which is situated near a small museum operated by the Willow Creek Historical Society.

mountain partridge *Nfld* See **rock ptarmigan**. Cp. **mountain grouse**.

1883 HATTON & HARVEY *Newfoundland* 234: There is another kind . . . an Alpine species, inhabiting only the highest and barest ridges, and called the "mountain partridge."

mountain pony a small, sure-footed pony of the Rockies. See also **mountain cayuse**.

1922 *Beaver* Feb. 37/1: . . . we could ride almost anywhere on mountain ponies, which were nearly as sure-footed as the goats. **1958** *Edmonton Jnl* 12 Aug. 15/7: It is this spirit which sends the Trail Riders into the mountains on spirited mountain ponies. . . .

mountain sheep† See **bighorn sheep**.

1824 (1955) BLACK *Journal* 98: The Mountain sheep & Goats often take the best windings to reach the Summits of the Mountains, but [are] often eccentric & choose entricacies not to be followed by man. **1965** *Star Wkly* 2 Jan. 37/1: . . . there was one 12-mile road snaking . . . down into a wilderness valley, frequented by mountain sheep and cougars and black bear, only to peter out into nothing.

mountain shrub See **mountain tea**.

1765 (1875) CAMPBELL *Hist.P.E.I.* 6: The Mountain Shrub and Maiden Hair are also pretty common, of whose leaves and berries the Acadian settlers frequently make a kind of tea.

mountain tea See **wintergreen**. See also **mountain shrub**.

1786 (1787) *Account N.S.* 20: Likewise the Indian, or mountain tea, and maiden-hair, an herb much in repute for the same purpose. . . . **1830** (1837) *Trans.Lit. & Hist.Soc.Que.* III 96: Mountain tea [is] a very small evergreen half-shrubby plant, with strong, shining, leathery leaves. **1964** WILSON *Barrett's Landing* 44: To supplement our meals . . . we ate berries, mountain teas (a leaf that tastes like wintergreen), and seaweed. . . .

mountain trout† See **mountain cutthroat**.

1914 STEELE *Forty Years* 89: Our food at this time consisted of pemmican and mountain trout. **1955** GOWLAND *Smoke* 153: The true mountain trout is speckled and does not grow very large, rarely, indeed, exceeding a pound and a half.

Mounte *n.* See **Montée**.

Mounted *n. Informal* the Royal Canadian (formerly, North West) Mounted Police, *q.v.*

1885 (1964) *Alta Hist.Rev.* Summer 23/1: All the mounted and two guns came back. **1919** FRASER *Bulldog Carney* 67: "You amuse me, Sergeant; you're unusual, even for a member of that joke bank, the Mounted." **1956** EVANS *Mountain Dog* 35: "We'll leave that to Corporal Sparling of the Mounted to decide."

Mounted Police the Royal Canadian (formerly, North West) Mounted Police, *q.v.*

1878 *Sask.Herald* (Battleford, N.W.T.) 25 Aug. 1/2: Shoal Lake has been created the headquarters of the Mounted Police for that district, instead of Pelly, the ancient capital. **1955** BIRNEY *Long Table* 194: The next month, when the Mounted Police tried to "skim the Reds off a camp" in Saskatoon, there was a battle whose fame had already reached a self-occupied Toronto. . . . **1963** *Calgary Herald* 4 Oct. 48/4: An old Mounted Police stable may also be seen from the

Mounted Policeman a member of the Royal Canadian (formerly, North West) Mounted Police, *q.v.* See also **horseman** (def. 2), **Mountie, M.P., redcoat** (def. 2), **redjacket, scarlet coat, yellowlegs**, and **yellow stripe**.

1900 LONDON *Son of Wolf* 113: The door opened, and a mounted policeman of the Northwest Territory entered, followed by two half-breed dog-drivers. **1963** SYMONS *Many Trails* 25: [There were] a few Mounted Policemen and some half-breed horse breakers. . . .

Mounted Rifles *Hist.* a name proposed for the force known as the North West Mounted Police, *q.v.*, now the Royal Canadian Mounted Police.

1963 *Globe and Mail* (Toronto) 26 Aprl 7/5: But the United States received news of the proposed "Mounted Rifles" with alarm.

Mountie or **mountie** ['maunti] *n. Informal* See **Mounted Policeman**.

1914 *Eye Opener* (Calgary) 12 Dec. 3/4: Ketchen, the Mountie, not having had to saw his own wood, was easily placated. **1936** MACKENZIE *Living Rough* 202: There is some talk of the mounties stopping all the stiffs from riding the freights. **1964** *Kingston Whig-Standard* (Ont.) 10 Nov. 3/2: There's some talk of putting the Mounties on the case. **1966** *Ibid.* 29 July 6/8: They are not allowed to take it back on the reservation and if they do go into the woods, the mounties charge them for drinking in a public place.

mourriac *n.* See **moyaque**.

mouse *n. Obs.* See **moose**.

mouse ear the soft, feltlike bud of the pussy willow.

1910 MCCLUNG *Second Chance* 327: Mouse ears came out on the willows that bordered the river, and a bunch of them was proudly carried to Libby Anne. . . .

mouth comb in a fire-drill, the socket held in the mouth and accommodating the vertical spindle. See picture at **fireboard**.

1943 MILLER *Lone Woodsman* 188: Out of his fire bag Dan took the Ojibway socket with the mouth comb, a thong with grip sticks on its ends, his drill, fire board and curls of yellow birch mixed with shredded cedar bark.

mouture *n. French, Hist.* See quote. See also 1815 quote at **moulin banal**.

1808 (1809) GRAY *Letters* 347: They are to perform certain annual services to their lord, and they must carry to his mill all the corn which they wish to have ground, of which he retains a fourteenth part, as *mouture,* or miller's fee.

mowi(t)ch ['mowitʃ] *n.* [< Chinook *mow-wich;* cf. Nootka *muwich*] *B.C.* **1** a deer. Also spelled *mowitz.*

c1846 (1849) ROSS *Adventures* 346: Small deer . . . Wow-wich [sic] **1869** *Mainland Guardian* (New Westminster, B.C.) 22 Sep. 3/2: The deer made violent struggles for liberty, and the accused and a tillicum being near, they fired and shot the deer, thus enabling Mr. Herring to take the "mowitch" into his boat. **1915** CUMMING *Skookum Chuck* 36: Some times he would be hunting mowich (deer), or driving off the coyotes. **1964** *Penticton Herald* (B.C.) 17 Sep. 1/5: [Headline] Mowich on Road Cause of Mishap.

2 the flesh of the deer used as food.
1958 TERRY *Chilcotin* 38: . . . twelve hours a day in the saddle, mowitch and bannock to eat, a makeshift tent and blanketless bed. . . . **1963** SYMONS *Many Trails* 83: . . . the good breakfast of fried mowitch and bannock [was] being cooked by Henry's klootch.

mowya ['maujə] *n.* [< Algonk.: Cree *mowja*] *North* wet snow.
1939 (1951) TWEEDSMUIR *Hudson's Bay Trader* 96: There is the soft mowya that clogs the runners of your sledge and wears down men and dogs. **1942** *Beaver* Dec. 36/1: . . . he was forced to turn back on account of the *mowja* (deep snow).

moyaque ['mɔiak *or* 'mojak] *n.* [< Cdn F < Algonk.: Micmac *mooe-ak* sea duck] See 1956 quote. See also **muniack**. Various spellings.
1760 PICHON *Cape Breton* 103: The coast round these islands swarms . . . with all sorts of wild fowl, as bustards, crevans, moyaques. . . . **1854** *Trans.Lit.& Hist. Soc.Que.* IV 334: Among the sea-birds are Mermettes, Moyocks. . . . **1956** MCATEE *Folk-Names* 17: Common Eider [is also called] . . . mooyak, mojak (. . . Gulf of St. Lawrence) . . . moyac . . . traces back to moyaque, Denys, 1672. "Labr.," N.S., N.B., Que.). . . .

mozo-mish ['mozə,mɪʃ] *n.* [< Algonk.; cf. Ojibwa *monosomish* moon shrub] See 1912 quote. Also spelled *moose misse* and *mozemize.*
1861 *Cdn Naturalist* Apr. 126: Mozo-mish [is] very abundant, forming a large part of the underwood in rocky woods. **1912** (1913) HODGE & WHITE *Indians of Canada* 200: Indian mozemize, or moose misse.—The American mountain-ash or dogberry (*Sorbus americana*).

M.P. See **Mounted Policeman**.
1923 WALDO *Down Mackenzie* 104: It makes the resolute, debonair "M.P." excessively weary to read and to see what is done with his uniform and his professional activity by the tribe of ink-slingers and film-doctors. **1927** *Cdn N.W.Hist.Soc.Pubs.* I 2 71: The Stobart Company hired him in 1877, to build houses at Duck Lake, including the M.P. barracks and flour mill. **1957** *Arctic Spotter* Nov. 6/2: Unfortunately for my vision of gallant politicos risking their lives for their constituents, the Chief's next few sentences revealed the fact that "M.P." was his term for "Mounty."

M.P.P. or **MPP** Member of Provincial Parliament. See also **M.L.A.**
☞ *In modern use confined largely to Ontario.*
1826 *Colonial Advocate* (York [Toronto]) 9 Feb. 2/4: John J. Lafferty, Esq. M.P.P. was called to the chair. . . . **1855** (1965) HAMILTON *Cdn Quotations* 158/1: How many Canadian M.P.P.'s could obtain third class certificates from the most lenient of our educational examination boards? **1884** *Brandon Mail* (Man.) 27 Mar. 4/3: Instead of their proposing to take bribes for the sake of drawing out bribers, we are almost confident it will be proved the M.P.P.'s were willing to be bribed, if they only saw the cash coming. **1918** JENKINS *Cdn Civics* ii: A member of a provincial legislature employs the form M.P.P. (that is, Member of Provincial "Parliament"). It may be observed that we do not now apply the term "parliament" to a provincial legislature. Therefore, it would be more correct, if we wrote M.L. (Member of the Legislature) or M.P.L. (Member of Provincial Legislature), but these forms have never been adopted. **1964** *Star Wkly* 12 Dec. 7/2: An MPP represents 3,566 people in P.E.I., while in Nova Scotia, he speaks for 17,720.

muca-much *n.* See **muck-a-muck**.

Muche Manito(u) See **Matchi Manitou**.

muck *n.* **1** *Placer Mining* topsoil that must be removed before mining can begin; also, pay dirt (def. 1).
1897 LEONARD *Klondike* 180: The top "muck" . . . is, when thawed out, about two-thirds water and one-third sediment. **1959** *Ont.Mines Accident Rep.* July 1: The searchers moved up to the 600 level and located his body on the rim of the pass beneath about a foot of fine muck.
2 *Hardrock Mining* broken rock, either ore or waste.
1960 *Sun* (Vancouver) 4 June 2/4: . . . 150 vertical feet of muck in the stope above had settled gently down over the mule, the string of cars—and our only way out. **1963** *Western Miner* July 13/1: Nels claimed that in his heyday he could lift a full shovel of muck with one hand, face the muck car, swing the loaded shovel between his legs, throw the muck up over his hard hat and land it in the car.

muck (out or **up)** *v.* **1** *Placer Mining* remove muck (def. 1).
1910 SERVICE *Trail of '98* 238: "One . . . got a job . . . down de shaft muckin' up and fillin' de buckets." **1957** GOWLAND *Return to Canada* 124: It seems that but few of those who mucked, sweated, froze, and starved for the yellow stuff ever had any lasting benefit from it.
2 *Hardrock Mining* remove muck (def. 2).
1959 *Ottawa Citizen* 15 Jan. 21/4: The miners . . . who contracted to work the mine were "mucking" (taking out blasted rock) from the floor of the vertical shaft. . . . **1964** *North* May-June 7: Mining in the pits will constitute benching of the ore-body in 35-foot lifts by drilling large diameter down-holes and blasting, then mucking with two 3½ cu.yd. shovels. . . .

muckaluck, muckluck, etc. *n.* See **mukluk** (def. 1).

muck-a-muck ['mʌkə,mʌk] *n.* [< Chinook Jargon] *Pacific Coast and Northwest* food. See also **hyiu muckamuck** and **makmak**.
1863 *Norfolk Reformer* (Simcoe, C.W.) 8 Jan. 3/1: On arriving back as far as Lytton or Lilooet, there was employment for all those who wished to avail themselves of the opportunity, at the rate of $40 per month, and "muca muc," as the Indian name implies. **1895** SOMERSET *Muskeg* 167: "Yes," they would say, "yes, all kinds of muck-a-muck at McLeod; jam, cake, biscuits—yes, ev'ything—you see by-'n-by; plenty plenty muck-a-muck, you see." **1915** CUMMING *Skookum Chuck* 18: Perhaps he had bought all his luxuries on jaw-bone from one store while he paid cash for his muck-a-muck in another. **1963** SYMONS *Many Trails* 74: "Hi-ya tillicum," he greeted me. "You plenty muck-a-muck stop."

muck-a-muck ['mʌkə,mʌk] *v.* [Chinook Jargon] *Pacific Coast* eat. See also **make muck-muck**.
[*c*1846 (1849) ROSS *Adventures* 347: Eat . . . mack-amack] **1927** PHILIP *Painted Cliff* 153: "I hate to bother you," apologized Foghorn from the doorway, "but there's a feller here wants to muck-a-muck."

mucker ['mʌkɚ] *n. Mining* **1** a person who removes muck (def. 1 or 2). See also **mud-rat**.

1900 *Lardeau Eagle* 28 Mar. 1/4: ... the muckers, ore sorters, rawhiders, four-horse teamsters, office men are all hard at work. 1960 McNAMEE *Florencia Bay* 32: Harry was a mucker from a gold-mine at Wells with a disinclination to stay underground when the grass was green.

2 See **mucking-machine.**
1956 *Ont. Dept of Mines, Fatal Accidents* Apr. 2: The mucker was hoisted clear of the bottom timber by 10 feet, to where it might normally have been anchored, when it suddenly fell down the 32 feet to the bottom.

mucking contest a contest in which miners compete in shovelling a measured quantity of broken rock (usually a ton) into a mine car in the shortest time. See **muck,** *n.* (def. 2).
1958 *Nelson Dly News* (B.C.) 2 Sep. 2/6: Races, horseshoe pitching, a mucking contest, a ball game and many other side-shows [took place].

mucking-machine *n. Hardrock Mining* a mechanical shovel for removing muck (def. 2).
1956 *Ont. Dept of Mines, Fatal Accidents* Feb. 4: Three cars of muck and a mucking machine had been left at the station by the two miners on that level, who had returned to the drift face. 1964 CRATE *Hardrock Mining* 4: Times are changing, and a mucker to-day is the operator not of a muckstick, but of a mechanical shovel known as a *mucking-machine.*

muckluck, mucluc(k) *n.* See **mukluk.**

muckmuck *n.v.* See **muck-a-muck.**

muck-stick *n. Hardrock Mining, Slang* a shovel.
1958 *Northern Miner* 27 Nov. 33/3: Dan, you move more dirt with a mid-iron than you ever did with a muck stick. 1963 *B.C. Digest* July-Aug. 46/2: The last I saw of him he was drunk and on a muck stick (shovel).

mud *n. North* muskeg, bog mud, etc. applied to the runners of a dog-sled so that it freezes into a smooth-sliding surface. See also **mud,** *v.* (def. 2), **mud runner,** and **shoeing.**
1942 *Beaver* Mar. 44/1: For generations the Eskimos have used "mud" as a shoeing on the runners of their sleds. North mud is muskeg or decayed mosses and vegetable matter. 1946 MANNING *Igloo* 63: "It's hardly worth while patching the [komatik] mud since it's so mild."

mud *v.* **1** †chink the exterior walls of a house or cabin with mud. See also **mudding.** Also *mud up.*
1914 DOUGLAS *Lands Forlorn* 151: It was thoroughly well mudded inside and out, and the inside was papered with the leaves of illustrated magazines that Hornby had given us. 1930 ROLYAT *Fort Garry* 199: "Better they was muddin up their 'ouses afore a frost. Las' year they leaves them unmudded and nigh froze."

2 *North* apply mud to dog-sled runners. See also **earth** and **mud,** *n.*
[1852 RICHARDSON *Arctic Exped.* 289: He first coated the runners with earth or clay tempered with water, coat after coat freezing as rapidly as it was applied.] 1942 *Beaver* Mar. 44/2: Many trips to the mudhole are necessary before the sled is completed, and when several men are mudding together, the first one finished will often help his companion.

mud bomber an aircraft fitted out to carry and drop chemical mud on forest fires to extinguish them.
1964 *Calgary Herald* 11 July 19/4: The B.C. Forest Service's mud bombers and helicopters got their first workout when they controlled a fire started by lightning at high altitude near Yahk Thursday night.

mud box *Placer Mining* See quote.
1942 WIEDERMANN *Cheechako* 211: Every miner has a mud box in his cabin. This is a watertight wooden box about six feet square and about two feet high, which is filled with warm water with which to pan out the pay dirt. The mud box has a twofold purpose. It not only enables a miner to pan out pay dirt in order to see how the gold is running, but it also enables him to get sufficient gold to purchase provisions and supplies on a trip to Dawson, without having to wait for the regular spring clean-up.

mud-cabin *n. Obs.* See quote.
1829 MACTAGGART *Three Years* II 243: It is a singular fact, too, with the Irish, that if they can get a *mud-cabin,* they will never think of building one of wood.

mud chimney a primitive chimney made of rolls or bricks of mud, usually reinforced with sticks. Cp. **clay cat.**
1924 *Beaver* Mar. 215: ... the dwellings were in a most dilapidated state—mud chimneys down. ...

mudded sled *North* a sled of which the runners have been treated with mud, *q.v.*
1942 *Beaver* Mar. 55/2: Natives have now finished using mudded sleds.

mudding *n.* the chinking of walls with mud. See also **mud,** *v.* (def. 1).
1896 RUSSELL *Far North* 2: The autumnal "mudding" was poorly done, and the second wash with muddy water, which is usually applied after the frosts have come, failed to fill the cracks.

muddy *v.* See **mud,** *v.* (def. 1).
1930 ROLYAT *Fort Garry* 233: Early in the autumn Don had "muddied" well the walls outside. Later he had banked them up with snow evenly.

Muddy (Little) York *Hist.* Toronto, Ont., formerly York, Upper Canada. See also **Little York** and note.
1853 *Hamilton Gaz.* (C.W.) 15 Sep. 2/7: At a recent sederunt of the civic daddies of *Muddy Little York,* this magnificent luminary of the North American continent thus expressed himself: "I look upon Editors as a contemptible set, and do not care for any of them." 1958 *Weekend Mag.* 21 June 12/1: His family emigrated to Toronto, known then as "muddy York," about 1818, where his father set up as a wine merchant. 1965 *Kingston Whig-Standard* (Ont.) 9 Jan. 9/8: ... he wrested the leadership of the old Family Compact from the Anglican Tories of muddy York and made it into the Conservative party.

Muddy (Little) Yorker *Obs.* a native or resident of Muddy (Little) York, *q.v.*
1854 *Hamilton Gaz.* (C.W.) 23 Mar. 3/1: Knowing the special interest you take in the doings of us "Muddy Little Yorkers," I hasten to certiorate you of a "passage at arms" which occurred here this day.

mudfall *n.* a mudslide.
1962 DICKIE *Great Golden Plain* 220: It took them five days to make sixteen miles, through mudfalls and up perpendicular rock points.

mud-fish *n. Esp.Nfld, Obs.* See 1819 quote. Cp. **green fish.**

1762 (1869) BROWN *Cape Breton* 345: We have nothing left us but a precarious right, subject to cavil and insult, to the morue verte, or mud-fish, a commodity not marketable in Portugal, Spain, or Italy, but only fit for our own home consumption. **1808** *Quebec Gaz.* 30 June 1/2: For Sale . . . Dried Cod Fish at 15s. per Cwt. Mud ditto, 10s. per do. **1819** ANSPACH *Hist.Nfld* 441: It frequently happens that some of the fish, taken towards the close of the fishing season, is not fit to be put on-board for exportation . . . It is called mud-fish; though this appellation belongs more properly to another kind, expressly prepared for the English market, where it is generally preferred. This last is split not quite open, but only down to the navel; it is then salted and washed in the usual manner, and barrelled up in a strong pickle of salt boiled in water. **1832** MCGREGOR *Brit.Amer.* I 232: . . . mud-fish, or green fish, is generally understood to be cod-fish, either wholly or partially split and pickled.

mud-flat† *n.* See **flat** (def. 1).

1922 FOOTNER *Huntress* 134: The only breaks in the endless panorama of cut-banks, mud-flats, willows, and grass were occasional little inlets, gay with aquatic flowers. **1959** *Time* (Cdn ed.) 23 Feb. 10/3: Built on mud flats in the Mackenzie River delta, Aklavik was a quagmire in summer, had no water supply, no airfield or much possibility of building one.

mud pilot *North, Slang* See quote.

1934 GODSELL *Arctic Trader* 265: The captains of the whaling vessels always took care to keep between the ice pack and the shore, and for this reason were often contemptuously referred to as "Mud-Pilots."

mudpup ['mʌd,pʌp] *n.* [< Am.E *mudpup* a kind of salamander] *B.C., Slang, Hist.* a young Englishman sent out to Western Canada to learn farming. See 1957 quote.

1955 *Maclean's* 2 Apr. 80/1: When the war [W.W. I] started the Mud Pups joined up to the last man and the bachelor population of Duncan vanished overnight. **1957** BARRATT *Coronets* 8: Mudpups were unwanted younger sons whose parents gave a premium to have them taught farming. **1958** TERRY *Chilcotin* 29: Charlie Steeman came to Riske Creek from Anahim. J. J. Barker, ranchhand. E. J. Stanger, mud pup.

mud-rat *n. Placer Mining, Slang, Obs.* See **mucker** (def. 1).

1910 SERVICE *Trail of '98* 238: Turning the windlass over the shaft was a little tough mud-rat, who excited in me the liveliest sense of aversion.

mud room in a school or house, a room just inside the entry where one removes and leaves overshoes and rubbers, to avoid tracking mud and snow through the building.

1964 *Calgary Herald* 13 Feb. 16/5: Mrs. Turner suggested one of the most common places of theft occurrences in the school is in the mud room.

mud runner *North* a dog-sled runner coated with mud, *q.v.*

1938 *Beaver* Mar. 9: At noon a brief halt is made for icing the runners of the sled. In the coldest weather "mud runners" are used. **1963** *Chatelaine* Apr. 57/2: He's the one who mixes up a bucket of mud that he uses to repair the six-inch frozen-mud runners which still make the best shoeing for a dog sled in wintertime.

mud shoe *West* See quote.

1954 *Ghost Pine* 119: A chap who was boarding at our

place while breaking a particularly wet piece of ground, made oval shaped hardwood mud shoes which he fastened to his horses' shoes to keep the horses from miring in soft ground.

muffin *n.* [< *muffin* small biscuit or cake] *Slang, Hist.* See 1865 quote.

1854 (1956) HENDERSON *Life of Oliphant* 50: I had a charming muffin yesterday. She is engaged to be married, so don't be alarmed. **1865** RUSSELL *Canada* 131: The fair Canadians may have been too kind in accepting the name and position of "muffins" from the young Britishry; but the latter cannot say that they have suffered much in consequence. A muffin is simply a lady who sits beside the male occupant of the sleigh— *sola cum solo.* **1873** FITZGERALD *Wickets* 118: We were then told that the term "muffin" is not in good odour at the present day; that no lady will admit she ever was or ever could be a muffin. . . . No lady owned to ever having been a muffin, at least not until she knew her young man well enough to tell him so. **1965** STEVENS *Incompleat Canadian* 202: . . . at the beginning of the winter season each young man chose "a muffin" —a "steady date" for the season—an arrangement terminated by mutual consent in the following spring. . . .

muffinage *n. Obs.* being partnered with a muffin, *q.v.*

1865 RUSSELL *Canada* 58: It may end in an introduction, and a condition of "muffinage." And what that is we must tell you hereafter.

muffle ['mʌfəl] *n.* [< F *mufle* muzzle] See **moose nose.** See also **moufle.**

1791 (1937) CAMPBELL *Travels* 97: I bought 20 lb. of Moose meat, and a Muffle, as it is called. . . . **1873** (1952) *Beaver* June 30/2: A banquet of baronial proportions was decreed—Buffalo tongues and humps . . . the muf[f]les of Moose-deer, the tails of Beaver. . . . **1958** WILSON *Treasury* 158: Muffle—the great proboscis of the lordly moose appearing as an article of food is terrifying to say the least.

mug-up† ['mʌg,ʌp] *n.* [< Brit. dial.] *Esp.North* a hot drink, usually accompanied by a light meal or snack.

1933 MERRICK *True North* 233: Back at the tent we had a mugup, lashed up and said good-bye to the Indians. **1936** *Cdn Geog.Jnl* XII 61/1: They would stop for a "mugup" of tea every little while. **1962** *B.C.Digest* Oct. 60/2: "I had to cook—270 meals in addition to the between meal "mug-ups."

mug-up† ['mʌg,ʌp] *v.* [< n.] *Esp.North* have a mug-up, *q.v.*

1936 STRINGER *Wife-Traders* 152: They fell into the habit of stopping more often to "mug-up" along the trail. **1950** HAMBLETON *Abitibi* 94: René was just "mugging up" when the shaggy terrier leaped from the bush, landed on his shoulders and sent the blackened tea pail flying.

mukduk *n.* See **muktuk.**

mukluk ['mʌklʌk] *n.* [< West Esk. *muklok* large, or bearded, seal] **1** a type of warm knee-high boot worn by the Eskimos and Indians of the Northwest Territories and the Yukon. See 1931 and 1958 quotes. See also **Eskimo boot** and **snowshoe** (def. 3). Cp. **kamik.** Also spelled *mackaluck, mucklu(c)k.*

1898 *Medicine Hat News* (Alta) 8 Dec. 5/4: Her parkee, made of Caribou, it is a lovely fit./And she's all right from muck-a-luck unto her dainty mit./This lovely Klooch is fond of Hooch, and makes it very well. 1909 SERVICE *Cheechako* 45: In cabin or dance-hall, camp or dive, mucklucks or patent shoon;/On velvet tundra or virgin peak, by glacier, drift or draw. . . . 1924 DORRANCE *Never Fire First* 42: She still wore her trail *muckluks* of fur, clumsy looking as a squaw's sacking. . . . 1931 LEBOURDAIS *Northward* 62: For cold, dry weather the best mukluks have reindeer skin tops; for wet weather they are, both tops and soles, of sealskin, tanned especially so that they will turn water. 1947 GILLHAM *Raw North* 93: These mukluks are usually of seal soles, and uppers of the same material in the summer months, or moose, caribou, or even canvas for winter. 1958 *Edmonton Jnl* 24 June 3 10/8: Sealskin mukluks, or boots, or sometimes the Indian's mukluks of duffel with moosehide soles, complete the ensemble. 1966 *Globe and Mail* (Toronto) 24 Jan. 17/8: I went back into the house [and] donned my hunting pants, Eskimo mukluks (with handy drawstrings) and a sweater.

Mukluks

2 any of several kinds of winter footwear resembling this original boot, such as those worn by Canadian soldiers on winter exercises and those styled by manufacturers for city wear.

1961 *Canada Month* Dec. 29/3: [Caption] Bank clerk Jean Sauve, like most Whitehorse folk, finds nothing beats native parka and mukluks for warmth. 1964 *Star Wkly* 5 Dec. 36/1: The group set out, clad in . . . nylon wind pants, mukluks, light parkas and camouflage suits. 1966 *Kingston Whig-Standard* (Ont.) 27 Apr. 26/1: . . . the Canadians' [soldiers'] mukluks and sleeping bags were superior to anything in use. The mukluk, a rubber-soled boot with a calf-high outer nylon cover, has a thick woollen inner boot that keeps feet warm in the coldest of weather.

3 *Figurative use.*

1963 *Globe and Mail* (Toronto) 9 Mar. 8/4: Edmontonians finally have an answer to Calgary's Stampede. It is called Muk-Luk Mardi Gras. 1964 *Calgary Herald* 20 Feb. 5/2: Organizers couldn't get a mukluk in the door to form branches or national groups.

mukluked ['mʌk,lʌkt] *adj.* [< n.] shod in mukluks (def. 1).

1910 LONDON *Burning Daylight* 30: He was no more sober than the crowd above which he now towered—a wild crowd, uncouthly garmented, every foot moccasined or muc-lucked, with mittens dangling down from necks. . . .

muktuk ['mʌktʌk] *n.* [< Esk. *maktak*] *Arctic* See

blackskin. Also spelled *maktak*, *mukduk*.
[1836 HUISH *Last Voyage* 701: Skin of a whale Mak tuk.] 1909 CAMERON *New North* 220: The wedding breakfast consisted of seal-meat, frozen rotten fish, and muktuk (whale-meat). 1940 *Beaver* Mar. 25/2: All were chewing *muktuk*—the outer protective skin of the whale—with great enjoyment. 1942 *Ibid.* Mar. 7/1: The protective "cork" or outer covering of the whale, whether it is bowhead, white whale or narwhal, is highly prized and regarded as a delicacy by the Eskimo. This muktuk is eaten raw or cooked and has the flavour characteristic of shell fish. 1966 *Star Wkly* 12 Mar. 10/1: The Eskimos love muktuk and eat it raw. It's rather rubbery but doesn't taste bad at all—a bit like hazel nut.

mule deer† the Rocky Mountain mule deer, *Odocoileus hemionus hemionus.* See also **jumper**[1] (def. 2), **jumping deer** (def. 2) and **muley.**
1892 (1908) DAWSON & SUTHERLAND *Geography* 30: The best known of the larger land animals of Canada . . . are . . . mule-deer, in the Rocky Mountain region only. . . . 1966 *Globe and Mail* (Toronto) 7 May 41/2: At the same time a count in March indicated an average of 32 surviving calf elk a 100 cows, 48 mule deer fawns a 100 does and 40 whitetail fawns a 100 does.

mule scraper See **scraper.**

mule-skinner† *n. Esp.West, Hist.* a mule-team driver. See also **skinner** (def. 1).
1889 MACLEAN *Indians* 198: There are four different occupations in the country the men engage in, which are called bull-whackers and mule-skinners, applied to freighters who drive oxen or mules, broncho-busters and cow-punchers. 1962 FRY *Ranch on the Cariboo* 160: I'd the repertoire of a mule-skinner, developed behind a wide variety of knotheaded horses.

mule trail a trail used by pack-animals.
1859 *Brit.Colonist* (Victoria) 29 Jan. 1/4: A good wagon road to Fort Yale, and a mule trail thence equal to the best in California, and which can be kept open at all seasons, can be made at a moderate expense.

mule train† a train of mules used for packing goods.
1859 *Brit.Colonist* (Victoria) 21 Oct. 3/1: Goods are reported scarce on the Upper Fraser; and mule-trains eagerly looked for by the hardy miners who anxiously desire to lay in a supply of provisions for the winter. 1957 *Beaver* Spring 44/2: A good mule could cover the distance from Yale to Quesnel in a month, having leapt like a mountain goat through the treacherous Fraser Canyon carrying a 250-lb load—at $1.00 a lb.— and most "mule trains" made money.

muley ['mjuli] *n. B.C., Slang* See **mule deer.**
1959 *Alaska Sportsman* Aug. 16/3: She was carrying two beautiful goat robes and the antlers, cape and hams of a giant mulie. 1964 *B.C.Digest* Oct. 16/1: The big muley buck had spent the last two days in the same draw, coming out only at night.

mulligan ['mʌləgən] *n.* [prob. < the name *Mulligan*] a stew of meat, or sometimes fish, and vegetables.
1904 *Yukon Midnight Sun* (Dawson) 10 Jan. 3/4: All the roadhouses served big Christmas dinners and most of them made a mulligan, giving a free lunch and warm welcome to all. 1955 HOBSON *Nothing Too Good* 138: "That's what's good for me, a great beeg vegetable mulligan with feesh in it." 1963 *Sun* (Vancouver) 31 Aug. 19/1: Fish and game mulligan [will be served] today.

mulligan-mixer *n. Esp.Lumbering, Slang* a camp cook, especially in a logging camp.
1925 *Cdn Labor Advocate* (Vancouver) 21 Aug. 6/5: After several days existing out of cans we got a professional "mulligan mixer," who hailed from the sound of "Bow Bells," and who had all the Whitechapel disgust of cleanliness.

mulligan wagon *Esp.Lumbering, Slang* See **crummy.**

mullnet(te) *n.* See **mulnette.**

mulnette or **mulnet** ['mʌl,nɛt] *n.* [origin uncertain] *Lumbering, Hist.* a kind of raft made of square timbers.
1859 (1956) WATERS *Mr.Vessey* 56: The piles of timber which they land on the shore above the influence of the tide they call mulnettes. **1896** GOURLAY *Hist.Ottawa* 116: Tows, cribs, mullnets and loose in single [pieces], almost all forms were used to get the pieces floated to form the rafts for market.

mulnette ['mʌl,nɛt] *v. Lumbering, Hist.* make or build into a mulnette.
1902 (1957) GUILLET *Valley of the Trent* 268: Being at the time engaged in the various branches of the timber trade, our practice was to mulnette the square pine, load it, all that it would float, with pipe staves . . . take all down the river and sell it at the Trent. . . .

multiple-member constituency in certain provinces, a riding in which more than one parliamentary or legislative seat exists.
1964 *Calgary Herald* 23 Apr. 1/8: The CCF picked up two seats on the completion of counting in the multiple-member Saskatoon constituency.

muniack ['muni,æk] *n.* [< Algonk.] See **moyaque.**
1853 *Trans.Lit.& Hist.Soc.Que.* IV 205: A duck, called the muniack, remains about the shore [of Anticosti Is.] all the winter. **1956** MCATEE *Folk-Names* 17: Common Eider [is also called] . . . moignac (Que. . . .) . . . mouniac (Que.); mourriac (Nfld., "Labr.") . . . moyak ("Labr.").

municipal council *Hist.* the governing body of a municipality such as a township or district.
1842 *Bytown* [Ottawa] *Gaz.* 29 Dec. 2/3: We may here promise, that we at first viewed the establishment of these local Municipal Councils, (or what some individuals have termed "Rural Parliaments") with no small degree of doubtfulness as to their well working in this country, where the population is composed of such materials as we have. **1882** *Brandon Dly Mail* (Man.) 28 Dec. 2/1: The idea of enacting a law enpowering municipal councils to levy rates in aid of free public libraries is not a new one. **1958** ATKINSON *History of Penticton* 40: Mr. Barnes was a member of the Municipal Council in 1909.

municipal district *Alta and Territories* a large rural municipality. See also **MD.** Cp. **rural municipality.**
1841 *Montreal Transcript* 24 Dec. 2/2: The same Gazette also contained a proclamation regulating the Election of certain Councillors in the Municipal Districts of Quebec . . . and Sydenham. **1864** *Nor'Wester* (R.R.S.) 13 Apr. 2/5: A circle with a radius of 50 miles from Fort Garry, or, to express it in other words, a circle of one hundred miles in diameter, with that Fort for a centre, correctly enough describes the Municipal District of Assiniboia. **1945** BROWN *Cdn Democracy* 134: Municipal districts cover the more thickly populated parts of the Province [Alta] and in size they average about thirty townships. **1964** *Calgary Herald* 10 Mar. 21/3: A weather modification plebiscite will be held in the Municipal District of Kneehill if the MD solicitor approves a proposed contract. . . .

municipality *n. N.S.* a division of rural government corresponding to a county.
1948 ANGLIN *Canada Unlimited* 66: In the first place, each province is divided into large rural municipalities. These are known as . . . counties in Ontario (subdivided into townships); counties in Quebec (divided into townships and parishes); counties (and parishes) in New Brunswick; and in Nova Scotia simply municipalities.

Munito *n.* See **Manitou.**

munyasse *n.* See **mooneas.**

muscallunge *n.* See **muskellunge.**

muscle mud See **mussel mud.**

muscovadoey [,mʌskə'vadoi] *adj. Eastern Townships* (*Que.*) of snow, having the consistency of muscovado, or raw sugar.
1923 WILLIAMS *Spinning Wheels* 60: The snow itself is of the coarse consistency known as moscovadoey.

mush [mʌʃ] *v.* [< Cdn F *marche (donc)!* q.v.] *Esp.North* **1** *imper.* move ahead! go on! (a command to sled dogs to advance). See also **march,** *v.* (def. 2a) and **marche.** Also *mush on.*
1897 *Medicine Hat News* (Alta) 30 Sep. 7/4: It is laughable to hear the driver yell, "Mush, Mush," at them, and if they don't get in and dig you generally hear something stronger. **1913** WILLIAMS *Wilderness Trail* 161: "Mistisi, mush on, you fiend, or I'll break your neck." **1958** *In Flight* Fall 1/3: Dog sled racing is a sport which is as Canadian as the command "Mush!" **1963** SYMONS *Many Trails* 198: And hurry! Hurry! Before it is too late—mush, mush on—the whip cracks hysterically.

2 a. travel by or with a dog-sled.
1862 (1942) KENNICOTT *Journal* 130: "My dogs are *dogs!* and we will *mouche* very likely after all." **1912** POCOCK *Man in the Open* 8: He tucked me up warm on the komatik, he hitched up the huskies, and mushed, way up the tickle, and through the soft bush snow, and at sunup we made his winter tilt on Torngak Creek. **1966** *Kingston Whig-Standard* (Ont.) 25 Feb. 12/1: There hasn't been so much excitement over sled-dogs in the north since Leonard Sepala mushed through the land of the midnight sun. . . .

b. travel on foot or on snowshoes. See also **march,** *v.* (def. 1), **musher** (def. 1), and **mushing** (def. 1). Also *mush on.*
1898 (1930) ROBERTSON *Yukon Memories* 210: You think all the while you are nearing the top, and "mush on," like viewing a ship at sea. **1921** MARSHALL *Snowshoe Trail* 244: Then she lighted a candle and put on her snowshoes. She mushed across the little space of snow to the men's cabin. **1936** MACKENZIE *Living Rough* 41: They told me of the mobs that used to mush over the Chilkoot Pass to the Yukon and then on down to the Klondike. **1958** *Alaska Sportsman* Dec. 16/3: Here [B.C.] a moose mushed along leaving a plowed record of his passing. **1966** *Globe and Mail* (Toronto) 24 Jan. 17/8: I then struck out to mush to the nearest bus stop.

c. of dogs, pull a sled under the command of a driver.
1898 (1936) *Western Miner* Mar. 22/2: The holder must be ready to "mush" behind the crack of the driver's whip. **1913** WILLIAMS *Wilderness Trail* 163: . . . he crushed back all the battle-fury in his pounding heart, and mushed as he had never mushed before. **1963** *Globe and Mail* (Toronto) 11 May 20/5: Siberian huskies from nearby Stittsville mushed in hauling authentic sourdough Mr. Yukon in a red flannel shirt and mountain-sheep vest.

d. mush it, travel by dog-sled; drive a dog team.
1923 *Beaver* Dec. 90/1: I have mushed it in the far north at 40 degrees below.

3 a. drive (dogs); urge (a dog team) on by whip and command. See also **march,** *v.* (def. 2b).
1900 LONDON *Son of Wolf* 19: Blindly . . . she took the gee-pole and whip, and "mushed" the dogs out on the trail. **1954** *North Star* (Yellowknife) Apr. 2/2: A James Oliver Curwood thriller, recently shown at our local theatre, "Back to God's Country", has its points as entertainment but shows drivers mushing dog teams in matters of hours between northern points that are from hundreds to thousands of miles apart. **1965** *Kingston Whig-Standard* (Ont.) 8 Feb. 7/5: Another time he mushed a team of wolves down Broadway in New York.

b. transport by dog-sled.
1953 SWANSON *Haywire Hooker* 58: By the lore of that Northland's legend they "cremated Sam McGee":/But the man who mushed that frozen corpse I'm a-telling you boys was me. **1962** *B.C. Digest* Oct. 29/1: The old prospectors had already begun to mush their outfits by dog sleds. . . .

4 *Slang* See **mush on** (def. 3).

mush [mʌʃ] *n.* [< *v.*] *Esp. North* a trip or journey, especially by dog-sled. Cp. **march,** *n.*
1910 SERVICE *Trail of '98* 341: I was still weak from my illness and my long mush had wearied me. . . . **1924** DORRANCE *Never Fire First* 53: "You see, when Oliver gets back from this inconsiderate mush of his, I'll become quite useless as your handmaiden. . . ." **1965** *Kingston Whig-Standard* (Ont.) 8 Feb. 8/6: It's "Mush, Mush" time for Owner-driver Vern Zoschke and his Dogs.

musher ['mʌʃɚ] *n.* [< *mush,* v. + *-er*] *Esp. North*
1 a traveller on foot or snowshoe. See also **mush,** *v.* (def. 2b) and **mushing** (def. 1).
*c*1900 (1963) *Western Miner* Mar. 30/1:
Way up north there's a railroad,
That was built on a track of gold;
It followed the tracks of the mushers,
Where they grasped the rocks for a hold.
1921 MARSHALL *Snowshoe Trail* 212: A musher in soft wet snow can only go at a certain pace. Any attempt to quicken the pace results only in a fall. The shoe cannot be pushed ahead as when the snow is well-packed or crusted. It has to be deliberately lifted, putting the leg tendons to an unnatural strain. **1958** BERTON *Klondike* 16: The volunteer was no hardened musher, but a steamboat man named George Williams, who with an Indian companion set off on a terrifying journey.

2 See **dog-driver.**
1922 PRINGLE *Tillicums* 22: I was to go with a dog-driver or "musher" named Stewart. **1944** CLAY *Fur Thieves* 121: [He gave] a brief account of the mysterious mushers

on the lake, with their white dogs, and white clothes. **1965** *Kingston Whig-Standard* (Ont.) 8 Feb. 8/5: Vern Zoschke . . . topped a field of 11 "mushers" to win the Kingston Winter Carnival's dog sled racing competition. **1966** *Ibid.* 25 Feb. 12/1: . . . Paul Ben Kassi [is] the 53-year-old veteran musher from Old Crow [Y.T.].

mush-ice† *n. North* rotten ice. See also **rotten.** Cp. **mush snow.**
1900 LONDON *Son of Wolf* 165: Then he put Tom Dixon in charge of his mines . . . promised to be back before the first mush-ice ran, and took passage on an up-river steamer. **1935** MOWERY *Resurrection River* 270: In crossing a small upland river that morning they had broken through the rotten "mush ice" and lost their packs, guns, and almost their lives. **1940** FINNIE *Lure of North* 99: The Coppermine River began to freeze over and a ribbon of mush-ice spread out into the gulf. **1966** PATTERSON *Trail* 86: They came . . . poling and tracking against the slowly drifting mush ice of the fall. . . .

mushing ['mʌʃɪŋ] *n.* [< *mush,* v. + *-ing*] *North*
1 a. travelling on foot or snowshoe. See also **mush,** *v.* (def. 2b) and **musher** (def. 1).
1899 (1930) ROBERTSON *Yukon Memories* 114: Nevertheless there is a lingering feeling that the monotonous mushing along has not been devoid of its pleasures, even amidst petty annoyances of ill-kept houses. **1910** SERVICE *Trail of '98* 109: The air was clear and cold, ideal mushing weather, and already parties were beginning to struggle into Bennett.

b. mushing the trails, following a migratory pattern of life. Cp. **pitch,** *v.* (def. 1).
1923 BARBEAU *Indian Days* 161: Weaning the red man out of his inveterate habit of "mushing the trails" has become a settled policy, and the aid of the mounted police has been more than once invoked.

2 the practice or skill of driving dogs. See also **mush,** *v.* (def. 3a) and **musher** (def. 2).
1910 WHITE *Stampeder* 217: The strain . . . had been more wearisome than a day of Yukon mushing, but dinner and a bath refreshed him. **1938** SULLIVAN *Cycle of North* 58: Pinasse fumbled in the pocket of his capote, pulled out an envelope and . . . began to speak, his throat husky from mushing. **1966** *Kingston Whig-Standard* (Ont.) 25 Feb. 12/1: . . . Wilfred Charles is regarded as a sure-pop betting cinch to retain the mushing title. . . .

mush on 1 See **mush,** *v.* (def. 1). **2** See **mush,** *v.* (def. 2b). **3** *Slang* leave town; vamoose.
1899 *Klondike Nugget* (Dawson, Y.T.) 3 June 2/2: C. Smith didn't "mush on" when requested by the police to do so, and showed his objection to the introduction of the new order for keeping the sidewalks clear by using abusive language. **1910** SERVICE *Trail of '98* 112: "Mush on, there," he repeated truculently; "you're not wanted 'round here' Mush! Pretty darned smart." **1938** BLACK *Seventy years* 98: After his death it was easy to round up the members of his gang, who were either imprisoned or told to "Mush on!"

mushrat ['mʌʃ,ræt] *n.* [either a blend of *muskrat* and *musquash* or a dial. var. of *marsh rat,* q.v., influenced by these words] *East* **1** See **muskrat.**
1943 RADDALL *Pied Piper* 47: "An' I'm goin' to play hell with you, you game-poachin', fish-spearin', wood-stealin' ol' mushrat!" **1954** BRUCE *Channel Shore* 18: Stan was carrying on . . . talk of mushrats and rabbit-snaring. *Ibid.* 117: . . . Grant went on to talk a little answering Bill's questions about how it would be later on. November and the mushrat season open. . . .

2 *Slang, Derog., Obs.* See quote.
1901 CONNOR *Man from Glengarry* 19: For the Glengarry men [of the Ottawa Valley] who handled only square timber, despised the Murphy gang as sawlog-men; "log-rollers" or "mushrats" they called them, and hated them as Irish "Papishes" and French "Crapeaux."

mushratting ['mʌʃˌrætɪŋ] *n.* the hunting of muskrats. See also **mushrat**, *n.* and **ratting**.
1952 *Beaver* Mar. 43/1: Spring mush-ratting is followed by blueberry picking, and wild rice gathering.

mush snow a heavy wet snowfall; heavy, wet snow. Cp. **mush-ice**.
1917 CURWOOD *Barree* 231: It was the wanderer's intention to swing over into the country of the Great Slave, a good eight hundred miles to the north and west, before the mush snows came.

muskallunge *n.* See **muskellunge**.

muskamoot *n.* See **muskimoot**.

muskanongé(e) or **muskenonge** *n.* See **maskinonge**.

musk beaver *Obs.* See **muskrat** (def. 1).
1772 *Phil.Trans.Roy.Soc.* LXII 370: Musk-Beaver . . . Musquash . . . frequents the plains, builds a house like the beaver, brings forth from 5 to 7 young at a time, and feeds on poplars, willows, and grass. **1795** (1911) HEARNE *Journey* 380: Though I have before said, that the Musk beaver generally build their houses on the ice, it is not always the case.

musk-beef *n. Obs.* the flesh of the musk-ox used as food. See also **musk-bull meat**.
1857 MCDOUGALL *Voyage* 376: A substantial warm meal, composed of pea-soup, bread-dust, and a pound (each) of musk-beef, was made on the occasion, no second bidding was required to "fall to."

·musk buffalo *Obs.* See **musk-ox** (def. 1).
1791 (1889) MCKENZIE *Reminiscences* 36: Keep for me one of the small musk buffalo horns in its natural state. **1812** (1890) KEITH *Letters* 103: The musk buffaloe, although very short limbed, is comparatively swift, daring and dangerous.

musk-bull meat *Obs.* See **musk-beef**.
1852 RICHARDSON *Arctic Exped.* 297: He distributed among them the remains of the dried meat brought from Fort Simpson, and a quantity of musk-bull meat, which was too strong for his own men, but which the natives relished greatly.

musk cattle *Obs.* musk-oxen. See **musk-ox** (def. 1).
1896 WHITNEY *On Snow-Shoes* 263: Many years ago, they say, a woman strayed into the Barrens among the musk cattle, and eventually became one.

musk-cow *n. Obs.* a female musk-ox (def. 1).
1829 (1935) STRANG *Pioneers in Canada* 29: Having now entered on Hood's River . . . they got on tolerably well . . . the hunters ever and anon bringing in a deer [caribou] or musk-cow, which kept them above absolute want, though always on the brink of it. **1896** WHITNEY *On Snow-Shoes* 222: I had walked for some time when I realized that, other than going south, I had not the remotest idea in what precise direction I was travelling, or just where that musk-cow lay.

muskeg ['mʌskɛg] *n.* [< Algonk.; Cree *muskāk* swamp] **1** an organic bog which is a brown to black mixture of water and living and dead vegetation often covered with a carpet of sphagnum or other

mosses and often of considerable depth. See also **muskeg swamp** (def. 1), **pothole** (def. 4), and **sink-hole** (def. 1).
[**1775** (1951) *Sask. Jnls* 3 Sep. 6: We passed over one Carrying Place of 1/4 Mile called Muskake or swampy carrying Place, also lead Canoes over two falls.] **1806** (1897) COUES *New Light* I 287: We passed through three abominably ugly mashquegies, in which our horses were nearly knocked up. **1824** (1955) BLACK *Journal* 73: He saw no Tracks on that side & Le Prise from the other says he could not make out to walk at all between the Lake & the mountains being a Muskegue & much water. **1933** THOMPSON & EDGAR *Cdn Ry Development* 238: In summer this type of country becomes almost impassable; but when winter freezes the swamps and muskegs, and a layer of snow covers everything, progress proves much easier. **1964** *Beaver* Spring 33/1: The muskegs were stunted spruce, labrador tea, and reindeer moss.

2 terrain made up of or characterized by such bogs. See also **muskeg swamp** (def. 2).
1860 HIND *Red River Exped.* I 162: He was two days dragging his canoe through the Muskeg, which is here nine miles broad. **1880** GORDON *Mountain and Prairie* 231: To the north of the Fort a large extent of territory is covered by muskeg, swamp, lakelet and stream. **1961** *Edmonton Jnl* 5 Aug. 10/7: A group of CPR officials . . . attended the ceremonies in honor of the man who as managing director of the railway company helped push it through the rocks and muskeg of northern Ontario. . . .

3 the substance (humus, vegetation, etc.) of which such bogs consist. See also **muskeg soil**.
1884 *Brandon Blade* (Man.) 28 Feb. 3/2: There is not much farming land in this section of the line, but what there is is good, the remainder of the land is principally sand and muskeg, and also some fine timberlands. **1905** OUTRAM *Cdn Rockies* 290: The trail being spongy and full of muskeg we travelled in the water on the firm gravel of the lake-bottom for a full mile to its north-east corner. **1966** *Imperial Oil Rev.* June 8/1: . . . most of the muskeg in Canada started accumulating about 10,000 years ago, when the last glacier retreated.

4 loosely: **a.** *Prairies* See **pothole** (def. 3a).
1875 *Canadian Mthly* 372/1: His neighbour regards the prairie as smiling for the husbandman; its "muskegs" as offering the choicest food for his stock. **1953** MOWERY *Mounted Police* 125: Moving slowly, the [buffalo] were heading for a swamp country to the north where they could find green pasture in the muskeg flats.

b. a swamp or mud-hole.
1897 *Slocan Pioneer* (B.C.) 28 Aug. 3/2: The whole thing is a perfect gamble, there are no surface indications whatever, and the coarsest gold has been found in the most unlikely places, a good deal of it in black muck, under a muskeg. **1910** FRASER *Red Meekins* 84: These muskegs was all made by beavers dammin' up streams, so they dry out. **1942** RADDALL *His Majesty's Yankees* 35: To be sure we raise a few cattle in our small salt meadows and cut wild hay from the muskegs for our work oxen. . . .

5 *Figurative use.*
1934 (1965) HAMILTON *Cdn Quotations* 137/2: His mind is a muskeg of mediocrity. John MacNaughton, on a Canadian professor: Queen's Quarterly, 1934, 362. **1963** *Globe and Mail* (Toronto) 12 Jan. 17/3: Mrs.

Held's . . . lively prose makes the jargon and collocations of most social scientists and philosophers look like an intellectual muskeg.

Muskeg, the *n.* See **Muskeg Express** (def. 1).
1928 FREEMAN *Nearing North* 377: The only regular train over the Hudson Bay railway is a mixed freight and passenger, appropriately called "The Muskeg." **1938** *Beaver* Sep. 20/2: It's best not to count too much on "The Muskeg."

muskeg country terrain characterized by muskegs (def. 1).
1883 *Edmonton Bull.* 6 Jan. 1/2: He travelled from Lac la Biche to Fort McMurray overland through a timbered and muskeg country which is seldom penetrated by whitemen. **1919** FRASER *Bulldog Carney* 30: Toward evening the trail gradually swung to the east skirting muskeg country.

Muskeg Express (Limited) Special 1 the mixed train running on the Hudson Bay Railway, *q.v.* See also **Muskeg, the** and **muskeg railway** (def. 1).
1933 THOMPSON & EDGAR *Cdn Ry Development* 212: Sir William Whyte looking down from his office window on this proceeding used to frequently laugh over it, nevertheless the "Muskeg Limited," as the train became known, occupied its own peculiar place in Winnipeg transportation, and the nickname is worthy of preservation. *Ibid.* 304: The turn of the tide occurred in 1923 when the first 118 miles were rehabilitated, and a train, humorously dubbed "The Muskeg Special," including passenger and freight cars mixed, was run once a week over part of the line. **1952** MOWAT *People of Deer* 7: In its own good time, the Muskeg Express brought us out of the forests and within sight of the ice filled waters of Hudson Bay, and to the end of a journey.

2 the mixed train running on the muskeg railway (def. 2).
1934 GODSELL *Arctic Trader* 179: The "Muskeg Limited," a conglomeration of dirty red box-cars, flat-cars, and one very rickety old-fashioned coach with a caboose tacked on to the rear, at length backed protestingly into the station. **1943** *Beaver* Mar. 29/1: Then came the railway from Edmonton to Waterways, the "Muskeg Express" as it was sometimes called. **1962** ONSLOW *Bowler-Hatted Cowboy* 129: . . . I took the bus to Dawson Creek and caught the evening train to Edmonton. 'The muskeg Special' took me to Edmonton.

muskeg grass or **hay** a kind of swamp grass.
1896 WHITNEY *On Snow-Shoes* 137: . . . the foregoer of the [buffalo] herd must have been a veritable Moses leading his followers to a promised land of—I suppose— muskeg grass. **1910** FRASER *Red Meekins* 142: . . . the carpeted muskeg itself would feed the conflagration . . . the wild grass, the muskeg hay, the short wolf willow . . . all were fuel.

muskeg railway 1 See **Hudson Bay Railway.** See also **Muskeg, the,** and **Muskeg Express** (def. 1).
1956 BERTON *Mysterious North* 171: All the while, below us, the slender ribbon of the Canadian National's "muskeg railway" stretched off toward Churchill on Hudson Bay.

2 the Alberta and Great Waterways railway, connecting Edmonton and Waterways, Alberta. See also **Muskeg Express** (def. 2).

1932 *Cdn Geog.Jnl* IV 305/1: Fort McMurray is the jumping-off port for the north, and there is a "muskeg railway" winding its slow length along the interminable miles from Edmonton.

muskeg school a school where persons whose work takes them into the muskeg learn how best to cope with the problems such terrain presents.
1964 *Globe Mag.* 14 Nov. 13/3: . . . Radforth worked with Ontario Hydro to set up its first muskeg school in the Parry Sound district where there is an abundance of organic terrain.

muskeg soil See **muskeg** (def. 3).
1952 PUTNAM *Cdn Regions* 453/1: A prosperous dairy industry could develop if accessible markets were found and if the dense forest and muskeg soil could be cleared and drained cheaply.

muskeg swamp 1 See **muskeg** (def. 1).
1895 SOMERSET *Muskeg* 22: Now for the first time we made the acquaintance of the muskeg swamp, and from this time forward hardly a day passed to the end of the journey when we did not curse this particular abomination. **1897** (1898) CHARLTON *H.B.Railway* 7: They and the other Indians agree that the whole country on the James Bay slope, after leaving the height of land a short distance, is timbered, except a narrow belt of muskeg swamps some distance below the Long Portage Falls on the Missanabie. **1928** FREEMAN *Nearing North* 370: Canada's boom cut its swath across two-thirds of a continent, overflowing into the mountain valleys of the Rockies and the muskeg swamps of the Athabaska. c**1963** *New Sounds* 11/1: The hauling roads, many of which are muskeg swamps during the summer months, become frozen in late fall and are immediately prepared for the winter haul. The main, all-weather roads are built to meet logging operation standards only.

2 See **muskeg** (def. 2).
1957 *Arctic Spotter* Dec. 25/2: As we left the railroad village of Ilford, the coniferous forests of Northern Manitoba gradually disappeared and the land began to take on a barren look—low scrub, muskeg swamp and rounded weatherworn rock. **1958** WATTERS *B.C.Cent. Anthol.* 269: I took the trail with him on that wild trip . . . through such a country as you never saw of mountains, streams and miry muskeg swamp. . . .

muskeg tea *North* **1** See **Labrador tea** (def. 1a). Also **tea muskeg.**
1859 (1863) PALLISER *Journals* 147: We encamped after passing the Long Muskeg, where we got a supply of the muskeg tea (*Ledum palustre*) which makes a capital beverage in absence of a better **1938** SULLIVAN *Cycle of North* 81: . . . others brought . . . leaves of the tea muskeg that they had got from Yellowknife Indians near the Bay.

2 See **Labrador tea** (def. 1b).
1863 (1931) CHEADLE *Journal* 66: [We were] taken into Chief's lodge . . . Pipe sent around . . . Meat and muskeg tea. Fat & water as cordial after. **1863** (1958) WATTERS *B.C.Cent.Anthol.* 280: We had tea too . . . "the tea muskeg" used by the Indians.

muskeg vehicle any vehicle designed to travel over muskeg (def. 2).
[**1958** BERTON *Klondike* 233: A man named Texas Smith arrived with a device designed to cross muskeg, snow, mud, and mountain; its wheels were wooden wine barrels, and it was topped off with a sleeping-platform.] **1964** *Globe Mag.* 14 Nov. 13/1: "Everybody seems to be inventing machines," an Ontario Hydro official says. "We're always testing new ones, but what we really need is a combined rock and muskeg vehicle."

1966 *Imperial Oil Rev.* June 9/1: A muskeg vehicle must be light, rugged, powerful, with good suspension systems. It should be able to steer without imparting high stresses on the muskeg.

muskeg water the brownish water that characterizes streams fed by or flowing through muskeg (def. 2).
1936 *Beaver* Mar. 43/2: There, at the mouth of a tiny trickle of muskeg water that registered but 58 against 72 for the water in the Cedar proper, we found a fisherman's paradise. **1944** CLAY *Fur Thieves* 21: ". . . one has to be careful 'bout drinkin' from every Dick-and-Harry bit o' water that comes along on the trail. But even muskeg water is all right when boiled."

muskegy ['mʌskɛgi] *adj.* [< *muskeg* + -*y*] characterized by swampy terrain, or muskeg.
1875 *Canadian Mthly* Sep. 371/2: He speaks of an Arctic December whose piercing frosts the warmest rays of June cannot overtake; of prairie—vast "muskegy" stretches with not even a spring to slake the traveller's thirst—whose monotony is relieved only by impudent gophers, and where black-fly bull-dogs torment by day and mosquitoes by the million at night. **1875** (1897) YOUNG *Manitoba* 291: From that point to Lake Winnipeg, about fifteen miles, we passed over a marshy, muskegy region.

muskellunge ['mʌskə,lʌndʒ] *n.* [< Algonk.: Ojibwa; cf. *maskinonge*] See **maskinonge**.
☛ *Spellings vary greatly in early writings. See 1963 quote at* **maskinonge**.
1794 (1911) SIMCOE *Diary* 215: . . . I reached the spot where they were catching maskalonge, a superior kind of pike, and pickerall. **1896** *Trans.Roy.Soc.Can.* II 2 138: He gives us himself amongst the various forms— muscalonge, muskellunge and muskallonge. . . .
1966 *Canadian* 30 Apr. 18: [Caption] Muskellunge are the meanest, roughest fresh-water fighters in Canada. . . .

muskemoot *n.* See **muskimoot**.

muskie† ['mʌski] *n.* [< *muskellunge*, q.v.] *Slang or Informal* See **maskinonge**. Also spelled *musky*.
1928 *Game Fishes of Canada* 12: The next most definite cult among the anglers are those who devote themselves to muskies. **1966** *Canadian* 30 Apr. 13/1: He spent an hour or so making notes with oils of the colors of a muskie that a friend had caught in Ontario's Rice Lake.

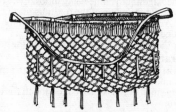

A muskimoot

muskimoot ['mʌskə,mut] *n.* [< Algonk.: Cree] a fairly large bag made of netted babiche (def. 1), often used by hunters to carry game. Also spelled *maskimute, muskemoot, muskymoot,* etc.
[**1791** LONG *Voyages* 200: *English* Bag *Algonkin* Maskimout *Chippeway* Muchcomat] **1803** (1897) COUES *New Light* I 226: [It was] loaded with his private baggage, cassetêtes, bags, kettles, and mashqueminctes. **1896** RUSSELL *Far North* 137: They could see that I had a little flour, a luxury the last pound of which had been consumed at that post months before, and I heard them speculating as to the probability of the various

muskimoots containing tea and tobacco. **1909** CAMERON *New North* 314: The fancy bag in which you carry your calling cards and little friendly gifts up here is a "musky-moot"; the more formidable receptacle, which gives your friends warning that you may stay a day or two, is a "skin-ichi-mun." **1913** *Geog.Board of Can.Rep.* App. 55: Especially noteworthy are the muskemoots . . . made of babiche.

muskinoonj *n.* See **maskinonge, muskellunge.**

musk-ox ['mʌsk,ɑks] *n.* -**ox** or -**oxen.** [see 1744 quote] **1** a bovine ruminant, *Ovibos moschatus,* having characteristics of both the ox and the sheep but having shaggy, dark brown to black hair, found in the Arctic regions. See also **Churchill buffalo, musk buffalo, musk cattle,** and **musk-cow.**
1744 DOBBS *Hudson's Bay* 18: Betwixt these Rivers is a kind of Ox, called the *Musk ox,* which smells at some Time in the Year so strong of Musk, that it cannot be eat. **1896** WHITNEY *On Snow-Shoes* 224: The musk-ox . . . seems to be the missing link between the ox and the sheep. **1965** SYMINGTON *Tuktu* 19: No vehicle less flexible than a dog team can travel such country, and no major herbivore other than the caribou and muskox can find sustenance in it.

2 the flesh of the musk-ox used as food.
[**1795** (1911) HEARNE *Journey* 31: . . . . the flesh of the musk-ox is not only coarse and tough, but smells and tastes so strong of musk as to make it very disagreeable when raw, though it is tolerable eating when properly cooked.] **1857** MCDOUGALL *Voyage* 354: The tables themselves were literally covered with roast-beef (musk-ox), beef-steak pie, preserved meats, plum puddings, apple and cranberry tarts, and especially, several jugs of "Richard's" home-brewed beer.
1941 DE PONCINS *Kabloona* 202: As for musk-ox, such meat was less to my taste, and I never want to eat it again.

muskrat† *n.* [ult. < Algonk. by folk etymology; cf. **musquash**] **1** an aquatic rodent, *Ondatra zibethica,* common to many parts of North America and widely trapped for its valuable fur. See also **marsh rat, mushrat** (def. 1), **musk beaver, musquash** (def. 1), **rat** (def. 1), and **water-rat.**
1703 LAHONTAN *New Voyages* I 110: In this place we kill'd some Musk-Rats. . . . **1883** *Selkirk Herald* (Man.) 2 Nov. 3/3: On one occasion I saw one attack a horse, while the settlers assured me that in some places the muskrats climb trees and hang from the branches, lying-in-wait for the passer by, whom they attack and sometimes destroy leaving nothing but the boot nails. **1966** *Globe and Mail* (Toronto) 9 May 7/1: They used to get together to chew over pemmican and offer up incantations to the great god Scouse for the preservation of the fertility of the muskrat and things like that.

2 the valuable fur of the muskrat. See also **musquash** (def. 2), **rat** (def. 2), and **rat skin.**
[**1796** (1911) SIMCOE *Diary* 315: We . . . slept well without mosquitoes, but the smell of muskrat skins, which had been drying in the house, was disagreeable.] **1805** *Quebec Gaz.* 25 July 2/1: Also received this day by the Schooner Corlotte from Restigouche . . . 845 Prime Martin Skins, A few Beaver and Otter do. 182 Muskrat do. *c*1902 LAUT *Trapper* 191: Next to musk-rat the most plentiful fur taken by the Indian, though not highly

esteemed by the trader, will be that of the rabbit or varying hare. **1963** *North* Sep.-Oct. 36: Coming home from the trapline, the toboggan will hold . . . furs, which include lynx, marten, mink, beaver, muskrat, fox, weasel and squirrel.

3 the flesh of the muskrat used as food. See also **musquash** (def. 3) and **rat** (def. 3).
[**1760** PICHON *Cape Breton* 102: Their porcupines, otters . . . and musk-rats, are . . . very good eating. . . .]
1852 (1923) MOODIE *Roughing It* 292: They very hospitably offered me a dishful of this odious mixture, which the odour of the muskrat rendered everything but savoury; but I declined, simply stating that I was not hungry. **1911** BICKERSTETH *Open Doors* 69: On this occasion he was out, but two saucepans were steaming on the stove, one labelled "beef," the other "muskrat à la mode." **1966** BERTON & BERTON *Cent.Food Guide* 17/2: Lumberjacks ate everything from muskrat to porcupine [sic].

4 See **talk muskrat.**

muskrat cabin, hut, or **lodge** See **muskrat house.**
1806 (1897) COUES *New Light* I 338: These villages at a distance appear like a cluster of mole-hills, or muskrat cabins. **1855** (1956) ROSS *Fur Hunters* 105: In this direction, we likewise passed a considerable lake in which there were several muskrat lodges. **1960** *News of the North* 14 Jan. 11/2: Perching like an abandoned muskrat hut in this mess is his touque.

muskrat house the living quarters of a muskrat, built on islands in and around a muskrat swamp, *q.v.* See also **living-house, lodge** (def. 1b), **muskrat cabin, rat-house,** and **wash,** *n.* (def. 2). Cp. **pushup.**
1872 DASHWOOD *Chiploquorgan* 115: I had observed some musk-rat houses at one end of the lake. . . .
1930 BEAMES *Army* 55: The sloughs near by swarmed with muskrat houses, or dams, as the settlers call them—domes of reeds and flags rising several feet above the ice. **1958** MACGREGOR *North-west of 16* 26: Around their banks and on little islands were muskrat houses.

muskrat rancher a man who breeds muskrats for their fur.
1961 *Time* (Cdn ed.) 25 Aug. 9/2: Tom Lamb carved out an empire of his own—as a fur trader, muskrat and beaver rancher. . . .

muskrat spear See 1939 quote. See also **rat spear.**
1914 STEELE *Forty Years* 219: . . . and the Indians rushed forward and drove muskrat spears into the poor fellow's body, tearing them out again to increase his torture. **1939** *Beaver* Dec. 24/1: I was interested in the large supply of muskrat spears which the men said we had to take. These were two and a half inch spears attached to nine inch rods of iron made by Company blacksmiths from rod iron brought from England.

muskrat stretcher See **stretcher.**

muskrat swamp a swamp or marsh where muskrats live. See also **rat marsh.**
1921 *Beaver* Mar. 16/2: All that is required to transform these muskrat swamps into a fine farming country is for our government to take the matter up. **1956** KEMP *Northern Trader* 56: Here the women and children would stay throughout the winter, but the men would set up their trapping camps miles off in the muskrats swamps.

musk-sheep *n. Obs.* See **musk-ox.**
1892 DAUNT *Land of Moose* 303: . . . we suddenly came upon the musk-sheep in a little sheltered valley where the dwarf willows surrounded a large pool.

muskwa [ˈmʌskwa] *n.* [< Algonk.: cf. Cree *maskwa* black bear] a bear.
[**1743** (1949) ISHAM *Observations* 20: a Black Bear Mus qua] **1951** ANGIER *At Home* 129: "Easy," Brad cautioned, suddenly alert. "That sounds like a young mus-kwa." **1956** KEMP *Northern Trader* 181: Muskwa was standing there, waiting for me. And I smacked right into him!

musky[1] [ˈmʌski] *n. Obs.* See **muskeg.**
1873 (1904) BUTLER *Wild North Land* 358: Crossing the Athabasca, near the point where it receives the Rivière la Biche, a region of presumed musky or swamp would be encountered.

musky[2] *n.* See **muskie.**

muskymoot *n.* See **muskimoot.**

muspike [ˈmʌs‚paɪk] *n.* [< *muskellunge* + *pike*] a hybrid game fish which did not become established. Cp. **splake.**
1954 *Ont. Dept Lands & Forests News Release* 28 Dec. 2: Another interesting experiment has been the crossing of the pike and the maskinonge to produce the second hybrid, the muspike.

musqua *n.* See **muskwa.**

musquash [ˈmʌskwɑʃ] *n.* [< Algonk.: cf. Ojibwa *miskwasi*] **1** See **muskrat** (def. 1).
1763 (1791) LONG *Voyages* 41: The country every where abounds with wild animals, particularly bears, moose . . . wolves, musquashes. . . . **1769** (1898) *N.B.Mag.* I 73: We have sent all the furs and everything received except about 60 lbs. Castor and a quantity of Musquash skins that could not be brought down. **1957** FISHER *Pemmican* 28: He doesn't know a beaver from a musquash.

2 See **muskrat** (def. 2).
1680 (1945) *H.B.C.Minutes* 29: 10 Musk Quash 16 Beaver peeces Valued att 15s. **1765** *Quebec Gaz.* 20 June 3/1: To be Sold at Public Vendue, On Friday Morning next . . . 675 Racoons . . . 1590 Musquash, 364 lbs. Indian half dress'd Deer, with some other Peltries. **1919** LOCKE *New France* 22: These are known to us as muskrats, the Algonquin name being mooskovesson, from which we get the name of the fur, musquash. **1957** *Beaver* Autumn 41/1: Of all pelts brought in—which included fox, marten, mink, musquash . . . wolverine or "skunk bear"—beaver remained supreme.

3 See **muskrat** (def. 3).
1909 CAMERON *New North* 272: Musquash in the spring is said to be tender and toothsome, but that overpowering smell of musk proved too much for our determination.

mussel mud† *Maritimes* sea mud used as fertilizer. See also **oyster mud.**
1825 *P.E.I.Register* (Charlottetown) 23 Aug. 1/1: Plenty of manure [is] at hand, either kelp, seaweed, mussle-mud. . . . **1861** SUTHERLAND *Geography P.E.I.* 27: These rivers have abundance of muscle mud, so valuable as manure. **1915** (1916) *Commission of Conservation* 71: This mussel-mud, as it is called is a very valuable fertilizer and, up to two years ago, the immense shell-mud deposits of St. Peter bay were practically untouched. . . . **1965** STEVENS *Incompleat Canadian* 110: The land [in P.E.I.] was not mined to exhaustion; instead the sea enriched it; "mussell-mud," heavy with lime, was dredged laboriously from the

coves and inshore waters; a herring was planted in every potato hill.

Mutchee Manitou See **Matchi Manitou.**

muthoy *n.* See **methy.**

muzzle-loader *n. Slang* See **muzzle-loading bunk.**
1919 *Camp Worker* 28 June 7/2: Then in other camps you have "muzzle-loaders":—Bunks arranged crosswise of the bunkhouse (double deckers also). As the name signifies, you have to crawl into them head first, and out feet first. *Ibid.* 30 Oct. 2/2: Bunks are double and double-deckers, and some muzzle loaders.

muzzle-loading bunk *Slang* a kind of bunk placed in banks at right angles to the wall so that the user must crawl in head first and out feet first (as in charging a muzzle-loading gun). See also **cannon bunk, muzzle-loader,** and **shotgun bunk.**
1947 SAUNDERS *Algonquin* 36: When he went to bed in the "muzzle-loading" bunks that lined the walls of the shanty, he stuck his knife in a niche of the wall at his head. **1959** *Globe and Mail* (Toronto) 29 June 27/3: Times have changed mightily since those days of the bucksaw, the horse, the log bunkhouse, and the "muzzle-loading" bunks in which men slept side by side under a long "canvas" made of wool army blankets sewn together.

mystery *n. Slang* See quote.
1892 DWIGHT *Life in N.W.M.P.* 32: Breakfast was served at a quarter to eight, when the remains of the previous day's dinner was made do service in the shape of hash, or "Mystery," as it was commonly called, together with dry bread and coffee.

mystery picket *Esp.B.C.* See **citizen picket.**
1963 *Canada Month* Apr. 29: In its battle with the B.C. government, organized labor thought it had got around the law by using "mystery pickets." **1963** *Sun* (Vancouver) 18 May 2/4: Mrs. Nan Bulbrook . . . told the Sun Friday she was hired as a mystery picket for the diamond drillers' union. **1965** *Ibid.* 1 Nov. 2/4: About 130 painters and carpenters refused to cross a mystery picket line thrown up today at the Matsqui Institution for drug addicts.

mystery picketing *Esp.B.C.* the practice of employing citizen pickets, *q.v.* See also **mystery picket.**
1966 *Sun* (Vancouver) 9 July 6/1: Management uses the injunction most often to curb picketing in wildcat strikes, mystery picketing, and mass picketing in legal strikes.

nacaishe *n.* [< Algonk.] *Obs.* See **goldeye**. Also spelled *mac(c)aysh*.
1793 (1933) MACDONELL *Diary* 116: The [Assiniboine] River is stocked with the following fish viz—Sturgeons . . . and Nacaishe. The men call these latter Lacaiche. . . . **1872** MCDONALD *Peace River* 5: Stopped on shore at the *Passe* . . . when we got a few "gold-eyes" (a kind of fresh herring about a foot long, with bright iris, large and yellow—Indian name Nacaish). **1897** COUES *New Light* I 444n: The lacaishe is the moon-eyed toothed herring . . . it occurs elsewhere in the quasi-French form la quesche; but all these are corruptions of the Indian nacaysh.

namacush *n.* See **namaycush**.

namapeth *n.* [< Algonk.; cf. Cree *namew* fish] *Obs.* the white sucker, *Catostomus commersonii*.
1784 PENNANT *Arctic Zoology* cxcii: The . . . Sucker Carp is a new species of which there are two varieties, the Mitheo-Mapeth of the Indians . . . and the White [carp], or Namapeth. . . . **1795** (1911) HEARNE *Journey* 327: The only species caught in those parts are trout . . . two sorts of barble (called by the Indians Na-may-pith,) . . . and a few perch.

namaycush ['næməˌkuʃ] *n.* [< Algonk.; cf. Cree *namēkus,* dim. of *namew* fish] See **lake trout**. Also spelled *namacush*.
[**1743** (1949) ISHAM *Observations* 22: Sammon Ne ma cu sheeck] **1775** (1951) *Sask.Jnls* 11 Nov. 21: Sent three men to the Nets from which . . . we received . . . a Namaycoose or kind of Sammon of 16 lb. weight and one Pike. **1852** RICHARDSON *Arctic Exped.* 288: The meshes will not admit the heads of the larger trout (*namaycush*), which weigh from 30 lbs. to 50 lbs. **1928** *Beaver* Sep. 58: The larger lakes, often of great depth, are the abode of the famed namaycush, the salmon trout of the lakes. . . . **1947** TANNER *Outlines* I 434: In the lower George River, the sea-trout and the salmon, and higher up the brook trout, ouinanishe and namacush are caught.

name-mask *n.* among certain Indians of the B.C. coast, a carved wooden mask worn during the name-giving ceremony.
1953 *Cdn Geog.Jnl* Dec. 252/1: The men followed the chiefs to war, made weapons, canoes, houses, totem-poles, name-masks. [Caption] The name-mask here illustrated was collected by the Indian agent at Meltakatla in 1912.

Nanabozho ['nænəˌbozo] *n.* [< Algonk.: Ojibwa] a supernatural giant, creator-magician and tribal hero of the Ojibwas.
1861 (1888) MCDOUGALL *G.M.McDougall* 83: To give the Ojibway idea, Nam-a-bush-you had shook his blanket, the old giant was mad. **1953** LOWER *Voyages* 16: There is a splatter of islands out from Nipigon House which were thrown into their present positions by Nan-i-bo-zhoo, the tribal hero of the Ojibways. . . . **1963** *Weekend Mag.* 9 Nov. 54/1: Tales of Nanabozho . . . is Ojibway lore about the tribe's creator-magician who turned himself to stone and, according to legend, now lies in Lake Superior off the Lakehead ports as the Sleeping Giant.

Nanook ['nanuk] *n.* [< Esk. *nanuq*] the polar bear. Also spelled *Nannook, nanook, nanuk*.
[**1824** NIAGUNGITOK *Esquimeaux Words* 26: Nenuk Bear (white)] **1854** (1892) KANE *Arctic Explor.* 232: It seemed as if the controversy was adjourned; and Nannook evidently thought so; for she turned off to our beef-barrels, and began in the most unconcerned manner to turn them over and nose out their fatness. **1922** FLAHERTY *Eskimo Friends* 168: Nanook, leading the fleet of kayakers, slowly paddled toward the harbour's mouth. **1963** *Weekend Mag.* 10 Aug. 17/1: . . . Eetuk suddenly whirled around and hissed, "Nanook!" He had spotted a polar bear.

nanuk or **nanuq** *n.* See **Nanook**.

nap(h)tha launch *Obs.* a motor launch using naphtha as fuel.
1906 LAWSON & YOUNG *Hist.B.C.* 90: Upon returning to the city [Victoria] they go, perhaps to one of the boat houses and secure seats in a naptha launch. **1923** WILLIAMS *Spinning Wheels* 182: There have been times when . . . skimming away in little naptha launches . . . has seemed an enviable lot.

Naskapi sled *Lab., Obs.* a type of sled associated with the Naskapi Indians.
1779 (1792) CARTWRIGHT *Journal* II 418: I put my gown, great-coat, and hatchet upon my Nescaupick sled, which was drawn by the two men, a bloodhound, and a Newfoundland dog.

national park† a tract of land held and maintained by the federal government so that people may enjoy its scenic and other attractions. Cp. **provincial park**.
1888 (1890) ST. MAUR *Impressions* 58: The National Park, which the Government is making here, is a tract of country about twenty-eight miles square, including some grand mountains and splendid scenery, amongst which they are laying out roads and riding-paths. **1958** *Edmonton Jnl* 23 July 29/1: O'Brien ffrench had been a Mountie in Canada in his youth, returned to his home in England and came back to Banff to stake claim to the only freehold property within the national park, just before the last war.

National Policy *Hist.* the policy of the Conservative party under Sir John A. Macdonald, which stressed protective tariffs and was the basis of a successful appeal to the electorate in 1878. See also **N.P.**
1870 *Cdn Illust.News* 26 Mar. 322/2: Dr. Tupper . . . has acquired a new source of popularity . . . by his vigorous advocacy of what he has . . . called a "national policy". . . . **1873** (1953) LEBOURDAIS *Nation of North* 74: That this House is of the opinion that the welfare of Canada requires the adoption of a National Policy, which, by a judicious readjustment of the tariff, will benefit and foster the agricultural, the mining, the manufacturing and other interests of the Dominion. **1965** *Kingston Whig-Standard* (Ont.) 13 Dec. 4/6: The Gordon policies for control on foreign investment and a government development corporation to buy into private enterprise, were corollaries to the Conservative Party's "National Policy" of the 1800's on which our present tariff structure and protection for Canadian industry is still based.

National Progressive Party See **Progressive Party**.
1946 LOWER *Colony to Nation* 497: By the beginning of 1920 [the rural interests] had been brought together into the *National Progressive Party,* under the leadership of T. A. Crerar, also a former Liberal and an ex-member of the Union Government.

1953 LEBOURDAIS *Nation of North* 226: The National Reconstruction Party [in 1935] . . . had all the advantages of a crusade still in its first flush.

national reserve *Obs.* See **national park.**
1916 WOOD *Tourist's N.W.* 492: On either side of the railway from the Pass to Parkgate the Dominion has set aside territory to the extent of 4400 square miles for a national reserve, which in scenic attraction and in wealth of hot springs rivals the Rocky Mountains Park.

National Union (Party) See **Union Nationale.**
1940 MACCORMAC *Canada* 162: The Liberal party which had enjoyed thirty-nine years of unbroken rule left office amid the odor of scandal and was succeeded by the overwhelmingly Conservative "National Union party" under the premiership of Maurice Duplessis. **1962** *Weekend Mag.* 9 June 15/1: A writer has told of "telegraphing" 20 votes in Montreal . . . on behalf of a National Union candidate.

native *n.* **1** an Indian or Eskimo.
1773 (1908) COCKING *Journal* 118: By marks we find the Natives up the other branch, have not passed downwards yet. **1856** BALLANTYNE *Young Fur-Traders* 60: This is the trading-store. It is always recognisable, if natives are in the neighbourhood, by the bevy of red men that cluster round it, awaiting the coming of the store-keeper or the trader. . . . **1951** BULIARD *Inuk* 316: The company nowadays certainly does give help to the natives, in the form of loans, gifts, and medicine, and it has assumed the responsibility for distributing government relief and family allowances among the Eskimos. **1959** *News of the North* 18 Dec. 1: [Heading] Native Housing Employs Many.

2 *Obs.* a half-breed, *q.v.*
1857 (1860) HIND *Red River Exped.* I 178: The term "native," distinguishing the half-breeds from the European and Canadian element on the one hand, and the Indian on the other, appears to be desired by many of the better class, who naturally look upon the epithet "half-breed" as applied to a race of Christian men, scarcely appropriate.

native *adv.* in the manner of an Indian or Eskimo.
1926 *Beaver* Dec. 46/2: When on a long journey in the north, he travels "native," which accounts for his success on these arduous trips and his popularity with the Eskimos.

native (Canadian) Indian *Esp.B.C.* a Canadian Indian, as opposed to an East Indian or a person from India.
1905 WIGHTMAN *Our Cdn Heritage* 159: In the past they have contributed the most of the food to the native Indians. **1959** *Native Voice* Sp.ed. 8: The Chief was allotted a seat at Westminster Abbey to witness the Coronation ceremony, marking the first time a Native Canadian Indian has been accorded such an honor. **1965** *Star Wkly* 30 Jan. 13/1: Most of Toronto's Negroes live there, and a few native Indians.

natural gas any combustible gaseous mixture formed in the earth's crust and obtained from natural fissures or bored wells.
1825 *Cdn Courant* (Montreal) 17 Dec. 1/5: This is undoubtedly the first attempt which has ever been made to apply natural Gas to so extensive and useful a purpose. **1897** TYRRELL *Sub-Arctics* 36: The first object of special interest passed was a natural gas flow, occurring on the left bank about fifteen miles below the Rapid. **1957** *Commonwealth* 13 Nov. 2/3: It is always a

new thrill to see natural gas come to the smaller communities in our province. **1966** *Globe and Mail* (Toronto) 1 Aug. 1/1: The lonely Yorkshire moors appear to hold a potential natural gas fortune for Canadian prospectors.

naygog *n.* [< Algonk.] *Obs.* See 1849 quote.
1849 ALEXANDER *L'Acadie* II 223: We were provided with an Indian fish spear, called a naygog; it is a singular instrument, but an effectual one for its purpose. Two crescents of light wood are tied at the end of a pole, and they open and close partially on a iron spike fixed between them, this last pierces the fish, and the half circles hold him. **1886** *Indian* (Hagersville, Ont.) 3 Mar. 47/1: It is not lawful to catch or kill any of the above-named fish by means of spears, grapple hook, negog or nishigans at any time.

NDP or **N.D.P.** the New Democratic Party, *q.v.*
1961 *Edmonton Jnl* 4 Aug. 17/3: The big hall broke into bedlam at that point, and with amazing speed the NDP organizers produced mimeographed songsheets complete with Tommy Douglas lyrics. Joe Glazer, Union troubador, led the delegates with his guitar. **1966** *Globe and Mail* (Toronto) 1 Aug. 10/2: The NDP failed to come close in any riding [in Alberta].

NDPer *n.* a member or supporter of the NDP.
1962 *Canada Month* Jan. 14/3: Travel Grant for NDPers.

neaps [nips] *n.pl.* [< Cdn F *nippes* < F "old clothes"] pieces of duffle, animal fur, etc. put round the feet as protection against the cold. See also **duffle neaps.** Cp. **nipper**[1]. Also **nippes.**
[**1634** *Relations des Jésuites* 48: . . . pour les garnir contre le froid, ils se seruent ordinairement d'vne peau de Lieure, ou d'vne piece de quelque couuerture, pliée en deux et trois doubles. Ils mettant auec cela du poil d'Orignac. **1820** (1922) HARMON *Journal* 416: The long soft hair [of the buffalo], the natives put into their shoes, about their feet, which supplies the place of socks; and it is fully as warm.] **1840** (1956) KOHL *Kitchi-Gami* 340: In the severe cold the "nippes" can be introduced into the mocassins to keep the feet warm more easily than in our unyielding boots. **1941** *Beaver* Sep. 38/2: Neaps—Strips of duffle wound around the feet next to the skin, which snowshoers prefer to woollen socks, as the skin is not chafed and the strips are more easily dried before the camp fire.

Near North See quotes.
1952 PUTNAM *Cdn Regions* 37/1: They thrive in the "Near North" or border area of the Shield. *Ibid.* 319/1: The "Near North" or southern fringe of Northern Ontario is a strip of lowland stretching for 300 miles from the Ottawa River to Lake Superior.

neche or **nechie** *n.* See **nitchie.**

neck *v.* **1** pull a sled with the traces passing over the shoulder near the neck.
1937 ANDREWS *Wrangell* 47: Men dragging sleds straggled up the river, "necking" it to the "pot of gold at the Rainbow's end". **1954** BERTON *I Married Klondike* 55: As we drove along we overtook brawny young men "necking" heavy sleighloads of provisions home from town (the traces passed around their necks).

2 See **track,** *v.* (def. 1).
1940 MARSHALL *Arctic Village* 84: At other times you

neck the boat up the river, that is, walk along the river bar some distance ahead of the boat, tugging against a rope which is attached on one end to the bow and the other to the stern.

neck log in a type of deadfall (def. 1), the log that falls on an animal's neck and kills it. See **drop-log**. Cp. **throat log**.
1743 (1949) ISHAM *Observations* 162: . . . a Long piece which goes on that which is called a neck Log. . . .

necktie social *Obs*. a party where each partner for the evening wore matching ties.
1892 *Medicine Hat Times* (Alta) 18 Aug. 1/5: The novelty of a necktie social drew a large crowd of pleasure seekers to the Reading Room on Tuesday evening.

nectuk *n*. See **netchek**.

nee-che or **nee-chee** *n*. See **nitchie**.

needle bar *North* a kind of long ice-pick for cutting water holes in ice. Cp. **ice-chisel**.
1956 KENNEDY *Gt Slave Lake* 11: The edges of the hole must be free of rough projections which would catch in the net, and many fishermen use an "ice chisel"— which is much like the needle bar except that the sharpened end is chisel-like—to finish the hole, but others use only the needle bar. 1960 *Weekend Mag*. 8 Oct. 28/3: I dug down through three feet of ice with a needle bar. . . .

needle ice needle-like formations of ice crystals. See quotes. Cp. **candle**.
1896 RUSSELL *Far North* 174: Dog Shoes . . . are used in lake travel, late in winter, when the sharp granular snow soon renders the dogs' feet raw and bleeding, or in spring when traveling upon the needle ice, after the snow has disappeared. 1951 BULIARD *Inuk* 246: The husky's feet are tough, their soles thick, and it is only after days of packing over sharp stones or of pulling over the spring "needle ice" that his (feet) show some sign of damage.

neejee *n*. See **nitchie**.

neestau or **neestow** ['nisto] *n*. See **neshtow**.

negog *n*. See **naygog**.

negrohead *n*. See **niggerhead**.

negrohead tobacco† See **niggerhead tobacco**.
1889 (1892) PIKE *Barren Grounds* 29: The Hudson's Bay negrohead tobacco is in my opinion much improved, as well as economized by a mixture with either of these substances (kinikinik or the inner bark of red willow). 1896 RUSSELL *Far North* 107: A laborer's ration is four fresh fish a day, or four pounds of half-dry, or three pounds of dried caribou meat; one and one-half pounds of tea, and two pounds of negro-head tobacco each month; forty pounds of white pressed sugar, and one hundred pounds of flour each year.

nekik [nə'kik] *n*. [< Algonk.: Ojibwa *nekeek*] the otter.
[1781 (1934) TURNOR *Journal* 343: This is called the Ne-keek Wine-e-cap or Otter Carrying place.] *c*1902 (1912) LAUT *Trapper* 251: All trapped between latitude thirty-five and sixty is good fur; and the best is that taken toward the end of winter when scarcely a russet

hair should be found in the long over-fur of nekik's coat.

nemaycoose, nemakuse *n*. See **namaycush**.

Neocaledonian *adj*. *Obs*. Nova Scotian.
1789 *N.S.Mag*. I 5/2: But at last, when he had enrolled some two or three hundred knights, who . . . had purchased . . . several millions of Neocaledonian acres. . . .

neshtow ['nɛʃto] *n*. [< Algonk.: Cree] See quotes. Also *neestau, neestow, nistow*.
1909 CAMERON *New North* 56: At 5:30 next morning we hear the familiar "Nistow! Nistow!" of the awakened camp. This word literally means "brother-in-law," but it is the vocative used by the Cree in speaking to anybody he feels kindly toward. 1922 *Beaver* May 12/2: We soon became fast Friends and called one another Neshtow (meaning brother-in-law), an Indian term of endearment. 1935 *Cdn Geog.Jnl* Aug. 127/1: In the sleeping cars officials of fur-trading companies sat cheek by jowl with dark-skinned "neestaus," weather-tanned trappers, Assyrian peddlers. [1965 *Time* (Cdn ed.) 14 May 17/3: [They] will spend the summer on Indian reserves in a social aid project called Neestow (Cree for "brother-in-law").]

netchek ['nɛtʃɛk] *n*. [< Esk.] a small seal, as the ring seal or the harbor seal, *qq.v*. Cp. **netschewuk**. Also spelled *netsek, netserk, netsik, nutchook*, etc.
[1852 RICHARDSON *Arctic Exped*. 494: Small seal Labrador Eskimo netsi-arksuk; netsek.] 1854 (1892) KANE *Arctic Explor*. 154: The netsik will not perforate ice of more than one season's growth, and are looked for, therefore, where there was open water the previous year. 1934 *Beaver* Dec. 52/1: He will remember the happy faced Eskimos, the huskies and their howling, the netchek-seals, the caribou. . . . 1942 TWOMEY & HERRICK *Needle to North* 173: Bob's sealskin pants were made from the soft, dull, dark-mottled *netchek*, and every little hair in them glistened as he bent over the flaming stove. 1958 *Evening Telegram* (St John's) 17/1: Those were "netserk" or ringed seals which remain here all the year round and on which the Eskimo depends for his clothing.

net-hole *n*. a hole through which fish are netted in ice fishing, *q.v*. See also **basin hole**.
1934 GODSELL *Arctic Trader* 82: Then, as the sun was almost setting, they came upon net-holes surrounded with spruce boughs, a sure sign of the proximity of Indians.

netminder *n*. *Informal* in hockey and lacrosse, a goalkeeper.
1931 *Vancouver Province* 17 Jan. 7/1: Scribner . . . tried to pull the netminder to one side. . . . 1966 *Globe and Mail* (Toronto) 20 June 19/1: Leafs peppered Brampton's starting netminder . . . continuously in the first 20 minutes. . . .

netschewuk *n*. *Eskimo* See **hood seal**. Cp. **netchek**.
1882 GILDER *Schwatka's Search* 175: The nets-che-wuk, "bladder-nosed" seal, has a skin which is a grade or two superior to the netchuk, and is much larger. 1916 HAWKES *Lab.Eskimo* 31: Netci°'vuk . . . commonly known as the Hood or Bladder-nose seal.

netsek, netserk, netsik, netsuk *n*. See **netchek**.

Neutral *n*. *Hist*. a French-speaking settler of eighteenth-century Acadia, so-called because of his disinterest in the wars between the English and French.

1755 (1895) RICHARD *Acadia* II 39: Some reflections on the situation of the inhabitants, commonly called Neutrals, and some methods proposed to prevent their escape out of the colony, in case, upon their being acquainted with the design of removing them, they should attempt to desert over to the French. **1786** (1787) *Account N.S.* 96: . . . most of the lands around the head of the Bay are very good, having been formerly possessed and cultivated by the ancient French colonists, distinguished by the name of Neutrals. . . .
1895 RICHARD *Acadia* II 250: A petition from one town on the coast asks to have the Neutrals removed to the interior, as they have a powder-house there, and were afraid they would blow them up. **1963** MORTON *Kingdom of Canada* 135: Then [1755] . . . the rulers of Nova Scotia turned to deal firmly with the long evasive, long neutral Acadians.

neutral school *Que.* a non-sectarian school not offering religious instruction as part of its regular curriculum but permitting such instruction by a special teacher or clergyman on an extra-curricular basis for parents who desire it.
1961 *Canada Month* 6 Oct. 28/2: Quebec's 96-member legislative assembly will soon face a storm beside which the rumpus over "neutral" schools will look like a polite difference of opinion. **1966** *Globe and Mail* (Toronto) 1 Jan. 5/2: Paul-Emile Cardinal Leger . . . spoke out yesterday on two key Quebec subjects—neutral schools and civil marriage.

New Britain *Hist.* the Ungava peninsula, especially the Labrador coast.
1748 DRAGE *Voyage* I 70: The South Shore which was named New-Britain by Mr. Hudson, but is now mostly known by the Name of the Labrador Shore, and Terra Corterealis, hath several Inlets along the Coast.
1819 ANSPACH *Hist.Nfld* 327: These straits are so called from an island lying on the eastern coast of New Britain, and forming the northern entrance of the River Saint Lawrence from the sea. **1963** DAVIES *Northern Quebec* xv n: When James Clouston referred to the [Ungava] peninsula in his journal of 1819-20 he used the seventeenth-century term, New Britain.

New Brunswick pound *Hist.* a monetary unit established in New Brunswick in pre-Confederation times.
1949 LAWSON *N.B.Story* 190: . . . in New Brunswick there was also the New Brunswick pound which was worth only four dollars, whereas the English pound or pound sterling was worth $4.86. . . .

New Caledonia *Hist.* 1 Nova Scotia.
1754 JEFFERYS *Conduct* 8: De Laet calls the peninsula New Caledonia, not New Scotland, into which Charlevoix has changed it. . . .

2 the name given by Simon Fraser (in 1808) to what is now the central and northern parts of the interior of British Columbia, which comprised a department of both the Northwest Company and the Hudson's Bay Company and was one of the great areas of the fur trade. See also **Siberia of the fur trade.**
1815 (1890) KEITH *Letters* 129: Mr. James Stuart after crossing to the Columbia is again returned to his old quarters, New Caledonia. **1905** (1954) *B.C.Hist.Qtly* 156: New Caledonia was a name given by the Highlanders of the Northwest Company to the east-central portion of the present province of British Columbia, comprising Fraser, McLeod, Stuart Lakes. **1963** *Canada Month* May 14/1: Gold was found in

the mid-1850s at several points in New Caledonia, a fur-trading reserve whose only white inhabitants were a few score servants of the Hudson's Bay Company.

3 the name given in 1858 to the British colony comprising much of the mainland of present-day British Columbia.
1858 (1907) *Letters of Queen Victoria* 376: If the name of New Caledonia is objected to as being already borne by another colony or island claimed by the French, it may be better to give the new colony west of the Rocky Mountains another name. **1921** *Cdn Hist.Rev.* II 352: Objection had been taken to the name of New Caledonia, by which title the mainland was usually designated, although New Caledonia was more properly the northern interior of British Columbia.
1958 *Maclean's* 10 May 13/2: For this is a province of extremes and it comes as no surprise to learn that this country of New Caledonia, which is steeped so thoroughly in the past, is now being tagged as The Land of the Future.

New Canadian an immigrant settled in Canada who has become or intends to become a Canadian citizen.
1904 KENNEDY *New Canada and the New Canadians* [Title] **1922** (1939) GIBBON *Canadian Mosaic* ix: The New Canadians, representing many lands and widely separated sections of Old Europe, have contributed to the Prairie Provinces a variety in the way of church architecture. **1946** LOWER *Colony to Nation* 409: The colonizers still were nearly all Anglo-Saxons, mostly from the east, with smaller groups of Icelanders and Mennonites: as late as 1901, there was no such phrase as "new Canadian." **1966** *Globe and Mail* (Toronto) 26 Jan. 4/1: The provincial Government will make special grants to school boards teaching English to New Canadian students. . . .

New Canuck *Slang* See **Canuck** (def. 2) and **New Canadian.**
1960 *Mine-Mill Herald* Oct. 6/3: [Headline] "New Canuck" Says His Piece.

New Company *Fur Trade, Hist.* See **X.Y. Company.** See also **New North West Company.**
1801 (1920) *Beaver* Oct. 31: Told them [Indians] to take all their provisions to the New Co. as we have got a sufficiency. . . . **1935** [see quote at **Old Company** (def. 2)].

new cut *Obs.* a strip cut through the forest, the felled trees being placed at the roadside to leave a primitive road about 30 feet wide.
1830 MOORSOM *Letters N.S.* 338: I felt too happy to be released from the execrable "new cuts," that may some day perchance deserve the name of roads, through this part of the country—to detain you long upon them.

New Dem *Slang* See **New Democrat.**
1962 *Kingston Whig-Standard* (Ont.) 13 Nov. 3/1: Can the 15 New Dems who voted Tory last Tuesday be the political kin of those who met in Regina in July, 1933.

New Democrat a member or supporter of the New Democratic Party.
1961 *Edmonton Jnl* 4 Aug. 2/6: [Headline] New Democrats Adopt Plank in Favor of NATO Alignment **1966** *Globe and Mail* (Toronto) 25 June 3/2: The New Democrats also took two [seats] from the Liberals.

New Democratic Party a political party formed in 1961 in place of the Co-operative Commonwealth Federation and with the support of a considerable portion of organized labor. See also **NDP.**
1961 *Edmonton Jnl* 4 Aug. 29/7: All that is changed are the initials, was the remark made by Senator David A. Croll (L—Ontario) when asked to comment on the New Democratic Party in an interview Friday. **1966** *Globe and Mail* (Toronto) 25 June 3/1: The voters [in Manitoba] ... gave the New Democratic Party four more seats for a total of 11.

New Denmark *Hist.* a name given to the west shore of Hudson's Bay.
1835 ROSS *Last Voyage* 20: The ice prevented Monk from running along the western coast of Greenland, he consequently steered for Hudson's Strait, and finding the coast of America in lat. 63 deg. 20 min., he took shelter in a harbour, which he called *Monks' Winter Harbour* (probably the Chesterfield inlet of our maps.) The surrounding country they named *New-Denmark.* **1932** KENNEY *Ft Churchill* 12: "Munck named the surrounding country 'New Denmark,' and Churchill harbour 'Jens Munck's Winter-haven,' or, adopting an English word, 'Jens Munck's Bay.'"

New England of Canada *Hist.* the Eastern Townships of Quebec, first settled by New England immigrants.
1952 PUTNAM *Cdn Regions* 195/1: From this as well as because of the hilly landscapes, the Eastern Townships have been called "the New England of Canada."

New England Planter *Hist.* a pre-Loyalist immigrant to Nova Scotia from the New England colonies. See also **Planter.**
1931 SEARY *Romance* 119: Some settlers came from Plymouth, the landing place of the Pilgrim Fathers and their arrival ... was done more quietly and with less pomp than that which attended the settlement of the New England planters "up the valley".... **1952** PUTNAM *Cdn Regions* 116/1: Four years later the area was granted to the "New England Planters" whose descendants still make up a large part of the population.

Newf [njuf *or* nuf] *n. Slang* See **Newfie** (def. 2).
1958 *Evening Telegram* (St John's) 8 May 4/5: "Of course he couldn't have passed me ... the ill bred Newf that I am...."

Newfie ['njufi *or* 'nufi] *n. Slang* **1** Newfoundland.
1945 PUGSLEY *Saints* 81: "This certainly is a change after those winters off Sydney and Newfie," said one. **1965** *Globe and Mail* (Toronto) 29 Jan. 7/6: Nobody in Newfie ... underestimates Joey Smallwood's abilities as a propagandist.

2 a native or resident of Newfoundland.
1958 *In Flight* Summer 8/1: Cod fishing has, of course, long been synonymous with Newfoundland, but today the canny 'Newfies' are no longer putting all their economic eggs in one basket. **1966** *Kingston Whig-Standard* (Ont.) 15 Jan. 3/1: ... Carter is one of those delightfully independent Newfies who refuses to bow and scrape before the powerful Mr. Pickersgill.

Newfie Bullet an ironic name for the train running through the interior of Newfoundland.
1965 *Globe and Mail* (Toronto) 7 Dec. 6/4: A couple of weeks back, I described a rail trip (on the famous Newfie Bullet) through the great dead heart of the island-province.

Newfiejohn ['njufi,dʒɑn *or* 'nu-] *n.* [< *Newfie,* q.v. + *St. John*('s)] *Slang* (*esp.Navy*) St. John's, Newfoundland.
1945 PUGSLEY *Saints* 32: There is something grimly exciting about St. John's, or "Newfiejohn," as the Navy calls it. *Ibid.* 106: Before long we were gliding through the familiar small cleft in the mountainous shore into Newfiejohn harbor.

Newfound Island *Obs.* an early name for Newfoundland.
1892 (1908) OXLEY *Young Nor'Wester* 60: Its name was probably given by Cabot during his first voyage, as is is met with shortly thereafter as *Terra Nova* and "New Islande," which soon passed into "Newfound Island," and then to its present form.

Newfoundland [nju'faundlənd *or* nu-] *n.* one of a breed of dog probably developed from crossing dogs from Europe with the Newfoundland dog (def. 1). See also **Newfoundland dog** (def. 2).
1880 (1893) YOUNG *Indian Wigwams* 132: I ... imported, through the aid of dear friends, St. Bernards and Newfoundlands in their place.... **1963** *Globe and Mail* (Toronto) 23 Mar. 32/4: The Newfoundland is one of the few breeds of dogs which claim this country as point of origin.... **1965** *Weekend Mag.* 9 Jan. 20/2: He was a Newfoundland—an aristocrat to start with.

Newfoundland dog 1 one of a breed of dog, the probable ancestor of the modern Newfoundland, *q.v.* See also **New Foundlander.**
*c*1766 (1964) *Nfld Qtly* Spring 30/3: I was told indeed at Trepassy lived a man who had a distinct breed which he called the original Newfoundland dogs.... **1771** (1911) TOWNSEND *Cartwright's Journal* 8 Apr.: [The wolf] travelled at such a rate with the trap upon one of his fore feet, that they had much difficulty to overtake him. though assisted by a couple of stout Newfoundland dogs. **1829** MACTAGGART *Three Years* II 72: Newfoundland dogs are rare to be met with ... they are chiefly found on the coast of Labrador: the settlers there obtain them from the Esquimaux. **1964** *Cdn Geog. Jnl* Mar. 93/1: The contents of one killer whale's stomache [sic]: fourteen seals, twelve porpoise and a Newfoundland dog!

2 See **Newfoundland.**
1818 CHAPPELL *Voy. of Rosamond* 141: The Newfoundland dog is an animal well known in England, for its attachment to the water; but the true breed has become scarce, and is rarely to be found, except upon the coast of Labrador. **1954** *Charlottetown Patriot* 26 Aug. 5/2: Burly good-natured Newfoundland dogs, this island's most famous export, are fast disappearing from Newfoundland and one of the world's best-known breeders says it is because of federal registration regulations.

Newfoundlander *n.* See **Newfoundland dog** (def. 1).
1779 (1792) CARTWRIGHT *Journal* II 423: The bloodhound and Newfoundlander, which were in the sled, ran vehemently at the deer.... **1894** ASHLEY *Tan Pile Jim* 106: ... Towzer was along ... For all he was a full-blooded Newfoundlander, whose preferences ran to water, he was competently up to snuff whenever he could get a chance to go into the woods....

Newfoundland grape *Local* the blueberry.
1942 GOUGH *New World Horizons* 179: The blueberries

or "Newfoundland grapes," that I picked when the train stopped at Grand Falls were delicious.

Newfoundland Ranger Force See **Labrador Ranger Force.**

1965 JENNESS *Eskimo Admin.* III 62: . . . the Newfoundland Ranger force or rural police, also contributed to the ferment and slow revolution that was taking place in northern Labrador. . . .

New France *Hist.* the former French possessions in North America.

1582 HAKLUYT *Divers Voyages* 25: It was written vnto me by Sebastian Gaboto, our countrie man Venetian, a man of great experience, and very rare in the art of Nauigation and the knowledge of Cosmographie: who sayled along and beyonde the lande of Newe Fraunce, at the charges of King Henrie the seuenth, king of Englande. *c*1665 (1885) RADISSON *Voyages* 93: The ffrench planters in Newfrance came up to live among this nation. **1708** CLARK *New Description* 174: Another part of this Tract, is called *Canada*, from the River of that Name that Waters it; and *New France*, from a Colony of French that settled there, who at their first arrival were gladly received by the Natives, with Singing and Dancing. **1963** MORTON *Kingdom of Canada* 33: The English had thus infringed in Acadia and Hudson Bay the title to the lands Champlain sought to make French, and had blocked the development of New France for three costly years.

New Ireland *Hist.* See 1907 quote.

1784 *N.B.Mag.* III 45: The separation of the province [of Nova Scotia] into two governments is determined upon in the cabinet. That of St. Johns which is to be called New Ireland, has been offered by General Fox. **1875** CAMPBELL *Hist.P.E.I.* I 54: We find that in the year 1780, an act for altering the name of the island from St. John to that of New Ireland was passed in the assembly with a suspending clause. **1907** *U of T Stud.Hist.& Econ.* II 223: The name of New Ireland was proposed at different times for each of these new provinces. The Legislature of Prince Edward (Island) in 1780 adopted the name, but the Sovreign disapproved.

New Lights† *Hist.* 1 a fundamentalist evangelical sect first established in Cornwallis, N.S., during the 1780's by Henry Alline.

1832 MCGREGOR *Brit.Amer.* II 465: Let us leave abstract points of Christian doctrine to theological disputants, and the raving of *new lights*. . . . **1934** DENNIS *Down in N.S.* 278: Congregationalists, Presbyterians, New Lights, Methodists, Baptists, Episcopalians, all held their meetings in by-gone days in the old Meeting house [in Shelburne, N.S.]. . . . **1949** *Cdn Hist.Rev.* Mar. 75: Professor Clark has brought together the variations on these Protestant themes in all of what is now Canada from 1760 to 1900, from the New Lights to the Salvation Army.

2 *Attributive uses.*

1816 MARSDEN *Narrative* 49: . . . many thought I was too legal, and certainly they had cause to think so, if the following doctrines industriously propagated in the settlements by some new-light preachers were genuine. . . . **1934** DENNIS *Down in N.S.* 99: It was here in Cornwallis that Henry Alline established the first of his "new light churches.—It was built in 1786 on what was known by the euphonious name of "Jaw-bone Corner." **1949** *Cdn Hist.Rev.* Mar. 75: Meanwhile Henry Alline, the New Light evangelist, was shattering the less sedate Dissenting congregations of the Nova Scotian out-ports and back country.

New Manitoba *Hist.* that part of the old Keewatin district added to the province of Manitoba in 1912.

1912 SANDILANDS *West.Cdn Dict.* 31: New Manitoba. In 1912 the province was extended northwest to the 60th parallel and eastward to a line drawn from the northeast angle to the original boundaries of the Province to the most northeasterly portion of Island Lake, thence northward to intersect with the southern shores of Hudson Bay in longitude 89 degrees. **1918** KITTO *New Manitoba* 7: The portion added to the old province is variously known as "Northern Manitoba" or "New Manitoba."

new milk *Fur Trade, Obs.* See **English milk.**

1803 (1897) COUES *New Light* I 203: . . . the Indians were anxiously awaiting me, to taste the 'new milk', as they generally call rum when speaking in a ceremonious style. . . .

New Nation *Hist.* the Métis of the Red River Settlement (a name they themselves adopted).

1870 (1941) *Beaver* June 17/1: This execution was published in the *New Nation* newspaper. . . . **1885** BRYCE *Old Settlers* 6/2: They looked upon themselves as a separate people, and headed by their Scoto-French half-breed leader, Cuthbert Grant, called themselves the New Nation. **1964** *Western Wkly* 24 June 3/2: During the troubled days of the Red River Insurrection, the Nor-Wester was seized by Louis Riel and used for the printing of the "New Nation's" proclamations.

New North West (or **N.W.) Company** *Fur Trade, Hist.* See **X.Y. Company.**

1798 (1957) *Ont.Hist.* 74: In the course of the day we passed the mouth of the River Rouche [Rouge], where the Americans are building some ships of burden, in order to engage in the North West trade, in conjunction with some English merchants, under the name of the New N.W. Company. **1947** *Beaver* Mar. 33/1: . . . the break in 1799 between Sir Alexander Mackenzie on the one hand and Simon McTavish and William McGillivray on the other—a break that resulted in Mackenzie leaving the North West Company and later reorganizing the New North West Company.

New Ontario that part of the present province of Ontario formally added in 1912; Northern Ontario. See also **Greater Ontario.**

1900 *Canadian Mag.* Sep. 490/2: I saw a map of our Province the other day, with the respective sizes of Old and New Ontario indicated, and truly it was an eye-opener. **1908** NICHOLSON *In Old Quebec* 102: We are still in the "banner province" of the Dominion, for the vast country to the north and West of Lake Nipissing and the French River is known as "New" or "Greater Ontario." **1936** LOWER *Settlement* 11: This geographical peculiarity . . . has caused Northern or "New" Ontario to be regarded almost as a separate province.

New Party 1 a Canadian political party of the early 1890's.

1890 *Grip* (Toronto) 18 Jan. 36/2: This was from *The Canadian Nation*, the New Party organ. *Ibid.* 29 Mar. 212/2: Canada's New Party held its second annual convention in this city last week. . . .

2 a name used for the New Democratic Party, *q.v.*, during the months prior to its official founding in 1961.

1961 *Edmonton Jnl* 1 Aug. 5/6: The New Party

returned to its convention huddle Tuesday, still seeking an official name, a national leader and a policy platform on which its labor, farm, and socialist supporters can agree.

New Quebec Northern Quebec, specifically that part of the Ungava peninsula that became part of the province in 1912.

1952 PUTNAM *Cdn Regions* 212/1: Officially known as New Quebec, the former territory of Ungava became part of the province in 1912. **1964** *Globe and Mail* (Toronto) 7 Mar. 8/3: New Quebec geographically represents more than half of the province's area, and an unknown proportion of its resources.

newsagent *n.* the person on a railway train who sells papers, magazines, refreshments, etc.

1880 *Great Western Railway Advert.Bull.* 26 May 4/7: For sale by the news agents. Try them. . . . **1912** BICKERSTETH *Open Doors* 141: The main passenger trains in this country are provided with a newsagent, a loquacious individual who continually walks from one end of the train to the other selling papers, tobacco, and candies. **1958** *Edmonton Jnl* 24 June 1 14/4: The Commons Monday heard a complaint that persons suffering from communicable diseases are allowed to travel alongside the sandwich-dispensing news agents on the CPR's Kettle Valley run in British Columbia.

News Boy's Address *Obs.* See **New Year's Address.**

1808 *Cdn Courant* (Montreal) 4 Jan. 4/1: The News Boy's Address, To the Patrons of the Canadian Courant. **1827** *U.E.Loyalist* (York [Toronto]) 6 Jan. 1: [Heading] The gazette and U.E. Loyalist News Boy's Address to His Patrons, 1827.

New Scotland *Hist.* an early name for Nova Scotia.

*c***1621** (1891) *Trans.Roy.Soc.Can.* IX 2 83: It is very important that all our beloved subjects who inhabit the said Province of New Scotland or its borders may live in the fear of Almighty God. . . . **1891** *Ibid.*: It was in all future time to have the name of New Scotland or, as it appears in the courtly Latin of the original, Nova Scotia. **1922** *Dalhousie Rev.* I 375: The Province was incorporated in one entire free barony which was to be called in all future time by the name of "New Scotland."

New Wales *Hist.* an early name for the western shore of Hudson's Bay, in the vicinity of Forts York and Churchill.

1748 ELLIS *Hudson's Bay* 47: His own Name he left to the Bay, where he wintered, and adjacent Country he called *New-Wales.* **1932** KENNEY *Ft.Churchill* 6: Cape Churchill, the promontory to the eastward, he seems to have named "Northerland" head, and the district to the south "New Wales."

New West *Hist.* the Northwest Territories (def. 1b), especially the Prairie Provinces, opened up for settlement in the late 19th century.

1966 *Sask.Hist.* Spring 41: In 1881 Major Bell set out from Brandon, Manitoba, on foot to view some of the country through which the Canadian Pacific Railway would pass. By this time the idea of establishing a large farm in the "New West" had been fixed firmly in his mind.

New Year's Address *Obs.* a greeting, usually in

rhyme, issued by newspaper carrier-boys to their patrons on the first day of each year, at which time they expected a Christmas box. See also **News Boy's Address.**

[**1767** *Quebec Gaz.* 1 Jan. 1/1: The New-Year Verses Of the Printers Lad, who carries about the Quebec Gazette to the Customers.] **1805** *Ibid.* 3 Jan. 1/1: The New Year's Address of the Boy who carries the Quebec Gazette to the Subscribers. **1826** *Novascotian* (Halifax) 4 Jan. 1/1: New Year's Address, to the Patrons of the Novascotian. **1868** *St.Catharines Constitutional* 2 Jan. 1/5: The Carrier Boy's New Year's Address to the Readers of the Constitutional.

New Year's (Day) levee See **levee** (def. 1).

1948 BORRETT *Historic Halifax* 158: The New Year's levees were traditional ceremonies dear to the hearts of loyal old Halifax. On that first day of the year . . . our people by hundreds pass through the entrance. There they move in regular lines through the stately room to pay their respects to their sovereign's representative, the Lieutenant-Governor. **1964** *Calgary Herald* 2 Jan. 8/1: The traditional custom of the New Year's Day levee was marked again in Canada's provincial capitals Wednesday.

New-Year Verses See **New Year's Address.**

New York currency† *Hist.* See **York currency.** *Abbrev.* N.Y.C., *q.v.*

1826 (1832) PICKERING *Inquiries* 51: It is run into various fanciful shapes in moulds . . . selling from 4d. to $6\frac{3}{4}$d. per pound, or 6d. to 1s. New York currency (in which trade is generally done in the Western part of the province), while in the eastern, it is in Halifax currency, 18s. sterling to the pound, or 5s. to the dollar. **1905** SCHERCK *Pen Pictures* 67: It was not until 1820 that the Halifax, or Provincial currency, became at all general, private and store accounts being mostly kept in New York currency previous to that time, public and school accounts in Halifax currency.

N.F. the province of Newfoundland.

1807 *Quebec Gaz.* 22 Oct. 3/2: On passing the Parade his Excellency was saluted by the two flank companies of the Royal N.F. Fencibles. . . . **1935** *Beaver* Dec. 12/2: The crew of twenty-five men escaped and rowed in dories 180 miles to St. John's, N.F.

niche or **nichi(e)** *n.* See **nitchie.**

nickel† *n.* the Canadian five-cent piece.

☛ *Although called a* **nickel,** *after United States practice, for many years, the Canadian five-cent piece was until the 1920's a small silver coin; since this was withdrawn from use, a larger coin of nickel alloy has been in circulation, except during World War II when it was temporarily displaced by a bronze coin.*

1883 *Brandon Dly Mail* (Man.) 14 Feb. 4/1: If they were put up for ornament they do not fill the bill worth a nickle. **1966** *Maclean's* 2 May 46/4: Here in Lloydminster, we still dial for a nickel. **1967** *Globe and Mail* (Toronto) 21 Apr. 5/8: A Queen's University student's contention that there are no such coins in Canadian law as pennies, nickels, dimes and quarters was rejected yesterday by an amused Ontario Supreme Court Judge.

nickel belt the Sudbury Basin in Northern Ontario, site of the world's most productive nickel mines.

[**1958** *Encyc.Can.* IX 431/2: Since 1953 [the Sudbury District] has been divided for federal purposes into two single-member ridings: Sudbury, comprising mainly the city of Sudbury, and Nickel Belt.] **1967** *Globe and Mail* (Toronto) 9 Mar. 22/1: He was . . . the son of a red-haired Irish miner and a patient Algonquin Indian mother . . . from Falconbridge, 260 miles up in the nickel belt.

nidgé *n.* See **nitchie.**

nigger *n. Hist.* See 1963 quote.
1852 (1923) MOODIE *Roughing It* 340: Some twenty or thirty little fires were burning briskly in different parts of the blackened field, and the old fellow was watching the slow progress of his silent "niggers," and replacing them from time to time as they smouldered away. **1899** MACKAY *Pioneer Life* 167: It was a Zorra man who wrote . . . to . . . Scotland, declaring that he had a hundred "niggers" working for him. He meant the fire used on the tree. . . . **1963** GUILLET *Pioneer Farmer* I 320: To save the work of chopping the trees into lengths small fires, in some districts called niggers, were placed on top of the trunks at intervals . . . and kept burning until they had burned their way through.

nigger† *v. Hist.* burn through the trunk of a tree by using a nigger, *q.v.*
1905 SCHERCK *Pen Pictures* 49: To save the time and labor of cutting the fallen trees into lengths for being drawn together by the oxen, they were often "niggered." **1909** ROSS *History of Zorra* 18: I've seen those old settlers "niggar" the fallen logs—that is, they would build a small fire on top of the fallen logs . . . and keep it burning until it was burnt through.

niggered *adj. Hist.* of trees, burned with a nigger, *q.v.*
1909 ROSS *History of Zorra* 18: When the trees were trimmed out, cut or "niggared," the ground would be staked out for a bee. . . .

niggerhead *n.* **1** *Fur Trade* See **niggerhead tobacco.**
1922 *Beaver* Sep. 16/1: I'll bet ye a pound of niggerhead that Old Joe's followin' us. . . . **1956** CRATE & WILLIAMS *We Speak for the Silent* 3: Groceries—particularly tea and "niggerhead" (a trade-tobacco for smoking and chewing)—are his more necessary "luxuries."

2 *North* **a.** See 1898 quote. See also **hummock** (def. 3), **tête-de-femme,** and **woman's head.**
1898 *Hints for Intending Klondikers* 18: But let him disembark and go inland and he will find the ground covered with what are locally known as "niggerheads," which consist of columns of decayed coarse grass peculiar to this region. They are formed by the annual growths of grasses decaying and falling down, while year after year the roots of the growing grasses bind this together into an almost solid column, which stands upon a bed of mud. **1938** *Beaver* June 40/1: Unless the train stopped near a creek, we had to scoop up water from the ditch or between the "niggerheads." **1958** BERTON *Klondike* 44: They poled up the Klondike for two miles, left their boat in a backwater, shouldered their packs, and began to trudge through the wet mosses and black muck and the great clumps of grass "niggerheads" that marked the mouth of Rabbit.

b. such mounds of grass collectively.
1909 SERVICE *Cheechako* 20: By muskeg hollow and nigger-head it wandered endlessly. . . . **1953** MOWERY *Mounted Police* 124: When he emerged from the niggerhead twenty minutes later, he was soaking wet and plastered with mud, but he had two tender young mallards in his sack.

niggerhead tobacco *Fur Trade, Hist.* a slender, twisted plug of tobacco once common in the old Northwest. See also **head, negrohead tobacco, niggerhead** (def. 1), **North West twist,** and **thistle twist tobacco.**
1860 *Nor'Wester* (R.R.S.) 28 June 4/5: After that I would smoke half a plug of "nigger-head tobacco." **1910** FRASER *Red Meekins* 98: A chaw of niggerhead tobacco'd be more in his line. **1936** *Beaver* Mar. 7/2: It is probably the lineal descendant of the nigger-head tobacco used in the Indian trade years ago, and as it came in ropes it was sold by the inch.

niggering *n. Hist.* the practice or process of using niggers, *q.v.*, to burn through the trunk of a tree.
1852 (1923) MOODIE *Roughing It* 339: Thus, after felling the trees, instead of chopping them into lengths, for the purpose of facilitating the operation of piling them preparatory to burning, which would have cost him too much labour, he resorted to the practice of "niggering," as it is called; which is simply laying light pieces of round timber across the trunks of the trees, and setting fire to them at the point of contact, by which means the trees are slowly burned through.

nigger wool a coarse grass or sedge, *Carex filifolia*, of the prairies, used widely in mulching to combat soil erosion. Cp. **prairie wool.**
1952 PUTNAM *Cdn Regions* 351/2: The characteristic species of the short grass are: June grass . . . blue grama . . . nigger wool. . . .

nightfishing *n.* the practice of fishing at night with the aid of a jacklight (def. 1) or other source of light to attract the fish.
1832 (1953) RADCLIFF *Letters* 175: The method . . . usually preferred is *night-fishing,* which is effected thus: Two sportsmen take their stations in a light skiff, one at the bow, with a spear in hand, the other at the stern. **1900** LONG *Wilderness Ways* 32: And when I had been out late on the lake, night-fishing . . . I would listen with childish anticipation for Killooleet's welcome as I approached the landing.

night-herd† *n. West* the job of preventing cattle from straying from the herd at night.
1955 HOBSON *Nothing Too Good* 71: At 4:00 A.M. Simrose and Rob came in from their night-herd shift and shook Stobie and myself awake for our turn round the cattle. **1963** SYMONS *Many Trails* 57: Usually everyone did a two-hour spell of night herd, or "guard" as it was sometimes called. . . .

night-herd† *v. West* prevent cattle from straying from the herd at night.
1903 *Eye Opener* (High River, Alta) 22 Aug. 1/3: What we would call roughing it is following the round-up and night-herding in wet weather, working on a threshing outfit in Manitoba or working for one's board on the farm of a Methodist Manitoban farmer. **1955** HOBSON *Nothing Too Good* 65: I took a chance and told the boys that there was no use night herding since there was not little time to sleep. **1963** SYMONS *Many Trails* 37: . . . we certainly did not propose to night herd.

night-herder† *n.* one who night-herds, *q.v.*
1945 GARD *Johnny Chinook* 41: The crew consisted of the wagon boss, six bull whackers, the night herder, and last but not least, the cook. **1955** MCCOWAN *Upland*

Trails 18: [He is] Mortal scared of a bear and an awful headache to a night-herder but a grand horse on a long steep trail.

Ninety-eighter *n. Hist.* a person who took part in the Klondike goldrush of 1898.
1955 HARDY *Alta Anthol.* 158: Today the journey takes four or five days by car; but when the Ninety-eighters began their foot-wearying pack-horse trek, they reached their destination two years later . . . if at all.

Ninety-two Resolutions *Hist.* See 1963 quote.
1836 *Vindicator* (Montreal) 18 Mar. 3/2: To the Poll, then, Reformers of Quebec and register your votes for Painchaud and the Ninety-two Resolutions. **1963** MORTON *Kingdom of Canada* 239: In Lower Canada, Papineau's party . . . embodied their grievances and their proposals for reform in the Ninety-two Resolutions which were approved by the Assembly in 1834.

Ninna-bo-jou *n.* See **Nanabozho.**

Ninoo *n. Obs.* See **Nanook.**

nip *n. Arctic* See 1850 cite. Cp. **nipped.**
1850 (1851) SNOW *Voyage* 107: At the far end of the "nip," that is, the place where two floes had met and crushed up parts of themselves into heavy hummocks, it was more loose, and it seemed to me that by a little exertion they might be made still looser, if some pieces were pushed out into the open water there, instead of working close to the ship where no room was.
1857 MCDOUGALL *Voyage* 68: At the time of the fog clearing, we were shut out from a comparatively large body of water, in shore of the ship, by a stubborn nip about 300 yards in length, and although Sunday, this was attacked by a party of men from each ship.

nipko(o) ['nɪpko *or* 'nɪpku] *n.* [< Esk.; cf. East Esk. *nikku* dried meat] See 1955 quote.
1937 *Beaver* June 30/1: The dried [caribou] meat (*nipko*) is put up during the spring migration of the bucks northwards, the meat being cut into strips and set in the sun to dry. **1942** *Ibid.* Mar. 5/2: Driftwood fires sizzle and smoke in front of every tent, wooden racks sag under the weight of dried strips of unpalatable looking seal meat, the age-old *nipkoo* that provides a welcome tid-bit in times of plenty and safeguards against famine when times are hard.
1955 ADTIC *Glossary*: nipko, *n.* An Eskimo term for jerky. Nipko is usually made of caribou meat, but may be of beluga or narwhal.

nipped (in) *adj. Arctic* of ships, caught and held, and sometimes, especially with older wooden vessels, utterly crushed, by the coming together of two ice-floes. Cp. **nip.**
1850 (1852) OSBORN *Arctic Jnl* 72: Penny had passed a long way inside of the spot the steamers had been beset and nipped in; and he witnessed a sight which, although constantly taking place, is seldom seen—the entire dissolution of an enormous ice-berg. **1861** *Nor'Wester* (R.R.S.) 1 Feb. 1/1: In the autumn of 1859 the Kitty, of Newcastle, was nipped in the ice and lost in Hudson's Bay, while taking stores out to York Factory.
1909 CAMERON *New North* 292: Two years ago the ships bound for "Outside" got nipped in early ice and were forced to winter at Herschel all unprepared.
1937 *Beaver* June 13/2: The "Fort James," a Company schooner, was "nipped" in the ice at Tuktuk, on the Western Arctic coast, 4000 miles from the nearest dry-dock.

nipper[1]† *n. Maritimes* a thick woollen mitten or wrap-around, used by fishermen to protect hands and wrists from the friction of the running lines. Cp. **neaps.**
1955 WALLACE *Roving Fisherman* 48: "Guess we'll haul back," said Jim at last, slipping a pair of woollen "nippers" over his hands and standing up in the bow of the dory.

nipper[2] *n. Mining* the person responsible for getting equipment and material from the station to the work-place, that is, the spot where the mining operation is being carried out. See also **call-boy** and **king-nipper.**
☛ *Clearly an extension of the British* **nipper** *"helper" (usually a youngster, from which is derived the slang sense "boy, lad").*
1963 *Western Miner* July 13/1: Only difference was when the nipper came down with the second bucketful of starters, that damned spot had grown up two inches. **1964** CRATE *Hardrock Mining* 4: Another occupational term that bears the stamp of British origin is "nipper," a nipper being originally a boy brought into the coal mines, usually as his father's helper. To-day the nipper is an expediter of materials used in the mine.

nippes *n.pl.* See **neaps.**

nipping-machine *n. Mining* See quote.
1964 CRATE *Hardrock Mining* 4: Because the nipper transports material from the drift to the raise, stope or *sub-level* by means of a small compressed-air hoist usually called a *tugger*, a machine that came into general use during the '30's, it has received the alternative name of *nipping-machine*.

nistow ['nɪsto] *n.* See **neshtow.**

nitchie or **Nitchie** ['nɪtʃi] *n.* [< Algonk.; cf. Ojibwa *anishinābe* Indian, friend] Also spelled *neche, nechee, nee-che, neejee,* etc. **1** *Obs.* in Indian parlance, especially of another Indian, a friend.
[**1768-82** (1904) LONG *Voyages* 303: Neejee . . . Friend]
1837 (1923) JAMESON *Rambles* 290: Thus, one man addressing another says "nichi" or "neejee," my friend. **1852** (1881) TRAILL *Cdn Crusoes* 188: While she called Louis, "Nee-chee," or friend. . . . **1857** (1863) PALLISER *Journals* 52: Our Indian guide . . . to whom we had given the name Nichiwa, or friend.

2 an Indian (now often derogatory).
1850 BIGSBY *Shoe and Canoe* II 161: I sallied forth, and found the Nidges loading the canoes, drest in their best. **1903** (1913) CULLUM *Devil's Keg* 178: A neche was leisurely cleaning up round Lablache's store. . . . **1930** BEAMES *Army* 131: "Have to see if I can dig up a Nitchie an' trade whitefish for tobacco or something," he concluded. **1960** *Canada's Story in Song* 127: They leave their homes on starving pay to take the nitchies' lives.

3 a small Indian pony; cayuse, *q.v.*
1915 CHICANOT *Polyglot Vernacular* 88: "Nitchie" is an alternate name for Indian and is also applied to the small native ponies.

nob stick *Obs.* See **lobstick** (def. 1).
1896 WHITNEY *On Snow-Shoes* 321: In the afternoon some of the Indians crossed the river, and, on one of the highest points, made two "lop," "lob," or "nob" sticks, as they are variously called in honor of Spencer and myself.

1963 *Albertan* (Calgary) 23 Dec. 3/1: But the problem was solved by pushing off or compacting the snow with the Nodwell, thus permitting the frost to penetrate the ground. 1964 *Calgary Herald* 11 Mar. 28/4: Calgary-built Nodwell track-vehicles are being used to supply troops with food, gas and equipment in the field. . . .

The Nome hitch

Nome hitch *North* See 1941 quote. See also **snooge**. Cp. **fan hitch** and **tandem hitch**.
1941 *Beaver* Mar. 11/2: In the Western Arctic, the "Nome" hitch is used instead of the "fan" hitch. In this arrangement the dogs pull two and two along a centre trace, with a single lead dog. 1943 *Ibid.* Mar. 36: [Caption] Note the Eskimo style dog harness, and the Nome hitch, seldom used with a toboggan.

nomination day a day fixed by law for the filing of nominations for elective offices.
1869 *Cdn Illust. News* 30 Oct. 3/1: Nomination day for the North Riding of Renfrew is fixed for the 2nd November. 1963 *Kingston Whig-Standard* (Ont.) 6 May 4/6: The simplest solution would be for Parliament to change the rules it has made and order that Nomination Day for all candidates be three weeks before Election Day instead of two.

non-capital murder murder for which the maximum punishment is life imprisonment. Cp. **capital murder**.
1962 *Kingston Whig-Standard* (Ont.) 14 Feb. 14/1: [He] changed his plea to guilty of non-capital murder . . . and was sentenced to life imprisonment. 1963 *Maclean's* 23 Mar. 2/3: The next day, the farmers were charged with noncapital murder and rounded up again. Then warrants were issued for the union men.

non-commissioned officer *Maritimes, Obs.* the white-throated sparrow.
1849 ALEXANDER *L'Acadie* II 60: It [the peabody bird] is also called the non-commissioned officer, as its note is like that of one calling for "pen and ink, pen and ink, pen and ink. . . ."

non-import *n. Cdn Football* an American player who, by virtue of having played in the Canadian league for four years, is no longer to be counted as one of the limited number of imported players allowed each team. Cp. **import** (def. 2).
1964 *Winnipeg Free Press* 19 June 36/5: . . . Americans only had to live here four years to qualify as non-imports. 1966 *Globe and Mail* (Toronto) 29 June 40/3: . . . it was the Rough Riders that pressed for a new definition of non-imports. . . .

nonny-bag ['nɑni,bæg] *n. Nfld* See **nunny-bag**.
1918 GRENFELL *Labrador Doctor* 90: Our sealers carry dry oatmeal and sugar in their "nonny bags," which, mixed with snow, assuage their thirst and hunger as well.

non-potlatcher *n. B.C.* an Indian opposed to the potlatch system, *q.v.*
1961 LA VIOLETTE *Survival* 94: When the writer was in Alert Bay in 1946, Indian informants claimed that the agent had divided the reserve into two major sections: the area for "potlatchers" to live in and the area for "non-potlatchers." This was not confirmed.

non-separatist *n.* with reference to French Canada, an opponent of the withdrawal of Quebec from Confederation.
1961 *Canada Month* 6 Oct. 40/1: . . . if the Lesage government is aggressively autonomist—though non-separatist—this is at least in part a response to the nationalistic temper of Quebec. . . .

non-treaty *n.* See **non-treaty Indian**.
1945 *Beaver* Mar. 12/1: . . . a population of some four hundred Chipewyans and one hundred Crees, the latter being mixed treaties and non-treaties.

non-treaty *adj.* of Indians, not living under the terms of a treaty (def. 1a). Cp. **out of treaty**.
1945 GARD *Johnny Chinook* 228: An interesting legend exists among this little band of Nontreaty Chippewas. 1963 *Cdn Geog. Jnl* Jan. 32/2: Farther west, the Indians waited for news of the Métis progress. The Crees on Poundmaker's reserve in the Eagle Hills south of Battleford were restless and hungry. So were the Assiniboines just west. Equally disgruntled were the non-treaty Crees of the Big Bear's band, who had put in a lean winter. Both chiefs were notable for keeping the peace.

non-treaty Indian an Indian who is not living under the terms of a treaty (def. 1a). See also **non-treaty,** *n.* and *adj.* Cp. **treaty Indian**.
1878 *Sask. Herald* (Battleford, N.W.T.) 18 Nov. 2/2: When they leave the hunting grounds to attend the annual payments the non-treaty Indians invade them, killing and racing away the game, so that when they return home they find no game, and their families consequently suffer. 1964 DUFF *Indian History* 70: The generalization, often heard, that the Indians of British Columbia are "non-treaty" Indians is not wholly true.

No. 1 hard Manitoba (wheat) See **Manitoba**.

Nootka cypress [< *Nootka* Sound, Vancouver Island] See **yellow cedar**.
1935 WALLACE *Encyclopedia* II 170/2: The yellow cypress . . . is known under various names . . . yellow cedar . . . canoe cedar, Nootka cypress and others and is confined to the Pacific coast. 1956 *Native Trees* 78: YELLOW CEDAR [is also called] Yellow cypress . . . Nootka cypress, canoe cedar.

Norseman *n. Trademark* a light airplane formerly much used in bush-flying throughout the North.
1943 *Beaver* Mar. 21/2: The plane was a Canadian Airways "Norseman." 1954 LONGSTRETH *Force Carries On* 146: A Norseman nine-passenger, single-engine, bush-type aircraft which can operate on wheels, floats, or skis, is based at Fort Smith, N.W.T. 1961 *Time* (Cdn ed.) 25 Aug. 9/3: It was near spring breakup, and before rescue arrived, the Norseman sank to the lake bottom.

North *n.* See **North Country**.
1793 (1933) MACDONELL *Diary* 77: This is called *les Rochers du Grand Callumet,* and here I saw for the first time, *tripe de Roche,* (rock weed)—which the men tell me is the last resource men have to subsist on in the inhospitable regions of the dreary north, and it has been Know[n] to keep men alive for months, boiled in water. . . . 1937 *Beaver* June 5/2: . . . the North is

always there like a presence; it is the background of the picture without which Canada would not be Canada. **1954** BERTON *I Married Klondike* 7: The clergymen on board made a fairly good cross section of the church in the North, as I was to see it in the years that followed.

North American Chinaman or **Chinese** *Slang, Derog., Hist.* among goldseekers in the Cariboo, a person from the Canadas; a Canadian. See also **oatmeal Chinaman.**

1932 MATHEWS *Early Vancouver* 320: Canadians acquired a reputation for "horning in", and simultaneously the epithet "North American Chinamen". **1952** (1965) HAMILTON *Cdn Quotations* 29/1: North American Chinamen—Pre-Confederation British Columbia term used to describe the "Canadians" who were unpopular because of their thriftiness. **1958** WATTERS *B.C.Cent.Anthol.* 408: . . . Englishmen, Canadians . . . jostled the Celestials, as everyone called the Chinese. Canadians were not too popular either; they were often called North American Chinese because they sent their money back to the Canadian provinces.

North canoe *Fur Trade, Hist.* a birchbark canoe 25 to 35 feet long, 5 to 6 feet wide, and 2 to 2½ feet deep, capable of carrying some 1½ to 2 tons of goods, a crew of 8 or 9, and 2 or 3 passengers, used primarily on the waterways north and west of Lake Superior. See also **canoe** (def. 1), **canoe** (def. 3), **canot du nord, light northern canoe, Northwest canoe, N.W. canoe,** and **six-fathom canoe.**

1819 WENTZEL *Letters* 134: Sir Alexander MacKenzie has suggested that one north canoe with Canadian voyageurs, and six small Indian canoes, would be a fitter outfit for the route from Fort Chipewyan to the Coppermine River. **1821** (1900) GARRY *Diary* 118: Our Canoes are much smaller than the Montreal Canoe and are called the "North Canoes" which Designation "North Men" is given to the Men who from long Experience and being more inured to the Changes of Climate and Fatigue and Privations are more hardy. **1879** ROBINSON *Great Fur Land* 31: The North canoe . . . is a light graceful vessel about thirty-six long, by four or five broad, and capable of containing eight men and three passengers. **1957** FISHER *Pemmican* 250: David stood in what was called a north canoe; twenty-five foot long and from four to five feet wide, it could carry a crew of eight or nine men and their supplies, as well as three passengers.

North Country the extensive, largely inhospitable regions of northern Canada, especially the Far North, *q.v.* See also **North, Northland,** and **Northlands.**

1896 WHITNEY *On Snow-Shoes* 150: So long as you have tea and tobacco you are entire master of the situation; for there is nothing you cannot obtain with one or the other of these North Country luxuries, and, moreover, there is no peace for you so long as either remains. **1965** *Kingston Whig-Standard* (Ont.) 7 Feb. 7/4: [He] had made himself a living legend with his periodic forays out of Ontario's north country. . . .

Northeast(ern) Territory *Hist.* prior to 1912, a name given to the entire Labrador peninsula. See 1892 quote.

1892 (1908) DAWSON & SUTHERLAND *Geography* 141: NORTH-EAST TERRITORY By this name is known the whole of the Labrador peninsula (120,000) square miles north of the province of Quebec, and west of the Atlantic coast-strip, which is politically attached to Newfoundland under the name of Labrador. **1961** *Cdn Geog.Jnl* Jan. 34/2: Major J. D. Moodie of the North West Mounted Police was appointed Acting Commissioner of the unorganized Northeastern Territories.

Northern *n.* See **northern pike.**

1956 KEMP *Northern Trader* 216: About the time I had knocked off a dozen more Northerns and had wallowed through Lesson Thirteen, Elsie decided to borrow Wally's dogs and go with me to La Ronge for the mail. **1964** *Western Wkly* 1 July 6/4: [Advert.] LAKE OF THE WOODS Thousands of other smaller lakes—Fishing, hunting, Recreation. Always top angling for Walleyes, Northerns, Bass, Lake Trout.

Northern Allowance a bonus paid to persons employed in the Far North as compensation for the high cost of living.

1954 *North West Territories Teachers Association Rev.* Dec. 3: Whereas the cost of living becomes considerably higher the farther north you go be it requested therefore, that some adjustment be made, either in the form of an increase in the Northern Allowance or the inclusion of a ration system for those teachers who are serviced by aeroplane and/or water only.

northern canoe See **North canoe.**

1938 *Beaver* Dec. 13/1: The northern canoe carried a crew of five or six men, apart from passengers. **1954** CAMPBELL *Nor'Westers* 44: Each northern canoe held twenty-five ninety-pound packs instead of the sixty loaded into the Montreal canoes . . . Even fewer packs were carried in the Athabaska canoes, so as to make better time on the four-thousand mile Rainy-Fort Chipewyan round trip between spring thaw and autumn freeze-up.

Northern Department *Hist.* the largest of the administrative divisions of the Hudson's Bay Company. See 1956 quote.

1824 (1931) SIMPSON *Fur Trade* 6: I do not conceive that the business of the North[n] Deptm[t] requires at any time exceeding Twenty Clerks whose Education & abilities should lead them to expect preferment in the Service, while there are Thirty Four commissioned Gentlemen attached thereto. **1956** INNIS *Travellers West* 3: The Hudson Bay Company's Northern Department extended from Hudson Bay to the Rocky Mountains and from the United States Boundary to the Arctic Ocean. **1963** MACLEOD & MORTON *Cuthbert Grant* 83: On July 5 [1823] the Council of the Northern Department of Rupert's Land appointed Grant . . . to be clerk in Lower Red River for three years at a salary of not more than £120.

Northerner *n.* **1** a resident or native of the North, especially the Far North, *q.v.* See also **Northman** (def. 2). Cp. **North Country.**

1936 STEELE *Policing the Arctic* 211: Every Northerner knows that a backward glance over the trail just traversed often helps in keeping direction, especially if the trail ahead lies through unknown country. **1963** *Maclean's* 23 Feb. 42/4: Northerners figure that one wolf will kill fourteen caribou in a year, and as the number of wolves has gone up, the number of caribou has gone down.

2 See **Northern Indian** (def. 1a).
1900 OSBORN *Greater Canada* 202: A few Chippewyans or Northerners still dwelt in the more northerly districts of the Territories. **1932** KENNEY *Ft Churchill* 56: The woman interpreter, who seems to have been the dominating figure in the whole affair, announced to the Northerners that a factory would be built at Churchill, and explained how they should catch and prepare the furs for the trade.

3 one of the Haida of the north B.C. Coast. Cp. **Northern Indian** (def. 2).
1927 MCKELVIE *Black Canyon* 31: The Northerner leisurely approached the roaring furnace until the heat must have blistered his flesh. . . . **1959** *Programme of the 12th Annual Indian Pow Wow* (Capilano Indian Reserve, North Vancouver, B.C.) 25 July 2/1: Now the Northerners were reputed to be a fierce and bloodthirsty lot, and here was a situation which demanded craft and cunning if the women and children and old people were not to fall under the butchering onslaught of our enemies.

northern hare See **varying hare.**
1866 KING *Sportsman in Can.* 25: The common Hare of Canada, or Northern Hare (Lepus Americanus), though one of those generally denominated throughout the country a "rabbit," is in its habits and anatomy a true hare, and presents the following very distinctive characteristics of the species:—its legs are much longer than those of the common rabbit; there is a greater disproportion between the length of the fore and hind legs; and the eye is yellow.

Northern Indian 1 a. a Chipewyan, so named in the Churchill region of Hudson Bay by the English traders to distinguish them from the Crees further south. See also **Northerner** (def. 2) and **Northward Indian.**
1689 (1929) KELSEY *Papers* 26: Found an old Canoe of these northern Indians. . . . **1715** (1932) *Beaver* Sep. 100: To Day I made a feast for the home Indians to know how many were willing to make a peace with the Northern Indians. . . . **1821** (1900) GARRY *Diary* 195: Among the Northern Indians or Chipewyans Pictures of any kind are in great Estimation for they generally consider them as Charms and frequently request them from us in the Fall of the Year to ensure Success during the Winter. **1963** *Beaver* Winter 5/2: . . . through [this area] the boundary line between the Northern Indians and their traditional enemies the Eskimos ran at this time.

b. a member of any of the Athapaskan tribes of the Northwest.
1834 (1909) CAMERON *New North* 111: . . . they are travelling on strange lands to kill grief, not an unusual custom among the Northern Indians. **1850** (1910) BURPEE *Yukon* 10: Again I have made frequent enquiries of the "Gens du large," of the Northern Indians, who visit the Arctic sea coast. . . . **1914** DOUGLAS *Lands Forlorn* 143: We saw none of that harsh treatment of their women supposed to be the custom of the Northern Indians. **1921** HAWORTH *Trailmakers* 27: Two years before, with two white companions, he had started with some of the northern Indians, but in a few weeks the Indians grew weary of the journey and plundered the white men of most of their possessions.

2 an Indian of the north coast of British Columbia, especially of the Haida. See also **Northern People** and **Northman** (def. 3). Cp. **Northerner** (def. 3).
1860 *Brit.Colonist* (Victoria) 3 Apr. 3/1: The Northern Indians are expecting a large number of their friends

from above, and as soon as they arrive, threaten to exterminate the Flat-heads. *Ibid.* 21 June 2/3: Tuesday evening saw a renewal of hostilities between the Hyter and Stickeen tribes of Northern Indians. **1927** MCKELVIE *Black Canyon* 44: Sometimes, though, they join to fight the Northern Indians.

3 one of the Montagnais and Naskapi Indians of the Ungava peninsula.
1963 DAVIES *Northern Quebec* xxxii: . . . between Eastmain River and Richmond Gulf, lived other Algonkian Indians of a more primitive and independent nature, the Northern Indians of the Eastmain and Whale River journals, who were less inclined or less able to become regular fur-trappers. . . .

Northern Messenger See 1959 quote.
1944 (1945) *Beaver* Mar. 22/1: All in all the [New Year's] evening was a great success, and especially so when the "Northern Messenger" via CBA came in clear and distinct, and all of us received messages. **1959** *Northern Affairs Bull.* Sep.-Oct. 12/1: THE NORTHERN MESSENGER, a program of messages to the police, missionaries, weathermen and others stationed in the North from their families and friends "outside", has been broadcast weekly throughout the winter every year since 1933. It is the oldest continuous radio program on CBC.

Northern Nation *Obs.* the Northern Indians (def. 1a).
1723 (1923) *Beaver* Mar. 234/1: . . . he being one of those that was Imploy'd to make the Peace with: the Northern Nation for wch. he was made a Capn: and Expects Greater Privileges Still than I can well afford him. . . .

Northern People *Hist.* See **Northern Indian** (def. 2).
1923 BARBEAU *Indian Days* 141: When the "Northern People" repaired to Fort Union for the barter of furs, in the autumn of 1843, the first . . . was no other than old Tchatka.

northern pike† a large species of pike, *Esox lucius,* found in northern waters. See also **brochet, jackfish, Northern,** and **white pike.**
1952 WILSON *Chibougamau* 71: The Great Northern Pike (Brochet) can reach forty pounds in weight. American anglers sometimes call this fish a 'muskie' for it resembles the muskellonge. **1961** *Edmonton Jnl* 12 Aug. 4/3: . . . commercial fishing was influential in the development of Lac La Biche itself. In its busiest days, 500,000 pounds of whitefish, pickerel, northern pike and tullibee were marketed from its waters in a single year.

northern service officer a federal government officer in charge of a district in the Far North. See also **N.S.O.**
1955 *Edmonton Jnl* 4 Jan. 7/6: The first phase of the program calls for construction of a two-room school which can be enlarged, housing for a northern service officer, a technical instructor and a school teacher, a warehouse, garage-workshop, mess hall, bunk house and power house. **1964** JENNESS *Eskimo Admin.* II 129: Teachers in Eskimo schools . . . were expected to perform welfare work after school hours; but the added burden proved impracticable, and today special "welfare officers" and "northern service officers" carry out those duties.

Northland *n.* See **North Country.**
1880 GORDON *Mountain and Prairie* 172: In the remoter
north-land competition will be powerless for many
years to come, and both soil and climate will protect
them from the inroads of colonisation. **1958** *Beaver*
Autumn 58/2: The Northland can be variously defined.
It may be the area north of 60°, the southern edge of the
Canadian Territories or north of 55° at the base of
Hudson Bay. **1964** *Naicam Sentinel* 26 Mar. 4/2: . . .
the finished articles are to be packed and sent out to
our missionary families in the northland.

Northlander *n.* **1** a native or resident of the North
Country, *q.v.* See also **Northland.**
1919 ROYAL *Trail of a Sourdough* 12: " 'Twas a night in
the middle of winter, A night such as Northlanders
know. . . ."

2 an Eskimo.
1960 *Kingston Whig-Standard* (Ont.) 9 May 5/7:
. . . cooked meat is greatly preferred by the Innuit, or
people, as the northlanders call themselves.

Northlands *n.pl.* See **North Country.**
1948 *Cdn Geog.Jnl* 149/2: Muskegs are so much the
predominating features of many districts that the word
itself seems to carry with it a savour of the northlands.
1961 *Ibid.* Jan. 3/1: This article is an endeavour to
outline some features with respect to . . . our Northlands.

Northland string See **babiche** (def. 1).
1896 WHITNEY *On Snow-Shoes* 88: The woman . . .
scrapes and tans the moose and caribou hides, from the
latter of which she afterwards makes *babiche*
(Northland string) by cutting it into strips an eighth of an
inch wide.

Northman *n.* **1** *Fur Trade, Hist.* See **winterer**
(def. 2a). See also **Man of the North** (def. 1).
1793 (1933) MACDONELL *Diary* 93: The North men while
here live in tents of different sizes pitched at random. . . .
1894 BEGG *Hist.of B.C.* 102: To the north-men, as the
employés who wintered in the forest were called, were
attached more than seven hundred native women and
children, victualled at the Company's expense.
1938 GODSELL *Red Hunters* 55: Beyond Grande Portage
the freighting was taken over by the boastful,
hard-drinking, hard-fighting Northmen whose duty it
was to convey the goods to the distant wilds of
Saskatchewan and the Athabasca. **1957** FISHER *Pemmican*
136: It had been said that no other northman could
blow up such a wind of brag or sweeten insults with such
wild honey. . . .

2 See **Northerner** (def. 1).
1953 *North Star* (Yellowknife) Oct. 3/2: The northmen
of the forts, the trappers and wanderers of the barrens,
speak from lifetimes of experience and an intimate
concern with things northern.

3 See **Northern Indian** (def. 2).
1958 WATTERS *B.C.Cent.Anthol.* 112: The northmen they
feared were the dreaded Haidas of the Queen Charlotte
Islands.

North Shore 1 the eastern part of New
Brunswick, fronting on the Gulf of St. Lawrence
and Northumberland Strait.
1812 *Montreal Herald* 25 Apr. 2/1: A petition of sundry
inhabitants of the North shore, below Cape Tourmente,
in the county of Northumberland, was presented to the

House, and ordered to remain on the table. **1892** (1908)
DAWSON & SUTHERLAND *Geography* 86: The . . . seven
towns are the principal ones on the eastern shore, often
locally called the "north shore," of the province.
1965 *Globe and Mail* (Toronto) 5 Jan. 7/2: . . . new
mining and smelting developments on New Brunswick's
North Shore . . . are changing the whole economic face
of that part of Canada.

2 that part of southeastern Quebec lying on the
north shore of the Gulf of St. Lawrence and the St.
Lawrence River.
1824 *Canadian Mag.* III 380: The whole North Shore of
the St. Lawrence, from Quebec to its mouth, and the
Labradore Coast, offers to the Geologist and
Mineralogist a field for research, such as we believe
cannot be met with in any other country. **1952** PUTNAM
Cdn Regions 211/1: The North Shore extends over 655
miles from Tadoussac to Blanc-Sablon at the Strait of
Belle Isle and inland to the height of land which forms
the boundary of the Coast of Labrador. **1963** *Maclean's*
16 Nov. 56/4: . . . nearly everyone I met on the staff of
the QNS & L was a North Shore oldtimer. . . .

3 the north shore of Burrard Inlet, opposite
Vancouver, B.C.
1958 *Citizen* (Vancouver) 4 Dec. 8/4: A resident of
North Vancouver since 1945 . . . his writing has helped
put the North Shore on the nation's map. **1965** *Globe
and Mail* (Toronto) 9 Jan. 1/7: The snow was so high
in the upper reaches of West Vancouver and other
North Shore municipalities that there were fears of
flooding. . . .

Northward Indian *Obs.* See **Northern Indian**
(def. 1a).
1743 (1949) ISHAM *Observations* 155: Among'st the
Northward Indians, and Ehuskemay's they have neither
of these beast's. **1785** (1954) *Moose Ft Jnls* 305: He has
even gone and taken one of our best young hunters
away with him to Moose clandestinely, and one of our
young Women and her young Boy obliged to fly in the
night time with the No'ward Indians as he was going
to take her likewise.

Northwest *n.* Also spelled *North-West, North-*
west, northwest, etc. **1** *Hist.* **a.** the vast region north
and west of Lake Superior, as known by the fur
traders and explorers. See also **Canadian Northwest,**
Great West, Northwestern Territory, Northwest
territory, and **pays d'en Haut.**
1775 (1901) HENRY (Elder) *Travels* 236: I was now [at
the Grand Portage] in what is technically called the
north-west; that is, the country north-west of Lake
Superior. **1871** (1883) BUTLER *Great Lone Land* 109: The
men who went out to the North-west as *voyageurs* and
servants in the employment of the rival companies from
Canada and from Scotland hardly ever returned to their
native lands. **1963** *Beaver* Winter 33/1: . . . the Canadian
government had yet to face the problem of actually
establishing order in the great North West.

b. See **Northwest Territories** (def. 1b).
1860 *Nor'Wester* (R.R.S.) 14 Feb. 2/3: What true
Canadian can witness the tide of immigration now
commencing to flow into the vast territories of the
North-west without longing to have a share in the first
settlement of that great and fertile country. **1908** MAIR
Mackenzie Basin 15: The year 1857 was an eventful one
in the annals of "The North-West," the name by which
the Territories were generally known in Canada.
1958 *Northern Miner* 27 Nov. 25/2: At eighteen Uncle
Dan had left his Ontario village for the "North West."
This was a vague wilderness near a place called
Winnipeg, where you could file on a homestead of 160
acres of bald prairie.

2 the general region making up the present Yukon and Northwest Territories (def. 2b) and adjacent areas of the western provinces.

517

**North-West Angle
Northwestern**

2 the general region making up the present Yukon and Northwest Territories (def. 2b) and adjacent areas of the western provinces.
1914 BICKERSTETH *Open Doors* XV: This is far from being a true picture of life as it is lived in the far North-West. **1952** PUTNAM *Cdn Regions* 498/1: The Northwest is a vast region occupying about ten per cent of the area of Canada. **1961** *Edmonton Jnl* 17 July 3/1: Alberta farmers, caught in drought-parched areas, are also increasing the demand for homestead land in the northwest.

North-West Angle the farthest northwesterly point of the Lake of the Woods, established as part of the Canada-U.S. border by the Treaty of Paris in 1783.
1815 BOUCHETTE *Lower Canada* 589: [From] north-west angle of the Lake of the Woods.... **1871** *Wkly Manitoban* 18 Feb. 2/6: A good cart road to the North-West Angle had been so nearly finished when he left, that by next week, it would be complete. **1877** GRANT *Ocean to Ocean* 67: At sunset the North-west Angle was reached. This point, though far North of the 49th degree—the boundary line between the Dominion and the United States, is claimed by the Republic, and their claim is sustained by an evident verbal mistake in the Treaty that defines the boundary. "North-west" has been inserted instead of "South-west." **1963** MORTON *Kingdom of Canada* 173: From Lake Superior the line was to follow the fur traders' route to the north-west angle of the Lake of the Woods....

Northwest canoe *Hist.* See **North canoe.**
1793 (1911) SIMCOE *Diary* 209: I went to-day for the first time in the North-West canoe. **1823** (1954) *B.C. Hist.Qtly* XVIII 160: An ordinary Northwest canoe, manned by five men, carries about 3,000 pounds, and seldom draws, when laden, more than eighteen inches of water. **1905** (1954) *B.C.Hist.Qtly* XVIII 208: The usual route with northwest canoes, via Saskatchewan Fort Assiniboine and Athabaska river, took us to the source of the latter, where is Jasper House (so named frome Jasper Hawse, a northwest company's clerk in the early part of the century). **1963** MACLEOD & MORTON *Cuthbert Grant* 27: On the same day ... forty-two colonists left for Canada in North West canoes....

Northwest cart *Obs.* See **Red River cart.**
1890 *Grip* (Toronto) 15 Feb. 98/1: Two official languages [would be] "as useless as two tongues on a North-West cart." And yet the vehicle in question requires two tongues just as much as the Governmental Machine of the Territories does.

North West Company *Hist.* a fur-trading syndicate with its headquarters at Montreal, organized between 1775 and 1783 and absorbed by the Hudson's Bay Company in 1821. See also **Lords of the North, Montreal Company, North West Fur Company,** and **N.W. Company.** Also spelled *Northwest Company.*
1788 (1951) ROE *North Amer.Buffalo* 845: A request from the Northwest Company for a grant of land one acre in width from Lake Superior to Long Lake. **1807** *Quebec Gaz.* 22 Oct. 4/1: Without resorting to the usual frauds of promises never intended to be fulfilled, the North West Company has explored an immense region, and penetrated even to the Pacific Ocean. **1891** *Trans.Roy.Soc.Can.* X 2 114: If potlatching and old-fashioned dancing did not at once fall into desuetude, it was because both were countenanced by the North-West Company and, later on, the Hudson Bay Company. **1963** MORTON *Kingdom*

of Canada 170: The pooling of interests in the northwest was accompanied by similar combinations at Montreal, and by 1778 men were commonly speaking of "the North West Company."

North-West Council *Hist.* an appointive council responsible for the affairs of the Northwest (def. 1a).
1923 *Beaver* Apr. 289/2: All the territory outside of Manitoba was under a governing body called "The North-West Council." **1958** *Encyc.Can.* VII 369/2: This act [Northwest Territories Act, 1875] provided for a resident Lieutenant-Governor and an appointed North-West council invested with both executive and legislative powers.

North West Currency *Hist.* See **Grand Portage Currency.**
1806 (1897) COUES *New Light* I 397: ... two skins, or 12 livres North West currency, making 24 livres Quebec currency, or one pound Halifax currency.

Northwester *n.* **1** *Hist.* **a.** a wintering partner (def. 1) or employee of the North West Company, *q.v.* See also **Montreal man, Northwest pedlar,** and **Nor'Wester** (def. 1b).
1791 (1889) MCKENZIE *Reminiscences* 36: It would be unbecoming a North-Wester to appear below so unprovided in that line. **1827** (1829) MACTAGGART *Three Years* I 191: ... when a mutiny appears about anything, the best way to have peace, is just to take the North-Wester's plan—dash into the mob, and knock the first down you meet, with a whack beneath the ear, when quietness is restored in a twinkling. **1860** *Nor'Wester* (R.R.S.) 15 Oct. 1/5: Among those present we also noticed Mr. Dease and other veteran North Westers. **1938** *Beaver* Dec. 10/1: Clarke was an ex-Northwester, first man into the Athabasca for the Hudson's Bay Company, and the founder of Fort Wedderburn.

b. (*plural*) the North West Company collectively. See also **Nor'Wester** (def. 1c).
1816 (1818) HALL *Travels* 143: The fur-traders, or North-westers, as they are familiarly termed, take the lead in society, for they give the best dinners. **1855** (1956) ROSS *Fur Hunters* 7: The Tartars never held the Grand Lama in higher estimation than the Canadians did the North Westers in those days. **1958** ATKINSON *Hist.of Penticton* 19: The North West Co. which had crossed the Rockies to establish Fort McLeod in 1805 had extended South to Kamloops also by 1812. Astor sold out to the North Westers in 1813.

2 a native or resident of the Northwest Territories (def. 1b). See also **Nor'Wester** (def. 2).
1882 *Edmonton Bull.* 8 July 4/1: Pain killer, the former standby of the North-Westers[,] was entirely at a discount. **1889** *Grip* (Toronto) 15 Jan. 4/1: More power to the elbows of our sturdy North-Westers....

Northwestern *adj.* of or pertaining to the Northwest Territories (def. 2). See also **Nor'Western.**
1900 OSBORN *Greater Can.* 130: "Nine months' winter and three months late in the fall;" even so the writer had heard the North-Western year defined by one of these gentry, who are in the habit of describing the Dominion as "that little ice-house up there." **1948** ONRAET *Sixty Below* 179: The scene was typically North-Western. The men wore beaded belts and

moccasins, rainbow-coloured shirts and bright silk scarves and tasselled vests.

Northwesterner *n. Obs.* See **Northwester** (def. 2).

1924 DORRANCE *Never Fire First* 74: "We're hitting the trail," explained the missionary. "We've just pitched camp and are about to make muck-muck. As North westerners never pack grub for idle hands to eat, we'd better strip off our coats and get into action."

Northwestern iron See **Northwest iron**.

Northwestern Territory *Hist.* See **Northwest** (def. 1a).

1953 LEBOURDAIS *Nation of North* 43: Lying to the north and west of Rupert's Land, as the Hudson's Bay Company domain was called, was an immense tract generally referred to as the North-Western Territory. This the Hudson's Bay Company had held under lease from the British government from 1821 to 1859.

Northwesters *n.pl.* See **Northwester** (def. 1b).

North West Field Force *Hist.* See quote.

1963 *Globe Mag.* 23 Feb. 10/4: The oldest is 106, the youngest 31, and included are seven veterans of the North West Field Force which took part in putting down the Riel Rebellion in 1885.

North West Fur Company *Hist.* See **North West Company**.

1798 (1957) *Ont.Hist.* XLIX 67: The great North West fur company buys up annually 5000 bushels of Indian corn. **1964** *Herald Mag.* 8 Aug. 4/1: This North West Fur Co. member founded Fort of the Forks there.

Northwest gun *Hist.* a light musket carried as trading goods by the North West Company. See also **Nor'Wester** (def. 1d), **Nor'West gun**, and **N.W. gun.** Cp. **fuke.**

1791 LONG *Voyages* 69: Suspecting the bad spirit was still in them, and that they were only gone a short distance to drink the rum, we prepared for an attack, loading twenty eight north-west guns and a brace of pistols, and sat down by the fire expecting their return to compleat the design my fortunate arrival had hitherto prevented. **1956** *Alta Hist.Rev.* Spring 5: Insofar as I have been able to determine, the name "North West gun" first came into use among traders in western Canada and the United States about the year 1800.

Northwest (or Northwestern) iron *Obs.* See **shaganappi** (defs. 1 and 2).

1890 *Trans.Roy.Soc.Can.* VIII 2 105: The last, but not the least, important product of the buffalo was shaganappi, or as it was often called "North-West Iron." [**1910** HODGE *Bulletin* II 518/1: *Shaganappi*, or "Northwestern Iron" was an important factor in the economic development of the N.W. . . . .]

North West livre *Hist.* a unit of Grand Portage Currency, *q.v.* See also **livre** (def. 2).

1950 OGDEN *Journals* xvi n: £ (Sterling) was worth 26⅔ Montreal livres or 13⅓ North West livres. £ Halifax Currency equalled 24 Montreal livres or 12 North West livres. **1955** RICH in BLACK *Journal* xxxiii: The debit entries show that during 1813 and 1814 he sent home 682 North West Livres or just over £50 Sterling to his mother in Scotland.

North West Mounted Police *Hist.* a federal police force organized in 1873 to bring law and order to the Northwest, the name after 1904 being the Royal North West Mounted Police and after 1920 the Royal Canadian Mounted Police, *q.v.* See also **Northwest Police, N.W. Mounted Police,** and **N.W.M.P.**

1887 *Grip* (Toronto) 25 June 3/2: The North-West mounted police requires the immediate attention of the proper authorities. **1913** (1957) *Sask.Hist.* X 1 31: It is reported that the North West Mounted Police are to be provided with motor cars for use in tracking down criminals. **1963** SYMONS *Many Trails* 52: The North-West Mounted Police commonly used to send constables to ride with the wagons, sometimes for months.

North West Mounted Policeman *Hist.* a member of the North West Mounted Police.

1958 BERTON *Klondike* 237: In the annals of the Peace River Route from Edmonton there is a complete record of one party that did get through to the Klondike. These were not gold-seekers but North West Mounted Policemen.

North West Mountie *Hist., Informal* See **North West Mounted Policeman.**

1938 CASH *I Like B.C.* 69: He served with the North West Mounties in their Scarlet and Gold days.

Northwest passage† **1** *Hist.* the long-sought route through or round North America to the Orient; a navigable passage connecting the Atlantic and the Pacific oceans.

[**1555** (1869) BROWN *Cape Breton* 12: For beinge in Englande in the dayes of Kyng Henry the Seventh, he furnysshed two shippes at his owne charges, (as sum say) at the kynges, whom he persuaded that a passage might bee fownde to Cathay, by the north seas, and that spices might bee brought from thense soner by that way, then by the vyage the Portugales use by the sea of Sur.] **1576** (1889) HAKLUYT *Voyages* XII 35: To proue by experience of sundry mens trauiles the opening of this Northwest passage, whereby good hope remaineth of the rest. **1748** ELLIS *Hudson's Bay* 75: Surely I need not tell you from hence what is said here with great Joy, of the Discovery of a North West Passage, made by two *English* and one *Frenchman* lately represented by them to his Majesty at *Oxford,* and answered by a Royal Grant of a Vessel to sail into *Hudson's-Bay,* and thence into the *South-Sea.* **1801** MACKENZIE *Voy.from Montreal* v: The first voyage has settled the dubious point of an practicable North West passage; and I trust, that it has set that long agitated question at rest, and extinguished the disputes respecting it forever. **1963** MORTON *Kingdom of Canada* 13: The term North-West Passage . . . had now assumed the meaning it was henceforth to bear, of a way around or through the continent of North America.

2 the route round the north of Canada through the Arctic seas.

1921 HAWORTH *Trailmakers* 183: The crew, however, traveled over the ice and joined an eastern searching party and thus made the Northwest Passage, though not all of it by ship. **1954** *Peoples of the N.W.T.* 28: No record of exploration in the north, however brief, would be complete without a mention of the first successful voyage through the Northwest Passage by Amundsen in 1903-06, or of Larsen's passage in a single season in 1944 in the R.C.M. Police Schooner, "St. Roch". **1961** *Canada Month* Dec. 41/3: He was the first man to physically explore the commercial potential of the Northwest Passage. . . .

Northwest pedlar *Fur Trade, Obs.* See **Northwester** (def. 1). See also **pedlar** (def. 1b).

1777 (1951) *Sask.Jnls* 7 Feb. 118: He was informed by the Pedlers That they had received a Packet over Land from the Northwest Pedlers this Winter which gave an Account of Twenty-eight Packs of Furrs having been Traded there.

Northwest Police *Hist*. See **North West Mounted Police.**
1897 BALLARD *Klondyke Mines* 13: A liberal supply of arms and ammunition should be taken, not that there is any special danger to human life, as the Northwest Police are famous for keeping order, but to give you a day's sport now and then, and possibly a supply of fresh meat. **1900** LONDON *Son of Wolf* 192: The door was flung open, and a man, clad in the scarlet tunic of the Northwest Police, waded knee-deep among the furious brutes, calmly and impartially dispensing soothing justice with the butt end of a dog-whip.

Northwest Rebellion *Hist*. **1** an uprising of Métis, *q.v.*, and some early white settlers in the Red River area in 1870, led by Louis Riel and caused by encroachment on prairie lands by the Canadian government. See also **Half-breed Rebellion, Rebellion** (def. 2a), **Red River Insurrection, Red River Rebellion,** and **Riel rebellion** (def. 1).
☛ *The term* **Northwest Rebellion,** *normally applied to the uprising of 1885 (see def. 2), is rarely used today with reference to the unrest in the Red River Settlement in 1869-70, the term* **Red River Insurrection** (*or* **Rebellion**) *being preferred by historians. However, the terms* **Northwest Rebellions** *and* **Riel Rebellions** *are sometimes used for convenience in referring to both events.*
1884 *Prince Albert Times* (Sask.) 11 Jan. 6/1: A second North West Rebellion, if it comes to that, would be a much more serious thing than the first one was. **1885** GEMMILL *Companion* 105: In session 1877 moved for an inquiry into the case of Prof. O'Donoghue, charged with having aided in the North-West Rebellion.
2 a second uprising of Métis, Crees, and white settlers, caused by the continued expansion of Canadian influence and settlement into the Saskatchewan region, nominally led by Louis Riel. See also **Half-breed Rebellion, Half-breed Uprising, Rebellion** (def. 2b), **Riel rebellion** (def. 2), and **Saskatchewan Rebellion.**
1946 LOWER *Colony to Nation* 410: The North West Rebellion of 1885 was put down with reasonable speed because the force sent out could travel by the almost completed Canadian Pacific Railway. **1958** *Cut Knife Grinder* (Sask.) 29 May 2/3: The hill was the scene of a battle during the Northwest Rebellion of 1885.

Northwest Staging Route *Hist*. a series of airports established between Edmonton and Whitehorse during World War II.
1944 *Beaver* June 5/1: . . . the Government . . . developed and improved this particular route to Yukon by the building of a line of airports at Fort St. John, Fort Nelson, Watson Lake and Whitehorse, and so the present airway known as the Northwest Staging Route came into being. **1958** *Edmonton Jnl* 2 Oct. 1/7: With the quiet switch of the last airports of the wartime Northwest Staging Route. . . .

Northwest Territories 1 *Hist*. **a.** See **Northwest** (def. 1a) and **Northwest territory.**
b. the early administrative districts which later became Saskatchewan and Alberta. See also **Northwest** (def. 1b) and **N.W.T.** (def. 1).

1880 GORDON *Mountain and Prairie* 246: The district around Edmonton is one of exceptional fertility and promise, the most promising indeed of all the North-West Territories. **1963** MORTON *Kingdom of Canada* 372: The government was therefore able to . . . carry out reforms in the administration of the North-West Territories. These now consisted of three, Assiniboia, Saskatchewan, and Alberta, organized in 1882, as well as the unorganized territory which was to become the districts of Athabaska, Franklin, Mackenzie, Ungava, and Yukon in 1895.
2 a. *Hist*. the unorganized extra-provincial districts of the North and Northwest prior to 1920.
1913 SANDILANDS *West.Cdn Dict*. 31/2: Northwest Territories comprise all British Territories in North America and all Islands adjacent thereto not included within any province or the Yukon Territory and the colony of Newfoundland. **1933** *Cdn Hist.Rev.* XIV 29: In 1895, by order-in-council, the dominion government defined the boundaries of the four districts into which the North-west Territories were divided.
b. from January 1, 1920, the division of northern Canada between the Yukon Territory and Hudson Bay, including Baffin Island and the islands in James Bay, Hudson Bay, Hudson Strait, and the Canadian Archipelago; the districts of Franklin, Keewatin, and Mackenzie. See also **N.W.T.** (def. 2). Cp. **Northwest** (def. 2).
1923 WALDO *Down Mackenzie* 84: Her daughter was for five years the only white girl in the Northwest Territories. **1962** *Canadian* June 39/2: The Slavey Indian tribe at Fort Providence in the North West Territories asked Anne to handle the sale of the porcupine quill work. **1965** *Maclean's* 21 Aug. 24/1: [Caption] Pale, prim and profuse: the Northwest Territories' Mountain Avens.

Northwest Territories Council a body responsible for the government of the Northwest Territories (def. 2b), now consisting of twelve members, of whom seven are elected and five appointed.
1962 *Canada Month* Nov. 16/3: To eight of the elders of the Eskimo Community of Rankin Inlet, it seemed the Northwest Territories Council was making a big fuss about nothing. **1965** *Kingston Whig-Standard* (Ont.) 11 Jan. 20/3: Granting residents of the eastern Arctic the right to vote for their own members of the Northwest Territories Council could mean the start of a language problem for the Parliament of the North.

Northwest territory (or territories) *Hist*. See **Northwest** (def. 1a).
1807 (1809) GRAY *Letters* 152: I had the pleasure of seeing both an arrival and departure of canoes from and to the north-west territories. **1860** *Nor' Wester* (R.R.S.) 28 Mar. 2/4: The North-West territory lies open before us—a field white for the harvest. **1880** MORRIS *Treaties* 9: One of the gravest of the questions presented for solution by the Dominion of Canada, when the enormous region of the country formerly known as the North-West Territories and Rupert's Land, was entrusted by the Empire of Great Britain and Ireland to her rule, was the securing the alliance of the Indian tribes and maintaining friendly relations with them. **1957** *Beaver* Spring 13/1: Macdonald . . . had taken a long time to consent to the incorporation of Rupert's Land and the North-West Territory in a Canadian Union.

North West turkey See **turkey**.

North West twist *Hist.* See **twist**. See also **niggerhead tobacco**.
1815 (1944) *Beaver* Mar. 38: I have got an excellent lot of Tobacco for the Indian trade which belonged to Mr. Astor . . . [who] held every ounce of North West Twist in the country. **1819** *Kingston Chron.* (U.C.) 16 Apr. 1/1: Orders for North West twist, and Carrot Tobacco, must be given in from 3 to 4 months, previous to its being wanted. . . . **1944** *Beaver* Mar. 38/1: This tobacco was evidently that known as "North West Twist". The North West Company for a number of years had imported its tobacco from the other side of the border rather than from Lisbon via London.

North woods the vast forests in the north of Canada; the Canadian taiga.
1947 ROWLANDS *Cache Lake* 15: . . . no man in his right mind faces a north woods winter without having his wood cut and stacked. **1953** LOWER *Voyages* 142: Here begin the "North Woods," as the Americans call the bush. **1958** MCCULLOCH *Woods Words*: No-see-um—An almost invisible fly found in the north woods, has a terrific bite.

Norway pine See **red pine**.
1793 (1933) MACDONELL *Diary* 77: It is shaded at the top by fine groves of Norway Pine whose stalks grow up fifty feet frequently without branches. **1854** KEEFER *Ottawa* 64: Red pine . . . is often, but improperly, called "Norway" pine. **1956** *Native Trees* 14: Red Pine [is also called] Norway pine. . . .

Norwegian snowshoe *Obs.* a ski.
1885 MOBERLY *Rocks and Rivers* 58: We . . . concluded to make some "Norwegian snowshoes." These snowshoes are made about eight or ten feet in length, and four or five inches in width; they are quite thin and light, and on flat ground or down hill, glide along easily and swiftly.

Nor'Wester *n.* **1** *Fur Trade* **a.** *Obs.* a man experienced in the fur country. Cp. **winterer** (def. 2).
1716 (1965) *Letters from Hudson Bay* 66: I would desire you to send as many old Norwesters over as you can and them men that you send that are not Norwesters let them be lusty strong stout fellows for that place requires none but such. **1854** KEEFER *Ottawa* 58: The wolverine . . . is as fond of beaver tail as an old nor'wester. . . .
b. *Hist.* See **Northwester** (def. 1a).
1953 LOWER *Voyages* 25: . . . Frenchman and Nor'Wester were paddling up through the lakes to the *pays d'en haut*.
c. *Hist.* (*plural*) See **Northwester** (def. 1b).
1885 *Trans.Roy.Soc.Can.* III 139: The plan of the Nor'Westers was first to induce the settlers to leave Red River and settle in Canada, and after that, or along with that, to drive out those refusing to accept their offer. **1963** *Herald Mag.* 14 Dec. 1/1: In September of 1799, the Nor'Westers went to the confluence of the Clearwater and the North Saskatchewan and built Rocky Mountain House.
d. *Hist.* See **Northwest gun**.
1922 *Beaver* Oct. 6/1: This again [flint-lock] was superseded by the "Norwester", a single-barreled percussion muzzle-loader—with the stock running the full length of the barrel. **1941** *Ibid.* Sep. 38/2:

Nor'Wester—In later years referred to the single barrel, full stocked percussion gun which replaced the flint-lock.
2 *Obs.* See **Northwester** (def. 2).
1884 *Nor'Wester* (Calgary) 7 Oct. 1/6: The Rev. gentleman is no tenderfoot, but an old nor'wester who has been over the rockies years ago, and his sketch of his travels was very interesting.
3 *Lakehead* See quote.
1963 *Maclean's* 18 May 40/3: I have never forgotten our first sight of them—halfway up the side of one of the "Nor'westers," our local outcropping of the Pre-Cambrian shield, extending along the southwest. . . .

Nor'Western *adj. Obs.* See **Northwestern**.
1900 OSBORN *Greater Can.* 74: There are no conventions in a new country—in Nor'Western parlance, "there's nobody holding you"—and with those newly released from conventions liberty is apt to become license, unless hard work all the time is absolutely required.

Nor'Westers *n.pl.* See **Nor'Wester** (def. 1c).

Nor'West gun *Fur Trade, Hist.* See **Northwest gun**.
1907 HUNTER *Cdn Wilds* 14: The outfit mostly consisted of tobacco, powder, ball, flints, possibly one or two nor'west guns, white, blue and red strouds for the men's leggings, sky blue second cloth for the squaws' skirts. . . .

Nor'West trader *Obs.* See **Northwester** (def. 1a).
1854 *Hamilton Gaz.* (C.W.) 14 Sep. 1/8: It wur as fine a five-point Mackinaw as ever kivered the hump-ribs o' a nor-west trader.

Nose *n. Slang, Obs.* a Conservative (def. 2).
1923 WILLIAMS *Spinning Wheels* 278: The next blue book is a thick one of over six hundred pages. The wide margins are copiously illustrated with youthful political caricatures of the Goodfellows and the Noses (the latter soubriquet bestowed on account of the protruberant feature of their chief [Sir John A. Macdonald]) engaged in all the imaginable and unimaginable stages of punitive combat. . . .

no-see-em or **no-see-um†** **(fly)** [no'siəm] *n. Informal* a tiny winged insect, *Culicoides* sp., that has a nasty bite; also, sometimes a sandfly, *q.v.* See also **punkie**.
1903 WHITE *Forest* 154: The midge, again, or punkie, or "no-see-'um," just as you please, swarms down upon you suddenly and with commendable vigour, so that you feel as though red-hot pepper were being sprinkled on your bare skin. . . . **1928** FREEMAN *Nearing North* 247: The needle-prick of an unobtrusive "no-see-um" reminded that the season of the venomous little sand-fly was not yet over. **1957** *Commentator* (Trail, B.C.) 26 Aug. 7/2: But we had plenty of company, both in the form of humans and no-see-um flies. **1964** *Atlantic Advocate* July 67/1: For quite a long way after that the going was downhill, but near the bottom we struck swampy ground, a paradise for no-see-'ems, those minute flies whose burning bites are inversely related to their size.

nose-hangar *n.* a structure used in winter to protect an airplane engine from extreme cold and bad weather.
1947 *Beaver* Sep. 20: [Caption] The first winter nose hangar and the first machine [plane] at Hudson [Ontario, 1927].

nose-hobbling *n.* See quote.
1965 *B.C.Digest* June 50/3: One of these practises (of handling and transporting wild horses) was "nose-

hobbling." In this, the nostrils are slit and wired shut so as to nearly close off the air passages. This facilitates handling since the gasping, choking horse is too weak to fight but still conveniently able to stagger on his own legs.

notary ['notəri] *n.* [< F *notaire*] *Que.* See 1962 quote.
1923 SCOTT *Witching of Elspie* 21 : My companion was a notary from St. Basil who was well acquainted with the monks and their institution. **1962** *Canada Month* Nov. 14/1 : . . . Quebec is a province where the notary has the same training as the barrister and enjoys exactly the same powers, except for the right of pleading in court. **1965** *Globe and Mail* (Toronto) 29 Jan. 4/1 : A notary who drew up legal papers for the deposit of $60,000 . . . said yesterday he was not told the purpose of the deposit.

notch† *n.* a narrow pass between hills; defile; gap.
1827 (1829) MACTAGGART *Three Years* I 171 : What are the Rocky Mountains?—have they been fully explored?—is there not a large notch or breach in them beyond Lake Superior? **1930** BEAMES *Army* 140 : By the first he discovered a short cut through a notch between two hills that eliminated seven miles of the crooked and treacherous Moose River.

nothing game *Slang* a league game the outcome of which has no bearing on the final standings in the league.
1963 O'BRIEN *Hockey* 76 : If a row broke out in this "nothing" game, it could mean loss through suspension of the Rocket for the playoffs. . . .

Nova Scotia Knight *Hist.* See **Baronet.**
1864 *St.Catharines Constitutional* 11 Feb. 1/5 : Those who have the courage to be candid will be inclined to admit that in their minds a haze of uncertainty has hovered for a long time as to the exact meaning of the words "U.E. Loyalists," as well as that of "Nova Scotia Knights."

Nova Scotia nightingale *Obs.* the marsh or pickerel frog, *Rana palustris.*
1830 MOORSOM *Letters N.S.* 163 : The marsh-frog, the "Nova Scotia Nightingale," as he is sometimes termed, unceasingly uplifts the voice of melody in chanting the praises of his helpmate.

nowluk *n.* See **oonock.**

N.P. *Hist.* See **National Policy.**
1879 *Morning Chron.* (Halifax) 3 July 2 : The Collector of Customs . . . is now occupying . . . a position given him for his support to their cause and his support of the great N.P. **1887** *Grip* (Toronto) 5 Feb. 3/1 : Professor Blake has accomplished a difficult task of swallowing the N.P. sword. . . . **1925** *Dalhousie Rev.* V 70 : It was in the very early days of the N.P.

N.S.O. or **NSO** See **northern service officer.**
1958 *Edmonton Jnl* 24 June 4 11/6 : NSOs are the senior field representatives of the department of northern affairs. They are stationed at several points in the Arctic, and their main job is to act as neighbors and friends to the Eskimos, to help them adjust to the changing way of life in which they find themselves involved as the frontiers are pushed back.

nuisance ground(s) *West* See 1958 quote.
1889 (1964) *Herald Mag.* 11 Jan. 8/6 : What seems to be a well-grounded complaint has been made by the people living east of the Elbow River in reference to dumping of filth in to the old cellar holes along the main road and in some cases on the road, instead of taking it to the nuisance ground. **1958** *Edmonton Jnl* 29 July 2/3 :

In Banff, the best place to see bears is the "nuisance grounds"—the preferred title [for the] garbage dump.

nunatak ['nunə‚tæk *or* 'nʌnə‚tæk] *n.* [< Esk.] an isolated mountain-peak or hill rising above glacial ice.
1958 *Time* (Cdn ed.) 20 Jan. 46/3 : It painfully threaded through a line of nunataks (mountain peaks almost submerged in ice), and reached ice with fewer crevasses on the high plateau behind. **1960** *Cdn Geog.Jnl* July 34/1 : The only possible ice-free areas in the islands may have been the highest peaks that may have projected above the icefield surface as nunataks. **1961** *Ibid.* Aug. 45/1 : Geological studies were begun, with visits to surrounding nunataks.

nunny-bag ['nʌni‚bæg] *n.* [< Brit. dial. *noony* dinner + *bag*] *Nfld* a kind of haversack, often made of sealskin. See also **nonny-bag.**
1842 JUKES *Excursions in Nfld* II 146 : Having determined to return, we hung up in the tilt a "nunny bag" full of bread. **1961** *Maclean's* 28 Jan. 47/2 : He clawed through his nunny-bag till he found a bit of oatmeal. . . .

nursing station *North* a small emergency hospital in charge of a trained resident nurse and visited periodically by a doctor.
1930 *Beaver* June 16 : . . . the small old hospitals . . . are becoming what we call nursing stations with only a summer visiting medical and surgical staff. . . . **1961** (1964) JENNESS *Eskimo Admin.* II 86n : The typical Nursing Station measures from 60 to 90 feet long and from 25 to 35 feet wide. At one end are the quarters of the nursing personnel, at the other accomodation for four patients, and in between a kitchen and a combination waiting-room and office. **1964** *Camsell Arrow* Summer 60/2 : Their "hospitals" are small nursing stations in Northern Alberta.

nutchook *n.* See **netchek.**

N.W. canoe See **North canoe.**
1793 (1933) MACDONELL *Diary* 97 : These N.W. canoes are about half the size of the Montreal or Grand River Canoes and when loaded to the utmost can carry a Tun and a half.

N.W. Company *Hist.* See **North West Company.** Also *N.W. Co.* and *N.W. Coy.*
1795 (1918) DAVIDSON *North West Co.* 234 : The profits arising yearly from a share in the N. W. Co. have been various these eleven years past. . . . **1799** *U.C.Gaz.* (York [Toronto]) 9 Mar. 4/2 : We hear, that the N.W. Company, has given Twelve Thousand Pounds towards, making Yonge-Street a good road, and that the N.W. commerce will be communicated through this place. **1820** (1955) BLACK *Journal* xxxvii : There is a possibility that I may be obstructed in my Rout as the N.W. Coy a band of unprincipled Lawless Marauders stick at nothing however desperate to gain their ends.

N.W. gun *Obs.* See **Northwest gun.**
1811 (1950) THOMPSON *Journals* 147 : Account of the Goods now with us . . . 8 NW Guns.

N.W. Mounted Police See **North West Mounted Police.**
1902 (1957) *Sask.Hist.* X 12 : The N.W. Mounted Police, a governmental military force, effectually protects the people and their property, at the same time performing the duties of sheriffs and constables.

N.W.M.P. See **North West Mounted Police.**
1881 *Edmonton Bull.* 29 Oct. 1/2: Recruits for the
N.W.M.P. are being brought in by way of Winnipeg.
1963 *Herald Mag.* 14 Sep. 1/1: In 1874 Rev. John
McDougall was sent to explain to the chief why the
NWMP had come to the West.

N.W.T. 1 *Obs.* See **Northwest Territories** (def. 1b).
1876 *Descriptive Catalogue of Econ.Min.* 23: North
Saskatchewan River, N.W.T. **1898** *Medicine Hat News*
(Alta) 20 Jan. 4/1: In the Banana Belt section of the
N.W.T. there is nothing to thaw this January. **1903** *Eye
Opener* (High River, Alta) 22 Aug. 1/3: Tell them to go
plumb to Okotoks, Alberta, N.W.T.

2 See **Northwest Territories** (def. 2b).
1953 *North Star* (Yellowknife) Oct. 2/2: We have been
given to understand, however, that since the present
N.W.T.'s Council Election Ordinance contains no
provision for by-elections, none can be held; though we
are well aware, as are the powers at Ottawa, that this
can be remedied by a simple Order-in-Council.
1966 *News of the North* 21 July 11: [Caption] Officer
Cadet Douglas Robertson of Yellowknife, N.W.T.
has successfully completed the Basic Aircrew
Indoctrination Course at Canadian Forces Base[,]
Centralia, Ontario.

N.Y.C. *Obs.* New York Currency. See **York
Currency.**
1798 *U.C.Gaz.* (York [Toronto]) 26 May 3/2: Way
passengers to be taken up at six-pence N.Y.C. per mile.

oakjook n. See **oogruk**.

oakjuk n. See **oogruk**.

oak opening† a relatively open tract of light, sandy soil supporting only a few oak trees in contrast to heavily wooded surroundings. See also **oak plain** and **plain** (def. 2). Cp. **opening**.
1852 (1881) TRAILL *Cdn Crusoes* 123: The black squirrel, for a succession of years, was very rarely to be met with on the plains, while there were plenty of the red and grey in the "oak openings." **1939** *Cdn Hist. Rev.* XX 282: The general results of the foregoing would seem at first sight to point to the "groves," "open woods," "oak openings," parklands, or whatever name one may give them, being more pronounced on the western borders of this huge territory than on the Atlantic slope.

oak plain *Obs*. See **oak opening**.
1799 SMYTH *Topogr. Descr. U.C.* 25: To the westward ... are oak plains, where the Indians cultivate corn. **1883** (1917) *London Hist. Soc. Trans.* VIII 26: At first it was oak plains, where the soil is sandy, but good for wheat, then pine flats, where we saw some of the handsomest pine trees I had ever seen.

oatmeal Chinaman *Slang, Derog., Obs*. See **North American Chinaman**.
1963 MORTON *Kingdom of Can.* 336: As in Red River, the Canadians had made themselves disliked by their drive and pertinacity, and earned the designation of "oatmeal Chinamen" from the easy-going colonists because of their readiness to work hard for the going wage.

oatmeal savage *Slang*. a Scotsman.
1954 *Ghost Pine* 106: We wondered ... had the strange emigrants from Grand Old Scotland come up to expectations ... somewhere beneath the blanket protections, was Mabel Young, no doubt wishing that those oatmeal savages would hasten away.

oats n. pl. [trans. of Cdn F *avoine* in this sense] *Fur Trade, Hist*. See **wild rice**.
1778 (1790) UMFREVILLE *Hudson's Bay* 57: ... it abounds with excellent fish and wild fowl; and oats, rice and cranberries in the swamps. **1804** (1933) FARIES *Diary* 206: Richard brought a parcel of dried Meat, today, the Indians had not yet made any Oats. **1931** NUTE *Voyageur* 80: Wild rice ... was usually called "oats" by the traders, and was bought by the sack from squaws, who gathered it in the lakes and marshes in the late summer.

O.B.U. See **One Big Union**.
1919 *Camp Worker* 17 May 5/3: At Medicine Hat the Federated Railway Trades have unanimously endorsed the O.B.U. **1963** MORTON *Kingdom of Canada* 431: The O.B.U. sought to establish by strike action the right to collective bargaining. ...

O Canada the title and opening words of one of Canada's national songs or anthems, composed in 1880 by Calixa Lavallée (1842-91), the original French words being by Hon. Sir Adolphe Routhier (1839-1920) and the most generally known English words being written in 1908 by the Hon. R. Stanley Weir (1856-1926).
1916 BRIDLE *Sons of Canada* 232: He swept himself off his own feet with the heroic strains of "O Canada." **1957** HUTCHISON *Canada* 282: The frogs' spring song was a recognized national anthem long before "O Canada" was written. **1958** *Encyc. Can.* VII 250/1: "O Canada" [was] originally a *chant national* of French-speaking Canadians, nowadays with accepted versions in both French and English. ...

occupation ticket *Obs*. See **location ticket**.
1790 (1905) *Ont. Bur. Arch. Rep.* III 95n: There are still extant several occupation tickets for Lots in the New settlement of which the Board have no entry in their Register.

ochima n. See **ogema**.

offside ancestor *Slang* a non-white ancestor; an Indian ancestor.
1921 MACKAY *Window-Gazer* 244: "Well, if Indian blood can give one a skin like hers, I could do with an offside ancestor myself!"

off-the-act Indian an Indian who is not classed as a registered Indian, *q.v.*, and to whom the Indian Act does not apply.
1958 HAWTHORN *Indians of B.C.* 67: A small group of off-the-Act Indians and people of mixed descent lives off the reserve but find acceptance only in Indian society.

ogama n. See **ogema**.

ogema(h) [ˈodʒə‚mɑ] n. [< Algonk.; see note]
☛ *This term has enjoyed wide use for many years throughout the Indian country, apparently being borrowed from several Algonkian languages in several dialectal forms, for the spelling and pronunciation variants are numerous. The main sources appear to be Cree okemaw, ukemaw and Ojibwa ojimaw, with the meanings of def. 1 below. The spellings recorded include huchemaw, ochima, hogama, oghema, ogima, oogamou, okema, okemow, okimow, okomow, ookemow, ookima, otsima. All of these variants have been cross-referred to this entry for convenience, the above entry-word being somewhat more frequently encountered, although the most recent evidence seems to favor the Cree forms of the* o(o)kemow *type.*

1 chief; war chief; great man.
[**1743** (1949) ISHAM *Observations* 16: A Captain or Chief U'ke maw. **1791** (1904) LONG *Voyages*: [Vocab.] Ojémaw, or Ókemaw Chief] **1820** (1922) HARMON *Journal* 356: A person appointed to head a war party, is called a chief, or O-ke-maw. He must have given distinguished proof of his bravery, prudence and cunning, in former war expeditions, in order that he should be considered qualified to fill this post. **1877** GRANT *Ocean to Ocean* 63: To show due respect to so great an O-ghe-mah, a newspaper was spread before him as a tablecloth, and a plate of fried pork placed on it, with a huge slapjack or thick pancake made of flour and fat. ... **1915** SPECK *Hunting Territories* 5: The chief, *ogima*, was a man chosen for life ... on account of his strength and wisdom.

2 of white men: **a.** an important official; master; boss.
1875 (1888) MCDOUGALL *G.M.McDougall* 218: At every point I met with a most cordial reception from our Indian friends, who were all delighted to hear that the "Great Ogeemah" was going to treat with them for their lands. **1885** *Prince Albert Times* (Sask.) 24 July 4/1: The news—which would immediately have spread like wild fire—of the defeat of the "okomow" of the police, would in all probability have induced the revolt of thousands instead of hundreds of Indians.

1955 SHIPLEY *Anna* 32: "Okemow," they said, which she knew meant Master. "We must portage here."
1963 MCTAVISH *Behind the Palisades* 89: . . . the product was classified as "Bourgeois" pemmican, suitable only to the palates and supposedly refined tastes of the "Ookimows" (chiefs) among the pale faces.

b. in fur trade parlance (often ironically), chief trader; boss.
1916 BRIDLE *Sons of Can.* 254: . . . this "Ougamou" of the dog-whip . . . worked out the gospel of success and self-help as no man ever did in that part of North America. **1954** BEZANSON *Sodbusters* 78: In his own estimation he was very much the Okema, but that didn't hurt his business with the natives . . . accustomed to meeting that attitude in the Company's trading posts. **1956** KEMP *Northern Trader* 228: Now the Ookemow is leaving, who will write letters for us—to the Indian Agent, to the Bishop, to the fish and game authorities?

oghema *n.* See **ogema**.

ogima *n.* See **ogema**.

ogjuk *n.* See **oogruk**.

Ogopogo [ˌogo'pogo] *n.* [< a name from a British music-hall song, applied first to the monster in 1912] a famed monster reported as being seen from time to time in Okanagan Lake, B.C.
1936 CROSS *Cross Roads* 71: Ogopogo's head is slightly reminiscent of Henry VIII, he has a torso like an accordeon, and a tail like a shillelagh. **1952** *Sun* (Vancouver) 2 Aug.: Ogopogo is no newcomer to the Okanagan. Long before the white men came the Indians knew him as Naitaka or Lake Demon—a dread monster with a carnivorous appetite. . . . **1964** *Cdn Geog.Jnl* Mar. 91/1: Here . . . according to hundreds of British Columbians who claim they've seen them—[are] a number of friendly sea monsters, including "Ogopogo."

oguk(e) *n.* See **oogruk**.

oil-borer *n. Hist.* an oil driller.
1909 CAMERON *New North* 58: Floating as we float, it is no longer a marvel to us that the North holds so many scientific men and finished scholars—colonial Esaus serving as cooks, dog-drivers, packers, trackers, oil-borers.

oil camp *North* a location where an oil company is drilling for oil.
1923 WALDO *Down Mackenzie* 191: About a mile down the river was an oil camp (of the Imperial Oil Company) with a derrick.

oil coal See **Stellar coal**.

oilers *n.pl.* waterproof clothing, originally oilskins but now often made of a kind of rubberized fabric. See also **oilies**.
1924 FLAHERTY *Eskimo Friends* 6: We peered with dismay from the lost shelter of the outer bar to the tumbling steamy wastes ahead, but old Puggie, donning oilers and sou'wester, grimly smiled the fact that we were caught, and settled down to the helm for a day of it. **1957** *Beaver* Spring 8/2: The big *Canadien* straightened up in his oilers and said proudly, "Yes, and [I'm doing the work of] six trucks, too." **1964** CRATE *Hardrock Mining* 6: I have mentioned perhaps 20% of the words peculiar to Canadian hardrock mining and

will mention one more—"*oilers*" the word applied to the waterproof suit (jacket and trousers) worn by miners when working in wet places.

oil fever excitement caused by desire to profit from an oil discovery, as in Petrolia, Ontario, about 1860.
1860 (1960) *Ont.Hist.* June 80: Let us remember the land fever and take care to avoid a complaint of a somewhat similar character under the name of "oil fever."

oilies ['ɔɪliz] *n.pl.* See **oilers**.
1923 MACMECHAN *Sagas of Sea* 148: In the night of 4th January, 1922, Matthew Munro . . . cast on a lee shore in a blizzard, swam off in his sea-boots and "oilies" with a line and dragged the five men of his crew to safety.

oil sands† See **Alberta tar sands**.
1954 BEZANSON *Sodbusters* 191: A railway was also being promoted to build to Ft. McMurray in the oil sands belt on the Athabasca. **1957** *Aklavik Jnl* Feb. 1/1: The Royalite Oil Co has announced that it will soon begin construction of an oil separation plant at the Athabaska oil sands a few miles from Waterways which will cost fifty million. **1964** *Calgary Herald* 22 Feb. 16/7: One time it [tar sands] was the accepted term, now it would appear "oil sands" is more accepted, although this is also open to criticism.

Ojibwa snowshoe See 1860 quote. See picture at **snowshoe**. See also **galley**.
[**1860** (1956) KOHL *Kitchi-Gami* 337: On any intersected terrain covered with stones, or on lakes or rivers, where the ice has packed, and is not quite covered with snow they have extremely long snow-shoes, turning up at the front end like the head of a skate or the prow of a ship. They are frequently six feet long, and easily glide over any obstacles on the road.] **1916** *Trans.Roy.Soc.Can.* X 1 314: It is somewhat peculiar in shape and is possibly a transition between the Ojibwa and Montagnais snowshoe. **1941** *Beaver* Mar. 28/1: The Ojibway snowshoe is the most familiar type, for this is the usual shape of the factory made shoe.

Oka (cheese) *n.* a kind of cheese cured by painting with brine, made by the Trappist monks of Oka, Quebec.
1936 *Cdn Geog.Jnl* XII 218/2: The Oka cheeses are given their peculiar flavour in the process of curing. **1964** LEE *Foods and Textiles* 72: Oka and Ermite are also typically Canadian cheeses.

okema, okemow, okimow, okomow ['okə,ma, 'okə,mau] *n.* See **ogema**.

olachen *n.* See **oolichan**.

olallie [o'lali] *n.* [< Chinook Jargon "berry"] Also spelled *olellie, olilie, ollala, ollallie,* etc.
1 any of several berries, especially the salmonberry, *q.v.* Cp. **soapolallie** (def. 1).
1855 (1956) ROSS *Fur Hunters* 80: . . . his bark platter [was] filled top heavy with the most delicious melange of bear's grease, dog's flesh, wappatoes, olelllies, amutes, and a profusion of other viands, roots and berries.
1863 *Norfolk Reformer* (Simcoe, C.W.) 2 Apr. 3/1: Their food is principally fish, and bread made from a species of berries and moss, which they term *Olally sapolel,* signifying berry bread. **1915** CUMMING *Skookum Chuck* 18: How he calculated to feed two with the one basket of o-lil-ies (berries) . . . did not seem to worry the community, as such things were taking place every day . . . and the klootchman always seemed to survive the ordeal. **1954** *B.C.Hist.Qtly* XVII 262: Olallie juice

was given a baby after he was weaned, and wild-strawberry leaves dried and powdered was an effective remedy for his sore mouth.

2 the bush such berries grow on. Also *olalie bush*.
1922 JOHNSON *Legends* 5: . . . the ollallie bushes were heavy with blossom. **1925** ANDERSON *Trees and Shrubs* 128: The Service-berry or June-berry . . . is called Saskatoon . . . and I have heard it alluded to as the Oolalie in this Province [B.C.]. **1948** HOLLIDAY *Valley of Youth* 167: . . . the snake fences [are] half hidden by wild rose, hawthorn and ollala.

olalliechuk [oˈlɑliˌtʃʌk] *n.* [< Chinook Jargon *olalie* berry + *chuck* water] *Pacific Coast* a native-made wine made from berries; homebrew. Cp. **chuck**[1] and **olallie**. Also spelled *olalla chuck* and *ollaliechuck*.
1958 *Native Voice* Sp.ed. 30/2: [It is] a receptacle into which during these feast-rejoicings and tribal conferences are poured many gallons of a sacred beverage dubbed "olalla chuck". . . . **1966** *Islander* 27 Feb. 6/2: . . . the Indian potlatch was only a . . . heathen festival, where people gathered to feast on native food with ollaliechuck. . . .

old bachelor *Obs*. See quotes.
1763 (1901) HENRY (Elder) *Travels* 124: There are beavers, called, by the Indians, *old bachelors,* who live by themselves, build no houses, and work at no dams, but shelter themselves in holes. **1829** MACTAGGART *Three Years* II 228: . . . the beavers leave their dams, and betake themselves to the banks of solitary rivers, and live, as the Indians report, *old bachelors*.

Old Canada *Hist*. Upper and Lower Canada prior to Confederation.
1872 *Canadian Mthly* 198/1: The farmer emigrant can make his choice from the richly-wooded land of old Canada and the maritime Provinces, or from the vast prairies of Manitoba and the North-west. **1915** PRESTON *Strathcona* 49: Donald A. Smith, who was then in Old Canada, hurried off . . . to Fort Garry, where he arrived long before the military expedition could possibly put in an appearance.

Old Canadian 1 *Obs*. a French Canadian.
1807 (1809) GRAY *Letters* 165: The descendants of the Old Canadians constitute at least nine-tenths of the population of Lower Canada.
2 a long-term resident or citizen of Canada, as opposed to a New Canadian, *q.v.*
1959 *Maclean's* 18 July 19/2: To what extent have New Canadians been grabbing jobs away from "Old" Canadians?

Old Chieftain *Hist*. See **Old Tomorrow**.
1965 *Kingston Whig-Standard* (Ont.) 9 Jan. 10/1: The political career of the Old Chieftain is traced in this story by a Canadian Press reporter.

Old Colony Newfoundland.
1931 *Beaver* June 211: Our deepest sympathy is extended to the many throughout the Old Colony who have been bereaved as a result of this disaster.

Old Compact *Obs*. See **Family Compact** (def. 1).
1853 *Hamilton Gaz.* (C.W.) 24 Nov. 2/5: Of all the "alliances" yet formed, or yet attempted to be formed, perhaps that now in process of incubation between the extreme "Clear grits" and the extreme "Old Compact" is the most "unholy."

Old Company 1 See **Hudson's Bay Company**.
1900 WILLSON *Great Fur Co.* 664: "What does 'H.B.C.'

mean?" Returned the native grimly: "That's the old Company, Here before Christ." **1909** CAMERON *New North* 7: No man or woman can travel with any degree of comfort throughout Northwest America except under the kindly aegis of the Old Company. **1953** LOWER *Voyages* 35: The Hudson's Bay Company—"the old Company"—had outposts only at Kapiskau and Attawapiskat, none further north.
2 See quote.
1935 *Trans.Roy.Soc.Can.* III 2 44: This was the period [1804] when the XY, or "New Company," was being absorbed by the "Old Company," from which it had broken off, and both became the North West Company.

Old Country† the country of one's origin (other than Canada), especially the British Isles. See also **Old Land** and **other side**.
1825 *Novascotian* (Halifax) 9 Feb. 57/3: Things in the old country are all regulated on a fixed principle. . . .
1887 (1888) LEES & CLUTTERBUCK *British Columbia* 42: . . . so many of the people one meets hail from the "old country"—as Canadians and also Americans almost always call the British Isles. . . . **1905** (1954) *B.C.Hist. Qtly* XVIII 207: The last decade or so of my life in the company's service as I have said, was passed at different posts in the above western department. I went no more either to Canada or the Old Country.
1959 *News of the North* 3 Sep. 8/3: I'm back to the work-a-day world after a pleasant vacation in Europe. All the wonders of the "old country" were nice to see. . . .

Old Dominion the province of Newfoundland.
1959 *Press* Apr. 18: The loggers of the "Old Dominion" fight to reduce their working hours from 60 a week to 54, their day from 10 to 9 hours. . . .

Old Eph(raim) See **Ephraim**.

Old Family Compact See **Family Compact** (def. 1).
1897 DURAND *Reminiscences* 47: His *Courier* paper was ably conducted in the Old Family Compact cause.

old home week *Informal* a time of festivity when former residents of a community or members of a family return for the celebrations.
1938 CURTIN *Yukon Voyage* 249: We are allowed off the boat now, and it is like old home week, for it seems as if half the population of Montana is here. **1959** *Ottawa Citizen* 8 July 9/3: This will be "old home week" for hundreds of former residents of this busy commercial center . . . as townspeople celebrate the town's 100th birthday.

Old Lady of Lime Street the Hudson's Bay Company, *q.v.*, so called from the address of its London (England) head office.
1934 GODSELL *Arctic Trader* 165: . . . I paid a visit to the Old Lady of Lime Street, as the London office was affectionately known.

Old Land† See **Old Country**.
1919 FRASER *Bulldog Carney* 261: . . . the amber fluid that trickled through the spiggot transported, mentally, the Englishmen back to the Old Land. **1922** STEAD *Neighbours* 102: "That's why we need some of you people from the Old Land to mix with ours," said Jean.

old-line party either the Liberal or the Progressive

Conservative Party, as opposed to more recently founded smaller parties on the Canadian political scene. See also **old party.**

1963 *Kingston Whig-Standard* (Ont.) 4 Mar. 3/6: . . . when he turns his oratorical thunder against the "old-line parties," almost all the thunderbolts are aimed at Lester Pearson and his followers.
1963 *Globe and Mail* (Toronto) 26 Mar. 7/1: Hamilton, the city that bucked the Golden Horseshoe swing to Liberalism in the last election, is the question mark to both old line parties in this one.

old log *Lumbering* a log that has lain underwater for some time, having sunk during an earlier drive, retrieved for drying out and processing as lumber.
1964 *Cdn Geog.Jnl* Feb. 73/2: Lumber from these "old" logs dries 20 per cent better than lumber cut in the bush. . . .

Old Ontario 1 See 1952 and 1963 quotes.
1909 *Gow Ganda Tribune* (Ont.) 17 Apr. 6/2: Teamster Anderson . . . was offered, two weeks ago, sixteen hundred dollars to take sixteen tons of left-over freight into Gow Ganda, but was compelled to turn the offer down because of a disinclination on the part of his men to turn back and miss the "seedin' " in their "Old Ontario" homes. **1952** PUTNAM *Cdn Regions* 213/2: South of this line is "Old Ontario" or Southern Ontario, the region which was first settled and which is distinguished on the map by an irregular division into counties and townships which were surveyed on base lines laid out more or less parallel to the shores of the St. Lawrence River and the Great Lakes. **1963** SYMONS *Many Trails* 23: She was born . . . in old Ontario, in the days when it was Upper Canada. . . .
2 the old-fashioned speech characteristic of certain rural districts in Southern Ontario.
1959 *Weekend Mag.* 10 Oct. 63/2: "He's et nine," said Hortense, who also speaks Old Ontario.

Old Original *Hist.* a member of the first contingent of the First Canadian Division of World War I.
1959 *Legionary* Apr. 7/1: April 22, 1915, is nevertheless an important date in the annals of this country, for on that day the Old Originals, the men of the First Contingent of the 1st Canadian Division . . . achieved immortal renown for their brave stand against the German gas attack at St. Julien near Ypres.

old party See **old-line party.**
1963 *Kingston Whig-Standard* (Ont.) 7 Feb. 4/3: There is always a danger that the voters, influenced by Socred and N.D.P. arguments, will conclude that there is little to choose between the "old parties" and will vote for a new party. Even Ontario showed its lack of confidence in the old parties by electing a farmer government.

Old Quebec that part of Quebec which was formerly known as Lower Canada, especially the communities of the St. Lawrence Valley.
1952 PUTNAM *Cdn Regions* 178/1: New highways are not the only problem, however, traffic between the cities of Old Quebec grows denser year by year and the old routes need constant rehabilitation.

Old Régime *Hist.* the period of French rule in Canada prior to 1758.
1904 RAND *Cdn Verse* 25: In the glimmering light of the

Old Régime / A figure appears like the flushing gleam / Of sunlight. . . . **1913** PARKER *Money Master* 94: Jean Jacques Barbille had come of the people of the Old Régime. **1960** *Press* Dec. 13: . . . at the downfall of the old regime in 1758, there were already bands of Metis as well as Indians living in the valley of the Red.

old settlers' scrip *Hist.* See **land-scrip** (def. 2).
1963 STANLEY *Louis Riel* 260: Your petitioners would humbly represent that their rights to a participation in the issue of the half-breed or old settlers' scrip are as valid and binding as those of the half-breed and old settlers of Manitoba. . . .

old squaw (duck)† a common duck, *Clangula hyemalis,* of the northern hemisphere. See also **cockawee, hound,** and **Siwash duck.**
1853 [see quote at **cockawee**]. **1890** *Trans.Hist.& Sci. Soc.Man.* 39 10: Thousands of "Old Squaws" were seen apparently feeding and otherwise disporting themselves in the waters of Franklin Bay. **1963** *Kingston Whig-Standard* (Ont.) 8 Feb. 11/2: Large numbers of Old Squaw ducks were sighted during the survey.

old T.O. See **T.O.**

Old Tomorrow *Hist.* Sir John A. Macdonald (1815-1891), first Prime Minister of Canada, so called because of his practice of putting off difficult decisions that time might be expected to make unnecessary. See also **Old Chieftain.**
1881 (1965) HAMILTON *Cdn Quotations* 128/1: Old Tomorrow would be just the name for Sir John. **1891** *Grip* (Toronto) 11 July 24/2: Punch sympathizes with Canadian Sorrow / For him known lovingly as "Old-To-morrow." **1959** SHIPLEY *Scarlet Lily* 156: "But the Prime Minister isn't called 'Old Tomorrow' for nothing!" Bruce boasted with pride. "He'll carry us safely out of this yet." **1965** *Kingston Whig-Standard* (Ont.) 9 Jan. 12/4: They nicknamed him "Old Tomorrow" for his procrastination.

old winterer *Fur Trade, Hist.* See **winterer** (def. 2).
1830 (1953) *Beaver* Dec. 50/2: The provisions for the Crew were Pork & Biscuits: from which circumstances the young recruits are called "Pork Eaters" to distinguish them from the old Winterers, who fed chiefly on "Pemican." **1908** LAUT *Conquest N.W.* II 14: Reports were received on the past season, men and plans arranged for the coming year, weak leaders shifted to easy places, strong men, "old winterers," "the crafty wolves of the North," dispatched to the fields where there was to be the hardest fighting against either Indians or English, and English always meant Hudson's Bay.

ollala, ollalie *n.* See **olallie.**

ollaliechuck *n.* See **olalliechuck.**

ollo, oloo *n.* See **ooloo.**

omiak, omyak *n.* See **oomiak.**

One Big Union *Esp.West* a labor organization formed at Calgary in 1919 on an industrial rather than a craft basis; also, a member of this organization. *Abbrev.* O.B.U., *q.v.*
c1921 *To the Lumber Workers* 2: You may say: "Well, if I join the One Big Union, I can't get a job. I can't hold my job, for the boss don't want O.B.U.'s." **1963** MORTON *Kingdom of Canada* 431: In the western provinces a radical industrial union took shape, the Canadian One Big Union, or O.B.U.

one-to-four jar a sealer, *q.v.*, containing jam made from one part of sugar to four parts of berries.
1903 RICHARDSON *Colin* 81: "But when Kearstie came t' clear th' table afore me an' th' childer was cut loose on th' remains, she mistook th' one t' four jar for th' pound fer pound. . . ."

onion *n*. *Obs*. See **wild onion**.
1808 (1950) THOMPSON *Journals* 11: [There were] very many Ducks—plenty of Onions.

on the blanket See **blanket** (def. 1c).

on the outside See **outside**, *n*. (def. 1b).

oodjuk *n*. See **oogruk**.

oodloo *n*. See **ooloo**.

oogamou *n*. See **ogema**.

oogruk ['ugrək] *n*. [< Esk.] *North* the bearded seal, *Erignathus barbatus barbatus*.
☛*The variant spellings of this word, which are almost as numerous as the references, are entered and cross-referred to this somewhat arbitrarily chosen entry-word. These variants include oakjook, oakjuk, ogjuk, oguk, oodjuk, oogyuk, ookchuk, ookgook, ookjuk, udjuk, ugluk, ugjuk.*
[**1836** HUISH *Last Voyage* 701: Seal, large Oguké.] **1852** RICHARDSON *Arctic Exped.* 494: Seal, largest kind uksuk; oguk. **1864** HALL *Life with Esquimaux* II 22: Most of the meat and blubber we deposited *en cache,* and the ookgook we left on the ice. **1909** CAMERON *New North* 255: As the four fingers dropped into the sea they changed respectively into beluga the white whale, nutchook the common seal, oogzook the big seal, and ibyl the walrus. **1959** *Beaver* Spring 56/1: Then there would be feasting, and everybody helped themselves to walrus, dried oogruk (bearded seal), whale blubber, and rotted fish. **1964** *North* July 45: As we proceeded the "oodjuki" could be seen resting on a fairly large sized piece of ice, with its nose at the edge just above the water.

oogyuk *n*. See **oogruk**.

ookchuk *n*. See **oogruk**.

ookemow *n*. See **ogema**.

ookgook *n*. See **oogruk**.

ookima *n*. See **ogema**.

ookjuk *n*. See **oogruk**.

An Ookpik

Ookpik ['ukpɪk] *n*. [< Esk. *ukpik* snowy owl] *Trademark* a doll resembling an owl, first made of sealskin by an Eskimo in 1963, subsequently adopted as a symbol in Canadian handicrafts exhibits abroad, and now being mass-produced under permit for general sale. Cp. **Sikusi** and **Toonik** (def. 3).
1964 *Calgary Herald* 17 Jan. 1/2: Ookpik . . . was originally "invented" by an unnamed Eskimo at Fort Chimo eight months ago, and northern affairs included

him in their handicraft catalogue. . . . **1966** *Kingston Whig-Standard* (Ont.) 22 Jan. 14/3: We plan to use Ookpik, a distinctively Canadian symbol, and hope the idea may catch on nationally.

ooksook ['uksuk] *n*. [< West Esk. *uqsuq*] seal blubber.
1864 HALL *Life with Esquimaux* I 289: A portion of seal's liver, raw and warm from its late existence in full life . . . This, with a slice of *ooksook* (blubber), was handed to each, and I made away with mine as quick as any of the old adepts. **1934** GODSELL *Arctic Trader* 265: . . . she did not have to worry as to where her next feed of seal meat, or ookchuk, was coming from. . . . **1942** TWOMEY & HERRICK *Needle to North* 186: For in winter there is only the flame of *ooksook* in the *kudliak,* which gives a fair light, a lot of smoke and bad odor and a heat that is very low.

oola *n*. See **ooloo**.

oolalie *n*. See **olallie**.

oolichan or **oolachan** ['uləkən] *n*. [< Chinook Jargon *ûlakân*] a small fish, *Thaleicthys pacificus,* of the smelt family, native to the Pacific coast. See also **candlefish, fathom-fish, lampfish,** and **Skeena turkey.** Also spelled *eulachon.*
☛ *The spelling variants recorded for this word are numerous; see 1953 quote for samples.*
1811 (1849) ROSS *Adventures* 97: There is a small fish resembling the smelt or herring, known by the name of ulichan, which enters the river in immense shoals, in the spring of the year. **1834** (1963) TOLMIE *Physician* 275: The canoes were laden with . . . dried herring spawn which they are to barter for Oolaghans. **1869** *Mainland Guardian* (New Westminster, B.C.) 29 Sep. 2/1: We are told that the Indians, when prostrated by disease sometimes in the worst stages of debility, go up to their sanitorium at the mouth of the Naas River, where they continue to live on oolachans until they are perfectly cured. **1926** MCKELVIE *Huldowget* 2: They came today for the oolichan fishing. **1953** *Beaver* Mar. 40/2: Oolikan, olachan, eulachon, uthlecan, hollikan and hoolican—spell it as you wish. . . . **1965** *Fisherman* 19 Mar. 2/5: Robichaud said commercial exploitation of eulachons was banned by regulation.

oolichan grease See **oolichan oil**. See also **grease trail**.
1880 DAWSON *Queen Charlotte Is.* 110: The oil is carefully stored away, and used as a condiment to dried fish or berries, instead of the oolachen grease, which by this tribe of Haidas is not much in request. **1966** *Islander* 27 Feb. 6/2: There was [at the potlatch] also a great deal of oolachan-grease and soapollalie.

oolichan oil a clear, edible oil rendered from the oolachan and long a highly valuable food and trade item among the Coast and Inland Indians of British Columbia. See also **fish oil** and **oolichan grease**.
1869 *Mainland Guardian* (New Westminster, B.C.) 29 Sep. 2/1: The oolachan oil is clearer, purer, and more agreeable to the palate than that obtained from cod liver, and from its tonic qualities is more readily assimilated in the stomach of an invalid. **1963** *Beaver* Autumn 40/1: This Grease Trail was so named because along it the Nass tribes carried much oolachan (candle-fish) oil or grease to the Upper Skeena River country.

ooloo or **ulu** ['ulu] *n*. [< Esk. *ulu*] an Eskimo woman's general purpose knife, having a crescent-shaped blade and a handle of bone, ivory, wood, etc. See also **woman's knife**.

[**1824** NIAGUNGITOK *Esquimeaux Words* 25: Ollo Chopping knife] **1864** HALL *Life with Esquimaux* I 291: The first-mentioned article being too small for my dimensions, one of the Innuit women slit them down with her oodloo till they did fit, after a fashion. **1940** *Beaver* Mar. 24: The women then take their semicircular knives or "ooloos," and flench the hide from the blubber, which the men load into the drums. **1964** *Nat.Geog.* May 718/2: Some Eskimo women want their favorite ulu to be buried with them. **1966** *North* July-Aug. 45/2: [Caption] A gas lamp hangs from the centre of the tent. Mother sits chewing, her ooloo in her hand. Bannock is slowly cooking in an iron pot hung above an old camp stove.

An ooloo

oomiak or **umiak** ['umi,æk] *n*. [< Esk. *umiaq*] a skin boat, 30-40 feet long, 4-5 feet wide, and 3 feet deep, having a flat bottom and narrowing at bow and stern, used for carrying freight and passengers and traditionally rowed by Eskimo women. See also **luggage-boat**, **skin boat** (def. 1), and **woman's boat**.

[**1578** BEST *Trve Discovrse* III 63: They haue one sort of greater boates where in they can carrie aboue twentie persons, and haue a Mast with a Sayle thereon, which Sayle is made of thinne Skinnes of bladders, sowed togither with the sinewes of fishes.] *c*1743 (1957) *Hudson's Bay Co. Calendar:* Several Oomiaks or Women's boats filled with women and children were also alongside.... **1824** LYON *Private Journal* 40: The mistress of the oomiak lent him a small whalebone scoop to bale his boat out. **1908** TYRRELL *Sub-Arctics* 126: There were thirty-six of them, all women and children, piled into one of their "oomiacks," or skin boats. **1963** *Beaver* Winter 24/2: Their umiaks were made of walrus or bearded seal skins and they also had sealskin kayaks.

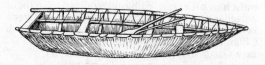

An oomiak

oomiak-tupek *n*. a kind of tupek, *q.v.*, having the appearance of an inverted oomiak, used by certain Eskimos.

[**1865** HALL *Arctic Researches* 549: The Innuit name of it is *Oo-mi-en-wa*, from its resemblance to an inverted oo-mi-en.] **1958** *Evening Telegram* (St. John's) 25 Apr. 8/8: And her husband, the provider, must at all times be properly shod and dressed. Often I heard her sewing machine from the depths of the oomiak-tupek as our komatik passed along.

oonar *n*. See **oonock**.

oonock or **oonok** ['unək] *n*. [< Esk. *unaq*] See 1933 quote.

1882 GILDER *Schwatka's Search* 166: In this way he can usually approach near enough to shoot his prey with a rifle, or strike it with a seal spear or oo-nar. **1933** MERRICK *True North* 155: In it he mentioned the word "oonock." It is an Eskimo implement, used for harpooning seals. **1941** *Beaver* Sep. 38/2: Oonok—The Company's staff who follow the sport of seal hunting in the spring are all familiar with this spearhead and its shaft.

open *n*. See **opening**.

1832 (1953) RADCLIFF *Letters* 91: I have been occupied in getting as many acres as I can cleared and prepared for cropping. Sixteen are already under operation, which will make a good open about the house. **1942** RADDALL *His Majesty's Yankees* 2: But when he came to the edge of the open he hesitated warily and whined. **1958** *Edmonton Jnl* 28 July 4/3: ... the animal seemed to distrust the bald opens of the marsh and its pace increased to get quickly around the watery obstacle.

open *adj*. **1** *Fur Trade* of skins, removed by slitting along the underside and down each leg so as to be cured by stretching flat. See also **split**, *adj*. (def. 1). Cp. **cased**.

1783 (1918) DAVIDSON *North West Co.* 269: Exports [included] ... Cassed Catts 5536, Open Catts, 4197 ... Tygers 26 ... Castoreum 1106 lb. **1864** *Nor'Wester* (R.R.S.) 20 May 3/4: Opossum were only saleable at very low rates say ... open good 6 to 9d. ... *c*1948 *Sask.Fur Marketing Service* 15: Two methods of skinning, the "open" and the "cased," are practised for all fur-bearing animals. Badger, beaver and bear are skinned "open," and all other animals, generally speaking, are skinned "cased."

2 of land, available to homesteaders, *q.v.*, or for leasing; not yet legally taken up by settlers.

1922 STEAD *Neighbours* 52: "But immedjut north-west, cornerin' right against this quarter, 'cept for the road allowance, is the south-east quarter of Twenty-two, which is open." **1954** *Ghost Pine* 57: When haying season came around I was really up against it. By that time the only open lands left for haying were a good four or five miles from the ranch.

open-and-shut day See quote.

1966 RADDALL *Hangman's Beach* 230: It was what fishermen called an open-and-shut day, with patches of black cloud, patches of sunshine, and occasional showers of rain.

open car(r)iole *Obs*. a cariole (def. 1) having no cab as protection from the weather.

1769 (1931) BROOKE *Emily Montague* 91: This is the first day I have ventured in an open carriole; we have been running a race on the snow.... **1791** (1911) SIMCOE *Diary* 58: From whence I went in an open carriole (which is a sort of phaeton body on a sledge or runners, shod with iron instead of wheels) to Woodfield....

opening† *n.* an open space in wooded country or one where trees are few. See also **open**, *n.* and **open woods.** Cp. **oak opening.**

1824 (1931) SIMPSON *Fur Trade* 64: The country here is very pleasant well wooded & Hills plains and beautiful openings coming to the view at every reach.
1952 PUTNAM *Cdn Regions* 434/2: Grassy openings are found also in the intermountain sections, throughout the northern Cordillera.

open spring *Nfld* a spring season in which the shores are virtually free of sea ice.

1933 GREENE *Wooden Walls* 35: . . . in what the Newfoundlanders call an "Open Spring," the ice will be swept so far east . . . that the thankful land will be seen rejoicing. . . .

open town *Esp.North* a town not controlled by the company whose employees make up most of the residents. Cp. **company town.**

1964 *North* May-June 42: The owner, Pine Point Mines Ltd., agreed that this should be an open town, and consequently its layout had to make the best possible use of land for phased industrial, commercial, residential, and public uses around a single-enterprise economy.

open water *Esp.North* **1** See **break-up** (def. 1).

1922 *Beaver* Jan. 33/1: We remained at Mountain House until open water in the spring. **1931** GREY OWL *Last Frontier* 57: After open water on until early in June, the spring hunt is in full swing on the frontier. . . . **1956** KEMP *Northern Trader* 50: When open-water came, I had had enough of everything.

2 See **break-up period.**

1922 *Beaver* Sep. 9/1: When the open water came, I got one hundred and thirty-two beaver and two otter. **1924** *Ibid.* May 291: At open water, goods were freighted by large birch-bark canoes. . . .

open woods bush land where the trees are not very close together. See also **opening.**

1939 *Cdn Hist.Rev.* XX 282: The general results of the foregoing would seem at first sight to point to the "groves," "open woods," "oak openings," parklands, or whatever name one may give them, being more pronounced on the western borders of this huge territory than on the Atlantic slope.

opportunity store or **shop** a store where used clothing and certain other items are available at reduced prices, often run for charitable purposes, for community-sponsored organizations, etc.

1966 *Weekend Mag.* 13 Aug. 13/1: Vaguely I remembered a colleague having sold suits to an opportunity store. **1966** *Kingston Whig-Standard* (Ont.) 22 Sep. 26/1: . . . the books [are] being sorted at 60 Brock street, opposite the Opportunity Shop. . . .

opting out (formula) See quotes.

1966 *Globe and Mail* (Toronto) 12 Aug. 7/6: The federal Government met that complaint at Quebec City by offering the opting-out formula; any province could accept full responsibility for administration of what had previously been a shared program, and Ottawa would reduce its taxes to allow the province to raise the money to run the program. *Ibid.:* But opting-out did not go far to meeting Quebec's new mood of confidence and desire to be master of its own house.

Order of Good Cheer (or **Times**) [trans. of F *L'Ordre de bon Temps*] *Hist.* a convivial fraternity organized by Champlain in 1604 to promote recreation and relaxation in the first French colony

in Canada, at St. Croix Island in 1604 and from 1605 at Port Royal, Nova Scotia.

[**1926** WRONG *History of Can.* 34: Champlain aroused the spirit of rivalry by founding the "Ordre de Bon Temps."] **1934** DENNIS *Down in N.S.* 141: . . . every fortnight as his turn came round, each of the party went hunting and fishing to secure by rod and by musket the fish of the sea and the game of the forest to provide for the table of the Order of Good Cheer. **1965** MACBEATH & CHAMBERLIN *New Brunswick* 39: They formed a club which they called "The Order of Good Times."

Oregon† *n. Hist.* See **Oregon country.**

1846 *Niagara Chron.* (C.W). 7 Jan. 1/1: Of late, the Eagle, soaring high over the "snow-capped" hills of Oregon, Said he, and winked his *hawkish* eye, "This here I'll lay my talons on." **1963** MORTON *Kingdom of Canada* 268: The Democrats took up . . . a demand for the whole of Oregon up to Russian Alaska.

Oregon country or **territory**† *Hist.* the vast region lying between California and Alaska on the Pacific coast of North America, that part south of the 49th parallel being ceded to the United States by Great Britain in 1846.

1843 *Bytown* [Ottawa] *Gaz.* 23 Feb. 2/4: England being rather unwilling to lend more money or goods to folk who won't pay, and the other European nations being equally untractable and surly, Jonathan has been compelled to carry his wonderful spirit of enterprise to the Oregon country . . . the Indians and bears of that civilized region not having yet found him out. **1853** *Trans.Lit.& Hist.Soc.Que.* IV 306: As to the rights of the Hudson's Bay Company to the Oregon territory, and the country lying between Canada and Russian America, these rights consist only in the company having a license to hunt and trade there, which will expire in 1859, and which gives them no territorial claim whatever. **1953** LEBOURDAIS *Nation of North* 16: In 1812, the Hudson's Bay Company bought the Astoria post from Astor, which helped to bolster the British claim to what was becoming known as the "Oregon Country." **1963** MORTON *Kingdom of Canada* 268: The Oregon territory, jointly occupied since 1818, furnished the pretext.

Oregon dispute† See **Oregon question.**

1921 *Beaver* July 16/1: When the negotiations between the Hudson's Bay Company and the United States government were under way to settle the Oregon dispute, the Company claimed 160,000 acres of land as being farmed and grazed by them. **1963** MORTON *Kingdom of Canada* 268: These changes were the settlement of the Oregon dispute with the United States and the abolition of the Corn Laws in the United Kingdom, both in 1846.

Oregon jay a jay, *Perisoreus obscurus obscurus,* resembling the Canada jay, *q.v.,* for which it is sometimes mistaken.

1910 FERGUSON *Janey Canuck* 93: He has several names, such as Hudson's Bay bird, Oregon jay, and moose bird.

Oregon pine† See **Douglas fir.**

1877 (1956) DIXON *Lumber Industry* 24/1: This British Columbia wood is known in Australia, New Zealand, and Great Britain as "Oregon Pine" though Oregon does not export it to these markets.
1932 WINSON *Weather and Wings* 51: The Great

Douglas fir is a "spruce" which is named "false hemlock" by the scientists, who give it a Greek prefix "pseudo", meaning false, followed by a Japanese term, "Tsuga", meaning hemlock. This is to describe a "spruce" or "fir" which the lumbermen persist in calling "Oregon Pine"! **1958** *Maclean's* 10 May 54/3: Among [the Douglas Fir's] early aliases in the common-name category were Oregon Pine ... Yellow Fir, and even Spruce Fir.

Oregon question the dispute (1818-1846) between Great Britain and the United States over the Oregon country, settled by division at the present British Columbia-Oregon border. See also **Oregon dispute** and **Oregon treaty.**
1846 *Niagara Argus* (C.W.) 7 Jan. 2/4: The Oregon Question absorbs all others.... **1881** BEGG *Great Cdn N.W.* 29: These troops were probably sent to defend the frontier line owing to the fuss made by the Americans at the time on the Oregon question. **1908** LAUT *Conquest N.W.* I 140: But perhaps the most notoriously absurd part the [Hudson's Bay] Company ever played internationally was in connection with what is known as "the Oregon question."

Oregon territory† See **Oregon country.**

Oregon Treaty the 1846 treaty settling the Oregon question, *q.v.*, officially called the Washington Treaty.
1931 *Beaver* Sep. 273: ... the boundary trouble between the U.S.A. and Great Britain, when the U.S.A. claimed the territory as far as the 54th parallel, a trouble which terminated with the Oregon Treaty of 1846. **1946** *Ibid.* Mar. 8/1: June of this year [1946] will mark the centenary of the Treaty of Washington, popularly known as the Oregon Treaty of 1846.

orignal [ɔrin'jal; *French* ɔri'ɲal] *n.* [< Cdn F < F *orignac* < Basque *orenac* deer, stag] *Now Rare* See **moose** (def. 1). See also **horiniack.** Also spelled *orignale,* (earlier) *oriniack.*
1665 (1885) RADISSON *Fourth Voyage* 187: The beare, the castors, and yᵉ Oriniack shewed themselves often, but to their cost; indeed it was to us like a terrestriall paradise. **1703** (1905) LAHONTAN *New Voyages* I 103: ... the hunting of Orignals or Elks.... **1792** (1911) SIMCOE *Diary* 79: Capt. Shaw gave me a description of the moose deer, which we call here "Orignale," and of which we eat the moufle. **1829** *Trans.Lit.& Hist.Soc.Que.* I 252: Also a man who discovers the Ravages of the Orignal fixes his mark, and tho' he go in pursuit of something else should another Indian kill his Orignal, the skin belongs to the Discoverer. **1963** *Field and Stream* Sep. 100/1: [Advert.] If you've ever hankered for the antlers of an *orignal* or a *chevreuil* on your trophy wall, French Canada is the place to bag 'em.

orignal butter *Obs.* See quote.
1760 PICHON *Cape Breton* 102: They gather the fat that comes upon the surface, and from thence extract five or six pounds of a kind of tallow, as white as snow, and as firm as wax. This is their provision when they are upon the chace; they call it *cacamo,* and we *orignal butter.*

oriniac(k) *n.* See **orignal.**

Orkneyman† *n. Fur Trade, Hist.* a native of the Orkney Islands of Scotland serving in the fur trade, especially with the Hudson's Bay Company.

1775 (1934) HEARNE *Journal* 191: I have interfered so far as to ask what encouragement they required to which the Orkneymen seem'd to intermate that 12L per annum would enduce them to be active & useful. **1842** *Trans. Lit.& Hist.Soc.Que.* IV 1333: The animals frequenting this country [include] ... the Common Hare of Canada, called Rabbits, by the Orkney men in the service of the Hudson's Bay Company.... **1936** *Beaver* Dec. 4/1: In the year 1799 about five hundred and thirty persons were employed by the Hudson's Bay Company, at their fur trade posts in North America, of whom four hundred and sixteen, or approximately seventy-eight and a half percent of the total, were Orkneymen. **1957** FISHER *Pemmican* 24: He had heard that ... there were ... a few red-faced Orkneymen, a few Moravian sisters and brothers.

Orthodox Doukhobor one of a sect of Doukhobors that does not subscribe to acts of terrorism. See 1963 quote. Cp. **Sons of Freedom.**
1954 *Comox District Free Press* (Courtenay, B.C.) 13 Jan. 1/3: Subjects discussed by the four speakers will be origins of the Doukhobors; religion, the three different sects, the Sons of Freedom, the Independents and the Orthodox; and possible solutions to the problem. **1963** *Globe and Mail* (Toronto) 21 Feb. 4/5: The leader of Canada's Orthodox Doukhobors yesterday said his followers did not feel obliged to obey government authority, but still opposed Doukhobor terrorism often mistakenly attributed to them.

ortolan ['ɔrtələn] *n.* [< Cdn F < F; ult. < L *hortolanus* gardener] *Rare* See **snow bunting.**
1760 PICHON *Cape Breton* 74: Lastly, you meet here, as well as in other parts of the island, great plenty of game, particularly ortolans, and white rabbets of a most delicate taste. **1760** JEFFERYS *Descr.New France* 39: This little creature has a very charming outside, and for its relish well deserves the name of Ortolan. **1956** MCATEE *Folk-Names* 67: Snow Bunting [also known as] ortolan (This name, originally denoting a European species of bunting, a gastronomically famous bird, has been applied to a number of other species used for food. The present species was formerly sent to market in large numbers. Nfld.)....

Osborn's caribou [< Henry F. *Osborn,* 1857-1935, U.S. zoologist] a large race of caribou (def. 1), *Rangifer tarandus osborni,* of northern British Columbia and the southern Yukon, now regarded as identical with the woodland caribou, *q.v.*
1916 WOOD *Tourist's N.W.* 347: You will not get any wapiti or deer there, but ... you could hardly fail to get specimens of moose, Osborn's caribou, Stone's sheep, and mountain goats, with a good chance of a grizzly or black bear or a wolf or fox. **1921** MARSHALL *Snowshoe Trail* 178: There is no animal in all North American fauna, even the bull elk, that presents a more splendid figure than that huge member of the deer family, Osborn's caribou. **1960** *Beautiful B.C.* Spring 6: The Spatsizi is the summer haunt of the Osborne caribou who come to browse on the rich plant life.

Oswego tea or **bitter** bee balm, *Monarda didyma,* or wild bergamot, *M. fistulosa,* both used by Indians and early settlers for their medicinal properties.
1793 (1911) SIMCOE *Diary* 176: The mountain is covered with a sweet, purple flower, the roots of which, infused in brandy, make a wholesome cordial. It is called Oswego bitter. **1955** HARDY *Alta Anthol.* 199: The flowers of Purple Bergamot, found growing alongside many Alberta roads, were once employed to concoct a

famous Indian cure-all called Oswego Tea.

other side, the the British Isles. See also **Old Country.**
1887 *Grip* (Toronto) 8 Jan. 6/2: You shake your head and he concludes that you are from the other side I suppose. **1962** *Canada Month* Apr. 48/2: Strangely enough the chap from "the other side" is, off duty, the best friend a man could have.

otsima *n.* See **ogema.**

Ottawa ['atə,wa] *n.* [< Cdn F *Outouan* < Algonk.; cf. Cree *atāweu* trader; originally the name of an Algonkian tribe living in southern Ontario] the government of Canada, the capital of which is Ottawa, Ontario.
[**1869** *Niagara Mail* (Ont.) 15 Dec. 2/3: The Ottawa Government is taking a wise step in sending . . . peacemakers to Red River. . . .] **1887** *Senate Report* XXI App. 95: Washington has been most successful in those experiments, and there is no reason why Ottawa should not be equally successful. **1957** *Financial Post* 2 Nov. 57/1: With the coming to office of the Conservative Government, these airlines are hopeful for [a] bigger slice of the cake than Ottawa had been allowing them. **1966** *Globe and Mail* (Toronto) 12 Aug. 7/5: In fact, Ottawa was unable to satisfy either the expectations or the needs of the provinces.

Ottawa River canoe *Hist.* See **Montreal Canoe** and picture.
1918 DAVIDSON *North West Co.* 217: The North canoes were about half the size of the Montreal or Ottawa River canoes, and when loaded to their utmost capacity could carry a ton and a half. *Ibid.* 218: Fewer men were required to carry a North canoe than an Ottawa or Grand River canoe.

Otter *n. Trademark* a famous light monoplane much used in bush flying, *q.v.*, in the Canadian North, manufactured by DeHavilland Aircraft of Canada Ltd.
1955 *Herald-Tribune* (Grande Prairie, Alta) 4 Mar. 3/7: . . . a ski-equipped Otter plane picked up the four passengers. . . . **1965** *Kingston Whig-Standard* (Ont.) 11 Jan. 5/8: A baby girl was born to Mrs. Iris Adjukak Saturday in a single-engine . . . Otter aircraft on an emergency flight from Coppermine, N.W.T. . . .

otterboard *n.* a board for stretching otter skins. Cp. **stretcher.**
1771 (1792) CARTWRIGHT *Journal* I 123: In the afternoon the sawyers were picking oakum, and the furriers making otterboards.

otter rub See **rubbing place.**
1933 MERRICK *True North* 75: [We] set traps on two otter rubs.

otterskins *n.pl. Slang, Obs.* See quote.
1900 OSBORN *Greater Can.* 44: Money is often spoken of as "otter-skins;" and the settler speaks of his house as a "tepee," even if he has never seen the Indian's circular tent to which that name rightly belongs.

ou [u] *interj.* See **hew,** *interj.*
1909 (1962) WHALLEY *Hornby* 36: They [sleigh dogs] are guided by shouting the words 'ou' to go to the right or 'shaw' to go to the left, and 'marche' straight ahead.

ouananiche ['wanənɪʃ] *n.* [< Cdn F < Algonk.: Montagnais *wananish* little salmon] a species of small fresh-water salmon, *Salmo salar ouananiche,*
native especially to Lake St. John and certain other lakes in Ontario and Quebec. See also **Atlantic salmon** (def. 2). Also spelled (older) *wananish, wananiche,* etc.
1808 (1890) MCKENZIE *King's Posts* 444: A sort of fish resembling salmon, one and a half feet long, called by the Indians *Winanis,* are found in it, though not in great numbers. **1889** MASSON *Les Bourgeois* I 84: A species of salmon, probably the "Wananish," so plentiful in Lake St. John, P.Q.: some say it is found in the Mackenzie River only. **1907** MILLAIS *Newfoundland* 202: Here we took out our rods and fished, although the worst time of the day for such an operation, and soon had enough ouananiche to feed our men for another day. **1966** *Globe and Mail* (Toronto) 15 Jan. 29/5: I . . . tied into my first ouananiche with him on Trout Lake near North Bay [Ont.].

ouimiack *n.* See **oomiak.**

ouk *interj.* [? < Esk.] *Lab.* a command to a sled-dog to wheel to the right. See also **hew,** *interj.*
1924 MATHEWS *Wilfred Grenfell* 94: The leader is a well-trained dog, who runs at a distance of about 70 feet from the driver. He is trained to go to the right when the driver shouts "ouk," and to the left when "ra" is called.

oulachan *n.* See **oolichan.**

Our Lady of the Snows See **Lady of the Snows.**

ourogan *n.* See **rogan.**

out *adv. North* to the more settled part of the country. See also **outside,** *adv.*
1910 SERVICE *Trail of '98* 467: ". . . It's the life, it's the land. A hard life and a hard land." "Why don't you go out?" **1959** *Edmonton Jnl* 31 July 4/3: On them he managed to thread his way out of the confusing maze of the Athabasca delta on his periodic trips "out" for supplies.

outarde [u'tard] *n.* [< Cdn F < F "bustard"] a wild goose, especially the Canada goose, *q.v.*
1791 (1911) SIMCOE *Diary* 59: I eat part of a metiffe, a bird between a wild goose (the outarde) and a tame one. **1825** *Gleaner* (Niagara-on-the-Lake, U.C.) 16 Apr. 2/1: The road is good on the ice from St. Ann's to Montreal —nevertheless the outarde has made its appearance: several, freshly killed, were exposed in our market this day. **1904** RAND *Cdn Verse* 17: Our own Outarde revisits well-known haunts,/And the loud quack rings out anew from sea to shore. **1959** MCATEE *Folk-Names* 8: Eastern Canada Goose . . . [is also called] outarde (Spelled also oultarde, outard, outarte = bustard. Early use Cartier, 1535 *fide* Ganong, 1910. This name was applied by early French explorers to a New World bird that reminded them of the great bustard of Europe; however, the two birds are only superficially alike, are unrelated, and have entirely different habits. Nfld., Que.). . . .

outcabin *n. Esp.North* a temporary shelter such as might be used by a trapper out tending his line. See also **outcamp** (def. 1).
1935 *Cdn Geog.Jnl* XI 129/2: The routine of the trap line, with its long cold nights spent at the makeshift "outcabins," called for greater and greater effort, and more and more the heavier work devolved upon Miller.

1954 PATTERSON *Dangerous River* 216: Then try it all day in zero weather over miles of mountain country, and come home at night to a cold cabin or, better yet, to an open camp such as we had, scattered around Deadman's Valley; for we built no out-cabins.

outcamp *n.* **1** See **outcabin.**
1948 ONRAET *Sixty Below* 96: I had a little rice and bacon in one of my out-camps. 1952 *Beaver* Sep. 23: As we were on our way to the outcamp of another trapper . . . he said a wolverine had been stealing from a cache of meat.

2 a fishing or hunting camp far back in the bush.
1963 VARDY *Labrador:* [Tourist Folder] Fly-out trips to the Shabogamo River . . . where out camps are located, cost an addition $155.00 per person. . . .

outfit *n.* **1** *Fur Trade* **a.** the annual shipment of trading goods and supplies sent by a fur company to its trading posts collectively; also, any part of this shipment dispatched to or received by any particular post. Cp. **returns.**
1761 (1901) HENRY (Elder) *Travels* 41: Michilimackinac is the place of deposit, and point of departure, between the upper countries and the lower. Here, the outfits are prepared for the countries. 1802 (1890) MASSON *Les Bourgeois* II 462: The present copartnership or concern shall commence with the outfit of the year one thousand eight hundred and three and shall continue remain and be carried on for the space and term of twenty years hereafter. 1829 (1909) CAMERON *New North* 304: The White Beads asked for the trade with the Loucheux are not according to the order sent, 15 pounds only of the quantity received . . . are of the proper size, the remainder being the same as those in outfit 1825 so much complained of. 1860 *Nor'Wester* (R.R.S.) 14 Mar. 4/3: As the Company's out fit for the fur-trade has been lost with the Kitty, very little, if any, of their goods in store this winter at York Factory, will be taken to this place. 1922 FOOTNER *Huntress* 22: "He build a house at Nine-Mile Point and a stable. Say he goin' to keep stopping-house for freighters when they bring in the company's outfit in the winter." 1963 SPRY *Palliser* 13: . . . and so to the prairies by York boat, with the company's brigades that carried the yearly outfit of trade goods by river and portage from Hudson Bay to the remote trading-posts far inland.

b. the trading goods and supplies taken into the interior by fur-company employees such as traders and runners, by free traders, etc.
☛ *It is quite possible that* **outfit** *was first used by the Hudson's Bay Company in 1670 to designate the annual shipment of trading goods and supplies to its factories in Rupert's Land (see 1933 quote at def. 2a); it seems probable, moreover, that most modern senses of the term derive from this early fur-trade usage.*
1761 (1901) HENRY (Elder) *Travels* 11: Arrived again in Montreal, bringing with me my outfits. 1765-75 (1933) POND *Narrative* 47: All my outfits had Dun well. 1824 *Canadian Mag.* II 293: On his arrival in Montreal, and finding no supply of the articles he wanted . . . he was under the necessity of making a second journey to Albany for . . . the necessary supplies, named in the language of the trader, an out-fit. 1920 FOOTNER *Fur-Bringers* 52: "He say: We got get white man on our side. We got get white man who knows all outside ways. He bring an outfit in and trade wit' us."

1956 KEMP *Northern Trader* 11: . . . the men gave us the perfunctory Indian handshake sized up the outfit and passed a few inconsequentials.
2 *Fur Trade* **a.** the fiscal year of the Hudson's Bay Company. See 1933 quote. Cp. def. 1a.
1791 (1947) *Beaver* Dec. 11/2: . . . the difficiency in the order for the carrot tobacco arises from the great overplus we have for the ensuing outfit. . . . 1874 (1956) ROSS *Athabasca* 16: The Athabasca accounts for the Outfit were closed and the Packet given over to the care of Mr. Moberly. 1913 COWIE *Adventurers* 280: The end of each business year—called "Outfit"—was May 31, upon which date the inventory of everything belonging to the Company at the fort was taken. 1933 *Beaver* Sep. 7/1: Since the incorporation of the Company in 1670, the word "outfit" has meant one trading year. That is, Outfit No. 1 was the trading year ending 1671 . . . and Outfit 263 is the trading year ending in 1933.
1956 KEMP *Northern Trader* 17: Looking at the piece so marked, you would know that it was for "Outfit" 1908, or the Company's fiscal year.

b. in fur trader's parlance, a year.
1833 (1947) HARGRAVE *Correspondence* 124: I had thought of getting away in one or two outfits. 1935 (1964) JENNESS *Eskimo Admin.* II 51: Altogether sixteen deaths occurred during the outfit and only four births that I know of.

3 a. equipment and supplies required for an expedition or other undertaking, such as might be engaged in by prospectors, miners, trappers, fishermen, etc.
1822 (1928) CORMACK *Narr.Nfld* 109: The fishermen, or planters, as they are called, obtain their outfits . . . from the merchants at Fortune Bay. 1860 *Brit.Colonist* (Victoria) 4 Feb. 2/3: Considerable activity is displayed among the miners in town, preparing their outfits for the upper Fraser. 1878 *Sask.Herald* (Battleford, N.W.T.) 30 Dec. 3/1: "We had a hull outfit, traps, grub, 'munition, pizen, an' we wor jest a-goin' to rake in a little pile. . . ." 1931 GREY OWL *Last Frontier* 12: . . . a toboggan loaded with a tent, stove, blankets, and a few provisions, drawn by dogs. This outfit will be set up every night on top of the snow. . . . 1963 STANLEY *Louis Riel* 265: . . . they were adventurous types, men with sufficient means to provide themselves with the "outfit" necessary to start upon their homesteads. . . .

b. the equipment necessary for a specific job or activity.
1910 SERVICE *Trail of '98* 183: There were crap-tables . . . roulette and faro outfits. 1912 POCOCK *Man in the Open* 90: Once a week I take my little pack outfit up to the Sky-line claim for a load of peacock copper. 1914 BINDLOSS *Intriguers* 237: I see your cooking outfit's still lying around. 1962 FRY *Ranch on the Cariboo* 14: These were simple rigs for hauling hay and, like everything else about our outfit back in the outpost meadows, were made almost entirely of jack-pine wood.

4 a.† a group of persons travelling together or otherwise associated in a common endeavor.
1887 (1888) LEES & CLUTTERBUCK *British Columbia* 70: It was gratifying to reflect that we were now an "outfit". . . . 1905 OUTRAM *Cdn Rockies* 428: A few hours later the "outfit" commenced the return journey from these mountain solitudes to prosaic civilization, and a last farewell was said to this strangely-fated camping-ground. 1939 O'HAGAN *Tay John* 76: He often hired out with outfits going west to the mountains, or north to the Peace. 1954 PATTERSON *Dangerous River* 259: Outfit can refer either to the equipment of an expedition or to the expedition party itself or to any body of men, e.g. "the whole outfit was tired and hungry." 1961 MITCHELL *Jake and the Kid* 176: "You

take the hockey outfits—Peewees, Juniors, Intermediates—ain't a year Wing didn't put up the money for their uniforms."

b. a company or firm.
1912 FOOTNER *New Rivers* 231 : The poll was held in the store of the French outfit, a low, rambling log shack, outside and in, the most picturesque post in the North. **1958** ELLIOTT *Quesnel* 184 : Sixty outfits cutting pit-props in the area for the coal mines of Wales invaded the town.

c.† *West* a ranch or those working for it.
1913 KELLY *Range Men* 13 : . . . some of the cattle carrying the brand of the outfit they worked for. **1963** SYMONS *Many Trails* 15 : And the journey had been briefly broken . . . when we passed a sheep outfit on the move.

5 a. a vehicle and its team, as a sled and dogs, a chuckwagon and horses.
1890 *Trans.Roy.Soc.Can.* VIII 2 103 : Genereaux, an old Hudson Bay man, in passing with a dog-train betwixt two thickets of timber, was suddenly pounced upon by one of these morose animals [a buffalo bull], which tossed dogs, sled and all into the air, and made a wreck of the outfit. **1928** FREEMAN *Nearing North* 136 : But turning, driving, slowly, drifting, keen of eye and steady of hand, the consummate old veteran put the unwieldy outfit through without so much as a kiss-off from one of the foam-masked niggerheads. **1964** *Albertan* (Calgary) July 15/6 : He's driving two chuckwagon outfits [and] will probably outride for a couple more. . . .

b. a machine, rig, or set of machinery for a specific job.
1954 *Ghost Pine* 81 : Another well-remembered thresher was a big steam outfit with a tremendous capacity. . . . When used for breaking, this outfit would pull from 12 to 14 breaking plows each 14 inches wide. Nearly every homesteader in Ghost Pine worked on this outfit at some time or other. **1954** TYRE *Saddlebag Surgeon* 58 : At harvest's end the owner of the outfit sold his machine and departed without paying his men.

outfit *v.* **1 a.** obtain or supply with an outfit (def. 3a).
1900 LONDON *Son of Wolf* 133 : "I'll send word down for a couple of the boys to outfit and pole a boat up the Yukon. We'll cross the divide and raft down the Indian River to meet them." **1909** CAMERON *New North* 96 : From its red sands, tamarak swamps, and mossy muskeg one almost expects to see arise the form of those great of old who outfitted here, making Chipewyan the base of their northward explorations. **1928** PERRY *Two Reds* 64 : They were here to be outfitted at the store. Here they drew clothing and supplies against their "time," and thus place themselves in debt to their employer for at least a month's work. . . . **1947** *Beaver* Dec. 19/2 : Everything was spent ; some of them [Indian trappers] at the end of the trade might still be in debt. But they had to be outfitted again. **1967** *Cdn Geog.Jnl* Jan. 21/1 : The trading post became a village from which prospectors outfitted and pushed off further into the wilds.

b. stock ; supply the needs of.
1910 FRASER *Red Meekins* 63 : "If I'd saved all the truck I'd found in camps, I'd have enough to outfit a museum. . . ."

2 act as an outfitter (def. 1).
1958 *Alaska Sportsman* Dec. 14/3 : Joe . . . outfits from Kluane Lake, one hundred and fifty miles northwest of Whitehorse on the Alaska Highway.

outfit number *Fur Trade* a number marked on all packages shipped as part of an outfit (def. 1a).
[1943 *Beaver* June 44 : This summer, all bales and boxes going to the Company posts from the Fur Trade depots bear the number 274—that is, the 274th outfit of trade goods sent out since the incorporation of the Company in 1670.] **1948** *Ibid.* Dec. 29/1 : [The] bale is compressed and sewn up, and the post manager marks on it the outfit number . . . the district letter . . . and the post number.

outfitter *n.* **1** a guide and manager of an expedition, as a hunting or exploring party in the wilderness.
1905 OUTRAM *Cdn Rockies* 271 : Of course Bill Peyto was my outfitter, but his growing business needed so much of his attention that he could not spare the time to spend eight or nine weeks away from his headquarters. **1921** MARSHALL *Snowshoe Trail* 11 : I will be accompanied by Mr. Lounsbury's uncle, Kenly Lounsbury, and I wish you to secure the outfit and a man to cook at once. You will be paid the usual outfitter's rates for thirty days. **1958** *Weekend Mag.* 26 Apr. 8/1 : Reinhold Eben [is a] game guide and outfitter at Slave Lake. . . . **1965** *Kingston Whig-Standard* (Ont.) 16 Sep. 18/1 : [They] were granted the outfitters' franchise for the area—25,000 square miles surrounding the Godlin Lakes . . . 275 miles northeast of Whitehorse.

2 a person who sells outfits (def. 3a).
1921 LAUT *Cariboo Trail* 15 : Ragged, poor, roofless, grubstaked by 'pardner' or outfitter on a basis of half profit, the prospector stands as the eternal type of the trail-maker for finance.

outgoer *n. North* a person on the point of going outside, *q.v.*
1909 CAMERON *New North* 319 : The outgoers are a cosmopolitan and a happy "bunch". . . .

out-harbo(u)r *n.* See **outport** (def. 1).
1818 CHAPPELL *Voy.of Rosamond* 27 : From this it will appear evident, that those merchants, who reside constantly at *St. John's,* receive a double profit : the first arising from their foreign exports of salted *cod;* and the second, from the articles which they supply to the *out-harbour* settlers, in return for this commodity. **1896** ROBERTS *Camp-Fire* 145 : In the winter of 1888 a fire took place in the out-harbor where I was then living, and a large part of the winter's stores was destroyed.

outlander *n. Esp.North* a person from another region, tribe, etc. ; stranger. Cp. **outsider.**
1936 STRINGER *Wife-Traders* 163 : She spoke with the indulgence of an outlander who had watched an Innuit mother quiet her baby with a "comfort" made from a wad of cotton soaked in seal-blood. **1959** MOWAT *Desperate People* 102 : Pommela, alone of the People, guessed something of what the arrival of the outlanders at Ennadai might really mean. . . .

outlands *n.pl.* See **back country** (def. 2) and **backwoods.**
1960 *Star Wkly* 1 Oct. 51 2 : Unfortunately the lure of high wages and easy living in our cities far outweighs the privations and toil of settling in Canada's outlands, and yet this is required today. **1961** *Press* July 7 : "Guaranteed Employment" can take the New Party into the outlands of darkest Quebec and into the underprivileged, low-standard coves and concessions of the Atlantic Provinces. . . .

outlet *n.* a store for selling beer or liquor.
1958 *Edmonton Jnl* 1 Aug. 5/1: Retention of the local-option system of establishing new outlets was recommended. **1962** *Ottawa Citizen* 6 June 1/1: Mayor Charlotte Whitton has questioned the legality of a proposed brewers retail outlet. . . .

out-mission *n.* an outlying mission station.
1937 *Beaver* Dec. 62/1: The [missionary] vessel [*Our Lady of Lourdes*] had a heavy programme and established two new out-missions. . . .

out of treaty of an Indian, not in receipt of treaty money, *q.v.* See also **non-treaty,** *adj.* Cp. **treaty Indian.**
1956 KEMP *Northern Trader* 34: The fact is, that like most of his compatriots in the North, Abraham lived like an Indian, spoke only Cree, and he was a "half-breed" merely by virtue of having had, somewhere in the dim past, a white man as an ancestor. That, and his preference to remain "out of Treaty."

outport† *n.* **1** *Nfld* any port other than St. John's, especially one of the many small, isolated fishing villages on the coasts of Newfoundland and Labrador. See also **out-harbo(u)r.**
1820 (1956) FAY *Life and Labour* 138: Almost every fifth fisherman is what is termed a 'Planter,' particularly in the outports of the Island. **1918** GRENFELL *Labrador Doctor* 75: . . . men from far-away outports had been . . . collecting at the capital. . . . **1966** *Weekend Mag.* 23 Apr. 2/2: When I was a boy growing up in a Newfoundland outport, we had no sources of entertainment from the outside world. . . .

2 *Maritimes* a small coastal fishing village.
1835 *Novascotian* (Halifax) 17 Dec. 371/3: Now Halifax is . . . fed by the outports, and they begin to have enough to do to feed themselves—it must larn to live without em. **1865** *Islander* (Charlottetown) 10 Feb. 3/1: In the outports there has been little work except what was afforded by means of the Road Grant of 1st Session. **1953** RADDALL *Tidefall* 18: Run the whole thing from an outport, where I don't have much taxes to pay; place where I can refit my vessels at my own wharf, on my own slips. . . .

outporter *n.* *Nfld* a native or resident of an outport (def. 1). See also **bayman.**
1905 DUNCAN *Grenfell's Parish* 67: There is the Newfoundland 'outporter'—the small fisherman of the remoter coast, who must depend wholly upon his hook and line for subsistence. **1958** *Kingston Whig-Standard* (Ont.) 17 Dec. 27/7: . . . many outporters still follow the custom of starting [Christmas Day] off with a breakfast of fish.

outpost *n.* **1** *Fur Trade, Hist.* a trading post in the interior; especially a temporary trading station dependent on a larger and more permanent post. See also **winter outpost.** Cp. **flying post** and **winter post.**
1802 (1897) COUES *New Light* I 204: [I] made up the assortment of goods for the outposts, equipped the summer men, clerks, etc. **1820** (1938) SIMPSON *Athabasca Jnl* 104: There is an Outpost from Fort Vermillion about to be established close to Colville House. . . . **1913** COWIE *Adventurers* 191: For instance, Egg Lake was an outpost of Fort Pelly, and Waterhen of Manitobah Post. There was an outpost of Shoal

River at Duck Bay. **1965** *Maclean's* 24 July 34/2: Norway House was the Old Jack River outpost of the Selkirk settlers.

2 See **outpost hospital.**
1955 HARDY *Alta Anthol.* 212: Accident and emergency cases—for which, in previous years, there was often little hope—received immediate treatment at the nearest Outpost.

outpost hospital *Alta, Hist.* See quote.
1955 HARDY *Alta Anthol.* 212: In Alberta, after World War I, it set up "outpost hospitals" for the brides and families of soldier-settlers in the outlying reaches of the province . . . The Outpost Hospital of those days was no figure of speech. It was a strategically located unit, with four to six beds for men and women patients, plus a miniature maternity ward full of clothes-basket-cribs for the new arrivals.

outpost meadow a large open space in a mountain valley far enough from the home ranch to justify the building of temporary quarters for the crew cutting and stacking the annual crop of hay. Cp. **meadow**[2].
1962 FRY *Ranch on the Cariboo* 14: These were simple rigs for hauling hay and, like everything else about our outfit back in the outpost meadows, were made almost entirely of jack-pine wood.

outride *v.* function as an outrider.
1964 *Albertan* (Calgary) July 15/6: He's driving two chuckwagon outfits [and] will probably outride for a couple more. . . .

outrider *n.* in a chuckwagon race, *q.v.*, one of the four riders who load the wagon, direct the horses during the starting turns, and gallop with the outfit to the finish line.
1955 HARDY *Alta Anthol.* 169: There are four outriders to each of the four outfits in every heat. When the starting-horn blows, one outrider holds back the team of horses fighting to be on its way. Another throws the stove in the rear of the chuckwagon. The remaining two pitch the flies and poles into the covered wagon. Now, the four entries are off. . . . **1964** *Albertan* (Calgary) 7 July 1/2: . . . three crack-ups . . . saw all drivers, outriders and horses come out unscathed. . . .

outside or **Outside** *n.* **1 a.** originally among fur traders and now generally in the North, the settled, civilized parts of Canada; civilization. See also **go outside.** Cp. **inside,** *n.*
1827 (1927) *Beaver* Dec. 141: He was to bring in the last letters from outside which we could expect until next spring. **1898** *Yukon Midnight Sun* (Dawson) 11 June 5/2: Many of these are men who have just arrived from the outside, sold their outfits at good profits and are going out, disgusted with the country. **1941** DE PONCINS *Kabloona* 13: Only the Arctic existed for them; and everything that lay below the Mackenzie River, was to them the remote, the virtually non-existent "Outside." **1964** *Star Wkly* 26 Dec. 7/3: These people—the shopowners, clerks, trappers and prospectors of the far-north community—see him as their representative "outside."

b. on the outside, in the civilized parts of Canada; in those parts other than the North. Cp. **outside,** *adv.*
1898 *Yukon Midnight Sun* (Dawson) 25 July 3/1: On the outside last winter when the item that flour sold in Dawson for $125 a sack appeared in the papers the public gave a greater squirm of surprise and astonishment than it did when hearing of some fabulous

strike on Eldorado. **1964** *Calgary Herald* 22 July 35/5: We don't look down on people for the slight mistakes they make the way they do on the outside.

2 that part of Canada away from the isolated interior valleys of the western mountains.
1919 FRASER *Bulldog Carney* 245: "When I'd just got enough sowbelly to see me to the outside I pulled my freight." **1965** *Star Wkly* 2 Jan. 37/2: The only communication with the "outside" was the CPR telegraph at Carmi.

outside *adj. North* of or having to do with the outside (def. 1a).
1896 WHITNEY *On Snow-Shoes* 40: Gairdner had annoyed me a great deal, and no doubt we had worried him not a little, breaking in upon the even and lethargic tenor of his monotonous life with our "outside" (as the great world is called by the denizens of this lone land) hustling ways. **1922** FOOTNER *Huntress* 189: "No bannock and sow-belly; no sir! Real raised outside bread and genuine cow-butter from the mission. Green stuff from the mission garden. . . ." **1958** BERTON *Klondike* 307: "Expense! . . . Don't show your ignorance by using that cheap Outside word."

outside *adv. North* away from or beyond the northern parts of Canada; in or to the outside (def. 1a). See also **out**. Cp. **inside**, *adv.*
1896 RUSSELL *Far North* 50: To "go in," by the way, is to descend the Athabasca; to return to civilization is to "go outside." **1923** WALDO *Down Mackenzie* 246: I had thought that life beyond the 65th parallel or so was life beyond the pale: but I was now to learn that the Arctic Circle is the inner circle, and the real outsider is—of course—the one who lives "Outside." **1955** *Whitehorse Star* 24 Feb. 2/1: One of the outstanding characteristics of the Yukon is the general indifference to what is going on Outside. This lack of interest in the world is one of the very first impressions that meets a stranger from anywhere south of North. **1964** *Herald Mag.* 11 Jan. 1/6: . . . we have far less trouble with drinking than I have experienced "outside."

outside collar *North* See quote. See picture at **sled dog**.
1924 MASON *Arctic Forests* 32: The "outside" collar, made of smooth cow-hide and shaped to the neck, like a horse collar, enables the dog to carry the full pressure on the sides of the neck and leaves his breathing free. A well-fitting collar should be just tight enough to be pushed over the skull without hurting the dog . . . To get it off, the skin has to be pulled away from under it. If it is too loose the dog gets a sore shoulder.

outsider *n. North* a person of or from the settled part of Canada; a non-resident of the North. See also **outside**, *n.* (def. 1a). Cp. **insider**.
1923 WALDO *Down Mackenzie* 247: Lo! the poor Outsider, what he loses, what he misses! **1958** *Edmonton Jnl* 24 June 3 8/3: Few "Outsiders" have any idea of the tremendous amount of administrative work done in the Northwest Territories and Yukon, by the R.C.M.P. **1961** *Cdn Geog.Jnl* Jan. 16/2: At the port were five white persons—the Anglican missionary, his wife and three at the Hudson's Bay Company post; they had not seen outsiders since the annual summer visit of the ship. . . .

out West in or to the Prairie Provinces of Canada.
1888 (1890) ST. MAUR *Impressions* 173: All ponies and dogs "out West" seem shy of women. **1920** GIBBON *Conquering Hero* 32: . . . the cook . . . taught him recipes which would be useful when he had to "batch" again out West. **1961** *Maclean's* 29 July 36/1: ". . . I've worked freights that have carried more passengers

than the passenger runs did, especially out west in the Depression."

out-winterer *n. Fur Trade, Obs.* a trader or agent who wintered on the trail with Indian hunting parties. Cp. **derouine**.
1862 *Nor'Wester* (R.R.S.) 16 Apr. 2/4: He gets his reports from Sinclair's men, who are constantly on the road among the out-winterers, half-breeds, and Indians.

overflow *n. Esp.North* water covering all or part of the frozen surface of a river or lake, having been forced by expansion through cracks and fissures in the ice. See also **overflowing**.
1863 (1956) INNIS *Travellers West* 158: All this time I was wading in the water and keeping the sled from upsetting; but when he continued his profanity I couldn't stand it any longer so just dumped him right out into the overflow and went on. **1938** *Beaver* Sep. 18/2: . . . we followed the trail with our feet. Then we ran into overflow, and there was no trail. **1940** MARSHALL *Arctic Village* 82: The rivers are generally the easiest routes for winter travel because they always have solid ice underneath, because they are windswept, and because the overflows reduce the amount of snow. On the other hand, overflows also make the rivers the most hazardous travelling.

overflow *v. Esp.North* of water in rivers and lakes, rise under pressure of expansion through cracks and fissures to cover the ice on the surface.
1901 (1964) *North* Nov.-Dec. 4/2: Day and the other returned at once lest the river should overflow and render the ice trail impassable. **1940** MARSHALL *Arctic Village* 83: The colder it is, the more the river freezes to the bottom, and consequently the more it overflows.

overflowing *n.* See **overflow**, *n.*
1887 (1932) *Beaver* Dec. 139: [You will] find the snow not only deep, but overflowings underneath.

overhale *n.* [var. of *overhaul*] *Fur Trade, Obs.* an inventory.
1776 (1951) *Sask.Jnls* 344: . . . you are to make a strict overhale of all the Goods, Stores and Provisions at that place. . . . **1780** (1934) HEARNE & TURNOR *Journals* 279: 28th Monday assisted Mr Hutchins in makeing an overhale of the Provisions and Stores of which the following is the very alarming account. . . . **1785** (1954) *Moose Ft Jnts* 302: You'll therefore after everything is lodged at your settlement take an exact overhale of the Trading Goods, Provisions, and stores.

Overlander *n. Hist.* one of a group of people from the Canadas who, in 1862, undertook a long and arduous journey overland from Ontario to the Cariboo goldfields in British Columbia. Cp. **Argonaut**. Also *Overlander of '62*.
1916 LAUT *Cariboo Trail* 55: . . . some of the Overlanders had narrowly escaped a massacre. **1950** HUTCHISON *Fraser* 88: The most remarkable immigrants of all deserve to be remembered—the Overlanders of '62, the men (and one pregnant woman) who walked to Cariboo across the Rocky Mountains and ran the Fraser on rafts in the strangest movement of those times. **1958** KELSEY *B.C.Rides a Star* 191: Starving, almost naked, penniless, the "Overlanders" settled down on small farms and millsites to found Kamloops' sawmilling, agricultural and other industries. **1963** *Cdn Geog.Jnl* Oct. 112/3: Among those who heard the call

of "Gold in the Cariboo!" were the Overlanders, a company that toiled across the prairies in covered wagons, and on foot through the Rockies at Yellowhead Pass.

Overlander Special a special train which each year takes a party of Maritimers overland on a tour of Canada.
1958 *Edmonton Jnl* 2 Aug. 22/6: More than 100 members of the "Overlander Special," a group of Maritimers touring Canada, were entertained . . . at Edmonton.

overparka n. *North* See **atigi** (def. 2 and picture).
1951 GILLIS & MYLES *North Pole* 89: She wore the usual bulky over-parka or *attigi* of white duck. . . .
1958 *Edmonton Jnl* 24 June 3 10/8: When it is warm [the Eskimo] wears a parka of duffel, with an overparka of windproof material purchased at the trading posts.

overplus n. *Fur Trade, Hist.* See 1965 cite. See also **overtrade**.
1712 (1958) RICH *Hudson's Bay Co.* I 27: . . . and as for the standard [of trade] as it is you will find your overplus considerable if you please for to look in your books. **1959** *Ibid.* II 102: . . . much of the trouble came from the "Overplus system" whereby the traders gave short measure and cheated the Indians . . . by the sleight of hand practised on them. **1965** *Letters from Hudson Bay* 27n: The "overplus" was the margin by which the Company's traders improved upon the terms of barter with the Indians laid down in the standard of trade. Had the standard been strictly followed the number of beaver skins taken in a year (together with other goods made beaver) would have equalled the beaver-equivalent of goods expended at the Company's factories. . . . In practice the number of skins taken exceeds the number expended in every year in this period for which a record survives.

overseer n. See quotes. Cp. **reeve**.
1954 TYRE *Saddlebag Surgeon* 243: A couple of men I half expected to see laid low with the financial jitters were Oliver Onerheim, the reeve of the municipality, and Louis Anderson, the overseer of the village.
1960 WARD *Government in Canada* 25: In a city, the executive is the city council, headed by the mayor; in a county, the county council headed by a warden; in a township, the township council headed by a reeve or an overseer.

oversnow adj. having to do with or intended for travelling over snow during winter.
1946 *Beaver* June 3/1: The plan [Exercise Muskox] called for a small force of a dozen tracked over-snow vehicles to make a 3200 mile trek. . . . **1949** *Report of DME Test Team* IE 1: It is a different story, however, with mobile detachments accompanying oversnow convoys. **1963** *Kingston Whig-Standard* (Ont.) 13 Feb. 21/3: [The RN110 is] used primarily for oversnow operations although it is capable of traversing rough ground, mud and muskeg with ease.

overtrade n. *Fur Trade, Hist.* See **overplus**.
1727 (1965) *Letters from Hudson Bay* 121: We observe in the Accounts you sent us, that your over Trade hath been every year very small compared with that of our other Factories. . . . **1965** *Ibid.* 121n: For a definition of "overtrade" or "overplus," see *supra* p. 27. . . .

owner-elector or **owner-voter** n. *B.C.* a person or corporation owning real property within a municipality and thus entitled to vote on money by-laws in municipal elections. Cp. **resident elector.**
1958 *Sun* (Vancouver) 11 Apr. 26/1: For all general purposes, there are two categories of voters—one is owner voters, the other is resident voters, but all must be citizens of Canada. **1958** *Citizen* 4 Sep. 7/3: Owner-Electors may vote at whichever *one* of the Polling Stations is most convenient.

oxhide shoe *Obs.* See **beef shoe.**
1944 *Beaver* Sep. 19: Most of the shoes meant for the voyageurs and canoemen were of local manufacture. Some of them were called . . . oxhide shoes.

ox-pusher n. *Slang, Hist.* See **bull-driver.**
1955 HARDY *Alta Anthol.* 78: And so Frank Oliver, the "ox-pusher," buying the first lot ever sold in Edmonton —for $25, in trade—threw up a log shack and began a trading business.

ox-skin n. *Obs.* a buffalo hide.
1775 (1901) HENRY (Elder) *Travels* 259: It [the community] consists of thirty families, lodged in skins of a circular form, and composed of dressed ox-skins, stretched upon poles twelve feet in length, and leaning against a stake driven into the ground in the centre.

ox-sled or **ox-sleigh** n. *Obs.* a low sled or stoneboat that slid on wooden runners made from shaped logs, pulled by an ox or by oxen.
1825 (1916) SELLAR *Narrative* 103: Walked to Toronto [to buy a] logging-chain and an ox-sled.
1844 (1963) GUILLET *Pioneer Farmer* II 25: Searching in the woods for a tree with a proper turn near the root to make a pair of runners for an ox sled. . . .
1896 GOURLAY *Hist.Ottawa* 41: In winter several small grists could be taken on one ox sleigh. **1957** *Beaver* Autumn 26/2: It was there that I met the first ox-carts, or rather "ox-sleds," that I have ever seen in Newfoundland.

oyster day *Maritimes* an annual occasion for consuming vast quantities of oysters and liquor during neighborly visits within the community.
1849 ALEXANDER *L'Acadie* I 111: . . .but this like "oyster day," perhaps only happens "once a year."

oyster mud *Maritimes* dense mudlike deposits of the remains of generations of bivalves and crustaceans, rich in lime and valuable as fertilizer. See also **mussel mud.**
1904 CROSSKILL *P.E.I.* 66: The Island possesses one advantage which is unique and very valuable. I refer now to its thick beds of 'mussel mud' or 'oyster mud' which are found in all bays and river mouths.

oyster saloon† *Obs.* a public house where one could drink liquor and eat oysters; oyster bar.
1863 *Norfolk Reformer* (Simcoe, C.W.) 5 Nov. 2/5: The intellect of the youth, I suppose, requires that such school as an oyster saloon for perfect development, but I should think, Sir, that week-day evenings were sufficient for this education; but the proprietors of the den aforesaid seem to think otherwise. **1864** *Islander* (Charlottetown) 12 Aug. 2/5: On landing the first sign swinging out half way across the street, is "Oyster Saloon", where they can be served up to your liking. **1883** *Brandon Dly Mail* (Man.) 7 Feb. 4/1: After carousing around for some time they left there and proceeded to an oyster saloon.

pacificator justice *Hist.* in Lower Canada, an unofficial arbitrator working outside the constituted authority during the political unrest of the 1830's.

1840 WILLIS *Cdn Scenery* I 82: . . . an organization was formed of *pacificator* justices, to compose differences without recourse to the constituted authorities, and in whose decisions all true patriots were required to acquiesce.

Pacific Coast that part of Canada bordering on the Pacific Ocean; the West Coast; now, especially, British Columbia.

1836 BACK *Arctic Land* 481: The country nearer the Pacific coast is frequented by a fox more closely resembling the European than the Canis fulvus of the eastern territory does. **1888** *Dominion Illust.* 51/1: We secured a foothold on the Pacific coast through the offer of British Columbia to join the Confederacy. **1958** *Kootenaian* (Kaslo, B.C.) 3 July 4/1: In this year of British Columbia's Centennial it is interesting to look back and marvel at the slender margin by which the decision was made here on the Pacific Coast to complete the structure of Canada, to make this Dominion truly "From Sea to Sea." **1966** *Sun* (Vancouver) 14 Nov. 20/3: Columbus and Westminster Royals made a patch to get into the Pacific Coast Soccer League on the weekend.

Pacific Northwest that part of North America lying west of the Rockies and north of the Columbia River, especially, in Canada, British Columbia.

1938 CASH *I Like B.C.* 100: The Provincial Library at the Parliament Buildings is quite one of the most interesting in the Pacific Northwest. **1954** *Comox District Free Press* (Courtenay, B.C.) 26 May 4/2: Fishermen coming to this district can have the best fishing to be found anywhere in the Pacific Northwest. **1955** *Vancouver Province* 6 Jan. 17/6: The huge housing construction program in the U.S. this year—expected to be the biggest in history—should mean big business for B.C. and other Pacific Northwest lumber-producing areas.

Pacific Province 1 *Obs.* either of two former colonies on the Pacific Coast: British Columbia and Vancouver's Island, *q.v.*

1862 *Nor'Wester* (R.R.S.) 14 May 1/2: Such an enterprise would draw an immense amount of travel to our shores, create strong bonds between Canada and the Pacific Provinces, and eventually lead to the settlement of many of the fortunate gold diggers in our midst.

2 in modern use, British Columbia.

1871 *Wkly Manitoban* 11 Mar. 2/4: Liberal, even munificent, as these stipulations are in favor of the Pacific Province, yet they are all deemed necessary to the project of a Pacific Railroad. **1921** *Cdn Hist.Rev.* II 352: . . . it was Queen Victoria who bestowed the title of British Columbia upon the Pacific Province. . . .

Pacific railway *Hist.* the transcontinental railway completed in 1885 and later known as the Canadian Pacific Railway, linking eastern Canada with the Pacific Coast.

1859 *Brit.Colonist* (Victoria) 13 July 1/2: He alluded to the Pacific Railway, and believed that it was more likely to be built within 15 years than was the Grand Trunk railway 10 years ago. **1883** *Prince Albert Times* (Sask.) 3 Jan. 4/2: Many persons still doubt that this will be the permanent terminus of the Pacific Railway. **1963** MORTON *Kingdom of Canada* 330: It was known . . . that Canada proposed a Pacific railway. . . .

Pacific Scandal *Hist.* a scandal that engulfed the administration of Sir John A. Macdonald during 1872-3, associated with the charter granted the Canadian Pacific Railway Company.

1946 LOWER *Colony to Nation* 357: It was this reorganized company which came to grief in the "Pacific Scandal" of 1873, the episode that also destroyed Macdonald's government. L. S. Huntingdon, a Liberal M.P. from Quebec, in the spring following the election of 1872, made most serious charges of corruption against Macdonald and of bribery against Sir Hugh Allan, who was virtually alleged to have bought the new charter from the Conservative government in return for campaign funds. **1966** *Kingston Whig-Standard* (Ont.) 8 Jan. 4/5: In 1872-73 his [Macdonald's] administration was defeated as a result of the "Pacific Scandal."

Pacific slope the drainage basin of rivers flowing to the Pacific.

1852 RICHARDSON *Arctic Exped.* 100: It had not until lately crossed the Rocky Mountain range, nor is it known on the Pacific slope, except in a very few places. **1905** *Eye Opener* (Calgary) 28 Jan. 2/2: Over on the Pacific Slope, to say nothing of the cities across the line, you get a schooner of beer for a nickel, with a hot lunch thrown in. **1945** PUGSLEY *Saints* 60: We were now on the Pacific Slope, rolling down to the sea.

pack *n.* **1** *Fur Trade* **a.** *Hist.* See **piece** (def. 1).

1774 (1934) HEARNE *Journal* 122: By the Masters account . . . 65 or 70 Packs or Caggs, called by them Pieces, are put on board each Canoe. . . . **1794** (1889) MACDONELL *Journal* 288: Paid Mary . . . for lacing 14 pairs of snowshoes, and then buffalo skins she dressed and cut into cords for the packs, and for cutting ten more skins into thongs that were dressed to her hand, 15 plues. **1961** *Cdn Geog.Jnl* July 5: All the trading goods and the furs had been made up into "pièces," each weighing about ninety pounds. A voyageur quickly slung one of these on his back, with a tumpline over his forehead pulling his head back. Into the hollow thus formed he tossed a second ninety-pound pack which pushed his head forward.

b. a bundle of furs, usually 90 pounds, especially one baled in a pack press, *q.v.*, and tagged and numbered as to contents and year. See also **package** (def. 2).

1784 (1790) UMFREVILLE *Hudson's Bay* 21: Sixty packs has been made this winter in his quarter, but four of his men have been eat by the savages through extremity of hunger. **1896** WHITNEY *On Snow-Shoes* 7: For many years the town will be . . . the outlet for the numberless "packs" fathered by the great Hudson's Bay Company. **1961** PHILLIPS & SMURR *Fur Trade* II 330: [He] fined him thirty packs of beaver, which was just the quantity he had.

2 See **ice-pack.**

1851 SNOW *Voyage* 385: A pack is a body of drift-ice, of such magnitude that its extent is not discernible. A pack is open when the pieces of ice, though very near to each other, do not generally touch, or close when the pieces are in complete contact. **1962** *Weekend Mag.* 5 May 4/3: We crashed headlong into the pack and hoped to drift through.

pack *v.* **1** *Fur Trade* prepare a bale of furs by means of a pack press, *q.v.*
1697 (1929) KELSEY *Papers* 94: Saturday ye 7th . . . pact ye rest of ye beaver. . . . **1874** (1956) ROSS *Athabasca* 15: . . . they have been dried and re-packed by Mr. Spencer, but as the fur mould and the pack press at his post are very bad . . . Mr. Spencer has had a great deal of trouble in repacking. . . .

2† a. of men, carry (goods, supplies, etc.), especially on the back. See also **pack in** and **packing.** Cp. **backpack,** *v.*
1862 *Islander* (Charlottetown) 12 Sep. 2/2: The mules cannot get nearer than the Forks of Quesnelle, so the stores have to be packed by men from there to the mines. **1898** *B.C.Hist.Qtly* XVI 1952 89: At the other side is the Nyaline Hill, which has only a very narrow pack trail, so that we must pack our stuff up on our backs for 3/4 of a mile. . . . **1923** *Beaver* Oct. 22/1: . . . the wife has to pack about three times as much as her husband or the dogs, and quite often has to pack a baby as well. **1959** *Native Voice* July 6/4: When they went into the mountains, Annie would pack his blankets, axe and shovel.

b. of animals, carry goods or supplies; serve as a pack animal. Cp. **pack dog.**
1922 *Beaver* Nov. 58/1: Throughout Alaska and Northern British Columbia [dogs] are trained to pack, just as are mules.

3 a. load or burden with packs of goods or supplies.
1860 *Brit.Colonist* (Victoria) 17 Dec. 3/2: Large trains of packed Indians were leaving for Boston Bar and the Forks. **1913** FOOTNER *Jack Chanty* 71: Four Indian lads completed the party. This was barely sufficient to pack the horses and make camp. **1959** *Native Voice* July 6/4: It took two years to train Annie, packing her light at first and by gradually increasing the weight he got her accustomed to a heavy pack.

b. transport on pack animals.
1889 WITHROW *Our Own Country* 543: . . . the miners "packed" on mule trains the whole outfit necessary for their operation and sustenance.

c. use for transporting goods or supplies.
1951 HOBSON *Grass* 102: Out at the corrals, Lester Dorsey . . . helped Pan finish the heavy job of shoeing and rockpacking the broncs we were going to pack. **1957** *Beaver* Summer 35/2: One mare had never before been packed, and she caused an endless amount of trouble. . . .

4 serve as a guide and bearer (for). See also **packer** (def. 2b).
1880 GORDON *Mountain and Prairie* 85: The son of the chief of the Achwilgate tribe . . . was anxious simply to hire as one of those who should "pack" for us. **1958** COUTTS *Dawson Creek* 78: . . . others either left the country or settled down to a life of prospecting and wild horse bickering, packing hunters through the mountains. . . .

'pack *n.* *Elliptical* See **shoepack.**
1931 GREY OWL *Last Frontier* 181: And here is where my hard-soled 'packs came in.

package *n.* *Fur Trade, Hist.* **1** See **piece** (def. 1)
1800 (1897) COUES *New Light* I 7: I gave out to all their respective loading, which consisted of 28 packages per canoe, assorted for the Salteur trade on Red River. . . .
1922 *Beaver* Mar. 35/1: Each package weighed ninety pounds, and was constructed as near as possible to fit on either side of a pack saddle.

2 See **pack,** *n.* (def. 1b) .
1894 BEGG *Hist.of B.C.* 104: . . . it was not uncommon in some of the passes of New Caledonia to see a train of two hundred horses, each laden with two packages of furs, winding with the narrow trail round cliffs and through passes, on their way to canoe navigation.

packboard *n.* a frame of light metal or wood shaped to fit the back and suspended therefrom by shoulder straps, used for packing loads.
1956 EVANS *Mountain Dog* 125: He rested his pack board on a windfall and took out his compass. **1963** *Placer-Mining B.C.* 40/1: The pack-board is superior to the pack-sack; it keeps the back moderately cool and on it can be lashed almost any sort of load and, what is most important, the correct balance for the load is easily attained.

pack-carrying dog See **pack dog.**
1908 MAIR *Mackenzie Basin* 170: . . . we rapidly advanced to about 300 yards from their position, when we halted and unloaded our twelve Eskimo pack-carrying dogs and sent them at the herd. . . .

pack cord *Fur Trade, Obs.* a strong cord, usually of leather, for tying up packs of fur and other large packages.
1806 (1930) FRASER *Journal* 154: Will you be able to send me over some green skins for windows and Babich and plenty pack cords. . . . **1810** (1897) COUES *New Light* II 583: Women all busy stretching buffalo hides to make pemmican bags and pack cords. **1831** (1944) *Beaver* Sep. 17/1: That Gentlemen in charge of Districts and Posts be directed . . . to collect large quantities of . . . Pack cords . . . as these articles are absolutely necessary for the trade in many parts of the country, and cannot be purchased in Europe or Canada.

pack dog a dog trained to carry a pack or other burden strapped to his back. See also **pack-carrying dog.** Cp. **packer** (def. 3).
[**1775** GRAHAM *Observations* 312: The Rivers that Water their Country have no communication with Churchill river for which reason it reduces them to the necessity of bringing their bundles on their backs and the Dogs are loaded like packhorses.] **1913** COWIE *Adventurers* 323: Besides the cart and the travois, pack-ponies were also used; also pack dogs, the latter bearing frequently burdens mountains high in comparison with their size. These also are still in everyday use amongst the Indians of the woods. **1955** HOBSON *Nothing Too Good* 113: He could use him on this trap line as a pack dog.

packer *n.* **1 a.†** a person who transports goods by means of pack horses or mules; one who operates a freighting business using a pack-train, *q.v.*
1859 *British Colonist* (Victoria) 6 June 2/3: The arrival of over one hundred pack mules from the Chilliwak country, where they have been wintering, and offers by the packers to take freight to Lytton city for eighteen cents, has failed to revive trade. **1958** TERRY *Chilcotin* 7: Tom Hutchinson was a packer and worked with a pack train of 300 mules between Yale and Barkerville.

b. a person who transports goods and supplies to remote places by truck or other vehicle.
1952 INNES *Campbell's Kingdom* 22: . . . I was wakened with the news that the packer was in from Come Lucky and would be leaving after lunch. I was taken out and introduced to a great ox of a man who was loading

groceries into an ex-army truck.

2 a. a person who transports goods on his own back. See also **packman.**

1873 GRANT *Ocean to Ocean* 356: We could see that continuous labour for one or two years in solitary wilderness . . . as surveyor, transit-man . . . or even packer, is a totally different thing from taking a trip across the continent. . . . **1921** HEMING *Drama of Forests* 320: Upon the first his companion placed two more packs; then, stooping beneath the weight of 240 pounds, the packers at a jog-trot set off uphill and down, over rugged rocks and fallen timber, through fern-covered marsh and dense underbrush. **1956** KEMP *Northern Trader* 35: From that day forward I drew double wages, and under Abraham's tutelage I was to become—of sorts—a canoeman, a packer, and a whitewater man. **1961** *Cdn Geog.Jnl* Jan. 15/2: One packer . . . [called] "the human derrick," actually a man of light stature, was quite a character. . . .

b. a person who packs (def. 4) for hunting expeditions, etc.

1965 *Kingston Whig-Standard* (Ont.) 16 Sep. 18/1: Burrell left Sindre in June . . . to supervise the . . . training of 15 local Indians as guides and packers.

3 a pack animal. Cp. **pack dog.**

1908 LAUT *Conquest N.W.* II 270: Getting two or three of the wise old bell-mares, that are in every string of packers, at the end of a long rope, the canoemen shot across the whirl of mid-stream and got footing on the opposite shore. **1944** MARTIN *Cdn Wilderness* 13: In spring and fall when it is impossible to haul your supplies, dogs come in handy as packers.

4 a fishing vessel that carries the catch of smaller vessels to the cannery.

1954 EVANS *Mist* 20: The packer had a gillnet boat tied up alongside, bow and stern, with only its pilot house above water. **1958** *Fisherman* 24 Oct. 4/5: In with 75,000 pounds of dogfish from the west coast last week was the packer Annie Tuck.

packet *n. Fur Trade, Hist.* **1** a parcel or package of mail, instructions, business documents, etc. Also spelled *pacquet.*

1679 (1948) *H.B.C.Letters Outward* 1: We are glad to heare of your safe arrivall . . . & have received the Packets you have sent us. . . . **1778** (1951) *Sask.Jnls* 222: . . . three Young North River Indians came with the pacquet, which they have had in their care since the Fall. **1783** (1954) *Moose Ft Jnls* 21: Two gone with a paquet to Albany. **1874** (1956) ROSS *Athabasca* 16: The Athabasca accounts for the Past Outfit were closed and the Packet given over to the care of Mr. Moberly.

2 a party carrying mail and other special deliveries between trading posts by dog-sled, canoe, etc. See also **packet man** and **packet party.**

1861 *Nor'Wester* (R.R.S.) 19 Feb. 4/1: The last packet from the far north brought us the following most interesting and most valuable communication from the Rev. W. W. Kirby. . . . **1956** KEMP *Northern Trader* 43: "The Packet," a canoe-brigade in the summer or a string of dog teams in the winter, carried in the mail and brought out the fur.

packet box *Fur Trade* a strong box used for carrying mail, post records, and other valuables.

1921 HEMING *Drama of Forests* 175: Before long the Factor's letters were sealed and carefully deposited in the packet box, which was lashed on the tail of the sled, the forepart of which was packed with blankets, flour,

tea, and pork for the packeteers, and frozen whitefish for the dogs. **1924** *Beaver* Sep. 438: [At ship time in the North] After the first greetings are over, enquiry is for the "packet box" with the most important item, the mail.

packet carrier *Hist.* See **packet man.**

1939 *Beaver* Dec. 25/1: Kipling. . . was an experienced hunter, trader and a man of high standing in the service of the Company. He was the famous "packet carrier" from Fort Garry to Norway House, which was a most responsible position.

packeteer *n. Hist.* See **packet man.**

1784 (1954) *Moose Ft Jnls* 27: Tradesmen at their separate employs, Hunters, Trappers, fishermen, and pacqueteers as before. **1943** *Beaver* Mar. 30/1: Mail packets were operated on a time-table, just as are mail flights by aeroplanes to-day. "Packeteers" were never armed.

packet Indian *Fur Trade, Hist.* an Indian serving as a packet man, *q.v.*

1916 TYRRELL in THOMPSON *Narrative* 30: The Hudson's Bay Company had established a very useful line of communications between their several factories by means of what were called Packet Indians; these were each of two Indian men, who left each Factory with letters to arrive at the next Factory about the expected time of the arrival of the Ship at such factory.

packet man *Fur Trade, Hist.* one of the men making up a packet (def. 2). See also **packet carrier, packeteer,** and **packet Indian.**

1779 (1934) TURNOR *Journal* 215: . . . no Packet having been received . . . began to get my things in readiness to proceed . . . being fearfull now of waiting any longer for the Packet men. . . . **1896** RUSSELL *Far North* 104: I reached the post the next day and learned that the returned packet men had heard that two buffaloes had been killed by the Smith Indians in the fall. **1938** GODSELL *Red Hunters* 117: I left York Factory with the packet-men on my way Outside for medical attention. . . .

packet party *Fur Trade, Hist.* See **packet** (def. 2).

1923 *Beaver* Aug. 414: The packet party is usually made up of two trains of eight to ten dogs each, the clerk in charge and two native *voyageurs.*

pack ice† thick sea ice that has been driven and packed into large masses by winds and currents. Cp. **ice-pack.**

1850 GOODSIR *Baffin's Bay* 108: As long as there was a chance of procuring whales in Prince Regent's Inlet, he might have persevered, deep as his ship was in the water, and great as the risk would have been in pushing through the heavy pack-ice we had fallen in with. **1965** *Kingston Whig-Standard* (Ont.) 3 Apr. 4/5: About 300,000 of these seals are killed on the pack ice every spring by the Canadian and Norwegian sealing fleets. . . .

pack in carry in one's supplies, especially on the back; deliver goods by packing, *q.v.* See also **pack,** *v.* (def. 2).

1923 STRINGER *Empty Hands* 30: While still unable to spare men to bring up his thirty-foot shallow-draught paddle-wheeler, which had arrived at the rail-head in sections, he had been compelled to "pack" in effeminate double-walled silk tents. . . . **1943** MILLER *Lone Woodsman* 24: Or would it (the river) be all choked with wind-thrown trees, so that he would have to abandon the canoe and pack in? **1957** LARGE *Skeena* 61: Provisions were packed in by pack train in the summer.

packing *n.* the transport of goods on the backs of men or animals. See also **pack,** *v.* (def. 2) and **pack in.**
1859 *Brit.Colonist* (Victoria) 19 Feb. 1/3: Packing, which has gone along steadily all the time, amounts to about 25 cts. per lb. to Fraser, which nothing but competition can reduce, the present number of working animals there not exceeding 50 in all. **1914** DOUGLAS *Lands Forlorn* 193: This was my first experience of packing with dogs, and the amount of weight they were able to carry fairly astonished me.

packing press See **pack press.**

pack line See **tumpline** and picture.
1956 INNIS *Fur Trade* 13: The absence or weak development of pottery and basketry, the use of snowshoes and toboggans in winter and the birch-bark canoe and the packline in summer ... were characteristic cultural features [of Indians in the Saguenay area, early 17th century].

packman† *n.* See **packer** (def. 2a).
1909 NURSEY *Isaac Brock* 45: Brock would watch these packmen as, thus handicapped with a load weighing from two to five hundred pounds, they set out across the rough portage, singing, and at a dog trot, following each other in quick succession.

pack mantle See **mantle.**

pack press *Fur Trade* a press used in making up packs (def. 1b) of fur. See also **fur press** and **jackscrew.** Also *packing press.*
1777 (1951) *Sask.Jnls* 141: The Carpenter & one man employed making the packing Press. **1822** (1940) *Minutes of Council* (H.B.C.) 380: The packing presses ... are extremely inconvenient and out of repair the machinery complex and the operation tedious. **1874** (1956) ROSS *Athabasca* 15: ... the fur mould and pack press at this post are both very bad and not the same size as the presses at the other posts. ...

packsack† *n.* a sack of strong material used for carrying supplies, personal belongings, etc. when on the trail, usually carried on the back and supported by shoulder straps and, often, a tumpline, *q.v.* Cp. **pacton** (def. 1).
1920 *Rod and Gun in Can.* Nov. 715/1: I note in the last issue ... a good old-time packsack illustrated by Mr. Haines. **1926** SULLIVAN *Northern Lights* 61: Carcajou—the wolverine and glutton—stared at the pack-sack, then slid down and began tearing it. ... **1960** *Beaver* Autumn 57/1: These Nile men were rather the shanty-boy variety of Canadian riverman, just as much at home on certain Canadian rivers as Jean Baptiste had ever been but more skilled with the raft, the pike and the peavey than with the paddle and packsack.

pack-sack citizen *Slang* a person who stays in a place for only a short time, living, as it were, out of a packsack.
1966 *Globe and Mail* (Toronto) 18 Jan. B5/7: [The logger] was a pack-sack citizen and appeared on Skid Row streets complete with dirty Stanfields and caulk boots which would be later hocked for the last bottle.

packstrap *n.* See **tumpline** and picture.
1897 TYRRELL *Sub-Arctics* 70: When our duties permitted and occasion required we both took a turn at the pack-straps, as we did on this portage. **1956** KEMP *Northern Trader* 25: Where our canoemen tied their packstraps around a hundred-pound piece, piled another hundred-pound piece atop it, squatted down cross-legged while they adjusted the headband, heaved themselves up and jogged off, I shambled down the portage with scarcely seventy pounds.

packton *n.* See **pacton.**

pack-trail† *n.* a trail used by pack-trains, *q.v.*
1858 (1921) LAUT *Cariboo Trail* 13: There is a pack-trail from Hope, but it cannot be travelled till the snow is off the mountains. **1921** *Beaver* Mar. 26/1: In making packtrails through the country all these marshy spots have to be bridged with corduroy. ... **1965** *Ibid.* Autumn 54/1: Along the pack trail we met trappers coming out of the bush ... with their winter's catch of furs.

pack-train† *n.* a line of animals employed in packing, *q.v.*, together with the men in charge.
1862 MAYNE *Four Years in B.C.* 148: From thence pack-trains could make Alexandria, or the mouth of the Canal River ... in 14 or 15 days. **1965** *Beautiful B.C.* Summer 9/1: He ... operated a pack train for the Hudson's Bay Company.

pack trip† an expedition in which all supplies and equipment are packed (def. 2).
1962 FRY *Ranch on the Cariboo* 219: ... they wondered what Pete had to offer in the way of a real pack trip into the hills.

packy *adj.* of snow, of such consistency as to be readily pressed into snowballs.
1952 BUCKLER *Mountain and Valley* 62: The snow was so packy it left a track right down to the grass roots.

pacquet *n.* See **packet.**

pacqueteer *n.* See **packeteer.**

pacton ['pæktən] *n.* [< Cdn F *paqueton* small pack] Also spelled *packton* and *paqueton. Fur Trade, Hist.* **1** a small pack of personal belongings rigged for carrying on the back. Cp. **packsack.**
[**1744** POTIER (au Detroit) in *Glossaire*: Il prit son paqueton et tout son drigail et fricassa le camp.] **1828** (1872) MCDONALD *Peace River* 44: [There were] the usual "agrès" for the canoes, besides the men's own pactons. **1860** (1956) KOHL *Kitchi-Gami* 168: Du Roy ... hung the while on his back, while fastening the broad band of the "paqueton" round his head. ... **1944** *Beaver* Sep. 18/1: Each spring, the food supplies, gathered in Montreal, filled the packs (called *paquetons*) in the large birch-bark canoes.

2 See **piece** (def. 1). See also **pack,** *n.* (def. 1a).
1804 (1911) LAROCQUE *Journal* 308: Sent 6 pactons of furs containing kitts, 57 wolves, 4 foxes, 7 beavers, 5 bags of corn and a horse. **1806** (1897) COUES *New Light* I 276: Grand Noir brought me a paqueton of beavers to induce me to show charity to his son-in-law. **1827** (1912) ERMATINGER *Express Jnl* 82: Embark ... taking with us all the furs at this place, say 7 Packtons.

paddle *n.* a canoe journey; a spell of paddling, as opposed to lining, portaging, etc.; also, the distance that can be covered by canoe in a specified time.
1754 (1907) HENDAY *Journal* 325: Othenume Lake is a

good day's paddle either way; and the woods around it are tall and well grown timber. **1784** (1954) *Moose Ft Jnls* 337: We have had two Pedlars paddling about from Lake to Lake within one Day's Paddle of our Place, but with what design I am at a loss to guess, as they had no Trading Goods with them. **1914** DOUGLAS *Lands Forlorn* 97: But we had good going, with an uninterrupted ten-mile paddle for a start. **1922** *Beaver* Apr. 21/1: . . . I was on my way up the river with an Indian and bark canoe and a heavy paddle ahead of us.

paddling song *Hist*. See **boat song.**
1793 (1933) MACDONELL *Diary* 92: . . . our canoe went well and the crew sung paddling songs in a vociferous manner. **1844** (1955) LEFROY *Magnetic North* 136: . . . they arrived in Toronto singing French paddling songs all up the street. . . . **1955** STANLEY in *Ibid.* xxiii: The two half-breeds who accompanied him were in a state of exhilaration and intoxication, bellowing their paddling songs at the tops of their voices as they were accustomed to do on arrival at the trading-posts in the western territories.

Padlock Law *Que., Hist*. See quotes.
1946 LOWER *Colony to Nation* 528: Urged on by many among his own people, by strong pressure, it may be assumed, from certain circle[s] in the church, and nothing loath himself, Mr. Duplessis enacted, in 1937, the notorious "Padlock Law." Under its authority the Attorney-General could, without court action, close for one year premises suspected of being used to propagate "communism" (the word was not defined). **1958** *Encyc. Can.* II 299/1: Provincial legislation which remained in effect for some years [included] the Quebec Padlock Law of 1937 (it was found to be *ultra vires* by the Supreme Court of Canada in 1957). . . .

pageesee ['pagisi] *n*. [< Algonk.] See **pagessan** (def. 3).

pagessan ['pagə,san] *n*. [< Algonk.: cf. Cree *pukēsēwuk* they throw (gamble) with dice]
☛ *For convenience several apparent cognates are listed under this entry. See note at* **platter.**
1 See **platter.** Also spelled *pukessan*.
1819 (1823) FRANKLIN *Journey* 67: The game most used amongst them, termed pukesann, is played with the stones of a species of *prunus*. . . . **1860** (1956) KOHL *Kitchi-Gami* 83: Some time ago I seated myself by some Indians who were playing at pagessan.
2 See **hand game.**
1908 MAIR *Mackenzie Basin* 50: On the island our Cree half-breeds enjoyed the first evening's camp by playing the universal button-hiding game called Pugasawin, and which is always accompanied by a monotonous chant and the tom-tom. . . .
3 See **lahal.**
1965 WILSON *No Man Stands Alone* 64: That night the Indians rounded off the day by playing Lahal, sometimes called Slahal or Pageesee.

pail smudge a smudge pot, consisting of a pail filled with burning wood and covered with damp leaves, hay, etc., which sends up clouds of smoke to repel insects.
1955 HARDY *Alta Anthol*. 119: We girls and Mother looked like wild witches, our long hair flying, our faces smudged with dirt, as we huddled over a "pail smudge" of wormwood in the centre of the wagon.

paintbrush† *n*. See **Indian paint-brush.**
1916 WOOD *Tourist's N.W.* 443: About 8 miles from Field the scene has so changed in character that meadow-banks of wild forget-me-nots and crimson

paint-brush, white violets, columbine, yellow daisies and purple asters tempt one to stray afield.

painted cup† See **Indian paint-brush.**
1852 (1881) TRAILL *Cdn Crusoes* 23: The high sloping hills . . . were clothed with . . . scarlet enchroma, or painted cup. . . . **1909** CAMERON *New North* 143: One day we gathered careopsis, pretty painted-cups, the dandelion in seed, shinleaf (*Pyrola elliptica*), our old friend yarrow, and golden-rod. **1930** JONES *Wild Flowers* Plate 268: PAINTED CUP . . . Often feeds on roots of other plants: hence it can do with scanty leaves.

painter ['pentɚ] *n*. [dial. var. of *panther*] See **cougar.**
1796 (1911) SIMCOE *Diary* 339: An American said he guessed it was the painters (so they call panthers). . . . **1844** MARRYAT *Settlers in Canada* 38: . . . he laughed and told them that painters were a species of panther, not spotted, but tawny-coloured, and at times very dangerous. **1962** *B.C.Digest* Oct. 45/1: In every-day language the species is known as cougar, puma, painter, panther, mountain lion, catamount and simply lion.

painter's brush† See **Indian paint-brush.**
*c*1902 LAUT *Trapper* 87: Ah! what is that little indurated line . . . winds in an out among the devil's-club and painter's-brush . . . and heather? **1938** GODSELL *Red Hunters* 263: . . . two of the ladies succeeded in gathering bouquets of . . . flaming painter's brush.

painter's flower See **Indian paint-brush.**
1908 LAUT *Conquest N.W.* II 63: Once across the divide, the men passed from the bare snow uplands to the cloud line, where seas of tossing mist blotted out earth, and from cloud line to the Alpine valleys with larch-grown meadows and painters' flowers knee deep, all the colors of the rainbow.

paleface† *n*. a white man.
☛ *Although widely held to be an Indian term for Europeans, the word may well be an invention of English-speaking writers of Indian tales.*
1843 *Montreal Transcript* 31 Aug. 1/5: The dog of a pale face returned evil for good. **1922** JOHNSON *Legends* 6: The only shadow on the joy of it all was war, for the tribe of the great Tyee was at war with the Upper Coast Indians, those who lived north, near what is named by the Pale-face as the port of Prince Rupert. **1955** COLLARD *Cdn Yesterdays* 282: "Pale face," he said, "could you tell me what the big wigwam is for?"

paleface† *adj*. See **pale-faced.**
1860 *Nor'Wester* (R.R.S.) 28 Feb. 3/2: We entered his name on our list, and were almost tempted to write the word 'Esquire' after it; for with amplitude which many of our "paleface," delinquent subscribers would do well to imitate, he at once paid his money. **1959** *Sun* (Vancouver) 16 July 23/2: Another attraction for paleface visitors will be the famed Indian Longhouse, built last year by Capilano Indians as their centennial project. **1964** *North* July 41/1: She had four beautiful children, all girls, blue-eyed and at the paleface end of a series in which she and her father were the mixed blood and full Indian elements respectively.

pale-faced *adj*. white (as opposed to Indian); non-Indian. See note at **paleface,** *n*.
1839 *Western Herald* (Sandwich [Windsor], U.C.) 11 Sep. 217/2: To mix his blood with that of his pale-faced betrayer, and hold by sufferance, the land it was

his right to rule. **1895** *Aurora* Feb. 2/2: The climax was reached when Kak-wa-ke won the vice-president's trophy, beating five of his "pale faced" opponents in succession. **1959** *Native Voice* May 1/5: So it is doubtful if their condition would be worsened by extending to them the same privileges accorded to their pale-faced brethen.

paleman *n. Obs.* See **paleface,** *n.*
1808 *Cdn Courant* (Montreal) 15 Feb. 1/3: Ten thousand moons ago . . . before the palemen . . . rushed on the wings of the wind to ruin this garden of nature . . . a race of animals existed . . . cruel as the bloody panther. . . .

pale oil the highest quality of oil rendered from seal blubber.
1832 MCGREGOR *Brit.Amer.* I 225: The first that runs off the seal blubber is the virgin, or pale oil, and the last the brown oil. **1966** *Cdn Geog.Jnl* Apr. 133/1: The resultant oil, classified according to colour and quality as "pale oil," "straw oil," and "dark oil," sells for an average of about 50 cents per gallon.

Palliser('s) triangle See 1952 quote.
[**1863** PALLISER *Journals* 7: This central desert extends, however, but a short way into British territory, forming a triangle having for its base the 49th parallel from longitude 100° to 114° W with its apex reaching the 52nd parallel of latitude.] **1937** *Beaver* Mar. 51/1: The famous Palliser triangle (indicating the portions not suitable for cultivation) may be compared with the map recently published by a well-known statistical firm. **1952** PUTNAM *Cdn Regions* 368/2: In 1857 The British Colonial Office sent Captain John Palliser to examine and report upon the area. During the years 1857 to 1860, he travelled from Lake Superior to beyond the Rocky Mountains. As a result of his explorations, he divided the plains into two parts, a "fertile belt" and the "true prairie" which he regarded as a semi-arid desert. The latter area, according to him, embraces most of what is now the southern parts of both Saskatchewan and Alberta. In spite of the fact that it is an irregular, five-sided area, it is often referred to as "Palliser's triangle." **1958** *Edmonton Jnl* 20 June 15/1: The affected area includes the eastern half of what is called Palliser's Triangle, 28,000,000 acres of semi-arid country stretching from Manitoba to the Rocky Mountain foothills.

pamima *n.* See **pembina.**

pan *n.* **1** See **ice-pan** (def. 1). Cp. **pan-ice.**
1771 (1792) CARTWRIGHT *Journal* I 78: I attempted to cross over at a place where the ice lay in small pans, and appeared to be firm. . . . **1841** *Trans.Lit.& Hist.Soc.Que.* IV 48: Upon the pans were many hundreds of young seals, just pupped. **1966** *North* July-Aug. 26: Jimmy managed . . . to hook him with a sealing hook . . . and eventually to haul the youngster on to a larger pan after paddling to it. . . .
2 *Sealing, Nfld* a stack of sealskins marked with a flag or pennant to show the owner and left for later recovery. See also **pan,** *v.* (def. 2).
1907 MILLAIS *Newfoundland* 41: We didn't form 'pans' (piles) of seals as they do now, but stuck pretty close to the vessel and hauled two seals a man. *a***1960** (1965) LEACH *Songs* 208: They killed and panned a heavy load with flags in every pan. . . . **1965** *Nfld Qtly* Spring 8/1: . . . they have to work sometimes half the night picking

up the day's kill from the pans, and stowing them below.
3 *Placer Mining* **a.†** a shallow, circular vessel used for separating gold from gravel, etc. See also **pan,** *v.* (def. 1).
1881 *Edmonton Bull.* 28 Feb. 2/2: [The gold and sand] is put in a good pan with quick silver, and as the sand is washed out the gold amalgamates with the quick silver, forming a pasty mass. **1957** GOWLAND *Return to Canada* 112: A pick, shovel and pan, stood outside, implements which had probably been there for the last fifty years.
b. a panful of gold-bearing gravel.
1860 *Brit.Colonist* (Victoria) 27 Oct. 2/2: Two bits to the pan is an excellent prospect. **1936** ARMSTRONG *Yukon Yesterdays* 29: she carried on, and then, in washing another pan, she obtained about twenty cents.
4 one of the broad curved surfaces of a moose's antlers.
1925 CLARKE *Chris in Canada* 10: . . . he had a spread of forty-seven inches, pans as broad as a tea-tray, with eighteen points. "Yes, sir, a record moose for these parts."

pan *v.* **1†** *Placer Mining* **a.** separate gold from gravel or pulverized rock by washing the gravel in a pan (def. 3). See also **panning** and **pan out** (def. 1).
1870 *Mainland Guardian* (New Westminster, B.C.) 2 Apr. 1/3: The only mining done was by Sylvester and Black, who had panned and rocked about $40 from the edge of the Discovery ground. **1910** FRASER *Red Meekins* 19: Little Joe . . . panning the powder in the fry pan, showed St. John a fairy-like thread of gold lying along the edge of the white grit. **1960** *Weekend Mag.* 8 Oct. 28/1: They had panned one or two colors and they wanted to get down to bedrock to see if she would pay, so they set to sinking a shaft. **1963** *Herald Mag.* 23 Nov. 3/4: A few flakes of gold panned from Bonanza Creek in Klondike Valley, Aug. 17, 1896. . . .
b. search for gold in this way.
1937 ARMSTRONG *Upper Yukon* 179: Between intervals I did some prospecting in the cut, panning along the face. . . . **1957** *Kingston Whig-Standard* (Ont.) 18 Sep. 25/1: The man looked like a sourdough and was panning for gold among the gravels of Bonanza Creek whose rich finds in 1896 set off the Yukon gold rush. **1959** *Native Voice* July 6/4: She was very intelligent, watching him closely while she panned a stream, with her sharp, beady eyes, occasionally shooting out her big paw when she saw him digging in the gravel. **1965** *Cdn Geog.Jnl* Apr. 117/3: . . . McNeeley found a quartz stringer, which, when panned, showed a small tail of gold.
c. mine (gold) in this way.
1948 ONRAET *Sixty Below* 40: He only asked where it was and said he came from Peace River town on his way to Buffalo Creek to pan gold. **1957** *Beaver* Spring 43/1: He had been panning gold on the Fraser bars for many months, and now he had made his stake.
2 *Sealing, Nfld* kill and stack in pans (def. 2). See also **panned.**
1916 DUNCAN *Billy Topsail* 236: . . . all day long they killed and sculped and towed and panned the fat—all smothered in blood. **1933** GREENE *Wooden Walls* 37n: They reached the far-off . . . [sealing ice] and started panning. . . . *a***1960** (1965) LEACH *Songs* 208:
> The *Neptune,* ruler of the Sea, she rides in court today,
> Filled up with white-coats to the hatch and her colors flying gay.
> They killed and panned a heavy load with flags on every pan,
> While bats did rattle on their heads, the murder then began.

pana or **panar** *n. Eskimo* See **snow-knife**.

1942 TWOMEY & HERRICK *Needle to North* 170: They jabbered a little, testing the snow with a sharp jap of the *pana*, and then continued testing on down the ridge. **1958** *Evening Telegram* (St. John's) 24 Apr. 17/4: Using a "panar" or snow-knife, he quickly cut snow blocks from the hard-packed cover of sea ice.

panage *n. Cdn French* a set of antlers.

1897 GREENOUGH *Cdn Folk-Life* 19: The caribou shed their horns usually in November, and the man who buys a fine *panage* to ornament his dining room has some ground to suspect that the animal was killed when he ought not to have been.

panbina *n.* See **pembina**.

pancake *n.* **1** See **pancake ice**.

1850 GOODSIR *Baffin's Bay* 17: The undulation of the sea still continuing, these enlarged pieces strike each other on every side, whereby they become rounded, and their edges turned up, whence they obtain the name of cakes or pancakes; several of these again unite; and thereby continue to increase, forming larger flakes, until they become, perhaps, a foot in thickness, and many yards in circumference.

2 *Slang* See **cow flap**.

1960 BUBLITZ *Dotted Line* 22: . . . the folks around us told me the cows had left lots of "pancakes" around. When dried out, they make quick, hot fires.

pancake ice† See 1958 quote. See also **pancake** (def. 1).

1850 GOODSIR *Baffin's Bay* 136: It was very cold, and the snow scarcely melting when it fell in the water; "pancake ice" began to form, and it looked very like as if we were going to be frozen up. **1958** *Manice* 5: Pancake Ice: Pieces of newly formed ice usually between one and six feet in diameter. The raised rims and the circular appearance are a result of the almost constant rotation and collision of the cakes against one another, as the result of wind and swell.

pan-ice *n.* ice that has broken away in pans (def. 1) or floes from a large ice field.

1916 DUNCAN *Billy Topsail* 139: When he was within two fathoms of the pan-ice a foot broke through and tripped him flat on his face. **1964** *Weekend Mag.* 7 Mar. 14: [Caption] Pan ice shrouds the rocks near Hacketts Cove on Nova Scotia's Atlantic coast.

panned *adj. Sealing, Nfld* killed and stacked in pans (def. 2). **1** See also **pan**, *v.* (def. 2).

1878 *North Star* (St. John's) 13 Apr. 3/2: When she left the ice the *Tiger*, with 2,000 on board, was alongside a sufficient number of panned seals to fill her. **1901** *Canadian Mag.* Jan. 196/2: The stealing of panned seals has been a fruitful source of litigation, and of a good deal of hard swearing. **1965** LEACH *Songs* 203n: . . . panned seal skins flattened and piled for easy transport over the ice and for stowing in the vessel.

2 of a ship, loaded with pans (def. 2) of seal skins.

*a***1927** (1965) LEACH *Songs* 203: All panned and safely stowed below, with colors waving gay, / The *Southern Cross* she left the ice, bound up for home that day.

panner *n.* a prospector who seeks gold by panning.

1948 ONRAET *Sixty Below* 40: Some rivers have enough gold for a good experienced panner to make fair wages. **1963** *Placer Mining B.C.* 25: Another plan is to punch two small holes on each side through the lip of the pan and thread two wire handles through them. In this way the panner's hands can be kept out of the water to some extent.

543

panning† *n. Placer Mining* **1** mining gold by washing gravel in a pan (def. 3). See also **pan**, *v.* (def. 1).

1948 ONRAET *Sixty Below* 41: We drove a long pole in the bottom all ready for John to tie to after his day's panning along the sand bars. **1965** *Cdn Geog.Jnl* Dec. 205/3: Stir the concentrates in the bottom . . . and take out any gold by panning.

2 the yield in gold from such mining.

1900 OSBORN *Greater Canada* 2: After the first news of preliminary "pannings" on Eldorado and Bonanza Creeks was brought to Canada by Mr. Ogilvie . . . every Western scribbler was hard at work inventing circumstantial lies.

pan out† **1** *Placer Mining* **a.** See **pan**, *v.* (def. 1a).

1859 BALLANTYNE *World of Ice* 89: It was the Kablunak's custom, when the ice cleared away, to pan out a few bags of gold-dust there. **1868** (1962) ANDERSON *Sawney's Letters* 33:
The bakin' board hangs on the wa',
Its purposes are twa-fold—
For mixing bread wi' yeast or dough
Or panning oot the braw gold!
1961 ROUGH *Totem Trail* 12: From time to time he hauls the sluice box to the bank and pans out the black sand with a gold pan to extract the gold.

b. yield (in gold).

1877 GRANT *Ocean to Ocean* 271: John Glen calculated . . . that he might strike a new bar or gulch that would pan out as richly as Williams' Creek, Cariboo. . . . **1921** HAWORTH *Trailmakers* 267: The Colonel had told them that a cubic foot of gravel would pan out twenty dollars in gold, and there were so many thousand cubic feet in the top layer of each claim.

2 *Informal* turn out; work out in practice.

1884 *Brandon Blade* (Man.) 24 Jan. 4/3: If the domineering Attorney-General "pans out" well during the coming session he will probably be the man. **1890** *Grip* (Toronto) 1 Mar. 158/1: What's the brilliant scheme that has panned out so well? **1919** FRASER *Bulldog Carney* 20: ". . . first guesses about a feller most gener'ly pans out pretty fair." **1929** *Nova Scotia Miner* (Glace Bay) 28 Dec. 1/3: How has all this talk panned out?

pan prospect *Placer Mining* a prospect estimated on the basis of preliminary panning.

1901 (1954) *North* Nov.-Dec. 4/2: Here [on Goldbottom Creek] he found a two cent pan "prospect."

panther† *n.* See **cougar**.

1764 (1901) HENRY (Elder) *Travels* 145: . . . a panther, which one of the young men had seen. **1833** *Liberal* (St. Thomas, U.C.) 29 Aug. 1/2: The villagers are aroused by the report that a panther had been seen in the neighborhood. **1959** *Kingston Whig-Standard* (Ont.) 2 May 11/7: Panthers—also known as cougars—were once rampant in Eastern Canada. . . .

paper birch See **white birch** (def. 1).

1903 WHITE *Forest* 274: Probably a trifle further along there would be a point of high land and delightful little paper-birches. **1966** *Kingston Whig-Standard* (Ont.) 26 Jan. 4/3: After the Indians taught white men its many uses, pioneers called it the Canoe or Paper birch.

paper town 1 *Hist.* a town projected but not always actually founded.

1819 EVANS *Tour* 228: On this river . . . is General

Simcoe's paper town called London [Upper Canada].
1883 *Brandon Blade* (Man.) 22 Nov. 10/1: Passing
through lively scenery . . . we arrive at Menota once
famous in the days of paper towns as Dobbin City.

2 a town or city where paper manufacturing is the
dominant industry.
1957 HUTCHISON *Canada* 307: Logging camps, mills,
paper towns, the new aluminum town of Kitimat, the
copper mines of Britannia, the salmon canneries, the
milkshed of Fraser Valley . . . pour their products into
Vancouver.

paper township *Hist.* See quote. Cp. **paper town**
(def. 1).
1945 CALVIN *Saga* 2: But, later on, a great part of the
so-called private property consisted of tracts in the
wilderness taken up by the colonists purely for the
timber growing on them, and not for settlement—
"paper townships," they were called.

paperweight *n. Slang, Obs.* See quote.
1963 *Herald Mag.* 21 Dec. 7/1: . . . some of the old
Western slang is worth repeating: . . . "tent pegs,"
(frozen beef steak ribs); "baked wind pills," (baked
beans); "paper weights,"(hot biscuits); "keg angels,"
(whisky traders).

Papineau *n. Obs.* See **habitant penny.**

Papineau party *Hist.* a popular name for the
radical reform group led by Joseph Papineau,
1786-1871, in opposition to the administration in
Lower Canada, opposition which reached a high
point in the Rebellion of 1837. Cp. **Parti Rouge.**
1832 *Canadian Courant* (Montreal) 1 Aug. 2/5: The
Papineau Party has been defeated at St. Hyacinthe, and
Mr. Poulin returned. **1899** *Rev.Hist.Pubs* III 91: They
represent an interesting view of the state of feeling among
the Papineau party, the keen sense of injustice which
lent vigour to the reform movement, and the
intemperate, visionary impulsiveness which produced
the armed rebellion itself.

Papineau Rebellion or **Revolt** *Hist.* a popular
name for the Rebellion of 1837 in Lower Canada,
where the rebels were led by Joseph Louis Papineau.
1838 *Montreal Gaz.* 17 Jan. 3/3: . . . at the time this
discussion on the affairs of Canada took place in the
House of Commons, no intelligence of the Papineau
Revolt in the Lower Province, nor McKenzie's
insurrection in the Upper could have reached England.
1838 *Western Herald* (Windsor, U.C.) 28 Aug. 213/1:
Why are Hume, Roebuck, Leader, Moleworth, and
others, who . . . encouraged . . . the Mackenzie and
Papineau Rebellions, allowed to go unpunished?
1899 GARDNER *Names* 513: When the Papineau
Rebellion nearly wrecked the ship of state, / Upon the
field of battle many comrades met their fate.

papoose [pə'pus] *n.* [< Algonk.] Also spelled
(older) *pappoose, papouse,* etc. **1**† a child or baby
of American Indian parents.
1816 MARSDEN *Narrative* 43: The Micmac Indians call a
child papoose, a wife squaw, and a husband sanop.
1852 (1881) TRAILL *Cdn Crusoes* 270: She had gone down
to the spring for water, and on her return was surprised
at the sight of a squaw and her family of three
half-grown lads, and an innocent little brown papoose.

1963 SYMONS *Many Trails* 79: The term papoose is
commonly used among the natives to denote children
of almost any age, but still I had expected a much
younger patient.
2 a beaver cub; young beaver.
1680 *H.B.C. Minutes* 27: the Men imployed in Sorting
the Beaver have found . . . 342 Stage Pappoes. . . .
1861 DE BOILIEU *Labrador Life* 82: The beaver is a social
kind of animal, living in communities or families,
generally consisting of five—father, mother, and three
"papouses" (so the young beavers are called).

papoose bag See **moss bag.**
1957 FISHER *Pemmican* 333: She was dressed for a
journey and over her back was little David in a papoose
bag.

papoose board† See **cradle-board** and picture.
1935 *Cdn Geog.Jnl* Feb. 99/1: Many of the villagers
have . . . relics of the old times [including] carved
papoose-boards and pipes. . . . **1958** *Weekend Mag.*
26 Apr. 37/1: Mrs. Gilbert decided that a papoose
board was the answer. She called Chief Poking Fire at
the Caughnawaga Indian Reservation and ordered one.

papoose-carrier *n.* See **cradle-board.**
1959 SHIPLEY *Scarlet Lily* 196: The old mother . . .
smoked contentedly, keeping one eye . . . on the
papoose-carrier in which a month old baby was laced.
1961 *Camsell Arrow* Summer 33: Kathleen snoozes in
her papoose-carrier lightly carried by her mother.

paquet *n.* See **packet.**

paqueton *n.* See **pacton.**

parc *n.* See **park** (def. 1).

parchment *n. Hist.* **1** See **parchment beaver.**
1679 (1945) *H.B.C. Minutes* 16: Resolved Upon Debate
that all our Beavor both Coat and Parchment shall be
exposed at the same time to Publique sale. . . .
1697 (1929) KELSEY *Papers* 75: Received some goods
into yᵉ trading room &c told into the warehouse 38 coat
beaver 26 half and 12 whole parchment. **1958** *Beaver*
Spring 15/1: This was the *castor sec,* the dry beaver or
"parchment" which normally came in great quantities
from Canada. . . .
2 an animal hide that has been dehaired, stretched,
and dried, used for making such things as babiche,
window panes, packstraps, and pemmican bags.
See also **parchment skin** and **skin** (def. 2). Cp.
parfleche (def. 1).
1749 *Short State of North America* 27: One Parchment
Mouse [moose], & two Beavers. **1819** (1939)
ROBERTSON *Correspondence* 68: The windows for want
of parchment were covered by damaged bale cloths.
1871 (1883) BUTLER *Great Lone Land* 340: During five
days our course lay through vast expanses of stiff
frozen reeds, whose corn-like stalks rattled harshly
against the parchment sides of the cariole. . . . **1952**
Beaver Dec. 29/1: The sale of dressed moose and
caribou hides, parchment, babiche, deer sinews and
moccasins also helped. . . .

parchment beaver *Fur Trade, Hist.* See 1957
quote. See also **castor sec, dry beaver,** and
parchment (def. 1). Cp. **coat beaver.**
1682 (1946) *H.B.C.Minutes* 37: Ordered the beavor
and skins be put up as Foll. at the Sale The Coate
Beavor . . . the parchment beavor . . . the halfe beavor.
. . . **1774** (1934) HEARNE *Journal* 115: This day 11
Cannoes of Grass River Indians came and pitch'd by
us, of whome I traded some Moose flesh and a few
Parchment Beaver. **1824** (1931) MERK *Fur Trade* 208:
We could therefore have had no Market for fine

Beaver but that for the Hatters, for whose use it is of little more value than the ordinary Parchment Beaver. **1957** *Beaver* Winter 14/2: Parchment beaver was a skin taken from the animal and stretched and dried.

parchment canoe *Obs.* a temporary boat consisting of a frame covered with parchment (def. 2), often used by Indians who, at the end of their trip, removed the skins and sold them to traders. Cp. **bull boat.**
[**1754** (1907) HENDAY *Journal* 329: The Indian Men made temporary Canoes of Willows, covered with parchment Moose skins.] [**1801** (1933) MCLEOD *Diary* 171: I gave Fallardeau (the free man) two Parchment Skins to make a Canoe with to drive down the Red River.] **1858** (1860) HIND *Assiniboine Exped.* I 442: These great prairie-rivers are generally crossed and often descended in "bull-boats" or "parchment canoes" by the Indians, for great distances.

parchment skin *Hist.* See **parchment** (def. 2).
1680 (1945) *H.B.C.Minutes* 21: And as for the Parchmt. skinns it appearing that there are several sorts of those Skinns some whereof may be fitt for the Rushia Mkt. **1791** (1934) FIDLER *Journal* 528: A Parchment skin is sometimes used for the purpose of Cooking in by them. **1862** *Nor'Wester* (R.R.S.) 16 Apr. 2/5: They succeeded in getting just two parchment-skins and when the Indians had no more to barter, they took the whiskey from the men and made them run for their lives. **1957** FISHER *Pemmican* 188: Those who had come from the distant posts had carioles, sleds of birch boards twelve feet long, the sides covered with parchment skins painted with bright colors.

parchment window *Hist.* a window pane of parchment (def. 2), widely used in cabins in the Northwest (def. 1a).
1775 (1934) HEARNE & TURNOR *Journals* 182: Mild clowdy weather; the Carpenter Employed nailing on a set of new Parchment windows. . . . **1860** (1870) SOUTHESK *Saskatchewan* 346: The cottage, built of massive logs plastered with mud, and lighted by firmly fixed parchment windows, admitted no communication with the outer air. . . . **1885** (1921) *Beaver* July 7/2: We were at one time reduced to such dire straits that we were obliged to eat our parchment windows. . . .

Parent Country or **State** *Hist.* Great Britain.
1793 *U.C.Gaz.* (York [Toronto]) 6 June 2/1: . . . those . . . that have vainly endeavoured to disturb the laws of our Parent Country have been discovered and crushed. **1805** *Quebec Gaz.* 3 Jan. 2/1: The Petitioners are looking forward to the aid of the Provincial Legislatire. . . . for establishing and improving the fisheries, the great source of wealth to the Parent State, the Colonial Husbandman, and Merchant. **1828** *Cdn Freeman* (York [Toronto]) 17 Jan. 2/1: Under the excellent Constitution derived from the wisdom and liberality of our Parent State, you are again convened.

paresseux *n.* [< Cdn F < F *paresseux* lazy] *Obs.* a sluggish stream; deadwater; backwater.
1804 (1933) FARIES *Diary* 196: After breakfast we walked up to the dead water—met a canoe with four men a little above the paresseux from Lac des Chiens.

parfleche ['parflɛʃ] *n.* [< Cdn F *parflèche* < F *parer* parry + *flèche* arrow, from its use as a shield] **1 a.** a sheet of rawhide, especially buffalo hide, from which the hair has been removed. Cp. **parchment** (def. 2).
1827 (1912) ERMATINGER *Express Journal* 110: . . . we embarked with crews and cargoes as follows: viz . . . 1

545

parchment canoe
paring bee

pack Parfleches . . . . **1830** (1948) MCLOUGHLIN *Letters* 8: [There is] also the necessity while the Buffaloes are fat to make appichimons[,] Parfleches & Lodges so as to make themselves independent. . . . **1957** FISHER *Pemmican* 52: He found another squaw pounding and stretching a parfleche to soften it. . . .
b. *Figurative use.*
1957 FISHER *Pemmican* 209: The old man's face was a parfleche of seams.
2 a container made from a sheet of rawhide, usually buffalo hide, folded into a kind of envelope and laced to make an efficient bag.
1829 (1948) MCLOUGHLIN *Letters* 44: Copy of Requisition forwarded to Mr J Work . . . . 60 Parfleches [saddle bags] . . . . **1887** (1888) LEES & CLUTTERBUCK *British Columbia* 299: A real parfleche is merely a hide, with holes punched all round its edges, into which all your small oddments are bundled. . . . **1929** MOBERLY *When Fur Was King* 35: A horse was worth about twenty madebeaver; a good robe, two; a dressed hide, one; a parfleche full of fine fat, dried buffalo ribs and bosses weighing around forty pounds, one made beaver. . . . **1963** *Beaver* Summer 33/2: But in the lodges that are entered for the best tipi contest, the traditional prevails and here are to be seen priceless treasures; decorated parfleches (rawhide bags made something like an envelope). . . .

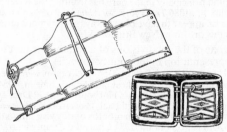

A parfleche (def. 2)

parfleche bag or **pouch** See **parfleche** (def. 2).
1909 PARKER *Northern Lights* 108: The Indian life is to the white life as the parfleche pouch—to this.
1938 GODSELL *Red Hunters* 33: Here braves . . . stored . . . commodities in painted parfleche bags for the forthcoming journey to York Factory.

parfleched *adj.* covered with parfleche (def. 1a). Cp. **parfleche trunk.**
1940 NIVEN *Mine Inheritance* 61: I saw her bending over another parflèched box in front of the tent and taking out two long, gleaming knives.

parfleche trunk a rectangular box covered with parfleche (def. 1a) often colorfully painted. Cp. **parfleched.**
1952 *Beaver* June 6/1: . . . the hides were manufactured into robes or were divested of their hair and made into teepee covers, clothing, moccasins, *parflèche* trunks and shields.

paring bee or **frolic** *Hist.* See 1931 quote. See also **bee.**
1830 PICKERING *Emigration* 72: . . . a paring "bee," or "be," [is] an assemblage of neighbours invited to one house, to prepare apples for drying. **1846** *St.Catharines Jnl* (C.W.) 19 Feb. 1/3: That night we had a parin'

little hooker was pretty well "parish rigged."

bee.... **1931** SEARY *Romance* 177: Another sort of frolic was the "paring frolic," when young men and girls gathered to pare and slice apples, that they might be dried out and kept throughout the winter. **1933** GUILLET *Early Life in U.C.* 195: A paring bee produced large numbers of strings of dried apples, and these were suspended from the ceiling of kitchen or attic.

parish† *n.* **1** in Quebec, a subdivision of a county which functions both as an ecclesiastical and political unit.
1775 *Quebec Gaz.* 21 Sep. 3/1: The Rebels have sent circular Letters to some of the Parishes above, upon the South Shore, threatening them with execution. **1844** *St.Catharines Jnl* (C.W.) 24 Oct. 1/4: All these clearings were made by squatters, who emigrated from the Parishes of Malbaie and St. Paul's Bay. **1963** *Globe and Mail* (Toronto) 27 Mar. 13/5: In the rural parish of St. Leon, 554 persons cast votes in the federal election June 18.

2 in New Brunswick: **a.** *Hist.* in colonial times, the jurisdiction of a town designated as the municipal seat.
1811 *Kingston Gaz.* (U.C.) 20 Aug. 3/2: The bridges, from the lower part of the parish up to St. Joseph [N.B.]... were most of them carried away. **1832** MCGREGOR *Brit.Amer.* II 318: These are also to be found principally in the parishes fronting the River St John.... **1886** *Trans.Roy.Soc.Can.* IV 2 65: Town and parish appear to have been always synonymous terms in this province [New Brunswick].

b. one of the subdivisions of a county, the unit of representation in the county councils.
1907 BAIRD *Roger Davis* 190: The elections were over— the report from the farthest parish had come in. **1954** *Fundy Fisherman* (Black's Harbour, N.B.) 22 Dec. 4/3: Collection of current and back taxes from parishes and towns for the first eleven months of this year amounted to 87.6 per cent of the 1954 Charlotte County warrant. **1958** *Encyc.Can.* VII 289/1: Each of the 15 counties is organized as a municipality; the unit of representation in the county councils is the parish.

3 *Hist.* in Prince Edward Island, one of the subdivisions into which the counties of the Island were originally divided.
1904 CROSSKILL *P.E.I.* 16: The parish lines are but little recognized, the more general sub-division being by lots or townships of which there are 67 running numerically from west to east. **1907** *U of T Stud.Hist.& Econ.* II 235: Prince Edward island was divided into "Counties," "Parishes," "Lots," and three towns with royalties and commons attached.

4 *Hist.* the smallest of the municipal districts proposed in the plan for subdividing New Scotland in the early 17th century. See also **hundred.**
1922 *Dalhousie Rev.* I 377: The country was divided into two provinces, each province into several dioceses, each diocese into ten baronies, and each barony into six parishes.

parish-rigged *adj. Atlantic Provinces* of a sailing vessel, fitted out for operating in local coastal waters only.
1955 WALLACE *Roving Fisherman* 408: She had no sidelights and in the matter of essential equipment the

parish school See **parochial school.**
1964 *Winnipeg Tribune* 21 Feb. 2/13: Since 1890, when the Manitoba legislature withdrew support for separate parish schools, Roman Catholic parents have protestingly paid both for the private schools their children attend and for the public schools they do not.

park *n.* **1** *Obs.* a fenced enclosure into which animals, especially buffalo, were driven to be slaughtered; a pound.
☛ *Meanings 1, 2, and perhaps 3 are derived from French* **parc** *through the French Canadians* (*coureurs de bois and voyageurs*), *who were the first to see these topographical features of the western prairies and mountains.*
*c*1797 (1819) MCDONNELL *Red River* 280: A good runner frequently goes before the band with the hair of his robe outwards and half bent, so as to represent a buffalo and, by that means, decoys them into the park which has a small door to make him a passage out. **1804** (1820) HARMON *Journal* 111: In order to kill them [buffalo], the Natives in large bands... drive them into parks and kill them at their leisure.

2† See **hole** (def. 1).
1900 FRASER *Mooswa* 59: When the young Spruce are growing, and would choke up the park, we strip the bark off and they die, and the open is still with us. **1954** PATTERSON *Dangerous River* 150: The place was what the old mountain men used to call a hole or a park—it was a little country of its own.

3 See **parkland** (def. 1).
1905 OUTRAM *Cdn Rockies* 53: Then came park country, rich green pasturage and dark forest belts, with a winding coal-black stream-bed meandering in the most abandoned manner through it all. **1952** PUTNAM *Cdn Regions* 397/2: The climate is drier and the vegetation grades from park to treeless steppe.

4 a national park or a provincial park, *qq.v.*
1905 OUTRAM *Cdn Rockies* 31: The Rocky Mountain Park stretches from the great wall that overhangs the foothills to the Divide, where it is joined by the almost equally extensive Yoho Park Reserve embracing a vast tract on the Pacific slope. **1940** *Cdn Geog.Jnl* Feb. 78/1: The Canadian Government, full conscious of the value of this alpine wilderness as a national asset, has... set aside for recreational purposes and for preservation for future generations, seven large park areas embracing 8,720 square miles of the most easily accessible and picturesque parts of the Rockies and Selkirks.

parka ['pɑrkə *or (def. 1)* 'pɑrkɪ] *n.* [< Aleutian Esk. *purka* skin; outer coat < Russian "hide or pelt" < Samoyed] **1** *North* See **atigi** (def. 2 and picture). See also **parkee.**
[**1784** PENNANT *Arctic Zoology* clv: Their clothing is chiefly of Deer skins, with large hoods, made in the form of loose jackets, scarcely reaching lower than half the thigh; where it was almost met by a great wide-topped boot.] **1852** RICHARDSON *Arctic Exped.* 493: English[,] Parka[:] Kutsutchewak. atkuk.
1897 WILSON *Yukon* 61: The women's *parka* differs slightly from that worn by the men, being cut up at the sides some ten inches and rounded at the bottom like a skirt. **1913** HAWKES *Inviting-in Feast* 15n: During the early occupation of Alaska by Russian fur-traders, several words of Kamchatkan origin were introduced, and incorporated in the native languages, among them being *parka*. It should be pronounced *pārkī*, but it being sanctioned by general use, I have retained the usual form. **1936** MACKENZIE *Living Rough* 67: At the north end of the street there was an Eskimo

encampment on the sand pit, and men, women and children dressed in reindeer parkas and mukluks were loitering all over the streets. **1966** *Kingston Whig-Standard* (Ont.) 17 May 19/1: [Headline] Parka is Baby-sitter for Eskimo Children.

2 a garment of wool, heavy cotton, nylon, etc. fashioned as a jacket or, less often, as a pullover, and usually shorter than the original Eskimo type. Cp. **capote** (def. 1).

1897 HAYNE *Pioneers* 103: The great charm about this particular outfit is that it is very warm—the parka is leather-lined—and really marvellously light. **1910** LONDON *Burning Daylight* 42n: *Parka;* a light, hooded, smock-like garment made of cotton drill. **1965** *Globe Mag.* 11 Dec. 10/1: One truly Canadian garment—a most practical one—is the parka, which originated centuries ago with the Eskimo.

parkade [par'ked] *n.* [< *park* (*arc*)*ade*] a building of several storeys serving as a parking area for motor vehicles.

1958 *Edmonton Jnl* 24 June 4 7/8: 700 tons of A.I.M. Reinforcing Steel were supplied and fabricated for the new Hudson Bay Co. "Parkade" now under construction in downtown Edmonton. **1958** *Lethbridge Herald* (Alta) 31 May 1/1: A young woman threatened . . . to jump from the top of a six-storey parkade in downtown Calgary. . . .

park belt See **parkland** (def. 1).

1947 TAYLOR *Canada* 163: There are said to be about 20 million acres of satisfactory arable lands in the Park Belt, and it is predominantly a wheat-growing region. **1958** *Unity Herald* (Sask.) 21 May 2/3: The Red Backed Cutworm is native to the Park Belt and to some extent horticultural crops a little further south.

parkee, park(e)y, or **parki** ['parki] *n.* See **parka** (def. 1).

☛ *These spelling variants testify to a pronunciation often heard in the North.*

1899 PALMER *Klondyke* 14: . . . three figures in parkees looking like hooded night-shirts began in earnest their journey. **1940** MARSHALL *Arctic Village* 98n: This word is usually spelled *parka,* but I am spelling it the way it is always pronounced. The parky is a loose-fitting garment which is slipped over the head and comes down to about the knees. **1947** *Beaver* June 41/1: Their parkis came down to a V fore and aft. . . . [Yukon Indians].

parkette *n.* a small park in a city, rarely larger and often smaller than a block, usually containing flower beds and one or more park benches.

1958 *Weekend Mag.* 9 Aug. 4/3: I was told that the parks and parkettes . . . had all been deeded to the community. . . .

parkha *n.* See **parka.**

parki ['parki] *n.* See **parka** (def. 1) and note at **parkee.**

parkland(s) *n.* **1** the lightly wooded, grassy belt of rich land lying between the open prairie and the northern forests in the three Prairie Provinces; also, similar but smaller areas of lightly wooded rolling grasslands, as the Peace River country. See also **park** (def. 3), **park belt,** and **parkland belt.** Cp. **fertile belt.**

1907 KENNEDY *New Canada* 182: Very soon the park lands of the north were all behind us, and the rolling, dry, illimitable plain stretched out to the horizon in

547

parkade
park warden

front. **1913** COWIE *Adventurers* 198: As we went on the poplar groves became more sparsely scattered over "the parklands". . . . **1960** *Maclean's* 9 Apr. 55/1: Hundreds of families abandoned their farms and . . . crowded the roads in their desperation to reach the parklands or forest belt to the north. . . .

2 lands set aside for public parks, national parks, etc.

1957 *Financial Post* 29 June 23/3: Every major Canadian city knows it should be providing 10 acres of parkland for every 1,000 people. **1958** *Maclean's* 10 May 8/1: We do, of course, sometimes set aside tracts of country for recreation and so forth—and we say these are in perpetuity; but this phrase only seems to mean until the parkland is needed for logging, or mining, or to take the waters backed up from some great dam. **1966** *Kingston Whig-Standard* (Ont.) 13 Jan. 8/3: The excellent camping facilities in Ontario's many parklands need more selling—and at a higher price.

parkland belt See **parkland** (def. 1).

1952 PUTNAM *Cdn Regions* 352/1: Between the open prairie and the forest lies the aspen grove or "Parkland" belt. This is a tall grassland formation interspersed at frequent intervals with small "bluffs" or groves of trees, indicative of an increased moisture supply. **1953** *Cdn Geog.Jnl* XLVI 240/1: This fact would seem to urge caution in the extension of irrigation northward into the parkland belt.

parklike *adj.* having the characteristics of parkland (def. 1). See also **parky²**.

1873 (1904) BUTLER *Wild North Land* 232: Thus, trotting through a park-like land of wood and glade and meadow, where the jumping deer glanced through the dry grass and trees, we gradually drew near the Rocky Mountains. **1963** SYMONS *Many Trails* 166: Had these great hills been once semi-prairie or park-like. . . .

park lot See 1833 quote. See also **town park.** Cp. **town lot** and **pasture lot.**

1806 *U.C.Gaz.* (York [Toronto]) 8 Mar. 4/3: To be Sold . . . Park Lots No. 17, 18 and 19 in the First Concession of York. **1833** (1838) NEED *Six Years in Bush* 47: When a reservation for a town is made by Government, a number of lots are laid out contiguous to the town itself, each of which contains about 10 acres, these are termed "Park lots," and prove of great use to the inhabitants when the town begins to increase in wealth and population. **1955** *Manitoulin Expositor* 26 May 15/3: . . . the Canadian Pacific Railway Company are now the owners of the Park Lots ten (10) and Nineteen (19) through which the extension of Vankoughnet Street must pass.

park ranger a government official responsible for the maintenance and patrolling of a national or provincial park. See also **park warden.**

1912 (1914) BICKERSTETH *Open Doors* 150: Next day, after seeing the park ranger about the burial place, the doctor and I went down with four labourers on a hand-car to a place where there is a flat stretch of land near the Athabasca River. **1958** *Kingston Whig-Standard* (Ont.) 7 June 12/1: . . . two park rangers tramped on snowshoes for five days and nights . . . tracking a wolf pack. **1965** *Cdn Geog.Jnl* Sep. 85: [Caption] Park Ranger . . . "light up" at a campsite on Keats Lake.

park(s) warden See **park ranger.**

1953 *Cdn Geog.Jnl* June 254/1: There is a telephone line along the entire route and contact with the outside world can be made at any of the park warden stations. **1955** GOWLAND *Smoke* 165: We were discussing a well-known parks warden who had recently died, and I mentioned that he had gone to the happy hunting-grounds. **1966** *Globe and Mail* (Toronto) 29 Aug. 6/4: Some of the jobs most suitable for Indians are:... fire rangers, timber cruisers, scalers ... lumbermen, game wardens ... park wardens and guides....

parky[1] *n.* See **parkee.**

parky[2] *adj.* See **parklike.**
1955 HOBSON *Nothing Too Good* 43: Cow tracks fanned out through the parky poplar country leaving a messy swath many yards wide.

parla ['parlə] *n.* [ult. < L *palla* cloth, covering] *North* (originally used in the fur trade) See quotes. **1872** MCDONALD *Peace River* 42: If overtaken ... the heavy "parla" (red canvas oilcloth) used to be thrown over the goods as a storm deck. **1941** *Beaver* Sep. 38/2: Parla A tarpaulin. **1955** ADTIC *Glossary*: parla, n. A tarpaulin or other heavy weather-proof covering.

Parliament Hill 1 the hill on which the Parliament buildings in Ottawa stand. See also **Parliament Square.**
1898 EDGAR *Canada and Capital* 6: Above the Chaudière, for a couple of miles, the river is very wide, and is broken with rapids and studded with islands so that, seen from Parliament Hill in the sunlight, it has the effect of a sparkling lake. **1958** *Lethbridge Herald* (Alta) 31 May 6/4: Thousands of tourists are visiting Ottawa to see the 1,000,000-odd tulips adorning the lawns of Parliament Hill, the National War Memorial and the 27-mile driveway along the Rideau canal for the annual tulip festival. **1965** *Kingston Whig-Standard* (Ont.) 3 Mar. 34/6:... the federal government traffic laws apply to the Parliament Hill area....
2 on (or **at**) **Parliament Hill,** in the Government or Parliament of Canada; in the House of Commons and/or the Senate. See also **Hill.**
1908 BROWN *Lady of the Snows* 54: It was opening day at Parliament Hill. **1916** BRIDLE *Sons of Canada* 26: ... the people on Parliament Hill are all wrong again. **1966** *Globe and Mail* (Toronto) 17 Jan. 7/2: It is widely known on Parliament Hill that [he] has been in touch with the House leaders of the third parties....

Parliament of the North See **Northwest Territories Council.**

Parliament Square *Obs.* See **Parliament Hill** (def. 1).
1891 *Grip* (Toronto) 18 Mar. 249/1: One day ... Sir John happened to meet the vigorous financier on Parliament Square. *Ibid.* 30 May 346/1: Members devoted attention to fixing up of lawn tennis, base ball, and cricket grounds on Parliament Square.

parlo(u)r *n.* See **beer parlo(u)r.**
1959 *Press* July 9: The woman with whom she stayed took her out to a card game in a club and afterwards they gave Reva her first beer in a nearby parlour. **1962** *Alta Hist.Rev.* Autumn 11/1:... saloons ... at times euphemistically described as "parlors," have always been numerous factors in every western town....

parochial school† a private school receiving no tax support, especially, in present-day use, such a school maintained by Roman Catholics. See also **parish school.** Cp. **separate school** (def. 3).
1860 *Nor'Wester* (R.R.S.) 14 Feb. 2/1: The Parochial Schools of our Protestant population speak for themselves, and I am sorry that they should have found disparagement at the hands of your correspondent. **1955** *Western Star* (Corner Brook, Nfld) 10 Mar. 2/3: An amendment to the Municipal Act ... would allow municipalities to exempt parochial schools from taxation "in whole or in part." **1964** *Calgary Herald* 11 Feb. 15: Premier Roblin Monday proposed a partial solution to the dilemma of Manitoba's parochial schools—leave their status unchanged but permit their students to share the services of tax-supported public schools. **1966** *Time* (Cdn ed.) 12 Aug. 12/1: Though traces of clannishness remain in Manitoba's parochial schools ... younger generations [of Canadian Ukrainians] have steadily struck down barriers.

Parry's ground squirrel [< Charles C. *Parry*, died 1890, American botanist] a ground squirrel, *q.v., Spermophilus undulatus parryi*, native to the northern parts of Canada.
[**1908** MAIR *Mackenzie Basin* 358: [A golden eagle] was once observed by us hunting a Parry's *Spermophile*, or marmot, near Langton Harbour, Franklin Bay.] **1911** SETON *Arctic Prairies* 224: Parry's Ground squirrel was found at nearly all points, including the large islands. **1965** SYMINGTON *Tuktu* 44: The Parry's ground squirrel—the "sik-sik" of the Eskimo, is common in some localities.

Parti Rouge *Cdn French, Hist.* a radical political party of Lower Canada, founded about 1850 and first led by Louis Joseph Papineau, which was later to become the Quebec wing of the Liberal Party. See also **Rouge party.** Cp. **Papineau party.**
1908 TRACY *Tercentenary History* III 885: In the French Province this [radical] element was called "Le Parti Rouge." **1916** MACMECHAN *Popular Government* 138: The "Clear Grit" party in Upper Canada was moving straight towards republicanism, and so was Papineau's *Parti Rouge*. **1924** *Cdn Hist.Rev.* V 256: Charles Joseph Laberge, one of the founders of the *Parti Rouge*, canvassed Canada East in favour of annexation. **1952** (1965) HAMILTON *Cdn Quotations* 177/2: French Canadians First! Parti Rouge plank, withdrawn in 1850.

partner *n. Fur Trade, Hist.* See **wintering partner** (def. 1).
1811 (1918) DAVIDSON *North West Co.* 284: The humble petition of Messers. McTavish Fraser and Co ... on behalf of themselves and the Agents and Other partners of the North West Company of Canada. **1918** *Ibid.* 226: The highest rank among the persons engaged in the actual trading was that of partner. The partners had charge of the trading posts, at least of the more important ones. **1957** FISHER *Pemmican* 143: In the same week a group of North West partners were lounging in their Beaver Club in Montreal....

partridge *n.* **1** any of various grouse found in Canada, especially the ruffed grouse, *q.v., Bonasa umbellus.* See also **birch partridge.**
1578 BEST *Trve Discovrse* III 67: Our men haue eaten of their Beares, Hares, Patriches, Larkes, and of their wild foule, and find them reasonable good meate, but not so delectable as oures. **1626** VAUGHAN *Golden Fleece* III 24: I knew one Fowler in a winter, which

killed aboue 700. Partridges himselfe at *Renoos*.
1775 (1951) *Saskatchewan Jnls* 15 Dec.: Two men daily hunting Partridges & Rabbets, but small success being scarce, particularly Rabbets. **1849** ALEXANDER *L'Acadie* II 127: In deep and retired places in the woods it was interesting to creep upon and watch the partridge, or more properly the ruffed grouse drumming on a prostrate log.... **1958** WATTERS *B.C.Cent.Anthol.* 274: Occasionally we were lucky enough to kill a partridge or skunk, and this formed a welcome addition to the rubaboo.

2 the ptarmigan, *Lagopus lagopus*. See also **willow ptarmigan.**
1696 (1929) KELSEY *Papers* 51: Some of our men went a hunting & brought home 4 patridges & some came home from yᵉ fourteens & brought 20 trouts.
1742 (1852) COATS *Geography of H.B.* 128: I observed that the hares, rabbits, foxes, and partridges, in September and the beginning of October, change their native colour to a snowy white. **1835** WIX *Journal* 97: The partridge, or ptarmigan, were also very numerous upon these hills, searching for a species of cranberry, which is called here, the partridge-berry. **1964** VARDY *Western Nfld:* [Folder] Caribou, moose and bear roam the more open sections of the country and partridge are plentiful on the barrens.

partridgeberry *n.* **1** a trailing evergreen shrub, *Mitchella repens,* having roundish leaves and white blossoms. See also **twinberry.**
1748 ELLIS *Hudson's Bay* 169: There are great variety of Shrubs and Plants ... Shrubs bearing red and black berries, which the Partridges feed on, therefore called Partridge Berries. **1853** *Anglo-American Mag.* II 183/1: That elegant little plant Mitchella repens, sometimes called partridge-berry and also twin-berry, from the scarlet fruit having the appearance of being double. **1964** *Globe and Mail* (Toronto) 11 Dec. 6/5: Then and there, he told you about the partridgeberries.

2 the edible red berry of this plant. See also **pheasantberry.**
1770 (1792) CARTWRIGHT *Journal* I 30: We landed opposite Grove Island, and walked upon the low hills, where we found plenty of partridge berries. **1835** WIX *Journal* 97: The partridge, or ptarmigan, were also very numerous upon these hills, searching for a species of cranberry, which is called here, the partridge-berry. **1954** *Fishermen's Advocate* 17 Sep. 1/2: Partridge berries jumped to 70 cents a gallon from 45 cents a few days after the season opened.

partridge hawk 1 the gyrfalcon, *Falco rusticolus*.
1772 *Phil.Trans.Roy.Soc.* LXII 382: Speckled partridge hawk, at Hudson's Bay. The name is derived from its feeding on the birds of the grouse tribe, commonly called partridges, at Hudson's Bay. **1882** *Trans.Roy. Soc.Can.* I 4 53: The last named is known as the partridge or winter hawk.... **1956** MCATEE *Folk-Names* 22: Gyrfalcon [is also called] partridge hawk ("Labr.," Hudson Bay)....

2 the goshawk, *Accipiter gentilis*.
1959 MCATEE *Folk-Names* 20: Goshawk [is known as] partridge hawk (As a predator on the ruffed grouse and allies. Nfld., "Labr.", Sask.); speckled partridge hawk ("Hudson Bay," Forster, 1772)....

pas d'ours [for Cdn F *patte d'ours*] See **bear-paw.**
1827 (1912) ERMATINGER *Express Jnl* 77: Passed several camps of Indians in course of the day and traded 7 pairs of Pas d'ours for our journey across the mountains....

passenger pigeon† a migratory wild pigeon, *Ectopistes migratorius,* which appeared in immense flocks during August up to the late 19th century, becoming extinct by 1914. See also **pigeon, wild pigeon,** and **wood pigeon.**
1852 RICHARDSON *Arctic Exped.* 127: This falcon is not rare throughout the Mackenzie, where it preys on the passenger pigeons and smaller birds. **1908** CLARKE *Sixty Years* 39: But the bird most missed is the passenger pigeon. **1962** *Kingston Whig-Standard* (Ont.) 4/6: The prairie chicken, once numbered in hundreds of thousands, may follow the passenger pigeon which darkened the sky in huge flocks.

pasture lot† *Esp.Maritimes, Obs.* a lot outside the limits of a newly established town, used for pasturing cattle. Cp. **park lot.**
1763 (1905) *Ont.Bur.Arch.Rep.* III lvi: ... Town and pasture lots [are] convenient to each Tenement. **1828** MCGREGOR *Maritime Colonies* 3: The plot of a town, containing a certain number of building and pasture lots, is reserved in each county. **1861** BAGSTER *Progress P.E.I.* 50: Charlottetown Common and Pasture Lots cover an area of 7300 acres.

pataroon *n. Obs.* See **pateroon.**

patch *n.* **1**† See 1851 quote.
1851 SNOW *Voyage* 385: A patch is a collection of drift or bay-ice, of a circular or polygonal form. In point of magnitude, a pack corresponds with a field, and a patch with a floe. **1852** SUTHERLAND *Baffin's Bay* II 312: There was a patch of ice between us and the island, which probably may have assisted to increase the refraction in that direction, although it was exceedingly powerful in every other direction.

2 *Esp.Nfld* a herd of seals. See also **seal patch.** Cp. **main patch.**
1878 *North Star* (St. John's) 6 Apr. 2/6: Other reports state that a portion of the fleet ... tried their fortunes in search of a more northerly patch than the *Falcon* and *Arctic* fell in with. **1916** DUNCAN *Billy Topsail* 234: Next day Cap'n Saul found the herds—a patch of harps and new-whelped young. **1933** GREENE *Wooden Walls* XV: CUT. the course selected by each Captain, as the best or shortest ice passage to the Patch. **1958** *Evening Telegram* (St. John's) 6 May 4/4: Captain Jackman had struck his patch, killed his load, and left another half a load on the ice....

patch fox See **cross-fox.**
1861 BAGSTER *Progress P.E.I.* 86: Should he be a RED [fox], his skin is worth half a dozen geese; if a PATCH he is worth a cow; if a BLACK PATCH, or a SILVER GREY, he is worth a horse; and if a real BLACK, a horse and sleigh and harness, whip and all, is not too high an estimate. **1942** BOSANQUET *Saddlebags* 48: The most common of these [variations] is the "cross" or "patch" fox, which is yellow with a dark cross or patch across the shoulders.

patch-log′ *v. Lumbering* engage in patch logging, *q.v.*
1953 *Harmac News* Oct. 7/1: Conversion of these operations to truck logging meant spending over two and a quarter million dollars ... but the Company will be able to patch-log more effectively and roads will be thrust into places which were formerly hard to reach and which will prove invaluable for fire patrols.

patch logging a system of logging by which only patches of lumber in a stand are cut down, the surrounding trees being left intact to ensure natural reseeding of the cutover patch.
1958 LYONS *Milestones* 224: Often "patch" logging is carried out which ensures that surrounding standing trees will drop seed in remote areas requiring special attention. **1958** *Maclean's* 10 May 55/2: Unless patch logging is employed, so remaining stands can naturally reseed cutover areas, the fir is like a baseball pitcher whose throw can't quite reach the plate. **1963** MCKINNON *Forest Activities 1* 1: The illustration shows a "patch" logging operation.

patent† *n*. **1** the right or title to a piece of land received as a grant or as a homestead (def. 2a). Cp. **patented land**.
1765 *Quebec Gaz.* 4 July 1/1: For the Great Seal to every Patent for vacant and unappropriated Land, not exceeding One Hundred Acres, Twelve Shillings. The Governor's Fees. **1883** *Prince Albert Times* (Sask.) 28 Dec. 3/1: I know men in Prince Albert who've grown quite gray, On their farms—but their patents are coming some day, When they've gone where there ain't any farming. **1912** (1914) BICKERSTETH *Open Doors* 97: If the homesteader has arrears of taxes against him he cannot get his patent, even though he has fulfilled the other conditions. **1966** *Sask.Hist.* Spring 54: . . . the Company had been unable to conform to the conditions as set out in the Order-in-Council dated March 2, 1885, and thus had not been able to acquire the patents for the land.

2 See **patented land**.
1798 *Quebec Gaz.* 31 May 3/1: I have seized and taken in execution . . . A Lot of land, consisting of two hundred superficial acres, being Lot No. 10, in the first concession of the Seigniory of Saint Armand, commonly called Dunn's Patent.

patented land† land whose title was conferred by grant. See also **patent** (def. 2). Cp. **patent** (def. 1).
1885 *Wkly Manitoba Liberal* 6 Nov. 1/5: The piles are being driven for the bridges on our railway. And those having patented land with oak timber on it are having quite a bonanza. **1955** *Northern Mail* 13 Apr. 1/1: . . . a contentious question loomed of compensation for farmers who hold patented land, leases or permits in the Saskeram area.

patentee *n*. *Hist.* a person receiving title to land through a patent (def. 1).
1763 (1906) *Ont.Bur.Arch.Rep.* IV 18: For every Fifty Acres of Land account plantable, each Patentee shall be obliged, within three years after the Date of his Patent, to clear and work three Acres at the least. **1913** *London & Middlesex Hist.Soc.Trans.* 57: His name, apparently, first appears in Canadian records as the original patentee of lot 120, in the 5th concession of the Township of Walsingham.

patent fence See **Russell fence** and picture.
1958 *Kingston Whig-Standard* (Ont.) 19 Apr. 6/1: Half of the Windward Slope's fencing is wire and the other half very old-fashioned . . . "patent" fence of weather-beaten cedar, pine, and ash split rails.

patent inside(s) a sheet or sheets of newsprint having one side printed and the other left blank for printing by local newspapers.

1879 *Winnipeg Dly Times* 22 Apr. 3/1: The Free Press patent insides did not arrive Saturday in time, so the Monday paper is double size. **1885** *Neepawa Star* (Man.) 28 Aug. 3/1: The Portage Liberal has changed its make up and is now a six column quarto, patent insides. **1903** *Eye Opener* (High River, Alta) 25 July 1/1: It has just occurred to us that the reason we become so intolerably sick after a jamboree is because, unlike most other country editors, we don't use a patent inside.

patent ready print sheet *Obs.* See **patent inside**.
1895 *Rat Portage* [Kenora] *News* (Ont.) 26 Apr. 3/1: The News has enlarged to eight pages, having adopted the patent ready print sheet issued from Hamilton.

pateroon *n*. [< Cdn F *patron(ne)* < F "captain of a coastal vessel"] Also *patron*. *Fur Trade, Obs.*
1 a commander; boss.
1748 DRAGE *Voyage* I 169: As there could be but few Snow-Shoes got . . . these they could procure were assigned to those of every Tent that hunted . . . there being seven persons in a Tent (including the Pateroon, or he who commands, and also a Boy) two of the People were Kept to Hunting, which term they give to going a Shooting of Partridge. . . .

2 See **steersman**.
1774 (1934) HEARNE & TURNOR *Journals* 122: . . . the Pataroon or Steersman of each Cannoe has 50£ Pr annom. . . . **1784** (1954) *Moose Ft Jnls* 207: So terribly have we been afflicted with sickness I was forced to send up to Henley for hands from the building to navigate my second Boat thither and then was obliged to Hire 11 Indians & send Geo. Sutherland as Pateroon. **1809-11** (1904) BRADBURY *Travels* 184: . . . our *patron*, or steersman . . . conducted the first boat, and directed our motions.

path *n*. *Lab.* See **trapline** (def. 2b).
1933 MERRICK *True North* 22: Sometimes he farms out his paths to another hunter.

pathmaster *n*. *Hist.* See **roadmaster** (def. 1).
1799 *U.C.Gaz.* (York [Toronto]) 29 June 3/2: The public are much indebted to Mr. John McDougal, who was appointed one of the path-masters at the last town meeting, for his great assiduity and care in getting the streets cleared of the many and dangerous (especially at night) constructions therein. **1886** *Indian* (Hagersville, Ont.) 9 June 126/2: A crying evil here is the inability of the pathmasters, and in consequence our roads are poor and rough. **1959** *Maclean's* 20 June 83/2: The name was changed about 40 years ago because Gottlieb Watts, town pathmaster, could not spell it.

Pat Jones *Local* See quote.
1966 *Cdn Geog.Jnl* Apr. 133/2: Locally they [harp seals] are known by the quaint name of "Pat Jones," a rather amusing adaptation of the French "pattes jaunes"— yellow legs. [La Tabatiere, P.Q., near Labrador boundary on Gulf of St. Lawrence]

patlatch *n*. See **potlatch**.

Patriot *n*. *Hist.* **1 a.** See 1958 quote. See also **rebel** (def. 1) and **Sympathizer**.
1837 *Patriot* (Toronto) 22 Dec. 3/2: For the attainment of these important objects, the patriots now in arms under the standard of Liberty, on NAVY ISLAND, U.C. have established a Provisional Government. . . . **1881** RATTRAY *Scots in Brit.N.A.* II 502: It had been for some time apparent to the Governor and the Colonial Office that the "patriots" were not to be satisfied by concessions. **1958** *Encyc.Can.* VIII 130/2: Patriots, a term generally applied to supporters of the Rebellion of 1837-38. . . .

b. one of the American sympathizers with the Canadian rebels of 1837-38, who mounted several abortive raids against Canada in the latter year. See also **Hunter.**
1838 *Bytown* [Ottawa] *Gaz.* 13 June 2/4: On Wednesday Last there was a "pretty considerable" kind of kick-up, on the frontier, caused by a ridiculous rumour, that 15,000 rebels and "Patriots" were about to cross over into Canada and lay waste the country. **1926** *Cdn Hist. Rev.* VII 19: In ordinary conversation the members of the order were referred to as "Hunters" or as "Patriots." **1953** RADCLIFF *Letters* x: When the news arrived from Detroit of Dr. Theller's preparations to attack Upper Canada with a strong contingent of American "Patriots," Radcliff led his regiment to meet them. . . . **1958** *Encyc.Can.* VIII 130/2: Patriots, a term generally applied to supporters of the Rebellion of 1837-38 but more specifically to American sympathizers who actively aided the rebels in exile and participated in several abortive raids against the British colonies in 1838.

2 See **Patriote.** Also spelled *patriot.*
1838 *Western Herald* (Sandwich, U.C.) 20 Oct. 253/3: The acquittal of the murderers of the ill-fated Chartrand by a "patriot" Jury, has elicited the deepest hatred and prejudice against the French inhabitants in the bosoms of the loyal British party. **1863** (1873) LEMOINE *Maple Leaves* 251: The sundering of the colonial tie, for attempting which, the "Patriots" of 1837 were gibetted by the score, when not exiled or plunged in dungeons, seems of late years, to have been considered by many Imperial statesmen, but a question of time or expediency. **1900** *Canadian Mag.* Dec. 115/2: From this the coins are called "Habitant pennies," but among the French Canadians, "Papineaus," because the Hon. L. J. Papineau, the leader of the patriots, affected this costume. **1952** (1965) HAMILTON *Cdn Quotations* 175/2: The Patriots. From the French "patriotes," the name assumed by Papineau's followers in Lower Canada who were associated in the rebellion of 1837.

Patriot army *Hist.* the combined forces of exiled rebels and American sympathizers which proposed to attack Canada in 1838. See also **Patriot** (def. 1) and **Patriot War.**
1838 *Gazette* (Montreal) 31 Jan. 2/1: Since writing the above we have ascertained that the man who was left on the island had hid himself for the purpose of getting rid of the "patriot army." **1841** MCLEOD *Upper Canada* 198: From this a proclamation was issued, setting forth the object of the Patriot army—promising a bounty of three hundred acres of wild land to all volunteers who should serve during the struggle, and a reward of £500 was offered for the apprehension of Sir Francis Head.

Patriote *n. Hist.* a follower of Louis-Joseph Papineau and a supporter of the Ninety-two Resolutions, *q.v.,* which set forth the political grievances of the rebels in Lower Canada. See also **Patriot** (def. 2). Also spelled *patriote.*
1904 DECELLES *Papineau* 69: During Papineau's struggle his friends assumed the name of Patriotes and their opponents were called Bureaucrats. **1915** WALLACE *Family Compact* 118: The Declaration . . . proclaimed the duty of every Upper-Canadian Reformer to co-operate heartily with Papineau and his French-Canadian patriotes. **1963** MORTON *Kingdom of Canada* 243: The result was to create distrust of Gosford's intentions among the now excitable Patriotes, as the followers of Papineau were beginning to be called.

Patriot War *Hist.* the several unsuccessful raids

carried out against Canada by the Patriots (def. 1) of 1838. See also **Patriot army.**
1861 CROIL *Dundas* 109: There is no doubt however that this *Patriot War,* as it was significantly termed by them, was winked at by American officials in high places. **1937** *Cdn Hist.Rev.* XVIII 46: The place of the Coburg conspiracy in the Patriot war is plain enough. **1947** DUMBRILLE *Deep Doorways* 6: One bleak November day Richard was called upon to protect his country in the last engagement of the Patriot War.

patro ['pætro] *n.* [< Cdn F < F *patronage* in similar sense] a youth club. See quote.
1959 *Ottawa Citizen* 11 Sep. 16/3: Pius XII Patro . . . will be a recreation centre for boys of the city and is expected to contribute much to prevent juvenile delinquency . . . The patro will be for boys and youths from 7 years of age to 20 years.

patrol *n.* See **road grader.**
1964 *Naicam Sentinel* 26 Mar. 2/3: . . . if it is not possible to borrow this money, we will purchase the patrol on a rental purchase basis . . . That the Secretary be instructed to advertise for 3 patrol operators, one for each of the patrols to be stationed at Pleasantdale, Lac Vert and Naicam.

patrol cabin an overnight stopping place for the convenience of rangers and others who patrol the bush.
1963 SYMONS *Many Trails* 165: . . . blazing narrow trails . . . was undertaken, as well as the putting up of some tiny patrol cabins.

patrol doctor a government doctor who makes regular circuits among the Indians and Eskimos.
1964 JENNESS *Eskimo Admin.* II 44: [There was] established at Pangnirtung a permanent medical post whose first incumbent, the patrol doctor . . . examined over 500 Eskimos. . . .

patron *n.* See **pateroon.**

Patron *n. Hist.* See **Patrons of Industry.**
1894 *Cdn Farmers' & Sun* (London, Ont.) 2 Jan. 2/2: The Patrons refuse to be bound to either political party, and the bold partisans cannot comprehend that it is possible for men to be neither Grits nor Tories. **1963** MORTON *Kingdom of Canada* 382: The Patrons did everything the Grangers did, but they added a special emphasis on co-operation.

Patrons of Industry *Hist.* a farmers' organization founded in 1891 and enjoying considerable political support for a number of years.
1905 BIGGAR *Oliver Mowat* II 499: Another and more important factor in this election was an association of farmers, which had been established in 1891 under the name of the "Patrons of Industry." **1962** *New Democrat* Oct. 3/2: In 1894 the Patrons of Industry elected 14 members to the Ontario legislature.

patroon *n.* See **pateroon.**

pause *n.* See **pose.**

pay *n. Placer Mining* **1** See **paystreak** (def. 1).
1863 *Nor'Wester* (R.R.S.) 16 Sep. 3/4: The Barker Company have struck pay again. **1958** LINDSAY *Cariboo Story* 35/1: "They . . . sunk a second shaft; when they got through the clay they had pay and they

had it all the way down to bedrock. . . ."
2† a profitable yield of gold.
1863 *Islander* (Charlottetown) 18 Dec. 2/1: For
instance, on Williams Creek, the chief mining stream
and the centre of trade, there are about 20 shafts taking
out rich pay. **1900** OSBORN *Greater Canada* 85: One
consequence of the "Cariboo rush" was to drain all the
other placer-mining camps in the province, even those
diggings which were returning good "pay" being
forsaken, and allowed to fall into the hands of Indians
and the inevitable Chinaman.
3 See **pay dirt** (def. 1).
1942 WIEDERMANN *Cheechako* 225: "That's only
chicken feed compared to what we've got in those pay
dumps out on the creek," retorted Hinkley.
1966 *Beautiful B.C.* Spring 34/2: . . . even today the
fortunate vacationer [in Atlin] may have the chance to
witness actual operations as miners "work the creeks"
for "colour" and "pay."

pay dirt† **1** *Placer Mining* gold-bearing gravel.
See also **pay** (def. 3), **pay gravel,** and **poor man's
gold.** Cp. **paystreak** (def. 1).
1863 *Nor'Wester* (R.R.S.) 22 July 3/5: The "Gumboots"
or Welsh Company, struck the pay-dirt in their new
shaft and took out twenty-four ounces in about three
hours, in coarse gold. **1881** *Progress* (Rat Portage
[Kenora], Ont.) 30 Apr. 3/2: The pay dirt, or gold
bearing gravel, varies from eight inches to four feet in
depth. **1966** *Islander* 27 Feb. 13/3: . . . fire swept
Barkerville down to the pay dirt. . . .
2 deposits of any kind rich enough to merit mining.
1953 *North Star* (Yellowknife) May 1/29 Biggest event
at Uranium City and environs since Gunner Gold
struck pay-dirt has been the organization of the
stabilized mining camps by Mine-Mill. **1957** *Beaver*
Spring 8/2: Red dust—"pay dirt"—covers every
window sill.

pay gravel See **pay dirt** (def. 1).
1897 BALLARD *Klondyke Mines* 3: What is known as
"pay gravel" lies below the bottom of the creeks, and is
obtained by sinking a shaft through the frozen ice, mud
and debris to the bed-rock, where the richest gravel is
encountered. **1898** *Yukon Midnight Sun* (Dawson)
9 Dec. 1/6: He has prospected several buckets of pay
gravel which went $21.

paying streak See **paystreak** (def. 1).

Pays d'en Haut *Cdn French, Hist.* See **Northwest**
(def. 1a), **up-country,** and **Upper Country** (def. 1).
1912 ROE *Whispering Hills* 154: These were the great
Nakonkirhirinons from that limitless region of the Pays
d'en Haut. **1931** *Beaver* Dec. 335: One of the conditions
of acceptance for membership [in the Beaver Club] was
that the applicant or invited member must have passed
a winter in the *Pays d'en Haut.* . . . **1963** MORTON
Kingdom of Canada 48: Soon indeed they would have to
take goods inland as the trade in the *pays d'en haut,*
the up country, became fiercely competitive.

Pays Sauvages *Cdn French, Hist.* See **Indian
country** (def. 2). Also spelled *pays sauvages.*
1834 (1963) TOLMIE *Physician* 262: When a person has
resolved to settle in the "pays sauvage" . . . the sooner
he takes a wife the better. **1952** (1954) JENNINGS *Strange
Brigade* vii: They came each year into the Pays
Sauvages . . . the great wide wilderness of mighty
mountains on the west and frozen muskeg in the

north. . . . **1960** *Press* Dec. 13: The Nor'westers . . .
took their trade goods into the Pays Sauvages, the
Pays d'en Haut of the Red River country and
beyond. . . .

paystreak *n.* **1†** *Placer Mining* a profitable deposit
or stratum of gold-bearing gravel. See also **pay**
(def. 1). Cp. **pay dirt** (def. 1) and **pay zone.** Also
paying streak.
[**1860** *Brit.Colonist* (Victoria) 2 June 1/2: Many have
already returned and their accounts are singularly
consistent, viz., that "good diggings are scarce,"
"paying streak thin," "provisions very high". . . .]
1898 *Yukon Midnight Sun* (Dawson) 10 Sep. 3/1: On
Fritz Miller's discovery claim it pays about $25 to the
shovel, and as the center of the creek is reached the
pay-streak increases in value. **1936** ARMSTRONG *Yukon
Yesterdays* 41: Early in February we struck the rich
paystreak very nearly off the boundary of the claim!
1963 *Placer Mining B.C.* 8/1: The gold concentration
or paystreak may have been formed in pre-glacial,
interglacial, or postglacial times, or paystreaks of all
three periods may lie in different parts and at different
levels in a single valley.
2 *Slang* See quote.
1924 MASON *Arctic Forests* 45: The only bacon the
traders sell is of very inferior quality, generally
"sow-belly," "pay-streak," etc.

pay treaty See **treaty money.**

pay zone *Hardrock Mining* a profitable stratum or
vein of mineral-bearing ore. Cp. **paystreak** (def. 1).
1966 *Sun* (Vancouver) 30 May 6A/1: . . . Pyramid
Mines reported it had cut 62 feet of pay zone . . . on its
prospect at Pine Point in the Northwest Territories.

P.C. Progressive Conservative, *q.v.*
1955 *Edmonton Jnl* 4 Jan. 1/7: He has been PC member
of the legislature for Lanark since 1937 and highways
minister since 1943. **1963** *Globe and Mail* (Toronto)
13 Mar. 8/1: At the provincial level, the PCs have
complete nominations in all provinces except Quebec. . . .

pea-bouncer *n. Slang* See quote.
1955 GILLESPIE *Bluenose Skipper* 14: . . . the cook wore
a "pea-bouncer"—better known today as a "derby". . . .

Peace, the *n.* See **Peace River Country.**
1954 BEZANSON *Sodbusters Invade the Peace* [Title].
1958 *Edmonton Jnl* 7 Aug. 34/1: Mr. Alden . . . has been
travelling the Peace for the past 10 years visiting
isolated points. . . .

peace belt† *Hist.* among Indians, a wampum
belt, *q.v.,* symbolizing peace. Cp. **war belt.**
1926 MAIR *Masterworks* XIV 207: The colour of the . . .
peace belt [was] white. . . .

peace calumet *Obs.* See **calumet of peace.**
1862 *Nor'Wester* (R.R.S.) 9 Oct. 3/1: Well, this party
was plundered by the very Assiniboines, in whose camp
our hunting-gentlemen were now smoking the peace
calumet.

peace pipe† *Hist.* See **calumet of peace.**
1865 *Nor'Wester* (Winnipeg) 23 Oct. 2/1: "Well, this
injun came to my house last spring, and sittin down on
the flore, sed, Nee-che giv me sum tobbaccer." "Well,
I giv nee chee some tibaccer and he fille his pees pipe and
smoked it very peecably like." **1958** *Nelson Dly News*
(B.C.) 25 Aug. 8/1: Twenty Indians gathered about a
fire of sweet grass inside the teepee and following a
prayer in Sioux, a peace pipe was passed.

Peace River Block See 1954 quote.
1940 *Beaver* Mar. 46/2: We passed through Peace River Block in British Columbia, which contains about three million acres of fine land. **1954** BEZANSON *Sodbusters* 64: MacDonnell, Dominion Land Surveyor, had recently finished surveying a line around three and a half million acres straddling Peace River, lying between the Alberta-British Columbia boundary and the Rockies, a grant of land ceded to the Dominion Government by the Province of British Columbia in a railway deal made years before. It was then designated The Peace River Block, and although it long since passed back to British Columbia so its boundaries have become meaningless, it is still referred to in the press, hence by many people, as The Peace River Block. **1963** *Calgary Herald* 20 Sep. 14/1: The section showing a reduction from 1962 is in the Peace River Block.

Peace River country or **district** the extensive area of rolling plains in the valley of the Peace River, in both northern Alberta and British Columbia. See also **Peace, the.**
1924 *Beaver* Mar. 213: The Canadian Pacific Railway is now operating through to the Peace river district. . . . **1958** *Edmonton Jnl* 24 June 4 10/1: The Peace River country is Canada's largest concentration of people north of the 55th parallel. **1966** *Maclean's* 19 Feb. 20/1: In the Peace River country, past and present, fact and folklore, are all intertwined and part of the same story.

peacock copper bornite, a copper-iron sulphide with a purplish tarnish, as in peacock feathers.
1897 *Slocan Pioneer* (B.C.) 4 Sep. 1/6: The Michigan claim on Toad mountain is showing up well, some very fine gray copper and peacock copper having been encountered which give promise of good returns. **1912** POCOCK *Man in the Open* 90: Once a week I take my little pack outfit up to the Sky-line claim for a load of peacock copper. It runs three hundred dollars to the ton in horn silver, and looks more like jewels than mineral.

peaconk *n.* See **pekan.**

pear *n.* [cf. Cdn F *poire sauvage* in this sense] *Obs.* See **serviceberry** (def. 2). See also **Indian pear** and **poire.**
1620 MASON *Briefe Discovrse* A iv[r]: The Countrie fruites wild, are cherries small, whole groaues of them, Filberds good, a small pleasant fruite, called a Peare. . . . **1793** (1933) MACDONELL *Diary* 116: The wild plumb, and Grape, the pair, choak and sand cherries, Summer berry and the Raspberry are also natives of this [Assiniboine] country. **1804** (1897) COUES *New Light* I 247: Pears ripe at Portage des Chiens.

peasoup ['piˌsup] *n.* [through long association with pea soup; see 1833 quote] *Slang, Derog.* a French Canadian (def. 1). See also **peasouper.**
[**1833** (1955) CRAIG *Early Travellers* 82: We left in bark canoes early one morning, and were paddled up to Dow's great swamp by Canadian voyageurs, hardy fellows who can accomplish 100 miles a day, on pea-soup and pork . . . lighten their labours with their simple boat songs.] **1896** PARKER *Lavilettes* 60: "Yes, an' dey call us Johnny Pea-soups." **1912** HEENEY *Pickanock* 22: "Pea-soup! I never drink with the likes of you, Pauquett!" ejaculated Bill. . . . **1945** MACLENNAN *Two Solitudes* 49: The soldier edged against him. "Listen, you goddam peasoup, you're too fast with your mouth." **1965** *Globe and Mail* (Toronto) 13 Oct. 6/3: It reminded me of a problem I encountered . . . when . . . describing our childhood forays in Ottawa between pea-soup and English-speaking gangs.

peasouper ['piˌsupɚ] *n. Slang, Derog.* See **peasoup.**
1962 *Maclean's* 2 June 51/2: And *then* we can highstick those peasoupers. **1966** *Globe and Mail* (Toronto) 19 Apr. 6/6: . . . their [French Canadians'] waspish counterparts in Quebec always refer to "pea-soupers" or "Joes." The word "Frog" in that connection went out of fashion 50 years ago.

A peavey

peavey† ['pivi] *n.* [origin uncertain] a strong pole or lever, 5 to 7 feet long, the end of which is furnished with a point of iron or steel and a hinged semicircular hook, used by loggers for directing logs in a drive (def. 1), during booming operations, etc. Also spelled *peevie, peevy.*
☛ *This tool was almost certainly devised in the woods of New Brunswick and Maine, where the first large-scale lumbering operations were carried out on this continent. The claim has been advanced, but not proved, that a J. B. Peavey of Bangor, Maine, was the inventor.*
1911 KNOWLES *Singer* 261: Peavy and cant-hook fell upon it, sharp saws. . . . **1938** CASH *I Like B.C.* 67: Indomitable, if cursing, under blazing sun and smoke-blackened night, they worked with shovel, axe, peevie and hose. **1963** MORTON *Kingdom of Canada* 221: In New Brunswick . . . developed the river drive of the squared timber and the masts down the river, the lumber camp, the lumberjack, the peavey, the term "Main John" for the woods boss. **1964** *Atlantic Advocate* July 60/2: Using bulldozers, the Irving company can put 28 to 30 million feet of logs into the river in one area in three or four days where it used to take 200 to 300 men pushing and straining with peaveys two to three weeks to do the same job.

pecan, peccan(t) *n.* See **pekan.**

pechause *n.* See **pichou.**

peddler *n.* See **pedlar.**

pedlar or **peddler** *n. Slang, Derog., Hist.* **1** *Fur Trade* in the usage of the men of the Hudson's Bay Company: **a.** a coureur de bois (def. 1), especially one who competed for trade in Rupert's Land, *q.v.*, thus being considered an interloper. See also **French pedlar.** Cp. **master pedlar.**
*c*1752 (1852) COATS *Geography of H.B.* 41: Nor is it in the power of man to prevent it growing worse and worse, without we could fall on a way to send our people amongst the Indians, to live and hunt, and marry and mix, and encounter and drive those pedlars back into their own lakes. **1764** (1954) WALLACE *Pedlars* 3: . . . in 1764 the Hudson's Bay Company factor at Severn House reported "several murders committed by the Indians on the pedlars up country". . . . **1908** LAUT *Conquest N.W.* I 365: To stand on the rights of monopoly conferred by an ancient charter while "interlopers and pedlars," as the Company called them—ran away with the profits of that monopoly, was like standing on your dignity with a thief while he picked your pockets. **1947** *Cdn Hist.Rev.* Dec. 430: The "Pedlars" and the

Nor'Westers quickly spread into the Rocky regions of the Shield, into the prairies and into the woodlands beyond. **1961** PRICE & KENNEDY *Renfrew* 27: Company men referred to the Montreal traders as the "Pedlars." The latter, first trading individually or in small groups, joined forces in 1776 as the North West Company.

b. after 1776, a member of the North West Company, *q.v.* See also **Northwest pedlar.**
1777 (1954) *Moose Ft Jnls* 345: To me it appears a matter of much consequence to our Welfare as it may happen & Time may prove us only to be fighting about a few Home Guards or Shore Indians, rather confounding the Company's Interest more than we annoy the Inland Pedlars. **1784** (1954) *Ibid.* 204: They acknowledged they had been with the Pedlars not knowing any body was here 'till the Spring, indeed their Cloathing and Powder plainly showed that (the latter a much better kind than our's is). **1921** HAWORTH *Trailmakers* 57: But the pedlars were keen business men and by carrying their goods right to the Indians they soon greatly diminished the number of aborigines who made the long journey to the Bay to trade. **1957** FISHER *Pemmican* 6: Far away yonder Jim Dugald was worrying his ass off about the pedlars. **1963** *Beaver* Summer 13/2: He . . . gave a further display of immaturity by openly espousing the cause of the pedlars from Montreal.

2 *Fur Trade* an American trader.
1860 (1956) KOHL *Kitchi-Gami* 168: The American pedlars . . . could afford us no assistance. . . .

3 *Nfld* See quote.
1964 *Nfld Qtly* Summer 25/2: The "peddler"—not a man with a pack on his back, but a trading schooner from St. Johns, the American Mainland, or even England—became in the 18th century, a competitive nuisance to the regular supplying merchant in Newfoundland harbours. . . .

peeshew *n.* See **pichou.**

peevee or **peevie** *n.* See **peavey.**

peewee *n.* **1** a player of the 8-12 age group in organized sports for boys.
1958 *Cut Knife Grinder* (Sask.) 6 Feb. 1/5: On Wednesday evening the Cut Knife PeeWees were hosts to the Unity team and defeated them in a hard fought game. . . . **1961** MITCHELL *Jake and the Kid* 176: ". . . You take the hockey outfits—Peewees, Juniors, Intermediates—ain't a year Wing didn't put up the money for their uniforms. . . ." **1962** *Kingston Whig-Standard* (Ont.) 28 Dec. 9/5: In the mosquito and peewee age-bracket, the fee is optional.

2 *Lumbering* an undersized log.
1965 *Western Wonderland* April 22/1: . . . the nine sorting categories [of logs] . . . are: hemlock, sawlogs . . . peewees . . . and, lastly, boomsticks.

Peg, the *n.* *Slang* Winnipeg, Manitoba.
1910 *Eye Opener* (Calgary) 5 Mar. 2/6: Mr. Hurte thereupon lit a cigar and launched into a most amusing account of his doings in the Peg. **1936** CROSS *Cross Roads* 49: . . . you have left Portage la Prairie behind, and are close to Winnipeg itself. The immediate approach to the 'Peg via Canadian National is slower and more interesting. . . .

pekan ['pɛkən] *n.* [< Cdn F *pékan, pécan*(*t*)

< East Algonk.; cf. Abnaki *pĕkanē*] Also spelled *pecan.* **1** See **fisher.**
1760 JEFFERYS *Descr.New France* 37: The fur of this animal, as also that of the Pekan . . . are what is called the . . . lesser furs. **1829** RICHARDSON *Fauna* I 52: The Pekan . . . Wejack, or Fisher [of the] Fur Traders. **1846** HATHEWAY *Hist.N.B.* 65: Foxes, Loup Cerviers, Wild Cats, Racoons, Porcupines, Peaconks or Fishers, Woodchucks or Ground Hogs, Saple or Martins, Minks, Squirrels and Hares, are native animals of the country. **1963** SYMONS *Many Trails* 177: It was one of the loveliest and rarest of fur-bearers—a pekan or fisher.

2 the fur of the fisher.
1784 (1790) UMFREVILLE *Hudson's Bay* 20: The Indians here offered us a few skins to trade . . . eight otters, one peccant, two beaver. . . . *c*1902 (1912) LAUT *Trapper* 189: Of otter and mink and pekan there will be plenty, for these fish-eaters are most easily taken before midwinter frost has frozen the streams solid.

pembina (berry) ['pɛmbənə] *n.* [< Cdn F < Algonk.: cf. Cree *nipiminān*; see 1853 quote] See **highbush cranberry.** Various early spellings.
☛ *Though* **pembina** *is established as the popular spelling, the form* **pimbina** *is often preferred by botanists.*
☛ *For another meaning, see note at* **mooseberry.**
1760 JEFFERYS *Descr.New France* 41: The *Pemine,* another plant peculiar to this country, is a different shrub, growing along the sides of rivulets, and in meadows, which also bears a clustering fruit of a very sharp and stringent taste. **1800** (1897) COUES *New Light* I 58: . . . others went in search of fruit, of which they found great plenty, such as red plumbs, panbinas, and grapes. **1853** REID *Young Voyageurs* 31: The name, however, by which it is known among the Indians of Red River is "anepeminan," from "nepen," summer, and "minan," berry. This has been corrupted by the fur traders and voyageurs into "Pembina": hence, the name of a river which runs into the Red and also the name of the celebrated but unsuccessful settlement of "Pembina," formed by Lord Selkirk many years ago. **1921** HEMING *Drama of Forests* 11: The girls join their mothers in picking berries . . . swampberries, saskatoonberries, pembinaberries, pheasantberries, bearberries, and snakeberries. **1958** MacGREGOR *North-West of 16* 188: . . . Pembina berries . . . we also called high-bush cranberries. **1966** *North* Nov.-Dec. 14: Luckily for him, it was the fall of the year and these [berries] were plentiful, especially the pembina or high-bush cranberry. . . .

pemmican ['pɛməkən] *n.* [< Algonk.: < Cree *pimii* fat, grease + *-kān* prepared] **1** beaten or pounded meat mixed with melted animal fat and, sometimes, berries, the preparation being sewn in a skin bag to form a hard, compact mass that would keep for a long time under almost any conditions. See also **taureau** (def. 3). Cp. **beat meat** and **pounded meat.**
☛ *Of great importance in the fur trade, pemmican was made from the flesh of buffalo (and at times from that of caribou, moose, etc.) and in preparations of varying quality and composition. Consequently, numerous compound terms were in use, as* **deer pemmican, berry pemmican;** *the qualifier being self-explanatory, few such terms have been entered here.*
1743 (1949) ISHAM *Observations* 156: Pimmegan as the Natives styles itt, is some of the Ruhiggan fatt and cranberries mixd. up togeather, and Reckon'd by some Very good food by the English as well as Natives.

1817 CHAPPELL *Voyage to Hudson's Bay* 194: Their crews encamp on the banks every night; and they generally land also to cook their meals, except when they are compelled to subsist on *pemmican,* a sort of dried, husky compound, composed of pounded venison and deer's fat mixed together. *Ibid.* 195: *Pemmican . . .* requires no cooking, and is sometimes rendered more palatable by the addition of berries. 1875 SOUTHESK *Saskatchewan* 176: I got some "sheep" pemmican from these hunters, and thought it very good—rather sweet and perhaps a bit richer, than the common buffalo pemmican. 1886 SCUDDER *Winnipeg Country* 87: But pemmican for breakfast, pemmican for dinner, pemmican for supper, is beginning to pall; and we can only move up and down the sea-beach, for beyond us is the inevitable muskeg. 1966 *Globe and Mail* (Toronto) 9 May 7/1: They used to get together to chew over pemmican and offer up incantations to the great god Scouse for the preservation of the fertility of the muskrat and things like that.

2 *Fur Trade, Hist.* **a.** a rawhide bag containing 90 pounds of pemmican. See also **taureau** (def. 2). 1824 (1955) BLACK *Journal* 185: A Pemican put into a Sand bank here two months ago is not in the least spoiled. 1825 (1931) SIMPSON *Fur Trade* 148: Half a Doz Pemicans is all that is required for the Voyage Westward which the Crew can carry on their backs and coming East a couple Bags may be transported in like Manner.

b. See **taureau** (def. 1). See also **pemmican bag.** 1944 *Beaver* Dec. 16/2: These sacks are known as *taureaux . . .* or pemmicans.

pemmican bag or **sack** *Fur Trade, Hist.* See **taureau** (def. 1). See also **pemmican** (def. 2b). 1810 (1897) COUES *New Light* II 582: Women all busy stretching buffalo hides to make pemmican bags and pack cords. 1887 *Senate Journal* XXI App. 66: The pemmican itself, packed in skins, would afford a very efficient means of defence, if necessary, by throwing up an entrenchment with earth and pemmican bags. 1940 NIVEN *Mine Inheritance* 263: . . . one of the labourers had brought some things down in an old pemmican-sack and emptied them into a canoe.

pemmican boat or **canoe** *Fur Trade, Hist.* a boat carrying pemmican (def. 1) and other supplies to a trading post. 1820 (1938) SIMPSON *Athabasca Jnl* 55: I have therefore to request the favor of your sending to Isle a la Crosse by the Pemican Canoes the undermentioned skins and sinews, vizt.: 350 skins 7 50 lbs. Sinews, and a quantity of Shaganapy lines. 1821 *Ibid.* 264: Perhaps you will be able to resolve this point by the return of Mr. Oxley or by the Pemmican Canoe in Spring. 1929 (1931) MERK *Fur Trade* 149: The pemmican boats, to which Simpson refers, reached Cumberland House on June 2, and the expedition under the command of the clerk Fraser proceeded northward to Methye Portage. 1963 MACLEOD & MORTON *Cuthbert Grant* 26: Macdonell had . . . planted his battery in 1814 to block the pemmican-boats on the Assiniboine.

pemmican house *Fur Trade, Hist.* a storehouse for pemmican (def. 1). 1921 MCKENZIE *Men of H.B.C.* 22: On the other side of the square, in an equally long row, built in the same style, were warehouses, ration houses, dry meat and pemmican houses, pork and beef houses, and a well appointed dairy.

pemmicanize ['pɛməkən͵aɪz] *v. Obs.* make into pemmican (def. 1).

1887 *Senate Journal* XXI App. 4: The weight of evidence herewith submitted indicates a greater measure of advantage to be obtained by the drying, salting, smoking, freezing or pemmicanizing of this food product for the use of the Indians and Whites near fishing waters, and for the rationing of western Indians. *Ibid.* 112: The less fatty animals, as the rabbit, may be and are dried and smoked for after use, and they might be with equal facility pemmicanized if the Indians or others had sufficient beef tallow to supply the natural want of fat.

pemmican post or **station** *Fur Trade, Hist.* a meat post, *q.v.,* where pemmican (def. 1) was prepared and stored for supplying to the trading posts. [1810 (1916) THOMPSON *Narrative* 143: Cumberland House . . . serves as the general Depot for all the dried Provisions made of the meat and fat of the Bison under the name of Pemican, a wholesome, well tasted nutritious food, upon which all persons engaged in the Furr Trade mostly depend for their subsistence during the open season.] 1935 *Cdn Geog.Jnl* Feb. 60/2: . . . a long rest was ordered near a cluster of log huts, the winter headquarters of the Métis hunters from Fort Qu' Appelle—the Company's "pemmican post" a hundred miles to the north-east. 1953 *Ibid.* Apr. 129/2: In the early days when Churchill was a fur highway, Green Lake . . . was a pemmican station.

pemmican-pounder *n.* a tool used by the Plains Indians for beating meat. 1961 *Edmonton Jnl* 5 Aug. 5/3: Stone axes, scrapers, pemmican-pounders, arrowheads and flints were discovered.

pemmican station See **pemmican post.**

pemmican straight *Fur Trade, Hist.* See quote. See also **pemmican** (def. 1). 1926 *Beaver* Sep. 135: The kind largely in vogue with the voyageurs was "pemmican straight." This was un-cooked, and was eaten after mixing it with a little flour and frying it in a pan. The appetite had to be sharp and there had to be nothing else to eat to make "pemmican straight" seem palatable.

penalty box in hockey or box lacrosse, a special bench outside the playing area, where penalized players are required to sit out the time of their banishment from the game. See also **sin bin.** 1931 *Vancouver Province* 17 Jan. 7/1: . . . two Vancouver players [were] in the penalty box. . . . 1963 *Calgary Herald* 11 Nov. 9/2: Alex Faulkner was in the penalty box serving a major penalty for high-sticking Montreal's Ralph Backstrom and drawing blood. 1966 *Globe and Mail* (Toronto) 29 June 19/2: Finegan . . . entered the penalty box and threw a glove on the playing surface.

penalty killer *Hockey* a player whose task is to keep the opposition from scoring while his team is short-handed as a result of one or more penalties, by keeping control of the puck, checking opposition players closely, etc. See also **time killer.** 1962 *Kingston Whig-Standard* (Ont.) 14 Dec. 10/1: Not only was Westfall one of the best defencemen in the league, a good point man on the power play and a

amphibious machines currently in production to get sportsmen way back in.

penalty killer of the first order, but he took over a left wing position just before his departure. . . .
1966 *Hockey News* 1 Jan. 13/2: He is an accomplished man on the power play and is among the top penalty killers in the league.

penalty-killing *n. Hockey* the function or activity of a penalty killer, *q.v.*
1963 *Kingston Whig-Standard* (Ont.) 6 May 11/4: Winger Bill Glashan stepped up from his penalty-killing role to score twice for Flyers. **1963** *Hockey Illust.* Dec. 38/2: I'm sure that if I took him off penalty killing and put him on the power play he'd score 40 goals a year. **1966** *Hockey News* 1 Jan. 13/1: Eight Amerks had a hand in the amazing penalty-killing feat.

penalty shot *Hockey* a penalty permitting a designated player of the non-offending team to play the puck from centre ice and take one shot at the opposing goal, all other players except the defending goalkeeper remaining out of the play.
1962 *Time* (Cdn ed.) 2 Mar. 10/2: [He] added an even unlikelier goal on a rarely called penalty shot. . . .
1965 *Weekend Mag.* 6 Mar. 4/1: For a time I thought the penalty shot would become extinct through lack of application.

penguin ['pɛngwɪn] *n.* [? < Breton "white head" (cf. Welsh *pen* head, headland + *gwyn* white), in reference to an island; see 1578 quote] **1** *Obs.* the now-extinct great auk, *Alca impennis,* once found in vast numbers in Newfoundland coastal islands.
[**1578** (1883) HATTON & HARVEY *Newfoundland* 15: In about two months sailing they fell in with Cape Breton—from thence they sail'd N.E. to Penguin Island which is very full of Rockes and stones and great Birds white and gray colour as big as Geese.] **1620** WHITBOURNE *Discovrse* 9: The Penguines are as bigge as Geese, and flye not, for they haue but a little short wing, and they multiply so infinitly, vpon a certaine flat Iland, that men driue them from thence vpon a boord, into their boates by hundreds at a time. **1819** ANSPACH *Hist.Nfld* 393: They were known by the name of *penguins,* according to some writers from the Welsh, in which language the word signifies *white-head,* the penguin having a remarkable white spot on one side of its otherwise black head. **1958** *Evening Telegram* (St. John's) 29 Apr. 4/2: "Penguins," as our great auks were called, were chased to extermination.

2 *Nfld* the common cormorant.
1959 MCATEE *Folk-Names* 5: Common Cormorant . . . penguin. (This term, applied to the Great Auk, has, since the extermination of that bird, been given to a variety of the larger sea fowl. Nfld.)

3 See **Penguin.**

Penguin *n. Trademark* a tracked oversnow vehicle of the snowmobile type, much used in the North, built by the Bombardier Co. of Valcourt, P.Q.
1949 *Report of DME Test Team* I 2: In addition to the Penguin and oversnow equipments used in the convoys, two Penguins . . . worked up and down the trail. . . .
1963 *Imperial Oil Rev.* Feb. 21/1: Then in 1943, Armand devised the "Penguin," a heavily-armoured amphibious Bren carrier. **1966** *Kingston Whig-Standard* (Ont.) 3 June 13/1: The penguin in this case was one of those

Pennsylvania Dutch† one of the substantial number of settlers of German origin coming into British North America from Pennsylvania during and after 1776.
1831 *Cdn Freeman* (York [Toronto]) 19 May 2/3: Let Mackenzie stick to the Central Committee, the Saddlebags, & the Pennsylvania Dutch of the Home District—the moment he separates from them he's a gone duck. **1887** HIGGINS *Life of J.Gould* 24: They were commonly called "Pennsylvania-Dutch"; most of them were members of the Society of Friends, or Quakers, and all were an excellent class of settlers. **1958** *Encyc. Can.* VIII 144/1: [They were] more commonly known as Pennsylvania Dutch because of the mistranslation of the German *Deutsch* as "Dutch" rather than "German," came originally from Palatinate Germany.

penny† *n.* See **cent.**
☞ *Although both* **penny** *and* **copper** *have long been used in Canadian informal speech, many Canadians still associate the former with usage in the United States, where it has been used for "cent" for over a century.* **1902** CONNOR *Glengarry* 166: "Six pennies and two dimes," was Hughie's disconsolate reply. **1920** *Cdn Hist.Rev.* Mar. 351: Our children call cents "pennies" (thus showing that the half is at least equal to the "nickel"), and our pretty five cent silver pieces they call "nickels," after their ugly American equivalents. **1967** *Kingston Whig-Standard* (Ont.) 16 Mar. 1/7: He noted that in the French language, Canada's official language along with English, there is no slang equivalent to penny and nickel.

penny-dog *n. Slang* a penny stock.
1959 *Financial Post* 7 Feb. 42/2: Bibis Yukon is another "penny dog" in a revival campaign. **1959** *Maclean's* 29 Aug. 48/1: Playing the penny-dogs is like playing the horses.

people *n. Fur Trade, Hist.* See 1945 quote. Cp. **commissioned gentleman.**
1694 (1929) KELSEY *Papers* 39: Today 3 of us was sent over ye river . . . to keep an Eye abroad our people wen[t] a rafting also. **1748** DRAGE *Voyage* I 169: . . . two of the People were Kept to Hunting, which term they give to going a Shooting of Partridge. . . . **1800** (1820) HARMON *Journal* 27: At these places, most of the property was taken out of the canoes, and carried across the Portages, on the backs of the people. **1945** *B.C. Hist.Qtly* Jan. 61n: In the records of the Company, any employee from the rank of clerk up, was termed a gentleman. Labourers, hunters, and the like, were referred to as the "people."

pequam *n.* See **pekan.**

percentage woman *Yukon, Hist.* See 1936 quote.
1902 *Yukon Midnight Sun* (Dawson) 20 Sep. 3/4: The new ordinance to abate percentage women went into effect last evening and the dance halls were notified by Constable H. H. Mallet, commonly known as "Blondie," that they must at once do away with this practice and obey the law. [**1936** ARMSTRONG *Yukon Yesterdays* 48: When a drink or a bottle of wine was served a girl and her partner, she was given a small circular disc with the amount of the percentage marked on it; this she usually secreted in her stocking and later on that night, or next day, it was cashed at the bar.]

permafrost ['pɜrmə,frɒst] *n.* [< *perma*nent +

frost] See 1957 quote. See also **perma-ice. Cp. dry permafrost.**

557

**permafrost line
Peterhead launch**

[**1742** (1852) COATS *Geography of H.B.* 130: The frost is never out of the ground; how deep, we cannot be certain.] **1946** *Beaver* Sep. 46/2: Permafrost . . . is a pressing geologic problem, for most of the North is characterized by it. **1957** *Maclean's* 14 Sep. 23/1: This enemy has been with us always, but only in 1943 was given an English name: permafrost. The Russians call it *vechnaia merzlota*, or "perennially frozen ground." **1966** *Cdn Geog.Jnl* July 23/1: "Left-over ice pushed up by the spring break-up," explained Capt. Brinkie, "sitting on the permafrost; it'll stay there 'til freeze-up."

permafrost line *North* the line marking the southern boundary of permafrost.
1957 *Maclean's* 14 Sep. 91/1: It is only an accident of geography that the 1,670-mile-long Alaska Highway rarely broached the permafrost line or it might not have been finished by November 1942. **1965** SYMINGTON *Tuktu* 23: The "permafrost line" runs in a very irregular line from the Ontario shore of Hudson Bay northwestward, passing north of Reindeer Lake and Lake Athabasca and along the north shore of Great Slave Lake.

permafrost pit *North* a storage pit for food, making use of the refrigeration properties of the permafrost.
1958 *Edmonton Jnl* 17 Sep. 2/6: Storage of abundant summer catches will be encouraged in permafrost pits. . . .

perma-ice *n.* See **permafrost.**
1947 *Beaver* June 20/1: Perma-ice is to be found throughout the year about one and one-half feet below the surface, filling the low, grass areas with muskeg water. . . .

permit *n.* **1** a licence to buy and consume a specified amount of liquor, often for medicinal purposes only, in areas where the sale of spirits is otherwise illegal.
1883 *Prince Albert Times* (Sask.) 10 Oct. 3/2: After an interim of half a year you receive another permit. **1934** GODSELL *Arctic Trader* 189: Permits are issued by Ottawa, upon application, to every responsible white resident entitling him to import for medicinal purposes only two gallons of liquor each year. **1964** JENNESS *Eskimo Admin.* II 36: [It] prohibited the importation of liquor into the [N.W.] Territories except for "medicinal" purposes, and then only by holders of government permits: and it had restricted the quantity a permit-holder might import each year to . . . two gallons.
2 a. the quantity of liquor one is permitted to buy with the government permit.
1883 *Prince Albert Times* (Sask.) 10 Oct. 3/2: I do not refer to clergymen, lawyers or doctors, neither to whites generally nor to half-breeds universally, but to a class that is always ready to drink any and every permit, no matter who it is that pays the piper. **1928** FREEMAN *Nearing North* 142: The term "permit" as used in the North has no reference, as one might suppose, to hunting or fishing or mining licenses, but is rather the popularly accepted euphemism for the monthly case of liquor each legal resident is permitted to import from the nearest licensed vendor. **1947** GILLHAM *Raw North* xiv: The Canadian Government allows each individual of the white population one permit of strong drink a year—two gallons.
b. liquor; a bottle of liquor.
1909 CAMERON *New North* 109: It has been a full day, and by the way the "permits" are opening up in the

settlement when we come back, promises to be a full night. These men have waited a whole year for a drink, and now the lids can't come off quick enough. **1953** MOWERY *Mounted Police* 38: "You lie natural and easylike," Nat growled at the man, whom he had once raided for selling "permit" to Indians. **1966** PATTERSON *Trail* 134: It was a wonderful dinner . . . and he was able to add to it, for in his load were two or three "permits" —bottles of rum. . . .

permit runner *West, Hist.* See **whisky runner.** See also **permit** (def. 2b).
1953 MOWERY *Mounted Police* 177: During his years with the Mounted he had sneaked up on many a nest of "permit" runners. . . .

peshew, peshoo *n.* See **pichou.**

pesogan [pə'sogən] *n.* [< Algonk.: Cree] dried fungus used as punk. Various spellings.
1743 (1949) ISHAM *Observations* 136: This posogan when once Light is Very Difficult to put out, if not tak'n in time, and if not put out will Clow and Bur'n tell quite Consum'd to ashes and never Blaze. **1795** (1911) HEARNE *Journey* 278: The Indians, both Northern and Southern, have found by experience, that by boiling the pesogan in water for a considerable time, the texture is so much improved, that when thoroughly dried, some parts of it will be nearly as soft as spunge. **1819** MCKEEVOR *Hudson's Bay* 51: The perogan [sic], or tinder, the Indians make use of, is a kind of fungus that grows on the outside of the birch tree. **1959** *Beaver* Winter 36: The bit of tinder wedged in the board below this bow-drill fire-maker is dried bracket fungus, called "pus-sag-on."

Peterborough (canoe) *n.* [< *Peterborough,* Ont.] a widely used wooden canoe patterned on the birchbark canoe, *q.v.,* and manufactured in Lakefield, Ontario, by the Peterborough Canoe Company. Also spelled *Peterboro.*
1895 *Rudder* 215: Eleven paddling canoes—eight Peterboro's and three Rushton—and the Cruiser, complete the fleet. **1897** TYRRELL *Sub-Arctics* 20: On the evening of the last day of May we launched our handsome "Peterboroughs" in the great stream, and commenced our long canoe voyage. **1958** BERTON *Klondike* 277: Here . . . light Peterborough canoes [were] packed over the passes on men's shoulders. . . . **1966** *Cdn Geog.Jnl* Sep. 78/3: . . . John Stephenson . . . later came up with the excellent cedar rib craft known the world over as the Peterborough Canoe.

Peterhead (boat) *n.* [< *Peterhead,* Scotland] *North* a decked launch or large whaleboat equipped with a single sail and a modest motor, widely used in the Eastern Arctic and patterned on a type of whaler deriving from Peterhead, Scotland.
1940 *Beaver* Mar. 6/1: . . . when our Peterhead boat had been fully provisioned with tea, coffee, canned goods . . . we started. . . . **1959** *Ottawa Citizen* 12 Dec. 38/5: Simonee got his boat, a one-masted schooner with engine, a modified version of the type known widely in the north as a peterhead and costing about $8,000. **1966** *Cdn Geog.Jnl* Mar. 94/1: . . . usually only the larger fully-decked "Peterhead" boats are used for travelling.

Peterhead launch or **schooner** See **Peterhead.**
1942 TWOMEY & HERRICK *Needle to North* 319: A trim Peterhead launch was moving toward us. **1958** *Cdn*

Geog.Jnl July 88/2: Staff members have cruised by Peterhead schooner, trap and whale boats, along the coasts of southern Baffin Island. . . .

petite bosse *Cdn French* See 1944 quote. Cp. **boss**.
1808 (1897) COUES *New Light* I 446: Buffalo are cut up into the following 20 pieces by the hunter: 1 grosse bosse; 1 petite bosse; 2 depouilles; 2 shoulders; 2 lourdes épaulettes [shoulder pieces]; 2 fillets; 2 thighs; 2 sides; 1 belly; 1 heart; 1 rump; 1 brisket; 1 backbone; 1 neck. The tongue usually belongs to the hunter. **1944** *Beaver* Dec. 16: To begin with, the *petite bosse* is taken off. This is a small hump, weighing about three pounds, which is found above the neck where it is attached to the main hump.

petite morue *Cdn French* See **tommy-cod**.
1808 (1809) GRAY *Letters* 267: The Canadians call them *petite Morue;* the English call them *Tommy cod*. **1832** MCGREGOR *Brit.Amer.* II 481: Bass, sturgeon, eels, and petite morue, are also brought to market. . . . **1866** KING *Sportsman in Canada* 315: The Tom-Cod, the Petite Morue Fraiche . . . of the French Canadians, is peculiar I believe to North America.

Petit Nord *Cdn French, Hist.* See **French shore** (def. 1).
1715 (1883) HATTON & HARVEY *Newfoundland* 134: One of these peninsulas points northerly and . . . is called Petit Nord by the French. **1818** CHAPPELL *Voyage of Rosamond* 113: Those lands that border on the Straits of *Belle-isle* were called Le Petit Nord by the people of that nation; and most of the harbours then received the *French* appellations, which a greater number of them retain to the present day. **1932** *Cdn Hist.Rev.* XIII 269: The French right to use the coast was restricted to the northern zone called by the French "le Petit Nord" and by the English after this time the "French Shore."

pew [pju] *n.* [< F *pieu* < L *palus* pole] *Esp.Nfld* a long-handled, pronged device used for forking fish from boat to wharf or stage.
1835 WIX *Journal* 22: Also a large species of fish, called the horse-mackarel, resembling that fish in every particular, but ten feet in length, had been killed here last summer, by a girl with a "pew," or fork used for throwing fish from the boats on the "stages." **1861** De BOILIEU *Labrador Life* 29: The fish are not taken out by hand, but by an instrument called a "pew," which is a prong with one point. Should a fish be damaged in the body, it is deteriorated in value; so great care is taken to stick the pew through the head of the cod, and thus to land it on the stagehead, where it undergoes the first process of salting. **1883** (1889) WITHROW *Our Own Country* 83: . . . the fish are flung one by one from the boat to the floor of the stage, with an instrument resembling a small pitchfork, and called a "pew."

pheasant *n.* 1 See **sharp-tailed grouse**.
1743 (1949) ISHAM *Observations* 124: Pheasants are likewise smaller than in England. . . . **1823** FRANKLIN *Journey* 680: The bird now under consideration is well known and common in the neighborhood of the Hudson's Bay settlements, where it is called the Pheasant or Sharp-tailed Grouse. **1896** WHITNEY *On Snow-Shoes* 298: Then there [is] the prairie-chicken, or the sharp-tailed grouse . . . which in the North Country is called pheasant. **1959** MCATEE *Folk-Names* 25: Sharp-tailed Grouse [is also called] pheasant ("Hudson Bay" . . .).

2 See quote.
1959 MCATEE *Folk-Names* 24: Ruffed Grouse [is also called] pheasant (N.B., "Keewatin," Sask., B.C.); pine pheasant (Eastern Canada). . . .

pheasantberry *n.* See **partridgeberry** (def. 2).
1921 HEMING *Drama of Forests* 11: The girls join their mothers in picking berries . . . swampberries, saskatoonberries, pembinaberries, pheasantberries, bearberries, and snakeberries.

piblokto [pəb‚lɑkto] *n.* [< Esk.] a form of hysteria among Eskimos, especially among women, occurring during the dark winter.
1959 *Camsell Arrow* Jan.-Feb. 74/1: There is a strange Eskimo madness—piblokto. Men and women are seized with uncontrollable frenzies during which they do all sorts of weird and violent things. . . .

pica *n.* See **pika**.

picaneau *n.* [< Cdn F < Algonk.; see 1897 quote] *Obs.* See **piccanan**. Also spelled *picano, pic(c)onou*, etc.
1804 (1897) COUES *New Light* I 242: We take large fat picaneau in our sturgeon nets; they are excellent eating, but too oily, and tend to increase the disease [diarrhea]. **1804** (1933) CONNOR *Diary* 255: [We] took 3 large Piconoes in our Net. **1897** COUES *New Light* I 444n: *Piccanan, picconou*, etc. are forms of the Cree name of a certain sucker, *Catostomu lesueuri*. **1933** GATES *Five Traders* 255n: Connor's "picanoes" should be *piconou*, listed by Taché as the Cyprinus (Catastomus) sueurii. It is a fish belonging to the family of carp.

picano, pic(c)onou *n.* See **picaneau**.

piccanan *n.* [< Cdn F < Algonk.; see 1897 quote at **picaneau**] *Obs.* a large, oily fish of the sucker family, *Catostomus* sp. See also **picaneau**. Also spelled *picanon, piccanon*, etc.
1800 (1897) COUES *New Light* I 41: We found some Indians, who had many sturgeon and various kinds of small fishes, such as catfish, piccanan. . . . *c*1804 (1890) GRANT *Sauteux Indians* 310: The *picanon* is a large fish, about 15 lb weight, remarkable for its oily quality, and peculiar to Ted Lake, about 100 miles west of *Lac La Pluie*. **1952** (1954) JENNINGS *Strange Brigade* 196: At the same time there were catfish and sturgeon of immense size in the river, as well as pike, piccanon. . . .

pichew *n.* See **pichou**.

pichou [pə'ʃu] *n.* -x or -s. [< Cdn F < Algonk.; cf. Cree *peshewah*] Also spelled *pechause, peeshew, peshew, peshoo, pichew*, etc. 1 See **Canada lynx**.
1743 (1949) ISHAM *Observations* 142: Catt's are a fierce creature to Look at, and about as big as a small sheep . . . they style these (peshue). . . . **1836** BACK *Arctic Land Exped.* 155: Now *Peeshew* is the Cree name for a lynx or cat, and the lake in question is accordingly marked on the map as Cat Lake. **1896** RUSSELL *Far North* 240: They should have been at their maximum during the winter of 1893-4 but in the Great Slave Lake region, where I then was, the "pishew" or "link" was by no means common. **1911** SETON *Arctic Prairies* 23: True to their religion, the half-breeds seized their rifles, the bullets whistled harmlessly about the "Peshoo"—whereupon he turned and walked calmly up the slope, stopping to look at each fresh volley, but finally waved his stumpy tail and walked unharmed over the ridge.

2 the fur of the Canada lynx.
1786 (1918) DAVIDSON *North West Co.* 269: Exports [included] . . . Kitts 296, Pichoux 882. . . . **1806** (1930) FRASER *Journal* 112: They brought 22 Beaver skins, 2 carcassause and six Pechause belonging to the chief. . . .

pick or **picker** *n. Informal* a pickerel.
1948 ONRAET *Sixty Below* 97: Next, three fish nets . . . suitable for white fish, trout, pike, pickers and conie.
1958 *Edmonton Jnl* 8 Aug. 12/2: Most of the picks were duped by a No. 8 Len Thompson black and orange. . . .

picking bee *Hist.* See quote. See also **bee**.
1905 SCHERCK *Pen Pictures* 177: The wool was then picked over by the women and girls, to get out any burs or lumps of dirt that might have adhered to it, "pickin' " bees being frequently made for this purpose.

picnic shelter a shelter erected at a roadside picnic ground or camping ground for the accommodation of motorists and others.
1959 *Cdn Geog.Jnl* Feb. 55/1: Picnic shelters have been constructed for the convenience of picnickers during inclement weather and thirty-two of these are now in use.

pie *n.* See **Canada jay**.
1959 [see quote at **magpie**].

piece [pis] *n.* [< Cdn F *pièce*] *Fur Trade, Hist.* **1** a pack of goods or furs weighing about 90 pounds. See also **fur pack, Indian pack, pack** (def. 1a), **package** (def. 1), and **pacton** (def. 2).
1761 (1901) HENRY (Elder) *Travels* 15: The freight of a canoe . . . consist of sixty *pieces*, or packages of merchandize, of the weight of from ninety to a hundred pounds each. **1840** (1955) BLACK *Journal* lxix: All their *aim is* to get through the voyage as quick as possible their cry is the *D——l take the hindermost* helter, skelter, bing, bang, the pieces here & there on the portage, pieces containing the most brittle ware are as tenderly dashed on the rocks' as two or three pieces of bar iron fasted together. **1874** (1956) ROSS *Athabasca Brigade* 11: Shipped the Battle River furs, amounting to 22 pieces. . . . **1965** *Cdn Geog.Jnl* Dec. 203/2: . . . it takes but little imagination to see the colourfully dressed voyageurs packing their heavy "pièces" . . . along the rocky river bank.
2 See quote.
1941 *Beaver* Sep. 38/2: Piece . . . At some posts . . . referred to the number of skins a hunter brought in.

piece-log canoe *Obs.* See **dugout canoe**.
1853 STRICKLAND *Canada West* I 272: A large piece-log canoe was furnished by Mr. W. F. Gooding, our Goderich store-keeper, who was one of the party, which consisted of nine persons, including myself.

piece meat *Fur Trade, Obs.* See 1933 quote.
1800 (1933) MCLEOD *Diary* 132: . . . all our piece meat is almost entirely out, & I should be very Sorry to be oblidged to make use of the little pounded meat we have at present. **1933** GATES *Five Traders* 132n: Piece meat refers to the meat that was cooked and eaten within a comparatively short time, instead of being pounded and dried. The pounded meat . . . was called pemmican.

pie social a social event to which women bring pies to sell to raise money for some charitable purpose. See also **social**.
1925 MONTGOMERY *Emily Climbs* 255: There was a concert and "pie social" at Derry Pond one Friday night and Ilse had been asked to recite. **1963** *Kingston Whig-Standard* (Ont.) 23 Jan. 112: The Women's Institute held a successful euchre and pie social in the hall recently.

pig *n. Lumbering* See quote.
1961 PRICE & KENNEDY *Renfrew* 50: Loads might be nine or ten feet in height with a "pig" or large log on top to weigh down on chains and bind the load.

pigeon† *n.* **1** *Hist.* See **passenger pigeon**.
1743 (1949) ISHAM *Observations* 125: Its Very Rare to see any Pidgeons or doves, in these parts, or Downe by the sea side, tho in Land some hundred miles are Very Numerious, once in 12 Year I did see some millions of them, which Came from the Southwd. flying in Ranges as the Geese does, &c. **1794** (1954) WALLACE *Pedlars* 85: . . . Pidgeons I understand are sometimes pretty plentiful [Lake Timiskaming, Ont.], for about 3 Weeks in Summer. . . . **1873** (1877) GRANT *Ocean to Ocean* 56: Frank caught a large pickerel and M-shot a few pigeons, giving us a variety of courses at dinner. **1959** MCATEE *Folk-Names* 41: Passenger Pigeon. Extinct; last positively identified in the wild, 1907, Pigeon, wild pigeon (general). . . .
2 *East* the Black Guillemot, *Cepphus grylle*.
1959 MCATEE *Folk-Names* 40: Black Guillemot [is also called] pigeon (Nfld., "Labr.," Que.); sea pigeon (Nfld., "Labr.," Que, P.E.I., N.S., N.B.); . . . wild pigeon (. . . Nfld., "Labr."). . . .

pigeonberry† *n.* **1** one of several berries, especially the fruit of the *Cornus canadensis,* a dogwood.
1822 (1928) CORMACK *Narr.Nfld* 21: The surface is bespangled . . . by . . . the crackerberry, bearing a cluster of wholesome red berries, sometimes called pigeon-berries. **1898** *N.B.Mag.* I 50: Children, too, may have romped and shouted there, and plucked the bright red pigeon berries, which seemed to be larger and richer there than any other place. **1958** MACGREGOR *North-west of 16* 62: . . . the bright red pigeon-berries, and the piles of spruce cones shelled out by the squirrels. . . .
2 the shrub these berries grow on.
1868 *Cdn Naturalist* III 409: Among the most common plants which overspread the burned ground . . . are . . . the pigeonberry (Cornus canadensis); and the red strawberry. **1952** PUTNAM *Cdn Regions* 49/1: On the forest floor [in B.C.] are found pigeon-berry (*Cornus canadensis*). . . .

pika† ['paɪkə *or* 'pikə] *n.* [< Tungus (E. Siberia) *piika*] a small mammal of the genus *Ochotona,* found in the western mountain region. See also **coney², little-chief, Little Haymaker, rock rabbit, whistler** (def. 2), and **whistling hare**.
1852 RICHARDSON *Arctic Exped.* 111: The little Pika, or tail-less hare, occupies the grassy eminences, and lays up a stock of hay for winter use. **1964** *Wildlife Rev.* May 17:
Upward o'er the whitened lumps
The furry-footed pika jumps
A tiny rabbit-track he leaves
A tiny rabbit—that he is.

pike *n.* See **pike-pole** and picture.
1960 *Beaver* Autumn 57/1: These Nile men were rather the shanty-boy variety of Canadian riverman, just as much at home on certain Canadian rivers as Jean Baptiste had ever been but more skilled with the raft, the pike and the peavey than with the paddle and packsack.

piked pole *Obs.* See **pike-pole**.
1849 ALEXANDER *L'Acadie* II 84: After saluting the master lumberer, who was superintending his sturdy people at work among the logs, rafting them, with their piked poles, or gaffs, and handspikes, I asked him what quantity of timber . . . had gone down this spring. . . .

pike-perch *n.* See **walleye pike**.
1866 KING *Sportsman in Canada* 324: Though Pickerel is a term often applied to young Pike, it is also used to designate a fish properly called the Pike-perch, or Sandre (*Lucioperca Canadensis*), the *Piccarel* of the French Canadians. . . . **1880** BELL *Churchill and Nelson* 6c: The pike-perch from York Factory he identifies as *Stizostethium Canadense*. **1915** (1916) *Commission of Conservation* 87: This fish [European carp] . . . has driven out certain other fish, such as the pike-perch or yellow pickerel and the bass. **1959** CARL *Fresh-Water Fishes B.C.* 147: WALLEYE *Stizostedion vitreum* (Mitchill) [also called] Pike-perch/Doré.

A pike-pole

pike-pole *n. Lumbering* See 1945 quote. See also **pike**.
1830 *Palladium* 29 Aug. 244/1: How delightful to . . . devote the livelong day to punching alligator-gars on the belly with a pike-pole! **1945** CALVIN *Saga* 68: First of all, men walking over the loose timber, in their spiked boots, sorted out with their long pike-poles (which were like twenty-foot boat-hooks with a sharp point and hook) the longer, thinner pieces to make the bottom tier. . . . **1964** *Dly Colonist* (Victoria) 27 Sep. 36/2: . . . a powered boom scooter rides herd on logs in the water where the timber used to be shoved around by a man with caulk boots, a pike pole and the agility of a cougar.

piled meat [< F *piler* crush, grind] *Fur Trade, Obs.* See **beat meat**. See also **pounded meat**.
1797 (1964) CHABOILLEZ *Journal* 155: The Cache . . . contained . . . Seven Bladders Grease & Six Pans Pilled Meat. . . . **1798** *Ibid.* 196: [I] gave them twelve pieces dryed Meat & 6 Double Hand-Full Piled Meat. . . . **1798** *Ibid.* 203: [We] are very short of Provisions— finished the Peal Meat & Grease—gave a Tonneau Pimetegan to the People. . . . . .

Pile o' Bones *Hist.* See 1953 quote.
1936 CROSS *Cross Roads* 27: Regina was once known as Pile of Bones. . . . **1953** MOON *Saskatchewan* 22: Some of them [buffalo bones] lay near Wascana Creek a few miles away from the high butte, gave the district the name Pile O' Bones. It became Regina, capital of the Province, Queen City of the Prairies. **1954** TYRE *Saddlebag Surgeon* 62: We spent two nights at Pile o' Bones, the capital of the Territories, which later was to be renamed Regina in honour of Queen Victoria.

pilgrim† *n. Slang* **1** *Northwest* a newcomer or tourist, as opposed to an established resident; greenhorn. Cp. **cheechako**.
1870 *Cariboo Sentinel* (Barkerville, B.C.) 21 May 4/1: "It scares off the gaim and drives off the fraters and bullwhackers and pilgrims. . . ." **1963** *Weekend Mag.* 6 Apr. 26/1: He complains at some length about pilgrims, the local [Yukon and Alaska Highway] name for tourists, and their driving habits. **1964** *Press* Feb. 2: His [poker] "stakes" are made at the expense of his fellows, "pilgrims," and "plow-jockeys" fresh from the farm, who pay to learn. . . .

2 *West* See 1962 quote.
1885 *Nor'Wester* (Calgary) 12 Feb. 3/1: Cattle have come through in good condition, without losses even in the pilgrim herds, much less in those that are to the manor born, so to speak. **1897** *Medicine Hat News* (Alta) 1 Apr. 4/1: Pilgrim cattle that can rustle through their first winter in such a season as we have just come through can withstand any weather which we may in future have in the stock country. **1962** *Alta Hist.Rev.* Autumn 16/2: In stockmen's language . . . Newly imported . . . cattle are "pilgrims," also applied to those unable to "rustle" or hunt for food.

piling *n. Hist.* in clearing land, putting logs and brush in piles for burning. Cp. **burning** (def. 1) and **plan-heap**.
1845 BEAVAN *Life in Backwoods N.B.* 46: . . . the wife . . . toiled with him in piling and fencing as well as in planting and reaping. **1931** SEARY *Romance* 177: There were "piling bees" for piling logs, "husking bees" for husking Indian corn. . . .

piling bee *Hist.* See **piling**. See also **bee**.

pilled meat See **piled meat**.

pilot *n. Obs.* **1** *Fur Trade* See **conductor** (def. 1).
1800 (1820) HARMON *Journal* 26: One or two Guides or Pilots are attached to each brigade.

2 an experienced person acting as a guide and leader for immigrant trains.
1834-43 (1955) RUSSELL *Journal* 91: We found the Camp consisting of about 60 men under the direction of Mr. Dripps James Bridger[,] Pilot.

pilot lot *N.S., Hist.* a lot granted to a ship's pilot to encourage him to settle in a region where his services were in demand.
1934 DENNIS *Down in N.S.* 351: "There were a lot of pilot lots around here, too. I've heard my father say you couldn't get charts in those days like you can now, so there were lots of pilots then. You can still see the remains of the stone walls which they built around their lots in the woods."

pimbina *n.* See **pembina**.
1957 [see quote at **mooseberry**].

pim(m)ecan, pim(m)ican, pimmicum, pimmikan, pimmikon, etc. *n.* See **pemmican**.

pine grosbeak a large grosbeak, *Pinicola enucleator,* common in the northern parts of Canada.
1772 *Phil.Trans.Roy.Soc.* LXII 402: [The] Pine Grosbeak . . . visits the Hudson's Bay settlements in May. . . . **1823** FRANKLIN *Journey* 675: The Pine Grosbeak, as well as two species of Cross bills, all natives of cold countries, have much red in their plumage when young, which turns to orange as they advance in age. **1955** MCCOWAN *Upland Trails* 47: This [the eradication of the Lodgepole Leaf Miner] should prove welcome news to the Pine squirrel and the Pine grosbeak.

pineman *n. Lumbering, Hist.* a logger (def. 1) of white pine.
1945 CALVIN *Saga* 51: . . . was it first made by the Ottawa River pine men?

pine marten See **marten.**
1772 *Phil.Trans.Roy.Soc.* LXII 370: Pine Marten . . . feeds on mice, rabbits, &c. though it will not touch a dead mouse which is put as a bait in a trap, and therefore the inhabitants are obliged to make use of a partridge's head, or the like, for that purpose. **1867** LORD *At Home in Wilderness* 313: Two or three different kinds of fall-traps are employed to catch pine martens. **1955** MCCOWAN *Upland Trails* 106: Although largely carnivorous in habit the Pine marten at times eats freely of this fruit [Mountain ash].

pine partridge *Now Local* the spruce partridge, *q.v.*
1808 (1809) GRAY *Letters* 246: A species of partridge, called the *pine partridge* (from its living on certain parts of the pine tree, of which it tastes very strongly), alone remains—but it is very rarely seen. **1959** MCATEE *Folk-Names* 24: Spruce Grouse [is also called] pine partridge (Alta.). . . .

pine pheasant See **pheasant** (def. 2).

pinery *n.* a stand of pine trees, especially one exploited for timber.
1783 (1905) *Ont.Bur.Arch.Rep.* III cxx: There are two fine pineries two or three miles from the water's edge where large masts may be procured. **1882** *Progress* (Rat Portage [Kenora], Ont.) 18 Mar. 2/1: Its timber . . . possesses an economic value far exceeding the pineries on the upper lakes. **1952** PUTNAM *Cdn Regions* 138/1: Its "pineries" formed the source of much of the timber which came down the Ottawa River.

Pinetree Line a coast-to-coast system of radar stations across southern Canada, equipped to detect and warn of approaching aircraft or missiles.
1956 *Time* (Cdn ed.) 10 Dec. 16/3: At 13 stations in eight provinces along Canada's coast to coast Pinetree Line, reservists . . . stood ready to scramble aircraft aloft to intercept any unidentified planes that turned up on the screens. **1963** *Calgary Herald* 31 Dec. 1/5: It will be one of five Western Canada sites of the Pinetree line . . . which will become operational at the same time.

Pinetree radar system See **Pinetree Line.**
1958 *Time* (Cdn ed.) 24 Mar. 12/3: Canada's Pinetree radar system, backstop of the nation's electronic defenses, will take on a supplementary chore this spring.

pinger ['pɪŋgɚ] *n. Placer Mining, Slang* See quote.
1958 WATTERS *B.C.Cent.Anthol.* 559: Each pinch of dust was one dollar and it was pure, whereas in other gold everything above a pinger—that is, everything above something that pinged in the pan—was coarse gold, and a lot of this coarse gold had hidden quartz in it. So a thousand in dust was the real McCoy.

pingminton ['pɪŋmɪntən] *n.* [< *ping*pong + bad*minton*] See second quote.
1958 *Edmonton Jnl* 14 June 19/8: Pingminton registrations for boys and girls 12 to 15 take place next week at the playground. Pre-school craft classes begin next week. *Ibid.* 26 June 11/7: A new, but already a popular game on Edmonton's playgrounds is "Pingminton," a mixture between table-tennis, volleyball and badminton. Players use over-size table tennis bats to hit a regular badminton bird over a volleyball net.

pingo ['pɪŋgo] *n.* **-es** or **-s.** [< Esk. *pinguq*] **1** *North* a large mound of ice covered with soil forced up by the pressure of expanding ice in the subsoil.

1941 *Beaver* June 9/1: We . . . made an expedition to the "pingos" or "bingos," those strange mounds that are landmarks on the coast. . . . **1957** *Maclean's* 14 Sep. 93/1: And what causes the "pingoes," strange mounds of pure clear ice fifty to a hundred and fifty feet high. **1966** *Cdn Geog.Jnl* Feb. 42: Since then only a few pingos have risen above the even surface.

2 See **demoiselle** and picture.
1958 *CBC Times* (Prairie ed.) 23-29 Mar. 1: Wind erosion has caused the hard sandstone cores of these pingos to be whittled away to fantastic shapes in the Red River Badlands of the Drumheller Canyon in Alberta.

pink *n.* See **pink salmon.**
1935 HALLIDAY *Potlatch and Totem* 155: After the close of the sockeye season, what are commonly known as humpback salmon were caught; these are the fish which are now canned under the technical name of 'pinks.' **1964** CARL *Marine Fishes of B.C.* 30: Pinks are taken commercially in purse-seines and gill-nets. . . .

pink-eye *n. Slang* cheap inferior whisky. See also **redeye.**
1900 OSBORN *Warders of West* 778: As his capital consisted of a yoke of oxen, a waggon, six four-gallon kegs of pink-eye and a Winchester rifle, he certainly received a fair interest on his investment. **1953** MOWERY *Mounted Police* 95: At Bender's joint, the price of a pint of pink-eye was a day's hard labor in a mine-head.

pinkie *n. Slang* **1†** See quote.
1958 *Maclean's* 27 Sep. 63/3: Pinkie [in St. John's, Nfld] is a cheap wine highly regarded by waterfront connoisseurs, a chaser for screech.

2 *Local* See quote.
1962 *Maclean's* 30 June 39/1: Vancouver police last year started issuing "pinkies," tickets that give motorists a gentle warning of infraction rather than require them to pay a fine.

pink salmon a species of Pacific salmon, *Oncorhynchus gorbuscha,* characterized by pinkish flesh. See also **hone, hook-nosed trout, humpback salmon, hunchback salmon,** and **pink.**
1952 PUTNAM *Cdn Regions* 447/1: The humpback or pink salmon weighs, on the average, four pounds. Most of these fish are canned . . . but they are not so highly prized as the sockeye because of their less appealing colour. **1963** *Sun* (Vancouver) 28 Mar. 29/1: The cutthroats could start feeding on the first hatches of pink salmon fry in the sloughs and lower reaches of the rivers.

pink tea a social gathering attended chiefly by women.
1886 *Wkly Manitoba Liberal* 26 Nov. 8/3: The Pink Tea held under the auspices of the Women's Christian Temperance Union on last Friday evening passed off quite pleasantly. The ladies in charge were all fittingly attired with pink caps and aprons and some of the gentleman patrons wore pink ties. **1923** STEELE *Spirit-of-Iron* 320: Hector liked to talk to the clergyman, because Northcote knew life as few men know it . . . no pink-tea preacher, shivering at the sight of sin. . . . **1952** *North Star* (Yellowknife) Dec. 2/1: That those who knew us best gave us their support is evident while the voters to whom we were only a name mentioned disparagingly at

the clique's pink teas and in their favorite publication, tended to avoid us as the plague.

pink tea social *Obs.* See **pink tea.**
1889 *Rat Portage* [Kenora] *News* (Ont.) 22 Mar. 4/2: The Ladies Aid Society of Knox Church will give a pink tea social, in the music hall, on Thursday 28th inst.

pinnated grouse† See **prairie chicken** (def. 1).
1823 FRANKLIN *Journey* 679: This species is an inhabitant of woody countries only, in which it differs from the Pinnated grouse of America, better known to the Sportsmen of the New World under the appellation of the Prairie hen and Heath hen. **1884** *Trans.Hist.& Sci. Soc.Man.* 14 13/1: It is supposed that at one time it ranged much further to the south than at present, but that it is retreating before the pinnated grouse . . . which has already entered Manitoba by the Red River Valley. **1966** *Kingston Whig-Standard* (Ont.) 21 Jan. 11/2: . . . on Manitoulin Island . . . they met our fifth grouse, the pinnated grouse, or prairie chicken. . . .

pintailed grouse See **sharp-tailed grouse.**
1819 (1823) FRANKLIN *Journey* 45: Several golden plovers, Canadian gros-beaks, cross-bills, woodpeckers, and pin-tailed grouse, were shot to-day. **1958** MACGREGOR *North-west of 16* 174: In those days, pin-tailed grouse, which we called prairie chicken, were plentiful.

pinto man [< Sp. *pinto* painted (pony) + *man*] *West, Slang* See **Métis.**
1910 FRASER *Red Meekins* 162: I guess the pinto man got Lord Happy, poor fellow.

pioneer *n.* **1†** a settler who helps to open up a part of a country.
1833 (1926) LANGTON *Early U.C.* 32: . . . such is the uncertainty in which we poor pioneers are left. **1965** *Islander* 14 Feb. 2/1: Pioneers . . . conceived the idea of a plank road between the two villages. . . .
2 a railway track-laying machine that works at the head of steel (def. 1).
1913 BICKERSTETH *Open Doors* 216: After two or three lengths of rail have been laid in this way, the pioneer gives two short hoots, the two locomotives behind give a few puffs, and the pioneer and the whole train advance some twenty or thirty feet; the pioneer then gives one hoot as a signal for the train to stop.

pioneer fringe the frontier of settlement in the North and Northwest.
1952 PUTNAM *Cdn Regions* 374/1: To the north there is a broad pioneer fringe but the transition from wilderness to agricultural landscape is quite abrupt on both eastern and western boundaries. *Ibid.* 414/1: In Saskatchewan, the agricultural settlement of the "Pioneer Fringe" has penetrated about halfway through the commercial forest belt.

pipe¹ *n.* [< Cdn F] *Fur Trade, Hist.* **1** a spell of travelling or rowing between rest periods at which a pipe was smoked; the distance that could be travelled in such a spell. See also **smoke** (def. 3b) and **spell** (def. 1).
1793 (1933) MACDONELL *Diary* 92: Leaving pointe au père we paddled two pipes and put to shore to give the men time to clean themselves, while we breakfasted. . . .
1824 (1931) MERK *Fur Trade* 37: Thence by Horses to Buffalo Dung Lake (1 pipe across) in Two Days. . . .

1908 LAUT *Conquest N.W.* II 306: "Five pipes" are the long portages. **1957** FISHER *Pemmican* 251: The distance of a portage was reckoned at so many pipes.
2 a rest period between spells of travelling. See also **smoke** (def. 3a), **smoke-up,** and **spell** (def. 2).
1806 (1960) FRASER *Letters and Journals* 193: . . . the men are better off and better pleased than if they ate a little at every Pipe. **1933** ROLYAT *Wilderness Walls* 40: The code of voyaging had made provisions for two full meals only in twenty-four hours, one early in the morning, the second on establishing camp for the night (and a "pipe" of five minutes at intervals, if one smoked).
3 a space of time. See also **smoke** (def. 3c).
1848 (1859) BALLANTYNE *Hudson's Bay* 76: The men used to row for a space of time, denominated a *pipe,* so called from the circumstance of their taking a smoke at the end of it. **1933** GATES *Five Traders* 92n: The "pipe" was one of the units of time commonly used by the Canadians. It was apparently a flexible unit, for there seems to be no agreement as to the length of time it covered. **1953** MOWERY *Mounted Police* 53: This evening we pitch off. We leave *hyas* quick—in half a pipe.

pipe² *n.* **1** See **calumet of peace.** See also **pipe of peace.**
1809 MACKENZIE *Mississouri Indians* 387: To-morrow I am to adopt one of the Shawyens for my son, and am to offer them a "pipe" on which the Gros Ventres will put all their goods and the Shawyens their horses. **1954** MACGREGOR *Shining Mountains* 157: Solemnly the pipe was passed around.

2 *Fur Trade, Obs.* **put on the pipe,** put up for trade by agreement entered into through a ceremonial smoking of a calumet.
1809 MACKENZIE *Mississouri Indians* 387: According to our manner of trade we aught to expect at least two hundred horses as we have that number of guns, besides other articles, to put on the Pipe.

pipe keeper See quote.
1925 *Beaver* Mar. 81: . . . so great was the faith that some tribes had in the sacred pipes that special tents were provided for their safety, as well as a pipe keeper, for no unchaste person might handle them. . . .

pipe of peace See **calumet of peace.** See also **pipe²** (def. 1) and **pipe-stem.**
1665 (1885) RADISSON *Fourth Voyage* 207: It was not in common pipes, but in pipes of peace and of the warrs, that they pull out very seldom, when there is occasion for heaven and earth. **1824** (1931) SIMPSON *Fur Trade* 55: They then smoke a Pipe of Peace and part with professions of Friendship but their treaties are no sooner ratified than broken as the moment the conference is over and we turn our backs they are ready to pillage each others Women and Horses and cut each others throats. **1960** BUBLITZ *Dotted Line* 34: There was the smell of burning sweet grass; and the pipe of peace was offered to dancers and guests alike.

pipe-stem *n. Obs.* See **calumet of peace.** See also **pipe of peace.**
1772 (1954) WALLACE *Pedlars* 10: Wabunashi Desired me to let you know that he Dwoe knot go to See you this Springe But Send his pipe Stem. . . . **1805** (1897) COUES *New Light* I 270: His gun and bow and arrows were lying near him, but he performed all his antics with his pipe-stem instead of his weapons. **1861** (1925) KANE *Wanderings* 23: . . . and which he desired might be represented to him, through the agent, accompanied with a pipe-stem of peace richly ornamented. **1880** MORRIS *Treaties* 230: The ceremonies, however, still went on; four pipe-stems were carried about and

presented to be stroked in token of good feeling and amity. . . .

pipestone *n.* any of various types of stone suitable for making tobacco pipes or calumets.
1761 (1901) HENRY (Elder) *Travels* 24: [The] name is derived from the pièrre a Calumet, or pipe-stone, which here interrupts the river, occasioning a fall of water. **1885** *Trans.Roy.Soc.Can.* III 2 91: His materials were the . . . black pipestone of Lake Huron; the . . . white pipestone procured on St. Joseph Island, and the . . . red pipestone of Coteau des Prairies. **1956** LEECHMAN *Native Tribes* 125: . . . tobacco pipes, which were of a soft black stone or of a bright red stone which they got from a special pipestone quarry in Minnesota.

pipe-talk *n. Obs.* a discussion with Indians solemnized by the smoking of a pipe, or calumet.
1864 *Nor'Wester* (R.R.S.) 16 Sep. 3/3: We must have some organisation—no use smoking pipes with Indians —be ready with something else, and then a pipe-talk may mean somewhat.

pipshi *n. Eskimo* See quotes. Also spelled *pipshy.*
1771 (1792) CARTWRIGHT *Journal* I 138: I was greatly pleased with their method of curing codfish without salt; this, in that state, they call *pipshy.* **1953** *Cdn Geog.Jnl* Apr. 160: [Caption] When I visited the other tents from time to time, the people would give me *pipshi* (dried fish) and I would hand round my tobacco.

pipsissewa† [pɪp'sɪsəwɑ] *n.* [< Algonk.: Cree] Prince's pine, *Chimaphila umbellata.* See quotes.
1830 (1837) *Trans.Lit.& Hist.Soc.Que.* 94: Pipsessawa [is] a small evergreen shrubby plant, six or eight inches high, with leaves of a deep green colour . . . one of the articles of Pharmacy among our aborigines. **1903** SETON *Animal Heroes* 191: Margat went out and gathered a lapful of pipsissewa to make tea, of which Corney was encouraged to drink copiously. **1930** JONES *Wild Flowers* Plate 201: PIPSISSEWA. Prince's Pine . . . June-July. **1958** *Encyc.Can.* X 346/2: Represented in Canada by . . . varieties of pipsissewa or prince's pine. . . .

pishew *n.* See **pichou.**

pishimore *n.* See **appichimon.**

piskun ['pɪskən] *n.* [< Algonk.: Blackfoot *pis'kun* deep blood kettle] *Hist.* a type of buffalo jump, *q.v.*, surrounded by steep cliffs, used by Plains Indians in slaughtering buffalo.
1928 (1936) *Cdn Hist.Rev.* XVII 69: Place-names of Alberta—Jumping Pond, west of Calgary, should properly, of course, be Jumping *Pound.* The Blackfoot original, *Nimapiskan,* contains the root form, *piskan.* **1950** STEELE *Ghosts Returning* 19: Then came the Stone-Hearts killing us with great sicknesses . . . shutting us up on reserves, like bulls in a piskun. . . . **1952** HOWARD *Strange Empire* 295: The *piskun* was a communal enterprise and the buffalo thus slain were distributed equally.

pitch *n.* **1**† a plot of land selected and occupied by a settler.
1808 (1809) GRAY *Letters* 275: As we approached the American boundary, we found a few settlements, what the Americans call a pitch. **1928** PERRY *Two Reds* 30: He cleared off a pitch and started a little farm and worked in the woods in the winter. . . .

2 a.† a sloping stretch in the course of a stream.
1811 (1897) COUES *New Light* II 207: There are many below this which cannot properly be termed rapids, being merely pitches of the river, where the water runs

over sloping beds of rocks and gravel. **1916** WOOD *Tourist's N.W.* 498: The one hundred and ten miles of river between Hinton and Whitecourt was swift, but easily navigable, except for a series of short choppy "pitches," where high waves made some danger. **1945** CALVIN *Saga* 74: . . . in the main "pitch" (drop) of Lachine rapids, for instance, the dram bent to the shape of the great waves. . . .

b. a small waterfall or rapids.
1834 (1926) LANGTON *Early U.C.* 102: You cannot take a boat upon your shoulders and carry it over any obstacle such as Cameron's Falls or the pitch at Bobcajewonunk, and in coming up even a practicable rapid in a boat you may indeed put out your whole strength. . . . **1872** DASHWOOD *Chiploquorgan* 20: The salmon here stand almost always on the ledges of rocks at the top of the rapids and "pitches", as a small fall is called. Some of these pitches are too steep to pole up but most of them can be run. . . . **1946** FERGUSON *Mink, Mary and Me* 23: At the first rapid—a mean, rock-studded seventy-yard pitch—Mary caught her breath and exclaimed: "Surely, you can't take the canoe up there!"

3 *Lumbering, Hist.* of water in a stream, the point of greatest volume, as the peak of the spring runoff.
1883 FRASER *Shanty* 271: It is an anxious time . . . for upon a favorable and early start, with a good "pitch of water," may depend the whole success of the "drive" . . . If the ice "hangs on" too long the water may fall— in fact, it is falling every day after a certain pitch. . . .

pitch *v.* **1** travel from one camping place to another; move on, especially in stages, camping en route. See also **pitching, pitching track,** and **pitch on.** Also *pitch along.*
1691 (1929) KELSEY *Papers* 9: Wee pitched again & Gott to the River Afore[d] where they appointed to meet us. **1774** (1934) HEARNE *Journal* 127: . . . they are to Pitch this way as soon as Possible. **1857** (1863) PALLISER *Journals* 45: . . . we determined to pitch along the base of the hill to the westward. . . . **1929** MOBERLY *When Fur Was King* 96: Little remaining for the men to do I paid off four of the Iroquois and sent them to join their families, who were pitching along from Lac Ste. Anne.

2 *Fur Trade, Obs.* See **pitch off** (def. 1).
1743 (1949) ISHAM *Observations* 19: to pitch or go from the fort &c. En ko po me pe chu. **1754** (1907) HENDAY *Journal* 336: 16 tents of different Natives pitched from us different ways. **1779** (1952) *Cumberland House Jnls* 279: Mr. Hansom informs me that they are all pitched away towards the Barren Ground. . . .

pitcher plant an herb, *Sarracenia purpurea,* whose leaves form into pitcher-shaped receptacles that entrap insects, adopted as the floral emblem of Newfoundland. See also **Indian cup.**
1819 ANSPACH *Hist.Nfld* 362: Another still more remarkable plant, found in the woods of Newfoundland, is the *Saracenia,* commonly called side-saddle flower, or pitcher-plant. **1898** CONNOR *Black Rock* 295: Our days were spent driving about among the hills, or strolling through the maple woods, or down into the swamp, where the pitcher plants and the swamp lilies and the marigold waved above the deep moss. **1965** *Maclean's* 17 Apr. 23/2: Newfoundland: The Pitcher Plant was recommended by Queen Victoria, adopted in 1954.

pitch-hole *n.* **1** *Ont. and Que.* See **cahot.**
1902 CONNOR *Glengarry* 86: . . . the deep snow packed hard into a smooth track . . . except where here and there pitch-holes or *cahots* came. **1924** BLAKE *Chez Nous* 51: He is not over-considerate, is the road-master; he puts you to no end of trouble for a trifle of a drift; and there are pitch-holes opposite his own place, too. **1946** LOWER *Colony to Nation* 63n: The Canadian peasants made a short one-horse sleigh that pounded and made pitch-holes—*cahots*—in the winter roads. The English began to object to this practice, but the more they tried to get the French to change, the larger the pitch-holes became.
2 a deep pothole (def. 2a) (especially in a road or trail) that causes a vehicle to pitch and toss.
1936 CROSS *Cross Roads* 106: So Charlie's horses jogged on with us along a road that was three feet above the normal altitude . . . and into pitch holes that jarred one's innards terribly. **1957** *Kingston Whig-Standard* (Ont.) 19 Sep. 25/5: . . . one looks back to the horse-drawn cutter of yesteryear . . . as we drove through the numerous pitch holes which formed between McMichael's Hill and the city limits. . . . **1962** DICKIE *Great Golden Plain* 288: . . . all must be loaded skillfully so as not to slide or roll off as the cat train rocks and plunges over the hummocks and pitch holes in the ice and snow roads.

pitch in *Fur Trade* bring in a season's fur catch to a post for crediting against debt (def. 1); visit a post to replenish supplies. Cp. **pitching-off debt.**
1934 GODSELL *Arctic Trader* 68: As soon as the Indians had all "pitched in" we packed the furs and pressed them into ninety-pound bales for convenience in transportation. **1956** KEMP *Northern Trader* 127: There would be the Christmas and the Easter seasons, the season when our trapping families "pitched-in" to the post.

pitching *n. Obs.* a stage in a journey when camp is made. See also **pitch,** *v.* (def. 1).
1792 (1934) FIDLER *Journal* 26 Nov.: Very little wood this pitching.

pitching-off debt *Fur Trade* the debt (def. 1) run up by a trapper at a trading post before leaving for the hunting grounds. See also **pitch off** (def. 1).
1956 KEMP *Northern Trader* 117: I showed him [an Indian] his account and told him that with his "pitching off" debt he would owe not less than a thousand dollars.

pitching track or **trail** *North and Northwest* a trail used over many years by Indians moving from one region to another. See also **pitch,** *v.* (def. 1).
1858 (1860) HIND *Assiniboine Exped.* II 51: The term "pitching track" is applied to an Indian trail from one part of the country to another. **1895** SOMERSET *Muskeg* 83: The pitching trail by which for the first few days after leaving Dunvegan we had travelled did not take us far. **1908** MAIR *Mackenzie Basin* 69: As a rule they [the half-breeds] had been born on the "pitching track," in the forest, or on the prairies. . . . **1929** MOBERLY *When Fur Was King* 53: . . . "pitching trails" [were so called] for the reason that whole camps travelled them and pitched . . . where feed was plentiful. . . .

pitch off 1 *Fur Trade* set out on a journey or a hunting expedition. See also **pitch,** *v.* (def. 2), **pitching-off debt,** and **pitch up.**

1825 (1950) OGDEN *Journals* 81: I am informed 35 Tents have pitched off some days Since in quest of Beaver. . . . **1913** COWIE *Adventurers* 293: Being too inexperienced . . . to find the main trail on which the people had pitched off, I wasted some time following different tracks. . . . **1957** *Beaver* Spring 30: Early in the fall, some "pitch-off" great distances—to the Wathamun River and beyond, eight or ten days north from the post.
2 *Obs.* shoot down.
1832 (1953) RADCLIFF *Letters* 157: Our alarm was that they [a herd of deer] would run over *us;* but they stopped short, and we pitched off two of them. Having bled and collected together those that we have shot, we parted company. . . .

pitch on *Obs.* See **pitch,** *v.* (def. 1).
1859 KANE *Wanderings* 419: . . . they were a party of 1500 warriors from 1200 lodges, who were then "pitching on" towards Fort Edmonton; that is they were making short journeys, and pitching their tents on towards Edmonton, leaving few behind capable of bearing arms.

pitch pine any of several species of pine that yield pitch, especially *Pinus rigida* found in parts of Eastern Canada. See also **cypress** (def. 2).
1827 (1829) MACTAGGART *Three Years* I 172: Let the local names be given, as . . . pitch pine. . . . **1887** (1888) LEES & CLUTTERBUCK *British Columbia* 308: . . . all that is needful [is] to keep a supply of "pitch-pine" chips ready. **1958** *Native Trees* 18: Under the most favourable conditions the pitch pine will reach a height of 60 feet and a diameter of 2 feet, usually, however, it is a small tree about 30 feet high and 6 to 8 inches in diameter.

pitch up See **pitch off** (def. 1).
1922 *Beaver* May 8/1: I sent word to the Iroquois advising them to "pitch up" in different directions hunting, and when short of ammunition or other supplies to come to Jasper House.

pitlamp *n. B.C.* a kind of jacklight (def. 1), so called because of its resemblance to a miner's pitlamp. See also **pitlamp,** *v.* (def. 1).
1967 *Vancouver Province* 21 Feb. 19/6: Stanton said his association wants to commend the fisheries department for banning "pit lamps" but believes the order should be made permanent.

pitlamp *v. Esp.B.C.* **1** engage in pitlamping, *q.v.*
1967 *Wildlife Rev.* Mar. 27/2: Frank Greenfield . . . once jailed a man for pitlamping deer. . . .
2 *Slang* dismiss from employment, especially because of union activity.
1966 *Sun* (Vancouver) 30 May 30A/3: A pit-lamped logger was one who had just been fired.

pitlamper *n. Esp.B.C.* a person who engages in pitlamping, *q.v.*
1967 *Wildlife Rev.* Mar. 27/2: Frank caught the pitlamper in the act [and] turned him over to the police at Nanaimo. . . .

pitlamping *n. B.C.* See **jacklighting.** See also **pitlamp,** *n.* and *v.* (def. 1).
1924 SHERMAN *Nature Stories* 61: Pit-lamping and hunting with dogs, in addition to natural enemies . . . have been the cause of its rapid disappearance. **1957** BARRATT *Coronets* 45: "That there Blotton had me arrested for pitlamping." **1963** *Sun* (Vancouver) 27 Sep. 33/8: Five Salmon Arm hunters were fined a

total of $2,500 and costs Thursday in police court on charges of pit-lamping (using a light to attract game at night).

placotte *n.* [< Cdn F < F *plats de côtes* cutlets] *Obs.* rib(s); cutlet.
1800 (1897) COUES *New Light* I 84: The grass was long and I lay quiet until a favorable opportunity offered as he [a buffalo] presented his placotte. **1806** *Ibid.* I 343: They have a peculiar way of roasting meat. A placotte is suspended from the roof of the hut exactly over the fire.... **1953** MOWERY *Mounted Police* 38: An Indian squaw, too old to excite quips from the crowd, was peddling fresh buffalo *placottes*.

plain(s) *n.* **1** See **prairie** (def. 2a).
1775 (1951) *Sask.Jnls* 19: In the Afternoon a Canoe with fourteen of the Pedlers men arrived on their way to the upper Settlement in Sas-kach-i-wan River, to be sent into the Plains to be supported.... **1784-1812** (1916) THOMPSON *Narrative* 183: By a Plain I mean lands bearing grass, but too short for the Scythe; where the grass is long enough for the Scythe, and of which Hay can be made, I name meadows. **1859** *Nor'Wester* (R.R.S.) 28 Dec. 2/5: The prey they fail to find elsewhere is supplied by the buffalo slaughterings on the Plains, where thousands of indifferent carcasses are left every summer and autumn by the hunters. **1958** *Time* (Cdn ed.) 25 Aug. 10/2: ... these scrubs [wild horses] of the plains are mostly too runty, too unreliable and too fierce to slip profitably into any man's harness or saddle.
2 *Hist.* See **opening.**
1799 *U.C.Gaz.* (York [Toronto]) 21 Sep. 4/3: Part of these valuable lands lie in the plains and part in the woods. **1825** (1832) PICKERING *Inquiries* 41: It is a dry sandy soil, thinly wooded with low whiteoaks, and is what is here termed plains. **1926** LANGTON *Early U.C.* xxxix: At this time ... there was but one inhabitant of Peterborough [1825], Adam Scott, who had a mill on the Plains....

plain(s) buffalo a species of buffalo (def. 2) native to the great plains, a smaller species than the wood buffalo. See also **prairie buffalo.**
1890 *Trans.Roy.Soc.Can.* VIII 2 96: The annual migration of the plain buffalo at one time an interesting feature of its life and movement.... **1963** *Maclean's* 23 Feb. 42/3: And can the decline be stopped or must the barren lands be swept clear of people, leaving the few remaining caribou to become a curiosity like the plains buffalo.

plain(s) grizzly *Hist.* a large bear, *Ursus horribilis,* once found on the prairies.
[**1827** (1914) DOUGLAS *Journal* 269: Saw a huge grisly bear ... and a number of small plain wolves.] **1959** *Town Crier* 13 Oct. 5/3: The huge beasts are believed to be remnants of the plains grizzlies which once moved with the buffalo herds across the prairies and were thought to be extinct before the turn of the century. **1965** SYMINGTON *Tuktu* 43: The barren-ground grizzly is similar to the plains grizzly, a buffalo killer common on the prairies before settlement.

plain ground *Obs.* See **prairie country.**
1777 (1951) *Sask.Jnls* 117: Then they [Indians] pitched away, and have been moving in the Plain Ground ever Since.

plain(s) hunt *Hist.* See **buffalo hunt.**
1861 *Nor'Wester* (R.R.S.) 15 Aug. 3/2: When the plain-hunt fails, the farmer's produce is entirely relied on; when the crops fail, the hunters find ample market; but when both succeed, the market is at once overstocked. **1890** *Trans.Roy.Soc.Can.* VIII 2 100: Immense numbers ... had been annually slaughtered in the great plain hunt of the Red River half-breeds, a system ... organized early in this century, and continued in full force down to about 1869, after which it began to languish.

plain(s) hunter *Hist.* See **buffalo hunter.**
1831 (1963) MACLEOD & MORTON *Cuthbert Grant* 108: The plains hunters have had a very successful season and the quantity of [country] provisions they have brought home is immense. **1860** *Nor'Wester* (R.R.S.) 28 Apr. 4/5: Its population is about 1,200, exclusive of the plain-hunters, who reside there only occasionally. **1930** ROLYAT *Fort Garry* 59: The Desjardins were quite wealthy plain hunters. . . .

Plain(s) Indian a member of any of several tribes of Indians inhabiting the prairies, as the Blackfoot, Assiniboine, and Plains Cree. See also **horse Indian** (def. 2) and **Prairie Indian.**
1697 (1929) KELSEY *Papers* 88: ... about four a clock some plain indians arrived at the fort.... **1844** (1955) LEFROY *Magnetic North* 142: The plains Indians are in a state of warfare, and there is a certain degree of danger in a single boat or canoe passing through their country. **1878** *Sask.Herald* (Battleford, N.W.T.) 23 Sep. 1/4: He considers the success of this attempt of the Plain Indians to settle down to the routine of the whiteman's life ... as most successful and gratifying. **1957** *Beaver* Spring 55/1: For the pedestrian Plains Indians, without a horse, the dog was a beast of burden.

plain(s) hare See **jack-rabbit.**
1963 SYMONS *Many Trails* 17: [Cottontails are] quite different from the long-legged plains hares and the varying hares, which we miscall snowshoe rabbits.

plainsman *n. Hist.* a man who lived on or was familiar with the prairies in early times.
1801 (1920) *Beaver* Dec. 7/1: Jas. Ruchan began yesterday to make plainsmen's coat for Ind.... **1887** *Senate Journal* XXI App. 74: I have heard plainsmen, who were all their lives on the plain, say that it is impossible to have a cross between the buffalo and domesticated cattle. **1939** *Cdn Hist.Rev.* XX 286: After a careful examination of the two, I confess that my faith in the average plainsmen's tradition—whether red or white— is very weak. **1963** MACLEOD & MORTON *Cuthbert Grant* 95: He would use this skilled plainsman against the American traders who were making incursions on Hudson's Bay Company territory.

plains provisions *Obs.* See 1950 quote.
1950 *Beaver* Sep. 5/1: Even in Kildonan, where agriculture was most highly developed, the purchase of "plains provisions" (buffalo meat) was a necessary part of providing the means of existence. **1963** MACLEOD & MORTON *Cuthbert Grant* 1: His buffalo hunters supplied them with "plains provisions"—practically the only food obtainable in the country.

plain(s) wolf *Obs.* See **coyote** (def. 1). See also **prairie wolf.**
1827 (1914) DOUGLAS *Journal* 269: Saw a huge grisly bear ... and a number of small plain wolves.

plan-heap *n. Hist.* in clearing land, a planned

procedure for felling trees for burning (def. 1) in such a way that as many as possible fall near or across each other so that an efficient burn results. Cp. **piling.**

1825 (1916) SELLAR *Narrative* 97: Jabez had shown us how to make plan-heaps, and we so fell the trees, which will save hard work when we come to burn. **1853** STRICKLAND *Canada West* I 95: If you succeed in getting a good burn for your fallow, the chances are, if your plan-heaps are well made, that they will be mostly consumed. **1905** CARTER *Dundas* 47: Much skill could be displayed in felling the timber by causing as many trees as possible to fall beside or over one another so as to form what were called "plan heaps."

plank boat *Hist.* a rude, flat-bottomed boat made of rough boards.

1958 *Edmonton Jnl* 24 June 3 2/2: Rafts, canoes, plank boats and paddle-wheelers plied the only route—the Yukon River and its tributaries.

planked road *Hist.* See **plank road.**

1849 *Journal and Express* (Hamilton, C.W.) 22 June 3/7: For Sale, a farm of 220 acress—100 cleared, Good Dwelling, Orchard, Barns, &c., situated 99 miles from Hamilton, on the Planked road, and 44 from the Grand River. **1956** ANDREWS *Glory Days* 23: [Caption] Planked road of A. & M. Logging Co. Ltd . . . shown running from timber to log dumps and around point.

A Kwakiutl plank house

plank house among Coast Indians, a long rectangular communal dwelling, built of cedar, housing several families, and used at times for ceremonial affairs. See also **longhouse** (def. 2), **ranch²** (def. 2a), **rancherie** (def. 2), and **ranch-house²** (def. 1).

1952 DUFF *Upper Stalo* 47: My information on Stalo plank-house types adds very little that is new to our knowledge. . . . **1955** JENNESS *Indians of Canada* 339: Each Bella Coola village contained from two to twenty plank houses built in a row facing the water front; and each house sheltered from two to ten families.

plank road *Hist.* a road made of rough-hewn planks laid across timbers running end-to-end at right angles to the planks. See also **planked road, plankway,** and **timber road** (def. 1).

1839 *Western Herald* (Windsor, U.C.) 16 May 95/1: On Wednesday we had the pleasure of a five or six continous miles on a Plank road, leading from Toronto to Kingston, which we understand is to be carried on as far as the Rouge. **1848** *Sun* (Picton, C.W.) 26 Sep. 2/5: Planks roads, it is said, were first made in Russia; and their first trial in America was in Canada, where they were made by Lord Sydenham, who from

a long residence in Russia, had become well acquainted with them. **1905** SCHERCK *Pen Pictures* 57: A plank road ran between Trenton and Belleville, a distance of twelve miles. **1965** *Islander* 14 Feb. 2/1: And in the Queen Charlotte Islands there is nothing left of a 14-mile plank road built more than 40 years ago.

plank sidewalk a sidewalk built of planks; a boardwalk.

1844 *Kingston Chron.and Gaz.* (C.W.) 3 Oct. 1/6: The first mile of Macadamized road ever made in Canada West, was that on Yonge Street, North of Toronto, by the same Engineer who first projected plank roads and plank side walks, which have since been so extensively adopted. **1914** BINDLOSS *Intriguers* 72: Following the deeply rutted street, which had a narrow, plank sidewalk, they reached the Imperial Hotel. . . . **1958** *Fisherman* 10 Oct. 6/2: . . . plank sidewalks were built [in Barkerville, B.C.] high above the muddy road.

plank village a village in which the buildings are made of wooden planks.

1965 *Globe and Mail* (Toronto) 26 May 3/1: That is the difference between the Indian district and the white people's district, two ends of the same plank village squeezed between a river and a swamp. . . .

plankway *n. Hist.* See **plank road.**

1849 ALEXANDER *L'Acadie* I 141: The plank-way, on which is the travelling for rough-shod horses only, is 16 feet wide. **1965** *Islander* 14 Feb. 2/2: Yet in spite of these hazards this 14-mile plankway may well hold a record: for its 30-year history is unmarred by death or injury.

plant *v. North, Obs.* See 1869 quote.

*a*1869 (1942) KENNICOTT *Journal* 99: When a sled can not keep up and take its proper place in the brigade at each spell, it is said to be "planted," which is considered something very disgraceful. **1896** RUSSELL *Far North* 97: I had traveled over eight hundred miles, on my own snow-shoes, in company with different parties of natives, each of which had tried to "plant" me.

plantation *n.* 1† *Hist.* See 1927 quote.

1620 WHITBOURNE *Discovrse* A3: The purpose thereof, is, with your Gracious allowance, to beget a disposition in all your Maiesties Subiects, for a Plantation in the New-found-land, grounded vpon reason of industry, both generally and particularly profitable to the Vndertakers and Posterities. **1793** REEVES *Hist.Nfld* 20: Upon full consideration of all these circumstances, their Lordships proposed, that all plantations in Newfoundland should be discouraged; and, in order thereunto, that the commander of the convoy should have commission to declare to all the planters, to come voluntarily away. **1842** BONNYCASTLE *Newfoundland* II 162: . . . all the original English settlements in America having received the official designation of plantations. . . . [for full quote see **planter** (def. 1a)] **1927** WALLACE *Windships* 27: Prior to 1860, vessels constructed in British North America were registered as being "British Plantation Built"— the term "Plantation" meaning "Colony."

2† *Obs.* a farm or holding of farm land.

1764 *Quebec Gaz.* 23 Aug. 4/2: The said Seigneurie [is] capable of containing upwards of 500 Plantations in more than 3 Concessions Depth on each Side the River. . . . **1837** *Times* (Halifax) 18 July 229/3: Convenient Plantation Lots were laid out in the most eligible situations, and advertised for Sale at Public Auction.

3 *Fur Trade, Obs.* the land and buildings of a

Hudson's Bay Company.

1696 (1929) KELSEY *Papers* 47: Our people shot 2 Geese
near ye plantation. **1773** (1908) COCKING *Journal* 118:
But what I am most surprised at, they [Montreal traders]
keep no watch in the night; even when the Natives
are lying on their plantation. **1775** (1951) *Sask.Jnls* 14:
The Men [at Cumberland House] employed Cutting &
Setting up Firewood in Piles to clear the Plantation. . . .
1923 *Beaver* Sep. 453: Beef, potatoes, and pork were
raised on the "plantation," as it [York Factory] was
called in those days. **1941** *Ibid.* Sep. 38/2: Plantation
—The first establishments were referred to as such.
History does not record if there were any piccaninnies
on deck.

4 *Lumbering* a reforested tract of land in an area
previously cut over.

1928 PERRY *Two Reds* 11: Derosier . . . agreed not to set
foot upon the Harris plantations. . . . **1963** MCKINNON
Forest Activities 2 13: A ten-year-old plantation of
Douglas fir. These trees were two years old when
planted in the spring of 1948 and twelve years old
(twelve growing seasons) when photographed in the
winter of 1957.

planter *n. Nfld and Lab.* **1 a.** *Obs.* a settler in the
colony, or plantation (def. 1), of Newfoundland.

1620 WHITBOURNE *Discovrse* 17: And it may be feared,
that such a Planter, growing to h2ue strength, your
subiects shall be (if not prohibited) yet at least hindered
of their trading and fishing there, or constrained to take
their fish of the Planters, and at their prices, which may
fall ovt to be a notable differuice [sic] to your Maiestie,
and the vtter ouerthrow of your subiects trade hither.
1626 VAUGHAN *Golden Fleece* III 15: And likewise the
Planters themselues may fish for Cod there a moneth
before our Englishmen can arriue thither, and also
after they are gone they may fish almost all the yeare
after. **1712** (1907) *U of T Stud.Hist.& Econ.* II: Planters
being very backward in paying he got only one hundred
quintals of fish this season. **1793** REEVES *Hist.Nfld* 15:
His majesty ordered . . . That no planter should cut
down any wood, or should plant within six miles of the
sea shore. **1842** BONNYCASTLE *Newfoundland* II 162:
Next, the middle-man or planter, as he is most absurdly
called,—probably from all the original English
settlements in America having received the official
designation of plantations; but the Newfoundland
planter has had in reality as little to do with cultivating
the soil as an Esquimaux.

b. See 1861 and 1937 quotes.

1714 (1793) REEVES *Hist.Nfld* 89: By this irregular
proceeding the strongest man gets all; and the rest of
the creditors nothing; so that the next year a planter is
forced to hire himself out for a servant. **1793** *Ibid.* 39:
He expresses astonishment, how the planters and
inhabitants could procure hands from England to fish
for them, considering how ill they used them.
1841 *Nfld House of Assembly Jnl App.* 25: Petitioners
deeply regret the situation they are placed in, as regards
the Merchants, Planters, and themselves, in the persons
of Suppliers, Masters, and Servants, for want of an
established law to protect [them]. **1861** DE BOILIEU
Labrador Life 32: The man who prosecutes, or
speculates in, the fishery, is called the Planter; and his
mode is generally to hire his men by the voyage, giving
them food and lodging, with the use of a boat, for half
their labour, retaining, however, the cod-livers for
himself. **1937** DEVINE *Folklore* 37: Those immigrants
who settled in Newfoundland and had means enough
to build their own fishing rooms, "ship" men, and issue
supplies to other fishermen, were called "planters". . . .
1958 *Evening Telegram* (St. John's) 5 May 3/3: One

important aspect of the fishery is that young
Newfoundlanders are now shipping with Labrador
skippers, a complete reversal of former years. These
"planters" . . . have their own gear . . . including power
operated pumps in their premises and need workers to
make up their crews on share and wage basis.

2 a. a small trader.

1771 (1792) CARTWRIGHT *Journal* I 156: I sent
Shuglawina on shore there, with a letter to Guy's father,
who is a planter, lives in that place, and keeps several
cows. **1808** (1890) MCKENZIE *King's Posts* 407: The
[Labrador] coast is inhabited by Esquimaux and a
mixture of English, Irish and Canadians, commonly
called "planters," who trade with the Eskimaux and
carry on salmon and cod fisheries along the Straits of
Belisle. **1905** WALLACE *Labrador Wild* 37: The coast
people who occasionally trade in a small way are known
as "planters."

b. a businessman who provides advances to
fishermen in return for the catch.

1875 *North Star* (St. John's) 18 Dec. 3/6: The
Inspector, therefore, who does work in a slovenly
fashion inflicts injury, not only upon a particular
merchant or supplier, but upon merchants, planters,
fishermen and the whole community. **1905** DUNCAN
Grenfell's Parish 73: The "planter," who advances the
salt to cure the fish, takes the catch at the end of the
season, giving in exchange provisions at an incredible
profit. **1918** GRENFELL *Labrador Doctor* 137: The planters,
or men who give advances to come and fish around the
mouth of Hamilton Inlet, were to ship their fish on a
steamer coming direct from England and returning
direct. . . . **1964** *Nfld Qtly* Spring 27/1: . . . sharemen
were and are sometimes chargeable with a part of
certain items . . . when a Labradorman's voyage of fish
has to be "made," i.e. sun dried, by the planters. . . .

c. *Obs.* See **freeman** (def. 1a).

1842 *Trans.Lit.& Hist. Soc.Que.* IV 87: The Planters
or freemen, are composed of persons who have come
out in the service of the different mercantile
establishments [sic] and at the expiration of their
engagements have remained in the country, hunting and
fishing, on their own account, receiving the necessary
supplies from the nearest establishment, and giving in
the produce of their hunt, &c., in return.

d. See **liveyere** (def. 1).

1905 WALLACE *Labrador Wild* 37: In Hamilton Inlet,
west of Rigolet, all of the trappers and fishermen are
called planters. **1947** TANNER *Outlines* II 727: The
resident white fishermen of the outer coast are . . . also
termed "planters" or "settlers." [for full quote see
liveyere (def. 1)]

e. a fisherman who visits the coast during the fishing
season.

1944 *Beaver* Sep. 21/1: . . . more fishing crews arrive
for the summer. These fishermen are known as
"Planters." They have their homes and fishing premises
scattered around various communities and at the end
of the season . . . they heave for home. **1956** FAY *Life
and Labour* 230: The Transient or "Visiting" Fishermen
. . . are of two types 1. The planters or "stationers," who
fish from the shore. 2. The "floaters" or "schoonermen."

Planter *n. Hist.* See **New England Planter.**

1952 PUTNAM *Cdn Regions* 89/2: The "Planters"
established agricultural colonies in 1760-1 at Truro . . .
Annapolis . . . and Sackville, for the most part on lands

formerly occupied by the exiled Acadians. **1957** WRIGHT *Blomidon Rose* 94: Consider, for instance, this word Planters, which is used for the New Englanders who came to settle in the Minas Basin area in the year 1760.

plastic (or plastic-foam) igloo a prefabricated igloo, intended to be used in the Arctic as a more permanent substitute for the traditional snowhouse. **1957** *Camsell Arrow* Christmas 65/2: Included in the Howe's cargo is a new plastic igloo, which will be tested to determine whether it is more practical than the traditional snow house. **1957** *Kingston Whig-Standard* (Ont.) 19 Sep. 3/3: And the plastic-foam igloo—which like all igloos resembles a large overturned mixing bowl—also lets light in.

platform skin *Arctic* an animal skin used to cover a sleeping platform or ledge in an igloo. **1946** *Beaver* Mar. 36/2: . . . all snow adhering to the sleeping-robes, platform skins, and clothing was carefully beaten off. . . .

platter *n.* usually, **game of the platter.** See 1792 and 1921 quotes. See also **bowl and beans** and **pagessan.**
☛ *Variations of this ancient game are widely played among the Indians to the East of the Rockies, lahal, q.v., being usual among the Indians of British Columbia. Other games of chance played among the Indians include the hand game, the moccasin game, the stick game, and the two-stick game, qq.v. Writers referring to these games do not always use the terms unambiguously; nor do they describe the many variations clearly.*
1760 JEFFERYS *Descr.New France* 76: This game, which shall be called the game of the Platter, can only be played between two persons, each of which has six or eight little bones, somewhat resembling, both in size and figure, the stones of apricots. [**1792** (1801) MACKENZIE *Voyages* 142: The instruments of it consist of a platter or dish made of wood or bark and six round or square but flat pieces of metal, wood, or stone, whose sides or surfaces are of different colours. These are put into the dish, and after being for some time shaken together are thrown into the air and received again in the dish with considerable dexterity, when by the number that are turned up of the same mark or colour the game is regulated. If there should be equal numbers, the throw is not reckoned; if two or four, the platter changes hands.] **1800** (1897) COUES *New Light* I 153: . . . I remained an hour with the worthless vagabonds, who do nothing but play at the game of the platter. **1921** HAWORTH *Trailmakers* 70: The quarrel in this instance arose out of a gambling game called "the platter," of which many of these western Indians were extremely fond. It was played with a platter or dish of wood or bark and with six round or square flat pieces of metal, wood, or stone, whose sides were painted different colors.

played out 1 of a mine or goldfield, worked out; exhausted of minerals.
1864 (1962) ANDERSON *Sawney's Letters* 8: . . . "Freend, be advised, and turn aboot,/For Cariboo is noo 'play'd out!'." **1880** GORDON *Mountain and Prairie* 166: When the Cassiar mines were opened, and Omenica was "played out," he turned back to Fort St. James. **1958** ELLIOTT *Quesnel* 54: Omineca [mines] played out. Fortunately Cassiar was discovered in 1874, but it too had seen its best days by 1876.

2 of animals or men, worn out; over-fatigued. See also **play out.**
1888 (1890) ST. MAUR *Impressions* 193: His pony was about "played out." **1956** KEMP *Northern Trader* 68: Another night camp seemed unbearable, but what could we do with a couple of played-out horses?

playoff *n.* one of a series of games played by two or more teams in a league to determine which is the champion.
1939 *Beaver* June 25/2: He had a son with the St. Boniface Seals and at that time was very interested in the fact that they were in the Dominion Junior Hockey Championship play-offs. **1965** *Kingston Whig-Standard* (Ont.) 23 Apr. 10/8: It was Ferguson's second tally of the series and his third of the playoffs.

play out of animals or men, become worn out or over-fatigued. See also **played out** (def. 2).
1897 TYRRELL *Sub-Arctics* 249: When we . . . were in the neighborhood of a fishing station at the mouth of Berens River, poor Pierre played out. . . . **1924** FLAHERTY *Eskimo Friends* 93: The dogs almost played out before we reached the crest.

plaza *n.* See **shopping plaza.**
1959 *Ottawa Citizen* 11 July 21/7: Two plazas with parking facilities and offices for Customs and Immigration and bridge authority offices are to be built. . . . **1965** *Kingston Whig-Standard* (Ont.) 4 Jan. 13/6: Police have gleaned a further description . . . from witnesses who had seen the man at the plaza prior to the murder.

plew *n.* See **plu.**

ploughing match a competition among farmers to determine who is the most skilful at ploughing. Also spelled *plowing match.*
1909 ROSS *Hist.of Zorra* 57: Besides the annual meet in October, prizes were awarded . . . at plowing matches. **1927** DICKIE *How Canada Grew Up* 47: The Society organised fairs and ploughing matches, fenced the burying-ground, bought a pall for use at funerals. **1945** HAIG *Brave Harvest* 57: Even plowing matches came into the picture.

P.L.S. *Obs. or Hist.* Provincial Land Surveyor.
1899 GARDNER *Names* 493: This township was named after James Dickson, P.L.S. **1909** HUNTER *Simcoe County* I 46: In order to have it made right, several of them applied to the County Council, which sent a memorial to the Lieut-Governor-in-Council to have it done, recommending Henry Creswicke, P.L.S., to make and complete the survey.

plu [plu] *n.* **-s** or **-es.** [< Cdn F < F *pelu* skin, pelt] Also spelled *plew, plue,* and (erroneously) *plus,* the last form being a plural form, used along with *plews, plues. Fur Trade, Hist.* **1** a prime beaver skin or other fur of equivalent value. See also **made beaver** (def. 1).
☛ *The plu was the standard unit of value used in the fur country by the North West Company, the made beaver being the equivalent unit with the Hudson's Bay Company.*
1800 (1933) MCLEOD *Diary* 143: The Iroquois . . . Makes us signes he & his 7 friends have 400 Plues. **1804** (1933) FARIES *Diary* 218: In the afternoon Young Jourdin arrived . . . with 27 Plus and left as many at the lodge. **1826** (1931) MERK *Fur Trade* 280: The Servants attached to the Sanke Expedition brought Two thousand one

hundred and eighty eight plus in Beaver weighing Two thousand eight hundred and seventeen pounds, and Seventy nine plus in Otters. **1963** *Albertan* (Calgary) 4 May 8/7: All other skins were graded in value to the beaver standard of the "plus" [sic].

2 a unit of value of one made beaver applied to goods other than furs.
1794 (1889) MACDONELL *Journal* 288: Tranquille bought a slave woman—i.e., taken in war . . . for two horses and 20 pluëz in goods. **1811** (1889) WENTZEL *Letters* 106: At this date we received only seven plues of fresh meat and were upon this little suply no less than eight months, of course it was but two meals.

plug *v. Slang* arrange the kernels (of grain) in such a way that inferior or frozen grain is concealed and an unduly high grade allowed by the elevator man.
1910 MCCLUNG *Second Chance* 206: The temptation to "plug" the wheat was strong, and so much of it was being done that the elevator men were suspicious of every one.

plus or **plues** [pluz] *n.pl.* See **plu.**

pocamogan *n.* See **pogamagan.**

pocket borough† a riding which is traditionally so strong in support of a given party that the candidate running there is virtually certain of being elected.
1927 DICKIE *How Canada Grew Up* 154: He [Baldwin] had a "pocket borough", as it was called, a safe Reform seat in the fourth riding of York. **1953** LEBOURDAIS *Nation of North* 70: Then, in the conscious rectitude of one with the power and wealth of the Hudson's Bay Company behind him, sitting himself in a pocket-borough, he indulged in a few homilies concerning political morality. **1963** *Press* Sep. 6: When McKenzie King was defeated in Prince Albert they found a "pocket-borough" for him in Glengarry.

pocket-pop *n. Fur Trade, Slang* a pocket pistol.
1825 (1918) DAVIDSON *North West Co.* 302: Mr. H . . . lost no time in firing one of his pocket-pops . . . and he succeeded in wounding the infamous Scoundrel in the groin. . . .

pogamagan *n.* [< Algonk.: Ojibwa or Cree] *Obs.* See **casse-tête** and picture. Various spellings.
*c*1787 (1916) THOMPSON *Narrative* 330: . . . they dashed at the Peeagans, and with their stone Pukamoggan knocked them on the head. **1789** (1801) MACKENZIE *Voyages* 37: The pogamagan is made of the horn of the rein-deer, the branches being all cut off, except that which forms the extremity. *c*1804 (1890) GRANT *Sauteux Indians* 332: In war, they use the pocomagan, a very destructive weapon; it consists of a piece of wood, a foot and a half long, curved at one end, with a big heavy knob, in which is fixed a piece of long sharp iron. **1859** KANE *Wanderings* 304: . . . one chief . . . dashed madly into the midst of his enemies, dealing death around him with his poke-a-mau-gun or war club. **1912** (1913) HODGE & WHITE *Indians of Canada* 107/1: [The] carved, often flattened, club . . . includes the flat curved club with a knobbed head (Alg. *pogamoggan,* Fr. *cassetête*) belonging to some Sioux, and to the Chippewa, Menominee, and other timber Algonquians.

pogey or **pogy** ['pogi] *n.* [originally, hobo slang for "workhouse"].
☛ *Though the ultimate origin of this term is obscure, it became current in Canada and was in general use throughout the Depression in a variety of applications, all related to the widespread public-relief programs.*

Slang **1** a hostel providing lodging for indigent persons at public expense, supervised by the local relief agency.
1936 MACKENZIE *Living Rough* 269: I was in the Pogey a couple of nights. It stinks. **1959** *Maclean's* 15 Aug. 21/1: . . . lean and hungry alley-cat men swung down from the freights and headed for a fifteen-cent mission meal or the innumerable pogies and scratch houses for a ten-cent cot.

2 a. a local relief centre; welfare office.
1936 MACKENZIE *Living Rough* 269: You ought to see the lousy Pogey (relief centre) they have here [Toronto]. **1953** LEBOURDAIS *Nation of North* 211: Thousands of self-respecting workmen, bricklayers, stone-masons, carpenters, machinists, and other artisans, sat at home while their wives made the dreary pilgrimage to the "pogie." **1955** BIRNEY *Long Table* 291: . . . the drab files would dwindle in front of the Pogey and swell outside the Recruiting Office.

b. food, clothing, shelter, etc. provided for the indigent by the public relief agencies.
1955 BIRNEY *Long Table* 190: "I'll never get a Pogey pair [of shoes] unless we raid the goddam joint." **1959** *Citizen* 10 Dec. 10/2: It will be far less of a burden for the taxpayer to provide work and wages clearing up the backlog of unfinished public works than to dole out "pogy" to the unemployed who have exhausted their U.I. benefits. **1964** BARKER *Ice Road* 49: During the winter we lived on turnips, potatoes, canned clams and the pogy, and Mother and I would hook rugs for the tourist trade.

3 unemployment-insurance payments.
1960 *Maclean's* 2 Apr. 54/2: Today unemployment-insurance payments are often referred to as pogey. But pogey in the depths of the Thirties meant something as different from present-day unemployment insurance as panhandling is from drawing money from your bank account. The word expresses by its very sound, the sometimes harsh and always meagre allowances doled out to the unemployed. **1961** *Time* (Cdn ed.) 31 Mar. 9/2: Said a jobless Hamilton steelworker, father of six children: "Why should I sweat for $40 a week? I'm getting more than that from the pogey (i.e., unemployment insurance), the welfare and the baby bonus."

point *n.* **1 a.** a wedge or tongue of land projecting into a river or lake, especially at a bend.
1784 (1790) UMFREVILLE *Hudson's Bay* 13: . . . a passage opens between a high sandy bank and the point of an islet. . . . **1825** (1950) OGDEN *Journals* 11: . . . we passed two Small Rivers & encamped in a fine point of woods. **1863** PALLISER *Journals* 10: The alluvial flats . . . are often well timbered, but from the manner in which the river winds from side to side, the "points," as they are termed, are seldom more than two or three miles in extent.

b. a similar projection into the prairie (def. 2c).
1800 (1897) COUES *New Light* I 99: The small wood and brush are entirely destroyed [by rubbing buffalo], and even the grass is not permitted to grow in the points of wood. **1857** (1863) PALLISER *Journals* 38: . . . the bends of the river are marked by clumps of wood, which are known in the country by the name of "points," which applies also to any projecting angle of wood whether it be caused by the bend of a river or not. **1871** *Wkly Manitoban* 11 Feb. 2/5: As for going into the points for

shelter, it was too big an operation for the party to attempt, and so they had to camp by the road side.

2 one of the markings woven into Hudson's Bay blankets (def. 1a).

See quotes. See also **point blanket.**

1780 (1935) *Beaver* June 47: [They] had misunderstood him about the price of the pointed plankets as the points were known to every Indian to be the price to be paid for each as 2½ points, 2½ beaver, 3 points, 3 beaver, etc. **1935** *Ibid.*: The "point" on the blanket in its present standardized form is comparatively modern, being introduced in 1850. Prior to that date blankets for the Hudson's Bay Company were made with the bar only by individuals in their own homes, each maker putting a distinctive mark, a "point" on his product to show the size and weight. These "points" were usually in coloured wools and usually about one inch long. **1944** *Ibid.* 43/2: To sum up the actual facts: 1. All Hudson's Bay "Point" Blankets are one hundred percent wool. 2. Back in 1779, the points signified the exchange value in terms of beaver—one beaver per point. 3. Nowadays the points refer to the size (not the weight per square foot) and the only sizes sold are 3½ point (63 × 81 ins.) and 4-point (72 × 90 ins.). **1954** RICH in *Moose Ft Jnls* 371: Originally the points and staves of the blankets were blue, but the colour was changed to red in 1786.

3 *Hist.* **a.** *Lacrosse* one of the players playing out in front of the goalie; a defenceman. Cp. **cover-point.**

1967 *Globe and Mail* (Toronto) 16 May 39/9: Actually, the goaltender led a charmed life. Most of the danger was involved with the fellow who played between point and cover-point.

b. *Hockey* one of the defencemen on a seven-man team. Cp. **cover-point.**

1895 *Rat Portage* [Kenora] *News* (Ont.) 11 Jan. 1/2: Each team is composed of seven players, namely: goal-keeper, point, cover-point, and four forwards. **1900** *Greenwood Miner* (B.C.) 26 Jan. 9/1: The puck was in the vicinity of the Boundary goal for most of the first half of the game, and the Rossland team shot time and again but could not get the puck past MacPherson, the Boundary's clever point. **1965** *Canadian Wkly* 2-8 Jan. 7/2: The team lined up in a T-formation with the two defencemen (called "point" and "cover-point") in single file in front of the goal, then the rover, then the centre, with wing-men to right and left.

4 *Hockey* See 1964 quote.

1963 *Hockey Illust.* Dec. 22/2: Kent Douglas shot the puck from the point. **1964** *Globe and Mail* (Toronto) 7 Dec. 22/1: The change was Armstrong for Bathgate on the point, that quaint hockey designation meaning a station just inside the enemy blue-line when a penalty has reduced the enemy's personnel. **1966** *Ibid.* 10 Jan. 20/1: He kills penalties, plays the point on the power play and when all our other defensemen got hurt, he hung in there, holding our blueline together.

5 *Placer Mining* See 1913 quote.

1913 OGILVIE *Yukon* 231: Steam at a pressure of about forty pounds to the inch was carried in flexible hose, and applied through "points," that is, a section of half-inch iron pipe five or six feet long, into one end of which a steel plug is inserted. In this are bored two or three holes one-eighth of an inch in diameter, through which the steam issues against the frozen gravel, and thaws it at an astonishing rate. **1936** ARMSTRONG *Yukon Yesterdays* 64: These steel pipes or points were about

five or six feet in length and when they had been driven in the full distance, they were allowed to "sweat" for seven or eight hours, by means of which several tons of gravel was thawed.

point blanket a well-known make of blanket produced for the Hudson's Bay Company and having marks, or points (def. 2), woven into the fabric. See also **four-point blanket, pointed blanket, three-point blanket, two-and-a-half point blanket,** and **two-point blanket.**

☞ *Commonly known as Hudson's Bay blankets (def. 1a) these blankets have long been used in the fur trade with the Indians.*

1783 (1954) *Moose Ft Jnls* 152: I have enclosed instructions for your Guidance and the Standard of the point Blankets I now send you. **1859** *British Colonist* (Victoria) 5 Feb. 3/1: His Excellency Gov. Douglas was pleased to accede to their demand for pay, and gave Chief Edensaw, of Queen Charlotte's Island a due bill; "Good to Edensaw for twenty-five 3 pt. best Blankets, on their departure from the Island." **1954** RICH in *Moose Ft Jnls* 371: Amongst the innovations were Point Blankets which were made for the first time for the Hudson's Bay Company in 1780 by Thomas Empson of Witney, Oxfordshire. The first order consisted of 100 each of 1, 1½, 2, 2½ and 3 points, making a total of 500 Point Blankets. The "points" were known to every Indian familiar with the Company's competitors as representing the price, e.g. a 2½ point blanket was exchanged for 2½ beavers. **1960** *Camsell Arrow* Jan.-Mar. 26: The other familiar product, which is known to white men, too, is the famous "point" blanket.

point-blanket coat See **Hudson's Bay blanket coat.**

[**1935** *Beaver* June 47: The original mackinaw coats were made from Hudson's Bay "Point" blankets. . . . (See **Mackinaw coat** for full quote.)] **1955** *Penticton Herald* (B.C.) 17 Mar. 8/1: All rigged out in handsome Hudson's Bay point-blanket coats are the famous and fabulous Vees.

pointed blanket *Hist.* See **point blanket.**

1779 (1935) *Beaver* June 47: . . . Read a letter from . . . dated 20th December accepting . . . p.pc. for the blankets and duffels ordered last week. Sends samples of five different sorts of Pointed blankets with their respective prices per pair. Ordered that Mr . . . be directed to make one hundred pairs of each sort of the said blankets. **1780** (1954) *Moose Ft Jnls* 356: We now send . . . pointed Blankets of different sizes . . . to be delivered to him, as he may want this year. **1956** *Beaver* Summer 50: It can be no coincidence that while Maugenest was in London enquiries were put in hand for *Pointed* blankets.

A pointer (def. 1)

pointer *n.* **1** *Lumbering* a sturdy flat-bottomed boat about 20 ft. long, pointed fore and aft and having a shallow draft, specially designed for use in river drives. See also **bonne, driveboat, lumberboat, pointer boat,** and **river pointer.**

1901 CONNOR *Man from Glengarry* 13: Swiftly the pointer shot down the current, the swaying bodies and swinging oars in perfect rhythm with the song that rose and fell with melancholy but musical cadence.
1950 HAMBLETON *Abitibi Adventure* 140: They would use "pointers," twenty-foot heavily built craft with steeply sloping sides, which seemed very tippy but actually were the most practical craft ever devised for Canadian logging. 1961 PRICE & KENNEDY *Renfrew* 156: At the suggestion of J. R. Booth, who wanted a useful river craft, John Cockburn in 1883 designed the "pointer," a sharp-pointed boat that is still widely used in the lumbering business. Jack Cockburn, grandson of the designer, makes them today in Pembroke; he is the only commercial builder of "pointers" in Canada. Largest ones are 55 feet long, weigh up to 2,000 pounds and carry eight tons. They draw such a small draft that Cockburn says they "will float on a heavy dew."
1964 *Cdn Geog.Jnl* Feb. 67/3: If you ask Emmett Chartrand about the driving boat or "pointer" he has a faraway look when he answers, "—used them, wore them out, broke them."

2 *Esp. Fur Trade* an inland freight bateau of shallow draft. See also **bateau** (def. 3) and **Hudson's Bay pointer.** See also **York boat** and picture.
1936 *Beaver* Dec. 61/2: In the interval we remained in the pointer, making periodic trips to the post by canoe for supplies and to salvage what we could.
1966 PATTERSON *Trail* 226: He got one twenty-four-foot, shallow-draft riverboat built, square-sterned for a four horsepower outboard, sweeping up and fining to a pointed bow. A "pointer."

-pointer See **four-pointer.** See also **point blanket.**

pointer boat See **pointer** (def. 1 and picture).
1964 *Cdn Geog.Jnl* Feb. 67/1: The distinctive pointer boat has been synonymous with the river drive for more than 100 years.

pointman *n. Hockey* the player taking up position at the point (def. 4) during a power play, *q.v.*
1962 *Kingston Whig-Standard* (Ont.) 23 Oct. 12/2: It's the job of the wingmen to take the pointmen.

point player See **pointman.**
1963 *Hockey Illust.* Dec. 73/1: Max Bentley must be rated as possibly the best point player since the days of Charlie Conacher.

poire [pwa:r] *n.* [< Cdn F *poire sauvage,* literally, wild pear] *Hist.* **1** See **serviceberry** (def. 2). See also **pear.**
1789 (1801) MACKENZIE *Voyages* 107: There were plenty of berries, which my people called *poires*; they are of a purple hue, somewhat bigger than a pea, and of a luscious taste. 1830 (1837) *Trans.Lit.& Hist.Soc. Que.* III 126: In the country parts this small fruit is dignified with the name of poire, more from its fine flavor, it is presumed, than from any resemblance to pears. 1843 (1955) LEFROY *Magnetic North* 62: The poire is mixed up in large quantities with a fine pemmican for the use of the officers and this makes what is called berry pemmican of which I never got any however, as none was made last year; the berry was scarce. 1951 O'MEARA *Grand Portage* [Glossary]: Poire [is] a large purple berry that was the most delicious of all.

2 See **serviceberry** (def. 1).
1807 (1890) KEITH *Letters* 66: Upon the south side of the river, the country is pretty level and covered with fir . . . and bois rouge; there are poire, gooseberry and

raspberry bushes. . . . 1852 RICHARDSON *Arctic Exped.* 428: *Amelanchier canadensis* . . . is *La Poire* of the voyageurs. . . .

3 the wood of the serviceberry (def. 1).
1890 *Trans.Roy.Soc.Can.* (1 ser.) VIII 2 101: The arrow was half the length of the bow, and was made from the Saskatoon, or poire.

poisson doré *Cdn French* See **doré.**
1775 (1901) HENRY (Elder) *Travels* 265: There are also pickerel, called *poissons dorés* (gilt-fish), and sturgeon. 1832 MCGREGOR *Brit.Amer.* II 481: The fish most esteemed is the poisson d'orée, a kind of pickerel, but it is rare. 1845 TOLFREY *Sportsman* I 250: In this, as well as all the smaller rivers in Lower Canada, will be found a voracious and very delicate fish called the *Poisson Doré.*

poisson inconnu *Cdn French* See **inconnu.**
1789 (1801) MACKENZIE *Voyages* 63: . . . the net . . . contained three of the poissons inconnus. 1908 MAIR *Mackenzie Basin* 116: The poisson inconnu, a species of salmon which ascends from the Arctic Ocean, is not found, he says, above this stream [the Salt River].

poke[1] *n.* †**1** a bag or small sack especially one used in carrying gold dust or nuggets.
1910 SERVICE *Trail of '98* 347: Then the girl will pry him loose from his poke. . . . 1958 BERTON *Klondike* 91: In two hours he took out two hundred and seventy-eight dollars in fine dust which had sifted out of miners' pokes slapped onto the bar above.

2 a sleeping bag.
1936 MOWERY *Paradise Trail* 27: . . . he dressed quickly, hung the canvas poke in a balsam for convenient reference that evening, and hurried to the cabin.
1953 MOWERY *Mounted Police* 154: The sergeant cooked thick caribou collops on the primus plate and made scones, and they ate. After they had put out the primus and lighted the sea-oil lamp, they leaned back on their pokes.

poke[2] [pok] *n.* [see note] *North* **1** See **dan** (def. 1).
☛ *This word appears to have come into northern use via Eskimo* **poq, puq** *bag; perhaps borrowed from early whalers in this sense.*
1931 LEBOURDAIS *Northward* 73: Formerly the Eskimos killed walruses with spears. The spear would not kill them outright, of course, but attached to it was a long sealskin line at the end of which was fastened an inflated sealskin bag called a pok.

2 See **dan** (def. 2).
1924 *Beaver* Aug. 405: On a large staging we see a number of seals, pokes of seal oil, a green polar bear skin and other . . . articles. 1946 JENNESS *Material Culture* 7: . . . these pokes when filled with blubber weighed from 150 to 200 pounds.

poke-check *n. Hockey* a defensive play made by holding the stick low along the ice and poking the puck out of the puck-carrier's control.
1945 FONTAINE *Happy Time* 45: The crowd was frantic. The score was tied. I was [in imagination] Frank Nighbor, Canada's immortal poke-check genius.
1964 *Maclean's* 2 May 46/1: To me some of the most fascinating moves in hockey . . . are poke-checks, or well timed interceptions, or expeditions of forechecking, and I'd like to see them pointed up more in the commentary.

poke-check v. *Hockey* make use of a poke-check, *q.v.*
1966 *Hockey News* (Montreal) 1 Jan. 13/2: He poke-checks and sweep-checks like the oldtimers, and makes few mistakes.

poke-checking n. *Hockey* the practice or skill of using the poke-check, *q.v.*
1963 O'BRIEN *Hockey* 60: At that point the defenceman will likely resort to poke-checking. . . .

pokelogan ['pokə,logən] n. [< Algonk.; cf. Malecite *pekelāygan* stopping place] *Maritimes* See 1855 quote. See also **bogan**[1]. Also spelled *pokologan*.
1818 LOCKWOOD *Nova Scotia* 98: At the head of this bay, is good shelter in a place called Pok-logan.
1855 HALIBURTON *Nature* II 404: A poke-loken is a marshy place or stagnant pool connected with a river.
1896 (1913) HODGE & WHITE *Indians of Canada* 66/1: Exactly the same thing the Indians call a pokelog—a still creek or bay branching from a stream. **1913** *Ibid.* 66/1: He thinks *bogan*, like *logan* . . . a corruption of *pokologan*. Both words, Ganong notes, are in good local use and occur in articles on sporting, etc.

Polar Bear Express See quote.
1966 *Globe and Mail* (Toronto) 12 Aug. 6/5: . . . on Sunday, June 19, he went on the first trip of the famous Polar Bear Express, an Ontario Northland [Railway] train which goes from Cochrane to Moosonee [Ontario].

polar hare See **Arctic hare**.
1823 FRANKLIN *Journey* 664: The Polar hare appears to vary much in size, and consequently in weight.
1866 KING *Sportsman in Canada* 26: In this respect it differs from the Polar-hare, the finer and softer fur of which is in winter pure white to the roots. **1911** SETON *Arctic Prairies* 231: It was only a Polar Hare, the second we had seen; but its very scarceness here, at least this year, gave it unusual interest.

pole n. See **setting-pole**.
1808 (1950) THOMPSON *Journals* 15: . . . every Inch must be gained by the Pole or the Line. . . . **1950** WHITE in THOMPSON *Journals* 15n: The pole and line were used ordinarily in *ascending* a stream with a swift current. The poles were usually ten feet in length, made of good ash and shod with an iron ferrule at each end.

pole v. propel a boat or canoe by means of a pole.
1827 (1912) ERMATINGER *Express Jnl* 94: [We] hauled and poled up the Lower Flats and reached the Lower Burntwood portage at 10. . . . **1961** *Cdn Geog.Jnl* July 5: Attacking a rapid upstream, the voyageurs would . . . paddle the canoe, "demi-charge," line or pole the canoe, make a "décharge," or portage.

pole bridge† See **corduroy road**.
1871 *Wkly Manitoban* 28 Jan. 2/6: He never disturbed Mr. Shepherd's equanimity, whose care and supervision extended to the most minute details, even to that of relaying in bitter cold the pole bridges across the dangerous sloos [sloughs] on the road. **1926** *Dalhousie Rev.* V 205: We cross another of those earth-covered pole bridges, and climb a diminutive, slaty hill.

pole bunk a rudimentary bed, or bunk, made of poles.
1955 HOBSON *Nothing Too Good* 136: The only open space on the floor where there was room enough to unroll my bed was next to Larkie's pole bunk. **1962** FRY *Ranch on the Cariboo* 63: Roger and I shared a badly built pole shack with room in it for two narrow pole bunks, nothing more.

pole camp *Lumbering, B.C.* a logging camp producing poles and posts for use in farming, construction, etc.
1954 EVANS *Mist* 169: He said that a fellow with a truck stood a good chance of getting hauling jobs around the Junction, as well as at the mills and pole camps farther down the river. **1965** *Islander* 14 Feb. 4/1: . . . our pole camp was closed for the winter [and] I had nothing else to do, so I gave trapping a whirl.

polecat† n. See **skunk**.
1778 (1962) *Hist.& Geog.Teaching Materials* 58: The articles which they [Nootka Indians] offered to sale were skins of various animals, such as bears, wolves, foxes, deer, racoons, polecats, martens, and in particular, the sea otters. . . . **1786** *Account N.S.* 63: The pole-cat, whose stinking properties have become proverbial, is of two or three kinds. . . . **1896** ROBERTS *Camp-Fire* 326: We were just about to hazard some guess, allowing for an owl, or polecat, or other night prowler. . . . **1966** *Sun* (Vancouver) 7 Jan. 4: [Headline] There's a Poverty of Polecats in Nova Scotia.

police camp *Obs.* See **police post**.
1897 TYRRELL *Sub-Arctics* 26: The police camp was the only other one in the neighborhood. . . . **1910** HAYDON *Riders of Plains* 114: The serviceable portion of the lumber from which the old buildings had been constructed was conveyed to the Police camp at Maple Creek, to be used in the erection of a post there.

policeman n. **1** *Obs.* See **Indian constable**.
1886 (1961) LA VIOLETTE *Survival* 53: The Chiefs are all strongly in favor of the continuance of the Potlach; the Policemen who are neither paid nor uniformed by the Department [of Indian affairs] I could not depend upon to act in this case and are besides mostly subordinate to the local Chiefs.
2 *Hockey, Slang* a rugged, aggressive player whose function is to intimidate opposing players and thus prevent them from roughing up his team-mates. See also **hockey cop**.
1963 *Maclean's* 9 Mar. 22/1: The role of policeman in the NHL is a comparatively modern one. It can probably be traced to the stricter enforcement of rules in the last ten years. . . .

police post a place where a detachment of Royal Canadian Mounted Police is stationed.
1929 JOHNSTON *Beyond Rockies* 107: Jean Ledoux trekked three days to the nearest police-post. **1964** JENNESS *Eskimo Admin.* II 8: The government established a police post there [Pangnirtung] in 1923. . . .

police town See **police village**.
1903 *U of T Stud.Hist.& Econ.* 76: It provided for the establishment of volunteer fire companies in the several police towns, and the granting of certificates to the efficient members exempting them from militia duties during peace.

police trustee a member of the board of trustees of a police village, *q.v.*
1852 (1853) STRICKLAND *Canada West* II 271n: A police trustee must be entered on the village roll, for rateable

property, in his own right or that of his wife as proprietor or tenant for £100.

police village *Esp.Ont.* an unincorporated village administered by an elective board of trustees. See also **police town.**
1852 (1853) STRICKLAND *Canada West* II 270n: In police villages the elections take place on the second Monday in January, for the choice of three police trustees. **1861** *Nor'Wester* (R.R.S.) 31 Aug. 1/1: Some villages are not incorporated, and these are not entitled to any representative in the county council. They are usually called police villages, and are governed by three trustees, chosen by the people, one of whom is chosen inspecting trustee, or head of the council. **1962** *Globe and Mail* (Toronto) 12 Dec. 7/3: This northeastern corner contains the police village of Malton, the Malton airport, and the Avro and Orenda factories. **1966** *Cdn Almanac* 406: A police village is run by a Board of Trustees elected by the residents.

poling *n.* the practice of using a setting-pole, *q.v.*
1811 (1950) THOMPSON *Journals* 141: ... the poling [was] very bad. **1905** (1954) *B.C.Hist.Qtly* XVIII 161: The hardest work is at muddy portages, and in getting through muddy lakes, where the water is low, and the bottom too soft for "poling." **1965** *Cdn Geog.Jnl* June 190/2: The steep climb up is achieved by a bruising marathon of poling, tracking, portaging, and wading. ...

poling-boat *n. North* See 1940 quote.
1900 LONDON *Son of Wolf* 163: But in the morning Madeline shook the dust of the Lower River from her moccasins, and with her husband, in a poling-boat, went to live on the Upper River.... **1940** MARSHALL *Arctic Village* 84: The most common boat on the rivers of the North is the poling boat which penetrates where the larger vessels could not go. Typically the poling boat is from ten to twenty feet long, from three to five feet wide on top, and has a narrow bottom eighteen to thirty inches wide. It has a nose shaped something like a shovel which is raised high above the water so that it does not bury in the current. **1958** BERTON *Klondike* 437: And so a man in a poling-boat can drift downstream for mile after mile without seeing any sign of human-kind. ...

poling bottom a firm bottom to a shallow river or lake, permitting the use of a setting-pole, *q.v.*
1954 PATTERSON *Dangerous River* 123: There were stretches of sheer cliff, with no poling bottom, here we could make our way up the river only by poling horizontally against the rock. **1956** EVANS *Mountain Dog* 46: Where the rocks had fallen, the bottom pitched steeply, and gave treacherous poling bottom.

pollack ['pɑlək] *v.* [origin uncertain] *Slang* look for usable or salable items that others have discarded, as in a dump or a junk shop.
1963 *Weekend Mag.* 31 Aug. 27/1: "Well, sir, in one of the villages up near the Point, I was pollacking around. And what did I find, stuck away in a corner, but this lovely fan."

poll captain in an election, a person charged with the responsibility of getting out the vote for a particular party in a given area.
1963 *Maclean's* 9 Mar. 1/3: In every riding in the nation the poll captains of the various parties are out harassing and cajoling the voters.

polygloo *n. Trademark* See quote.
1959 *Ottawa Citizen* 17 July 17/5: Two Eastview boys ... pay a visit to the "Polygloo".... The prototype is a

forerunner to a fibreglass igloo that may some day become fashionable in the Arctic.

pomme de glace [< Cdn F "apple of ice"] *Obs.* See quote.
1827 *Novascotian* (Halifax) 24 Feb. 72/3: The following list is but a small part of the contents of the nursery.... Apples—Rhode Island Greening ... Bourassa ... Pomme D'Glace or Transparent....

pomme de neige [< Cdn F] *Obs.* See **snow apple.**
1807 (1809) GRAY *Letters* 150: The apples are particularly good—The *Pomme de Neige,* so called from its being extremely white, and from its having the granulated appearance of snow, when broken; it dissolves, almost entirely, in the mouth like snow.... **1853** STRICKLAND *Canada West* II 204: ... last year gave me upwards of a hundred bushels of ... the Ribstone pippin, Newtown pippin, Pearmain, Pomme-de-gris, Pomme-de-neige and many other sorts equally good.

pomme gris [< Cdn F "gray apple"] *Obs.* a once-popular eating apple native to Canada. Also spelled *pomme grise.*
1806 *Quebec Gaz.* Oct. 4/1: [There are] 30 Barrels Pommes Grises, Bourassas, and Fameuses.... **1827** (1829) MACTAGGART *Three Years* I 42: ... vegetables they have in great abundance, and fruit—beautiful apples called pomgrees. **1864** *Canada Farmer* 1 July 188/2: The varieties most cultivated are the Fameuse, St. Lawrence, Pomme Gris, and Bourassa, yet under the existing mode of culture, these are not hardy enough.

ponask ['ponæsk *or* 'punæsk] *v.* [< Algonk.: Cree] cook game or fish by splitting it and holding it on a stick or spit over an open fire. See also **ponasking.** Also spelled *poonask.*
1922 *Beaver* March 39/2: As we had no kettle ... we were forced to "ponask" the fish on a pointed stick before a bright fire. **1934** GODSELL *Arctic Trader* 46: She had, therefore, taken the heart, impaled it on a stick, and ponasked it as one would roast a duck. **1963** MCTAVISH *Behind the Palisades* 90: While the kettles would be boiling their meat, they [Indians] would be "Poonasking" strips of meat and delicacies like leg-bones in front of the fire. ...

ponasking ['ponæskiŋ *or* 'punæskiŋ] *n.* [cf. *ponask*] See 1963 quote. See also **ponask.** Also spelled *poonasking.*
1944 CLAY *Fur Thieves* 31: Thus were the two pieces of duck held up to the blaze and heat. "That's called 'ponasking,' Dave," said the old trapper.... **1963** MCTAVISH *Behind the Palisades* 90: "Poonasking" is a method of cooking before a campfire by splitting meat or game, impaling on a pointed stick, where it is quickly roasted from the intense heat.

pond *n.* **1** *Maritimes* See **barachois** (def. 1).
1760 PICHON *Cape Breton* 26: We left this pond to those who were rash enough to venture being lost there, and entered into an *auniguen,* which brought us east south-west for above four-hundred fathoms to the pond of Marcochet. **1954** BRUCE *Channel Shore* 292: Under the bridge, a creek slips down to lose itself in the brackish water of the pond, a narrow salt lagoon lying inside the channel beach.

2 *Esp.Nfld* a lake.
1693 (1929) KELSEY *Papers* 3: This wood is poplo ridges with small ponds of water.... **1772** (1792) CARTWRIGHT

Journal I 253: From the head of the pond, a good otter-path led into Twelve-o'clock Harbour. **1872** DASHWOOD *Chiploquorgan* 269: . . . towards sundown we reached a large lake or "pond," as they are termed by the natives [in Nfld], fifteen miles long and five broad . . . in this "pond" the beach, which extended about sixty yards from the water to the forest, was formed of the finest white sand. **1948** *Cdn Geog.Jnl* Mar. 49/1: Everyone knows what a lake is and there are lakes of all sizes from coast to coast, but if you happen to reside in the Eastern Townships of Quebec you may find your *lake* is called a *pond*. The generic term, pond, migrated across the boundary with stout settlers from Vermont and New Hampshire, who settled much of this district a hundred and fifty odd years ago. **1964** *Ibid.* Apr. 136: . . . at Goodyear's Cove . . . the salt sea laves one side of a *barachois* not twenty yards from a freshwater pond.

3 *Lumbering* an expanse of quiet water where logs, often retained by a boom, are penned till needed. See also **boom pool, log pond, log pool,** and **lumber dam.** Cp. **holding boom** and **hot pond.**
1829 MACTAGGART *Three Years* II 87: The timber-merchants regret that they were not found to answer; as they had cleared their ponds and cover of lumber. . . . **1839** *Bytown* [Ottawa] *Gaz.* 12 June 3/2: [He] incautiously ventured with a pike-pole on a floating log in the pond, at the dam-head. **1947** ENGLEBERT *Men and Trees* 19: The mill operation starts when the boom man pokes the nose of a floating log in the pond on to the jackladder. This moving chain is equipped at intervals with steel grips, called log dogs. . . . **1964** *Atlantic Advocate* July 56/2: The whole operation is done electrically; from the pond to the main mill, through the trading and cutting, to the electronic recording of each parcel for shipment.

4 a. *Obs.* a deep, still pool in a stream.
1832 (1953) RADCLIFF *Letters* 124: The village . . . is . . . on a high bank of the river Credit, where what is termed the *Pond* of that river begins. **1849** ALEXANDER *L'Acadie* II 216: Its rapids prevent its freezing, except in the still water, or "ponds," as the lumberers call them. . . .

b. See **beaver pond.**
1954 EVANS *Mist* 203: "I will let my ponds make me an increase for next year when prices should be higher."

pond beaver a beaver that builds a beaver dam, as opposed to a bank beaver, *q.v.*
1918 (1919) SCHULTZ *Rising Wolf* 121: There were many beavers, pond beavers and bank beavers, along the stream.

pont *n. Cdn French* See **ice-bridge** (def. 1a).
1808 (1809) GRAY *Letters* 255: A variety of circumstances must combine to form a *pont;* when many very large masses of ice happen to come in contact, and fill the whole space between one side of the river and the other, then become stationary. **1850** ROY *Hist.of Canada* 214: When the ice does form, it is called a *pont;* there is always a kind of jubilee, and people are to be seen in every direction sleighing, sliding, skating, and running.

pool *n.* **1** *West* a co-operative grain-marketing organization among farmers.
1920 (1945) HAIG *Brave Harvest* 211: All pool members should receive the same price for the same grade of wheat, after adjustment of freight charges at terminals. **1940** MACCORMAC *Canada* 234: The depression hit the pools hard but they have survived and are apparently in the West to stay. **1957** *Time* (Cdn ed.) 2 Sep. 12/3: Wheatmen and their marketing "pools," as well as the government's own Wheat Board, ignore census data, rely on information supplied by grain elevator agents at 2,000 shipping points across the prairie provinces.

2 *Attributive use.* See **pool train.**
1959 *Ottawa Citizen* 24 April 25/2: The treasures were moved . . . from the Bank of Montreal to Union Station and a pool baggage car bound for Toronto.

pool (passenger) train a train operated over a line of track by more than one railway company.
1959 *Kingston Whig-Standard* (Ont.) 28 Sep. 1/5: His death was the fifth caused by the collision in which a CNR freight ripped open the side of a dining car on a pool passenger train being shunted in the yards. **1965** *Globe and Mail* (Toronto) 10 Nov. 19/8: At one time the pool trains ran over the CNR to Brockville and then by CPR tracks to Ottawa. . . . As at the end of October, the pool trains ceased to exist and the two railways went on their separate ways.

poonask *v.* See **ponask.**

poor man's camp, claim, or **diggings**† *Placer Mining* See 1947 quote.
1896 *Kootenaian* (Kaslo, B.C.) 20 June 3/1: This is a condition, too, that invites investments for the reason that it is a "poor man's camp." **1900** OSBORN *Greater Can.* 16: It is already evident that the average Klondike creek or gulch mine cannot be regarded as "poor man's diggings" in the sense that the California placers were so regarded. **1947** TAYLOR *Canada* 435: Such deposits are called *alluvial* or *placer* deposits: and since they are easily mined they are sometimes described as 'poor man's fields.'

poor man's gold *Placer Mining* See **pay dirt** (def. 1).
1921 HAWORTH *Trailmakers* 266: Quartz . . . lacks the romantic interest that attaches to "poor man's gold," that is, "pay dirt" on a river bar. **1938** CURTIN *Yukon Voyage* 19: Gold! Lots of it! Placer Gold! Poor man's Gold!

poor man's route or **trail** *Placer Mining, Hist.* a route to a goldfield that is safe and cheap for stampeders (def. 1).
1897 *B.C.Mining Jnl* (Ashcroft) 18 Sep. 1/2: It is not only a "poor man's route," but a really good cattle road, and in my opinion a route by which prospectors or miners who wish to pass their own freight through can use to great advantage. **1900** OSBORN *Greater Can.* 6: Though some of these routes are practicable enough, and may be justly called "poor man's trails," owing to the abundance of fish and game in the country through which they pass, their great length is against them. **1952** MACGREGOR *Twelve-Foot Davis* 310: "Edmonton," chorused the boosters, "The Poor Man's Route to The Yukon!"

poplar bluff *West* See **bluff** (def. 3a).
1875 *Canadian Mthly* Dec. 376/2: Near the Red and Assiniboine rivers the prairie is one great level dotted with poplar bluffs. . . . **1961** *Cdn Geog.Jnl* Jan. 12/2: In Spring . . . prairie crocuses bloomed, ruffed grouse could be heard drumming in poplar bluffs. . . .

poplo *n. Obs.* See **popple.**
1693 (1929) KELSEY *Papers* 3: This wood is poplo ridges with small ponds of water. . . . **1952** MALKUS *Little*

Giant 63: The ground, Henry noted, began to be dry with wood—poplo, birch and ash. . . .

popple† ['pɑpəl] *n.* [var. of *poplar*] *North* See 1956 quote.

1903 WHITE *Forest* 195: We started out afoot soon after dinner, through a scattering growth of popples. . . . **1941** *Beaver* Sep. 38/2: Popple—Why the humble poplar tree should be so distorted in name is not known. **1956** *Native Trees* 90: Trembling Aspen *Populus tremuloides* Michx. [is also called] . . . popple. . . .

porcelain(e) *n.* [< Cdn F] *Obs.* See **wampum** (def. 1).

*c*1665 (1885) RADISSON *Voyages* 49: When we came neere our dwellings we mett severall gangs of men to our greatest disadvantage, for we weare forced to sing, and those that came to see us gave porcelaine to those that most did us injury. **1760** JEFFERYS *Descr.New France* 52: . . . for [affairs] of less importance, they make use of brooches, or necklaces of porcelain, skins, coverings, maize, or Indian corn. . . .

Porcupine River Husky See **Mackenzie River husky.**

1928 (1956) DAVIS *Modern Dog Encyc.* 66/1: Another breed [of husky] was called the "Porcupine River" or "Mackenzie" Husky. These were the best freight dogs I have ever seen, being far superior, much larger and stronger than the Eskimo.

pork duck the common goldeneye, *Bucephala clangula.*

1907 HUNTER *Cdn Wilds* 229: The French-Canadians call this duck the diver and the half-breeds of Hudson Bay the pork duck. **1956** MCATEE *Folk-Names* 14: Common Goldeneye [is also called] . . . pork duck ("Keewatin"). . . .

porkeater ['pɔrk,itər] *n.* [trans. of Cdn F *mangeur de lard*] **1** *Fur Trade, Slang, Derog., Hist.* **a.** in early use, an engagé, *q.v.*, of the North West Company who signed on to man the canoes plying between Montreal and the Grand Portage, so called because pork was the staple of their diet, as opposed to the pemmican and coarser foods endured by winterers and others who ventured into the interior. See also **comers and goers, grand voyageur, mangeur de lard** (def. 1), and **Montreal canoeman.**

☞ *The term (def. 1a) originated with the North West Company, later senses developing after the merger with the Hudson's Bay Company in 1821.*

1793 (1933) MACDONELL *Diary* 94: Between two and three hundred yards to the East of the N.W. Fort beyond the Pork eaters camp is the spot Messʳˢ David and Peter Grant have selected to build upon. . . . **1821** (1918) DAVIDSON *Fur Traders* 302: Mr. K. recommends . . . the absolute necessity of forwarding 7 or 8 Canoes of pork eaters [and] Winterers . . . with full ladings. **1956** INNIS *Fur Trade* 239: In 1767 wages of "porkeaters" (men who were hired for the trip from Montreal to Grand Portage and return) were roughly 350 livres for a guide, 300 to 320 for foremen and steersmen and 240 livres for middlemen.

b. See 1961 quote. See also **mangeur de lard** (def. 2)

1820 (1823) FRANKLIN *Journey* 281: There is a pride amongst 'Old Voyagers', which makes them consider being frost-bitten as effeminate, and only excusable in a "Pork-eater," or one newly come into the country. **1844** (1955) LEFROY *Magnetic North* 116: It is the young hands "porkeaters" that they persecute the worst.

1961 JONES *Trappers* 67/2: Voyageurs were of two classes: a beginner was called a "pork-eater"; an experienced man who spent the cold months at an interior post was called a "winterer."

c. any canoeman or boatman. See also **voyageur** (def. 1).

1829 (1948) MCLOUGHLIN *Letters* 69: By this opportunity I send you all you requested . . . and four Pork eaters. **1831** (1947) HARGRAVE *Correspondence* 71: . . . sixteen men drowned in this river . . . six of Mr. Harriot's pork eaters and one belonging to [Ft. Colville]. **1859** KANE *Wanderings* 34: The men who usually work this brigade of [H.B.C.] canoes are hired at Lachine, and are called by the uncouth names of mangeurs du lard, or pork-eaters. . . .

2 *Hist.* a volunteer for the force raised in Lower Canada to oppose the Patriotes, *q.v.*, during the Rebellion of 1837-8.

1873 LEMOINE *Maple Leaves* 261: The first paid corps raised, consisted of laborers, mechanics and tradesmen, chiefly Irish, and were called the Porkeaters, forming a regiment of about 600 strong; able, resolute fellows, who, on being equipped, at first presented a motley, awkward squad.

porpoise *n.* the beluga or white whale, *q.v.*

1897 TUTTLE *Golden North* 213: Aside from the walrus hunt, Mr. Spencer is developing a large porpoise, or white whale fishery, on the very shores of Churchill harbor, where, with his nets and traps, he took last season, one hundred and ninety of these mammals, of immense size. **1931** CONNOR *Rock and River* 4: . . . the "porpoises" were thrashing the water in their furious chase on the shoals of herring and smaller fish that fled before them.

portage ['pɔrtɪdʒ *or* pɔr'taʒ] *n.* [< Cdn F < F] **1 a.** on a waterway, a place where both canoe (or other vessel) and cargo are carried from one lake or river to another or around rapids, falls, or other obstructions. See also **carriage** (def. 2) and **carrying-place.**

[**1698** HENNEPIN *New Discovery* [trans.] I 75: The Portage was two Leagues long.] **1761** (1901) HENRY (Elder) *Travels* 23: In this distance there are four carrying-places, besides three or four *decharges* or *discharges,* which are places where the merchandise only is carried, and are therefore distinguishable from *portages* or *carrying-places,* where the canoe itself is taken out of the water, and transported on men's shoulders. **1826** *U.E.Loyalist* (York [Toronto]) 2 Dec. 213/3: The longest portage on the route is about 13 miles in length, and occupied us seven days. **1966** *Globe and Mail* (Toronto) 11 July 15/2: Others tore down one of the overnight shelters . . . and prepared the canoe for an emergency trip by water and portage to the main camp. . . .

b. See quote. See also **portage railroad.**

1908 *London & Middlesex Hist.Soc.Trans.* II 40: It may be noted that early railroads were looked upon simply as portages to connect navigable waters. **1965** STEVENS *Incompleat Canadian* 121: The first [railway] line, fourteen miles of tracks between the St. Lawrence and Richelieu rivers, was intended as a *portage* for goods.

2 a. the act or process of carrying canoes, boats, supplies, etc. at such a place. See also **carriage** (def. 1) and **traverse**[1], *n.* (def. 4).

1897 TYRRELL *Sub-Arctics* 80: Towards the centre of it was discovered a peninsula, which is connected with the west shore only by a very narrow neck of land, across which a portage was made. **1965** *Cdn Geog.Jnl* Dec. 202/3: During the portage . . . Champlain stopped to watch a party of Indians perform their traditional ceremony. . . .

b. make a portage, carry craft and cargo at such a place.
[1698 HENNEPIN *New Discovery* [trans.] I 74: . . . we were oblig'd to make our Portage. . . .] **1808** (1960) FRASER *Letters and Journals* 92: They made several portages . . . the rest of the men carried the baggage. **1964** CARROLL *Shy Photographer* 9: He made the portage . . . without once stopping.

3 the act or process of carrying boat and cargo across ice, from open water to open water. See also **portage,** *v.* (def. 3).
1849 (1852) RICHARDSON *Arctic Exped.* 311: On the 16th, by making a number of portages over the ice, we rounded Point Mackenzie and entered Back's Inlet, which was partially open. **1965** *Maclean's* 16 Oct. 56/4: The men carried a boat, and where the ice of the lake gave way the four of them entered the boat and proceeded to the next floe. Half a dozen times they made this cold portage before reaching the American shore.

4 the route across a height of land, or watershed, often involving many carrying-places.
1905 (1954) *B.C.Hist.Qtly* 161: Hudson's Bay men . . . apply the term "portage," in a larger sense, to the higher land between water systems. . . . **1933** MERRICK *True North* 28: . . . their interests demand that they get along as fast as possible, lest the lakes on the portage freeze up. **1961** *Edmonton Jnl* 12 Aug. 4/3: The "Little Divide" separates the . . . Athabasca and Churchill River systems, and the three-mile portage between Lac La Biche and Beaver Lake was used as long ago as 1798 by Hudson's Bay Company and North West Company explorers. So long as the fur traders plowed the waters of the Northwest, the "Little Divide" saw the comings and goings of brigades bound for the Mackenzie River or Hudson Bay.

5 *Obs.* the obstruction around which a carry is made.
1826 (1829) MACTAGGART *Three Years* I 328: Not so the Canadian voyagers; they have no curiosity, but pass the portage without looking to right or left. **1829** *Ibid.* 281: This river might be made navigable at no great expense, were the portages *locked* with *dry-stone* locks, the stone laid on edge and well puddled behind.

6 a journey by dog-sled, specifically one taking an overland route as opposed to a coastal route over sea-ice (def. 1).
1882 GILDER *Schwatka's Search* 58: Inuits always prefer to move by portages when they have heavy loads and plenty of food on the sledges, and such had been the custom on all the previous sledge journeys made by "Esquimau Joe" in company with white men. **1905** (1954) *B.C.Hist.Qtly* XVIII 161: Hudson's Bay men . . . apply the term "portage," in a larger sense, to . . . the transport effected by dog sleighs in winter. **1951** BULIARD *Inuk* 93: They tell us that travel around the coast is impossible. The sea ice is too rough. We will have to go overland and take potluck with a three or four day portage.

7 *North* See **land-crossing.**
1951 BULIARD *Inuk* 238: But while crossing a portage we got lost inland, and, tired of the rocks, made for the sea. To reach the ice we had to unhitch the dogs from the sled and carry the sled downhill, over the rocks, then go back for the dogs.

8 *Maritimes, Hist.* See **portage road** (def. 2).
☛ *The usual local pronunciation of this word was* ['pɔrtæʃ]. *See quote below and those at* **portage man** *and* **portaging crowd.**
1925 CLARKE *Chris in Canada* 9: ". . . Of course the road goes on. But it arn't a highway after it enters the woods. It's called a portage" (he pronounced it portash) "and goes right through to the Nashwaak and the Miramichi. Nothin' but woods and lakes. . . ."

portage *v.* [< Cdn F < F] **1 a.** carry (canoe, supplies, etc.) at a portage (def. 1a).
1864 GORDON *Vacation Tour* 508 [*OED*]: [We encountered] some falls where we were compelled to portage the canoes. **1914** DOUGLAS *Lands Forlorn* 109: We tried to explain by signs that we would like him to come back to our camp and help us to portage our stuff. **1966** *Globe and Mail* (Toronto) 11 July 15/5: [Caption] Pat Hall . . . leads way as canoe is portaged through the bush.

b. *Hist.* transport by means of a portage road (def. 1a).
1909 NURSEY *Isaac Brock* 65: To portage these goods around Niagara Falls kept fifty or more farmers' waggons busy every day during the summer.

2 *Maritimes, Obs.* carry or pack through the bush. See also **portaging crowd.** Cp. **portage road** (def. 2).
1872 DASHWOOD *Chiploquorgan* 60: . . . we left the lake and portaged our horns, skins [etc], nearly twenty miles to a lumber camp, which we were fortunate enough to find occupied by a party of lumberers.

3 a. make a portage (def. 2a or 3). See also **carry,** *v.* (def. 1).
1897 TYRRELL *Sub-Arctics* 237: After carefully considering the situation, we concluded to portage across the island of ice and launch on the other side. **1912** FOOTNER *New Rivers* 80: Landing, we looked over the rapids as far as we could see them and decided to portage. **1965** *Cdn Geog.Jnl* June 184/3: In the forest, water levels are more stable and a portage path becomes well established, indicating whether, where, and how far to portage.

b. *Figurative use.*
1959 *Weekend Mag.* 18 July 20/1: Governor George Simpson portaged into view at the head of the fur traders of 1825, stopping off at Jasper House en route to the virgin forests of Oregon.

4 a. circumvent (a rapids, waterfall, etc.) by carrying craft and cargo.
1900 LONDON *Son of Wolf* 133: "Why, we'll pole up . . . and portage the White Horse Rapids and the Box Cañon."

b. cross (land) by carrying craft and cargo.
1908 LAUT *Conquest N.W.* I 218: By canoe, this land could be portaged, and Iberville was probably the first man to blaze the trail across the swamp, which has been used by hunters from that day to this.

portage bay a sheltered cove where a portage landing, *q.v.*, is to be found.
1954 PATTERSON *Dangerous River* 70: Then it sloped gently off into the river in a natural ramp, and we got into the canoes again and whirled across the river to the portage bay. **1955** RICH in BLACK *Journal* lxx: The

Finlay here issues from the canyon mouth into the portage bay with, at high water, a most tumultuous uproar. . . .

portage collar *Fur Trade, Obs.* See **tumpline**. See also **collier**.

1931 NUTE *Voyageur* 47: For portaging, a sort of harness, called the "portage collar," was used. This consisted of a strap of leather about three inches wide, to which smaller straps were attached of sufficient length to tie around the packages.

portage landing or mouth the point where a portage path, *q.v.*, begins.

1944 CLAY *Fur Thieves* 63: A half-dozen fine mallards lay in the bottom of the canoe when they finally beached at the second portage-mouth. **1964** *Weekend Mag.* 11 July 18/2: Because of a poorly-marked map they slipped by a vital portage landing off the Isaac river. . . .

portage man *Lumbering, Maritimes, Hist.* a logger who worked on the portage roads (def. 2).

1930 *B.C.Lumberman* May 56/3: But gone are all the "portash" men/ And gone the swampers too.

portage path a path followed by persons making a portage (def. 2a). See also **portage road** (def. 1c), **portage route**, and **portage track**.

1831 *Trans.Lit.& Hist.Soc.Que.* II 293: After a little searching we found a portage-path which led to a small lake. **1965** *Cdn Geog.Jnl* June 184/3: In the forest, water levels are more stable and a portage path becomes well established, indicating whether, where, and how far to portage.

portager *n.* one who portages; one skilled in portaging.

1897 TYRRELL *Across Sub-Arctics* 9: He was highly recommended, not so much as a canoeman, but as being an expert portager of great experience in northern travel, and also a Eskimo linguist. **1955** *Beaver* June 21/1: From him I first learned to use the portager's tumpline correctly. . . .

portage railroad *Hist.* See 1958 quote. See also **portage, n.**(def. 1b) and **portage road** (def. 3).

1946 LOWER *Colony to Nation* 278: [Caption] Early Portage Railroads: The Champlain and St. Lawrence Railroad, 1836. [**1958** *Encyc.Can.* VIII 404/2: The history of railways in Canada begins in 1832 with . . . the Champlain and St. Lawrence Railroad . . . conceived as a portage link in the water route from the St. Lawrence River to New York.]

portage road 1 a. a road used for portaging boats and cargo by means of vehicles.

1801 *Niagara Herald* (Niagara-on-the-Lake, U.C.) 4 July 1/1: Whoever shall find the same and leave it at either the public houses on the portage road from Queenston to Chippawa, shall receive five dollars for their trouble. **1868** SMALL *Chronicles* 157: Grain portage roads . . . are called for in consequence of the break in lake navigation, caused by the Niagara Falls. **1952** PUTNAM *Cdn Regions* 497/1: At Fort Fitzgerald, Alberta, goods are transhipped on trucks and trailers over the portage roads to the head of northern water transportation at Fort Smith. **1963** MORTON *Kingdom of Canada* 194: The Rangers began the road system Simcoe planned: the portage road, or Dundas Street, from Burlington . . . to . . . the Thames.

b. *Hist.* an overland route for York boats and other heavy boats, often equipped with roller-ways.

1852 RICHARDSON *Arctic Exped.* 31: Owing to the shallowness of the streams, and badness of the portage roads over the heights between Lake Superior and Rainy Lake, the transport of goods requires to be performed in canoes, with much manual labor, and is, consequently, very expensive. **1897** LADUE *Klondyke Nuggets* 23: It would be better if the traveller should portage here, the miners having constructed a portage road on the west side and put down roller-ways in some places on which they roll their boats over. **1928** FREEMAN *Nearing North* 380: The rotting logs of the old portage road of the *voyageurs* are covered by the high fill which forms the southern approach to the bridge.

c. See **portage path**.

1831 *Trans.Lit.& Hist.Soc.Que.* II 290: To surmount these, a good portage road has been formed north of the channel, through a stony hard-wood tract, in which three small lakes are crossed. **1903** CARR-HARRIS *White Chief* 26: . . . the nearer or right passage led by a winding route to a rocky cove at the beginning of the portage road. **1961** GREENING *Ottawa* 85: . . . the main street of this community [Pembroke] was for some time a portage road.

2 *Maritimes, Hist.* a trail or path through the bush; a bush road, especially a logging road. See also **portage, n.** (def. 8 and note). Cp. **portage, v.** (def. 2).

1815 BOUCHETTE *Lower Canada* 587: There is an Indian footpath or portage road of eleven miles to the Grand River, which flows into the River St. John. **1902** *Gun and Rod in N.B.* 91: Perhaps the best district for partridges and woodcock is that between Bass River and Tabusintac, in the vicinity of the Miramichi highway, and the portage roads leading off it.

3 *Hist.* See **portage railroad**.

1916 SKELTON *Railway Builders* 37: This portage road promised to shorten materially the journey from Montreal to New York. **1946** LOWER *Colony to Nation* 281: It became a portage road across from Lake Ontario to the Georgian Bay.

portage route See portage path.

1905 WALLACE *Labrador Wild* 65: On Monday morning George took an axe and cut us a portage route from our camp through the swamp a mile and half to the foot of a steep hill. **1958** *Cdn Geog.Jnl* July 82/2: . . . he found a portage route from the east end of Lake Athabasca. . . .

portage sling *Fur Trade, Obs.* See tumpline.

1808 (1897) COUES *New light* II 478: The four middlemen tackled themselves to the towing-line by means of their portage slings.

portage strap *Fur Trade* See tumpline and picture. See also portage collar.

1827 (1912) ERMATINGER *Express Jnl* 103: Passengers, pieces and baggage being as follows . . . 1 bale portage straps . . . ½ Maccaron. . . . **1857** (1863) PALLISER *Journals* 24: The voyageur carried two of these pieces at each trip backwards and forwards across the portage on his back; they are held by a long leather strap called a portage strap, the peculiarity of which is its being broad in the middle, where it is adjusted to the man's forehead leaving him the free use of his arms in passing the brush. **1948** *Beaver* June 21/2: The simple voyageur Leger lost only a three-point blanket . . . a portage strap, a pair of French shoes, and a cotton shirt.

portage track or **trail** See **portage path.**

1894 WINSOR *Cartier to Frontenac* 258: The party began
to carry the material . . . along the portage track for
twelve miles. **1896** (1898) RUSSELL *Far North* 14: I left
the portage trail to hunt in the bush, found it almost
impossible to manage my small snow-shoes in the soft
snow and took them off only to find myself sinking
waist deep in the snow! **1921** HAWORTH *Trailmakers* 15:
In 1615 Champlain ascended the rapids-filled Ottawa,
crossed a portage track worn smooth by untold
generations of moccasined feet following the great
aboriginal route between East and West, [and] reached
the broad expanse of demon-infested Lake Nipissing.
1965 *Cdn Geog.Jnl* Sep. 88: [Caption] Park Rangers . . .
keep the portage trails open.

portage work See **portaging.**

1905 (1954) *B.C.Hist.Qtly* XVIII 217: It was a large
party, heavily laden, and, in the absence of help, the
portage work at the Dalles of the Columbia river would
have taken a long time.

portaging *n.* the carrying of canoes or boats and
their cargoes at a portage (def. 1a).

1854 KEEFER *Ottawa* 34: . . . it must be high wines, 40
o.p., condensed for convenience of portaging, and in
color and in character veritable blue ruin. **1918**
DAVIDSON *North West Co.* 217: In speaking of portaging,
Landmann said that a canoe weighed fifteen hundred
pounds and that six men were expected to reverse,
shoulder, and carry it. **1965** *Cdn Geog.Jnl* June 184/3:
Portaging on the Barrens is different from portaging
through trees.

portaging crowd *Lumbering, Maritimes, Hist.* a
group of loggers in town from the portage roads
(def. 2) for a visit. See also **portage,** *v.* (def. 2).

1930 *B.C.Lumberman* May 56/2: Just one more night at
Colpaw's with the old "portashing" crowd.

portash, portashing *n.* See **portage, portaging.**

Port Colborne fair lead [after Port Colborne,
Ontario, at the western end of the Welland Canal,
where the lead was first devised] See quote.

1959 *Kingston Whig-Standard* (Ont.) 12 May 1/2: The
Port Colborne fair lead is a revolving pulley in the ship's
side through which a line is put ashore. The pulley
turns as the ship moves through a lock or up and down
in the lock so the line can move easily from the power
winch on deck.

pose [poz] *n.* [< Cdn F "a laying or setting down"
< F *poser* set down, deposit] *Fur Trade, Hist.*
1 one of several stopping places established on a
long portage (def. 1a). See 1933 quote. See also
rest (def. 1) and **stage,** *n.* (def. 5b).

1793 (1933) MACDONELL *Diary* 96: The Portage is full
of hills is divided by the voyageurs into sixteen Poses
or resting places. . . . **1860** (1956) KOHL *Kitchi-Gami* 59:
This rocher de Otamigan is in a swamp close to one of
these poses. **1933** GATES *Five Traders* 97n: A pose was
not merely a resting place; it was also a temporary
depot, and all the packs were brought to the first pose
before any were carried to the second. This arrangement
was designed as a security against possible Indian raids.
Inasmuch as the same places were used as poses by all

who passed, it came to be the common thing to measure
the length of a portage by the number of poses along
the trail. The distance between two poses varied
between six to eight hundred yards, depending upon
conditions on the trail. **1961** *Cdn Geog.Jnl* July 5: . . . he
puts down his load at a place known as a "posé" [sic].
2 the distance or track between two such stopping
places. See also **lift** (def. 1), **rest** (def. 2), **stage,** *n.* and
stopping-place (def. 3).

1798 (1916) THOMPSON *Narrative* 294: A Rest, or Pose,
is the distance the cargo of a canoe is carried from place
to place and then rest. **1824** (1931) SIMPSON *Fur Trade*
62: The Portage . . . is crossed in two poses or lifts; at
each end of the pose a guard is stationed for the security
of the property while the people transport the Canoes
and Baggage. **1929** (1931) MERK *Fur Trade* 11: Such a
load was carried by the voyageur at a kind of a dog
trot, by "poses" or "lifts" of 500 to 800 yards if the
portage was a long one.

posogan *n.* See **pesogan.**

posse ['possi] *n. West* a group of riders on well-
trained horses who perform in processions, at
fairs or stampedes, etc., usually for some charity.

1958 *Edmonton Jnl* 2 Aug. 23/5: The Jasper Rodeo . . .
program includes the Edmonton Sheriff's Posse musical
ride. . . . **1961** *Ibid.* 3 July 21/4: Adding to the show was
the Edmonton posse, comprising 16 matched palomino
horses. . . . The posse also gave performances Saturday
and Sunday and was greatly enjoyed by the large crowd.

possible sack† [< Am.E < Sp. *posibles* wealth,
means] *West and Northwest, Hist.* a canvas or
leather bag in which a person's belongings are
kept.

1866 LORD *Naturalist* I 79: . . . setting to work, I
overhauled my 'possible sack,' found a few coarse
hooks, a bit of gut, and some thread. **1892** DAUNT *Land
of Moose* 65: So saying, the old trapper unsheathed his
shining knive, and separated the "mouffle," or
overhanging upper lip of the moose, and placed it in his
possible sack. **1952** (1959) HAYCOX *Earthbreakers* 319:
All he carried was gun, powder flask and possible sack.

post *n. Fur Trade* a trading post (def. 1), especially
one belonging to the Hudson's Bay Company.

1789 *Quebec Gaz.* 1 Nov. 2/1: We still expect a very
considerable quantity of Furrs and Peltries from the
most distant Posts of the Upper Country, which cannot
arrive to admit of the Vessels sailing before the 25th.
1820 (1938) SIMPSON *Athabasca Jnl* 2: The officers
selected for the several Posts, are perfectly competent
for the charge. . . . **1960** *Press* Dec. 13: The title was,
however, except for a few isolated posts on the great
Bay itself, generally not "pushed" so long as the
French held Quebec. . . .

postage stamp province *Hist.* See quotes.
See also **prairie province** (def. 1).

1935 MORICE *Red River Insurrection* 332: A province
named Manitoba [was] erected [containing 13,928
square miles]. [Footnote] This was to form what was long
known as the postage stamp province. [**1953** LEBOURDAIS
Nation of North 64: The province of Manitoba had
been set up, a small square patch in the midst of the
Northwest Territories, like a postage stamp on the map
of North America.]

post-and-rail (fence)† *n.* a fence made of rails
set lengthwise between vertical posts, usually in
pairs side by side.

1824 *Canadian Mag.* III 100: Post-and-rail fences have
a neat light appearance, and occupy but little space.

1954 BRUCE *Channel Shore* 57: Across the field to the west . . . Richard at least had serviceable post-and-rail.

post cariole *Obs.* See **cariole** (def. 1a).
*a*1820 (1838) HEAD *Forest Scenes* 147: I hired a post cariole, or small sleigh drawn by one horse, to take me hence to Quebec.

post-house *n.* **1**† *Hist.* one of a number of government-licensed inns equipped with livery and a fixed tariff of rates per mile for hire of horses by travellers.
1778 *Quebec Gaz.* 5 Nov. 1/1: It is His Excellency the Governor's pleasure, that Post-houses be established by Lorette, Champigny, St. Ange and the upper Concessions of St. Augustin, in order to avoid the inconveniences which attend travelling the lower road by Cap-rouge. **1923** WILLIAMS *Spinning Wheels* 23: . . . earlier when Kingston was still a fur trading post . . . a line of post-houses extended from Quebec to Montreal and the water *route* between the latter and Toronto was accomplished in Government *bateaux.* . . .
2 *Fur Trade* the manager's house at a post, *q.v.*
1913 (1917) CURRAN & CALKINS *Northland* 73: When on our former trip to the country, we usually slept aboard the yacht or at the post houses, consequently we were not brought into such close touch with the dogs as on this occasion. **1942** TWOMEY & HERRICK *Needle to North* 23: Sick natives must get to the post-house before August and wait until the little boat brings him.

postkeeper *n. Fur Trade* See **post manager**.
1953 LOWER *Voyages* 20: . . . old "Colonel" Millar, the postkeeper . . . had come through Hudson's Straits in 1870. . . .

post-Loyalist *n. Hist.* See **late Loyalist**. Cp. **Pre-Loyalist**.
1948 ANGLIN *Canada Unlimited* 18: The Americans thought . . . the Loyalists would have had time to regret their previous decision and the great flood of "post-Loyalists" who had followed them to British North America looking for new land and opportunities would be ripe for revolt. **1957** *Culture* XVIII 246: During the next thirty years [1795-1825] . . . increasing numbers of post-Loyalist settlers [came] into Upper Canada, where they settled along the shores of Lakes Erie and Lake Ontario.

post manager *Fur Trade* the person in charge of a post, *q.v.* Cp. **factor**.
1920 *Beaver* Nov. 2/2: . . . Mr. Brabant received orders . . . to report at Chipewyan as post manager.
1965 *Globe and Mail* (Toronto) 24 May 4/1: [Caption] . . . bales of silken, goaty-smelling beaver skins [are] purchased by Hudson's Bay post manager Marshall Campion. . . .

postmaster *n. Fur Trade* See 1829 quote.
1829 (1940) *Minutes of Council* (H.B.C.) 236n: Post Masters Are a Class which ranks in the Service between Interpreters and Clerks. They are generally persons who while filling the office of common Labourers brought themselves into particular notice by their steadiness honesty and attention and were in due times raised from the "ranks" and placed in charge of small Posts at Salys from 35 to £45 p. Annm.
*c*1840 (1889) MACKENZIE *Missississouri Indians* 319: I do not see the use of so much Greek and Latin for these postmasters, since neither artificial nor natural acquirements are of any avail. **1953** LOWER *Voyages* 33: The postmaster at Attawapiskat . . . was minus the toes on his right foot.

postmastership *n. Fur Trade* the position and status of postmaster.
1889 MASSON *Les Bourgeois* I 319: These postmasterships, necessarily of late creation, were intermediate positions in the Hudson Bay Company's service between the clerks—the "commissioned gentlemen" —and the men, and were generally given to educated half-breeds.

post native *Fur Trade* See **home-guard** (def. 1b).
[**1913** COWIE *Adventurers* 194: Lamack was counted among the Saulteaux Indians frequenting the post. On the Bay he would have been called one of the "Homeguards," for he never went far from it, and was available for odd trips or work which haughtier, or lazier, hunters would not condescend to perform.]
1955 JENNESS *Indians of Canada* 257: "Post" natives disregarded and undermined the prestige of the chiefs and elders. . . .

Posts of the Western Sea *Hist.* See quote.
1954 WALLACE *Pedlars* xi: In the later days of the French Régime in Canada, the French built on the Red, the Assiniboine, and the Saskatchewan Rivers a series of trading-posts known as "the Posts of the Western Sea."

potashery *n. Hist.* See **ashery**.
1799 *Canada Constellation* (Niagara-on-the-Lake, U.C.) 8 Nov. 4/1: For field ashes, 9d. at the potashery, and 6d. if he goes for them. **1832** DOYLE *Hints on Emigration* 48: When timber is burned if a potashery be near, the sale of the ashes will produce a smart sum. **1930** *Cdn Hist.Rev.* XI 39: The only buildings were . . . two saw-mills, a carding shop, a potashery. . . .

pot au beurre *Cdn French, Slang, Hist.* See **butter tub**.
[**1814** (1954) WALLACE *Pedlars* 75: [trans. from French of the *Narrative* of Gabriel Franchere] Behind all this is . . . a *jail*, not less necessary than the rest. The voyageurs give it the name of *pot au beurre*—the butter tub.] **1900** BRYCE *History of H.B.C.* 157: The voyageurs give the last [building] the name "Pot au beurre." **1927** ELLIOTT *Hugh Layal* 159: The "Pot au Beurre," the half-breeds called it [the Butter Vat] and its fame was known even in Montreal. **1954** CAMPBELL *Nor'Westers* 103: There was, too, a jail—the *pot au beurre,* or buttertub, the *voyageurs* called it—where unruly young men cooled off after some of the worst brawls.

pot-bow *n.* a piece of wood used in suspending a pot over an outdoor fire. See also **chiploquorgan** and **picture**.
1945 RICHARDSON *We Keep a Light* 182: Consequently a certain element in the district had been accustomed to having their own way about coming and going over the Island, making use of wood for pot-bows, gathering the berries and shooting the ducks . . . and they were reluctant to admit our rights as owners.

pot-cover *n. Nfld* See quote.
1906 LUMSDEN *Skipper Parson* 57: There was a clumsy imitation [of snowshoes] in use, made of wood, called "pot-covers," which they wore with long boots. *Ibid.* 63: We soon got disgusted with the "pot-covers," and left them hanging on a tree.

poté *n.* See **pottie**.

pothead[1] *n.* See **caa'ing whale**.

1863 *Islander* (Charlottetown) 14 Aug. 2/3 : Large numbers of Potheads are in the Bay, which probably accounts for the squid panic. Brigus, Nfld. **1964** *Cdn Geog.Jnl* Mar. 92/3 : . . . entire herds of 40-foot pothead whales have been known to run aground on the beaches to escape his vicious attacks.

pothead[2] *n.* See quote.

1958 *Edmonton Jnl* 31 July 25/4 : The pothead was being replaced Thursday . . . The [cable] terminal, known as a pothead, has been in use about five years.

pothead whale See **pothead**[1].

pothie *n.* See **pottie**.

pothole *n.* **1 a.**† See **kettle**[1] (def. 2).

1880 GORDON *Mountain and Prairie* 162 : Its rocky sides have been rent and peeled by the current, here scooped into great pot-holes, there seamed with broad fissures, now broken into jagged edges, now worn into smooth curves. **1921** HAWORTH *Trailmakers* 75 : More than a century after Mackenzie passed, I myself stood at this spot and saw some of these interesting "pot holes." **1956** KEMP *Northern Trader* 209 : This pothole-in-the-making is near the foot of the rapid and in very deep water, but the whirling rock can be heard as it grinds itself away.

b. a circular depression in any rock surface.

1913 (1917) CURRAN & CALKINS *Northland* 37 : The trail is only about three hundred feet long and crosses rough rocks, in which many pot-holes have been worn, hence the name [Kettle Portage]. **1959** LEISING *Arctic Wings* 295 : A good thirty feet above the high-tide mark on the rocks, we came to a square stone building nestled in a rock pothole.

2 a.† a hole in a road, especially one caused by water erosion or frost damage. See also **pitch-hole** (def. 2).

1953 (1958) WALKER *Pardon My Parka* 53 : We . . . took a right-angle turn down a narrow little lane with ruts and potholes that nearly shook the car apart. **1963** *Kingston Whig-Standard* (Ont.) 20 Feb. 30/1 : "Ottawa is a city famous for its potholes, and also for its pot bellies," said Kingston Labor Council's new President as he took office Tuesday.

b. an airpocket which causes an aircraft to bump.

1963 *Sun* (Vancouver) 7 May 11 : [Headline] 68 Survive Wild Ride [as] Airliner Hits Pothole in the Sky.

3 *West* **a.** See 1902 quote. See also **muskeg** (def. 4), **pothole lake,** and **slough** (def. 1). Cp. **sink-hole** (def. 2).

1902 (1956) *Sask.Hist.* IX 1 31 : In natural depressions of the soil, of course, water had gathered and formed so-called "pot-holes"—circular basins of a swampy nature, generally shallow. The "potholes" usually have a heavy growth of wild hay, though occasionally one was met with in which the vegetation was stunted, because of the presence of some alkali. **1955** HOBSON *Nothing Too Good* 92 : We held the cattle on the pothole for two days, with two of us riding twelve-hour shifts around them. **1963** *Globe and Mail* (Toronto) 13 Mar. 17/1 : Show me the man who doesn't get the shivers when half-a-dozen greenhead mallards start sideslipping into the pothole in front of him. . . .

b. an artificial dam or reservoir. See also **dugout** (def. 3).

1957 *Maclean's* 25 May 27/3 : Today any southern Albertan can catch a creelful of trout simply by driving or strolling to the nearest government-planted pothole, a term loosely used on the prairie to embrace, in this case, any small landlocked lake, or dam. **1957** *Fish and Game* June 9/1 : With its growing irrigation, power and agricultural demands for impounding water Alberta is becoming a land of man-made lakes and pot-holes filled with millions of fighting trout, where once there were only windswept expanses of gently-rolling prairie.

4 *North* See **muskeg** (def. 1).

1921 MARSHALL *Snowshoe Trail* 64 : The breath of the horses was a steam cloud ; the potholes in the marsh were grey and lifeless with ice. **1950** HAMBLETON *Abitibi* 133 : There were, so far as the Indians could recall, no large lakes, but the ground was swampy, muskeg and full of potholes in the summer-time. **1959** BODSWORTH *Strange One* 134 : They [geese] need pothole muskeg—muskeg that's full of small lakes and ponds with little islands in them.

5 *B.C.Interior* See **hole** (def. 1).

1955 HOBSON *Nothing Too Good* 69 : Our plan had been to throw the cattle into Chinee Lake pothole this night. . . . **1962** FRY *Ranch on the Cariboo* 143 : It was in Bridge Lake country that Bill Wilson . . . had his pothole homestead. . . .

6 See **hell-hole**.

1965 *Kingston Whig-Standard* (Ont.) 10 May 6/2 : Rumor also suggests that the most interesting of the underground potholes fell victim to progress, having been in the path of the right-of-way for the railway when it was built.

pothole easement a payment made to prairie farmers to induce them to permit ducks to breed freely in sloughs on their property.

1962 *Globe and Mail* (Toronto) 23 Feb. 3/1 : The solution would be a pothole easement—paying the farmer to leave his own pothole alone.

pothole fishing angling in prairie potholes in which trout have been planted.

1957 *Maclean's* 25 May 56/1 : . . . you can only judge the success of pothole fishing by the new gleam in the Albertans' eyes. Pothole fishing is reuniting the family. Families sometimes camp by a pothole all weekend.

pothole lake or **slough** See **pothole** (def. 3a).

1938 ELLS *Northland Trails* 85 : It is a land of . . . mysterious pot-hole lakes and ponds with neither inlets nor outlets. **1958** *Edmonton Jnl* 28 July 4/3 : We stopped the car to watch waterfowl on a pothole slough by the road and suddenly spotted a young buck deer, trotting toward us and the pothole.

pothole meadow See **slough meadow**.

1955 HOBSON *Nothing Too Good* 69 : . . . the pothole meadows were still some five miles away from the spruce clump.

pothole shooting *West* hunting ducks near potholes or sloughs, where they feed and breed.

1964 *B.C.Digest* Oct. 4/2 : However, it is not too great a distance to the Merritt-Douglas Lake pothole shooting which looks good this season.

potlatch ['pɑtlætʃ] *n.* [< Chinook Jargon < Nootka *patshatl* gift ; a giving] *Esp.Pacific Coast* **1** *Obs.* a gift of goods or money ; donation ; handout. See also **cultus potlatch** and **return potlatch**. Also spelled *potlach*.

1860 *Brit.Colonist* (Victoria) 17 July 2/2: A Tongass Indian on Sunday afternoon accosted a man named John Garretson, on Humboldt Street, with the demand; "Patlatch quarter." **1883** *Brandon Blade* (Man.) 1 Nov. 4/2: Indians from various parts of the valley are already coming to ... find out how much "potlatch" the various growers will pay in the way of potatoes, beef, pasturage, and "tillicum" money, beside what they earn. **1884** CHITTENDEN *Queen Charlotte Is.* 14: The Indian, generally ... steals into your presence without warning, handles whatever he sees without permission, smokes if you allow it, and seldom, especially if a middle-aged or old woman, leaves you without begging a potlatch. **1935** HALLIDAY *Potlatch and Totem* 5: The word *potlatch* is a Chinook word, and signifies 'a gift.' The real Indian word used in this connection is not *potlatch* but *passapa,* and while it means a gift, it also means a gift with an elastic string attached to it, so that it will come back with interest.

2 a. *Hist.* See 1964 quote. See also **donation feast** and **winter festival.** Cp. **private potlatch.**
☞ *Although the potlatch was most highly developed among the Kwakiutl of British Columbia, it played, in one form or another, an important part in the culture of the Indians of the Pacific Coast from Oregon to Alaska and of those in the Interior of B.C. and the Northwest. The practice was outlawed in 1884 by the Potlatch Law, q.v.*
1873 (1877) GRANT *Ocean to Ocean* 318: His reputation mounted to an extraordinary height because of so magnificent a potlatch, and he stood a good chance of the Tyeeship.... **1876** (1961) LA VIOLETTE *Survival* 34: I questioned the chief respecting a "Potlache" which he had held at his place during the previous winter, and ascertained that himself and two of his headsmen had given away in presents to their friends 134 sacks of flour, 150 pairs of blankets, together with a quantity of supplies and provisions.... **1880** DAWSON *Queen Charlotte Is.* 126B: The potlatch besides being a means of combining labour for an industrial 'bee', for purposes in which individual effort is insufficient, is also a method of acquiring influence in the tribe, and in some cases, as we have seen, of attaining even to the chieftaincy. **1955** JENNESS *Indians of Canada* 341: Most potlatches took place in the autumn, after the people had stored away their food and before the secret society began its winter dances. **1964** DUFF *Indian History* 58: A potlatch was a large gathering to which important people were invited in order to witness some event, such as a young person assuming a new name or the completion of a new house and erection of a totem pole. On such an occasion the host would display his wealth and present gifts to his guests. The more he gave away, the more prestige he acquired.
b. a modified festival and ceremony taking the form of a present-giving party after the passing of the Potlatch Law *q.v.* See also **give-away dance.** Cp. **tea-dance.**
1958 HAWTHORN *Indians of B.C.* 280: The exceptions include the rare contemporary potlatch of the mid-Coast, with its dances and privilege displays.... **1964** *Western Miner* Apr. 27/1: The little Indian village of Mooseide below Dawson held its annual Potlach around Christmas time [c1910]. The Indian Chief came to Dawson with his dog teams and took Mr. Dines and his orchestra and instruments to play for their big dance of the year. **1966** *Islander* 27 Feb. 7/2: It is considered very rude to leave your seat at a potlatch....
c. See **potlatch system.**

1926 MCKELVIE *Huldowget* v: The potlatch—a peculiar banking system—has been banned, and the bartering of coppers has been declared illegal. **1961** LA VIOLETTE *Survival* 36: An important facet of the entire system of potlatch debts and credits along with native enforcement of payment, was demolished for Mr. Duncan's newly-converted Christians: they were withdrawn from participation and accessibility.

d. (used attributively) designating articles used during the potlatch.

1890 BOAS *Masks* 9: Masks must not be used in summer and during daylight, except *potlatch* masks. **1900** LONDON *Son of Wolf* 222: "Then made I preparation for the wedding, and the people that lived even to the east came for the food of the feast and the potlatch token." **1961** LA VIOLETTE *Survival* x: ... I was impressed with the amount of talk among the coastal Indians about the land title question and about "getting back those potlatch goods," as Guy Williams expressed it.... **1962** *Wildlife Rev.* 12 July: [Caption] The Potlatch Dish. **1966** *Islander* 27 Feb. 6/1: Birger and I were listening to the Indian's potlatch drum.

3 *Hist.* a party given by fur traders for the distributing of gifts to Indians. See also **regale** (def. 3).
1891 *Trans.Roy.Soc.Can.* X 2 115: The Hudson Bay Company ... the better to keep the natives under subjection, gave themselves every year a kind of tobacco potlatch, in connection where with the traditional differences of rank among the receivers were scrupulously observed. **1957** FISHER *Pemmican* 40: Potlatch was a Chinook term meaning a free feast with gifts and was generally taken by the Indians to mean the Christmas season.

4 *Informal* a party or celebration.
1900 LONDON *Son of Wolf* 24: Then he [a white trapper] mingled with the men and maidens, and that night gave a *potlatch.* **1924** DORRANCE *Never Fire First* 30: He ... sent for the makings of a "party," or potlatch. **1936** STRINGER *Wife-Traders* 55: "You know as well as I do that these people had one of their pot-latches last night. And that's something I've been trying to stop." **1948** HOLLIDAY *Valley of Youth* 156: ... the main purpose of these gatherings seemed to be the potlatch, a sort of gambling orgy.... **1954** EVANS *Mist* 131: "Police or no police, what a potlatch that will be!"

5 a fair or carnival held on an Indian reserve and featuring canoe races, games, and dances, often held to raise funds for local causes.
1958 *Native Voice* Sp.ed. 4: The Princess [Margaret] attended a Potlach at Courtenay arranged by President Robert Clifton of the Native Brotherhood of British Columbia. **1959** *Sun* (Vancouver) 13 May 27: [Caption] Tom-toms and smoke signals are announcing the second annual Squamish Indian Potlatch, May 23 and 24. *Ibid.* 25 May 21/5: The squall and a dangerously rough ebb tide marred the international canoe races that marked the wind-up of the two-day potlatch sponsored by the Squamish tribe.

6 *Figurative uses.*
1963 *Sun* (Vancouver) 16 Aug. 26/1: In the international cutthroat competition between East and West, have we got to such a desperate position ... where, in order to win at all costs we are willing to throw our children into the potlatch fire? **1964** *Press* Feb. 13: Certainly the two-party leadership potlatch was not

potlatch
potlatch system

without its shadows cast before. **1964** *Family Herald*
12 Mar. 15/1: Recently I talked to a farm couple who
are happier than a sweepstake winner at a potlatch.

potlatch ['pɑtlætʃ] *v.* [< n.] *Esp.Pacific Coast*
1 a. give with the expectation of a return gift.

1870 *Mainland Guardian* (New Westminster, B.C.)
27 Apr. 3/3: Willingly would we potlatch a couple of
ordinary blankets for one of their iktas. **1966** *Islander*
27 Feb. 6/1: Potlatch means give away—but not quite.
because a return was in order, of more than the gift and
of something that often might be quite unusual.
b. give freely.
1909 SERVICE *Cheechako* 92: And it seems to me ...
that the man who potlatched the whiskey and landed
me into the hole/ Was Grubbe that unmerciful
bounder, Grubbe of the City Patrol. **1945** *B.C.Hist.
Qtly* Oct. 245: Chief Wattle-kainum potlatched all his
wealth to save the white man's life. ... **1962** NICHOLSON
West Coast 267: He still has his gasboat and fishes on
and off, but only catches sufficient to eat and potlatch to
the older Indians, some of whom are in their nineties.

2 a. hold or take part in a potlatch (def. 2a).
1899 (1961) LA VIOLETTE *Survival* 78: To potlatch or
not to potlatch is the question which is agitating the
minds of Indians of Nass River district. ...
1927 MCKELVIE *Black Canyon* 22: "By Jove, the Songhees
are up to something, I think they're going to potlatch."
1961 LA VIOLETTE *Survival* 87: At Alert Bay, in 1946, the
late Mrs. Stephen Cook reported to the writer that "my
sons have been chased from the fishing grounds because
they would not potlatch." **1966** *Islander* 27 Feb. 7/1:
... the Owekenos cleaned up on the Bella Bellas, by
inviting the Bella Bellas to potlatch with them one
evening in a strange house, built half underground,
with entrance by a ladder leaning downward inside.
b. *Informal* hold a party. See also **potlatch,** *n.*
(def. 4).
1957 FISHER *Pemmican* 137: "By the way, this
[Christmas] season do we potlatch at our post or at
yours?"

potlatched ['pɑtlætʃt] *adj. Pacific Coast* obtained
at a potlatch (def. 2a).
1966 *Islander* 27 Feb. 6/1: Birger's father ... [sold]
potlatched goods for cash over the counter of his store.

potlatcher ['pɑtlætʃɚ] *n.* [< *potlatch*, v. + *-er*]
Pacific Coast **1** a person giving a potlatch (def. 2a).
See also **potlatch-giver.**
1961 LA VIOLETTE *Survival* 98: William Scow, one of the
Kwakiutl potlatchers convicted in 1922, now Chief
Scow ... is considered to be one of the outstanding
Indian leaders in all Canada. ...

2 a person attending a potlatch.
1961 LA VIOLETTE *Survival* 90: Whereas earlier
potlatchers travelled only in canoes ... the increased
use of the gasoline engine provided easier access to
isolated villages.

potlatch-giver *n. Pacific Coast* See **potlatcher**
(def. 1).
1955 JENNESS *Indians of Can.* 344: ... there was more
... wanton destruction of both food and property for
no other purpose than to enhance the prestige of the
potlatch-giver.

potlatch hall or **house** *Pacific Coast* a
communal hall for holding potlatches (def. 2).
1926 MCKELVIE *Huldowget* 190: The trial will be held
in the old potlatch hall. **1954** *B.C.Hist.Qtly* XVIII 53:
Perhaps all had plank houses ... but Chowitsut also
had a "potlatch house" at the Portage. ...
1966 *Islander* 27 Feb. 7/1: There were signs of life ...
in the potlatch house. ...

potlatching ['pɑtlætʃɪŋ] *n. Esp.Pacific Coast*
1 a. *Hist.* the holding of potlatches (def. 2a).
1882 (1961) LA VIOLETTE *Survival* 35: The question of
"potlaching" has engaged the most serious attention.
1964 DUFF *Indian History* 59: Potlatching also changed
in character. Among the Kwakiutl at least, it became
a substitute for war. ... During the 1850's and 1860's
warfare decreased and potlatching increased.
b. the holding of potlatches (def. 2b).
1958 HAWTHORN *Indians of B.C.* 66: Potlatching is
carried on at burials. As this was described to us it was
merely a large, somewhat drunken party with no gift
giving, but this report was from the Sisters and is
probably not a full account.

2 *Hist.* the holding of potlatches (def. 3).
1891 *Trans.Roy.Soc.Can.* X 2 114: If potlatching and
old-fashioned dancing did not at once fall into
desuetude, it was because both were countenanced by
the North-West Company and, later on, the Hudson
Bay Company. **1922** *Beaver* May 4/1: Smoking,
drinking, potlaching, and Sunday work were
prohibited. **1923** *Ibid.* Oct. 23: They will all come up the
river again and spend several days potlatching.

potlatching ['pɑtlætʃɪŋ] *adj. Pacific Coast* of or
having to do with potlatches (def. 2a).
1961 LA VIOLETTE *Survival* 21n: Philip Drucker ... is
of the opinion that in the great dramatic productions
which incorporated the tamanawas (medicine dance)
and the potlatching activity, the "corpse" was a
simulation. ... *Ibid.* 81: [In January, 1915] Charles
Nowell, a Kwakiutl of Alert Bay, sent a list of names of
each copper to Mr. Clements, a member of the House
of Commons, with the symbolic potlatching value of
each sheet of copper metal indicated, the coppers
varying in value as do banknotes.

Potlatch Law *Hist.* a federal law forbidding the
potlatch (def. 2a) on the ground that the
institution was wasteful and disruptive. See quote.
1961 LA VIOLETTE *Survival* 43: The Potlatch Law as it
came to be called ... remained on the statutes of
Canada [from April 19, 1884] until the Indian Act
was revised completely in 1951. ...

potlatch system *Pacific Coast* the system of
holding reciprocal potlatches (def. 2a) and thus
incurring the accompanying debts and obligations
of this social institution among the Coast Indians.
See also **potlatch,** *n.* (def. 2c).
1955 JENNESS *Indians of Can.* 344: Practically identical
with that of the other tribes ... was the potlatch
system of the Kwakiutl, except that there was more
rivalry between the heads of clans, and consequently
more extravagance and wanton destruction of both
food and property for no other purpose than to enhance
the prestige of the potlatch-giver. **1958** HEALEY *Alert
Bay* 41: The potlatch system was a powerful spur to
ambition, but finally the privilege of giving began to be
abused and distorted until it resembled a huge octopus,
which held all customs and habits of the Indians in its
embrace. **1961** LA VIOLETTE *Survival* 78: ... almost
annually deputations had gone to Victoria to try to

secure . . . the maintenance of the potlatch system. **1966** *Sun* (Vancouver) 3 Oct. 31/1: . . . some of us grieve the suppression and near extinction of the potlach system. . . .

pottie ['pɑti] *n.* [< Cdn F; prob. from *petit* little (see 1773 quote), perhaps influenced by Cdn F *potée* person of little worth] *Fur Trade, Slang, Hist.* **1** a member of the X.Y. Company, *q.v.* See also **Little Company** and **Little Potties.**
[**1773** (1954) WALLACE *Pedlars* 12: We had one Peter Pangman, a petty pedlar, down here [York Factory] to spy out the Market. . . .] **1800** (1933) MCLEOD *Diary* 145: [They] cannot keep their own Indians from going to trade with our people, who are so near a little Poté opposition & short of Goods at the same time. **1800** (1890) MCKENZIE *Journal* 390: Last night, he gave a large keg to the Montagners . . . but as soon as he was out of sight they went to the Potties to take credits. **1897** COUES *New Light* I 223n: The "X.Y. Co.," [was] also styled in derision the "Little Company" (whence probably the nickname "Potties," by Indian corruption of F. Les Petits, "Little Ones.") **1954** CAMPBELL *Nor'Westers* 96: Meantime Simon McTavish was taking strong measures to meet the opposition from the X.Y. "potties."
2 a member of the Hudson's Bay Company, *q.v.* See quote.
1821 (1938) SIMPSON *Athabasca Jnl* 214: My services would be required as a bully in Athabasca to fight with and beat the servants of the H.B. Coy. (usually nick named "putties" by the N.W. Coy.).

poudre *n. Cdn French* See **poudrerie.** Also *la poudre.*
1791 (1911) SIMCOE *Diary* 71: There is little wind here, except with a snowstorm of fine snow. The French call it poudre or powdered snow, and to travel with that blowing in one's face is very disagreeable.
1832 MCGREGOR *Brit.Amer.* I 129: The Canadians and Acadians call this kind of drift *La Poudre.* **1901** PARKER *Right of Way* 83: It was a goodly scene . . . the flowery tracery of frost hanging like cobwebs everywhere; the poudre sparkle in the air. . . .

poudre day See 1909 quote. See also **poudre** and **poudrerie.**
1873 (1904) BUTLER *Wild North Land* 149: The sun, which on one of these "poudre" days in the North seems to exert as much influence upon the war of cold and storm as some good bishop was wont to exercise over the belligerents at Cressy or Poictiers . . . muffled himself up in the nearest cloud and went fast asleep until the fight was over. **1909** PARKER *Northern Lights* 232: A day like this is called a poudre day; and woe to the man who tempts it unthinkingly, because the light makes the delicate mist of frost shine like silver. For that powder bites the skin white in short order, and sometimes reckless men lose ears, or noses, or hands under its sharp caress. **1951** O'MEARA *Grand Portage* 186: It was a real "poudre" day. Only a few inches of dry, fine snow lay on the prairies, just enough to provide easy sledding for the dogs. . . .

poudrerie *n. Cdn French* See quotes. See also **poudre** and **snow-smoke.**
1760 PICHON *Cape Breton* 7: A circumstance that considerably adds to the horror of this season, is a kind of meteor seldom observed in other countries, and which the inhabitants distinguish by the name of poudrerie or powdering. It is a species of very fine snow, which insinuates itself into every hole and corner, and even into the minutest crevices. **1837** *Montreal Transcript* 3 Jan. 2/2: The whole of Sunday and Monday our city was enveloped in poudrerie, extremely unpropitious to

the custom of making visits. . . . [**1887** *Trans.Hist.& Sci. Soc.Man.* 28 4/2: In speaking of the climate near Hudson's Bay he uses the word poudrerie, adding in a parenthesis: "C'est ainsi qu'on appelle une petite neige qui s'insinue partout." This most expressive name for a storm of fine, hard, drifting, powdery snow has not yet been recognized in France.] **1951** BULIARD *Inuk* 45: The real northern blizzard has no match anywhere, and for it the old "coureur de bois" invented the word poudrerie.

pound *n.* **1** *Hist.* **a.** an enclosure or trap into which deer or caribou were driven for slaughtering by the Indians. See also **deer-pound.** Also spelled *pond.*
1770 (1911) TOWNSEND *Cartwright's Jnl* 22: [Caribou] walk along them [hunting fences], until they are drawn into the pound. . . . **1824** (1955) BLACK *Journal* 41: In walking about at this place I saw an Old Pond for ensnaring Reindeer &c & two Winter Encampments.
b. See **buffalo pound.**
1772 (1908) COCKING *Journal* 109: We are preparing to proceed tomorrow, to be in readiness for pounding Buffalo at an Archithinue [Blackfoot] pound. **1776** (1901) HENRY (Elder) *Travels* 299: . . . the chief led his hunters to its southern end, where there was a pound or enclosure. The fence was about four feet high, and formed of strong stakes of birch-wood, wattled with smaller branches of the same. **1879** *Sask. Herald* (Battleford, N.W.T.) 10 Feb. 2/3: At the Crossing, about nine miles from here, the Crees have made a pound for killing buffalo, but it remains to be seen if it will be a success. **1962** DICKIE *Great Golden Plain* 56: The Indians built a pound, an enclosure surrounded by a four-foot fence made of birch stakes interlaced with branches. An alleyway, funnel-shaped and with a wide mouth, was built in the same way to lead up to the pound.
2 *Hist.* See **buffalo jump.**
1792 (1934) FIDLER *Journal* 12 Nov.: [We saw] an old Blood Indian Pound for buffalo. c**1902** LAUT *Trapper* 74: The Indians hunted buffalo by driving them over a precipice where hunters were stationed on each side below, or by luring the herd into a pound or pit by means of an Indian decoy masking under a buffalo-hide. **1957** FISHER *Pemmican* 90: And what a sight it was to see the squaws rush in with hatchets and knives . . . until the whole pound under the precipice was wet with blood. . . . **1965** *Cdn Geog.Jnl* Feb. 59/3: As they plunged over the bluff into the pound below, strategically placed marksmen would dispatch them with arrows at close range.
3 *Obs.* See 1784 quote.
1784 PENNANT *Arctic Zoology* cxcvii: In the salt pile, the fish are spread one upon another, with a layer of salt between. Thus they remain till they have taken salt; and then are carried, and the salt is washed from them by throwing them off from shore in a kind of float called a Pound.

pound[1] *v. Obs.* trap in a pound (def. 1 or 2).
1772 (1908) COCKING *Journal* 109: We are preparing to proceed tomorrow, to be in readiness for pounding Buffalo at an Archithinue [Blackfoot] pound. **1776** (1951) *Saskatchewan Journals* 10 Mar.: Henry informed me that . . . the Indians have been of late very successful in Pounding Buffalo, and are continually bringing the meat in Fresh the Masters not being able to prevail on them to dry it.

pound² *v. Hist.* prepare meat for pemmican by pounding it to powder between two stones, an Indian practice adopted by the white man in the old Northwest. See also **pounded meat.**

1770 (1911) HEARNE *Journey* 89: We agreed to stay here for a day or two, to dry and pound some of the carcases to take with us. **1834** (1963) DAVIES *Northern Quebec* 251: Busily employed drying and pounding meat to render it more portable. **1921** HAWORTH *Trailmakers* 35: Here they remained for about ten days, drying and pounding caribou meat and cutting light tepee poles for use on the Barren Grounds, where no poles could be found.

pounded fish *North* fish that has been dried and powdered by being pounded between two stones to make it easier to store and carry.

1921 HEMING *Drama of Forests* 293: The friends and relations had given a plentiful store of fresh, dried, and pounded fish.

pounded meat *Hist.* the flesh of the caribou, buffalo, or other game cut into thin slices, dried in the sun or over a fire, and pulverized between two stones, the resulting powder being the basic ingredient of pemmican. See also **beat meat, piled meat,** and **pound²,** *v.*

1775 (1934) HEARNE *Journal* 177: . . . one Cannoe came with some Dry'd & Pownded Meate, and return'd emediately after trading. . . . **1896** (1898) RUSSELL *Far North* 163: While at the Dog Rib camps at the edge of the Barren Ground, I saw large quantities of pounded meat, grease, and tongues eaten, and all was hospitably shared with me, yet they refused to sell any of these luxuries if carried away from the camp. **1956** KEMP *Northern Trader* 93: The meat so acquired would either be dried, converted into pounded meat, or mixed with fat and cranberries and made up as pemmican.

powahgen or **powargan** [pəˈwɑgən] *n.* [< Algonk.] **1** a spirit, especially an evil spirit. *c*1863 (1888) MCDOUGALL *G.M.McDougall* 144: The pagan believes that his "Genius" instructs him in the hours of sleep, and the consequence is frequently awful. A Plain Cree, with whom I am acquainted, dreamed that his Puh-wah-gun, demanded three human victims, and he actually murdered three of his own tribe. **1939** *Beaver* Dec. 26/2: They had powogans (evil spirits) cut out of bark, roots, metal and charms of every description. **1956** LEECHMAN *Native Tribes* 48: They believed that there was a spirit, called a po-wah-gen, in every animal and tree. . . .

2 See **medicine bag.**

1934 GODSELL *Arctic Trader* 42: Still a pagan he worshiped his powargan, or medicine bag, the spirits in the woods and waterfalls around him, and appeased the evil manitous with offerings of tobacco and colored cloth. . . .

power *n. Obs.* a waterfall used as a source of power, as at a mill site.

1908 CLARKE *Sixty Years* 44: Less than a mile up the Irvine [River] were two other "powers," while down the Grand itself . . . was a fall taking in the waters of the combined streams.

power grader an engine-driven road-grading machine.

1926 (1966) *Cariboo Observer* 12 May 1/3: A power grader, the first of its kind seen in this district, arrived here on Tuesday for the department of public works, and has been placed at work on the main Cariboo Road, between the rancherie and Dong Prairie.

power play *Hockey* a special combination of players which is iced by a team whenever its opponents are shorthanded.

1962 *Maclean's* 6 Jan. 24/1: In these days of . . . screened shots and five-man power plays . . . it's a rare bird who holds up even for a single season. . . . **1966** *Hockey News* 1 Jan. 13/2: He is an accomplished man on the power play and is among the top penalty killers in the league.

power scow *North* a scow driven by an inboard motor.

1923 WALDO *Down Mackenzie* 156: It was not of the Captain's volition that the oil-burning power-scow was merely lashed alongside as so much dead weight to be carried, instead of helping. **1954** PATTERSON *Dangerous River* 106: Starke and Stevens had a power scow and Jack didn't think it could get up the Nahanni.

power toboggan See **motor toboggan** and picture.

1963 *Globe and Mail* (Toronto) 14 Jan. 7/7: [He] drowned . . . when his power toboggan broke through five inches of ice on the Grand River. *Ibid.* 2 Mar. 30/2: Fishermen . . . were getting to the choice spots the easy way, using skidoos, power toboggans and aircraft.

power-wagon *n.* See quote.

1949 (1958) WATTERS *B.C.Cent.Anthol.* 104: On December 19, Nurse Wilson had set out from Fort St. John in a power-wagon (a radio-and winch-equipped, four-wheeled drive vehicle), together with Indian Agent Galibois. . . . From the radio on the power-wagon, reports went out that brought planes with more antitoxin. . . .

powmagan *n. Obs.* See **pogamagan.**

1808 (1960) FRASER *Letters and Journals* 99: Their arms consist of bows and arrows, spears and clubs, or horn Powmagans.

powogon *n.* See **powahgen.**

pow-wow† [ˈpau,wau] *n.* [< Algonk.] **1** among Indians: **a.** a conference or gathering to discuss business or to engage in some ceremonial or rite.

1871 (1883) BUTLER *Great Lone Land* 165: A lot of half-naked redskins came out of the trees, and the pow-wow commenced. **1965** *Cdn Geog.Jnl* Sep. 79/3: Colonel Wolseley . . . attended a pow-wow at Fort Frances . . . with Crooked Neck, the principal Ojibwa chief [in 1870].

b. the noise and hubbub accompanying such a gathering.

1841 MCLEOD *Upper Canada* 242: The signal to board was given—the terrifying pow wow raised—the woods re-echoed the howl. **1920** *Beaver* Nov. 7/2: The pow-wow . . . was everlastingly heard during the afternoon. . . .

c. See quote.

1908 LAUT *Conquest N.W.* I 350: Four hundred miles down stream, the Blackfeet Indians were met and with great pow-wow of trading turned their furs over to the crafty Assiniboines to be taken down to York.

d. See **give-away dance.**

1952 *Beaver* Dec. 28/2: In some localities, notably the Lake of the Woods district they still held their "pow-wows" or give-away dances, at which they vied with each other in the giving away or exchanging of their treasured possessions, and to which they came adorned in their finest bead-work moccasins, belts and fire bags.

2 *Informal* among whites: **a.** a conference or meeting.

1883 *Brandon Dly Mail* (Man.) 8 Jan. 2/2: The Reform pow-wow which has recently been inflicted upon the people of Toronto gives at least some assurance that the Reform party is still in existence. **1958** *Edmonton Jnl* 20 June 2/3: The 15th annual pow-wow is expected to consider the federal Indian Act and proposed amendments now before Parliament. **1962** *Press* Nov. 9: . . . he turned up in London at a periodical pow-wow initiated by one Cyrus Eaton. . . .

b. a chat or discussion.

1903 *Eye-Opener* (High River, Alta) 21 Nov. 1/1: Being anxious to die rich, I have decided, after a prolonged pow-wow with my wife, to start in the newspaper business at Leduc, an alleged town twenty miles south of Edmonton. **1950** STEELE *Ghosts Returning* 22: "Run into him at the blacksmith's, gittin' a loose shoe put right. With him an hour. Had quite a pow-wow. Told me he was aimin' to have supper with Aunt Zina."

c. a social gathering, usually featuring a campfire after dark.

1943 *Crag and Canyon* 13 Aug. 1/3: A new slate of officers was presented by J. Murray Gibbon at the annual pow-wow held Monday night in the big pow-wow tent on the grounds of Banff Springs Hotel. **1958** *Edmonton Jnl* 19 July 2/3: The ride will end with a chuckwagon-style supper and grand pow-wow on the grounds of Banff Springs Hotel . . . and the Association's annual meeting.

3 *B.C.* a fair or exhibition held by Indians.

1959 *Programme of the 12th Annual Indian Pow Wow* (Capilano Reserve, North Vancouver, B.C.) 25 July 4/3: I wish to express my sincere thoughts to all my friends and our wonderful supporters of the Capilano Indian Pow-wow, and I want to thank you all who have contributed one way or another and have made our All Indian Show a success in the past eleven years. **1964** DUFF *Indian History* 104: The Indian "pow wows" held in recent years at North Vancouver, the "Indian Days" at Kamloops, and other gatherings such as the Williams Lake stampedes are similar occasions for Indians to enjoy renewed social contacts and gain recognition as Indians.

pow-wow† ['pauˌwau] *v.* [< n.] *Informal* converse; chat.

1951 ANGIER *At Home* 72: "It'll cheer me up vastly to have some hot lap with you later, though, and powwow a bit. Got to look at a couple of traps above here. . . ." **1954** BEZANSON *Sodbusters* 31: Roberts powwowed with the chief a while.

praire *n. Obs.* See **prairie** (def. 1).

prairie ['prɛri] *n.* [< Cdn F < F] **1** a meadow.

1734 (1866) BELL *Hist.of Canada* II 497: General Census of New France.—1734 . . . Prairies 17,657. **1760** JEFFERYS *Descr.New France* 13: The channel which separates the two islands is called La Riviere des Prairies, or, the River of the Meadows. . . . **1800** (1922) HARMON *Journal* 32: Yesterday and to-day, our way has been through prairies, interrupted occasionally, by small groves of wood. **1870** *Cdn Illust.News* 7 May 423/3: The country is . . . thickly wooded, except about the terraces of the Fraser, and occasional small prairies. . . . **1952** *Beaver* June 18/2: The Chinook wind was singing over those high prairies. . . .

2 a. extensive rolling grasslands, specifically those

found in western Canada; also, the region covered by these grasslands. See also **plain** (def. 1), **prairie country, prairie region,** and **Prairies** (def. 1). Cp. **Prairie,** *n.*

1856 BALLANTYNE *Young Fur-Traders* 23: . . . I've had to fight with red-skins and grizzly bears, and to chase the buffaloes over miles and miles of prairie. . . . **1911** (1914) BICKERSTETH *Open Doors* 27: The country north-west of Edmonton is not prairie, such as one finds in Manitoba, Saskatchewan, and Southern Alberta. **1965** *Maclean's* 19 June 40/4: The first of the trunk roads takes off . . . round the foothills' flanks to the prairie beyond.

b. the grassy plains of Western Canada collectively.

1872 *Wkly Manitoban* 18 Mar. 3/2: He could remember when vast herds of buffalo covered the prairie from the foot of the Rocky Mountains to Fort Garry. **1960** BUBLITZ *Dotted Line* 10: My living on the prairie was a full course I could not get in any college in any land.

c. *North* treeless barren ground; tundra.

1843 (1955) LEFROY *Magnetic North* 41: Although prairie, it is not quite destitute of underwood. . . . **1951** GILLIS & MYLES *North Pole* 15: I went for a long walk on the barren prairie back of the rocky beach.

d. a vast, barren expanse.

1939 (1951) TWEEDSMUIR *Hudson's Bay Trader* 155: He [a seal] was lying beside a crack, enjoying the evening sunlight that was gilding the great motionless prairie of floe ice.

Prairie *n.* See quote. Cp. **prairie** (def. 2b).

1936 DENTON & LORD *World Geography* 80: The central plain of the Saskatchewan is roughly 800 miles in length by 300 miles in width, and is known throughout Canada as The Prairie.

Prairie *adj. or attrib.* of or having to do with the Prairie Provinces, *q.v.*

1940 MACCORMAC *Canada* 231: The purchasing power of prairie farmers was cut down to less than a third. **1963** *Globe and Mail* (Toronto) 2 Feb. 1/9: Airline flights from most southern Prairie points were cancelled. **1965** *Ibid.* 5 Jan. B5/2: And the third Prairie partner—Manitoba—is making significant advances. . . .

Prairie Bubble *Hist.* See 1952 quote.

1900 OSBORN *Greater Canada* 61: The bursting of the prairie Bubble of 1881-82, the issue of transferable scrip to the half-breeds, the payment of huge Government subsidies to railway companies in land instead of cash—for all these blunders a penalty has been imposed. **1952** (1965) HAMILTON *Canadian Quotations* 185/1: The Prairie Bubble. A term used to describe the inflation of western land values, followed by collapse in 1882.

prairie buffalo† See **plain buffalo.**

1908 MAIR *Mackenzie Basin* 178: Mr. P. Deschambeault remembers seeing, in the early fifties of the last century, two fine albino examples of the prairie buffalo. . . . **1934** GODSELL *Arctic Trader* 186: During recent years some six thousand prairie buffalo have been shipped by rail from Wainwright, Alberta, to Fort McMurray. . . .

prairie cart† *Obs.* a crude two-wheeled vehicle similar to the Red River cart, *q.v.*

1880 GORDON *Mountain and Prairie* 255: The primitive prairie-cart is the conveyance most frequently employed but it is well, if possible, to have saddle-horses for the sake of comfort, and to leave the carts for tents, camp outfit, baggage, etc.

prairie chicken† **1** a grouse, *Tympanuchus cupido americanus,* common on the southern prairies. See also **chicken, heath cock, pinnated grouse, prairie fowl, prairie grouse, prairie hen,** and **squaretail** (def. 2).
1854 *Hamilton Gaz.* (C.W.) 23 Jan. 2/4: Among the edible furnished under their supervision, were 75 hams, 150 Turkeys, 400 Chickens, 250 Prairie Chickens . . . and 100 Smoked Tongues. **1958** *Edmonton Jnl* 27 Oct. 4/3: . . . there's a colony of true prairie chicken living here. . . . **1966** *Kingston Whig-Standard* (Ont.) 21 Jan. 11/2: At one time the prairie chicken lived in the southern counties of Essex and Kent [Ont.].

2 See **sharp-tailed grouse.**
1874 (1961) *Alta Hist.Rev.* Winter 13/2: The country about us teemed with ducks, prairie chickens, and prairie plovers. . . . **1908** MAIR *Mackenzie Basin* 99: . . . we found it to be a wide and beautiful table-like prairie, begirt with aspens, on which we flushed a pack of prairie chickens. **1963** *Canadian Wkly* 30 Mar. 18/4: . . . Saskatchewan is the only province to adopt an official emblem in addition to a flower: in 1945 the prairie chicken, or sharp-tailed grouse, by enactment was made an emblem of Saskatchewan.

3 *Esp.B.C., Slang* a newcomer, especially a farmer from the prairies.
1919 *Camp Worker* 3 Oct. 3/3: They would be good camps to send these prairie chickens to, and any other man who does not believe in union principles. **1953** SWANSON *Haywire Hooker* 36: So a brand-new deck was toted in,/ And eight of us sat in,/ Four of them were fallers,/ And the foreman Joe McGlinn./ The other a prairie chicken/ Who had come to the woods to toil. . . . **1961** *Sun* (Vancouver) 4 July 1/1: Clod-hopper, we call him, and stubble-jumper. And when he drives his fat new Buick to the Coast to winter among us we brand him "prairie chicken". . . .

prairie chip† See **buffalo chip.**
1935 *Cdn Geog.Jnl* Mar. 109/2: "Prairie chips," the "bois de vache" of the Métis—dried dung of the buffalo—had replaced wood in the portable and resourceful kitchens. **1961** *Alta Hist.Rev.* Winter 23/2: We used "prairie chips" altogether.

prairie country See **prairie** (def. 2a). See also **plain** (def. 1).
1853 *Trans.Lit.& Hist.Soc.Que.* IV 298: The prairie country of the Saskatchewan is roamed over by countless herds of the buffalo, also by the reindeer and the beautiful antelope. **1922** *Beaver* Oct. 15/1: During that time there had been two half-breed rebellions in the prairie country. . . .

prairie crocus See **crocus.**
1922 STRINGER *Prairie Child* 304: . . . prairie-crocuses [are] soft blue and lavender and sometimes mauve. **1955** *News-Optimist* 27 Apr. 4/4: We've heard much about the prairie crocus and now, like most westerners, we too will watch for the clumps of tiny and colorful florets each spring. **1963** SYMONS *Many Trails* 166: In early May I found prairie crocuses (anemones) there. . . .

prairie dog 1 *Obs.* See **kit fox** (def. 1a).
1823 FRANKLIN *Journey* 658: The Fulvous-necked Fox . . . is the Prairie Dog of the French settlers in America.

2† a marmot, *Cynomys ludovicianus,* once common on the southern prairies.
1833 TYLER *Progress of Discovery* 339: . . . the wistonwish or prairie marmot . . . is called prairie dog by Sergeant Guss and Lieut. Pike and it is also the barking squirrel of Lewis and Clarke. **1887** ROBERTS *Western Avernus* 8: . . . looked at me as if he were a prairie dog of yonder town of quaint, brown, sleek-furred marmots, whose cry is like that of chattering angry birds. **1961** *Maclean's* 29 July 23: "I've seen me . . . lying at the edge of a field in Saskatchewan spying on the prairie dogs. . . ."

prairie-dog town or **village**† one of the large communities of the gregarious prairie dog (def. 2).
[**1853** REID *Young Voyageurs* 214: The "dogs" live in large settlements, many hundreds of them in one place.] **1890** *Our Forest Children* Jan. 125/2: There was a prairie dog town close to the agency. **1957** FISHER *Pemmican* 71: He had ridden it hell for leather over badger holes and prairie dog villages. . . .

prairiedress *n. Obs.* See quote.
1910 HAYDON *Riders of Plains* 345: One pattern, which was considered to be the best fitted for [North West Mounted] Police work, was what was termed a "prairiedress," which was to consist of "dark brown cord or velveteen breeches, long boots and spurs, a heavy flannel shirt, over which a stable jacket could be worn when required, and a broad-rimmed hat of soft felt to complete the outfit."

prairie elk See **wapiti.**
1930 ROLYAT *Fort Garry* 102: . . . these dusky people with the freshness of plain winds still on their faces [moved] about with the grace of prairie elk. . . .

prairie fire a great grass-fire that sweeps across tinder-dry prairie (def. 2a).
[**1813** *Kingston Gaz.* (U.C.) 14 Sep. 3/1: We have been a prairie of fire to the white men.] **1859** *Nor'Wester* (R.R.S.) 28 Dec. 2/5: Unless driven in by extensive prairie fires, as in the present year, they for the most part give us a pretty wide berth. **1960** BUBLITZ *Dotted Line* 11: He rode to Gull Lake to inform us that our home and belongings had been burned by a terrible prairie fire. **1965** *Kingston Whig-Standard* (Ont.) 4 Jan. 13/2: Much to the organizer's astonishment the idea caught on like a prairie fire.

prairie fowl† *Hist.* See **prairie chicken** (def. 1).
1886 *Indian* (Hagersville, Ont.) 14 Apr. 77/1: Grouse, pheasants, prairie fowl, or partridge, [shall not be taken] between the first day of January and the first day of September. **1952** JENNINGS *Strange Brigade* 200: They put up pickled fish and jellied venison, made pemmican and salted bear hams, pressed goose and duck and prairie fowl. . . .

prairie fox† **1** a variety of the red fox, *Vulpes fulva,* found on the prairies.
c**1902** (1912) LAUT *Trapper* 259: His cousin with the black fore feet, the prairie fox, who is the largest and strongest and scientifically finest of his kind, has more value as a fur.

2 See **kit fox** (def. 1a).
1948 RAND *Eastern Rockies* 107: Kit Fox. *Vulpes velox* (Also called Prairie Fox).

prairie gopher See **prairie squirrel.**

prairie grouse See **prairie chicken** (def. 1).
1852 (1955) CRAIG *Early Travellers* 176: For common shooting, there is plenty of quail, woodcocks, snipes, wild-foul . . . also prairie grouse in abundance within three days' travelling. **1918** SCHULTZ *Rising Wolf* 127: [We saw] coveys of sage hens and prairie grouse.

prairie hare *Obs.* See **jack-rabbit.**
1866 KING *Sportsman in Can.* 32: The Prairie Hare . . . is one of the largest hares of the continent, weighing from seven to eleven pounds, and is of a grey colour tinged with yellow, the entire under parts dusky white.

prairie hen† **1** See **prairie chicken** (def. 1).
1823 FRANKLIN *Journey* 679: This species is an inhabitant of woody countries only, in which it differs from the Pinnated grouse of America, better known to the Sportsmen of the New World under the appellation of the Prairie hen and Heath hen. **1909** PARKER *Northern Lights* 336: A prairie hen rustled by with a shrill cluck. **1959** MCATEE *Folk-Names* 25: Common Prairie Chicken [is also called] prairie chicken (General; often shortened to "chicken"); prairie hen (General); square tail . . . square-tailed grouse (Man.).

2 See **sharp-tailed grouse.**
1853 REID *Young Voyageurs* 206: Basil had already arrived with a fine prairie hen (*Tetrao cupido*) which he had shot. . . . **1959** MCATEE *Folk-Names* 25: Sharp-tailed Grouse [is also called] pintail grouse . . . prairie chicken (Sometimes "chicken" alone. Ont., Man., Sask., Alta., B.C.); prairie hen (Sask.); sharptail (Man.); willow grouse (Y.T.).

3 *Figurative use.*
1922 STRINGER *Prairie Child* 37: I'm merely a submerged prairie-hen with the best part of her life behind her.

Prairie Indian See **Plain Indian.**
1853 *Hamilton Gaz.* (C.W.) 31 Mar. 2/3: These prairie Indians are dependent most entirely on the buffalo for subsistence. **1957** FISHER *Pemmican* 79: Prairie Indians have the buffalo and that is all they need. . . .

prairie itch a form of dermatitis caused by a fresh-water hydra encountered in certain sloughs on the prairie (def. 2a). See also **salt-water itch.**
1904-8 (1955) *Sask.Hist.* Winter VIII 18: Our experience with the prairie itch was a case in point. **1961** MITCHELL *Jake and the Kid* 105: I had the measles and the prairie itch once and the mumps on both sides. I had the black crowing, Ma says, but I never had the worst of all.

prairie-land *n.* **1** See **Prairies** (def. 1).
1873 (1904) BUTLER *Wild North Land* 44: A horse, a flint gun, some white cloth and beads, could purchase the hand and heart of the fairest squaw in Prairie land. **1887** *Press* Dec. 13: . . . the Hudson's Bay Company . . . laid claim to the vast prairieland. . . .

2 *Attributive use.* See **prairie** (def. 2b).
1913 (1965) HAMILTON *Cdn Quotations* 131/1: Softly the shadows of prairie-land wheat / Ripple and riot adown to her feet. . . .

prairie level or **steppe** See 1952 quote.
1873 (1904) BUTLER *Wild North Land* 343: The depression, or slope, of the prairie level toward the north continues, with marked regularity, throughout the whole of British America. **1884** *Moose Jaw News* (District of Assiniboia [Sask.]) 1 Feb. 3/2: Beyond this region, distinguished for the almost inexhaustible fertility of its soil, we cross the Second Prairie Steppe, which has an elevation of 1,600 feet above the sea level.

1952 PUTNAM *Cdn Regions* 342/2: From east to west these are . . . the Manitoba Lowland or First Prairie Level, with an elevation of less than 1,000 feet above sea level . . . the Saskatchewan Plain or Second Prairie Level, with an average elevation of 2,000 feet above sea level . . . the Alberta Plain or Third Prairie Level, which rises gradually from about 2,500 feet above sea level to nearly 4,000 feet at the foothills of the Rocky Mountains. **1963** SPRY *Palliser* 61: They were now near . . . the long, low hill that is the edge of the next upward prairie "step."

prairie lily† the wild orange-red lily, *Lilium philadelphicum.* See also **range-lily.**
1958 *Weekend Mag.* 7 June 38: Prairie lily, an orange-red tiger lily, was chosen as Saskatchewan's emblem in 1941. It blooms in June and July, and is nowhere more abundant than on the prairies. **1963** SYMONS *Many Trails* 166: In June I was again reminded of the southland by the orange prairie lilies.

prairie oyster† **1** a raw egg swallowed whole or drunk in vinegar, brandy, etc.
*c***1923** GIBBONS *Sourdough Samaritan* 301: What would be good for him? he meditated, confusedly. A "prairie oyster"? . . . He made and gulped down the concoction shuddering . . . That egg had seen better days!

2 *Figurative use.*
1952 *Trail Riders' Bull.* Spring 6/2: I thought the world was my oyster, but it proved to be a prairie oyster.

prairie post *Fur Trade, Hist.* a trading post established on the prairie (def. 2a).
1908 MAIR *Mackenzie Basin* 100: When it is remembered that, in the old buffalo days, the daily ration per head at the company's prairie posts was eight pounds of fresh meat, which was all eaten, its equivalent being two pounds of pemmican, the enormity of this Gargantuan feast may be imagined.

prairie potato† See **prairie turnip.**
1891 *Cdn Indian* Mar. 168: The prairie potato . . . yields when dry a light, starchy flour, and is often cut into thin slices and dried for winter. **1912** [see quote at **Indian turnip** (def. 1)].

prairie province **1** *Hist.* Manitoba. See also **postage stamp province.**
1876 HAMILTON *The Prairie Province* [Title]. **1881** *Progress* (Rat Portage [Kenora], Ont.) 12 Nov. 4/1: The editor of the Woodstock (Ont.) *Sentinel-Review,* proposes with all the seriousness of a provincial scribe, to get up a huge excursion of marriageable girls in Ontario to proceed early next spring to the prairie province. **1916** SKELTON *Day of Laurier* 97: The Winnipeg Board of Trade denounced the policy of "crushing and trampling upon one hundred thousand struggling pioneers of the prairie province to secure a purely imaginary financial gain to one soulless corporation." **1965** HAMILTON *Cdn Quotations* 130/2: The Prairie Province. From the title of the book [see 1876 quote] which gave the phrase general circulation; after 1905 it was extended to include Saskatchewan and Alberta in "The Prairie Provinces."

2 one of the Prairie Provinces, *q.v.*

Prairie Provinces, the See 1952 quote. See also **Prairies** (def. 2).
[**1878** *Sask.Herald* (Battleford, N.W.T.) 23 Sep. 2/4: In our Prairie Province the nomination day is fixed for

the 19th, and the elections for the 26th of the same month.] **1908** BROWN *Lady of the Snows* 221: ... the majority ruled, but the minority clamored from the prairie provinces.... **1952** PUTNAM *Cdn Regions* 340/1: Manitoba, Saskatchewan and Alberta are known as the "Prairie Provinces" because they include the Canadian section of the vast grass-covered interior plains of North America. **1965** *Globe and Mail* (Toronto) 5 Jan. B5/1: All three Prairie provinces are particularly unhappy about the special incentives being offered to attract industrial enterprises.

prairie region See **prairie** (def. 2a).
1860 *Nor' Wester* (R.R.S.) 14 Jan. 4/3: An unbroken navigation of 20 miles extends by Rainy River and Lake of the Woods to within sixty miles of the prairie region. **1963** *Sask.News* Sep. 4: The current issue depicts ... a typical "dugout" and wind-charger of the prairie region, and a modern harvesting scene in the wheat belt.

prairie rose† a pink climbing rose, *Rosa setigera,* of the prairie (def. 2a).
1910 WARD *Canadian Born* vi:
  Put me somewhere west of Selkirk
  When the prairie roses bloom
  Where you run clean out o' fences
  And a man has elbow room.
1963 *Cdn Geog.Jnl* Aug. 54/2: Later the hardy prairie rose makes its appearance and fills the air with its sweet scent.

prairie-rover *n. West, Obs.* See **bad man** (def. 1).
1909 PARKER *Northern Lights* 316: There had been great excitement over the capture and subsequent escape of a prairie-rover....

prairies *n.pl.* See **prairie.**

Prairies *n.pl.* **1** the region of the prairie (def. 2a).
See also **Great Plain** and **Prairie land.**
[**1776** (1901) HENRY (Elder) *Travels* 267: The Plains, or as the French denominate them, the Prairies, or Meadows, compose an extensive tract of land or country....] **1852** *Anglo-American Mag.* I 293/2: Now the life of a Canadian settler ... is pleasure itself compared with what must be endured in Australia, California, or the Western Prairies. **1966** *Time* (Cdn ed.) 12 Aug. 11/2: [Manitoba] offered ... homesteads ... to all who would try their luck on the empty Prairies.

2 See **Prairie Provinces.** See also **Prairie,** *adj.*
1907 BINDLOSS *Winston of the Prairies* [Title]
1958 *Edmonton Jnl* 24 June 1/1: [This is the] weather pattern for the Prairies. **1965** *Globe and Mail* (Toronto) 5 Jan. B5/1: Proponents of the plan also believe joint action would help the Prairies to counter the industrial incentives being offered by bodies like Quebec's General Investment Corp.

prairie schooner† *Hist.* any of various types of wagon used by settlers in the westward migration of the nineteenth century. See also **prairie wagon** and **tilted wagon.**
1880 GORDON *Mountain and Prairie* 255: The light waggon, covered with a cotton awning that gives it the name of "prairie-schooner," from its fancied resemblance to a sail-boat [and] the two-horse spring waggon ... are the greatest favourites. **1914** STEELE *Forty Years* 108: All freight ... was brought ... in ox waggons, commonly called prairie schooners. These

were very large and hauled by spans of ten pairs of oxen.... **1964** *Calgary Herald* 10 July 19/8: Other reminders of the past included ... a Conestoga wagon, or prairie schooner. **1966** *Weekend Mag.* 8 Jan. 31: [Caption] These prairie schooners brought Canadians back from Montana to homesteads in the Peace River Country.

prairie smoke† See **crocus.**
1958 *Weekend Mag.* 7 June 38/1: Earliest of spring flowers, Manitoba's crocus grows so profusely in places that it looks like a low-lying mist. Hence its nickname: the "Prairie smoke."

prairie squint a squint characteristic of many western farmers who work long hours in the sun.
1963 SYMONS *Many Trails* 92: He wears a grey felt hat, beneath which his tanned face is puckered in the "prairie squint"....

prairie squirrel or **gopher** the Richardson ground squirrel, *Spermophilus richardsonii.*
1872 (1873) GRANT *Ocean to Ocean* 113: No sound broke the stillness except the chirp of the gopher, or prairie squirrel, running to his hole in the ground. **1955** MCCOWAN *Upland Trails* 140: The prairie gopher rarely, if ever, drinks water, a special provision of Nature causing the starchy food in the stomach to be converted into liquid.

prairie steppe See **prairie level.**

prairie turnip† See 1892 quote. See also **biscuit root, bread-root, buffalo root, Indian bread-root, Indian carrot, Indian turnip** (def. 1), **meadow turnip, prairie potato, turnip of the plains,** and **wild turnip** (def. 2).
[**1820** HARMON *Journal* 327: They find a root in the plains, that is nearly a foot long, and two or three inches in circumference, which is shaped like a carrot, and tastes like a turnip, which they pound fine, and then dry it in the sun.] **1857** (1863) PALLISER *Journals* 38: ... the root which receives the name of the Prairie Turnip by the half-breeds, who, with Indians, use it as food, and sometimes crush it into a kind of flour and make bread from it. The root is very dry and almost tasteless, and even when boiled for a great length of time does not become soft, and is at best but insipid unnutritious trash. **1892** BRYCE *Glimpses of Past* 9: After this he took to eating what the Canadians (French voyageurs) call the turnip of the plains. This is the root of one of the Pea family (psoralea esculenta), "Pomme blanche," or "Pomme de Prairie" or "Prairie turnip." **1956** LEECHMAN *Native Tribes* 110: The prairie Indians also ate service berries, wild cherries, red willow berries, prairie turnips, bitter root, and wild rose haws.

prairie wagon† *Hist.* See **prairie schooner.**
Also *prairie immigrant wagon.*
1888 *Dominion Illust.* 127/2: The Indian dogs or huskies haul the portable canvas house—like the top of a prairie immigrant wagon on runners.... **1909** CAMERON *New North* 72: He [the Mountie] brands stray cattle, interrogates each new arrival in a prairie-waggon ... herds wood bison on the Slave....

prairie wolf† See **coyote** (def. 1).
1836 BACK *Arctic Land* 481: The prairie wolf, the kit-fox and various marmots are peculiar to the plains. **1963** SYMONS *Many Trails* 121: Mishagunis—that's what the Crees call him, the grey jackal of the plains which we call in English the prairie wolf, but more often in corruption of its Aztec name, coyote—locally pronounced kī-yiut' or koy-yo'té.

prairie wool See 1953 quote. See also **buffalo wool** (def. 2). Cp. **nigger wool**.
1934 BETTANY *Valley of Lost Gold* 284: She loved . . . every blade of prairie wool . . . the sunflowers which covered the alkali flats. . . . **1953** *Cdn Geog.Jnl* June 245/1: The sheep crop the "prairie wool"—that excellent hard forage composed of spear-grass, bunch-grass and buffalo-grass. **1964** *Calgary Herald* 25 May 23/1: Solidly entrenched along road allowances, coulee banks and pastures of prairie wool they have multiplied. . . .

prairion or **prairillon** *n. Hist.* [< Cdn F *prairillon,* dim. of *prairie*] a small tract of grassland; a small meadow.
1811 (1897) COUES *New Light* II 700: The country about the house is in general wooded with small prairions at intervals of a mile or more. **1833** (1963) TOLMIE *Physician* 192: Our course lay through rich & level prairies and prairions or smaller plains, separated from each other by belts of wood. . . . **1953** MOWERY *Mounted Police* 125: A little stream wound down the valley center, widening here and there into ponds and small green prairillons. In one of these meadows, about two-thirds of a mile away, a herd of two thousand buffaloes were pasturing on the aromatic bunch grass.

pre-Confederation *adj. or attrib.* relating to the period prior to 1867, when Confederation, *q.v.,* was established.
1899 GARDNER *Nothing But Names* 5: When one observes how slight is the knowledge of the present-day school-boy regarding the public men of the pre-Confederation period, it is possible to estimate the mystery which will surround some of the township names in northern Ontario half a century after the completion of the surveyor's work. **1966** *Globe and Mail* (Toronto) 1 Apr. 29/8: [He] wants to know how come John Robarts calls himself Prime Minister instead of Premier of Ontario (because pre-Confederation practice sanctions it).

pre-empt *v.* **1** *Obs.* take over (land) by legal claim for purposes of engaging in mining operations.
1866 *Cariboo Sentinel* (Barkerville, B.C.) 25 June 2/2: "Have we as colored men the right to pre-empt ground for mining purposes?"

2† purchase or establish the right to purchase public lands by pre-emption (def. 1).
1869 *Mainland Guardian* (New Westminster, B.C.) 1 Dec. 2/1: In British Columbia there are vast districts of rich arable land which can easily be pre-empted. **1913** SANDILANDS *West.Cdn Dict.* 23/1: In certain districts a homesteader in good standing may pre-empt a quarter-section alongside his homestead. **1963** *Beaver* Autumn 51/1: More than a thousand acres were pre-empted and they set to work to establish their way of life.

pre-emption† *n. Hist.* **1** the right to purchase public land under stipulated conditions and on the basis of a prior claim, such as established settlement or the ownership and improvement of adjacent land.
1827 *U.E.Loyalist* (York [Toronto]) 6 May 396/2: The first hundred purchasers of Town Lots, when they have erected a habitable house, will, at any time within twelve months from the date of their purchase be entitled to the pre-emption or privilege to purchase a Lot of Twenty-Five Acres, in the immediate vicinity of the Town, at the low rate of 7s 6d. per acre.
1933 SPINKS *B.C.Frontier* 110: Some of the land had

already been pre-empted, and pre-emption amounted to an agreement by the government to sell the land to the pre-empter.

2 (a piece of) land available for or acquired by purchase under such a right.
1871 *Mainland Guardian* (New Westminster, B.C.) 9 Mar. 3/1: Pre-emptions are being recorded daily, showing that the influx of new settlers is rapidly on the increase. **1881** *Edmonton Bull.* 26 Nov. 4/1: Pre-emptions outside of the Canadian Pacific Railway belt shall be sold at the uniform price of two dollars per acre, to be paid in one sum at the end of three years from the date of entry. **1911** SMITH *Is It Just?* 16: About two miles from Poplar Grove was the preemption of Mr. Guy Pierce, another Englishman, but one who belonged to that class rather contemptuously regarded by their neighbors as remittance men." **1963** *B.C.Digest* Nov.-Dec. 38/2: Topping . . . pre-empted a townsite on Trail Creek with the help of a partner called Hanna. From his pre-emption grew the city of Trail.

pre-emptor† *n.* one who acquires land by pre-emption (def. 1).
1860 *Brit.Colonist* (Victoria) 12 Jan. 2/1: Pre-emptors run the risk of having to pay twice the amount required by the American government for wild land. **1962** NICHOLSON *West Coast* 265: . . . a kindly Norwegian pre-empter . . . assisted them in re-sawing and whittling the boards down to the proper dimensions by hand.

prêle [prɛl] *n.* [< Cdn F < F < *l'aprêle* < Ital. *asperella,* dim., ult. < L *asper* rough] See 1897 quote.
1813 (1897) COUES *New Light* II 752: [There were] sand-banks on which grow coarse grass, prêle. . . . **1859** (1863) PALLISER *Journals* 150: Leaving the horses to feed on a fine meadow of the "Prele" or goose grass . . . I started to explore the valley. . . . **1897** COUES *New Light* II 667n: Goosegrass is properly *Polygonum aviculare* and other species of the same genus, but what Henry means is the equisetaceous plant known to the voyageurs as prele, a name he uses beyond for horsetails of the genus *Equisetum.* **1925** ANDERSON *Trees and Shrubs* 149: [The] Horse-tail, or, as it is called by the French-Canadians, "Prele," used to be considered excellent horse-feed, and when possible the Hudson's Bay Company's brigades were halted where it was abundant.

pre-Loyalist *adj. Hist.* of or pertaining to the period prior to the arrival of the Loyalists in Canada. See also **Pre-Loyalist**.
1896 *Trans.Roy.Soc.Can.* II 2 222: Probably for Joel Bonny, a pre-loyalist settler in this region. **1907** *U of T Stud.Hist.& Econ.* II 249: A number of districts, [including] the pre-Loyalist Barrington, were given an opportunity. . . .

Pre-Loyalist *n. Maritimes, Hist.* a settler arriving prior to the American Revolution, especially a New Englander who settled in Nova Scotia prior to 1776. Cp. **late Loyalist** and **United Empire Loyalist**.
1934 DENNIS *Down in N.S.* 172: . . . Bear River's pioneers came from Granville, Annapolis and Digby. These pre-loyalists were joined later by a number of Loyalists from the United States. **1946** LOWER *Colony to Nation* 103: When asked about their origins, it must

not be suggested to them [people of the Annapolis Valley, N.S.] that they are "Loyalists": they are of an older breed; "Pre-Loyalists," they will proudly say.

premier *n.* **1** the chief executive of a provincial government (in modern use in Canada, usually distinguished from the prime minister). See also **provincial premier** (def. 1).
1853 *Hamilton Gaz.* (C.W.) 3 Oct. 2/6: In the prosecution of this singularly dignified scheme—we shall say nothing of its abstract honesty—the Premier scruples not to employ the influence which his position invests him with. **1917** MILLER *New Era* 197: Why did Honoré Mercier, as Premier of Quebec, place a reference to the Pope in the preamble to his Jesuits Estates Bill? **1965** *Globe and Mail* (Toronto) 6 Jan. 2/8: Opposition Leader John G. Diefenbaker will attend, as will former Ontario premier Leslie Frost and his wife.

2 See **prime minister** (def. 1).
☞ *This application is obsolescent in Canada, the title of premier being nearly always used to refer to the chief executive of a province.*
1883 *Brandon Dly Mail* (Man.) 29 Jan. 2/1: It says that several of those roughly classed as Ministerialists will in all probability vote "no confidence" in the present Premier. **1916** BRIDLE *Sons of Canada* 14: It is of prime importance to remember how . . . so impersonal a figure ever came to be Premier of Canada. . . .

present *n. Obs.* one of an annual issue of gifts to the Indians, made by the government or the fur companies with the intent of maintaining the goodwill of the recipients.
*c*1820 (1838) HEAD *Forest Scenes* 175: It being the season of the year when "the presents," as they are termed, are given to the Indians, these people were walking about the streets in crowds, all in holiday apparel, and animated by anticipation of what they were to receive—blankets, blue cloth, guns, powder and shot, &c.

present of rum See quote. Cp. **present.**
1808 (1964) INNIS *Fur Trade* 236: . . . these Indians are not like those of the cold and mountainous regions in want of manufactured goods, their principal inducement to perform the services . . . is the present of rum, which they receive at stated periods.

president *n. Hist.* a person charged with administering the affairs of a province during the absence of the governor general or lieutenant-governor or in the interim between the departure of one governor and the arrival of his successor. In full, *President of the Council* or *Province.*
1797 (1906) *Ont.Bur.Arch.Rep.* IV 191: By a Proclamation of His Excellency Peter Russell, President of the Province of Upper Canada, dated the eleventh day of October one thousand seven hundred and ninety-seven, the meeting of the Legislative Council and House of Assembly stands prorogued to the thirtieth day of November, next ensuing. **1842** *Bytown* [Ottawa] *Gaz.* 22 Sep. 3/2: Mr. Sullivan continues as President of the Council, Mr. Daly Secretary for Canada East, and Mr. Harrison holds the same office for Canada West. **1891** EDGAR *Ten Years of U.C.* 127: In Upper Canada, General Brock was acting Lieutenant Governor, or President of the Council, during the absence in England of Mr. Francis Gore.

pret or **prey** *n.* [< Cdn F *prêt;* cf. F *prêt* soldier's five-day pay allowance] *Obs.* a ration of food; rations; share.
1800 (1890) MCKENZIE *Journal* 395: The "Red Knife" brought us 25 pieces of fish . . . . Gave the prey to them as usual. **1869** KENNICOTT *Journal* 115: A dog's "prey" is half of a man's, and the same as a wife's— that is, four pounds of fresh meat, one and a half pounds of dry meat, two fresh white fish or two pounds of dry fish. **1896** WHITNEY *On Snow-Shoes* 88: The woman . . . yield's the lion's share of the scanty larder when he is at home luxuriating in smoke and sleep, and, when he is away, gives her children her tiny pret (allowance) of fish and goes hungry without a murmur. **1896** (1898) RUSSELL *Far North* 272: The inhabitants of the country, especially those in charge of the "pret" become expert in judging the condition of whitefish.

prickly beaver *Obs.* the American porcupine, *Erethizon dorsatum.*
1824 (1955) BLACK *Journal* 61: Our Indian Guides travelling with their little dogs who at one time raised their puny voices some distance before & a deer or a Bear was anticipated, but it turned out a Porcupine the first of these prickly Beavers we have met with. . . .

Prima Vista *Hist.* the name given by John Cabot to what is now Newfoundland.
1584 (1877) HAKLUYT *Discourse on Western Planting* 126: In which mappe, in the chapiter of Newfoundelande, there in Latyn is put down, besides the yere of our Lorde, even the very day, which was the day of St. John Baptiste; and the firste lande which they saw they called Prima Visa or Prima Vista. **1752** ROBSON *Hudson's Bay* 2: John and Sebastian Cabot sailed from Bristol, and discovered Newfoundland, or Prima Vista, in 1494. **1873** LEMOINE *Maple Leaves* 170: The navigator above mentioned called the Island of Newfoundland "Prima Vista" as being the first land seen by him.

prime *adj. adv. Fur Trade* designating skins that are in undeteriorated winter growth of hair and full thickness of hide. Cp. **unprime.**
[**1825** (1950) OGDEN *Journals* 48: . . . the weather is now becoming very warm. Still the Beaver are in their Prime.] **1859** (1870) SOUTHESK *Saskatchewan* 307: The fur of our fox was "prime,"—as the phrase is here,— that is to say, he was in his complete winter coat, which had not been worn long enough to become torn or rusty. **1913** COWIE *Adventurers* 225: . . . in the fur book the names of each kind of skin and whether large or small, prime or common, were written alphabetically. **1965** *Islander* 14 Feb. 13/3: A wolverine, prime-furred, is as sleek and glossy as a marten.

prime minister **1** the chief executive of the government of Canada; the first minister of the federal government and, in practice, the leader of the party in power. See also **premier** (def. 2) and note.
1853 *Hamilton Gaz.* (C.W.) 3 Oct. 2/6: The Prime Minister of her Majesty's Canadian Government, associates himself with a Toronto stock jobber, to raise the wind on a parcel of civic debentures. **1965** *Globe and Mail* (Toronto) 6 Jan. 2/8: He said the Prime Minister accepted with the proviso that he would attend if something did not turn up.

2 the chief executive of a provincial government, now usually referred to as *premier* (def. 1).
1885 GEMMILL *Companion* 13: [He] was Prime Minister of Can. from May, 1862, to March, 1864; and first Prime Minister of his native Province after

Confederation. **1960** *Gulf Islander* (Galiano, B.C.)
23 July 5: The "Sorry for the Inconvenience" signs
and the king-size coloured pix of our "Prime Minister"
(by Royal assent & chop-stick OK) all added to the
gay mood of the assemblage.... **1966** *Globe and Mail*
(Toronto) 1 Apr. 29/8: [He] wants to know how come
John Robarts calls himself Prime Minister instead of
Premier of Ontario (because pre-Confederation practice
sanctions it).

Prince Edward's Island *Hist.* Prince Edward
Island.
1806 (1809) GRAY *Letters* 21: To the southward of our
course lies Prince Edward's Island, near the coasts of
Nova Scotia and New Brunswick. **1815** BOUCHETTE
Lower Canada 55: On its south side is the Island of St.
John, otherwise called Prince Edward's island.

Prince Rupert's Land See **Rupert's Land.**
1844 HOWSE *Cree Language* [Title page]: By Joseph
Howse, Esq. F.R.G.S. and resident twenty years in
Prince Rupert's Land, in the service of the Hon.
Hudson's Bay Company. **1930** ROLYAT *Fort Garry* 18:
Once he had gone into Canada, a distant country in the
East ruled by the same sovereign who ruled Prince
Rupert's Land, Queen Victoria, superior in authority
even to the Governor of the Hudson Bay.

private potlatch *Pacific Coast* the distribution of
property and gifts at small gatherings without the
customary ceremony, to circumvent the Potlatch
Law, *q.v.* Hence, *private potlatcher.* Cp. **potlatch,** *n.*
(def. 2a).
1961 LA VIOLETTE *Survival* 90: Perhaps even more central
to the Indian interests was the discovery of a way to
potlatch in spite of the law. It could be done through
private potlatches and by disjointing the potlatch.
Ibid. 97: The system of wardship and the legal
procedures as experienced by the accused Indians and
by the surreptitious and private potlatchers could
bring about no satisfactory redress in grievances for the
Indians.

private trade *Fur Trade, Hist.* the practice among
company officers and, at times, other employees
of trading with the Indians on a private basis.
1671 (1942) *H.B.C.Minutes* 5: That Capt. Guillam &
all others imployed this voyage bee examined what
private trade hath been by them or any of them in the
Countrey, or by the mariners under them....
1821 (1938) SIMPSON *Athabasca Jnl* 212: Chastellain &
Lamallice I find are renewing their old practice of
carrying on Private Trade with the Indians. **1942** *H.B.C.
Minutes* 5n: ... both captains and the crews and the
Frenchmen took part in private trade on their own
accounts, and ... the Company conducted a steady
campaign against the practice.

production line *Hockey, Slang* a forward line
that scores a large number of goals.
1963 *Kingston Whig-Standard* (Ont.) 21 Jan. 10/5:
Every team in the National Hockey League has its
scoring stars and its production line.

Progressive *n. Hist.* a member or supporter of
the Progressive Party, *q.v.*
1940 MACCORMAC *Canada* 190: In the federal field the
Progressives flattered but to deceive. In 1921 they were
returned second only to the Liberals. **1961** *Edmonton
Jnl* 4 Aug. 18/1: Clear Grits, Unionists, Progressives,
United Farmers, Bloc Populaire, and now the CCF,
are part of the ancestral lore of politics—parties with
a past but without a future.

Progressive Conservative a member or

supporter of the Progressive Conservative Party.
See also **Conservative** (def. 2) and **P.C.**
1955 *Tweed News* 14 Apr. 1/4: From all indications the
East Hastings Progressive-Conservative Association
convention at Madoc ... will be a wide-open affair.

Progressive Conservative Party the current
name, since 1942, of the Canadian political party
descended from the Conservative Party, *q.v.*, of
Sir John A. Macdonald and succeeding leaders;
also, any of the several related provincial parties.
1965 *Globe Mag.* 8/2: [They] bolted to join the
Progressive Conservative party....

Progressive Party *Hist.* a political party having
substantial support among liberals and farmers in
the 1920's. See also **National Progressive Party**
and **Progressive.**
1946 LOWER *Colony to Nation* 506: [Chronology] 1921
[the] Progressive Party takes 65 seats. **1950** MORTON
The Progressive Party in Canada [Title].
1958 *Encyc.Can.* IV 103/1: This decision revealed the
dual nature of the Progressive Party; the majority were
low-tariff Liberals; a small but zealous minority were
group-government doctrinaires determined to keep free
of caucuses and Party politics.

prompt trade *Fur Trade, Hist.* a transaction in
which the customer at a trading post simply
turned over his furs for their exact value in goods.
1913 COWIE *Adventurers* 226: In the Indian debt book
every article had to be strictly itemized ... and even in
what was called "prompt trade" ... it was better to
make a balancing entry in his current account....

prongbuck† *n.* See **pronghorn.**
1867 LORD *Wilderness* 262: I believe I once saved my
own, and several men's lives, by following the tracks of
Prongbuck to their drinking places. **1947** *Beaver* Mar.
36: The Pronghorn Antelope, sometimes called the
Prongbuck, is a ruminant somewhat smaller ... than
the Whitetailed Deer.

pronghorn (antelope) *n.* See **antelope** (def. 1).
See also **prongbuck.** Also *pronghorned antelope.*
1823 FRANKLIN *Journey* 667: [The] Pronghorn, which is
generally called a goat by the Canadians, resorts to the
neighbourhood of Carleton-house to bring forth its
young. **1836** BACK *Arctic Land* 482: The moose deer,
reindeer, wapiti ... and the prong-horned antelope,
also inhabit New Caledonia. **1963** *Calgary Herald*
25 Oct. 14/7: The Provincial Government will allow
you to take one of the most desirable game animals in
North America—The Pronghorn Antelope.

proof line *Obs.* See **base line.**
1810 (1909) *London & Middlesex Hist.Soc.Trans.* II 12:
I proved every concession line that I ran by measuring on
the said proof line, and can safely say that the operation
is very correct. **1853** *Canadian Watchman* (Toronto)
9 Apr. 117/4: He was last seen alive in the Tavern ... on
the Thursday night previous, and in a very intoxicated
state left for home by the 8th concession east of the
proof-line, across which runs a very dangerous creek.

propeller† *n. Hist.* a steamboat propelled by a
turning screw, used largely on the Great Lakes.
1853 (1854) KEEFER *Montreal* 20: Now, it is in our
power by constructing a canal, to enable that

prospecting *n.* the searching of an area for mineral deposits.

propeller to proceed directly into Lake Champlain instead of stopping at Ogdensburgh.... **1870** *Cdn Illust.News* 26 Mar. 334/1: In those days, there being no propellers or ferries of any kind, nearly every farmer along the river had his boat.... **1961** *Cdn Hist.Rev.* June 133: A relatively minor incident which provides a small window into Confederate activities, the subject of this study—the affair of the propeller Georgian, a vessel owned by a neutral British subject.

proprietor *n. Fur Trade, Hist.* See **wintering partner** (def. 1).
1800 (1820) HARMON *Journal* 41: Every summer, the greater part of the Proprietors and Clerks, who have spent the winter in the Interiour, came here [Grand Portage] with the furs which they have been able to collect. **1821** (1938) SIMPSON *Athabasca Jnl* 214: [We] accompanied one Cameron a N.W. Proprietor to their establishment at Pembina.... **1918** DAVIDSON *North West Co.* 16: The remaining shares were held by the proprietors, who were obliged to winter and manage the business of the concern with the Indians, the respective clerks and others. These proprietors were not supposed to be under any obligation to furnish capital, or even credit.

prospect† *n. Mining* **1** a mining area or claim appearing to have attractive mineral deposits; a site that a prospector works.
1859 *Brit.Colonist* (Victoria) 8 Jan. 2/2: At this place I prospected and found some excellent prospects. **1928** WALDEN *Dog-Puncher* 27: On his way from his "prospect" to the "outside" this man saw his fellow men for the first time at the mines. **1958** *Northern Miner* 20 Nov. 28/3: Black Crow Mines is exploring a 21-claim gold prospect in Davis Twp., Sudbury area, Northern Ontario.
2 the quantity of gold panned on a prospect.
1860 *Brit.Colonist* (Victoria) 27 Oct. 2/2: Two bits to the pan is an excellent prospect. **1870** *Mainland Guardian* (New Westminster, B.C.) 23 Apr. 3/3: On French creek the Cosmopolitan co., on Thursday last, got a prospect of two ounces to nine car-loads of dirt, although their tunnel is not yet fairly in the channel.

prospect† *v. Mining* search an area of mineral deposits.
1859 *Brit.Colonist* (Victoria) 29 Aug. 3/1: The coast was prospected for some sixty miles ... but without success, except finding in the interior an old pick where some former explorers had been blasting for quartz gold. **1953** *North Star* (Yellowknife) Jan.-Feb. 1/1: Last summer, six parties prospected in northern Saskatchewan under that province's prospectors' assistance plan.

prospect hole or **shaft†** *Placer Mining* a shaft sunk in searching for minerals.
1897 *Medicine Hat News* (Alta) 30 Sep. 7/5: It takes about 30 days to sink a prospect hole to bedrock, say about 25 feet deep. **1900** OSBORN *Greater Canada* 13: The grabbing of a half of all diggings discovered after a certain date by a Government which "has never dug a single prospect shaft" and is doing nothing whatever to help the prospector, is deeply resented. **1962** *B.C. Digest* Oct. 28/2: ... the prospector ... will ... study and locate the creek wash, the formations and surface indications, so as to know where to sink his prospect holes in the winter.

1868 HEATHERINGTON *Gold Fields N.S.* 23: Though the prospecting license was accorded, its terms were so illiberal that Mr. Campbell and his friends had to abandon the project, for which tools, machinery, miners, and a vessel to transport them had already been purchased. **1952** *North Star* (Yellowknife) Nov. 3/2: ... transportation facilities outside of that radius are extremely difficult, a factor which may hamper further extension of prospecting on a large scale.

prospector *n.* **1†** a person who prospects for minerals.
1897 *Slocan Pioneer* (B.C.) 28 Aug. 3/3: If you saw men shaking $50,000 drafts under the noses of ragged old prospectors and getting refused, you would know how different it is to what you think. **1954** PATTERSON *Dangerous River* 143: I had looked in at his old cabin at the mouth of the Flat to pick up a gold pan and a prospector's pick I had left there in his care.
2 See **cruiser** (def. 1).
1933 CAMERON *Twigs* 117: Lumber prospectors had ascended the Castor in canoes before the district had been surveyed.

prospector canoe *North* See quotes.
1957 *Cominco Mag.* Feb 11/2: We used 17-foot prospector canoes, cedar strip with canvas cover. **1964** *Canadian Wkly* 13 June 10/1: Reg Treacy and I ... had fought our 17-foot prospector canoe through heavy swells.

prospector's stew a stew made with squares of bacon, potatoes, onions, etc.
1962 *B.C.Digest* Oct. 61/2: Because the hunters are interested in the more basic trail cookery, I make them a "Prospector's Stew" occasionally....

Prospector's Toboggan *Trademark* See 1959 quote.
[**1910** FRASER *Red Meekins* 251: ... so the body was placed on a rough prospector's toboggan, drawn by six train dogs.] **1959** *Alaska Sportsman* Aug. 39/3: Although this toboggan has apparently been discontinued by the Peterborough Canoe Company, their catalog does list a Prospector's Toboggan, which ... is very popular in the [Canadian] northern countries especially with prospectors. The hood bent in a long curve rises easily when it strikes a log or other obstruction.... These toboggans are made with three slats of selected birch or maple to a width of fifteen inches at the front or shoulder, tapering to thirteen and one-half inches at the tail.

prospect shaft See **prospect hole.**

protracted meeting *Hist.* a series of religious services held all day long for several days.
1832 *Patriot and Farmer's Monitor* (Kingston, U.C.) 10 Apr. 2/6: It is now required of the Episcopal Methodist preachers, to make the public acquainted with their motives for establishing Protracted Meetings. **1848** *St.Catharines Jnl* (C.W.) 4 Jan. 2/4: The Association is the result of a "retreat" or protracted meeting which has recently been held in Longueuil. **1909** PARKER *Northern Lights* 255: They dreaded to meet Laura; they kept away from the "protracted meetings," but were eager to hear about her and what she said and did.

prove† *v. Mining* demonstrate that a prospect has the hoped-for mineral deposits.

1900 OSBORN *Greater Canada* 89: The old-time placer-miners seldom or never looked for quartz-veins; for they lacked the scientific knowledge to "prove" such discoveries, and also they knew it was impossible to bring in the necessary machinery for working them when proved. **1954** BEZANSON *Sodbusters* 144: "Do you think there is a chance for the strike at Porcupine Lake to really prove gold in paying quantities in Ontario?"

prove out See **prove up**.
1959 *Globe and Mail* (Toronto) 23 July 2/1: It took him four years, and one proved-out and sold homestead, to get the money.

prove up† carry out the improvements, *q.v.*, required to gain the patent on homesteaded land. See also **proving up**. Cp. **improve** (def. 1).
1911 (1914) BICKERSTETH *Open Doors* 41: Finally, after many anxieties and hardships, they manage to fulfil the homestead conditions and "prove up"—that is, get their patent. **1963** SYMONS *Many Trails* 141: The other cause of delay was the reluctance of a great many homesteaders to prove up. . . .

prove up on See **prove up**.
1922 STEAD *Neighbours* 222: "At least it should take as long to get married as to prove up on a homestead," Jake remarked. . . . **1945** GARD *Johnny Chinook* 311: They had managed to prove up on a homestead . . .

province *n.* **1** *Hist.* any one of the principal administrative subdivisions of British North America.
1764 *Quebec Gaz.* 9 Aug. 3/1: [He is] Captain General and Governor in Chief in and over His Majesty's Province of Quebec. . . . **1786** *Account N.S.* 65: The north side of the Province, beyond the bay of Funday, is best stocked with them. . . . **1838** *Western Herald* (Sandwich [Windsor], U.C.) 3 Jan. 4/1: There is close at hand a numerous and determined band of Potawatomies, and other Indians, who left in disgust the American Territory, and sought an asylum in our Province. **1863** WALSHE *Cedar Creek* 334: This is with reference to the hundred and thirty representatives in the Lower house of the Provincial Legislature. The members of the indissoluble Upper House, or Legislative Council, are also returned at the rate of twelve every two years, by the forty-eight electoral divisions of the Province [Upper Canada].
2 since Confederation, any one of Canada's major political subdivisions.
[**1867** (1967) *Globe and Mail* (Toronto) 13 Mar. 7/1: It will be recollected that under the Quebec scheme, New Brunswick had a special advantage over the other Provinces.] **1958** *Saturday Night* 27 Sep. 6/3: The Dominion can protect a citizen from arbitrary arrest in a criminal case. But that wouldn't stop a province declaring him insane and throwing him into a provincial mental home. **1964** *Atlantic Advocate* 56/3: Much remains to be done, in "The Province of Newfoundland and Labrador," as it is now to be called, and in the other Atlantic Provinces too. **1966** *Globe and Mail* (Toronto) 25 June 5/1: . . . Ontario is only one of 10 provinces subject to the limiting factor of federal trade and agriculture policies.

Province of Canada *Hist.* the official name of the entity formed by the union of Upper and Lower Canada from 1841 to 1867, the two parts being known officially as Canada West and Canada East respectively.

1841 *U.C.Gaz.* (Toronto) 9 Feb. 1/1: Upon, from and after, the 10th day of this present month of February, the Provinces of Upper Canada and Lower Canada shall form and be one Province, under the name of the Province of Canada. **1948** ANGLIN *Canada Unlimited* 25: Durham also recommended that Upper and Lower Canada be merged into a single "Province of Canada." This was done by the Act of Union of 1840, which provided one government for "Canada East" and "Canada West," as they came to be known, with each of the old provinces electing an equal number of members to the assembly.

province paper *Obs.* See **provincial bank-note**.
1825 *Novascotian* (Halifax) 20 July 237/2: There is no such act, and neither dollars, doubloons nor even Province Paper are legal tender.

provincial *n.* **1** *Now Rare* a native of one of the provinces of Canada. See also **provincialist** (def. 1).
1853 SLEIGH *Pine Forest* vi: I consider the word "Life" to apply to all that relates to the social and political condition of the Provincials. **1859** *Brit.Colonist* (Victoria) 2/1: There were many provincials at Queenborough who were competent mechanics, and who ought to have had the privilege of tendering. **1923** MACMECHAN *Sagas of Sea* 103: NOVA SCOTIA has need of another Hakluyt to record the traffics and discoveries, the disasters and the heroic deeds of the seafaring provincials.
2 See **provincial policeman**.
1936 MOWERY *Paradise Trail* 4: On his flight across the provinces he had outwitted city cops a-plenty and slipped out of several tight squeezes with the Provincials; but these Mounteds were bad eggs. **1963** *Kingston Whig-Standard* (Ont.) 1 June 6/1: Cpl. Denis G. (Denny) Jones, one of the most popular "provincials" every to serve here, was transferred after being promoted from constable.

provincial *adj.* **1** *Hist.* of or pertaining to one of the provinces of British North America.
1795 *Quebec Gaz.* 8 Jan. 3/1: His Excellency the Governor General has been pleased to appoint Charles Thomas Esquire, for the notary and Clerk of the Court of King's Bench, and also Clerk of the Provincial Court for the District of Three Rivers. **1849** ALEXANDER *L'Acadie* I 35: In Canada, in 1814, it was found necessary to intermingle the newly arrived regulars with the Glengarry light infantry, a provincial corps, to show them how to cover themselves, and to teach them, in short, wood-craft. **1963** MORTON *Kingdom of Canada* 201: A considerable number of them [American immigrants], being Quakers and Mennonites, were pacifists, and had been granted exemption from military service by provincial law.
2 of, associated with, or under the jurisdiction of a province, as opposed to the federal government, of Canada.
1868 *Niagara Mail* (Niagara-on-the-Lake, Ont.) 7 Oct. 2/2: The first, second and third prize on wheat was taken by Niagara—beating the country wheat that took the prize at the Provincial exhibition. **1904** CROSSKILL *P.E.I.* 79: The provincial fair at Charlottetown in connection with horse races under the auspices of the Driving Park Association, is, from an agricultural point of view, superior to any show of the kind in the Maritime

Provinces. **1919** *One Big Union Bull.* 13 Sep. 2/2: The heavy iron-barred gate of the Provincial Jail swung open and the men filed in. **1962** *Bad Lands of Red Deer River* 40: Since the project originated, the hatchery has produced almost 100 million fish yearlings, fingerlings and eyed-eggs for planting in provincial waters.

provincial bank-note *Hist.* any of the currency notes issued by several of the provinces in colonial times. See also **province paper.** Cp. **Halifax currency** and **provincial currency.** Also *provincial note.*
1829 MACTAGGART *Three Years* I 320: The money in circulation [in Canada] is chiefly what is called dollar bills, being provincial bank-notes.... **1946** LOWER *Colony to Nation* 517: Nova Scotians in the 18th century had their struggle with their "provincial notes," another form of unredeemable paper.

Provincial Building *P.E.I.* the building in which the Legislative Assembly convenes.
1860 *Islander* (Charlottetown) 6 Jan. 3/2: The above Term commenced its sittings on Tuesday last, the 3rd January, at the Provincial Building, in Charlottetown. **1957** HUTCHISON *Canada* 72: Some Islanders refused to recognize that alternative and had a habit of fastening black crepe to the doors of the Provincial Building on Dominion Day, the new nation's anniversary.

provincial currency *Hist.* See **Halifax currency.**
1804 *Quebec Gaz.* 2 Aug. Supp. 4/1: The Rents ... will be ... twenty-five shillings Provincial currency, or eight bushels of good, clean and merchanable Wheat ... per annum. ... **1905** SCHERCK *Pen Pictures* 67: It was not until 1820 that the Halifax, or Provincial currency, became at all general, private and store accounts being mostly kept in New York currency previous to that time, public and school accounts in Halifax currency.

provincial flag a flag officially adopted by a province.
1965 STANLEY *Canada's Flag* 87: Those provinces which have their own provincial flags include Nova Scotia, New Brunswick, Prince Edward Island, Quebec, Ontario, Manitoba, Newfoundland and British Columbia. **1966** *Globe and Mail* (Toronto) 1 Aug. 1/8: [Caption] Young Quebeckers want B.C. to drop its provincial flag.

provincialist *n.* **1** *Obs.* See **provincial** *n.* (def. 1).
1844 *Bytown* [Ottawa] *Gaz.* 14 Mar. 2/4: Antithetically however, let it be recorded that poor By was an anxious, persevering, generous hearted officer, and like most men valued here for having done us Provincialists anygood, was most ungraciously received at home.
2 *Hist.* a person who advocated the dominance of provincial rights at the expense of a strong central government.
1882 *Brandon Dly Mail* (Man.) 30 Dec. 2/1: This is where issue is joined by Federalists on the one hand and Provincialists on the other, and the more violent of the Provincialists are the malcontents who do not believe in constitutional means to secure a just interpretation, but who wish not only to be expounders of the constitution but violators of it.

provincial legislature the legislature of any Canadian province. See also **provincial parliament.**

1799 SMYTH *Topogr.Descr.U.C.* 72: It received its present name by an act of the Provincial Legislature.
1863 WALSHE *Cedar Creek* 334: This is with reference to the hundred and thirty representatives in the Lower House of the Provincial Legislature. **1955** *Shawinigan Standard* 12 Jan. 2/1: The usefulness of the Senate can and should be restored, says The Financial Post. If it is not, that institution must surely go the way of similar bodies in the provincial legislatures, which have now all but disappeared.

Provincial Marine *Hist.* See 1934 quote.
1811 *York* [Toronto] *Gaz.* 4 July 3/4: Our Provincial Marine command the interior waters. **1934** *Beaver* Dec. 26/1: When the government of Canada, at the close of the eighteenth century, by formation of the quasi-naval establishment known as the Provincial Marine, began ship navigation on the Great Lakes for the benefit of commerce generally, fur traders immediately took advantage of the service. The accommodation was provided on Lakes Ontario, Erie, Huron and Michigan.

provincial note See **provincial bank-note.**

provincial park a large tract of wild land preserved for the enjoyment of the people and maintained by the provincial government. Cp. **national park.**
1953 MOON *Saskatchewan* 70: A Provincial park with swimming pool, golf course and fishing is built about an enchanted lake. **1963** *Globe and Mail* (Toronto) 21 Feb. 5/1: Public beaches in provincial parks account for only 30 of the 3,300 miles of Great Lakes shoreline in Ontario.

provincial parliament See **provincial legislature.**
1795 (1824) *Canadian Mag.* II 242: At the conclusion of this session the term, "Provincial Parliament," was for the first time made use of by the Governor in Chief, Lord Dorchester, on proroguing the two houses. **1853** STRICKLAND *Canada West* II 6: Dr. Dunlop was the first representative for the Huron District in the Provincial Parliament.... **1953** *North Star* (Yellowknife) July 3/1: However, Canadian law and tradition demands that no one hold seats in two legislatures, and the N.W.T.'s Council is regarded as a legislature, equivalent to a provincial parliament.

provincial police a police force maintained by a province to enforce the laws of the province in areas lacking municipal police protection. See also **provincial policeman.**
☞ *Only Ontario and Quebec retain such forces at present.*
1878 *Herald* (Ottawa) 24 Jan. 1/4: Two whiskey informers, who have lately been giving evidence in several cases, and who were under the protection of the Provincial Police, bolted last night. **1930** *Cdn Labor Defender* Oct.-Nov. 3: The "Progressive" government of Alberta retaliated by rushing in fresh forces of Provincial Police and "Specials." **1965** *Globe and Mail* (Toronto) 10 Mar. 1/6: Provincial police said the single-engined plane ... struck the lines with its undercarriage....

provincial policeman a member of the provincial police, *q.v.* See also **provincial,** *n.* (def. 2).
1955 BIRNEY *Long Table* 223: ... a quirt [was] brought swinging down on his head from the height of a provincial policeman's horse. **1963** *B.C.Digest* 43/1: Nov.-Dec. ... the Provincial Policeman ... tried to bar her path.

provincial premier See **premier** (def. 1).
1890 *Grip* (Toronto) 22 Mar. 196/2: Provincial Premier is highly popular with everybody.... **1961** *Time* (Cdn ed.) 25 Aug. 7/3: Last week, when ten provincial premiers gathered anew in the "cradle of Confederation," Charlottetown was again in festive mood....

provincial rights the rights of the several provinces to exercise control in those areas designated as being under provincial jurisdiction in the British North America Act.
1882 *Progress* (Rat Portage [Kenora], Ont.) 20 May 2/1: The future may be made more secure by a better consideration of provincial rights in the exercise of federal rights. **1916** SKELTON *Day of Laurier* 63: It was in Quebec that the first issue as to provincial rights arose. **1953** LEBOURDAIS *Nation of North* 80: Litigation was almost constant between the Macdonald administration and Mowat's Ontario government over the question of "provincial rights."

proving up the carrying out of the commitments required to prove up, *q.v.*, a homestead.
1958 MACGREGOR *North-west of 16* 67: Carrying out these obligations and getting title to the land was termed "proving up." **1963** *Alta Hist.Rev.* Spring 32: ... first things come first, and these are proving up a homestead and building up his capital.

provincial county *Hist.* a municipal unit in Upper Canada which was not qualified as a county proper but which was expected soon so to qualify. Cp. **reputed township**.
1958 *Encyc.Can.* IX 9/1: Renfrew remained united with Lanark until 1861, when it became a provisional county, with its seat at Pembroke. **1961** PRICE & KENNEDY *Renfrew* 59: In 1861 ... the Governor General made Renfrew a "Provisional County." T. P. French ... became provisional warden.

provincial district See **district** (def. 1).
1892 (1908) DAWSON & SUTHERLAND *Geography* 132: KEEWATIN ... is a large provisional district extending indefinitely northward from Manitoba. **1910** HAYDON *Riders of Plains* 1: The great north-west of Canada ... comprises the enlarged provinces of Saskatchewan and Alberta (the former provisional districts of Athabasca and Assiniboia having been merged into them), and, to the north, the extensive Yukon territory. **1952** PUTNAM *Cdn Regions* 4/2: The district of Yukon, as it exists on present day maps, was defined in 1897 and, in 1920, the present outlines of the provisional districts of Mackenzie, Keewatin and Franklin came into force.

provincial government *Hist.* **1** a temporary government set up by the rebels in Upper Canada in 1838.
1838 *Montreal Transcript* 2 Jan. 1/1: Proclamation by William Lyon MacKenzie, Chairman pro tem of the Provisional Government of the State of Upper Canada. **1940** MACCORMAC *Canada* 134: Taking refuge on Navy Island in the Niagara River after an unsuccessful attack on his home town, Mackenzie proclaimed a provisional government and hoisted a flag bearing two stars and a new moon.
2 a temporary government set up during the Red River Insurrection in 1870 by Louis Riel's New Nation, *q.v.*
1870 *Wkly Manitoban* 12 Nov. 2/5: Has he actually appointed the first President of the Provisional Government to be Justice of the Peace? **1957** *Beaver* Spring 19/1: On November 2nd Riel and his men

seized Upper Fort Garry and set about forming a provisional government.

provisional territory See **district** (def. 1).
1884 *Prince Albert Times* (Sask.) 1/4: Agent's office, Swift Current, Assa., containing 32,290 square miles more or less, being composed of part of the Provisional territory of Assiniboia, and more particularly described as follows.... **1897** TUTTLE *Golden North* 119: Two new provisional districts or territories have recently been erected in the far northwest by the Canadian government. The first is that called Mackenzie....

provisional warden *Hist.* the chief executive of a provisional county, *q.v.* Cp. **county warden**.
1961 PRICE & KENNEDY *Renfrew* 59: In 1861 ... T. P. French ... became provisional warden.

provision post *Fur Trade, Hist.* See **meat post**.
1896 (1898) RUSSELL *Far North* 70: Rae was for many years the best provision post in the Mackenzie District, and furnished thousands of pounds of meat for the river transport.

pryor (pole) ['praɪɚ] *n.* [origin unknown] *Lab.* See 1941 quote. Cp. **jone**.
1774 (1792) CARTWRIGHT *Journal* II 29: Having filled up the boat with ... pryor-poles and killick-rods, at high water we sailed home. **1861** DE BOILIEU *Labrador Life* 86: A long pole fastened to one corner of the net and a short one to the other corner (the former called a "pryor" and the latter a "bobber") show where the net is. **1941** *Beaver* Sep. 38/2: Pryor Pole—a long pole attached to a seal net and floating in an upright position marking the site of the net in deep water.

puagun ['pwɑgən] *n.* [< Algonk.; Ojibwa *pwahgan;* cf. Cree *ospwakun* pipe] a tobacco pipe. See also **spwagan** and **uspogan**.
1860 HIND *Assiniboine Exped.* II 137: Nothing appears to contribute so largely to the comfort and enjoyment of Indians ... as the pwahgăn of the Ojibway, the uspwägăn of the Cree, or the pipe of the English. **1926** SULLIVAN *Northern Lights* 149: Murchison reddened, glanced at his mother, then took one puff and held out the puagun to its rightful owner. **1938** SULLIVAN *Cycle of North* 135: Then a fighting man brought and filled the great soapstone puagun, the pipe with its yard-long stem and strange, straight bowl, that had been handed down from father to son for more years than even the oldest of them knew.

public school† a tax-supported school for the education of children, especially, in modern use, an elementary school; also, the building in which such a school is held.
1789 *Nova Scotia Mag.* I 80/1: This seminary is erected in consequence of a law of this Province, intitled, "An Act for establishing a public school, in the town of Halifax." **1872** *Canadian Mthly* June 483/1: Public Schools ... are distinguished from those which until recently were entitled Grammar Schools, and were intended to afford instruction in the elements of the classical languages as well as the mother tongue. **1889** WITHROW *Our Own Country* 344: The Educational system of Ontario is one of the best in the world. It consists of Public Schools, High Schools and the University, an organic whole, each part fused into the other. **1957** *Northland News* 7 Jan.: ... to interview Mr. Hamilton, architect, regarding the construction of

a twelve-roomed public school. . . . **1966** *Kingston Whig-Standard* (Ont.) 31 Aug. 6/2: . . . public or separate school levies must be added on to the general levy.

puck [pʌk] *n.* [< Brit. dial. var. of *poke*] a disk of hard, black rubber used in ice hockey.
1895 *News* (Rat Portage [Kenora], Ont.) 11 Jan. 1/2: The puck is about the size of a blacking box, m⌐de of rubber. **1931** *Vancouver Province* 8 Jan. 10/2: Joe Martin drew Doran out and netted the puck home with a tricky shot. **1963** O'BRIEN *Hockey* 32: All this fits in with the name, puck. Just how it came to be called that, or by whom, nobody knows.

puck carrier *Hockey* the player in possession of the puck during play.
1957 *Maclean's* 28 Sep. 1/2: The top scorers in the League are the best puck carriers. **1965** *Weekend Mag.* 6 Mar. 41/1: Incidentally, if the goaler has been removed and a puck carrier is tripped or fouled from behind with no opposition between him and the empty net, no penalty shot is called.

puckchaser *n. Hockey, Slang* a hockey player. See also **puck-pusher** and **puckster**.
1958 *Evening Telegram* (St. John's) 29 Apr. 19/6: . . . the Harbour Grace puckchasers made that lead stand up as they took a 3-1 win from Coley's Point. . . . **1966** *Kingston Whig-Standard* (Ont.) 28 June 9/1: It was class and the poetry of motion that set Jackson apart from most of the world's great puckchasers.

puck-handling *n. Hockey* See **stickhandling**.
1965 *Kingston Whig-Standard* (Ont.) 15 May 9/6: . . . Flyers dominated the game with superior skating, checking, passing and puck-handling.

puck-off *n. Hockey, Obs.* See **face-off** (def. 1).
1896 *Times* (Niagara-on-the-Lake, Ont.) 20 Feb. 1/4: Play was called, Bishop getting the best of the puck off and carried the rubber down to St. Catharines goal by a neat combination.

puck-pusher *n. Hockey, Slang* See **puckchaser**.
1897 *Medicine Hat News* (Alta) 25 Feb. 1/5: . . . we have a club which can hold its own with the puck pushers from almost anywhere.

puck sense *Hockey* intuitive ability to play hockey.
1966 *Hockey News* (Montreal) 1 Jan. 13/2: An intangible part of Melnyk's all-round prowess is something called "puck sense."

puck shy *Hockey* of goalies, afraid of being hit by a puck.
1965 *Globe and Mail* (Toronto) 29 Dec. 24/2: I think the new rule could cause a goalie to become puck shy.

puckster ['pʌkstər] *n.* [*puck* + *-ster*] *Hockey, Slang* See **puckchaser**.
1955 *Toronto Dly Star* 11 Apr. 18/5: Moncton Hawks, as optimistic a band of pucksters as ever came down the Allan Cup hockey trail, had little left on which to hang their hopes after 60 minutes' jousting with the K-W Dutchies here Saturday night. **1963** *Calgary Herald* 20 Nov. 17/2: Hockey registration and practice for juveniles B and midget B pucksters will be held . . . at 7.30 p.m.

pugasawin *n.* [< Algonk.] *Obs.* See **pagessan** (def. 2).

puhwahgun *n.* See **powahgen**.

pukamoggin *n.* See **pogamagan**.

pukesann *n.* See **pageesee** (def. 1 and note).

pull-out *n.* See **Hudson's Bay start**.

pull out leave; quit; withdraw.
1884 *Prince Albert Times* (Sask.) 8 Aug. 3/1: Striking camp one morning we pulled out for MacLeod. **1956** KEMP *Northern Trader* 126: The previous manager had pulled out just before we arrived.

pull whistle *Lumbering* work as a whistle-punk, *q.v.*
1956 ANDREWS *Glory Days* 31: Bob Swanson went into the woods pulling whistle for John Coburn in 1919.

A pulphook

pulphook *n. Lumbering* a sickle-shaped hand hook used in working with pulpwood.
1944 KOROLEFF *Woodcutter's Handbook* 15/2: Pulphooks are best when shaped not too open or too closed. **1967** *Toronto Dly Star* 17 Mar. 11/2: Give them axes, pulphooks, teams of horses and send them into the bush.

pulp mill a mill producing pulp for paper.
1958 *Edmonton Jnl* 24 July 3/6: The subject of the study was Hinton, bustling pulp mill town 185 miles west of Edmonton, where North Western Pulp and Power Ltd. has invested $60,000,000 in its plant, woodland operations, roads, utilities and equipment. **1964** *B.C. Digest* Dec. 25/1: There are rumours of a pulpmill coming to this area in the foreseeable future, and these beavers are practising cutting pulpwood. **1965** *Western Wonderland* April 22/1: This [group of logs] is rafted to B.C.Forest Products pulp mill at Crofton, V.I.

puma† *n.* See **cougar**.
1844 MARRYAT *Settlers in Can.* 165: Alfred who was in advance, perceived that a puma (catamount, or painter, as it is usually termed), had taken possession of the deer. . . . **1953** MOWERY *Mounted Police* 126: If they had seen or winded a predatory animal, a wolf or puma, the cows would have bunched together and stood their ground. . . .

pumpkin pine See **white pine** (def. 1).
1832 BAILLIE *Account of N.B.* 42: There are three varieties of this species of pine, called by the workman the Pumpkin, the Black-bark, and the Sapling. . . . **1956** *Native Trees* 6: Eastern White Pine [is also called] pumpkin pine . . . Quebec pine.

punch *v. West* drive (cattle) while on horseback; work as a cowboy (def. 1).
1885 *Nor'Wester* (Calgary) 12 Feb. 3/2: It would pay the stockmen to keep men out during the winter to punch the cattle out of the brush in fine weather. **1955** HOBSON *Nothing Too Good* 47: I wrote out a check, on brown wrapping paper, to Little Thomas and his wife for their superb job of punching cows.

punch donkey *Lumbering, Slang* work as a donkey jammer, *q.v.*

1956 ANDREWS *Glory Days* 49: Skid greaser and bull skinner in the Oregon woods at 18, Stub Dillon could do anything in the woods from setting a charge of powder to punching a donkey. . . .

puncher *n.* 1† See **cowboy** (def. 1).
1912 WHITE *Wildcatters* 137: . . . the mare could tell a rider from a lubber the minute he put foot in the stirrup. Ben had decked him out in puncher's garb. The lariet was correctly coiled at the saddle-horn. 1950 STEELE *Ghosts Returning* 30: Jean thanked the gorgeous young puncher and rapturously admired not only the fellow's horse but the fellow himself, while John attended to the menial task of getting down and looking over team and harness.
2 *Lumbering, Slang* See **donkey jammer.**
1942 SWANSON *Western Logger* 17: . . . I toot my signal with ease,/ To keep the puncher a-guessing, with a crew he can never just please. 1953 SWANSON *Haywire Hooker* 21: The lunches were crappy, the hotcakes were lousy,/ The puncher was nervous, the whistle punk drowsy. . . .

pung† [pʌŋ] *n.* [reduction of *tom pung* < *tow-pung*, ult. < Algonk. and related to *toboggan*, q.v.] *Maritimes* See 1896 quote.
1896 ROBERTS *Camp-Fire* 121: . . . they were getting snugly bundled into the warm, deep "pung," as the low box-sleigh with movable seats is called. 1946 BIRD *Sunrise* 132: Then the storm had become so bad that he could not drive the horse, and somewhere the animal had left the road. He had been upset from the pung and the horse had vanished. 1952 BUCKLER *Mountain and Valley* 171: He remembered the time Chris had persuaded his mother to let him, David, go to the pung races on the lake. . . . 1965 MACBEATH & CHAMBERLIN *New Brunswick* 312: Fathers, like most businessmen, preferred the buggy, or the pung in winter.

punk *n. Lumbering, Slang* See **whistle-punk.**
1942 SWANSON *Western Logger* 14: The punk! The useless, lazy streak—/ Ruins my ears with his whistle's squeak. 1953 SWANSON *Haywire Hooker* 18:
I've been having my troubles of lately,
And it's all on account of my punk;
He ran off with another hook-tender,
And took with him all of my junk.

punk *v. Lumbering, Slang* work as a whistle-punk, *q.v.*
1942 SWANSON *Western Logger* 17: And I hate to punk on a "cold deck" or to help on a "rig-up" crew—/ It's then I can't sit on my "fanny," for there's jobs they will find me to do.

punkie† ['pʌŋki] *n.* [< Algonk.; see 1798 quote; cf. Ojibwa *penkī* small] See **no-see-em.**
1798 (1957) *Ont.Hist.* 77: . . . we had, to sustain, [inconvenience] from immense numbers of those small and almost imperceptible insects, called by the Delaware Indians, mocpungies, by our German brethren punks, and by the English Sandflies.] 1867 LORD *Wilderness* 273: The tiny insect called . . . *Punkees* and *mosquito* (little fly) . . . belongs to the order *Diptera*. 1903 WHITE *Forest* 154: The midge, again, or punkie, or "no-see-'um," just as you please, swarms down upon you suddenly and with commendable vigour, so that you feel as though red-hot pepper were being sprinkled on your bare skin. . . .

punt *n. Nfld* See 1906 quote.

1792 CARTWRIGHT *Journal* Glossary: Punt. A small boat. 1861 DE BOILIEU *Labrador Life* 161: The punt loaded with our game, homeward we hie for breakfast; and a jolly meal it is, the allowance being a duck a man. 1906 LUMSDEN *Skipper Parson* 55: If confined to the Arm and when the day was fine, a punt (in Newfoundland a keeled rowboat of peculiar native construction) and one man sufficed; if out in the bay to Deer Harbor, a "cod-seine skiff" and half a dozen men might be needed. 1954 *Fishermen's Advocate* 24 Dec. 10/1: I got out in the punt and pushed off for a picture of the boat.

pup *n. Esp.Yukon* a small tributary stream of a creek.
1897 HAYNE *Pioneers* 154: The Bonanza was panning out nearly as richly as its "pups." 1942 WIEDERMANN *Cheechako* 187: Finally we reached our claim. It was at a point where a ravine, or "pup" as they called it up North, called Caribou, formed an intersection with Dominion Creek. 1958 BERTON *Klondike* 55: They had little faith in their property, but on an impulse they walked up the pup in a group and sank their pans into the sand.

pure Indian *Obs.* See **fullblood.**
1836 (1935) STRANG *Pioneers in Canada* 80: This supposition was soon after agreeably confirmed by the discovery . . . of a cache . . . with a note written by Thomas Hassel, a pure Indian, who had been educated at Red River, and engaged by me as an interpreter.

purgatory ledger *Fur Trade, Hist.* See quote.
1934 GODSELL *Arctic Trader* 150: A "Purgatory Ledger" was a book in which a post manager or trader entered unauthorized debts to Indians which he was afraid to show in the regular books and statements. The debt remained "in Purgatory" until the Indian made a good hunt when it was entered as "Barter."

purple sandpiper a shore bird, *Erolia maritima*, common in the North, so called because of its winter feathers of purplish black over underparts of white.
1908 MAIR *Mackenzie Basin* 330: Sir John Richardson many years ago stated that it bred extensively on Melville Island and on the shores of Hudson Bay. 1942 TWOMEY & HERRICK *Needle to North* 227: Very few white men have seen what we saw—the mating of the purple sandpiper. 1959 MCATEE *Folk-Names* 32: Purple Sandpiper [is also called] Big Beachy bird (Nfld., "Labr."). . . .

push *n. Esp.West, Slang* See 1942 quote. Cp. **side-push** and **straw-push.**
1930 *B.C.Lumberman* May 50/2: "the push jest told me that the yarder went and broke down today. . . ." 1942 HAIG-BROWN *Timber* 252: PUSH. A word used for the camp foreman and occasionally for lesser foremen. 1953 SWANSON *Haywire Hooker* 21: "Well, I'll tell you," says Pete, "I'd a made her I think/ But the push, the damn fool, couldn't lay off the drink."

pushing pole or **stick** *North* a long pole or stick used to push a dogsled whenever the dogs need help from the driver.
1896 (1898) RUSSELL *Far North* 103: One of my dogs had injured his shoulder on the way to Providence, and I had to turn him out of the harness and help the others with the pushing stick. 1921 HEMING *Drama of Forests* 176: When the sleighing grew heavy, the drivers used long pushing poles against the ends of the sleds to help the dogs. 1938 *Beaver* Sep. 17/1: The dogs were soft,

the going bad because of a thaw, but, using pushing poles, we came just after dark to . . . the bottom of the lake.

push-pole *n*. 1 *North* See **pushing pole**.
1913 (1917) CURRAN & CALKINS *Northland* 316: The going next day was good for some time, and we again let the dogs pull our toboggan, assisting them with the push-pole.

2 See **setting-pole**.
1931 NUTE *Voyageur* 184: Each canoe was manned by two men, each supplied with a push-pole, *pique de fond* in the voyageur's vocabulary.

pushup *n*. a breathing-hole made in the ice by muskrats and kept open by means of tufts of grass and other vegetation stuffed in the opening. See also **rat-hill**. Cp. **muskrat house**. Also spelled *push-up*.
1937 CONIBEAR *Northland Footprints* 354: ". . . There's no danger of catching her either; she [a fox] didn't go near the push-ups." **1948** *Beaver* Mar. 32: After the surface of the lake is frozen over, the muskrat starts to build his push-ups, which he keeps open so that he may come up to feed. From the bottom of the lake he gathers vegetation which he pushes up through a hole in the ice. As the vegetation freezes the push-up is formed. Constant movements up and down keep the hole open, but if it should freeze too much he just uses those very sharp teeth of his to cut away the ice and make the hole bigger. This he can do only from the top and bottom edges, and so he learns to keep his hole fairly large. **1956** KEMP *Northern Trader* 58: With two quick motions of his trapping hatchet, old Napão knocked the pushup apart and clubbed the squirming rat on the head. **1959** LEISING *Arctic Wings* 65: He was more at ease with a bullwhip out on the trail than cooped up like a rat in a push-up, shoving a pen in his office at Fort Smith.

puskaway *n*. [< Algonk.; cf. Cree *puskaweyao* he leads him astray] *Obs.* See quote.
1864 *Nor' Wester* (R.R.S.) 10 June 1/2: Fond of gambling, in fact all kinds of pastime, a favorite sport of theirs is the Game of Ball or as they call it Pusk-a-way—the delight alike of children, the women, and the men.

pusky ['pʌski] *n*. [< Algonk.; cf. Cree *pukanisīwuk* party] *West* a party.
☛ *Perhaps derived from the name of a gambling game, the featured attraction of many such parties. Cp.* **pageesee** *(def. 2 and note) and* **potlatch** *(def. 4).*
1903 (1913) CULLUM *Devil's Keg* 128: He said he would pay for everything—all we could eat and drink—and that the pusky should be held the night after to-morrow. He will come himself and dance the Red River Jig.

pusse, pussi *n*. See **pussy**.

pussoggin *n*. See **pesogan**.

pussy *n*. [origin uncertain] *Eastern Arctic, Obs.* See quotes.
1852 *Arctic Miscellanies* 89: ". . . I am as much puzzled . . . as was our good old King Talua (may his spirit revel in the land of blubber and pussis!) when the first white men first came among us." [**1852** RICHARDSON *Arctic Exped.* 494: A seal, general name Labrador Eskimo puese (P. pue-sit).] **1860** (1865) HALL *Arctic*

Researches 161: Tookoolito informed me to-day that the words pickaninny, for infant; cooney, for wife; pussy, for seal; Husky, for Inuit; smoketute, for pipe, and many other words, are not Esquimaux, though in use among her people.

puttie *n*. See **pottie**.

pwahgan *n*. See **puagun**.

quadruped snowshoe *Obs.* a snowshoe worn by horses, mules, etc. and made of an ore sack packed with hay.

1897 *Slocan Pioneer* (B.C.) 25 Dec. 1/3: The principal use of the quadruped snowshoe is to break trails for rawhiding.

quaking aspen the aspen poplar, *Populus tremuloides.*

1791 (1937) CAMPBELL *Travels* 101: Here I observed a great number of aspen trees, vulgarly called the quaking ash, because of the singular quality of the leaves keeping in almost perpetual motion. The Indian name of it is woman's tongue, for they say if one leaf be set in motion all the rest begin, and then there is no such thing as stopping them. **1955** MCCOWAN *Upland Trails* 105: The Aspen poplar, being widely distributed, has in consequence, many names, of which Quaking aspen and trembling aspen are the most common.

quaking bog or **swamp** a tract of land made up of spongy peat which quakes when walked or driven on. Cp. **muskeg.**

1958 (1860) HIND *Assiniboine Exped.* II 61: [We] entered a region of swamp, ridge and quaking bog of very formidable character. **1908** MAIR *Mackenzie Basin* 39: The hunters described the inland country as a wilderness of sand-hills, surrounded by quaking-bogs, muskegs, and soft meadows. **1965** *Islander* 14 Feb. 2/1: But between these two outposts there were 14 miles of quaking swamp and muskeg which could engulf man and beast....

qualha *n.* See **qualla.**

qualla ['kwɑlə] *n.* [< Salishan *kw'alux* striped] *Pacific Coast* See 1962 quote.

1869 *Mainland Guardian* (New Westminster, B.C.) 25 Sep. 2/1: The Qualhas . . . run during September and October.... [**1952** DUFF *Upper Stalo* 62: Dog salmon or chums (*O.keta*) appeared in mid-September and remained until December. They were called *kwalux,* "striped."] **1962** *Co-op Grocery News Bull.* 1 Aug. No. 5340 1: Formerly known as dog salmon, the chum, with the scientific name *Oncorhynchus Keta,* has also been called the qualla, keta and calico salmon. It is caught all along the coast of British Columbia.

quanker ['kwɑŋkɚ] *n.* [imitative] See quote.

1945 RICHARDSON *We Keep a Light* 173: This he does by going to the stairdoor and squawking loudly on the small horn-like instrument made to entice ducks, and called a "Quanker."

quar ice or **water** [< Brit. dial. *quar* congeal, coagulate] See quotes. Also spelled *quarr, quor.*

1933 MERRICK *True North* 253: At one point we had to climb a steep ice cliff formed by the seepage of water from above, "quarr water" they call it. **1941** *Beaver* Sep. 39/1: Quor. Water oozing from the ground through snow and freezing on the surface. **1955** ADTIC *Glossary*: quar ice. A Labrador term for ice formed in spring from melt water draining on to a beach, ice foot or fast ice where it refreezes. Quar ice is often brownish in color and difficult to detect; it is slippery and may be a serious obstacle to foot and sled travel.

quarter *n.* **1 a.** *Hist.* a quarter of a Spanish dollar, *q.v.* See also **quarter-dollar** (def. 1).

1799 *Canada Constellation* (Niagara-on-the-Lake, U.C.) 30 Aug. 3/1: We are told . . . that cut quarter dollars are heavier, and . . . more valuable than round quarters. **1854** *Hamilton Gaz.* (C.W.) 4 May 2/6: . . . the erstwhile consumptive treasury . . . became plethoic with donated yorkers and quarters.

b. a quarter of a Canadian dollar; a twenty-five-cent piece. See **dollar** (def. 2). See also **quarter-dollar** (def. 2).

[**1860** *Brit.Colonist* (Victoria) 27 Mar. 2/2: The warm spring sun has the effect of drying up the mud . . . much to the disgust of all respectable boot-blacks, who have reaped a large harvest of quarters during the last winter.] **1897** *Slocan Pioneer* (B.C.) 18 Dec. 3/4: One would think twice in the east before paying twenty-five cents for a pie, but when you get a genuine pie here with crisp flaky crust, just the kind your mother used to make, you think it cheap at a quarter. **1967** *Globe and Mail* (Toronto) 21 Apr. 5/8: A Queen's University law student's contention that there are no such coins in Canadian law as pennies, nickels, dimes and quarters was rejected yesterday by an amused Ontario Supreme Court Judge.

2† *Esp.West* See **quarter-section.**

1871 *Wkly Manitoban* 25 Mar. 3/3: In the survey of any and every township the deficiency or surplus, as the case may be, resulting from the convergance of meridians, shall be set out and allowed in the quarter section on the west boundary, the areas of which shall in the survey be returned accordingly at their actual contents. **1963** SYMONS *Many Trails* 25: Amos had filed on a quarter by the creek, and had a small log shack sheltered against a cut bank....

3 *Cdn Football* one of the four periods into which a regulation game is divided.

1958 *Edmonton Jnl* 12 Aug. 6/7: . . . Edmonton never seriously threatened in Ottawa territory until the fourth quarter.

quarter beaver *Fur Trade, Obs.* a one-year-old beaver.

1743 (1949) ISHAM *Observations* 147: They are four years before the Come to the full growth, Distinguishing by Whole, ¾ ½ and ¼ beaver.

quarter blood Indian See **quarter-breed.**

1897 DURAND *Reminiscences* 218: On the corner of John and Main streets west, Bailey's bakery stood, where William Johnson Kerr, the giant quarter-blood Indian, assaulted W. L. McKenzie in 1832 at night.

quarter-breed† *n.* the offspring of a white person and a person half Indian.

1862 *Nor'Wester* (Winnipeg) 22 Oct. 2/4: The name is given equally to those who may have a White father and Halfbreed mother, or vice versa, and who are, thus, quarter-breeds—if we accept the reason of the name. **1903** (1913) CULLUM *Devil's Keg* 156: Thoughts of this wild, quarter-breed girl filled his brain as he sat in his little office.... **1935** *Cdn Geog.Jnl* Nov. 297/1: Inside the schoolhouse a French Quarter-Breed was calling the dances....

quarter-dollar *n.* **1** *Hist.* See **quarter** (def. 1a).

1801 *U.C.Gaz.* (York[Toronto]) 12 Dec. 3/3: As there are a number of counterfeit pieces of money in circulation in this town, the public is requested to be on its guard in receiving dollars, quarter dollars, &c. **1958** RADDALL *Rover* 15: The Spanish *pesos* were silver pieces each worth eight *reals.* Hence they were commonly called "Pieces of eight," and Canadian and American traders in the olden times spoke of a half-dollar as "four bits" and a quarter-dollar as "two bits."

2 See **quarter** (def. 1b).

1888 (1890) ST. MAUR *Impressions* 64: Round these springs have lately been erected small bathing-houses, where hot baths can be obtained, the water being brought in pipes from the springs; a quarter-dollar is charged for a bath.

quarter-section† *n. Esp.West* one quarter of a surveyed section of land, that is, 160 acres, the area of the usual homestead grant in the West. See also **quarter** (def. 2).
1842 (1955) CRAIG *Early Travellers* 134: Many years ago the whole province was laid out in sections, and quarter sections, dividing the whole country like a "damboard." **1880** GORDON *Mountain and Prairie* 279: Any person who is the head of a family, or who has attained the age of eighteen years, is entitled to be entered on these unappropriated lands for a homestead of a quarter-section. **1958** *Herald-Tribune* (Grand Prairie, Alta) 10 Feb. 22/1: The quarter section was surrounded by a fence eight poles high with stakes held together by willow wands. . . .

quartz claim† *Mining* a claim having a quartz vein of gold or other ore.
1859 *Brit.Colonist* (Victoria) 22 Aug. 2/1: Considering the wide distribution of quartz over the Island, it is desirable that a law should be made regulating the taking up and working of quartz claims. **1897** *B.C. Mining Jnl* (Ashcroft) 16 Jan. 1/5: Several quartz claims have been located and recorded within the past few days on Tyaxion creek.

quartz fever *Obs.* enthusiasm for quartz mining.
1869 *Mainland Guardian* (New Westminster, B.C.) 1 Sep. 3/5: The quartz fever continues, and several new reefs had been located; so that the test mill will have plenty to do when it arrives.

quartz gold *Mining* gold found in mineralized quartz as opposed to placer or alluvial gold.
1859 *Brit.Colonist* (Victoria) 29 Aug. 3/1: The coast was prospected for some sixty miles . . . but without success, except finding in the interior an old pick where some former explorers had been blasting for quartz gold.

quartz lode *Mining, Esp.B.C.* a lead or vein of mineral-bearing quartz.
1869 *Mainland Guardian* (New Westminster, B.C.) 8 Sep. 3/3: Several new quartz lodes were spoken of that promise well.

quartz mine† *Mining* a mine in which gold or other mineral is found in quartz rock.
1900 OSBORN *Greater Canada* 87: Nearly all the great quartz-mines of North America—and without a quartz-mine no really permanent mining settlement is possible—have been discovered by tracing alluvial deposits of gold to their point of origin in the mother rock.

quartz mining† the practice of mining mineral-bearing quartz.
1880 GORDON *Mountain and Prairie* 146: Quartz-mining has as yet received little attention in British Columbia. **1963** *Western Miner* Mar. 38/3: . . . the special committee drafting proposed amendments to the "Yukon Quartz Mining Act" has mailed its final recommendations to the Hon. Walter Dinsdale. . . .

quawk [kwɑk] *n.* [< Esk. *quaq* frozen meat] *Arctic* uncooked frozen meat or fish.
1942 *Beaver* Dec. 18/2: The [caribou] rump is usually eaten as kwark, or frozen meat. **1947** GILLHAM *Raw North* 117: The fish are thus eaten without cooking, and the mess is called quawk.

Quebec Act *Hist.* the act of the British Parliament by which Canada was governed from 1774 to 1791. See also **Quebec Bill** (def. 2).
1789 *Quebec Herald* 6 July 290/2: Some years after the Quebec Act passed, a bachelor in this city got so much enamoured with the venal charms of a fair lady, that he changed his religion, and stipulated a genteel dower in her favour, in consideration of marriage. **1899** GARDNER *Names* 176: Cramahe administered the government during Sir Guy Carleton's absence from the country 1770-74, the period in which the Quebec Act was under consideration. **1963** MORTON *Kingdom of Canada* 161: But the events were to give the Quebec Act a finality which would have surprised its drafters.

Quebec Bill *Hist.* **1** See **Quebec currency.**
1772 *Quebec Gaz.* 28 May 3/1: I am sure that you will meet with many that will go for Payment of the Quebec Bills now Hawking about here for Sale.

2 See **Quebec Act.**
1787 (1905) *Ont.Bur.Arch.Rep.* II 23: The new-comers from the States have again raised a cry for a House of Assembly, and wish to put an end to the "Quebec Bill," under which the great body of the people, the Canadians, live happily. **1806** (1809) GRAY *Letters* 60: By the Quebec bill of 1774, the clergy are authorised to receive tythes from people of their own persuasion, but not from Protestants.

Quebec burner See **Quebec heater** and picture.
1964 *Maclean's* 7 March 15/2: His phones were in the basement beside a lighted Quebec burner.

Quebec Conference or **Convention** *Hist.* a conference held in Quebec City in 1864, at which plans for Confederation were drawn up.
1864 *Islander* (Charlottetown) 18 Nov. 1/5: Report of the Quebec Conference on the Question of Colonial Union. **1865** *Ibid.* 17 Feb. 2/3: The examples I have given—examples worthy of imitation—have been set at defiance by the Quebec Convention, nor will any impartial person say that the deviation has been for the better. **1964** *Calgary Herald* 17 Mar. 31/4: The resolution said the visit, because of its connection with the centenary of the 1864 Charlottetown and Quebec conferences leading to confederation, makes the Queen a propaganda instrument on behalf of confederation. . . .

Quebec currency *Hist.* one of the standards of currency in use in British North America in colonial times. See also **Quebec Bill** (def. 1).
1765 (1905) *Ont.Bur.Arch.Rep.* III 417: Quebec Currency . . . Exchange at 33⅓ p.ct. . . . **1793** *U.C.Gaz.* (York [Toronto]) 18 Apr. 4/2: All advertisements inserted in it and not exceeding 12 lines will pay 4s. Quebec Currency. . . . **1909** HUNTER *Simcoe County* I 12: For £101, Quebec currency, those five chiefs "gave, granted, etc.," that tract of land butted and bounded as follows. . . .

Quebecer *n.* See **Quebecker.**

Quebec heater a type of heating stove having a tall, cylindrical firebox. See also **Quebec burner.**
1927 *Toronto Dly Star* 8 Oct. 2: Dominion Circulation "Quebec" Heater . . . gets the heat into every corner of the house. **1942** *Gazette* (Glace Bay, N.S.) 2 Oct. 14: If

you require plenty of heat, a Quebec Heater is the answer to your needs. **1964** *Maclean's* 2 Dec. 35/1: They were apt to fall out of love and drive home thinking of things like Quebec heaters and hot chocolate.

A Quebec heater

Quebec horse See **Canadian horse.**
1964 *Gazette* (Montreal) 13 June 6/4: These hardy Quebec horses were suited not only to these hazards of broken ice, and the jolts of the rough roads . . . they endured one of the most exacting needs of all-impatient fast driving.

Quebec Jersey See **Canadian cattle.**
1936 MACEWAN & EWEN *Cdn Animal Husbandry* 54: . . . they [Canadian cattle] probably sprang from ancestors which also gave rise to the Channel Islands' breeds—Jersey and Guernsey. The Canadian has been dubbed the "Quebec Jersey." **1941** MACEWAN *Farm Live-Stock* 252: . . . such names as "Quebec Jersey" and "Black Jersey," sometimes heard with reference to the Canadian breed [of cattle] may have more significance than is usually supposed. **1958** FRANDSEN *Dairy Handbook* 338/2: Canadian (Quebec) Jerseys—said to be the same as French-Canadian [cattle].

Quebecker [kwə'bɛkɚ *or* kə'bɛkɚ] *n.* a native or resident of Quebec, especially a French Canadian. Cp. **Quebecois.**
1836 *Bytown* [Ottawa] *Independent* 24 Feb. 3/2: We think the Quebecers are not such flats as to pay for measuring timber, merely because they receive it; if they do, it is more than we would be willing to accuse them of. **1837** *Montreal Transcript* 14 Jan. 2/2: The match . . . was played on Tuesday last, at Three Rivers, when the Quebeckers proved victorious. **1901** *Rev. Hist.Pubs* V 104: The Dauphin whose birth gave such joy to the Quebeckers of 1730 never ascended the throne, but he was the father of three kings. **1965** *Globe and Mail* (Toronto) 5 Jan. B5/6: [It] will provide a greater degree of economic control by Quebeckers.

Quebec marmot *Obs.* See **groundhog** (def. 1).
1754 (1787) PENNANT *Supplement* 54: The Wenusk, or Quebec Marmot, feeds on coarse grass. **1849** ALEXANDER *L'Acadie* II 320: List of Animals . . . in New Brunswick . . . Arctomys Empetra Wood chuck, Quebec Marmot.

Quebecois [kebɛ'kwa] *n.* [< Cdn F] **1** a French-Canadian native or resident of Quebec. Cp. **Quebecker.**
1873 LEMOINE *Maple Leaves* 171: The County and town of Joliette preserve the name of another distinguished Canadian, a Québecquois, Louis Joliette, who was chosen by Frontenac to accompany Father Marquette in his exploration of the Mississippi. **1962** *Maclean's* 17 Nov. 4/1: He lashed out at editors of French-

language newspapers who had wailed about the "stupidity" of rural Québecois in the last federal election. **1965** *Kingston Whig-Standard* (Ont.) 9 Jan. 22/2: . . . the Quebecois drawn into federal government must revise their code of political ethics. . . .
2 the variety of French spoken in Quebec.
1963 *Maclean's* 6 Apr. 23/1: Like many people who matured in Quebec after World War II she has spent much of her time as a young adult in France. Without being affected, her French sounds more Parisian than what we who don't speak French well call Quebecois.

Quebecois *adj.* of or pertaining to French-speaking Quebec or Quebecois (def. 1).
1954 RADDALL *Muster of Arms* 135: She was speaking in English but the mind behind the tongue was Quebecois, drawing its thoughts from old deep sources. . . . **1963** *Sun* (Vancouver) 22 Mar. 4/1: This is a startling discovery for a Quebecois newspaperman travelling across Canada.

Quebec pine See **white pine** (def. 1).
1837 *Bytown* [Ottawa] *Gaz.* 28 June 2/3: The demand for timber was so languid, at 17 d. a 17¼ l. per foot, for Quebec pine. **1956** *Native Trees* 6: Eastern White Pine [is also called] Quebec pine.

Québecquois *n. adj.* See **Quebecois.**

Quebec Resolutions *Hist.* the resolutions passed at the Quebec Conference, *q.v.*, as proposals for Confederation.
1873 (1905) BIGGAR *Oliver Mowat* II 510: This was a provision in the Quebec resolutions; but Mr. Caldwell, then Colonial Secretary, objected to it. **1963** MORTON *Kingdom of Canada* 321: So rapidly and fiercely did the storm build up that Tupper did not venture to put the Quebec Resolutions before the Assembly.

Quebec Scheme *Hist.* the scheme of government proposed for a confederated Canada at the Quebec Conference and embodied in the Quebec Resolutions, *q.v.*
1867 *Islander* (Charlottetown) 15 Mar. 2/1: It will be recollected that under the Quebec Scheme, New Brunswick had a special advantage over the other Provinces. **1928** *Cdn Hist.Rev.* IX 8: By that time, the public would have had a better opportunity to appreciate the merit of the Quebec scheme.

Queen Charlotte Island caribou See quotes; *Rangifer arcticus dawsoni.*
1946 ANDERSON *Cdn Mammals* 178: Queen Charlotte Island caribou . . . long considered to be extinct, but Cowan . . . is confident that the animal is still to be found. . . . **1956** LEECHMAN *Native Tribes* 273: [The Haida] lived almost entirely on the coast of their island home, seldom going inland except occasionally to hunt bears and the rare Queen Charlotte Island caribou, which may now be extinct.

Queen City 1 Toronto, Ontario. See also **Queen City of the West** (def. 2).
1852 *Wkly Leader* 22 Sep. 3/5: Out of respect to an enlightened humanity, notwithstanding the influence of fogeys and *foggieism*, I am compelled once more to return to the social geniality of the "Queen City." **1887** *Grip* (Toronto) 14 May 10/2: . . . in the presence of the peach-blow complexion, brilliant eyes and

juno-like form of our Queen City girls, they fade into positive homeliness. **1958** *Evening Telegram* (St. John's) 7 May 8/2: [He went] to the Queen City where he made a home large enough to accommodate four or five boarders and his wife and three children. **1963** *Kingston Whig-Standard* (Ont.) 5 Feb. 10/1: In 1921 . . . University of Toronto . . . "swamped" the McGill Redmen . . . by 11 to 0 in a sudden-death game at the Queen City.

2 See Queen City of the Plains.
1892 *Medicine Hat Times* (Alta) 13 Oct. 1/6: Winnipeg is known as "The Prairie City"; Regina as "The Queen City." **1957** *Ottawa Jnl* 14 Aug. 6/3: Moose Jaw . . . was years ahead of the Queen City when it built its warm-water natatorium and it was not until the post-World War II era that Regina caught up with the construction of out-door pools.

3 Victoria, B.C. Also *Queen City of British Columbia.*
1900 *Canadian Mag.* May 11/1: Of course, the Queen City has its Chinatown, its parks, and its share of good hotels, just like Vancouver. **1908** DORR *Sunset Shore* 15: . . . over at our right the Queen City of British Columbia, Victoria, the city of eleven lakes. . . .

Queen City of the Plains Regina, Saskatchewan. See also **Queen City** (def. 2).
1882 *Edmonton Bull.* 16 Sep. 1/1: After toasting and luncheon had been partaken of, Pile of Bones, alias Leopold was christened Regina. Great oratorical powers were displayed in wishing success to the queen city of the plains. **1965** *Cdn Geog.Jnl* Feb. 59/1: This is true of much of the country in the vicinity of Regina, the "Queen City of the Plains."

Queen City of the West *Hist.*
☛ *In both senses,* **West** *refers to Canada West,* q.v. *See also* **Western Canada.**
1 Hamilton, Ontario.
1849 *Journal of Education for U.C.* I 702: We have much pleasure in referring pointedly to the following indication of cordial interest in our Public Schools as evidenced by the Corporate authorities of the Queen City of the West. **1854** *Hamilton Gaz.* (C.W.) 3/3: In fact a stranger would suppose it was some back alley, instead of one of the central streets of the Queen City of the West. Hamilton.
2 See Queen City (def. 1).
1852 *Anglo-American Mag.* I 2/1: The "Queen City of the West" hold out no charms for the disciple of Monkbarns, and yet she has seen changes and vicissitudes in her time. **1908** NICHOLSON *In Old Quebec* 96: In the early evening we are set down at Ontario's capital, the "Queen City of the West."

queen crab a species of crab, *Chionoecetes opilio,* found on the East Coast.
1966 *Kingston Whig-Standard* (Ont.) 27 July 36/1: Similar to but smaller than the famous king crab of the Pacific, the species found on the East Coast was recently given the name North Atlantic Queen crab by the fisheries departments. . . . Chief feature of the queen crab is its lobster-like flavor.

Queen's Birthday See **Victoria Day.**
1859 *Brit.Colonist* (Victoria) 25 May 2/3: Yesterday was the Queen's Birthday and it was generally observed as a holiday. **1959** *Maclean's* 29 Aug. 45/2: During the stop at Kingston on May 24, the children had their

first introduction to one of the colonial customs, the celebration of the Queen's birthday.

Queen's Bush *Hist.* See 1958 quote.
1852 *Elora Backwoodsman* 15 Apr. 1/2: The now important tract of country a few years since appropriately named the "Queen's Bush," but to which that name is no longer applicable, is without the means of bringing its necessities and wishes before the public; and receives a much smaller share of attention than it deserves. **1958** *Encyc.Can.* VIII 383/2: Queen's Bush [is a] name commonly applied during the period of Ontario's colonization to a tract of approximately 2,000,000 acres of land near Lake Huron and Georgian Bay, just north of the so-called Huro n Tract.

Queen's Park the Ontario government or legislature, so called after the park in which the buildings stand.
[**1893** YEIGH *Ont.Parliament* 108: No better situation could have been chosen for a public building than the southern end of the Queen's Park.] **1954** *Pictou Advocate* 3 June 1/1: All in all, the highway situation in Queen's Park is far from wholesome, if you believe the average man on the street in Toronto. **1966** *Globe and Mail* (Toronto) 6 Apr. B1/2: Thirteen hundred Ontario farmers marched on Queen's Park yesterday, demanding higher prices for farm products.

Queen's post *Hist.* See **King's post** (def. 1).
1850 ROY *Hist.of Canada* 219: There is at present one of the Queen's Posts, and the Hudson's Bay Company have large stores here for the purposes of the fur-trade.

Queen's Printer† **1** *Hist.* the publisher of a newspaper authorized by the government to print laws and proclamations as well as the debates and proceedings of Parliament. See also **King's Printer** (def. 1).
1806 *Islander* (Charlottetown) 24 Feb. 1/4: The Bill was concocted Good Friday, by the Hon. the late Queen's Printer and others, who, not having attended their places of worship, and, consequently, feeling the want of something to do, amused themselves by preparing the measure, altering the whole character of the representative branch of the Legislature. **1860** *Nor'Wester* (R.R.S.) 28 June 3/1: We shall have made half a dozen volumes of Reports of Committees for the benefit of the Queen's Printers, and at the cost of the Queen's lieges. **1885** GEMMILL *Companion* 217: While in the Commons he proposed the abolition of the office of Queen's Printer, and letting all Departmental printing by tender, which has greatly reduced the annual expenses.
2 (in modern use) the printer of all government documents, federal and provincial. See also **King's Printer** (def. 2).
1958 *Edmonton Jnl* 30 Sep. 4/3: Publication by the Queen's Printer in Ottawa of a new Alberta Gazeteer gives Albertans an opportunity to dwell on the romantic associations aroused by more than 6,500 place names. **1961** *Time* (Cdn ed.) 8 Sep. 17/2: The Queen's Printer is better known to ordinary Canadians as a peerless source of information on everything from dietetics to how to get rid of the purple-backed cabbage worm.

quickhatch *n.* [< Algonk.: Cree *kwekwuhakao*] *Obs.* See **wolverine** (def. 1).
1683 (1946) *H.B.C.Minutes* III 145n: Quickahash (wolverine) 8 which cost £0 10 0. **1748** ELLIS *Hudson's Bay* 42: The Quick-Hatch or Wolverene is another very extraordinary Beast of the Size of a large Wolf.

1836 BACK *Arctic Land* 489: The quickèhatch, or wolverene, is another inhabitant of the high latitudes—its remains having been found in Parry's Islands, near the 75th parallel. 1952 *Beaver* Sep. 22/1: Sometimes this animal is called skunk-bear because its size, build and colour suggest a cross between the two. The French named it *carcajou,* the English *quickhatch,* names derived from the Cree *kwekwuhakayo.*

quick-kick *n. Cdn Football* a punt made on a first or second down, when the defending team least expects such a play, the aim being to catch the defenders with no backs in a position to field the ball quickly.
1963 *Calgary Herald* 11 Nov. 8/6: Fred Burket completed the scoring with a single off a quick-kick.

quickwater† *n.* a stretch of a stream that has sufficient fall to create a marked current but where there are no rapids. Cp. **dead water.**
1905 MOTT *Jules* 260: Nearer and nearer sounded the quick water of the thoroughfare between Lac des Rochers and the dead-water of Rivière du Renard. 1958 *Montreal Star* 22 Oct. 14/3: On the subject of water also there is the definition of quickwater (it isn't in the dictionary). It used to be used in the Maritimes, a term designating water running rapidly but not broken by rapids.

quill *n. Fur Trade, Hist.* a quill, especially a goose quill, used as a token by traders bartering with Indians.
1801 MACKENZIE *Voy.from Montreal* ciii: The chief, when he proposes to make a feast, sends quills, or small pieces of wood, as tokens of invitation to such as he wishes to partake of it. 1833 (1932) MCLEAN *Notes* 137: The trader, on receiving the Indian's hunt, proceeds to reckon it up . . . giving the Indian a quill for each beaver; these quills are again exchanged at the counter for whatever articles he wants. 1934 *Beaver* June 9: So the old gentleman now asked for the promised skins. He was handed one hundred marked goose quills, representing that number of skins. After checking them over in bunches of ten, he entrusted twenty to his eldest grandson . . . to be held in reserve for ammunition.

quill pig or **quilly pig** the porcupine.
1924 SHERMAN *Nature Stories* 200: . . . those Quill Pigs were determined to capture that camp, which had been pitched in the dead centre of their salt-lick. 1943 MILLER *Lone Woodsman* 83: Looking up they saw a large brown animal clinging to the trunk of a tree. "Quilly-pig!" Dan whooped. . . .

quilting *n.* See **quilting bee.**
1896 GOURLAY *Hist.Ottawa* 12: They used to have quiltings too in these primitive times. . . .

quilting bee a social gathering of women at which quilts are made. See also **bee** and **quilting.**
1842 WILLIS *Cdn Scenery* II 4: Then there are logging-bees, husking-bees, chopping-bees, and quilting-bees. 1955 *Flin Flon Dly Miner* (Man.) 17 Mar. 9/1: The Baptist Mission Circle will meet for a Quilting Bee at the church suite, on Thursday, March 17 at 7.30 p.m. 1959 *Press* Dec. 6: Amongst the homesteaders, logging bees, barn raisings, quilting bees, the sharing of game, the trading of work (a day for a day), the rotating harvest crews were the factors that made for existence, progress and at least some degree of good living.

quilting frolic or **match** *Hist.* See **quilting bee.**
1836 *Novascotian* (Halifax) 3 Feb. 37/2: I won't consent to Sall's goin to them huskin parties and quiltin frolicks along with you no more, on no account, for you know how Polly Brown and Nancy White. . . . 1934 DENNIS *Down in N.S.* 240: "It's a French dish," I was told, "but the English are crazy over it. Years ago when they met at the homes for a dance they'd always have rappé pie, or, if there was ever a quilting-match, there'd always be rappé pie."

quincajou *n.* [< Cdn F < Algonk.: Cree; cf. *quickhatch*] *Obs.* See **carcajou** (def. 1).
1760 PICHON *Cape Breton* 101: As there is no species of animal, but that hath its natural enemy, besides man, that of the orignal is the quincajou. 1823 *Canadian Mag.* I 496: The rosomack or glutton of the north of Europe, is the same animal with the carcajou or quincajou of North America.

quinnat† ['kwɪnət] *n.* [< Salishan *t'kwinnat*] *Pacific Coast* See **Chinook salmon.**
1907 LAMBERT *Fishing in B.C.* 73: They are the king salmon or quinnat, a large fish running up to over 80 lb., known also as the spring salmon. . . . 1947 TAYLOR *Canada* 345: The Quinnat or spring salmon weighs from 18 to 30 pounds, and its colour is darker than that of the sockeye.

quint *n.* [< Cdn F < F] *Que., Hist.* See 1905 quote.
1808 (1809) GRAY *Letters* 347: On transfer of the seigneurie, they pay a fifth part of the value, called the Quints. 1905 *Ont.Bur.Arch.Rep.* III xlix: A form of succession duty insured to the Crown, known as quint, amounting to one fifth of the value of the fief, payable on every mutation of ownership by sale or inheritance.

quintal† ['kwɪntəl or 'kæntəl] *n.* [< MF < Med.L, ult. < Arabic] *Esp.Nfld* **1** a quantity of fish, especially cod, weighing 112 pounds.
1712 (1907) [see quote at **planter** (def. 1a)] 1715 (1883) HATTON & HARVEY *Newfoundland* 61: The cod fishery was in a thriving condition, 386,274 quintals of cod having been made in that year, of which two-thirds had been caught and cured by the resident inhabitants. 1815 *Kingston Gaz.* (U.C.) 2 Dec. 4/1: Just arrived, 100 Quintals dry Cod Fish. 1907 MILLAIS *Newfoundland* 152: This effective trap is hauled up twice a day, and generally it will contain anything from 1 to 150 quintals of fish. 1958 *Evening Telegram* (St. John's) 6 May 4/3: There are places . . . where thousands of quintals of fish spoil because there is no salt. 1964 *Nfld Qtly* Spring 27/1: . . . a prior pre-quintal charge is reserved from the entire voyage's value for this labour called "fish-making". . . .

2 a container for packing and shipping dried and salted cod, holding 112 pounds.
1824 *P.E.I.Register* (Charlottetown) 29 Dec. 2/4: Cleared out from the customs house here . . . 27·534 quintals of Cod Fish, 93 casks of salmon, 344 tons of Oil. 1953 BANFILL *Labrador Nurse* 36: The successful progressive fisherman needs nets, bobbers, trawls, quintals, salt, traps, a motorboat.

quintering ['kwɪntərɪŋ] *n.* [origin unknown] *Sealing, Nfld.* See quotes.
1937 DEVINE *Folklore* 39: [Quintering means] killing scattered seals while the ship is moving through loose ice, the men going over the side for the purpose.

1966 *Weekend Mag.* 19 Mar. 36/3: "Quintering" is
still believed to be carried out in Cabot Strait between
Cape Breton Island and Newfoundland. In this type of
hunting a ship moves through the loose floating ice
and the younger and more agile members of the crew
line up at the bow. When they see a seal they hop from
the deck on to the ice, club the seal and hook it through
the jaw. It is then hauled back to the ship on a line.

quiquahatch, quiquehatch, quiquihatch *n.*
See **quickhatch.**

quor *n.* See **quar ice.**

rabascaw *n*. See **rabiscaw.**

rabbit *n*. See **varying hare.**
1696 (1929) KELSEY *Papers* 59: Today our hunters kill'd 30 patridges and 3 Rabbits. **1743** (1949) ISHAM *Observations* 128: Rabbits in some parts are Very plenty. **1872** DASHWOOD *Chiploquorgan* 88: There is a species of hare . . . mis-called a rabbit, which is numerous, but hardly eatable, as they feed altogether on the shoots of the fir trees. In winter they turn white. **1954** BEZANSON *Sodbusters* 19: Rabbits had been everywhere throughout the district in teeming abundance and that meant abundant food for fur bearers, most of whom practically live off rabbits.

rabbit dance 1 See quote.
1952 *Beaver* Mar. 44: The rabbit dance is a remembrance dance. It perpetuates the time . . . when the Indians heard the evil spirit come crashing through the bush to annihilate them. Pretending they were rabbits, they leaped, cavorted and hopped, accordingly. The ruse was successful. The evil one passed, leaving them unharmed.
2 *North* See **Wahpooskow.**
1921 HEMING *Drama of Forests* 167: As the afternoon wore on the Rabbit Dance began, and was soon followed by the Hug-Me-Snug, the Drops of Brandy, and the Saskatchewan Circle, and—last but not least—the Kissing Dance. **1928** FREEMAN *Nearing North* 329: Everything from the Red River jig and the "Rabbit dance" to the fox trot and tango were danced with verve and abandon.

rabbit(-skin) robe See **rabbit-skin blanket.**
1915 SPECK *Hunting Territories* 28: When I saw the dance, the chief had a woven rabbit skin robe over his head and shoulders. **1940** *Beaver* Sep. 14/2: In the shade of the trees near the water's edge, an Indian woman was seen weaving a rabbit-robe. . . .
1963 SYMONS *Many Trails* 79: Within lay the injured child, among a collection of shabby blankets and rabbit-skin robes.

rabbit-skin blanket a warm blanket or robe made by cutting the skins of rabbits, or hares, into long strips and weaving them together, long used by the Indians and adopted by others in the Northwest. See also **rabbit robe.**
1793 (1801) MACKENZIE *Voyages* 248: They were clad in leather, and had some beaver and rabbit-skin blankets. **1921** *Beaver* May 18/2: It was fortunate that he had a rabbit skin blanket and that the weather was not extremely cold. . . . **1963** MCTAVISH *Behind the Palisades* 90: The rabbit skin blanket was . . . porous yet close, light and warm, and the best covering to keep man comfortable underneath that was ever used in a cold country.

rabibou *n*. See **rubaboo.**

Rabisca [rə'bıskə] *n*. [< Cdn F] *Fur Trade, Hist.* (an aphetic alteration of) Athabasca. See also **Athabasca Department. Cp. rabiscaw.**
1913 COWIE *Adventurers* 129: . . . the challenge was generally addressed to "les meilleurs" of the offending district, the men of which were known by such nicknames as "Les Blaireaux," or badgers of Saskatchewan; "Les Cygnes," or Swans of Swan River; "Les Rabisca," of Athabasca; or "Les Gens de la Grande Riviere," of Mackenzie River. **1941** *Beaver* Sep. 39/1: Rabisca brigade—The Athabasca fleet of York Boats.

rabiscaw [rə'bıskɑ] *n*. [cf. *Rabisca*] *Fur Trade, Hist.* See quotes.
1919 *Cdn Field Naturalist* May 24: An offshoot of the Algonkian canoe was the "rabiscaw" of the Hudson Bay Company, an extra large birch-bark craft designed to meet the standards of the fur trade. A prominent feature was the high, upturned bow and stern decorated with gaudy designs. **1920** *Geog.Rev.* Aug. 57: The canoe commonly used was the large birch-bark "rabiscaw" with high, rounded ends and about 33 feet long and 4½ feet wide, or, as the canoemen would describe it, "the five-and-a-half fathom variety."

raccoon† [rə'kun] *n*. [< Algonk.] a fur-bearing mammal, *Procyon lotor,* of North America; also, the fur of this animal.
1764 *Quebec Gaz.* 19 July 2/2: On the 10th Day of August next, will be sold a large Quantity of Furrs, consisting of Beavers, Otters, Martins, Racoons, Foxes. . . . **1765-75** (1933) POND *Narrative* 32: These Wood aford Partreages . . . Rackcones, sum Wild Pigins. **1811** *U.C.Gaz.* (York [Toronto]) 6 Apr. 4/1: The highest price in Cash for Pot and Pearl Ashes, Flour, Beaver, Racoon and Musk-rat Skins. **1955** MCCOWAN *Upland Trails* 128: . . . the rest of the somnolent brotherhood [are] respectively, the bear, the raccoon, the skunk, the woodchuck, the chipmunk, and the bat.

racer *n. Obs.* See **buffalo runner** (def. 1). See also **buffalo racer.**
1820 (1922) HARMON *Journal* 332: . . . when a herd of buffaloes is seen at no great distance off, thirty of forty or more young men mount their racers, which are well trained to this business, and surround them. . . .

racing snowshoe a long slender snowshoe resembling the Ojibwa snowshoe, *q.v.,* used in snowshoe races.
1966 *Globe and Mail* (Toronto) 18 May 6/1: I asked about his racing snowshoes. They are 11 inches wide and an inch or two more than three feet long. He strings them himself.

rackcone, rackoun, rac(k)oon *n*. See **raccoon.**

racket ['rakət *or* ra'kɛt] *n*. a snowshoe, *q.v.* See **raquette.** See also **Indian racket.**
☛ *Though* racket *is an English form and has existed for some three centuries side by side with the French form, it is now virtually obsolete in this sense. Like* racquet, *q.v., its use in modern times seems to have been confined to Labrador.*
1665 (1885) RADISSON *Fourth Voyage* 202: They are broad, made like racketts, that they may goe in the snow and not sinke when they runne after the eland or other beast. **1760** PICHON *Cape Breton* 133: . . . notwithstanding they . . . are even better able to skip over snowy mountains with their legs than we with our rackets, yet he used to run them down. **1823** *Canadian Mag.* I 496: They use rackets or snow-shoes, by means of which they walk on the snow without sinking. **1906** LUMSDEN *Skipper Parson* 53: Schooners, skiffs, punts, snowshoes ("rackets," in common parlance), were ordinary dependences.

racquet ['rakət *or* ra'kɛt] *n*. See **raquette.** See also **racket** and note.
1933 MERRICK *True North* 137: It's a good thing Kay is

handy with the racquets or she would have dropped on the way.

racquet *v.* travel on racquets, *q.v.*
1953 MOWERY *Mounted Police* 186: At one o'clock the next afternoon, through a still, bright cold of sixty-odd degrees below zero, three men loped out of the southeast prairie and racqueted into the open quadrangle of the Police post.

racquette *n.* See **raquette**.

Rad *n. Slang, Obs.* See **Radical**.
1836 *Dundas Wkly Post* 16 Feb. 2/2: What! nasal Bidwell, a party man, We know he is a RAD most hearty, But in Lot-street, say who can, He never countenanced a PARTY. **1852** *Hamilton Gaz.* (C.W.) 16 Feb. 3/2: We have recently seen several of the Walsingham Rads in the ancient garb—can't say it looks bad—rather antique to be sure, but we think the very antiquity adds a shade of respectability.

radial *n. Hist.* one of a number of interurban electric railways operated in southern Ontario from the 1890's to the 1940's, so called because the lines radiated from Toronto.
1916 BRIDLE *Sons of Canada* 191: When he foisted the hydro-radial scheme on the municipalities in January 1916, he had come to the point where he would make hydro-electric compete with all systems of radial and inter-urban lines in that part of Ontario. **1921** *Rod and Gun in Can.* Aug. 34/1: The radial roads between Brantford and Hamilton, Brantford and Paris and Brantford and Port Dover carried out the hunters by the hundreds.... **1966** *Globe and Mail* (Toronto) 12 Sep. 16: [Caption] The radials: commuter dream of the auto killed. *Ibid.*: [Caption] In the 20s, the plans of Ontario Hydro's founder ... to expand the network of York County's radial cars were thwarted.

Radical *n. Hist.* a member of the Radical party, *q.v.* See also **Rad, Radical Reformer,** and **rebel** (def. 1).
1833 *Cdn Correspondent* (York [Toronto]) 1 June 3/1: We are the friends of justice, freedom, and independence, and these virtues we shall always respect and reverence whether they be found in a Radical, a Whig, or a Tory. **1839** (1955) CRAIG *Early Travellers* 124: We have here Tories, Whigs, and Radicals, so called; but these words do not signify exactly what we mean by the same designations at home. **1937** *Cdn Hist.Rev.* XVIII 32: In general the Reformers were either not Radicals or felt constrained to change their allegiance—outwardly at least—upon the crushing of the revolt.

Radicalism *n. Hist.* the principles espoused by a Radical, *q.v.*
1824 *Wkly Register* (York [Toronto]) 8 July 226/2: We must give this little Hero of Radicalism ... full credit for the boldness of his attempts to perpetuate a species of political malignity.... **1837** *Times* (Halifax) 4 Apr. 110/3: We hold the Radicalism of Nova Scotia to be the Radicalism of Papineau and Bidwell, in the Canadas. **1885** DENT *U.C.Rebellion* I 107: Rolph, though a man of equable mind, and by no means constitutionally inclined towards Radicalism, had much better opportunities for mixing with the people than had Colonel Talbot.

Radical party *Hist.* the radical wing of the Reform party, *q.v.*, in Upper Canada.
1836 (1926) LANGTON *Early U.C.* 160: Several of the old bureaucracy ... have yielded to the Radical party and deserted Sir Francis in his struggle with the House of Assembly, and their places in the Executive Council have been filled up by better men. **1849** *St.Catharines Jnl* (C.W.) 20 Dec. 3/2: He disclaims the spurious Conservatism recognized as the guiding star of Canadian Tories, and objects to the democratic ideas of the extreme Radical party.

Radical Reformer *Hist.* a member of the Radical party, *q.v.* See also **Radical** and **Reformer** (def. 1).
1833 *Liberal* (St. Thomas, U.C.) 18 July 3/4: Some of them will, no doubt, turn Radical Reformers, at least by profession, to secure a return to Parliament. **1899** GARDNER *Names* 449: He was the first to use the term "Clear Grit" as applied to the Radical Reformers since 1850.

radio blackout *Esp.North* See quotes.
1951 GILLIS & MYLES *North Pole* 154: "At times we had complete radio black-outs and for two-and-three-day periods Joe would be unable to 'get out' at all." **1958** *Evening Telegram* (St. John's) 29 Apr. 13/6: Once when, because of peculiar meteorological conditions a "radio blackout" occurred at Cape Hay, for nearly ten days....

radome ['redom] *n.* [*radar* + *dome*] a rigid, domed structure housing radar equipment, the antennae revolving within the dome.
1957 *Kingston Whig-Standard* (Ont.) 28 Feb. 7/1: The radomes house electronic search equipment in the various air attack warning stations and are primarily protection for the complicated radar apparatus. The new, rigid dome developed in the U.S., will require less maintenance. **1957** *Time* (Cdn ed.) 25 Nov. 49/1: Arctic blizzard, blowing against radome and insulated Atwell shelters during long winter night, adds to loneliness of 20-man DEW line auxiliary warning station on Boothia Peninsula.

raft *n.* **1**† *Lumbering* a number of pieces of timber pinned, bound, or otherwise kept together to facilitate transport by water. See also **boom,** *n.* (def. 3b) and **timber raft.**
[1697 (1929) KELSEY *Papers* 95: two of ym brought their rafts wth ym[;] ye other came aground.] **1790** (1961) PERKINS *Diary* 10 July: I git a Raft of plank boards &c., from the falls, & have the Clapboard, that were Counted yesterday, Spread to dry. **1829** (1832) PICKERING *Inquiries* 113: ... some squatters have made clearings and settled, for making rafts. **1849** (1926) LANGTON *Early U.C.* 205: The process is to break up the raft and commit the spars to the stream. About an hour after that perhaps two or three sticks reach Peterborough, the rest are left sticking here and there on rocks, dams and islands. **1892** (1908) DAWSON & SUTHERLAND *Geography* 155: The logs are generally [B.C. coast] brought from the places where they are cut ("logging camps") to the shore on "skid-ways," after which they are formed into rafts and these are towed to the various mills. **1965** STEVENS *Incompleat Canadian* 38: The process of getting the logs off the snags and sandbars and of marshalling them into rafts involved the now almost forgotten art of "birling," wherein the rivermen, pikes or peavies in hand, worked logs out of shallows by spinning them under their sure feet.

2 *Lumbering, Hist.* a large assemblage of square timbers, spars, etc. arranged in any of several ways according to the conditions of the waterways used. See also **lumber raft.**

☛ *Such rafts, of varying construction, were for more than a century a common sight moving toward Quebec on the Great Lakes and the St. Lawrence River and its tributaries, especially the Ottawa. No attempt has been made here to distinguish the differing types of rafts, although the quotations touch on the subject. See also* **crib** (*def. 1a*), **dram, float** (*def. 1*) **traverse²,** *and* **withe.**
1796 (1911) SIMCOE *Diary* 346: I walked to the Seigneurie House [and] examined a raft lying in the Chateauguay River and thought its construction very curious. **1807** (1809) GRAY *Letters* 211: The rafts of oak timber and staves are of a different form. **1846** BONNYCASTLE *Canada and Canadians* I 70: A raft a quarter of a mile long . . . is curious enough; but to see it in drams, or detached portions, sent down . . . the timber slides of the Ottawa . . . is still more so. **1864** (1955) CRAIG *Early Travellers* 284: To understand how the thing works, you must know that a "raft" consists of 30 or 40 separate "cribs," that is, subdivisions or small rafts, each crib complete in itself, and all bound together by cords and withes. **1945** CALVIN *Saga* 70: . . . an average [St. Lawrence River] raft of the 1870's might contain twelve to sixteen drams— occasionally more. **1961** PRICE & KENNEDY *Renfrew* 51: The last raft of timber went down the mighty Ottawa in 1909. **1963** *Cdn Geog.Jnl* Nov. 159/1: The last raft of square timber went down the St. Lawrence [from the Lower Lakes], running the rapids, in 1911. **1964** *Ibid.* Feb. 70/1: The raft was a great floating community of up to 250 lumberjacks. At one end would be the cook's shanty with its fireplace built on sand and ashes.

A raft (def. 2)

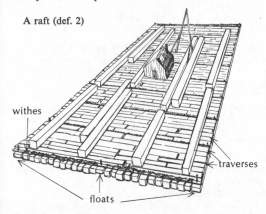

withes

traverses

floats

3 of ice, an ice formation resulting from large cakes of ice being lifted by pressure on top of other ice. See also **raft,** *v.* (def. 3).
1944 *Beaver* Mar. 17/2: . . . the ice was a mass of hummocks with rafts over twenty feet in height. **1964** *North* July 39/2: Now in November, it [the river] was nearly choked; a mad race of water in the middle flung rafts of ice to the sides, burrowed under ice bridges, and showed in roils and slicks as far as could be seen. Soon a man could drive right across.

raft *v.* **1** travel along or cross (a river) by means of a raft.
1689 (1929) KELSEY *Papers* 30: This morning tryed to gett over yᵉ mouth of it but could not so . . . went up yᵉ river to Raft our selves over. **1873** (1888) MCDOUGALL *G.M.McDougall* 191: . . . rapid and dangerous rivers have been rafted. . . . **1900** LONDON *Son of Wolf* 133:

"I'll send word down for a couple of the boys to outfit and pole a boat up the Yukon. We'll cross the divide and raft down the Indian River to meet them."
2 *Lumbering* **a.** drive (logs, timber, etc.) by means of a raft (def. 1 or 2); transport in the form of a raft by water. See also **rafting** (def. 1).
1743 (1949) ISHAM *Observations* 171: For our firing we . . . Rafted home . . . two piles [of wood] of 160 yds. Curcumference. . . . **1818** PALMER *Journal* 237: One of the men . . . had been with a company, cutting lumber in Upper Canada, and rafting it down to Quebec. **1829** MACTAGGART *Three Years* II 207: Let them seek up the Black River to the Manicogan Lake, and raft down into English Bay. **1874** *Canadian Mthly* Oct. 344/2: The timber intended to be rafted down to Quebec, is taken from the booms, say in Toronto bay, and built up in drams. **1965** *Western Wonderland* Apr. 22/1: [Caption] This [group of logs] is rafted to B.C. Forest Products pulp mill at Crofton, V.I.
b. *Obs.* engage in rafting (def. 1).
1829 MACTAGGART *Three Years* II 170: . . . about a year ago, as they were rafting down the lake, one of their hands, a Canadian, went ashore to shoot pigeons. . . .
c. fashion into a raft (def. 2). See also **raft up** and **rafting up.**
1846 (1957) GUILLET *Valley of the Trent* 204: To insure the proper working of the slides, I propose . . . that the person in charge of the slides be instructed . . . to allow no timber to pass out of that Boom except in Cribs properly rafted for running the slides.
1853 STRICKLAND *Canada West* II 281: . . . they also [drill] a mortice-hole through it at both ends of the timber, which was made on purpose to pass the withes through when rafting them. **1854** KEEFER *Ottawa* 66: If the stream in which the timber is hauled out is not navigable for cribs, "driving" is resorted to—the loose sticks with the "floats" and "traverses" for rafting it are allowed to float down, followed by the lumbermen in canoes and along shore. . . . **1872** DASHWOOD *Chiploquorgan* 106: When the timber has been driven down to large rivers or lakes, it is rafted; then it is wharped, or towed by steamers to the saw mills. . . . **1945** CALVIN *Saga* 9: With the help of a neighbour he cut square timber, probably oak, rafted it . . . ran his little raft to Quebec and sold it.
3 See 1883 quote. See also **raft,** *n.* (def. 3), **rafted ice, rafter,** *v.,* and **rafting** (def. 2).
1883 HATTON & HARVEY *Newfoundland* 301: Or, under pressure of the storm, it frequently happens that the ice is "rafted," as the sealers call it; that is the fragments are piled in layers one over the other to the height of thirty or forty feet, being lifted by the swell and hurled forward as if from large catapults. **1939** *Beaver* Mar. 13/2: On the sea and large lakes ice seldom forms smoothly. Early storms break it and pack it in confusion, and pressure causes it to "raft." **1958** *Evening Telegram* (St. John's) 28 Apr. 2/3: And there Bozo is now, surrounded by pack ice which is being rafted by tides and frost into a jumble of pressure-ice.

rafted ice ice that has been caused to raft (def. 3). See also **raftered ice** and **rafting ice.**
1897 TYRRELL *Sub-Arctics* 92: Toward the north end of the lake we passed great piles of rafted ice on the shore. **1922** FLAHERTY *Eskimo Friends* 93: On the tenth of April we came face to face with a gigantic pile of

rafted ice. **1959** *Globe and Mail* (Toronto) 13 Apr. 1/5: Capt. Knight reported rafted ice up to 15 feet thick. . . .

rafter† *n.* **1** *Lumbering, Obs.* See **raftsman.**
1864 (1955) CRAIG *Early Travellers* 283: At the bottom of each separate "shute" there is a wooden platform or "apron" upon which the rafters are precipitated, and so preserved from diving down under the surface by the impetus of their fall.
2 a person who rafts (def. 1).
1954 BEZANSON *Sodbusters* 161: Rafters kept coming quite a while. They all finally got tired waiting for God to freeze the rivers again, and came down on rafts.

rafter *v. Nfld* See **raft,** *v.* (def. 3).
1861 DE BOILIEU *Labrador Life* 100: It is a sad sight to see a ship on the weather edge of ice not enabled to work off; for when the ice begins to rafter she is thrown up, falls over, and becomes like corn between two millstones, and is literally ground up. **1924** FLAHERTY *Eskimo Friends* 99: Then for two days a tumultuous army floated by—miles and miles of ice, raftering and rearing and overriding us it fought its way to the sea. **1964** *Nfld Qtly* Spring 16/3: Evidently, just like frozen masses of ice raftered . . . the crust of the earth broke and travelled southward. . . .

raftered ice *Nfld* See **rafted ice.**
1916 DUNCAN *Billy Topsail* 130: It was six miles from the edge of the raftered ice to the first island. . . .

raft foreman *Lumbering, Hist.* the raftsman, *q.v.*, in charge of a raft (def. 2).
1945 CALVIN *Saga* 77: . . . all the raft foremen were French. . . .

rafting *n.* **1** *Lumbering, Hist.* the practice, business, or work of transporting (timber) by means of rafts (def. 2). See also **raft,** *v.* (def. 2).
[**1697** (1929) KELSEY *Papers* 95: our 3 boats went to ten shilling creek to rafting. . . .] *c***1778** (1964) *Atlantic Advocate* July 59/1: Each March the King's Purveyor certified the number and sizes of the sticks that had been brought to the stream, "trimmed four-square and fit for rafting." **1829** MACTAGGART *Three Years* II 170: . . . the chap [a raftsman] was got weary of rafting, and his comrades suspected he meant to clear out. **1844** *Ottawa Advocate* 23 Apr. 3/1: Already has the rafting of Timber down the noble Ottawa for the Quebec Market commenced. **1961** GREENING *Ottawa* 103: The crib was the type of raft usually found on the Ottawa and its tributaries, while the dram was used for rafting operations on Lake Ontario and the section of the St. Lawrence above Montreal. **1963** *Cdn Geog. Jnl* Nov. 165/3: . . . years after St. Lawrence rafting ceased, one could see, along the southeast coast of England, groynes built of rock-elm timber. . . .
2 of ice, the process of forming into rafts (def. 3).
1918 GRENFELL *Lab. Doctor* 78: On them swept the floe, crashed into the fixed ice, shattered its edge, rose up out of water over it, which is called "rafting," forced itself on the unfortunate ship. . . .

rafting-channel *n. Lumbering, Obs.* See **snye** (def. 1b).
1827 (1829) MACTAGGART *Three Years* I 128: Passing the east end of Merrick's Mill-dam . . . is a *snie*, which has been converted into a rafting channel.

rafting ice See **rafted ice.**
1883 (1889) HATTON & HARVEY *Newfoundland* 95: When they are in danger from "rafting" ice, or fragments of floes . . . the self-sacrificing affection of the mothers leads them to brave all dangers. . . . **1966** *Weekend Mag.* 19 Mar. 34/1: Each year . . . seals congregate on the rafting ice pressing in around the shores of Canada's Magdalen Islands. . . .

rafting up *Lumbering, Hist.* fashioning (timber) into a raft (def. 2). See also **raft,** *v.* (def. 2c).
1883 FRASER *Shanty* 340: The rafting-up process is an arduous and stirring piece of work. . . . **1926** MAIR *Masterworks* XIV liii: I loved the river life . . . the "drive" in spring and the "rafting-up" at Arne Prior or elsewhere, the timber being formed into cribs, securely withed and chained, and united into enormous rafts. . . . **1945** CALVIN *Saga* 67: This very brief description of the work of "rafting up" timber has taken no account of the human side. . . .

raftsman *n. Lumbering, Hist.* a person employed in the rafting (def. 1) of timber. See also **rafter** (def. 1).
1776 (1845) MAYER *Memoirs* 67: A small current begins here, and the raftsmen are not obliged to row. **1818** PALMER *Journal* 237: He gives the Canadian raftsmen a bad character for idleness . . . and says, that in the greatest dangers, such as passing rapids, they will leave their oars, and fall on their knees to pray to some favourite saint! **1961** GREENING *Ottawa* 113: By this date there [was] a grist mill which provided flour for the raftsmen and shantymen. . . .

raft up *Lumbering, Hist.* See **raft,** *v.* (def. 2c).
1883 FRASER *Shanty* 340: . . . the timber is floated in single pieces down all the numerous tributaries of the Ottawa, and then "rafted-up" at "the mouth" of each.

rag *v. Hockey* retain control of the puck by superior stickhandling and deceptive play, the object being to waste time while killing a penalty or protecting a lead.
1963 O'BRIEN *Hockey* 29: . . . replacements were few and speed lagged at the end or when players "ragged" the puck in mid-ice to kill off penalties. **1964** *Kingston Whig-Standard* (Ont.) 12 Dec. 10: [They] controlled the puck, ragging it so skillfully that the crowd roared with approval.

ragged jacket *Nfld* a harp, *q.v.*, seal more than six weeks old.
1880 (1964) *Nfld Qtly* (St. John's) 4/1: The young when first born, are called by the Newfoundland sealers "White Coats," later during the first moult, "Ragged Jackets". . . . **1883** HATTON & HARVEY *Newfoundland* 95: At the end of six weeks, the young shed their white woolly robe, which has a yellowish or golden lustre, and a smooth, spotted skin appears, having a rough, darkish fur. They [harp seal] have now ceased to be "White-coats," and become "ragged-jackets."

rail fence† any of several kinds of fence made of rails split from logs, as the snake fence, *q.v.*
See picture in next column. See also **straight rail fence.**
1815 *York* [Toronto] *Gaz.* 14 Jan. 4/2: The Land good and well watered; the cleared part, of which 19 Acres are clover, &c. meadow, is mostly under a new rail fence. **1961** *Weekend Mag.* 5 Aug. 27/1: And on the far left-hand corner, on a rail fence, was a smaller sign. . . .

railhead *n.* **1 a.** the farthest point to which track has been laid on a railway line. See **head of steel** (def. 1).

1909 PARKER *Northern Lights* 316: There had been great excitement over the capture and the subsequent escape of a prairie-rover, who had robbed the contractor's money-chest at the rail-head on the Canadian Pacific Railroad. **1939** O'HAGAN *Tay John* 164: The railhead by this time had been hammered through the mountains, past Solomon's Flats, across Yellowhead Pass, along the north shore of Yellowhead Lake, and down into the dim Canyon country of the Fraser.

b. the terminus of a railway line. See **end of steel** (def. 1a).

1916 BRIDLE *Sons of Can.* 53: If any man in America knew the rail-head value of such commodities it was this man Shaughnessy.... **1921** HAWORTH *Trailmakers* 224: ... it was eight degrees below zero the second night after we reached railhead at Peace River Landing. **1964** *North* May-June 27: It will eliminate the circuitous and time-consuming haul to Great Slave Lake and Mackenzie via the railhead at Waterways....

2 a major railway terminus; a distribution centre for railway traffic, freight, etc.

1950 SUTTON *Footloose* 52: Moncton is many things— a railhead, an industrial center, a factory town—but it is no resort for tourists. **1958** *Edmonton Jnl* 1 Aug. 31/1: Civic officials have said it would be impractical to raze sections of the main railhead building, which is nearly two blocks long. **1963** *Herald Mag.* 23 Nov. 3/4: The 110-mile route takes the train from its railhead....

railiner ['reɪ,laɪnɚ] *n.* [*rail* + *liner*] See **dayliner.**
1958 *Edmonton Jnl* 24 June 2 3/2: Go CNR RAILINER between Edmonton and Calgary....

rail portage See quote. See also **portage,** *n.* (def. 1a). Cp. **portage,** *n.* (def. 1b) and **portage railroad.**
1965 *Islander* 14 Nov. 13/3: ... Babcock Lake brought us to the first of the two short rail portages.... the parks branch have provided two short stretches of wooden rail line through the bush and a hand car which can be loaded and pushed.

rail speeder See **speeder** (def. 1b).
1958 *Maclean's* 4 Jan. 19/2: There I climbed on a rail speeder for the ten-mile lap to where we were cutting.

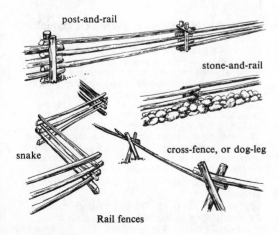

post-and-rail

stone-and-rail

snake

cross-fence, or dog-leg

Rail fences

railway belt See 1958 quote. See also **railway lands** Cp. **mile-belt.**
1880 GORDON *Mountain and Prairie* 271: It does not apply to the railway belt.... **1939** *B.C.Hist.Qtly* July 184: ... the Canadian Pacific Railway was under construction, and along its route, and within the ... "Railway Belt," prospectors were quite ... busy.... [**1958** *Encyc.Can.* II 203/2: These provisions [1880] included ... a grant of 25,000,000 acres of land to be given in alternate sections of 640 acres in a belt 24 miles deep on each side of the railway (deficiencies in fertile land to be made up in other regions)....] **1963** MORTON *Kingdom of Canada* 363: [They received] a block of land in the Peace River to compensate for alienated or rocky land in the "railway belt" granted by the original terms of union.

railway cache a protected storing place used by the Hudson's Bay Company as a pick-up and delivery point on northern railways.
1934 GODSELL *Arctic Trader* 110: ... a remarkable story ... savage Indians threatening the safety of the trading-posts in the North, and bearing down Lake Winnipeg towards Selkirk, looting Hudson's Bay railway caches as they came.

railway dump the fill constituting the built-up embankment of a railway bed.
1954 HAMILTON *Prairies* 14: ... sometimes, too, I seem to see the railway dump winding along the lake bank, and the men busy with pick and shovel....

railway lands See **railway belt.**
1880 GORDON *Mountain and Prairie* 297: Let an entire township be settled at this rate, and even if the railway lands be occupied, there will be only sixty-four families in the township of thirty-six square miles. **1910** WARD *Canadian Born* 93: And it is precisely here that the railway lands are selling at a higher price for the moment than anywhere else, and that settlers are rushing in.

railway town or **village** a town or village located on a railway.
1881 BEGG *Great Cdn N.W.* 106: The railway is constructed to a point on the eastern side of the river opposite Selkirk, so that there is every chance of its becoming a railway town, if not a railway centre. **1952** PUTNAM *Cdn Regions* 403/1: The cultural landscape is characterized by the huge rectangular wheat fields and by the beaded strings of railway villages, each with its cluster of grain elevators.

rain *v.* make rain; cause rain to fall (as a rainmaker claims to do).
1961 MITCHELL *Jake and the Kid* 151: There was a little piece saying that Jake Trumper was going to rain on Tuesday next at Tincher's back forty where the ground rose between the correction line and Government Road.

rainbow (trout)† *n.* a steelhead which lives permanently in fresh water. See **steelhead** and note.
1905 OUTRAM *Cdn Rockies* 277: An ample supper of splendid rainbow-trout witnessed to a part of the afternoon's occupation. **1907** LAMBERT *Fishing in B.C.* 5: The feeding-grounds of the rainbow are the eddies and the back-washes in swift-running rivers.... **1966** *Islander* 27 Feb. 2/2: ... here live some of the largest rainbow trout in the world ... along with the

kokanee on which the rainbows feed themselves to their fine, fat, fit condition.

raintest *n.* See quote.
1942 HAIG-BROWN *Timber* 252: RAINTEST. A stiff, heavy material from which the Coast logger's winter coat and pants are usually made. To some extent, and for a limited time only, water-repellent. Some loggers use a dressing of parawax to increase this tendency.

raise *n.* an increase in pay or salary.
1869 ANDERSON *Sawney's Letters* 44:
In a short time I made a "raise,"
And bought into a claim,
And there they made me engineer,
Or carman—'tis the same—
1904 *Eye Opener* (Calgary) 4 Aug. 1/4: The public is under the impression that the Mounted Police recently got a raise in pay of 35¢ a day. **1916** BRIDLE *Sons of Can.* 6: A factory hand who wanted a raise of pay ... must be inquired into by Macdonald.

raise a cache See **cache** (def. 1c).

raise a white-ash breeze *Obs.* See **white-ash breeze.**

raise camp *Fur Trade, Obs.* See **break camp.**
1824 (1950) OGDEN *Journals* 5: ... the Kootonnies & Flat Heads are likewise here waiting our arrival intending to raise Camp together.... **1855** (1956) ROSS *Fur Hunters* 244: The next morning on raising camp, I ordered Martin's horses to be loaded and we set off....

raising *n.* **1†** the setting up of the frame of a house, barn, etc.
*a*1820 (1838) HEAD *Forest Scenes* 194: When the trees are all notched, nothing remains but to lay them in their places one upon the other, or "raising" as it is called. **1906** CONNOR *Doctor* 33: I have never done anything but carry pins and braces at a raising all my life. **1961** *Alta Hist.Rev.* Spring 9/1: Reed was a skilled carpenter, and famous as a "barn-raiser." ... When all were ready, the day of the "raising" was advertised far and near....
2 *Hist.* See **raising bee.**
1826 *U.E.Loyalist* (York [Toronto]) 16 Dec. 231/4: Assisting at a Raising in Waterford Village ... he fell down in an Appoplectic fit ... and immediately expired. **1836** *Cdn Temperance Advocate* June 16/1: Men who stated as their only reason for not joining, was that they could get no men to come to a raising without spirits, have been told to try, and if none will come the members of the Temperance Society will do the work. **1946** BIRD *Sunrise* 154: "The frame's all hewed now, and there's three loads of boards. Pa's goin' to—to call a raisin' after the grain's in."

raising bee *Hist.* a community-work project and social affair at which neighbors pooled efforts to raise the frame of a house, barn, etc. See also **bee** and **raising.** Cp. **barn-raising** and **house-raising.**
1832 DOYLE *Hints on Emigration* 45: This kind of work is called a raising Bee, and in the same way assistance is mutually given in beating out the Indian corn from its husks, in what is called a husking Bee. **1879** *Winnipeg Dly Times* 12 Apr. 4/4: A number of "raising bees" have taken place in the Pembina Mountain District lately. **1964** GUILLET *Pioneer Days* 10: Some settlers were able to hire workmen to build

their houses, though the "raising bee" was much more usual.

raising pole See following **pole.**

raising tree *Lumbering* See 1963 quote.
1963 MCKINNON *Forest Activities 1* 6: Often the first tree topped is used only for a raising tree to raise the final spar tree.

rake stand See quote.
1927 DICKIE *How Canada Grew Up* 168: Now came a genius who invented the automatic self-rake reaper. He devised the rake stand with its four rotating rakes that knocked the grain on to the knives, leaving its heads lying one way upon the table till this fourth rake came round and by the use of a trip travelling on a track lower than the others, kept its teeth pointed down and so swept the bundle off the table for men to bind with straw.

ral *n.* [? < Irish Gaelic *raille*] *Nfld* vagabond, trickster. See quotes.
1954 BRIFFETT *Newfoundland* 89: This [1816-17] became known as the "Winter of the Rals" (rowdies) when bands of half-starved men robbed the terrified people who had anything left to steal. **1955** ENGLISH *Newfoundland* 34: ral [means] a disorderly fellow. **1965** MacNUTT *Atlantic Provinces* 156: The winter of 1817-18 was long remembered as the "Winter of the Rals," or the Rowdies.

Ralliement des Créditistes, le *Cdn French* the official name of the Social Credit group from Quebec in the House of Commons in the 1960's. See also **Creditiste, Rally,** and **Social Credit Rally.**
1963 *Globe and Mail* (Toronto) Oct. 29/1: ... ending a parliamentary crisis, when le Ralliement des Creditistes, maverick Social Credit group from Quebec, withdrew threatened legislation blockade.

Ralliement National *Cdn French, Que.* a political party supporting the principle of separatism, *q.v.* Abbrev. RN, *q.v.*
1966 *Globe and Mail* (Toronto) 23 Aug. 7/3: Gilles Gregoire [is] the new leader of the right-wing separatist party, the Ralliement National....

Rally ['ræli] *n.* [< Cdn F *Ralliement*] *Informal* See **Ralliement des Créditistes.**
1965 *Globe Mag.* 10 Apr. 5/4: Laurent Legeault, president of the Rally, is still an enthusiast of this idea....

rampart *n.* (*usually plural*) *Northwest* **1** a high, precipitous stretch of river bank, as found on either side of a steep gorge; also, the gorge itself.
1851 (1853) CAMPBELL *Two Journals* 112: Tuesday 17th. Yesterday and today we have been passing through what they call the ramparts—rocks and steep banks along the river.... **1910** FRASER *Red Meekins* 32: Cast high on a rampart by a thrust of the waters lay the stern half of their canoe.... **1940** *Beaver* June 29/1: ... after forty miles more came to the ramparts, a large canyon or gorge where for seven miles the river flows between perpendicular cliffs of limestone from one hundred to two hundred feet high. The channel is very deep here—three hundred feet in places.
2 **Ramparts,** the name given locally to several such gorges.
1910 BURPEE *Yukon* 36n: The Ramparts is "a local name employed by the traders to designate a contracted walled valley or cañon." (The term has been

applied to similar conditions on the Mackenzie, the Yukon and the Porcupine.) **1929** *Beaver* June 213: The Company moved up the Porcupine river to the Ramparts. **1965** *Cdn Geog.Jnl* June 190/1: The scenery till well down near the Ramparts [Mackenzie R.] is dull. . . .

3 the precipitous terrain adjacent to such gorges.
1942 SWANSON *Western Logger* 36: Born of ramparts in the Rockies, silver-capped with ancient snows,/ Melting glaciers there are feeding the mighty Fraser as it grows. **1958** BERTON *Klondike* 11: Into the brooding hills known as the Lower Ramparts, where the river channels were gathered into a single rustling gorge.

ram pasture *Slang* **1** the sleeping quarters of a gang or crew of men, as an open bunkhouse.
1912 POCOCK *Man in the Open* 226: Instead of Jesse's whistling, Mick's barking, the altercations in the new ram-pasture where our cowboys live . . . our yard was filled with the exact opposite. **1925** *Cdn Labor Advocate* (Vancouver) 7 Aug. 6/3: One large "ram pasture" for the men to sleep in, full of bedbugs.

2 *Fur Trade, Hist.* See **bachelors' hall.**
1921 *Beaver* June 4/2: . . . I was sitting in the bachelors' hall, commonly known as the Ram Pasture. . . .

rampike ['ræm,paɪk] *n.* [cf. Brit. dial. *rampick, ranpike;* origin obscure, but probably from shape] a tall, dead tree, especially one that is blackened and branchless from being caught in a forest fire. See also **deadwood, snag** (def. 2b) and **stub.**
1840 GOSSE *Canadian Naturalist* I 179: . . . those tall stumps of Canada [are] known by the elegant name of rampikes. **1853** STRICKLAND *Canada West* II 198: . . . the recently burnt fallow, with its blackened stumps and rampikes did not contribute much to improve the landscape. **1883** FRASER *Shanty* 20: In backwoods parlance these are called "rampikes," and make you think of the crowbars which the Titans may have used to pry up the rocks, with which they tried to pelt Jupiter out of Heaven. **1963** *Kingston Whig-Standard* (Ont.) 16 Feb. 17/6: In due course, the area of forest is ruined, the rampikes fall, the little streams run through chaos.

rampike country See **brulé** (def. 1).
1908 MAIR *Mackenzie Basin* 146: Farther up, the right bank rose bare to the sky-line with a mere sprinkling of small aspens, indicating what the appearance of the "rampike" country would be if again set ablaze, and converted from a burnt-wood region to a bare one.

Ram Skidder *Trademark* See quote.
1963 *Imperial Oil Rev.* Feb. 19/1: Bombardier also has other special machines such as the Ram Skidder, for skidding whole trees. . . .

ranch[1]† *n.* [< Am.E < Am.Sp. *rancho* small farm < Sp. "camp"]
☛ *The word* **ranch** *has been used in Western Canada in various ways, and it is difficult, indeed impossible, to determine the specific senses of many occurrences. In general,* **ranch** *refers to rangeland, with or without buildings; the owners of such land; the living-quarters on such land; and, at times, any farm at all.*

1 *West* **a.** *Esp.B.C.* a farm or homestead.
1865 *Cariboo Sentinel* (Barkerville, B.C.) 6 June 1/1: . . . on the ranches at Williams Lake a great deal of land has been laid down with the same crop. **1872** (1873) GRANT *Ocean to Ocean* 289: Between this point and Kamloops there are now ten or eleven farms or "ranches," as they are termed on the Pacific slope.

1966 BAITY *Wilderness Welfare* 173: Irvin Johnston . . . still ran the ranch in there and his mother stayed with him. I found the ranch all right, but they weren't there.

b. the land and buildings of an extensive holding devoted primarily to the raising of livestock. See also **ranch**[1], *v.* (def. 1).
1869 *Mainland Guardian* (New Westminster, B.C.) 1 Oct. 3/1: Flynn & Co., in the creek below Boyd & Heath's Ranch, are ground sluicing. . . . **1884** *Nor'Wester* (Calgary) 27 May 1/5: I little doubt but that other able and unselfish managers of cattle ranches are of the same opinion. **1923** STEELE *Spirit-of-Iron* 171: [He] landed in at my husband's ranch one day . . . and asked for work. **1966** *Cariboo Observer* 15 Sep. 9/4: Mr. Jim Clarke who works at the Twin Ranches has returned to New Westminster to visit with his parents before potato picking time.

c. the living quarters on a homestead or cattle ranch. See also **ranch-house**[1] (def. 1). Also spelled (older) *ranche.*
1888 (1890) ST. MAUR *Impressions* 43: The ranche was a nice log-house, the inside being match-boarded with the red Douglas pine, which gave an air of comfort to the nicely-arranged rooms. **1889** WITHROW *Our Own Country* 504: The Word was spoken in little huts . . . in the crowded stopping-place by the way, in ranches to the assembled cowboys, in shacks where lonely bachelors lived. **1906** BINDLOSS *Alton* 113: It was some time later when Nellie Townshead stood by a window of her father's ranch. Jean-clad stock breeders and axemen hung about the clearing. . . .

d. the owners or lessees of a cattle ranch.
1958 *Encyc.Can.* VIII 411: All ranches own some land, such as native-hay land . . . choice range . . . and sites suitable for buildings.

2 a. See **fur farm** (def. 1). See also **ranch**[1], *v.* (def. 3).
1928 (1953) *Fur Trade Jnl* Mar. 27/1: Any person who has the courage of his convictions should not hesitate to pay $200.00 or more per pair for good ranch bred stock from a reliable ranch. **1953** *Ibid.* 25/3: There are always a few sick mink, even on the best of ranches.

b. See **fur preserve** (def. 2).
1938 *Beaver* June 61/2: A good year for growth of aquatic and marsh vegetation is expected. This has a very important bearing on the success of the ranch.

c. *B.C.* See **fruit ranch.**
☛ *In this sense,* ranch *is now applied only to commercial orchards covering many acres.*
1953 LOWER *Voyages* 146: The Okanagan with its pleasant little towns and fruit ranches—everything is a ranch in B.C. . . . constitutes a good big stretch of settled countryside. **1966** *B.C.Digest* Oct. 48/3: In a few years young orchards extended along the east bench from Penticton to Naramata and south from Ellis Creek along the shores of Skaha Lake. . . . For nearly three decades the ranch was the only refuge between Okanagan Mission and Osoyoos or Keremeos.

3 See **ranch-house**[1] (def. 2).
1965 *Sun* (Vancouver) 25 Aug. 43/5: [Advert.] LUXURY RANCH . . . only $39,900 for this fabulous one-floor bungalow. **1966** *Globe and Mail* (Toronto) 4 Aug. 28/2: [Advert.] Executive prestige ranch . . . Lavishly landscaped.

ranch[1]† *v.* [< **ranch**[1], n.] **1** *West* engage in

farming, especially in raising livestock. See also
rancher (def. 1). Also *ranch it.*
1891 *Grip* (Toronto) 11 Apr. 238/2: . . . a cousin who
was ranching it out west sent me an invitation. . . .
1904 CONNOR *Prospector* 119: So I drifted round, dug
for gold a little, ranched a little, just like now, gambled
a little, sold whisky a little, nothing very much.

2 exploit as rangeland for raising livestock.
1965 SYMINGTON *Tuktu* 13: If the central Arctic were
being systematically "ranched" with caribou herds, the
value of these herds would probably be not less than a
hundred million dollars.

3 breed and raise (animals) on a fur farm (def. 1).
See also **ranch**[1], *n.* (def. 2a), **ranched, rancher**
(def. 2), and **ranching** (def. 2).
1931 *Beaver* June 223: Ranching foxes is one of the
most interesting occupations there is. . . . **1964** *Fur
Trade Jnl* Oct. 12/3: [Advert.] We do NOT offer to
ranch your chinchillas for you—or offer to purchase
back your reproduction.

ranch[2] *n.* Also (older) spelled *ranche. Pacific
Coast* **1** See **rancherie** (def. 1).
☞ *These older meanings of* **ranch** *appear to be derived
from* **rancherie** *and to have their genesis in the
communal nature of the plank house, q.v., of the Pacific
Coast Indians.*
1863 *Norfolk Reformer* (Simcoe, C.W.) 8 Jan. 3/1: On
our route we arrived at a "ranche" for the purpose of
taking in wood but was obliged to remain until
morning, and arrived at the Fort at 9 o'clock a.m.
1869 *Mainland Guardian* (New Westminster, B.C.)
20 Nov. 1/4: The ranch contained over a hundred souls,
many of whom talked a little English. **1937** ANDREWS
Wrangell 39: . . . he went back home to the "Ranche"
to sleep off the effects of the debauch. **1948** HOLLIDAY
Valley of Youth 146: On the outskirts of [Enderby, B.C.]
was an Indian reserve, on the reserve was the
"rancherie"—Chinook for Indian village or ranch. . . .

2 *Obs.* **a.** See **plank house.**
1872 POOLE *Queen Charlotte Is.* 134: . . . her papa had
built his ranche (house) within a mile of ours, and had
come to reside. . . .

b. See quotes. See also **road ranche.**
*a*1860 BALLANTYNE *Over Rocky Mountains* 87: "Is it
far up the valley?" asked Will Osten of the landlord
of the last ranche, or inn (a small hovel) in which they
had passed the night. **1872** POOLE *Queen Charlotte Is.*
178: One Wallace it was who kept the ranche or hotel
there. . . .

ranch[2] *v.* [< *ranch*[2], n.] *Pacific Coast, Obs.*
live together as bachelors; live communally.
☞ *Apparently derived ultimately from* rancherie, *q.v.
See note at* **ranch**[2] *(def. 1).*
1871 *Mainland Guardian* (New Westminster, B.C.)
5 Apr. 4/1: Many young men, of good education, what
is termed "ranch" together; they live economically, in
accordance with their means; but because they do so,
they cannot vote.

rancharee, rancharie *n.* See **rancherie.**

ranch bungalow See **ranch-house**[1] (def. 2).
1966 *Globe and Mail* (Toronto) 30 June 30/5:
[Advert.] Rustic 7 room ranch bungalow on ½ acre
lot, trees galore!

ranche *n.* See **ranch**[1] and **ranch**[2], *n.* and *v.*

ranched *adj.* raised on a fur farm (def. 1). See also
ranch[1], *v.* (def. 3).
1965 *Fur Trade Jnl* Aug. 13/1: Ranched mink continue
to dominate the market. . . . **1966** *North* Mar.-Apr.
34/2: Trapping gets underway in most parts of the
country around the same time as the pelting of ranched
mink. . . .

rancher *n.* **1** a person who owns or operates a
ranch for raising livestock. See also **ranch**[1], *n.*
(def. 1b) and *v.* (def. 1) and **ranchman** (def. 1).
1882 *Edmonton Bull.* 7 Jan. 2/2: Remember in a dry
fall a box of matches, well-applied, will put both
large and small ranchers on an even footing. **1908** *Eye
Opener* (High River, Alta) 8 Aug. 1/5: The branch lines
connecting the outlying ranches would be of untold
convenience to ranchers living at a distance, saving
them many a long trip over our bum roads.
1965 *Beautiful B.C.* Summer 14/2: One rancher is said
to have brought 400 horses overland all the way from
New Mexico.

2 an operator of a fur farm (def. 1). See also **ranch,**[1]
n. (def. 2a) and *v.* (def. 3).
1928 (1953) *Fur Trade Jnl* Mar. 26/3: Now these
ranchers are aware that there is an ever increasing
number of people who wish to procure this information
free of all study, risk and cost, which would at once
put them on a competitive basis by getting a start with
wild stock. **1946** WOOD *Rockies* 54: Fortunes have been
made in a few years' time out of mink ranching. . . .
1965 *Fur Trade Jnl* Aug. 7/2: Ranchers who breed
mink find that they have to spend a great amount in
order to feed the mink correctly.

3 the owner of a ranch (def. 1a).
1966 BAITY *Wilderness Welfare* 170: . . . they [Indians]
kept their credit good with the fur traders and
ranchers who advanced them grub against their winter's
catch of furs and haying wages.

4 See **ranch-house**[1] (def. 2).
1965 *Sun* (Vancouver) 8 Aug. 47/7: [Advert.] RANCHER
. . . close to Burnaby Park and swimming pool.

rancheree *n.* See **rancherie.**

rancheria† [ˌræntʃəˈriə] *n.* [< Am.E < Sp.
ranchería] See **rancherie** (def. 1a).
1860 *Brit.Colonist* (Victoria) 25 Feb. 3/2: Fire at the
Indian Rancheria. **1862** *Islander* (Charlottetown)
16 May 2/2: Four miners, recently returned from
Victoria, on their way to Cariboo, having got on a
"bend", adjourned about midnight to an Indian
rancheria hard by. **1966** BAITY *Wilderness Welfare* 170:
I rode through the Indian rancheria while the Indians
were inside the cute little white church attending early
morning mass.

rancherie [ˈræntʃəˌri] *n.* [< *rancheria,* q.v.] *B.C.*
1 a. a village or settlement of Indians, especially
the settled part of an Indian reserve. See also
ranch[2] (def. 1) and note.
1858 (1937) *B.C.Hist.Qtly* Oct. 249: We then came
to . . . a beautiful valley of some thousand acres, on
which was situated a large Rancharee of Indians. . . .
1872 JOHNSON *Very Far West* 197: "I'd take a dozen
Injuns straight out of the rancherie, an' make a
better government out of 'em than they've got up thar."
1929 JOHNSTON *Beyond Rockies* 169: To the west is the
wretched-looking rancherie where there are three score
Indians—mostly squaws and children, for the men are
away hunting and getting ready for the trapping

season by this time. **1963** SYMONS *Many Trails* 61 : So here I was, having come up the Cariboo Road with horses I had bought at the Indian rancherie at Clinton.

b. *Hist.* a settlement of other non-whites, specifically Kanakas, *q.v.*

1947 ROBINSON *Esquimalt* 55 : A small rancherie, known as Kanaka Ranch, adjoined Viewfield farm toward the west. . . . This was the home of a small colony of Kanakas. **1958** *Sun* (Vancouver) 20 Jan. 35/2 : By a civil servant's error, Kanakas with Indian wives living at the "Kanaka rancherie" on Coal Harbor and working at the inlet mills were allowed to pre-empt and improve a part of the Morton-Brighouse-Hailstone land [in 1868].

2 See **plank house** and picture. See also **ranch-house²** (def. 1).

1885 MOBERLY *Rocks and Rivers* 22 : Here night overtook us when opposite an Indian village, composed of several large rancheries, and a few hundred Indians. **1963** *Alaska Sportsman* Jan. 9 : [Caption] Elliott's "Haidah Rancherie" shows the type of dwelling used . . . before "booze, bullets and bacteria" devastated the indigenous peoples.

rancher's friend *West* See **Chinook wind.**

1899 *Medicine Hat News* (Alta) 21 Dec. 4/3 : The ice on the rink was nearly in shape, but on Monday one of the "rancher's friends"—a chinook—struck the Banana Belt and has spoiled hockey prospects for the present.

ranch hand *West* a person employed on a ranch, especially a cattle ranch.

1951 GILLIS & MYLES *North Pole* 6 : . . . a minister to the spiritual needs of the husky ranch-hands in Alberta's godless foothills. **1953** MOON *Saskatchewan* 66 : Over the next decade twenty-five ranch hands worked there at once.

ranch-house¹ *n.* **1** the principal dwelling on a ranch (def. 1b). See also **ranch¹,** *n.* (def. 1c).

1955 GOWLAND *Smoke* 202 : The ranch-house was only a few miles from the cabin, and . . . I became a fairly frequent visitor. **1957** HUTCHISON *Canada* 264 : . . . every ranch-house stove [was] red-hot, the washing as solid as iron on the line.

2 a style of one-storey house characterized by long, low spaciousness. See also **ranch¹,** *n.* (def. 3), **ranch bungalow,** and **rancher** (def. 3).

1958 *Town Crier* (North Vancouver, B.C.) 10 Nov. 6/4 : . . . far up the mountains where we used to pick wild berries, there are fancy new homes and ranch houses. **1965** *Maclean's* 24 July 47/2 : . . . an appreciably smaller percentage of Canadians than Americans make the ranch-house, two-car, gadget-filled world portrayed by the slick magazines.

ranch-house² *n.* [cf. *rancherie* (def. 2)] *Pacific Coast* **1** See **plank house** and picture.

1958 HEALEY *Alert Bay* 9 : [Caption] [Kwakiutl] Ranch house under construction.

2 an Indian house, especially a communal dwelling on a rancherie (def. 1). See also **ranch²** (def. 2a).

1907 SERVICE *Songs of a Sourdough* 78 : . . . And who would dream as I speak/In a tribal tongue like a rogue unhung, 'mid the ranch-house filth and reek,/I could roll to bed with a Latin phrase and rise with a verse of Greek ? **1947** ROBINSON *Esquimalt* 55 : A small rancherie, known as Kanaka Ranch adjoined Viewfield farm toward the west. Old residents of Esquimalt still remember the decrepit old ranch house near the sea end of Constance avenue. . . .

ranching *n.* **1** *West* See 1958 quote.

1888 (1890) ST. MAUR *Impressions* 35 : Calgary is the centre of the great ranching country, and one of the chief outfitting places for the mining districts. **1953** MOON *Saskatchewan* 73 : It was good ranching land in the early days on the arrival of the mounties . . . and the pioneer rancher of the Cypress Hills. . . . **1958** *Encyc.Can.* VIII 407 : Ranching. The raising of livestock by grazing the native grasslands on a relatively extensive basis is confined to two large areas of Western Canada : (1) Southern Alberta together with southwestern Saskatchewan and (2) the southern interior plateau of British Columbia.

2 the raising of any of various animals for commercial purposes. See also **ranch¹,** *v.* (def. 3).

1959 *Argosy* (Cdn sec.) July 28/3 : Tom introduced rat ranching (muskrat, that is) to the North Country, and his workings covered 54,000 acres at Moose Lake, 320,000 acres in Saskatchewan Province. **1963** *Cdn Geog.Jnl* June 189/1 : . . . the Canadian government was prompted to purchase, in 1929, a herd of 3,000 reindeer from Alaska to start reindeer ranching in the Canadian Arctic. **1965** *Fur Trade Jnl* Aug. 6/3 : Looking ahead, we feel the rewards of fur ranching—of all kinds— will increase.

ranching town See **cowtown.**

1897 *Medicine·Hat News* (Alta) 28 Jan. 1/6 : The rather distressing situation of the woman and children—one a babe in arms—appealed at once to the whole-souled munificence of the "ranching town."

ranchland *n.* *West* land used or suitable for ranching (def. 1). Cp. **rangeland.**

1953 *Cdn Geog.Jnl* Sep. 87/1 : It curves . . . into the weird Badlands, and through ranchland that is semi-desert with short bunch-grass and spiny cactus. **1964** *Beautiful B.C.* Summer 22/2 : At Williams Lake . . . are stock yards and large lumber yards in a country that has vast areas of ranch land.

ranchman *n.* *West* **1** See **rancher** (def. 1).

1887 (1888) LEES & CLUTTERBUCK *British Columbia* 101 : . . . a ranchman came down and mentioned that he had a letter to send . . . by the returning boat. . . . **1910** HAYDON *Riders of Plains* 299 : Attired in plain clothes, he watched the country closely until his suspicions fell upon a certain ranchman.

2† a person who works on a cattle ranch; cowboy.

1884 *Nor'Wester* (Calgary) 27 May 1/6 : The citizen of leisure was there, and the ranchman, and the person who calls himself a ranchman, and other hundred varieties, including the typical English, who smoked, talked and "yer knowed" until he was black in the face. **1898** CONNOR *Black Rock* 43 : There were . . . ranchmen in wide cowboy hats and buckskin shirts and leggings. . . . **1962** *Alta Hist.Rev.* Autumn 16/2 : A ranchman's overalls are made of "Montana broadcloth," otherwise known as "duck". . . .

Rand Formula [< Ivan C. *Rand,* b. 1884, judge of the Supreme Court of Canada] See 1966 quote.

1959 *Time* (Cdn ed.) 23 Mar. 15/3 : That year [1945] he also successfully arbitrated the bitter 99-day Ford Motor Co. of Canada strike by proposing the Rand formula, now widely adopted in Canadian industry. . . . **1963** *Oily Bird* Feb. 5/1 : Our demand for the Rand Formula is a most important and justified demand and it is my sincere hope that this year our Union is going to fight for it. **1966** *Kingston Whig-Standard* (Ont.) 20 Aug. 1/1: Mr. Justice Rand was the originator of the Rand formula, which requires all employees to pay union dues but makes actual membership in the union voluntary.

range† *n.* **1** *Maritimes, Hist.* one of a series of lots often ranged back from a river bank. Cp. **concession** (def. 1).
1832 BAILLIE *Account of N.B.* 104: . . . many lots in the rear are all thickly settled, even to the fifth tier or range from the River St. John, and several settlements are formed along the boundary line. **1860** *Islander* (Charlottetown) 24 Feb. 1/4: Five instead of ten schools would be sufficient for that range section of the country. **1916** *P.E.I.Register* (Charlottetown) 19 Jan. 4/2: [He chose] No. 10, in the 6th range on the banks of a beautiful navigable river.

2 a. *Que.* a row of concessions (def. 1).
1789 *Quebec Gaz.* 17 May 4/1: The whole said piece of land . . . is bounded in front partly by the river Richelieu, behind by the range of concessions. *Ibid.*: In another piece of Land at the end of the above mentioned of three arpents in front by one arpent in depth, or there about joining the road of the second range.
b. *Que., Ont.* a row of lots comprising a concession (def. 2); also, such a concession as a unit. See also **rank.**
1790 (1905) *Ont.Bur.Arch.Rep.* III 65: The first project . . . was to have the townships laid out into 8, 10, 12, or more ranges of Lots called Concessions, according to the depth of the Township. **1833** *Trans. Lit.& Hist.Soc.Que.* III 226: Some thirty years ago, this and the adjoining townships were surveyed and laid out into ranges and lots. **1954** *Fundy Fisherman* (Black's Harbour, N.B.) 3 Mar. 1/1: The second stretch will include all the waters in front of Crown Land extending from a point opposite the south-east angle of Lot No. 22 in the province of New Brunswick, Range 2 of Patapedia township in the province of Quebec, upstream to the mouth of Tom Ferguson's Brook. **1958** *Weekend Mag.* 20 Dec. 3/1: "Doctor," he said, "I come from the sixth range of Laval (a small village among the Laurentians, in the Montmorency river district), and I want you to come with me at once. . . ."

3† *West* See 1952 quote. See also **range line.**
1885 *Neepawa Star* (Man.) 28 Aug. 2/3: A real ghost roams about township 14, range 15, and is occasionally very destructively inclined, having destroyed all the cabbages and other garden truck belonging to an ex-Captain. **1952** PUTNAM *Cdn Regions* 372/1: Each meridional row of townships is called a "range" and these are numbered from east to west, beginning at each principal meridian. **1958** MACGREGOR *North-west of 16* 8: The square bordering it on west was called Township 1,Range 2. . . .

4† (*often plural*) *Esp.West* See **rangeland.**
1890 ST. MAUR *Impressions* 36: The cattle are fat and sleek, though they have had nothing but what they could find on the "range" all winter. **1913** WILLIAMS *Wilderness Trail* 59: Here on the prairie, the crust was the result of the soft Chinook west winds that came across the ranges, and melted the snow swiftly—only to let it freeze again into a sheathing of armor-plate. **1962** *Alta Hist.Rev.* Autumn 13/1: They had a general

round-up [of people] of the hull range. **1963** *B.C. Digest* Oct. 30/3: It is true that in some instances there are now fewer animals on some ranges than there were a few years ago—but today we no longer see the winter kills that were common on overpopulated ranges.

range *v.* See **cruise,** *v.* (def. 2).
1910 FERGUSON *Janey Canuck* 235: With Walter Barrie, his guide, he was ranging timber up north.

rangeland *n.* extensive areas of grassland suitable for grazing. See also **range,** *n.* (def. 4). Cp. **ranchland.**
1958 *Albertan* (Calgary) 12 Aug. 20/8: Members will be able to see the contrasts between heavily and lightly used rangeland along nearby areas. **1963** *Sun* (Vancouver) 29 May 19/1: The tent, and its successor, got pitched in high forest, on rock, above the treeline, in open rangeland . . . and on sandy beaches.

rangeland jockey *Slang* See **cowboy** (def. 1).
1957 *Maclean's* 9 Nov. 44/2: But he did wonder how a sawed-off Indian, a rangeland jockey, could have found the one he carried.

range-lily *n.* *West* See **prairie lily.**
1920 STRINGER *Prairie Mother* 232: I told him of our range-lilies . . . and buffalo-beans . . . and prairie-roses and crocuses. . . .

range line† *West* the principal meridian forming the boundary between rows of townships. See also **range,** *n.* (def. 3).
1925 GROVE *Settlers* 304: When he reached the Range Line, he was six miles south of his farm. **1955** *Star City Echo* (Sask.) 4 May 1/3: The road to Brooksby on the range line is impassable in places. . . . **1963** SYMONS *Many Trails* 89: Every six miles between meridians are other north-south lines called range lines.

ranger *n.* **1** *Nfld* See **harbo(u)r seal.**
1771 (1792) CARTWRIGHT *Journal* I 136: At one o'clock this morning the rinders returned . . . and informed me that they . . . had killed an otter, a porcupine, and a ranger. **1861** DE BOILIEU *Labrador Life* 97: The next kind is a small and beautiful animal, called the Ranger, which remains on the coast all the winter, and is sometimes found about the bays during the summer months. **1958** CAMERON *Cdn Mammals* 55: The dark markings are responsible for another name often applied to him—"leopard seal." To most fishermen he is known as the "bay seal," but in Newfoundland he bears the unusual name "ranger."

2 *Hist.* **a.**† a soldier in a regiment originally trained and equipped for defending the frontier against Indian raids. Cp. **Canadian ranger** and **Voltigeur** (def. 1).
☛ *This term has been preserved in the names of certain Canadian regiments, as the Queen's Rangers, the Simcoe Rangers, etc.*
1793 *U.C.Gaz.* (York [Toronto]) 1 Aug. 4/2: A few days ago, the first division of his Majesty's corps of Queens Rangers left Queenstown for Toronto (now York), and proceeded in Batteaux round the head of Lake Ontario. . . . **1827** *U.E.Loyalist* (York [Toronto]) 11 Aug. 88/1: He formerly belonged to the old Queen's or Simcoe's Rangers, and when they were reduced at the Peace of 1778, he remained in New Brunswick. **1922** *Beaver* Jan. 17/2: A. E. Dodman . . . was presented with a silver cigarette case by the officers and men of the 172nd Rocky Mountain Rangers. . . . **1942** RADDALL *His Majesty's Yankees* 5: The Micmacs had called my father Hawk . . . since the days when he and his rangers fought them up and down the length of

Nova Scotia. **1958** *Encyc.Can.* VIII 413/2: After serving with distinction, the rangers became part of the British Regular Army, until disbanded in New Brunswick in October 1783. In 1791 the corps was reorganized by Simcoe and taken to the new province of Upper Canada, of which he was Lieutenant Governor.

b. a member of the Labrador Ranger Force, *q.v.*

1954 BRIFFETT *Newfoundland* 147: In 1935, Newfoundland introduced a Ranger Force, modelled very closely on the plan of the Royal Canadian Mounted Police. Each ranger wore as his badge a caribou head.... **1965** JENNESS *Eskimo Admin.* III 59: ... at the outset of its [Newfoundland Commission of Government] rule, it had created a rural police force to maintain order and uphold the laws of Newfoundland in every part of the territory, and at various outposts on the Labrador coast it had stationed "Rangers" from that force, three in the northern region and five in the southern.

3 *Maritimes, Obs.* a variety of the black bear, *q.v.* See quote.

1846 HATHEWAY *Hist.N.B.* 64: The common Ant Bear has very short legs, and is considered less destructive among the stock than the long-legged ranger, with a brown nose and a white spot in his breast.

4 See **fire-ranger** and **forest ranger**.

1837 *Bytown* [Ottawa] *Gaz.* 13 Apr. 3/3: The Ranger would require to be particularly well qualified for the execution of his duty ... he would require to be an active, persevering, enterprising traveller, equally expert as a woodsman and a canoe man. **1898** EDGAR *Canada and Capital* 152: The protection given to the deer has attracted many more wolves to the Park, and the rangers have opened active war upon them. **1965** *Cdn Geog.Jnl* Sep. 82/3: ... protective efforts—be they on the part of rangers . : . or the public at large—remain a constant necessity....

ranger station the headquarters of a ranger or group of rangers (def. 4).

1955 GOWLAND *Smoke* 176: We unloaded our tools, tents, pots, pans and other items, which included part of the paraphernalia that would be required and which was always kept ready in store at the Ranger Station. **1963** SYMONS *Many Trails* 187: ... we started down the Carrot River from the Mountain Cabin ranger station....

range wolf *West, Slang, Obs.* See **bad man** (def. 1). See also **prairie-rover**.

1912 POCOCK *Man in the Open* 181: "Of course these or'nary, no-account, range wolves reckoned my friends would wait for day before they attempted tracking."

rank *n.* [< Cdn F < F *rang* row] *Que.* See **range** (def. 2).

1957 (1960) NELSON *Northern Lights* 307: Back there [in Quebec] on what they call the "ranks" the houses are not far from each other, as they are on our [Manitoba] plains....

rapee pie See **rappé pie.**

rapid(s)† ['ræpɪd(z)] *n.* (*usually plural*) [prob. < Cdn F *rapide(s)* < F *rapide* fast, rapid] See 1792 quote. Cp. **shoot,** *n.* (def. 1).

1770 (1792) CARTWRIGHT *Journal* I 73: The rattles and rapids in the river are now broken up. **1792** (1911) SIMCOE *Diary* 99: The term "rapid" is meant to describe shallow water, strong currents and a rocky bottom, which causes the whole surface of the water to appear foaming and white, like breakers at sea. **1829** MACTAGGART *Three Years* I 238: Would they examine the rapids with care, and not the still sheets, the truth would be guessed much nearer. **1965** *Cdn Geog.Jnl* June 186/1: On our 1964 trip, since the maps were fairly recent, only about half of the rapids were shown.

rapide couvert *Cdn French* See 1931 quote.

1808 (1889) FRASER *Journal* 170: This morning, our men put on their best clothes ... so that we might appear to more advantage to the eyes of the new Indians we were to meet at the rapide couvert. **1931** NUTE *Voyageur* 239: The leader of the expedition [Fraser] describes the worst of these dangers, the famous rapide couvert where the channel of the great river contracts to about forty yards and is nearly enclosed by overhanging walls of stone.

rapids boat *Northwest* a specially equipped river boat of shallow draft used on the Mackenzie River for marking safe channels by buoys and markers, a constant task because of the shifting sandbanks. Cp. **sturgeon-head.**

1948 *Beaver* Mar. 20/2: Here [are] the rapids boats—sturgeon-head boats they were called, "something between a scow and a York boat" with blunt, rounded bows.... **1958** *Edmonton Jnl* 24 June 3 18/3: The branch, with Headquarters at Fort Smith, N.W.T., does this through two methods; by means of its own rapids boats and through the cooperation of the captains of all river vessels.

rappé pie ['rape] [< Acadian F *tarte râpée* (also *pain râpé*), literally "grated pie"] *Maritimes* a rich, nourishing dish popular among Acadians and others in the Maritimes. See 1951 quote. Also *rappie pie, rapee pie, rawpi pie.*

1934 DENNIS *Down in N.S.* 240: "It's a French dish," I was told, "but the English are crazy over it. Years ago when they met at the homes for a dance they'd always have rappé pie, or, if there was ever a quilting-match, there'd always be rappé pie." **1951** PHINNEY *Recipes* 78: Rapee pie (Tarte à la râpure)—Acadian dish: 12 large potatoes; 3 large onions; 5 lb. chicken, or black duck, or rabbit; 1/2 lb. pure lard; salt and pepper.

raquette [ra'kɛt *or* 'rakət] *n.* [< Cdn F < F "tennis racket"] a snowshoe. See also **racket** and note and **racquet,** *n.* and *v.* Also spelled (older) *racquette.*

c1665 (1885) RADISSON *Voyages* 66: We found snowes in few places, saving where the trees made a shaddow, wch hindred the snow to thaw, wch made us carry the raquetts wth our feete, and sometimes wth the hands. **1760** JEFFERYS *Descr.New France* 57: The texture of the raquette or snow-shoe, consists of straps of leather about two lines in breadth, bordered with some light wood hardened in the fire. **1849** ALEXANDER *L'Acadie* II 19: Next morning, with three pairs of socks and mocassins, we essayed snow-shoeing; and it was ludicrous to witness the mishaps of those who figured on the broad racquettes for the first time.... **1965** *Cdn Geog.Jnl* Feb. 62/2: The "raquettes" of today are strung, usually, with especially prepared cowhide, rather than the original deerhide or gut of the 17th century....

rascho, rasho *n.* See **richeau.**

rat *n. Northwest* **1** See **muskrat** (def. 1).
1584 (1877) HAKLUYT *Discourse on Western Planting* 27:
There is greate store of . . . bevers, squirrells, badgers,
and ratts excedinge greate, and divers other sortes of
beastes for huntinge. **1824** (1955) BLACK *Journal* 153:
Saw no appearance of the Otter, Rat or Mink [n] or
have we yet seen any in the Rocky mountains. . . .
1962 *Favorite Recipes* 9: Get a "Y" shaped stick and
put the rat on it and roast slowly over an open fire.

2 See **muskrat** (def. 2).
1800 (1933) MCLEOD *Diary* 130: The first paid his Debt,
the next, gave 40 Ratts *en present*, &. [telling] me he
expected at least a Keg, &. a little stronger than I
generally made it. **1944** MARTIN *Cdn Wilderness* 48:
I have caught both good and poor rats in both lakes and
streams, and from my observations I am forced to
believe that it is the food which makes the pelt
wherever he is, and in the northwest we get the best rats
from the lakes or marshes. **1962** (1964) INNIS *Fur Trade*
298: Rats were made up into uniform packages of 600
rats and 2 large beaver.

3 See **muskrat** (def. 3).
1882 *Edmonton Bull.* 18 Feb. 3/2: They are living
principally on rats and jackfish from Buffalo Lake.
1962 *Favorite Recipes* 11: Duck . . . is good to eat when
tired of roasted rat when hunting rats in the
springtime.

rat *v. Northwest* trap muskrats. See also **ratting**.
1931 *Nat.Geog.* Aug. 155/1: The 154 men, women, and
children ratting in the Crow Flats took out more than
51,000 muskrat skins alone. **1949** LEECHMAN *Indian
Summer* 64: [She] was ratting on the Old Crow Flats,
the wide area of lakes and marsh from which the
Vanta-kutchin get their name.

rat canoe *Northwest* See **ratting canoe**.
1947 GILLHAM *Raw North* 121: When I was near the
Mackenzie Delta one spring, I met three Eskimos in
their tiny rat canoes, heading out for the coast.

Rate Bill system *Hist.* in Upper Canada, the
system whereby school taxes were levied through
charging the parents for each individual child
attending school.
1899 MACKAY *Pioneer Life* 242: Long and loud was the
controversy between what was called the "Rate Bill"
system and the "Free School" system.

rat-hill *n. Northwest* See **pushup**.
1937 CONIBEAR *Northland Footprints* 291: She came . . .
investigating a willow that Jones had stuck on a
mound he had made in the snow where no rat-hill was.

rat-house *n. Northwest* See **muskrat house**.
1903 SETON *Animal Heroes* 177: Only a few bounds it
was from wood shelter to the great rat-house, but she
was an hour in crawling that small space. **1965** *North*
Nov.-Dec. 26/1: Norman McDonald and Freddy
Frost . . . went to Crow Flat to . . . stake rat house.

rat hunt *Northwest* a special hunt for muskrats
during peak season. Cp. **ratting**.
1825 (1931) SIMPSON *Fur Trade* 150: The Rat hunts have
likewise failed in consequence of the lowness of the
Waters, but the returns in Beaver are very fair about
3,000. **1957** *Beaver* Spring 10/2: When the trappers
returned from the rat hunt, my wife and I enquired
among the women to see if any of the others knew the
art. . . .

rat hunting *Northwest* See **ratting**.
1966 *Beaver* Winter 54/1: When the snow began to melt
in the spring, all the different Indians started back to
their own countries for rat [muskrat] hunting.

rat lodge *Northwest, Obs.* See **muskrat house**.
1883 *Edmonton Bull.* 3 Feb. 1/1: Rat catching is not
brisk now as the snow is so deep in most places that the
rat lodges in the ponds cannot be seen.

rat marsh or **swamp** *Northwest* See **muskrat
swamp**.
1938 *Beaver* Mar. 48/1: Canoes and dogs are both
necessary during spring travel in the rat marshes of
Cumberland House. **1956** KEMP *Northern Trader* 65:
When you face up to it and find you can't—not even
after another trip to the Cumberland rat-swamps with
Elsie keeping the home-fires burning—you'll turn to
anyone who will offer you salvation.

rat money *Northwest* cash received for muskrat
skins.
1959 LEISING *Arctic Wings* 131: . . . the people of
Aklavik just strolled about jingling "rat money" in
their pockets, relaxed, and soaked up the sun.

rat skin *Northwest* See **muskrat** (def. 2).
1817 (1939) ROBERTSON *Correspondence* 10: The
remainder of my life will be spent in fighting windmills
and gathering rat skins. **1940** *Beaver* Mar. 11/1:
Gambling among the Indians may sometimes involve
stakes ranging from rat skins to wives.

rat-skin cap *Northwest* a warm peakless cap made
from muskrat skin and often having earflaps.
1848 BALLANTYNE *Hudson's Bay* 59: A small rat-skin
cap covers his head, and his legs are cased in the
ordinary blue cloth leggins. **1965** *Islander* 11 July 10/1:
. . . the earflaps on their rat skin caps [were] pulled well
down.

rat skinning *n. Northwest* the practice or skill of
removing the skins from muskrats.
1958 *Cdn Geog.Jnl* Jan. 4/2: There are also ice-fishing
contests, snowshoe marathons . . . and displays of such
special skills as trap-setting and rat-skinning.

rat spear *Northwest* See **muskrat spear**.
1939 *Beaver* Mar. 45/2: A hunter tied his paddles
lengthwise to the bars of his canoe, poked his rat spear
and a nice pole . . . in with them. **1956** KEMP *Northern
Trader* 57: Napao then took his rat spear, three feet
long, barbed and affixed it to a slender pole, and
probed the house till he found a spot where the wall
was the thinnest.

rat swamp See **rat marsh**.

ratting *n. Northwest* See 1949 quote. See also **rat,
v.** and **rat hunting**. Cp. **rat hunt**.
1939 *Beaver* June 54/2: The ratting season is in full
swing in the Mackenzie delta and reports indicate that
a good catch is expected. **1949** LEECHMAN *Indian
Summer* 65: "Ratting" is the local term for trapping
and shooting muskrats, which are the main source of
income. . . . **1957** *Aklavik Jnl* Apr. 8/2: Elias Kolinik
and Roger Kunuk in town recently by dogs report
ratting poor due to much overflow.

ratting canoe *Northwest* a small native boat
especially designed for hunting muskrats in
swamps and marshes. See also **rat canoe** and
ratting.
1962 SLOBODIN *Kutchin* 14: . . . a child armed with a
.22 rifle, paddling or portaging the light, narrow
ten-foot ratting canoe.

rattle *n. Nfld* a small waterfall in the course of a mountain stream, so called because of the rattling roar such tumbling water makes.

1770 (1792) CARTWRIGHT *Journal* I 73: The rattles and rapids in the river are now broken up. **1861** DE BOILIEU *Labrador Life* 166: In the different bays are brooks, and in these brooks are "rattles," as they are termed, or, more properly speaking, "falls," though none are of any great magnitude.

ravage ['rævɪdʒ] *n.* [< Cdn F] See **yard**, *n.* (def. 1).

1846 (1955) CRAIG *Early Travellers* 160: ... the guide ... told us we were at the place for stopping that night, and within two miles of the "Ravage," or moose-yard. ... **1941** BUCHAN *Sick Heart River* 156: "Yards they call them down East—but the Hares call 'em RAVAGES—Got the name from the French missionaries."

rawhide *n.* 1† a whip made of rawhide.

1852 MOODIE *Roughing It* 163: "Yesterday, I forgot to take the oxen out of the yoke, and Musther William tied me up to a stump, and bate me with the raw hide." **1902** CONNOR *Glengarry* 15: ... the master [laid] two swift, stinging cuts from the rawhide over ... Bob's back.... **1944** EVATT *Snow Owl's Secret* 85: "... Dog like sound of whip. Make music in ears." The factor scratched his head. "Yes, that is true; the huskies do like the sound of the singing rawhide."

2 *B.C., Hist.* an untanned hide used in rawhiding, *q.v.*

1897 *Slocan Pioneer* (B.C.) 8 May 1/2: At a considerable cost a rawhide and pack trail has been constructed from the town of Brandon to the Two Friends mine, on said creek. **1913** COWIE *Adventurers* 213: [They] were hauled outside by an ox hitched to a rawhide instead of a cart or sled, which served the purpose better. **1958** HARRIS & HAWTHORNE *New Denver* 6/1: In olden days they used to sack all the ore and then pack it in winter on raw hides or sleighs to the wharfs.

rawhide *v. B.C., Hist.* engage in rawhiding, *q.v.*

1897 *Slocan Pioneer* (B.C.) 25 Dec. 1/5: The trail to the Two Friends was broken this week and Allen's pack train started rawhiding ore to the wharf. **1952** *Cdn Geog.Jnl* Sep. 131: [Caption] Raw-hiding ore in the Lardeau in 1914.

rawhider *n. B.C., Hist.* a person engaged in rawhiding, *q.v.*

1896 *Kaslo Claim* (B.C.) 22 Feb. 1/3: Yesterday the Madison slide came down and the Reco rawhiders only escaped by the skin of their teeth. **1900** *Lardeau Eagle* (B.C.) 28 Mar. 1/4: ... the muckers, ore sorters, rawhiders, four-horse teamsters, office men are all hard at work.

rawhiding *n. B.C., Hist.* the practice of transporting goods, especially ore, in winter by wrapping them in dressed but untanned hides, hair out and head forward, the lashed package being drawn by rope tugs over the snow and ice. See also **rawhide** (def. 2).

1896 *Kaslo Claim* (B.C.) 4 Jan. 1/3: There is some snow now, just enough for rawhiding. **1897** *Slocan Pioneer* (B.C.) 25 Dec. 1/3: The principal use of the quadruped snow shoe is to break trails for rawhiding.

rawhiding train *B.C., Hist.* a line of rawhides (def. 2) carrying ore and being hauled from the mine to the wharves.

1897 *Slocan Pioneer* (B.C.) 25 Dec. 1/2: A first view of a rawhiding train has a tendency to cause cold shivers to run up and down the spinal column, as it strikes one as looking like a long parade of dead bodies.

razoo *v.* [origin unknown] *Slang, Obs.* raise the emotions of, as enthusiasm, annoyance, etc.

1890 *Grip* (Toronto) 18 Jan. 40/1: Shall I razoo old Mowat on the Separate School business? *Ibid.* 19 Apr. 265/1: [Parliament] is dependent on the whip's razoo round.

R.C.M.P. or **RCMP** See **Royal Canadian Mounted Police.**

1933 *Cdn Labor Defender* Jan.-Feb. 3/1: The delegation of twenty-five workers and farmers proceeds to the Parliament Buildings and are there met by a cordon of R.C.M.P. **1963** *Kingston Whig-Standard* (Ont.) 23 Apr. 20/3: More than 200 RCMP, steel-helmeted and armed with rifles, lobbed tear gas shells to quell the rioting.

read *v. North* especially in **read (the) water,** scan the surface (of a stream, river, etc.) from a canoe or boat for signs of shoals, sandbars, snags, and other sources of danger. Cp. **river sense.**

1921 HAWORTH *Trailmakers* 206: As Brennan had lost one eye and could not see any too well out of the other, he was glad to have one of us ride in his canoe and read water for him. **1944** *Beaver* Sep. 30/2: The skeptics did not know that my Indian canoeman ... had few peers in "reading bad water". **1964** *Imperial Oil Rev.* Dec. 18/1: "How do you get to be a pilot, Jerry?" The reply is soft-voiced. "Takes a long time, maybe 30 years; got to learn to read the water." **1965** *Islander* 14 Nov. 13/1: The swift opaque glacial waters present a problem for the bowman to read the river properly and avoid the shallow rocks and snags lying ahead.

rear *v. Lumbering* follow after a log drive gathering up stray logs and getting them through to the mill. See also **rearing.**

1957 *Bush News* (Port Arthur, Ont.) June 2/1: Along the shore are clumps of hung-up logs which will be reared through in the Fall.

rear admiral *Nfld, Hist.* the title given to the captain of the third ship to arrive in a harbor at the beginning of a fishing season, a position carrying with it numerous benefits. Cp. **fishing admiral.**

1765 *Quebec Gaz.* 31 Oct. 2/1: The Master of the third arriving British Fishing Ship asaforementioned (besides being Rear-Admiral of the Harbour) shall enjoy in common with the first and second Ships, the eclusive Privilege of trafficking with the Savages. **1883** HATTON & HARVEY *Newfoundland* 44: ... the masters of the second and third vessels were to be vice-admiral and rear-admiral. ...

rearguard *n. Hockey, Slang* a player on the defence, *q.v.*

1963 *Globe and Mail* (Toronto) 21 Jan. 16/3: Back in action after a hand injury ... was Leaf rearguard Allan Stanley.

rearing *n. Lumbering* the activity of following after a log drive to gather stray logs and get them through to the mill. See also **rear.**

1957 *Bush News* (Port Arthur, Ont.) June 2/1: We arrived at Camp 3-G, which is staffed by about 10 men during the drive months . . . and about 25 men during the Fall rearing operations. **1963** SYMONS *Many Trails* 184: . . . the last men with their cook will form the nucleus of the "rearing" crew—that is, the crew which will bring up the rear of the drive, taking care to roll into the water any logs left stranded on the banks. . . .

rebel *n. Hist.* **1** a supporter of the radical political position which led to the abortive rebellions of 1837-38 in Upper and Lower Canada. See also **Patriot** (def. 1a) and **Radical**.
1828 BIDWELL *Tor.Pub.Lib.MSS B104* 137: The rebels had just got into position, and were waiting for the word to advance, when Baldwin and Rolph arrived at Gallows Hill with the flag of truce. **1833** *Liberal* (St. Thomas, U.C.) 17 Jan.2/4: I have heard of his talk before; he wants the States to have this fine Province, and until he and all such Yankees and Rebels are banished from the country there will be no peace in it. **1863** (1930) *Cdn Hist.Rev.* XI 42: We were plundered by the rebells on the day and night previous to the battles fought on the 7th. and 9th. of November 1837.
2 a supporter of Riel in the Northwest Rebellions, *q.v.*
1870 *Wkly Manitoban* 12 Nov. 2/5: It is the favoritism shown to "Rebels" that I object to. **1871** *Ibid.* 15 Apr. 2/2: "Rebel" is popularly understood to mean a Riel man, without meaning that such a man is necessarily a rebel.

Rebellion *n. Hist.* **1** the abortive rebellion of 1837-38 in Upper and Lower Canada. See also **Upper Canadian Rebellion.**
1838 *Western Herald* (Windsor, U.C.) 3 Jan. 6/3: Rebellion has been overwhelmed, too, in our Sister Province, without extraneous assistance. **1858** *Brit. Colonist* (Victoria) 11 Dec. 4/3: . . . Louis J. Papineau [was] Speaker of the Lower House and originator of the Rebellion of 1837. **1957** HUTCHISON *Canada* 152: When William Lyon Mackenzie . . . led his mob of country bumpkins to the barricades of Gallows Hills in the Rebellion of 1837 and fled to sanctuary in the United States, he had unconsciously altered the history of the world.
2 a. See **Northwest Rebellion** (def. 1).
1871 *Wkly Manitoban* 22 Apr. 2/1: He speaks of the "Rebellion," like other ignorant and thoughtless people, but we imagine that he would find it rather difficult to make out that charge. **1885** GEMMILL *Companion* 74: Went to the North West in 1860, and was leader of the Canadian party at the time of the Rebellion of 1869-70.
b. See **Northwest Rebellion** (def. 2).
1927 *Cdn North-West Hist.Soc.Pubs* I ii 41: I . . . was not in any other way connected with the Rebellion . . . as I was located in the town of Battleford.

Rebellion Losses Bill *Hist.* See 1955 quote. See also **Rebel Rewarding Bill.**
1851 *Voice of the Fugitive* (Sandwich [Windsor], C.W.) 18 June 2/2: The House has been officially notified that the seat of Government will be removed to Quebec early during the next Autumn, which measure . . . has been accelerated by the necessity that exists for further legislation as to the Rebellion Losses Bill. . . .
1955 COLLARD *Cdn Yesterdays* 291: In the spring of 1849 the debates grew wild with anger. The

Government had introduced the Rebellion Losses Bill, a measure that would give compensation from the public treasure to those who had suffered property losses during the political rebellion of 1837-38.

Rebellion Losses Commission *Hist.* the government commission established to make judgments on claims submitted by citizens claiming damages under the Rebellion Losses Bill of 1848.
1853 *Hamilton Gaz.* (C.W.) 2 Feb. 3/1: The rebellion losses commission terminated their labors on Saturday last, on which day, we understand, the report was forwarded to Quebec.

Rebel Rewarding Bill *Hist.* See **Rebellion Losses Bill.**
1852 *Hamilton Gaz.* (C.W.) 27 Apr. 2/7: If he made any allusion to eggs . . . the Rebel-rewarding Bill . . . or the fact that a worn out, traitorous dispensator of pills, formed part of the Provincial Cabinet, it did not reach the ear of the short hand writer. *Ibid.* 14 Oct. 3/1: Bitter was the pill which the honest and loyal denizens of Canada were forced to swallow when the thrice-infamous Rebel Rewarding Bill was crammed down their loathing throats.

réchaud *n.* See **richeau.**

reclaimed lake See quote.
1963 *Kingston Whig-Standard* (Ont.) 5 Mar. 6/2: He pointed out that the best catches came from what are known as "reclaimed" lakes. These lakes have been restocked with trout following a drop in the number of species in them.

Recollet *n.* **1** *Hist.* a member of a French order of Franciscan monks who came to New France in 1615 and played an impressive part in missionary work among the Indians, especially the Hurons.
1760 JEFFERYS *Descr.New France* 6: Opposite to this, is the convent of the Recollets. . . . **1766** *Quebec Gaz.* 27 Oct. 2/1: On Tuesday last the Reverend Mr. Vessiere, who a few days since left the Order of the Recollets . . . subscribed the Declaration against Popery. **1952** HOWARD *Strange Empire* 314: In this he acted on flat defiance of the "Liberal" Archbishop of Quebec, and in opposition to the well-established Sulpician Society and the Recollets (Franciscans).
2 *Obs.* the waxwing, *Bombycilla cedrorum.*
1792 (1911) SIMCOE *Diary* 141: The Governor went to the Landing, and I went to the fort to see Capt. Darling's stuffed birds . . . the Recollet, a light brown with a tuft on its head and the tips of the wings scarlet, like sealing wax. . . .

Reconstructionist *n. Hist.* a supporter of the Reconstruction Party, *q.v.*
1935 *Daily Colonist* (Victoria) 6 Oct. 3/2: Reconstructionists speak in support of Percival E. George at Margaret Jenkins School on Monday. . . .

Reconstruction Party *Hist.* a reformist political party organized by the Hon. H. H. Stevens, a disaffected Conservative, in 1935. See also **National Reconstruction Party** and **Stevens' Party.**
1935 *Daily Colonist* (Victoria) 8 Oct. 1/8: The Reconstruction Party nominated in today's eight seats but stayed out of Kootenay West, Yale and Skeena last Monday. **1946** LOWER *Colony to Nation* 518: It was much more surprising when people all over the country began to display interest in a movement known as the "Reconstruction Party" sponsored by Mr. Stevens, on the basis of the revelations of the Price

Spreads Inquiry. **1959** STEWART & FRENCH *Ask No Quarter* 218: The Reconstruction Party under H. H. Stevens took a brief canter in Canadian politics at this time, and there was a move towards a "League for National Government."

rectory *n. Hist.* in colonial times, a Church of England benefice, the stipend for which came from an endowment fund built up from the sale of the Clergy Reserves, *q.v.*, an arrangement which proved to be one of the principal grievances of the Reformers of the period.
1828 *U.E.Loyalist* (York [Toronto]) 12 Jan. 262/2: This construction was viewed as being of a forced nature, and inapplicable to the more definite construction, which the Law itself gives—such as "Parsonages"—"rectories"—"Clergy of the Church of England"—"duly ordained according to the rights [sic] of the said Church." **1832** (1953) RADCLIFF *Letters* 118: ...a church is about to be built in Adelaide, and a Mr. Conin ... is appointed to the situation. Those clerical appointments are now called Rectories, and will become most desirable settlements for zealous and unambitious clergymen. **1855** *Hamilton Gaz.* (C.W.) 21 May 3/1: I firmly believe that the Church would do better, make better progress, and be in a far healthier position than she now is, were the rectories not in existence.

red *n.* **1** See **Red** (def. 1). **2** See **Red** (def. 2). **3** *Fur Trade* the pelt of a red fox.
1933 MERRICK *True North* 117: "I got—oh—'bout twenty martens, thirty minks, forty weasels, 139 muskrats, two crosses and a red." **1936** *Beaver* Dec. 38/1: To the Hudson's Bay Company's store the hunters brought their fox pelts—whites, crosses, silvers and reds—which they had accumulated since freeze-up.
4 See **sockeye.**
1958 WATTERS *B.C.Cent.Anthol.* 143: Many an ex-handliner can recall the "bad year" when reds brought three cents a pound.... **1964** *Fisherman* 2 Oct. 4/1: It is believed to be the first time the Japanese have actively fished for immature reds, and the effect of such fishing pressure may well be felt by Canadian and US salmon fishermen next year.

Red† *n. Slang* **1** a North American Indian.
1878 *Sask.Herald* (Battleford, N.W.T.) 30 Dec. 3/2: "An' we knew old Tom was rite, so we lit up agin, an' then we diskivered four reds in the teepee."
1921 HAWORTH *Trailmakers* 92: But the instinct for killing sometimes led both Whites and Reds to engage in useless slaughter.
2 See **Liberal.** See also **Rouge** (def. 2). Cp. **Blue** (def. 1).
1875 *Canadian Mthly* Dec. 533/2: The downfall of Sir George Cartier, the union between the [ultramontanes] and the Reds of Quebec, and the formation of the League in Ontario, give a new complexion to the soi-disant Liberalism of the Globe. **1962** *Chronicle-Herald* (Halifax) 10 Aug. 4/8: Since Confederation we have heard the same old story, have changed from red to blue and blue to red.

red-back *n. West, Slang* a Hereford steer, cow, etc.
1962 FRY *Ranch on the Cariboo* 25: ... I was alone with a stream of red backs moving just a mite too fast for comfort.

red-barked willow *Obs.* See quote. Cp. **red-osier dogwood.**
1858 (1860) HIND *Assiniboine Exped.* I 315: The Indians of the prairies generally use the inner bark of the *Cornus*

sericea, the red-barked willow as they term it. We also saw them smoke the inner bark of the dog-wood, *Cornus alternifolia.*

redberry *n. Lab.* a shrub, *Vaccinium* sp., bearing edible red berries.
1933 MERRICK *True North* 39: All the hills are covered with blueberries and redberries. **1953** BANFILL *Lab. Nurse* 53: Before the blueberries are finished the famous Coast redberries, clinging to the mossy, rocky slopes, begin to ripen.

red brother† a North American Indian.
1832 (1953) RADCLIFF *Letters* 129: After a residence of six weeks with my Red Brothers, I prepared to return homeward, and felt much regret in parting from them, so marked was their kindness to me, and so good-natured their attention. **1896** (1898) RUSSELL *Far North* 58: ... now they brought the best of goods to give their red brothers at ridiculously low prices.

Red Chamber 1 See **Senate Chamber.** Cp. **Green Chamber.**
1905 *Eye Opener* (Calgary) 25 Feb. 1/6: The innocent hawbuck who imagines that the red chamber is full of dignity and high thoughts has never listened to the debates from the galleries, for the ultra-prudish newspapers suppress the graphic and staggering parts of the debate which create the atmosphere. **1966** *Globe and Mail* (Toronto) 19 Jan. 7/1: The House of Commons is sometimes called the Green Chamber and the Senate the Red Chamber because the carpet, the leather chair bottoms, and the desk blotters are all green, whereas in the Senate they are red.
2 the Senate (def. 1) itself.
1955 *Chatelaine* Apr. 13: Canada's first woman senator is Mrs. Norman F. Wilson, who shattered a fifty-year-old tradition that had preserved the Red Chamber as an exclusively men's club when she stepped over the threshold in 1930. **1958** *Kootenaian* (Kaslo, B.C.) 3 Apr. 3/1: Senator Gladstone is a quiet, intelligent, educated man who has run the gamut from printer to rancher and ultimately a member of the Red Chamber in his 71 years of life. **1965** *Globe and Mail* (Toronto) 6 Dec. 6/5: ... Mr. Pearson ... could make no better beginning than to appoint to the Red Chamber 12 such Canadians.

red-chamber club *Slang* See **Red Chamber** (def. 2).
1963 *Canada Month* Jan. 15/1: ... Diefenbaker picked out an obscure railway conductor from Kenora as the next member of the red chamber club.

Red Chevron a Canadian veteran of the First World War (1914-18) who served at the Second Battle of Ypres.
1959 *Legionary* April 7/1: Forty-four years ago this month—on April 22, 1915—Canadian soldiers who today are known by the honoured name of "Red Chevrons" received their baptism of fire in the Second Battle of Ypres.

Red Children *Hist.* **1**† the Indians of Canada considered as wards of the Crown.
1814 *Montreal Herald* 2 Apr. 1/2: Listen. Open your eyes to your Children, to your Red Children that are in the West. **1871** *Wkly Manitoban* 5 Aug. 2/4: She wishes her Red Children, as well as her White people, to be happy and contented.

2 the Indians in Rupert's Land, *q.v.*, considered as wards of the Hudson's Bay Company.

1896 RUSSELL *Far North* 58: Then the whole story would be repeated—how the Company had always looked after its red children and fed them when the fishery failed, how they brought them goods when others could not, and goods of a quality far superior to those of the opposition, which was not going to be in the country another year anyway.

redcoat *n.* **1** *Hist.* **a.**† a British soldier stationed in Canada.

1837 (1930) *Cdn Hist.Rev.* XI 235: No sooner, however, the disaffected here found that the "Red Coats" were all gone than they began to muster their strength, and on the 4th of December broke out into open Rebellion. **1870** *Wkly Manitoban* 24 Dec. 1/3: Bad treatment of the French half-breeds is still continued by the "redcoats" at Fort Garry. **1958** *Kootenaian* (Kaslo, B.C.) 3 Apr. 2/2: Color of the scarlet jackets worn by RCMP was chosen in deference to the wishes of the plains Indians, who had regarded the "Red Coats" of the earlier British Army garrisons in the west as friends and protectors.

b. in Indian parlance, a white man, especially one identified with officialdom.

1833 *Brit.Colonial Argus* (St. Catharines, U.C.) 5 Oct. 2/2: Fired by their wily suggestions, the high and jealous spirit of the Indian chiefs took the alarm, and they beheld with impatience the "Red Coat," or "Saganaw," usurping . . . those possessions. . . . **1918** SCHULTZ *Rising Wolf* 246: The fierce chief asked many questions about the Red Coats' trading post, and the price in beaver skins of different articles.

2 See **Mounted Policeman.** See also **redjacket.**

1893 CREIGHTON *North West Mounted* 402/2: The Indians often came into conflict over encroachments upon each other's hunting grounds, and were quick to appeal to the red-coats as arbiters and protectors. **1912** FOOTNER *New Rivers* 20: He must have led rather a lonely life, because the only times he could really relax were with his fellow-redcoats. **1963** *Maclean's* 20 Apr. 14/3: The redcoats' professional skill is such that a score of foreign countries have sought their guidance in police problems.

red cod a reddish rock fish, *Sebastodes ruberrimus,* found in Pacific Coast waters.

1859 *Brit.Colonist* (Victoria) 20 July 1/2: [There are] rock cod, bank cod, red cod, shore cod. **1960** *Fisheries Fact Sheets* 70 1: Other more brightly coloured species, usually termed "red-cod," such as the red snapper . . . occur at depths from thirty to over one hundred fathoms.

redcrested woodpecker *Obs.* the pileated woodpecker, *Dryocopus pileatus.*

1828 MCGREGOR *Maritime Colonies* 28: The birds common on the island are the following, which remain during the whole year . . . Large redcrested Woodpecker, Red-headed Woodpecker. . . .

red deer *Hist.* **1**† See **whitetail deer**; also, the skin of this animal.

1584 (1877) HAKLUYT *Discourse on Western Planting* 27: There is greate store of stagges, redd dere, fallowe dere, beares, and other suche like sorts of beasts. . . . **1749** *Short State of North America* 19: There are now no Deer-Skins now imported, except a few Moose, Elk,

and Red Deer dreess'd. **1898** EDGAR *Canada and Capital* 147: In the short season of fifteen days, from the first to the fifteenth of November, it is wonderful how many red deer are killed in Ontario. **1916** PARKER *World for Sale* 30: But the red man no longer set up his tepee in these secluded groves; the wapiti and red deer had fled to the north never to return. . . .

2 See **wapiti.**

*c*1665 (1885) RADISSON *Voyages* 41: They weare waited on by a sort of yong men, bringing down dishes of meate of Oriniacke, of Castors, and of red deer mingled with some flowers. **1793** (1801) MACKENZIE *Voyages* 237: They are not so large as the elk of the Peace River, but are the real red deer, which I never saw in the north. **1857** (1863) PALLISER *Journals* 56: It was not until we came to the west of San Joseph that we found Red Deer (wapite), and then very scarce. **1952** (1954) JENNINGS *Strange Brigade* 105: There were also red deer or biche. . . . **1966** *Globe and Mail* (Toronto) 19 July B1/3: Red Deer was named by settlers who mistook the elk for a species of Scottish red deer.

red dog-willow See **red-osier dogwood.**

1937 CONIBEAR *Northland Footprints* 194: The tearing winds of September plucked them [leaves] from swamp-willow, red-dog willow—from which, perhaps, the first tobacco was made—grey wolf-berry, high-bush cranberry . . . and poplars black and white.

red dogwood See **red-osier dogwood.**

1954 CONSTANTIN-WEYER *Half-Breed* 15: The half-breed then seated himself . . . and filled his red-clay pipe with Kenik-Kenik, the bark of red dogwood.

Red Ensign a red flag with a Union Jack in the upper corner next to the staff and the Canadian coat of arms on the fly, used as the national flag of Canada until replaced in 1965 by the official red-and-white flag with a maple-leaf design.

1912 CONNOR *Corp.Cameron* 229: High over a noble maple in the centre of the grassy meadow floated the Red Ensign of the Empire, which, with the Canadian coat of arms on the fly, by common usage had become the national flag of Canada. **1964** *Calgary Herald* 27 Feb. 2/1: It is a sad commentary on our maturity as a nation that the Red Ensign is recognized as Canada's flag by everyone but Canadians themselves.

redeye† *n.* *Slang* cheap liquor, especially whisky. See also **pink-eye.** Cp. **Calgary redeye.**

1900 OSBORN *Greater Canada* 151: They generally paid the Indians in liquor—the vilest of "red-eye"—but, if possible, they paid them only with blows. **1945** GARD *Johnny Chinook* 129: "You're not sure whether it's genuine red-eye or snake poison." **1962** *Alta Hist.Rev.* Autumn 16/1: Under the general term liquor we have "Old Alky" . . . "red-eye" . . . for whiskey. . . .

Red Fife (wheat) *Hist.* the first variety of wheat to be produced in Canada, developed in the 1870's, near Peterborough, Ontario, by David Fife (?1804-1877). See also **Fife wheat.** Cp. **White Fyfe.** Also *Red Fyfe.*

1883 *Prince Albert Times* (Sask.) 3 Oct. 6/2: Bestir yourselves, farmers, in this matter, try it and be convinced, and by all means give the "red fyfe" the preference. **1936** DENTON & LORD *World Geography* 85: Dr. Charles E. Saunders, the Dominion cerealist, had been experimenting for several years, trying to produce a new wheat which would ripen earlier than Red Fife. **1965** BERTON *Remember Yesterday* 71: [Caption] The year is 1905. . . . These casual labourers . . . are part of a vast army recruited back east to help harvest the early-maturing Red Fife wheat, which is changing the face of the prairies.

redfish *n*. **1** See **kokanee**.
1888 (1890) ST. MAUR *Impressions* 167: In some of the small streams which flow into the Kootenay Lake, is found what the miners call red fish: they are from 3 to 6 inches long, rather flat and very good food. **1958** WATTERS *B.C.Cent.Anthol*. 392: In addition . . . there were the little speckled trout, known as "redfish," for which we whipped the mountain torrents. **1964** *Globe and Mail* (Toronto) 22 Dec. 3/4: Officials . . . say the fish being transplanted from British Columbia . . . is known as the kokanee, the kickaninny, the silverfish, or the redfish, depending on where you're fishing for it, and at what time of year.
2 a large rose-colored food fish of the genus *Scorpaenidae,* common in the waters of the East Coast; ocean perch.
1954 *Fundy Fisherman* (Black's Harbour, N.B.) 3 Mar. 1/3: Newfoundland east coast redfish vessels have concentrated on the larger redfish of the eastern edge of the Grand Bank. **1963** *Canadian Wkly* 4 May 15/2: Two fish stories this week, the first about redfish. If you're eating these anywhere but Newfoundland, you probably call them ocean perch.

Red Fyfe (wheat) See **Red Fife**.

Red Indian [see 1891 quote] **1** *Hist*. a member of the Beothuk people, a now-extinct race inhabiting Newfoundland during the early settlement period. See also **Red Man** (def. 2).
[**1770** (1792) CARTWRIGHT *Journal* I 18: These Indians are called Red, from their custom of painting themselves, and everything belonging to them, with red ochre, which they find in great plenty in various parts of the island.] **1819** *Kingston Chron*. (U.C.) 13 Aug. 3/1: On Sunday last, the curiosity of the good people of this town, was gratified by an unexpected visit from one of the Red Indians—a native tribe, so called from the pigment of red earth with which they colour their bodies. **1891** *Trans.Roy.Soc.Can*. IX 2 124: The name Red Indians . . . is the translation of the Micmac name for them, Maquajik, which means redmen or red people. **1964** *Nfld Qtly* Summer 12/3: The Journal takes us back to pioneer days in Labrador and Newfoundland to a day when the wigwams of the Red Indians could be seen on the shores of Exploits Bay.
2 erroneously, any North American Indian. See also **Red Man** (def. 1) and **redskin**.
☛ *The association of red skin with the North American Indian no doubt derives from early references to the Beothuks of Newfoundland, who made a practice of coating their bodies with ochre, as reported by John Cabot in the closing years of the fifteenth century. This popular misconception gave rise to such synonyms as* Red Man *and* redskin *alongside* Red Indian.
1852 *Arctic Miscellanies* 45: The tribes of Mongolian extraction . . . finding the more southern portions of North America already tenanted by the warlike and vindictive Red Indians . . . were driven to take up their permanent abodes in the regions of everlasting snow. . . . **1897** YOUNG *Indian Trail* 11: Romantic missionary work among the red Indians will soon be a thing of the past. **1957** *Chronicle-Herald* (Halifax) 16 Aug. 29/8: Since then I have always liked the Red Indians.

redjacket *n*. See **Mounted Policeman**. See also **redcoat** (def. 2).
1909 CAMERON *New North* 94: In among the half-breed populace stalk policeman and priest, red jacket keeping the dark-skinned people straight in this world and black robe laying out conditions for the world to come. **1953** MOWERY *Mounted Police* 133: The other eight changed their minds about sneaking up on the lone, grim redjacket in the little sink-in.

red-line *n*. *Hockey* the red line marking mid-ice and important in regulations governing offsides.
1963 O'BRIEN *Hockey* 53: Then [in 1943/44] came the red-line across mid-ice.

red liquor *Slang, Obs*. See **redeye**.
1897 *Slocan Pioneer* (B.C.) 8 Sep. 3/2: Lotta had been dallying beyond a reasonable length of time with red liquor of some kind and when the jag reached fighting proportions she proceeded to run the town.

Red Man 1† See **Red Indian** (def. 2) and note.
1840 WILLIS *Cdn Scenery* I 54: . . . when they saw themselves outnumbered by the Red-men, they retired. . . . **1965** *Cdn Geog.Jnl* Apr. 115/1: The Red Men, believing that the creature was "Matchi Manitou" —the evil spirit—slew it and its blood flowed into the lakes, dyeing the water red.
2 *Hist*. See **Red Indian** (def. 1).
1955 ENGLISH *Newfoundland* 9/2: They [Beothucks] were described as of ordinary height—yet there are recorded instances of giant Red Men of seven feet in stature.

red-osier dogwood a shrub, *Cornus stolonifera,* with conspicuous red stems, the inner bark of which was often used in the making of kinnikinik (def. 1). See also **barouge, bois rouge, red dog-willow, red dogwood,** and **red willow**.
1938 (1950) STANWELL-FLETCHER *Driftwood Valley* 112: He pointed out how the moose tracks, the first we had seen since early December, followed willow-grown portions of the river-bank, as the moose browsed on young twigs of willow and red-osier dogwood. Twigs and strips of dogwood bark are used by the Indians as a scent for beaver traps. **1939** GROVE *Two Generations* 29: A lane bordered with . . . red-ozier dogwood . . . led through the very centre of the place. . . .

red paint *Slang, Obs*. See **redeye**.
1909 SERVICE *Cheechako* 75: The smooth Beau Brummels of the bar, the faro men, are there;/The tinhorns and purveyors of red paint. . . .

Red Parlo(u)r *Hist*. **1** a room in the Queen's Hotel, Toronto, where Sir John A. Macdonald held many of his conferences while in that city.
1891 BIGGAR *Sir John Macdonald* 220: A meeting of manufacturers interested in the National Policy was called by Sir John, in the campaign of 1882, and was held in the "Red Parlor" of the Queen's Hotel, Toronto. *Ibid*. 275: [quoting Toronto *World,* January, 1891] "After a busy day's work he [Macdonald] left Monday morning for Toronto, arriving here next morning. The Red Parlor was visited by scores of friends and workers during the day." **1891** *Grip* (Toronto) 20 Sep. 178/2: The spectacle of manufacturers in the Red Parlor is a piece of brazen effrontery which could not be witnessed outside the Dominion of Canada.
2 *Transferred use* the business men and politicians who became identified with the conferences in this room.

1891 *Grip* (Toronto) 24 Jan. 50/2: Probably nobody in the country is more thoroughly aware of this than the members of the Dominion Government, and yet they are bound to fight for it till the last cartridge is gone, because they think it better politics to put their faith in the Red Parlor, than in the cause of the people.

red pine 1 a tree, *Pinus resinosa,* of eastern and central Canada. See also **Norway pine.**
1767 *Quebec Gaz.* 8 Dec. 3/1: They are hereby forbid to cut down . . . White Pine, Red Pine, Cypress, or White Oak Trees, on the lands above described. **1854** KEEFER *Ottawa* 64: Red pine . . . is often, but improperly, called "Norway" pine. **1963** *Globe and Mail* (Toronto) 13 Mar. 20/1: Here is also a stand of red pine valuable as a seed orchard [Algoma district, north of Lake Superior].
2 the wood of this tree.
1814 *Kingston Gaz.* (U.C.) 5 Jan. 3/2: Required for His Majesty's Navy, 20,000 Feet of Red Pine. . . . **1962** *Forest Conservation* 27/2: In the Maritime Provinces, red pine and red spruce are the most extensively used. . . .

Red River *Hist.* See **Red River Settlement.**
1824 *Montreal Herald* 3 Nov. 2/5: In Red River the climate is healthy; the soil productive; the plains abound with Buffaloes; the waters with excellent fish. **1957** *Beaver* Spring 16/2: But the appointment of McDougall did not for a moment imply that Macdonald regarded Red River as an administrative monopoly of Canadians, still less of Ontarians.

Red River belt *Hist.* See **sash.**
1909 NURSEY *Isaac Brock* 112: Then unwinding his own parti-colored, closely-woven Red River belt, "Would the great white *shemogonis* (warrior)," he whispered, "accept the simple sash of the Shawanese in return?"

Red River boat *Hist.* See **York boat** and picture.
1892 *Wkly Manitoban* Dec. 402/1: It was away back in the sixties, when every pound of goods was carried to the Northwest in Red River boats, and a long slow trip it was. **1927** LONGSTRETH *Silent Force* 22: "E" (Troop) followed, to be succeeded early the next day by "F" with all but the heaviest stores which Red-River boats would take to Dufferin.

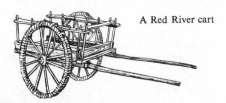

A Red River cart

Red River cart *Hist.* a sturdy two-wheeled cart constructed entirely of wood, the parts being fixed by wooden pins and lashed with shaganappi (def. 1); the wheels were some five feet in diameter and about three inches broad at the rim; the axle carried a simple box equipped with a railing for carrying the load, about 1,000 pounds. As a rule, the carts travelled in trains or brigades and the ungreased wheels gave forth ear-piercing shrieks and squeals which could be heard for miles across

the prairie. See also **Red River wagon** and **trail-cart.**
[1802 (1897) COUES *New Light* I 205: We have . . . a new sort of cart, which facilitates transportation, hauling home meat, etc. They are about four feet high and perfectly straight; the spokes are perpendicular, without the least bending outward. These carts carry about five pieces, and are drawn by one horse.] **1857** (1863) PALLISER *Journals* 38: The Red River cart is one admirably suited to the exigencies of the country. . . . **1885** [see quote at **shaganappi harness**]. **1894** TAYLOR *Woman in Mackenzie Delta* 47/2: After the first half-day we saw no sign of life on the way except the freighters, who, with their lines of Red River carts and ponies, were carrying the "pieces" for the northern outfit to the Landing. **1966** *Star Wkly* 12 Mar. 17/2: . . . Frank Oliver trudged overland from southern Ontario, hauling a printing press by Red River cart, to found the Edmonton Bulletin.

Red River colony *Hist.* See **Red River Settlement.**
1859 *Brit.Colonist* (Victoria) 3 Oct. 1/2: Within the last year, a great deal of land has been taken up in and around the Red River colony. **1952** PUTNAM *Cdn Regions* 373/2: The pioneers of the Red River colony dug their fields by hand, later using an oxdrawn wooden plough with an iron point.

Red River fever *Hist.* See 1889 quote.
1883 *Brandon Blade* (Man.) 15 Nov. 4/1: The doctors insist that for the low Red River fever it is an indispensable medicine. **1889** DONKIN *Trooper* 41: In fact it is the typho-malarial scourge known as Red River fever in Manitoba, jungle fever in India . . . and Rocky Mountain fever in British Columbia. **1945** HAIG *Brave Harvest* 40: Aunt Alice's heart sank. The Red River fever!

Red River frame (building) *West, Hist.* See 1921 quote.
1882 *Edmonton Bull.* 29 July 4/1: They are of the style known as Red River frame and are for use as storehouses [at Ft. Dunvegan]. **1915** MCCLUNG *Times Like These* 209: They built a house, which in those days of sod roofs and Red-River frames seemed quite palatial . . . In ten years they built another house, and it had everything, back-stairs, dumb-waiter, and laundry shoot. . . . **1921** *Beaver* Feb. 15/2: The "big house" was a two-and-a-half storey building, with a large kitchen behind, built from the same plan as the officers' dwellings in Fort Garry, and known as a Red River frame building. **1963** MACLEOD & MORTON *Cuthbert Grant* 93: There on the western limit of his seigniory, Cuthbert Grant built the great log house, in the Red River frame style, which was to be his home for the rest of his life.

Red River granite *Slang, Obs.* See quote.
1886 SCUDDER *Winnipeg Country* 48: The biscuit . . . has received the soubriquet of "Red River granite." These wonderful objects, as large as sea-biscuit, are at least three-quarters of an inch in thickness, and against them the naturalist's geological hammer is always brought into requisition.

Red River horse *Obs.* See **cayuse.**
1871 (1873) BUTLER *Great Lone Land* 92: . . . a Red River cart is a very limited conveyance, and a Red River horse . . . an animal capable of wonders.

Red River Insurrection *Hist.* See **Northwest Rebellion** (def. 1).
1870 *Wkly Manitoban* 19 Nov. 4/4: A pamphlet lately published in Montreal, entitled "The Red River

Insurrection," has come to hand at a most opportune moment. **1942** *Beaver* Dec. 26/2: ... the Red River Insurrection broke out, and as there was some danger of the returns from Forts Pelly and Ellice, being seized by Riel, Campbell took upon himself the responsibility of sending them through the States to the Company post at Georgetown. **1966** *Ibid.* Spring 50/1: Without the fort [Fort Garry], the Red River insurrection would almost surely have been short-lived.

Red River jig 1 a vigorous dance popular in the old Northwest. See also **Jig** and **Red River reel.**
1872 *Canadian Mthly* Oct. 305/1: The principal dance, in fact the only one, is called a Red River jig, which somewhat resembles a horn-pipe, male and female participating in it.... **1942** *Beaver* Dec. 17/2: Gethon's explanation of the origin of the Red River Jig was that he (Fred) learned the jig from his father, who in turn had learned it in Winnipeg after it had been brought west from Montreal soon after the advent of the 1800's. **1962** *Calgary Herald* 8 Oct. 12/1: The "Thumper" intercepted two Jackson passes and promptly dazzled Ottawa tacklers with something resembling a cross between the Charleston and the Red River Jig.
2 the tune to which the jig is danced.
1900 OSBORN *Greater Canada* 147: After that saddest and most haunting of all melodies, a fiddle would be pulled out of its moose-skin bag, and the stirring strains of the "Red River Jig" would bring everybody to their feet. **1954** CONSTANTIN-WEYER *Half-Breed* 44: ... he played the Red River jig. To this day, it is still a national air of the half-breeds. ...

Red River maple See **Manitoba maple.**
1887 *Senate Report* 80: Is that what is called the Red River Maple? Yes; the Red River or ash-leaved maple. **1955** *Beaver* Spring 10: These maple trees in Manitoba, called ash leaved and Red River maple, or box elder, have been given the botanical name, *Acer negundo.*

Red River of the North *Hist.* the Red River of southern Manitoba.
1859 *Brit.Colonist* (Victoria) 27 July 2/1: A newspaper is about to be started, under Canadian auspices, at the Selkirk settlement, on the Red River of the North. **1869** (1873) BUTLER *Great Lone Land* 4: But far away in the farthest West ... along a river called the Red River of the North, a people, of whom nobody could tell who or what they were, had risen in insurrection.

Red River Rebellion *Hist.* See **Northwest Rebellion** (def. 1).
1884 *Prince Albert Times* (Sask.) 18 July 1/5: Now in the days of the Red River rebellion ... Mr. Riel may have been the best man they had for the purpose, although the event justified at least a doubt upon this head. **1934** *Cdn Hist.Rev.* XV 376: Why ... was not this area left in the status of a territory? The reason was the Red River Rebellion of 1869-70. **1946** LOWER *Colony to Nation* 351: There is some evidence for believing that the surveyors not only trespassed but talked boastfully too about Canada taking over, making suggestions that the *Metis* would have their lands taken away from them. Here was a major cause of the so called Red River "Rebellion" of 1870. **1958** *Encyc.Can.* VII 362/2: The outcome of the Red River Rebellion was the creation, prematurely, of the province of Manitoba. ...

Red River reel See **Red River jig** (def. 1).
1922 *Beaver* Aug. 34/1: ... the old time Red River reel was danced to the tune of the fiddle. ...

Red River salmon *Slang, Obs.* See quote.

1952 HOWARD *Strange Empire* 335: There was still "Red River salmon"—catfish—and bread and strong black tea.

Red River Settlement *Hist.* the colony established by Lord Selkirk in the valley of the Red River in Manitoba in 1812. See also **Red River, Red River colony, R.R.S., Selkirk** (def. 1), **Selkirker,** and **Settlement.**
1815 *Kingston Gaz.* (U.C.) 8 July 3/1: It is said that Captain D'Orsennons with a considerable party, left Fort William in the Autumn, and reached Fort Douglas in Red River settlement about the 10th January. **1935** MORICE *Red River Insurrection* 34: The colony of Assiniboia, as it was officially called, or the Red River Settlement, as it was popularly known, was made up of a population of about 11,500 souls divided into sections: French or Catholics, and English, generally Protestants, the former slightly predominating.

Red River wagon *Hist.* See **Red River cart** and picture.
1956 *Family Herald* 29 Mar. 42/1: That's the Old Missouri Wagon Trail which was used between the States and Canada for traffic by buffalo hunters, trappers, cattle, and Red River wagon.

red salmon *Pacific Coast* See **sockeye.**
1859 *Brit.Colonist* (Victoria) 12 Oct. 2/2: Several parties on the Fraser river have given up fishing for this season, owing to the red salmon not striking in. **1964** *Fisherman* 2 Oct. 4/1: Unable to meet their quotas with mature red salmon, the Japanese mothership fleet moved back toward the abstention line. ...

red sash *Obs.* a type of woven belt similar to the L'Assomption sash, *q.v.*
1849 ALEXANDER *L'Acadie* II 38: There were also a warm waistcoat with sleeves, comforter for the neck, Canadian red sashes to gird up the loins, and enable one the better to hold out. ...

redskin† *n.* See **Red Indian** (def. 2) and note.
1832 (1929) *Selected Stories* 40: "The great chief of the Ottawas knows that the Saganaw has promised the redskins a feast," returned the Governor. **1955** COLLARD *Cdn Yesterdays* 283: The judge replied: "There is where they lock up the redskins who refuse to pay the beaver skins they owe the merchants."

red spring *Pacific Coast* a red-fleshed variety of the spring salmon, *q.v.*
1966 *Fisherman* 6 May 14/3: [Advert.] SMOKER WANTS PRIME, FAT, large red springs, net or troll.

red spruce 1 a species of spruce, *Picea rubens,* found in eastern Canada.
1801 MACKENZIE *Voyages from Montreal* cxxvi: Close-grained wood is, on that account, the best; but theirs are made from the red or swamp spruce fir tree. **1952** PUTNAM *Cdn Regions* 27/2: The dominant and characteristic tree [of the Acadian forest] ... is red spruce ... which is found throughout this region and, apparently, to no great extent anywhere else.
2 the wood of this tree.
1777 *Quebec Gaz.* 17 Apr. 2/1: The sleepers of all bridges shall be of cedar; the logs covering the sleepers, shall be of ash or red spruce, well squared and pinned to the sleepers. **1962** *Forest Conservation* 27/2:

In the Maritime Provinces, red pine and red spruce are
the most extensively used. . . .

redthroated diver or **loon** a small loon, *Gavia
stellata,* found throughout the north of Canada.
1795 (1911) HEARNE *Journey* 430: Redthroated Divers
. . . are also called Loons in Hudson's Bay; but they are
so far inferior to the two former, that they seldom weigh
more than three or four pounds. **1896** (1898) RUSSELL
Far North 150: Red-throated loons and cacawees were
the most abundant of the water birds. **1956** SCHERMAN
Spring 313: Two red-throated loons had created a large
sloppy nest on its edge some weeks earlier.

red tide a micro-organism which when ingested by
clams and mussels renders them poisonous to man.
1958 HEALEY *Alert Bay* 73: The name of this plankton
is *goniolax satapella,* known to fishermen as "red tide"
because at one stage of its life it turns red. **1965** *Globe
and Mail* (Toronto) 2 June 9/1: Police said it was
believed they were victims of red tide poisoning that
sometimes occurs in shellfish off the coast. **1965** *Dly
Colonist* (Victoria) 30 Oct. 7/3: The fisheries department
has ordered special closure on clam harvesting in a
number of areas still affected by the poisonous red tide
that hit the coast last summer.

red trout See 1966 quote.
1898 EDGAR *Canada and Capital* 146: A few hours on
the rail . . . will take the fisherman to numerous streams
and lakes well stocked with maskinonge and bass, or
with red and grey trout. **1966** *Globe and Mail* (Toronto)
24 Sep. 31/3: . . . salmon and ouananiche literally rub
fins with great lakers and scarlet speckled trout, the
so-called red trout of Quebec.

Red Wig *Slang, Hist.* See **Knight of the Red Wig.**
1833 *Liberal* (St. Thomas, U.C.) 23 May 1/1: The
Common's house groaned and the Council responded,/
To think with Red Wig you so long corresponded.
1833 *Colonial Advocate* (York [Toronto]) 28 Mar. 1/2:
 Red-wig and I are turn-coats baith
 Tho' not on the same pin—
 Red Wig has turned him inside out,
 But I've turned outside in.

red willow See **red-osier dogwood.**
1743 (1949) ISHAM *Observations* 135: Their is a willow
they styl, (misqu pemeque,) or red willow, which makes
an Excellent Dye upon bone, Ivory, Quills, or cloth &c.
1873 GRANT *Ocean to Ocean* 164: [We saw] the
creeper which the Indians make into kinni-kinnick,
when they can't get the bark of the red willow to mix
with their tobacco. **1958** WATTERS *B.C.Cent.Anthol.*
352: Dry red willow flames well. . . . It is the antithesis
of smudge-fire smoke. . . .

red-winged oriole *Obs.* a red-winged blackbird,
Agelaius phoeniceus. Cp. **soldier bird.**
1772 *Trans.Linnean Soc.* XII 673: Red-winged
Oriole . . . is well known from the deperadations it
commits on the crops of Indian corn. It was formerly
called the Red-Winged Starling. **1823** FRANKLIN
Journey 673: In company with the Red-winged Orioles
they attack the fields of maize, and destroy often a great
part of the crop.

reef *v. Slang* in hockey, etc., bodycheck (an
opponent) so heavily as to knock [him] down.
1963 O'BRIEN *Hockey* 72: On the other hand, a
defending player who "lines up" an opponent and
reefs him into the boards is sure bait for the sin-bin.

reefer† ['rifɚ] *n.* [a shortening and alteration of
refrigerator] *Slang* a refrigerator car or truck; also,
a walk-in refrigerator.
1942 SWANSON *Western Logger* 54: reefer—a refrigerator
box car. **1963** *North* May-June 14/1: Price had been
showing them how to can the local fruit and prepare
it for freezing in the Indian Affairs reefer.

reels *n.pl.* See **fire-reels.**
1957 *Kingston Whig-Standard* (Ont.) 28 Sep. 1/5:
[Toronto CP release] Sixty firemen and 14 reels
responded to the alarms. . . .

reeve *n.* in Ontario and the western provinces, the
chairman of a village, township, or municipal-
district council, an elective office except in Alberta
(see 1945 quote). See also **town-reeve** and **township
reeve.** Cp. **overseer.**
1852 (1853) STRICKLAND *Canada West* II 271n: Counties
—the several township, village, and town councils in
each county, choose their reeves, and deputy reeves
where the population admits of it, and these form the
county council. **1884** *Brandon Blade* (Man.) 17 Jan. 8/3:
The Reeve, in a few well chosen remarks, dwelt on the
duties and responsibilities devolving on them as servants
of the people. **1945** (1950) BROWN *Cdn Democracy*
134: The Reeve [of an Alberta Municipal District] is
chosen by the Councillors from the Council and holds
office for one year. **1965** *Victoria Dly Times* 20 July
11/8: The reeve said the general principle of regional
planning is good but the mechanics need improving.
1966 *Globe and Mail* (Toronto) 15 Jan. 9/1: He had
been challenged only once, in 1962, when he beat a
suburban reeve by four votes.

reeveship *n.* the office and responsibilities of a
reeve.
1873 *Woodstock Sentinel* (Ont.) 12 Dec. 3/2: The all
absorbing question in town this week, has been, Who
wrote the letter to the Excise Department that caused
Mr. McWhinnie's involuntary retirement from the
candidature for the Reeveship? **1964** *Kingston
Whig-Standard* (Ont.) 10 Dec. 6/3: Warden Brown . . .
declined to contest the reeveship this year. . . .

reflector (oven) *n.* a type of oven of highly
polished metal, used for baking before an open
campfire by reflected heat.
1835 *Novascotian* (Halifax) 1 Oct. 288/1: The house of
every substantial farmer had three substantial
ornaments, a wooden clock, a tin reflector, and a
Polyglot Bible. **1914** DOUGLAS *Lands Forlorn* 154: Our
bannocks we baked in a reflector oven before the open
fire and we actually got to like them better than the
usual bread of civilisation as we found when we got
back. **1955** GOWLAND *Smoke* 153: A reflector can be
made from any piece of shiny tin large enough for the
job, though I used one of highly polished steel.
1957 LEWIS *Buckskin Cookery* I 38: Trout or salmon, or
bread can be cooked in a reflector oven if time is no
particular object.

Reform *adj. Hist.* of or pertaining to the
Reformers (def. 1).
1834 *Brit.Amer.Jnl* (St. Catharines, U.C.) 24 June 3/2:
We are at a loss to conceive why the Reform electors
of this riding have tho't it necessary, or expedient, to
nominate two candidates in opposition to each other.
1896 *Kootenaian* (Kaslo, B.C.) 6 June 3/1: Meanwhile
the Reform hosts are putting up a magnificent fight,
and if success does not crown their labors it will not be
for lack of hard work and the utmost enthusiasm.

1957 *Beaver* Spring 16/2: Macdonald was never
permitted to forget the fact that his government was a
coalition and that his Reform colleagues must have their
share of places and preferments.

625

**Reformed Doukhobor
regale**

Reformed Doukhobor See **Sons of Freedom.**
1958 *Edmonton Jnl* 2 Aug. 24/5: Mr. Sorokin six years
ago left the Kootenay district where the Freedomites,
who call themselves Reformed Doukhobors, make
their homes.

Reformer *n. Hist.* **1** in Upper and Lower Canada,
a member of a political group advocating a greater
measure of responsible government and other
reforms, the movement being among the
antecedents of the present Liberal Party, *q.v.* See
also **Radical Reformer** and **Reform party.**
1832 *Liberal* (St. Thomas, U.C.) 18 Oct. 3/3: It is not an
uncommon thing to hear Reformers, besides their other
numerous and equally appropriate titles, distinguished
by the appellation of Mackenzieites. 1853 *Mackenzie's
Wkly Message* 22 Sep. 3/4: The faithfulness with which
I stood by Lower Canada Reformers for thirty years
ruined my worldly prospects, injured my constitution,
impoverished my family in a foreign land, and covered
me with obloquy. 1909 TOWNLEY *Opinions* 215: Suppose,
for instance, some bigoted old Conservative storming,
when approached by a prospective son-in-law of
Liberal tendencies, "What! my daughter marry a
Reformer! When her mother and I and our people
before us have always been good Conservatives, and
she has been brought up in the same faith! Never, sir!"
1963 MORTON *Kingdom of Canada* 241: This, perhaps
the most pregnant sentence in Canadian political
history, was written by a moderate Reformer.

2 in Nova Scotia, a supporter of the Reform
movement led by Joseph Howe in the 1830's and
40's.
1837 *Times* (Halifax) 6 June 2/2: The eager and
determined manner in which the Reformers pushed
their violent measures at the commencement of the last
Session, plainly shows how all obstacles to their views
would be disposed of. 1963 MORTON *Kingdom of Canada*
257: Thomson intervened tactfully and persuaded
Campbell to take some Reformers into the executive
council [of Nova Scotia].

Reform party *Hist.* Reformers (def. 1) as a
political group. See also **Saddlebag party.**
1833 *Liberal* (St. Thomas, U.C.) 19 Sep. 2/4: When this
singular affair is sifted, the country must see there is
but little cause of triumph . . . and if the Reform party
be silent, the partizans of Government should be still.
1887 *Grip* (Toronto) 18 June 3/1: Mr. Blake has been
obliged by ill-health to withdraw . . . from the
leadership of the Reform Party. 1946 LOWER *Colony to
Nation* 235: It was partly by its (the western peninsula
which was predominantly of American extraction) vote
that in 1824 an Assembly was elected which contained
a number of "reformers." The name was beginning to
be used loosely for all who did not approve of things
as they were, but was not yet a party label. The
"reformers" of 1824 lacked cohesion and a platform:
they formed only a loose opposition group, not an
official opposition. Yet they were the fathers of the
Reform party and through it of the Liberal party.

refter *v.* See **rafter.**

refugee *n.* **1** *Maritimes, Hist.* See 1946 quote.
1786 *Account N.S.* 42: The best harbours are already
occupied by the loyalists and refugees, who have
settled there [N.S.] from other places. . . . 1845 BEAVAN
Life in Backwoods N.B. 67: . . . here . . . is seated the
owner of the dwelling . . . one of that fast declining
remnant—the refugees. 1946 LOWER *Colony to Nation*
105: During the [American] Revolution, scattered
individuals and families . . . made their way to Nova
Scotia . . . referred to, somewhat contemptuously, as
"refugees." 1956 RADDALL *Wings* 65: They came up
here to Nova Scotia with the other refugees.
2 *Obs.* See **United Empire Loyalist.**
1783 *Quebec Gaz.* 4 Mar. 2/1: All Issues of Provisions
to the Refugee Loyalists and disbanded Troops will
cease on the 10th day of April next, except at Quebec,
Sorel, and the Quarters at la Chine.

regale *n.* [< Cdn F *régale* < MF "pleasure,
festive occasion"] *Fur Trade, Hist.* **1** a ration of
rum, brandy, etc. issued to company employees
embarking on, during, or following an arduous
journey by canoe, York boat, etc.
☛ *This practice seems to have been established by the
North West Company, being taken over by the Hudson's
Bay Company following the amalgamation of 1821 and
varying somewhat in character as time passed.*
1797 (1964) CHABOILLEZ *Journal* 143: Gave the
People their Regals, & Mr. McGillivray set off.
1800 (1897) COUES *New Light* I 8: All were merry over
their favorite regale, which is always given on their
departure, and generally enjoyed at this spot, where we
have . . . plenty of elbow-room for the men's antics.
1832 COX *Adventures* II 332: At Christmas and New
Year they are served out with flour to make cakes and
puddings, and each man receives half pint of rum. This
they call a *regale,* and they are particularly grateful
for it. 1859 KANE *Wanderings* 258: In the Hudson's Bay
Company's service no rations of liquor are given to the
men, either while they are stopping in fort or while
travelling, nor are they allowed to purchase any; but
when they are about commencing a long journey, the
men are given what is called a regale, which consists of
a pint of rum each. This, however, they are not allowed
to drink until they are some distance from the post,
where, those who are entitled to get drunk may do so
without interfering with the resident servants of the
establishment. 1908 LAUT *Conquest N.W.* II 9: At the
hardest places and the hardest pace, the bourgeois
unbends and gives his men a *régale,* which means rum.
1929 MOBERLY *When Fur Was King* 58: . . . the head
guide came for the grand "regale," or feast, which
consisted of a quart of rum for the steersman, a pint for
the bowsman & half a pint for each of the others.
1941 *Beaver* Sep. 36/2: In York Boat days the regale of
rum afforded an occasion for conviviality. 1957 FISHER
Pemmican 81: "Had one," John said, meaning regale,
which was a cup of brandy or rum.

2 a. a party or feast that followed the issuing of
extra rations, usually including liquor, on a festive
occasion, as at Christmas, New Year's, or on the
arrival of special guests or important visitors.
1820 (1938) SIMPSON *Athabasca Jnl* 90: . . . none [rum]
must be sold to the people unless it is a Pint to each
after their Xmas regale. 1844 (1955) LEFROY *Magnetic
North* 92: After this they have a "régale" of which I
must not lower your idea by revealing what it consists
in, but one item is always a glass of wine if there is any.
1928 FREEMAN *Nearing North* 175: By way of
appreciation custom decrees that he then provide the
traditional "regale" and distribute gifts to the
deserving. 1947 (1957) MCKELVIE *Ft Langley* 34:
McMillan seized upon the advent of All Saint's Day,
November 1, as an excuse for a regale.

b. See 1941 quote.
1833 (1963) TOLMIE *Physician* 236: The men have also received a "regale" of pork, potatoes, molasses & rum & are at present loudly chaunting their voyaging songs.... **1941** *Beaver* Sep. 39/1: Regale—Extra rations issued at Christmas and New Year, including in former years a noggin of rum.
3 a free issue of rum, brandy, etc. to Indians, especially on special occasions. See also **potlatch,** *n.* (def. 3). Cp. **rum** (def. 2b).
1908 LAUT *Conquest N.W.* II 325: The régale pacified the discontent, and the Indians marched off without so much as the firing of a gun. **1913** COWIE *Adventurers* 307: This impost was intended also as special punishment to the Company for ceasing to give them [Indians] the old and highly appreciated presents of rum as "regales" on state occasions. **1952** HOWARD *Strange Empire* 265: Squaws could get in on the "regale" if they chose, but they frequently were too busy hiding the weapons in anticipation of the inevitable bloody brawl. **1957** FISHER *Pemmican* 246: But this year there was no feasting at either post, though the chiefs received more than their usual regale of rum and tobacco.

regale *v.* [< *n.*] *Fur Trade, Obs.* treat to a regale (def. 2).
1819 (1941) *Beaver* Dec. 19/2: ... the whole Inmates of our Garrison assembled in the Hall ... and were regaled ... with a few flaggons Rum and some Cakes.... **1830** (1909) CAMERON *New North* 110: In the evening they have the use of the hall to dance, and are regaled with a beverage.

Regina Manifesto See 1962 quote.
1957 *Commonwealth* 2 Oct. 8/5: A year later, 1933, a convention was held under the same auspices in Regina, when the famous "Regina Manifesto" was drafted. **1962** DICKIE *Great Golden Plain* 282: In 1932 when the Co-operative Commonwealth Federation was founded, Woodsworth was chosen as its leader. A year later the C.C.F. as it was commonly called, adopted the Regina Manifesto, an advanced program of social services, economic planning, and public ownership.

regional school See **consolidated school.**
1963 *Kingston Whig-Standard* (Ont.) 1 Feb. 21/1: The regional school has become a familiar feature of Canada's rural landscape. *Ibid.* 21/4: In roughly the same period of time New Brunswick has set up 145 regional schools, secondary and elementary....

registered Indian See 1964 quote. See also **Indian** (def. 1b), **legal Indian,** and **treaty Indian.** Cp. **Indian Register.**
1964 DUFF *Indian History* 46: The first [definition], which refers to what are usually called "registered Indians," is the legal definition used by the Indian Affairs Branch for the people who come under the jurisdiction of the *Indian Act;* that is, those whose names are included on the official Indian Register, either on a Band List or a General List. **1966** *Victoria Dly Times* 26 July 3/6: A council exclusively for registered Indians would be "prejudicial and discriminatory," Walter Currie, a director of the National Indian Council, said here Monday.

rehab ['rihæb] *n.* [shortening of *rehabilitation*] *Informal* (used attributively) of or having to do with the rehabilitation program introduced by the Department of Veterans Affairs following World War II.
1949 PETERSON *Chipmunk* 33: The car was completely theirs though; he'd paid cash for it out of his rehab money.... **1961** *Camsell Arrow* Summer 11: The rehab staff gave us good counselling and it is easier now. **1964** *Canadian Wkly* 28 Nov. 12/3: By then I had a wife and child and my army rehab allowance was $90 a month.

rehabilitation grant a sum of money granted to all honorably discharged Canadian veterans following World War II, used by many for completing their education.
1956 RADDALL *Wings* 30: After I got my discharge from the army I took a forestry course at U.N.B., on my rehabilitation grant.

reindeer *n. Esp.North* See **caribou** (def. 1). See also **deer.**
1793 (1937) CAMPBELL *Travels* 105: ... at the root of almost every tree may be seen the marks of Moose ... or Keraboo Deer. **1806** (1960) FRASER *Letters and Journals* 188: La Malice killed a Rein Deer that was crossing the River.... **1936** ARMSTRONG *Yukon Yesterdays* 22: He was dressed in a reindeer "parkey"[,] fur cap and "Much-luck" boots.

reindeer lichen *Obs.* See **caribou moss.**
1770 (1792) CARTWRIGHT *Journal* I 8: [Caribou] find there many extensive tracts of land destitute of wood, and covered with plenty of Reindeer Lichen ... and other herbage.

reindeer moss† See **caribou moss.**
1772 (1919) STURTEVANT *Edible Plants* 177: Reindeer moss, says Kalm ... grows plentifully in the woods around Quebec. **1822** (1928) CORMACK *Narr.Nfld* 27: We soon found ... beautiful lichens or reindeer moss. **1964** JENNESS *Eskimo Admin.* II 35: ... studied the terrain ... for two years, and reported ... that it carried an abundance of reindeer moss.

reindeer pass See **deer-pass.**
1939 *Beaver* June 27/1: Franklin had taken his advice finally, and gone into winter quarters at Great Bear Lake near the reindeer passes, where the Yellowknives could secure and dry a supply of meat....

remittance farmer *Hist.* a remittance man (def. 1) who runs a farm.
1893 LEGGE *Sunny Manitoba* 198: It is much to be regretted that the consumption of spirits, made more fiery by abominable adulteration, appears to be on the increase; but this is chiefly amongst the "remittance farmer" class, with whom "whisky-sprees" have become an institution. **1957** *Toronto Dly Star* 9 Feb. 6/2: Such words as concession road, separate school ... remittance farmer and suitcase farmer are used by Canadians every day and are considered good English.

remittance fellow *Hist.* See **remittance man.**
1910 FRASER *Red Meekins* 139: "Once me an' a young remittance feller went out chasin' a mine."

remittance man *Esp.West* **1** *Derog., Hist.* a person living in Canada on money remitted from his family in the Old Country, usually to insure that he did not return home to become a source of embarrassment.
1896 BODDY *Ocean, Prairie and Peak* 87: There is a lass of men who are called ... "Remittance-men" ...

always expecting a remittance in a few posts from the old country. **1911** SMITH *Is It Just?* 16: About two miles from Poplar Grove was the preemption of Mr. Guy Pierce, another Englishman, but one who belonged to that class rather contemptuously regarded by their neighbors as "remittance men." **1957** *Beaver* Autumn 51/1: "In the '80s," a Western pioneer recalled, "remittance men were as plentiful as gophers and just as unpopular." **1964** *Maclean's* 16 May 27/1: Contrary to popular belief, there were actually few remittance men on the [N.W.M.P.] force. . . .

2 *Figurative uses.*
1912 POCOCK *Man in the Open* 83: "The timber wolf I trimmed out because he wasted around like a remittance man." **1963** *Calgary Herald* 26 Dec. 24/4: Although the fairy shrimp is a fascinating creature to biologists, he is a sort of a remittance man of the animal world performing no very useful function in nature's scheme of things.

remitter *n. Obs.* See **remittance man.**
1896 BODDY *Ocean, Prairie and Peak* 87: There is a class of men who are called "Remitters" or "Remittance-men."

rente *n. Cdn French, Hist.* See **cens et rentes.**

renversé *n. Cdn French* See **windfall** (def. 2).
1809 (1897) COUES *New Light* II 569: They came through dreadful country . . . covered with thick woods, brules, and renverses. **1860** (1956) KOHL *Kitchi-Gami* 409: At times, when a violent storm has raged, whole districts in the forests for miles round will be covered with over-blown trees. Thus is formed what the French Canadians call a "renversi."

represent *v.* See **Representation Day.**

representation commissioner See quote.
1963 *Calgary Herald* 17 Dec. 11/6: With approval from all parties, a bill to establish the office of a representation commissioner, whose chief task will be to reshape Canada's electoral boundaries, breezed through second reading in the Commons.

Representation Day *B.C., Obs.* a day requiring all miners to "represent" their claims (occupy and work them in good order) following a winter layoff period when the law governing jumping claims was not enforced, it being a requirement that no unoccupied claim be protected from jumpers for a period longer than seventy-two hours.
1870 *Cariboo Sentinel* (Barkerville, B.C.) 21 May 2/4: Representation Day—yesterday the general laying over of claims ceased, and all miners possessing claims were required to represent them.

Republic of Madawaska See quote.
1958 *Time* (Cdn ed.) 15 Sep. 16/3: French-Canadian mill town of Edmundston, in the northwest corner of New Brunswick, is the capital of what its inhabitants call, for lack of a better name, "The Republic of Madawaska". . . . [Fn.] So named in the early 1800s by the first settlers of Madawaska county who found themselves virtually isolated from—and ignored by— the government of New Brunswick.

Republic of Manitoba *Hist.* See 1958 quote.
1870 *Wkly Manitoban* 12 Nov. 4/2: Dr. Schultz . . . signalised his return to Fort Garry, by entering the house of the editor of the New Nation, Mr. [Thomas] Spence, the ex-president of the first Manitoba Republic, going into the bed-room and actually attacking the naked man with a horse-whip! **1946** LOWER *Colony to*

Nation 352: How loose things were becoming in the territories is evidenced by the remarkable conduct of one Spence, a resident of Portage la Prairie, who one fine day in 1869 came out with a modest proclamation announcing that he had set up the Republic of Manitoba. [**1958** *Encyc.Can.* IX 378/1: In 1867 Spence . . . had the [Portage la Prairie] council reorganized to form the government of New Caledonia, soon more appropriately renamed Manitobah; the new body was derisively called "the Republic" by the Red River *Nor'Wester.*]

reputed township *Obs.* an area generally accepted as a township or planned as one, but not yet officially so designated. Cp. **provisional county.**
1793 *U.C.Gaz.* (York [Toronto]) 18 July 1/2: . . . the said Inhabitants-Householders [are] to choose and nominate two fit and discreet persons to serve the office of Town-Warden for such Parish, Township, reputed Township or Place.

reservation† *n.* See **Indian reserve.** See also **reserve** (def. 2).
☛ *This term is nowadays characteristic of the United States,* **reserve** *being the more usual Canadian term.*
1859 (1959) *Native Voice* Feb. 5/4: Has the Government of this Island the power to remove the Indians (by purchase) from that piece of outside Victoria Harbour known as the Indian Reservation. **1966** *Kingston Whig-Standard* (Ont.) 29 July 6/8: They are not allowed to take it back on the reservation and if they do go into the woods, the mounties charge them for drinking in a public place. . . .

reserve *n.* **1** a tract of land set aside for a specific purpose by the government. See also **Clergy Reserves** and **Huron Tract.**
1791 (1905) *Ont.Bur.Arch.Rep.* III xciv: Those already settled there complain much of what they suffer in the loss of Cattle and Hogs by the Indians at present settled in the Reserve. **1841** WARD *River St.John* 64: The land in the rear is chiefly ungranted, except that which is reserved for timberlands such as the great Prince William Reserve. **1889** WITHROW *Our Own Country* 600: About midnight I stopped off at Banff Springs, where there is a Government reserve of ten miles by twenty-six, which is being converted into a national park and health resort. **1961** *Alta Hist.Rev.* Winter 1/1: I was range-riding on the Buffalo Reserve at Wainwright on patrol with my favourite saddle horse "Frost."

2 See **Indian reserve.** See note at **reservation.**
1832 BAILLIE *Account of N.B.* 79: The Richibucto River is also well and thickly settled, to the head of the tide excepting in a large tract reserved for Indians, which reserve is a great drawback on the prosperity of the place. **1862** *Nor'Wester* (R.R.S.) 14 May 3/3: We purpose, merely, to ask for a Reserve of Land for ourselves—that, all; and that it might not seem a request of my own alone, I have asked my people to come forward and show that the desire for a reserve is general. **1908** MAIR *Mackenzie Basin* 57: These reserves are holdings you can select when you please, subject to the approval of the Government, for you might select lands which might interfere with the rights or lands of settlers. **1965** *Kingston Whig-Standard* (Ont.) 22 Feb. 7/2: Even the word "reserve" is a bit touchy with the department [of Indian Affairs].

Reserve(s) *n. Hist.* See **Clergy Reserves.**
1836 *Royal Standard* (Toronto) 17 Dec. 3/2: He
believed the Church of Scotland had ever as good a
right to the Reserves as the Church of England.

reserve agent See **Indian superintendent.**
1964 *Globe and Mail* (Toronto) 30 Dec. 8/5: The council
[declined] an offer by reserve agent Fred Hall....

residence lot a parcel of land suitable for
building a house on.
1882 *Edmonton Bull.* 21 Jan. 3/1: Prices range from
$30 to $60 advances on residence lots to $100 on those
on Broadway and Mainstreet, while cornerlots on
either of the above streets are still higher. **1897** *Slocan
Pioneer* (B.C.) 5 June 4/2: If you want to get in on the
ground floor, you should not lose a moment's time in
buying a cheap residence lot at Brandon.

resident elector or **voter** *B.C.* a British subject
over 21 years of age who has resided in a
municipality for more than six months prior to a
municipal election, exclusive of owner-electors, *q.v.*
1958 *Citizen* (North Vancouver) 18 Sep. 2/3:
Tenant-electors and resident-electors have until
September 30 to get on the 1959 voters' list, Reeve
Sam McCrea pointed out today. **1958** *Sun* (Vancouver)
11 Apr. 26/1: For all general purposes, there are two
categories of voters—one is owner voters, the other is
resident voters, but all must be citizens of Canada.

residential school *North* a boarding school
operated or subsidized by the federal government
to accommodate students, especially Indians and
Eskimos, attending classes at a considerable
distance from their homes. See also **hostel** (def. 2),
hostel school, and **Indian residential school.** Cp.
hostel (def. 1), **Indian boarding school,** and **Indian
day school.**
1954 *North Star* (Yellowknife) Feb. 4/2: Prior to that,
there were no educational facilities for Metis and whites
in the area, and Treaty Indians went to residential
schools at Sturgeon Landing and Prince Albert.
1965 *Globe and Mail* (Toronto) 2 Sep. W1/5: In
comparison with public schools for whites, the Indian
day and residential schools were of poor quality.

resident voter See **resident elector.**

resources road See **access road** (def. 1).
1958 *Edmonton Jnl* 18 Sep. 2/5: At the western
boundary of Wood Buffalo Park, the federal road will
link up with a resources road to be built jointly by the
federal and provincial governments....

rest *n. Obs.* **1** See **pose** (def. 1).
1784 (1790) UMFREVILLE *Hudson's Bay* 24: Got our
things over the portage at two more rests, then entered
a lac about one mile long.
2 See **pose** (def. 2).
1798 (1916) THOMPSON *Narrative* 294: In this hilly
country ... a Rest may be from five hundred to six
hundred yards.

Restigouche salmon a much esteemed variety
of Atlantic salmon, associated with the
Restigouche River in New Brunswick.
1958 *Maclean's* 24 May 1/1: The prized Arctic Char,
a well-known but little-tasted delicacy in most of

Canada, is going to start muscling into gourmet circles
once sacred to Lake Winnipeg goldeye and Restigouche
salmon. **1962** *Commercial Letter* Oct. 2/2: Thus the
famous Restigouche salmon has given international
recognition to the Restigouche River in New
Brunswick.

resting place *Obs.* See **pose** (def. 1).
1793 (1933) MACDONELL *Diary* 96: The Portage is ...
divided by the voyageurs into sixteen Poses or resting
places....

resting pole See **rest-stick.**
1922 *Beaver* Oct. 59/2: ... it was not unusual to see the
mother, with perhaps 150 pounds on her back, back up
to one of the resting poles placed at frequent resting
places, rest her pack against the pole, pull her baby down
from the top and commence to nurse the child.

rest-stick *n.* a sturdy stick or pole used to take
the weight of a pack off the bearer's shoulders and
forehead while he is resting on the trail. See also
resting pole.
1943 MILLER *Lone Woodsman* 14: Dan cut a rest-stick
and adjusted the tump strap across his forehead, so as
to relieve his shoulders for the canoe load.

returned man or **soldier** a veteran returned from
overseas service.
1915 *Eye Opener* (Calgary) 11 Dec. 2/3: An army of
returned soldiers—all real men—who have been away
fighting for the Empire are not going to return with their
bodies wrecked and their nerves shattered and allow
themselves to be told what is right and what is wrong
by a bunch of stay-at-home aldermen or freak
legislators. **1917** *Grit* (Toronto) 11 Dec. 3/3: He has
been engaged by the publicity agents of the Hon.
Frank Cochrane, along with the other returned men....
1957 *Globe and Mail* (Toronto) 7 May 6/2: He ... told
us that 85 per cent of them were returned men, many of
whom had been unfitted for ordinary employment by
war. **1958** *Edmonton Jnl* 24 June 3 11/4: To the
northeast, in the Blueberry Mountain District lies an
area of good farmland ... where many returned
soldiers and others settled a number of years ago.

returning officer† See 1945 quote.
1793 *U.C.Gaz.* (York [Toronto]) 1 July 4/2: An Act to
provide for the appointment of Returning Officers for
the several Counties within this Province. **1945** (1950)
BROWN *Cdn Democracy* 41: The returning officer in each
constituency ... must arrange for polling stations, must
appoint a deputy returning officer to conduct the
election and count the votes in each polling station,
and when he receives the statement of votes from each
deputy returning officer he must add them up and
proclaim which candidate is elected. **1963** *Kingston
Whig-Standard* (Ont.) 5 Mar. 16/6: Among them are
Chief Electoral Officer Nelson Castonguay and the
returning officers in the 263 electoral districts.

return(ing) potlatch *B.C., Hist.* a potlatch
(def. 1) held to pay back with interest gifts
received at earlier potlatches.
1885 (1961) LA VIOLETTE *Survival* 46: Mr. Lomas was of
the opinion that the enforcement of the new Indian Act
should be delayed so that each band could be allowed
a special licence to hold just one "returning 'Potlatch'
with the distinct understanding that no additional
property shall be lent." *c***1886** (1961) *Ibid.* 50: Now if
Dr. Powell will try to get permission for him to hold
his return Potlatch, Lohah will be lifted up above the
others....

returns *n.pl. Fur Trade, Hist.* See 1963 quote. Cp.
outfit, *n.* (def. 1a).

1694 (1929) KELSEY *Papers* 33: [I] shall be more able to yive you a large Epistle yᵉ next Return hoping to receive a line or two from your honour. . . . **1761** (1901) HENRY (Elder) *Travels* 41: Here [Michilimackinac], the outfits are prepared . . . and here, the returns, in furs, are collected and embarked for Montréal. **1908** MAIR *Mackenzie Basin* 183: . . . there was still much work to be done in the way of transport of outfit and returns between Anderson and Fort Good Hope. . . . **1963** MCTAVISH *Behind the Palisades* 84: "Returns" was the opposite of "Outfit," and was the generic name for furs, and all trade results which were returned to the Old Country in exchange.

revanche du berceau *French* See **Revenge of the Cradle.**
1967 *Globe and Mail* (Toronto) 1 Apr. 8/3: The pronatality suggestions are merely a revival of the traditional "revanche du berceau" (the revenge of the nursery) which led past generations of the nationalist elite of Quebec to imagine that high birth rates could outstrip the hordes of immigrants who were flocking to Eastern Canada early in this century.

Revenge of the Cradle [trans. of F *revanche du berceau*] See quote. See also **revanche du berceau.**
1964 *Winnipeg Tribune* 6 Feb. 6/6: Quebec's answer was a high birthrate, epitomized in the title of an article in a French Canadian nationalist magazine in the 'twenties, "The Revenge of the Cradle."

Revillon (Frères) *n. Hist.* See **French Company** (def. 2).
1914 BINDLOSS *Intriguers* 42: I was in Revillons' . . . where they supply especially light handsleds, snowshoes, and patent cooking cans. **1922** *Beaver* July 8/1: A clerk from Revillon Freres told of a wonderfully sagacious dog he had. **1956** KEMP *Northern Trader* 92: In so far as Revillons were concerned, the policy of giving "debt" had been completely eliminated.

Rhinoceros Party a pseudo-political party which ran candidates in Montreal ridings during federal elections of the 1960's, the objective being to make the electors aware of purported inadequacies in the old-line parties.
☞ *The name appears to be derived from an incident in Rio de Janeiro, where, in 1959, a rhinoceros named Cacarecto, on loan from an Argentinian zoo, was elected as a councillor on a write-in vote. Though he was disqualified for not having Brazilian citizenship, the people were understood to have indicated their dissatisfaction with the official nominees.*
1964 *Globe and Mail* (Toronto) 8 Feb. 8/4: Many people, however, are intrigued by the platform and pronouncements of a fifth and new group which might be called an anti-political party and which has also formally entered candidates in both ridings. This is the Rhinoceros Party, founded and headed by a Montreal physician, Dr. Paul Ferron, who is the party candidate in St. Denis. **1967** *Kingston Whig-Standard* (Ont.) 16 May 5/7: The candidates [include] Outremont-St. John—F.L.M. Bonnier, Rhinoceros Party.

ribbon farm a long, narrow holding of land fronting on a river, such as the farms of old Quebec along the St. Lawrence River and those in the Red River Settlement. See also **river lot** (def. 2) and **strip farm.**
1962 DICKIE *Gt Golden Plain* 84: The Kildonan settlers were given ribbon farms on the west bank of the Red

River, north of the earlier arrivals. Each farm had a narrow frontage on the river and ran back two miles, with a two-mile-wide strip of pasture and hay land behind for the use of all.

Ribbonite *n. Hist.* a member of a society of teetotallers, who wore blue ribbons.
1884 *Nor'Wester* (Calgary) 7 Oct. 3/1: If the Ribbonites are trying to run this district, the license men must be up and doing, and have a say on that point.

Ribbon-man† *n. Hist.* See **Shiner.**
1829 MACTAGGART *Three Years* I 291: The Irish have frequent *rows*, and carry the spirit of party with them wherever they go; the *orange* and *ribbon-men* have dreadful recounters. **1933** CAMERON *Twigs* 218: Bytown was then infested with a class of people called Shiners, or, as they were sometimes called, Ribbon men; rough characters that neither feared God nor regarded man. . . .

ribstone ['rɪb,stoʊn] *n.* [trans. from Cree] See 1965 quote. See also **medicine stone.** Cp. **buffalo stone.**
1928 *Place Names of Alberta:* Ribstone; lake and creek, Battle River, 45-1-4; on Palliser map, 1865; in Cree *as-sin-i-kos-pike-ganit;* a large stone bears marks resembling a man's ribs. **1959** *Within Our Borders* June 4: Two rocks, carved and chiselled so as to resemble the ribs of a buffalo, are marked by the cairn. The ribstones are believed to have had a sacred significance to the Indians of this area for more than a thousand years. According to the legend associated with the stone carvings, Indians sacrificed buffalo on the stones at the commencement of each hunt, in the belief that such sacrifices would ensure success. **1965** WORMINGTON & FORBIS *Archaeology Alta* 170: Ribstones are boulder petroglyphs . . . three to five feet in length . . . composed of tough resistant quartzite, probably transported to Alberta from the Canadian Shield by glacial action.

rice *n.* See **wild rice.**
1665 (1885) RADISSON *Fourth Voyage* 215: We had there a kinde of rice, much like oats. It grows in the water in 3 or 4 foote deepe. **1775** (1901) HENRY (Elder) *Travels* 242: The rice grows in shoal water, and the Indians gather it by shaking the ears into their canoes. **1963** *Sask.News* Nov. 1: [Caption] Kitchener Halkett illustrates dexterity required in brushing rice kernels into canoe bottom using set of wooden batons.

rice bed, field, grounds, or **pond** the shallows of a lake where wild rice grows.
1831 *Trans.Lit.& Hist.Soc.Que.* II 260: About the great rice pond, and the channel leading from it to the Musk-rat lake, the lands are fertile. **1850** BIGSBY *Shoe and Canoe* II 317: It is very long . . . with frequent marshes and productive rice-grounds. **1852** (1881) TRAILL *Cdn Crusoes* 198: The extensive rice-beds on the lake had now begun to assume a golden tinge which contrasted very delightfully with the deep blue waters. . . . **1905** DAWSON *St.Lawrence* 365: It is collected by the women, who pole their bark canoes into the rice fields when the grain is ripe, and reaching out draw over the heads, on both sides, and beat out the grain into the canoe.

richeau or **rechaud** [rəˈʃo *or* rəˈʃu] *n.* [< Cdn F < F *réchaud* portable warming oven; cf. F *réchauffer* warm over] *Hist.* a palatable dish of pemmican mixed with flour and vegetables, when

available, and warmed over a fire. See also **infidel
dish** and **rousseau.** Cp. **rubaboo.**

☛ *This term had many spelling variants, including*
rasho, richot, rouchou, rousseau, rusho(o), rowshow.
1848 BALLANTYNE *Hudson's Bay* 190: They call it
richeau; it is uncommonly rich, and very little will
suffice for an ordinary man. **1879** *Sask.Herald*
(Battleford,N.W.T.) 13 Jan. 3/2: He labors hard now
in the river's bed,/Enjoying his three square meals a
day,/And getting fat on richeau, spuds, and bread.
1914 STEELE *Forty Years* 70: . . . the other was called by
the plain hunters a "rechaud." It was cooked in a frying
pan with onions and potatoes or alone. **1938** GODSELL
Red Hunters 202: While the white man was making a
fire of buffalo chips and preparing a meal of richeau,
the Indian . . . wandered far afield. . . . **1963** MCTAVISH
Behind the Palisades 89: When flour was procurable,
the trippers disintegrated the solid pemmican in a
frying pan by heat, added flour, pepper or salt, and made
a dish fit for the gods called locally "Rushoo". . . .

Richibucto goose *Maritimes* salted shad, as
prepared in Richibucto, Kent County, Nova
Scotia. Cp. **Digby chicken.**
1939 BARTON & THOMAS *In New Brunswick* 175: For
instance, should you see Richibucto goose noted on
your hotel menu, do not let the appetizing thought
mislead your palate into expecting the breast of one
of the numerous honkers that frequent the bay.

richôt *n.* See **richeau.**

rick-a-dick *n. Obs.* See quote. Cp. **sloven.**
1959 *Cdn Geog.Jnl* Jan. 3/2: As late as the 1870's
"rick-a-dicks," long trucks with shafts at one end and
wheels in the centre and used almost exclusively for the
trucking of flour in barrels, fish, and other products,
were a common sight on Halifax streets.

ride *v. Obs.* See quote.
*a*1820 (1838) HEAD *Forest Scenes* 309: Still I was in
ignorance, till I found, that for an old woman to ride,
meant the same as to say that she practised the
profession of a midwife.

ride and tie *Hist.* See 1958 quote.
*c*1862 (1958) LINDSAY *Cariboo Story* 38/1: They were to
ride and tie the horse they brought from Beaver Lake,
which I think they did. **1888** (1890) ST. MAUR
Impressions 229: Packed one horse, and we went
"ride and tie" on the other. **1958** MCCULLOCH *Woods
Words* Glossary: *Ride and Tie*—A system whereby
two men and one horse could cover a lot of ground.
One man rode ahead, tied the horse, and walked on.
The second man reached the horse, got on, rode past
the first man to an agreed point, where he tied the
horse and walked on himself.

Rideau Hall since 1868, Government House in
Ottawa, the residence of the Governor General of
Canada.
1869 *Cdn Illust.News* 30 Oct. 3/1: . . . His Excellency
will return to Rideau Hall at the end of the week.
[**1903** CARR-HARRIS *White Chief* 227: [In 1838] a small
dinner party [was] given by the "Laird of Bytown,"
The Hon. Thomas MacKay, at his new residence,
Rideau Hall. . . .] **1958** *Encyc.Can.* IV 424/2: The
official residence of the Governor General in Ottawa
is Government House, sometimes known as Rideau
Hall.

Rider of the Plains *Hist.* a member of the North
West Mounted Police, *q.v.*
1878 *Sask.Herald* (Battleford, N.W.T.) 23 Sep. 4/3:
Ring out . . . ring out the marching call for the Riders of
the Plains. **1910** HAYDON *Riders of the Plains* 92:
Several weeks later, when the snows had melted, a
search party found the body of the Rider of the Plains.
1955 HARDY *Alta Anthol.* 63: Around the world, the
famed "Riders of the Plains" have been popularized,
eulogized, even glamorized, in prose and poem.

ride the rapids See **shoot,** *v.* (def. 1).
1929 JOHNSTON *Beyond Rockies* 175: Some "ride" the
rapids, I believe.

riding ['raɪdɪŋ] *n.* [Brit.E "an administrative
division of a county, esp. Yorkshire" < ME
thriding < ON *thrithjungr* a third part; the *th-* was
lost by assimilation to the previous *-t* or *-th* in
the compounds *East Thriding, North Thriding, West
Thriding*] **1** *Hist.* in Upper Canada, a subdivision
of a county, set up primarily for election purposes.
See note at **county.**
1792 (1906) *Ont.Bur.Arch.Rep.* IV 180: The said county
of Glengarry, bounded as aforesaid, shall be divided
into two ridings. **1853** *Elora Backwoodsman* (C.W.)
21 Apr. 2/5: When I do seek the votes of the electors
of the north riding, I shall fearlessly submit my
qualifications and character to the judgment of all who
can cast aside their personal feelings and look only to
the public good

2 See **electoral district.**
1890 *Grip* (Toronto) 29 Mar. 213/1: In that riding the
New Party had only 50 pledged members, but pulled
nearly 800 votes. **1900** *Prospector* (Lillooet, B.C.)
16 Mar.4/1: The east and west ridings of Lilooet have
a few names mentioned, but before the time comes a
dark horse will no doubt appear in both fields.
1957 *Maclean's* 6 July 36/2: At one time Spadina
regularly returned J. B. Salsberg as an LPP [Communist]
member to the Provincial Legislature, a habit that
inspired a waggish reporter to tag it the "Little Red
Riding." **1958** *Edmonton Jnl* 2 Aug. 3/4: Mr. Brundsen
. . . represents one of two southern Alberta ridings
containing irrigated sections. . . . **1966** *Toronto Dly
Star* 30 Apr. 67/5: Opposition Leader Diefenbaker
scored the new electoral map for Saskatchewan for
lumping wheat farmers and city dwellers together in
common ridings.

Rielite [ri'ɛl,aɪt] *n. Hist.* a supporter of Louis Riel.
See also **Northwest Rebellion.**
1887 *Grip* (Toronto) 7 May 3/2: This is the same Col.
Ouimet who led the Riel bolters last session; this is the
same Government that denounced all Rielites as
essentially traitors, knaves and rebels.

Riel rebellion or **(up)rising** *Hist.* **1** See
Northwest Rebellion (def. 1).
1897 YOUNG *Indian Trail* 100: It was the time of the
first Riel Rebellion in Manitoba, and although we were
living far north of the actual scene of the rebellion, yet
our supplies had in so great a measure been cut off, that
we were existing on very scant rations. **1920** *Cdn Hist.
Rev.* I 158: The force which put down the Riel
Rebellion of 1870 was not a Canadian, but an Imperial
force. **1947** *Ibid.* Dec. 432: . . . following the first Riel
rising [1870] the more recalcitrant group migrated to
the Saskatchewan River Valley. . . .

2 See **Northwest Rebellion** (def. 2).
1885 *Qu'Appelle Vidette* (Sask.) 2 Apr. 3/1: The sole
subject of conversation here is the Riel rebellion, and
everyone seems anxious for the latest news.

1958 *Herald-Tribune* (Grand Prairie, Alta.) 10 Feb. 21/2: When he came to Canada from Ireland in 1882, one of his early jobs was to help repair a grist mill wrecked by insurgents during the Riel rebellion.
1962 *Sask.News* 19 June 4/1: Interest in the old march, an integral part of the [1885] Riel uprising, was spurred recently. . . .

riffle† *n.* [origin obscure; cf. *ruffle, ripple*] **1 a.** an obstruction in a watercourse, as a shallows, rapids, or sandbar. See also **rift** and **ripple** (def. 1). Cp. **shoot,** *n.* (def. 1).
1859 (1964) INNIS *Fur Trade* 315: Some of the boats at that season came up from York in 18 days with forty pieces so that it could not have been so low as the year the rif[f]les came up. . . . **1912** FOOTNER *New Rivers* 141: Every little riffle caused us to start up and seize a paddle, and it became necessary to go ashore for undisturbed sleep. **1938** *Beaver* Mar 14: The river became swifter and shallower, and, at low water stages, riffles and scattered boulders broke its course. **1954** BRUCE *Channel Shore* 13: Just west of that riffle a log bridge crossed the brook. . . . **1956** EVANS *Mountain Dog* 40: Above one of the riffles, a good-sized trout—a rainbow—rose to a small blue dragonfly

b. a stretch of ruffled water caused by such an obstruction; the place where such an obstruction is. See also **rip** and **ripple** (def. 2).
1869 *Mainland Guardian* (New Westminster, B.C.) 8 Sep. 3/3: The citizens of Quesnelmouth had subscribed $450 for the widow of the late unfortunate Frank Roberts, who was drowned at Spanish Riffle.
1894 ASHLEY *Tan Pile Jim* 197: But the moment they [the logs] drifted into the riffles, and plunged into the foaming rapids, they began to act in the most scandalous manner. **1963** *Weekend Mag.* 21 Dec. 6/1: It was at a riffle called the Figure Eight . . . that we almost came to grief.

c. *Northwest* a fast-moving stretch of water over a relatively smooth bed. See 1955 quote. See also **chute** (def. 2), **dalle** (def. 2), **flat rapid, run,** *n.* (def. 1), and **slide** (def. 1b).
1908 MAIR *Mackenzie Basin* 132: Presently . . . we entered a succession of the sweetest little rapids and riffles imaginable. . . . **1952** *Beaver* June 13/1: There were so many memories—the sudden rush of white water in the riffles . . . the swirl and struggle of the arctic grayling and those gigantic Dolly Vardens of the Flat River. **1954** PATTERSON *Dangerous River* 312: riffle—a chute or slide of water in a river, usually in shingle or broken rock and not in solid rock. **1963** PATTERSON *Far Pastures* 181: One could slide down a riffle [in a canoe] —which is a chute through or around a shingle bar. . . .

2 *Placer Mining* the transverse barriers placed across the bottom of a sluice-box, *q.v.*, to arrest the particles of gold.
1900 LONDON *Son of Wolf* 128: . . . there would come a time when those dumps would pass through his sluice-boxes, depositing in the riffles, in the course of half a dozen days, several hundred thousand dollars.
1927 MCKELVIE *Black Canyon* 105: The gold, being heavier than the sand and small stones, settled to the bottom to be caught by cleats or riffles, while the lighter material was carried away. . . . **1965** *Cdn Geog.Jnl* LXXI 205/1: Riffles are cross pieces of wood, two inches square and set about two inches apart with nails left projecting so the riffles can easily be removed.

riffle *v.* [< *n.*] ruffle; cause to form into wavelets or ripples.

1903 WHITE *Forest* 211: Suddenly you make out the bottom . . . and the big suckers and catfish idling over its riffled sands. . . . **1954** BRUCE *Channel Shore* 13: As Hazel walked down the crooked hauling-road, her ears caught the slight rushing murmur of the Black Brook, riffling across a stretch of stony bottom. **1958** *Happy Motoring* XIX 4 5/1: So land-locked and cliff-flanked is the Inlet that the surface waters are rarely riffled by wind and so make a perfect mirror.

rift† *n.* [? < *riff,* obs.var. of *reef*] *Obs.* See **riffle** (def. 1a).
1760 JEFFERYS *Descr.New France* 18: The navigation is very troublesome, on account of the many rifts and portages or carrying places. **1827** (1829) MACTAGGART *Three Years* I 153: These rifts, as they are called, otherwise small ripples, continue about a mile.

rig *v.* *Lumbering* make a tree ready to function as a spar tree, *q.v.*, attaching guy lines to it and equipping it with the main line (def. 3) and other lines which run into the bush for the moving of logs. See also **rigger.**
1942 HAIG-BROWN *Timber* 254: This [a spar tree] may be a standing tree, topped and rigged, or a tree brought in from elsewhere and raised for the purpose.

rigger *n.* *Lumbering* See 1942 quote. See also **high-rigger.**
1942 HAIG-BROWN *Timber* 253: RIGGER. "The Rigger" is the high or head rigger or high climber, all terms for one and the same job. He has a crew consisting of a second rigger, several "extra riggers" and his engineer. He and his second rigger do the spectacular job of climbing and topping the spar trees and, in the case of a skidder, the back trees. What is a good deal more important, they are responsible for the proper rigging of a tree, its support with guy lines, the way the blocks are set and how the lines run out in the woods.
1963 *Press* Apr. 9:
There's where you'll hear the mainline hum
Through the bull-block, hanging high,
As the friction locks on the big main drum
And the rigger hollers, "Hi."

rigging crew a crew of riggers, *q.v.*
1906 *Log of the "Columbia"* June 8/1: He . . . had stood the taunts of his riggan crew a number of times without paying any attention. **1932** *Lumber Worker* Sep. 4/2: Then the question of new methods of struggle was raised [for] . . . rigging crew, fallers and buckers, boommen . . . in logging camps. . . . **1942** SWANSON *Western Logger* 54: rigging crew—crew which handle rigging (yarding).

rigging goat See quote.
1942 HAIG-BROWN *Timber* 251: Goat or "rigging goat." Term applied to a small general purpose donkey engine, especially the one used by the "rigging up crew" to raise spar trees and rig them with the necessary guy lines and blocks.

rigging leverman *Lumbering* the engineer on a rigging crew.
1942 HAIG-BROWN *Timber* 251: Engineer [is] used of any man who is running a steam-boiler—thus for yarding and loading and rigging levermen as well as for locomotive engineers.

rigging-slinger *n.* *Lumbering* the lead hand of a crew of riggers, *q.v.*

1906 *Log of the "Columbia"* June 7/1: "I've been . . . riggan-slinger for this layout for over 8 years an' . . . they put on a bloomin' blue nose, who hasn't been on the coast over a year." **1965** *Sun* (Vancouver) 17 June 35/2: We always need hooktenders, rigging-slingers . . . and experienced woodsmen.

right-of-way *n.* **1**† a strip of land granted or sold to a company for the construction of a railway, power line, etc.
1911 (1914) BICKERSTETH *Open Doors* 51: Then the right-of-way cutters, who cut down and burn the timber and brush to a width of a hundred feet. **1966** *Imperial Oil Rev.* June 9/1: Hydro uses muskeg vehicles . . . in maintenance work along its right-of-way.
2 *Esp.West* See **road allowance** (def. 1).
1895 *Times* (Niagara-on-the-Lake, Ont.) Apr. 1/3: The right-of-way for the new road has been procured for almost the entire distance. **1957** *Commonwealth* 4 Dec. 23/1: Right-of-way maintenance has been improved, and all right-of-ways are now mowed. **1963** *Calgary Herald* 19 Oct. 21/3: . . . modern highways would not carry heavy traffic loads if the soft "black dirt" on right of ways had not been excavated and replaced with firm aggregate.

rim *n. Placer Mining* See **rimrock**, *n.* (def. 1).
1869 (1962) ANDERSON *Sawney's Letters* 37: He hammers at the rock, / Believin' its a rim, / When ten to ane 'tis naething / But his fancy's whim. . . .
1963 *Placer Mining* 20/1: The first shallow diggings gave way to drifting on bedrock, then to hydraulicking, and finally to sniping operations along the rims or on weathered bedrock.

rim-ice *n.* See **ice-shelf** (def. 2).
1902 LONDON *Daughter of Snows* 288: Nor, though the water was open, did she find a clear way, for the river was full of scattered floes which had crumbled down from the rim-ice. **1928** FREEMAN *Nearing North* 349: The big freighting canoes had been launched into a basin cracked out of the rim ice and were being loaded for the voyage.

rimrock *n. Esp.West* **1** an outcropping or ridge of rock, especially one that once formed the bank of a stream. See also **rim.**
1860 *Brit.Colonist* (Victoria) 22 May 3/1: There is every reason to believe that it is equal to the hill-diggings in California, because this has the appearance of rimrock. **1884** *Nor'Wester* (Calgary) 8 July 3/2: Work is at present being advanced on the rim rock and the dirt pans out from $1.50 to half an ounce in the crevices. **1958** *Globe and Mail* (Toronto) 3 June 15/3: Proof of the depth and force of this meltwater torrent can be studied today in the whirlpool potholes on the rimrock of the river's 80-foot limestone shoreline. **1964** BERTON *Golden Trail* 16: Each claim by law extended five hundred feet down the valley, and extended from rim-rock to rim-rock.
2 See 1963 quote.
1912 POCOCK *Man in the Open* 154: "By dusk I'll be on top of the cliffs, and make my fires back from the rimrock, where them robbers won't see the glare."
1963 SYMONS *Many Trails* 63: By pushing the cattle up over the rimrock—as they call the crest of the hills—to scatter out for the summer, the ranchers are able to conserve the bunch-grass hillsides nearer home for their winter range. **1966** PATTERSON *Trail* 66: . . . mountain goat were . . . moving in single file along some trail below the rimrock. . . .

rimrock *v. West, Slang* **1** drive (cattle) into a corral, enclosure, etc.
1955 HOBSON *Nothing Too Good* 188: With the Vanderhoof stockyards only seven days away, I had a strong feeling that if any outfit could rimrock this drive into the cattle cars, this was the one that would do it.
2 hedge in; cut off; entrap. See also **rimrock,** *n.* (def. 2).
1951 HOBSON *Grass* 114: He had spotted a band of at least twenty wild horses . . . rimrocked by a heavy snowfall in a high valley beyond Tatla Lake. *Ibid.* 59: "You've got me to thank, boy, for saving you from being rimrocked by a bunch of females in that town."

rind† *n. Nfld* the bark of trees. See also **rinding.**
☛ *Although this is in general an archaic, if not obsolete, word for* bark, *it is still current in Newfoundland and Labrador, and, locally, in Nova Scotia.*
1620 WHITBOURNE *Discovrse* 30: The rindes of these trees serue to couer their Stages, and necessary roomes, with turfes on them; so that in a fvv yeeres, I feare, that most of the good timber trees neere the Sea-side, vvere men vse to fish, vvill be either felled, spoyled or burned. **1771** (1792) CARTWRIGHT *Journal* I 133: At nine I went myself with three hands in the skiff to Stage Cove, and carried all the rinds which were below the house. **1829** (1964) *Nfld Qtly* Summer 28/1: Winter's work . . . This metonymous term is the quantitative one for the total of sticks, lumber, rinds and so forth that a man would produce while living with his family away from his settlement "in the woods for the winter."
1966 *Weekend Mag.* 23 Apr. 7/1: [Old Song]
　　Sods and rinds to cover yer flake,
　　Cake and tea for supper,
　　Codfish in the spring o' the year,
　　Fried in maggoty butter.

rind *v. Nfld* remove the rind, *q.v.*, from. Hence, **rinder.** See also **rinding.**
1620 WHITBOURNE *Discovrse* 30: For our Nation, vpon their arriual yeerly to that Countrey, doe cut downe many of the best trees they can finde, to build their stages and roomes withall fortheir necessary occasions; hewing, rinding, and destroying many others that grow within a mile of the Sea, where they vse to fish. **1771** (1792) CARTWRIGHT *Journal* I 129: Two of them joined rinders, and the other two ground hatchets. **1793** REEVES *Hist.Nfld* 35: The trees were rinded, and the woods destroyed. . . .

rinding *n. Nfld* See 1792 quote. See also **rind,** *n.* and *v.*
1633 *Commission for well Gouerning* 11: . no person [shall] . . . worke any detriment or destruction . . . by Rynding. . . . **1792** CARTWRIGHT *Journal* II Glossary: Rinding. The action of taking the bark from the trees. In this part of the world [Labrador], one length only, of six feet, is taken off the lower part of the trunk of a tree. The chief use of rinds is, to cover the roofs of houses, and piles of fish.

ring† *v. Obs.* See **girdle.**
1808 (1809) GRAY *Letters* 275: Instead of cutting down the trees, the Americans very frequently ring them, as they term it, which is cutting a section of the bark quite round: soon after which the tree decays. **1836** (1923) JAMESON *Rambles* 50: . . . a deep gash is cut through the bark . . . quite round the bole of the tree . . . This is technically called ringing timber.

ring dollar *Hist.* See **holey dollar** and picture.
1899 *P.E.I.Mag.* Mar. 21: Another coin of interest, in that it possesses a local history of its own, is the "Ring Dollar."

ring(ed) seal a seal, *Phoca hispida,* characterized by ringlike white spots on the body, found in northern regions. See also **jar** and **silverjar.** Cp. **netchek.**
1880 (1964) *Nfld Qtly* Spring 4/2: ... it appears not to advance as far northward as the "Ringed Seal".... **1937** *Beaver* Mar. 9/2: After the business of getting this one out, another ringed seal about one hundred pounds, we felt it was time for a cup of hot tea.... **1964** JENNESS *Eskimo Admin.* II 62: They still knew how ... to draw the victim on to the surface of the ice, if it was a common ring seal....

rink *n.* **1** See **hockey rink** (def. 1).
1896 *Times* (Niagara-on-the-Lake, Ont.) 27 Feb. 1/4: The Niagaras know every inch of the rink and so know just how to toss the puck around from one end of the rink to the other in order to score. **1965** *Globe and Mail* (Toronto) 5 Jan. 27/1: They meet at the rink, choose sides and ply their skills without a financial charge.
2 See **arena.**
1916 BRIDLE *Sons of Can.* 263: There had been ... none on the scale of this memorable event that packed the old Mutual Street rink.... **1964** *Globe and Mail* (Toronto) 16 Dec. 6/1: This, to a man who helped fill the rinks for nine years.
3 a building in which curling, *q.v.,* is played.
1920 *Beaver* Nov. 21/2: ... get together and join themselves into one large curling association and all curl at one rink. **1960** BLONDAL *Candle* 195: Even the rink, center of all winter life, was closed.

rinkhouse *n.* a small, heated cabin near an outdoor rink, used by persons putting on or taking off skates.
1962 *Kingston Whig-Standard* (Ont.) 27 Dec. 13/3: [He] found one man trying to get a fire going in a rink house on Weller Avenue to warm himself.

rink rat *Slang* a boy or young man who helps with the chores around a hockey rink, often in return for free skating, free admission to hockey games, etc.
1957 *Kingston Whig-Standard* (Ont.) 25 Feb. 11/6: [Headline] Rink Rats, Belles [a hockey team from Belleville] in Post-game Battle. **1964** *Winnipeg Free Press* 19 June 37/3: [Headline] Rink Rat Became Harvard Bookworm **1965** *Victoria Dly Times* 20 July 10/6: I was a rink rat at the Forum [in Vancouver] in the days before the Zamboni (the motorized monster that cleans and resurfaces the ice between periods in hockey games).

rinkside *n.* the space behind the boards surrounding a hockey rink, especially the seats along the boards. Hence, **rinksider,** *n.*
1916 BRIDLE *Sons of Can.* 26: The genial boss ... sits in his fur-lined greatcoat at the rinkside. **1931** *Vancouver Province* 8 Jan. 10/2: Players were spilled in all directions and frequently gave the "rinksiders" evidence of pugilistic prowess.

rip† *n.* See **riffle** (def. 1b).
1903 WHITE *Forest* 89: We ... had weathered the rips of white water to shelter on the other side.... **1909** ROBERTS *Backwoodsman* 60: At last, when the bateau had run a dozen of these noisy "rips," Mandy

Ann grew surfeited with terror and thought to comfort herself.

rip *v.* of water, rush through or over a riffle (def. 1a). See also **rip,** *n.*
1953 LOWER *Voyages* 61: Where the water ripped down past the points too quick for paddling, we had to wade her up.

ripple† *n.* **1** See **riffle** (def. 1a).
1811 (1950) THOMPSON *Journals* 189: ... no strong Rapids but many Ripples. **1827** (1829) MACTAGGART *Three Years* I 153: These rifts, as they are called, otherwise small ripples, continue about a mile. **1933** MERRICK *True North* 121: By the ripple rapid, water has flowed over the snow and made a smooth rink....
2 See **riffle** (def. 1b).
1916 DUNCAN *Billy Topsail* 264: In the gravel-bottomed ripple, the water was too swift, too deep, for an overbalanced boy to regain his feet....

river boot See **caulked boot** (def. 1).
1954 *Proud Procession* 69: Each man got ready a pair of heavy river boots with spikes in the soles ... and sharpened his peavey.

river-boss *n. Lumbering* the logger in charge of a drive (def. 1).
1895 PARKER *Adventurer* 120: [He] was startled and sorry when it turned out that Dugard, the river-boss, was married. **1912** HEENEY *Pickanock* 255: ... the river "boss" and his "gang" ... came with their cant-dogs and pike-poles and cork-shoes.... **1931** CONNOR *Rock and River* 30: "Ah! You have run logs with them. In what capacity?" "I have been a river boss."

riverbottom† *n.* See **interval.**
1912 CONNOR *Corp.Cameron* 373: Raven is just ahead in the woods there alone and the Indian is further back with a bunch of ponies down in the riverbottom. **1963** *Placer Mining B.C.* 7/1: He may also be reworking bars or sections of riverbottom which are only exposed at low water or taking up bedrock which has been made workable by recent weathering.

river cake *Lab.* See **galette.**
1933 MERRICK *True North* 54: The tale unfolds to the accompaniment of a scraped frying pan and a flipped river cake.

river claim† *Placer Mining* See **creek claim.**
1899 *Yukon Midnight Sun* (Dawson) 3 Jan. 1/4: A river claim shall be situated only on one side of the river, and shall not exceed 250 feet in length, measured in the general direction of the river.

river drive *Lumbering* See **drive,** *n.* (def. 1).
1920 *Rod and Gun in Can.* Nov. 646/1: ... we were enjoying the sights we saw along the line: the lakes, rivers, the river-drives ... also the logs in the rivers. **1963** MORTON *Kingdom of Can.* 221: In New Brunswick ... developed the river drive of the squared timber and the masts.... **1964** *Cdn Geog.Jnl* Feb. 72/2: In remote areas along the Petawawa ... the colourful river drive is as much a part of the 1960's as it was of the 1860's.

river-driver *n. Lumbering* See **driver** (def. 1).
1853 *Anglo-American Mag.* II 180/2: A few blows ... with the axe ... the log snaps in an instant ... and ere

our bold river-driver is jerked half-way to the top of the cliff, scores of logs . . . rush beneath his feet. . . . **1963** *Canada Month* Nov. 22/1: The lumber trade furnished employment for thousands of lumber jacks, river drivers, and sailors.

river-driving *n. Lumbering* See **driving** (def. 1).
1913 PARKER *Money Master* 187: It was a river-driving and lumber case for which many witnesses had been called. . . . **1948** *Ont.Timberworker* 30 May 6/5: In the Summer months concrete "aprons" could be constructed at the worst of these bad spots, and other improvements made, that would make river driving a safer and easier task.

river flat(s)† See **bottom.**
1908 MAIR *Mackenzie Basin* 84: Descending a very long and crooked ravine, we reached the river flat at last. . . . **1933** *Beaver* Sep. 37/2: . . . *S.S.Saskatchewan,* a river steamboat greatly addicted to sticking on river flats. . . .

river foreman *Lumbering, Obs.* See **raft foreman.**
1945 CALVIN *Saga* 75: A letter [came] to Quebec office, from the first of the river foremen. . . .

river-hog *n. Lumbering* See **driver** (def. 1).
1953 MOON *Saskatchewan* 215: All winter they had been reaping the timber harvest and the most colourful of them, the river hogs, steered the logs . . . into the main stream of the North Saskatchewan when the breakup came. **1956** KEMP *Northern Trader* 114: But he seemed a friendly sort of river-hog, for he was grinning affably. **1964** *Outdoorsman* Dec. 1/2: One may see a visitor with a misty look in his eye; an old blacksmith, top loader, barn boss, teamster, cookie or river hog who has returned to a fleeting glimpse of an era long gone by.

river landing *Lumbering* See **ice-landing.**
1955 *Bush News* (Port Arthur, Ont.) Feb. 7/3: . . . hauling is going along nicely and about two-thirds of the wood has been hauled to river landings.

river lot 1 a lot fronting on a river.
1780 *Quebec Gaz.* 27 Apr. 3/1: To be Sold by Auction . . . a River lot situate in the Lower-town of Quebec in St. Peter's Street. **1882** *Prince Albert Times* (Sask.) 8 Nov. 6/1: It is to be hoped that the government will carry out the same policy here, in the North West, as has been established in Manitoba, with regard to river lots.

2 See **ribbon farm.**
1900 OSBORN *Greater Can.* 146: The long "river-lots" [were] newly clad in a silken wind-blown vesture of green. . . . **1963** STANLEY *Louis Riel* 3: Peter began the first surveys [on the Red River], dividing the land into narrow river lots, as in the old province of Quebec.

riverman *n.* **1** a man who spends much of his life working on a river as a boatman, canoeman, etc. and is therefore knowledgeable about its ways.
1912 FOOTNER *New Rivers* 45: The paddles supplied with our boat were an insult to a riverman, and the little camp-stools on which we were supposed to sit were not only useless, but positively dangerous in broken water. **1966** *Globe and Mail* (Toronto) 18 July 15/8: The plaque on the memorial will read: "In memory of Tom Parris—riverman, woodsman, natural philosopher and friend of the people of Oxtongue Lake."

2 *Lumbering* See **driver** (def. 1).

1903 WHITE *Forest* 136: . . . a riverman and spiked boot and a saw-log can do more work than an ordinary man with a rowboat. **1966** *Kingston Whig-Standard* (Ont.) 2 June 38: [Caption] Rivermen keep the flow of logs moving downstream during logging drive down the Loup river north of Joliette, Que.

3 *Lab.* a man who lives along a river, trapping, fishing, etc.
1933 MERRICK *True North* 115: The old rivermen always wash their hands before they mix bread. . . .

river pointer *Lumbering* See **pointer** (def. 1 and picture).
1952 WILSON *Chibougamau* 44: River pointers and barges would be too slow and unwieldy in the sudden squalls and gales that sweep the Chibougamau region.

river rat† *Lumbering, Slang* See **driver** (def. 1).
1917 (1942) *Highroads to Reading* 345:
> So leap away you river rats,
> From landin' down to sluice;
> There's logs to run, there's peavey fun
> To break the timber loose.

river road See **ice-road** (def. 2).
1829 MACTAGGART *Three Years* II 202: When the snow falls deep, before the ice has had time to freeze to any considerable thickness, the river roads remain dangerous all the season; because after they have got their covering of snow, say three feet deep, the ice below cannot continue to thicken by the frost. **1955** COLLARD *Cdn Yesterdays* 302: Some experienced travellers on the river-roads even carried "choke-ropes."

river sense See quote. Cp. **read.**
1928 FREEMAN *Nearing North* 50: They navigate simply by that product of instinct, memory and experience called river sense.

R.M. *West* See **rural municipality.**
1958 *Progress* 28 May 5/2: Notice is hereby given that the Assessment Roll of the R.M. of Hazel Dell No. 335, for the year 1958 has been prepared and is now open to inspection. . . . **1964** *Naicam Sentinel* 26 Mar. 2/3: A meeting of the council of the Rural Municipality of Pleasantdale No. 398 was held in the R.M. office . . . .

R.M.C. Royal Military College.
1947 DUMBRILLE *Deep Doorways* 132: Matthew was crazy; he could have finished at R.M.C. and amounted to something. **1963** *Kingston Whig-Standard* (Ont.) 7 Mar. 10/1: Dates were arranged for all 98 RMC cadets by a special office at the academy. . . .

R.N.W.M.P. *Hist.* See **Royal North West Mounted Police.**
1904 *Eye Opener* (Calgary) 4 Aug. 1/3: In applying for a batch of R.N.W.M.P. he did so in the expectation that they would succeed in affecting a capture of the men who had become a menace to his railroad. **1955** MCCOWAN *Upland Trails* 6: Calgary [was] so named by Colonel James Farquharson Macleod of the R.N.W.M.P. in 1876. . . .

roach (knife) [rotʃ] *n.* [< *roach-bellied* < *roach* a variety of carp having a curved back] *Fur Trade, Hist.* a kind of knife the blade of which folded into a curved handle. See also **Rochbury.**
☛ *Although the earliest available references appear as* **Rochberry, Rochbary,** *and* **Rochbury knife,** *the term* **Roach-belly'd knives** *also appears very early. Only* **roach knife** *appears after the 17th century. Since* **Rochbury** *does not appear to have been a place name, the given etymology seems most likely.*

[**1683** (1946) *H.B.C.Minutes* III 171: Ordered that Mr.
Sam Banner provide . . . 1000 Rochbury large Ditto. . . .
[Fn] (1946) In A.6/3, fo.42d., there is a reference to
these knives as "Roach belly'd knives," a name
presumably descriptive of their shape.] **1728** (1965)
Letters from Hudson Bay 137: Likewise send us no small
long knives nor small roach knives . . . they being so
weak that the natives does not care for trading
them. . . . **1825** (1954) PATTERSON *Dangerous River*
162n: . . . the 1825 invoice of goods sent to York
Factory [lists] scalping and roach knives. . . . **1829** *Ft
Langley Jnl* 12 Aug.: 8½ doz. Roach Knives.

road allowance 1 a strip of land between surveyed
concessions, ranges, sections, etc., retained by the
municipality for the construction of a road. See
also **right-of-way** (def. 2).
[**1822** GOURLAY *Upper Canada* I 122: The allowance
for the front road was generally 60 feet and for the
other concession roads 40 feet.] **1844** *Niagara Chron.*
(Niagara-on-the-Lake, C.W.) 29 May 2/2: A bill was
introduced . . . entitled "An act to close up the Road
Allowance between Lots Nos. 42 and 43 . . . in the
township of Cayuga. . . ." **1882** *What Farmers Say* 12:
The whole country is divided into townships containing
36 sections of one mile square, or 640 acres in each
section, together with road allowance of . . . 116 feet
in width between all townships and sections.
1930 BEAMES *Army* 185: There were, of course the road
allowances, but these had been laid out geometrically
in straight lines that took no account of hills and
swamps. **1965** *Maclean's* 3 July 26/3: In rare cases . . .
the trail has been routed along unused, overgrown, road
allowances. . . .

2 See quote.
1958 *Edmonton Jnl* 14 Aug. 23/2: . . . they were in the
habit of assuming that the beautifully kept property
was crown land, and they camped, and roamed far
inland from the legal road allowance, as it is called,
along the shore. . . .

road ban *Esp.Prairies* a temporary prohibition
against making use of unpaved roads during the
wet period in spring. Also **ban**.
1957 *Melville Advance* 17 Apr. 5/4: Road bans were
placed on the following provincial highways. . . .
1958 *Cut Knife Grinder* (Sask.) 17 Apr. 7/5: The roads
are nicely dried up in the district, the ban is lifted and
farmers, generally, are getting seed and machinery
ready for a start on the land in the next few days.

road camp 1 a camp for accommodating men
engaged in building roads.
1889 *Rat Portage* [Kenora] *News* (Ont.) 30 Aug. 2/1:
The Government Rainy River Road Camp recently
removed from near the mouth of the river back to near
Fotherham & McQuarrie's mill, and they are now
setting a road from this point to Grassy river. **1962** FRY
Ranch on the Cariboo 148: I might even find a meal at
the road-camp cookhouse. . . . **1964** *Globe and Mail*
(Toronto) 17 Nov. 31/8: . . . a gang in a road camp went
down to the lake in the dead of winter, cut a hole in the
ice and dunked the unfortunate cook several times.

2 *Lumbering* See quote.
1964 *Powell River News* 7 May 3/4: Today, many
of the larger operations are what the logger refers to as
"road camps"—not only is there no bunkhouse, but
no cook-house either. The modern logger employed in
a road camp leaves home each morning and returns to
his family every night.

road cheque a cheque issued by the Department
of Highways for work done on roads and trails.

1963 PATTERSON *Far Pastures* 15: I rode out of town the
evening of train day with my share of the road cheque
in my pocket.

road commissioner *Hist.* See **roadmaster** (def. 1).
1825 *Novascotian* (Halifax) 5 Jan. 4/1: The Hammond's
Plain gentry had better look out, be more obedient to
the road commissioner, and take care to perform their
labour according to law; or else The bailiff will come
with a gang at his tail, and t'will be Down with your
dust, Sir; and d— you, to jail. **1858** *Brit.Colonist*
(Victoria) 11 Dec. 3/3: Mr. McKay was in favor of
road commissioners. **1908** CLARKE *Sixty Years* 99:
I . . . had previously served as pathmaster or road
commissioner, as it was then entitled. . . .

road company *Hist.* in Upper Canada, a private
company which undertook the building of roads
for the government.
1849 *Wkly Globe* 7 Dec. 93/5: The Act of last session
regarding the formation of Road Companies, begins to
bear fruit. **1850** *Watchman* (Port Hope, C.W.) 12 Dec.
2/3: Another Road Company has been formed which
has determined upon extending and completing the
Plank Road to the boundaries of the Townships of
Clarke and Cavanagh.

road-cutter *n. Lumbering, Hist.* See **swamper**
(def. 1).
1854 KEEFER *Ottawa* 64: A cheaper class of men,
generally the "greenhorns," are employed as road
cutters. **1896** GOURLAY *Hist.Ottawa* 90: . . . how
delightful is that operation, to a fellow that began his
career as a cook or road cutter in a shanty. . . .
1961 PRICE & KENNEDY *Renfrew* 48: Each gang working
together in the wood—logmakers, road cutters . . .
—took a lunch in a cotton bag.

road district *N.S.* a district in which roads come
under local control.
1829 (1830) MOORSOM *Letters N.S.* 241: Personal labour,
for a certain number of days annually, is obligatory
on the inhabitants of every road-district, for each of
which a surveyor is appointed, who superintends the
execution, and receives the composition of the more
wealthy.

road donkey *Lumbering* See **roader**.
1943 SWANSON *Lumberjack* 56: . . . some genius [about
1900] invented the road donkey or roader. This
contraption was a steam engine with a vertical boiler,
the engine being geared to a set of big drums on which
could be wound a mile or more of one-inch cable,
thereby pulling the logs along the now heavier and
better-built skid roads in long strings dogged together.
1953 SWANSON *Haywire Hooker* 71: [Caption] Here is
shown a road donkey making up a turn for the locie.

roader ['rodɚ] *n.* [< *(skid) road* + *-er*] *Lumbering*
a donkey engine having a very long cable on a
drum, used for skidding logs out of the bush. See
also **road donkey**.
1919 *Camp Worker* 2 June 3/3: [There were] Two . . .
skidders, one yarder, one swing, one ground swing
and one roader, and not very high ball. **1958** HEALEY
Alert Bay 34: A small outfit consists of two or three
donkey engines; one, a roader, and one or two yarders.

road grader a vehicle equipped with a heavy
blade, used for maintaining unpaved roads and,

often, for snow-ploughing. See also **patrol** and **road patrol.**

1899 *Medicine Hat News* (Alta) 25 May 1/4: The road grader is at work this week and is turning up the streets in great shape. **1966** *Western Producer* 24 Nov. 23/4: [Advert.] WANT—SNOW WING FOR ROAD GRADER. Geo. Shave, Breton, Alta.

road hockey a form of hockey played on a road or street by children using hockey sticks and, usually, a ball. See also **shinny** (def. 1b) and **street hockey.**

1965 *Kingston Whig-Standard* (Ont.) 28 Dec. 24: [Caption] Road hockey was back in style Monday as these youngsters proved in a rough game played in Portsmouth during the afternoon. **1966** *Ibid.* 16 Apr. 6/1: . . . local youngsters on their Easter vacation have been taking advantage of the warm weather to play road hockey.

roadhouse *n. West and Northwest, Hist.* a rest house or lodge, often of simple character, used by wayfarers. See also **road ranche, stopping-house,** and **way-house.**

1909 SERVICE *Cheechako* 32: In their road-house down by the river-trail they waited and watched for prey. . . . **1922** PRINGLE *Tillicums* 71: The roadhouse was a low, log building about fifty feet long and twenty wide. **1936** ARMSTRONG *Yukon Yesterdays* 33: Every few miles we stopped at a road-house where food of sorts and liquor were disposed of at high prices. **1962** FRITH *Lost Stagecoach* 13: My ranch house used to be a stopping place or roadhouse for this stagecoach.

road inspector *Hist.* See **roadmaster** (def. 1).

1817 *Montreal Herald* 25 Jan. 3/1: It is therefore the duty of the road inspector, immediately to order the lumber to be removed from the King's high-way. . . . **1863** *Nor'Wester* (R.R.S.) 14 Oct. 1/3: What would the Candians think of our system, under which Councillors are also Judges, . . . Road Inspectors, &c.

road-maker *n. Lumbering, Hist.* See **swamper** (def. 1).

1891 OXLEY *Chore-Boy* 50: . . . he would much rather be a chopper, or teamster, or road maker. . . . **1961** PRICE & KENNEDY *Renfrew* 50: The head-swamper or road-maker extended the roads into the forest as work progressed so teamsters could haul back to the roll-way.

roadmaster *n.* **1** an elected municipal official responsible for public roads, paths, bridges, etc. See also **pathmaster, road commissioner,** and **road inspector.**

1825 *Kingston Chron.* (U.C.) 7 Jan. 3/3: Bulls and Oxen to run at large—Fences 5 feet high. Road Masters to be Judges of Fences. **1865** *Nor'Wester* (R.R.S.) 13 May 2/2: We had occasion to notice, on a recent visit to the lower part of the Settlement, two broken bridges, and upon informing the road-master, we received an explanation of the cause in the one case, and a promise of immediate attention to the other. **1924** BLAKE *Chez Nous* 51: He is not over-considerate, is the roadmaster; he puts you to no end of trouble for a trifle of a drift; and there are pitch-holes opposite his own place, too.

2† a person in charge of the maintenance of the track in a division of a railway.

1883 *Brandon Dly Mail* (Man.) 20 Feb. 2/1: Last autum Supt. Egan, instructed all road-masters to have section men all along the line construct snow fences running parallel with the track. . . . **1966** *Kingston Whig-Standard* (Ont.) 1 Sep. 3/2: The roadmaster came down on his track speeder and gave us a fatherly talking to.

road patrol *West* See **road grader.**

1958 *Cut Knife Grinder* (Sask.) 3 Apr. 1/6: In the Rural Municipality of Cut Knife, the burgesses were asked to vote upon Bylaw 12 authorizing the Council to purchase a new road patrol. . . .

road ranche *West, Obs.* See **roadhouse.** See also **ranch²** (def. 2b).

1902 *Eye Opener* (High River, Alta) 11 July 1/2: Find yourself somewhere out in the West at a lonesome "road ranche" and want to hire a team of horses to continue the journey. . . .

road-scraper *n.* See **scraper.**

1853 STRICKLAND *Canada West* I 308n: [The road] has been ploughed on each side, and the earth, so raised, thrown up in the centre by the means of a road-scraper or turnpike shovel, worked either with horses or oxen.

roaring game† *Orig.Scottish* See **curling.**

☞ *First recorded as* **roaring-play** *(Robert Burns, 1786), the game was so called from the hollow, rumbling noise made by a curling stone (formerly made of iron) sliding over an outdoor rink of natural ice on a pond, river, etc. Since little noise is made by a modern granite stone on an indoor rink of artificial ice, the name is often erroneously associated with noise made by the players, for example the instructions shouted by the skip to the sweepers.*

1864 (1964) GUILLET *Pioneer Days* 212: . . . although the day turned out one of the most severe that we have had this winter, the "roarin' game" was kept up with much spirit. . . . **1882** *Prince Albert Times* (Sask.) 20 Dec. 6/1: Two rinks have been cleared of snow, opposite Mr. Johnston's store, and every fine day the knights of the broom may be seen enjoying themselves in mysteries of the "roarin game." **1962** *Canada Month* Apr. 26/2: . . . it at least indicates the tremendous (and growing) enthusiasm for the "Roarin' Game" right across Canada.

robaboo *n.* See **rubaboo.**

robe *n.* [< Cdn F < F "ankle-length garment"] **1** *Fur Trade, Hist.* **a.** See **beaver coat.**

☞ *In early use, the term* **robe** *was current among the Montreal traders, a borrowing from the French Canadians, the Hudson's Bay Company usage being* **coat, blanket,** *etc.*

1794 (1929) MCGILLIVRAY *Journal* 42: They bestow the best part of the Lodge covered with clean robes on a Stranger. **1801** (1933) MCLEOD *Diary* 169: A band of Stone Indians came here. they seem to have a few, very few Robes, or wolves. . . . **1965** *Canadian Wkly* 19 Mar. 9/2: Natural wear and tear on the skin side of these [beaver] robes soon loosened the roots of the long guard hairs on the fur and they dropped out.

b. See 1848 quote. See also **buffalo robe.**

1825 (1935) *Trans.Roy.Soc.Can.* III 2 176: Buffalo tongues, 9d. each; prime robes, 5s. each. . . . **1848** (1859) BALLANTYNE *Hudson's Bay* 36: The hide of the bison,—or as it is called by the fur traders, the buffalo—when dressed on one side and the hair left on the other, is called a robe. Great numbers are sent to Canada, where they are used for sleigh wrappers in winter. In the Indian country they are often used instead of blankets. **1860** *Nor'Wester* (R.R.S.) 28 Sep. 3/1: I find that she has brought down over 200 tons of goods of every kind, and returned with 50 tons—mostly robes. **1873** (1904) BUTLER *Wild North Land* 59: Not less than 30,000 robes had already found their way to the Red River, and fully as many more in skins of parchment or in leather had been traded or consumed in the thousand wants of savage life. **1934** *Cdn Hist. Rev.* XV 10: There never was any progressive "extermination" in Canada for robes alone, in the way that there was in the United States.

2 similarly prepared hides or pelts of other animals, especially when used as a wrap or covering.
1897 TYRRELL *Sub-Arctics* 123: I produced a telescope, a jack-knife, and an old shirt, and offered them for the three remaining [muskox] robes. **1904** ROBERTS *Watchers of Trails* 352: ... and over the broad, low seat were blankets with one heavy bearskin robe. **1934** BETTANY *Valley of Lost Gold* 40: ... with a team and cutter, fur robes, hot stones at her feet ... their continued journey had been warm and comfortable by comparison.

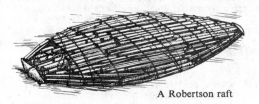

A Robertson raft

Robertson raft *Lumbering, Hist.* a huge, cigar-shaped raft of as many as 22,000 logs, devised by Hugh Robertson of Saint John, N.B., in 1886 and in use for several decades in the lumbering industry for transporting logs in the Atlantic and Pacific.
1965 *Canadian Wkly* 2 Jan. 15/3: [Caption] This Robertson raft on the Columbia river was so long only half of it was shown in stereoscopic picture taken in 1902. *Ibid.*: [Caption] The raft in the photograph below was a Robertson raft built in 1902. ...

robidoo *n.* See **rubaboo.**

robin† *n.* a large red-breasted thrush, *Turdus migratorius,* native to North America. Also *robin red-breast.*
[**1620** MASON *Briefe Discovrse* Aivᵛ: Their particulars too tedious to relate, all good meate ... black birds with redd breastes....] **1778** (1792) CARTWRIGHT *Journal* II 335: ... one of [the traps] had a robin red-breast in it. **1779** *Ibid.* 454: I shot a loon, took a duck's nest ... and found a robin's nest. **1909** CAMERON *New North* 68: For instance, little Robin Red-Breast ... has successively lived through three tags, "Turdus migratorius," "Planesticus migratorius," "Turdus canadensis." **1934** BETTANY *Valley of Lost Gold* 44: "In spring-time, these bushes will be covered with marsh blackbirds—you'll see. Plenty of meadow larks and robins, too." **1966** *Vancouver Province* 19 Nov. 1/5: Drury said the robin had been sitting in a mountain ash tree in his front yard for over a month before being rescued.

Robin Nodwell *Trademark* a wide-tracked vehicle for use in rough roadless areas, manufactured by the Robin-Nodwell Manufacturing Co. in Calgary, Alberta. See also **Nodwell.**
1963 *Kingston Whig-Standard* (Ont.) 13 Feb. 21/1: Robin Nodwell [RN-110] sounds like the name of a

movie star. It is not a Hollywood actor, but a tracked carrier which turns in a stellar performance as it chews its way through mud and snow. The vehicle consists of a passenger cab on top of two 40-inch-wide treads. It has a speed of 15 miles per hour, can carry up to five-and-one-half tons of cargo, and can climb grades up to 60 per cent.

robin redbreast See **robin.**

robin run See quote.
1923 WILLIAMS *Spinning Wheels* 83: [Maple] Syrup and sugar made from the first or "robin run" are superior to that found in either of the succeeding runs, known respectively as the "frog" and "bud."

robin snow (or **storm)**† a late snowstorm, coming at about the time the robins, heralds of spring, are due to return. See also **smelt storm.**
1947 ROWLANDS *Cache Lake* 109: Once in a while we have a snow flurry [in May]—"robin snow," we call it. **1955** *Hants Journal* 9 Mar. 1/5: Others call it the "Robin Storm," presumably on the theory that the ... robins [sneak up] into the trees, under the cover of the snow.

Rochbury (knife) *n. Fur Trade, Obs.* See **roach** and note. Also spelled *Rochberry, Rochbary.*
1682 (1946) *H.B.C.Minutes* 2 Dec. 53: 734 Rochberry Knives £6 12*s* 6*d.* **1683** (1946) *Ibid.* 7 Dec. 172: And have Agreed wth. him for the prices following ... Rochbury large 2*s.* 8*d.* p. Doz. Ditto Small 22*d.* p. Do. **1684** (1946) *Ibid.* 29 Apr. 297: [Invoice of goods] 500 large Rochbary knives S.B. 500 ditto small. **1684** (1957) *Beaver* Winter 17/1: Some idea of the amount of trading that went on in the earliest years may be derived from studying the outfit for 1684. In that year there were received at York Fort the following: ... 3000 jack-knives 3000 large "Rochbury" knives 2000 small knives. ...

rock *n.* the stone used in curling, *q.v.*
1911 KNOWLES *Singer* 296: Every man of them held his breath as the flying rock came to the port. **1965** *Globe and Mail* (Toronto) 5 Jan. 27/9: Mrs. Salter forced an extra end by counting a two on the eight end as she made a takeout and stayed with her final rock.

rock (out) *v. Placer Mining* wash gravel with a rocker, *q.v.*
1870 *Mainland Guardian* (New Westminster, B.C.) 2 Apr 1/3: The only mining done was by Sylvester and Black, who had panned and rocked about $40 from the edge of the Discovery ground. **1898** *Klondyke Miner* (Dawson, Y.T.) 1 Oct. 3/1: The layman on a Rich Hill claim is rocking out the refused dirt of last year's lay and is making $100 a day. **1937** ANDREWS *Wrangell* 37: Four miners from up on the Stikine came down with $500 each rocked out on the bars.

rock-bottom sluice-box *Placer Mining* See quote. See also **sluice-box** and picture.
1964 *Dly Colonist* (Victoria) 5 July Mag.sec. 3/3: [Hiram F.] Smith ... is credited with originating the "rock bottom" sluice box, a great aid in the recovery of fine gold.

rock chuck See **yellow-bellied marmot.**
1963 *Sun* (Vancouver) 20 June 25/1: On the Interior beat, two of my cronies and I flyfished our best lick, on Salmon Lake last weekend after mornings of rock 'chuck (marmot) hunting.

rock doctor *Mining, Slang* a geologist.
1952 KNOTT *Harnessing* 2/2: Then the Indian brought back the rock doctor a sample of iron ore of extremely high grade and led him to the place in Ungava where he had found it. **1964** CRATE *Hardrock Mining* 5: Another "doctor" is the rock-doctor, a term originally applied to a geologist holding a doctor's degree, but now generally applied to all geologists.

rock elm a tree, *Ulmus thomasi,* of eastern Canada; also, the tough wood of this tree.
1830 *Trans.Lit.& Hist.Soc.Que.* III 84: The timber of this variety . . . is known by the name of Rock Elm. **1952** PUTNAM *Cdn Regions* 138/2: Rare species in the upper St. Lawrence are basswood and rock elm. **1955** *Bush News* (Port Arthur, Ont.) Feb. 3/5: Southern Ontario . . . is sending . . . rock elm timbers to Britain. . . .

rocker[1]† *n. Placer Mining* a contrivance used to separate gold from gravel. See also **cradle-rocker, rock,** *v.,* and **rocking.**
1859 *Brit.Colonist* (Victoria) 8 Jan. 2/2: I saw the product of many of the rockers, and found that the daily yield to each rocker was from ten dollars to two ounces; in some instances a much larger yield. **1927** MCKELVIE *Black Canyon* 105: Each night the rockers were "cleaned up" and the gold was collected, the finer particles being separated from the metallic black sands by the use of mercury. **1965** *Cdn Geog.Jnl* Dec. 206/2: [Caption] A rocker set up to rework old tailings at Cedar Creek.

rocker[2] *n. North* See **rock ptarmigan.**
1883 *Trans.Roy.Soc.Can.* I 4 52: It is the rocker and not the willow bird which has the slender beak. **1942** TWOMEY & HERRICK *Needle to North* 149: The rattling cry of the rockers echoed from the encircling tundra plateaus above us and from the sloping hillsides.

rockerthon *n.* [a blend of *rocker* rocking chair + mara*thon*] *Esp.Que.* a competition to see who can rock longest in a rocking chair.
1955 *Western Star* (Corner Brook, Nfld) 10 Mar. 10/4: Just like the rockerthon mania in some parts of Quebec, the sizzling race for the National Hockey League scoring championship . . . has the Montreal fans in a sweat. . . .

rock grouse *Obs.* See **rock ptarmigan.**
1823 FRANKLIN *Journey* 682: Captain Sabine has distinguished the Rock Grouse from the Ptarmigan as a distinct species. **1853** REID *Young Voyageurs* 427: The habits of the "rock" and "willow" grouse are very similar. **1959** MCATEE *Folk-Names* 25: Rock Ptarmigan [is also called] rock grouse ("Hudson Bay"). . . .

rock-hog *n. Mining, Slang* a tunnel-worker; tunneller; also, sometimes, a driller. See also **rock worm.**
1935 MOWERY *Resurrection River* 261: "You've been awful durned good to us rock-hogs." **1954** LYSENKO *Yellow Boots* 190: They spoke of dynamite and flying rock responsible for the death of many a "rock-hog."

rocking *n. Placer Mining* the practice of using a rocker, *q.v.*
1859 *Brit.Colonist* (Victoria) 3 Apr. 2/1: In proof of the latter the lowest sum named by any miner as the product of a day's rocking is three to five dollars, for nearly two hundred miles along Fraser river. **1900** *Prospector* (Lillooet, B.C.) 21 Dec. 4/2: There are quite a few Chinamen all along the river who make a few dollars rocking. **1936** ARMSTRONG *Yukon Yesterdays* 71: We could always get enough water to operate two or three "rockers" but when our claims were being worked on a fairly large scale the rocking system could no longer be economically applied.

rocking-chair money *Slang* See quote.
1959 *Globe and Mail* (Toronto) 22 Apr. 7/1: The somewhat less sophisticated people of the Maritimes have a happier name for Unemployment Insurance . . . "Rockin' Chair Money."

rock maple *Esp.Maritimes* the sugar maple (def. 1); also, the hard wood of this tree.
1774 ROBINSON & RISPIN *Journey N.S.* 34: This town . . . affords a great store of fine timber . . . white and black ash; white mapple; rock mapple (a very fine wood for household furniture). . . . **1832** BAILLIE *Account of N.B.* 46: The rock maple [is] . . . a very hard wood, but not durable in exposed situations. . . . **1954** BRUCE *Channel Shore* 213: Here there were . . . hills clothed with white maple and rock maple. . . . **1957** HUTCHISON *Canada* 51: As we left the shipyard, he was climbing like an aged cat about the framework of oak and rock maple.

rock moss *Hist.* See **rock-tripe.**
1801 MACKENZIE *Voy.from Montreal* cxxvii: Its chief vegetable substance is the moss, on which the deer feed; and a kind of rock moss, which, in times of scarcity, preserves the lives of the natives. **1957** FISHER *Pemmican* 141: He also had tripe-de-roche or rock moss, which some Indians boiled and ate with relish but which David thought tasted exactly like rock moss.

rock partridge *Obs.* See **rock ptarmigan.**
1743 (1949) ISHAM *Observations* 123: Rock partridges is the smallest, and black from the Eye to the bill and white all over else in the winter, Excep't the tail, having 14 black feathers with a Litle white at the End and the Rest which is 14 more all White. **1795** (1911) HEARNE *Journey* 416: Rock Partridges . . . like the Willow Partridge, change their plumage in summer to a beautiful speckled brown; and at that season are so hardy, that, unless shot in the head or vitals, they will fly away with the greatest quantity of shot of any bird I know.

rock pigeon *Obs.* See **passenger pigeon.**
1846 TAYLOR *Narrative* 62: Rock pigeons are sometimes very numerous in Canada.

rock ptarmigan a chubby, partridge-like fowl, *Lagopus rupestris,* of the Barren Grounds. See also **mountain partridge, rocker**[2], **rock grouse, rock partridge,** and **white grouse.**
1882 *Trans.Roy.Soc.Can.* I 4 52: . . . lastly there appears to be only the rocker or rock ptarmigan (*Lagopus rupestris,* Leach). **1883** HATTON & HARVEY *Newfoundland* 234: There is another kind called the rock ptarmigan . . . an Alpine species, inhabiting only the highest and barest mountain ridges, and called the "mountain partridge." **1927** (1937) CHRISTIAN *Unflinching* 66: Jack shot 1 Rock Ptarmigan on ridge by his traps. **1964** *Nat.Geog.* May 715/1: Two species of ptarmigan—the willow and the rock—frequent Banks Island and supplement the Eskimos' diet.

rock rabbit† See **pika.**
1927 PHILIP *Painted Cliff* 69: Rock-rabbits shrilled, darting amongst the rubble. . . . **1962** *Field, Horse &*

Rodeo Nov. 15/3: The Pika (or Rock Rabbit) spends most of the daylight hours cutting and gathering vegetation.

rock rose *B.C.* See 1958 quote.
1950 LYONS *Mighty Fraser* 127: The Rock Rose, Sandhill Rose or Bitterroot (Lewisia rediviva), is also a well-known plant throughout arid regions. . . .
1958 ATKINSON *Hist.of Penticton* 14: . . . the Rock Rose or Bitterroot (*Lewisia Rediviva*) . . . is a low growing plant bearing a single beautiful shell-pink bloom close to the ground, which opens only in the sunlight.
1963 *Beaver* Autumn 53/1: The rolling hills, cactus and rock roses . . . flooded the dry land with character and colour.

rock-tripe *n.* [< Cdn F *tripe de roche*] an edible lichen of the genus, *Umbilicaria* (or, less often, the genus *Gyrophora*), having circular, leathery, gray-to-brownish thalli often attached to certain rocks by a threadlike holdfast. See also **rock moss, rock weed,** and **tripe de roche.**
1853 REID *Young Voyageurs* 384: On reaching the rock, they saw what Norman had meant by the words *tripe de roche* (rock-tripe). It was a black, hard crumply substance that nearly covered the surface of the rock, and was evidently of a vegetable nature.
1944 CLAY *Fur Thieves* 69: Often they speeded past high banks, where the rock-tripe and lichens had been scraped off by voyageurs, leaving their names and dates etched in white against the dark of the remaining vegetation. **1952** MOWAT *People of Deer* 37: Sometimes she scrabbled through the drifts on hilltops and found a few wizened bearberries or a handfull of rock-tripe, a kind of moss.

rock weed See **rock-tripe.**
1793 (1933) MACDONELL *Diary* 85: These figures are made by scratching the Rock weed (moss) off the Rocks with the Point of a knife or some other instrument.
1821 (1938) SIMPSON *Athabasca Jnl* 319: Our people . . . for three days past have subsisted chiefly on rock weed.
1915 SPECK *Myths* 15n: The "rock weed," *wakwund* (rock tripe) is often eaten in the bush when other foods fail. It is scraped off the rocks with a flat stick into a blanket, then washed and boiled and eaten. The water becomes a little slimy, but it makes a nourishing soup.

rock whistler *Obs.* See **hoary marmot.**
1866 LORD *Naturalist* II 195: A dinner off roasted rock-whistler, washed down with a pull at the crystal stream, is a repast not to be despised.

rock woodchuck See **yellow-bellied marmot.**

rock worm *Mining, Slang* See **rock-hog.**
1918 COPELAND *Swinging Lanterns* 101: Vein sampling engineers, grubstakers, rock-worms, mine captains, prospectors and agents in coats of "astrachan goose" . . . strut about and add to their kit, each man jack of them probably thinking he has a "nose for ore" and inside information.

Rocky Mountain bean *Obs.* See quote.
1851 JOHNSTON *Notes* I 268: Among the horticultural productions there were two which were new to me. One was the Rocky Mountain bean which had pods from 12 to 18 inches in length, growing in pairs, and about the thickness of a common French bean. The seed has the appearance of a small kidney-bean.

Rocky Mountain bighorn See **Rocky Mountain sheep.**
1915 (1916) *Commission of Conservation* 101: The first animal in importance, from the sportsman's viewpoint, is the Rocky Mountain big-horn. **1964** *Calgary Herald* 9 July 5/2: He climbed to the top of our present Sheep

Mountain . . . where he found a large Rocky Mountain bighorn ram. . . .

Rocky Mountain deadshot *B.C., Slang* a pancake.
1921 LAUT *Cariboo Trail* 105: The fare consisted of ham . . . slapjacks, known as 'Rocky Mountain dead shot,' in maple syrup that never saw a maple tree and was black as a pot. . . . **1950** HUTCHISON *Fraser* 85: On the stagecoach route you started from Yale at dawn after a breakfast of ham, eggs and flapjacks known, for their digestive properties, as "Rocky Mountain deadshot."

Rocky Mountain dew *West, Slang* whisky.
1962 *Alta Hist.Rev.* Summer 10/1: "What! No Rocky Mountain Dew, no Old Alky, or to give you the straight tip, seein' you're a pilgrim, none of the Old Creatur, eh?"

Rocky Mountain feathers *B.C., Slang* See quote.
1962 *Maclean's* 18 July 44/2: It was a windless and comfortable twenty below as I started a fire with a handful of "Rocky Mountain feathers"—dry shavings —made that morning before we left our previous camp.

Rocky Mountain fever *West* See quotes. See also **mountain fever.** Also *Rocky Mountain spotted fever.*
1889 DONKIN *Trooper* 41: In fact it is the typho-malarial scourge known as Red River fever in Manitoba, jungle fever in India . . . and Rocky Mountain fever in British Columbia. **1965** *Winnipeg Tribune* 12 June 10/8: Ticks in Manitoba and northwestern Ontario do not carry fearsome diseases, such as Rocky Mountain spotted fever which is carried by ticks in the western areas.

Rocky Mountain goat a goatlike mammal, *Oreamnos montanus,* found in the western mountains and related to the European chamois. See also **goat** (def. 1b), **mountain goat, white sheep** (def. 1), and **wild goat** (def. 2).
1888 (1890) ST. MAUR *Impressions* 55: Upon the grass slopes of Castle Mountain, which stood high above us, are sometimes to be seen the Rocky Mountain goat.
1958 *Beaver* Spring 28/1: Upon the trapper in the frozen silence of the north the Dall sheep and the Rocky Mountain goat look down. . . .

Rocky Mountain mutton *Obs.* the meat of the Rocky Mountain sheep, *q.v.*
1824 (1955) BLACK *Journal* 144: The Old Slave arrived with a load of Rocky Mountain mutton on his back which proves good but not bulky, but he says its an Askayis i.e. a young one but at any time this kind of meat neither resembles the Scotch or the English mutton in appearance Taste or flavor, it more resembles Beef.

Rocky Mountain sheep a sheep, *Ovis canadensis,* found in the western mountains. See also **argali, bighorn sheep, Rocky Mountain bighorn,** and **sheep.**
[**1794** (1911) SIMCOE *Diary* 243: There are a kind of large sheep on the Rocky Mountains, their horns the size of a cow's.] **1821** (1900) GARRY *Diary* 203: 1 Horn, Rocky Mountain Sheep. **1892** (1908) DAWSON & SUTHERLAND *Geography* 30: Of mammals found in Canada which are not known elsewhere in the world

except to the southward in the same Nearctic region . . . the following may be mentioned: Rocky Mountain goat, Bighorn, or Rocky Mountain sheep. . . .
1964 *Calgary Herald* 5 May 32/3: Waterton Lakes National Parks officials have weighed, measured and marked 30 Rocky Mountain and Bighorn sheep this spring. . . .

Rocky Mountain spotted fever See **Rocky Mountain fever.**

rodeo† ['rodɪo] *n.* [< Am.E < Sp. "round up"] See **stampede,** *n.* (def. 2).
1922 STRINGER *Prairie Child* 112: And with them they brought a quartet of rampageous young buckaroos who promptly turned our sedate homestead into a rodeo. **1962** *Canada Month* May 38/1: Riding and roping competitions had been held at various territorial expositions throughout the West but it wasn't until 1912 that rodeo competition became a specialized commercial venture.

rodney ['rɑdnɪ] *n.* [origin obscure; cf. Brit.dial. "something small, inferior, or mean"] *Nfld* a small, open type of fishing boat that sometimes carries a sail.
1916 DUNCAN *Billy Topsail* 155: And 'twas for Tom West's little rodney that the seven last men o' Ragged Run was jumpin'. **1930** SMALLWOOD *Newfoundland* 266: Often he'd take us to sail in his rodney,/Out over the water. . . .

rogan ['rogən] *n.* [< Cdn F (*h*)*ouragan* < Algonk.; cf. Ojibwa *onagan* bowl] See 1923 quote. See also **birchbark rogan** and **birch rogan.** Cp. **mocock.**
[**1693** (1955) *Beaver* Spring 13/2: 20 livres de sucre et des petits houragans.] **1743** (1949) ISHAM *Observations* 188: A Roggan. Slawee. **1791** FIDLER *Journal* 523: We are obliged to roast all & make water by immersing red hot stones into a roggan of Snow. . . . **1820** (1963) DAVIES *Northern Quebec* 57: He had a wooden roggin which would hold about five gallons. **1887** *Senate Journal* XXI App. 142: At Fairford and the Little Saskatchewan . . . the Indians dry the whitefish by the fire and then pound it to pieces, and then put it into birch rogans, to keep for the winter use as food. **1923** WALDO *Down Mackenzie* 76: There were rogans— small bowls or buckets—of birch-bark, water-tight, pitched with spruce gum and sewed with spruce roots, the workmanship as delicate as in a fine Panama hat. **1957** *Beaver* Winter 27/2: [Caption] The bark rogan at bottom right bears the artist's signature, "P. Rindisbacher."

roll *v.* **1** place tobacco into a small rectangle of paper and make a cigarette by rolling the paper round the tobacco with a deft motion of the fingers and thumbs. See also **rollings, twist,** *v.,* and **twisting.**
1892 (1896) PARKER *Pierre* 129: He slowly rolled a cigarette and replied: "He says it's a scandal that I live at Fort Anne." **1960** MCNAMEE *Florencia Bay* 59: "Looks sixty. Thin face. Dark. Looks a little Indian but not our kind of Indian. Rolls his own. . . ."

2 roll one's blanket (or **bundle**), *Lumbering, Slang* quit the job.
1953 SWANSON *Haywire Hooker* 34:

Rolled my bundle, hiking down the trail,
When—Through the night came a donkey's wail,
'Twas the crew, out yarding, crazy as a loon
And they logged another million by the silvery moon.
1956 ANDREWS *Glory Days* 43: [If] he didn't like the donkey puncher . . . he would roll his blanket and head for town.

roller *n. Lumbering* a logger who piles logs on a skidway (def. 2a), so called because the logs are then rolled up.
1942 KOROLEFF *Skidding of Wood* 18: [Caption] Roller is piling wood with a "jack". . . .

rollie *n. Slang* a cigarette rolled by hand. See also **roll,** *v.* (def. 1).
1963 *Ubyssey* 11 Oct. 5/1: Wrapped in the top-quality cigarette paper of good photography and production, the cigarette is nevertheless un-disguisable. It's a "rollie" using dung for tobacco.

rolling prairie† a stretch of undulating plains, as in parts of the Prairie Provinces.
1841 (1931) *Beaver* Mar. 180: . . . the country behind [Fort Edmonton] consist of rolling prairie. **1880** GORDON *Mountain and Prairie* 228: After leaving the river the road passes for the most part through a beautiful tract of country, rolling prairie alternating with woodland. **1905** WIGHTMAN *Cdn Heritage* 147: Northward from the Thompson for one hundred miles is another region of rolling bench lands . . . in a surprising manner maintaining a dryness far north into the Chilcotin rolling prairie country west of the Fraser. . . . **1936** (1960) STANLEY *Western Canada* 358: The rolling prairie, like the South African veldt, offered extensive cover to the defending force. . . .

rollings *n.pl. Slang* See **makings.** See also **roll,** *v.* (def. 1).
1956 KEMP *Northern Trader* 89: The tobacco was medium cut, suitable for pipe or the "rollings." **1965** *Sun* (Vancouver) 31 Dec. 27/1: [Headline] "Rollings" are Safer . . . Dr. E. R. Thretewie . . . said . . . that home-made cigarettes burn at a lower temperature . . . [which] reduces the amount of cancer-producing substances produced.

roll tobacco *Hist.* large tobacco leaves twisted into a rope one inch in diameter and then wound into a large (70 lb.) roll and sold by the inch or foot
1684 (1946) *H.B.C.Minutes* 211: . . . to Bespeake of Mr. Lassells the whole quantity of role tobacco that is to be Shipt of the Next Expedition. **1743** (1949) ISHAM *Observations* 86: Let the young men have Roll tobacco cheap. . . . **1811** (1916) THOMPSON *Narrative* 460: Ignace, carrying two rolls of Tobacco, preferred wading across the brook to passing on a single tree; when almost across he stumbled; the rolls of Tobacco fell (each seventy pounds) and were swept away by the current. **1929** MOBERLY *When Fur Was King* 35: One and a half feet of Canadian roll tobacco sold for one . . . made-beaver.

rollway *n. Lumbering, Hist.* **1**† an assembly point between the cutting area and the water's edge, where logs were piled for a time before being transported to the brow (def. 1).
1883 FRASER *Shanty* 58: They are a mazy labyrinth of road network, each one of which is a blind alley whose terminus is some "rollway" where a collection of logs or square timber has been made, ready to be drawn away by the teamsters. **1964** *Cdn Geog.Jnl* Feb. 67/1: The big log was skidded to the trail, to a secondary depot or "rollway."

2 See quote.
1912 SANDILANDS *West.Cdn Dict.* 44/1: Stack, a pile of lumber; a rollway of logs decked on the banks of the river ready for the drive.

room *n. Nfld* **1** *Hist.* See 1954 quote. See also **ship-room.**
1620 WHITBOURNE *Discovrse* 30: [They] doe cut downe many of the best trees they can finde, to build their stages and roomes.... **1954** BRIFFETT *Newfoundland* 32: A man's fishing property—flakes, stages and stores— was known as his room. **1964** *Nfld Qtly* Summer 15/2: A fishing establishment employing about twelve or more producers would divide them into a fishing crew and a smaller shore crew, the latter remaining [at] the "room" to "put away" (split and slat) the "voyage of fish," and later to "make" (sun-dry) it.
2 See quote.
1948 *Cdn Geog.Jnl* Mar. 110/1: Fishing off Labrador is carried on by fishermen who leave Newfoundland in May or June and reside at "rooms" (buildings used by the fishermen) on various parts of the Labrador coast until the close of the season.

root bread *Obs.* a breadlike substance made from the camas bulb by the Indians of the Pacific Coast.
1809 (1950) THOMPSON *Journals* 58:... traded abt 40 Skins, Some Root Bread, Salmon....

root-catcher *n. Slang, Obs.* a botanist.
1832 MCGREGOR *Brit.Amer.* I 199: The names of the almost innumerable places within this great bay [Trinity] would puzzle the most genuine root-catcher that ever existed.

root doctor *Obs.* a herbalist.
1821 (1955) CRAIG *Early Travellers* 65: "My dear good lady," cried the doctor, "I'll bet a pint of spirits I'll *raise* you in five days, and make you so *spry*, that you'll dance upon this floor."—"Oh!" said the woman, "if I had but the *root* doctor that used to attend our family at Connecticut; he was a dreadful *skeelful* man."
1846 (1957) *Ont.Hist.* XLIX 38:... when he was off Jeffery without my knowledge sent to Fingal for a famous *Root* Doctor who came and after minutely examining her, gave her some powder which removed the fever in a very short space of time....

root-house *n.* a space wholly or partly underground where vegetables, especially root vegetables, are stored during the winter.
1832 (1953) RADCLIFF *Letters* 47: When we had completed the house, we raised a barn ... with an ice-house, root house, and summer dairy beneath it....
1852 (1881) TRAILL *Cdn Crusoes* 261:... and when they were digging for the site of the root-house below the bank, which they had just finished, they had met with charred wood, at the depth of six feet below the soil....
1961 MITCHELL *Jake and the Kid* 28: "Bin a real fine summer fer vegetables," he said then. "Too bad yer ma don't have no root house."

rose raspberry *Obs.* a shrub, *Rubus odoratus.*
1830 (1837) *Trans.Lit.& Hist.Soc.Que.* III 117: Rose Raspberry—a handsome spreading shrub, three or four feet high, bearing large reddish purple flowers, resembling a single rose.

rosomack *n.* [origin unknown] *Obs.* See **wolverine** (def. 1).
1823 *Canadian Mag.* I 496: The rosomack or glutton, though not so numerous, is a more dangerous enemy.

Ross *n.* See **Ross's goose.**
1958 *Edmonton Jnl* 17 Sep. 18/2: Meanwhile, the Ross —or little snow goose—nests above the Arctic Circle on the Perry river....

Ross rifle [< Sir Charles *Ross,* 1872-1942, Canadian engineer and soldier] *Hist.* a rifle designed and manufactured in Canada and issued to Canadian troops overseas during World War I.
1917 *Grit* (Toronto) 7 Dec. 4/5: Think of the Ross Rifle, the lame horses, the sham shoes, the Allison rake-off.... **1963** *Military Arms of Canada* 43: The Ross Rifle was a straight pull bolt action rifle that was made in calibre .303 British and .280 Ross for the Canadian Government. Although the first agreement to manufacture them was made by Sir Charles Ross in 1901, the first delivery was not made to the military until 1905. **1964** *Star Wkly* 20 June 3/3: This was the Canadian-made Ross rifle, an excellent target rifle which in action turned out to be an unqualified disaster.

Ross's goose [< Bernard R. *Ross* (d. 1874), a factor of the Hudson's Bay Company] a smallish white goose, *Chen rossii,* that breeds in the Far North. See also **galoot, horned wavey,** and **scabby-nosed wavey.**
1908 MAIR *Mackenzie Basin* 320: At Fort Chipewyan, Athabasca, however, Ross's goose is the *last* to arrive in the spring, but is among the first to return in the autumn. **1947** GILLHAM *Raw North* 175: He kindly interpreted for me while I interviewed his natives regarding the whereabouts of the Ross's goose.

rot oil *Nfld* See quote.
1964 *Nfld Qtly* Spring 26/1: [Cod-liver oil] was often further differentiated as "rotted cod oil" or "rot oil," indicative of its method of manufacture which was to merely store the cod livers in casks or vats.

roto-thresh (combine) *n.* a rotary combine invented by the Streich Brothers of Clandeboye, Manitoba, in the 1950's which separates chaff from grain by a blast of air through a rotating drum.
1964 *Family Herald* 12 Mar. 13/2: The flow of material through the roto-thresh combine closely parallels that of a conventional machine—up to a point. *Ibid.* 13/3: To date, we haven't found any grain or seed which the roto-thresh couldn't handle.

roto-threshing *n.* threshing with a roto-thresh.
1964 *Family Herald* 12 Mar. 13/1: Their new system is called "roto-threshing" and 12 years of field tests and structural alterations prove that it works.

rotted cod oil See **rot oil.**

rotten *adj.* See 1958 quote. See also **green ice** and **mush-ice.**
1665 (1885) RADISSON *Voyages* 133: We cutt the ice wth hattchetts & we found places where [it] was rotten, so we hazarded ourselves often to sinke downe to our necks. **1795** (1911) SIMCOE *Diary* 266: At Jacques Cartier the ice was so rotten I was obliged to go a league higher to cross the river with safety.... **1849** ALEXANDER *L'Acadie* II 31: Thence we proceeded to Montreal, which we reached after four days and three nights of most unpleasant travel, and even dangerous, on account of exposure to the rotten ice....

1916 DUNCAN *Billy Topsail* 120: [The ice] had yielded somewhat—it must have gone rotten—in the weather of the day. **1958** *Manice* 5: Rotten Ice. Old ice which has become honeycombed in the course of melting and which is in an advanced stage of disintegration.

rotting *adj.* See **rotten.**
1910 HAYDON *Riders of Plains* 204: After the close of navigation it took two months to make the ice fit to travel upon, and for one month before the river and lakes again opened the rotting ice was fraught with terrible dangers. **1954** PATTERSON *Dangerous River* 290: The creek ice was also rotting at the edges where it touched the warm, sunny bank on which I was lying. **1966** *Cdn Geog.Jnl* July 23/2: The rotting ice of earlier years floated low in the water, black, ugly and pock-marked with saucer-like holes.

rotunda *n. Esp.West* a lobby, concourse, foyer, or main hall of a hotel, railway station, college building, etc.
1905 *Eye Opener* (Calgary) 28 Jan. 3/1: The hotels have no drinking-water tanks in their rotundas for the use of guests or local patrons—for obvious reasons. **1924** DORRANCE *Never Fire First* 134: The scene in the rotunda of Montreal's impressive Windsor Station was as lively as it was metropolitan. **1958** *Edmonton Jnl* 19 June 33/3: Place and Date of Sale [is] Rotunda, Fifth Floor, Natural Resources Building, Edmonton, Alberta. **1964** *Calgary Herald* 15 May 25/3: Vibrations of calypso music rocked the rotunda at McCall Field Thursday....

rouchou *n.* See **richeau.**

rouge [ruʒ] *n.* [extended use of an English football term of obscure origin] *Cdn Football* **1** a play in which the team receiving a punt behind its own goal line is unable or unwilling to carry the ball back into the field of play, thus conceding a point to the opposition. See also **single** and **touch-in-goal.** Cp. **safety touch** (def. 1).
1895 *Outing Mag.* XXVII 249/2: A "rouge" occurs when a man ... touches the ball down behind his own goal.... **1954** *Globe and Mail* (Toronto) 11 Dec. 25/5: Other Canadian features which aroused interest were the rouge and the fact that kicks must be run back.... **1966** *Weekend Mag.* 27 Aug. 20/2: If only our rouge were added to the American game, football ... wouldn't leave a thing to be desired as a game.
2 the single point conceded on such a play.
1964 *Kingston Whig-Standard* (Ont.) 27 Oct. 9/3: The above article [1895] mentions the only peculiarly Canadian feature of football which endures namely the single point, either the "rouge" or the "touch in goal."

rouge [ruʒ] *v.* [< n.] *Cdn Football* **1** concede a rouge.
1904 CONNOR *Prospector* 38: No sooner has the McGill captain kicked off then the ball is returned and again McGill is forced to rouge.
2 force to concede a rouge.
1958 *Edmonton Jnl* 6 Aug. 11/6: [Caption] Cameron Rouged by Moran on Etcheverry Kick.

Rouge [ruʒ] *n.* [< Cdn F] **1** *Hist.* a member of the Rouge party, *q.v.* Cp. **Bleu.**
1856 *Niagara Mail* (Niagara-on-the-Lake, C.W.) 24 Sep. 2/2: De Witt having retired from the contest with Mr. Renoud a no party candidate, that gentleman is to be opposed by Mr. Boutre, a Rouge. **1865** *Leader* (Toronto) 12 Jan. 2/1: By spreading their gold fine, the Rouges are attempting to give to a feeble demonstration an imperial aspect. **1963** MORTON *Kingdom of Canada* 291: By [1852] the political scene in Canada had altered considerably. The growing conservatism of Lafontaine and Baldwin had stimulated the rise of the Rouges in Canada East and of the Clear Grits in Canada West.
2 in present-day Quebec, a Liberal, especially with reference to federal politics. See also **Red** (def. 2). Cp. **Bleu.** Also *rouge.*
1958 *Winnipeg Free Press* 4 June 23/1: Politics in French Canada are at last returning to the pattern of the days before Riel—the days of the Rouges and the Bleus. **1963** *Globe and Mail* (Toronto) 24 Mar. 7/7: What they really mean is that the Quebec voters' traditional loyalties have been strained to the limit and that the real tug of war no longer is between the rouges and the bleus—the Liberals and the Tories— but between the "old" and the "new" parties. **1965** KILBOURN *Making of Nation* 36/1: As the Rouge he was, he [Laurier] could poke fun at the classical colleges as "hotbeds of conservatism."

Rouge party *Hist.* the political party made up of the moderate reformers in Quebec (Canada East) during the 1850's and 60's, merging with the Liberals after Confederation. See also **Parti Rouge** and **Rouge** (def. 1).
1854 *Hamilton Gaz.* (C.W.) 14 Sep. 2/6: It would appear that such a course was the only one left, unless to allow the Clear Grits and Rouge party to assume the reins of government, which to both legitimate Reformers and Conservatives would have been infinitely worse. **1916** SKELTON *Day of Laurier* 14: He had been one of the original members of the Rouge party.

rough-barked poplar See **Balm of Gilead.**
1887 *Senate Journal* XXI App. 180: The ash-leaved poplar, the rough barked poplar or Balm of Gilead ... would be found to grow rapidly.... **1959** LEISING *Arctic Wings* 91: Often we found patches of rough-barked poplar, or balm of Gilead, growing straight to sixty feet with three-foot butts.

rough country See **lumbering counties.**

rough ice *North* See quote.
1963 MCTAVISH *Behind the Palisades* 202: When the river freezes in the fall, the ice by successive tides is forced up in piles on either side of the river, and generally gets the name of "rough ice," being virtually small icebergs.

roughing *n.* in hockey and lacrosse, an infraction of the rules whereby one or more players engage in shoving, punching, etc., thus earning a minor penalty.
1958 *Herald-Tribune* [Grande Prairie, Alta] 28 Feb. 5/6: Bryan McCurdy ... and Bill Oakford ... went off together for roughing and slashing at the 18:55 mark. **1963** *Kingston Whig-Standard* (Ont.) 22 Jan. 8/7: [They] were sent to the penalty box for roughing, elbowing and slashing after a minor tussle at centre ice....

rough sledding See **tough sledding.**
1954 KELLEY *Black Donnellys* 57: Damnation—had he somehow, unknowingly, revealed himself? If so, he could sure expect some rough sledding ahead.

roundup† *n.* **1** the periodic bringing together of range livestock for branding, shipping, etc.

round-up this year they should have had 13,000 head of
cattle, and they only counted 5,000. **1963** SYMONS
Many Trails 43: So the roundup was organized, and
the riders went out keen with the excitement of the
chase.

2 a bringing together of persons, usually by some
authority, such as the police.
1926-27 *Battleford Hist.Soc.* I 23: A few of the wildest
and most independent Indians had, in one way and
another, evaded the "round up" of the police and
American cavalry. **1955** McCOWAN *Upland Trails* 18:
"There was one thing you could be sure of with Baldy
and that was that as sure as there was a mornin'
round-up, he would be away without leave, more than
likely up on some mountain top lookin' at the sunrise."

round up 1 bring (livestock) together in a
roundup (def. 1).
1882 *Edmonton Bull.* 18 Mar. 3/2: It is thought when
the herds are rounded up in the spring a good many will
be missing of which no account has been received.
1966 PATTERSON *Trail* 9: ... the men went back over
the trail to try to round up the strays.

2 bring people together in a roundup (def. 2).
1955 *Herald-Tribune* (Grande Prairie, Alta.) 4 Mar.
7/4: The culprits have been rounded up and tried at
High Prairie.

3 fetch; collect; bring together. See also
roundup (def. 2).
1936 STRINGER *Wife-Traders* 127: ... Slim Downey
was to fly back to Iviuk Inlet as soon as he could after
the freeze-up, leaving the white woman and her friend
to round up Owen Winslow....

rousseau ['ruso *or* ru'so] *n. Hist.* See **richeau.**
1886 SCUDDER *Winnipeg Country* 90: Hereafter,
cracker dust and dirt takes the place of flour as one of
the ingredients of rousseau. **1964** *Beaver* Summer 54/1:
Frying the pemmican in its own fat resulted in what
was called rousseau (or rechaud or richot) and to it
might also be added some flour or a suitable wild plant
or berries.

rover *n. Hist.* in hockey and lacrosse, a fourth
forward on a team.
1963 *Kingston Whig-Standard* (Ont.) 5 Feb. 10/2:
... [in 1911] the forward line composed of Hunt at
centre, the late "Bouncer" Brouse at rover, Leo
Millan on the left rail [left wing] and Reg Boyer on the
right, made their highly rated opponents look ridiculous.
1965 *Canadian Wkly* 2-8 Jan. 7/2: The team lined up in
a T-formation with the two defencemen (called "point"
and "cover-point") in single file in front of the goal,
then the rover, then the centre, with wing-men to right
and left.

rowraddy or **rue-raddy** *n.* [origin unknown]
North, Obs. See **tracking belt.**
1850 (1851) SNOW *Voyage* 133: Little was there to dread,
however; for, independent of the thickness of the ice,
each man had for safety his tracking belt, called by
them "rowraddy".... **1853** (1892) KANE *Arctic Explor.*
66: Each man had his own shoulder-belt, or "rue-
raddy," as we used to call it, and his own track-line,
which, for want of horse-hair, was made of Manilla
rope; it traversed freely by a ring on a loop or bridle,
that extended from runner to runner in front of the
sledge.

rowshow *n.* See **richeau.**

Royal Canadian Mounted Police since 1920, a
police force under the jurisdiction of the federal

government of Canada, formerly the North West
Mounted Police, *q.v.* See also **Mounted, Mounted
Police, R.C.M.P., Royal Mounted,** and **Silent
Force.**
1927 LONGSTRETH *Silent Force* 344: "All right,
Captain," says Blakeney ... "but we are members of
the Royal Canadian Mounted Police and I'm also a
customs and excise officer, and I'm going to seize your
ship and cargo and detain you and your men on board."
1962 *Globe Mag.* 3 Feb. 8/2: ... this was made all the
more important by our arrangement to rendezvous
with a Royal Canadian Mounted Police boat on the
other side.

royal commission any investigation by a person
or persons commissioned by the Crown to inquire
into some matter on behalf of the federal or a
provincial government and to make a report
recommending appropriate action.
1834 *Cdn Correspondent* (York [Toronto]) 3 Sep. 1/2:
We have alluded to these points only for the purpose of
enabling the reader to judge what little hopes we have
of improving the condition of the country from the
Legislative Council or the Royal Commission. **1891** *Grip*
(Toronto) 7 Mar. 151/2: The "royal commission"
fake is always available as a means of gaining time by
holding out the hope of action without any definite
promise which commits the Government to do anything.
1963 *Kingston Whig-Standard* (Ont.) 24 Jan. 3/3:
Liberal leader Pearson's speech in the Commons last
month, calling for a royal commission inquiry into
bilingualism and biculturalism in the federal sphere,
found much favor in Quebec, where the Grits hope to
capture the Social Credit seats that cost them victory
last June.

Royalist† *n. Hist.* **1 a.** a person loyal to the British
Crown during the American Revolution.
1775 *Quebec Gaz.* 19 Oct. 3/1: On reading in your
paper an account of the skirmish between the Rebels
and Royalists at Montreal ... I have endeavoured to
give you as true and perfect an account as possible....

b. See **United Empire Loyalist.**
1785 (1943) HUNTER *Diary* 65: The Royalists have
settlements along Lake St. Francis and up to Cataraqui.
1818 LOCKWOOD *Nova Scotia* 25: Two royalist families,
in 1783, settled it from South Carolina....

2 a supporter of the Crown in the Rebellion (def. 1)
of 1837-38.
1837 *St.Catharines Jnl* (U.C.) 7 Dec. 3/1: The main
body of the Royalists were ordered to halt, and
opening to right and left, allowed the field-pieces to
pass to the front ... the second discharge of which
spread such terrour and confusion in the Rebel ranks,
that they broke and fled in all directions.

Royal Mounted See **Royal Canadian Mounted
Police.**
1924 DORRANCE *Never Fire First* 96: If it is true, as
Kipling says, that "single men in barracks don't grow
into plaster saints," it is doubly true of the same in
lonely detachment shacks of the Royal Mounted
scattered about the Arctic foreshore.

Royal North West Mounted Police an
earlier (1905-1920) name for the Royal Canadian
Mounted Police. See also **R.N.W.M.P.**
1906 (1957) *Sask.Hist.* X 31: The escort, furnished by

the Royal North-West Mounted Police, furnished the color to set off the function, the officers in their handsome uniforms and the men in the wellknown redcoats. **1959** STOREY *Prairie Harvest* 44: The following morning Mike had a visit from the Royal Northwest Mounted Police.

Royalty *n. Hist.* See 1904 quote.
1823 *P.E.I.Register* (Charlottetown) 27 Sep. 3/4: To be Sold by Private Contract, the following valuable Real estates situate in Charlotte-town and Royalty. **1833** *Cdn Correspondent* (York [Toronto]) 14 Sep. 2/6: In the 67 Townships of the Island: in Charlottetown, Georgetown, with their Royalties; and in Panmure, Boughton, Rustico, St. Peter's and Governor's Islands, we find the total population amounts to Males, 16,840, Females, 15,452. **1904** CROSSKILL *P.E.I.* 16: At the time of Holland's survey, a capital town in each county was laid out, the supposed most suitable site for a future city being selected—and to each of these town sites was attached a royal domain or district called a "Royalty," and also a Common. The intention was that the man who held a lot in the town should be allowed a lot in the Royalty for pasturing purposes; and the Royalties accordingly for a distance of two miles from the town were divided into pasture lots—Princetown and Georgetown Royalties into 8 acre lots and the Charlottetown Royalty into 12 acre lots.

R.R. 1 See **R.R.S.**
1862 *Nor'Wester* (R.R.S.) 19 Mar. 2/4: Being a subscriber to a foreign Weekly Paper I pay,—First, for subscription 8s. Second, U.S. and R.R. postage 6s. 6d.
2 See **rural route.**
1963 *Globe and Mail* (Toronto) 9 May 5/1: [The] body was discovered by Cecil Lane of RR 3, Watford, a farmer on whose land the cottage stands.

R.R.S. *Hist.* See **Red River Settlement.** See also **R.R.** (def. 1).
1825 (1926) *Cdn Hist.Rev.* VII 309: Districts not permitted dealings or Barter accounts with R R S (Buffalo Wool Co. included) without the authority of Council.... **1860** *Nor'Wester* (R.R.S.) 14 Apr. 4/5: We are particularly at this stage of our existence, anxious to enlarge our dwellings, and all such articles as are conductive to man's comfort while here below but it is difficult to do so, owing to the extravagant prices of R.R.S. nails at 1s. 6d. per lb. Cm. Contry Salt 16s. per bushel or 32 qts.

rub *n.* See **rubbing place.**
1933 MERRICK *True North* 76: A rub is a smooth, worn shoot-the-chutes down the side of a bank where the otters play, running up and sliding down like children....

rub(b)aboo ['rʌbə,bu] *n.* [ult. < Algonk., prob. through Cdn F; cf. Ojibwa *nempūp* soup, broth; Cree *apū* soup] **1** See 1964 quote. See also **burgoo** and **ruhiggan burgoo. Cp. richeau.**
☛ *The precise origin of this widely used term of earlier days is obscure; it may have been influenced by* **burgoo,** *used by the English traders in much the same sense.*
1821 (1900) GARRY *Diary* 151: Our Men are now eating Rababoo made of Pemican and Flour. **1863** *Nor'Wester* (R.R.S.) 22 July 2/5: There ... is scarcely enough firewood to cook the snipe you shoot, or to make the "rubaboo" kettle boil.... **1909** BRYCE *Lord Selkirk's Colonists* 87: There was this year plenty of buffalo meat

and the Scotch women soon learned to cook it into "Rubaboo," or "Rowschow," after the manner of the French half-breeds. **1930** ROLYAT *Fort Garry* 7: How he had relished that first meal at home, consisting chiefly of rubaboo and bannock buttered with buffalo marrow fat. **1964** *Beaver* Summer 54: There was the soup or stew called rubbaboo in which a lump of pemmican was chopped off and put in a pot of boiling water. If it was available, flour was added and possibly wild onions, sometimes a little sugar, occasionally a vegetable and a scrap of salt pork.
2 *Fig.* a miscellany; a mixed bag.
*c*1862 (1966) *B.C.Digest* Dec. 48/2: I must tell now why I call these writings a Rubbaboo Journal. Any queer mixture gets that name among the voyageurs. When I try to speak French and mix English, Slavy and Louchioux words with it, they tell me "that's a rubbaboo." And when the Indians attempt to sing a voyaging song, the different keys and tunes make a "rubbaboo." **1963** *Weekend Mag.* 9 Nov. 55: Another follow-up is Rubaboo 2 (Gage) an anthology of Canadian stories and poems.

rubber *n. Hockey, Slang* a puck, *q.v.*
1895 *Rat Portage* [Kenora] *News* (Ont.) 11 Jan. 1/2: The forwards immediately close in and the rubber flys from player to player with the speed of lightning. **1955** *Glaslyn Chron.* 27 Jan. 1/2: The local boys really played hockey when they managed to keep the rubber in the St. Thomas zone a great portion of the remaining time.

rubber bum *Slang* See quote.
1961 *Maclean's* 29 July 34/3: Tom Briggs is one of the older hoboes who have switched from the railways to become "rubber bums"—hitch-hikers on long-distance trucks.

rubber-chicken circuit *Slang* the tour made by an after-dinner speaker, the dinners being noted for tough chicken as the main course.
1959 *Maclean's* 23 May 1/1: Next year's rubber-chicken circuit is being sewed up by three Toronto women with a public-speaking agency called Canadian Celebrity Bureau.

rubber ice *Esp.North* thin, flexible ice, especially elastic young sea ice. Also called *rubbery ice.*
1916 DUNCAN *Billy Topsail* 120: What the frost had accomplished since dusk could be determined only by trial. "Soft as cheese!" Doctor Luke concluded. "Rubber ice," said Billy. **1920** STRINGER *Prairie Mother* 231: I had no wish to slide on rubber-ice just for the sake of seeing it bend. **1951** BULIARD *Inuk* 210: Sea ice two or three inches thick will bear a man's weight, though it is tricky. We call it "rubber ice," for it is supple and yields beneath your feet without breaking, but there are weak patches.

rubbing place See 1958 quote. See also **otter rub** and **rub.**
1770 (1792) CARTWRIGHT *Journal* I 28: We observed many signs of porcupines and several rubbing places.... **1861** DE BOILIEU *Labrador Life* 79: The mode adopted is to bury the traps in the "rubbing place," and cover them lightly with soil, particular care being taken not to disturb any part, but as near as possible to keep the place as it is. **1958** WILSON *Treasury* 238: [Glossary] Rubbing place—an otter slide.

rubby ['rʌbi] *n.* [< *rubbing* alcohol] *Slang*
1 rubbing alcohol used as a drink, especially when flavored with cheap wine or rum.

1961 *Maclean's* 29 July 36/1 : A gallon of wine and two bottles of rubby and you can throw a party in the jungles that'll last all night.

2 a person who drinks rubbing alcohol, shaving-lotion, etc., often flavored with cheap wine or rum; hence, an alcoholic, especially a derelict. See also **rubbydub.**

1950 PALMER *Montreal Confidential* 102 : The police department has probably given up keeping score of rubbies they have fished out of the river. . . . **1965** *Sun* (Vancouver) 18 Oct. 35/6 : Most of the dinner guests were men off the street, rubbies, derelicts, the jobless, alcoholics, the lost ones, residents of Vancouver's Skid road.

rubbydub ['rʌbi,dʌb] *n.* [< *rubby*, q.v. + *dub* clumsy, stupid person] See **rubby** (def. 2).

1950 PALMER *Montreal Confidential* 101 : If the bum looks a bit plastered don't stop . . . Chances are he's a "rubby-dub" and his mind is no doubt clouded with smoke. **1957** *Maclean's* 25 May 68/2 : "We've got everything here from ex-cons to rubby-dubs," says Scott Raebould, one of Elliot's six provincial policemen. **1964** *Time* (Cdn ed.) 12 June 14/2 : He is apt to notice . . . a sunblinded rubbydub who has just lurched out of the Metropole Tavern.

rubi(e)boo *n.* See **rubaboo.**

rub noses *Arctic* See 1945 quote.

1829 (1935) STRANG *Pioneers in Canada* 18 : . . . and when the principal [Eskimo dancer] had pretty well exhausted himself, he walked gravely up to him, and, taking his head between his hands, rubbed noses with him, amidst the plaudits of all present. **1945** LEECHMAN *Eskimo Summer* 240 : Before they had much contact with white men, the Eskimos used to rub noses on meeting old friends after a protracted absence. This is seldom done now, though I did see it at Pangnirtung on the east coast of Baffin Island. It is not the vigorous, nose-smashing rubbing that the cartoonist seems to expect, but a gentle approaching of one face to the other, as though they were about to kiss. The noses barely touch, if at all, and there is a gentle intake of breath, as though sniffing. The lips make no contact at all. **1963** RICHLER *Incomparable Atuk* 51 : "You're not talking to a stage Eskimo. Like I don't rub noses anymore, you know."

rue-raddy *n. Obs.* See **rowraddy.**

ruffed *n.* See **ruffed grouse.**

1963 *Sun* (Vancouver) 3 Dec. 23/1 : Most alarming decline of all is in grouse, with the tally dropping almost 50 per cent . . . Most of the drop was in ruffeds, though blue, sharptail and franklin were all down. This is what biologists mean when they speak of the cyclic population CRASH of grouse.

ruffed grouse a partridge-like game bird, *Bonasa umbellus*, occurring in many subspecies across Canada. See also **birch partridge, Canadian partridge, partridge** (def. 1), **white-flesher, willow, willow grouse** (def. 2), and **willow pheasant.**

1795 (1911) HEARNE *Journey* 407 : The Ruffed Grouse . . . is the most beautiful of all that are classed under that name. **1966** *Kingston Whig-Standard* (Ont.) 21 Jan. 11/1 : The ruffed grouse, commonly called partridge, is the one that startles you in the woods with its explosive take-off.

ruffled grouse See **ruffed grouse.**

1853 REID *Young Voyageurs* 109 : I knew it was not that, but the drumming of the ruffled grouse.

1869 *Mainland Guardian* (New Westminster, B.C.) 10 Nov. 3/2 : We only succeeded in getting . . . two blue grouse . . . and one ruffled grouse . . . which we cooked for supper and found delicious. **1959** MCATEE *Folk-Names* 24 : Ruffed Grouse [is also called] ruffled grouse. . . .

rugby *n.* See **rugby-football** and note.

1898 CONNOR *Black Rock* 2 : He was . . . the prince of half-backs on the Rugby field. . . . **1916** BRIDLE *Sons of Can.* 121 : None but a cynical materialist could make odious comparisons more odious between these two great colleges—particularly in the matter of either revenues or rugby. **1966** *Globe Mag.* 20 Aug. 87/3 : The West adopted the forward pass and used it before the Canadian Rugby Union legalized it. . . .

rugby-football *n.* a distinctive Canadian variety of football developed in the late nineteenth century from English rugby or rugger. See also **football.**

☛ **Rugby football,** *often* **rugby** *at the popular level, has, except among some older Canadians, gradually been displaced since the 1930's by the characteristically American term* **football,** *the Canadianism being confined largely to official league titles.*

1910 (1965) *Canadian* 27 Nov.-24 Dec. 8/1 : Smirle Lawson will not play half-back . . . on the Toronto University rugby-football team this fall. **1924** SHERMAN *Nature Stories* 106 : The hungry and infuriated class of cannibals would fall upon him like a mob of Rugby football players. **1958** *Edmonton Jnl* 24 June 21/1 : . . . the groups chiefly interested . . . are . . . the junior rugby football league. . . .

ruhiggan *n.* [< Algonk.] *Obs.* See **beat meat.**

1743 (1949) ISHAM *Observations* 77 : Accordingly being willing to Satisfy my Curiosity, I sitts downe upon a Bundle of Ruhiggan which was handed to me; when Looking round me I see them all sett to work, some a picking, & some a trussing of Geese. **1754** (1934) HENDAY in HEARNE & TURNOR *Journals* 4 : . . . they have neither victuals nor drink, Except a Little Ruhigan, they are very Lazey, not one stick of wood anigh their house. . . .

ruhiggan burgoo *Obs.* See **rubaboo.**

1743 (1949) ISHAM *Observations* 132 : Their is a Sort of mawse which grows upon the Rocks, which is of a Brownish Colour, which the Indians Eats frequent, they wash itt clean, then Boil itt for a considerable time till itts tender, then mixing itt with Ruhiggan Burgoe or other Victuals, and Reckon itt Good Eating.

rum *n.* **1** a generic term for spiritous liquor, often personified as in *demon rum.*

1800 *U.C.Gaz.* (York [Toronto]) 5 Apr. 3/2 : Many have labored to calumniate Rum, and render it unpopular, by dwelling on some of its supposed bad effects. **1851** *Voice of the Fugitive* (Sandwich [Windsor], C.W.) 5 Nov. 2/5 : Rum and Negro hate [are] the two great public evils of our time. . . . **1918** MACKAY *Trench and Trail* 15 : . . . no one will rejoice more than Oscar Dhu to see the demon rum utterly destroyed in Canada ere many moons. **1957** *Prairie Overcomer* Dec. 444/2 : Of these two foes we cannot say whether *Rome* or *rum* is the greater adversary of the pure Gospel.

2 *Fur Trade, Hist.* **a.** spiritous liquor used in the Indian trade. See also **Indian liquor** and **rum trade.**

1797 (1964) CHABOILLEZ *Journal* 167: The Corbeaux . . . killed Six Cows which I paid him Eighteen Skins in Rum. **1819** (1941) *Beaver* Dec. 19/2: . . . the whole Inmates of our Garrison assembled in the Hall . . . and were regaled . . . with a few flaggons Rum and some Cakes. . . . **1861** *Nor'Wester* (R.R.S.) 1 Aug. 3/5: This decision will prove an auxiliary to us, as the use of rum has hitherto greatly retarded our work. **1871** *Wkly Manitoban* 27 May 4/1: He had been drinking "much rum," and got awfully mad. **1963** SPRY *Palliser* 105: A great many Indians were camped round the fort, waiting for Mr. Brazeau, whom Hector had met on his way to Edmonton, to come back with a supply of rum.

b. a gratuity paid, after 1821, to Indian trappers by the Hudson's Bay Company in place of the traditional regale (def. 3).

1907 HUNTER *Cdn Wilds* 260: [The Indian trapper] was at liberty, after paying his debt, to trade whatever he fancied out of the shop to the extent of his "rum." But unless he paid his debt in full, the "Rum" he was entitled to went towards his account.

rummage *n.* [< *v.*] *Nfld, Obs.* a hunting or fishing expedition. See also **rummage,** *v.*

1770 (1792) CARTWRIGHT *Journal* I 56: [I left] my attendant behind, to join the other man, and pass the night in the woods; in order that they might finish the rummage of that brook to-morrow.

rummage *v.* [< Brit.dial. "ransack"] *Nfld, Obs.* See 1819 quote. See also **rummage,** *n.*

1770 (1792) CARTWRIGHT *Journal* I 56: The other furrier accompanied me in rummaging for beavers. **1819** ANSPACH *Hist.Nfld* 376: Thus prepared, he fearlessly ranges about, or according to the technical term, rummages in search of his game. **1835** (1836) WIX *Journal* 60: Such tracks, being only of persons who have been "rummaging," or searching for firesticks of timber in the woods, may, again and again have raised deceptive hopes, respecting their leading immediately to some habitation or settlement.

Rummy *n.* [< *rummy* drunkard] *Slang, Obs.* a political opponent of the temperance movement.

1853 *Cdn Watchman* (Toronto) 19 Mar. 93/4: The Rummies gathered from all parts of the neighborhood, to have a last look at—the establishment. **1908** *Observer* (Cowansville, Que.) 3 Dec. 1/6: If we do run and win we will make the rummies run at Ottawa.

Rumocrat *n. Slang, Obs.* See **Rummy.**

1852 *Cdn Watchman* (Toronto) 4 Oct. 194/1: The same spirit, the same energy, the same determination, though at the expense of a few more lives, to perpetuate the horrid traffic, obtains among the Rumocrats from Sarnia to Gaspe. **1853** *Ibid.* 19 Mar. 93/2: But lo! the rumocrats attempted to lynch Bro. Nowatt, as soon as he left the Hall.

rum trade *Hist.* See quote. See also **rum** (def. 2a).

1922 *Beaver* May 6/1: . . . Mr. Swanson had misunderstood my meaning, that "to drink with the Indians" was the common expression for a "rum trade" in which the Indian got the rum and his white brother got the furs.

run *n.* **1** See **riffle** (def. 1c).

1796 (1911) SIMCOE *Diary* 345: There is a place called "the run" near the locks, which is like going down the stream of an overshot mill, and I really thought we should never have risen out of it. **1856** BALLANTYNE *Young Fur-Traders* 65: . . . just as he said it, we came in sight of the first run, foaming and boiling like a kettle of robbiboo. **1928** FREEMAN *Nearing North* 275: As I had sensed from mid-stream, the run could have been made in safety down either side, but only by putting in at the right places above.

2 *Hist.* See **buffalo run** (def. 1).

1858 (1860) HIND *Assiniboine Exped.* I 300: . . . fresh [buffalo] tracks were seen, and skulls and bones in large numbers, the remains of last year's "run". . . . **1872** (1877) GRANT *Ocean to Ocean* 136: The half-breed would not exchange the pleasure of one such "run" for a whole year's profitable farm work. **1913** COWIE *Adventurers* 217: I was told they each killed twenty-eight buffalo in a run. **1963** MACLEOD & MORTON *Cuthbert Grant* 14: After a run, their women had hard days of work before them, cutting and drying the meat. . . .

3 See **drive** (def. 1).

1894 ASHLEY *Tan Pile Jim* 197: The different logging gangs had combined their forces for the drive, or run, and every one was on the alert to see that his part of the work was done to the best of his ability. **1959** TAYLOR *Canada and Neighbours* 37/2: When the first 'run' is over, some of the men go back upstream and collect any of the logs left behind that bear their company's stamp.

4 See **ice-run.**

1900 LONDON *Son of Wolf* 104: We struck the Yukon just behind the first ice-run . . . and the tribe only a quarter of an hour behind. But that saved us; for the second run broke the jam above and shut them out.

5 *Nfld* See quotes.

1918 GRENFELL *Labrador Doctor* 70: [We] had turned in from sea through the last "run" or passage between islands. **1952** PUTNAM *Cdn Regions* 44/2: Between [the islands] and the mainland, and among the islands themselves, is a veritable maze of waterways to which Newfoundlanders have applied a number of curious geographic names such as "tickle," "run," "reach," "arm" and "sound."

6 of animals, a period of abundance, from a trapper's or hunter's point of view. See also **run,** *v.* (def. 6).

1937 *Beaver* Mar. 7/2: . . . although the brief run of white fox around Churchill appeared to be over, tracks in the snow out here showed there were yet some foxes in the country.

7† *Maple Industry* the flow of sap from the trees in a sugar bush during the late winter or early spring. See also **sap run.**

1826 (1916) SELLAR *Narrative* 124: In the afternoon there was a fair run . . . the large kettle had been slung and the fire started. **1853** STRICKLAND *Canada West* II 309: I found it necessary to sit up all night and drive the kettles, in consequence of the large accumulation of sap from two good runs. **1959** TAYLOR *Canada and Neighbours* 77/1: This first "run of sap" makes the best syrup, and so is usually sold in this liquid form.

run *v.* **1** See **shoot,** *v.* (def. 1).

1781 (1934) TURNOR *Journal* 351: The Canadians run this fall down, enter on the south side and cross directly to the north. **1869** *Cdn Illust.News* 30 Oct. 6/3: The Prince "ran the Slides," visited the Upper Ottawa, and enjoyed a few days hunting. . . . **1965** *Cdn Geog.Jnl* June 184/3: Occasional portaging is the price paid for the fun of running rapids.

2 *Hist.* take part in a buffalo run (def. 1). See also **runner**[1] (def. 2).

1765-75 (1933) POND *Narrative* 59: I Have Sean them [ponies] Run [buffalo] with those of Natrall Nostrals and Cum in Apearantley Not the Least Out of Breath. **1820** (1823) FRANKLIN *Journey* 114: Mr. Heriot, to shew us the mode of hunting on horseback, or as the traders term it, running of the buffalo, went in chase of a cow, and killed it after firing three shots. **1963** STANLEY *Louis Riel* 5: There could be no room for selfish individualism when the métis ran the buffalo. . . .

3 *Lumbering* move or transport logs from the cutting area by skidding, driving, towing, etc.
1847 (1945) CALVIN *Saga* 50: In 1847 the firm advanced to Allan Edgar four cents per cubic foot on a lot of timber which was "to run to Belleville," down the Moira River; it was to be rafted and sold on the same terms as the Grant lot of the year before. **1958** HEALEY *Alert Bay* 33: Trees were chosen to be felled that could be run to the water without too much difficulty. **1961** GREENING *Ottawa* 104: Running and guiding the logs down the rapids was a very dangerous business in the days before the construction of the slides and runways.

4† a. put forward (as a candidate); endorse.
1844 *Pilot* (Montreal) 5 Apr. 1/2: The Tories could not run a single candidate, but are forced to give their support to one of the two Reformers, in three of the Wards. **1860** *Brit.Colonist* (Victoria) 14 Jan. 2/2: When the poll closed two of the high priests of the H.B. Company expressed great regret that they had not attempted to run three candidates, instead of two. **1958** GRIFFIN *British Columbia* 71: In the provincial election of 1898 they ran Ralph Smith . . . as an independent labor candidate . . . in Nanaimo and elected him. . . .

b. stand for public office; enter an election as a candidate.
1851 *Toronto Mirror* 28 Nov. 2/8: Why not bring out a second progressive Reformer Candidate to run with Mr. O'Neill? **1958** *Edmonton Jnl* 24 June 2 6/4: Ralph Walker . . . said Monday he is considering running for leader of the provincial Liberals.

5 function as a forerunner, *q.v.* See also **runner**[1] (def. 3).
1893 YOUNG *Indian Wigwams* 281: One Night, Sowanas . . . complained of a swelling in one of his knees which made it impossible for him to keep running ahead of the trains at the rapid rate we wished to travel. **1896** (1898) RUSSELL *Far North* 44: On the following day, the tenth from Grand Rapids, as Aleck was able to run again, I occupied the cariole myself.

6 of animals, be abundant at a special time. See also **run,** *n.* (def. 6).
1921 HAWORTH *Trailmakers* 255: On some rounds, particularly in November and March, when fur is running, he will do better; on others not so well.

7 follow a trapline (def. 1) to gather the catch, check and reset the traps, etc.
1913 WILLIAMS *Wilderness Trail* 19: He said that he and partner, the murdered man, had been met by Charley Seguis while running their trap-line. . . . **1956** EVANS *Mountain Dog* 61: His father had mushed the dogs out to Pitchpine for supplies, and he had offered to run the line by himself. **1966** *North* Mar.-Apr. 41/1: They prefer to trap a small area to extinction and then move their tent to a new area and begin all over, rather than run a lone line and move their traps frequently during the season.

8 *Slang, Obs.* **run one's face,** buy on credit. See also **jawbone.**

1870 *Cariboo Sentinel* (Barkerville, B.C.) 14 May 4/1: Thy equals to obtain/I know not way, nor place/ Unless to cloth my legs,/I run my face.

9† **run ice,** of rivers, choked with running ice, *q.v.*
1897 TYRRELL *Sub-Arctics* 234: The channel of open water to the north was running full of heavy ice, making it quite impossible to use the boat. **1960** *North* July-Oct. 20/1: . . . the best hunting is in the fall when the Mackenzie is running ice, ruling out the possibility of a crossing.

runner[1] *n.* **1† a.** one of two longitudinal pieces on which a sled or sleigh glides over the snow or ice. See also **sleigh runner** and **sleigh shoe.**
1788 *Quebec Gaz.* 27 Nov. 2/1: In every other part of America, sleighs and sleds are otherwise constructed, the runners are from nine to twelve inches high and are drawn by cross bars or hooks made fast to the upper part of the runners. **1829** *Brockville Gaz.* (U.C.) 9 Jan. 3/4: . . . we observed on Saturday a skiff fixed on runners coming from Long Island. **1965** SYMINGTON *Tuktu* 50: The caribou provided the interior people with . . . bone and antler to shoe the wooden sled runners. . . .

b. *Hist.* a light, fast sleigh, often used in racing.
1836 (1935) STRANG *Pioneers in Can.* 67: By 8 a.m. each man had his runner laden with something less than a hundred pounds' weight. . . . **1898** CONNOR *Black Rock* 50: But he left behind him his 'runners.' He had not yet thrown up the game.

2 *Hist.* **a.** See **buffalo runner** (def. 1). See also **run,** *v.* (def. 2).
1810 (1897) COUES *New Light* II 619: I had purchased another horse from him for 20 pints of liquor; this was a runner. **1849** (1932) MCLEAN *Notes* 375: The "runner" is tended with all the care which a cavalier of old bestowed on his war steed. . . . **1955** MCCOWAN *Upland Trails* 15: With the passing of the buffalo, the days of the runner were also numbered.

b. See **buffalo runner** (def. 2). See also **run,** *v.* (def. 2).
1858 (1863) PALLISER *Journals* 90: Breakfast finished, our "runners" saddled and mounted. . . . **1862** *Nor'Wester* (Winnipeg) 11 Sep. 2/5: In these expeditions the "runners"—ie. a select band of the best equipped, best-mounted, most experienced and most daring horsemen—are of course the only ones in danger. . . .

3 See **forerunner.** See also **run,** *v.* (def. 5).
1867 GIBBS *Notes on Tinneh* 309: The man was a famous runner . . . despite the disadvantage of small tripping snow-shoes. . . . **1921** *Beaver* June 27/2: The "runner's" duty is to travel in front of the dogs picking out and breaking the trail. It is also his duty to clear away with an axe any trees which may have been blown across the road. **1934** GODSELL *Arctic Trader* 35: There was also Donald Flett, a wonderful runner and a dog-driver of renown.

runner[2] *n.* [trans. of Cdn F *coureur* (*derouine*) runner on the move; see **derouine**] *Fur Trade, Hist.* a company employee, often an Indian, who made fur-buying trips to the Indian hunting camps in the forest. See also **fur-runner** and **tripper** (def. 3). Cp. **derouine.**
1820 (1938) SIMPSON *Athabasca Jnl* 136: We are sadly in want of runners all over the Country. **1830** (1931) MERK *Fur Trade* 323: Ever since your departure we have

had 32 Men 2 Clerks, the Interpreter & One Runner employed in that way & a few days after your departure the Tariff fell to One Beaver p Blanket. **1960** *Press* Dec. 13: . . . the mixed bloods . . . [lived] as canoemen and runners for the fur-trade, as buffalo hunters and makers of pemmican. . . .

running ice ice that is moving swiftly through the water, carried by the current. See also **run**, *v.* (def. 9).
1913 OGILVIE *Yukon* 44: In this it satisfactorily succeeded, when running ice put a stop to further mining operations. **1922** CODY *King's Arrow* 101: [The canoe] had battled with running ice. . . .

running shoe a strip of metal attached to a runner (def. 1a).
1940 MARSHALL *Arctic Village* 81: Both [sleds] were invented by the natives, though the whites have added iron running shoes and brakes.

runoff† *n.* the water that flows from a particular area, especially following the spring thaw.
1925 GROVE *Settlers* 81: Belated rains which, in the bush, had fallen on frozen ground had caused an abundant run-off. **1962** *Field, Horse & Rodeo* Nov. 11/3: Lots of it will be left for cover, not primarily for game birds but because it is needed for shelter for his stock, for snow traps for moisture and to control run-off. But the wildlife will greatly benefit.

runway† *n.* **1** See 1849 quote.
1849 ALEXANDER *L'Acadie* II 9: Knapp and his sons mustered their dogs, and the hunters went off to place themselves in pairs, at the "runways," or tracks where the deer usually pass, and towards which they would be driven by the dogs. *c*1902 LAUT *Trapper* 133: He sets no more snares across that runway, for the rabbits have had their alarm. **1948** *Sask. Fur Marketing Service* 31: Blind sets are successfully made in runways between racks and fallen trees near their dens. . . .
2 the channel or bed of a watercourse.
1909 CAMERON *New North* 57: The bowsman points to a rude cross on the right bank where a small runway makes in. . . . **1930** BEAMES *Army* 257: Ted passed by the poplar bluff and down across the old corduroy road through the runway, still used in wet springs.

Rupert ['rupərt] *n.* [< *Rupert's House*, a trading post named after Prince Rupert; see **Rupert's Land**] See quote.
1935 *Beaver* Dec. 64/3: The Rupert's House canoe factory has been going full blast for the summer and J.S.C. Watt has turned out approximately sixty canoes during the season. Two new models, an eighteen-foot "Rupert" and a sixteen-foot "Rupert," have been developed and are now on display in the Winnipeg Fur Trade depot.

Rupertia *n.* [< *Rupert's Land,* q.v.] *Obs.* a name once suggested for what is now Winnipeg.
1860 *Nor'Wester* (R.R.S.) 28 Sep. 4/3: The name of the metropolis should be a surname for all your expected pilgrim-children: a cognomen of the first and highest rank—nothing less comprehensive than "Rupertia." **1861** *Ibid.* 15 Nov. 2/4: An estimable clergyman lately suggested RUPERTIA as a suitable one.

Rupert's bird [< *Rupert's Land,* q.v.] *Obs.*
See **Canada jay.**

1891 (1892) PIKE *Barren Grounds* 123: This bird is common throughout the wilder parts of Canada, and has acquired many names in different places; in the mountains of British Columbia he is the Hudson's Bay bird or grease bird, and far away to the East the moose bird, caribou bird, Rupert's bird, and camp robber.

Rupert's Land *Hist.* the territory granted by charter in 1670 to the Hudson's Bay Company and surrendered to the Government of Canada in 1870 for a compensation of £300,000, understood as comprising all land watered by rivers flowing into Hudson Bay and so named because Prince Rupert was first governor of the Company. See also **Prince Rupert's Land.**
1670 (1900) OSBORN *Greater Canada* 187: And further we will and grant by these presents, for us, our heirs and successors, unto the said Governor and Company, and their successors . . . that the said land be from henceforth reckoned and reputed as one of our plantations or colonies in America, called "Rupert's Land." **1748** ELLIS *Hudson's Bay* 78: One would have imagined, that after this considerable Settlements suitable to the Design of the Charter should have been made and *Rupert's* Land, for so his Majesty directs the new Plantation to be called, should by this Time have become none of the least considerable Colonies in *America.* **1862** *Nor'Wester* (R.R.S.) 2 Apr. 2/3: It is too late in the day for toryism—and foreign readers will understand what Rupert's Land toryism means—too late, we say, for it to sneer. **1966** *Modern Instructor* Mar. 440: When the purchase of Rupert's Land was completed, the Canadian Government continued the investigation of the region in order to decide the route of the railway and to encourage settlement.

rural municipality one of several divisions into which certain provinces are broken down for administrative purposes. See 1945 quote. Cp. **municipal district.** See also **R.M.**
1861 *Nor'Wester* (R.R.S.) 15 Aug. 1/4: Such was the state of things in Canada until 1841, when the Canadian Legislature passed an act (4 & 3 Vic. cap 10) to extend the municipal system to districts (now counties) and other rural municipalities. **1904** *U of T Stud. Hist. & Econ.* II 140: The council of a rural municipality is made up of a reeve and not less than four nor more than six councillors, the number being fixed by by-law. **1945** (1950) BROWN *Cdn Democracy* 84: One of the reasons for the apparent confusion is that rural municipalities go by different names in different provinces. In Nova Scotia they are called municipalities; in New Brunswick, counties and parishes; in Quebec, counties, townships and parishes; in Ontario, counties and townships; in Manitoba and Saskatchewan, rural municipalities; in Alberta, municipal districts; and in British Columbia, districts. **1964** *Naicam Sentinel* (Sask.) 26 Mar. 2/3: A meeting of the council of the Rural Municipality of Pleasantdale No. 398 was held in the R.M. office Wednesday.

rural parliament *Obs.* See quote.
1842 *Bytown* [Ottawa] *Gaz.* 29 Dec. 2/3: We may here promise, that we at first viewed the establishment of these local Municipal Councils, (or what some individuals have termed "Rural Parliaments") with no small degree of doubtfulness as to their well working in this country, where the population is composed of such materials as we have.

rural route a mail-delivery route outside an urban area. See also **R.R.** (def. 2).
1956 *Chatham Dly News* (Ont.) 14 June 2/6: Entrants

will be accepted from Thamesville and surrounding rural routes. **1965** *Globe and Mail* (Toronto) 15 Oct. 7/1: George Harris Hees of Bay Street, Toronto, St. James Street, Montreal, and, within the last month, of Rural Route 5, Cobourg.

rush† *n.* See **gold rush.**
1859 *Brit.Colonist* (Victoria) 30 Sep. 2/2: Mr. A. has the impression that there will be a great rush for the upper country next year, as there is no doubt of it being highly auriferous. **1963** *Placer-Mining B.C.* 18/1: In 1908 and again in 1932 there were small "rushes" into the creek.

rusho(o) *n.* See **richeau.**

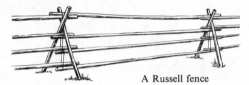

A Russell fence

Russell fence [< the name of its patenter] See 1953 quote. See also **patent fence.** Also spelled (erroneously) *rustle fence.*
1932 JAMIESON *Cattle in the Stall* 75: There was the rustle fence, with boom on top and centre. . . .
1953 *Cdn Geog.Jnl* Dec. 226/2: The Russell fence has the unusual distinction of having been patented and Russell, the inventor, succeeded, in some cases at least, in collecting royalties from people who built fences on his model. It consists of pairs of crossed posts, set in post holes as in the stake-and-rider and the dog-leg, but the rails are hung from the crotches and from each other in wire loops. This makes a very strong fence with few rails and the work of repairing it is made much easier. *Ibid.* 227: [Caption] Cowboys of the Chilcotin district, B.C., appreciate the uses of a Russell fence. **1964** *Sun* (Vancouver) 11 Feb. 4/3: Many members declare the proto-type Cariboo gate to be horizontal, loose jackpine poles with large knobby knots which must be pried in and out of the interstices of a Russell Fence.

Russian Indian *Hist.* an Indian, as a Tlingit, from the territory in Alaska which was long under Russian control.
1885 (1921) *Beaver* July 7/2: . . . we passed a winter of constant danger from the savage Russian Indians. . . .
1955 MCKELVIE *Pageant of B.C.* 45: In 1836 a party was sent to locate a post on the lake (Dease), but, fearful of the "Russian Indians," the men were seized with panic and fled.

Russian poplar a species of poplar introduced on the prairies for windbreaks and bluffs to control soil erosion.
1963 SYMONS *Many Trails* 94: Separated from the farmyard by a fine grove of Manitoba maples and Russian poplars . . . stands an eight- or ten-roomed house. . . .

Russian potato *B.C.* a variety of potato growing wild in the Cariboo region, said to have been first obtained from Russian traders in New Caledonia (def. 2) and planted during the goldrush days of the 1860's.
1966 *Williams Lake Tribune* 21 Sep. 3/8: The Likely district grows wild and tame cherries, apples, plums, blackberries, large gooseberries, Russian potatoes, sugar maples, also cedars many hundreds of

years old. . . . **1966** *B.C.Digest* Dec. 19/1: We have been given some potato tubers which we were told were Russian potatoes and which were originally grown in British Columbia by early settlers in Likely.

Russian sheeting *Hist.* See 1963 quote.
1786 (1959) PRESTON *Kingston* 120: [Goods handled] *Up* Tobacco . . . Russian Sheeting, Strouds. . . .
1817 (1964) PAYETTE *Northwest* 425: The 10p[s] of inferior Russia[n] Sheeting are packed under mark 18 in Bale No. 165. . . . **1963** MCTAVISH *Behind the Palisades* 235: The tarpaulins to cover the freight [of a York boat] . . . were made of a singularly light but strong flaxen material which went by the name of Russian sheeting. They were made at the Factory and waterproofed by a special treatment of raw linseed oil to insure pliability.

Russian thistle† a European prickly herb, *Salsola kali tenuifolia,* introduced into N. America in the 1870's, a costly pest, especially in the grain-growing areas.
1915 HENRY *Flora of B.C.* 113: SALSOLA (Russian Thistle) A bushy annual with fleshy or spiny leaves and sessile axillary flowers; calyx 5-parted. . . .
1954 TYRE *Saddlebag Surgeon* 232: Another jolly feature of the dust storms was the great amount of Russian Thistle that travelled with the drifting soil. **1963** *Herald Mag.* 19 Oct. 3/3: With practically no vegetation remaining except Russian thistles, the premises gave the impression of poverty, desolation and desert.

rustle fence See **Russell fence.**

Ruthenian *n. Hist.* **1** See **Galician** (def. 1).
1909 CAMERON *New North* 388: Up in Edmonton the Galicians (Ruthenians?) have just organised a corps of volunteer militia to serve the Canadian country of their adoption. **1929** ENGLAND *Immigrant* 56: Ruthenians are an intensely nationalistic and independent people. **1935** WALLACE *Encyclopedia* III 3/2: The Ruthenians who came chiefly from the Polish province of Galicia, but partly also from Bukowina in Roumania are commonly known in Canada as Galicians.

2 See **Galician** (def. 2).
1909 CONNOR *Foreigner* 14: . . . Slavs from Little Russia and from Great Russia, the alert Polak, the heavy Croatian, the haughty Magyar, and occasionally the stalwart Dalmation from the Adriatic, in speech mostly Ruthenian. . . .

Ryanite ['raɪə,naɪt] *n.* [< Henry *Ryan,* early circuit preacher in Upper Canada] *Hist.* See 1959 quote.
1883 RYERSON *My Life* 88: The Ryanite controversy turned chiefly on the refusal at first of the American General Conference to separate the Canada work from its jurisdiction. **1897** DURAND *Reminiscences* 114: In 1826 to 1830, in Hamilton, and generally in Upper Canada, there were four divisions—the Episcopal Methodists, in connection with the American body; the Ryanites, as they were called, or Canadian Wesleyans of that day; the New Connexion body, who had a church on Main, near Walnut Street; and the Old Primitives—the extremists, or some called them English ranters. **1959** PRESTON *Kingston* 330n: Henry Ryan was "Received on Trail" in Vergennes, Vt., in 1800 and served in the Bay of Quinte 1805, 1806. He was located in 1827 and in 1829, with James Jackson,

founded a rival to the Methodist Episcopal Conference
which he called the Canadian Wesleyan Methodist
Church, also known as the Ryanites.

rye *n*. See **Canadian whisky.**
1860 *Grumbler* (Toronto) 19 May 3/3: And, tho' the
crowd may smile at me, I'll take some neat "old rye."
1918 *Eye Opener* (Calgary) 2 Feb. 1/4: Entering into
a heated altercation with your pastor with regard to the
relative merits of Rye and Scotch is considered bad form.
1964 *Time* (Cdn ed.) 31 Jan. 7/1: Accepting a rye and
ginger, Mike Pearson then went back to writing out
a personal report. . . .

Ryersonian [,raɪər'soniən] *n*. *Hist*. a supporter of
Egerton Ryerson 1803-1882, Upper Canadian
Methodist leader and Reformer (def. 1). See also
Saddlebag.
1830 *Canada Freeman* 22 Apr. 3/1: Those Christian
Pharisees, the Ryersonians, govern our elections and
we must go with the tide. **1833** *Patriot* (York
[Toronto]) 28 June 2/4: Methodist preachers—as the
cant term "Ryersonian" designates—have used every
effort to procure the signatures of children to political
grievance petitions, and even prostituted the pulpit to
such work.

Ryersonian *adj*. of or pertaining to Egerton
Ryerson or his supporters and their views. See also
above entry.
1832 *Canada Freeman* 5 Apr. 2/4: It is a pity such men
should be exposed to the wily hypocrisy of Ryersonian
cant. **1833** *Liberal* (St. Thomas, U.C.) 6 June 2/2: The
Ryersonian methodists, as they are sometimes called,
are bound by their religion to be true to the government
under which they live, and there is no reason to doubt
their sincerity.

Ryersonianism *n*. *Hist*. the body of opinion held
by Egerton Ryerson and his followers. See also
Ryersonian, *n*.
1853 *Hamilton Gaz*. (C.W.) 27 Oct. 2/7: Should
Ryersonianism continue to spread its baleful influence,
however, a proposition similar to the one made by Mr.
Gamble, will come to be regarded, twenty years hence,
as the most presumptuous and insensate utopianism.

Sabine('s) gull [< Sir Edward *Sabine,* Brit. explorer, d. 1883] a small Arctic gull, *Xema sabinii,* having a forked tail, gray head, and black collar.
1852 SUTHERLAND *Baffin's Bay* II 88: Sabine and ivory gulls, and other birds, such as ducks, brent geese, &c., were on their flight up the Channel.
1958 *Evening Telegram* (St. John's) 6 May 30/5: Few people have the opportunity to see Sabine's Gulls as they rarely come south even in the winter.

sablefish *n.* a large dark gray or black food fish, *Anoplopoma fimbria,* of the Pacific Coast. See also **black cod** and **skilfish.**
1960 *Fisheries Fact Sheets* 62 1: The blackcod or sablefish is a member of the skilfish family. **1964** CARL *Marine Fishes B.C.* 49: Most [sablefish] are smoked and sold under the name of "black cod."

Sable Island pony a wiry, wild pony of a distinctive type found on Sable Island in the Atlantic off the coast of Nova Scotia.
1962 *Maclean's* 19 May 80/2: The typical Sable Island pony, Lawlor says, "is a brightly colored bay with black points. There are also a few blacks."
1964 *Canadian Wkly* 13 June 9/1: [We] mentioned P.E.I.'s Big Jim Prendergast . . . and his efforts to save the Sable island ponies.

sac à commis, saccacommi(s), etc. See **sagakomi.**

sachem† ['setʃəm] *n.* [< Algonk.] the chief of an Indian tribe. See also **sagamore.**
1721 (1925) *Cdn Hist.Rev.* VI 36: For this purpose their missionaries are constantly employed, frequent presents are made to the Sachems or King's of yᵉ several Nations, and incourragement given for Inter-marriages between the French and Natives.
1845 *Literary Garland* II June 254/2: When round the solemn council fire,/The sage and sachem hold a talk,/ And tell the braves in wild attire,/ To lift the buried tomahawk. **1960** MCNAMEE *Florencia Bay* 184: Charlie . . . could have been a chief with sachems planning a nocturnal raid.

sackay commis See **sagakomi.**

sack ship *Atlantic Provinces, Hist.* a large vessel employed in carrying supplies from Europe to the East Coast fisheries, returning with cargoes of fish.
1957 *Nfld Qtly* June 7/2: . . . the sackships had come very early in the spring [with] supplies. . . . **1965** *Cdn Geographer* IX 1 3: . . . fishing ships and "sack" ships came to Cape Breton's coves and harbours each year in substantial numbers. **1965** MACNUTT *Atlantic Provinces* 14: Its larger vessels, now known as "sack ships," appeared on the scene at St. John's, taking no part in the catching of the cod, and serving primarily as freighters and transporters.

saddle and notch See **saddle notch.**

Saddlebag or **saddlebag** *n.* [cf. **saddlebag preacher**] *Hist.* in Upper Canada, a Reformer (def. 1), specifically a Ryersonian, *q.v.*
1831 *Canada Freeman* (York [Toronto]) 19 May 2/3: Let Mackenzie stick to the Central Committee, the Saddlebags, & the Pennsylvania Dutch of the Home District—the moment he separates from them he's a gone duck. **1832** *Patriot and Farmer's Monitor* (Kingston, U.C.) 27 Mar. 1/1: A few Catholic bigots in Town, (old boys at home who are well known as the tools of the saddlebag faction) opposed this meeting;—

others intimidated by the opposite faction kept out of sight. **1833** *Colonial Advocate* (York [Toronto]) 21 Mar. 3/1: [He asked] the Editor not to mention his name in full, as the saddlebags would be displeased with his change of opinion.

saddlebag doctor *Hist.* See **saddlebag surgeon.**
1957 GUILLET *Valley of the Trent* xl: There were [in Upper Canada] circuit-riding clergymen, saddle-bag doctors, and self-sacrificing mid-wives.

saddlebag itinerant *Hist.* See **saddlebag preacher.**
1933 SLATER *Yellow Briar* 80: ". . . that's the hoarseness the saddle-bag itinerants get with their roaring and noisy preaching."

Saddlebag party *Hist.* the Reform party, *q.v.,* in Upper Canada in the 1830s. See also **Saddlebags Parliament.**
1833 *Liberal* (St. Thomas, U.C.) 7 Mar. 3/3: "I hold in my hand," said John Brown, "a resolution, that will—G-d d-m them all, d-m Mackenzie, d-m the Methodists, and d-m the whole saddle-bag party."

saddlebag preacher *Hist.* in colonial times, an itinerant Methodist preacher who carried his requirements in his saddlebags; a circuit rider. See also **saddlebag itinerant.** Cp. **Saddlebag.**
1953 RADCLIFF *Letters* xvi: Thomas Radcliff properly paid tribute to the work of the Methodist saddle-bag preachers. Had he been in the country long when he wrote, he almost certainly would have referred also to the Methodist camp meetings, which impressed all who observed them for the first time. **1958** *Encyc.Can.* IX 120/1: Called to the ministry, [Egerton] Ryerson was [a] saddle-bag preacher. . . . **1967** *Kingston Whig-Standard* (Ont.) 8 Mar. 27/2: Mr. Bates . . . was a saddle-bag preacher during the early years of the 19th century.

Saddlebags Parliament *Hist.* the Parliament dominated by the Saddlebag party, *q.v.*
1830 *Canada Freeman* (York [Toronto]) 28 Oct. 3/1: Here lies the remains of the Saddlebags Parliament, the ranting, hypocritical, and corrupt offspring of the Central Committee, which, while living, had the Bible, religion, and morality on its lips, while its "inside was full of rapine and iniquity."

saddlebag surgeon in the early days of settlement in the West, a doctor who did his rounds on horseback, carrying his instruments, medicines, etc. in his saddlebags. See also **saddlebag doctor.**
1954 TYRE *Saddlebag Surgeon* 4: Another card . . . came from a former patient who remembered the pioneer years before the turn of the century, when the saddlebag surgeon rode through blizzard and downpour to sod shanties on the prairie. . . .

saddle notch a saddle-notched joint. See also **saddling.**
1930 BEAMES *Army* 12: He disdained the clumsy "squaw notch," where one log sits simply in a shallow groove cut in the one below, and fitted them neatly into place with the "saddle notch," a triangular ridge cut to fit closely into a deep V in the log above. One grade higher

is the dovetail, or "square corner," but that takes time and requires a good axeman at each end of the log.
1948 HOLLIDAY *Valley of Youth* 139: But the real little log cabin ... would be rather low with the logs crossed at the corners, "saddle" and "notch" style. ...

saddling *n*. the use of saddle-notched joints. See also **saddle notch.**
1912 HEENEY *Pickanock* 45: His shanty was made of small white pine logs ... crossed at the corners of the building, where they were made to fit one astride the other by a process known among the lumber men as "saddling."

safety touch *Cdn Football* **1** a play in which a player of the team in possession of the ball intentionally touches it to the ground behind his own goal line, thus conceding two points to the opposing team. Cp. **rouge** (def. 1).
1904 CONNOR *Prospector* 38: With a brilliant series of passes the 'Varsity quarters and halves work the ball through the McGill twenty-five line, and by following hard a high punt, force the captain to a safety touch.
1958 *Edmonton Jnl* 7 Aug. 7/2: Flying wing Jack Hill ... booted three converts while guard Don Walsh picked up two points on a safety touch.

2 the two points conceded on such a play.
1964 *Kingston Whig-Standard* (Ont.) 24 Nov. 9/1: [He] should have crossed the goal line where he would have been grassed for a safety-touch.

sagakomi *n*. [< Algonk.; cf. Ojibwa *sagākomin* smoking-leaf berry] *Obs.* Also spelled *sac a comis, saccacommi(s).*
☛ *The long accepted etymology of the French variant* **sac à commis** (**sac** *pouch* + **commis** *clerk—see 1889 quote at def. 1 and 1823 quote at def. 2) is a folk etymology, perhaps based on a pun.*
1 the leaf of the bearberry (def. 1), used alone or mixed with tobacco for smoking. See also **bearberry** (def. 3).
1703 LAHONTAN *New Voyages* II 53: They are forc'd to buy up Brasil Tobaco, which they mix with a certain Leaf ... call'd *Sagakomi*. **1830** (1837) *Trans.Lit.& Hist.Soc.Que.* III 91: ... Saccacommi [is] frequently used to smoke in lieu of tobacco, by the traders' engaged in the fur countries. ... **1890** MASSON *Les Bourgeois* II 102: *Graine d'ours,* bear berry, also called *sac à commis,* [is a] creeping plant which is smoked, and which the clerks put in their sacs. ... **1912** (1913) HODGE & WHITE *Indians of Canada* 402/1: Sagakomi. The name of a certain smoking mixture, or substitute for tobacco [as] bearberry ... or other shrubs the leaves and bark of which are used for the same purpose.

2 See **bearberry** (defs. 1 and 2a).
1823 FRANKLIN *Journey* 741: Jackashey-puck ... has received the name of *Sac à Commis,* from the trading clerks carrying it in their smoking bags. **1836** BACK *Arctic Land* 257: We passed many sand-hills, variegated by the ... plant called ... by the traders, "sac a commis". ... **1912** (1913) HODGE & WHITE *Indians of Can.* 402/1: Sagakomi [is] the bearberry bush. ...

Sagalie (or Saghalie) Tyee [< Chinook Jargon *sagalie* above + *tyee* chief] *Pacific Coast* the Christian God. Also spelled *Saggali Tyee, Segali Tyee.*

[**1833** (1963) TOLMIE *Physician* 242: After breakfast [I] was requested to "wawa saccgali." Gave them an account of the Creation. ...] **1922** JOHNSON *Legends* 9: Then the Sagalie Tyee smiled on his Indian Children. **1963** SYMONS *Many Trails* 80: "You good mans ... You go Saggali Tyee [God]." **1964** DUFF *Indian History* 89: Coast Salish groups who do not remember this name refer to the deity by a name which translates into "Chief Above," and this is an exact equivalent of the term for God used by missionaries and Indians in the Chinook jargon—"Saghalie Tyee."

sagamité [sə'gɑmə,te] *n*. [< Cdn F < Algonk.; cf. Cree *kisakumitew* it is a hot liquid and Ojibwa *kisagamite* the broth is hot] Also spelled *sagamite, sagamity, shag(g)amitie,* etc. **1** a broth or soup of boiled meat, fish, etc.
☛ *Although the entered form is that derived from Algonkian through Cdn French, the word was undoubtedly borrowed independently by the English traders from the Crees of the Hudson's Bay region. Early spelling variants are numerous. See also further note at def. 2.*
[**1633** *Relations des Jésuites* 41: les Sauuageais aiment for le sagamité le mot de Sagamiteou en leur langue signifie proprement l'eau, ou de brouet chaud: maintenant ils estendent sa signification a toute sorte de potage, de bouille, choses semblables.] *c*1665 (1885) RADISSON *Voyages* 40: Then my father made a speech shewing many demonstrations of vallor, broak a kettle full of Cagamite with a hatchet. **1748** DRAGE *Voyage* I 216: From the Meats they boil they have the Advantage of the Broth, which they call Sagamite, and in Winter Weather set it out in the Kettle to freeze till it becomes Ice, and so portable Soop. **1791** LONG *Voyages* 61: Among several of the tribes of Indians, pap is made of saga[m]ite, from a root they call toquo, of the bramble kind; this is washed and dried, afterwards ground, or pounded, and made into a paste, which being baked is pleasant to the taste, but of a very astringent quality. **1938** GODSELL *Red Hunters* 54: On the long carrying places campfires were kindled while the packers toiled and kettles of sagamité were slung above them for the evening meal.

2 a kind of porridge made from Indian corn, long associated with the Hurons.
☛ *Although long in use among the corn-growing Hurons to refer to hominy, or corn porridge, this word originated among the non-farming Algonquins, who used it to refer to hot liquid, such as soup or broth. The Hurons may have borrowed it directly from the Algonquins, adapting it to their own purposes; or they may have learned it from the French missionaries, who would in that case have borrowed it from the Algonquins somewhat earlier.*
[**1632** (trans. 1939) SAGARD *Journey to Hurons* 57: I could not yet eat their sagamité ... being unaccustomed to it. ...] **1760** JEFFERYS *Descr.New France* 91: Of this vegetable [corn] is made what they call sagamite ... is received from the women. ... **1916** WAUGH *Iroquois Foods* 91: Probably no corn or other food is referred to so frequently as hominy, or sagamité, as it was more familiarly known to the early French. **1963** *Beaver* Autumn 17/2: Their [Hurons'] sagamité, a kind of corn porridge that drew excruciatingly long faces from the early Frenchmen, was, nevertheless, remarkably nourishing.

sagamore† ['sægə,mɔr] *n*. [< Algonk.] *Hist.* **1** See **sachem.** Also figurative.
1842 *Montreal Transcript* 27 Jan. 2/3: The chief was called a Sachem, or Sagamore; he wore no badge of rank, and often possessed no more wealth than others.

influential Sagamore was not the only cross.
2 any important person.
1942 RADDALL *His Majesty's Yankees* 96: "The Old One
is dead. They cut his head to a meat. Then the red-coat
sagamore stood with thy father in the house door and
commanded the ship men to take their dead and go. . . ."

saganash ['sægə,næʃ *or* 'sægə,nɑʃ] *n.* [< Algonk.;
cf. Ojibwa *shākenāsh*] in Indian parlance, a white
man, especially an Englishman, or Britisher.
Cp. **Shagalasha.** Also spelled *saganaw, saganosh,
sag(g)inosh, sagonosh.*
1784 (1790) UMFREVILLE *Hudson's Bay* 47: The old
man . . . affected much regard for me as being a
Sagonosh. . . . **1791** LONG *Voyages* 101: . . . the young
warrior . . . wished . . . to praise the goodness of the
Saggonash. **1832** (1929) RICHARDSON in *Selected Stories*
40: The great chief of the Ottawas knows that the great
father of the Saganaws has a big heart to make presents
to the red-skins. **1863** *Nor' Wester* (R.R.S.) 28 Oct. 2/5:
Two of these gentry . . . were very particular in their
enquiries as to what hay was owned by "Saganash"
(the English). **1904** WHITE *Silent Places* 68: I know the
language of the saganash. **1935** *Cdn Geog.Jnl* Mar.
107/2: [They were] cheered with ammunition, calico
and tea and assurances of friendship from the White
Chief of the Saganosh. . . .

saganaw *n.* See **saganash.**

sage or **sagebrush**† *n.* a bluish-gray shrubby plant
of the genus *Artemisia,* as *A. tridentata,* of the arid
regions of the West.
1857 (1863) PALLISER *Journals* 54: Here we . . . met
with the sage. . . . **1859** (1958) WATTERS *B.C.Cent.Anthol.*
246: I climbed mountains and got covered with
wood-ticks as I ploughed through the sage-brush and
greasewood. . . . **1953** CUSHMAN *Stay Away Joe* 6: [He]
sat perfectly still . . . staring out across the foothills
studded with sage and jackpine. . . . **1963** *Canada
Month* May 14/1: South of Cariboo lies the Dry Belt,
an area of stunted jack-pine, sagebrush, sand and
cactus.

sage bush or **grass** See **sage.**
1872 (1873) GRANT *Ocean to Ocean* 300: The cattle had
eaten off all the bunch-grass within three or four miles
of the road, and a poor substitute for it chiefly in the
shape of a bluish weed or shrub called "sage grass" or
"sage bush" had taken its place. **1908** MAIR *Mackenzie
Basin* 435: Another nest taken under the same
conditions along Frenchman's River, Province of
Saskatchewan, on 21st June, was built of the outer
bark of sage bush. . . .

sage cock See **sage grouse.**
1959 MCATEE *Folk-Names* 25: Sage Grouse [is also
called] sage cock (The bird's range is practically that of
the sage brushes (*Artemesia*) upon which it freely feeds.
Sask.) sage grouse, sage hen (Sask.).

sage fowl *Rare* See **sage grouse.**
*c*1890 (1904) RAND *Cdn Verse* 18: Beneath the brushwood Sagefowl snugly lie. . . .

sage grass See **sage bush.**

sage grouse† or **hen** *West* a species of grouse,
Centrocerus urophasianus, found in arid regions
where sage is plentiful. See also **sage cock** and
sage fowl.
1871 (1877) GRANT *Ocean to Ocean* 283: British
Columbia boasts of having seven or eight varieties of

the grouse kind, the most abundant being the sage
hen . . . and the spruce partridge or fool-hen, that is
oftener knocked over with a stick than shot.
1952 PUTNAM *Cdn Regions* 39/2: In the very dry parts of
the Okanagan there is a desert fauna including the
pocket gopher . . . sage grouse. . . . **1956** *Sask.News*
12 June 4/1: The display includes the six native grouse
species in the province: pinnated grouse (the true
prairie chicken); sharp tailed grouse; sage grouse; ruffed
grouse; ptarmigan; and spruce grouse or "fool hen."
1958 *Beaver* Autumn 53/2: A field notebook sketch of
a sage hen (a large grouse) to which were added
complete data.

Saggali (or Saghalie) Tyee See **Sagalie Tyee.**

sagonosh *n.* See **saganash.**

Saguenay ['sægə,ne] *n.* [< Cdn F < Algonk.]
See 1958 quote.
[**1582** (1850) HAKLUYT *Divers Voyages* 11: The people of
Saguinay doe testifie that vpon their coastes Westwarde
there is a sea, the ende whereof is vnknowne vnto them.]
1754 JEFFERYS *Conduct* 73: Canada . . . lay to the west
of the country to Saguenay (so called from the river
which still bears that name) which therefore lay
between it and the mouth of the river [St. Lawrence]. . . .
1848 LANMAN *Adventures* 183: In speaking of the
Saguenay, I must not omit to mention its original
proprietors, a tribe of Indians . . . known as the
Mountaineers. **1958** *Encyc.Can.* IX 125/1: The
Saguenay [is] a term used to designate a vast region
in Quebec, extending between 48° N. and 51° N. from
the St. Lawrence River to the height of land that
constitutes the watershed between Hudson Bay and the
St. Lawrence.

Saint Jean *Hist.* See **St. John's Island.**
☞ **St. John's Island** *and other entries in which* **Saint**
*is commonly written in its abbreviated form, will be
found in their alphabetical places under* **St.**
1926 WRONG *History of Canada* 109: Above all, she
[France] retained the two large islands off the coast,
Saint Jean—now Prince Edward Island—and the
island of Cape Breton.

salal [sə'læl] *n.* [< Chinook Jargon < Chinook
klkwu-shala] Also spelled *sallal. Pacific Coast*
1 a small evergreen shrub, *Gaultheria shallon.*
1825 (1914) DOUGLAS *Journal* 104: Gaultheria Shallon
[is] called by the natives "Salal" " not "Shallon."
1900 *Canadian Mag.* May 8/1: The glossy foliage of
the sallals with their delicate pink flowers, and the
star-eyed, scarlet-fruited pigeon berries, all contribute
vivid spots of colour to the soft-toned pictures of the
woods. **1962** *Canadian Wkly* 30 June 6/3: Salal's an
evergreen shrub used by florist's in bouquets instead of
fern, and it has an edible berry . . . that gourmets use
to make a jelly to eat with game.

2 See **salal-berry.**
1833 (1963) TOLMIE *Physician* 230: Have supped on
Sallal & at dusk, shall turn in. **1964** *Islander* 16 Aug.
2/3: [She] asked me if I had ever tasted salal or
Oregon grape jelly.

salal-berry *n.* the edible, purplish berry of the
salal (def. 1). Also spelled *sallal berry.*
1867 LORD *Wilderness* 249: Of these the Service berry
. . . and the Sallal berry . . . may be specified as being the

most useful. **1952** *Tsimshian* 17: Crab-apples, cherries, currants, huckleberries, salmon-berries, salal-berries, soapberries, and saskatoons, were all gathered to be eaten fresh or dried for use during the winter.

saleshop *n. Hist.* a retail store of the Hudson's Bay Company.
1907 HUNTER *Cdn Wilds* 10: Where most of the old prairie posts stood in the old days, the company now have "Sale Shops" for the whites. . . . **1957** *Beaver* Autumn 38/1: The "Saleshop" classification marked a modest type of urban transition, from fur trade to general store operation.

salmonberry† *n.* the red-flowered raspberry, *Rubus spectabilis,* of western North America; also, the berries of this shrub. See also **olallie.**
1884 *Brandon Blade* (Man.) 28 Feb. 3/3: Right on the top of this moss there is . . . the wild strawberry, raspberry, salmon berry, cranberry. **1888** (1890) ST. MAUR *Impressions* 138: . . . salmon-berries, blueberries, and cranberries . . . are what attract the bears. **1954** *B.C.Hist.Qtly* XVIII 45: One informant's account . . . tells how a trading-ship gave the Lummi a keg of rum; the Lummi poured it over a great feast-dish filled with salmonberries and ate the rum-soaked berries with their spoons. **1960** *Time* (Cdn ed.) 7 Mar. 11/1: The Victoria Natural History Society delightedly announced that a few lucky members had spied . . . sturdy buds of salmonberry. . . .

salmon fence *B.C., Hist.* a fence enclosing a pound for trapping salmon, built by Indians.
1956 EVANS *Mountain Dog* 85: During supper, Peter asked Moses to tell him about those old Indian salmon fences.

salmonier *n.* [< F *saumonier*] *Obs.* a salmon fisherman. See also **salmon post.**
1770 (1792) CARTWRIGHT *Journal* I 14: When the salmoniers visited their nets this morning, they found that the Indians had stolen one fleet. **1770** (1911) TOWNSEND *Cartwright's Jnl* 26: We took a walk . . . to look at a new beaverhouse, in which the salmoniers had killed four beavers.

salmon of the lakes *Obs.* See **lake trout.**
1827 (1829) MACTAGGART *Three Years* I 172: What are the local names of the fishes? Let *black bass, mosquenonge, fresh water herrings, salmon of the lakes,* &. be examined.

salmon post *Obs.* the base of a salmon-fishing crew.
1770 (1792) CARTWRIGHT *Journal* I 14: Upon landing at the salmon-post, I found the crew to consist of three men; and, from several circumstances, they had little opportunity of enriching their employers.

salmon stand *Obs.* a pool or quiet water in a river, where salmon rest during upstream migrations; a salmon pool.
1845 TOLFREY *Sportsman* I 75: The Major smiled at the question, and gave me to understand it was a nickname of his own for the first sheet of smooth water—the first salmon-stand in fact below the bridge, where the fish reposed themselves after their fatigue of ascending the numerous scurs and rapids between Jacques Cartier and the St. Lawrence. . . . **1872** DASHWOOD

Chiploquorgan 76: The bottom is gravel and sand, so the salmon "stands," vary more or less with the spring freshets, new pools being formed and old ones silted up or changed.

salmon trout 1 See **lake trout.**
☛ **Lake trout** *is the usual term nowadays. For another earlier term, see* **salmon of the lakes.**
[**1620** MASON *Briefe Discovrse* A iv ᵛ: The South part is not so mountanous nor so woodie . . . hauing pretty Groues and many fresh laks replenished with Eeeles & Salmon-Troutes great, and in great plentie.]
1749 DRAGE *Voyage* II 32: With a setting Net placed in the Creek, we took daily great Number of Jacks and Salmon Trout. **1838** TRAILL *Backwoods* 161: One of the small lakes of the Otanabee is called Trout Lake, from the abundance of salmon-trout that occupy its waters. **1948** ONRAET *Sixty Below* 72: You might look down from a canoe and see bull trout and salmon trout chasing one another forty feet below, and that's beating Great Bear River outside Fort Norman.

2 See **Dolly Varden trout.**
1882 *Edmonton Bull.* 25 Feb. 4/2: Mountain trout are plentiful in all the streams and salmon trout in the mountain lakes. **1912** FOOTNER *New Rivers* 100: We trolled for and caught the fine salmon trout that the Indians call sapi.

salmon wheel See **fish wheel.**
1889 WITHROW *Our Own Country* 534: The man who invented the western river salmon wheel was a genius. The laziest fisherman who ever baited a hook could ask for no easier way of landing fish.

saloon† *n.* See 1871 quote.
1844 *St.Catharines Jnl* (C.W.) 10 Oct. 2/4: Mr. B's garden will soon be as celebrated as his well-furnished and well-managed Saloon. **1871** (1883) BUTLER *Gt Lone Land* 71: Several new saloons (name for dram-shops, gaming-houses, and generally questionable places) were being opened for the first time to the public, and free drinks were consequently the rule. **1957** *Cdn Geog. Jnl* Oct. 166/2: Within a short time 1,000 people were working on Wild Horse River, and a town, named Fisherville, with saloons, restaurants, and a brewery developed rapidly.

salt-banker *n. Maritimes* a banker (def. 1) carrying enough salt to preserve the caught fish at once, thus making possible protracted stays on the fishing grounds. Cp. **salt fishing.**
1955 GILLESPIE *Bluenose Skipper* vii: I would like to acknowledge . . . the help given by the details of fishermen's duties aboard a salt-banker suggested in a short story by Thomas H. Raddall. . . . **1961** *Atlantic Advocate* Jan. 38: It was marked by the loss of a Nova Scotia salt-banker which had raced her way into the hearts of the nation

salt-bulk *n. Nfld* See **bulk.**
1861 DE BOILIEU *Labrador Life* 31: The cod is now placed in what is called salt-bulk, where it may remain any period of time; for, so long as fish is being caught in the bay, so long will the "drying" and "washing"—which constitute the final process—be delayed. **1964** *Nfld Qtly* Summer 27/1: This well-known method [pickling] of producing the most palatable codfish, was perhaps then a new departure, to get a better price from the traditional saltbulk style.

salt-burnt *adj. Nfld* See quote. Cp. **broken fish.**
1832 MCGREGOR *Brit.Amer.* I 231: If too much salt have been used, the fibres break in drying, and the

[cod] fish easily falls to pieces. In this state, it is called salt-burnt, and is unfit for market.

salt-chuck ['sɑlt,tʃʌk] *n*. [< *salt* + Chinook Jargon *chuck* water] *B.C., Informal* the ocean, including all salt-water inlets, canals, and bays affected by tidewater. See also **chuck**[1] (def. 2b).
*c*1857 (1927) MCKELVIE *Black Canyon* vii: "Hist . . . Before sun up you white men go . . . to salt-chuck (ocean). Indian kill all white men in canyon." **1874** HORETZKY *Canada* 132: A thick heavy mist hung over the valley, completely hiding the Cascade range which we had now to enter and pass through before reaching the "salt-chuck." **1938** CASH *I Like B.C.* 61: And unless you are camped near a log dump—which means where a logging company is dumping logs into the salt chuck —you have quite a time gathering enough. **1966** *Sun* (Vancouver) 30 May 30A/3: They . . . felled the big ones [trees], rolled them up to a thousand feet to the salt chuck and herded them into booms from leaky boats.

salt-chucker ['sɑlt,tʃʌkɚ] *n*. [< *salt-chuck*, q.v. + *-er*] *B.C., Informal* a salt-water angler. See also **'chucker.**
1958 WATTERS *B.C.Cent.Anthol.* 216: It is the spirit that counts, and that spirit extends to trying to make life happier for thousands of scattered salt-chuckers. **1963** *Sun* (Vancouver) 20 July 15/1: Now, however, with an average of almost two fish per short outing of a few hours each trip, I'm wearing the saltchucker's smug smirk.

salter *n*. a member of a cod-pickling crew who washes the fish and salts it.
1760 PICHON *Cape Breton* 109: The salter immediately draws it aside, and places it with the skin undermost. **1954** *Fundy Fisherman* (Black's Harbour, N.B.) 3 Mar. 1/2: The Gaspe cure salt fish is salted in deep tubs, the salter usually carting both the fish from the splitting table and the salt from the salt bin to these tubs.

salt fishing fishing over long periods from a vessel having enough salt to preserve the catch for an entire trip. Cp. **salt-banker.**
1960 *Atlantic Advocate* Nov. 29: "You can't beat 'em for salt fishing," declares Mr. Ritcey.

salt goose *Hist*. goose meat pickled in salt. See also **goose hunt.**
1898 (1957) *Beaver* Autumn 13/1: While here [York Factory] we some days had "salt goose" instead of beef for dinner. **1941** *Ibid*. Sep. 39/1: Salt Goose [was] . . . a staple article of diet, the daily meat ration being one goose per man. Some years the numbers preserved were phenomenal.

salt grass *Pacific Coast* See 1952 quote.
1917 PHILLIPPS-WOLLEY *Songs* 31: Through gray salt grass the April breezes creep. . . . **1952** PUTNAM *Cdn Regions* 26/1: Especially noteworthy are the saline sloughs and lakes around which salt tolerant plants are found such as spike grass (*Distichlis spicata*), salt grass (*D. stricta*). . . .

salt hay *Esp.Maritimes* hay from salt-water tidal marshes, as *Juncus gerardi*. See also **salt-water grass.**
1822 (1960) MCCULLOCH *Stepsure Letters* 55: . . . he had just exchanged her [a mare] with a couple of tons of salt hay, for an excellent young horse. . . . **1934** DENNIS *Down in N.S.* 273: "It's salt hay," said the driver. "Oxen and cattle like it for a relish. We gather it from the meadows near the salt water. Salt hay is different

from English hay. It has to be dried and dried and dried." **1963** WICKENS *Mary* 154: The swamp was lush with rank grass, known as salt hay because the water of the swamp was brackish.

salt-house *n*. *Nfld* the building in which fish are processed for salt-curing.
1832 MCGREGOR *Brit.Amer*. I 228: Generally covered over and attached to it [the stage], or rather on the same platform, is the salt-house. . . .

saltie ['sɑlti] *n*. [< *salt* (water) + *-ie*] *Great Lakes, Slang* **1** an ocean-going vessel, as opposed to a lake boat, *q.v.*
1959 *Ottawa Citizen* 29 Apr. 53/1: Sixty or more ocean ships—called "salties" by lake seamen—and inland ships were expected to be in transit today. **1966** *Kingston Whig-Standard* (Ont.) 5 Jan. 19/7: The only saltie to visit Kingston that year, the 17,170 ton Malmanger of Norway, sailed with her holds only half full of grain.
2 a sailor on such a vessel.
1962 *Canada Month* Sep. 17/1: Once free of the Great Lakes, the salties figure they rule the roost.

salt lick† **1** *Obs*. See **salt spring**. See also **lick** (def. 1).
1793 (1833) *Cdn Literary Mag*. May 82/2: We crossed two or three rivulets through a thick wood, and over a Salt Lick, and stopped at four o'clock to give the Indians time to make a small wigwam. **1832** RADCLIFF *Letters* 155: [Finding the deer] is best to be effected at the *salt licks*, or springs, whither they resort to drink.
2 a place where the ground contains particles of salt and other minerals, resorted to by wild animals. See also **lick** (def. 2) and **licking place.**
1828 *U.E.Loyalist* (York [Toronto]) 2 Sep. 112/1: Found, thirteen feet below the surface of the earth, on Simpson's job, Welland Canal, in the old salt lick . . . a deer's horn. . . . **1955** GOWLAND *Smoke* 65: By some mysterious kind of forest telegraph, all the hoofed creatures for miles around learnt about that salt, a commodity that is rare in the mountains, where the salt licks are not only few, but also far between.
3 a place, such as a hollow log or a hole at the base of a tree, where salt is placed by a hunter as a lure for game.
1903 CARR-HARRIS *White Chief* 184: I reckon there's only two ways to shoot a moose: one is to coax him within range by imitating the call of his mate; the other way is to make a salt lick for him.

salt pile *Nfld, Obs*. **1** See **bulk.**
1784 PENNANT *Arctic Zoology* cxcvii: In the salt pile, the fish are spread one upon a other, with a layer of salt between. Thus they remain till they have taken salt; and then are carried, and the salt is washed from them by throwing them off from shore in a kind of float called a Pound.
2 a pile of green seal hides salted to keep them from deteriorating.
1900 LONDON *Son of Wolf* 232: And with them I went to the rich beaches of Copper Island, where our salt-piles became high with skins.

salt plains arid, unproductive saline earth; specifically, a tract of such soil lying some 40 miles northeast of Fort Smith, N.W.T.

the mud and floats upon the surface. **1925** *Beaver* Sep. 184: It was customary to send the sheep to the marsh to graze, the salt water grass being ideal for fattening.

salt-water itch *West* See **prairie itch.**
1957 MOWAT *Dog* 30: We slithered about on the surface, acquiring painful sunburns and bad cases of salt-water itch.

Salt Water Siwash *B.C., Hist.* an Indian who lived on the Pacific Coast, as opposed to an inland Indian. See also **Coast Indian.**
1963 SYMONS *Many Trails* 67: They perished almost to a man in the massacre which followed—a crime committed by the warlike and murderous Salt Water Siwashes.

salty *n.* See **saltie.**

saluting *n. Maritimes* See **shivaree** (def. 1).
1952 BUCKLER *Mountain and Valley* 51: That was the skirt she'd worn the night of Joseph's saluting. Her feet had moved so lightly they'd made her lead the Lancers and the Eights.

samp† [sæmp] *n.* [< Algonk.; cf. Narraganset *nasaump* cornmeal porridge] See **supon.**
1916 WAUGH *Iroquois Foods* 92: Roger Williams [1643] applies the name of nasaump (samp) to "a kind of Meale Pottage, unpartch'd." He further remarks that "the English samp is corn, beaten and boiled and eaten hot or cold with milk or butter." [**1923** WILLIAMS *Spinning Wheels* 275: The queer old iron kettle in which sanap [sic] pudding was boiled was the one that swung from the crane. . . .] **1943** MILLER *Lone Woodsman* 168: A savory stew steamed near the fire in an iron kettle; a copper one held tea; there was a great bowl of white samp, the corn rinds having been leached off by soaking in wood ashes before boiling.

sample room a hotel or other room rented to commercial travellers and other salesmen who wish to display samples of their goods for viewing by prospective customers.
1887 *Grip* (Toronto) 21 May 10/2: . . . one of the drug travellers insisted . . . that the clerk . . . had, in the north sample room, first nicknamed Albendis "Chippy." **1897** *Inland Route to the Yukon* 21: The Dominion Hotel . . . Sample Rooms for Commercial Travellers. **1898** *Yukon Midnight Sun* (Dawson) 11 June 7/2: The Aurora Sample Room . . . We have the finest brands of Wines, Liquors and Cigars in the city.

Samson (fox) *n.* [< *Samson*, the Israelite judge, who destroyed the Philistines' grain by letting loose foxes with torches tied to their tails (Judges 15, 4-5)] *Fur Trade* a red fox lacking guard hairs, giving its fur a burnt appearance.
1921 (1955) RUSSELL *Carlton Trail* 99: Foxes that were burned like these were what we called "Samsons," and were useless. **1933** MERRICK *True North* 305: He said he weren't goin' to . . . go clear into Canada [from Labrador] to trap a few weasels and samson foxes.

sanap *n.* See **samp.**

sandberry *n. Obs.* See **sand cherry.**
1804 (1890) CAMERON *Nipigon Country* 241: Some years there are many pigeons, which are very fat and palatable when they feed on berries, very plentiful here some years such as: strawberries, raspberries, blueberries, gooseberries, sandberries, cranberries, small cherries and abundance of wild currants of different colours.

1851 (1908) MAIR *Mackenzie Basin* 116: These natural pans, or salt plains, he describes . . . as "bounded on the north and west by a ridge between six and seven hundred feet high." **1882** *Prince Albert Times* (Sask.) 6 Dec. 1/4: We proceeded on our stage to the salt plains in our new conveyance comfortably enough untill towards evening we met with a mishap which delayed us for some time. **1927** *Cdn N.W.Hist.Soc.Pubs* I iii 19: The weather was ideal while mosquitoes were numerous and attentive, especially on the Salt Plains. . . .

salt-rising *n.* sourdough (def. 1a) kept as a leavening agent for future batches of baking.
1833 (1846) TRAILL *Backwoods* 137 [DA]: [The wife of a Canadian settler] must know how to manufacture *hop-rising* or *salt-rising* for leavening her bread. **1852** *Elora Backwoodsman* (C.W.) 30 Sep. 3/1: Butter and bread she is too modest to say much about, but she does venture a complaint about . . . salt-rising being rather uncertain, and not to be depended upon for the making of the other. **1951** ROBINS *Cdn Humour* 202: Course the cook made salt-risin bread, but he couldn't get nobody to touch it after he got good on pancakes.

salt slob *Nfld* See **slob.**
1953 BANFILL *Lab.Nurse* 126: For two days we had travelled from early morning until dark over soft ice covered with a thin crust of salt slob.

salt slough *West* a pond or small lake that is alkaline.
1908 LAUT *Conquest N.W.* I 341: Instead of brackish swamp water or salt sloughs, were clear-water lakes. **1957** MOWAT *Dog* 30: I enjoyed myself at Manitou, which is one of the saltiest of the west's salt sloughs.

salt spring a small spring or stream containing salt from local deposits and used by animals as a source of salt. See also **lick** (def. 1), **salt lick** (def. 1) and **salt-water creek.**
1822 GOURLAY *Upper Canada* 146: There are likewise salt-licks or springs. **1851** (1908) MAIR *Mackenzie Basin* 116: Several salt springs issue at its foot, and spread over the plain. **1867** *Cdn Naturalist* III 173: These island marine plants have only as yet been detected on . . . the borders of large swamps or in the immediate vicinity of salt springs and "salt licks."

salt struck *Nfld, Hist.* of cod, sufficiently impregnated with salt as to be adequately pickled. See also **struck.**
1957 *Cdn Geog.Jnl* Oct. 129/2: The fish were left in the stage until they became "salt struck", then the family removed the fish from salt, washed them, piled them to press out excess water and finally spread them several times for complete sun-drying on the green-bough-covered (longer) framed "flakes" which are still such a prominent feature of the Newfoundland coastal settlements.

salt-water creek *Obs.* See **salt spring.**
1787 *Account N.S.* 208: In several places, in the vicinity of the lakes [Ontario and Erie], are found salt water creeks, probably impregnated by the veins of rock-salt, sometimes found in the bowels of the earth. . . .

salt-water grass See **salt hay.**
1832 BAILLIE *Account of N.B.* 62: Bay Vert takes its name from the quantity of salt water grass which grows in

sand cherry† either of two low-growing shrubs, *Prunus pumila* or *P. p. besseyi;* also, the fruit of either of these shrubs.
1793 (1933) MACDONELL *Diary* 116: The wild plumb, and Grape, the pair, choak and sand cherries, Summer berry and the Raspberry are also natives of this [Assiniboine] country. **1795** (1911) SIMCOE *Diary* 348: [I] gathered cardinal flowers, a beautiful purple flower, sand cherries and some raspberries. **1827** (1914) DOUGLAS *Journal* 290: *Prunus* . . . found sparingly on gravelly places and lime stone rocks on Red River, called by the voyageurs Sand-Cherry. **1956** *Native Trees* 216: One species, the sand cherry, *Prunus pumila* L., is a low, often prostrate shrub. **1958** *Encyc.Can.* IX 200/1: Sand Cherry (*Prunus besseyi*) [is] a well-known, low-growing, shrubby fruit found wild in the Prairie Provinces.

sandflower *n. West* See **crocus.**
1884 *Trans.Hist.& Sci.Soc.Man.* 14 14/2: Next after the hips their most important food in May is the sandflower (Anemone Patens), which purples with its millions the prairies from the Great Lakes to the Rockies.

sandfly *n.* any of several small winged insects with a sharp bite, especially *Phlebotamus* sp. Cp. **no-see-em.**
1717 (1932) KNIGHT *Journals* 147: To Sett in, y^t is, the Musketos & horse flyes; but ye 3^d is worse than ye other 2, for here is now Such Swarms of Small Sand flyes that wee can hardly See the Sun through them, & where they light is Just as If a Spark of fire fell & raises little lump wch Smarts & burns So that wee cannot forbear Rubbing of them as cases Such Scabbs that our hands & faces is nothing but-Scabbs. **1867** (1876) LORD *Wilderness* 282: The male sand-fly is not a blood-sucker, but lives on flowers. **1921** HEMING *Drama of Forests* 282: One night those almost invisible torments, the sand flies, caused us—or rather me—much misery until Granny built such a large fire that it attracted the attention of the brutes, and into it they all dived, or apparently did—just as she said they would—for in less than half an hour not a single sand fly remained.

Sand Hills a region in southeastern Alberta, long sacred to the Plains Indians, often a euphemism for death. See 1957 quote.
1838 (1947) HARGRAVE *Correspondence* 273: People may say it is a pity that so many Indians are gone to the Sanday Hills. **1949** MACGREGOR *Blankets and Beads* 113: . . . Nothing marks the spot where some mighty chief or minor brave sleeps, while his spirit travels the trails of the Great Sand Hills. **1957** *Camsell Arrow* Christmas 77/1: The sun dance site is in the heart of the 50-mile-square Blood reserve about 40 miles south of Lethbridge. There are situated the sacred sand hills and the happy hunting grounds for departed spirits. **1959** SLUMAN *Blackfoot Crossing* 13: Little Tree would have to go unadorned to the Sand Hills, for her daughter could not part with the red glass beads.

sandwich *n. Hockey, Slang* a defensive play in which an attacking player is simultaneously bodychecked by two opponents, especially defencemen.
1963 O'BRIEN *Hockey* 42: Time and time again . . . he'd get caught squarely in the "sandwich."

sapa *n.* See **sapi.**

sap-boiler *n.* See **sugar-kettle.**
1966 *Kingston Whig-Standard* (Ont.) 19 Mar. 6/8: [Caption] Here Neil Parks . . . throws wood into his stove to keep the sap boiler steaming.

sap-boiling *n.* See **sugaring-off.**
1885 HAIGHT *Country Life* 5: . . . the sap-boiling was under the direction of my mother, who mustered all the pots and kettles she could command, and when they were properly suspended over the fire on wooden hooks, she watched them, and rocked me in a sap-trough.

sap-bucket *n.* **1** *Hist.* See **sap-trough.**
1897 DURAND *Reminiscences* 83: Sap troughs, hundreds, were prepared, deepened to receive the maple sap. . . . These troughs or sap buckets were carefully emptied into pails or tubs, and the precious sap carried to the boiling pots. **1923** WILLIAMS *Spinning Wheels* 87: "I can't never pay fer them sap-buckets now." **1960** *Cdn Geog.Jnl* Nov. 171: [Caption] An exhibit of maple sugar-making equipment in the Dalziel Barn museum [included] . . . sap buckets and maple sugar moulds. **1967** *Kingston Whig-Standard* (Ont.) 16 Mar. 6/6: [Advert.] Auction Sale . . . sap buckets and pans; 100 bales of hay; coaloil lamps. . . .

2 See **sap-carrier.**
1909 ROSS *Hist.of Zorra* 30: His sap-troughs—there being no sap buckets in those days [1853]—were full, as there was a good run of sap that spring. **1947** WELLS *Owl Pen* 89: It is time . . . to get . . . sap buckets down from the beams of the woodshed.

sap-bush *n.* See **sugar bush.**
1885 HAIGHT *Country Life* 5: The sap-bush was not very far away from the house. . . .

sap-carrier *n. Maple Industry* a wooden receptacle equipped with a handle and used for carrying sap from the tree to the sugar house. See also **sap-bucket** (def. 2).
1953 *Cdn Geog.Jnl* May 180/2: Sap buckets and sap carriers, in fact all the tribe of buckets, keelers, piggins and other containers made of staves, came a little later to Upper Canada.

sap-house *n.* See **sugaring-hut.**
1940 *Dalhousie Rev.* XX 223: . . . a stove [was] placed in a special building known as a "sap house." **1966** *Kingston Whig-Standard* (Ont.) 18 Mar. 6/1: But who can be bored sitting around a sap house in a beautiful day in March. . . .

sapi ['sɑpi] *n.* [< Athapaskan] *Northwest* See **Dolly Varden trout** and **salmon trout** (def. 2).
1824 (1955) BLACK *Journal* 52: He knew only of 3 Fishing Lakes in this quarter[:] Bears Lake a small round Lake in which they take Sapa. . . . **1912** FOOTNER *New Rivers* 100: As we were . . . frying sapi steaks, our camp received two canoe-loads of visitors. **1929** JOHNSTON *Beyond Rockies* 172: Going down river, for many miles the only living souls we saw were a few Indians camping on the river bank with their "sapi" (big trout) hanging on poles to dry for winter supplies. **1955** RICH in BLACK *Journal* 52n: Sapi or Dolly Varden (*Salvelinus alpinus malma*) [is] a sub-species of the arctic char.

sapin ['sæpɪn *or* sa'pa] *n.* [< Cdn F < F] See **balsam** (defs. 1 and 2).

1807 WENTZEL *Letters* 90: The habitations of these people are built in oblong figure, of pieces of wood placed upon one another, the roof of which is thatched with sapin and the sides cemented or rather calked with moss. **1846** (1955) CRAIG *Early Travellers* 157: The Indians trampled down the snow for a resting-place, made a seat of sapins—the tops of fir trees, and brought us deliciously cold and pure water from a stream close by.... **1931** CONNOR *Rock and River* 96: Down the course marked out by "sapins" and back again amid the cheering throngs, the procession moved at a moderate pace.

sap run See **run,** *n.* (def. 7).

1966 *Kingston Whig-Standard* (Ont.) 18 Mar. 6/1: Every year ... a reporter must ... trudge down a muddy lane to somebody's sugar bush and do a story on the annual sap run.

sap-shed *n.* See **sugaring-hut.**

1966 *Kingston Whig-Standard* (Ont.) 18 Mar. 6/6: ... small plastic tubing ... feeds the sap directly from the trees to a storage basin outside the sap shed.

sap tank See **sugar-kettle.**

1960 *Cdn Geog.Jnl* Nov. 171: [Caption] The exhibit of maple-sugar-making equipment [contained] a sled for transportation of the sap tank....

sap-trough *n. Maple Industry, Hist.* a container, usually of wood, used for catching the maple sap running from the spile, *q.v.,* in a tree. See also **sap-bucket** (def. 1).

1852 (1881) TRAILL *Cdn Crusoes* 152: Is it to be like the big sap-trough in the sugar-bush at home? **1909** ROSS *Hist.of Zorra* 30: His sap-troughs ... were full, as there was a good run of sap that spring. **1964** GUILLET *Pioneer Days* 99: The Mohawk Indians commonly used a hollowed-out basswood log for a sap trough, the log being burned out as much as possible and then cleaned out with a stone adze.

sap weather See **sugar weather.**

1955 *Tweed News* 14 Apr. 2/4: Sap weather may be here, but syrup makers are getting a very poor run of sap. **1963** *Kingston Whig-Standard* (Ont.) 26 Mar. 13/2: Yes, "Sap weather" is really the only sure sign of spring.

SARAH beacon [*S*earch *A*nd *R*escue *A*nd *H*oming] a three-pound battery-operated homing device designed and produced in Canada for use as safety equipment in aircraft.

1963 *Weekend Mag.* 4 May 34/2: The R.C.A.F. reports also keep harping on the usefulness of the SARAH beacon homing equipment.

sarce *n.* See **sauce.**

sarskutum *n. Obs.* See **saskatoon.**

sarviceberry *n.* See **serviceberry.**

sash *n. Hist.* a belt or waistband, often of worsted and of bright design, as the L'Assomption sash, *q.v.,* characteristic of French Canada and long identified with the voyageurs and Métis. See also **belt** (def. 2), **ceinture, Indian sash, Red River belt,**

scarf-belt, and **voyageur sash.** See picture at **L'Assomption sash.**

1791 (1911) SIMCOE *Diary* 71: The habitants call it [a hooded coat] a capitshaw, and their coats are tied round with a coloured worsted sash. **1801** (1933) MCLEOD *Diary* 159: ... Cadottes ... overtook them before noon ... [and] they restored the Sash.... **1961** *Cdn Geog.Jnl* Jan. 35/2: Then he gave to each of the older men a suit of underwear and the younger, a toque, pair of mittens and a sash.

sash-belt *n.* See **sash.**

1880 (1893) YOUNG *Indian Wigwams* 155: ... I managed to fasten the end of the sled-rope which I held in my hand to my sash-belt, which was tied tightly around my moose-skin coat....

sashed *adj.* wearing a sash.

1922 (1958) WATTERS *B.C.Cent.Anthol.* 60: ... a white man dressed as Thompson was to come up the lake in a canoe manned by sashed voyageurs....

Saskatchewan [sə'skætʃə,wan *or* -wən] *n.* [< Cree *kisikatchewin* swift current, fast-flowing river] *Hist.* **1** (often with *the*) the extensive prairie country in the vicinity of the Saskatchewan River. [**1754** (1954) MACGREGOR *Shining Mountains* 42: Paddled two miles up the River, and then came to the Keiskatchewan River on which the French have two houses....] **1827** *Gore Gaz.* (U.C.) 15 June 62/4: The botanist, during the absence of the exploring party from the Fort has been engaged in investigating the vegetable productions of the Taskatoohawin country. **1853** *Trans.Lit.& Hist.Soc.Que.* IV 298: The prairie country of the Saskatchewan is roamed over by countless herds of the buffalo, also by the reindeer and the beautiful antelope. **1884** *Prince Albert Times* (Sask.) 14 Mar. 4/1: The Saskatchewan brigade left Edmonton as soon as possible after the opening of navigation, and arrived at York in the latter end of July.

2 See 1882 and 1889 quotes.

1882 *Prince Albert Times* (Sask.) 13 Dec. 3/1: To sum up the Saskatchewan district includes Battleford, Carleton, and Prince Albert. **1889** WITHROW *Our Own Country* 447: This vast region (the North-West Territory) has been provisionally organized by the Dominion Government for purposes of administration into four districts, named respectively Assiniboia, Saskatchewan, Alberta and Athabasca. **1958** *Encyc. Can.* IX 212: 1882—The District of Saskatchewan is created.

Saskatchewan berry See **saskatoon berry.**

1963 *Kingston Whig-Standard* (Ont.) 20 July 13/3: There is quite a history to the Saskatchewan berry; it grows in profusion on the banks of the Red and Assiniboine rivers.

Saskatchewan Rebellion *Hist.* See **Northwest Rebellion** (def. 2).

1963 MORTON *Kingdom of Canada* 370: The Saskatchewan Rebellion was a sad affair, and it was to have even sadder consequences; consequences which began to work out their evil course when on November 16 [1885], after all appeals had failed, Riel was hanged at Regina. **1963** *Beaver* Winter 1963 42/2: ... in 1885 he saw more adventure and this time some action during the campaigns of Riel's Saskatchewan Rebellion.

saskatoon [,sæskə'tun] *n.* [< Cree *misāskwatomin* fruit of the tree of many branches] Many spellings in 19th century: *saskatome, saskatoom, saskatum, saskootum, suskatum,* etc. **1** See **saskatoon berry** (def. 1). See also **misaskatomina** (def. 1).

[**1800** (1820) HARMON *Journal* 81: Different kinds of berries are now ripe, such as strawberries, raspberries, and what the Canadians call *paires*, which the Natives denominate Mi-sas-qui-to-min-uck.] [**1820** (1823) FRANKLIN *Journey* 88: Under the name of *meesasscootoomeena* it is a favourite dish at most of the Indian feasts, and mixed with pemmican, it renders that greasy food actually palatable.] **1821** (1900) GARRY *Diary* 150: Walked about two miles through a Wood, [saw] Strawberries, Raspberries ... Sasquetuin. ... **1955** HARDY *Alta Anthol.* 434: Jake went right on with his Saskatoon pie, eating it real careful with his knife and fork. **1961** *Edmonton Jnl* 1 Aug. 1/1: Sunday morning for breakfast we had ... saskatoons, raspberries, and cranberries.

2 See **saskatoon bush**. See also **misaskatomina** (def. 2).

1810 (1950) THOMPSON *Journals* 119: Vegetation is much advanced[;] the Sarskutum &c are in blossom. ...
1883 *Selkirk Herald* (Man.) 24 Aug. 2/2: There is also ash leaved maple, cherry, saskatoon, plum and hazel, of a small size. **1956** *Native Trees* 212: The serviceberries, also known as juneberries, shad-bushes, and, in the West, the Saskatoons, are deciduous species with simple alternate leaves and slender unarmed twigs.

3 the wood of the saskatoon bush, *q.v.*

1890 *Trans.Roy.Soc.Can.* VIII 2 101: The arrow was half the length of the bow, and was made from the saskatoon. ... **1952** HOWARD *Strange Empire* 298: The saskatoon or choke-cherry-wood arrow was often driven clear through the body of the buffalo.

saskatoon berry 1 the edible, purplish berry of the saskatoon bush, *q.v.* See also **Saskatchewan berry, saskatoon** (def. 1), **serviceberry** (def. 2), and **summerberry**.

1859 KANE *Wanderings* 149: A small bag of pemmi-kon made in the usual way, except that it contained Sasketome berries, was stolen, and a search being made for its recovery, a part of it was found in one of the men's bags. **1889** *Regina Jnl* 1 Aug. 1/6: Saskatoon berries are ripe and fairly abundant. **1963** *Kingston Whig-Standard* (Ont.) 20 July 13/3: The Saskatoon berry ... has a wonderful color and a tantalizing tartness.

2 See **saskatoon bush**.

1930 JONES *Wild Flowers* Plate 61: Saskatoon-Berry. *Amelanchier canadensis.* A tree or tall shrub.
1955 MCCOWAN *Upland Trails* 85: Be that as it may, the fact remains that the Saskatoon-berry is one of the best known plants, whether on the prairies or in the mountain regions.

saskatoon bush a species of serviceberry (def. 1), *Amelanchier alnifolia,* common in the West and prized for its succulent berries. See also **saskatoon** (def. 2), and **saskatoon berry** (def. 2).

1880 GORDON *Mountain and Prairie* 186: There is here a great profusion of saskatum, or service-berry bushes, and the bears, being exceedingly fond of these berries, come out upon the high sloping banks to enjoy them. **1895** SOMERSET *Muskeg* 33: Daukhan said that the bears were very plentiful, and that he thought it would be a good hunting year, as the saskatoon bushes would bear a large crop of berries. **1959** SHIPLEY *Scarlet Lily* 188: While Skipper munched the sweet green grass growing by the chokecherry and saskatoon bushes. ...

saskatoon tree See **saskatoon bush**.
1952 MACGREGOR *Twelve-Foot Davis* 17: Saskatoon trees, six, eight or ten feet high in the spring, provided a border of snowy white around every copse.

saskatoon willow *Obs.* See **saskatoon bush**.
[c**1804** GRANT *Sauteux Indians* 309: [There is] a fine fruit not larger than a currant, tasting much like a pear and growing on a small tree about the size of a willow.] **1889** *Our Forest Children* Dec. 99/1: Their bows are of cherry-wood, strung with a leathern thong, and their arrows of the Saskatoon willow, winged with feathers, and pointed with scrap-iron, filed to a sharp point.

Sasquatch ['sæskwætʃ] *n.* [< Salish *se'sxac*] See 1958 quote.
1929 *Maclean's* 1 Apr. 61/1: "The strange people of whom there are but few now—rarely seen and seldom met—" said the old hunter, "are known by the name of Sasquatch, or 'the hairy mountain men'." **1958** *Encyc. Can.* IX 233/1: Known originally to the Indians—most of whom believe in this mysterious race—as Saskehavas (wild men), they are called by the whites Sasquatch (hairy men). They are described by Indians who claim to have seen them as hairy monsters between 7 and 9 feet tall, of subhuman appearance, with wide flat noses and abnormally long arms. **1966** *Globe Mag.* 11 June 3/3: Most villagers relate every Sasquatch sighting to the amount of alcohol they insist must have been consumed immediately prior to the monster's appearance.

sasqueetum or **sasquetuin** *n. Obs.* See **saskatoon**.

sass *n.* See **sauce**.

sastrugi [sə'strugi] *n.pl.* [< Russian *zastrugi* (pl. of *zastruga*)] ridges of hard-packed snow, formed by the wind and at times attaining a height of four feet.
1851 (1852) OSBORN *Arctic Jnl* 164: The snow ridges, called Sastrugi by the Russians, run ... in parallel lines, waving and winding together. ... **1853** (1884) MCCORMICK *Voyages* II 75: For this purpose, I fixed upon the softest wreath, or sastrugi, of snow at hand to cut a trench deep enough to hold the two dogs, my companion, and myself. ... **1939** TWEEDSMUIR *Hudson's Bay Trader* 96: There is sastrugi, when the snow lies in hard patches furrowed and fluted by the wind, like ribbed sea sand. It was sastrugi that hampered Captain Scott's sledges and contributed to his heroic failure to return from the Pole. **1963** *North* Mar.-Apr. 13/1: While sledging through the fog, he had noted "hard sastrugi" and "ice rollers". ...

sauce† *n. Hist.* **1** stewed or preserved fruit, pumpkin, etc. Cp. **short sauce**.
☞ *Earlier dialectal variants current in North America account for such forms as* **sarce** [sas] *and* **sass** [sæs], *which occur frequently in writings of the 19th century. The term doubtless came to Canada in these meanings along with settlers from the New England speech area.* **1822** *U.C.Gaz.* (York [Toronto]) 2 May 22/2: For several weeks I was a good deal puzzled by persons coming, as they said, "to trade for some of my notions,"—"some of my little notions,"—They "guessed they could trade some pumpkin sarce for a few of my little notions." **1853** (1959) MOODIE *Life in Clearings* 148: "Oh, dear, yes; she lost all her clothes, and three large jars of preserves she made about a week ago, and sarce in accordance!" **1926** *Dalhousie Rev.* V 96: They will dry and shrink to a fraction of their original size, and be stored in crocks for the

manufacture of "sass" in those barren spring months when the bounties of autumn have been dissipated by the hunger of winter.

2 dried apples, hung on strings in colonial days. See 1926 quote at def. 1. Cp. **paring bee.**
1852 (1923) MOODIE *Roughing It* 112: Not know what sarce is? You are clever! Sarce is apples cut up and dried, to make into pies in the winter. **1863** WALSHE *Cedar Creek* 113: ". . . What's them strings of yallow stuff that are hangin' out of the rafthers, an' are like nothin' I see in all my days 'cept savin's?" / "Sarce," answered Mrs. Logan . . . "So ye calls apples 'sarce!' "

sauce garden or **patch** *Maritimes, Local* a vegetable garden. See also **short-sauce garden.**
1835 *Novascotian* (Halifax) 10 Dec. 365/2: They vegitate like a lettuce plant in a sauce garden. . . .
1942 RADDALL *His Majesty's Yankees* 172: ". . . But— hey!—look there, Mister Carson!—swear if there ain't a brindle cow in your sarce patch!"

sauger ['sɔːɡɚ] *n.* [origin unknown] a species of pike-perch, *Cynoperca* (syn. *Stizostedion*) *canadense,* similar to the walleye, *q.v.* See also **horn-fish.**
1882 JORDAN & GILBERT *Synopsis Fishes N.A.* 526: *Stizostedium canadense* . . . Sauger; Sand-pike; Gray-pike; Horn-fish. **1929** (1937) TONER *Fishes of East.Ont.* 17: Hubbs and Brown (1929) referred Lake Ontario sauger to the subspecies *S.c. canadense.* **1955** *Northern Mail* 15 June 3/3: . . . even boys have been put to work owing to the large quantity of boxes required for the large daily catches of pickerel and . . . saugers. . . .
1964 *Commercial Letter* Mar. 7/2: The most important catch in terms of value is the pickerel, followed by whitefish, sauger (a pickerel-like fish) and pike.

sault [suː] *n.* [< Cdn F, a 17th c. form, *sault* leap, jump; Mod. F *saut*] a waterfall or rapids. Also spelled (earlier) *saut.*
☞ *This old term occurs largely in place names nowadays.*
1600 HAKLUYT *Voyages* III 234: The Captaine prepared two boats to goe vp the great River to discouer the passage of the three Saults or falles. **1665** RADISSON *Voyages* 231: Being come nigh the Sault, we found a place where 2 of these men sweated, & for want of covers buried themselves in the sand by the water side to keepe their bodyes from the flyes . . . wᶜʰ otherwise had kill them wᵗʰ their stings. **1761** (1901) HENRY (Elder) *Travels* 15: . . . the Sault of Saint-Louis . . . is the highest of the *saults, falls,* or *leaps,* in this part of the Saint-Lawrence. **1785** HUNTER *Diary* 73: Boats are often lost in these dreadful rapids of the Long Saut. **1836** *Bytown* [Ottawa] *Gaz.* 30 June 2/3: . . . Mr. Ralph Lowe, while shad-fishing . . . at the head of the long Sault, overreached his stroke, and pitched headlong into the rapids. **1922** FLAHERTY *Eskimo Friends* 2: The rugged granites over which the Mattagami breaks, long "saults," smoking falls, and canyon-slots through the hills, give way about halfway down to a vast muskeg plain. . . . [**1953** MOWERY *Mounted Police* 63: For the sake of speed they were constantly taking white-water *sautes* which looked like suicide. . . .] **1958** *Cdn Geog. Jnl* Nov. 173/2: Stopped by a sault in their upward progress, the missionaries returned. . . .

sault [suː] *v.* [< *n.*] *Obs.* shoot (def. 1) a rapids, riffle, etc. Also spelled *saut.*
1800 (1897) COUES *New Light* I 29: I perceived the canoe on the N. side coming off to sault the rapids.
1821 (1900) GARRY *Diary* 129: This is a very dangerous Rapid, and so many fatal Accidents have attended the Sauting of it that it has been interdicted to the Servants of both Companies.

Saulteur liquor [< *Saulteur* Saulteaux, the western branch of the Ojibwa Indians] See quote. See also **Indian liquor.**
1799 (1897) COUES *New Light* I 3: ". . . I gave my two men . . . a 9-gallon keg of Saulteur liquor to each man." **1897** *Ibid.* 3n: Alcohol or "high wine" diluted to suit an Ojibway Indian's stomach, as regarded from a commercial rather than digestive standpoint. Indians already debauched would not stand so much water as fresh tribes could be induced to exchange beaver skins for, and hence a difference in recognized degrees of dilution in different cases. On the Red and Assiniboine rivers, about 1800, it was no uncommon thing for an Indian to give five or six prime beavers for a quart of "Salteur liquor"—a gill or two of alcohol, the rest water.

saupon [sauˈpɒn] *n.* [< Algonk.: ? Micmac; cf. Massachusetts *saupáum*] See **supon.**
1947 BIRD *Judgment Glen* 68: . . . Hester learned . . . the art of making saupon of Indian corn-meal. . . .
1950 BIRD *This is N.S.* 72: There had been a hotel then famed for three different things, its nickname of "The Apostles," its supper dish called "saupon," and the way the girls who worked there got married.

saut *n.* See **sault.**

savanna(h)† [səˈvænə] *n.* [< earlier *zavana* < Sp. < Arawakan (Taino) *zabana,* undoubtedly influenced by Cdn F *savane* used in this sense] *Atlantic Provinces* a tract of peat bog; a boggy barren. See also **caribou plain.**
[**1760** JEFFERYS *Descr.New France* 44: All these Indians . . . are comprehended by French authors, under the general appellation of *Savanois,* from the nature of the country they inhabit, which is low, swampy, and ill-wooded, those drowned barren lands, being called *Savanes* in Canada.] **1849** ALEXANDER *L'Acadie* II 245: I paced and took angles along indifferent roads, climbed steep ascents, and crossed the great savannah of some 40 miles long, which would afford an almost inexhaustible supply of peat. . . . **1883** HATTON & HARVEY *Newfoundland* 137: These savannas are composed of fine, black, compact peat-mould, formed by the growth and decay of mosses, and sustain countless herds of reindeer. **1952** PUTNAM *Cdn Regions* 83/1: Many of these [bogs] are treeless and are locally known as "savannas."

savanna(h) grouse *Maritimes, Obs.* probably the spruce partridge, *q.v.* See also **savanna.**
1849 ALEXANDER *L'Acadie* II 243: Savannah grouse, which we saw with young broods, were so tame in these solitudes . . . that they ruffled up to us to defend their offspring which perched on the low bushes.

savoyan *n.* [< Cdn F *savoyane, saouiyane* < Algonk.; cf. Cree *utesaweyan* dye (root)] *Obs.* an evergreen herb of the crowfoot family, *Coptis trifolia;* goldthread.
[**1739** (1965) *Letters from Hudson Bay* 290: As to the Tysowian . . . it was very good and gathered in the proper season . . . the Indians use to dye their quills with the root. . . .] **1807** WENTZEL *Letters* 80: The dyes made use of by the Indians to stain porcupine quills and

feathers, which are the only things they stain, are the roots of a plant which the Canadians call *Savoyan;* its colour is of an orange cast. **1907** HODGE *Bulletin* I Glossary: Savoyan—A name of the goldthread . . . the savoyane of Canadian French.

sawdust nobility See **lumber king**.
1956 RADDALL *Wings* 31: In each of these ghost towns there must have been a little group of mill and timber owners, a sawdust nobility of the Oak Falls kind. . . .

sawlog *n.* a log suitable for processing in a sawmill.
1799 SMYTH *Topogr.Descr.U.C.* 32: The saw logs are conveyed to this mill in a very remarkable manner. **1826** *U.E.Loyalist* (York [Toronto]) 5 Aug. 1/3: Upon Saw Logs of the proper length to be cut into Deals, Two pence upon each Log. **1883** FRASER *Shanty* 271: The square timber and sawlogs are lying many tiers deep on the ice, or piled up on the bank. . . . **1964** *Cdn Geog.Jnl* Feb. 66/3: A.R.M. Lower . . . describes a typical sawlog gang as "two sawyers and three choppers, the latter's duties being at first to fell and to top the limbs, the sawyers cutting into lengths."

sawlog nobility *Facetious, Obs.* members of the legislature, so called because of their abilities at sleeping through sittings, that is, at "sawing logs," or snoring.
1836 *Vindicator* (Montreal) 15 July 3/2: Our made Governor gave his party notice of the dissolution of the House at an early day, and appointed the election immediately after it and generally promulgated, which gave the sawlog nobility time to electioneer one month before the virtuous intelligence of the people knew that a new election would take place.

sawmill burner a conical furnace for burning excess sawdust at a sawmill.
1964 *Time* (Cdn ed.) 13 Nov. 18/2: But this year, where once there was only campfire smoke on the trail, the Cariboo horizon was dotted also by the smoke from sawmill burners.

saw-off *n. Slang* **1** in politics: **a.** *Hist.* an arrangement by which one party agreed, after an election, to drop charges of corruption against another if the second party would make a similar agreement.
1908 *Observer* (Cowansville, Que.) 19 Nov. 1/6: This is the month for election protests. Next month will be the month of election sawoffs. **1953** LEBOURDAIS *Nation of North* 67: Sometimes "saw-offs" were arranged, when protest proceedings were withdrawn by mutual consent.

b. an arrangement between two parties by which one agrees not to enter a candidate in a certain riding if the other agrees not to enter a candidate in a different riding.
1963 *Leader-Post* (Regina) 11 Oct. 29/1: "If you're certain you can elect three members by a saw-off with the Conservatives, go ahead."

2 any arrangement by which one concession is balanced against another.
1909 PARKER *Northern Lights* 258: What's up? Someone getting married—or a legacy, or a saw-off? **1910** FRASER *Red Meekins* 274: "I orter been satisfied with savin' that feller's life as a saw-off to some wuss things I've did. . . ." **1963** *Maclean's* 4 May 12/1: So-called "permissible concentrations" and "protection guides" are merely saw-offs between political, military or economic expedience, on one hand, and medical fact on the other. **1966** *Globe and Mail* (Toronto) 25 Jan. 3:

[Headline] Alberta hopes for sawoff on medicare with Ottawa.

saw-whet† *n.* See **Acadian owl**. See also **sawyer** (def. 2).
1845 BEAVAN *Life in Backwoods N.B.* 13: . . . the snow begins to melt on the roads, and the "saw whet," a small bird of the owl species, makes its appearance. . . . **1965** *Wildlife Rev.* Spring 25: Adult saw-whets are not aggressive and usually perch close by the nest and watch when an intruder happens along.

sawyer *n.* **1** *Obs. or Hist.* See 1784-1812 quote.
1784-1812 (1916) THOMPSON *Narrative* 187: A Sawyer, for want of a Greek name, is a large tree torn from the Banks by the current, and floated down to some place too shoal to allow the root to pass[;] here it rests, but the tree itself is in the current below it. It's buoyancy makes it float, but being fast the current buries it, to a certain depth, from which the . . . lightness of the wood causes it to rise . . . again it is buried, and again it rises, and thus continues to the great danger of everything that comes it's way. . . . **1837** *St.Catharines Jnl* (U.C.) 20 July 2/1: They would be hemmed in by sunken rafts, "snags," and "sawyers," that could be placed at an hour's notice.

2 *Ont.* See **Acadian owl**. See also **saw-whet**.
1822 GOURLAY *Upper Canada* I 174: The *Sawyer* or *Whetsaw* is so named from the sound of his voice, which resembles the whetting of a saw. **1956** MCATEE *Folk-Names* 44: Saw-whet owl [is called] sawyer (Ont.). . . .

3 *Lumbering* a logger employed in cutting felled trees into sawlogs, *q.v.*
1891 OXLEY *Chore-Boy* 67: . . . the "sawyers" . . . cut [the trees] into convenient lengths. . . . **1919** *Camp Worker* 30 Oct. 2/5: Prices vary from 11 cents to 18 cents per log for sawyers and 20 cents to 25 cents per log for teamsters, swampers, etc. **1964** *Cdn Geog.Jnl* Feb. 66/3: A.R.M. Lower . . . describes a typical sawlog gang as "two sawyers and three choppers. . . ."

A sawyer's fence

sawyer's fence a type of fence made of slabs, log ends, and other waste lumber from a mill placed at an angle to the ground, each piece being supported by a pair of crossed stakes.
1958 SYMONS *Fences* 24: This very odd-looking fence arrived in Canada with the advent of saw mills, and was commonly known as a sawyer's fence. It was supported by crossed stakes driven firmly into the ground.

scab *n. West, Slang* a saddle.
1951 HOBSON *Grass* 89: Throw down that cayuse and cinch my scab down good and hard on him, and I'll be out.

scabbard *n.* a guard for a skate blade, usually of rubber or plastic, often used when skates are being worn while walking to or from the skating area.

1963 *Calgary Herald* 21 Nov. 18/3: Rubber scabbards are very good to put on your blades when you pack them in your equipment bags. . . .

scabby-nosed wavey See **Ross's goose**. Cp. **wavey**.
1945 *Beaver* Sep. 17/2: . . . the Ross goose is in some quarters known as "galoot" and as "scabby-nosed wavy," nasty derogatory names. . . . **1956** MCATEE *Folk-Names* 10: Ross's Goose [is also known as the] scabby-nosed wavey ("N.W.T.," Alta.). . . .

scale† *v. n.* See 1963 quote.
1902 WHITE *Blazed Trail* 48: Not a log do I scale for ye, Jimmy Bourke. **1963** MCKINNON *Forest Activities I* 11: All timber cut for commercial use in British Columbia must be "scaled" (measured for wood volume) immediately by an official or licensed scaler. From the "scale" is determined the amount of tax "stumpage" or "royalty" to be paid to the Government. The official scale of timber in British Columbia is recorded in cubic measure.

scaler† *n. Lumbering* a person employed to scale timber.
1936 *B.C.Lumber Trade* 22: On the Coast, official scalers are now charged with the work of grading logs under the provision of the "Forest Act" . . . an Official Scaler holds the balance between logger and manufacturer. **1956** EVANS *Mountain Dog* 24: Hal knew that a summer at scaler's wages meant university for sure this fall. **1963** *Maclean's* 2 Dec. 19/4: On the American side the scaler calculates the proportion of rot, and the man is paid for the rest.

scallop dragger or **scalloper** *Maritimes* a fishing vessel equipped to drag for scallops.
1962 *Chronicle-Herald* (Halifax) 10 Aug. 19/1: A 95-foot scallop dragger was launched . . . Thursday. . . . *Ibid.* 19/2: The keel of a 100-foot scalloper . . . is standing by ready to be laid. . . .

scalp† *n.* **1** *Hist.* **a.** the hair and skin from the crown of the head, taken as a trophy. See also **scalp-lock** (def. 1) and **tophair.**
1743 (1949) ISHAM *Observations* 93: If one of a family Dies . . . They put . . . a painted Stick up . . . with the sculp of their Enemies, when they go to warr, which no Indians whatsoever takes away. **1955** JENNESS *Indians of Can.* 279: Whoever slew an enemy carried home the scalp for the victory dance, and thereafter enjoyed the privilege of wearing an eagle feather in his hair.
b. in **raise** (or **lift**) **a scalp,** See **scalp,** *v.* (def. 1).
*c*1804 GRANT *Sauteux Indians* 336: He then instantly pretends to make a circular incision with his knife around the head to raise the scalp, which he attempts to take with his teeth, after which he gives the whoop and dances around the circle. **1909** PARKER *Northern Lights* 265: He'll lift his scalp, and make a monk of him.
c. *Figurative uses.*
1884 *Nor'Wester* (Calgary) 6 May 2/2: The HERALD is not satisfied with condemning the mining regulations in toto but is after Mr. Hilliard's scalp. **1912** CONNOR *Corp.Cameron* 243: He could not win, of course, for McGee, the champion of the city police force, had many scalps at his girdle. **1955** *North Shore Leader* 18 Mar. 1/3: . . . for the fans who have been "crying for their scalps" all winter, here is your chance to show us that you can do a better job.
2 *Nfld* See **sculp,** *n.* (def. 2).

scalp *v.* **1** *Hist.* of Indians, cut off a victim's scalp (def. 1a). See also **scalping.**
1749 DRAGE *Voyage* II 46: An *Indian* who kills an *Eskemaux* scalps him; then takes and rounds a bit of willow, sowing the Scalp to it, and hangs one or two . . . on a Stick at the End of his Canoe. . . . **1861** *Nor'Wester* (R.R.S.) 31 Aug. 2/4: Some were for scalping us—others for horse-whipping us; but the good old chief would not allow us to be molested at all. **1930** *Cdn Hist.Rev.* XI 34: [They] used every means available to keep the Indians from scalping their victims. . . .
2 *Esp.Nfld* See **sculp,** *v.*

scalp cry *Hist.* a piercing cry given by an Indian after scalping an enemy.
1900 OSBORN *Greater Can.* 143: Even when the struggle between French and British for the possession of Canada was finally settled at the Heights of Abraham, and the *aw-oh-aw-oh-aw-oh* (the last syllable an octave higher than the rest, and prolonged till the chest was empty of air) of the [Iroquois] war-whoop or scalp-cry ceased to be heard in the East, men still fought over parcels of furs.

scalp dance *Hist.* See 1929 quotes.
1791 LONG *Voyages* 35: The dances among the Indians . . . [include] the scalp dance. *a*1929 LAUT in *Selected Stories* 72: That evening the united bands kindled an enormous campfire and with the scalps of the dead flaunting from spear heads danced the scalp dance, re-enacting in pantomime all the episodes of the massacre to the monotonous chant-chant of a recitative relating to the foray. **1929** JEFFERSON *Saskatchewan* 88: In this [Indian] order of things the Scalp Dance was a prime factor. The hair of a dead enemy was the first thing taken, indeed it was not necessary that the enemy be dead, so long as he was unable to resist the mutilation.

scalper *n.* **1** *Hist.* See **scalping-knife.**
1800 (1897) COUES *New Light* I 97: I . . . gave out to the Indians . . . an assortment of small articles gratis, such as one scalper, two folders. . . . **1824** (1955) BLACK *Journal* 162: Saw one of our Files stamped M & Co & one of the blades of our Scalpers L imprinted.
2 *Slang, Obs.* an Indian.
1845 TOLFREY *Sportsman* I 178: . . . and having shy'd his bolster at me, and desired the Indian to leave the room, I followed the scalper's example, fearing some more substantial article of bed-room furniture than the ticking and feathers might follow the bolster.

scalping† *n. Hist.* the practice or art of removing an enemy's scalp (def. 1a).
1768-82 (1791) LONG *Voyages* 22: If a blow is given with the tomahawk previous to the scalp being taken off, it is followed by instant death; but where scalping only is inflicted, it puts the person to excruciating pain, though death does not always ensue.

scalping-knife† *n. Hist.* a sharp knife used by Indian warriors to scalp their defeated enemies, an important item of trading goods in the fur country. See also **scalper** (def. 1).
1768-82 (1904) LONG *Voyages* 128: I gave him two gallons of rum . . . [and] a scalping knife. . . .
1883 *Prince Albert Times* (Sask.) 3 Oct. 4/1: It is now against the law to carry a scalping knife, and besides the Indians are no longer savages—they all now go to Sunday School. **1929** MOBERLY *When Fur was King* 36: . . . a bunch of seed beads or a scalping-knife [sold for]

one, a small country-made axe two, and a larger axe four made-beaver.

scalp-knife *n. Obs.* See **scalping-knife.**
1892 (1896) PARKER *Pierre* 217: They stood as their forefathers in battle, almost naked, with crested head, gleaming axe, scalp-knife, and bows and arrows.

scalp-lock *n. Hist.* **1** See **scalp,** *n.* (def. 1).
1848 *St.Catharines Jnl* (C.W.) 6 Jan. 3/1: I'll cause . . . the plundered scalp-locks of the pigmy and giant to flutter in ghastly bloody glory. . . . **1900** OSBORN *Greater Canada* 142: Indeed, there were times when the gathering of scalp-locks was to all intents and purposes a branch —and that not the least lucrative branch—of the commerce in peltries. **1934** *Cdn Geog.Jnl* Oct. 182/2: . . . their leggings and the arms of their shirts [were] fringed with ermine tails, or scalp-locks taken from the heads of enemies slain in combat.

2 a long tuft of hair worn by some Indian warriors with otherwise cropped or shaven heads as a challenge to their enemies. See also **fore-lock.**
1859 KANE *Wanderings* 5: He was the first Indian I had seen whose hair had been pulled out, all except the scalp-lock; this custom is common amongst many tribes of Indians, though not universal amongst any. **1925** *Beaver* June 141: The Indian is naturally a brave man . . . wearing his scalp-lock as an emblem of defiance. **1965** STEVENS *Incompleat Canadian* 11: [The Canadian Indians] shaved their heads either in whole or in part; in the east and on the plains they retained the scalp-lock.

scalp-shirt *n. Hist.* a ceremonial shirt embellished with scalps taken in battle.
1934 *Cdn Geog.Jnl* Oct. 182/2: On occasions of ceremony the men would wear scalp-shirts of light elk skin, having broad bands of porcupine quill-work embroidery down the arms and across the shoulders. . . .

scalp-traffic *n. Hist.* See quote.
1900 OSBORN *Greater Canada* 23: Many of them engaged in the infamous scalp-traffic—a peculiar branch of the fur trade inaugurated by the French commanders and prosecuted on the other side only by way of reprisal— and collected scalps among their Indian friends as methodically as they had formerly collected beaver-skins.

scare-wolf *n. West, Obs.* a device similar to a scarecrow, used to frighten wolves from carcasses of large game left by hunters for retrieving later.
1853 REID *Young Voyageurs* 127: "I left a 'scare-wolf' over both the [buffalo] bulls, however, and I guess we'll find them all right in the morning." **1892** DAUNT *Land of the Moose* 64: . . . the two trappers butchered the carcass and returned to camp, staggering under the weight of as much meat as they could carry. The hide was suspended to a pole cut from the ill-fated poplar; in which position the hunters hoped it would act as a sufficient scare-wolf.

scarf-belt *n. Hist.* See **sash.**
1893 YOUNG *Indian Wigwams* 60: Then his [the Metis'] moccasined feet and brilliant-colored scarf-belt, beaded cap, fire-bag and leggins, and distinct Indian face seemed to so ally him to the native tribes that too many never for a moment thought he could have any grievances to be redressed.

scarlet coat *Hist.* See **Mounted Policeman.**
1900 OSBORN *Warders of West* 778: The task of introducing British law and order into this remote corner of the empire was carried to completion without bloodletting, the scarlet coats looking too much like business for the wolfers to show fight.

Schenectady boat *Hist.* a kind of bateau in use on the St. Lawrence River in the late eighteenth and early nineteenth centuries, so called because similar to a class of boats identified with Schenectady, N.Y.
1798 *U.C.Gaz.* (York [Toronto]) 10 Mar. 3/3: Taken up, Some time last fall, in the mouth of the Niagara River, by the subscriber, a three hand Schenectady Boat. [**1806** (1904) LEWIS & CLARK *Journals* V 390: Those boats are from Canada in the betteaux form and wide in proportion to their length, their length [being] about 30 feet and the width 8 feet & pointed bow and stern, flat bottom and rowing six ores only the Skenackeity form.] **1905** SCHERCK *Pen Pictures* 33: The Durham and Schenectady boats used on the St. Lawrence before the days of the steamboat were only a form of bateaus.

schnoose [ʃnus] *n.* See **snoose.**

schnye *n.* See **shnye.** Cp. **snye.**

school area *Ont.* See **school district.**
1966 *Kingston Whig-Standard* (Ont.) 31 Aug. 6/4: Some increase was experienced in the township's own school area rate because of plans to build a new central school next year.

school board a group of persons (usually elected) who are responsible for the administration of the public elementary and secondary schools in a given area. See also **board of trustees** (def. 1).
1826 *Colonial Advocate* (York [Toronto]) 9 Feb. 3/2: But what good is it that there is one when the university or school board, keep the township as a block in the way of population and improvement. **1923** *Beaver* Nov. 41: He was . . . chairman of the Fort Qu'Appelle school board. **1966** *Globe and Mail* (Toronto) 26 Aug. 6/3: In fact, school boards need not be elected but can be appointed by the appropriate council or councils.

school commissioner† *Obs.* a member of a school board, *q.v.* See also **school trustee.**
1841 *Bytown* [Ottawa] *Gaz.* 23 Dec. 2/3: It behoves the inhabitants of the various Townships to watch carefully who they may appoint as School Commissioners. **1845** *Literary Garland* II 48/2: I cannot too earnestly exhort the School Commissioners . . . to take steps immediately to profit by this aid. . . .

school committee† *Obs.* See **school board.**
1813 *Kingston Gaz.* (U.C.) 28 July 1/3: Solomon Johns, one of the members of the School Committee of Ernest Town . . . on several occasions assumed the settlement of accounts due to the subscriber.

school crossing-guard a person employed to shepherd children across busy streets on their way to and from school.
1965 *Kingston Whig-Standard* (Ont.) 8 Feb. 7/6: He . . . worked as a school crossing guard until he retired 15 years ago.

school district† *Esp.West* (in modern use) an area designated as a unit for the local administration of public schools. See also **district** (def. 2), **school area,** and **school unit.** Cp. **school board.** *Abbrev.* S.D., *q.v.*

1825 *Novascotian* (Halifax) 30 Mar. 109/3: Such salary together with the expense of building and maintaining a school House, shall be raised and levied by and upon every inhabitant of each respective school district. . . . 1873 *Wkly Manitoban* 19 Apr. 4/2: The religion of the majority of ratepayers in any School District shall determine the designation of the District as Protestant or Roman Catholic, and any School dissenting from this shall be termed a Separate School. 1957 *Record-Gaz.* (Peace River, Alta) 19 Dec. 6/5: Nomination and acceptance forms may be obtained from the secretary of your school district. . . . 1960 WARD *Government in Can.* 7: Scattered throughout the city are public schools and high schools, all operated by the school boards that are the government of the Saskatoon school district.

school division 1 *Obs.* See **school district.**
1842 *Bytown* [Ottawa] *Gaz.* 30 Dec. 3/1: Can any one feel surprised to hear some Townships complaining of the inadequacy of the School Fund, when it is known they have divided their Townships into Fourteen School Divisions, and thus frittered down to a mere pittance what might otherwise have been an essential service in supporting four or five respectable schools.
2 *Esp.Alta* an administrative unit made up of several school districts, *q.v.*
1958 *Edmonton Jnl* 20 June 1/8: Ratepayers and trustees at Spirit River [Alta] in the Peace River country are demanding an RCMP investigation of the area's school division.

school lands† *Hist.* land put aside by the Crown, the income from which was to be used to support schools. See also **school reserve, school section** (def. 2), and **school township. Cp. Clergy Reserves.**
1832 *Brockville Gaz.* (U.C.) 12 Jan. 3/3: It is therefore most important to the contentment and welfare of the people of this Province that, the School Lands amounting to Five hundred and forty-nine thousand two hundred and seventeen Acres, be applied to the purposes for which they were originally intended. 1883 *Brandon Dly Mail* (Man.) 2 Jan. 2/2: Thousands of acres of school lands lie scattered all over our Province, locked up and unavailable, while our children are growing up without those advantages these lands were intended to confer. 1952 PUTNAM *Cdn Regions* 372/2: Another factor in the land pattern was the reservation of certain parcels as school lands.

schoolmarm (tree) *n. Lumbering, Slang* See 1942 quote.
1939 O'HAGAN *Tay John* 217: It was a pine. Long ago its trunk had been broken off by a slide or by the wind. Two stout branches had grown up instead, lightly tufted, to form a crotch. It was what the men there call a "school-marm tree." It stood sturdy, rather than tall, stark and black against the sunset. To me in those moments it had no phallic form. It was a figure, arms upflung. 1942 SWANSON *Western Logger* 54: school marm—a forked log or tree. 1959 *Press* 6 Dec. 6: . . . and the only "school marm" he saw was a forked tree.

school question See **Manitoba School Question.**
1916 BRIDLE *Sons of Canada* 81: Most of the politics of Manitoba in those days grew out of the school question. . . . 1935 MORICE *Red River Insurrection* 332: This bore on the school question and events have proved but too clearly that, in this respect, the

Westerner was more far-seeing than the Ottawa legists, who seemed otherwise to be animated by the best of intentions.

school reserve *Hist.* See **school lands.**
1820 *Kingston Chron.* (U.C.) 24 Mar. 3/4: . . . an English Episcopalian Church should be built . . . on a piece of ground called the School Reserve, on the Carrying Place, for the Townships of Ameliasburgh. 1826 *Colonial Advocate* (York [Toronto]) 9 Feb. 3/1: Four miles below the big Otter you enter the township of Houghton which is a school reserve. . . . 1883 *Prince Albert Times* (Sask.) 16 May 2/1: These with the odd numbered sections, the school and Hudson's Bay reserves, form such a large part of the country that it will be quite impossible for the district to come in any sense of the term "settled."

school section 1 a subdivision of a school district, *q.v.* See also **section** (def. 1). *Abbrev.* S.S., *q.v.*
1849 *Journal of Education for U.C.* I 41/1: Some would prefer a uniform rate bill upon all the children residing in a school-section (the school sections reserving the power of the Trustees to excuse any for good reasons) whether in attendance or not. 1903 *U of T Stud.Hist.& Econ.* II 107: Each organized township divides its districts into school sections. . . . 1959 STEWART & FRENCH *Ask No Quarter* 94: Agnes automatically organized in terms of schools and school sections. She aimed at a public meeting in each school section at least once a year. . . .
2 *West, Hist.* See **school lands.**
1881 *Edmonton Bull.* 5 Nov. 3/2: As the surveys in Manitoba are made it is found that sections which should be available for school sections are already occupied, it is said, in not a few instances by the Syndicate for station grounds and other purposes. 1912 BICKERSTETH *Open Doors* 96: When the district is developed, and the land goes up in value, these two sections, which are called school sections, are sold, and the proceeds go to the Education Department. 1963 SYMONS *Many Trails* 91: . . . Sections 11 and 29 in each township were set aside for schools, and were commonly called school sections.

school township *Hist.* a township set aside as school lands, *q.v.*
1819 *U.C.Gaz* (York [Toronto]) 1 Apr. 53/4: Notice is hereby given that Sealed Proposals will be received at this Office . . . for surveying the School Townships of Hughton and Westminster, in the District of London, the former containing about 27,000 and the latter 62,000 acres of unsurveyed land. 1829 *Kingston Chron.* (U.C.) 5 Dec. 2/5: I would suggest an early inquiry in the reservation of what are termed the school Townships, in order to ascertain how far the intention of their original appropriation might now be put in execution.

school trustee† a member of a school board, *q.v.* See also **trustee.**
1850 *Journal of Education for U.C.* III 75/1: May we hope the Bill about to be submitted to the House will secure the appointment of their School Trustees in cities as well as in the country. 1966 *Islander* 27 Feb. 6/2: My father and Mr. Gibson were school trustees.

school unit See **school district.**
1958 *Kelvington Radio* (Sask.) 5 June 4/3: The Sturgis School Unit invites applications for the position of Assistant to the Secretary-Treasurer.

school van *West.* a small bus for taking children to school.

1957 *Herald-Tribune* (Grande Prairie, Alta) 17 Dec.
9/5: Effect on Improvement Districts would be
recommendations for school van routes, service roads
and other public works projects necessary for the
development of fringe areas. . . . **1958** *Edmonton Jnl*
31/5: The request was for a north-south auxiliary road
one mile west, presently used by the school van in dry
weather to be brought to market road standard and the
present market road discontinued as such.

scoocoom *n*. See **skookum**.

scoop *n*. See 1853 quote. See also **trough**.
1825 (1916) SELLAR *Narrative* 97: Having no sawed
lumber or shingles, [we] will have to cut basswood
staves and scoops. [**1853** STRICKLAND *Canada West* I
30n: A shanty is a building made with logs, higher in
the front than in the back, making a fall to the roof,
which is generally covered with troughs made of pine
or bass-wood logs; the logs are first split fair in the
middle, and hollowed out with the axe and adze.
A row of these troughs is then laid from the front or
upper wall-plate, sloping down to the back plate, the
hollowed side uppermost. The covering troughs is [sic]
then placed with the hollow reversed, either edge resting
in the centre of the under trough.] **1891** OXLEY *Chore-
Boy* 48: The scoops are small logs hollowed out on one
side and flat on the other. . . . **1935** SULLIVAN *Great
Divide* 388: He . . . stared at his ceiling of cedar
scoops. **1964** *Cdn Geog.Jnl* Feb. 65/1: Two long
timbers from one end to the other, supported the
scoops.

scoop *v*. **1** hollow out scoops with an adze or axe.
See also **scooped**.
1863 WALSHE *Cedar Creek* 127: You chop and I'll
scoop for a start. **1947** SAUNDERS *Algonquin* 33: . . . some
of the others were able to scoop out the logs into long
wooden tiles for the roof.

2 roof with scoops.
1896 GOURLAY *Hist.Ottawa* 72: Shanties could easily
be raised and scooped and made tight, but many were
not content with shanties.

scoop-bearer *n*. See quotes. See also **scoop**, *n*.
1891 OXLEY *Chore-Boy* 48: Next day they laid long
timbers across the top of the wall, resting them in
the middle on four great posts they called
"scoop-bearers." **1961** PRICE & KENNEDY *Renfrew* 43:
These scoops, supported by two long timbers ("scoop
bearers") that stretched from one gable to the other,
were laid side by side, hollow side up, sloping from the
low peak to the eaves [of the shanty].

scooped *adj*. **1** hollowed out into a scoop, *q.v*. See
also **scoop**, *v*. (def. 1).
1896 GOURLAY *Hist.Ottawa* 139: The Garlick settlement
claimed the first schoolhouse, scooped log, and
respectable. . . . **1964** *Cdn Geog.Jnl* Feb. 64/3: A
camboose was made of the forest at hand, of large pine
logs for the sides and "scooped" cedar for the roof.

2 roofed or fashioned with scoops, *q.v*. See also
scoop, *v*. (def. 2).
1896 GOURLAY *Hist.Ottawa* 6: . . . picture to yourself
a shanty 14x20, and 8 feet high scooped, standing in a
clearing. . . . *Ibid*. 121: His school house was a log
shanty, roof scooped, floor and benches, home-made
basswood. . . .

scoop-out *n*. See **dugout** (def. 3). Cp. **scoop-up**.
1958 KELSEY *B.C.Rides a Star* 81: Every day the skies
grew higher and bluer, the enclosing fields greener, the
light so golden it even gilded the brackish water of
pasture scoop-outs.

scoop roof a roof made of scoops, *q.v*. See also
log-trough roof.
[**1866** (1957) GUILLET *Valley of the Trent* 366: The house
was of the rudest description of "shanty," with
hollowed basswood logs fitting into each other
somewhat in the manner of tiles for a roof instead of
shingles.] **1964** *Cdn Geog.Jnl* Feb. 65/1: The scoop roof
was made by placing one layer of cedar logs with the
scooped side up and a second layer over them with the
scooped side down.

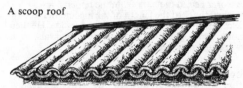

A scoop roof

scoop-up *n*. See quote. Cp. **scoop-out**.
1929 JOHNSTON *Beyond Rockies* 203: With the
exception of one or two good wells, the farmers rely
for domestic water on ice cut from the rivers and
"scoop-ups," as they call the sloughs which are made
by damming some depression to hold rain-water or
the flow from small streams.

scoot [skut] *n*. [< v. go suddenly and fast] a boat
equipped with runners, driven by an airscrew, and
designed to operate on ice or water. See also
iceboat (def. 3), **ice-scooter**, and **snow-scoot**. Cp.
snowplane.
1958 *Citizen* 31 Dec. 4/7: A scoot is a craft used for
winter travel, primarily among the Thirty Thousand
Islands of Georgian Bay [Ont.]. **1961** *Maclean's* 7 Jan.
27/2: . . . a scoot is a small craft driven by an aircraft
motor and propeller that can travel over ice or through
water.

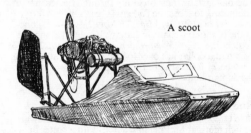

A scoot

scootewahbo *n*. See **scuttaywabo**.

score† *v*. *Lumbering, Hist*. mark and, sometimes,
roughly trim (a log) for hewing into square timber,
q.v. See also **scorer** and **wane**.
1835 (1838) HALIBURTON *Sam Slick* 12: I hope it won't
be long afore he has the wainy edge scored off. . . .
1891 OXLEY *Chore-Boy* 67: . . . the "scorers" . . .
stripped off the branches and slab sides from the tree
trunks set aside for square timber. . . . **1964** *Cdn Geog.
Jnl* Feb. 67/1: When the bark had been peeled off, the
log was "scored."

scorer† *n*. *Lumbering, Hist*. See 1947 quote. See
also **score**.
1853 STRICKLAND *Canada West* II 280n: [Rossing
involves] taking off the bark a few inches in width

along the entire length of the trunk on the space that is to be lined, so that the black mark may be more distinctly seen by the scorers. **1854** KEEFER *Ottawa* 65: In squaring large trees much of the finest timber is blocked off by scorers and lost. **1947** (1963) SAUNDERS *Algonquin* 30: The fitter came first, selecting trees large enough to make a stick, and sound from top to base. The faller laid axe to tree, making it fall in the most convenient direction for the next operation. The log maker took over next, trimming the log of its branches, and cutting off the top to a specified length. After him the scorer peeled the bark from the upper sides, stretched the cord the length of the log and marked the thicknesses to be sliced off to make a flat side. He then "scored" each side with an axe at close intervals, so the hewer could hew to the line.

Scotch half-breed a half-breed having a Scots father and an Indian mother. See also **improved Scotsman** and **Scotch Métis**.
1861 *Nor'Wester* (R.R.S.) 1 Aug. 3/2: He soon got tired of their slow movements, and went ahead ... with ... James Bruce, a Scotch Half-breed.... **1952** HOWARD *Strange Empire* 384: As soon as she learned of the Batoche incident he sent to Prince Albert for Thomas McKay, a Scotch half-breed and Hudson's Bay Company agent, to be his go-between in negotiations for release of the prisoners and goods taken by the Métis.

Scotch Line a concession road, *q.v.*, near Perth, Ont., where many Scots settled in the early nineteenth century. See **line**, *n.* (def. 3b). See also **Scotch Settlement. Cp. English Line.**
1828 *Brockville Gaz.* (U.C.) 26 Dec. 3/4: We are sorry to learn that a teamster of the name of M'Pherson from the Scotch line, lost his span of horses and sleigh on Tuesday last, by their breaking through the ice in attempting to cross the Rideau lake at Oliver's ferry. **1842** *Bytown* [Ottawa] *Gaz.* 26 May 2/4: [It was] one of the best of the roads in Lanark [County] along the Scotch line.... **1958** *Northern Miner* 27 Nov. 22/2: We even had a dollar left over for a livery rig to attend the strawberry festival at Burnbrae, three miles east on the Scotch Line....

Scotch Métis See **Scotch half-breed**.
1896 (1898) RUSSELL *Far North* 165: Kenneth Stewart, a Scotch métis at McPherson, acted as interpreter in preparing a Loucheux vocabulary.

Scotch Settlement or **Townships** a region in eastern Ontario, part of the present counties of Lanark and Renfrew, settled in the 1820's by Scotsmen. See also **Scotch Line**.
1815 *Montreal Herald* 15 Apr. 3/1: We need no other proof to be convinced of this policy than to cast our eyes at the Scotch townships in the eastern districts of U.C. **1817** *U.C.Gaz.* (York [Toronto]) 3 July 107/2: Those who are in doubts of succeeding, need only travel to some of the Scotch Townships in Upper Canada, and ask their countrymen how they were enabled to render themselves so comfortable. **1903** RICHARDSON *Colin* 1: To the pioneers in other parts of the forest this district became known as "the Scotch Settlement."

Scotch Yankee *Obs.* See quotes.
1821 (1955) CRAIG *Early Travellers* 62: ... it is a remarkable circumstance, that, in Upper Canada, the *Ne plus ultra* of vanity, impudence, and rascality, is thought to be comprised under the epithet *Scotch Yankey*. **1832** MCGREGOR *Brit.Amer.* II 190: I quite agree with Mr Howison, when he says, "that the *ne plus ultra* of impudence, rascality, and villainy, is comprehended in the epithet *Scotch Yankee*." [applied here to Gaelic settlers of N.E. Nova Scotia].

Scott Act [< Sir Richard William *Scott*, 1825-1913, prominent lawyer and legislator] See 1958 quote.
1883 *Prince Albert Times* (Sask.) 24 Jan. 6/2: The Scott Act, in the lower provinces especially, and we believe also in Ontario, has proved a perfect farce. **1958** *Encyc.Can.* IX 246/2: He was father of ... the Canada Temperance Act of 1878, sometimes known as the Scott Act.

scout *n.* a person employed to search out promising mineral properties and to check on the activities of competitors.
1924 DORRANCE *Never Fire First* 246: Already I've been spotted as a scout for a gold-dredging outfit with designs on the Cheena. **1952** INNES *Campbell's Kingdom* 88: ... I asked him to drop a word here and there among the oil-company scouts. **1963** *Albertan* (Calgary) 23 Dec. 3/4: Scouts of competing oil companies would have an extremely hard time spying on the project.

scoutaywaubo *n. Hist.* See **scuttaywabo**.

A scow

scow† *n.* [Am.E < Du. *schouw*] a crude, oblong, flat-bottomed boat of shallow draft, much used in colonial days on the St. Lawrence and the Lower Lakes and in later times on the lakes and rivers of the Northwest.
1795 (1911) SIMCOE *Diary* 289: I saw some of the vessels which are built on this lake and rigged like scows, a large flat bottomed boat. **1807** (1809) GRAY *Letters* 202: A scow is a vessel with four sides, an oblong square, in length forty to fifty feet, in breadth thirty to forty, and from four to five feet deep, flat-bottomed. **1898** *Yukon Midnight Sun* (Dawson) 1 Aug. 3/2: The cargo on a 100-foot scow consisted principally of whiskey and fair doves, and the number of women coming up was probably equal to that of the men. **1957** *Beaver* Autumn 40/1: Our scow, based at Fort George and always manned there by an all-Indian crew, was 40 feet long with an eight foot beam. In the bow a rough wooden capstan provided a means of winding through the worst of the white water in the canyons. At the stern a sweep, as long as the scow itself, was the chief navigational aid.

scow brigade *Hist.* a fleet of scows transporting Hudson's Bay Company outfits (def. 1) to the trading posts of the North country. See also **brigade** (def. 1).
1928 FREEMAN *Nearing North* 137: McMurray held its place through being the point at which the scow brigade transshipped cargo to the river steamer.

1932 (1967) *Cdn Geog.Jnl* Mar. 92/3: The present story is of a journey down the Athabaska in [1914] the last year in which the scow brigades carried northward to Lake Athabaska the season's freight for Chipewyan and the Slave and Mackenzie river posts. **1952** *Beaver* June 43/1: The last of the scow brigades was that which ran from Pagwa down the Pagwachuan River, to the Kenogami, and so into the Albany and down to James Bay.

scow ferry *Hist.* a scow serving as a ferry across a river, a use to which scows were frequently put.
[**1830** MOORSOM *Letters N.S.* 299: The usual mode of the country is here pursued, the ferry-boat being a large punt or "scow," with the raised sides to prevent horses from stepping into the water.] **1896** GOURLAY *Hist.Ottawa* 141: Earlier the road from Burrit's Rapids to Kemptville had been opened and a scow ferry at the latter was available for crossing.

scow-house *n. Pacific Coast* a kind of floathouse, *q.v.*
1924 SHERMAN *Nature Stories* 243: Skookum Charlie was an Indian boy of the Lillooet tribe, who had been sent by his father to live with an uncle residing in a scow-house on the waterfront of Vancouver.

scowman *n.* a man employed on a scow, *q.v.*
1833 (1926) LANGTON *Early U.C.* 41: The scowmen were not far off, under a cedar tree. . . . **1921** HEMING *Drama of Forests* 172: Besides the regular post servants there were others employed such as: voyageurs, among whom were the guides, canoe-men, boatmen, and scowmen; then, again, there were fur-runners, fort hunters, and packeteers.

scrape *n.* See **hunting scrape**.

scraper† *n.* See 1935 quote. See also **road-scraper, slip** (def. 2), **slip-scraper,** and **slush-scraper**.
1826 (1832) PICKERING *Inquiries* 68: Along the "street" they are getting them up, and ploughing the sides, and with a kind of large shovel, having a handle, (called a scraper) and a yoke of oxen, the dirt is drawn into the centre and rounded, which is called "turnpiking." **1903** RICHARDSON *Colin* 97: I was holding the scraper for Jock, the drover, that week. . . . **1935** SULLIVAN *Great Divide* 200: They strolled eastward over the newly-graded embankment. Nearby, a siding was being built in earth, and scrapers were at work, great open steel scoops with sharp, flat mouths drawn by two horses; behind projected long, stout handles so that the mouth could be tilted and bite into the soil, when, full to the muzzle, they were dragged up and tipped on the grade. **1953** CUSHMAN *Timberjack* 79: There was a bulldozer at his Belle Creek camp, but it needed new bearings. He put some horse scrapers to work. **1959** STOREY *Prairie Harvest* 5: There was a thin layer of darkish soil at the top and under it an anaemic-looking white sand as far down as the mule scrapers had gone.

scrapping-hitch *n. West, Slang, Obs.* a brawl.
1900 OSBORN *Warders of West* 781: Scrapping-hitches and other forms of the free North-Western fight became so frequent that the railway men in charge sent in an urgent message to the authorities a few dozen [NWMP] troopers. **1900** OSBORN *Greater Canada* 46: . . . there were seasons of the year . . . when the little village under the walls of Fort Garry was a pandemonium of drunken, gambling "breeds," but nothing worse than a black eye or a bitten thumb, or a kick "between the long ribs and the short," ever befell those who took a hand in these "scrapping-hitches."

screech [skritʃ] *n.* [ult. < Scottish dial. *screigh* whisky, presumably from its effect on those who

overindulge] *Esp.Nfld, Slang* **1 a.** a potent dark rum.
1957 HUTCHISON *Canada* 24: He is little addicted to the Island's national drink called "Screech." **1958** *Maclean's* 27 Sep. 63/3: Pinkie is a cheap wine highly regarded by waterfront connoisseurs, a chaser for screech. **1965** *Globe and Mail* (Toronto) 7 Dec. 6/4: A couple of shots of Newfie Screech or Big Dipper and you get a crying jag on. . . .

b. See 1958 quote.
1958 *Maclean's* 27 Sep. 63/3: Screech is a mixture of rums now sold by the liquor board under a new label that displays a map of the island and the legend "Newfoundland's Famous Screech." **1959** *Globe and Mail* (Toronto) 25 May 21/5: The most favored libation is a dark, evil-looking rum prophetically labelled "Screech."

2 any cheap, potent liquor or wine.
1945 PUGSLEY *Saints* 231: [The rating] gets hold of some bootleg scotch—"high life," they call it on the West Coast, and "screech" in Newfie—and then he's away to doing something that may easily end him up in Cells or Detention. **1957** DALZEL *Settlers* 44: Early on the great morning of the 22nd July [1948] "Grandpa" set out to take charge of the local polling station, with a forbidden bottle of "screech" in his pocket.

scrip *n. Hist.* **1 a.**† See **land-scrip** (def. 1).
1850 *Wkly Globe* 11 Oct. 59/3: Some years ago, the plan was adopted of issuing scrip in settlement of these claims, which was made transferable, and entitled holders to land at the current value for the amount borne on its face. **1954** BEZANSON *Sodbusters* 81: With his family using their homestead rights, plus a scrip or two of a half-section each, they could gain a big farm for an expenditure of a comparatively little besides their labour.

b. See **land-scrip** (def. 2).
1878 (1963) STANLEY *Louis Riel* 261: . . . the half-breed, having no idea whatsoever of thrift, or of the necessity of making provision for the future by locating his scrip and securing the land for the benefit of his family, would, as our experience in Manitoba proves beyond all doubt, sell the scrip for whatever he could get for it, which in most cases would be a mere trifle. **1885** *Neepawa Star* (Man.) 31 July 2/1: The volunteers will now be able to draw their scrip and sell it for $40 and get themselves a new suit. **1956** *Calgary Herald* 1 Sep. 38/4: Script was a certificate given all half-breeds, born before 1885, upon request. It was transferable for about 240 acres of land, The federal government inaugurated the system in 1889 on the recommendation of a royal commission that studies the restless condition of the half-breeds in the West. **1957** *Ibid.* 1 Mar. 1/1: Judge Buchanan listed three reasons why this protest was "a nullity" from the start. . . . They charged "forebearers" of the 122 [Indians] in question took "script" rather than "scrip," which is the proper spelling.

2 *Hist.* See **money-scrip**.
1885 *Nor'Wester* (Calgary) 14 May 2/1: The scrip called for by this certificate, amounting to $240, will be payable to bearer, will specify the name of the person in whose favor it is granted . . . said scrip will be accepted at par in payment of Dominion lands. **1929** JEFFERSON *Saskatchewan* 122: The Scrip, when

issued, would at once be thrown on the market, bought for next to nothing and a great amount of money put into circulation. **1956** *Sask.Hist.* IX 2: To métis children born before July, 1870, was given the choice between a "scrip" valued at $240, which they could either negotiate or use for the purchase of federal lands, and a "land scrip" which authorized them to pick out a piece of property of 240 acres on unoccupied Dominion lands.

scrip certificate *Hist.* See **land-scrip** (def. 2).
1908 MAIR *Mackenzie Basin* 74: It was indeed a gala time for the happy-go-lucky Lakers, and the effects of the issue and sale of scrip certificates were soon manifest in our neighbourhood.

scrip land *Hist.* land available to persons holding land-scrip (def. 2).
1955 HARDY *Alta Anthol.* 464: Scrip land was available forty miles to the north-west, and on this they settled immediately.

scrip millionaire *Hist.* a person who speculated in land-scrip (def. 2), buying at a very low price from the halfbreeds and selling at a handsome profit to settlers.
1947 *Cdn Hist.Rev.* Dec. 432: But the scrip soon found its way into the pockets of the "scrip millionaires"....
1963 *Alta Hist.Rev.* Aug. 12/2:... some, in what are now Alberta and Saskatchewan, owned mostly by "scrip millionaires" who feared such a plan... would prevent them amassing more riches....

script *n.* See **scrip.**

scrip tent *Hist.* a marquee in which scrip (def. 1b or 2) was issued to those entitled to it.
1908 MAIR *Mackenzie Basin* 68: The "scrip tent," as it was called, a large marquee fitted up as an office, had been pitched with the other tents when the camp was made, and in this the half-breeds held a crowded meeting to talk over the terms, and to collate their own opinions as to the form of scrip issue they most desired.

scrub pine a popular name for any one of several species of *Pinus,* especially the jackpine, *q.v.*
1791 (1934) TURNOR *Journal* 373: Small scrub Pine and Juniper on right hand side. **1877** GRANT *Ocean to Ocean* 46: The wood on this lake is heavier than on Shebandowan: poplars, white birch, red, white and scrub pine, all show well. **1956** *Native Trees* 16: Jack Pine [is also called] scrub pine....

sculp [skʌlp] *n.* [var. of *scalp*] **1** *Obs.* scalp (def. 1). **2** *Sealing, Esp.Nfld* See 1842 quote. See also **fat** (def. 1b). Also, *scalp.*
[**1832** MCGREGOR *Brit.Amer.* I 224: The pelts, or scalps, are carried to the vessels, and packed closely in the hold....] **1842** JUKES *Excursions in Nfld* I 273: The legs or "flippers," and also the head, are then drawn out from the inside, and the skin is laid out flat and entire, with the layer of fat or blubber firmly adhering to it, and the skin in this state is called the "pelt," and sometimes the "sculp." **1956** STORY *Nfld Dial.Dict.* 3: Words originating in Newfoundland [include] sculp: skin of a seal with the blubber attached. **1966** *Cdn Geog.Jnl* Apr. 133/1: The sculps (the seal skin plus the attached blubber) are piled between layers of snow in the storage shed.

sculp [skʌlp] *v.* [var. of *scalp*] *Sealing, Esp.Nfld* remove the sculp (def. 2) (from). See also **sculping** (def. 1).
[**1832** MCGREGOR *Brit.Amer.* I 224:... the weather often is such as to leave no time to scalp the seals on the ice, and the carcasses are then carried whole to the vessel.] **1842** JUKES *Excursions in Nfld* I 274: Having killed or at least stunned all they see within a short distance, they skin, or, as they call it, "sculp" them.... **1923** PRATT *Nfld Verse* 22: Fast as our arms could swing we slew them,/Ripped them, "sculped" them, roped and drew them/To the pans....

sculping ['skʌlpɪŋ] *n.* **1** the process of removing the skin and adhering fat from a seal. See also **sculp,** *n.* and *v.*
1883 HATTON & HARVEY *Newfoundland* 92: This process is called "sculping"—a corruption, no doubt, of scalping.

2 a similar process in whaling.
1894 MORRIS *Sketches* 24: We were taken over to the oil house, where was moored a large whale, sixty-nine feet long, and already undergoing the process of sculping. **1897** TUTTLE *Golden North* 209: On the approach of the vessel, the whale is made fast to her side, tail forward, so that the large open mouth will not fill with water in case of the advance of the ship, and the work of sculping is begun. This is done under the superintendence of an official called "the Inspectioneer."

sculping knife *Sealing* See 1842 quote.
1842 JUKES *Excursions in Nfld* I 274: Having killed... all they see within a short distance, they skin... them with a broad clasp-knife, called a sculping knife. **1883** HATTON & HARVEY *Newfoundland* 312: Instantly the sculping-knife is at work, the skin with the fat adhering is detached with amazing rapidity from the carcase which is left on the ice still quivering with life, while the fat and skin alone are carried off. **1956** STORY *Nfld Dial.Dict.* 5: From the seal-fishery we get such words as:... sculp... to which we add sculping knife....

scun(n) [skʌn] *v.* [var. of *scan*] *Nfld* See quotes.
1918 GRENFELL *Lab.Doctor* 76: [They]... go up... in the forebarrel to "scun" the ship—that is, to find the way or leads through the ice. **1956** STORY *Nfld Dial. Dict.* 5: From the seal-fishery we get... scunn, to direct a sealing vessel from the barrel, hence scunner, assistant to the master of a watch....

scunner ['skʌnɚ] *n.* [< *scun,* v.] *Nfld* See 1956 quote. See also **barrelman.**
1924 MATHEWS *Wilfred Grenfell* 114: Up aloft in a conning tower is Dr. Grenfell with the "scunner" as he is called.... **1953** MILLS *Folksongs of Nfld*: We found that Stephen was at the wheel, and Jimmie was the Scunner. **1956** STORY *Nfld Dial.Dict.* 5: From the seal-fishery we get... scunn, to direct a sealing vessel from the barrel, hence scunner, assistant to the master of a watch....

scurvy grass a herb of the mustard family, *Cochlearia officinalis,* common in northern regions and formerly used in treating scurvy.
1743 (1949) ISHAM *Observations* 132: Scurvy Grass has been found at this place Lately, growing by the Sea shore amongst the Rocks. **1811** (1947) *Beaver* Sep. 30/1: A sallad of scurvy grass was made for supper. **1960** MOWAT *Ordeal by Ice* 65: They found sorrel and scurvy-grass in great abundance.

scuttaywabo ['skʌtə,wɑbo] *n.* [< Algonk.; cf. Cree *iskotawāpō* < *iskota* fire + *wāpō* water] spiritous liquor; firewater. Various spellings.

[**1743** (1949) ISHAM *Observations* 39: Brandy Scut ta wop pou] **1768-82** (1904) LONG *Voyages* 151: I thanked her for her song, and giving the husband a bottle of scuttaywabo, left them together to enjoy their heart's delight.... **1853** STRICKLAND *Canada West* II 69:... the traders... paid their victims, by way of barter, a villainous compound, yclept New England rum, or, as the Indians call it, skitawahbo. **1913** COWIE *Adventurers* 317: They had all been preparing to take advantage of the "skoot-e-wha-bo," which Zenith had been mixing with swamp water in the state of dilution most profitable to him since his arrival. **1951** O'MEARA *Grand Portage* 33: Full of scuttaywabo and boisterous spirits, they milled about....

S.D. See **school district.**

1958 *Rosetown Eagle* 22 May 8/3:... a bus route [may] be established to serve the Aluvia S.D. commencing with the 1958 fall term.

sea boil *Lab.* See **water-pup.**

1905 GRENFELL *Harvest* 132: The industry they pursue especially exposes them to accident, and in particular to cuts, sea-boils and ulcers.... **1918** GRENFELL *Labrador Doctor* 63: "I never gets sea boils," one old chap told me the other day. **1932** GRENFELL *Forty Years* 95: Friends were at first surprised when I began commending the brass chains worn round the wrist against Water Pups which are sea boils.

sea-flea *n.* a tiny, one-man speedboat driven by a powerful motor and much used for racing, so called because it skims the surface of the water.

1958 *Saturday Night* 24 May 2/3: If your predictions about the boat-boom are correct—and I'm afraid they are—it shouldn't be long before we can cross from island to mainland by hopping from one sea-flea to the next, like Eliza crossing the ice. **1959** *Globe and Mail* (Toronto) 18 June 8/6: Seven distributors are lining the southwest corner of the plaza with boats, ranging from sea fleas to cabin cruisers....

sea-ice *n.* **1** masses of ice in the sea; ice formed from frozen salt water.

1924 MATHEWS *Wilfred Grenfell* 60: Bitterly cold in winter, Labrador has a short and lovely time when the snow and sea-ice melt.... **1946** *Beaver* Mar. 37/1:... one of those cracks which generally divides [sic] the inshore ice, anchored to the rocks below, from the main body of floating sea ice.

2 *Nfld* See **ice,** *n.* (def. 1).
1952 RADDALL *Nymph* 23: "When I was your age I'd been to Spain and Italy... in schooners and square-riggers... and before that I'd been out to the sea-ice five seasons with the swilers."

seal, to talk See **talk seal.**

sealapack ['silə,pæk] *n.* [< Esk. *silapak*] a white outer garment, often worn as camouflage by Eskimo hunters. See also **snowshirt.** Also spelled *seelapak, sil(l)apak.*

1942 *Beaver* Dec. 37/2: The cold pierced through his thin sillapak so that all night he jumped about to prevent the fatal drowsiness which precedes death from creeping upon him. **1952** *Ibid.* Dec. 10/2: Sometimes the hunter dons a white "seelapak" to make himself even less conspicuous.... **1959** *Weekend Mag.* 22 Aug. 9:... a tightly-woven poplin of cotton and nylon takes the place of the wind-blocking fabric Eskimos first used for the outer garment known as a sealapack.

seal beef the flesh of the seal.

1953 MOWERY *Mounted Police* 146: A hunter led the

Yellow-striped *kabluna* into his igloo and tendered him a heaped-up bowl of seal beef.

sealer[1] *n. Esp.Nfld* **1** See **seal hunter** (def. 1).

1770 (1792) CARTWRIGHT *Journal* I 76: After breakfast we set off homewards, being accompanied by two of the sealers. **1842** BONNYCASTLE *Newfoundland* II 129: The sealers are seen coming from all parts of the country to St. John's, with their bundle of spare clothing over their shoulders, supported by a stick, six or eight feet long, which is to serve as a bat or club to strike the seal on the nose, where he is very vulnerable.... **1966** *Weekend Mag.* 19 Mar. 38/1: At the end of a hunting day the sealers leave the ice with their skins and the female seals—thousands of them—crawl back on to the ice to the carcasses of their young.

2 a ship engaged in hunting seals. See also **seal hunter** (def. 2) and **soiler.**
1829 *Brockville Gaz.* (U.C.) 5 June 2/4: The crews of 10 sealers, lost in the ice, had been brought into St. John's.... **1962** *Canada Month* May 12/1: Men from the sealer *Algerine* pack together pelts from seals they have caught on the last winter's ice.

sealer[2] *n.* a glass jar, usually holding a pint or a quart, in which jam, fruit, vegetables, etc. are preserved.

1932 JAMIESON *Cattle in the Stall* 12: Just take in a great half-gallon sealer and get it filled—for about half a dollar! **1959** *Weekend Mag.* 15 Aug. 39/2: I went into the fruit cellar, turned on the light and was actually picking up two quart sealers of icicle pickles....

sealery ['siləri] *n.* See **seal fishery.**

1905 GRENFELL *Harvest* 121: After the sealery, however, comes the really busy time.

seal fishery *Esp.Nfld* the annual hunt for seals at the ice (def. 1). See also **sealery** and **seal hunt.**

1808 *York* [Toronto] *Gaz.* 30 July 4/1: The Seal fishery upon the ice at Newfoundland, has been very fortunate, four vessels engaged in that business, caught no less than 8344, and other have been equally successful. **1819** ANSPACH *Hist.Nfld* 351: The stated period for the seal-fishery, so as not to injure the cod-fishery, does not admit of any delay; otherwise the voyage would be lost, and it is this very ice that brings the seals near these coasts. **1928** *Beaver* Mar. 193/2: Preparations for the S.S. *Nascopie* proceeding to the seal fishery are now well under way.... **1947** *Ibid.* Sep. 3/1: There she wintered, and the following spring was again engaged in the seal fishery, from which she brought back 32,000 skins.

seal gaff See **gaff.**

seal gun See **sealing gun.**

1942 TWOMEY & HERRICK *Needle to North* 55: Yes, it was a good seal gun; yes, it would kill the seal all right.

seal hole See **aglu.**

1836 HUISH *Last Voyage* 701: Seal-hole Ag-loo. **1942** TWOMEY & HERRICK *Needle to North* 75: Opposite the north end of Paint Islands we were all laughing for once, because the lead dog had bolted off to a seal hole, followed pellmell by all the others, and the drivers had been completely taken by surprise.

seal hook a hook set on a line for catching seals.

[**1864** HALL *Life with Esquimaux* II 241: The two women

started off, each with dog and hook, to hunt for seal igloos.] **1958** *Alaska Sportsman* Dec. 10/1 : They had [a] seal line . . . and [a] seal hook on [the] end. **1964** *Globe and Mail* (Toronto) 4 Nov. 1/4 : The practice of setting out lines with seal hooks will be prohibited.

seal hunt See **seal fishery.**
1883 (1889) WITHROW *Our Own Country* 88 : During the seal hunt of 1872, one hundred men perished, fifty of these having gone down in a single vessel called the *Huntsman,* on the coast of Labrador. **1933** GREENE *Wooden Walls* 1 : The Seal Fishery of Newfoundland, or more properly the Seal Hunt . . . is a commercial enterprise unique of its kind and singular in its location. . . . **1947** *Beaver* Sep. 3/1 : Her [Nascopie's] first transatlantic voyage began shortly afterwards, when she sailed from St. John's, Newfoundland, to take part in the annual seal hunt. **1955** *Western Star* (Corner Brook, Nfld) 12 Mar. Back sec. 2/1 : Judging from the number of departmental scribes NOT contributing to this page this week, we are wondering if they managed to "stow-away" on some of the ships that sailed for the 1955 seal hunt at the icefields a few days ago.

seal hunter 1 *Esp.Nfld* a person taking part in the seal fishery, *q.v.* See also **ice-hunter, sealer** (def. 1), and **swiler.**
1832 MCGREGOR *Brit.Amer.* I 224 : . . . the hardy Newfoundland seal-hunters seem even to court those terribly sublime and hazardous adventures.
1906 LUMSDEN *Skipper Parson* 111 : Think of a few of the "unnumbered hardships" of our friend the Newfoundland seal-hunter.
2 See **sealer¹** (def. 2).
1889 WITHROW *Our Own Country* 89 : [Caption] Seal Hunter in Snow-Storm.

seal-hunting sermon See quote.
1906 LUMSDEN *Skipper Parson* 110 : "The seal-hunting sermon," as it was called, was an institution, being a discourse specially adapted to the men and the hour, preached the Sabbath before sailing.

seal igloo See **aglu.**
1864 HALL *Life with Esquimaux* II 241 : The two women started off, each with dog and hook, to hunt for seal igloos.

sealing *n.* the hunting of seals. See also **ice-hunting.**
1777 (1792) CARTWRIGHT *Journal* II 256 : It is rather too shoal for sealing, yet I must try it, since there is not better hereabouts. **1951** BULIARD *Inuk* 105 : And when I've said Mass, I go sealing if the wind is east and the ice is moving, or hunting Arctic hares, if the wind is in the west.

sealing club See **gaff.**
1853 INGLEFIELD *Summer Search* 190 : I am informed, that for hundreds of miles the fields of ice are studded with seals, which in the case of the young ones are so tame as to be approached with a "sealing" club, with which they are killed.

sealing dog *Esp.Nfld* a veteran seal hunter (def. 1).

1916 DUNCAN *Billy Topsail* 218 : It was even held by some old sealing dogs that the floes had gone to the east in a spurt of westerly weather. . . .

sealing fleet the fleet of vessels engaging in the seal fishery, *q.v.*, in a given year.
1906 (1964) JENNESS *Eskimo Admin.* II 18 : The *Neptune,* the largest and most powerful ship of the Newfoundland sealing fleet, was chartered. . . . **1961** *Maclean's* 28 Jan. 17 : That year, 1914, the twenty ships of the sealing fleet sailed early in March.

sealing gaff See **gaff.**

sealing ground(s) a place where seal hunting is carried on.
1921 *Beaver* Jan. 16/1 : Our nine dogs . . . displayed a fierce eagerness to reach the sealing grounds. . . . **1964** JENNESS *Eskimo Admin.* II 9 : . . . they [the Eskimo] deserted their expendable villages and moved to other sealing-grounds.

sealing gun a harpoon gun used in hunting seals. See also **seal gun** and **swiling gun.**
1872 DASHWOOD *Chiploquorgan* 271 : Such a herd [of caribou] being discovered in a plain, an army of pot hunters, armed with sealing guns, issue forth and surround the deer. **1889** WITHROW *Our Own Country* 88 : Some of the men . . . carry a long sealing-gun on their shoulders. **1957** HUTCHISON *Canada* 10 : It was not likely, he supposed, that I had ever seen in Canada the like of this sealing gun used by his grandfather.

sealing-post *n. Obs.* a station where sealing was carried on.
1775 (1792) CARTWRIGHT *Journal* II 117 : I went off for Blackguard Bay to look for a sealing-post.

seal lamp See **kudlik** and picture.
1951 GILLIS & MYLES *North Pole* 161 : . . . I made out the central feature of this snow igloo, the seal lamp. . . .

seal line *North* a tough cord made of sealskin.
1946 *Beaver* Sep. 3/2 : . . . he instructed his wife and family to build themselves a new igloo . . . then to prepare and fix a hangman's noose of seal line to the roof of the old one. **1951** GILLIS & MYLES *North Pole* 145 : We like the folks to have what they want directly— boots, mitts, seal line, dog food. . . .

seal-meadow *n. Obs.* See quote. Cp. **patch** (def. 2).
1819 ANSPACH *Hist.Nfld* 422 : Their next object is to reach a seal-meadow by sailing or cutting through the intermediate field of ice; they then run their vessel into it, the crew disperses, and whilst the gunners fire at the largest seals, the others assail the rest with clubs.

seal oil† oil from rendered seal fat.
1829 MACTAGGART *Three Years* I 315 : Seal oil would produce good gas, and so would that of *porpoise* and *grampus.* . . . **1958** *Edmonton Jnl* 24 June 3 16/6 : Usually, a seal oil lamp, a rectangular soapstone receptacle which is filled with seal oil and has a wick made of moss, is used for heating. **1965** MACNUTT *Atlantic Provinces* 215 : Large vats for the manufacture of seal oil were to be seen at Fogo, Twillingate, Greenspond, and Trinity, and in the ports of Conception Bay.

seal-oil lamp See **kudlik** and picture.
1850 (1852) OSBORN *Arctic Jnl* 16 : Along one side of the abode a sort of bed-place extended for its whole length, forming evidently the family couch ; for on one end of it, with her head close to a large seal-oil lamp, was the sick woman. **1958** *Annual Pictorial Rev.* 62 : [Caption] The kettle for tea is heating over the kudlik or seal-oil

lamp. **1967** *Time* (Cdn ed.) 17 Mar. 16/1: . . . while clay abounds in the Arctic, there was . . . no heat other than the low flame of seal oil lamps.

seal patch See **patch** (def. 2).

1883 HATTON & HARVEY *Newfoundland* 86: The steamers . . . can double and beat about in search of the "seal-patches"; and when the prey is found they can hold on to the ice-fields. . . .

seal patrol a patrol of the sealing grounds by government officers whose job it is to enforce hunting regulations.

1964 *Globe and Mail* (Toronto) 4 Nov. 1/6: Seal patrols will be intensified in the coming season.

sea of mountains *B.C.* the western mountains.

1880 GORDON *Mountain and Prairie* 114: Were it not for the lofty summits that here and there stretch up in the background, one would have little idea that he was in a country that has, for the most part, been fitly described as a "sea of mountains." **1952** PUTNAM *Cdn Regions* 475/2: The "sea of mountains," topped by ice fields and snow capped peaks . . . form one of the most scenic regions in North America.

sea pie a kind of meat pie, formerly served in the logging camps of the Ottawa Valley.

1947 SAUNDERS *Algonquin* xii: And he must also feel . . . when he has eaten sea pie in the camboose camp . . . that this is a place he must know well. . . . *Ibid.* 38: After that, the Sunday meat dish, called "sea pie," was augmented by buns sweetened with blackstrap.

search-and-rescue unit a unit of the Royal Canadian Air Force equipped and trained to search for and aid persons in downed aircraft or on marine craft in distress.

1958 *Time* (Cdn ed.) 25 Aug. 8/3: Luckily for the survivors of crashes or forced landings, the Royal Canadian Air Forces' Search and Rescue Units are on a round-the-clock alert to find them.

searchmaster *n.* the officer in charge of an organized search conducted by a search-and-rescue unit.

1956 *Kingston Whig-Standard* (Ont.) 11 Dec. 1/7: The RCAF searchmaster in charge of the hunt for the missing Trans-Canada Air Lines plane . . . said today a search plane . . . may have sighted "what could have been wreckage." **1963** *Weekend Mag.* 4 May 4/1: The searchmasters have good reason to complain if a search is prolonged unnecessarily.

sea smoke See quote.

1958 *Manice* 7: Frost Smoke—(*Arctic Sea Smoke, Sea Smoke, Water Smoke*) . . . thick fog rising from the sea surface when relatively warm water is exposed to an air temperature much below freezing. Frost smoke frequently appears over newly-formed cracks and leads.

seat of one's pants in **fly by the seat of one's pants,** in the manner of a seat-of-the-pants flyer.

1966 PATTERSON *Trail* 215: And they flew (as, indeed, they had to fly, for there were few aids to navigation) "by the seat of their pants." **1966** *Globe and Mail* (Toronto) 21 Feb. 17/8: What [they] are trying to find out is why and how a good bush pilot can fly "by the seat of his pants."

seat-of-the-pants flyer or **flier** a pilot, especially a bush pilot, *q.v.,* who flies by experience and knowledge of weather and terrain rather than by maps and instruments.

1958 *Kingston Whig-Standard* (Ont.) 14 May 34/2:

Jacklin is no "seat of the pants" flyer; rather, he is one of the most careful members of a careful fraternity. He knows his meteorology inside out, and has made enough forced landings in the Barrens to know what to do if something goes wrong. **1966** *Star Wkly* 12 Mar. 17/1: . . . the famous bush pilots of 30-odd years ago [were] the seat-of-the-pants fliers who began the modern opening of Canada's northern wilderness.

seat-of-the-pants flying flying after the fashion of a seat-of-the-pants flyer.

1966 *Globe and Mail* (Toronto) 21 Feb. 17/8: As more and more instruments and greater refinements in aircraft came into use, seat-of-the-pants flying became something that was looked upon with the same kind of suspicion as that displayed toward rule-of-thumb measurements.

sea trout 1 in the Atlantic Provinces, a variety of trout that spawns in fresh-water rivers.

1830 MOORSOM *Letters N.S.* 327: It is remarkable for the immense shoals of trout (usually called sea trout) which frequent it in spring and autumn. **1872** DASHWOOD *Chiploquorgan* 79: Sea trout frequent more or less all the rivers in North America. These fish are not the same species as the sea trout of the English and Irish coast; they are shorter and thicker fish, more spotted on the back, and with a yellowish tinge on the belly. **1958** *Evening Telegram* (St. John's) 7 May 3/8: Sea trout are beginning to put in an appearance in Newfoundland rivers. *c*1963 *Touring P.E.I.* 52: After you pass a body of water known as Fullerton's Marsh, a good spot for sea trout, you arrive at Mount Herbert.

2 on the Pacific Coast, the steelhead, *q.v.*

1947 *Game Trails in Canada* Aug. 18/1: Right now in English Bay you will find the Sea-trout beginning to run and both blue-backs and cohoe being caught. **1960** MCNAMEE *Florencia Bay* 162: "Steelheads. Sea trout. That big one must be about fifteen pounds."

sea unicorn *Hist.* the narwhal, *Monodon monoceros.*

1577 (1966) FROBISHER *Baffin Island,* quoted in *Star Wkly* 12 Mar. 10/2: On this west shoare we found a dead fishe floating, whiche had in his nose a horn streight and tourquet of length two yards lacking two ynches, being broken in the top, where we might perceive it hollow . . . We supposed it to be a sea unicorne. **1578** BEST *Trve Discovrse* 15: This horne is wreathed and strayte, like in fashion to a Taper made of waxe, and maye truely be thoughte to be the sea Unicorne. **1748** ELLIS *Hudson's-Bay* 68: It is a thing out of Question, that all Sorts of Fish, but more especially the larger Sorts, such as Sea-Unicorns and Whales, are found in great Numbers in these Northern Parts. **1897** TUTTLE *Golden North* 219: The narwhal, or sea unicorn, is valuable for its oil and ivory.

sec *n. Hist.* See **castor sec.**

1964 *Wildlife Rev.* May 22: The hat formula, however, was rigid—it had to be three Gras to one Sec.

second *n. Hist.* **1** *Fur Trade* the clerk next senior to the factor, *q.v.,* of a post.

1913 COWIE *Adventurers* 112: All were placed at table in order of seniority, we apprentice clerks being . . . near the foot, where the kindly "second" . . . presided. . . .

2 See **second chief.**

second chief *Hist.* the second-in-command of an Indian band. Also *second.*

1836 (1923) JAMESON *Rambles* 75: Peter Jones, otherwise Kahkewaquionaby, a half-caste Indian, is the second chief and religious teacher.... 1862 (1888) MCDOUGALL *G.M.McDougall* 95: Mas-ke-pe-toon, the head chief, set before us a kettle full of the choicest flesh. O-nah-tah-me-nah-oos, his second, placed his tent at our service. 1962 SLOBODIN *Kutchin* 72: To the traders, and later to the Canadian Government, a second chief was a man who, in return for emoluments and enhancement of power, would assume responsibility for the probity, from the White man's viewpoint, of his fellows.

second growth a growth, especially of trees, after the original cover has been removed by logging.
1880 GORDON *Mountain and Prairie* 211: Their valleys are frequently wooded, sometimes with patches of the original forest, but usually with second-growth timber such as is commonly found on the prairie. 1891 OXLEY *Chore-Boy* 35: ... their way ran through ... the scrubby "second growth".... 1925 GROVE *Settlers* 57: When he rounded this bluff which, to the south, trailed off into smaller second-growth of poplar, skirting the Marsh, a great piece of good luck befell him. 1965 *Wildlife Rev.* Mar. 19/2: Cougars travel over long ranges and are found in various ecological types of terrain such as slash, mature forest and second growth.

section *n.* 1 See **school section** (def. 1).
1849 *Journal of Education for U.C.* I 59/1: The practice is less prevalent than formerly, of forming selfish and unwarrantable designs upon the teacher on his entrance into a Section. 1871 *Wkly Manitoban* 22 July 2/2: Now it is to be hoped that the examining Boards appointed by the Sections, will inaugurate something different from this effete way of doing things. 1902 CONNOR *Glengarry* 45: The two years of Archibald Munro's régime were the golden age of the school, and for a whole generation "The Section" regarded that period as the standard for comparison in the following years.

2† *Esp.West* one square mile of land (640 acres). See also **half-section** and **quarter-section**.
1842 (1955) CRAIG *Early Travellers* 134: Many years ago the whole province was laid out in sections, and quarter sections, dividing the whole country like a "damboard." 1873 (1877) GRANT *Ocean to Ocean* 76: ... the whole of the Province has been surveyed, divided off into townships, sections and sub-sections.... 1957 MOWAT *Dog* 56: Paul owned two sections on the shores of an immense slough known as Middle Lake that lies well to the east of Saskatoon. 1963 SYMONS *Many Trails* 90: ... there are 36 sections to a township, so you will understand why the homesteader who cuts hay or timber in violation of certain regulations commonly boasts that the hay, or timber it was, came off "section 37."

section line *West* 1 the survey line setting off a section (def. 2).
1871 *Wkly Manitoban* 17 June 2/2: In exceptional cases, the rectangular system of survey admits of such subdivisions as to enable him to include all his improvements, whether or not they are on different sides of a section or quarter-section line. 1911 BICKERSTETH *Open Doors* 21: In time, there will be regular Government roads cut through the bush along the section lines every two miles east and west, and every mile north and south.

2 a road running along the survey line separating sections. Cp. **concession road.**

1957 *Maclean's* 28 Sep. 102/3: ... he stays strictly at home, except to go to the polls on election day and to walk up and down the section lines around home.

secure *v. Obs.* See **cache,** *v.* (def. 2).
1808 (1960) FRASER *Letters and Journals* 62: Went a shore ... and secured a bale of salmon for our return.

Sedna ['sɛdnə] *n.* [< Esk.] See 1956 quote.
1896 MACLEAN *Savage Folk* 99: The Supreme Being of the Eskimo is a woman, named Sedna. 1936 STRINGER *Wife-Traders* 175: But tomorrow I go with Ootah to the Hill of the Winds. And there, maybe, Sedna who rules the shadows of the Great Whale Spirit will tell me what to do. 1956 LEECHMAN *Native Tribes* 191: Some of the more important [Eskimo] nature spirits have names and their position in the world of supernatural beings is well known and explained in legends.... Sedna, another feminine being, is in charge of all the seals and other sea animals and it is she the hunter must thank or blame for his success or failure.

seelapak *n.* See **sealapack.**

Segali Tyee See **Sagalie Tyee.**

seigneur ['sinjɚ] *n.* [< F] Also spelled *seignior*. *Hist.* in French Canada: 1 the legal holder of a seigneury (def. 1a).
1766 *Quebec Gaz.* 27 Oct. 3/1: She was villainously seduced by one Moses Hazen, Esq; (who stiles himself Seignior of some Ground adjacent to St. John's) to swerve from her Duty. 1769 (1878) LEMOINE *Chronicles of St.Lawrence* 208: Representations ... have been made to us by the ... Seigneur of Crane and Goose Islands ... that by his title he has the exclusive right to shoot on these said Islands. 1833 (1955) CRAIG *Early Travellers* 107: [Mr. Frazer said] he was so tired of his solitary life that he intended to leave his farm and retire to some property he possessed on the river Du Lout, situated in a district of which he was Seigneur. 1963 MORTON *Kingdom of Canada* 98: Settlement of the land has ... been the obligation imposed on the seigneurs in New France.

2 the holder of a seigneury (def. 1b).
1962 DICKIE *Great Golden Plain* 44: ... M. Leduc, a fur trading seigneur, who took him to his manor house, revived him with hot food and drink, and kept him up half the night by the great fire in the hall, telling him wild tales of the Canadian fur trade at Michilimackinac.

seigneuress [ˌsinjɚˈrɛs] *n.* [< F] *Hist.* the wife of a seigneur (def. 1).
1769 (1931) BROOKE *Emily Montague* 28: I paid my respects wherever I stopped, to the seigneuress of the village; for as to the seigneurs, except two or three, if they had not wives, they would not be worth visiting. 1792 (1911) SIMCOE *Diary* 90: ... we dined and slept at the house of Madame Hamelin, the seigneuresse of this village [Grondines, L.C.].... 1882 LEMOINE *Quebec* 440: It contained the boudoir and sleeping apartments of some of the fair seignioresses of Beauport in the house which Robert Giffard the first seignor built there more than two centuries ago.

seigneurial [sinjɚˈriəl] *adj.* [< F] of or relating to a seigneur or seigneury. Also spelled *seigniorial*.
1765 *Quebec Gaz.* 14 Feb. 3/1: To be Sold, the Lands and Seigniory of Neuville ... with all the seigniorial Rights thereunto annexed. 1832 *Cdn Courant* (Montreal) 22 Dec. 2/4: We hesitate not to say, that should their example be generally followed throughout the country, the whole Seignorial fabric would be crushed to the

slavish charges and requirements. **1962** *Time* (Cdn ed.)
10 Aug. 9/2: There was fine French-Canadian food,
based on fish and venison, in seigneurial times. . . .

seigneury ['sinjəri] *n.* [< F] Also spelled
seigniory. **1** *Hist.* in French Canada: **a.** a tract of
land granted under conditions of feudal tenure by
the French Crown, the seigneurial rights obtaining
until 1854. See also **barony** (def. 2) and **fief.**
1703 (1905) LAHONTAN *New Voyages* I 34: [There is] a
seigniory or manour. **1711** (1920) *Cdn Hist.Rev.* I 52:
Two Leagues further [is] a Seigniory called St Ann
where there is about forty men. **1764** *Quebec Gaz.*
23 Aug. 4/2: The entire Seigneurie is offered to be sold
for 38,000 livres. **1846** HATHEWAY *Hist.N.B.* 71: . . . a
large grant of land on the Western bounds of this
Province, called the Seigniory, [is] situate for an extent
of two leagues round the Tamasquatta Lake. . . .
1964 *Weekend Mag.* 26 Dec. 15/1: Frank Jarvis . . . now
lives on the site of the Dower House of the Hurtubise
seignory in Westmount. . . .

b. a large land grant in the hinterland, exploited for
furs, fish, etc.

1789 *Quebec Herald* 2 Feb. 104/2: For Sale . . . the
fief or seigniory of Point au Pere situate in the Parish
of Rimousky, containing three quarters of a league in
front, the best adapted in the Province for the Indian
trade. **1808** MCKENZIE *King's Posts* 451: After sailing
thirty one leagues along high, steep, rugged rocks on
the one hand and nothing but the open sea the most of
the way on the other, we arrived at the Head Post of the
seignory the next day. **1840** (1860) MURRAY *Brit.Amer.*
I 62: The French, when forming stations for the fur-
trade at its western extremity, were tempted by the fertile
banks of the Detroit, between Lakes Erie and St. Clair,
and established a number of seigniories similar to those
on the St. Lawrence in Lower Canada. **1956** *Beaver*
Summer 20/2: We steamed out of a sparkling white
fog one day into another of the Montagnais centres—
Mingan, which means "wolf," and which was once part
of an ancient French seigniory. **1966** *Canadian* 29 Jan.
13/1: Grant . . . survived a murder trial in Quebec
and, by 1824, had become the holder of the West's only
seigniory.

c. the manor or house of a seigneur (def. 1). See
also **seigneury house.**

1896 PARKER *Lavilettes* 3: Behind the Manor
Casimbault and the Seigneury, thus flanking the
Church at reverential distance, another large house
completed the acute triangle, forming the apex of the
solid wedge of settlement drawn about the Church.
1938 (1939) GIBBON *Canadian Mosaic* 24: In the country
districts and in Montreal and Quebec there are old
Manors and houses with shelving roofs and gables to
remind us of the Seigneuries.

2 *Hist.* one of the townships of early Lower
Canada, especially as represented in the legislature,
so called because coterminous with a seigneury
(def. 1a).

1828 *Loyalist* (York [Toronto]) 27 Sep. 123/3: It has
been stated by one of the witnesses, that under the
proposed division, a disproportionate increase would
have been given to the Representatives from the
Seigneuries. **1835** *Vindicator* (Montreal) 4 Aug. 2/2:
In some of the seigniories there are separate schools for
girls. **1903** *U of T Stud.Hist.& Econ.* II 5: They were
not to be referred to as townships, but as royal
seigneuries. **1929** CUDMORE *World's Commerce* 230:
Farther east they founded "free" townships instead of
feudal seigneuries to the south of the St. Lawrence and
on the lower Ottawa.

3 *Que.* See quote.
1966 *Cdn Forest Industries* 17/2: He [Premier Lesage]
said unexploited free-hold forests in private hands—
known as "seigniories"—will also be expropriated.

seigneury house *Obs.* See **seigneury** (def. 1c).
1796 (1911) SIMCOE *Diary* 345: There is a good
Seigneurie House falling into ruins.

seignior(y), seigniorial, etc. See **seigneur(y),**
seigneurial.

Seigniorial (Tenure) Bill *Hist.* the legislation
passed by the government of United Canada in
1854 to abolish seigneurial tenure.

1855 (1926) LANGTON *Early U.C.* 216: . . . Lemieux
commands more votes among the Franco-Canadians
than any other person in Upper Canada, and his
appointment stops a mischievous re-agitation of the
Seigniorial Bill question. **1855** *Hamilton Gaz.* (C.W.)
10 May 3/1: The Maine Liquor Law—which is likely
to have as long a lease of Parliamentary attention as
the celebrated Seignorial Tenure Bill—again occupied
the House to-day to the exclusion of almost everything
else. [**1963** MORTON *Kingdom of Canada* 295: The new
ministry [1854] at once carried the secularization of
the Clergy Reserves and the abolition of seigniorial
tenure, with compensation. . . .]

self-dumper *n.* *Lumbering* a huge barge that dumps
its load of logs into the water when it arrives at its
destination.

1964 *Beautiful B.C.* Fall 40/1: [Caption] The era of
huge log booms is being superseded by huge log
barges of the type shown above. This is a self-dumper.

Selkirk *n.* *Hist.* **1** an early name for the Red River
Settlement, *q.v.*, founded by Lord Selkirk, 1771-
1820. See also **Selkirk Settlement.**
1862 *Nor'Wester* (R.R.S.) 2 Aug. 4/1: The people of
Selkirk have been left entirely to themselves, and without
any stimulus from abroad have hitherto been content to
continue in their old pathway, which has produced
contentment and plenty, if not wealth.

2 See **Selkirker** (def. 2).
1957 FISHER *Pemmican* 217: The pedlars [were] shrewder
and more ruthless than the Selkirks. . . .

Selkirker *n.* *Hist.* **1** a settler at Selkirk (def. 1).
See also **Selkirk settler.**
1862 *Nor'Wester* (R.R.S.) 19 Mar. 3/5: The Selkirkers
are getting stirred up, and we look for a large emigration
towards the mountains. **1952** HOWARD *Strange*
Empire 48: Several hundred more Selkirkers, most of
them Swiss, followed in the next five years, after stops
of varying periods in Pembina.

2 a man of the Hudson's Bay Company, identified
with Lord Selkirk, 1771-1820, who, with his
brother, had bought control of that company about
1810, before embarking on his plan to found the
Red River Settlement, *q.v.*
1961 JONES *Trappers* 87/1: [Caption] Fort William . . .
became headquarters of the North West Company in
1801, replacing the post at Grand Portage . . . the fort
was perched at the edge of the western fur country that
was to be so bitterly contested by the Nor'Westers

and the determined Lord Selkirk's Hudson's Bay men, called Selkirkers.

Selkirk Settlement *Hist.* See **Selkirk** (def. 1).
1859 *Brit.Colonist* (Victoria) 27 July 2/1: A newspaper is about to be started, under Canadian auspices, at the Selkirk settlement, on the Red River of the North. **1871** (1873) BUTLER *Great Lone Land* 111: . . . these hardy fellows traversed the forests and frozen lakes upon snow-shoes, and, entering from the Lake of the Woods, suddenly appeared in the Selkirk Settlement, and took possession of Fort Douglas.

Selkirk settler See **Selkirker** (def. 1).
1923 *Beaver* Dec. 78-79: The Selkirk settlers . . . were for the most part Highland Scots Presbyterians. **1963** STANLEY *Louis Riel* 5: [The métis] subtly suggested that the Selkirk settlers had come to rob them of their heritage. **1965** *Maclean's* 24 July 34/2: Norway House was the old Jack River outpost of the Selkirk settlers.

Senate *n.* **1** the upper house of the Canadian Parliament. See also **Red Chamber** (def. 2) and **Upper House** (def. 2).
[**1864** *Nor'Wester* (R.R.S.) 21 Nov. 3/3: The Confederation conference has decided in reference to members of the Legislative Council to the new Confederacy, that they be selected from the members of the Legislative Councils of the several provinces instead of being elected by the people.] **1867** *St.John Jnl* (N.B.) 1 Mar. 2/9: The Upper House is to be styled "Senate," and the Lower House "House of Commons." **1906** *Eye Opener* (Calgary) 8 Dec. 3/2: As a home for decayed Politicians, run on purely benevolent lines at $2,500 per, the senate could lay claim to being a success. **1964** *Globe Mag.* 28 Nov. 12/2: Tardif said Diefenbaker had been warned the Senate would resign in a body if she were appointed.
2 See **Senate Chamber.**

Senate Chamber the chamber in the Parliament Buildings where the Senate convenes. See also **Red Chamber** (def. 1).
1870 *Cdn Illust.News* 12 Mar. 298/1: The Senate Chamber is ninety by forty-five feet, and the ceiling over sixty feet high. **1887** *Grip* (Toronto) 17 Apr. 9/2: That he will be able to do good service in the Senate chamber, his large experience as well as an intimate knowledge of all parts of the Dominion are a sufficient guarantee.

senator *n.* **1** *Hist.* in colonial times, a member of a legislative council (def. 1) or assembly.
1825 *Colonial Advocate* (York [Toronto]) 20 Jan. 2/5: Our leading senator, Mr. Attorney General, mounted on a highly mettled charger, was estimating the damage done, with the scientific glance of a veteran architect. **1832** *Novascotian* (Halifax) 5 Dec. 390/1: In a few weeks the Senators of New Brunswick and Prince Edward Island will be in Session. . . .
2 a member of the Senate, *q.v.*
1867 *Islander* (Charlottetown) 8 Mar. 2/5: The Senate, shall, subject to the provisions of this Act, consist of seventy-two members, who may be styled Senators. **1887** *Grip* (Toronto) 2 Apr. 1/2: Mr. Sanford, of Hamilton, has been made a senator. This is the reward of his sneaking disertion of the reform party. He has sold himself to the Tory corruptionists for the sake of a paltry bribe in the shape of a senatorship—a thing

which any man of sense now regards as exceedingly small pay for dirty work. **1915** PRESTON *Strathcona* 107: The Senators are expected to review Bills from the Lower House with judicial calm and free from party bias. **1966** *Globe and Mail* (Toronto) 11 Jan. 3/4: J. W. Comeau, 89, Canada's oldest senator, yesterday submitted his resignation to Governor-General George Vanier.

senior citizen an elderly person, especially one beyond the normal retirement age.
1957 *Commonwealth* 2 Oct. 3/2: Nowadays doddering derelicts (I'm one) are lovingly called Senior Citizens, with $46 a month for doing nothing. **1960** *Vancouver Province* 23 Dec. 15/7: At the other end of the temporal scale we find the elderly subjected to the indignity of being called "a senior citizen." A senior citizen is somebody who is old and can't afford it. Better to be called "a dirty old man." At least you have color. **1966** *Kingston Whig-Standard* (Ont.) 31 Aug. 35/2: The residents have no opposition to senior citizens units on the land—"fill it full of senior citizens homes if you want."

senior government a provincial government or the federal government (or both), as opposed to a municipal government.
1958 *Citizen* 4 Dec. 8/3: He favors a pay as we go policy with all council business open to press and to public, and states that a greater portion of school costs should be paid for by Senior governments. **1959** *Ibid.* 8 Jan. 2/1: Senior governments have been criticized for delaying payments to the North Shore Union Board of Health.

senior matric See **senior matriculation.**
1939 GROVE *Two Generations* 79: "Why not take senior matric with me?" **1965** *Sun* (Vancouver) 21 Aug. 3/7: Senior matric has been replaced by the new college program at King Edward. . . .

senior matriculation in certain provinces, the successful completion of a secondary-school course (usually including an extra year of study) satisfying the requirements for university entrance. Cp. **junior matriculation.**
☞ *A distinction between senior and junior matriculation used to be more widespread in Canada than it is now. Senior matriculation sometimes entailed a twelfth year of schooling, as it used to in Alberta, and sometimes a thirteenth year, as it still does in Ontario.*
1945 PUGSLEY *Saints* 236: . . . the cadet's course [is] equivalent to Senior Matriculation. . . . **1946** LOWER *Colony to Nation* 413: In Ontario, where the "honours Courses" of the Universities exerted an influence present nowhere else, high schools gave a sound education and had already built up their courses to five years for "senior" matriculation. **1964** *Maclean's* 25 July 38/3: Requirements for grades vary from province to province . . . some provinces have junior and senior matriculation, some do not.

separate church school *Obs.* See **separate school** (def. 3a).
1852 *Hamilton Gaz.* (C.W.) 7 Oct. 3/1: They deem it to be necessary to petition the Colonial Legislature, to, permit the establishment of separate Church Schools, and that the assessments paid by Churchmen for the support of Common Schools, be applied to the maintenance of such as are in connexion with the Church, wherever such appropriation is practical and desired.

separate high-school See quote. See also

separate school (def. 3a) and **separate secondary school.**

1964 *Calgary Herald* 4 Mar. 34/2: Once a separate high school district was set up, the Roman Catholic separate school supporters would pay taxes only to support the separate high schools. They would not pay taxes to support the public high schools in their area.

separate parish school See **separate school** (def. 3a).

1964 *Winnipeg Tribune* 21 Feb. 13/2: Since 1890, when the Manitoba legislature withdrew support for separate parish schools, Roman Catholic parents have protestingly paid both for the private schools their children attend and for the public schools they do not.

separate school 1 *Que., Obs.* a school for girls.

1835 *Vindicator* (Montreal) 4 Aug. 2/2: In some of the seigniories there are separate schools for girls. **1835** *Missiskoui Standard* (Frelighsburg, Que.) 28 Apr. 3/3: When the Assembly passed this most important law . . . they seemed to consider us, for having (may I say?) the misfortune of being protestants and of another descent, as beneath those of their own origin and religion, and therefore unworthy of having a separate school, like those for our sisters and daughters.

2 *Hist.* a segregated school for Negroes.

1857 (1963) *Ontario Hist.* June 88: Separate schools and churches are nuisances that should be abated as soon as possible, they are dark and hateful relics of Yankee Negrophobia. . . . **1903** *U of T Stud.Hist.& Econ.* II 108: Protestant and coloured separate schools may be authorized by the council of a township, town or village, upon the application of five or more heads of families. **1963** *Time* (Cdn ed.) 22 Nov. 14/1: In 1927, the legislature created a separate school district in the area for "all residents other than white persons in the district"—and did not repeal the legislation until 1960.

3 a. a school for children belonging to a religious minority in a particular district, operated by a school board elected by the minority ratepayers and financed by taxes imposed on them by the board as well as by grants from the provincial Department of Education. Such schools are under the jurisdiction of the Department and follow the same basic curriculum as that laid down for public schools. See also **separate church school, separate high-school,** and **separate parish school.** Cp. **parochial school.**

☛ *This situation obtains substantially in Quebec, Ontario, Saskatchewan, Alberta, and the Territories at the present time. Except in Quebec,* **separate school** *has come to refer almost exclusively to schools for Roman Catholics. See def. 3b and note.*

1852 *Dundas Warden* (C.W.) 28 May 2/7: The law makes provision for Separate Schools, to meet an exigency—namely, the anticipated intrusion of the religious dogmas of a majority upon a minority. **1895** BOURINOT *How Canada is Governed* 245: The term "separate school" applies also to Protestants and coloured persons, but as a matter of practice the exception to the general principle of the [Ontario] common school system is confined chiefly to Roman Catholics. **1902** (1957) *Sask.Hist.* X 1 12: Catholics may have separate schools, which receive the same financial subsidies as the public schools, provided they employ teachers with certificates and conform with the prescribed curriculum of studies. **1958** *Encyc.Can.* III 378/2: In Ontario, Saskatchewan and Alberta, separate schools and public schools alike are under the provincial control of a single department of education. **1966** *Toronto Dly Star* 30 Apr. 63/1: There are 54,128

Roman Catholic children in public schools in Metropolitan Toronto despite the existence of 107 separate schools in Toronto and the suburban municipalities.

b. a denominational school, especially one operated for and by Roman Catholics.

☛ *Although* **separate school** *is not an official designation in six of Canada's provinces, either because such schools as defined in def. 3a have never existed or because they have been discontinued, the term is widely used in the general sense of the above definition, and has been for over a century.*

1872 *Canadian Mthly* July 64/1: The Roman Catholics spoke frankly and sincerely for their separate schools, the New Brunswickers for their local liberties; in all other quarters strategical considerations manifestly prevailed. **1873** *Wkly Manitoban* 19 Apr. 4/2: The religion of the majority of ratepayers in any School District shall determine the designation of the District as Protestant or Roman Catholic, and any School dissenting from this shall be termed a Separate School. **1891** *Grip* (Toronto) 18 July 43/1: St. John has outgrown the wretched Separate school system, having abolished it fifteen years ago . . . with the happiest result to all, and especially to the Catholic people. **1909** O'DONNELL *Manitoba* 65: One of the most important measures passed in the first session of the Manitoba Legislature was "The School Act," being an Act to establish a system of education in the Province, and establishing Public Schools; the dual system having been inaugurated—Catholic and Protestant, not separate schools as they have generally been called. **1949** LAWSON *N.B.Story* 207: The Roman Catholics still [in 1872] wanted to have separate schools, and they were willing to pay for these themselves, but they objected to paying in addition the taxes to support the common schools. **1955** *Northern Mail* 23 Mar. 2/2: Added to this, of course, is the fact that numerous children are educated at the Separate School, without charge to the ratepayers. **1964** *Winnipeg Tribune* 21 Feb. 13/3: Rejecting the idea of tax-supported separate schools which exist in every other province except British Columbia, Roblin suggested instead [for Manitoba] what he called a "program of shared services." Under his plan, separate schools would affiliate themselves loosely with the public school system.

separate-school board a board, usually elective, of trustees responsible for the separate schools (def. 3a) in a given area.

1917 MILLER *New Era* 251: In 1866 the Separate School Board [of Ottawa] formed itself into two committees, one to control the French-speaking, the other the English-speaking schools. **1960** WARD *Government in Can.* 75: The Roman Catholic citizens who support the separate schools elect a Separate School Board of their own.

separate-school district the area within which a separate-school board, *q.v.*, has responsibility.

1884 *Prince Albert Times* (Sask.) 8 Feb. 2/1: The proposed ordinance makes provision for the establishment of "separate school districts," that is for the establishment of Protestant and Roman Catholic schools. **1964** *News of the North* 19 Mar. 7: [Advert.] A special meeting of the ratepayers of the Yellowknife Roman Catholic Separate School District No. 2 has been called to consider the operating budget for the 1964-5 school term.

separate-school question the political problem of deciding whether denominational schools should be allowed to exist beside the public schools, both getting support from public funds. Cp. **Manitoba School Question.**

[**1868** (1941) PATTERSON *N.S.History* 109: The Separate Schools story has been ingeniously distorted and lied about and there is no use for any person who does not speak Gaelic trying to go among them or influence them.] **1958** *Encyc.Can.* III 381/1: Another controversial issue associated with the separate school question concerned bilingual schools. **1963** *Canada Month* April 18/2: The Ontario separate-school question played a notable role in French Canada's lack of enthusiasm for World War I.

separate-school system 1 a school system permitting denominational schools to exist alongside public schools, each with its own board and each supported by public funds. See also **separate school** (def. 3a).

1882 *What Farmers Say* 11: Educational interests on the Separate School system are very carefully attended to, there being as many as 102 Protestant schools, with an attendance of over 5,000 children, and 27 Catholic schools with over 2,500 children. **1963** *Calgary Herald* 13 Dec. 4/1: He was not objecting to the continued existence of the separate school system, but he did emphasize that . . . the religious minority must be prepared to pay for all the costs entailed.

2 (by extension) a system of Roman Catholic parochial schools in provinces where no provision is made for separate schools (def. 3).

1966 *Citizen* (Prince George, B.C.) 12 Oct. 1/3: A veteran Ontario school inspector has termed "regrettable" the British Columbia government's policy of not assigning taxes to the separate school system.

separate secondary school See **separate high-school.**

1963 *Globe and Mail* (Toronto) 9 Mar. 11/4: It called for increased financial aid for separate schools from the Provincial Government and the establishment of separate secondary schools and teachers colleges.

separate teachers college a teachers college for training teachers for separate schools (def. 3a).

1963 *Globe and Mail* (Toronto) 9 Mar. 11/4: It called for increased financial aid for separate schools from the Provincial Government and the establishment of separate secondary schools and teachers colleges.

separatism *n.* the political concept of a province withdrawing from Confederation and existing as a separate and independent state; also, advocacy of or support for this concept.

1961 *Canada Month* 6 Oct. 36/1: Separatism is not new to Quebec. **1963** *Maclean's* 7 Sep. 14/1: Separatism, of course, is still a long way from obtaining the support of the majority. There are still many people in the boondocks who haven't ever heard of it. **1966** *Globe and Mail* (Toronto) 14 Jan. 5/2: Where does Quebec's special status end and separatism take over?

separatist *n.* a supporter of separatism.

1961 *Time* (Cdn ed.) 29 Dec. 9/1: The shock troops on the battlefield are Quebec's separatists, who want nothing less than to secede from Canada and establish an independent Republic of Quebec. **1963** *Canada Month* May 15/3: The cracks [in Confederation] are small yet, and the separatists of B.C. are not organized. But neither were the separatists of Quebec a few years ago. **1966** *Globe and Mail* (Toronto) 23 Aug. 7/6: Mr. Caouette's suggestion that Mr. Gregoire should resign from federal politics now that he has become a separatist, means the end of that alliance.

separatist *adj.* consisting of or pertaining to separatists or separatism.

1916 BRIDLE *Sons of Can.* 103: On the whole, we may conclude that it is Henri Bourassa, the creator of the separatist party, who really wants the Nationalist idea to prevail. **1962** *Kingston Whig-Standard* (Ont.) 13 Feb. 3/3: Mr. Leblanc said representatives of the news media have a responsibility to understand some of the reasons for the current "separatist movement" in Quebec.

Separatist party *Hist.* in British Columbia, a political group opposed to Confederation.

1894 BEGG *Hist.of B.C.* 426: The "Standard," the organ of the Separatist party, in describing the closing scenes of 1875, brings in an ode, the production of a local poet . . . James MacBraire Smith.

servant *n. Hist.* an employee of the Hudson's Bay Company, specifically one other than an officer holding a commission from the company. See also **Company man.**

1690 (1752) ROBSON *Hudson's Bay* App. 19: If any two or three of our servants shall shew their forwardness to go upon new discoveries, we require you to encourage the undertaking, and upon their good success, to allow them such advance of wages or gratuity for their pains, as you in your discretion shall find convenient. **1775** (1934) HEARNE *Journal* 193: These losses together with their payment not only runs away with all the Profit, but renders the Company's Servants the make game and laughing stock of every trader from Canady. **1880** GORDON *Mountain and Prairie* 230: The Fort at lesser Slave Lake consists of shop, store-houses and dwellings of the Company's servants, ranged in a quadrangle. **1960** *Press* Dec. 13: The traders and their "servants" liked the land and the free life and, mingling with the Indians and with Metis bands, within a generation formed a new and dominant element, the mixed bloods. . . .

serviceberry† *n.* **1** any of several bushes or shrubby trees of the genus *Amelanchier*. See also **Indian pear** (def. 2), **juneberry** (def. 1), **poire** (def. 2), **saskatoon bush,** and **shadbush.**

[**1793** (1801) MACKENZIE *Voyages* 179: The trees are spruce . . . service tree, bois-picant, &c. . . .] **1860** (1956) KOHL *Kitchi-Gami* 185: . . . the English call it "service . . . berry". . . . **1956** *Native Trees* 212: The serviceberries, also known as juneberries, shad-bushes, and, in the West, the Saskatoons, are deciduous species with simple alternate leaves and slender unarmed twigs.

2 the fruit of any of these plants. See also **Indian pear** (def. 1), **juneberry** (def. 2), **pear, poire** (def. 1), **saskatoon berry** (def. 1), **shad berry,** and **Siwash berry.**

1853 REID *Young Voyageurs* 356: The berries have received different names in different parts of America. They are known as "shadberries," "June-berries," "service-berries," and by the Canadian voyageurs they are called "le poire."

1879 ROBINSON *Great Fur Land* 117: The best form of pemmican, made for table use, generally has added to it ten pounds of sugar per bag, and saskatoon or service berries. . . . **1964** *Beaver* Summer 53/1: For variety sometimes dried fruits such as chokecherries, saskatoon or service berries might be added.

service centre a town or city which acts as a distribution point for food, clothing, etc. in a sparsely populated region such as a national park, a summer-cottage area, etc.
1963 *Calgary Herald* 20 Sep. 1/3: He said he wanted to get more private investment into the parks and make the towns of Banff and Lake Louise "service centres" for the adjacent parks of Jasper, Yoho, and Kootenay.

service college See **services college.**

serviced land land lying within an urban area and serviced with public utilities, especially sewers, water, and gas mains.
1966 *Kingston Whig-Standard* (Ont.) 8 Jan. 1/6: Kingston is bound to benefit—although there is not too much serviced land left—from an increase in . . . loan interest rates.

service road See **access road** (def. 1).
1965 *Time* (Cdn ed.) 23 Apr. 17/2: This spring, with amenities ranging from modern bunkhouses to service roads . . . [they] are clearing the rich land in earnest.

services college one of three institutions of higher learning, The Royal Military College of Canada, Le Collège Militaire Royal de St-Jean, and Royal Roads, where cadets (and some officers at the graduate level) take university instruction in courses leading to degrees in Arts, Science, and Engineering. Also called (unofficially) **service college.**
1953-54 *Royal Military College Calendar* 15: The purpose of the Canadian Services Colleges is to instruct young men in the skills and qualities essential to continued development after graduation as officers in the Active or Reserve Forces. . . . **1963** *Globe and Mail* (Toronto) 12 Jan. 6/1: The Commission found that to graduate an officer from one of Canada's three Service colleges cost $47,000. . . .

service vote in an election, that portion of the total vote which is cast by persons in the armed services who are absent from their home ridings, these voters casting their ballots on a designated day prior to election day, the results of the balloting being made public some time after the general election results.
1962 *Chronicle-Herald* (Halifax) 11 Aug. 4/1: Even if it is administratively impossible to camouflage the service vote completely . . . surely arrangements could be made whereby the ballots of servicemen were counted on election night. . . . **1963** *Globe and Mail* (Toronto) 27 Mar. 8/5: The results of the service vote likely will be known on Saturday or Sunday following the April 8 general election.

service voter a member of the armed services who casts a ballot in the service vote, *q.v.*
1963 *Kingston Whig-Standard* (Ont.) 19 Mar. 18/1: For this election there are 141,210 eligible service voters. **1963** *Globe and Mail* (Toronto) 27 Mar. 8/6: Service voters far from their home constituencies . . . are told the political affiliation of each candidate.

service voting voting in the service vote, *q.v.*
1963 *Globe and Mail* (Toronto) 27 Mar. 8/6: The

London office handles service voting at 146 polling places in Western Europe, Egypt, Palestine, the Congo and Indochina.

serviette† *n.* a table napkin.
☛ *Though by no means native to Canada, this British term is characteristic of Canadian usage as opposed to the American* **napkin,** *which is also heard in Canada.*
*c*1902 LAUT *Trapper* 250: He may even use a fresh hide to handle the traps, as a waiter uses a serviette to pass plates. There must be no man-smell, no man-track near the otter traps. **1956** KEMP *Northern Trader* 29: I admired his cut glass, his silver and his spotless serviettes.

sessional indemnity See **indemnity** (def. 1).
1900 OSBORN *Greater Canada* 105: But Canada, having no large leisured class, and being a country of such magnificent distances that the M.P. cannot attend to his business as well as his legislation, is obliged to pay the workers on her political machinery, with the result that politics have come to be looked upon as a profession . . . and the average partisan gets to Ottawa for the sake of his sessional indemnity and what he can make by means of his position. **1950** WARD *House of Commons* 114: . . . if membership [in Parliament] is to be a full-time occupation, it is high time that the sessional indemnity be frankly regarded as an annual salary for work performed. **1963** *Globe and Mail* (Toronto) 12 July 8/2: Increases in sessional indemnities and expenses that the Quebec Legislature has just approved put it in a class by itself. The indemnity for a single session is $10,000 plus a tax-free $5,000 expense allowance.

set *n.* **1** a snare or trap. See also **variation set.**
1912 ROE *Whispering Hills* 74: But what is all this beside that which waits the runner of the trail at every "set" in those many miles. **1965** *Islander* 14 Feb. 4/3: . . . whenever he got within a hundred yards or so of a "set" he left the trail. . . .
2 *West* the field or other area to be worked by a stook-threshing outfit.
1922 STEAD *Neighbours* 140: Sometimes, to finish a "set" we would burn a straw pile and work by its light. . . . **1963** SYMONS *Many Trails* 111: Following the machinery were the stook teams, which loaded the sheaves from the field and drew them to the "set" where the separator had been levelled and located.

setting *n. Lumbering* See quote.
1942 HAIG-BROWN *Timber* 253: SETTING. The whole of the area logged from a single spar tree. **1966** *Sun* (Vancouver) 12 Jan. 25/1: When you go to the camp, the bullbucker takes you out and shows you your quarter of the setting. . . .

setting-pole† *n. Hist.* a long pole, often tipped with iron or steel, used for pushing or guiding a canoe or other boat in narrow or shallow streams. See also **canoe pole, pole,** and **push-pole** (def. 2).
1768-82 (1791) LONG *Voyages* 75: Where the water is shallow, the canoes must be forced upward with long setting poles. . . . **1798** (1918) DAVIDSON *North West Co.* 217: Each canoe was provided with a mast and lug-sail, and also each man had a ten-foot setting pole, of good ash, shod with an iron ferrule at each end. . . . **1853** STRICKLAND *Canada West* I 261: . . . for, although the spring floods were considerably abated, the water ran with great rapidity, and in some places was up to our middles; but with the help of a strong setting-pole,

we got over with safety. **1933** GATES *Five Traders* 81n: The setting poles were thrown away at the height of land since they were not necessary on the journey downstream.

settlement *n.* **1 a.** a community, especially in its early stages of development.
1769 (1931) BROOKE *Emily Montague* 208: ... there is a settlement within a few leagues, on which there is an extreme agreeable family.... **1814** *Montreal Herald* 21 May 2/1: I wish Lord S ... was in his grave before he thought of this settlement, or I in mine before I came to it. **1958** *Time* (Cdn ed.) 10 Nov. 18/2: From one settlement near the Henik Lakes, a mother with five small children headed across the barrens on foot in 40-below zero weather.... **1966** *Ibid.* 18 Nov. 16/2: For EPA's pilots, that just adds to the challenge of flying mail to 43 remote Newfoundland and Labrador settlements....
b. *N.S., Hist.* See **township** (def. 1a).
1907 *U of T Stud.Hist.& Econ.* II 235: The term "Settlement" was used with few exceptions in eastern Nova Scotia in place of "Township," the common term in the western part.
c. in the Northwest, an officially designated community.
1953 *North Star* (Yellowknife) Oct. 1/1: At many posts, camps and settlements where an organic community exists the people decided which candidate they wished to favor and cast their votes for him. **1954** *Ibid.* Aug. 2/3: ... most of the natives there lived a nomadic life travelling far from the settlement, fishing, hunting and trapping in order to live.... **1965** *Time* (Cdn ed.) 14 May 20/3: ... the houses will bring Indian and Metis children to settlement schools....
2 *Obs.* a trading post of a fur company.
1775 (1951) *Saskatchewan Jnls* 23 Oct.: In the Afternoon a Canoe with fourteen of the Pedlers men arrived on their way to the upper Settlement in Sas-kach-i-wan River.... **1778** (1954) *Moose Ft Jnls* 368: I shall be ready to go up again as soon as the River breaks up and to be down again at Ship time so that I may have an opportunity of knowing what is the Companys Intentions in regard to this settlement.

Settlement *n. Hist.* See **Red River Settlement**.
1815 (1963) MACLEOD & MORTON *Cuthbert Grant* 29: It is hereby promised that peace & amity shall hereafter ever exist between the people of this Settlement and the Half Breeds.... **1883** *Trans.Hist.& Sci.Soc.Man.* II 3/1: Having spent a year in "the settlement," as Assiniboia was called up to only a few years ago, he left his native land for England in 1842, and though ardently attached to it never had the privilege of seeing it again. **1929** JEFFERSON *Saskatchewan* 15: The "settlement" (that is, the Red River Settlement) on each side of the river continues for six or eight miles below Selkirk.

settlement duty one of several obligations assumed by settlers occupying land on location tickets, *q.v.*, or under a Homestead Law, *q.v.* See also **settler's duty** and **settling duty**.
1819 *U.C.Gaz.* (York [Toronto]) 15 July 113/4: Locations of Two Hundred Acres will be made, upon their undertaking to begin their Settlement Duty within One Month after receiving the Certificate of Location, and continuing the same, until a Dwelling House be

erected, and Ten Acres cleared adjacent to the Road, and one half of the Road in front of the Location also cleared. **1840** *Montreal Transcript* 24 Dec. 407/1: Settlers will be required to clear, and place once under crop, one third of the land located, and to reside on the land until this settlement duty is performed.
1882 *Prince Albert Times* (Sask.) 15 Nov. 2/1: The usual homestead and pre-emption can be secured, and in addition to this the odd numbered sections can be obtained at two dollars per acre, without subjecting the purchaser to the settlement duties required in the railway belt. **1909** HUNTER *Simcoe County* 51: In all cases the settlement duty was insisted upon.

settlement-duty certificate *Hist.* a certificate testifying that settlement duties have been fulfilled.
1853 STRICKLAND *Canada West* I 89: A magistrate ... told me that a Yankee chopper came to him one day and demanded to be sworn on a settlement duty certificate....

settlement-duty road *Hist.* a road built by pioneers as part of their settlement duties.
1853 STRICKLAND *Canada West* I 174: The place I had selected to watch for them was an old settlement duty-road which had been cut out some years before....

settlement officer a government official who advises newly arrived immigrants and directs them to their place of settlement.
1964 *Calgary Herald* 31 July 21/2: [They] were greeted today by city officials and Earl Kellar, settlement officer with the department of immigration....

settlement road *Hist.* See **colonization road**.
1961 PRICE & KENNEDY *Renfrew* 113: The following data ... contains some interesting sidelights on ... the building of the "settlement roads."

settler *n.* **1** a person who settles in a new country or in another part of the same country, usually on the frontier.
1755 (1895) RICHARD *Acadia* II 100: In order to save as many of the Acadian cattle as possible, I have given some of them among such of the English settlers as have the means of feeding them. **1852** *Toronto Mirror* 30 Jan. 3/3: Although the upper part hasn't as yet any settlers upon it, a great many clearings are to be found on the lower part. **1960** *Sask.News* 12 Apr. 2/1: The settlers called them "dugouts."
2 *Lab.* **a.** See quote.
1947 TANNER *Outlines* II 727: The resident white fishermen of the outer coast are ... also termed "planters" or "settlers." [for full quote see **liveyere** (def.1)]. **1964** *North* July 4/1: But since the Labrador settlers ... have always lived with and worked alongside Eskimos, there was not the antagonism that might have occurred in a white community "outside" if 150 strangers had suddenly moved in with them.
b. See quote 1947.
1947 TANNER *Outlines* II 727: ... the term "settler" [for livyer] should be eliminated because it may give rise to confusion; in the coastal district north of Makkovik this is the term given to some semi-settled half-breeds of white and Eskimo. **1959** *Northern Affairs Bull.* May-June 21: Hopedale—[Labrador, has] about 200 people. Very few, if any, are pure Eskimo, nearly all are "Settlers," mainly Eskimo speaking, but most can speak English.
3 a small farmer and part-time logger and trapper in Northern Ontario, especially a French-speaking Canadian. See also **colonist** (def. 3).

1963 *Maclean's* 23 Mar. 2/1 : The farmers' hold on the land is so tenuous [because of poverty] that even though some have been here [N.Ont.] thirty years, they are still called "settlers."

settler's duty *Hist*. See **settlement duty.**
1963 *Sask.News* Sep. 1 : Claiming the land as their own, the two immediately set about settlers' duties, digging a well and erecting a claim shanty.

settlers' effects See 1913 and 1967 quotes.
1913 SANDILANDS *West.Cdn Dict*. 40/1 : Settlers' effects include a host of things which the immigrant is allowed to convey into the Dominion duty free and at a cheap rate of transportation. 1927 (1928) ROSE *Stump Farm* 177 : Very seductive rates are offered on settlers' effects and a very low rate on farm produce and grain to be shipped out of the country. 1967 *Canadian Almanac & Directory* 774/1 : Settlers' effects including household furnishings, aircraft . . . for personal use. . . are admitted duty free. . . .

settle up 1 occupy (as a settler) or be occupied (by settlers).
1859 *Brit.Colonist* (Victoria) 4 July 1/2 : By that means the trader would have followed the miner, and settled up the country, and thousands who have left our shores would have remained to add millions to our productive wealth. 1921 *Beaver* Mar. 4/2 : The country began to settle up very rapidly and business with the Hudson's Bay Company assumed . . . large proportions. . . .
2 pay a debt; honor a commitment.
1910 SERVICE *Trail of '98* 17 : "All right, I'll settle up with you later on." 1964 *Nfld Qtly* Spring 27/1 : Down to 45 years ago, a planter would often "ship" a girl as a house servant by a brief formal agreement written out and filed in his merchant's office, the servant thereafter drawing her small needs from the shop on credit, and her account being credited and the planter's account per contra debited, at settling up time with her agreed very small wage.

settling duty *Hist*. See **settlement duty.**
1825 (1927) DICKIE *How Canada Grew Up* 42 : The settler must clear five acres upon each hundred granted to him, open a road in front of his lot, and build a loghouse of certain dimensions. These settling duties, if performed within eighteen months after location ticket has been issued entitle the emigrant to a deed from the Government which makes the lot his forever.
1827 *Colonial Advocate* (York[Toronto]) 14 June 1/1 : I wish to contract with some person or persons to do the settling duties for me in Lot No 32 in the first concession of Garrafraza, containing 200 acres.
WM.L.MACKENZIE.

Seventy-Two Resolutions *Hist*. See 1958 quote.
1868 SMALL *Chronicles* 198 : After sitting some eighteen days in Quebec, the result of their deliberations was the famous "Seventy-two Resolutions," which in accordance with the final resolution, were authenticated by the signatures of the Delegates, and were ordered to be submitted by each delegation to its own government. 1958 *Encyc.Can*. VIII 379/2 : The main work of the [Quebec] conference was embodied in the Seventy-Two Resolutions that were drawn up as an outline for the proposed federal union. These later became the basis of negotiations at the London Conference in 1866-67 and eventually formed the core of the BNA Act.

sewage lagoon See 1958 cite.
1958 *Progress* (Preeceville, Sask.) 28 May 1/6 : Northwest of town the earthwork for the sewage lagoon has been largely completed. Looking like a large rectangular coliseum (less seats) the basin has been scooped out, built up and packed to provide a reservoir for sewage from town. 1964 *North* May-June 44/2 : It was decided that the company should act for the Territorial Government and install in 1963 the essential services-roads, street-lighting, water and sewer lines, water treatment plant and sewage-lagoon.

sewel† *n*. [var. of *shewel*, something to scare] *Hist*. or *Obs*. See 1792 quote.
1770 (1911) TOWNSEND *Cartwright's Journal* 20 : Where any open places intervened [in a hunting fence], they [Beothuks] made use of a sort of sewell, made of narrow strips of birch rind, tied together in the form of a wing of a paper kite. 1792 CARTWRIGHT *Journal* II viii : Sewel [is] a device to turn deer, particularly applied to the feathered line. 1891 *Trans.Roy.Soc.Can*. IX 2 133 : In places where the trees grew too stunted, or were too scattered to be available for fences, they placed "sewels," poles on which attached tassels of birch bark flutter and frighten the deer.

sewellel† [səˈwɛləl] *n*. [< Chinook *shewallal* a robe from the skins of the *ogwoollal* mountain beaver] a mammal of the western mountain regions, *Aplodontia rufa*. Also called *Mountain beaver*.
1953 *Cdn Geog.Jnl* Oct. 133/1 : The largest of the mouse-like rodents, so called, is the mountain beaver or sewellel. It looks more like a tailless muskrat than a beaver; dark brown, flat headed, with small ears, strong digging claws on its front feet, and almost no tail.

sewer trout *Slang* trash fish.
1958 WELLS *Georgian Bay* 104 : Bass there are, and pickerel, and muskenonge, not to mention such sewer trout as catfish, dog fish and pike.

Seymo *n*. *Obs*. See quotes at **Suckemo.**

shack *n*. [< Brit.dial. *shackety, shackling,* etc. rickety, rundown] a rude dwelling, especially one of wood, usually in a rundown condition. See also **shanty,** *n*. (def. 3b).
[1821 (1955) CRAIG *Early Travellers* 64 : There is indeed a good deal of cleared land on some of the farms; but miserable log-huts, ill-ploughed fields, shackling barns and unpruned orchards, are to be seen everywhere, disfiguring the face of the country, and showing too accurately the character of those who inhabit it.] 1884 *Prince Albert Times* (Sask.) 13 June 1/2 : The "shack" of my neighbor, the side stable near it,/ And e'en the old shanty that stood on the plain. 1958 *News of the North* 25 Dec. 17/2 : Not a stable indeed, for stables are rare, but shacks we do have—in Yellowknife.

shack *v*. live in a shack.
1884 *Prince Albert Times* (Sask.) 13 June 3/2 : Of all the enjoyments Prince Albert can number, there's none equals shacking on a *pre-emption* claim. 1954 BRUCE *Channel Shore* 16 : Men had sailed east from here to the Cape Breton coast, to shack on the beaches and fish the waters off Petit de Grat. . . .

shackanappe *n*. See **shaganappi.**

shacker *n.* See quote. See also **shackman.**
1962 *Alta Hist.Rev.* Autumn 17/1: . . . a chief topic of conversation among local politicians was as to whether or not "shackers" would be permitted to vote at an election, a "shacker" being a person who occupies a temporary residence commonly known as a shanty or "shack."

shackie *n.* [< *shack* + *-ie*, presumably influenced by *shanty*] a cheap and hastily constructed house, store, etc.
1958 KELSEY *B.C.Rides a Star* 80: Learning in advance that the highway was to be built, they rushed in to buy up properties around the business district on which to build shackies to rent for exhorbitant sums.

shackman *n.* a person who lives in a shack. See also **shacker.**
1957 HUTCHISON *Canada* 123: The shackman . . . adds a clumsy porch as if he were building for the ages.

shack-tent *n.* See **log tent** (def. 2).
1956 KEMP *Northern Trader* 62: In fact, the only time any part of me was warm was when we were in the shack-tent at night with a huge box stove blood-red and roaring, a kettle of fish boiling on top of it.

shacktown *n.* a community, or section of a town, etc., that is comprised of shacks, *q.v.* See also **shantytown.**
1923 STEELE *Spirit-of-Iron* 105: Where little shack-towns rose, it knew there should be cities. **1960** *North* July-Oct. 39/1: The Eskimos who are not employed are gradually concentrating their numbers at almost every DEW site in the western Arctic with the subsequent build-up of "shacktowns" erected with discarded materials from the dumps. **1965** *Globe and Mail* (Toronto) 12 Jan. 7/3: True, there are highly visible shack-towns . . . the French Line up in Lanark and, over a larger area of the Shield, the Ozarks of Ontario.

shad† *n.* a north American food fish, *Alosa sapidissima,* of the Atlantic Coast.
1774 (1945) ROBINSON & RISPIN *Journey N.S.* 31: They caught . . . forty barrels of fish, which they call chad, and which they sell for four dollars per barrel, of thirty-two gallons. . . . **1866** KING *Sportsman in Can.* 301: The Shad . . . can barely be classed among the game fish of the country, for they are chiefly taken in "brush fisheries." **1962** *Commercial Letter* Oct. 5/2: Shad are caught in the nets when the tide is in.

shad berry *Maritimes* See **serviceberry** (def. 2). See also **shadbush.**
1801 (1820) HARMON *Journal* 81: The last [berries] . . . exactly resemble, in shape and taste, what in the New England states are called shad berries. **1859** (1870) SOUTHESK *Saskatchewan* 86: M'Kay calls them Shad (?Shade) berries, the Indian name is Meesasskatoom.

shadbush *n. Esp.Maritimes* See **serviceberry** (def. 1). See also 1932 quote.
1822 (1928) CORMACK *Narr.Nfld* 19: On the skirts of the forest, and of the marshes, are found shadbush, and the red choke-berry. . . . **1932** WINSON *Weather and Wings* 66: On the eastern side of the Rockies this June-berry is called the Saskatoon-berry; on the Atlantic shores it is the shad-bush. **1956** *Native Trees* 212: The serviceberries, also known as juneberries, shad-bushes,

and, in the West, the Saskatoons, are deciduous species with simple alternate leaves and slender unarmed twigs.

shade *n.* a simple shelter consisting of several upright poles, a lattice roof, and brush or rush-mat roofing.
1808 (1890) MCKENZIE *King's Posts* 453: The buildings consist only of a dwelling house, a store and a shade. **1808** (1960) FRASER *Letters and Journals* 121: The Chief made a harangue & then invited us to his *shade,* where we were treated with great hospitality. **1954** *Ghost Pine* 38: On July 1, a community picnic was held on Sarcee Butte. A big shade was made, covered with brush. A good crowd turned out.

shad-fly *n. Maritimes* one of several flies, especially the May fly. See also **shad-worm.**
1825 *Canadian Mag.* IV 474: Among the curious phenomena of Canada, is the ephemeral Spring fly, called . . . by the English the Shad Fly, as they are supposed to indicate the approach of the fish.

shad-waiter *n. Obs.* See **mooneye.**

Shagalasha ['ʃægə,læʃə] *n.* [< Algonk.; cf. Ojibwa *shākanāsh* Englishman] in Indian parlance, a Mounted Policeman, *q.v.* Cp. **saganash.**
1923 STEELE *Spirit-of-Iron* 29: "I thank the Great White Mother and the One Above who rules us all because they have sent to us the Shagalasha, the red-coats, to save us from the bad white man and from ourselves. The Shagalasha are our friends." **1936** MOWERY *Paradise Trail* 15: . . . Colonel French and his band of red-coated Shagalasha had not yet come riding across the plains from old Fort Garry, bringing order and justice to the North-West Territories. **1953** MOWERY *Mounted Police* 122: "If you make enemy of the Shagalasha too, then you will have no place on earth to pitch your tepee."

shaganappi ['ʃægə,næpi] *n.* [< Algonk.; cf. Woods Cree *pishaganabii* < *pishagan* what is flayed + *abii* cord]
☛ *Earlier spellings are exceptionally varied for this widely used term.*

1 a thong of rawhide. See also **babiche** (def. 1) and **Northwest iron.**
[**1743** (1949) ISHAM *Observations* 46: Shag, a nap, pee or a string of Leather tauk' a miss.] **1749** DRAGE *Voyage* II 40: These Bales are . . . tied up with Shackanappe in a close compact Manner. **1825** (1926) *Cdn Hist.Rev.* VII 318: Shaganapie pack Cords lb 1d. **1872** (1873) GRANT *Ocean to Ocean* 187: The triangular shaped load is bound in one by folds of shaganappi twisted firmly but without a knot, after a regular fashion called the "diamond hitch." **1938** *Beaver* Dec. 19/2: I take three poles, put them together, and tie them at one end with shaganappi. **1956** INNIS *Fur Trade* 295: The packsaddle became an important part of the equipment with plenty of shaganappi for diamond hitches and knots.

2 rawhide.
1880 GORDON *Mountain and Prairie* 164: One outfit consisted of a small pack-saddle, shaped something like a diminutive saw-horse . . . and girt with a broad belt of shaganappi. **1909** BRYCE *Lord Selkirk's Colonists* 237: To add to its oddity, the shafts are heavy, straight beams, between which is harnessed an ox, the harness of rawhide (shaga-nappi) without buckles. **1963** *B.C. Digest* Oct. 22/1: The harness, made of raw buffalo-hide, the "shaganappi" of the North-west, served good purpose while it was kept dry, but when wet the story was quite different.

3 See **shaganappi pony.**

[**1886** BOULTON *N.W.Rebellion* 55: The term "shaganappi" came to be applied by the new settlers to everything in connection with a Red River outfit.]
1889 DONKIN *Trooper* 9: These native quadrupeds, in the Far West, are called cayeuses, or shagganappis.
1930 BEAMES *Army* 159: The half-breed whipped up his shaganappies and whirled away down the lake.
1956 KEMP *Northern Trader* 20: Farm horses or shaganappies, the searing cold and outside camps were too much for them.

shaganappi [′ʃægə‚næpi] *adj.* [< n.] *West, Slang* of little worth; inferior; hasty; badly organized. See 1941 and 1962 quotes at **shaganappi pony.** See also **haywire,** *adj.* (def. 2).
1900 FRASER *Mooswa* 35: Have patience, little shaganappi (cheap) Bird. **1961** MITCHELL *Jake and the Kid* 2: "At the Rabbit Hill school concert last night, folks heard a shaganappy speech. It give everybuddy from Crocus to the correction line the heartburn." *Ibid.* 107: "Thinka anybuddy havin' a shaganappy thing like that in their house!"

shaganappi cayuse See **shaganappi pony.**
1938 GODSELL *Red Hunters* 171: ... between these two places there streamed a constant caravan of wagons drawn by shagganapi cayuses. ... **1953** MOWERY *Mounted Police* 109: A shaganappi cayuse and rider broke through the willow thicket, splashed recklessly across the creek, and galloped up to him.

shaganappi harness or **hitchings** *Hist.* gear made of shaganappi (def. 2), as for hitching oxen or ponies to carts.
1871 (1883) BUTLER *Great Lone Land* 234: "Shanganappi harness is tough stuff and a broken sled is easily set to rights. ..." **1885** *Selkirk Herald* (Man.) 17 Jan. 4/2: Huge wheels, out of all proportion to the carrying capacity, with felloes roughly cut from native wood ... shaganappi fastening everywhere, shaganappi "hitchings"; not a grain of iron in its whole anatomy— such was the far-famed Red River Cart in its palmy days.

shaganappi line 1 *Obs.* See **shaganappi,** *n.* (def. 1).
1820 (1931) SIMPSON *Fur Trade* 58: Any dressed skins, sinews, and Shaganapy lines that can be spared, you will send here, for New Caledonia; and also whatever Babiche is not required for your own District.
2 *Hist.* a freight line of wagons and shaganappi ponies, *q.v.*
1879 *Sask.Herald* (Battleford, N.W.T.) 24 Mar. 1/3: Very Latest—(By Shaganappi Line).—Five per cent duty on tobacco, and tobacco at Fort McLeod $2.50 per pound.

shaganappi pony See **cayuse.** See also **shaganappi** (def. 3), **shaganappi cayuse,** and **shag pony.**
*c***1902** LAUT *Trapper* 198: In place of the ox sometimes was a "shagganippy" pony, raw and unkempt, which the imps lashed without mercy or the slightest inconvenience to the horse. **1909** BRYCE *Lord Selkirk's Colonists* 308: The stage coach, the Red River cart, and the shaganappi pony are things of the past, and several railways with richly furnished trains connect St. Paul and Minneapolis with the City of Winnipeg. **1941** COTTER *Fur Trade Glossary:* Shaganappie Pony. A small under-size horse, generally with the harness the last word in knots, hitches and splices. ... **1962** *Alta Hist.Rev.* Autumn 14/2: A "cayuse" is an Indian pony, also called a "shagnappi" (literally, common or ordinary); this word is, however, usually applied to rawhide.

shaganappi rope *Hist.* a rope made of braided shaganappi (def. 1).
1930 ROLYAT *Fort Garry* 117: "I thought of the long shaganappi rope in me bag—I ripped it out and tied it to Adam's bridle. ..."

shaganash *n.* See **saganash.**

shaggamitie *n.* See **sagamité.**

shag pony *West* See **shaganappi pony.**
1918 MOORHOUSE *Deep Furrows* 65: ... every morning, after sucking a couple of eggs for a breakfast, E. A. Partridge took to loping across the prairie on a "Shag" pony.

shake† *n.* a large unplaned shingle, usually hand-split, used for roofing and siding.
1898 (1966) PATTERSON *Trail* 95: Murton ... got at the building while Kirkendale split and dressed jack-pine shakes: "940 shakes was my record day." **1922** PICKTHALL *Bridge* 278: Presently she heard him, wrenching furiously at the loose flimsy cedar "shakes" of which the shack was built. ... **1963** *Beaver* Summer 10/2: Giant beams, fifty feet long, were swung onto the ceiling frame and a roofing of long cedar shakes laid over them.

shaked *adj.* constructed of shakes.
1955 HOBSON *Nothing Too Good* 98: A ten-horse, twenty-eight-foot-square, log barn with dirt floor and high-shaked roof with haymow was contracted for a hundred and fifty dollars. **1960** MCNAMEE *Florencia Bay* 68: On a promontory, on the other side of Lost Shoe Creek from Dumont's cabin, was a shaked-roofed weather-beaten shed.

shaking tent or **lodge** See **conjurer's lodge.**
1935 JENNESS *Parry Island* 49: His parents then consulted a conjuror ... who interpreted the dream through the spirits of the shaking lodge, and restored the boy to health. **1965** *Beaver* Summer 35/2: It is said that one old man at Nemiscau is capable of performing the shaking tent rite and on occasion still does.

shalloway *n.* [origin uncertain] *Obs.* a small sailing vessel used in coastal waters.
1774 (1792) CARTWRIGHT *Journal* II 14: Hooper's shalloway having sprung her foremast, when she was out with captain Scott, I sent the boat-builder to make her a new one. **1776** *Ibid.* 132: The ice was cut about the shalloway to day, to prevent it from lifting her.

shaman† *n.* among the Indians and Eskimos, a medicine-man or angakok, *qq.v.*
1852 RICHARDSON *Arctic Exped.* 217: When the shaman was sent for to cure a sick person, he shut himself into a tent with his patient, and, without tasting food, sung over him for days together. **1964** *Cdn Geog.Jnl* May 162: However, the shaman (medicine man) is still a force in the community, with the power that is held by superstition.

shamateur [′ʃæmətʃɚ] *n.* [*sham* + *amateur*] *Sports, Slang* a so-called amateur, especially a hockey player, who in fact receives payment for his services.

1966 *Globe and Mail* (Toronto) 20 Apr. 28: [Headline] Weslock no shamateur; juniors get TV money.

shamateurism ['ʃæmətʃə,rɪzəm] *n.* [< *shamateur* + *-ism*] *Sports, Slang* See quote.
1963 *Globe and Mail* (Toronto) 4 Mar. 1/3: "Shamateurism"—outright deception involving payment for so-called amateur performance—is an acknowledged system in hockey.

shanks *n.pl.* [cf. Brit.dial. *shank* leg of a stocking] *Esp.Maritimes* leggings made from the hide, peeled off and cured, from the hind legs of a moose, caribou, etc. See also **moose-shanks.** Cp. **hock-moccasin.**
1943 DENNIS *Cape Breton* 165: Footwear was of home manufacture and consisted of moccasins, or more often shanks. **1952** BUCKLER *Mountain and Valley* 100: The Rothesays down the road ... wore moose shanks with the hair still on them. ...

shanty ['ʃænti] *n.* [< Cdn F *chantier,* q.v.] **1** *Hist.*
a. a crude hut used as a dwelling by lumbermen in the bush. See also **chantie** (def. 2) and **log shanty** (def. 1).
☞ *Although the most probable source of* **shanty** *is Cdn F* chantier, *especially in lumbering contexts, the possibility remains that a similar word, derived from Irish Gaelic* sean tig *hut, may have been introduced by Irish immigrants into Upper Canada, where the term seems first to have enjoyed currency; it may well be, therefore, that two different words of similar form contributed to the generalization of this term and its derivatives in Canada during the nineteenth century. Cp. note at* **shebang.**
1822 (1932) MCLEAN *Notes* 30: We arrived ... and finding a quantity of timber collected on the ice, concluded that the shanty must be close at hand.
1826 *Colonial Advocate* (York [Toronto]) 25 May 2/3: Like kings they can live in a shantie/ And sleep upon green hemlock boughs. **1849** ALEXANDER *L'Acadie* II 22: We took up our position for the night in a deserted lumberer's shanty of logs, a considerable part of the roof of this small square hut being wanting, to favour the passage of the smoke. **1923** (1929) *Selected Stories* 84: The afternoon began to wear away, and long after the time when they should have started for the shanty, Monique was staring at the pine-trees. **1963** MORTON *Kingdom of Canada* 246: In Lower Canada ... scores hid out in the sugaring huts and loggers' shanties in the bush.

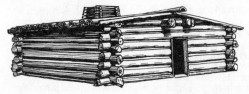

A shanty (def. 1b)

b. a specially designed log bunkhouse used by a gang of loggers. See also **camboose** (def. 3), **camp** (def. 1c), **log shanty** (def. 2), and **lumber shanty** (def. 1).

1829 MACTAGGART *Three Years* I 242: As these people live in huts in the woods ... which huts are houses only for a season, they are called *shanties,* and hence, *shantymen.* ... **1883** FRASER *Shanty* 23: Monahan's shanty ... is a capital specimen ... of backwoods architecture. **1961** *Ont.Hist.* Sep. 197: This [museum] ... includes a full-size replica of a logging shanty or camboose camp. ...

c. a boarding-house or bunkhouse erected at a work camp for the accomodation of miners, loggers, etc. See also **sleeping camp.**
1861 (1965) GAETZ *Diary* 65: There are now upwards of 600 persons at work at the gold fields. A number of "shanties" have been erected for the accomodation of the "diggers". ... **1905** SCHERCK *Pen Pictures* 89: The camp was situated in the woods, and consisted of board shanties sufficient to accomodate 500 people. **1945** CALVIN *Saga* 147: Straight ahead was "the shanty," where the Indians lived. ...

2 *Hist.* **a.** a camp at which logging (def. 2) is carried on. See also **camboose camp** (def. 2), **chantier** (def. 2), **logging camp,** and **lumber shanty** (def. 2).
1829 MACTAGGART *Three Years* I 242: In these shanties they pass the time pretty well, considering them to be made up of Highlandmen, Irishmen, and Yankees. **1834** *Vindicator* (Montreal) 3 Jan. 2/4: Last winter in a "shanty" at Lassomption a few American sleighs (dragged by one horse) tracked a road for themselves, which was free from Cahots. ... **1911** KNOWLES *Singer* 247: At dinner time ... most o' the men's working close to the shanty, so they come in for dinner. **1960** *Ont.Hist.* Dec. 229: In the early period of the trade, the shanty was an unruly haven of the "rugged individual."

b. See quote.
1829 MACTAGGART *Three Years* I 242: ... but there is something more attached to the name *shanty* than mere hut, in the lumberman's dictionary. Thus, so many men, oxen, so much pork, flour, &c. compose a *shanty.*

c. the gang of loggers who work together and live in the same dwelling.
1883 FRASER *Shanty* 30: So the very next day the two confederates who were causing all the trouble in the other shanty, were ordered ... to go to work in Larry's shanty, and their place was supplied by two of his best and most peaceful men. **1902** (1957) GUILLET *Valley of the Trent* 269: Every man in the shanty, cook included, got on the piece [a monster mast] and danced ... to the music of the fiddle for the two miles' distance between the shanty and the landing place at the forks of the Ouse.

d. **go to shanty,** enter the bush in winter to work as a logger in the shanties (def. 2a).
1870 *Cdn Illust.News* 5 Feb. 210/2: The stalwart lumbermen "go to shanty" without the slightest dread of cold. ... **1947** SAUNDERS *Algonquin* 33: Paddy Farrell of Pembroke, who for many years was a "walking boss" for camps operated by the Gillies Company, recalls the first time he ever "went to shanty." **1964** *Cdn Geog.Jnl* Feb. 64/1: What it was that took thousands of men up the Opeongo Line, can only be guessed or dimly felt by those of us who never "went to shanty."

e. **put in shanty,** establish a logging camp.
1945 CALVIN *Saga* 65: In the busy years, the firm often "put in shanty" in the Rideau Lakes area ... to cut floats and traverses. ...

3 a. *Hist.* a crude one-room dwelling of logs patterned after the shanty (def. 1a) and much used

by the pioneers, usually to serve as a temporary dwelling until a more substantial house could be built.
1833 (1926) LANGTON *Early U.C.* 20: I incline myself to the regular routine; a wigwam the first week; a shanty till the loghouse is up; and the frame, brick or stone house half a dozen years hence, when I have a good clearing and can see which will be the best situation. **1842** WILLIS *Cdn Scenery* II 64: The shanty is a sort of primitive hut in Canadian architecture, and is nothing more than a shed built of logs, the chinks between the round edges of the timbers being filled with mud, moss, and bits of wood. . . . **1961** *Ont.Hist.* Mar. 8: A shanty [as opposed to a cabin or a house] had just two openings, one for a door and one in the roof to permit the smoke to escape.

b. See **shack,** *n.*
1842 WILLIS *Cdn Scenery* II 63: Behind the town . . . is a wide space which I call the "squatters' ground," it being entirely covered with shanties, in which the poor immigrants, commuted pensioners, and the like, have located themselves and families. **1852** *Anglo-American Mag.* I 362/1: Our readers, who are acquainted with Toronto, will remember the corner of Bay and King Streets, which used to be disfigured by some wooden shanties of two stories. **1880** GORDON *Mountain and Prairie* 240: The telegraph office was a very rude shanty, but to one who had for months been cut off from tidings of friends and of the world it seemed like a temple of science. **1965** *Maclean's* 3 July 23/1: [They] saw a bearded fellow hoeing a garden beside a shanty below.

shanty *v. Hist.* work as a logger in a shanty (def. 2a). See also **shantying.**
1903 RICHARDSON *Colin* 85: As he had shantied most of his life, he professed to have learned the French language during his shanty life. **1963** GUILLET *Pioneer Farmer* I 314: Particularly were the young men of the northerly townships sent shantying, and in spring and summer many of them remained to float the great rafts. . . .

shanty biscuit *Obs.* See **shanty cake.**
1961 PRICE & KENNEDY *Renfrew* 49: There was also generally a barrel of shanty biscuit (hardtack) on hand for use before the cook got his bread baked, in emergencies and on journeys.

shanty-boy *n. Hist.* See **shantyman** (def. 1).
*c*1850 (1960) FOWKE *Story in Song* 189: . . . Give the shanty boys whiskey and nothing goes wrong. **1912** HEENEY *Pickanock* 14: Luke Hanley and his companions . . . chatted for a time with "shanty-boys" met during former winters in the woods. . . . **1963** *Cdn Literature* Spring 29: Thus the shantyboys preserved and spread folk songs of many types. . . .

shanty bully *Obs.* See quote.
1883 FRASER *Shanty* 338: . . . nor have I the slightest sympathy or consideration for the recognized "professional" shanty bully—the man who, in liquor or sober, in the shanty or on the drive, is always ready for a fight and trying to provoke one.

shanty cake *Obs.* a kind of unleavened bread made of coarse flour and resembling hardtack, used in earlier days in the bush cabins and camps. See also **shanty biscuit** and **shanty loaf.**
1849 ALEXANDER *L'Acadie* I 244: The child was alive and well, and eating a piece of shanty cake (of coarse flour). . . . **1853** STRICKLAND *Canada West* II 195: He made us extremely welcome, and gave us a hearty supper of pea-soup and shanty cake, and plenty of hot toddy. . . .

shanty camp See **shanty** (def. 2a).
1957 *Northland News* 4 Oct. 2/1: In five years, it has grown from a rough-hewn shanty camp . . . to a modern town. . . . **1967** *Cdn Geog.Jnl* Mar. 82/3: The disappearance of the shanty camps also meant the loss of a ready market for fresh vegetables and dairy products. '

shanty farming *Hist. or Obs.* farming carried on to supply provisions and draft animals for the shanties (def. 2a). See also **depot farm.**
1958 *Encyc.Can.* IX 9/2: The big operators relied to a large extent on what became known as "shanty farming." Hay and oats fetched good prices, while farm horses and farm labour were hired to the shanties.

shanty fashion *Obs.* in the manner of loggers.
1903 RICHARDSON *Colin* 55: As he always followed the most extreme shanty fashion, his attire usually included a pair of long boots, which were studded with heavy nails and furnished with copper toes, red leather tops, and lugs hanging loosely on either side.

shanty fire *Hist.* See **camboose** (def. 2). See also **camboose fire.**
1852 (1881) TRAILL *Cdn Crusoes* 223: At night, when the canoes had all retired to the camp on the north shore, and all fear of detection had ceased for the time, they lighted up their shanty fire, and cooked a good supper, and also prepared sufficiency of food for the following day. **1947** SAUNDERS *Algonquin* 35: Visitors who bask in the warmth of the famous central fireplace at the Seigneury Club in the Province of Quebec, likely do not know that French-Canadian lumbermen long enjoyed the same kind of comfort from the old shanty fires.

shanty foreman *Obs.* the boss of a gang of loggers.
1883 FRASER *Shanty* 24: Jim himself is a capital type of the shanty foreman.

shantying *n. Hist.* living and working in a shanty (def. 2a). See also **shanty,** *v.*
1824 *Canadian Mag.* III 202: Such is the usual routine of what is called Shantying in Canada, and such is the plan followed by those who take out squared Timber. **1883** FRASER *Shanty* 59: John, after an experience of thirty years shantying in this country, could go blindfold through its most intricate windings. **1947** SAUNDERS *Algonquin* 38: Nowadays pie forms a standard part of at least two meals a day in most lumber camps, but all these varieties of food have been introduced since the early days of shantying in the Park.

shanty knot *Obs.* a hitch or knot such as used by the men in the shanties (def. 2a).
1903 RICHARDSON *Colin* 56: They were supported by a red, white, and blue sash, which Goarden had tied about his waist in a specially constructed shanty knot.

shanty lad See **shantyman.**
1903 RICHARDSON *Colin* 341: On the break-up in the spring, Goarden followed "the drive" down to Quebec, where, true to the practice of the average "shanty lad" . . . he had gone on a spree. **1964** *Edmonton Jnl* 11 July 3/6: The raw shanty lad . . . came out of the backwoods of Quebec at the age of 14. . . .

shanty life *Hist.* life in the shanties (def. 2a).
1854 KEEFER *Ottawa* 54: I . . . propose to give you a slight episode of shanty life. . . . **1891** OXLEY *Chore-Boy* 35: "I haven't much fear of you, my boy . . . even if you do find shanty life a good deal rougher than you may have imagined." **1960** *Ont.Hist.* Dec. 229: This violent reaction to freedom was accentuated by the strict regimen of shanty life.

shanty loaf See **shanty cake.**
1845 BEAVAN *Life in Backwoods N.B.* 14: The sugar-maker's bark-covered hut contains his bedding and provisions, consisting of little save the huge round loaf of bread, known as the "shanty loaf"—his beverage or substitute for tea is made of the leaves of wintergreen, or the hemlock boughs which grow beside him, and his sweetening being handy bye, he wants nothing more.

shantyman ['ʃæntiˌmæn] *n.* **1** *Hist.* a man who lived and worked in a shanty (def. 2a). See also **chantie-man, shanty-boy,** and **shanty lad.**
1824 *Canadian Mag.* III 406: You make a great fuss about the high price of labour, but you don't consider the high price the shanty men pay you for what you raise off your farms. **1896** GOURLAY *Hist.Ottawa* 20: Joe Veleau kept a hotel in the woods . . . patronized by shantymen. **1964** *Cdn Geog.Jnl* Feb. 63/2: Equally significant . . . is the story of early roads by which shantymen reached their camboose camps.
2 See **Shantyman missionary.**
1962 *Globe and Mail* (Toronto) 6 Jan. 9/5: The firefighters' chief at Ignace [Ont.] did not need to think twice. "If they're shantymen, they can take care of themselves," he said.

Shantyman missionary a lay missionary belonging to the Shantymen's Christian Association, which carries out evangelical work among loggers and miners in bush camps across Canada.
1962 *Globe and Mail* (Toronto) 6 Jan. 9/1: A Shantyman missionary once cut a miner's hair to get a receptive audience.

shantyman's smallpox *Obs.* See quote.
1965 STEVENS *Incompleat Canadian* 38: Feet rather than fists were the principal weapons and many a riverman, beaten down in the onset, carried on his face and chest for the rest of his life the scars of "shantyman's smallpox"—the pits and punctures of caulks and cleats.

shanty-mug *n. Obs.* See quote.
1947 SAUNDERS *Algonquin* 36: Each man was provided with a small tin bowl, a "shanty-mug" from which he drank his soup or his tea, and a tin plate.

shanty queen *Lumbering, Slang* See quote.
1942 SWANSON *Western Logger* 54: "shanty queen"— logger's wife, living in a shack in camp.

shanty road See **logging road.**
1895 (1929) *Selected Stories* 192: He crossed shanty roads, trod heaps of brush, forced his way through the tops of felled pines. . . . **1896** GOURLAY *Hist.Ottawa* 138: Shanty roads, those cut for lumbering, were the only roads for years.

shanty song a folksong about the men who worked in the shanties (def. 2a); also, a song favored by shantymen (def. 1).
1947 SAUNDERS *Algonquin* 43: Like a well-known shanty song that tells the story of young Munroe . . . this French-Canadian shantyman lies buried by the shores of the river where he met his death.

shanty tea *Obs.* the potent, black, tea brewed by the shantymen, characterized by its souplike consistency.
1854 KEEFER *Ottawa* 62: Shanty tea is as unlike the delicate infusion over which ladies are said to imbibe such nice discrimination of character, as the oil of peppermint is to the essence.

shantytown† *n.* ['ʃæntiˌtaʊn] *n.* See **shacktown.**
1900 *Canadian Mag.* May 9/2: [It is a] shanty town of rough-hewn logs, warmly mudded-up. . . .
1928 FREEMAN *Nearing North* 53: He apologized for Dunvegan, assuring me that I must understand that Water Holes was no such tumble-into-the-river shanty-town but a real up-and-coming emporium of commerce. **1965** *Globe and Mail* (Toronto) 2 Sep. W1/1: The failures are inscribed on . . . denizens of shanty towns and slums who drifted away from their hunting grounds in search of a more comfortable life. . . .

share *n. Esp.Nfld, Hist.* that portion of the value of a catch of fish or seals due to each shareman, *q.v.*
[**1877** *Belford's Mag.* (Annual II) 782: The cook is an important personage and is well paid—on some of the . . . [fishing] vessels he receives as much as eighty dollars a month and a share in the profits—but then he is hard worked, especially on a banker.] **1965** MacNUTT *Atlantic Provinces* 18: . . . after the Peace of Utrecht, the West Countrymen discarded the old system of fishing "by shares" and adopted the payment of wages, usually in truck.

share *v. Esp.Nfld, Hist.* receive as the right of a shareman, *q.v.*
1964 *Nfld Qtly* Spring 28/1: . . . she [a sealer] made three full loads of seals one spring, her men sharing $303, the biggest "bill" ever made in a wooden wall at the ice.

shareman *n. Esp.Nfld* a man shipping as a fisherman or sealer for a share of the catch, providing his own provisions and receiving no wages. Cp. **berth money.**
1820 (1956) FAY *Life and Labour* 138: . . . sharemen are frequently indigent planters who have fallen into debt with their merchant and who cannot afford to raise their own boats. **1964** *Nfld Qtly* Spring 27/1: . . . sharemen were . . . sometimes chargeable with a part of certain items usually the burden of the company planters, e.g., salt, motor boat, fuel, etc. . . .

sharp-tail *n.* See **sharp-tailed grouse.**
1958 *Beaver* Autumn 49/1: Swathing was unknown, and sharp-tails had lots of stooks to sit on. **1964** *B.C. Digest* Oct. 28/3: . . . sharp-tails [are] frequently encountered in the Chilcotin. **1966** *Globe and Mail* (Toronto) 15 Jan. 29/1: . . . the far northern wilderness [is] the home of the ptarmigan and the sharptail. . . .

sharp-tailed grouse a species of grouse, *Pedicetes phasianellus,* found in the West and North. See also **pheasant, pintailed grouse, prairie chicken** (def. 2), and **prairie hen** (def. 2).

1785 PENNANT *Arctic Zoology* 306: Sharp-tailed
Grouse. 1795 (1911) HEARNE *Journey* 408: Sharp-tailed
Grouse . . . are always found in the Southern parts of
the Bay, are very plentiful in the interior parts of the
country, and in some Winters a few of them are shot
at York Fort. 1896 (1898) RUSSELL *Far North* 48: The
sharp-tailed grouse and a few species of small deer were
common in the bush covering the foothills.
1966 *Kingston Whig-Standard* (Ont.) 21 Jan. 11/2: Up
in the Hudson Bay region we have the sharp-tailed
grouse and the willow ptarmigan. . . .

shave *v*. **1** *Fur Trade* shear off close to the skin.
1803 (1897) COUES *New Light* I 221: 129 Shaved and
Parchment Skins. 1933 MERRICK *True North* 218: For
the fur ears on caps they use skins that have been cut
and shaved by mice. . . . *Ibid*. 258: A dream about a
fox meant, "mice are shaving your fur in some trap
to-night."

2† *Slang, Obs*. discount (a note), often at excessive
interest. See also **shaver.**
1839 *Montreal Transcript* 20 July 135/2: The Notes of
the Bank of Upper Canada can still be "shaved" at the
Agent's Office at a discount of 1½ percent.

shaver† *n. Slang, Hist.* a person who discounted
notes, usually at excessive interest. See also
shave (def. 2).
1836 *St.Catharines Jnl* (U.C.) 15 Dec. 3/2: It is said
that . . . discounts at the ordinary rates are but
sparingly granted, the shavers, many of whom are
Directors . . . are amply supplied with funds, which
they lend out at the enormous interest of four or five
percent. per month. . . . 1841 *Bytown* [Ottawa] *Gaz.*
25 Nov. 1/3: During all this time Brokers were in
demand and Shavers made their harvest. 1946 LOWER
Colony to Nation 517: The Albertans fought the "St.
James Street gang" as dauntlessly as the people of
Upper Canada, a century before, had fought the
"Montreal shavers."

shaving mill *Maritimes, Hist.* See 1950 quote.
1782 (1961) PERKINS *Diary* 153: Mr. McLeod goes out
in the New Shaving mill to make Discovery but See
nothing. 1950 BIRD *This is N.S.* 139: Many stories were
told of the "shaving mills" then in operation, a
"shaving mill" being an open boat filled with men who
were out to plunder either side during the American
revolution.

shaving parlo(u)r *Obs.* a barber shop.
1909 TOWNLEY *Opinions* 37: One does not have to go
poking around to gather information regarding
"shaving parlors" in Canadian cities.

A shay

shay [ʃe] *n.* [< E *Shay,* who built the first such
locomotive in Michigan in 1874] *Lumbering* See
1942 quote.
1936 *B.C.Timber Trade* 74: Elk River Timber Co.,
Ltd. . . . Camp: Quinsom, Union S.S. . . . 75 Miles of
Track; 5 Locos; 4 Shays; 1 Porter. 1942 HAIG-BROWN
Timber 253: SHAY. A geared locomotive, slow but

powerful and adapted to heavy hauling. Shays of about
70 tons are commonly used in hauling logs from the
landing to the mainline. 1953 *Harmac News* Oct. 8/1:
However, railroad locies were in use much earlier in the
Alberni Valley. A 42-ton Shay was hauling logs for
Wiest Logging in 1914.

shearboom *n.* See **sheer-boom.**

shebang [ʃə'bæŋ *or* ʃi'bæŋ] *n.* [perhaps < Cdn
F *cabane* < F "hut"] *Slang* **1** a low drinking
establishment frequented by the loggers and
rivermen of Lower and Upper Canada. See also
bush tavern and **caboose** (def. 6b).
☛ *Although this term is usually assumed to derive from
Cdn F* **cabane,** *it seems possible, in view of the Canadian
sense, that Irish* **shebeen** *of similar meaning was the
source, especially since Irishmen were prominent among
the shantymen with whom the term is associated. Cp.
note at* **shanty.**
1901 PARKER *Right of Way* 49: Yet there were people
who called the tavern a "shebang"—slander as it was
against Suzon Charlemagne, which every river-driver
and woodsman and habitant who frequented the place
would have resented with violence. 1907 (1908) SINCLAIR
Raw Gold 68: There was a sort of sheebang—you
couldn't call it a hotel if you had any regard for the
truth—on the outskirts of Walsh for the accommodation
of wayfarers without a camp-outfit. . . .
1963 GUILLET *Pioneer Farmer* I 314n: Less picturesque
were the *shebangs* dotted along the rivers, where
squaws and whiskey awaited the shanty boys and their
winter pay.

2† **the whole shebang,** the entire lot; everything;
all the things involved.
☛ *Here too, the Newfoundland context of the early
quote suggests possible Irish influence.*
c1885 (1960) FOWKE *Story in Song* 166: . . . We met a
heavy sou'west gale that washed away our boat,/It
washed away our quarter deck, our stanchions just as
well,/And so we set the whole "she-bang" a-floating in
the gale. 1920 STRINGER *Prairie Mother* 254: It would
. . . be a God-send . . . to have somebody . . . keep the
cobwebs out of the corners and the mildew off his
books and save the whole disintegrating shebang from
the general rack and ruin which usually overtakes
empty mansions. . . . 1959 *Weekend Mag.* 18 July 39/2:
[He] became managing director of the whole shebang
in six years. . . .

shed *n.* See **shed tent.**

shed grizzly *Placer Mining* See **grizzly head.**
See picture at **grizzly** (def. 3).
1965 *Cdn Geog.Jnl* Dec. 207: [Caption] A portable
placer-pump delivers water to a metal trough through
which discharges the gravel onto a shed grizzly.

Shediac (oyster) *n.* an oyster from Shediac,
New Brunswick.
1825 *P.E.I.Register* (Charlottetown) 8 Jan. 3/2: We
know the Shediac oysters are excellent, that the beds
grow very fast, and would in two years or less, afford
supplies through the winter season. 1835 *Novascotian*
(Halifax) 3 Dec. 355/1: "Mrs. Pugwash . . . would you
like a dish of superior Shittyacks for supper." *Ibid.:*
". . . where have you been all your days, that you never
heard of our Shittyack Oysters—I thought everybody
had heard of them."

shed tent See **lean-to** (def. 1a). Also *shed*.

1849 ALEXANDER *L'Acadie* II 41: I accordingly got three sheds of striped ticking made to put up to windward, the two for the men (five men in each shed) were twelve feet long, ten broad, and seven deep, the sides were made by cutting a square of seven feet ticking diagonally, each half or right angle triangle forming a side for the shed, which was supported on two forked poles, or "crutches," seven feet high and a ridge pole resting on them, which with four or five other poles, which rested slanting on the ridge pole, were cut every day, the thick layer of fir twigs, laid upside down for softness, forming the carpet of the shed. *c*1902 LAUT *Trapper* 119: In this case he uses the *abuckwan*—canvas—for a shed tent, with one side sloping to the ground, banked by brush and snow, the other facing the fire, both tent and fire on such a slope that the smoke drifts out while the heat reflects in. **1913** WILLIAMS *Wilderness Trail* 188: Because of the storm, shed-tents had been set up, and the men were gathered under them for the night.

shee(fish) [ʃi] *n*. [? < Athapaskan (Chipewyan)] See **inconnu.**

1795 (1911) HEARNE *Journey* 249: Their flesh, though delicately white, is very soft, and has so rank a taste, that many of the Indians, except they are in absolute want, will not eat it. The Northern Indians call this fish Shees. **1959** *Columbia* July 21/1: Within minutes, I had three shee fish, each about two feet long, flopping on the bank.

Sheela [ˈʃilə] *n*. [< Esk.] See **Sila.**

sheep *n*. See **Rocky Mountain sheep.**

1822 *U.C.Gaz.* (York [Toronto]) 25 Apr. 14/1: We learn on the authority of a gentleman who has traversed the Rocky Mountains from the north branch of the Columbia to the Athapescow that numerous flocks of these sheep inhabit that region. **1957** HUTCHISON *Canada* 256: Yet a crew of men ... had replaced the original habitants of this waste, the sheep and goat, and were boring straight down through the stone spires of the continent to its underlying pool of oil.

sheepherder† *n. West* a person who looks after flocks of sheep in the range country. Cp. **sheepman.**

1903 SETON *Animal Heroes* 139: At dawn the next day a sheepherder seeking lost Sheep discovered her from a neighboring hill. **1953** *Cdn Geog.Jnl* June 245/1: ... the majority of Alberta sheep are out on range in care of a "sheepherder." (Not a "shepherd" in the West, where terms vary from traditional phrases.) **1963** SYMONS *Many Trails* 58: ... the men who are the backbone of the range sheep industry [are] the sheepherders, as we call the Scottish, Mexican, or Basco (Basque) shepherds.

sheep-hook *n. West* a shepherd's crook.

1953 *Cdn Geog.Jnl* June 247/1: By six o'clock, the herder takes in hand his "tin dog" (cans strung on a wire to get the sheep's attention) and "sheep-hook" (crook).

sheepman† *n. West* the owner of a sheep ranch. Cp. **sheepherder.**

1897 *Medicine Hat News* (Alta) 1 Apr. 4/1: In spite of all this the cattlemen and sheepmen are getting their herds through with but a trifling loss. **1964** *Calgary*

Herald 25 Feb. 25/5: Coyotes Termed Serious Problem to Sheep Men.

sheep shower sheep sorrel, *Rumex acetosella.*

1957 LEWIS *Buckskin Cookery* I 22: Sheep Shower, which grows around fields and looks like the shamrock, is tasty to nibble on.

sheep valuer *N.S.* a municipal officer who assesses the harm done by dogs to sheep, a dog tax being levied to provide his services.

1955 *Wkly Monitor* 4 May 2/3: List of Ward Officers ... Cattle Reeves ... Fence Viewers ... Sheep Valuers. ...

sheer-boom† *n. Lumbering* a small boom having one end anchored to the shore and the other swinging out into the stream to direct logs into a holding boom, *q.v.* See also **lead boom** and **log-guard.**

1896 ROBERTS *Camp-Fire* 179: The section of the sheer-boom thus peculiarly adorned was called the wing-boom. **1958** *Evening Telegram* (St. John's) 6 May 19/1: J. D. Roberts, woods manager, pointed out that the portion which broke was the lead or "sheer" boom and not the main holding boom ... into which the floating logs are funnelled by the lead booms.

sheet *n. Curling* the strip of ice on which a game of curling is played.

1921 *Beaver* Nov. 27/1: The ... curling club has been fortunate in securing two sheets of ice for the coming season. ... **1953** *Cdn Geog.Jnl* Apr. 138/2: Curling has become an extremely popular sport since the dozen white men in the settlement built the two-sheet rink out of slabs in 1944. **1963** *Maclean's* 26 Jan. 16/2: One [curling rink] in Calgary has forty-eight sheets of ice.

sheet-iron stove a light, portable stove made of sheet iron. Cp. **airtight burner.**

1888 *Dominion Illust.* 127/2: The Indian dogs ... haul the portable canvas house ... with a sheet iron stove and a supply of fire wood to the "basin holes". ... **1930** BEAMES *Army* 8: They pitched their tent and set the sheet-iron stove up in front of it.

shelf *n*. See **ice-shelf** (def. 2).

1933 MERRICK *True North* 256: Kay and Donald were going along one behind the other when a big section of the shelf they were on cracked off and started floating down the river.

shell-bird *n. Nfld* the merganser, *Mergus* sp.

1770 (1792) CARTWRIGHT *Journal* I 40: They returned with three shellbirds and a saddle-back. **1959** MCATEE *Folk-Names* 5: That is shell-bird, a name used for the mergansers ... [in] Nfld.

shell ice *North* a formation of ice which once covered water but which stands alone as a shell, the water having receded.

1924 MASON *Arctic Forests* 235: The sled and I fell through the shell ice on to the gravel beach about seven feet below. **1963** *North* May-June 42/2: Snow covered the ground in the morning, and a thin border of shell ice clattered on the lake shore.

shell wampum *Hist.* See **wampum** (def. 1).

1926 MAIR *Masterworks* XIV 207: European traders substituted porcelain for shell wampum and degraded its value. ...

shelterbelt† *n*. a stand of trees or shrubs which functions as protection against wind and rain and which reduces the risk of serious soil erosion.

1894 *Trans.Roy.Soc.Can.* XII 4 143: . . . the failures in the shelter-belts and plantations have gradually been made good by planting with hardier sorts.
1964 *Kingston Whig-Standard* (Ont.) 5 Dec. 7/1: To protect their fields, many farmers of the Quinte area started planting trees as windbreaks and shelterbelts.

shelter kitchen a roofed shelter equipped with a fireplace and tables, intended for the convenience of tourists at roadside campgrounds.
1965 *Maclean's* 19 June 17/1: Along its hundred-and-forty-mile length there are well-spaced campgrounds with log shelter kitchens and fireplaces.

she-ny *n.* See **shnye.**

sheriff *n.* an appointed official who enforces certain court orders, such as evicting persons for failure to pay rent and escorting convicted persons to prison.
1822 (1940) *Minutes of Council* (H.B.C.) 31: RESOLVED That William Kemp be appointed Sheriff for the District of Ossiniboia. . . . 1849 ALEXANDER *L'Acadie* I 56: The Sheriff was one of the most singular characters at this time in Kingston. 1890 *Grip* (Toronto) 11 Oct. 227/1: Capital punishment is the penalty fixed by law for murder in this country, and the sheriff is the officer appointed to carry out the sentence of the court. 1963 *Calgary Herald* 23 Sep. 22/1: He relieved as sheriff and clerk of the court at *Red Deer* and *Hanna,* and was in charge of the sheriff's office at *Vegreville* for six years before moving to *Fort Macleod* in 1938.

sheriff's sale a sale of property or goods conducted by a sheriff following a court order for seizure and sale to satisfy a judgment.
1809 *Quebec Gaz.* 18 Jan. 3/1: Mutation Fines are . . . due to the Crown on Property acquired at Sheriff's Sales. 1841 WARD *River St.John* 77: The entire concern, which cost £20,000, was disposed of at a Sheriff's sale in December last for £1100. 1883 *Brandon Dly Mail* (Man.) 9 Jan. 4/1: There will be a sheriff's sale of goods and chattels belonging to the late firm of Hambly & Miller, barbers, etc., on Saturday next. 1966 *Globe and Mail* (Toronto) 6 Sep. 30/1: [Notice] Sheriff's Sale of Lands—Under and by Virtue of an Execution issued out of the Ninth Division Court of the County of York to me directed against the lands and tenements of . . . Plaintiff. . . .

she-she-qui *n.* See **shishiquoi.**

Shield *n.* See **Canadian Shield.**
1936 *Cdn Geog.Jnl* XII 164/2: However in hollows in the Shield there are many areas with a fair covering of soil still preserved. 1965 SYMINGTON *Tuktu* 18: In many regions the gnarled outcrops of the Shield are visible. . . .

Shiner or **shiner** ['ʃaɪnɚ] *n.* [see 1960 quote] *Hist.* one of the many Irish laborers in Bytown [Ottawa] during the 1830's and 1840's, employed first in the building of the Rideau Canal and later as shantymen, (def. 1). See also **Ribbon-man** and **Shiners' War.**
1835 *Dundas Wkly Post* (U.C.) 18 Aug. 3/1: Three of the Bytown shinners [sic] have been arrested for an attack on a female while picking berries. 1836 *Cdn Temperance Advocate* June 16/1: The Bytown Society . . . gives an awful description of the intemperance of the town in summer, on account of the shanty men and raftsmen—last year denominated "shiners." 1960 *Ont. Hist.* Dec. 228: The term, "Shiner," has been variously described as derived from "cheneur" or "oakman," the black silk hats "shiners," worn by greenhorns arriving

in Bytown, or from the newly-minted half crown coins with which the lumberers were paid. 1964 *Cdn Geog.Jnl* Feb. 71/2: Then the chances that Shiner and Canadien would be fighting on the street . . . were good indeed.

Shiners' War *Hist.* a protracted donnybrook involving the Shiners and other loggers, such as Canadiens, and resulting from the bellicose attitude of the former.
[1896 GOURLAY *Hist.Ottawa* 142: The Shiners . . . were at enmity with the Canadian French nearly as much as with their Protestant fellow craftsmen, wishing the monopoly of the shanty business to be in their own hands, if that had been a possibility.] 1960 *Ont.Hist.* Dec. 228: The so-called "Shiners' War" was waged between 1837 and 1845 in the woods, along the slides and in the streets of Bytown. 1964 *Cdn Geog.Jnl* Feb. 70/3: In these years [1837-45] the so-called "Shiners' War" turned the future capital of Canada into a brawling, barbarous camp.

shinigbee ['ʃɪnɪg,bi] *n.* [< Esk. *sinnigbi(k)*] *North* a type of sleeping-bag, *q.v.*
1897 TYRRELL *Sub-Arctics* 144: The "shin-ig-bee," or Eskimo sleeping bag, is an article essential to the comfort of the traveller when making long overland journeys during the cold winter season. 1909 CAMERON *New North* 248: Lothario, one night, crossed the icy gully, entered the igloo of his elect, seized her in her *shin-ig-bee,* or sleeping-bag and lifted the dear burden over his back.

Shining Mountains the Rocky Mountains.
1784 PENNANT *Arctic Zoology* cxxxix: This exalted situation is part of the Shining Mountains, which are branches of the vast chain which pervades the whole continent of America. 1873 (1904) BUTLER *Wild North Land* 314: In the first years of the new century men penetrated the gorges of the shining mountains and reached the great river of the west. 1963 SPRY *Palliser* 121: The unending, curved horizon was becoming monotonous. Now, at last, there were the Shining Mountains.

shinner *n.* See **Shiner.**

shinney *n.* See **shinny.**

shinnia *n.* [< Algonk.; cf. Cree *shōneyā*] *West, Obs.* See quote.
1962 *Alta Hist.Rev.* Autumn 14/2: Money is known under a variety of appelations some of which are now rarely used [including] "shinnias" . . . "otter-skins" and "the velvet."

shinny ['ʃɪni] *n.* [< Scottish dial. *shinny, shinty* game played with a ball and curved sticks, perhaps < the whack of stick against shin] **1 a.** a loosely organized game of ice hockey, played on ice without referees. See also **shinty.** Cp. **millpond hockey.**
1847 (1953) HEWITT *Hockey Night* 2: Most of the soldier boys [in Kingston, Ont.] were quite at home on skates. They could cut the figure eight and other fancy figures, but shinny was their first delight. 1964 *Star Wkly* 5 Dec. 21/1: No shinny stuff for these boys . . . taught in big league style by Richard Caouette. 1965 *Globe and Mail* (Toronto) 5 Jan. 27/1: A scrambly production usually held without benefit of referees, shinny is popular among youngsters. 1965 *Kingston*

Whig-Standard (Ont.) 4 Jan. 13/1: They knew how difficult it was to obtain an adequate sheet of ice in Kingston for neighborhood "shinny."

b. See **road hockey.**

1902 CONNOR *Glengarry* 272: [Playing] shinny in the snow upon the roadway in front of the school was none too exciting. **1910** MCCLUNG *Second Chance* 56: ... the boys and girls were playing "shinny," which is an old and honourable game, father or uncle of hockey. **1963** *Kingston Whig-Standard* (Ont.) 6 Mar. 7/8: But the boy playing shinny in the street may be dreaming of the NHL.

2 *Slang* See **hockey.**

1963 *Globe and Mail* (Toronto) 12 Jan. 27/7: Shinny lore has it that the schedule is much tougher in the second half. **1966** *Globe and Mail* (Toronto) 23 Mar. 30/1: This prompted the Canadian ... to rise with drink in hand and deliver a half-hour defense of good old shinny.

shinplaster† ['ʃɪn,plæstər] *n.* [a contemptuous name based on the small size of the bill] **1** *Slang, Obs.* one of several denominations, from one dollar downward, of paper bills issued in the United States in 1837 and circulated for a time in Canada.

1837 *Montreal Transcript* 26 Aug. 2/2: As a constant reader of your invaluable paper, I have the opportunity of observing that you, of all others, pay the most satisfactory attention to the subjects of specie payments, copper currency, Upper Canada bank affairs and shin plasters. **1837** *Ibid.* 29 Aug. 2/1: Shin Plasters.—Much has been said and written a'propos to this beautiful currency, while the public have been in full enjoyment of all its varieties. **1838** *Western Herald* (Sandwich [Windsor], U.C.) 31 Jan. 22/3: Whoever will apprehend the said robber, or will give such information as will lead to the recovery of the above munitions of war, will receive the above reward in current shinplasters from Uncle Sam.

2 *Hist.* a Canadian banknote worth twenty-five cents. See 1966 quote.

1887 *Grip* (Toronto) 2 Apr. 10/2: I will give further particulars on receipt of a shin-plaister. **1913** SANDILANDS *West.Cdn Dict.* 40/2: Shin-plaster, a 25-cent or quarter-dollar note, a curiosity not often seen nowadays. **1961** *Sun* (Vancouver) 9 Jan. 8/7: A rare 25-cent "shinplaster" was among $80 in bills stolen from the home ... by a thief who forced a bedroom window, police said. **1966** *Citizen* (Vancouver) 22 Oct. 1/7: Frank Howard, New Democratic Party MP for Skeena has asked Finance Minister Sharp to bring back the shinplaster for Canada's centennial year. The shinplaster was 25-cent paper money issued by Canada in 1870, 1900 and 1923.

3 *Slang* a dollar (def. 2).

1963 *Globe and Mail* (Toronto) 29 Apr. 3/4: When the Canadian shinplaster plunged to a devaluated discount, the churl's reactionary conservatism crumbled, economically as well as politically.

shin-tangle *n. Slang* See quote.

1905 OUTRAM *Cdn Rockies* 176: Farther down, we encountered thick woods and a dense undergrowth (which is often designated by the expressive term "shin-tangle"), and, as every leaf was dripping with the heavy rain, we soon were saturated from head to foot.

shinty *n. Rare* See **shinny** (def. 1a).

1926 MAIR *Masterworks* XIV lii: ... in winter shinty,

an old Scotch game, played on the ice, resembling hockey [was played].

ship fishery *Esp.Nfld., Hist.* See **green fishery.**

1963 MORTON *Kingdom of Canada* 12: But from earliest times the fishery developed in two modes, that of the wet fishery and that of the dry. The former was carried on from ships on the Banks where the fish were taken, cleaned and heavily salted on board. In this "wet" or ship or banks fishery, there was little resort to the shores of Newfoundland.

Shippigan turkey *Maritimes* See quote.

1939 BARTON & THOMAS *In New Brunswick* 175: Richbucto goose is salt shad. Just as ... Shippigan turkey is salt cod.

shipping paper *Nfld, Hist.* See quote.

1964 *Nfld Qtly* Summer 14/2: In mid-18th century, the custom became a legal requirement in Newfoundland for fishing masters, merchants and planters, when employing immigrant servants (whether "youngsters" or experienced fishermen) all generically "servants," to have a written employment agreement executed to reserve return passage money from the wages. The agreement was called a shipping paper and it came to be used for native Newfoundlanders as well.

ship-room *n. Nfld, Hist.* See **room** (def. 1).

1829 (1956) FAY *Life and Labour* 144: As the Sedentary ousted the Transitory Fishery, Ship Rooms became permanent—replacing the Fishing Admiral's stations, secured by 1st arrival. **1883** HATTON & HARVEY *Newfoundland* 55: To defray the cost of building a prison at St. John's and at Ferryland, he ordered a rate to be collected, which was assessed on the boats and ship-rooms.

shiptime *n. North* the time that the supply ship arrives in the summer after break-up (def. 1).

1778 (1954) *Moose Ft Jnls* 368: I shall be ready to go up again as soon as the River breaks up and to be down again at Ship time so that I may have an opportunity of knowing what is the Companys Intentions in regard to this settlement. **1938** *Beaver* Mar. 21/1: I can well remember my first "ship-time" the following year, when the Nascopie was so late we had given her up. **1951** GILLIS & MYLES *North Pole* 13: All at once I found myself in the midst of that great gala of the Eastern Arctic, "ship-time." **1956** *Beaver* Winter 52/1: Time to plan the spring work—but why do that; shiptime is far away and now is really the time for that rest.

shiretown *n. Maritimes* See **county town.**

1756 (1932) *Cdn Hist.Rev.* June 193: It is further proposed that when the Towns become very large and populous, the most considerable should be made Shire Towns, and have the right of electing One or more Members. **1841** WARD *River St.John* 11: The latter is the shire-town of the county, and was materially injured by the great fire of 1825. ... **1962** *Chronicle-Herald* (Halifax) 10 Aug. 14/1: Liverpool, the shiretown of Queens County, occupies the site of an Indian village.

shishigwan *n.* See **shishiquoi.**

shishiquoi ['ʃɪʃə,kwɑ] *n.* [< Cdn F < Algonk.; cf. Montagnais *shishikwan*] a rattle used by the Indians in medicine rituals and to accompany singing and dancing. See also **medicine rattle.** Numerous spellings.

1763 (1901) HENRY (Elder) *Travels* 116: In his hand, he had his *shishiquoi*, or rattle, with which he beat time to his *medicine song.* **1801** MACKENZIE *Voy.from Montreal* ciii: While the company are enjoying their meal, the chief sings, and accompanies his song with the tambourin, or shishiquoi, or rattle. **1819** (1922) HARMON *Journal* 324: If the patient is very ill, [the conjuror] attends him at least every morning, and sings and shakes his che-che-quy, for an hour or two. . . . **1903** CARR-HARRIS *White Chief* 17: Pieces of bear-steak, which had been sizzling before the fire, were then served, while the Chief entertained his guests with strange monotonous songs, accompanied by the "shishiquoi," or rattle. **1935** JENNESS *Parry Island* 64: Instead of a tambourine, they used a disk-like rattle (shishigwan) of parchment 6 to 9 inches in diameter. . . .

A shishiquoi

Shittyack *n. Obs.* See **Shediac**.

shivaree ['ʃɪvəˌri] *n.* [< Cdn F < F *charivari*, q.v.] Also spelled *chivaree, chivari(e)*, etc. **1 a** noisy celebration to serenade a newly married couple. See also **charivari** and **saluting**.
1827 (1829) MACTAGGART *Three Years* I 41: The natives . . . and settled residents wed as becomes them, and at their weddings they have what is called Shirevees [sic], a parading kind of a show, with sleighs if in winter, or a two-wheeled sort of gig, if in summer. **1905** *Eye Opener* (Calgary) 25 Feb. 1/5: Girl given away by father . . . Shivaree big drunk for cowboys. Honeymoon trip to Banff. **1962** ONSLOW *Bowler-Hatted Cowboy* 248: Rumour had it that our neighbours intended to give us a "Shivaree." This is a courtesy visit paid to newly married couples at night. It is a delightful old custom aimed at embarrassing the happy pair by catching them in bed.
2 *Slang* any noisy affair or activity, as a final series in baseball, a hockey playoff, a gala celebration, etc.
1963 *Globe and Mail* (Toronto) 11 May 27/8: The San Franciscans, in winning the Western shivaree, averaged 8,500 fans in the final seven games. . . . **1966** *Cdn Forest Industries* Oct. 50/3: One of the highlights of this year's Squamish shivaree was the exhibition put on by . . . the Wickheim brothers from Sooke.

shivaree ['ʃɪvəˌri] *v.* hold a shivaree for; serenade with a shivaree (def. 1).
1910 MCCLUNG *Second Chance* 350: "Well, anyway, when Bill and the girl got married, the boys came to 'shivaree' them. . . ." **1965** *Sask.Hist.* Spring 45: . . . in most communities it was the rare [newly married] couple who were not "shivareed."

shnay *n.* See **shnye**.

shnye [ʃnaɪ] *n.* an older and now local form of snye, *q.v.* Also spelled *schnye, she-ny, shnay*.
1873 (1904) BUTLER *Wild North Land* 162: One night's delay, and again we were on the endless trail; on along the great silent river . . . amidst the great diamond-shaped islands where the snow lay deep and soft in "shnay" and "batture." **1896** (1898) RUSSELL *Far North* 73: We continued through the winding *chenals* (anglicized as schnys), among low islands, where we ran uncomfortably close to sunken rocks. **1909** CAMERON *New North* 70: A narrow channel is called a "she-ny," evidently a corruption of the French *chenal*.

1961 PRICE & KENNEDY *Renfrew* 70: . . . around Bryson and Campbell's Bay [Ottawa Valley] . . . one still hears the expression "The Shnye"—seemingly holding onto the "ch" of "chenal."

shodding *n. North* See **shoeing**.
1941 *Beaver* Mar. 10/2: Last, but not least, he takes along a small piece of bear skin for icing the runners of the sled, a fifteen inch jackplane for smoothing down the shodding and perhaps some spare mud.

shoe *n.* **1** See **snowshoe** (def. 1 and picture).
1748 DRAGE *Voyage* I 168: These Shoes, as well as the Manner of Cloathing in Winter, is after the Example of the Indians, and the Shoes are made by the Indians for the People at the Factory. **1900** LONDON *Son of Wolf* 6: At every step the great webbed shoe sinks till the snow is level with the knee. **1964** *Western Wkly Supp.* 29 Jan. 3/1: . . . great differences in terrain (heavy timber, muskeg, open plains, mountainous slopes) evolved many forms of shoe to meet such widely contrasting conditions.
2 See quote.
1949 LAWSON *N.B.Story* 14: When the water was too shallow for the canoe to float, the Indian covered its bottom with "shoes" or splints of cedar, and dragged it over the wet stones.

shoe *v.* travel on snowshoes.
1924 DORRANCE *Never Fire First* 127: The sergeant heard the native shoeing back. . . .

'shoe *n.* See **snowshoe hare**.
1963 *Kingston Whig-Standard* (Ont.) 1 Feb. 11/4: 'Shoes breed anywhere from three to five times a season with usually three or four young in each litter.

shoeing *n. North* See **mud**, *n.* See also **shodding**.
1897 TYRRELL *Sub-Arctics* 229: This made travelling hard for the team, as it caused the ice glazing to melt from the sled, and the mud shoeing to wear and drag heavily upon the track. **1933** MERRICK *True North* 219: With runnered sledges, komatiks and catamarans, different kinds of shoeing have varying advantages and defects.

shoepack† ['ʃuˌpæk] *n.* [< Am.E by folk etymology < Lenape (Delaware) *shipak* < *machtschipak* inferior shoe, as opposed to a moccasin] **1** a variety of moccasin having uppers of thick, oiled leather that extend above the ankle and, often, a stiff sole. See also **Canadian shoe**. See also **larrigan** and picture.
1853 STRICKLAND *Canada West* II 286: Shoe-packs, a species of mocassin peculiar to the Lower Province, cow-hide boots, and a *bonnet rouge* for the head, complete the costume of the Canadian lumberman.
1912 FOOTNER *New Rivers* 197: . . . while I was still enduring the pain of *mal de raquette* his shoe-packs had worn through and his feet were imperfectly tied up in pieces of canvas. **1946** LOWER *Colony to Nation* 215: . . . the habitants . . . shod their feet, not in honest English boots, but with cowhide made up after the fashion of the Indian moccasin ("shoe-packs").
1956 RADDALL *Wings* 85: Much better to have walked in, straight from the canoe, with the worn shoepacks, the shirt and breeches stained with balsam and smudged by campfires, the black bird's-nest of beard.
2 a kind of boot having high, laced uppers of

heavy oiled leather and thick soles, often of hard rubber. See also **beef boot** and **Canada boot**.

1882 LEMOINE *Quebec* 201: ... he came pounding along Notre Dame street, in Montreal, in his red shirt and tan-colored *shupac* boots, all dripping wet. ...
1904 ROBERTS *Watchers of Trails* 353: Inside their high-laced, capacious "shoe-packs" were several pairs of yarn socks. **1940** MARSHALL *Arctic Village* 101: It is only in the fall and the spring that the snow is soggy, and in those seasons shoepacks with rubber bottoms and leather uppers replace the moccasins. **1962** ALLEN *Peace River Country* 36: Harold stared at a disk of melting snow on one of his dubbined shoepacks.

shoot *n.* **1**† a falls or rapids. See also **chute** (def. 1). Cp. **rapid** and **riffle**, *n.* (def. 1a).

1772 (1792) CARTWRIGHT *Journal* I 195: I went up the river, and visited all the traps; I brought the upper-most one down, and tailed it above the shoot.
1792 (1934) TURNOR *Journal* 463: The head of the Island all a rapid with three heavy shoots which cannot be shot in going down but must carry ¼ mile.
1836 (1926) LANGTON *Early U.C.* 174: Formerly, we used to unload at McConnell's, drag the scow up the shoot, load again. ... **1860** *Nor' Wester* (R.R.S.) 15 Oct. 4/2: By dint of a good deal of enquiry I ascertained that ... "Bear-shoot" was so named from a bear crossing the river in sight of the crew at another "shoot" below.

2 *Lumbering, Hist.* See **slide**, *n.* (def. 1a).

1868 SMALL *Chronicles* 155: More than 20,000,000 cubic feet of timber come down the "shoots" of the Ottawa in this manner each year.

shoot *v.* **1** navigate a rapids, riffle, etc. in a canoe, boat, or raft. See also **run**, *v.* (def. 1).

1689 (1929) KELSEY *Papers* 30: [We] were forct to shoot 3 Desperate falls[;] yᵉ Raft stuck upon two of yᵐ but gott safely over. ... **1793** (1933) MACDONELL *Diary* 72: ... the guides who shoot the Canoes down the long sault and *Carrillon* Rapids have their huts erected.
1849 ALEXANDER *L'Acadie* II 304: Then I made a rapid run to Canada West, to visit my relations there, and returning by the Rapids of St. Lawrence, the Long Sault, etc. (which is exciting to "shoot" in a steamer, rolling down as it does majestically, with the angry water roaring and tumbling, and rushing about it. ...
1958 *Edmonton Jnl* 20 June 1/5: It was believed the boat overturned when the men attempted to shoot some rapids.

2 *Ottawa Valley, Hist.* ride a crib of logs down a slide (def. 1a). See also **shoot**, *n.* (def. 2).

1864 (1955) CRAIG *Early Travellers* 285: They say that there is considerable danger in shooting these slides, but it is much exaggerated. **1883** FRASER *Shanty* 340: Shooting the slides on cribs is capital sport; in its excitement and velocity it reminds you of tobogganing. **1964** *Cdn Geog.Jnl* Feb. 69/1: Cribs could shoot the slides along the upper Ottawa at places like Calumet and Chaudière.

shopping mall See **shopping plaza**.

shopping plaza a concentration of stores, usually in or near a suburban residential district, where there is adequate room for parking, spacious walks, etc.; shopping centre. See also **mall** and **plaza**.

1957 *Ottawa Jnl* 6 Aug. 1/1: The break-ins were compared with the noisy June 3 "tow-truck" robbery

at another grocery store in the shopping plaza.
1960 *Maclean's* 16 July 39/1: Elliot Lake residential zones are two miles from the shopping plazas. ...
1966 *Kingston Whig-Standard* (Ont.) 28 Jan. 15/7: The Kingston Planning Board Thursday approved ... construction of a nine-store shopping plaza. ...

shore brook See **shore lead**.

1933 MERRICK *True North* 285: At a spot where the shore brook was narrow we got ashore on stepping-stones of ice. ...

shore dance *Esp.Maritimes* a dance held on the shore.

1920 MONTGOMERY *Rilla* 17: "Miss Oliver, shall I wear my white dress tonight or my new green one? The green one is by far the prettier, of course, but I'm almost afraid to wear it to a shore dance for fear something will happen to it."

shore fishery See **dry fishery**. See also **shoreman**.

shore-floe *n. Esp.North* See **shore-ice** (def. 1).

1954 *Labrador and H.B.Pilot* 3: LAND ICE (shore floe or ice foot) is field or floe ice attached to the coast.

shore-ice *n.* **1** *Esp.North* sea ice that is anchored to the shore and extends seaward in a great shelf. See also **board-ice, ice-belt, ice-foot** (def. 1), **ice-ledge, ice-lip, ice-shelf** (def. 1), **inshore ice, land-floe, land-ice,** and **land pack.**

1752 ROBSON *Hudson's-Bay* 58: At York-fort and Churchill-river I have observed that the ice did not break off close at the shore, but gradually; the first field leaving the shore-ice two or three miles broad, the second less, and so on till it was cleared away.
1864 HALL *Life with Esquimaux* I 283: From the breaking up and consequent absence of the sea ice, which had occurred two days before my arrival, we were obliged to follow the shore-ice, walking on what Dr. Kane called the "ice-foot." **1936** (1955) STRINGER *Wife-Traders* 169: But a lead, widening in the shore-ice, still cut the two fur-clad figures off from the mainland.
1953 *Beaver* June 22: They walked across the shore ice, perhaps as far as two miles, and when they came to open water, made their camp there on the ice.

2 See **ice-shelf** (def. 2).

1811 (1950) THOMPSON *Journals* 187: Glush of Ice &c driving—Shore Ice where no Current, but weak. ...
1922 PICKTHALL *Bridge* 251: It hollowed the shore-ice into great milky bubbles. ...

3 *North* See **ballacater**.

1958 *Manice* 6: Shore Ice—Sea ice that has been beached and pushed ashore by wind and waves.

Shore Indian *Obs.* See **Home Indian**.

1777 (1954) *Moose Ft Jnls* 345: To me it appears a matter of much consequence to our Welfare as it may happen & Time may prove us only to be fighting about a few Home Guards or Shore Indians, rather confounding the Company's Interest more than we annoy the Inland Pedlars.

shore lead See quote. See also **shore brook**. Cp. **flaw lead**.

1958 *Manice* 7: Shore Lead—A lead between floating ice and the shore or between floating ice and fast ice.

shoreman *n. Nfld* a fisherman in the dry fishery, *q.v.*, or shore fishery.

1771 (1792) CARTWRIGHT *Journal* I 133: We got one raft on shore there, and I fixed on the place for the stage, flakes, and the shoremen's house. **1832** MCGREGOR

Brit.Amer. I 223: ... the crews ... collect together, with all assistance from the shoremen, and ... fix on two lines far enough apart to allow their largest schooners to pass. **1958** *Evening Telegram* (St. John's) 9 May 12/4: With ... shoremen bringing in record catches for this time of year, the Burin plant is taxed to capacity. **1964** *Nfld Qtly* Summer 15/1: Shoreman. A fishing establishment employing about twelve or more producers would divide them into a fishing crew and a smaller shore crew, the latter remaining [at] the "room" to "put away" (split and salt).

shoreyer or **shorier** ['ʃɔrjɚ] *n.* [< *shore* + *-yer;* cf. *liveyere;* see 1957 quote] *Nfld* the eider duck, *Somateria mollissima.*
1958 HARRINGTON *Sea Stories* 167: Coombs and Rex reached the island without mishap and immediately loaded their guns and went after the salt water ducks or "shoriers," killing twenty in a very short time. **1959** MCATEE *Folk-Names* 16: Common Eider [is also called] shoreyer (As frequenting the shore. "Labr.")

shorthand Chinook See **Chinook shorthand.**
1958 *Beaver* Winter 29/2: Somehow the Indians learned to read shorthand Chinook, much more quickly than ordinary writing. ...

short-log camp *West* a logging camp where the timber, usually pine, is cut into logs of not more than 20 feet.
1962 *B.C.Digest* Oct. 12/2: In the early 1900's he made the rounds of the short log camps in the East Kootenays playing the fiddle in the bunk houses in the evening.

short-logger *n.* a logger in a short-log camp, *q.v.*
1919 *Camp Worker* 30 Oct. 2/5: The short loggers can force the same living conditions that the coast members are forcing if only they will get together and stick together.

short order† **1** a meal or dish that can be prepared quickly and is cooked to order.
1899 *Klondike Nugget* (Dawson, Y.T.) 17 May 4/2: [Advert.] Short orders at all times. The Regina.
2† (used attributively) designating, preparing, or selling such meals.
1896 *Kootenaian* (Kaslo, B.C.) 2 May 1/4: You can snooze in the morning with the assurance that you can get a nice short order breakfast until noon at the Hotel Slocan. **1912** FOOTNER *New Rivers* 21: Above the track stretched a row of log shacks calked with clay, and hanging out over the doors such rakish, home-made signs as: "Dad's Stopping-house"; "Short Order Resterant"; "Pool-room"; "The Old Man's Place," etc. **1966** *Saturday Night* April 14/2: The girl went away and held a hurried conference first with the short-order cook, then, on his advice, went to seek someone in the kitchen.

short sauce† *Obs.* See quote. Cp. **sauce.**
1833 (1955) DOMETT *Cdn Journal* 46: You eat "short sauce" (apple sauce in vulgar English) with a two-pronged fork.

short-sauce garden† *Obs.* See **sauce garden.**
1835 *Novascotian* (Halifax) 29 Oct. 315/2: Do you see that snug looking house there, said he, with a short sauce garden afore it, that belongs to Elder Thomson.

shot claw *Maritimes* See quote.
1965 RICHARDSON *Living Island* 202: There were also several gnarled, plate-sized "shot" claws, for lobsters shoot—suddenly discharge with a snap—one or both claws to facilitate escape. ...

shotgun bunk *Slang* See **muzzle-loading bunk.**
1963 *B.C.Digest* July-Aug. 46/3: Most of them [bunkhouses] had what were called shotgun bunks. Those were on tiers of three high and placed close beside each other. The only way to get in was to crawl in the bottom like going into a tunnel.

shot rock[1] pieces of rock that result from blasting.
1961 *Cdn Geog.Jnl* Jan. 16/1: The shot rock was then loaded by hand into small cars. ...

shot rock[2] *Curling* the rock that is lying in scoring position at a given time.
1964 *Calgary Herald* 20 Mar. 16/8: Dagg hit the shot rock and stayed. ... **1966** *Globe and Mail* (Toronto) 2 Mar. 26/9: Mrs. Cooke ended the suspense by curling her final rock through a maze of stones to take out Ontario's shot rock. ...

shotsmith *n. Curling, Slang* a skilled curler.
1963 *Calgary Herald* 31 Dec. 21/3: Chernoff, the slick shotsmith ... experienced one of those nights, the kind that send many a curler in the direction of the gas pipe.

shove *n.* **1** See quote.
1829 MACTAGGART *Three Years* I 28: Sometimes the soil on the breasts of the hill will shove down with all its trees to the plains below. The spots where these shoves have taken place, are plainly seen from the river, and have a singular appearance.
2 *Hist.* **a.** See **ice-shove** (def. 2). See also **shoving of the ice.**
1837 *Montreal Transcript* 6 July 3/1: It will be remembered that during the unprecedented "shove" in the spring of 1836, this tree withstood a tremendous pressure, and its upper branches were filled with immense masses of ice. **1955** COLLARD *Cdn Yesterdays* 305n: The "shove" menaced anyone still trying to cross the St. Lawrence on the ice-roads, and year by year there would be rescues or casualties.
b. a thrusting forward of river ice under pressure, an action causing ridges on the ice surface and the building up of masses of ice on the shores. Cp. **ice-shove** (def. 2) and **bourdigneau.**
1842 *Montreal Transcript* 29 Dec. 2/4: Sleighs were crossing as early as the 23d instant, a little below Longueuil, and on that day the ice in that quarter made a "shove" for some distance, although fortunately no person was then on the ice. **1898** *Trans.Roy.Soc.Can.* IV 3 7: Before the revetment wall was constructed these shoves drove the ice-fields up the sloping beach to such a height beyond top bank that they broke by their own weight and piled a rampart of ice thirty feet high in front of the buildings they could not reach and out of which the terrified inmates escaped (in this ice) by the third story windows.

shove *v. Hist.* of ice, thrust forward under pressure causing pressure ridges in the ice or causing it to break up in spring. See also **ice-shove** (def. 2) and **shove,** *n.*
1836 *Montreal Transcript* 29 Dec. 2/2: The ice refouléd for the first time about 9 o'clock yesterday morning, and about one it shoved for the second time, when it remained stationary till dark. **1836** *Vindicator* (Montreal) 22 Apr. 3/3: The ice opposite the town shoved yesterday, but it is now steady again.

shovel *n.* **1** of a moose, the broad, flat part of the antler.

[1853 REID *Young Voyageurs* 341: [The moose's] horns flattened out to the breadth of shovels, weighed over sixty pounds.] 1966 *Cariboo Observer* 3 Nov. 15/2: [Caption] Most average size adults could stretch out quite comfortably in the shovels of the huge bull moose.
2 of a caribou, one of the small, flattened forward tines of the antler.
1911 ROGERS *Wild Animals* 324: There is a round beam and six broad, flattened "shovels" of several points on a typical antler. The "armchair" form is worn by the barren-ground caribou, the extra long round beam of each antler curving backward, then rising and pointing its tines ahead, while two broad, short-stemmed "shovels" go straight forward over the face. 1939 (1955) PATTERSON in BLACK *Journal* 93: The brow tines extend down over the muzzle, the tip expanding into a broad, vertical "shovel" bearing small points on its margin.

shoving of the ice *Hist*. See **ice-shove** (def. 2) and **shove**, *n*. (def. 2).
1853 (1854) KEEFER *Montreal* 12: The rise of water in winter and the shoving of the ice, prevent the erection of warehouses on the wharves.... 1863 WALSHE *Cedar Creek* 370: [Heading] SHOVING OF THE ICE

show *n. Mining* See **showing**.
1958 LINDSAY *Cariboo Story* 18/1: It was a bedrock show with the gravel loaded with the coarsest gold Bill or anyone else had ever seen. 1964 *Western Miner* Apr. 52/3: "Would like to dispose of a molybdenum show—cash quit claim—staked last fall. This show is written up in the report "Molybdenum in B.C.," and is located ... at Malaka, a whistle-stop just out of Sicamous...."

showing *n. Mining* an indication of the presence of minerals in sufficient quantity to suggest a possible site for a mine. See also **show**.
1936 LOWER *Settlement* 140: ... although they [prospectors] often found encouraging "showings," no mines could be operated so far from civilization until rail transport was secured. 1965 *Western Miner* June 57: [Caption] Claim post on Ruddock Creek main showing.

show the white feather *Obs*. See quote.
1853 STRICKLAND *Canada West* I 175: Indeed, I had often heard, that if they show the white feather, as putting up their tail is called by Canadian sportsmen— they[deer] are not hit.

show up *Mining* prove to have a showing, *q.v.*
1900 LONDON *Son of Wolf* 14: I think that bench claim will show up.

shupac *n. Obs*. See **shoepack**.

shutout *n. Hockey* a game in which a team's goalie prevents the opposing team from scoring; also, the credit given a goalie for such an achievement.
1955 *Edmonton Jnl* 4 Jan. 10/4: ... a few hours later he secured that elusive shutout that had escaped him so far this season. 1966 *Hockey News* (Montreal) 9 Apr. 20/5: Toronto ... led team totals in shutouts with eight....

shut-out *v*. in hockey, prevent the opposing team from scoring throughout an entire game.

Siberian *n.* **1** See **Siberian husky**.
2 See **Siberian wolf**. **3** See quote.
1965 CRAMOND *Big Game* 133: ... Vancouver Island wolves ... are sometimes referred to as "Siberians."

Siberian husky a breed of medium-sized working dog originally from Siberia, characterized by a brush tail and a thick coat of black, tan, or gray and white markings. Also *Siberian*.
1944 CLAY *Fur Thieves* 137: "But let's get back to the Yukon and Alaska. They drive 'nother kind o' dog there—called the Siberian. It was originally bred an' raised in Siberia, is smaller in size than a huskie, more stockily built, more heavily furred, an' is nearly always white...." 1950 HAMBLETON *Abitibi* 74: In their equipment was included a two-dog team, made up of Siberian huskies, blue-eyed beauties trained for generations to pull their hearts out and to survive the utmost rigors of the north. 1966 *Kingston Whig-Standard* (Ont.) 28 Feb. 10/1: [He drove] his team of Siberian huskies to smashing victory in the three-day Yukon Sourdough Rendezvous Derby.

Siberian wolf *North* a misnomer for the Arctic wolf, *q.v.* Also *Siberian*.
1921 *Beaver* Feb. 14/2: Today there is a herd of about two hundred and fifty animals [buffalo] in the MacKenzie River valley. They have not increased in numbers. The Siberian wolves get among them continually and destroy many of the calves.
1951 ANGIER *At Home* 39: "Wolves," he breathed. "Big Siberians. We're lucky, hearing them so close the first night."

Siberia of the fur trade *Hist*. See **New Caledonia** (def. 2).
1960 RAMSAY *Barkerville* 1: The country went under the general heading of "New Caledonia," a name given to it by Simon Fraser of the North West Company in 1808, but to the servants of the Hudson's Bay Company, the successors to the N.W.Co., it had a far more sinister name—"the Siberia of the fur trade"—on account of its remoteness from civilization....

sick convener the member of a club, lodge, ladies auxiliary, etc. who is responsible for visiting sick fellow members, sending them flowers, etc.
1958 *Oshaworker* 4 Sep. 4/3: Sick convener has been real busy, 5 of our sisters have been in hospital, sorry to say.

sick-train *n. Hist*. a dog-sled party whose job it is to run sick or wounded persons out of the bush.
1913 WILLIAMS *Wilderness Trail* 156: Because of fast traveling, the sick-train had no fresh meat.

side *n. Lumbering* See 1942 quote. See also **two-side camp**. Cp. **strip**.
1925 *Cdn Labor Advocate* 16 Oct. 11/4: On some of the sides the men have to walk from a mile to two miles before they arrive at their destination to start work at 7:30. 1942 HAIG-BROWN *Timber* 253: SIDE ONE, TWO, etc. Most large logging camps run two or more sides—that is, two or more entirely separate operations, each on its own spur of track, having its own facilities for rigging trees, yarding logs and loading.
1953 SWANSON *Haywire Hooker* 34: "If you can't yard three million," he says, "to every side,/You'd better roll your bundle and go take a ride."

side bark *Hist.* sheets of thin birch bark for forming the sides of canoes, as opposed to bottom bark, *q.v.*

1822 (1940) *Minutes of Council* (H.B.C.) July 27: That the following prices be allowed for Country produce . . . Birch Bottom Bark 3*s.* and side Do. 1*s.* 6*d.* **1922** *Beaver* July 11/2: [The bark] is trimmed evenly for its whole length, and is then ready to receive the "side bark," which is thinner than that first applied.

sideboards *n.pl. Hockey* See **boards** (def. 1).

1963 *Kingston Whig-Standard* (Ont.) 4 Mar. 13/1: Slow, miserable labor, pitching up to ten or a dozen tons of snow over the sideboards of a rink, after a big snowstorm!

side-channel *n. Northwest* See **snye** (def. 2a).

1899 PALMER *Klondyke* 74: The flat-bottomed river steamers continued on their course until the ice in the river led them to seek a slough or side-channel for safety. **1928** FREEMAN *Nearing North* 138: McMurray's steamer landing is located on a quiet-flowing side channel . . . which in the North is dubbed a "sny."

side-chute *n. Northwest* See **snye** (def. 2a).

1928 FREEMAN *Nearing North* 316: Now he would head through a side-chute not twenty feet in width, to come out on a serpentine channel that bent back almost into itself before suddenly losing its identity in a lake so shallow that the wind was skimming the north side of it dry of water.

side dam *Hist.* a dam built at the side of a rapids to build up a reservoir of water for floating logs down a slide (def. 1a).

1883 FRASER *Shanty* 313: At that time . . . [the rapids] were in their natural state, but now they have been improved by side dams and slides that their passage is comparatively easy.

side-gulch *n.* a blind gulch or gully leading into a larger one.

1900 OSBORN *Greater Canada* 117: But for the folly of a tenderfoot (who had no respect for old miners' lore), the millions lying hid in the affluent creeks and side-gulches might never have been brought to light.

sideline *n. Hist.* **1 a.** the line marking the side boundary of a concession (def. 2) and running at right angles to the concession line (def. 1).

1834 (1926) LANGTON *Early U.C.* 91: The concession lines run N.17 1/2W. and the side lines I am told are not exactly perpendicular. **1836** *Correspondent and Advocate* (Toronto) 3 May 1/3: The following petitions were read: . . . of Thomas Fleming, of Charles Williams and twenty-seven others, inhabitants of the first concession . . . Township of Hallowell . . . praying that certain sidelines may be surveyed.

b. the side boundary of a lot.

1852 (1923) MOODIE *Roughing It* 344: We sat down to rest ourselves before commencing the operation of "blazing," or marking the trees with our axes, along the side-line of my lot.

2 See **side-road** (def. 2).

1887 *Grip* (Toronto) 4 June 7/2: . . . we missed the lane leading to the Colonel's house, and turned into a side line where a wheel came off the buggy. . . . **1896** GOURLAY *Hist.Ottawa* 34: The concessions and sidelines in these townships were 66 feet wide. The plan was to plant a post in the centre of the road and one on each side 33 feet from it. These were the corner posts. Then 120 rods from these three more posts were driven into the ground dividing the first double lot of 200 acres from the next, and so it proceeded throughout. **1909** ROSS

Hist.of Zorra 27: Another [school] was in the south-west corner of the sideline and the fourth concession south of Embro. . . .

side-push *n. Lumbering, Esp.West, Slang* See second quote. Cp. **push** and **strip boss.**

1942 HAIG-BROWN *Timber* 246: Things are in a bit of a jackpot up there and it needs a good side-push to straighten it out. *Ibid.* 251: [The hooktender] is sometimes called the "side-push," implying that he is sub-foreman in charge of the whole operation of one "side" of a multiple-operation camp.

side-road *n.* **1** a secondary road, often unpaved, leading to a main highway.

1854 KEEFER *Ottawa* 72: The municipalities have taxed themselves too heavily for the main road . . . to be able to build also the side roads. **1931** MONTGOMERY *Tangled Web* 6: Uncle Pippin . . . drove away beside his meek white horse down the narrow, leisurely red side-road. . . . **1959** *Maclean's* 20 June 17/2: Now we go round by Tinchers', take the side road and go east two miles, then back to the correction line where it hits the Candy place.

2 in Ontario, a road built along the side boundaries of a concession (def. 2) at right angles to a concession road, *q.v.* See also **sideline** (def. 2).

1873 *Woodstock Sentinel* (Ont.) 5 Dec. 3/4: To Joseph Whaley for pine timber for culvert on first side road, $1.00. **1947** WELLS *Owl Pen* 32: . . . I carried the big shelf a long mile from the ploughed side-road, down the drifted concession line to Moonstone creek. **1966** *Globe and Mail* (Toronto) 7 May 41/1: . . . the best catches [were] at Claremont . . . Bruce's Mill (between Highway 7, and Gormley sideroad in Markham Township) and the Heart Lake area near Brampton.

side-saddle flower *Nfld* See **pitcher plant.**

side sleigh *Nfld, Hist.* See quote.

1964 *Cdn Geog.Jnl* Mar. 89/1: [Caption] This unique side sleigh from Newfoundland was a status symbol for several generations. A foot pedal brake was a convenience for the driver who stood at the dashboard or sat on a "box." Passengers sat facing the ditch, ready to be tossed into a snowdrift rather than into oncoming traffic, in case of accident.

sidewalk† *n.* a walkway, usually paved, beside a street or road.

1826 *U.E.Loyalist* (York [Toronto]) 1 July 39/4: Some regulation with respect to the improvement of the sidewalks, may be considered as necessary. **1869** CANNIFF *Settlement U.C.* 61: When the town of York was incorporated as a city, in 1834, under the name of Toronto, it had not a single sidewalk within its limits. **1960** BLONDAL *Candle* 13: For a moment the hand sleigh made sharp whistling noises against the sheath of snow on the sidewalk.

sidewinder *n. Lumbering, Slang* a type of shay, *q.v.*

1942 SWANSON *Western Logger* 54: shay [is also called] . . . sidewinder. . . .

siffleur ['sɪflɚ] *n.* [< Cdn F "whistler"] Also spelled *siffler, siffleu* (in older use). **1** *B.C.* **a.** See **hoary marmot.**

[1703 LAHONTAN *New Voyages* I 110: [We saw] little beasts called Siffleurs or Whistlers. . . .] **1824** (1955) BLACK *Journal* 81: The Whisle . . . seems to sound a retreat & into their dens [;] nor will they Whisle when near their habitations—from the singular powers of whistling of this animal, the Canadians have given them the appropriate appellation of Siffleu or the Whistlers. **1858** (1863) PALLISER *Journals* 94: . . . the only animal which we have seen is the siffleur, whose shrill whistle we heard for the first time close to our encampment. . . . **1890** *Cdn Record of Science* Jan. 52: We observed moose and reindeer . . . wolverines, siffleurs. . . . **1966** PATTERSON *Trail* 73: . . . there . . . the Sikannis . . . could snare the marmot, the siffleur . . . the little haunter of the barren heights.

b. the flesh of the hoary marmot used as food.
1808 (1960) FRASER *Letters and Journals* 86: They gave us a *siffleur* which is the first fresh meat we tasted since our departure. **1825** (1955) SIMPSON in BLACK *Journal* lxxviii: He saw very few Indians who barely existed on Fish & Siffler. **1949** *Cdn Alpine Jnl* May 32: They dined on "delicious siffleur" which tasted on the tongue like "very delicate mutton or the fat of sucking pig." **1963** SPRY *Palliser* 253: Hector's party also tried dried siffleur and goat meat, but found it was . . . rather highly flavoured. . . .

c. the skin of the hoary marmot.
1824 (1955) BLACK *Journal* 138: The Thecannies with their Siffleu Robes look like as many half drowned Rats crawling amongst the willows copiously bedaubed with mud & mire.

2 *North, Obs.* a ground squirrel, *q.v., Spermophilus undatus.*
1853 REID *Young Voyageurs* 226: The larger [marmots] were of greyish yellow above, with an orange tint upon the throat and belly. These were the "tawny marmots," called sometimes "ground-squirrels," and by the voyageurs, "siffleurs," or "whistlers." **1896** (1898) RUSSELL *Far North* 151: I collected a few siffleux, one of which I boiled to test the quality of its flesh; it tasted much as a house rat *looks. Ibid.* 249: Ground squirrels or "siffleux" as they are known to the Company's people, are a characteristic feature of the barren portions of Arctic America.

Siftonism ['sɪftən,ɪzəm] *n.* [Sir Clifford *Sifton*, 1861-1929] *Hist.* the views and policies of Sir Clifford Sifton while Attorney General of Manitoba, especially with regard to his opposition to separate schools in the 1880's. See also **Manitoba School Question.**
1882 *Brandon Mail* (Man.) 23 Dec. 2/1: Such picayunish tactics are very self-evident assurance that Siftonism is below par in the western portion of the constituency. **1953** LEBOURDAIS *Nation of North* 138: Nevertheless, the result in Manitoba was mainly due to causes far deeper than a revolt against Siftonism.

Sifton's Sheepskins *Hist.* the so-called Galicians, *q.v.,* who entered Canada in the 1890's under the immigration policy of Sir Clifford Sifton, 1861-1929, then Liberal Minister of the Interior. See also **men in sheepskin coats.**
[**1900** (1965) HAMILTON *Cdn Quotations* 175/2: Peasants in sheepskin coats. Phrase used by Conservative Party speakers, election November 1900; a reference to the type of immigrants preferred by Clifford Sifton.]

1916 BRIDLE *Sons of Canada* 82: "Sifton's sheepskins" the Conservative critics called them. **1955** HARDY *Alta Anthol.* 111: Today, the Alberta descendants of Sifton's Sheepskins number nearly 100,000 and they form the third largest racial group.

sight *v.* evaluate (timber) for commercial purposes. See also **cruise,** *v.* (def. 2).
1919 ROGERS *Joan at Halfway* 28: He's been off in the woods sighting timber, but you'll see more of him later along. . . .

sighting-in range a free range equipped with rests and targets supplied by a forestry department and used by hunters to test their rifles before going into the bush.
1962 *Wildlife Rev.* Dec. 9: The opening of a sighting-in range at Maiden Creek some 12 miles north of Cache Creek has been welcomed with enthusiasm by sportsmen. **1963** *B.C. Digest* Oct. 33/1: For this reason they built a sighting-in range on the Cariboo Highway, sixteen miles north of Cache Creek.

Sigiutl *n.* See **Sisiutl.**

signal fire or **smoke** See **smoke** (def. 2).
1820 (1963) DAVIES *Northern Quebec* 60: Made a signal smoke which was answered at Seal Lake. **1949** MACGREGOR *Blankets and Beads* 36: When they did find them [buffalo], they set signal fires to apprise the camp the way to come.

signiorial, signiory, etc. See **seigneurial, seigneury,** etc.

sik-sik *n. Eskimo* See **Parry's ground squirrel.**
1965 SYMINGTON *Tuktu* 44: The Parry's ground squirrel —the "sik-sik" of the Eskimo, is common in some localities.

Sikusi [si'kusi] *n.* [< Esk.; cf. *sikku* ice] *Trademark* See quote. See also **snowsnake** (def. 2). Cp. **Ookpik.**
1965 *Globe and Mail* (Toronto) 4 Mar. 2/5: The newcomer, Sikusi, (pronounced see-koo-see) is described as an iceworm. He, she or it is about 18 inches long, has horns and a long lolling tongue, and generally looks like a shaggy bottle-brush. Sikusi was created by a group of Eskimo women at Tuktoyaktuk, a community at the mouth of the Mackenzie River. Like Ookpik, the design will be registered and manufacturers will pay a royalty for its use.

Sila ['silə] *n.* [< Esk.; cf. *sila* atmosphere, intelligence] See quote. Also spelled *Sheela.*
1931 *Beaver* Dec. 347: The great Goddess Sila, whose spirit controlled the elements, was in a kindly mood. . . . **1956** LEECHMAN *Native Tribes* 191: Sheela . . . controls the weather and can bring on storms or hold back winds as she wills. . . .

silapak *n.* See **sealapack.**

Silent Force See **Royal Canadian Mounted Police.**
1927 LONGSTRETH *The Silent Force* [Title]. **1937** *B.C. Hist. Qtly* July 202: The "Silent Force" in its inimitable way has penetrated to the outposts of civilization, carrying with it law and order. . . .

Silent Land See **Silent Places.**
1929 MOBERLY *When Fur Was King* 237: The Silent Land produces valuable medicinal plants in great variety.

Silent Places the Canadian North.
1903 WHITE *Forest* 123: One can no longer wonder at the taciturnity of the men who dwell here; nor does one

fail to grasp the eminent suitability to the country of its Indian name—the Silent Places. **1909** CAMERON *New North* 31: Then he convoyed forty Indian witnesses ... to Edmonton to tell what they knew about the crime committed in the silent places. **1934** GODSELL *Arctic Trader* 4: I ... was conquered by the romance of the Silent Places. ...

Silk Train† *Hist.* See quote.
1955 HARDY *Alta Anthol.* 124: A generation ago the Silk Trains—those crack C.P.R. flyers that roared from the West Coast ports to New York City loaded with raw silk from Japan—were one of the biggest thrills of the year to bug-eyed kids along the western tracks.

sillapak *n.* See sealapack.

silver *n.* **1** See **silver fox** (def. 1).
1771 (1792) CARTWRIGHT *Journal* I 91: I went down the river, where I observed ... a brace of silvers. **1956** KEMP *Northern Trader* 138: Those two little traps of mine had bagged a silver.

2 See **silver-fox skin**.
1933 MERRICK *True North* 313: ... he showed me a beautiful cross fox and a silver. **1944** CLAY *Fur Thieves* 229: ... there hung a trapper's dream in furs! Red foxes, cross foxes, silvers; marten and mink; otter; wolf and wolverine; bundles of weasel skins; and many others!

silverberry (plant) *n.* a silvery-gray shrub, *Elaeagnus argentea,* common in the west. See also **silver oleaster** and **wolf-willow.**
1880 GORDON *Mountain and Prairie* 157: The banks ... are green with grass, kinnikinnick, juniper ... and the beautiful silverberry plant. **1955** MCCOWAN *Upland Trails* 83: Closely related to the Silverberry and common everywhere in the Rockies is a thornless and highly ornamental shrub known locally as Soapberry, but sometimes called Buffalo-berry.

silver birch See 1956 quote.
1856 BALLANTYNE *Young Fur-Traders* 129: Before him lay ... here and there the bright stem of a silver birch ... and solitary specimens of the spruce fir. **1956** *Native Trees* 134: White birch *Betula papyrifera* Marsh [is also called] silver birch.

silver dollar 1 *Hist.* See **dollar** (def. 1).
1826 *Colonial Advocate* (York [Toronto]) 9 Feb. 3/3: I higgled for a whole half hour with farmer B——o before I bought his fat pig, and brought him down at last a silver dollar. **1836** *Bytown* [Ottawa] *Gaz.* 15 Dec. 3/2: A Silver Dollar t'other day/Flat on a Paper Dollar lay. **1913** PARKER *Money Master* 329: It was gold louis abroad and silver dollars at home—that was the standard.

2 a silver coin first issued by the Canadian government in 1935 and having the value of one dollar.
1958 *Encyc.Can.* III 15/2: Silver dollars have been issued every year since 1935, except during the war years of 1940 to 1944.

silver fir 1 *Obs.* See **balsam** (def. 1). See also **silver pine.**
1775 (1792) CARTWRIGHT *Journal* II 58: They feed on nothing but rinds the whole winter, and by so doing kill a prodigious number of trees of all sorts; though they prefer the silver-fir to all others.

2 See **balsam** (def. 4).
1925 ANDERSON *Trees and Shrubs* 26: This fir [balsam fir] is also known as the White or Silver Fir from the appearance of its smooth grey bark, dappled with

white. **1956** *Native Trees* 68: Amabilis fir [is also called] silver fir. ...

silver fox 1 a color phase of the red fox, *Vulpes fulva,* characterized by black fur having silvery-white guard hairs, *q.v.,* dispersed over the back, found rarely in nature but nowadays bred on fox farms. See also **silver** (def. 1), **silver-gray,** and **silver-hair.**
1770 (1792) CARTWRIGHT *Journal* I 76: On Niger Sound we saw a good silver fox. **1861** *Cdn Naturalist* VI 16: My own theory is that the silver fox is the offspring of two silver parents; the cross of a silver and red; the red of two reds; and the different shades being caused by fresh inter-breeds. **1946** *Beaver* Mar. 3/1: ... in the wilds the silver fox is a rare phenomenon—probably two, or at the most, three per cent of red fox litters. **1964** *P.E.I.Tourist Guide:* [Folder] It is also the birthplace of the silver fox industry.

2 See **silver-fox skin.** See also **silver-gray.**
1820 (1823) FRANKLIN *Journey* 83: A silver fox, white fox, or otter, are reckoned two beavers, and a black fox, or large black bear are equal to four. **1921** *Beaver* Apr. 8/2: The silver fox is the choicest of all foxes, and now that sea otters are almost extinct, it may be considered the most valuable of all furs. **1947** GILLHAM *Raw North* 77: A pair of silver fox mittens dangled from ornate cords around his neck.

silver-fox skin or **pelt** the fur of the silver fox. See also **silver** (def. 2) and **silver fox** (def. 2).
☞ *These skins, being rarely found in nature, have long been highly valued. Nonetheless, the claim made by the author of the 1900 quote has been challenged by reputable authorities.*
1900 OSBORN *Greater Can.* 110: Furs were so numerous that for a flint-lock musket (worth, say, 15*s.* in England) the Indians were expected to pay a pile of fine furs—such as *silver* fox-skins—standing as high as the weapon placed with the stock on the ground. **1913** WILLIAMS *Wilderness Trail* 183: One year, he brought in three of the six silver-fox skins taken that winter in the whole of Canada. **1928** (1953) *Fur Trade Jnl* 27/1: Highest price received for one fine half-silver —$525.00 which is the highest price obtained this year for a silver fox pelt sold in Canada.

silver frost *Maritimes* See **silver thaw** (def. 2).
1828 *P.E.I.Register* (Charlottetown) 14 Oct. 4/3: A phenomenon appears frequently during winter, known here by the appellation of Silver Frost. **1889** LIGHTHALL *Songs* 409: [Title] The Silver Frost by Barry Straton

silver-gray (fox) *n.* a variation of the silver fox, *q.v.,* characterized by the presence of many silver hairs, which give it a grayish appearance.
1773 *Quebec Gaz.* 26 Aug. 3/1: ... they daily expect an eminent Merchant who ... has at length resolv'd ... to purchase ... Silver Grey Foxes, to a very large Amount. **1897** TUTTLE *Golden North* 212: The Indians (Chippewayans) come in the early spring, to trade, bringing with them the valuable skins of the otter, the deer and the marten, the mink, the silver-gray fox, etc. **1908** BROWN *Lady of the Snows* 204: At the fox-hunt they caught a silver grey and two reds. ...

silver-hair *n. Obs.* See **silver fox** (def. 1).
1861 DE BOILIEU *Labrador Life* 76: The "silver-hair" is the same size as our common fox, with a beautiful jet-black fur for the ground, which on each end is tagged with about an inch of "silver tinge," which glitters like jewels in the sun and snow.

silverjar (seal) *n. North* **1** an adolescent ring seal, *q.v.* See also **jar.**
1956 SCHERMAN *Spring* 40: The adolescent ringed seal, from one to four months old, called silverjar, is preferred because its hide brings three dollars at the trading post.

2 the silvery pelt of this seal.
1956 SCHERMAN *Spring* 259: The legs of the boots were of silverjar with the fur outside—the dressy boots of the Eskimo women. **1957** *Aklavik Jnl* Mar. 4/2: Silver-Jar Seal skins (young in May, June and July) bring $3.50 locally.

silver(y) oleaster *Obs.* See **silverberry.**
1830 *Trans.Lit.& Hist.Soc.Que.* III 88: Silver Oleaster [is] a spreading shrub about three or four feet high, of very unusual appearance. **1852** RICHARDSON *Arctic Exped.* 123: The . . . silvery oleaster (*Elaeagnus argentea*) . . . and Amelanchier grow on banks that in Europe would be covered with gorse and broom.

silver pine See **balsam** (def. 1).
1824 (1955) BLACK *Journal* 133: The descent is steep & covered with such a luxuriance of brush wood and a kind of Silver Pine (the Canadians name Sapin before mentioned) degenerated into a low shrub growing in feathery branches rising from a low Knotty root. . . .
1883 *Edmonton Bull.* 24 Feb. 3/1: The sides of the mountains for a considerable height are well timbered with spruce, poplar, silver pine, and hemlock.
1956 *Native Trees* 64: Balsam Fir [is also called] silver pine . . . Canadian fir.

silver salmon *Pacific Coast* See **coho.**
1884 CHITTENDEN *Queen Charlotte Is.* 8: I have seene fine silver salmon at the mouth of the Ya-koun River.
1907 LAMBERT *Fishing in B.C.* 73: They are . . . the silver and blue-back salmon, which are known as the cohoe and sockeye. . . . **1955** MCKELVIE *Pageant of B.C.* 142: The main source of food supplies, for both men and dogs, was the silver salmon.

silver thaw *Esp.Atlantic Provinces and B.C.* **1** a freezing rain that covers all exposed surfaces with glistening ice. See also **glitter** (def. 1), **ice-storm** (def. 2), and **ver glas.**
1770 (1792) CARTWRIGHT *Journal* I 73: There was a silver thaw in the morning, and it rained freely: very mild weather all the rest of the day. **1806** STEWART *P.E.I.* 103: . . . a freezing rain, or as it is commonly called, a silver thaw, sometimes happens on these occasions. . . . **1872** DASHWOOD *Chiploquorgan* 134: On my return . . . I witnessed for the first time a silver thaw in all its beauty—one of the most lovely sights in North America. **1948** MAIDEN *Lighted Journey* 26: [Caption] The silver thaw of 1933 created havoc with power lines and disrupted all traffic in the Fraser Valley.
1952 RADDALL *Nymph* 216: It was what Nova Scotians called a "silver thaw," a condition that covers the world outdoors with a glaze of ice, making a glassy fairyland of woods and parks, coating every branch and twig and glittering in the next day's sunshine like an enormous crystal chandelier.

2 the coating of ice resulting from such freezing rain. See also **glitter** (def. 2), **silver frost,** and **ver glas.** Cp. **ice-storm.**
1842 BONNYCASTLE *Newfoundland* I 339: Fruit trees and shrubs are seriously injured by this silver thaw, which very fortunately is rare. **1955** *Evening Telegram* (St. John's) 14 Mar. 3/5: Motorists whose cars were covered with the "silver thaw" this morning found that most of it had melted by 11 o'clock, though in areas such as Torbay the glitter was still falling.

3 *Obs.* See quote.
1835 (1836) WIX *Journal* 25: The country at this time presented an appearance quite different from that presented by the vegetation when affected by a moistness of the atmosphere which is afterwards operated upon by sudden frosts, and is improperly denominated here, a silver thaw.

silvertip (grizzly) *n.* a variety of grizzly bear, *q.v.*, found in the western mountain region, characterized by hairs having silver tips.
1897 TUTTLE *Golden North* 96: There are four species of bear in the region. These are the grizzly, brown, black, and small kind called the "silver-tip." The latter are of a gray color and are very fierce. **1922** *Beaver* July 27/2: The large silver tip grizzly in the Rockies, however, is as a rule always ready to attack. **1957** FISHER *Pemmican* 3: That was the trouble with a silver tip; the awful beast would attack anybody anytime. . . .
1960 NELSON *Northern Lights* 715: This is the country of the silvertip grizzly and the gigantic lobo wolf, vicious 200 pound animals who pack together for the kill.

silver trout *B.C.* **1** See **Kamloops.**
1907 LAMBERT *Fishing in B.C.* 43: Every local fisherman speaks of having caught a red side or a silver trout, and firmly believes they are distinct species. . . .
1922 *Beaver* Feb. 37/1: The streams and rivers were full of trout—mountain, silver and speckled.

2 See **kokanee.**
1937 *Kootenay and the City of Nelson, B.C.* 6/2: The Kokanee or "Silver Trout," which is in reality a landlocked Sockeye salmon, abounds in the larger lakes of the district. . . .

silvery oleaster See **silver oleaster.**

sin bin *Hockey, Slang* See **penalty box.**
1958 *Herald Tribune* (Grande Prairie, Alta) 11 Mar. 5/3: [The] game saw 37 minutes spent in the sin-bin. . . .
1966 *Hockey News* Aug. 12/3: Then, Ted Harris joined Fergy in the sin bin and Ron Ellis scored for the Leafs.

singing house among Eskimos, a special building where communal singing and dancing take place. Cp. **dance house** and **snowhouse** (def. 2).
1916 HAWKES *Lab.Eskimo* 59: Old missionary accounts speak of snow-houses 16 feet high and 70 feet across, which the heathen Eskimo built to celebrate their winter festivals in. These ceremonial houses probably corresponded to the qaggi or singing-house of the Baffin-islanders.

single (point) *n. Cdn Football* See **rouge,** *n.*
1958 *Edmonton Jnl* 8 Aug. 13/4: Gary Shreider kicked two converts and Ron Quillian booted a single.
1966 *Globe Mag.* 20 Aug. 7/2: Capozzi listed seven major rules differences between the Canadian and the U.S. games [including] single point if punt not run out of end zone. . . .

single buggy a small buggy drawn by one horse.
1912 CONNOR *Corp.Cameron* 259: On occasion Perkins
would hitch up in the single buggy Dexter, the fiery
young colt, too fiery for any other to drive, and, as a
special attention to his employer's daughter, would
drive her to the service.

single canoe *Fur Trade, Hist.* See quote. Cp.
express canoe and **small canoe.**
1929 (1931) MERK *Fur Trade* 346: Besides North canoes,
there were in use in the fur trade half canoes and single
canoes. . . .

single car(r)iole See **cariole** (def. 1).

single-jack *n. Mining* a relatively small hammer
used in single-jacking, *q.v.* Cp. **double-jack.**
1961 *Press* 1 Sep. 11: The mechanization of mines in
1890—the replacing of hand-steel, single-jack and
double-jack, by drilling machines—had created new
problems. . . . **1964** *Vancouver Times* 3 Nov. 17/4: The
miner, working either a double-jack or single-jack job,
might worry about the sprags. . . .

single-jacking *n. Mining* See quote. Cp.
double-jacking.
1964 *Vancouver Times* 3 Nov. 17/6: Single jacking is a
[drilling] job where one man handles both the chisel
[drill steel] and a small hammer.

single-line hitching *North* See **tandem hitch.**
1924 *Beaver* Aug. 410: In the extreme north, single-line
hitching, and fan hitching is in general use. . . .

single relief the welfare allowance granted a man
appearing on the relief-office records as being
single.
1955 BIRNEY *Long Table* 210: "If yer not married on
them cards ye get single relief, no matter how many
wives you've got or kids either."

sink-hole *n. West* **1** See **muskeg** (def. 1).
1910 WARD *Canadian Born* 18: Elizabeth had ample
time during the ensuing sixteen hours for inquiry as to
the nature of sink-holes. *Ibid.*: "A sink-hole, well it's as
you may say—a muskeg."
2 See quote. Cp. **pothole** (def. 3a).
1963 SYMONS *Many Trails* xviii: [A] sinkhole [is] a
small depression in the prairie, usually with alkaline
springs below it and therefore having no herbage.

siscoe *n.* See **cisco.**

siscowet *n.* See **cisco.** See also **siskawet.**

sish (ice) [sɪʃ] *n.* [imitative, influenced by *slush*
and *swish*] *Esp.Nfld* See 1918 quote. See also **swish
ice.** Cp. **frazil** and **slur ice.**
1887 BOND *Skipper George* 116: [There was] a slight
coating of "sish" or ice-scum on the harbour.
1909 GRENFELL *Adrift on Ice-Pan* 7: Then the wind
suddenly fell, and I noticed that I was travelling over
loose "sish," which was like porridge and probably
many feet deep. **1918** GRENFELL *Labrador Doctor* 110:
"Sish" ice is made up of tiny bits formed by the
pounding together of the large pans by the heavy seas.
1924 MATHEWS *Wilfred Grenfell* 144: This "sish" ice was
now simply falling to bits, for the wind-pressure had
disappeared. **1933** GREENE *Wooden Walls* 32: . . . each
one [icepan] will be rimmed around by the splashing
of the "sish."

Sisiutl [sɪsˈjutəl] *n.* [< Kwakiutl] See 1888 quote.
Also spelled *Sigiutl.*

1888 BOAS *Houses of Kwakiutl Indians*: Another figure
that is frequently represented in the carvings of these
tribes is the Sisiutl, the fabulous double-headed snake
that can adopt the shape of any fish. **1958** *Family
News-Advertiser* (Vancouver) 22 Oct. 1/4: [Caption]
SIGIUTL—double-headed snake.

siskawet [ˈsɪskə,wɛt] *n.* [< Cdn F *sisquoette*
< Algonk. Ojibwa *pemitewiskawet* that which has
oily flesh] a variety of lake trout, *q.v.*
1837 (1923) JAMESON *Rambles* 344: . . . there is a fish . . .
in the upper part of Lake Superior, called the skevát, so
exceedingly rich, luscious and oily, when fresh, as to be
quite uneatable. **1841** *Patriot* (Toronto) 1 Mar. 2/3:
The varieties usually taken for pickling are, Trout,
Pickerel, White Fish and Sisquoette. **1860** (1956) KOHL
Kitchi-Gami 325: The siskawet is a fish bearing some
resemblance to the salmon-trout. **1959** WOODING
Angler's Book 108: The Lake Trout has a long,
somewhat slender body (exception is the "Siskowet,"
which is fat and deep-bodied).

sister colony *Hist.* one of the British North
American colonies, regarded as having equal
status with other such colonies.
1822 *Montreal Herald* 23 Oct. 4/4: It may truly be said
that in this important particular, a Sister Colony is
permitted to exercise over Upper-Canada, a more
obnoxious authority than Great Britain exerts over her
Colonies. **1858** *British Colonist* (Victoria) 11 Dec. 2/2:
It is consequently a much more delicate task for us to
comment on the administration of public affairs here,
than it would be in our sister Colonies, where the
Governor is not held responsible for acts done by the
advice of his ministers. **1897** *Trans.Roy.Soc.Can.* III
2 19: It is now quite clear that this large colony [Nfld],
which has been placed as a sentinel at the portals of
Canada, must, ere long, fall into line with its sister
colonies in North America.

sister province 1 *Hist.* See **sister colony.**
1789 *Nova Scotia Mag.* I vii: The Editor conceives, that
the Nova-Scotia Mag. might be made highly conducive
to the improvement of this and the sister Provinces. . . .
1819 *Kingston Chron.* (U.C.) 19 Mar. 2/3: It is
presumed that our Sister Province would go hand in
hand with us in improving the navigation of her
portion of the river. **1849** GESNER *Ind.Resources N.S.*
11: Nova-Scotia is rivalled in steam navigation by the
sister province New Brunswick, where the coal
employed is imported from Great Britain.
2 one of the provinces of Canada.
1891 *Grip* (Toronto) 25 July 50/2: The Sister Provinces
were also happy in their choice of welcomes.
1953 LEBOURDAIS *Nation of North* 188: Saskatchewan,
in 1915, Ontario, Alberta, Nova Scotia, Manitoba, New
Brunswick and British Columbia, in 1916, passed
prohibition laws; while, in 1918, Quebec fell in line with
its sister provinces.

sit hard *Nfld* of ducks, remain on a nest of eggs
until the last possible moment as danger approaches.
1958 *Evening Telegram* (St. John's) 1 May 21/4: Eider
Ducks and Old Squaws were "sitting hard" on their
eggs and flushed practically in our faces.

Sitka deer [< *Sitka* (Alaska) < Tlingit] a smaller
subspecies, *Odocoileus hemionus sitkensis,* of the
blacktail deer, *q.v.*

1945 RAND *Mammals of Yukon* 76: The Yukon form [of the Black-tail deer] . . . is Sitka deer. . . . **1952** PUTNAM *Cdn Regions* 39/2: The Pacific coast with its mild humid climate and luxuriant forests is inhabited by . . . the Sitka deer. . . .

Sitka grouse a race of sooty grouse, *Dendragapus fuliginosus sitkensis,* found on the Pacific slope.
☛ *See* **Sitka deer** *for origin of* **Sitka.**
1952 PUTNAM *Cdn Regions* 39/2: Some birds of the coastal forest are: Sitka grouse . . . red-breasted sapsucker. . . .

Sitka spruce 1 a tall spruce, *Picea sitchensis,* found on the Pacific slope in British Columbia. See also **Menzies spruce** and **tideland spruce.**
☛ *See* **Sitka deer** *for origin of* **Sitka.**
1906 DEFENBAUGH *Lumber Industry* 63: . . . in the interior of British Columbia . . . extending to the coast, the giant of the species is found in the Menzies or Sitka spruce. **1962** *Kingston Whig-Standard* (Ont.) 2 Oct. 15/5: A 150-foot golden Sitka spruce, believed to be the only one of its kind in the world, stands in a forest on the Yakoun River in British Columbia.
2 *Fig.* the logging camps of B.C.
1928 PERRY *Two Reds* 163: "Just the morning after you left for the Sitka spruce. . . ."

Siwash ['saɪwaʃ] *n.* **Siwash** or **Siwashes.**
[< Chinook Jargon < F *sauvage* savage, the term used by voyageurs for Indians] *Pacific Coast and Northwest* **1** a native Indian. See also **Siwash Indian.**
☛ *In present-day use, this term has deteriorated to such a degree that it might well be labelled as derogatory slang. See def. 2.*
1851 *Kamloops Jnl* (B.C.) 29 Mar.: Late in the evening Mr. John Simpson with 2 returning Siwashes reached this [post] from Langley. **1865** *Cariboo Sentinel* (Barkerville-Williams Creek, B.C.) 22 July 4/1: A Siwash walking blindfold from Yale to the Meadows by the usual route would be able to tell more correctly the condition of the country than your friends will learn from the columns of your contemporary. **1901** (1958) WATTERS *B.C.Cent.Anthol.* 37: . . . Father Rohr . . . addressed the kneeling siwashes, the priest speaking in the Chinook, and the interpreter rendering his speech in the native tongue. **1938** CURTIN *Yukon Voyage* 43: We call the natives Siwashes, as do all the white people we have met here, but this is only slang. **1958** BERTON *Klondike* 41: Instead he wanted to be an Indian in a land where the natives were generally scorned by the white man and the word "Siwash" was a term of opprobrium. **1963** SYMONS *Many Trails* 73: . . . most ranchers in the interior loosely refer to all Indians as Siwashes.
2 *Slang* of whites: **a.** *Derog.* See 1913 quote.
1882 *Edmonton Bull.* 3 June 4/3: Does this great chieftain think new settlers are a community of Siwashes or cringing dependants that his aggressive actions are to be unrestrained by any power or his word doubted in the slightest particular. **1913** SANDILANDS *West.Cdn Dict.* 41/2: Siwash, a mean, contemptible person; a term of address that is meant to give offence, as "You Siwash." **1920** FOOTNER *Fur-Bringers* 9: "You ornery worthless . . . Siwash! Change your face or you'll give a dog distemper!"

1964 BERTON *Golden Trail* 23: "Shall we go up and stake?" one of them asked the other. "I wouldn't go across the river on that old Siwash's word," was the reply.
b. (familiar use) fellow; old-timer.
1921 DURKIN *Lobstick Trail* 166: . . . Tuck Roberts entered. Kirk glanced round, then leaped to his feet. "Tuck, you old siwash!" Kirk cried and threw his arms about him.
3 See **Siwash tongue.**
1936 MOWERY *Paradise Trail* 14: "That's what Saghelia means in Siwash—the purty land . . . paradise."
4 See **Siwash duck.**

Siwash ['saɪwaʃ] *adj.* **1** of or having to do with the Siwash (def. 1).
1860 *Brit.Colonist* (Victoria) 26 July 1/2: The Indians in this neighborhood, though sufficiently numerous, are on the whole, an industrious and peaceably disposed branch of the Siwash family. **1887** (1932) MATHEWS *Early Vancouver* 51: The Siwash rancherie below the Hastings Mill was the scene of another disgraceful disturbance on Thursday night.
1912 MCGREGOR *Wisdom of Waloopi* 21:
Should you ever meet a siwash spook,
Ask, if you please, in your best Chinook,
The fate of Legai—what course he took,
And how did his choice pan out.
1964 BERTON *Golden Trail* 15: . . . they all began to do a war dance around the pan. It was, as Carmack said later, a combination of Scotch horn-pipe, Indian fox-trot, syncopated Irish jig, and Siwash hula-hula.
2 *Slang, Derog.* **a.** See quote.
1961 LA VIOLETTE *Survival* 113: At least on the coastal areas of the northwest portion of Canada and the United States, and to some extent in the interior, one often hears siwash also used as an adjective, meaning "no good." It is applied to Indians in that sense as well as dogs, coffee, and a variety of other things.
b. mean; stingy.
1923 GIBBONS *Sourdough Samaritan* 187: "Can't yeh get none off a' him a' tall? Come Christmas time he oughtn't t' act siwash if he is a sheeny. . . . Jes' three er four mebbe'd fix us up?"

siwash ['saɪwaʃ] *v.* [< n.] *Pacific Coast and Northwest* **1 a.** travel light, establishing siwash camps, *q.v.*, or sleeping in the open without prepared shelter. See also **siwashing.**
1938 (1950) STANWELL-FLETCHER *Driftwood Valley* 111: With fresh memories of bitter cold nights when we had siwashed under trees, I dressed for this trip more warmly. **1951** ANGIER *At Home* 189: When I used to siwash up here winters with the mail, I had to break out a new snowshow trail practically every trip.
b. siwash it, See quote.
1931 HENDRYX *Outlaws* 193: I'll not try to put up my tent. I've got a good warm bed [bedroll], and I'll Siwash it for the rest of the night, and put up the tent later. Good night!
2 *Slang* **a.** prohibit from obtaining liquor; put on the Indian list, *q.v.* See also **interdict,** *v.* (def. 2).
☛ *This term now applies to any person placed on the interdict list,* q.v., *in B.C.*
[**1922** MURPHY *Black Candle* 217: The Siwashes are Indians in British Columbia. They can't get whiskey because they are Indians.] **1948** HOLLIDAY *Valley of Youth* 292: The Dasher had been siwashed for a period, and . . . he had hidden supplies in various places so that

he would have something to fall back on that was more palatable than painkiller or Jamaica ginger.
1957 BARRATT *Coronets* 9: "Hit's against the law ter ell wisky to the Siwashes . . . So wen a wite man gets so's no one will sell him drinks—well folks say e's been siwashed."

b. deny access to prohibited drugs.
1922 MURPHY *Black Candle* 217: He always gave it [morphine] to me in the end, but I have had to get on my knees first. . . . Tai told them to Siwash me.

c. See quote.
1965 *Native Voice* Dec. 4/2: Twenty years ago when a white man was struck off the voters' list he was being turned into an Indian—"siwash" they call it.

3 *Lumbering, Slang* run (a cable, line, etc.) around anything but a proper block. See also **Siwash fashion** (1938 quote). Cp. **Siwash**, *adj.* (def. 2a).
1942 SWANSON *Western Logger* 28:
   The slumber of ages silence was broken
   By cursing and laughter of loggers a jokin',
   And fallin' of pines, and snappin' of lines,
   As "haulback" that's "siwashed" pulsingly whines.
1943 SWANSON *Lumberjack* 56: In ground lead logging, at first the main line rubbed or *siwashed* around a stump in order to spool it onto the drum, but when the *bull block* was invented, ground lead logging prospered by leaps and bounds, and its inventor, "Tommy" Moore, was crowned with a wreath of salal and made immortal among loggers who know their stuff.

Siwash berry *B.C.* See **serviceberry** (def. 2).
1887 (1888) LEES & CLUTTERBUCK *British Columbia* 117: . . . a blue berry . . . growing on a bush often several feet in height . . . is known as the Service or Siwash (the latter word meaning Indian) berry . . . and is good.

Siwash blanket *Pacific Coast and Northwest* a low ceiling of clouds covering the sky.
1926 *Beaver* June 108: A Siwash blanket means that on account of the clouds it will be warmer than it would be if the sky were clear.

siwash camp *Northwest* See quote. See also **siwash**, *v.* (def. 1).
1924 MASON *Arctic Forests* 28: All Indians, and many white men, build what is known as a "siwash" camp. The snow is scraped away with a snowshoe to leave a rectangular patch of bare ground. Round this the camper builds a windbreak two or three feet high of young spruce-trees at the back and sides, and lines the camp with the soft boughs of green spruce. In front he builds a large fire of dry logs, and if the night is particularly cold he builds another screen behind the fire so as to enclose the camp completely and throw the heat back. If it looks like snow he generally erects a slanting frame to stretch the sled-canvas over his head.

Siwash dog or **pup** *B.C. and Northwest* See 1924 quote. Cp. **giddee.**
1910 LONDON *Burning Daylight* 13: "Get down to the ground, you-all, Malemutes, huskies and Siwash purps! Get down and dig in! Tighten up them traces!"
1924 MASON *Arctic Forests* 52: The Indian or 'Siwash' dog is a mixture of every known breed in existence, with husky predominating. **1936** MACKENZIE *Living Rough* 33: "Yeah, you'd have got out of there in a hurry too, if you's had a pack of lousy Siwash dogs after you."

Siwashdom *n. Pacific Coast, Obs.* the "uncivilized" native state.
1870 *Mainland Guardian* (New Westminster, B.C.) 16 Apr. 3/3: In front sit a few klootchmen in their blankets, little removed from the first degree of siwashdom.

Siwash duck *B.C.* **1** See **old squaw.**
1956 MCATEE *Folk-Names* 16: Old Squaw [is also called] Siwash, Siwash duck (For the Siwash Indians, B.C.). . . .
2 a scoter, *Melonitta* sp. or *Oidemia nigra.*
1959 MCATEE *Folk-Names* 17: White-winged Scoter [is also called] Siwash, Siwash duck (Eaten by the Siwash Indians, so named for them. B.C.). . . .
1966 *Dly Colonist* (Victoria) 20 Mar. 11/4: It is a rare occurrence for a Siwash duck, as the species [surf scoter] is commonly called, to be found on such a shoreline. . . .

Siwash fashion or **style** *B.C. and Northwest* **1** after the manner of Indians.
1923 WALDO *Down Mackenzie* 217: Promenade around in a single file/And the lady in the lead in the Siwash style. **1957** *Maclean's* 9 Nov. 51/1: And so, even in a foreign land a foreign intruder had had his head smashed in the Siwash fashion. *Ibid.* 52/2: "How would you like to do your courting Siwash style?"
2 See **siwash**, *v.* (def. 3).
1938 CASH *I Like B.C.* 187: We pried and he heaved with the tow rope round what you couldn't by the wildest stretch of imagination call the boulder's waist, windlassed Siwash fashion around a neighbouring fir.

Siwash goose *Pacific Coast* the Western grebe, *Aechmophorus occidentalis.*
1956 MCATEE *Folk-Names* 3: Western Grebe [is also called] Siwash goose (used as food by the Siwash Indians, hence their "goose." B.C.). . . .

Siwash house *Fur Trade, Pacific Coast, Hist.* See **Indian hall.**
1965 *Islander* 4 Apr. 4/3: . . . he shooed Jennie and little Louis off to the Siwash house (a log cabin on the foreshore reserved for visiting Indians). . . .

Siwash Indian *Pacific Coast and Northwest* See **Siwash**, *n.* (def. 1).
☞ *This term is a tautological formation which does not refer to an Indian of any specific tribe.*
1889 WITHROW *Our Own Country* 553: . . . a Negro, a Chinaman, and a Siwash Indian prepared dinner on the steamer for a company representing many countries, provinces and States. **1926** DILL *Long Day* 202: The Mounted Police handled the Government stores and to facilitate their transport a large number of Siwash Indians were employed. **1934** *Beaver* Sep. 50/2: The Nisqually and other Puget Sound Siwash Indians with whom trade was established were friendly and helpful. **1957** *Arctic Spotter* Nov. 6/1: The water-trail ended at a camp of Siwash Indians at the northern end of the lake.

siwashing ['saɪwɑʃɪŋ] *n. B.C. and Northwest* the practice of travelling light, living Indian fashion on the trail. See also **siwash**, *v.* (def. 1).
1928 WALDEN *Dog-Puncher* 75: I made the back trip without tent and stove, having sold mine on the creeks. This is the way they used to travel in the early days, and it was called "siwashing." **1938** (1950) STANWELL-FLETCHER *Driftwood Valley* 108: The day after our siwashing trip, we lounged about the cabin, luxuriating

in a paradise of warmth and rest. We'd had enough for a long time of winter camps and travels.

Siwash list *B.C., Slang* See **interdict list.** See also **Indian list** and **siwash,** *v.* (def. 2).
1966 ST. PIERRE *Quarter Horse* 101: The glass shattered against the wall. "You are now on the Siwash list," said the tapman, rising again from behind the counter.

Siwash logger *Lumbering, Pacific Coast, Slang* See **beachcomber** (def. 2).
1908 GRAINGER *Woodsmen* 66: "I'm a Siwash logger, am I? Well I *am* a Siwash logger."

Siwash pudding *B.C.* See quote.
1957 LEWIS *Buckskin Cookery* I 13: "Siwash Pudding" (Indian) Boil dried saskatoons. Thicken with flour. Add sugar.

Siwash purp See **Siwash dog.**

Siwash rhubarb *B.C.* a dish made with Indian rhubarb, *q.v.*
1957 LEWIS *Buckskin Cookery* I 22: "Siwash Rhubarb" (Indian) Use only the hollow stalk with the flower on it. Skin it, and cut it in pieces. Boil in salted water. Serve with butter, salt and pepper.

Siwash slipper *Northwest, Obs.* See **moccasin** (def. 1).
1899 (1930) ROBERTSON *Yukon Memories* 120: Two good pairs of German socks, a pair of Esquimaux or "Siwash" slippers [are among essential clothing].

Siwash sock *Northwest* See **duffle sock** (def. 1).
1900 LONDON *Son of Wolf* 148: Their Siwash socks were similarly conditioned, and when these had been thawed and removed, the dead-white tips of the toes ... told their simple tale of the trail. **1912** LONDON *Smoke Bellew* 93: The siwash socks and heavy woolen stockings were sheaths of ice.

Siwash style See **Siwash fashion.**

Siwash sweater *Esp.West* See **Cowichan sweater.**
1945 *Beaver* Dec. 19/1: In a good year the Siwash sweaters may retail for a gross sum of $10,000, half of which is taken in by one small store on the highway leading into Duncan. [**1948** ONRAET *Sixty Below* 100: The Siwashs on the west coast of British Columbia make the best kind [of sweater] from unspun yarn.]

Siwash tongue *Pacific Coast and Northwest* any native Indian language, especially the Chinook Jargon, *q.v.*
1902 LONDON *Daughter of Snows* 73: Even Dave Harney ... waxed facetious over the newcomers—*chechaquos,* he called them, having recourse to the Siwash tongue. ...

Siwash trot *Pacific Coast* a slow, leisurely trot.
1965 *Maclean's* 16 Oct. Leisure Living 14/4: Abruptly, cheerfully, he reined the bay horse left and kicked it into a Siwash trot.

Siwash waptoo *Pacific Coast* See **wapatoo.**
1925 ANDERSON *Trees and Shrubs* 134: The corm of this water-plant is known amongst some of the natives as "Siwash Waptoo," signifying Indian potato. ...

Siwash wind *Pacific Coast, Local* a fresh blow; brisk wind.

1888 (1890) ST. MAUR *Impressions* 145: We started with what the Indian called a "siwash" wind.

six bits† *Slang* seventy-five cents. See also **bit** (def. 1) and note.
1899 *Greenwood Miner* (B.C.) 8 Sep. 3/1: Some of them have since had indigestion, caused by the six-bit attachment to the menu at Kamloops and other places. It must be remembered that editors in agricultural districts live principally upon ozone, carboniferous vegetables and eat their pie off a boiler plate, with patent medicine and salad, consequently when they strike a country where it costs six-bits for a jag of ordinary grub, their amazement at seeing their savings for years disappear in a day or two's gastronomical pleasure is a sight too sad for ordinary mortals to witness with dry eyes. **1942** SWANSON *Western Logger* 11: With a six-bit tip to the "hair-decked lip" he was whisked on high to his floor,/ And the "hop" took his grip, stood there for the tip, with his hand on the numbered door! **1966** BAITY *Wilderness Welfare* 42: All I figure on now is to find a high bar some place where I can make six bits or a dollar a day till low water.

six-fathom canoe *Hist.* See **North canoe.**
1921 HEMING *Drama of Forests* 10: Canoes of the largest size, thirty-six feet, are called six-fathom or "North" canoes.

Six Nations the original Five Nations, *q.v.,* together with the Tuscarora nation, which joined the confederacy in the early eighteenth century (1722), many of whom remained loyal to the British Crown, moving north to reservations in Canada, especially that on the Grand River near Brantford, Ontario.
1765 *Quebec Gaz.* 18 July 3/1: The Six Nations ... we are assured having agreed to the Particulars recommended to them by the King's Orders. **1783** (1905) *Ont.Bur.Arch.Rep.* III cxx: Captain Joseph Brant, with several Indians of the Six Nations went up to Cataraqui Falls and made excursions into the woods. **1886** *Indian* (Hagersville, Ont.) 3 Feb. 2/2: Certain of the chiefs of the Six Nations have, it seems, passed a resolution declaring that the Indians do not want the franchise. **1959** *Time* (Cdn ed.) 16 Mar. 18/1: For weeks Joseph Logan, 81, one of the deposed chiefs ... talked up their plan among the 6,400 members of the Six Nations who live on and near the Grand River reserve.

Skeena turkey [< *Skeena* River, B.C.] *Pacific Coast and Northwest, Slang* See **oolichan.**
1953 *Beaver* Mar. 44/1: Before the coming of the railway to Prince Rupert, oolachan was considered a delicacy, "the Skeena turkey."

skeleton car *Lumbering* See 1942 quote.
1936 *B.C.Lumber Trade* 73: ELCO Logging Co. Ltd. Youbou, B.C. ... Three Sides; Three High Leads; ... 45 Skeleton Cars. ... **1942** HAIG-BROWN *Timber* 253: SKELETON CAR. A railroad car made up of two sets of four wheels joined by a heavy timber across which the steel bunks are set to carry the logs. A car to serve the same purpose is made by simply setting bunks on the deck of a flat car, but the skeleton car is more common.

skeleton sleigh *Hist.* a light, fast sleigh, popular with the sporty set.
1955 COLLARD *Cdn Yesterdays* 232: Next comes a stunner—a skeleton sleigh, red as fire, drawn by a trotter black as coal. ...

skeleton tent See quote.
1965 *Maclean's* 19 June 17/1: A few skeleton tents, that is to say, poles arranged in the shape of an Indian

wigwam, told us we were following a hunting track made by Indians evidently a long time ago.

701

skevat
skid

skevat *n. Obs.* See **siskawet**.

ski *n.* one of a pair of runners attached to aircraft for landing on snow and ice, especially common on bush planes in the North. See also **winter ski**.
1936 *Cdn Geog. Jnl* XII 35/1: Here again Winter holds the winning cards, both in point of length of season, and the fact that a plane on skis can carry a heavier load than one on pontocns. **1942** TWOMEY & HERRICK *Needle to North* 39: The big two-foot skis, twelve or fourteen feet long, had polished oak runners, golden-colored when they caught the light. **1966** *Commercial Letter* Jan.-Feb. 7/1: The airplane, equipped with skis in winter and pontoons in summer, has broadened knowledge of northern resources and given immense impetus to their development.

skid† *n. Lumbering* **1 a.** one of two or more long poles or logs, often notched or spiked, used as a ramp for raising logs onto a skidway (def. 2a), a sleigh, etc. See also **skidder** (def. 1).
1889 WITHROW *Our Own Country* 397: The logs are loaded on the sleds by being rolled up an inclined plane formed by a pair of "skids". . . . **1943** KOROLEFF *Pulpwood Skidding* 22: Two . . . skids, one on each side of the pile are placed at a convenient angle, and the logs are rolled or pushed up them by hand. **1966** BAITY *Wilderness Welfare* 134: The trees had to be . . . cut into log length and peeled, then skidded in with the team. I rigged up a set of lines and skids to roll them up, one on top of the other, each one notched into the one beneath it.

b. one of two or more long poles or logs, often peeled, placed against a bank or hillside and used as a runway for rolling logs to a beach, *q.v.*, or booming ground, *q.v.*
1902 (1957) GUILLET *Valley of the Trent* 269: . . . teamsters bringing forward their peeled skids gave evidence of the effort yet to come before the monster [a mast] would begin its head-long rush for the landing berth. . . . **1924** BINDLOSS *Green Timber* 178: In fact, if possible, the logs ought to run down [to the river] on skids.

c. one of several long poles or logs forming a bed for a skidway (def. 2a).
1896 ROBERTS *Camp-Fire* 204: First a layer of logs is deposited parallel with the river's edge. Across these, at right angles, are laid a few light poles, technically termed skids. [See **skidded landing** for full quote.] **1966** *Cdn Forest Industries* Aug. 28/3: Piles averaging about 0.65 cunits are made as large as possible on skids of non-merchantable wood.

d. *Hist.* one of a number of transverse poles or logs, usually peeled and greased, forming a road over which logs were dragged from the cutting area. See also **skidroad** (def. 1).
1929 (1956) DIXON *Lumber Industry* 21/3: This meant cutting and placing skids under the logs so the skidding team could haul them to the main skid road. **1942** HAIG-BROWN *Timber* 254: Skid Road . . . is a survival of horse-and-bull-logging days, when roads were built with greased cross skids and the logs hauled directly over these by the teams. **1964** DUFF *Indian History* 86: At times there were shortlived demands . . . for dogfish oil, which was used in huge quantities by early loggers to grease their skids.

e. *Hand-logging* See quote.
1925 WHITE *Skookum Chuck* 201: Tim proceeded methodically to fall and trim several trees of nearly a foot diameter. He cut them into lengths and thrust the skids at various points beneath the raised log. Over and over again he tested their bearing on the ground and the solidity of the support on which their ends rested; for they must sustain the full weight of the log when the jack should be removed.

f. *Slang* **put the skids under,** cause to lose ground, decline, or fail (that is, cause to go downhill).
1922 JENKINS *Timber Pirate* 95: Gildersleeve and his associates put the skids under them by manipulating the market, so that the United States plant manufacturing the North Star's paper-making machinery went into bankruptcy.

g. *Slang* **hit the skids,** lose ground, decline, or fail.
1963 PATTERSON *Far Pastures* 38: The upshot of all this was that the cause of education rather hit the skids in the Clear Hills . . . country. **1966** *Sun* (Vancouver) 18 Apr. 5/4: "Hitting the skids," also "greasing the skids," are both derivatives of the term [skid road].

h. *Slang* **grease the skids** make easier; make things run more smoothly.
1966 [See quote at def. 1g].

2 See **skidway** (def. 2a).
1928 PERRY *Two Reds* 109: . . . the break-out had been set for the following day. The big skid had been completed and they were going to try it out. **1945** CALVIN *Saga* 58: Usually it [the timber] was hauled over snow-roads and left on skids on the beach ready to be rolled down to the water.

3 *Slang, Hist.* See **skidroad** (def. 1).
1918 MACKAY *Trench and Trail* 112: I am call' de "Skookum Kid," Rosemarie; / I'm grease lightning on de skid Yes siree. . . .

skid† *v. Lumbering* **1** slide or drag logs down a prepared slide. Cp. **skid,** *n.* (def. 1b).
1884 *Prince Albert Times* (Sask.) 7 Mar. 3/1: [They were] skidding logs. . . . **1912** SANDILANDS *West. Cdn Dict.* 41/2: Skid, to slide a lumber log down an incline to the skidway, where the logs are temporarily stacked until the big drive. **1950** HALLMAN *Canadians at Work* 46: Sometimes the logs are skidded down a chute on a steep hill [to the water or beach].

2 a. drag or haul logs from a cutting area along a skid trail, *q.v.*, or skidroad (def. 1) with horses, oxen, etc.
1888 (1890) ST. MAUR *Impressions* 258: . . . two men skidding with a team will, if timber grows fairly thick . . . pile eighty logs in a day. **1939** O'HAGAN *Tay John* 182: . . . Olaf Johansen, the big Swede . . . with a crew had been on the place all winter skidding the logs down from the hillsides. . . . **1966** *Cdn Forest Industries* Nov. 45/1: The grandaddy of all lumbering stamps, Newfoundland's 1897 issue featuring cattle skidding logs, was one of a 14-stamp set commemorating the 400th anniversary of its founding.

b. See quote.
1966 *B.C. Logging* 8/1: In both regions [B.C. Coast and Interior] . . . "donkeys" [donkey engines] were used to skid logs along the ground.

c. haul, drag, or transport logs with a skidder (def. 3c).

1964 *Cdn Geog.Jnl* Feb. 72/2: Trees are felled with power saws . . . and a tractor used to skid the logs to the trail. **1966** *Cdn Forest Industries* Oct. 10: [Advert.] Working out of Port Arthur, Ontario, he skids, forwards and loads pulpwood.

3 skid a road, make a skidroad (def. 1). Cp. **corduroy,** *v.*
1959 MILLS *Songs of the Maritimes* 3/2: He said "You look quite happy, all in your little abode. A pox upon the devil, boys! Why didn't you skid the road!"

Skid Blvd. *Slang* See **skidroad** (def. 5).
1963 *Globe and Mail* (Toronto) 29 Apr. 3/4: . . . their humble hovel on Skid Blvd. has been warmed by a coaliverous furnace. . . .

skidded landing *Lumbering* See **skidway** (def. 2c). See also **landing** (def. 1a).
1896 ROBERTS *Camp-Fire* 204: The 'skidded' landing is a much more business-like affair. In this kind of structure the logs are placed systematically. First a layer of logs is deposited parallel with the river's edge. Across these, at right angles, are laid a few light poles, technically termed skids. On these another layer of logs parallel to the water, and so on to the completion of the structure.

skidder *n. Lumbering* **1** a logger employed in building and piling a skidway (def. 2a). See also **skid,** *n.* (def. 1a).
1910 FERGUSON *Janey Canuck* 96: Further on the skidders were at work. They roll the logs up a spiked incline by means of canthooks. **1961** PRICE & KENNEDY *Renfrew* 48: Each gang working together in the woods—logmakers, road cutters, teamsters and skidder—took a lunch in a cotton bag.

2 *Hist.* a logger who built or maintained the skidroad (def. 1).
1956 ANDREWS *Glory Days* 14: These were . . . the skidders who cut short hemlock logs and embedded them crosswise [to make skidroads]. . . .

3 a. a teamster or driver employed in hauling logs from a cutting area.
1957 *Beaver* Spring 40/2: The work goes on the year round and men work in teams of two—a cutter, with his power saw and axe, and a skidder, who bundles the logs and skids them to the road with his horse.

b. See 1942 quote. See also **skidding** (def. 2) and **skidding line.** See picture at **skyline.**
1919 *Camp Worker* 2 June 3/3: [There were] two Ledgerwood [sic] skidders, one yarder, one swing, one ground swing and one roader, and not very high ball. **1942** HAIG-BROWN *Timber* 254: SKIDDER. A yarding machine with a tight sky line, and for this reason able to haul from greater distances than the ordinary yarder with its endless slack sky line.

c. a powerful vehicle used for drawing or hauling logs from a cutting area. See also **skitter.**
1965 *Weekend Mag.* 2 Oct. 3/3: Then it [the "harvester"] lays the denuded trunk on the ground and another machine, called a "skidder," takes it to a landing area where it is cut into pulpwood lengths. **1966** *Cdn Forest Industries* Oct. Back cover: [Advert.] The wheeled skidder has proven its reliability. . . .

skidding† *n. Lumbering* **1** the process of hauling logs from a cutting area. See also **skid,** *v.* (def. 2).

1929 (1956) DIXON *Lumber Industry* 21/3: This meant cutting and placing skids under the logs so that the skidding team could haul them to the main skid-road. **1958** *Maclean's* 10 May 55/1: Oxen were succeeded by horses, and then the skidding of the big logs was done with ship's winches; then came logging railroads, and then huge diesel jobs roaring over fancy logging highways, and cars that rode on cables strung between spar trees, and called skyhooks.

2 the process of yarding logs by means of a skidder (def. 3b).
1966 *B.C.Logging* 8/2: Skidding and slackline operations are examples of the skyline method.

skidding line *Lumbering* See quote. See also **skidding** (def. 2). See picture at **skyline.**
1942 HAIG-BROWN *Timber* 254: A wheeled "bicycle" or carriage runs along this [the skyline], bringing the logs from the woods when drawn by the skidding line, carrying the chokers back out to the waiting chokerman when drawn by the "receding line," which corresponds to the "haulback" of the yarder.

skidding road or **trail** *Lumbering* See **skid trail.**
1942 KOROLEFF *Skidding of Wood* 6/1: Main skidding trails should lead to skidway on as favourable a grade as possible. **1966** *Cdn Forest Industries* Oct. 10: [Advert.] During this time Gill's Cat D4D Tractor roughs out and finishes more than 20 miles of main haul roads plus all skidding roads.

skid grease *Lumbering, Hist.* lubrication used on the skids of a skidroad (def. 1a).
1954 *B.C.Hist.Qtly* XVIII 64: Another item of increased importance was fish oil, especially dogfish-oil, which went to logging companies for skid grease.

Ski-doo or **Skidoo** ['ski'du *or* skı'du] *n.* *Trademark* a motor toboggan, *q.v.,* invented by the Bombardier Company of Valcourt, Quebec. See note at **skidoo.**
1961 *Time* (Cdn ed.) 29 Dec. 10/1: To hear the Eskimos tell it, the Ski-doo is the greatest thing to hit the north since stripped blubber. **1963** *Imperial Oil Rev.* Feb. 20/1: Many mounties, particularly around Churchill, now use the Skidoo for another ironic task; rounding up for destruction stray dogs put out of work by their successor, the mighty little Skidoo. **1964** *Star Wkly* 19 Dec. 13/1: The first of these open-air snowmobiles was the Skidoo, originated by the late Armand Bombardier of Valcourt, Que., seven years ago and intended to make life easier for trappers, foresters and Arctic missionaries.

skidoo or **ski-doo** [skı'du] *n.* [< *Ski-doo,* q.v.] See **motor toboggan** and picture. See also **Ski-doo.**
☛ *This form is fast replacing the original trade name, for the word is becoming something of a generic name for motorized toboggans; the pronunciation is doubtless influenced by that of* **skidoo** *"go away fast," the connotations of which, along with those of* **ski** *and* **do,** *were implied by the manufacturer in coining the term.*
1963 *Globe and Mail* (Toronto) 2 Mar. 30/2: Fishermen . . . were getting to the choice spots the easy way, using skidoos, power toboggans and aircraft. **1966** *Islander* 20 Mar. 16/1: Today's prospector is likely to be seen loading his "skidoo" for his journeys into the wilds. That's a type of snowmobile using tank-like tracks and short ski-runners for steering. **1966** *Beaver* Winter 29/2: A trapper with a fast skidoo is able to cover his lines in a third of the time that it took him to do it by dog-team.

skidooing *n.* driving, or riding in, a motor toboggan, *q.v.,* especially a skidoo.

1966 *North* Nov.-Dec. 38n: . . . a Northerner by choice, she now substitutes skidooing under the Midnight Sun for surfing on sub-tropical seas.

skidoo race a winter sport in which motorized toboggans compete against each other over a cross-country course.

1963 *News of the North* 31 Mar. 1/3: We also are looking forward to a large participation in our new events in the Fiddling and Old timer's jigging contest, and also in the Go Cart and Skidoo races on the ice. **1966** *Kingston Whig-Standard* (Ont.) 11 Feb. 13: [Caption] Gene Bougie . . . takes his ski-doo flying over an obstacle during the International Ski-Doo Race held in Vernon, B.C.

skidroad *n.* **1** *Lumbering, Hist.* a prepared road having greased skids (def. 1d) over which logs were dragged by teams of mules, oxen, or horses. See also **jumper road** and **skidway** (def. 1a).

*c*1889 (1956) DIXON *Lumber Industry* 22/1: They used [about 1864] to have a lot of mules at Moodyville to draw the logs down the skid-roads. . . . **1900** *Canadian Mag.* May 9/2: A shanty town of rough-hewn logs, warmly mudded-up, a band of glossy-coated horses to haul the sawn timber over the skid roads, the inevitable Chinese cook, and the very best of food are the chief adjuncts of a British Columbia logging place. **1937** MULHOLLAND *Forest Resources B.C.* 29: Hauling logs [by four-horse team] on a greased skid road.

2 *Lumbering* a slide or chute down which logs are skidded (def. 1) or dragged by a donkey engine. See also **skidway** (def. 1b).

1924 BINDLOSS *Green Timber* 159: Still the river is small and the channel is blocked by rocks. One would be forced to build a skid-road to easy water. **1958** HEALEY *Alert Bay* 34: A skidroad consisted of three logs let into cross pieces cut away to form a convex in which the logs rested.

3 *Lumbering* See quote.

1942 HAIG-BROWN *Timber* 254: SKID ROAD . . . Now applied to the line along which logs are hauled to the track from any given setting of blocks and rigging. Thus a spar tree, looked down on from the air, is the hub of a complete wheel of skid road "spokes."

4 *Lumbering* an improved logging road along which logs are hauled from the cutting area.

1966 *B.C.Logging* 9/1: A tractor, or rubber-tired skidder vehicle, with an attached metal arch and power winches for lines pulls several logs per trip on short hauls over skid roads to the landing.

5† *Orig.Lumbering, Slang.* Also spelled *Skid Road.* **a.** *Hist.* a low-class district of drinking and gambling houses, brothels, hotels, hiring halls, etc. catering to lumberjacks, seamen, miners, and construction workers.

1906 *Log of the "Columbia"* 8/1: "We'll likely see him in town." "Sure, Mike. He'll be in the Skid road, somewhere." **1966** *Sun* (Vancouver) 18 Apr. 5/4: When the loggers came to Vancouver to blow their stakes they congregated in the area bounded by Carrall and Cordova streets. This area soon became known as the "skid road."

b. a city district characterized by cheap lodging houses, second-hand stores, low-class beer parlors and cafes, mission soup-kitchens, etc. and frequented largely by derelicts, transients, petty criminals, and unskilled workers. See also **skid row** (def. 1).

☛ *The original* **skidroad** *(def. 5a) was Yesler's Way in Seattle, Wash., built in 1852. Certainly the term was in use in British Columbia before 1900, having been used of the Vancouver derelict district for many years. The districts so named in Seattle and Vancouver appear to have grown up near the terminus of actual skidroads (def. 1), becoming gathering places for loggers when unemployed or seeking amusement. After the logging operations receded inland, the name for these districts was retained, becoming a general term for such districts even in cities having no connection with logging.*

1936 MACKENZIE *Living Rough* 206: When I got out I went up to a mission flophouse on the skid-road. **1963** *Vancouver Province* 12 Jan. 1/1: I remember, Mr. Mayor, one cold night 14 years ago when a young Indian girl tried to end her life by jumping out the window of a skidroad hotel. There was interest in cleaning up the skidroad then, too. . . .

6 *Figurative use.* See quote.

1964 *Western Wkly Supp.* 18 Mar. 4/3: These operations [by beavers] often result in unmistakable skid-roads, chutes and canals being developed to expedite their enterprise.

skidroad *v. Lumbering* See **skid**, *v.* (def. 1). See also **skidroad**, *n.* (def. 2).

1958 HEALEY *Alert Bay* 34: The usual method was to skidroad the logs out with this machine [donkey engine].

skid row† [alteration of *skidroad*] *Slang* **1** See **skidroad** (def. 5b).

1950 PALMER *Montreal Confidential* 58: There are tattooing parlors, Skid Row beaneries, and you can get a haircut for a few cents. **1961** *Press* Feb. 11: Two hoboes on skidrow in Vancouver picked a paper up out of the street. **1966** *Sun* (Vancouver) 18 Apr. 5/4: Toronto, New York and other large cities may have a "skid row" but any older generation native Vancouverite winces at the term when applied to our city.

2 on skid row, down and out; in impoverished circumstances.

1965 *Globe and Mail* (Toronto) 2 Sep. W1/4: "A lot of Indians on skid row are the former pupils of church schools," I was told by an Ontario Indian leader. . . .

skid trail *Lumbering* a trail cut through the bush for dragging or hauling logs from the cutting area. See also **skidding road.**

1966 *B.C.Lumberman* June 27/2: Keep skid trails cut well ahead of the skidders, and not too far apart.

skidway *n.* **1** *Lumbering* **a.** *Hist.* See **skidroad** (def. 1).

1892 (1908) DAWSON & SUTHERLAND *Geography* 155: The logs are generally brought from the places where they are cut ("logging camps") to the shore on "skid-ways," after which they are formed into rafts and these are towed to the various mills.

b. See **skidroad** (def. 2).

1922 (1928) PERRY *Two Reds* 111: The logs seemed to leap from position and bounce down the skidway. They plunged like live things into the water.

2 *Lumbering* **a.** a bed or inclined platform of two or more timbers on which logs are piled at a brow (def. 1). See also **skid**, *n.* (def. 2).

1910 FERGUSON *Janey Canuck* 97: The men at "the dump" were piling the logs on huge skidways. . . . **1912** SANDILANDS *West.Cdn Dict.* 45/2: Swamper, the man who cuts and clears the roots from the narrow trails through the forest from the standing timber to the skidway at the edge of the logging road. . . . **1930** BEAMES *Army* 65: When the logs had been cut, they pulled them out of the bush with their teams and piled them on a skidway ready for loading and hauling to the mill. **1961** PRICE & KENNEDY *Renfrew* 50: Logs were skidded to the road and laid up on skidways from where they were loaded on sleighs.

b. the area where logs are thus piled.
1942 KOROLEFF *Skidding of Wood* 6/1: Main skidding trails should lead to skidway on as favourable a grade as possible. . . . **1948** *Ont.Timberworker* 15 Aug. 1/2: Bucking of the trees into desired pulpwood lengths is done by means of a power saw mounted on sawing table at skidway.

c. the skids (def. 1c) and the logs piled on it. See also **skidded landing**.
*c*1963 *New Sounds* 9/1: This unit [a sort of tractor] goes into the forest to get a load of tree length logs, winches the wood to its arch and delivers it to roadside piles of logs called skidways. **1967** *Globe and Mail* (Toronto) 14 Mar. B7/8: . . . trees containing stem rot are difficult to separate once they are in skidways or fed to slashers.

3 an inclined ramp of poles or logs used to move canoes, boats, etc. from a higher to a lower position or vice versa.
1923 SCOTT *Witching of Elspie* 52: "I'm thinking we'll have to make some new skidways afore we haul up the boats for the winter, and you and Luke had better edge up the axes in a way." **1954** PATTERSON *Dangerous River* 93: Loading up next morning, with the canoe rocking and slapping about in the waves, was not easy in spite of a log skidway that I had made. **1956** EVANS *Mountain Dog* 27: He cut green alder poles and laid them for a skidway, then the three of them slid the finished canoe to the water's edge.

skiffer *n. Maritimes* a person who fishes from a skiff, close inshore.
1945 RICHARDSON *We Keep a Light* 244: Most of the big boats fish the more distant grounds, leaving the inner places for "skiffers" and men in other small craft.

skil *n.* See **skilfish**.

skilfish ['skɪlˌfɪʃ] *n.* [< Haida *squil* + *fish*] *Pacific Coast* See **sablefish**. Also *skil*.
1897 TUTTLE *Golden North* 124: One of the most delicious of deep water fish is the skil, or black cod, as it is sometimes called. **1907** HODGE *Bulletin* I Glossary: Skil [is a] local name of the black candle-fish (*Anoplopoma fimbria*), an excellent food fish of the waters of the N. Pacific Coast. . . . **1964** CARL *Marine Fishes B.C.* 48: The sablefish . . . is smoked and sold under the name of "black cod". . . . The sablefish belongs to the skilfish family . . . the giant skilfish . . . may attain a weight of 200 pounds.

'Skim [skɪm] *n. North, Slang, Derog.* See **Eskimo** (def. 1). See also **'Skimo**.
1924 DORRANCE *Never Fire First* 23: Things have come to a pretty pass in the territories when the 'Skims get to biting the hands that are feeding them.

skim diggings *Placer Mining* See 1913 quote.
1897 LEONARD *Gold Fields Klondike* 23: There was a general fear that these might be only "skim diggins." **1913** OGILVIE *Yukon* 138: . . . all mining done in the territory was on the bars and banks of the streams, and most of this was known as skim diggings, that is, only the two to four feet of the surface was worked. . . .

skimmings *n.pl. Placer Mining, Obs.* See quote.
1881 *Edmonton Bull.* 28 Feb. 2/2: A fresh supply [of fine gold] comes down every freshet, and forms what is called skimmings, but is washed out of the banks by the high water.

'Skimo ['skɪmo] *n. Slang* See **Eskimo** (def. 1). See also **'Skim** and **Suckemo**. Also spelled *Skimau*.
[**1817** CHAPPELL *Voyage to H.B.* 92: *Esquimaux*, or *Skimaux*, is an expression of the Cree and other inland *Indians*, signifying "eaters of raw flesh" and they have bestowed this appellation on the maritime *Indians*, in contempt, as there has always been a most deadly hatred between them.] **1956** BERTON *Mysterious North* 182: "[The] bird-watchers . . . used to rush out of the tents with nets, and the 'skimo kids would all look at them and shout: 'Clazy! Clazy!' Before they was through they had all the 'skimos working for them, too."

skimobile ['skɪməˌbil] *n.* [*ski* + auto*mobile*] See **bombardier** and picture.
1955 *Kingston Whig-Standard* (Ont.) 6 Apr. 25/3: With the advent of snowmobiles and skimobiles, most dog teams are now used for dog races.

skin *n. Fur Trade* **1** a unit of value originally equivalent to one made beaver, *q.v.*, or, in some areas, to one martin (def. 2b), and varying in real worth from district to district.
1708 (1957) *Beaver* Winter 14/1: One with the other 10 good skins; that is, Winter Beaver; 12 Skins of the biggest sort, 10 for the mean, and 8 for the smallest. [Oldmixon of HBC on the exchange rate of guns.] *c*1787 MCKENZIE *Reminiscences* 16: I sent Leonard yesterday with two Indians who took 54 skins credit from me; as they do not go your way, I do not send you an account of their credits. **1825** (1931) SIMPSON *Fur Trade* 160: I pressed those indolent rascals to Guide us to Brandon House and offered them the value of 100 Skins for that Service but they declined it with a variety of excuses. **1858** (1863) PALLISER *Journals* 116: The value of the skin differs in different parts of the country, thus a skin in Swan River district is about 2s., and in Upper Saskatchewan it is about 2s. 3d. Again, at Forts Shepherd and Colville, where the influence of the gold begins to be felt, it is 8s. 4d. **1909** CAMERON *New North* 70: From here northward the terms "dollars" and "cents" are unheard. An article is valued at "three skins" or "eight skins" or "five skins," harking back to the time when a beaver-skin was the unit of money. The rate of exchange to-day is from four skins to two skins for a dollar. **1956** KEMP *Northern Trader* 41: These men each had a handful of six-inch hardwood sticks. One man bought a pound of tea, worth at Brochet a dollar and a half. Told that the tea was worth "three skins," the man drew the requisite number of sticks from his hand and laid them on the counter.

2 *Obs.* See **parchment** (def. 2).
1859 (1870) SOUTHESK *Saskatchewan* 52: "Robes," it must be understood [are buffalo] skins with the hair on, as distinguished from those dressed without hair, which are simply known as "skins."

skin boat 1 See **oomiak** and picture.
1811 (1947) *Beaver* Sep. 30/2: Our skin boat . . . was
seized by the vortex, and received a rapid twist. . . .
1830 (1963) DAVIES *Northern Quebec* 115: . . . saw six
kyaks and two large skin boats full of people.
1908 TYRRELL *Sub-Arctics* 126: There were thirty-six
of them, all women and children, piled into one of their
"oomiacks," or skin boats. **1966** *Cdn Geog.Jnl* Sep.
85/3: . . . the drawing made by an old lady called
Pisiolak . . . shows a large skin boat or umiak being
rowed through monster-infested waters.

2 See **kayak**[1] and picture.
1841 *Trans.Lit.& Hist.Soc.Que.* IV 45: After their
expulsion from the Gulf Shores, they occasionally
made predatory excursions against the French—coming
into the Straits, early in the Spring, in skin-boats,—
burning fishing rooms, boats, &c., killing the guardians
or making them fly. **1942** TWOMEY & HERRICK *Needle to
North* 270: Not only was he notable to us, the strangers,
as the first native hunter to venture with a skin boat
among the moving ice floes, but he was notable in
almost every way.

3 *Northwest* See 1956 quote. See also **skin canoe**
(def. 2).
1924 MASON *Arctic Forests* 40: The skin boat is used for
bringing meat from the hunting grounds when the
river is impossible for a raft. The uncured skins are
sewn together with sinew and stretched around a spruce
frame with the hair inwards. **1947** *Beaver* June 10/1: In
the springtime, skin boats are made and the hunters
come in down the Nahanni or down the Beaver River,
with their catch of fur, hunting beaver on the way.
[**1956** LEECHMAN *Native Tribes* 217: Some canoes
consisted of a wooden framework covered with skins,
not unlike the Eskimo umiak. They were used for
bringing loads of furs out of the woods and, when the
Indians reached their destination they took the skins
off the framework . . . but left the wooden frames lying
on the beach.] **1963** PATTERSON *Far Pastures* 251:
. . . they built skinboats out of moosehide and departed
down the Beaver . . . to Nahanni Butte. . . .

skin boot See **kamik**.
1940 *Beaver* Sep. 17/2: In the Eastern Arctic one speaks
of skin-boots or *kumik* never mukluks. . . .

skin canoe 1 *Obs.* See **bull boat**.
1801 (1897) COUES *New Light* I 175: Maymiutch came
down Park river in a skin canoe, with 25 beaver skins.
1858 (1863) PALLISER *Journals* 11 Oct.: Crossed the
river in a skin canoe at sunrise.

2 *Northwest* See **skin boat** (def. 3).
1801 (1933) MCLEOD *Diary* 168: . . . Fallardeau . . .
intends making a Skin Canoe to drift down with the
Ice in hopes of being able to kill a few Beaver. . . .
1825 (1931) SIMPSON *Fur Trade* 156: The object of
bringing so many Horses is to carry our little Baggage,
live on them if Game fails and make Skin Canoes of
their Hides if we find it necessary on account of Indians
Sickness or any other cause to go down the
Assiniboine River after reaching its heads instead of
Crossing the Red River plains. **1922** *Beaver* June 19/2:
In spring we made another large skin canoe and
travelled . . . to Fort Assiniboine and on to Fort
Edmonton.

3 *North* See **kayak**[1] and picture.
1882 GILDER *Schwatka's Search* 78: In summer they
kill a few reindeer from their kyacks, or skin canoes,
while crossing the big lakes in their migrations.
1898 *Trans.Roy.Soc.Can.* IV 2 97: When the sagas
mentioned skin canoes as being used by the inhabitants
of Vinland, it was thought to settle the question of the
site, at least as far as latitude was concerned.

skin carosse *Obs.* See **cariole** (def. 3).
1867 GALTON *Art of Travel* 128: If it [the wind] does
so, no thickness is of any avail in keeping out the cold;
hence the advantage of skin carosses, buffalo robes,
leather sheets, and macintosh rugs.

skin ice *North* thin ice, newly frozen.
1924 FLAHERTY *Eskimo Friends* 121: There was skin
ice over the harbour on several snapping clear days
before September closed. **1937** *Beaver* March 9/2: The
water was calm in the lee of the collar ice, with skin ice
forming in the little bays.

skin lodge† See **teepee**. See also **lodge** (def. 2a).
1910 HAYDON *Riders of Plains* 172: The old skin lodges
were fast disappearing, to give place to neatly
constructed log houses, whitewashed and comfortably
furnished. **1934** GODSELL *Arctic Trader* 121: Across the
river . . . were pitched scores upon scores of conical
skin lodges. . . .

skinner *n. Slang* **1** *Hist.* a teamster, so called
because he figuratively skins his horses, mules,
etc. with his whip. See also **mule-skinner.**
1910 FERGUSON *Janey Canuck* 91: The teamsters are
called "skinners." I met them all on the log road.
1953 *Beaver* June 44/2: The [stage] drivers, or
"skinners," as they were called, wore coonskin coats
with an eight-foot red sash, braided by Quebec
habitants, tied around the waist. **1954** HAGELL *Grass
was Free* 3: A single line attached to the next leader's
bit and passed back along the teams to the teamster or
"skinner."

2 See **catskinner** (def. 1).
1958 *Edmonton Jnl* 24 June 4 6/2: In one day, a skinner
can cut one mile of trail, three miles of trail or ten feet
of trail depending entirely on what he hits.

skinning knife a knife used for skinning animals.
1929 MOBERLY *When Fur was King* 39: At length
Running Wolf drew his heavy skinning knife and
stepping out in front of me, began to brandish it before
my face.

skin stretcher See **stretcher** and picture.
1942 TWOMEY & HERRICK *Needle to North* 310: Near
almost every doorway stood the native skin stretcher,
a semi-circular wooden frame somewhat resembling
a half wagon wheel.

skin tent *Obs.* a tent made of the skins of deer,
moose, buffalo, etc., as certain wigwams, teepees,
or tupeks.
1743 (1949) ISHAM *Observations* 91: One of these [log]
tents 14 foot Long 7 foot wide 3 foot high will
conveniently stove 14 men, they are not so subject to
smoak as the skin tents, and Reckon'd much warmer.
1848 BALLANTYNE *Hudson's Bay* 47: Over the poles (if
he is a good hunter, and has plenty of deer-skins) he
spreads the skin tent, leaving an opening at the top for
the egress of the smoke. **1887** *Trans.Roy.Soc.Can.* V
106: The dwellings of the Innuit are the skin-tent and
the snow-hut. **1951** BULIARD *Inuk* 300: And so, after a
few moments of instruction in that stifling skin tent, to
the music of the maddening, gnattering insects outside,
Komayak the shaman became a Christian.

skin way by basing transactions on the skin
(def. 1) as a unit of barter.

1938 GODSELL *Red Hunters* 74: In spite of the passing of the centuries trading was still very primitive, and was conducted "skin way."

skipertogan ['skɪpɚˌtogən] *n*. [< Algonk.; cf. Cree *kuskipitakun*] *Hist*. See **fire-bag**.
1748 DRAGE *Voyage* I 163: To their Belt, with which they tie up their Coats, they have a bag hanging behind them, which they call a Skipper Toakin, containing a wooden Tinder-box, a Flint, and a Steel. **1795** (1911) HEARNE *Journey* 48: They first begged me to lend them my skipertogan to fill a pipe of tobacco. **1819** MCKEEVOR *Hudson's Bay* 63: He . . . desires them to bury him with his gun, shot-pouch, kettle, as also his skippertogan, containing his flint, steel, and touch-wood. c**1902** LAUT *Trapper* 129: And somewhere, in side pockets or hanging down his back, is his *skipertogan*—a skin bag with amulet against evil, matches, touchwood, and a scrap of pemmican.

skiplane ['skiˌplen] *n*. an airplane equipped with skis, *q.v*.
1941 *Beaver* March 49/1: . . . generally it is necessary to prepare runways before a skiplane can safely come down.

skippertogan or **skipper toggy** See **skipertogan**.

skip rock *Curling* one of a team's last two rocks of an end, usually curled by the skip.
1963 *Calgary Herald* 31 Dec. 21/5: . . . Glen Kemp, throwing skip rocks for Irving, narrowly missed his . . . last-rock takeout. . . .

skirtings *n.pl. Obs*. See quote. Cp. **road allowance** (def. 1).
1849 ALEXANDER *L'Acadie* I 243: . . . having no money to buy land, they turned up the soil on the cleared sides of the roads, called the skirtings, among the stumps, there they sowed corn and planted potatoes.

ski-scooter *n*. See **motor toboggan** and picture.
1963 *Maclean's* 20 Apr. 4/3: The same man asked . . . why Eskimo hunters and fishermen couldn't get government subsidies on motorized ski-scooters since white farmers get subsidies on farm equipment.

ski-sled *n*. See **motor toboggan** and picture.
1965 *Globe and Mail* (Toronto) 14 Dec. B5/2: A white Christmas would probably see him arriving on a motorized ski-sled. . . .

skitawahbo *n*. See **scuttaywabo**.

skitter *n. Lumbering* See **skidder** (def. 3c).
1964 *Atlantic Advocate* July 60/2: Horses are now being replaced by mechanical skitters, four-wheeled machines powered by diesel or gasoline with a winch and cable on the back. The skitters drag the trees to the yards where the timber is sawn into log or pulpwood lengths.

ski-wheel *n*. See quote. Cp. **ski**.
1958 *Edmonton Jnl* 24 June 3 17/8: A pilot on ski-wheels who runs into trouble will pick a lake or river, set down parallel to the shore, and ski neatly up onto the beach before his aircraft loses its forward momentum and sinks.

skookum ['skukəm] *adj*. [< Chinook Jargon < Chahalis *skukm*] *Pacific Coast and Northwest* powerful; strong; big; brave. See also **hyiu-skookum** and **skookum tumtum**.

1891 SETON-KARR *Bear Hunting* 83n: For instance he believed that a bear would hold out its paw towards a man at a distance and feel whether he was *skookum*—brave. **1953** SWANSON *Haywire Hooker* 33: When first I hit the camp, the "Push" he says to me/ "We've got some skookum donkeys and a tough spar-tree,/ It's good level yarding out there in the brush. . . ." **1955** HOBSON *Nothing Too Good* 152: "I don't know why I gotta work hard all year and feed that skookum ugly face for nothing." **1965** *Islander* 14 Nov. 5/1: The girls provided us with a skookum bacon and egg breakfast complete with toast and coffee.

skookum box *Pacific Coast and Northwest* a brig. See also **skookum-house**.
1908 GRAINGER *Woodsmen* 13: [On shipboard] there too was the skookum box—That is, the *strong room* or lock-up.

skookumchuck ['skukəmˌtʃʌk] *n*. [< Chinook Jargon *skookum* strong + *chuck* water] *B.C*.
1 white water; swift current; rapids.
1887 (1888) LEES & CLUTTERBUCK *British Columbia* 184: Accordingly we arranged to meet at Skookumchuck Creek ("the stream of the rapid torrent"). **1922** JOHNSON *Legends* 87: If so, you have listened to the call of the Skookum Chuck, as the Chinook speakers call the rollicking, tumbling streams that sing their way through the canyons with a music so dulcet, so insistent, that for many moons the echo of it lingers in your listening ears. . . .
2 tidal rapids; tide rip.
1940 PINKERTON *Three's a Crew* 102: Skookum chuck means tidal rapids. **1958** LINDSAY *Cariboo Story* 6/2: But eastward across the skookumchuck on the mainland up the Fraser River . . . the . . . tribes watched beside their game trails. . . . **1958** WATTERS *B.C.Cent.Anthol*. 216: Sometimes as many as six services are held on a Sunday and between any two such services may be miles of stormy water and a couple of *skookum chucks*. . . .

skookum-house *n. Pacific Coast and Northwest* jail; prison. See also **skookum box**.
c**1870** (1873) LUNDIN-BROWN *Klatsassan* 153: . . . it was only after much *waw-waw* (parley) and sundry threats of the skookkum-house (gaol) . . . that one of them was got to undertake to carry him. **1907** CROSBY *An-ko-me-nums* 131: Turning to Tom I said, "I might have had you put in the 'skookum house' " (as they call the jail), "but I want you to do better. . . ." **1965** *Islander* 9 May 6/2: In 1872, Frederick Brent was appointed Justice of the Peace and a skookum-house (jail) was built on his land.

skookum tumtum *Chinook Jargon* **1** See quotes.
c**1862** (1935) STRANG *Pioneers in Canada* 248: The title of "Scokum tum-tum Siwash," or "Strong-hearted Savage," which he was much given to insist upon as being one of his special designations, often seemed to me not inaptly to describe him. **1884** CHITTENDEN *Queen Charlotte Is*. 65: . . . they had inquired . . . if I had a skookum tumtum (a stout heart). . . . **1958** *Beaver* Winter 27/2: *Heehee tumtum* was a merry heart, and a sad one, *sick tumtum*. The word came not from tummy, but from the beat, or thump of the heart, and conveyed mental attitudes. *Skookum tumtum* naturally meant brave.
2 See quote.
1915 CUMMING *Skookum Chuck* 19: The cultus Indian was at Lillooet when this skookum tumtum (good thought) occurred to him.

skunk† *n.* [< Algonk.] **1** See 1958 quote. See also **polecat.**

☞ *The name also applies to related animals, as the little spotted skunk,* Spilogale gracilis, *found in southern B.C.* [1620 MASON *Briefe Discourse* A iv^v^: The Beastes are Ellans, Follow-deare, Hares, Beares harmeles, Wolues, Foxes, Beauers, Catnaghenes excellent, Otteres, and a small beast like a Ferret whose excrement is Muske.] 1743 (1949) ISHAM *Observations* 20: a Sculk She cow wuck. 1792 (1911) SIMCOE *Diary* 141: Among the animals there was a skunk like a polecat, with black and white marks. 1872 DASHWOOD *Chiploquorgan* 185: The skunk ... is often met with, the body eighteen inches long; in colour white with a black streak down the middle. 1958 *Encyc.Can.* IX 326/2: Skunk (*Mephitis mephitis*), a member of the weasel family, the size of a large house cat. Black, with two white stripes on its back, the skunk is well known for its ability to throw a jet of scent up to a distance of 15 feet.

2 the fur of this animal.
1880 *Edmonton Bull.* 13 Dec. 3/1: Skunk, bear beaver and otter are in good demand for local use, and good lots will bring big prices. 1956 KEMP *Northern Trader* 106: Too, there were foxes and bear hides, skunk, ermine, and wolf.

3 the flesh of this animal used as food.
1921 HEMING *Drama of Forests* 278: In a fourth [pot] bubbled choice pieces of beaver, muskrat, lynx, and skunk.

4 *Figurative uses.*
1848 *Ottawa* [Bytown] *Advocate* 13 June 3/3: "Well sur, it was agreed between thim that the writher was to go at it in the colliams o' the *Packet;* and play Skunk agin the office-howldhers wud the intinshun of pisenin thim out cumplately." 1883 *Brandon Blade* (Man.) 4 Oct. 10/3: There is an odor of skunk in the First ward that cannot be eliminated until there is a new civic Council and a change in the duplex. 1903 (1913) CULLUM *Devil's Keg* 159: "... Damned scoundrel' slidin' from yer flannel face is like a coyote roundin' on a timber wolf, an' a coyote ain't as low down as a skunk...."

5 a. *Slang* a mean, contemptible person; a "stinker."
1825 *Colonial Advocate* (York [Toronto]) 3 Mar. 2/5: In reply to Mac's first astounding epistle, out came this government skunk, opened his infernal water recess, and discharged on the Queenston hero such a torrent that even at thirty miles off, it offended the delicate senses of my beloved sister, Miss Griselda. 1954 CONSTANTIN-WEYER *Half-Breed* 126: "... But you, Pierre Lavallée, you bloody pest, you dirty skunk!..."

b. a smelly, slow, inferior locomotive.
1953 MOON *Saskatchewan* 39: Known at times in the past as the "shuttle" and the "skunk" because of the form of locomotion, it may be near the bottom rung of the railway ladder.

skunk *v. Slang* fail or cause to fail (in an attempt to get or achieve something).
1961 *Sun* (Vancouver) 10 Jan. 10/1: We could almost taste the steelhead Sunday after finding the little "Q" (river) so prime but we were skunked. 1963 *Ibid.* 20 June 25/1: One of my partners boated and released an eight-incher and the other worthy, who fished less than us, was skunked.

skunk-bear† *n.* See **wolverine** (def. 1).
1911 ROGERS *Wild Animals* 112: The wolverine, largest of all the weasels, looks more like a bear and a skunk combined. "Skunk-bear" is one of his many nicknames. 1957 *Beaver* Autumn 41/1: Of all pelts brought in—which included ... wolverine or "skunk bear"—beaver remained supreme.

skunk cabbage 1† a variety of arum, *Symplocarpus foetidus,* of eastern North America, characterized by its giving off a strong odor when bruised.
1860 *Trans.Lit.& Hist.Soc.Que.* IV 20: Those which are commonly called the FIRST FLOWERS of spring, are the Mayflower, the Skunk Cabbage, and the Hepatica. 1959 MACLENNAN *Watch* 262: April had turned into May and the world was bright and clear: cool air and warm sun, a powder of buds on the hardwoods, fields of skunk cabbage green against the heavy viridian of spruce and fir....

2 a plant of the Rocky Mountain region, *Lysichiton camtschatensis,* so called because of its resemblance to the skunk cabbage of the East. See also **skunk lily.**
1869 *Mainland Guardian* (New Westminster, B.C.) 20 Nov. 1/5: Barnston skinned the "bar" and cutting off a ham, plastered it thickly with mud, skunk cabbage leaves, and more mud, then put it in the fire for an hour and a half, when we found it a dish fit for a king. 1960 *Time* (Cdn ed.) 7 Mar. 11/1: The Victoria Natural History Society delightedly announced that ... skunk cabbage also had made their appearance—ten days to two weeks ahead of schedule.

skunk lily See **skunk cabbage** (def. 2).
1938 CASH *I Like B.C.* 66: Charred and blackened ugliness everywhere ... Occasionally a patch of bracken, brightly green, freakishly untouched by fire. Skunk lilies in a marshy pool.

skunk oil *Slang* See quote.
1955 *Maclean's* 19 Mar. 54: Skunk oil [is] ... low grade fuel producing more odor than power.

sky *n. Obs.* See **Sky Blue.**
1821 (1939) ROBERTSON *Correspondence* 175: The skyes bundled in with everything that was proposed.

sky agent *Slang* See **sky-pilot.**
1903 RICHARDSON *Colin* 78: "It all comes uv thet confounded travellin' sky agent a-stayin' here for supper."

Sky Blue *Fur Trade, Hist.* an officer of the Hudson's Bay Company, so called from the color of the uniform. See also **Blue** (def. 2) and **sky-blue.** Cp. **Grey.**
1821 (1939) ROBERTSON *Correspondence* 175: The sky blues ... swelled at the word "commission." 1830 (1947) HARGRAVE *Correspondence* 47: I have even beat up the quarters of some of the old Sky Blues on their own territories. 1955 RICH in BLACK *Journal* lxxxiii: Black instantly took offence and, in accordance with his pledge, proceeded to act "as honestly and zealously for" the flouted Sky Blues as he had once "acted honestly and zealously against them": he challenged Douglas to a duel.

sky-blue *adj. Hist.* representative of or identified with the Hudson's Bay Co. See also **Sky Blue.**

1849 (1932) MCLEAN *Notes* 386: His old friends of the Hudson's Bay, or "sky-blue" party, were gradually received into favour.... [**1913** COWIE *Adventurers* 116: ... we had donned the sky-blue capotes and wrapped the red sashes around our waists....]

sky-climber *n. Slang* a religious person.
1911 KNOWLES *Singer* 110: "Now ... if there's any indiwidual here ... that really wants to go to heaven, let 'em stand up on their hind legs'—an' he waited—an' the sky-climbers jes' gripped their seats tighter'n death an' hung on."

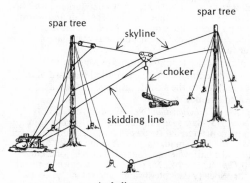

spar tree
spar tree
skyline
choker
skidding line

A skyline system

skyline *n. Lumbering* See 1942 quote. See also **high-lead** and **high-line logging**.
1925 PHILIP *Crimson West* 144: Preparing the "spar-tree" for "high-lead," or "sky-line" rigging, is the most spectacular and thrilling performance in the logging industry. **1942** HAIG-BROWN *Timber* 254: SKY LINE. In the case of a skidder, a heavy cable stretched from the spar tree out to a "back tree" at the far edge of the setting. A wheeled "bicycle" or carriage runs along this, bringing the logs from the woods when drawn by the skidding line, carrying the chokers back out to the waiting chokermen when drawn by the "receding line," which corresponds to the "haulback" of the yarder. In the case of a yarder the sky line is the same as the main-line, going from the spar tree through a block attached to a tree stump at the back of the setting, and is itself coupled directly to the haulback line. **1956** ANDREWS *Glory Days* 49: Matt [Hemmingsen] was also the man who rigged up the first skyline system ever used in the woods. This was in 1914 at Wardroper Bay on Cowichan Lake.... **1963** *Press* Apr. 9:

> There's where the donkeys puff and strain
> As they pull the logs on the road
> And the skyline moans, as if in pain
> As it bears its heavy load.

sky-pilot *n. Slang* a clergyman; missionary; chaplain. See also **sky agent**.
1889 MACLEAN *Indians* 201: ... The "Sky-pilot" and "Gospel-grinder" dispense "soul-grub" to the cow-boys and adventurous settlers among the foot-hills of the Rocky Mountains.... **1907** *Eye Opener* (Calgary) 26 Jan. 3/1: A couple of partially crazy sky pilots ... spoke in a most disparaging and insulting manner of the Mormons of Alberta.

1955 HARDY *Alta Anthol.* 90: When Alberta was young, a missionary was also hunter, doctor, teacher, civilizer, counsellor and friend, prophet and statesman. They were a sturdy breed, most of those early "sky pilots."

slack *n. Obs.* thread.
1852 MOODIE *Roughing It* 113: I guess if you won't lend me the gown, you will let me have some black slack to quilt a stuff petticoat, a quarter of a pound of tea and some sugar; and I will bring them back as soon as I can. **1863** WALSHE *Cedar Creek* 100: A store where everything was sold, from a nail or a spool of 'slack' to a keg of spirits or an almanac....

Slackers *n. Naval Slang* Halifax, Nova Scotia, so called because of the relatively slack discipline ashore following duty at sea.
1945 PUGSLEY *Saints* 126: The war suddenly felt a whole lot closer than it ever had back in "Slackers" or Newfie.

slahal [slə'hɑl] *n.* [see 1863 quote] See **lahal**.
1863 GIBBS *Chinook Dict.* 24: Sla-hal, n. Chinook [not Jargon] Etlaltlal. A game played with ten small discs, one of which is marked. **1965** WILSON *No Man Stands Alone* 64: That night the Indians rounded off the day by playing Lahal, sometimes called Slahal or Pageesee.

slapshooting *n. Hockey* the practice or skill of making slapshots.
1963 O'BRIEN *Hockey* 83: "... why don't you, as coach, order him to cut down on his slapshooting?"

slapshot *n. Hockey* a fast, not always accurate, shot made by hitting the puck after bringing the stick through a short, powerful arc.
1962 *Globe and Mail* (Toronto) 28 Dec. 33/1: ... Mahovlich, who unleashed one of his slap-shots from about twenty feet, saw it stopped by Gordie Howe.... **1966** *Canadian* 29 Jan. 7/2: What occurs to almost every veteran hockey fan who's seen the Russians play, is how closely their play resembles the Canadian game of 20 ... years ago; shorter passes, no slapshots, no head-manning the puck.

slash *n.* **1 a.** *Hist.* See **slashing** (def. 1b).
1825 (1916) SELLAR *Narrative* 102: ... we have been here scarce three months and there is a great slash. **1840** GOSSE *Cdn Naturalist* 297: The first quarter of a mile lay through a very rough slash.... **1849** ALEXANDER *L'Acadie* I 272: After various difficulties ... getting with our horses into "slashes" or parts of the forest cut down ... we at last reached the small wooden hostel.... **1959** STEWART & FRENCH *Ask No Quarter* 24: My Grandmother Campbell was brave and bonny. She could work in the slash with the men and rush home a few minutes early to prepare the bannocks and bacon.

b. the felled trees, brush, etc. on a piece of land in process of being cleared. See also **slashing** (def. 1c).
1841 *Bytown* [Ottawa] *Gaz.* 17 Feb. 1/3: To end of month clearing up old "slash," which term has previously been defined. **1917** MILLER *New Era* 85: In Quebec and British Columbia, settlers who desire to burn their slash must now obtain permits from the Government forest ranger, who supervises the burning.... **1944** MOWAT *Carrying Place* 35: They cleared, stumped and ploughed three quarters of the eight hundred acres, and burned huge pyramids of slash and trunks that lit the autumn skies at night.... **1954** RADDALL *Muster of Arms* 226: "Late in the fall he piled the old dry slash from his choppin's around the stumps, and set it afire, and burned the stumps off."

c. a tract of land from which trees have been
cleared for a townsite.

709

**slash
slashing**

1961 ROUGH *Totem Trail* 20: In 1912, there was nothing
there [Usk, B.C.] except a slash along the Skeena River
and construction of the right-of-way of the Grand
Trunk Pacific. . . .

2 downed timber and other debris left in a forest by
wind and storm. See also **slashing** (def. 2) and
windfall (def. 2).

1920 *Rod and Gun in Canada* Nov. 303: I figured
that by the time I hit the bush I could see in the
distance, I should have covered at least two miles of
the goldarnedest blowdowns, slash and other debris
that a man ever set eyes on. **1942** RADDALL *His Majesty's
Yankees* 210: "Ye can strike a spark there that'll set the
whole province aflame like a fire in dry slash. . . ."
1965 *Wildlife Rev.* Mar. 19/2: Cougars travel over long
ranges and are found in various ecological types of
terrain such as slash, mature forest and second growth.

3 a. *Lumbering* a tract of land littered with debris
following logging operations. See also **timber slash.**
1923 WILLIAMS *Spinning Wheels* 154: . . . raspberries are
found oftenest in what are called "slashes" in the woods,
where the older timber has been cut down, and the new
has not yet grown up to replace it. **1956** RADDALL
Wings 87: . . . there'd been some damage from fire in
the old slash afterward. **1963** *Sun* (Vancouver) 23 Nov.
21/1: The rolling hills along the Kootenay, Bull and
Elk rivers are parklike with their copses of fir,
tamarack, poplar and willow . . . left standing in old
log slashes or burns.

b. the debris left after a logging operation. See also
slashing (def. 4).
1945 CALVIN *Saga* 173: The timber-maker did not fell
a tree to save it from fire—rather he left "slash" in the
forest which greatly increased the risk of fire. **1966** *B.C.
Lumberman* June 32/3: . . . it has been a common
practice to burn slash . . . ever since the introduction
of high-lead logging.

4 *Hockey* an instance of slashing (def. 4).
1965 *Globe and Mail* (Toronto) 3 Dec. 14/1: . . . press
box witnesses saw the infraction as more of a hook or
slash.

slash *v.* clear land of trees and brush. See also
slashing (def. 1).
1821 (1960) MCCULLOCH *Stepsure Letters* 20: . . . he had
slashed down a large piece of wood; and now he
determined to raise a crop which would do something
for him in the fall. **1889** WITHROW *Our Own Country*
362: The native forest had been "slashed" in that
particular locality, and workmen passed from point to
point by the help of the fallen trees. . . . **1931** *Beaver*
Sep. 276: . . . and five acres of virgin land were slashed,
grubbed, broken, and double-disced, in readiness for
the prospective occupant. **1962** FRY *Ranch on the Cariboo*
66: Sometimes we built fence or slashed brush to
extend the yard.

Slasher *n. Slang, Hist.* See 1961 quote.
1922 CODY *King's Arrow* 25: You are employed by the
slashers to spy upon the King's men, engaged in the
lawful business of cutting masts for His Majesty's
navy. They are well named, for they are slashing
everywhere. *Ibid.* 156: "Micmac; all sam' Slasher.
Fight King George." **1961** *Press* Apr. 6: Who can tell
who were the "SLASHERS," a derogatory name applied
to an insurrectionist group in Western Nova Scotia
(now New Brunswick) in the late 18th century? They
. . . tried to enforce squatters' rights and fought the
parcelling out of what they regarded as their own land
to the United Empire Loyalists.

slasher *n. Lumbering* See 1963 quote. See also
slash saw.
1948 *Ont.Timberworker* 15 Aug. 3/1: The crews on the
Slashers and in camps where Slashers operate, (with
the exception of the cutters who are paid piece-work
rates) receive a bonus. **1963** WILKINSON *Abitibi* 4:
Slasher. A series of saws that cut 8' or 16' logs into 4'
length, the size utilized in the pulp mill process.

slash fence *Obs.* a fence made from slash
(def. 1b).
1896 GOURLAY *Hist.Ottawa* 6: This was the brush or
slash fence.

slash fire a fire in slash (def. 3b).
1964 *Sun* (Vancouver) 10 Apr. 23/1: . . . most of it has
been logged off, much of it recently, this completely
unspoiled Gold Valley is in startling contrast to the
vast area of the north bank of the Fraser that is seared
by power saws and slash fires.

slashing *n.* **1** *Hist.* **a.** See quotes. See also **slash,** *v.*
1834 FERGUSSON *Practical Notes* 42: A mode of chopping
is in use hereabouts, termed slashing. It consists in
merely prostrating the trees, without any further
operation for a season, and then at leisure consuming
the whole by fire. It is a cheap method, and may be
done for four dollars an acre, instead of twelve; but its
success depends upon the kind and condition of the
wood. **1899** MACKAY *Pioneer Life* 167: There were three
ways by which the first settlers cleared the land. The
first was called "slashing." The farmer slashed the
trees down in winnows, and let them thus lie on the
ground for three or four years. Then in dry weather he
would set fire to the winnows, and soon the whole
slashing of ten or twelve acres would be a great mass of
smoke and flame. **1963** GUILLET *Pioneer Farmer* I 309:
Another easy and cheap method was "slashing" . . .
felling the trees and allowing them to stay where they
fell for a season or two.

b. a tract of land prepared for clearing in this way.
See also **slash,** *n.* (def. 1a).
1905 SCHERCK *Pen Pictures* 49: In order to hasten the
clearing of the land, and save labor, the farmer would
often convert part of his woods into a "slashing," by
chopping the trees down, and allowing them to remain
for a few years in this fallen condition, to be acted upon
by decay. **1912** CONNOR *Corp.Cameron* 269: At the
"slashing" the wagon ruts faded out and the road
narrowed to a single cow path. . . .

c. See **slash,** *n.* (def. 1b).
1957 BARRATT *Coronets* 42: The men had waited for a
day when the wind blew away from the buildings to
fire our slashings.

2 See **slash,** *n.* (def. 2).
1928 TAVERNER *Belvedere, Alta* 104: Mountain Bluebird.
Not uncommon in the burnt spruce and slashings, but
scarce elsewhere.

3 *Lumbering* See **slash,** *n.* (def. 3b).
1964 *Islander* 20 Sep. 5/2: Another small fire was
burning in slashing on the west side of Reef Point.

4 the operation of clearing away brush and trees,
as in making way for a road, power line, etc.
1955 HOBSON *Nothing Too Good* 54: Two Nazko Indian
friends of mine from Trout Lake country, and Peter

were willing to contract the slashing job for a hundred dollars. **1960** ELLIOTT *Klondike* 2n: The slashing had been completed from Quesnel to Telegraph Creek, but by 1898 would be of questionable character. **1965** *Star Wkly* 13 Feb. 6/3: Bob had . . . run a slashing crew . . . and had been a mine manager.

5 *Hockey or Lacrosse* the illegal action of striking or swinging at an opposing player with the stick.
1958 *Herald-Tribune* (Grande Prairie, Alta) 28 Feb. 5/6: Bryan McCurdy . . . and Bill Oakford . . . went off together for roughing and slashing at the 18:55 mark. **1965** *Globe and Mail* (Toronto) 27 Dec. 22/1: He dismissed Shack for a two-minute sin of slashing, rather than a five-minute sentence for spearing. . . . **1966** *Ibid.* 20 June 19/2: Finegan [was] upset by a slashing call in the second period. . . .

slashing camp a work camp for a crew engaged in slashing (def. 4).
1955 *Crag and Canyon* 8 Apr. 1/1: Further complaint was made that peddlars had been selling clothing in the slashing camps without license and travelling on closed roads.

slash saw See **slasher.**
1881 *Progress* (Rat Portage [Kenora], Ont.) 15 July 1/5: The upper story or saw floor contains one large circular for dimension stuff, two slash saws. . . .

slaughter (down) *v. Obs.* of trees, cut down, especially wastefully.
1830 MOORSOM *Letters N.S.* 277: The timber is found about fifteen miles up the Shelburne River, where large quantities of it are (in the phraseology of the woodsmen,) "slaughtered down," and floated with the stream, when the waters rise with the freshets in the spring.

slaughter sale See quote.
1888 (1890) ST. MAUR *Impressions* 12: A "Slaughter Sale" of dry goods or a "Slaughter Sale of Babies' Buggies" were startling announcements over shop windows; these were, I found, the terms used for clearing sales, dry goods, meaning silks, muslins, &c; babies buggies an Americanism for children's perambulators.

slave beaver *Obs.* See quote.
☞ *The reference is to an old myth to the effect that certain beavers, introverts perhaps, were enslaved by their more vigorous fellows.*
1795 (1911) HEARNE *Journey* 245: With respect to the inferior, or slave-beaver, of which some Authors speak, it is, in my opinion, very difficult for those who are best acquainted with the economy of this animal to determine whether there are any that deserve that appellation or not.

slave killer See quote.
1956 LEECHMAN *Native Tribes* 305: Among some of the west coast people there were actually special stone clubs known as "slave killers" which were used for this purpose.

Slave Kit *North* a heated mobile sled in which are stored the tools, equipment, battery bank, etc. that may be needed on a cross-country journey by a train of vehicles.

1949 *Report of DME Test Team* IA 1: The team's tool kits were stowed behind the seats in the Penguin and fast moving spare parts were kept in the Slave Kit.

Slave Market *Slang* an office of the National Employment Service.
1960 *Voice of the Idle Worker* 8 Feb. 2/2: And the chances are, that he will be a regular customer at the SLAVE MARKET for a few months.

slay *n.* See **sleigh.**

sled *n.* **1** See **dog-sled** and picture. See also **sledge.**
1577 (1889) HAKLUYT *Voyages* 92: They . . . keepe certeine doggs not much unlike Wolues, whiche they yoke . . . to a sled. . . . **1778** (1934) TURNOR *Journal* 216: The ice being rough and the snow deep [I] was obliged to haul our sleds the dogs not being able. **1858** (1863) PALLISER *Journals* 120: It was with great difficulty . . . that we got the sleds up the bank, which was 240 feet high. . . . **1956** TOLBOOM *Arctic Bride* 87: Still the teams continued to arrive. The grind of sled runners, the pit-patter of dogs' feet and the swish of the long whips.

2 *Obs.* See **cariole** (def. 2a).
1784 (1954) *Moose Ft Jnls* 89: Anthony King sewing sleds and making traces for the Dogs.

3 See **stoneboat** and picture.
1872 DASHWOOD *Chiploquorgan* 89: Every man can handle an axe, mend his waggon, and build his own "sled"—a kind of rough sleigh, for hauling timber and other heavy stuff. **1934** DENNIS *Down in N.S.* 214: The *Black Hawk* . . . was built on Butler's Hill, some distance from the shore. It was conveyed to the shore by fifty oxen, after first being lowered onto a huge sled.

4 *North* See **caboose** (def. 5b).
1952 PUTNAM *Cdn Regions* 497/2: Tractors pulled large sleds slowly over this winter road to Hay River settlement. . . . **1957** *Kingston Whig-Standard* (Ont.) 29 March 13/5: A cat-swing is a convoy of three tractors and their sleds. A bunkhouse for the men is among the cargo-laden sleds.

sled anchor *North* an anchor used to moor a dog-sled, *q.v.* See also **sled** (def. 1).
1946 *Beaver* March 36/1: They just threw the sled anchor and brought up. . . . **1951** BULIARD *Inuk* 96: Before I pulled up my sled anchor, I turned and yelled at them a vigorous "Ilanitok!" . . . "We shall see each other again!"

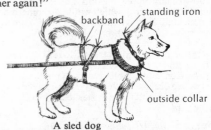

A sled dog

sled dog 1 a dog, as an Eskimo dog, *q.v.* used to pull a sled (def. 1), especially in the North. See 1577 quote at **sled** (def. 1). See also **hauler, sledge-dog,** and **sleigh dog.**
1692 (1929) KELSEY *Papers* 21: Now as for a woman they [Indians] do not so much mind her for they reckon she is like a Slead dog or Bitch when she is living & when she dies they think she dyes to Eternity. . . .
1777 (1792) CARTWRIGHT *Journal* II 277: . . . finding my sled-dog lame, I deferred my journey and went to Pinchgut Point and Alder Head. **1910** HAYDON *Riders*

of Plains 270: For the ten sled dogs 30 lb. pemmican and 500 lb. fresh deer meat was needed, giving an average of 3 lb. per dog per day. **1966** *Kingston Whig-Standard* (Ont.) 28 Feb. 10/2: Even Whitehorse city dogs, jealously maddened by the adulation that the visiting sled-dogs were receiving, fell upon Washington's two huskies and reduced them to a state, nigh onto hamburger.

2 See 1896 quote. See also **steer-dog**.
1896 RUSSELL *Far North* 15: The "sled dog," usually the heaviest in the team is trained to swing the head of the sled away from obstacles; it is important that he should be well trained when following a crooked track through the forest. **1903** LONDON *Call of Wild* 55: Dave was wheeler or sled dog; pulling in front of him was Buck, then came Sol-leks; the rest of the team was strung out ahead, to the leader, which position was filled by Spitz. **1921** HEMING *Drama of Forests* 81: Off they went, the two leading dogs pulling the wolf along from in front, while the sled-dog nipped him from behind and encouraged him to go ahead.

sledge† *n.* See **dog-sled** and picture. See also **sled** (def. 1).
1703 (1905) LAHONTAN *New Voyages* I 406: Sledges are a conveniency for travelling, built . . . upon two pieces of wood. . . . **1811** (1820) HARMON *Journal* 214: Our goods were drawn on sledges by dogs. **1924** FLAHERTY *Eskimo Friends* 28: A sledge or more of natives had arrived.

sledge cover *Obs.* See **sled wrapper**.
1852 SUTHERLAND *Baffin's Bay* II 4: The sailmakers had to make . . . sledge-covers eight, of which two were for dog sledges . . . forty sets of dog harness. . . .

sledge-dog *n.* See **sled dog** (def. 1).
1864 HALL *Life with Esquimaux* II 238: Their mother was an excellent sledge-dog of our team.

sled (or **sledge**) **line** a line used in the trappings of a dog-sled, especially to lash down the load.
1896 WHITNEY *On Snow-Shoes* 214: Every man in the party but myself was more or less severely snow-blind, one or two so badly as to necessitate their holding on to a sledge-line for guidance. **1896** RUSSELL *Far North* 121: One of them grasped the sled line to show me how to straighten up the load, and tugged and hauled and tugged again without producing the slightest effect. **1905** (1910) HAYDON *Riders of Plains* 264: The skin is made into boots, clothing, and sled lines; the fat used as oil for their stone lamps—the meat as a rule is eaten raw.

sled rail See **gee-pole**.
1925 *Beaver* Dec. 23: When all was ready and we were seated and hanging onto the sled rail, the rope was let go and we shot out like a stone from a catapult.

sled road or **trail 1** *Obs.* See **winter road** (def. 2a).
1826 (1916) SELLAR *Narrative* 110: Spent three days on the sledroad and the three families joined in the work.

2 a way for dog-sleds, especially a train of such sleds.
1870 *Wkly Manitoban* 10 Dec. 2/4: In a day or so a sled-road will be open to the Lake of the Woods, and by the first of January, the main road will be cut through. **1924** MASON *Arctic Forests* 233: A practised man can chop a sled-trail through an apparently impassable jam surprisingly quickly.

sled-sheet *n.* See **sled wrapper**.
1928 WALDEN *Dog-Puncher* 116: A wind-break of a sled-sheet or boughs was then constructed. . . .

sled-team *n.* a dog-team, *q.v.* often including the driver and fore runner, *q.v.*, as well as the dogs.
1910 HAYDON *Riders of Plains* 213: In olden days in the winter a sled team used to leave Fort Garry in Manitoba and proceed along the Red River to Lake Winnipeg. **1914** BINDLOSS *Intriguers* 130: . . . Clarke's friends were unable to find food enough for sled-teams. **1928** FREEMAN *Nearing North* 311: A 'bred' fisherman by the name of Colin Mackenzie assured me that the most terrible mess-up he had ever seen occurred when two six-dog sled-teams got to fighting in a canoe containing a score of sturgeon lines.

sled-tender *n.* *Lumbering, Obs.* See quote.
1891 OXLEY *Chore-Boy* 66: . . . the "sled-tenders" . . . saw that the loads [of logs] were well put on. . . .

sled trail See **sled road**.

sled train *North* See **cat-train**.
1952 PUTNAM *Cdn Regions* 161: Logs are hauled by sled trains to the frozen rivers where they are piled to await spring break-up. **1963** MORTON *Kingdom of Can.* 447: New means were already being rapidly developed in the sled trains drawn by caterpillar tractors (the "cat swings") over winter roads, and above all in the development of "bush flying."

sled wrapper *North* a sheet of canvas or tarpaulin used to cover up the load on a dog-sled. See also **sledge cover, sled-sheet, toboggan sheet, toboggan wrapper,** and **wrapper**.
1933 MERRICK *True North* 226: It proved to be . . . a big, dome-shaped *meetchwop* of canvas sled wrappers and tents and skins over a frame of bent willows. **1941** *Beaver* Mar. 10/2: Lashing ropes for the load are necessary, sled wrappers are used in the Eastern Arctic. . . .

sleep† *n.* in Indian and Eskimo parlance, a day, that is the time between one time of sleeping and the next; the distance travelled in this lapse of time.
[**1743** (1949) ISHAM *Observations* 63: How many nights have you been a comming (or how many nights did you sleep.)] **1896** WHITNEY *On Snow-Shoes* 182: The one "sleep" did not bring us up to the caribou, but it took us north to the lodge of another Indian who had been more fortunate than we. **1938** *Beaver* June 30/2: I was warned to take more "gas" or we would never get back by motor; the lake was "seven sleeps long." **1951** GILLIS & MYLES *North Pole* 37: ". . . attempt the journey of seven or eight sleeps for a visit, a sleep meaning one day's travel and one night's rest on the trail."

sleeper *n.* **1** *Lumbering, Obs.* See **bedding timbers**.
1863 WALSHE *Cedar Creek* 103: Sam explained the structure when the waggon had done bumping over it: trunks of trees had been laid along the road as "sleepers" in three continuous lines. . . .

2 *Maritimes* a large root or other piece of wood partially buried in the soil.
1954 BRUCE *Channel Shore* 140: The thing Grant had noticed from the first was that if the plough-point caught in a boulder, Stewart would go at the rock with his hands. If a sleeper needed shifting he would strain at the heavy timber without waiting for help.

3 *Cdn Football* See **sleeper pass**.
1966 *Globe Mag.* 20 Aug. 7/3: But it took an imaginative play . . . to sound the knell of the sleeper.

sleeper pass or **play** *Cdn Football* a play in which a player moves to the sidelines as if moving off the field during a group substitution, then moves ahead on a quick play to receive a pass unchallenged by a defending player. See also **sleeper** (def. 3).
1966 *Globe Mag.* 20 Aug. 7/3: Part of Canadian football folklore is the sleeper pass Keith Spaith threw . . . in 1948. *Ibid.* The sleeper play was one casualty.

sleep in† lie in; stay in bed longer than is customary.
1935 *Beaver* Dec. 66/2: On Sundays the chief guide usually allows his voyageurs to sleep in, which means that instead of getting up at four o'clock they get up about six-thirty. **1959** *Maclean's* 15 Aug. 23/1: Saturday morning the boys and I let Merna and Willa sleep in while we go to see Demi-tasse, as we had made a beauty-parlor appointment for him.

sleeping-bag *n.* a warmly lined bag made of skins, blanketing, canvas, nylon, etc., used mainly when camping. See also **shinigbee** and **sleeping poke**.
[**1821** (1900) GARRY *Diary* 97: First, Canvas which forms the Cover of the Bed and our Seat in the Canoe. Then a Bed of Blankets sewn together which form an Article of Trade in the Interior; on these two fine Blankets as Sheets and above this a coloured Blanket as a Coverlid.] **1850** (1852) OSBORN *Arctic Jnl* 147: Friday morning, at seven o'clock, we rolled up our beds, or rather sleeping-bags, stowed the sledge, drank boiling hot chocolate, and gnawed cheerily at frozen pork and biscuit. **1905** DUNCAN *Grenfell's Parish* 134: Many a night the doctor must get into his sleeping bag and make himself as comfortable as possible in the snow, snuggled close to his dogs, for the sake of the warmth of their bodies. **1966** *Kingston Whig-Standard* (Ont.) 27 Apr. 26/2: Canadian [army] sleeping bags have an easily inflatable rubber air mattress, flannel inner cover, down-filled main bag and a nylon outer cover.

sleeping-bench *n.* See **sleeping-platform**.
1938 *Beaver* Dec. 17/1: New deerskins were laid out on the sleeping bench and everything in good order. **1958** *Edmonton Jnl* 24 June 3 16/7: [They sat] on the fur rugs of the sleeping benches.

sleeping-caboose *n. West, Hist.* See **caboose** (def. 4a).
1963 SYMONS *Many Trails* 117: Some outfits had sleeping-cabooses and fed their own men from a cook-wagon. . . .

sleeping camp See **shanty** (def. 1c).
1898 CONNOR *Black Rock* 2: The grub camp, with cook-shed attached, stood in the middle of the clearing; at a little distance was the sleeping-camp with the office built against it, and about a hundred yards away . . . stood the stables, and near them the smiddy. **1935** SULLIVAN *Great Divide* 195: The sleeping camps were marquees with hewn log floors and four-foot log walls, a box stove in the centre. . . .

sleeping-platform *n. Northern Arctic* the bench or platform inside an igloo, used for sleeping and usually at the original snow level, the remaining space being an excavation where cooking and eating and other activities are carried on. See picture at **igloo**. See also **sleeping-bench, sleeping-stage**, and **snow platform**.
1940 FINNIE *Lure of North* 121: There were two sleeping-platforms, one on either side of a pit in which were the stoves and cooking utensils. **1956** TOLBOOM *Arctic Bride* 206: Not one speck of snow was allowed to fall on the sleeping platform. About half the floor space of a snow-house is taken up by the bench on which one sleeps. It is usually the original snow level.

sleeping-poke *n.* See **sleeping-bag**.
1935 MOWERY *Resurrection River* 161: Craig . . . unrolled Patricia's sleeping poke on the bunk, and spread his own on the floor beside the stove.

sleeping robe *North* a fur robe used as a blanket.
1896 WHITNEY *On Snow-Shoes* 159: When the sledges are loaded with the requisite supply of wood and the sleeping-robes there is no room left for provisions. **1946** FERGUSON *Mink, Mary and Me* 95: The sleigh was loaded with fish for the dogs and for bait; scents for fox, mink, and lynx; my sleeping robe and duffel bag, with extra socks, mittens, moccasins, babiche, and cord; kettle, frying pan, rifle, and ax.

sleeping-stage *n.* See **sleeping-platform**.
1936 (1955) STRINGER *Wife-Trader* 203: . . . she stooped to replace the duly aired blankets on the sleeping-stage. Then she restored the snow-beater to its hook.

sleeping toque *n.* a nightcap resembling a long stockinglike tuque (def. 1).
1943 MILLER *Lone Woodsman* 6: Into them [duffel bags] went his red . . . Hudson's Bay blanket . . . and a sleeping toque.

sleigh† *n.* [< Am.E < Du. *slee* (< *slede*)] **1** a winter vehicle on runners, drawn by horses or oxen and used for work or pleasure.
1764 *Quebec Gaz.* 27 Dec. 2/1: Every Owner . . . of any Sled or Slay, used either for the Carriage of Goods or Persons, shall cause at least Six Horse Bells to be affixed to the Horse Harness. . . . **1831** (1953) RADCLIFF *Letters* 13: . . . the others being cleared away, the oxen and sleigh can ply without difficulty. **1957** HUTCHISON *Canada* 248: First I drove an unloaded sleigh ahead to break trail, then a loaded sleigh or two, and finally the cattle.

2 See **dog-sled** and picture.
1845 *St.Catharines Jnl* (C.W.) 23 Oct. 3/1: Being frozen in we were obliged to take dogs and sleighs for Fort Asiniboe, where they arrived the 4th of December. . . . **1948** ONRAET *Sixty Below* 93: If there is only one tent, it would have to be pitched every night, struck every morning and hauled around on the sleigh all day.

3 a. a small sled pulled by hand. See also **handsled** and **handsleigh** (def. 1).
1791 (1934) FIDLER *Journal* 522: I very fortunately fell into a fresh sleigh track which I supposed to belong to the woman & the boy particularly as I could see only the footsteps of two people. **1811** (1950) THOMPSON *Journals* 144: Showers of Snow—made a small Slays & hauled the Goods full 2½ miles. . . . **1913** WILLIAMS *Wilderness Trail* 148: With remarkable ingenuity, he fashioned a small sleigh, some four or five feet long.

b. a small sled used by children for coasting, *q.v.* See also **coaster**[1] and **handsleigh** (def. 2).
1805 *Quebec Gaz.* 27 June 4/1: . . . the practice of Sliding on small sleighs and skaits in the streets of this city in the winter season is found to be extremely dangerous to passengers and a very great nuisance. . . . **1837** *Times* (Halifax) 17 Jan. 19/1: Allow me to call the

attention of the Magistrates to the danger pedestrians are exposed to from the practice of boys riding down the streets with such velocity on sleighs. **1852** MOODIE *Roughing It* 165: All his spare time he spent in making little sleighs and toys for her, or in dragging her in the said sleighs up and down the steep hills in front of the house, wrapped up in a blanket. **1966** *Eaton's Christmas Catalogue* 96: The Grand Prix sleigh . . . The sleigh that features the exclusive flexible steering. Constructed of heavy-gauge steel and select Canadian hardwoods.

4 See **stoneboat** and picture.

1902 (1957) *Sask.Hist.* X 1 18: The usual mode of hauling water among the halfbreeds is to put a water barrel upon a sleigh, attach a team and drag the water home, as near the kitchen door as possible, where it stands until the supply is exhausted, when more is brought in the same way.

sleigh *v.* **1** ride in a sleigh; travel by sleigh.

1849 ALEXANDER *L'Acadie* II 30: We sleighed across the ice of the Ottawa, which was rapidly becoming unsafe. . . . **1852** *Hamilton Gaz.* (C.W.) 19 Aug. 3/2: We used also to sleigh down the hill by Robert Hamilton's house, but we are not allowed to do that now. **1913** OGILVIE *Yukon* 108: In the month of April they sleighed up to the Stewart. . . .

2 transport by sleigh.

1825 *Colonial Advocate* (York [Toronto]) 14 Apr. 46: On my way down I saw a great many oak logs squared, and lying near the road, waiting sleighing.

sleigh-bed *n. Hist.* (a modern term) for a style of bed current in the first half of the 19th century, characterized by an outward curl at the top of the headboard and footboard.

1950 BIRD *This Is N.S.* 48: She is immensely proud of his [Thos. C. Haliburton's] place in Nova Scotia history, and enjoys showing visitors around, upstairs to the old fourposters and "sleigh beds" or down to the basement and its great fireplace.

sleigh-bell† *n.* (*usually plural*) one of a number of small ball-like metal bells attached to a sled or to the harness of the animal pulling it.

1811 *Kingston Star* (U.C.) 8 Jan. 3/2: But little snow has fallen; and with the exception of a very few days, the sound of sleigh bells has not been heard. **1851** *Toronto Mirror* 26 Dec. 2/7: But, hark! there goes the merry sleigh bells, reminding us that we are in Canada. **1955** COLLARD *Cdn Yesterdays* 23: I learned in this beautiful neighbourhood to appreciate the charms of a bright Canadian winter day and to take delight in the cheerful music of your sleigh-bells.

sleigh carriage *Obs.* See **cutter** (def. 1).

1846 TAYLOR *Narrative* 32: In winter when . . . sleigh carriages are in full action, there is such a jingling of bells, as would almost lead the mind to fancy that every star in the firmament had a tongue in motion.

sleigh club *Obs.* a club made up of persons interested in sleighing (def. 1).

1830 MOORSOM *Letters N.S.* 104: From a dozen to twenty of the members of the sleigh club may be seen . . . making a tour of the streets to the open-mouthed admiration of all the little truant ragamuffins. . . .

sleigh-cutter *n. Obs.* See **cutter** (def. 1).

1846 TAYLOR *Narrative* 33: Sleigh-cutters are a simple but elegant carriage, without wheels, embellished with buffalo skins, which hang over the sides, lined with cloth of various dazzling colours, scolloped out, van-dyke shape, and squirrel skins attached to various parts of the robes.

sleigh dog† See **sled dog** (def. 1 and picture).

1897 YOUNG *Indian Trail* 140: My splendid dogs obtained from Hamilton, Montreal and elsewhere, had increased and multiplied, until now I had a number of the finest sleigh dogs in the country. **1965** *Globe and Mail* (Toronto) 15 Jan. 33/8: [The wolf was] intent upon following the tracks of Andy's sleigh dogs.

sleighing† *n.* **1** riding or driving in a sleigh (def. 1) for pleasure. See also **carioling.**

1807 *U.C.Gaz.* (York [Toronto]) 28 Feb. 3/1: This is January twenty,/ When we have been sleighing plenty. . . . **1813** (1955) CRAIG *Early Travellers* 42: Sleighing is another amusement, of which the people are very fond, and for which they are well prepared, as it respects horses, sleighs, clothing, and furs. **1834** (1926) LANGTON *Early U.C.* 60: The sleighing, about which we hear so much, is . . . unpracticable for us who have no beaten track. . . . **1927** MCARTHUR *Friendly Acres* 200: At the present time sleigh bells are used because they add to the charm of sleighing.

2 the quality or condition of the snow with regard to travelling by sleigh.

1807 (1891) EDGAR *Ten Years of U.C.* 20: It is very cold weather here and very excellent sleighing, and very fine skating for the boys who have skates. **1914** DOUGLAS *Lands Forlorn* 184: . . . we decided to bring the second loads of stuff to this point at once before the sleighing got any worse.

sleighing party† a group of persons riding together in a sleigh or in several sleighs as a form of recreation. See also **sleigh-ride** (def. 2).

[**1769** (1931) BROOKE *Emily Montague* 87: Emily . . . wants me, every time we make a carrioling-party, to invite all the Misses of Quebec. . . .] **1883** FRASER *Shanty* 46: No doubt it would be impracticable to prepare beans in the proper way on the sleighing parties. . . . **1937** CLARK *So What?* 48: "I haven't been on a sleighing party," cried Jim, "for thirty years!"

sleighing season or **time** the time of year for sleighing (def. 1).

1829 MACTAGGART *Three Years* II 7: . . . it is only in the sleighing season that he has a chance of seeing his mistress. **1833** (1926) LANGTON *Early U.C.* 50: And now farewell until sleighing time. **1837** *Times* (Halifax) 17 Jan. 18/3: The sleighing season having set in, the knights of the whip have begun the campaign in good earnest.

sleigh meet *Obs.* a gathering of persons in sleighs for social intercourse, races, etc.

1849 ALEXANDER *L'Acadie* I 183: Twice a week we had sleigh meets, when curricles, and tandem, and cutters, or sleighs of one horse power, turned out with steeds gaily decked with party-coloured streamers, and alive with bells.

sleigh rack See **sloop** (def. 2).

1962 FRY *Ranch on the Cariboo* 86: One cow . . . remained at the Blaze with a last pitiable forkful of hay, she would have to be moved on a sleigh rack.

sleigh-ride *n.* **1**† a ride in a sleigh.

1860 *Islander* (Charlottetown) 14 Dec. 2/5: The first snow fell on Tuesday last, but the principal part of it was nearly washed away by the rain in the evening—not, however, before a few indulged in a sleigh ride.

1961 *Chatelaine* Mar. 39/2: [Caption] . . . Fergus takes Calum on sleigh ride, led by family Labrador, past warehouse of Hudson's Bay post father runs.

2 See **sleighing party.**
1896 *Times* (Niagara-on-the-Lake, Ont.) 1/3: The young people of St. Andrew's Church, went on their annual sleigh-ride to the county gaol in St. Catherines, on Tuesday evening. **1956** YOUNG *Flood* 19: He was big and blonde and so was she and they ski'd and went on sleigh-rides and talked in hearty shouts. **1955** BLAKELEY *Nova Scotia* 178: Sleigh rides were popular too. When the snowy roads were well packed down, a group of young people might organize a sleigh ride. Crowded into the long box of a bob sled and bundled up with rugs, the party would ride for miles along the snowy roads. . . .

sleigh-ride party *Obs.* See **sleighing party.**
1896 *Times* (Niagara-on-the-Lake, Ont.) 27 Feb. 1/2: Sleigh-ride parties are all the rage.

sleigh-riding *n.* **1** the pastime of riding in a sleigh.
1819 *Kingston Chron.* (U.C.) 30 Apr. 3/1: As far as I have been able to discover, the only amusements which the Province affords . . . are Dancing and Sleigh-riding. **1845** BEAVAN *Life in Backwoods N.B.* 140: Nothing can be more exhilarating than sleigh-riding . . . the bells ringing gladly out.
2 the practice of coasting down hills on a sleigh (def. 3b).
1966 *Caribou Observer* 24 Nov. 6/1: The above areas for sleigh riding will be designated by signs.

sleigh road or **track** a winter road built or laid out for the use of sleighs.
1834 *Cdn Courant* (Montreal) 15 Jan. 2/5: There is a good sleigh road opposite to Longieuil three miles below the city. **1853** STRICKLAND *Canada West* I 261: It was only seven miles to the mill by a new cut-out sleigh-track through the township of Goderich. . . . **1955** HOBSON *Nothing Too Good* 119: The Pan Meadow was over a hundred and fifty sleigh-road, deep-snow miles from Quesnel and the nearest doctor.

sleigh robe a warm robe, often of buffalo or other skins, used by sleigh passengers to keep warm.
1811 *U.C.Gaz.* (York [Toronto]) 1 Feb. 1/3: The Subscriber has for Sale Sleigh Robes & Matts on Commission. **1955** COLLARD *Cdn Yesterdays* 230: Dr. Lapthorn Smith could be seen driving his little tandem, with his sleigh robes of Japanese fox, which were much admired.

sleigh runner† See **runner** (def. 1a).
1834 (1926) LANGTON *Early U.C.* 80: The next day one of our sleigh runners, being worn out by the bare roads, gave way and detained us so long that we could only reach a miserable farmhouse in Brock. **1962** FRITH *Lost Stagecoach* 157: There was a . . . set of sleigh runners from a winter freight wagon. . . .

sleigh shoe† *Obs.* See **runner** (def. 1a).
1819 *Kingston Gaz.* (U.C.) 11 Dec. 3/3: The subscriber . . . has on hand . . . a few pair of Cast Iron Sleigh-shoes . . . which will sell at a very reduced price for cash or produce. **1827** *Colonial Advocate* (York [Toronto]) 14 June 2/2: I went over the works and saw . . . sleigh shoes . . . bull wheels and mill spindles for flouring mills &c.

sleigh slide a hill of snow for children to coast down on sleighs and toboggans.
1957 *Record-Gaz.* 19 Dec. 10/5: Motion passed that the recreation director put up a sleigh slide for the children in the park.

sleigh track See **sleigh road.**

sleighwaggon *n. Obs.* a heavy sleigh (def. 1) used for winter work.
1826 (1832) PICKERING *Inquiries* 69: A yoke of oxen . . . perhaps a horse or a "span;" a sleighwaggon, plough and harrow . . . [are] all their riches except their land.

sleigh wrangler *North, Slang* See **dog-driver.**
1951 ANGIER *At Home* 110: There were a lot of disgruntled sourdoughs in Hudson Hope that particular holiday, but the sleigh wrangler wasn't feeling any pain.

sleugh or **slew** *n.* See **slough.**

slick *n.* a smooth, unruffled patch on the surface of fast moving water.
1964 *North* July 39/2: Now in November it [the river] was nearly choked; a mad race of water in the middle flung rafts of ice to the sides, burrowed under ice bridges, and showed in roils and slicks as far as could be seen. Soon a man could drive right across.

slicker† *n.* an oilskin raincoat.
1911 BICKERSTETH *Open Doors* 28: I had a Mexican saddle; my pack fastened behind and a slicker (oilskin coat) in front. **1957** *Mine-Mill Herald* Oct. 10/2: The agreement also provides for seniority, free slickers for underground, and sets the board at $2.50 during life of the contract.

slicker-pants *n.pl.* oilskin pants.
1921 MARSHALL *Snowshoe Trail* 28: What you want is a good pair of slicker pants, both of you, and plenty of wool inside.

slidage *n. Lumbering, Obs.* **1** facilities for by-passing rapids and falls by means of slides (def. 1a).
1845 *Bytown* [Ottawa] *Gaz.* 19 June 2/6: We consider it clearly and imperatively the duty of the Government to improve the slidage of this place.
2 *Obs.* See **slide dues.**
1883 FRASER *Shanty* 347: . . . timber licenses, Government dues, slidage . . . have been draining his pockets for the last twelve months.

slide *n.* **1 a.** *Lumbering* an artificial sluiceway down which logs or cribs may be directed to avoid rapids, falls, or other obstructions in a river. See also **chute** (def. 3). **log slide, shoot,** *n.* (def. 2), **timber chute,** and **timber slide.**
1836 *Bytown* [Ottawa] *Gaz.* 21 July 2/5: On Saturday last the new slide, to facilitate the passing of the Chaudier falls was opened, and the first crib run. **1875** *Canadian Mthly* Jan. 54/2: The first slide, on the north side of the Ottawa, was built in 1829 by Philemon Wright, and was subsequently purchased by the Government for $40,000. **1891** OXLEY *Chore-Boy* 141: At one side of the fall a "slide" is built—that is, a contrivance something like a canal, with sides and bottom of heavy timber, and having a steep slope down which the water rushes in frantic haste to the level below. **1948** *Ont.Timberworker* 30 May 6/5: No "improvements" are noticeable, unless the old 1800 foot slide to by-pass Aubrey Falls, or the rotting dam above the Falls, can be called improvements. **1964** *Cdn Geog.Jnl* Feb. 69/2: Shooting the slides on cribs took many a lumberjack's life.

b. See **riffle,** *n.* (def. 1c).

2† a. the mass of earth, rocks, etc. deposited by a landslide.

1866 (1962) ANDERSON *Sawney's Letters* 14: On prospeckin' I still was bent;/Had shares in a' the kintra side,/In shafts gaun' doon thro' slum and slide. ... **1908** MAIR *Mackenzie Basin* 39: The men had to cope with the swift current, bordered by a series of steep gumbo slides, where the tracking was hazardous. ... **1957** *Arctic Spotter* Nov. 6/3: ... at the foot of the slide lay ten dead wild sheep, which appeared either to have been tumbled by the avalanche or to have been hit by an aircraft.

b. See **slide course.**

1916 WOOD *Tourist's N.W.* 349: ... the growth on these slides varies ... according to the exposure; and while one slide may be quite green, another may have snow on it.

3 See **toboggan slide.**

1870 *Cdn Illust.News* 26 Mar. 330/3: Our illustration shows ... a fair sprinkling of pleasure-seekers trying to enjoy the national toboggan adown its steep slides. **1898** EDGAR *Canada and Capital* 130: The perfection of tobogganing is found on the artificial slides which are raised to a dizzy height, with a wide, deep trough, coated with snow and ice, pitching toward the ground at a fearful angle. **1927** *Beaver* Dec. 107: The slides are specially constructed of ice sides. ...

4 *Nfld* See **catamaran,** *n.* (def. 2b).

[**1665** (1885) RADISSON *Fourth Voyage* 221: We overloaded our slide on that rotten ice. ...] **1906** LUMSDEN *Skipper Parson* 65: Said he, "We're all right now, sir. Here's an old slide-path." **1937** DEVINE *Folklore* 50: To swamp a road or path is to build one with a bedding of boughs to be used in hauling slide loads of wood in winter. **1957** *Nfld Qtly* June 50/2: And the old dog Rex was harnessed next and hitched fast to the slide.

5† See 1948 quote. See also **sliding** (def. 1).

1920 SCHOOLING *Hudson's Bay Co.* 61: The animals [otters] may be seen sliding down and climbing up again for hours on end, evidently in a state of keen enjoyment. Trappers take advantage of this habit to capture the otters at their slides. c1948 *Sask. Fur Marketing Service* 33: The best place to make a set is where the otter amuse themselves sliding down steep banks until they have made a "slide."

slide course the part of a mountain side over which an avalanche or landslide has passed, recognizable as an area bearing a growth of grass and shrubs rather than trees. See also **slide** (def. 2b).

1956 EVANS *Mountain Dog* 67: He saw a blur of white up one of the these green slide courses and recognized it for a mountain goat.

slide dues *Hist.* a charge made for running timber down a slide (def. 1a). See also **slidage** (def. 2).

1846 (1957) GUILLET *Valley of the Trent* 205: [He] recommends another boom beeing thrown across the River at the Mouth of the Trent to insure also collection of the Slide dues. **1933** GUILLET *Early Life in U.C.* 236: Along the larger streams many of the slides were constructed by the government and a small charge was made for their use; in 1861, for example, the "slide dues" collected in Canada amounted to $55,546.

slidemaster *n. Hist.* the person in charge of a slide (def. 1a).

1849 (1957) GUILLET *Valley of the Trent* 205: Why not appoint a proper practical Superintendant ... Capable of Conducting the repairs of slides ... [and] doing all the Duty required as Slide Master. **1961** PRICE & KENNEDY *Renfrew* 45: [Caption] Slidemaster's house and log slide ... at Fitzroy Harbour.

sliding *n.* **1** *Obs.* See **slide** (def. 5).

1770 (1792) CARTWRIGHT *Journal* I 50: Arriving at the head of Long Pool, I met with the sliding of an otter.

2 See **coasting.**

1805 *Quebec Gaz.* 27 June 4/1: Whereas the practice of Sliding on small sleighs and skaits in the streets of this city in the winter season is found to be extremely dangerous to passengers and a very great nuisance, it is therefore ordered that if hereafter any person be found so sliding or skaiting he shall pay a fine of five shillings or be admitted to the House of Correction for a time not exceeding eight days. **1923** WILLIAMS *Spinning Wheels* 288: In skating and sliding ... you have no ulterior thoughts, are hardly conscious of being. ...

sling-ding *n. Fisheries, Maritimes* a weight, as a rock, a piece of iron or lead, or a sock or mitten full of stones, attached to the first end of a trawl to be set, its function being to moor the end of the line.

1955 WALLACE *Roving Fisherman* 68: These "sling-dings," so-called, were made fast to the first end, and when the whole tub of 2,100 feet of line was payed out into the water, an anchor would be used on the last or tub end.

slink *n.* [< Brit.dial. *slink,* adj., lean, weak, inferior] *Esp.Nfld* an immature or undernourished cod.

1771 (1792) CARTWRIGHT *Journal* I 132: We had three slinks in the net. **1955** WALLACE *Roving Fisherman* 40: "The slinks and the scrod don't git a chanst. ..."

slip *n.* **1** *Nfld, Obs.* a noose or snare for catching deer and other large game.

1772 (1792) CARTWRIGHT *Journal* I 199: We fresh tailed the deertrap and the slip by Atkinson Pond, and returned home over the Barrens.

2 See **scraper.**

1961 *Cdn Geog.Jnl* Jan. 14/1: Slips were the forerunners of the modern scrappers [sic] in common use today.

slip-scraper *n.* See **scraper.**

1961 *Cdn Geog.Jnl* Jan. 14: [Caption] Grading with slip scrappers [sic] and mules, 1910. **1965** SHEPHERD *West of Yesterday* 35: At work, the Black and Schumann outfit consisted of an elevating grader with twelve dump wagons. This was the mainstay of the outfit, but in addition there was a wheel-scraper outfit, a fresno gang, and some slip-scrapers.

slip-string *n.* the thong which fastens a snowshoe to the foot. See also **snowshoe lashing.**

1913 WILLIAMS *Wilderness Trail* 162: Crying to Jean to go on, he halted and stooped over his snowshoes, the slip-strings of which had loosened.

slitheroo *n.* [< its viscous character] *Slang, Obs.* an early type of insect repellent.

1896 ROBERTS *Camp-Fire* 24: The flies and mosquitoes were swarming, but we inflicted upon them a crushing defeat by the potent aid of "slitheroo." This magic fluid consists of Stockholm tar and tallow spiced with pennyroyal, and boiled to about the consistency of treacle. It will almost keep a grizzly at bay.

slob (ice) *n. Orig. Nfld* a mass of densely packed pieces of heavy, sludgy ice, especially sea ice. See also **dirty ice** and **salt slob**. Cp. **slur ice** and **slush ice**.

1835 WIX *Journal* 16: After attending and assisting at a marriage which he was solemnizing, I crossed through the "slob ice," which was very thick in Conception Bay, to Port de Grave, four leagues, in three hours. **1878** *North Star* (St. John's) 30 Mar. 3/1: The bay here was caught over last week, and a string of "slob" made its appearance across the mouth, but the heavy sea of Thursday broke it all up. **1930** *Keewatin* 37: The first ice is called "slob," which is of a slushy nature and gathers along the coast in bays and shallow water. The "slob" checks wave action and permits young ice to form out from the shore. **1957** *Beaver* Autumn 27/2: Two or three times, when crossing lakes, we got bogged down in surface "slob" and most of the passengers had to walk through slush. . . . **1964** *Calgary Herald* 17 Mar. 44/1: Heavy slob ice is beginning to put the squeeze on the east and northeast coasts of Newfoundland. . . .

slob water *Nfld* slushy water, a mixture of broken ice and snow. Cp. **slob**.

1952 BANFILL *Lab.Nurse* 102: Once more, we clung to the komatic and headed homeward very thankful that we did not have to hike six miles through icy slob water. . . .

sloo *n*. See **slough**.

sloop *n*. [? prob. < *sloop* boat; cf. **stoneboat**]
1 *Lumbering* a single sleigh (def. 1) used for hauling logs.

1955 *Bush News* (St. Catharines, Ont.) Feb. 7/3: At the present rate, it's expected that the haul will be finished by March 1. Some 250 persons are engaged in the operation plus 55 teams for the horse-haul, and several tractors, sloops, trucks and jammers. **1966** *Globe and Mail* (Toronto) 6 Jan. 5/4: The six, square-timbered barns that surround the farmhouse . . . [contain] a museum of pioneer equipment—cutters, wagons, broad axes, double sleighs, and a single sleigh known as a scoop [sic].

2 *B.C.* a hayrack mounted on runners. See also **sleigh rack**.

1962 FRY *Ranch on the Cariboo* 15: . . . nothing counted then but . . . pitching out the raked-up bunches onto the sloops, hauling sloop load after sloop load alongside the derrick poles. *Ibid.* 62: He'd send us out to load our sloops while he'd open the stack, spreading the emergency top he'd built at the onset of the storm.

slooper *n. Hist.* **1** a Hudson's Bay Company employee engaged as a skipper for a sailing craft operated by Eskimo crews for local tripping around Hudson Bay.

1784 (1954) *Moose Ft Jnls* 187: I am afraid I shall not be able to supply the Sloopers with their Summer's Stock for I shall have no Indians here to Hunt this Spring. **1939** *Beaver* Sep. 30/2: . . . the Company brought out Orkneymen as sloopers, carpenters, and coopers.

2 a crewman on such a vessel.

1843 *Standing Rules* (H.B.C.) 94: That from & after the close of the Current Outfit, the Wages of Mechanics on new Engagements will be as follows. Sloopers £23 Stg. **1913** COWIE *Adventurers* 75: . . . all the steerage passengers were obliged to assist on deck, while those engaged as "sloopers"—seamen—. . . berthed with the crew. . . . *Ibid.*: That year [1867] all the sloopers . . . had been drafted for service at Moose Factory.

slough† [slu] *n*. **1** *Prairie Provinces* See **pothole** (def. 3a).

☛ *This meaning of* **slough**, *invariably pronounced* [slu], *is peculiar to the West and Northwest, roughly between the Lakehead and the Rockies. In B.C. the term, usually pronounced* [slu], *has taken on other meanings. In the East* **slough**, *usually pronounced* [slaʊ] *if used at all, is for most people a book word.*

1860 *Nor'Wester* (R.R.S.) 14 Feb. 4/2: These sloughs are temporarily filled up with hay, a couple of loads of which being thrown into them, make a kind of floating bridge on the top of the mud—perfectly safe, economical, and expeditious. **1909** CAMERON *New North* 30: In front of the old camp-fire was a little slough or lake, and this seemed a promising place to look for evidence. **1948** *Cdn Geog.Jnl* Mar. 150/1: On the prairies everything is a slough (pronounced slew): you cut hay in the slough, the little morainic lake is a slough, and so is the bleak waste of shining alkali on black mud. . . . It is not readily apparent how this name came to the prairies. It seems to have been in common use in England in the time of Bunyan (John not Paul) and his "Slough of Despond"; but appears to have skipped over all the swamps between the Atlantic and Lake Winnipeg to find an abiding home on the prairie. **1962** *Globe and Mail* (Toronto) 23 Feb. 3/1: Prairie grain growers often regard a pothole or pond or slough on their land as a soggy nuisance.

2 *B.C.* **a.** See **slough meadow**.

1860 *Brit.Colonist* (Victoria) 13 Mar. 2/3: This slough will be worked until the river commences to rise, when it will have to be abandoned for high-water diggings. **1887** (1888) LEES & CLUTTERBUCK *British Columbia* 357: . . . one morning the lodge was pitched by a little brook, in a pretty grassy valley libelled under the name of mud slough. **1905** OUTRAM *Cdn Rockies* 277: The sloughs were full of water, the trails thick with soft and sticky mire.

b. See **slough-creek**.

1858 *Brit.Colonist* (Victoria) 18 Dec. 2/3: A trail had to be made over high mountains, through ten inches of snow, wade sloughs waist deep; the cold was intense, and the underbrush thick and passed with difficulty. **1955** HOBSON *Nothing Too Good* 96: At the Pan Meadow . . . two small, mud-bottomed creeks merged into a long, dangerous slough where several springs bubbled up out of the mud.

c. an inlet; lagoon.

1859 *Brit.Colonist* (Victoria) 17 Dec. 3/2: At Old Langley, the slough is entirely frozen up. The main channel is open down to New Langley. **1887** (1888) LEES & CLUTTERBUCK *British Columbia* 74: The water therefore was falling rapidly, and leaving on either side huge marshy lagoons known as sloughs (pronounced sloo). **1963** *Sun* (Vancouver) 28 Mar. 29/1: The cutthroats could start feeding on the first hatches of pink salmon fry in the sloughs and lower reaches of the rivers.

3 *Northwest* See **snye** (def. 2a).

1880 GORDON *Mountain and Prairie* 143: At the same time there are many sloughs, or "slews" so-called, where part of the river flows by some devious and half-hidden course, that might, when they blend again with the main current, be mistaken for tributary streams. **1899** PALMER *Klondyke* 74: The flat-bottomed river steamers continued on their course until the ice in the river led them to seek a slough or side-channel for safety. **1960** NELSON *Northern Lights* 322: For two hours we flew across . . . a land of great rivers, green little sloughs, and broad empty valleys. . . .

slough-creek *n. B.C.* a widening in a creek to create a mud-bottomed, swampy stretch. See also **slough** (def. 2b).
1958 *Wildlife Rev.* May 26/1: Ho! ye ditchers, ye drainers, go ye slow/Till I walk once more where the slough-creeks go. . . .

slough grass† *West* any of several coarse grasses, *Muhlenbergia* spp., growing in the sloughs of the Prairies or of the interior of B.C.
1930 BEAMES *Army* 26: Billy ran up a bunk of poles in a corner, with tough willow sticks for springs, and an armful or two of coarse slough grass for a mattress. **1951** HOBSON *Grass* 41: We sat around . . . talking of range cows and tough trails, slough grass and swamp meadows. . . .

slough hay *West* **1** See **slough grass.**
1934 BETTANY *Valley of Lost Gold* 264: In the tall slough hay beside them[,] orange lilies raised their heads waist high. . . . **1948** ONRAET *Sixty Below* 135: I have often seen them kneeling on their forelegs to feed in comfort on short willows and slough hay.

2 hay from slough grass, *q.v.*
1955 *Sentinel-Courier* 31 Mar. 4/1: FOR SALE—Baled slough hay, wire tied, $10.00 per ton. **1957** *Beaver* Autumn 19/1: The Indian agent put up a wing next to the school and at last the Jordens could occupy a real bedroom—one made of boards and covered with long slough hay and clay.

slough meadow *B.C. Interior* a low-lying meadow subject to flooding during spring runoffs and productive in hay. See also **meadow², pothole meadow, slough** (def. 2a), and **swamp meadow.**
1955 HOBSON *Nothing Too Good* 69: This little slough meadow was nearly four miles beyond the cattle.

slough water *West* water, often brackish and alkaline, taken from a pothole (def. 3a). See also **slough** (def. 1).
1920 WINLOW & POCKLINGTON *Mornin'-Glory* 46: If you once drink slough water you know you will never like any other. **1948** *Cdn Geog. Jnl* Mar. 150/1: You shoot ducks in a slough and may also unfortunately drink slough water. **1965** *Wildlife Rev.* Mar. 4: Since none of the Plains Indians had seen a sea, they weren't too sure what was being looked for and in response to descriptions such as "water which no man drinketh," led the explorers to more slough water than sea water.

sloven ['slʌvən] *n. Atlantic Provinces* See 1895 and 1964 quotes.
1895 (1944) WENTWORTH *Am. Dial. Dict.*: sloven, *n.* A low truck wagon. 1895 e. Canada N.B. N.S. Newfoundland 1934. . . . **1941** MacLENNAN *Barometer Rising* 11: Grinding on the cobblestones behind a pair of plunging Clydesdales came one of Halifax's most typical vehicles, a low-swung dray with a high driver's box, known as a sloven. **1956** PARTRIDGE *Chaplet of Grace* 47: With the ebb we'll be sitting on the bottom of the harbour & the Market Slip will have so little water that slovens will be out in the center of it, loading & unloading. **1964** *Atlantic Advocate* Aug. 79: As evening approached the horses were hitched to a long, low wagon, known in our country as a "sloven," and the apples were hauled to the house.

slow ice *Hockey* ice that is covered with ice particles skinned off the surface by the players' skates, the effect being to impede movement thus slowing down the game.
☞ *Slow ice also refers to ice that is not frozen as hard as it might be as a result of defective freezing apparatus or because the surroundings are at too high a temperature, as is often the case late in the spring.*
1963 O'BRIEN *Hockey* 54: It was ruled that ice surfaces had to be re-flooded between periods to prevent "slow ice" from developing.

slow time standard time, as opposed to daylight-saving time when the clocks are advanced an hour. Cp. **fast time.**
1953 MOON *Saskatchewan* 14: The school board wanted the school to stay on slow time.

slue *n.* See **slough.**

sluice† *n. Placer Mining* See **sluice-box.**
1869 *Mainland Guardian* (New Westminster, B.C.) 9 Oct. 3/2: The Indians fully bear out Price's own story . . . of the Indian taken . . . in the act of robbing their sluices. **1965** *Cdn Geog. Jnl* Dec. 205/3: The sluice can be partially sunk in a stream and wedged with rocks.

sluice† *v.* **1** *Placer Mining* wash gold in a sluice-box, *q.v.*
1937 ANDREWS *Wrangell* 37: "Buckskin" Miller still sluiced on his ground. . . .

2 *Lumbering* of logs, drive through a sluice in a river.
1949 LAWSON *N.B. Story* 221: Tobique's white with foam./Once again the mighty drives/Are sluicing grandly home. **1957** *Bush News* (St. Catharines, Ont.) June 2/5: Sawlogs are also sorted from the wood being sluiced from the Kenogamisis into Long Lake.

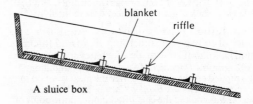

A sluice box

sluice-box† *n. Placer Mining, Hist.* a long box or trough containing riffles (def. 2) by means of which gold is separated from gravel. See also **long tom, rock-bottom sluice-box, sluice,** *n.,* and **sluicing-box.**
1869 *Mainland Guardian* (New Westminster, B.C.) 28 Aug. 3/2: He was busy fixing his sluice-boxes and had evidently dropped on a good thing. **1962** FRITH *Lost Stagecoach* 157: There was a small, battered piano . . . an old sluice box; and a "cradle rocker" from some long-forgotten gold claim.

sluice-fork† *n. Placer Mining, Obs.* a device used to break up lumps of gravel in a sluice-box, *q.v.*
1860 *Brit. Colonist* (Victoria) 14 July 1/2: If you come, bring the following articles: The whip-saw and six

files, two cross-cut files, your hand saw, a sluice-fork, and shovel ... a pair of gum boots for William, and an axe, for they are worth here $6 each.

sluice-fork v. *Placer Mining, Obs.* use a sluice-fork, *q.v.*
1860 *Brit.Colonist* (Victoria) 11 Sep. 3/2: The day before I left, Black & Co., (four men—two shoveling, one bailing, and one sluice-forking) took out eighteen ounces and two dollars.

sluicing n. *Placer Mining* the action or practice of separating gold from gravel in a sluice-box, *q.v.*
1859 *Brit.Colonist* (Victoria) 29 Aug. 3/1: The unusual dry weather this summer has so shrunk the smaller streams that sluicing in several places has been suspended and the miners are now actually praying for rain.
1913 OGILVIE *Yukon* 122: ... Quartz Creek, up which he went a day and a half, where he put up a dam to raise water for sluicing. ...

sluicing-box n. *Placer Mining* See **sluice-box** and picture.
1897 TUTTLE *Golden North* 77: The boat was hauled up on a bar, her engines detached from the wheels, and made to drive a set of pumps manufactured on the ground, which supplied water for a set of sluicing boxes. **1909** SERVICE *Cheechako* 66: The riffles of his sluicing-box were choked with speckled earth,/And night and day he worked that lay for all that he was worth.

slum [slʌm] n. [shortening of *slumgullion*, q.v.] *Placer Mining* thick slippery mud, or gumbo, found in the creek valleys of the B.C. interior. See also **Cariboo slum.**
1866 (1962) ANDERSON *Sawney's Letters* 14: On prospeckin' I still was bent;/Had shares in a' the kintra side,/In shafts gaun' doon thro' slum and slide. ... **1870** *Cariboo Sentinel* (Barkerville, B.C.) 19 Mar. 2/2: At the depth of three feet he struck a bed of dry slum, nine feet thick. **1958** ELLIOTT *Quesnel* 162: The creek had never been properly bottomed and E. Edens ... sank a shaft ninety feet only to hit slum.

slumgullion [ˌslʌmˈgʌljən] n. [< Am.E a fanciful coinage for something viscid and thick, as mud] a kind of stew made of whatever is available.
1902 LONDON *Daughter of Snows* 45: "Slumgullion," she replied curtly, and thereafter the meal went on in silence. **1919** FRASER *Bulldog Carney* 247: When the bacon was cooked the chef lifted it out on the point of his knife and stirred some flour into the gravy, adding water, preparing the well-known delicacy of the trail known as slumgullion. **1966** PATTERSON *Trail* 10: ... we ate what we called slumgullion—cheese, macaroni, and everything, all thrown into the same pot.

slur ice [cf. Brit.dial. *slur* thin, washy mud] *Maritimes* a thin mixture of mushy ice and water, found especially near shore. Cp. **sish** and **slob.**
*c*1965 RICHARDSON *Living Island* 209: Soon the waves, thickened by snow and slur ice, become too heavy to crest and break, although the sea grumbles along the shore.

slusherman n. *Mining* See quotes.
1958 WATTERS *B.C.Cent.Anthol.* 259: The slushermen take over, drawing the broken ore down through chutes, dropping it into mine cars. **1964** CRATE *Hardrock*

Mining 4: In some working places a scraper operated by cables attached to a drum is used to move the broken rock. It is termed a *slusher* and the man who *slushes out* is a *slusherman.*

slush hole *North* a patch of rotten, *q.v.*, ice on the surface of a lake or river.
1962 DICKIE *Great Golden Plain* 288: Worse than the pitch holes are the slush holes on the lakes, for the cat skinners (drivers) prefer the level lakes to the rough land, even though the slush and air holes on the lakes are dangerous.

slush ice 1 See 1897 quote. Cp. **slob.**
1897 *Times* (Niagara-on-the-Lake, Ont.) 9 May 8/1: There was an ice-bridge across the river, and below it what we call slush ice—soft sticky stuff—a great deal harder to work a boat through than good hard ice would be. **1922** PRINGLE *Tillicums* 99: Grayling are caught in the fall when slush ice is running in the river. **1954** BEZANSON *Sodbusters* 200: One crack, and further along at the mouth of a river ... slush ice, might have delayed us for days if the new railway grade ... hadn't enabled us to crawl along the shore for the necessary detour. **1962** *B.C.Digest* Oct. 28/3: ... our boats were nearly smashed while going down a sharp bend in the river. Slush ice packed in around us so tight that the sides were bent in, the boards cracked and started to leak.

2 See **green ice.**
1964 *B.C.Digest* Dec. 6: Keep in mind though, that slush ice is only half as strong as clear, blue ice. ...

slush-scraper n. See **scraper.**
1960 *Sask.News* 12 Apr. 2/1: The pioneers scooped out shallow basins at the end of sloughs, where spring run-off could collect. To dig these, the farmer hitched his steadiest team to a slush-scraper. ...

small canoe *Hist.* See quotes. Cp. **express canoe** and **single canoe.**
1798 (1964) CHABOILLEZ *Journal* 204: [I] sent two men in a small Canoe for their Skins. **1860** *Nor' Wester* (R.R.S.) 14 Feb. 2/5: Two sorts of boats are in use— the larger called "north canoes," thirty feet long, and carrying four or five tons; the others, "small canoes," very light, and carrying but three persons. **1922** *Beaver* June 5/2: Canoes are built of varying sizes in two distinct classes; the small canoe, used by the individual Indian, in length fifteen to eighteen feet, for hunting or for moving the family from place to place; and the big canoe, or what today is designated a freighter, for the transport of goods or passengers.

small furs *Fur Trade, Hist.* the pelts of small animals, such as mink, fox, squirrel, and wolverine. Cp. **great furs.**
1682 (1948) *H.B.C.Letters Outward* 41: ... wee now againe repeate *that you Use your Utmost* endeavors to procure as many small furrs of all sorts as you can, for they turne us to a good account. ... **1743** (1949) ISHAM *Observations* 50: Ho! what they are all small fur's I suppose. **1832** (1947) HARGRAVE *Correspondence* 94: Small Furs, have failed, and Indians ... suffered much from starvation. **1835** (1945) *B.C.Hist.Qtly* Jan. 49: Since he went off ... he has traded about 450 beaver & land Otters beside some small furs. ...

smart-assed adj. *Slang* overly clever; smart alecky.
1960 BLONDAL *Candle* 191: "... a lot of smart-assed novelists would have you believe they're dirt-common."

smash *n.* [cf. *smash* a kind of cocktail] *Slang* a drink of liquor. See also **snort.**

1959 *Maclean's* 15 Aug. 28/2: ". . . so I had a couple of smashes and marched in." **1966** *Globe and Mail* (Toronto) 15 Mar. 35/8: . . . every time you wanted a smash the check girl would hand the coat to you over the counter, so you could get your mickey without actually taking the coat out.

smell for water use a divining rod to locate a spring.

1960 *Sun* (Vancouver) 11 Apr. 3/1: "That's right," said the Gulf Islander. "He witches for wells." In the language of the trade, smelling for water.

smelt storm *Maritimes* See **robin snow.**

1955 *Hants Jnl* 9 Mar. 1/5: Last Tuesday we had what some old-timers call the "Smelt Storm," a mixture of snow and rain with the thermometer [sic] hovering around the freezing point . . . presumably on the theory that the smelt sneak up the rivers . . . under cover of the snow.

smoke *n.* **1** See **smudge** (def. 1).

1689 (1929) KELSEY *Papers* 26: [There was] abundance of Musketers & at night could not gett wood Enough for to make a smoke to Clear ym. . . . **1717** (1932) KNIGHT *Journals* 118: The Musketos was so thick . . . they was forc'd to make a Great Smoke as they could hardly fetch thare breath's. . . . **1849** ALEXANDER *L'Acadie* II 165: In the evening the mosquitoes were excessively annoying till we made "smokes" with wet moss. **1872** (1883) BUTLER *Great Lone Land* 95: My host "made a smoke" and the cattle came close around.

2 a column of smoke from a dampened fire, intended as a signal or taken as a sign of the presence of other men. See also **signal fire** and **smoke talk.**

1717 (1932) KNIGHT *Journals* 140: Our Indian Tells me that he did see a Great Smoke to the Norward. **1858** (1860) HIND *Assiniboine Exped.* I 394: Once or twice "smokes," which, from their being soon answered in another quarter, we presumed to be signals, and might be raised by the Blackfeet in the distant prairies, appeared on the west side of the river. **1954** PATTERSON *Dangerous River* 36: They thought now that he must be somewhere ahead of them, but they never could find him though they did their best, making big smokes and firing rifles from time to time.

3 a. See **pipe**[1] (def. 2).

1869 (1942) KENNICOTT *Journal* 55: Smoke [is] A canoe man's resting spell.

b. See **pipe**[1] (def. 1).

1875 (1922) MACOUN, *Autobiography* 120: I said to one of the men, "How far have we to go now?" He considered solemnly for a few moments and then said, "Five smokes."

c. See **pipe**[1] (def. 3).

1921 HEMING *Drama of Forests* 303: Then the brigade would paddle incessantly for about two hours; then they would "spell," and paddles were laid aside "one smoke." **1929** MOBERLY *When Fur Was King* 199: We separated a little, however, so that all should not be killed at once. To go the distance took us many smokes.

4 See **smoke drift.**

1963 MCKINNON *Forest Activities* 3: [The lookouts] are manned 24 hours a day during the fire season, have two-way radios or telephones, a fire-finder for obtaining a bearing on a "smoke". . . .

smoke-alley *n.* a glass marble having a translucent, smoky appearance.

1953 *North Star* (Yellowknife) Oct. 3/1: [Advert.] It's OUR Birthday! But we're giving the gifts—October 8, 9, 10th FREE coasters to adults . . . FREE smoke-alleys and pencils to the children. . . .

smoked *adj. Slang, Obs.* of Indian blood; Indian. See also **Smoked Scotchman** and **smoky.**

1826 (1829) MACTAGGART *Three Years* I 330: There are no females here, except an old, smoked, Canadian's wife—no other woman is to be seen. . . .

smoke drift a drift of smoke seen at a distance as evidence of a forest fire. See also **smoke** (def. 4).

1962 *Sask.News* 19 June 3/1: . . . smaller smoke drifts are often easiest seen in the wee, small hours. . . .

Smoked Scotchman *North, Slang* See **improved Scotsman.**

*a*1960 NELSON *Northern Lights* 516: They married . . . among the Indians, and to this day some of the finest names in Canadian history are perpetuated in Indian tents along the Athabasca and the Mackenzie, and their bearers are known locally as Smoked Scotchmen.

smokehole *n.* the hole in the top of a teepee through which the smoke escapes.

1896 RUSSELL *Far North* 118: We were destined to spend the next day in the blankets, with the clouds of powdery snow settling down through the smokehole of our lodge upon us. **1954** EVANS *Mist* 154: At night they would lie by the fire under the smoke-hole while he told the little fellow old, old stories of their grounds.

smoke smudge See **smudge** (def. 1).

1958 *Edmonton Jnl* 12 Aug. 2/4: I didn't have any matches to start a fire or to make a smoke smudge and there were times when I thought the mosquitoes would eat me up. **1958** MACEWAN *Fifty Mighty Men* 309: The scores of smoke smudges set out on his land on August nights failed to spare the crops from early frost but they served a purpose inasmuch as homesteaders thereabouts were spared from pursuing the same futile technique.

smoke talk in Indian parlance, smoke signals. See also **smoke** (def. 2).

1953 MOWERY *Mounted Police* 22: Back at the camp the Tzuhl-Tinnehs were making "smoke talk" with wet moss and blankets.

smoke-up *n. North* See **pipe**[1] (def. 2). See also **smoke** (def. 3a).

1956 KEMP *Northern Trader* 122: After each rapid there would have to be a detailed post-mortem. Smoke-ups would be plentiful.

smoking bag *Obs.* See **fire-bag.**

1800 (1933) MCLEOD *Diary* 131: The Frênes wife (being Drunk) fell on a Knife she had in a smoking bag at her girdle. . . . **1822** (1932) MCLEAN *Notes* 31: Here we borrowed a "smoking bag," containing a steel, flint, and tinder.

smoky *n. Slang, Derog.* an Indian. See also **smoked.**

[**1885** *Prince Albert Times* (Sask.) 13 Feb. 1/5: "Mother Smoke," a squaw, was tried for having in her possession a buck-saw and axe belonging to a half-breed, but was discharged.] **1953** MOWERY *Mounted Police* 53:

Clad in breechclout and moccasins, Itai-Po was no reservation "smoky" but thoroughly an Indian. *Ibid.* 112: While Prawl did not particularly care for this Chippewa band, he disliked to see them accused of crimes that other Smokies might have committed.

smudge† [smʌdʒ] *n.* **1** a fire which gives off dense, acrid smoke from having damp moss, green grass or leaves, etc. heaped on its flames. See also **mosquito-smudge, smoke** (def. 1), **smoke smudge, smudge bonfire,** and **smudge fire**:
1801 (1897) COUES *New Light* I 287: The women closed the openings of the cabins, and made a smudge inside. **1880** GORDON *Mountain and Prairie* 257: The little enclosure, some ten feet square [is] fenced in to contain the extensive "smudge" of grass and leafy boughs, around which the horses gather on summer evenings to secure in the smoke a respite from the mosquitoes. **1959** *Weekend Mag.* 5 Sep. 3/2: The man replied that he was making smudges to keep away mosquitoes.

2 See **smudge pot**.
1829 MACTAGGART *Three Years* I 185: ... they keep a *smudge* always at the threshold of the door of the dwelling. **1921** (1923) HEMON *Chapdelaine* [trans.] 88: "Telesphore ... make us a smudge. Take the old tin pail." **1961** *Alta Hist.Rev.* Spring 23/1: Flies and mosquitoes were in millions. Everywhere, when driving to town, one had to have a "smudge" in the wagon to ward them off.

3 See 1941 quote.
1939 GROVE *Two Generations* 32: If there had been a moon, a person coming over the hills would have seen that smudge as a perfectly level sheet closing the bowl like a lid. **1941** *Beaver* Sep. 39/2: Smudge—An acrid smoke from green grass or turf for keeping mosquitoes away from a certain area.

smudge bonfire See **smudge** (def. 1).
1923 WALDO *Down Mackenzie* 116: One sees the horses, after a trip—coming in red with blood, perhaps—released for rest, huddling to windward of smudge bonfires, or in default of these standing in a forlorn group together to get in one another's shade.

smudge can See **smudge pot**.
1954 BEZANSON *Sodbusters* 134: A smudge can was my constant companion in or in front of the house.

smudge fire See **smudge** (def. 1).
1909 BINDLOSS *Lorimer* 3: The dun smoke of a smudge-fire shows that Harry is in prairie fashion protecting our stock, and I see it drifting eastward across the dusty plain, with the cattle seeking shelter from mosquitoes under it. **1956** KEMP *Northern Trader* 92: We had to build a big smudge fire for each dog.

smudge pen See quote. See also 1880 quote at **smudge** (def. 1).
1954 BEZANSON *Sodbusters* 134: I burned ten cords of wood each summer in a big smudge pen near the stable to keep the animals from being eaten alive.

smudge pot a can, pail, etc., often with a perforated bottom, used to build a smudge (def. 1). See also **smudge** (def. 2) and **smudge can**.
1947 FREEDMAN *Mrs.Mike* 103: We had to keep smudge pots going, and all day long they huddled about them. **1957** HUTCHISON *Canada* 274: We used to keep a smudge pot on the tongue of the wagon for the horses— they'd go plumb crazy without it—and another by us on the seat.

smudging *n. Obs.* the process of warding off mosquitoes and other winged insects by means of a smudge (def. 1).
1829 MACTAGGART *Three Years* I 184: Nothing will keep them at bay but the strong *smudging smoke* of fire. ...

snag *n.* **1** a large branch or tree trunk, usually submerged, having one end embedded in the bottom of a river or lake. See also **deadhead**.
1784-1812 (1916) THOMPSON *Narrative* 188: The Snag is ... always under water, so that it is not seen, and cannot be avoided; several boats have been sunk by them. ... **1887** (1888) LEES & CLUTTERBUCK *British Columbia* 186: The real risk is from snags, which are very numerous, and in spite of the utmost care cannot always be guarded against. ... **1928** FREEMAN *Nearing North* 290: Many a snag was bumped by boat or motor, but never hard enough to do any harm. **1965** STEVENS *Incompleat Canadian* 38: The process of getting the logs off the snags and sandbars and of marshalling them into rafts involved the now almost forgotten art of "birling," wherein the rivermen, pikes or peavies in hand, worked logs out of shallows by spinning them under their sure feet.

2 a. the stump of a cut or fallen tree.
1920 WINLOW & POCKLINGTON *Mornin'-Glory* 176: At the rink the enthusiastic country boy enjoyed the vast expanse of ice with no snags to interrupt his skating. **1963** *Sun* (Vancouver) 3 Dec. 25/1: ... he was eight feet from his horse, yet his chaps, hat and bloodstained gloves were found more than 80 feet away, in a neat pile behind a snag.

b. See **rampike**.
1953 MOWERY *Mounted Police* 78: In the dead quiet of ... that night ... a dead spruce snag ... crashed full length to the ground. ... **1961** *Sun* (Vancouver) 14 Aug. 4/4: The fire was put out mostly by rain but we cut down smouldering snags and dug out hot spots on a very steep hillside for several days, a dirty and unspectacular job. **1963** MCKINNON *Forest Activities* 12: Cross cut saw for falling snags and trees on fire-line. ...

snag rubbers *Maritimes* rubber boots with the tops trimmed or cut down.
1934 DENNIS *Down in N.S.* 349: He never dresses up. He wears an old pair o' snag rubbers and common pants. He's what we call independent.

snake *n.* See **snowsnake** (def. 1 and picture).
1966 *Globe and Mail* (Toronto) 21 Feb. 5/7: The throwers ... hold the snake in their right hand, take a run of 15 feet or so and launch the snake into the trough, which is from 10 to 18 inches deep.

snakeberry *n. B.C.* See 1952 quote.
1921 HEMING *Drama of Forests* 11: The girls join their mothers in picking berries, which are plentiful and of great variety—raspberries ... bearberries, and snakeberries. **1952** PUTNAM *Cdn Regions* 49/1: On the forest floor are found pigeon-berry ... snakeberry (*Clintonia borealis*) ... and heather moss. ...

snake fence† a kind of rail fence, *q.v.*, in which the rails, often of split cedar, in panels of six or eight, interlock with each other in a zigzag pattern, being sometimes supported by crossed-rail uprights. See also **worm fence** and **zigzag fence**.
1844 MARRYAT *Settlers in Can.* 53: ... a herd of cattle were grazing on a portion of the cleared land; the other was divided off by a snake-fence, as it is termed, and

was under cultivation. **1904** ROBERTS *Watchers of Trails* 239: He had just come out of the woods and up to the snake fence of split rails which bounded the pasture. **1962** *Kingston Whig-Standard* (Ont.) 6 Dec. 4/6: Even the disappearance of the old wooden "snake fences" on the farms, and their replacement by wire or electric fences, is an example of man's "progress" in the destruction of bird life.

snake rail-fence See **snake fence.**
1918 LOWREY *Young Canada Boys* 77: And then when they looked down those first winrows which looked like a "snake (rail) fence," their chagrin was complete, but they soon learned the trick of keeping them straight. **1958** SYMONS *Fences* 48: One of the early Canadian fences most popular in the east was the snake rail fence.

snake room *n.* **1** *Hist.* See 1912 quote.
1910 FRASER *Red Meekins* 76: "Who turned on that gas?" he growled. "Talk 'bout the snake room in any booze joint; this's got 'em all skinned for no rest." **1912** SANDILANDS *West.Cdn Dict.* 42/1: Snake-room, a side room or a basement where saloon-keepers accommodate doped or drunken people until they recover their senses, presumably a place where they "see snakes."

2 *Slang* a beer parlor, *q.v.*; bar.
1961 *Maclean's* 7 Jan. 62/1: . . . drinking and curling are synonymous [and] many a good rink has lost a crucial Brier game or two in a hotel snake-room.

snake-stick *n.* See **snowsnake** (def. 1b and picture).
1900 FRASER *Mooswa* 124: . . . he darted down the Slide as an Indian throws the snake-stick over the snow.

snake-whip *n.* See **black-snake whip.**
1900 FRASER *Mooswa* 194: In the morning, François, taking his loaded snake-whip, hammered the Huskie dogs into a submission sufficient to permit of their being harnessed.

snap *n.* *Cdn Football* a pass which puts the ball into play from scrimmage, the ball being passed through the centre lineman's legs to another player, usually the quarterback. See also **snapout.**
1958 *Edmonton Jnl* 7 Aug. 7/2: . . . London kicker Legg fumbled a snap on the third down. . . . **1963** *Albertan* (Calgary) 19 Nov. 11/6: A poor snap prevented the convert. **1966** *Kingston Whig-Standard* (Ont.) 20 Sep. 11/3: Only once did he back away after coming up behind centre for the snap.

Snap-apple night *Hist.* See quote.
1912 SANDILANDS *West.Cdn Dict.* 42/2: Snap-apple night, Hallowe'en.

snapout *n.* See **snap.**
1964 *Kingston Whig-Standard* (Ont.) 24 Nov. 9/1: . . . he fumbled a bounding snapout on a third down.

snapper (broom) *n.* *Curling* See first quote.
1966 *Globe and Mail* (Toronto) 22 Mar. 29/1: The snappers are Canadian-made brooms—in some areas they are illegal in Canada . . . with a strip of leather in the centre. The leather gives a crackling noise when it strikes the ice, thus the name. *Ibid.*: The . . . rink were given permission . . . to continue using their snapper brooms.

snapping *n.* *Cdn Football* the action of putting the ball into play with a snap, *q.v.*
1965 *Globe and Mail* (Toronto) 14 Jan. 24/4: I'll get somebody else to do the snapping.

snapshot *n.* *Hockey* a shot made by a quick action of the wrist, directing the puck suddenly and accurately at the goal.
1963 *Globe and Mail* (Toronto) 21 Jan. 16/3: Hull responded by taking a quick pass from Balfour and scoring on a quick snap-shot.

sneak *n.* *Slang, Obs.* **make one's sneak,** make one's getaway; duck out.
1890 *Grip* (Toronto) 27 Dec. 411/1: Lawyer Flyman made his sneak early—said he had important business. . . . **1891** *Ibid.* 31 Jan. 68/2: So I'll just write "Liar" on his . . . card and quietly make my sneak.

snie, snigh *n.* See **snye.**

snipe *v.* *Placer Mining* comb through old diggings for overlooked gold. See also **sniper** (def. 1) and **sniping.**
1909 SERVICE *Cheechako* 122: I panned and I panned in the shiny sand, and I sniped on the river bar;/But I know, I know, that it's down below that the golden treasures are. . . .

sniper *n.* **1** *Placer Mining* a person who snipes.
1963 *Placer Mining, B.C.* 7/1: The sniper then takes over, cleaning and scraping pockets and even rewashing old boulder-piles. **1966** BAITY *Wilderness Welfare* 39: . . . the bars had been left for the sniper to work in his slow, laborious way for whatever he could make.

2 *Lumbering, Hist.* See 1956 quote.
1906 *Log of the "Columbia"* June 8/1: "He ought to be chased out of the woods," said Jim, the sniper. **1956** ANDREWS *Glory Days* 14: These were . . . snipers who shaped the butt ends so they [logs] wouldn't hang up on the skids. . . .

sniping *n.* *Placer Mining* See 1965 quote.
1897 HAYNE *Pioneers* 93: There is a little "snipping" [sic]—*i.e.* working old bars—on Forty Mile Creek, but it does not pay much. **1963** *Placer Mining B.C.* 7/1: Chinese miners were particularly adept at sniping and have worked in most camps and on most creeks . . . Sniping and bar-combing are continuously being carried out by individuals who would rather do this than work for wages, and the number so engaged increases in hard times. **1965** *Cdn Geog.Jnl* Dec. 206/3: "Sniping," usually done by the individual, is studying an area and selecting sections of bedrock for working or reworking old tailings.

snipping *n.* See **sniping.**

snooge [snudʒ] *n.* [origin unknown] *Nfld* a way of hitching sled dogs, called Nome hitch, *q.v.*, in the western Arctic. See picture at **Nome hitch.**
1957 *Beaver* Autumn 28/1: They [sled dogs] can also be driven on a "snooge" which is a single long trace with the dogs harnessed to short ones leading off from it at intervals.

snoose [snus *or* ʃnus] *n.* [< Mod.Scand. *snus,* shortening of *snustobak(k)* snuff] a kind of snuff, prepared damp and in grated form, usually chewed; chewing snuff. See also **Copenhagen snoose.** Also spelled *schnoose, snoosh, snooze.*
1912 FOOTNER *New Rivers* 21: Loud were the lamentations of the foreigners when his "snooze" gave

out, "snooze" being the local familiarity for snuff.
1958 *Maclean's* 10 May 55/1: The pioneers with their
oxen and their skid roads greased with Whale blubber
and their lower lips packed with snoose could hardly
be expected to know the tree's very virtues were one of
the seeds of its destruction. **1965** *Sun* (Vancouver)
22 Apr. 51/7: [Caption] ". . . just before ya face the old
lady ya shove a wad of schnoose in yer mouth . . . she'll
never smell yer breath."

snoosh [snuʃ] *n*. See **snoose**.

snooze [snuz] *n*. See **snoose**.

snort *n*. *Slang* a drink of liquor. See also **smash**.
1912 SANDILANDS *West.Cdn Dict*. 42/2: The sporting
Canadian asks his friend, "Will you have a snort?"
1912 BICKERSTETH *Open Doors* 171: I take a snort now
and again, Parson—any harm, eh? **1948** MOIR *Sinners
and Saints* 74: "Say boys! Let us go in and have a snort
before dinner!" **1954** HAGELL *Grass Was Free* 34: "You
know yourself there's a time when a snort of powerful
scotch or rye comes in mighty useful. . . ."

snow *n*. **1**† in Indian parlance, a winter
(representing a year).
1811 (1849) ROSS *Adventures* 324: A common mode of
counting with them [Okanagans] is by snows or
winters. **1923** *Beaver* Sep. 454: He . . . was born some
forty odd "snows" ago.

2 See **snow apple**.
1878 *Cdn Horticulturist* Mar. 42: . . . Fameuse or
Snow, St. Lawrence, and Duchess of Oldenburg, are
quite reliable, and deserve all the praise they get.
1949 DE LA ROCHE *Wakefield* 320: In bunks, like
sleepers, lay the apples, Spies, greenings, russets,
Tolman sweets, snows, pippins. . . .

snow apple [trans. of Cdn F *pomme de neige*,
q.v.] a juicy fall apple having crisp, white flesh and
red skin when ripe. See also **snow** (def. 2) and
fameuse (def. 1).
1865 *Leader* (Toronto) 11 Jan. 4/1: Fameuse, Snow
Apple (Pomme de Neige) [is] excellent when well
developed, bears abundantly, and needs rich soil and
good culture. **1952** BUCKLER *Mountain and Valley* 208:
David's excitement was mixed with the thought of . . .
setting off in the ox wagon to pick Snow apples in the
township orchard. . . . **1959** BARBER & MCPHERSON
Christmas in Can. 24: The apple-jelly was bright red in
color, for snow apples were now sold in Mr Lundy's
store. . . .

snowball party See quote.
1953 MOON *Saskatchewan* 85: At year's end here
[Willow Bunch] they have snowball parties. Which
means a man calls on his neighbour to extend greetings
and the two of them go to a third's house and
gradually the calling group grows like a snowball
rolling down hill.

snow beater a short curved piece of wood or
antler used by the Eskimos to knock loose snow
from their fur clothing.
1936 STRINGER *Wife-Traders* 203: . . . she stooped to
replace the duly aired blankets on the sleeping-stage.
Then she restored the snow-beater to its hook beside
the door. **1946** *Beaver* Mar. 36/2: . . . all snow adhering
to the sleeping-robes, platform skins, and clothing was
carefully beaten off with snow beaters. . . .

snowbird *n*. **1** the snow bunting, *q.v.*, or, less often,
the slate-colored junco, *Junco hiemalis*.
1749 DRAGE *Voyage* II 60: A few Days before our
leaving the Creek, we saw several Flocks of snow Birds.
1792 (1934) FIDLER *Journal* 546: The Snow Birds made
their first appearance, an unerring harbinger of Spring.
1861 BAGSTER *Progress P.E.I.* 90: Prince Edward Island
has . . . her birds of color, such as the Blue-bird . . . the
Snow-bird, and the Cherry-bird. **1958** *Time* (Cdn ed.)
28 Apr. 16/1: While the limited supply lasted, Cheneau
could fill the orders of favored customers for the
succulent little sparrow-sized snowbirds, whose flavor
has delighted French and French Canadian gourmets
[for centuries]. **1963** SYMONS *Many Trails* 179: As I
rode nearer, the snowfield turned to a blizzard of flying
snowbirds.

2 See **Canada jay**.
1959 MCATEE *Folk-Names* 51: Grey Jay [is also called]
snow bird (From being seen in the snowy season.
"Labr."). . . .

snowblind *n*. a bank or heap of snow behind which
an Eskimo hides while hunting.
1924 FLAHERTY *Eskimo Friends* 61: Behind him,
crouching over his snowblind, arms folded on knees
and harpoon in lap, sat an Eskimo.

snow-blind *adj*. affected by snow-blindness, *q.v.*
Cp. **ice-blind**, *adj*.
1748 ELLIS *Hudson's Bay* 189: They frequently become
Snow-blind, in the Spring of the Year, at which time I
have been informed, a Film grows over the Pupil of the
Eye, which I was likewise told these People are so
ingenious as to cut away with the Sharp Point of a
Gun-Flint. **1896** WHITNEY *On Snow-Shoes* 214: Every
man in the party but myself was more or less severely
snow-blind. . . . **1962** *Weekend Mag*. 5 May 4/2: Hunt
was snow-blind and both men collapsed with chest
pains, headaches and fatigue.

snow-blindness *n*. a painful inflammation of the
eyes caused by over-exposure to the glare of the
sun on expanses of snow and ice and resulting in
temporary blindness accompanied by gritty
sensations under the eyelids, excessive watering,
and, in early stages, double vision.
1748 ELLIS *Hudson's Bay* 137: This Invention prevents
Snow-Blindness, a very grievous and painful Distemper,
occasioned by the Action of the Light, strongly reflected
from the Snow upon the Eyes, more especially in the
Spring, when the Sun is pretty high. **1811** (1950)
THOMPSON *Journals* 143: Vallade ill of Snow Blindness.
1937 WHITTAKER *Arctic Eskimo* 116: Snow-blindness is
treated by flooding the eyes with smoke of burning
heather, or sometimes by tying a louse to a thread and
putting it in the eye to scratch the inflamed surface. **1965**
SYMINGTON *Tuktu* 20: By early March dark glasses must
be worn to prevent snow-blindness.

snow blockade on a road or railway, a blocking
of traffic caused by a heavy snowfall.
1869 *Niagara Mail* (Niagara-on-the-Lake, Ont.)
17 Mar. 2/4: [Headline] The Snow Blockade.
1884 *Gateway Express* (Emerson, Man.) 18 Feb. 3/1:
Thursday's train did not get in until nine o'clock this
forenoon, snow blockades being the cause, and still
the "beautiful" falls. **1896** *Kaslo Claim* (B.C.) 4 Jan.
3/1: The snow blockade does not affect the Royal
Cafe. [**1958** *Evening Telegram* (St. John's) 2 May 4/7:
Push plows are being used. This is the second blockade
of the line by snowdrift within the past two weeks.]

snowblockaded *adj. Obs.* snowed-in; isolated by much snow.

1884 *Brandon Blade* (Man.) 7 Feb. 8/1: His experience, on reaching the eastern end of his journey, was that he was just getting into the cold, snowblockaded country.

snowblower *n.* a machine that clears snow from roads, sidewalks, etc. by drawing it in and then blowing it some distance away. See 1966 quote.

1955 *Hamilton Spectator* (Ont.) 25 Jan. 24/3: Were appalled by the possibly $500,000 worth of cement mixers, road rollers, street sweepers, snow blowers, and other city equipment stored outdoors at the Elgin Street yard.... **1962** *Kingston Whig-Standard* (Ont.) 14 Feb. 1/7: Snowblowers were at work this morning clearing the runways. **1966** *Time* (Cdn ed.) 11 Feb. 12/3: It took twenty years of tinkering before [Arthur] Sicard perfected his idea, and in 1927 the city of Outremont [Quebec] bought Sicard's first prototype snowblower for $12,500.

snowboot *n.* a warm, waterproof boot, usually well lined, for winter wear.

*a*1820 (1838) HEAD *Forest Scenes* 20: I had provided myself, according to the custom of the place, with snow-boots made of Brussels carpeting, which buttoned over my boots, reaching above my ancles, with soles of rough felt. **1885** (1963) STANLEY *Louis Riel* 325: The men and officers were in the regular British uniform supplemented with snow boots, fur caps and gloves and most of them with hideous red comforters around their necks. **1962** *Globe and Mail* (Toronto) 23 Mar. 23/8: I donned my parka and my snowboots and journeyed up to Lake Simcoe....

snowbridge *n.* a stretch of packed snow forming a bridge over a river, crevasse, etc.

1890 *Moose Jaw Times* (Sask.) 20 June 1/4: Every observant passenger on the Canadian Pacific Railroad has noticed the snow bridge on the Illecillewaet, but there are records of ice bridges also. **1935** EVANS *Reindeer Trek* 231: Three of the dogs had passed over a frail snowbridge across a narrow but bottomless canyon.

snow-broth *n. Slang, Obs.* See quote.

1912 SANDILANDS *West.Cdn Dict.* 42/2: Snow-broth, snow and water mixed; hence very cold liquor.

snow-bucking engine *Obs.* a railway engine equipped with a snowplough for clearing snow from the track.

1897 *Medicine Hat News* (Alta) 15 Apr. 1/5: The engines which were sent to "buck" the snow on the Soo line have been returned. It is quite needless to say that snow bucking engines were not required on this division during the past winter.

snow-bug *n. Slang* See **motor toboggan** and picture.

1964 *Star Wkly* 19 Dec. 14/1: ... snowmobile owners are likely to get their fun ... going on snow-bug hikes in the bush.

snow-buggy *n. Slang* See **motor toboggan** and picture.

1965 *Kingston Whig-Standard* (Ont.) 27 Dec. 17: [Caption] [They] were roaring through the snow at speeds ... approaching 35 miles-an-hour on the ... new snow buggy.

snow bunny *Slang* a young woman who makes herself conspicuous at ski resorts by the color and attractiveness of her winter garb.

1964 *Star Wkly* 19 Dec. 39/1: December used to be a dull month, but that was before our pretty Canadian snow bunnies gave up hibernation and started brightening up the Canadian snow scene.

snow bunting an Arctic sparrow, *Plectrophenax nivalis.* See also **ortolan, snowbird,** and **white bird** (def. 1).

1772 (1908) COCKING *Journal* 108: Saw a few Snow-buntings. **1795** (1911) HEARNE *Journey* 385: Snow Buntings, universally known in Hudson's Bay by the name of the Snow Birds ... make their appearance about ... the beginning of April, when they are very fat, and not inferior in flavour to an ortolan. **1883** HATTON & HARVEY *Newfoundland* 234: The finches include the American pine grosbeak, the American crossbill, the snow bunting.... **1964** *North* July 40/1: Flocks of snow buntings chattered across his way....

snow cat See quote. Cp. **cat³.** (def. 1).

1960 *Maclean's* 2 Jan. 15/2: ... the snow is brushed and groomed between one day's skiing and the next by tread-driven machines called snow cats.

snow-cloth *n. North* See **sod-cloth.**

snow-cock or **-hen** *n.* See **willow ptarmigan.**

1912 SANDILANDS *West.Cdn Dict.* 42/2: Snow-cock, a snow-partridge. **1959** MCATEE *Folk-Names* 25: Willow Ptarmigan [is also called] snow hen (Que.)....

snow-creek *n.* a small stream formed by melting snow during the spring runoff.

1963 *Maclean's* 18 May 40/3: I have never forgotten our first sight of them ... in the last week of May when the hillsides were still running with little snow-creeks.

Snow Cruiser *Trademark* See **cruiser** (def. 4) and **motor toboggan** (and picture). Cp. **skidoo** and note.

1964 *Star Wkly* 19 Dec. 13/2: Today the Skidoo has Canadian-made competitors with names like Snow Cruiser and Jus-ski and imported rivals like the Autoboggan, Arctic Fox and Arctic Cat, all of them thriving on the discovery that these winter workhorses can also provide winter fun. **1965** *Kingston Whig-Standard* (Ont.) 5 Feb. 11/1: Cam Moulds received a snow cruiser for Christmas—complete with trailer. **1966** *Cdn Geog.Jnl* Sep. 79/3: Outboard Marine makes ... [the] Snow Cruiser ... a small motorized toboggan on rubber tires and skis, a variation of the original snowmobile invented by Armand Bombardier of Quebec ten years ago.

snow-cruising *n.* driving, or riding in, a motor toboggan, *q.v.*

1966 *B.C.Digest* Dec. 10: [Advert.] '67 is the BIG YEAR for SNOW CRUISING ... and you have 3 fabulous OMC Snow Cruisers to choose from!

snow-crust *n.* See **crust.**

1824 (1955) BLACK *Journal* 14: They left the Fort in March on the snow crust. *c*1902 LAUT *Trapper* 220: The heat of the sun told him the directions; and when the sun went down, the crooning west wind, bringing thaw and snow-crust, was his compass. **1955** GOWLAND *Smoke* 201: Once the snow was broken the cattle got their noses underneath and then moved along, feeding and breaking the snow crust upwards with their heads.

snowcut *n.* a gully made by a snow-plough in clearing a way through a large snowdrift.

1959 *Ottawa Citizen* 8 Jan. 19/5: He recollected a winter working on the railway when 30 or 40 cattle were killed by a train in a snowcut.

snow-dag *n.* See **snow-knife.** Cp. **dag.**
1936 BLAKE *Barren Lands* 155: Nilgar and his assistant architect eyed the spot and made a rough estimate of the size the house was to be. Then they set to work to cut snow bricks. Their implement was a flat piece of copper, double-edged and fastened to a wooden handle. It was called a snow-dag.

snow devil a whirling column of snow sucked up in a vortex by the wind. Cp. **dust devil.**
1954 PATTERSON *Dangerous River* 263: There was the same damned wind and the same mad-looking snow devils whirled up the surface of the river. 1959 *Maclean's* 31 Jan. 42/2: During the long night of Feb. 7, the great wind born of the polar ice came seeking to the south across five hundred miles of tundra plain . . . to send snow devils dancing like dervishes across the ice.

snow-eater† *n.* See **Chinook wind.**
1912 SANDILANDS *West.Cdn Dict.* 42/2: Snow-eater, a Chinook or warm wind which rapidly melts the snow. 1951 ANGIER *At Home* 83: Such periods (of cold) are often followed by summery chinook winds which the Indians call *snow-eaters.* 1959 TAYLOR *Canada and Neighbours* 158/1: The warm west wind which brings this sudden change is known as . . . a "snow-eater."

snowed in filled in, covered, or blocked by snow.
1857 MCDOUGALL *Voyage* 331: The fore and after parts of the upper deck were now snowed in, to the depth of nine inches on the starboard side. 1896 (1898) RUSSELL *Far North* 46: That afternoon we passed two recently ditched locomotives and learned that three trains were snowed in ahead of us. 1955 GOWLAND *Smoke* 203: I have seen a little cul-de-sac valley littered with skulls of perhaps a hundred cattle which had become snowed in and could not get out.

snowed out postponed because of heavy snow making activity impracticable.
1964 *Weekend Mag.* 25 July 29/2: In 1962, for example, the race was "snowed out."

snow-eyes *n.pl. Obs.* See **snow goggles.**
1748 ELLIS *Hudson's Bay* 137: If their Clothes and other Necessaries are well contrived, their Snow-Eyes, as they very properly call them, are no less so. 1772 (1792) CARTWRIGHT *Journal* I 201: He was afterwards employed in making his sled, while I was engaged in making a pair of snow-eyes. 1819 MCKEEVOR *Hudson's Bay* 31: For the purpose of guarding off the intense light reflected from the snow, they make use of a very ingenious kind of spectacle, or snow-eyes, as they call them.

snow fence a fence erected on the windward side of a road or railway to prevent obstruction through drifting.
1872 (1873) GRANT *Ocean to Ocean* 261: The high mountains not only protect the valleys from much of the cold, but . . . also act as natural snow fences. 1876 FLEMING *Intercolonial* 110: Should the adjoining lands be cleared of their timber, a snow fence becomes a necessity, and a thick belt of brush would prove extremely well for that purpose. 1963 *Weekend Mag.* 7 Dec. 8/3: But I saw farmers . . . mending snow fences. . . .

snow fencing material used for snow fences, especially an easily handled combination of slats and wire which can be rolled up when not in use.
1953 *Cdn Geog.Jnl* XLVI 68/2: Still others made cribs out of snow fencing and piled the grain in the open fields. 1961 *Time* (Cdn ed.) 29 Dec. 10/3: [He] testified that Stelco returned $36,823 in over-payments to intermediaries . . . largely for snow fencing. . . .

snowfly *n.* the first fall of snow.
1962 FRY *Ranch on the Cariboo* 270: "Why, if I contract the Anthony [job] it'll start raining tomorrow and it won't quit till snowfly."

snow glasses See **snow goggles.**
1930 *Beaver* Mar. 368: . . . the light of the sun becomes so great that snow glasses become a necessity. . . . 1954 PATTERSON *Dangerous River* 278: Soon snow glasses were making their appearance and shady hats, while others ringed their eyes with charcoal, thus achieving a . . . clownish, appearance.

Snow goggles

snow goggles *North* slotted goggles of wood, bone, ivory, etc., worn as protection against snowblindness, especially by Eskimos. See also **snow-eyes, snow glasses,** and **travelling spectacles.**
1882 GILDER *Schwatka's Search* 92: All three wore spectacles, not snow goggles, but, as the interpreter said, all the same seko (ice). 1941 *Beaver* Mar. 13/1: Snow goggles are useful for flat stretches of country where there are no trees. 1952 HOWARD *Strange Empire* 400: Some had been issued snow goggles but some had not, or had lost them.

snow goose a white goose, especially *Chen hyperborea.* See also **white goose.** Cp. **wavey.**
1795 (1911) HEARNE *Journey* 441: The skin, when stripped of its feathers, is of the same colour as the Snow Goose, and is equally good eating. 1963 *Globe and Mail* (Toronto) 13 Mar. 2/1: . . . the cost is nothing compared to the thrill of seeing great honkers sweep in on their blind, of hearing and seeing the Cree Indians talk the language of the blue and snow geese and coax them right down to their shotgun muzzles.

snow-hen *n.* See **snow-cock.**

snowhouse *n. Arctic* **1** See **igloo** (def. 1a and picture).
1771 (1792) CARTWRIGHT *Journal* I 96: I looked at my traps down the river, and then proceeded to Lyon Head, where I visited my Indian friends in their snowhouse. 1819 *Christian Recorder* (York [Toronto]) Mar. 35/2: The Esquimaux now began to build a snow-house about thirty paces from the beach. 1966 *Globe and Mail* (Toronto) 5 Jan. 25/3: The Eskimos in the area [Boothia Peninsula] . . . stay in tents in the summer and snowhouses in the winter.

2 a building made of snow blocks and intended for communal gatherings. Cp. **dance house** and **singing house.**
1962 *Weekend Mag.* 5 May 4/2: This kept up . . . until a large section of the snow house roof caved in from the heat of the gathering. 1964 *Kingston Whig-Standard* (Ont.) 23 Dec. 16/4: At Pelly Bay . . . great snow

houses are erected and the drummer goes to the middle of a stage. . . .

snow hut *Arctic* See **igloo** (def. 1a and picture).
1823 *Literary Gaz.* 25 Oct. 673/3: This was a tribe of about fifty Esquimaux who were erecting their snow-huts, and taking up their residence at a short distance from the vessels. **1958** *Encyc.Can.* IV 38/1: Umiak and kayak have already disappeared from most regions, snow hut and stone lamp seem likely to follow in their wake. . . .

snow igloo *Arctic* See **igloo** (def. 1a and picture).
1921 HAWORTH *Trailmakers* 235: Their clothing was of skins, and in summer they lived in skin tents and in winter in snow igloos, in the building of which they were very expert. **1952** STANWELL-FLETCHER *Tundra World* 218: She's been stormbound in tents and snow igloos; when their small son was only four, they were lost in a storm once for days in the ice of Hudson Bay, but kept alive by building an igloo and eating one of their loved dog team.

snow-knife *n.* a knife about 15 inches long having a broad, straight blade and used primarily for cutting snow blocks for igloos (def. 1a). See also **pana** and **snow-dag.**
1850 (1852) OSBORN *Arctic Jnl* 161: My supporters . . . consisted of old Abbott, armed with a snow-knife, and some men who ran, because they saw o thers doing so. **1930** *Beaver* Mar. 362: The pieces [of snow] are made to have a slight inclination inwards and are fitted close together by the skilful use of the snow knife. **1958** *Evening Telegram* (St. John's) 24 Apr. 17/4: Using a "panar" or snow-knife, he quickly cut snow blocks from the hard-packed cover of sea-ice. **1966** *Beaver* Winter 32/2: They had no snow knife to build a shelter, no food, and one pair of mitts between them.

snow-lily *n.* See **avalanche lily.**
1910 WARD *Canadian Born* 123: They dismounted and explored the great camps of workmen in the pass; they watched the boiling of the stream, which had carved the path of the railway; they gathered white dogwood, and yellow snow-lilies, and red painter's brush.

snow-melter *n. Prairies* See quote.
1960 *Sask.News* 12 Apr. 2/2: Livestock ate snow or drank water from snow-melters, made by propping a metal trough on bricks. The farm lads preferred to fire the melter with flax straw. . . .

snowmobile ['snoməˌbil] *n.* [< *Snowmobile,* a trademark < *snow* + auto*mobile*] **1** a large tracked vehicle designed to carry persons and goods across country over snow and ice. See also **snow tractor.** Cp. **bombardier.**
1934 *Beaver* June 60/3: . . . this season a . . . Snowmobile is being shipped to Coronation Gulf for inspection work next winter. **1935** *Ibid.* June 60/3: Mr. Gibson travelled as far as Kugaryuak by snowmobile, where engine trouble developed and he took to the slower but surer dog-team pending repairs. **1953** MOON *Saskatchewan* 9: In the heart of Moosomin, Bob Fudge has a snowmobile manufacturing plant, possibly the first anywhere. His experimentation period began in the late 1920's. In the early 1930's, when contraction rather than expansion was the rule, he began production. His early work had trials. Just when things were going nicely, a rural municipal convention passed a resolution branding snowmobiles a "menace" to horse-drawn vehicles. **1961** GREENING *Ottawa* 154: In winter a great deal of timber is transported by snowmobiles and trailers to the depots and waterways. . . . **1963** *Calgary Herald* 20 Sep. 26/1: The

snowmobile clattered along the road marked by rows of empty oil drums to the Eskimo village. . . .
2 See **motor toboggan** and picture.
1963 *Kingston Whig-Standard* (Ont.) 2 Mar. 10/8: Those who didn't travel to fishing spots by snowmobile or other powered equipment had to go by snowshoe. **1964** *Star Wkly* 19 Dec. 13/2: These sports-car model snowmobiles cost from $600 to $1,500, depending on power and accessories—which even include mufflers. **1966** *Globe and Mail* (Toronto) 1 Jan. 23/1: I would put the snowmobile down as the greatest single factor in the public use of the winter outdoors. . . .

snowmobile club a club made up of owners of motor toboggans, *q.v.*
1964 *Star Wkly* 19 Dec. 14/1: Quebec has 35 snowmobile clubs which compete almost every winter weekend in local, regional and provincial competitions. **1966** *Globe and Mail* (Toronto) 1 Jan. 23/1: It is a handy, practical guide on how to start a snowmobile club and keep it running.

snowmobile race a cross-country race in snowmobiles (def. 1) or motor toboggans, *q.v.*
1953 MOON *Saskatchewan* 202: During the 1930's snowmobile races were held. . . . **1965** *Kingston Whig-Standard* (Ont.) 4 Jan. 13/8: He admitted there will be a . . . snowmobile race. . . .

snowmobiling ['snoməˌbiliŋ] *n.* the sport of travelling or racing in motor toboggans, *q.v.*
1964 *Star Wkly* 19 Dec. 14/1: We'd like to see a broader approach to snowmobiling as a family-style sport.

snow moss *Obs.* See **caribou moss.**
c1752 (1852) COATS *Geography of H.B.* 82: There is some snow moss in the valleys, which, I am told, the dear are fond of; and nature produces nothing in vain.

snow-mushroom *n.* a mushroom-shaped cap of snow that forms on trees, stumps, etc. in regions where snowfall is heavy and constant.
c1902 LAUT *Trapper* 195: At a certain altitude in the mountains, much frequented by game because undisturbed by storms, snow falls—falls—falls, without ceasing, heaping the pines with snow mushrooms, blotting out the sun, cloaking in heavy white flakes the notched bark blazed as a trail. **1921** HEMING *Drama of Forests* 180: Among the branches huge "snow-bosses" were seen, and "snow-mushrooms" of wondrous shape and bulk were perched upon logs and stumps. [**1957** HUTCHISON *Canada* 265: Midwinter in the Rockies and . . . every stump bears a mushroom of snow.]

snow pants *Arctic* pants of sealskin, caribou skin, etc., worn by Eskimos and others in the North.
1948 ONRAET *Sixty Below* 100: The ordinary snow pants and parka are made with the least possible openings.

snow partridge See **snow-cock.**
1912 [see quote at **snow-cock**]. **1959** MCATEE *Folk-Names* 25: Willow Ptarmigan [is also called] snow partridge (Alta.). . . .

snowplane *n. Rare* an early type of bombardier, *q.v.*, which, driven by a propeller, or airscrew, travelled over snow and ice on skis. Cp. **snowmobile** (def. 1).

1953 MOON *Saskatchewan* 9: Bob Fudge's manufacturing is not confined to snowplanes.

snow platform See **sleeping-platform.**
1966 *Beaver* Winter 27/1: I don't feel nostalgic about the vanishing igloo with its snow platform and seal oil lamp.

snowplough or **snowplow**† *n.* any of various devices for clearing snow off roads, railway tracks, etc.; in modern use, usually, a vehicle equipped with a blade for this purpose.
1849 ALEXANDER *L'Acadie* II 138: [Settlers] are of course indispensable along a road at intervals, to keep it clear of snow in winter, by means of the simple snowplough, like the letter A laid on the ground and drawn by horses or bullocks. 1854 *Hamilton Gaz.* (C.W.) 7 Dec. 2/7: In consequence of a snow plough being in front of the Express engine, and it blowing a heavy storm at the time, the Engineer did not perceive the warning. 1895 *Times* (Niagara-on-the-Lake, Ont.) 5 Dec. 1/1: The snow-plough made its first appearance on the street this morning. 1966 *Globe and Mail* (Toronto) 24 Jan. 17/8: How many even knew where to find someone with a snowplow for hire?

snow-plough club a group of persons in rural areas banded together to share the work and expense of keeping local roads open in winter.
1964 *Naicam Sentinel* 26 Mar. 2/4: . . . Snow Plow Clubs wishing for a special levy for Snow Removal must submit a petition. . . .

snow probe or **sounder** *Arctic* See quotes.
1946 MANNING *Igloo* 73: The snow probe, a rigid but slender rod of brass about three feet long with a terminal knob of ivory used to test the snow, was carried in one of the gun bags. 1946 JENNESS *Material Culture* 105: The main purpose of the snow sounder was to test the depth and compactness of snow with a view to the construction of a snow-hut . . . The implement was a straight, slender rod of antler roughly three feet long, usually shod at the bottom with a peg of bone or musk-ox horn.

snow-road *n. Hist.* See **winter road** (def. 2).
1829 MACTAGGART *Three Years* II 103: When sleighs, in the *snow-roads*, form one *cahot* or wave, others follow directly in regular succession; for the heave they make when descending from the crown of the cahot, creates a valley beyond. 1883 FRASER *Shanty* 22: . . . as they are in the vicinity of the mill, they can be drawn direct to it on the snow-roads, just when they are cut. . . . 1945 CALVIN *Saga* 52: . . . letters to him in 1876 . . . are full of questions about the condition of his snow-roads in the bush, about the prospect for "driving" on the streams in the spring. . . .

snow-scoot *n.* See **scoot** and picture.
1963 *Globe and Mail* (Toronto) 1 Apr. 1/1: They were using a snow-scoot, a propeller-driven sled equipped with a pull-type, rather than the usual pusher propeller.

snow scooter See **motor toboggan** and picture.
1964 *Star Wkly* 19 Dec. 13/1: The odd little snow scooters you see cavorting about . . . represent the

newest phenomenon to revolutionize Canadian sport, family living—and business. 1966 *Kingston Whig-Standard* (Ont.) 17 Jan. 18/5: . . . their snow scooter plunged through the ice on Mitchell Bay [Ont.].

snow-shed *n.* a sloping shed or roof, now usually of reinforced concrete, constructed over a railway track or a highway so that avalanches may pass harmlessly overhead without blocking the way or endangering lives.
1872 (1873) GRANT *Ocean to Ocean* 252: On each side of the valley are mountains that act as natural snow-sheds. 1887 (1888) LEES & CLUTTERBUCK *British Columbia* 380: These snow-sheds are huge wooden constructions, with a slanting lean-to roof, designed to shoot the avalanches over the track. . . . 1964 *Herald Mag.* 29 Feb. 1/1: The chief defences are the snow sheds (which carry slides harmlessly over the road in the Illecilliwaet Valley) and the avalanche warning system.

snowshirt *n. Arctic* See **sealapack.**
1934 GODSELL *Arctic Trader* 286: Throwing back his *ahtegi* hood . . . he handed me a letter which he drew from within his snowshirt. 1941 *Beaver* Mar. 9/2: For storms, a white cotton snowshirt worn over the two parkas is useful, especially if it has a draw string around the face, and a sash around the waist makes all snug. 1956 GODSELL *Mad Trapper* 66/1: Their *ahtegis* and snow-shirts belted about their waists . . . they whipped up their huskies and headed for the Rat. . . .

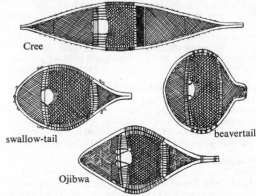

Cree

swallow-tail   beavertail

Ojibwa

Snowshoes

snowshoe *n.* **1** one of a pair of webbed frames for walking on top of deep snow. See also **racket, raquette, shoe** (def. 1) and **web.**
1680 (1945) *H.B.C.Minutes* 67: Mar. Letton to Deliver 4 dressed Mouse skins to Thos. Garland to make Snowe Shooes. 1760 JEFFERYS *Descr.New France* 57: The texture of the raquette or snow-shoe, consists of straps of leather about two lines in breadth, bordered with some light wood hardened in the fire. 1872 DASHWOOD *Chiploquorgan* 70: The moose, being started from his yard, is followed by the men on snow shoes, sometimes accompanied by dogs, who head the animal and bring him to bay. 1966 *Globe and Mail* (Toronto) 19 Jan. 29/7: [He] went out on his snowshoes to check some sets he had made for rabbits . . . on the south shore of Lake Athabasca.

2 See **horse snowshoe** and picture.
1964 *Western Wkly* 29 Jan. 3/3: [Caption] When the snowshoe comes loose, intelligent horses stop until it is adjusted.

3 See **mukluk** and picture.
1960 *Camsell Arrow* Jan.-Mar. 70/2: "We call these

snow shoes but white people call them mukluks," he said.

snowshoe *v.* travel on snowshoes (def. 1). See also **snowshoeing.**
1921 HEMING *Drama of Forests* 161 : When we reached God's Lake, for a while we snowshood down the centre, until at the parting of our ways we said goodbye, for the Indians were heading directly for Fort Consolation. **1963** *Weekend Mag.* 2 Feb. 6/1 : They had to snowshoe to the Little Island Lake where, in the autumn, they had built a lean-to. **1964** *Star Wkly* 5 Dec. 35/2 : So far, he has snowshoed himself to near exhaustion, been lost, hungry and marooned in the wilderness. . . .

Snowshoe *n.* See **snowshoe hare.**
1887 (1888) LEES & CLUTTERBUCK *British Columbia* 261 : The Snowshoe is an animal perhaps unknown to some of our readers. He is the largest kind of alpine hare. . . . **1963** *Kingston Whig-Standard* (Ont.) 1 Feb. 11/4 : Most common in the area are the Snowshoe and the Cottontail. The southern boundary of the 'shoe territory has been gradually moving northward out of Southern Ontario. . . .

snowshoe babiche See **snowshoe netting.** See also **babiche** (def. 1).
1956 EVANS *Mountain Dog* 55 : All he found beside the bed was a short length of snowshoe babiche.

snowshoe club a club made up of persons interested in snowshoeing, *q.v.*, as recreation.
☞ *Such groups are especially popular in Quebec nowadays.*
1881 (1882) LEMOINE *Quebec* 521 : That the Quebec-Snow-Shoe Club may long continue to enjoy the benefit and influence of your agreeable company is the heartfelt desire of us all. **1927** *Beaver* Dec. 107 : . . . numerous snowshoe clubs exist in the cities of Canada. **1962** *Maclean's* 6 Jan. 26/1 : French Canada's 90 snowshoe clubs have about 15,000 members. A few of them own snowshoes.

snowshoed *adj.* shod with snowshoes (def. 1); wearing snowshoes.
1896 WHITNEY *On Snow-Shoes* 213 : Had it been less serious I should have been amused by the spectacle of a snow-shoed Indian chasing the fleetest quadruped on earth. **1942** TWOMEY & HERRICK *Needle to North* 120 : By and by, when it was again silent, we heard the shuffling sound of snowshoe'd feet, and the ringing, steady blows of the axe.

snowshoe evil *Obs.* See **mal de raquette.**
1763 (1901) HENRY (Elder) *Travels* 69 : I was now troubled with a disorder, called the snow-shoe evil, proceeding from an unusual strain on the tendons of the leg, occasioned by the weight of the snow-shoe, and [which] brings an inflammation.

snowshoe fever See **mal de raquette.**
1952 (1954) JENNINGS *Strange Brigade* 127 : By the end of our first fortnight on the trail we had developed several cases of snowshoe fever, which is a painful swelling of the ankles and lower legs, brought on by the unaccustomed use of the racquets.

snowshoe frame the wooden frame of a snowshoe (def. 1).
1772 (1955) MCCOWAN *Upland Trails* 152 : The Indians were employed . . . in preparing small staffs of birch-wood . . . which they convert into snow-shoe frames when the winter sets in. **1801** (1933) MCLEOD *Diary* 157 : . . . Roy is getting wood for Snow Shoe frames. . . . **1954** EVANS *Mist* 201 : Matt had a pair of snowshoe-frames which he had long meant to fill and

this morning . . . he brought in the bucket of rawhide which he had put to soak behind the kitchen stove.

snowshoe hare the varying hare, *q.v.*, so called because of the heavy winter feathering on its feet; also, in some areas, the Arctic hare, *q.v.* See also **'shoe, Snowshoe,** and **snowshoe rabbit.**
1936 *Natural Hist.* Nov. 290 : In the "Good Rabbit Years," when the woods were overrun with snowshoe hares, and the lynx and foxes that preyed upon them were plentiful, the beaver were left practically untouched. **1965** *Kingston Whig-Standard* (Ont.) 5 Feb. 11/1 : On the long drive . . . we noticed a number of snowshoe hares on the highway.

snowshoeing *n.* the practice or pastime of travelling or racing on snowshoes (def. 1). See also **snowshoe,** *v.*
1789 (1882) LEMOINE *Quebec* 86 : Your success in killing [moose] depends on the number of people you have to pursue and relieve one another in going first (which is the fatiguing part of snowshoeing). . . . **1887** *Grip* (Toronto) 5 Mar. 1/2 : Snow-shoeing consists chiefly in tumbling down and picking one self up; and the wise snow-shoer will leave this latter task to some one else. . . . **1966** *Globe and Mail* (Toronto) 18 May 6/1 : He was named King of the Trappers in Edmonton . . . defeating all comers at load-carrying . . . and snowshoeing.

snowshoe lameness See **mal de raquette.**
1947 ROWLANDS *Cache Lake* 32 : *Mal de raquette,* or snowshoe lameness, is something you have to watch out for at this time of year.

snowshoe lashing the harness by which a snowshoe is attached to the foot.
1925 GRAHAME *Bompas* 29 : If the snow-shoe lashings . . . are too tight on the limbs, or if the feet are held too stiffly, a very painful affliction of the muscles supervenes, known as the snow-shoe sickness.

snowshoe line 1 *Obs.* See **snowshoe netting.**
1831 (1944) *Beaver* Sep. 17 : That Gentlemen in charge of Districts and Posts be directed to use their utmost endeavours to collect large quantities of . . . Snowshoe Line . . . as these articles are absolutely necessary for the trade in many parts of the country, and cannot be purchased in Europe or Canada.

2 See **snowshoe lashing.**
1934 GODSELL *Arctic Trader* 291 : . . . pushing our feet into the snowshoe lines we hit the trail once more.

snowshoe lines See **snowshoe lashing.**

snowshoe marathon a long-distance race on snowshoes (def. 1).
1958 *Cdn Geog.Jnl* Jan. 4/2 : There are also ice-fishing contests, snowshoe marathons, . . . and displays of such special skills as trap-setting and [musk]rat-skinning.

A snowshoe needle

snowshoe needle See 1941 quote.
1784 (1954) *Moose Ft Jnls* 64 : Armourer making Fish darts and Snow Shoe needles for Abbittibby.

1933 MERRICK *True North* 103: In it he carries a few matches, a few candles and cartridges, a spare pair of sox, his pencil, an awl and crooked-knife, a snowshoe needle, sewing materials . . . and other cherished encumbrances. **1941** *Beaver* Sep. 39/2: Snowshoe Needle—A bone or metal needle four inches in length, sharp at both ends and with a hole in the centre. An expert Indian woman will work this like a shuttle and turn out beautiful netting in a pair of snowshoes.

snowshoe netting the thongs of rawhide, or babiche, which are used to web snowshoes (def. 1). See also **snowshoe babiche** and **snowshoe line** (def. 1).
1774 (1934) HEARNE & TURNOR *Journals* 119: Traded a little Meat and some Parchment Deerskins for Snow shoe Netting. **1878** (1921) *Beaver* July 4/2: That Factor Belanger be instructed to forward . . . 50 lbs. large snowshoe netting, 50 lbs. small snowshoe netting.

snowshoer *n.* a person who travels on snowshoes (def. 1).
1884 *Brandon Blade* (Man.) 21 Feb. 8/3: The snowshoers then having lighted their torches, started on their way to the summit of Mount Royal.
1921 HEMING *Drama of Forests* 185: No snowshoer could be found who was swift enough to break a trail for those dogs and no horse ever overtook them.

snowshoe rabbit See **snowshoe hare.**
1903 LONDON *Call of Wild* 90: And leap by leap, like some pale frost wraith, the snowshoe rabbit flashed on ahead. **1964** *Sun* (Vancouver) 15 July 19/1: Snowshoe rabbits (hares) bounded across the road in our truck headlights going in, and again in the bright blue, dewless morning. . . .

snowshoe race a competition in cross-country snowshoeing, *q.v.*
1957 *Aklavik Jnl* Apr. 3/1: Snowshoe races will be run for both men and women. **1966** *Globe and Mail* (Toronto) 18 May 6/1: . . . last winter in a snowshoe race he ran five miles through soft snow to win in a few seconds over 35 minutes. . . .

snowshoe runner a person skilled at making fast time while travelling on snowshoes (def. 1).
1921 HEMING *Drama of Forests* 174: All crowded round the voyageur, who . . . was famed as a snowshoe runner throughout the wilderness stretching from the Canadian Pacific Railroad to the Arctic Ocean.

snowshoe sickness See **mal de raquette.**
1841 (1937) *Beaver* Sep. 32/2: . . . the snow shoe sinks much deeper before the track is formed, and retains upon it a great quantity of snow . . . which forces the foot dreadfully in a long journey, and often occasions the *mal de raquette,* or snow shoe sickness, which is extremely painful. **1954** PATTERSON *Dangerous River* 259: [Glossary] . . . snowshoe sickness [is] much the same as the navy's 'immersion foot', or trench foot.

snowshoe trail a trail followed by persons snowshoeing.
1914 DOUGLAS *Lands Forlorn* 157: We had snow-shoe trails strung all over the country for a radius of ten miles, and under our thorough patrolling we missed very little of what went on among the animals.
1965 *Islander* 14 Feb. 4/3: So I dug a hole three feet

deep in my snowshoe trail half a mile south of the camp. . . .

snowslide *n. Obs.* a hill used for tobogganing or sleighing.
1852 (1881) TRAILL *Cdn Crusoes* 251: Warm and glowing from head to foot, with cheeks brightened by the delightful exercise, they would remain for hours enjoying the amusement of the snow-slide. . . .

snow-smoke *n.* See **poudrerie.**
1924 FLAHERTY *Eskimo Friends* 145: By daybreak we were off again, helter-skelter down a steep slope, a-crash through the tidal ice, then off straight north through twisting snow-smoke on an unending sweep of frozen sea.

snowsnake† *n.* **1 a.** an Indian game played with a straight wooden rod having a weighted head resembling that of a snake, this rod being slid over a smooth field of snow or down specially constructed runways. See also **snake.** Also *snowsnakes.*
1888 *Trans.Roy.Soc.Can.* VI 2 44: If this is the game spoken of by other writers as "Snow-snakes," there is nothing in the [Abenaki] name to so indicate.
1935 JENNESS *Parry Island* 95: In winter the children . . . vied with each other in the widely-spread game of snow-snake. **1956** LEECHMAN *Native Tribes* 42: Another game, seldom seen now, called "snow snake," was played in winter. . . . **1966** *Globe and Mail* (Toronto) 21 Feb. 5/6: One of the oldest winter sports among the Indians of the Iroquois country . . . snowsnakes is beginning a revival after a slowdown of several years.

A snowsnake

b. the rod used in this game. See also **snake-stick.**
1932 JAMIESON *Cattle in the Stall* 179: Did you ever see a snow snake? **1958** *Encyc.Can.* V 263/2: Snowshoes, hickory walking sticks, and snowsnakes (used in a traditional game) as well as a few masks are still made on various reserves. **1966** *Globe and Mail* (Toronto) 21 Feb. 5: [Caption] Fred Green of Ohsweken examines highly polished snowsnake. Made from maple, ash, oak or hickory, snakes range from 4 to 9 feet in length.

2 *North* See **Sikusi.**
1958 *Cdn Geog.Jnl* Jan. 4/2: Each year there is a competition for the invention of a strange new northern animal—a contest in which clever taxidermists are apt to carry off the honours with such fantastic creations as the "snow snake" (a snake with a coat of fur).

snowsnake racing See **snowsnake** (def. 1).
1932 JAMIESON *Cattle in the Stall* 179: . . . it is very probable that within a few years the pastime of snowsnake racing will be a rival to skiing or snowshoeing.

snow sounder See **snow probe.**

snowspoon *n. North* a wooden shovel about four feet long, used by Indians for excavating holes in the snow when camping on the trail.
1942 TWOMEY & HERRICK *Needle to North* 97: One with the snowspoon and one with a snowshoe, two Indians shoveled out a depression a little larger than our tent floor and about eighteen inches deep.

snow tractor a kind of snowmobile (def. 1).

1936 *Cdn Geog.Jnl* Jan. 34/2: Somebody began to work on the idea of snowmobiles and snow tractors. **1947** *Beaver* Sep. 20/1: When the department got around to finding out about snow tractors, the weather threatened to break. **1948** *New Deal for Sask.Fisheries* 20: ... replacing the old-fashioned dog team and sled [are] ... motor toboggans and "snow tractors" which attain a speed up to 35 miles per hour and manoeuver in almost any kind of terrain.

snow trail a trail through the snow.
1957 *Beaver* Spring 40/1: The tractor led to better roads—first by opening snow trails to ease the work for horses and then, with bulldozers on bigger tractors, to the construction of all-season roads. **1966** *Globe and Mail* (Toronto) 8 Feb. 10/7: ... more than 2,000 women travel the rugged snow trails over their traplines in northern forests.

snow trap 1 *North, Obs.* a fox trap built of blocks of snow and baited, the fox jumping in after the bait but being unable to jump out again.
1856 BALLANTYNE *Young Fur-Traders* 191: Now, then, what say you to going farther out on the river, and making a snow trap for white foxes?
2 a number of trees, bushes, etc. left standing to trap drifting snow. See quote.
1962 *Field, Horse & Rodeo* Nov. 11/3: Lots of it will be left for cover, not primarily for game birds but because it is needed for shelter for his stock, for snow traps for moisture and to control run-off. But the wildlife will greatly benefit.

snow-village *n.* a community of Eskimos living in snowhouses, *q.v.*
1962 *Weekend Mag.* 5 May 4/2: We arrived at a snow-village one evening and heard quite a commotion in the largest house.

snow-water *n.* **1** water from melted snow, used for drinking and other purposes.
1771 (1947) *Beaver* Mar. 10/2: No springs near; drink snow water nine months of the year. In summer keep three draught horses to haul water & draw stones.
1864 HALL *Life with Esquimaux* I 286: We had nothing by which to make snow-water, and we had vainly searched the rocks for some. **1913** WILLIAMS *Wilderness Trail* 56: Taking care to avoid the space beneath it, the man built his little fire, and boiled snow water. **1966** BAITY *Wilderness Welfare* 210: We would ... boil a pot of snow water tea, and sit on a log. ...
2 melted snow, often that lying on the surface of sea ice.
1924 MATHEWS *Wilfred Grenfell* 147: His tremendous sealskin boots that reached right up to his hips he took off, shook out the ice and snow-water, and tied them firmly one on the back of each of the two dogs.
1956 TOLBOOM *Arctic Bride* 144: A little warm snow water still lay in the rocky basins on top of the hills. ...

snow-wing *n.* a large, curved blade used for thrusting snow from the path of the vehicle carrying it.
1963 *Albertan* (Calgary) 23 Dec. 3/4: A heavy oilfield tandem truck is equipped with a snow wing travelling up to 15 miles an hour while clearing the road and carrying a load at the same time.

snow-yard *n. Obs.* See **yard,** *n.* (def. 1a).
1873 (1904) BUTLER *Wild North Land* 205: Hunting the moose in summer and winter is one thing—killing him in a snow-yard, or running him down in deep snow is another.

snowy owl a large white owl, *Nyctea nyctea,* native to the Arctic regions, ranging in winter south into the United States. See also **white owl.**
1795 (1911) HEARNE *Journey* 401: The beautiful species of White or Snowy owl is common in all parts of Hudson's Bay, as far north as the Copper-mine River. **1890** *Trans.Hist.& Sci.Soc.Man.* 39 18: Unfortunately, while we slept, a Snowy Owl devoured the captured female, together with her four eggs. **1955** *Fishermen's Advocate* 4 Mar. 6/6: He soon discovered the trouble: a huge snowy owl on the roof-top aerial.

snye or **sny** [snaɪ] *n.* **snyes** or **snies.** [< Cdn F *chenail* channel; cf. Mod.F *chenal*] **1** *Esp.Ottawa Valley* **a.** a side-channel, especially one that bypasses a falls or rapids, rejoining the main river downstream and thus creating an island. See def. 1c.
1827 (1829) MACTAGGART *Three Years* I 136: At this place, there are numbers of islands formed by snies winding round the Falls. **1833** (1955) CRAIG *Early Travellers* 82: Below some of the other piers there are snies, or channels, into which the water furiously rushes, carrying with it entire trees, which again appear far below, mutilated and stripped of their branches. **1948** *Cdn Geog.Jnl* Mar. 150/2: The word *snye, sny* or *snie* has been used for many years to describe a channel behind an island, with slack current or partly dried, or some similar feature.

b. *Lumbering, Obs.* such a side channel used as a route for rafts and cribs of timber. See also **rafting-channel** and **timber snye.** Cp. **dry snye.**
1827 (1829) MACTAGGART *Three Years* I 128: In this snie, or rafting-channel, we propose to place three locks. ...

c. in place names.
1826 (1829) MACTAGGART *Three Years* I 114: This channel is called Gloucester Snie, and seems by Nature made to receive the Rideau Canal. ... **1831** *Trans.Lit. & Hist.Soc.Que.* II 248: This channel, popularly called the Mississippi Snigh, (chenal) leads from the backwater near its mouth, to the foot of the rapids. **1961** PRICE & KENNEDY *Renfrew* 70: ... around Bryson and Campbell's Bay [in the Ottawa Valley] ... one still hears the expression "The Shnye". ...

2 *Northwest* **a.** a narrow, meandering, sluggish side-channel of a river, usually shallow and often coming to a dead end. See also **back-channel, side-channel, side-chute,** and **slough** (def. 3).
1873 (1904) BUTLER *Wild North Land* 162: ... the snow lay deep and soft in "shnay" and "batture." **1908** MAIR *Mackenzie Basin* 40: Much of [the tracking] is in the water, wading up "snies," or tortuous shallow channels ... floundering in gumbo slides ... and finally tottering to the camping-place sweating like horses. ...
1963 PATTERSON *Far Pastures* 201: ... two miles at least of bush and beaver dams, springs and snyes (which are subsidiary channels of the main river), deadfall, potholes and moose meadows.

b. See 1923 quote. Cp. **fast snye.**
1923 WALDO *Down Mackenzie* 45: We swung out slowly from the "snye" into the main stream of the Athabasca. The "snye" is the cut-off between two streams at their junction, making an island of what would otherwise be

a promontory. **1957** CALDER *Frozen North* 165: We skidded down the banks and on to the snye . . . the branch of the river encircling the island.

c. See landing snye.

1921 *Beaver* Aug.-Sep. 15/1: The Imperial Oil Company narrowly escaped the loss of their machines, which were lying on the snye at the back of the Fort awaiting favorable weather. . . . **1945** *Ibid.* Mar. 16/1: Fullerton saw the trouble and . . . chose a spot some distance away on a nearby snye, where he was able to sit [his plane] down without damage. **1958** *Edmonton Jnl* 24 June 3 18/3: In the early days of flying, when the bush pilots and their planes were opening up the north, the snye between the Athabasca and Clearwater rivers became one of the most important landing places.

d. in specific names of streams.

1939 *Beaver* Sep. 28/1: Up the narrow channel known as the Snye, the water is sometimes too low to float fully loaded barges. **1955** HARDY *Alta Anthol.* 134: Fifty feet above the frozen Snye—a tiny tributary of the Mackenzie River—the Rene nosed into the ice.

snye-dam *n. Lumbering, Obs.* a dam for holding water to be redirected through a snye (def. 1b).

1827 (1829) MACTAGGART *Three Years* I 127: . . . here [the river] is quite shallow, requiring all the water for the lock-chamber backed up from the snie-dam below.

soapberry *n.* **1** a shrub, *Shepherdia canadensis,* the berries of which have a high saponaceous quality. See also **buffalo berry** and **soapolallie bush.**

1905 (1954) *B.C.Hist.Qtly* XVIII 186: His account of his case was that for some time the doctor had given him a preparation of "soapberry," next a decoction of "Oregon grape". . . . **1957** CHRISTIE *Okanagan Falls* 42: One little shrub, the Indians' "soopolallie," . . . soap-berry to us, bears its gay red current-like berries now only for the birds to enjoy.

2 the edible red berries of this shrub. See also **bitter berry, brue, buffalo berry, hooshum,** and **soapolallie berry.**

1904 MORICE *Northern Interior of B.C.* 61: The soap-berries were ripening and most of 'Kwah's people were camped at the mouth of Beaver Creek. . . . **1923** *Beaver* Dec. 104: In Central British Columbia it [Indian ice cream] was made by working to a lather the dried soap berry. **1963** *Ibid.* Autumn 40/1: . . . the interior fresh-water Indians . . . readily gave soapberries, kinninnick leaves and bark for smoking, and skins in exchange [for oolachan oil].

soap hole *West* See quote.

1954 *Ghost Pine* 179: We had to watch for patches of quicksand called "soap holes."

soapolallie ['sopə,lɑli] *n.* [< Chinook Jargon *soap* soap + *olallie* berry] *B.C.* **1** a dessert or drink made from crushed soapberries (def. 2). See **1952** quote. See also **Indian ice-cream** and **soapsuds.** Cp. **olallie.**

☛ *The spellings of this term are very numerous:* soapal(l)al(l)i(e), soapalalla, soopal(l)al(l)y, sopelalee, sopolally, *etc.*

1895 *Canadian Mag.* Aug. 344/1: Walking over to the reservation . . . we were fortunate enough to see some Indians eating "soapolali." **1944** BARBEAU *Mountain Cloud* 199: Here are the stems of blackberries and the

wild fruit of the hills that gives sopelalee. **1952** *Tsimshian* 17: The soapberry . . . was mashed, formed into cakes, and dried in the sun. When required the cake was crumbled into water and soaked for awhile, then whipped into a foamy liquid of the consistency of thick soup. This drink was called "soopalally" and was considered a great delicacy. **1966** *Islander* 27 Feb. 6/2: There was [at the potlatch] also a great deal of oolachan-grease and soapollalie.

2 this substance used as a medicine.

1954 *B.C.Hist.Qtly* XVIII 262: Soopolallie made a mild laxative, and rattlesnake weed was used for more drastic purging.

3 See **soapolallie bush.**

4 See **soapolallie berry.**

soapolallie berry *B.C.* See **soapberry** (def. 2). See note at **soapolallie.**

1952 LYONS *Trees, Shrubs* 84: Soopolallie berries when rubbed between the hands make a soapy froth, hence the Indian name: (soop – soap; olallie – berry). **1963** *Sun* (Vancouver) 23 Sep. 6/1: Another name for them is soopallalie—which means soap berries.

soapolallie bush *B.C.* See **soapberry** (def. 1). Also spelled *soopolallie bush.* See note at **soapolallie.**

1937 (1950) STANWELL-FLETCHER *Driftwood Valley* 34: On drier, more open ridges [are] dense thickets of small Shepherdia, or soopolallie, bushes. **1953** FLUKE *Kwakiutl* 21: Another special feast food was made from the berries of the "soopolally" bush, which were dried and stored whole. **1957** CHRISTIE *Okanagan Falls* 42: One little shrub, the Indians' "soopolallie" . . . bears its gay red current-like berries now only for the birds to enjoy.

soapolallie ice-cream *B.C.* See **Indian ice-cream.** See also **soapolallie** (def. 1) and note.

1957 LEWIS *Buckskin Cookery* I 30: "SOAPALALLIE ICE CREAM" (Indian) Pick red soapalallie berries in season. Crush and add sugar. Beat with a spoon or fork until frothy. . . .

soapolallie stick *B.C.* a special paddle-like stick for whipping soapberries into a froth in making soapolallie (def. 1).

1923 BARBEAU *Indian Days* 186: . . . soaking them in water, [they] beat them [berries] up into a froth with a *sopolally* stick.

soapstone carving **1** an *objet d'art* created out of soapstone (steatite) by Eskimo craftsmen.

1964 JENNESS *Eskimo Admin.* II 114: The art trade is beset with so many uncertainties . . . that beautiful prints and attractive soapstone carvings are not a safe base on which to build a people's economy. . . .

2 the art or practice of making such objects.

1963 *Chatelaine* Apr. 58/4: Batiste never had the time for soapstone carving.

soapsuds *n.pl. Obs.* See **soapolallie** (def. 1).

1834 (1963) TOLMIE *Physician* 296: Slaves & young men . . . came in, each with a large box full of "Soapsuds," which he kept vigorously stirring with his naked arm, small sticks having been previously distributed, the guests set to work immediately to convey the contents of the boxes into their stomachs.

social *n.* a social gathering, often for the purpose of raising funds for a church or other organization. See also **box social** and **pie social.**

1870 *Mainland Guardian* (New Westminster, B.C.) 8 Jan. 3/4: A very pleasant Social was given by the ladies and friends in our new mission church on Christmas day. **1873** *Woodstock Sentinel* (Ont.) 12 Dec. 3/1: [They] intend giving an oyster social this Friday evening in the lecture room of their church.
1908 *Observer* (Cowansville, Que.) 8 Oct. 4/1: The stocking social to have been held by the ladies of the Methodist church has been indefinitely postponed.
1915 MCCLUNG *Times Like These* 112: ... they may ... augment the missionary funds by bazaars, birthday socials, autograph quilts and fowl suppers. ...
1958 *Herald-Tribune* (Grande Prairie, Alta) 11 Mar. 3/2: Last year, a March social was held in the Crystal Creek hall. ...

social convener or **convenor** the member of a club committee who is responsible for social activities and for seeing that refreshments are provided at meetings.
1955 *Pictou Advocate* (N.S.) 20 Jan. 1: Following the business meeting a social hour was enjoyed with delicious refreshments served by [the] Social Convener.
1955 *Hamilton Spectator* (Ont.) 25 Jan. 5/2: A committee consisting of the social conveners and the president was appointed. ... **1958** *Kelvington Radio* (Sask.) 5 June 1/6: Social Convenor, Mrs. Torrence.

Social Credit See **Social Credit Party**.
1935 *Calgary Typo News* 15 Mar. 1/1: We Wonder ... What is the policy of The Albertan? Liberal, Social Credit or Independent? **1962** *Maclean's* 28 July 44/2: He said this was not an important election for Social Credit. ...

Social Crediter a member or supporter of the Social Credit Party. See also **Socred** (def. 1).
1957 *Herald-Tribune* (Grande Prairie, Alta) 17 Dec. 12/5: ... the point the editor was making has been conveniently ignored by the Social Credit-ers. ...
1966 *Canadian* 30 Apr. 10/2: The Social Crediters peevishly decided to close Government House.

Social Credit League the organization in which the Social Credit Party has become institutionalized outside the political arena.
1958 *Maclean's* 10 May 97/4: He had had the foresight to copyright the name Social Credit, so that when the two factions separated Wicks and Savage took the name and formed the Social Credit League, pledged to political action. **1961** *Canada Month* Nov. 11/3: ... the B.C. Social Credit League offered alternative solutions to his problem. ...

Social Credit Party a Canadian political party formed in the 1930's, its policies being based on the economic theories of Major C. H. Douglas, 1878-1952, a British engineer. See also **Social Credit** and **Socred** (def. 2).
1958 *Time* (Cdn ed.) 15 Sep. 16/3: The leader of the badly mauled Social Credit party last week was right back where he started. **1963** *Canada Month* Mar. 18/1: It is perhaps a little ironic that the Social Credit Party has been attempting to use this same Baby Bonus as a means of political blackmail.

Social Credit Rally See **Ralliement des Créditistes**.
1963 *Globe and Mail* (Toronto) 23 Oct. 1/5: Mr. Speaker replied ... that it had been agreed during a morning conference that the term would be Ralliement des Creditistes in French and Social Credit Rally in English.

sockeye (salmon) ['sɑkaɪ] *n*. [by folk etymology < Coast Salish *suk-kegh* red fish] a species of Pacific salmon, *Oncorhynchus nerka,* that ranges from Alaska to Japan. See also **red** (def. 4) and **red salmon**.
1869 *Mainland Guardian* (New Westminster, B.C.) 25 Sep. 2/1: The most important from the latter point of view, is the Sockeye. **1880** DAWSON *Queen Charlotte Is.* 110B: These answer no doubt to the fish known on the Fraser River as the suck eye, and much prized.
1964 CARL *Marine Fishes B.C.* 34: Sockeye salmon usually live to be four or five years of age. ...

Socred *n*. **1** See **Social Crediter**.
1955 *Pictou Advocate* 24 Feb. 1/1: ... the addition of the British Columbia Socreds have [sic] given them just the monkey glands they needed to restore them!
1964 *Victoria Dly Times* 8 Feb. 1/1: This ... must be considered the boldest Socred move since the B.C. Electric take-over.

2 See **Social Credit Party**.
1962 *Canada Month* Feb. 21/2: ... Social Credit has been badly damaged by the highhanded methods of B.C.'s Socred government. **1966** *Globe and Mail* (Toronto) 15 Jan. 8/9: And there is the nagging knowledge of the Socred's grand Government House in British Columbia.

sod *n*. *Obs*. a furrow. Cp. **sod corn**.
1826 (1955) CRAIG *Early Travellers* 74: The quantity of seed required is only about one peck per acre; corn is sometimes planted on the furrow (or sod, as it is here called) of new ploughed grass land, and does very well.

sodbust ['sɑd,bʌst] *v*. [< *sod* + *bust* (dial.var. of *burst*)] *West, Slang* operate a farm; farm.
1966 *Maclean's* 19 Feb. 32/4: Up there [High Level, Alta] Canadian homesteaders are sod-busting in the space age.

sodbuster ['sɑd,bʌstɚ] *n*. [< *sodbust*, q.v. + *-er*] *Slang* a farmer, especially a farmer who raises field crops rather than livestock.
1922 STEAD *Neighbours* 126: "Between your fine words I figger that you pick up a dollar now an' again by tottin' these tenderfoot sod-busters out over the bald-headed." **1959** *Press* Dec. 6: It is on the subject of pioneers – trailbreakers, bushwhackers, sodbusters, homesteaders – that the slick "free enterprise" propagandist ... waxes most eloquent. ...

sod-cloth *n*. *North* See quote. See also **sod-flap**.
1942 TWOMEY & HERRICK *Needle to North* 98: The snow-cloth or sod-cloth—a canvas strip always sewed completely around the bottom of a Northern tent— was pulled well out and banked heavily with snow.

sod corn† *Obs*. corn planted in one furrow and covered with the turf from the next, and so on. Cp. **sod**.
1838 *Bytown* [Ottawa] *Gaz.* 19 Sep. 1/3: The sod corn does not make more than half a crop, and is cut up, stalks and all together is stacked for fodder stock.

soddy† *n*. *West, Slang* **1** a rude dwelling consisting of an excavation, often in the bank of a coulee, etc., roofed with sods. See also **sod house** (def. 2).

1958 *Northern Miner* 27 Nov. 25/3: ... he sold out his quarter section and his "soddy," a half-buried hovel made of tough prairie sod and roofed with poplar poles and more sod. **1958** STEGNER *Making Paths* 38: A soddy that poked its low brow no higher than the tailings of a gopher's burrow would have suited me better. **1966** *Islander* 24 Apr. 13/2: It wasn't much of an abode, but it was better than some of the soddies, further south, where pioneers had dug a hole in the ground and covered it over with sods and earth.

2 See **sod shack.**

1965 SHEPHERD *West of Yesterday* 37: The true soddy had four sod walls. The building material came from a twelve- or fourteen-inch furrow ploughed from a dried-up slough bottom.

sod-flap *n.* See **sod-cloth.**

1942 TWOMEY & HERRICK *Needle to North* 224: The sod-flap, corresponding to the snow-cloth, we next weighted down with piles of fine gravel, and at last had on Flaherty Island a neat and windproof shelter.

sod house *West* **1** See **sod shack.**

1953 MOON *Saskatchewan* 12: Of course, his wife wouldn't want him to stay in a sod house with litter and mice in the bed.

2 See **soddy** (def. 1).

1965 SHEPHERD *West of Yesterday* 37: Sometimes the sod house was, in fact, an excavation in a coulee bank.

sod hut *West* See **sod shack.**

1921 HAWORTH *Trailmakers* 247: Year after year more "claims" were taken up, more "sod huts" were built, more of the land was broken for crops. **1963** *Calgary Herald* 14 Dec. 5/1: [Greetings] to people who once lived in log cabins and to those who lived in sod huts.... **1967** *Century* (*Toronto Dly Star*) 13 Feb. 22/1: [In 1898] ... gophers dotted the prairie wool like tent pegs ... where my grandfather and my uncle would build a sod hut.

sod shack or **shanty** *West* a rude dwelling having walls of sods and a roof either of sods supported by wooden rafters or, sometimes, canvas. See also **soddy** (def. 2), **sod house** (def. 1), and **sod hut.**

1883 *Brandon Blade* (Man.) 1 Nov. 8/1: How different when the writer first saw it in April, '82, with one building and a sod shanty. **1951** CORMACK *Local Rag* 14: He had a small piece of land ... and his house was part sod shack and part teepee. **1963** SYMONS *Many Trails* 93: I decided on a sod shack, as being both warmer and cheaper than lumber.

softball *n.* a form of baseball in which a smaller playing field and a larger, softer ball is used.

1927 *Beaver* Sep. 80/2: ... the boys who play soft ball are well in the running for the Peden cup. **1964** *Calgary Herald* 11 July 19/3: An RCAF softball team from Alsask, Sask. captured the Cereal Softball Tournament this week.

soft birch *Obs.* the water birch, or mountain birch, *Betula occidentalis,* of the western mountain region.

1793 (1801) MACKENZIE *Voy.from Montreal* 155: The East side of the river consists of a range of high land covered with the white spruce and the soft birch.

soft sawder [< *soft* + *sawder* (var. of *solder*) blarney] *Slang, Obs.* flattery (an expression popularized by Judge Haliburton's stories of Sam Slick the Clockmaker).

1835 *Novascotian* (Halifax) 3 Dec. 355/1: The "soft sawder" of the Clockmaker had operated effectually on the beauty of Amherst, our lovely hostess of Pugwash's Inn. **1863** WALSHE *Cedar Creek* 136: "That fellow's a master of soft sawder when he chooses: but did you see how he clutched the hard cash, after all?"

soiler *n.* [dial.var. of *sealer*] *Obs.* See **seal hunter.**

1842 BONNYCASTLE *Newfoundland* II 128: From the middle of February until November, they are fully occupied in attending to the fisheries, the fitment of the seal fishing vessels or *soilers,* as they are vernacularly called, beginning early in the year.

soil miner or **robber** *West, Slang* See **land-miner.**

1920 STRINGER *Prairie Mother* 119: All this talk of mine about wheat sounds as though I were what they call out here a Soil Robber, or a Land Miner, a get-rich-quick squatter who doesn't bother about mixed farming or the rotation of crops, with no true love for the land.... **1958** *Alaska Highway News* 30 Jan. 2/1: It is well known that soil miners have put a lot of the farms definitely in the dust bowl class.

sol [sɑl] *n.* [< F; cf. Mod.F *sou*] *Hist.* a French unit of currency formerly in circulation in Quebec. Cp. **sol marqué.**

1777 *Quebec Gaz.* 22 May 3/1: It is this day ordered by the said Court, that the assize and price of Bread be as follows, viz. The white Loaf weighing 4 lbs. at eighteen sols or 9d. The brown Loaf weighing 6 lb. at eighteen sols or 9d. **1930** *Cdn Hist.Rev.* XI 130: His debt of six hundred and twenty-two livres, twenty sols, may have been a factor in determining the unusual length of the agreement. **1964** TAYLOR *Cdn Coins* 19: In Canada, the sol had a value of about one penny, 20 sols making one livre, the 12 denier piece being equivalent to one sol.

soldier *n. Hist.* See 1784-1812 quote.

1784-1812 (1916) THOMPSON *Narrative* 358: In every large camp the Chiefs appoint a number of young men to keep order ... these are called Soldiers, they are all young men lately married, or are soon to be married, they have a Chief, and are armed with a small wooden club. They have great power and enforce obedience to the Chiefs. **1859** (1863) PALLISER *Journals* 135: The Blackfeet chiefs paid us a visit, accompanied by their soldiers. **1874** (1880) MORRIS *Treaties* 93: We are also ready to give the Chief's soldiers, not exceeding four in each band, a present of ten dollars, and next year and every year after, each chief will be paid twenty-five dollars, and his chief soldiers not exceeding four in each band, will receive ten dollars. **1929** JEFFERSON *Saskatchewan* 64: After a sufficient number [of Indians] had assembled, the first thing done was forming a band of "soldiers" or police. These practically chose each other, gathering into their company all the likely young men with those others who, it was known, could be relied on in an emergency.

soldier (black)bird† the redwinged blackbird, *Agelaius phoeniceus.* See also **field officer** and **swamp blackbird.** Cp. **red-winged oriole.**

1958 WATTERS *B.C.Cent.Anthol.* 155: In a bush a few early soldier blackbirds talked to each other ... Then the male flew. His red epaulettes shone finely. **1959** MCATEE *Folk-Names* 60: Red-Winged Blackbird [is also called] soldier bird (. . . Ont.); soldier blackbird (Ont., Man.)....

soldier grant a land grant made to a veteran under the legislation for rehabilitating soldiers after World War I. See also **Soldier Settlement Board.**
1929 JOHNSTON *Beyond Rockies* 193: . . . returning from overseas . . . they took up homesteads and soldier grants, 320 acres each.

Soldier Settlement See **Soldier Settlement Board.**
1956 KEMP *Northern Trader* 59: Things were tough on the homestead, and I had to repay a Soldier Settlement loan.

Soldier Settlement Board a federal government board having charge of settling veterans on land grants following World War I. *Abbrev.* S.S.B., *q.v.*
1921 *Beaver* Dec. 18/1: . . . according to the report of the Soldier Settlement Board, 25,443 of his brothers-in-arms have forsaken the cities . . . and gone to the soil. . . . **1951** CORMACK *Local Rag* 76: The original Soldier Settlement Board . . . was bringing out veterans of the 1914-18 war . . . to settle on western farms.
1965 SHEPHERD *West of Yesterday* 87: Tom got a position with the Soldier Settlement Board.

soldier-settler *n. Hist.* a veteran of World War I who settled on land granted under the terms of the Soldier Settlement Board.
1965 SHEPHERD *West of Yesterday* 87: Later on he was stationed at Swift Current, where he inspected land bought by soldier-settlers.

soldiers' lodge *Hist.* See **war lodge** (def. 2). See also **soldier.**
1936 (1960) STANLEY *Birth of Western Canada* 196: The war chief was independent of the civil chief. He held his position by virtue of physical prowess and military reputation, and might, at any time, gather a number of young men around him, set up a "soldiers' lodge" and make forays against hereditary foes. **1936** *Ibid.* 366: The Assiniboines in his camp [Poundmaker's] had set up a "soldiers' lodge," and . . . were anxious to join the métis at Batoche.

soldiers' tent *Obs.* See **war lodge** (def. 1). See also **soldier.**
1913 COWIE *Adventurers* 308: Warriors' Council Lodge (always called "Soldiers' Tent" by traders). . . .

solid Grit a dyed-in-the-wool Liberal.
1891 *Grip* (Toronto) 28 Feb. 134/2: Non-Party Fellow (*to Solid Grit*) – "Did you go to hear Sir John the other night?"

sol (or sou) marqué *Hist.* See 1952 quote. Cp. **sol.**
1764 *Quebec Gaz.* 4 Oct. 1/1: It is hereby further Ordained and Declared . . . That from the Date of the Publication hereof, all Sols Marqués, whether old or new, shall pass only as Farthings. **1896** PARKER *Lavilettes* 54: "I'll bet he's got nothing more than what he went away with, and that wasn't a sou markee!"
1952 (1965) HAMILTON *Cdn Quotations* 138/2: It's not worth a sou marquee. Phrase common in the Maritime provinces meaning, of trifling value; a reference to French Guiana sous which, counterstamped by other West Indian colonies, were sometimes carried north to Canada.

Solomon Grundy or **Gundy** [by folk etymology < *salmagundi*, perhaps influenced by the nursery rhyme about Solomon Grundy] *N.S.* pieces of

salted herring marinated in vinegar, pickling spices, and onions.
1959 *Maclean's* 28 Mar. 27/1: [Lunenburg] is continentally famous for its cooking and for its dozens of local recipes, including solomon gundy, hodge podge (cooked mixed fresh vegetables), dandelion beer, krishelo (patties made from curds, cream and caraway seeds). . . . **1964** *Ibid.* 16 Nov. 27/3: There's another good herring dish, too, called Solomon Grundy, which I've never eaten outside Nova Scotia.

sonobuoy ['sonə,bɔɪ] *n.* [alteration of *sonar* + *buoy*] See quote.
1966 *Globe and Mail* (Toronto) 11 Jan. B4/1: Sonobuoys are underwater detection devices used by the Canadian armed forces.

Sons of Freedom an extremist sect of the Doukhobors, called Community Doukhobors and dedicated to protesting against the government by disrobing, arson, bombings, and other forms of violence. See also **Community Doukhobor, Freedomite,** and **Reformed Doukhobor.** Cp. **Orthodox Doukhobor.**
1929 ENGLAND *Immigrant* 54: It is important to distinguish between the independent Doukhobors and the Community Doukhobors known as the "Sons of Freedom." **1963** *Globe and Mail* (Toronto) 12 Jan. 1/4: The provincial [B.C.] health department today ordered an inspection of the snow-covered and almost waterless tent camp of the Sons of Freedom Doukhobors. . . .

Sons of Liberty *Hist.* See **Fils de la Liberté.**
1837 *Patriot* (Toronto) 22 Dec. 3/3: In Lower Canada, Divine Providence has blessed the arms of the Sons of Liberty—a whole people are there manfully struggling for that freedom without which property is but a phantom, and life scarce worth having. . . .
1841 MCLEOD *Upper Canada* 251: The sons of liberty were shot, like dogs by martial law in the roads or reserved for a more cold blooded sacrifice.
1916 MACMECHAN *Popular Government* 4: These might prove, as thought . . . one of the leaders of the "Sons of Liberty" in Lower Canada, so many Lexingtons, with a Saratoga and a Yorktown to follow.

Soo, the [su] *n.* an abbreviation of Sault Ste. Marie, Ont.
1887 (1888) LEES & CLUTTERBUCK *British Columbia* 47: In due course we arrived at Sault St. Marie, which is pronounced *Soo,* and indeed is now pretty commonly spelt and alluded to as "the Soo." **1964** *Globe and Mail* (Toronto) 28 Dec. 5/1: The Soo's population is expected to reach 100,000 by 1980.

soopolallie ['supə,lɑli] *n.* See **soapolallie.**

sooty fox See **blue fox.**
1853 REID *Young Voyageurs* 411: The "sooty fox" is a variety of the "Arctic," distinguished from it only by its colour, which is of a uniform blackish brown.
1863 (1873) LEMOINE *Maple Leaves* 240: . . . our distinguished travellers would shoot . . . ptarmigan, blue or sooty foxes . . . and musk ox after camping on the shores of the Copper Mine and Great Slave Lake.

sopelalee, sopalali(e), sopolally, etc. *n.* See **soapolallie.**

soul-catcher *n. Pacific Coast* See quote.
1955 JENNESS *Indians of Canada* 333: Peculiar to the medicine-men of the Haida, Tlinkit, and Tsimshian was the use of a special "soul-catcher," a bone tube, generally carved, for capturing the wandering souls of the sick and restoring them to their bodies.

sou marquee *Hist*. See **sol marqué.**

sourdough *n. Esp.Northwest* **1 a.** fermenting dough, often a piece held over from a previous baking, used as a starter in baking bread, biscuits, etc. See also **sourdough starter.**
☞ *Sourdough was a staple in the camps and cabins of prospectors and others during the gold-rush days in the Cariboo and the Klondike.*
1864 (1962) ANDERSON *Sawney's Letters* 11:
Gie my respecks to ye're guid wife;
If ever I get back to Fife,
I'll teach her hoo to mak loaf bread,
Wi' sour dough. . . .
1900 LONDON *Son of Wolf* 103: "Boys, it would have done your hearts good to see that whole tribe fighting drunk—and all because of a glorious ferment of sugar and sour dough." **1951** ANGIER *At Home* 75: Dudley went on, by mixing three-fourths of the sourdough with a tablespoon of melted fat and a cup of flour into which a teaspoon of baking soda had been well stirred.
1962 *B.C.Digest* Oct. 23/3: The grub supply was getting low as to variety . . . No sugar, baking powder, sour-dough or fruit.
b. (used attributively) made of sourdough. See also **sourdough bread.**
1935 *Cdn Geog.Jnl* XI 18: [Caption] Sourdough bannock, that effervescent and toothsome standby of the early miner, still plays a part in the mining of placer gold in Cariboo. **1938** *Beaver* June 41/2: These sour dough hot cakes, made right on top of the stove by the men of the north, have no equal anywhere. **1962** *B.C. Digest* Oct. 61/3: As breakfasts vary with hotcakes, sourdough biscuits, muffins and toast, most of the bread is used for sandwich lunches. **1966** *Kingston Whig-Standard* (Ont.) 28 Feb. 10/2: For the adults, there was legal gambling, sourdough flapjacks and the town was awash with bottled spirits. . . .
2 a. *Hist.* a prospector or miner who crossed the White, Chilcoot, or Dyea passes into the Yukon gold-fields before 1898, so called because his staple was sourdough bread, *q.v.*
1899 *Klondike Nugget* (Dawson, Y.T.) 17 May 4/2: Good judges among the sour doughs predict that the river will clear this week. **1963** *Herald Mag.* 23 Nov. 3/4: The narrow-gauge railway . . . follows the shore of Lake Bennett, following a path beaten so hard by the thousands of sourdoughs that the gold trail is still visible today.
b. a prospector, especially an experienced one who spends a lot of time in the wilderness.
1901 *Klondike Miner* (Grand Forks, Y.T.) 18 Oct. 3/1: It means longs walks, and plenty of them; but walking has no terrors for the "sourdough" when he is only talking about it. **1957** *Kingston Whig-Standard* (Ont.) 18 Sep. 25/1: The man looked like a sourdough and was panning for gold among the gravels of Bonanza Creek whose rich finds in 1896 set off the Yukon gold rush. **1963** *Toronto Dly Star* 20 Mar. 18/1: But a rank

greenhorn can have just as much fun making like a sourdough with a basic prospector's kit, a set of mineral samples and a layman's geological guide.
c. any old hand in the Yukon or the Northwest Territories; an old-timer, as opposed to a greenhorn, or cheechako, *q.v.*
1898 *Klondike Nugget* (Dawson, Y.T.) 20 July 1/4: The usual strong expletives had been used expressive of their meeting and Mr. Chee Chaco was not looking for information from his old friend Mr. Sour Dough.
1944 CLAY *Fur Thieves* viii: Trapper Top is the prototype of Canadian Sourdoughs the Northland over!
1954 BERTON *I Married Klondike* 84: I was now a sourdough, according to the accepted definition, for I had watched the river freeze up in the fall and break to pieces with a grinding roar in the spring.
3 See **sourdough bread.**
1935 *Cdn Geog.Jnl* XI 18: These sourdoughs are started from yeast, potato water and flour—whole wheat preferred. **1958** *Edmonton Jnl* 24 Nov. 31/4: . . . and celebrated New Years by making sourdough to eat with beans.

sourdough banquet or **party** *Northwest* a meal eaten on the trail, consisting primarily of sourdough bread, *q.v.* Cp. **sourdough supper.**
1919 ROYAL *Trail of a Sourdough* 14: So I cooks up a sourdough banquet,/And eats till my brain was a haze; **1924** DORRANCE *Never Fire First* 74: "So this is what you meant by a sour-dough party," observed Mrs. Morrow. . . .

sourdough beard a full beard grown on the occasion of some festivity, such as the 60th anniversary of the Yukon gold-rush, the Klondike Days in Edmonton, etc.
1958 *Edmonton Jnl* 24 June 3 2/2: . . . the men have been busily engaged growing "sourdough" beards.

sourdough boy *Northwest, Obs.* See **sourdough** (def. 2c).
1900 LONDON *Son of Wolf* 182: Grizzled "sour-dough boys," day-laborers at the mines . . . either patronized the spruce-looking tenderfeet and lied eloquently,— the "sour-dough boys" being specially created to toy with the truth,—or gave them savage looks of indignation because of their ignorance.

sourdough bread *Esp.Northwest* bread made with dough started with sourdough (def. 1a). See also **sourdough** (def. 3).
1900 LONDON *Son of Wolf* 204: Prince bared his womanly arms and kneaded sour-dough bread. . . .
1964 *Weekend Mag.* 27 June 22/3: Last summer the bakery just couldn't keep up with the demand for old-fashioned sourdough bread.

sourdough kettle *Northwest* a container in which sourdough (def. 1a) is kept.
1933 MERRICK *True North* 166: We have a permanent sourdough kettle hanging on a nail above the stove. From this we mix up pancake batter and the crisp, yeasty cakes are a little more satisfying than bread.

sourdough party See **sourdough banquet.**

sourdough starter *Northwest* See **sourdough** (def. 1a).
1963 *Western Wkly Supp.* 27 Feb. 10/2: [Advert.] SOURDOUGH STARTER, AUTHENTIC. Made in the Yukon . . . a legend in the North. Makes Sourdough hotcakes, bread and muffins. Lasts a life time . . . Send $1.00 to Yukon Yarter, Box 177, Watson Lake, Yukon Territory, Canada.

sourdough stiff *Northwest, Slang, Obs.* See quote.
1899 PALMER *Klondyke* 135: Jim, in the language of the Klondyke, was a "sour-dough stiff" . . . A "sour-dough stiff" will, under no circumstances, eat baking powder bread.

sourdough supper a special supper held to celebrate an anniversary of the Yukon gold-rush, presumably featuring bread, hotcakes, muffins, etc. baked with sourdough. Cp. **sourdough banquet**.
1958 *Edmonton Jnl* 24 June 3 2/1: Old time teas, fashion shows, sourdough suppers . . . and dedication services in Yukon churches to commemorate the pioneers of the rush to the land of gold, are planned.

southern *adj. North* of or relating to the southern parts of Canada; associated with the settled parts of the country. See also **outside,** *n.* (def. 1a) and *adj.*
1958 *Edmonton Jnl* 24 June 4 19/5: The freeze-drying process . . . is a method of reducing the weight of "southern" meat such as beef or pork to about one third. **1965** SYMINGTON *Tuktu* 78: Trapping should be encouraged . . . so that money is available for "southern food" like flour, lard, and vitamin-rich supplements.

Southern Department *Hist.* the extensive administrative division of the Hudson's Bay Company extending from James Bay southward to the Canadas and including the East Main.
1822 (1931) MERK *Fur Trade* 189: In the Southern Department (where there is a great want of Talent) I think Mr. Haldane might be useful particularly at Temiscamingue but here he devotes himself more to Legislating than to business. **1927** *Beaver* Mar. 66: . . . Moose Factory, then [c1835] the headquarters of what was known as the Southern Department.

Southern Indian *Obs.* **1** among Hudson's Bay Company men: **a.** a Cree, as opposed to the Chippewyans, or Northern Indians (def. 1a), who lived to the north and west of the Churchill River.
1689 (1929) KELSEY *Papers* 28: . . . his Country people was gone far to yᵉ northward for fear of yᵉ southern Indians. . . . **1768** DRAGE *Prob.N.W.Passage* 138: [We] walked a great Way in an *Indian Path,* and saw several marked trees, as is practised among the Southern Indians.
b. the language of the Crees.
1744 DOBBS *Hudson's Bay* 95: Mr. Thompson, the Surgeon, who could speak some of the Southern Indian Tongue, was endeavouring to learn their Language, and to teach them English. **1795** (1911) HEARNE *Journey* 341: During their stay at the Fort they made a considerable progress both in the Southern Indian and the English languages.
2 probably a Naskapi Indian of the Labrador, as opposed to an Eskimo.
1773 (1792) CARTWRIGHT *Journal* I 278: I understand that the southern Indians never kill any whales, but either purchase whalebone from the northern tribes, or cut it out of a dead whale when they chance to meet with one, which often happens.

South Shore 1 in Quebec, the south shore of the St. Lawrence River and Gulf of St. Lawrence.
1775 *Quebec Gaz.* 21 Sep. 3/1: The Rebels have sent circular Letters to some of the Parishes above, upon the South Shore, threatening them with Military

Execution. . . . **1853** (1854) KEEFER *Montreal* 15: . . . and there seems nothing for the ancient and modern capital, but emigration to the South shore, unless indeed she is content with the North shore timber coves, her citadel, a political menagerie every alternate four years, and the dining of American tourists. **1966** *Gazette* (Montreal) 29 Jan. 39/8: Among the projects the group plans to support are: the Richelieu Canal . . . and a port on the South Shore.
2 in Nova Scotia, the southeast shore of the peninsula, roughly from Halifax to Yarmouth, including the region some distance in from the actual shore.
1831 *Novascotian* (Halifax) 20 July 230/1: I have not heard how it is on the south shore. **1952** PUTNAM *Cdn Regions* 81/1: The Bay of Fundy and the South Shore are among the foggiest coasts on earth. **1962** *Chronicle-Herald* (Halifax) 8 Aug. 4/6: . . . There are areas in Nova Scotia to visit other than the Cabot Trail and the South Shore.

sow *n.* a female bear, especially one with cubs.
1958 *Alaska Sportsman* Dec. 8/3: I might unwittingly corner one [a bear] or stumble on a sow with cubs. . . . **1962** FRY *Ranch on the Cariboo* 6: We closed in on the sapling to hold the hostage cub, knowing without it the old sow wouldn't go far. **1963** *B.C.Digest* Nov.-Dec. 4/3: If the sow and two cubs that had been seen in the areas were killed by the baits[,] the trophy fees alone on those animals[,] had non-resident hunters taken them[,] would more than compensate for the loss of a steer.

Sowegian [sə'widʒən] *n.* [prob. an altered blend of *S*wede + Nor*wegian*] *West, Slang, Derog.* a Scandinavian.
1930 BEAMES *Army* 187: "No Sowegians in mine," he declared. "Bunch of damn thieves."

Spadina Strip See **Strip.**

Spam medal *Slang* the Canadian Volunteer Service Medal, issued to all persons who volunteered for service in World War II, so called after a kind of processed pork that figured prominently in the diet of soldiers in the field.
1959 *Legionary* Mar. 11/1: As all of us overseas at the time were volunteers, it meant that everybody wore one and so, in patronizing fashion, we tagged it the Spam Medal.

Spanish dollar† *Hist.* a silver dollar long circulated in Canada and other parts of America during colonial times, being gradually displaced by American and, later, Canadian money. See also **dollar** (def. 1). Cp. **half-dollar** (def. 1) and **holey dollar.**
1766 *Quebec Gaz.* 1 Dec. 3/1: Their respective copies will be delivered . . . on payment of Two Spanish Dollars for each. **1825** *Novascotian* (Halifax) 20 July 237/2: His Majesty has ordered that a tender and payment of British silver money to the amount of 4s 4d shall be considered as equivalent to the tender and payment of one Spanish dollar. **1958** *Encyc.Can.* III 175: In Nova Scotia all sorts of coins had circulated from earliest days, but the Spanish dollar, which was obtained through the trade with the West Indies, was one of the commonest coins and at one time was even imported by the British Government to pay its troops.

Sparrow *n. Slang* an Englishman, especially a Cockney. See also **Chirper.**

1912 SANDILANDS *West.Cdn Dict.* 43/2: Sparrow, an immigrant from London, England. **1918** MOORE *Clash* 306: So long as we continue to drink its [racial doctrine's] intoxicating waters we shall never dwell in harmony with the French Canadians, nor any other nationality, not even with the men whom we called "bronchos" and "sparrows" before the war. **1966** *Sun* (Vancouver) 22 Mar. 12/8: Canadians have not been slow to find nicknames for themselves and others. Among them are: Spud Islander, pea souper . . . and, for the Englishman . . . sparrow.

spar tree *Lumbering* a clean, sound tree (from 90 to 200 feet high), topped, firmly guyed, and rigged with a high-lead or skyline, *qq.v.*, used in hauling logs from the cutting area to the yarding area. See pictures at **high-lead system** and **skyline.** See also **high-line logging.**

1925 PHILIP *Crimson West* 144: Preparing the "spar-tree" for "high-lead," or "sky-line" rigging, is the most spectacular and thrilling performance in the logging industry. A standing tree is trimmed of top and branches then strengthened with guys. With the pull coming from this altitude, the advantage over the straight ground pull is enormous as logs are lifted high in [the] air over all impedimenta. **1942** HAIG-BROWN *Timber* 248: ". . . You get in there and run a decent camp where spar-trees don't break and men don't get . . . blacklisted for no reason. . . ." **1963** MCKINNON *Forest Activities 1* 6: Often the first tree topped is used only for a raising tree to raise the final spar tree.

speaking wire See quote.

1880 MORRIS *Treaties* 10: . . . surveyors passed through the territories—and the "speaking wires," as the Indian calls the telegraph, were erected.

speak white See **white,** *adv.* (def. 2).

speak with a forked tongue See **forked tongue.**

spear *v. Hockey* check an opposing player by thrusting the blade of the stick into some part of his body, especially his stomach. See also **spearing.**

1963 *Globe and Mail* (Toronto) 14 Mar. 7/7: Defense star Doug Harvey confessed: "I spear any forward who runs interference and sticks too close." **1964** *Maclean's* 21 Mar. 49/4: At one point, Brewer the Leafs' bad man, speared Stan Mikita, which is to say he rammed the business end of his hockey stick into Mikita's stomach. **1966** *Globe and Mail* (Toronto) 1 Jan. 21/2: It was said he speared Phil Goyette so severely that [he] will need a month to convalesce.

spear grass any of several species of tough, irritating grass, such as *Poa pratensis* or *Stipa columbiana.*

1881 (1957) *Sask.Hist.* X 67: Spear grass, which is something like wild oats, works right through boots, stockings, trousers, and everything. **1952** PUTNAM *Cdn Regions* 24/2: The most typical montane landscape . . . is a scattered parklike stand of ponderosa pine amidst a steppe vegetation of bunch grass . . . spear grass. . . . **1953** *Cdn Geog.Jnl* June 245/1: The sheep crop the "prairie wool"—that excellent hard forage composed of spear-grass, bunch-grass and buffalo-grass.

spearing *n. Hockey* an illegal check made with the blade of the stick. See 1965 quote. See also **spear,** *v.*

1963 *Albertan* (Calgary) 10 Dec. 11/2: "Spearing is dangerous, too, but there's more high-sticking," Thompson said. **1965** *Globe and Mail* (Toronto) 30 Dec. 14/1: Spearing is defined in Rule 78 of the NHL code as "stabbing an opponent with the point of the stick blade while the stick is being carried with one or both hands."

special (constable) *n.* a man sworn in for temporary duty as a constable, especially with the R.C.M.P.

1889 *Rat Portage* [Kenora] *News* (Ont.) 31 May 4/3: Our brave and heroic (?) special returned to Fort Francis a sad and lugubrious looking man, and if you wish to see a tear drop glisten in his eye ask the simple question, "where is Jumbo." **1946** *Beaver* Dec. 22/2: The next day every civilian in the fort was sworn in as a special constable by my father, who was a justice of the peace. **1959** MOWAT *Desperate People* 278: I had a companion on my walk, an Eskimo special constable of the R.C.M.P. **1960** *Press* 15 Nov. 10: Organization of the specials began on May 6th under Major Lyall. Many of the specials were returned soldiers.

Speech† *n.* See **Speech from the Throne.**

1830 *Niagara Herald* (Niagara-on-the-Lake, U.C.) 21 Jan. 2/4: This Speech, without the usual varnish of affection, is a plain, dignified and business-like production. **1953** LEBOURDAIS *Nation of North* 239: Nothing was said in the Speech about going to war.

Speech from the Chair *Obs.* the message of the sovereign to a colonial council and assembly through the governor.

1778 *Quebec Gaz.* 6 Aug. 1/1: The members of the House of Assembly now convened in their legislative capacity, beg leave to assure you of their satisfaction in your obliging Speech from the Chair.

Speech from the Throne† a statement read at the opening of a session of Parliament by the Governor General, or at the opening of a provincial legislature (or, formerly, a colonial legislative council) by the Lieutenant-Governor, as representative of the Crown, reviewing the state of affairs and summarizing the legislation proposed for the session by the Cabinet. See also **Speech** and **Throne Speech.**

1811 *Kingston Star* (U.C.) 8 Jan. 2/2: We, his Majesty's most dutiful and loyal subjects, the Legislative Council of the Province of Lower Canada, in Provincial Parliament assembled, beg leave to return your Excellency our most humble thanks for your Speech from the Throne. **1849** *Examiner* (Toronto) 24 Jan. 2/1: The Members of the Legislative Council being assembled . . . His Excellency opened the second Session of the Third Parliament of the Province of Canada, with the following Speech from the Throne. **1871** *Wkly Manitoban* (Winnipeg) 18 Mar. 2/1: Already a 'Speech from the Throne' in Red River Settlement. Who, two or three years ago would have believed it a possibility! **1962** *Canada Month* Feb. 18/3: Indeed the Speech from the Throne which opened it failed notably to come to grips with the vital issues.

speeder *n.* **1 a.** a small motorized vehicle used by railway employees for line maintenance. See also **gas-car, jigger** (def. 3), **track car,** and **track speeder.** Cp. **hand-car.**

1905 OUTRAM *Cdn Rockies* 152: . . . the cow-catcher or the top of a box car is the choicest of propelling methods, unless one can get a ride on a hand-car or a speeder, with opportunity to slacken speed or stop whenever one desires. **1947** SAUNDERS *Algonquin* 128: ... the husband, apparently a section man, had rushed up the tracks on a three-wheeled "speeder" to bring Molly back to help. **1963** *Calgary Herald* 14 Nov. 2/4: A gas-driven speeder got away from workers and scooted 20 miles along the CP's main line through northwestern Ontario before it was stopped.

b. *Lumbering* a small track car used especially for carrying foremen, company officials, and minor supplies on a logging railway. See also **rail speeder**.
1942 SWANSON *Western Logger* 8: ... I'm pining to sit on a "speeder," a "locie," or car on the track. **1960** SWANSON *Railroad Logging* 5: Another innovation developed in the logging railroad industry was called the "speeder."

2 *Hist.* See quote.
1912 SANDILANDS *West.Cdn Dict.* 42/1: A low sleigh is known as a cutter, and a high sleigh is a speeder.

speeding-up or **speed-up (system)** *n.* any condition or situation tending to increase production through increased labor output; also, a point or bonus system, as the Bedaux system, designed to achieve this end.
1919 *Camp Worker* 28 June 6/2: Fellow-Workers. Let us abolish the speeding-up system as speedily as possible. **1930** *Canadian Needleworker* 10 Sep. 1/1: More and more workers are thrown out of industry as a result of the terrific speed-up system that the dress-makers are faced with. **1932** *Lumber Worker* Sep. 4/2: The question of the united front tactics in mobilizing [sic] the lumber and sawmill workers in struggle against wage cuts, speed up, for increase in pay was thoroughly discussed. **1957** *Herald-Tribune* [Grande Prairie, Alta] 17 Dec. 10/2: The "speed-up," so bitterly complained of by unions in Canada and the United States, is the normal state of affairs in Russia.

spell *n. Esp.North* **1** See 1873 quote. See also **pipe¹** (def. 1).
1848 (1859) BALLANTYNE *Hudson's Bay* 76: Each spell lasted for nearly two hours, during which time they rowed without intermission. **1873** GRANT *Ocean to Ocean* 118n: The term "spell" is commonly used, all over the plains, to indicate the length of journey between meals or stopping places; the latter are sometimes called spelling places, by half-breeds and others. **1953** OSGOOD *Winter* 145: About every five miles the Indians rest their dogs, making tea where firewood is available. Generally at the end of the fourth spell you will find a suitable place to spend the night.

2 See **pipe¹** (def. 2).
1869 (1942) KENNICOTT *Journal* 99: When a sled can not keep up and take its proper place in the brigade at each spell, it is said to be "planted," which is considered something very disgraceful. **1896** WHITNEY *On Snow-Shoes* 52: His train was invariably so far behind as to delay us ten to fifteen minutes at every "spell" (rest), which meant a loss of from six to eight miles in a day's travel. **1913** FOOTNER *Jack Chanty* 253: Riding down the hill they made their noon spell on the site of Camp Trangmar. **1953** OSGOOD *Winter* 145: Some spells may be only three or four miles apart and others eight to ten but they will average roughly five.

spell *v.* **1** *Esp.North* **a.** stop for a spell (def. 2).
1912 FOOTNER *New Rivers* 208: We "spelled" twice a day to eat, making four meals in all, a general rule on the trail. **1927** (1937) CHRISTIAN *Unflinching* 87: Here we spelled and had a cup of tea and frazzled hide with a little bit of sugar.

b. give a rest to (dogs) for a specific time.
1921 HEMING *Drama of Forests* 177: Now the brigade was halted, in voyageur parlance, "to spell the dogs one smoke." **1922** *Beaver* Sep. 17/2: Soon they came to the place where the men ahead of them had stopped to "spell" their dogs.

2 *Nfld Dial.* See quotes.
1920 GRENFELL *Le Petit Nord* 150: There is an old story about a foreigner who once asked, "How do you spell 'swile'?" The answer the fisherman gave him was, "We don't spell [carry] 'em. We mostly hauls 'em." **1933** MERRICK *True North* 155: "How do you spell it?" [wood] "Sometimes I spells it in my apron, Sir, and sometimes I spells it in my arms." **1944** WENTWORTH *Am.Dial.Dict.* 146/2: To spell (gather) a yafful (armful) of crunnocks (kindling). 1921 Newfoundland.

spelling-place *n. Esp.North* a place where one takes a spell (def. 2).
1872 (1873) GRANT *Ocean to Ocean* 153: Our first "spelling-place" to-day was Stony Lake. **1912** FOOTNER *New Rivers* 216: We made twelve miles before turning in that night, and reached our last spelling-place of the way over.

Spencer's twist *Hist.* a kind of tobacco that was prominent among the trading goods carried by the fur traders.
1794 (1889) MACDONELL *Journal* 287: The fifteen men sent to Pine Fort returned with 4 rolls Brazil tobacco, 1 roll Spencer's twist.... **1800** (1933) MCLEOD *Diary* 146: I gave a roll of Spencer's Twist Tobacco ... with Mr. McDonell's cheese to his two men.... **1912** ROE *Whispering Hills* 99: Packs of furs went up the main way and loads of merchandise went down ... guns ... and many a foot of Spencer's Twist at one beaver foot....

spiceberry† *n.* the creeping wintergreen, *Gaultheria procumbens,* of eastern Canada.
1852 (1881) TRAILL *Cdn Crusoes* 186: The little creeping wintergreen, with its scarlet berries, that grows on the dry flats or sandy hills, which the Canadians call spice-berry, she showed them was good to eat.... **1952** BANFILL *Lab.Nurse* 38: Before the bagh apple has run its course, green blueberries, spice berries and moss blackberries make it necessary to continue the castor oil.

spider† *n.* a frying pan having long metal legs to hold it above coals or an open fire.
1836 *St.Catharines Jnl* (U.C.) 3 Nov. 1/3: Twenty Tons Hollow Ware ... including Pots, Kettles, Spiders, Griddles.... **1913** OGILVIE *Yukon* 300: Cooking was mostly done in frying-pans, called spiders....

spiked *adj. Mining, Slang* made to look richer in mineral content than is the case; salted.
1960 MCNAMEE *Florencia Bay* 52: Then the promoter who, on the strength of spiked assays, had floated a company.

spiked boot *Lumbering* See **caulked boot**.
1903 WHITE *Forest* 136: ... a riverman and spiked boots and a saw-log can do more work than an ordinary man with a rowboat. **1945** CALVIN *Saga* 68: ... men walking over the loose timber, in their spiked boots, sorted out with their long pike-poles ... the longer, thinner pieces....

spike-pitcher *n.* the member of a threshing crew

who forks the sheaves from the load into the separator of the machine. Cp. **stook pitcher.**
1958 MACGREGOR *North-west of 16* 217: In the fall of 1919, Henry ter Horst gave me the job of spike-pitcher on his machine.

spiker *n.* See **spike-pitcher.**
1955 HARDY *Alta Anthol.* 433: "Go by a field an' see alla them spikers an' field pitchers working without no pants. . . ."

spile *n. Maple Industry* a small tube or spout of wood or metal inserted in a maple tree to carry the running sap into a pail or other receptacle.
1845 *Bytown* [Ottawa] *Gaz.* 20 Mar. 1/3: A spout, or spile as it is termed, is inserted about two inches below this incision with the same gouge. **1947** WELLS *Owl Pen* 89: It is time . . . to get the rusty spiles and sap buckets down from the beams of the woodshed. **1966** DUNCAN *Black Creek* 26: Holes were bored in the trees with an auger and into these wooden spouts or "spiles" were inserted.

spill *v.* [var. of *spile*] *Rare* fit with a spile, *q.v.*
1863 WALSHE *Cedar Creek* 230: "I'll just bring up the potash kettle on the sled Monday, an' we'll spill the trees."

spinning frolic *Obs.* See quote.
1828 MCGREGOR *Maritime Colonies* 73: If a good wife has a quantity of wool or flax to spin, she invites as many of her neighbours as the house can well accommodate; some bring their spinning wheels, others their cards; they remain all day at work, and after drinking abundance of tea, either go home or remain to dance for some part of the night: this is called a spinning frolic.

spirit duck the bufflehead, *Bucephala albeola.* See also **conjuring duck** (def. 1).
1785 PENNANT *Arctic Zoology* 558: Spirit Duck . . . Inhabits North America, from Hudson's Bay to Carolina. **1862** *Nor' Wester* (R.R.S.) 5 Mar. 4/2: Among other I noticed the eggs and parent birds of the . . . spirit duck. . . . **1956** MCATEE *Folk-Names* 15: Bufflehead [is also called] . . . spirit duck.

spirit stone *Obs.* See **medicine stone.**
1789 (1801) MACKENZIE *Voy. from Montreal* 29: Their declivities were . . . sprinkled with white stones . . . called by the Indians *manetoe aseniah*, or spirit stones.

spirit-wrestler† *n.* [a literal trans. of Russian *dukhoborets*] See **Doukhobor.**
1916 BRIDLE *Sons of Can.* 91: Mavor investigated the spirit wrestlers and other forms of communities of similar character in Russia and advised that these people be immigrated into the north-west prairies. **1953** MOWERY *Mounted Police* 165: Does anybody know what happened with that bunch of spirit-wrestlers that was a-wandering around our district looking for the Promised Land?

splake [splek] *n.* [< *speckled* + *lake* trout] a hybrid game fish of the trout family, developed by Canadian biologists. See also **Wendigo trout.** Cp. **muspike.**
1954 *Chicago Tribune* 18 Apr. ii 7/5: [Canadian] Biologists who developed the fish . . . had named it

Splake. **1957** *Fish and Game* 30 Aug. 24/2: In 1953, the Ontario Department of Lands and Forests stocked 3,600 splake in Chrysler Lake. **1966** *Kingston Whig-Standard* (Ont.) 3 June 13/6: The splake, Canada's newest game fish, is being put to the use for which it was specifically bred—combatting the ravages of the sea lamprey in the Great Lakes.

splashing pole a pole used for scaring fish into a net.
1954 EVANS *Mist* 214: She coiled her line, laid it on the gravel, then took his axe to cut herself a splashing pole.

split *adj.* **1** *Fur Trade, Obs.* See **open,** *adj.* (def. 1). See also **split-skin** and **split-skinning.**
1776 (1951) *Saskatchewan Jnls* 67: . . . their Furrs are generally Beaver & Split Cats with a few Wolves & Martin's. **1921** HEMING *Drama of Forests* 230: All split skins are stretched on rectangular frames—all save beaver skins which are stretched on oval frames.
2 of logs, roughly split with an axe to form building timbers, planks, fence rails, etc.
1829 MACTAGGART *Three Years* II 205: The mail coac hes or waggons are often in this predicament, when the passengers instantly jump off, and having obtained split rails of the fence, they lift it up by sheer force. **1962** FRY *Ranch on the Cariboo* 146: So while we . . . gathered spruce boughs to lay on a corner of the split-pine floor for a bed, I told Bill what I was up to.
3 of fish, split along the belly from head to tail, gutted and ready for salting.
1890 *Grip* (Toronto) 5 Apr. 233/2: Always "high line," he was always the first "filled up" with the split mackerel of the North Bay.

split-rail fence† a fence made of split rails, such as a snake fence, *q.v.*
1958 KELSEY *B.C. Rides a Star* 56: Perpendicularly or diagonally laid logs of farm homes and buildings and split-rail fences do more than identify Bulkley and Endako Valleys as frontier country. **1964** *Maclean's* 2 Dec. 13/1: Farmers just outside Toronto drove their sleighs right across those picturesque split-rail fences that caught all the snow. . . .

split-skin *v. Fur Trade* See quote. See also **split** (def. 1) and **split-skinning.**
1921 HEMING *Drama of Forests* 230: To split skin an animal such as wood-buffalo, moose, wapiti, caribou, deer, bear, beaver, wolf, or wolverine, the skin is cut down the belly from throat to tail and also on the inside of each leg to the centre cut, and then the pelt is peeled off both ways toward the back.

split-skinning *n.* the practice of skinning an animal by cutting down the belly from throat to tail and up the inside of each leg to the belly cut, then peeling the skin off upward toward the back. See also **split** (def. 1). Cp. **case-skinning.**
1921 HEMING *Drama of Forests* 230: In the forest there are several different ways of skinning animals: one is called "case skinning" and another is called "split skinning."

splitter *n. Esp. Nfld* See 1784 quote. Cp. **header.**
1784 PENNANT *Arctic Zoology* cxcvii: He then shoves the fish to the splitter, who stands opposite to him; his business is to split the fish, beginning at the head, and opening it down to the tail; at the next cut he takes out the larger part of the back-bone, which falls through the floor into the water. **1840** (1860) MURRAY *Brit. Amer.* II 126: This structure is provided with one or more tables,

round which, invested in leathern aprons, are seated three important personages, the cutthroat, the header, and the splitter. **1944** *Beaver* Sep. 22/2: He [the header] then passes the fish to the splitter, who takes out the sound bone or backbone in quick stroke of his knife. **1965** STEVENS *Incompleat Canadian* 105: ., . in turn they received the attention of the header, the splitter and the cleaner.

splitting cuff *Esp. Nfld* See quote.
1965 LEACH *Songs* 5: On his left hand the splitter wears a "splittin' cuff," a kind of fingerless wool mitten; with this hand he grasps the upper part of the back bone and then runs the blade of his slightly curved, squarish knife longitudinally, first down one side of the vertebra and then back up the other, separating the backbone and the upper ribs from the flesh.

spool bed† a design of bed having spool-like turnings as part of the design of the headboard and footboard, popular in the nineteenth century.
1947 WELLS *Owl Pen* 38: There was . . . the old spool bed that we had found in a junk shop in a neighbouring town. **1956** RADDALL *Wings* 34: The white spool bed, the hooked rug in two colors on the floor [were familiar]. **1958** *Maclean's* 24 May 27/2: Above it is a storeroom cluttered with fishing tackle, skates, dismantled spool beds . . . a broken parlor organ.

spoon canoe See quote.
1907 CROSBY *An-ko-me-nums* 141: The canoes of the Pacific coast are of the type usually called "dugouts" . . . [including] a "spoon canoe," flat-bottomed and nearly straight with hardly any bow or stern.

spot fire 1 See 1942 quote.
1942 HAIG-BROWN *Timber* 254: SPOT FIRE. Sparks and burning embers of a forest fire, caught by its up-draft and driven by the following wind, set small fires far ahead of the main fire. These are the fire fighter's main concern once he has a good fire trail built.
2 an isolated forest fire, limited to a relatively small area.
1964 *Islander* 27 Sep. 4/2: In a little open area, maybe the scene of an ancient lightning spot-fire, I came upon the remains of a caribou banquet.

spotted alder See **swamp alder** (def. 1).
1817 (1897) DURAND *Reminiscences* 106: [The following trees are found near Ancaster, Upper Canada] . . . swamp oak . . . black and spotted alder. . . .
1829 MACTAGGART *Three Years* I 99: In the marshes, alder, spotted alder, willow shrub, and a variety of thorn appear. . . . **1963** SYMONS *Many Trails* 164: . . . there were thickets of mountain maple, hazel, and spotted alder.

spring *n.* See **spring salmon.**

spring bird the song sparrow, *Melospiza melodia.*
1749 DRAGE *Voyage* II 8: Upon the Eighth, there came several large Flocks of what they call Spring-Birds, as they always come in the Beginning of that Season.
1832 MCGREGOR *Brit.Amer.* I 109: The birds most generally known in America [include] . . . red-hooded winter bird . . . musquito hawk . . . yellow bird, spring-bird . . . spotted godwait, or yellow-legs. . . .
1959 MCATEE *Folk-Names* 66: Song Sparrow [is also called] spring bird (N.B.).

spring break-up See **break-up.**

spring-burn *n. Obs.* in clearing land, the occasion in spring for burning trees felled during winter.

1845 BEAVAN *Life in Backwoods N.B.* 18: . . . the first dry "spell" is looked forward to most anxiously to burn off the land which has been chopped during the winter. It is bad policy, however, to depend for the whole crop on this "spring burn" as a long continuance of wet weather may prevent it. **1853** STRICKLAND *Canada West* II 197: . . . the dry weather enabled me to get a spring-burn of five acres. . . . **1863** WALSHE *Cedar Creek* 303: The garden stuff planted on Robert's spring-burn ground had flourished. . . .

spring cart See **spring wagon.**
1880 GORDON *Mountain and Prairie* 292: The H.B. Company's agent furnished us with horses, and secured for me a spring cart from one of the settlers.
1928 LEROSSIGNOL *Beauport Road* 155: Surely too, the bones of the fathers must have turned in their graves as the gayly-painted buggy rattled past the quiet churchyard, where nothing more frivolous than a spring cart had ever been seen before.

spring fallow *Obs.* See **fallow.**
1883 FRASER *Shanty* 77: The real origin of our appalling forest fires is traceable . . . to the *settlers of the country,* either in their spring or summer fallows in clearing the land, or, occasionally, in making potash.

spring fly *Obs.* the May fly, *Ephemera* sp.
1825 *Canadian Mag.* IV 474: Among the curious phenomena of Canada, is the ephemeral Spring Fly. . . .

spring herring† *Maritimes* See **alewife.**
1861 BAGSTER *Progress P.E.I.* 96: We are inclined to believe that what are called Fall herring, is as much a different species of herring from the Spring herring, as Winter wheat differs from Summer wheat.
1924 MATHEWS *Wilfred Grenfell* 58: In addition to the cod, the people fish for the bait fishes—the spring herring, the caplin (a small fish about the size of a smelt)—the squid and whelk—without which the cod-fishing could not be carried on.

spring hunt 1 See 1921 quote.
1784 (1954) *Moose Ft Jnls* 170: Should you be successful in your Spring Hunt a few Geese at this time of scarsity would essentially promote the Company's Interest. . . . **1921** HEMING *Drama of Forests* 258: The Indians divide their annual hunt for fur into three distinct hunting seasons: the fall hunt—from autumn until Christmas; the winter hunt—from New Year's Day until Easter; and the spring hunt—from Easter until the hunters depart for their tribal summer camping ground. **1948** ONRAET *Sixty Below* 85: Just keep track of it and pay me when your spring hunt is over. **1966** *Beaver* Winter 54/1: After the spring hunt, they all went to a big meeting place.
2 the skins taken in the spring hunt.
1778 (1951) *Sask.Jnls* 218: . . . Mr. Tomison who I intent to send off again shortly with more trading Goods to wait for the Indians spring hunt, and to intercept them from going to the Canadian traders. **1826** (1931) MERK *Fur Trade* 276: By so doing the Spring hunt would not be lost and Winter quarters could be found with the assistance of our Hunters to join the party and proceed at the opening of the Season to the Country beyond the Claminitts from whence Mr McDonald returned. **1956** KEMP *Northern Trader* 401: They had already spent their Treaty money but each had a credit from his spring hunt.

spring-pole *n. Fur Trade* a kind of set (def. 1) that consists of a resilient sapling having a snare or trap attached to the top and being bent over so that when the trap is sprung, the caught animal is hoisted in the air. See also **twitch-up**. Cp. **tossing-pole**.
1924 *Beaver* June 325: The animals caught are almost always immediately choked to death by the action of the spring pole when the snare is pulled. **1956** KEMP *Northern Trader* 58: [It is] more humane than a mink dangling from another trap on a spring pole.

spring salmon *Pacific Coast* a mature Chinook salmon, *q.v.* See also **red spring, white, n.** (def. 3), and **white spring.** Also *spring*.
1869 *Mainland Guardian* (New Westminster, B.C.) 25 Sep. 2/1: Then come what are called the Spring Salmon which arrive from the sea during May, and after an interval, in August. **1916** WOOD *Tourist's N.W.* 344: Prince Rupert and Port Simpson see splendid fishing for spring salmon in early March and for cohoes in the summer. **1964** CARL *Marine Fishes B.C.* 28: A few mature [Chinook salmon] may enter the larger rivers in late spring or early summer (hence the name "spring salmon"). . . . **1965** *Daily Colonist* (Victoria) 3 Aug. 7/3: Today . . . sees him with a 14:4-pound spring from Becker Bay. . . .

spring wagon a light wagon, the box of which rides on springs. See also **spring cart**.
1850 BIGSBY *Shoe and Canoe* II 53: Jonathan it was, and he brought us good news,—that we must walk some couple of miles to a farm-house, where a spring-waggon, well filled with straw, would be ready to carry us on to Kingston, then eight or nine miles distant.
1880 GORDON *Mountain and Prairie* 255: The light waggon . . . the two-horse spring waggon similar to the ordinary "democrat" waggon of Ontario, and the double buck-board are the greatest favourites.
1950 STEELE *Ghosts Returning* 84: The ground about the stables was so jammed with strange horses, democrats, buckboards and spring wagons that they could hardly reach them.

sprucebark canoe *Hist.* a kind of canoe made by the Indians of the western mountains.
[**1876** LORD *Wilderness* 191: The 'Kallispellem' canoes used by the Columbia River Kootanie and other inland Indians, are made of large sheets of bark, stripped from the spruce fir or cedar tree (*Thuja gigantia*).]
1928 FREEMAN *Nearing North* 194: The abandoned sprucebark canoe I reconditioned and launched upon the Mackenzie disintegrated and swamped within a hundred yards. **1957** HUTCHISON *Canada* 287: He told me many tales of his people, of Father Morice . . . of the hunt, the autumn salmon hordes, the sprucebark canoes of his boyhood.

spruce-bark tea See **spruce tea**.
1958 BERTON *Klondike* 369: None of its citizens were ordinary, for almost every one of them knew how to . . . treat scurvey with spruce-bark tea, how to carry a pack on a tumpline, and how to navigate fast water.

spruce barrens *Maritimes* See **barren** (def. 1b).
1849 ALEXANDER *L'Acadie* II 124: [We] saw some good land and some spruce barrens or swamps. I wondered . . . what end these spongy plains could answer, producing neither trees nor grass, but only wet moss on a sandy

bottom. . . . **1925** MONTGOMERY *Emily Climbs* 35: [I wonder] who is sleeping in my old room there, and if any one is loving the little birches and playing with the Wind Woman in the spruce barrens. . . .

spruce beer a drink made from boiling tender spruce shoots, straining off the liquid, adding sugar or molasses, fermenting with yeast, and allowing to cool, widely used among pioneers and still made in some places. Cp. **spruce tea**.
1741 (1852) COATS *Geography of H.B.* 112: I have given them, ever since our English beer has been expended, spruce beer and brandy, the only means used here to prevent the scurvy. **1816** (1818) HALL *Travels* 208: . . . we stopped to bait our steed, and selves a few miles beyond, at a solitary log hut in the centre of a forest; where, besides oats, we found excellent spruce beer made on the spot, and gingerbread cakes, as the sign specified, being underwritten "Cakes and Beer." **1928** LEROSSIGNOL *Beauport Road* 32: He continued all the long morning, only stopping now and then to take a drink of spruce beer from the stone jug under the fence, or to sharpen his scythe. . . . **1963** *Globe and Mail* (Toronto) 6 July 8/3: Spruce beer, ice cream, bands and abstract art are features of a promotion in which Montreal has been engaged during the past few years to brighten the city's image for visitors.

spruce feathers See **feathers**.

spruce-fir *n.* any of a number of firs, as the balsam, *q.v.*
1760 PICHON *Cape Breton* 14: The spruce-fir is of the resinous kind, but does not produce a sufficient quantity for general use. **1829** MACTAGGART *Three Years* I 97: The spruce-fir is very common, and furnishes materials for spruce-beer, a beverage of high request among the Canadians; and spruce knees, which are the roots of this tree, are found to be a good substitute for crooked oak, in boat and ship-building. **1905** OUTRAM *Cdn Rockies* 255: . . . as thunder-clouds looked threatening, at once prepared an elaborate nest, hollowed amongst the roots of a large spruce fir, and filled in with small trees and branches.

spruce game *Obs.* See **spruce partridge**.
1770 (1792) CARTWRIGHT *Journal* I 22: I met with three spruce-game, and knocked all their heads off, at separate shots, with my rifle.

spruce grouse† See **spruce partridge**.
1937 (1950) STANWELL-FLETCHER *Driftwood Valley* 13: Several times we've scared up coveys of spruce grouse along the trail. **1966** *Kingston Whig-Standard* (Ont.) 21 Jan. 11/1: The spruce grouse is so retiring . . . that few people get to see one.

spruce gum† a resinous secretion of the spruce, used for caulking canoes, chewing, in medicine, etc.; also, a globule of this substance as found on the tree. See also **Canada balsam** (def. 1).
1896 (1898) RUSSELL *Far North* 216: Wisagatchak soon tired of the manner of traveling and told the fox to bring him some clear spruce gum. **1909** (1926) ROBERTS *Backwoodsman* 136: While none were observing her she had gleefully clambered out over the solid mass, looking for spruce-gums. **1953** FLUKE *Kwakiutl* 27: When done by a skilled wood-worker, little or no caulking was necessary to make the box water-tight. Knot-holes and other defects were plugged with shredded cedar-bark saturated with hot spruce-gum.

spruce-gum tea See **spruce tea**.
1962 *Chronicle-Herald* (Halifax) 10 Aug. 15/2:

MacDonnell's party suffered from scurvy, allayed in part by drinking spruce gum tea.

spruce harvester See quote.
1964 *Islander* 27 Sep. 36/3 : The most spectacular of the new machines ... is a 30-ton giant called the spruce harvester, which can strip the limbs from a tree, top it, fell it, bunch the loose branches, and stack the trunk— and all in 50 seconds.

spruce hen See **spruce partridge.**
1913 ROTHROCK *Collin's Overland Exped.* 11 Jan. : Spring and fall we shot many ducks and geese, and in early winter grouse, spruce hens, and ptarmigan.... **1959** LEISING *Arctic Wings* 31 : I had to confess that I had not seen the spruce hen until the shot bird came tumbling out of the tree.

spruce partridge a grouse, *Canachites canadensis,* dark gray barred with black, found in swampy woods. See also **bush partridge, Canada grouse, fool hen, pine partridge, spruce grouse, spruce hen, wood grouse,** and **wood partridge.**
1771 (1935) *Cdn Hist.Rev.* 57 : There are more spruce Partridges in the woods than I have seen anywhere in this country. **1829** MacTAGGART *Three Years* II 235 : He had been in Davis Straits frequently at the whale-fishing : there are no trees on that coast, but plenty of eagles and spruce partridges. **1963** *Calgary Herald* 4 Oct. 27/7 : Spruce partridge and Franklin's grouse season has been open since Aug. 31.

spruce tea an infusion of boiled tender spruce shoots, used for the prevention of scurvy. See also **bush tea, green-spruce tea, spruce-bark tea,** and **spruce-gum tea.** Cp. **hemlock tea** and **spruce beer.**
1783 (1899) *N.B.Mag.* II 320 : Some chocolate is wanted for our Masting Camp for at present we use Spruce Tea which causes some murmuring. *c*1862 (1958) LINDSAY *Cariboo Story* 32/2 : ... We all called him Doctor Spruce after this in honor of the great medicine in spruce tea which save us from a lot of suffering and death.... **1956** *Beaver* Summer 18 : I lashed out strong laxatives all round and ordered spruce tea to be brewed and administered constantly.

spruce tonic See **spruce tea.**
1932 WINSON *Weather and Wings* 51 : The leaves or needles of a hemlock are used for "spruce" tonic.

spruce-tuck *n.* See **tuckamore.**
1923 (1924) STRINGER *Empty Hands* 207 : She followed the trail through a slashing of brush, over spruce-tuck and brakes, along a rocky hillside....

spruceway *n.* a road made of spruce planks. See also **plank road.**
1965 *Islander* 14 Feb. 2/3 : The spruceway served Graham Island well for 30 years....

spud (in)† *v.* begin to drill an oil well.
1952 (1956) INNES *Campbell's Kingdom* 108 : On Tuesday morning, Garry spudded in. **1958** *Edmonton Jnl* 6 Oct. 25/1 : ... at the time the wildcat was spudded, crew members were taking bets among themselves that it would be a dry hole. **1960** *North* July-Oct. 45/2 : [The] foreman ... spudded (began drilling) in March 1....

spudgel† ['spʌdʒəl] *n.* [< Brit.dial.] *Nfld* a small bucket affixed to the end of a staff, for bailing boats.
1775 (1792) CARTWRIGHT *Journal* II 73 : The boat proved so leaky, that the spudgel was scarce ever out of hand. **1937** *Beaver* June 23/1 : The engine did not require a water intake, but pumped the water out of the boat, which with the help of a spudgel kept the level sufficiently low.

Spud Island *Slang* Prince Edward Island, so called because it is famous for its potatoes.
*c*1939 CHAMPION *On the Island* 25 : Has any other district in the world acquired so many descriptive names ? Prince Edward Island, St. John's Island ... Spud Island.... **1961** *Telegram* (Toronto) 19 May 7/1 : This is your day across the land. The day of the southshore schoonerman, prairie wheatgrower, "l'Acadie" market gardener, "Spud Island" farmer....

Spud Islander *Slang* a native or resident of Prince Edward Island.
1957 *Globe Mag.* 29 June 4/2 : [Caption] Spud Islanders are known throughout Canada for the quality of their potatoes.

spwagan *n.* [< Algonk. : Cree *ospwakun*] *Obs.* See **puagun.**
1848 (1859) BALLANTYNE *Hudson's Bay* 51 : They sat gravely on the floor, smoking their spwagans in silence.

spymobile ['spaɪmə‚bil] *n.* [*spy* + auto*mobile*] See quote.
1966 *Globe and Mail* (Toronto) 10 Aug. 5/4 : Metro police are experimenting with a small machine, known as a spymobile to some officers ... to cut down the incidence of break-ins and burglaries. The machine is a little motorcycle that is claimed to be the most silent in the world ... called a Velocette.

squadron *n. Fur Trade, Obs.* See quote.
1800 (1820) HARMON *Journal* 26 : The whole squadron, which consists of thirty canoes, is divided into three brigades.

square *n. Slang* See **square meal.**
1869 (1962) ANDERSON *Sawney's Letters* 45 : And I went to "Bob," the "Wake-up's,"/And had a bully "square".... **1927** LONGSTRETH *Silent Force* 77 : This unusual trip came to an end at last with a reception at Fort Walsh and a "square" of buffalo and bannock, and just in time. **1964** *Outdoorsman* III 7/1 : She'll get 'em out in the bush and prove that all that Hydro pap don't stop a GOOD gal from putting three good squares a day on the table.

square awl See **Indian awl.**
1922 *Beaver* July 10/2 : It requires but three tools to build a canoe : an axe, a "crooked knife," and a square or Indian awl.

squared timber *Lumbering, Hist.* See **square timber.**
1824 *Canadian Mag.* III 202 : Such is the usual routine of what is called Shantying in Canada, and such is the plan followed by those who take out squared Timber. **1959** *Cdn Geog.Jnl* Feb. 53/2 : Tools and implements used in the early days of the logging and squared timber era are on display.

square fipper *Nfld Dial.* See **square-flipper.**
1784 PENNANT *Arctic Zoology* 161 : The Seal-hunters in Newfoundland have a large kind, which they call the Square Phipper, and say weighs five hundred pounds. **1842** JUKES *Excursions in Nfld* I 312 : The "square fipper" ... is, however, very rare ; and we did not see one or hear of one being seen this season.

square-flipper (seal) *n.* See **bearded seal.** See also **square fipper** and **square fripper.**
1832 MCGREGOR *Brit.Amer.* I 108: Five kinds ... come down to the coasts of Labrador, Newfoundland, and to the Gulf of St. Lawrence: the harp seal ... the hooded seal ... the square flipper, the blue seal, and the jar seal. **1873** *Maritime Mthly* Aug. 145: On that day they shot a large square-flipper seal which served them for food for twelve days. **1939** (1951) TWEEDSMUIR *Hudson's Bay Trader* 152: A great square-flipper broke the water and set us dragging the dogs to a halt and reaching for a rifle. **1957** *Beaver* Spring 49/1: They were immensely strong and could carry off a square-flipper seal single-handed.

square fripper *Nfld Dial.* See **square-flipper.**
1774 (1792) CARTWRIGHT *Journal* II 38: A square phripper was caught in a net to-day, but got away as one of the people was clearing him out. **1861** DE BOILIEU *Labrador Life* 91: Now these seals are not like the Square Frippers, but are seen in large parties.

square needle See quote.
1955 SHIPLEY *Anna* 81: [It is] commonly called a "square" needle although actually three-sided, the sort used by Indian women when embroidering deer or moose-hide garments.

square phipper See **square fipper.**

square phripper See **square fripper.**

squaretail *n.* **1** the brook trout, *Salvelinus fontinalis.*
1936 *Beaver* Dec. 65/2: We had no fire scares and caught as many two-pound "squaretails" as we could eat, though we had to work hard for them. **1952** WILSON *Chibougamau* 71: Someone told me that a nine-pound squaretail was once caught up there.... **1963** *Sun* (Vancouver) 26 June 18/1: And those Mile High trout at this particular time proved the deepest-feeding, surface-hatingest squaretails I've run into.
2 See **prairie chicken** (def. 1). Cp. **sharp-tailed grouse.**
1958 *Edmonton Jnl* 27 Oct. 4/3: I mean square-tails, or pinnated grouse. **1959** MCATEE *Folk-Names* 25: Common Prairie Chicken [is also called] square-tail (The tail is evenly rounded, not pointed ... Man., Sask.); square-tailed grouse (Man.).

square timber *Lumbering* in the early days of Canadian logging, the staple export of timbers squared in the shanties and rafted to the Quebec timber coves for shipment. See also **squared timber, stick**[1] (def. 1a), and **timber.**
1765 *Quebec Gaz.* 8 Aug. 2/1: For every Load containing forty cubick Feet of sound merchantable square Timber of all Kinds (the Timber not to be less than ten Inches square) Twelve Shillings. **1892** (1908) DAWSON & SUTHERLAND *Geography* 104: The logs then go either to some saw-mill, or are shipped in the form of "square timber" without further treatment. **1947** (1963) SAUNDERS *Algonquin* 29: All these companies were cutting "square timber", the product of a particular way of cutting logs, and trimming them for market. Only the soundest and straightest red or white pine could be used to make a "stick" of timber. When such a tree was felled, trimmed of its branches, and cut flat

on four sides, it made one timber, or stick, perfectly square, and measuring the same at the top and both ends. **1964** *Cdn Geog.Jnl* Feb. 66/3: To make "square timber" only giant pines, 3 to 5 feet at the base and approximately 125 feet high, were used.

square timbering *Hist.* See quote.
1960 *Ont.Hist.* Dec. 222: Square timbering was the most simple and profitable business for the lumbermen of the Ottawa. ...

squash† [skwɑʃ] *n.* [< Am.E < Algonk. by shortening; cf. Narraganset *askútasquash*] a plant of the genus *Cucurbita;* also, the fruit of this plant.
1821 HOWISON *Sketches* 247: The vegetable best adapted for this purpose is the squash or gourd. **1952** BUCKLER *Mountain and Valley* 23: "I'll put my squash on the outside row, this year," Ellen said. ...

squat† *v.* occupy land without title to it; settle on public land without applying for legal title.
1829 MACTAGGART *Three Years* I 277: Squire Wright built his *town* on an island of this kind. Mrs. Firth squatted on one too, unknown to herself.... **1861** *Nor'Wester* (R.R.S.) 19 Feb. 2/5: Throughout the Settlement Indians squat on settlers' lands and burn up their carefully-preserved firewood or their fencing, and complaint is useless. **1958** *Sun* (Vancouver) 21 Apr. 7/3: By 1873 ... and J. L. Lockhart were squatting on mill-grant lands along False Creek.

squat-shack *n. Slang* the shack of a squatter.
1955 BIRNEY *Long Table* 193: "I holed up in a squat-shack on the Fraser with a old Wobbly sidekick till I used up the few bucks I had."

squatter† *n.* a person who squats.
1829 (1832) PICKERING *Inquiries* 113: ... some squatters have made clearings, and settled, for making rafts. **1958** *Sun* (Vancouver) 20 Jan. 35/2: They were shortly legally dispossessed, but remained as squatters.

squatters' rights† the rights of a squatter to remain on the public land he has occupied.
1883 *Brandon Dly Mail* (Man.) 24 Feb. 4/2: The infernal row you are all making up there about grievances, monopolies, squatter's rights, etc., has together with your last spring's floods and Winnipeg speculations, cooled off the Manitoba fever prevalent in Ontario last year. **1954** BEZANSON *Sodbusters* 135: "Squatter's rights" have been recognized in America since the early days of settlement simply because the urge to acquire land drove people way beyond surveyed boundaries. **1961** *Press* Apr. 6: They ... tried to enforce squatters' rights and fought the parcelling out of what they regarded as their own land to the United Empire Loyalists.

squaw† [skwɑ] *n.* [< Algonk.; cf. Cree *iskwāo* woman] **1** an Indian woman, especially a wife.
☛ *Although* squaw *is the normal and acceptable English term for an Indian woman, it is used in some contexts, especially by white men, with derogatory connotations. Moreover, the term is often resented by Indians who are not Algonkian-speaking, for it is to them an English word, one having no significance in their own languages.*
[**1743** (1949) ISHAM *Observations* 8: a Woman Es' qu 'u] *c*1745 (1898) *N.B.Mag.* I 73: At this place ye Squaws came down to the edge of the river, dancing and behaving themselves in the most brutish manner that is possible for human kind and taking us prisoners by the arms, one squaw on each side of a prisoner, they led us up to the village and placed themselves in a large circle

round us. **1827** (1829) MACTAGGART *Three Years* I 173: A Highlandman and a *squaw* beget an infernal progeny. **1911** SETON *Arctic Prairies* 281: "If you go I will run off into the backwoods with the first wild Indian that wants a squaw." **1957** *Maclean's* 7 Dec. 40/3: "We'll have a bunch of squaws to clean the fish and put it in packages."

2 an Eskimo woman.
1964 *North* July 48/1: A clear picture of that old squaw is beyond description.

3 *Fig., Derog.* See quote.
1891 EDGAR *Ten Years of U.C.* 230: Tecumseh, it is said, rose from the council, dashed his sword on the table, and denounced Porter as a miserable old squaw.

squaw axe† *Hist.* a small hatchet used by Indian women in their work.
1948 *Beaver* Dec. 6/2: The history of hatchets and axes [must include] the half axe, the broad axe, the squaw axe and the almost endless variations of the metal tomahawks.

squawberry *n.* **1** a kind of blueberry, *Vaccinium stamineum.*
1852 (1881) TRAILL *Cdn Crusoes* 60: At present we have plenty of ... squawberries ... and birdcherries. **1852** *Anglo-American Mag.* I 418/2: The partridge leads her young brood forth to feed upon the soft luscious fruits of the huckleberry and squaw-berry.

2 See **bearberry**.
1872 (1873) GRANT *Ocean to Ocean* 156: The sasketoon are simply what are known in Nova Scotia as Indian pears, and the kinni-kinnick creeper is our squaw-berry plant. **1947** DICKIE *Gay Adventurers* 42: When he [a snowshoe hare] curled up for a good night of rest, looking out through the leafless boughs of his squawberry, he saw the moon very white on the surface of the water.... **1957** FISHER *Pemmican* 161: Dried elderberry, or squawberry or wild currant he did not care for....

3 See **partridgeberry**.
1912 (1913) HODGE & WHITE *Indians of Can.* 438/1: After the squaw [has] been named [the] Squawberry (the partridge berry)....

squaw boot a type of moccasin having tops of soft buckskin, usually intricately beaded or embroidered.
1952 HOWARD *Strange Empire* 336: The older women wore bright shawls, retaining their dull dark dresses, but the girls liked colorful calico; and all the women had beaded ornaments and lavishly embroidered "squaw boots."

squaw dance *Orig.Northwest* in mining towns, a dance attended by white men and, mainly, by Indian women.
1864 (1963) *Beaver* Autumn 52/2: Oregon Jack gave a squaw dance at which everybody got very drunk, I believe.... **1958** BERTON *Klondike* 21: One of the main amusements, apart from the saloons, was a folk rite known as the "squaw dance."

squawfish *n.* a fairly large fish of the interior of British Columbia, *Ptychocheilus oregonense.*
1887 (1888) LEES & CLUTTERBUCK *British Columbia* 147: [We] fished with fair success for the white-fish and the squaw-fish which abound.... **1907** LAMBERT *Fishing in B.C.* 42: The squaw fish, also, will take the fly sometimes, but more often the minnow or grasshopper; its flesh is white and tasteless. **1962** *Wildlife Rev.* July 16/1:

Trout ... lie on the cool bottom along with hordes of squawfish and other piscatorial neighbours. ...

squaw hitch *B.C.* a type of hitch used for lashing a pack to a pack animal. Cp. **diamond hitch**.
1887 (1888) LEES & CLUTTERBUCK *British Columbia* 232: Other hitches there are of less fame than this [Diamond hitch], notably the "Squaw Hitch," a comparatively simple affair.... **1955** GOWLAND *Smoke* 22: There were some who swore by another hitch called the Squaw, but except for certain shaped loads I always found the diamond the best, and, once used to it, I rarely had to halt and re-pack while on the way.

squaw horse or **pony** *West* a quiet or spiritless cayuse, *q.v.*
1954 BEZANSON *Sodbusters* 22: He got an ancient, flea-bitten "squaw pony" for John. It had been relegated to that lowly estate because of lack of spirit and pokey gait. **1955** EWERS *Horse* 34: The horses of the Blackfoot ... were sometimes termed "cayuses" or "squaw horses" by the white residents of the country.

squawman† *n.* **1 a.** a white man married to an Indian woman, especially a man who thereafter follows Indian ways.
1884 *Nor'Wester* (Calgary) 17 June 3/1: It is the whisky man and the squaw man that defeat the benevolent aims of the government. **1928** WALDEN *Dog-Puncher* 55: A saloon-keeper proposed marriage to the girl; but because he was twitted as a future squaw-man he crawfished. **1958** BERTON *Klondike* 13: They took Indian wives, but in no sense did they resemble the "squawmen," who were looked down upon by their fellows.

b. a white man married to an Eskimo woman.
1936 (1955) STRINGER *Wife-Traders* 83: And the peace of mind of any such squaw-man was most assuredly coming at a price.

2 See 1912 quote.
1896 WHITNEY *On Snow-Shoes* 125: If there is caribou or moose meat or fish at the lodge, it goes to the hunters, who must face the storms and withstand the hardships of travel; but the "squaw men," the old men, and certainly the women and children, more than once during the year owe their very lives to the rabbit. **1912** (1913) HODGE & WHITE *Indians of Can.* 438/1: [A] squaw man [is] an Indian who does woman's work.

squaw notch See quote.
1930 BEAMES *Army* 12: He whetted his axe once more to a razor-like keenness, and began to notch them into place. He disdained the clumsy "squaw notch," where one log sits simply in a shallow groove cut in the one below, and fitted them neatly into place with the "saddle notch"....

squaw pole 1 a pole cut in the bush for use in a temporary shelter and left behind on breaking camp. See also **lodgepole** (def. 1).
1966 *Kingston Whig-Standard* (Ont.) 6 Feb. 4/5: The peaked lodge differed in having a ridge pole like a modern tent, supported by squaw poles lashed together.

2 See **chiploquorgan** and picture.
1966 BAITY *Wilderness Welfare* 113: I took the axe and cut a slender pole, stuck one end in the ground and leaned it out over the fire. I rescued the teetering pot and hung it on the end of my newly erected squaw pole.

squaw pony See **squaw horse.**

squaw tale *Obs.* See quote.
1912 SANDILANDS *West.Cdn Dict.* 44/1: Squaw tale, an old woman's story, a prophecy of evil, a very unintelligent anticipation of events that will never occur.

squaw tea See **Labrador tea** (def. 1).
1910 FERGUSON *Janey Canuck* 264: The marshes stand thick with Labrador tea, known in these parts as "squaw tea." **1910** FRASER *Red Meekins* 142: . . . the carpeted muskeg itself would feed the conflagration; the woven woof of squaw-tea shrub, first cousin to the wintergreen, with its coral berries. . . .

squaw winter† *Northwest* **1** See quote.
1912 (1913) HODGE & WHITE *Indians of Can.* 438/2: Squaw winter . . . a term in use in parts of the Canadian North West to designate a mild beginning of winter.
2 a spell of wintry weather occurring in early fall, especially when followed by an Indian summer, *q.v.*
1935 MOWERY *Resurrection River* 64: In the middle of September a short "squaw winter" had blown down from the coastal hills, killing all greenery and bringing a six-inch snow. Though the snow had quickly melted and the weather had faired up a little, the lazy golden days of summer were definitely gone. . . . **1953** MOWERY *Mounted Police* 31: A short "Squaw Winter" ten days ago had turned the Alberta Plains sere and dusty, but the cold snap had passed and the Indian Summer afternoon was warm and lazy, with the prairie sky a smoky blue and heat waves dancing over the hard-packed sod of the Police quadrangle. **1955** HIEMSTRA *Gully Farm* 210: The snow and the cold, squaw winter, as the old-timers called it, lasted for about a week, then the sun came out, the snow melted, and we had Indian summer.

squaw wood† *West and Northwest* easily gathered fuel for fires, such as small, dry sticks, pine cones, and cow chips, *q.v.*
[**1944** ADAMS *Western Words*: squaw wood. A slang name for dried cow chips also used in speaking of small, dry, easily broken sticks when used for fuel.]
1954 PATTERSON *Dangerous River* 259: Squaw wood, some people call it contemptuously, but I felt most grateful to it that night as I toasted myself at the glowing fire.

squid [skwid] *n.* [origin uncertain] a cephalopod of the genus *Loligo;* cuttlefish.
1578 (1959) HAKLUYT in REID *Sourcebook of Cdn Hist.* 28: . . . and [there is] another . . . called the Squid. . . .
1622 WHITBOURNE *Discovrse* 42: The other followes the Capling, which is a fish like the Smelt: And the third followes the Squid, which is a fish something like the Cuddell. **1954** FOWKE *Folk Songs* 53: The squid is a species of cuttle-fish about ten inches long which is used as bait for larger fish. **1958** *Evening Telegram* (St. John's) 2 May 5/2: [We were] waiting for the first squid to strike our jiggers.

squid-jigging *n. Nfld* the practice of catching squid for bait, using a jig, *q.v.*

1905 DUNCAN *Grenfell's Parish* 105: Jack had told me much of the lore of lobster-catching and squid-jigging. **1958** *Evening Telegram* (St. John's) 2 May 5/2: Says Mr. Scammel, "Every greenhorn who goes squid-jiggin' knows what it is like to get the 'juice' right in the eye."

squid-jigging ground(s) *Nfld* the place where fishermen jig (def. 1) for squid. See also **jigging ground.**
1936 (1966) *Weekend Mag.* 23 Apr. 4/1: All sizes and figures, with squid lines and jiggers,/They congregate here on the squid-jiggin' ground. **1958** *Beaver* Summer 24/2: They usually occurred when a herd of potheads wandered within spotting distance of boats on the cod or squid jigging grounds.

squirrel whisky *Slang* a potent alcoholic liquor, often homebrew.
1912 FOOTNER *New Rivers* 39: We received many invitations to partake of squirrel whiskey, but seeing the results before our eyes, we would as soon have drunk bichloride of mercury.

S.S. See **school section** (def. 1).
1874 *Woodstock Sentinel* (Ont.) 2 Jan. 1/9: The final examination off S.S. No. 4 . . . was held on Fri. the 19th ult.

S.S.B. See **Soldier Settlement Board.**
1951 CORMACK *Local Rag* 76: The Evans family was our first experience with S.S.B. folks.

stag boot a cut-down high boot.
1950 CREIGHTON *Lunenburg County* 15: Don't wear grey mittens or stag boots on board a fishing vessel. . . .
1964 *Chronicle-Herald* (Halifax) 4 Sep. 14/3: Jack boots are fine; but no stag boots are allowed. . . .

stage† *n.* **1** *Esp.Nfld* a waterside shed for gutting, heading, and salting fish to be dried on flakes, *q.v.* See also **cod-stage, fishing stage** (def. 1), and **fish stage** (def. 2). Cp. **stagehead.**
1620 WHITBOURNE *Discovrse* 22: Such Stages and Houses, that the first arriuers into an Harbour finde standing, wherein men set diuers necessaries, and also salt their fish, some men haue vsed to pull downe, or taken their pleasures of them: by which vnfit disorders of some first arriuers there yeerely, those which arriue after them, are sometimes twenty dayes and more to prouide boords and timber, to fit their boates for fishing. **1818** LOCKWOOD *Nova Scotia* 39: . . . at its mouth the islands afford shelter to fishermen and small vessels, as well as a means of erecting their stages.
1883 HATTON & HARVEY *Newfoundland* 136: Fishing hamlets line the shores, with their rough stages and fish flakes for landing and drying the cod. **1957** *Cdn Geog. Jnl* Oct. 129/2: The fish were then washed and then placed under salt in pounds erected for the purpose in a crudely constructed waterside shed called a "stage."
1962 MOWAT *Black Joke* 11: Down to the stage with ye and we'll do some proper work.
2 See **flake.**
1842 BONNYCASTLE *Newfoundland* I 295: To a stranger, and especially a female, the task of walking over these impending stages, often the only path, appears a very nervous one, as the boughs are not placed close, nor wattled in, but left separated as much as possible, to admit the passage of air to the underside of the drying fish.
3 *North* See **drying stage** (def. 2).
1887 *Senate Jnl* XXI App. 184: During summer the fish are best smoked and dried, and in fall and winter are

hung on a stage and kept frozen. **1908** MAIR *Mackenzie Basin* 40: Innumerable ice-cold creeks poured in from the forest . . . and the frequent marks on trees, informing passing hunters of the success of their friends, and the number of stages along the shore for drying meat, indicated a fine moose country. **1913** COWIE *Adventurers* 224: We found Jacob Bear with a big stage laden with whitefish, hung, in tens by the tail, to freeze for winter's use. **1956** KEMP *Northern Trader* 223: We built a big raftered stage of poplar logs and cut the sticks necessary for the hanging of the fish.

4 *North, Hist.* a platform raised high off the ground, as in a tree, where meat and other food might be put out of the reach of predatory animals. See also **cache**, *n.* (def. 2 and picture) and **staging** (def. 2).
1715 (1965) *Letters from Hudson Bay* 51n: Wee were all forcd to leave the factory & to take our Selves to ye Woods & to gett on trees & Stages for Six Days. . . .
1743 (1949) ISHAM *Observations* 141: . . . of all the beast's in the Country, their is none so much an Enemy to the Indians, as these Creatures [wolverines] are; by breaking their stages op'n and getting all their provender away. . . . **1800** (1897) COUES *New Light* I 91: We then arranged camp . . . and made a suitable stage nearby, to hold fresh meat, etc. **1922** *Beaver* Mar. 39/2: Passing a considerable amount of "jerked" meat on a stage, I entered the wigwam. *Ibid.* Apr. 5/2: [They went] to haul in some three hundred buffalo cows which had been previously killed and put up on stages. **1940** NIVEN *Mine Inheritance* 45: Here and there on the way between Point Douglas and Pembina he saw to the erection of stages, platforms raised high on poles above the prairies on which food could be left beyond the reach of leaping wolves.

5 *North* **a.** See **pose** (def. 2).
1830 (1963) DAVIES *Northern Quebec* 107: . . . thence into the sixth and seventh lakes by portages each a stage long. . . . **1933** MERRICK *True North* 58: We generally make stages of about a quarter of a mile and get everything to that point before carrying on to the next stage.

b. See **pose** (def. 1). See also 1933 quote above.
1931 GREY OWL *Last Frontier* 67: This, then, is not the end, only a stage.

stage *v.* **1** place on a stage (def. 3).
1956 KEMP *Northern Trader* 225: They had staged over four thousand fish. . . .

2 *Hist.* place on a stage (def. 4).
1929 MOBERLY *When Fur Was King* 67: After the last of these trains had departed a brigade of sixty horse-sleds and thirty dog-trains was sent to the Beaver Hills to haul in three hundred buffalo cows previously killed and staged out of the reach of predatory animals.

3 *Hist.* place (a corpse) on a burial-tree, *q.v.*
1858 (1860) HIND *Assiniboine Exped.* I 308: Mr. West saw an Indian corpse staged about ten feet above the ground.

stage or **staged** *adj.* of furs, inferior by virtue of dark blue patches on the skin. See 1943 quote. See also **stagey.**
1680 (1945) *H.B.C.Minutes* 27: . . . the Men employed in Sorting the Beaver have found 302 Stage Skinns. . . .
1784 (1954) *Moose Ft Jnls*: The Honourable Company have complyed with my proposal for altering the standard of Otters, and have accordingly ordered their prime Otters in future to be rated at 2 Beaver each and the dammaged and Staged at one Beaver each.
1859 *Kamloops Jnl* 19 July: St. Paul sent me a Staged Skin for Tea. **1933** MERRICK *True North* 248: . . . by the beginning of April the mink and marten skins

are almost stage. They will bring less than half what they would have if caught in January. **1842** (1948) MCLOUGHLIN *Letters* 70n: Mr. N. E. Beynes, Assistant Manager of the Fur Department of the Hudson's Bay Company, states that "A 'staged' or 'stagey' skin is one with dark blue patches on the pely (i.e. leather). The condition occurs when the animal is taken out of season, when, in the case of most animals, the fur and pelt are not at their best."

stagehead *n. Nfld* See 1819 quote. See also **stage,** *n.* (def. 1).
[**1779** (1792) CARTWRIGHT *Journal* II 446: We found the head of the stage raised up about five inches, many of the posts, shores, and stouters gone. . . .] **1819** ANSPACH *Hist.Nfld* 430: The place where the operation of curing the cod-fish is performed, is a stage or covered platform erected on the shore, with one end projecting over the water, which is called the stage-head, and which is fortified with stouters, or very strong shores, to prevent the stage from receiving any damage from ships or boats. **1944** *Beaver* Sep. 20/2: Boats are made shipshape, and temporary wharves or "stageheads" set out on the beaches for the splitting and dressing of the cod. **1958** HARRINGTON *Sea Stories* 127: Miss Butt was carried down to the stagehead, taken off in a rowboat and put aboard the vessel.

stage sleigh or **sled**† *Hist.* a sleigh for transporting people or goods along a stage route.
1912 POCOCK *Man in the Open* 132: On the stage sleigh from Ashcroft this person got froze, which mostly happens to a tenderfoot, who'd rather freeze like a man than run behind like a dog. **1955** COLLARD *Canadian Yesterdays* 200: At two o'clock on the morning of the appointed day the musical bells of the stage sled, the French-Canadian carriole, came sounding down his street and stopped before his door.

stagey *adj.* See **stage,** *adj.*
1784 (1954) *Moose Ft Jnls* 197: 'Twill be necessary for you to use every means in your power to prevent the Canadians from . . . employing Indians to Trade their indifferent and stagey Furrs from these articles, & then sell 'em again to the Natives for prime Furrs.
1941 *Beaver* Sep. 39/2: Stagey An unprime skin.

stagged (off)† *adj.* of pants, cut down from original size.
1925 *Cdn Labor Advocate* (Vancouver) 18 Sep. 6/5: A logger wearing "stagged pants" as a substitute for "plus fours," tripping lightly o'er the green with a popular society flapper as his caddy would be an inspiring sight, and a good advertisement of the democratic principles of the "Hoosiers." **1953** MOON *Saskatchewan* 215: . . . they [the lumberjacks] wore pants stagged off or rolled half way to the knee so as not to be confused with mere city dwellers. **1956** KEMP *Northern Trader* 114: He had the mackinaw shirt and stagged-off pants, the black felt hat, and the high caulked boots, and the bulge in his cheek was probably a wad of Shamrock.

staging *n.* **1** *Esp.North* See **drying stage** (def. 2). See also **stage,** *n.* (def. 3).
1889 WITHROW *Our Own Country* 543: . . . on many prominent points were Indian stagings for drying and smoking the salmon. . . . **1896** RUSSELL *Far North* 273: The fish are hung in the fishery in "sticks" upon staging,

to dry and freeze; a stick, an inch in diameter is thrust through the tail and they are hung heads downward in bunches of ten.

2 See **stage**, *n*. (def. 4).

1947 ROWLANDS *Cache Lake* 205: Their traps, snowshoes, and hunting sleds have been cached all summer on stagings at last winter's camping places. . . .

3 *Maritimes* a pier for unloading fishing boats. Cp. **stagehead**.

1956 RADDALL *Wings* 10: And then on the steel curve you saw . . . the scatter of gray weathered cottages and fish sheds, the small wharves and stagings and the boats. . . .

stag jacket a short, warm jacket of Mackinaw cloth, tight at the waist and roomy at the shoulders, a style favored by loggers, trappers, etc. Cp. **stag shirt**.

1954 PATTERSON *Dangerous River* 206: I had on good winter clothes: over these I had pulled a pair of khaki "bib" overalls as windbreak, and on top of all came a heavy mackinaw stag jacket with double shoulders.

stag shirt a shirt of heavy woollen cloth, similar in design to a stag jacket, *q.v.*

1951 ANGIER *At Home* 220: He laced on his outer pair of mooseside moccasins, then scuffed into rubbers while buttoning a kersey stag shirt.

stake† *n*. See **grubstake**, *n*. (def. 3).

1887 ROBERTS *Western Avernus* 47: And now he was trying to make a "stake," or a sum sufficient to take him back. . . . **1912** SANDILANDS *West.Cdn Dict.* 44/1: Stake, the little pile of earnings which is due to the harvester, the lumberjack and others at the end of the season's work. **1966** *Islander* 21 Aug. 5/1: They [loggers] seldom worked more than a few months in one place, just long enough to gather a stake, which they spent in a few days in town. . . .

stake (off or **out)** *v*. **1 a.** *Mining* mark or indicate the boundaries of (a claim) with stakes. See also **staking** (def. 2).

1860 *British Colonist* (Victoria) 2 June 1/1: . . . the flats . . . are all staked off, and claims are changing hands at very high prices. . . . **1913** FOOTNER *Jack Chanty* 176: The three claims were staked out before you came into the country. **1955** *Cdn Mining Reporter* 8 Apr. 1/5: The Company staked 110 claims (4400 acres) in the area. . . .

b. *Lumbering* lay claim to a timber berth by marking out its boundaries with stakes prior to registering the claim.

1908 GRAINGER *Woodsmen* 78: Now Billy Hewlitt was a "timber-cruiser"—a man who sought for forest timber, to stake it. . . .

2 See **grubstake**, *v*. (def. 1c).

1919 FRASER *Bulldog Carney* 226: . . . I'll get Jeanette to stake me to a couple of days' grub. . . . **1960** *Sun* (Vancouver) 19 Apr. 4/2: About one in ten is a boomer, seldom staying in a town longer than was required to stake himself for a move to the town beyond.

staker *n*. a person who stakes (def. 1a) a mining claim.

1898 *Yukon Midnight Sun* (Dawson) 15 Aug. 1/3: He also said that until after September 1st no one but the

original staker has any business upon these claims. **1954** *North Star* (Yellowknife) Aug. 2/1: Though a few stakers were "made," it was generally the brokers and speculators who skimmed off the cream.

stakey ['steki] *adj*. [< *stake*, n., q.v.] *Slang* adequately provided with money. Also *staky*.

1919 *Camp Worker* 28 June 7/1: If they hold a job for a month they have done something out of the ordinary, and as a consequence, they are never very staky, and the question of funds comes first in most cases. **1960** *Weekend Mag.* 8 Oct. 28/1: I wasn't going to go in, because at the time I wasn't stakey. . . . **1964** *Press* Feb. 2: He is stakey now, and exuberant. . . .

staking *n*. **1** the provision of a grubstake (def. 2).

1957 *Bay News* July 3/2: He has to use his own judgement in the staking of a trapper to grub and ammunition in the lean years.

2 the marking of mining claims by means of stakes. See also **stake**, *v*. (def. 1a).

1952 *North Star* (Yellowknife) Nov. 3/2: There, the mineral claims map sheet is completely filled, so far as staking is concerned. **1958** *Northern Miner* 25 Dec. 13/5: . . . at least three staking parties [are] known to be busy taking up ground at the present time.

staking bee See **staking rush**.

1956 *Northern Miner* 29 Nov. 113/1: A new nickle find . . . has stirred the Shiningtree area of Northern Ontario, where a fair sized staking bee seems to be under way.

staking rush a movement of persons intending to stake claims for mining purposes.

1953 *North Star* (Yellowknife) July 1/1: There are possibilities of an additional poll in the Marion River area, where a staking rush is now under way. **1964** *North* May-June 14: A miniature "staking rush" to the Pine Point area took place during the following winter. . . .

staky *adj*. See **stakey**.

Stampede *n*. the Calgary Stampede. See also **stampede**, *n*. (def. 2).

1919 *Eye Opener* (Calgary) 9 Aug. 4: Come to Calgary Stampede Week and have the time of your life. **1955** HARDY *Alta Anthol.* 164: Its name is Stampede, it was born in 1912, and it wouldn't think of living anywhere else. **1964** *Calgary Herald* 11 July 38/3: But three years is not the extent of his experience with the Stampede.

stampede ['stæmpid] *n*. [< Am.E < Am.Sp. *estampida*] **1† a.** a wild, unrestrained rush of animals, usually set in motion by fright.

1855 *Anglo-American Mag.* VI 45/2: If the animals become frightened they will start off in a regular stampede breaking down every barrier that stands in their way. **1929** MOBERLY *When Fur Was King* 178: One of the most thrilling and most terrifying sights of those early days was the stampede of a vast herd of buffalo before a prairie fire. **1963** SYMONS *Many Trails* 57: [The] stories one reads of stampedes and terrible nights with cattle may not all be true, but all could be; for a bunch of big steers are twice as "spooky" as a mixed bunch. . . .

b. a rush of people to get somewhere.

1854 KEEFER *Ottawa* 70: On the first appearance of a break up in March there is a regular stampede among the teamsters. . . . **1859** *Brit.Colonist* (Victoria) 18 May 2/4: Many of them speak in gloomy terms of mining and business prospects and predict a general stampede from the upper country. **1966** *Canadian* 30 Apr. 7/1: ... when the train pulled into the divisional point at Ignace, Ont., there was a stampede for the station saloon, where every bottle was seized.

c. a rush of people to a place where gold, silver, etc. has been discovered. See also **gold rush.**
1898 *Yukon Midnight Sun* (Dawson) 11 June 1/2: All the rest of the creeks of the district, some thirty or forty, which have had their stampedes and booms, and some of which may turn out very rich, are not expected to yield any money from the winter's work. **1965** *Cdn Geog.Jnl* Apr. 119/1: Not only was it the last of the old-fashioned stampedes in which dog teams and men vied for space along the narrow trail, but it also ushered in the air age of prospecting.

2 an exhibition of skills in various activities associated with ranching, such as riding, roping, and bull-dogging, also offering chuckwagon races, a grandstand show, etc. See also **rodeo.**
1912 SANDILANDS *West.Cdn Dict.* 44/1: Stampede ... a picturesque name for shows and exhibitions of the Wild West description. **1923** BARBEAU *Indian Days* 5: Picturesque stampedes take place every summer in the July celebrations at Banff. ... **1945** HAIG *Brave Harvest* 116: Later that year Miss Hind was in Calgary at the first stampede. **1964** DUFF *Indian History* 104: The Indian "pow wows" held in recent years at North Vancouver, the "Indian Days" at Kamloops, and other gatherings such as the Williams Lake stampedes are similar occasions for Indians to enjoy renewed social contacts and gain recognition as Indians.

stampede† *v.* [< n.] **1 a.** of animals, rush headlong in wild flight.
1888 (1890) ST. MAUR *Impressions* 181: We hoped to have gone, though it was a ride of over twenty miles, but all the ponies had stampeded except Adela's, and as they were nowhere to be found we had to give it up. **1914** BINDLOSS *Intriguers* 67: Last time we tried it the pony stampeded and the wheel went over my foot. **1963** SYMONS *Many Trails* 38: After days in the hot fly-time ... cattle stampeded over the prairie. ...
b. cause (animals) to rush away in wild flight.
1908 LAUT *Conquest N.W.* II 31: If a snow storm caught the travelers, it was an easy matter for marauding Indians to stampede the horses and plunder packs. **1949** MacGREGOR *Blankets and Beads* 36: As they approached the precipice, the Indians increased their pace and, with a final rush, stampeded the animals [buffalo] over the edge.

2 a. of persons, take part in a goldrush; take off in haste to a place where a strike has been reported.
1898 *Medicine Hat News* (Alta) 8 Dec. 5/4: On every new discovery she's sure to have a claim,/She stampedes like a whirlwind and she gets there just the same. **1898** LANDREVILLE *Appeal* 23: That the diggings along Birch Creek were deserted signifies nothing more than that miners are prone to stampede to any district which has the appearance of greater richness than the one wherein they are at work. **1951** ANGIER *At Home* 41: "The prospectors who stampeded through here around '98 on their way to the Yukon had a pretty good trick," Brad mentioned.
b. cause (persons) to rush unthinkingly into a course of action.
1912 POCOCK *Man in the Open* 104: At that the lady attracted attention by screaming, so the third shot stampeded poor Jones. **1917** *Grit* (Toronto) 11 Dec. 6/6: The Borden press is very nervous and will pull everything but a gun in order to stampede the voters to

the Borden camp. **1924** *Machinists' Bull.* Oct. 3/2: Efforts are being made by various agencies to use the present condition as a club to stampede the men and disgust them with their Organization.

3 enter (a region) in large numbers in search of gold.
1900 LONDON *Son of Wolf* 22: ... the country was stampeded and staked by a tidal wave of *che-cha-quas*. ... *Ibid.* 165: Besides, there drifted down the river ... ludicrous accounts of the *che-cha-quas* who had rushed in and were stampeding the whole country.

stampeder *n.* **1** a person who participates in a stampede (def. 1c).
1898 *Yukon Midnight Sun* (Dawson) 11 June 4/1: Mr. Frank P. Slavin, the well known ex-pugilist who rightfully earned the name of "Stampeder" last fall ... returned to this city Friday evening. ...
1936 ARMSTRONG *Yukon Yesterdays* 13: No wonder that hundreds of the weaker stampeders returned to the base to take the first steamer back home! **1963** *Beaver* Summer 42/2: Before the turn of the century, hordes of rushing stampeders ... had reason to curse the savage stretch of water. ...
2 *West* a horse, cow, or steer that is easily frightened and whose behavior is likely to start a stampede.
1954 HAGELL *Grass was Free* 59: Among them were stampeders, kickers, strikers and the odd one that would cow-kick or bite.

stampeding *adj.* rushing wildly in a headlong fashion.
*c***1902** LAUT *Trapper* 67: At fording-places on the Qu'Appelle and Saskatchewan ... carcasses of buffalo have been found where the stampeding herd trampled the weak under foot, virtually building a bridge of the dead over which the vast host rushed. **1956** EVANS *Mountain Dog* 118: Hal rapped the gunwale with his paddle and heard what he did not want to hear—the rumbling sound that only a very large school of stampeding salmon make.

stampeding pack *Obs.* a packsack carried by a stampeder (def. 1).
1900 LONDON *Son of Wolf* 181: ... it is known that several che-cha-quas and at least the Old-Timer kept their stampeding packs stored behind the bar, ready to hit the trail at a moment's notice. **1902** LONDON *Daughter of Snows* 173: St. Vincent was in sight, footing it at a lively pace, the regulation stampeding pack on his shoulders.

standing-bed berth *Lumbering, Obs.* one of a range of bunks lining the sides of a shanty (def. 2a). Cp. **muzzle-loading bunk.**
1853 STRICKLAND *Canada West* II 285: Standing-bed berths are constructed on the two sides and one end of the building [shanty], similar to those on board ship. ...

standing iron *North* the iron or twisted wire spike on the collar of a dog harness to which a string of ribbons, pompoms, or other decoration may be attached. See picture at **sled dog.** See also **collar iron.**
1934 GODSELL *Arctic Trader* 39: Bells jangled as the dogs proudly tossed their massive heads and shook their beribboned standing-irons in the gusty breeze.

1956 KEMP *Northern Trader* 104: Hitched tandem-wise to a high-curled toboggan, they were elegant in their standing irons, pompoms, and ribbons.

Stanfields *n.pl.* long underwear manufactured by Stanfield's Ltd., a knitting mill in Truro, Nova Scotia.
1966 *Globe and Mail* (Toronto) 18 Jan. B5/7: He [the logger] was a pack-sack citizen and appeared on Skid Row streets complete with dirty Stanfields and caulk boots which would be later hocked for the last bottle.

Stanley Cup the trophy emblematic of the professional hockey championship of the world, named for Lord Stanley, Governor General of Canada, 1888-93, who presented it in 1893.
1958 *Encyc.Can.* IX 395/2: To encourage Canada's winter sport he presented the Stanley Cup, originally intended to be held by Canada's most outstanding team each year. . . . **1962** *Canada Month* Apr. 13/2: But for Canada's reputation, the world championship is more important than all the Stanley Cup playoffs ever staged.

star(ch)igan *n.* [origin uncertain; prob. < Algonk.] *Esp.Lab.* a kind of Indian dwelling.
1920 GRENFELL & SPALDING *Le Petit Nord* 94: Light snow has fallen during the night, and every "starigan," every patch of "tuckamore" is "decked in sparkling raiment white." **1923** (1924) STRINGER *Empty Hands* 342: . . . the thing that had looked so like a lodge-pole starchigan was nothing more than a tumble of blow-downs carried over the cliff-edge in a snow-slide.

States† *n.pl. Elliptical* the United States of America.
1785 (1943) HUNTER *Diary* 75: They made up a court at Johnstown, tried him, and condemned him to be flogged round the town and sent back to the states.
1852 (1923) MOODIE *Roughing It* 232: There was a runaway nigger from the States came to the village, and set up a barber's pole and settled among us.
1955 *Western Star* (Corner Brook, Nfld) 10 Mar. 11/2: All set to take the States by storm is Canada's National Ballet Company, who on their opening night in New York will present a new ballet, "Offenbach in the Underworld."

states-general *n.* a proposed body of representatives from all sectors of French Canada, to discuss constitutional and other matters of vital interest to French Canadians.
1963 *Globe and Mail* (Toronto) 9 May 5/5: He was speaking . . . for the creation of a special Legislature committee to study the possibility of calling a French-Canadian states-general to discuss constitutional questions.

station† *n. Nfld* temporary quarters established on shore during the fishing season. See also **fishing station** (def. 1) and **stationer.**
1892 (1908) DAWSON & SUTHERLAND *Geography* 63: These islands are employed as stations by the French fishing fleet. . . . **1905** GRENFELL *Harvest* 113: At the end of the voyage with all the fish, split and salted, stowed away in the hold, this solitary crew returns to the station.

stationer *n. Nfld* See 1952 quote. See also **station.** Cp. **floater** (def. 2).

1905 GRENFELL *Harvest* 113: The men that have remained are called "stationers"; the others are green-fish catchers. **1952** PUTNAM *Cdn Regions* 52/2: The migratory fishermen fall into two classes: the "stationers" who establish temporary quarters on shore, and the "floaters" who operate from their schooners and follow the fish from place to place. **1954** *Fishermen's Advocate* (Port Union, Nfld) 7 Jan. 1/4: The catch on the Labrador coast was also lower than last year, due to the reduction in the number of stationers and floaters engaged in the fishery.

stationman *n. Hist.* See 1887 quote.
1887 ROBERTS *Western Avernus* 101: The grading was here of an easy character . . . consequently it was let out to small parties of working men, or "station men" as they are called, who were paid by the piece and not by the day. **1961** *Cdn Geog.Jnl* Jan. 16/2: Materials from the cuts were pushed by stationmen . . . over a track of poles to build adjacent embankments.

statute labo(u)r† *Hist.* road work and other duties required of settlers by law as part of settlement duties, *q.v.*
1833 *Cdn Correspondent* (York [Toronto]) 12 Jan. 2/5: A general commutation of statute labour would, we think, be a desirable measure in itself—even if it were commuted for one half its real value, and the proceeds usefully applied under proper restrictians it would still prove advantageous to the public. **1903** RICHARDSON *Colin* 84: . . . the older men were engaged at a "by-the-day" pace, in making some improvements to the road. It was the season for doing the statute labour.

stave grub(b) See **grub**, *n.*

steady *n. Nfld* See 1792 quote.
1792 CARTWRIGHT *Journal* II Glossary: Steady in a river. A part where the bed widens, inclining to a pond, and there is no perceptible stream. **1842** JUKES *Excursions in Nfld* II 241: I understand from a salmon-fisher, the only person inhabiting the neighbourhood, that a succession of "steadies," with occasional rapids, may be met with for twelve miles farther. **1912** ROGERS *Sport* 261: The brooks and shallow steadies were now full up from the heavy rains, so we pole where we had to portage coming in. **1963** VARDY *Labrador*: [Tourist Folder] The falls on County Cat are 3 and 8 miles from the forks and beyond the falls are a series of steadies which are reported to hold large numbers of salmon.

steam alligator *Lumbering* an alligator (def. 2) driven by steam engines.
1947 SAUNDERS *Algonquin* 73: There they would be made into booms, and dragged by means of the steam alligator, still to be seen at Baysville, to the starting point of the haul over the height of land.

steam canter *Lumbering, Hist.* See quote.
1964 *Atlantic Advocate* July 59/2: They had [c1870] patent edgers, endless haul-ups, jump-up saws, steam canters to roll the logs on the saw carriage, transfer chains.

steamjetting *n. North* See quote.
1957 *Maclean's* 14 Sep. 91/2: The simplest passive method for building on permafrost is a framework of logs called a "mudsill." Heavier structures usually are placed two feet up on piles, which are sunk into the permafrost by an ingenious technique known as "steamjetting." Hollow pipes are driven into the permafrost under pressure of fifty to eighty pounds of steam. This quickly thaws about a foot all around the pipe. Wooden posts, sometimes greased or tar-papered

to resist the upthrusting tendency of the permafrost, are then driven in butt down and left to refreeze solidly before the weight of the building is put on them.

steam jigger See quote. Cp. **jigger** (def. 3) and **speeder** (def. 1a).
1948 HOLLIDAY *Valley of Youth* 259: The railway did have a funny little contraption known as the "steam jigger"; a miniature flatcar on which there were two seats and a small steam engine, with which they ran a passenger service of sorts. . . .

steam scow *Obs.* a scow driven by a steam engine.
1833 *Canadian Courant* (Montreal) 24 July 2/5: When he had an effort to push through a Steam Scow, a thousand difficulties arose from miscalculation and very bad work on the south end of the Canal, that baffled the Colonel so, he was glad to leave it.

steel *n.* **1 a.** railway track. See also **end of steel.**
1888 *Dominion Illust.* 18/3: The fourth and last episode was the building of the Canadian Pacific Railway—that long, strong bright link of steel which binds the fair little island on the Atlantic coast with her bigger sister on the shores of the Pacific. **1963** *Maclean's* 16 Nov. 54/2: But even such lowly creatures as laborers . . . followed the progress of the steel the way the captain of the *Queen Elizabeth* measures off his daily mileage.
b. a length of railway track.
1909 BEMISTER *Stories* 104: As the steels were laid, the camp moved on from time to time, with its great crowds of men, most of them ready for a fight at any moment.
c. a railway line.
1912 (1914) BICKERSTETH *Open Doors* 110: The C.N.R. steel arrived in Edmonton in 1906, and the day the last rail was laid the property went for 24,000 dollars. **1928** FREEMAN *Nearing North* 137: With the coming of steel it consolidated its position through becoming the terminal at which (at near-by Waterways) the steamer meets the railways. **1938** *Beaver* Sep. 18/2: From Norway House, Buck went to "Steel" at Mile 137 on the Hudson Bay Railway. **1953** LOWER *Voyages* 64: Since there was no radio in those days, anyone going into the bush anywhere was cut off from the outside world as soon as he left "the steel."
2 *Northwest* a steel drum of or for oil, gasoline, etc.
1959 LEISING *Arctic Wings* 233: I asked . . . about the availability of my two steels of aviation gasoline.
3 *West Coast* See **steelhead.**
1961 *Sun* (Vancouver) 7 Feb. 22/1: Vedder River—[they] hooked 10 steels in high-ish, somewhat-colored water Sunday, landed only two. **1967** *Sun* (Vancouver) 20 June 19/1: Most Cheakamus steels are five-year, rather than the usual four-year-old fish . . . .

steel-end *adj.* of or relating to the end of steel (def. 1a). See also **steel** (defs 1a and 1b).
1936 MOWERY *Paradise Trail* 5: . . . it was one of the few cars which Gary had seen in the little steel-end town.

steel gang the workmen responsible for laying the tracks in railway building.
1910 WARD *Canadian Born* 109: But they were watching it and as soon as the 'steel gang' of a projected railway came within measurable distance they meant to claim their sections and work their land together.
1958 *Kingston Whig-Standard* (Ont.) 14 Oct. 7/6: In the old days, it kept a steel gang hopping to lay 90 rails a day. **1963** *Maclean's* 16 Nov. 57/1: The steel gang lived in railway cars, pulled up by a locomotive along one or two miles of the track they had laid that day.

steelhead *n.* a fish, *Salmo gairdnerii,* of the Pacific coast, which spawns in fresh water after two or three years in the sea. See also **iron-nose, rainbow, sea trout** (def. 2), **steel** (def. 3), and **steelie.** Cp. **Kamloops.** Also *steelhead trout.*
☞ *The* **steelhead** *is sometimes erroneously regarded as a rainbow trout that has spent some time in the sea. Actually the reverse is true, the rainbow trout being a steelhead that spends its entire life in fresh water.*
1896 *Province* (Victoria) 28 Mar. 210/2: Still this did not prevent my good friend Duncan Campbell from landing a fine steelhead with a march brown just opposite the Quamichan rancherie. . . . **1955** *Vancouver Province* 6 Jan. 15/4: Steelhead trout are British Columbia's number one game fish, but their habits and life history are still pretty much of a mystery. **1966** *Dly Colonist* (Victoria) 27 Feb. 8/2: . . . the sand pool . . . at this time of year is often filled with cutthroat trout and sometimes is holding water for steelhead.

steelheader *n.* one who fishes for steelheads.
1948 *Game Trails in Canada* Feb. 25: The average steelheader that lands one in three seems quite content with his quotient, but I don't think it's quite good enough. **1964** *Vancouver Province* 14 Feb. 18/1: The Gold River has blanked many a good steelheader—and it is tough to fish.

steelheading *n.* fishing for steelhead.
1958 *Vancouver Province* 4 Nov. 16/5: Bud reports steelheading still poor . . . Largest steelhead Bud saw was a 22 pounder taken by a Yank. . . . **1963** *B.C. Digest* Apr. 28/1: Steelheading in the Valley is good from November to May with Steelies to twenty-five pounds. **1966** *Dly Colonist* (Victoria) 27 Feb. 8/1: He is also 10 minutes from the Campbell River tyee grounds, but our story today is about steelheading.

steelhead rod an especially long, resilient rod used in fishing for steelhead.
1963 *Sun* (Vancouver) 22 Mar. 15/1: This man is easily identified as belonging to our first category of fishermen, the "veteran" who is marked by his Cowichan Indian sweater, hip waders and long, willowy steelhead rod.

steelhead trout See **steelhead.**

steelie *n. Pacific Coast, Informal* See **steelhead.**
1958 *Sun* (Vancouver) 28 Jan. 14/1: Jackie Francks [is] a veteran of two year's persuit [sic] of steelies. . . . **1963** *B.C. Digest* Apr. 28/1: Steelheading in the Valley is good from November to May with Steelies to twenty-five pounds.

steel-layer *n.* See **steel man.**
1913 (1914) BICKERSTETH *Open Doors* 215: About half a mile ahead of the pioneer come the surveyors, who stake out the line, putting in centre stakes, which are the only guide the steel-layers have to go by.

steel man a worker on a steel gang, *q.v.*
1942 HAIG-BROWN *Timber* 254: . . . the steel men . . . lay ties and steel. . . . Like the graders in British Columbia, these are often northern Italians.

steel-worker *n.* See **steel man.**
1912 (1914) BICKERSTETH *Open Doors* 157: There are a number of steel-workers here, all men who have been making good wages for years, and yet they have not saved a cent.

steer-dog *n. Esp.North* in a dog-team, the dog hitched nearest to the sled or toboggan, his task being to guide the vehicle, keeping it clear of anything that might obstruct it. See also **boss dog, sled dog** (def. 2), **steerer** (def. 2), **steering dog,** and **wheel dog.**
1873 (1904) BUTLER *Wild North Land* 103: Upon my assuming charge of the train, an ominous tendency to growl and fight on the part of my steer-dog told me something was wrong. **1896** WHITNEY *On Show-Shoes* 102: The steer-dog keeps the sledge upon a slanting track, and guides it through trees and rocks. **1953** OSGOOD *Winter* 65: ... a steer dog or wheel dog hitched nearest the toboggan.

steerer *n.* **1** *Fur Trade, Obs.* See **steersman.**
1800 (1897) COUES *New Light* I 49: Etienne Charbonneau; Voyageur, steerer, or helmsman.
2 See **steer-dog.**
1963 MCTAVISH *Behind the Palisades* 202: Of the remaining three [dogs] ... Wolf, the steerer, showed symptoms of the disease.

steering dog See **steer-dog.**
1913 COWIE *Adventurers* 247: The beautiful and benevolent Beaver was the steering dog (next the sled); the leader or foregoer was Seresto. ...

steersman *n. Fur Trade, Hist.* in the canoes and boats of the fur brigades, the foreman of a crew, usually the most skilled boatman and the highest paid. See also **pateroon** (def. 2). Cp. **bowsman.**
1774 (1934) HEARNE *Journal* 122: The Pataroon or Steersman of each Cannoe has 50£ pr annom, the foreman £40 and the rest of the Crew 20 and 25£ according to their goodness. **1821** (1900) GARRY *Diary* 131: As he had dreamt, the Canoe was lost, but the Steersman who remained with the Canoe fortunately saved himself. **1905** (1954) *B.C.Hist.Qtly* XVIII 161: The bowman and steersman usually carry or superintend the carrying of the canoe. **1929** (1931) MERK *Fur Trade* 13: Bowmen and steersmen were crew leaders in North canoes and inland boats [respectively]. **1963** *Beaver* Winter 23/2: With him were ... his Iroquois steersman ... Indian paddlers and interpreters.

Stellar coal a kind of soft coal found in 1798 near present-day Stellarton, Nova Scotia. Also called *oil coal.*
1918 DRUMMOND *Mining in N.S.* 130: ... the sample is now classed to be that of an oil coal, having to all appearance, the characteristics of Stellar Coal. **1954** SHERWOOD *Out of the Past* 11: The name of Stellarton comes from the fact that a singular bed of coal exists there. The coal is known as "Stellar" or "oil" coal because when burning it gives off sparks like stars. **1958** *Encyc.Can.* IX 402/2: ... the town [Stellarton] was named for its so-called stellar coal, which during combustion emits sparks resembling stars.

stem *n.* an Indian ceremonial pipe. Cp. **calumet of peace.**
1806 (1897) COUES *New Light* I 371: Two Crows [took] the lead with the stem of ceremony, which he continually held out before him, never allowing it to touch either his own or any other horse. **1913** COWIE *Adventurers* 275: Amongst the things sent out to meet Loud Voice was his great ceremonial calumet and

decorated stem. ... **1951** O'MEARA *Grand Portage* 308: [Glossary] Stem: Indian ceremonial pipe.

stemmo ['stɛmo] *n.* [< Algonk.; cf. Cree *chistamaw*] tobacco. Also spelled *stemow, stimu.*
[**1743** (1949) ISHAM *Observations* 39: tobacco in Generall che stem mo] **1927** (1933) MERRICK *True North* 107: P.S. here is 1/2 fig of stimu for your nose warmer. **1952** *Beaver* Sep. 4/1: ... I found myself selecting at Battleford an assortment of trade goods: blankets, strouds, prints, *stemow* (tobacco). ... **1953** MOWERY *Mounted Police* 156: Ogohko stuffed his pipe with still more of the sergeant's precious, dwindling *stemmo*. ...

Stevens' Party *Hist.* See **Reconstruction Party.**
1935 *Dly Colonist* (Victoria) 12 Sep. 6/2: Plans by the Stevens' Party organizers in this section today disclosed that a convention for the nomination of a candidate will be held in Duncan on Tuesday, September 17. ...

stick¹ *n.* **1** *Lumbering* **a.** *Hist.* a piece of square timber, *q.v.* See also **timber stick.**
1806 (1903) CARR-HARRIS *White Chief* 92: One stick only remained on the rock, with Martin clinging to one end and me to the other. **1854** KEEFER *Ottawa* 39: The rude and insecure manner in which the sticks of timber are retained in a crib, although sufficient to carry them in safety through the navigable rapids, forbids the attempt to pass them down the *chûtes* or higher falls. **1947** SAUNDERS *Algonquin* 12: Down the Ottawa ... floated the great square "sticks" of timber in thousands; and all along its shores lay heaps of "slash," while great gashes in the forest showed like wounds. **1964** *Atlantic Advocate* July 59/1: Each March the King's Purveyor certified the number and sizes of the sticks that had been brought to the stream, "trimmed four-square and fit for rafting."
b. a tree suitable for logging.
1829 MACTAGGART *Three Years* I 248: *Sticks,* or *pines* suitable for making masts of, are rare, and not to be found in the forest but by very intelligent lumbermen. ... **1849** ALEXANDER *L'Acadie* II 152: Our guides ... now left us with a small present, having come so far to see our forest-camp and to try and discover "sticks" for lumber. **1863** WALSHE *Cedar Creek* 221: "I daursay now, that stick's standing about a thousand years. ..."
c. a log.
1849 ALEXANDER *L'Acadie* II 73: Some "sticks" thrust others to the edge of the rapids. ... **1907** BAIRD *Roger Davis* 152: My duties as clerk were ... to record the number of sticks, large and small, hauled to the river each day. **1964** *Nfld Qtly* Summer 28/1: Winter's work [means] the total of sticks, lumber, rinds and so forth that a man can produce while living with his family away from his settlement "in the woods for the winter."
2 *Esp.North* **stick of fish,** a group of ten fish skewered on a rod to be hung on a stage (def. 3) for freezing or drying for later use. See also **stick³,** *v.* (def. 2).
[**1804** CAMERON *Nipigon Country* 298: We then pierce the fish with the point of a knife through the bone, at about two inches from the tail and string them by tens on a twisted willow branch, then hang them on poles, with their heads down, in a shady place.] **1887** *Senate Journal* XXI App. 56: It is quite a common thing, when an Indian has preserved nothing for himself, to go to a Hudson's Bay Company's man and ask for "a stick of fish." **1944** CLAY *Fur Thieves* 77: Ten fish were threaded on each of the sticks—to make what is called, in North Country vernacular, "a stick of fish." Each "stick"was worth about a dollar. And the sticks were hung on the

racks to freeze in the chill autumn air. **1956** KEMP *Northern Trader* 225: One canoe we filled with sticks of fish....

stick² *n.* [< Chinook Jargon *stik* wood, tree, forest] *B.C. and Northwest* **1** woods; bush. See also **stick country** and **Stick Indian**.

*c*1857 (1927) MCKELVIE *Black Canyon* vii: One night this young woman suddenly appeared and said in a subdued voice, "Hist!... Before sun up you white men go. Go back in the stick (forests) far, far, far."

2 (attributive uses) of, related to, or located in the stick country, *q.v.*

1951 HOBSON *Grass* 97: Now you fellows figure we're stuck, but let me tell you a real stick man's never stuck. **1955** HOBSON *Nothing Too Good* 128: He was batching it out on this lonely, stick ranch.

stick³ *v.* **1** *Lumbering* See **hang up** (defs. 1a and 1b).

1827 (1829) MACTAGGART *Three Years* I 115: Farther up the river... is a noted ridge of rocks, called the Hog's Back, from the circumstance of raftsmen with their wares sticking on it in coming down the stream. **1849** (1926) LANGTON *Early U.C.* 205: The process is to break up the raft and commit the spars to the stream. About an hour after that perhaps two or three sticks reach Peterborough, the rest are left sticking here and there on rocks, dams and islands. **1854** KEEFER *Ottawa* 67: The whole year's labor is thus lost from the timber "sticking" as it is called, unless heavy rains should come to the rescue....

2 *Esp.North* prepare sticks of fish for drying or freezing. See also **stick¹** (def. 2).

1942 *Beaver* Mar. 23/1: Now for sticking: Willow sticks are cut about four-foot long and pointed at one end.... The white [fish] is slit through near the tail, just above the vertebral column....

Stick *n.* [< *stick²*, *q.v.*] See **Stick Indian**.

1897 WILSON *Yukon* 64: The "Sticks" are probably the most stalwart of any [Indians]. **1902** LONDON *Daughter of Snows* 369: "It is the Stick talk of the Upper White," La Flitche stopped long enough to explain. **1910** HAYDON *Riders of Plains* 206: The Chilkats traded with the Sticks, who in turn traded with the natives of the Coppermine River in the interior. **1937** ANDREWS *Wrangell* 21: These Indians were of the "Stick" tribes, a name used by the Thlingits and other coast tribes for the people of the interior.

stick-boy *n.* **1** *Hockey* the person charged with looking after the hockey sticks used by a team.

1955 *North Shore Leader* 8 Apr. 4/3: Everyone on the Beaver team from the stick boy to the trainer is presently overjoyed.... **1963** *Kingston Whig-Standard* (Ont.) 5 Feb. 10/6: His father was a professional hockey player in Quebec and Cammy was a stick-boy, which is comparable to being a bat boy in baseball.

2 *Cdn Football* one of the two persons responsible for moving the yard sticks during a game.

1963 *Calgary Herald* 29 Oct. 8/1: The stick boys are....

stick chimney *Obs.* a chimney having walls made of logs set in mortar, the whole being covered with plaster, used where stones were not ready to hand.

1825 (1916) SELLAR *Narrative* 92: There may be stones on our land, but there are none in sight. Jabez says we will have to put up with stick chimneys.

stick country *B.C. and Northwest* the wooded country of the interior. See also **stick²** and **sticks** (def. 1). Cp. **bush country** and **Stick country**.

1955 HOBSON *Nothing Too Good* 67: This is particularly true in a wooded or stick country, where trails are narrow and cattle are spooky. **1963** SYMONS *Many Trails* 63: It appears to be all timbered "stick country," covered with aspen, poplar, and lodgepole pine....

Stick country *B.C. and Northwest* the wooded country of the Stick Indians, *q.v.* Cp. **stick country**.

1926 *Dalhousie Rev.* VI 58: Many an Indian from the remote "Stick" country, above the canyons, brought his fox skins, his mink and bear, from the coast his sea-otter and fur seal, and throwing them down on the floor of Cunningham's store would ask to know their value. **1958** BERTON *Klondike* 41: By that time Carmack could speak both the Chilkoot and the Tagish dialects, and was exerting considerable influence over the Stick Indians from the interior or "Stick" country.

stick-fire *n.* See quote.

1943 MILLER *Lone Woodsman* 69: An Indian stick-fire was the medicine this time. He smashed a number of dead balsam poles... till he had a circle of clubs all around the fire. Their ends were pushed together as they burned away.

stick game 1 See 1793 quote.

1793 (1801) MACKENZIE *Voyages* 311: We all sat down... and our guide and one of the [Carrier] party prepared to engage in play. Each had a bundle of about fifty small sticks neatly polished, of the size of a quill, and five inches long; a certain number of these sticks had red lines around them, and as many of these as the players might find convenient were curiously rolled up in dried grass, and according to the judgment of his antagonist respecting their number and marks he lost or won.

2 See **lahal**.

1963 *Citizen* (Vancouver) 13 June 3/5: Performances include the Swai-Swai dance, Lahal or stick game, Salish Mask dance, medicine, paddle and masked dances. **1965** *Beaver* Autumn 54/1: They had sold their furs and we watched them [Beaver Indians] play the "stick" game which was accompanied by the roll of a drum. **1966** ST. PIERRE *Quarter Horse* 162: The Indians will work okay. They had a big stick game here and as usual it ended up with nobody winning... so everybody is now broke.

stickhandle *v.* *Hockey* carry a puck forward and around opponents by deft and deceptive movements of the stick; control the puck while moving forward on an irregular course.

1931 *Vancouver Province* 3 Jan. 7/3: Hayes... stickhandled past the entire Wanderers' team and beat Sinclair with a pretty shot. **1966** *Canadian* 29 Jan. 5/3: Some of the most exciting moments... come during the killing of penalties, when the defending team, not allowed to ice the puck into the attacking team's end, must stickhandle or pass to waste... time.

stickhandler *n.* *Hockey* a player who handles his stick skilfully. See also **stickhandle**.

1958 *Rosetown Eagle* 29 May 10/1: One writer giving a thumb nail sketch of the championship team says "Dick (the man) Elliot, plugger type, stick handler, back-bone of the team, who can score from any angle." **1963** *Hockey Illust.* Dec. 72/2: Gainor was one of the most tricky stickhandlers of all time.... **1965** *Globe* *and Mail* (Toronto) 6 Nov. 34/3: "The only good stickhandlers nowadays are the rink rats," said [Bob] Davidson.

stickhandling *n. Hockey* skilful use of a hockey stick. See **stickhandle.** See also **puck-handling.**
1955 *Western Star* (Corner Brook, Nfld) 14 Mar. 9/1: ... he got a breakaway and made a marvelous stickhandling play forcing the attack ... straight down center ice. **1963** *Albertan* (Calgary) 10 Dec. 12/1: Lloyd Turner ... doesn't like the slap shot because it is not accurate, and it does away with stickhandling.

Stick Indian [see note below; cf. **stick²**] *B.C. and Northwest* an Indian from the bush country of the interior, originally so called by the Indians of the Pacific Coast. See also **stick²** and **Stick.** Cp. **stick Indian.**
☞ *In the Chinook Jargon, stick meant anything of wood, from a ship's mast to a forest; hence "Stick" Indians were the forest dwellers as opposed to the people of the coast.*
1887 DAWSON *Tribes of Yukon* 14: They are classed with the "Stick Indians," by the coast tribes, and have been assumed to be Tinné, but their language very clearly shows that they are in reality of Thlinkit people.
1913 OGILVIE *Yukon* 24: Coast Indians ... found their profits from fur trade with the interior, or "Stick Indian" as he was known, because he came from the land of forest.... **1958** BERTON *Klondike* 283: All along the banks were camped the Stick Indians, dirty, ragged, and sick-looking, smoking salmon and offering to buy or sell everything and anything from those who floated by. **1963** SYMONS *Many Trails* 72: ... snowshoes are known only as a strange accoutrement of the "Stick Indians," who inhabit the area north from the Blackwater basin, and with whom the Chicotin sometimes come in contact.

stick Indian *Pacific Coast, Slang, Derog.* a native from the backwoods; an Indian ignorant of city ways. Cp. **bush Indian** (def. 2) and **Stick Indian.**
1954 EVANS *Mist* 12: "Talk about your stick Indian." "You said that before. What's it mean, stick Indian?" "Straight out of the bush. Hillbilly. Get it?" *Ibid.* 176: Instead he looked wooden-faced and scared ... like some stick Indian. **1956** EVANS *Mountain Dog* 96: To him they were not "characters" or stick Indians, or any of the slighting things that Belile and others of his kind called them.

sticks *n.pl.* [cf. **stick²**] **1** *B.C. and Northwest* the bush; wooded interior country. See also **stick country.** Cp. **Land of Little Sticks.**
1913 OGILVIE *Yukon* 24: Coast Indians ... found their profits from fur trade with the interior, or "Stick Indian" as he was known, because he came from the land of forest, or "sticks".... **1938** (1950) STANWELL-FLETCHER *Driftwood Valley* 132: "Wolf very wise, judt like man. I think you neber see him in sticks [forest], only open country, sometimes." **1954** EVANS *Mist* 258: Back in the sticks is no place for her, that's for sure. **1962** FRY *Ranch on the Cariboo* 77: Christmas Day the cows have to be fed, like any other day, and chances are you're away out in the sticks somewhere like this.

2 *Slang* any place distant from urban areas; back-country.
1936 MACKENZIE *Living Rough* 203: You're away out in the sticks and they expect you to work for twenty cents

a day. **1958** *Globe and Mail* (Toronto) 16 July 7/5: The company's decision not to migrate uptown or to the suburbs was a reversal of the out-to-the-sticks movement which has been marked in some U.S. cities by building of huge office buildings in farmers' fields.

stick-tie *v. Northwest* tie up (a dog) with a toggle and noose, after the fashion of the Stick Indians, *q.v.*
1912 LONDON *Smoke Bellew* 297: And when he stick-tied the dogs, instead of letting them forage free through the night, he knew that he had administered another jolt to the nervousness of Dawson.

still hunt See **still-hunting.**
[**1828** BIDWELL *Tor.Pub.Lib.MSS B104* 69: Under the guidance of Mackenzie, who did not conduct himself with the caution and reserve of a new member, the House went on a still hunt for grievances.]
1849 ALEXANDER *L'Acadie* I 266: A breeze is favourable for the still hunt, as it prevents the step of the hunter from being heard. c**1902** LAUT *Trapper* 124: A slight snowfall and the wind in his face are ideal conditions for a still hunt.

still-hunt *v.* engage in still-hunting, *q.v.* Cp. **creep.**
1863 WALSHE *Cedar Creek* 107: "... you see I'm often away trapping or still-hunting...." **1898** EDGAR *Canada and Capital* 147: The hunter ... still-hunts and stalks the deer among the rocks and trees. **1921** HEMING *Drama of Forests* 39: ... the follower should use great caution and circle down wind in order to still-hunt the hunter's trail in exactly the same way he would still-hunt a moose.

still-hunter *n.* one who engages in still-hunting, *q.v.*
1852 (1923) MOODIE *Roughing It* 193: " 'Tis old Brian B—, the still-hunter, and a near neighbour of your'n." **1885** *Indian* (Hagersville, Ont.) 30 Dec. 11/1: Now it is safe to say that not one-tenth of these were killed by the "stalker" or "still hunter." **1959** *Maclean's* 4 July 22: They had acquired this apparel from a man they respected as the best fly-fisherman, the best bird-shot and the best still-hunter in a region where standards in these activities were high.

still-hunting *n.* See 1939 quote. See also **creeping, still hunt,** and **still-hunt.**
1853 STRICKLAND *Canada West* I 178: Deer-hunting is a very exciting sport; but I prefer still-hunting (or deer-stalking, as it is called in the Highlands of Scotland) to driving them into the lakes and rivers with hounds. **1883** FRASER *Shanty* 146: In this respect it stands far ahead of still-hunting.... **1931** GREY OWL *Last Frontier* 87: Still-hunting is an art learned from the Indian, an accomplishment in which few white men excell.... **1939** GODSELL *Vanishing Frontier* 95: Still-hunting [is the] tracking down and creeping up on the moose through the deep, soft snow—a method necessitating all the arts of woodcraft.

stimu *n.* See **stemmo.**

stink hole See quote.
1953 MOON *Saskatchewan* 56: These [sodium sulphate plants] are built beside bleak, eye-burning lakes, or what used to be lakes. People used to call these places "stink holes," and still do, and because of the unpleasant odours, there is reason.

stint *n.* [< Brit.dial. *stint* a check; cf. OE *āstyntan* stop, check] *Lab., Obs.* a beaver dam.
1778 (1792) CARTWRIGHT *Journal* II 325: The stint was the longest and completest I ever saw....

St. James Street a Montreal street on which are located many banks and financial houses exerting great influence on Canadian business; hence, the moneyed interests of Quebec and Eastern Canada collectively. Cp. **Bay Street.**

1939 *Thunderbolt* Mar.-Apr. 5/1: The decisions made in St. James St. and Wall St. have more effect upon the lives of the people of Canada than have the trifling measures which our worthy representatives at Ottawa are able to secure. **1946** LOWER *Colony to Nation* 493: The northern prairie frontier . . . joined in with the general prairie agitations against the Winnipeg Grain Exchange, which for the western farmer is even more directly symbolical of metropolitanism than is "St. James Street." **1963** *Calgary Herald* 20 Sep. 4/6: Bay Street and St. James Street may well have been dilatory in examining the investment prospects offered by this province [British Columbia]. . . .

St. John's Island *Hist.* See 1889 quote. See also **Saint Jean.**

1786 (1787) *Account N.S.* 78: The situation of this country, considered in every point of view, is far more advantageous for Great Britain to be possessed of than any other on the whole Continent of North America, whether in respect to its connection with Canada, Newfoundland, Cape Breton, St. John's Island, and the fisheries, or to its being much nearer to the mother country than any other Province. . . . **1889** WITHROW *Our Own Country* 67: Prince Edward Island, known till 1798 as St. John's Island, is supposed to have been discovered by Cabot in one of his early voyages. **1958** *Encyc.Can.* VIII 318/1: The second was the decision, taken by the British in 1769, to separate the island (St. John's, as it was by now known) from Nova Scotia. . . .

St. Lawrence (apple) an eating apple having white flesh with pinkish streaks when ripe and greenish, red-streaked skin.

1864 *Canada Farmer* 1 July 188/2: The varieties most cultivated are the Fameuse, St. Lawrence, Pomme Gris, and Bourassa, yet under the existing mode of culture, these are not hardy enough. **1923** WILLIAMS *Spinning Wheels* 239: And to few of us is it given to see a striped Duchess, to taste a pink-veined St. Lawrence. . . .

St. Lawrence provinces *Rare* Ontario and Quebec.

1892 (1908) DAWSON & SUTHERLAND *Geography* 40: . . . the remaining native population is . . . distributed as follows: Newfoundland, none, or but a few Indian immigrants from Nova Scotia; Acadian provinces, 4000; St. Lawrence provinces (Ontario and Quebec), 30,000; Manitoba, North-West Territory and North-East Territory, 40,000; British Columbia 25,000; Eskimo, along the Arctic coast, 4000.

stog *v.* [cf. Brit. dial. *stog* stuffed with food; related to *stodge*] *Esp.Nfld* See 1937 quote. See also **stub,** *v.*

1835 WIX *Journal* 64: The structure of the winter tilt, the chimney of which is of upright studs, stuffed or "stogged" between with moss, is so rude, that in most of them in which I officiated the chimney has caught fire once, if not oftener, during the service. **1937** DEVINE *Folklore* 49: Stog—To chinse moss between the logs of a log house to keep out draughts.

stomach-robber *n. Slang* See quote.

1912 SANDILANDS *West.Cdn Dict.* 44/2: Stomach-robber, the cook in a lumber or construction camp; sometimes also called dough-slinger.

stone-and-rail fence *Hist.* a rail fence, *q.v.,* having the lower rails replaced by piled stones.

1963 GUILLET *Pioneer Farmer* II 21: Where stones had to be removed from the field the combined stone-and-rail fence . . . was very common.

A stoneboat

stoneboat† *n.* a low sledlike contrivance, sometimes having shaped log-runners, used for removing stones from fields and for other heavy hauling. See also **ground sleigh, sled** (def. 3), and **sleigh,** *n.* (def. 4).

1887 (1952) *United Church Observer* 15 Oct. 29/1: Then we loaded them on the stoneboat, drawn by the oxen. **1901** CONNOR *Man from Glengarry* 189: In the afternoon the colt was put through her morning experience, with the variation that the stone-boat was piled up with a fairly heavy load of earth and stone. **1963** SYMONS *Many Trails* 93: We brought out two hams . . . and between stoneboat loads of heavy sod we made great inroads into them. . . .

stone fence† *Slang, Obs.* a mixed drink, such as cider and brandy.

1853 STRICKLAND *Canada West* I 216: The Doctor, as he said, used to "improve" it, making what he called, a "stone fence," by inserting a small *soupçon* of brandy from a pocket-pistol, which he was too much in the habit of carrying about with him in hot weather.

stone-hooker *n. Hist.* a vessel employed in hooking and transporting stones for ballast. See also **hooker**[1] (def. 2).

1890 *Grip* (Toronto) 4 Oct. 214/1: [He] had taken passage on a stone-hooker for Oswego. **1924** (1933) SLATER *Yellow Briar* 241: . . . a still sadder misfortune befell Mrs. Johnstone, whose two sons were running a stone-hooker out of Port Credit in the fall of 1862. **1945** CALVIN *Saga* 154: In May, 1848, the firm was supplying a new centreboard, and "fixing the floor for the stone" in a little vessel—probably a "stone-hooker."

stone lamp See **kudlik** and picture.

1938 GODSELL *Red Hunters* 298: From a frame of willow sticks arising from another snow platform are suspended the stone cooking pots, beneath which a tray-shaped *kudlik,* or stone lamp, is placed. **1958** *Encyc.Can.* IV 38/1: Umiak and kayak have already disappeared from most regions, snow hut and stone lamp seem likely to follow in their wake. . . .

Stone sheep [< Andrew J. *Stone,* an American sportsman of Missoula, Montana, one of an expedition up the Stikine River for the American Museum of Natural History] a sub-species of the mountain sheep, *Ovis canadensis stonei,* found in northern British Columbia and adjacent parts of the Yukon. See also **gray sheep.** Cp. **bighorn sheep.** Also *Stone's (mountain) sheep.*

1916 WOOD *Tourist's N.W.* 347: You will not get any wapiti or deer there, but . . . you could hardly fail to get specimens of moose, Osborn's caribou, Stone's sheep, and mountain goats, with a good chance of a grizzly or black bear or a wolf or fox. **1921** HAWORTH *Trailmakers* 205: The following day I was lucky enough to kill a fine black bear and the next day two Stone's mountain sheep, or black sheep, so that we had an abundance of good meat. **1960** *Beautiful B.C.* I 46: [Caption] Stone sheep on a mineral lick in the Spatsizi district of northern British Columbia. **1966** *Commercial Letter* Jan.-Feb. 6/1: The Yukon big game season . . . enables the licence holder to take one of such big game as moose . . . Stone sheep, mountain goat or grizzly bear.

stook† [stuk] *n.* **1 a.** a structure of grain sheaves, sometimes set up end to end in five or six pairs (a long stook), sometimes in a circle with a crossed pair on top as a shed (a round stook). See also **stook,** *v.*
1835 (1926) LANGTON *Early U.C.* 148: [My grain], notwithstanding two or three bushels per acre loss by shedding, from the constanting shifting of the stooks . . . will yield nearly if not quite twenty-five bushels per acre fit to go to the mill. . . . **1905** SCHERCK *Pen Pictures* 176: After the grain had been bound it was gathered together and stood on end, two sheaves in a pair, in "stooks" or "shocks" of ten to twelve sheaves to dry. **1966** *Canadian* 30 Apr. 7/3: [You] lead your wagon along row after row of stooks, pitching them up onto the wagon.
b. a stack of bales of hay.
1958 *Department of Agriculture News Release* I-204 8 July: This machine consists of a platform pulled behind the hay baler and it leaves stooks of six bales.
2 in (the) stook, of grain, at the stage of harvesting when stooked.
1922 STEAD *Neighbours* 134: . . . the last sheaf of his six hundred acre crop was in stook. **1958** MACGREGOR *North-west of 16* 138: . . . after it had dried thoroughly in the stook. . . .

stook† *v.* set up in stooks (def. 1a).
1860 *Nor'Wester* (R.R.S.) 14 Sep. 3/2: There is great difficulty in procuring even a small number of Indian "helps" to use the sickle or follow up the work of the reaper by typing and "stooking" (which is the diminutive for "staking") the sheaves in the field.
1929 ENGLAND *Immigrant* 144: When I was at home I was herding cattle for a while then I was stooking at home helping my parents. . . . **1963** SYMONS *Many Trails* 109: Stooking grain—or as they call it in the States "shocking"—is a hard and monotonous job. . . .

stooker *n.* **1** one who puts up stooks (def. 1).
1909 ROSS *Hist.of Zorra* 60: A gang of nine men, four cradlers, four binders, and a stooker would be put in each section. **1962** ALLEN *Peace River* 43: In good years and bad he paid his stookers and threshers exactly twenty-five cents a day above the going wage. . . .
2 a machine which sets up stooks (def. 1b) of hay bales. Cp. **stook loader.**
1958 *Department of Agriculture News Release* I-204 8 July: A recent innovation known as the Hay Bale Stooker is a useful piece of haying equipment for smaller farms.

stooking† *n.* the practice or skill of setting sheaves of grain up in stooks (def. 1a).

1913 FRANCIS *Cdn Home Boy* 79: I had worked hard for the farmer, pitching and stooking. **1966** *Canadian* 30 Apr. 5: [Caption] Eight binders, giants of their day, move down the field and the men who do the stooking are pressed to keep up.

stook loader a mechanical contrivance which loads sheaves or bales into a wagon a stook at a time. See also **stook,** *n.* (defs 1a and 1b). Cp. **stooker** (def. 2).
1958 *Department of Agriculture News Release* I-204 8 July: A tractor equipped with a stook loader can lift all six bales and load them on a wagon. **1959** STOREY *Prairie Harvest* 118: Some of the big machines used stook loaders for picking up the sheaves.

stook pitcher a member of a harvesting crew who throws sheaves onto the stook wagon, *q.v.* Cp. **spike-pitcher.**
1963 SYMONS *Many Trails* 111: . . . a stook pitcher who already had his load on, connected the foot-wide drive belt. . . .

stook wagon a kind of rack for transporting stooks (def. 1).
1952 PUTNAM *Cdn Regions* 374/1: Finally, grouped about the outfit will be four or more teams of horses drawing flat-floored stook wagons.

stoop† [stup] *n.* [< Am.E < Du. *stoep* a small porch with benches] **1** a porch or veranda, nowadays especially one at the back door, often unroofed. See also **back stoop, front stoop,** and **long stoop.**
1792 (1955) CRAIG *Early Travellers* 7: Many of the houses have a balcony or piazza of wood, erected in front, covered, and floored with the same material. This, the inhabitants term a stoop. **1833** (1838) TRAILL *Backwoods* 142: The Canadians call the verandahs "stoups." **1885** *Neepawa Star* (Man.) 11 Sep. 3/3: He won't take "no" for an answer when parting with her on the stoop and asks for "just one." **1959** *Globe and Mail* (Toronto) 12 Mar. 25/9: . . . there are plenty of them [houses] which look pretty snug and homey, as though they might have a nice stoop on the back equipped with a comfortable rocker.
2 a platform, usually by the back door of a house, erected to enable a person to reach a clothes line.
1959 CREIGHTON *Bluenose Ghosts* 237: It came up behind the buildings and took to moaning like a person in pain, and it followed him to the platform (stoop). . . .
1964 *Maclean's* 2 Dec. 13/1: On clear washdays the women of the neighborhood came out onto little clothesline stoops in their husbands' old overcoats. . . .

stopper or **stopper-net** *n.* *Lab., Obs.* a type of net-trap placed permanently across narrow channels, for catching seals.
1771 (1792) CARTWRIGHT *Journal* II 184: The boats made only one trip each to-day; one of them to the shoal-nets; the other to the stoppers, and brought in sixty-three seals. **1861** DE BOILIEU *Labrador Life* 87: There is another method of catching the seal by what is called the stopper-net.

stopping-house *n.* *Hist.* a place providing accommodation for travellers; an inn, usually of a primitive sort. See also **keep-over.** Cp. **mile house** and **road house.**
1883 *Prince Albert Times* (Sask.) 18 Apr. 1/5: The road from Carrot River crosses the South Saskatchewan at this point where there is now a first class ferry and stopping house. **1912** FOOTNER *New Rivers* 235: None of

the stopping-houses along this trail have progressed beyond the most primitive stage. They provide a floor for you to sleep on and a fire-place, in some cases a stove for you to cook your food on; that is all. **1958** ELLIOTT *Quesnel* 177: . . . farmers have had to subsidize their land with stopping houses, by mining, freighting, railway construction, or, as at present, by logging.

stopping-place *n. Hist.* **1** See **stopping-house**.
1878 LEMOINE *Chronicles of St.Lawrence* 21: When being jolted in a two-wheeled post stage, without springs, over these villainous roads, the traveller will do well to fix beforehand the stopping places (for meals), as hostelries are few and far between. **1947** SAUNDERS *Algonquin* 31: At several places along the roads leading from the Ottawa in the Petawawa limits, there were "stopping places" where the teams could be fed and watered, and where the men could be put up for the night if necessary. **1960** BUBLITZ *Dotted Line* 13: On our journey to the homestead, we had to stop for the night at a "stopping place."

2 a settlement where stagecoaches and groups of travellers customarily stop for food and lodging, etc.
1909 CAMERON *New North* 28: At noon it clears, and . . . we "make tea" at Sturgeon Creek (the Namao Sepee of the Indians), the first of the "stopping-places" or Waldorf-Astorias of the wilderness. . . . **1961** *Edmonton Jnl* 5 Aug. 4/3: Among the stopping-places in the Edmonton district sixty years ago, North Cooking Lake was held in high esteem by persons travelling between Edmonton and such places as Beaverhill Lake, Ross Creek and other settlements to the southeast.

3 *Hist.* See **pose** (def. 2).
1954 CAMPBELL *Nor'Westers* 37: Over the year those French Canadian canoemen and their forbears had developed regular stopping-places along the nine-mile carrying-place. . . .

stops and starts *Hockey* a skating exercise intended to strengthen the muscles of the legs and feet and to improve a player's ability to change direction rapidly, involving alternate stopping and starting at the command of the coach, who usually controls the movement with whistle blasts.
1962 *National Hockey Annual* 25/3: Sometimes I get more tired just fore-checking for a minute or so because it's like stops and starts, than I do when I'm out there for four minutes.

store *n.* **1 a.**† a retail shop.
1764 *Quebec Gaz.* 18 Oct. 2/2: Alexander Mackenzie & John Grant, Have to sell at their Store, in the Low-Town of Quebec, A Great Variety of Goods. . . . **1827** (1829) MACTAGGART *Three Years* II 221: The towns are full of shops, or what are called stores. **1966** *Cariboo Observer* 15 Sep. 13/1: The new store has a total area of over 20,000 sq. ft. with approximately 13,000 sq. ft. devoted to sales area and the balance to stockroom.

b. *Hist.* See **store pay**.
1832 (1833) SOCKETT *Emigration* 7: I have 5 *s.* a day, and 2 *s.* 6 *d.* per day in store, what they call it: you must take clothes, shoes, hats, or any thing that your master works for, and I take 15 *s.* a week paid in money.

2† *Maritimes* See **fish house** (def. 1).
1959 CREIGHTON *Bluenose Ghosts* 104: He was at the shore in the store (fish house) and when he went outside a sea gull flew very low.

storekeeper *n.* **1**† the owner of a store or shop.
1834 (1926) LANGTON *Early U.C.* 52: The first is confined

almost entirely to storekeepers and married men in old and well settled townships. . . . **1836** (1926) *Ibid.* xi: The storekeeper in Canada holds a very different rank from the shopkeeper of the English village. The storekeepers are the merchants and bankers of the places in which they reside.

2 the man in charge of a fur company's trading post. See also **trader** (def. 3).
1856 BALLANTYNE *Young Fur-Traders* 60: This is the trading-store. It is always recognisable, if natives are in the neighbourhood, by the bevy of red men that cluster round it, awaiting the coming of the store-keeper or the trader. . . . **1923** WALDO *Down Mackenzie* 79: I tell you, those H.B. storekeepers don't have an easy time of it. **1966** *North* July-Aug. 50/1: He wonders what happened to the storekeeper who used to help him with anything he wanted, especially nets, shells.

store meat *North* the kind of meat obtainable in a butcher's store, as opposed to meat obtained by hunting.
1953 *North Star* (Yellowknife) Oct. 3/2: Moreover, repeating rifle or no, the natives seldom waste meat nor, at present prices of "store meat," does the white hunter.

store pay *Hist.* See quotes. See also **store** (def. 1b).
1842 BONNYCASTLE *Canadas* II 180: A quintal of fish . . . is worth 12 *s.* 6 *d.* in hard cash, or 14 *s.* 6 *d.* store pay, the latter being the usual mode of payment. Store pay in Canada signifies what the storekeeper values his goods at in settling with the working classes, and of course varies with the demand and supply. **1898** CONANT *U.C.Sketches* 43: Wheat at that time [1812] could only be sold for one-half cash and one-half store-pay. **1905** CARTER *Dundas* 51: The store-keeper bought the settlers' produce but would give them only trade in return, or what was known as "store pay."

store-teeth *n. Slang* false teeth; dentures.
1890 *Grip* (Toronto) 21 June 4 7/2: And so on . . . through a long catalogue of the fair one's charms, including "ripe red lips," "teeth of pearl," (store-teeth, presumably). . . . **1958** *News of the North* 27 Mar. 3/3: [He] is just about ready to partake of solid food once again and is snapping his store-teeth in anticipation.

stoup *n.* See **stoop**.

stouter ['stautə] *n.* [< *stout* strong + -*er*] *Nfld* See 1819 quote.
1779 (1792) CARTWRIGHT *Journal* II 446: We found the head of the stage raised up about five inches, many of the posts, shores, and stouters gone, and the ice a solid bed under it. . . . **1819** ANSPACH *Hist.Nfld* 430: . . . the stage-head . . . is fortified with stouters, or very strong shores, to prevent the stage from receiving any damage from ships or boats. **1964** ENGLISH *Newfoundland* 34: Strouters [sic], posts at the end of a fishing stage.

stove cake See **galette**.
1941 *Beaver* Sep. 37/2: Stove cakes is another name for these hurry-up trail creations.

stove horse in a pack train, the horse laden with the packers' camp outfit, gear, etc.
1938 *Beaver* Sep. 46/1: At last when all were loaded, the "stove horse" was led in advance, followed by the

natural leader, the horse that had won this position and fought for it against all comers.

strad [stræd] *n.* [? a shortening of *straddle*] *Maritimes* See quote.
1955 WALLACE *Roving Fisherman* 373: Before anchoring I had had the cable parceled and served with canvas and bagging along the part stretching from the hawse-pipe to the water—the "strad" as fishermen call it.

straight-combine *v.* harvest with a combine while the grain is still standing in the field. Hence **straight-combining**, *n.*
1959 *Herald Mag.* 1 Aug. 6/5: On the basis of 35 acres of grain straight combined for every foot of cutter bar the harvesting will take some time. *Ibid.*: The great superiority of swathing over straight combining is that it can and should be done before the crop attains uniform maturity.

straight rail fence See 1932 quote. See also **rail fence** and picture.
1932 JAMIESON *Cattle in the Stall* 75: There was the rustle fence, with boom on top and centre; the straight rail fence, made with post planted in the ground, and stake bound alongside with tree wires to contain the rails—bottom, centre and top. **1953** *Cdn Geog.Jnl* Dec. 226/1: The straight rail fence is used a great deal today. Posts are erected at suitable intervals and the rails are simply nailed into place. These fences have become practicable only since the invention of the wire nail.

stranger *n. Nfld, Obs.* a species of duck.
1776 (1792) CARTWRIGHT *Journal* II 178: We brought in a beaver, a goose, a bottle-nosed diver, five ducks, four strangers, and three hundred and seventeen eggs.
1777 (1792) *Ibid.* 257: After breakfast I went in a skiff with two hands round the harbour, took up all the traps, and shot two strangers.

straw-and-pole barn *West* a barn constructed of poplar poles and roofed with straw.
1959 STOREY *Prairie Harvest* 28: Pending the arrival of the lumber for the house, Henry worked on the straw-and-pole barn he had planned.

strawberry festival or **frolic†** a social gathering, usually under church auspices, at which strawberries are served.
1879 *Morning Chronicle* (Halifax) 9 July 2/4: The members of the Sewing Society in connection with Granville St. Church, intend to hold a Strawberry Festival, in the vestry, Queen Street, on Thursday, July 10th. **1942** RADDALL *His Majesty's Yankees* 129: I took it and didn't know what to do with it, any more than I'd know that day of the strawberry frolic. **1954** BRUCE *Channel Shore* 28: Up-shore there were box-socials and strawberry festivals and small white box-like churches at Currie Head and Leeds.

strawberry tea a social gathering at which tea and strawberries are served, the purpose of the function being to raise money for charity work.
1957 *Camsell Arrow* Christmas 53/3: The women had sold 300 tickets for their strawberry tea to earn around $100. **1963** *Gulf Islander* (Galiano, B.C.) 4 July 5/1: The spacious grounds of The Glade were dotted with tea tables on Wednesday afternoon June 19th when the United Church Women held their Strawberry Tea....

straw-line *n. Lumbering* See quotes. See also **grass-line** (def. 1) and **tenas.**
1942 SWANSON *Western Logger* 55: straw line—small line to pull haulback. **1942** HAIG-BROWN *Timber* 254: STRAW LINE. The lightest size of steel cable commonly used in the woods. It is dragged out by riggers, passed through blocks and brought back to the drums of the donkey. Then the heavier cable is attached, the straw line wound on to the drum and the heavy cable thus drawn into place.

straw oil *Nfld* a medium grade of seal oil.
1966 *Cdn Geog.Jnl* Apr. 133/1: The resultant oil, classified according to colour and quality as "pale oil," "straw oil," and "dark oil," sells for an average price of about 50 cents per gallon.

straw-push *n. Lumbering, Slang* the assistant to the foreman of a logging crew, construction gang, etc. Cp. **push.**
1964 *Press* Feb. 12: The straw-push . . . instructed me not to come out after lunch and had me wait upon the superintendant.

stream *n. North, Obs.* an oblong field of drift-ice, *q.v.*
1850 (1851) SNOW *Voyage* 100: The streams became thicker, and occurred oftener.... **1850** GOODSIR *Baffin's Bay* 12: On Friday, the 20th of April, we passed through the first "streams" of ice we had seen. **1852** SUTHERLAND *Baffin's Bay* II 257: Suppose that late in the season . . . a piece of wood had been dropped by a ship in Lancaster Sound, at the commencement of an easterly gale, and that it had alighted on a bit of ice at the edge of a "stream," the gale would carry the ice westward into Barrow Straits, at the rate of three or four miles an hour, and before its termination the bit of wood might be at Cape Hotham or Cape Riley, still reposing upon the ice and waiting a fair wind to drift it up Wellington Channel.

stream-driver *n. Lumbering, Esp.N.B.* See **driver** (def. 1).
1904 ROBERTS *Watchers of Trails* 352: The man was Steve Williams, best axe-man and stream-driver in the camp; the boy, young Steve, his eldest son, who was serving as "cookee," or assistant to the camp cook. **1949** LAWSON *N.B.Story* 222: In those days a good stream-driver was a king of the woods.

stream-driving *n. Lumbering, Esp.N.B.* See **driving** (def. 1).
1845 BEAVAN *Life in Backwoods N.B.* 8: Larger pieces of wood or timber are floated singly down the stream nearest to the place whence they are cut. This operation is called stream-driving, and commences as soon as the rapid melting of the snow and ice has so swollen the small streams as to give them power to force and carry the huge pieces of timber.... **1896** ROBERTS *Camp-Fire* 203: The task the lumbermen are now engaged upon is termed "stream driving"; and laborious, perilous work it is. ...

Streamers *n.pl.* See quote.
1912 SANDILANDS *West.Cdn Dict.* 45/1: Streamers, the Aurora Borealis, Northern Lights.

streetcar† *n.* a conveyance used primarily for carrying passengers and equipped to run on rails set in the street.
1887 *Grip* (Toronto) 5 Feb. 6/2: Toronto law is plain and hard—no streetcars out on Sunday.... **1960** NELSON *Northern Lights* 304: "The Transcontinental! For

Winnipeg!" cried the nun, grasping her little cross. "And you say that as I might say I'm going to take the streetcar...."

street hockey See **road hockey.**
1964 *Globe and Mail* (Toronto) 15 Dec. 41/8: . . . he brought a fresh approach to street hockey when he began trying to teach his son Frank how to shoot a puck.

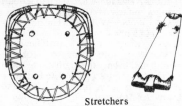
Stretchers

stretcher *n. Fur Trade* a device, such as a willow wand fashioned into a hoop, or a thin board of appropriate shape, used by trappers to stretch their pelts to dry. See also **fur stretcher** and **skin stretcher.**
[**1810** (1950) THOMPSON *Journals* 95: . . . he accordingly gave up 32 Seasoned Beaver . . . 1 seasoned but badly stretched Otter. . . .] **1921** HEMING *Drama of Forests* 231: After that, it is taken off the stretcher and rubbed together between the hands and pulled between two people. **1931** GREY OWL *Last Frontier* 230: [They were] whittling out muskrat stretchers with crooked knives. . . . **1948** ONRAET *Sixty Below* 103: Marten stretchers are about three feet long and four inches wide, the whole length tapering off from the shoulders to a point at the nose. **1965** *Globe and Mail* (Toronto) 17 Feb. 31/7: [Caption] Beaver pelts hang in stretchers (left) to dry.

stretcher board *Fur Trade* See **stretcher.**
1956 EVANS *Mountain Dog* 64: His father's condition must have been desperate for him to have burned his stretcher boards.

strike *n. Slang, Obs.* **on the strike,** attempting to pick up someone of the opposite sex without proper introduction.
1891 *Grip* (Toronto) 8 Aug. 86/2: These juveniles . . . are as a rule "on the strike,"—which is something I very strongly disapprove of.

striking party *Maritimes, Hist.* See quote.
1929 MacQUEEN *Skye Pioneers* 71: On the eve of that day [New Year's] "striking parties" composed of young folk of the district, armed with sticks . . . arrived at a house [and] surrounded it . . . to the accompaniment of music from the sticks beating the log walls. . . .

string *n. Lumbering, Obs.* See **string measure.**
1945 CALVIN *Saga* 39: In the 1870's a typical contract for waney pine might call for the timber to be not less that 15 feet long averaging 22 feet, and 20″ average "string."

string bog a series or chain of muskegs (def. 1), as opposed to a continuous expanse of bog.
1963 *Cdn Geog.Jnl* Mar. 77/1: Above Grand Falls [Labrador], however, the undulating surface of the interior plateau is largely covered by muskeg, string bogs, and interconnected lakes. . . .

stringer *n.* **1** a log or timber set across a stream to serve as a foot-bridge. See also **crossing-stringer.**
1896 GOURLAY *Hist.Ottawa* 105: With the current running so swiftly from such a deep volume of water, it

was no easy thing for women to pass on flatted stringers, nor even for men. **1923** WILLIAMS *Spinning Wheels* 54: When she came to the river the bridge was gone, swept away, and only the "stringers" spanned the black flood.
2 a chain along which a number of snap hooks are spaced, used for stringing caught fish, each being attached through a gill to one of the hooks.
1965 *Kingston Whig-Standard* (Ont.) 5 Feb. 11/2: It was one of these summer dog days when the stringer was bare.
3 *Lumbering* See quote. See also **dram.**
1945 CALVIN *Saga* 67: Space was left for "stringers," which were pieces of timber hauled lengthwise of the dram up upon the traverses and withed down to them; the "stringers" thus enclosed, and prevented the possible escape of, the un-withed cross tier in rough weather or in the rapids.

string measure *Lumbering, Hist.* a system for measuring waney pine to determine the average circumference for reckoning purposes.
1945 CALVIN *Saga* 37: This difficulty was solved by a method known as "string measure." *Ibid.* 52: There was bit timber to be had at first; the 1873 cut was over 21″ string measure.

string-team *n. B.C., Hist.* a pack-train, *q.v.,* of mules or horses, capable of making better time than oxen.
1912 POCOCK *Man in the Open* 91: . . . I tote the cargoes over there by sleigh. There my contract ends, because Tearful George takes on with his string team down to the railroad. **1930** MacINNES *Rockies* 177: String-teams . . . carried less freight, never more than fifteen tons.

Strip, the *n.* a richly cosmopolitan section of Spadina Avenue in Toronto, noted for its markets, flophouses, and polyglot atmosphere; the section of Spadina between Wellington and College Streets. Also *Spadina Strip.*
1957 *Maclean's* 6 July 33/1: The many-tongued enclave known as the Strip is cut off from the midtown section by a near-Gothic stone pile that straddles the Avenue just north of College Street. . . .

strip *n. Lumbering, Esp.Ont.* the cutting area of a logging operation. Cp. **side.**
1955 *Bush News* (Port Arthur, Ont.) Feb. 7/3: The tractor-drawn sloops and often the horses are used mainly to haul short distances from strip to transfer point with trucks carrying the pulpwood the balance of the distance.

strip boss *Lumbering* the man in charge of the cutting operation on a strip. Cp. **side-push.**
1957 *Beaver* Spring 41/2: While they still come up through the ranks, starting as cutters or strip bosses, and serving as assistant foremen, they get ahead by their mental ability rather than with their fists. **1957** *Bush News* (Port Arthur, Ont.) June 3/1: Other buildings in the camp include a garage, cookery and administration building which also serves as living quarters for the foreman, clerk, strip boss and the scaling crew.

strip cruise *Lumbering* a timber survey in which the cruiser counts or estimates the number of trees

suitable for logging on each side of a pre-set compass line.
1953 *Cdn Geog.Jnl* Feb. 59/1: By running strip cruises through the area, it is possible to determine the amount of timber that can be cut immediately for either pulp or sawlogs.

striped blanket *Obs.* See **point blanket**.
1800 (1933) MCLEOD *Diary* 132: I sent 4 men for the four red Deer that are in our Hunters lodges, to whom I sent some Amunition &. to the *Petit Corbau* a Strip'd Blanket.

striped maple† a small maple, *Acer pensylvanicum,* found in central and eastern Canada. See also **goosefoot maple, moose maple,** and **moosewood** (def. 1).
1822 (1928) CORMACK *Narr.Nfld* 14: . . . the striped maple [is] known as the moose-wood of Canada. . . .
1956 *Native Trees* 244: The striped maple, like the mountain maple with which it is frequently associated, is a tall shrub or small tree. . . .

striped marmot or **spermophile** a gopher, *q.v.,* *Spermophilus tridecemlineatus,* having stripes down its back.
1819 (1823) FRANKLIN *Journey* 45: Mr. Black killed a small striped marmot. [**1908** MAIR *Mackenzie Basin* 264: Richardson found this species [striped spermophile] quite common at Carleton House, Saskatchewan.]

striped squirrel *Obs.* See **chipmunk**.
1793 (1933) MACDONELL *Diary* 116: The . . . following animals are native of it [the Assiniboine River country] . . . Grizzly . . . large ground squirrels of two kinds . . . Kits, the common red wood squirrel, and the striped Swiss. . . . **1812** (1889) KEITH *Letters* 103: There are . . . no great number of bears, and those mostly black, with a few brown; few otters and striped squirrels.
*a*1820 (1838) HEAD *Forest Scenes* 242: I shot . . . a striped squirrel, a harmless little creature, somewhat less than the English squirrel.

strip farm See **ribbon farm**.
1909 CONNOR *Foreigner* 12: Those dour and doughty pioneers of peoples had planted on the Red River their homes upon their little "strip" farms. . . .

strip road *Lumbering* See **logging road**. See also **strip**.
1955 *Bush News* (Port Arthur, Ont.) Feb. 7/4: At the first it was tough hauling due to lack of snow for levelling the strip roads, but since the 15th, it has been described as excellent. . . .

strong cold in Indian parlance, the depth of winter; any very low temperature.
1953 CUSHMAN *Stay Away Joe* 218: [They] pulled their mackenaw jackets more tightly against . . . the strong cold, as the old men said. . . . **1956** KEMP *Northern Trader* 62: . . . Old Napao wasn't keen about fine-fur trapping until the Strong Cold of January was past.

strong medicine See **medicine**.
1942 CAMPBELL *Thorn-Apple Tree* 26: And the testing of the braves! That had been strong medicine.
1944 *Beaver* Sep. 15/2: These strange [medicine] men have nearly altogether died off, and I know of none of them now living who used to make what they called 'strong medicine" in the late seventies.

strong wood(s) [trans. of Cdn F *bois fort(s),* used by the voyageurs] forest; heavy woods; big trees. See also **strong woods country, thickwood,** and **thickwood country.** Cp. **stick²**.
[**1794** (1929) MCGILLIVRAY *Journal* 34: Soon after their departure 2 tribes of Assinoboines arrived . . . called Strong Wood & . . . Grand River Assiniboine.]
1800 (1897) COUES *New Light* I 83: We had a quarter of a mile of strong wood to pass through. . . .
1859 MCDONALD *Autobiog.Notes* 17: The new fort was upon the margin of a fine hummock of pine, upon a rising hill or bank, with the noble Sascatchewan in front, its banks covered with strong wood for perhaps a mile in breadth and twenty in length along the river.
1921 HEMING *Drama of Forests* 264: The Indians of the Strong Woods are very superstitious in relation to the otter. **1953** MOWERY *Mounted Police* 16: Calling themselves the "Skunk Bears," they ranged through the northern Strong Woods and the southern Barrens in winter, robbing lonely white men and *métis,* playing carcajou to trap lines, and occasionally resorting to murder itself.

strong wood buffalo *Obs.* See **wood buffalo**.
1810 (1897) COUES *New Light* II 639: We had scarcely left camp when we fell in with a herd of strong wood buffalo.

strong wood reindeer *Obs.* See **woodland caribou**.
1861 *Cdn Naturalist* Dec. 438: The Strong-wood Reindeer inhabit the thickly wooded parts of the District, particularly among and in the vicinity of the mountain ranges.

strong woods country See 1921 quote. See also **strong wood**.
1801 MACKENZIE *Voy.from Montreal* xvii: The strong woods and mountain countries afforded a refuge to those who fled from the contagion. . . . **1921** HEMING *Drama of Forests* 15: The several zones of the Canadian wilderness are locally known as the Coast Country—the shores of the Arctic Ocean and Hudson Bay; the Barren Grounds—the treeless country between Hudson Bay and the Mackenzie River; the Strong Woods Country—the whole of the enormous belt of heavy timber that spans Canada from east to west; the Border Lands—the tracts of small, scattered timber that lie between the prairies and the northern forests; the Prairie Country; the Mountains; and the Big Lakes. **1922** *Beaver* May 7/2: [Caption] "Huntsman's prize in the "strong woods" country of northern Ontario.

stroud(s)† [straud(z)] *n.* [< *Stroud,* Gloucestershire, the original place of manufacture] Also *Stroud(s).* **1** a heavy woollen cloth in several colors, much used in the North during three centuries for making blankets, leggings, capotes, etc. See also **Hudson's Bay strouds** and **strouding.** Cp. **duffle**.
1680 (1945) *H.B.C.Minutes* 54: . . . to pay George Small Clothier 65 *li.* 5s. for 9 peeces of Stroud water Reds.
1794 (1929) MCGILLIVRAY *Journal* 33: She also requested to be wrapt up in a fathom of fine Strouds that she might appear with decency before her ancestors in the land of Spirits. **1808** *Cdn Courant* (Montreal) 4 Jan. 3/3: Will be sold on Monday next, the 11th instant, at Alex. Henry's Auction Room—at One o'clock, 45 Pieces Blue Strouds, 100 Pieces of 2½ point Blankets. **1896** WHITNEY *On Snow-Shoes* 61: "Duffel" is a thick blanket stuff, which, together with "strouds," a similar though more closely spun material, the Hudson's Bay Company introduced and

christened. **1954** PATTERSON *Dangerous River* 21: Red Pant, the Indians called him, because he always wore great, heavy work pants of scarlet stroud.
1963 MCTAVISH *Behind the Palisades* 107: . . . we used plain white gartered leggings, reaching halfway to the thigh, made from a very strong material called Strouds.
2 (*usually plural*) See 1923 quote.
1749 *Short State of North America* 19: [If] Duffields, Strouds, Blankets . . . which would serve them for Coverings Cloaths . . . were carried to them. . . .
1923 WORK *Journal* 23n: Strouds were bolts of different coloured blanket cloth which was traded to the Indians. **1952** *Beaver* Sep. 4/1: . . . I found myself selecting at Battleford an assortment of trade goods: blankets, strouds, prints. . . .

stroud blanket a blanket of stroud (def. 1).
1763 (1901) HENRY (Elder) *Travels* 116: Before him, on a new stroud blanket, was placed a basin of water. . . .

strouding ['straudɪŋ] *n.* [< *stroud*] See **stroud** (def. 1).
1896 (1898) RUSSELL *Far North* 93: His leggins, of blue strouding, reached above the knee and had a broad stripe of beadwork along the outer seam, reaching from the ankle to the gay-colored garter.

stroud leggings *North* warm, heavy leggings or trousers made of stroud (def. 1).
[**1896** RUSSELL *Far North* 171: Men's leggins . . . are sometimes made of white strouds. . . .] **1934** GODSELL *Arctic Trader* 39: Donald Flett and a dozen other drivers, all clad in fringed and decorated buckskin capotes, blue stroud leggings and fur caps, were scurrying here and there. . . . **1952** *Beaver* Dec. 28/1: Stroud leggings of hip length were also frequently worn.

stroud trousers See **stroud leggings**.
1936 STRINGER *Wife-Traders* 14: On one arm of his chair he saw, for the first time, a pair of stroud trousers fringed with white fox and with stripes down the outer seams.

struck *adj. Nfld* See quote. See also **salt struck**.
1944 *Beaver* Sep. 23/1: Around the end of August, when fish is under salt long enough to be properly "struck" (hardened by salt), the drying commences.

stub *n.* See **rampike**.
1924 SHERMAN *Nature Stories* 65: I saw them [woodpeckers] entering dark holes in lofty dead trees, or branchless stubs, impossible for a small boy to climb.
1933 MERRICK *True North* 140: . . . every mile or two there is a broken-off stub. . . . **1965** *Cdn Geog.Jnl* Sep. 88: [Caption] Park Rangers . . . keep the portage trails open. Here they get rid of a "widow-maker," a dead stub hung up over the trail.

stub *v. Hist.* See 1831 quote. Hence **stubbing,** *n.* See also **stog**.
1831 (1953) RADCLIFF *Letters* 18: The chimney is then built with mud, if stones be scarce. The *stubbing* afterwards takes place, which means the filling up [of] the vacancies between the logs with slips of wood, mud and moss. **1961** *Ont.Hist.* Mar. 13: The spaces between the logs were chinked or "stubbed" with wooden wedges, stones, branches or just plain straw mixed with mud or clay.

stubble-jumper *n. Slang* a prairie farmer.
1961 *Sun* (Vancouver) 4 July 1/1: The prairie farmer, to those of us who don't know him well, is a stock comic character. Clod-hopper, we call him, and stubble-jumper. . . . **1966** *Kingston Whig-Standard* (Ont.)

28 Feb. 10/1: The new champion dog-musher of the Yukon is a stubble-jumper from Brandon, Manitoba.

stump *n.* **1** *Obs.* **in the stumps,** of towns, in a region recently cleared of trees.
1849 ALEXANDER *L'Acadie* I 142: Some idea may be formed of the newness of the "location" of London "in the stumps," when I say that two or three bears from the woods sauntered through the streets at night when we were there, and one of them on passing looked curiously at a sentry.
2 on the stump, of timber, not yet logged.
1956 RADDALL *Wings* 44: ". . . my uncle Geoffrey marrit a Hagget girl that owned five thousand acres o' prime white pine timber on the stump."

stump *v.* remove the stumps from, as in clearing land.
1820 (1823) JOHNSTONE *Travels in P.E.I.* 26: But, though none of it should produce any grass worth naming, it must remain in this state till it can be stumped or partly so. **1932** JAMIESON *Cattle in the Stall* 32: Many a day he toiled strongly, clearing his land from bush, stumping it, picking off the stones . . . making roads and raising what crops he could in the meantime.

Stump Act or **Law** *Hist.* a law requiring the removal of stumps from cleared land.
1800 *U.C.Gaz.* (York [Toronto]) 4 Jan. 3/3: I should at the same time think it, a singular happiness, if they could by any means be thrust into the "Stump Act." **1800** *Canada Constellation* (Niagara-on-the-Lake, U.C.) 4 Jan. 3/2: The stump law, although framed for the particular benefit of York, meets with such universal approbation that it is expected considerable exertion will be made to extend it through the province.

stumpage *n. Lumbering* **1 a.** a price paid for the right to cut standing timber. See also **timber tariff**.
1821 (1960) MCCULLOCH *Stepsure Letters* 21: But my cousin . . . had an excellent lot of it [standing timber]; and Jack and a few more of the youngsters agreed to pay him stumpage and make one job of the whole. **1922** *Dalhousie Rev.* II 91: The land is very expensive, and the stumpage, of course, is high.
b. a tax or royalty paid to the government on each tree taken out of a timber berth. See also **stumpage dues** and **timber dues**.
1854 KEEFER *Ottawa* 54: The first step necessary for a lumberman is to secure his limits, which is done by an application for a license to cut timber on Crown lands at a certain stumpage. **1963** MCKINNON *Forest Activities I* 11: All timber cut for commercial use in British Columbia must be "scaled" (measured for wood volume) immediately by an official or licensed scaler. From the "scale" is determined the amount of tax "stumpage" or "royalty" to be paid to the Government. **1966** *B.C.Forest Industry* 12/1: Then, standing trees sold at a price per tree and the practice was to count the stumps after cutting to determine the total sum owing to the government. Thus, the origin of the term "stumpage."
c. the right to cut standing timber. Cp. **timber rights**.
1954 BRUCE *Channel Shore* 63: ". . . Instead've foolin' around, why don't you get stumpage on a lot of places?

Put in a crew and go after pulpwood big? You could make a go of it. . . ."

2 See 1912 quote.

1912 SANDILANDS *West.Cdn Dict.* 45/1: Stumpage, standing trees, as viewed by the lumberman in his trade calculations; the amount of standing timber available for cutting. **1928** PERRY *Two Reds* 7: "I'll bet you an even thousand acres of my white-pine stumpage north of Lac Bleu that I can do it."

stumpage dues or **costs** See **stumpage** (def. 1b).
1896 ROBERTS *Camp-Fire* 96: Having no stumpage dues to pay, they could afford a little extra outlay for the difficult hauling [of stolen lumber]. **1963** *Weekend Mag.* 7 Dec. 9/1: It is estimated that . . . the farmer has paid his stumpage costs to the government. . . .

stumper *n. Hand-logging* See quotes.
1908 GRAINGER *Woodsmen* 60: Many trees they noticed . . . would drop right into water from the stumps when felled; a thought that made their hearts feel light. For "stumpers" are the most profitable trees that hand-loggers can hope to get; they need so little time and work. **1940** PINKERTON *Three's a Crew* 102: Stumper [is] a tree—having been felled by a handlogger—which does not stop from stump to sea.

stump farm *Slang* See **stump ranch.**
1936 MACKENZIE *Living Rough* 213: . . . I guess he had been trying to make a living so long on a stump farm that he was bitter and disillusioned.

stump farmer *Slang* See **stump rancher.**
1938 CASH *I Like B.C.* 68: A stump farmer, who had been making a pretty good thing of selling fresh eggs and milk to the Company, packed up and sent out hens, pigs and horse. **1964** *Dly Colonist* (Victoria) 4 Sep. 4/5: The first thing a . . . stump farmer did was to buy a cow. She could usually find enough to eat among the stumps until the farmer could clear a few acres for pasture. . . .

stump fence See 1932 quote.
1932 JAMIESON *Cattle in the Stall* 73: Which fence came first? One might suppose the stump fence, that fantastic but effective barrier of pine roots turned on edge and laid in a line with their earthy-filled faces showing all one way. It gave the impression of a stockade. . . . **1939** CHAMPION *On the Island* 181: "Ugly as a stump fence" is a well-known phrase, fraught with meaning for any Canadian. **1963** GUILLET *Pioneer Farmer* I 326: Stump fences, mute evidences of many an arduous stumping bee, still dot the countryside.

stumping *n.* **1** *Obs.* See quote.
1845 BEAVAN *Life in Backwoods N.B.* 140: In the days of the early settling of the country, marriages were attended with a ceremony called stumping. This was a local way of publishing the banns, the names of the parties and the announcement of the event to take place being written on a piece of paper, and inserted on the numerous stumps bordering the corduroy road. . . .

2 the job of removing stumps when clearing land.
1896 GOURLAY *Hist.Ottawa* 228: The best thing they can do will be to . . . encourage the draining, stumping, removing stones and levelling of their fields. **1933** GUILLET *Early Life in U.C.* 283: The stump fences which are still a characteristic feature of the rural landscape recall many an old-time stumping bee.

stumping (or **stump) machine** a device for pulling stumps in clearing land for farms or roads.
1825 *U.C.Gaz.* (York [Toronto]) 20 Oct. 6/1: As there are many persons wishing to see my Stump Machine in operation, I propose to work with it on Thursday the tenth day of Nov. next, on my farm in Trafalgar, near the lake shore. **1905** SCHERCK *Pen Pictures* 50: The best device for ridding the land of pine stumps was the stumping machine. **1921** (1923) HEMON *Chapdelaine* [trans.] 70: . . . the other three men handled the stumping-machine with the aid of Charles Eugene. The pyramidal scaffolding was put in place above a large stump and lowered, the chains which were then attached to the root passed over a pulley, and the horse at the other end started away quickly, flinging himself against the traces and showering earth with his hoofs. **1963** GUILLET *Pioneer Farmer* I 325: In the eighteen-forties stumping machines came into use in older settled districts along the front, their owners sometimes contracting to remove stumps, large and small, for 50 cents each.

stumping powder low-percentage dynamite used to uproot stumps.
1930 *B.C.Lumberman* May 39: [Advert.] Polar Stumping Powder plays a big part in British Columbia's great logging camps. **1942** CASH *Million Miles* 95: He's given me an idea of how you estimate the number of sticks of stumping powder you need to blow up a certain-sized stump. **1961** MITCHELL *Jake and the Kid* 59: "She—she shore was mad—she . . . went up like stumpin' powder."

stump land land from which the timber has been cut.
1928 PERRY *Two Reds* 9: The seven big tracts Harris bought in the Travoy were for Gwen; likewise the stump land which went with the stumpage. He had already begun to reforest them with white pine.

Stump Law See **Stump Act.**

stump machine See **stumping machine.**

stump polisher *B.C., Slang* See **stump rancher.**
1936 MACKENZIE *Living Rough* 202: Some of them stump-polishers and prairie hoosiers sure worked, but some of them weren't long in B.C. before they got educated.

stump ranch *B.C., Slang* an undeveloped bush ranch, *q.v.,* having the trees logged off and, often, having grass sown between the stumps for grazing cattle. See also **stump farm.**
1919 *Camp Worker* 3 Oct. 3/3: They imagine we are going to divide up their old stump ranches they have lived on for many years, which are all mortgaged to some bank or trust company. **1958** WATTERS *B.C.Cent. Anthol.* 141: The lads . . . were raised on . . . threadbare stump ranches. **1961** *Sun* (Vancouver) 7 Feb. 4/1: Somewhere he has a stump ranch, a little mining claim, a few range cows or a bit of timber he can hand-log.

stump rancher *B.C., Slang* the owner of a stump ranch, *q.v.* See also **stump farmer** and **stump polisher.**
1963 SYMONS *Many Trails* 7: I [was] a stump rancher in the Peace River country. . . . **1964** *Fisherman* Oct. 8/5: [How] many stump ranchers with a hundred fathoms of cork line and a pitch fork dragged a hundred or so spawning salmon home on the rope [?]

stump-ranching *n. B.C., Slang* operating a stump ranch, *q.v.*

flotsam of the ocean adopted such respectable
occupations as fishing and stump-ranching.

sturgeon (boat) *n. Northwest, Hist.* See
sturgeon-head.
1908 MAIR *Mackenzie Basin* 32: . . . the population
being mainly mechanics . . . constructed scows, small
barges, called "sturgeons," and the old "York," or
inland boat, carrying four or five tons. **1943** *Beaver*
March 29/1: York boats . . . were supplemented by
shovel-nosed scows called "sturgeon boats," which
could carry still greater loads.

sturgeon-head (boat) *n.* [so called because the
shape of the bow and stern resembled the shovel-
snout of a sturgeon] *Northwest, Hist.* a freight
boat about 55 feet long and 11 wide, with a draught
of little more than two feet, capable of carrying
10-12 tons and propelled by poles and/or oars, or,
in later days, an outboard motor. See also **sturgeon,
sturgeon-head scow,** and **sturgeon scow.** Cp. **rapids
boat.**
1889 (1892) PIKE *Barren Grounds* 6: These inland boats,
as they are termed, are extraordinary specimens of
marine architecture, classified according to shape as
York boats, sturgeon-heads, and scows. . . . **1892** (1948)
Beaver June 45/2: The same sturgeon-head boats of the
downward trip were in readiness, loaded with bales of
furs. **1928** FREEMAN *Nearing North* 213: A large
sturgeon-head boat powered with an outboard motor
put out to meet the steamer as we came abreast of the
fishing camp. **1948** *Beaver* Mar. 20/2: Here the rapids
boats—sturgeon-head boats they were called,
"something between a scow and a York boat" with
blunt, rounded bows. . . . **1964** INNIS *Fur Trade* 364n:
Goods were sent to Athabasca Landing, taken up the
river by steamboat and then hauled in a sturgeon-head
to Lesser Slave Lake post and carried by trail to Peace
River.

sturgeon-head scow *Northwest, Hist.* See
sturgeon-head.
1921 HEMING *Drama of Forests* 308: In summer there
were the canoe, York boat, sturgeon-head scow, and
Red River cart brigades.

A sturgeon-nosed canoe

sturgeon-nosed canoe *B.C.* a type of bark
canoe formerly associated with the Kootenay
Indians. See also **canoe** (def. 1).
[**1808** (1960) FRASER *Letters and Journals* 123: The men
described it ["a small canoe, narrow at both ends"],
un canot puit au bec d'Eturgeons [which] could carry no
more than two at a time.] **1955** JENNESS *Indians of Can.*
360: Some of them [Chilcotin] pointed the ends of their
bark canoes to correspond with the "sturgeon-nosed"
canoes of the Interior Salish and Kootenay. . . .

sturgeon (-nosed) scow *Northwest, Hist.* See
sturgeon-head.
1921 HEMING *Drama of Forests* 52: When tracking their
six-fathom canoes, or "York boats," or "sturgeon
scows," the voyageurs of the north brigades use very
long lines, one end of which is attached to the bow of
the craft while to the other end is secured a leather

harness of breast straps called *otapanapi* into which
each hauler adjusts himself. **1948** *Beaver* Mar. 21/1:
[Caption] Screw steamers and sturgeon-nosed scows at
Fort Smith.

sub-farmer *n.* [cf. **fermier**] *Fur Trade, Hist.* a
lessee of lands in the King's Domain, *q.v.*
1947 *Cdn Hist.Rev.* Dec. 405: Riverin and Guillemin,
who were Sub-Farmers from 1710 to 1719, were
particularly vicious.

subscription assembly *Obs.* an evening of
dancing and other social activities organized by
subscription.
*a*1820 (1838) HEAD *Forest Scenes* 60: . . . on returning
to the inn, I found a card lying on my table from the
managers of a subscription assembly, which was to be
held the same evening in the town.

subtrader *n. Fur Trade, Hist.* See quote.
1961 JONES *Trappers* 67/2: Any voyageur became the
accepted term for the subtrader who worked for the
"bourgeois," the man with enough capital to pay for a
trading license and to invest in a quantity of items for
barter.

Suckemo *n. Obs.* See **Eskimo** (def. 1). See also
'Skimo. Cp. **chimo.**
1852 RICHARDSON *Arctic Exped.* 202: The sailors
of the Hudson's Bay Company's ships, and the
Orkney men in the employment of the Company,
still call them [Eskimos] *Suckemos* or *Seymos.*
1869 HARTWIG *Polar World* 290: The seamen of the
Hudson's Bay ships, who trade annually with the
natives of Northern Labrador and the Savage Islands,
have long called them "Seymos" or "Suckemos,"
names evidently derived from the cries of "Seymo," or
"Teymo," with which they greet the arrival of the ships;
they speak of themselves simply as "Innuit," or men.

sucker *n.* **1** one of a number of fresh-water fish of
the family *Catostomidae,* which are bottom feeders
having mouths so shaped as to give the appearance
of being engaged in sucking.
1748 ELLIS *Hudson's Bay* 186: At the Mouths of the
Rivers . . . are Plenty of fine Salmon, Trout, and
another which is a tolerable good Fish resembling a
Carp, called a Sucker. **1849** (1956) COLVILLE *Letters* 2:
At Dunvegan . . . the people had lived for some
time . . . upon a species of fish called "suckers," which
when dried . . . in the sun contain very little more
nourishment than a pine shingle. . . . **1925** *Beaver* Mar.
109: Despise not the suckers, ye who have not known
What gnawing hunger is. . . . **1960** *Fisheries Fact Sheets*
47 1: The common white sucker . . . is one of about 16
species of the sucker family found in Canada.

2† *Slang* **a.** a gullible person; a fool.
1838 *Patriot* (Toronto) 29 May 1/2: It's true that pigs
has their troubles like humans—constables catches 'em,
dogs bites 'em, and pigs is sometimes as done-over
suckers as men. **1896** *Kootenaian* (Kaslo, B.C.)
23 May 4/1: In camps like Rossland, where the fever is
on, and where the "sucker," with well lined purse, is
standing on every corner inviting the wildcat's claws,
the temptation is indeed great, even to the "reputable
stock broker." **1961** *Press* Feb. 14: Think it over
carefully and have yourself scratched off the list of
perennial suckers!

b. play (one) for a sucker, deceive by easy means; take advantage of (one's) gullibility.

1890 *Grip* (Toronto) 10 May 298/1: Mr. Boodlefaker adds, "You bet I ain't going to be played for a sucker." **1958** *Weekend Mag.* 29 Nov. 2/3: A wife complains that her husband is "so gullible that everyone plays him for a sucker"....

suckering *n.* fishing for suckers in rivers during the spring run.

1947 WELLS *Owl Pen* 111: The first Canadians went suckering as gleefully as they went sugaring.

sucker run the spring migration of large numbers of suckers ascending fresh-water rivers to spawn. See also **run,** *n.* (def. 6b).

1924 (1933) SLATER *Yellow Briar* 119: In the spring spawning season, he had bought him a wagon-box full of fish in the sucker run.... **1960** *Fisheries Fact Sheets* 47 1: The end of winter, with melting ice and snow and increased stream flow, is the signal for the sucker run.

suckeye *n.* See **sockeye.**

sucking-carp *n.* *Obs.* See **sucker** (def. 1).

1852 RICHARDSON *Arctic Exped.* 101: During the whole summer, in the eddies between the islands in this part of the lake, multitudes of fish may be taken with hooks and by nets, such as trout, white-fish, pike, sucking-carp, and inconnu.

sucrerie *n.* *Cdn French* See **sugary.**

sugar *n.* See **maple sugar.**

1780 *Quebec Gaz.* 27 Jan. 3/1: There is on it an excellent Maple Sucrerie, capable of producing annually from 300 to 600 w. of Sugar. **1786** *Account N.S.* 22: The sugar, when cold, is of a reddish brown colour, somewhat transparent, and very pleasant to the taste. **1832** MCGREGOR *Brit.Amer.* II 592: *Sugarie* is a plot of forest lands in which maple-trees abound, and where sugar is made from the sap.

sugar *v.* See **sugar off.**

1863 WALSHE *Cedar Creek* 235: "Uncle Zack'll be here first thing in the mornin' to sugar the syrup, and he says yo're to have a powerful lot o' logs ready chopped for the fires...."

sugar boiler *Maple Industry* **1** See **sugar-kettle.**

1853 STRICKLAND *Canada West* II 299: The common way in use by the settlers is, to suspend their sugar-boilers over the fire from a thick pole, by means of iron chains....

2 in sugaring-off, the person in charge of the sugar-kettle, *q.v.*

1853 STRICKLAND *Canada West* II 303: Great attention must now be paid by the sugar boiler.

sugar-boiling camp *Obs.* See **sugar-camp.**

1853 STRICKLAND *Canada West* II 34: ... I found the remains of a very large [Indian] sugar-boiling camp upwards of thirty feet in length by sixteen wide....

sugar bush a grove of sugar maples. See also **bush** (def. 4), **maple bush, maple grove, sap-bush, sugar grove, sugar orchard,** and **sugary** (def. 1).

1804 (1933) CONNOR *Diary* 274: Henries Squaw & family Came from the Sugar Bush. They say the Maples give no more water. **1852** (1923) MOODIE *Roughing It* 265: The whole block of land was almost entirely

covered with maple trees, and had originally been an Indian sugar-bush. **1901** CONNOR *Man from Glengarry* 83: Taking each a bundle of spiles and an ax, the boys set out for the part of the sugar bush as yet untapped, and began their work. **1966** *Kingston Whig-Standard* (Ont.) 18 Mar. 6/1: Every year ... a reporter must ... trudge down a muddy lane to somebody's sugar bush and do a story on the annual sap run.

sugar-bush maple See **sugar maple** (def. 1).

1863 WALSHE *Cedar Creek* 381: ... groups of "sugar-bush" maples stood and....

sugar-bush party See **sugaring-off party.**

1903 RICHARDSON *Colin* 206: ... many invitations came to them and their sisters to participate in dances, sugar-bush parties, and other pastimes.

sugar cabin See **sugaring-hut.**

1945 MACLENNAN *Two Solitudes* 155: "... Do you think he's in the sugar cabin?" **1958** *Encyc.Can.* VI 377/2: ... maple products are now produced in sugar cabins, where evaporators over furnaces permit the rapid conversion of sap into sugar.

sugar-camp *n.* *Maple Industry* the place in a sugar bush where sugaring-off (def. 1) takes place, including the building and equipment. See also **camp** (def. 4), **maple camp,** and **sugary** (def. 2). Cp. **sugaring-hut.**

1845 BEAVAN *Life in Backwoods N.B.* 13: A visit to a sugar-camp is an interesting sight to a stranger.... **1905** SCHERCK *Pen Pictures* 191: In the modern "sugar camp" things are much more convenient than formerly. **1963** MACLEOD & MORTON *Cuthbert Grant* 107: It was not easy to get around the country to the sugar camps....

sugarer *n.* See **sugar-maker.**

1923 WILLIAMS *Spinning Wheels* 84: ... the sugarers linger on—till the sun drops behind the distant peaks....

sugar grove See **sugar bush.**

1896 GOURLAY *Hist.Ottawa* 166: ... the aborigines began to see their sugar groves would disappear....

sugar-house *n.* See **sugaring-hut.**

1923 WILLIAMS *Spinning Wheels* 77: And in the gold and ruddy glow ... was a little unpainted sugar-house, sitting sedately among the gray-liveried maples. **1964** *Family Herald* 12 Mar. 16/4: Plastic pipe lines bring them within range of the sugar house.

sugar-hut *n.* See **sugaring-hut.**

1805 (1933) CONNOR *Diary* 272: ... this forenoon [two] Squaws arrived from the Sugar Huts intoxicated.... **1836** *Vindicator* (Montreal) 6 May 2/3: Two young persons of the name of Scott, were nearly killed in their sugar hut (*Cabane*) by the fall of a Maple. **1863** (1873) LEMOINE *Maple Leaves* 247: And if, perchance, camped for the night out on the mountain brow in a deserted sugar-hut, you hear the terrible hooting of the great horned owl, fear nothing; it is not the evil one.

sugarie *n.* See **sugary.**

sugaring *n.* See **sugar-making.**

1826 (1916) SELLAR *Narrative* 123: Gordon is preparing for sugaring, making spouts and buckets. **1947** WELLS *Owl Pen* 111: The first Canadians went suckering as gleefully as they went sugaring.

sugaring-hut *n.* *Maple Industry* a building where sugaring-off (def. 1) takes place. See also **boiling-down shack, boiling place** (def. 1), **cabane** (def. 1),

sap-house, sap-shed, sugar cabin, sugar-house, and sugar-hut. Cp. sugar-camp.
1963 MORTON *Kingdom of Canada* 248: In Lower Canada ... scores [of rebels] hid out in the sugaring huts and loggers' shanties in the bush.

sugaring-off *n. Maple Industry* **1** the process of boiling maple sap to make syrup and sugar through evaporation and crystallization. See also **maple-sugar making, sap-boiling, sugar-making,** and **sugar off.**
1836 (1846) TRAILL *Backwoods* 237 [DA]: The best rule I can give as to the sugaring-off ... is to let the liquid continue at a fast boil. **1885** HAIGHT *Country Life* 43: Each day's run was finished, if possible, the same night, when the sugaring-off took place. **1954** BEATTIE *Along the Road* 2: The sweet smell of sugaring-off was carried on the west wind. **1966** DUNCAN *Black Creek* 26: The sap was boiled in iron kettles ... until it was time for "sugaring off."

2 See **sugaring-off party.**
1901 CONNOR *Man from Glengarry* 102: She was glad, too, that her aunt had fixed the sugaring-off for a time when she could be present. **1903** CARR-HARRIS *White Chief* 121: Whereupon Mrs. Bancroft ... resolved, when the spring days should come, to have a "sugaring-off".... **1905** CARTER *Dundas* 51: Happy were the experiences of "sugaring-off," when the youth from the neighborhood, the boys and the girls, assembled at the sugar-camp to have a good time.

sugaring-off party a party held in the sugar bush at the time of sugaring-off (def. 1). See also **sugar-bush party, sugaring-off** (def. 2), **sugaring party, sugar-party,** and **taffy-pull** (def. 2).
1959 *Maclean's* 4 July 40/1: Barn-raisings, corn-huskings, quilting bees and threshings were community occasions and so were the sugaring-off parties.... **1962** *Ibid.* 6 Oct. 71/1: The Beauce is probably the best maple syrup district in Canada and undoubtedly has the best sugaring-off parties.

sugaring party See **sugaring-off party.**
1955 *Star* 15 Apr. 3/1: [Advert.] Camp available for sugaring parties.

sugaring season or **time** See quotes. See also **maple season, sugar-making season,** and **sugar-time.**
1953 *Cdn Geog.Jnl* May 180/2: Such troughs of basswood, pine, cherry or butternut, some of them holding three to four gallons, were standard equipment for catching the sap of the maple tree during the hectic spring sugaring season. **1956** LEECHMAN *Native Tribes* 41: Among the Ojibwas, the annual sugaring time, when the maple sap was running in the spring, and the wild rice harvest in the autumn, were two occasions for large gatherings of the people.

sugar-kettle *n. Maple Industry* a large cauldron used to contain the maple sap that is boiled in sugaring-off. See also **sap-boiler, sap tank,** and **sugar boiler** (def. 1).
1852 (1923) MOODIE *Roughing It* 427: The very first day a terrible accident happened to us; a large log fell upon the sugar-kettle—the borrowed sugar-kettle—and cracked it, spilling all the sap, and rendering the vessel, which had cost four dollars, useless. **1927** DICKIE *How Canada Grew Up* 166: Here he [Daniel Massey, Bond Head, UC, 1846] made ploughs, scufflers, sugar kettles and repairs for threshers.

sugar lodge *Obs.* a wigwam or other structure in an Indian sugar-camp.
1804 (1933) CONNOR *Diary* 272: Bellaire came from the Sugar Lodges. reports that the Maple Trees give no Juice.

sugar-maker *n. Maple Industry* one who engages in making maple sugar. See also **sugarer.**
1804 (1933) CONNOR *Diary* 272: [I] sent Déseve with a Bag of Oats to my Sugar Makers. **1845** BEAVAN *Life in Backwoods N.B.* 14: The sugar-maker's bark-covered hut contains his bedding and provisions.... **1899** MACKAY *Pioneer Life* 171: In early spring there was the sugar making. Not infrequently would the sugar-makers remain in the woods most of the night boiling down the sap.

sugar-making *n.* See **sugaring-off** (def.1). See also **sugaring.**
1767 (1901) HENRY (Elder) *Travels* 211: Sugar-making continued till the twelfth of May. **1853** STRICKLAND *Canada West* I 166: The chopping now begins, and may be followed without any interruption until the season for sugar-making commences. **1923** WILLIAMS *Spinning Wheels* 78: There is a quaint old Indian legend, according to which the Redman is held responsible for the manifold labors attendant upon the sugar-making industry. **1963** GUILLET *Pioneer Farmer* II 5: Indian sugar-making was an ancient and very primitive process, and the resulting sugar poor and dirty.

sugar-making season See **sugaring season.**
1852 (1881) TRAILL *Cdn Crusoes* 256: And many pleasant days they passed during the sugar-making season.

sugar maple 1 a maple tree, *Acer saccharum,* found in Canada from Lake Superior eastward and commercially valuable for its hard wood and for its sap, which is used in making maple sugar and syrup; also, its wood. See also **curly maple, rock maple, sugar-bush maple,** and **sugar tree.**
1796 (1911) SIMCOE *Diary* 298: I walked to Major Smiths lot, on which I gathered keys of the sugar maple and partridge berries. **1830** MOORSOM *Letters N.S.* 267: These trees are of the description called rock or sugar-maple, and in the back-settlements have great value in furnishing a luxury which the young settlers would otherwise be unable to procure. **1902** ROBERTS *Kindred of Wild* 220: ... the sap was beginning to flow from the sugar maples.... **1956** *Native Trees* 252/2: The sugar maple is one of the most valuable commercial hardwoods in Canada, and is especially desirable where strength and resistance to wear are necessary.

2 *West, Hist.* the Manitoba maple, *q.v.,* used for sugar-making by the Indians and fur-traders.
1820 (1823) FRANKLIN *Journey* 87: The sugar maple, elm, ash, and the arbor vitae, termed by the Canadian voyagers cedar, grows on various parts of the Saskatchewan. **1887** *Trans.Roy.Soc.Can.* V 3 39: The *Negundo* is the "sugar maple" of our Northwest, and sugar is there frequently made from its sap by Indians and others. **1933** GATES *Five Traders* 165n: Sugar maples were rare as far north as the Swan River, but Monseigneur Taché speaks of a variety of maple peculiar to the country from the sap of which sugar similar to that of sugar maple could be made.

sugar-maple grove *Obs*. See **sugar bush**.
1802 *Niagara Herald* (Niagara-on-the-Lake, U.C.)
13 Feb. 4/1: There is an excellent sugar-maple grove
on the farm.

sugar-maple rum *Obs*. an alcoholic liquor made
from maple sugar or syrup.
1829 MACTAGGART *Three Years* I 180: Sugar-maple rum
may be made of excellent quality....

sugar off *Maple Industry* convert maple sap to
syrup by evaporation or to sugar by evaporation
and crystallization. See also **sugar**, *v*., and **sugaring-
off** (def. 1).
☞ *Maple sap is boiled to make syrup; to make sugar,
further boiling is required before the syrup is ready to
crystallize on cooling. Although* **sugar off** *and*
sugaring-off *may have originally referred only to the
second stage of this process (see 1852 quote), they have
been commonly used with reference to the whole
activity of boiling down maple sap.*
1826 (1916) SELLAR *Narrative* 124: Under his teaching
Ailie quickly learned to sugar off, and did it over the
kitchen fire in the biggest pot. **1836** ROLPH *Brief
Account* 126: The kettles should also, while warm,
receive a thin coat of whitewash, and when dry, the sap,
put in and kept boiling till it is "sugared off." **1852**
(1923) MOODIE *Roughing It* 427: While Jenny was
engaged in boiling and gathering the sap in the bush, I
sugared off the syrup in the house, an operation watched
by the children with intense interest. **1905** SCHERCK
Pen Pictures 189: Sitting on logs, out in the woods
beside the boiling kettles, the watchers had often a
weary wait into the night for the time to "sugar off."
1957 *Kingston Whig-Standard* (Ont.) 2 Mar. 7/5: Many
thousands of maple trees will be tapped, filling sap pails
which, when collected by sleigh, are taken to the
evaporating pans and sugared off, producing the golden
brown maple syrup, unrivalled for its taste and aroma,
and blocks of maple sugar. **1965** STEVENS *Incompleat
Canadian* 48: He caught gaiety everywhere—coasting
parties on the frozen rivers, canoemen shooting the
rapids, families sugaring-off in the woodlot....

sugar orchard See **sugar bush**.
1923 WILLIAMS *Spinning Wheels* 81: In Canada the
sugar bushes or orchards, as they are variously called,
occupy chiefly the south-eastern section of the
Province of Quebec.

sugar-party *n*. See **sugaring-off party**.
1903 CARR-HARRIS *White Chief* 135: The other was her
brother's most intimate friend, who had assisted in
releasing her from her perilous position the night of the
sugar party. **1967** *Kingston Whig-Standard* (Ont.)
29 Mar. 7/1: Thursday ... will bring Loughboro's
Centennial old time sugar party at Perth Road.

sugar pemmican *Hist*. See **sweet pemmican**.
1951 O'MEARA *Grand Portage* 138: Sugar pemmican.
Pemmican with maple sugar added.

sugar plantation *Obs*. See **sugar bush**.
1896 GOURLAY *Hist.Ottawa* 166: They expressed
astonishment that their great father King George ...
would ... permit anyone to cut down their sugar
plantations and chase away their game.

sugar sand† See quote.
1951 *Canadian Woods* 225/1: As the liquid becomes
syrupy it turns an amber colour, and the mineral
matter is deposited on the bottom or sides of the pan
as "sugar sand." This precipitate is composed largely
of calcium malate or malate of lime.

sugar shanty *Obs*. See **sugaring-hut**.
1853 STRICKLAND *Canada West* II 311: I have even
known my sugar-shanty made the rendezvous of a
picnic party, to my small discomfiture.

sugar snow *Obs*. a fall of snow accompanied by a
slight fall in temperature which delays the leafing
of the maple trees, thus producing a longer run
of sap.
1826 (1916) SELLAR *Narrative* 124: Gordon awakened us
by shouting "A sugar snow." There had been a light
shower of it during the night, and the air was soft.
Holes were rebored and there was a fine run of sap.

sugar-time *n*. See **sugaring season**.
1826 (1916) SELLAR *Narrative* 124: The fine weather
had made him tired of the town [Toronto] and recalled
the sugar-time of his youth.

sugar tree† *Obs*. See **sugar maple** (def. 1).
1786 *Account N.S.* 21: ... amongst them none is more
useful to the inhabitants, than a species of maple,
distinguished by the name of the sugar tree....
1832 (1953) RADCLIFF *Letters* 137: ... but where's the
use of my telling you anything about it [preparing
maple sugar], as you have no sugar trees at home.

sugar weather spring weather, characterized by
cold nights and warm days, that starts the sap
running in maple trees and ushers in the sugaring
season, *q.v*. See also **sap weather**.
1826 (1916) SELLAR *Narrative* 124: Have had no sugar-
weather this week; frosty with strong winds, and some
snow. **1851** JOHNSTON *Notes* I 303: In Upper Canada,
from its proximity to the lakes probably, the sugar
weather is more variable, and the crop less certain than
in Lower Canada. **1903** RICHARDSON *Colin* 214: ... the
inhabitants, taking advantage of the ideal sugar weather
which had arrived, all began to "tap." **1942** CAMPBELL
Thorn-Apple Tree 97: When the March sun began to
honeycomb the snow, and the sun was warm on the
south side of the house, then came sugar-weather.

sugar woods *Obs*. See **sugar bush**.
1799 (1936) RUSSELL *Correspondence* III 219: They
proposed to meet ... with all the Chiefs that could
then be collected, the greatest part being out on their
hunting grounds and Sugar Woods.

sugary *n*. [trans. of Cdn F *sucrerie*] *Hist*. **1** See
sugar bush.
[**1780** *Quebec Gaz*. 27 Jan. 3/1: There is on it an
excellent Maple Sucrerie....] **1832** MCGREGOR *Brit.Amer*.
I 88: The maple ground occupied by a party is termed a
"sugarie".... **1898** EDGAR *Canada and Capital* 43: They
feared the destruction of the forests and game, of
sugaries and beaver huts and all their means of
subsistence. **1903** CARR-HARRIS *White Chief* 10: ... we
shall endeavour to protect your beaver and fishing-
grounds; but as for the sugaries, we must make use of
them, because the land has already been given us....

2 See **sugar-camp**.
1836 *Vindicator* (Montreal) 6 May 2/3: On Monday
week, a squall blew down a great many trees, and as
numbers of persons were at the time employed in the
Sugaries, several accidents followed.

suicide squad *Cdn Football* the backs who are required to catch and run back punts.
1958 *Edmonton Jnl* 31 July 6/5: The Vancouver native . . . had been a regular member of the suicide squad (punt returns) all three years.

suitcase farmer *West, Slang* See quote.
1956 *Saturday Night* 13 Oct. 15/1: Further, the wheat-marketing problem means the end of the "suitcase farmer," who has been accustomed to spend only a few weeks on his land each spring and summer for seeding and harvesting.

sulky (plough)† *n. Hist.* See 1959 quote.
1888 *Dominion Illust.* 98/3: There the prairie farmer sits on a comfortable spring seat, on his "sulky" plough, and, possibly in white shirt sleeves, holds the reins and drives. **1959** STOREY *Prairie Harvest* 67: He explained that a sulky was a one-furrow, three-wheel plow on which the plowman rode.

sulky sleigh *Nfld, Obs.* a horse-drawn sleigh which takes two persons in seats arranged tandem fashion. Cp. **tandem sleigh**.
1835 (1836) WIX *Journal* 14: Being driven in a sulky sleigh as far as the new road to Topsail Beach, upon the commencement of which the Legislature have lately expended a small sum.

summer beaver *Fur Trade, Hist.* unprime fur from beavers caught out of season. See also **dry summer beaver** and **fat summer beaver**.
1743 (1949) ISHAM *Observations* 51: Your coate is bad & half summer Beaver. **1785** (1954) *Moose Ft Jnls* 273: James Robinson is here now and informs me that [he] . . . traded 13 summer Beaver, and 24 musquashes with him. **1790** (1934) HEARNE & TURNOR *Journals* 323: They brought a few Summer Beaver, some dry, and a little fresh Moose flesh. . . .

summerberry *n. Hist.* See **saskatoon berry** (def. 1).
1793 (1933) MACDONELL *Diary* 116: The wild plumb, and Grape, the pair, choak and sand cherries, Summer berry and the Raspberry are also natives of this [Assiniboine] country. **1940** NIVEN *Mine Inheritance* 21: On the last day of August—the year of 1812—we drew in to the bosky bank of Red River, otherwise known as Summerberry River. . . . **1952** (1954) JENNINGS *Strange Brigade* 200: . . . they picked quantities of summerberries and wild rice and made jelly of the first and sacked the latter in rawhide bags.

summer cottage a summer residence, usually at a resort or some place close to water.
1840 *Montreal Transcript* 22 Dec. 402/2: Some owners of lots also propose putting up summer cottages. **1958** *Edmonton Jnl* 28 June 25/1: Schools and universities are closing their doors for the next few months and many Canadian households will begin the annual exodus to summer cottage or camp.

summer cottager one who lives in a summer cottage.
1962 *Chronicle-Herald* (Halifax) 10 Aug. 12/4: Two half days a week they go to the beach where they teach summer cottagers to swim. **1963** *Globe and Mail* (Toronto) 9 Feb. 28/1: Of all those who use the outdoors today the persons who get the least consideration are summer cottagers.

summer express *Fur Trade, Hist.* the summer trip of the express (def. 1). Cp. **winter express**.

1890 MASSON *Les Bourgeois* II 387: This was the summer express, hurrying down to Grand Portage with the result of the winter work. **1918** DAVIDSON *North West Co.* 219: The summer express hurried down to the place of rendezvous. . . .

summer lodge *Arctic* See **tupek**.
1850 (1852) OSBORN *Arctic Jnl* 13: Most of them had moved for a while into their summer lodges, which consisted of little else than a seal-skin tent, clumsily supported with sticks. **1897** TYRRELL *Sub-Arctics* 135: . . . his summer lodge is made of oil-tanned seal or deer-skins, neatly sewn together, and supported by poles . . . or pieces of drift-wood spliced together. **1963** *Beaver* Winter 23/2: The first Eskimo summer lodges were found the next day.

summer man *Fur Trade, Hist.* **1** an employee engaged for the summer only.
1801 (1897) COUES *New Light* I 181: I sent off the canoes with the remaining property, the summer men, etc., for Panbian river. . . .
2 See **summer master**.
1825 (1926) *Cdn Hist.Rev.* Dec. 313: Interpreters [are] to act as summer men & all other duties when required from £15 to £25 according to age & capacity. **1829** (1948) MCLOUGHLIN *Letters* 10: I need not say that the Summer Man at Okanagan should be directed to be particularly careful of the provisions left there.

summer master *Fur Trade, Hist.* a person in charge of a trading post for the summer only. See also **summer man** (def. 2).
1913 COWIE *Adventurers* 228: Many of these journals were kept by a "summer master," who was quite often a very illiterate laborer, who could barely scrawl phonetics in the book during the real master's absence on the annual voyage to and from headquarters with the furs and for the outfit.

summer parka *North* See **amoutik**.

summer road See 1957 quote. Cp. **winter road** (def. 2a).
1820 (1890) WILCOCKE *Death B.Frobisher* 224: With the summer road they were acquainted and that, therefore, they followed. **1909** *Gow Ganda Tribune* (Ont.) 17 Apr. 6/2: What will be the cry on the summer roads when we reach those points where the dense forest and rocks obstructs the view ahead . . . ? **1957** *Ont.Hist.* XLIX 6: This was evidently a "summer road," *i.e.* one which could be used at all seasons of the year by either sleighs or wheeled vehicles; a "winter road" was meant to be used by sleighs only, and therefore the construction cost was much less than for a summer road.

summer skin *Fur Trade, Obs.* See **summer beaver**.
1776 (1951) *Sask.Jnls* 92: One Canoe came, brought a few Summer Skins and a little dried Moose Flesh.

summer work *Placer Mining* the opening of pits and cuts and the sluicing of gravel, that is, open-cast mining, beginning in June and ending in mid-September.
1898 LANDREVILLE *Appeal* 64: During the last season of "summer work" $1.50 an hour was the universal price of ordinary unskilled labour in this District.

sun bug *Obs.* a cicada.
1826 *Colonial Advocate* (York [Toronto]) 9 Feb. 3/2:

On the poplar trees in the prairies I saw hundreds of insects much resembling the locust, the country people call them sun bugs.

sunker *n. Nfld* See 1962 quote.
*a*1923 (1955) ENGLISH *Newfoundland* 51:
We'll rant and we'll roar like true Newfoundlanders,
We'll rant and we'll roar on deck and below,
Until we see bottom inside the two sunkers,
When straight up through the channel to Toslow we'll go.
1962 MOWAT *Black Joke* 33: This was not the main entrance but a shortcut or "inside" passage full of sunkers (as reefs and shoal rocks are called in Newfoundland).

sun parlo(u)r *Informal* the western part of Southern Ontario lying on the north shore of Lake Erie, noted for its advanced growing season, which makes it a prominent producer of tobacco and early vegetables.
1959 *Star Wkly* 22 Aug. 2/1: But one place where all three combine to bring on quick, bountiful crops is in the sun parlor of Southern Ontario, centred around the town of Leamington, in Essex county....

superintendent *n.* See **Indian superintendent.**
1958 HAWTHORN *Indians of B.C.* 171: They expect this to happen, because of support the Indian superintendent has offered. **1965** *Kingston Whig-Standard* (Ont.) 22 Feb. 7/5: "Superintendent" is the title given to the government official in charge of each reserve agency.

supon† [sə'pɑn] *n.* [< Am.E < Du. *sappaen* mush < Algonk.; cf. Massachusett *saupáum* softened by water] cornmeal mush; hasty pudding. See also **samp** and **saupon.** Also spelled *supawn* and (older) *supporne.*
1852 (1881) TRAILL *Cdn Crusoes* 183: We shall have a glorious summer, mon ami, no doubt, and a fine flourishing crop, and Kate is a good hand at making supporne. **1905** (1946) TALMAN *Narratives* 2: I well remember when "sup-on" and milk was our morning repast. **1958** GOGO *St.Lawrence* 236: This sup-on is made of Indian corn, ground and boiled for several hours, then eaten with milk, butter, sugar, etc.

supply cache or **house** See **cache,** *n.* (def. 4).
1905 MOTT *Jules* 161: A voyageur showed him to the supply-house, and he got some pemmican, tea and bread, and a blanket. **1955** HOBSON *Nothing Too Good* 98: Smaller log buildings such as a meathouse, a supply cache on stilts and an outhouse were constructed at thirty dollars per building.

supply road a road built for trucks carrying supplies into a bush camp, mining property, etc. at some distance from public roads. Cp. **access road** (def. 1).
1963 *Albertan* (Calgary) 23 Dec. 3/3: The 85-mile supply road will be held open all through the winter.

supply teaching acting as a substitute teacher in such schools as may require help.
1957 *Kingston Whig-Standard* (Ont.) 24 Jan. 17/6: She told the students something of the practice and supply teaching possible while at college.

supporne *n.* See **supon.**

surrogate *n. Nfld, Hist.* a magistrate appointed from among the captains at the fisheries. See also **floating surrogate.**
1793 REEVES *Hist.Nfld* 154: The governor conferred on them the title of surrogates, an idea taken from the admiralty-law; to which, and which alone the naval governors were in the habit of looking, and under which it had long been a notion, that the fishery, as an admiralty concern, ought to be regulated. **1818** CHAPPELL *Voyage of Rosamond* 215: The Admiral always selects the best-informed Captain for the fulfillment of this arduous service; and the Surrogate has power to levy fines under the amount of fifty or sixty pounds.

surrogate court *Nfld, Hist.* the court held by a surrogate, *q.v.*
1818 CHAPPELL *Voyage of Rosamond* 49: For the adjustment of the latter cases, an officer of the Navy is annually appointed to hold a Surrogate Court in the out-harbours.

surrogating *n. Nfld, Hist.* the process of moving from station to station holding surrogate court, *q.v.*
1793 REEVES *Hist.Nfld* 154: The time of surrogating was looked forward to as a season when all wrongs were to be redressed against all oppressors; and this naval judicature was flown to by the poor inhabitants and planters, as the only refuge they had from the west country merchants, who were always their creditors, and who were generally regarded as their oppressors.

surround† *n.* a method of hunting animals such as antelope, caribou, buffalo, etc. by surrounding them and keeping them penned in while as many as possible were slaughtered.
[**1811** (1950) THOMPSON *Journals* 188: ... abt Dusk they arrived, havg killed 8 Chevruil but complain they are too few to surround them well being only 22 reckoning Boys.] **1907** MILLAIS *Newfoundland* 221: Work in the interior then closes for the year, though in February many of the Indians travel inland a day's journey to the main herd of the wintering caribou, and conduct a "surround." **1956** LEECHMAN *Native Tribes* 112: The use of the pound seems to have been largely dropped when the Indians got rifles and horses, for they then adopted another way of hunting, called the surround.

suskatoom, suskatoomina *n. Obs.* See **saskatoon.**

swallow-tail snowshoe a kind of snowshoe common among the Indians of the northeast of Canada, used for travel through deep, soft snow and underbrush. See picture at **snowshoe.** See also **elbow snowshoe.** Cp. **beavertail snowshoe.**
1916 *Trans.Roy.Soc.Can.* X 1 314: [Caption] Swallow-tail type. **1965** *Beaver* Summer 33/1: One is relatively broad, rounded in front and pointed in back. This type is sometimes referred to as the "swallow-tail" snowshoe.

swamp *n. Local* a woodlot; bush (def. 2).
1965 *Kingston Whig-Standard* (Ont.) 16 Jan. 7/2: In Prince Edward County, practically all land, except for wet areas, has been cleared and so today, when people talk about swamps, they usually mean woodlots, even if they happen to be on relatively dry land.

swamp *v.* **1**† cut a road or trail through bush country, especially for hauling lumber.
1872 DASHWOOD *Chiploquorgan* 104: ... the "swampers" ... "swamp"—cut roads—to the felled trees to enable the "teamster" and his assistants to haul

them on a "Bob sled".... **1888** (1890) ST. MAUR
Impressions 81 : The brushwood was so thick that we
had to "swamp it" out with an axe.... **1954** BRUCE
Channel Shore 27 : [He] had swamped a hauling-road
into the middle of the stretch that lay south of the
shore road. **1958** *Cdn Geog.Jnl* Jan. 16/1 : [He] is still
there ... sixty wagon-miles north of Anahim Lake
[B.C.] over a trail he "swamped out."

2 *Nfld* See quote.
1937 DEVINE *Folklore* 50 : To swamp a road or path is
to build one with a bedding of boughs to be used in
hauling slide loads of wood in winter.

3† haul or skid (def. 1), especially along a road that
has been swamped (def. 1). See also **swamping road.**
1959 LEISING *Arctic Wings* 92 : It had been a few years
since I jockeyed a caterpillar tractor but in a half hour
I was turned loose and began to swamp the cut logs
through the muskegs and tangled brush to the mill.

swamp alder 1 the speckled alder, *Alnus rugosa,*
common in wet areas from Saskatchewan to Nova
Scotia. See also **spotted alder.**
1852 (1923) MOODIE *Roughing It* 291 : The inner bark of
the swamp-alder, simply boiled in water, makes a
beautiful red. **1925** GROVE *Settlers* 305 : [The] hedgerows
of swamp alder which bordered the fields reminded
[him] of the Marsh as it had been. **1952** (1954) JENNINGS
Strange Brigade 123 : ... to our left, lay the woodsy
thickets, the tall stands of spruce and fir and hemlock
and cedar, patched and slashed by clumps of tangled
swamp alder....

2 a variety of this species found in Nova Scotia and
the Eastern United States.
1947 BIRD *Judgment Glen* 270 : She talked of ... the
virtues of the bark of swamp alder, of wild ginger for
stomach-ache.... **1956** *Native Trees* 144 : The type form
of this species is the common swamp alder, *Alnus
rugosa* ... found in Canada only in western Nova
Scotia.

swamp ash one of several ash trees, especially
Fraxinus nigra, the black ash.
1801 MACKENZIE *Voy.from Montreal* lxviii : The greatest
proportion is shaded with large trees, such as the liard,
the swamp-ash, and the willow. **1861** SUTHERLAND
Geography P.E.I. 58 : The swamp Ash ... is prized by
the Indians, by whom its wood is used in making
baskets, &c. **1956** *Native Trees* 276 : Black ash [is also
called] Swamp ash....

swamp birch *Maritimes* See **wire birch.**
1956 *Native Trees* 138 : Wire Birch [is also called] ...
swamp birch.

swamp blackbird See **soldier bird.**
1793 (1911) SIMCOE *Diary* 184 : After we entered we
rowed some distance among low lands covered with
rushes, abounding with wild ducks and swamp black
birds, with red wings. **1956** MCATEE *Folk-Names* 60 :
Red-winged blackbird [is also called] swamp
blackbird ("Swamp" in the sense of marsh, General).

swamp-boot *n. Obs.* See **larrigan.**
1810 (1955) CRAIG *Early Travellers* 29 : A pair of
moccasins, or swamp-boots, complete the lower part of
his dress.

swamp buggy *North* a tracked vehicle capable of
pulling a heavily loaded trailer over rough and
boggy terrain.
1966 *North* July-Aug. 14/2 : And when the usually
dependable swamp buggy breaks down, it's back to the
dog team.

swamp cat a tracked vehicle for pulling cat-
trains, *q.v.*
1957 *Kingston Whig-Standard* (Ont.) 27 Mar. 7/2 : One
swamp cat made a 300-mile journey through the
roughest Ungava territory, proving it possible to haul
supplies in this manner—but not proving the method
to be economically wise.

swamp elm a common species of elm, *Ulmus
americana,* found from central Saskatchewan to
the Maritimes; white elm.
1830 (1837) *Trans.Lit.& Hist.Soc.Que.* III 83 : It is
known in market by the name of Swamp Elm.
1916 BRIDLE *Sons of Can.* 5 : He was a timberjack in the
hardwood bush of western Ontario, about to notch a
five-foot swamp elm which he and his mate would
afterwards bring down with a crosscut saw. **1956** *Native
Trees* 182 : White Elm [is also called] swamp elm....

swamper† *n.* **1** *Lumbering* a logger employed in
cutting roads and, often, in trimming branches
from felled trees. See also **road-cutter** and
road-maker.
1872 DASHWOOD *Chiploquorgan* 104 : A crew of
lumberers have different occupations assigned to them;
... the "swampers," who "swamp"—cut roads....
[See **feller** for full quote.] **1908** GRAINGER *Woodsmen*
84 : We came to where the "swampers" were at work
chopping limbs and brush, preparing the cut logs for
hauling. **1956** ANDREWS *Glory Days* 14 : These were the
swampers who cleared the brush for the skid roads....
1967 [see quote at **choreboy**].

2 a. *Hist.* See quote.
1960 DOWNS *Wagon Road* 43 : [Caption] Many drivers
were accompanied by a "swamper," who was usually
a young fellow apprenticed to the teaming business.
The swamper looked after the horses, including
rounding them up in the morning, usually about four
o'clock, and in general assisted the teamster with the
over-all duties of freighting.

b. a truck-driver's helper.
1959 *Sun* (Vancouver) 17 July 25/7 : He told the court
he had gone into the office and left the job to his
swamper and returned without noticing the tarp was not
in place.... **1963** *Ibid.* 28 Feb. 1/5 : A wood truck
swamper was charged $25 each for two stolen kisses
Wednesday.

swamp fire marsh gas, methane, which at times
burns in swampy areas; will-o'-the-wisp.
1903 WHITE *Forest* 172 : Like swamp-fire, it lured the
imagination always on and on and on through the
secret waterways of the uninhabited north.
1954 LYSENKO *Yellow Boots* 146 : Behind them the
swamp fire, like a gigantic Jack o'lantern, bumped and
danced and ran around the sky, then finally, as it
reached the ground, evaporated into the night air.

swamping *n. Lumbering* the work done by a
swamper (def. 1).
1908 GRAINGER *Woodsmen* 113 : "I'll take you off
swamping and give you a job barking up at the head of
the new skid-road." **1943** KOROLEFF *Pulpwood Skidding*
70 : The only swamping a teamster should normally be
required to do is the clearing of a by-pass around a
deteriorated section of a trail, or perhaps to swamp a
short cut....

swamping axe a wide, double-bitted axe used in swamping and other rough work.

1947 *Game Trails in Canada* Aug. 16/1: The broad axe holds its own as the typical equipment of the tie-cutter and the relatively short and thick "swamping axe" gives promise of forever remaining the essential, all-purpose tool.

swamping road See **logging road**. See also **swamp**, *v.* (def. 3).

1900 LONG *Wilderness Ways* 124: I turned into an old swamping road which gave me a bit of open before and behind.

swamp larch *Obs.* See **tamarack, *n.***

1852 (1881) TRAILL *Cdn Crusoes* 77: The Indian name of the flexible roots of the tamarack, or swamp larch [is watappe, here war-tap]. . . .

swamp maple the red maple, *Acer rubrum,* found on moist sites in the southern part of Canada from Lake Superior eastward.

1800 WELD *Travels* I 381: The swamp maple . . . yields a much greater quantity of sap . . . but this sap does not afford so much sugar as that of the curled maple. **1956** RADDALL *Wings* 130: The shores had a fringe of swamp maples and in a few more weeks when their leaves were turning scarlet it would be a very pretty place.

swamp meadow *B.C.* See **slough meadow.**

1951 HOBSON *Grass* 41: We sat around . . . talking of range cows, and tough trails, slough grass and swamp meadows. . . .

swamp out 1 See **swamp**, *v.* (def. 1).

2 clean out thoroughly, especially with water and a mop; swab.

1964 *Press* Feb. 8: Two old warehouses were rented at the end of Market Street, swamped out with disinfectant [and] rigged with three tier bunks. . . .

swamp rabbit See **marsh rabbit.**

1951 ANGIER *At Home* 139: The succulent dark meat of the little water animal is actually hard to equal— especially when it's sliced, moist and steaming from the oven, as musquash or swamp rabbit. **1956** KEMP *Northern Trader* 59: The muskrat had become a "swamp rabbit," and he cost a lot more than he had in the Cumberland swamps.

swamp tea *North* **1** See **Labrador tea** (def. 1a).

1807 (1889) WENTZEL *Letters* 80: The large wood is the red and white pine, cypress, birch, poplar and liard; the under wood is the elder, willow, red wood, and swamp tea, none of which, except the red wood, bear fruit.

2 See **Labrador tea** (def. 1b).

1821 (1823) FRANKLIN *Journey* 481: Our meal at night consisted of scraps of deer skins and swamp tea, and the men complained of their increasing debility.

sweat-bath *n.* **1** a bath such as that taken for reasons of health by certain Indians, the bather sitting naked in a hut or lodge and perspiring freely in the steam caused by water being dripped onto hot rocks, the process sometimes being completed by a plunge into an adjacent lake or stream.

[**1800** (1820) HARMON *Journal* 64: They sweat themselves in this manner, they say, in order that their limbs may become more supple, and they more alert, in pursuing animals, which they are desirous of killing.] **1940** NIVEN *Mine Inheritance* 117: "I am at least clean again, bodily clean, I mean. I've been having sweat-baths." **1952** *Beaver* Dec. 27/1: They [Swampy Cree] used the sweat bath in cases of illness.

2 See **sweat-house.**

1958 WELLS *Georgian Bay* 65: Having seen the Indian Village with its longhouse, torture stake, sweat bath, and storage pits, all maintained, except for the vermin and filth, exactly as they would have been maintained in Champlain's day, the visitor should then proceed to the Huronia House Museum. **1965** WILSON *No Man Stands Alone* 56: At nearly every Indian camp you will find a sweat bath, Built like a tiny tent with its frame of willows covered by skin or blankets, it is usually located close to a small creek or river.

sweat factory *Slang, Obs.* See **sweatshop.**

1904 *Independent* (Vancouver) 23 July 4/2: Manchester's Sweat Factory in New Westminster is still running full blast.

sweat-house *n.* a hut, wigwam, etc. used for taking sweat-baths (def. 1), originally a practice of Indians. See also **sweat-bath** (def. 2), **sweating bath,** and **sweat lodge.**

1887 (1888) LEES & CLUTTERBUCK *British Columbia* 259: We have passed many of these sweat houses at various places. . . . **1935** JENNESS *Parry Island* 72: Facing the entrance, at the distance of a few yards, was a domed sweat-house for the candidate's purification. **1957** LEWIS *Buckskin Cookery* I 46: Build a sweat-house by making a dome shaped tee-pee of willow hoops, large enough for a person to crouch down inside, preferably beside a creek or river. . . .

sweating bath or **booth** See **sweat-house.**

1872 (1873) GRANT *Ocean to Ocean* 190: We passed one or two deserted tents, and "sweating booths," but no Indians. *c***1902** LAUT *Trapper* 152: The man-smell is as acute to the beast's nose as the rank fur-animal-smell is to the man's nose; and the first thing that an Indian who has had a long run of ill-luck does is to go to a native "sweating-bath" and make himself clean.

sweating house *Obs.* See **sweat-house.**

1743 (1949) ISHAM *Observations* 96: . . . they then take about 20 Large stones, and heat them hott in the fire, in another tent, when hott, they put them into their hutt or swetting house. . . . **1820** (1824) FRANKLIN *Journey* I 115: The ceremony took place in a sweating house . . . erected for the occasion by the worshipper's two wives.

sweat lodge† See **sweat-house.**

1891 *Cdn Indian* July 294: The other was sitting by the child tending it, and squatting inside the sweat lodge were the five medicine men. **1963** SYMONS *Many Trails* 137: The crossed, bent-over willows so often seen in the bush are the frameworks of Indian sweat lodges.

sweatshop† *n. Slang* a factory where workers are employed at low wages for long hours of toil. See also **sweat factory.**

☛ *The term derives from the practice of "sweaters" in the highly competitive middle-man shops in the garment industry driving underpaid needlewomen and tailors, often immigrants.*

1903 *Bond of Brotherhood* 12 June 4/1: No more strikes, No more lockouts, No more hold ups, No more unions, Healthy niggers sound in wind and limb well broke to handcuffs, two pair of genuine sweat shop overalls given with each piece of ebony. **1916** BRIDLE *Sons of*

against the labour unions, why was he so hostile to the
Jews? 1963 *Canada Month* Nov. 17/2: In those days
[the Montreal garment industry] was considered the
sweatshop industry.

sweatshop conditions working conditions
similar to those obtaining in sweatshops.
1930 *Cdn Needleworker* 15 Oct. 1/4: Wages are cut, the
standard of living is reduced daily, and the sweat shop
conditions are sapping the life blood of the workers.
1953 LEBOURDAIS *Nation of North* 224: This led to
sweat-shop conditions in a number of industries.

Swede *n. Slang, Often Derog*. See 1958 quote.
See also **Sowegian**.
1934 BETTANY *Valley of Lost Gold* 29: "No. I used to go
with Charles to Kaisersdorf, sometimes, and I've been
to the Swede settlement west of the hills. . . ."
1958 BERTON *Klondike* 53: Another trudged up Bonanza
as far as Twenty Above, then shrugged his shoulders.
"I'll leave it to the Swedes," he said, using the classic
term of derision, for Scandinavians were alleged to work
ground that no other man would touch.

Swede bucksaw See **Swede-saw**.
1951 HOBSON *Grass* 21: Here is the list: . . . 2 curved-
backed, take-down model Swede bucksaws. . . .

Swede-saw *n*. [see note] a type of saw having a
bow-like tubular frame and a sharp blade with
many cutting teeth, especially efficient in cutting
pulpwood and any soft, green wood. See also
Swede bucksaw, **Swedish saw**, and **Swedish violin**.
Cp. **Swedish fiddle**.
☞ *It has been suggested that this term may have received
its name because the original blades were of Swedish
steel. It is also possible that the name was applied
derisively because the saw was associated with Swedish
lumbermen, as may well be the case with* **Swedish
fiddle**, **Swedish violin**, *etc. See also* **Swede**.
1950 HAMBLETON *Abitibi* 120: It looked just like any
other "Swede saw," with its tubular metal frame,
painted blue, and a thin, keen blade which was kept
taut by a clamp. **1956** GOWLAND *Sikanaska Trail* 25:
Withdrawing my axe from its scabbard and taking the
"Swede" saw from beneath the pack cover, I assembled
it and surveyed my task. **1959** LEISING *Arctic Wings* 91:
There were evenings when my neck was so bloody
[from bulldog bites] it looked as if someone had been
trying to hack off my head with a dull Swede-saw.

Swedish fiddle *Lumbering, Slang* a long crosscut
saw used by buckers, *q.v.* Cp. **misery fiddle**,
homesteader's fiddle, and **Swede-saw**.
1942 SWANSON *Western Logger* 55: swedish fiddle—a
bucking saw.

Swedish saw See **Swede-saw**.
1960 MCNAMEE *Florencia Bay* 15: In all he had twelve
loads to carry, tent, kitbag, bedroll . . . Swedish saw, a
small tarpaulin. . . .

Swedish violin *Lumbering, Slang* See **Swede-saw**.
Cp. **Swedish fiddle**.
☞ *This term is clearly a variant of* **Swedish fiddle**,
here applied to the one-man **Swede-saw**.
1950 HAMBLETON *Abitibi* 90: Fathers and even
grandfathers in the smallest towns packed their clothes,
sharpened their pet two-pound bush axes and in many
cases carried their own "Swedish violins," or light,
tubular framed bucksaws, especially adapted for fast
cutting of pulpwood.

sweep-check *n. Hockey* a check made by a
player crouching low while sweeping the ice
surface in an arc with his stick, thus deflecting the
puck from the blade of the opposing player's stick.
See also **hook-check**.
1963 *Kingston Whig-Standard* (Ont.) 17 Jan. 14/2:
According to Jack Adams a Fort William player named
Rochon invented the hook or sweep check which
Nighbor and Jack Walker adopted. . . .

sweep-check *v. Hockey* make a sweep-check.
See also **hook-check**.
1966 *Hockey News* (Montreal) 1 Jan. 13/2: He poke-
checks and sweep-checks like the oldtimers, and
makes few mistakes.

sweep-checker *n. Hockey* a player who is skilled
in using the sweep-check.
1963 *Kingston Whig-Standard* (Ont.) 17 Jan. 14/2:
[He] was . . . one of the best sweep-checkers in NHL
history. **1966** *Ibid*. 16 Apr. 9/1: Nighbor was the most
skilful sweep-checker the sport has ever known. . . .

sweep-checking *adj. Hockey* skilled in using the
sweep-check.
1966 *Kingston Whig-Standard* (Ont.) 16 Apr. 9/1:
. . . Jack Walker [was] one of the original sweep-
checking forwards. . . .

sweeper *n*. a tree that has been undermined by the
current of a stream so that it has fallen either partly
or entirely into the water although usually still
moored to the bank by its roots. Cp. **sawyer** (def. 1).
1888 (1890) ST. MAUR *Impressions* 95: . . . we glided
through the water at about ten miles an hour,
sometimes rushing . . . within few inches of a sweeper,
as they call the trees which hang across the river just
clear of the water. . . . **1929** JOHNSTON *Beyond Rockies*
191: "Where are them sweepers, Charlie?" (sweepers
being the river term for drifting trees, which may in a
moment upset the craft of an unwary skipper).
1954 PATTERSON *Dangerous River* 48: From a wooded
bank nearby came the thudding lash of "sweepers"—
trees that have been undercut by the floods into the
river, but which still cling with their roots to the bank,
lashing and beating at the water which drives through
their branches. **1963** *Alta Hist.Rev.* Aug. 2/1: Care was
needed to avoid the odd "sweeper" (a tree leaning out
over the water close to the surface).

sweep gang *Lumbering, Hist*. See quote.
1966 *Globe and Mail* (Toronto) 6 Dec. 36/1: Over the
rest of the long route to Ottawa, sweep gangs aboard
river craft called pointers broke the jams and picked up
stray logs.

sweep-head *n. Obs*. the deck or platform
occupied by the sweepman, *q.v.*, on a scow equipped
with a tail-sweep, *q.v.*
1902 LONDON *Daughter of Snows* 89: "Bear witness,
O my comrades, what a hard-bit gang were we,—/The
servants of the sweep-head, but the masters of the sea!"

sweepman *n*. the man operating the sweep on a
river scow. Cp. **tail-sweep**.
1940 MARSHALL *Arctic Village* 83: [A scow] is manned by
a crew of six, among whom the most highly skilled job
is that of the sweepman who steers the boat from the
rear by means of a huge oar.

sweet corn any of several varieties of Indian corn which are sweet to the taste.

1809 MACKENZIE *Mississouri Indians* 383: Many, incited by Indian hospitality, came with the best their humble huts could afford, such as fresh and dried fruit, sweet corn prepared in different manners, green pumpkins and beans, meats green and dried. **1952** PUTNAM *Cdn Regions* 160/1: The chief crops are tomatoes, sweet corn, green peas, cabbage and cauliflower which are either sold fresh on the city markets or sold to canning plants.

sweet pemmican *Hist.* pemmican into which maple syrup had been mixed. See also **sugar pemmican.**

1873 (1904) BUTLER *Wild North Land* 161: It seems positively ridiculous now, how one could regard the possession of flour and sugar, of sweet cake and sweet pemmican, as some of the most essential requisites of life.

swift (fox)† *n.* See **kit fox** (def. 1a).

1853 REID *Young Voyageurs* 8: There, too, may be seen the . . . "swift fox." *c*1902 LAUT *Trapper* 259: The hairs are coarse, horsey, indistinctly marked, and the fur is of small value to the trader; so dainty little swift, who looks as if nature made him for a pet dog instead of a fox, is slighted by the hunter.

swile [swaɪl] *n. Nfld Dial.* a seal. See also **swiler** and **swiling gun.**

☞ *See note at* **swiler.**

1883 HATTON & HARVEY *Newfoundland* 305: The food of the men is none of the daintiest and no one who is at all squeamish about what he "eats, drinks, and avoids" need attempt to go "swile huntin'." **1907** MILLAIS *Newfoundland* 39: "Lard God Almighty, send a swile fer daddy, an' send a swile fer mamma, and a swile fer Uncle Jim, an' wan fer Uncle Jim's wife, an' a swile fer little Tommy, an' one each fer Jarge an' Mary, an' a swile fer each of Cousin Will's family, not forgettin' a swile fer Aunt Jane what's a pore widder." **1916** DUNCAN *Billy Topsail* 152: "Ay," says Sam; "but I wants t' bludgeon another swile afore I dies." **1932** GRENFELL *Forty Years* 96: The "swiles" [seals] had "stuck in," and all hands were out on the ice, eager to capture their share of these valuable animals.

swiler ['swaɪlɚ] *n. Nfld Dial.* See **seal hunter** (def. 1). See also **swile.**

☞ *Also spelled* **swoiler** *to indicate the regional pronunciation* ['swɔɪlɚ] *and similar variants.*

1883 HATTON & HARVEY *Newfoundland* 88: In the last week of February, the roads leading from the various out-ports of St. John's, begin to be enlivened by the appearance of the sealers, or, as they are called in the vernacular, "swilers," their enterprise being designated "swile huntin'." **1958** HARRINGTON *Sea Stories* 118: She sailed on the 1st of March, 1872 with Skipper Ned Dower in command, and a crew of able "swoilers." **1966** *Globe and Mail* (Toronto) 8 Mar. 1/2: Mr. Robichaud, bundled in parka and bright yellow toque, mingled with a group of blood-spattered swilers, questioning them closely on their killing methods.

swiling gun *Nfld Dial.* See **sealing gun.** See also **swile.**

☞ *See note at* **swiler.**

1906 LUMSDEN *Skipper Parson* 90: "If the Canadians come down here to take our country I'll get down my "swiling gun," and we'll go out and meet 'em."

swim-up *n.* See quote.

1958 *Wildlife Rev.* 30: During their early stages, advanced fry or alevins are often called "swim-ups" since they begin to swim to the surface for food.

swing *n.* **1** *North* a train of sleighs or freight canoes, so called because they move, or swing, over a certain route in periodic trips.

1941 *Beaver* June 56/1: . . . it was the first mechanized swing to be seen here for ten years. **1943** *Ibid.* Mar. 17/1: As the swing of silent canoes glided downstream . . . the Indian guide stood erect in the bow. . . .
1956 KEMP *Northern Trader* 211: He would build big thirty-horse barns for every day he would be on the road; he would put the freight through in swings.

2 *North* See **cat-train.** See also **cat-swing.**

1941 *Beaver* June 56/1: Great amazement was shown by the Indians when the Armstrong and Low swing from Flin Flon arrived here [Lac du Brochet, Man.] in March. **1952** KNOTT *Harnessing* 15/2: Six drivers, two brakemen and a cook make up the crew of a three-tractor "swing" which may be hauling eight or nine sleighs carrying some 100 tons of supplies. **1957** *Kingston Whig-Standard* (Ont.) 29 Mar. 13/5: For the last three years the company has sent its swings over ice-covered lakes and snow-covered portages in temperatures often near 50 below zero. **1958** *CBC Times* (Prairie ed.) 23-29 Mar. 6/4: The train is called a "swing"; each swing consists of three or more tractors, each dragging four or five sleighs. One of the sleighs is used as a caboose for eating and sleeping.

3 *West* See **swing-out.**

1961 MITCHELL *Jake and the Kid* 68: "Weasel Tail, I says to him, you . . . herd 'em with a hundred drags behaind and two hundred swings to the side. . . ."

swing boss *North* the foreman in charge of a cat-swing, *q.v.*

1959 *Argosy* (Cdn sec.) July 28/3: One tractor stripped its forward gears so that the swing boss had to drive the final ninety miles backwards, looking over his shoulder.

swing-out *n. West* a cowboy who rides well out to the side of a herd to keep the animals from spreading. See also **swing** (def. 3).

1962 *Canadian Wkly* 1 Sep. 9/2: All went out to herd the cattle into the branding corral, Donnie riding as a swing-out at the side . . . swinging a rope and the way his father always did, . . . spooking stray cows and calves out of the willow brush.

swish ice *Nfld* See **sish.**

1835 WIX *Journal* 23: We have plenty of work for the ice-pounder in this cove and in the bay, as it was full of a species of ice, significantly called by the people, "swish-ice," which, when struck with the oar, makes a sound similar to that of straw when thrashed with a stick.

swoiler *n.* See **swiler.**

syllabic *adj.* of or pertaining to any one of several syllabic systems of writing devised for the use of Indians and Eskimos. See also **Cree syllabics** and picture. See also **syllabics.**

1852 RICHARDSON *Arctic Exped.* 70: They have already taught many of their pupils here to read and write a stenographic syllabic character, first used by the late Reverend Mr. Evans, a Wesleyan missionary, formerly resident at Norway House. **1897** YOUNG *Indian Trail* 83:

As I journeyed among these wonderful people, I carried as part of my outfit, a number of these syllabic Bibles. . . . **1945** LEECHMAN *Eskimo Summer* 143: The syllabic script has proved a blessing indeed to the Eskimos. **1965** *Maclean's* 24 July 34/2: Once more Evans examined his syllabic alphabet.

syllabics *n.pl.* See **Cree syllabics** and picture. See also **syllabic.**
1861 *Nor'Wester* (R.R.S.) 15 Mar. 3/5: The whole Bible is in course of publication in the Cree language and in the syllabics of the Rev. J. Evans, under the superintendence of the Rev. W. Mason. **1896** RUSSELL *Far North* 99: They wanted . . . pencils and paper for writing letters in syllabics when sending for supplies. . . . **1936** *Beaver* Sep. 15/2: Syllabics are not "Indian writing," as some suppose, but were concocted by the white man for the use of the Indians, and we must take off our hats to the originator for his ingenuity in inventing so simple and yet so adaptable a form of writing the Indian language. **1965** *Maclean's* 24 July 25/1: And their descendants have been reading the syllabics of James Evans ever since.

Sympathizer *n. Hist.* any of certain residents of Upper Canada who, during 1837-8, sought to sever the British connection and join the province to the United States. See also **Patriot** (def. 1a).
1838 (1841) MCLEOD *Upper Canada* 269: Sealed tenders will be received at this office, until 12 o'clock, noon, Dec. 6th, 1838, from persons who may be willing to contract for the hanging of such sympathisers, patriots, rebels, Yankees, and other vagabonds, as have been taken, or may be taken in arms, during the present disturbances, the tenders to express the rate per dozen, York currency, at which the due execution of the law will be performed. **1849** ALEXANDER *L'Acadie* I 159: . . . monied men in Rochester, Buffalo, and other towns along the frontier, subscribed handsomely in 1837-38 to aid the wicked attempts of the "Sympathizers" on the peace of Canada. **1850** BIGSBY *Shoe and Canoe* II 48: Half a mile still further east, near one or two windmills, a sharp fight took place in 1837, between the British troops and a party of American Sympathisers.

syndic ['sɪndɪk] *n.* [< Cdn F *syndic d'habitations*] *New France, Hist.* See 1963 quote.
1886 *Trans.Roy.Soc.Can.* IV 2 46: They declared that, having regard to the smallness of the population, it would be better to appoint a syndic. **1960** RYERSON *Founding of Canada* 122: The syndics, elected annually, were allowed to attend the governing council, make representations on matters affecting their constituents, but not to debate or vote. **1963** MORTON *Kingdom of Canada* 44: The administration of the colony was made less autocratic, and syndics, or representatives of the people of Quebec and Montreal [1647] were allowed to appear before the council on the business of their electors.

syrup *n.* See **maple syrup.**
1766 (1916) WAUGH *Iroquois Foods* 141: They [Abenaki Indians] were contented to let it [maple sap] boil a little, to thicken it something, and make a Sort of Syrup. **1845** BEAVAN *Life in Backwoods N.B.* 15: The great treat is the candy made by dashing the boiling syrup on the snow where it instantly congeals, transparent and crisp, in sheets. **1955** *Tweed News* 14 Apr. 2/3: Sap weather may be here, but syrup-makers are getting a very poor run of sap.

tabac *n. Cdn French* a strong, dark homegrown tobacco smoked by many French Canadians.
1856 BALLANTYNE *Young Fur-Traders* 63: Peter Mactavish gave Louis a hearty shake of the hand before proceeding to supply his wants, which were simple and moderate, excepting in the article of *tabac,* in the use of which he was im-moderate, being an inveterate smoker. . . . **1899** PARKER *Lane* 152: . . . he ogled her, and smoked his strong *tabac,* and tried to sing. **1901** (1903) DRUMMOND *J.Courteau* 127: Dere's only wan kin' of tabac for me,/An' it grow on de Rivière des Prairies—/Dat's w'at I smoke. **1923** WILLIAMS *Spinning Wheels* 31: . . . they [habitant women] smoked clay pipes filled with *tabac Canayen* [*Canadien*].

tabanask [tə'banɑsk] *n.* [< Algonk.; cf. Cree *otābānāsk* toboggan] *North* See **cariole** (def. 2a and picture). See also **toboggan,** *n.* (def. 4).
[**1887** *Trans.Roy.Soc.Can.* V 2 114: In winter the flat-sled (*tabaskhan*) [sic] is used for bearing the household and other valuable effects.] **1933** MERRICK *True North* 135: John claims old Mathieu will make him a better *tabanask* than that, but I don't believe him. **1938** *Beaver* Sep. 17/2: From behind us came a speeding dog team—three flying huskies drawing on a diminutive *tabanask*. . . .

tabogan *n.* See **toboggan.**

Tadoussac Trade See **King's Domain.**
1948 *Beaver* June 32/2: This vast territory was variously known as the "Tadoussac Trade," the "King's Domain," or simply the "King's Posts."

taffy ['tæfi] *n.* [< var. of *toffee*] **1** maple-syrup candy, often made by pouring the syrup over the snow so that it hardens in brittle sheets. See also **lateer** and **maple candy.** Cp. **taffy-pull** (def. 2).
[**1826** (1916) SELLAR *Narrative* 124: It was a big play for the youngsters, and their shouting when Jabez poured sap on the snow and it turned to candy, might have been heard a mile away.] **1901** CONNOR *Man from Glengarry* 105: Ladies and gentlemen, the program for this evening is as follows: games, tea, and taffy, in the order mentioned. **1903** CARR-HARRIS *White Chief* 128: . . . the gentlemen served each lady with a block of hard snow upon which had been poured some of the boiling [maple] sugar, which immediately hardened into "lateer," or "taffy."
2 See **maple syrup.**
1903 RICHARDSON *Colin* 225: . . . it was announced that the taffy was ready, so everybody got a lump of snow or ice and the McNabb boys went about with large dishes full of hot taffy, which they lifted out in ladlesful, pouring it on each one's snow or ice.

taffy-on-a-stick *n.* [a pun on *taffy* flattery, blarney and *taffy* sweet candy] *Slang* romantic nonsense.
1890 *Grip* (Toronto) 8 Mar. 170/2: Are you really pining to see ox-carts wobbling over prairie roads with a decided French accent, or is it only taffy-on-a-stick you are giving us.

taffy-pull *n.* **1** a social affair at which taffy is made from maple syrup or other syrups, as sugar-molasses. See also **taffy-social.**
1895 *Rat Portage* [Kenora] *News* (Ont.) 29 Nov. 5/2: A taffy pull will be given by Rev. Father Blais . . . to the children of Mount Carmel Convent. **1926** *One Big Union Bulletin* (Winnipeg) 19 Aug. 5/6: We had planned a taffy pull but the ball game was so prolonged that we succeeded in making fudge. **1949** *Cominco Mag.* Jan. 8/3: This first Christmas party at Rossland was a taffy pull and everyone had a wonderful time. **1963** DILLMAN *Wee Folk* 54: So the evening went, ending with dancing and a taffee pull for the younger elves.
2 See **sugaring-off party.**
1905 SCHERCK *Pen Pictures* 189: It frequently brought the young folks together in gatherings called "taffy pulls." **1942** BOSANQUET *Saddlebags* 186: But the glories of the maple syrup season reached their consummation at Johnny Tait's taffy-pull.

taffy social *Obs.* See **taffy-pull** (def. 1).
1886 *Indian* (Hagersville, Ont.) 28 Apr. 90/2: The taffy social given by Sabbath School No. 2, Oneida, on Friday evening last . . . was an unqualified success, there being a good attendance to enjoy the lengthy and interesting program.

Tahltan (bear) dog ['taltən] [< *Tahltan* an Athapascan people of N.W. British Columbia] See **bear dog.**
1904 (1958) *Alaska Sportsman* Dec. 19/3: [Yukon locale] She [a Tahltan woman] believed she was a hundred and ten years old, yet she lived in her tent with only a Tahltan bear dog for company. **1956** *Beaver* Summer 41/1: It is natural . . . that a Tahltan dog should retain a strong instinct for hunting. **1963** *Islander* 8 Sep. 2/1: Richardson's Hare Indian Dog is undoubtedly of the same breed as those we find in B.C. and the Yukon. Here they are often called Tahltan Bear Dogs, because the Tahltan Indians used them in bear hunting; they even refer to them as "our" dogs. **1965** WILSON *No Man Stands Alone* 82: . . . I saw the Tahl-Tan Bear Dogs. They looked like a cross between a fox and a fox-terrier.

taiga ['taɪga *or* 'taɪgə] *n.* [< Russian < Turk.; cf. Turk. *dag* mountain] See quotes.
1947 TAYLOR *Canada* 7: It is clear from Fig. 41 that an environment marked by an almost universal cover of coniferous forest is the most widespread feature in Canada. This cool, temperate forest the geographer calls Taiga. **1960** *Cdn Geog.Jnl* Jan. 9/1: The sub-arctic, on the other hand, is a forested zone generally referred to as the *taiga* or the northern coniferous forest, or simply as the boreal (northern) forest. **1965** SYMINGTON *Tuktu* 17: The second zone, and a more important one to the caribou, is the taiga, where stunted timber and shrubbery struggle to survive in a cold, dry climate.

tail (a trap) *v. Esp.Nfld* See 1941 quote.
1770 (1792) CARTWRIGHT *Journal* I 30: I tailed a couple of traps for otters, but did not find many rubbing places. **1819** ANSPACH *Hist.Nfld* 378: The common expression for fixing properly this engine of destruction is, *to tail a trap.* **1941** *Beaver* Sep. 39/2: Tailing a trap. To set a trap.

tail-buoy *n.* one of the floats attached to the far end of a herring net.
1954 BRUCE *Channel Shore* 23: There in the shadowed calm before sunrise men leaned across the gunnels of flats, grasped the tail-buoys of herring nets. . . .

tail-less hare *Obs.* See **pika.**
1858 (1863) PALLISER *Journals* 100: [We saw] the little Pika or tailless hare. . . .

tail-line *n. North* a strong leather line attached to the rear of a dog-sled, permitting the driver to pull back on the sled when going downhill and enabling him, when the line is allowed to drag behind the sled, to retrieve the outfit should the dogs bolt or should his grip on the sled be dislodged. See also **tail-rope.** Cp. **headline.**
1858 (1863) PALLISER *Journals* 121: In effecting this descent . . . we untackled the dogs, and each held on by the "tail line" of his "sled" and, sitting in the snow, dragged behind to prevent its acquiring impetus. **1896** WHITNEY *On Snow-Shoes* 186: Whenever we began a descent and I called "W-h-o-a!" Foro, the foregoer, invariably broke into a run, starting up the other dogs, and dragging me after them, hanging to the tail-line. . . . **1922** *Beaver* Aug. 12/1: Fortunately, I had trailing [behind the dog-sled] a long tail-line of buffalo raw-hide, which I at once grabbed. **1963** SPRY *Palliser* 182: The party had to go down an exceeding steep 400-foot bank that night . . . and each held on by the tail line of his sled. . . .

tailor-made *n. Slang* a cigarette that is made in a factory, as opposed to one that a smoker rolls for himself. See also **tailor-made,** *adj.* Cp. **makings.**
1942 HAIG-BROWN *Timber* 131: Johnny fumbled for tobacco pouch and cigarette papers, then remembered the pack of tailor-mades in his pocket, took it out and lit one. **1960** MCNAMEE *Florencia Bay* 135: "You smoke tailor-mades, Johnnie?"

tailor-made *adj. Slang* of cigarettes, made in a factory. See **tailor-made,** *n.*
1939 O'HAGAN *Tay John* 179: He offered me a tailor-made cigarette, his initials upon it. **1955** HOBSON *Nothing Too Good* 162: How about a tailormade coffin nail? **1959** STOREY *Prairie Harvest* 120: Rynold would have burned the school down for a "tailor made" cigarette. **1967** *Globe and Mail* (Toronto) 30 May 29/8: I mean tailor-made, ready-rolled . . . cigarets.

tail-rope *n. North* See **tail-line.**
1931 GREY OWL *Last Frontier* 53: On the down grade, tail ropes are loosed, and men bear back with all their weight. . . . **1948** ONRAET *Sixty Below* 75: "The son of a bitch, I got tangled in me tail-rope, and had a runaway."

tail-sweep *n. Hist.* a long oar for steering a scow, much used on the rivers of the Northwest at the turn of the century. Cp. **sweepman.**
1909 CAMERON *New North* 74: . . . the runaway [barge] with tail-sweep set has turned the next corner of the Athabasca.

takanogan *n.* See **tikinagan.**

take *v.* of a body of water, freeze solidly from shore to shore. Cp. **throw ice.**
1781 *Quebec Gaz.* 11 Jan. 2/1: It is universally asserted that, since the settlement of this country by Europeans, it has not before been known to take so early as the month of December, to so often so late as March. **1825** *Kingston Chron.* (U.C.) 4 Feb. 3/2: On Saturday night last, the ice took between Kingston and Long Island, and since [then] the foot passengers have been crossing. **1881** *Edmonton Bull.* 28 Mar. 1/2: Ice took in the Saskatchewan on the 19th of November, and the first fall of snow was two inches on the 26th of that month. **1931** NUTE *Voyageur* 79: Seines were set in the water just before the ice "took" on the lake or river.

take off the cauldron *Obs.* in Indian parlance, make peace.

1840 WILLIS *Cdn Scenery* I 16: Thus to throw up the hatchet, or to put on the great cauldron is to begin a war; to throw the hatchet to the sky, is to wage open and terrible war; to take off the cauldron, or to bury the hatchet is to make peace. . . .

take to the bush *Slang* make oneself scarce; leave town.
1957 *Maclean's* 7 Dec. 47/1: They would be raising their hands to him on Saturday, each with a rock, if he didn't take to the bush Friday night.

take treaty See **treaty** (def. 1b).

talik ['tælik] *n.* [< Russian] See quote.
1957 *Maclean's* 14 Sep. 93/1: How can layers of unfrozen earth exist in the permafrost? These layers, known by their Russian name *talik*, frequently have streams and springs flowing through them.

talkie-tooter *n. Lumbering, Slang* See quote. Cp. **whistle-punk.**
1966 *Dly Colonist* (Victoria) 3 Aug. 28/2: The whistle punk is being replaced by the talkie-tooter, an electronic device worn on the belt of the chokerman. When a log is ready to be yarded in, after the choker is set, the chokerman just presses the talkie tooter. It sends an electronic signal to the receiving set on the donkey and sounds a whistle.

talk muskrat or **musquash** *North, Slang* discuss the fur trade.
1880 GORDON *Mountain and Prairie* 137: Listen to them when several of them are together "talking muskrat," (to use their own term for discussing the business of the Company,) and they have scarcely a good word for the service. **1921** HEMING *Drama of Forests* 6: After the two traders had finished "talking musquash"—fur-trade business—they began reminiscing on the more picturesque side of their work.

talk (to) seal *North* stalk a seal by creeping up on it while making seal-like noises.
1865 HALL *Arctic Researches* 580: The bear lies down and crawls by hitches toward the seal, "talking" to it, as the Innuits say, till he is within striking distance, then he pounces upon it with a single jump. **1897** TYRRELL *Sub-Arctics* 151: The seal takes the Eskimo, who is able to talk seal perfectly, to be one of its kinsmen; and indeed there is a great deal of resemblance between the genera, for both are similarly clothed, and the Eskimo's living largely upon the flesh and oil of the seal, is similarly odorous.

talk white See **white,** *adv.* (def. 2).

Tallow Company *Hist.* an unsuccessful joint-stock cattle company formed in the early 1830's at the Red River Settlement for the purpose of raising range cattle on the prairie. Also *Tallow Concern.*
1834 (1947) HARGRAVE *Correspondence* 159: You will hear that Tallow Concern is at an End and all the Cattle sold by auction. . . . **1913** KELLY *Range Men* 110: A new company, called the "Tallow Company" was formed.

tamanaos *n.* See **tamanawous.**

tamanawous [tə'mɑnəwəs] *n.* [< Chinook Jargon *ta-mah-no-us* magic, luck, shaman, anything supernatural, prob. < Interior Salish] *Pacific*

Coast See **medicine-man** (def. 1a). Also spelled *tamanaos.*
1862 MAYNE *Four Years in B.C.* 262: He was communing with the "To-man-na-was" or familiar spirit. *c*1865 (1960) CRONIN *Cross* 126: . . . It was a favourable time to show these Indians that I did not fear them, nor their tamanaos (witch doctors). . . . **1956** RELANDER *Drummers* 142: Smohalla—seer . . . medicine man or tamanawous—proved to be a rather undersized Indian. . . .

tamarac(k) *v. Informal* **tamarac(k) 'er down,** dance with great gusto.
1961 PRICE & KENNEDY *Renfrew* 50: . . . on a Saturday night . . . the lads would "tamarac 'er down" on the old pine floor. **1964** *Cdn Geog.Jnl* Feb. 66/1: Yet on Saturday nights the gay spirit of the French Canadian or Irish lumberjack would forget the toil of the week and "tamarac 'er down" to the music of fiddles, mouth organs or bones.

tamarack ['tæməræk] *n.* [< Algonk. cf. *hackmatack*] **1** the larch, especially *Larix laricina.* See also **hackmatack.**
1815 BOUCHETTE *Lower Canada* 260: On the north-west and north-east sides are found some swamps, abundantly covered with . . . tamarack. . . . **1873** (1962) WINSLOW-SPRAGGE *G.M.Dawson* 69: This was a regular muskeg covered with wiry grass and moss, with small groves of tamerac here and there. **1963** *Maclean's* 16 Nov. 57/1: . . . in autumn the green of the spruces . . . is gently tinted by the yellowing tamaracks.
2 the wood of the larch.
1828 *Brockville Gaz.* (U.C.) 19 Sep. 3/4: Wanted, 500 Cords Hemlock, Tamarac, or Dry white Pine Wood. **1953** BANFILL *Lab.Nurse* 73: Outside, I found some green, wet tamarack which smouldered, then caught to a blaze.

tamarack muskeg or **swamp** a low-lying wet tract where tamarack flourish.
1831 *Trans.Lit.& Hist.Soc.Que.* II 295: A still channell . . . winds for a mile or two through a tamarac swamp. . . . **1943** MILLER *Lone Woodsman* 65: This valley was filled with a black spruce and tamarack swamp. **1956** KEMP *Northern Trader* 191: The whole river there was grass-lined and swampy, with a big tamarack muskeg stretching away to the north.

tandem *n.* **1** *Hist.* See **tandem sleigh.**
1846 (1927) DICKIE *How Canada Grew Up* 190: There was a very gay muster of carioles; some tandems with showy robes and ornamental harness; handsome family conveyances; snug little sleighs, very low and narrow, for two people. . . . **1923** SCOTT *Witching of Elspie* 209: . . . Mrs. Bagg was convinced that she saw Captain Sabervois' tandem prancing through the street. . . .
2 See **tandem hitch.**

tandem hitch *Esp.North* a method of harnessing sled-dogs in single file, used in country where there are obstructions, as in the bush. See also **single-line hitching** and **trapper hitch.** Cp. **fan hitch** and **Nome hitch.**
1928 WALDEN *Dog-Puncher* 34: A freight team was harnessed single file in what is now called the "tandem hitch". . . . **1936** *Beaver* Mar. 39/2: This arrangement is known as "the fan" in contradistinction to the method of single file hitch used in the forest and referred to as "the tandem."

The tandem hitch

tandem sleigh *Hist.* a two-seater pleasure sleigh pulled by two horses hitched in single file. See also **tandem** (def. 1). Cp. **sulky sleigh.**
1828 (1830) MOORSOM *Letters N.S.* 105: One of my brother officers was lately passing in his tandem-sleigh . . . when a youngster . . . dashed between the legs of the leader, but luckily without doing or receiving any injury. **1955** COLLARD *Cdn Yesterdays* 134: . . . he arrived at a remote mission in a tandem sleigh, nearly buried in coverings and with his wife's "cloud" or scarf wrapped around his face as a respirator.

tanky ['tæŋki] *n. West, Hist.* the man in charge of the steam engine and team in a steam-threshing crew.
1965 SHEPHERD *West of Yesterday* 55: Shortly after 1910, the steam threshing outfit began to find its rule challenged by the newer and smaller gasoline threshing outfits. These could be operated by a combined engineer-separator man. This did away with the wages of a separator man, the tanky and his team.

tanley *n. North, Obs.* See quote.
1879 ROBINSON *Great Fur Land* 126: . . . the steersman occupies the stern-sheets, while the crew by arranging the mast and oars lengthwise over the boat, and stretching oil-clothes over the framework so formed, turn the vessel into one long, snug tent in which they can rest in comfort. This device is called a "tanley," the word being corrupted from the French, "tendre-le."

tapis ['tæpi] *n.* [< Cdn F < F "carpet, rug"] *North* a blanket worn by sled-dogs.
1896 RUSSELL *Far North* 16: The collars are surmounted by variegated pompons and the dog blankets or tapis, are elaborately beaded or embroidered. **1908** MAIR *Mackenzie Basin* 187: The dogs were also dressed with worsted or silk-fringed tapis of fine cloth, richly braided and embroidered, and banded with brass or silver-plated round bells. **1938** GODSELL *Red Hunters* 36: Within the warehouse were piled furs . . . and the usual assortment of carrioles, toboggans, dog harness and beaded tapis.

tarboggin *n.* See **toboggan.**

tar sands See **Alberta tar sands.** Also *tar sand-bed.*
1897 TYRRELL *Sub-Arctics* 36: Just at this place commence the wonderful tar sand-beds of the Athabasca, extending over an enormous area. **1905** WIGHTMAN *Our Cdn Heritage* 144: The remarkable tar sands, lignite beds and gas deposits of Athabasca give promise of wondrous richness when fully developed. . . . **1964** *Calgary Herald* 22 Feb. 16/7: I'll bet, unless you are closely associated with the tar sands of northern Alberta, you have all sorts of preconceived idea[s] of this natural phenomenon—mostly wrong.

Taskatoohawin *n. Obs.* See **Saskatchewan.**

taureau ['tɔro] *n.* [< Cdn F < F "bull"] *Fur Trade, Hist.* **1** a strong bag made of buffalo

rawhide sewn hair side out, used as a container for
90 pounds of pemmican (def. 1). See also **bag**
(def. 1) and **pemmican bag**.

775 **tax-sharing agreement
tea plant**

1794 (1889) MACDONELL *Journal* 276: I cut off 20 sacks
or *taureux* to put pemican in, and gave them to Minie
to sew. **1944** *Beaver* Dec. 16/2: These sacks are known
as *taureaux* (*bulls*) or pemmicans. **1951** O'MEARA *Grand
Portage* 116: The pemmican [is] mixed and stored in
heavy taureaux. . . .

2 the bag and its contents. See also **bag** (def. 2) and
pemmican (def. 2a).
1795 (1889) MACDONELL *Journal* 294: Started them for
the Forks with 138-137 taureaux of pemican.
1860 *Nor'Wester* (R.R.S.) 15 Nov. 3/3: The grease is
ladled out onto the buffalo-skin, and meat and grease
being thoroughly incorporated [it] is all shovelled into
the bag, pressed down, sewn up, and the "Taureau" is
made. **1890** *Trans.Roy.Soc.Can.* VIII 2 104: A sack or
"toreau" of pemmican, as it was called, consisted of
nearly equal quantities of tallow and dried meat, the
latter being pounded on the bull hides with stone
hammers, axe heads or flails.

3 See **pemmican** (def. 1).
1807 (1889) WENTZEL *Letters* 90: This is our staple article
of provisions when travelling, it is called *taureau* or
Pimecan. **1821** (1938) SIMPSON *Athabasca Jnl* 278: . . . it
may be well to have the Toreau in store.
1927 WOOLLACOTT *Mackenzie* 52n: It [pemmican] was
a staple food among the fur-traders on long journeys,
when fish, fresh, dried, or frozen, or game could not be
had. Also known as "taureaux."

tax-sharing agreement See **equalization**.
1961 *Edmonton Jnl* 4 Aug. 5/1: He rejected demands of
three premiers for one more federal-provincial
conference before new tax-sharing agreements go into
effect.

tea-bag *n.* a bag for carrying provisions; a grub-
bag, *q.v.*
1896 RUSSELL *Far North* 161: If a crooked knife, a tea
bag, or anything that is in the heap is needed, everything
is tumbled about until it is found. **1937** CONIBEAR
Northland Footprints xii: . . . give him a large piece of
bannock from your tea-bag. . . .

teaberry *n.* See **wintergreen**.
1796 (1911) SIMCOE *Diary* 335: Rode very pleasantly
through the pine plains; gathered tea berries.
1861 SUTHERLAND *Geography P.E.I.* 56: To this family
belong the Cranberry, red and grey; the Blue berry;
the Teaberry; the Whortleberry. **1958** *Edmonton Jnl*
7 Aug. 4/3: . . . we knew when it was time to go to the
swamp for handfuls of dainty pink Mayflowers and
taste-treats of the sharp tea-berries.

tea bross [< Scottish *brose* oatmeal seasoned with
salt and butter and moistened with hot water or
milk] See quote. Cp. **brewis**.
1965 *Globe and Mail* (Toronto) 26 May 3/7: Nobody is
starving in the village across Store Creek, although the
poorer Indians are eating bannock (flour-and-water
pancakes) and drinking tea bross (tea broth with lard,
oatmeal and sugar) while whites eat steak and bacon
and eggs.

tea-dance *n. Northwest* a social gathering held by
Indians, so called because in the early days the
Hudson's Bay Company contributed tea, bannock,
etc., the dance itself being a kind of single-file
stomp done to the beat of skin drums. See also
tea revel. Cp. **potlatch**, *n.* (def. 2b).

1885 GOWANLOCK & DELANEY *Camp of Big Bear* 119:
When the Indians held their tea-dances or pow-wows
in times of peace, the squaws and children joined in and
it was a very amusing sight to watch them. **1923** WALDO
Down Mackenzie 219: The Mackenzie River tea-dance
is not one of your penurious, parsimonious affairs at
which wafers are brought in on a tray and the tipple is
served by the thimbleful. **1929** JEFFERSON *Saskatchewan*
33: Tea is brewed in an immense kettle, as strong as
circumstances warrant, and "painkiller," or in default
of that luxury, chewing tobacco, stirred thoroughly
through it. This concoction is handed round to the
company in the cups with which each comes provided.
This dance, the white men call "The Tea Dance". . . .
1940 *Beaver* Sep. 46/1: The tea dance was nothing more
than an excuse for men and women to get the best of
taboos: during a tea dance, one could talk to the other
fellow's wife. . . . **1965** *News of the North* 29 July 5/4:
The ceremony was marked by a tea dance, in which
everyone joined. . . .

tea-dance *v.* take part in a tea-dance, *q.v.*
1964 *Camsell Arrow* Summer 60/4: High point of their
four months in the north was the invitation to join the
Indians "tea dancing" Anne said.

tea-fee *n. Lab.* a person's share of tea from a
communal container.
1963 *Maclean's* 16 Nov. 60/2: When we broke for
lunch, they'd scoop the tins into the drum to get their
own tea-fee, or whatever it was.

team-boat† *n. Obs.* **1**† See **horse-boat**.
1825 *Novascotian* (Halifax) 20 July 237/1: Two boys
were brought up to this office on Thursday last, and
bound over to the sessions, for having exposed
themselves improperly the night previous on the Market
slip, while the Team boat was approaching the wharf.
1835 (1838) HALIBURTON *Sam Slick* 11: . . . like a horse
that refused to draw, he is put into the team boat. He
finds some afore him, and others behind him; he must
either draw or be dragged to death.

2 See quote.
1950 BIRD *This is N.S.* 196: This type of ferry passed
from the scene in 1816, being supplanted by a team-boat
—two boats united by a platform with a paddle wheel
between.

teamster *n.* **1**† a driver of a team of horses or other
draft animals.
1807 *U.C.Gaz.* (York [Toronto]) 28 Feb. 3/2: Tailors,
tinkers, parsons, pedlars, Sawyers, teamsters, smiths
and fiddlers, Rich and poor, or high and low, Hop, and
swear—for want of snow. **1964** *Outdoorsman* III 1/3:
One may see a visitor with a misty look in his eye; an
old blacksmith, top loader, barn boss, teamster, cookie
or river hog who has returned to a fleeting glimpse of an
era long gone by.

2 *Obs.* one of a team of sled-dogs.
1860 *Nor'Wester* (R.R.S.) 14 Mar. 4/5: Here I had to
make an exchange of dogs, my teamsters from
Athabaska being used up.

tea muskeg *North* See **muskeg tea**.

tea plant *Obs.* See **Labrador tea** (def. 1a).
1853 REID *Young Voyageurs* 208: "You may try [to
draw some birch sap for sweetening] while I go in
search of the tea-plant."

tea revel *Obs.* See **tea-dance**.
1895 SOMERSET *Muskeg* 1: Often above the roaring of
the rain we heard the beating of the tom-tom through
the night, while the Indians gambled or held a tea revel.

tea wheat *Obs.* See 1832 quote.
1830 *P.E.I.Register* (Charlottetown) 23 Feb. 1/2: The
Committee received from Miramichi . . . fifteen
bushels of the celebrated Tea Wheat. . . . **1832** MCGREGOR
Brit.Amer. II 315: Some years ago, a person, on opening
a chest of tea, found in one corner a small quantity of
wheat; how it got there no one can tell. Whether in
London, on the chest being opened by the East Indian
Company, or in China, is equally uncertain; but the
seed was sown in New Brunswick; it grew and
flourished better than any previously sown. The produce
was preserved, sown again, and multiplied so rapidly,
that it is, at the present time, the kind of seed-wheat
generally sown, and known by the distinction of "tea
wheat."

teepee† ['tipi] *n.* [< Siouan *ti* dwell + *pi* used for;
Assiniboine *tipi*] a conical tent in which poles
spread at the ground and joined at the top are
covered with buffalo hide (originally), canvas, etc.,
used primarily by the Plains Indians. See also
skin lodge and **wigwam** (def. 1b). Also spelled
tepee and *tipi*.
1743 (1949) ISHAM *Observations* 45: a tent Built ti pee
[Assiniboine] **1870** *Huron Expositor* (Seaforth, Ont.)
4 Mar. 2/3: One "buck" was found alive afterwards, in
his tepee, who had killed two of his squaws with his
knife and piled their dead bodies over himself to hide
him. **1914** DOUGLAS *Lands Forlorn* 27: Every teepee had
three or four dogs stretched out in the coolest place or
prowling around looking for something to chew, or
else the chance of a fight. **1963** *Beaver* Summer 33/2:
The traditional buffalo-hide covering of tipis has given
way to canvas but there is still much work in making
them.

teepee pole one of the poles used in making the
framework of a teepee, *q.v.* Also *teepee tent pole*.
1897 TYRRELL *Sub-Arctics* 68: But in this we were
disappointed, and, instead of Indians, found only old
forsaken "tepee" poles and blackened fire-places.
1957 *Beaver* Autumn 43/1: Not a person had intruded
during the interval, not even Indians, and everything
was unchanged, even to the teepee poles that still rested
against the spruce trees as we had left them.
1965 *Islander* 14 Feb. 5/1: Three poles about three
inches in diameter at the butt and, say, eight feet long
are set up like teepee-tent poles to form a tripod,
securely tied together at the apex.

teepee ring *West* See **tent ring**.
1956 LEECHMAN *Native Tribes* 10: We find . . . on the
prairies, tipi rings, circles of stones that once were used
to hold down the edges of the skin tents.
1965 WORMINGTON & FORBIS *Archaeology Alta* 195: The
number of tipi rings found in some areas also suggests
the presence of a fairly large population.

telegraph *v.* [< Cdn F *télégrapher*] *Que., Slang*
vote more than once in an election by impersonating
other voters, usually ones who are dead, sick, late,
or away from home. See also **telegraphed,
telegrapher,** and **telegraphing**.
1962 *Weekend Mag.* 9 June 15/1: A Montreal M.P.

tells of being approached recently by a man who
offered to telegraph votes for him "I voted against you
seven times in the last election . . . let me even it up this
time."

telegraphed *adj. Que., Slang* of votes, cast
illegally by impersonation. See also **telegraph**.
1961 *Globe and Mail* (Toronto) 13 Apr. 10/1: The
disqualification part of the case hangs on 78 alleged
telegraphed votes passed on behalf of Mr. Chartrand in
the last provincial election.

telegrapher *n.* [< Cdn F *télégraphe*] *Que., Slang*
a person who telegraphs, *q.v.*
[**1957** *Le Devoir* (Montreal) 31 Oct. 1/2: On rapporte
que dans Notre-Dame-de-Grâce les "télégraphes" ont
été très nombreux et des plus discrets.] **1960** *Maclean's*
13 Aug. 2/1: There was a way to hand the slip to the
DRO . . . so he would know we were "telegraphers."
1962 *Weekend Mag.* 9 June 16/1: In an Eastern
constituency a candidate once lent his fur coat to a
decrepit telegrapher so that he might look more like
the prosperous man he was impersonating.

telegraphing *n.* [< *telegraph*, v.] *Que., Slang*
See 1960 quote. See also **telegraph**.
1960 *Maclean's* 13 Aug. 271: What the red-shirted
young man was telling us was how to impersonate
legitimate voters—a practice known as telegraphing in
Montreal politics. . . . **1963** *Gazette* (Montreal) 15 June
14/4: The slips being done away with are those given to
a voter by the enumerator which must be presented at
the poll on election day. Their main purpose is to
prevent the telegraphing of votes.

telephone room *Slang* a room serving as a
temporary headquarters of persons selling
dubious or worthless stocks by telephone; bucket
shop.
1959 *Kingston Whig-Standard* (Ont.) 2 May 11/3:
eventually the Ontario Securities Commission drove
most of the telephone room boys out of Ontario—but
like gophers they popped up elsewhere. . . .

temperance beer *Hist.* non-alcoholic beer or,
sometimes, near beer.
1882 *Edmonton Bull.* 8 July 4/1: temperance beer.
1916 *Eye Opener* (Calgary) 8 July 3/2: Sold honestly
and in an open and aboveboard manner, temperance
beer will just fill the bill nicely and keep the boys
satisfied and contented.

temperance colony *Hist.* one of a number of
colonies established in the Northwest Territories
(def. 1b) by persons subscribing to total
abstinence.
1882 *Edmonton Bull.* 26 Aug. 2/2: Part of the
Temperance Colony for the South Branch has arrived
in Winnipeg. **1883** *Prince Albert Times* (Sask.) 21 Mar.
1/5: A large number of the residents of Yorkville, Ont.,
leave for the North West this month, a few for the
temperance colony, and others the pioneer company
party of the Saskatchewan Homestead Company.
1927 *Cdn North-West Hist.Soc.Pubs* I iii 25:
Saskatoon may claim its origin in a temperance colony
with John N. Lake as its leader.

tenant-elector *n. B.C.* a rent-paying resident
having the right to vote in municipal elections.
1958 *Citizen* 18 Sep. 2/3: Tenant-electors and
resident-electors have until September 30 to get on the
1959 voters' list, Reeve Sam McCrea pointed out today.
1958 *B.C.Federation of Labour*, 3rd Convention (Oct.
21-24) Res. 37: . . . tenant electors and resident electors

desiring to have their names entered on Municipal
Voters Lists must make statutory declaration. . . .

777

tenas
terminal

tenas ['tɛnæs] *n.* [< adj.] *Lumbering, B.C.*
See **straw-line.**
1942 HAIG-BROWN *Timber* 254: [The straw line is also]
called "tenas" from the chinook word meaning "little."

tenas ['tɛnæs] *adj.* [< Chinook Jargon ? <
Nootka *t'an'as* child, baby] *Pacific Coast* small;
little. See also **tenas-man.**
1922 JOHNSON *Legends* 66: His tribes-people called him
the Tenas Tyee (little Chief) and they loved him.
1927 PHILIP *Painted Cliff* 25: We'll build a tenas cabin/
On the shore of Canim Lake.

tenas-man ['tɛnæs,mæn] *n.* [< Chinook Jargon
tenas little + E *man*] *Pacific Coast* a youth; boy. See
also **tenas,** *adj.*
1870 *Mainland Guardian* (New Westminster, B.C.)
16 Apr. 3/3: In the crowd behind are a few dusky
natives in Boston clothing, while there trip about a few
Tenass-men, some with the remains of an old coat and
beaver hat, and some [in] almost naked savagedom.
1913 ROTHROCK *Collin's Overland Exped.*: August 10,
having engaged three Indians and a "tenas man" to
help up the . . . rapids, we started for Lake Trembleur.

tenderfoot† *n.* -**foots** or -**feet.** *Orig.West* See
cheechako, *n.*
1880 *Great Western Railway Advert.Bull.* 26 May 1/8:
He was evidently a "tenderfoot," but . . . he made a
strong effort to appear as if he had been born with a
contempt for civilization. . . . **1909** CAMERON *New North*
50: . . . the Indians still point out . . . the site . . . where
Sergeant Anderson rescued a dozen tenderfoots from
drowning. **1959** SHIPLEY *Scarlet Lily* 16: He . . . earned
for himself among half-breeds and Indians . . . epithets
reserved for blundering tenderfeet.

tend hook *Lumbering* direct the hooking up of
logs for ground-lead or high-line skidding, usually
a foreman's responsibility. See also **hooktender.**
1908 GRAINGER *Woodsmen* 21: . . . I was tending hook
there. . . . **1918** MACKAY *Trench and Trail* 112: I can
"team" or "tend de hook,"/I can "bark" or "fall" or
"buck". . . . **1942** HAIG-BROWN *Timber* 50: Dann's
tending hook and Jerry's slinging rigging for him.

tent *n.* **1** *Hist.* See 1932 quote. See also **lodge**
(def. 2b) and **wigwam** (def. 2).
1689 (1929) KELSEY *Papers* 29: Rain'd very hard so
came to & made a tent of moss. . . . **1783** (1934) *Beaver*
Mar. 25/1: Made a Platform and Erected another [log]
Tent which we covered over with feather Edge boards
then stowed the Furs in the inside of all & came away
with Heavy Hearts. **1800** (1897) COUES *New Light* I 100:
To Indians came . . . to ask me to send a large canoe for
what they had collected at their tents. **1932** KENNEY
Ft Churchill 117: . . . "tent" in the parlance of Hudson's
Bay journals was applied to a small hut or shanty of any
construction. . . .
2 *Hist.* a family group or household of Indians or,
less often, Eskimos. See also **lodge** (def. 3).
1690 (1929) KELSEY *Papers* 2: Some of the home Indians
came upon their track And for old grudges & their
minds to fill Came up with them Six tents of w^ch, they
kill'd. **1795** (1911) HEARNE *Journey* 148: The three men
who had been sent as spies met us on their return, and
informed my companions that five tents of Esquimaux
were on the west side of the river. **1862** *Nor'Wester*
(R.R.S.) 9 Oct. 3/1: Here they fell in with a large

body of Assiniboines—60 tents of them—and had to
manage with great skill and courage to escape being
plundered or killed. **1963** MACLEOD & MORTON *Cuthbert
Grant* 79: . . . as there were on the track some thirty
tents of Indians who were likely to give trouble, Grant
volunteered to act as guide.

Tenth Province Newfoundland, so called because
it was the tenth province to join Confederation,
doing so in 1949.
1955 *Evening Telegram* (St. John's) 12 Mar. 19/4: The
Newfoundlanders won one game in the championships
—their 3rd win, the Tenth Province entered its first
team in 1950.

tent peg *West, Slang, Obs.* See quote.
1963 *Herald Mag.* 21 Dec. 7/1: . . . some of the old
Western slang is worth repeating . . . "tent pegs,"
(frozen beef steak ribs); "baked wind pills," (baked
beans); "paperweights," (hot biscuits); "keg angels,"
(whisky traders).

tent ring a ring of stones used to hold down a tent,
such as a teepee or tupek, often remaining in
position after the tent has been removed. See also
Indian teepee ring, teepee ring, and **tupek ring.**
1945 *Beaver* Mar. 39/2: When a tent is struck and the
owner moves on, the ring of stones which held it down
lies there for years to come, and these tent rings are
found today scattered even more widely and
plentifully than are the old igloos. **1955** JENNESS *Indians
of Can.* 320: Men and women who had been prominent
in their communities, they [Blackfoot] laid out on
hill-tops inside their tents, after weighing down the
edges of the skin with stones. Many of the "tent rings"
still visible on the prairies are, therefore, burial-rings,
not the sites of ancient camps. **1958** *Evening Telegram*
(St. John's) 29 Apr. 13/3: My large tent needed more
rocks to hold it down firmly that the usual tent ring
supplied. **1967** *Cdn Geog.Jnl* Mar. 85/1: In the valleys
of the Dubawnt . . . and Back Rivers . . . only their
stone tent rings remain, mute witnesses to the fact that
people once lived there.

tent-town *n.* a town of tents and other temporary
shelters such as one might find near a gold strike.
1923 STEELE *Spirit-of-Iron* 108: So he came in touch
with all the vice, wretchedness and stark tragedy
abounding in the tent-towns and construction camps.
1965 *Globe and Mail* (Toronto) 26 May 3/2: . . . near
this town of acculturated Indians there is a tent-town
of marginal people and transients.

tepe or **tepee** *n.* See **teepee.**

tepee² ['tipi] *adj.* [< Esk. *tipi*] *Arctic* strong
smelling; rotten.
1882 GILDER *Schwatka's Search* 33: I became so faint
for the want of food that I had to get some tepee walrus
from the natives, and I ate it with a keen appetite.

terminal *n.* **1** *Obs.* a final examination.
1896 ROBERTS *Camp-Fire* 260: This examination was
open only to those declaring themselves competitors
for the scholarship. It was generally expected throughout
the college that the winner would be Bert Knollys, who,
without effort, had gained a slight lead in the first two
terminals, and whose ability in classics was
unquestioned.

2 See quote.
1959 *Globe and Mail* (Toronto) 4 May 10/2: A terminal is a warehouse, in fact a deluxe warehouse.

terminal elevator a large grain elevator which serves as a storage bin at a trans-shipping point where carloads of grain are received from country elevators, *q.v.* See picture at **elevator.** See also **grain elevator** (def. 2).
1921 *Dalhousie Rev.* I 237: These two farmers' companies own and operate 632 country elevators and 4 terminal elevators at the head of the lakes.
1924 *Beaver* Mar. 212: The establishment this year of the big terminal elevator in Edmonton is proof of this. . . . **1953** LEBOURDAIS *Nation of North* 124: By 1916, the farmers of the three prairie provinces owned over 500 country elevators, in addition to terminal elevators at the head of the lakes with a capacity of 3,000,000 bushels.

tern schooner *Maritimes* a three-masted schooner, often used for fishing in former times.
1923 MACMECHAN *Sagas of Sea* 144: The Parks are a substantial, sea-faring clan, fishermen, masters of tern schooners, owners of large comfortable houses.
1954 BRUCE *Channel Shore* 87: The story of . . . Rob Currie, who had sailed his tern schooner down the Channel, long and long ago. . . .

Terra Nova [< L] *Hist.* Newfoundland.
1576 (1889) HAKLUYT *Voyages* XII 44: But no such conflicts of streames, or contrary courses are found about any part of Labrador, or Terra noua, as witnesse our yeerely fishers, and other saylers that way.
1902 *U of T Stud.Hist.& Econ.* II 11: St. John's, Newfoundland, is policed by the "Terra Nova Constabulary," a body controlled by the general government. **1933** GREENE *Wooden Walls* 37: . . . the hardy sons of Terra Nova . . . every Spring beseech the Jowlers of the Fleet for a berth to the Ice. . . .

Terre Neuve *French, Hist.* See **Terra Nova.**
1955 ENGLISH *Newfoundland* 26/1: In the month of June, 1534, Jacques Cartier of St. Malo explored the west coast of Terre Neuve.

terrier *n.* [< Cdn F < F *terrier* of earth] *Obs.* See **bank beaver.**
1784 PENNANT *Arctic Zoology* 103: There is a variety of the beaver kind, which wants either the sagacity or the industry of the others, in forming dams and houses. These are called *Terriers.* They burrow in the banks of rivers, and make their holes beneath the freezing depth of the water, and work upwards for a great number of feet. Beavers which escape the destruction of a community, are supposed to become Terriers.
1823 *Canadian Mag.* I 494: These solitary beavers are called terriers. They are easily distinguished by their dirty tattered robe; for the hair of the back is rubbed off by the friction of the earth. **1824** (1955) BLACK *Journal* 152: Another Beaver Lodge at this place but these Lodges contain only 1 or 2 Beavers & appear to be Terrines or Terriers i.e. having only a hole or Burrow in a Bank. . . .

territorial *adj.* of or having to do with the territories, *q.v.*
1953 MOON *Saskatchewan* 18: [Dec. 18, 1901] That day the Territorial Grain Growers' Association was formed.

1958 *Edmonton Jnl* 24 June 1/6: Appointment of . . . as judge of the Territorial Court of the Yukon was announced in Ottawa Tuesday. **1963** MORTON *Kingdom of Canada* 351: Beyond the boundaries of Manitoba lay the North-West Territory, governed by the Lieutenant-Governor of Manitoba with the aid of a territorial council, and from 1873 under the new Department of the Interior.

territory *n.* (*usually plural*) one of the vast, sparsely populated regions which are part of Canada but lack the status of provinces, being administered by the federal government through a council, a term used in the last century of the extensive lands between Ontario and British Columbia, but especially of the prairies during the settlement period, and nowadays of the Yukon Territory, *q.v.*, and the Northwest Territories (def. 2b).
1881 *Edmonton Bull.* 14 Feb. 2/1: In other parts of the Territories in winter every wind is cold but the coldest of all is that from the west, which brings the blizzards —the terror of the plains. **1890** *Grip* (Toronto) 15 Feb. 98/1: Two official languages [would be] "as useless as two tongues on a North-West cart." And yet the vehicle in question requires two tongues just as much as the Governmental Machine of the Territories does. **1957** *Aklavik Jnl* Mar. 2: As the white men advanced they brought their law with them and imposed it on the natives of the Territories. **1966** *Globe and Mail* (Toronto) 26 Aug. 8/2: [She] will establish the first residence . . . operated for girls in the territories.

tête-de-femme [tɛːt də'fam] *n.* [< Cdn F *tête-de-femme* < F "woman's head"] *Northwest* See **niggerhead** (def. 2a). See also **woman's head.**
1800 (1897) COUES *New Light* I 131: We took our course directly homeward . . . passing through trembliers, willows, tetes-de-femme, and small meadows. **1824** (1955) BLACK *Journal* 131: The valley and sides of the mountain as usual is soaked in snow water & from the number of knotty tufts of matted Grass & Moss Roots, the Canadians call Tetes de fammes is fatiguing to walk in. . . . **1890** *Trans.Roy.Soc. Can.* VIII 2 98: These wallows are sometimes confounded by new-comers with the têtes des femmes as they are called, or rough depression and hummocks caused by fire penetrating and interlacing the sod.
1955 BARNETT *World We Live In* 215/2: "Têtes de femmes"[,] small grass-covered hummocks of frozen earth, are often found in densely vegetated marshes in the north.

tettymeg *n.* See **titimeg.**

teyma *n.* See **tima.**

thaw-up *n.* See **break-up** (def. 2).
1925 GROVE *Settlers* 63: Winter went by; the thaw-up came. Breaking and seeding, on a share of the crop.

Theiscatchiwan *n. Obs.* See **Saskatchewan.**

thickwood(s) *n.* (*usually plural*) *Hist.* See **strong wood.**
1754 (1907) HENDAY *Journal* 343: Strong gale with Snow and Sleet. Obliged to move into thick woods.
*a*1855 (1956) ROSS *Fur Hunters* 137: All had now retreated for shelter to the thick woods, so that we were more than once on short allowance and on these emergencies had to regale ourselves on wolf's flesh. . . . **1870** *Cdn Illust.News* (Montreal) 7 May 426/1: Ten year's residence in the North-West . . . has made him at home . . . on snow-shoes, in the thickwood, or the boundless prairie. . . . **1957** HARRIS *Cariboo Trail* 137:

The gold-seekers had arrived at the fort after making their way through the thickwoods and the wild Blackfoot hills. . . .

thickwood buffalo See **wood buffalo**.
1890 MAIR *American Bison* 95: The thickwood buffalo . . . differs strikingly from all the others though some writers seem to think it is the offspring of animals detached by accident from the great herds.

thickwood country *Hist.* heavily forested country. See also **strong wood** and **thickwood**.
1825 (1931) SIMPSON *Fur Trade* 159: The Muschetoes . . . are of a different kind to those found in the Thick Wood & Swamps countries . . . their Sting occasioning inflammation & Swelling. **1861** (1863) PALLISER *Journals* 10: The lower or main Saskatchewan river . . . flows entirely through thickwood country, which is often low and marshy. . . .

thistle twist tobacco *Fur Trade, Hist.* See **niggerhead tobacco**.
1952 *Beaver* Dec. 28/2: Thistle Twist tobacco, commonly known as "niggerhead," was also widely used [c1905], sometimes being mixed with the bark of the red willow which the Indians called *kinnikkinick*.

thitabebee *n.* [imitative] *Obs.* the chickadee, genus *Parus* (or *Penthestes*).
1838 TRAILL *Backwoods* 173: Nor are our Canadian songsters mute: the cheerful melody of the robin, the bugle-song of the black bird and thrush, the weak but not unpleasing call of the little bird called Thitabebee, and a wren, whose note is sweet and thrilling, fill our woods.

Thompsonite *n.* a Social Credit member of the House of Commons supporting Robert Thompson, former leader of the non-Quebec wing of the party. Cp. **Caouettiste**.
1965 *Globe Mag.* 8/2: . . . two of these so-called Thompsonites later bolted to join the Progressive Conservative party. . . .

Thor [θɔr] *n.* [< Scand. god of thunder and war] *West, Slang* See quote.
1961 *Maclean's* 29 July 36/1: ". . . They've got a new drink now on the west coast called Thor—fifty percent rubby-dub and fifty percent B.C. Vin Supreme. A gallon of wine and two bottles of rubby and you can throw a party in the jungles that'll last all night."

Thousand Islands a widely known vacation region between Brockville and Kingston in the St. Lawrence River.
1785 (1943) HUNTER *Diary* 80: They may well call this place the Thousand Islands for the river is full of them and many of them the most beautiful objects that it is possible to imagine. *a*1820 (1838) HEAD *Forest Scenes* 343: We had a pleasant voyage down this noble river, where the "Thousand Islands" present a beautifully romantic prospect of land and water. . . . **1923** MACMECHAN *Sagas of Sea* 5: You must recall the camp on the headland, the run down the Bay of Quinte, the thridding [threading] of the Thousand Islands and what we found there. **1966** *Kingston Whig-Standard* (Ont.) 20 Aug. 6/1: Business in the 1000 islands area has picked up again.

three-dollar bill 1 *Obs.* a provincial bank-note, *q.v.*, worth three dollars.
1813 *Kingston Gaz.* (U.C.) 7 Sep. 3/3: . . . the above sum [shall] be struck off in the following manner, viz. The sum of twelve hundred & fifty pounds in three

Dollar Bills, two hundred and fifty pounds in Dollar bills, and two hundred and fifty pounds in half Dollar Bills.
2 *Figurative use* (in expressions indicating that something is non-existent, scarce, or spurious).
1953 *North Star* (Yellowknife) Mar. 2/1: Then there is the abolition of radio license fees; but radio licenses are as scarce as $3 bills in the Territories! **1967** *Globe and Mail* (Toronto) 17 Apr. 6/1: "[The] remark [made] recently by Ralph Cowan, 'a phony three dollar bill,' in connection with this being a bilingual country . . . is true."

three-point blanket *Hist.* a grade of point blanket, *q.v.*
1798-1800 (1935) *Trans.Roy.Soc.Can.* III 2 46: The Indian trade articles include . . . ceintures, three-point blankets. . . . **1878** *Sask.Herald* (Battleford, N.W.T.) 7 Oct. 1/3: Good three-point blankets stood steadily at one dollar apiece. **1948** *Beaver* June 21/2: The simple voyageur Leger lost only a three-point blanket . . . a portage strap, a pair of French shoes, and a cotton shirt.

Three Rivers stove *Obs.* a kind of cooking stove manufactured at Three Rivers, Quebec, from local bog-iron.
1835 *Dundas Wkly Post* 1 Dec. 3/3: Three Rivers Stoves [are] so well known to be superior to the imported Stoves, that they command better prices, and the Canadians in Lower Canada give them a preference to any other. **1840** *Montreal Transcript* 29 Sep. 259/3: Sales by Auction . . . 10 Cooking stoves, 10 do do Three Rivers. **1841** *Journal and Express* (Hamilton, C.W.) 3 Feb. 2/2: The Subscriber has just received Single and Double Three Rivers Stoves, assorted size; which he offers for sale at reasonable prices.

throater *n. Maritimes* See 1950 quote. See also **cut-throat** (def. 1).
1923 MACMECHAN *Sagas of Sea* 146: He had learned the fisherman's strenuous trade, as "flunkey," "trouter" [throater], "header". . . . **1950** CREIGHTON *Lunenburg County* 133: Boys of ten began as throaters, and then became headers, cutting the particular parts of the fish so designated. **1952** PUTNAM *Cdn Regions* 99/2: In addition to the dory-men, each vessel carries a captain, salter, throater, header and cook, a total complement of nineteen to twenty-five men.

throat log *Obs.* one of the principal pieces, the other being the neck log, *q.v.*, of a type of trap, or deadfall (def. 1), made of logs.
1743 (1949) ISHAM *Observations* 162: Take for this Log trap . . . a piece of wood on the front, which goes across and Serves as a throat Log—and a Long piece which goes on that which is called a neck Log. . . . **1784-1812** (1916) THOMPSON *Narrative* 49: For a Marten, a throat log, of about 4 feet . . . is first laid in the snow. . . .

Throne Speech See **Speech from the Throne**.
1955 *Toronto Dly Star* 2 Feb. 6/2: An experimental program for the treatment of drug addicts was announced in this year's Throne speech at the opening of the British Columbia legislature. **1963** *Globe and Mail* (Toronto) 18 May 9/1: Chief Justice Robert Taschereau read the Throne Speech in the absence of Governor General George Vanier, who is recovering from a mild heart attack.

through *n. Obs.* in clearing land, a parcel of one acre assigned to a crew of four choppers and a teamster, their responsibility being to log (def. 1) that area in a day.

1902 (1957) GUILLET *Valley of the Trent* 273: If . . . any gang should have fallen upon a piece of bad fortune in the way of an extra heavy "through" as the acre parcels were called, his more fortunate comrades as a rule assisted him to finish. Severe contests for who would have his "through" completed first often occurred, yet owing to difficulties in timber or the nature of the ground in the various "throughs" the best men and the best oxen did not in all cases succeed in being the first done.

throw *v.* lift a canoe from the ground, over the head, and onto the shoulders for portaging.
1963 *Canada Month* Nov. 23/2: . . . I was proud to demonstrate my ability still to "throw" a canoe.

throw a diamond hitch See **diamond hitch** (def. 2).

throw ice *North* See quote. Cp. **take.**
1910 SERVICE *Trail of '98* 337: I was just in time to see the last boat go out. Already the river was "throwing ice," and every day the jagged edges of it crept further towards midstream.

throw the hatchet to the sky *Obs.* in Indian parlance, wage total war.
1840 WILLIS *Cdn Scenery* I 16: Thus to throw up the hatchet, or to put on the great cauldron is to begin a war; to throw the hatchet to the sky, is to wage open and terrible war; to take off the cauldron, or to bury the hatchet is to make peace. . . .

thrum-cap ['θrʌm,kæp] *n.* [< *thrum cap* a cap of cloth embroidered with thrums (waste ends of the warp); see 1958 quote] *Esp.Atlantic Provinces, Obs.* (*except in place names*) a small island, especially one having a conical appearance with a tuft of trees in the centre; also a shoal of similar shape.
1832 BAILLIE *Acct of N.B.* 120: Opposite to this point an islet or thrum-cap, (as these are termed), was once considered available for the purpose of drawing fish. . . . *Ibid.*: Another thrum-cap island contiguous to the above is of no value whatever. **1934** MACMECHAN *Late Harvest* 4: And on the outer Thrum Cap shoal he ran her hard aground. **1958** *Names* Dec. 202: The toponymic frequency of thrumcap is due to the ubiquity of a type of headgear [worn] among sailors of the Maine and Canadian coasts a century and a half ago and the presence of certain islands resembling it in shape and appearance.

thunderbird *n.* **1 a.** a mythical bird which, according to the legends of many Indian peoples, created the thunder with its beating wings and the lightning with its flashing eyes. Cp. **hohoq.**
1878 (1926) MOSER *Reminiscences* 86: The noise of thunder is explained by the fact that the thunder-bird takes hold of a whale and in a struggle with the monster of the deep causes all thundering reports. **1929** MOBERLY *When Fur Was King* 202: I think, my nephew, that it must have been one of the holes of the big snake that feeds the Thunder Bird. **1959** *Native Voice* Jan. 7/2:

The legend of the Thunderbird was told to us.
1963 SYMONS *Many Trails* 150: [They] do not see the Thunder Bird . . . under whose wings the people tremble.

A carving of

a thunderbird

b. a representation or symbol of this mythical bird, commonly met with on the totem poles of Pacific Coast tribes, in designs on clothing, and in various art forms.
1958 *Native Voice* Sp.ed. 18/1: On top of this totem is perched the great Thunder-bird, having on his breast a man's face, denoting that these two mystic beings were interchangeable at will. **1964** LEE *Foods and Textiles* 287: The knitting [of the Cowichans] was beautifully patterned with thunderbirds and other designs. . . .

2 in Indian parlance, an airplane.
1936 (1955) STRINGER *Wife-Traders* 103: Few of them, he remembered, were familiar with the "thunder-bird" of the white man. **1956** GOWLAND *Sikanaska Trail* 172: ". . . Maybe Indian he have no automobile or thunderbird, but he go places faster than white man and still stop where he is."

thunderbird cape *Pacific Coast* See **button blanket.**
1964 *Canadian Wkly* 4-10 Jan. 9/3: He's also made a full-length thunderbird cape, in flaming scarlet and blue, studded with tiny mother-of-pearl buttons.

thunder-stick *n. Hist.* in Indian parlance, a pistol, musket, rifle, etc.
1965 *Cdn Geog.Jnl* Apr. 115/1: Long, long ago, according to the legend, many years before the white man came to shatter the silence of the wilderness with his thunder stick, a band of Indian huntsmen came upon a great animal foraging along the shore of a lake far to the north and west of the sweet-water sea that is now called Lake Superior.

Thursday-night soldier *Slang, Derog.* a member of the militia or reserve army, which usually parades one night a week.
1949 PETERSON *Chipmunk* 289: "Well, I'll be a son of a whore, what're you s'posed to be, a Thursday night soldier."

ticamang *n.* See **tickameg.**

ticcanagon, tickamegan, etc. *n.* See **tikinagan.**

tickameg ['tikə,mɛg] *n.* [< Algonk.: Cree *utikumāk*] *Hist.* See **whitefish.** See also **atikameg** and **titimeg.** Also spelled *tickomeg.*
1743 (1949) ISHAM *Observations* 169: Tickomegg which is like a herring is also very Numerious. . . . **1816** (1939) ROBERTSON *Correspondence* 94n: There is an excellent fishing Weir which supplies . . . a good number of Tickameg. **1963** STANLEY *Louis Riel* 18: Without doubt Louis shared in the . . . feasts of galettes, tickameg (whitefish), buffalo steaks and boiled tea. . . .

ticket (of location) *n. Hist.* See **location ticket** (def. 1).

1789 (1905) *Ont.Bur.Arch.Rep.* VIII 316: There being then no land Board instituted those tickets . . . to give the Settlers the satisfaction of knowing the number of their Lots. **1840** *Montreal Transcript* 24 Dec. 407/1: An assignment, or attempt to assign any ticket of location, will also be considered as a forfeiture of all right in the Locatee or Assignee. **1896** GOURLAY *Hist.Ottawa* 50: The Government gave them [in 1798] claims they called tickets, to land. . . . **1909** HUNTER *Simcoe County* I 51: Upon presenting a certificate of service from the head adjutant general, each claimant of this class became entitled to receive a ticket of location.

tickle ['tɪkəl] *n.* [perhaps < Brit. (western) dial. *stickle* rapids, riffle] *Atlantic Provinces* (*esp.Nfld*)
1 a. a narrow strait between an island and the mainland or, sometimes, between two islands. See also **tittle.**

1770 (1792) CARTWRIGHT *Journal* I 64: There is a narrow tickle of twenty yards, between this island and the continent; across which a net is fixed, to stop the seals from passing through. **1896** *Trans.Roy.Soc.Can.* II 2 210: Tickle [is used] at Miramichi, for a narrow passage between island and shore. **1907** MILLAIS *Newfoundland* 43: "It was moonlight, and a' travelled nine miles over pretty rotten stuff to the north island, and then nine miles more across the tickle to the next." **1962** *Time* (Cdn ed.) 12 Jan. 10/1: [The ferries] suspend operations when winter winds pack ice into the three-mile "tickle" between the island and the inner landing at Portugal Cove. **1966** *Weekend Mag.* 23 Apr. 2/2: . . . we complained bitterly that "our bonnies lay over the ocean," when we knew very well that they lived across the "tickle."

b. a narrow entrance into a harbor; sometimes, the narrows and the harbor together.

1842 BONNYCASTLE *Newfoundland* II 241: Tickle . . . often occurs in the Newfoundland charts, and means a small safe harbour—whence derived, I cannot say. **1891** PACKARD *Labrador Coast* 183: The best spots to dredge are the patches of shelly bottoms situated at the inner end of a "tickle" leading out from a deep harbor, where the tides and currents have no power. **1962** MOWAT *Black Joke* 41: The run through the narrow channel, or "tickle," out of Milltown Bay was fast and uneventful.

2 *North* See **lead,** *n.*

1908 LAUT *Conquest N.W.* I 53: Carried with the current southward from Greenland, sometimes slipping into the long "tickles" of water open between the floes, again watching their chance to follow the calm sea to the rear of some giant iceberg . . . *The Discovery* came to Ungava Bay, Labrador, in July.

tickle-ace *n. Nfld* the kittiwake, *Rissa tridactyla.*
1956 FAY *Life and Labour* 64: We walk gingerly between the nests, which are so close together that it is hard to avoid trampling on the eggs—of gannet, puffin, tar, tickleace (kittiwake) and small pigeon. **1965** *Nfld Qtly* Spring 12/1: The kittiwake, commonly called tickle-ace in Newfoundland is actually a medium-sized gull.

tickomeg *n.* See **tickameg.**

tideland spruce† *West Coast* See **Sitka spruce** (def. 1).
1906 DEFENBAUGH *Lumber Industry* 63n: The *Picea sitchencis,* known . . . also as the tideland spruce. **1956** *Native Trees* 46: Sitka Spruce [is also known as] tideland spruce. . . .

tide line a line etched near the top of a glass for use in a beer parlor, intended to show the level to which the glass must legally be filled.
1965 *Globe and Mail* (Toronto) 7 Jan. 5/4: The tide line, introduced in 1959, will be broken by the initials LCBO.

tie *n.* a wooden beam used as a transverse support for a railway track.
1854 *Hamilton Gaz.* (C.W.) 27 Mar. 3/1: The deceased came to his death by being run over by the Locomotive Oxford, on the Line of the Great Western Railway, on Wednesday last, having previously laid himself between the ties on the track. **1961** *Cdn Geog.Jnl* Jan. 18/1: Treated track ties are expected to have a life of fifty or more years.

tie-camp *n. Lumbering* a camp for the cutting and shaping of ties, *q.v.*
1881 *Progress* (Rat Portage [Kenora], Ont.) 5 Nov. 4/1: About fifty choppers arrived by Wednesday's train, en route for the tie camps. **1959** *Press* Aug. 14: Now even the native son may be *scotch* with his money . . . be *gyped* by the confidence-man (or work *gippo* in a tie-camp). . . .

tie-pass ['taɪ,pæs] *n.* [< *tie,* q.v. + *pass* card or slip entitling bearer to free passage on a train] *West, Slang* a trip on foot along a railway track.
1912 CONNOR *Corp.Cameron* 406: I shall have to work my passage on handcars and doubtless by tie pass. **1918** KENDALL *Benton* 45: "Out of town by the first train that comes in—East or West. . . ." "We ain't got the price," was the somewhat aggrieved answer. "Then take a 'tie pass,' d--n you," said the Sergeant grimly.

tiger† *n. Fur Trade, Obs.* a wild cat, especially the cougar, *q.v.* See also **tiger cat.**
1744 DOBBS *Hudson's Bay* 41: The Elks, Stags, Rain-Deer, Bears, Tygers, wild Beeves, Wolves, Foxes, Beavers, Otters, Corcajeu, &c. are the Employment of the Men. **1783** (1918) DAVIDSON *North West Co.* 269: Exports [included] . . . Cassed Catts 5536, Open Catts 4197 . . . Tygers 26 . . . Castoreum 1106 lb. **1808** (1950) THOMPSON *Journals* 20: . . . on the east Side he killed a Specius of the Tiger. . . .

tiger cat *Obs.* See **tiger.**
1791 LONG *Voyages* 146: Soon after they untied him, and brought him to the war-kettle to make his death-feast; which consisted of dog, tyger-cat, and bear's grease, mixed with wild oats, of which he was compelled to eat. **1832** MCGREGOR *Brit.Amer.* II 8: The wild animals are the moose, carriboo, bear, loup-cervier, tiger-cat. . . .

tigers of the plains *Hist.* the Blackfoot or, sometimes, the Sioux. Cp. **Ishmaels of the prairie.**
1913 (1963) MACLEOD & MORTON *Cuthbert Grant* 1: They protected . . . the agricultural settlers of the Red River Colony from molestation by the bloodthirsty "Tigers of the Plains" and other warlike tribes. **1955** HARDY *Alta Anthol.* 48: From the pages of his accurate journal, and through his eyes, we glimpse for the first time the immensity of prairies and parklands, the famous Blackfoot—"tigers of the plains". . . .

tiger trout See quote.
1965 *Globe and Mail* (Toronto) 20 Nov. 33/4: A fish
with a catchy name—tiger trout—caused some
excitement for a while recently in Manitoba. It is a
brightly hued fish a la brook trout, with vivid
yellow-orange fins and similar gaudy markings on the
spots along the sides.

tikameg *n.* See **tickameg**.

tikinagan [ˌtɪkəˈnɑgən] *n.* [< Algonk.: Cree
tikinakun] See **cradle-board**. See also **moss bag**.
☛ *This word has been spelled in many ways, most of
which are entered in the dictionary as cross-references.*
1860 (1956) KOHL *Kitchi-Gami* 7: In fact, you may roll
an Indian tikinagan over as much as you please, but
the child cannot be injured. **1941** LEWIS *Poems* 322:

Fished and caught nothing;
While the young chieftain
Tugged at her breasts
Or slept in the lacings
Of the warm tickanegan.

1957 *Beaver* Autumn 53/2: But snowshoes of birch
wood and babiche, tikinaguns (cradle boards) and dry
tanned moccasins will be seen for quite a while yet.
1965 *Globe and Mail* (Toronto) 26 Nov. 7/1: Four
hundred men, women and children, including babies in
tiknagans [sic] on their mothers' backs, moved through
the neon-lighted streets of Kenora. . . .

tillicum [ˈtɪləkəm] *n.* [< Chinook Jargon
tilikum people, person < Chinook *tilikum*
Indians] *Pacific Coast and Northwest* **1** (one's)
people.
*a***1855** (1956) ROSS *Fur Hunters* 35: . . . a woman who
happened to be in the canoe, bawled out to the men,
"Alke, Alke, Tilla-kome, Tilla-kome" "Stop, stop, a
man! a man!" **1859** *Brit.Colonist* (Victoria) 30 Apr. 2/2:
Four Haidah Indians, on Thursday afternoon, came to
the house of Mr. Oxner, Colquitz Farm, and after
agreeing to work for him, one left, when the rest said
they preferred to go with tilekum. **1913** JOHNSON
Shagganappi 138: "Tillicums," he said facing the crowd,
"this boy has danced no tribal dance . . . " "Bring ten
dollars of the white man's chicamin (money). . . ." **1922**
JOHNSON *Legends* 35: I saw her graceful, high-bowed
canoe heading for the beach that is the favourite
landing-place of the "tillicums" from the Mission.

2 friend; buddy; pal.
1869 *Mainland Guardian* (New Westminster, B.C.)
9 Oct. 3/2: The Indians fully bear out Price's own
story in relation to stealing the gold, and the rescue from
the courthouse at Kootenay, by his tillicums, of the
Indian taken there by the Prices when caught in the
act of robbing their sluices. **1903** *Yukon Sun* (Dawson)
1: Our old tillicum, Foxy Granpa was onetime mayor
of a town of 3 or 4000 dollars, so granpa said.
1922 PRINGLE *Tillicums* 99: Six old "tillicums" were
gathered in Jordan's cabin on Gold Run. **1962** FRY
Ranch on the Cariboo 215: I had come to know him
when he worked at Holmwood, for he and Rupert
Duck were tillicums from away back.

tillicum money [< *tillicum* (def. 2) + *money*]
Pacific Coast, West bonus money; gratuity;
buckshee money.
1883 *Brandon Blade* (Man.) 1 Nov. 4/2: Indians from
various parts of the valley are already coming to . . .
find out how much "potlatch" the various growers will

pay in the way of potatoes, beef, pasturage, and
"tillicum" money, beside what they earn.

tilt *n.* **1 a.** *Esp.Lab.* a temporary shelter of canvas,
sealskins, etc.; tent.
[**1753** (1768) DRAGE *Prob.N.W.Passage* 132: Entering
the Harbour they saw Shallops built after the
Newfoundland Manner, at Anchor, with Buoys and
Cables, a Mast, a square Yard athwart, with a Sail
bent, a tilt made of seal Skins abaft.] **1771** (1911)
TOWNSEND *Cartwright's Jnl* 78: [I made] a tilt with
some seal skins which I borrowed. . . . **1891** PACKARD
Lab.Coast 141: On every square rod of flat rock on the
steep sides of the harbor was a Newfoundlander's "tilt"
or summer house. **1907** MILLAIS *Newfoundland* 95:
When the black bear enters a tilt or wigwam, it opens
and scatters everything within, whilst it has a curious
habit of never departing by the way of entry,
preferring to scrape a hole in the side of the shelter by
way of exit. **1942** RADDALL *His Majesty's Yankees* 156:
Some had canvas tilts, and in these were the
regiment's women and children, a mixed lot like the
men.

b. *West, Hist.* the canvas covering of a prairie
schooner, *q.v.* See also **tilted wagon**.
1859 (1870) SOUTHESK *Saskatchewan* 8: We set out in
a . . . waggon and four . . . a stout canvas tilt and
curtains protecting us around and overhead.
1942 NIVEN *Flying Years* 133: Mrs. Fraser was still in
the wagon . . . craning from the hooped open front of
the tilt to see him. . . .

A tilt (def. 2a)

2 *Esp.Lab.* **a.** a log hut or cabin used by
fishermen or trappers and characterized by a
sloping roof that overhangs the door. Cp. **tilt-
back**.
1770 (1792) CARTWRIGHT *Journal* I 46: In our return
we found two old furriers' tilts, and snow death-falls;
which appeared to be of Canadian construction.
1958 HARRINGTON *Sea Stories* 34: In a fisherman's
"tilt" or hut, McKay's observant eye noticed a piece of
bright yellow stone on the mantelshelf. **1966** *Beaver*
Summer 16/1: The tilt was a trapper's winter quarters
and the slanted gable was a protection against heavy
snowfall, helping prevent the entrance becoming
snowbound.

b. any simple dwelling, especially one made of
wood.
1842 BONNYCASTLE *Newfoundland* II 259: [He] killed
a cow at Broad Cove Gastors, with several sheep, goats,
and fowls, having been repeatedly seen by the poor
people, from the doors of their tilts, in the woods. . . .
1849 MCLEAN *Notes* II 161: The planters, as they are
designated, live in houses which they call "tilts,"
varying in shape and size according to the circumstances
of the owner. **1905** DUNCAN *Grenfell's Parish* 77:
They live in little "tilts"—log huts of one large square
room, with 'bunks' at each end for the women-folk,
and a 'cockloft' above for the men and lads.

tilt-back *n. Nfld, Obs.* See quote. Cp. **tilt** (def. 2).
1819 ANSPACH *Hist.Nfld* 468: Tilt-backs, or linneys, are sheds made of studs, and covered either with boards or with boughs, resembling the section of a roof, fixed to the back of their dwellings towards the wind.

tilted wagon *West, Hist.* See **prairie schooner.** See also **tilt** (def. 1b).
1942 NIVEN *Flying Years* 133: Mr. Fraser was clambering down from the first tilted wagon as they came outside, and his greeting was a hearty chesty laugh at the expression on Angus's face.

tima ['tima] *n.* [< Esk.] See **chimo.** Also *teyma, timah.*
1795 (1911) HEARNE *Journey* 156: *Tima* in the Esquimaux language is a friendly word similar to *what cheer?* **1914** DOUGLAS *Lands Forlorn* 204: The Eskimos saw us before we got to the rapids, and hailed us with as much pleasure as we did them; there was a great shouting of "Teyma!" and waving of arms.

timber *n. Lumbering* See 1945 quote. See also **square timber.**
1844 *Ottawa Advocate* 23 Apr. 3/1: Already has the rafting of Timber . . . for the Quebec market commenced. **1874** *Canadian Mthly* Oct. 344/2: The timber intended to be rafted down to Quebec, is . . . built up in drams. **1945** CALVIN *Saga* 35: In the Quebec export trade the word "timber" had, and still has, a specific meaning not assigned to it by the dictionary. Timber meant tree-trunks brought by the broad-axe to four flat sides. This "stick" tapered slightly, like the tree it had been cut from; for this reason its sides were always measured in the middle of its length. **1961** PRICE & KENNEDY *Renfrew* 51: The timber was floated in single pieces down all the numerous tributaries of the Ottawa and then "rafted up" at the mouth of each.

timber *interj. Lumbering* See 1912 quote.
1912 SANDILANDS *West.Cdn Dict.* 47/1: Timber-r-r! the long-drawn melodious call of the sawyers in a lumber camp when the tree is about to fall. **1942** HAIG-BROWN *Timber* 255: "Timber" is the traditional warning cry of fallers from coast to coast. **1962** *Field, Horse & Rodeo* Nov. 7/2: From the time the first tall tree is felled on the Atlantic seaboard to make a mainmast for the Royal Navy, the cry of "Timber!" has spread westward.

timber agency *Lumbering, Hist.* the jurisdiction of a timber agent, *q.v.*
1882 *Edmonton Bull.* 11 Feb. 4/1: The Indian agency for the Upper Saskatchewan was placed here, the timber agency for a still larger district has been established.

timber agent *Lumbering, Hist.* an agent appointed by the federal government to regulate the use of timber on government land.
1881 *Edmonton Bull.* 3 Dec. 2/2: The appointment of a timber agent for the territories, with residence at Edmonton, has given every satisfaction, as it is in the interest of the people as well as of the government that the use of timber should be regulated so as to prevent waste. **1898** *Yukon Midnight Sun* (Dawson) 8 Aug. 2/2: The timber agent has been beset by all kinds of fraudulent schemes. . . .

timber baron See **lumber king.**
1961 PRICE & KENNEDY *Renfrew* 87: Where once a timber baron guided the life of a town, now diversified industry has assumed priority. . . .

timber-beast *n. Lumbering, Slang* See **logger** (def. 1).
1919 *Camp Worker* 26 Apr. 5/2: A large number of our city folk imagine that a "timber beast" has just about as much need for a brain as a Canadian soldier in Siberia has for refrigeration machinery. **1942** HAIG-BROWN *Timber* 145: "You want to watch it," Alec said, "or that kid will turn out a worse timber beast than his dad." **1966** *Islander* 21 Aug. 4/3: In the early days of the industry these men were rough, tough, and a wild, usually uneducated class, some of whom with actual pride gave to themselves the name TIMBER BEASTS.

timber berth See **timber limit** (def. 1a).
1837 *Times* (Halifax) 17 Jan. 22/1: The selling of Crown lands by auction—and the disposal of the timber berths of the same process, thereby preventing settlement of the country, inasmuch as the poor settler would not be able to compete with the capitalist. **1957** *Camsell Arrow* Christmas 68/3: Last year, the mission bought a sawmill and set it up on a timber berth just north of the Sunchild reserve buildings.

timber-boss *n. Lumbering* the foreman of a logging operation.
1910 MCCLUNG *Second Chance* 248: The timber-boss took Ned aside. . . .

timber butcher *Lumbering* a careless or unscrupulous logging company.
1925 HENDRYX *Oak and Iron* 214: Together they looked upon tens of thousands of acres of barren waste, where the timber butchers and the fire that followed in their wakes, roaring through the uncleared slash, had skinned the gaunt land to the bone.

timber chute *Lumbering, Hist.* See **slide** (def. 1a).
1933 GUILLET *Early Life U.C.* 237: At some timber chutes, notably that at the Cedars on the St. Lawrence, rafts and men were sometimes temporarily submerged during their progress. **1965** *Cdn Geog.Jnl* Sep. 85: [Caption] A vestige of the early lumbering period: old timber chute at Moose Bay, Crooked Lake.

timber claim *Esp.B.C.* See **timber limit** (def. 1a) and **tree claim.**
1926 *Cdn Labor Advocate* 15 Apr. 2/2: Every timber claim that has been logged off in B.C. during the past fifteen years is a veritable fire trap. **1954** EVANS *Mist* 147: The timber claim they were after was only three miles down the road. . . .

timber concession *Lumbering* See **timber limit** (def. 1a).
1961 GREENING *Ottawa* 112: During the 1840's and 1850's many lumber operators . . . began to lease timber concessions . . . along the Ottawa. . . . **1963** *Globe and Mail* (Toronto) 18 May 8/3: All that was needed was an exchange of Crown land for timber concessions held in the eastern areas of the province. . . .

timber cove *Lumbering, Hist.* one of a number of coves on the St. Lawrence River, near Quebec, where square timbers, staves, spars, etc. for export were stored in booms for trans-shipping after being rafted down from the lumber camps. See also **cove** (def. 1), **timber-ground,** and **timber-yard.**
1853 (1854) KEEFER *Montreal* 15: . . . she is content with the North shore timber coves. . . . **1945** CALVIN *Saga* 89:

The Quebec timber coves were the goal of all timber which came down the Great Lakes and the St. Lawrence, and they were the starting point for the export of that timber to Britain.

timber crib *Lumbering* See **crib** (def. 1a).
1896 GOURLAY *Hist.Ottawa* 67: They had to walk from the foot up to the head of the rapids in running their timber cribs.... **1947** SAUNDERS *Algonquin* 36: One of the heroic figures in the annals of those days, was the cook who continued working in his cookhouse on a timber crib, as the whole affair went sliding down one of the Ottawa chutes.

timber-cruise *n. Lumbering* a survey of a tract of forest to determine the quality and quantity of timber on it. See also **cruise**, *n.* (def. 2).
1933 MERRICK *True North* 319: The people in Mud Lake remember the lumbermen by ... their timber cruises and gigantic booms of wood as though it were yesterday. **1956** RADDALL *Wings* 33: "Someone offered me a job on a timber cruise up in the north Ontario bush." **1958** *Kootenaian* (Kaslo, B.C.) 12 June 8/1: A PWA helicopter ... is employed by the B.C. Forest Service on a timber cruise of the Kootenay Lake area.

timber-cruiser *n. Lumbering* See **cruiser** (def. 1).
1908 GRAINGER *Woodsmen* 78: Now Billy Hewlitt was a "timber cruiser"—a man [who] sought for forest timber, to stake it.... **1947** SAUNDERS *Algonquin* 29: The man who determined the direction and extent of new operations was the timber cruiser. **1965** *Cdn Geog.Jnl* Dec. 207/2: One timber cruiser of my acquaintance ran across an old cabin far in the bushland.

timber-cruising *n. Lumbering* the work of a cruiser (def. 1). See also **cruising, timber-hunting,** and **woods-cruising.**
1908 GRAINGER *Woodsmen* 83: ... Higgs and I went timber-cruising up Coola Inlet. **1954** BRUCE *Channel Shore* 189: He had learned to map land and figure the cordage of standing trees during three seasons with a timber-cruising outfit in the west end of the county.... **1958** *Vancouver Province* 12 May 8/4: The public will see firefighting equipment—and be given explanations of timber cruising and timber sale inspections. **1961** *Sun* (Vancouver) 14 Aug. 4/4: When a helicopter did turn up it was taken over for most of a day by a local logging interest to go timber cruising.

timber drive *Lumbering* See **drive**, *n.* (def. 1).
1954 *Proud Procession* 401: "Don't you see the 'Main John' striding in the Lead? / Clear-eyed strong and fearless, kith of Bluenose breed; / First to bring a timber-drive through the wild Grand Falls...." **1957** HUTCHISON *Canada* 101: He had heard only vague rumors of the old timber drives in the days of Peter Emberley.

timber dues *Lumbering* See **stumpage** (def. 1b).
1883 FRASER *Shanty* 87: ... how easily this could be balanced in the treasury accounts by the smallest additional fraction upon the timber dues. **1936** LOWER *Settlement* 77: To Crown timber dues was added ... "timber-berth" arrangement, by which lumbermen obtained the sole right to cut on specified areas for a given time.

timberfall *n. Obs.* See **deadfall**, *n.* (def. 2).
1958 WATTERS *B.C.Cent.Anthol.* 189: ... these two

grizzlies were together, they even had a home—maybe still too sleepy to know where they were, still wrapped in a dream of their timberfalls and wild blueberries in the Cordilleras....

timber fever a feverish desire or drive to be successful in lumbering.
1964 *Cdn Geog.Jnl* Feb. 62/1: [They] soon found themselves carried by timber fever into the mainstream of the logging industry.

timber-ground *n. Lumbering, Obs.* See **timber cove.**
1815 BOUCHETTE *Lower Canada* 407: Westward of this place is another inlet called Ritchie's Cove, and to eastward another spacious timber-ground called Atkinson's, in each there are convenient booms and other securities.

timber grove *Obs.* a stand of timber.
1854 KEEFER *Ottawa* 60: The hay cutters then proceed to the timber grove to make ready for the choppers, hewers and scorers....

timber-harvester *n. Lumbering* See quote.
1965 *Cdn Geog.Jnl* Sep. 86/2: ... the record all too often indicates that governments have been prone to favour the "sound" economic arguments of timber-harvesters....

timber-harvesting *n. Lumbering* See quote.
1965 *Cdn Geog.Jnl* Sep. 86/1: It may also be that top park administrators, many of whom have been trained as professional foresters, are too apt to apply the terminology and techniques of timber-harvesting to areas in which the primary use is recreational.

timber-hunting *n. Lumbering, Obs.* See **timber-cruising.**
1849 ALEXANDER *L'Acadie* II 176: Lumberers would be glad, too, of the chance of "timber hunting." *Ibid.* 180: He was communicative, and told, among other things, how he had been lost for five days in the woods of the Oromoocto, when timber-hunting....

timberjack *n. Lumbering* See **logger** (def. 1).
1916 BRIDLE *Sons of Canada* 5: He was a timberjack in the hardwood bush of western Ontario.... **1928** PERRY *Two Reds* 51: But Martin Legrand had the frequent opportunity to meet one or two of those particularly vicious timber jacks of the Canadian woods.... **1953** CUSHMAN *Timberjack* 127: "You boys hired out to be timberjacks. That's good enough for me."

timber jam *Lumbering* See **jam**, *n.* (def. 2).
1887 (1888) LEES & CLUTTERBUCK *British Columbia* 186: ... on one of the huge timber jams which so often occurred we passed close to a wolverene.... **1910** LONDON *Lost Face* 133: Then, crossing a timber jam on the frozen bed of the Teelee, the sled suffered a wrenching capsize....

timber king See **lumber king.**
1925 *Cdn Labor Advocate* (Vancouver) 9 Oct. 6/4: The timber kings of the Pacific Northwest are holding what the "British Columbia Lumberman" is pleased to call the "Loggers' Parliament." **1952** PUTNAM *Cdn Regions* 202/2: Founded in 1800 by Philemon Wright, an early "timber king," Hull and Ottawa were the chief centre of the square timber trade and the succeeding lumber trade during the 19th century.

timberland festival a social gathering at which there are demonstrations and competitions in birling, chopping, sawing, and other logging skills.

persons thronged the festival grounds [of Hinton, Alta] . . . on the final day of a three-day timberland festival.

timber lease *Lumbering* a lease to cut logs and remove them from Crown lands, *q.v.*
1925 GROVE *Settlers* 217: . . . he took out a timber lease on government land, so as to provide work in the bush for the rest of the winter.

timber licence *Lumbering* a licence permitting one to cut timber on a timber limit, *q.v.*, on payment of certain dues to the government. Cp. **timber rights.**
1936 LOWER *Settlement* 77: To Crown timber dues was added "timber licence," "timber-limit," or "timber-berth" arrangement, by which lumbermen obtained the sole right to cut on specified areas for a given time.
1966 *Cdn Forest Industries* Nov. 55/1: Amendments made to the Forest Act in 1965 now permit: Application of the cost of timber sales to the timber licence as a whole, or to cutting permits issued pursuant to the licence.

timber limit 1 *Lumbering* **a.** a tract of forested land the bounds of which have been established by the government, which leases or sells the rights to fell and remove timber. See also **berth** (def. 1), **limit, lumber claim, timber berth, timber claim,** and **timber concession.** Cp. **coal limit.**
1854 KEEFER *Ottawa* 56: No timber limits are without water—for it is by water alone that the timber can reach its market, and wherever there is or has been water, there you are sure to find Beaver meadows. **1896** GOURLAY *Hist.Ottawa* 113: Now a timber limit is a fortune without touching it with your hand. **1961** PRICE & KENNEDY *Renfrew* 39: The practice of the government was to grant "timber limits" or "berths" to lumbermen by yearly licences or leases for a longer period.
b. a tract of forested land suitable for commercial lumbering; a stand of timber.
1890 *Grip* (Toronto) 8 Feb. 83/2: A Journal of this city is greatly agitated lest, by disputing our timber limits and other assets, the Ontario Government shall bring the province to direct taxation. **1909** CONNOR *Foreigner* 335: . . . he imparted full and valuable information in regard to Wakota, its possibilities as a business centre, its railroad prospects, its land values, its timber limits. . . . **1960** *Ottawa Citizen* 18 June 38/5: . . . A Blackfoot Indian band in 1892 surrendered a timber limit in Alberta.
2 See **timberline** (def. 1).
1898 JENNINGS *Routes to Yukon* 9: The whole valley and slopes to the timber limit are clothed with cotton-wood, spruce and alder trees. **1905** OUTRAM *Cdn Rockies* 338: Soon I found myself alone, passing through the sparse, stunted trees that verge the timber-limit, and approaching a wide, verdant upland.
3 See **timberline** (def. 2).
1914 BINDLOSS *Intriguers* 108: We want to get as far north as the timber limit. . . . **1936** *Cdn Geog.Jnl* XII 62/2: The timber limit is the boundary line between the Indian and the Eskimo.

timber line or **timberline** *n.* **1** on a mountain, the line beyond which trees do not grow. See also **timber limit** (def. 2) and **treeline** (def. 1).
1887 (1888) LEES & CLUTTERBUCK *British Columbia* 121: At last I got to timber-line, and from this point upwards the mountain was bare. . . . **1947** *Cdn Alpine Jnl* June 102: This offered an easy way up . . . to a beautiful park

area near timberline. **1965** WILSON *No Man Stands Alone* 39: The flat tops of the mountains soon gave way to more jagged peaks that rose far above timberline.
2 *North* the line north of which trees do not grow; the line where the Barrens begin. See also **first timber, timber limit** (def. 3), **tree limit,** and **treeline** (def. 2).
1896 WHITNEY *On Snow-Shoes* 287: How well I remember that birch-tree! And how delighted I was, for I knew by that sign the timber-line was very close. **1934** GODSELL *Arctic Trader* 288: We had a warm camp that night, as we were still within the timber line. **1965** SYMINGTON *Tuktu* 10: With the winds of late September . . . the scattered deer bunch into groups once more and move toward the timberline.

timber-maker *n. Lumbering* See **logger** (def. 1). See also **make timber.**
1945 CALVIN *Saga* 173: The timber-maker did not fell a tree to save it from fire—rather he left "slash" in the forest which greatly increased the risk of fire. **1946** LOWER *Colony to Nation* 209: The timber merchants . . . [bought] square timber and deals from the timber-makers and the lumbermen . . . [to] ship them to England.

timberman *n. Lumbering* See **lumberman** (esp. def. 1a).
1889 WITHROW *Our Own Country* 527: The trees, where the timbermen have not culled out the finest, are most picturesque. **1945** CALVIN *Saga* 47: The timber-man . . . picked out the most heavily forested land he could find, provided the timber could be got to the water. **1963** LINDSAY *B.C.Outlaws* 7: This is a statement made by people who should be in a position to know. Among them is J. E. Duffy, a prominent timberman who recently became interested in timber limits at Quatsino.

timber permit See quote.
1912 SANDILANDS *West.Cdn Dict.* 47/1: Timber permit. A homesteader, on application and the payment of a nominal fee, can obtain a permit to cut for his own use a stated number of lineal feet of timber on Government lands.

timber pirate *Hist.* See **bogus settler.**

timber raft *Lumbering, Hist.* See **raft,** *n.* (defs 1 and 2).
1816 (1818) HALL *Travels* 118: . . . the frequent sail, or heavy timber-raft, "floating many a rood," prepare the mind, by a succession of pleasing objects, for the enjoyment of the scene which awaits it. **1832** MCGREGOR *Brit.Amer.* II 241: . . . our eyes and imagination feast on . . . timber-rafts, *bateaux,* and the white canoe of the savage. . . . **1955** COLLARD *Cdn Yesterdays* 158: There were also a number of Irish immigrants and Norwegians, and some twenty voyageurs who were going above Montreal to bring a timber raft down to Quebec.

timber rights See quote. Cp. **stumpage** (def. 1c) and **timber licence.**
1900 *Canadian Mag.* May 18/1: The Ontario Government sells "timber rights" to lumbermen to cut all timber over ten inches in diameter.

timber road 1 *Hist.* See quotes. See also **plank road.**

1844 *Kingston Chron.* (C.W.) 26 Sep. 2/1: In 1832, models of Plank and Timber Roads were submitted to Sir John Colborne, with estimates of the cost of each, by Mr. Cull, Civil Engineer, who had been recommended to Sir John Colborne. **1844** *Kingston Chron.* (C.W.) 3 Oct. 1/6: The model of a third description of timber road was also submitted to the Government and laid on the table of the House of Assembly, during the period of Sir Francis Head's residence in Canada.

2 *Lumbering* See **logging road**.
1883 FRASER *Shanty* 58: These timber roads are often exceedingly bewildering even to old experienced bush-rangers.... **1896** GOURLAY *Hist.Ottawa* 139: Roads by which supplies were got to the shanties and timber roads connecting shanties with rivers and creeks, were long their only roads.

timber shanty *Lumbering, Hist.* See **shanty** (def. 2a).
*c***1885** (1894) MILES *Boy Life* 310: The "prog" [supplies] he spoke of was then cached, or stored, in an abandoned timber shanty about fifteen miles from our tent.... **1945** CALVIN *Saga* 41: The accounts are ... for ... all the usual costs of a timber shanty.

timber ship *Lumbering, Hist.* See quote.
1903 CONANT *Life in Canada* 109: [In Quebec] the thirteen Canadian prisoners were put on board a timber ship and sent to England. **1963** MORTON *Kingdom of Canada* 199: There the great timbers were loaded on the "timber ships," old ships at the end of their days, and freighted to the British Isles.

timber slash See **slash** (def. 3a).
1958 *Sun* (Vancouver) 18 Nov. 14/1: It had already been logged and was merely a snag-studded, burnt-log-littered timber slash....

timber slide *Lumbering, Hist.* See **crib navigation** and **slide** (def. 1a).
1836 *Bytown* [Ottawa] *Gaz.* 21 July 2/5: This improvement with many others (amongst the rest a timber slide at the Chats,) the country owes to the enterprise of George Buchannan, Esq. of Arnprior, having been erected under his direction and at his expence. **1889** WITHROW *Our Own Country* 412: The great caldron of the Chaudiere, in which the strongest dram would be broken like matchwood, is passed by means of the Government timber slides—long sloping canals, with timber sides and bottoms, down which the drams glide with immense rapidity. **1963** *Globe Mag.* 9 Feb. 4/2: At Richmond Landing on the Ottawa River just where loggers later erected timber slides, the ancient scenes will be created.

timber snye *Lumbering, Obs.* See **snye** (def. 1b).
1845 *Bytown* [Ottawa] *Gaz.* 19 June 2/6: Had the Government Slide in the Timber Snie, so long talked of, been in operation, at least two of the cases, would have been obviated.

timber-spec *n. Slang, Obs.* the risks of being in the lumbering business.
1845 BEAVAN *Life in Backwoods N.B.* 128: ... our neighbour, the embarrassed lumber-man, who was still wooden-headed enough to like anything of the timber-spec, got out the frame by contract, himself giving most generously five pounds' worth of work towards it.

timber stick *Lumbering, Obs.* See **stick**[1] (def. 1a).
1845 BEAVAN *Life in Backwoods N.B.* 83: ... howsomever I got to the shore, and hewed out a canoe from one of our own timber sticks.... **1883** FRASER *Shanty* 340: The timber "sticks" are bound together, according to size and length, into cribs....

timber tariff See **stumpage** (def. 1b).
1961 PRICE & KENNEDY *Renfrew* 39: Robert Sherriff ... became the first collector of government timber tariffs.

timber thief *Hist.* See **bogus settler**.

timber wolf a large, usually gray, wolf, *Canis lupus occidentalis,* found in the northern forest.
1860 *Nor'Wester* (R.R.S.) 28 Feb. 4/2: We also saw a large timber wolf (not a wolf made of wood, but a gentleman who inhabits prairies and wooded country). **1921** HEMING *Drama of Forests* 148: Everybody has read, at one time or another, harrowing stories of the great timber-wolves of our northern forest forming themselves into huge packs and pursuing people all over the wilderness until there is nothing left of the unfortunate community save a few odds and ends of cheap jewellery. **1965** SYMINGTON *Tuktu* 37: The darker wolves of the timber are like the timber wolves found throughout the great boreal forest from Labrador to British Columbia.

timber-yard *n. Lumbering, Obs.* See **timber cove**.
1829 MACTAGGART *Three Years* II 87: When at Quebec, I went and saw the Timber-yard on the Isle of Orleans....

time *n. Esp. Atlantic Provinces* See 1963 quote.
1950 CREIGHTON *Lunenburg County* 109: Are you going to the time tonight? **1963** *Time* (Cdn ed.) 30 Aug. 10/2: Older Newfoundland songs are still sung at evening "times" (a square dance and church social)....

time killer *Hockey* See **penalty killer**.
1966 *Hockey News* 1 Jan. 13/2: [The] time killers started early that night as Red Armstrong was whistled off at 2:24 of the first period.

tin-cow *n. Esp.West, Slang* See quotes.
1889 MACLEAN *Indians* 199: Some of the old timers feast occasionally on hardtack covered with dope—butter—and in their tea or strong coffee they use the tin-cow—condensed milk. **1910** FERGUSON *Janey Canuck* 92: The condensed milk ... is correctly known as "tin cow." **1962** *Alta Hist.Rev.* Autumn 15/2: In the commissariat department [are] "dope" (butter) ... "tin-cow" (condensed milk)....

tin dog *West, Slang* See quote.
1953 *Cdn Geog.Jnl* June 247/1: By six o'clock, the herder takes in hand his "tin dog" (cans strung on a wire to get the sheep's attention) and "sheep-hook" (crook).

tinette *n.* [< F] *Obs.* a kind of wooden pail in which butter was packed and carried; a butter tub.
1927 DICKIE *How Canada Grew Up* 92: With butter it was even worse. The settlers brought it to the Company's store in small quantities, some more, some less; not in firkins, tinettes or kegs, but in open dishes, covered with a towel, a napkin or a cabbage leaf. **1955** (1965) COLLARD *Call Back Yesterdays* 222: I still can see in the cool larder the curls of butter scooped from the 20 lb. tinnet [sic]....

tinker *n. Atlantic Provinces* **1** the razor-billed auk, *Alca torda.* See also **turr** (def. 1).
1771 (1792) CARTWRIGHT *Journal* I 133: From this place they brought fifteen ducks, a tinker, a white-fox,

and eighty-seven eggs. **1905** DAWSON *St.Lawrence* 150:
It is sometimes called tinker, and sometimes turre.
1965 *Chronicle-Herald* (Halifax) 15 Feb. 4/6: Had this
officer possessed the minimum requirements of
knowledge, he would have promptly identified the bird
as a Razor-billed Auk, a sea-bird about crow size which
is locally called "Tinker."

2† the common mackerel, *Scomber scombrus,*
caught off the Atlantic coast.
1899 *Yarmouth Telegram* (N.S.) 7 July 3/1: They made
a small haul of tinkers.

tinker duck See **tinker** (def. 1).
1916 HAWKES *Labrador Eskimo* 33: Small birds,
particularly the little sea-pigeon (pitchulu'x) and
"Tinker" ducks are secured in summer with the bird
dart or net. . . .

tin pants *Slang* heavy work pants of canvas
soaked with a waterproofing solution, as of
paraffin wax, formerly much worn by loggers.
1927 PHILIP *Painted Cliff* 10: As to his costume it was
altogether grotesque, consisting of a grayed and torn
buckskin shirt without a collar, a pair of "tin pants" so
covered with patches that little was left of the original
material. **1948** (1956) ANDREWS *Glory Days* 25: . . . his
face and neck were tanned and wrinkled like an old
pair of logger's tin pants. He wore congress shoes.

tipi *n.* See **teepee.**

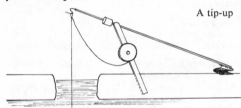

A tip-up

tip-up *n.* in ice-fishing, a device for supporting a
line and indicating when a fish is hooked, as a
pole balanced on a fulcrum so that one end, which
often has a flag attached, is raised upright when
a fish pulls on the line.
1923 WILLIAMS *Spinning Wheels* 247: Fishing through
the ice . . . With the aid of what they call "tip-upses"
several lines can be used simultaneously.

titimeg ['tɪtə,mɛg] *n.* [< Algonk.; var. of *tickameg,*
q.v.] See **whitefish.** Various spellings.
1748 ELLIS *Hudson's Bay* 185: Up the Rivers and Lakes,
they have . . . two very delicious kinds of Fish; the one
called by the French, White Fish, but by the Indians and
English, Titymagg; the other . . . Muthoy. **1749** (1963)
Beaver Winter 8/2: The bottom is covered with fine
muscles, and sea-eggs, and clamms . . . and other
shell-fish, which allures those shoals of fish . . . salmon,
titimegg, and lake fish, which abounds in every place
within the gulph. **1823** FRANKLIN *Journey* 710: The
Cree name of this fish is attihhawmegh, which is
corrupted into tittameg by the traders. The Canadian
voyagers term it poisson blanc. **1905** (1954) *B.C.Hist.
Qtly* XVIII 169: There is an excellent food fish in the
lakes of that region—the white fish ("titimeg" or
"atikameg," as the Crees called it) which averages about
1½ pounds in weight.

tittle ['tɪtəl] *n. Maritimes* See **tickle** (def. 1).
1896 *Journal of Amer.Folklore* II 32: In two or
three instances in Nova Scotia and New Brunswick we

have such a place known as a *tickle,* but commonly as a
tittle, which I deem a corruption of it.

T.O. ['ti'o] *n. Local, Slang* Toronto, Ontario.
1964 *Globe and Mail* (Toronto) 23 Dec. 24/1: Old T.O.,
where Bay Street is Canada's original hardened artery,
where the intersection of King and Yonge is the
double-crossroads of the country. **1965** *Ibid.* 6 Jan. 6/4:
Let's take it as one more piece of evidence that old
T.O.—fish and chips, suet pudding, gloomy Sunday—
is fast becoming one of this world's gay and glittering
cities. . . . **1966** *Ibid.* 24 Jan. 6/4: . . . K-W [Kitchener-
Waterloo] has the same zestiness as old T.O.

toag *n.* See **togue.**

tobaccomik [tə'bækə,mɪk] *n.* [< *tobacco* + Esk.
komik that tickles or itches] *Arctic* in Eskimo
parlance, tobacco, especially snuff.
1924 FLAHERTY *Eskimo Friends* 113: Never did Eskimo
so quickly gulp down the few scraps of food we had to
spare, and the tobaccomik and tea we gave them they
held close with trembling hands, when finally they bade
us "chimo" and strode off through the gloom.
1936 (1955) STRINGER *Wife-Traders* 8: "Me good friend
of Kablunak Winslow," he explained to the old man . . .
"Tomorrow, maybe, I have tea and tobaccomik for
your people."

toboggan [tə'bagən] *n.* [< Cdn F *tabagan(e)*
< Algonk.; cf. Mikmac *tobagun, tobakun*
handsled].
☞ *Although the modern spelling of this word is
standardized, earlier writers used varied forms:* **tabagan,
taboğan, tarbogan, tarboggin, tob(b)agan, tobogan,** *etc.*

1 a. See 1820 quote. See also **Indian sled** and
toboggan sleigh.
[**1691** LE CLERCQ *Gaspésie* 70: tabaganne] [**1791** (1904)
LONG *Voyages* 240: *English* Slay, an Indian carriage
Chippeway Tarbinnáck.] *a***1820** (1838) HEAD *Forest
Scenes* 64: A tobogin is a small sleigh . . . of very simple
construction, and capable of conveying from 100 to 140
pounds of clothes or other baggage. It is made of
quarter-inch plank, about a foot and a half broad and
eight feet long; the forward end is bent upwards, so as
the more readily to pass over any obstructing body.
1866 KING *Sportsman in Can.* 62: The camp supplies . . .
are transferred to tarboggins, or light hand-sledges,
which are drawn after the hunters by their dusky
attendants. **1955** MCCOWAN *Upland Trails* 151:
Algonquins and Iroquois found wooden toboggans
handy in hauling food and fuel. **1966** *Kingston
Whig-Standard* (Ont.) 6 Feb. 4/5: Toboggans were made
of hardwood. . . .

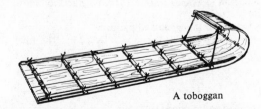

A toboggan

b. any similar small freight sled adapted from that
of the Indians, sometimes equipped with flat steel
runners.

1846 (1955) CRAIG *Early Travellers* 156: With their snow-shoes loosely tied on, and their tobogin dragged from over the shoulder, they can get over a long journey without fatigue. **1867** (1876) LORD *Wilderness* 231: If . . . the snow is soft, then I like the flat sleigh, usually styled a "tobogan," the better of the two. **1871** *Brit.Colonist* (Victoria) 25 Mar. 3/2: Tabogans of all sizes and shapes are to be seen here, some of wood, others of sheet iron with and without runners. **1883** FRASER *Shanty* 127: So next morning they started, each man dragging behind him a large toboggan on which the meat was to be loaded. **1963** *North* Sep.-Oct. 37/1: This is hard on the toboggan, because the hard crust causes wear and tear. Steel runners are usually bolted to the undersides, and these take the weight and tear. It is also easy to run, regardless of weight. The only problem with steel runners is that they can't be used in the cold weather. A toboggan with runners does not always stay on the trail.

2 a similar sled used for coasting down snow-covered hills for fun and sport. See also **tobogganing.**

1846 (1927) DICKIE *How Canada Grew Up* 191: One of the great amusements for visitors is to climb up to the top of this cone and slide down again in a tarboggin. **1853** *Anglo-American Mag.* I 243/1: Again, in moon-lit evenings . . . civilians, military, married or unmarried, spend the greater part of the night sliding down a hill in a species of sleigh called by the Indians Tobaggan. **1935** JENNESS *Parry Island* 95: In winter the children coasted down the slopes on small toboggans. . . . **1955** *Crag and Canyon* 8 Apr. 4/3: They shipped me down the mountain in a toboggan. . . .

3 a large runnerless sled pulled by one horse. See also **cariole,** *n.* (def. 2b).

1954 TYRE *Saddlebag Surgeon* 170: Another device that added new zest to the sport was riding the teetering deck of a horsedrawn toboggan. **1960** NIX *Mission* 79: John [led] the way on snowshoes; Eliza next in a long coffin-like toboggan pulled by a horse, then another toboggan carrying kit and "everything else" lashed to it. . . .

4 *North* See **cariole,** *n.* (def. 2a and picture). See also **tabanask.**

1881 *Progress* (Rat Portage [Kenora], Ont.) 30 Apr. 4/2: The dogs broke through the ice and the toboggan started to go down, and they had to scramble to solid ice. **1927** LONGSTRETH *Silent Force* 275: The trail came out again on the Peel, and three miles on, they found two more sets of dog-harness and a toboggan. **1952** STANWELL-FLETCHER *Tundra World* 125: Beside one tent was a tiny flat toboggan with high, caribou skin sides—just big enough for a baby or a big doll. **1963** SYMONS *Many Trails* 171: . . . I picked up my toboggan rope, spoke quietly to the dogs and continued my journey.

5 See **motor toboggan** and picture.

1964 *Globe and Mail* (Toronto) 19 Dec. 26/5: The other type of toboggan seems faster in the open going. . . . **1967** *Globe and Mail* (Toronto) 29 Mar. 5/8: The abandoned toboggan was discovered Saturday on the lake ice.

toboggan [təˈbagən] *v.* [< n.] Various early spellings; see note at **toboggan,** *n.* **1** ride on a toboggan; engage in tobogganing, *q.v.*

1846 (1927) DICKIE *How Canada Grew Up* 191: . . . they tarboggined, slid and trudged about merrily in the deep,

dry snow. **1913** WILLIAMS *Wilderness Trail* 87: "She went tobogganing out behind the fort at ten o'clock, with the missionary's wife."

2 transport on a toboggan (def. 1).

1907 HUNTER *Cdn Wilds* 58: After the hunting of big game it rests with the women and children to cut up the meat and toboggan it to camp.

3 slide like a toboggan (def. 2).

1928 FREEMAN *Nearing North* 352: Deeply loaded, both [canoes] had literally tobogganed on the rocks all the way down the steep shallow rapid. **1938** (1950) STANWELL-FLETCHER *Driftwood Valley* 143: Once we found otter tracks leading along a bank to a deep slide where they tobogganed down to a small rushing creek. **1964** *Maclean's* 2 Dec. 12/2: . . . their youngsters, in the absence of snow, do belly floppers on the terrazzo floors and toboggan around on shopping carts.

toboggan bag *Obs.* a bag to hold the goods to be conveyed on a toboggan (def. 1).

*a*1820 (1838) HEAD *Forest Scenes* 64: . . . the required articles could be procured; namely, a couple of tobogins, two tobogin bags, a canteen, havresac. . . . A set of small holes are bored in each side [of the toboggan]; and the tobogin bag when full is then laced tightly on the machine by means of a cord.

toboggan car(r)iole *North* See **cariole,** *n.* (def. 2a and picture).

1942 *Beaver* Dec. 40/2: . . . we nestled down into the toboggan carrioles.

toboggan chute See **toboggan slide.**

1964 *Globe and Mail* (Toronto) 15 Dec. 32/3: . . . winter fun-seekers will take to . . . two new toboggan chutes.

tobogganer [təˈbagənə] *n.* [< *toboggan,* v. + *-er*] See **tobogganist.**

1878 *Cdn Gentleman's Jnl* 8 Mar. 1/5: In fact, there has been so little snow this winter that the tobogganers have not had a good time. **1958** *Liberty* Jan. 62/1: [Caption] Heavy mustachios kept these tobogganers warm on the banks of the old Canal at Cardinal, Ontario [in 1882].

tobogganing [təˈbagəniŋ] *n.* the pastime of sliding on a toboggan (def. 2). See also **toboggan,** *v.* (def. 1) and **tobogganist.**

1849 ALEXANDER *L'Acadie* I 186: . . . an amusement of which Canadian boys, and sometimes ladies too, are passionately fond . . . is called "tobogganing." **1887** *Grip* (Toronto) 8 Jan. 7/1: I cannot conceive what there is in tobogganing to so fascinate the adult portion of both sexes in our 1886 humanity. **1966** *Star Wkly* 12 Mar. 19/1: The Gettys go in for backyard barbecues [and] tobogganing in the North Saskatchewan ravines. . . .

tobogganing hill a hill used for tobogganing, especially one provided with artificial slides.

1885 *Selkirk Herald* (Man.) 24 Jan. 3/2: The official programme for that day is: Morning—Opening of the toboggan slides; afternoon . . . grand opening of the Montreal tobogganing hill.

tobogganing party See **toboggan party.**

1883 *Brandon Dly Mail* (Man.) 29 Jan. 4: Tobogganing parties is the popular thing just now. **1890** *Regina Jnl* 23 Jan. 1/3: The youth and beauty of the town are enjoying the evenings, when not too cold, at skating, tobogganing parties, etc.

tobogganing slide See **toboggan slide.**

1884 *Prince Albert Times* (Sask.) 21 Mar. 1/4: The tobogganing slide is again in good condition.

tobogganist *n.* a person who engages in tobogganing, *q.v.* See also **tobogganer.**
1884 *Moose Jaw News* (Sask.) 22 Feb. 1/4: We are sorry yesterday's mildness was accompanied by a high wind, to the disappointment and grief of several of our tobogganists.... **1964** *Globe and Mail* (Toronto) 15 Dec. 32/4: Tobogganists were free to use the remainder of the golf course.

toboggan party a social affair where the people present engage in tobogganing, *q.v.* See also **tobogganing party.**
1887 *Grip* (Toronto) 8 Jan. 7/1: Jack Templeman ... announced his attention of escorting me to a toboggan party. **1958** *Liberty* Jan. 62/1: [Caption] Ontario Toboggan Party: 1882.

toboggan sheet *North* See **sled wrapper.**
1931 GREY OWL *Last Frontier* 37: Here, with his toboggan sheet for a windbreak ... he can make some kind of a stand....

toboggan-sled *n.* See **cariole,** *n.* (def. 2a and picture).
1905 MOTT *Jules* 16: He had no dogs with him on this trip, but drew the toboggan-sled, which was already well laden with skins, by a thong over his shoulder. **1912** LONDON *Smoke Bellew* 335: Women and children were departing with dogs harnessed to empty toboggan-sleds....

toboggan sleigh See **toboggan,** *n.* (def. 1 and picture).
*c*1902 LAUT *Trapper* 196: Wrapping her husband in robes on the long toboggan sleigh, the squaw placed her younger child beside him and with the other began tramping through the forest drawing the sleigh behind.

toboggan slide an artificial runway built on a hill for the use of tobogganists, *q.v.* See also **slide** (def. 3), **toboggan chute,** and **tobogganing slide.**
1884 *Brandon Blade* (Man.) 21 Feb. 9/2: The several Toboggan Slides were illuminated every evening, and the Snowshoe Clubs invited all strangers in the city to participate in their tramps. **1950** SUTTON *Footloose* 98: In winter the entire length of the terrace becomes part of an illuminated toboggan slide....

toboggan trail *North* a trail travelled by carioles (def. 2a).
1963 SYMONS *Many Trails* xi: ... he travelled the gleaming canoe routes by summer, by winter the drifted and tortuous toboggan trails.

toboggan wrapper See **sled wrapper.**
1938 *Beaver* Sep. 17/1: We ... boiled a great pot of beans, and spread them one bean deep over a toboggan wrapper and opened the door wide until the beans were frozen.... **1947** *Ibid.* Dec. 20/2: We did not put up a fly unless it looked like snowing, and then we cut some poles and with our toboggan wrappers made a fly. **1954** BERTON *I Married the Klondike* 116: Here was a toboggan wrapper and the remains of more dogmeat.

tockey *n. Obs.* See **toggy.**

toe-hole *n.* the open space somewhat forward of the central point of a snowshoe, necessary for the tipping action of the snowshoer's foot when walking or running. See also **eye.** See picture at **snowshoe.**
1933 MERRICK *True North* 227: They [the snowshoes] are beautifully knit with a pattern of binding at the toe-hole, as though it grew there under their fingers, irresistibly.

tog [tɒg] *n.* [shortening of *tautog* < E. Algonk.] *Maritimes, Slang* a valuable food fish, the tautog, *Tautoga onitis,* of the Atlantic Coast. Cp. **togue.**
1957 *Kingston Whig-Standard* (Ont.) 29 Oct. 6/2: The tog, often mistaken for a bass, is a heavy stout fish with a high dorsal ridge and a blunt nose.

toggle *n. North* **1** on a dog harness, a kind of button or fastener, such as a piece of bone, attached to the end of an individual dog line so that it can be passed through a ring when the dog is being hitched to the main line of a fan hitch, for example.
1867 (1876) LORD *Wilderness* 232: ... by 'toggles' I mean round pieces of bone made small enough to slip through the bone ring.... **1918** GRENFELL *Lab. Doctor* 88: The dogs' traces should be of skin, and fastened with toggles or buttons to the bow-line. **1940** *Cdn Geog.Jnl* Feb. 108/1: One unavoidable though minor drawback to the fan hitch arises from the inclination of the animals (dogs) to intermittently shift places; this results in the braiding of the numerous traces forward of the toggle, with the necessity of "clearing" after every few hours of travel.

2 See quote.
1932 JAMIESON *Cattle in the Stall* 74: These [logs in a log fence] were bound by a wooden toggle—a grooved piece, shaped above and below to lie across the logs and hold them in place.

3 a stick to which the end of a trap chain is attached, intended to restrict the movements of a trapped animal by catching on snags, trees, etc. as the creature attempts to make off.
1937 CONIBEAR *Northland Footprints* 278: He fastened the trap on a heavy spruce stick, called a "toggle," driving the ring on it.... He buried the stick and chain....

toggy ['tɒgi] *n.* [< Algonk.: Cree *miskotaki* coat; perhaps influenced in early use by older cant *toge(man)*, ult. < L *toga* cloak, loose coat] *Fur Trade, Hist.* a calf-length greatcoat of skins, usually beaver, worn by Indians and traders in the Hudson Bay country. See also **beaver coat** and **beaver tockey.** Also spelled *tockey* and *toggey.*
1743 (1949) ISHAM *Observations* 212: All the Indians was gone for their Winter Quarters Except some women who I Keep for to Dress beavr. for tockey's for their own use.... **1774** (1795) HEARNE *Journey* 119: This day I gave each of the People a Dresst Moose Skin to mak them a Toggey for the Winter. **1821** (1900) GARRY *Diary* 203: I painted leather Toggy with Porcupine Epaulets and trimmed with the Otter Skin. **1957** *Beaver* Winter 14/2: Coat beaver—supple, greasy skins worn as "toggies" by Indians—were the kind preferred by hat makers.

togony *n.* [< Algonk.; cf. Cree *māstuchakunis*] *Obs.* See **coyote** (def. 1).
1857 (1863) PALLISER *Journals* 63: I saw great numbers of the case wolf (mischechogonis or togonie) prowling about. This is the wolf proper to the partially wooded country, and is about twice the size of a fox, with a tail

shaped like the brush of that animal. **1913** COWIE *Adventurers* 250: There were two kinds of wolves, the smaller being those known today by the familiar name of coyote, and then called "togony," an abbreviation of the longer Cree word.

togue [tog] *n*. [< E. Algonk.] *Maritimes* See **lake trout**. Cp. **tog**.
1849 GESNER *Ind.Resources N.S.* 119: Togue. . . . Common in the large lakes of New Brunswick, and Canada, have only been observed in lake Rosignol in the county of Liverpool. **1902** ROBERTS *Kindred of Wild* 63: . . . the daring fisher [fish-hawk] arose, grasping in his victorious claws a large "togue" or gray lake trout. **1928** *Game Fishes of Can.* 32: The "Mountain trout," "gray trout," "mackinaw trout," "togue" and the salmon trout of the big lakes are all merely lake trout. *c***1954** *Nova Scotia. Canada's Ocean Playground* 28: Land locked salmon and deep-feeding togue are taken in several lakes during the summer months.

tolerance *n*. [< Cdn F] *Que*. See quote.
1960 *Ottawa Citizen* 15 July 9/4: Quebec's new attorney-general has announced a crack-down on "tolerances"—unlicensed liquor serving establishments which he says were allowed to operate under the former Union Nationale government. "Tolerances" are bars or taverns operating openly, usually in rural areas, but without permits to sell liquor.

tollibee or **tolliby** *n*. See **tullibee**.

toll plaza the area at the entry to a toll road, or bridge where the tolls are collected.
1960 *Gazette* (Montreal) 29 Jan. 17/1: More than 5,000,000 cars . . . have passed through the Montreal-Laurentian toll plaza . . . since it was opened. . . .

tolt [tolt] *n*. [< Brit.dial. *toll* clump or ridge of trees] *Nfld* an isolated hill rising abruptly from a plain; monadnock.
1905 DAWSON *St.Lawrence* xxiv: Many detached peaks, locally called "tolts" rise abruptly from the plain. **1946** TAYLOR *Newfoundland* 33: Near Holyrood is a striking tolt (or monadnock), the so-called Butterpot, which is a relic of one of Iwenhofel's peneplains. **1964** *Cdn Geog.Jnl* Apr. 138: When we drove east from Deer Lake, it was through . . . forest interspersed with lakes and sudden small mountains called "tolts."

tomahawk† ['tamə,hɑk] *n*. [< Algonk.] **1** originally, a light Indian war-club (cp. **casse-tête**); in later use, a light hatchet often used as a weapon.
1755 (1907) HENDAY *Journal* 347: A Captive Girl aged about 17 years was knocked on the head with a Tomahawk by a Man's wife in a fit of jealousy: No notice was taken as such game is common amongst them. **1888** (1890) ST. MAUR *Impressions* 156: The punishment given to squaws who have given offence to the tribe, is to fell a large pine-tree with nothing but a small tomahawk. **1960** JENNESS *Indians of Can.* 298: The offensive weapons on both sides were clubs and bows and arrows; for tomahawks were not used, apparently, prior to contact with Europeans.
2 bury the tomahawk. See **hatchet** (def. 4).
1814 *Niagara Chron.* (U.C.) 8 Apr. 1/4: Therefore, my Red Children, let the war cry cease to be heard—let the Tomahawk be buried—and let us once more smoke the pipe of peace with him. **1836** *Bytown* [Ottawa] *Gaz.* 16 June 3/4: Let us, like true Patriots, and good fellows,

"bury the Tomahawk"—concentrate our conservative strength—and as mariners intent on weathering the storm, let us devote our undivided attention to the safety of the Constitution. [**1845** *Literary Garland* II June 254/2:
When round the solemn council fire,
The sage and sachem hold a talk,
And tell the braves in wild attire,
To lift the buried tomahawk.]

tomahawk ['tamə,hɑk] *v*. **1**† strike with a tomahawk; kill with a tomahawk.
1778 (1930) *Cdn Hist.Rev.* XI 32: Seeing by the fate of their comrades what they had to expect, the next on his left sang his death song, and was in turn tomahawked. **1910** HAYDON *Riders of Plains* 56: In the darkness of night this wretch rose up, tomahawked the helpless women and children, and disappeared with their scalps. **1963** MACLEOD & MORTON *Cuthbert Grant* 49: The wounded were knifed and tomahawked, the dead stripped and ripped up after the Indian fashion.
2 prevent bills from passing into law.
1832 *Colonial Advocate* (York [Toronto]) 26 Jan. 3/2: The Legislative Council have . . . tomahawked Mr. Bidwell's bill for dividing intestate property equally among the children. **1836** *Vindicator* (Montreal) 1 Apr. 2/2: Of 32 Bills sent up in the last 12 days, they contrived . . . to "tomahawk" 21, which is equal to nearly 70 per cent. **1883** RYERSON *My Life* 94: His Majesty's Royal assent would have been given to that bill had it not . . . fallen into company with some ruthless vagrant . . . who had slandered, abused, and tomahawked it at the foot of the throne.
3 *Figurative uses*.
1834 *Brit.Amer.Jnl* (St. Catharines, U.C.) 22 July 3/2: The above communication, as far as the composition is concerned, is "prose run mad," or the King's English tomahawked and scalped, in both sense and grammar. **1852** *Elora Backwoodsman* (C.W.) 14 Oct. 3/1: It seems to be the general impression that McKirdy, the innocent, is to be tomahawked [sacrificed] to save Scott, the guilty.

tomalki [tə'mælki] *n*. [< *toma(to juice)* + *alky* alcohol] *Slang* See quote. Cp. **Calgary redeye**.
1952 WILSON *Chibougamau* 62: One of the drinks sold by the bootlegger was known as "Tomalky," a vile mixture of cheap alcohol and tomato juice. . . .

tom-cod† *n*. **1** See 1784 quote.
1779 (1792) CARTWRIGHT *Journal* II 476: At sunset we hauled the seine by the stage, but took only a few . . . small tom-cods. **1784** PENNANT *Arctic Zoology* cxcvi: The bait is small fish of all kinds: Herring, Capelin, Lance, Tom Cod, or young Cod. . . . **1838** HALIBURTON *Sam Slick* 65: "The Endgians . . . used to make a sort o' fish flakes, and catch herrin' and tom cods . . . and put 'em on the flakes, and then crawl onder themselves." **1943** DENNIS *Cape Breton* 23: I go through the quaint village of Poulamon—named from the Acadian French word for the small cod-fish or "tom-cod."
2 a. See **tommy-cod**.
1828 MCGREGOR *Maritime Colonies* 34: Trout, smelt, tom-cod, and perch, are caught in winter with a hook and line, through a hole in the ice. **1860** *Islander* (Charlottetown) 13 July 2/4: We presume the intention of fishing trout, tom-cods and smelts would warrant the issuing of a license, under which a farmer's marshes might be thrown open. **1866** KING *Sportsman in Canada* 315: The Tom-Cod, sometimes called also the Frost-fish . . . the Petite Morue Fraiche, Tacaud, and Gode Mollet of the French-Canadians, is peculiar I

believe to North America. **1944** *Beaver* June 42/1: Tom-cod . . . may be had all the year round by jigging.

b. a related fish, *Microgadus proximus,* of the Pacific Coast.
1960 *Fisheries Fact Sheets* 63 1: The gray cod is readily distinguishable from its relatives the tomcod and whiting, by the long barbel on the lower jaw.

3 *North* any of several small fish of the cod family, as *Boreogadus saida* or *Eleginus navaga,* found in Arctic and sub-Arctic waters, or the loche, *q.v*
1928 WALDEN *Dog-Puncher* 244: . . . tom-cod . . . are small cod, and our method was to catch them through holes in the ice. **1948** *Beaver* Sep. 11: Nulaiyuk who controls the spirits of the mammals of the sea . . . down to even that of the lowly tom cod. **1953** MOWERY *Mounted Police* 146: Two of the hunters untoggled the bow lines of his huskies, and others brought frozen tomcod for the team. **1956** SCHERMAN *Spring* 41: Soon, however, they discover that shrimps are easy to catch and later they realize that tomcod and sculpin taste quite as good as milk.

tomey-cod *n.* See **tommy-cod.**

tommy-cod *n.* **1** a small food fish, *Microgadus tomcod,* of the St. Lawrence River and adjacent waters. See also **frost fish, petite morue,** and **tom-cod** (def. 2a).
1808 (1809) GRAY *Letters* 267: The Canadians call them *petite Morue;* the English call them *Tommy cod.*
1818 *Description P.E.I.* 6: The Fish of this Island are, cod, herrings . . . eels, smelts, tomy-cod, elwives, &c.
1822 (1955) HARVEY *Island of St.John* 152: There are also bass, haddock, sturgeon, perch, flounders, eels, tomey-cod, alewives &c. **1833** *Vindicator* (Montreal) 25 Jan. 1/3: Tommy-cods are plenty; the river nearly froze over, but as the d--l would have it, thawed again. **1952** BANFILL *Labrador Nurse* 174: In quick succession, we flicked tommy cod and gasperos from the holes.
1961 *Maclean's* 7 Jan. 25/1: . . . now [winter carnivals] they're coming back . . . with . . . a tommy-cod derby at Ste Anne de la Perade, Que. . . . **1965** *Star Wkly* 2 Jan. 21/1: Each winter the [Ste.Anne river] is home to millions of tommycod, small fish of the cod family that come from the St. Lawrence to spawn.

2 See **loche.** See also **tom-cod** (def. 3).
1936 *Cdn Geog.Jnl* XII 142: Both "La Loche" and "Mithey" signify the humble tommycod.

tompline *n.* See **tumpline.**

tom-rocker *n.* *Placer Mining* a kind of cradle operated by one man and used to wash gold from gravel.
1936 MOWERY *Paradise Trail* 29: His equipment was of the simplest—a shovel, two buckets and a tom-rocker, which sat over at the creek edge, convenient to water.

tomy-cod *n.* See **tommy-cod.**

tongue *n.* See 1850 quote.
1850 SNOW *Voyage* 385: A tongue is a point of ice projecting nearly horizontally from a part that is under water. Ships have sometimes run aground upon tongues of ice. **1850** OSBORN *Arctic Jnl* 41: The object always is, in fastening to an iceberg, to look for a side which is low and sloping without any tongues under water.
1853 INGLEFIELD *Summer Search* 9: I felt at first extremely solicitous about the screw, dreading that some of the floe pieces which had long projecting tongues under water would catch it.

tookto(o) *n.* See **tuktu.**

tool push(er) *Oil Drilling* the foreman of a drilling crew.
1957 *Herald-Tribune* (Grande Prairie, Alta) 19 Dec. 9/3: Keith Brown, tool push for Can-American Drilling Co., and three assistants, negotiated the iron behemoth over treacherously icy roads on a ten-ton tandem truckbed. **1960** *North* July-Oct. 45/2: [The] tool pusher . . . spudded (began drilling) on March 1. . . .

Toonik or **Tunik** ['tunɪk] *n.* [< Esk.] **1** See **Tunit.**
1942 TWOMEY & HERRICK *Needle to North* 198: No one really knows who lived on the islands when the Eskimos came, or where the women came from by which the race has persisted, but it seems probable that even two hundred years ago there may have been Tuniks still living on the islands, for these ancient people survived on Southampton Island until 1902.

2 a creature of Eskimo folklore (probably derived from legends about the Tunit, *q.v.*). Cp. **Torngak.**
1965 *Toronto Dly Star* 16 Oct. 35/4: Toonik are prominent in Eskimo folklore from the western Arctic to the east. In the west they were giants but by the time the stories (or the Toonik themselves) had made it to Baffin Island, they had shrunk to the size of elves.

A Toonik

3 *Trademark* a sealskin doll made by Eskimos for selling as a novelty. It has red eyes, a pot belly, and long fangs. Cp. **Ookpik.**
1965 *Toronto Dly Star* 16 Oct. 35/6: Toonik now has his copyrights and has made a trip south to potential markets.

toothache grass a species of grass, *Ctenium aromaticum,* having an aromatic flavor and formerly used as a remedy for toothache.
1796 (1911) SIMCOE *Diary* 335: I walked down the hill in the evening and gathered . . . toothache plant, like toothache grass.

top *v.* *Lumbering* cut the top off a standing tree, usually one to be used as a spar tree, *q.v.*
1942 HAIG-BROWN *Timber* 254: This [a spar tree] may be a standing tree, topped and rigged, or a tree brought in from elsewhere and raised for the purpose.
1953 SWANSON *Haywire Hooker* 33: . . . I've topped a spar up in Aberdeen,/ I've polled the logs down the Old Lachine. **1963** MCKINNON *Forest Activities 1* 6: Often the first tree topped is used only for a raising tree to raise the final spar tree.

topeck, topek, topick *n.* See **tupek.**

tophair *n.* *Hist.* See **scalp** (def. 1a).
1962 *Field, Horse & Rodeo* Nov. 27/1: "My girl will not look at me until I have brought back a Blackfoot tophair," the young man grinned.

toque [tuk] *n*. **1** See **tuque** (def. 1 and picture).
1888 (1890) ST. MAUR *Impressions* 265: [He] was . . .
made picturesque by a red cap "toque," sash and red
duffel overall stockings. **1945** HAIG *Brave Harvest* 170:
They were matched by toques and mittens, and tied in
with gay voyageur sashes streaming like banners
against the snow. **1965** *Kingston Whig-Standard* (Ont.)
13 Dec. 19/4: The toque has become carnival's symbol
and again this year prizes will be awarded for the most
distinctive.

2 See **tuque** (def. 2 and picture).
1906 (1958) WATTERS *B.C.Cent.Anthol.* 7: . . . with his
toque pulled down . . . he looked for all the world like
one of the small gnomes we children used to see pictures
of. **1966** *Globe and Mail* (Toronto) 8 Mar. 1/2: Mr.
Robichaud, bundled in parka and bright yellow toque,
mingled with a group of blood-spattered swilers,
questioning them closely on their killing methods.

tora or **toreau** *n*. See **taureau**.

Tornat *n.pl.* See **Tornit**.

Torngak ['tɔrngɑk] *n*. [< Esk.] a spirit or devil.
See also **Eskimo devil, Torngarsuk**, and **Tornit**.
Cp. **Toonik** (def. 2). Also spelled *Torngark*.
[**1744** DOBBS *Hudson's Bay* 203/2: Devil, To-nu-ock.]
1823 *Literary Gaz.* 25 Oct. 675/1: He called to his
assistance Torngak, his Familiar and a friendly spirit,
in company with whom he journeyed to the realms
below, to combat with the Evil Genius. **1894** *Trans.Roy.
Soc.Can.* XI 2 125: Those who neglect these precautions
aɪe liable to some misfortune, perhaps even the loss of
their lives; besides, the Torngak of the air might be
provoked on their account to raise stormy weather.
1916 HAWKES *Labrador Eskimo* 14: Near Cape Chidley
. . . are the Tornga'it or "Spirit Mountains," a wild
and impressive group believed by the Eskimo to be the
abode of To'rngak. . . .

Torngarsuk ['tɔrngɑr,suk] *n*. [< Esk. *torngak*
spirit + *-suk* great] great spirit; the chief Torngak,
q.v.
1847 PRICHARD *Researches* I 189: There dwells the great
spirit Torngarsuk, and his mother, under a joyous and
perpetual summer, where a shining sun is obscured by
no night. . . . **1909** CAMERON *New North* 254: The
Eskimo pray to Sidne; but it is wise to propitiate Atti or
Tornarsuk. . . . **1916** HAWKES *Labrador Eskimo* 14n:
Near Cape Chidley . . . are the Tornga it, or "Spirit
Mountains," a wild and impressive group believed by
the Eskimo to be the abode of To'rngak, or
Tornga'rsoak, "The great To'rngak," the chief spirit
consulted by their shamans.

Tornit ['tɔrnət] *n.pl.* [< Esk.] the plural form of
Torngak, *q.v.* Various spellings.
1887 *Trans.Roy.Soc.Can.* V 2 37: This being is unknown
among the central Eskimo, and numerous spirits, the
tornait, take his place. **1897** TYRRELL *Sub-Arctics* 167:
These wizards are said to be taught from youth by one
of the deputy chief friends, named "Tornat," and some
of them are supposed to have great power with the
spirits. **1912** (1913) HODGE & WHITE *Indians of Can.*
461/2: TORNIT. A fabulous race which the central
Eskimo believe to be akin to themselves, but much
taller and stronger, having very long arms and legs and
being able to toss huge boulders as though they were
pebbles. The Akudnirmiut call them Tuniqdjuait.

1949 LEACH *Dict.of Folklore* I 453/2: The fabulous
creatures of Eskimo mythology known as the Tornit
are giants. . . .

Toronto couch [< *Toronto,* Ont.] See
Winnipeg couch.
1962 *Maclean's* 30 June 6/2: I recall back home in
Winnipeg some 30 years ago, we had . . . at least five
of what we used to call "Toronto couches" out on the
verandah. . . .

Toronto lily *Obs.* probably the wild orange lily,
Lilium philadelphicum.
1793 (1911) SIMCOE *Diary* 196: I walked on the sand
bank and gathered seeds of Toronto lilies.

Toronto Purchase *Hist.* See quote.
1958 *Weekend Mag.* 21 June 12/1: Only a decade before
[the Mississaugas] had sold some 250,880 acres of land
extending west from Scarboro Bluffs, for the grand sum
of 10 shillings. This was known as the "Toronto
Purchase" and seems to have been a pretty good
bargain.

Toronto the Good Toronto, Ontario.
1898 CLARKE *Of Toronto the Good* [Book Title].
1936 CROSS *Cross Roads* 63: Toronto is known as
Toronto the Good, because of its alleged piety. My
guess is that there's more polygamy in Toronto than
Baghdad, only it's not called that in Toronto. **1965** *Globe
and Mail* (Toronto) 14 Jan. W1/1: Tucked behind Bloor
Street, east of Avenue Road, is an area that owes more
to the Champs Elysees than to Hogtown, more to
Greenwich Village than to Toronto the Good.

Tory† *n*. **1** *Hist.* a supporter of the British Crown
during the American Revolution.
1775 *Quebec Gaz.* 19 Oct. 3/1: Yesterday I hear a
New-England man say "that he had never been on the
Parade, because his conscience would fly in his face were
he to assist, or make show of assisting the Torys in their
attempt to thwart the endeavours of the Patriots to give
Liberty to this Province." **1778** *Quebec Gaz.* 5 Mar.
Supp. 2/1: A party of General Parson's troops having
found out the residence of a number of Tories, alias
cow and horse thieves alias free booters, were so
successful as to take 47 of them, who are all properly
disposed of.

2 *Hist.* in colonial times, a person who supported
the British connection and opposed the desires of
the Liberals and Reformers for a greater measure
of self-government, the influential group among
such persons being known, in Upper Canada, as
the Family Compact (def. 1). See also **Tory**, *adj.*
(def. 1) and **Toryism** (def. 1).
1832 *Liberal* (St. Thomas, U.C.) 13 Dec. 3/2:
According to the doctrine of the Tories of Upper
Canada, freedom of thought is *treason*—freedom of
speech is *rebellion*—and liberty of forcing opinions and
acting under them is becoming traitorous and
yankefied. **1838** HALIBURTON *Sam Slick* 287: "Now, if
they had a good set of liners, these blue-nose tories and
radicals would be for everlastingly abotherin' of
government with their requests and complaints."
1897 DURAND *Reminiscences* 127: In fact, the talent in
papers was with the Tories, and in that day [1831] York
had many. **1963** MORTON *Kingdom of Canada* 241: [In]
1830 Ogle R. Gowan, a Tory and an Orangeman, seems
to have published a pamphlet calling for "responsible
government."

3 a member or supporter of the Progressive-
Conservative Party, *q.v.*, and its predecessors, as
the Conservative Party, *q.v.*, descended from the

right-wing groups of colonial times. See also **Tory**, *adj*. (def. 2) and **Toryism** (def. 2).

1905 *Eye Opener* (Calgary) 25 Nov. 1/1: The Macleod Advance (Liberal) says that the Opposition is a no-Tory-ous party. **1936** (1965) HAMILTON *Cdn Quotations* 49/2: Never did we see such an assemblage of long-visaged Tories. **1966** *Saturday Night* June 7/3: Later you say that, if the positions were reversed, with Turner the Tory and Chambers the Grit, Turner would still have won.

Tory *adj*. **1** *Hist*. of or having to do with the Tories (def. 2) of colonial times.

1836 *Bytown* [Ottawa] *Gaz*. 16 June 1/5: Under the auspices of a Tory House of Assembly, emigration was fertilizing our remotest townships, with an influx of settlers possessing intelligence, capital, and British feelings. **1963** MORTON *Kingdom of Can*. 282: Thus the Tory opposition felt they had grounds for objecting to the measure. . . .

2 of or having to do with the Tories (def. 3).

1890 *Grip* (Toronto) 11 Jan. 40/2: Partyism is what is ruining this country. The Grit and Tory machines are always truckling to Rome. The N.P. is a fraud. What Canada wants is commercial unions. **1958** *Maclean's* 4 Jan. 32/4: Tory Whip L. E. Cardiff later privately thanked Sinclair for his temporary silencing of Fulton.

Toryism *n*. **1** in colonial times, the political influence of the Tories (def. 2) and all they stood for.

1833 *Liberal* (St. Thomas, U.C.), 14 Mar. 4/1:
    The Tories ne'er in Parliament
    Again their jobs shall vend,
    And with them once for aye—
    The name of Toryism shall end.
1852 *Huron Signal* (Goderich, C.W.) 6 Jan. 2/5: The easy going "good old times of Toryism" may now be numbered with the things that were, and never again will such be seen in Huron.

2 the Tories (def. 3) and their policies and principles.

1887 *Grip* (Toronto) 18 June 5/2: I'll stick to that every day of the week, and Toryism will be knocked out in the second round. **1915** PRESTON *Strathcona* 88: The fall carried with it a cloud upon the reputation of the great chief, which, though Canadian Toryism of to-day would gladly forget, time cannot altogether remove. **1959** *Maclean's* 29 Aug. 2/4: It's still easy enough to tell a member of the CCF from a member of the Albany Club, that shrine of Toronto Toryism. . . .

Toryized *adj*. *Obs*. induced to adopt the principles of Toryism (def. 1).

1852 *Welland Advocate & Rev*. (Port Robinson, C.W.) 13 Feb. 2/7: The last rumor is that Joseph Couchon and his lately Toryized friends have now won over Mr. Morin.

Tory party *Hist*. the Tories (def. 2) as a political group.

1832 *Liberal* (St. Thomas, U.C.) 2 Nov. 3/2: Why is he Sheriff of New-Castle District, and a pampered meanial of the Tory party? **1836** *Novascotian* (Halifax) 20 Jan. 17/2: "They have two parties here, the Tory party and the opposition party, and both on 'em run to extremes." **1963** MORTON *Kingdom of Can*. 284: This firm stand [in 1849] stopped the rot completely in the Tory party. . . .

tossing-pole *n*. *Fur Trade* a kind of trap in which a pole is fixed on a fulcrum, a weight being placed on one end and on the other a snare by which a

trapped animal is hoisted into the air. Cp. **spring-pole**.

1907 HUNTER *Cdn Wilds* 97: Instead of the [lynx] snare being tied to a tossing pole, it is simply tied to a stout birch stick, 3 or 4 feet long, by about 2 inches in diameter. **1921** HEMING *Drama of Forests* 144: It had not been disturbed, but a little farther on we saw the form of a dead lynx hanging from a tossing-pole above the trail. **1923** STRINGER *Empty Hands* 142: ". . . This lynx I knocked over when he was trying to get a rabbit still kicking on one of my tossing-poles. . . ."

tote-bag *n*. See **grub-bag**.

1905 MOTT *Jules* 21: Then he cut some chunks from a piece of caribou-meat, which he got out of his tote-bag.

tote-load *n*. a load, such as a wagonload of supplies.

1952 BUCKLER *Mountain and Valley* 146: When Joseph came home . . . there were ten-dollar bills . . . but those all went for the country rates, the tote-load of flour and feed, things like that.

totem ['totəm] *n*. [< Algonk.; cf. Ojibwa *ototeman* his brother-sister kin] **1 a**. among certain Indian peoples, a spirit in the form of a creature or plant with which a group, such as a family, and its members are identified, and which is supposed to watch over each of them.

1768-82 (1791) LONG *Voyages* 86: The evening previous to the departure of the band, one of them, whose totam was a bear, dreamed that if he would go to a piece of swampy ground, about five days march from my wigwaum, he would see a large herd of elks, moose, and other animals; but that he must be accompanied by at least ten good hunters. **1896** WHITNEY *On Snow-Shoes* 97: Any animal or bird dreamed of used to be, and is yet in a minor degree, taken as the dreamer's totem. **1916** WOOD *Tourist's N.W.* 385: Personal totems are acquired by dream or vision, or by direct contact with the object when hunting. **1956** LEECHMAN *Native Tribes* 38: A child was of the same clan, and had the same totem, as its mother, and never of the same clan or totem as its father, but in some tribes these rules were just the other way. . . .

b. a graphic representation of such a creature or plant.

1804 CAMERON *Nipigon Country* 247: All those who are of the same mark or totem consider themselves as relations, even if they or their forefathers never had any connexion with each other, or had seen one another before. **1844** MARRYAT *Settlers in Canada* 38: "Why, Ma'am, a totem is an Indian's mark, and you know I am almost an Indian myself. All the Indian chiefs have their totems. One is called the Great Otter, another the Serpent, and so on, and so they sign a figure like the animal they are named from." **1956** LEECHMAN *Native Tribes* 38: A totem is the badge or emblem of the clan, often an animal, and it is from this animal that the clan claims to be descended. **1966** *Islander* 27 Feb. 6/2: You also saw totem birds with strange sad eyes.

2 the kinship group represented by this symbol.

1804 CAMERON *Nipigon Country* 246: These are divided into the following totems or tribes from which they take their family names: the Moose, reindeer, Bear, Pelican, Loon, Kingfisher, Eagle, Sturgeon, Pike, Sucker, Barbue tribes and a few of the Rattlesnake tribe. **1880** DAWSON *Queen Charlotte Is*. 134: The members of the different totems are generally pretty equally divided in each tribe. **1891** *Cdn Indian* Apr. 198: No one may marry in his or her totem; children follow the totem of the mother, save in very exceptional cases to strengthen the totem of a father, when his number has been reduced.

3 See **totem pole.**
1891 *Cdn Indian* July 287: A remarkably fine totem, thirty-five feet high and well carved, has recently been donated to the museum of McGill University.
1958 *Camsell Arrow* Christmas 63/1: Carvings on the 100-foot totem tell the legend of the Kwakiutl nation and its ten tribes.

totem crest See **crest.**
1891 *Cdn Indian* Apr. 197: The designs are carefully and symetrically drawn, are often hereditary, and represent the totem crest of the wearer; the face, however, is never tattooed.

totemism ['totə,mizəm] *n.* the traditions associated with totems (def. 1).
1768-82 (1791) LONG *Voyages* 87: This idea of destiny, or, if I may be allowed the phrase, "totamism," however strange, is not confined to the Savages ... many instances might be adduced from history, to prove how strong these impressions have been on minds above the vulgar and unlearned. **1896** WHITNEY *On Snow-Shoes* 96: They lean to an inferior species of "totemism," although no religious ceremony was ever attached to its acceptance. **1916** WOOD *Tourist's N.W.* 385: The essential element of totemism is "the concept of a ghostly helper or tutelary spirit."

totem pole among certain West Coast Indian tribes, a pole, often a standing tree trunk, which has been carved and painted with the family crests, personal exploits, etc. of the owner. See also **totem** (def. 3) and **totem post.** Cp. **house-post.**
[**1808** (1960) FRASER *Letters and Journals* 98: Upon the boards and posts are carved beasts and birds, in a curious but rude manner, yet pretty well proportioned.]
1890 *Cdn Indian* Dec. 70: The rank of the chiefs is denoted by the height of their totem poles, and there are frequent quarrels among them on the subject.
1940 *Beaver* June 48: Totem poles are not, as is commonly supposed, pagan gods or demons. **1964** DUFF *Indian History* 54: One well-known authority ... believes that much of what is commonly believed to be aboriginal in coast Indian culture, such as the clan system, the use of crests, and the carving of totem poles, did not exist before the time of contact, but was in a sense a product of the fur trade.

totem-pole culture a culture of which totem poles form an essential part.
1932 *Cdn Hist.Rev.* XIII 412: There were, not so long ago, no totem-pole culture, no exogamic groups whose law was to marry outside the clan, no totemic emblems, in the very districts where these features are now the most typical.

totem post See **totem pole.**
1882 (1888) DAWSON *Haidas* 404/2: The door is usually an oval hole cut in the base of the grotesquely covered post, forty or fifty feet high, which we may call the totem post, but which to the Haidas is known as *kechen*.
1897 TUTTLE *Golden North* 134: ... the village is marked by several totem-posts curiously carved.

tote road† See **1912** cite.
1887 ROBERTS *Western Avernus* 71: On this "toat" or freight-road the wagons went east during one part of the day and west during the other. **1912** SANDILANDS *West.Cdn Dict.* 47/2: Tote road, the trail or road over which provisions and supplies are conveyed to a working camp. **1942** *Gazette* (Glace Bay, N.S.) 21 Sep. 1/8: The problem was not solved until fully ten minutes later when Jerome appeared coming down the tote road with his dog bounding ahead of him. **1965** *Cdn Geog.Jnl* Sep. 82/1: For years the winter woods rang with the sound of the axe and the crash of falling trees, while tote roads were hacked out for horse-drawn sleds, and sluice-ways built for the spring run of logs.

tote-sleigh *n.* See quote.
1912 SANDILANDS *West.Cdn Dict.* 47/2: Tote-sleigh, a sled on which provisions and supplies are carried to a lumber camp.

tote-team *n.* the team used in bringing supplies into a logging or other camp.
1910 FERGUSON *Janey Canuck* 107: A "tote" team will take him out to the hospital tomorrow. **1963** PATTERSON *Far Pastures* 166: ... the driver of a lumber camp tote-team found Mrs. Marston sitting on a large boulder that lay by the main trail. ...

tote wagon a wagon used to haul supplies to a logging or other camp.
1964 *Islander* 27 Sep. 3/1: Here he gained employment ... at the same wage as tie cutting, but better grub, fetched to the camp by tote wagon, with a cook to prepare it.

tot lot a playground for very young children.
1958 *Edmonton Jnl* 16 June 15/4: Despite heavy showers in the morning, the Rosedale tot lot held its official opening underneath the grandstand of Renfrew Ball Park, Saturday. *Ibid.* 19 Sep. 3/6: Tot lot apparatus is proposed for Strathearn. ...

tot rink a skating rink restricted to small children.
1962 *Kingston Whig-Standard* (Ont.) 27 Dec. 13/3: In Lions park ... there is a tot rink and a larger rink.

touchdown† *n. Cdn Football* a major score, currently valued at six points, achieved when the ball is downed by a player of one team behind the goal-line of the opposing team; also, the act of scoring in this way.
1904 CONNOR *Prospector* 36: The McGill captain, with Pepper hanging desperately to his hips, drags himself over the line and secures a touchdown for McGill.
1958 *Edmonton Jnl* 7 Aug. 9/3: The two touchdowns, both unconverted, put the Stampeders ahead 12–0. ...

touch-in-goal *n. Cdn Football, Hist.* See **rouge,** *n.* (def. 1).
1964 *Kingston Whig-Standard* (Ont.) 27 Oct. 9/3: The above article [1895] mentions the only peculiarly Canadian feature of football which endures namely the single point, either the "rouge" or the "touch in goal."

tough sledding *Slang* hard going. See also **rough sledding.**
1908 BEACH *Barrier* 127: "Now them kind of places is all right for married men but they're tough sleddin' for single ones, and after a while a feller gets awful careless about himself." **1938** BLACK *Seventy Years* 169: Of course it was not all easy going, and there were times of "tough sledding," but there were no tragedies.

touladi [tuləˈdi] *n*. [< Cdn F < Algonk.; Micmac] See **lake trout**. Various older spellings.
1846 HATHEWAY *Hist.N.B.* 61: The Toledi . . . weighs from five to twenty-five pounds, has two strong rows of teeth round its mouth like a Shark, flat, sharp and hooking, will bite off an ordinary cod line, and is a very voracious fish. **1855** MONRO *New Brunswick* 181: These waters, as also those of the Temiscouta and Madawaska, are well supplied with Tulidi, a fresh water fish, weighing from seven to ten lb., of delicious flavor —with white fish, and large trout. **1896** *Trans.Roy.Soc. Can.* II 2 135: The Mackinaw trout of the great lakes [is] the *kokomesh* of the Montagnais Indians and the *touladi* of the country of the Micmacs and Abenaquis. **1957** *Field and Stream* May 90/2: . . . a fourth kind of trout called touladi . . . the French-Canadians say, is a natural cross between the lake trout and brook trout.

touque *n*. See **tuque**.

tourist (sleeping-) car See quotes. Cp. **colonist car.**
1899 *Medicine Hat News* (Alta) 26 Jan. 8/2: On the first of February or at an early date a new schedule of rates for tourist car accommodation will come into effect on the C.P.R. **1902** (1956) *Sask.Hist.* IX 1 28: The tourist cars are comfortably arranged though much less elegant than the first class cars. At one end of the car a small room contains a stove where passengers may prepare tea and warm such victuals as they have brought with them. At night they may occupy a berth in the tourist sleeping car by paying $1.50 extra, but they are expected to furnish their own bedding. **1912** SANDILANDS *West.Cdn Dict.* 48/1: Tourist car, the class of railway car between the Pullman and the colonist, about equalling the second-class accommodation on Old-Country lines.

tourquie *n*. See **turkey**.

tow *n*. *Lumbering* a collection of boomed logs rigged for towing. See also **log tow** and **tow timber.**
1851 (1957) GUILLET *Valley of the Trent* 265: I wish it mey [sic] come with the first Tow in cribs. **1891** OXLEY *Chore-Boy* 137: The logs . . . were now handed over to the care of a company which gathered them up into "tows" and with powerful steamers dragged them down the river until the sorting grounds were reached. . . . **1912** FERGUSON *Open Trails* 140: As I stand watching the bridge, one section of it opens to let a tug through with a tow of logs. **1965** *Victoria Dly Times* 12 Aug. 21/5: . . . logs totalling about 1,000,000 board feet . . . were lost from a tow early today.

towboater *n*. *Lumbering* a person employed on a tugboat that hauls log booms, barges, etc.
1965 *Star Wkly* 5 June 16/2: Although towboaters are paid for 12 months a year . . . they spend only a little over five on the water.

tower *n*. See **fire tower.**
1965 *Star Wkly* 23 Jan. 37/3: He works in the summer months as a fire spotter at the Montgomery Lake tower in the Petawawa forestry reserve.

towerman *n*. See **fire-spotter**. See also **fire tower.**
1962 *Sask.News* 19 June 2/1: Quickly the towerman sights the base of the smoke in his firefinder; a bearing is read off, double checked for accuracy, then plotted on a map.

towline† *n*. See **tracking line.**
1796 (1911) SIMCOE *Diary* 345: They used great exertion in poling and drawing with a tow line and pushing the boat. . . . **1821** (1900) GARRY *Diary* 97: Here the skill of

the Voyageurs now shows itself; at one moment using their Poles, then their Paddles, then jumping into the Water, now using the Tow Line which if it was to break would end in certain Destruction to all. **1958** BERTON *Klondike* 216: By October these had reached the Copper River and were engaged in an upstream struggle with poling-boat and towline.

town council the elected municipal officers who administer a town.
1863 WALSHE *Cedar Creek* 336: The town-council consists of five members, one of whom is town-reeve; the town-reeves form the county council; and the presiding officer elected by them is called the warden. **1955** *Northern Light* (Bathurst, N.B.) 5 May 9/1: He felt that the nine-man Town Council was carrying the load for all the taxpayers. . . .

town father a member of a town council, *q.v.*
1883 *Selkirk Herald* (Man.) 4 May 3/1: The Town Fathers held a caucus meeting on Monday last for the purpose of informally discussing matters of municipal interest. **1889** *Regina Jnl* 5 Dec. 5/2: The Town Fathers for '90 are doubtless of the same opinion as Ex-President Cleveland, and believe that the office should seek the man, and not the man the office.

townie *n*. *Nfld* See 1964 quote.
1958 *Kingston Whig-Standard* (Ont.) 17 Dec. 27/5: But what can you expect, he says, when "townies" [build] spacious living rooms and small kitchens? **1964** *United Church Observer* Sep. 12/3: They call the St. John's man a "townie" while the outporter is a "bayman."

town limit(s) the area of jurisdiction of a town council.
1848 *Ottawa Advocate* 13 June 3/1: We have been given to understand that residents outside of the town limits, are in the habit of wantonly impounding the Cows of those living in the town; simply because a township regulation has been passed to that effect. **1960** *Rainy River Record* 11 Feb. 1/2: The licensing of peddlers and certain vending machines in the town limits will be given close study by council.

town lot† *Hist.* a surveyed parcel of land within the boundaries of a town. Cp. **park lot.**
1784 (1905) *Ont.Bur.Arch.Rep.* VIII 75: When situation for a town shall be determined upon, the persons who now settle upon farm lots, and who are mechanics, will each be allowed a town lot. **1898** LANDREVILLE *Appeal* 78: The price demanded for this absurd excuse for a serviceable highway to the Klondike [includes] the right to engage in nearly every form of trade short of vending town-lots on the stars. **1922** STRINGER *Prairie Child* 81: Dinky-Dunk, who is a born dickerer, has been trading some of his ranch-stock for town-lots on the outskirts of Buckhorn. **1952** PUTNAM *Cdn Regions* 278/1: The actual founder of the village was George Hamilton, who, in 1813, laid out his farm in town lots and named the streets after the members of his family.

town meeting *Hist.* See **township meeting.**
1793 *U.C.Gaz.* (York [Toronto]) 8 Aug. 4/2: They appointed a Town Meeting to be held at Newark on Saturday the 17th instant, for the purpose of electing the Town and Parish Officers, as directed by the late act of this Legislature. **1833** *British Colonial Argus* (St. Catharines, U.C.) 16 Nov. 3/1: The inhabitants of each and every township at their annual town meeting, shall

nominate, choose and appoint five commissioners, to be
called commissioners of township schools, of whom
three shall be a quorum. **1909** HUNTER *Simcoe County*
I 265: In this way, the township councils throughout
this county were first organized [Municipal Act, 1849],
and the "town meeting" for choosing officers, as well as
the District Council itself, thus came to an end.

town park *Obs.* See **park lot.**
1789 (1905) *Ont.Bur.Arch.Rep.* III 75: The Boards shall
not issue any certificate for more than one Town lot of
one acre, or one town lot and one town park of twenty-
four acres together, to the same person. **1790** *Ibid.* 74:
Town park for a minister, 24 acres.

town plot† *Obs.* See **townsite.**
1794 (1959) PRESTON *Kingston* 347: ... a certain Part of
these Lotts ... shall be reserved ... together with the
Water Lotts, and the vacant Ground beyond the Limits
of the Town Plot. ... **1801** *U.C.Gaz.* (York [Toronto])
21 July 4/3: To Be Sold ... the Lots Nos. 12, 13 and
14, in the 1st and 2nd concessions of Charlotteville,
immediately beyond the Town Plot, containing 1200
Acres. **1863** WALSHE *Cedar Creek* 136: "Why, there's a
far better site for a town plot on my land. ..."

town-reeve *n.* See **reeve.**
1850 *Wkly Globe* 15 Feb. 131/3: The following is a list
of the names of the Town Reeves and Deputy Town
Reeves, from several Townships composing the County
Council. **1903** *U of T Stud.Hist.& Econ.* II 85: The
town reeve was to preside at all meetings of the councils,
or, in his absence, the deputy reeve.

township *n.* **1**† **a.** *Maritimes, Hist.* an early land
division of approximately six square miles. See also
settlement (def. 1b).
1756 (1932) *Cdn Hist.Rev.* June 190: ... perhaps a
Division of the Province into Districts or Townships,
may be the more eligible method. ... **1764** (1899) *N.B.
Mag.* I 264: I have been trying ... to have my choice in
the Townships of this River, the land and title as good
as any in America, confirmed by the King in answer to
our petition. **1818** LOCKWOOD *Nova Scotia* 59: A fire
getting into the woods ... spread over the greater part
of Halifax township, consuming an immense quantity
of valuable wood. ... **1907** *U of T Stud.Hist.& Econ.* II
248: This right the townships (or settlements, as they
were sometimes called) continued to enjoy until 1879.
1957 WRIGHT *Blomidon Rose* 96: As first comers, they
had the choice of township sites.
b. the administration of such a settlement,
considered as a corporate body.
1765 (1875) CAMPBELL *Hist.P.E.I.* 6: It may be proper
to observe that very few houses mentioned in the
explanation of the Townships are good for anything,
and by no means tenantable, except one or two at St.
Peter's, kept in repair by the officers. **1823** *P.E.I.
Register* (Charlottetown) 13 Sep. 3/2: ... the first
parcel [of land] being sold ... brought more than was
required to satisfy the judgment against the
Township. ...

2 *Ont.and Que.* **a.** *Hist.* See **district** (def. 1).
1763 (1906) *Ont.Bur.Arch.Rep.* IV 18: It is our Will and
Pleasure, that each Township do consist of about
Twenty Thousand Acres, having, as far as may be,
natural Boundaries extending up into the Country, and
comprehending a necessary part of the River St.
Lawrence, where it can be conveniently had.

b. one of the subdivisions of a county, *q.v.*
1793 *U.C.Gaz.* (York [Toronto]) 25 July 1/2: ... the
said Assessors shall cause the same to be affixed on the
Church door or some other place of public resort in the
said Parish, Township, reputed Township, or Place for
general inspection. **1815** BOUCHETTE *Lower Canada* 245:
The most exact content of ten miles square, the usual
dimensions of an inland township, as prescribed by the
warants of survey, is 61,000 acres, exclusive of the usual
allowance of five acres on every hundred for highways.
1842 WILLIS *Cdn Scenery* II 56: The township forms a
square, and is divided into 16 concessions, in each of
which are 6,400 acres. These concessions are subdivided
into lots of 200 acres of which there are 32 in each.
1933 CAMERON *Twigs* 259: During the greater part of his
pastorate of seventeen years he filled the position of
superintendent of public schools for the township.
1966 *Kingston Whig-Standard* (Ont.) 31 Aug. 6/4: The
school ... will replace all existing public school
accommodation in the township. ...

c. the municipality of such an area, considered as a
corporate body.
1957 *Temiskaming Speaker* (New Liskeard, Ont.)
17 Jan. 5/1: ... Coleman is open to receive tenders for
Garbage Collection in and for the Township. ...
1962 *Cdn Saturday Night* Aug. 29/2: There will be
action and counter-action, with demands that the
township take over.

3 *West* a land-survey division comprising thirty-six
sections (def. 2) of one square mile each.
1893 (1908) DAWSON & SUTHERLAND *Geography* 130:
Each of these (divisions) is known as a "township," and
contains 36 square miles or "sections" which are further
subdivided into "quartersections" of 160 acres. The
same system of survey extends over the North-West
Territory. **1929** MOBERLY *When Fur Was King* 225: As
each township was surveyed the [Hudson's Bay]
Company secured in it one and three-quarter sections
until the total acreage had been allotted, their sections
being numbers 8 and three-fourths of 26 out of the
thirty-six sections into which each township was
divided. **1952** PUTNAM *Cdn Regions* 371/1: With the
exception of a few early settled areas such as the Red
River and Saskatchewan River settlements, the land of
the Prairie Provinces is divided into practically square
townships, each containing thirty-six sections of as
nearly one mile square as is permitted by the
convergence of the meridians.

township clerk *Ont.and Que.* the secretary of a
township council, *q.v.*
1891 *Grip* (Toronto) 24 Jan. 51/2: Deacon Punkin, in
presence of the township clerk, has subscribed to the
following solemn affirmations. ... **1947** WELLS *Owl Pen*
75: A dozen times a day ... I hung on the telephone,
pestering council members, reeve and deputy reeve, and
township clerk, in an effort to get our road ploughed. ...
1957 *Temiskaming Speaker* (New Liskeard, Ont.) 17 Jan.
5/1: Tenders are to be in the hands of the Township
Clerk on ... February 11, 1957.

township council *Ont.and Que.* the body of
elected officers who are responsible for the
administration of a township.
1896 GOURLAY *Hist.Ottawa* 120: After the organization
of township and county councils, Arthur Allen, Esq.,
was Reeve of Osgoode. ... **1945** (1950) BROWN *Cdn
Democracy* 89: A township council consists of a reeve
and four councillors. **1966** *Kingston Whig-Standard*
(Ont.) 20 Aug. 6/7: Mr. Hannah expressed appreciation
to ... the township council. ...

township line 1 *Ont.and Que.* the boundary of a township (def. 2a).

1819 *Gleaner* (Niagara-on-the-Lake, U.C.) 28 Oct. 742/1: His Grace . . . walked for several miles along the township line . . . and appeared to be much gratified with the improvements. **1952** PUTNAM *Cdn Regions* 286/1: The street pattern of London is the usual, rigid grid, oriented with the township lines.

2 *West* the boundary of a township (def. 3).

1962 ONSLOW *Bowler-Hatted Cowboy* 114: Jim knew roughly where the township line ran. We had often come across old stumps that had been cut with an axe. . . . **1963** SYMONS *Many Trails* 89: Commencing with the United States boundary are imaginary east-west lines also six miles apart, numbered 1, 2, 3 etc. from north to south. These are called township lines.

township meeting *Hist.* in Upper Canada, a public meeting held annually by citizens of a township to appoint officers and decide on affairs concerning the township (discontinued in 1849 after the passing of the Municipal Act). See also **town meeting.**

1835 *Brit.Amer.Jnl* (St. Catharines, U.C.) 8 Jan. 3/1: As the Township Meeting of the inhabitants of Wainfleet . . . they formed themselves into a publick body for the purpose of changing the name of the village of *Marshville* to that of some more congenial name. **1836** *Bytown* [Ottawa] *Independent* 10 Mar. 2/1: The people of every township ought to be aware of any sharks, who, under false pretenses, goes round with petitions, and practice that treachery on the unsuspecting farmers, which often militates against their real interests, and compels them to call a Township Meeting to disapprove of all that the cunning ones had accomplished. **1887** HIGGINS *Life of J.Gould* 137: The township meeting for 1835 was held at Thompson's tavern on the 5th concession, at which place the township meetings continued to be held for many years.

townshipper *n.* a person from the rural districts. See also **township** (def. 2b).

1903 RICHARDSON *Colin* 59: "Some young bloods wuz frum th' town wearin' dickeys an' standin' collars. Frum th' first thar wuz bad blood atwixt th' townshippers an' th' town gang. . . .''

township reeve See **reeve.** See also **town-reeve.**

1852 *Elora Backwoodsman* (C.W.) 29 July 3/3: A meeting of the inhabitants of the Township of Nichol, was held at St. Andrew's Tavern in Fergus, on the 10th of July, in accordance with a requisition to the Township Reeve.

Townships *n.pl.* See **Eastern Townships.**

1810 *Kingston Chron.* (U.C.) 20 Nov. 3/2: This grand passage to the Townships, will give to the city of Quebec some hope of independence, in procuring the necessary supplies for the growing population. **1923** WILLIAMS *Spinning Wheels* 110: As a rule the Englishman in the Townships seldom dabbles in politics. . . . **1952** PUTNAM *Cdn Regions* 149/1: They were better off for transportation here along the river, and moreover they looked upon the townships as a stronghold of the English Protestants.

townsite *n.* a tract of surveyed land set off for the establishing of a town. See also **town plot.**

1821 *Cdn Courant* (Montreal) 17 Jan. 1/2: There are about fourteen acres cleared for a Town site but not a single house in a finished state. **1897** TUTTLE *Golden North* 151: The streets are sixty-six feet wide and the

whole plat has been regularly entered with the Dominion Government, by Joseph Ladue, its proprietor, as a town site. **1964** *Herald Mag.* 8 Aug. 4/1: That was probably much the same observation as made by New Englander Peter Pond in 1787 when he surveyed the bog sliced up by huge, navigable rivers leading to the Arctic from today's townsite.

townsite reserves *West* land reserved for the establishing of a town.

1884 *Moose Jaw News* (Sask.) 11 Jan. 1/5: The opening of the Mile Belt and Town Site Reserves, when it comes, cannot fail to stimulate the lumber trade in our town.

town warden *Hist.* See 1793 quote. Cp. **county warden.**

1793 *U.C.Gaz.* (York [Toronto]) 18 July 1/2: . . . the said Inhabitants-Householders [are] to choose and nominate two fit and discreet persons to serve the office of Town-Warden for such Parish, Township, reputed Township or Place. **1886** *Trans.Roy.Soc.Can.* IV 2 59: The act also provided for two town-wardens. . . . These wardens were a corporation to represent the whole inhabitants of the township or parish, with the right to let or sell property, to sue and be sued. **1909** HUNTER *Simcoe County* I 257: Chief of these officers were the wardens, or townwardens, as they were sometimes called.

tow timber *Lumbering* logs towed in rafts or booms (def. 3a) from one place to another. See also **tow.**

1927 DICKIE *How Canada Grew Up* 158: Lumbering began in Tracadie soon after 1800. At first the people worked at preparing white pine tow timber. This could not be shipped from Tracadie, but had to be formed into rafts and towed along the shore to Miramichi to be exported.

track *v. Esp.North* 1 draw or lead a canoe, boat, scow, etc. through rapids, shallows, or other difficult stretches of water by means of a line or lines running from the craft to a man, or men, on the bank or shore. See also **cordelle,** *v.,* **line,** *v.* (def. 2), **neck** (def. 2), **tracker** (def. 1), **tracking** (def. 1), and **trackline,** *v.*

☞ *This practice, especially common in the Northland and called by several names, as* **lining** *and* **cordelling,** *varies in detail according to time and place, type of craft, kind of obstacle, and direction and nature of current. For example, canoes are often tracked by means of lines attached to both bow and stern. Loaded York boats and sturgeonhead boats, qq.v., were laboriously hauled through otherwise impassable stretches of the Mackenzie River by gangs of men equipped with special harness attached to long, heavy rope lines. Much information relating to the various conditions of tracking is to be found in the many quotations offered for this and related entries.*

1691 (1929) KELSEY *Papers* 5: We went through a little creek were we were forc'd to track our Cannoes into a little Island within wch is great ponds of water. **1796** (1963) *Beaver* Autumn 23/1: . . . they were to track the canoe up by a line, walking on shore, while I steered it. . . . **1827** (1912) ERMATINGER *Express Jnl* 94: Tracked the whole day, except 1 hour stopt for breakfast. **1860** (1964) INNIS *Fur Trade* 331: They come and track with the York and Oxford House Indians during the time of tripping in the summer. . . . **1935** *Beaver* June 31/2: The tide carried us upstream about sixteen miles, but from there on . . . the current was too swift and we had to "track." **1957** *Ibid.* Autumn 40/1: The Fort George post . . . received its outfit by the traditional Hudson's Bay Company method of tracking scows up river, with crews of Indians harnessed to the line.

2 *Hist.* haul or drag a scow, York boat, etc. over a portage using logs as rollers.
1909 CAMERON *New North* 154: [Caption] Tracking a Scow across Mountain Portage.

track-beater *n. North* See **forerunner.**
1908 MAIR *Mackenzie Basin* 190: He was a wonderful little animal; he never seemed tired or weary; he was always ready and willing to follow the track beater, or the sled ahead of him; for three-fourths of the entire journey he acted as foregoer or leader of his own team. **1921** HEMING *Drama of Forests* 175: . . . the Indian track-beater [was] hurrying far ahead while the half-breed dog-driver loped behind the sled.

track-beating *n. North* moving ahead of a dogsled on snowshoes to make a passable track for the team. See also **trail-breaking.** Cp. **forerunner.**
1921 HEMING *Drama of Forests* 160: Our domestic outfit was loaded upon two hunting sleds in the hauling of which we all took turns, as well as in relieving each other in the work of track-beating.

track-breaker *n. North* See **forerunner.**
1897 TYRRELL *Sub-Arctics* 221: In soft snow it is necessary for the guide or track-breaker to wear very large shoes, that he may not sink too deeply, but those who follow in his trail get along with the more ordinary size.

track car See **speeder** (def. 1a).
1959 *Weekend Mag.* 7 Mar. 7/2: Struck by a train during a blinding snowstorm, the man was delivered to the doctor on a speeder (track car) unconscious. **1965** *Islander* 11 July 10/3: There they put the dead man on a track car and pumped their way to Nichol, where they flagged a freight.

tracker *n. Esp.North* **1** a person who tracks (def. 1).
1908 MAIR *Mackenzie Basin* 33: The non-arrival of our trackers was serious, as we had two scows and a York boat, with a party all told of fifty souls, and only thirteen available trackers to start with. **1954** BEZANSON *Sodbusters* 58: A lone tracker must attach his line with great care as to the angle of tension when pulling, for that is his method of steering.
2 See **forerunner.**
1921 HEMING *Drama of Forests* 205: Two trackers on large snowshoes had already gone ahead to break the trail.

tracking *n.* **1** *Esp.North* the action or activity of one who tracks, *q.v.* See also **lining** and **warping.**
1775 (1951) *Saskatchewan Jnls* 3: Our Distance about 24 miles, at 22 Miles Tracking. . . . **1847** (1947) *Beaver* June 39/2: . . . tracking was equally laborious, and the water too deep in most places for using poles. **1938** *Ibid.* Mar. 16: . . . tracking has become a lost art. The name applies to the method of hauling a boat against the current from the shore by means of a long

rope attached to it in such a manner that the boat was almost in a state of balance—the current tended to force it out while the pull of the rope counteracted this. **1965** *Cdn Geog.Jnl* June 190/2: The steep climb up is achieved by a bruising marathon of poling, tracking, portaging, and wading. . . .
2 See quote.
1866 KING *Sportsman in Can.* 51: Moose hunting lasts throughout the autumn and winter, and there are several different methods of pursuing the sport, as "calling," "driving," "creeping," and "tracking," or hunting on snow-shoes, sometimes called "crusting."

tracking beach *Esp.North* See **tracking ground.**
1851 (1853) CAMPBELL *Two Journals* 6 June: . . . with river bounded on either side with hills and rocks affording good tracking beach. . . . **1952** *Beaver* Dec. 33/1: . . . I rounded a bend into a beautiful reach, free from driftpiles and with a good tracking beach. **1954** PATTERSON *Dangerous River* 47: You can make time up river that way, with a light load, just as fast as you can walk, as long as you've got a good tracking beach.

tracking belt *North, Obs.* a shoulder belt attached to a track-rope, *q.v.*, to increase pulling power. See also **rowraddy.**
1850 (1851) SNOW *Voyage* 133: Little was there to dread, however; for, independent of the thickness of the ice, each man had for safety his tracking belt, called by them "rowraddy," so fastened to the trackrope that he could not well fall through any hole without first letting himself loose.

tracking crew a group of men employed as trackers (def. 1).
1922 FOOTNER *Huntress* 139: The tracking crew was on the opposite bank.

tracking ground 1 *North* a river bank along which trackers walk when hauling a canoe, boat, etc. See also **hauling place, tracking beach,** and **tracking trail.** See note at **track,** *v.*
1777 (1951) *Sask.Jnls* 150: This day we proceeded on the Tracking ground. **1778** (1934) HEARNE & TURNOR *Journals* 200: . . . we have passed all the tracking ground which is so exceeding bad that no person is able to track that cannot walk without shoes. . . . **1847** (1910) MURRAY *Yukon* 36: . . . there is good "tracking ground" all the way unless the water is very high. **1922** *Beaver* July 10/1: [It is] treacherous tracking ground where men . . . hang on by their hands and feet. . . .
2 a stretch of shallow or fast water where canoes, boats, etc. must be moved by tracking (def. 1).
1949 MacGREGOR *Blankets and Beads* 186: There are . . . two other swift stretches on the Saskatchewan, and these are referred to as the "tracking ground." *Ibid.* 196: When the tracking ground was reached, the men had to get out and walk along the shore line pulling the boats. . . .

tracking line *Esp.North* a strong line or rope used in tracking (def. 1). See also **cordelle,** *n.*, **dragline, hauling-line, line,** *n.* (def. 1a), **main line** (def. 1), **towline, tracking-rope, track-line** (def. 2), and **whale line.**
1784 (1954) *Moose Ft Jnls* 257: Tracking lines are made in the same manner as I am told Mr. Turnor made one here in your time, it's so simple a contrivance that any body that has seen Rope makers at work, or can twist three threads together can do it. **1840** (1951) *Beaver* Sep. 35/1: . . . a tracking line was attached to the boat, and the men towed her along the Shore. **1953** LOWER

Voyages 25: The banks of the Albany are wide and smooth, and it is therefore easy to walk along, a dozen or fifteen men on the tracking line, towing the boat. **1964** INNIS *Fur Trade* 305: Old tracking line or bale cords were used for buoy lines, for trout lines and for mending nets.

tracking-rope *n. Obs.* See **tracking line.**
1872 BALLANTYNE *Pioneers* 98: Being lifted on the shoulders of some of the men, the tracking-rope was fastened to the bow. . . .

tracking shoe *North, Hist.* a special type of heavy moccasin or beef shoe, *q.v.*, issued by the Hudson's Bay Company to its boatmen for use in tracking (def. 1) over rough or wet ground.
1830 (1940) *Minutes of Council* (H.B.C.) 266: That Gentleman in charge of Districts & Posts be directed to use their utmost endeavors to collect large quantities of . . . tracking Shoes . . . as they are articles absolutely necessary for the trade in many parts of the country and cannot be purchased in Europe or Canada. **1913** COWIE *Adventurers* 213: The duty of . . . making a certain number of tracking shoes for the voyageurs . . . was all that was required of the women of the fort. **1964** INNIS *Fur Trade* 305: In Mackenzie River district, tracking shoes and moccasins were ordered, 120 pairs (60 with tops) in one year.

tracking trail See **tracking ground.**
1932 (1967) *Cdn Geog.Jnl* Mar. 97/2: Occasionally it was found advisable to row across the river to get the best tracking trail. . . .

track-line *n.* 1 See **track-rope.**
1853 (1892) KANE *Arctic Explor.* 66: Each man had his own shoulder-belt, or "rue-raddy," as we used to call it, and his own track-line, which, for want of horse-hair, was made of Manilla rope; it traversed freely by a ring on a loop or bridle, that extended from runner to runner in front of the sledge.

2 See **tracking line.**
1938 ELLS *Northland Trails* 27: Gone are the trackers, coiled are the track-lines. **1947** TAYLOR *Canada* 350: The left-hand sketch shows two 40-foot York boats being hauled up-river by track-lines. **1963** PATTERSON *Far Pastures* 199: I picked up the trackline—a hundred feet of light line, one end fastened to the ring in the bow, the other to the rear seat. We shoved the canoe out on it and I started to steer it with the line down the riffle.

trackline *v.* See **track,** *v.* (def. 1). See also **tracking line.**
1925 HENDRYX *Oak and Iron* 222: ". . . we picked up them scows for twenty dollars at Fort McMurray, an' we tracklined 'em up with a crew of Injuns. . . ."

track-rope *n. North, Obs.* a heavy rope used for dragging or hauling sleds, boats, etc. See also **track-line** (def. 1).
1850 SNOW *Voyage Prince Albert* 133: . . . each man had for safety his tracking belt . . . so fastened to the track-rope that he could not well fall through any hole without first letting himself loose. **1854** (1892) KANE *Arctic Explor.* 106: . . . a large sled with broad runners . . . was taken down, scraped, polished, lashed, and fitted with trackropes and *rue-raddies*—the lines arranged to draw as near as possible in a line with the centre of gravity.

track speeder See **speeder** (def. 1a).
1966 *Kingston Whig-Standard* (Ont.) 1 Sep. 3/2: The roadmaster came down on his track speeder and gave us a fatherly talking to.

tractor brigade *North* See **cat-train.** Cp. **fur brigade.**
1958 *Edmonton Jnl* 24 June 4 2/3: The tractor brigades started operating out of Grimshaw for the far north.

tractor caboose *North* See **caboose** (def. 5b).
1935 *Beaver* June 61/3: They stayed weeks at the terminus, during which time they built tractor cabooses, but due to some hitch over fishing permits they were obliged to withdraw for the present.

tractor-log *v. Lumbering* haul (logs) by tractor.
1965 *Star Wkly* 13 Feb. 7/1: We high-lead-logged the slopes of the Iskut, tractor-logged the river bottom [and] built a road up the south shore. . . .

tractor road or trail *North* a road used by cat-trains, *q.v.* See also **cat trail** and **tractor-train road.**
1946 *Beaver* June 4/2: . . . the force [Exercise Muskox] set out across the lake to reach the winter tractor trail. . . . **1948** ONRAET *Sixty Below* 35: Our next big rapids were hundreds of miles down at Fort Fitzgerald and there was a good tractor road round it.

tractor swing *North* See **cat-train.**
1959 *Argosy* (Cdn sec.) July 27/1: . . . he was at Churchill, waiting for an Easter Sunday snowstorm to stop, so he could fly north to oversee his tractor swing on the ice of Hudson Bay.

tractor train *North* See **cat-train.**
[**1936** *Cdn Geog.Jnl* XII 34/2: Presently, weird-looking tractor-like machines, drawing veritable young freight trains on bob sleighs, were creeping through the northern bush, over lake and stream and muskeg. . . .] **1941** *Beaver* June 56/2: The contractors hauled . . . some eight hundred tons of supplies . . . by tractor train through heavily timbered country. . . . **1965** *Time* (Cdn ed.) 26 Feb. 10/3: A tractor train crawled most of the forty miles from Stewart, only to be turned back by the threat of a new avalanche.

tractor-train road or trail *North* See **tractor road.**
1947 *Beaver* June 19/1: He stated that these animals probably came down from the barren lands near Churchill following the winter tractor-train roads. . . . **1958** *Edmonton Jnl* 24 June 3 10/3: . . . Mills Lake . . . was the terminus of the winter tractor-train trail which fed the Canol pipeline project. . . .

trade *n. Fur Trade* 1 a. a quantity of furs to be offered in return for goods or credit.
1800 (1897) COUES *New Light* I 154: The Crees had brought a good trade . . . three black bear skins and a few foxes.

b. (attributive uses) designating articles or goods made or bought to be exchanged for furs. See also **trade gun, trading goods, trading gun,** etc.
1922 FLAHERTY *Eskimo Friends* 12: The women wore native trousers of deerskin and parkas of trade cloth edged with red, blue, and yellow tapes with pewter beads and spoons and large Canadian pennies dangling and jingling from the ends of them. *Ibid.* 120: Trade candy, of colours dazzling to the eye, and black plug tobacco went far to break down their reserve. **1941** *Beaver* June 26/2: The sashes collected among the Indians, in the past fifty years, form a group distinctly apart from the trade sashes of the Hudson's Bay

Company. **1953** MOWERY *Mounted Police* 65: ... he
... put the string on a flat rock, along with a fine
hunting knife and a pound of trade tobacco. **1964**
Wildlife Rev. May 21: With the appearance of the
"trade kettle" on the scene, Indian mobility increased
tremendously.

2 *Nfld* See 1964 quote.
1828 (1964) *Nfld Qtly* Summer 27/2: ... the Trade had
its commencement in this country about 24 years
ago.... **1964** *Ibid.* 27/2: The noun "trade" in old
Newfoundland usage, not yet entirely dead, means
commercial firm, e.g. Bowring's Trade for Bowring
Brothers, Ltd.

trade *v. Fur Trade* **1** exchange furs for goods or
credit.
1697 (1929) KELSEY *Papers* 84: 3 cannoes came to the
fort and some sayled haing tradded told Beaver into
the warehouse. **1723** (1923) *Beaver* Mar. 234/2: the Inds.
yᵗ came here last traided this morning. **1835** (1923)
B.C.Hist.Qtly VIII 139: The Indians brought in some
deer & traded a few beaver. **1951** GILLIS & MYLES
North Pole 120: "Dress up warmly and come see Jimmy
trade," suggested John.

2 trade out of, obtain (something) from someone by
exchanging something of less value than what is
received.
1942 (1945) GARD *Johnny Chinook* 341: After which he
traded them out of their fur....

trade goods† *Fur Trade* See **trading goods.**
1921 HAWORTH *Trailmakers* 202: This post was so
remote that seven years would elapse between the time
trade goods left London for Fort Selkirk and the time
the furs obtained in exchange arrived. **1957** *Beaver*
Winter 13/1: In time, the commodities used in the
purchase of furs, or in any other dealings with the
natives, came to be known as "trade goods."

trade gun *Fur Trade, Hist.* See **Indian gun.**
1896 RUSSELL *Far North* 81: The Indians' guns were of
the pattern known in the country as "trade guns."
They were of small bore, long, single- or double-
barrelled, muzzle-loaders of light weight. **1921** *Beaver*
June 2/1: ... the old-time "trade gun" (which came to
be a primary item in an Indian trapper's equipment)....

trade jargon See **Chinook Jargon.**
1896 RUSSELL *Far North* 141: The Indians conversed
with the Eskimos in the trade jargon of the coast, which
included even Kanaka words in its vocabulary.

trader *n. Fur Trade* **1** See **fur trader.**
1775 (1934) HEARNE *Journal* 193: These losses together
with their payment not only runs away with all the
Profit, but renders the Company's Servants the make
game and laughing stock of every trader from Canada.
1897 TYRRELL *Sub-Arctics* 106: About us were to be
seen evidences of communication with traders, such as a
large tin kettle, two old guns and a pair of moleskin
trousers. **1955** *Western Star* (Corner Brook, Nfld) 14
Mar. 5/2: Long after he had made his desperate journey
into the wilderness did the trappers, the settlers and the
traders come.

2 *Obs.* See **carrier.**
1776 (1934) HEARNE & TURNOR *Journals* 189: [Primeau]
who is his linguist, trader, a Pataroon, and everything
... has but 25£ a year.... **1795** (1911) HEARNE *Journey*
84: I have often heard it observed, that the Indians who

attend the deer-pounds might, in the course of a winter,
collect a vast number of pelts, which would well
deserve the attention of those who are called carriers or
traders.

3 See **storekeeper** (def. 2).
1823 (1963) MACLEOD & MORTON *Cuthbert Grant* 84:
[He was] a tolerable clerk[,] good trader[,] active and
steady[;] will be extremely useful in Red River on
account of his influence with the Half breeds. **1856**
[see quote at **storekeeper** (def. 2)]. **1948** ONRAET *Sixty
Below* 93: All the traders carry 30-30 in stock, and if a
man was to run short in the bush for any reason,
chances are that the first person he'd meet—white,
Indian or half-breed—would have 30-30. **1960** (1963)
MACLEOD & MORTON *Cuthbert Grant* 57: [Trans.]
Good Trader, join our dance.
There's Fraser's nose; one glance
Tells us that he will like our little ball.

trade room *Fur Trade, Hist.* See **trading room.**
1867 LORD *Wilderness* 56: In many of the *Posts* the trade
room is cleverly contrived, so as to prevent a sudden rush
of Indians, the approach from outside the pickets being
through a long, narrow passage, only of sufficient width
to admit one Indian at a time, the passage being bent
at an acute angle near the window, where the trader
stands. **1942** NIVEN *Flying Years* 106: The whisky
smugglers have forts such as none of the old Northwest
forts were like—double-walled, some of them. And do
they let their customers into the trade-rooms even in
small groups? No, sir!

trade store or **shop** *Fur Trade* See **trading store.**
1907 HUNTER *Cdn Wilds* 18: The sum total [of the furs]
being arrived at[,] the amount of his outfit and supplies
being deducted[,] he [the trapper] was given a "bon" on
the trade shops for his credit balance. **1951** BULIARD
Inuk 313: In the same way the buyer's color was an
infallible price test at the trade store, where the Copper
Eskimo paid prices three times as high as those the
white man paid.

trade token *Fur Trade, Hist.* See **beaver** (def. 5a
and picture).
1957 *Beaver* Autumn 41/1: We still issued some trade
tokens, when the red men brought in a bunch of pelts.

trade whisky *Fur Trade, Hist.* See **Indian liquor.**
1952 HOWARD *Strange Empire* 261: "Trade" or "Injun
whiskey" as distributed on the Northwestern frontier
was made of one gallon of raw alcohol to three gallons
of water. For color and "flavor" the trader added a
pound of tea or a pound of rank black chewing tobacco,
some Jamaica ginger and a handful of red peppers.

trading chief *Fur Trade* See **chief.**
1966 *Beaver* Winter 54/1: The trading chief of the
Mountain Indians got all kinds of stuff from the trader
and he made a feast. In those days all the trading chiefs
got feasts from the Hudson's Bay.

trading coat *Fur Trade, Obs.* See **captain's coat.**
1783 (1954) *Moose Ft Jnls* 155: Sibley you'll keep close
employed in fitting up the new House & Leask in
making Trading Coats.... **1784** *Ibid.* 32: Two Taylors
at work for the men and one making trading coats.

trading fort *Fur Trade* See **fort.**
1952 *North Star* (Yellowknife) Oct. 1/1: The place is ...
Yellowknife, Hay River and the settlements and trading
forts up and down the great water system that joins in
the Mackenzie and empties its waters into the Arctic
Ocean. **1958** *Edmonton Jnl* 9 Aug. 4/3: His congregation
could be found wherever he happened to be at any
time. Stony Indians to the south, Crees to the north and
the few whites at the trading forts were his congregation.

trading goods *Fur Trade* the guns, ammunition, tobacco, blankets, etc. that the fur traders carried in stock to exchange for furs. See also **goods** and **trade goods**.

1777 (1954) *Moose Ft Jnls* 156: We are much concerned to Discover that so many of Our Trading Goods are given away & applied under the Article of Expences especially as they rise so high in Proportion to the Returns in Made Beaver from each Factory. **1913** COWIE *Adventurers* 289: I was ordered to go out to meet him with a fresh supply of trading goods. . . . **1954** *Moose Ft Jnls* xviii: In addition to trading goods to be taken up and furs to be brought down, food for the whole distance had to be carried.

trading gun or **piece** *Fur Trade, Obs.* See **Indian gun**.

1804 (1933) FARIES *Diary* 201: [He] told us he had but 15 trading pieces. . . . **1821** (1938) SIMPSON *Athabasca Jnl* 408: The Trading Guns (marked Wilson) are not to be compared with those of "Barnets" make which the N.W. Companies import. . . .

trading house *Fur Trade, Hist.* See **trading post** (def. 1).

1772 (1908) COCKING *Journal* 101: . . . in the afternoon passed by an old Trading house, belonging to the French pedlars before the conquest of Quebec. . . . **1816** (1818) HALL *Travels* 104: The only habitation beyond it, is a trading house of the North-west Company, who drive a pretty gainful traffic with the Indians of the neighbourhood, taking their furs at a shilling each, and selling them those commodities custom has rendered necessaries, at their own price. . . . **1864** *Nor'Wester* (R.R.S.) 10 June 1/1: . . . the green in front of the Trading House was covered with the swarthy devils in all manner of paint and adornment—drums, pipes, hatchets and knives. **1949** LAWSON *N.B.Story* 137: In order to cultivate friendly relations with the Indians and guard against the attempts of the enemy to wean them away, it was decided to establish an Indian trading-house for them at a little cove above the Reversing Falls.

trading outfit *Fur Trade* See **outfit** (def. 1a).

1852 (1966) *Beaver* Winter 9/2: Their Vessel . . . had $1500 on board in Gold and Silver and a complete trading outfit. . . . **1957** *Ibid*. Winter 50/1: York . . . forwarded into the interior the trading outfits brought to its vast warehouse by sea from London.

trading(-post) permit *Fur Trade* a permit issued to an applicant wishing to establish a trading post and who undertakes to meet certain stipulated conditions.

1934 (1964) JENNESS *Eskimo Admin*. II 57: . . . it has been decided to grant you a trading permit for this location upon the distinct understanding that the company will comply with the under-mentioned terms. . . . Trading post permit No. 405 authorizing your company [HBC] to establish this trading post is enclosed and we would be glad to receive assurance that the conditions enumerated above will be complied with. A fee of one dollar is charged for this permit.

trading post 1 *Fur Trade* a building or a group of buildings serving as a trading centre for a fur company in a certain region. See also **post, trading house,** and **trading station**.

1821 (1900) GARRY *Diary* 133: At half past three we started and at half past four arrived at Bas de la Riviere where the North West had a trading Post, now become Hudson Bay's. **1907** HUNTER *Cdn Wilds* 209:

At these places are trading posts where they barter and sell their winter's catch, get new supplies for another year, and load their canoes again in September for another nine or ten months in the Far North Wilds. **1965** *Globe and Mail* (Toronto) 17 Feb. 31/7: In the bay areas, many live up to 500 miles from a trading post. . . .

2 See **trading store** (def. 2).

1965 *B.C.Digest* August 69/1: Stan opened a trading-post and garage at this out of the way location 30 years ago.

trading room *Fur Trade* the room in a trading post (def. 1) where the actual bartering takes place. See also **Indian shop, Indian storehouse, trade room, trading shop,** and **trading store** (def. 1). Cp. **Indian hall**.

1697 (1929) KELSEY *Papers* 75: Received some goods into yᵉ trading room &c told into the warehouse 38 coat beaver 26 half and 12 whole parchment. c**1775** (1947) *Beaver* June 46/1: . . . in the evening the drum is beat upon the works to give notice the trading room is going to be shut. . . . **1848** BALLANTYNE *Hudson's Bay* 38: Thus an Indian arrives at a fort with a bundle of furs, with which he proceeds to the Indian trading-room. **1921** HAWORTH *Trailmakers* 159: If, in spite of all these precautions, the Indians either in the trading room or Indian room grew so violent as to be really dangerous, the traders could fire down upon them from loopholes in the ceiling. **1964** *Calgary Herald* 15 May 26/1: Completed phases include . . . Rocky Mountain House stockade (the trading room will also be built this year).

trading rum See **Indian liquor**.

1878 *Sask.Herald* (Battleford, N.W.T.) 23 Sep. 1/2: The Indians of Edmonton . . . have succeeded in manufacturing beverage that will make them drunk and just as sick as the old fashioned trading rum or any other liquor as formerly compounded and sold to them.

trading shop See **trading room**.

1867 (1876) LORD *Wilderness* 55: The trading shop, and store of goods employed in bartering with the savages, adjoins the trader's house, although not actually part of it.

trading station *Fur Trade, Obs.* See **trading-post** (def. 1).

1896 RUSSELL *Far North* 160: The inhabitants of the trading stations during the winter of '93-'94 were upon the verge of starvation themselves, and certainly could not have relieved the natives in case of famine. **1897** TYRRELL *Sub-Arctics* 213: For nearly two hundred years it had been the practice of the Hudson's Bay Company to send out from England every year one or two small sailing vessels with supplies to their trading stations on Hudson Bay.

trading store 1 *Fur Trade* See **trading room**. See also **trade store**.

1856 BALLANTYNE *Young Fur-Traders* 60: This is the trading-store. It is always recognisable, if natives are in the neighbourhood, by the bevy of red men that cluster round it. . . . **1957** *Beaver* Spring 27: Save for such innovations as the radio and the outboard motor and a greater variety of merchandise in the two trading stores, the people live much the same life as they have done for generations.

2 a store operated by a private merchant who engages in a certain amount of barter, usually in a frontier community. See also **trading post** (def. 2).
1880 GORDON *Mountain and Prairie* 135: A small single-storied dwelling made of hewn logs, little better than the rude farm-house of a Canadian backwoodsman, a trading-store as plain as the dwelling, a smoke-house for curing and storing fish and meat, and a stable constitute the whole establishment. **1909** CAMERON *New North* 340: The settlement boasts two churches, two mission schools, and two trading stores. . . .

trail† *n.* a way, especially a footpath, through wild country or bush.
1858 *Brit.Colonist* (Victoria) 27 Dec. 3/2: The man . . . had no right to the privilege of using the trail for his walks. . . . **1862** MAYNE *Four Years in B.C.* 105: At the present day the trail—which is the name given in the country for any sort of path—is so improved that I believe mules travel by it. **1909** BEMISTER *Stories* 103: The Indian's [sic] called their path through the bush and over the prairie, a trail, and for many years these were the only paths on the great prairies. **1965** *Maclean's* 3 July 23/1: . . . the trailmakers have been greeted with a surprising degree of co-operation from the landowners . . . whose permission had to be obtained for routing the trail across their land.

trail axe a light, short-handled axe, or hatchet, carried by persons on the trail, used for cutting away underbrush, chopping wood for fires, etc. See also **tripping axe**.
1954 PATTERSON *Dangerous River* 226: I . . . hit the high spots back to camp, knocking what ice I could off my snowshoes with the back of my trail axe as I went. **1959** LEISING *Arctic Wings* 37: We packed the sled with . . . a trail ax, and our two guns lashed well forward on top of the load.

trail biscuit See **bannock**.
1959 SLUMAN *Blackfoot Crossing* 8: . . . the fruits of Little Stree's industry [were] pemmican and trail biscuit.

trail blaze See **blaze**, *n.* (def. 1).
1965 *Maclean's* 3 July 30/3: [I] peered at Nadjiwon's trail blazes. . . .

trailblazer† *n.* **1** See **trailman**.
1942 HAIG-BROWN *Timber* 218: "You never were much of a trail blazer. Could a man make it up to the lake, cut across to the South Fork and get out down to the Beach by Sunday night?" **1948** MOIR *Sinners and Saints* 74: The crowd of idle fellows got a great kick out of the old "trail blazer."

2 See **trail-cutter**.
1958 ATKINSON *Hist.of Penticton* 20: Let us join the trail blazers as they marked out a route. **1965** *Maclean's* 3 July 22/1: . . . Mac Kirk [was] one of the Owen Sound trailblazers. . . .

3 one who leads the way into new fields; pathfinder. See also **trail-breaker** (def. 3) and **trail-maker** (def. 1).
1955 *Western Star* (Corner Brook, Nfld) 14 Mar. 5/2: He was the trail-blazer, the pathfinder in whose wake the tide of empire rolled westward. **1963** *B.C.Digest* Nov.-Dec. 35/1: It [gold] drew men from all walks of life, converting them into trail-blazers and town founders.

trail-breaker *n. North* **1** See **forerunner**.
1931 GREY OWL *Last Frontier* 53: "Dinner," say the trail breakers; well, they ought to know, they are bearing the brunt of the work. **1963** *Beaver* Winter 15/1: Boys of about thirteen are usually the trail breakers of the group [Naskapi Indians], which constantly moves in the eternal search for food. . . .

2 See quote. Cp. **trail shoe**.
1931 GREY OWL *Last Frontier* 64: . . . slipping with deft ankle movements into the bridles of an immense pair of trail breakers (large snowshoes), [he] is away.

3 See **trailblazer** (def. 3).
1959 *Press* Dec. 6: It is on the subject of pioneers—trailbreakers, bushwhackers, sodbusters, homesteaders—that the slick "free enterprise" propagandist . . . waxes most eloquent. . . .

trail-breaking *n. North* See **track-beating**.
1942 *Beaver* Dec. 42/2: So it was that we engaged the aid of another guide . . . for trail-breaking. . . .

trailbuilder *n.* **1** See **trail-cutter**.
1965 *Maclean's* 3 July 23/1: According to one story, a party of trailbuilders came to a gulch with steep limestone cliffs surrounding it and saw a bearded fellow hoeing a garden beside a shanty below.

2 a bulldozer moving ahead to break a trail for a party in the bush.
1949 ROBERTS *Mackenzie* 213: The large trailbuilder necessarily was always in the lead.

trail-cart *n. Hist.* See **Red River cart** and picture.
1916 BRIDLE *Sons of Can.* 69: . . . York boats and trail-carts were being superceded by freight trains and passenger coaches.

trail cook one who cooks for parties on the trail.
1951 ANGIER *At Home* 31: Brad was telling me last night that you've got the reputation of being the best trail cook in the North.

trail-cutter *n.* a person who cuts or breaks a trail through the bush. See also **trailblazer** (def. 2), **trailbuilder** (def. 1), and **trail-maker** (def. 3).
1858 *Brit.Colonist* (Victoria) 11 Dec. 2/4: The majority of the Lillooet trail cutters would have remained had it not been grossly mismanaged. . . . **1958** *Edmonton Jnl* 24 June 4 6/1: Normally, the trail-cutters work a four-month season in the winter; when spring comes and the ground begins to thaw, they must get out—and fast.

trail-horse *n.* a horse adept in making his way along tortuous, rocky trails in the mountains.
1905 OUTRAM *Cdn Rockies* 287: My old "Nigger," unsurpassed as a trail-horse, clever in fallen timber, excellent at fording streams, sure-footed on grassy slopes or rough, stony ground, dependable at all times when one is on his back, was utterly depraved when he was cast loose and would lead the other horses into mischief if any were practicable.

trail-maker *n.* **1** See **trailblazer** (def. 3).
1921 LAUT *Cariboo Trail* 15: Ragged, poor, roofless, grubstaked by "pardner" or outfitter on a basis of half profit, the prospector stands as the eternal type of the trail-maker for finance.

2 See **trailman**.
1930 BEAMES *Army* 280: Billy, though an unexcelled trail maker in an unsettled wilderness, had the not uncommon peculiarity among pioneers of becoming confused in a network of roads.

3 See **trail-cutter**.

been greeted with a surprising degree of co-operation from the landowners . . . whose permission had to be obtained for routing the trail across their land.

trailman *n.* a man knowledgeable about life on the trail in wild country. See also **trailblazer** (def. 1) and **trail-maker** (def. 2).

1858 *Brit.Colonist* (Victoria) 27 Dec. 3/2: The man . . . was no trail-man but a stranger. . . . **1905** OUTRAM *Cdn Rockies* 271: He could only accompany us as far as the Saskatchewan, leaving the camp in charge of Jim Simpson and Fred Ballard, both experienced hunters and trailmen, and both excellent cooks.

trail musher See **sourdough** (def. 2b).

1910 FRASER *Red Meekins* 23: "That's what every trail musher says when he brings in a find, 'gold-bearin' quartz.''

Trail of '98 *Hist.* any of several long, hard trails to the Yukon, followed by stampeders during the gold rush of 1898-99.

1910 SERVICE *The Trail of Ninety-Eight* [Title].
1938 BLACK *Seventy Years* 159: The hydraulic outfit was installed at Excelsior Creek, where I had staked my first claims when I came over the Trail of '98. **1958** *Edmonton Jnl* 18 July 19/8: These "successful" men landed in the Klondike with little more than the ragged clothes they wore, their 20 to 40 horses, tons of supplies and equipment with which they left Edmonton strung along mountain slopes and in the woods of the Trail of '98.

trail ride a trip through the mountains on horse-back, taken by a party of tourists, campers, etc., led by experienced trailmen, *q.v.*

1943 *Crag and Canyon* 13 Aug. 1/3: As in the Trail Ride, the ladies boasted substantial numerical majority over the male hikers. **1958** *Edmonton Jnl* 19 July 2/3: Friday's ride was preceded by a gathering highlighted by the showing of trail ride and other films.

trail shoe *North* See quotes. See also **tripping shoe.** Cp. **trail-breaker** (def. 2).

1924 MASON *Arctic Forests* 33: The trail shoes are small, to break down the soft snow for the dogs to follow and run on the broken trail. **1955** BEAVER *Yukon Trader* 146: Her snow-shoes were the short, narrow birch webs called "trail shoes" and were not built for deep snow. **1966** PATTERSON *Trail* 61: Reed and the Indian moved swiftly over the trodden, blood-stained snow on their light trail shoes. . . .

trail-sled *n. Maritimes* a flat horse-drawn sled used for hauling wood from the bush.

1952 BUCKLER *Mountain and Valley* 5: . . . Joseph tied a bag of straw on the trail-sled for a seat and took him to the woods for the first time.

trail work *North* the hauling of freight on tractor roads, *q.v.*

1963 *Kingston Whig-Standard* (Ont.) 13 Feb. 21/3: [The RN110] is used in the north for trail work and winter hauling.

train[1] *n.* [< Cdn F < F *traîne* woodcutter's cart] *Obs.* a low runnerless sled used in early Quebec for hauling goods to market and for similar purposes. See also **traineau** (def. 1). Also spelled *traine.*

1783 *Quebec Gaz.* 22 May 2/1: No person shall come with traines, carts or other carriages, loaded with hay, straw or wood within the limits of the market-place on market days, but shall resort to the parade near the parish church. **1788** *Ibid.* 27 Nov. 2/1: Had reason and common sense been consulted . . . the sleigh and sled of

Vermont and New-York or the cariole and train of Canada would have been pronounced best, most convenient and most useful. **1813** *Montreal Herald* 31 Dec. 3/3: The evil complained of will never be remedied, until the use of double sleighs or trains [is banned]. . . . **1819** *Cdn Courant* (Montreal) 5 Feb. 3/1: If the habitant considered the train better suited to work in his woodland, let him continue. **1841** *Bytown* [Ottawa] *Gaz.* 11 Nov. 2/1: No cariole, train, berline, or other winter carriage, (excepting the sleigh above described) shall be used unless the horse or horses shall be harnessed thereto in the manner above mentioned.

train[2] *n.* [< Cdn F *traîne sauvage* toboggan; cp. **traineau**] **1 a.** *Obs.* See **cariole** (def. 2a and picture). Also spelled *traine.*

1789 MCKENZIE *Reminiscences* 33: I make traines, bend snow-shoe frames, and with perseverance, I'll perhaps learn to handle the *couteau croche.* **1801** (1897) COUES *New Light* I 169: I sent two men to Portage la Prairie with two trains and four dogs. **1918** DAVIDSON *North West Co.* 246: A train, or *traineau,* was a sledge made of a thin board, ten or twelve inches wide, and eight or ten feet long. It was bent up at one end, by which it was dragged on the snow or ice. **1933** GATES *Five Traders* 219n: These *traines* were usually drawn by dogs, but at this post horses were used.

b. See **dog-team.**

1801 (1897) COUES *New Light* I 175: Another of my men brought in six young wolves he had found in one hole; they were very tame, and we proposed to keep them for the trains, as they are of the large species. **1820** (1938) SIMPSON *Athabasca Jnl* 102: A Thousand to fifteen hundred livres is no unusual price for a good train, say 3 dogs. **1956** KEMP *Northern Trader* 53: . . . eating nothing but pail candy, he once ran a hundred-mile relay race against four trains of dogs.

c. *Hist.* a dog-sled and the dog-team together. See also **dog-train** (def. 1).

1806 (1960) FRASER *Letters and Journals* 203: . . . the first trip he made . . . on the snow with trains. **1858** (1860) HIND *Assiniboine Exped.* II 83: I engaged a half-breed of the name of Cline . . . to organize my trains. **1939** *Beaver* June 24/2: Back in the train age again, Brownie strained in his collar. . . .

2 *Obs.* See **travois** (def. 1 and picture).

1834-43 (1955) RUSSELL *Journal* 52: . . . seven of 8 [Indians] had been badly wounded which they dragged away on trains to their village. **1859** (1870) SOUTHESK *Saskatchewan* 63: A dog happened to pass drawing a "train" after the common Indian fashion.

train[3] *n.* **1** *Hist.* **a.** See **dog-train** (def. 4).

1900 LONDON *Son of Wolf* 209: An hour later, the train had taken on the likeness of a black pencil crawling in a long, straight line across a mighty sheet of foolscap. **1913** WILLIAMS *Wilderness Trail* 157: In ten minutes, a goodly supply of frozen rabbits had been packed on the north-bound train. . . .

b. a number of wagons drawn by teams of oxen, employed in hauling freight.

1945 GARD *Johnny Chinook* 41: Six teams to the train, twelve yoke to the team, with the three wagons swinging and creaking along behind, and the sixteen-foot bull whips popping like pistol shots. **1962** *Alta Hist.Rev.* Autumn 14/1: The whole train, consisting of five or six "strings" of twenty bulls yoked to three "prairie-schooners" . . . [is] superintended by a "wagon-boss."

2 *North* See **cat-train.**
1958 WATTERS *B.C.Cent.Anthol.* 421: Two tractor drivers manoeuvered their cats into position to pull the two "trains"....

train boss *North* the foreman in charge of a cat-train, *q.v.*
1953 MOON *Saskatchewan* 229: The cat-skinners, as the train bosses are called, like it when the temperature is between forty and sixty degrees below zero.

train dog *Hist.* a dog employed in a dog-team, *q.v.* See also **train²** (def. 1b).
1881 *Edmonton Bull.* 21 Feb. 3/2: The government's train dogs at Fort Saskatchewan made a raid on S. Taber's meat house one day last week and made away with the greater portion of his stock of beef. **1910** FRASER *Red Meekins* 251: ... so the body was placed on a rough prospector's toboggan, drawn by six train dogs. **1938** ELLS *Northland Trails* 19: Nearby crouched the train dogs—waiting....

traine¹ *n.* See **train¹.**

traine² *n.* See **train².**

traineau ['treno *or* tre'no] *n.* **-eaux.** [< Cdn F < F *traîneau* sled; cp. **train²**] *Hist.* **1** See **train¹.**
1791 (1911) SIMCOE *Diary* 54: I was amused by seeing several dogs of all sizes drawing traineaux or sleds with wood. **1845** TOLFREY *Sportsman* I 262: The common country *traineau*, as used by the *Habitans*, is open to the same objection; and from the floor of the vehicle, if I may so express myself, being so close to the surface over which it passes the loose snow is driven before it in heaps, and the hillocks so formed are termed by the Native *cahôts*. **1903** CARR-HARRIS *White Chief* 23: Traineaux drawn by French ponies, and toboggans, loaded with furs and drawn by several dogs in tandem, were frequently seen in the streets [of Montreal].... **1928** LEROSSIGNOL *Beauport Road* 87: There was a certain disadvantage, too, in the traineau, where there was only room for one, while Jean walked or ran behind, guiding the dogs.
2 See **cariole** (def. 2a and picture).
1820 (1823) FRANKLIN *Journey* 125: We passed ... Train Lake, which received its name from being the place where the traders procured the birch to make their sledges, or traineaux. **1888** (1890) ST. MAUR *Impressions* 26: The dogs which draw the traineaux are also fed with them, one dried fish being the daily allowance for each dog. **1931** CONNOR *Rock and River* 96: At the tail of the gorgeous procession came ... a dog team hitched to a luxuriously appointed traineau, driven by a Hudson's Bay trapper in all his glory. **1933** GATES *Five Traders* 219n: A *traine* or *traineau* in the Northwest was a sledge or sleigh about seven feet in length, the front end of which was turned up in a picturesque fashion to enable it to pass over bushes and low obstructions.

traineau man *Obs.* See **dog-driver.**
1891 *Cdn Indian* Mar. 179: Many are the interesting stories told of the adventures of old traineau men.

train-leader *n. North* See **leader** (def. 2).
1900 FRASER *Mooswa* 148: ... the Train-leader is a big Huskie Dog, and he'll chew ... the Wolf into little bits....

train road *Obs.* a winter road (def. 2a) kept open for sleighs hauling freight, logs, etc.

1896 GOURLAY *Hist.Ottawa* 165: They had considerable trouble with teams and their wide double sleighs on the train roads, keeping one animal in the snow alternately to keep from wearing one out.

tramp *n. Obs.* an organized hike held by a snowshoe club.
1884 *Brandon Blade* (Man.) 21 Feb. 9/2: The several Toboggan Slides were illuminated every evening, and the Snowshoe Clubs invited all strangers in the city to participate in their tramps. **1884** *Prince Albert Times* (Sask.) 21 Mar. 1/2: The snow shoe club had the best tramp of the season on Tuesday evening.

trans-Canada *adj.* spanning Canada from Atlantic to Pacific.
1916 WOOD *Tourist's N.W.* 315: The Island Automobile Club of Victoria, with the co-operation of motor organisations throughout the Dominion, is promoting a campaign for the improvement and construction of roads which it is proposed shall in combination form a trans-Canada motor route. **1963** *Maclean's* 2 Nov. 56/4: ... for every twenty French Canadians you encounter in my house or yours, fifteen can affirm that they have been treated to the discreditable "speak white." I harvested it three times in the course of my trans-Canada tour.

Trans-Canada *n.* See **Trans-Canada Highway.**
1963 *Maclean's* 20 Apr. 22/3: "This summer the wife and I are going to drive the Trans-Canada for two weeks." **1963** *Sask.News* Oct. 1/3: The Trans-Canada campsites are established on a cost-sharing plan between the Federal and Provincial governments.

Trans-Canada Highway the joint federal-provincial highway (and alternate routes) extending from St. John's, Nfld, to Victoria, B.C.
1953 LOWER *Voyages* 142: West of Hearst, the Trans-Canada highway cuts back slightly to the south and enters the Canadian Shield again. **1962** *Time* (Cdn ed.) 10 Aug. 10/3: Their goal [was to] travel the Trans-Canada Highway end to end for the first time.

transcontinental *n.* **1** either of the two railways that cross Canada.
[**1877** ST. JOHN *Sea of Mountains* I 163: We say that in the first place, without the trans-continental railway British Columbia is of no use to Canada, nor Canada to British Columbia.] **1907** *Eye Opener* (Calgary) 18 July 3/3: Dealing with the immense expenditure on the G.T.P. transcontinental in excess of the original estimates, the Toronto News puts the case very fairly, as follows.... **1955** *Shawinigan Standard* 12 Jan. 2/2: Yet the grain that train carries moves for exactly the same number of cents per bushel, a rate fixed by the rigid agreement shortly after the first trans-continental opened for business.
2 a train on a trans-Canada run.
1920 GIBBON *Conquering Hero* 147: ... at Winnipeg the transcontinental was boarded by one Bill Panns, a rancher on his way back to the foothills after two years in a German prison. **1964** CARROLL *Shy Photographer* 6: "You heard the one about the squaw on the trans-continental?"

trans-provincial *adj.* crossing a province.
1916 WOOD *Tourist's N.W.* 316: A trans-provincial highway is building through southern British Columbia from the mountains, via Cranbrook, Nelson, Penticton (foot of Okanagan Lake) and Princeton, to Hope in the Fraser River Valley. **1952** PUTNAM *Cdn Regions* 338/1: They have not, for instance, been able to get the Ontario Government to construct adequate transprovincial highways.

trap berth *Nfld* an area marked off by a trap fisherman, *q.v.* and claimed for his own use.

1905 GRENFELL *Harvest* 122: ... the Government has had to pass a law forbidding any mark to be put out claiming a "trap berth," as it is called, before a certain day and hour.

trapboat *n. Nfld* a boat, 25 to 35 feet long, having low sides and capable of carrying a cod-trap, *q.v.* See also **trapskiff**.

1922 *Beaver* Feb. 9/2: Two boats were in tow, a big trap boat and a dory. **1954** BRIFFETT *Newfoundland* 149: The ship also carried food for the people, trapboats, empty barrels, and salt for preserving the codfish.

trap fisherman *Nfld* a person fishing with a trapboat, *q.v.*, and cod-traps, *q.v.*

1904 (1929) *Selected Stories* 245: "... Sure, 'tis sugar I wants t'me tea—not black-strap. 'Tis what I laarned," he added, proudly, "when I were a trap fisherman."

trap house *Fur Trade* a small structure usually built against a tree trunk or bank and used for housing bait, a trap for small animals being set inside the entrance. See also **house** (def. 3).

1931 GREY OWL *Last Frontier* 23: ... on nearly every occasion on which a valuable animal entered a trap house, the rabbits were there first. ... **1933** MERRICK *True North* 141: From here on we stopped about every fifteen minutes to dig out a trap, bait it, set it and fix the trap house if necessary. **1958** *Native Voice* Nov. 5: [They] had trap houses on the banks of Seton Creek.

trapline *n. Fur Trade* **1** a series of traps set and maintained by a trapper who periodically runs the line, removing the trapped animals and resetting the traps. See also **line,** *n.* (def. 5), **marten road,** and **trap road.**

1913 WILLIAMS *Wilderness Trail* 19: He said that he and his partner, the murdered man, had been met by Charley Seguis while running their trap-line. ... **1938** ELLS *Northland Trails* 19: As best she could, Rose Marie took up the double duty of trap-line and of teepee. **1965** *Globe and Mail* (Toronto) 6 Jan. 1/2: Make and use a bow and arrow, run a trapline, learn to drive a dog sled, and take part in a seal hunt.

2 a. the route or trail followed by a trapper maintaining his series of traps. See also **fur path** (def. 1), **fur trail** (def. 1), and **trapping path.**

1921 HAWORTH *Trailmaker* 263: Some trap lines are very long, seventy, eighty, ninety, or even a hundred miles, but there are short ones also. **1929** JOHNSTON *Beyond Rockies* 179: In winter Charlie is away a good deal on his twenty-mile circular trap-line. **1966** *Toronto Dly Star* 30 Apr. 65/6: Because trappers have long trap-lines the animal may lie caught in the trap for days. ...

b. the general area in which a trapper has trapping rights. See also **fur path** (def. 2) and **path.**

1931 *Beaver* Dec. 349: ... in a few days they will disperse to their trap lines. ... **1958** *Edmonton Jnl* 16 Oct. 4/3: ... as this area was his registered trapline—36 square miles. **1961** *Chatelaine* Mar. 62/3: For the annual Treaty Party an Indian agent, a Mountie, a government officer and a doctor come to pay the treaty money, and the Indians for miles around gather from their trap lines.

3 the trapper's way of life.

1931 GREY OWL *Last Frontier* 20: A man who has successfully overcome the difficulties, and endured the privations of the trap-line for a few years, can no more quit it than the confirmed gambler can leave his gaming. **1953** *North Star* (Yellowknife) Mar. 3/5: When the Red Cross reporter visited them some three weeks later

---

they were both sitting up chatting happily, looking forward to getting out of hospital and back to the trap-line.

4 a trail connecting a series of traps.

1954 PATTERSON *Dangerous River* 156: The clearing was a more open and orderly place than when I had last seen it—and, in addition to this, a lot of trapline had been cut out.

trapline cabin *Fur Trade* See **trapping cabin.**

1951 HOBSON *Grass* 64: Thomas Squinas was camped with a group of relations at his trapline cabin on a wild hay meadow a few miles west of Sugarloaf. **1956** EVANS *Mountain Dog* 59: There'll be salt up at the trap-line cabin in the basin. **1966** BAITY *Wilderness Welfare* 2: We did, however, have enough money to buy my trapper's license [and] enough grub ... to stock my trapline cabins for the winter.

trap net† See **cod-trap.**

1905 GRENFELL *Harvest* 121: ... we always race as hard as we can, to get a good place to put our trap net down.

trap out *Fur Trade* exhaust the supply of fur-bearing animals through trapping.

1936 *Cdn Geog.Jnl* XII 49/2: An Indian never "traps out" his territory, like many white trappers, but always leaves enough fur-bearing animals to insure the permanent value of the locality. **1956** LEECHMAN *Native Tribes* 225: Trapping is not as profitable as it was, for much of the country is becoming trapped out.

trapper canoe See quote.

1958 *Maclean's* 30 Aug. 33/1: The trapper canoes weigh about thirty-five pounds and sometimes have runners fitted to them for scooting across ice.

trapper hitch *North* See **tandem hitch** and picture.

1939 *Beaver* Sep. 27/1: [Caption] Karl Johnson's team, trapper hitch.

trapping cabin *Fur Trade* a simple cabin serving as quarters for a trapper. See also **trapline cabin** and **trapping camp** (def. 2).

[**1921** HAWORTH *Trailmakers* 256: In cases where two trappers go into partnership, they lay out a much longer trap line and have a central cabin at which they meet on certain appointed days.] **1954** PATTERSON *Dangerous River* 57: He had built a trapping cabin close to the springs some years previously. **1964** JENNESS *Eskimo Admin.* II 25: ... spent their days in the solitude and isolation of their individual trapping cabins and tents.

trapping camp *Fur Trade* **1** an Indian camp used as headquarters during a hunt.

1938 *Beaver* Sep. 17/1: Each day there were fewer tepees on the reservation, for one by one the families were paddling away through the early snow flurries to their winter trapping camps. **1947** GILLHAM *Raw North* 47: However, long before time to leave for their trapping camps, they gather in Fort Resolution, drink their rum ... and play poker. **1965** *Globe and Mail* (Toronto) 17 Feb. 31/7: In each district, the Department of Lands and Forests keeps a close watch on the trapping camps.

2 See **trapping cabin.**

1954 PATTERSON *Dangerous River* 132: I strolled across the creek and into the spruce where there was an old trapping camp and cache. **1956** KEMP *Northern Trader*

105: In all my years in the North never once have I been "lousy." That includes nights . . . far north of the Churchill in moss-chinked trapping camps. . . .

trapping-grounds *n.pl. Fur Trade* an area where Indians carry on trapping and hunting. Cp. **hunting grounds.**
1903 WHITE *Forest* 207: The Ojibway family . . . searches out new trapping-grounds. . . . **1907** MILLAIS *Newfoundland* 226: The sanctity of their trapping-grounds is considered inviolate by the Micmacs. **1956** EVANS *Mountain Dog* 9: When his father sold his furs from their Kelta Lake trapping grounds, there would be candy and treats all round.

trapping line, path, or **trail** *Fur Trade* See **trapline** (def. 2a).
1896 RUSSELL *Far North* 102: Our course was toward the south, for two days, along François' trapping trail, where he found a few martens and a fisher in his traps and a dozen hares in snares. **1921** HEMING *Drama of Forests* 213: He had admonished them that only white men and half-breeds would use dogs to haul a sled on a trapping path. **1936** *Beaver* June 32/1: In mid afternoon I came upon a trapping trail which I resolved to follow, thinking it might lead me out of the maze. **1964** *Indian News* July 4/3: "I could never forget my poor late father's and my older brother's labours on their trapping lines in Northern Quebec to earn me my education."

trapping track *Obs.* See **trapline** (def. 1).
1896 RUSSELL *Far North* 105: During the month Mr. Hidgson and I maintained a "trapping track," or rather, a line of poisoned baits, thirty miles in length.

trap road See **trapline** (def. 1).
1907 HUNTER *Cdn Wilds* 154: I have found no fewer than three martens when visiting my trap road a day after the wolverine had passed.

trapskiff *n. Atlantic Provinces* See **trapboat.**
1958 *Beaver* Summer 23/2: Even in sheltered coves the punts, dories and trapskiffs . . . threatened to snap free and go careening along the hollows and crests to the open sea. . . . **1963** *Maclean's* 5 Oct. 5/2: One pilot landed in the teeth of a northeaster to rendezvous with a father who had wrapped his baby in oilskins and rowed across the open water·in a trap skiff. **1964** *Atlantic Advocate* June 82/3: Meanwhile, Gillis with two men and a boy, started after the fugitives in a small boat while four other men followed in a trapskiff.

trauvoy *n.* See **travois.**

travail or **travaille** *n.* [< Cdn F; cf. **travois**] *Hist.*
1 See **travois** (def. 2 and picture).
1801 (1897) COUES *New Light* I 190: Chamanau arrived from the hills, bringing his deceased wife on a travaille to be buried here. **1880** GORDON *Mountain and Prairie* 292: When the last and only cart breaks down the usual resource is to make a "travail." **1921** HAWORTH *Trailmakers* 144: At the rear of any band of Indians on the march there was likely to be a number of these travailles, drawn usually by old, broken-down ponies.

2 See **travois** (def. 1 and picture).
1808 (1863) PALLISER *Journals* 81: I have got Indian "travails" for the dogs, consisting of two poles joined together at an acute angle, which rests on the dog's neck, while the ends trail on the ground ten feet behind him, and kept apart by a few cross bars close behind his tail,

on which the load is strapped. **1879** ROBINSON *Great Fur Land* 225: The vehicles to which dogs are harnessed in, the Fur Land are of three kinds—the passenger sledge or dog-cariole, the freight-sledge, and the travaille.

travelling box or **case** *Fur Trade, Hist.* See 1840 quote. Cp. **cassette.**
1800 (1820) HARMON *Journal* 29: I gave him the keys of our travelling box and basket, that he might have the means of making a supper. . . . **1840** (1951) *Beaver* Sep. 34/1: The travelling case is lined with a baize and divided into several compartments, the upper part containing places for knives, and forks, spoons, glasses, cups and saucers, a cruet stand &c. and the lower part is fitted with large Chrystal flaggons, for wine and other liquids, and also contains a tea pot, and cases for tea and sugar. **1929** *Ibid.* Sep. 253: . . . the old chief . . . noticed my travelling box, which lay open on the floor. . . .

travelling igloo *North* See quote.
1942 *Beaver* Mar. 8/1: During the course of this inland trapping, small "travelling" igloos are built sufficiently large to accommodate two men. . . .

travelling spectacles *Obs.* See **snow-goggles** and picture.
1681 (1945) *H.B.C. Minutes* 173: Ordered that Mr. John Bridgar bespeake 10 Dozen of Travelling specktacles.

travel permit area in a fire district, *q.v.*, any area entry to which requires, at certain times of the year, a travel permit, this restriction being intended to reduce the risk of forest fires.
1953 *Cdn Geog.Jnl* Feb. 52/1: The main portion of the fire district is set aside as a "travel permit area."

traverse[1] *n.* [< Cdn F < F "way across"] **1 a.** *Hist.* an open stretch of water, as a widening in a river or a course across a lake, where canoes or boats are required to leave the shelter of the shoreline. See also **crossing.**
1789 (1963) *Beaver* Summer 55: From this stop Mackenzie sailed west-northwest "to the foot of a traverse, the opposite Land bearing South-West. . . ." **1860** (1956) KOHL *Kitchi-Gami* 181: No one ever yet attempted this "traverse" in small boats.

b. especially in **make a traverse,** the journey, often dangerous, across such an open stretch. See also **traverse,** *v.* (def. 1).
1793 (1933) MACDONELL *Diary* 108: Started at sunrise, made the traverse to the entrance of the Red River Streight. **1821** (1900) GARRY *Diary* 127: We had here a Traverse to make of about 3 Leagues. **1872** MCLEOD in MCDONALD *Peace River* 42: If overtaken . . . in a long traverse . . . across large bays and big lakes, the heavy "parla" (red canvas oilcloth) used to be thrown over the goods as a storm deck. . . . **1943** MILLER *Lone Woodsman* 11: "You watch yourself, and wait for a good day afore ye make that traverse!" **1963** *Cdn Geog.Jnl* May 157/3: And following their example, we each stepped from the canoe wearing a cedar sprig in his hat; for this was the voyageur's way of telling the world a man had made his first traverse. . . .

2 *Hist.* **a.** on the prairies, a stretch of open land between bluffs which were used for shelter, the open prairie being hazardous in winter.
1799 (1897) COUES *New Light* I 2: My route lay directly across an open plain for 15 or 20 miles. About the middle of the traverse I was suddenly seized with a violent colic; the pain was so great that I could not keep my saddle. **1880** GORDON *Mountain and Prairie* 293:

East of this, there is a treeless plain or "traverse," as such tracts are called, probably because when once entered they must be crossed ere good camping-ground can be reached.

b. the journey across such a stretch of open prairie. See also **traverse,** *v.* (def. 2).
1913 COWIE *Adventurers* 207: The trading and hunting parties sent out over these treeless prairies had many a battle with the blizzard in crossing them in winter by "traverses" occupying days between the infrequent patches where wood was to be found.

3 *Obs.* a ford.
1826 (1914) DOUGLAS *Journal* 237: We could cross the river on a fallen tree and the horses could swim at an old traverse, a little below. **1827** (1912) ERMATINGER *Express Jnl* 119: The traverses today were deep and the current strong which obliged us to ford hand in hand for personal safety.

4 See **portage,** *n.* (def. 2).
1963 *Beaver* Autumn 31/2: . . . even then passengers and freight made a traverse across country over a height of land. . . .

traverse¹ *v. Obs.* **1** make a traverse (def. 1b).
1784 (1790) UMFREVILLE *Hudson's Bay* 28: Then [we] traversed over to a rocky face of the bank. . . .

2 make a traverse (def. 2b).
1857 (1863) PALLISER *Journals* 40: [We] attempted to traverse the next stretch of plain, but finding this traverse too long for our horses, we stopped short of the woods.

traverse² *n. Lumbering, Hist.* a log used as one of the crosspieces of the framework of a crib, dram, or other raft. See also 1854 quote at **float** (def. 1). See also **raft,** *n.* (def. 2, picture, and note).
1854 KEEFER *Ottawa* 66: If the stream in which the timber is hauled out is not navigable for cribs, "driving" is resorted to—the loose sticks with the "floats" and "traverses" for rafting it are allowed to float down, followed by the lumbermen in canoes and along shore. . . . **1945** CALVIN *Saga* 149: At the foot of the Island [were] piled rafting materials—withes, toggles, floats and traverses. **1961** GREENING *Ottawa* 103: The crib was a small raft made up of about twenty-five strips of timber lying parallel to one another in a frame consisting of two round logs and traverses fastened to them by wooden pins.

traverse³ *n.* [< Cdn F] *Hist. or Obs.* See **travois.**
1921 HAWORTH *Trailmakers* 144: The Plains Indians . . . evolved a rude sort of conveyance known by the French as a *travois,* but variously called *travail, travaille, traverse,* and *travee.*

travoie *n.* See **travois.**

travois [trə'vɔɪ, 'trævwa, *or* tra'vwa] *n.* [< Cdn F (dial.var. of *travail*) < F *travail* one of the shafts by which a wheeled vehicle is drawn] *Hist.* **1** a simple wheel-less conveyance originally used by the Indians and made of two poles on which was a platform or net for holding a load, the contrivance being pulled by a dog. See also **dog travail, dog travois, train²** (def. 2), and **travail** (def. 2).
[1793 (1933) MACDONELL *Diary* 114: They make each Dog haul a trunk[?] (made of two sticks tied close together right over the dogs head, the other end which drags upon the ground as far asunder as a pair of Cart wheels, upon which they put from 50 to 100 lbs weight according to the dog's strength) both summer and winter.] **1888** *Our Forest Children* Oct. 27 26/1: We kept

overtaking and passing . . . women and men . . . dogs also with "travoies" carrying smaller loads. **1960** RYERSON *Founding of Can.* 28: They harnessed dogs as draft-animals, to draw the travois, a device made of trailing poles held together with webbing. **1962** DICKIE *Great Golden Plain* 56: The procession began with the road-breakers, a group who marched first to tramp down the snow for the dogs, who followed drawing the family possessions on travois.

Travois (defs. 1 and 2)

2 a larger conveyance of similar design, drawn by a horse or pony, the shafts often being teepee poles. See also **horse travail** and **travail** (def. 1).
1888 *Our Forest Children* 27 Oct. 26/1: We kept overtaking and passing parties of them, women and men, astride on their ponies with baggage behind them, on the "travoie". . . . **1927** LONGSTRETH *Silent Force* 79: As they were pulling down their lodges, they were attacked by the followers of Crow's Dance, who fired guns, cut the lodges, upset the travois, killed nineteen dogs, and knocked the men down. **1963** SYMONS *Many Trails* 158: We knew our women would find our trail and follow with the travois ponies.

3 a. any of a number of similar simple drags.
1897 *To Klondyke via Edmonton* 15: Another conveyance which is highly recommended by those who have used it is a species of travois which is manufactured here for use instead of packsaddles. **1903** RICHARDSON *Colin* 216: . . . another barrel was needed for gathering the sweet material. This barrel was usually fastened tightly to a "trauvoy" or "jumper." **1935** SULLIVAN *Great Divide* 369: ". . . Some of these guns are so heavy that they are drawn by horses on strong travois: when they speak it is like thunder, and they kill more than two miles away."

b. *Lumbering* a kind of horse- or ox-drawn drag consisting of two poles or shafts bent so that their ends rode flat along the ground, 4 cross-pieces being fixed to these poles to serve as a bed for a platform to carry a load or the butt of a log being skidded to the bank. See also **bogan²** and Cp. **jumper¹** (def. 1b) and **crotch.**
1961 PRICE & KENNEDY *Renfrew* 75: Spencer Allen forwarded lumberman's supplies over this road in the early 1840's by means of a "travois."

4 *Lumbering* a logging road or skid road along which a travois (def. 3b) was pulled.
1928 PERRY *Two Reds* 53: August was not done when the axemen and sawyers started into the woods, as

usual, over the travoys which radiated from the village of Travoy and up the Coulogne and Black Rivers for the cuttings.

travois pole a pole, usually a teepee pole, used as one of the shafts of a travois (def. 2).
1942 NIVEN *Flying Years* 113: . . . Angus could see the Stoneys trooping on their way, befeathered with dragging travois-poles. **1963** SYMONS *Many Trails* 158: No tree grew for travois poles, and I could not haul the meat.

travois trail *Hist.* a track created by the passing of many travois.
1955 HARDY *Alta Anthol.* 121: This travois trail was clearly defined with three well-worn paths. In the centre the cayuse walked, wearing a deep rut in the prairie grass, while on each side were the slightly lighter markings where the two poles dragged on each side of the cayuse.

travoy *n.* See **travois.**

treacle *n. Obs.* See **maple syrup.**
1835 (1927) DICKIE *How Canada Grew Up* 104: I only wish you had been here to see your sister and the girls making sugar in the woods, sometimes up to their knees in snow, but they made one hundred and fifty pounds of sugar and sixty pounds of treacle.

Treasury Board See quote.
1963 *Globe Mag.* 23 Feb. 4/4: The inner cabinet, of course, is the real power bloc. This consists of six members who meet under the name of the Treasury Board.

treasury branch in Alberta, a banking office, in effect, a savings bank, chartered by the provincial government.
1964 *Time* (Cdn ed.) 25 Dec. 7/3: Despite an earlier threat to set up a provincially chartered "near-bank" system on the model of Alberta's treasury branches . . . Bennett vowed to fight on in Ottawa. . . .

treaty *n.* **1 a.** one of a number of official agreements between the federal government and certain Indian bands whereby the Indians forego their right to certain lands, except for stipulated reserves, and accept treaty money, *q.v.*, a supply of rations, and other kinds of government assistance, including protection and supervision. See also **Indian treaty** (def. 1).
1878 *Sask.Herald* (Battleford, N.W.T.) 21 Oct. 2/2: They have not yet come into the treaty, and being industrious and frugal, claim that they are better off and more independent, and less apt to suffer from want, than those bands that have done so. **1959** SHIPLEY *Scarlet Lily* 211: It's amazing how eagerly the Crees welcome treaty. They see it as an end to starvation, and ask for school teachers, missionaries, and farm instructors to be sent to their reservations. . . . **1965** *Globe and Mail* (Toronto) 26 May 3/4: . . . Indians who have treaties (about half of Canada's total of 207,000) get treaty money of $4 or $5 a year.
b. take (the) treaty, of Indians: **(i)** accept the conditions laid down by treaty (def. 1a).
1880 *Edmonton Bull.* 20 Dec. 2/1: As a considerable number of half-breeds have taken the treaty the population will not appear to be as numerous as it

really is. **1938** *Beaver* June 64/1: Many of the former nomads feel that the time has come for them to consider the benefit of taking treaty and having land set aside for their exclusive use. **1963** SYMONS *Many Trails* 140: Since this was written the Saulteaux bands which I knew have been persuaded to "take treaty."
(ii) receive treaty money, *q.v.*
1883 *Selkirk Herald* (Man.) 13 Apr. 2/3: We referred recently to the fact that very few of the inhabitants of the reserve were taking "treaty." **1928** FREEMAN *Nearing North* 86: Thanks again to that hypothetical Scotch progenitor—one so remote, as it chanced, that this particular descendant still "took treaty" and was not rated as a 'breed—he was far from being an ordinary Indian. **1939** *Beaver* Mar. 41/2: Today its echoes are still heard, when every year the Indians assemble at various Hudson's Bay posts to "take treaty." **1962** SLOBODIN *Kutchin* 41: Although the money itself is of little importance, its acceptance, i.e., "taking treaty," has legal and social significance, as marking those who are members of the band, in the terms of White man's law.

2 See **Treaty Day.**
1883 *Selkirk Herald* (Man.) 13 July 2/3: Two days are generally taken up in making the payments, and as the aborigines receive rations of flour and bacon in addition to the money, it is not to be wondered that they should regard the "Treaty" as a most pleasant and remunerative time. **1909** CAMERON *New North* 372: Two days ago, at the treaty at Lesser Slave, when a smiling couple drew five dollars for a baby one day old, a Cree bystander dubbed the baby "dat little meal-ticket!"

3 See **treaty money.**
1896 RUSSELL *Far North* 30: Every man, woman and child, receives an annual "treaty" of five dollars in cash. **1959** *News of the North* 25 June 3/3: Treaty was paid at Fitzgerald June 22 and at Fort Smith June 23.

4 See **treaty Indian.**
1945 *Beaver* Mar. 12/1: . . . a population of some four hundred Chipewyans and one hundred Crees, the latter being mixed treaties and non-treaties. **1949** *Native Voice* July 4/1: The Indians of Canada are divided into two categories, treaty and non-treaty. **1956** CRATE & WILLIAMS *We Speak for the Silent* 2: The reason they [the Métis] are referred to here is that a minority living the life of Indians, often poverty stricken, have been made "Treaty" in order to provide them with even the few amenities given members of native bands.

treaty agent the government agent on a treaty party (def. 1).
1956 KEMP *Northern Trader* 22: At these points, the Treaty Agent would pay each man, woman, and child the required five dollars in cash, the Chiefs and Councillors receiving proportionately more.

treaty annuity *Obs.* See **treaty money.**
1881 *Edmonton Bull.* 3 Jan. 3/2: He brought the money to pay the Stoney Indians their treaty annuity.

treaty card See 1933 quote.
1933 *Beaver* June 53: . . . each head of a family in turn coming before the paymaster and producing his treaty card on which is written his name, band number and number of members in the family. **1956** KEMP *Northern Trader* 27: . . . the cash box was opened, the Treaty card made out, and the Indian handed his five dollars.

treaty coat *Hist.* a resplendent coat given to certain Indian chiefs at the original taking of treaty (def. 1a). Cp. **captain's coat.**
1964 *Calgary Herald* 6 Jan. 8/1: . . . One can sense the proud dignity of Old Sun of the Blackfoot as he greets

a NWMP corporal in the original treaty coat given him by the government at the signing of the Blackfoot treaty in 1877. . . .

treaty commissioner *Hist.* an official of the Dominion government who was empowered to establish treaty (def. 1a) with the Indians.
1885 *Battleford Hist.Soc.Pubs* I-III 51: The Treaty Commissioners then returned to Winnipeg. **1952** HOWARD *Strange Empire* 271: Then the chiefs called at the council tent to pay their respects to the treaty commissioners and to say good-by.

Treaty Day the day on which treaty (def. 1a) was originally taken out by a group of Indians; nowadays, any day on which treaty money, *q.v.*, is paid. See also **Indian treaty** (def. 3), **treaty** (def. 2), **treaty payment** (def. 2), and **treaty time.** Cp. **treaty party** (def. 2).
1908 MAIR *Mackenzie Basin* 40: The next day was treaty day, and we were still a long way from the treaty post. **1962** SLOBODIN *Kutchin* 41: Treaty Day, in late June or early July, has become perhaps the most inclusive and celebrated of the yearly band assemblies, and the occasion for ceremony, feasting, and sports.

treaty district *Hist.* one of the administrative districts into which the Northwest was divided to facilitate the arranging of treaties (def. 1a).
1878 *Sask.Herald* (Battleford, N.W.T.) 21 Oct. 2/1: A careful estimate places the total Indian population of this treaty district at about 7,000 souls.

treaty Indian an Indian who is in receipt of treaty money, *q.v.*, or who adheres to a treaty (def. 1a). See also **registered Indian** and **treaty** (def. 4). Cp. **enfranchised,** *adj.*, **non-treaty Indian** and **out of treaty.**
1881 *Edmonton Bull.* 7 Feb. 4/1: The best wheat that has been brought to mill this season was raised at White Fish Lake by treaty Indians. **1923** WALDO *Down Mackenzie* 180: The dogs brought in by the treaty Indians were in a terrible condition—the extreme of emaciation in many harrowing instances. **1957** *Star Wkly* 17 Aug. 43/1: Being a Canadian treaty Indian I am not eligible to vote but, if I could, I'd be proud to vote Conservative. **1965** *Globe and Mail* (Toronto) 26 Jan. 39/7: Paul Mocassin [is] a treaty Indian from the Cochin Reserve. . . .

treaty lands land settlements accepted in lieu of treaty money, *q.v.*, by Indians electing to do so. See also **land-scrip.**
1958 *Sun* (Vancouver) 28 Jan. 3/5: The bill would make it impossible to strike off Indian band registries the names of half-breeds or heirs of Indians who collected scrip or received treaty lands in the past.

treaty list See **Indian Register.**
1957 *Aklavik Jnl* Apr. 5/2: To-day a man enrolled on the Treaty Lists for decades as an Indian . . . may suddenly find that he and his family *are Indians no longer*.

treaty medal *Hist.* a medal presented to band chiefs and councillors on the occasion of a treaty (def. 1a) being entered into.
[**1885** (1964) *Alta Hist.Rev.* Summer 20/1: He [Chief Beardy] and his councillors soon came in, and their medals and treaty money were taken from them.] **1939** *Beaver* Mar. 39/2: From then on, most treaty medals were made of solid silver. **1957** *Camsell Arrow* Christmas 79: He was the favored son of the old chief and it was 50 years ago that the father gave him his treaty medal to save and keep.

treaty money the annual cash payment (usually $5.00) received by Indians whose names are entered in the Indian Register, *q.v.* See also **Indian treaty** (def. 2), **treaty** (def. 3), and **treaty payment** (def. 1).
1878 *Sask.Herald* (Battleford, N.W.T.) 7 Oct. 1/3: About 700 Indians were present to receive treaty money, and about $8,700 were paid out. **1910** WARD *Canadian Born* 34: Then I went exploring to the north, and took a Government job at the same time—paying treaty money to the Indians. **1965** *Globe and Mail* (Toronto) 26 May 3/4: . . . Indians who have treaties (about half of Canada's total of 207,000) get treaty money. . . .

treaty party 1 the party representing the government on the occasion of treaty payments (def. 1), usually comprising a government agent, a doctor, and a member of the Royal Canadian Mounted Police.
1909 CAMERON *New North* 116: Trailing the scow is a York-boat carrying the treaty party and Mr. Harris. **1922** *Beaver* July 8/1: The treaty party were camped in a large marquee in front of the Company house. **1956** KEMP *Northern Trader* 174: When the Treaty Party doctor came up, he agreed that the drug stock was inadequate.
2 the occasion, usually a festive one, on which an annual treaty payment (def. 1) is made. Cp. **Treaty Day.**
1956 KEMP *Northern Trader* 23: I considered the Treaty parties of other years—the long line of canoes, the officials riding in splendor; the flag flying in the lead canoe and the throng of gun-firing Indians waiting expectantly on shore. **1961** *Chatelaine* Mar. 62/3: For the annual Treaty Party an Indian agent, a Mountie, a government officer and a doctor come to pay the treaty money, and the Indians for miles around gather from their trap lines.

treaty payment 1 an annual payment of treaty money, *q.v.*
1864 *Nor'Wester* (R.R.S.) 1 Oct. 2/5: All is quiet here though we have a great many Indians waiting not very patiently for the treaty payment. **1936** STEELE *Policing the Arctic* 132: Far off, on the lake, they saw the Dog Ribs, Yellow Knives and other Indians hurrying in boats and canoes to Fort Resolution for the treaty payments. **1962** *Maclean's* 1 Dec. 46/2: "My friend been collecting treaty payments on his name. . . ."
2 a day on which such payments are made. See also **Treaty Day.**
1921 *Beaver* Mar. 21/1: My duties were to follow the treaty payments. Wherever the government had a treaty with the Indians, each member of an Indian family received $5 per year, councillors $15 and chiefs $25, in addition to fish nets, tea, tobacco and seeds. **1952** *Ibid.* Dec. 28/1: . . . moccasins were worn the year around, the fancy beaded or silk embroidered variety being much in evidence during Christmas festivities and at Treaty Payment.

treaty point *Hist.* a stated place where a treaty commissioner had agreed to meet Indians who wished to take treaty.
1908 MAIR *Mackenzie Basin* 66: There were, of course, many Indians who did not or could not turn up at the various treaty points that year [1889], viz., the Beavers

of St. John, the Crees of Sturgeon Lake, the Slaves of Hay River . . . and the Dog-Ribs, Yellow-Knives, Slaves, and Chipewyans, who should have been treated with at Fort Resolution, on Great Slave Lake.

treaty rights the rights guaranteed to Indians in their treaties (def. 1a) with the federal government.
1886 *Indian* (Hagersville, Ont.) 8 Sep. 194/3: Of the 43 who did not vote the most of them were the pagan chiefs and warriors who had been told that if they did so, they would endanger other treaty rights and be struck off the Indian pay list. **1965** *Kingston Whig-Standard* (Ont.) 16 Sep. 18/1: The region is almost inaccessible . . . and has previously been hunted only by Indians, who have treaty rights. **1966** *Globe and Mail* (Toronto) 21 July 5/1: . . . Mr. Thompson said treaty rights are "part of our civil rights in Canada."

treaty roll See **Indian Register.**
1934 GODSELL *Arctic Trader* 320: The Canadian Government looks upon all Indians as minors, regardless of the extent of white blood in their veins, provided they are registered on the treaty rolls as "Indians."

Treaty Shore *Hist.* See **French shore** (def. 1).
1920 GRENFELL & SPALDING *Le Petit Nord* 15: North of it is called the French or Treaty Shore, or as the French themselves much more quaintly named it, "Le Petit Nord."

treaty time the time at which treaty money, *q.v.*, is paid. See also **Treaty Day.**
1947 *Beaver* June 15/1: All the flags which the chiefs had received from the Dominion Government at "treaty time," they had destroyed. . . .

treaty tobacco tobacco distributed to Indians as part of the supplies accompanying treaty payment.
1908 MAIR *Mackenzie Basin* 55: . . . here was a gathering of commonplace men smoking briar-roots, with treaty tobacco instead of "weed" . . . .

treaty trip a journey taken by a treaty party (def. 1) in making annual treaty payments.
1942 *Beaver* Dec. 34/1: We were watching (on film) . . . the doctor's "treaty" trips up the Bay.

tree claim *Obs.* See **timber claim.**
1880 GORDON *Mountain and Prairie* 271: Not long ago an excellent act was passed, entitling settlers to "tree-claims" not exceeding 160 acres, for which patents would be issued at the end of eight years, provided that a certain area had been planted in trees, tree-seeds or cuttings, and that there were a certain number of living and thrifty trees to each acre.

tree faller See **faller.**
1966 *Williams Lake Tribune* 29 Dec. 2/1: Charles (Chuck) Fraser, tree faller for T and B Logging Co. at Tatlayoko, failed to respond to frantic efforts by firemen operating a respirator.

tree-grouse *n.* See **fool hen.**
1888 (1890) ST. MAUR *Impressions* 80: Tree-grouse . . . are somewhat larger than the Scotch grouse, perch in the trees, and if alarmed, when on the ground, run, but if in a tree, they remain perfectly still. . . . **1905** OUTRAM *Cdn Rockies* 214: Both the ptarmigan and tree-grouse, or foolhens, are remarkable for their freedom from fear.

tree limit See **timber line** (def. 2).

1952 STANWELL-FLETCHER *Tundra World* 14: The Indian population, roughly, extends as far north as the tree limit, beyond that the Eskimos begin.

treeline *n.* **1** See **timber line** (def. 1).
1905 *Eye Opener* (Calgary) 29 July 4/1: Although several attempts have been made before to scale its mighty height of over two miles, the highest point ever reached before was the tree line. . . . **1952** PUTNAM *Cdn Regions* 432/2: The tree-line varies in the Coast Forest, but is reached at about 5,000 feet in the south and 4,000 feet in the north. **1958** *Beaver* Autumn 22/1: They were staying . . . not far from the tree-line.

2 See **timber line** (def. 2).
1942 TWOMEY & HERRICK *Needle to North* 5: No one had described the inland conditions of Ungava at the tree-line after snow fall. **1965** *Globe and Mail* (Toronto) 24 May 1/3: Ontario south of the treeline and along the coasts of Hudson Bay and James Bay is thinly settled by the Indians who call themselves Omooskekowak— people of the Muskeg, or Swampy Cree.

tree-platform *n.* See **burial-tree.**
1966 *Kingston Whig-Standard* (Ont.) 6 Feb. 4/6: Some tribes took their dead to a tree platform and left them there. . . .

tremble *n.* [< Cdn F < F] *Obs.* See 1957 quote. See also **tremblier.**
1806 (1960) FRASER *Letters and Journals* 241: The hangard is not yet finished, the wood is scarce and far off, and almost all tremble. **1957** FISHER *Pemmican* 25: The French called the aspen trembles or tremblers. . . .

tremblier *n.* [< Cdn F *tremblière* < F *tremblaie* place where poplars are planted] *Obs.* a grove of poplars. See also **tremble.**
1800 (1897) COUES *New Light* I 131: We took our course directly homeward . . . passing through trembliers, willows, tetes-de-femme, and small meadows. **1806** *Ibid.* 294: Having passed through several ugly trembliers, we came to what is called the Grande Trembliere [Tremblaie]. . . . Through this wood the road was horrid. . . .

trench [trɛntʃ] *n.* [prob. < Cdn F < F *tranche* cold chisel] *Fur Trade, Obs.* See **ice-chisel** and picture. See also **trenching** and **trenching-tool.** Also spelled *tranch.*
1794 (1929) MCGILLIVRAY *Journal* 31: . . . they begin to trade [and] they obtain the large Keg at 30 Beavers . . . 1 p Trenches 3 [Beavers]. **1812** (1890) KEITH *Letters* 109: They make use of . . . iron trenches for fishing or working beaver. **1825** (1950) OGDEN *Journals* 108: . . . some of the Trappers started with Trenches and the remainder to visit their Traps and returned in the evening without success their Traps fast in the Ice and did nothing with their Trenches in fact they know not the use of them nor do they appear to wish to learn. . . . *c***1835** (1932) MCLEAN *Notes* 113: . . . the moment they [dogs] discover a retreat, [they] begin to bark and jump on the ice; the hunter then cuts a hole with his trench. . . . **1844** (1937) *B.C.Hist.Qtly* Jan. 49: . . . it was customary formerly to loan Guns, Axes, Tranches, Moose Skins and Traps to the Indians. . . .

trench *v.* hunt beaver by trenching, *q.v.*
[1907 HUNTER *Cdn Wilds* 8: These [sticks] . . . the Indian drove across the creek after he had cut a trench in the thin ice from shore to shore. This was to prevent the beaver from going down the creek.] *Ibid.* 88: I . . . describe a small lake that Wa-sa-Kejic and I went to trench in December.

trenching *n.* *Fur Trade* a method of trapping beaver by means of a trench cut across a frozen

river with a long ice-chisel, a row of stakes being driven through the trench to prevent the escape of the beaver while the beaver house is opened from the top, the various escape hatches also being closed by stakes. See also **chisel** and **trench**, *n.v.*
1892 MARTIN *Castorologia* 144: It has been shown that in winter the methods employed in hunting, placed the beaver entirely at the mercy of the Indian, but when extreme measures were instituted, the creeks and streams were closely staked across, a method called "trenching," whereby every inhabitant of the colony was imprisoned from the first move. **1907** HUNTER *Cdn Wilds* 88: Describing the mode of killing beaver would not be complete unless we explained that of "trenching." This method . . . is largely practiced by the Indians after the lakes and rivers are frozen over.

trenching-tool *n. Fur Trade, Obs.* See **trench**, *n.*
1763 (1901) HENRY (Elder) *Travels* 125: The most common way of taking the beaver is that of breaking up its house, which is done with trenching-tools, during the winter, when the ice is strong enough to allow of approaching them.

trenchliner *n.* a backhoe trench-digging machine.
1958 *Progress* (Preeceville, Sask.) 28 May 1/6: A centre of interest in town during the week was the trenchliner working on Pheasant Street. Digging a trench as deep as 13 feet the huge machine inched its way. . . .

triangle country the dry belt of southern Saskatchewan and Alberta, also known as Palliser's Triangle, *q.v.*
1953 MOON *Saskatchewan* 55: Old Charlie Willhoft . . . came to this triangle country in 1910.

trigger-puller *n. Hockey, Slang* a high scorer.
1963 O'BRIEN *Hockey* 75: . . . while many are called to the N.H.L., only a chosen few become trigger-pullers.

trillium *n.* See **white trillium**.
1796 (1911) SIMCOE *Diary* 335: I walked down the hill in the evening and gathered . . . tryliums, which resemble lilies. . . . **1852** (1881) TRAILL *Cdn Crusoes* 23: The high sloping hills . . . were clothed with . . . the large pure white blossoms of the lily-like trillium. . . . **1955** MCCOWAN *Upland Trails* 136: Through the quiet woods of Ontario such early flowers as Spring Beauty, Hepatica, and Trillium are lifting their pretty heads above the brown coverlet of fallen leaves.

trip *v. North* travel through the bush by trail or canoe; take to the trails. See also **tripper** (def. 2b).
1913 FOOTNER *Jack Chanty* 52: . . . most of the time he is tripping; long hikes from Abittibi to the Skeena, and from the edge of the farming country clear to Herschel Island in the Arctic, generally alone. **1933** MERRICK *True North* 251: An old trapper once said of outsiders who were tripping up Grand River, "Gone' to the Grand Falls fer pleasure heh? They'd go to Hell fer a pastime."

tripe *n. Rare* See **tripe de roche**.
1853 REID *Young Voyageurs* 386: [The] lichen became reduced to a soft gummy pulp, and Norman thickened the mess to his taste by putting in more snow, or more of the "tripe," as it seemed to require it.

tripe de roche [< Cdn F] *North* See **rock-tripe**.
[**1665** (1885) RADISSON *Voyages* 142: The kittle was full wth the scrapings of the rocks, wch soone after it boyled became like starch, black and clammie & easily to be swallowed.] **1768** (1901) HENRY (Elder) *Travels* 214: I found a very high rock, and this was covered with a

lichen, which the Chipeways call *waac,* and the Canadians, *tripe de roche.* **1836** (1947) HARGRAVE *Correspondence* 240: A small box of Tripe de Roche is forwarded to your address. **1936** *Beaver* Sep. 22/2: That is good when you journey to meet them, but when you are behind—then comes the misery of empty bellies and "tripe de roche." **1963** *Ibid.* Summer 16/2: [They are] preparing a camp and gathering tripe de roche, main food of the starving men on the return journey.

triplex *n.* a building containing three self-contained apartments or suites. Cp. **duplex**.
1962 *Maclean's* 10 Mar. 37/1: They wanted to build three triplexes. "Definitely not," Reeve Fred Hall told Norman.

tripman *n. Fur Trade, Hist.* a man other than a permanent employee, taken on for single trip with a brigade (def. 1). See also **tripper** (def. 1) and **voyageur** (def. 1c). Cp. **freeman** (def. 1b) and **yearly servant**.
*c***1830** (1889) *Trans.Hist.& Sci.Soc.Man.* 33 4/1: Several instances have occurred within the last season of tripmen and others forming engagements with different individuals at the same time. **1865** *Nor'Wester* (R.R.S.) 8 June 2/2: Scores of tripmen are away to the interior on lengthened voyages in the Hudson's Bay Company's service and that of private freighters. **1963** *Cdn Geog.Jnl* Apr. 118/3: Around their heads they wore the almost symbolic band of the tripman [of the York boats], a simple piece of calico to keep the perspiration from sliding down . . . into their eyes.

trip money *Fur Trade, Obs.* the money paid to a tripman, *q.v.*, for his services.
1798 (1927) *Beaver* June 18: . . . as they will receive double Trip Money for this Duty [they] will increase their wages considerably.

tripod set *Fur Trade* See quote. Cp. **variation set**.
1965 *Islander* 14 Feb. 5/1: Perhaps a description of the "tripod set" will show how the wolverine's trait of persistence can contribute to his downfall . . . Three poles about three inches in diameter at the butt and, say, eight feet long are set up like teepee-tent poles to form a tripod, securely tied together at the apex. From the apex the bait is suspended, wired solidly to the peak of the tripod. It must also be wired downward to each of the three poles so it is practically immovable. . . .

tripper *n.* **1** *Fur Trade, Hist.* See **tripman**.
1834 (1947) HARGRAVE *Correspondence* 171: The Indian Trippers invariably deliver their goods here in better condition than the Red River freemen. . . . **1893** YOUNG *Indian Wigwams* 54: To carry out his contract he used to hire hundreds of Indians and half-breeds as boatmen, or "trippers" as they are generally called. **1908** MAIR *Mackenzie Basin* 143: On the 11th we set off for Athabasca landing, accompanied by a little fleet of trippers' and traders' canoes. . . . **1963** MCTAVISH *Behind the Palisades* 89: When flour was procurable, the trippers integrated the solid pemmican in a frying pan by heat. . . .

2 a. *Esp.Fur Trade* a man in charge of a train of dogs, a packet, or a swing (def. 1).
1874 (1925) GRAHAME *Bompas* 27: Here are our "trippers," as they are called, and all ready to start, and my Bishop in his fur cap and warm wraps which I have made for him. **1934** GODSELL *Arctic Trader* 36:

. . . and Alex Budd, head dog-driver and tripper for the Company. . . . **1938** *Beaver* Sep. 17/1: Eleven or twelve hours a day on the trail is the aim of the winter tripper, and when the sun sets at 3.30, one must roll out early if one is to keep to this program and still get camp started before dark.

b. *Esp.North* a person who travels the bush trails. See also **trip.**

1896 RUSSELL *Far North* 96: Our first day's travel was up the Mackenzie where we experienced some difficulty in finding sufficient fuel, the dry timber having been used by the many trippers hauling fish from Big Island to Providence. **1912** FOOTNER *New Rivers* 56: The tenderfoot is betrayed by his fire just as surely as the experienced tripper is made known by his. **1944** CLAY *Fur Thieves* 53: "Some tripper must have lost it." "Tripper?" muttered Tom. "Trippers never use this old route now. Perhaps some hunter."

3 *Fur Trade, Hist.* See **runner²**.

1921 HEMING *Drama of Forests* 173: But before the fort-hunter had returned with the telescope, the snowy veil suddenly thinned and revealed the gray figure of a tripper coming up the bank. **1938** GODSELL *Red Hunters* 23: Soon the ubiquitous French fur trader, "tripper" and trapper roamed everywhere.

tripping *n. Fur Trade, Hist.* **1** See **derouine.** See also **tripper** (def. 3).

1820 (1938) SIMPSON *Athabasca Jnl* 89: McDougald who is a good trader and understands the language will be usefully occupied in tripping after the N.W.Indians. . . . **1934** GODSELL *Arctic Trader* 35: Not only were dog-teams kept for tripping to the Indian camps for furs but others were employed in carrying the mail. . . . **1962** SLOBODIN *Kutchin* 59: Trading groups . . . existed during "the Old Days," in relation to the Euro-American practice of "tripping for fur." Post managers would send men and trade goods into areas where it was known or supposed that there were concentrations of natives.

2 the activity or business of transporting goods, furs, etc. from one place to another. See also **voyaging** (def. 2).

1832 (1964) INNIS *Fur Trade* 309: . . . in the Course of Summer three Trips is made from the Factory with 80 pieces p. Boat, the Boats are larger than usual for this Tripping Business. **1861** *Nor' Wester* (R.R.S.) 1 Apr. 4/1: Some of them had been employed in . . . road-making, house-building, tripping and the like. . . . **1907** HUNTER *Cdn Wilds* 70: The laborers . . . about the post got nothing in the way of imported provisions except when at the hard work of tripping. **1963** SPRY *Palliser* 96: All travel about the fort, called "tripping," was now done with dogs.

tripping axe *Fur Trade, Hist.* See quote. Cp. **trail axe.** See also **tripping** (def. 2).

1955 *Beaver* Spring 10/1: He would have felt more at home for this task [tapping Manitoba maple trees] with a "long tripping axe" such as was used in the early days.

tripping kit *Fur Trade, Hist.* the gear used in tripping (def. 2). See also **agrès** (def. 1).

1921 HEMING *Drama of Forests* 302: In the storeroom the voyageurs gathered up the "tripping" kit of paddles, tents, axes, tarpaulins, sponges.

tripping (snow)shoe *Esp.North* See **trail shoe.**

1896 WHITNEY *On Snow-Shoes* 129: . . . the snow was deep, and breaking trail excessively hard, especially with tripping-shoes on which you sank to the knee, and with the toe of which you barked your shins as you raised your foot after every step to shake off the shovelful of accumulated snow. **1896** RUSSELL *Far North* 182: There is a pair of small or "tripping" snowshoes . . . intended for use on hard snow, either upon Lake Winnipeg or in traveling behind a loaded sled through the bush. **1921** HEMING *Drama of Forests* 179: The other men wore Chipewyan "tripping shoes" about three feet long—the only style of Canadian snowshoes that are made in "rights and lefts."

triservice *adj.* designating all three branches of the Canadian Forces—navy, army, and air force.

1963 *Kingston Whig-Standard* (Ont.) 30 Apr. 17/1: Royal Canadian Navy cadets at the tri-service college [RMC] will be . . . seeing Hawaii. **1965** *Islander* 14 Feb. 2/4: . . . the motto . . . exemplifies the [Postal] Corps' mission, a tri-service function. **1966** *Globe and Mail* (Toronto) 1 Aug. 7/2: Traditional army commands and area headquarters were disbanded and replaced by 12 tri-service district headquarters.

trou *n.* [< Cdn F < F "hole"] *Obs.* See 1912 quote.

1827 (1912) ERMATINGER *Express Jnl* 119: Start at ½ past 4 p.m. Breakfast at the trou at 8. **1912** *Trans.Roy.Soc. Can.* VI 2 119n: The place called the "Hole" (trou) is at the confluence of the Whirlpool and Athabasca rivers. Ross says it is so called "from the depth of the water at the edge of the bank. . . ."

trough *n.* See **scoop,** *n.*

1834 (1961) *Ont.Hist.* Mar. 26: . . . trees have to be split and hollowed out into troughs to form the roof. . . . **1863** WALSHE *Cedar Creek* 127: The Yankee took the adze from his hand . . . and set about hollowing troughs very rapidly. **1961** *Ont.Hist.* Mar. 8: The walls are chinked with "slats and moss" and roofed with "wooden troughs." The interpretation for the wooden troughs for roofing is perfectly clear. They consisted of halved cedar logs hollowed out and laid alternately with the trough up and inverted. . . .

trousseau tea a tea-party at which a bride shows off her trousseau to her friends and accepts gifts for adding to it.

1930 MCCLUNG *Be Good* 24: We went today to another Trousseau Tea—Mrs. Burns, (No, she is not getting married; she is going to New York.) **1951** ROBINS & RAY *Cdn Humour* 185: ". . . I don't believe there is any reference in Westermarck to such ceremonies as showers and trousseau teas which appear to be purely indigenous rites—"

trouter *n.* dial.var. of throater, *q.v.*

truck system† *Atlantic Provinces* a credit system under which a fisherman, logger, trapper, etc. gets his outfit and supplies for the season as an advance and is committed to trade only with the merchant extending the credit, all or most dealings being in kind.

1849 ALEXANDER *L'Acadie* II 170: And some of those men who work saw mills "grind the faces of the poor," by the truck system of payment, and by the two and three hundred per cent of profit they demand for necessaries. . . . **1872** DASHWOOD *Chiploquorgan* 247: The truck system is universal in the country [Nfld], and the fishermen, after paying all expenses of outfit and provisions for the season, have but little left in cash. **1918** GRENFELL *Labrador Doctor* 59: But the trader knew that the truck system creates slippery, tricky men. . . . **1965** MACNUTT *Atlantic Provinces* 18: Strong men might contend against it but the "truck system" . . . became entrenched in Newfoundland and later extended itself to the lumbering and agricultural industries. . . .

trunk-hole n. Nfld See quote.
1819 ANSPACH Hist.Nfld 430: The header . . . takes it in his left hand, and with the right, draws out the liver which he throws through a hole into a cask under the table; next, the guts, which he throws through the trunk-hole in the floor of the stage into the sea.

trunk line See trunk road.
1965 Maclean's 19 June 39/1: There is one filling station at the junction of the main north-south road and the Highwood trunk line.

trunk road an access road (def. 1), so called
because smaller forest trails branch from it. See also **trunk line.**
1952 North Star (Yellowknife) Oct. 4/2: [We favour] Government extension of and responsibility for trunk roads in the Territories. **1961** Edmonton Jnl 8 Aug. 25/2: In the afternoon the cavalcade travelled the forestry trunk road known as The Loop. . . . **1965** Maclean's 19 June 17/1: A trunk road curves 50 miles through Highwood Valley . . . to the prairies.

trust n. Fur Trade, Obs. See debt (def. 1).
1713 (1947) Cdn Hist.Rev. Dec. 402n: One Cannowe Came from ye Northard for trust which was granted. **1783** (1954) Moose Ft Jnls 14: One canoe of uplanders came in for trust.

trust v. Fur Trade, Obs. extend credit to. See also
debt (def. 4).
1774 (1934) HEARNE & TURNOR Journals 125: This day I Trusted the Indians in all about 200 Beaver in Amanition and other Necessaries, to help support them Dureing the Winter. **1791** LONG Voyages 152: . . . he asked me to trust him a gun, blanket, and ammunition; but I refused him.

trustee n. See school trustee.
1849 Journal of Education for U.C. I 41/1: Some would prefer a uniform rate bill upon all the children residing in a school-section (the school sections reserving the power of the Trustees to excuse any for good reasons) whether in attendance or not. **1895** BOURINOT How Canada is Governed 248: High school trustees and members of boards of education cannot hold posts in the municipal councils of the municipality or county in which those schools are situated. **1963** Kingston Whig-Standard (Ont.) 5 Mar. 17/4: At least one trustee of the Kingston Board of Education doesn't like the rating policy of the Ontario Secondary School Teachers Federation.

Tsonoqu(o)a [tsə'nokw(o)ə] n. [< Kwakiutl] Pacific Coast See quotes.
1941 CARR Klee Wyck 51: "Who is that big carved woman?" I repeated. "D'Sonoqua." No white tongue could have fondled the name as he did. "Who is D'Sonoqua?" "She is the wild woman of the woods." "What does she do?" "She steals children." "To eat them?" "No, she carries them to her caves. . . ." **1956** LEECHMAN Native Tribes 318: Tsonoquoa, the wild woman of the woods, was a Kwakiutl being, who wandered through the woods with a basket in which to put the children she caught; then she would carry them off to kill them and eat them. **1964** SPECK Kwakiutl Art 7: This great shaggy giantess figure of the Tsonoqua people has many aspects in Kwakiutl carving and painting. Always depicted as huge and dark with lips pursed to utter a cry, she is the figure of many conflicting stories.

T to T Club Slang See quote.
1962 Kingston Whig-Standard (Ont.) 6 Dec. 4/1: It appears that a new cult has sprung up in Ottawa which correspondents there refer to as the "T to T Club" (so-called because it is made up of members who find it "convenient" to attend Parliament only from Tuesday to Thursday).

tuckamore ['tʌkə,mər] n. [cf. Brit. dial. tuck
loose, tangled straw, etc.] Nfld See quotes. See also **spruce-tuck** and **tucking bush.**
1895 PATTERSON Dial.of Nfld 39: Tuckamore, a clump of spruce . . . matted together. **1920** GRENFELL Le Petit Nord 47: In this northern part even that little is rendered almost impenetrable in the summer-time by the thick under-brush, known as "tuckamore," and the formidable swarms of mosquitoes and black flies. **1955** (1963) ENGLISH Newfoundland 35: tuckamore [means] a low clump of trees.

tucking bush Nfld See quote. See also **tuckamore.**
1842 JUKES Excursions in Nfld II 13: "Tucking bushes" . . . consist of a kind of dwarf juniper or other fir-tree, with very thick short stumps and strong flat inter-lacing branches . . . Where it is not possible to avoid them by going round, I think 200 yards of "tucking bushes" in an hour would be quick work, and certainly much severer toil than six miles of plain ground.

tugger n. See quote.
1964 Vancouver Times 3 Nov. 5/2: The king-nipper is boss of the nippers, men who transport materials in the mine with a compressed air hoist known as a tugger.

tuggy n. See toggy.

tuktu ['tʌktu] n. [< Esk.] Arctic Also spelled
tuktoo. **1** See caribou.
[**1748** ELLIS Hudson's Bay 256: . . . upon giving them to understand, that we wanted Tuktoa, which in their Language signifies Venison, they . . . brought us some which had been cured after their manner, by drying.] **1865** HALL Arctic Researches 285: When the feet of tuktoo are wet, they can go much faster over the mountain rocks. **1924** FLAHERTY Eskimo Friends 91: "Tooktoo," said he, and advanced his three fingers before our incredulous eyes. **1965** Globe and Mail (Toronto) 27 Dec. 21/2: . . . men of the Canadian Wildlife Service fear that tuktu, the beast with the handsome antlers, may soon be remembered only in illustrations. . . .

2 See quote.
1864 HALL Life with Esquimaux I 176: So complete was his happiness, that he told me I should have the choice of his two wives, all his tuktoo (reindeer furs) that I might need, and sealskin for making boots, with other articles in abundance.

tuladi or tulidi n. See touladi.

tullibee ['tʌlə,bi] n. [< Cdn F toulibi < Algonk.;
cf. Cree otonabi] a species of whitefish, q.v., Leucichthys tullibee. See also **mongrel whitefish.**
1789 (1889) MCKENZIE Reminiscences 33: I rise with the sun and, after debarbouilling mon visage, I take a walk to my traps, return to the house, eat Tollibees about nine. **1823** FRANKLIN Journey 711: The Cree name of this fish, ottonneebees, has been corrupted by the traders into tullibee. **1918** KITTO New Manitoba 58: Pike is a coarser fish though very common, and tullibee is an

inferior species of whitefish. **1961** *Edmonton Jnl* 12 Aug.
4/3: In its busiest days . . . whitefish, pickerel, northern
pike, and tullibee were marketed from its waters
[Lac La Biche]. . . .

tumbleweed† *n. West* a plant, as *Amaranthus
graecizans,* whose upper part breaks off from the
root in autumn and is driven about by the wind.
1922 STEAD *Neighbours* 276: . . . many a detour I made
with pounding heart, to find only a prairie boulder or a
lump of tumbleweed blown into a wolf willow. **1961**
MITCHELL *Jake and the Kid* 178: That essay just rolled
along like tumbleweed. I put down all about how Jake
can tell the weather and witch water wells.

tump† [tʌmp] *n.* [< Algonk.; cf. Abenaki
mādumbī pack strap] See **tumpline.** See also
tump strap.
[**1829** MACTAGGART *Three Years* II 225: The voyageurs,
who are chiefly Canadians, fix the *pieces* on their backs
with a thong of leather, a broad piece coming over the
head, against which the brow leans. . . .] **1947** *Beaver*
Dec. 50/2: [Caption] . . . with the tump on one's head
as shown, the result would be a very sore neck.

tump† [tʌmp] *v.* [< n.] *Obs.* haul by means of a
tumpline.
1855 HALIBURTON *Nature* I 268: A man passed . . .
tumping . . . an immense bull moose on a sled.

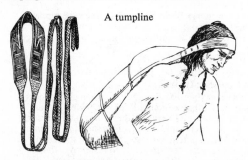

A tumpline

tumpline† [ˈtʌmp͵laɪn] *n.* [< *tump,* q.v. + *line*]
a kind of harness for carrying heavy loads, drawing
on a tracking line, etc., consisting of a leather strap
that is broad at the middle and tapers at both ends,
the broad band being placed around the forehead
(or chest) and the two ends attached to the pack or
other load. See also **carrying-strap, collier, forehead
strap, headstrap, Hudson's Bay harness, pack line,
packstrap, portage strap**, and **tump.**
[**1809** (1890) JOHNSTON *Lake Superior* 165: Carrying
the canoes, goods and provisions . . . is done by means of
leather straps or thongs the middle of which is broad
and fitted to the forehead of the carrier.] **1854** KEEFER
Ottawa 69: . . . the "tump-line" will never again
compress his swollen and weary temples. . . . **1922**
Beaver July 10/1: The hardy voyageur of the paddle
and tumpline, or "Hudson's Bay harness" as it is termed
in York boat parlance. **1965** *Ibid.* Autumn 55/1: Since
few of us had used a tumpline . . . before, the first move
of three miles . . . was something to remember. . . .

tump pack a backpack carried with the aid of a
tumpline.
1953 MOWERY *Mounted Police* 154: He capped the little
beehive igloo with a block of snow and then crawled in

at the tunnel entrance, with his tump pack and eider
sleeping poke.

tump strap See **tump,** *n.*
1910 FRASER *Red Meekins* 105: Suddenly a turmoil in
the distance caused Meekins to slip the tump strap from
his forehead, drop his pack, and stand rifle in hand,
waiting. **1943** MILLER *Lone Woodsman* 14: Dan cut a
rest-stick and adjusted the tump strap across his
forehead, so as to relieve his shoulders for the canoe
load.

tumtum [ˈtʌm͵tʌm] *n.* [< Chinook Jargon, in
allusion to a beating heart] *West Coast* heart;
affection; mind; opinion.
1869 ANDERSON *Sawney's Letters* 38: But he has aye the
grit, / Tho' his "tum-tum" may be sair, / For anither
year is coming. **1872** POOLE *Queen Charlotte Is.* 314: . . .
she had shown a good tumtum (heart) in assisting the
needy. **1874** (1926) MOSER *Reminiscences* 17: His
Lordship stepped forward . . . saying he knew by what
he had heard the tom-tom of the whole tribe. **1915**
CUMMING *Skookum Chuck* 22: Peter soon realized that
his wife was eating at his table and living in another
man's tum-tum. . . . **1963** SYMONS *Many Trails* 78: "Me
hyu sick tum-tum. My papoose going mamaloosh I
t'ink."

tundra† [ˈtʌndrə] *n.* [< Russian < Finno-Ugric;
cf. Lapp *tundar* hill] See **Barren Ground.** See also
tundra lands.
[**1900** OSBORN *Greater Canada* 164: From the hunter's
point of view "Caribou-land" would be an exceedingly
apt name for the *tundri* of Greater Canada.] **1909**
SERVICE *Cheechako* 45: On velvet tundra, or virgin peak,
by glacier, drift or draw. . . . **1939** *Beaver* June 34/1: To
catch the strains of this music in the brooding stillness
of the tundras, saturated with the mellow radiance of the
midnight sun, is a rare and delightful experience. **1965**
SYMINGTON *Tuktu* 18: In many regions of both the taiga
and tundra, the granite hills of Pre-Cambrian rock
dominate the landscape. . . .

tundra deer See **caribou** (def. 1).
1963 *Maclean's* 23 Feb. 42/1: Then a winter came when
"Man's Man" could not find even one of the tundra
deer to kill.

tundra lands or **plain** See **Barren Ground.** See
also **tundra.**
1940 *Cdn Geog.Jnl* Feb. 94/1: It is characterized by
level tundra plain, or desolate mountainous country,
normally destitute of trees of any kind, though often
relieved by scrubby bushes of birch and willow a few
inches high. **1947** TAYLOR *Canada* 288: The Tundra
lands to the east of the Mackenzie basin are known
locally as the "Barren Lands" or the "Arctic Prairies."
1959 *Maclean's* 31 Jan. 42/2: . . . the great wind . . .
came . . . to the south across five hundred miles of tundra
plain. . . .

tundra wolf See **Arctic wolf.**
1958 *Edmonton Jnl* 16 July 7/6: The council was told a
wolf-killing program to help boost flagging caribou
herds had accounted for about 5,000 tundra wolves in
five years. **1965** SYMINGTON *Tuktu* 37: The whiter tundra
wolves have obviously adapted to Arctic conditions.
They are imposing beasts, long-legged, broad-footed,
and deep-chested, and carry a heavy coat of long
creamy white or pure white fur.

Tunik *n.* See **Tunit.**

Tunit or **Tunnit** [ˈtunɪt] *n.* [< Esk.] a word used
by the Eskimo to indicate "a people earlier than

themselves," possibly either Dorset or Thule culture Eskimos. See also **Toonik** (def. 1).
1918 GRENFELL *Lab.Doctor* 66: It appears that a larger race of Eskimos called "Tunits," to whom the present race were slaves, used to be on this section of the coast. At Nakvak there are remains of them. 1936 *Beaver* June 11/2: The ancient Eskimos—the Tunnits—are said to have been somewhat fierce and warlike, but this may be only garbled folklore. 1966 *Cdn Geog.Jnl* Sep. 86/2: He [said] . . . that the inukshuks were built to commemorate a notable Eskimo victory over the Tunits, the ancient inhabitants of the Island [Baffin].

tunnel boat See 1942 quote.
1921 *Beaver* May 12/1: An interesting addition to the H.B.C. fleet of northern river transport vessels is the new "tunnel" boat, launched at Vancouver, March 26th. 1942 *Ibid.* Mar. 17/1: On the Dease River, gasoline propelled "tunnel" boats (that is, boats fitted with a propeller that is retractable into a tunnel) replaced the scows. . . . 1958 *Arctic Spotter* Feb. 17/3: On stern-wheel river steamboat, three shallow-draft power boats (Called 'tunnel-boats'), and twelve barges, were built.

Tunnit *n.* See **Tunit.**

tupek or **tupik** ['tupək] *n.* [< Esk. *tupiq*] *Arctic* a tent of skins, used as a summer dwelling. See also **Eskimo tent, skin tent, summer lodge,** and **wigwam** (def. 1c). Cp. **oomiak-tupek.** Various spellings.
[1577 (1889) HAKLUYT *Voyages* XII 93: Their houses are tentes, made of Seale skins, pitched vp with 4. Firre quarters, foure square, meeting at the toppe, and the skinnes sewed together with sinewes, and layd thereupon: they are so pitched vp, that the entraunce into them, is alwayes South, or against the Sunne.] [1836 HUISH *Last Voyage* 702: Tent Too-pik.] 1860 (1865) HALL *Arctic Researches* 169: On my way, . . . just outside the angeko's tupic, I noticed an oar of a kia[k] stuck upright in a drift of frozen snow. 1895 TABOR *In Rugged Labrador* 97/1: We were visiting an encampment of half a dozen "tupeks," and one morning, some of our "Huskie" friends volunteered to go with us in the boats for wood. 1959 LEISING *Arctic Wings* 321: Occasionally he called our attention to one or more Eskimo tupiks, or skin tents, at the deltas of small rivers.

tupek ring See **tent ring.**
[1749 DRAGE *Voyage* II 220: We saw also at our first landing a round of Stones, which we supposed had been the Foundation of one of the Eskemaux Tents.] 1936 STEELE *Policing the Arctic* 259: They . . . descended that stream for ten miles camping on its low swampy shores, among many caribou and snow geese, old Eskimo cairns and tupik rings. 1936 *Beaver* June 9/1: Tupik rings of old encampments are to be seen at all favourable points.

tuque [tuk] *n.* [< Cdn F; dial.var. of F *toque*] **1** a long knitted bonnet of wool, resembling a stocking tied at the foot end, often tasselled and made in more than one color, associated with French Canada through the voyageurs, woodsmen, etc. See also **toque** (def. 1).
1882 LEMOINE *Quebec* 521: The locket and chain which were presented to Mr. A. Holloway were made by Mr. G. Seifert, the locket having upon it a pair of crossed snow-shoes and tuque with a monogram of the club beautifully raised on the one side. 1914 STEELE *Forty Years* 99: Alexis had for a head covering a tuque, or thick woollen cap, commonly used in the woods in winter. 1938 *Beaver* June 24/2: The Fort is filled with

gay young French-Canadians in red tuques, coloured sashes, beaded leggings, and they all talk Cree. 1964 *Family Herald* 12 Mar. 16/3: Nicholson's red tuque and beard are basis for "Tuque Rouge" brand syrup he manufactures.

Tuques (def. 1 and 2)

2 a similar but shorter woollen cap usually having a round tassel on the top. See also **toque** (def. 2).
1912 SANDILANDS *West.Cdn Dict.* 48/2: Tuque (pronounced tuke), a woollen cap worn by a child, usually running to a peak, which ends with a tassel, said peak and tassel hanging down by the side of the head when the tuque is in use. 1958 *Weekend Mag.* 6 Dec. 63/2: On the second floor, he walked briskly through the boys' shirts, boys' windbreakers, boys' suits, pants, tuques, socks. 1961 *Time* (Cdn ed.) 31 Mar. 12/3: Finished at last, Tommy pulled on a Montreal Canadiens' tuque, grabbed his stick and skates and ran outside to play hockey.

turkey *n. West* the little brown crane, *Grus canadensis.* See also **wild turkey.**
1795 (1911) HEARNE *Journey* 423: They are generally esteemed good eating, and, from the form of the body when fit for the spit, they acquire the name of the North West turkey. 1955 MCCOWAN *Upland Trails* 23: In some quarters these lanky birds have been locally known as "turkeys" although one even slightly familiar with the long-legged creatures is at a loss to account for this misleading name. 1956 MCATEE *Folk-Names* 26: Brown Crane [is also called] wild turkey (Often shortened to "turkey." Man., Sask., Alta.).

turning harp See **harp.**
1880 (1964) *Nfld Qtly* Spring 4: . . . the yearlings and two year olds are called "Young Harps" or "Turning Harps" and also Bedlimers (or Bedlamers). . . .

turnip of the plains *Obs.* See **prairie turnip.**
1805 (1892) PRITCHARD *Letters* 9: I this day found a plant, whose root the Canadians call the turnip of the plains: But not having a knife or axe to make a stick, I had no hope of digging them up; the root being at least a foot in the earth, and the ground extremely hard. 1827 (1914) DOUGLAS *Journal* 284: *Psoralea* sp . . . this is the Turnip of the Plains of the voyageurs, the roots of which are used by the Indians both boiled and raw.

turnout *n. West* the time in spring when cattle are turned out to forage for themselves.
1962 FRY *Ranch on the Cariboo* 59: Only days after turnout, we had bear trouble on the range about halfway to the meadow.

turnpike *n.* See **turnpike road.**

turnpike† *v. Hist.* make in the manner of a turnpike road, *q.v.* See also **turnpiking** (def. 1).

1826 *U.E.Loyalist* (York [Toronto]) 1 July 39/4: Many others are undergoing the same process, and several are prepared for it, by being first turnpiked and allowed time to settle. **1863** WALSHE *Cedar Creek* 98: "I see they've turnpiked this road since I was on it before." **1927** DICKIE *How Canada Grew Up* 162: The great public roads built by the Government were turnpiked.

turnpike company† *Obs.* a company organized to build or maintain turnpike roads.
1812 *Montreal Herald* 11 Apr. 2/1: Consequently, this turnpike company cannot take possession of any lawful road now existing, but must keep their own apart. **1828** *Loyalist* (York [Toronto]) 8 Nov. 174/2: It has been suggested, that a Turnpike Company for the improvement of Yonge Street From York to Lake Simcoe, would be attended with much disadvantage to that portion of the Country, through which the Street passes.

turnpike road† *Hist.* See 1927 quote. See also **turnpiking** (def. 2). Also *turnpike*.
1807 *Quebec Gaz.* 25 Feb. 6/1: . . . turnpike road. **1852** (1881) TRAILL *Cdn Crusoes* 354: The traveller . . . passes along on that smooth turnpike road that leads from Coburg to Cold Springs, and . . . Gore's Landing. . . . **1927** DICKIE *How Canada Grew Up* 162: In building a turnpike the road allowance was cleared and the stumps removed, sometimes by a machine worked by horses. Ditches were dug on either side and the earth thrown up on the road to form a causeway; the surface was then levelled in a rude way. Drains were built where the ground was swampy and streams were spanned by bridges.

turnpike shovel *Obs.* See **scraper.** See quote at **road-scraper.**

turnpiking *n. Obs.* **1** the making of a turnpike road, *q.v.* See also **turnpike,** *v.*
1826 PICKERING *Inquiries* 68: Along the "street" they are getting them up, and ploughing the sides, and with a kind of large shovel, having a handle, (called a scraper) and a yoke of oxen, the dirt is drawn into the centre and rounded, which is called "turnpiking." **1863** WALSHE *Cedar Creek* 98: "There," said the Canadian, pointing to a ploughed line along each side of the road, whence the earth had been thrown up in the centre by a scraper; "that's turnpiking." **1903** CONANT *Life in Canada* 146: Sometimes the turnpiking is only half completed, or again the gravel has been left in great heaps, which give to your carriage the motion of a vessel at sea as it passes over the lumps.

2 See **turnpike road.**
1830 *Colonial Advocate* (York [Toronto]) 10 June 3/3: The turnpiking is entirely too narrow for two teams to pass each other.

turr [tɜ·] *n.* [prob. imitative] *Esp.Nfld* **1** the razor-billed auk, *Alca torda.* See also **tinker** (def. 1).
1853 *Trans.Lit.& Hist.Soc.Que.* IV 334: Among the sea birds are *Mernettes, Moyocks,* Gulls, Murrhs or *Calculots,* Turrhs, Paraquets, Penguins, and divers others. **1964** *Imperial Oil Rev.* Apr. 23: Turrs are black and white seabirds the size of ducks. Newfoundlanders had a long battle with Ottawa over their right to shoot turrs.

2 *Nfld* the murre, *Uria aalge* or *U. lomvia.*
1960 TUCK *The Murres* 34: A common vernacular name for the murre in Newfoundland is "turr." It is used for either species and especially for a bird in winter plumage.

twenty-cent piece *Hist.* a silver coin (valued at twenty cents) of which 750,000 only were minted in the Canadas, the series being discontinued in 1858.
☛ *Similar coins were issued in Newfoundland (1865-1912) and in New Brunswick (1862 and 1864).*
1865 *Guelph Advertiser* (C.W.) 30 Mar. 1/6: The first witness [said] he had a 20c. piece in his hands, and he told me he could find a way to make such money. **1916** WOOD *Tourist's N.W.* 320: The 20-cent piece is easily confused with the silver quarter of both Canada and the United States. **1964** TAYLOR *Cdn Coins* 43: When the decimal system was adopted a twenty-cent piece was struck, as it was considered a convenient unit and a decimal of one hundred (the dollar). It was also equivalent to the shilling in Halifax currency. However, before any more were required, it was decided to follow the United States practice and use a twenty-five cent piece instead.

twillick or **twilleck** ['twilək] *n.* [imitative] *Nfld* either the greater yellowlegs, *Totanus melanoleucus,* or the lesser yellowlegs, *T. flavipes.*
1842 JUKES *Excursions in Nfld* I 141: On going back to the wigwam we shot a couple of "twillecks," a grey long-legged bird, about the size and shape of a plover. **1907** MILLAIS *Newfoundland* 86: The greater yellowshank . . . locally known as 'Twillik,' is very common in all the Newfoundland rivers during the summer and autumn. **1956** MCATEE *Folk-Names* 31: Lesser Yellow-legs [is also called] twillick (Sonic. Nfld., "Labr."). . . . .

twinberry *n.* See **partridgeberry.**
1823 HALIBURTON *General Descr.N.S.* 36: Plants [include] Twin berry. . . . **1853** *Anglo-American Mag.* II 183/1: That elegant little plant Mitchella repens, sometimes called partridge-berry and also twin-berry, from the scarlet fruit having the appearance of being double.

Twin Cities 1 See 1912 quote.
1912 SANDILANDS *West.Cdn Dict.* 48/2: Twin Cities, when spoken of in Canada, usually refer to Port Arthur and Fort William, neighboring cities and ports in Ontario, situated on Thunder Bay, Lake Superior. **1952** PUTNAM *Cdn Regions* 333/2: Two-thirds of this population is urban however, and concentrated in the twin cities of the "Lakehead," Fort William and Port Arthur.

2 Kitchener and Waterloo in western Ontario.
1952 PUTNAM *Cdn Regions* 283/1: The "Twin Cities" constitute an exceedingly well built and prosperous appearing urban area.

twinflower† *n.* a plant, *Linnaea borealis,* whose sweet-smelling flowers are in pairs.
1860 *Trans.Lit.& Hist.Soc.Que.* IV 4 31: Linneus, whose enthusiasm for flowers was such that he went down upon his knees and thanked God that he had lived to see a furze bush in full flower, has given his name to our lovely twin flower (Linnea Borealis) which is now in full bloom. **1963** *Maclean's* 18 May 30/1: . . . mushroom smells can vary from . . . frankly fetid to a fragrance as sweet as twinflower. . . .

twist *n. Fur Trade, Hist.* tobacco prepared in twisted ropes, prominent among the trade goods of the fur companies. See also **North West twist.**
1776 (1901) HENRY (Elder) *Travels* 320: Tobacco, when sold, fetched one beaver-skin per foot of Spencer's twist. **1944** *Beaver* Mar. 39/2: As more and more natives became cigarette smokers, carrot and twist (or "niggerhead") are going into the discard. **1957** FISHER *Pemmican* 87: The man was chewing twist and browning his sandy stubble with it.

twist (up) *v. Slang* See **roll,** *v.* See also **twisting.**
1966 ST. PIERRE *Quarter Horse* 21: Smith twisted a cigarette for the old man and continued speaking gently, as he did so. **1967** *Globe and Mail* (Toronto) 30 May 29/8: [He] smiled at her as he twisted up a [cigarette] with one hand. . . .

twister *n.* a kind of doughnut made by folding a six-inch roll of dough in half and twining the two halves around each other.
1886 *Indian* (Hagersville, Ont.) 26 May 119/2: The "youngster" thinks a good, fluffy, fat twister is more than twice as good as the little rings and balls, "'cause there are several mouthfuls in one." **1903** RICHARDSON *Colin* 226: But they all ate to their hearts' content, Mrs. McNabb and the girls having brought a liberal supply of "twisters" and cakes for the guests.

twisting *n. Slang* a cigarette rolled by hand. See also **twist,** *v.* Cp. **tailor-made.**
1966 ST. PIERRE *Quarter Horse* 23: He lit his own twisting and blew fragrant blue smoke into the quiet air. . . .

twitch-up† *n.* See **spring-pole.**
1923 STRINGER *Empty Hands* 76: "I knocked this fellow [an animal] over with a club. I had better luck there than I did with my twitch-ups. I set out three last night, in their runs beyond the second muskeg. But my root-fibre wasn't strong enough. It was broken in both loops that were sprung." **1924** SHERMAN *Nature Stories* 247: The bait stick and horizontal stick were then adjusted . . . and the twitch-up was complete.

two-and-a-half-point blanket a grade of point blanket, *q.v.*
1824 (1955) BLACK *Journal* 140: Made a present to the old man of a 2½ pt Blanket to make him a Coat. **1887** *Trans.Roy.Soc.Can.* V 2 76: A somewhat inferior quality, known in the Hudson's Bay Company parlance as a "two and a-half point" blanket, is the standard. . . . **1905** (1954) *B.C.Hist.Qtly* 182: The [beaver's] skin was larger than a Hudson's Bay Company's 2½ point blanket.

two-bit† *adj. Slang* cheap; inferior.
1915 CUMMING *Skookum Chuck* 18: And it must not be forgotten that Johnny had a seven and a half Stetson hat while all Peter could afford was a two bit cap. **1955** BIRNEY *Long Table* 259: "You and your two-bit ILO aint a damned bit better than the Stalinists."

two bits† *Slang* twenty-five cents. See also **bit** (def. 1) and note.
1860 *British Colonist* (Victoria) 27 Oct. 2/2: Two bits to the pan is an excellent prospect. **1912** FOOTNER *New Rivers* 36: The first thing that struck us as out of the common was the sight of several inanimate bodies sprawled in the mud of the trail . . . The instrument of havoc was "squirrel whiskey" at two bits a drink. **1964** *Islander* 30 Aug. 6/2: . . . they would cross the Fraser to Hope in a gasboat (fare, two bits). . . .

two Canadas *Hist.* from 1791 to 1841, Upper Canada and Lower Canada, *qq.v.*; also, after 1841, Canada West and Canada East, *qq.v.*, although technically one province.
1811 *Montreal Herald* 19 Oct. 1/1: An institution such as is now contemplated, would be desirable to a country so rapidly advancing in resources and improvement as the two Canadas. **1838** HALIBURTON *Bubbles* 226: The foundation of this complaint appears to be, that thirteen years ago a bill for the union of the two Canadas was brought into Parliament by the then government, which, had it passed into a law, would

have made English the single official language of both. **1953** LEBOURDAIS *Nation of North* 11: There [Kingston], in a structure built for a hospital, members from the two Canadas met in parliament for the first time.

two-cent prospect *Placer Mining* the minimum prospect (about two cents per pan) considered worth working.
1913 OGILVIE *Yukon* 124: Here he found a two-cent prospect, that is, two cents of gold to a pan.

two-member constituency a riding (def. 2) represented by two members of Parliament or of the legislative assembly. See also **dual-member constituency.**
1964 *Globe and Mail* (Toronto) 14 Nov. 3/6: . . . they wish to retain the historic two-member constituencies of Halifax and Queens, in P.E.I.

two-point blanket a grade of point blanket, *q.v.*
1905 (1954) *B.C.Hist.Qtly* XVIII 168: There were two special seasons—the spring and the autumn—in which the trade was carried on . . . the standard being six beaver skins for a gun, and four skins for a "two-point" blanket, or six skins for a "three-point" blanket.

two-side camp *Lumbering* a logging camp having two operations underway simultaneously. See also **side.**
1925 *Cdn Labor Advocate* (Vancouver) 11 Sep. 6/4: About two hundred men are employed here, a two-side camp. **1942** HAIG-BROWN *Timber* 253: The full operation of a two-side camp, including grading, track laying and maintenance, falling and bucking, rigging, yarding, loading, hauling, calls for the employment of about 250 men with the cookhouse and camp staff.

two-sticker *n.* See **jackboat.**
1895 *St.Nicholas* Apr. 448/2: . . . the gashers [were] dashing in and out among the punts and jacks (stoutly built two-stickers larger than gashers). **1931** *Cdn Geog. Jnl* II 391/1: Our "two-sticker with a kicker" lies in Sandy Bay harbour, Nova Scotia, outward bound for Labrador, that terra incognito even to the Maritimers.

two-way player in hockey, lacrosse, etc. a player who is effective both on offence and defence.
1963 *Hockey Illust.* Dec. 33/3: All three were two-way players.

tyee ['taɪ,i] *n.* [< Chinook Jargon "chief, boss, champion"; cf. Nootka *tāyī* older brother] *Esp.B.C.*
1 the chief of an Indian tribe or band. Cp. **medicine tyhee.**
1792 (1958) HEALEY *Alert Bay* 15: The Ty-ee, or chief, of the village paid us an early visit. . . . **1816** (1896) WILSON *Adventures* 174: The boy was considered as a Tyee, or chief, being the only son of Tootoosch, one of their principal chiefs. . . . **1880** GORDON *Mountain and Prairie* 117: We were surprised to find, at the head of Stewart Lake, a well-stocked farm, owned and worked by the Indian "tyhee." **1963** *B.C.Digest* Oct. 54/2: A British officer . . . may have told the Chief that he was now the great Tyee of the country. The Indian took the words literally and elevated himself to top position.
2 any important person; boss.
1866 LORD *Naturalist* I 161: Having handed my letters of introduction from his Excellency the Governor to the chief trader, I was presented to the chiefs as a Hyas

tyee (great chief), one of "King George's" men. **1902**
MCEVOY *From the Gt Lakes* 181: You find they [Chinese
immigrants] understand the financial market as well as
anybody, and that numbers of the lower orders are
absolutely subject to their "tyee" who lords it over
them. **1927** PHILIP *Painted Cliff* 14: J. B. Smith is the
high-muck-a-muck, the tyee of the mining business of
British Columbia. . . . **1957** FISHER *Pemmican* 210:
"Tiye," David said . . . indicating himself, telling the old
man that he, David, was a chief, a master.

3 a Chinook salmon, *q.v.*, especially one over a
specified weight. See 1958 quote. See also **tyee
chinook** and **tyee salmon.**

1912 ROGERS *Sport* 53: Mac was a good boatman, and
the way he followed the tyee in the eight-knot current
did him credit. **1958** KELSEY *B.C.Rides a Star* 137:
Technically, a tyee, or champion, is a spring salmon,
but in Campbell River's sport fishing circles the title
applies to a salmon of thirty pounds or over. At Saanich
and other Provincial fishing grounds, a salmon of
twenty pounds or more is accepted as a tyee. **1966** *Dly
Colonist* (Victoria) 27 Feb. 8/1: He is also only 10
minutes from the Campbell River tyee grounds, but our
story today is about steelheading.

tyee chinook See **tyee** (def. 3).
1961 *Sun* (Vancouver) 17 Aug. 23/1: Record tyee
chinook is a 92-pounder on rod and reel, a 126½-
pounder by net. . . . **1963** *Ibid.* 6 Aug. 12/1: Fletcher
reports a friend drew a blank Sunday at Britannia . . .
another ordinarily good tyee chinook hangout at this
time. . . .

tyee klootchman *Obs.* a female ruler, specifically
Queen Victoria.
1872 POOLE *Queen Charlotte Is.* 311: The most frequent
questions used to refer to *Tyhee Klootchman* and her
Papoose, that is to Queen Victoria and her children.

tyee salmon See **tyee** (def. 3).
1907 LAMBERT *Fishing in B.C.* 74: The king or tyee,
quinnat, spring or chinook salmon (*O. tschawytscha*) is
the most important from the sportsman's point of view,
but owing to the white or very pale pink flesh not so
useful to the canner. **1961** *Canada Month* 6 Oct. 15/1:
. . . Alberni Inlet [is] famed for its big Tyee salmon.

tyeeship *n. Obs.* the rank and responsibilities of a
tyee (def. 1).
1872 (1877) GRANT *Ocean to Ocean* 318: His reputation
mounted . . . and he stood a good chance of the
Tyeeship. . . .

tyhee *n.* See **tyee.**

Tyndall (lime)stone a kind of blue-gray
limestone quarried near Garson, Manitoba and
famous as a building stone for ornamental purposes
since production began in 1896.
1926 *Beaver* Mar. 57: One hundred and fifty thousand
cubic feet of Tyndall stone will be used for facing the
building. This stone is quarried and cut . . . at Tyndall,
Manitoba. **1952** PUTNAM *Cdn Regions* 399/2: On the
south shore of the lake, stand the Saskatchewan
Legislative Buildings, constructed of Tyndall limestone
and surrounded by landscaped gardens. **1958** *Encyc.
Can.* IV 321/1: The area is a centre for the production of
limestone, known as Tyndall stone. . . .

tysowian *n. Obs.* See **savoyan.**

1798 *U.C.Gaz.* (York [Toronto]) 6 Apr. 1/2: List of Letters remaining with J. Edwards, esq. at Newark, (U.C.) for the accomodations of the person to whom they are addressed. **1906** *Ont.Bur.Arch.Rep.* IV ii: After the reunion of Upper and Lower Canada into the Province of Canada, the *Canada Gazette* was re-issued beginning with No. 1 dated 2nd October, 1841 and was published at Kingston U.C.

udjuk, ugiuk, ugjuk *n.* See **oogruk.**

U.E. 1 United Empire. See quotes.
1790 (1905) *Ont.Bur.Arch.Rep.* II 7: That the Board will take course to inform the Loyalists (U.E.) of the resolves of Council this in favor and direct the Clerk to refund any fees received from persons of that description. **1909** *London and Middlesex Hist.Soc. Trans.* II 7: The following year an order in Council granted 200 acres of land to all children of Loyal Subjects during the late war, with the honorable distinction that they and their descendants should add the letters U.E. to their names for all time.

2 See **United Empire Loyalist.**
1789 (1905) *Ont.Bur.Arch.Rep.* III lxxxvi: And the said U.E. is hereby authorized to occupy and improve the said Lands. . . . **1838** *Patriot* (Toronto) 15 May 3/4: Many of them are sons of the sons of that portion of inhabitants who emigrated to this country, and whose loyalty cannot be doubted, called U.E.'s. **1884** *Echo of Niagara* (Ont.) 18 May 2/2: The people of Niagara should celebrate with the U.E.'s and make this a mammoth celebration.

3 See **U.E. rights.**
1834 (1926) LANGTON *Early U.C.* 75: I am not surprised at your feeling uneasy about my U.E.'s, as the low price must have given you some fears as to the validity of the title, but be assured they are groundless. . . .

U.E. (or U.E.L.) grant *Hist.* See **U.E. rights** (def. 1).
1852 (1923) MOODIE *Roughing It* 236: The farm . . . forms a part of our U.E. grant. **1905** *Ont.Bur.Arch.Rep.* III lxix: The U.E.L. grants were to be free of all expense.

U.E.L. See **United Empire Loyalist.**
1887 HIGGINS *Life of J.Gould* 118: This class of settlers had no objection whatever to be classed as U.E.L.'s notwithstanding that their sympathies were altogether with the "patriots." **1899** *Rev.Hist.Pubs* III 138: The frequency with which U.E.L. occurs after the names of the first Canadian members of their respective families is characteristic of the country. **1958** *Encyc.Can.* X 185/1: In 1897 the United Empire Loyalists' Association of Ontario was incorporated with the object of uniting the descendants of the UEL's and preserving the historical records of these settlers.

U.E.L. grant See **U.E. grant.**

U.E. list *Hist.* the official register of those persons entitled to be called United Empire Loyalists, *q.v.*
1798 *U.C.Gaz.* (York [Toronto]) 29 Dec. 2/3: All Loyalists . . . whose names have been enrolled upon the U.E. Lists . . . may continue to consider themselves entitled to receive from this Government, Two Hundred Acres of Land free from the payment of Fees and other Charges. **1822** GOURLAY *Upper Canada* I 13: As the sons and daughters of those whose names are on the U.E. list become of age, they petition the lieutenant-governor, in council, stating the facts and verifying them by their own oath, and the affidavite of one witness, and upon such petitions obtain orders for the land, which they locate in some of the new townships, and then take out their patents without cost. **1958** *Encyc.Can.* X 184/1:

A list of these Loyalists, known as the Old U.E. list, was drawn up, and in Upper Canada additions to this list were made by Lieutenant-Governor Simcoe.

U.E. Loyalist See **United Empire Loyalist.**
1797 (1932) RUSSELL *Correspondence* I 125: The Board direct that no fees whatever shall be taken from the U.E. Loyalists for any application to the Council respecting land. **1819** *Kingston Chron.* (U.C.) 2 July 3/2: The Sons and Daughters of U.E. Loyalists being entitled to gratuitous grants of 200 Acres, must apply to the Lieutenant Governor-in-Council. **1885** DENT *U.C. Rebellion* I 60: The grants to the children of U.E. Loyalists were the constant subjects of bargain and sale, and wrought great evil to the Province without producing any corresponding benefit to the recipients. **1926** LANGTON *Early U.C.* xxv: There was, of course, plenty of prejudice against republicanism among the U.E. Loyalists, who had inherited an abhorrence of the United States government.

U.E. rights *Hist.* **1** the land grant of 200 hundred acres to which all Loyalists on the U.E. list, *q.v.*, were entitled, including the rights of sons and daughters of grantees to claim that grant at a later date. See also **U.E.** (def. 3), **U.E. grant,** and **United Empire Rights.**
1835 *U.C.Gaz.* (York [Toronto]) 1 Jan. 293/3: It is the intention of the Government in granting the privileges commonly called U.E. Rights, to confer upon the children of those brave men, who during the American Revolution adhered to the Crown, a Lot of Land on which they might comfortably reside, as a mark of distinction for their Loyal Services. **1837** *Bytown* [Ottawa] *Gaz.* 16 Aug. 2/4: All holders of U.E. Rights and other claims, who shall be willing actually to settle in the said Townships, shall, upon producing a certificate of their actual settlement . . . be entitled to locate their claims in the said settlement. **1838** *Western Herald* (Sandwich [Windsor], U.C.) 7 Oct. 245/1: The allowance to Officers, duly certified at the Crown Lands Office, will be received in payment by the Agent, also U.E. and Militia, Military, and other Land Rights, on the production of Certificates of unlocated authorities from the Surveyor General's Office.

2 the actual land or holding obtained under such a grant; also, the location ticket for such land.
1833 (1926) LANGTON *Early U.C.* 14: . . . I am at present partly in treaty for certain U.E. rights, which I can procure at 3/9 to 5'-, and, if I come to any arrangement upon the subject the cost of my land will be materially diminished. *Ibid.* 19: Besides this I have bought two U.E. rights of 200 acres each at 3/9; one of which I have resold at a profit of £12 10, and the other I have located immediately adjoining my other land but in the township of Verulam. **1861** CROIL *Dundas* 135: U.E. rights became a staple article of commerce, and were readily bought up by speculators, almost as fast as they came into the hands of the rising generation.

U.E.-right ticket a location ticket (def. 1) for land obtained under U.E. rights (def. 1).
1896 GOURLAY *Hist.Ottawa* 50: The Government gave them claims they called tickets, for land, but the people not paying much attention to the U.E.L., pronounced them all in a word "Ueright tickets."

U.F.A. United Farmers of Alberta. See **United Farmers.**
1918 MOORHOUSE *Deep Furrows* 261: [In 1916] President H. W. Wood, of the United Farmers of Alberta . . . inaugurated "U.F.A. Sunday"—one Sunday in each year to be set aside as the Farmer's own particular day, with special sermons and services.

U.F.O. United Farmers of Ontario. See **United Farmers.**
1920 *Rod and Gun in Can.* 629/2: We shall probably hear of him as a combined U.F.O. and Home-Rule candidate at no distant date! **1946** LOWER *Colony to Nation* 497: . . . in Ontario in the fall of 1919, a farmers' slate of candidates was put up (the "U.F.O." or United Farmers of Ontario) and to everyone's surprise it swept the province.

uglit *n.pl. Eskimo* See **échoueries.**
1966 *Cdn Geog.Jnl* Mar. 90/2: In only a few instances have walrus herds been seen on sandy or rocky beaches, but these have always been adjacent to *uglit*.

ugloo *n.* See **aglu.**

ukamaw *n.* See **ogema.**

Uke [juk] *n.* [shortening] *Slang* Ukrainian.
1955 BIRNEY *Long Table* 195: "They got their Ukes to let us sleep on the floor of the Ukrainian Labor Temple." **1959** *Kingston Whig-Standard* (Ont.) 15 Sep. 10/4: Coach Milt Schmidt today said the only certainty on his Boston Bruins hockey team is the Uke line—Bronco Horvath, Vic Stasiuk and Johnny Bucyk.

ula *n.* See **ooloo.**

ulaken or **ulekun** *n.* See **oolichan.**

Ultra ['ʌltrə] *n.* [shortening] *Hist.* See **Ultramontagne.**
1963 STANLEY *Louis Riel* 31: Between the *Rouges* and the *Ultras* there could be no compromise, no common meeting ground. . . .

Ultramontagne [,ʌltrə'mɑntən] *n.* [< Cdn F] *Hist.* in Quebec, from 1870 to 1900, a member of an extreme right wing of the Conservative Party, a militant group of French-speaking and Catholic Quebecois whose political aims embodied religion and nationalism. See also **Ultra.** Also spelled *Ultramontane.*
1904 DECELLES *Cartier* 79: In this case the danger sprang from among the most advanced Conservatives of his following, those whom Protestants called Ultramontanes, and loyal Conservatives nicknamed Castors. **1963** STANLEY *Louis Riel* 218: Taschereau . . . had stood aside from the efforts of the Ultramontagnes to establish a Catholic political party in Canada.

ultramontagne *adj.* of or having to do with the Ultramontagnes. Also spelled *ultramontane.*
1890 *Grip* (Toronto) 26 July 50/2: He may still be a true liberal in his mind, of course, but the sort of politics he has had on tap for a good while back tastes like the real ultramontane vintage. **1916** SKELTON *Day of Laurier* 167: Up and down the province of Quebec he was denounced by the ultra-montane leaders. **1963** MORTON *Kingdom of Canada* 357: In the new ultramontagne creed in Quebec, Catholicism helped the growth of *nationalisme*, that is, nationalism as an emotional and practical union of race, language, family and faith.

Ultramontagnism *n. Hist.* the policies of the Ultramontagnes. Also spelled *Ultramontanism.*
1881 RATTRAY *Scots in Brit.N.A.* 594: Some of [his] best speeches have been published in pamphlet form, as well as one brochure on Canada from 1849 to 1859, and another on the effects of Ultramontanism in Canada. **1891** *Grip* (Toronto) 1 Aug. 69/2: [The] truly loyal Orangeman, while loudly professing his desire to fight Jesuitism to the death, is always found on election day voting for the retention in office of the Lantevins, Chapleaus, Thompsons and other sworn defenders of Ultramontanism. . . .

ulu *n.* See **ooloo.**

umiak *n.* See **oomiak.**

UN or **U.N.** See **Union Nationale.**
1961 *Time* (Cdn ed.) 24 Nov. 16/1: . . . [the] chief U.N. organizer for St. Johns . . . held court in the local provincial police headquarters. **1963** *Globe and Mail* (Toronto) 26 Mar. 7/8: The UN leader came back into power stronger than ever.

underbrush† *n.* the shrubs and small trees forming the low growth of a wooded area.
1824 *Canadian Mag.* III 246: Every year we are . . . very particular upon the first fall of snow to sow my grass seed upon the lands intended for mowing or pasturage, and also to have a quantity of wood land under-brushed, and the underbrush piled for better accomodation of cutting our fire wood. **1942** CAMPBELL *Thorn-Apple Tree* 28: Then he picked his way carefully . . . slipping sideways through the tangle of underbrush.

underbrush *v.* cut down underbrush and clear it away. See 1824 quote at **underbrush,** *n.*
1835 (1926) LANGTON *Early U.C.* 144: This week all hands, guests and all, were underbrushing. **1964** GUILLET *Pioneer Days* 122: . . . after underbrushing the piece of land the workers proceeded with logging.

underbrushed *adj.* cleared of underbrush.
1841 *Bytown* [Ottawa] *Gaz.* 17 Feb. 1/4: Clearing part of the underbrushed land for winter wheat.

underbrushing *n.* the action or process of removing underbrush, as in clearing land.
1853 STRICKLAND *Canada West* II 182: As soon as the underbrushing was finished, I hired another man and commenced cutting out a sleigh road to Peterborough. **1863** WALSHE *Cedar Creek* 99: A man in a red shirt, who was engaged in underbrushing at a little distance, said that "the town" was only a mile away. . . . **1933** CAMERON *Twigs* 124: That process . . . called "underbrushing," was continued over a space about twenty yards wide, up the steep bank of the creek to the high level land.

underground railroad or **railway**† *Hist.* a system set up by abolitionists in the United States to conduct Negro slaves to freedom, one of its branches leading into Canada.
1852 *Voice of the Fugitive* (Sandwich, C.W.) 22 Apr. 1/3: I was formerly, while residing East, a conductor of a car on the Underground Railroad, I felt a desire to get the perusal of said paper, so that I might be able to keep track of the progress that is being made by a portion of mankind who were so unfortunate as to receive their birth in a land of slavery. **1965** *Victoria Daily Times* 11 Aug. 18/5: Amherstburg was the main debarking point 100 years ago for the "Underground Railway," the terminus of the smuggling of Negro slaves into Canada from the U.S.

underground route *Hist.* See **underground railroad.**

1852 *Voice of the Fugitive* (Sandwich, C.W.) 1 July 2/4: Some noble specimens of humanity have come in by the underground route from Kentucky.

Ungava [ʌnˈgævə] *n.* [< Esk.] the general area lying between Northern Labrador and Hudson Bay; specifically, the peninsula lying between the Bay and Ungava Bay.
1835 (1963) DAVIES *Northern Quebec* 243: . . . the Ungava mountaineers would have no objection to attach themselves to this post. **1952** KNOTT *Harnessing* 5/2: Ungava, in Eskimo, means "Far Away," and it is the far away lands across the top of Canada that attract this country's new pioneers. **1965** *Maclean's* 24 July 2/4: Conditions are even worse now than in the early '50s, when there was heavy air traffic to the DEW Line, Ungava and other regions.

unification *n.* the policy or action of completely merging the traditional navy, army, and air force into one combined force having a unified command and common uniform, rank structure, and pay rates. Cp. **integration.**
1966 *Globe and Mail* (Toronto) 1 Aug. 7/8: Many naval officers share his view that while integration of the three forces is a worthy objective, unification is not. **1966** *Kingston Whig-Standard* (Ont.) 28 Sep. 8/2: Neither is the military, by and large, opposed to unification. The argument of opponents of unification is that it is being rushed.

Union *n. Hist.* **1** the uniting of Upper and Lower Canada, finally effected by the Union Act, *q.v.* See also **United Canada.**
1822 *Kingston Chron.* (U.C.) 22 Nov. 3/4: Meetings friendly to the Union have been held in St. Armand's and Frelighsburgh, in Lower Canada, but we have no room for their resolutions. **1824** *P.E.I. Register* (Charlottetown) 26 June 4/4: A rumour has been in circulation for a few days past, that it was the intention of His Majesty's Ministers to submit to Parliament a Union of the British Provinces in North America, and to place at their head a Royal Duke as Vice-Roy. **1844** *Kingston Chron.and Gaz.* (C.W.) 3 Oct. 2/6: Our late Parliamentary majority, to govern United Canada, having doubled the expenditure of the two provinces before the Union. **1963** MORTON *Kingdom of Can.* 258: In the Union there was also to be equal representation of the two sections which were the old Upper and Lower Canada, now Canada West and Canada East.

2 See **Confederation.**
1859 *British Colonist* (Victoria) 5 Feb. 3/2: Except union is adopted British Columbia [may] be a long time without free institutions. **1885** GEMMILL *Companion* 388: Manitoba (1870), British Columbia (1871), and Prince Edward Island (1873), have all been admitted to the Union, but there is no authoritative arrangement as regards precedence. **1953** LEBOURDAIS *Nation of North* 26: Tilley again formed a government, and in the elections that followed, with the aid of much Canadian money, the union forces won.

Union Act *Hist.* the act of the British Parliament uniting Upper and Lower Canada into United Canada, *q.v.*, passed July 23, 1840 and effective February 5, 1841. See also **Union** (def. 1) and **Union Bill.**
1882 RATTRAY *Scots in Brit.N.A.* II 491: He opposed the Union Act because he thought it unjust to the bulk of the French Canadian population. **1899** GARDNER *Names* 180: This county, which was at the time of the Union Act of 1840 known as the north riding of Northumberland, takes its name from the town of Peterborough.

Union Bill *Hist.* a bill for the uniting of Upper Canada and Lower Canada, *qq.v.*, first drawn up in 1822 and eventually passed in 1840 as the Union Act, *q.v.*
1822 *Cdn Courant* (Montreal) 12 Oct. 3/2: The meeting is for the express purpose of taking measures to lay before the mother country a statement of the necessities of these provinces to a political point of view, and to petition for the passing of the Union Bill. **1840** *Patriot* (Toronto) 18 Aug. 2/2: The prominent object of interest is, of course, the Union Bill. **1904** DECELLES *Papineau* 53: In spite of Ellice's protests, the Union Bill was well and duly shelved in 1823, and filed away in the records of Downing street, whence it was to be brought forth eighteen years later. **1923** *Dalhousie Rev.* III 290: As for the Union Bill, so pregnant a proof of race conflict, with twenty-five troublous years of agitation to follow, the histories dismiss it briefly.

Union Government *Hist.* the coalition that governed Canada from 1917 to 1920. See also **Unionist** (def. 3) and **Unionist Party.**
1917 *Grit* (Toronto) 7 Dec. 1/1: The so-called Union Government is a truce rather than an alliance. **1953** LEBOURDAIS *Nation of North* 188: To round out the picture, in December 1917, the Union government, by order-in-Council, prohibited the importation and manufacture of liquor anywhere in Canada. **1963** MORTON *Kingdom of Canada* 433: In adition to laying the foundation of the Canadian National Railways, the Union Government carried two other measures of permanent significance. . . .

Unionist *n. Hist.* **1** a person in favor of union among the provinces of British North America, especially of Upper and Lower Canada.
1823 *Wkly Register* (York [Toronto]) 6 Feb. 28/1: It is probable, that the Unionists are to be found chiefly, if not wholly amongst the mercantile classes of the community. **1840** *Bytown* [Ottawa] *Gaz.* 3 Sep. 3/1: As regards Canadian politics in particular, I am a Unionist in every sense of the word. **1904** DECELLES *Papineau* 52: After quoting . . . from the Unionist petition, Papineau exclaims: "Are not these accents of rage and hatred?"

2 a supporter of Confederation, *q.v.*
1869 *Cdn Illust.News* 20 Nov. 34/2: The elections in Newfoundland have resulted adversely to Confederation. Twelve Antis and five Unionists have been returned, and five Constituencies remain to be heard from. **1875** CAMPBELL *Hist.P.E.I.* 177: The Honorable W. H. Pope, the colonial secretary—who was always a decided unionist—spoke effectively for an hour in its favor. **1953** LEBOURDAIS *Nation of North* 161: Two weeks before polling day, even with the aid of their two disreputable election Acts, the Unionist campaign managers were still not sure of success.

3 during World War I and later, a supporter of the principle of a coalition government. See also **Union Government.**
1916 BRIDLE *Sons of Canada* 235: Most of these adventurous souls, of whom the newspapers keep any account, go into politics. A majority of them become Unionists, speak often on platforms—sometimes quite badly, sometimes well—write books, engage in social reform, get taken up by the aristocracy, perhaps themselves acquire titles along the way. **1961** *Edmonton Jnl* 4 Aug. 18/1: Clear Grits, Unionists, Progressives . . . are part of the ancestral lore of politics—parties with a past but without a future.

Unionist Party *Hist.* the political party supporting the Union Government, *q.v.*
1917 *Grit* (Toronto) 11 Dec. 1/2: The so-called Unionist Party are harping on the election note that the boys at the front must not be deserted—as though anybody ever thought of deserting them. **1953** LEBOURDAIS *Nation of North* 174: In the federal field, T.A. Crerar and the group who had followed him out of the Unionist party had been busy organizing the Progressive party, drawing its strength mainly from the prairie provinces.

Union Nationale in Quebec, a provincial political party, long under the leadership of Maurice Duplessis, 1890-1959, and identified with conservative French-Canadian nationalism. See also **National Union** and **UN.**
1946 LOWER *Colony to Nation* 556: During the Quebec provincial election of the summer of 1944 the Union Nationale and Bloc Populaire had deluged the province with flysheets.... **1957** *Kingston Whig-Standard* (Ont.) 19 Sep. 25/2: Union Nationale candidates won handily over Liberals in Compton, Chateauguay and Megantic. **1966** *Globe and Mail* (Toronto) 11 Jan. 5/6: Opposition Leader Daniel Johnson of the Union Nationale calls it [an election] for April.

union school *Hist.* an elementary school serving two adjacent districts, townships, etc. See also **union section.** Cp. **consolidated school.**
1832 MCGREGOR *Brit.Amer.* II 512: ... we now find at Montreal a royal grammar school, a classical academical institution ... a parochial school, a union school.... **1849** *Journal of Education for U.C.* I 71/1: Examination of the Paris Union School ... took place on Saturday the 31st ultimo, much to the credit of Mr. Meston, the Teacher, who was lately a Student in the Normal School, Toronto. **1884** *Prince Albert Times* (Sask.) 14 Mar. 3/2: A union school district is about to be formed in the neighborhood of Pembina Crossing. **1890** *Medicine Hat Times* (Alta) 31 July 1/4: At the last meeting of the Board of Education, it was decided to bring the matter of establishing a kindergarten system in the Union Schools ... before the Assembly at its next meeting. **1896** GOURLAY *Hist.Ottawa* 25: Two or three were union schools with Huntley ... one on the Huntley side, two on the March side....

union section *Hist.* a school section embracing parts of two or more adjacent townships. See also **union school.**
1849 *Journal of Education for U.C.* I 78/1: Of the Union Sections 2 are composed of parts of four Townships, 5 of parts of three Townships, and 29 of parts of two Townships. **1903** *U of T Stud.Hist.& Econ.* II 107: Sometimes adjoining sections in different townships unite to form what is called a union section.

United Assembly *Hist.* See **United Legislature.**
1840 *Montreal Transcript* 13 Oct. 282/1: ... many of the public officers in both provinces are candidates for seats in the United Assembly.

United Canada *Hist.* the political union of Upper and Lower Canada, lasting from 1841 to 1867. See also **Union** (def. 1), **Union Act,** and **United Province.**
[1836 *Bytown* [Ottawa] *Gaz.* 17 Nov. 3/2: From this, the embryo Capital of the United Canadas, tho' at present the most remote part of Your Excellency's Government, a humble devotee to the luxury of idleness, purposes by one or two addresses to unfold to your attention the sentiments of an usually silent portion of Her Majesty's subjects.] **1844** *Kingston Chron.and Gaz.* (C.W.) 3 Oct. 2/6: Our late Parliamentary majority, to govern United Canada, having coupled the expenditure of the two provinces before the Union. **1958** *Encyc.Can.* IX 246/2: ... Scott represented Ottawa in the legislature of United Canada....

United Church 1 the United Church of Canada, a Protestant church formed in 1924-1925 of Methodists, Presbyterians, and Congregationalists.
1925 DAVIS *United Churches B.C.* 364: Columbian College has become the property of the United Church. **1957** WRIGHT *Blomidon Rose* 159: On a Sunday, especially at the union services of the Baptist and United Churches.... **1965** *Victoria Dly Times* 31 July 22/8: The United Church Observer predicts final union of the Anglican and United Churches will come in "less than 10 years" and calls for "rush approval" on the proposed plan.
2 a church building belonging to the United Church of Canada.
1958 *Citizen* 30 Nov. 1/4: Mrs. E. Rands will open the annual Fall bazaar of St. Andrew's United Church. **1962** ALLEN *Peace River* 38: [There was] the yellow steeple of the United Church poking skyward at the top of the street.... **1963** *Globe and Mail* (Toronto) 30 May 6/3: A letter from L. E. O'Connor [was received] after some reflections of mine about a United Church with a pool table in its basement.

United Empire Loyalist† one of a large number of persons loyal to the British Crown during the American Revolution, many of whom came to the eastern provinces of Canada as settlers during the Revolution and for some years afterwards. See also **British Loyalist, Empire Loyalist, French Loyalist, Loyalist** (def. 1a), **refugee** (def. 2), **Royalist** (def. 1b), **U.E.** (def. 2), **U. E. L., U.E. Loyalist,** and **Yankee,** *n.* (def. 2b). Cp. **late Loyalist, post-Loyalist,** and **Pre-Loyalist.**
1826 *Colonial Advocate* (York [Toronto]) 4 May 10: There is, as we all know, a certain feeling among many of the native and immigrant United Empire Loyalists of this day, which teaches them to consider themselves much better subjects, nay even a superior race to their American brethren who by their later immigration cannot lay claim to the same rights. **1892** (1908) DAWSON & SUTHERLAND *Geography* 44: It is estimated that within two years of the recognition of the United States 20,000 refugees, known as "United Empire Loyalists," found new homes in Acadia.... **1963** *Canada Month* May 19/1: He was born in 1900 on a farm near Hastings, New Brunswick of United Empire Loyalist stock.

United Empire men *Obs.* See **United Empire Loyalist.**
1841 MCLEOD *Upper Canada* 14: These two classes formed the first permanent settlement of Upper Canada, and were distinguished from other British emigrants, by the term of *United Empire Men,* or, as they are now generally known, U.E. Loyalists.

United Empire Rights *Hist.* See **U.E. rights** (def. 1).
1834 (1926) LANGTON *Early U.C.* 54: United Empire rights are also sources of considerable profit, but as our sapient Parliament has been legislating about them lately I know not how they may answer for the future.

United Farmers one of several political groups growing out of farmers' organizations at the provincial level. See also **U.F.A.** and **U.F.O.**

1918 MOORHOUSE *Deep Furrows* 301: [In] January 14th, 1909 . . . amalgamation took place at Edmonton under the name, "United Farmers of Alberta." *Ibid.* 302: [The] United Farmers of Ontario [were formed in] 1914. **1958** MACGREGOR *North-west of 16* 220: Both the Wheat Pool idea and the United Farmers of Alberta movement gathered momentum in the years after the war. **1959** STEWART & FRENCH *Ask No Quarter* 159: That summer [1931] . . . The United Farmers of Canada (Saskatchewan Section) approved a series of resolutions favouring "social ownership and co-operative production" and agreed that direct political action was necessary to achieve their aims. **1966** *Globe and Mail* (Toronto) 12 Aug. 15/5: The victory of the United Farmers in the 1919 election changed the picture.

United House *Obs.* See **United Legislature.**
1841 *Montreal Transcript* 23 Jan. 457/5: The United House will contain some thirty representatives of French Canadian constituencies.

United Legislature or **Parliament** *Hist.* the legislature of United Canada, *q.v.* See also **United Assembly.**
1839 *Montreal Transcript* 15 Aug. 2/1: Under these circumstances, although troops may suppress any attempt at rebellion, yet as they do not vote at elections there remains no doubt of the character of the first United Legislature. . . . **1845** *St.Catharines Jnl* (C.W.) 16 Jan. 3/3: On the first session of the United Parliament a pledge was given that all funds arising from the sale of lands would be so employed.

United Province(s) *Hist.* See **United Canada.**
1841 *U.C.Gaz.* (Toronto) 9 Feb. Extra 1/2: . . . the Governor of Canada . . . will to-morrow assume the Executive functions over the United Provinces. **1909** HUNTER *Simcoe County* I 219: The general election for the first parliament of the United Provinces was held in the spring of 1841, the union having been formally proclaimed February 10th of that year. **1967** *Globe Mag.* 28 Jan. 7/1: Brown's solution to the problems of the United Province was: break it up.

unknown fish See **inconnu.**
1947 *Beaver* Dec. 24/1: The "Unknown fish," or "conny" as it is more often called, looks like an overgrown whitefish and turns the scales between twenty and forty pounds.

unlocated *adj. Obs.* of lots or land, not yet located (def. 2a). Cp. **unpatented.**
1790 (1905) *Ont.Bur.Arch.Rep.* III 59: The board received 10 petitions for the many lots of the 12 unlocated ones outermost in the new Settlement, at the mouth of the Strait of Detroit. **1883** *Prince Albert Times* (Sask.) 11 July 2/1: His duty cannot be, as is generally supposed, to show immigrants the unlocated lands in the District, because all or very nearly all of the surveyed belt has been taken up.

unpatented *adj. Hist.* pertaining to lands which had not been taken up or on which land duties and payments had not been completed. Cp. **unlocated.**
1879 *Canadian Mthly* II 476/2: Its lands are, to a large extent, unpatented, and in the hands of the Crown in Ontario. **1909** HUNTER *Simcoe County* I 59: The government in 1863 resumed and offered for sale unpatented and unimproved lands in the Township of Flos.

unprime *adj. Fur Trade* of furs, not prime, *q.v.*
1921 *Beaver* May 2/2: . . . it was important that animals should be left unmolested while reproducing and during the season when pelts were unprime.

unprospected *adj.* not surveyed by prospectors; not investigated for minerals.
1898 *Yukon Midnight Sun* (Dawson) 1 Aug. 3/3: Within a radius of fifty miles of Dawson there is practically no little unprospected territory, and much of this ground has been thoroughly prospected. **1901** (1953) LEBOURDAIS *Nation of North* 103: As yet there are between one and three million square miles of country in Canada practically unprospected. . . . **1958** *Edmonton Jnl* 24 June 3 2/2: The territory is still relatively "unprospected". . . .

Unsatisfied Judgment Fund a fund established by a provincial government for the purpose of settling claims against uninsured drivers.
1964 *Calgary Herald* 8 Apr. 3/6: Motorcyclists and operators of scooters and tote-goats licenced in Alberta will have to pay $20 into the Unsatisfied Judgment Fund if they cannot produce liability insurance. . . .

uomiak *n.* See **oomiak.**

U-Paddle *n.* See quote.
1967 *Cdn Geog.Jnl* May 154/1: The last four or five years have seen an extraordinary growth of (allegedly) holiday travel north of the tree line, a development which the Hudson's Bay Company greatly facilitated in 1964 by instituting a canoe-rental service based on the best Tilden principles and called "U-Paddle." Though the rental fleet has close to thirty canoes, so popular has this northern travel become that the canoes are all reserved a year ahead.

up-country *n. Hist.* See **Northwest** (def. 1a). See also **Upper Country** (def. 1). Also *Up Country.*
*c*1902 LAUT *Trapper* 84: Only the most daring hunters would sign contracts for the "Up Country," or *Pays d'en Haut* as the French called it. **1954** CAMPBELL *Nor' Westers* 6: Each man who had been on one of those long exciting trips to the interior, the *pays d'en haut* or up-country, had faced starvation. **1963** MORTON *Kingdom of Canada* 65: The upshot was a compromise in 1669 . . . when it was agreed to prohibit the taking of liquor into the woods but to permit its use in Montreal and other settlements, including trading posts in the up country. . . .

upland boat *Fur Trade, Hist.* See **bateau** (def. 3).
1922 *Beaver* June 6/1: . . . in 1780 and probably previous to that date "upland" boats were in use on the Moose river for carrying goods to the posts south of that place.

uplander *n. Fur Trade, Hist.* See **upland Indian.**
1697 (1929) KELSEY *Papers* 67: Y^e uplander & his wife went away. **1787** (1963) DAVIES *Northern Quebec* xxviii: . . . the uplanders are not agreeable to assist us with any part of the goods. . . . **1965** *Letters from Hudson Bay* xxiii: The traders divided the Indians into two broad classes, the "Home Guards" and the "Uplanders."

upland Indian *Fur Trade* an Indian, especially a Cree, from the interior, as opposed to those in the vicinity of the Hudson's Bay posts. See also **uplander.** Cp. **home-guard.**
1697 (1929) KELSEY *Papers* 67: Likewise an upland Indian & his wife came to ye fort from up this river wch traded some beaver. **1744** DOBBS *Hudson's Bay* 47: There were about 100 Upland Indians came in their Canoes to

trade, and about 200 Northern Indians, who brought their Furs and Peltry upon Sledges. **1790** UMFREVILLE *Hudson's Bay* 56: In the month of March, the Upland Indians assemble on the banks of a particular lake. . . . **1924** FLAHERTY *Eskimo Friends* 5: We were provided with an open "York" boat and a crew, one Captain John Puggie, a half-breed post servant, and three upland Indians, one of whom . . . was Chief of the Moose River Crees.

Upper Canada *Abbrev.* U.C., *q.v.* **1** *Hist.* **a.** from 1791 to 1841, the official name of the province lying west of the Ottawa River and north of Lakes Ontario and Erie. See also **Upper Country** (def. 2) and **Upper Province** (def. 1). Cp. **Lower Canada** (def. 1a).
1791 (1911) SIMCOE *Diary* 69: Dec. 26—This day the division of the Province of Quebec into Upper and Lower Canada, and the new constitution given to the former, was announced by proclamation. **1838** HALIBURTON *Bubbles* 82: Sufficient has now been said to show you that the evils of Canada have their origin in the defects of the constitutional act, which by substituting French for English laws, by securing to them an overwhelming majority in the assembly, and in separating them from Upper Canada, have had the effect of making them a French and not an English colony. **1964** *Canada Month* Jan. 27/2: And before the age of railways and steam navigation, connections were not easy between Upper Canada and the colonies situated along the Atlantic seaboard.
b. from 1841 to 1867, the popular name for Canada West, *q.v.* Cp. **Lower Canada** (def. 1b).
1860 *Grumbler* (Toronto) 24 Mar. 3/3: Frenchmen will not stand quietly by and see their rights and liberties trodden under foot by a ranting, howling Clear Grit from Upper Canada. **1917** MILLER *New Era* 231: French was used freely . . . in schools in Upper Canada wherever there was a French-speaking population.
2 *Esp.Maritimes* Ontario. See also **Upper Province** (def. 2). Cp. **Lower Canada** (def. 2).
1889 WITHROW *Our Own Country* 291: Niagara is the Plymouth Rock of Upper Canada, and was once its proud capital city. **1956** RADDALL *Wings* 84: . . . it was a joke in Oak Falls that whenever Senator Sam was away in Upper Canada sounding off about the green forest the plate on his office door at home was just as green. **1958** *Herald-Tribune* 11 Mar. 2/4: Met a friend of earlier days, who pounds a typewriter for one of the strong partisan newspapers of Upper Canada. . . . **1964** WILSON *Barrett's Landing* 40: Papa says that this is because nobody in Upper Canada knows how to salt herring properly. **1966** *Globe and Mail* (Toronto) 14 Jan. 45/4: Upper and Lower Canada came together with a head-table flourish last night amid the rocking rhythms of old Canadian folk music. . . .

Upper-Canada *adj.* of or relating to Upper Canada.
☛ *For convenience, no attempt has been made here— or in the following two entries—to subdivide the quotations according to the political divisions of the time. See* **Upper Canada,** *where such distinctions have been made.*
1805 *Quebec Gaz.* 6 June 3/1: For Sale by the subscriber on reasonable terms, about 60,000 feet Upper Canada Pine Planks. **1836** *Cdn Temperance Advocate* Aug. 30/3: There happened to be . . . Upper Canada Merchants

present, who all drank water, affording good evidence of the progress of Temperance principles. **1856** (1926) LANGTON *Early U.C.* 283: Of the five Upper Canada Ministers three don't conceal their desire to divide the endowment. . . . **1957** *Time* (Cdn ed.) 2 Sep. 14/3: Halifax businessmen remembered once-booming sugar refineries, shoe factories and cotton mills bought by "Upper Canada interests" and later closed down. . . .

Upper Canadian a native or resident of Upper Canada. See note at **Upper-Canada.**
1822 *Kingston Chron.* (U.C.) 23 Nov. 3/4: They should learn not to asperse the well-tried loyalty of the Upper Canadians. **1849** *Wkly Globe* 2 Nov. 71/4: Once resolved that it had to leave Montreal, Kingston was the only place which could possibly have been selected as the permanent seat; it would have been unjust to take the Lower Canadians *always* so far West as Toronto—it would have been equally unjust to take the Upper Canadians *always* so far East as Quebec. **1871** *Wkly Manitoban* 28 Jan. 2/2: He frowned constantly and persistently on all the Ontario residents here, and to this day, out of nearly twenty appointments made, there is not one single Upper Canadian. **1966** *Kingston Whig-Standard* (Ont.) 26 Aug. 9/4: Premier Robarts wishes Nova Scotians would stop referring to persons who live in Ontario as Upper Canadians.

Upper-Canadian *adj.* of or having to do with Upper Canada or Upper Canadians. See note at **Upper Canada,** *adj.*
1824 *Wkly Register* (York (Toronto)) 27 May 173/2: This paper of motley, unconnected, shake-bag, periods; this unblushing, brazen faced Advocate, affects to be a Queenston and Upper Canadian Paper, whereas it is to all intents and purposes, and radically, a Lewiston and genu-wine Yankee paper. **1841** *Montreal Transcript* 23 Jan. 475/5: The Upper Canadian delegation will necessarily be divided in opinion and feeling on most subjects, and there is no chance of their ever being so united on any more question of Lower Canadian law, as to vote in solid phalanx for any unfair demand made by the British party. **1864** *Nor'Wester* (Winnipeg) 21 Nov. 2/3: In remodelling the present order of things Provincial, we notice with unfeigned pleasure that the Upper Canadian Delegates kept a sharp eye to the interests of this North-West territory. **1938** *Cdn Hist. Rev.* XIX 11: When at his desk the average Upper Canadian editor wrote editorials which more than compensated for the times they were omitted, if invective be a virtue in editorial writing. **1963** MACLEOD & MORTON *Cuthbert Grant* 69: This [acquittal] undoubtedly was arranged, as the handling of the transfer of the cases to the Upper Canadian courts suggests.

Upper-Canadian Rebellion *Hist.* the abortive rebellion of 1837-38 in Upper Canada, undertaken by extremist radicals under the leadership of William Lyon Mackenzie. See also **Rebellion** (def. 1).
1885 DENT *U.C. Rebellion* I 222: All the references to the Upper Canadian Rebellion to be found in current histories are traceable, directly or indirectly, to Mackenzie himself.

Upper Chamber See **Upper House** (def. 2).
1891 *Grip* (Toronto) 16 May 310/2: The *Telegram* literally suggests that the best thing that Senators could do would be to unanimously skip two sessions and allow a grateful country to declare vacant every seat in the Upper Chamber.

Upper Country 1 *Hist.* See **Northwest** (def. 1a). See also **up-country.**
1761 (1901) HENRY (Elder) *Travels* 41: Michilimackinac is the place of deposit, and point of departure between

the upper countries and the lower. **1789** *Quebec Gaz.*
1 Nov. 2/1: We still expect a very considerable quantity
of Furrs and Peltries from the most distant Posts of the
Upper Country, which cannot arrive to admit of the
Vessels sailing before the 25th. **1803** (1947) *Beaver* 34/2:
... God knows I'm not very tame especially on arriving
from the Upper Country. **1918** DAVIDSON *North West
Co.* 21n: McGill, writing in 1785, stated that he
estimated the value of the Upper Country trade—in
which he included the country from the mouth of the
Ohio and on the rivers falling into the Mississippi to as
far north as Lake Arabaska—at £180,000 currency.

2 *Hist.* Upper Canada (def. 1), especially that part
lying west of York (Toronto).
1797 *U.C.Gaz.* (York [Toronto]) 18 Jan. 1/2: It
[Queenston] may justly be stiled the emporium of the
upper country, and bids fair for becoming the most
populous town in this province. **1832** (1915) *London &
Middlesex Hist.Soc.Trans.* VI 31: If I should take it to
the Upper Country, I should have to pay a heavy price
for its transfer, as where if I settled the family in or near
York I should be allowed to retain the furniture as the
carriage of it would not be heavy. **1927** DICKIE *How
Canada Grew Up* 7: Those who settled in Upper
Canada were business men and farmers. Their interests
were less literary, and it was a little later before books
began to be written in the "Upper Country."

3 *B.C.* See quote.
1925 ANDERSON *Trees and Shrubs* 10: "The Upper
Country" and "The Upper Mainland" have the same
meaning. *Ibid.* 62: This climber [white clematis] is
common throughout the Upper Country....

Upper House 1 a. *Hist.* in colonial times, a
legislative council (def. 1).
1792 (1955) CRAIG *Early Travellers* 10: The Chief Justice
is the Speaker of the Upper House, and a Mr.
McDonnell of the Lower. **1863** WALSHE *Cedar Creek*
334: The members of the indissoluble Upper House, or
Legislative Council, are also returned at the rate of
twelve every two years, by the forty-eight electoral
divisions of the Province.

b. See 1963 quote. See also **legislative council**
(def. 2).
1963 *Globe and Mail* (Toronto) 25 Feb. 8/1: Abolition
of Quebec's Legislative Council—only provincial
Upper House remaining in Canada—and more pay for
members of the Legislative Assembly were among the
proposals adopted as the Quebec Liberal Federation
ended its annual convention yesterday. **1966** *Ibid.* 1 Dec.
4/5, 6: The 24-member council is Quebec's Upper
House and if the Union Nationale Government and the
Liberal Opposition stick to their promises it may be
abolished this session.

2 See **Senate**. See also **Upper Chamber**.
1958 *Edmonton Jnl* 26 June 1/7: ... the same resolution
is now before the Upper House for approval. **1965** *Globe
and Mail* (Toronto) 6 Dec. 6/4: As blatantly as any
Prime Minister before him, Mr. Pearson continued to
send to the Upper House party bagmen....

Upper Lake *Rare* Lake Superior, largest and most
northerly of the Great Lakes, *q.v.*
*c*1752 (1852) COATS *Geography of H.B.* 51: 'Tis caled
Superior, or Upper Lake, by the Europeans; I suppose,
from the descent of the waters falling into the Hurons
and Illinease, and other lakes of Canada, at the streight
of St. Maria, where is a fall caled Sauteures.

upper laker a lake boat that plies the Upper Lakes,
q.v.
1963 *Weekend Mag.* 21 Dec. 18/3: There were upper
lakers, canallers, packets, side-wheelers and schooners.

Upper Lakes 1 *Obs.* See **Great Lakes**.
☛ *This early usage may have resulted from considering
these lakes in relation to the St. Lawrence River and
Lake Champlain.*
1780 (1959) PRESTON *Kingston* 14: Mr Cornwall late
Master Builder on the upper lakes came [as a]
Passenger in the Vessel ... Fn. Cornwall was master
builder of ships on Lake Ontario. **1803** (1912) *Trans.
Roy.Soc.Can.* VI 2 5: Both the North-West Companies
(Old North-West Co. and X Y Company. Ed.) have
vessels in the Upper Lakes (neither of them on
Ontario)....

2 Lakes Huron and Superior, and, sometimes,
Michigan, the most northerly of the Great Lakes,
q.v. See also **Upper Lake**. Cp. **Lower Lakes**.
1850 BIGSBY *Shoe and Canoe* II 1/3: Although it will be
described in the Appendix, I may here advert to the
singular fact that all the superfluous waters of the
great upper lakes pass through it, while in one place it
is only 115 yards broad. **1959** *Globe and Mail* (Toronto)
18 June 8/4: Upper Lakes Shipping hopes to have a
new bulker, Seaway Queen, on hand after her maiden
trip to the Upper Lakes for ore.

upper posts *Fur Trade, Obs.* the fur posts in the
Northwest (def. 1a).
1788 (1959) PRESTON *Kingston* 132: [We] beg leave to
suggest the Removal of the place of Depot for the
Upper Posts; from Carleton Island to Kingston....
1860 *Nor'Wester* (R.R.S.) 28 July 3/2: If the weather is
at all favorable, the brigade will arrive at Edmonton
about the 20th September, from whence the outfits will
be forwarded to the upper posts, reaching their
destinations about the end of October.

Upper Province *Hist.* **1** See **Upper Canada**
(def. 1a).
1792 (1955) CRAIG *Early Travellers* 13: In the course of a
century, the Upper Province may become a fruitful
source of history. **1825** *P.E.I.Register* (Charlottetown)
22 Nov. 3/1: Canada is generally a level country,
particularly the Upper Province. **1938** *Cdn Hist.Rev.*
XIX 11: The *True Patriot*, published in London,
lamented that the press of Canada generally, but more
particularly of the upper province, was more degraded
than the press of any other country.

2 Ontario. See also **Upper Canada** (def. 2).
1899 *Yarmouth Herald* (N.S.) 17 Mar. 3/1: He says he
wants to see the world, and intends to go through
Dalhousie college on his return home and then go into
journalistic work in the upper province.

Upper Provinces *Hist.* Upper Canada and
Lower Canada, *qq.v.*
1829 MOORSOM *Letters N.S.* 202: Live-cattle are often
sent to Halifax market, at a price which hardly repays
the farmer, while salt provisions are imported from
Ireland, or from the upper provinces.

Upper School *Ont.* See quote. Cp. **middle
school**.
1953 *Globe and Mail* (Toronto) 21 May 7/3: Ontario
has had a fifth year in its secondary school program for
a long time. It has gone under different names—the
one best known to older people was the Upper School—
but is now known far and wide as Grade 13.

Upper Town the part of a town on high ground
some distance from the waterfront, usually
residential in character. Cp. **Lower Town** (def. 1).

1764 *Quebec Gaz.* 5 July 3/2: The House [is] situate in
the Upper Town of Montreal. . . . **1848** LANMAN
Adventures 156: There is but one street leading from the
Lower to the Upper Town and that is narrow and very
steep, and the gate way is defended by a number of large
cannons. **1958** *Encyc.Can.* VIII 376/1: Quebec . . . is
topographically divided into . . . the upper town and the
lower.

Uskemau, Uskemaw, Uskimay *n. Obs.* See
Eskimo.

usp(w)ogan *n. Obs.* See **puagun.**
1852 RICHARDSON *Arctic Exped.* 271: The use of the
Uspogan, or Calumet, which forms so important a part
of every ceremony among the Eythinyuwuk, was not
an original practice of the Tinne, but was introduced
to that people by Europeans along with tobacco.
1858 (1860) HIND *Assiniboine Exped.* II 137: Nothing
appears to contribute so largely to the comfort and
enjoyment of Indians . . . as the pwahgăn of the
Objibway, the uspwägăn of the Cree, or the pipe of the
English.

Usquamay, Usquemay, Usquemow *n. Obs.* See
Eskimo.

U.S.Section *Obs.* union school section. See also
union school and **union section.**
1863 *Elora Observer* (C.W.) 24 July 3/5: The Trustees of
U.S. Section Pell and Pilkington, are prepared to receive
Tenders for the erection of a Brick School House in
the Village of ALMA, Up to Saturday, July 25th, Noon.

utilidor [ju'tɪlə,dər] *n.* [< trademark] *North* See
1958 quote.
1957 *Maclean's* 14 Sep. 92/2: At many outposts such as
Churchill, Norman Wells and Frobisher ingenious
insulated conduit boxes called "utilidors" are used to
convey water, sewage and heating pipes to their
destinations. The idea is that the warmth from the
heating pipes is just enough to keep the other two pipes
from freezing. But utilidors are not used in old Aklavik,
mainly because [of] the cost of installing them. . . .
1958 *Edmonton Jnl* 16 July 30/3: Pipelines carrying the
heating water, domestic water and sewer lines will be
carried in insulated boxes called "utilidors," which will
be above ground. **1965** *Islander* 10 Oct. 7/2: . . . buildings
on stilts are connected together by a labyrinth of
"utilidors," the flumes that house the hot water, heat
and sewage pipes. These flumes are also on stilts and the
combination gives Inuvik a most unusual appearance.

utility *n. North* a caboose (def. 5b) for use as a
lavatory for the crew of a cat-train, *q.v.*
1958 WATTERS *B.C.Cent.Anthol.* 42: First was the "Meal
Train" with the kitchen, the diner, the utility and three
sleepers. In the other group were the office, two sleepers,
the workshop and the fuel sloop.

van *n.* **1** *Lumbering* a large chest containing numerous small articles for sale to persons working in a lumber camp. Cp. **wanigan** (def. 1c).

1883 FRASER *Shanty* 115: This "van" is a very peculiar institution of shanty life. It is an immense chest, made of the strongest wood, ribbed with iron bands, and secured with a mighty padlock, of which the foreman and clerk only possess each a key. **1947** SAUNDERS *Algonquin* 39: From the "Van" you could purchase mitts and socks if necessary, as well as tobacco and matches. . . . **1961** PRICE & KENNEDY *Renfrew* 46: Each man bought a small butcher knife for himself from the "van" for 25 cents.

2 *North* See **caboose** (def. 4b).

1920 FOOTNER *Fur-Bringers* 282: A private letter from the Landing tells of a wonderful van on runners that Ambrose Doane is building there to house his bride on their long journey north.

van *v.* *Alta* transport (children) to school by bus.
1954 RUSSELL *Living Earth* 197: They can van their pupils in to composite schools. . . . **1958** *Edmonton Jnl* 24 June 3 12/2: Several hundred children from the Barrhead district are vanned into centralized schools here each day.

Van-Columbia *n. Hist.* a proposed name for the united colonies of Vancouver Island, *q.v.*, and British Columbia.

1859 *Brit.Colonist* (Victoria) 6 June 2/1: Our salvation lies in union, for by that means we would have a fair chance to make Victoria the political capital of Van-Columbia.

Vancouver (or Vancouver's) Island *Hist.* a crown colony established on Vancouver Island in 1850 and united with mainland British Columbia in 1866. Also *Vancouver*.

[**1835** ROSS *Last Voyage* 34: The island which forms the western boundary of the inlet, and on which Nootka is situated, is named *Vancouver's* or *Quadra's Island*.] **1853** *Trans.Lit.& Hist.Soc.Que.* IV 308: Vancouver's Island, which is destined to become the England of the North Pacific, should be made another province, with the large gold-bearing island of Queen Charlotte attached to it as a dependency. **1862** *Nor'Wester* (Winnipeg) 2 Apr. 4/1: It will be said that to govern Vancouver at Quebec will be impossible, from any of knowledge of affairs there, but same will apply in a lesser degree to the Red River. **1918** *Archives of B.C.* No. II 5: Thus it is that the little Colony of Vancouver Island, though it existed as such only for the short period of seventeen years, (1849-66), plays no inconsiderable part in the early history of Canada on the Pacific. **1958** KELSEY *B.C.Rides a Star* 122: That rivalry became hostility when Vancouver Island Colony's citizens, to rid themselves of a new and unpopular governor, clamored for union with British Columbia.

Van Doos ['væn'duz] [< F *vingt-deux* twenty-two] *Informal* the Royal 22nd Regiment, a famous infantry regiment made up mostly of French-Canadians.

1958 *Edmonton Jnl* 7 Aug. 1/5: At the station she inspected a 100-man guard of honor mounted by the Van Doos and the regiment's 61-piece regimental band. **1964** *Dly Colonist* (Victoria) 1 Oct. 4/1: They [Canadian Guards] will replace the Royal 22nd Regiment, the "Van Doos," which have completed their allotted six months spell abroad.

var *n.* [< dial.var. of *fir*] *Atlantic Provinces* the balsam fir; also, its wood. See **balsam** (defs 1 and 2). Also spelled *varr* (obs.).

1793 (1937) CAMPBELL *Travels* 57: The men set to work,

and . . . cut the crops of a species of ever green wood, which they call varr [in New Brunswick]. **1842** BONNYCASTLE *Newfoundland* II 266: For some distance, too, the bark of the spruce pine, (pinus balsamifera) called var in Newfoundland, probably from a west of England corruption of fir, was taken off, it being one of the customs of the Boeothics to use the inner bark as food. **1904** CROSSKILL *P.E.I.* 85: The woodman's axe, forest fires and the fore-time prosperous ship-building industry have swept away the "Forest primeval," leaving but insignificant growths of the cone-bearing, soft wood species, the commonest being the balsam, fir or var, and spruce. **1959** *Atlantic Advocate* Jan. 74: In the feel of drawknife in wood, smoothing a shingle out of straight-grained var, there was something that smoothed the mind.

variation set *Fur Trade* See quote. See also **set** (def. 2). Cp. **tripod set**.

1965 *Islander* 14 Feb. 13/2: I had made a "variation set": two tall spruces grew about four feet apart and I had strung a twisted, three-strand haywire cable from one to the other as high up as I could reach, stapling each end securely and testing it by swinging my weight on it. In the middle of this cable, halfway between the trees, I fastened the bait. On the ground below I set two traps, each about a foot from each tree base.

varve, varvoe, varvon *n. Obs.* See **varveau**.

varveau ['varvo] *n.* **-x** or **-s.** [< Cdn F < F *varveau, verveau* fish trap] *Pacific Coast* **1** *Obs.* See quote.

1828 (1872) MCDONALD *Peace River* 31: Indians here and there along the river, with *verveux* (sweep nets) at each lodge.

2 *Hist.* a woven basket, about 6 feet long, used by certain Indian bands in fishing with a barrier, *q.v.*, the basket being attached over an opening in the weir. Also spelled *varvo(e)*, *varvou, verveau, vervo*, etc.

1832 (1948) MCLOUGHLIN *Letters* 272: I think that in twelve days I will send a party after you so that you may go to the Verveau and the men I send will go to you wherever you are. . . . **1833** (1932) MCLEAN *Notes* 152: Gaps are left in the works [barrier] of sufficient size to admit the *varveaux*, or baskets, in which the fish are taken. **1860** *Kamloops Jnl* (B.C.) 3 Apr.: Tahow arrived from Sevwright River and states that the Varvoux there and Barrier is complete. **1905** (1954) *B.C.Hist.Qtly* XVIII 169: A particular tribe . . . captured this [white-] fish by means of a pouch-basket ("vervoe") placed in the running stream. . . . **1953** *Beaver* Mar. 22/1: The salmon —sockeye—were caught in traps called weirs or "varvoes," "varvons," or "varves" in the journals.

varying hare† a species of hare, *Lepus americanus,* especially common in the North, so called because its fur is brown in summer and white in winter. See also **Arctic rabbit, bush rabbit, jack-rabbit, northern hare, rabbit, snowshoe hare,** and **wapoose.**

1784 PENNANT *Arctic Zoology* 95: The hind legs are longer in proportion than those of the common Hare or varying Hare. **1896** RUSSELL *Far North* 239: The graders assert that the marten is subject to periodic murrains, as is the varying hare, but when these periods occurred and whether at seven year intervals they did not know. **1963** SYMONS *Many Trails* 17: [Cottontails are] quite different from the long-legged plains hares and the varying hares, which we miscall snowshoe rabbits.

vase *n.* [< Cdn F < F, ult. < Gmc] *Fur Trade, Obs.* a muddy, boggy tract, especially a portage (def. 1a) through such terrain.
[**1760** (1901) HENRY (Elder) *Travels* 29: We reached the Portage a la Vase . . . Their name describes the boggy ground of which they consist.] **1793** (1933) MACDONELL *Diary* 81: Leaving this lake we have three portages running called the vases. The men will have the first vase to be some perches longer than the *Grand Callumet.* . . . **1821** (1900) GARRY *Diary* 105: We then passed through a Succession of small Lakes and at 9 encamped on the last Vase. **1933** GATES *Five Traders* 81: The propriety of the name Portages des Vases, or Muddy Portages, was attested to by Henry the elder, who noted the term with understanding in 1760, and by Bigsby, who passed that way more than half a century later.

vejack *n.* See **wejack**.

velvet duck the white-winged scoter, *Oidemia deglandi.*
1823 FRANKLIN *Journey* 699: It [the Black Duck] is smaller than the Velvet Duck, but, like that bird, is chiefly black. **1872** POOLE *Queen Charlotte Is.* 264: . . . I bagged several . . . velvet duck, all of which [were] good eating. **1956** MCATEE *Folk-Names* 17: White-winged scoter [is also called] velvet duck (From its soft plumage. Nfld., N.S., N.B.). . . .

ventes *n. Hist.* See **lods et ventes**.

verglas *n. Cdn French* See **silver thaw**.
1808 (1809) GRAY *Letters* 301: During the thaw, a very extraordinary effect is produced, sometimes, on the trees. The Canadians call it *ver-glas. Ibid.* 302: I see every day the effects of the last *ver-glas.* **1863** WALSHE *Cedar Creek* 310: . . . perhaps you could tell me the cause of the *ver glas?* What makes that thin incrustation of ice over the trunk and every twig . . . ?

verrandis *n. Obs.* See **verrangue**.

verrangue *n.* [< Cdn F < F *varangue* rib of a boat] *Fur Trade, Obs.* in a canoe, one of a series of semi-hoops set at right angles to the gunwales to give structural support to the form. Also spelled *verengue.*
1806 (1930) FRASER *Journal* 118: Buyson was employed making verangues for a small canoe, and Mr. Stuart banded the large one but did not render all the verangues. **1814** (1897) COUES *New Light* II 838: Men preparing wood for canoes . . . making maiters, verrangues, etc. **1862** *Cdn Naturalist* May 134: It is used for the thin hoops or *verrandis* [sic] and lining of bark canoes.

verveau or **verveu** *n. Obs.* See **varveau**.

vest-pocket trawler *Maritimes* See quote.
1963 *Kingston Whig-Standard* (Ont.) 2 Mar. 4/3: In that year [1947], the first five New Brunswick draggers, or vest-pocket trawlers, made their appearance on the Gulf of St. Lawrence.

Vets Affairs *Informal* the Department of Veterans' Affairs.
1949 PETERSON *Chipmunk* 138: It was like trying to get something out of Vets Affairs in the government.

vice-admiral *n. Nfld, Hist.* See 1915 quote. Cp. **fishing admiral**.
1714 (1793) REEVES *Hist.Nfld* 89: I had several complaints from the inhabitants and others, of injustice done them by the admirals, vice-admirals, &c. . . . **1765** *Quebec Gaz.* 31 Oct. 2/1: The Master of the 2d arriving British Fishing Ship, in any Harbour as above mentioned, shall (besides being Vice-Admiral of the Harbour) have the exclusive Right to all the Salmon Fishery in that Harbour, during that Season. **1915** WOOD *All Afloat* 161: They came from all seafaring peoples, and had no other form of justice than what could be enforced by 'fishing admirals' who won their rank by the order of their arrival on the Banks—admiral first, vice-admiral second, rear-admiral third.

Victoria Day a national holiday, May 24th, established in 1845 to celebrate Queen Victoria's birthday, now also celebrating the birthday of Queen Elizabeth II and since 1952 observed on the first Monday preceding May 25th. See also **Queen's Birthday.**
1904 *Eye Opener* (Calgary) 30 Apr. 4/2: The Calgary Fire Brigade have prepared a good fat programme of sports for Victoria Day. **1955** *Hamilton Spectator* (Ont.) 25 Jan. 10/8: The Victoria Day celebration in the park, the open air jamboree, had been successful; the supervised playground where 60 pupils had been taught handicrafts and enjoyed the use of new equipment, might be the envy of any city, he said.

vigilance committee† *Hist.* a committee of citizens set up to watch over and protect the interests of a community, faction, etc., often according to their own definition of "interests."
1836 (1866) CHRISTIE *Lower Canada* IV 299: In most of the places of these meetings Vigilance Committees have been formed and the registration commenced, and in some of them, delegates have been named to the proposed general meeting. **1897** *B.C.Mining Jnl* (Ashcroft) 17 July 3/1: Knots of people can be seen at every street corner considering the advisability of holding a mass meeting and forming a vigilance committee for the purpose of dealing in a summary manner with the jumpers. **1921** LAUT *Cariboo Trail* 30: When word came of this murder the vigilance committee of Yale formed a rifle company of forty. . . .

Virginia(n) deer the white-tailed deer, *Odocoileus virginianus.*
1784 PENNANT *Arctic Zoology* cxl: A plain . . . swarming with . . . Stags and *Virginian Deer* . . . occupies an amazing tract, from the great lakes of *Canada*, as low as the gulph of *Mexico*. **1888** (1908) MAIR *Mackenzie Basin* 485: . . . the third shows the southern limit of the feeding-ground of the musk ox and the reindeer, the northern range of the wolverine, otter, beaver, black bear, and Virginia deer . . . . **1958** *Edmonton Jnl* 28 July 4/3: Its spike antlers were in the swollen velvet of summer, arched forward to identify it as a "Virginia" or white-tailed deer.

visiting fisherman *Nfld* a fisherman who comes to the banks of Labrador only with the fishing season. See also **Labradorman** (def. 1). Cp. **liveyere** (def. 1).
1956 FAY *Life and Labour* 230: The Transient or "Visiting" Fishermen . . . are of two types 1. The planters or "stationers," who fish from the shore. 2. The "floaters" or "schoonermen."

vitico *n.* See **Weetigo**.

Voltigeur [voltɪ'ʒœr] *n.* [< Cdn F < F *voltigeur* horseman, sharpshooter < *voltiger* leap]

Hist. **1** in French Canada, a militiaman; a specialist in bush warfare. See also **ranger** (def. 2a).

1812 *Quebec Gaz.* 23 Apr. 3/1: The Voltigeurs. This Corps now forming under the command of Major De Salaberry, is completing with a dispatch worthy of the ancient warlike spirit of the country. **1836** *Vindicator* (Montreal) 8 Jan. 2/3: A handbill has been extensively posted in different parts of this city, calling a meeting of the Canadians this evening at Rasco's, for the purpose of forming a company of Voltigeurs. **1896** GOURLAY *Hist.Ottawa* 116: His three hundred men were the Canadian fencibles and Voltigeurs. **1963** MORTON *Kingdom of Canada* 204: To these were added the ... Voltigeurs of Lower Canada under a Canadian officer of the British Army, Colonel Charles de Salaberry. ...

2 See 1955 quote.

1894 BEGG *Hist.of B.C.* 238: Mr. J. W. McKay, who was at the time in charge of the coal works at Nanaimo, was ordered to take twenty-one voltigeurs, and secrete them near the mouth of the river to watch the Indian village that no one should leave during the night. **1955** MCKELVIE *Pageant of B.C.* 157: Vancouver Island had an active armed militia, which under the name "Victoria Voltigeurs" played an important part in the protection of the Colony from Indian attack. It was organized about 1850. ...

voluntary statement *Que.* See 1965 quote.

1957 *Kingston Whig-Standard* (Ont.) 7 Nov. 31/2: He was freed on $23,000 bail and ordered to appear for voluntary statement Nov. 13. **1965** *Ibid.* 19 Oct. 1/3: In Quebec, no charges are laid in violent deaths until after a coroner's inquest. After charges are laid, a preliminary hearing is held and then comes voluntary statement, a stage in Quebec legal procedure where the defence can present evidence aimed at getting the charges dismissed before trial.

voyage[1] *n. Nfld* the complete catch for a season by any man or company of men, as trappers, fishermen, etc.

1771 (1792) CARTWRIGHT *Journal* I 137: I went to Seal Island, where Hezekiah Guy and company delivered to me two thousand seven hundred and five gallons of seals' oil; thirty-two fox, and four otter skins; one wolf and one deer skin, with two bags of feather; being part of their winter's voyage. **1964** *Nfld Qtly* Spring: [A] prior pre-quintal charge is reserved from the entire voyage's value to pay for this labour called "fish-making". ...

voyage[2] *n.* [influenced by Cdn F use in this sense] *Fur Trade, Hist.* a trip inland with a fur brigade, *q.v.*; a journey as a voyageur (def. 1a).

1789 (1889) MCKENZIE *Reminiscences* 29: I had a very favorable voyage into the country until a short distance from *Ile à la Crosse* when one of the canoes got injured and sunk. **1828** (1872) MCDONALD *Peace River* 9: The other five men of each of the canoes ... with the assistance of the ten Indians in carrying the loading, were able to move everything in one haul (trip, "*voyage*" is the usual term). ...

voyage[2] *v.* [see *n.*] **1** *Fur Trade, Hist.* make a trip inland with a fur brigade, *q.v.*

1820 (1922) HARMON *Journal* 10: Those ... in the habit of voyaging this way, are obliged to say their prayers more frequently perhaps than when at home. ... **1924** *Beaver* Mar. 235: He used to voyage as guide in the York boats to Heron Bay.

2 travel in the wilderness by canoe.

1853 REID *Young Voyagers* 19: The river upon which they are voyaging runs due northward into the great lake Winnipeg.

voyage (or **voyaging**) **allowance** *Fur Trade, Hist.* See **allowance**.

1913 COWIE *Adventurers* 500: 'Luxuries'—in the ante-steam transport days this fur-trade term was applied to the voyaging and wintering allowances given to the officers and missionaries, and consisted of mustard, pepper, pimento, Hyson and Souchong tea, sugar, rice, raisins, currants, vinegar and flour, also of wine and spirits in non-interdicted districts. **1929** MOBERLY *When Fur Was King* 82: This was the winter allowance, but in addition, the officer in charge of the brigade on the annual trip to York Factory, with the clerks who accompanied him, was made a voyage allowance.

voyager *n.* [< Cdn F *voyageur*] **1** *Hist.* See **voyageur** (def. 1a).

1765-75 (1933) POND *Narrative* 29: Scars a Voiger but stops hear and Puts a small Sum in the Box. **1853** (1955) CRAIG *Early Travellers* 188: Canadian voyagers formed another motley group, with their half Indian dresses, bronzed faces, and flaringly-striped cotton shirts. **1965** *Wildlife Rev.* Mar. 5: These [Coureurs de Bois] were a hardy breed of voyagers and woodsmen.

2 See **voyageur** (def. 4b).

1925 GRAHAME *Bompas* 14: But winter was rapidly closing in upon them and threatening the daring voyagers. **1959** LEISING *Arctic Wings* 16: ... Father Le Treste pointed to the small, original mission church that had been built in 1862 by the first Oblate missionary priest in those parts, Father Lacombe, known as the black-robed voyager.

voyage seal *Nfld, Obs.* See **harp**.

1861 DE BOILIEU *Labrador Life* 93: The principal seal of the coast is termed the Voyage seal, while the males are distinctively called Harps, or Blackbacks. When the first of these Voyage seals is caught on the coast a great sensation is the result, for this one, it appears, is the precursor of thousands, and a good "harvest" may be expected.

voyageur [ˌvɔɪəˈʒɝ; F vwajaˈʒœr] *n.* [< Cdn F] ☞ *Although the form* **voyageur** *is almost always preferred to the English* **voyager**, *it is often printed in italics, even when reference is being made to present-day travellers. The word is, however, considered fully a part of Canadian English by most persons who have occasion to use it.*

1 *Fur Trade, Hist.* **a.** one of the canoemen or boatmen, usually a French Canadian, Orkneyman, Indian, or Métis, who crewed the vessels of the inland fur trade. See also **Canadian voyager, Canadian voyageur, engagé, porkeater** (def. 1c), and **voyager** (def. 1).

1793 (1933) MACDONELL *Diary* 95: A full allowance to a voyageur while at this Poste is a Quart of Lyed Indian Corn or maize, and one ounce of Greece. *a*1820 (1838) HEAD *Forest Scenes* 343: The subject treated of the hardihood of the Voyageurs, the troubles and difficulties they encounter. ... **1908** MAIR *Mackenzie Basin* 96: One by one these old voyageurs are passing away, and with them and their immediate successors the tradition perishes. **1935** *Beaver* Dec. 15/1: Indian voyageurs were always used on the Rupert river canoe transport system and, apart from supervision by the factor in charge of the trading post, there were no white supervisors actually on the route, for native supervisors (head guides they were called) were developed from among the outstanding Indians or their chiefs. **1965** *Cdn Geog.Jnl* Dec. 203/2: ... it takes but little imagination to see the colourfully

dressed voyageurs packing their heavy "pieces" . . .
along the rocky river bank.

b. any of those journeying into the wilderness of
the Northwest, both engaged servants and company
officers.

1815 BOUCHETTE *Lower Canada* 92: The male inhabitants
of this and three or four other seigniories in this part of
the district are mostly voyageurs. **1829** MACTAGGART
Three Years I 180: My dear friend Mr. Fleming . . . and
a party of *voyageurs* discovered a notch, which led them
through from the Great Lakes to Black River, which falls
into the Columbia. **1935** MORICE *Red River Insurrection*
344: The Rev. Mr. Young shows us "soldiers, voyageurs
and Indians—who had abstained from all intoxicants so
advantageously to themselves. . . ." **1962** *Sask.News* 2
Oct. 1: [Caption] Immense Squaw Rapids power project
is transforming a voyageur's highway into a fluid
"power line."

c. See **tripman**.

1860 *Nor'Wester* (R.R.S.) 14 May 3/5: The voyageurs
are subjected to slavish hardships, and owing to the
difficulty of procuring men for the tripping to Hudson's
Bay, and the generally disagreeable nature of the whole
business, master-freighters are fast giving it up. **1896**
WHITNEY *On Snow-Shoes* 93: The voyageur considers he
is travelling well if he makes two fires during the day, at
which he drinks tea, and sleeps thirty or thirty-five miles
nearer his destination every night. **1914** STEELE *Forty
Years* 15: More than 700 voyageurs, whites and Indians
had been hired in different parts of Ontario and Quebec,
selected on account of their great skill in handling boats,
canoes. . . . **1958** BERTON *Klondike* 232: But Heming
neglected to consider that the traders traveled light in
canoes and with dog-teams piloted by relays of Indians
and voyageurs. . . .

2 *Hist.* a boatman on the St. Lawrence River and
tributary waters.

1824 *Canadian Mag.* II 306: From their dialect I soon
discovered them to be a mixture of Americans (ycleped
Yankies), Canadians (voyageurs), Dutch and Irish men.
1832 MCGREGOR *British America* II 571: The Canadian
boatman, or voyageur, is naturally polite, and always
cheerful. . . . **1863** WALSHE *Cedar Creek* 374: Sometimes
they had open water in lanes and patches; sometimes a
field of jagged ice, whereupon the merry-hearted
voyageurs jumped out and dragged the canoe across to
water again. . . .

3 *Hist.* a soldier in the Voyageur Corps, *q.v.*

1812 *Kingston Gaz.* (U.C.) 24 Nov. 2/3: On the morning
of the 20th instant, a company of Voyageurs consisting
of 45 men, including officers, were surprised at St.
Regis, and taken prisoners. **1848** (1866) CHRISTIE *Lower
Canada* II 41: The north west company raised a corps of
Voyageurs, which, however, was disbanded in the
ensuing scoring. **1893** *Trans.Hist.& Sci.Soc.Man.* XLIII
13: It is the account of a gentleman in the Canadian
Voyageurs—the corps that had so distinguished itself
in the war against the United States in 1812-15. **1954**
WALLACE *Pedlars* 82: [Aeneas Cameron] was in 1812
appointed paymaster of the Corps of *Voyageurs* raised
by the North West Company for service in the War of
1812.

4 a. a person who travels the northern wilderness as
trapper, canoeman, dog-driver, etc.; an
experienced woodsman.

*a*1820 (1838) HEAD *Forest Scenes* 358: . . . many
persons . . . having an additional object in locating

settlers in distant points along their thread of settlement,
for the protection of the voyageurs and encouragement
of the trade. **1912** WHITE *Wildcatters* 188: It was
Beteric, known as the voyageur. He was hunter, trader,
trapper, and guide all in one. **1913** WILLIAMS *Wilderness
Trail* 237 "Thought I was done for in that storm, boys,"
said the aged *voyageur* wagging his head. **1963** *Beaver*
Summer 16/2: The ten-man party consisted of himself
and King, five Scottish and native-born voyageurs, and
three artillerymen.

b. any traveller of the rivers and trails of the
wilderness, especially by canoe. See also **voyager**
(def. 2).

1853 REID *Young Voyageurs* 23: There they had
commenced their canoe voyage—in other words became
"voyageurs"—for such is the name given to those who
travel by canoes through these wild territories. **1879**
ROBINSON *Great Fur Land* 31: The North canoe [is]
the ideal craft of the summer voyageur. . . . **1909**
CAMERON *New North* 222: The barter consummated,
these Northland voyageurs [Eskimos] had their yearly
dance and sing-song and orgy of delight. **1966** *Globe and
Mail* (Toronto) 9 Aug. 27/7: [Caption] Rough waters
briefly force Ontario voyageurs offstroke in the first
80-mile lap of the Canadian Centennial canoe race
from Fort St. James, B.C., to Victoria.

voyageur air See **Canadian boat-song**.
1828 (1872) MCDONALD *Peace River* 1: . . . the free use
of the paddle and one of its accompanying "voyageur
airs."

Voyageur Corps *Hist.* a regiment of
predominantly French-Canadian boatmen raised
by the North West Company for service in the War
of 1812. See also **voyageur** (def. 3).

1963 MACLEOD & MORTON *Cuthbert Grant* 21:
Commissions such as Archibald Norman Macleod held
in the Voyageur Corps, although it was already
disbanded [1814], were obtained for others.

voyageur route any of the routes followed by the
fur brigades, *q.v.*, of earlier days, especially that
from Montreal to the Grand Portage.

1948 ANGLIN *Canada Unlimited* 16: The first trans-
Canada transport system was launched by these new
traders long before the days of railroad and airline—the
voyageur route to the Northwest. **1963** *Canada Month*
Nov. 23/3: My friend has retraced most of the old
voyageur routes and has paddled Lake Superior in his
canoe. He is a true *coureur de bois*.

voyageur sash See **sash**.

1945 HAIG *Brave Harvest* 170: They were matched with
toques and mittens, and tied in with voyageur sashes
like banners against the snow.

voyageur song See **Canadian boat-song**.

1807 (1809) GRAY *Letters* 155: They strike off, singing
a song peculiar to themselves, called the *Voyageur
Song*: one man takes the lead, and all the others join
in a chorus. **1860** (1934) *Beaver* Dec. 50/2: . . . the fleet
of canoes darted out from an island to meet him . . . to
the inspiring cadences of a voyageur song. **1962** *Cdn
Forum* Dec. 213/2: The forty-two delightful jongleur
and voyageur songs contained in this volume are the
works of a man who has devoted his life to preserving
the folklore of Canada's early French settlers.

voyaging *n.* **1** *Fur Trade, Hist.* travelling on
voyages (see **voyage**[2]); employment as a voyageur
(def. 1).

1793 (1933) MACDONELL *Diary* 117: [He] knows the
Road well having seen twenty years voyaging in the
Hudson's Bay Service. **1855** (1956) ROSS *Fur Hunters*

81: The mode of voyaging at that particular period varies according to the transportation, of the climate, the face of the country, or the peculiar habits of the tribes. **1933** ROLYAT *Wilderness Walls* 40: The code of voyaging had made provision for two full meals only in twenty-four hours.... **1952** (1954) JENNINGS *Strange Brigade* 147: As much as possible the men of our contingent were spread among the crews, both in order to reduce the deadweight load of the passengers and so that they might learn the tricks of voyaging: of wielding a paddle and packing over a carry....

2 *Fur Trade, Hist.* See **tripping** (def. 2).

1841 (1966) *Beaver* Winter 50/2: Voyaging on the boats to York Factory . . . is so laborious that some kill themselves by it, and many are sprung and so disabled that it makes old men of them before they come to the prime of life. *a*1869 (1942) KENNICOTT *Journal* 99. In boat voyaging the signal to the crew to stop rowing or hauling the line for a spell is the steersman's cry of "illiume!" which means in voyaging lingo "light your pipes!" **1921** HEMING *Drama of Forests* 10: Some Indians engage in "voyaging" or "tripping" for the traders—taking out fur packs to the steamboats or railroads, by six-fathom canoe, York boat, or sturgeon-head scow brigades, and bringing in supplies.

1935 *Beaver* Dec. 66/2: When living his natural life of trapping in the winter and voyaging in the summer, as he still does at the isolated northern posts, he is happy and takes a great delight and interest in his work.

3 travelling as a voyageur (def. 4b).

1956 RADDALL *Wings* 7: After some miles of this casual voyaging we heard a rattle in the woods and began to meet patches of foam.

voyaging *adj. Hist.* **1** of, for, or having to do with voyageurs (def. 1).

1820 (1938) SIMPSON *Athabasca Jnl* 37: . . . as ancient voyaging customs must be respected, I have indulged the people with a bottle of rum.... *a*1869 (1942) KENNICOTT *Journal* 99: . . . the steersman's cry of "illiume!" . . . means in voyaging lingo "light your pipes!" [See **voyaging,** *n.* (def. 2) for full quote.] **1935** *Beaver* Dec. 16/1: Rations and equipment are assembled; canoes, paddles and other gear thoroughly overhauled; voyaging rations apportioned and all other necessary preparations made.

2 of or having to do with a voyage (see **voyage²**).

1823 (1955) BLACK *Journal* 1: Had we been provided with Voyaging Animals we could have reached the point of destination.

voyaging allowance See **voyage allowance.**

wabbano ['wɑbən‚o] *n.* [< Algonk.; cf. Ojibwa *wāpano* I am a conjurer,Cree *wapun, wabun* dawn] Various spellings. **1** *Hist.* **a.** among certain Indians, a ritual that involves singing, dancing, and conjuration, usually held in the spring and fall.
1800 (1897) COUES *New Light* I 124: He has given my hunter an elegant drum, trimmed with all the symbols of the wabbano medicine. **1802** (1897) *Ibid.* 199: The Indian tribes, having finished the grand medicine, are making the wabbano. **1905** MOTT *Jules* 143: Outside the noise had increased, and the babel of voices came to them distorted and strange, mingled with curses and the sounds of the Indian wobbano songs. **1931** GREY OWL *Last Frontier* 22: [We have] for neighbours a people who carry drums to celebrate the Wabeno and wear charms to ward off evil spirits....

b. See **boisson.**
1951 O'MEARA *Grande Portage* 112: The great wabbano went merrily on. **1957** FISHER *Pemmican* 50: They would all have a grand wabbano and they would relive in pantomime and song their feats of heroism in battle....

2 See quotes.
*c***1804** GRANT *Sauteux Indians* 363: The Wabanoe is another order of imposters who pretend, by virtue of their medicine bags, to baffle all the secret machinations of their most inveterate enemies, and even to kill them at pleasure without being detected. **1852** RICHARDSON *Arctic Exped.* 267: A society named Wabuno is said to have been formed among the Chippeways, for the practice of certain nocturnal orgies called Wabunsi.... **1935** JENNESS *Parry Island* 32: If a man were very ill, and all remedies had failed to heal him, the wabeno might place him beside the fire before the ceremony....

wabby *n.* See **whabby.**

wabeno *n.* See **wabbano.**

wachee or **watchee** [wɑ'tʃiə] *interj.* [< Cree *wacheyā* < E *what cheer*] *North* a long-established greeting. See also **whacheer.** Various spellings.
1872 BALLANTYNE *Pioneers* 18: ... he wiped his greasy right hand on his legging and extended it, exclaiming, "Watchee!" by which he meant, what cheer? **1922** *Beaver* Sep. 18/1: "Watchea," said a low voice. Jerking off a heavy mitten, the newcomer extended his hand. **1955** SHIPLEY *Anna* 11: All were exchanging the friendly greeting of the North—"Wacheya." **1964** CARROLL *Shy Photographer* 4: "Watchee!" cried Shorty to Mad Pierre, using the Swampy Cree greeting.

Waconda(h) *n.* See **Wakanda.**

wahboos(e) *n.* See **wapoose.**

Wahkonda(h) *n.* See **Wakanda.**

wahpoos *n.* See **wapoose.**

Wahpooskow *n.* [cf. **wapoose**] *North* See quote. See also **rabbit dance** (def. 2).
1908 MAIR *Mackenzie Basin* 139: The dances were the customary reels, and, of course, the Red River Jig. I was sorry, however, to notice a so-called improvement upon this historic dance; that is to say, they doubled the numbers engaged in it, and called it "The Wahpooskow."

wah-wah *n.* See **wawa².**

wainy *adj.* See **waney.**

wait-a-while match *Hist.* See quote.
1965 *Islander* 7 Mar. 2: Perhaps I should stop to explain the "wait-a-while" match. In the early days matches were Chinese; they came in wooden blocks, split part way down, from which the matches were stripped one by one. At the end of each matchstick a dab of red phosphorus ignited the sulphur along a quarter inch of the stick and it was necessary to wait-a-while, after striking, for the sulphur to burn and the matchstick to take fire. They had a lovely smell.

wakan *n.* See **Wakanda.**

Wakanda† [wɑ'kɑndɑ] *n.* [< Siouan; cf. *wakan* spirit] among certain Plains Indians (as the Assiniboines) the Great Spirit, *q.v.* Various spellings.
[**1776** (1901) HENRY (Elder) *Travels* 305: They believe ... in spirits, gods, or *manitos,* who they denominate *wakons.* **1934** *Cdn Geog.Jnl* IX 183/1: The Assiniboines, while ostensibly believing in a Wacondah, or Master of Life, were originally practically sun-worshippers, as were all the Indians of the Plains. **1943** MILLER *Lone Woodsman* 47: "I thank Thee, Wahkondah," he muttered, humbly. **1955** JENNESS *Indians of Can.* 171: The Algonkians called both this higher force and its individual manifestations *manito,* the Iroquoians *orenda,* and some Siouan tribes *wakanda.*

Wakonda *n.* See **Wakanda.**

walking boss a foreman or superintendent of a series of construction camps, logging operations, etc.
1881 *Progress* (Rat Portage [Kenora], Ont.) 20 May 1/5: Mr. D. J. McDonald, the walking boss on this division, is pushing the work ahead rapidly for the number of men he has. **1919** *Camp Worker* 17 May 6/3: When we arrived Kelly's walking boss ... told us Whalen did not have any work there for us. **1947** (1963) SAUNDERS *Algonquin* 33: Paddy Farrell of Pembroke, who for many years was a "walking boss" for camps operated by the Gillies Company, recalls the first time he ever "went to shanty." **1961** *Cdn Geog.Jnl* Jan. 14/1: During summer travel was on foot. The contractors' representatives were one "lone clerk" at each cache and a "walking boss" in charge of say fifty miles of work.

walking portage See quote.
1937 *Beaver* Sep. 10/2: There is a portage here; a walking portage. The passengers get out and walk, the Indians ... run the loaded canoes through the rough water.

walleye (or walleyed) pike† the pickerel, *Stizostedion vitreum,* of the Great Lakes system. See also **doré** and **pike-perch.**
1936 *Beaver* Mar. 42/2: On the Savant and Pashkokogan rivers we had tried our fly rods on wall-eyed pike. **1966** *Canadian* 30 Apr. 13/1: They are not great fighters, but a good-sized walleye can give you a workout.

wallow† *n.* See **buffalo wallow.**
1884 *Brandon Mail* (Man.) 6 Mar. 3/1: The wallows are saucer-like depressions in the ground, made by the buffaloes rubbing themselves.... **1952** HOWARD *Strange Empire* 253: These beasts normally were healthier than domestic cattle, but sometimes huge sores appeared inexplicably on their bodies and they thrashed about madly in their wallows, the shallow circular pits in the prairie in which they rolled to shed their matted winter coats.

wampum† ['wɑmpəm] *n.* [< Algonk.:
Narraganset *wampompeag* strings of white (things)]
Hist. **1** a bead or beads of shell, *Venus mercenaria,*
later also of porcelain, important as a kind of
currency among eastern Indians. See also **porcelain,
shell wampum,** and **wampum bead.**
1789 (1918) DAVIDSON *North West Co.* 267: [They are
paid] In Strouds . . . Wampum, and other trinkets. . . .
1863 HIND *Exploring Labrador* I /5: In 1637 the
Abenakis ascended the St. Lawrence as far as Three
Rivers, to trade porcelain beads (wampum) with the
Algonquins, for beaver skins. **1963** *Commercial Letter*
Jan. 2/1: The first settlers to the North American
Continent found wampum, a form of shell money, in
use among the Indians as an article of adornment and
a means of exchange. It consisted of beads made from
the inner whorls of certain shells. The beads were
polished and strung together in belts and sashes.
Different colours stood for different values. The unit
of the money was the fathom, consisting of 360 white
beads and at one time was worth sixpence, or about
fourteen cents. Wampum was also used as a pledge of
peace and friendship and for other solemn occasions.
Here again the colours were significant, white stood for
health, richness and peace, purple and black stood for
sorrow and sympathy.
2 See **wampum belt.**
1835 (1947) SAUNDERS *Algonquin* 23: Baddeley gave him
a "wampum of acknowledgment which would enable
him to secure a gun or a pair of blankets at Toronto. . . ."
1908 BROWN *Lady of the Snows* 57: "And to see us
exchange wampums and chiefs as hostages, or kiss the
hatchet and bury it as we spoke," added another.

wampum bead† *Hist.* See **wampum** (def. 1).
*c*1804 (1890) GRANT *Sauteux Indians* 316: They put
great value on wampum beads and wear several strings
of them about the neck, or suspended from the hair and
ears. **1955** JENNESS *Indians of Can.* 139: Practically the
only objects open to theft were the strings of wampum
beads that served both as ornaments and currency. . . .

wampum belt† a belt of wampum (def. 1), often
worked in significant designs, used by Indians as a
reminder of a treaty or agreement, etc. See also
wampum (def. 2).
1765-75 (1933) POND *Narrative* 43: As I Aprocht . . . I
Perseaved . . . Sum Pa[i]nted Dogs and also a Grate
Number of Wampam Belts with a Number of Silver
Braslets and Other Articels in the Indan way. **1845**
BEAVAN *Life in Backwoods N.B.* 95: From his wampum
belt he took a roll of the bark of the birch tree. . . . **1934**
GODSELL *Arctic Trader* 171: This was confirmed by the
presentation of a beaded wampum belt upon which the
ideas conveyed in the speech were depicted in minute
figures, a black band across the background representing
the cloud which had temporarily marred the relationship
between the Indians and the Company.

wampum-keeper *n. Hist.* an Indian chief
responsible for the care and interpretation of
wampum belts. See also **wampum reader.**
1883 *Trans.Roy.Soc.Can.* I 4 68: It ranked also among
the ancient traditions of the Wampum keepers. . . .
1956 LEECHMAN *Native Tribes* 79: The affairs of the
League [of the Iroquois] were debated several times a
year in the Council, which consisted of fifty chiefs. . . .
Some of these chiefs . . . held special positions, such as
the speaker, the fire-keeper, the door-keeper, and the
wampum-keeper whose duties were like those of a
recording secretary.

wampum reader *Hist.* See **wampum-keeper.**
1887 *Trans.Roy.Soc.Can.* V 2 3: The two songs that I
send are from Sapial Selmo, the wampum reader of the
Wabanakis.

wampum shell *Obs.* See **wampum** (def. 1).
1800 (1933) MCLEOD *Diary* 146: I gave a roll of Spencer's
Twist Tobacco &. 14 Quarts Powder, 10 Wampum
Shells with Mr. McDonell's cheese to his two men. . . .

wananish *n.* See **ouananiche.**

wandering seal *North* See **harbo(u)r seal.**
1882 GILDER *Schwatka's Search* 169: In some parts of
the Arctic, as at Iwillik (Repulse Bay), there is a species
called "wandering seal," which in the spring are known
to come upon the ice in great numbers, usually through
a large crack, and move quite a distance from the open
water.

wane *n. Lumbering* **1†** See quote. See also **waney,
waney pine,** etc.
1945 CALVIN *Saga* 37: Waney timber is only partly
squared—broad slightly rounded corners called "wanes"
are left, from which the bark is removed.
2 a piece of timber so processed.
1958 GOGO *St.Lawrence* 184: Tree-trunks partly squared
with broad rounded corners left where the bark has
been cut away are called wanes.

wanegan *n.* See **wanigan.**

waney† *adj. Lumbering, Hist.* cut in such a manner
as to leave wanes, *q.v.*
1945 CALVIN *Saga* 37: Oak was sometimes cut "waney";
birch usually. . . . When "waney" was used as an
adjective to describe timber other than pine, the kind of
wood was always named—waney oak, waney ash.
1947 SAUNDERS *Algonquin* 30: At a later date "waney"
timber was made by the same method, only in this
operation the edges of the log were left rounded instead
of squared off. In this way, the good outside boards,
that were previously wasted, were sliced off at the mill
into narrower pieces than the actual square would have
involved. **1963** *Forest Conservation* 6/2: [Caption] A
raft of "waney" timber on the Ottawa River about 1908.

waney boardwood *Lumbering, Hist.* See **waney
pine.**
1945 CALVIN *Saga* 37: [Waney pine] was also called
(especially at Quebec and in Britain) board pine or
waney boardwood.

waney cut *Lumbering, Hist.* a manner of trimming
logs so as to leave a wane, *q.v.*
1945 CALVIN *Saga* 38: The waney cut was used for the
best of the pine; that is, the lower part of a first-class tall
pine would make one good waney stick, its upper part
would make a piece (or two) of square timber. *Ibid.* 51:
Do these things . . . perhaps mean that Canfield, or
Calvin and Breck, had invented the waney cut?

waney pine *Lumbering, Hist.* pine trees cut and
trimmed so as to leave wanes, *q.v.* See also **board
pine, waney,** and **waney boardwood.**
1945 CALVIN *Saga* 50: Waney pine appears first in the
Garden Island records, in a letter from Calvin and
Breck to D. D. Calvin and Company, Quebec, July 6th,
1860. . . .

wangan (boat) ['wɑngən] *n.* [var. of *wanigan,*
q.v.] **1** *Lumbering, Orig.N.B.* a scow or raft
equipped to accommodate loggers while engaged
in a drive (def. 1b). See also **wanigan** (def. 3).

1959 MILLS *Songs of the Maritimes* 3/2: . . . the men slept in tents on the shore, getting their meals from the cook's scow or "wangan" that was moored off-shore. . . . **1959** *Maclean's* 4 July 38/4: . . . behind the drive come the Wangan boats which are house-carrying scows powered by outboards and crewed by about twenty men. **1961** MACLENNAN *Seven Rivers* 163: Within three weeks the Wangan boat men clear the river of stray logs all the way from Beechwood to Maugerville. . . .

2 running the wangan See quote.
1912 (1913) HODGE & WHITE *Indians of Can.* 509: "Running the wangan" is the act of taking a loaded boat down the river, from station to station, particularly in swiftly flowing water.

wanigan ['wɑnəgən] *n.* [< Algonk.; cf. Abnaki *waniigan* trap; container for odds and ends]
1 *Lumbering* **a.** See 1935 quote.
1902 WHITE *Blazed Trail* 323: Outside the cook and cookee were stowing articles in the already loaded wanigan. **1935** WALLACE *Encyclopedia* VI 257/1: Wanigan, a receptacle in which small supplies or a reserve stock of goods are kept.

b. See quote.
1912 (1913) HODGE & WHITE *Indians of Can.* 508/2: wanigan . . . a large chest in which lumbermen of New Brunswick, Maine and Minnesota keep their spare clothing, pipes, tobacco, etc. Called also *wongan-box,* and spelled *wangun* and *wangan.*

c. a store operated by a logging company; commissary. See also **van,** *n.* (def. 1).
1966 *Sask.Hist.* Winter 27: The company ran little stores in the office called wannigans where you could get anything that was required in the line of clothing for bushwork.

2 *Lumbering* See quote.
1912 (1913) HODGE & WHITE *Indians of Can.* 508/2: Wanigan . . . a place in a lumber camp where accounts are kept and men paid.

3 *Lumbering* See **wangan.**
1912 (1913) HODGE & WHITE *Indians of Can.* 508/2: Wanigan . . . a boat used on the rivers of New Brunswick and Maine for the transportation of the entire personnel of a logging camp, along with the tools of the camp and provisions for the trip.
1957 *Bush News* (Port Arthur, Ont.) 1 June 1/1: Three wanegans, a floating mess hall and cook shack, and six drive camps are maintained to keep the wood moving.

4 *North* **a.** See **caboose** (def. 4b).
1955 HARDY *Alta Anthol.* 161: Log houses, built hastily by the early gold-rush pioneers, nestle beside the luxurious main hotel and the "wanigans"—the one-room houses on skids. **1966** *Islander* 20 Feb. 7/3: While sleeping in a wanigan, a hut on sleds, I was awakened . . . by native children shouting. . . .

b. See **caboose** (def. 5a). Also spelled *wanegan, wangan, wannegan, wannigan,* etc.
1949 *Report of DME Test Team* I 1: With the availability of Wannegans for living, the convoy was restricted only by weather and equipment breakdowns from travelling day and night. *Ibid.* II 1: The Wannegan has a sled mounted house type body made of light gauge metal, and heavily insulated for use in sub zero temperatures. **1955** ADTIC *Glossary*: wanigan . . . a small housekeeping shed mounted on runners and hauled behind an oversnow vehicle.

5 a warm, short laced boot.
1966 *Eaton's Fall & Winter Catalogue* (West ed.) 41/5: Natural sheepskin wannigans for wear under overboots. Leather soles, heels. . . .

wanigan-box *n.* See **wanigan** (defs. 1a and 1b).

wannigan *n.* See **wanigan.**

wapati *n.* See **wapiti.**

wapato ['wɑpə,to] *n.* See **wapatoo.**

wapatoo ['wɑpə,tu] *n.* [< Chinook Jargon *wappato*] *West* a tuberous root, *Sagittaria latifolia.* See 1942 quote. See also **Indian potato, Siwash waptoo,** and **wild potato.** Also spelled *wap(p)ato.*
1811 (1832) COX *Adventures* 128: . . . we also got a quantity of excellent roots, called by the natives wappittoo; in size, they resemble a small potato, for which they are a good substitute when roasted or boiled. **1813** (1897) COUES *New Light* II 777: . . . the natives . . . will not hunt them; their sole employment is digging roots, such as commass . . . and waptoe . . . and stealing beaver from traps when opportunity offers. *a*1855 (1956) ROSS *Fur Hunters* 80: . . . his bark platter [was] filled top heavy with the most delicious melange of bear's grease, dog's flesh, wappatoes, olellies, amutes, and a profusion of other viands, roots and berries. **1942** *Sun* (Vancouver) Aug. 3/2: In the shallow water of ponds and marshes can frequently be found a plant called "arrowhead"; the tuberous roots of the arrowhead were much used as food by the Indians in the west, who called the plant "wapatoo." The roots (bulbs) were boiled like potatoes or sometimes roasted in hot ashes.

wapiti ['wɑpə,ti] *n.* [< Algonk.: Cree; cf. *wapitā* it is white, (the animal name having reference to the white, i.e., light-colored, rump)] the North American elk or stag, *Cervus canadensis.* See also **biche, Canadian stag, elk** (def. 2), **gray moose** (def. 2), **prairie elk, red deer** (def. 2), **waskesew,** and **wewaskish.**
1824 *Wkly Register* (York [Toronto] 26 Feb. 61/1: These animals, whose aboriginal name is that of Wapeti, are known to the settlers in North America by the name of elk. **1872** DASHWOOD *Chiploquorgan* 136: The wapiti, the king of the red deer tribe, inhabits the regions bordering on the Rocky Mountains; it is also found in British Columbia and on Vancouver's Island. **1958** CAMERON *Cdn Mammals* 5: The North American elk or wapiti is one of the most sociable of our antlered mammals. . . .

wapiti deer See **wapiti.**
1823 FRANKLIN *Journey* 666: All the other names given to the Wapiti deer have led to much confusion respecting them. **1902** ROBERTS *Kindred of Wild* 101: The wapiti deer had migrated to safer ranges. . . .

wapoose [wɑ'pus] *n.* [< Algonk.: Cree *wāpūs* rabbit] *North* a hare or rabbit, especially the varying hare, *q.v.*
[**1743** (1949) ISHAM *Observations* 20: A hair or Rabbit Wap puss. **1791** LONG *Voyages* 203: *English* Hare *Algonkin* Wapoos *Chippeway* Wapoos.] *c*1902 LAUT *Trapper* 240: There are . . . wahboos, whose snowy coat is put to the indignity of imitating ermine with a dotting of black cat for the ermine's jet tip. **1931** GREY OWL *Last Frontier* 42: The leaping progression of Wapoose the white rabbit . . . shows everywhere. **1963** *Camsell Arrow* Autumn 85: The moose, the deer, the lordly elk, / "Wappus" the rabbit fleet . . . / To us was [sic] all good meat.

war belt *Hist.* among Indians, a wampum belt, *q.v.* symbolizing a declaration of war. Cp. **peace belt**.

1793 (1937) CAMPBELL *Travels* 192: Two Ibawa Indians came down express from Detroit to Niagara, carrying with them a war belt, and . . . it was the intention . . . to wage war against the British. . . . **1926** MAIR *Masterworks* XIV 207: The colour of the war-belt was purple or red. . . . **1965** *Can.Hist.Rev.* June 109n: In December [1775] the Iroquois delegation told Philip Schuyler that Johnson after offering them a war belt and hatchet had invited them to "feast on a Bostonian and drink his blood—an ox being roasted for this purpose and a pipe of wine given to drink."

warbird *n.* the scarlet tanager, *Piranga olivacea*.

1816-37 (1956) MCATEE *Folk-Names* 61: This bird is very generally known in Canada by the name of War-bird, as much I suppose from its colour as from its having been seen in unusual numbers immediately preceding the late war with the United States. **1836** TRAILL *Backwoods* 214 [DA]: . . . the American war-bird [is] a very beautiful creature . . . in plumage. **1866** KING *Sportsman in Can.* 111: In succession arrive the scarlet war-bird, its gorgeous hues glancing among the green leaves of the forest. . . . **1956** MCATEE *Folk-Names* 61: Scarlet Tanager [is also called] war bird. . . .

war bonnet or **cap** a headdress used by Indians at war.

1808 (1897) COUES *New Light* I 435: Upward of 100 willows, about six feet long, with a fork about the middle, were stripped of their bark, and stuck in the ground. This, I am told, is for the purpose of hanging up their war-caps before attacking an enemy. **1923** *Beaver* Dec. 107: They rode in irregular formation, with their eagle-feather war bonnets blowing in the breeze. . . . **1957** *Camsell Arrow* Christmas 85: For himself he fashioned a war bonnet, and named it the "Red Pheasant."

war canoe 1 *Hist.* a large Indian canoe, often associated by white men with war.

1824 (1931) SIMPSON *Fur Trade* 98: They appoint a time for Meeting and the Belligerents go to the scene of action in their War Canoes, the neighbouring tribes or Nations observing a strict neutrality. **1852** (1881) TRAILL *Cdn Crusoes* 367: The Indians say, that before their fathers had tools of iron and steel in common use, a war canoe was the labour of three generations. It was hollowed out by means of fire, cautiously applied, or by stone hatchets; but so slowly did the work proceed that years were passed in its excavation. **1955** MCKELVIE *Pageant of B.C.* 156: . . . a flotilla of war-canoes, carrying several hundred armed and painted natives, swept around a river bend. **1965** STEVENS *Incompleat Canadian* 14: The huge Nootka war canoes, with prows more resplendent than any clipper ship figurehead . . . bespoke . . . exact craftmanship. . . .

2 a large canoe used in races.

1955 DAWSON *Ahoy There!* 126: An Indian youth answered our questions: "No, she's not a war canoe. She's a racer. We're taking her to Victoria to race there. . . ." **1959** *Sun* (Vancouver) 25 May 21/3: The Indian war canoes did most of their fighting against a treacherous rain squall and choppy water Sunday. **1967** *Globe and Mail* (Toronto) 4 May 4: [Caption] Sailors from HMCS Saskatchewan switch from warship to war canoe during practice in Victoria harbor yesterday to race against Indian team later this month.

war cap See **war bonnet**.

war captain† *Hist.* See **war chief**. See also **captain** (def. 3).

1882 LEMOINE *Quebec* 460: Each family has its chief, or war captain; he is selected by choice. **1955** JENNESS *Indians of Can.* 278: The chief of a band was generally . . . its war captain.

war chief *Hist.* See 1856 quote. See also **war captain** and **warrior chief**.

1760 JEFFERYS *Descr.New France* I 55: The war-chief is no more than a spectator in it, with his pipe in his mouth. . . . **1823** *U.C.Gaz.* (York [Toronto]) 20 Feb. 46/1: Arrived at this place on Thursday last, Sakianahawie, the great war chief of Delaware village. **1856** (1923) BROADUS *Cdn Prose and Verse* 212: Besides being captain in common with the others, he was styled the great war chief or head of the camp; and on all public occasions he occupied the place of president. **1960** BARBEAU *Indian Days* 67: Bear's-Paw, war chief. Bear's Paw's mother went hunting porcupine, carrying her axe on her back.

war club *Hist.* See **casse-tête** and picture.

1808 (1889) FRASER *Journal* 200: The Natives seeing our difficulties assumed courage and began to make their appearance from every direction, dressed in their coats of mail and looking like so many wolves, and brandishing their war clubs. **1921** HAWORTH *Trailmakers* 95: The poor mother actually did recover the child and was running off with both children, when she was felled to the ground by a blow on the head with a war club.

Ward *n.* *Local* under the old ward system in Toronto, an area in the west-central part of the city, formerly populated by low-income immigrants from Europe.

1964 *Maclean's* 21 Mar. 17: The mayor is an astute Jewish lawyer from Augusta Avenue in what used to be called snootily "the ward". . . . **1967** *Globe and Mail* (Toronto) 8 Mar. B12: [Caption] Outdoor used clothing market was a well-attended event in Toronto's "The Ward" around 1900.

war dance *Hist.* a dance performed before a raid or battle; also, a dance simulating a battle.

*c*1751 (1852) COATS *Geography of H.B.* 56: Accordingly, the poor Esqowenow declares the war-dance in the year 1748, and away they go with great alacrity, and succeeded, and brought seven alive and thirteen scalps in great tryumph. **1869** *Cdn Illust.News* 30 Oct. 6/3: A feature in the amusements of the day was the "war dance" of the Indians in full costume. **1935** JENNESS *Parry Island* 100: War Dance: a number of men decked themselves in fighting array and with their bows and arrows, clubs and knives staged a mimic battle. **1966** *Cdn Geog.Jnl* Sep. 90/1: "White men call this our War Dance. It is not a War Dance. It is not intended to rouse hate against anybody. It is for the warriors of our past. It is a farewell to warriors before battle, and a welcome for warriors after battle."

warden *n.* **1 a.** See **warden of the forests**.

1827 *Gore Gaz.* (Ancaster, U.C.) 13 Apr. 27/1: Persons wishing to contract for Clearing and Forming a Road . . . through . . . the Canada Company's . . . Guelph Block, may inspect the plan . . . at the Warden's Office in Galt. **1841** *Montreal Transcript* 24 Dec. 2/1: Must the taxes be demanded by suit at law? or is the failure to pay, a forfeiture such as to warrant the Treasurer, or Warden, or A. B. or C. to declare the land lapsed?

b. See **warden of the plains.**

2 See **county warden.** Cp. **town warden.**

1841 *Bytown* [Ottawa] *Gaz.* 11 Nov. 1/2: And be it enacted, that there shall be a district council in each such district as aforesaid, which district council shall consist of a warden and councillors, to be appointed and elected as hereinunder provided. **1861** *Nor'Wester* (R.R.S.) 31 Aug. 1/1: The head of every county and provisional corporation is designated the warden . . . so the head of every township and village, the reeve. **1945** (1950) BROWN *Cdn Democracy* 90: The elections for all councils are held annually, and each county council appoints after the election one of its number as a presiding officer, who is called the warden. **1966** *Globe and Mail* (Toronto) 12 Jan. 25/7: His uncle . . . was a former warden of the county and in 1887 a great-uncle . . . was also a warden.

3 a.† a government officer responsible for seeing that game laws are observed; a game warden.

1938 CASH *I Like B.C.* 130: The warden heard him give an unearthly scream, but he never saw him again though he searched for hours. **1955** GOWLAND *Smoke* 149: As proof of his fitness to continue as warden he challenged the superintendent to a thirty-mile hike on snowshoes with an eighty-pound pack, guaranteeing to beat him by five miles.

b. *Maritimes* someone employed to keep poachers from fishing in leased waters.

1954 *Fundy Fisherman* (Black's Harbour, N.B.) 3 Mar. 1/1: The lease will be sold subject to the stipulation that the lessees are required to supply sufficient wardens to protect their waters.

4 at certain Canadian universities, a faculty member in charge of a students' residence, students' union, etc.

1958 *Kingston Whig-Standard* (Ont.) 16 Sep. 11/2: Some of the students residing in the new men's residence at Queen's are shown chatting with the warden. . . .

warden of the forests *Obs.* in colonial times, an official of a land company who was responsible for disposing of Crown Lands for settlement. See also **warden** (def. 1a).

1828 *Gore Gaz.* (Ancaster, U.C.) 9 Feb. 199/2: Dr. Dunlop—Warden of the Forests of the Canada Company—arrived in Bytown on the 18th and is busy disposing of the Crown Reserves in that vicinity. . . .

warden of the plains *Hist.* in the Red River Settlement, an official having charge of the keeping of law and order on the plains, as during the buffalo hunts.

1828 (1963) MacLEOD & MORTON *Cuthbert Grant* 101: The Council resolved [in July 1828] "That Mr. Cuthbert Grant be appointed Warden of the Plains of Red River at a salary of £200 p. Annum and that the Duties of his Office be the prevention of illicit Trade in Furs within that District under the direction of Chief Factor McKenzie." **1861** *Nor'Wester* (R.R.S.) 15 July 3/1: It was judged necessary that Mr. Grant, the under sheriff and warden of the plains should accompany them to prevent any further outbreak. **1966** *Canadian* 29 Jan. 13/2: As Warden of the Plains, Councillor of Assiniboia, Sheriff and Magistrate, doctor, fighter, teacher, judge and drinker, Grant brought peace to Western Canada.

wardenship *n.* the office and obligations of a warden (def. 2).

1882 *Brandon Dly Mail* (Man.) 23 Dec. 4/2: The candidates for the Wardenship so far as they have been named are the Rev. Geo. Roddick, the present Warden, Mr. W. F. Clegg and Councillor W. Scott. His chances for the Wardenship are considered good. **1908** CLARKE *Sixty Years* 233: He had filled [local] offices from the wardenship down during his residence in Campbell-ford, and was highly popular.

war dress *Hist.* clothing worn by Indians when at war.

1809 MACKENZIE *Missisouri Indians* 380: The chief was mounted on a milk-white horse and dressed in his war dress and haranguing the Shawyens as he was coming along. **1922** *Beaver* Feb. 35/1: . . . the Blackfoot appeared before him in full war dress. . . .

war eagle† the golden eagle, *Aquila chrysaetos,* so called because its feathers were highly valued for war bonnets, *q.v.*

1859 KANE *Wanderings* 267: The kee-yeu, or war eagle, on the east side of The Rocky Mountains [is] supposed to be the maker of thunder. **1934** *Cdn Geog.Jnl* IX 188: The long-tailed ornate war-bonnets are characteristic of the Plains Indians living in the vicinity of the mountains where war eagles have their nests.

war hoop See **war-whoop.**

war lodge *Hist.* among certain Indian tribes: **1** a teepee or lodge erected as the headquarters of the war chief, *q.v.,* during a state of war. See also **soldiers' tent** and **warriors' lodge** (def. 1).

1893 CREIGHTON *North-West Mounted* 403/2: Surrounding the war lodge erected in the centre of the camp, he arrested and took away the head chief, Crow's Dance. . . . **1927** LONGSTRETH *Silent Force* 80: Moving up a ravine until near the camp, they struck in toward the war-lodge at a sharp trot.

2 a war chief, *q.v.,* and his warriors, who held authority in a tribe during war. See also **soldiers' lodge** and **warriors' lodge** (def. 2).

1910 HAYDON *Riders of Plains* 81: The Salteaux had been camping with the Assiniboines and were desirous of moving away, but to this Crow's Dance would not agree, as he had formed a "war lodge" and given orders that no one should leave the camp without the permission of his warriors.

war party† *Hist.* a number of Indians on the warpath (def. 2a).

1794 (1929) McGILLIVRAY *Journal* 39: He reports that a War party has been formed among the Crees. **1963** LINDSAY *B.C.Outlaws* 23: The successes of Tellot's and Klattasine's war party stirred the blood of the powerful Chilcotin tribes. . . .

warpath† *n. Hist.* **1** See **war-road.**

1858 (1860) HIND *Assiniboine Exped.* II 28: The following are celebrated "war-paths," where hunting is generally disallowed. . . .

2 on the warpath, a. of Indians, on an expedition of war.

1861 *Nor'Wester* (R.R.S.) 1 Aug. 2/3: A number of the Sioux have started on the war-path, to avenge the recent slaughter of their brethren at St. Joseph. **1953** LEBOURDAIS *Nation of North* 78: In all, about 1,000 Indians and Métis were on the warpath, although many additional thousands might have been drawn into the quarrel, which is what terrified people in isolated prairie homesteads.

b. *Figurative uses.*

1954 PATTERSON *Dangerous River* 106: The famous mosquitoes of South Nahanni were starting to get on the warpath so I went out to fix my bed and stake out my mosquito net. **1955** HOBSON *Nothing Too Good* 45: I knew that Letcher and Joe were more or less on a periodic grievance match against each other, but it had never occurred to me that the boys would pick this time to go on the warpath.

3 take the warpath, *Figurative use.*

1923 MACMECHAN *Sagas of Sea* 77: Evidently she [a ship] lost no time in taking the war-path.

warping *n.* See **tracking** (def. 1).

1836 (1926) LANGTON *Early U.C.* 174: Formerly we used to unload at McConnell's drag the scow up the shoot, load again, and by dint of poling, warping, wading and lifting her over occasional obstacles with handspikes we got her up somehow. **1913** COWIE *Adventurers* 126: The "Tracking Grounds" now being passed, we entered into the fight with the rushing river by poling, warping and portaging.

war pipe *Hist.* among Indians, a pipe symbolic of war. Cp. **calumet of peace.**

1768-82 (1791) LONG *Voyages* 76: Previous to their going to war, the head chief calls a council, and each chief has a belt of wampum, and a war pipe: the belt to remind them of former transactions relative to the nation they intend to commence hostilities against, and the pipe to smoke at the council fire. **1949** MACGREGOR *Blankets and Beads* 41: The war pipe had been circulated, and one or two minor attacks made on the traders.

warrior chief *Hist.* See **war chief.**

1955 JENNESS *Indians of Can.* 137: It was these warrior chiefs indeed, not the sachems, who won most fame and honour during the Revolutionary war.

warriors' lodge *Hist.* **1** See **war lodge** (def. 1).

1913 COWIE *Adventurers* 308: In this camp of the allies each tribe had set up a Warrior's Lodge of its own.

2 See **war lodge** (def. 2).

1913 COWIE *Adventurers* 306: . . . the Warriors' Lodge had to be supported by contributions, voluntary and otherwise, from the camp at large.

war-road *n. Hist.* a route followed by Indian war parties. See also **warpath** (def. 1) and **war-track.**

1800 (1897) COUES *New Light* I 78: It is the common war road of the Sioux at this season. **1826** (1931) MERK *Fur Trade* 285: A party less than Fifty could not trap with safety, it being in the vicinity of the great War road in fact of all the War tribes. **1858** (1860) HIND *Assiniboine Exped.* II 29: The "War-road" near the Elbow of the South Branch of the Saskatchewan, on the flanks of the Grand Coteau, [is that] of the Blackfeet and Plains Cree.

war song *Hist.* a song sung by Indians prior to or during battle.

1768-82 (1791) LONG *Voyages* 46: When the repast is over, the war song is sung. . . . **1885** *Battleford Hist. Soc.Pubs* I-III 53: They came up the road singing war songs, riding around in circles and lying on the sides of their horses, shooting under the horses' necks. **1952** HOWARD *Strange Empire* 546: The Crees, however, say that while the other seven shrieked war songs as the hoods were lowered over their heads, Wandering Spirit hummed a love song to his wife.

war-track or **war-trail** *n. Hist.* See **war-road.**

1825 (1950) OGDEN *Journals* 23: . . . the War tribes appear determined that we Shall not want for their Company this year [;] it cannot be otherwise as we are

following the main War track. . . . **1873** (1904) BUTLER *Wild North Land* 64: They were somewhat startled too, for the Blackfeet bands were said to be on the war-trail. **1913** KELLY *Range Men* 94: [The] young Indian bucks in the war-trail season [are] often inclined to bully. . . .

war-whoop† *n.* **1** a blood-curdling yell uttered by Indians engaged in or about to engage in battle.

1768-82 (1791) LONG *Voyages* 21: The Savages immediately rushed from their ambush, and setting up the war-hoop, fell upon the enemy, scalped seven of them, and took five prisoners, whom we painted like ourselves. **1805** *Quebec Gaz.* 26 Dec. The war-whoop's echo and the slave's sad throes / are hush'd in music, pleasure, and repose. **1929** JEFFERSON *Saskatchewan* 110: . . . the war-whoop . . . is produced by yelling in falsetto, and at the same time rapidly slapping the open mouth with the palm of the hand.

2 *Figurative use.*

1958 *Camsell Arrow* Jan.-Feb. 31: The occasional war whoop entered the fray, but this came . . . from assorted visiting warlike tribesmen from Scotland, Newfoundland and the Prairie Provinces.

wascaysou *n. Obs.* See **waskesew.**

wash [wɑʃ] *n.* [< Algonk.; cf. Cree *wate* lair; see note below]

☛ *The above etymology is based on the fact that* **wash** *in this sense occurs only in trapping contexts in North America. Furthermore, the following quotes suggest fairly wide use of Cree and Ojibwa forms of a parent Algonkian word with the basic meaning of "lair."*

[**1772** (1908) COCKING *Jnl* 105: Leaving the river on one hand, came to some high land named Mikisew Wache, or Eagle hills, where we pitched. **1773** *Ibid.* 115: . . . all the Natives were pitched further on, toward Waskesew-Wachee. . . .] **1860** (1956) KOHL *Kitchi-Gami* 104n: Wisch is the pure Ojibbeway orthography and pronunciation of the word. The French voyageurs have accepted it in their language, and turned it into "wasch" or "waschi." **1921** HEMING *Drama of Forests* 113: The hunter must make the best of his two short opportunities; that is, unless he already knows where the bear will "den up," and is counting on killing him in his o-wazhe—or as the white hunters and traders call it "wash"—his den.

1 a. an underwater exit from a beaver lodge.

1763 (1901) HENRY (Elder) *Travels* 124: It [a beaver lodge] is always entirely surrounded by water; but, in the banks adjacent, the animal provides holes or washes, of which the entrance is below the surface, and to which it retreats on the first alarm. *c*1804 GRANT *Sauteux Indians* 343: But should the beavers get into any of those numerous holes or washes which they dig around their habitations, they can often baffle the united efforts, both of dogs and hunters. **1907** HUNTER *Cdn Wilds* 88: This was done to scare the beaver out into the lake and make them resort to their washes [which] . . . have their entrances under water.

b. the beaver lodge itself, including the escape routes.

1810 (1890) KEITH *Letters* 91: When two or more Indian work a beaver lodge, the one who draws the beaver out of his lodge or wash gives it to some other one present. [**1860** (1956) KOHL *Kitchi-Gami* 104: Here he saw a "wisch," or beaver house.] **1908** MAIR *Mackenzie Basin* 253: It is not an uncommon experience for hunters to find one or more beavers dead of disease in their houses or "washes."

2 See **muskrat house.**
1908 MAIR *Mackenzie Basin* 245: . . . many thousands of the animals [muskrats] perished miserably under the ice and in their frozen up "washes". . . .

3 a bear's den.
1921 HEMING *Drama of Forests* 113: [A bear's] wash may consist of a hollow tree or a hollow log, a cave, or any suitable shelter formed by an uprooted tree.
1947 ROWLANDS *Cache Lake* 99: Once it came back with a full-grown wolf and another time it dug a bear out of his wash and drove him right to the cabin.

wash *v. Placer Mining* **1†** separate gold from gravel by using water. See also **wash out.** Cp. **wash up.**
1862 (1958) LINDSAY *Cariboo Story* 39/1: I got some drifters and started to wash. The black sand was hard to get out of the gold. **1913** FOOTNER *Jack Chanty* 144: For it was on that very little stream he had washed his gold, and there his claims were situated. **1963** *Placer Mining B.C.* 24: Panning is a simple method of recovering placer gold, but it becomes laborious if any yardage is washed.

2 mine by the placer method.
1900 LONDON *Son of Wolf* 22: All summer he fought mosquitoes and washed the sure-thing bars of the Stuart River for a double grub-stake. **1959** *Native Voice* July 6/3: Henry said it was up to him to make a good showing and find the best places for the kids to "wash". . . .

washing *n.* the proceeds from placer mining.
1862 *Nor'Wester* (R.R.S.) 24 Sep. 3/3: A small section of the party remained where they were, being satisfied from sundry washings, that there is gold in the Saskatchewan River, but the river being very high they could not "prospect" to advantage.

wash out *Placer Mining* See **wash,** *v.* (def. 1).
1898 (1952) *B.C.Hist.Qtly* XVI 95: On Eldorado Creek I have seen from No. 36 over 100 lbs., (no mistake, *not* oz) of gold, washed out in 24 hours. Of course this does not go on the year thro', it takes months of very expensive labour to get ready for the "Wash-up." **1964** *Edmonton Jnl* 11 July 3/6: He washed out $165,000 in three months at the No. 16 Gold Stream mine.

wash-up *n. Placer Mining* **1** the process by which gold is recovered by cleaning the riffles, sluice-boxes, etc. after gravel is washed, *q.v.* See also **wash up.**
1897 *B.C.Mining Jnl* (Ashcroft) 22 May 1/3: No good mine ever opened not barring the famous Bloomfield, with its record of $115,000 in a single washup is the equal of this property. **1900** LONDON *Son of Wolf* 165: So, after the wash-up he weighed in a couple of hundred pounds of dust. . . .

2 the quantity of gold obtained by this process.
1869 *Mainland Guardian* (New Westminster, B.C.) 16 Oct. 3/1: On Rock creek the Flume Co. had reached flood ground again, and expected a large wash-up.

wash up *Placer Mining* clean out the riffles, sluice-boxes, blankets, etc. in which gold has been caught in the process of washing the gravel. See also **wash-up.** Cp. **wash,** *v.*
1868 (1962) ANDERSON *Sawney's Letters* 34: "Now say, what have you 'wash'd up'?" "Small wages. . . ." **1896**

MCNAUGHTON *Overland to Cariboo* 154: In 1875 the Van Winkle Company, on Lightning Creek, washed up fifteen hundred ounces of gold, as the result of six days' work.

waskesew ['wɑskə,su] *n.* [< Algonk.: Cree *wawaskāsiw*] Various spellings.

1 See **wapiti.**
1754 (1907) HENDAY *Journal* 328: The young men hunting, killed several Moose and Waskesew. **1772** (1908) COCKING *Journal* 101: Red Deer plenty hereabouts named Waskesew. **1857** (1863) PALLISER *Journals* 54: [We] killed a fine wapite stag. . . the wawaseshu of the Crees. . . . **1913** COWIE *Adventurers* 304: The beautifully antlered and magnificent was-cay-sou [is] known variously by the English as red deer and elk. **1920** *Beaver* Dec. 40/1: Red deer—called by the Assiniboines "waskesaw" were in myriads. **1954** MacGREGOR *Shining Mountains* 60: "Wawaskesiw" of the Crees was what we call elk or wapiti.

2 the hide of the wapiti, *q.v.*
1716 (1965) *Letters from H.B.* 65: There is three Wascashus sent home that's writ upon that I would desire you to give to three several leather dressers to dress. . . .

wasscashu *n.* See **waskesew.**

watap [wɑ'tɑp] *n.* [< Algonk., perhaps through Cdn F; cf. Ojibwa *watappi,* Cree *wutupe*] the fine roots of various evergreen trees, especially of the white spruce, used by the Indians as a thread or string in sewing. Also spelled *watape, wattap.*
1761 (1901) HENRY (Elder) *Travels* 14: The small roots of the spruce-tree afford the wattap, with which the bark is sewed [for a canoe]. **1798** (1918) DAVIDSON *North West Co.* 217: Each canoe had . . . a few Hambro lines [and] a bundle of watap. . . . **1808** (1889) FRASER *Journal* 194: Their hats, which are made of wattap, have broad rims and diminish gradually to the top, some make use of cedar bark painted different colours, resembling ribbon for hats. **1821** (1900) GARRY *Diary* 93: Around this the Bark is sewed by the slender and flexible Roots of the young Spruce Tree called Wattape and also where the pieces of Bark join so that the Gunwales resemble the Rim of an Indian Basket. **1961** *Beaver* Autumn 31: [Caption] Makakons, chief of the Barrières . . . is making watap from the roots of the white spruce, to be used in sewing a canoe.

watap kettle *Obs.* a watertight vessel woven of or sewn with watap, *q.v.,* used by Indians for cooking.
1793 (1801) MACKENZIE *Voyages* 313: When she had finished her operation, she filled a watape kettle nearly full of water, and poured the roes into it. **1812** (1890) KEITH *Letters* 115: They live principally upon fish, and are not over delicate in their manner of preparing and dressing it, particularly with their wattap kettles, and very few of the Natives can afford copper or brass kettles of any size suitable for a family. **1824** (1955) BLACK *Journal* 161: From the Pot Hook they seem to have Kettles or a Kettle also Watap Kettles Wooden & Bark dishes.

watchee, watcheer *interj.* See **wachee** and **whacheer.**

watching waiter *Obs.* See **deadman** (def. 1).
1896 MCDOUGALL *Saddle, Sled, and Snowshoe* 274: From the ends of the fence bundles of willows were placed on end at regular intervals for a mile or more, their outside terminals being fully a mile apart. These were called "watching waiters."

water-bomber *n.* See **fire bomber**.
1961 *Canada Month* 6 Oct. 42/3: The Grove and Tsus fires, they claim, could have been kept small if water bombers and helicopters had been available from the beginning.... **1965** *Victoria Dly Times* 12 Aug. 21/2: They included two [forest fires] caused by lightning ... one of which was knocked out by a Mars waterbomber....

water-bombing *n.* fighting forest fires by means of fire bombers, *q.v.*
1959 *Time* (Cdn ed.) 17 Aug. 13/3: Ontario has a new gadget that makes water-bombing more efficient than ever: snorkel-like water intakes on tanks attached to the aircraft floats that enable the planes to load up as they taxi along lake surfaces.... **1965** SYMINGTON *Tuktu* 78: Airborne crews in planes equipped for water bombing seems to be the only method that can work.

A water drum

water-drum *n.* See 1956 quote.
1923 BARBEAU *Indian Days* 120: When the storm was about to break out, at midnight, a deep sound from the seer's lodge startled the people, a sound like that of a large water drum. **1935** JENNESS *Parry Island* 72: ... the leaders, marching near the lodge, beat the water-drum and chanted a song. **1956** LEECHMAN *Native Tribes* 45: There was also a water drum made like a small barrel with a skin head at one end. The barrel was partly filled with water which gave the drum a queer echoing note that carried a long way.

water-hole *n.* **1** a hole cut in ice, especially one cut in a river or lake as a source of fresh water.
1749 DRAGE *Voyage* II 14: This thickness of Ice, was caused by the over-flowing of the Tides, which came up through the Cracks of the Ice, or by the Water Holes which were cut in the Ice, for freshening the Meat. **1852** RICHARDSON *Arctic Exped.* 289: In the winter, Albert built a snow wall very neatly round the water-hole by which the fort was supplied, to keep off the snow-drifts, cut steps through the ice down to the water, and then fitted to the aperture a light snow-lid, that could be easily removed. **1883** *Prince Albert Times* (Sask.) 14 Feb. 5/1: On Saturday evening an ox got into a water hole that had been cut to an enormous and dangerous size, with an utter disregard to life and property. **1955** HOBSON *Nothing Too Good* 101: One morning we opened the water holes and fed the cattle early, then struck south through the bush.
2 See **air-hole** (def. 2).
1897 TYRRELL *Sub-Arctics* 158: The new ice being thin, the walruses break up through it at any place, and sport about in the water-holes which they make. **1921** HEMING *Drama of Forests* 260: In order to keep the water-hole from freezing, [muskrats] build a little house of reeds and mud over it.

water-horse *n.* [origin unknown] *Nfld* **1** newly washed fish.
1777 (1792) CARTWRIGHT *Journal* II 242: Fourteen quintals of fish were washed, the water horse was carried off, and the green fish were spread. **1819** ANSPACH *Hist. Nfld.* 446: ... bulk of fish left to drain after being washed and previous to its being spread for drying, is called the water-horse, a name which sets at defiance all

penetration and learning of the deepest etymologist.
1861 DE BOILIEU *Labrador Life* 36: ... the water-horse is carried on hand-barrows, and placed, back downwards, on "flakes".... **1944** *Beaver* Sep. 23/1: When a fine day does appear, it is not always suitable for drying "water horse"....
2 *Nfld* a pile of newly washed fish. Cp. **bulk**.
1818 CHAPPELL *Voy.of Rosamond* 128: The fish are then ... piled up to drain; and the heap ... is styled "a water-horse". **1832** MCGREGOR *British America* I 230: The fish is then ... piled in a long heap, called by the unintelligible name of "water-horse," for the purpose of draining. **1840** MURRAY *Brit.Amer.* II 126: Further to complete the draining, they are piled in long heaps, bearing the odd name of water-horses. **1861** DE BOILIEU *Labrador Life* 36: This pile is called a water-horse.

water-line *n.* *Obs.* a waterway as a route followed by travellers in boats, canoes, etc.
1830 MOORSOM *Letters N.S.* 294: The greater part of this water-line is a chain of lakes, one of which, under the name of Lake Rossignol, they describe as extending for thirty miles in a direction at right angles to the course of their route.

Waterloo copper or **harp** *Hist.* See quotes. Cp. **Wellington copper**.
1819 *Kingston Chron.* (U.C.) 29 Jan. 1/2: We, the subscribers, will receive, as small change, the various species of Coppers, which have heretofore been current here, except those denominated Brock Coppers, and Waterloo coppers. **1820** *Ibid.* 8 Sep. 1/3: Such immense quantities of ... spurious Coppers have been imported ... that it has become absolutely necessary to [prohibit] the circulation of the Waterloo Harp, the Half penny tokens, having Britania on the one side and a ship on the other, and Montreal ship coppers.

water lot a piece of land fronting on a lake, river, etc.
1791 (1905) *Ont.Bur.Arch.Rep.* III 64: With respect to the granting of these concessions to the proprietors of the water Lots without discrimination some strange language it is said has been held out. **1859** *Brit. Colonist* (Victoria) 20 May 1/2: Proclamations are issued about towns, town lots and water lots, rules and regulations, as though it was the all important subject. **1965** MACNUTT *Atlantic Provinces* 193: Contrary to custom, he [Baillie] demanded payment for the use of "water lots" on the rivers and harbours where merchants constructed wharves and booms.

water oats *Obs.* See **wild rice**.
1853 REID *Young Voyageurs* 18: It is the wild rice, "the water oats" (*Zizania aquatica*), the food of millions of winged creatures, and thousands of human beings as well.

water privilege† *Hist.* **1** a site on a river, creek, etc. suitable for building a mill run by water power. Cp. **mill site**.
1833 (1917) *London Hist.Soc.Trans.* VIII 26: All the villages in Canada are situate on creeks, and the finding of a water privilege is the first requisite in the formation of a village. **1852** (1923) MOODIE *Roughing It* 103: There is a fine water privilege not a stone's-throw from the door. **1863** WALSHE *Cedar Creek* 136: " ... Why, there's a far better site for a town plot on my land, Holt." "Ay, and a better water privilege too...." **1897** DURAND *Reminiscences* 49: The town of Ancaster

is beautifully situated on a mountain ridge, had good water privileges . . . and many fine stores.

2 the right to hold and make use of such a site.
1835 (1838) HALIBURTON *Sam Slick* 5: "Then, there is that water privilege, worth 3,000 or 4,000 dollars. . . ."
1849 ALEXANDER *L'Acadie* II 170: It would be advisable, for the sake of further settlements, that the water privileges, so much abused on this and other rivers, be purchased back by the Government, or be abolished by some means or other; say by lateral mill races.

3 *Placer Mining* the right to set up a dam to provide water for a sluice.
1860 *Brit.Colonist* (Victoria) 21 Aug. 3/1: A Mr. Whitworth has also recorded a water privilege on the creek about a mile below the forks, and proposes bringing water to a bar near the mouth of it.

water-pup *n.* [origin unknown] *Atlantic Provinces* a painful kind of boil caused by an organism found in sea water. See also **sea boil**.
1912 POCOCK *Man in the Open* 27: ". . . the bo's'n got a water-pup on his neck."

water-rat *n.* See **muskrat** (def. 1).
*c***1902** LAUT *Trapper* 271: The water-rat has tried to hide in the under-tangle; and the ermine has not only dived in pursuit but headed the water-rat back from the safe retreat of his house. **1944** CLAY *Fur Thieves* 109: "Mr. Weasel is a good swimmer! He can catch a water-rat, out-divin' an' out-swimmin' him with ease. . . ."

water rice† *Obs.* See **wild rice**.
1821 (1900) GARRY *Diary* 123: The Water was covered with Lilies and Water Rice. The latter plant is not unlike the Oat in Appearance.

water sky *Arctic* sky having the relatively dark appearance natural to the underside of cloud cover over open (unfrozen) sea. Cp. **land sky**.
[**1752** ROBSON *Hudson's Bay* 45: I noted this in my journal, and concluded that these black watry clouds must be generated in places where the waters are not frozen; for when I observed them at west-by-south, I turned immediately to the east, where I knew was an open sea, and found that the clouds in that point had exactly the same appearance.] **1850** SNOW *Voyage* 73: In the western horizon, too, there was evidently, as the mate said, a water sky; though it was impossible to say how far we might actually find a clear sea in that direction if we went there. **1851** OSBORN *Arctic Jnl* 247: On the afternoon of the 28th of August a strong water-sky and heavy bank showed the sea to be close at hand to the south, as well as a strong breeze behind it. **1958** *Manice* 8: Bare land and open water reflect little or no light and for this reason the clouds above these surfaces are relatively dark (*Land Sky, Water Sky*).

water smoke *North* See quote.
1958 *Manice* 7: Frost Smoke—(Arctic Sea Smoke, Sea Smoke, Water Smoke). A thick fog rising from the sea surface when relatively warm water is exposed to an air temperature much below freezing. Frost smoke frequently appears over newly-formed cracks and leads.

water snow See quotes.
1941 *Beaver* Sep. 39/2: Water Snow . . . is found beneath the surface and generally in granular form. **1955** ADTIC *Glossary*: water snow. Granulated snow with a high water content, giving more water on melting than ordinary snow. Also called "cooking snow."

water taxi a small boat that functions as a short-trip carrier.
1956 TALLBOOM *Arctic Bride* 131:—each establishment possessed both a boat and an Eskimo servant, which comprised an unique form of water taxi. **1958** HEALEY *Alert Bay* 94: Three water-taxi outfits operate out of Alert Bay to supply speedy service to all outlying points. **1965** *Cdn Geog.Jnl* Apr. 116: [Caption] Prospector's water taxi on the Limestone River, 1928.

water turkey the cormorant, *Phalacrocorax* sp.
1938 *Beaver* Sep. 13/1: The cormorants, known also as shags and water turkeys, are large black divers nearly the size of a wild goose, known to the Crees as crow ducks.

water witch(er)† See 1947 quote.
[**1829** MACTAGGART *Three Years* II 5: Water may attract the willow to a certain extent, which may account for the Dutchman's art in discovering spring-wells with a forked stick.] **1885** HAIGHT *Country Life* 101: There were certain persons, I do not remember what they were called, whether water doctors or water witches, who professed to be able . . . to tell where a well should be sunk. . . . **1947** WELLS *Owl Pen* 24: "Yeah, I'm a witcher." "A what?" "A water witcher," he explained. "I witch for water—I find water. I dig wells."

wattap(e) *n.* See **watap**.

wau-wau *n.* See **wawa²**.

wavey or **wavy** ['wevi] *n.* [< Algonk.; cf. Ojibwa *wewe* and Cree *wehwew* goose] a wild goose, especially the snow goose, *q.v.* See also **blue wavey, horned wavey, wavey goose, wawa¹**, and **white wavey**.
☛ *Although* **wavey** *is ultimately derived from an Algonkian onomatopoeic word for a goose, the present form may have been influenced by that of the Canadian French borrowing of the same term.*
1743 (1949) ISHAM *Observations* 120: . . . the white geese . . . they [Crees] style wappawawewuck) which the English call's weywey's. **1820** (1823) FRANKLIN *Journey* 234: On the way back Hepburn and Keskarrah shot several waveys. . . . **1965** *Globe and Mail* (Toronto) 24 May 4/1: Even children can talk goose language. They call the wavies down to the hunter's guns.

wavey goose See **wavey**.
1902 PATTILLO *Moose-Hunting* 98: Canadian and wavy geese by the tens of thousands made the stubble fields their feeding ground. . . . **1955** *Crag and Canyon* (Banff, Alta) 6 May 5/3: [I saw] Four Wavey geese, or greater snow geese, in Ike Mill's pasture. **1965** *Globe and Mail* (Toronto) 24 May 4/1: April in the Cree dialect of this area is Niskapesim, goose month. That means Canada geese; and September is Wawaypesim, wavy goose moon ("wavy" being English-Cree slang for blue and snowy goose).

wawa¹ ['wɑwə *or* 'wɑwɑ] *n.* [var. of *wavey*, q.v.] See **wavey**. Also spelled *wa-wa, wawey*.
1785 (1954) *Moose Ft Jnls* 115: The Indians having received the last Powder and shot, they seem inclined to take as the Waways are realy very scarce. . . . **1872** (1883) BUTLER *Great Lone Land* 125: We will get the mecuhaga (Blueberry) and the "wa-wa". . . . **1903** SETON *Woodmyth* 30: . . . his cunning was like that of the Wa-wa of many snows.

wawa² ['wɑwɑ] *n.* [< Chinook Jargon] *Pacific Coast, Now Slang* talk; speech; language; words. See also **Kinchotch wawa**. Various spellings.
1860 *Brit.Colonist* (Victoria) 23 June 2/2: The Hyters

are to visit the Governor at some future time for a "waw-waw." *c*1870 (1873) LUNDIN-BROWN *Klatsassan* 153: . . . it was only after much waw-waw (parley) . . . that one of them was got to undertake to carry him. **1927** PHILIP *Painted Cliff* 22: "I seen hyak that I ain't got no chance o' gettin' the best in an exchange o' gay reparty with a jane that slings the wau-wau like she does." **1942** *B.C.Hist.Qtly* Jan. 11: Father Le Jeune . . . commenced to publish the *Wawa* . . . on May 2, 1891. The last issue of the magazine was dated September, 1904.

wawa[2] ['wɑwɑ] *v.* [< n.] talk; speak.
[**1833** (1963) TOLMIE *Physician* 242: After breakfast [I] was requested to "wawa saccgali." Gave them an account of the Creation. . . .] **1936** MOWERY *Paradise Trail* 121: "Stop talking about that damned bum!" Hugh flared out. "You've been wa-waning [sic] about him all afternoon." **1940** *B.C.Hist.Qtly* July 196: . . . to follow the hounds . . . and later to ride many hundreds of miles over mountain trails to hold Court, to wa-wa with the Indians, to visit mines. . . .

wawaskesiw *n*. See **waskesew**.

waw-waw *n*. See **wawa**[2].

way-house *n*. *Hist*. See **roadhouse**.
1928 WALDEN *Dog-Puncher* 32: There were two "way-houses" on this line, afterwards called "road-houses," where we were furnished wood, water, and shelter, but nothing else; we carried our own provisions, did our own cooking, and provided our own bedding.

wayside *n*. a railway station intermediate between major stations; a way station.
1963 *Time* (Cdn ed.) 8 Mar. 13/2: Alighting for 10 to 30 minute stops in such waysides as Capreol, Hornepayne [Ont.] . . . he was greeted by friendly crowds.

web *n*. See **snowshoe** (def. 1 and picture).
1923 *Beaver* Jan. 145: . . . it is said they still enjoy an occasional zestful tramp on the "webs" over leagues of new Manitoba snow. **1956** KEMP *Northern Trader* 148: As you proceed, the slush on your webs freezes. The webs become heavier to lift.

wedge-board *n*. *Fur Trade* a type of stretcher, *q.v.*, used for pelts removed by case-skinning, *q.v.*
1900 FRASER *Mooswa* 67: Even Muskrat and Pisew go on a wedge-board when they are skinned. You, Beaver, and Muskwa, and Mooswa have your skins stretched by iron thorns on the side of a Shack.

weed *n*. *Esp.Northwest, Slang* See **kinnikinnick** (def. 1).
1908 MAIR *Mackenzie Basin* 55: [Here] was a gathering of commonplace men smoking briar-roots, with treaty tobacco instead of "weed."

weeghteko *n*. See **Weetigo**.

weendigo ['wɪndə,go] *n*. See **Wendigo**.

weenusk ['winəsk] *n*. [< Algonk.: Cf. Cree *wénusk*] See **groundhog** (def. 1).
1754 (1787) PENNANT *Supplement* 54: The Wenusk, or Quebec Marmot, feeds on coarse grass. **1784** (1954) *Moose Ft Jnls* 374: The Comparative of Furrs &c to Beaver The Standard . . . Weenusk [Skins] 2 [as] 1 [beaver]. **1897** TUTTLE *Golden North* 221: . . . the following list [shows] the catch for one season in and about Cumberland House: . . . Otter 424, Wolverine 175, Weenisk 1. **1933** *Beaver* Dec. 28/1: . . . it was into one of these holes that the weenusk scuttled as I made my exit. . . .

Weesakachak, Weesarkejauk, Weesukeechak *n*. See **Wesakachak**.

Weetigo ['wɪtɪ,go *or* 'wɪtɪ,go] *n*. [< Algonk.: Cree *wītiku* evil spirit; cannibal] **1** See quotes. See also **Wendigo** (def. 1). Various spellings.
☞ *The concept denoted by* Weetigo *and* Wendigo *varies from a personified Evil Spirit to a supernatural creature of which there are many, all having fearful characteristics including an insatiable appetite for human beings.*
[**1743** (1949) ISHAM *Observations* 5: The Devil Whit te co]. **1748** ELLIS *Hudson's Bay* 193: They likewise acknowledge another Being, whom they call *Wittikka*, whom they represent as the Instrument of all Kinds of Mischief and Evil; and of him they are very much afraid; but however we know of no Methods made use of by them to appease him. **1908** MAIR *Mackenzie Basin* 76: One Pahayo—"The Pheasant"—had gone mad and threatened to kill and eat people. Of course, this was attributed to the Weeghteko, by which he was believed to be possessed, a cannibal spirit who inhabits the human heart in the form of a lump of ice, which must be got rid of by immersion of the victim in boiling water, or by pouring boiling fat down his throat. **1943** *Beaver* Mar. 18/1: Among the unearthly inhabitants of the Cree spirit world are the dreaded witikos, cannibalistic creatures which fly through the night, breathing flame, in search of victims to satisfy their craving for human flesh. **1956** BERTON *Mysterious North* 10: There are others, all kin to these . . . the Weetigo of the Barrens, that horrible, naked cannibal, his face black with frostbite, his lips eaten away to expose his fanglike teeth. . . . **1963** SYMONS *Many Trails* 197: Above, the northern lights rush like squadrons *en echelon,* their cold silken banners faintly rustling, to do battle with the dark *weetigoes.*

2 usually **weetigo**, a man turned cannibal and believed possessed by an evil spirit. See also **Wendigo** (def. 2a). Various spellings.
[**1798** (1916) THOMPSON *Narrative* 260: The word Weetego is one of the names of the Evil Spirit and when he gets possession of any Man, (Women are wholly exempt from it) he becomes a Man Eater, and if he succeeds, he no longer keeps company with his relations and friends, but roams all alone through the Forests, a powerful wicked Man, preying upon whom he can, and as such is dreaded by the Natives.] **1908** MAIR *Mackenzie Basin* 129: But here, too, many years ago, a priest was murdered and eaten by a weeghteko, an Iroquois from Caughnawaga. **1929** MOBERLY *When Fur Was King* 114: He was sure he had now run upon a real weetigo (cannibal) and, being a plucky man, determined to hunt and kill him.

Wehndigo *n*. See **Wendigo**.

weh-ti-go *n. adj*. See **Weetigo**.

weiner (or wiener) roast† a social affair at which frankfurters are roasted (or, more often, boiled) over an open fire, usually after dark, the group engaging in singing and other forms of entertainment.
☞ *Dictionaries usually prefer to give the spelling as* wiener, *thus preserving the etymological development from* Wien *Vienna, where this type of (Vienna) sausage originated. However, the spelling* weiner *is often met in North America, where it seems general in the combination* weiner roast.
1947 *Game Trails in Can.* Aug. 28/3: The weiner roast in the evening [of the picnic] was a feature. **1957** *Commonwealth* 2 Oct. 5/4: . . . to end the two

enjoyable days, [there was] a weiner roast for the children. **1961** *Edmonton Jnl* 3 July 31/1: The group drove to the provincial campsite where a weiner roast proved a welcome break in the sight-seeing. **1966** *Kingston Whig-Standard* (Ont.) 27 Apr. 7/5: Many will remember . . . the corn and weiner roast and . . . the Christmas eve gathering after carol singing.

wejack ['widʒæk] *n.* [< Algonk.; cf. Cree *uchāk* and Ojibwa *uchik;* perhaps influenced by Ojibwa *wachashk* muskrat. Cp. **woodchuck**] Various spellings. **1** See **fisher** (def. 1). See also **woodshock**.

1743 (1949) ISHAM *Observations* 21: a wejack Shar qua she wuck. **1755** (1907) HENDAY *Journal* 345: In the evening we came to a Creek where were plenty of Wejacks. **1829** RICHARDSON *Fauna* I 52: The Pekan . . . Wejack, or Fisher [of the] Fur Traders. *c*1902 LAUT *Trappèr* 251: This is wuchak the fisher, or pekan, commonly called "the black cat"—who, in spite of his fishy name, hates water as cats hate it. **1956** KEMP *Northern Trader* 57: When Wuchusk comes up through a tunnel from the water and makes for his bed, he will step in the trap.

2 *Obs.* See **fisher** (def. 2).
1749 *Short State of North America* 27: Two Vejacks [are valued] as one Beaver. **1777** (1951) *Saskatchewan Jnls* 11 Apr.: To William Tomison 15½ Beaver in Trading Goods as necessaries for Trapping forty-five Martins and one Wejeck.

Wellington copper or **token** *Hist.* a copper coin having the value of half a penny, in circulation in the early nineteenth century. See also **Brock copper** and picture. Cp. **Waterloo copper**.
1848 *Examiner* (Toronto) 1 Nov. 2/4: The old 'Brock' and 'Wellington' coppers are familiar to the recollection of the old settlers: they once formed our only copper circulation although 4 or 5 of them would not balance a British penny! **1891** *Trans.Roy.Soc.Can.* IX 2 55: There were many other coins, especially "Wellington tokens" imported into Nova Scotia, but it is impossible to separate them from those imported into the other provinces.

Wendigo ['wɛndɪ,go] *n.* [< Algonk.; Ojibwa *windigō* evil spirit; cannibal] **1** See **Weetigo** (def. 1 and note). Also spelled *Weendigo, Windigo,* etc.
1830 JAMES *Narrative* 316: The Muskegoes, who inhabit the low and cheerless swamps on the borders of Hudson's Bay, are themselves reproached by the other tribes as cannibals, [and] are said to live in constant fear of the Weendegoag. **1847** NEVINS *Two Voyages* 115: When Windego saw him, he was very angry, and said, "What do you mean, boy, by coming out and making that noise? I am going to eat you." **1863** HIND *Exploring Labrador* I 58: These Montagnais think . . . that the Wendigoes are great cannibals, twenty and thirty feet high. They think that they live on human flesh, and that many Indians who have gone hunting, and have never afterwards been heard of, have been devoured by Wendigoes. **1963** *B.C.Digest* Nov.-Dec. 14/3: Some of the old accounts of Wendigos in the northwest describe apparitions more in accord in description and behaviour with the Sasquatch . . . than with the traditional wendigo or weetigo of the Cree-Algonkinian tribesman.

2 usually **wendigo, a.** See **Weetigo** (def. 2). Also spelled *weendigo, windigo,* etc.

1859 KANE *Wanderings* 60: The Weendigoes are looked upon with superstitious dread and horror by all Indians, and any one known to have eaten human flesh is shunned by the rest; as it is supposed that, having once tasted it, they would do so again should they have an opportunity. **1860** *Nor'Wester* (R.R.S.) 28 Mar. 2/1: Thick Foot's brother had killed his grandson, a boy ten or twelve years of age, being apprehensive that said boy was becoming a "Windigoo." **1921** HAWORTH *Trailmakers* 30: A weendigo, as one who was known to have been guilty of making such a terrible repast was called, was always thereafter not only detested but shunned. **1949** MACGREGOR *Blankets and Beads* 108: The Weentigo, an Indian who had killed his companion and eaten him, was an object of dread and superstition to the Indians everywhere.

b. turn wendigo, become a maneater.
1886 *Indian* (Hagersville, Ont.) 3 Feb. 8/2: Delirium, resulting from fevers, etc., was a thing they entirely misunderstood, and looked upon it as a symptom of the approach of irresistible cannibalism, or "turning windigo," and it became their duty to knock such patients on the head. **1934** GODSELL *Arctic Trader* 41: Upon a spruce bed in one of the birch-bark lodges lay the young squaw Sap-was-te, raving in delirium; possessed, said Pe-ce-quan the Medicine Man, by evil spirits; liable at any moment to turn "Weendigo," or cannibal, and endanger the lives of every member of the band.

3 *Figurative uses.*
1936 *Beaver* Sep. 49/2: The bird with the canoe is the tribal softie; the others sling three or four hundred pounds of goods on a headband and stagger after the canoe bearers as if the Wendigo himself were on their heels. **1948** ONRAET *Sixty Below* 38: Charlie laughed; I laughed; we both laughed to beat the windigo. **1956** MOWAT *Lost in Barrens* 50: "And should you see any signs of Eskimos you will abandon this camp as if the devil Wendigo was on your heels, and flee into the south."

4 See **Wendigo trout.**

Wendigo trout See **splake.** Also *Wendigo.*
1954 *Ontario Dept Lands and Forest News* 28 Dec. 2: At the same time, research experts of the Department have scored with their crossing of the speckled and lake trout to produce the famous hybrid "Splake" or "Wendigo." **1958** *Ottawa Jnl* 3 May 42/5: Anglers fortunate enough to fish one of the many specially selected lakes in which Wendigo Trout or splake were introduced last year, will again have the thrill of taking and keeping these fighting beauties. **1963** *Globe and Mail* (Toronto) 25 May 29/2: I don't like the name splake. It is harsh, has no appeal or romance. Some years ago a province-wide contest was held to suggest a better name for this hybrid. The winning name was Wendigo trout, but that was as far as it ever got.

Wenigo ['wɛnə,go] *n.* See **Wendigo.**

wenusk *n.* See **weenusk.**

Wesakachak [wə'sɑkə,tʃɑk] *n.* [< Algonk.: Cree *wesukāchak*] See 1784-1812 quote. Various spellings.
1784-1812 (1916) THOMPSON *Narrative* 85: There is an important being, with whom the Natives appear better acquainted with than the other, whom they call "Weesarkejauk" (the Flatterer); he is the hero of all their stories, always promising them some good, or inciting them to some pleasure, and always deceiving them. **1857** (1863) PALLISER *Journals* 64: It is called Manitoe's Rest by the Crees, and is one of the many knolls of the kind that have Indian superstition attached

to them, generally about a mythical person called Wee-suk-ee-chak. **1944** CLAY *Fur Thieves* 18: Wesakachak, an Indian spirit, went to the king beaver o' the colony and asked him to destroy the dam an' let the water go. **1963** SYMONS *Many Trails* 136: ... the legendary Cree Weesakachak appears to be the same sort of go-between with the Great Spirit ... the Kisa (or Kitche) Manito—as the hero of the poem.

West, the *n.* 1 *Hist.* See **Western Canada.**
1836 *Bytown* [Ottawa] *Gaz.* 25 Aug. 2/5: Emigrants are now pouring into the "West" in greater numbers than ever.

2 the western part of Canada, generally that part west of the Great Lakes. See also **Western Provinces.**
1863 *Nor'Wester* (R.R.S.) 19 Aug. 2/5: Before leaving Red River, I had heard of the fertile West—the garden of the continent—the Oasis strip, and so on; all applying to the very country we have passed through. **1909** PARKER *Northern Lights* 21: His people in the East, who had thwarted his youth, vexed and cramped him, saw only evil in his widening desires, and threw him over when he came out West—the scallywag, they called him, who had never wronged a man or—or a woman? **1940** MACCORMAC *Canada* 223: It has become obvious that the West was too hastily settled, that its good land, far from being limitless, has already been largely taken up.

West Block the block of offices comprising the most westerly of the Parliament Buildings in Ottawa. See also **block** (def. 7b) and **Western Block.** Cp. **Centre Block, East Block.**
1958 *Encyc.Can.* VIII 123/1: The original East Block and West Block, housing departmental staffs, are still in use. **1963** *Time* (Cdn ed.) 20 Sep. 10/2: But the experts around the U-shaped table in the West Block's room 308 were slightly out of place. ...

West Coast the western coast of Canada, especially southwestern British Columbia, including Vancouver Island and, usually, the Queen Charlotte Islands.
1856 *Canada West and H.B.C.* 6: On the west coast the case is even worse than in the interior; for while the exclusive right of trade exercised by the Hudson's-Bay Company keeps off from the coast all British vessels, those of the United States trade there with the natives, without let or hindrance, and, in consequence, spirits and firearms are ordinary articles of barter, and the fierce passions of savage life are developing and increasing, instead of being subdued under the influences of civilization and religion. **1962** *Chronicle-Herald* (Halifax) 10 Aug. 17/1: Early in the century he went to the West Coast where he was employed as an engineer.

Western boat *Nfld, Hist.* a schooner-rigged vessel having a 40-50 foot keel and a 14-15 foot beam, used on the fishing banks.
1951 *9th Census of Canada* IX Fisheries D-3: Western boats ... Bateaux de la côte Ouest. **1958** HARRINGTON *Sea Stories* 28: George Harvey owned a fishing vessel of a fair size-one of the so-called "Western boats" of the period. **1966** *Weekend Mag.* 23 Apr. 4/1: [Old folk song] Take me back to my western boat, / Let me fish off Cape St. Mary's, / Where the hag-downs sail and fog-horns wail. ...

Western Block *Obs.* See **West Block.**
1898 EDGAR *Canada and Capital* 57: The original structures consisted of the Parliamentary and Library buildings, and of the Eastern block as they now exist, and part of the Western block.

Western Canada *Hist.* the present Western Ontario. See also **West** (def. 1).
1849 ALEXANDER *L'Acadie* I 56: ... in travelling in a stage coach in Western Canada, he had found himself in company with three passengers. ... **1853** STRICKLAND *Canada West* I 155: The mischances consequent upon being lost in the woods, which were so frequent in the early settlement of Western Canada, are of rare occurrence now. **1858** (1955) CRAIG *Early Travellers* 230: Want of time prevented me from extending my journey through the whole length of Western Canada to Sarnia upon the River St. Clair. ...

Western Department the administrative division of the Hudson's Bay Company extending westward from the Rocky Mountains.
1956 INNIS *Fur Trade* 297: On the Pacific coast or in the Western department goods were brought from England by Cape Horn to the depot at Fort Vancouver (later, 1843, Victoria).

Westerner *n.* a native or resident of the West (def. 2).
1897 TYRRELL *Sub-Arctics* 100: Opportunities for excitement were seldom neglected by our dare-devil young Westerner. **1958** *Edmonton Jnl* 24 June 1/4: B.C.'s Attorney-General Robert Bonner Monday joined the parade of westerners to Ottawa.

western flowering dogwood a species of dogwood, *Cornus nuttalli,* native to the Pacific Coast, the floral emblem of British Columbia.
1958 *Weekend Mag.* 7 June 38: Found only in British Columbia, the western flowering dogwood is a natural emblem for the province. A tree from 20 to 60 feet high, it is covered with large flowers in April and May, carries clusters of bright red fruit in the autumn.

Western Ocean *Maritimes* See quote.
1958 HARRINGTON *Sea Stories* 3: The Maranee spent the next three weeks ... beating about the Western Ocean (a sailor's term for the northwest Atlantic).

Western Province 1 *Hist.* Canada West, *q.v.,* now Southern Ontario.
1846 TAYLOR *Narrative* 39: Toronto lies in the home district, and is the capital of the Western Province of the United Canadas. **1866** KING *Sportsman in Canada* 29: ... but I have myself seen and shot it at the Short Hills, in the Western Province, which is about 43°15', and it is common still further south in many parts of the State of New York. ... **1916** MACMECHAN *Popular Government* 57: In the western province the Tory and Orange opposition was equally violent towards a measure which was deemed to favour the French.

2 *Obs.* Manitoba.
1864 *Nor'Wester* (R.R.S.) 18 Aug. 1/1: North-western extension is a doctrine ... which has long been advocated in the Western province.

3 See **Western Provinces.**

Western Provinces the provinces of Canada west of Ontario, especially Manitoba, Saskatchewan, and Alberta. See also **West** (def. 2).
[**1871** *Wkly Manitoban* 29 Apr. 2/3: Then, as to the power to make special provisions in behalf of the Western Provinces, the 146th section of the British North American Act, 1867, is liberal, almost unqualified, in its grant of power.] **1914** BINDLOSS

Intriguers 86: Files of papers and a large map of the Western Provinces hung on one wall. . . . **1957** *Representative* 19 Dec. 2/2: In the three western provinces a swing to either of the two major parties would have placed this part of the country in a position of political power equal to that which is often attributed to Ontario or Quebec. . . . **1964** *Canada Month* Jan. 27/2: As for the western provinces, we know that they only came into being after Confederation.

Western settlements *Hist.* the settlements in the western part of Upper Canada (def. 1).
1818 *U.C.Gaz.* (York [Toronto]) 15 Oct. 177/4: A Treaty is on foot with our Indian neighbors for the purchase of new Territory, including certain tracts, which serve by their intervention to disconnect our Western Settlements. **1935** WALLACE *Encyclopedia* III 138/1: Hesse, a judicial district created in 1788 in the so-called "Western settlements" of the old Province of Quebec [later Lower and Upper Canada].

western white birch a variety of white birch, *q.v.*
1956 *Native Trees* 136: The name western white birch is misleading, as this tree grows in both Eastern and Western Canada. **1962** *Forest Conservation* 13/1: Other common tree species are lodgepole pine, aspen, and western white birch.

western white oak See **Garry oak.**
1894 *Trans.Roy.Soc.Can.* XI 4 15: There are no trees on Vancouver Island that are peculiar to it, and only one which is not found on the mainland—the western white oak. **1956** *Native Trees* 170: Garry Oak [is also called] western white oak.

western white pine See 1956 quote. See also **white pine** (def. 3).
1954 LYONS *Trees, Shrubs* 16: Western white pine [is also called] White Pine. . . . **1956** *Native Trees* 8: The western white pine [*Pinus monticola*] occasionally reaches a height of 250 feet and a diameter of 8 feet, but is more often 90 to 110 feet high and 2 to 3 feet in diameter.

West India *Obs.* **1** See **West India fish.**
2 *Lumbering* a size of stave measuring 3½′ long by 4″ broad and ¾″ thick.
1821 (1957) GUILLET *Valley of the Trent* 255: I . . . have seized the same—amounting to about Six thousand Pipe Staves—five thousand feet Square Oak timber, and four thousand West India staves. . . . **1945** CALVIN *Saga* 83: Though there were other sizes, for example the heavy "pipe stave," the two which were common in the Quebec export trade were the "standard" and the "West India."

West India fish *Esp.Nfld, Hist.* the lowest grade of cod for export. Also *West India* and *West Indies.*
1818 CHAPPELL *Voy.of Rosamond* 130: West-India fish: the refuse of the whole. These last are invariably sent for sale, to feed the Negroes of the Caribee Islands. **1832** MCGREGOR *British America* I 232: First, the merchantable, which are those of the finest quality and colour; second, the Madeira, which are nearly equal to the first; third, West India fish. . . . **1883** HATTON & HARVEY *Newfoundland* 291: [The fish] are "culled" or sorted into four different kinds called Merchantable (the best), Madeira, West India . . . and Dun, or broken fish, which will not keep and is intended for home use. **1936** (c1960) FOWKE *Canada's Story in Song* 207: Seven dollars for large fish, and five for your

small, / Pick out your West Indies and wait till the fall. . . .

West India stave See **West India** (def. 2).

West Indies See **West India fish.**

West Main *Hist.* the western shore of Hudson Bay. Cp. **Eastmain.**
1680 (1933) *Beaver* Sep. 13/2: In 1680 Governor Nixon was ordered "to keep on said factory where it now is upon Hayes Island in Moose river and there to keep our chief strength to prevent the encroachment of the French too far upon the West Main". . . .

Westmount ['wɛst,maunt] *n.* a district in Montreal, on the western slope of Mount Royal, long favored by wealthy English-speaking Montrealers.
1916 BRIDLE *Sons of Can.* 3: While other money barons of Montreal build modern castles in Westmount, Macdonald kept his terrace. . . . **1962** *Maclean's* 8 Sep. 15/2: In Canadian, Westmount, *n.*, means that part of English Montreal that once dominated much of the country's economy and still dominates most of Quebec's.

West Shore *Nfld* See **French shore** (def. 1).
1841 *Nfld House of Assembly Jnl* App. 49: The West Shore . . . is not liable to fogs nearly so much as the S.E. and S., where they are not only exceedingly dense, but may continue for weeks together.

wet fishery *Esp.Nfld* See **green fishery.**
1963 MORTON *Kingdom of Canada* 12: But from earliest times the fishery developed in two modes, that of the wet fishery and that of the dry.

Wetigo, Wittako *n. Obs.* See **Weetigo.**

wewaskish *n.* [< Algonk.; var. of *waskesew,* q.v.] See **wapiti.**
1795 (1911) HEARNE *Journey* 259: The same may be said of all the Indian-dressed leather, except that of the wewaskish, which will wash as well as shammy-leather, and always preserve its softness. **1832** MCGREGOR *British America* I 102: The species of deer called by the Indians we-was-kish, has been confounded, even by Mr. Pennant with the moose deer, and by others with the cariboo. **1853** REID *Young Voyageurs* 165: It is called in different districts or by different authors . . . *red deer, wapiti,* and *wewashkish.*

Weymouth pine [after Thomas Thynne (d.1714), 1st Viscount of *Weymouth*] See **white pine** (def. 1).
1770 (1792) CARTWRIGHT *Journal* I 10: The arrows are made from Weymouth pine; they are slender, light, perfectly straight, and about three feet long. **1832** BAILLIE *Acct of N.B.* 41: The white, yellow, or Weymouth pine, is the monarch of our forest, growing to the height of 130 feet. . . . **1956** *Native Trees* 6: Eastern white pine [is also called] white pine, Weymouth pine. . . .

whabby or **wabby** ['wabi] *n.* [perhaps Brit. dial. *wabbly* an unfledged bird] *Nfld* See 1956 quote.
1770 (1792) CARTWRIGHT *Journal* I 31: The rest of the party killed four grouse, one curlew, one auntsary, and a whabby. **1956** MCATEE *Folk-Names* 2: Red-throated Loon [is also called] . . . whabby (Spelled also wabby, waby, and wobby. Possibly derived from "wobble," a name for the extinct Great Auk which alluded to the bird's awkwardness on land. Early use Cartwright 1792. Nfld., "Labr.", Que.). . . .

whacheer or **what cheer** [wɑ'tʃir] *n.* [< English greeting, *what cheer,* borrowed by the Crees] *North* a long-established greeting. See also **wachee.** Also spelled *watcheer.*

[**1578** (1889) HAKLUYT *Voyages* XII 206: They haled one another according to the manner of the Sea, and demaunded what cheare? & either partie answered ye other, that all was well.] **1743** (1949) ISHAM *Observations* 47: How do you do friend [is, in Cree] Watcheer Coshock. **1858** (1860) HIND *Assiniboine Exped.* II 141: Among the Plains Cree, with whom the Scotch employes of the Hudson's Bay Company early established communication, the first address is generally "whacheer! whacheer!" **1934** GODSELL *Arctic Trader* 31: . . . the Chief Factor proceeded to shake each squaw and Indian by the hand, saying "Watcheer?" **1963** MCTAVISH *Behind the Palisades* 67: Next came the Indian men . . . who gravely shook hands, said "What Cheer" the common seaman's salutation, engrafted in the Cree language from constant repetition. . . .

whacker† *n.* See **bullwhacker** (def. 1).
1954 HAGELL *Grass was Free* 2: The perverse obstinacy of the cattle, however, was a trial to the whackers. . . . **1962** *Field, Horse & Rodeo* Nov. 29/1: Soon the settlers were joined by a young man, Lincoln Bastedo, who had been a whacker on the bull train express that plied between Winnipeg and Edmonton.

whaleback *n.* **1** See 1952 quote. See also **whaleback hill.**
1934 BETTANY *Valley of Lost Gold* 165: "I couldn't find any quartz on this land of ours—nor schists. To-day I found both." "On the whale-back?" "Yep." **1952** PUTNAM *Cdn Regions* 219/1: The drumlins are special features of the ground moraine and are composed of the same kinds of boulder as the till plains. They occur in groups which may contain anywhere from ten to many hundreds, with their crests all trending in the same direction. A group of drumlins looks very much like a school of huge whales basking on the surface and they are often locally termed "whalebacks."
2† a type of freighter used for carrying grain or ore on the Great Lakes, having a cigar-shaped hull and low, convex deck.
1936 DENTON & LORD *World Geography* 103: [Caption] "Whale-Backs" and other Grain-Carriers Waiting to Load Wheat at Fort William Elevators. **1957** HUTCHISON *Canada* 197: Even on the newly built "whalebacks" a seaman must slither over an open deck between bow and stern. **1966** *Kingston Whig-Standard* (Ont.) 27 Apr. 5/4: The John Erikson, the last of the Great Lakes whaleback grain carriers, was donated Tuesday to the City of Hamilton [Ont.]. . . .

whaleback hill See **whaleback** (def. 1).
1967 *North* Mar.-Apr. 9/2: The short cut over the point of Kinnakjuak was ruled out with its two crossings of pressure ice and the whaleback hill.

whale line *Fur Trade, Obs.* a heavy rope or line often used for tracking boats or canoes. See also **tracking line.**
1784 (1954) *Moose Ft Jnls* 247: "We shall be greatly distressed next Spring unless you or East Main can assist us with some ½ inch and ¾ inch whale line." **1913** COWIE *Adventurers* 120: . . . hauling, inch by inch, against the force of a rapid or fall with a whale or "main" line.

whaway *n. Obs.* See **wavey.**

Wheat Belt the large tract on the Prairies, *q.v.*, mainly given over to the growing of wheat.
1875 *Canadian Mthly* July 3/1: There are, no doubt, considerable portions of the North-West Territories external to the Wheat Belt which are capable of producing cereals. **1905** OUTRAM *Cdn Rockies* 30: The winters are much milder than in the wheat belt, and the warm "Chinook" winds melt the snow at frequent intervals, enabling cattle and horses to forage for themselves. **1965** *Cdn Geog.Jnl* Feb. 59/1: . . . Canada's "Wheat Belt" is generally pictured as a flat featureless expanse of prairie with nothing rising higher than a country grain elevator.

Wheat Board a government body having the function of regulating the buying and selling of wheat.
1923 *One Big Union Bulletin* 22 Mar. 4/4: It is commonly reported that the farmers of the three prairie Provinces intend to nationalize the disposition of grain by the establishment of a Compulsory Wheat Board. **1953** *Cdn Geog.Jnl* Feb. 67/2: . . . we got it from the Wheat Board and the private grain trade. **1963** MORTON *Kingdom of Canada* 463: Equally significant was the creation of the Canadian Wheat Board, also in 1935, with the statutory task of disposing of the annual wheat crop.

wheat miner *West, Slang, Derog.* a farmer who grows wheat exclusively and intensively, often without proper regard for soil conservation. Cp. **land-miner.**
1953 *Cdn Geog.Jnl* Feb. 69/2: It was the fashion, a few years ago, to sneer at the "wheat miners" of the prairies.

wheat pool 1 a co-operative formed by western farmers to handle their own grain.
1930 (1945) HAIG *Brave Harvest* 215: One thing, which was very marked in all the conversations about wheat and flour, was the unanimity of belief [in Britain] that Canada's wheat pools . . . had been fatal in Canada's grain trade. **1957** *Maclean's* 17 Aug. 25/1: Early in the century prairie farmers, impatient with the monopoly and abuses of a few private grain-handling companies, founded United Grain Growers and the three Wheat Pools. The UGG and Wheat Pool buildings now stand on Main near Portage, representing 280,000 prairie farmers and two thirds of the grain handled in Canada. **1958** MACGREGOR *North-west of 16* 220: . . . the Wheat Pools had their start at this time in little meetings in country schools all over the province.
2 the total annual amount of wheat handled by such a co-operative.
1958 *Edmonton Sun* 5 June 12/1: The wheat board's final payment to prairie farmers on the 1956-57 wheat pool will be announced in a few days, it was learned Tuesday.

wheat province any one of the three Prairie Provinces, especially Manitoba and Saskatchewan.
1928 FREEMAN *Nearing North* 372: Pressure from the wheat provinces began to tell politically by 1925, but neither then nor since has there been much save more or less open opposition in evidence from Ontario, Quebec, British Columbia and the Maritime Provinces.

wheel-barrow outfit *Slang, Derog.* See quote.
1912 FOOTNER *New Rivers* 66: It appeared that at this end of the road there were no "Gyppos" or "wheel-barrow outfits," as they call the independent freighters, and the contractors . . . refused to carry a pound that was not their own.

wheel-dog *n.* of a dog team, the dog nearest the sled in a tandem hitch, *q.v.*, or either of the two

dogs nearest the sled in a fan hitch, *q.v.* See pictures at **fan hitch** and **tandem hitch.** See also **steer-dog** and **wheeler.**
1922 PRINGLE *Tillicums* 85: I put a smaller dog named Mike in the lead and hitched Steal up next the sleigh as my "wheel-dog." **1941** *Beaver* March 11/2: The wheel dogs—those nearest the sled—and the leader are allowed a trace six feet long, the others being about five feet. **1965** WILSON *No Man Stands Alone* 29: I firmly believe that the "wheel-dog," next to the sled, can upset one any time he wishes.

wheeler *n.* See **wheel-dog.**
1900 LONDON *Son of Wolf* 209: . . . the dogs whined; and He of the Otter Skins talked with his whip to a recalcitrant wheeler. **1903** LONDON *Call of the Wild* 55: Dave was wheeler or sled dog, pulling in front of him was Buck, then came Sol-leks; the rest of the team was strung out ahead, single file, to the leader. . . .

wheeskyjaun *n.* See **whisky-john.**

whelping ice *Nfld* See 1918 quote.
1918 GRENFELL *Lab.Doctor* 75: Then there is the clearer, heavy Arctic ice, with here and there huge icebergs frozen in; and again the smoother, whiter variety known as "whelping ice"—that is the Arctic shore ice, born probably in Labrador, on which the seals give birth to their pups. **1958** HARRINGTON *Sea Stories* 119: The sailing vessels always left some days ahead of the steamers, as the former found it hard going through the ice; even so it was the 17th of March before the *Elsie* got into the "whelping ice" and "struck the fat."

whig *n.* **1** *Hist.* in colonial times, a person in favor of self-government.
1833 *Cdn Correspondent* (York [Toronto]) 1 June 3/1: We are the friends of justice, freedom, and independence, and these virtues we shall always respect and reverence whether they be found in a Radical, a Whig, or a Tory. **1838** (1955) CRAIG *Early Travellers* 124: We have here Tories, Whigs, and Radicals, so called; but these words do not signify exactly what we mean by the same designations at home. **1942** RADDALL *His Majesty's Yankees* 256: If the scattered farms at Cobequid could send so resolute a company, surely we might expect a large force from the stout Whigs of Truro.

2 *Rare* a member or supporter of the Liberals; a Grit, *q.v.* See also **Whiggism.**
1963 *Ubyssey* 27 Sep. 13/5: [Headline] WHIGS INVADE BROCK HALL Liberal leader Ray Perrault and twelve Liberal candidates from greater Vancouver will be on Campus Friday.

whiggery *n. Obs.* the principles of the Whigs (def. 1).
1842 (1882) RATTRAY *Scots in Brit.N.A.* II 449: I also leave my late brother's watch to my brother Sandy, exhorting him at the same time to give up whiggery, radicalism, and all other isms that do most easily beset him.

Whiggism *n. Rare* the principles and policies of the Liberal Party of Canada. See also **Whig** (def. 2).
1908 BROWN *Lady of the Snows* 118: " . . . You know Whiggism is a scheme of practical expediency, a working policy with a chance of being realized, and they can do so without violating any principles. . . ."

whigwam *n.* See **wigwam.**

whigwham *n. Obs.* See **wigwam.**

whim stick *Lumbering, B.C.* See quote.
1906 BEARD *Field and Forest* 124: In the Rocky, Cascade and Selkirk mountains, the lakes and streams have their shores plentifully supplied with "whim sticks," logs of fine dry timber, which the freshets have brought down from the mountain sides, and which the rocks and surging torrents have denuded of bark. These whim sticks are of all sizes, and sound and perfect as kiln-dried logs.

whisk-e-jonish *n. Obs.* See **whisky-john.**

whiskey (in compounds) See **whisky.**

whisky blanc [< Cdn F "white whisky"] *Esp. Que.* a drinkable dilution of ethyl alcohol, distilled from cereals. See also **alcool** and **white whisky.**
1897 DRUMMOND *Habitant* 31: " . . . he was glad for get de chance drink some good w'sky blanc." **1918** MACKAY *Trench and Trail* 15: I am glad to hear that whisky blanc does not "cut the figure" in French festivities now that it did twenty years ago. . . . **1945** MacLENNAN *Two Solitudes* 49: Once Marius has seen . . . a man in Saint-Marc who was drunk on *whiskey-blanc.* **1965** *Kingston Whig-Standard* (Ont.) 15 Apr. 17/2: He . . . took a nip of whisky blanc from a reporter to thaw out.

whisky-boy *n. Hist.* a person responsible for dispensing the liquor at a barn raising, logging bee, etc. See also **grog-boss.**
1903 CONANT *Life in Canada* 83: Old men to-day tell me that there were mere lads then, and were the "whiskey-boys" at these loggings. **1933** GUILLET *Early Life in U.C.* 288: The amount of whisky distributed at bees by the "whiskey-boys," "grogmen" or "grog-bosses" was so great that there are records of as much as eighty gallons consumed at one bee.

whisky feast *Hist.* See **boisson.**
1907 CROSBY *An-ko-me-nums* 130: I turned around through the village and found [the Indians] had had a "whiskey feast." And, oh! What a sight! Nearly all drunk—men, women and children.

whiskyite ['hwɪski,aɪt *or* 'wɪs-] *n. Rare* a person who favors the legal sale of spiritous liquor.
1908 *Cotton's Wkly* 31 Dec. 5/3: The majority of the voters of Sweetsburg cling to their licensed barroom almost as closely as they would to a long lost brother and the Cowansville whiskyites know this.

whisky-jack ['(h)wɪski,dʒæk] *n.* [alteration of *whisky-john,* q.v.]
1 See **Canada jay.**
1743 (1949) ISHAM *Observations* 23: a white Whisker jack or a Jay Like [bird] wap pis ka John *or* wap pa whisker John. **1795** (1911) HEARNE *Journey* 405: The . . . Whisky-Jack . . . is very familiar, and . . . so much given to pilfering, that no kind of provisions it can come at, either fresh or salt, is safe from its depredations. **1888** (1890) ST. MAUR *Impressions* 251: They are called by the men Whisky-Jacks . . . they are pretty birds about the size of a jay and of a bluish-grey colour. **1965** *Beaver* Autumn 55/1: They . . . [Indian trappers] had lived on Canada jays, commonly known as whiskey jacks.

2 *Obs.* See **whisky trader.**
1907 (1908) SINCLAIR *Raw Gold* 9: "There'll be heaps uh fun in the Cypress Hills country when they [the NWMP] get t' runnin' the whisky-jacks out."

whisky-jay *n.* See **Canada jay.** See also **whisky-john.**

1908 LAUT *Conquest N.W.* I 118: Whiskey jays became noisier and bolder than in winter. **1956** RADDALL *Wings* 44: "[he was] crazy as a whiskey-jay."

847

**whisky-john
whistler**

whisky-john ['(h)wɪskɪ,dʒən] *n.* [< Algonk.; cf. Cree *weskuchanis* little blacksmith (from sooty color)] See **Canada jay.** See also **whisky-jack.**

[**1772** FORSTER *Trans.Linnean Soc.* XII 673: They are named by the natives Whisky-Jonish, which has been changed by the English into Whisky-Jack.] **1821** (1823) FRANKLIN *Journey* 315: Some young ravens and whiskey-johns made their appearance at this time. **1889** CHURCH *Making a Start* 183: ... we shot a partridge and a wood-grouse, also a "whisky-John".... **1963** *Weekend Mag.* 16 Nov. 41/1: His names, all Canadian, are: whisky jack, whisky john, moose bird, meat bird, camp robber, meat hawk and lumberjack.

whisky johnny *Rare* See **Canada jay.** See also **whisky-john.**

1922 FLAHERTY *Eskimo Friends* 3: Even in the forest places, the cawing of some "Whisky Johnny" for bits of bannock and bacon rind, and the forlorn cries of "Poor Canada" were the only sounds.

whisky peddler† *Hist.* See **whisky trader.**

1923 STEELE *Spirit-of-Iron* 108: So he came in touch with all the vice, wretchedness and stark tragedy abounding in the tent-towns and construction camps. He knew all the thieves, 'rollers,' roughs, shell-game experts, whiskey-peddlers, and ladies of doubtful reputation by sight and most of them by name. **1953** MOWERY *Mounted Police* vii: The white population consisted of a handful of fur traders, frontier badmen, and a few vicious whisky-peddlers, with their rotgut and blaze-belly.

whisky post *West, Hist.* an establishment operated for the illicit selling of whisky to Indians. See also **whisky-trading post.**

1954 *Proud Procession* 410: Other whiskey posts were built also, but Whoop-up remained the centre and from it terror spread in all directions. **1957** MACEWAN *Eye Opener Bob* 31: A few miles to the west of town was the site of the old Fort Spitzee, one of the lawless whiskey posts....

whisky rancher *West, Slang, Hist.* See **whisky trader.**

1936 MOWERY *Paradise Trail* 15: ... British Columbia, New Caledonia then, was a raw wild region, its whole interior almost an unknown land ... in its foothills Blackfeet warred with Piegan, and the whisky ranchers preyed on both....

whisky runner *West, Hist.* See **whisky trader.** See also **permit runner.**

1890 (1929) *Selected Stories* 108: Sergeant Fones, he dreams perhaps Old Aleck sells whisky against the law to men you call whisky runners, sometimes to Indians and half-breeds.... **1927** LONGSTRETH *Silent Force* 14: Whiskey-runners had conjectured that the Crees on Lake Winnipeg would prove a soft thing.

whisky smuggler *West, Hist.* See **whisky trader.**

1916 BRIDLE *Sons of Can.* 217: The north-west was a greater land than either. It was an empire of Indians, half-breeds, cowboys, furposters, mounted policemen, cart-freighters, dog-drivers, whisky-smugglers, and missionaries. **1955** HARDY *Alta.Anthol.* 42: These whisky smugglers didn't care about the effect of liquor on the Indians who, crazed with firewater, killed parties of white men and fought with each other.

whisky trader *Esp.West, Hist.* a person trading or selling whisky, especially as an illicit business,

to the Indians. See also **free trader** (def. 2b), **keg angel, whisky peddler, whisky rancher, whisky runner,** and **whisky smuggler.**

1802 *Niagara Herald* (U.C.) 13 Feb. 3/3: The chiefs of the Grand River Indians at a late meeting, taking into consideration the consequences of whisky traders coming among their nations, have resolved that no indulgence for that purpose shall be given. **1859** *Brit. Colonist* (Victoria) 1 July 2/1: The other day a whiskey trader entered Sooke harbor, and stopped near a fishing station and enquired if they were Boston men. **1910** HAYDON *Riders of Plains* 157: Few Indians were proof against the wiles of the illicit whisky traders. **1965** *Maclean's* 19 June 15/1: By the middle of the nineteenth century the trail was being used by beaver trappers and wolfers, by gold seekers and missionaries and whisky-traders.

whisky-trading post *West, Hist.* See **whisky post.**

1965 *Maclean's* 19 June 15/1: His mission was to find and report on whisky-trading posts....

whisky white *Obs.* See **whisky blanc.**

1889 LIGHTHALL *Songs* 151: So I jes' turns into the bar an' calls / For finger of whisky white....

whisky-wine *n. Que.* See **caribou** (def. 4).

1899 PARKER *Lane* 177: "Whiskey-wine is meat and drink to me—I was born on New Year's Day, old coffin-face. Whiskey-wine day, they ought to call it..." **1901** PARKER *Right of Way* 49: When he coolly walked into the great room, where a half-dozen of them were already assembled, drinking white "whisky-wine," he had no intention of setting himself right.

whistle-punk *n. Lumbering, B.C.* a person who relays the shouted signals of the hooktender, *q.v.,* to the donkey operator by blowing a whistle or operating an electric whistle (an occupation now largely displaced by electronic devices). See also **punk.** Cp. **talkie-tooter.**

1930 *B.C.Lumberman* Apr. 48/1: Shall honest hook-tenders and whistle punks be clocked while they eat? **1958** *Sun* (Vancouver) 25 Nov. 1/5: No settlement had been reached Monday in the labor dispute over introducing a radio signal device to replace "whistle punks" in the north-island ... operations. **1958** *Globe and Mail* (Toronto) 30 May 3/3: "I should truly love to see that because very shortly every whistle punk in British Columbia would have two Cadillacs in his garage." **1966** *Dly Colonist* (Victoria) 3 Aug. 28/2: The whistle punk, used throughout the last half-century of logging in B.C. was usually a young fellow, just learning the art of logging.

whistler *n.* **1** See **hoary marmot.**

1703 LAHONTAN *New Voyages* I 110: [We saw] little beasts called Siffleurs or Whistlers.... **1819** (1922) HARMON *Journal* 377: There is a small animal, found only on the Rocky Mountain, denominated, by the Natives, Quis-qui-su, or whistlers, from the noise which they frequently make, and always when surprised, strongly resembling the noise made by a person in whistling. **1866** LORD *Naturalist* II 195: The Redskin is the whistler's most implacable enemy; he never tires of hunting and trapping the little animal, delighting to use his jacket in the fabrication of rugs. **1953** *Cdn Geog.Jnl* Oct. 136/1: The whistler's annual life cycle consists of an 8 months' winter sleep interrupted by 4 months of eating and basking in the summer sunshine.

1965 WILSON *No Man Stands Alone* 67: The name Whistler comes from their shrill whistle when frightened.

2 See pika.

1939 *Beaver* Mar. 46/2: We found here a peculiar little animal, native to the region, called a whistler or coney.

3 a. See whistling swan.

1853 REID *Young Voyageurs* 49: That [swan] which is best known is the "whistler".... **1938** (1950) STANWELL-FLETCHER *Driftwood Valley* 179: Several large companies comprising seventy and eighty swans have gone over. We are sure these were the whistlers because of their distinctly higher, more whistling-like notes. **1964** *B.C. Digest* Oct. 23/3: The flock that winters on the North Thompson east of Kamloops have been identified as whistlers.

b. See quote.

1959 MCATEE *Folk-Names* 8: Lesser Canada Goose [is locally called] whistler (Sask.).

4 See quote.

1958 WATTERS *B.C.Cent.Anthol.* 340: It was the kind of slide oldtimers called a "dry" or "Whistler." The kind that often follows a fresh snowfall on crust, gathering force and volume with lightning speed, bending or snapping off stray trees like matchwood.

whistle stop† a small, unimportant town or village, so called because trains indicated by a whistle whether or not a stop was to be made.

1957 HUTCHISON *Canada* 217: The railway traveler sees only the dismal villages of the main line, the whistle stops around a wooden grain elevator, a skating rink, and a garage. **1958** *Edmonton Jnl* 11 Aug. 1/2: At whistle stops in Nova Scotia's Annapolis Valley ... she left her train to mingle with crowds on station platforms. **1964** *Globe and Mail* (Toronto) 19 Dec. 26/2: At this whistle stop on the way to James Bay ... they take the place of the family car.... **1966** *Canadian* 30 Apr. 7/2: Station agents at these whistle stops also came in for their share of chivvying and those who failed to accept the banter in good humor ran the risk of being shanghaied aboard the train and not released until hundreds of miles from home.

whistle-wing *n.* See whistling duck.

1852 (1881) TRAILL *Cdn Crusoes* 241: The silence of the forest was unbroken, save by the ... whirring sound of the large white and grey duck, (called by the frequenters of these lonely waters the whistlewing,) as its wings swept the waters in flight.... **1907** HUNTER *Cdn Wilds* 225: The whistler, whistle-wing, great head, garrot or brass-eyed is one of the few ducks that to my knowledge, builds its nest in trees. **1956** MCATEE *Folk-Names* 14: Common Goldeneye [is also called] ... whistle-wing....

whistling badger *Rare* See hoary marmot.

1905 (1954) *B.C.Hist.Qtly* 182: An interesting small animal is one of the American badgers, the whistling badger, or "siffleur"....

whistling duck any of several ducks that make a whistling sound in flight, especially the golden eye. See also whistle-wing.

1823 HALIBURTON *General Descr.N.S.* 31: The following catalogue contains a list of the known birds of the Province with their popular names. Horned Owl ... Whistling Duck.... **1935** JENNESS *Parry Island* 80: Do not give bear meat or the meat of the whistling duck to the sick....

whistling frog *Obs.* the spring peeper, *Hyla crucifer,* of eastern North America.

1833 *Canadian Mag.* Mar. 196: I have had frequent opportunities of examining this little creature, which is commonly called, by way of distinction, "the whistling frog," but is in reality a toad, of small size, and reddish brown colour.

whistling hare See pika.

1960 *Cdn Audubon* Jan.-Feb. 27/3: For a creature so small, the pika has many names: Coney, Rock Rabbit, Calling Hare, Whistling Hare, and others.

whistling john *Obs.* See Canada jay. See also whisky-john.

1850 BIGSBY *Shoe and Canoe* I 241: We were visited here by two of the birds called "Whistling John."

whistling marmot See hoary marmot.

1921 LAUT *Cariboo Trail* 28: A whistling marmot pops up from the rocks and pierces the stillness. **1935** EVANS *Reindeer Trek* 234: What a mighty struggle to reach the top! Pressing, digging, sinking, wallowing, even burrowing like the whistling marmots! **1963** SPRY *Palliser* 245: They found their way ... into the valley of a river that Hector named Siffleur—the French name for the whistling marmots.

whistling pig See hoary marmot.

1936 MOWERY *Paradise Trail* 28: Higher up the slope, in an area of rocky open, a colony of "whistling pigs," perched prominently on their den boulders, were whistling sociably at one another.... **1966** PATTERSON *Trail* 73: ... there ... the Sikannis ... could snare the marmot, the siffleur, the "whistling pig," the little haunter of the barren heights.

whistling swan† a wild swan, *Olor columbianus,* which breeds in northern Canada and Alaska. See also whistler (def. 3).

1882 *Trans.Roy.Soc.Can.* I 4 51: The whistling swan ... breeds near Churchill and on the islands towards the eastern side of Hudson's Bay. **1962** *Globe and Mail* (Toronto) 7 Apr. 29/4: Nothing is more thrilling ... than the high double or triple notes of the leader of a flock of whistling swans....

white *n.* **1**† See white man (def. 1).

1789 (1959) PRESTON *Kingston* 152: ... I would have you Act as if you were Certain of it, keeping the report as Secret as possible, that no unnecessary alarm may be spread amongst either Whites or Indians. **1810** (1957) GUILLET *Valley of the Trent* 254: He has constantly a gang of drunken vagabonds about him, of vagrant whites & Indians, constantly fighting among themselves and abusive to others. **1818** PALMER *Journal* 213: ... skins and furs ... are brought down from the interior by Indians and whites in the service of the [N.W.] Company. **1835** (1944) *B.C.Hist.Qtly* Jan. 137: It is probable they [Indians] will not be thoroughly quiet until they be chastised and be made to feel the strength and power of the Whites. **1963** *Maclean's* 6 July 22/1: The main reason is that the Mistassini Indians ... as yet have no white problem. **1965** *Globe and Mail* (Toronto) 26 May 3/5: Most Moosonee whites do nothing to harm the Indians ... and nothing to help them.

2 See whitefish.

1942 *Beaver* Mar. 22/2: Whites, as they're popularly called, also lend themselves to hanging. And they're just about the right size and shape for thawing out before a winter fire.

3 *Pacific Coast* See spring salmon. See also white spring.

1958 WATTERS *B.C.Cent.Anthol.* 143: Many an ex-hand-liner can recall the "bad year" when reds brought three cents a pound; pinks two, and the half-cent whites went overboard all along the coast.

white *adj.* **1**† of or associated with the white man (def. 1), as opposed to the Indian.
1785 (1943) HUNTER *Diary* 55: We saw several white children and handsome white squaws. **1811** (1950) THOMPSON *Journals* 169: A fine day—At 7.40 AM we set off—all the White Hunters in company. **1965** SYMINGTON *Tuktu* 59: ... most missionaries tried to teach their charges how to cope with the "white" culture and economy. ...

2 *Slang* **a.**† decent, fair; honest. See also **white Indian** and **white man** (def. 2).
1904 CONNOR *Prospector* 117: "You're line ain't mine, but you're white." **1923** STEELE *Spirit-of-Iron* 115: "God, you're ... the first white policeman I've ever met."

b. *Slang* pertaining to English-speaking persons. See also **white,** *adv.* (def. 2) and **white man** (def. 3).
1959 STOREY *Prairie Harvest* 102: The children ... made it difficult for the bohunk children whenever they were in the minority in the "white" schools.

white *adv. Slang* **1** fairly; decently.
1899 *Greenwood Miner* (B.C.) 8 Sep. 3/1: Over at Nelson the people used the editors white, and gave them a take so that everyone regretted the coming of "30."
1909 SERVICE *Cheechako* 28: Just a dollar to help me out, I know you'll treat me white; / I'll do as much for you some day. ...

2 *Derog.* in **speak** or **talk white,** like an English-speaking Canadian. See also **white,** *adj.* (def. 2b).
1912 POCOCK *Man in the Open* 37: "Sounds like Injun languages," says he, "can't you talk white?" **1963** *Maclean's* 2 Nov. 58/1: I refuse to look forward to a future time when one of my children will come home hurt because he has been ordered to "speak white." **1964** *Globe Mag.* 28 Nov. 15/4: Every English Canadian who ... says "speak white" to a French compatriot, is equally totalitarian and Fascist. **1966** *Saturday Night* Apr. 14/3: As we toasted the action later that day in the prize bottle of Scotch, Yves had to agree that "speak white in Toronto," if it had been true, was certainly not true now.

white-ash breeze *Obs.* of canoes, boats, etc., propulsion by means of paddles or oars, as opposed to wind-filled sails.
1853 STRICKLAND *Canada West* I 272: We must raise a white-ash-breeze (meaning that we must have recourse to our paddles) or we shall not see the Nine-Mile Creek this day, I can tell you. **1854** KEEFER *Ottawa* 47: [They] bring her [a steamboat] alongside the island and transfer passengers and freight into flat bottomed boats—to the slow but certain influence of a "white ash" breeze.

whiteback *n. Nfld* See **whitecoat.**
1901 *Canadian Mag.* Jan. 196/1: The young Harps or "Whitebacks" are covered with an unspotted soft fur, only less white than the snow on which they lie.

white bass See 1963 quote.
1821 (1900) GARRY *Diary* 134: ... the river [is] full of Cat-fish and White basse. **1872** DASHWOOD *Chiploquorgan* 81: There are numbers of white bass and sturgeon in many of the large rivers. **1963** *Globe and Mail* (Toronto) 3 Aug. 21/1: The proper name of this fish is white bass (Lepibema chrysops) and though the average caught weighs less than a pound, weights up to three pounds are not uncommon. As the name indicates this fish is silver in color, the back dark green or grey,

the belly white. The eyes are tinted with yellow and five to seven horizontal dark stripes mark the flanks.

white bear 1 a polar bear.
1600 (1889) HAKLUYT *Voyages* XII 24: The soile is barren in some places, and yeeldeth litle fruit, but it is full of white beares, and stagges farre greater than ours. **1717** (1932) KNIGHT *Journals* 145: Wee See the White Bear as broke our Netts. **1823** *Canadian Mag.* I 394: The great white bear takes refuge in the most icy climates, and lives where scarcely any other animal can find substance. **1953** MOWERY *Mounted Police* 149: [He had] several livid weals across his left cheek where a white bear once had clawed him.

2 *Now Rare or Obs.* a light-gray color phase of the grizzly bear, *q.v.*
1791 LONG *Voyages* 95: The large white bear commonly called the grizly bear, is a very dangerous animal. **1921** HEMING *Drama of Forests* 309: As long as there's danger o' white bears bein' round you'll never again find Old Billy Brass tryin' to sleep beside a big fire. **1952** (1954) JENNINGS *Strange Brigade* 105: There were also red deer or *biche,* and white bears and white partridges, or ptarmigan, which were very fine eating but not so plentiful as other kinds.

3 See **Kermode bear** (def. 2).
1964 *Wildlife Rev.* Dec. 20: [Caption] This is the only British Columbia white bear ever kept in captivity. **1966** *B.C. Digest* Dec. 20/2: The white bear had disappeared by the time we got there. ...

white birch† **1 a.** a species of birch, *Betula papyrifera,* found in many parts of Canada. See also **canoe birch** and **paper birch.**
1793 (1801) MACKENZIE *Voyages* 179: The trees are spruce, red-pine, cypress, poplar, white birch. ... **1863** WALSHE *Cedar Creek* 253: One woman was stripping a large white birch of its bark with a sharp knife. ... **1966** *Kingston Whig-Standard* (Ont.) 26 Jan. 4/3: The white birch is a lady of the forest ... always dignified and serene.

b the heavy, straight-grained wood of this tree.
1774 ROBINSON & RISPIN *Journey N.S.* 34: This town ... affords great store of fine timber ... birch, white yellow and black. ... **1908** NICHOLSON *In Old Quebec* 29: The principal kinds of timber are spruce, balsam, fir, white birch, cypress and pine.

2 See **wire birch.**
1853 REID *Young Voyageurs* 134: [The] "white birch" (*B. populifolia*) [is] a worthless tree of some twenty feet in height, and less than six inches in diameter. The bark of this species is useless. ... **1956** *Native Trees* 138: Wire Birch [is also called] white birch. ...

white bird 1 See **snow bunting.**
1760 JEFFERYS *Descr. New France* 39: The best musician of all the Canadian groves, is a sort of ortolan, the plumage of which is of an ash-colour on the back and white on the belly, whence it is called the white-bird. ... **1959** MCATEE *Folk-Names* 67: Snow Bunting [is also called] white bird ("Labr.") ... *Oiseau blanc* (White bird. Que.). ...

2 See **willow ptarmigan.**
1939 *Beaver* June 46/2: The "white birds" ... as the Indians call them, were seen at each thicket of willows. ... **1959** MCATEE *Folk-Names* 25: Willow Ptarmigan [is also called] white bird (Ont., "N.W.T."). ...

white buffalo 1 an albino buffalo.

1793 (1889) MACDONELL *Journal* 285: The men were in chace of a white Buffalo all day but could not get within shot of him. **1800** (1897) COUES *New Light* I 159: White buffalo are very scarce. **1953** MOWERY *Mounted Police* 117: Against the far wall of the teepee the Sioux chieftain was sitting on a white buffalo robe. . . .

2 *Obs.* See **Dall sheep.**

1789 (1801) MACKENZIE *Voy. from Montreal* 40: Our conductor informed us that great numbers of bears, and small white buffaloes, frequent those mountains, which are also inhabited by Indians.

whitecaps *n. pl. Obs.* See quote.

1902 (1957) GUILLET *Valley of the Trent* 271: In the rank condition in which wheat grew in those days [1830's] the flail left great quantities of chaff known as "whitecaps" and which was objected to by the wheat buyers.

white carp *Obs.* the carp sucker, *Carpiodes carpio.*

1784 PENNANT *Arctic Zoology* cxcii: The *Cyprinus Catastomus* of Dr. *Forster,* or *Sucker Carp,* is a new specie: of which there are two varieties, the *Mitheo-Mapeth* of the Indians, marked with a broad stripe of red along the lateral line, and found on the sea coast, and the White [carp], or *Namapeth,* with larger scales, and wholly of a whitish color: very scarce in the salt water, but in such plenty in the inland lakes and rivers, as to be even burdensome to the nets. **1789** (1801) MACKENZIE *Voy. from Montreal* xli: There are trouts of three kinds . . . sturgeon, pickerel, pike, red and white carp. . . .

white cedar† a species of cedar, *Thuja occidentalis,* found from southern Manitoba eastward; also, the soft, brittle wood of this tree.

1760 PICHON *Cape Breton* 84: There are two kinds of cedar trees, white and red; the white is the largest, and serves to make shingles. . . . **1864** *Cdn Naturalist* II 330: This building, made of squared timbers of white cedar . . . placed upon each other was in good preservation. **1966** *Kingston Whig-Standard* (Ont.) 6 Feb. 4/6: White birch, white cedar . . . and a half a dozen other tree species had their special uses.

white coal water used to generate hydro-electric power; also, the power so generated.

1885 *Neepawa Star* (Man.) 21 Aug. 2/1: Nor should those intrusted with the people's money, committed to their care in confidence for judicious expenditure for the public good, embezzle, in any way, the least portion of that money, under colour of black coal or white coal, ditch contracts, or any other pretext whatever. **1954** *Fundy Fisherman* 3 Mar. 4/4: Here is Ontario screaming about power shortage. But Monsieur Maurice [Duplessis] always has a measure or so of "white coal" to peddle.

whitecoat *n. Esp. Nfld* a young harp seal, *q.v.,* so called because of its furry, white coat. See also **whiteback** and **white harp.** Cp. **beater.**

1778 (1792) CARTWRIGHT *Journal* II 300: He afterwards crossed the island to Sandwich Tickle, where he saw abundance of harps, and two whitecoats. **1876** *North Star* (St. John's) 15 Apr. 2/6: The writer took eighty "white coats" on the 22d, averaging 47 lbs. each. **1966** *Globe and Mail* (Toronto) 9 Mar. 3/5: About 500 men swarmed through the herds . . . killing and skinning the 4-day-old whitecoats.

white crane See **whooping crane.**

1743 (1949) ISHAM *Observations* 125: Browne crains are but small in comparison to a white Craine, which is Very Large, some being 10 foot and ½ high from the claw to the Bill. . . . **1852** RICHARDSON *Arctic Exped.* 61: Very rarely during the summer a flock of white cranes passes over Fort Simpson, in latitude 62° N. **1877** GRANT *Ocean to Ocean* 127: On our way to dinner, two large white cranes rose swanlike from a wet marsh near the road. **1911** (1955) MCCOWAN *Upland Trails* 21: Ernest Thompson Seton, while camping at Lake Chipewyan as early as 1911, mentions hearing "the glorious trumpeting of the White crane," adding "It has less rattling croak and more whoop than that of the Brown crane."

White Dall sheep See **Dall sheep.**

1957 *Yukon* 24: The world's record White Dall sheep and Canada's all-time finest moose trophy were taken in the Yukon. **1966** *Commercial Letter* Jan.-Feb. 6/1: The Yukon big game season . . . enables the licence holder to take one of such big game as moose, caribou, White Dahl or Stone sheep, mountain goat or grizzly bear.

White Eskimo See **blond Eskimo.**

1928 FREEMAN *Nearing North* 176: It was he who brought out the first story of the so-called "White Eskimo" of Victoria Island.

White Fathers See quote.

1902 (1957) *Sask. Hist.* X 2 59: It was in charge of two Fathers of the Canons of the Immaculate Conception, usually called the "White Fathers" in this part of the country.

White Fife See **White Fyfe.**

whitefish *n.* a widely distributed North American food fish, *Coregonus* sp., especially *C. clupeaformis.* See also **atikameg, herring salmon, tickameg, titimeg,** and **white,** *n.* (def. 2).

1744 DOBBS *Hudson's Bay* 62: Here is a great Fishery for white Fish, the richest and best Fish in the World, being so luscious that all Sauce spoils it. **1872** DASHWOOD *Chiploquorgan* 41: In this stream we speared some white-fish, a species peculiar to North America, and excellent eating. . . . **1965** *Globe and Mail* (Toronto) 14 Jan. W10/5: These unwanted species clutter the lakes . . . affecting the highly regarded whitefish and lake trout.

white-flesher *n.* See **ruffed grouse.**

1827 (1914) DOUGLAS *Journal* 265: [I] killed a pair of White Fleshers and a hen of a different species. **1857** (1863) PALLISER *Journals* 64: This afternoon we shot several of the *ruffed grouse,* which is called here the white flesher; its meat being as white as the breast of a fowl, while that of all the other grouse in the country is dark. **1956** MCATEE *Folk-Names* 24: Ruffed grouse [is also called] . . . white-flesher ("Keewatin," B.C.). . . .

white fox 1 See **Arctic fox.**

1696 (1929) KELSEY *Papers* 54: "3 indians came to the fort one of which was the french Captain they brought nothing but 2 white fox skins." **1749** DRAGE *Voyage* II 16: In the Beginning of the Month, the white Foxes began to appear in great Plenty; and many of them were catched. **1862** *Cdn Naturalist* May 138: White Foxes have been killed on the south shore of Great Slave Lake, and a single blue one on the North shore. **1963** *Kingston Whig-Standard* (Ont.) 25 Apr. 14/6: Eskimos trap white foxes, but he said he had received word that at one point only four foxes had been taken. . . .

2 the commercially valuable fur of this fox.
1784 (1954) *Moose Ft Jnls* 28: Recd. one white Fox the first I have got this year.... **1820** (1823) FRANKLIN *Journey* 83: A silver fox, white fox, or otter, are reckoned two beavers and a black fox, or large black bear are equal to four. **1964** *Calgary Herald* 22 July 17/6:... the price of white fox has risen to $25 from $10 in the 1950's.

white-fox economy *North* an artificial economic pattern of Eskimo life dominated by the drive to supply the demand for the fur of the Arctic fox.
1965 SYMINGTON *Tuktu* 70: When the white man came the "white fox economy" began to govern the seasonal movements of most coastal Eskimos.

white-front *n.* See **white-fronted goose.**
1959 MCATEE *Folk-Names* 9: White-fronted Goose [is sometimes called] white-front (There is a white patch about the base of the bill. Alta.).

white-fronted goose a grayish-brown goose, *Anser albifrons,* having a white face and a black-blotched breast and breeding in the Canadian Arctic. See also **gray goose** (def. 2), **gray wavey,** and **laughing goose.**
1908 MAIR *Mackenzie Basin* 321: American white fronted goose ... This fine goose is fairly abundant some seasons at Fort Chipewyan.... **1939** *Beaver* Mar. 18/1: Also to be found in the goose flocks are Canada Geese, White Fronted Geese and other less well known species such as the Ross Goose. **1959** [see quote at **white-front**].

White Fyfe (wheat) a strain of fast-ripening wheat formerly in wide use in Canada. Cp. **Red Fife.**
1883 *Moose Jaw News* (Sask.) 2 Nov. 4/3: The wonderful report from the Roman Catholic Mission at Edmonton which appeared in our columns over a week ago, stating that four acres of white Fyfe wheat had actually yielded the enormous quantity of 91¼ bushels to the acre, has been confirmed. **1888** *Trans.Roy.Soc. Can.* VI 4 75: Under the exceptional conditions named all the variations sown ripened prematurely, Red Fyfe and White Russian in 84 days, and White Fyfe in 83 days.

white goose See **snow goose.**
1779 (1792) CARTWRIGHT *Journal* II 452: He also told me, that they had met with white-geese.... **1850** (1910) BURPEE *Yukon* 11: White geese are also passengers here, and there are like-wise black geese.... **1959** MCATEE *Folk-Names* 9: Lesser Snow Goose [is also called] white goose (general)....

white governor *Fur Trade, Obs.* See 1828 quote.
1828 (1872) MCDONALD *Peace River* 3: White Governor [is] a *soubriquet* of the man at the head of a boat brigade. **1830** (1921) *Beaver* Apr. 11/2: The White Governor arrived with two boats of MacKenzie River.... **1834** (1947) HARGRAVE *Correspondence* 171: Our living is good; the white Governor having knocked over a few Deer, and I killed an Ox....

white grouse† See **white partridge.**
1823 FRANKLIN *Journey* 681: The White Grouse of the countries round Hudson's Bay, are inhabitants of the plains, where bushes of willows abound, on the buds of which they support themselves. **1929** *Beaver* Dec. 305: ... the white grouse is another useful addition to the larder.... **1959** MCATEE *Folk-Names* 25: Rock Ptarmigan [is also called] white grouse ("Hudson Bay"). *Ibid.*: Willow Ptarmigan [is also called] white grouse ("Hudson Bay," B.C.)....

white hare See **Arctic hare.**
1938 GODSELL *Red Hunters* 40: The dull boom of seven cannon reverberated through the dead air of the Barrens, startling the white hares and Arctic foxes.

white harp *Nfld* See **whitecoat.**
1923 PRATT *Nfld Verse* 20: In the stretch of that field— "white harps" to spare / For a dozen such fleets....

white-head *n.* See **bald eagle.**
1853 REID *Young Voyageurs* 421: [The] golden eagle ... does not migrate, like its congeners the "white-head" and the osprey, to more southern regions.

white-headed eagle See **bald eagle.** See also **white-tailed eagle.**
1793 (1801) MACKENZIE *Voy.from Montreal* 341: The white-headed eagle ... is common in the interior parts. **1908** MAIR *Mackenzie Basin* 361: The white-headed eagle is noted as "common to the Arctic coast" by Mr. Ross. **1956** MCATEE *Folk-Names* 22: Bald Eagle [is also called] ... white-headed eagle (Rather general).

white heather a shrub, *Cassiope tetragona,* having mosslike foliage and found in the Arctic regions.
1936 *Beaver* Mar. 37/1: On caribou hunting expeditions into the interior, the Eskimo relies on certain forms of vegetation for fire, of which the commonest is the white heather ... called by the Eskimos "Keyukta." **1952** PUTNAM *Cdn Regions* 23/1: On the upland north of Great Bear Lake ... are found ground birch ... Labrador tea ... white heather....

white Indian See **good Indian.** See also **white,** *adj.* (def. 2a).
1918 LOWREY *Young Canada Boys* 98: " ... gar, he wuz a white Injun an' thet loyal yuh couldn't look crossey'd ut the old Union Jack when he wuz around.... "

white kloochman *Pacific Coast* See **white squaw.** Cp. **kloochman** (def. 1).
1859 *Brit.Colonist* (Victoria) 13 July 3/2: A novel case was presented in court this morning by the appearance of something wrapped up in a blanket gliding into court, which on being unwrapped turned out to be the celebrated white klootchman. **1958** *Wildlife Rev.* Apr. 3/2: Andy Paull, president of the North American Indian Brotherhood, said "White Kloochmen knit poor sweaters.... "

white man† **1** a person of non-Indian blood, especially a European or one of European origins. See also **white,** *n.* (def. 1).
1802 (1935) STRANG *Pioneers in Can.* 180: It is, however, imprudent for us to venture thus far without fire-arms, for every white man, when in a savage country ought at all times to be well armed. **1840** *Bytown* [Ottawa] *Gaz.* 20 Feb. 1/5: When the white man came into our country our forefathers took him by the hand, and gave him land on which to pitch his wigwam. **1965** *Kingston Whig-Standard* (Ont.) 22 Feb. 7/2: Residents of Tyendinaga reserve still use the term "white man" when referring to his neighbors off the reserves. To the department, "non-Indian" is the phrase preferred.
2 a man of honest, loyal behavior; a good man. See also **white,** *adj.* (def. 2a).
1892 PARKER *Pierre* 244: Shon had won the reputation of being a "white man," to say nothing of his victories

in the region of gallantry. **1923** STEELE *Spirit-of-Iron* 115: "God, you're a white man, Mr. Adair," declared the gambler, as they parted. . . .

3 *Slang* a white, English-speaking Canadian, especially as opposed to an immigrant from central Europe, the Orient, etc. See also **white,** *adj.* (def. 2b).

1900 *Lardeau Eagle* (B.C.) 28 Mar. 1/3: Good miners and machine men can find work in any white man's mining camp. . . . **1953** LOWER *Voyages* 17: With him, the "white men" ate; afterwards the "bohunks" could go in if they wished.

white maple 1 the mountain maple, *Acer spicatum,* found in Canada from Saskatchewan eastward to Newfoundland.

1774 (1945) ROBINSON & RISPIN *Journey N.S.* 34: This town . . . affords a great store of fine timber . . . white and black ash; white mapple; rock mapple (a very fine wood for household furniture). . . . **1861** SUTHERLAND *Geography P.E.I.* 58: Acerines or Maples, include . . . the White Maple, whose wood is soft and little esteemed; and the Striped Maple or Moose Wood. **1959** *Native Trees* 242: Mountain maple [is also called] white maple, dwarf maple.

2 the silver maple, *Acer saccharinum.*

1899 PENHALLOW *Herbacious Plants* 52: White or Silver. Maple. Leaves very deeply 5-lobed with the sinuses rather acute, silver-white (and when young downy) underneath. . . . River banks; N.B., Q. and Ont.; most common southward and westward. **1959** *Native Trees* 258: Silver maple [is also called] white maple. . . .

white mother *Hist.* in Indian parlance, the Queen of England; specifically Queen Victoria.

1876 (1877) ST. JOHN *Sea of Mountains* I 321: I hope that you will understand that your white mother and the Government of Canada are fully prepared to protect you in the exercise of your religion. . . . **1919** FRASER *Bulldog Carney* 289: " . . . They'll obey the Police generally, because they know the 'Redcoat' is an agent of the Queen, the White Mother who feeds them; but, being drunk, the young bucks will be hostile."

white-out *n.* **1** *Esp.Arctic* a meteorological phenomenon in which the light from a cloudy sky is balanced by that reflected off the snow on the ground, resulting in a dazzling whiteness and the neutralization of all significant features of the landscape, including shadows and the horizon. Cp. **gray-out.**

1958 *Evening Telegram* (St. John's) 26 Apr. 23/1: There is no sense of direction during a "white-out," as the compass is not effective in that part of the Arctic. **1965** *Dly Colonist* (Victoria) 9 Jan. 1/3: . . . Gibson flew into a "white-out"—a condition existing in snow or haze when no horizon can be seen. . . .

2 *North* See quote.

1965 SYMINGTON *Tuktu* 20: Even more dangerous to aviators [than grey-out] is the white-out that occurs when the whole landscape is obscured by mist or drifting snow, and visibility drops to yards, sometimes very suddenly.

white owl See **snowy owl.**

1743 (1949) ISHAM *Observations* 23: a White owl wap pa ho *or* wap pa cullu. **1864** *Nor'Wester* (R.R.S.) 18 Feb. 3/3: He also referred to the white snow birds . . .

and the white owls, which were to be seen in great quantities. . . . **1953** MOWERY *Mounted Police* 81: A white owl brushing over his head brought him to his feet with an oath.

white partridge a rock or willow ptarmigan, *qq.v.,* in winter plumage. See also **white grouse.**

1684 (1885) RADISSON *Voyages* 272: Our men repair'd this Losse, having kill'd some more Deere and 4,000 white Partridges, somewhat bigger than those of Europe. **1748** ELLIS *Hudson's Bay* 37: The white Partridge is of a middle Size, between our common Partridge and the Pheasant, shaped much like the former, except that its Tail is somewhat longer. **1843** (1955) LEFROY *Magnetic North* 69: The white partridges and pheasants are so tame that I have shot them close to the fort. . . . **1952** (1954) JENNINGS *Strange Brigade* 105: There were also . . . white partridges, or ptarmigan, which were very fine eating but not so plentiful as other kinds.

white pike *Obs.* See **northern pike.**

1898 JENNINGS *Routes to Yukon* 14: I learned that Teslin Lake . . . is well stocked with trout, white ("Dagolly") pike, and "Inconnu" fish, of which I had evidence when there.

white pine† **1 a.** a tall, stately pine, *Pinus strobus,* of eastern Canada, much used for shipmasts in colonial days and providing the basis for the lumber industry. See also **buckwheat pine, pumpkin pine, Quebec pine,** and **Weymouth pine.**

1767 *Quebec Gaz.* 8 Dec. 3/1: They are hereby forbid to cut down . . . White Pine . . . on the lands above described. **1853** STRICKLAND *Canada West* I 257: Generally speaking, the white or American pine, from its vast length of trunk, contains a larger number of cubic feet than any other tree in the Canadian forest. **1966** *Kingston Whig-Standard* (Ont.) 6 Feb. 4/6: But the white pine, tallest and stateliest of all the trees in Ontario, was held the most worthy of worship.

b. the light, soft wood of this tree.

1828 *Brockville Gaz.* (U.C.) 19 Sep. 3/4: Wanted, 500 Cords Hemlock Tamarac, or Dry white Pine Wood. **1947** SAUNDERS *Algonquin* 61: He would have to make his own [shingles] with a drawknife and some chunks of "corky" white pine. . . .

2 See **lodgepole pine.**

1894 *Trans.Roy.Soc.Can.* XI 4 13: Ascending the slope on the west side of the valley we come at once into a belt of the western hemlock and white pine which is characteristic of all the mountains from here to the Coast Range. **1956** *Native Trees* 24: Lodgepole Pine [is also called] white pine. . . .

3 *Lumbering* the western white pine, *q.v.,* especially with reference to its wood.

1959 *Native Trees* 8: Western white pine [is also called] white pine. . . . **1966** *B.C.Forest Industries* J10: SPECIES CUT, ALL PRODUCTS, 1964, CONVERTED TO F.B.M. . . . Totals, Coast . . . White Pine 3,717,638.

white poplar† a species of poplar, *Populus tremuloides,* found throughout Canada; trembling aspen. See also **whitewood** (def. 1).

1908 MAIR *Mackenzie Basin* 81: It was well timbered, in some places, with the finest white poplar I had yet seen. **1954** EVANS *Mist* 19: At home there was the wide and sunny freedom of his valley, with birches and white poplars between the belts of jackpine.

white sheep 1 See **Rocky Mountain goat.**

1825 (1948) MCLOUGHLIN *Letters* 21: I have taken the liberty of sending a few Curiosities collected . . . along the Coast. Among them you will find two Skins of what our people call the White Sheep of the Rocky Mountains, but it resembles more a Goat with Black Horns. **1888** PHILLIPPS-WOLLEY *Sportsman's Eden* 133: English sportsmen call it the Rocky Mountain goat; natives in the cascades call it "the white sheep"; naturalists. . . call it an antelope. . . .

2 See Dall sheep.
1958 CAMERON *Cdn Mammals* 26: The white or "Dall" sheep occur in northern British Columbia, the Yukon and Northwest Territories. . . . **1954** PATTERSON *Dangerous River* 195: So the river was useless to us, and over . . . on the north bank and up Trowel Tail's Creek, the beavers could proceed with their logging, and the white sheep could come down to their licks unmolested.

white spring (salmon) *Pacific Coast* a spring salmon, *q.v.*, having white flesh. See also **white**, *n.* (def. 3).
1869 *Mainland Guardian* (New Westminster, B.C.) 25 Sep. 2/1: There is also a white Spring Salmon, known by the name Pocke, used principally fresh for home consumption. **1958** *Fisherman* 10 Oct. 7/4: The fisherman knew how long he could fish sockeye, then he could take in the chum salmon run in September, also the white springs.

white spruce a species of spruce, *Picea glauca,* found from the Rockies to Newfoundland, much used for pulpwood and lumber. See also **cat spruce.**
1770 (1792) CARTWRIGHT *Journal* I 30: About four miles above, are several small low islands, on which grow many fine white, and black spruces. **1852** RICHARDSON *Arctic Exped.* 415: On the borders of Great Bear Lake, four hundred years are required to bring the stem of the white spruce to the thickness of a man's waist. **1962** *Forest Conservation* 27/2: [There are] minor quantities of balsam fir, white spruce, and Norway spruce.

white squaw *Obs.* a white woman. See also **white kloochman.**
1785 (1943) HUNTER *Diary* 55: We saw several white children and handsome white squaws. **1888** (1890) ST. MAUR *Impressions* 183: He had only come to have a look at us on the way down the trail, "white squaws" being still a curiosity in the Kootenay valley.

whitetail† *n.* See **whitetail deer.**
1875 (1888) MCDOUGALL *G.M.McDougall* 220: . . . the Stoney hunts the wild goat, and the big horned sheep, the black tail, the white tail, and the graceful antelope. **1964** *Globe and Mail* (Toronto) 12 Dec. 8/9: Until current studies give a reasonably accurate estimate of the number of whitetails in New Brunswick . . . it is impossible to say whether worried sportsmen . . . are right. **1966** *Ibid.* 7 May 41/2: At the same time a count in March indicated an average of 32 surviving calf elk, a 100 cows, 48 mule deer fawns, a 100 does, and 40 whitetail fawns, a 100 does.

whitetail(ed) deer the Virginia deer, *Odocoileus virginianus.* See also **red deer** (def. 1) and **whitetail.**
1887 *Senate Jnl* XXI App. 85: There is just the black tailed deer, the white tailed deer, and the antelope. . . . **1963** *Globe and Mail* (Toronto) 9 Feb. 28/4: A whitetail deer has a life expectancy of 16 years under favorable conditions, but few last that long.

white-tailed eagle *Obs.* See **white-headed eagle.**
1748 ELLIS *Hudson's Bay* 39: There are likewise in this Country some very curious Birds, with respect to their Size and Strength; such as *White Tailed Eagles,* about the Bigness of a Turkey-Cock. [**1821** (1900) GARRY *Diary* 127: We met at every moment the White-headed Eagle with a white Tail.]

whitetailed ptarmigan a ptarmigan, *Lagopus leucurus,* native to the mountainous areas of the West and Northwest.
1852 RICHARDSON *Arctic Exped.* 112: The willow and white-tailed ptarmigans bear the designation of *Kasbah* or *Kampbah,* in the Slave or Chepewyan tongue. **1950** STANWELL-FLETCHER *Driftwood Valley* 320: Above the last clumps of bushes, in the open rocky meadows, are the flocks of white-tailed ptarmigan and the little larks. **1959** MCATEE *Folk-Names* 25: White-tailed Ptarmigan [is also called] Rock ptarmigan (B.C.).

white trillium any of several trilliums having a flower resembling a lily, especially *Trillium grandiflorum,* the floral emblem of Ontario. See also **trillium.**
1952 PUTNAM *Cdn Regions* 26/2: A few of the common species are . . . baneberry . . . white trillium. . . . **1958** *Weekend Mag.* 7 June 39: White trillium of Ontario is also known as wake robin. It blooms in April and May, and its flowers usually all face the same way. **1961** *Telegram* (Toronto) 19 May 17/1: White trilliums are at the peak of their blooming.

white trout See **lake trout.**
1744 DOBBS *Hudson's Bay* 52: They have Pike, Trout, perch, and white Trout in great Perfection in all their Rivers. **1831** *Trans.Lit.Hist.Soc.Que.* II 292: The most noted fish is called the white trout, which is caught in abundance . . . frequently forty pounds in weight. It is of a light silver hue, and cream coloured in the flesh, but in shape and flavor resembles the common speckled trout, which is also plentiful in the same water. **1947** SAUNDERS *Algonquin* 19: . . . the white or lake trout he learned could be caught in great abundance both in the winter and in the summer.

whitewashed American *Slang* See quote.
1926 DILL *Long Day* 147: This particular story concerns a "white-washed American," *i.e.,* a native of Canada who had been naturalized in the United States and then secured repatriation in his own country.

white-water man 1 an expert at handling a canoe in rapids and riffles (def. 1b).
1921 HEMING *Drama of Forests* 298: . . . Oo-koo-hoo, the famous white-water-man . . . actually did keep the bow of that canoe ahead of all others—no matter where or when the other crews contested for the honour of leading the Fur Brigade. **1931** GREY OWL *Last Frontier* 70: They are the "white water men," to whom the thunderous roar of rapids, and the smell of spray flying in the face, are as the intoxication of strong drink. **1956** EVANS *Mountain Dog* 45: Had he lost the sure judgment a white-water man must have?

2† *Lumbering* See **driver** (def. 1).
1958 *Evening Telegram* (St. John's) 28 Apr. 5/5: "Watch her haul" is the ringing yell of white water men as they pry loose the piles of winter piled wood. . . .

white wavey a white goose, such as the snow goose, *q.v.,* or the lesser snow goose, *Chen hyporborea hyperborea.* See also **greater snow goose, lesser snow goose,** and **wavey.**
[**1781-1801** (1959) MCATEE *Folk-Names* 9: Lesser Snow Goose . . . white way-way ("Hudson Bay." Latham 1781-1801).] **1882** *Trans.Roy.Soc.Can.* I 4 51: They do not associate either with the large blue or white wavies. **1932** SUTTON *Southampton Is.* 11: He found great

numbers of swans nesting at Cape Low [1902] . . . and during the fall of that year saw quantities of white and blue wavies. **1959** MCATEE *Folk-Names* 9: Lesser Snow Goose [is also called] White Wavey. . . .

white whale the beluga, *Delphinapterus leucas,* of the North Atlantic and Arctic Oceans. See also **porpoise.**
1688 (1932) KENNEY *Ft Churchill* 18: That Churchill River Bee Settled this yeare with a Good Shipp a Competent Cargo for Trade and Materials for White Whale ffishings. **1784** PENNANT *Arctic Zoology* cxc: The fishery of the Beluga, or White Whale, is attended with more success. **1826** *U.E.Loyalist* (York [Toronto]) 2 Dec. 213/3: They had a wide prospect of salt water free from ice, and abounding in seals and white whale. **1964** JENNESS *Eskimo Admin.* II 7: Even Churchill came within their [Eskimos'] summer range; right down to the end of the seventeenth century they journeyed there to hunt the white whales off its river mouth. . . .

white whisky See **whisky blanc.**
1901 PARKER *Right of Way* 23: Rouge Gosselin flung off his glass of white whisky, and threw after it another glass of cold water. **1897** PARKER *Pierre* 156: He was lodging with Louis Charron, a small farmer . . . who sold whisky—"white whisky"—without a license.

white whisky-john *Rare* the northern shrike, *Lanus borealis.* Cp. **whisky-john.**
1823 FRANKLIN *Journey* 674: Lanus excubitor, from its baring a general resemblance in plumage to the Canada Jay, it has obtained among the settlers round Hudson's Bay the name of White Whisky-John. **1959** MCATEE *Folk-Names* 57: Northern Shrike [is also called] white whiskijohn (From its paler colour and slight similarity to the grey jay or whiskey-john. "Hudson Bay").

white-wing *n.* **1** *N.S.* the willet, *Catoptrophorus semipalmatus.*
1950 BIRD *This is N.S.* 121: From May to August visitors to Chebogue see those large showy shore birds, the "Willets," locally known as "white-wings," and it is said that Yarmouth is the only place in the east where these rare birds may be seen. **1956** MCATEE *Folk-Names* 31: [The] Willet [is also called] . . . white-wing (When lifted, the wings have a percurrent white band bordered on each side by blackish, N.S.).
2 *Prairies* the lark bunting, *Calamospiza melanocorys.*
1963 SYMONS *Many Trails* 30: . . . they began to see birds which were strange to them—small black ones with white wing patches, which the children at once called white wings, not knowing that they were lark buntings.

white-winged crossbill† a crossbill, *Loxia leucoptera,* of eastern North America.
1908 MAIR *Mackenzie Basin* 400: White-winged cross bill. **1956** MCATEE *Folk-Names* 63: White-winged Crossbill [is also called] spruce bird (As feeding on the seeds of that tree. Nfld.). **1966** *Weekend Mag.* 8 Oct. 24: [Caption] White-winged Crossbill . . . One of the finch family. Crossed bill lets them open evergreen cones.

white wolf a white color phase of the common wolf, *Canis lupus.*
1821 (1823) FRANKLIN *Journey* II 50: We saw . . . a number of deer, and, occasionally, a solitary white wolf. . . . **1853** REID *Young Voyageurs* 416: It was also

of a snow-white colour, with long hair, bushy tail, and short erect ears, but its aspect was not to be mistaken. It was the great *white wolf.*
1855 (1956) ROSS *Fur Hunters* 50: The white wolf skin in season is esteemed an article of royalty; it is one of the chief honours of the chieftainship and much used by these people in their religious ceremonies, and the kind of wolves are not numerous. **1892** DAUNT *Land of the Moose* 92: "Wal, I follered that buffler like a white wolf. I wur determined to hev that buffler, boys, and so I glued myself to his tail, an tore arter him. . . ."

whitewood *n.* **1**† any of several poplars, as Balm of Gilead and white poplar, *qq.v.*
1760 JEFFERYS *Descr.New France* 41: White-wood, a species of the poplar which grows among maples, and the bitter cherry tree, are very plentiful. **1860** *Nor'Wester* (R.R.S.) 17 Dec. 3/1: Portage la Prairie was once famous for white wood, but now it would be with the greatest difficulty that a sufficient quantity of logs could be obtained to give even one hundred sound boards. **1905** (1954) *B.C.Hist.Qtly* XVIII 183: As an ungent for scratches and sores, they [the Indians] know the value of a decoction of the gum-laden buds of the whitewood, or "Balm of Gilead poplar," mixed with deer fat in proper proportion.

2 See **basswood.**
1852 RICHARDSON *Arctic Exped.* 422: . . . white-wood, or bass-wood, is a familiar ornamental and useful tree in the United States and Canada. **1956** *Native Trees* 264: Basswood [is also called] whitewood.

3 *West Coast* See quote.
1965 *Cdn Forest Industries* July 8/3: The latest mission from Canada to the U.K. was that on western white spruce [Picea glauca]. The demand for whitewood has sparked off a greater interest in this species from the B.C. Interior.

whiting *n. Lab., Obs.* See 1792 quote.
1792 CARTWRIGHT *Journal* II x: Whitings [are] Trees which have been barked and left standing. **1836** WIX *Journal* 60: Even the sight of a "whiting" in the woods, that is, of a tree stripped of its bark for the uses of the fishery . . . seem to remind the lone traveller of the link which binds him to the rest of his species.

whole beaver *Fur Trade, Obs.* the skin of a full-grown four-year-old beaver; hence, a unit of value based on such a skin. See also **made beaver** and **skin** (def. 1).
1743 (1949) ISHAM *Observations* 147: [Beaver] are four years before they Come to the full growth, Distinguished by Whole, ¾, ½ and ¼ beaver. . . . **1802** (1897) COUES *New Light* I 195: Crow . . . came down Tongue river with 36 whole beavers in a skin canoe. **1821** (1964) INNIS *Fur Trade* 319: Beaver, whole or full grown 30 = 30 Whole Beaver. . . .

whooper† *n.* See **whooping crane.**
1955 *News of the North* 18 Nov. 5/3: This year it was twins in the whooping crane families of Canada—two sets—six little whoopers in all. **1963** *Vancouver Province* 15 Feb. 4/1: And the future of the whooper again hangs in the balance.

whooping crane† a species of crane, *Grus americana,* which nests in western Canada. See also **white crane** and **whooper.**
1795 (1911) HEARNE *Journey* 422: Hooping Crane. This bird visits Hudson's Bay in the Spring, though not in great numbers. **1961** *Cdn Geog.Jnl* Jan. 6/1: Another

feature within [Wood Buffalo Park] is the nesting ground of the almost extinct whooping crane.

whoop-up *n.* [from the verbal phrase *whoop* (*it*) *up*, enjoy oneself in a boisterous way] *Esp.West* a noisy party or other celebration.
1913 COWIE *Adventurers* 319: As soon as the general "whoop-up" began, all the traders . . . packed up their outfits snugly and retired. . . . **1953** CUSHMAN *Stay Away Joe* 22: "Ain't you going to have no dance, no rodeo, whoop-up?" **1964** *Albertan* (Calgary) 7 July 15/1: Welcome . . . to all . . . who've [made] it to our annual whoop-up.

Whoop-up *n. Hist.* Fort Whoop-up, in southern Alberta, principle centre for the illicit whisky trade with the Indians. See also **whisky trader.**
1888 MCDOUGALL *G.M.McDougall* 192: Father . . . travelled . . . from the Cree camps to . . . the mountains in Bow River, south-eastward to Fort Benton, on the Missouri, taking in the famous Whoop-up country by the way. **1927** LONGSTRETH *Silent Force* 46: Fort Whoop-Up had been built by Trader Hamilton for the purpose of whooping-up the interchange of whiskey and buffalo robes and it was the centre of demoralization in a land of tolerance. **1958** BERTON *Klondike* 25: He had built the most famous of the whisky forts on Canadian territory, ruled it like a feudal baron, and dubbed it "Whoop-Up," thereby giving a name to the great block of untamed Indian country that straddled the Montana-Alberta border.

wickiup† ['wɪki,ʌp] *n.* [< Algonk.; cf. Sauk *wikiyap;* cp. Cree *weke* lodge] a rude shelter, as a lean-to, *q.v.*; originally a brush or mat-covered shelter among certain Algonkian Indians. See also **meetchwop.** Cp. **wigwam** (def. 1a).
1897 COUES *New Light* III 1025: Wickiup, now a common name throughout the West, of any rude temporary shelter like a hut or hovel, is said to be from an Algonquian word rendered mikiouaps [error for *wikiouaps*], meaning a conical leather lodge, wigwam, or tepee. **1912** ROE *Whispering Hills* 380: I have not always lived so. Time was when I had my own wickiup, when I lay by my own night-fire and played with the braids of a woman's hair. **1920** STRINGER *Prairie Mother* 39: ". . . . I'd gone kiting off to prairie-ranch and a wickiup with a leaky roof." **1923** GIBBONS *Sourdough Samaritan* 75: "This really won't do," he chided himself as he strode back in the frigid moonlight to his primitive wickiup. **1961** *Camsell Arrow* Summer 30: Don has already told his boys . . . how to build a brush "wickiup" shelter, and even . . . how to make fire without a match.

wickiup roof a roof of brush, bark, reeds, etc. such as might be used on a wickiup (def. 1).
1951 HOBSON *Grass* 163: Above the poles we built a crude bark wickiup roof.

widow-maker *n.* **1** *Esp.Lumbering, Slang* a loose limb, rampike, *q.v.*, or dead tree which is apt to fall and injure somebody.
1965 *Cdn Geog.Jnl* Sep. 88: [Caption] Park rangers . . . get rid of a "widow-maker," a dead stub hung up over the trail.

2 *Hardrock Mining* **drill widow-maker.** See quote.
1964 *Vancouver Times* 3 Nov. 17/6: A miner drilling widowmaker is one so careless that he neglects to use a water attachment on his drill to dampen down quartz dust, thus leaving himself vulnerable to the mining lung disease, silicosis.

wife of the country *Hist.* See **country wife.**
1948 *Beaver* Dec. 9/2: McTavish was soon settled in his new environment with his "wife of the country" . . . and his children.

wig *n.* [see note] *Obs.* See **boss.**
☛ *Although Brit.dial.* wig < *ME* wigge, *a wedge or wedge-shaped cake, has been suggested as the source of this term, it is quite probable that a simple transfer of* wig *(hairpiece) is involved, for the heavy mane of the buffalo extended down over the hump so as to suggest a head and wig.*
1820 (1823) FRANKLIN *Journey* 115: The meat which covers the spinal processes themselves, after the wig is removed, is next in esteem. . . . **1833** TYLER *Progress of Discovery* 354: The hump or wig (of a bison) as it is sometimes called, has a fine grain. . . .

wigwam† ['wɪgwɑm] *n.* [< Algonk.; cf. Abenaki *wīkwām,* Ojibwa *wīkuwān* dwelling, lodge] **1 a.** a kind of dwelling used by Indians from Manitoba to the Atlantic Provinces, characterized by an arched or conical structure of poles covered with hides, bark, rush mats, etc. See also **lodge** (def. 2a) and **skin tent.** Cp. **wickiup.**
1770 (1792) CARTWRIGHT *Journal* I 29: There we found another whigwam which we concluded had been lately inhabited, as we saw the fresh footmarks of the Indians on the sand. **1890** *Cdn Indian* Oct. 23: The Ojebways, Wood Crees and other Bush Indians live in wigwams, the framework made with sticks, with either conical or dome-shaped roofs, covered with long sheets of birch bark sewn together with fibres, and laid on diagonally. **1965** *Globe and Mail* (Toronto) 9 Jan. 2/4: When autumn leaves turned red and brown the Micmacs set up their winter wigwams. . . .

b. See **teepee.**
1875 (1888) MCDOUGALL *G.M.McDougall* 218: Here I met with a deeply interesting people, the Plain Stoney; they had seventy leather wigwams. **1927** LONGSTRETH *Silent Force* 119: The fenceless West, the figured wigwams, the last wide freedom of that land when it was a community of antelope and Indians and the Police were ten years old, can never be quite lost till Russell's pictures fade. **1965** *Maclean's* 24 July 25/2: Before the white man came to Canada, the Indians had no written language beyond the symbols on their totem poles and the sign-and-picture drawings that decorated their wigwams.

c. See **tupek.**
1861 DE BOILIEU *Labrador Life* 216: Our next halt was at an Esquimaux wigwam.

2 a temporary dwelling built by white men in the bush. See also **camp** (def. 1a) and **tent** (def. 1).
1771 (1935) *Cdn Hist.Rev.* XVI 57: The Canadians had 3 wigwaums here in different places all of which appeared to be made in the winter or spring. **1829** MACTAGGART *Three Years* I 244: To know them [shantymen], we must visit their wigwams afar in the depth of the forest. . . . **1849** ALEXANDER *L'Acadie* II 20: [On the ridge-pole] rested at an angle of 45 degrees other poles, and on them were carefully disposed "hemlock feathers," or small branches of the hemlock-pine, broken off and laid like thatch on the sloaping roof of our wigwam. . . . **1939** GROVE *Two Generations* 37: . . . he searched for and found half-rotten poles and planks; and, by leaning them together, he built a cone-

shaped shelter in which they squatted.... The warmth of this wigwam seemed all the more welcome because of its contrast to the weeping wetness of nature outside.

3 *Figurative or transferred uses.*

1836 *Vindicator* (Montreal) 1 Apr. 2/1: Also, the Bills which originated in the Legislative Council, and were sent down to the Assembly, caused no little sensation in the Life Legislative Wigwam. **1844** MARRYAT *Settlers in Can.* 58: "I mean, Miss, that if he don't like company so near him, he must shift and build his wigwam further off." **1846** *Cdn Freeman* (St. Thomas, C.W.) 1 Aug. 2/5: Another Gaol will necesarily have to be built to replace the old wigwam, now in a state of delapidation. **1912** POCOCK *Man in the Open* 9: We'd build her a stand-up wigwam of firewood, so it wouldn't be lost in the snow, we'd tote her grub from the fort, the loads of fish, and the fall salmon. **1956** RADDALL *Wings* 35: [I had] a wigwam of blanket over the electric lamp ... lest my grandmother see the glint beneath the door.

wigwam *v.* See **winter.**
1908 LAUT *Conquest N.W.* I 216: It had been no play, this fur-trade raid, and now Iberville was back from his scouting, having seen with his own eyes that the English fur traders were really wigwamming on the bay.

wigwam shanty *Obs.* See **wigwam** (def. 2).
1829 MACTAGGART *Three Years* I 52: When night drew on, two of the axe-men were sent off to rig the wigwam *shanty* by the side of the swamp.

wigwam village an Indian encampment.
1897 YOUNG *Indian Trail* 43: The great Canadian Pacific Railway ... has not only brought trade to their wigwam villages, but also the missionary with the Bible to their very doors. **1913** CURRAN & CALKINS *Northland* 255: Now, instead of the wigwam village on the field to the west of the Post houses, there were only a few piles of poles and here and there a cache of such articles as would not be required during the winter.

wild-and-woolly† *adj.* characterized by uncouth, untamed behavior.
☛ *The term* **woolly** *has been variously accounted for. One view is that many pioneers wore sheepskin coats with the wool out, thus earning the epithet; another is offered in the 1910 quote below.*
1900 OSBORN *Warders of West* 778: The ... wolfer ... was ... about as rough and tough a customer as one could have hoped *not* to meet anywhere in the wildest and wooliest parts of the west. **1903** (1913) CULLUM *Devil's Keg* 5: Breaking the wild and woolly broncho is thrilling, and he needs no other tonic.... [**1910** FERGUSON *Janey Canuck* 233: The Padre contends that the West is called "woolly" because of our storms, and urges, in defence of his opinion, that in Alaska the winds are called "woollies."] **1914** BICKERSTETH *Open Doors* v: Nearly fifty years ago a young Presbyterian minister, James Robertson, born 1839, swore that, God helping him, he would never allow the Canadian Prairie to become a "wild and woolly West." **1958** LINDSAY *Cariboo Story* 10/1: While the colony on Vancouver Island was law-abiding, the miners ... were a wild and wooly bunch of extroverts.

wild asparagus *Obs.* milkweed, *Asclepias syriaca.*
1792 (1911) SIMCOE *Diary* 140: I send you some seeds of the wild asparagus. It may be eaten when very young; afterwards it becomes poisonous. The milky cotton in the seed vessels is very pretty, and makes excellent pillows and beds. I hope it will grow enough to stuff a muff. **1860** *Trans.Lit.& Hist.Soc.Que.* IV 4 41: In the spring the Habitans bring into town a vegetable called wild Asparagus.

wild cat 1 one of several varieties of lynx, especially the Canada lynx, *q.v.*
1749 DRAGE *Voyage* II 5: Upon the thirty-first, some of the People searching a Rabbet Snare, found only a Part of a Rabbet, the other Part being eat by a wild Cat, whose Track was perceptible in the Snow. **1789** *Quebec Herald* 27 Apr. 201/2: The animal which the ancients called the Lynx, known in Siberia by the name of the Ounce, is only called the WILD CAT in Canada. **1895** PARKER *Adventurer* 165: The cry of wild cats was no new thing to them. **1953** WOODLEY *Bible in Canada* 206: The bank was very steep—I had not gone very far before I met a lynx or wildcat.

2 the flesh of the lynx used as food.
1765 (1875) CAMPBELL *Hist.P.E.I.* 9: Here they live on the ... game which they frequently kill, as hares and partridges, lynxes or wild cats, otters, martins.... **1880** YOUNG *Indian Wigwams* 135: One day as we rose from a rather poor breakfast which consisted principally of a piece of cooked wild cat, Mrs. Young said to me.... **1897** YOUNG *Indian Trail* 139: During the other six months we lived principally upon game, such as— venison, bear's meat, beaver, wild-cat....

3 the fur of the lynx.
1828 *Methodist Mag.* 74: There various furs for caps are found: ... beaver, coon, wild cat....

wild celery 1 an aquatic plant, *Vallisneria spiralis,* having long, ribbonlike leaves; tape grass. Cp. **eel grass.**
1853 REID *Young Voyageurs* 244: The canvass-back ... feeds upon the roots of ... a species of "tape-grass" ... botanically called *"Valisneria,"* after the Italian botanist, Antonio Valisneri.... Its roots are white and succulent, and bear some resemblance to celery—hence the plant is known among duck-hunters as "wild celery." **1962** *Weekend Mag.* 5 May 11/1: Greedily they suck up the wild celery, water lilies and swamp-grass roots. **1957** LEWIS *Buckskin Cookery* I 35: Groups of Indian women gather berries; also wild celery, the roots of rushes, and the inner bark of the poplar—all which they eat raw.

2 See 1925 quote.
1925 ANDERSON *Trees and Shrubs* 128: WILD CELERY. *Lomatium utriculatum, Nutt.* In the very early spring, in fact as soon as the snow is off the ground, the young sprouts ... are sought for amongst the broken rocks on hillsides which constitute the natural habitat of this plant.... It is a good imitation of the cultivated Celery, but becomes rather pungent as it grows old.

wild cherry any of several species of cherry, *Prunus* sp., common in eastern North America; pincherry.
1769 (1931) BROOKE *Emily Montague* 57: ... the wild cherry, of which the woods are full, is equally charming in flower and in fruit.... **1852** RICHARDSON *Arctic Exped.* 425: *C. pennsylvanica,* wild red cherry, the Pasis-so-wey-minan of the Chippeways, and Pasi-a-wey-minan of the Crees. produces a small sour red fruit. **1943** MILLER *Lone Woodsman* 154: The north shore of the pond had sunny and indented banks, where moisture-loving viburnums and wild cherries and the northern hawthorn disputed for sunlight....

wild geranium *West* the cranesbill, *Geranium* sp.
1888 (1890) ST. MAUR *Impressions* 273: It grows in luxuriant clumps of fiery red, and is commonly called wild geranium from its flaming red leaves. **1958** STEGNER *Making Paths* 38: I could . . . see the beaten footpath, leading gray and dusty between grass and cactus and the little orange flowers of the false mallow that we called wild geranium, until it ended, its purpose served, at the hooked privy door.

wild ginger See 1830 quote.
1830 (1837) *Trans.Lit.& Hist.Soc.Que.* III 102: Wild Ginger [is] a small perennial herbaceous plant, with a few broad kidney-shaped leaves on long footstalks and in pairs [*Asarum canadense*]. **1947** BIRD *Judgment Glen* 270: She talked of . . . the virtues of the bark of swamp alder, of wild ginger for stomach-ache. . . .

wild goat 1 *Obs.* See **antelope**.
1754 (1907) HENDAY *Journal* 336: Saw several wild goats. [**1853** REID *Young Voyageurs* 100: Norman called it "a goat," and stated that this was its name among the fur-traders, while the Canadian voyageurs give it the title of "cabree."]

2 See **Rocky Mountain goat**.
1807 (1890) KEITH *Letters* 66: Large animals consist of the moose deer, and the wild goat; the latter is to be found only upon the Rocky Mountains, and is much the same as in Europe, though smaller and without beard. **1875** (1888) MCDOUGALL *G.M.McDougall* 220: . . . the Stoney hunts the wild goat, and the big horned sheep, the black tail, the white tail, and the graceful antelope.

wild goose See **Canada goose**.
1744 DOBBS *Hudson's Bay* 52: The wild Geese come to these Rivers from the Southward in the Middle of April, as soon as the Swamps are thawed. **1897** TYRRELL *Sub-Arctics* 102: It is commonly said that the breeding place of the wild goose has never been discovered, but here, at any rate, was the breeding place of these. **1959** MCATEE *Folk-Names* 8: Eastern Canada Goose (*Branta canadensis canadensis*) [is also called] wild goose (universal). . . .

wild grape 1 any of several species of wild grape, *Vitis* sp., common in eastern Canada.
1798 (1957) *Ont.Hist.* XLIX 79: The wild grapes and plums, which are here in great abundance along the banks of the rivers and creeks, are much superior to those of Pennsylvania. **1826** (1832) PICKERING *Inquiries* 57: The blossoms of the wild grapes, growing about the fences, perfume the air with their pleasant odour; something like mignionette. **1952** PUTNAM *Cdn Regions* 26/2: The vegetation also includes . . . service berry . . . wild grape. . . .

2 *Pacific Coast* either of two small evergreen shrubs, *Mahonia agnifolium* or *M. nervosa;* Oregon grape.
1905 (1954) *B.C.Hist.Qtly* XVIII 175: . . . from a bush of what they call "wild grape," on the high bank of the river . . . emerged the fore part of a large black bear.

wild land(s)† *Hist.* land that has not been settled on or developed in any way.
1791 (1906) *Ont.Bur.Arch.Rep.* III xciii: Others of them . . . were under the necessity of purchasing land of . . . those persons claiming large Tracts under Indian Titles at the enormous price of £100 for 100 acres of wild land. **1851** *Toronto Patriot* 22 Aug. 3/4: The undersigned also offers . . . Wild Lands in Collingwood, Enniskillen, &c., too numerous to mention. **1918** KITTO *New Manitoba* 75: Under stress of breaking land, erecting buildings and fences, digging wells and carrying out the endless tasks incidental to converting a piece of "wild"

land into a home and a farm, the farmer was forced to forgo many of the activities that more leisure time would permit. **1967** *Cdn Geog.Jnl* Mar. 78/1: [He] asked the government agent how much capital would be needed [in 1856] for a family to settle down on wild land in that part of the country [Renfrew, Ont.].

wild oats [trans. of Cdn F *folle avoine*] *Hist.* See **wild rice**.
1744 DOBBS *Hudson's Bay* 36: All around its Banks, in the shallow Water and Marshes, grows a kind of wild Oat, of the Nature of Rice; the outward Husk is black, but the Grain within is white and clear like Rice; this the Indians beat off into their Canoes, and use for Food. **1765-75** (1933) POND *Narrative* 36: But Just in the Canoe track the Wilde Oates were so thick that the Indans Could scarse Git one of thare Small Canoes into it to Geather it. . . . **1933** GATES *Five Traders* 206n: Wild rice was ordinarily called "oats" or "wild oats" by traders and voyageurs. **1944** *Beaver* Sep. 18/1: Such items as these appear in the accounts: "5 kegs of wild oats of Kam."

wild onion a plant of the genus *Allium*, as *A. acuminatum* of the Pacific Coast.
1808 (1889) FRASER *Journal* 173: Soon after, our new friends . . . brought different kinds of roots, wild onions formed into syrup, excellent dried salmon, and some berries. **1852** MOODIE *Roughing It* 334: They come here to collect the best birch-bark for their canoes, and to gather wild onions. **1909** MORICE *Great Déné Race* 598: . . . the wild onion . . . is eaten, roots and leaves, either raw or slightly roasted in the ashes. **1954** PATTERSON *Dangerous River* 126: He glared sourly at a piece of dried moose meat that sat stiffly on his plate, surrounded by a mess of dried potatoes and wild onions.

wild ox *Obs.* See **buffalo**, *n*. (def. 2).
1775 (1901) HENRY (Elder) *Travels* 281: Our supper was made on the tongues of the wild ox, or buffalo, boiled in my kettle, which was the only one in camp.

wild parsnip 1 *Obs.* See **cow parsnip**.
1793 (1925) ANDERSON *Trees and Shrubs* 127: Sir Alexander Mackenzie . . . frequently alludes to this plant under the name of "Wild Parsnip." . . . "The Wild Parsnip, which luxuriates on the borders of the lakes and rivers, is a favourite food of the natives."

2 the poisonous water hemlock, *Cicuta maculata*.
1829 *Brockville Gaz.* (U.C.) 3 July 2/4: On Saturday, John . . . died from the effects of eating a poisonous root called the wild parsnip. **1884** *Nor'Wester* (Calgary) 17 June 1/6: Fifteen children of the Blackfeet were poisoned by eating wild parsnips and four of them died from the effects of the same. **1932** WINSON *Weather and Wings* 51: Frequently the poison is described further as being "wild-parsnip," "cowbane," "water parsnip," "wild carrot," or "wild parsley."

wild pigeon† *Hist.* See **passenger pigeon**.
1765-75 (1933) POND *Narrative* 32: These Wood afford Partreages . . . Rackones, sum Wild Pigins. **1830** *Gleaner* (Niagara-on-the-Lake, U.C.) 8 May 29/2: Large flocks of the wild pigeon have been passing in the neighborhood of the city since Sunday the 12th instant. **1868** *Cdn Naturalist* III 413: The wild pigeon has its favourite resort in the barrens during a greater part of the summer. **1908** CLARKE *Sixty Years* 34: Wild

pigeons . . . were offered at figures which would be startling to people with modern ideas of value. **1959** MCATEE *Folk-Names* 41: Passenger Pigeon [was also called] wild pigeon (general). . . .

wild potato 1 *Obs.* See **wapatoo.**

1801 (1897) COUES *New Light* I 183: Esquebois . . . a root about the thickness and length of a man's finger, which may be termed the wild potato or pomme de terre of this country; it has a thin skin of a yellowish color, the inside perfectly white, and when boiled is tolerably good eating. They are also eaten raw, but are then of a windy nature, and sometimes cause a severe colic.

2 See quote.

1925 ANDERSON *Trees and Shrubs* 134: Spring Beauty. *Claytonia lanceolata,* Pursh. The so-called "wild potato" is the tuberous root of this beautiful Claytonia, which belongs to the Portulaca family. The tuber is quite small, sweet, and agreeable in flavour. It is boiled for use.

wild red cherry See **wild cherry.**

wild rice See 1963 quote. See also **Canadian rice, crazy oats, folle avoine, Indian rice, menominee, oats, rice,** and **wild oats.**

1748 ELLIS *Hudson's Bay* 170: By the Sides of Lakes and Rivers there is abundance of wild Rice, which if cultivated, would make good Food. **1791** LONG *Voyages* 75: I . . . took an Indian slay, loaded with wild rice and dried meat, and two of his Canadians to assist me. **1863** WALSHE *Cedar Creek* 306: Here were some hundreds of yards of shallow water, filled with the tall graceful plant, named by the Jesuits "folle avoine," and by the English "wild rice." **1963** *Sask.News* Nov. 4/1: Scientifically speaking, wild rice is Zizania Aquatica and isn't rice at all. The "rice" term was applied to it by early settlers because the grains resembled rice and it grew in shallow water on lake shores.

wild rose any uncultivated rose, *Rosa* sp., as *R. acicularis,* the floral emblem of Alberta.

1853 REID *Young Voyageurs* 168: They [wapiti] are especially fond of a species of wild rose . . . which grows in the countries they frequent. **1889** DONKIN *Trooper* 86: The luscious perfume of . . . wild rose, and all the healthy ozone of this sunset land, comes scampering on the western breeze. **1909** CAMERON *New North* 88: Wood violets, wild roses, false Solomon-seal, and the wild sarsaparilla are everywhere. . . . **1958** *Weekend Mag.* 7 June 37: The wild, or prickly, rose, Alberta's emblem since 1930, is the most widely distributed native rose in Canada. In winter, it bears red berries.

wild tea See **Labrador tea** (def. 1a).

1929 MOBERLY *When Fur Was King* 237: The Silent Land produces valuable medicinal plants in great variety. The wild tea found there was in common use by both natives and Hudson's Bay Company men before the imported article was obtained. **1938** SULLIVAN *Cycle of North* 120: The plains are carpeted with the profuse blossom of the wild tea, whose velvety-pointed leaf brings comfort by many a camp fire.

wild turkey *West* See **turkey.**

1930 *Cdn Geog.Jnl* I 32/1: The Sandhill Crane, improperly called Wild Turkey on the prairies, is to-day seldom seen, though a few years ago its hoarse trumpeting was a familiar sound overhead during the migration

period. **1963** SYMONS *Many Trails* 186: [We have] seen the wild turkeys leave the cultivated and . . . drouth-stricken prairies. . . .

wild turnip 1 *Obs.* jack-in-the-pulpit, *Arisaema triphyllum.* See also *Indian turnip* (def. 2).

1796 (1911) SIMCOE *Diary* 328: I gathered a great many plants [including] dewberries; wild turnip, which cures a cough—it is like aram.

2 See **prairie turnip.**

1879 *Battleford Hist.Soc.Pubs* I-III 58: Their women are also at work early and late every day digging wild turnips and gathering berries. **1887** *Senate Jnl* XXI App. 170: I was surprised to see that there was no mention made . . . of the root known by us as the wild turnip or buffalo root. **1930** ROLYAT *Ft Garry* 154: And they had seen Mistress Currie sitting down on the ground outside the fort eating wild turnips, with some squaws.

willow *n. B.C.* See **ruffed grouse.**

1961 *Vancouver Province* 1 Sep. 11/1: Willows or ruffed grouse have a more confined area of migration or movement and are much more inclined to stay close to river and stream beds. . . .

willow bird See **willow ptarmigan.**

1882 *Trans.Roy.Soc.Can.* I 4 52: We then enter on the home of the willow grouse, willow ptarmigan, or willow bird (*Lagopus albus,* Aud.). . . . **1884** *Trans.Hist.& Sci. Soc.Man.* 14 14/1: To illustrate the usefulness of the rose, I append a table of observations on the contents of the crop of the . . . Birch and willow birds. **1959** MCATEE *Folk-Names* 25: Willow Ptarmigan [is also called] willow bird (Ont., "Keewatin"). . . .

willow grouse 1 See **willow ptarmigan.**

1823 FRANKLIN *Journey* 681: The White Grouse of the countries round Hudson's Bay . . . have acquired the appellation of Willow Grouse, or Partridges among these others. **1866** KING *Sportsman in Can.* 154: The Ptarmigan, Willow-grouse, or White-grouse (*Lagopus albus*) is mentioned by Dr. Hall as one of the birds of the Montreal district. . . . **1959** MCATEE *Folk-Names* 25: Willow Ptarmigan [is also called] willow grouse ("Keewatin," "N.W.T."). . . .

2 *Esp.B.C.* See **ruffed grouse.**

1907 MILLAIS *Newfoundland* 274: The Newfoundland willow grouse . . . fly in large bodies from one district to another, and often visit the outer islands of the east coast. . . . **1960** *Gulf Islander* (Galiano, B.C.) 23 July 1/1: In the fir tree behind us we listened to the resonant call of the willow grouse. . . .

3 *Local* See quote.

1959 MCATEE *Folk-Names* 25: Sharp-tailed Grouse [is also called] willow grouse (Y.T.).

willow partridge 1 See **willow ptarmigan.**

1743 (1949) ISHAM *Observations* 123: the willow Partridge which is Larger than those above mention'd is the same colour Excep't the black from the Eye to the Bill. . . . **1896** WHITNEY *On Snow-Shoes* 298: One, the willow-partridge, is a very handsome bird, with a black throat and head and scarlet eyebrows, and a brownish body handsomely mottled with orange. **1959** MCATEE *Folk-Names* 25: Willow Ptarmigan [is also called] willow partridge (. . . "Keewatin").

2 See **ruffed grouse.**

1959 MCATEE *Folk-Names* 24: Ruffed Grouse [is also called] willow partridge (Man.).

willow pheasant *B.C.* See **ruffed grouse.**

1906 *Log of the "Columbia"* Aug. 12/1: . . . here a flock of downy, brown baby "willow" pheasants scampered across the road. . . .

willow ptarmigan a widely distributed ptarmigan, *Lagopus lagopus albus*. See also **partridge** (def. 2), **snow-cock, snow partridge, white bird** (def. 2), **willow bird, willow grouse** (def. 1), and **willow partridge** (def. 1).

1896 RUSSELL *Far North* 260: Willow Ptarmigan . . . were not easily distinguishable at a little distance from the balls of snow which are common in the willow tops. **1947** *Beaver* Mar. 12/2: The old-timers on the Bay owed a lot to the willow ptarmigan. **1966** *Kingston Whig-Standard* (Ont.) 21 Jan. 11/1: Up in the Hudson Bay region we have the sharp-tailed grouse and the willow ptarmigan. . . .

winanishe *n*. See **ouananiche**.

windbreak *n*. **1** anything used as a temporary barrier to break the force of the wind, especially when camping.

[**1772** (1792) CARTWRIGHT *Journal* I 211: In the evening we enclosed the fire with a fence of boughs to keep off the wind. . . .] **1897** TYRRELL *Sub-Arctics* 222: The snow was cleared away from the inside of the windbreak. . . . **1908** LAUT *Conquest N.W.* 225: The nights now became bitterly cold, and there were no more old lodges—only a windbreak made of the canoe and the deerskin. **1930** BEAMES *Army* 117: They drew the sleighs up to form a windbreak. . . .

2 a row or clump of trees serving as protection against the wind and, often, as a means of preventing soil erosion.

1884 *Moose Jaw News* (Sask.) 10 Oct. 1/6: Lesser windbreaks are planted where larger are difficult to establish. **1927** HAMILTON *Maritime Provinces* 128: The two-hour run from Halifax to Truro was through country [of] rolling hills and rocky ledges, scattered farms with their wind-breaks of spruce trees. . . . **1964** *Kingston Whig-Standard* (Ont.) 5 Dec. 7/1: To protect their fields, many farmers of the Quinte area started planting trees as windbreaks and shelterbelts.

windbreaker *n*. a wind-resistant jacket that fastens to the neck and has close fitting cuffs and waist.

1934 *Beaver* June 6/2: The wind-breakers and coats are shown by a series of photographs. **1942** *Gazette* (Glace Bay, N.S.) 24 Sep. 3/1: Gear should include a windbreaker, an ice chisel or spud, strainers for cleaning the slush around the hole made in the ice, and above all warm clothing should be worn. **1964** *Weekend Mag.* 11 July 18/3: They chose . . . a sweater each, windbreakers and rain capes.

wind-charger *n*. a generator driven by a windmill, the electricity generated being used to charge storage batteries; also, the windmill itself.

1946 MANNING *Igloo* 156: . . . we could hear the wind tearing past, and the high screaming whine as it met the wires of the radio masts and wind-charger. **1949** MACGREGOR *Blankets and Beads* 20: Everywhere is to be seen the wind-charger, which generates the farmer's electricity by the wind. **1963** *Sask.News* Sep. 4: [Caption] The current issue . . . depicts . . . a typical "dugout" and wind-charger of the prairie region, and a modern harvesting scene in the wheat belt.

wind chill the rate at which exposed human skin cools under given conditions of temperature and wind speed. When the wind chill count is 2,400, exposed flesh begins to freeze.

1949 *Report of DME Test Team* IE 1: Even on milder days (−20°F) with a strong wind, the wind-chill factor prevents sustained periods of work. **1957** *Kingston*

Whig-Standard (Ont.) 1 Mar. 3/2: Army officials here at Fort Churchill, Man. say that . . . all animal life in the district heads for shelter when the wind chill climbs to 1,750. **1958** *Edmonton Jnl* 19 Sep. 4/1: The thermometer might read ten below zero but the weather report would point out that due to the "wind chill" it was as cold outside as it would be at forty below zero in still air. **1962** *Time* (Cdn ed.) 5 Jan. 7/1: The Calgary *Herald* obligingly broke out a kind of cold weather discomfort index called a wind chill index. Based on studies at the joint U.S.-Canadian Weather testing station at Churchill, the wind chill index goes on the theory that, just as in summer when it is not the heat but the humidity, in winter it is not the cold but the wind. Thus the wind chill index measures both; a temperature of −30° with little or no wind is not as bad as a temperature of, say, 20° above zero with a 20-m.p.h. wind.

Windego *n*. See **Wendigo**.

windfall *n*. **1 a.** a tree blown down by the wind.

1823 *P.E.I. Register* (Charlottetown) 16 Aug. 3/2: The Road is to be cut ten feet wide and opened straight; the trees to be cut down level with the ground and removed, with all windfalls and obstructions. **1958** *Edmonton Jnl* 7 Aug. 4/3: We investigated the groves and woodlot to find which old trees had been felled by the winter storms, and to clear out brush and windfalls from the pathways.

b. such trees collectively. See also **down timber** and **wind-throw timber**.

1849 ALEXANDER *L'Acadie* II 186: . . . we had to cut our way through, and to climb over . . . the prostrate trees, windfall, entangled with second growth of birch, fir. . . . **1965** *Beaver* Autumn 55/2: . . . for two days I walked and crawled over windfall which was strewn to a depth of five feet.

2 a tract of land strewn with trees toppled by the wind. See also **renversé** and **slash,** *n*. (def. 2).

1829 MACTAGGART *Three Years* II 5: Winds are seldom severe; sometimes, however, they lay waste extensive belts of the forest of thirty miles at a stretch, and from a quarter to a mile broad; these are called Windfalls. **1834** (1926) LANGTON *Early U.C.* 110: . . . about ten or twelve acres of this will be light chopping, principally young timber on an old windfall or burn and will have to lie a summer before burning. **1947** *Beaver* Sep. 35/1: In a windfall we saw a large bull with wide-spread flat, irregular antlers. . . .

windflower *n*. *West* any of several anemones. See also **crocus**.

1952 LYONS *Trees, Shrubs* 117: The widespread anemones or wind flowers generally have a vasal group of toothed or lobed hairy leaves and one or two leaf whorls on the slender stem. **1963** SYMONS *Many Trails* xix: [The] windflower . . . is commonly called by this name in the cattle country, and crocus on the more eastern prairie.

Windigo(o) *n*. See **Wendigo**.

windlass press *Fur Trade, Hist*. a type of fur press, *q.v*.

1941 *Beaver* Sep. 37/2: Various sorts [of fur presses] were used—the jack screw press, the lever and tackle, the windlass press. . . .

wind pants See quote.

1966 *Kingston Whig-Standard* (Ont.) 27 Apr. 26/1: The [Canadian army's] windproof parkas and special nylon wind pants are used by some other countries. . . .

wind-shell *n.* a light, unlined outer garment serving as protection from the wind.
1965 *Globe and Mail* (Toronto) 29 Apr. 3/5: [Caption] Mother carries baby in fur-trimmed hood of kooletuk, the blanket-cloth parka under her nylon wind-shell.

wind-throw timber *Lumbering, B.C.* See **windfall** (def. 1b).
1966 *B.C.Logging* 3/1: They [B.C.Prov.Dist.foresters] also can sell in their local areas wind-throw timber and stands threatened with destruction by disease or insects.

winehound *n. Slang* a derelict who drinks cheap wine. See also **rubby** (def. 2).
1961 *Maclean's* 29 July 34/2: . . . from any figure must be subtracted a lot of derelicts and itinerants who are not real hoboes—hometown drifters, winehounds, "mission" stiffs who seldom stray from the source of free meals and beds. . . .

wing *n.* **1** *Cdn Football* formerly, any of the six men on the line, three on each side of the snap, or the flying wing (the only position for which the term is in current use). The three men on the right and the left were known respectively as the *inside wing,* the *middle wing,* and the *outside wing.*
1895 (1964) *Kingston Whig-Standard* (Ont.) 27 Oct. 9/3: . . . the wings which are seven in number correspond to the American guards, tackles and ends and the extra man is called a flying wing. **1964** *Ibid.* 27 Oct. 9/4: . . . the forward pass was introduced [c1931], shortly followed by the wholesale importation of U.S. coaches who promptly substituted the U.S. names of "guards," and "tackles" for the Canadian "wings," and also changed the term "union" to "conference."
2 in hockey and lacrosse, either of the two players on the left and right of the centre man of a forward line. See also **winger.**
1902 CONNOR *Glengarry* 311: Dan . . . passed swiftly to the waiting Red who immediately shot far out to his alert wing, and then rushing down the center . . . scored another goal. . . . **1958** *Liberty* Jan. 6/3: The same goes for hockey, in which a good left-handed wing, or defense man, is an asset to a team.
3 *Fishing* See quote.
1938 CURTIN *Yukon Voyage* 131: On top of the ice was a latticelike affair made of seventeen strips of wood, each about fifteen feet long, laid side by side nearly two inches apart, and held in place by fourteen cross pieces and bound together by strips of wood. This is . . . what is called a wing, and is let down into the water through the trench to steer the fish into the trap.

wing-boom *n. Lumbering* a line of logs attached to each other by chains at either side of a sheer-boom, *q.v.*
1896 ROBERTS *Camp-Fire* 179: The section of the sheer-boom thus peculiarly adorned was called the wing-boom. Just above the upper end of the wing-boom, at a place widened out a few feet to receive it, was built a little shanty known as the boom-house.

winger *n.* See **wing** (def. 2).
1955 *Daily News* (St. John's) 9 Mar. 10/1: The sharp-shooting winger was the turning point in the game as he

took advantage of a Grand Falls penalty to change a 2-2 tie into a 5-2 Bell Island lead in little more than half a minute. **1962** *Kingston Whig-Standard* (Ont.) 28 Dec. 10/7: The big Toronto winger had taken a commanding four-point lead going into Thursday night's game.

Winnipeg couch a simple, inexpensive couch which could be opened out into a double bed. See also **Toronto couch.**
1954 RUSSELL *Living Earth* 233: . . . he sat on the Winnipeg couch that stood at one end of the room. . . . **1958** *Vancouver Province* 11 Sep. 1/1: The Winnipeg couch was a fine oldtimer, built of solid iron and coil springs in those days when Canadians fell into bed with their boots on. **1966** *Maclean's* 5 Mar. 21/2: Then he opened a door and I saw them—twenty unshaven, hollow-eyed men lying under grey blankets on low Winnipeg couches opened up into beds.

Winnipeg goldeye See **goldeye.**
1954 *Fundy Fisherman* (Black's Harbour, N.B.) 8 Dec. 4/4: Here are smoked kippers from Scotland, shelled oysters from New York, fresh shrimps from Texas, cohoes, a sort of herringy fish done in henna shades to look like a first cousin to Winnipeg Goldeye, chilled salmon from British Columbia. **1958** *Edmonton Jnl* 22 Sep. 4/3: . . . you are ready to do some specialized cooking that will make goldeyes from the river equal the famed Winnipeg smoked goldeyes once featured by train dining cars. **1964** *Commercial Letter* Mar. 7/2: Manitoba's most famous fish, the goldeye, which often appears on distant menus as "Winnipeg goldeye," has in recent years been playing a decreasing role commercially.

Winnipeg smoked goldeye See **Winnipeg goldeye.**

winnish or **winnonish** *n.* See **ouananiche.**

winter *v. Fur Trade, Hist.* spend the winter in the interior. See also **winterer** (def. 2).
1776 (1951) *Sask.Jnls* 17: These Canoes it seems belonged to two French Men (new Adventurers this way), who had proposed to have Wintered with the rest. . . . **1803** (1890) MASSON *Les Bourgeois* II 233: I can assure you it is with great difficulty I can hold my pen, but I must tell you that the X.Y. sends in to the Nipigon this year, therefore, should I leave my bones there, I shall go to winter. **1918** DAVIDSON *North West Co.* 95: Turning north by Beaver River, he built a fort at Lac La Biche and wintered. **1954** WALLACE *Pedlars* 82: He had signed the North West Company agreements of 1802 and 1804, but I could find no information as to where he had wintered. . . .

winter (or **wintering) allowance** *Fur Trade, Hist.* certain special supplies allowed by a fur company for an officer or employee wintering in the interior. See also **allowance.**
1825 (1926) *Cdn Hist.Rev.* Dec. 3/7: Winter allowance 25 lb Flour 20 lb Sugar 10 lb Grease. **1913** COWIE *Adventurers* 500: " 'Luxuries'—in the ante-steam transport days this fur-trade term was applied to the voyaging and wintering allowances given to the officers and missionaries, and consisted of mustard, pepper, pimento, Hyson and Souchong tea, sugar, rice, raisins, currants, vinegar and flour, also of wine and spirits in non-interdicted districts." **1929** MOBERLY *When Fur Was King* 82: This was the winter allowance, but in addition, the officer in charge of the brigade on the annual trip to York Factory, with the clerks who accompanied him, was made a voyage allowance.

winter beaver *Fur Trade, Hist.* beaver skins taken with their winter growth of hair, or when prime, *q.v.* See also **dry winter beaver** and **fat winter beaver.**

1708 (1948) *Beaver* Sep. 46: Oldmixon, in his *British Empire in North America,* published in 1708, had this to say about the price for guns in the 1680's or thereabouts: "One with the other 10 good skins; that is Winter Beaver." **1735** (1899) WILLSON *Great Company* 238: The beaver . . . was classified into eight varieties. The first was the fat winter beaver, slain in winter, which was valued at five shillings and sixpence a pound. **1944** *Beaver* Mar. 37/1: The report [1686] . . . approves of the establishment of the standard of trade at half a pound [of Brazil tobacco] for a winter beaver.

winter bird See **winterer** (def. 4).

winter canoe *Obs.* See **ice-canoe.**

1830 *Brockville Gaz.* (U.C.) 12 Feb. 3/2: On Friday one of the winter canoes used in crossing the Saint Lawrence . . . was upset just at the moment it was launched into a small opening between the floating ice.

winter carnival an organized winter social activity featuring winter sports, beauty contests, ice-sculpture, etc. See also **ice carnival.**

1905 WIGHTMAN *Our Cdn Heritage* 38: The ice palaces and winter carnivals, once so popular in the chief cities of the Dominion . . . have aided in this work of peculiar education to a surprising degree. . . . **1958** *In Flight* Fall 12/2: Many Canadian centres stage colorful Winter Carnivals each year. **1963** *News of the North* 31 Mar. 1/1: With less than two weeks remaining, plans are . . . nearing completion with regard to Yellowknife's Ninth Annual Dog Derby and Winter Carnival.

winter club a club providing members with facilities for skating, curling, and other social activities during the winter.

1958 *Citizen* 11 Dec. 5A/3: The North Shore Winter Club [announces that] Family Membership will be increased from the present $350.00 to $400.00. **1962** *Canada Month* Apr. 26/2: By the time the curling season opened in November, Fredericton had a handsome five-sheet rink called Capital Winter Club.

winter dance *Pacific Coast, Hist.* a ceremonial performance given by one of the Dancing Societies of the Kwakiutl and other coastal tribes during the winter months. Hence, *winter dancing.*

1955 JENNESS *Indians of Can.* 341: Most potlatches took place in the autumn, after the people had stored away their food and before the secret society began its winter dances. **1964** DUFF *Indian History* 102: When the missionaries swept out heathenism, they included the social forms that supported it—potlatches, winter dances, and the systems of class and rank. *Ibid.* But potlatching and winter dancing did not die easily. . . .

winterer *n.* **1** *Nfld, Obs.* a fisherman who wintered at a fishing station; a settler as opposed to a seasonal fisherman. Cp. **liveyere** (def. 1).

1766 *Quebec Gaz.* 4 Aug. 1/1: I hereby forbid all Persons from Quebec . . . to winter on the Coast of Labradore, within my Government; and if any such Winterers are met with there, they are immediately on Sight hereof to quit it, as they will answer to the Contrary at their Peril. . . . *c*1766 (1964) *Nfld Qtly* Spring 31/3: The whole of winterers in the whole island are reckoned at 10,000.

2 *Fur Trade, Hist.* **a.** a seasoned fur trader or voyageur who spent his winters in the fur country. See also **hivernant, homme du nord, Man of the North** (def. 1), **Northman** (def. 1), **old winterer,** and **winterman.**

1801 MACKENZIE *Voy. from Montreal* xxviii: The latter . . . are called North Men, or Winterers; and to the last class of people were attached upwards of seven hundred women and children, victualled at the expence of the company. **1821** (1918) DAVIDSON *Fur Traders* 302: Mr. K. recommends . . . the absolute necessity of forwarding 7 or 8 Canoes of pork eaters [and] Winterers . . . with full ladings. *c*1902 LAUT *Trapper* 12: The elder Stuart was a rollicking winterer from The Labrador, with the hail-fellow-well-met air of an equal among the mercurial French-Canadians. **1961** JONES *Trappers* 68/2: The Indians were so partial to the voyageurs that at least one Englishman, Alexander Henry the Elder, disguised himself as a French winterer in a successful effort to escape being killed.

b. See **wintering partner** (def. 1).

1804 (1890) MASSON *Les Bourgeois* II 493: The debts due by Winterers of the said Old and New Companies shall be assumed by the said joint concern according to the mode of evaluing the same by the said Old Company. *a*1855 (1956) ROSS *Fur Hunters* 8: On the arrival once every year of the winterers at Fort William the voyageurs and common men in every grade were in the habit of receiving from their employers a regale gratis. **1947** *Beaver* Dec. 8/2: John Frobisher, who was essentially a "winterer" . . . asked to supervise the hiring of the canoemen. . . .

c. See **wintering partner** (def. 2).

1833 (1963) TOLMIE *Physician* 185: The surplus funds . . . are subdivided into 85 shares . . . which are received by the "Winterers" viz 1 share to a Trader and 2 to a Factor. . . . **1864** *Nor'Wester* (R.R.S.) 16 Sep. 3/3: Let the "winterers" look out for themselves, as we must for ourselves. **1952** HOWARD *Strange Empire* 33: Winterers [are] the partners working in the field as post factors, who shared the profits but had no voice in determining policy.

3 *Hist.* See quote.

1914 STEELE *Forty Years* 43: There were two classes of [Indian] hunters, one that lived by the chase, called winterers, [who] usually arrived from their winter quarters and encamped west of the fort.

4 See quotes. See also **winter hawk.**

1853 REID *Young Voyageurs* 425: It is known by the name of "jerfalcon," or "gyrfalcon," but its zoological name is *Falco Islandicus.* "The Indians here," interposed Norman, "call it by a name that means 'winter bird,' or 'winterer'—I suppose, because it is one of the few that stay in these parts [Arctic] all year round, and is therefore often noticed by them in winter time. . . ." **1959** MCATEE *Folk-Names* 22: Gyrfalcon [is also called] winterer. . . .

winter express *Fur Trade, Hist.* the winter trip of the express (def. 1). Cp. **summer express.**

*c*1799 MCKENZIE *Reminiscences* 29: About Christmas, Mr. MacKenzie paid us a visit which he extended to the departure of the winter Express in February. **1825** (1931) MERK *Fur Trade* 255: You will also receive ten horses and by the winter express we hope to be able to forward sixteen more to make up the number to one hundred for New Caledonia. **1858** (1863) PALLISER *Journals* 72: . . . writing letter for England, which leave today by the winter express which the Company sends with their accounts at this season to Red River. **1918** DAVIDSON *North West Co.* 219: The winter express left the farthest posts in the north about the end of November, passed through the whole country on sledges and snow-shoes and reached Sault St. Marie in March. [See **express** (def. 1) for full quote.] **1933** GATES *Five Traders* 149n: The Northwest traders organized their winter expresses or couriers with great care, and the resulting system of communication was one of the picturesque features of the life of the wilderness.

winter festival *Pacific Coast, Hist.* See **potlatch** (def. 2a). Cp. **winter dance**.
1942 *Highroads to Reading* 117: They are thus a visible reminder of the tales and legends that were recited at the winter festival or potlatch.

winter field *West* See **winter range**.
1963 SYMONS *Many Trails* 47: The open grass land adjoining is generally fenced off for winter range—the term winter field is now the correct one, even if the area contains thousands of acres.

winter fish 1 *Nfld* See quote.
1822 (1928) CORMACK *Narr.Nfld* 106: The cod caught in October, November, and December are called winter fish. *Ibid.* 107: There are no winter fish caught in Newfoundland except on the south-west coast.

2 *North* See quote.
1956 KEMP *Northern Trader* 133: In early October, Mooneas asked me what I was going to do about fish. He meant winter fish, dog-feed. I knew we would require some "hung fish"—semi-dried fish—for winter travel.

winter grounds *Fur Trade, Obs.* See **wintering ground** (def. 2).
1825 (1948) MCLOUGHLIN *Letters* 7: ... it might prevent his returning to his winter grounds and the Concern would in a great measure lose the hunts of this party for a Season.

winter hawk *North* See **winterer** (def. 4).
1882 *Trans.Roy.Soc.Can.* I 4 53: The [gyrfalcon] is known as the partridge or winter hawk.... **1959** MCATEE *Folk-Names* 22: Gyrfalcon [is also called] winter hawk ("Hudson Bay").

winter hunt among Indians, the hunt carried out in winter, the most productive hunting season.
1820 (1938) SIMPSON *Athabasca Jnl* 46: The Chipewyans also frequently pass this place in the course of their Winter Hunt. **1921** HEMING *Drama of Forests* 258: The Indians divide their annual hunt for fur into three distinct hunting seasons: the fall hunt—from autumn until Christmas; the winter hunt—from New Year's Day until Easter; and the spring hunt—from Easter until the hunters depart for their tribal summer camping ground. **1954** PATTERSON *Dangerous River* 284: They had gone in from South Nahanni ... to the Beaver after freeze-up, and they were making their winter hunt in there.

winter hunting grounds *Hist.* See **wintering ground** (def. 2).
1953 LOWER *Voyages* 36: The half-breed usually did not go out to the winter hunting grounds, but earned his living in second rank company employment.

winter ice *North* See 1958 quote.
1954 *Labrador and H.B.Pilot* 12: In Hudson Strait ice is derived from three sources: Baffin Bay or Arctic ice, Foxe Channel, and "winter ice" formed locally. **1958** *Manice* 5: Winter Ice: Sea ice more than 8 inches thick formed and developed in one winter. Winter ice is therefore one year old or less.

wintering ground(s) *Fur Trade, Hist.* **1** the region in which a fur trader carried on his business throughout the winter in the fur country.
1763 (1901) HENRY (Elder) *Travels* 74: He told me, that he had just returned from his *wintering-ground*, and I asked after his health.... **1843** *Standing Rules* (H.B.C.) 16: An extra allowance for the wintering grounds of 25 lbs. flour, 20 lbs. Sugar and 10 lbs. Grease in addition to the ordinary rations. *a*1855 (1956) ROSS *Fur Hunters* 111: In MacMillan's wintering ground everything went on in its successful train.

2 the region where the winter hunt, *q.v.*, is carried on. See also **winter grounds** and **winter hunting grounds**.
1765-75 (1933) POND *Narrative* 44: ... we Come to the Planes of the Dogs [Prairie du Chien] so Cald the Grate Plase of Rondavues for the traders and Indans Before thay Dispars for thare Wintering Grounds. **1820** (1938) SIMPSON *Athabasca Jnl* 104: Mr. Laronde had equipped twelve hunters ... and sent them to their wintering grounds.

wintering house *Fur Trade, Hist.* See **winter post**.
1806 (1897) COUES *New Light* I 418: "We ... came to the old wintering houses of 1801-02, at the White Mud." **1850** BIGSBY *Shoe and Canoe* II 99: Other traders have wintering-houses in this neighbourhood, on the west side of a low promontory, from ten to thirteen miles long. **1934** *Beaver* Mar. 45: ... at holiday festivities held in wintering houses in the heart of the Indian country.

wintering partner [cf. Cdn F *hivernant*, q.v.] *Fur Trade, Hist.* **1** a stock-holding partner in the Montreal-based fur companies, especially the North West Company, *q.v.*, who represented the company the year round at the trading posts in the fur country. See also **bourgeois** (def. 2a), **master pedlar, partner, proprietor,** and **winterer** (def. 2b). Cp. **agent** (def. 2).
1802 (1890) MASSON *Les Bourgeois* II 466: The said partners shall assume and be stiled Agents of the North West Company and shall be aided and assisted in all occasions by the Wintering partners whose duty it shall also be to attend in a particular manner to the Business in their respective Departments. **1834** (1948) *Beaver* Dec. 14/2: I think I have heard it said that they belonged to the Wintering partners of the old North West Company. **1940** NIVEN *Mine Inheritance* 26: Within the palisade were several small houses, one, we discovered later, for the wintering partner (as the North West Company called those who, in the Hudson's Bay, were styled factors).... **1963** MACLEOD & MORTON *Cuthbert Grant* 10: Wills ... was one of the six wintering partners of this concern [XY Co.]....

2 a comparable officer in the Hudson's Bay Company. See 1905 quote. See also **bourgeois** (def. 2b) and **winterer** (def. 2c).
1905 (1954) *B.C.Hist.Qtly* XVIII 190: The chief factors and chief traders ... were known as the "Wintering Partners" of the company. The profits of the fur trade were divided into 100 parts. Of these, 60 parts were appropriated to the stockholders and 40 to the "Wintering Partners." These last were divided into 85 shares, of which two were held by each chief factor and one by each chief trader. The "clerks" ... were paid by salary. **1921** *Beaver* Nov. 37/2: The commissioned officers in the country were called "Wintering Partners" and received among them two-fifths of the net profits of the concern. **1954** CAMSELL *Son of North* 4: It was a

sad blow to the prestige of the officers when in 1887, after several years of hard times during which the profits received by the "wintering partners" were small, they decided to go on a regular salary basis. **1963** *Beaver* Winter 51/1: The Hudson's Bay Company people, whom I took to be the equivalent of the old wintering partners, disappointed me by not staging one of the wild debauches I had read about in northern novels.

wintering post *Fur Trade, Hist.* See **winter post.**
1913 COWIE *Adventurers* 191: Of the above some were only wintering posts, abandoned for the summer. **1953** MOON *Saskatchewan* 20: Qu'Appelle Fort was established sometime after 1885 or soon after as a wintering post or outpost from Fort Ellice. . . .

wintering share *Fur Trade, Hist.* the share of stock held by a wintering partner (def. 1).
1806 (1964) PAYETTE *Northwest* 299: . . . nothing in the said Account current shall be taken . . as influencing . . . the question now in agitation respecting the two Wintering Shares relinquished or given up by John Finlay and Peter Grant. . . .

wintering station *Fur Trade, Hist.* See **winter post.**
1819 (1963) DAVIES *Northern Quebec* 7: We met . . . an Indian in a canoe laden with goods and provisions and intended to form a wintering station. . . . **1918** DAVIDSON *North West Co.* 204: In about two weeks they would be on their way back to their wintering stations.

winterkill† *n.* **1** death (of plants, animals, fish, or birds) brought on by extreme winter conditions.
1853 STRICKLAND *Canada West* I 53: Late sown wheat is more liable to winter-kill and rust. **1958** *Edmonton Jnl* 16 Aug. 27/8: [Many] . . . streams . . . have been depleted by winter-kill of resident fish. **1964** *Kingston Whig-Standard* (Ont.) 5 Dec. 7/2: Windbreaks . . . often save crops from winterkill.

2 an instance of such killing.
1963 *B.C. Digest* Oct. 30/3: . . . today we no longer see the winter kills that were common on overpopulated ranges.

winterkill† *v.* die or cause to die through exposure to extreme winter conditions.
1863 *Islander* (Charlottetown) 9 July 2/4: St. John Morning Telegraph—The hay crop this year will be much below the average owing to excessive "winter killing." **1957** *Farm News Press Clip Sheet* 16 Oct. 1/1: Such shrubs as the tender roses . . . require protection as those portions above the snow line winter kill rather severely. **1964** *Kingston Whig-Standard* (Ont.) 5 Dec. 7/2: A farmer near Adolphustown reported 90 per cent of his Hudson winter wheat winter-killed on an open field. . . .

winter madness *Esp. North* a state of mental unbalance caused by isolation in remote northern outposts. Cp. **bushed**[1] (def. 1) and **cabin fever.**
1957 LARGE *Skeena* 50: Little wonder that 'winter madness' crept into the cabins and more than one operator had to be taken out for psychiatric treatment.

winterman *n. Fur Trade, Hist.* See **winterer** (def. 2a).
1956 INNIS *Fur Trade* 193: In 1774, Waden signed a license for Jos. Le Clair to take 2 canoes and 13 men . . . a Lawrence Ermatinger, 4 canoes, 32 men, of whom 17 were wintermen. . . .

winter moccasin an outsize moccasin roomy enough to accommodate duffle wrappers or heavy socks. See also **winter shoe.**

1896 RUSSELL *Far North* 27: Winter moccasins are made large enough to contain a square piece of duffel or old blanketing in lieu of socks. **1959** SLUMAN *Blackfoot Crossing* 4: He wore winter moccasins pulled high over bright plaid trousers.

winter outpost *Fur Trade, Hist.* See **outpost** (def. 1).
1913 COWIE *Adventurers* 191: Fort Ellice had a regular winter outpost at Riding Mountain, besides flying posts wherever the buffalo were numerous. . . . **1956** KEMP *Northern Trader* 17: The red [thumbtacks] represent the Company's permanent, year-round establishments; the blue ones, the winter posts and outposts.

winter packet *Fur Trade, Hist.* the winter mail and mail delivery; the mail carried by the winter express, *q.v.*
1831 (1947) HARGRAVE *Correspondence* 79: . . . our Winter Packet being now preparing to Travell on to your Quarter, I will not let it go without acknowledging the receipt of your friendly epistle. **1850** (1852) RICHARDSON *Arctic Exped.* 316: . . . the winter packet arrived and I received your instructions respecting the establishment of an Indian party on the Coppermine. . . . **1938** *Beaver* June 58: The subject is, "The Winter Packet from York Factory Arriving at Fort Garry." **1954** CAMSELL *Son of North* 7: Mail came in twice a year, once in summer with the York boat brigade which brought in the supplies and once in winter with dog teams which carried letters only. The "winter packet," as it was called, left Fort Garry early in the winter.

winter partner *Fur Trade, Hist.* See **wintering partner** (def. 1).
1938 SIMPSON *Athabasca Jnl* xxxi: With complete immunity from any effective Hudson's Bay jurisdiction, the winter partners could afford to keep their own legal weapons in reserve.

winter post *Fur Trade, Hist.* a trading post used only in winter. See also **wintering house, wintering post, wintering station,** and **winter trading post.** Cp. **outpost** (def. 1).
1824 (1931) MERK *Fur Trade* 231: Resolved . . . That the winter post of Athabasca River under the Management of William McIntosh C. F. be kept up for ensueing summer attached to the Saskatchewan District. **1897** TYRRELL *Sub-Arctics* 59: It was Mr. Reed with his party returning from Fort Fond du Lac (now a small winter post only) to Chippewyan with the last winter's trade. **1953** LOWER *Voyages* 38: From the landing they were "toted" up stream three or four miles and put in the winter post.

winter range† *West* a region suitable for the grazing of cattle, sheep, or horses in winter. See also **winter field.** Cp. **winter rustling.**
1883 *Edmonton Bull.* 17 Feb. 2/1: The partial failure of the Calgary country as a winter range this year is likely to cause capitalists to look with a less covetous eye on the stock ranges of the Bow and Belly rivers. **1965** *Wildlife Rev.* June 15/1: Helicopters were used last winter in the study of ungulate winter ranges in the Kootenay and Fraser River region (from Macalister to Prince George).

winter road 1 *Hist.* See **winter trail.**
1801 MACKENZIE *Voy. from Montreal* 84: One of the natives who followed us, called it the Winter Road

River. **1820** (1890) WILCOCKE *Death B.Frobisher* 233: The winter road through the woods from Rabbit Point to Moose Lake, had the men been acquainted with it, would have brought them to the post in two days. **1860** *Nor'Wester* (R.R.S.) 28 Apr. 3/3: On returning with the mail packet, winter overtook them in the Abbittibbe Lake, when they abandoned their canoe, and not knowing the usual winter road, they were obliged to follow the course of the river.

2 a. a secondary road used only when the ground is frozen, usually because the terrain is impassable at other times, formerly used by sleighs. See also **snow-road.** Cp. **summer road.**
1808 (1809) GRAY *Letters* 254: The country people who first form the winter roads on the snow, direct their *Carioles* by the nearest course where the snow is most level; and they go in as straight a line as possible, to the place to which they are destined. **1842** *Bytown* [Ottawa] *Gaz.* 6 Oct. 3/2: We fear the French Canadians will not feel satisfied with being deprived of their good Winter Roads, which they were just beginning to enjoy under the Sleigh Ordinance. **1937** *Beaver* June 81/3: The winter road from St. Felicien, Lake St. John, to Chibougamau, was completed in time to permit of a considerable tonnage being freighted for mining interests before "break-up." **1957** *Ont.Hist.* XLIX 6: This was evidently a "summer road," i.e. one which could be used at all seasons of the year by either sleighs or wheeled vehicles; a "winter road" was meant to be used by sleighs only, and therefore the construction cost was much less than for a summer road. **1964** *Maclean's* 2 Dec. 12/2: It's carried out on a scale that would have been almost inconceivable a quarter of a century ago when "winter roads" were a political issue as debatable as socialized medicine.

b. *Lumbering* a road swamped (def. 1) through the bush and used for hauling logs during the winter months. See also **snow-road.**
1847 (1957) *Ont.Hist.* XLIX 2: As an instance of the importance of these roads, some enterprising Lumbermen on the Upper Madawaska have penetrated, at their own expense, the Townships in the rear of Victoria District [i.e. Hastings County], by winter roads, by means of which they are able to obtain supplies, delivered at their shanties, at Bytown prices. **1902** CONNOR *Glengarry* 86: . . . the winter road by which they hauled saw-logs to the mill, cut right through the forest, where the deep snow packed hard into a smooth track, covering roots and logs and mud holes, and making a perfect surface for the sleighs, however heavily loaded, except where here and there pitch-holes or cahots came. **1947** SAUNDERS *Algonquin* 31: To this day some of their winter roads may still be picked out from the air, but on the ground they have become so overgrown they are hard to find, except where the "corduroy" of logs over a gully or soft ground lies rotting among the second growth.

3 *Obs.* See **ice-road** (def. 2).
1829 MACTAGGART *Three Years* II 202: The *winter roads* are not those followed in summer: those of winter, are along the edges of the frozen rivers. **1886** *Trans.Roy. Soc.Can.* IV 3 88: These [fissures] are often a source of trouble to lumbermen and other travellers on the ice, since wooden bridges require to be thrown across them where they intersect the winter roads, their width being often from five to ten feet.

winter rustling of cattle, horses, etc., winter foraging by pawing through snow to get to the grass beneath.
1963 SYMONS *Many Trails* 63: This "winter rustling," as they call it on the prairies, becomes "bunch-grassing it" in the Chilcotin.

winter shoe *Obs.* See **winter moccasin.**
1821 (1938) SIMPSON *Athabasca Jnl* 278: . . . get all the Leather that can be collected . . . made up into Winter Shoes. . . .

winter ski See **ski.**
1938 (1950) STANWELL-FLETCHER *Driftwood Valley* 161: The plane was equipped with winter skis, and . . . made a "beautiful landing" on the south end of Bear Lake.

winter trader *North* a trader who serves trappers and hunters during the winter season.
1957 *Aklavik Jnl* Mar. 8/2: Because of the presence of caribou nearby all winter traders in Aklavik are out of the standard calibre shells, 30-30, 300.

winter trading post *Fur Trade, Hist.* See **winter post.**
1921 *Beaver* Dec. 5/1: In the summer of 1867 he was assistant . . . and in the fall was sent to establish a winter trading post at Water Hen river. . . .

winter trail *North* a route used in winter, especially by dog drivers. See also **winter road**(def. 1).
1922 *Beaver* Aug. 12/1: The winter trail cut straight across country. . . . **1953** BANFILL *Labrador Nurse* 235: We were the first to try this winter trail, so Norman and his team went ahead of us over the first bay. **1966** PATTERSON *Trail* 120: . . . he saw the empty winter trail running on into the south-west. . . .

winter work *Placer Mining, Hist.* the recovery of gold- or platinum-bearing gravel through burning (def. 3) and drifting.
1898 LANDREVILLE *Appeal* 37: Prospects and "winter work" indicate that there are on said three creeks about thirty other claims which will yield an average of $35 per cubic yard of the dirt handled in a summer cut thirty feet wide in the richest portion of the deposit. **1898** *Yukon Midnight Sun* (Dawson) 22 Aug. 3/6: He has bought No. 25 above on Bonanza, and will direct the winter work and add it to the gold dust producers.

wire *n.* a telegram.
1904 CONNOR *Prospector* 305: Shock drew a blank sheet toward him and set himself to compose a wire. **1906** *Eye Opener* (Calgary) 5 May 3/1: If you fall into a crevasse and are never heard of again, your friends will be notified by wire free of charge. **1955** *Penticton Herald* (B.C.) 9 Mar. 2 4/1: Lil interrupted to quote a wire she received from Grant, sent just after the great moment Sunday.

wire birch a small species of birch, *Betula populifolia,* native to the Maritimes, southern Quebec and eastern Ontario. See also **gray birch** and **swamp birch.**
1917 (1920) *Native Trees* 68: Betula Populifolia, Marsh. Common names: White birch, grey birch, wire birch, poplar leaved birch. **1946** BIRD *Sunrise* 55: Henry loaded his musket with care and led the way to the tip of the bog barren. He cut a strip of bark from a "wire birch" and rolled it cornerwise into a horn. . . . **1956** RADDALL *Wings* 12: Then came the long reach of scrub woods, wire birch and poplar mostly, with blossoming clumps of Indian pear, like patches of snow on the slopes. . . .

wishakapucka *n.* [< Algonk.; cf. Cree *wesukipukosu* bitter herbs] *Obs.* See **Labrador tea** (def. 1a).

1743 (1949) ISHAM *Observations* 134: Plants of Physicky Herb's Several are growing in these parts one of Which they styl (wishakapucka) which is used as a perge or fomentation. . . . **1748** DRAGE *Voyage* I 234: They hold in great Esteem . . . an Herb which they call *Wiseaca Pucca* or *Bitter Herb.* **1748** ELLIS *Hudson's Bay* 169: The Plant, by the Indians called Wizzekapukka, used by them, and the English as a Medicine, in nervous and scorbutic Disorders; it's most apparent and immediate Effect, is promoting Digestion, and causing a keen Appetite. **1795** (1911) HEARNE *Journey* 40: The land was entirely barren, and destitute of every kind of herbage, except wish-a-capucca and moss. **1857** (1858) *Report from the Select Committee* 373: It was formerly imported into this country [England] by the Hudson's Bay Company under the name of Weesukapuka. . . .

wishakapucka tea *Obs.* See **Labrador tea** (def. 1b).
1743 (1949) ISHAM *Observations* 134: . . . the English in these parts makes a Drink of itt, going by the Name of wishakapucka tea, being of fine flavour, and reckoned Very wholesome. [**1795** (1911) HEARNE *Journey* 165: There is plenty of Wishacumpuckey, (as the English call it, and which they use as tea). . . .]

wiskajon, wiskatjan, wisky jan *n.* See **whisky-john.**

wiskey-jack *n.* See **whisky-jack** (def. 1).

Witake *n. Obs.* See **Weetigo.**

witch-pole *n. Maritimes, Obs.* See quote.
1849 ALEXANDER *L'Acadie* II 80: There is a singular story connected with the Upper St. John's, regarding witch-poles. [Fn.] Lieutenant Simmons had lately been in a canoe with an old Indian hunter, on one of the lakes of the St. Francis River, and they came to two smooth and green poles, without branch or leaf, and apparently growing out of the bottom; they stood eight feet above water. On sounding, the depth was found to be 30 feet, and on shaking one pole, the other also moved. The hunter said these poles had been there since his childhood, and always had stood there since two witches had come up the lake to fish, and thrusting their poles to the bottom to make fast their canoe, they had grown there.

withe† *n. Lumbering, Hist.* See 1854 quote. See also **raft,** *n.* (def. 2, note, and picture), **withe,** *v.,* and **withing.**
1854 KEEFER *Ottawa* 67: The cribs are lashed together by means of "withs"; these are formed by taking young birchen trees about the size of whip stalks and fastening their butts firmly, by means of wedges, into an auger hole bored into a stump, then commencing at the points and twisting them . . . until the whole of the fibre is separated and the twig becomes as pliant as a rope. **1945** CALVIN *Saga* 160: Up to this time [1854], the withes had been softened for use by manpower, by rolling them on drums between pairs of six-foot wheels such as were used for steering the river-steamers. **1963** *Cdn Geog.Jnl* Nov. 160/2: From the tough elastic nature of the withes and their being evenly and snugly tied, a really extraordinary strength was developed in the whole fabric of the bottom of the dram.

withe *v. Lumbering, Hist.* fasten with withes, *q.v.*
1829 MACTAGGART *Three Years* I 242: When they are passing a *breaking-up rapid,* they live in these lairs, until the raft is *new withed,* and fixed on the still-water below. **1896** GOURLAY *Hist.Ottawa* 137: Oak rafts had to be floated by the lightest material and the ends grubbed and withed to the traverses, and were not loaded on. **1945** CALVIN *Saga* 68: Cribs were brought to it [timber afloat in booms] to be "stowed" and withed and made into drams.

withing *n. Lumbering, Hist.* the process of lashing the pieces of a lumber raft together with specially made withes, *q.v.*
1963 *Cdn Geog.Jnl* Nov. 160/2: When a bottom was completed the next step was "withing"; each piece of timber in the "bottom" and the traverse as it passed above it were tied together by a withe (a small white birch sapling softened between power-rollers) twisted up tight by a lever or "toggle."

witiko *n.* See **Weetigo.**

wizzekapukka *n.* See **wishakapucka.**

wobbano *n.* See **wabbano.**

Wobbly† ['wɑbli] *n.* [see 1923 quote] *Labor Slang* a member of the International Workers of the World (I.W.W.).
1923 (1936) MENCKEN *Amer.Language* 190: The origin of *wobbly* is thus given by Mortimer Downing, a member of the I.W.W. in its heyday: In Vancouver, in 1911, we had a number of Chinese members, and one restaurant keeper would trust any member for meals. He could not pronounce the letter *w,* but called it *wobble,* and would ask: "You I. *Wobble Wobble* ?" and when the card was shown credit was unlimited. Thereafter the laughing term among us was I. *Wobbly Wobbly.* **1963** *Press* Dec. 5: Grogan could find no sympathetic ear to listen to the Old Wobbly Theory, indeed it seemed that he himself was dead.

wolfberry *n.* the snowberry, *Symphoricarpos occidentalis.*
1909 CAMERON *New North* 143: Another day brought to the blotting-pads . . . the flower of the wolf-berry, fireweed, and ladies'-tresses. **1910** FERGUSON *Janey Canuck* 199: The trail runs through fields aflame with golden-red asters, "Black-eyed Susans," wolf-berry, and big, white convolvuli that stare at us with wonder-wide eyes. **1937** CONIBEAR *Northland Footprints* 194: The tearing winds of September plucked them [leaves] from swamp-willow . . . grey wolf-berry, high-bush cranberry. . . . **1952** LYONS *Trees, Shrubs* 72: Wolfberry . . . has leaves usually not hairy beneath. Stamen and styles are longer than petals. Sporadic occurrence.

wolf certificate *Obs.* a certificate issued by a county and entitling the bearer to a bounty payment for killing a wolf.
1853 STRICKLAND *Canada West* I 185: According to an act of the Provincial Parliament, six dollars must be paid by the county treasurer for every wolf-certificate signed by a magistrate.

wolf dog *North* a sled-dog having wolf ancestry. Cp. **Eskimo dog** and **malemute.**
1896 MCNAUGHTON *Overland to Cariboo* 47: A large number of wolf-dogs were prowling about . . . They were precisely the same as those used by travellers in the Arctic. . . . **1925** *Beaver* Mar. 107/1: It was a splendid sight, their coming in, Indians and great wolf dogs with bells on. **1953** BANFILL *Lab.Nurse* 19: Higher up on the rocks, the mossy grass knolls were dotted with tethered wolf dogs.

wolfer† *n. West, Hist.* See 1930 quote. See also **wolf hunter** and **wolver.**
1879 *Sask.Herald* (Battleford, N.W.T.) 24 Feb. 1/2: Five good carcasses, the remains of three that had been

devoured, and three crows, recently fell to the share of one "wolfer." **1930** MACINNES *Rockies* 66: Even more disreputable than the whisky traders were the wolfers. They made their living by hunting the wolves that preyed upon the herds of bison. **1965** *Maclean's* 19 June 15/1: By the middle of the nineteenth century the trail was being used by beaver trappers and wolfers, by gold seekers and missionaries and whisky-traders.

wolf-fire *n.* See quote.
1899 MACKAY *Pioneer Life* 223: The light at the top was the mycelium of the fungus which, it is well known, develops on the decaying wood of the spruce and some other kinds of trees under certain climatic conditions, and shines at night with a pale, soft phosphorescence. It is frequently called by the country people "fox-fire," and sometimes "wolf-fire."

wolf hunter *Hist.* See **wolfer.**
1964 *Imperial Oil Rev.* Dec. 16/1: Here [Cypress Hills] in 1873 a party of drunken wolf hunters from Montana massacred a band of peaceful Assiniboines.

wolf jaw actinomycosis, a disease common in cattle.
1950 CREIGHTON *Lunenburg County* 101: . . . I was able to cure lumps on an animal's jaw—wolf jaw it was called.

wolf-juice *n. Slang* See quotes.
1963 *Maclean's* 16 Nov. 65/1: . . . soon after I introduced him to wolf-juice, a beverage made with hundred-percent grain alcohol. *Ibid.* 65/2: . . . I was in no fit state to do anything except hurry home and seek solace in a jar of wolf-juice.

wolf range *Obs.* See quote.
1884 (1957) GUILLET *Valley of the Trent* li: . . . at this point the country is entirely uninhabited and is a "wolf range," so called on account of the numerous bands of wolves that roam through the unbroken forests. . . .

wolf-willow *n. West* any of several shrubs, especially the silverberry, *q.v.*
1889 DONKIN *Trooper* 86: The luscious perfume of wolf-willow and wild rose . . . come scampering on the western breeze. **1929** MOBERLY *When Fur Was King* 193: Flat on their bellies, taking advantage of every bit of cover, each tuft of grass, each tiny island of wolf-willow, they slipped forward. . . . **1955** MCCOWAN *Upland Trails* 82: The name of this common but handsome shrub is Silverberry (*Elaeagnus argentea*), better known to prairie residents as Wolf willow, a name probably bestowed upon it by some early fur-trader or settler who noted that the Prairie wolf constantly found concealment amongst these grey shrubs. **1963** SYMONS *Many Trails* 108: . . . a vagrant breeze from the open prairie brought to me the sweet, almost cloying scent of the silver wolf-willow. . . .

wolver *n. Hist.* See **wolfer.**
1903 SETON *Animal Heroes* 113: The ranchmen offered a bounty for each Wolf killed, and every cowboy out of work, was supplied with traps and poison for wolf-killing. The very expert made this their sole business and became known as wolvers. **1954** HAGELL *Grass was Free* 44: The big cattle killer, the prairie lobo, was now under almost as strict control as the reservation Red Man, and the wolver was being forced to turn to other more remunerative forms of making grub stake.

wolverine† *n.* **1 a.** a large fur-bearing animal,

Gulo luscus, of the northern forests and tundra, noted for its guile and craftiness. See also **beaver-eater, carcajou** (def. 1a), **glutton, Indian devil** (def. 1), **mountain devil, quickhatch, skunk-bear,** and **wolverine devil.**
1743 (1949) ISHAM *Observations* 141: Wolvereen's, or Quequahatches . . . are very Glomsay and Slow footed, and cou'd not have imagin'd they shou'd Kill Deer as they do, not by running them Downe, no! they Gett in a tree and as the Deer passes, they spring upon their back's, gett hold of their Neck and their hang and Suck their blood, tell the Deer trops [sic]. . . . **1872** DASHWOOD *Chiploquorgan* 186: The wolverine . . . often called "Indian Devil," is very rarely met with in the Maritime provinces of Canada. **1965** *Islander* 14 Feb. 5/1: All the time I thought it was all hooey about wolverines robbing traps. . . .

b. the valued fur of this animal.
1749 DRAGE *Voyage* II 3: These Skins in the Hudson's Bay Company Sales, are called Wolverins, and they are so named at the Factories. **1957** *Annual Pictorial Rev.* 71: [Caption] Note the hood of wolverine . . . .

c. the flesh of the wolverine used as food.
1926 (1937) CHRISTIAN *Unflinching* 58: Having no fish we had foxes for supper and they certainly seemed exceptionally good with a little bit of flour added and warmed up in Wolverine fat. **1954** PATTERSON *Dangerous River* 228: I supped off muscular chunks of wolverine and a thick mess of rolled oats and beans cooked in wolverine soup.

2 in figurative uses, with reference to persons having crafty, destructive, or gluttonous characteristics.
1923 SCOTT *Witching of Elspie* 76: "There now," she said, "you good-for-nothing wolverine, think of that." **1960** *Star Wkly* 13 Aug. 25/2: The jumble of sunniness and wolverine temper, affection and calculation that lies behind the expressionless smile of Jack Kent Cooke is headed for the United States.

wolverine devil See **wolverine** (def. 1a).
1957 HARRIS *Cariboo Trail* 142: "No, them Injins know plenty, I figger, about . . . wolverine devils."

woman's (or women's) boat See **oomiak** and picture.
1774 LA TROBE *Mission Labrador* 14: The Esquimaux can go much more conveniently from place to place in their Kajaks and women's boats, when the water is open, than on their sledges over the ice, and are not so much exposed to the cold. **1853** INGLEFIELD *Summer Search* 19: Their kyacks, and their light canoes, are principally employed in fishing operations, and a larger vessel, which is called a woman boat (being the only kind in which their women can venture), is used where whales are to be attacked, or fish in large quantities taken. **1954** *Peoples of the N.W.T.* 17: The umiak, or women's boat, was used to move families and their belongings from point to point by sea. This open boat, sometimes large enough to carry 30 people with their possessions and dogs, was built of driftwood lashed together with seal skin thongs and covered with seal skins.

woman's head [see **tête de femme**] *Obs.* See **niggerhead** (def. 2a).
1823 FRANKLIN *Journey* 768: This, and the other species of Dicrana, form dense tufts on the Barren Grounds, that are very troublesome to pedestrians, and obtain from the Indians the name of women's heads, because, they say, when you kick them they do not get out of the way. **1836** (1935) STRANG *Pioneers in Can.* 65: Our way lay through swamps, covered with what the Indians

call women's heads, which are round hummocks of moss-covered earth. . . . **1852** RICHARDSON *Arctic Exped.* 191: . . . the hassocks . . . bear, among the Chepewyan tribes, the name of "women's heads," and render the footing of pedestrians insecure and dangerous.

woman's knife *n.* See **ooloo** and picture.
1795 (1911) HEARNE *Journey* 169: The men's bayonets and women's knives are also made of copper. **1896** RUSSELL *Far North* 194: The "woman's knife" is made by the natives from saw blades; the pattern, which is that of a mincing knife and the manner of using remain the same as when made of stone; the women use them in cutting cloth, leather, or meat—in fact, for every purpose for which a knife may be employed.

wongan *n.* See **wanigan.**

wood *v.* *Obs. or Hist.* See **wood up.**
1892 (1948) *Beaver* June 42/2: Next day they spent three hours "wooding" five miles before reaching Fort Norman, where 150 "pieces" went ashore. **1922** *Ibid.* Apr. 21/2: Never was freight unloaded and the boat wooded in quicker time.

wood bison See **wood buffalo.**
1853 REID *Young Voyageurs* 7: There the fur-bearing animals exist in greatest plenty, and many others whose skins are valuable in commerce, as the moose, the wapiti, and the wood-bison. **1896** WHITNEY *On Snow-Shoes* 116: Little is known of the wood-bison, except that he is gradually going the way of the plains species, from the difficulty of maintaining an existence where climate, pasturage, and man are all against him. **1955** HARDY *Alta Anthol.* 258: The great buffalo herds the Indians hunted are gone from the prairies, but their cousins, the wood-bison, are thriving and increasing in the north-eastern corner of Alberta. Their home is Wood Buffalo Park—a refuge larger than all of Belgium—and this is indeed Canada's strangest national park, for it has been set aside much more for animals than for man.

woodboat *n.* *N.B., Hist.* See quote.
1965 MACBEATH & CHAMBERLIN *New Brunswick* 217: On the St. John River another answer was the woodboat—a rough, stubby-looking, slow, but popular little boat built chiefly along the river's lower shores. Woodboats were not all just alike, but most of them had a stoutly curved bow and a cut-off stern with a rudder.

wood buffalo a variety of bison, *Bison bison athabascae,* found in lightly wooded regions of northern Alberta and the Mackenzie District. See also **strong wood buffalo, thickwood buffalo, wood bison,** and **woodland bison.** Also spelled *woods buffalo.*
1810 (1897) COUES *New Light* II 622: Deschamps came in with two cows; a few are seen about Fish Lake, but they are the wood buffalo, more shy and wild than those on the plains. **1891** *Medicine Hat Times* (Alta) 23 July 1/5: The wood buffalo inhabits Athabasca and Peace River districts principally, and their numbers are comparatively small, so that their robes are seldom seen in this part of the country. **1958** *Edmonton Jnl* 24 June 4 1/3: Not quite as serious, but certainly a factor in economics, was the fact that the new buffalo which emerged was larger than the plains buffalo but smaller than the true wood buffalo. **1964** *Western Wkly* 1 July 3/1: These northern buffalo were known as the Wood Buffalo. Some biologists classify them as a separate species because of their somewhat larger size and darker colour.

wood buffalo country See 1946 quote.
1936 STEELE *Policing the Arctic* 139: Those deep drifts proved an equally severe handicap to Johnson and Gairdner, making March patrols to keep an eye on the wood-buffalo country. **1946** *Beaver* Mar. 47/2: . . . he explored the wood buffalo country between Peace River and Great Slave Lake. . . .

wood camp See **woods camp.**

wood caribou See **woods caribou.**

wood cat *Obs.* See **marten** (def. 1).
1768-82 (1904) LONG *Voyages* 77: The country everywhere abounds with wild animals, particularly bears . . . wood cats. . . . **1907** MILLAIS *Newfoundland* 280: We received a visit from Micky John and a little boy of nine . . . who were on their way to Sambadesta (St. John's Lake), where they meant to spend the fall trapping "wood-cats."

woodchuck† ['wood,tʃʌk] *n.* [< Algonk. See note] See **groundhog** (def. 1).
☛ *This word appears to have been derived by folk etymology from earlier* **woodshock,** *q.v., itself a folk etymology meaning fisher, q.v., from an Algonkian word of similar meaning, as Cree* o(t)chãk, *which also came into English as* **wejack,** *q.v. At some time in the eighteenth century the term* **woodshock** *appears to have been transferred from the fisher to the groundhog, in which sense the alteration* **woodchuck** *has become generalized.*
*a***1820** (1838) HEAD *Forest Scenes* 309: One of the men brought in an animal . . . called a wood-chuck, or ground-hog, about the size of a Chinese pig half grown and resembling a guinea pig in shape and species. **1958** *Cdn Red Cross Junior* Nov. 30/1: While digging, he came upon an animal's burrow, and following it to the end, we found a groundhog, or woodchuck.

wood-claim *n.* *B.C.* a small timber limit (def. 1a) such as might be used by a hand-logger.
1954 EVANS *Mist* 169: The other night she heard him tell Matt that if he cleared enough on the wood claim he would make a down payment on a truck.

wood deer *North* See **woodland caribou.**
1923 WALDO *Down Mackenzie* 89: They have the region to themselves except for the wood deer and the wolves.

wood duck See 1866 quote.
1832 (1953) RADCLIFF *Letters* 171: The *Wood Duck* is so termed from lighting in the trees; and is, of course, very easily shot. **1866** KING *Sportsman in Canada* 215: The Wood-duck (*Aix sponsa*) which is called also the "Summer duck" and "Tree duck" is not only one of the most beautiful of all its family, but is excelled in plumage by few of the feathered race. **1955** MCCOWAN *Upland Trails* 124: Often the vacant nest-chamber of a flicker is used by a Wood duck: sometimes the abandoned cradle of a Pileated woodpecker is occupied. **1962** *Chronicle-Herald* (Halifax) 8 Aug. 14/2: . . . the hunter must be able to distinguish between the wood duck and all other species.

wood gopher *West* See **bushy-tailed wood rat.**
1957 MOWAT *Dog* 165: . . . I shared the tenancy with a dozen chipmunks . . . three bushy-tailed wood gophers . . . and a baker's dozen of garter snakes. *Ibid.* 167: It was my owl . . . gripping the still-wriggling body of a wood gopher in its talons.

wood grouse† See **spruce partridge.**
1963 MCTAVISH *Behind the Palisades* 70: There was [York Factory, c1880] beaver . . . wood-grouse—pheasants we used to call them—trout. . . .

woodhawk *n. West, Hist.* See quote. See also **wooding stage.**
1965 SHEPHERD *West of Yesterday* 117: The water was shallow, hence only day [steamboat] travel was safe. Refuelling was done at woodhawks, supplies of wood piled in readiness at the river bank in strategic places.

wooding stage or **stop** *Hist.* a place where wood-burning steamers took on wood for fuel. See also **woodhawk** and **wood up.**
1888 (1890) ST. MAUR *Impressions* 226: We stopped to-day in the steamer at a wooding-stage, and to my surprise, were hailed from the bank. . . . **1928** FREEMAN *Nearing North* 156: Hardly were we well away from the wooding stop than a cry went up from a gesticulative half-breed that his partner "Frenchy" was missing.

wooding-up *n. Hist.* the taking on of wood for fuel by steamers. See also **wood up.**
1872 (1873) GRANT *Ocean to Ocean* 56: Captain Bell's style of wooding-up contrasted favorably with that of the captain of the *Frances Smith*. **1928** FREEMAN *Nearing North* 54: Awakened before daylight by a series of bumps, followed by the grind of the winch and the sound of shouted orders, I peered out to find the searchlight playing along a pile of cut spruce and the *Thomas* just mooring for its first wooding-up. **1939** *Beaver* Sep. 24/1: Slabs of bacon were thrown into the fire-box of the boiler until a wooding-up place could be reached. **1945** CALVIN *Saga* 146: . . . to go ashore from the ferry-boat you walked across their decks among wheel-barrows of the "wooding-up" gangs.

wood island [trans. of *islet de bois,* q.v.] *Obs.* See **bluff** (def. 3a).
1871 (1951) *Beaver* June 20/1: It [Red River country] is a vast prairie dotted here and there at intervals of about 10 or 15 miles with what are called Wood Islands.

woodland bison or **buffalo** See **wood buffalo.**
1891 *Cdn Indian* Aug. 307: With the exception of the Woodland buffalo, in the northern parts of Assiniboia or Saskatchewan, there is now probably not a native buffalo of the plains to be found. **1896** RUSSELL *Far North* 231: The wood buffalo, or—to use a more exact term—woodland bison, is described as larger and darker than the buffalo of the plains. **1909** CAMERON *New North* 147: Evidently the beautiful thick coat of the woodland bisons allows them to laugh at the mosquito. . . .
1947 GILLHAM *Raw North* 25: Near our campsite we discovered the tracks of many of the woodland buffalo, and the remains of a very smelly skunk.

woodland caribou a species of caribou (def. 1), *Rangifer tarandus,* of the forested areas of northern Canada. See also **Indian deer, wood deer, woodland reindeer,** and **woods caribou.** Cp. **Barren ground caribou.**
1853 REID *Young Voyageurs* 154: . . . he had killed three caribou, of the large variety known as "woodland caribou." These are a species of the reindeer (*Cervus tarandus*). . . . **1863** HIND *Exploring Labrador* I 213: The Caribou, or American Reindeer [is] sometimes called the Woodland Caribou, to distinguish it from

the Barren Ground Caribou. **1897** WILSON *Yukon* 53: The woodland caribou is found throughout the lake and upper river country. **1965** SYMINGTON *Tuktu* 44: The woodland caribou eats about the same forage as the barren-ground caribou. . . .

woodland reindeer *Obs.* See **woodland caribou.**
1852 RICHARDSON *Arctic Exped.* 290: Whether these be the same with the woodland reindeer, which inhabit the southern districts of Rupert's Land and the adjoining parts of Canada . . . has not been determined, no comparison having been instituted.

woodland wolf *Rare* See **timber wolf.**
1908 MAIR *Mackenzie Basin* 180: In some seasons the woodland wolf is more abundant than usual at certain points throughout the north.

woodlot *n.* **1** See **bush** (def. 2).
1922 PICKTHALL *Bridge* 230: Here and there some wood-lot rang to the sound of an axe. **1945** CALVIN *Saga* 168: A mixed lot . . . had come into Toronto by rail—gleanings from the wood-lots of "old" Ontario. **1965** *Kingston Whig-Standard* (Ont.) 6 Mar. 12/5: In the area north of the Bay of Quinte we have a few such woodlots, which have been cared for over several years. . . .

2 a relatively small holding of forested land which is used as a source of wood for commercial purposes.
1951 ANGIER *At Home* 102: We could hear the hollow ring of Dudley's ax from his woodlot a quarter-mile inland when we passed his cabin on our way to the river. **1954** EVANS *Mist* 127: After breakfast he took his axe and crosscut saw and put in the morning at the woodlot. **1963** *Globe and Mail* (Toronto) 26 Apr. 7/7: The next 10 recommendations deal with . . . use of woodlot products, building of windbreaks and snow fences.

wood partridge *North* See **spruce partridge.**
1691 (1929) KELSEY *Papers* 6: Went a hunting all Returning in the Evening having kill'd nothing but 2 wood partridges & one squirrel. **1743** (1949) ISHAM *Observations* 124: Wood partridges are not nigh so plenty as those afore mention'd . . . are Very fatt in the fall and good Eating, but in the Depth of winter are hardly worth Killing. **1896** WHITNEY *On Snow-Shoes* 298: Another, the wood-partridge, has brownish plumage, spotted with white and black. **1949** ROBERTS *Mackenzie* 135: Traders and clerks ventured into the surrounding country to shoot ptarmigan or wood-partridge.

wood pigeon *Obs.* See **passenger pigeon.**
1792 (1911) SIMCOE *Diary* 91: Talbot gave a shilling to liberate some wood pigeons I must have otherwise seen and heard fluttering most disagreeably. *a*1820 (1838) HEAD *Forest Scenes* 237: I soon perceived that a flock of wood pigeons had settled themselves all round about me. . . . **1897** DURAND *Reminiscences* 184: The wild wood pigeons used to visit us from the south in tens of thousands in my early life; so thick did they fly that they could be killed with clubs and sticks . . . of late, that is, for twenty or thirty years, they seem to have left us. **1959** MCATEE *Folk-Names* 41: Passenger Pigeon [was also called] wood pigeon ("Hudson Bay," Ont.).

wood-ranger *n.* **1** *Lumbering, Obs.* See **cruiser** (def. 1).
1842 *Bytown* [Ottawa] *Gaz.* 4 May 2/5: The house of a person who was acting as a kind of wood ranger to the party was set fire to in the night and himself and family narrowly escaped perishing. **1891** OXLEY *Chore-Boy* 5: An open space . . . presented itself to the keen eye of the woodranger traversing the trackless wastes of forest as a fine site for a lumber camp.

2 *Fur Trade, Hist.* See **coureur de bois** (def. 1).

1883 *Trans.Hist.& Sci.Soc.Man.* III 2/2: The inland voyageurs rejoiced in the name "coureurs des bois" or wood rangers, going as they did to Athabasca and the Rocky Mountains. **1905** DAWSON *St.Lawrence* 289: The others ... became the forerunners of the coureurs de bois, or wood rangers, who made the labours of the missionaries doubly difficult by their disorders and evil example. **1908** LAUT *Conquest N.W.* I 235: Taking on board one hundred and twenty woodrangers, Iberville sailed from Quebec on August 10, 1694.

wood rat 1 *Obs.* See **muskrat** (def. 1).

1760 JEFFERYS *Descr.New France* 37: The fur of this animal ... that of the otter ... the wood-rat ... and martin, are what is called the *Menüe Peleterie,* or lesser furs.

2 a rat of the genus *Neotoma* whose habitat is the bush, as the bushy-tailed wood rat, *q.v.*

1836 (1932) MCLEAN *Notes* 175: A most destructive little animal, the wood rat ... [is] of a grey colour, and of nearly the size and form of the common rat, but the tail resembles that of the ground squirrel. **1939** O'HAGAN *Tay John* 22: They had for food ... marmot, squirrels and wood-rats when times were bad.

wood road a road used for hauling wood, either from a woodlot or from a lumber camp.

1905 MOTT *Jules* 38: Across the clearing the two went; then down a wood road till it ended, and on into the woods. **1933** MERRICK *True North* 319: In the days of the lumbermen there were ... a bridge across the channel and a woodroad way in to the hills. **1954** BRUCE *Channel Shore* 89: In early winters he and James had cut firewood there and hauled it out over the wood road he had swamped, and up the main road, home.

woodrover *n. Obs.* See **coureur de bois** (def. 1).

1687 (1948) *H.B.C.Letters Outward* 280: His Most Christian Ma[jes]tie. hath last of all given his order to Prevent the Incurtions of whose which wee call Woodrovers or People without Tolleration. ...

wood-runner *n.* See **woods-runner.**

woods boss *Lumbering* See **woods superintendent.**

1928 PERRY *Two Reds* 44: "... he's a scrapper from way back. Sort of a bully in the village, I guess." "Derosier's woods boss," breathed Gwen. **1938** CASH *I Like B.C.* 172: He was amazed when on a side-hill in the depths of the forest he found the whole logging company, owner, woods' boss and engineer was a woman. **1952** (1965) HAMILTON *Cdn Quotations* 127: The Main John. Lumbermen's expression for woods bosses.... [See **Main John** for full quote.]

woods camp *Lumbering* See **logging camp.** Also *wood camp.*

1905 (1958) *B.C.Hist.Qtly* XVIII 221: A man, Camille, from one of these wood camps, on his way to the fort for a supply of provisions, placed, foolishly, a remnant of salt salmon he had with him on one of these wolf baits.... **1930** *Cdn Labor Defender* May 10: They organized a strike amongst the unemployed "Relief" workers who were herded in a winter wood camp in tents some 40 miles out in the country, with wages $2.00 per day for married men and $1.00 a day for single men. **1965** *Sun* (Vancouver) 17 June 35/4: MB and PR has begun construction of 350 homes on three of its west coast divisions in an attempt to wipe out the shacktown concept from its woods camps.

woods caribou See **woodland caribou.** Also *wood caribou.*

1873 (1904) BUTLER *Wild North Land* 108: Now and again a wood Cariboo crossed the track. **1897** TUTTLE *Golden North* 96: There are two species of caribou in the country. One—the ordinary kind—is found in most parts of the north. This much resembles and is generally spoken of as the reindeer. The other is known as the "Wood caribou," being a much larger and more beautiful animal. **1956** KEMP *Northern Trader* 191: It was a woods caribou, standing in midstream and nibbling at some grass that sprouted in the water.

woods-cruising *n. Lumbering* See **timber-cruising.**

1909 (1926) ROBERTS *Backwoodsman* 47: He brought him round this morning because he had to get off to woods cruising.

woodser *n. Fur Trade, Obs.* a fur-post employee whose task it was to obtain firewood and lumber in the woods. Cp. **chantier** (def. 3).

1777 (1951) *Sask.Jnls* 122: One Man came from the Woodsers for Provisions.

woodshock *n.* [< Algonk., alteration of Cree *o(t)chāk*] *Obs.* See **fisher.** See also **wejack.** Cp. **woodchuck.**

1719 (1965) *Letters from Hudson Bay* 75n: Marginal note in another hand: "has sent 14 wooskocks but not castoreum." **1784** PENNANT *Arctic Zoology* 82: This animal inhabits *Hudson's Bay* ... [where] they are called *Wejacks* and Woodshocks. ... **1836** BACK *Arctic Land* 491: The skins of the pekan are called "woodshocks" at the Hudson's Bay Company's sales. **1869** NARTWIG *Polar World* 316: The pekan, or woodshock ... generally lives in burrows near the banks of rivers, as it principally feeds on the small quadrupeds that frequent the water.

wood sled, sledge, or **sleigh** a low, sturdy sleigh drawn by oxen or horses and used to haul wood in winter.

1852 RICHARDSON *Arctic Exped.* 289: He was appointed to attend to the officers' fires, and immediately set about preparing his wood-sledge according to his own fashion. **1863** (1930) *Cdn Hist.Rev.* XI 41: Before the waggon was in use the whole crop of grain and hay had to be drawn in what was called a wood sled. **1885** HAIGHT *Country Life* 275: We left the house after dinner with a yoke of oxen and wood-sleigh freighted with pails and tubs to bring back our expected prize. **1954** BRUCE *Channel Shore* 16: Now it was nothing but a track for woodsleds in winter....

woods manager *Lumbering, Esp.Nfld* See **woods superintendent.**

1955 *Western Star* (Corner Brook, Nfld) 14 Mar. 6/4: ... our former woods manager had been selected for this most important position.... **1958** *Evening Telegram* (St. John's) 6 May 19/1: J. D. Roberts, woods manager, pointed out that the portion which broke was the lead or "sheer" boom and not the main holding boom....

woods-runner *n.* Also *wood-runner.* **1** *Fur Trade, Hist.* See **coureur de bois** (def. 1).

1716 (1965) *Letters from H.B.* 57: ... the French wood-runners ... are settled in that lake they call the Sea Lake [Lake Winnipeg]. ... **1743** (1949) ISHAM *Observations* 99: But to his Surprize about ½ a mile from his tent, he Imagin'd he see a parcill of wood Runners, or French Indians, with gun's upon their shoulder's a comming towards him.... **1908** LAUT *Conquest N.W.* I 157: Such luck as a French wood-runner deserting from Canada to the Hudson's Bay was promptly recognized by the order: "To Jan Ba'tiste Larlee, £1-5, a periwig to keep him loyal." **1916** WOOD *Tourist's N.W.* 366: Fifty years later, Pierre Radisson and Medard de Groseillers, "the most renowned and far-travelled wood-runners that New France had yet produced," reached the same sea by canoe-ways from the south. **1961** JONES *Trappers* 8: . . . a tough, colorful, sometimes cruel, always superbly skilled breed of men called by the French *coureurs de bois,* by the English woods runners, by the Russians *promyshlenniki,* and by the American trappers, free men, and mountain men.

2 See **bushman** (def. 2).
1953 MOWERY *Mounted Police* 17: A grim and taciturn man this Wilson was, but the best scout and most experienced woods-runner in all Mackenzie or Keewatin.

woods superintendent *Lumbering* the person supervising logging operations over a wide area in a timber limit (def. 1a); a company's manager of operations in a logging area. See also **Main John, woods boss,** and **woods manager.**
1964 *Powell River News* 7 May 5/5: Jack Kliever, Mahood's woods superintendent, said that westerly winds last year caused considerable damage to the company's log pond at the mouth of Kelly Creek.

woodsworker *n. Lumbering* See **bushworker.**
1955 *Bush News* (Port Arthur, Ont.) Feb. 3/1: During the eight years he's been in the bush he has developed into a first-rate woodsworker.

wood thrush a kind of thrush, *Hylocichla mustelina,* found in wooded areas of eastern Canada.
1833 *Trans.Lit.& Hist.Soc.Que.* III 225: The Hermit Thrust . . . although perhaps inferior to the Wood Thrush, is a cheerful and melodious songster, not uncommon here. **1903** WHITE *Forest* 125: If you symbolize the hermit thrush by the flute, you must call the wood thrush a chime of little tinkling bells.

wood-tick *n.* a kind of tick, *Dermacentor andersoni,* a cause of spotted fever, tick fever, or Rocky Mountain fever, *q.v.*
1859 (1958) WATTERS *B.C.Cent.Anthol.* 246: I climbed mountains and got covered with wood-ticks as I ploughed through the sage-brush and greasewood. . . . **1942** CASH *Million Miles* 57: Fitzpatrick, our eager Irish terrier, came home with a couple of woodticks in his ear. **1962** FRY *Ranch on the Cariboo* 243: The wood tick, occasionally seen in the Cariboo, is often a dreaded menace on the spring ranges of the dry belt: the Kamloops, Nicola and Okanagan country.

wood ticket *Hist.* a ticket given by steamer captains in return for wood taken on as fuel, the supplier later claiming payment at the steamship company's head office.
1945 CALVIN *Saga* 142: The captains carried books of "Wood Tickets," bound with stubs like cheque-books. . . .

wood up *Hist.* of a steamboat or locomotive, take on wood for fuel. See also **wood,** *v.,* **wooding stage,** and **wooding-up.**
1858 *Victoria Gaz.* 28 July 1/3: Some ten minutes inside the entrance from Fraser River, the word was passed to

"wood up!" and the *Umatilla* was headed into a quiet little cove . . . where all hands . . . sprang ashore . . . to cut and collect the required fuel. **1888** (1890) ST. MAUR *Impressions* 207: At one place . . . we drew near the bank to "wood up,"—as taking on board wood for the engines is called. . . . **1945** CALVIN *Saga* 141: Hundreds upon hundreds of cords of wood were hauled over the ice . . . to ensure that the firm's steamers might always be able to "wood up". . . . The railways, too, in these early days had to have wood available at frequent intervals along their lines—the passengers sometimes helped to "wood up" the tender.

wood wolf 1 See **brush wolf.**
1908 MAIR *Mackenzie Basin* 182: I think the wood wolf inhabiting the plains country is much smaller than the kind found further north, and also lighter in color. . . .

2 See **timber wolf.**
1922 *Beaver* Feb. 37/1: . . . we saw an exciting chase between a large wood wolf and a caribou.

woolly *adj.* See **wild-and-woolly.**

woolly dog *Pacific Coast, Hist.* a species of dog whose wool was used in weaving by the Coast Salish Indians.
[**1798** (1955) JENNESS *Indians of Can.* 68n: The dogs . . . much resembled those of Pomerania, though in general somewhat larger . . . so compact were their fleeces, that large portions could be lifted up by a corner without causing any separation. They were composed of a mixture of a coarse kind of wool, with very fine, long hair, capable of being spun into yarn.] **1887** (1894) BEGG *Hist.of B.C.* 217: . . . these "woolly dogs" seem to have become extinct. These Indians used to shear them, and make a sort of blanket out of the wool. **1956** *Beaver* Summer 39/1: A painting by Paul Kane, dated 1848, showing one of these dogs freshly shorn, with a woman in the background spinning, is the only illustration in existence of the so-called "woolly dog."

woolly Labrador tea *Rockies* See 1955 quote. Cp. **Labrador tea** (def. 1a).
1953 *Cdn Geog.Jnl* June 260/1: Woolly Labrador tea is perhaps most widespread . . . with bearberry a close second. **1955** MCCOWAN *Upland Trails* 82: The most widespread flowering shrub in Canada is in all probability that known as Labrador Tea. There are two varieties of this plant but the one best known in the Canadian Rockies is that known as Woolly Labrador tea, the glossy leaves having a rusty-red wool on the underside.

woolly-whipper *n. West and North, Slang* See **blizzard.**
1953 MOWERY *Mounted Police* 149: Here I footslog three hundred miles through an Arctic woolly-whipper . . . and you sit there fiddling with that silly doodad.

wooskock *n. Obs.* See **woodshock.**

work bee a voluntary co-operative undertaking to do some task requiring the efforts of a number of people. See also **bee.**
1958 *Cut Knife Grinder* (Sask.) 27 Mar. 1/1: A workbee was called on Tuesday . . . to start repairing the hall. **1961** *Edmonton Jnl* 4 July 28/2: Fifty men formed a work bee . . . to greatly improve conditions at the once popular picnic grounds.

worm fence† See **snake fence.**
1824 *Canadian Mag.* III 100: What is termed the Virginia worm fence, formed by split rails laid in a zig zag position with the ends of the rail crossing each

other occupies too much ground, and requires an enormous number of rails. **1954** BRUCE *Channel Shore* 57: It annoyed him now to see . . . the staked zig-zag of Alex Neill's worm fence.

wrangle† *v.* [see **wrangler**] *West* **1** take care of or be in charge of saddle or pack horses. See also **wrangler** (def. 1).
1939 O'HAGAN *Tay John* 15: After a while he got a job wrangling horses on a party sent out to the mountains to line the rivers into the contours of the land. **1952** INNES *Campbell's Kingdom* 16: He wrangles a bunch of horses and acts as packer for the visitors in the summer.
2 *Figurative use.* See quote. See also **dude** (def. 1).
1966 BAITY *Wilderness Welfare* 149: I guess Skie's whole grown up life had been spent around horses, and most of it wrangling dudes in the foothills of Alta.

wrangle field or **pasture** a fenced field into which saddle horses are turned loose to pasture.
1951 HOBSON *Grass* 195: Tommy picked up his hackamore and started for the wrangle pasture and I went happily to the cookfire with the delicacies. **1963** SYMONS *Many Trails* 37: I left one man . . . to take care of things and run a fence around a few hundred acres to make a "wrangle field" (pasture) for our twenty-odd head of saddle horses.

wrangler† *n.* [< Am.E < Mex. Sp. *caverango* hostler, prob. influenced by E *wrangle* quarrel, struggle] *West* **1** a person having charge of a bunch of saddle horses, pack horses, etc. See also **horse wrangler** and **wrangle.**
1912 POCOCK *Man in the Open* 54: Then I procured an extra special, cherry-red, silk scarf out of the wrangler's kit. **1963** SYMONS *Many Trails* 54: This band of loose horses was called the "cavvy," and required two "wranglers," one to drive them with the wagon by day and one to herd them by night.
2 a cowboy. See also **cattle wrangler.**
1962 *Canada Month* May 36/3: Many of the early cowboys were American wranglers who accompanied the herds and remained on the open ranges of the Canadian territories. . . . **1966** *Alta Hist.Rev.* Winter 13: [Caption] A wrangler attempts to catch a horse inside a rope corral at a roundup camp in the 1890's.

wrapper *n. Esp.North* See **sled wrapper.**
1896 RUSSELL *Far North* 89: Behind them a confused mass of dog harness, wrappers, and flat sleds formed a barrier to keep out a score or more of giddés. . . . **1924** MASON *Arctic Forests* 30: Others [toboggans] have the tanned leather wrapper with the head and tail lines. **1957** *Aklavik Jnl* Mar. 6/2: Sam Dick with wife and child were mostly scared Feb. 20th when a Cessna 195 landing at Tuk veered into their dog team and caught the wrapper of the sled in one ski.

wuchak or **wuchusk** *n.* See **wejack.**

wusquay *n.* [< Algonk.; cf. Cree *wuski-cheman*] *Obs.* a birchbark canoe.
1861 *Nor'Wester* (R.R.S.) 1 June 3/3: The Ven. Archdeacon Hunter and the Rev. Mr. Cowley might also be seen paying their visits in the same characteristic vehicle: the red man's wusquay.

X.Y. *Fur Trade, Hist.* **1** See **X.Y. Company.**
1804 (1933) FARIES *Diary* 219: I was informed by
Laverdure, that the X.Y. were preparing to go a
derouine. **1822** (1931) MERK *Fur Trade* 189: He devotes
himself more to Legislating than to business and has
the entire lead of McDonald, George Keith and Leith
his old XY partisans. **1944** *Beaver* Dec. 3/2: . . . the
groundwork was already laid when the heads of the
newly amalgamated companies, the North West and the
X.Y., met at their headquarters at Fort William.

2 a member of the X.Y. Company, *q.v.*
*c*1902 LAUT *Trapper* 55: In Canada the French sided
with the Nor'Westers and X.Y.'s, who had sprung up
in opposition to the great English Hudson's Bay
Company.

X.Y. Company *Fur Trade, Hist.* a Montreal-
based fur company formed in 1798 by disaffected
Northwesters and absorbed by the North West
Company in 1804, so called because its packs were
labelled XY to keep them distinct from those of its
competitor, which were marked N.W. See also
**Little Company, New Company, New North West
Company, pottie** (def. 1), and **X.Y.**
1800 (1922) HARMON *Journal* 15: There is also another
fort . . . belonging to the X. Y. Company, under which
firm, a number of merchants of Montreal and Quebec,
&c. now carry on a trade into this part of the country.
1803 (1912) *Trans.Roy.Soc.Can.* VI 2 5: Both the North-
West Companies (Old North-West Co. and X Y
Company. Ed.) have vessels in the Upper Lakes (neither
of them on Ontario). . . . **1966** *Alta Hist.Rev.* 14 5/2n:
The XY Company, or New Northwest Company, was
organized in 1798 by a number of independent traders to
compete with the N. W. Co. and H. B. Co. It
established a number of posts in Alberta before being
absorbed by the N. W. Co. in 1804.

Yangee or **Yengee** *n. Hist.* See quotes. Cp.
Yankee.
1844 MARRYAT *Settlers in Canada* 50: Then Indians and
Yangees (that is, English) both try to gain same object,
only try in not the same way. **1942** RADDALL *His
Majesty's Yankees* 138: The Micmacs and Malicetes had
never lost their love for the French king, their hatred
for the "Yengees," and they clung to the faith of bloody-
minded Father Le Loutre. . . .

Yankee† *n.* [prob.ult. < Du *Jan Kees* John
Cheese, a nickname, the *s* being taken as a pl.
inflection] *Slang* **1** a native or citizen of the
United States, originally a New Englander.
1775 *Quebec Gaz.* 5 Oct. 3/1: A party of ours pursu'd
them and took Ethan Allen their commander, 17
Yankeys, and 16 Canadians, prisoners. **1838** HALIBURTON
Sam Slick viii: It wipes up the blue-noses considerable
hard, and don't let off the Yankees so very easy neither.
. . . **1918** LOWREY *Young Canada Boys* 25: . . . his chum
whispered: "Put her there, Chuck, you old Canuck, we
are allies now. The days of Stoney Creek are passed.
We've buried the hatchet with both England and
Canada . . . I'm Yankee, Chuck, old boy, but we'll
always be allies, won't we ?" **1967** *Kingston Whig-
Standard* (Ont.) 6 Mar. 15/5: The trophies . . . are
still in "Yankee" hands after RMC was whipped in
hockey and pistol-shooting . . . and narrowly lost the
debating contest.

2 a. *Hist.* any United-States-born immigrant to
the British North American provinces.
1810 (1957) GUILLET *Valley of the Trent* 254: I take the
liberty of mentioning . . . that a worthless Yanky of
the name of Truman Napping, has without authority
set himself down in Seymour, where he has built a
House and vends liquor in the most disorderly manner.
1818 PALMER *Journal* 231: The drunkard said it [Upper
Canada] was "a d——d wild country, full of yankies
and agues. . . ." **1832** (1902) LUNDY *Diary* 10: The white
emigrants from the United States are all termed
"Yankees." **1851** *Voice of the Fugitive* 2 July 3/1: It
has been but a short time since a colored gentleman
was put on the Grand Jury in Toronto, C.W., which
appears to have been very offensive to some of the
"blue skin" yankees there, who complained and curled
up their noses at it. **1926** LANGTON *Early U.C.* xxv:
. . . there was also, quite apart from political feeling, a
general dislike of the "Yankees," as they were always
called, who had migrated to Canada. **1963** GUILLET
Pioneer Farmer I 22: The Loyalists . . . were not
generally highly regarded by their contemporaries . . .
who included them with other "Yankees" settled in the
province.

b. *Obs.* a United Empire Loyalist, *q.v.*, or one of his
descendants.
1823 *Gleaner* (Niagara-on-the-Lake, U.C.) 1 Nov. 3/3:
I mean the U.E. Loyalists, and their descendents, who
have been but too frequently insulted by the opprobrious
epithet of Yankee, opprobrious at least in this part of
the country. **1825** *Canadian Mag.* IV 214: The landlord
was demonstrating his claim to be considered a yankee
from having been [a]cross the line on a smuggling
expedition where he lost his whole adventure.

c. *Derog., Obs.* in Upper Canada, a supporter of
the Radicalism, *q.v.*, adopted by many post-Loyalist
American immigrants and others. See also
Yankee Democrat.
1832 *Liberal* (St. Thomas, U.C.) 20 Sep. 3/1: I have
heard such men endeavoring to intimidate the ignorant
and assailing the cupidity of the better informed, by
asserting that Canadian reformers are seeking to

overthrow the Government, are disloyal yankees, and such like. **1834** *Brit.Colonial Argus* (St. Catharines, U.C.) 11 Jan. 2/6: . . . the imputation . . . that the Editor of the British Colonial Argus is a "Yankee," is as FALSE as it is meant to be scandalous. **1836** (1926) LANGTON *Early U.C.* 170: There was astonishingly little fighting considering the number of wild Irishmen we brought down, but they were altogether too strong for the Yankees, who after giving their votes generally mounted their horses and made off.

3 speech characteristic of Americans, in early use with special reference to New England speech; American English.
1822 *U.C.Gaz.* (York [Toronto]) 2 May 22/1: I consider that it would be conferring a signal benefit on future travellers from England, in America, to put a complete Yankee Dictionary and Vocabulary into their hands, by the aid of which they could be at no loss to understand what must otherwise appear strange and unintelligible. **1835** (1838) HALIBURTON *Sam Slick* 1: "You did not come from Halifax, I presume, did you?" in a dialect too rich to be mistaken as genuine Yankee. **1872** *Canadian Mthly* Jan. 87/1: If a language distinct from that of English has been formed in the States, let it be called Yankee: or if that name is wanting in dignity, by some other name which correctly denotes the fact. **1918** MACKAY *Trench and Trail* 117:

> They return with finer clothes,
> Speaking "Yankee" through their nose!
> That's the way the Gaelic goes—
> Pop! goes the Gaelic.

Yankee *adj.* **1** native to the United States.
1811 *Cdn Courant* (Montreal) 4 Feb. 3/2: I say in plain words, that if . . . a Yankey Ox, Hog, Cod-Fish, &c. can be allowed to pass free into Quebec by Craig's Road, the same indulgence should be allowed those coming to this Market. **1835** *Novascotian* (Halifax) 1 Oct. 288/1: I had heard of yankee clock pedlars, tin pedlars. and bible pedlars. . . . **1863** WALSHE *Cedar Creek* 260: How insignificant was gentle Mrs. Wynn beside the Yankee woman's portly presence! **1926** MAIR *Masterworks* XIV lii: Woe to the Yankee boy, had he appeared amongst us then [on Training Day].
2 characteristic of or pertaining to the United States or Americans.
1825 *Novascotian* (Halifax) 18 May 164/2: He was certainly a queer fish, something of a wag; and dealt just as much in Yankee lingo as he did in bulls and calves. **1837** (1926) LANGTON *Early U.C.* 187: . . . there are plenty of cooking stoves of Yankee construction to be bought here with all the coppers, etc., for £10 or £12 and a great convenience they are. . . . **1913** WILLIAMS *Wilderness Trail* 269: The man had Yankee blood in him somewhere, for now he was chewing tobacco industriously, and staining the snow in front of the barricade. . . .
3 made in the United States.
1827 (1829) MACTAGGART *Three Years* I 172: . . . let it drive the Yankee whisky into the lakes. . . . **1845** BEAVAN *Life in Backwoods N.B.* 31: One of [Sam Slick's] wooden-made yankee clocks is here. . . . **1872** DASHWOOD *Chiploquorgan* 26: My head gear was a broad brimmed Yankee felt hat.

Yankee Democrat See **Yankee,** *n.* (def. 2c).
1832 *Brockville Gaz.* (U.C.) 10 May 2/1: It is really astonishing to observe the ignorance, the daring, and the insolence of the contemptible Yankee Democrat faction in this country.

Yankeedom† *n. Slang, Obs.* the United States.
1860 *Nor'Wester* (R.R.S.) 14 Apr. 4/5: They sell me good Brandy at 6s. 3d. per quart while Indifferent Whiskey brought from Yankeedom and watered with R.R. muddy water fifty per cent, is sold almost at the same rate or 24s. per gal. by Pedlars. **1861** *Ibid.* 15 Nov. 2/5: On Monday morning, when they did not present themselves at the hour of work, suspicion took a different form—namely, that the scamps had scampered to Yankeedom.

Yankeefied† *adj. Slang, Obs.* **1 a.** of things, so made as to be characteristic of the United States and its people. Also spelled *Yankified.*
1788 *Quebec Herald* 26 Jan. 87/2: Let Mr. Habitant bring his yankefied slays, and draw up the hills and down the hills of Canada. . . . **1827** (1829) MACTAGGART *Three Years* I 189: To think of persons like us . . . launched out to Canada to raw pork, Yankified rum, and a soft bed of leaves. . . . **1963** GUILLET *Pioneer Farmer* I 85: Isabella (Bird) Bishop . . . found that the *smart gals* could hold up their end with the best of the men when it came to the *Yankified* jargon of table conversation . . . at an inn.
b. of speech, so uttered as to suggest or characterize an American.
1824 *Colonial Advocate* (Queenston, U.C.) 28 Oct. 3/3: "Yea more, he declares, (not modestly, with an 'I suppose,' nor even with a mild Yankified 'I expect'). . . . " **1825** *Novascotian* (Halifax) 5 Mar. 81/2: "Nor before it either, I calculate," snuffled a yankiefied voice from the corner. **1863** WALSHE *Cedar Creek* 137: He [an Indian] answered when spoken to, not in Mohawk, or Cherokee, or Delaware, but in nasal Yankeefied English; nay, he seemed weakly garrulous.
2 sympathetic to or in support of American ways, political attitudes, etc.
1832 *Liberal* (St. Thomas, U.C.) 13 Dec. 3/2: According to the doctrine of the Tories of Upper Canada, freedom of thought is *treason*—freedom of speech is *rebellion*—and liberty of forcing opinions and acting under them is becoming traitorous and yankefied. **1852** (1923) MOODIE *Roughing It* 221: But from this folly the native-born Canadian is exempt; it is only practised by the low-born Yankee, or the Yankeefied British peasantry and mechanics. **1891** (1905) BIGGAR *Oliver Mowat* II 579: I am quite sure that the Reformers will not be Yankeefied by unrestricted reciprocity, and I hope the Conservatives will not be Yankeefied either by any such means.

Yankee fix *Slang, Obs.* a compromising situation.
1846 TAYLOR *Narrative* 75: A Canadian farmer some time ago was placed in what is termed a Yankee fix, having been detected in the very act of attempting to drown a cart load of manure in the lake.

Yankee gang *Obs.* a kind of gang saw.
1858 (1957) GUILLET *Valley of the Trent* 275: Nassau Mills . . . the largest and most complete mill in the Counties . . . has 2 "yankee gangs". . . .

Yankeeish† *adj. Slang, Obs.* like an American.
1832 (1953) RADCLIFF *Letters* 135: We've got a very good girl in my place—a little Yankeeish as they say—but we must give and make allowances.

Yankeeism *n. Slang* **1** the quality that characterizes the United States or its people in their speech, customs, political views, etc.

1822 *Scribbler* (Montreal) 18 July 33: There are a few symptoms of yankeeism in the language, such as the use of the words *grade* for degree, and *avails* for profits. **1833** (1917) *London Hist.Soc.Trans.* VIII 24: It has two newspapers. The one a violent Tory, the other a Liberal, and represented as favoring Yankeeism, which I think, from all I have seen, is not true. *a*1855 (1956) ROSS *Fur Hunters* 21: . . . such things were now looked upon as a useless relic of "Yankeeism". . . .

2 a word, expression, turn of phrase, etc. that is characteristic of the speech of Americans; Americanism.

1822 *U.C.Gaz.* (York [Toronto]) 2 May 22/2: All those who read this epistle . . . will contribute . . . such words and terms as may be fairly deemed true Yankeeisms. . . . **1853** *Hamilton Gaz.* (C.W.) 28 Feb. 2/6: The article on the Agricultural Bureau—a Yankeeism, by the way, which we abhor—is a sad attempt at an apology for a disgraceful and barefaced job. **1882** *Edmonton Bull.* 25 Nov. 2/3: To use a Yankeeism, it is eternally and perennially behind time.

Yankeeland *n. Slang* the United States.

1832 (1915) *London & Middlesex Hist.Soc.Trans.* VI 78: There are many who "guess" and "calculate" and "expect" from Yankee land. **1839** (1964) GUILLET *Pioneer Days* 198: . . . a party of strolling players from Yankee-land [were performing]. **1918** LOWREY *Young Canada Boys* 140: "They say that William Lyon Mackenzie hiself escaped tuh Yankeeland by dressin' up ez a woman in petticoats."

Yankee leave *Slang, Obs.* leave taken secretly or without permission; French leave.

1853 STRICKLAND *Canada West* I 211: When too late, he . . . found his best plan was to take a Yankee leave, and clear out, leaving his unfinished home as a legacy to his creditors.

Yankee lingo See **Yankee**, *n.* (def. 3).

1963 GUILLET *Pioneer Farmer* I 85: But if the beef was plentiful but tough, most British travellers thought many Upper Canadians equally so. . . in their *Yankee lingo*.

Yankee pedlar *Hist.* See **Boston pedlar**.

1937 *B.C.Hist.Qtly* Apr. 78: . . . the Company did not have a monopoly of the trade, as there are, in the Fort Langley Journal, 1827-1830, and other material, many complaints about the American vessels—the "Yankee Pedlars" as the Hudson's Bay Co.'s employees called them—selling goods to Indians at lower prices than those charged by the Company, and paying higher prices for furs. **1963** GUILLET *Pioneer Farmer* I 87: "Yankee" peddlers brought over the first scythes. . . .

Yankee shave *Slang, Obs.* an instance of sharp practice.

1853 STRICKLAND *Canada West* I 188: It was a clever trick, no doubt—a real Yankee shave. . . .

Yankee sleigh *Obs.* See **American sleigh**. See also 1788 quote at **Yankeefied** (def. 1a).

1811 *Cdn Courant* (Montreal) 4 Feb. 3/2: I say in plain words, that if a Yankey Sleigh . . . can be allowed to pass free into Quebec by Craig's Road, the same indulgence should be allowed those coming to this Market.

Yankee tea *Obs.* See **hemlock tea**.

1842 WILLIS *Cdn Scenery* II 77: . . . we agreed to try the Yankee tea—hemlock sprigs boiled.

Yankee-town *n. Obs.* York, Upper Canada, so called because it was said to be the political headquarters of the Radicals, who were accused of being Yankees (def. 2c).

1831 *Cdn Freeman* (York [Toronto]) 21 Apr. 2/4: This contest terminated in the election of Mr. Shade and the rejection of Caleb Hopkins, the saddlebag candidate, after the Ryersonians putting forth their strength, & their political priests using every exertion in favour of the old grog-boss from Yankee-town.

Yankee war *Obs.* the War of 1812.

1813 *Montreal Herald* 2 Jan. 1/2: By keeping my eyes open to the various movements of the military since the Yankee war commenced, I have learned what I did not know before.

Yankified *adj.* See **Yankeefied**.

yard *n.* **1 a.** a browsing area where a group of moose or deer in winter tread down the snow, remaining there for protection and warmth until the fodder within easy reach is exhausted. See also **deer yard**, **moose-yard** (def. 1), **ravage**, and **yard**, *v.* (def. 1).

1828 *U.E.Loyalist* (York [Toronto]) 17 May 416/1: . . . after much fatigue they reached the neighbourhood of the yard or beat of the moose-deer. **1904** ROBERTS *Watchers of Trails* 355: The deer and moose were in their well-trodden "yards," for the snow was deep. **1964** *Star Wkly* 5 Dec. 37/1: They [moose] trample down "yards" in the snow, for cover and feed.

b. the moose or deer so grouped.

1872 DASHWOOD *Chiploquorgan* 39: The yard consists of generally three or four animals. Cows and young bulls yard together, the old bulls alone [moose].

2 a place where musk-ox huddle together for warmth and protection.

1899 PARKER *Translation* 234: I have friends on the Far Off River who show me the yards where musk-ox gather. . . .

3† *Lumbering* an assembly point for logs, often at a brow (def. 1). See also **yard**, *v.* (def. 2).

1943 KOROLEFF *Pulpwood Skidding* 7: The load is then dragged [by horse] over the trails swamped by the cutters to a rollway or a yard. **1952** PUTNAM *Cdn Regions* 440/2: From the yard, logs are hauled by truck or rail to tide-water where they are dumped. In some instances, the yard may be at the water's edge and then the logs are rolled directly into the water.

yard *v.* **1** of moose and deer, stay or establish themselves in a yard (def. 1a). See also **yarded** (def. 1) and **yard up**.

1872 DASHWOOD *Chiploquorgan* 39: If once disturbed they [moose] will travel miles before yarding afresh. **1921** HEMING *Drama of Forests* 245: On account of its wide-spreading and concave hoofs the Woodland caribou does not have to "yard" as other deer do in winter time, for thus provided with natural snowshoes, the caribou can pass over the deepest snow with little trouble. **1958** CAMERON *Canadian Mammals* 11: In winter several moose may yard together. . . .

2† *Lumbering* pile (logs) at a yard (def. 3). See also **yarded** (def. 2), **yarder**, and **yarding** (def. 1).

1925 DAVIS *United Churches B.C.* 93: By this time the weather had grown very cold and frozen the lake solid where they were "yarding," and along whose shore the twenty bunkhouses floated on rafts. **1953** SWANSON *Haywire Hooker* 34:

> Never stopped for dinner, ate her as we ran,
> Killed six punks and a chokerman;
> Yarded two million and sent them down the line
> Before the whistle blew for quitting time.

1963 MCKINNON *Forest Activities 1* 7: After the logs have been yarded to the "side," a loader places the tongs on the log at a point somewhat behind its centre of gravity.

yarded (up) *adj.* **1** of moose or deer, grouped in a yard (def. 1a). See also **yard,** *v.* (def. 1).

1902 ROBERTS *Kindred of Wild* 256: A herd of deer well yarded, under the leadership of an old and crafty buck, will come safe and sleek through the fiercest wilderness winter. **1921** *Beaver* June 9/1: It can be readily understood how easy it was for the Indians . . . to kill every animal found "yarded up."

2 *Lumbering* of logs, piled in a yard (def. 3). See also **yard,** *v.* (def. 2).

*a***1954** FOWKE *Folk Songs* 81: While loading teams with yarded logs I received my deathly wound. **1954** BRUCE *Channel Shore* 204: The picture formed in Alan's mind: a low slab-sided bunkhouse somewhere out back with logs yarded shoulder high and more being snaked in.

yarder *n. Lumbering* **1** a donkey or other engine rigged to haul logs from the woods to the track, skidroad, or landing. See also **yard,** *v.* (def. 2).

1919 *Camp Worker* 2 June 3/3: [There were] Two Ledgerwood skidders, one yarder, one swing, one ground swing and one roader, and not very high ball.

2 a vehicle used for hauling logs to a yard (def. 3).

1955 *Bush News* (Port Arthur, Ont.) Feb. 7/1: About 1,100 men are involved on the haul plus 450 horses, 125 trucks, 47 tractors, 5 graders, 4 draglines and 4 yarders. *c***1963** *New Sounds* 9/1: Cable skidding of logs to the skidway is carried out by self-mobile, A-frame yarders mounted on runner-equipped platforms; or track-mounted, steel-boomed yarders.

yarder (or yarding) engineer an operator of a yarder, *q.v.*

1919 *Camp Worker* 26 Apr. 5/2: There are very few railroad camps in this neck of the jungles which do not boast of having the best yarding engineer that ever took the slack out of a bull-hook. **1960** *Sun* (Vancouver) 2 June 50/8: We invite enquiries from Hookers & Riggers, Head Loaders, Yarder Engineers, etc., who are available now. Call Don Stevenson at B.C. Forest Products. . . .

yarding *n.* **1** *Lumbering* the assembling and stacking of logs in yards (def. 3). See also **yard,** *v.* (def. 2).

1942 HAIG-BROWN *Timber* 252: Leverman, Yarding or Skidder. Operates the levers which control the yarding or skidding from the woods to the track. **1955** *Bush News* (Port Arthur, Ont.) Feb. 7/1: Marathon Corp of Canada . . . is progressing right on schedule in all phases. Tree length falling and yardings are complete. . . .

2 *West* See quote.

1939 *Beaver* Mar. 50/1: The movement of freight between Waterways and Lehman's Landing is locally known as "yarding." To accomplish this we had at times as many as three power boats and seven barges in operation. . . .

yarding engineer See **yarder engineer.**

yard up See **yard,** *v.* (def. 1).

*c***1902** LAUT *Trapper* 122: The moose herds are yarding up in some sheltered feeding-ground. **1958** CAMERON

Cdn Mammals 10: In winter, especially during periods of deep snows, the deer "yard up." **1964** *Star Wkly* 5 Dec. 37/1: Ezra Ames . . . said the moose had started to "yard up," which they do at this time of year, travelling [in] herds of up to 20 bulls, cows, calves and yearlings.

yea *interj.* See **chee.**

1921 *Beaver* Nov. 13/2: In all sections of Canada east of the Rockies the terms used in driving dogs were taken from the French language—*'marche',* commonly used as *'march',* to start; *'yea'* for *'gee'* and *'chaw'* for *'haw'.* In this country west of the mountains they tried to copy from the east, but made a failure. The terms they used are *'mush', 'gee'* and *'haw'.*

yearly servant *Fur Trade, Hist.* a person accepting employment with the Hudson's Bay Company on a year-to-year basis of engagement. Cp. **tripman.**

1923 *Beaver* June 337/1: At the age of eighteen [1880] Pierre engaged himself to the Hudson's Bay Company as a yearly servant.

Yellowback *n. Slang, Derog., Obs.* an Orangeman.

*c***1878** (1963) *Cdn Literature* Spring 40: Come all you gallant Irishmen who love your church and creed / I hope you'll pay attention to the few lines that you read, / Concerning your church and countrymen, your brothers, one and all / It's how we licked the Yellowbacks in the city of Montreal. [Reference to a riot, July 12, 1877.

yellow bear *Fur Trade, Obs.* See **cinnamon bear.**

1793 (1933) MACDONELL *Diary* 116: The . . . Assinibouan River is the part most abounding in all the north west, the following animals are natives of it . . . Grizzly, Black, Brown, and yellow [bears]. . . .

yellow-bellied marmot a species of marmot, *Marmota flaviventris,* closely related to the hoary marmot, *q.v.* See also **rock chuck.**

1958 CAMERON *Cdn Mammals* 58: Both the hoary and yellow-bellied marmots are found in our western mountains where they live among the rockslides of steep mountain slopes. **1963** *Sun* (Vancouver) 21 June 19/1: Three of us had some interesting though not too productive yellow-bellied marmot (rock woodchuck) hunting around Merritt last weekend.

yellow birch a species of birch, *Betula lutea,* found in central and eastern Canada; also, the hard wood of this tree.

1774 (1945) ROBINSON & RISPIN *Journey N.S.* 34: This town at the foot . . . affords great store of fine timber . . . birch, white, yellow, and black. . . . **1821** *Kingston Chron.* (U.C.) 24 Aug. 1/3: The wood to be of sound and merchantable quality, consisting of black or yellow Birch, Maple, or White Beech. **1956** *Native Trees* 130: Yellow birch takes its name from its yellowish bark. **1963** *Beaver* Autumn 17/1: Since the Crees . . . had no white ash . . . they used the more brittle yellow birch.

yellow cake semirefined uranium ore; uranium oxide concentrate.

1957 *Maclean's* 25 May 30/3: The wealth is "yellow cake," semi-refined uranium ore; over the next five years the . . . Eldorado Mining and Refining Company has guaranteed to buy more than a billion dollars worth. . . . **1962** *Time* (Cdn ed.) 10 Aug. 8/2: . . . Canadians plunged joyfully into a crash program to supply the heavy "yellow cake" . . . to the U.S. . . .

yellow cedar a species of evergreen, *Chamaecyparis nootkatensis,* of the Pacific Coast. See also **canoe cedar** (def. 2), **cypress** (def. 3), **Nootka cypress,** and **yellow cypress.**

1894 *Trans.Roy.Soc.Can.* XII 4 15: The coast forests are ... composed of spruce, hemlock and yellow cedar only. **1965** *Kingston Whig-Standard* (Ont.) 25 Jan. 23/6: A man stands beside a yellow cedar tree overlooking the Nimpkish Valley in British Columbia.

yellow cypress See **yellow cedar.**

1872 POOLE *Queen Charlotte Is.* 319: The players spread a mat, made of the inner bark of the yellow cypress, upon the ground.... **1956** *Native Trees* 78: Yellow cedar [is also called] yellow cypress....

yellowlegs *n.pl.* [from the yellow stripe down the sides of the breeches] *Slang, Derog.* See **Mounted Policeman.**

1918 KENDALL *Benton* 38: "Oh, you Harry! Say, wha's dat dere wit de yaller laigs?" **1955** BIRNEY *Long Table* 175: ... the American who had been in the fight, and who was now keeping lookout, pulled his bullet head in suddenly and yelled "Yellowlegs." **1959** STOREY *Prairie Harvest* 51: "You're her brother and I'm your friend. Even the damned yellow legs can't break that."

yellow stripe *Slang* See **Mounted Policeman.**

1953 MOWERY *Mounted Police* 147: Later came three Yellow-stripes looking for him, but again Mugwa was not there—neither in the village nor at the seal holes....

Yengee *n.* See **Yangee.**

York *n.* **1** *Obs.* See **York currency.**

1798 (1935) RUSSELL *Correspondence* II 115: We have some very good powdered Maple at 1/6 York of which any Quantity can be sent. **1849** ALEXANDER *L'Acadie* I 198: ... they would run back for change for a shilling York (sixpence) to pay for it, when the train would drive off, with much laughter. **1871** *North Wellington Times* (Elora, Ont.) 25 Aug. 2/2: We are willing to stake two and sixpence York, that the fat men will win.

2 See **York boat.**

1935 MOWERY *Resurrection River* 23: The water edge was cluttered with craft of every kind, from slender Indian birchbarks to big Yorks....

A York boat

York boat an inland freight boat, descended from the bateau, in common use from the early 1820's but used for tripping as early as 1790, and finally withdrawn from service entirely about 1930. See also **bateau** (def. 4), **Hudson's Bay bateau, inland boat** (def. 1), **Mackinaw boat** (def. 1), **pointer** (def. 2), **Red River boat,** and **York** (def. 2). Cp. **flat-boat.**

☛ *York boats, named after York Factory, were of varying size, the largest ones, used in the Northwest, being about 40 feet long and ten feet wide, of shallow draft with the stem and sternposts sloping at an angle of 45 degrees, open decked and equipped with a square sail and oars, which were pulled by eight oarsmen, the steering being done by means of a heavy stern-sweep; such boats were capable of carrying 110 pieces of 90 pounds each.*

1864 *Nor'Wester* (R.R.S.) 26 Apr. 2/5: Gentlemen of practical experience gave their opinion that the present York boats (bateaux) could be used for the transportation of goods from Lake of the Woods to Lake Superior with as little difficulty as is encountered between this place and York Factory. *c*1909 BRYCE *Lord Selkirk's Colonists* 71: The birch-bark canoe is a mere trifle on the portage, but the heavy York boat capable of carrying three or four tons is a clumsy lugger. **1963** STANLEY *Louis Riel* 196: Neither the Red River cart nor the York boat had entirely disappeared from the Manitoba scene [by 1873]. ...

York currency *Hist.* the standard of currency established at New York, where the dollar was set as equivalent to eight shillings, a unit of account used during much of the colonial period in Montreal, Quebec City, and Upper Canada. See also **New York currency, York** (def. 1), **York money, York pound,** and **York shilling.** Cp. **Halifax currency.**

1764 *Quebec Gaz.* 4 Oct. 1/1: From the Date of the Publication hereof ... Forty-Eight Sols Marqués shall be deemed to be equal to One Shilling Halifax; and Thirty of said Sols Marqués equal to One Shilling York Currency. **1789** *Quebec Herald* 13 Apr. 187/2: By a letter from Niagara we learn they are in great distress for want of the necessaries of life, wheat 20s. York currency per bushel, and difficult to be got at that price; cats &c. have been substituted for beef, &c &c. **1829** *Brockville Gaz.* (U.C.) 20 Nov. 3/1: Wheat, at present, commands but 5s. York currency, other grains in proportion. **1963** *Commercial Letter* Jan. 6/2: In 1777 Halifax currency was established as the official standard of the colony of Canada, but York currency continued in use in Montreal and in what was then known as Upper Canada. Later when Canada was formally divided into two provinces, Upper and Lower Canada, each was given jurisdiction over its own currency and York currency enjoyed recognition in Upper Canada. In 1821 the York unit was replaced by Halifax currency although it continued for many years as a popular unit of account with the rural population.

yorker *n. Hist.* a York shilling, *q.v.*

1852 (1923) MOODIE *Roughing It* 109: "What do you ask for it?" "Two Yorkers." **1908** CLARKE *Sixty Years* 33: I have seen currants sold at "three yorkers" (37½ cents) a pound....

Yorkite *n. Hist.* a person who supported the retention of York currency as a standard of exchange.

1835 *Brit.Amer.Jnl* (St. Catharines, U.C.) 5 Feb. 2/4: Hold, hold, says one of the Yorkites; if you lose the odd copper in breaking the York shilling to-day, you gain it to-morrow; what is fair for one side is fair for the other; if we take the odd copper, we give it in return.

York money *Obs.* See **York currency.**

1853 *Huron Signal* (Goderich, C.W.) 6 Jan. 2/4: In one place we make our calculations in York money—in another we have the American computation of dollars and cents; in a third place we use the ordinary currency.

York pound *Hist.* See quote. See also **York currency.**

1920 *Cdn Hist.Rev.* I 190: "York shilling" or "Yorker" was 12½ cents, the York pound, $2.50.

York shilling *Hist.* one shilling York currency, *q.v.*, (12½ cents). See also **yorker.**
1824 *Colonial Advocate* (Queenston, U.C.) 18 May 3/3: There was forty-four or forty-five dollars in York Bank notes, three half dollars, a watch with seal, and a York shilling found on the deceased. **1862** *Nor'Wester* (R.R.S.) 24 Dec. 4/2: The pressure became so great that the owner . . . at last commenced to charge a York shilling fee; and on Monday she did a handsome business in this way. **1920** *Cdn Hist.Rev.* I 190: There was no coin for the York shilling, but the English sixpence passed as such.

you *interj.* See **hew,** *interj.*

Youcon *n.* See **Yukon.**

Young Canada *Hist.* See **Young Canada party.**
1849 *Wkly Globe* 16 Nov. 77/76: There did not appear to be many French Canadians present, and those of them who took an active part, were gentlemen of "young Canada." **1920** *Cdn Hist.Rev.* I 147: D'Arcy McGee . . . by his fervent appeals to the younger generation of Canadians . . . gathered about him a rising nationalist school, a party of Young Canada. **1963** MORTON *Kingdom of Canada* 333: McDougall was something of a mentor to them, and his Young Canada was soon to be outshone by their Canada First.

Young Canada (or **Canadian**) **party** *Hist.* a political party formed in the early 1850's by young Canadians who had had enough of the bickering that was characteristic within the old-line parties and who wanted to advance the concept of Canadian nationhood as opposed to the then active movement toward annexation to the United States. See also **Young Canada.** Cp. **Canada First.**
1849 *Wkly Globe* 21 Dec. 98/6: Because their measures and appointments have not been shaped precisely according to the personal interests and desires of these men—we are to have a "young Canada party," with the *Examiner* as its organ! **1850** *Toronto Dly Express* 8 Apr. 2/1: Now, the "Young Canada" party and the Annexationists in the L.C. province can easily control 8 members, and the Conservatives 2 members, making from that section 10 Anti-Ministerial votes. **1853** *Hamilton Gaz.* (C.W.) 2 June 3/1: The Grits voted with the Ministry. The Young Canadian party joined the Conservatives.

young ice *North* See 1958 quote.
1835 WIX *Journal* 42: At eight, A.M., started through the "young ice" in a new punt, which was stained with blood from a recent freight of fresh-killed seals. **1931** LEBOURDAIS *Northward* 274: Young ice was making and it impeded our progress. **1958** *Manice* 5: Young Ice: newly-formed ice generally in the transitional stage of development from ice crust to winter ice; thickness 2 to 8 inches.

youngster *n. Nfld, Hist.* See 1792 quote.
1792 (1911) TOWNSEND *Cartwright's Jnl* 380: Youngster. A novitiate; a person in the first year, or early part of his servitude; one who has his business to learn. **1964** *Nfld Qtly* Summer 14/2: In mid-18th century, the custom became a legal requirement in Newfoundland for fishing masters, merchants and planters, when employing immigrant servants (whether "youngsters" or experienced fishermen) all generically "servants," to have a written employment agreement executed to reserve return passage money from the wages.

youth allowance See quote. See also **Family Allowance Act.**
1967 *Globe and Mail* (Toronto) 17 Mar. 1/7: Under the federal family allowance program, payments at present are $6.00 monthly for children under the age of 10 and $8.00 a month for children from 10 to 16. In September, 1964, the federal Government introduced a youth allowances program, providing $10 a month for 16-year and 17-year-old children still in school.

Y.T. See **Yukon Territory.**
1900 *Yukon Sun* (Dawson) 13 Feb. 3/1: Neither was I constantly informing the Canadian officials how much superior the U.S. laws were to those of the Y.T. **1958** *Edmonton Jnl* 2 Aug. 36/5: Sealed tenders . . . marked "Tender for repairs to Portion of Radio Range Road and Related Work at Snag, Y.T." will be received up to 15:00 hrs. . . .

Yukon ['jukɑn] *n.* [< Athapaskan: Kutchin *yuk, dyuk* river + *-on* great, big; cp. **Klondike**]
1 *Fur Trade, Hist.* a department of the Hudson's Bay Company in the region now known as the Yukon Territory, *q.v.* Usually spelled *Youcon.*
1851 CAMPBELL *Journal* 99: . . . the Youcon outfit which had been rendered there from Peel River last winter was loaded into the Youcon boat. **1861** *Nor'Wester* (R.R.S.) 19 Feb. 4/1: A few remarks therefore, may not be out of place, or unwelcome to your readers upon a journey that I have just made to the Youcon, with a short descriptive sketch of the character and habits of the Indian tribes of that part of the country.

2 *Hist.* from 1895 to 1898, a provisional district of the Northwest Territories.
1897 TUTTLE *Golden North* 119: Two new provisional districts or territories have recently been erected in the far northwest by the Canadian government. The first is that called Mackenzie, lying to the north of Athabasca, and extending westward to the summit of the Rockies. The second is called Yukon, and extends westward from the summit of the Rockies to the 141st degree of longitude, and northward from the northern boundary of British Columbia.

3 See **Yukon Territory.**
1910 BURPEE *Yukon* 19n: Youcon is one of several variants of the name now settled as Yukon, that form having been adopted by both the Canadian and American Boards on Geographic Names. The name was first applied by John Bell, of the Hudson's Bay Company, in 1846, as he understood it. **1957** *Yukon* 3: The Yukon, which gets its name from the Indian word "Yuckoo" meaning clear water, comprises the extreme northwestern part of the mainland of Canada, and has an area of 207,076 square miles, or 5.6% of the total area of the country. **1958** BERTON *Klondike* 4: The Russians were the first on the river, in 1834, but they cared not a hoot for gold; no more than the natives who had given the river its name of Yukon, meaning "The Greatest." **1965** WILSON *No Man Stands Alone* 134: "Guess you know the name 'Yukon' means 'Great River.' Well, you don't know nothin' about the Great River till you see that ice go."

Yukon boat *Northwest* a type of square-backed boat.
1851 CAMPBELL *Journal* 99: . . . the Youcon outfit which had been rendered there from Peel River during last winter was loaded into the Youcon boat. . . . **1924**

MASON *Arctic Forests* 41 : I know an Indian who sold a Yukon boat (some one else's) to three different people.

Yukon chimney or **stovepipe** *Esp.Northwest* a safety chimney consisting of two concentric sheet-metal cylinders joined at top and bottom by perforated collars which allow an exchange of air, thus preventing over-heating of the stovepipe, which passes upward within the inner cylinder. See also **Klondike chimney** and **Yukon pipe.**
1900 LONDON *Son of Wolf* 79 : The smoke curled up pathetically from the Yukon stovepipe. **1962** FRY *Ranch on the Cariboo* 73 : Centrally, one sees a typical small log cabin, chinked with mud, a Yukon chimney poked through the roof, a whiff of wood smoke trailing from it.

Yukon holly *Local* See **kinnikinik** (def. 2).
1954 BERTON *I Married Klondike* 131 : I followed a faint trail up the hill and my feet soon sank into thick carpet of bright bear berries and kinnikinnik, a green, red-berried creeper sometimes called Yukon holly.

Yukon pipe See **Yukon chimney.**
1962 FRY *Ranch on the Cariboo* 143 : I passed farmhouses where the smoke had yet to rise from the chimneys, then one or two where the first flush from lighting up belched out of the Yukon pipe.

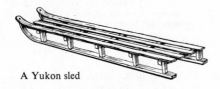

A Yukon sled

Yukon sled or **sleigh** *Northwest* a simple wooden platform mounted on turned-up runners of wood or metal, about ten feet long and sixteen inches wide (so as to be able to follow the narrow trails) and about four inches off the ground. Cp. **Klondike sleigh.**
1895 MUNROE *Snow-Shoes* 78 : They were to use the ingalik, or regular Yukon sledge, which is much lighter than the Eskimo, or coast sledge, but heavier and stronger than the Hudson Bay toboggan commonly used in the interior. **1898** *Hints for Intending Klondikers* 13 : In addition each man in the party will require a Yukon sleigh, a skeleton affair made from the best hard wood and shod with ground brass runners. **1924** MASON *Arctic Forests* 31 : The "Yukon" sled . . . is perfectly useless for cross-country travel, but it is useful for hauling wood, etc., on good trails, or for river travel in spring-time. **1940** MARSHALL *Arctic Village* 81 : With the Yukon sled there is no place to ride except on top of the load. **1962** (1964) INNIS *Fur Trade* 298 : Yukon furs were packed in smaller weights and in different moulds since they were taken on Yukon sleds. . . . **1965** *Sun* (Vancouver) 21 Apr. 37/2 : There he hitches up his dogs, to a toboggan for deep snow, to a Yukon sleigh for crust snow.

Yukon stove *Esp.Northwest* a kind of airtight burner, *q.v.*, identified with the Yukon. See also **Klondike stove.**

1898 HASKELL *Klondike* 75 : The "Yukon stove" is a small sheet iron box with an oven at the back and a telescope pipe. **1900** LONDON *Son of Wolf* 192 : . . . the lighted parchment window . . . told its own story of the home cabin, the roaring Yukon stove, the steaming pots of tea. **1924** DORRANCE *Never Fire First* 227 : There were three bunks along as many walls and a Yukon stove in the cell's centre. . . . **1958** WATTERS *B.C.Cent. Anthol.* 317 : . . . it required well over two hours to make the last two miles to our tent with its small Yukon stove.

Yukon stovepipe See **Yukon chimney.**

Yukon Territory a territory in Northwestern Canada, established June 13, 1898. See also **Y.T.** and **Yukon** (def. 3).
1913 OGILVIE *Yukon* 6 : About one-third of the total length [of the Yukon River] is in Yukon Territory. . . . **1963** *Canada Month* May 8/1 : From all over the Yukon Territory as well as the Outside, engineers, oilmen . . . railwaymen had come to see what wonders the future held for the Yukon. **1966** *Commercial Letter* Jan.-Feb. 2/1 : The Yukon Territory, which gets its name from the Indian word "yuckoo" meaning "clear water," forms the extreme northwest portion of the mainland of Canada. . . .

Yukon welcome the greeting "Chimo, Cheechakos!" See also **chimo.**
1964 *Edmonton Jnl* 11 July 1/2 : Thunder the Yukon welcome.

yuniak *n. Obs.* See **oomiak** and picture.
1897 HAYNE *Pioneers* 24 : Here we saw an Indian village, and were met by a yuniak or family canoe, made of walrus-hide, containing seven men and three women— all Indians, all dressed alike in salmon-skin, and all horribly dirty.

zabois ['zæbwa] *n.* [origin uncertain] *North* See quote.
1965 SYMINGTON *Tuktu* 42: Calves or even mature animals may bog down in muskeg or in gullies or "zabois" filled with soft, wet snow.

zastrugi *n.* See **sastrugi.**

zigzag fence† a snake fence, *q.v.,* usually one made of split rails.
1842 WILLIS *Cdn Scenery* II 99: The large logs are ... rolled away for ... making the zigzag log fences to keep off the cattle and sheep. ... **1849** ALEXANDER *L'Acadie* I 185: Our way led past small log or frame farm houses, separated from the road by the everywhere seen zigzag or snake fence. **1942** CARR *Book of Small* 114: The New Field had a snake fence around it, that is, a zigzag fence made of split cedar logs or of young sapling trees laid criss-cross, their own weight holding them in place so that they required no nails. Snake fences were extravagant in land and in wood, but wood and land were cheaper in Canada in early days than were nails and hinges.

zing party *Slang.* See **zing-ping.**

zing-ping *n. Slang* See quote.
1963 *Kingston Whig-Standard* (Ont.) 1 June 6/1: Gananoque—Latest kick among the younger set is "Zing" parties. The sect mixes the new flavored wine with grapefruit juice to produce "zing-ping" or as grampa would say "ring-a-ding, ding!"

zombie *n. Slang, Derog., Hist.* **1** See quotes.
1949 PETERSON *Chipmunk* 85: "Didn't I volunteer in the war? I wasn't a zombie...." **1953** LEBOURDAIS *Nation of North* 245: In October [1940], the first men were drafted for service under the N[ational] R[esources] M[obilization] A[ct]. Contemptuously referred to as "zombies," they were never taken seriously by the military authorities, and when, later on, they were needed overseas, they were found to be inadequately trained. **1963** MORTON *Kingdom of Canada* 481: ... a nasty distinction arose between the volunteers for service overseas and the conscripts for home defence, who were given the pungent nickname of "zombies," a West Indian word for impotent spirits.

2 a person who was not in the armed services.
1953 (1958) WALKER *Pardon My Parka* 78: "I lent my [golf] clubs to some zombie when I went to war and heaven knows where they are now."

zombie issue *Hist.* the controversy relating to the issue of conscription during World War II. Cp. **zombie.**
1964 *Telegram* (Toronto) 10 Oct. 7/8: I recommend it to soldiers of the time because of the clear treatment of the zombie issue.

Bibliography

The following bibliography is organized in two parts. The first embraces sources of quotations identified by author (or, rarely, editor) and/or title (if written anonymously), whether a book, an extract from a book, or an article in a newspaper, magazine, or other source. Book titles are often identified in the text by an abbreviated form, or short title, which, taken with the author's name and the date of publication, should be readily traced in the bibliography. The second part embraces periodicals cited in the dictionary by the year, title, and month of issue (or volume number) or day and month of the source, the usual practice of readers being to provide only this information for quotations drawn from periodicals, newspapers, and similar sources. In the case of periodicals now defunct, the inclusive dates of publication, in so far as the editors have been able to discover them, are given in parentheses at the end of the entry. Newspapers are not listed in the bibliography, their places of publication being given within parentheses in the text, immediately following the title.

Both parts of the bibliography are intended to direct the reader to the source cited, giving him such information as may be reasonably expected to achieve this end. Whenever more than one edition of a book has been read, all relevant publication dates have been given. Details as to how such have been presented in the text of the dictionary are set forth on p. *xix* under *Principles of Style*. Various notes and cross-references have been entered in the bibliography as aids to the reader.

The form outlined above has been dictated by the nature of the collected materials, which presented many difficult problems for those collating the bibliographical data. The main obstacle was that in the early stages of independent collecting by various persons no consistent pattern of providing bibliographical information was followed. As a result, the record is incomplete with respect to a few details relating to edition and place and date of publication, especially for very early writings. It must be added, however, that the search for such missing details goes on. For the present, the editors have offered the fullest information available from the resources at their disposal. They have, moreover, striven to achieve a sensible compromise between the opposed demands of completeness in detail and economy of space.

The "ABC" British Columbia Lumber Trade Directory & Year Book, 1936-1937. Vancouver: Progress Publishing Co., 1936.

ABERHART, Willam. National Monetary Reform — Canada's Urgent Need. Edmonton: Today & Tomorrow, c1940.

An Account of the Present State of Nova Scotia.... 2nd ed. Edinburgh: Creech, 1787. [First published, Edinburgh: Creech and Longman, 1786].

ADAMS, A. T. The Explorations of Pierre Esprit Radisson. Minneapolis, Minn.: Ross & Hains, 1961.

ADAMS, Ramon F. Come An' Get It — The Story of the Old Cowboy Cook. Norman, Okla.: Univ. of Oklahoma Press, 1952.

———. Western Words — A Dictionary of the Range, Cow Camp and Trail. Norman, Okla.: Univ. of Oklahoma Press, 1944.

ADTIC. Glossary. See Glossary of Arctic and Subarctic Terms.

ALEXANDER, Sir James E. L'Acadie or Seven Years Explorations in British America. 2 vols. London: Henry Colburn, 1849.

ALEXANDER, Jessie. Platform Sketches. Toronto: McClelland, Goodchild & Stewart, 1916.

ALLEN, Ralph. Peace River Country. Winnipeg: Harlequin Books, 1962. [First published, New York: Doubleday, 1958]

American Dialect Dictionary. See Harold WENTWORTH.

AMES, R. A. The Cheechako — A Novel of the Alaska-Yukon Gold Rush. New York: Lothrop, Lee & Shepard, 1958.

ANDERSON, Alexander C. The Dominion at the West. Victoria: Richard Wolfenden, 1872.

ANDERSON, James. Sawney's Letters and Cariboo Rhymes. Edited by W. E. Ireland. Barkerville, B.C.: Barkerville Restoration Advisory Committee, 1962. [First published, 1868; rev. ed., 1869]

ANDERSON, James R. Trees and Shrubs—Food, Medicinal and Poisonous Plants of British Columbia. Victoria: Department of Education, 1925.

ANDERSON, Rudolf M. Catalogue of Canadian Recent Mammals. National Museum of Canada Bulletin 102. Ottawa, 1946.

ANDERSON, W. A. Angel of Hudson Bay. Toronto: Clarke, Irwin, 1961.

ANDREWS, Clarence L. Wrangell and the Gold of the Cassiar. Seattle, Wash.: Privately printed, 1937.

ANDREWS, R. W. Glory Days of Logging — Action in the Big Woods — British Columbia to California. Seattle, Wash.: Superior Publishing Co., 1956.

ANGER, Harry D. Summary of Canadian Commercial Law. Rev. ed. Toronto: Pitman, 1942.

ANGIER, V., and B. Angier. At Home in the Woods — Living the Life of Thoreau Today. Toronto: McLeod, 1951.

ANGLIN, G. Canada Unlimited. Toronto: O'Keefe Foundation, 1948.

ANSPACH, Lewis A. A History of the Island of Newfoundland.... London: Privately printed, 1819.

Arctic Manual TM 1-240. Washington, D.C.: U.S. War Dept., 1942.

Arctic Miscellanies — A Souvenir of the Late Polar Search. 2nd ed. London: Henry Colburn, 1852.

ARMSTRONG, Nevill A.D. After Game in the Upper Yukon. London: John Long, 1937.

———. Yukon Yesterdays. London: John Long, 1936.

ARMSTRONG, R.W. The Salt of the Earth — A Study in Rural Life and Social Progress. Ottawa: Graphic Publishers, 1930.

ARNOLD, Oren A., and John P. Hale. Hot Irons — Heraldry of the Range. New York: Macmillan, 1940.

ARROWSMITH, A. A Map Exhibiting All the New Discoveries in the Interior Parts of North America.... London: A. Arrowsmith, 1824. [First published, 1795]

ASHLEY, B. Freeman. Tan Pile Jim or A Yankee Waif among the Bluenoses. Chicago: Laird & Lee, 1894.

ATKINSON, Christopher. The Emigrant's Guild to New Brunswick, British North America. Berwick-upon-Tweed: Warder's Office, 1842. [See next entry]

———. A Historical and Statistical Account of New Brunswick. 3rd ed. Edinburgh: Anderson & Bryce, 1844. [Revision of preceding entry]

ATKINSON, R. M. 50th Anniversary — Historical Souvenir of Penticton, B.C., 1908-1958 — On the Occasion of the City of Penticton's Golden Jubilee. Penticton, B.C.: Okanagan Historical Soc., 1958.

AUDUBON, John. American Ornithological Biography. 5 vols. Edinburgh: 1831-1839.

BACK. Narrative of the Arctic Land Expedition to the Mouth of the Great Fish River.... London: John Murray, 1836.

The Bad Lands of the Red Deer River. Drumheller, Alta: Board of Trade, 1962.

BAGSTER, C. The Progress and Prospects of Prince Edward Island. Charlottetown: John Ings, 1861.

BAILLIE, Thomas. An Account of the Province of New Brunswick. London: Rivington, 1832.

BAILLIE-GROHMAN, W.A. Fifteen Years' Sport and Life in the Hunting Grounds of Western America and British Columbia. London: Horace Cox, 1900.

BAIRD, Frank. Roger Davis, Loyalist. London: Religious Tract Soc., 1907.

BAITY, Earl. Wilderness Welfare — An Epic of Frontier Life. Vancouver: Mitchell Press, 1966.

BAKER, R.P. History of English-Canadian Literature to the Confederation.... Cambridge, Mass.: Harvard Univ. Press, 1920.

BALCH, F. H. The Bridge of the Gods — A Romance of Indian Oregon. Chicago: McClurg, 1890.

BALLANTYNE, Robert M. Hudson's Bay; or, Everyday Life in the Wilds of North America, during Six Years' Residence in the Territories of the Hon. Hudson's Bay Company. Boston, 1859. [First published privately, Edinburgh, 1848]

———. Over the Rocky Mountains. London: James Nisbet, 18—. [Usually cited as c1860]

———. The Pioneers — A Tale of the Western Wilderness. London: James Nisbet, 1872.

———. Ungava — A Tale of Esquimaux-Land. London: Dent, 1908. [First published, London: Nelson, 1858]

———. The World of Ice or, The Whaling Cruise of "The Dolphin."

———. The Young Fur-Traders. London: John F. Shaw, 1856.

BALLARD, Walter. The Klondyke Mines and the

Golden Valley of the Yukon. Jersey City, N.J.: Albert Datz, 1897.

BANCROFT, Hubert H. *History of British Columbia.* San Francisco: History Co., 1887.

BANFIELD, A. W. F. *The Barren-Ground Caribou.* Ottawa: Department of Resources & Development, 1951.

BANFILL, B. J. *Labrador Nurse.* Toronto: Ryerson, 1952; Philadelphia: Macrae Smith, 1953.

BANTING, F. G. "The History of Insulin," *Edinburgh Medical Journal,* Jan., 1929, pp. 1-18.

BARBEAU, C. Marius. *Assomption Sash.* National Museum of Canada Bulletin 93. Ottawa, 1938.

————. *Canadian Folk Songs.* The Columbia World Library of Folk & Primitive Music VIII. Toronto: Columbia Records, 1954.

————. *Haida Myths Illustrated in Argillite Carvings.* National Museum of Canada Bulletin 127. Ottawa, 1953.

————. *I Have Seen Quebec.* Toronto: Macmillan, 1957.

————. *Indian Days in the Canadian Rockies.* Toronto: Macmillan, 1923.

————. *Indian Days on the Western Prairies.* National Museum of Canada Bulletin 163. Ottawa, 1960. [Preface dated May, 1959]

————. *Mountain Cloud.* Toronto: Macmillan, 1944.

————. *Totem Poles.* 2 vols. National Museum of Canada Bulletin 119. Ottawa, 1959.

BARBER, Mary, and Flora McPherson. *Christmas in Canada.* Toronto: Dent, 1959.

BARCLAY, Charles. *Letters from the Dorking Emigrants who Went to Upper Canada.* London: Robert Best Ede, 1832.

BARKER, Burt Brown. *Letters of Dr. John McLoughlin.* Portland, Ore.: Binfords & Mort, 1948.

BARKER, H. T. "The Ice Road," *Atlantic Advocate,* Feb., 1964.

BARNEBY, W. Henry. *Life and Labour in the Far, Far West.* London: Cassell, 1884.

BARNETT, Lincoln. *The World We Live In.* New York: Time, 1955.

BARNHOUSE, Dorothy P. "Skipper for Keeps," in *Rubaboo 2,* pp. 49-60. Toronto: Gage, 1963.

BARRATT, Alyn R. *Coronets and Buckskins.* Boston, 1957.

BARRETT-LENNARD, C. E. *Travels in British Columbia. . . .* London: Hurst & Blackett, 1862.

BARTON, R. W., and L. J. Thomas. See L. J. THOMAS.

BEALE, Will. *Frontier of the Deep — A Tale of the Great Northeast.* New York: Burt, 1925.

BEAMES, John. *An Army without Banners.* Toronto: McClelland & Stewart, 1930. [First published, Boston: Little, Brown, 1929]

BEARD, D. C. *The Field and Forest Handy Book.* New York: Scribner, 1906.

BEATTIE, Jessie L. *Along the Road.* Toronto: Ryerson, 1954.

BEAULIEU, A., and C. Barton. *Applied Lumber Science — Being a Non-technical Analysis of the Methods Used in Producing and Selling the Lumber of the West Coast of North America.* Vancouver: Clarke & Stuart, 1939.

BEAVAN, Mrs. F. *Sketches and Tales Illustrative of Life in New Brunswick, North America.* London: George Routledge, 1845. [Cited as *Life in Backwoods N.B.*]

BEAVER, C. Masten. *Fort Yukon Trader — Three Years in an Alaskan Wilderness.* New York: Exposition Press, 1955.

BECK, J. M. "The Young Joseph Howe," *Atlantic Advocate,* Jan., 1965.

BECKER, Ethel. *Klondike '98 — Hegg's Album of the 1898 Alaska Gold Rush.* Portland, Ore.: Bindfords & Mort, 1949 and 1958.

BEEMAN, H. *For Our Bureau — Being the Bureau Ballads Contributed to Volumes One and Two of "Via Vancouver," the Journal of the Foreign Trade Bureau of the Vancouver Board of Trade.* Vancouver: Cowan Brookhouse, 1924.

BEGG, Alexander. *The Great Canadian North West — Its Past History, Present Condition, and Glorious Prospects.* Montreal: John Lovell, 1881.

————. *History of British Columbia from Its Earliest Discovery to the Present Time.* Toronto: William Briggs, 1894.

BELANEY, George Stanfield. See GREY OWL.

BELL, Andrew. *History of Canada from the Time of Its Discovery till the Union Year, 1840-41.* 2 vols. Montreal: Richard Worthington, 1866.

BELL, Robert. *Report on Explorations of the Churchill and Nelson Rivers. . . .* Montreal: Dawson, 1880.

BELLOT. *Journal.* 2 vols. 1855.

BEMISTER, George. *Railway Routes from Montreal.* Montreal: Burland-Desbarats, 1875.

BEMISTER, Margaret. *Stories from Prairie and Mountain.* Toronto: Copp, Clark, 1909.

BENNETT, O. J. *Cloth of Gold.* Abbotsford, B.C.: Trinity Memorial Church, 1950.

BENTLEY, R. *Naturalist . . . .* See J. K. LORD.

BERNIER, J. E. *Report on the . . . Expedition to the Arctic Islands and Hudson Strait. . . .* Ottawa: King's Printer, 1910.

BERRY, Gerald L. *Whoop-up Trail.* Edmonton: Allied Arts Products, 1953.

BERTON, Laura Beatrice. *I Married the Klondike.* Boston: Little, Brown, 1954.

BERTON, Pierre. *Centennial Food Guide — A Century of Good Eating Comprising an Anthology of Writings about Food and Drink over the Past Hundred Years.* Toronto: Canadian Centennial Publishing Co., 1966.

————. *The Golden Trail — The Story of the Klondike Rush.* Toronto: Macmillan, 1964.

————. *Klondike — The Life and Death of the Last Great Gold Rush.* Toronto: McClelland & Stewart, 1958.

————. *Mysterious North.* New York: Knopf, 1956.

————. *Remember Yesterday — A Century of Photographs.* Toronto: Canadian Centennial Publishing Co., 1965.

BESANT, Sir Walter, and James Rice. *The Golden Butterfly.* New York, 1888. [First published, London, 1876]

BEST, George. *A Trve Discovrse of the Late Voyages of Discoverie. . . .* 3 vols. London: Henry Bynnyman, 1578.

BETTANY, George, *Valley of Lost Gold.* London: Skeffington, 1934.

BEZANSON, A. M. *Sodbusters Invade the Peace.* Toronto: Ryerson, 1954.

BIARD, P. "Relation de la Nouvelle-France," in Vol. I of *Relations des Jésuites.* 1858.

BICKERSTETH, J. Burgon. *The Land of Open Doors —*

Being Letters from Western Canada. London: Wells Gardner, Darton, 1914. [Written, 1911-1914]

BICKET, James. *Canadian Curler's Manual.* 1840.

BIDWELL, Marshall Spring. *Letter to W. Warren Baldwin.* Toronto Public Library MSS B 104. [Written, 1828]

BIGGAR, Charles Robert Webster. *Sir Oliver Mowat.* 2 vols. Toronto: Warwick & Rutter, 1905.

BIGGAR, E. B. *Anecdotal Life of Sir John Macdonald.* Montreal: John Lovell, 1891.

BIGGAR, H. P. *Voyages of Jacques Cartier.* Public Archives No. 11. Ottawa, 1924.

BIGSBY, John J. *The Shoe and the Canoe.* 2 vols. London: Chapman & Hall, 1850.

BILBY, Julian W. *Among Unknown Eskimo.* Philadelphia: Lippincott, 1923.

BINDLOSS, H. *Alton.* New York: F. A. Stokes, 1906.

———. *Carmen's Messenger.* New York: F. A. Stokes, 1917.

———. *Green Timber.* New York: F. A. Stokes, 1924.

———. *The Intriguers.* New York: A. L. Burt, 1914.

———. *Lorimer of the Northwest.* New York: F. A. Stokes, 1909.

———. *Prescott of Saskatchewan.* Toronto: McLeod & Allen, 1913.

———. *Thurston of Orchard Valley.* Toronto: McLeod & Allen, 1910.

———. *Winston of the Prairies.* New York: F. A. Stokes, 1907.

BIRD, Will R., ed. *Atlantic Anthology.* Toronto: McClelland & Stewart, 1959.

———. *Despite the Distance.* Toronto: Ryerson, 1961.

———. *Here Stays Good Yorkshire.* Toronto: Ryerson, 1945.

———. *Judgment Glen.* Toronto: Ryerson, 1947.

———. *Sunrise for Peter, and Other Stories.* Toronto: Ryerson, 1946.

———. *This Is Nova Scotia.* Toronto: Ryerson, 1950.

BIRKET-SMITH, K. A. J. *The Caribou Eskimos.* 2 vols. Copenhagen: Gyldeddalske Boghandel, 1929.

BIRNEY, Earle. *Down the Long Table.* Toronto: McClelland & Stewart, 1955.

———. *Turvey — A Military Picaresque.* Toronto: McClelland & Stewart, 1949.

BLACK, Mrs. George. *My Seventy Years.* London: Nelson, 1938.

BLACK, Samuel. *Journal of a Voyage from Rocky Mountain Portage in Peace River . . . in 1824.* Edited by E. E. Rich. Hudson's Bay Record Society Publications XVIII. London, 1955.

BLAKE, Norman (joint pseud. of R. K. Gordon and H. C. Jamieson). *In the Grip of the Barren Lands.* London: Blackie, 1936.

BLAKE, W. H., translator. *Chez Nous.* See RIVARD.

———. *Maria Chapdelaine.* See L. HÉMON.

BLAKELEY, Phyllis R. *Nova Scotia — A Brief History.* Toronto, Vancouver: Dent, 1955.

BLANCHET, Guy. *Keewatin and Northwest Mackenzie.* Ottawa: King's Printer, 1930.

———. *Search in the North.* Toronto: Macmillan, 1960.

BLONDAL, Patricia. *A Candle to Light the Sun.* Toronto: McClelland & Stewart, 1960.

BLOUET, Paul. *John Bull & Co. — The Great Colonial*

Branches of the Firm: Canada, Australia, New Zealand and South Africa. New York: Cassell, 1894.

BLUMGARTEN, A. S. *Textbook of Materia Medica.* 5th ed. Toronto: Macmillan, 1931. [This edition first published, 1930]

BOAS, Franz. *Anniversary Volume. Anthropological Papers Written in Honor of Franz Boas.* New York: G. E. Stecbert, 1906.

———. "The Central Eskimo," *Sixth Annual Report* (1884-85). Washington, D.C.: Bureau of American Ethnology, 1888.

———. "Contributions to the Ethnology of the Kwakiutl," *Thirty-fifth Annual Report* (1913-14). 2 vols. Washington, D.C.: Bureau of American Ethnology, 1921.

———. "The Eskimo of Baffin Land," *Transactions of the Anthropological Society of Washington,* Vol. III (1883-85), 95-102; *Bulletin of the American Museum of Natural History,* Vol. XV (1901), Part I: New York, 1901.

———. "The Houses of the Kwakiutl Indians, British Columbia," *Proceedings of the United States National Museum,* 1888, pp. 197-213.

———. "Indians of British Columbia," *Popular Science Monthly* XXXII (1888).

———. *Masks and Head Ornaments,* 1890.

Boating Adventures in Canada. Peterborough, Ont.: Outboard Marine Corp., 1959. [Pamphlet]

BODDY, Alexander A. *By Ocean, Prairie and Peak....* London: Society for the Propagation of Christian Knowledge, 1896.

BODSWORTH, Fred. *The Strange One.* New York: Dodd, Mead, 1959.

BOHN, Eric. See PRICE-BROWN.

BOLLES, Frank. *From Blomidon to Smoky and Other Papers.* Boston: Houghton, Mifflin, 1894.

BOMPAS, William Carpenter. *Diocese of Mackenzie River.* London: Society for Promoting Christian Knowledge, 1888.

BOND, George John. *Skipper George Netman — A Story of Outpost Methodism in Newfoundland.* London: Woolmer, 1887.

BONNYCASTLE, Sir Richard H. *Canada and the Canadians, in 1846.* 2 vols. London: Henry Colburn, 1846.

———. *The Canadas in 1841.* 2 vols. London: Henry Colburn, 1842.

———. *Newfoundland in 1842.* 2 vols. London: Henry Colburn, 1842.

BORRETT, William C. "Historic Halifax," in *Tales Told under the Old Town Clock.* Toronto: Ryerson, 1948.

BOSANQUET, Mary. *Saddlebags for Suitcases — Across Canada on Horseback.* Toronto: McClelland & Stewart, 1942.

BOTWELL, Fred. "Trails of Yesteryear," *Alberta Historical Review,* Summer, 1956.

BOUCHETTE, Joseph. *Topographical Description of the Province of Lower Canada.* London: W. Paden, 1815.

BOULTON, Charles A. *Reminiscences of the North-West Rebellions — with a Record of the Raising of Her Majesty's 100th Regiment in Canada, and a Chapter on Canadian Social and Political Life.* Toronto: Grip, 1886.

BOULTON, D'Arcy. *Sketch of His Majesty's Province of Upper Canada.* London, 1805.

BOURINOT, Sir John G. *How Canada is Governed —
A Short Account of Its Executive, Legislative, with an
Historical Outline of their Origin and Development.*
Toronto: Copp Clark, 1895.

BOYD, William. *With a Field Ambulance at Ypres.*
Toronto: Musson, 1916.

BOYLE, Thomas. *Justice through Power.* Toronto:
Longmans, 1961.

BRADBURY, John. *Travels in the Interior of America,
1809-1811.* Edited by R. G. Thwaites. Cleveland, 1904.

BRAINARD, David L. *Six Came Back.* Edited by
Bessie Rowland James. New York: Bobbs-Merrill,
1940.

BRAMBLE, Charles A. *The Land of the Lobstick.*
Regina, 1920.

BRAULT, Lucien. *Ottawa, Old and New.* Ottawa:
Ottawa Historical Information Institute, 1946.

BRERETON, F. S. *A Boy of the Dominion — A Tale of
Canadian Immigration.* London: Blackie, c1935.

BRIDGES, William. *Wild Animals of the World.* Garden
City, N.Y.: Garden City Publishing Co., 1948.

BRIDLE, Augustus. *Sons of Canada — Short Studies of
Characteristic Canadians.* Toronto: Dent, 1916.

BRIFFETT, Frances. *The Story of Newfoundland and
Labrador.* Toronto: Dent, 1954.

BRINTON, Daniel G. *The American Race.* New York:
N. D. C. Hodges, 1891.

*British Columbia Commission on Indian Affairs. Report
of the Royal Commission on Indian Affairs for the Province of British Columbia.* Victoria: Acme Press, 1916.

British Columbia Directory for the Years 1882-1883.
Victoria: R. T. Williams, 1882.

British Columbia Federation of Labour, 3rd Convention.
Vancouver: Oct. 21-24, 1958.

British Columbia Forest Industries Yearbook, 1965-1966.
Vancouver: Mitchell Press, 1966.

British Columbia Forest Industry. Vancouver: Council
of the Forest Industries of B.C., 1966.

British Columbia Game Regulations, 1966-1967. Victoria:
Fish & Wildlife Branch, Dept of Recreation & Conservation, 1966.

British Columbia Logging. Vancouver: Council of the
Forest Industries of B.C., 1966.

British Columbia Lumber Trade. See *The "ABC" British
Columbia Lumber Trade Directory & Year Book, 1936-37.*

British Columbia Pilot. Vol. I, *Southern Portion of the
Coast of British Columbia.* 5th ed. Ottawa: Queen's
Printer, 1953. Vol. II, *Northern Portion of the Coast of
British Columbia.* Ottawa: King's Printer, 1930.

British Columbia Pulp & Paper. Vancouver: Council of
the Forest Industries of B.C., 1967.

BROADUS, E. K., and E. H. Broadus. *A Book of
Canadian Prose and Verse.* Toronto: Macmillan, 1923.

BROOKE, Frances. *The History of Emily Montague.*
Ottawa: Graphic Publishers, 1931; Toronto: McClel-
land & Stewart, 1961. [First published, London:
T. Dodsley, 1769]

BROWN, George W. *Canada in the Making.* Toronto:
Dent, 1953.

———. *Canadian Democracy in Action.* Toronto: Dent,
1950 and 1952. [First published, 1945]

BROWN, Margaret A. *My Lady of the Snows.* Toronto:
William Briggs, 1908.

BROWN, Richard. *A History of the Island of Cape
Breton.* London: Sampson Low & Marston, 1869.

BROWN, Robert. "On the Vegetable Products, Used
by the Northwest American Indians as Food and
Medicine, in the Arts, and in Superstitious Rites,"
Botanical Society of Edinburgh Transactions, Vol. IX
(1868), 378-396.

BROWNE, Patrick William. *Where the Fishers Go —
The Story of Labrador.* Toronto: Musson, 1909.

BRUCE, Charles. *The Channel Shore.* Toronto: Macmillan, 1954.

BRYCE, George. *Mackenzie Selkirk Simpson.* Makers
of Canada Series IX. Toronto: Oxford Univ. Press,
1926.

———. "Old Settlers of Red River," *Annual Report*
(1888). Winnipeg: Historical & Scientific Society of
Manitoba, 1889. [Apparently written in 1885]

———. *Our Indians.* Winnipeg: Manitoba Free Press,
1884.

———. *Remarkable History of the Hudson's Bay
Company.* Toronto: William Briggs, 1900.

———. *The Romantic Settlement of Lord Selkirk's
Colonists.* New York: Barse & Hopkins, 1910. [First
published, Toronto: Musson, 1909]

BRYCE, George, ed. *Glimpses of the Past in the Red
River Settlement, from Letters of Mr. J. Pritchard,
1805-1836.* Middle Church, Man.: Rupert's Land Indian
Industrial School Press, 1892.

BUBLITZ, Dorothea E. *Life on the Dotted Line.* New
York: Vantage Press, 1960.

BUCHAN, J. *Sick Heart River.* London: Hodder &
Stoughton, 1941.

BUCKLER, Ernest. *The Mountain and The Valley.* New
York: Holt, 1952.

BULIARD, Roger. *Inuk.* New York: Farrar, Straus
and Young, 1951. [Account of life in Canadian Arctic,
1934-1950]

BULL, William Perkins. *From Rattlesnake Hunt to
Hockey.* Toronto: Perkins Bull Foundation, 1934.

BUNTING, William H. *Report of a Special Inquiry into
Fruit Growing Conditions in Canada, 1911.* Ottawa:
King's Printer, 1912.

BURPEE, L. J., ed. *Canadian Eloquence.* Toronto:
Musson, 1910.

———. *Journal de Larocque de la Rivière Assiniboine
jusqu'à la Rivière "Aux Roches Jaunes" 1805.* Publications des Archives Canadiennes 3. Ottawa, 1911.

———. *Journal of the Yukon, 1847-1848.* See Alexander
H. MURRAY.

BURT, A. L. *The Romance of Canada.* With British
Columbia Supplement. Toronto, 1946.

BUSCHLEN, J. P. *A Canadian Bankclerk.* Toronto:
William Briggs, 1913.

BUTLER, W. F. *Far Out — Rovings Retold.* London:
William Isbister, 1880.

———. *Great Lone Land.* London: Sampson Low,
Marston, 1873 and 1883. [Written, 1872]

———. *The Wild North Land — Being the Story of a
Winter Journey, with Dog, across Northern North
America.* New York: A. S. Barnes, 1904. [Preface
dated 1873]

BUTTERWORTH, Hezekiah. *Log Schoolhouse on the
Columbia — A Tale of the Pioneers of the Great Northwest.* New York, 1890.

CADZOW, Donald A. *Native Copper Objects of the Copper Eskimo.* New York: Museum of the American Indian, 1920.

CAIRNES, D. D. *Moose Mountain District, Southern Alberta.* Geological Survey of Canada Mem. 61. Ottawa, 1914.

CALDER, Ritchie. *Men against the Frozen North.* London, 1957.

CALLAGHAN, Morley. "Rigmarole," in George E. NELSON, *Cavalcade of the North.* See below. [First published, 1935]

CALVIN, D. D. *A Saga of the St. Lawrence.* Toronto: Ryerson, 1945.

CAMERON, Agnes D. *The New North — Being Some Account of a Woman's Journey through Canada to the Arctic.* London: D. Appleton, 1909.

CAMERON, Austin W. *Canadian Mammals.* Ottawa: National Museum of Canada and Dept of Northern Affairs and National Resources, 1958.

———. *Guide to Eastern Canadian Mammals.* Ottawa: Queen's Printer, 1956.

CAMERON, D. G. *Twigs from the Oak and Other Trees.* Regina: Privately printed, 1933.

CAMERON, Duncan. "Nipigon Country, 1804 — With Extracts from His Journal," in Vol. II of L. F. R. MASSON, *Les Bourgeois . . . ,* pp. 229-300. See below.

CAMP, D. K. "The Tourist," *Atlantic Advocate,* July, 1959.

CAMPBELL, Duncan. *History of Prince Edward Island.* Charlottetown: Bremmer, 1875.

CAMPBELL, Grace. *The Higher Hill.* Toronto: Wm. Collins, 1944.

———. *Thorn-Apple Tree — A Romance of the Glengarry Settlers.* Toronto: Collins, 1942.

CAMPBELL, J. R. *A History of the County of Yarmouth, Nova Scotia.* St. John, N.B.: J. & A. McMillan, 1876.

CAMPBELL, Marjorie W. *The Nor'Westers — The Fight for the Fur Trade.* Toronto: Macmillan, 1954.

———. *The Saskatchewan.* Toronto: Rinehart, 1950.

CAMPBELL, Patrick. *Travels in the Interior Inhabited Part of North America, 1791-1792.* The Champlain Society Publications XXIII. Toronto, 1937. [First published, 1793]

CAMPBELL, Robert. *Journal of Robert Campbell* (1808-1851). Vancouver Public Library MSS. [Retyped from manuscript]

———. *Two Journals of Robert Campbell* (1808-1853). Vancouver Public Library MSS. [Retyped from manuscript; includes another version of above *Journal*]

CAMSELL, Charles. *Geology of the National Parks of Canada.* 1914.

———. *Son of the North.* Toronto: Ryerson, 1954.

Canada's Story in Song. See Edith FOWKE.

Canada West and the Hudson's Bay Company. London: William Tweedie, 1856.

Canada Year Book. Ottawa: Queen's Printer. [Published annually]

Canadian Almanac & Directory. Toronto: Copp Clark, 1966 and 1967. [Published annually]

Canadian Eskimo — People of the High Arctic. Ottawa: National Film Board, c1957.

Canadian Favourites. Ottawa: C.C.F. National Council, 1944.

Canadian North-West — Climate and Productions — A

Misrepresentation Exposed. 5th ed. Ottawa: Dept of Agriculture, 1883.

Canadian Prose. See *Selected Stories from Canadian Prose.*

Canadian Readers Book III. B.C. ed. Toronto: Gage, 1881.

CANNIFF, William. *History of the Settlement of Upper Canada — With Special Reference to the Bay of Quinte.* Toronto: Dudley & Burns, 1869.

CANUCK, Janey (pseud. of Emily Ferguson). *Open Trails.* Toronto: Cassell, 1912.

CARL, G. C. *Guide to Marine Life of British Columbia.* B.C. Provincial Museum Handbook 21. Victoria, 1963.

———. *Some Common Marine Fishes of B.C.* B.C. Provincial Museum Handbook 23. Victoria, 1964.

CARL, G. C., W. A. Clemens, and G. C. Lindsey. *The Fresh-Water Fishes of B.C.* Victoria: Department of Education, 1959.

CARLIN, Robert. *I Know Mine Mill . . . Do You?* Toronto: United Steel Workers, 1962. [Pamphlet]

CARMACK, George W. *My Experiences in the Yukon.* Seattle, Wash., 1933.

CARR, Emily. *The Book of Small.* Toronto: Oxford Univ. Press, 1942.

———. *Klee Wyck.* Toronto: Oxford Univ. Press, 1941.

CARR, Lucien. "The Food of Certain American Indians and Their Methods of Preparing It," *Proceedings of the American Antiquarian Society,* Vol. X (1895), 155-190.

CARR-HARRIS, Bertha Wright. *The White Chief of the Ottawa.* Toronto: William Briggs, 1903.

CARROLL, Jock. *The Shy Photographer.* New York: Bantam, 1964.

CARRUTHERS, Janet. "Land of the Ojibway," *Beaver,* Outfit 282 (March, 1952), 45.

CARTER. *Story of Dundas from 1784 to 1904.* Iroquois, Ont., 1905.

CARTWRIGHT, George. *Captain Cartwright and His Labrador Journal.* See C. W. TOWNSEND.

———. *A Journal of Transactions and Events, during a Residence of Nearly Sixteen Years on the Coast of Labrador. . . .* 3 vols. Newark: Allin & Ridge, 1792.

CARVER, J. *Travels through the Interior Part of North America in the Years 1766, 1767, and 1768.* London: Privately printed, 1778.

CASH, Gwen. *I Like British Columbia.* New York: Macmillan, 1938.

———. *A Million Miles from Ottawa.* Toronto: Macmillan, 1942.

Cash for Your Canada, United States, Great Britain, Coins and Bills. 9th ed. Winnipeg: Numismatic Guild of Canada, 1965.

CASHMAN, A. W. *The Edmonton Story — The Life and Times of Edmonton, Alberta.* Sketches from a radio series broadcast over CJCA. Edmonton, 1956.

CASSIDY, Harry. *Social Security and Reconstruction in Canada.* Toronto: Ryerson, 1943.

Catalogue of Canadian Forestry and Other Resource Films. Ottawa: Dept of Forestry, 1965.

Census of Canada, Ninth, 1951. Ottawa: Dominion Bureau of Statistics.

A Century of Progress in Our Forest Industries. Vancouver: Canadian Forestry Association of B.C., 1967.

CHABOILLEZ, Charles, "Journal, 1797-1798," in B. C. PAYETTE, *The Northwest.* See below.

CHALMERS, John W. *Horseman in Scarlet*. Toronto: Gage, 1961.

CHAMBERS, E. T. D. *The Ouananiche, and Its Canadian Environment*. New York: Harper, 1896.

CHAMPION, H. J. *Over on the Island*. Toronto: Ryerson, 1939.

CHAMPLAIN, Samuel de. *Carte de la Nouvelle France*. 1632.

———. *Works*. Edited by H. P. Biggar. Vol IV. Toronto: Champlain Society, 1932. [Cited as *Voyages*]

CHAPPELL, Edward. *Narrative of a Voyage to Hudson's Bay in His Majesty's Ship Rosamond — Containing Some Account of the North-eastern Coast of America and of the Tribes Inhabiting that Remote Region*. London: J. Mawman, 1817.

———. *Voyage of His Majesty's Ship Rosamond to Newfoundland* . . . . London: J. Mawman, 1818.

CHARLTON, W. A. *Hudson's Bay Railway Route*. Toronto: Warwick & Rutter, 1898.

CHARTRAND, Michael, Vernel Olson, and John Riddell. *The Real Cuba as Three Canadians Saw It*. Toronto: Fair Play for Cuba Committee, 1964.

CHATTERTON, W. Gordon. *Canada and Other Lands*. Toronto: Winston, 1955.

CHEADLE, W. P. *Journal, 1862-1863*. Ottawa: Graphic Press, 1931.

CHISHOLM, A. M. *The Land of Big Rivers — A Story of the North-West*. New York: Chelsea House, 1924.

CHITTENDEN, Hiram M. *The American Fur Trade of the Far West*. 2 vols. Stanford, Calif.: Academic Reprints, 1954. [First published, 3 vols, New York, 1902]

CHITTENDEN, N. H. *Official Report of the Exploration of Queen Charlotte Islands for the Government of British Columbia*. Victoria: Provincial Government, 1884.

CHRISTIAN, Edgar. *Unflinching — A Diary of Tragic Adventure*. London: John Murray, 1937.

CHRISTIE, James R., and Isabel MacNaughton. *The Story of Okanagan Falls*. Okanagan Falls, B.C.: Okanagan Falls Centennial Committee, 1957.

CHRISTIE, Robert. *A History of the Late Province of Lower Canada, 1791-1841*. 6 vols. Quebec: Carey, 1848-1866.

Christmas Tree Farming. Victoria: Department of Forestry, 1955.

CHURCH, Alfred J. *Making a Start in Canada — Letters from Two Young Emigrants*. London: Seeley-Service, 1889.

CLARK, Catherine. *The Golden Pine Cone*. Toronto: Macmillan, 1958.

CLARK, Christopher St. George. *Of Toronto the Good — A Social Study. The Queen City of Canada as It Is*. Montreal: Toronto Publishing Co., 1898.

CLARK, Ella E. *Indian Legends of the Pacific Northwest*. Berkeley, Calif.: Univ. of California Press, 1953.

CLARK, Gregory. *So What?* Toronto: Reginald Saunders, 1937.

CLARK, S. *A New Description of the World*. 2nd ed. London: Henry Rhodes, 1708.

CLARK, W. P. *The Indian Sign Language*. Philadelphia: Hammersley, 1885.

CLARKE. *All Aboard for Fun*. Philadelphia: National Publishing Co., 1906.

CLARKE, Charles. *Sixty Years in Upper Canada*. Toronto: William Briggs, 1908.

CLARKE, G. F. *Chris In Canada*. Toronto: Blackie, 1925.

CLAY, Charles. *Muskrat Man*. Toronto: Ryerson, 1946.

———. *Phantom Fur Thieves*. Toronto: Ryerson, 1944.

CLEMENS, W. A., and G. V. Wilby. *Fishes of the Pacific Coast of Canada*. Fisheries Research Board of Canada Bulletin No. 68. 2nd ed. Ottawa, 1961.

CLEMENT, W. H. *The History of Canada*. Toronto: Copp, Clark, 1897.

CLUTTERBUCK, J., and J. A. Lees. *British Columbia*. See. J. A. LEES.

COATS, Captain William. *The Geography of Hudson's Bay — Being the Remarks of Captain W. Coats, in Many Voyages to that Locality, between the Years 1727 and 1751*. Edited by John Barrow. London: Hakluyt Soc., 1852.

COCKING, Matthew. "An Adventurer from Hudson Bay — Journal of Mathew Cocking, from York Factory to the Blackfeet Country, 1772-73." Edited by L. J. Burpee. *Trans.Roy.Soc.Can.*, Vol. II (1908), Sec. 2, 89-121.

CODY, H. A. *The Frontiersman — A Tale of the Yukon*. Toronto: William Briggs, 1912. [First published, 1910]

———. *The King's Arrow — A Tale of the United Empire Loyalists*. Toronto: McClelland & Stewart, 1922.

———. *The Long Patrol — A Tale of the Mounted Police*. Toronto: William Briggs, 1912.

———. *Under Sealed Orders*. Toronto: McClelland & Stewart, 1917.

COLE, Carol C. *Downy Wing and Sharp Ears*. Toronto: Musson, 1923.

COLLARD, E. A. *Call Back Yesterdays*. Don Mills, Ont.: Longmans Canada, 1965.

———. *Canadian Yesterdays*. Toronto: Longmans, Green, 1955.

COLLINSON, Sir Richard. *Journal of H.M.S. Enterprise on the Expedition in Search of Sir John Franklin's Ships by Behring Strait, 1850-1855*. London: Sampson Low, Marston, Searle & Rivington, 1889.

COLVILLE, Eden. *Letters*. Edited by E. E. Rich. Hudson's Bay Record Society Publications XIX. Ottawa, 1956. [Written, 1852]

COMER, George. "Whaling in Hudson Bay, with Notes on Southampton Island," in F. BOAS, *Anniversary Volume*, pp. 475-484. See above.

The Commercial Fisheries of British Columbia. Victoria: Provincial Government, 1962.

A Commission for the Well Gouerning of Our People, Inhabiting in New-found-land. . . . London. Robert Barker, 1633.

Commission of Conservation. See next entry.

Conservation of Fish, Birds and Game — Proceedings at a Committee of the Commission of Conservation, Nov. 1 & 2, 1915. Toronto: Methodist Book & Publishing Co., 1916.

CONANT, Thomas. *Life in Canada*. Toronto: William Briggs, 1903.

———. *Upper Canada Sketches*. Toronto: William Briggs, 1898.

CONIBEAR, Kenneth. *Northland Footprints or Lives on Little Bent Tree Lake*. New York: Scribner, 1937.

CONNOR. Ralph (pseud. of C. W. Gordon). *Black*

Rock. London: Hodder & Stoughton, n.d. [First published, Toronto: Westminster, 1898]

———. *Corporal Cameron of the North West Mounted Police — A Tale of the MacLeod Trail*. Toronto: Westminster, 1912.

———. *The Doctor*. Toronto: Westminster, 1906.

———. *The Foreigner — A Tale of Saskatchewan*. Toronto: Westminster, 1909.

———. *Glengarry School Days*. Toronto: Westminster, 1902. [Cited as *Glengarry*]

———. *The Major*. Toronto: McClung & Stewart, 1917; New York: George H. Doran, 1917.

———. *The Man From Glengarry*. Chicago: F. H. Revell, 1901.

———. *The Prospector — A Tale of the Crow's Nest Pass*. New York: F. H. Revell, 1904.

———. *The Rock and the River — A Romance of Quebec*. Toronto: McClelland & Stewart, 1931.

———. *The Sky Pilot — A Tale of the Foothills*. Toronto: McClelland & Stewart, n.d. [First published, Toronto: Westminster, 1899]

———. *The Sky Pilot in Noman's Land*. Toronto: McClelland & Stewart, 1919.

CONNOR, Thomas. "Diary, 1804-1805," in C. M. GATES, ed., *Five Fur Traders of the Northwest*. See below.

CONSTANTIN-WEYER, M. *The Half-Breed*. Winnipeg: Harlequin Books, 1954.

———. *A Man Scans His Past*. Translated by Slater Brown. Toronto: Macmillan, 1929.

Constitution and Caucus of the Provincial Synod of Rupert's Land. 1947.

COOPER, Courtney Ryley. *Challenge of the Bush*. Toronto: McClelland & Stewart, 1929.

COOPER, J. Fenimore. *The Sea Lions or The Lost Sealers*. London: Co-operative Publishing Soc., 1849.

COPELAND, John Morison. *The Trail of the Swinging Lanterns*. Toronto: Addison & Mainprice, 1918.

CORMACK, Barbara V. *Local Rag*. Toronto: Ryerson, 1951.

CORMACK, W. E. *Narrative of a Journey across the Island of Newfoundland in 1822*. Edited by F. A. Bruton. London: Longmans, Green, 1928. [First published, 1822]

CORNEY, Peter. "Journal," *Literary Gazette*, 1821.

CORNISH, G. A. *Canadian Geography for Juniors*. B.C. ed. Toronto: Dent, 1930. [This edition first published, 1928]

CORNWALLIS, Kinahan. *The New Eldorado, or British Columbia*. London: Thomas Cautley Newby, 1858.

COTTER, H. M. S. "A Fur Trade Glossary," *Beaver*, Outfit 272 (Sept., 1941), 36-39.

COUES, Elliott, ed. *New Light on the Early History of the Greater Northwest — The Manuscript Journals of Alexander Henry, Fur Trader of the Northwest Company, and of David Thompson, Official Geographer and Explorer of the Same Company, 1799-1814*. 3 vols. New York: Francis P. Harper, 1897.

COUTTS, Margaret Ellen. *Dawson Creek, Past and Present — A Historical Sketch*. Dawson Creek, B.C., 1958.

COWAN, I. "The Fur Trade & The Fur Cycle, 1825-1857," *British Columbia Historical Quarterly*, Jan., 1938.

COWIE, Isaac. *The Company of Adventurers — A Narrative of Seven Years in the Service of the Hudson's Bay Company during 1867-1874 on the Great Buffalo Plains*. Toronto: William Briggs, 1913.

COWPER, Edith E. *Witch of the Wilds — A Story of Adventure in the Northern Snows*. London and Toronto: Nelson, 1925.

COX, Ross. *Adventures on the Columbia River*. New York: Harper, 1832. Also, in *Up the Columbia for Furs*. Edited by Cecil Dryden. Caldwell, Idaho: Caxton Printers, 1949.

COZZENS, Frederic S. *Acadia, or A Month with the Blue Noses*. New York: Derby & Jackson, 1859.

CRAIG, Gerald M. *Early Travellers in the Canadas, 1791-1867*. Toronto: Macmillan, 1955.

———. *Upper Canada — The Formative Years, 1784-1841*. Toronto: McClelland & Stewart, 1943.

CRAMOND, Mike. *Big Game Hunting in the West*. Vancouver: Mitchell Press, 1965.

CRATE, Chas. B. *The Language of Canadian Hardrock Mining*. Paper presented to the Canadian Linguistic Association, Charlottetown, June, 1964. Unpublished MS.

CRATE, Chas. B., and A. E. Williams. *We Speak For the Silent!* A Brief submitted to the Royal Commission on Canada's Economic Prospects. Yellowknife: Yellowknife District Miners' Union, Jan., 1956. [Mimeographed]

CREED, G. E. *Money — Master or Servant? The Democratic Way to Full Employment*. Hamilton-Toronto: League for Economic Democracy, 1944.

CREIGHTON, Helen. *Bluenose Ghosts*. Toronto: Ryerson, 1957.

———. *Folklore of Lunenburg County, Nova Scotia*. National Museum of Canada Bulletin 117. Ottawa, 1950.

CROASDAILE, Henry E. *Scenes on Pacific Shores*. London: Town & Country Publishing Co., 1873.

CROIL, James. *Dundas, or A Sketch of Canadian History, and More Particularly of the County of Dundas, One of the Earliest Settled Counties in Upper Canada*. Montreal: B. Dawson, 1861.

CRONIN, K. *Cross in the Wilderness*. Vancouver: Mitchell Press, 1960.

CROSBY, (Rev.) Thomas. *Among the An-ko-me-nums of the Pacific Coast*. Toronto: William Briggs, 1907.

CROSS, Austin F. *Cross Roads*. 2nd ed. Montreal: Southam Press, 1936.

CROSS, W. K., C. F. Coulson, and A. E. Loft. *British Columbia Land Bulletin Areas Source Book*. Victoria: Department of Education, 1966.

CROSSKILL, William Hay. *Prince Edward Island, Garden Province of Canada — Its History, Interests and Resources with Information for Tourists*. Charlottetown: Provincial Government, 1904.

Crown Zellerbach — Profile of a Corporation. San Francisco: Crown Zellerbach Corp., 1964. [Booklet]

CUDMORE, S. A. *History of the World's Commerce with Special Reference to Canada*. Toronto: Pitman, 1929.

CULLUM, Ridgwell. *The Devil's Keg — The Story of the Foss River Ranch*. London: Chapman & Hall, 1913. [First published as *The Story of the Foss River Ranch — A Tale of the Northwest*. Boston: L. C. Page, 1903]

———. *The Law of the Gun*. Toronto: William Briggs, 1918.

————. *The Tiger of Cloud River*. New York: A. L. Burt, 1929.

Cumberland and Hudson House Journals, 1775-78. Edited by E. E. Rich. Hudson's Bay Record Society Publications XIV. London, 1951. [Cited as *Saskatchewan Journals*]

Cumberland House Journals and Inland Journal, 1779-1782. Edited by E. E. Rich. Hudson's Bay Record Society Publications XV. London, 1952. [Cited as *Cumberland House Journals*]

CUMMING, R. D. *Skookum Chuck Fables — Bits of History through the Microscope.* Ashcroft, B. C.: Privately printed, 1915.

CURRAN, W. Tees, and H. A. Calkins. *In Canada's Wonderful Northland.* New York: Putnam, 1917. [Preface dated 1913]

CURTIN, W. R. *Yukon Voyage.* Idaho: Caxton, 1938.

CURTIS, Thomas. "A Narrative of the Voyage of Thos. Curtis to the Island of St. John's in the Gulf of St. Lawrence in North America, in the year 1775," in D. C. HARVEY, *Journeys to the Island of St. John or Prince Edward Island 1775-1835.* See below.

CURWOOD, James Oliver, *Barree, Son of Kazan.* Garden City, N.Y.: Doubleday, Page, 1917.

————. *The Danger Trail.* New York: Grosset & Dunlap, 1910.

————. *The Flaming Forest.* Winnipeg: Harlequin, 1957. [First published, New York: Cosmopolitan, 1921]

————. *A Gentleman of Courage — A Novel of the Wilderness.* Toronto: Copp Clark, 1924.

————. *The Grizzly King.* New York: Grosset & Dunlap, 1918. [First published, 1915]

————. *The Honor of the Big Snows.* New York: A. L. Burt, 1911.

————. *The Plains of Abraham.* Toronto: Doubleday, Doran & Gundy, 1928.

————. *The River's End — A New Story of God's Country.* New York: Cosmopolitan, 1919.

————. *Steele of the Royal Mounted.* Montreal: Pocket Books of Canada, 1946. [First published, 1911]

————. *The Valley of Silent Men — A Story of the Three River Country.* Toronto: Copp Clark, 1923.

CUSHMAN, Dan. *Timberjack.* New York: Fawcett, 1953.

————. *Stay Away Joe.* Toronto: Macmillan, 1953.

DALL, W. H. *Tribes of the Extreme Northwest. Contributions to North American Ethnology I.* Washington, D.C.: 1877.

DALZEL. See Peter Dalzel JOB.

DASHWOOD, R. L. *Chiploquorgan, or Life by the Camp Fire in the Dominion of Canada and Newfoundland.* London: Simpkin & Marshall, 1872. [First published, Dublin, 1871]

DAUNT, Achilles. *In the Land of the Moose, the Bear and the Beaver — Adventures in the Forests of the Athabasca.* London: Nelson, 1892.

DAVIDSON, Gordon C. *The North West Company.* Univ. of California Publications in History VII. Berkeley, Calif., 1918.

DAVIDSON, William McCartney. *Louis Riel 1844-1885.* Calgary: Albertan Publishing Co., 1955.

DAVIES, K. G., ed. *Northern Quebec & Labrador Journals & Correspondence (1819-1835).* Hudson's Bay Record Society Publications XXIV. London, 1963.

DAVIES, R. *A Mixture of Frailties.* Toronto: Macmillan, 1958.

DAVIS, E. A. *Review of the United Churches in British Columbia.* Vancouver: Joseph Lee, 1925.

DAVIS, H. L. *Winds of Morning.* Toronto: McLeod, 1952.

DAVIS, H. P. *The Modern Dog Encyclopedia.* Harrisburg, Pa.: Stackpole, 1949; reprinted, 1956.

DAVIS, T. *Using Our Language.* Toronto: Dent, 1958. [First published, 1942]

DAVYS, John. *The Voyages and Works of John Davis the Navigator.* Edited by Albert Hastings Markham. London: Hakluyt Society, 1880.

DAWLISH, P. (pseud. of S. L. Kerr). *The Race for Gowrie Bay.* London: Oxford, 1959.

DAWSON, George M. "The Haidas," *Harper's Monthly,* 1888.

————. "Notes and Observations on the Kwakiool People . . . ," *Trans.Roy.Soc.Can.,* Vol. II (1887).

————. "Notes on the Indian Tribes of the Yukon District," *Annual Report of the Geological Survey of Canada.* Ottawa, 1887.

————. *Report on an Expedition Made in 1887 in the Yukon District and Adjacent Northern British Columbia.* Montreal, 1888.

————. *Report on the Exploration between Lake Superior and the Red River Settlement. . . .* Toronto: Legislative Assembly, 1859.

————. "Report on the Queen Charlotte Islands," *Geological Survey of Canada, Report of Progress 1878-1879.* Montreal: Dawson, 1880.

————. "Sketches of the Past and Present Condition of the Indians of Canada," *Canadian Naturalist and Geologist,* Vol. IX (1879), No. 3.

DAWSON, G. M., and A. Sutherland. *Geography of the British Colonies.* Toronto: Macmillan, 1908 [First published, 1892]

DAWSON, J. W. *Acadian Geology.* 1st ed. Edinburgh: Oliver Macmillan, 1855.

DAWSON, R. M. *The Government of Canada.* Toronto: Univ. of Toronto Press, 1947, 1957, 1964.

DAWSON, Samuel Edward. *Hand-book for the Dominion of Canada.* Montreal, 1884.

————. *The Saint Lawrence, Its Basin and Border Lands.* New York: A. Stokes, 1905.

DAWSON, Will. *Ahoy There!* Toronto: Dent, 1955.

DAY, Holman F. *King Spruce.* New York: Harper, 1908.

DAY, Luella. *The Tragedy of the Klondike.* New York: Luella Day, 1906.

de BOILIEU, Lambert. *Recollections of Labrador Life.* London: Saunders, Otley, 1861.

DeCELLES, Alfred. *Sir Georges Etienne Cartier.* Toronto: Morang, 1904.

————. *Louis-Joseph Papineau.* Toronto: Morang, 1904.

DELANEY, Theresa. See Theresa GOWANLOCK.

de la ROCHE, Mazo. *The Building of Jalna.* Toronto: Macmillan, 1948.

————. *Mary Wakefield.* Boston: Little, Brown, 1949.

————. *Possession.* Toronto: Macmillan, 1923.

De MAR, Paul (pseud. of Pearl Foley). *The Gnome Mine Mystery.* London: John Hamilton, 1933.

DENISON, Merrill. *Klondike Mike — An Alaskan Odyssey*. Toronto: Collins, 1950. [First published, 1949]

DENNIS, Clara. *Cape Breton Over*. Toronto: Ryerson, 1943.

———. *Down in Nova Scotia — My Own, My Native Land*. Toronto: Ryerson, 1934. [Preface dated 1933].

DENNY, Sir Cecil. "Animals of the Early West," *Alberta Historical Review*, Spring, 1956.

DENNYS, N. B. *An Account of the Cruise of the St. George*. London: Saunders, Otley, 1862.

DENSMORE, Frances. "Uses of Plants by the Chippewa Indians," *Forty-fourth Annual Report* (1926-27). Washington, D.C.: Bureau of American Ethnology.

DENT, John Charles. *The Story of the Upper Canada Rebellion*. 2 vols. Toronto: C. Blackett Robinson, 1885.

DENTON, V. L., and A. R. Lord. *A World Geography for Canadian Schools*. Toronto: Dent, 1936.

DENYS, Nicolas. *Description Géographique et Historique des Costes de l'Amérique Septentrionale*. Paris: Claude Barbin, 1672.

Department of the Interior Annual Report (1877). Sessional Paper 11.

De PONCINS, Gontran. *Kabloona*. New York: Reynal & Hitchcock, 1941.

A Description of Prince Edward Island. 3rd ed. Bristol, England, 1818.

Descriptive Catalogue of Economic Minerals of Canada. Ottawa, 1876.

Descriptive Sketch of the Physical Geography and Geology of the Dominion of Canada. Montreal: Selwyn & Dawson, 1884.

De SMET, P. J. *Letters and Sketches*. . . . Philadelphia: M. Fithian, 1843.

———. *New Indian Sketches*. New York: D. & J. Sadlier, 1865.

———. *Oregon Missions*. . . . New York: Edward Dunigan, 1847.

DEVINE, Patrick K. *Devine's Folk Lore of Newfoundland in Old Words, Phrases, and Expressions, Their Origin and Meaning*. St. John's; Robinson, 1937.

DEWAR, Thomas R. *A Ramble round the Globe*. London: Chatto & Windus, 1894.

DICKIE, Donalda J. *The Canadian West*. Dent's Canadian History Readers VII. Toronto: Dent, 1926.

———. *The Great Golden Plain*. Toronto: Gage, 1962.

———. *How Canada Grew Up*. Toronto: Dent, 1927.

———. *Pages from Canada's Story*. Toronto: Dent, 1931.

DICKIE, Donalda J., et al. *Gay Adventurers*. Toronto: Dent, 1947.

Dictionary of the Chinook Jargon or Indian Trade Language, of the North Pacific Coast. Victoria: T. N. Hibben, 1899. [Photo-reprint, 1965]

DIESPECKER, Richard E. *Between Two Furious Oceans and Other Poems*. Toronto: Oxford, 1944.

DILL, W. S. *The Long Day — Reminiscences of the Yukon*. Ottawa: Graphic Publishers, 1926.

DILLMAN, M. A. *The Wee Folk — About the Elves in Nova Scotia*. 5th ed. Fredericton: Unipress, 1963. [First published, 1953]

DILLON, J. C. "Forest Protection in Ontario," *The Canadian Geographical Journal*, Vol. XLVI (Feb., 1953), 42-59.

DIXON, L. B. "The Birth of the Lumber Industry in British Columbia," *B.C. Lumberman*, 1956.

DOBBS, Arthur. *An Account of the Countries Adjoining to Hudson's Bay*. . . . London: J. Robinson, 1744.

DOBIE, James Frank. *Mustangs*. New York: Bantam, 1958.

———. *The Voice of the Coyote*. Boston: Little, Brown, 1950.

DOMETT, Alfred. *The Canadian Journal of Alfred Domett, 1833-1834*. Edited by E. A. Horsman and Lillian Rea. London, Ont.: University of Western Ontario, 1955.

DONER, Mary Frances. *The Host Rock*. Garden City, N.Y.: Doubleday, 1952.

DONKIN, John G. *Trooper and Redskin in the Far North-West*. London: Sampson Low, Marston, Searle & Rivington, 1889.

DONOVAN, Peter. *Late Spring*. Toronto: Macmillan, 1930.

DORR, J. W. *On the Sunset Shore — A Book of Poems and Rhymes*. Seattle, Wash.: Souvenir Publishing Co., 1908.

DORRANCE, James French. *Never Fire First*. New York: Macaulay, 1924.

DORSEY, G. A. "The Geography of the Tsimshian Indians," *American Antiquarian Society Transactions and Collections*, Vol. XIX (1897), 276-282.

DOUGHTY, A. G. *The Acadian Exiles — Chronicle of the Land of Evangeline*. Toronto: Glasgow, Brook, 1916.

DOUGLAS, A. F. *Logging and Vocational Training*. Vancouver: B.C. Loggers' Association, 1965.

DOUGLAS, David. *Journal Kept by David Douglas during His Travels in North America, 1823-1827*. . . . London: Wesley, 1914.

———. "Journal," in Vol. II of *Companion to the Botanical Magazine* (1836), edited by W. T. Hooker, pp. 134-137.

Douglas Day Observance Act. Victoria: Queen's Printer, 1960.

DOUGLAS, George M. *Lands Forlorn. A Story of an Expedition to Hearne's Coppermine River*. New York: Putnam, 1914.

DOWLING, D. B., et al. *Investigations in the Gas and Oil Fields of Alberta*. Geological Survey of Canada Memoir 116. Ottawa, 1919.

DOWNIE, William. *Hunting for Gold*. San Francisco: California Publishing Co., 1893.

DOWNS, Art. *Wagon Road North — The Story of the Cariboo Gold Rush in Historical Photos*. Quesnel, B.C.: Northwest Digest, 1960.

DOYLE, Martin. *Hints on Emigration to Upper Canada*. Dublin: William Curry, Junior, 1832. [Used pseudonym William Hickey].

DRAGE, Theodorus S. *The Great Probability of a North West Passage*. . . . London: Jefferys, 1768.

———. *An Account of a Voyage for the Discovery of a North-West Passage by Hudson's Streights, to the Western and Southern Ocean of America, Performed in the Year 1746 and 1747, in the Ship California, Capt. Francis Smith, Commander*. By the clerk of the *California*. 2 vols. London: Jolliffe, 1748 (Vol. I), 1749 (Vol. II).

DRIMMER, Frederick. *Scalps and Tomahawks — Narratives of Indian Captivity*. New York: Coward-McCann, 1961.

Drop in Anytime Neighbour. Quebec: Tourist Bureau, 1963.

DRUCKER, Philip. *Indians of the Northwest Coast.* American Museum of Natural History, Anthropological Handbook Number Ten. New York: McGraw-Hill, 1955.

DRUMMOND, R. *Minerals and Mining in Nova Scotia.* Stellarton, N. S.: Mining Record Office, 1918.

DRUMMOND, William H. *Habitant and Other French-Canadian Poems.* New York, 1897.

———. *Johnnie Courteau and Other Poems.* London: Putnam, 1903. [First published, 1901]

———. *The Voyageur and Other Poems.* New York: Putnam, 1905.

DUCHAUSSOIS, Father. *Among the Mackenzie River Eskimos, Northern Canada.* Annals of the Propagation of the Faith LXXXI (Dec., 1918).

DuCREUX, François. *The History of Canada or New France.* Champlain Society Publications XXX-XXXI. Toronto, 1951-52. [Written, 1664]

DUFF, Wilson. *The Indian History of British Columbia, Vol. I — The Impact of the White Man.* Anthropology in British Columbia Memoir 5. Victoria: Provincial Museum, 1964.

———. *Preserving British Columbia's Prehistory — A Guide for Amateur Archaeologists.* Victoria: Archaeological Sites Advisory Board, 1961.

———. *The Upper Stalo Indians of the Fraser Valley, British Columbia.* Anthropology in British Columbia Memoir 1. Victoria: Provincial Museum, 1952.

DUFFERIN and AVA, Marchioness of. *My Canadian Journal, 1872-8 — Extracts from My Letters Written Home while Lord Dufferin Was Governor General.* London: John Murray, 1891.

DUGMORE, A. R. *The Romance of the Beaver — Being the History of the Beaver in the Western Hemisphere.* . . . London: Heinemann, 1914.

DUMBRILLE, Dorothy. *Deep Doorways.* Toronto: Thomas Allen, 1947.

DUNCAN, Dorothy. *Bluenose, a Portrait of Nova Scotia.* New York: Harper, 1942.

DUNCAN, Dorothy Ellen. *Black Creek Pioneer Village.* Toronto: Metropolitan Toronto & Region Conservation Foundation, 1966.

DUNCAN, Norman. *Billy Topsail & Company.* Toronto: McClelland & Stewart, 1947. [First published, New York: F. H. Revell, 1910]

———. *Billy Topsail, M.D.* New York: Grosset & Dunlap, n.d. [First published, New York: F. H. Revell, 1916]

———. *Cruise of the Shining Light.* New York: Harper, 1907.

———. *Dr. Grenfell's Parish.* New York: F. H. Revell, 1905.

———. *Doctor Luke of the Labrador.* New York: F. H. Revell, 1904.

———. *Harbor Tales Down North.* New York: F. H. Revell, 1918.

———. *The Suitable Child.* New York: F. H. Revell, 1909.

DUNHAM, Mabel. *Grand River.* Toronto: McClelland & Stewart, 1945.

DUNN, John. *History of the Queen Territory.* London: Edwards & Hughes, 1844.

DURAND, Charles. *Reminiscences of Charles Durand of Toronto, Barrister.* Toronto: Hunter Rose, 1897.

DURKIN, Douglas. *The Lobstick Trail — A Romance of Northern Canada.* Toronto: Musson, 1921.

Dutch Oven: a Cook Book of Coveted Traditional Recipes from the Kitchens of Lunenburg. 2nd ed. Lunenburg, N.S.: Ladies Auxiliary of The Lunenburg Hospital Society, 1953.

DWIGHT, Charles P. *Life in the North-West Mounted Police and Other Sketches.* Toronto: National Publishing Co., 1892.

DYMOND, John Richardson. *The Trout and Other Game Fishes of British Columbia.* Ottawa: King's Printer, 1932.

The Eastern Townships — Information for Intending Settlers. Ottawa: Department of Agriculture, 1883.

EATON, Evelyn. *Quietly My Captain Waits.* New York: Literary Guild of America, 1940.

———. *The Sea is so Wide.* New York: Harper, 1943.

Eaton's Catalogue. Western ed. Winnipeg: T. Eaton Co. Ltd, 1963 and 1966. [Published twice a year]

Economic Minerals. See *Descriptive Catalogue of Economic Minerals of Canada.*

EDGAR, J. D. *Canada and Its Capital.* Toronto: George N. Morang, 1898.

EDGAR, Matilda. *Ten Years of Upper Canada in Peace and War, 1805-1815 — Being the Ridout Letters.* Toronto: William Briggs, 1890; London: Fisher Unwin, 1891.

EGGLESTON, Edward G. *The Hoosier Schoolmaster.* Reprint of 1892 rev. ed. New York: Books, Inc., 1948. [First published, 1871]

ELLIOTT, Gordon R. *Klondike Cattle Drive — The Journal of Norman Lee.* Vancouver: Mitchell Press, 1960.

———. *Quesnel — Commercial Centre of the Cariboo Gold Rush.* Quesnel, B.C.: Quesnel Branch of the Cariboo Historical Society, 1958.

ELLIOTT, T. R. *Hugh Layal, A Romance of the Up Country.* New York, 1927.

ELLIS, Henry. *A Voyage to Hudson's-Bay, by the Dobbs Galley and California, in the Years 1746 and 1747, for Discovering a North West Passage.* London: H. Whitridge, 1748.

ELLIS, Thomas. *A True Report of the Third and Last Voyage into Meta incognita: achieued by the worthie Capteine M. Martine Frobisher, Anno. 1578.* London: Thomas Dawson, 1578.

ELLS, S. C. *Northland Trails.* Toronto: Garden City Press, 1938.

Encyclopedia Canadiana. Ottawa: Canadiana Co., 1958.

ENGLAND, G. A. *Vikings of the Ice.* Garden City, N.Y.: Doubleday, Page, 1924.

ENGLAND, Robert. *The Central European Immigrant in Canada.* Toronto: Macmillan, 1929.

ENGLEBERT, R. *Men and Trees.* Vancouver: Vancouver Feature Publications, 1947.

English Dialect Dictionary. See Joseph WRIGHT.

ENGLISH, L. E. F. *Historic Newfoundland.* St. John's: Newfoundland Tourist Development Office, 1955 and 1959.

ERMATINGER, C. O. Z. *The Talbot Regime; or, The First Half Century of the Talbot Settlement.* St. Thomas, Ont.: Municipal World, 1904.

ERMATINGER, Edward. "Edward Ermatinger's York

Factory Express Journal — Being a Record of Journeys Made between Fort Vancouver and Hudson Bay in the Years 1827-1828," *Trans.Roy.Soc.Can.*, Vol. VI (1912), Sec. 2, 70-127.

ERSKINE, J. S. *Nova Scotia Prehistory*. Halifax, N.S., 1964.

The Eskimo. Ottawa: National Museum of Canada, 1939. [Pamphlet]

Esquimaux Indians. See *An Interesting Account*. . . .

ETCHES, John. *An Authentic Statement of All the Facts Relative to Nootka Sound*. . . . London: J. Debrett, 1790.

EVANS, Allen Roy. *Reindeer Trek*. Toronto: McClelland & Stewart, 1935.

EVANS, Estwick. *A Pedestrious Tour of Four Thousand Miles, through the Western States and Territories*. Concord, N.H.: J. C. Spear, 1819.

EVANS, Hubert. *Mist on the River*. Toronto: Copp Clark, 1954.

———. *Mountain Dog*. Philadelphia: Westminster Press, 1956.

EVARTS, H G. *Fur Brigade — A Story of the Trappers of the Early West*. New York: A. L. Burt, 1928.

EVATT, Harriet. *The Snow Owl's Secret*. New York: Bobbs-Merrill, 1944.

EWART, J. S. *Kingdom Papers*. Vol. I. Ottawa: Privately printed, 1912.

———. *The Manitoba School Question — An Historical Account of the Red River Outbreak in 1869 and 1870*. . . . Toronto: Copp Clark, 1894.

EWERS, John C. *The Horse in Blackfoot Indian Culture*. Bureau of American Ethnology Bulletin 159. Washington, D.C.: Smithsonian Institution, 1955.

———. "The Northwest Trade Gun," *Alberta Historical Review*, Spring, 1956.

FAIRLEY, Margaret, ed. *The Selected Writings of William Lyon Mackenzie, 1824-1837*. Toronto: Oxford, 1960.

FARIES, Hugh. "Diary, 1804-1805," in C. M. GATES, *Five Fur Traders* . . . , pp. 195-241. See below.

FARLAND (pseud.). *Poverty Be Damned*. 2nd ed. Winnipeg: Privately printed, 1938. [Pamphlet]

FAUGHNAN, Thomas. *Stirring Incidents in the Life of a British Soldier — An Autobiography*. Toronto: Hunter Rose, 1889. [First published, 1879]

Favourite Recipes. Inuvik: Anglican Church of Ascension, 1962.

FAY, C. R. *Life and Labour in Newfoundland*. Toronto: Univ. of Toronto Press, 1956.

FERGUSON, Chick. *Mink, Mary and Me — The Story of a Wilderness Trapline*. New York: M. S. Mill, 1946.

FERGUSON, Emily. *Janey Canuck in the West*. Toronto: Cassell, 1910.

———. *Open Trails*. See Janey CANUCK.

FERGUSON, J. D. *The Human Ecology and Social and Economic Change in the Community of Tuktoyaktuk, N.W.T.* Ottawa: Dept of Northern Affairs and National Resources, 1961.

FERGUSON, R. D. *Fur Trader — The Story of Alexander Henry*. Toronto: Macmillan, 1961.

FERGUSSON, Adam. *Practical Notes Made during a Tour in Canada and a Portion of the United States in MDCCCXXXI*. Edinburgh: William Blackwood, 1833.

FERGUSSON, C. B., ed. *The Diary of Adolphus Gaetz*.

See A. GAETZ.

FESSENDEN, E. J. *Centenary Study of Upper Canada*. Welland, Ont., 1892.

FETHERSTONHAUGH, R. C. *The Royal Canadian Mounted Police*. New York: Carrick & Evans, 1938.

FIDLER, Peter. *Journal of a Journey over Land from Buckingham House to the Rocky Mountains in 1792 & 1793*. Hudson's Bay Co. Archives. MS.

———. *Peter Fidler's Journal, 1791-1792*. Champlain Society Publications XXI. Toronto, 1934.

FINNIE, Richard. *Lure of the North*. Philadelphia: David McKay, 1940.

FISHER, Vardis. *Pemmican*. Montreal: Pocketbooks of Canada, 1957. [First published, New York: Doubleday, 1956]

Fisheries Fact Sheets. Ottawa: Dept of Fisheries.

FITZGERALD, Robert A. *Wickets in the West; or, the Twelve in America*. London: Tinsley, 1873.

FLAHERTY, Robert J. "The Belcher Islands of Hudson Bay," *Geographical Review*, Vol. V (1918), No. 66, 433-58.

———. *My Eskimo Friends — "Nanook of the North."* New York: Doubleday, Page, 1922; Garden City, N.Y.: Doubleday, Page, 1924.

FLEMING, Archibald Lang. *Dwellers in Arctic Night*. Toronto: Missionary Society of Church of England in Canada, 1928.

FLEMING, Sandford. *The Intercolonial — A Historical Sketch*. Montreal: Dawson, 1876.

FLUKE, A. F. *Déné*. British Columbia Heritage Series I, Our Native Peoples, Vol. IX. Edited by T. F. Fairey. Victoria: Dept of Education, 1953.

———. *Kwakiutl*. British Columbia Heritage Series I, Our Native Peoples, Vol. VII. Edited by T. F. Fairey. Victoria: Dept of Education, 1953.

FONTAINE, Robert. *The Happy Time*. New York: Simon & Schuster, 1945.

FOOTNER, Hulbert. *The Fur-Bringers — A Story of the Canadian Northwest*. London: Hodder & Stoughton, 1920.

———. *The Huntress*. London: Hodder & Stoughton, 1922.

———. *Jack Chanty — A Story of Athabasca*. Garden City, N.Y.: Doubleday, 1913.

———. *New Rivers of the North — The Yarn of Two Amateur Explorers*. New York: Outing Publishing Co., 1912.

———. *Two on a Trail — A Story of the Far Northwest*. Toronto: Musson, 1911.

———. *The Woman from "Outside."* New York: McCann, 1921.

Forest Conservation. Ottawa: Dept of Forestry, 1962.

Forestry Course I (Elementary). Textbooklet 2. Ottawa: Canadian Legion Educational Services, 1944.

Forestry Course II (Advanced). Textbooklet 1. Ottawa: Canadian Legion Educational Services, 1944.

Fort Langley Journal. British Columbia Provincial Archives. MS.

Fort Langley National Historic Park. Ottawa: Dept of Northern Affairs and National Resources, 1964. [Cited as *Fort Langley*]

FOSTER, A.H., and A. Grierson. *High Days and Holidays in Canada — Collection of Holiday Facts for Canadian Schools*. Rev. ed. Toronto: Ryerson, 1956.

FOWKE, Edith, and Richard Johnston. *Folk Songs of Canada*. Waterloo, Ont.: Waterloo Music Co., 1954.

FOWKE, Edith, Alan Mills, and Helmut Blume. *Canada's Story in Song*. Toronto: Gage, 1960.

FOWLER, Jacob. *Journal*. Edited by Elliot Coues. New York, 1898.

FRANCIS, S. A. *The Canadian Home Boy*. London: H. Williams & Son, 1913.

FRANDSEN, J. H. *Dairy Handbook and Dictionary*. Amherst, Mass.: Privately printed, 1958.

FRANKLIN, John. *Narrative of a Journey to the Shores of the Polar Sea in the Years 1819, 1820, 1821, and 1822*. London: John Murray, 1823.

FRASER, Sir John Foster. *Canada as It Is*. London, 1905.

FRASER, Joshua. *Shanty, Forest, and River Life in the Backwoods of Canada*. Montreal: John Lovell, 1883.

FRASER, Simon. "First Journal . . . from April 12th to July 18th, 1806," App. B of *Canadian Archives Report* (1929), pp. 109-145. Ottawa, 1930.

————. "Journal of a Voyage from the Rocky Mountains to the Pacific Coast, 1808," in Vol. I of L. F. R. MASSON, *Les Bourgeois . . .*, pp. 155-221. See below.

————. *The Letters and Journals of Simon Fraser, 1806-1808*. Edited by W. Kaye Lamb. Toronto: Macmillan, 1960.

————. "Letters from the Rocky Mountains from August 1st, 1806 to February 10th, 1807," App. C of *Canadian Archives Report* (1929). Ottawa, 1930.

FRASER, W. A. *Bulldog Carney*. Toronto: McClelland & Stewart, 1919.

————. *Mooswa and Others of the Boundaries*. Toronto: William Briggs, 1900.

————. *Red Meekins*. Toronto: McClelland & Stewart, 1921. [First published, 1910]

FRAYNE, Trent, and Peter Gzowski. *Great Canadian Sports Stories — A Century of Competition*. Toronto: Canadian Centennial Publishing Co., 1965.

FRAZER, P. "Syrup from Soft Maples," *Grain Growers' Guide*, Dec. 31, 1924, p. 23.

FRECHETTE, Louis. *Christmas in French Canada*. New York: Scribner, 1899.

FREEDMAN, B., and N. Freedman. *Mrs. Mike — The Story of Katherine Mary Flannigan*. Toronto: Longmans, Green, 1947. [First published, 1946]

FREEMAN, Louis R. *The Nearing North*. New York: Dodd, Mead, 1928.

FRENCH, M. P. *Boughs Bend Over*. Toronto: McClelland & Stewart, 1943.

FREUCHEN, P., and F. Salomonsen. *The Arctic Year*. New York: Putnam, 1958.

FRITH, Austin F. *The Lost Stagecoach*. Toronto: Gage, 1962.

From Wampum to Bank Notes. Toronto: G. H. Wood, 1966. [Booklet]

FRY, Alan. *The Ranch on the Cariboo*. New York: Doubleday, 1962.

Full Details of the Railway Disaster of the 12th of March, 1857, at the Desjardin Canal. . . . Hamilton, Ont.: William A. Shepard, 1857.

GAETZ, A. *The Diary of Adolphus Gaetz*, Edited by C. B. Fergusson. Halifax: Public Archives of Nova Scotia, 1965.

GALTON, Francis. *The Art of Travel; or, Shifts and Contrivances Available in Wild Countries*. 4th ed. London: John Murray, 1867.

The Game Fishes of Canada. Toronto: Canadian Pacific Railway, 1928.

GARD, Robert E. *Johnny Chinook — Tall Tales and True from the Canadian West*. Toronto: Longmans, Green, 1945.

GARDNER, Herbert Fairbairn. *Nothing but Names*. Toronto: Morang, 1899.

GARRIOCH, A. C. *The Far and Furry North — A Story of Life and Love and Travel in the Days of the Hudson's Bay Company*. Winnipeg: Privately printed, 1925.

GARRY, Nicholas. "Diary of Nicholas Garry, Deputy-governor of the Hudson's Bay Company from 1822-1835 — A Detailed Narrative of His Travels in the Northwest Territories of British North America in 1821 . . . ," *Trans. Roy. Soc. Can.*, Vol VII (1900), Sec. 2, 75-204.

GATES, Charles M., ed. *Five Fur Traders of the Northwest — Being the Narrative of Peter Pond, and the Diaries of John Macdonell, Archibald N. McLeod, Hugh Faries, and Thomas Connor*. Minneapolis, Minn.: Univ. of Minnesota Press, 1933.

GEIKIE, Sir Archibald. *Outline of Field-Geology*. 3rd ed. London: Macmillan, 1886.

GEMMILL, John Alexander. *Canadian Parliamentary Companion*. Ottawa, 1885.

A Genuine Account of Nova Scotia. London: P. Bowes, 1750.

Geographical Board of Canada Report. Ottawa: Queen's Printer. [Published annually]

GESNER, Abraham. *The Industrial Resources of Nova Scotia comprehending the Physical Geography, Topography, Geology, Agriculture, Fisheries . . . of the Province*. Halifax: A. & W. MacKinlay, 1849.

————. *A Practical Treatise on Coal, Petroleum, and Other Distilled Oils*. New York: Bailliere Brothers, 1861. [Preface dated 1860]

Ghost Pine. See Memoirs of the Ghost Pine Homesteaders.

Giant Yellowknife Agreement. Collective Bargaining Agreement between Giant Yellowknife Gold Mines Limited and Yellowknife District Miners' Union, Local 802, International Union of Mine, Mill and Smelter Workers. Yellowknife, 1953.

GIBBON, J. Murray. *Canadian Mosaic — The Making of a Northern Nation*. New York: Dodd, Mead, 1939. [First published, Toronto: McClelland & Stewart, 1938]

————. *The Conquering Hero*. Toronto: S. B. Gundy, 1920.

GIBBONS, Charles H. *A Sourdough Samaritan*. Toronto: Hodder & Stoughton, 1923.

GIBBS, George. *A Dictionary of the Chinook Jargon, or Trade Language of Oregon*. New York: Cramoisy Press, 1863.

————. *Notes on the Tinneh or Chepewyan Indians of British and Russian America*. Washington, D.C.: Smithsonian Institution, 1867.

GIFFEN, Naomi Musmaker. *The Roles of Men and Women in Eskimo Culture*. Chicago, Ill.: Univ. of Chicago, 1930.

GILBERT, Grove, and Albert Brigham. *Ontario High School Physical Geography*. Toronto: Macmillan, 1922. [First published, 1902]

GILBERTSON, Albert Nicolay. "Some Ethical Phases

of Eskimo Culture," *Journal of Religious Psychology,* Vols VI and VII (1913-14).

GILDER, William H. *Schwatka's Search.* London: Sampson Low, Marston, Searle, & Rivington, 1882.

GILLESPIE, W. J. *Bluenose Skipper.* Fredericton: Brunswick Press, 1955.

GILLHAM, Charles E. *Raw North.* New York: A. S. Barnes, 1947.

GILLIS, E., and E. Myles. *North Pole Boarding House.* Toronto: Ryerson, 1951.

Glossary of Arctic and Subarctic Terms. Adtic Publication A-105. Maxwell Air Force Base, Alabama: Arctic, Desert, Tropic Information Centre, Research Studies Institute, 1955.

GODMAN, John Davidson. *American Natural History* . . . 2 vols. Philadelphia: H. C. Carey & I. Lea, 1826.

GODSELL, Philip H. *Arctic Trader — The Account of Twenty Years with the Hudson's Bay Company.* New York: Putnam, 1934.

———. "The Mounties Handled the Hot Hootch," *Fury,* Dec., 1956, pp. 32-35, 57-60.

———. *Red Hunters of the Snows — An Account of Thirty Years' Experience with the Primitive Indian and Eskimo Tribes of the Canadian North-West and Arctic Coast.* . . . Hale, 1938; Toronto: Ryerson, 1938.

———. "Trailing the Mad Trapper of Rat River," *Fury,* March, 1956, pp. 8-11, 65-69.

———. *The Vanishing Frontier — A Saga of Traders, Mounties and Men of the Last North West.* Toronto: Ryerson, 1939.

GOETZ, A. L. *The Park Country: A History of Red Deer and District.* Vancouver: Wrigley, 1948.

GOGO, Jean L. *Lights on the St. Lawrence.* Toronto: Ryerson, 1958.

Gold Commissioner Report. Halifax: Provincial Government, 1863.

GOODMAN, A. E. *Klondyke Gold Fields, Yukon District.* Vancouver: Privately printed, 1897.

GOODSIR, Robert Anstruther. *An Arctic Voyage to Baffin's Bay and Lancaster Sound, in Search of Friends with Sir John Franklin.* London: John Van Voorst, 1850.

GORDON, C. W. See Ralph CONNOR.

GORDON, Daniel M. *Mountain and Prairie — A Journey from Victoria to Winnipeg, via Peace River Pass.* London: Sampson Low, Marston, Searle, & Rivington, 1880.

GOSSE, Philip Henry. *The Canadian Naturalist — A Series of Conversations on the Natural History of Lower Canada.* London: John Van Voorst, 1840.

GOUGH, John. *New World Horizons.* Toronto: Dent, 1942.

———. *The Story of British Columbia.* Toronto: Dent, 1952.

GOULD, D. F. *Beyond the Shining Mountains.* Portland, Ore.: Binfords & Mort, 1938.

GOULD, S. *Inasmuch — Sketches of the Beginnings of the Church of England in Canada in Relation to the Indian & Eskimo Races.* Toronto: Privately printed, 1917.

GOURLAY, John L. *History of the Ottawa Valley — A Collection of Facts, Events and Reminiscences for over Half a Century.* Ottawa: 1896.

GOURLEY, Robert F. *Statistical Account of Upper Canada.* 3 vols. London: Simpkin & Marshall, 1822.

GOWANLOCK, Theresa. *Two Months in the Camp of Big Bear — The Life and Adventures of Theresa Gowanlock and Theresa Delaney.* Parkdale: Times, 1885.

GOWLAND, John S. *Return to Canada.* London: T. Werner Laurie, 1957.

———. *Sikanaska Trail.* London: T. Werner Laurie, 1956.

———. *Smoke over Sikanaska — The True Story of a Forest Ranger.* London: T. Werner Laurie, 1955; Winnipeg: Harlequin Books, 1959.

GRAHAM, Andrew. "Observations." *Hudson's Bay Record Society Publications XII,* App. B, pp. 309-317. Edited by E. E. Rich. London, 1949. [Written, 1775]

GRAHAM, Angus A. *The Golden Grindstone—The Adventures of George M. Mitchell.* Edited by D. Thompson. London: W. Heinemann, 1951. [First published, Toronto: Oxford, 1935]

GRAHAM, Clara. *Fur and Gold in the Kootenays.* Vancouver: Wrigley, 1945.

GRAHAME, N. B. M. *Bishop Bompas of the Frozen North.* London: Seeley, Service, 1925.

GRAINGER, M. Allerdale. *Woodsmen of the West.* London: Edward Arnold, 1908.

Grand Trunk Railway of Canada. Book of Rules and Regulations. Montreal: M. Longmoore, 1865.

GRANT, Bruce. *American Indians Yesterday and Today — A Profusely Illustrated Encyclopedia of the American Indian.* Rev. ed. New York: Dutton, 1960.

GRANT, George M. *Ocean to Ocean — Sandford Fleming's Expedition through Canada in 1872.* London: Sampson Low, Marston, Searle, & Rivington, 1873; Rev. ed. New York: R. Worthington, 1877.

GRANT, P. "The Sauteux Indians about 1804," in Vol. II of L. F. R. MASSON, *Les Bourgeois* . . . , pp. 303-366. See below.

GRAY, Hugh. *Letters from Canada.* London: Longman, Hurst, Rees, & Orme, 1809. [Written 1806-1809]

GRAY, John M., and Frank A. Upjohn. *Prose of Our Day.* Toronto: Macmillan, 1940.

Great Western Railway Advertisement Bulletin. Toronto: M. T. Platt, 1880.

GREELY, A. W. "The Origin of Stefansson's Blond Eskimo," *National Geographic Magazine,* Dec., 1912, pp. 1225-1238.

———. *The Polar Regions in the Twentieth Century — Their Discovery and Industrial Evolution.* Boston: Little, Brown, 1928.

GREEN, William Spotswood. *Among the Selkirk Glaciers.* London: Macmillan, 1890.

GREENE, W. H. *The Wooden Walls among the Ice Flows — Telling the Romance of the Newfoundland Seal Fishery.* London: Hutchinson, 1933.

GREENING, W. E. *The Ottawa.* Toronto: McClelland & Stewart, 1961.

GREENOUGH, William P. *Canadian Folk-Life and Folk-Lore.* New York: George H. Richmond, 1897.

GRENFELL, Anne E. C., and Katie Spalding. *Le Petit Nord.* Boston: Houghton Mifflin, 1920.

GRENFELL, Wilfred T. *Adrift on an Ice-pan.* New York: Houghton, 1909.

———. *Forty Years for Labrador.* Boston: Lippincott, 1932.

———. *The Harvest of the Sea — A Tale of Both Sides of the Atlantic.* Toronto: F. H. Revell, 1905.

———. *Off the Rocks — Stories of the Deep-Sea Fisherfolk of Labrador.* Philadelphia: Sunday School Times, 1906.

———. *The Story of a Labrador Doctor — as Told by*

Himself. 14th ed. London: Hodder & Stoughton, n.d. [Written, 1918]

GREW, David. *The Ghost Mare.* New York: Coward-McCann, 1949.

GREY OWL (pseud. of G. S. Belaney). *The Adventures of Sajo and Her Beaver People.* London: Lovat Dickson, 1935.

———. *The Men of the Last Frontier.* London: Country Life, 1931.

GRIFFIN, H. *British Columbia — The People's Early Story.* Vancouver: Tribune, 1958.

GROVE, Frederick P. *Settlers of the Marsh.* New York: Grosset & Dunlap, 1925.

———. *Two Generations.* Toronto: Ryerson, 1939.

GUBERLET, Muriel Lewin. *Animals of the Seashore.* Portland, Ore.: Binfords & Mort, 1949. [First published, 1936]

A Guide Book Containing Information for Intending Settlers. Ottawa: Dept of Agriculture, 1883.

Guide to British Columbia for 1877-1878. Victoria: T. N. Hibben, 1877.

GUILLET, Edwin C. *Early Life in Upper Canada.* Toronto: Ontario Publishing Co., 1933.

———. *Pioneer Days in Upper Canada.* Rev. ed. Toronto: Univ. of Toronto Press, 1964. [First published, 1933]

———. *The Pioneer Farmer and Backwoodsman.* 2 vols. Toronto: Ontario Publishing Co., 1963.

———. *The Valley of the Trent.* Toronto: Champlain Society, 1957.

GUNN, S. W. A. *Totem Poles of British Columbia — A Complete Guide to the Totem Poles in Stanley Park, Vancouver, B.C.* Vancouver: W. E. G. Macdonald, 1965. [Booklet]

HADFIELD, Joseph. *An Englishman in America, 1785; Being the Diary of Joseph Hadfield.* Edited by Douglas S. Robertson. Toronto: Hunter Rose, 1933.

HAGELL, E. F. *When the Grass Was Free.* Toronto: Ryerson, 1954.

HAIG, Kennethe M. *Brave Harvest — The Life Story of E. Cora Hind, LL.D.* Toronto: Thomas Allen, 1945.

HAIG-BROWN, R. L. *Starbuck Valley Winter.* Toronto: Collins, 1948.

———. *Timber — A Novel of Pacific Coast Loggers.* Toronto: Collins, 1946. [First published, 1942]

HAIGHT, C. *Country Life in Canada Fifty Years Ago.* Toronto: Hunter Rose, 1885.

HAKLUYT, Richard. "Discourse of Western Planting," in Vol. II of *The Original Writings and Correspondence of the Two Richard Hakluyts.* Edited by E. G. R. Taylor. London: Hakluyt Society, 1935.

———. *Divers voyages touching the discoverie of America and the Ilands adiacent. . . .* Edited by John Winter Jones. London: Hakluyt Society, 1850. [Cited as *Divers Voyages*]

———. "A particuler discourse concerning the greate necessitie and manifolde comodyties that are like to growe to this Realme of Englande by the Westerne discoueries lately attempted," in Vol. II of *Collections of the Maine Historical Society, Second Series.* Edited by Charles Deane. Cambridge, Mass.: John Wilson, 1877. [Cited as *Discourse on Western Planting*]

———. *The Principal Navigations, Voyages, Traffiques, and Discoveries of the English Nation.* Edited by Edmund Goldsmid. 4 vols. Edinburgh: E. & G. Goldsmid, 1889. [Cited as *Voyages*]

HALIBURTON, Thomas Chandler. *The Attaché; or, Sam Slick in England.* London: Routledge, 1843.

———. *The Bubbles of Canada.* London: Richard Bentley, 1839. [Preface dated 1838]

———. *A General Description of Nova Scotia.* Halifax: Royal Acadian School, 1823.

———. *Nature and Human Nature.* Vol. II. London: Hurst & Blackett, 1855.

———. *Sam Slick, the Clockmaker — His Sayings & Doings.* Toronto: Musson, 1838.

———. *Sam Slick's Wise Saws & Modern Instances or What He Said, Did, or Invented.* 2 vols. London: Hurst & Blackett, 1853.

HALKETT, John. *Statement Respecting the Earl of Selkirk's Settlement upon the Red River, in North America. . . .* London: John Murray, 1817.

HALL, A. J. *The Gospel According to Saint Luke. Translated into the Kwā Gūtl Language, North of Vancouver Island.* London: British & Foreign Bible Society, 1894.

———. *The Gospel According to St. Matthew, Translated into the Qā-Gūtl (or Quoquols Language).* London: British & Foreign Bible Society, 1882.

HALL, Basil. *The Log-Book of a Midshipman.* London: Blackie, 1894.

HALL, Charles Francis. *Arctic Researches and Life among the Esquimaux.* New York: Harper, 1865.

———. *Life with the Esquimaux.* 2 vols. London: Sampson Low, Son, & Marston, 1864.

———. *Narrative of the Second Arctic Expedition.* Edited by J. E. Nourse. Washington, D.C.: Government, 1879.

HALL, Francis. *Travels in Canada and the United States in 1816 and 1817.* London: Longman, Hurst, 1818.

HALLIDAY, William M. *Potlatch and Totem, and the Recollections of an Indian Agent.* Toronto: Dent, 1935.

HALLMAN, Maynard. *Canadians at Work.* Toronto: Longmans, Green, 1950.

HAMBLETON, Jack. *Abitibi Adventure.* Toronto: Longmans, Green, 1950.

HAMILTON, D. E. *The Maritime Provinces.* Toronto: Gage, 1927.

HAMILTON, Fred. J. *A Trip over the Intercolonial.* Montreal: Gazette Printing House, 1876.

HAMILTON, James C. *The Prairie Province — Sketches of Travel from Lake Ontario to Lake Winnipeg. . . .* Toronto: Belford, 1876.

HAMILTON, Robert M. *Canadian Quotations and Phrases — Literary and Historical.* Toronto: McClelland & Stewart, 1952 and 1965.

HAMILTON, Z. M., and M. A. Hamilton. *These Are the Prairies.* Regina: School Aids and Text Book Publishing Co., 1954.

HANBURY, David T. *Sport and Travel in the Northland of Canada.* London: Edward Arnold, 1904.

Handbook of British Columbia. London: W. Oliver, 1862.

HANNAY, James. *The Life and Times of Sir Leonard Tilley.* St. John: Bowes, 1897.

HARDY, Campbell. *Forest Life in Acadie.* London: Chapman & Hall, 1869.

BIBLIOGRAPHY

————. *Sporting Adventures in the New World.* 2 vols. London: Hurst & Blackett, 1855.

HARDY, G. A. *Fifty Edible Plants of British Columbia.* British Columbia Provincial Museum Handbook No. 1. Victoria, 1942.

HARDY, W. G. *The Unfulfilled.* 1952. [First published, Toronto: McClelland & Stewart, 1951]

HARDY, William G., ed. *The Alberta Golden Jubilee Anthology, 1905-1955.* Toronto: McClelland & Stewart, 1955.

HARGRAVE, Letitia. *The Letters of Letitia Hargrave.* Edited by Margaret A. Macleod. Champlain Society Publications XXVIII. Toronto, 1947. [Cited as *Correspondence*]

HARKNESS, John Graham. *Stormont, Dundas and Glengarry — A History, 1784-1945.* Morrisburg, Ont.: Privately printed, 1946.

HARMON, Daniel Williams. *A Journal of Voyages and Travels in the Interiour of North America.* Andover, Mass.: Flagg & Gould, 1820; New York: Allerton Book, 1922.

HARRINGTON, Lyn. "Chinook Jargon," *Beaver*, Winter, 1958, pp. 26-29.

HARRINGTON, Michael. *Sea Stories from Newfoundland.* Toronto: Ryerson, 1958.

HARRIS, A. C. *Alaska and the Klondike Gold Fields.* 1897.

HARRIS, Christie. *Cariboo Trail.* Toronto: Longmans, Green, 1957.

————. *Raven's Cry.* Toronto: McClelland & Stewart, 1966.

HARRIS, Cyril. *Northern Exposure — A Nova Scotia Boyhood.* New York: Norton, 1963.

HARRIS, John. *Navigantium atque Itinerantium Bibliotheca.* Vol. I. London, 1744.

HARRIS, Nancy, and Frances Hawthorne. *New Denver —Eldorado of the Past.* New Denver, B.C.: New Denver Elementary School, 1958. [Booklet]

HARTWIG, Georg L. *The Polar World — A Popular Description of Man and Nature in the Arctic and Antarctic Regions of the Globe.* New York: Harper, 1869.

HARVARD, P. "Food Plants of the North American Indians," in *Bulletin 22*, pp. 98-123. New York: Torrey Botanical Club, 1895.

HARVEY, D. C. *Journeys to the Island of St. John or Prince Edward Island, 1775-1835.* Toronto: Macmillan, 1955.

HASKIN, Leslie H. *Wild Flowers of the Pacific Coast.* Portland, Ore.: Metropolitan Press, 1934.

HATHEWAY, C. L. *The History of New Brunswick, from Its First Settlement.* Fredericton: James P. A. Phillips, 1846.

HATTON, J., and M. Harvey. *Newfoundland, the Oldest British Colony.* London: Chapman & Hall, 1883.

HAVERLY, Charles E. *Klondyke and Fortune.* London: Southwood, Smith, 1898.

HAVERSON, James P. *Sour Sonnets of a Sorehead, and Other Songs of the Street.* Toronto: McLeod & Allen, 1908.

HAWKES, E. W. *The "Inviting-In" Feast of the Alaskan Eskimo.* National Museum of Canada Memoir 45. Ottawa, 1913.

————. *The Labrador Eskimo.* Geological Survey of Canada Memoir 91. Ottawa, 1916.

HAWKINS, Ernest. *Historical Notices of the Missions of the Church of England in the North American Colonies.* London: Fellowes, 1845.

HAWORTH, Paul Leland. *Trailmakers of the Northwest.* New York: Harcourt, Brace, 1921.

HAWTHORN, Audrey. *People of the Potlatch.* Vancouver: Vancouver Art Gallery, 1956.

HAWTHORN, H. B., C. S. Belshaw, and S. M. Jamieson. *The Indians of British Columbia — A Study of Contemporary Social Adjustment.* Toronto: Univ. of Toronto Press, 1958.

HAYCOX, Ernest. *Earthbreakers.* Montreal: Bantam Books, 1959. [First published, Boston: Little, Brown, 1952]

HAYDON, A. L. *The Riders of the Plains — Adventures and Romance with the North-West Mounted Police, 1873-1910.* Chicago: McClurg, 1910.

HAYES, Isaac I. *An Arctic Boat Journey, in the Autumn of 1854.* Rev. ed. Boston: James R. Osgood, 1871.

HAYNE, M. H. E. *The Pioneers of the Klondyke.* London: Sampson Low, Marston, 1897.

HAYS, H. R. *From Ape to Angel.* New York: Knopf, 1958.

HAYWOOD, William D. *Bill Haywood's Book — The Autobiography of William D. Haywood.* New York: International Publishers, 1958. [First published, 1929]

HEAD, Sir Francis Bond. *The Emigrant.* London: John Murray, 1847.

————. *A Narrative.* London: John Murray, 1839.

HEAD, Sir George. *Forest Scenes and Incidents in the Wilds of North America.* 2nd ed. London: John Murray, 1838. [First published, 1829]

HEALEY, Elizabeth. *History of Alert Bay.* Alert Bay, B.C.: Alert Bay Board of Trade, 1958.

HEALY, W. J. *Women of the Red River — Being a Book Written from the Recollections of Women Surviving from the Red River Era. . . .* Winnipeg: Russell, Lang, 1923.

HEARNE, Samuel. *Journey from Prince of Wale's Fort in Hudson's Bay, to the Northern Ocean in the Years 1769, 1770, 1771, and 1772.* Edited by J. B. Tyrrell. Champlain Society Publications VI. Toronto, 1911. [First published, London: Strahan & Cadell, 1795]

HEARNE, Samuel, and Philip Turnor. *Journals of Samuel Hearne & Philip Turnor between the Years 1774 and 1792.* Edited by J. B. Tyrrell. Champlain Society Publications XXI. Toronto, 1934.

HEATHERINGTON, Alexander. *. . . A Practical Guide for Tourists, Miners and Investors, and All Persons Interested in the Development of the Gold Fields of Nova Scotia.* Montreal: John Lovell, 1868.

Heaton's Guide to Western Canada. Toronto: Heaton Publishing Co., 1913.

HEENEY, Bertal. *Pickanock.* Toronto: Bell & Cockburn, 1912.

Hello Folks. Charlottetown: Abegweit Sightseeing Tours, 1964.

HEMING, Arthur. *The Drama of the Forests.* Toronto: Doubleday, Page, 1921; Toronto: Doubleday, Doran & Gundy, 1928.

HÉMON, Louis. *Maria Chapdelaine.* Translated by W. H. Blake. Toronto: Macmillan, 1923. [First published, 1921]

HENDAY, Anthony. "Journal of a Journey performed by Anthony Henday, to explore the Country Inland, and to endeavour to increase the Hudson's Bay Company's Trade, A.D. 1754-1755." Edited by L. J. Burpee. *Trans.Roy.Soc.Can.*, 3rd series, Vol. I (1907), Sec. 2, 321-364.

HENDERSON, Philip. *Life of Laurence Oliphant — Traveller, Diplomat, Mystic.* London: Hale, 1956.

HENDRYX, James B. *Blood of the North.* New York: Sun Dial Press, 1942. [First published, 1938]

————. *Oak and Iron.* London: Hutchinson, n.d. [First published, New York, 1925]

————. *The Long Chase.* New York: Dell, n.d. [c1960]. [First published as *On the Rim of the Arctic.* New York: Doubleday, 1948]

————. *Outlaws of Halfaday Creek.* Philadelphia: Blakiston, n.d. [c1944]. [First published, New York: Doubleday-Doran, 1931]

————. *The Yukon Kid.* Philadelphia: Blakiston, 1943. [First published, New York: Doubleday-Doran, 1933]

HENNEPIN, Louis. *Description de la Lousiane, nouvellement découverte ou sud' oüest de la Nouvelle France, par ordre du roy. Avec la carte du pays: Les Moeurs et La manière de vivre des sauvages.* Paris: La veuve Sebastion Huré, 1683.

————. *A New Discovery of a Vast Country in America.* London, 1698.

HENRY, Alexander (the Elder). *Travels and Adventures in Canada and the Indian Territories, between the Years 1760 and 1776. . . .* New York: I. Riley, 1809; Toronto: Morang, 1901.

HENRY, Alexander (the Younger). *Journals.* See Elliott COUES.

HENRY, J. K. *Flora of Southern British Columbia and Vancouver Island, with many References to Alaska and Northern Species.* Toronto: Gage, 1915.

HERIOT, George. *Travels through the Canadas.* London: Phillips, 1807.

HERRING, F. E. *In the Pathless West — With Soldiers, Miners, and Savages.* London: T. Fisher Unwin, 1904.

HEWITT, Foster. *Hockey Night in Canada.* Toronto: Ryerson, 1953.

HICKEY, William (pseud). See M. DOYLE.

HIEBERT, Paul. *Sarah Binks.* Toronto: Oxford, 1947.

HIEMSTRA, Mary. *Gully Farm.* Toronto: McClelland & Stewart, 1955.

HIGGINS, W. H. *The Life and Times of Joseph Gould, Ex-Member of the Canadian Parliament. Struggles of the Early Canadian Settlers, Settlement of Uxbridge, Sketch of the History of the County of Ontario, the Rebellion of 1837, Parliamentary Career, etc. Reminiscences of Sixty Years of Active Political and Municipal Life.* Toronto: C. B. Robinson, 1887.

High Days and Holidays. See A. H. FOSTER, and A. Grierson.

Highroads to Reading. Book 5. Toronto: Gage, 1942.

HIGINBOTHAM, J. D. *When the West Was Young.* Toronto: Ryerson, 1933.

HILL, A. S. *From Home to Home — Autumn Wanderings in the North-West in the Years 1881, 1882, 1883, 1884.* London: Sampson Low, Marston, Searle & Rivington, 1885.

HILL, S. S. *A Short Account of Prince Edward Island.* London, Madden, 1839.

HIND, Henry Youle. *Exploration in the Interior of the Labrador Peninsula, the Country of the Montagnais and Nasquapee Indians.* 2 vols. London: Longman, Green, Longman, Roberts, & Green, 1863. [Cited as *Exploring Labrador*]

————. *Narrative of the Canadian Red River Exploring Expedition of 1857, and of the Assiniboine and Saskatchewan Exploring Expedition of 1858.* 2 vols. London: Longman, Green, Longman, & Roberts, 1860.

HINDLEY, John I. *Indian Legends: Nanabush, the Ojibbeway Saviour; Moosh-kuh-ung, or the Flood.* Barrie, Ont., 1885.

Hints for Intending Klondikers. Kamloops, B.C.: Klondike Publishing Co., 1898.

History and Geography Teaching Materials. Vancouver: University of British Columbia, 1962.

History of Penticton. See R. M. ATKINSON.

HOBSON, Laura Z. *Gentleman's Agreement.* New York: Simon & Schuster, 1947.

HOBSON, Richmond P., Jr. *Grass beyond the Mountains.* Philadelphia: Lippincott, 1951.

————. *Nothing too Good for a Cowboy.* Philadelphia: Lippincott, 1955.

HODGE, F. W. *Handbook of American Indians North of Mexico.* Bureau of American Ethnology Bulletin 30. 2 vols. Washington, D.C.: Smithsonian Institution, 1907 (Vol. 1); 1910 (Vol. 2). [Usually cited as *Bulletin*]

HODGE, F. W., and J. White. *Handbook of Indians of Canada.* Ottawa: King's Printer, 1913.

HODGSON, R. G. *Successful Muskrat Farming.* 6th ed. Toronto: Fur Trade Journal of Canada, 1930.

HOIGHT, C. See C. HAIGHT.

HOLBROOK, Stewart H. *Holy Old Mackinaw — A Natural History of the American Lumberjack.* New York: Macmillan, 1938.

HOLLIDAY, C. W. *The Valley of Youth.* Caldwell, Idaho: Caxton Printers, 1948.

HOLMES, W. H. "Certain Notched or Scalloped Stone Tablets of the Mound Builders," *American Anthropologist*, Vol. VIII (1906), 101-108. [Cited as *Anthropological Papers*]

HORETZKY, Charles. *Canada on the Pacific — Being an Account of a Journey from Edmonton to the Pacific by the Peace River Valley, and of a Winter Voyage along the Western Coast of the Dominion. . . .* Montreal: Dawson, 1874.

HOWARD, Joseph Kinsey. *Strange Empire.* New York: Morrow, 1952.

HOWAY, Frederic W. *British Columbia — From the Earliest Times to the Present.* Vol. II. Vancouver: S. J. Clark, 1914.

————. *The Early History of the Fraser River Mines.* Victoria: Charles F. Banfield, 1926.

HOWISON, J. *Sketches of Upper Canada and Some Recollections of the United States of America.* Edinburgh, 1821.

HOWSE, Joseph. *A Grammar of the Cree Language.* London: Rivington, 1844.

Hudson's Bay Company Charter. "The Royal Charter Incorporating The Hudson's Bay Company, A.D. 1670," in *Minutes of the Hudson's Bay Company, 1671-1674*, App. A, pp. 131-148. See below.

HUGHES, Thomas. *A Journal by Thos. Hughes* (1787-1789). Edited by E. A. Benians. Cambridge: Cambridge Univ. Press, 1947.

HUISH, Robert. *The Last Voyage of Capt. Sir John Ross*. . . . London: John Saunders, 1836.

HUNTER, Andrew Frederick. *A History of Simcoe County*. 2 vols. Barrie, Ont.: Barrie County Council, 1909.

HUNTER, Martin. *Canadian Wilds — Tells about the Hudson's Bay Company, Northern Indians and their Modes of Hunting, Trapping, etc.* Columbus, Ohio: A. R. Harding, 1907.

HUNTER, Robert, Jr. *Quebec to Carolina in 1785-1786 — Being the Travel Diary and Observations of Robert Hunter, Jr., a Young Merchant of London.* Edited by Louis B. Wright and Marion Tinling. San Marino, Calif.: Huntington Library, 1943. [Usually cited as *Diary*]

HUTCHISON, Bruce. *Canada: Tomorrow's Giant.* New York: Knopf, 1957.

———. *The Fraser.* Toronto: Clarke, Irwin, 1950.

———. *The Hollow Men.* New York: Coward-McCann, 1944.

———. *The Incredible Canadian — A Candid Portrait of Mackenzie King: his Works, his Times, and his Nation.* Toronto: Longmans, Green, 1953.

HUYSHE, G. L. *The Red River Expedition.* London: Macmillan, 1871.

Illustrated Forest Activities. See F. S. McKINNON.

INGLEFIELD, E. A. *A Summer Search for Sir John Franklin.* London: Thomas Harrison, 1853.

Inland Route to the Yukon. Kamloops, B.C.: Kamloops Printing & Publishing, 1897.

INNES, Hammond. *Campbell's Kingdom — A Struggle against Powerful Interests.* London: Collins, 1952; New York: Bantam, 1956; London: Collins, 1956. [First published, New York: Knopf, 1952]

INNIS, Harold A. *The Cod Fisheries — The History of an International Economy.* Toronto: Ryerson, 1940.

———. *The Diary of Simeon Perkins, 1766-1780.* Champlain Society Publications XXIX. Toronto, 1948.

———. *The Fur Trade in Canada — An Introduction to Canadian Economic History.* New Haven: Yale Univ. Press, 1930; Toronto: Univ. of Toronto Press, 1956; New Haven: Yale Univ. Press, 1962, reprinted 1964.

INNIS, Mary E. *Travellers West.* Toronto: Clarke, Irwin, 1956.

An Interesting Account of those Extraordinary People the Esquimaux Indians, from Baffin's Bay, North Pole. . . . Sheffield, England: George Ridge, 1824.

Interior Salish. Victoria: Dept. of Education, 1952.

Intermediate Booming Grounds in British Columbia. Vancouver: Johnson, Walton, 1945. [Booklet]

IRVING, Washington. *Adventures of Captain Bonneville, U.S.A., in the Rocky Mountains of the Far West.* New York: Putnam, 1868.

———. *Astoria, or Anecdotes of an Enterprise beyond the Rocky Mountains.* New York: Putnam, 1868.

———. *Tour on the Prairies.* Philadelphia: Carey, Lea, & Blanchard, 1835.

ISHAM, James. "A Journal of the most material Transactions, and Copys of Letters between Mr. James Isham & Council at York Fort, and Capt. William Moor, Capt. Francis Smith and their Council during their Wintering in Haye's River Commencing 26 August, 1746, Ending 24 June, 1747," *Hudson's Bay Record Society Publications XII*, App. A, pp. 241-308. Edited by E. E. Rich. London, 1949. [Cited as *Journal*]

———. "Notes and Observations on a Book Entitled A Voyage to Hudson Bay in the Dobbs-Galley &c, 1746 & 1747. Wrote by Henry Ellis's," *Hudson's Bay Record Society Publications XII.* Edited by E. E. Rich. London, 1949. [Written, 1748. Cited as *Notes and Observations*]

———. "Observations on Hudson's Bay," *Hudson's Bay Record Society Publications XII.* London, 1949. [Cited as *Observations*]

It Blows, It Snows; A Winter's Rambles through Canada. Dublin: Brady, 1846.

JACOBS, Peter. *Journal of the Reverend Peter Jacobs . . . From Rice Lake to the Hudson's Bay Territory; and Returning. Commencing May, 1852.* Toronto: Anson Green, 1853.

JAMES, Edwin, ed. *Narrative of the Captivity and Adventures of John Tanner.* See John TANNER.

JAMESON, Anna. *Winter Studies and Summer Rambles in Canada.* Toronto: McClelland & Stewart, 1923. [Diary, 1836-37]

JAMIESON, Nina M. *The Cattle in the Stall — Sketches and Poems.* Toronto: Privately printed, 1932.

JAQUES, Edna. *Fireside Poems.* Toronto: Thomas Allen, 1950.

JEFFERSON, Robert. "Fifty Years on the Saskatchewan," *Canadian Northwest Historical Society Publications*, Vol. 1, No. V. Battleford, Sask., 1929.

JEFFERYS, C. W. *Canadian History Pictures.* Lesson Aids Service No. 2017. Victoria: British Columbia Teacher's Federation, 1963.

———. *The Picture Gallery of Canadian History.* 3 vols. Toronto: Ryerson, 1942-1950.

JEFFERYS, Thomas. *The Conduct of the French, with Regard to Nova Scotia.* London: T. Jefferys, 1754.

———. *Fishing Banks of Nova Scotia.* London: T. Jefferys, 1750.

———. *The Natural and Civil History of the French Dominions in North and South America: A Description of New France.* 2 vols. London: T. Jefferys, 1760.

JENKINS, C. C. *The Timber Pirate.* New York: George H. Doran, 1922.

JENKINS, H. F., *et al. Canadian Woods — Their Properties and Uses.* Rev. ed. Ottawa: Forestry Branch, Dept of Resources and Development, 1951.

JENKINS, R. S. *Canadian Civics.* B.C. ed. Toronto: Copp Clark, 1918.

JENNESS, Diamond. *Eskimo Administration I: Alaska.* Montreal: Arctic Institute of North America, 1962.

———. *Eskimo Administration II: Canada.* Montreal: Arctic Institute of North America, 1964.

———. *Eskimo Administration III: Labrador.* Montreal: Arctic Institute of North America, 1965.

———. *Eskimo Songs.* Ottawa: King's Printer, 1925.

———. *Indians of Canada.* National Museum of Canada Bulletin 65. Ottawa, 1932, 1955, 1960.

————. *The Life of the Copper Eskimos*. Ottawa: King's Printer, 1922.

————. *Material Culture of the Copper Eskimo*. Ottawa: King's Printer, 1946.

————. *Ojibwa Indians of Parry Island*. Ottawa: National Museum of Canada, 1935.

————. *The People of the Twilight*. New York: Macmillan, 1928.

————. *The Problem of the Eskimo*. Toronto: Univ. of Toronto Press, 1933.

JENNINGS, John. *The Strange Brigade — A Story of the Red River and the Opening of the Canadian West*. Montreal: Pocket Books of Canada, 1954 and 1955. [First published, Boston: Little, Brown, 1952]

JENNINGS, W. T. *Report on Routes to the Yukon*. Ottawa, 1898.

JEREMIAH, Eddie. *Ice Hockey*. New York: A. S. Barnes, 1942.

Jesuit Relations and Allied Documents — Travels and Explorations of the Jesuit Missionaries in New France, 1610-1791. Edited by R. G. Thwaites. 74 vols. Cleveland, Ohio: Burrow Bros., 1890-1901.

JOB, Peter Dalzel. *The Settlers*. London: Constable, 1957.

JOHNSON, Emily Pauline. *Legends of Vancouver*. Toronto: McClelland & Stewart, 1922.

————. *The Shagganappi*. Toronto: Ryerson, 1913.

JOHNSON, George. *Pulp Woods of Canada*. Ottawa, 1904.

JOHNSON, Lukin. *Beyond the Rockies*. See Lukin JOHNSTON.

JOHNSON, M. E. *Dayspring in the Far West — Sketches of Mission-Work in Northwest America*. London: Seeley, Jackson & Halliday, 1875.

JOHNSON, R. Byron. *Very Far West Indeed — A Few Rough Experiences on the North-West Pacific Coast*. London: Sampson Low, Marston, Low, & Searle, 1872 and 1873.

JOHNSON, R. F. "The Fish Trade," in *Canada and the West Indies Federation*, pp. 68-74. Edited by Philip A. Lockwood. Mount Allison Univ. Publication No. 2. Sackville, N.B., 1958.

JOHNSTON, C. M. *The Head of the Lake*. Hamilton, Ont.: Wentworth County Council, 1958.

JOHNSTON, James F. W. *Notes on North America, Agricultural, Economical & Social*. 2 vols. Edinburgh: Blackwood, 1851.

JOHNSTON, John. "An Account of Lake Superior, 1792-1807," in Vol. II of L. F. R. MASSON, *Les Bourgeois . . .*, pp. 135-174. See below.

JOHNSTON, Lukin. *Beyond the Rockies — Three Thousand Miles by Trail and Canoe through Little-known British Columbia*. Toronto: Dent, 1929.

JOHNSTONE, C. L. *The Young Emigrants — A Story for Boys*. London: Nelson, 1898.

JOHNSTONE, Walter. "A Series of Letters, Descriptive of Prince Edward Island, in the Gulph of St. Laurence . . .," in D. C. HARVEY, *Journeys . . .*, pp. 86-161. See above. [First published, Dumfries: J. Swan, 1822]

————. "Travels in Prince Edward Island . . .," in D. C. HARVEY, *Journeys . . .*, pp. 164-172. See above. [First published, Edinburgh: David Brown, 1823]

JONES, Evan. *Trappers and Mountain Men*. New York: American Heritage Publishing Co., 1961.

JONES, J. E. *Some Familiar Wild Flowers*. Toronto:

National Boys' Work Board, 1930.

JUKES, J. B. *Excursions in and about Newfoundland, during the Years 1839 and 1840*. 2 vols. London: John Murray, 1842.

JULIEN, Henri. "MSS, c1874." *Alberta Historical Review*, Winter, 1961.

Junior Division Physical Education. Grades 4, 5, and 6. Toronto: Ontario Dept. of Education, 1960.

KANE, Elisha K. *Arctic Explorations in Search of Sir John Franklin*. London: Nelson, 1892.

KANE, Paul. *Wanderings of an Artist among the Indians of North America, from Canada to Vancouver's Island and Oregon, through the Hudson's Bay Company's Territory and Back Again*. London: Longman, 1859; Toronto: The Radisson Society of Canada, 1925.

KEEFER, Thos. C. *Montreal* (1853) and *The Ottawa* (1854). Two lectures. Montreal: J. Lovell, 1854.

Keewatin and Northeastern Mackenzie — A General Survey of the Life, Activities, and Natural Resources of this Section of the Northwest Territories, Canada. Ottawa: King's Printer, 1930. [Booklet]

KEITH, George. "Letters to Mr. Roderic McKenzie 1807-1817," in Vol. II of L. F. R. MASSON, *Les Bourgeois . . .*, pp. 61-132. See below.

KEITH, Marian. *Treasure Valley*. Toronto: McClelland & Stewart, 1928.

————. *Yonder Shining Light*. Toronto: McClelland & Stewart, 1948.

KELLEY, H. J. *A Geographical Sketch of that Part of North America Called Oregon*. Boston: J. Howe, 1830.

KELLEY, T. P. *The Black Donnellys — The True Story of Canada's Most Barbaric Feud*. Toronto: Harlequin Books, 1954.

KELLY, L. V. *The Range Men — The Story of the Ranchers and Indians of Alberta*. Toronto: William Briggs, 1913.

KELLY, P. A. "Shipping," in *Canada and the West Indies Federation*, pp. 74-77. Edited by Philip A. Lockwood. Mount Allison Univ. Publication No. 2. Sackville, N.B., 1958.

KELSEY, Henry. *The Kelsey Papers*. Edited by Arthur G. Doughty and Chester Martin. Ottawa: Public Archives of Canada, 1929.

KELSEY, Vera. *British Columbia Rides a Star*. New York: Harper, 1958.

KEMP, H. S. M. *Northern Trader*. Toronto: Ryerson, 1956; New York: Bouregy & Curl, 1956.

KENDALL, Ralph S. *Benton of the Royal Mounted — A Tale of the Royal Northwest Mounted Police*. New York: John Lane, 1918.

————. *The Luck of the Mounted — A Tale of the Royal Northwest Mounted Police*. Toronto: S. B. Gundy, 1920.

KENNEDY, Clyde C., and Mrs. Carl Price. *Renfrew*. See Mrs. Carl PRICE and Clyde C. Kennedy.

KENNEDY, Howard Angus. *New Canada and the New Canadians*. London: Horace Marshall, 1907.

KENNEDY, W. A. *The First Ten Years of Commercial Fishing on Great Slave Lake*. Fisheries Research Board Bulletin No. 107. Ottawa, 1956.

KENNEY, J. F., ed. *Founding of Fort Churchill*. See J. KNIGHT.

KENNICOTT, Robert. "Biography of Robert Kennicott and Extracts from His Journal," *Transactions of* the *Chicago Academy of Science*, Vol. I, 133-224. Chicago, 1942. [Journal date, 1869]

KEPHART, Horace. *Camping and Woodcraft.* 2 vols. New York. Outing Publishing Co., 1916-1917.

KERBY, George W. *The Broken Trail — Pages from a Pastor's Experience in Western Canada.* Toronto: William Briggs, 1909.

KERR, S. L. See P. DAWLISH.

KILBOURN, Elizabeth. *Great Canadian Painting — A Century of Art.* Toronto: Canadian Centennial Publishing Co., 1966.

KILBOURN, W. *The Making of the Nation — A Century of Challenge.* Toronto: Canadian Centennial Publishing Co., 1965.

KING, C. *Saskatchewan Harvest — A Golden Jubilee Selection of Song and Story.* Toronto: McClelland & Stewart, 1955.

KING, Ethel. *Golden Memories . . . of the Town where the Turbulent Kicking Horse Meets the Mighty Columbia.* Golden, B.C.: The Golden Historical Branch of the Centennial Committee, 1958.

KING, W. Ross. *The Sportsman and Naturalist in Canada.* London: Hurst and Blacknell, 1866.

KINGSTON, W. H. G. *Captain Cook — His Life, Voyages and Discoveries.* London: Religious Tract Society, c1897.

KINNEY, E. *Westward and Other Poems.* Vancouver: D. A. Chalmers, 1923.

KIRBY, W. *The Golden Dog (Le Chien d'Or) — A Romance of Old Quebec.* Edited by E. C. Woodley. Toronto: Macmillan, 1937. [First published, Montreal: Lovell, 1877]

KIRK, Robert C. *Twelve Months in Klondike.* London: William Heinemann, 1899.

KITNEY, K. *Along Outdoor Trails.* [A regular column in the *Tribune* (Winnipeg)]

KITTO, F. H. See *New Manitoba District.*

Klondike and all About It. New York: Excelsior Publishing House, 1897.

To Klondike via Edmonton. 1897.

KNIGHT, J. *The Founding of Churchill, Being the Journal of Captain James Knight, Governor-in-Chief in Hudson Bay, from the 14th of July to the 13th of September, 1717.* Edited by James F. Kenney. Toronto: Dent, 1932.

KNOTT, L. L. *Harnessing the Giant.* Forward With Canada 6. Toronto: Northern Electric Co., 1952. [Booklet]

KNOWLES, R. E. *The Handicap — A Novel of Pioneer Days.* Toronto: F. H. Revell, 1910.

————. *The Singer of the Kootenay — A Tale of To-Day.* Toronto: F. H. Revell, 1911.

————. *St. Cuthbert's — A Novel.* Toronto: F. H. Revell, 1905.

————. *The Web of Time.* Toronto: F. H. Revell, 1908.

KOHL, J. G. *Kitchi-Gami — Wanderings round Lake Superior. . . .* Minneapolis, Minn.: Ross & Haines, 1956. [First published, Chapman & Hall, 1860; translated from German]

Kootenay and the City of Nelson, B.C. Nelson, B.C.: Nelson Board of Trade, 1937.

Kootenay Railway and Navigation Company Prospectus. 1888.

KOROLEFF, A. *Efficiency in Skidding of Wood and*

Handling of Horses. Montreal: Canadian Pulp & Paper Assn, 1942.

————. *Full-Tree Logging — A Challenge to Research.* Montreal: Pulp & Paper Research Institute, 1954.

————. *Woodcutter's Handbook. How to Cut More Pulpwood Safely without Greater Effort.* Montreal: Canadian Pulp & Paper Assn, 1944.

KOROLEFF, A., D. R. Stevens, and J. F. Walker. *Pulpwood Hauling with Horse and Sleigh.* Montreal: Canadian Pulp & Paper Assn, 1943.

————. *Pulpwood Skidding with Horses — Efficiency of Technique.* Montreal: Canadian Pulp & Paper Assn and Pulp & Paper Research Institute of Canada, 1943.

Kwakiutl. See A. F. FLUKE.

KYNE, P. B. *Cappy Ricks, or The Subjugation of Matt Peasley.* New York: Grosset & Dunlap, 1916.

[*Labrador and Banks Pilot*] *Sailing Directions for the Labrador and Banks Pilot.* Boston: William Norman, 1799.

Labrador and Hudson Bay Pilot — Comprising the Strait of Belle Isle to Cape Chidley and Hudson Strait and Bay. Ottawa: Dept of Mines and Technical Resources and Surveys, 1954.

Labrador Banks Pilot. London: Hydrographic Office, 1799.

LADUE, Joseph. *Klondyke Facts.* New York: American Technical Book Co., 1897.

————. *Klondyke Nuggets.* Montreal: John Lovell, 1897.

LAHONTAN, Louis Armand, Baron de. *New Voyages to North-America.* Edited by R. G. Thwaites. 2 vols. Chicago: McClurg, 1905. [First published, London: Bonwick, 1703; translated from French]

LAIDLAW, G. *Reports and Letters on Light Narrow-Gauge Railways.* Toronto: Globe Printing Co., 1868.

LAMB, W. K., ed. See Simon FRASER, *Letters and Journals.*

LAMBERT, R. S. *Exploring the Supernatural.* Toronto: McClelland & Stewart, 1955.

LAMBERT, T. W. *Fishing in British Columbia — with a Chapter on Tuna Fishing at Santa Catalina.* London: Horace Cox, 1907.

LAMORIE, Andrew (pseud.). *How They Sold Our Canada to the U.S.A.* Gravenhurst, Ont.: Northern Book House, 1963.

LANDREVILLE, M. *Appeal of Yukon Miners to the Dominion of Canada.* Ottawa: Mortimer, 1898.

LANGTON, W. A., ed. *Early Days in Upper Canada — Letters of John Langton from the Backwoods of Upper Canada and the Audit Office of the Province of Canada.* Toronto: Macmillan, 1926. [Written, 1833-69]

LANMAN, Charles. *Adventures of an Angler in Canada, Nova Scotia and the United States.* London: Richard Bentley, 1848.

LARGE, R. Geddes. *The Skeena, River of Destiny.* Vancouver: Mitchell Press, 1957.

LARGE, R., ed. See W. F. TOLMIE, *Journals.*

LAROCQUE. *Journal.* See L. J. BURPEE, *Journal de Larocque. . . .*

LATHAM, R. G. "On the Languages of Northern, Western, and Central America," *Transactions*, pp. 57-115. London: Philological Society, 1856.

LA TROBE, Benjamin. *A Brief Account of the Mission Established among the Esquimaux Indians on the Coast* of Labrador. . . . London: M. Lewis for the Moravian Brethern, 1774.

LAUT, Agnes C. *The Cariboo Trail — A Chronicle of the Gold-Fields of British Columbia*. Toronto: Glasgow, Brook, 1921.

———. *The Conquest of the Great Northwest — Being the Story of the Adventurers of England Known as the Hudson's Bay Company*. 2 vols. New York: Outing Publishing Co., 1908.

———. *Lords of the North — A Romance of the Northwest*. . . . Toronto: William Briggs, 1900.

———. *The Story of the Trapper*. New York: D. Appleton, 1912. [First published, Toronto: William Briggs, 1902]

LaVIOLETTE, F. E. *The Struggle for Survival — Indians Cultures and the Protestant Ethic in British Columbia*. Toronto: Univ. of Toronto Press, 1961.

LAWRENCE, Guy. "Forty Years on the Yukon Telegraph Service," *Alaska Sportsman*, Oct., 1958 to May, 1959.

LAWRENCE, J. W. *Foot-Prints; or, Incidents in Early History of New Brunswick*. St. John: J. & A. McMillan, 1883.

LAWSON, Jessie I., and Jean M. Sweet. *Our New Brunswick Story*. Toronto: Canada Publishing Co., 1949.

LAWSON, M., and R. Young. *A History and Geography of British Columbia — for Use in Public Schools*. Toronto: Gage, 1906.

LEACH, MacE. *Folk Ballads and Songs of the Lower Labrador Coast*. National Museum of Canada Bulletin 201. Ottawa, 1965.

LEACH, M. *Funk & Wagnalls Standard Dictionary of Folklore and Legend*. New York: Funk & Wagnalls, 1949.

LEACOCK, Stephen B. *Canada — The Foundations of Its Future*. Montreal: House of Seagram, 1941.

———. *Literary Lapses*. Montreal: Gazette Printing Co., 1910.

———. *Moonbeams from the Larger Lunacy*. 2nd ed. London: John Lane, 1917.

———. *Nonsense Novels*. London: John Lane, 1911.

LeBOURDAIS, D. M. *Metals and Men*. Toronto: McClelland & Stewart, 1957.

———. *Nation of the North — Canada since Confederation*. New York: Frederick A. Praeger, 1953.

———. *Northward on the New Frontier*. Ottawa: Graphic Publishers, 1931.

———. *Stefansson — Ambassador of the North*. Toronto, 1963.

LEE, Margaret Hitchie, M. Margaret E. Price, and Elizabeth Chant Robertson. *Food and Textiles*. Vol. I. Toronto: Gage, 1964.

LEECHMAN, Douglas. *Eskimo Summer*. Toronto: Ryerson, 1945.

———. "Good Fences Make Good Neighbours," *Canadian Geographical Journal*, Vol. XLVII (Dec., 1953), 218-235.

———. *Indian Summer*. Toronto: Ryerson, 1949.

———. *Native Tribes of Canada*. Toronto: Gage, 1956.

———. *Vanta Kutchin*. National Museum of Canada Bulletin 130. Ottawa, 1954.

LEES, J. A., and J. Clutterbuck. *B.C. 1887 — A Ramble in British Columbia*. London: Longmans, Green, 1888.

LEFOLII, Ken. *The Canadian Look — A Century of Sights and Styles*. Toronto: Canadian Centennial Publishing Co., 1967.

LEFROY, John Henry. *In Search of the Magnetic North — A Soldier-Surveyor's Letters from the North-West, 1843-1844*. Edited by George F. G. Stanley. Toronto: Macmillan, 1955.

LEGGE, Alfred O. *Sunny Manitoba — Its Peoples and Its Industries*. London: T. Fisher Unwin, 1893.

LEISING, W. A. *Arctic Wings*. Garden City, N.Y.: Doubleday, 1959.

LeMOINE, James M. *The Chronicles of the St. Lawrence*. Montreal: Dawson, 1878.

———. *Maple Leaves*. Quebec: A. Cote, 1873.

———. *Picturesque Quebec — A Sequel to Quebec Past and Present*. Montreal: Dawson, 1882.

LEONARD, J. W. *The Gold Fields of the Klondike*. London: T. Fisher Unwin, 1897.

LeROSSIGNOL, James E. *The Beauport Road — Tales of Old Quebec*. Toronto: McClelland & Stewart, 1928.

Letters from Hudson Bay 1703-1740. Edited by K. G. Davies. Hudson's Bay Record Society Publications XXV. London, 1965.

The Letters of Queen Victoria, 1837-1861. London: John Murray, 1907.

"Letters Outward, 1679-1694," *Hudson's Bay Record Society Publications XI*. London, 1948.

LEWELLIN, J. L. "Emigration — Prince Edward Island . . . ," in D. C. HARVEY, *Journeys . . .* , pp. 180-213. See above. [First published, Charlottetown: James D. Haszard, 1832]

LEWIS and CLARK. *Original Journals of the Lewis and Clark Expedition*. Edited by R. G. Thwaites. 8 vols. New York: Dodd, Mead, 1904.

LEWIS, C. E., ed. *Poems Worth Knowing*. Toronto: Copp Clark, 1941.

LEWIS, Gwen. *Buckskin Cookery — A Souvenir Cookbook Compiled of Recipes Donated by Old Timers and Natives of B.C. Volume I: The Pioneer Section. Volume II: The Hunting Section*. Quesnel, B.C.: Privately printed, Vol. I, 1957; Vol. II, 1958.

LEWIS, John. *George Brown*. Toronto: Morang, 1906.

LIGGETT, Walter W., ed. *Frozen Frontier*. Toronto: Harlequin Books, 1954.

LIGHTHALL, W. D., ed. *Songs of the Great Dominion — Voices from the Forests and Waters, The Settlements and Cities of Canada*. London: Walter Scott, 1889.

LINDSAY, F. W. *The B.C. Outlaws*. Quesnel, B.C.: Privately printed, 1963.

———. *The Cariboo Story*. Quesnel, B.C.: Privately printed, 1958.

LLOYD, J. A. T. *The Real Canadian*. London: Everett, 1913.

LOCKE, George H. *When Canada Was New France*. Toronto: Dent, 1920.

LOCKWOOD, Anthony. *A Brief Description of Nova Scotia*. London: Cadell & Davies, 1818.

LOFTHOUSE, J. *A Thousand Miles from a Post Office; or, Twenty Years' Life and Travel in the Hudson Bay Regions*. London, 1922.

LOGIE, Jack L., ed. *The Demon of the Okanagan*. Okanagan Centre, B.C.: Privately printed, 1928.

LONDON, Jack. *Burning Daylight*. New York: Macmillan, 1910.

———. *Call of the Wild*. New York: Macmillan, 1903.

———. *A Daughter of the Snows*. London: Nelson, n.d. [First published, New York, 1902]

———. *Lost Face*. New York: Macmillan, 1910.

———. *Smoke Bellew*. Toronto: Bell & Cockburn, 1912.

———. *Son of Wolf*. New York: Grosset & Dunlap, 1900.

———. *White Fang*. New York, 1907.

LONG, John. *Voyages and Travels of an Indian Interpreter and Trader*.... London: Privately printed, 1791.

———. *Voyages and Travels of an Indian Interpreter and Trader, 1768-1782*. Edited by R. G. Thwaites. Cleveland, Ohio: Clark, 1904.

LONG, William J. *Wilderness Ways*. Boston: Ginn, 1900.

LONGSTRETH, T. M. *The Force Carries On*. Toronto: Macmillan, 1954.

———. *The Silent Force*. New York: Century, 1927; New York: Appleton-Century, 1934.

LORD, John Keast. *At Home in The Wilderness — What to Do There and How to Do It — A Handbook for Travellers and Emigrants*. London: Hardwicke, 1867; 3rd ed. London: Hardwicke & Bogue, 1876.

———. *The Naturalist in Vancouver Island and British Columbia*. 2 vols. London: Richard Bentley, 1866.

LORNE, Marquis of. *The Canadian North-West — Speech Delivered at Winnipeg by His Excellency the Marquis of Lorne, Governor-General of Canada, after His Tour through Manitoba and the North-West, during the Summer of 1881*. Ottawa: Queen's Printer, 1882.

LOWER, A. R. M. *Colony to Nation*. Toronto: Longman's Green, 1946.

———. *Settlement and the Forest Frontier in Eastern Canada*. Canadian Frontiers and Settlement, Vol. 9. Toronto: Macmillan, 1936.

———. *Unconventional Voyages*. Toronto: Ryerson, 1953.

LOWREY, Harold C. *Young Canada Boys with the S.O.S. on the Frontier*. Toronto: Thos. Allen, 1918.

LUCAS, Sir Charles. *Historical Geography of Canada*. Part I. London: Oxford, 1923.

LUMSDEN, James. *The Skipper Parson on the Bays and Barrens of Newfoundland*. Toronto: William Briggs, 1906.

LUNDIN-BROWN, R. C. *Klatsassan and Other Reminiscences of Missionary Life in British Columbia*. London: London Society for Promoting Christian Knowledge, 1873.

LUNDY, Benjamin. *Diary* (1832). Ontario Historical Society Papers and Records XIX. 1902.

LYELL, C. *Travels in North America, in the Years 1841-1842 — with Geological Observations on the United States, Canada, and Nova Scotia*. New York: Wiley & Putnam, 1845.

LYON, George Francis. *The Private Journal of Captain G. F. Lyon of H.M.S. Hecla during the Recent Voyage of Discovery under Captain Parry*. London: John Murray, 1824.

LYONS, C. P. *Milestones on the Mighty Fraser*. Vancouver: Dent, 1950.

———. *Milestones on Vancouver Island*. Victoria: Milestone Books, 1958.

———. *Trees, Shrubs and Flowers to Know in British Columbia*. Toronto: Dent, 1952.

LYSENKO, Vera. *Yellow Boots*. Toronto: Ryerson, 1954.

McARTHUR, Peter. *Familiar Fields*. Toronto: Dent, 1925.

———. *Friendly Acres*. Toronto: Musson, 1927.

McATEE, W. L. *Folk-Names of Canadian Birds*. 2nd ed. National Museum of Canada Bulletin 149. Ottawa, 1956 and 1959.

MacBEATH, George, and Dorothy Chamberlin. *New Brunswick — The Story of Our Province*. Toronto: Gage, 1965.

MACBETH, Madge. *The Long Day*. Ottawa: Graphic Press, 1926.

MacBETH, R. G. *The Selkirk Settlers in Real Life*. Toronto: William Briggs, 1897.

MacCALLUM, Jean, and Jessie Lawson. *This is New Brunswick*. Toronto: Ryerson, 1951.

McCLUNG, Nellie. *Be Good to Yourself — A Book of Short Stories*. Toronto: Thomas Allen, 1930.

———. *In Times like These*. Toronto: McLeod, 1916. [First published, New York: Appleton, 1915]

———. *Painted Fires*. Toronto: Thomas Allen, 1925.

———. *Purple Springs*. Toronto: Thomas Allen, 1921.

———. *The Second Chance*. Toronto: William Briggs, 1910.

———. *Three Times and Out — A Canadian Boy's Experience in Germany*. Toronto: Thomas Allen, 1918.

MacCORMAC. *Canada: America's Problem*. New York, 1940.

McCORMICK, R. *Voyages of Discovery in the Arctic and Antarctic Seas*. 2 vols. London: Sampson Low, Marston, Searle, & Rivington, 1884.

MACOUN, John. *Autobiography of John Macoun. M.A.* Ottawa: Field-Naturalists' Club, 1922.

McCOURT, Edward. *Home is the Stranger*. Toronto: Macmillan, 1950.

McCOWAN, Daniel. *Animals of the Canadian Rockies*. Toronto: Macmillan, 1936.

———. *Upland Trails*. Toronto: Macmillan, 1955.

McCRACKEN, H. *The Beast that Walks like Man — The Story of the Grizzly Bear*. Garden City, N.Y.: Hanover House, 1955.

McCREA, R. B. *Lost amid the Fogs*. London: Sampson Low, Son, & Marston, 1869.

McCULLOCH, Thomas. *The Stepsure Letters*. Toronto: McClelland & Stewart, 1960. [First published as "Letters of Mephibosheth Stepsure," *Acadian Recorder*, 1821-23]

McCULLOCH, Walter Fraser. *Woods Words — A Comprehensive Dictionary of Loggers Terms*. Portland, Ore., 1958.

MACDONAL, W. L., ed. *A Book of Modern Prose*. See W. L. MACDONALD.

McDONALD, Archibald. *Peace River — A Canoe Voyage from Hudson's Bay to the Pacific, by the late Sir George Simpson . . . in 1828; Journal of the late Chief Factor, Archibald McDonald (Hon. Hudson's Bay Company) who Accompanied Him*. Edited by Malcolm McLeod. Ottawa: J. Durie, 1872.

MACDONALD, D. G. Forbes. *Lectures on British Columbia and Vancouver's Island*. London: Longman, Green, Longman, Roberts, & Green, 1863. [Preface dated 1862]

MACDONALD, E. M. *Recollections, Political and Personal*. Toronto: Ryerson, 1938.

McDONALD of Garth, John. "Autobiographical

Notes, 1791-1816," in Vol. II of L. F. R. MASSON, *Les Bourgeois . . .* , pp. 1-59. See below.

MacDONALD, Malcolm. *Down North.* Toronto: Oxford, 1943.

MACDONALD, W. L., ed. *A Book of Modern Prose.* Toronto: Dent, 1938.

MACDONELL, John. Diary, May 10th-Oct. 8th, 1793," in C. M. GATES, *Five Fur Traders . . .* , pp. 61-119. See above.

———. "Some Account of the Red River (about 1797) with Extracts from his Journal, 1793-1795," in Vol. I of L. F. R. MASSON, *Les Bourgeois . . .* , pp. 265-295. See below. [Cited as *Journal*]

McDONNELL, Alexander Greenfield. *A Narrative of Transactions in the Red River Country.* London: Macmillan, 1819.

McDOUGALL, George F. *The Eventful Voyage of H.M. Discovery Ship Resolute to the Arctic Regions in Search of Sir John Franklin. . . .* London: Longman, Brown, Green, Longman, & Roberts, 1857.

McDOUGALL, John. *George Millward McDougall — The Pioneer, Patriot & Missionary.* Toronto: William Briggs, 1888.

———. *Saddle, Sled and Snowshoe — Pioneering on the Saskatchewan in the Sixties.* Toronto: William Briggs, 1896; New York: Eaton & Mains, 1896.

McDOWELL, F. D. *The Champlain Road.* Toronto: Macmillan, 1939 and 1941.

McEVOY, Bernard. *From the Great Lakes to the Wide West — Impressions of a Tour between Toronto and the Pacific.* Toronto: William Briggs, 1902.

MacEWAN, Grant. *Between the Red and the Rockies.* Toronto: Univ. of Toronto Press, 1952.

———. *Calgary Cavalcade.* Edmonton: Applied Arts Centre, 1958.

———. *Eye Opener Bob: The Story of Bob Edwards.* Edmonton: Institute of Applied Art, 1957.

———. *Fifty Mighty Men.* Saskatoon: Modern Press, 1958.

MacEWAN, J. W. G. *The Breeds of Farm Live-Stock in Canada.* Toronto: Macmillan, 1941.

MacEWAN, J. W. G., and A. H. Ewen. *The Science and Practice of Canadian Animal Husbandry.* Toronto: Nelson, 1936.

McEWEN, Jessie. *Taltrees.* Toronto: Ryerson, 1949.

MACFIE, Matthew. *Vancouver Island and British Columbia.* London: Longman, Green, Longman, Roberts, & Green, 1865.

McGILLIVRAY, Duncan. *The Journal of Duncan M'Gillivray of the North West Company at Fort George on the Saskatchewan, 1794-1795.* Edited by A. S. Morton. Toronto: Macmillan, 1929.

McGREGOR, J. *Historical and Descriptive Sketches of the Maritime Colonies of British America.* London: Longman, Rees, Orme, Brown, & Green, 1828; London: Cadell, 1832.

MacGREGOR, J. G. *Behold the Shining Mountains.* Edmonton: Applied Art Products, 1954.

———. *Blankets and Beads—A History of the Saskatchewan River.* Edmonton: Institute of Applied Art, 1949.

———. *The Land of Twelve-Foot Davis — A History of the Peace River Country.* Edmonton: Applied Art Products, 1952.

———. *Northwest of 16.* Toronto: McClelland & Stewart, 1958.

MacINNES, C. M. *In the Shadow of the Rockies.* London: Rivington, 1930.

MacINNES, Tom. *Chinook Days.* [Vancouver], 1926.

MacKAY, Isabel E. *Blencarrow.* Toronto: Thomas Allen, 1926.

———. *The Window-Gazer.* Toronto: McClelland & Stewart, 1921.

MACKAY, W. A. *By Trench and Trail.* Vancouver, 1918.

MacKAY, W. A. *Pioneer Life in Zorra.* Toronto: William Briggs, 1899.

McKEEVOR, Thomas. *A Voyage to Hudson's Bay, during the Summer of 1812.* London: Sir Richard Phillips, 1819.

McKELVIE, B. A. *The Black Canyon — A Story of '58.* Toronto: Dent, 1927.

———. *Fort Langley — Outpost of Empire.* Toronto: Nelson, 1957. [First published, Vancouver: "Daily Province," 1947]

———. *Huldowget: A Story of the North Pacific Coast.* Toronto: Dent, 1926.

———. *Pageant of B.C. — Glimpses into the Romantic Development of Canada's Far Western Province.* Toronto: Nelson, 1955.

MACKENZIE, Alexander. *Voyages from Montreal on the River St. Laurence through the Continent of North America to the Frozen & Pacific Oceans in the Years 1789 & 1793 with a Preliminary Account of the Rise, Progress, & Present State of the Fur Trade of that Country.* London: T. Cadell, Junior, & W. Davies, 1801; Masterworks of Canadian Authors III. Edited by John W. Garvin. Toronto: Radisson Society, 1927.

MACKENZIE, Charles. "The Mississouri Indians, a Narrative of Four Trading Expeditions to the Mississouri, 1804, 1805, 1806, for the North-West Company," in Vol. I of L. F. R. MASSON, *Les Bourgeois . . .* , pp. 315-393. See below.

McKENZIE, James. "Extracts from His Journal 1799-1800," in Vol. II of L. F. R. MASSON, *Les Bourgeois . . .* , pp. 369-399. See below.

———. "The King's Posts & Journal of a Canoe Jaunt through the King's Domains, 1808," in Vol. II of L. F. R. MASSON, *Les Bourgeois . . .* , pp. 401-454. See below.

MACKENZIE, Kenneth. *Living Rough.* London: J. Cape, 1936.

McKENZIE, N. M. W. J. *The Men of the Hudson Bay Company, 1670 A.D. - 1920 A.D.* Fort William, Ont.: Times-Journal Presses, 1921.

McKENZIE, Roderick. "Reminiscences by the Honorable Roderick McKenzie being chiefly a synopsis of Letters from Sir Alexander Mackenzie," in Vol. I of L. F. R. MASSON, *Les Bourgeois . . .* , pp. 1-66. See below.

MACKENZIE, W. R. *The Quest of the Ballad.* Oxford: Oxford, 1919.

McKINNON, F. S. *Illustrated Forest Activities.* 3 vols. 1963.

McKISHNIE, Archie P. *Love of the Wild.* Chicago: M. A. Donohue, 1910.

———. *A Son of Courage.* Toronto: Thomas Allen, 1920.

———. *Willow, the Wisp.* Toronto: Thomas Allen, 1918.

McKOWAN, Evah May. *Graydon of the Windermere.* Toronto: McClelland & Stewart, 1920.

McLEAN, John. *Notes of a Twenty-five Years' Service in the Hudson's Bay Territory.* 2 vols. London: Richard Bentley, 1849; Champlain Society Publications XIX. Edited by W. S. Wallace. Toronto, 1932.

MacLEAN, John. *Canadian Savage Folk — The Native Tribes of Canada.* Toronto: William Briggs, 1896.

———. *The Indians of Canada — Their Manners and Customs.* London: C. H. Kelly, 1892. [First published as *The Indians. Whence Came They? Who Are They? Their Manners and Customs.* Toronto: William Briggs, 1889]

MacLENNAN, Hugh. *Barometer Rising.* Toronto: Collins, 1941. [Also, an extract read in George E. NELSON, *Cavalcade of the North.* See below.]

———. *Seven Rivers of Canada.* Toronto: Macmillan, 1961.

———. *Two Solitudes.* Toronto: Collins, 1945.

———. *The Watch that Ends the Night.* Toronto: Macmillan, 1959.

McLEOD, Archibald N. "Diary, 1800-1801," in C. M. GATES, *Five Fur Traders . . . ,* pp. 125-185. See above.

McLEOD, D. *A Brief Review of the Settlement of Upper Canada. . . .* Cleveland: F. B. Penniman, 1841.

MacLEOD, Margaret A., and W. L. Morton. *Cuthbert Grant of Grantown.* Toronto: McClelland & Stewart, 1963.

McLEOD, Robert R. *Markland or Nova Scotia — Its History, Natural Resources, etc.* Berwick, N.S.: Markland Publishing Co., 1903.

McLOUGHLIN, John. *Letters of Dr. John McLoughlin Written at Fort Vancouver, 1829-1832.* Edited by Dr. Burt Brown Barker. Portland, Ore.: Binfords & Mort, 1948.

MacMECHAN, Archibald. *Late Harvest.* Toronto: Ryerson, 1934.

———. *Old Provincial Tales.* Toronto: McClelland & Stewart, 1924.

———. *Sagas of the Sea.* Toronto: Dent, 1929. [First published, 1923]

———. *The Winning of Popular Government.* Toronto: Glasgow, Brook, 1916.

McMULLEN, John. *History of Canada.* Brockville, C. W., 1855.

McNAB, Frances. *British Columbia for Settlers—Its Mines, Trade & Agriculture.* London: Chapman & Hall, 1898.

McNAMEE, J. *Florencia Bay.* Toronto: McClelland & Stewart, 1960.

———. *My Uncle Joe.* Toronto: Macmillan, 1962.

McNAUGHTON, Margaret. *Overland to Cariboo — An Eventful Journey of Canadian Pioneers to the Gold Fields of British Columbia in 1896.* Toronto: William Briggs, 1896.

McNEIL, Grant. *Between the Red.* See Grant MacEWAN.

MacNEIL, Neal. *The Highland Heart in Nova Scotia.* New York: Scribner, 1948.

MACNUTT, W. S. *Atlantic Provinces — The Emergence of Colonial Society, 1712-1857.* Toronto: McClelland & Stewart, 1965.

MacQUEEN, M. A. *Skye Pioneers and "The Island."* Winnipeg: Stovel, 1929.

McROBERT, Patrick. "Tour Through Part of the North Provinces of America," *Penna. Mag. Hist. & Biog.,* Apr., 1935. [First published, Edinburgh, 1776]

MacTAGGART, John. *Three Years in Canada, 1826-1828.* 2 vols. London: H. Colburn, 1829.

McTAVISH, G. S. *Behind the Palisades — An Autobiography.* Victoria: E. Gurd, 1963.

McWILLIAMS, Margaret. *This New Canada.* Toronto: Dent, 1948.

Made in Canada. Toronto: Distillers-Seagrams, 1962.

MAIDEN, Cecil. *Lighted Journey — The Story of the B.C. Electric.* Vancouver: B.C. Electric, 1948.

MAIR, Charles. *Masterworks of Canadian Authors, XIV.* Toronto: Radisson Society, 1926.

———. "On the American Bison," *Trans. Roy. Soc. Can.,* Vol. VIII (1890), Sec. 2, 93-108.

———. *Through the Mackenzie Basin — A Narrative of the Athabasca and Peace River Treaty Expedition of 1899.* Toronto: William Briggs, 1908.

MALHIOT, F. V. *A Wisconsin Fur-Trader's Journal, 1804-1805.* Madison: Wisconsin Historical Collections, 1910.

MALKUS, Alida. *Little Giant of the North — The Boy who Won a Fur Empire.* Toronto: Winston, 1952.

MALLOCK. *When the Drive Comes Down.* 1942.

Manice. Manual of Standard Procedures and Practices for Ice Reconnaissance. Ottawa: Dept of Transport, Meteorological Branch, 1958.

MANNING, Mrs. Tom (Ella W.). *Igloo for the Night.* Toronto: Univ. of Toronto Press, 1946.

MARQUIS, T. G. *Canada's Sons on Kopje and Veldt — A Historical Account of the Canadian Contingents.* Toronto: Canadian's Sons Publishing Co., 1900.

MARRIOTT, Harry. *Cariboo Cowboy.* Victoria: Gray's Publishing Ltd, 1966.

MARRYAT, Fred. *Masterman Ready.* London: Nelson, 1912. [First published, London, 1841]

———. *Settlers in Canada—Written for Young People.* London: Blackie, n.d. [First published, London, 1844]

MARSDEN, Joshua. *The Narrative of a Mission to Nova Scotia, New Brunswick, and the Somers Islands; with a Tour to Lake Ontario.* Plymouth-Dock: J. Johns, 1816; 2nd ed. London: Kershaw, 1827.

MARSH, Donald B. "Canada's Caribou Eskimos," *National Geographic Magazine,* Jan., 1947, pp. 87-104.

MARSH, George. *Men Marooned.* Philadelphia: Penn Publishing Co., 1925.

MARSHALL, E. *The Snowshoe Trail.* New York: A. L. Burt, 1921.

MARSHALL, Marguerite. *Wilderness Nurse.* Montreal: Pocket Books of Canada, 1950. [First published, Philadelphia: Macrae Smith, 1949]

MARSHALL, Robert. *Arctic Village.* New York: Penguin Books, 1940.

MARTIN, H. E. *The Alberta Story.* Edmonton: Alberta Publicity Bureau, 1965. [Booklet]

MARTIN, Horace T. *Castorologia; or, The History and Traditions of the Canadian Beaver.* Montreal: Drysdale, 1892.

MARTIN, Joe. *Canadian Wilderness Trapping.* Toronto: Fur Trade Journal of Canada, 1944. [Booklet]

MARTIN, Quimby, and Collier. *Indians before Columbus.* Chicago: University Press, 1947.

MARTYR, Peter. *The Decades of the Newe Worlde or West India.* London: Richarde Eden, 1555.

MASON, J. Alden. *Notes on Northeastern Athabascan Culture (c1913).* National Museum of Canada MSS.

MASON, John. *A Briefe Discovrse of the Nevv-foundland.* Edinburgh: Andro Hart, 1620.

MASON, Michael H. *The Arctic Forests.* London: Hodder & Stoughton, 1924.

MASON, Winfield Scott. *The Frozen Northland.* Cincinnati: Jennings & Graham, 1910.

MASSON, Louis F. R., ed. *Les Bourgeois de la Compagnie du Nord-Ouest — Récits de Voyages, Lettres et Rapports inédits relatifs au Nord-Ouest canadien, avec une Esquisse historique et des Annotations.* 2 vols. Quebec: De l'Imprimerie Générale A. Coté et Cie, 1889-1890. [Most of the items in this collection are in English]

MATHEWS, Basil, *Wilfred Grenfell — The Master Mariner.* New York: George H. Doran, 1924.

MATHEWS, J. S. *Early Vancouver.* Vancouver Public Library MSS. 1932.

MATTHEWS, Jack. *Who Uses Our Woods Roads?* Toronto: Abitibi Power & Paper Co., 1962. [Pamphlet]

MAYER, B. *Memoirs.* London, 1845.

MAYNE, Richard Charles. *Four Years in British Columbia and Vancouver Island.* London: John Murray, 1862.

MEDSGER, Oliver Perry. *Edible Wild Plants.* New York: Macmillan, 1939.

Memoirs of the Ghost Pine Homesteaders. Three Hills, Alta: Ghost Pine Community Group, 1954.

Memorandum on Office of Lieutenant-Governor of a Province: Its Constitutional Character and Functions. Ottawa: Department of Justice, Nov., 1937.

MENCKEN, Henry L. *The American Language—An Inquiry into the Development of English in the United States.* New York: Knopf, 1919, 1921, 1923; 4th ed., with two supplements, 1936-48.

MENZIES, Archibald. *Journal of Vancouver's Voyage, April to October, 1792.* Archives of British Columbia, Memoir V. Victoria, 1923.

MERK, F., ed. *Fur Trade and Empire — Sir George Simpson's Journal, 1824.* Cambridge, Mass.: Harvard Univ. Press, 1931.

MERKEL, Andrew. *Schooner Bluenose.* Toronto: Ryerson, 1948.

MERRICK, Elliot. *Northern Nurse.* New York: Scribner, 1942.

———. *True North.* New York: Scribner, 1933.

MIDDLETON, Samuel H. *Kootenai Brown.* Lethbridge, Alta: Lethbridge Herald, 1954.

MILES, Alfred Henry, ed. *Fifty-two Stories of Life and Adventure for Boys.* London: Hutchinson, 1894.

MILLAIS, J. G. *Newfoundland and Its Untrodden Ways.* London: Longmans, Green, 1907.

MILLER, J. O., ed. *The New Era in Canada.* Toronto: Dent, 1917.

MILLER, Warren Hastings. *The Lone Woodsman.* Toronto: Winston, 1943.

MILLS, Alan. *Folksongs of Newfoundland.* Song Album No. FP 831. New York: Folkway Records and Service Corp., 1953.

———. *Songs of the Maritimes.* Song Album No. 8744. New York: Folkway Records and Service Corp., 1959.

Mining Explained in Simple Terms. Toronto: Northern Miner Press, 1955.

Mining Textbooklets: 1, *Geology & Mineralogy;* 2, *Prospecting in Canada;* 3, *Practical Mining.* Ottawa: Canadian Legion Educational Services, 1945.

Minutes of Council, Northern Department of Rupert's Land, 1821-1831. Hudson's Bay Record Society Publications III. London, 1940.

Minutes of the Council of Vancouver Island. Archives of British Columbia, Memoir No. II. Victoria, 1918.

Minutes of the Hudson's Bay Company, 1671-1674. Edited by E. E. Rich. Champlain Society Publications, Hudson's Bay Company Series V. Toronto, 1942.

Minutes of the Hudson's Bay Company, 1679-1684. Edited by E. E. Rich. 2 vols. Champlain Society Publications, Hudson's Bay Company Series VIII-IX. Toronto, 1945-1946.

MITCHELL, George, and Angus Graham. *The Golden Grindstone — The Adventures of George M. Mitchell, Recorded by Angus Graham.* Toronto: Oxford, 1935.

MITCHELL, J. See Patrick SLATER.

MITCHELL, W. O. *Jake and The Kid.* Toronto: Macmillan, 1961.

———. *Who Has Seen the Wind.* Toronto: Macmillan, 1947.

MOBERLY, H.J., in collaboration with W.B. Cameron. *When Fur Was King.* Toronto: Dent, 1929.

MOBERLY, Walter. *The Rocks and Rivers of British Columbia.* London: Blacklock, 1885.

MOIR, George T. *Sinners and Saints.* Victoria: G. L. Wooding, 1948.

MONRO, Alexander. *New Brunswick . . .* Halifax: Richard Nugent, 1855.

MONRO, James. *MSS. History and Description and State of the Southern and Western Townships of Nova Scotia in 1795.* Report of the Board of Trustees of the Public Archives of Nova Scotia, for 1946. Halifax, 1947.

MONTAGUE, S. R. *I Lived with the Eskimos.* New York: McBride, 1939.

MONTGOMERY, Lucy M. *Anne of Ingleside.* Toronto: McClelland & Stewart, 1939.

———. *Anne of Windy Poplars.* Toronto: McClelland & Stewart, 1936.

———. *Anne's House of Dreams.* New York: Stokes, 1917.

———. *Chronicles of Avonlea.* London: Simpkin, Marshall, Hamilton, Kent, 1912.

———. *Emily Climbs.* Toronto: McClelland & Stewart, 1925.

———. *Kilmeny of the Orchard.* London: George G. Harrap, 1925. [1936 reprint read. First published, Boston: Page, 1910]

———. *Pat of Silver Bush.* Toronto: McClelland & Stewart, 1933.

———. *Rainbow Valley.* Toronto: McClelland & Stewart, 1919.

———. *Rilla of Ingleside.* Toronto: McClelland & Stewart, 1920.

———. *A Tangled Web.* New York: Stokes, 1931.

Montreal Police Regulations. Montreal: James Lane, 1817.

MOODIE, Susanna (Strickland). *Life in the Clearings, to which Is Added this Author's Introduction to Mark Hurdlestone.* Edited by R. L. McDougall. Toronto: Macmillan, 1959. [First published, London: Bentley, 1853]

————. *Roughing It in the Bush.* Toronto: McClelland & Stewart, 1923. [First published, London: Bentley, 1852]

MOODY, Irene H. *Attar of Song and Other Poems.* Toronto: Macmillan, 1936.

MOON, Robert. *This is Saskatchewan.* Toronto: Ryerson, 1953.

MOON, T. J., J. H. Otto, and P. B. Mann. *Modern Biology.* Rev. ed. Toronto: Clarke, Irwin, 1954.

MOORE, P. H. *The Castle Buck—Hunting and Fishing Adventures with a Nova Scotia Guide.* Toronto: Longmans, Green, 1945.

MOORE, W. G. *A Dictionary of Geography.* Rev. ed. Harmondsworth, England: Penguin Books, 1958.

MOORE, William Henry. *The Clash — A Study in Nationalities.* Toronto: Dent, 1918.

MOORHOUSE, Hopkins (pseud. of Arthur H. J. Moorhouse). *Deep Furrows — Which Tells of Pioneer Trails along which the Farmers of Western Canada Fought Their Way to Great Achievements in Co-operation.* Toronto: George J. McLeod, 1918.

MOORSOM, William S. *Letters from Nova Scotia — Comprising Sketches of a Young Country.* London: Colburn & Bentley, 1830.

Moose Fort Journals, 1783-85. Edited by E. E. Rich. Hudson's Bay Record Society Publications XVII. London, 1954.

MORDEN, Robert. *A New Map of the English Empire in America.* 1719.

MORGAN, J. C. *The Emigrant's Note Book and Guide; With Recollections of Upper and Lower Canada, during the Late War.* London: Longman, 1824.

MORGAN, Margaret: *Jerry's Adventure.* Unpublished essay. 1964.

MORICE, Adrian G. *The Carrier Language (Déné family); A Grammar and Dictionary Combined.* Winnipeg: Privately printed, 1932.

————. *A Critical History of the Red River Insurrection after Official Documents and Non-Catholic Sources.* Winnipeg: Canadian Publishers, 1935.

————. "The Great Déné Race," *Anthropos,* Winnipeg, 1910.

————. *History of the Catholic Church in Western Canada, from Lake Superior to the Pacific* (1659-1895). 2 vols. Toronto: Musson, 1910.

————. *The History of the Northern Interior of British Columbia, Formerly New Caledonia* (1660-1880). Toronto: William Briggs, 1904.

MORLEY, P. F. *Bridging the Chasm — A Study of the Ontario-Quebec Question.* Toronto: Dent, 1919.

MORRIS, Hon. Alexander. *The Treaties of Canada with the Indians of Manitoba and the North-West Territories, Including the Negotiations on which They Were Based and Other Information Relating thereto.* Toronto: Belford's, Clarke, 1880.

MORRIS, Isaac C. *Sketches of Our Western Sea Coast.* St. John's: George S. Milligan, Jr., 1894.

MORSE, J. J. *Kamloops — The Inland Capital.* Kamloops, B.C.: Kamloops Museum Assn, 1958.

MORTON, A. C. *Report on the Gauge for the St. Lawrence and Atlantic Rail-Road.* Montreal: Canada Gazette Office, 1847.

MORTON, A. S. *A History of the Canadian West to 1870-1871 — Being a History of Rupert's Land (the Hudson Bay Company's Territory) and of the North-West Territory (Including the Pacific Slope).* Toronto: Nelson, 1939.

————. *Kingdom of Canada.* Toronto: McClelland & Stewart, 1963.

MORTON, B. R. See *Native Trees of Canada.*

MOSER, Charles. *Reminiscences of the West Coast of Vancouver Island.* Victoria: Acme Press, 1926.

MOTT, Lawrence. *Jules of the Great Heart — "Free" Trapper and Outlaw in The Hudson Bay Region in the Early Days.* Toronto: Copp Clark, 1905.

MOWAT, Angus. *Carrying Place.* Toronto: S. J. Reginald Saunders, 1944.

MOWAT, Farley. *The Black Joke.* Toronto: McClelland & Stewart, 1962.

————. *The Desperate People.* Boston: Little, Brown, 1959.

————. *The Dog who Wouldn't Be.* Boston: Little, Brown, 1957.

————. *Lost in the Barrens.* Boston: Little, Brown, 1956.

————. *Ordeal by Ice.* Toronto: McClelland & Stewart, 1960.

————. "Pals of My Childhood," *Saturday Evening Post,* April 13, 1957, pp. 134-138.

————. *People of the Deer.* Boston: Little, Brown, 1952; London: Readers Union, 1954.

MOWERY, William Byron. *Paradise Trail — A Novel of the Northwest.* Toronto: Better Publications of Canada, 1936.

————. *Resurrection River.* Boston: Little, Brown, 1935.

————. *Tales of the Mounted Police.* New York: Airmont, 1962. [First published as *Sagas of the Mounted Police.* Thomas Bouregy & Co., 1953]

MULHOLLAND, F. D. *The Forest Resources of British Columbia, 1937.* Victoria: B.C. Forest Service, 1937.

MUNN, H. T. *Prairie Trails and Arctic By-Ways.* London: Hurst & Blackett, 1932.

MUNN, H. T., and E. Sprigge. *Home is the Hunter.* London: John Lane, 1930.

MUNROE, Kirk. *Snow-Shoes and Sledges.* New York: Harper, 1895.

MUNSTERHJELM, Eric. *Fool's Gold.* 1957.

————. *Wind and the Caribou.* Toronto: Macmillan, 1953.

MURDOCH, Beamish. *A History of Nova-Scotia, or Acadie.* Vol. II. Halifax: James Barnes, 1866.

MURPHY, Emily Gowan (Ferguson). *The Black Candle.* Toronto: Thomas Allen, 1922.

————. *Janey Canuck in the West.* See Emily FERGUSON.

————. *Open Trails.* See Janey CANUCK.

MURRAY, Alexander H. *Journal of the Yukon, 1847-48.* Edited by L. J. Burpee. Publications of the Canadian Archives 4. Ottawa, 1910.

MURRAY, Hugh. *An Historical and Descriptive Account of British America.* 2 vols. New York: Harper, 1860. [Dated 1840]

MYLES, E., and E. Gillis. *North Pole Boarding House.* Toronto: Ryerson, 1951.

Native Trees of Canada. Forestry Branch Bulletin No. 61. Ottawa, 1920 and (5th ed.) 1956. [1st ed. (1917) by B. R. Morton, with notes by R. C. Lewis]

Natural Food Products. See *Journals of the Senate of Canada.*

NEED, Thomas. *Six Years in the Bush; or, Extracts from the Journal of a Settler in Upper Canada, 1832-1838.* London: Simpkin Marshall, 1838.

NELSON, George E., ed. *Cavalcade of the North.* Garden City, N.Y.: Doubleday, 1958.

———. *Northern Lights.* Garden City, N.Y.: Doubleday, 1960.

NEUBERGER, Richard L. "Boss of the Royal Mounted," *Holiday,* Dec., 1949, pp. 141-152.

NEVINS, J. B. *A Narrative of Two Voyages to Hudson's Bay.* ... London: Society for Promoting Christian Knowledge, 1847.

NEWBERRY, J. S. "Food and Fiber Plants of the North American Indians," *Popular Science Monthly,* Vol. XXXII (1887), 31-46.

New Canadian Geography. B.C. ed. Toronto: Gage, c1906. [First published, 1899]

New Deal for Saskatchewan Fisheries. 1948.

Newfoundland House of Assembly Journal. Appendix. 1841.

Newfoundland Statutes. Chronological Table of Statutes. 1951.

The New Manitoba District; Canada, Its Resources and Developments. Ottawa: King's Printer, 1918.

New Sounds. Abitibi Forest Products Ltd, c1963. [Pamphlet]

NIAGUNGITOK, George. *Vocabulary of Esquimeaux Words, Translated into English.* Sheffield: George Ridge, 1824.

NICHOLSON, Byron. *In Old Quebec and Other Sketches.* Quebec City: Commercial Printing Co., 1908.

NICHOLSON, G. *Vancouver Island's West Coast, 1762-1962.* Victoria: Privately printed, 1962.

NICOLLET, Joseph Nicholas. *Report Intended to Illustrate a Map of the Hydrographical Basin of the Upper Mississippi River.* Washington, D.C.: Blair & Rives, 1841.

NIVEN, Fred. *The Flying Years.* Toronto: Collins, 1942.

———. *Mine Inheritance.* London: Collins, 1940.

———. *The Transplanted.* Toronto: Collins, 1944.

———. *Wild Honey.* New York: Dodd, Mead, 1927.

NIX, James E. *Mission among the Buffalo.* Toronto: Ryerson, 1960.

Northern Affairs & National Resources Publication — Sectional Catalogue 11. Ottawa: Queen's Printer, 1963.

Northern Lights. See George E. NELSON.

North Georgia Gazette, and Winter Chronicle. Edited by Edward Sabine. London: John Murray, 1821.

NORTON, Claire. "Would You Starve?" *Nature Magazine,* Vol. XXXV (June, July, 1942), 295-297.

Nova Scotia — Canada's Ocean Playground. Halifax, 1954.

NURSEY, Walter R. *The Story of Isaac Brock — Hero, Defender and Saviour of Upper Canada.* Toronto: William Briggs, 1909.

NUTE, Grace Lee. *Voyageur.* New York: Appleton, 1931.

O'BRIEN, Andy. *Headline Hockey.* Toronto: Ryerson, 1963.

O'DONNELL, John H. *Manitoba as I Saw It—From 1869 to Date.* Toronto: Musson, 1909.

The Official Guide to the Klondyke Country. ... Chicago: Wabash Publishing House, 1897.

OGDEN, Peter Skene. *Oregon Historical Quarterly,* Vols. X and XI.

———. *Peter Skene Ogden's Snake Country Journals, 1824-25 and 1825-26.* Hudson's Bay Record Society Publications XIII. London, 1950.

———. *Peter Skene Ogden's Snake Country Journals, 1826-27.* Hudson's Bay Record Society Publications XXIII. London, 1961.

OGILVIE, William. *Early Days on the Yukon — The Story of Its Gold Finds.* Ottawa: Thorburn & Abbott, 1913.

O'HAGAN, Howard. *Tay John.* London: Laidlaw & Laidlaw, 1939.

OLDMIXON, John. *The British Empire in America — Containing the History of the Discovery, Settlement, Progress and State of the British Colonies on the Continent and Islands of America.* 2 vols. London: John Nicholson, 1708.

O'LEARY, Peter. *Travels and Experiences in Canada, the Red River Territory, and the United States.* London: John B. Day, 1877.

OLSEN, Sigurd. *Runes of the North.* New York: Knopf, 1963.

O'MEARA, Frederick A. *Report of a Mission to the Ottahwahs and Ojibwas, of Lake Huron.* London: Society for the Propagation of the Gospel, 1846.

O'MEARA, Walter. *The Grand Portage.* New York: Bobbs-Merrill, 1951; New York: Bantam, 1952.

ONRAET, Tony. *Sixty Below.* New York: Didier, 1948.

ONSLOW, John. *Bowler-Hatted Cowboy.* Edinburgh: Blackwood, 1962.

Ontario Department of Mines. Report on Fatal Accidents. Toronto, 1956.

Ontario — Great Ontario Adventure Vacations. Toronto: Dept of Tourism & Information, 1965.

Ontario High School Physical Geography. Toronto: Macmillan, 1902.

Ontario Mines Accident Report. 67th Annual Report Ontario Department of Mines. Toronto, 1959.

Opening Address, National Liberal Convention. By Hon. James Sinclair. Ottawa, Jan. 15, 1958.

Opportunities in the Forests and Forest Industries of B.C. 9th ed. Vancouver: Cdn Forestry Assn of B.C., 1964. [Booklet]

O'RELL, Max (pseud. of Paul Blouet). *John Bull & Co. — The Great Colonial Branches of the Firm: Canada, Australia, New Zealand and South Africa.* London: Frederick Warne, 1894.

ORMSBY, Margaret A. *British Columbia—A History.* Toronto: Macmillan, 1958.

OSBORN, E. B. *Greater Canada—The Past, Present and Future of the Canadian North-West.* London: Chatto & Windus, 1900.

———. "Warders of the West," *Cornhill Magazine*, June, 1900, pp. 774-787.

OSBORN, Sherard. *Stray Leaves from an Arctic Journal.* London: Longman, Brown, Green, & Longman, 1852. [Written, 1850-51]

OSGOOD, Cornelius. *Winter.* New York: Norton, 1953.

OSTENSO, Martha. *Wild Geese.* Toronto: McClelland & Stewart, 1925.

OUTRAM, James. *In the Heart of the Canadian Rockies.* New York: Macmillan, 1905.

OXENDEN, Ashton. *My First Year in Canada.* London: Hatchards, 1871.

OXLEY, J. Macdonald. *Chore-Boy of Camp Kippewa.* Philadelphia: American Baptist Publishing Society, 1891.

———. *The Wreckers of Sable Island.* Philadelphia: American Baptist Publishing Society, 1891.

———. *The Young Nor'-Wester.* Toronto: Musson, 1908. [First published as *Archie of Athabasca.* Boston: Lothrop, 1893; also as *Archie M'Kenzie — The Young Nor'-Wester.* London: Religious Tract Society, 1894]

PACKARD, Alpheus Spring. *The Labrador Coast — a Journal of Two Summer Cruises.* New York: N.D.C. Hodges, 1891.

PALLISER, John. *Journals, Detailed Reports and Observations Relative to the Exploration, by Captain Palliser . . . between the Western Shore of Lake Superior and the Pacific Ocean during the Years 1857, 1858, 1859, and 1860.* London: Eyre & Spottiswoode, 1863.

———. *Papers Relative to the Exploration by Captain Palliser of that Portion of British North America which Lies between the River Saskatchewan. . . .* Vol. I. London: Eyre & Spottiswoode, 1859.

PALMER, A. *Montreal Confidential.* Toronto: Export Publishing Enterprises, 1950.

PALMER, F. *In the Klondyke—Including an Account of a Winter's Journey to Dawson.* New York: Scribner, 1899.

PALMER, Joel. *Journal of Travels over the Rocky Mountains. . . .* Cincinnati: J. A. & U. P. James, 1847.

PALMER, John. *Journal of Travels in the United States of North America, and in Lower Canada, Performed in the Year 1817.* London: Sherwood, Neely and Jones, 1818.

Papers Relating to the Red River Settlement, 1815-1819. London, 1819.

Papers Relative to the Affairs of British Columbia. London: Eyre & Spottiswoode, 1859.

Papers Relative to the Exploration of the Country between Lake Superior and the Red River Settlement. London, 1859.

PARHAM, H. J. *A Nature Lover in British Columbia.* London: Witherby, 1937.

PARKER, Sir H. Gilbert. *An Adventurer of the North — Being a Continuation of* PIERRE AND HIS PEOPLE. London: Nelson, n.d. [First published, London: Methuen, 1895]

———. *The Lane that Had No Turning—and Other Tales Concerning the People of Pontiac; together with Certain "Parables of Prov."* New York: A.L. Burt, 1899.

———. *The Money Master — Being the Curious History of Jean Jacques Barbille, his Labours, his Loves and his Ladies.* New York: Harper, 1915. [Copyright, Hearst Magazines, 1913]

———. *Northern Lights.* Toronto: Copp Clark, 1909.

———. *Pierre and His People — Tales of the Far North.* New York: Stone & Kimball, 1896; Toronto: Copp Clark, 1897. [First published, London: Methuen, 1892]

———. *The Pomp of the Lavilettes.* New York: Lamson, Wolffe, 1896.

———. *The Power and the Glory — A Romance of the Great La Salle.* Toronto: Copp Clark, 1925.

———. *The Right of Way — Being the Story of Charley Steele and Another.* Toronto: Copp Clark, 1901.

———. *A Romany of the Snows — Second Series of* AN ADVENTURE OF THE NORTH. *Being a Continuation of* PIERRE AND HIS PEOPLE. New York: Stone & Kimball, 1896.

———. *The Translation of a Savage.* New York: Appleton, 1899. [First published, 1893]

———. *When Valmond Came to Pontiac — The Story of a Lost Napoleon.* Toronto: Copp Clark, 1898.

———. *The World for Sale.* Toronto: S. B. Gundy, 1916.

PARKER, Samuel. *Journal of an Exploring Tour beyond the Rocky Mountains. . . .* New York: Privately printed, 1838.

PARKMAN, Francis. "Champlain and His Associates," in *Pioneers of France in the New World.* Boston, 1865.

———. *The Jesuits in North America in the Seventeenth Century. Second Part of France & England in North America.* Cambridge, Mass.: Harvard Univ. Press, 1895. [First published, 1867]

PARRISH, Randall. *Beyond the Frontier.* New York: A. L. Burt, 1915.

PARTRIDGE, Basil. *Chaplet of Grace.* Philadelphia: Westminster Press, 1956.

PARTRIDGE, Eric. *Dictionary of Slang and Unconventional English.* London: Routledge & Kegan Paul, 1937 and 1949.

PATTERSON, G. "Notes on the Folklore and Dialect of Newfoundland," *Journal of American Folklore*, Vol. VIII (1895), 27-40.

PATTERSON, George. *More Studies in Nova Scotia History.* Halifax: Imperial Publishing Co., 1941.

PATTERSON, R. M. *The Dangerous River.* London: George Allen & Unwin, 1954; New York: Sloane, 1954.

———. *Far Pastures.* Sidney, B.C.: Campbell, 1963.

———. "Peace River Passage," *Beaver*, Outfit 287 (Winter, 1956), 15-19.

———. *Trail to the Interior.* New York: Morrow, 1966.

PATTERSON, W. J. *Dominion of Canada.* Montreal: D. Bentley, 1883.

PATTILLO, Thomas R. *Moose-Hunting, Salmon-Fishing, and Other Sketches of Sport — Being the Record of Personal Experiences in Hunting Wild Game in Canada.* London: Sampson Low, Marston, 1902.

PAYETTE, B.C., ed. *The Northwest.* Montreal: Privately printed, 1964.

PECKHAM, Sir George. *A True Reporte, of the late discoueries, and possession, taken in the right of the Crowne of Englande, of the New-found Landes. . . .* London: John Hinde, 1583.

P.E.I. See *Prince Edward Island.*

PEMBERTON, J. Despard. *Facts and Figures Relating to Vancouver Island and British Columbia.* 1860.

PENHALLOW, D. P. *A Manual of the More Common Herbaceous Plants of Quebec and Ontario — For Use in Connection with Groom's Botany.* Toronto: Copp Clark, 1899.

PENNANT, Thomas. *Arctic Zoology.* Vol. I. London: Henry Hughs, 1784. [Preface dated 1785]

————. *History of Quadrupeds.* 2 vols. London: B. & J. White, 1781.

————. *Supplement to the Arctic Zoology.* London: Henry Hughs, 1787.

Peoples of the Northwest Territories. Ottawa: Dept. of Northern Affairs and National Resources, 1954.

PERKINS, Simeon. *Diary of Simeon Perkins, 1790-96.* Toronto: Champlain Society, 1961.

PERLEY, Moses Henry. *Reports on the Sea and River Fisheries of New Brunswick.* 2nd ed. Fredericton: Queen's Printer, 1852.

PERRY, Clay. *The Two Reds of Travoy — An Adventure Story.* Toronto: Nelson, 1928.

PETERSON, Len. *Chipmunk.* Toronto: McClelland & Stewart, 1949.

PHILIP, Alex. *The Crimson West.* Toronto: Allen, 1925.

————. *The Painted Cliff.* Ottawa: Graphic Publishers, 1927.

PHILLIPS, Alan. *The Living Legend — The Story of the Royal Canadian Mounted Police.* Boston: Little, Brown, 1954.

PHILLIPS, C. E. *The Development of Education in Canada.* Toronto: Gage, 1957.

PHILLIPS, P. C., and J. Smurr. *The Fur Trade.* 2 vols. Norman, Okla: Univ. of Oklahoma Press, 1961.

PHILLIPPS-WOLLEY, Clive O. *Gold, Gold in Cariboo! A Story of Adventure in British Columbia.* London: Blackie, 1894.

————. *Songs from a Young Man's Land.* Toronto: Thomas Allen, 1917.

————. *A Sportsman's Eden.* London: Richard Bentley, 1888.

PHINNEY, Marguerite. *Famous Yarmouth Recipes.* 2nd ed. Yarmouth, N.S.: Ladies Auxiliary to Y.M.C.A., 1951.

PHIPPS, Constantine John (2nd Baron Mulgrave). *A Voyage towards the North Pole, undertaken by His Majesty's Command, 1773.* London: J. Nourse, 1774.

PICHON, Thomas. *Genuine Letters and Memoirs, Relating to the Natural, Civil, and Commercial History of the Islands of Cape Breton, and Saint John. . . .* London: J. Nourse, 1760.

PICKERING, J. *Emigration, or No Emigration: Being the Narrative of the Author (an English Farmer) from the Year 1824 to 1830.* London: Longman Rees, 1830. See also next entry.

————. *Inquiries of an Emigrant.* London: Wilson, 1832. [3rd ed. of preceding entry]

PICKTHALL, Marjorie. *The Bridge — A Story of the Great Lakes.* London: Hodder & Stoughton, [1922].

PIKE, Warburton. *The Barren Ground of Northern Canada.* London: Macmillan, 1892.

————. *Through the Subarctic Forest — A Record of a Canoe Journey from Fort Wrangel to the Pelly Lakes and down the Yukon River to the Behring Sea.* London: Edward Arnold, 1896.

PINKERTON, Kathrene Sutherland (Gedney). *Three's a Crew.* New York: Carrick & Evans, 1940.

————. *Wilderness Wife.* New York: Carrick & Evans, 1939.

PINKERTON, Robert E. *The Fourth Norwood.* Toronto: Copp Clark, 1923.

Placer Mining in British Columbia. 1863.

POCOCK, H. R. A. "The Laurentides," in W. D. LIGHTHALL, *Songs of the Great Dominion*, p. 355. See above.

POCOCK, Roger. *A Man in the Open.* Toronto: McLeod & Allen, 1912.

POIRIER, Pascal. *Glossaire Acadien.* Université Saint-Joseph, New Brunswick, 1953.

POLLARD, William C. *Life on the Frontier — A Sketch of the Parry Sound Colonists.* London: A. H. Stockwell, n.d. [c1900]. See also next entry.

————. *Pioneering in the Prairie West.* 2nd ed. of *Life on the Frontier.* Uxbridge, Ont.: Cave, 1925. [1926 edition read]

POND, Peter. "Narrative 1765-1775," in C. M. GATES, *Five Fur Traders. . . .* See above.

POOLE, Francis. *Queen Charlotte Islands — A Narrative of Discovery and Adventure in the North Pacific.* London: Hurst & Blackett, 1872. [Based on diaries, 1862-63]

POOLE, Michael. *The Secret of Lotos Island.* Toronto: Musson, 1939.

PORSILD, Alf Erling. *Illustrated Flora of the Canadian Arctic.* National Museum of Canada Bulletin 146. Ottawa, 1957.

PRATT, E. J. *Newfoundland Verse.* Toronto: Ryerson, 1923.

PRESTON, Jack (pseud. of J. P. Buschlen). *Finding His Balance; or, The Bank Clerk Who Came Back.* Toronto: Stevenson & Hevey, 1915.

PRESTON, Richard A. *Kingston before the War of 1812.* Champlain Society Publications (Ontario Series). Toronto, 1959.

PRESTON, T. R. *Three Years' Residence in Canada.* 2 vols. London: Richard Bentley, 1840.

PRESTON, W. T. R. *Strathcona and the Making of Canada.* New York: Condé, Nast, 1915. [First published as *The Life and Times of Lord Strathcona.* Toronto: McClelland & Stewart, 1914]

PRICE, Julius M. *From Euston to Klondike.* London: Sampson Low, Marston, 1898.

PRICE, Mrs. Carl, and Clyde C. Kennedy. *Notes on the History of Renfrew County.* Pembroke, Ont.: Renfrew County Council, 1961.

PRICE-BROWN, John. *In the Van; or, The Builders.* Toronto: McLeod & Allen, 1906.

PRICHARD, James Cowles. *Researches into the Physical History of Mankind.* 4th ed., London: Sherwood, Gilbert, & Piper, 1841, Vol. I; 1847, Vol. V.

Prince Edward Island, Canada — Road Map & Tourist Guide. Charlottetown: P.E.I. Travel Bureau, 1964.

PRINGLE, A. L. *The Home of Evangeline—Before and After Longfellow's Poem.* London: Angelus, 1911.

PRINGLE, George C. F. *Tillicums of the Trail — Being Klondike Yarns Told to Canadian Soldiers Overseas by a Sourdough Padre.* Toronto: McClelland & Stewart, 1922.

PRITCHARD, John. *Glimpses of the Past in the Red River Settlement — From Letters . . . 1805-1836.* Edited by George Bryce. Middlechurch, Man.: Rupert's Land Indian Industrial School Press, 1892.

Problems of American Geology. See W. N. RICE.

Proceedings of Committee. See *A Short Narrative....*

Prospecting in Canada. Ottawa: Canadian Legion Educational Services, 1944.

Prospectus. Victoria: Meteor Mining Co., 1966.

Proud Procession. 7th ed. Toronto: Dent, 1954.

"Provincial Elections Act," in *Revised Statutes of British Columbia.* Victoria, 1960.

Provincial Voters Act. See preceding entry.

PUGSLEY, Wm. H. *Saints, Sinners and Ordinary Seamen.* Toronto: Collins, 1945.

[*Pulp and Paper.*] *About Pulp and Paper — Canada's National Industry.* Toronto: Abitibi Power & Paper, n.d. [c1963]. [Pamphlet]

PURDY, Alfred W. *Emu, Remember!* Fredericton: Univ. of New Brunswick, 1956.

———. *The Enchanted Echo.* Vancouver: Clarke & Stewart, 1944.

PUTNAM, Donald F. *Canadian Regions: A Geography of Canada.* Toronto: Dent, 1952.

QUANCE, Frank. *The Canadian Speller — Grade 6.* Toronto: Gage, 1930.

QUAYSIDER (pseud. of James Evans). *Recollections; or, Incidents Culled from the Lives of Some of Our Sea-Faring Men.* Berwick-on-Tweed: Privately printed, 1908.

RADCLIFF, Thomas, ed. *Authentic Letters from Upper Canada.* Toronto: Macmillan, 1953. [First published, Dublin: William Curry, 1833]

RADDALL, Thomas Head. *The Governor's Lady.* Garden City, N.Y.: Doubleday, 1960.

———. *Hangman's Beach.* Garden City, N.Y.: Doubleday, 1966.

———. *His Majesty's Yankees.* Toronto: McClelland & Stewart, 1942; Garden City, N.Y.: Doubleday, 1942.

———. *A Muster of Arms and Other Stories.* Toronto: McClelland & Stewart, 1954.

———. *The Nymph and the Lamp.* Boston: Little, Brown, 1950; New York: Popular Library, 1952.

———. *Pied Piper of Dipper Creek and Other Tales.* Toronto: Copp Clark, 1943.

———. *Pride's Fancy.* Toronto: McClelland & Stewart, 1946.

———. *Roger Sudden.* Garden City, N.Y.: Doubleday, Doran, 1944.

———. *The Rover—The Story of a Canadian Privateer.* Toronto: Macmillan, 1958.

———. *Tidefall.* Toronto: McClelland & Stewart, 1953.

———. *Wings of the Night.* New York: Doubleday, 1956.

RADIN, P. *Some Myths and Tales of the Ojibwa of S. E. Ontario.* Geological Survey of Canada Memoir 48. Ottawa, 1914.

RADISSON, Pierre Esprit. *Voyages of Peter Esprit Radisson — Being an Account of his Travels and Experiences among the North American Indians, from 1652 to 1684.* Edited by Gideon D. Scull. Boston: The Prince

Society, 1885. [Sometimes cited as *Fourth Voyage*]

RAE, Herbert (pseud. of George H. R. Gibson). *Maple Leaves in Flanders Fields.* London: Smith, Elder, 1916.

RAE, John. *Correspondence with the Hudson's Bay Company on Arctic Exploration, 1844-1855.* Edited by E. E. Rich. Hudson's Bay Record Society Publications XVI. London, 1953.

———. "Journey from Great Bear Lake to Wollaston Land," *Journal Royal Geographical Society*, Vol. XXII (1852), 73-82. [Written, 1851]

———. "Recent Explorations along the South and East Coast of Victoria Land," *Journal Royal Geographical Society*, Vol. XXII (1852), 82-96. [Written, 1851]

RAMSEY, Bruce. *Barkerville — A Guide in Word and Picture to the Fabulous Gold Camp of the Cariboo.* Vancouver: Mitchell Press, 1960.

RAND, Austin L. *Mammals of the Eastern Rockies and Western Plains of Canada.* National Museum of Canada Bulletin 108. Ottawa, 1948. [Sometimes erroneously cited as 1945]

———. *Mammals of Yukon, Canada.* National Museum of Canada Bulletin 100. Ottawa, 1945.

RAND, Theodore H., ed. *A Treasury of Canadian Verse.* 2nd ed. Toronto: William Briggs, 1904. [First edition, 1900]

RANDALL, Jack, as told to Meigs O. Frost. *I'm Alone.* Indianapolis: Bobbs-Merrill, 1930.

RASMUSSEN, Knud. *Observations on the Intellectual Culture of the Caribou Eskimos.* Copenhagen: Gyldendalske Boghandel, 1930.

RATHBORNE, St. George. *Canoe Mates in Canada; or, Afloat on the Saskatchewan.* Chicago: Goldsmith, 1912.

RATTRAY, W. J. *The Scot in British North America.* 4 vols. Toronto: Maclear, 1880-1884.

READ, David B. *The Lives of the Judges of Upper Canada and Ontario from 1791 to the Present Time.* Toronto: Rowsell & Hutchison, 1888.

Real Estate and Business Trends in Metropolitan Vancouver and British Columbia. Vancouver: Vancouver Real Estate Board, 1960. [Published annually]

REEKS, Henry. *A List of the Flowering Plants and Ferns of Newfoundland with Meteorological Observations.* 1873.

REEVE, Winifred E. *His Royal Nibs.* New York: A. L. Burt, 1925.

REEVES, John. *History of the Government of the Island of Newfoundland.* London: J. Sewell, 1793.

Regional Index of British Columbia. Victoria: Bureau of Economics and Statistics, 1966. [Published at irregular intervals]

REID, J. H. S., et al. *A Sourcebook of Canadian History.* See J. H. STEWART REID.

REID, Mayne. *The Young Voyageurs; or, The Boy Hunters in the North.* London: Routledge, 1853.

REID, Wallace Q. *Bluewater Landing.* Toronto: Collins, 1945.

———. *The Doctor of the North.* Toronto: Collins, 1946.

RELANDER, Click. *Drummers and Dreamers.* Caldwell, Idaho: Caxton Press, 1956.

Report from the Select Committee on the Hudson's Bay

Company, together with the Proceedings of the Committee, Minutes of Evidence, Appendix and Index. Westminster, England, 1857.

Report of DME Test Team Operations, Fort Churchill, Manitoba, Winter Trials, Period 1948-49. Ottawa: Queen's Printer, 1949.

Report of the Expedition to Hudson Bay and Cumberland Gulf in the Steamship "Diana".... Ottawa: S. E. Dawson, 1898.

Report of the Government of British Columbia on the Subject of Indian Reserves. 1875.

Report of the Royal Commission on Indian Affairs for the Province of British Columbia. Victoria: Acme Press, 1916.

Reports of the Commissioners Appointed to Inquire into a Series of Accidents and Detentions on the Great Western Railway, Canada West, by Commission Bearing Date Nov. 3, 1854. Quebec, 1855.

Review of Historical Publications Relating to Canada. Univ. of Toronto Studies. Toronto: Univ. of Toronto Press, 1896-1918.

RICE, William North, et al. Problems on American Geology. New Haven: Yale Univ. Press, 1915.

RICH, E. E. The Hudson's Bay Company. Hudson's Bay Record Society Publications XXII. London, 1959.

RICHARD, Edouard. Acadia: Missing Links of a Lost Chapter of American History. 2 vols. New York: Home Book Co., 1895.

RICHARDSON, Evelyn M. (Fox). Desired Haven. Toronto: Ryerson, 1953.

———. From Norfolk to the Hawk. Halifax: Review Publishing Co., 1953.

———. Living Island. Toronto: Ryerson, 1965.

———. My Other Islands. Toronto: Ryerson, 1960.

———. No Small Tempest. Toronto: Ryerson, 1958.

———. We Keep a Light. Toronto: Ryerson, 1945.

RICHARDSON, Sir John. Arctic Searching Expedition. New York: Harper, 1852.

———. Fauna Boreali-Americana; or the Zoology of the Northern Part of British-America, Containing Descriptions of the Objects of Natural History Collected on the Late Northern Land Expedition, under Command of Sir John Franklin, R.N. London: J. Murray, 1829-37.

RICHARDSON, John "Wacousta," in Selected Stories from Canadian Prose. See below. [First published, 1832]

———. Canadian Prose. See preceding entry.

RICHARDSON, R. L. Colin of the Ninth Concession — A Tale of Scottish Pioneer Life in Eastern Ontario. Toronto: Morang, 1903.

RICHLER, Mordecai. Incomparable Atuk. Toronto: McClelland & Stewart, 1963.

... Rise, the True North. Ottawa: Department of Northern Affairs & National Resources, n.d. [c1962].

RIVARD, Adjutor. Chez Nous (Our Old Quebec Home). Translated by W. H. Blake. Toronto: McClelland & Stewart, 1924.

ROBBINS, John E. Canada Between Covers. An address to the Rotary Club of Ottawa, Jan. 7, 1957. MS.

ROBERTS, Sir Charles G. D. Around the Camp-Fire. Toronto: Musson, n.d. [First published, New York: Crowell, 1896]

———. The Backwoodsman. New York: Macmillan, 1926. [First published, 1909]

———. The Kindred of the Wild — A Book of Animal Life. 1953. [First published, Boston: L. C. Page, 1902]

———. More Animal Stories. Toronto: Dent, 1922.

———. Red Fox — The Story of his Adventurous Career. New York: Teen Age Books, 1957. [First published, Boston: L. C. Page, 1905]

———. The Watchers of the Trails — A Book of Animal Life. New York: A. Wessels, 1904.

ROBERTS, Dorothy. "The Dappled Mare," in Rubaboo, pp. 162-172. Toronto: Gage, 1962.

ROBERTS, Leslie. The Mackenzie. Rivers of America Series. Toronto: Rinehart, 1949.

ROBERTS, Morley. Western Avernus. London: Smith, Elder, 1887.

ROBERTSON, Colin. Correspondence Book, Sept., 1817-Sept., 1822. Edited by E. E. Rich. Hudson's Bay Record Society Publications II. London, 1939.

ROBERTSON, J. Ross, ed. The Diary of Mrs. Simcoe. See Elizabeth P. SIMCOE.

ROBERTSON, William Norrie. Yukon Memories. Toronto: Hunter Rose, 1930.

ROBINS, John D., ed. A Pocketful of Canada. Toronto: Collins, 1952. [First published, 1946]

ROBINS, John D. and Margaret V. Ray, eds. A Book of Canadian Humour. Toronto: Ryerson, 1951.

ROBINSON, D. J. Transactions of the Fifteenth British Columbia Natural Resources Conference, February 26-28, 1964, Victoria, B.C. Vancouver, 1964.

ROBINSON, Edward Colpitts. In an Unknown Land. London: Elliot Stock, 1909.

ROBINSON, H. M. The Great Fur Land; or, Sketches of Life in the Hudson's Bay Territory. London: Sampson Low, Marston, Searle, 1879.

ROBINSON, John, and T. Rispin. "Journey through Nova Scotia," in Report of the Board of Trustees of the Public Archives of Nova Scotia, pp. 26-57. Halifax: King's Printer, 1945. [First published, York, 1774]

ROBINSON, Leigh Burpee. Esquimalt, Place of Shoaling Waters. Victoria: Quality Press, 1947. [Cited as 1948]

ROBSON, Joseph. An Account of Six Years Residence in Hudson's Bay, from 1733 to 1736, and 1744 to 1747. London: J. Payne & J. Bouquet, 1752.

ROCHE, Bill, ed. The Hockey Book. Toronto: McClelland & Stewart, 1953.

ROE, F. G. The North American Buffalo — A Critical Study of the Species in Its Wild State. Toronto: Univ. of Toronto Press, 1951.

———. Some Notes on Professional Canadian Railroad Terms. 1965. MS.

ROE, Vingie E. The Maid of the Whispering Hills. Toronto: William Briggs, 1913. [First published, New York: Dodd, Mead, 1912]

ROGER, Charles. Quebec: As It Was, and As It Is.... Quebec, 1857. [Early editions, prior to 5th ed. of 1867, appeared under the name of Willis Russell]

ROGERS, Grace Dean. Joan at Halfway. Toronto: McClelland & Stewart, 1919.

ROGERS, Sir John G. Sport in Vancouver and Newfoundland. London: Bell, 1912.

ROGERS, Julia E. Wild Animals Every Child Should Know. New York: Grosset & Dunlap, 1911.

ROLPH, Dr. Thomas. A brief account together with observations made during a visit in the West Indies, and a tour through the United States of America in parts of the years 1832, 1833, together with a statistical account of Upper Canada. Dundas, U.C.: Privately printed, 1836.

ROLYAT, Jane. *The Lily of Fort Garry*. Toronto: Dent, 1930.

————. *Wilderness Walls*. Toronto: Dent, 1933.

ROLYAT. *Stump Farm*. See ROSE.

ROPER, Edward. *By Track and Trail — A Journey through Canada*. London: W. H. Allen, 1891.

RORKE, Louise R. *Lefty — A Story of a Boy and a Dog*. Toronto: Nelson, 1931.

ROSE, Hilda. *The Stump Farm — A Chronicle of Pioneering*. Boston: Little, Brown, 1931. [First published, 1928]

ROSS, Alexander. *Adventures of the First Settlers on the Oregon or Columbia River — Being a Narrative of the Expedition Fitted out by John Jacob Astor. . . .* London: Smith, Elder, 1849. [Preface dated 1846]

————. *The Fur Hunters of the Far West*. Edited by K. A. Spaulding. Norman, Okla: Univ. of Oklahoma Press, 1956. [First published, London: Smith, Elder, 1855]

————. *The Red River Settlement. . . .* London: Smith, Elder, 1856.

ROSS, Donald. *Daily Journal of Donald Ross, 1833-35*. Vancouver Public Library MSS.

ROSS, Donald. "Athabasca Brigade," in *Alberta Historical Review*, Spring, 1956.

ROSS, Sir John. *Last Voyage of Capt. J. Ross*. London, 1835.

————. *Narrative of the Recent Voyage of Captain Ross to the Arctic Regions . . . .* New York: Wiley & Long, 1835.

————. *Narrative of a Second Voyage in Search of a North West Passage, and of a Residence in the Arctic Regions during the Years 1829, 1830, 1831, 1832, and 1833*. London, 1835.

————. *A Voyage of Discovery Made under the Orders of the Admiralty, in His Majesty's Ships Isabella and Alexander, for the Purpose of Exploring Baffin's Bay and Inquiring into the Probability of a North-west Passage*. London: John Murray, 1819.

ROSS, Norman M. *Tree Planting on the Prairies of Manitoba, Saskatchewan and Alberta*. Forestry Branch Bulletin 1. 5th ed. Ottawa, 1913.

ROSS, Victor. *Petroleum in Canada*. Toronto: Southam Press, 1917.

ROSS, W. A. *History of Zorra and Embro — Pioneer Sketches of Sixty Years Ago*. Embro, Ont.: Courier, 1909.

ROSS. *Totem Trail*. See Stanley ROUGH.

ROTHROCK, J. T. *Collin's Overland Expedition*. Letter to E. O. S. Scholefield, West Chester, Pennsylvania, 1913. Experiences in British Columbia with an Exploring Party for the Western Union Telegraph Company's Russian Extension, 1865-1866. B.C. Provincial Archives MSS. Also in A. W. SHIELS, *Seward's Ice Box*, pp. 349-364. See below.

ROUGH, Stanley, *et al. Along the Totem Trail; Port Essington to Hazelton*. Kitimat, B.C.: Privately printed, 1961.

ROUSSEAU, Jacques. *Origine du motif de la double courbe*. Ottawa, 1956.

————. "L'origine et l'evolution du mot esquimau," *Les Cahiers des Dix XX*, pp. 179-198. Montreal, 1955.

ROWAND, John. "Letter of John Rowand, Chief Factor for H. B. Co. at Ft Edmonton to Governor (Geo. Simpson) and other Officials of the Northern Department H. B. Co., Jan. 1, 1840," *Alberta Historical Review*, Winter, 1963.

ROWLANDS, John J. *Cache Lake Country — Life in the North Woods*. New York: Norton, 1947.

ROY, Jennet. *The History of Canada*. Montreal: Armour & Ramsay, 1850.

ROYAL, Charles E. *The Trail of a Sourdough — Rhymes and Ballads*. Toronto: McClelland & Stewart, 1919.

Rules and Regulations Respecting the Fisheries of Newfoundland, 1907. St. John's: Herald, 1907.

RUSSELL, Frank. *Explorations in the Far North . . . Being the Report of an Expedition under the Auspices of the University of Iowa during the Years 1892, '93 and '94*. Iowa City: Univ. of Iowa, 1898. [Preface dated 1896]

RUSSELL, Osborne. *Journal of a Trapper, 1834-43*. Oregon Historical Society, 1955.

RUSSELL, Peter. *Correspondence 1796-1799*. 3 vols. Toronto: Ontario Historical Society, 1932, Vol. I; 1935, Vol. II; 1936, Vol. III.

RUSSELL, Ralph C. *The Carlton Trail*. Saskatoon: Modern Press, 1955.

RUSSELL, S. M. *The Living Earth*. Toronto: Longmans, 1954.

RUSSELL, Sir William Howard. *Canada: Its Defences, Condition, and Resources*. Boston: Burnham, 1865.

RUSSELL, Willis. *Quebec: As It Was and As It Is*. See C. ROGER.

RYERSON, Adolphus Egerton. *The Story of My Life . . . Being Reminiscences of Sixty Years' Public Service in Canada*. Edited by J. George Hodgins. Toronto: William Briggs, 1883.

RYERSON, Stanley B. *The Founding of Canada — Beginnings to 1815*. Toronto: Progress Books, 1960.

————. *French Canada — A Study in Canadian Democracy*. Toronto: Progress Books, 1943.

SAGARD-THÉODAT, Gabriel. *The Long Journey to the Country of the Hurons*. Edited by G. M. Wrong; translated by H. H. Langton. Toronto, 1939.

Sailing Directions. See *Labrador and Banks Pilot*.

St. JOHN, Molyneux. *The Sea of Mountains — An Account of Lord Dufferin's Tour through British Columbia in 1876*. 2 vols. London: Hurst & Blackett, 1877.

St. MAUR, Mrs. Algernon. *Impressions of a Tenderfoot during a Journey in Search of Sport in the Far West*. London: John Murray, 1890. [Journal, written 1888]

ST. PIERRE, Paul. *Breaking Smith's Quarter Horse*. Toronto: Ryerson, 1966.

SALVERSON, Laura G. *Lord of the Silver Dragon — A Romance of Lief the Lucky*. Toronto: McClelland & Stewart, 1927.

————. *The Viking Heart*. Toronto: McClelland & Stewart, 1923.

————. *When Sparrows Fall*. Toronto: Thomas Allen, 1925.

SANDILANDS, John, ed. *Western Canadian Dictionary and Phrase Book. . . .* Winnipeg: Telegram Job Printers, 1912 and 1913.

Saskatchewan Fur Marketing Service Report. Regina: Saskatchewan Marketing Services. [Published annually]

Saskatchewan Journals. See *Cumberland and Hudson House Journals*.

SAUNDERS, Audrey. *Algonquin Story*. Toronto: Ontario Department of Lands and Forests, 1947. [1963 reprint read]

SAUNDERS, Charles F. *Useful Wild Plants of the United States and Canada*. New York: McBride, 1920.

SAUNDERS, Margaret Marshall. *Esther de Warren — The Story of a Mid-Victorian Maiden*. New York: Doran, 1927.

SAUNDERS, William. *Agricultural Colleges and Experimental Farm Stations*. Ottawa: 1886.

SAVIGNY, Annie G. *A Heart-Song of To-Day* (*Disturbed by Fire from The "Unruly Member"*). Toronto: Hunter, Rose, 1886.

SCHERCK, M. G. See M. G. SHERK.

SCHERMAN, Katherine. *Spring on an Arctic Island*. New York: Little, Brown, 1956.

School Building Manual. Victoria: Dept of Education, 1954 and 1962.

SCHOOLING, Sir William. *The Governor and Company of Adventurers of England Trading into Hudson's Bay during Two Hundred and Fifty Years, 1670-1920*. London: Hudson's Bay Company, 1920.

SCHULTZ, Christian, Jr. *Travels on an Inland Voyage*. 2 vols. New York: Isaac Riley, 1810.

SCHULTZ, J. W. *On the Warpath*. Boston: Houghton Mifflin, 1914.

———. *Rising Wolf — The White Blackfoot; Hugh Monroe's Story of His First Year on the Plains*. Boston: Houghton Mifflin, 1919. [Copyright, 1918]

SCOGGAN, H. J. *Flora of Manitoba*. National Museum of Canada Bulletin 140. Ottawa, 1957.

SCOTT, Duncan C. *The Witching of Elspie — A Book of Stories*. Toronto: McClelland & Stewart, 1923.

SCOTT, F. R., and A. J. M. Smith, eds. *The Blasted Pine — An Anthology of Satire, Invective & Disrespectful Verse Chiefly by Canadian Writers*. Toronto: Macmillan, 1957.

SCOTT, J. M. *The Story of Our Prairie Provinces*. Toronto: Dent, 1958.

SCOTT, S. O., and D. A. Mulligan. "The Red River Dialect," *Beaver*, Outfit 282 (Dec., 1951), 42.

SCOULER, John. "Observations of the Indigenous Tribes of the North West Coast of America," *Journal of the Royal Geographical Society*, Vol. XI (1841), 215-250.

SCUDDER, Samuel Hubbard. *The Winnipeg Country*. Boston: Cupples, Upham, 1886. [Used pseudonym "A. Rochester Fellow"]

Sea Fisheries of Eastern Canada — Being the Proceedings of the Committee on Fisheries, Game, and Fur Bearing Animals of the Commission of Conservation held at Ottawa, June 4-5, 1912. Ottawa: Mortimer, 1912.

SEARY, V. P. *Romance of the Maritime Provinces*. Toronto: Gage, 1931.

SEEMAN, Berthold C. *Narrative of the Voyage of H.M.S. Herald. . . .* 2 vols. London: Reeve, 1853.

Selected Stories from Canadian Prose. Toronto: Macmillan, 1929.

SELLAR, Gordon. *The Narrative of Gordon Sellar, who Emigrated to Canada in 1825*. Toronto: Britnell, 1916.

Senate Journal. See *Journals of the Senate of Canada*.

Senate Report. See *Journals of the Senate of Canada*.

SERVICE, Robert. *Ballads of a Cheechako*. Toronto: William Briggs, 1909; New York: Barse & Hopkins, 1909.

———. *Harper of Heaven — A Record of Radiant Living*. New York: Dodd, Mead, 1948.

———. *Songs of a Sourdough*. Toronto: William Briggs, 1907.

———. *The Trail of '98 — A Northland Romance*. Toronto: Ryerson, 1910.

SETON, E. T. *Animal Heroes*. New York: Grosset & Dunlap, n.d. [First published, New York: Curtis Publishing Co., 1903]

———. *The Arctic Prairies — A Canoe Journey of 2,000 Miles in Search of the Caribou. Being the Account of a Voyage to the Region North of Aylmer Lake. . . .* Toronto: William Briggs, 1911; New York: International University Press, 1943.

———. *Trail of an Artist-Naturalist—The Autobiography of Ernest Thompson Seton*. New York: Scribner, 1941.

———. *Wild Animals I Have Known and Two Hundred Drawings*. New York: Grosset & Dunlap, n.d. [First published, New York: Scribner, 1898]

———. *Woodcraft Manual for Girls*. New York, 1919.

———. *Woodmyth & Fable*. Toronto: William Briggs, 1905. [Copyrights, 1901-1904]

SETON-KARR, Hayward Walter. *Bear Hunting in the White Mountains; or, Alaska and British Columbia Revisited*. London: Chapman & Hall, 1891.

SETTLE, Dionyse. "A true reporte of Capteine Frobisher his last voyage into the west and northwest regions. . .," in Vilhjalmur Stefansson, *Three Voyages of Martin Frobisher*. See below. [First published, London: Henrie Middleton, 1577]

SHACKLETON, Edward. *Arctic Journeys — The Story of the Oxford University Ellesmere Land Expedition, 1934-5*. London: Hodder & Stoughton, 1937.

SHAFFER, Mary. *Old Indian Trails*. Toronto: William Briggs, 1911.

SHARP, Paul F. *Whoop-up Country*. Minneapolis: Univ. of Minnesota, 1955.

SHEPHERD, George. *West of Yesterday*. Edited by John H. Archer. Toronto: McClelland & Stewart, 1965.

SHERK, Michael G. *Pen Pictures of Early Pioneer Life in Upper Canada*. Toronto: William Briggs, 1905.

SHERMAN, Ralph S. *Mother Nature Stories*. Toronto: Dent, 1924.

SHERWOOD, Roland H. *Out of the Past — Vignettes of Historical Significance in Pictou County*. Truro, N.S.: Coastal Publishers, 1954.

SHIELS, Archibald Williamson. *Seward's Ice Box*. Bellingham, Wash.: Union Printing Co., 1933.

SHIPLEY, Nan. *Anna and the Indians*. Toronto: Ryerson, 1955.

———. *The Scarlet Lily*. Toronto: Ryerson, 1959.

SHIRREFF, P. *A Tour through North America; Together with a Comprehensive View of the Canadas and United States, as Adapted for Agricultural Emigration*. Edinburgh: Oliver & Boyd, 1835.

SHORT, Luke. *Barren Land Murders*. New York: Fawcett Publications, 1951. [First published as a magazine serial, 1940]

A short narrative and justification of the proceedings of the committee appointed by the adventurers, to prosecute the discovery of the passage to the western ocean of

America, and to open and extend the trade, and settle the countries beyond Hudson's Bay . . . to which are annexed the report and petitions referred to in the narrative. London: J. Robinson, 1749.

A short state of the countries and trade of North America claimed by the Hudson's Bay Company under pretence of a charter for ever, of lands without bounds or limits, and an exclusive trade to those enbounded seas and countries. . . . London: J. Robinson, 1749.

SIMCOE, Elizabeth P. *The Diary of Mrs. John Graves Simcoe . . . 1792-6.* Edited by J. Ross Robertson. Toronto: William Briggs, 1911.

SIMCOE, John Graves. *The Correspondence of Lieut-Governor John Graves Simcoe, with Allied Documents Relating to His Administration of the Government of Upper Canada.* Edited by E. A. Cruickshank. 5 vols. Toronto: Ontario Historical Society, 1923-1936.

SIMPSON, Sir George. *Athabasca Journal.* See below, *Journal of Occurrences. . . .*

———. *Fur Trade.* See F. MERK, *Fur Trade and Empire.*

———. *Journal.* See F. MERK, *Fur Trade and Empire.*

———. *Journal of Occurrences in the Athabasca Department by George Simpson, 1820 and 1821, and Report.* Edited by E. E. Rich. Hudson's Bay Record Society Publications I. London, 1938. [Cited as *Athabasca Journal*]

———. *Part of Dispatch . . . from George Simpson, Esqr., Governor of Rupert's Land, to the Governor and Committee of the Hudson's Bay Co. of London, 1829.* Champlain Society Publications X. Toronto, 1947.

SIMPSON, John. *The Western Eskimo.* London: John Murray, 1875.

SIMPSON, Thomas. *Narrative of the Discoveries of the North Coast of America.* London: Richard Bentley, 1843.

Simpsons-Sears Catalogue. Vancouver: Simpsons-Sears Ltd., Fall, 1963. [Published twice a year]

Simpsons-Sears Fall Sale Catalogue. Western ed. Regina: Simpsons-Sears, 1966. [Published annually]

SINCLAIR, Bertrand William. *Burned Bridges.* Boston: Little, Brown, 1919.

———. *The Hidden Places.* New York: A. L. Burt, 1922.

———. *North of Fifty-Three.* New York: Grosset & Dunlap, n.d. [First published, Boston: Little, Brown, 1914]

———. *Raw Gold.* Chicago: M. A. Donohue, 1908. [Copyright, 1907]

SKELTON, Oscar Douglas. *The Day of Sir Wilfrid Laurier — A Chronicle of Our Own Times.* Toronto: Glasgow, Brook, 1916.

———. *The Railway Builders.* Toronto: Glasgow, Brook, 1916.

SLATER, Patrick (pseud. of John Mitchell). *The Yellow Briar — A Story of the Irish on the Canadian Countryside.* Toronto: Thomas Allen, 1933. [Written, 1924]

SLEIGH, B. W. A. *Pine Forests and Hacmatack Clearings; or, Travel, Life, and Adventure in the British North American Provinces.* London: Richard Bentley, 1853.

SLOBODIN, Richard. *Band Organization of the Peel River Kutchin.* National Museum of Canada Bulletin 179. Ottawa, 1962.

SLUMAN, Norma. *Blackfoot Crossing.* Toronto: Ryerson, 1959.

SMALL, H. Beaumont. *Chronicles of Canada.* Ottawa: G. E. Desbarats, 1868.

SMALLWOOD, J. R. *The New Newfoundland.* New York: Macmillan, 1930.

SMET, P. J. See P. J. De SMET.

SMETHURST, G. *A Narrative of an Extraordinary Escape Out of the Hands of the Indians, in the Gulph of St. Lawrence.* London, 1774.

SMITH, D. J. S. *The Citizen's Business — A Study of Law and Business Practice in British Columbia written for Young People.* Vancouver: Copp Clark, 1961.

SMITH, H. I. *Archaeological Collection from the Southern Interior of B.C.* Ottawa: King's Printer, 1913.

SMITH, J. Harry. *Newfoundland Holiday.* Toronto: Ryerson, 1952.

SMITH, Minnie. *Is It Just? A Tale of British Columbia Life.* Toronto: William Briggs, 1911.

SMITH, Philip H. *Acadia — A Lost Chapter in American History.* Pawling, N.Y.: Privately printed, 1884.

SMITH, William Loe. *The Pioneers of Old Ontario.* Toronto: Morang, 1923.

SMYTH, Sir David William. *A Short Topographical Description of His Majesty's Province of Upper Canada, in North America.* London: W. Faden, 1799.

SNOW, W. Parker. *Voyage of the Prince Albert in Search of Sir John Franklin. . . .* London: Longman, Brown, Green, & Longman, 1851. [Preface dated 1850]

SNYDER, L. L. *Arctic Birds of Canada.* Toronto: Univ. of Toronto Press, 1957.

SOCKETT, T., ed. *Emigration: Letters from Sussex Emigrants.* Petworth, England, 1833.

SOMERSET, H. Somers. *The Land of the Muskeg.* London: Heinemann, 1895.

SORELLE, Rupert P., and Charles W. Kitt. *Words — Spelling, Pronunciation, Definition, and Application.* Toronto: Gregg, 1929.

SOUTHESK, James Carnegie, Earl of. *Saskatchewan and the Rocky Mountains — Travel and Adventure through the Hudson's Bay Company's Territories, 1859-60.* Toronto, 1870; Edinburgh: Edmonston & Douglas, 1875.

SPECK, F. G. *Family Hunting Territories and Social Life of the Various Algonkian Bands of the Ottawa Valley.* National Museum of Canada Memoir 70. Ottawa, 1915.

———. *Myths and Folk-lore of the Timiskaming Algonquin and Timagami Ojibwa.* National Museum of Canada Memoir 71. Ottawa, 1915.

SPECK, Chief Henry. *Kwakiutl Art.* Vancouver: Indian Designs, 1964.

SPEDON, A. L. *Rambles among Bluenoses; or, Reminiscences of a Tour through New Brunswick and Nova Scotia.* Montreal, 1962.

SPINKS, William Ward. *Tales of the British Columbia Frontier.* Toronto: Ryerson, 1933.

SPOTTON, H. B., and A. Cosens. *Wild Plants of Canada.* Toronto: Gage, 1926.

SPROAT, Gilbert Malcolm. *Scenes and Studies of Savage Life.* London: Smith, Elder, 1868.

SPRY, Irene. *The Palliser Expedition — An Account of John Palliser's British North American Exploration Expedition, 1857-1860.* Toronto: Macmillan, 1963.

SQUIER, E. L. *On Autumn Trails and Adventures in Captivity.* Cleveland: International Fiction Library, 1923.

Standing Rules and Regulations of the Honble Hudson's Bay Company's Fur Trade Established by the Council for the Northern Department of Rupert's Land. Enacted in 1843.

STANLEY, George F. G. *The Birth of Western Canada.* Toronto: Univ. of Toronto Press, 1960. [First published, Longmans, Green, 1936]

———. *Canada's Soldiers — The Military History of an Unmilitary People.* Toronto: Macmillan, 1960.

———. *Louis Riel.* Toronto: Ryerson, 1963.

———. *The Story of Canada's Flag — A Historical Sketch.* Toronto: Ryerson, 1965.

STANLEY, George F. G., ed. *For Want of a Horse — Being a Journal of the Campaigns against the Americans in 1776 and 1777 Conducted from Canada by an Officer who Served with Lt. Gen. Burgoyne.* Sackville, N.B.: Tribune Press, 1961.

———. *In Search of the Magnetic North.* See John Henry LEFROY.

STANLEY, R. C. *The Story of Nickel.* Copper Cliff, Ont.: International Nickel Co. of Canada, 1932.

STANWELL-FLETCHER, Theodora. *Driftwood Valley.* Boston: Little, Brown, 1950. [Diary, written 1937-38]

———. *The Tundra World.* Toronto: McClelland & Stewart, 1952.

Statutes of British Columbia. Victoria: Queen's Printer, 1960.

STEAD, Robert. *The Cow Puncher.* Toronto: Musson, 1918.

———. *Dennison Grant — A Novel of To-day.* Toronto: Musson, 1920.

———. *Grain.* Toronto: McClelland & Stewart, 1926.

———. *The Homesteaders — A Novel of the Canadian West.* Toronto: Musson, 1916.

———. *Neighbours.* Toronto: Hodder & Stoughton, 1922.

STEARNS, W. A. *Labrador — a Sketch of Its Peoples, Its Industries, and Its Natural History.* Boston: Lee & Shephard, 1884.

STEELE, Harwood. *Ghosts Returning.* Toronto: Ryerson, 1950.

———. *Policing the Arctic — The Story of the Conquest of the Arctic by the Royal Canadian (formerly North-West) Mounted Police.* London: Jarrolds, 1936.

———. *Spirit-of-Iron (Manitou-pewabic) — An Authentic Novel of the Northwest Mounted Police.* Toronto: McClelland & Stewart, 1923.

STEELE, Samuel B. *Forty Years in Canada. Reminiscences of the Great North-West.* Toronto: McClelland & Stewart, 1914.

STEEVES, Dorothy G. *The Compassionate Rebel — Ernest E. Winch and His Times.* Vancouver: Boag Foundation, 1960.

STEFANSSON, Vilhjalmur. *Northwest to Fortune.* New York: Duell, Sloan & Pierce, 1958.

———. *Prehistoric and Present Commerce among the Arctic Coast Eskimo.* National Museum of Canada Bulletin 6. 1914.

———. *Three Voyages of Martin Frobisher — In Search of a Passage to Cathay and India by the North-West, A.D. 1576-8.* 2 vols. London: Argonaut Press, 1938.

STEGNER, Wallace. "The Making of Paths," *New Yorker,* Sept. 6, 1958, pp. 37-38.

STEPHEN, Alexander M., ed. *The Golden Treasury of Canadian Verse.* Toronto: Dent, 1928.

———. *The Voice of Canada — Canadian Prose & Poetry for Schools.* Toronto: Dent, 1927.

STEPHEN, Pamela. *Winged Canoes at Nootka, and Other Stories of the Evergreen Coast.* Vancouver: Dent, 1955.

STERNBERG, Charles H. *Hunting Dinosaurs in the Badlands of the Red Deer River, Alberta.* Lawrence, Kansas: Privately printed, 1917.

STEVENS, G. R. *The Incompleat Canadian — An Approach to a Social History.* Privately printed, 1965.

STEWART, Charles J. *A Short View of the Present State of the Eastern Townships in the Province of Lower Canada.* Montreal: Hatchard, 1815.

STEWART, John. *An Account of Prince Edward Island, in the Gulph of St. Lawrence, North America.* London: W. Winchester, 1806.

STEWART, Margaret, and Doris French. *Ask No Quarter — A Biography of Agnes Macphail.* Toronto: Longmans, Green, 1959.

STEWART REID, J. H., Kenneth McNaught, and Harry S. Crowe. *A Sourcebook of Canadian History.* Toronto: Longmans, Green, 1959.

STIRLING, Earl of. *Register of Royal Letters Relative to the Affairs of Scotland and Nova Scotia from 1615 to 1635.* 2 vols. Edinburgh, 1835.

STOCKWELL, C. H. *Geology and Economic Minerals of Canada.* 1957.

STOREY, Arthur G. *Prairie Harvest.* Toronto: Ryerson, 1959.

STORY, George M. *A Newfoundland Dialect Dictionary — A Survey of the Problems.* St. John's: Memorial Univ. of Newfoundland, 1956. [Booklet]

STRANG, Herbert, ed. *Pioneers in Canada—Explorers & Settlers in the Far North and West.* London: Hodder & Stoughton, 1935.

STRANGE, K. *With the West in Her Eyes — The Story of a Modern Pioneer.* Toronto: McLeod, 1945. [First published, 1937]

STRICKLAND, Samuel. *Twenty-Seven Years in Canada West; or, The Experience of an Early Settler.* Edited by Agnes Strickland. 2 vols. London: Richard Bentley, 1853.

STRINGER, Arthur J. A. *Empty Hands.* New York: A. L. Burt, 1924. [Copyright, 1923]

———. *Lonely O'Malley — A Story of Boy Life.* Toronto: McClelland & Stewart, 1924. [First published, Boston: Houghton, 1905]

———. *The Prairie Child.* Indianapolis: Bobbs-Merrill, 1922.

———. *The Prairie Mother.* Toronto: McClelland & Stewart, 1920.

———. *The Wife-Traders — A Tale of the North.* Winnipeg: Harlequin, 1955. [First published, Indianapolis: Bobbs-Merrill, 1936]

STUBBS, Philip. *Anatomie of Abuses.* London, 1583.

STURTEVANT, Edward Lewis. *Sturtevant's Notes on Edible Plants.* Albany, N.Y.: J. B. Lyon, State Printers, 1919.

STUTFIELD, Hugh E. M., and J. Norman Collie. *Climbs & Exploration in the Canadian Rockies.* London: Longmans, Green, 1903.

SULLIVAN, Alan. *The Cycle of the North.* London: Dent, 1938.

———. *The Great Divide — A Romance of the Canadian Pacific Railway.* London: Lovat, Dickson, & Thompson, 1935.

———. *Under the Northern Lights*. Toronto: Dent, 1926.

SUTHERLAND, George. *A Manual of the Geography and Natural and Civil History of Prince Edward Island*. Charlottetown: John Ross, 1861.

SUTHERLAND, Peter C. *Journal of a Voyage in Baffin's Bay and Barrow Straits . . . .* Vol. II. London: Longman, Brown, Green, & Longman, 1852.

SUTTON, George Miksch. *The Birds of Southampton Island*. Pittsburgh: Carnegie Institute, 1932.

———. *Eskimo Year — A Naturalist's Adventures in the Far North*. New York: Macmillan, 1934.

SUTTON, Horace. *Footloose in Canada*. Toronto: Rinehart, 1950.

SWANSON, Robert E. *A History of Railroad Logging*. Victoria: Dept of Commercial Transport, 1960. [Booklet]

———. *Rhymes of a Lumberjack — A Second Book of Verse*. Toronto: Thomas Allen, 1943.

———. *Rhymes of a Western Logger*. Vancouver: Lumberman Printing Co., 1942.

SWANSON, Robert E., and Dan Swanson. *Rhymes of a Haywire Hooker — A Book of Verse*. Vancouver: Lumberman Printing Co., 1953. [Used pseudonym "Seattle Red"]

SYMINGTON, Fraser. *Tuktu — A Question of Survival*. Ottawa: Queen's Printer, 1965.

SYMONS, Harry. *Fences*. Toronto: Ryerson, 1958.

SYMONS, R. D. *Many Trails*. Toronto: Longmans, Green, 1963.

TALBOT, Edward Allen. *Five Years' Residence in the Canadas*. 2 vols. London: Longman, Hurst, Rees, Orme, Brown & Green, 1824.

TALLBOOM. *Arctic Bridge*. See W. N. TOLBOOM.

TALMAN, J. J. *Basic Documents of Canadian History*. Toronto: Van Nostrand, 1959.

———. *Loyalist Narratives from Upper Canada*. Champlain Society Publications XXVII. Toronto, 1946.

TANNER, John. *Narrative of Captivity and Adventures during Thirty Years' Residence among the Indians in North America*. Prepared for the Press by Edwin James. New York, 1830; San Francisco, Calif.: California State Library, 1940.

TANNER, V. *Outlines of the Geography, Life & Customs of Newfoundland-Labrador — (The Eastern Part of the Labrador Peninsula)*. 2 vols. Cambridge: Cambridge Univ. Press, 1947.

TAVERNER, P. A. *Birds of Eastern Canada*. Rev. ed. National Museum of Canada Memoir 104. Ottawa, 1922.

———. *Birds of Western Canada*. National Museum of Canada Bulletin 41. Ottawa, 1928.

———. *Ornithological Investigations Near Belvedere, Alberta*. National Museum of Canada Bulletin 50. Ottawa, 1928. [Cited as *Belvedere, Alta*]

TAYLOR, G., D. J. Seiveright, and T. Lloyd. *Canada and Her Neighbours*. Rev. ed. Toronto: Ginn, 1959. [Sometimes cited as *Canada*]

TAYLOR, G. *Newfoundland — A Study of Settlements with Maps & Illustrations*. Toronto: Canadian Institute of International Affairs, 1946.

TAYLOR, Gladys. *Pine Roots*. Toronto: Ryerson, 1956.

TAYLOR, Griffith. *Canada — A Study of Cool Continental Environments and Their Effect on British and French Settlement*. London: Methuen, 1947; Toronto: Saunders, 1947. [Cited as *Canada*]

TAYLOR, H. C., and S. James. *Canadian Coins, Paper Currency, and Tokens*. Winnipeg: Canadian Numismatic Publishing Institute, 1964.

TAYLOR, James. *Narrative of a Voyage to and Travels in Upper Canada*. Hull, Que.: J. Nicholson, 1846.

TAYLOR, P. M. *Buckskin and Blackboard*. London: Darwin, Finlayson, 1955.

TEIT. *Tahltan Indians*. National Museum of Canada MSS. 1906.

TERRY, G. *History and Legends of the Chilcotin*. Williams Lake, B.C.: Privately printed, 1958.

THOMAS, Lowell J., and Rexford W. Barton. *In New Brunswick We'll Find It*. New York: Appleton-Century, 1939.

THOMAS, Lowell J., Jr. *Trail of Ninety-Eight*. New York: Duell, Sloan & Co., 1962.

THOMPSON, David. *Journals Relating to Montana and Adjacent Regions, 1808-1812*. Missoula, Mont.: Montana State University, 1950.

———. *Narrative of His Explorations in Western America, 1784-1812*. Edited by J. B. Tyrrell. Champlain Society Publications XIII. Toronto, 1916.

THOMPSON and Edgar. *Canadian Railway Development from the Earliest Times*. Toronto: Macmillan, 1933.

THOMSON, Edward W. "Old Man Savarin," in *Selected Stories from Canadian Prose*, pp. 192-207. See above. [First published in *Old Man Savarin, and Other Stories*. Toronto: William Briggs, 1895]

THOREAU, Henry David. *Maine Woods, 1864*. Boston: Riverside Edition, 1884-94.

THWAITES, R. G., ed. See *Jesuit Relations and Allied Documents*.

The Times Book of Canada. London: The Times, 1920.

To Klondike via Edmonton. 1897.

TOLBOOM, Wanda Neil. *Arctic Bride*. Toronto: Ryerson, 1956.

TOLFREY, Frederic. *The Sportsman in Canada*. 2 vols. London: T. C. Newby, 1845.

TOLMIE, William Fraser. *The Journals of William Fraser Tolmie — Physician and Fur Trader*. Edited by R. Large. Vancouver: Mitchell Press, 1963.

TOLMIE, W. Fraser, and George M. Dawson. *Comparative Vocabularies of the Indian Tribes of British Columbia . . .* Montreal: Dawson, 1884.

TONER, G. C. "Preliminary Studies of the Fishes of Eastern Ontario," in *Bulletin Eastern Ontario Fish and Game Protective Association, Supplement 2*. Gananoque, Ont., 1937.

Toronto Public Library MSS B104. See M. S. BIDWELL.

To the Lumber Workers. Sandon, B.C.: One Big Union, c1921. [Leaflet]

Touring Prince Edward Island—your Guide to Places of Interest, Scenic and Historic in Canada's Garden Province. Charlottetown: Provincial Travel Bureau, c1963.

TOWNLEY, Alice A. *Opinions of Mary*. Toronto: William Briggs, 1909.

TOWNSEND, Charles Wendell, ed. *Captain Cartwright and His Labrador Journal*. Boston: Dana Estes, 1911; London: Williams & Norgate, 1911.

TRACY, F. B. *Tercentenary History of Canada—From Champlain to Laurier*. 3 vols. Toronto: Collier, 1908.

TRAILL, Catherine Parr (Strickland). *The Backwoods of Canada — Being Letters from the Wife of an Emigrant Officer. Illustrative of the Domestic Economy of British America*. 3rd ed., London: C. Knight, 1838; Toronto: McClelland & Stewart, 1966. [Written, 1832-35. First published, London: C. Knight, 1836]

———. *The Canadian Crusoes — A Tale of the Rice Lake Plains*. Boston: Hall & Whiting, 1881. [First published, London: Hall, 1852]

TROW. "Manitoba and the North-West Territories in 1878," in R. C. RUSSELL, *The Carlton Trail*. See above.

Tsimshian. British Columbia Provincial Archives. MS. 1952.

TUCK, Esme. *A Brief History of Pouce Coupe Village and District, British Columbia, Canada*. Pouce Coupe, B.C.: Pouce Coupe Women's Inst., 1958.

TUCK, Leslie M. *The Murres*. Ottawa: Dept of Northern Affairs and National Resources, 1960.

TUFTS, Robie W. *Birds of Nova Scotia*. Halifax: Nova Scotia Museum, 1961.

———. "Migratory . . . Birds," *Chronicle-Herald* (Halifax), Feb. 5, 1965.

TUPPER, Sir Charles. *Recollections of Sixty Years in Canada*. Toronto: Bart-Cassell, 1914.

TURNER, D. B., ed. *Inventory of the Natural Resources of British Columbia*. Victoria: B.C. Natural Resources Conference, 1964.

TURNER, John P. *The North-West Mounted Police, 1873-1893*. Vol. II. Ottawa: Queen's Printer, 1956.

TURNER, Lucien M. *Ethnology of the Ungava District, Hudson Bay Territory*. Washington, D.C.: Smithsonian Institution, 1894.

TURNEY-HIGH, Harry Holbert. *Ethnography of the Kutenai*. American Anthropological Assn Memoir 56. Menasha, 1941.

TURNOR, Philip. *Journal*. See Samuel HEARNE and Philip Turnor.

TUTTLE, Charles R. *The Golden North — A Vast Country of Inexhaustible Gold Fields, and a Land of Illimitable Cereal and Stock Raising Capabilities*. Chicago: Rand McNally, 1897.

———. *Our North Land — Being a Full Account of the Canadian North-West and the Hudson's Bay Route, together with a Narrative of the Experiences of the Hudson's Bay Expedition of 1884 . . .* Toronto: C. Blackett Robinson, 1885.

TWEEDIE. "New Brunswick, Nova Scotia, & Newfoundland," *Dialect Notes*, 1895.

TWEEDSMUIR, John N. S. Buchan, 2nd baron. *Hudson's Bay Trader*. London: Clerke & Cockeran, 1951. [Diary, written 1938-39]

TWOMEY, Arthur C., and Nigel Herrick. *Needle to the North*. Boston: Houghton Mifflin, 1942.

TYLER, Patrick. *Progress of Discovery on the More Northern Coasts of America from the Earliest Period to the Present Time*. Edinburgh: Oliver & Boyd, 1833.

TYRE, Robert. *Saddlebag Surgeon*. Toronto: Dent, 1954.

TYRRELL, James W. *Across the Sub-Arctics of Canada — A Journey of 3200 Miles by Canoe and Snowshoe through the Hudson Bay Region*. Toronto: William Briggs, 1897 and 1908.

———. *Annual Report, Department of the Interior*, App. 26. Pt. III, pp. 17-18. 1901.

TYRRELL, Joseph B., ed. *Documents Relating to the Early History of Hudson Bay*. Champlain Society Publications XVIII. Toronto, 1931.

UMFREVILLE, Edward. *The Present State of Hudson's Bay, Containing a Full Description of that Settlement, and the Adjacent Country, and Likewise of the Fur Trade, with Hints for its Improvement . . .* London: Stalker, 1790.

United States War Department Arctic Manual. Washington, D.C., 1942.

UPTON, P. *The History of the Okanagan Mission. A Centennial Retrospect*. Okanagan Mission, B.C.: Centennial Committee, 1958.

VALLEE, F. G. *Kabloona and Eskimo in the Central Keewatin*. Ottawa: Dept of Northern Affairs & National Resources, 1962.

VAN DUSEN, Conrad. *The Indian Chief — An Account of the Labours, Losses, Sufferings and Oppressions of Ke-zig-ko-e-ne-ne (David Sawyer), a Chief of the Ojibbeway Indians in Canada West*. London: Nichols, 1867.

VARDY, O. *Labrador and Newfoundland*. St. Johns: Newfoundland Tourist Development Office, 1963.

———. *Western Newfoundland for Your Holiday*. St. John's: Tourist Development Office, 1964.

VAUGHAN, William. *The Golden Fleece Divided into Three Parts . . .* London: Francis Williams, 1626.

VAUGHAN, William. *The Importance and Advantage of Cape Breton*. London, 1746.

VINAY, J.-P. *Dictionnaire Canadienne — The Canadian Dictionary*. Concise Edition. Toronto: McClelland & Stewart, 1962.

WAAGEN, Mary E. *The Wayside Cross*. Toronto: Musson, 1929.

WADE, Mark S. *The Overlanders of '62*. Edited by John Hosie. Archives of B.C. Memoir 9. Victoria, 1931.

WALDEN A. T. *A Dog-Puncher on the Yukon*. London: T. Werner Laurie, 1928; Montreal: Louis Carrier, 1928.

WALDO, Fullerton. *Down the Mackenzie through the Great Lone Land*. New York: Macmillan, 1923.

WALDRON, Malcolm T. *Snow Man — John Hornby in the Barren Lands*. Boston: Houghton Mifflin, 1931.

WALKER, Frank N. *Sketches of Old Toronto*. Don Mills, Ont.: Longmans, 1965.

WALKER, Joan. *Pardon My Parka*. Winnipeg: Harlequin Books, 1958. [First published, Toronto: McClelland & Stewart, 1953]

WALLACE, D. *The Lure of the Labrador Wild*. 8th ed. New York: F. H. Revell, 1905.

WALLACE, Frederick W. *Captain Salvation*. Toronto: Musson, 1925.

———. *In the Wake of the Windships — Notes, Records, and Biographies*. Toronto: Musson, 1927.

———. *Roving Fisherman — An Autobiography*. Gardenvale, Que.: Canadian Fisherman, 1955.

———. *Salt Seas and Sailormen*. London: Hodder & Stoughton, 1922.

———. *The Shack Locker — Yarns of the Deep Sea Fishing Fleets*. Montreal: Industrial & Educational Press, 1916.

————. *Tea from China, and Other Yarns of the Sea.*
Toronto: Musson, 1926.

————. *Wooden Ships and Iron Men — The Story of the
Square-rigged Merchant Marine of British North
America* . . . Toronto: Hodder & Stoughton, 1924.
[First published, 1923]

WALLACE, William Stewart. *By Star and Compass —
Tales of the Explorers of Canada.* Toronto: Ryerson,
1953. [First published, Toronto: Oxford, 1922]

————. *The Encyclopedia of Canada.* 6 vols. Toronto:
University Associates of Canada, 1935.

————. *Family Compact — A Chronicle of the Rebellion
in Upper Canada.* Chronicles of Canada, Vol. 24.
Toronto: Glasgow Brook, 1915.

————. *A First Book of Canadian History.* Toronto:
Macmillan, 1928.

————. *The Pedlars from Quebec and Other Pares on
the Nor'Westers.* Toronto: Ryerson, 1954.

WALLACE, William Stewart, ed. *Documents Relating
to the North West Company.* Champlain Society Publications XXII. Toronto, 1934.

WALSHE, Elizabeth H. *Cedar Creek—From the
Shanty to the Settlement.* London: Religious Tract
Society, 1863.

WALWORTH, Arthur. *Cape Breton — Isle of Romance.*
Toronto: Longmans, 1948.

WARD, Edmund. *An Account of the River St. John,
with Its Tributary Rivers and Lakes.* Fredericton:
Sentinel Office, 1841.

WARD, Mary A. *Canadian Born.* London, 1910.

WARD, Norman. *The Canadian House of Commons.*
Toronto, 1950.

————. *Government in Canada.* Toronto: Gage, 1960.

WARKENTIN, John. *The Western Interior of Canada
— A Record of Geographical Discovery, 1612-1917.*
Toronto: McClelland & Stewart, 1964.

WASHBURNE, Heluiz Chandler. *Land of the Good
Shadows.* New York: John Day, 1940.

WASHINGTON, John. *Eskimaux and English Vocabulary, for the Use of the Arctic Expeditions.* London:
John Murray, 1850.

WATERS, Brian, ed. *Mr. Vessey of England.* New York,
1956.

WATSON, Ken. *Curling to Win.* Toronto: Stovel-
Advocate Publications, 1955.

WATSON, Robert. *My Brave and Gallant Gentleman —
A Romance of British Columbia.* Toronto: McClelland,
Goodchild & Stewart, 1918.

————. *The Spoilers of the Valley.* Toronto: McClelland
& Stewart, 1921.

WATSON, Sheila. *The Double Hook.* Toronto:
McClelland & Stewart, 1959.

WATSON, William R. *I Give You Yesterday.* Toronto:
Macmillan, 1938. [1940 edition read]

WATTERS, R. E., ed. *British Columbia — A Centennial
Anthology.* Toronto: McClelland & Stewart, 1958.

WAUGH, F. W. "Canadian Aboriginal Canoes," *Canadian Field Naturalist,* XXXIII (May, 1919), 23-33.

————. *Iroquis (!) Foods and Food Preparation.* Ottawa:
Government Printing Bureau, 1916.

WELD, Isaac. *Travels through the States of North
America, and the Provinces of Upper and Lower Canada,
during the Years 1795, 1796, and 1797.* Vol. I. 1800. [First
published, London, 1799]

WELLS, Kenneth McNeill. *Cruising the Georgian Bay.*
Toronto: Kingswood House, 1958.

————. *Cruising the North Channel.* Toronto: Kingswood House, 1960.

————. *Cruising the Trent-Severn Waterway.* Toronto:
Kingswood House, 1959.

————. *The Owl Pen.* Toronto: Dent, 1947.

WELLS, William B. *Canadiana — Containing Sketches
of Upper Canada, and the Crisis in Its Political Affairs.*
London: Privately printed, 1837.

WENTWORTH, Edward N. "Dried Meat — Early
Man's Travel Ration," in *Agricultural History,* XXX
(Jan., 1956), 2-10.

WENTWORTH, Harold, ed. *American Dialect Dictionary.* New York: Crowell, 1944.

WENTZEL, W. F. "Letters to the Hon. Roderick McKenzie, 1807-1824," in Vol. I of L. F. R. MASSON,
Les Bourgeois . . . , pp. 67-153. See above.

Western District Union. Convention Monograph (M.C.-
L & G) of Western District Union, International Union
of Mine, Mill and Smelter Workers (Canada). Vancouver, Jan., 1963. [Mimeographed]

WEST, John. *The Substance of a Journal during a Residence at the Red River Colony, British North America,
and Frequent Excursions among the Northwest American Indians, in the Years 1820, 1821, 1822, 1823.* London:
L. B. Seeley, 1824.

WESTLAND, Lynn. *Shooting Valley.* Winnipeg: Harlequin Books, 1953.

WHALLEY, George. *The Legend of John Hornby.*
London: John Murray, 1962.

*What Farmers Say of Their Personal Experiences in the
Canadian North-West.* 3rd ed. Ottawa: Dept of Agriculture, 1882.

WHEELER, Arthur O. *The Selkirk Mountains — a
Guide for Mountain Climbers and Pilgrims.* Winnipeg,
1912.

————. *The Selkirk Range.* Ottawa, 1905.

Where to Fish on Prince Edward Island. Charlottetown:
Tourist & Information Branch, c1963.

WHERRY, J. H. *The Totem Pole Indians.* New York:
Funk, 1964.

WHITBOURNE, Richard. *Discovrse and Discouery
of Nevv-fovnd-land.* London: Felix Kyngston & F. W.
Barrett, 1620.

————. *A Discovrse containing a Loving Invitation . . .
to all such as shall be Adventuerers . . . for the aduancement of his Maiesties most hopefull Plantation in the
Nevv-fovnd-land.* London: Felix Kyngston, 1622.

WHITE, Charles Langdon, and Edwin J. Foscue. *Regional Geography of Anglo-America.* 2nd ed. New York:
Prentice-Hall, 1954. [First published, 1943]

WHITE, Samuel A. *The Stampeder.* Toronto: William
Briggs, 1910.

————. *The Wildcatters — A Tale of Cobalt.* Toronto:
William Briggs, 1912.

WHITE, Stewart E. *The Blazed Trail.* Toronto: Morang,
1902.

————. *Call of the North.* New York: Triangle Books,
1941. [First published as *Conjuror's House,* 1902]

————. *The Forest.* New York: Nelson, 1903.

————. *The Riverman.* New York: Doubleday, 1919.
[First published, 1908]

BIBLIOGRAPHY   918

————. *The Silent Places.* Toronto: McLeod & Allen, 1907. [First published, Toronto: Morang, 1904]

————. *Skookum Chuck.* Toronto: S. B. Gundy, 1925.

————. *Stampede.* Garden City, N. Y.: Doubleday, Doran, 1910.

WHITEHOUSE, F. C. *Sport Fishes of Western Canada, and Some Others.* Toronto: McClelland & Stewart, 1946.

WHITNEY, Caspar. *On Snow-Shoes to the Barren Grounds.* New York: Harper, 1896.

WHITTAKER, Charles E. *Arctic Eskimo — A Record of Fifty Years' Experience & Observation among the Eskimo...* London: Seeley, Service, 1937.

WICKENS, A. Gordon. "Mary and the Patriarch," in *Rubaboo 2*, pp. 154-159. Toronto: Gage, 1963.

WIEDERMANN, T. *Cheechako into Sourdough.* Portland, Ore., 1942.

WIGHTMAN, Frederick A. *Our Canadian Heritage — Its Resources and Possibilities.* Toronto: William Briggs, 1905.

WILCOCKE, Samuel H. "Death of B. Frobisher," in Vol. II of L. F. R. MASSON, *Les Bourgeois . . .*, pp. 177-226. See above.

WILCOX, Walter. *The Rockies of Canada.* 3rd ed. New York: Putnam, 1909.

WILKIE, Sir David. *Sketches of a Summer Trip to New York and the Canadas.* Edinburgh, 1827.

WILKINSON, Anne. *Lions in the Way — A Discursive History of the Oslers.* Toronto: Macmillan, 1956.

WILKINSON, C. E. "*Abitibi*" — *Canadian Award Winning Film — Teaching and Discussion Guide.* Toronto: Abitibi Power & Paper Co., 1963.

WILLIAMS, Frank. *The Wilderness Trail.* New York: Grosset & Dunlap, 1913.

WILLIAMS, Helen E. *Spinning Wheels and Homespun.* Toronto: McClelland & Stewart, 1923.

WILLIS, N. P. *Canadian Scenery.* 2 vols. London: George Virtue, 1840-1842.

WILLSON, Beckles. *Great Company — A History of the Honourable Company of Merchants — Adventurers Trading into Hudson's Bay.* Toronto: Copp Clark, 1899.

————. "The Great Fur Company To-Day," *Cornhill Magazine*, Nov., 1900, pp. 660-668.

————. *Quebec — The Laurentian Province.* Toronto: Bell & Cockburn, 1912. [1913 edition read]

WILSON, Alexander. *American Ornithology.* 9 vols. Philadelphia: Bradford & Inskeep, 1808-1814.

WILSON, Amy V. *No Man Stands Alone.* Sidney, B.C.: Gray's Publishing, 1965.

WILSON, C., ed., *Northern Treasury.* Toronto: Nelson, 1958.

WILSON, Helen Dacey. *Tales from Barrett's Landing.* Toronto: McClelland & Stewart, 1964.

WILSON, John. *The Expulsions from the Ontario New Democratic Party.* Toronto: Committee to Defend Democracy in the NDP, 1963. [Pamphlet]

WILSON, L. *Chibougamau Venture.* Montreal: Chibougamau Publishing Co., 1952.

WILSON, V. *Guide to the Yukon Gold Fields.* Seattle: Calvert, 1897.

WILSON, William. *Newfoundland and Its Missionaries.* Cambridge, Mass.: Dakin & Metcalf, 1866.

WINDARD, Philip. "Early High River," *Alberta Historical Review*, IV (Summer, 1956), 15.

WINLOW, Alice, and Kathryn Pocklington. *The Mornin'-Glory Girl.* Toronto: McClelland & Stewart, 1920.

WINSLOW-SPRAGGE, Lois. *Life and Letters of George Mercier Dawson, 1849-1901.* Toronto, 1962.

WINSON, J. W. *Weather and Wings — Nature Essays.* Toronto: Nelson, 1932.

WINSOR, Justin. *Cartier to Frontenac—Geographical Discovery in the Interior of North America in Its Historical Relations, 1534-1700.* Boston: Houghton Mifflin, 1894.

WITHROW, W. H. *Our Own Country — Canada, Scenic and Descriptive.* Toronto: William Briggs, 1889.

WIX, Edward. *Six Months of a Newfoundland Missionary's Journal.* London: Smith, Elder, 1836. [Written, 1835]

WOOD, Kerry (pseud. of Edgar A. Wood). *Birds and Animals of the Rockies.* Hamilton: H. R. Larson, 1946.

WOOD, Ruth Kedzie. *The Tourist's Northwest.* New York: Dodd, Mead, 1916.

WOOD, William Charles Henry. *All Afloat—A Chronicle of Craft and Waterways.* Toronto: Brook, 1915.

WOODING, F. H. *The Angler's Book of Canadian Fishes.* Don Mills, Ont.: Collins, 1959.

WOODLEY, E. C. *The Bible in Canada — The Story of the British & Foreign Bible Society in Canada.* Toronto: Dent, 1953.

WOOLLACOTT, Arthur P. *Mackenzie and His Voyageurs — By Canoe to the Arctic and the Pacific, 1789-93.* London: Dent, 1927.

WOOLVERTON, Linus. *The Canadian Apple Grower's Guide.* Toronto: William Briggs, 1910.

WORCHESTER, J. E. *Todd's, Johnson's, and Walker's Pronouncing Dictionary.* Boston, c1837.

WORK, John. *Journal, Jan. to Oct., 1835.* British Columbia Provincial Archives, Memoir X. Victoria: Banfield, 1945.

————. *The Journal of John Work, a Chief Trader of the Hudson's Bay Co., during his Expedition from Vancouver Island to the Flatheads and Blackfeet of the Pacific Northwest.* Edited by William S. Lewis and Paul C. Phillips. Early Western Journals I. Cleveland, Ohio, 1923.

WORMINGTON, H. M., and Richard G. Forbis. "An Introduction to the Archaeology of Alberta, Canada," *Proceedings of the Denver Museum of Natural History*, No. XI (Aug., 1965), 170-172.

WRIGHT, E. C. *Blomidon Rose.* Toronto: Ryerson, 1957.

WRIGHT, Joseph, ed. *English Dialect Dictionary.* London: Henry Frowde, 1898-1905.

WRONG, George. *Ontario Public School History of Canada.* Toronto: Ryerson, 1926.

YALE, L. M., and J. G. A. Creighton. "Land of the Winanishe," *Scribner's Magazine*, Vol. V (May, 1889), 515.

YEIGH, Frank. *Ontario's Parliament Buildings.* Toronto: Williamson, 1893.

YOUNG, Egerton Ryerson. *By Canoe and Dog-Train Among the Cree and Salteaux Indians.* New York: Hunt & Eaton, 1891. [First published, Toronto, William Briggs, 1890]

————. *On the Indian Trail — Stories of Missionary Work among the Cree and Saulteaux Indians.* Toronto: F. H. Revell, 1897.

————. *Stories from Indian Wigwams & Northern Camp-Fires.* Toronto: William Briggs, 1893.

YOUNG, George. *Manitoba Memories . . . 1868-1884.* Toronto: William Briggs, 1897.

YOUNG, Katherine. *Stories of the Maple Land — Tales of the Early Days of Canada for Children.* Toronto: Copp Clark, 1898.

YOUNG, Scott. *The Flood.* Toronto: McClelland & Stewart, 1956.

Yukon, Its Riches and Romances. Ottawa: Dept of Northern Affairs & National Resources, n.d. [*c*1957] and 1962. [Booklet]

Yukon Telegraph Service. See G. LAWRENCE. *Forty Years on the Yukon Telegraph Service.*

Yukon Via Prince Albert. Prince Albert, Sask., 1898.

PERIODICALS

Acadiensis. St. John, N.B. Quarterly. (1901-08)

Advocate. Queenston, 1824. York and Queenston, 1824-33, as *Colonial Advocate.*

Agricultural History. Berkeley, Calif. Quarterly.

Aklavik Journal. Aklavik, N.W.T. Monthly.

Alaska Highway News. Fort St. John, B.C. Weekly.

Alaska Sportsman. Juneau, Alaska. Monthly.

Alberta Historical Review. Edmonton. Quarterly.

Alberta Home & School News. Calgary.

Alexandria Glengarrian. Alexandria, Ont. Weekly. (1884-1909) [1884-88, as *Glengarry Review*]

American Anthropologist. Lancaster, Pa. Bimonthly.

American Antiquarian Society Transactions and Collections. Worcester, Mass. Annual. (1820-1911) [1820-85, as *Archaeologia Americana Transactions and Collections*]

American Bureau of Ethnology. Annual Report.

American Journal of Physiology. Washington, D.C.

American Pioneer. Cincinnati. Monthly. (1842-43)

American Speech. New York. (Columbia Univ.) Quarterly.

Anglo-American Magazine. Boston, 1843. Toronto, 1852-55. New York, 1899-1902.

Annual Pictorial Review. Edmonton (Charles Camsell Indian Hospital).

Annual Report Smithsonian Institution. Washington, D.C.

Anthropological Records. Berkeley, Calif. Monthly.

Arctic Spotter. Edmonton. Monthly.

Argosy. Dayton, Ohio. Monthly.

Arthur Advocate, Mount Forest Express, Luther & Minto Journal. Arthur, Ont.

Ashcroft Journal and Lillooet District News. Ashcroft, B.C. Weekly.

Athabasca Echo. Athabasca, Alta. Weekly.

Athletic Life. Toronto. Monthly. (1895-96)

Atikokan Progress. Atikokan, Ont. Weekly.

Atlantic Advocate. Fredericton. Monthly.

.Aurora. Middle Church, Man.

Banner. Aurora, Ont. Weekly.

Barrie Gazette. Barrie, Ont. Weekly. (1868-1916)

Barrie Herald. Barrie, C. W. Weekly. (1852-57)

Barrie Magnet. Barrie, C. W. Weekly. (1847-54)

Bay News. Winnipeg. Monthly.

B.C. See *British Columbia.*

Beautiful B.C. Victoria. Quarterly.

Beaver. Winnipeg (Hudson's Bay Company). Quarterly.

Bee. Ottawa. Weekly.

Belleville Intelligencer. See *Ontario Intelligencer.*

Biz. Toronto.

Blackwood's Magazine. Edinburgh. Biannual.

Bond of Brotherhood. Calgary.

Bowmanville Canadian Statesman. See *Canadian Statesman.*

Bowmanville Star. Bowmanville, C. W. Weekly. (1854-57)

Bracebridge Northern Advocate and General Advertiser for the Free Grant Districts of Parry Sound. Bracebridge, Ont. Weekly. (1869-70)

Bradford Chronicle and General Advertiser. Bradford, C. W. Weekly. (1853-62)

Bradford South Simcoe Times. Bradford, Ont. Weekly.

Bradford Witness. See *Witness*.

Brampton Banner and Times. Brampton, Ont. Weekly. [1868-1902, as *Peel Banner*]

Brampton Progress. Brampton, Ont. Weekly. (1873-74)

Brandon Blade. Brandon, Man. Weekly. (1883-84)

Brandon Mail. Brandon, Man. Semiweekly. (1882-98)

Bridgewater Bulletin. Bridgewater, N.S. Weekly.

British-American Cultivator. Toronto. Monthly. (1842-47)

British American Journal. St. Catharines, U.C. Weekly. (1833-35) [1833-34, as *British Colonial Argus*]

British-American Register. Quebec. Weekly.

British Association for the Advancement of Science. London. (1898-1903)

British Canadian Review. Quebec. Monthly. (1862-63)

British Colonial Argus. St. Catharines, U.C. Weekly. (1833-34) [See *British American Journal*]

British Colonist. Toronto. Semiweekly. (1838-59)

British Colonist. Victoria. Semiweekly. [Became *Daily Colonist*]

British Colonist and St. Francis Gazette. Stanstead, Que. Weekly.

British Columbia Centennial Spokesman. Victoria.

British Columbia Digest. Quesnel, B.C. Bimonthly.

British Columbia Forest Industry Facts. Vancouver.

British Columbia Historical Quarterly. Victoria.

British Columbia Labour. Vancouver. Intermittent publication.

British Columbia Lumberman. Vancouver.

British Columbia Miner. See next entry.

British Columbia Mining Journal. Ashcroft, B.C. Weekly. (1895-99)

British Columbia Teacher. Vancouver. Monthly.

British Standard. Cookstown, Ont. Weekly. (1869-70)

Brockville Gazette. Brockville, U.C. Weekly. (1828-32)

Brockville Recorder. Brockville, Ont. Weekly.

Bush News. Port Arthur, Ont.

Bush News. St. Catharines, Ont.

Buzzer. Vancouver.

Bytown Gazette, and Ottawa and Rideau Advertiser. Bytown [Ottawa]. Weekly.

Bytown Independent and Farmers' Advocate. Bytown [Ottawa]. (1836)

Calgary Herald Magazine. See *Herald Magazine*.

Calgary Typo News. See *Typo News*.

Campbellton Tribune. Campbellton, N.B. Weekly.

Campus. Lennoxville, Que. (Bishop's University). Weekly.

Camp Worker. Vancouver. (1919)

Camsell Arrow. Edmonton (Charles Camsell Indian Hospital).

Canada Constellation. Niagara-on-the-Lake, U.C. Weekly. (1700-1800)

Canada Farmer. Toronto. Monthly. (1847 and 1864-76)

Canada Fisheries Research Board Journal. Toronto.

Canada Forward. Toronto. Weekly. (1926-27)

Canada Freeman. See *Canadian Freeman*.

Canada Month. Montreal. Monthly.

Canada Temperance Advocate. Montreal. Monthly. (1835-54)

Canadian. Toronto. Weekly.

Canadian Alpine Journal. Vancouver. Annual.

Canadian Audubon. Toronto. Bimonthly.

Canadian Aviation. Toronto. Monthly.

Canadian Boy. Toronto. Weekly.

Canadian Cattlemen. Winnipeg. Monthly.

Canadian Checkerist. Fortnightly. (1888)

Canadian Church Missionary Bulletin. Toronto.

Canadian Constellation. See *Canada Constellation*.

Canadian Correspondent. York, U.C. (1832-34)

Canadian Courant & Montreal Advertiser. Montreal. Semiweekly. (1807-34)

Canadian Farmer-Labor Advocate. Vancouver. Weekly. (1925)

Canadian Farmers' & Sun. London, Ont.

Canadian Field Naturalist. Ottawa. Quarterly.

Canadian Fisherman. Gardenvale, Que. Monthly.

Canadian Forest Industries. Don Mills, Ont. Monthly.

Canadian Forum. Toronto. Monthly.

Canadian Freeman. York, U.C., 1825-34. Chatham, C.W., 1848. Weekly.

Canadian Gentleman's Journal.

Canadian Geographer. Toronto. Quarterly.

Canadian Geographical Journal. Montreal & Ottawa. Monthly.

Canadian Girl. Toronto. Weekly.

Canadian Historical Review. Toronto. Quarterly.

Canadian Horticulturist. St. Catharines, Ont. Monthly. (1878-1913)

Canadian Illustrated Magazine. See *Canadian Illustrated News*.

Canadian Illustrated News. Montreal. Monthly. (1869-83)

Canadian Indian. Owen Sound, Ont. Monthly. (1890-91)

Canadian Journal of Corrections. Ottawa. Quarterly.

Canadian Journal of Linguistics. Toronto. Biannual. [Before 1961, as *Journal of the Canadian Linguistic Association*]

Canadian Journal of Science, Literature, & History. Toronto. Monthly. (1852-78)

Canadian Labor Advocate. Vancouver. Weekly. (1925-26)

Canadian Labor Defender. Toronto. Monthly. (1930-33)

Canadian Literary Magazine. York, U.C. Monthly. (1833)

Canadian Literature. Vancouver. Monthly.

Canadian Magazine. Toronto. Monthly. (1871-72)

The Canadian Mining Reporter. Toronto. Weekly. [After 1939, as *Canadian Financial and Mining Reporter*]

Canadian Monthly and National Review. (1872-78)

Canadian Naturalist and Geologist. Montreal. Monthly. (1856-1916) [After 1883, as *Canadian Record of Natural History & Geology*]

Canadian North West Historical Society Publications. Battleford, Sask. Occasional publication. (1926-31)

Canadian Peat Society. See *Journal of the Canadian Peat Society.*

Canadian Pulp and Paper Industry. Toronto. Monthly.

Canadian Record of Science, Including the Proceedings of the Natural History Society of Montreal & Replacing the Canadian Naturalist. Montreal. Monthly. (1884-1916)

Canadian Red Cross Junior. Toronto. Monthly. [Became *Junior Magazine.*]

Canadian Saturday Night. Toronto. Weekly. (1962-63)

Canadian Seaman. Vancouver. Bimonthly. (1944-45)

Canadian Statesman. Bowmanville, Ont. Weekly.

Canadian Temperance Advocate. See *Temperance Advocate.*

Canadian Tribune. See *Toronto Tribune.*

Canadian Unionist. Official Journal of the Canadian Congress of Labour. Hull, Que. Monthly (1927-56)

Canadian Watchman. Kingston, U.C. Weekly. (1830-32)

Canadian Weekly. Toronto.

Cariboo Observer. Quesnel, B.C. Weekly.

Cariboo Sentinel. Barkerville, B.C. Semiweekly & weekly. (1865-75)

Cataract Weekly. Grand Falls, N.B. Weekly.

CBC Times. Toronto, Winnipeg, and Vancouver. Weekly.

Champion. Toronto. Fortnightly.

Champlain Society Publications. Toronto. Occasional.

Chatelaine. Toronto. Monthly.

Chatham Banner-News. Chatham, Ont. Weekly. (1865-1921) [1865-1896, as *Chatham Banner*]

Chatham Journal. Chatham. Weekly.

Chauvin Chronicle. Chauvin, Alta. Weekly.

Christian Advocate. Park Ridge, Ill. Biweekly.

Christian Recorder. York, U.C. Monthly. (1819-21)

Christmas Echo. St. John's.

Chronicle. Kingston, U.C. Weekly. (1819-33)

Citizen. North Vancouver. Weekly.

Clinton New Era. Clinton, B.C. Weekly. (1865-1924)

Coast Guard. Shelburne, N.S. Weekly.

Cobourg Reformer. See *Reformer.*

Cobourg Sentinel. See *Sentinel-Star.*

Colborne Northumberland Pilot. See *Northumberland Pilot.*

Collections of the New Brunswick Historical Society. See *New Brunswick Historical Society Collections.*

Collingwood Enterprise. See *Enterprise-Bulletin.*

Collingwood Messenger. See *Messenger.*

Colonial Advocate, and Journal of Agriculture, Manufacture & Commerce. York, U.C. (1824-33)

Colonial Patriot. Pictou, N.S. Weekly. (1828-30)

Columbia. New Haven, Conn. (Knights of Columbus). Monthly.

Cominco Magazine. Trail, B.C. Monthly.

Commentator. Trail, B.C. Irregular publication. (1938-62)

Commercial Letter. Toronto (Canadian Imperial Bank of Commerce). Monthly.

Commonwealth. Regina. Weekly.

Comox District Free Press. Courtenay, B.C. Weekly.

Companion and Teacher. London, Ont.

Confidential Flash. Toronto. Weekly.

Cookstown British Standard. See *British Standard.*

Co-operative Consumer. A Journal of Co-operative Development and Education. Saskatoon. Semimonthly.

Co-op Grocery News Bulletin. Saskatoon (Federated Co-ops Ltd).

Cornwall Chronicle. Cornwall, Ont. Weekly.

Cornwall Economist. Cornwall, Ont. Weekly.

Cornwallis Ensign. Cornwallis, N.S. (H.M.C.S. Cornwallis). Weekly.

Cornwall Observer, and Eastern District General Advertiser. Cornwall, U.C. Weekly. (1832-48)

Correspondent & Advocate. Toronto. Weekly. (1832-37)

Country Guide. Winnipeg. Monthly.

Courant. See *Canadian Courant and Montreal Advertiser.*

Courier of Upper Canada. York. Weekly.

Cowichan Leader. Duncan, B.C. Weekly.

Crag & Canyon. Banff, Alta. Weekly.

Crowsnest. Ottawa (Queen's Printer). Monthly. (1948-65)

Culture. Quebec. Quarterly.

Cut Knife Grinder. Cut Knife, Sask. Weekly. (1943-58)

Dalhousie Gazette. Halifax. Weekly.

Dalhousie Review. Halifax. Quarterly.

Dauphin Herald & Press. Dauphin, Man. Semiweekly.

Dawson Creek Star. Dawson Creek, B.C.

Deer Park York Gazette. See *York Gazette* (Deer Park, Ont.).

Digby Courier. Digby, N.S. Weekly.

Distributor. Yellowknife, N.W.T. (Holy Trinity Church).

Dominion Illustrated. Montreal. Monthly. (1888-95)

Dominion Monthly. See *Dominion Illustrated.*

Duncan-Cowichan Leader. See *Cowichan Leader.*

Dundas Warden. Dundas, C.W.

Dundas Weekly Post. Dundas, U.C. Weekly. (1834-36)

Durham Standard, and County of Grey Advertiser. Durham, Ont. Weekly.

Echo of Niagara. Niagara-on-the-Lake, Ont. May 17, 1884.

Edmonton Sun. Edmonton. Weekly.

Elora Backwoodsman. Elora, Ont. Weekly.

Elora Express. See *Express.*

Emerson Journal. Emerson, Man. Weekly. (1895-1966)

Enterprise-Bulletin. Collingwood, Ont. Weekly.

Examiner. Toronto. Weekly. (1840-55)

Explorer. Toronto (United Church Publishing House & Baptist Publications). Weekly.

Express. Elora, Ont. Weekly.

Eye Opener. High River, Alta, 1902-04. Calgary, 1904-22. Weekly. [Irregular]

Family Herald. Montreal. Bimonthly.

Farmers' Journal. St. Catharines, U.C. (1826-35)

Farmer's Sun. Toronto. Weekly. (1892-1930)

Farming Today. Dearborn, Mich. (Massey-Ferguson Industries Ltd). Monthly. (1940?-57)

Farm News Press Clip Sheet. Ottawa (Dept of Agriculture).

Field, Horse & Rodeo. Calgary. Monthly.

Field and Stream. New York. Monthly.

The Financial Post. Toronto. Weekly.

Fish and Game. Calgary. Bimonthly.

Fisheries Research Board Journal. See *Canada Fisheries Research Board Journal*.

Fisherman. Vancouver. Three times monthly.

Fishermen's Advocate. Port Union, Nfld. Weekly.

Flash. See *Confidential Flash*.

Flin Flon Miner. Flin Flon, Man. Weekly. (1931-66)

Fort George Herald. See *Prince George Herald*.

Free Press Weekly Farmers' Advocate. Winnipeg. Weekly.

Free Press Weekly Prairie Farmer. See *Free Press Weekly Farmers' Advocate*.

Fundy Fisherman. Black's Harbour, N.B. Fortnightly.

Fur Market Bulletin. Vancouver. Occasional publication.

Fur Trade Journal of Canada. Bewdley, Ont. Monthly.

Game Trails in Canada. Vancouver. Monthly. (1939-41) [1937-39, as *Game Trails in British Columbia*]

Garland. Hamilton, U.C. Semimonthly. (1832-33)

Gateway Express. Emerson, Man.

Gauntlet. Calgary (Univ. of Calgary). Weekly.

Gentleman's Magazine. London, Eng. Monthly. (1731-1907)

Geographical Review. New York. Quarterly.

Gilbert Plains Maple Leaf. Gilbert Plains, Man. Weekly.

Glaslyn Chronicle. Glaslyn, Sask.

Gleaner. Huntingdon, Que. Weekly. [1863-1912, as *Canadian Gleaner*]

Gleaner. Niagara, U.C. Weekly. (1817-37)

Globe Magazine. Toronto. Weekly.

Gore Gazette, and Ancaster, Hamilton, Dundas & Flamborough Advertiser. Ancaster, U.C. Weekly. (1827-29)

Gow Ganda Tribune. Gow Ganda, Ont.

Granby Gazette and Shefford County Advertiser. Granby, Que. Weekly. (1855-78)

Great Western Railway Advertising Bulletin. Toronto. Occasional publication.

Greenwood Miner. Greenwood, B.C. Weekly. (1899-1901)

Grip. Toronto. Bi-annual. (1873-94)

Grumbler. Toronto. Weekly. (1858-1869)

Guelph Advertiser and County of Waterloo Advocate. Guelph, Ont. Weekly. (1848?-54)

Guelph Mercury. See *Guelph Weekly Mercury*.

Guelph Weekly Mercury. Guelph, Ont. (1854-1927)

Gulf Islander. Galiano, B.C.

Gun and Rod in New Brunswick. Montreal. Monthly.

Hamilton Enquirer. See *Ingersoll Enquirer*.

Hamilton Free Press. Hamilton, U.C. Weekly. (1831-37)

Hamilton Gazette. Hamilton, U.C. Semiweekly. (1835-56)

Hamilton Ingersoll Chronicle. See *Ingersoll Chronicle and County of Oxford Intelligencer*.

Hamilton Journal Express. See *Journal and Express*.

Hamilton Morn Banner. See *Reform Banner* . . . .

Hamilton News. See *Ingersoll News*.

Hamilton Times. Hamilton, Ont. (1858-1920).

Hansard's Parliamentary Debates. Ottawa. Daily (during session).

Hants Journal. Windsor, N.S. Weekly.

Happy Motoring. Toronto (Imperial Oil Ltd). Bimonthly.

Harbor Grace Standard. Harbor Grace, Nfld. Weekly.

Harmac News. Vancouver (MacMillan Bloedel Ltd). Bimonthly.

Harper's New Monthly Magazine. New York. Monthly.

Herald Magazine. Calgary. Weekly.

High River Times. See *Times* (High River, Alta).

Hockey Canada. Melville, Sask. Monthly.

Hockey Illustrated. New York. Monthly.

Hockey News. Montreal. Weekly.

Holiday. Philadelphia, Pa. Monthly.

Holiday Inn Magazine. Memphis, Tenn. Monthly.

Home and School News. Lethbridge, Alta.

Horizons. Toronto. Monthly.

Hudson's Bay Record Society Publications. London.

Hunter-Trader-Trapper. Columbus, Ohio. (1900-40)

Huntingdon Gleaner. Huntingdon, Que. Weekly.

Huntingdon Herald. Huntingdon, Que. Weekly. (1860-62)

Hunt's Merchants' Magazine. New York. Monthly. (1839-70)

Huron Expositor. Seaforth, Ont. Weekly.

Huron Signal. Goderich, Ont. Weekly.

Imperial Oil Review. Toronto (Imperial Oil Ltd). Bimonthly.

Independent. Vancouver. Weekly. (1899-1904)

Indian. Hagersville, Ont. Monthly. (1885-86)

Indian-Eskimo Association Bulletin. Toronto. Five times yearly.

Indian News. Ottawa. Quarterly.

In Flight. Montreal (Air Canada). Occasional.

Ingersoll Chronicle and County of Oxford Intelligencer. Ingersoll, Ont. Weekly. (1853-1921)

Ingersoll Enquirer. Ingersoll, Ont. Weekly. (1863-73)

Ingersoll News. Ingersoll, Ont. Weekly. (1867-68 ?)

Insider Reports. Toronto.

Irish Vindicator. Montreal. See *Vindicator*.

Islander. Victoria. Weekly.

Islander, or Prince Edward Island Weekly Intelligencer and Advertiser. Charlottetown, P.E.I. Weekly. (1842-72)

Jack Canuck. Toronto. Weekly.

Journal and Express. Hamilton, U.C. Weekly. (1836-58)

Journal of Education for Upper Canada. Toronto. Monthly. (1848-67)

Journal of the Canadian Linguistic Association. Beauceville, Que. Biannual. (1954-61) [Became *Canadian Journal of Linguistics*]

Journal of the Canadian Peat Society. Ottawa. Monthly. (1911-16)

Journal of the House of Assembly of Newfoundland. St. John's. Sessional.

Junior Magazine. Toronto. Monthly. [Formerly, *Canadian Red Cross Junior*]

Kaslo Claim. Kaslo, B.C.

Kelvington Radio. Kelvinton, Sask. Weekly.

The Killarney Guide. Killarney, Man. Weekly.

Kingston Chronicle. See *Chronicle.*

Kingston Herald. See *Upper Canada Herald.*

Kingston News. Kingston, Ont. Weekly. (1906-07)

Kingston Watchman. See *Canadian Watchman.*

Klondike Nugget. Dawson, Y.T.

Klondike Miner. Dawson, Y.T.

Klondike Miner. Grand Forks, Y.T.

Kootenaian. Kaslo, B.C. Weekly.

Labor Statesman. Vancouver (Vancouver & District Labour Council). Monthly.

Lardeau Eagle. Ferguson, B.C. Weekly. (1900-04)

Leader. Oak Bay. See *Oak Bay Leader.*

Leaflet. Vancouver (Pulp & Paper Workers of Canada). Monthly.

The Ledge. New Denver, B.C. Weekly. (1897-1904)

Legionary. Ottawa. Monthly.

Liberal. St. Thomas, U.C. Weekly.

Liberal. Hamilton, Ont.

Liberty. Toronto. Monthly.

Lightning Express. Elora, Ont. Weekly. [Became *Express*]

Literary Garland. Montreal. Monthly. (1838-52)

Literary Miscellany. Hamilton, U.C. Biweekly.

Log of the Columbia. Rock Bay, B.C. Irregular publication.

London Advertiser. London, Ont. Daily (1866). Weekly (1875-7).

London Historical Society Transactions. See next entry.

London & Middlesex Historical Society Transactions. London, Ont. Monthly.

Loyalist. York, U.C. See *United Empire Loyalist.*

Lumber Worker. Sudbury, Ont. Monthly. (1925-34)

Machinists' Bulletin. Winnipeg.

Mackenzies' Weekly Message. Toronto. (1852-60)

Maclean's Magazine. Toronto. Biweekly. [Since 1967, monthly]

Mainland Guardian. New Westminster, B.C.

Manitoba Liberal. Winnipeg. See *Weekly Manitoba Liberal.*

Manitoban. Winnipeg. Biweekly.

Manitoulin Expositor. Little Current, Manitoulin Island, Ont. Weekly.

Maple Ridge-Pitt Meadows Gazette. Maple Ridge-Pitt Meadows, B.C.

Maritime Monthly. St. John, N.B. Monthly. (1873-75)

The Marker. Kingston, Ont. (Royal Military College).

The Martlet. Victoria (Univ. of Victoria).

Meadow Lake Progress. Meadow Lake, Sask. Weekly.

Melville Advance. Melville, Sask. Weekly.

Mercury. Quebec. (1805-1903)

Messenger. Collingwood, Ont. Weekly. (1877-81)

Mine-Mill Herald. Toronto (International Union of Mine, Mill and Smelter Workers). Monthly.

Mine-Mill News. Sudbury, Ont. (Local 598, International Union of Mine, Mill and Smelter Workers). Biweekly.

Mirror. Toronto. See *Toronto Mirror.*

Missiskoui Standard. Frelighsburg, Que. Weekly. (1835-39)

Modern Instructor. Regina. Monthly.

Montreal Transcript. Semiweekly. (1836-65)

Moose Jaw News. Moose Jaw, Sask.

Mountaineer. Rocky Mountain House, Alta. Weekly.

Naicam Sentinel. Naicam, Sask. Weekly.

National Geographic Magazine. Washington, D.C. Monthly.

Native Voice. Vancouver. Monthly.

Natural History. New York (American Museum of Natural History). Monthly.

Nautical Magazine. Glasgow. Monthly.

Naval Chronicle. London. (1799-1818)

Naval Officers Association of Canada Journal. Monthly.

Neepawa Star. Neepawa, Man.

Neilburg Star. Neilburg, Sask.

New Brunswick Historical Society Collections. St. John. Occasional publication.

New Brunswick Magazine. St. John. Monthly. (1898-1899, 1904-1906)

New Commonwealth. Toronto. Monthly.

Newfoundland Quarterly. St. John.

New Frontiers. New York. Monthly.

New Party Newsletter. Ottawa.

News. Truro, N.S. Weekly.

News. Tweed, Ont. Weekly.

News & Sentinel. Amherst, N.S. Semiweekly.

Newsletter. Vancouver (MacMillan Bloedel Ltd). Monthly.

News of the North. Yellowknife. Weekly.

News-Optimist. North Battleford, Sask. Semiweekly.

News-Record. Clinton, Ont. Weekly. [Became *New Era*]

New Yorker. New York. Weekly.

Niagara Argus. Niagara, Ont. Weekly.

Niagara Chronicle. Niagara, Ont.

Niagara Mail. Niagara-on-the-Lake, C.W. (1840-70)

Niagara News. Niagara-on-the-Lake, C.W. Weekly. (1871-?)

Niagara Reporter. Niagara-on-the-Lake, U.C. Weekly.

Niagara Spectator. Niagara, U.C. Weekly.

Niagara Telegraph. Niagara, U.C. Weekly.

N.O.A.C. Journal. See *Naval Officers Association of Canada Journal.*

No Advance. Barrie, Ont.

North. Ottawa (Northern Administration Branch, Dept of Northern Affairs & National Resources). Bimonthly.

North American Notes & Queries. Quebec. Monthly. (1900-1901)

Northern Light. Bathurst, N.B. Weekly.

Northern Mail. The Pas, Man. Weekly.

Northern Miner. Toronto. Weekly.

North Hill News. Calgary. Weekly.

Northland News. Uranium City, Sask. Biweekly.

North Shore Leader. Newcastle, N.B. Weekly.

North Star. St. John's.

North Star. Yellowknife. Monthly.

Northumberland Pilot. Colborne, Ont. Weekly.

North Wellington Times. Elora, Ont.

Northwest Digest. Quesnel, B.C.

Northwest Territories Teachers Association Review. Fort Smith.

Nova Scotia Magazine. Halifax. Monthly. (1789-92)

Nova Scotia Miner. Glace Bay, N.S. Weekly.

Novascotian. Halifax. Weekly.

Oak Bay Leader. Victoria. Weekly.

Observer. Cowansville, Que.

Observer. Toronto. Weekly.

Occupational Health Bulletin. Ottawa. Monthly.

Oily Bird. North Burnaby, B.C. (O.C.A.W. Local 9-601). Monthly.

Okanagan Historical Society Reports. Vernon, B.C. Monthly.

One Big Union Bulletin. Winnipeg. Weekly. (1919-34)

Ontario Department of Lands and Forests News. Toronto.

Ontario Farmer. Toronto. Weekly. [1909-58, as part of *Farmers' Magazine*]

Ontario History. Toronto. Quarterly.

Ontario Timberworker. Sudbury, Ont., 1947-50. Port Arthur, Ont., 1951. Bimonthly.

Orange Lily. Bytown [Ottawa].

Oshaworker. Oshawa, Ont. (Local 22, United Automobile, Aircraft & Agricultural Implement Workers of America). Bimonthly.

Ottawa Advocate and Dalhousie and Sydenham Advertiser. Ottawa. Weekly.

Our Forest Children. Sault Ste. Marie, Ont. Monthly. (1887-90)

Outdoorsman. Campbellford, Ont.

Outing Magazine. New York. Monthly. (1882-1923)

Outlook. Middleton, N.S. Weekly.

Pacific Tribune. Vancouver. Weekly.

Packet. Bytown, U.C. Weekly. [After 1851, became *Ottawa Citizen*]

Palladium of British America and Upper Canada Mercantile Advertiser. Toronto. Weekly. (1837-39)

Patriot. Toronto. See *Toronto Patriot.*

Patriot and Farmer's Monitor. Toronto, Ont. Semiweekly.

Peace River Block News. Dawson Creek, B.C. Weekly.

Peace River Record. Peace River, Alta. Weekly. (1929-32)

Pennsylvania Magazine of History & Biography. Philadelphia, Pa. Quarterly.

Pentecostal Testimony. Toronto. Monthly.

Philosophical Transactions of the Royal Society. London. Monthly.

Picton Gazette. Picton, Ont. Semiweekly.

Pictou Advocate. Pictou, N.S. Weekly.

Playground Press. Burnaby, B.C. (Parks & Recreation Commission). Weekly.

Port Dover Maple Leaf. Port Dover, Ont. Weekly.

Powell River News. Powell River, B.C. Weekly.

Press. Vancouver. Monthly.

Prince Albert Times. Prince Albert, Sask. Weekly.

Prince Edward Island Magazine. Charlottetown. Monthly.

Prince Edward Island Register. Charlottetown. Weekly. (1823-30)

Prince George Herald. Prince George, B.C. Weekly. (1915-16)

Progress. Preeceville, Sask.

Progress. Rat Portage, Ont.

Progress-Enterprise. Lunenburg, N.S. Weekly.

Prospector. Lillooet, B.C.

Province. Victoria.

Qu'Appelle Vidette. See *Vidette.*

Quebec Gazette. Quebec. Weekly. (1764-1817)

Quebec Herald & Universal Miscellany. Quebec. Weekly and biweekly. (1788-93)

Quebec Mercury. See *Mercury.*

Queen's Quarterly; a Canadian Review. Kingston, Ont. (Queen's Univ.). Quarterly.

Rainy River Record. Rainy River, Ont. Weekly.

Rat Portage News and Lake of the Woods Mining Journal. Rat Portage, Man. (now Kenora, Ont.).

Record-Gazette. See *Peace River Record.*

Reform Banner & Railway Chronicles. Hamilton, C.W. Triweekly.

Reformer. Cobourg, U.C. Weekly. (1832-37)

Regina Journal. Regina. (1885-91)

Register. Berwick, N.S. Weekly.

Renfrew Mercury. Renfrew, Ont. Weekly.

Report and Collections of the Nova Scotia Historical Society. Halifax.

Reports of the Okanagan Historical Society. See *Okanagan Historical Society Reports.*

Representative. Leduc, Alta. Weekly.

Rod and Gun in Canada. Woodstock, Ont., Montreal, and Toronto (Canadian Forestry Association).

Royal Military College of Canada Calendar. Ottawa. Annual.

Royal Military College of Canada Review. Kingston, Ont. Semiannual.

Rosetown Eagle. Rosetown, Sask. Weekly.

Rudder. New York.

Sackville Tribune-Post. Sackville, N.S.

St. Catharines Constitutional. St. Catharines, Ont. (1850-71)

St. Catharines Journal. St. Catharines, Ont. Weekly. (1835-1915)

St. Nicholas. New York. Monthly.

Saskatchewan Fur Marketing Service Report. Regina (Saskatchewan Marketing Services). Annual.

Saskatchewan Herald. Battleford, N.W.T. (now Sask.).

Saskatchewan Highway News. Regina.

Saskatchewan History. Saskatoon (Saskatchewan Archives Board). Three issues a year.

Saskatchewan News. Regina. Fortnightly.

Saturday Evening Post. Philadelphia. Weekly.

Saturday Night. Toronto. Monthly.

Searchlight. Montreal.

Sechelt Peninsula Times. Sechelt Peninsula, B.C. Weekly.

Selkirk Herald. Selkirk, Man.

Sentinel-Courier. Pilot Mound, Man. Weekly.

Sentinel-Star. Cobourg, Ont. Weekly.

Shawinigan Standard. See *Standard*.

Skyline Trail. Montreal (Skyline Trail Hikers of the Canadian Rockies).

Slocan Pioneer. Slocan, B.C.

Spectator. Annapolis Royal, N.S.

Spectator. St. Catharines, U.C.

Spectator. St. David's, U.C. Weekly.

Spotter. Edmonton (R.C.A.F. Ground Observer Corps Detachment). Monthly. [After 1957, as *Arctic Spotter*]

Springhill Record. Springhill, N.S. Weekly.

Standard. Elliot Lake, Ont.

Standard. Shawinigan Falls, Que. Weekly.

Star. Val d'Or, Que. See *Val d'Or Star*.

Star City Echo. Star City, Sask. Weekly.

Star Weekly. Toronto.

Statesman. Brockville, U.C.

Statesman. Kingston, C.W.

Steel Labor (Cdn ed.). Indianapolis, Ind. Monthly.

Stettler Independent. Stettler, Alta. Weekly.

Story Hour. Toronto (United Church Publishing House). Monthly.

Summerside Journal. Summerside, P.E.I. Weekly.

Sun. Picton, C.W.

Temiskaming Speaker. New Liskeard, Ont.

Temperance Advocate. Brampton, Ont. Monthly. (1902-46)

Temperance Advocate. Toronto.

Thunder Bay Sentinel. Port Arthur, Ont. Weekly. (1875-95)

Thunder Bay Times. Prince Arthur, Ont. (now Port Arthur).

Thunderbolt. Toronto. (1939)

Time (Cdn ed.). Montreal. Weekly.

Times. High River, Alta. Weekly.

Times. Halifax.

Toronto Mirror. Weekly. (1842-66)

Toronto Patriot. Weekly. (1839-55)

Toronto Saturday Night. Weekly. (1887-1952) [Became *Saturday Night*]

Toronto Tribune. Weekly. (1875-86)

Tourist of Woods. Kingston, C.W.

Town Crier. North Vancouver, B.C.

Trade News. Ottawa (Dept of Fisheries). Monthly.

Trail Riders. Montreal (Trail Riders of the Canadian Rockies).

Transactions of the American Antiquarian Society. See *American Antiquarian Society Transactions and Collections*.

Transactions of the Linnean Society of London. London.

Transactions of the Literary and Historical Society of Quebec. Quebec. Irregular publication. (1829-61 and 1863-1924)

Transactions of the Manitoba Historical Society. (Historical and Scientific Society of Manitoba). Winnipeg. Annual.

Transactions of the Royal Society of Canada. Ottawa.

Traveller. Hallowell, U.C. Weekly. (1836-37)

Tribune. Windsor, N.S. Weekly.

Tribune Post. Sackville, N.B. Weekly.

Truro Weekly News. See *News* (Truro, N.S.).

Tweed News. See *News* (Tweed, Ont.).

Typo News. Calgary. Weekly. (1935)

U.B.C. Reports. Vancouver. Monthly.

Ubyssey. Vancouver (Univ. of British Columbia). Three times weekly.

UE Canadian News. Toronto (District Five Council, United Electrical, Radio & Machine Workers of America). Weekly.

Ukrainian Canadian. Toronto. Semimonthly.

United Church Observer. Toronto. Semimonthly.

United Empire Loyalist. York, U.C.

Unity Herald. Unity, Sask. Weekly.

Upper Canada Gazette. York, U.C. Weekly. (1793-1826)

Upper Canada Herald. Kingston, U.C. Weekly. (1819-51)

Val d'Or Star. Val d'Or, Que. Weekly.

Veterans' Advocate. Montreal. Monthly.

Vidette. Qu'Appelle, Sask. Weekly. (1884-99)

Vindicator. Quebec. Semiweekly.

Vindicator & Canadian Advertiser. Montreal. Semi-weekly. (1828-1937)

Voice of the Fugitive. Sandwich, C.W. Semiweekly. (1851-53)

Voice of the Idle Worker. Vancouver (Unemployed Workers' Alliance). Weekly.

Voice of the Rock. Yellowknife (Community Baptist Church).

Watchman. Port Hope, Ont.

Watchman. St. Catharines, Ont.

Watchman. St. Thomas, Ont.

Watchman. Toronto.

Weekend Magazine. Montreal. Weekly.

Weekly Globe. Toronto. [Became daily]

Weekly Leader. Toronto.

Weekly Manitoba Liberal. Portage La Prairie, Man. (1883-1930)

Weekly Manitoban and Herald of Rupert's Land and the Northwestern Territory. Winnipeg. (1870-74)

Weekly Monitor. Bridgetown, N.S.

Weekly Register. York. (1822-26)

Weekly Sun. Toronto.

Welland Advocate & Review. Port Robinson, C.W. Weekly. (1852)

Wentworth Historical Society, Papers and Records. Hamilton, Ont.

Western Canadian Lumber Worker. Vancouver (Regional Council No. 1, I.W.A.). Irregular publication.

Western Herald & Farmers' Magazine. Sandwich, C.W. Weekly. (1838-42)

Western Miner & Oil Review. Vancouver. Monthly. (1953-1963)

Western Star. Montreal. (1819)

Western Weekly. See *Western Weekly Supplement*.

Western Weekly Supplement. Ponoka, Alta.

Western Wonderland. Seattle, Wash. Monthly.

Whitehorse Star. Whitehorse, Y.T. Weekly.

Wildlife Review. Victoria. Semiannual.

Windsor Tribune. See *Tribune*. Windsor, N.S.

Wilkie Press. Wilkie, Sask. Weekly.

Within Our Borders. Edmonton.

Witness. Bradford, Ont. Weekly.

Wolfville Acadian. Wolfville, N.S. Weekly.

Woodstock Sentinel. Woodstock, Ont.

Yachting. New York. Monthly.

Yarmouth Herald. Yarmouth, N.S. Weekly.

York Gazette. York, U.C. Weekly. (1807-16)

York Gazette. Deer Park, Ont. Weekly. (1895—?)

York Weekly Post. York, U.C. Weekly. (1821-22)

Yukon Midnight Sun. Dawson City.

Yukon Sun. Dawson City.

READER'S NOTES